BEHAVIORAL HEALTH

BEHAVIORAL HEALTH

A Handbook of Health Enhancement and Disease Prevention

Edited by

JOSEPH D. MATARAZZO, Ph.D.
University of Oregon
Portland, Oregon

SHARLENE M. WEISS, R.N., Ph.D.
Healthy People, Inc.
Silver Spring, Maryland

J. ALAN HERD, M.D.
Sid W. Richardson Institute
Methodist Hospital
Houston, Texas

NEAL E. MILLER, Ph.D.
Rockefeller University
New York, New York

STEPHEN M. WEISS, Ph.D.
National Heart, Lung, and Blood Institute
Bethesda, Maryland

A Wiley-Interscience Publication

JOHN WILEY & SONS

New   York   •   Chichester   •   Brisbane   •   Toronto   •   Singapore

3

Published by John Wiley & Sons, Inc.

Library of Congress Cataloging in Publication Data:

Main entry under title:

Behavioral health.

   "A Wiley-Interscience publication."
   Includes index.
   1. Medicine and psychology. 2. Health. 3. Medicine,
Preventive. I. Matarazzo, Joseph D. [DNLM: 1. Behavioral
Medicine. 2. Preventive Medicine. WA 108 B4195]
R726.5.B424   1984   613   84–11906
ISBN 0–471–86975–9

Printed in the United States of America

10 9 8 7 6 5 4 3 2

CONTRIBUTORS

David Abrams
Memorial Hospital, Pawtucket
Brown University
Providence, Rhode Island

Elizabeth Adler
Stanford University
Palo Alto, California

Judith E. Albino
State University of New York
Buffalo, New York

Michael H. Alderman
Cornell University Medical College
Ithaca, New York

James K. Alexander
Baylor College of Medicine
Houston, Texas

Aaron Antonovsky
Ben-Gurion University of the Negev
Beershiba, Israel

Lynn Artz
Memorial Hospital, Pawtucket
Brown University
Providence, Rhode Island

William A. Ayer
American Dental Association
Chicago, Illinois

Paula Beaudin
Memorial Hospital, Pawtucket
Brown University
Providence, Rhode Island

Catherine S. Bell
Department of Health and Human Services
Washington, D.C.

Herbert Benson
Beth Israel Hospital
Harvard Medical School
Boston, Massachusetts

Göran Berglund
Sahlgrenska Hospital
University of Göteborg
Göteborg, Sweden

James E. Birren
Andrus Gerontology Center
University of Southern California
Los Angeles, California

Henry Blackburn
School of Public Health
University of Minnesota
Minneapolis, Minnesota

Steven N. Blair
University of South Carolina
Columbia, South Carolina
Institute for Aerobics Research
Dallas, Texas

Joan Borysenko
Beth Israel Hospital
Boston, Massachusetts

Neil Bracht
University of Minnesota
Minneapolis, Minnesota

George A. Bray
University of Southern California School of
    Medicine
Los Angeles, California

Prudence Breitrose
Stanford University
Palo Alto, California

Kelly D. Brownell
University of Pennsylvania School of
    Medicine
Philadelphia, Pennsylvania

John J. Burt
University of Maryland
College Park, Maryland

Liz Cabrera
Memorial Hospital, Pawtucket
Brown University
Providence, Rhode Island

Joseph P. Carbonari
University of Houston
Baylor College of Medicine
Houston, Texas

Raymond Carlan
University of Minnesota
Minneapolis, Minnesota

Richard Carleton
Memorial Hospital, Pawtucket
Brown University
Providence, Rhode Island

Margaret A. Chesney
SRI International
Menlo Park, California

Edward R. Christophersen
University of Kansas Medical Center
Lawrence, Kansas

Robert B. Cialdini
Arizona State University
Tempe, Arizona

Thomas J. Coates
University of California School of
   Medicine
San Francisco, California

Frances Cohen
University of California
San Francisco, California

G. H. Collings, Jr.
New York Telephone Company
New York, New York

Norman L. Corah
State University of New York
Buffalo, New York

Patricia H. Cotanch
Duke University Medical Center
Durham, North Carolina

Nicholas A. Cummings
Biodyne Institute
San Francisco, California, and Honolulu,
   Hawaii

Patrick H. Deleon
United States Senate Staff
Washington, D.C.

Nancy Marwick Demuth
The Johns Hopkins School of Hygiene and
   Public Health
Baltimore, Maryland

Robert A. Dershewitz
Michael Reese Hospital and Medical Center
The University of Chicago Pritzker School
   of Medicine
Chicago, Illinois

Rogelio Diaz-Guerrero
National University of Mexico
Cuernavaca, Morelos, Mexico

Richard M. Eisler
Virginia Polytechnic Institute and State
   University
Blacksburg, Virginia

John Elder
Memorial Hospital, Pawtucket
Brown University
Providence, Rhode Island

David Engstrom
University of California
Irvine, California

Richard I. Evans
University of Houston
Houston, Texas

George S. Everly, Jr.
Loyola College
Psychological Sciences Institute
Baltimore, Maryland

John W. Farquhar
Stanford University
Palo Alto, California

Robert H. L. Feldman
University of Maryland
College Park, Maryland

Andrea Ferreira
Memorial Hospital, Pawtucket
Brown University
Providence, Rhode Island

Howard M. Field
University of Iowa
Iowa City, Iowa

June A. Flora
Stanford University
Palo Alto, California

Stephen P. Fortmann
Stanford University
Palo Alto, California

Bernard H. Fox
National Cancer Institute
Silver Spring, Maryland

Elliot N. Gale
State University of New York
Buffalo, New York

Brenda S. Gillum
University of Minnesota
Minneapolis, Minnesota

Richard F. Gillum
University of Minnesota
Minneapolis, Minnesota

Lawrence W. Green
University of Texas Health Science Center
Houston, Texas

David Hamburg
Carnegie Foundation
New York, New York

William R. Harlan
University of Michigan Medical School
Ann Arbor, Michigan

Alfred E. Harper
University of Wisconsin
Madison, Wisconsin

L. Howard Hartley
Harvard Medical School
Boston, Massachusetts

William L. Haskell
Stanford University School of Medicine
Palo Alto, California

D. M. Hegsted
Harvard School of Public Health and New
    England Regional Primate Center
Harvard Medical School
Boston, Massachusetts

J. Alan Herd
Baylor College of Medicine
Houston, Texas

William Hettler
University of Wisconsin
Stevens Point, Wisconsin

Donald C. Iverson
Mercy Medical Center
Denver, Colorado

David Jacobs
University of Minnesota
Minneapolis, Minnesota

Richard Jessor
University of Colorado
Boulder, Colorado

S. Stephen Kegeles
University of Connecticut Health Center
Storrs, Connecticut

Phillip C. Kendall
University of Minnesota
Minneapolis, Minnesota

France Kittel
Universitaire Libre de Bruxelles
Brussels, Belgium

H. Asuman Kiyak
University of Washington
Seattle, Washington

F. G. Kline
University of Minnesota
Minneapolis, Minnesota

Patricia Knisley
Memorial Hospital, Pawtucket
Brown University
Providence, Rhode Island

Lloyd J. Kolbe
University of Texas Health Science Center
Houston, Texas

Lynn T. Kozlowski
Addiction Research Foundation
University of Toronto
Toronto, Ontario, Canada

Richard C. Labarba
University of South Florida
Tampa, Florida

Thomas Lasater
Memorial Hospital, Pawtucket
Brown University
Providence, Rhode Island

Robert L. Lemke
Trinity University
San Antonio, Texas

Sol Levine
Boston University School of Public Health
Boston, Massachusetts

Sandra M. Levy
National Cancer Institute
Silver Spring, Maryland

Edward Lichtenstein
University of Oregon
Eugene, Oregon

Carol Lindeman
University of Oregon Health Sciences Center
Portland, Oregon

Russell V. Luepker
University of Minnesota
Minneapolis, Minnesota

Adrian K. Lund
Insurance Institute for Highway Safety
Washington, D.C.

Nathan Maccoby
Stanford University
Palo Alto, California

James E. Maddux
Texas Tech University
Lubbock, Texas

Susan H. Marcus
Texas Christian University
Fort Worth, Texas

Joseph D. Matarazzo
University of Oregon Health Sciences Center
Portland, Oregon

Robin J. Mermelstein
University of Oregon
Eugene, Oregon

Neal E. Miller
Rockefeller University
New York, New York

Sheldon I. Miller
Sheppard and Enoch Pratt Hospital
Baltimore, Maryland

Maurice Mittelmark
University of Minnesota
Minneapolis, Minnesota

David M. Murray
University of Minnesota
Minneapolis, Minnesota

Murray P. Naditch
Control Data Corporation
Minneapolis, Minnesota

Peter E. Nathan
Rutgers University
New Brunswick, New Jersey

Neil B. Oldridge
McMaster University
Hamilton, Ontario, Canada

Chandra Patel
London School of Hygiene and Tropical
   Medicine
University of London
London, England

Terry F. Pechacek
University of Minnesota
Minneapolis, Minnesota

Eileen B. Peck
Department of Health Services
Sacramento, California

Gussie Peterson
Memorial Hospital, Pawtucket
Brown University
Providence, Rhode Island

Pekka Puska
National Public Health Institute
Helsinki, Finland

Paul M. Ribisl
Wake Forest University
Winston-Salem, North Carolina

Frederick P. Rivara
University of Tennessee Center for the
   Health Sciences
Knoxville, Tennessee

Michael C. Roberts
University of Alabama
Birmingham, Alabama

Leon S. Robertson
Yale University
New Haven, Connecticut

Judith Rodin
Yale University
New Haven, Connecticut

Antonio Rodriques
Memorial Hospital, Pawtucket
Brown University
Providence, Rhode Island

Todd Rogers
Stanford University
Palo Alto, California

Patricia Rosenberg
Memorial Hospital, Pawtucket
Brown University
Providence, Rhode Island

Paul Rozin
University of Pennsylvania
Philadelphia, Pennsylvania

John D. Rugh
University of Texas Health Science Center
San Antonio, Texas

Dale H. Schunk
University of Houston
Houston, Texas

Gary E. Schwartz
Yale University
New Haven, Connecticut

Ascher Segall
Boston University
Boston, Massachusetts

Phyllis E. Sensenig
Arizona State University
Tempe, Arizona

Arthur K. Shapiro
Mount Sinai School of Medicine
New York, New York

Elaine Shapiro
Mount Sinai School of Medicine
New York, New York

Wesley E. Sime
University of Nebraska
Lincoln, Nebraska

Scott K. Simonds
University of Michigan
Ann Arbor, Michigan

Everett L. Smith
University of Wisconsin
Madison, Wisconsin

Robert Snow
Memorial Hospital, Pawtucket
Brown University
Providence, Rhode Island

Douglas S. Solomon
Stanford University
Palo Alto, California

James R. Sorenson
Boston University School of Public Health
Boston, Massachusetts

Lee Stauffer
University of Minnesota
Minneapolis, Minnesota

George C. Stone
University of California
San Francisco, California

Bonnie R. Strickland
University of Massachusetts
Amherst, Massachusetts

Peter Suedfeld
University of British Columbia
Vancouver, Canada

C. Barr Taylor
Stanford University
Palo Alto, California

Calvin W. Taylor
University of Utah
Salt Lake City, Utah

Henry L. Taylor
University of Minnesota
Minneapolis, Minnesota

Carl E. Thoresen
Stanford University
Palo Alto, California

Barry S. Tuchfeld
Sheppard and Enoch Pratt Hospital
Baltimore, Maryland

Dennis C. Turk
Yale University
New Haven, Connecticut

Gary R. Vandenbos
American Psychological Association
Washington, D.C.

Jeffery T. Wack
Yale University
New Haven, Connecticut

Thomas A. Wadden
University of Pennsylvania School of
    Medicine
Philadelphia, Pennsylvania

Linda Weiner
Stanford University
Palo Alto, California

Philip Weinstein
University of Washington
Seattle, Washington

Sharlene M. Weiss
Healthy People, Inc.
Silver Spring, Maryland

Stephen M. Weiss
National Heart, Lung, and Blood Institute
Bethesda, Maryland

Arthur Weltman
Center for Sports Medicine and Health
    Fitness
St. Francis Medical Center
Peoria, Illinois

G. Terence Wilson
Rutgers University
New Brunswick, New Jersey

Peter D. Wood
Stanford University
Palo Alto, California

Anita M. Woods
Texas Research Institute of Mental Sciences
Houston, Texas

Logan Wright
Institute of Health Psychology for Children
Oklahoma City, Oklahoma

FOREWORD

During the past decade, a new awareness has dawned: much of disease and disability is related to human behavior, and therefore the role of behavior in keeping people healthy must be understood scientifically. In this direction lies the possibility of preventing much disease and promoting health. This promising approach affects the well-being of people everywhere.

A powerful stimulus for this line of inquiry comes from epidemiological and clinical studies over several decades making clear that health-damaging behavior adds a heavy load to the burden of illness in affluent, industrialized countries. The most common measure of burden of illness is mortality; other useful indices include potential years of life lost, in-patient days, primary care visits, days lost from work, limitation of major activities, and economic costs. However measured, behavioral factors weigh much more heavily than we thought one or two decades ago.

Indeed, the heaviest burdens of illness in the United States today are related to individual behavior, especially the long-term patterns of behavior often referred to as "life style." The Centers for Disease Control of the U.S. Public Health Service estimate that about half the mortality from the ten leading causes of death can be linked to life style. Known behavioral risk factors include cigarette smoking, excessive consumption of alcoholic beverages, illicit drugs, certain dietary habits, insufficient exercise, reckless driving, noncompliance with medication regimens, and maladaptive responses to stressful experience. Cigarette smoking and heavy alcohol intake are two of the best examples of behaviors that make a major contribution to the modern burden of illness.

Cigarette smoking is the single most important environmental factor contributing to early death in the United States. In a twelve-year follow-up on one million men and women in the United States, mortality rates were greater for smokers than for nonsmokers regardless of age or sex. There are several lines of evidence that cigarette smoking actually has a causal role in cardiovascular disease, cancer (lung, larynx, esophagus, pancreas, mouth, and throat) and respiratory disease (chronic obstructive lung disease, bronchitis, and emphysema). For example, the effect depends on the dose: greater morbidity and mortality occur with more cigarettes smoked, higher tar and nicotine content, greater inhalation of cigarette smoke, and earlier age of smoking initiation. Risk is reduced with quitting, although it may take many years to return to the risk levels of individuals who never smoked. Cigarette smoking is even dangerous to the unborn child. Women who smoke during pregnancy are at greater risk of having a low birth weight baby and other serious complications.

Alcohol abuse constitutes the most serious drug problem in America, affecting an estimated 13 million youthful and adult problem drinkers, their 40 million family members, and thousands of innocent bystanders who each year become the victims of alcohol-related accidents—particularly automobile accidents—and violence. The misuse of alcohol is a factor in more than 10 percent of all deaths in the United States and it cost the nation over $50 billion in 1980. As with smoking, alcohol use during pregnancy tends to be damaging to the fetus. Heavy drinking is an important causal factor in damage to the liver and brain as well as some cancers. In addition, alcohol abuse constitutes one of the main worldwide causes of work loss as well as family disruption.

Though these examples are formidable, a variety of others are provided in this book. Moreover, there are worse health problems in the poor, developing nations of Africa, Asia, and Latin America. Their problems are also strongly related to behavior involved in nutrition, sanitation, and reproduction as well as alcohol, smoking, and child care. Thus the world's health future turns out to be far more heavily behavior-related than we had understood only a decade or two ago.

The U.S. experience provides reason for hope in this regard. We began to address ourselves seriously to this problem in the early 1970s, in significant part through the initiative of our scientific community. This involves obtaining information on risk factors such as those predisposing to cardiovascular disease. It also involves the scientific study of behavior and its connection with biomedical research in order to change behavior for health. Indeed, one of the deeply significant changes of the twentieth century is the growing recognition that attitudes and methods of science can be employed in understanding human behavior. This cutting edge of science can foster the promotion of health in all countries.

One heartening feature of this new work is the emergence of a group of distinguished psychologists who have turned their attention to health problems. They constitute the principal contributors to this book. Psychology has been a path-breaking discipline in the scientific study of behavior, especially in elucidating principles of learning and of human relations. Bringing these principles to bear on health problems (and techniques to permit their objective study) offers much promise for future insight.

Moreover, psychologists have worked collaboratively with scientists in various branches of medicine and biology to enhance understanding of the complex links between behavior and health. One such domain is the study of psychophysiological reactions to stressful experience—a seminal influence in the field relating basic research in psychology and biology to clinical medicine and indeed to public health.

Altogether, this is an exciting and demanding time for the biobehavioral sciences. Opportunities for progress in basic knowledge are unprecedented, and their application to health problems is of great interest. The potential rewards, measured in terms of decreased mortality and morbidity or improved quality of life, are very encouraging. Yet the tasks are complex and difficult. Progress has often been slow and the obstacles formidable. But the threshold has now been passed and progress should come more rapidly. This book conveys the main thrusts of work in the field, illuminating the frontiers of research on health and behavior. Whatever else it may do, I certainly hope it will stimulate young scientists to pursue these lines of inquiry.

DAVID A. HAMBURG, M.D.
President
Carnegie Corporation of New York

PREFACE

A general lesson from the history of medicine is that prevention usually is much more effective, and especially more cost-effective, than are treatment and cure. In spite of this lesson, prevention—in the form of investment of resources relative to cure—often receives far less attention than it merits, primarily because its effects usually are not immediate. Once a person has acquired a disease, however, that patient and the medical community have immediate motivation for attempting a cure. Thus efforts at prevention should, as much as possible, be reformulated to emphasize the immediate benefits of health maintenance and health enhancement.

The Surgeon General's report *Healthy People* presents a challenge to us all. At the beginning of this century, the leading causes of death were influenza, pneumonia, diphtheria, tuberculosis, and gastrointestinal infections. Since then, the yearly death rate from these diseases has been reduced from 580 to 30 per 100,000 people. The burden of illness has shifted to deaths and disabilities in which behavior plays an important role, such as heart disease, cancer, cirrhosis of the liver, and injuries from accidents, violence, or poisons. This Surgeon General's report quotes two studies, one in Canada and another in the United States, which estimate that half the mortalities from the current ten leading causes of death in these countries can be traced to behavior and life style. It concludes that a major opportunity for further improvements in health is in the area of changing health-related behaviors. Stated more positively, this means helping citizens to establish and maintain health-preserving and health-enhancing behaviors while at the same time supporting legislation and other initiatives to accomplish the same goals at a societal level.

This book examines how behavioral health issues relate to particular life periods from prenatal to geriatric, the various models and strategies employed in the service of disease prevention and health promotion, and the settings in which such strategies are implemented. It also reviews the evidence for various risk factors that have behavioral life style correlates and examines the current state of the training of various health professionals to assist our citizens in achieving and maintaining healthy life styles. It is the hope of the editors and authors of this book that its readers will find it to be a comprehensive source of information pertinent to their needs.

While the clinical, epidemiological, and experimental evidence in support of the role of behavioral factors in health is becoming increasingly impressive, certain cautions should be borne in mind. Many health-destructive behaviors—such as smoking, overeating, and the abuse of alcohol and drugs—are extremely resistant to permanent change; therefore, the behavioral and biobehavioral sciences should be careful not to promise more than can be delivered. Large-scale programs to modify health-related behaviors should not be conducted without adequate support from pilot studies. Lest we discourage society's investment of the needed fiscal and human resources, we should avoid fads and be sure that there is sound evidence for the more healthful behaviors that are recommended. We must not conclude that because some is good, much more will be better; rather, we must adjust our aims according to what people (ordinary citizens, legislators, policymakers, and manufacturers) are willing and able to continue to do. Too frequently technically correct programs designed to achieve the optimal long-term physiological effect of diet, exercise, smoking cessation, or weight reduction fail because, on the one hand, they cannot be incorporated into a person's daily routine in a manner that will ensure continuing adherence and, on the other, the passage of facilitative legislation intrudes upon other values we hold equally dear. But with the alarmingly rapid rise in the cost of health care, which is forcing greater attention to be devoted to prevention, even modest advances reflecting fair compromises among such competing values may prove extremely cost-effective.

Finally, the recent efforts to integrate biomedical and behavioral science perspectives and techniques in the search for answers to the health issues discussed in this handbook demonstrate the creativity of biobehavioral approaches to complex problems. It is the hope of all of us who have been involved in producing this first handbook devoted to behavioral health that it will help lay the foundation for significant scientific advances in this emerging area.

Portland, Oregon

Silver Spring, Maryland

Houston, Texas

New York, New York

Bethesda, Maryland

June 1984

JOSEPH D. MATARAZZO

SHARLENE M. WEISS

J. ALAN HERD

NEAL E. MILLER

STEPHEN M. WEISS

CONTENTS

SECTION 1
BEHAVIORAL HEALTH: AN OVERVIEW

CHAPTER 1

BEHAVIORAL HEALTH: A 1990 CHALLENGE FOR THE HEALTH SCIENCES PROFESSIONS

JOSEPH D. MATARAZZO

Oregon Health Sciences University

The recent focus on enhancing health and wellness has helped spawn a major white-collar industry, which has attracted tens of thousands of new workers during the past 25 years and has helped give birth to hundreds of new companies and enterprises offering ways for healthy individuals to lose weight, stop smoking, tone flabby muscles, and improve their cardiovascular systems, as well as ways to inoculate them against stress at work and at home. This development in the direction of health enhancement represents a major break with the whole of the past history of humankind, in which survival and recovery from illness were paramount goals. The major health challenge faced by our earliest human ancestors was survival in a very hostile environment characterized by a perpetual shortage of food and an ever present danger from human and animal predators. After humans discovered the survival benefits of an agricultural society some ten thousand years ago, a host of infectious diseases associated with communal living became, after shortage of food, the second predominant cause of illness and death. Finally, in the past 300 years, great strides were made in reducing mortality and morbidity through significant advances in hygiene, public health, microbiology, control of the environment, and the capacity of the inhabitants of many countries to produce more food. As a result the patterns of illness, disability, longevity, and death have undergone considerable change. These changes have been especially evident in the twentieth century. They have been so dramatic in our country that the first sentence of the epochal first report by the Surgeon General of the United States on health promotion and disease prevention, forwarded to President Carter and the Congress by then Surgeon General Julius Richmond via then HEW Secretary Califano (1979a), states: "The health of the American people has never been better."

A number of factors contributed to this optimistic conclusion. First, as shown in Figure 1.1, since 1900 life expectancy in the United States has increased more than 50% for both males and females—for males from 46.3 years at birth in 1900 to 69.9 years in 1979, and for females from 48.3 to 77.8 years. Along with these differences in longevity for the sexes, life expectancy continues to vary among races, although marked improvements have occurred in all races. Specifically, since 1900 life expectancy for white Americans rose 56% (from 47.6 to 74.4 years) and for nonwhites 119% (from 33 to 70 years). Virtual eradication of infectious diseases such as influenza, rubella, whooping cough, and polio through immunization is the major factor associated with this remarkable increase in longevity.

As shown in Table 1.1, the major causes of death today are no longer infectious diseases

LIFE EXPECTANCY AT BIRTH: 1900-1978

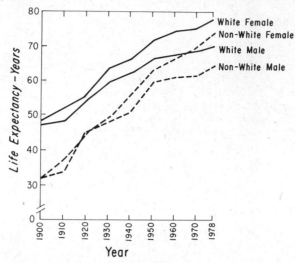

Figure 1.1 Life expectancy at birth for males and females and blacks and whites. (Adapted from Lunde, A. S. Health in the United States. *Annals of the American Academy of Political and Social Science,* 1981, **453**, 28–69.)

Table 1.1   Major Causes of Death and Associated Risk Factors, United States, 1977

Cause	Percentage of All Deaths	Risk Factor
Heart disease	37.8	Smoking,[a] hypertension,[a] elevated serum cholesterol,[a] diet, lack of exercise, diabetes, stress, family history
Malignant neoplasms	20.4	Smoking,[a] worksite carcinogens,[a] environmental carcinogens, alcohol, diet
Stroke	9.6	Hypertension,[a] smoking,[a] elevated serum cholesterol,[a] stress
Accidents other than motor vehicle accidents	2.8	Alcohol,[a] drug abuse, smoking (fires), product design, handgun availability
Influenza and pneumonia	2.7	Smoking, vaccination status[a]
Motor vehicle accidents	2.6	Alcohol,[a] no seat belts,[a] speed,[a] roadway design, vehicle engineering
Diabetes	1.7	Obesity[a]
Cirrhosis of the liver	1.6	Alcohol abuse[a]
Arteriosclerosis	1.5	Elevated serum cholesterol[a]
Suicide	1.5	Stress,[a] alcohol and drug abuse, gun availability

Source: Office of Disease Prevention and Health Promotion. Adapted from Harris, P. R., *Health United States 1980.* U.S. Department of Health and Human Services, Pub. No. (PHS) 81–1232. Washington, D.C.: U.S. Government Printing Office, 1981.
[a] Major risk factors.

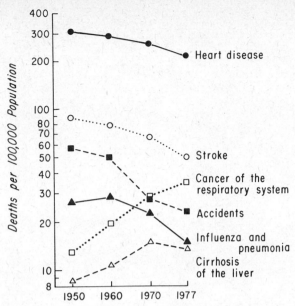

Figure 1.2 Age-adjusted rates for selected causes of death, United States, selected years 1950–1977. (Adapted from Harris, P. R. *Health United States 1980*. U.S. Department of Health and Human Services Pub. No. (PHS)81–1232. Washington, D.C.: U.S. Government Printing Office, 1981.)

and starvation. Rather, today's major killers of Americans are heart disease (37.8% of all deaths), cancer (20.4%), and stroke (9.6%). Deaths from heart disease and stroke increased during the first half of the twentieth century, but, as detailed by Thom and Kannel (1981) and Levy and Moskowitz (1982), this pattern has recently begun to reverse. Unfortunately, however, as revealed in Figure 1.2, whereas deaths due to heart disease and stroke (as well as accidents and influenza and pneumonia) have shown a small but steady decline in the United States since 1950, deaths due to cancer and cirrhosis have *increased* at an alarming rate during the same period. Furthermore, as shown in Figures 1.3 and 1.4, deaths due to motor vehicle accidents (especially for white males and females under 19 years of age) and deaths from lung cancer in both males and females have increased substantially since 1950. The data in Figures 1.3 and 1.4 are especially alarming to health professionals

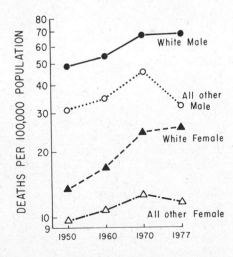

Figure 1.3 Death rates for motor vehicle accidents among persons 15–19 years of age, United States, selected years 1950–1977. (Adapted from Harris, P. R. *Health United States 1980*. U.S. Department of Health and Human Services Pub. No. (PHS)81–1232. Washington, D.C.: U.S. Government Printing Office, 1981.)

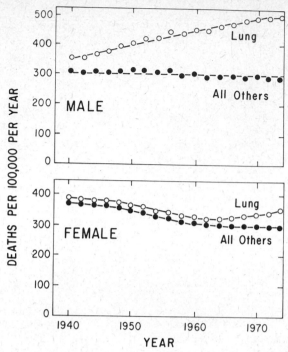

Figure 1.4 Annual mortality rates for cancers in the United States among white adult males and females. Open circles denote deaths from respiratory cancer only; filled circles denote deaths from all other types of cancers. (Adapted from Califano, J. A. Jr. *Healthy people: Background papers.* Washington, D.C.: U.S. Government Printing Office, 1979.)

in view of the now well-established findings that legislation requiring use of automobile seat belts and motorcycle helmets as well as educational programs to prevent smoking are effective in reducing the mortality (and morbidity) shown in these two figures (Harris, 1981; Jonah, Dawson, & Smith, 1982).

ENVIRONMENTAL AND BEHAVIORAL PATHOGENS

The evidence is strong that major discoveries in the biomedical sciences have played a crucial role in the dysfunctions that have shown significant *decreases* in mortality, whereas the by-products of twentieth-century industrial and lifestyle changes are associated with the *increases* in mortality for other conditions. Thus, as stated earlier, microbiological, chemical, and physical pathogens associated with acute and chronic infectious diseases caused by microorganisms were until recently the major sources of disability and death throughout human history. As is well known, the effects of these pathogens have been greatly ameliorated during the past two centuries through public health triumphs that have improved sanitation, purified food and water, and made related advances in microbiology, pharmacology, and therapeutics. A clear result has been considerable curtailment of the toll from infectious agents, viruses and other microbes, mutant cells, and pollutants as sources of disease and death. The most recent example of the beneficial effects of the science of immunology was the virtual elimination of small pox and poliomyelitis in this country by 1978 (Lunde, 1981). Furthermore, it appears that measles soon will be completely elimi-nated in the United States, although there are alarming early signs that today's young parents may be so uninformed about the crucial role played by immunization in eliminating these scourges that some of them are neglecting to protect their children by use of the simple and inexpensive preventive measures.

The shifts in the specific causes of death and disability (Table 1.1, Figure 1.2) that have paralleled the recent striking increases in longevity (Figure 1.1) enjoyed by inhabitants of the United States and other industrialized nations were so impressive that government leaders in a number of countries were impelled to underscore and highlight the significance of these changes in special reports to their nations. Both the Canadian Minister of National Health and Welfare (Lalonde, 1974) and the Surgeon General of the United States, communicating to his countrymen via the Secretary of Health, Education and Welfare (Califano, 1979a, 1979b), used the visibility and power of their respective offices to herald the need for a new focus on the continuing war against morbidity and mortality. As evidence of the nineteenth- and twentieth-century revolutionary advances against infectious diseases, Califano reported that whereas in 1900 580 deaths for every 100,000 U.S. citizens resulted from the five leading causes of death (influenza, pneumonia, diphtheria, tuberculosis, and gastrointestinal infections), deaths from these same causes number only 30 per 100,000 today.

Furthermore, as Lunde (1981, p. 32) records, significant declines in some of the leading causes of death occurred during only the last decade. Thus, from 1968 to 1978, age-adjusted death rates for a number of leading causes of mortality have registered the following declines: diseases of the heart, −23%; cerebrovascular diseases, −37%; influenza and pneumonia, −43%; cirrhosis of the liver, −10%; arteriosclerosis, −38%; diabetes mellitus, −29%; bronchitis, emphysema, and asthma, −47%; and nephritis and nephrosis, −28%. Unfortunately, deaths from cancer of the respiratory system have increased substantially during the same decade. Thus, as was shown in Table 1.1 and Figure 1.2, heart disease and cancer are the major causes of death in the United States today, followed by accidents, diabetes, arteriosclerosis, and suicide. These major causes of death are all ones in which behavioral pathogens— the personal habits and lifestyle behaviors of the individual—not the external pathogens of earlier epochs in human history, are the single most important etiologic factor.

In his introductory remarks, Califano (1979a) provides the essence of the full report to his nation in these pithy observations about Americans:

We are killing ourselves by our own careless habits.

We are killing ourselves by carelessly polluting the environment.

We are killing ourselves by permitting harmful social conditions to persist—conditions like poverty, hunger and ignorance—which destroy health, especially for infants and children.

You, the individual, can do more for your own health and well-being than any doctor, any hospital, any drug, any exotic medical device. (p. viii)

It may prove instructive to explore some of the developments that shifted the focus of interest in the microbial and related pathogens of death and disability from a hostile external environment to a host of self-initiating events associated with the lifestyle behaviors of the individual.

THE ROLE OF BEHAVIOR IN MORBIDITY AND MORTALITY

A new term—risk factor—has become commonplace in the lexicon of this country's professionals and laypersons during the past decade. Passages in the Old Testament and in even earlier written documents indicate that humans have long sensed the relationships between good health and such personal behaviors as regularity of meals and sleep, moderation in food and alcohol consumption, and physical activity and exercise. However, more precise quantification of these relationships occurred only very recently as a corollary of the partnerships that were formed between behavioral scientists and biomedical health specialists following the large post–World War II investments of public research and training funds that were deliberately targeted at furthering these alliances. Aspects of that recent history have been detailed elsewhere (Matarazzo, 1980, 1982). Epidemiology, cardiology, public health, and preventive medicine (and their corresponding disciplines in nursing and dentistry) are a few of the biomedical disciplines that appear to have gained considerably from the postwar contributions to their respective fields by medical sociologists, health psychologists, and representatives of several other behavioral science disciplines. Although these contributions have been many and varied, findings from research on the role of behavioral pathogens (risk factors) in morbidity and mortality have been so impressive that they have spawned a number of new health industries and have helped give new direction to the overall war on disease, disability, and death.

In his report to the U.S. Congress, Califano (1979a) stated that the 10 leading causes of death in our country today, in order starting from the most frequent killer, are heart disease, cancer, stroke, all accidents except motor vehicle, infectious diseases, motor vehicle accidents, diabetes, cirrhosis of the liver, arteriosclerosis, and suicide. Yet, as also suggested here in Table 1.1, Califano followed the enumeration of these 10 major killers with the equally important statement that, of these 10 causes, "at least seven could be substantially reduced if persons at risk improved just five habits: diet, smoking, lack of exercise, alcohol abuse and use of hypertension medication" (p. 14). The types of accumulating scientific evidence linking each of these habits (risk factors) with increased rates of death are shown in Figure 1.5. A comparable relationship between smoking and lung cancer, though not shown in the figure, was also demonstrated. Results such as those shown in Figure 1.5 could not be ignored; collectively, they offered powerful support for the role played by these five habits in the major causes of death of our citizens.

As just indicated, medical sociologists, epidemiologists, biomedical scientists, public health researchers, and psychologists played a prominent role in laying the groundwork for this startling conclusion and insight. Isolated observations had been published by a variety of investigators in and out of government—lung specialists; epidemiologists; statisticians from the American Cancer Society; medical sociologists; personality, clinical, and social psychologists; and a host of other types of biomedical and behavioral science investigators. However, these disparate reports took on a new meaning and a more clearly integrated

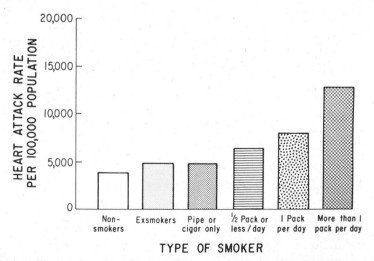

TYPE OF SMOKER

Figure 1.5 Age-adjusted rates of first heart attack for white males aged 30–59, United States, categorized by smoking status. (Adapted from Califano, J. A., Jr. *Healthy people: The Surgeon General's report on health promotion and disease prevention.* Washington, D.C.: U.S. Government Printing Office, 1979.)

direction, first, with the publication in 1964 of the first Surgeon General's Report on Smoking and, shortly thereafter, with a number of influential reports from high-level study groups specifically assembled by the National Heart, Lung and Blood Institute to review the state of scientific knowledge on the etiology of heart and lung disease and to chart directions for prevention and treatment. Considerable new sums of money were provided to the National Institutes of Health by succeeding administrations and Congress for research at the interfaces of the biomedical and behavioral sciences.

One result was that, in the brief period of two to three decades, a major new focus was grafted alongside the biomedical approaches that had characterized biomedically based medical care in the United States during the twentieth century (Matarazzo, 1980, 1982). This new focus, behavioral in its essential features, shared with the biomedical approach the belief that *prevention* of morbidity and mortality, not treatment, was the most cost-effective strategy that should be employed. Students of the history of the behavioral sciences since 1945 are aware that the research of literally thousands of individual behavioral scientists and epidemiologists was responsible for this new direction in the war on disease, disability, and death that emerged in the post–World War II period. Unfortunately, we can mention here the contributions of only a selected few of these behavioral and biomedical scientists.

LIFESTYLE RISK FACTORS AND MORTALITY

The research, surveys, and writings of a team of human population researchers made up of Lester Breslow, Nedra Belloc, Leonard Syme, and a number of colleagues (Belloc, Breslow, & Hochstim, 1971) at the Human Population Laboratory of the California State Department of Public Health in Berkeley constituted an important contribution to our knowledge of the role of personal lifestyle in physical health and dysfunction. In one of several interrelated papers, Belloc and Breslow (1972) presented the results of a 1965 survey of a representative probability sample of 6,928 American adults. The survey revealed that seven specific personal health practices were highly correlated with the physical health of these Americans:

1. Sleeping seven to eight hours daily;
2. Eating breakfast almost every day;
3. Never or rarely eating between meals;
4. Currently being at or near prescribed height-adjusted weight;
5. Never smoking cigarettes;
6. Moderate or no use of alcohol;
7. Regular physical activity.

Those adults who followed all or most of these seven "good" practices were found in the initial 1965 survey to be in better general health than those who followed none or few. An important follow-up paper by Belloc (1973) continued to probe the relationship between health status and these seven health practices by examining (using death records) the subsequent mortality experience of the same individuals during the next 5½ years. This subsequent investigation discovered 371 deaths in the original sample of 6,928 individuals. When the initial 1965 health practices were next compared with subsequent mortality over the next 5½ years, the striking results shown in Figure 1.6 emerged. Although the presence or absence of each of the seven health practices had shown only modest levels of intercorrelation across individuals when analyzed simply as pairs of behavior, summing the practices for each individual (as in Figure 1.6) showed a clear relationship to mortality at follow-up. Although levels of mortality increased with increasing age, as was expected, the results also made it strikingly clear that the proportions of both men and women in each age group who died were relatively smaller at each age level for those individuals who followed more of the seven healthier practices. Further analyses showed that this

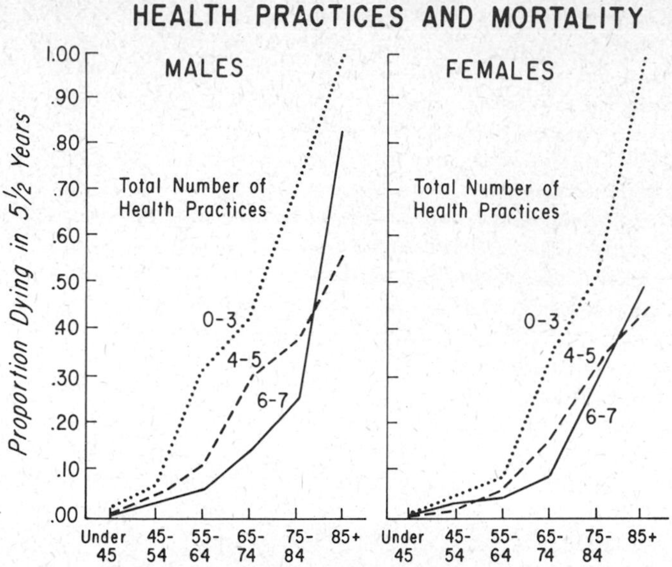

HEALTH PRACTICES AND MORTALITY

Figure 1.6 Age-specific mortality rates by number of health practices followed by subgroups of males and females. (Adapted from Belloc, N. B. Relationship of health practices and mortality. *Preventive Medicine,* 1973, **2,** 67–81.)

inverse relationship between number of health practices and mortality rates was independent of the individual's 1965 level of income and, except for a very small subsample, independent of 1965 health status, as assessed on a continuum of vitality from good health (without complaints) to severely disabled. In a follow-up survey conducted in 1974 with 4,864 of the 6,928 individuals initially surveyed in 1965, Breslow and Enstrom (1980) confirmed the effect on mortality of these seven health practices. Specifically, their 9½-year follow-up revealed that men who followed all seven health practices had a mortality rate only 28% of that of men who followed zero to three practices; the comparable rate for women who followed all seven practices was 43% of that of women who followed only zero to three health practices. They also found a remarkable stability in the health practices of each individual over that 9½-year period.

Breslow (1978a, 1978b) and his associates (Breslow & Somers, 1977) cited the findings from these earlier studies, as well as those from a number of studies involving controlled intervention trials that are currently under way in this and other countries, as evidence that new health initiatives stressing prevention of disease and health maintenance based on risk factors such as these are both desirable and cost-effective.

The paper by Breslow and Somers (1977) is especially impressive in that it lists a small number of demonstrably valid and cost-effective specific steps that can be taken to reduce the risks of morbidity and mortality significantly during 10 epochs of a person's life span. These steps include such health-enhancing measures as receiving each of seven immunizations, routine screening tests during infancy, control of smoking and obesity, and screening tests for hypertension and cancer (cervical, mammary, and gastrointestinal) for individuals between the ages of 40 and 59. This prescription for a more healthy life is a refreshing alternative to the heretofore recommended annual physical examination, which few Americans seek and which many practicing physicians, as well as increasing numbers of investigators, believe is ineffective for health promotion and monitoring.

The research of a number of medical sociologists and other health researchers also has contributed considerably to our understanding of illness and health. Thus, such heuristically powerful concepts as the health belief model, whose dimensions have been creatively explored by I. M. Rosenstock, Marshall Becker, Lawrence Green, and others, have done much to increase our understanding of humans who are ill or well. Although this work is not sufficiently germane to our interests here to warrant extended discussion, the interested reader will find excellent reviews in a number of sources (Green, Kreuter, Deeds, & Partridge, 1980; Maiman & Becker, 1974; Rosenstock, 1974).

One medical sociologist whose program of research is particularly germane to the present discussion is David Mechanic. After many years of study of the health practices of children and adults, Mechanic was able to ask a series of questions whose answers would do much to further our understanding of the relationships between behavior and health. Thus, for example, in common with the interests of Breslow and Enstrom (1980) discussed earlier, Mechanic asked such questions as (a) whether or not an individual's health attitudes and these attitudes' behavioral manifestations were stable over time (e.g., from childhood to adulthood) and (b) whether the health behaviors followed at one of these times (e.g., adulthood) were such that an individual found to be manifesting one positive health behavior would also evidence an increased probability of engaging concurrently in other positive lifestyle practices.

In a series of recent publications, Mechanic presents data bearing on both these questions. The original health practices data (utilizing measures somewhat like those used later by Breslow) were collected by Mechanic in 1961 from a sample of 350 pairs of mothers and their school-aged children who were surveyed in Madison, Wisconsin. In 1977, 16 years later, 333 of the children were located and resurveyed, and the retest responses provided Mechanic data for additional analyses, including information on the stability of health and illness behaviors. The 1961 data were obtained from mothers (home interviews), children, teachers, official school records, and the daily illness diaries completed by 198 of the 350 mothers. Because of the ages of the children (they were in grades 4 and 8 in 1961), the questions used in 1961 differed slightly in wording and in format from those used when these same children were reexamined as adults 16 years later.

Table 1.2 (from Mechanic, 1979) shows these differences in wording in the 1961 and the 1977 questions. The table also presents the correlations that were computed to reveal the stability of the answers to each of the six similar questions over the 16-year interval. These "stability of health response" correlations are shown in the diagonal of the table for 302 of the children initially studied. The rest of the values in the table are the correlations obtained on these same children when each of the answers to the six 1961 questions was correlated with each of the answers to every other question presented in 1977.

Although they may be a bit surprising to some health researchers, the results shown in the diagonal of Table 1.2 indicate that health-related attitude responses of children who were approximately 9 and 12 years old when first studied were only modestly correlated with the answers given by the same children as adults 16 years later. Specifically, only three of the six correlations shown in the diagonal were significant ($p < .05$) and their individual magnitudes were only modest at best. These modestly stable items were "take risks of injury" ($r = .20$), "get sick easily" ($r = .15$), and "continue usual activities when sick" ($r = .16$).

These modest diagonal values might suggest to some readers not familiar with personality and attitudinal research that the health attitudes and practices of preadolescent and adolescent children are not predictive of their own later adult health-related behavior and attitudes. In fact, a review of this vast literature by Epstein (1979) reveals just that; with rare exception, studies that have correlated objective, self-report responses on two occasions have obtained correlations below .30. Furthermore, measures of such self-report statements in the main have produced equally low correlations with overt measures of the same behavior. However, as Epstein shows, this state of affairs is not so bleak as it might at first appear. Rather, the issue is resolved by recognizing that most single items of behavior (such as the attitudinal statement items in Table 1.2) have a high component of measurement error and a narrow range of generality. In the studies Epstein reviewed, it was demonstrated that when such

Table 1.2 Correlations between Health and Illness Attitude Responses to Comparable Test-Retest Queries in 1961 and 1977 (N = 302)

1961 Questions	1977 Questions					
	(A) Tell close friends when don't feel well	(B) Take risks of injury	(C) Uncomfortable going to a doctor	(D) Deny pain	(E) Get sick easily	(F) Continue usual activities when sick
(A) Tell others when don't feel well	.08	−.01	.02	−.04	.07	−.05
(B) Not afraid to do things where could get hurt	−.08	.20*	.07	.10	.03	.10
(C) Dislike going to see a doctor	.03	−.05	.09	−.09	−.02	−.00
(D) Hide feelings when injured	−.02	.15*	−.00	−.02	−.04	−.06
(E) Get sick easily	.06	−.06	−.01	−.03	.15*	−.04
(F) Don't pay much attention to pain	−.18*	.15*	.03	.20*	.05	.16*

Source: Adapted from Mechanic, D. The stability of health and illness behavior: Results from a 16-year follow-up. *American Journal of Public Health*, 1979, **69**, 1142–1145.
N = 302.
* $p < .05$.

measures of behavior are averaged over an increasing number of events, the resulting stability coefficients for such behavior increase to high levels for all kinds of data, including objective behavior, self-ratings, and ratings by others, and that objective behavior can then be reliably related to such self-report measures, including standard personality inventories. Epstein's observation that it is normally not possible to predict single instances of behavior but, as also was shown in Figure 1.6, from the work of Belloc and Breslow, that it is possible to predict behavior averaged over a sample of situations and occasions, has important implications for study—not only for the risk factors of interest to us here but, as Epstein suggests, for behavioral research in general. Fortunately, Mechanic was aware of the findings in the types of research reviewed by Epstein, and, in time, Mechanic integrated some of his measures to yield a more robust and heuristically more predictive measure of health and risk status, rather than relying only on a single item dealing with health status.

Even viewed singly and in isolation, however, the items studied by Mechanic over a 16-year period and presented in Table 1.2 do provide useful information. Regarding the capacity of one health response to predict another health response 16 years later, the single item that yielded the greatest predictability was the youngsters' 1961 response to "don't pay much attention to pain." As shown in the last row of Table 1.2, that 1961 item is correlated with four of the six health responses assessed in 1977. These 1977 items and predictive correlations from this single 1961 item were (a) "tell close friends when I don't feel well" ($r = -.18$), (b) "take risks of injury" ($r = .15$), (c) "deny pain" ($r = .20$), and (d) "continue usual activities when sick" ($r = .16$). It is interesting that, as shown in the diagonal, items dealing with communicating (telling) their illness to others ($r = .08$) and disliking and experiencing discomfort in seeing doctors ($r = .09$) showed little stability over time between childhood and adulthood.

The questions used by Mechanic in the 1977 reexamination of his sample were not restricted to those reported here in Table 2 but included, in addition, queries relevant to 10 types of health and illness risk behaviors appropriate to an adult-aged sample of respondents. Included in 1977 were questions related to such risk factors as seat belt use, smoking, general risk taking, exercise, drinking, and related lifestyle factors. Answers to these 10 questions, intercorrelated by Mechanic in a search for commonalities, yielded the matrix shown in Table 1.3.

Table 1.3 Intercorrelations Among the Dependent Measures of Self-Reported Health and Illness Behaviors and Attitudes Reflected in the 1977 Study of the Adulthood Sample

	(2)	(3)	(4)	(5)	(6)	(7)	(8)	(9)	(10)
(1) Seat belt use	−.23*	−.07	.13*	.07	.02	.17*	−.09	.22*	.12*
(2) Smoke		.09	−.20*	−.10	.00	−.12*	.27*	−.26*	−.08
(3) Take risk			.08	.18*	.05	−.16*	.26*	.01	.09
(4) Exercise				.43*	−.05	.05	−.04	.21*	.27*
(5) Enjoy physical activity					−.03	.16*	.00	−.31*	.28*
(6) Release						.07	.05	−.17*	−.03
(7) Preventive health care							−.12*	.18*	.02
(8) Drinking behavior								−.04	−.09
(9) Perception of physical health									.28*
(10) Personal control over illness (I-E Health)									

Source: Adapted from Mechanic, D. The stability of health and illness behavior: Results from a 16-year follow-up. *American Journal of Public Health*, 1979, **69**, 1142–1145.
* $p < .05$.

As evidence that beauty is in the eyes of the beholder—and no doubt also reflecting my background in clinical psychology, with its long history of research (some reviewed by Epstein, 1979) that yields low-order correlations—I find both the number (22) and the magnitudes of statistically significant correlations in Table 1.3 impressive. However, reflecting his own experiences in health-related research, the conclusion drawn by Mechanic (1979) from the table is that the 10 varying dimensions of health and illness behavior tend to be only modestly correlated. In fact, Mechanic points out that no single dimension or small number of dimensions is related to the concept of individual responsibility for one's own overall health. He then addresses specific findings in the table, such as seat belt use (item 1) being substantially related to only two other risk factors—yielding an r of $-.23$ with smoking (item 2) and an r of .22 with a positive current perception of physical health (item 9). Mechanic also points out that the table shows that, besides correlating (negatively) with seat belt use, smoking also correlates with drinking ($r = .27$), the exercise of less preventive medical care ($r = -.12$), and a poorer perception of physical health ($r = -.26$).

Table 1.3 also reveals that persons who reported taking risks also reported enjoying physical activity ($r = .18$), drinking more ($r = .26$), and being less likely to engage in preventive medical care ($r = -.16$). Individuals who exercised more also reported enjoying physical activity ($r = .43$), having a high sense of personal control over illness ($r = .27$), having a positive view of their physical health ($r = .21$), being more likely to wear a seat belt ($r = .13$), and being less likely to smoke ($r = -.20$). Respondents who enjoyed physical activity also perceived their physical health as less negative ($r = -.31$), had a high sense of personal control over illness ($r = .28$), and engaged in preventive medical care ($r = .16$). Preventive health care, in turn, is related to a positive perception of physical health ($r = .18$) and less drinking ($r = -.12$). Additionally, Mechanic found that releasing oneself from activities when ill is related to a poorer perception of physical health ($r = -.17$), which, in turn, is related to a low sense of personal control over potential illness ($r = .28$).

I agree with Mechanic that these statistically significant findings are modest correlations and, thus, that they suggest that the 10 health and illness risk behaviors enumerated in Table 1.3 are not governed in each individual by a single complex of attitudes and responses related to health maintenance or promotion (or their lack). Nevertheless, given our relative ignorance in matters of lifestyle, the number of significant correlations in the table and the fidelity with which they match the expected direction of correlation impress me in terms of their potential to increase our knowledge of the factors associated with promotion of good health (or its lack). By themselves, the results obtained by Mechanic and reproduced here in Tables 1.2 and 1.3 might not be impressive. They assume more potential importance, however, when they are considered in the context of Belloc's related findings on similar risk factors (shown in Figure 1.6) and Epstein's literature review, which indicates that averages of single items over an increasing number of events will yield findings that are more stable and predictive than those from the components studied individually.

Mechanic's findings have led him to a search for just such a general orientation to health and wellness in his sample of 1961 (and 1977) respondents; his additional analyses of these survey responses provided him with heuristically interesting hypotheses. Mechanic and Cleary (1980) combined eight of the individual variables shown in Table 1.3 into a single index of degree of positive health behavior for each individual. Analysis of this person-specific risk index revealed such interesting findings as that the women in Mechanic's 1977 sample had a more positive index of health (were at less risk) than the men did, as assessed by a higher level of drinking and risk taking and a lower level of preventive medical behavior among men. It was also clear that some men are at little or no risk. Thus, those men who earned relatively higher scores for positive health behaviors reflected—to a larger degree than was true for similarly indexed women in this same sample—higher scores associated with three risk factors: physical activity, exercise, and less drinking. Several further analyses led Mechanic and Cleary to the conclusion that an adult's positive health behavior is a complex measure of lifestyle that reflects each individual's ability to anticipate potential problems related to health, to mobilize to meet them, and to cope actively.

Thus, although these findings by Mechanic and his associates indicate only correlations of modest to moderate strengths, they are, in my opinion, evidence that behavioral scientists are increasing our knowledge of risk factors in health and illness in important ways. In fact, as suggested by Epstein's (1979) literature review, the research programs of Mechanic and of Breslow and Belloc and their associates are moving in the direction that personality researchers also have found to have the highest potential for payoff. Indeed, research that studies behavioral and biomedical indices concurrently in the same individual is validating the insight achieved by Socrates (Kass, 1975) 24 centuries ago—that personality and lifestyle variables, on the one hand, and indices of physical health, on the other, are intimately correlated (see Breslow & Enstrom, 1980; Carmody, Matarazzo, Fey, & Connor, 1983).

RESPONSIBILITY FOR ONE'S HEALTH

Although health maintenance also is the responsibility of the state, as through appropriate legislation enforcing immunization against infectious diseases, outlawing pollution of the environment, prohibiting speeding on the highways, or controlling the sale of tobacco and mind-altering substances, the focus in this chapter is the role of individual behavior in health. As may be discerned so far, the studies published by Mechanic, Breslow, and other recent researchers in the health field have brought into prominence the issue of one's personal responsibility for health and illness and the costs that they extract both from the individual and from society. It is clear from examining the 10 major causes of death in the United States today (see Table 1.1) that, in the view of the biomedical and behavioral scientists who contributed to the Surgeon General's 1979 report, *Healthy People* (Califano, 1979a), lifestyle and related individual behavior is a strong if not the major etiologic factor in 7 of these 10 causes of death among Americans. Documentation of this changing pattern in the causes of morbidity and mortality was associated during the 1970s with the plea from many quarters that health was no longer an issue that could be left entirely in the hands of each individual.

In fact, as depicted in Figure 1.7, from information published by Gibson and Waldo (1981) and updated by more recent figures compiled by Waldo (1982), the cost of providing health care for Americans is currently consuming a full 10% of our country's gross national product; that is, the United States is now spending on the health care of its citizens 10 out of every 100 dollars of goods and services it produces annually. In 1981, these health

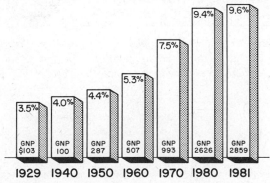

Figure 1.7 The percentage of the gross national product (GNP), expressed in billions of dollars, spent annually on total health care in the United States.

expenditures totaled almost $300 billion of a gross national product of approximately $3,000 billion. Conversely, in 1950 we spent only 4.4% of our gross national product of $286 billion, and in 1970 only 7.5% of that year's $993 billion GNP.

It is important that these spiraling costs of health care be put in proper perspective. First, the critics of these annually rising costs should remember that the concerns being voiced are not aimed at the defensibly high costs of surgical and medical care associated with new developments in biomedical science and technology. Rather, as I noted in a recent article (Matarazzo, 1982), a portion of the present high cost of health care in the United States has resulted because our citizens have opted to pay for coronary care and renal dialysis units, neonatal emergency care units, computerized axial tomography (CAT) scanners, and many other very costly diagnostic and critical-care life-support services. The criticisms presented in the Lalonde (1974) and Califano (1979a) reports to their respective nations, and by a host of biomedical and behavioral scientists concerned with the costs associated with health care, are not directed at such legitimate and, in the minds of most of us, defensible costs. Rather, the exhortation and criticism is directed at the inordinate and unnecessary costs associated with health conditions that arise from lifestyle and that are therefore preventable. The specific risk behaviors and practices that are preventable or changeable were identified in Table 1.1, along with the percentage of all deaths in which each such risk factor is implicated, either alone or collectively. Until the last several decades, with few notable exceptions, health care in the United States was paid for by the individual or his or her family. However, this direct payment mechanism changed with the advent of private health insurance, Medicare, Medicaid, and a host of private and public programs under which hospital and health services were paid by third-party payers. One result of these changes, among many, is that the expenses for health care are now more than ever before a collective, societal burden, rather than an expenditure paid for directly by the person receiving the service.

This being the case, and cognizant that this country's collective health expenditures consume 10 out of every 100 dollars of goods and services we produce in this country (which includes in its total 11 out of every 100 dollars Americans pay in federal taxes), it is not surprising that increasing numbers of influential members of the health care establishment have been speaking their minds on these issues. One critic, the physician and social philosopher Knowles (1977), was sufficiently disturbed by the fact that the larger society, rather than the individual, has to bear so much of the current costs of health care in the United States for the health conditions shown in Table 1.1 and Figure 1.2 that he wrote:

> Over 99 percent of us are born healthy and made sick as a result of personal misbehavior and environmental conditions. The solution to the problems of ill health in modern American society involves individual responsibility, in the first instance, and social responsibility through public legislative and private volunteer efforts, in the second instance. (p. 58)
>
> Most individuals do not worry about their health until they lose it. . . . I believe the idea of a "right" to health (guaranteed by government) should be replaced by the idea of an individual moral obligation to preserve one's own health—a public duty if you will. (p. 59)

Knowles then went on to discuss a number of specific changes in behavior (e.g., cutting out salt and high-cholesterol foods, getting adequate sleep, driving at the then recently mandated and less hazardous 55 mph, and so on) that each individual must make, personally, to cut the costs associated with each person's morbidity and mortality. Knowles clearly was aware of the research on risk factors that was accumulating in this country during the past two decades and he therefore also stressed, along with Breslow (1978a, 1978b) and others, that this nation's research priorities should be shifted immediately from biological to epidemiological, social, educational, environmental, and behavioral factors in health and illness. In 1979, the result in the United States of these and many related initiatives was *Healthy People: The Surgeon General's Report on Health Promotion and Disease Prevention*, which was crafted by Surgeon General Julius B. Richmond with the help of David Hamburg and the specialized personnel of the Institute of Medicine, National Academy of Science, and a host of other specialists to whom was made available the vast resource of statistical information gathered annually by the National Institutes of Health and many other data-gathering government agencies. The message to the nation in this 1979 report is underscored in two recent follow-up reports from the National Academy of Sciences—one published by its National Research Council (Adams, Smelser, & Treiman, 1982) and one published by its Institute of Medicine (Hamburg, Elliott, & Parron, 1982).

As will be discussed later, a similar initiative by the Surgeon General in 1964, directed at only one risk factor (smoking), achieved considerable success in reducing the projected costs of morbidity and mortality that public and private actuarial experts already had indicated would result from reduced smoking. The United States government acknowledged by publishing the 1964 report to the nation that, although smoking was a personal activity, its direct and indirect health-related costs extended beyond the individual smoker and were being borne collectively by the rest of American society. These increased expenses took the form of increased costs associated with premiums paid by individuals and by industry for health insurance, for industrial compensation to disabled workers, for unemployment benefits when a sick employee missed work, and so on. The result of that 1964 Surgeon General's report has been that 30 million Americans who formerly smoked have given up that habit following publication of the report. Furthermore, the percentage of new smokers taking up the habit has decreased for adult males and, although it showed an earlier upswing, recently is also on the downturn for adult females and boys and girls (Matarazzo, 1982).

What Knowles and other social critics have done was to extend this reasoning of unacceptable societal expenses beyond smoking to a number of additional risk factors. In the Foreword to the 1979 Surgeon General's report, which was sent to President Carter by then Secretary of Health, Education and Welfare Califano, there was no question of where the United States government stood on the issue of individual versus collective responsibility for the health of Americans. In the section immediately after the passages from his Foreword reproduced earlier in this chapter, Califano (1979a) continued with these explicit statements regarding the responsibility of each citizen:

> *This report underscores a point I have made countless times, again and again, in my thirty months as Secretary of Health, Education and Welfare: "You, the individual, can do more for your own health and well-being than any doctor, any hospital, any drug, any exotic medical device."*
>
> *Indeed, a wealth of scientific research reveals that the key to whether a person will be healthy or sick, live a long life or die prematurely, can be found in several simple personal habits: one's habits with regard to smoking and drinking; one's habits of diet, sleep and exercise; whether one obeys the speed laws and wears seat belts, and a few other simple measures.*
>
> *One study [see Figure 1.6 in this chapter] found that people who practiced seven of these simple habits lived, on the average, eleven years longer than those who practiced none of them.*
>
> *We can see certain signs that Americans are taking this message to heart: a growing national enthusiasm for exercise; signs that more and more people are having their blood pressures checked—fewer people, as a result, are dying from heart disease and stroke; and signs that cigarette smoking is declining, as more people recognize smoking for what it really is—slow-motion suicide.*
>
> *But we are a long way from the kind of national commitment to good personal health habits that will be necessary to change drastically the statistics about chronic disease in America.*

And meanwhile, indulgence in "private" excesses has results that are far from private.
Public expenditures for health care that consume eleven cents of every federal tax
dollar are only one of those results. . . .

There will be controversy—and there should be—about what role government should
play, if any, in urging citizens to give up their pleasurable but damaging habits. But
there can be no denying the public consequences of those private habits. (pp. viii–ix)

In the next section I will present more information on the prevalence of some of these
preventable medical conditions, on the levels of concern Americans voice about their health,
and on the degree of success individual Americans have had to date in giving up the
"pleasurable but damaging habits" to which our several Secretaries of Health, Education
and Welfare, as well as other influential government and nongovernment spokespersons,
have been referring.

ATTAINABLE GOALS: REDUCTIONS IN HEART DISEASE AND CANCER

The data in Table 1.1 show that 7 out of every 10 Americans who die this year will die
of either heart disease and stroke (37.8% and 9.6%, respectively, for a total of 47.4%) or
of cancer in all its forms (20.4%). It also is clear from Figure 1.4 that deaths from lung
cancer are increasing in both males and females and, as shown in Figure 1.2, have more
than doubled as a percentage of all deaths since 1950. Furthermore, Figure 1.2 also shows
that whereas deaths from heart disease and stroke have begun to decline during the same
period, their annual rates still outnumber deaths from every other cause. The additional
data presented here in Figures 1.8, 1.9, and 1.10 show that among healthy Americans,
the risks associated with the prevalence of cardiovascular disease, hypertension, and the
presence of abnormally high levels of serum cholesterol (a) dramatically increase with advancing age and (b) differentially affect the sexes and also blacks and whites, with blacks more
at risk for hypertension and females more at risk for cardiovascular diseases associated
with abnormally elevated levels of serum cholesterol. These latter facts notwithstanding,

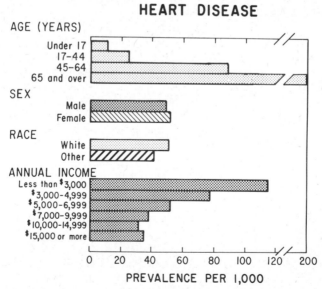

Figure 1.8 Heart disease incidence per 1,000 Americans, 1972. (Adapted from Lunde, A. S. Health
in the United States. *Annals of the American Academy of Political and Social Science,* 1981, **453,** 28–
69.)

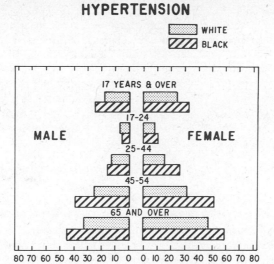

Figure 1.9 Hypertension in white and black Americans aged 17 to over 65. (Adapted fron Lunde, A. S. Health in the United States. *Annals of the American Academy of Political and Social Science,* 1981, **453,** 28–69.)

Figures 1.8, 1.9, and 1.10 reveal that the associated lifestyle risks for morbidity and mortality for these conditions are insidious over the life span, remaining "silent" in many of us into middle age (see, especially, the findings reported by Carmody, Matarazzo, Fey, & Connor, 1982). It is this fact—that the symptoms of developing heart disease and cancer often are not diagnosed until many years after a risky habit (e.g., smoking or improper diet) is begun—that has made the elimination or reduction of risk factors such a slow process. That 30 million Americans, with apparently relative ease for the majority of them (Matarazzo, 1982; Schachter, 1982), have successfully quit smoking since the 1964 Surgeon General's report leaves no doubt, however, that Americans will modify their health behavior if enough resources are put into the task of raising the level of consciousness of our total society about the risks involved. Until the last two decades, prevention of disease was

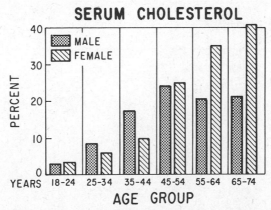

Figure 1.10 Serum cholesterol levels of 260/mg/100 ml and over in American males and females aged 18–74. (Adapted from Lunde, A. S. Health in the United States. *Annals of the American Academy of Political and Social Science,* 1981, **453,** 28–69.)

mainly a passive, one-shot affair (immunization) for many Americans. Prevention consisted mostly of acquiescing to the demands of our local public health departments and our schools that each child entering kindergarten present evidence of immunization against measles, polio, and a few other contagious diseases. From then on into adulthood, the only contact the majority of us had with measures to raise our level of consciousness about health and illness was by passive exposure to a few typically tepid lectures on hygiene, diet, and venereal disease usually given by a not very happy physical education teacher. As I will review in the next section, a dramatic change appears to have taken place during the past decade, as concepts of lifestyle, physical fitness, nutrition, and overall wellness have become part of the thinking and lifespace of increasing numbers of Americans.

AMERICANS' CHANGING ATTITUDES TOWARD HEALTH

Evidence of this increasing interest in issues of prevention is presented in the latest U.S. Surgeon General's report, *Health United States 1980,* forwarded by Secretary Patricia Harris to our president and Congress (Harris, 1981). Among considerable other data it includes two excellent sections (pp. 291–323) devoted to issues in prevention, which I will summarize here. The authors review a national poll, conducted by Louis Harris (1978), which revealed that today almost 50% of Americans describe themselves as much more concerned about preventive health than they were a few years ago. Among the general public 42% responded in that manner, whereas among top executives in industry and labor (two groups with considerable potential for influence) some 75% stated that preventive health is more important to them now than previously. Some 85% of these leaders in industry and labor stated further that our health system should give more emphasis to preventive and less to curative medicine. Apparently, these executives did not stop at merely voicing positive opinions. As evidenced in recently published descriptions of health promotion programs that have been initiated in companies ranging alphabetically from the American Telephone and Telegraph Company to the Xerox Corporation (Parkinson and Associates, 1982), in a mere four years these executives actually have installed well-crafted health promotion programs in many of this country's largest companies.

Furthermore, the 1978 Harris poll revealed that the diseases and conditions Americans fear the most today are cancer, heart disease, and accidents. In a concurrent survey published by Yankelovich, Skelly, and White (1979) Americans polled were shown a list of 30 possible health threats; they identified the extent of their fear (from most to least) of each of the greatest threats as follows:

Potential Threat	Percentage with This Fear
Industrial waste	59
Pollution	58
Marijuana	58
Cigarettes	55
Crash diets	55
Diet pills	52
Overweight	52
Pesticides	47
Tranquilizers	43
Cholesterol	42
Liquor	41
Nuclear power plants	40

It is of interest to our discussion here that, whereas the major risk factors to the health of Americans shown in Table 1.1 are included in the foregoing list of 12 subjectively felt threats, the perceptions of relative threat from industrial waste down to nuclear power plants are not completely in accord with the best scientific evidence of the reality of each threat, as was summarized in Table 1.1.

Yankelovitch et al. (1979) also sampled American adults' major fears by asking their respondents what specific health habits each would like to carry out in order to promote, by personal example, the good health of the other members of his or her own family. The responses were as follows:

Good Health Habit	Percentage Perceiving as Important
Stop smoking	29
Exercise regularly	19
Stay calm, not lose temper	18
Lose weight	15
Cut back on sweets	13
Eat more balanced diets	12
Go for physical checkups	9
Not put off going to doctor	9
Be more cheerful	9

Contrary to demonstrated evidence that some 50,000 Americans die on the highway annually, but consistent with research on seat belt usage showing that few Americans actually use seat belts (Jonah et al., 1982), this 1979 national survey revealed (by the absence of a seat belt item in the list) that Americans do not perceive the use of seat belts while driving to be one of their own important health habits.

Another finding from the Yankelovitch et al. poll was significant, however, for the information it reveals about how many Americans agree with Califano (1979a), Knowles (1977), and others that promoting health is each individual's own responsibility. This very gratifying finding was that about 60% of the adult family members polled believed that being healthy requires that the individual work at it and actively, rather than passively, take a preventive approach to health care. The reliability of this finding also is clear from other survey data compiled and published by the Division of Analysis, National Survey of Personal Health Practices and Health Consequences (Harris, 1981), as a means of annual follow-up to the initiatives launched by the 1979 Surgeon General's report (*Healthy People*). Figure 1.11 presents the responses to one of the questions asked a sample of Americans by their government during 1979. The question was: "How much control do you think you have over your future health?" The results reveal that slightly over 50% of American adults feel they have "a great deal of control" over their future health and another 30% to 40% believe they have "some control." Only 1 in 10 Americans is fatalistic and believes that he or she has no control over his or her future health status.

The answer to another question in that recent poll is consistent with this gratifying evidence of almost universal belief in the ability of American adults to exercise control over their own future health. Specifically, 92% of them agreed with the statement: "If we Americans ate more nutritious food, smoked less, maintained our proper weight, and exercised regularly, it would do more to improve our health than anything doctors and medicine can do for us." This finding suggests that Americans have a global awareness of the risk

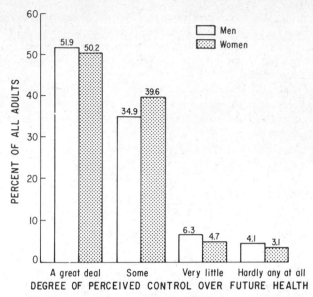

Figure 1.11 Responses of American adults aged 20–64 to a question about how much individual control they felt they had over their future health. (Adapted from Harris, P. R. *Health United States 1980.* U.S. Department of Health and Human Services Pub. No. (PHS)81–1232. Washington, D.C.: U.S. Government Printing Office, 1981.)

factors associated with their health, as listed in Table 1.1, although it is likely that only a very small number of our citizens are aware of the specific relative values of each of these risks, as documented in the various figures presented in this chapter.

Accumulating evidence suggests that, despite the popularity of smoking and obesity control clinics, most Americans do try to change their lifestyles on their own (and in fact succeed) without going to commercial firms for help (Matarazzo, 1982; Schachter, 1982). Fortunately, health education and health promotion programs and sources of information are increasing in number. In a nine-city survey conducted during 1977–1978 by the American Hospital Association (1978), a large number of urban Americans stated that they are interested in health information and health education programs. Nevertheless, a total of 62% of these respondents were unaware of the existence of such educational and informational programs in their city. Of the 38% who were aware of at least one such program, however, close to half reported they had participated in it. The programs mentioned most often were cardiopulmonary resuscitation (9% of the respondents) and first aid (6%). Of the respondents who knew about the existence of a health education program, their stated sources for that information were as follows: from the media (42%); from a friend or relative (16%); and from a personal physician (6%). When asked what types of educational and information programs would be of most interest to them, these urban Americans identified stress reduction and home accidents as the risk factors they most wished to learn about. The many programs in industrial firms described by Parkinson and Associates (1982) suggest that many more Americans will soon become aware of health promotion programs through their availability at the worksite, where many of us spend a third of each working day (Matarazzo, 1980, p. 814).

Of equal importance to our concerns in this discussion is the finding in the Yankelovich et al. (1979) survey that 46% of American adults reported having recently changed their lifestyle and that of their families in order to promote better health. In addition, a gratifying 70% of adults responded that following a good health routine is easy, inasmuch as "it just requires willingness and determination." Fortunately, in terms of both preventing illness and disability and promoting behavioral health, only the remaining 30% reported that "it takes too much dedication and discipline." It is interesting that, despite the pessimism expressed by this 30%, virtually all (between 95% and 98%) of 2,200 American respondents over the age of 30 queried by Flanagan (1978) in a study on the quality of life reported their desire "to be physically fit and vigorous, to be free from anxiety and distress, and to avoid bodily harm." The highly creative approaches currently being used by growing numbers of behavioral scientists who are developing quantitative indices for assessing the quality of life as perceived and reported by young and older American citizens hold considerable promise for improving the health and well-being of our citizens. Prototypes of such quantitative approaches have been described by Andrews and McKennell (1980), Flanagan (1982), Hunt and McEwen (1980), and Kaplan and Bush (1982).

The report of the Surgeon General forwarded to our nation by Califano (1979a) provided a blueprint for a 10-year health promotion program, detailing how Americans may achieve better individual and collective health by 1990. The statistics gathered concurrently by our government and by the private polls reviewed here provide clear proof that Americans today recognize more than ever before that smoking, excess weight, risky driving, stress, alcohol abuse, and lack of physical exercise are clear and potent threats to their health and that of their families and that these threats are ones that individuals can *control.* We next shall examine the extent to which this knowledge about these risks has led to a change in behavior of Americans.

RECENT CHANGES IN THE LIFESTYLE OF AMERICANS

The data that were reviewed in another section of the Surgeon General's report on the present status of health in the United States (Harris, 1981) are likely to be a pleasant surprise for many health professionals. These 1980 data showed that large numbers of Americans already appear to be eliminating, reducing, or otherwise changing for the better those lifestyle behaviors that constitute a risk factor in their own morbidity and mortality. The data, compiled from a wide variety of sources by the Division of Analysis, National Center for Statistics, are summarized in Figure 1.12.

As shown in the figure, between 1965 and 1979 there were large reductions in the United States in the percentage of current smokers among adult males (−28%), adult females (−13%), and teenage boys (−2%). Unfortunately, during the same period, possibly because of the skillfully crafted subliminal messages aimed directly at them (e.g., the advertising for Virginia Slims cigarettes—"You've Come a Long Way, Baby"), there was a corresponding large increase (+51%) in the percentage of teenage girls who were smoking. Such an alarming increase, in the presence of concurrent decreases among male and female adults and teenage boys, did not go unnoticed; although largely uncoordinated, a number of educational programs aimed at young girls were initiated by health groups of various types. Fortunately, as reviewed elsewhere (Matarazzo, 1982), more recent American Cancer Society data suggest a very positive new trend. Whereas smoking among girls increased from 1964 to 1974 (from 8.4% to 15.8%), the percentage of teenage girls smoking in the most recent American Cancer Society survey (*Sunday Oregonian,* 1981) showed a decrease back to 12.7%. Although this 1979 statistic shows a 51% increase over the 1968 figure (8.4%), it masks the important drop from 15.8% to 12.7% that occurred among teenage girl smokers between 1974 and 1978. In sum, then, the smoking data in Figure 1.12 indicate that smoking is a risk factor that Americans are reducing. In fact, as reported earlier in this chapter, 30 million American former smokers have quit smoking, and, based on the most recent surveys, the number of new smokers in all age groups continues on the downturn in both sexes and in all age groups. The reader interested in a more detailed analysis of the impact of the 1964 Surgeon General's report to the nation on this decline of cigarette use in the United States will find it in Remington (1980).

The summary statistics shown in Figure 1.12 are equally encouraging with regard to

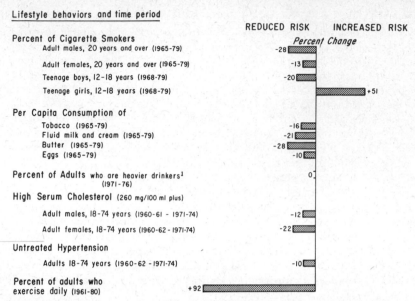

Figure 1.12 Recent changes in lifestyle behaviors that affect health. (Adapted from Harris, P. R. *Health United States 1980.* U.S. Department of Health and Human Services Pub. No. (PHS)81–1232. Washington, D.C.: U.S. Government Printing Office, 1981.)

most of the other risk factors discussed throughout this chapter. Americans have reduced their per capita consumption of fluid milk and cream (−21%), butter (−28%), eggs (−10%), and serum cholesterol (−12% for adult males and −22% for adult females). Furthermore, undoubtedly as a result of large-scale educational campaigns, fewer Americans with hypertension are going untreated (−10%). Finally—which will come as no surprise to anyone who drives or walks along our country's streets and parkways, which today are full of joggers, walkers, and bicyclists—between 1961 and 1980 a striking increase (92%) occurred in the proportion of Americans who exercise daily. I was unable to find the actual baseline figures on which this 92% increase was calculated—and it is important to record whether such an increase occurred, for example, from a baseline figure of only 10% who were exercising in 1961 or from a baseline of 30%—but the 92% increase is impressive nevertheless.

As discussed earlier in this chapter, in the 1979 Surgeon General's report (Califano, 1979a), the statement was made that of the 10 leading causes of death in the United States (see Table 1.1), "at least seven could be substantially reduced if persons at risk improved just five habits: diet, smoking, lack of exercise, alcohol abuse, and use of antihypertensive medication" (p. 14). Although, as just pointed out, the data summarized in Figure 1.12 represent only percentage change and thus do not indicate the actual base level figures of total Americans upon which each individual change is based, these relative change values still constitute robust evidence that Americans are changing. Furthermore, they are changing four of the five lifestyle behaviors that are causes of 7 of the 10 major killers of Americans. The four behavioral risk factors whose percentage incidence is decreasing are diet, smoking, lack of exercise, and use of hypertensive medication. Only the fifth important behavioral risk factor, alcohol abuse, has shown no change (see Figure 1.12). In regard to the decreases in the numbers of persons with untreated hypertension shown in Figure 1.12, it is important to note that the recently published results of the 10-year nationwide Multiple Risk Factor Intervention Trial (MRFIT) study contain very strong suggestive evidence that some of the newer drug treatments (diuretics) for hypertension produced a totally unexpected higher level of mortality compared to the mortality level found in the control group of patients, who continued to receive the standard health care in the community for hypertension (Kolata, 1982; MRFIT Research Group, 1982).

Admittedly, the data summarized in Figure 1.12, though impressive, are far from conclusive. Nevertheless, they present a more optimistic picture than was available a short decade ago. In addition, they are consistent with attitudes clearly expressed by adult Americans, reviewed in the last section, that our citizens (a) desire good health, (b) are to a surprising degree aware of the behaviors they must adopt or change to achieve this desired good health, and (c) as shown in Figure 1.11, are fully aware that it is they—along with health care providers, government, or others—who have a primary responsibility and control over their own good health or its lack. This being the case, we turn next to a consideration of some additional issues that are germane to the challenges that such newly appearing changes in the attitudes and lifestyles of Americans pose for behavioral and biomedical scientists working in the field of health promotion and disease prevention.

SALUTOGENESIS

A refreshingly lucid and well-written book by another medical sociologist (Antonovsky, 1979) is both provocative and timely. The book is unique in that, as one of its central themes, it concentrates not on the minority but on the majority of living persons (those who are healthy instead of ill at any given time) and asks why it is that so many of us remain healthy despite the presence of disease-producing pathogens in our bodies, in our feelings, and in our environment. In his analysis of this provocative question Antonovsky saw fit to coin a new word, *salutogenesis,* the entymological roots of which are the origins (*genesis*) of health (*saluto*). Instead of focusing on the numbers of persons per 100,000 population who die or are ill from each of several diseases, as I did in my earlier discussion of Figures 1.2, 1.3, and 1.4, for example, Antonovsky suggests we reverse our procedure and focus on the persons in that 100,000 who did not die or who are not ill or disabled. Antonovsky (1979, p. 37) writes: "Pathogenesis asks, Why does this person enter this particular state of pathology? (or the epidemiological equivalent of this question). Contrariwise salutogenesis asks, What are the factors pushing this person toward this end (pathology) or toward that end (health) of the continuum?"

Having posed these questions, Antonovsky's analysis next takes him on a long odyssey during which he evaluates society's definitions of and attitudes toward health and illness and the all-too-limited attention paid to date by biomedical and behavioral scientists, health educators, health providers, and society at large to the fundamental question that he believes is heuristically more important than most others: how people initially attain health, maintain it when they achieve it, and then institute steps to promote it throughout their lifetimes. Antonovsky's concern is with "dis-ease" in its various psychological and physical manifestations, not with "disease." He acknowledges the role of "life stressors" of the type studied by Holmes and Rahe (see Rahe & Gunderson, 1974) and others who have used the elegantly simple scale devised by Holmes and Rahe for quantifying such stress by use of "life change units." Antonovsky's focus, however, is on the standard deviations revealed by individual illness, not on the statistical mean (central tendency of a group of individuals) that comes out of such research. Specifically, he is concerned with the individual differences that occur such that among a number of persons experiencing equal units of life stress, one becomes ill and the other does not. After a detailed analysis of this empirical observation, Antonovsky concludes that persons who have a strong, well-ingrained sense of coherence in their lives are less apt to succumb to microbiological and psychological pathogens (stressors) than are those individuals who are under equal life stress but whose lifespace has less coherence. Before arriving at this conclusion, Antonovsky reviews an extensive literature from such diverse fields as sociology, cultural anthropology, child rearing, stress research, and behavioral medicine, to mention only a few. Although his view of a person's sense of coherence superficially resembles what others call the individual's locus of control (i.e., whether the individual or others control that individual's health status), Antonovsky (1979) means more than this by coherence. He states that a sense of coherence is "a crucial element in the basic personality structure of an individual" (p. 124). Furthermore, coherence reflects "a global orientation that expresses the extent to which one has a pervasive, enduring though dynamic feeling of confidence that one's internal and external environments are predictable and that there is a high probability that things will work out as well as can reasonably be expected" (p. 123). As but one example, Antonovsky integrates into his concept the findings of Holmes and Rahe by stating that "a radical change in one's structural situation—in marital status, occupation, place of residence—can lead to a significant modification in one's sense of coherence" (p. 125).

For purposes of this chapter, I am less concerned with Antonovsky's creative ideas about the genesis and maintenance of health than I am in the fact that he so forthrightly has captured and refocused our attention on healthy people rather than on those of us who are ill or dying. His book is thus part of today's dynamically changing zeitgeist in the health field—a changing climate that has as one of its important catalysts and elements the call by individuals at the highest levels of government in the United States and in Canada (Califano, 1979a; Lalonde, 1974) for a similar reordering of our priorities away from concern with the sources of morbidity and toward better exploitation and utilization of the sources of health.

Although Antonovsky coined the word *salutogenesis,* a term I find particularly attractive, whether one wishes to refer to the national goal toward which the zeitgeist seems to be taking us by his term, by *healthy people,* by a term such as *behavioral health* (on which I will expand later), or by any other term is relatively unimportant. My reading of today's climate (Matarazzo, 1980, 1982), especially as it is influenced by developments in medicine, in the behavioral sciences, in the sources of funds for research, teaching, and service delivery, and in the actual behavior of our citizens—as summarized here in Figure 1.12—is that the goal of keeping healthy people healthy is now a very pervasive one, with many adherents.

THE PROCESS: LIFESTYLE CHANGE

If salutogenesis (or behavioral health) is considered an appropriate individual and collective goal, it is then necessary to ask by what process or processes individuals might attain this goal. The earlier sections of this chapter, as well as the summary statistics in Figure 1.12, should leave no question that leaders from many quarters in the biomedical and behavioral sciences and leaders in the public and private sectors of our society appear to agree that origins of health for each individual are to be found in the lifestyle behaviors of each individual. The accumulating evidence is eloquent in its suggestion that the next frontiers to be mastered in health care lie at the interfaces of biology and behavior. Therefore, if we are to prevent morbidity and mortality and concurrently promote and maintain health in and for each citizen, the task will begin by helping our currently healthy children and their currently healthy parents (the majority of our citizens) in (a) not initiating the previously discussed behaviors that are antithetical to good health or (b), if already initiated, terminating them.

The data in Figure 1.11 clearly indicate that our citizens have a strong belief that, in matters of personal health, each person is the captain of his or her own ship and thus has control over its future course. Furthermore, the data in Figure 1.12 indicate that four of the five lifestyle behaviors cited by the Surgeon General as needing change are, in fact, being changed. Smoking is going down, our diets are being changed in ways that research suggests are more prudent, larger percentages of us are being treated for existing hypertension, and, finally, a larger percentage of us exercise daily. In my opinion, evidence for the means and processes by which each of us may strive individually to attain better health is now everywhere around us.

Because such lifestyle change may be accelerated by a bit more structure, our government sought the counsel of leaders from many areas of the biomedical and behavioral communities. As discussed earlier, this counsel helped produce three interrelated publications under the leadership of Surgeon General Julius B. Richmond, which were submitted to the president, Congress, and the nation by HEW Secretary Califano (1979a, 1979b) and his successor, HHS Secretary Harris (1980, 1981). These publications constitute a national "map," consisting of 15 specific goals we, as citizens of this nation, should strive to meet by 1990. These goals (Harris, 1980) are listed in Table 1.4. Each of these 15 goals has been translated into attainable targets in terms of specific numbers of us for whom this threat will no longer be salient in 1990 if we begin to change our lifestyle behavior. For example, such clearly stated targets as the following are included in the specific objectives to be obtained by 1990 or earlier in the single area of high blood pressure control:

a. By 1990, at least 60 percent of the estimated population having definite high blood pressure (160/95) should have attained successful long term blood pressure control, i.e., a blood pressure at or below 140/90 for two or more years. . . .

b. By 1990, the average daily sodium ingestion (as measured by excretion) for adults should be reduced at least to the 3 to 6 gram range. (In 1979, estimates ranged between averages of 4 to 10 grams sodium. One gram salt provides approximately .4 grams sodium.)

c. By 1990, the prevalence of significant overweight (120 percent of "desired" weight) among the U.S. adult population should be decreased by 10 percent of men and 17 percent of women, without nutritional impairment (from the 1974 levels of 14 and 24 percent, respectively). (Harris, 1980, p. 7)

The government volumes constitute a remarkable national commitment and represent, for the biobehavioral sciences, a set of challenges not unlike those undertaken earlier in this century to eradicate infectious diseases by the disciplines of microbiology, immunology, and public health. Fortunately, the current U.S. Secretary of Health and Human Services (Schweiker, 1982) also has committed himself to achievement of the same 1990 goals to which his predecessors challenged us as a nation.

Table 1.4   Fifteen Specific, Measurable Objectives for Producing Better Health for Americans by 1990

A. *Preventive Health Services*
  1. Control of high blood pressure
  2. Family planning
  3. Pregnancy and infant health
  4. Immunization
  5. Sexually transmitted diseases
B. *Health Protection*
  6. Control of toxic agents
  7. Occupational safety and health
  8. Accident prevention and injury control
  9. Fluoridation and dental health
  10. Surveillance and control of infectious diseases
C. *Health Promotion*
  11. Smoking and health
  12. Misuse of alcohol and drugs
  13. Nutrition
  14. Physical fitness and exercise
  15. Control of stress and violent behavior

The baseline data (1970–1980) on which these 1990 targets were based are admittedly far from adequate in every instance. Nevertheless, as a people we must begin somewhere, and the data currently available provide the best base possible. Few of us believed in 1964 that we could reduce as much as we have a habit as well ingrained and overlearned as smoking. Yet, as I have stated several times, 30 million Americans have succeeded in giving up this habit. In a review of the literature on smoking two decades ago, Matarazzo and Saslow (1960, pp. 506–507) pointed out that, although the figure was not known with certainty, the best of the studies they reviewed placed the number of American men who already had successfully quit smoking at just under 20% of those polled in a national sample of Americans. Impressive as that percentage was, the publication of the Surgeon General's 1964 report—targeted specifically at smoking as a risk factor—clearly increased the numbers of us who have succeeded in giving up smoking. As shown in Figure 1.12, even in the absence of equally well-coordinated and well-targeted campaigns against untreated hypertension and the other risk factors shown, Americans clearly are making significant progress on their own toward reducing their health risks through a number of equally important lifestyle behavioral changes. The data summarized here in Table 1.1 and Figures 1.2 through 1.10 suggest, however, that more needs to be done.

BEHAVIORAL HEALTH: A MOTIVATIONALLY SALIENT RUBRIC FOR HEALTH PROMOTION AND LIFESTYLE CHANGE

As indicated earlier, my acquaintance with the various changes in the zeitgeist in our society that have been described so far in this chapter recently led me to suggest a new term, *behavioral health,* in an effort to provide a bit of additional emphasis to these highly gratifying changes already in process toward the goal of better health. In particular, as discussed in greater detail elsewhere (Matarazzo, 1980, 1982), I was impressed by the developments in many different quarters that recently gave birth to the exciting new field called *behavioral medicine.* Although defined variously by different writers, the following definition of behavioral medicine, agreed upon by a subset of representative biomedical and behavioral scientists who already were working in this field, is the one that seems to have attracted the most followers:

> Behavioral medicine *is the interdisciplinary field concerned with the development and integration of behavioral and biomedical science knowledge and techniques relevant to health and illness and the application of this knowledge and these techniques to prevention, diagnosis, treatment and rehabilitation. (Schwartz & Weiss, 1978a, 1978b).*

I was present at both gatherings where this definition of behavioral medicine was developed, and I believe that the mere fact of its publication has done much in a surprisingly short period to provide the needed structure, the organizing philosophy and force, to more effectively marshall under one umbrella the many disparate and uncoordinated developments (Matarazzo, 1980) in this field that were taking place concurrently in medicine and in the behavioral sciences. There is no doubt in my mind that this published definition has played a large part in inspiring the current vitality in research, in training, and in service delivery in this new interdisciplinary field.

However, the relatively large-scale community intervention project on the current American diet that my colleagues and I launched in 1976 with a cross section of currently healthy individual American homemakers and their families (Carmody, Matarazzo, Fey, & Connor, 1982; Matarazzo, Connor, Fey, Carmody, Pierce, Brischetto, Baker, Connor, & Sexton, 1982) left me with a growing feeling that this definition of behavioral medicine did not emphasize strongly enough the powerful and, in the long run, most cost-effective of its elements—namely, the maintenance of health and the prevention of illness and dysfunction. Therefore, in September 1979, in my presidential address to the membership of the newly formed Division of Health Psychology (Division 38) of the American Psychological Association, I took the opportunity to articulate my concern that workers in behavioral medicine should put as much, if not more, of their effort toward promoting good health and preventing illness as they already were directing toward treating Americans who already were ill or disabled. To add what I felt was the needed emphasis on this concern and to stimulate further discussion, I used that forum to introduce the term *behavioral health* to refer to these two areas (prevention and maintenance) in the definition of behavioral medicine, which I felt needed greater focus and emphasis. Furthermore, drawing on my acquaintance with some of the many uncoordinated activities that were then occurring in the field of health, and with the hope of stimulating needed dialogue among scientists, practitioners, and applied workers in the field, I suggested the following definition to my colleagues in health psychology, with the hope that, in time, others would improve upon it:

> Behavioral health *is an interdisciplinary field dedicated to promoting a philosophy of health that stresses* individual responsibility *in the application of behavioral and biomedical science knowledge and techniques to the maintenance of health and the* prevention *of illness and dysfunction by a variety of self-initiated individual or shared activities. (Matarazzo, 1980, p. 813)*

I was pleased, of course, that my use of this term coincided with (a) the publication of the Surgeon General's newest report, *Healthy People*, which Califano (1979a) transmitted to the nation, and (b) the publication of the book by Antonovsky (1979), introducing his concept of salutogenesis, with its emphasis on a greater need for an understanding of the dynamics of health rather than of pathology. These two publications, and hundreds of others, provided clear evidence that the zeitgeist in our country was turning from an emphasis on illness to a focus on health.

Inasmuch as I was not aware at the time of my address on behavioral health that *Healthy People* was being compiled and would soon be published, I articulated my hope in that talk, and in another one in Chicago a year later (Matarazzo, 1980, 1982), that the rubric *behavioral health* might serve as a catalyst for the National Institutes of Health and other federal and private institutions to take the necessary steps to rebudget some of their monies for research, training, and delivery of service into areas that emphasize health rather than illness. Fortunately, such steps already were under way and, most important, have recently been given a high priority by our current U.S. Secretary of Health and Human Services (Schweiker, 1982).

BEHAVIORAL HEALTH: VAST OPPORTUNITIES FOR PSYCHOLOGISTS

For workers in my own discipline, I also suggested that academic, scientific, and applied psychologists from all areas of our specialty already have within their ranks highly trained scientists and other specialists with the potential to do their part in mapping some of the important landmarks in this beckoning and relatively unexplored frontier—the health-maintaining, health-enhancing, and illness-preventing behaviors of currently healthy people. I suggested that, whereas this potential talent clearly is being applied already to the field of behavioral medicine, its potential is as great if not greater for the newer field of behavioral health—helping willing and currently healthy children and adults remain healthy (Matarazzo, 1982).

Prevention of Smoking

Since the Surgeon General's report listing the 15 specific goals for the nation (given here in Table 1.4) had not yet been published, and to help interested psychologists begin to apply their talent to the field of behavioral health, I suggested that, building on its 100 years of experience in the study of individual behavior, including behavior change, there were four risk factors to which interested representatives from every subfield of psychology could now make a substantial contribution. One of these four areas in which current research indicates risks could be reduced is the further refinement of existing educational programs for elementary school children to help immunize such youngsters against beginning to smoke. Although far from totally successful in preventing our nation's children from beginning a habit with the known risks shown here in Table 1.1 and Figures 1.4 through 1.9, the research on crafting educational programs for immunizing youngsters against smoking already appears to be succeeding. Some of the programs report a prevention success rate for up to 50% of the grammar school children receiving this active behavioral immunization. These grammar school programs have been carried out by a number of different research teams made up of behavioral and biomedical scientists working in several American and Canadian cities. The results have been published by Arkin, Roemhild, Johnson, Luepker, & Murray (1981); Botvin, Eng, & Williams (1980); Evans (1982); Evans & Raines (1982); Evans, Rozelle, Mittlemark, Hansen, Bane, & Havis (1978); Evans, Rozelle, Maxwell, Raines, Dill, Guthrie, Henderson, & Hill (1981); Flay, d'Avernas, Best, Kersell, & Ryan (1983); Green, Heit, Iverson, Kolbe, & Kreuter (1980); Hurd, Johnson, Pechacek, Bast, Jacobs, & Luepker (1980); McAlister, Perry, & Maccoby (1979); McAlister, Perry, Killen, Slinkard, & Maccoby (1980); Telch, Killen, McAlister, Perry, & Maccoby (1982); and Williams, Carter, Arnold, & Wynder (1979).

It is important to point out that helping children not to begin smoking not only will reduce their adult risk for morbidity and mortality from heart disease, lung cancer, and stroke, but additional recent research findings also suggest that when the girls among these children become adults, such knowledge will help reduce the risk of developmental disability in the fetuses of what then will be fewer women who smoke during pregnancy. This finding that the fetus of a mother who smokes during her pregnancy appears to be at a considerable risk for a wide variety of deformities and disabilities is gaining wide acceptance as more and more investigators are focusing on mothers who smoke during pregnancy (Christianson, 1980; Johnston, 1981). Although the research findings are far from clear-cut, a review of the accumulating literature (Cushner, 1981) strongly indicates that, compared to the pregnancy outcome of a nonsmoking mother, the fetus of a smoking mother is smaller in birthweight, shows a greater incidence of perinatal mortality, and, after birth, shows more learning and developmental retardation. Such evidence is much too strong to be ignored by a pregnant woman who wishes to maximize the chances of producing a healthy baby.

Preventing Risks Associated with Alcohol

A second area with a high cost in morbidity and mortality is alcohol abuse. Research during the past two decades has made it clear that alcohol is implicated in some 50% of the 50,000 automobile fatalities that occur in the United States annually. Furthermore, accumulating and more recent research evidence (Cushner, 1981; Streissguth, Landesman-Dwyer, Martin, & Smith, 1980; Wilson, 1981) strongly suggests that pregnant women who drink socially (two or three drinks per day) likewise put their unborn fetuses at future risk for a wide variety of very serious developmental disabilities associated with a newly defined disorder, fetal alcohol syndrome. These disabilities, which affect a number of body and cognitive systems, have been reproduced in animal models that very closely parallel the human findings (Sulik, Johnston, & Webb, 1981).

It is refreshing to realize in relation to alcohol abuse by teenagers and adults that, whereas two decades ago those of us who treated end-stage alcoholic patients typically met with little success, reports published from many different treatment centers indicate that the prospect of success for such treatment by a variety of different modalities is considerably better today. This no doubt reflects in great part the considerable effort, both in targeted monies and in person-power, invested in this challenge by the National Institute on Alcohol Abuse and Alcoholism. Today we are not only successfully treating more patients (adults) with alcoholism before it results in physical disability (see Neubuerger, Miller, Schmitz, Matarazzo, Pratt, & Hasha, 1982), but, in areas with considerable potential for primary prevention, social psychologists such as Jessor and Jessor (1982) also are beginning to better understand the individual psychological, psychosocial, and interpersonal developmental processes that play a significant role in children beginning to drink (or use marijuana or engage in other less than healthy behaviors). Still other psychologists and behavioral scientists are using this and other empirical and theoretical knowledge to craft programs or intervention strategies that are aimed at preventing alcohol abuse before it occurs in youth (Collins & Marlatt, 1981; Mills, Pfaffenberger, & McCarthy, 1981).

As reviewed earlier in this chapter, Antonovsky (1979) believes that each individual develops a "sense of coherence," which is intimately associated with potential changes in his or her health status as a result of coping with life's changing internal and external stresses. In addition, the research conducted by Mechanic and his associates (Mechanic & Cleary, 1980) likewise has led this group to a search for a potentially discernible index of each person's level of risk taking—namely, a personal philosophy or orientation to life, which is uniquely characteristic of each individual and which, for our purposes here, may have as one of its by-products a person-specific, moderately pervasive orientation to health and wellness that may help provide a sense of direction for the individual in regard to positive (or risky) health behavior. This orienting individualized perspective, or set, helps determine how the individual will react to both old and novel situations that constantly present themselves. Approaching the same problem from an entirely different theoretical orientation, and based on the results of a study of a large sample of preadolescents and another sample of college students followed prospectively over 12 years of transition into young adulthood, Jessor and Jessor (1977, 1982) concluded that one element of this person-specific orientation toward healthy versus nonhealthy lifestyle behavior that we each develop during adolescence involves a personality dimension they call *conventionality-unconventionality*. One important insight the Jessors gleaned from repeated study of the developing attitudes and changing behavior of their sample of adolescents in transition is that the change in an individual's behavior from a healthy behavior to one that society labels as more deviant (e.g., the transition from nonsmoker to smoker, from nondrinker to drinker) is in many instances predictable, before the new behavior actually emerges, from close study of the course of that person's life to date. Their extensive findings led them to conclude that the "adolescent who is *less* likely to engage in problem behavior is one who values and expects to attain academic achievement, who is not much concerned with independence, who treats society as unproblematic rather than as an object for criticism, who maintains a religious involvement and a more compromising attitude toward normative aggression, and who sees little attraction in problem behavior relative to its negative consequences." The Jessors also conclude that the "adolescent *more* likely to be involved in problem behavior shows an opposite pattern: a concern with personal autonomy, a lack of interest in the goals of conventional institutions like church and school, a jaundiced view of the larger society, and a more tolerant view of transgression" (Jessor & Jessor, 1982). After presenting an interesting array of findings on the personal, psychosocial, and environmental measures that were used initially in studying their pre-high school and young college samples, in the most recent report this team of investigators used those earlier measures in an attempt to predict which of these teenagers would become problem drinkers in young adulthood (i.e., empirically at ages 24 and 28). They found that what distinguishes the adolescent who will be a problem drinker as a young adult from the one who will be a nonproblem drinker is not a predisposition toward problems with alcohol; rather, the person already has begun to exhibit a proneness toward problem behavior in adolescence that is generalized across a number of deviant behaviors, not solely alcohol abuse. These investigators (Donovan, Jessor, & Jessor, 1983) therefore conclude, in contrast to the more targeted focus and strategies of Collins and Marlatt (1981) and Mills, Pfaffenberger, and McCarthy (1981), that it may be more effective to focus prevention or intervention efforts on changing the total adolescent (his or her personality, social environment, and behavioral involvements) rather than attempting to influence specific aspects of alcohol use or other deviant behavior as the primary target.

Integration of Disparate Approaches

The findings from this still ongoing longitudinal study would appear to have considerable implication for a wide array of applications in prevention and behavioral health. To summarize, Breslow and Belloc and their associates (see Figure 1.6) and many other health researchers have begun to unravel in more precise terms the potential cost in morbidity and mortality to each individual, as well as to society, of the health-risk-increasing or health-enhancing behaviors we each carry out or fail to carry out. Antonovsky and Mechanic have identified what they believe is the existence in each of us of a core person-specific philosophy of life that appears to carry over, as one of its by-products, into a guiding framework for a set of attitudes, which translates into a set of behaviors (lifestyles) that are healthful or less healthful. Finally, researchers such as the Jessors and their associates are helping to identify the influences on this underlying core personality, or set, of each individual, which, when activated, leads to the manifestation of these healthful or less healthful behaviors. The Jessors are seeking to unravel and identify the complex interaction of the developing total personality, the perceived environment (especially perceived environmental supports), and the actual end-product behavior (e.g., the role played in the emergence of new behavior, such as drinking, by the presence of other deviant behaviors, such as cigarette smoking).

The fact that findings from the research of these three groups of investigators, each from a different behavioral or biomedical discipline, and from the research of hundreds of other scientists too numerous to mention, is directing our understanding into a more unified whole cannot help but be gratifying to the investigators involved. Juxtaposing the ideas of Antonovsky and Mechanic and the Jessors against the data in Table 1.1 and Figure 1.6 should suggest ideas for hundreds of masters theses and doctoral dissertations, as well as programs of researchable hypotheses for more experienced investigators. The Jessors, for example, have been studying the developmental dynamics that lead to an individual's use of marijuana. An interested investigator might therefore wish to ask whether or not it would make a difference in subsequent mortality if marijuana were added to the seven other risks studied by Belloc and Breslow and noted here in Figure 1.6. Conversely, Belloc and Breslow, as well as Mechanic and others, might wish to integrate their interests and research findings with those of the Jessors by asking such questions as whether the psychosocial developmental dynamics the Jessors have been studying in relation to the use of alcohol, marijuana, and cigarettes also apply in the same ways to the personal decisions to get 7 to 8 hours of sleep per day, never to eat between meals, to use health foods that are low in serum cholesterol and saturated fats (as do seemingly daily increasing numbers of our young people), or to stay fit by regular daily exercise. If they find that this is true, it would constitute additional evidence that, as Antonovsky is coming to believe, each of us develops a sense of coherence regarding our health, which makes us vulnerable or less vulnerable in the presence of similar stressors or, if we succumb and engage in such a behavior, determines whether or not such a risky behavior will lead to our continued health or to cellular change associated with morbidity. Additionally, some of the growing numbers of new investigators who are being attracted to research problems in the field of behavioral health would benefit considerably if they examined the relevance for their research of the equally provocative and heuristically attractive theories of Ajzen and Fishbein (1980) and Bandura (1982). Each of them has developed a theoretical model for relating an individual's intentions to his or her actual subsequent behavior; the models already have been applied in areas of health and behavior.

Although the ideas for new research directions that emerge from juxtaposition of these various theoretical views against the annually accumulating empirical findings would appear to number in the hundreds, space precludes further development of such considerations here. It does appear, however, that these and other extant empirical and theoretical publications already do constitute more than an adequate base for more cross-investigator studies and literature reviews which attempt to focus and, where possible, to integrate the research findings which have been published by scores of investigators working in isolation.

Promotion of Seat Belt Use

A third area of research that I recently suggested would profit from a fresh look by psychologists from every subspecialty (as well as investigators from many other disciplines) is the question of why Americans do not use seat belts while driving their automobiles. The data summarized here in Table 1.1 and Figures 1.2 and 1.3 offer eloquent testimony that if we buckled up we would reduce in number the 50,000 Americans who now die on our highways annually. Psychologists, especially those with experience in human factors and in human engineering, teamed up with engineers and scientists from many other disciplines and, as just two examples, played a role in World War II in helping young pilots learn to fly our airplanes more efficiently and, in 1969, in wedding man and machine into one integrated system to help put two astronauts on the moon. The effort required of such psychologists and others in applying their human factors knowledge to the design of a seat belt that Americans would use voluntarily seems to be a minor challenge in comparison with the achievement in space, which presented an infinitely more complex challenge. The brake in our automobiles is a highly motivationally salient device each of us uses voluntarily and automatically many times every day. Surely one among us can devise a seat belt system that is equally salient as a stimulus to an equally automatic part of our behavior. Even my brief perusal (Matarazzo, 1982) of the sparse literature on seat belt usage left no question in my mind that psychology has a vast store of accumulated knowledge on motivation and behavior change (Jonah et al., 1982) that it could apply to this problem that costs individuals and our society billions of dollars annually, not to mention the immeasurable human costs associated with the resulting morbidity and mortality.

Promotion of Diet Control

An examination of the risk factors shown in Table 1.1 and Figures 1.2 through 1.11 reveals many other opportunities that await academic, research, and professional psychologists, and others, who would like the challenges offered by the field of behavioral health. Acknowledging the complexity of the problem and therefore the need for the informed approach suggested by Miller, Fowler, and Bridgers (1982), and reviewed in considerable detail by Carmody, Fey, Pierce, Connor, and Matarazzo (1982), a fourth challenge that occurred to me is the research, training, and applied opportunities associated with the role of diet in the future well-being of currently healthy children and adults. Not only are exercise and other forms of weight control important in health but, as we also know, foods high in serum cholesterol play a large role in future heart disease, stroke, and arteriosclerosis. Among other groups, the National Heart, Lung and Blood Institute became aware of this relationship early and provided support for several large-scale community intervention projects designed to help clarify the role diet plays in the future health of currently healthy samples of Americans. As reviewed elsewhere (Carmody, Fey, Pierce, Connor, & Matarazzo, 1982; Hollis, Connor, & Matarazzo, 1982; Matarazzo, 1982) such prospective intervention studies are being carried out in Houston, Stanford, and Portland, and in nationally coordinated multiple-risk studies in numerous other American cities. The insights into morbidity and mortality associated with the so-called more prudent diets that these studies might produce will, at most, set the stage for still additional research. Thus, if eating less butter or sugar or meat is found in a small targeted sample to reduce the risk of morbidity and mortality, we must determine how that knowledge can be used most efficiently to raise the level of awareness of larger numbers of individual Americans so that such knowledge will be translated into meaningful and enduring changes in the daily diets of increasing numbers of us. Is the type of food we each ultimately learn to enjoy and adopt as our daily family diet determined as much as or less than other risk behaviors by the three influences (person, environment, concurrent behavior) being studied by the Jessors (or the other theorists discussed above)? Will presenting such knowledge on the role of one's daily diet on later morbidity and mortality to young children help immunize them against future cardiovascular dysfunctions, as now seems to be the case in the immunization studies reviewed earlier that had potential smoking as their target behavior? Hundreds of other research questions could, should, and no doubt will be asked by investigators in a number of behavioral science and biomedical disciplines.

Funding Priorities

To help ensure that such questions are asked in ways that will increase the likelihood of our making progress against diseases and dysfunctions associated with lifestyle, it seems to me that public and private funds should now be targeted in relatively large amounts away from the areas of illness and dysfunction and into areas more focused on behavioral health. I believe that not only research monies should be so targeted but also monies for predoctoral and postdoctoral training, which is designed to produce the needed new investigators as well as needed new teachers in the various biomedical and behavioral science disciplines (Matarazzo, 1980, 1982, 1983; Stone, 1979). Larger sums of public and private monies are also required to carry out many different types of demonstration projects and related applications that use this accumulating knowledge on the role of lifestyle in keeping healthy people healthy.

HEALTH EDUCATOR AND BEHAVIORAL SCIENTIST: A MARRIAGE WHOSE TIME HAS COME

I also believe we must make more creative and efficient use than we now do of the currently available personnel in other disciplines that have a role to play in the field of behavioral health. I therefore offer a suggestion that may facilitate the better use of interested personnel from several such disciplines, among many others, that until now have tended to work in isolation from each other.

As but one more isolated example of the current zeitgeist in this country, an entire issue of the journal *Health Education* (May/June 1981) was devoted to "The Behavioral Sciences and Health Education." In one of the articles, a health educator and a psychologist, Dwore and Matarazzo (1981), joined forces to provide a brief review of selected elements of the pertinent histories of each of their disciplines and then suggested that the behavioral sciences and health education can relate to each other in one of three ways. First, they may continue as at present on the same university campus (in the college of education and in the liberal arts college), with little contact and articulation but with considerable duplication and overlap of the coursework they each offer their essentially nonoverlapping student bodies (an option to continue their benign neglect). Second, given the new emphasis now under way and discussed throughout this chapter, these two disciplines can compete with each other for larger resource allocation by claiming primacy in areas of common interests; faculties thus can duplicate the coursework from other areas and practitioners can continue to develop their own methodologies without assistance from colleagues in other disciplines (the option of costly competition). The third option, the one Dwore and Matarazzo imply is the most cost-effective for society and most advantageous to each group, is for the two disciplines to show greater, mutually enriching collaboration—through jointly taught, interdisciplinary classes and seminars, collaborative research, increased interprofessional stimulation by visiting faculty exchanges, and jointly undertaken community action projects, to name but a few possibilities.

To such a marriage, psychology, as one of the behavioral sciences, could bring the rich legacy of over 100 years of research on individual differences, on motivation, on learning, on persuasion, and on attitude and other forms of behavior change. (It should go without saying that representatives of sociology and anthropology and the other behavioral sciences also could bring collaboratively to health education the fruit of the best of the research knowledge and experience from their respective fields.) To this same collaborative effort and partnership, health educators could contribute the best products of their many years of experience in teaching about and doing research on health behavior, not only in the elementary school, high school, and college classroom but also in larger scale community intervention projects, such as those associated with hypertension case finding, treatment, and prevention. An excellent example of what health educators have to offer is the skillfully crafted and implemented school curriculum project recently described by Green, Heit, Iverson, Kolbe, and Kreuter (1980). A second example, the role of physical fitness in good psychological health, is presented in an excellent literature review by Folkins and Sime (1981).

The behavioral science and health education authors of the remaining articles in the special issue of *Health Education* offered many additional ideas for ways in which representatives from health education and from the behavioral sciences could pool their resources to their mutual advantage and, of course, that of society. A mature collaboration between disciplines, characterized by mutual respect and sharing, would add considerable impetus to this nation's efforts to meet the 15 specific health goals that have been established for 1990 (see Table 1.4). A doctoral program in health behavior offered by faculty consisting of psychologists and health educators, recently introduced at the University of Maryland (Matarazzo, 1983), is an example of how these two disciplines can pool the best ingredients from their fields to provide graduate education for the leaders of tomorrow.

OTHER HEALTH PROFESSIONALS AND BEHAVIORAL SCIENTISTS

The reader no doubt will have sensed that it is equally wasteful for behavioral scientists in colleges of arts and sciences not to team up in collaborative research and application with their colleagues in colleges of nursing. Highly trained nurses working in our public schools, in industry, in private practice, and in many other settings come into daily contact with large numbers of healthy children and adults, and, because of their high-quality education and their interest in prevention, are one of today's major underutilized resources for maintaining the health of currently healthy Americans. I recently offered the opinion (Matarazzo, 1983) that it is time for behavioral scientists in our universities to team up with their colleagues in our schools of nursing as well as schools of dentistry and public health. How else will we meet the nation's 1990 goals? As described throughout this chapter, the last decade has witnessed a mutually rewarding partnership between the behavioral sciences and medicine. During the next decade, we should expand such partnerships to these other professions.

BIOMEDICAL SPECIALIST AND BEHAVIORAL SCIENTIST: A MARRIAGE THAT IS BEGINNING TO BEAR FRUIT

I need not devote much more space to the collaboration between biomedical and behavioral scientists because evidence that this marriage, consummated only a decade or two ago, is thriving and is everywhere about us. It is found in the publications emanating from the highest levels of our government (e.g., *Healthy People*), in editorials and articles in the most prestigious journals in the biomedical specialties and in the behavioral sciences, and in the dozens of textbooks and handbooks devoted to behavioral medicine that are accumulating in annually increasing numbers.

My purpose is not to present here as I did earlier (Matarazzo, 1980) my perception of the many varied forces and tributaries that have fed into what today is the thriving, integrative, and cross-disciplinary activity called behavioral medicine. Rather, by assigning this collaboration to a section of its own I would like again, as I did earlier in this chapter, to underscore the need for these many behavioral science and biomedical disciplines to also direct some of their remaining vast reservoirs of talent into the equally important area of behavioral health. The field of preventive medicine has been with us for many years. Appropriate to the state of scientific knowledge at those times, most of its effort and its greatest successes were associated with wiping out a number of deadly infectious diseases and dysfunctions associated with pollution, coal dust, tuberculosis, and numerous other pathogens found in our everyday environment. It is clear to me that one of the important remaining frontiers for biology (preventive medicine) to conquer as we approach the twenty-first century is the role of lifestyle in illness and in health. Research in the various behavioral sciences during the past several decades has produced what now appears to be a critical mass of new information, plus tested technologies for modifying behavior, such that the goal of behavioral health for millions more of our citizens by the year 1990 is both justified and attainable. The interested reader will find an overview of some of the new directions in prevention being explored by psychologists working at the interfaces of modern public health and psychology in the six articles commissioned for a recent special issue of *American Psychologist* by DeLeon and Pallak (1982, pp. 934–965).

The 15 specific goals established for our nation with the help of our biomedical, behavioral science, and other health profession communities are a public prescription for the behavioral health of its citizens. If sufficient public and private funds for research, training, and application are added to this prescription, and if leaders in our universities, scientific communities, and professions rise to meet this 1990 goal for our nation, we shall meet it a decade from now no less successfully than, in 1969, we met President John F. Kennedy's 1963 goal that our nation would place a man on the moon by 1970.

Behavioral pathogens are as important in illness and dysfunction as are microbial pathogens. Many leaders in our country have acknowledged this important relationship. It therefore falls upon those of us in the various health sciences and health professions who wish to accept the vast challenges offered us by the identification of these new types of pathogens to do so forthrightly and with confidence. In doing so, however, we should not overlook the equally important behavioral immunogens (good health practices) also discussed throughout this chapter.

REFERENCES

Adams, R. McC., Smelser, N. J., & Treiman, D. J. *Behavioral and social science research: A national resource (Part I)*. Washington, D.C.: National Academy Press, 1982.

American Hospital Association. *Health—A national survey of consumers and business.* Chicago: Author, 1978.

Ajzen, I., & Fishbein, M. *Understanding attitudes and predicting social behavior.* Englewood Cliffs, N.J.: Prentice-Hall, 1980.

Andrews, F. M., & McKennell, A. C. Measures of self-reported well-being: Their affective, cognitive, and other components. *Social Indicators Research,* 1980, **8,** 127–155.

Antonovsky, A. *Health, stress, and coping.* San Francisco: Jossey-Bass, 1979.

Arkin, R. M., Roemhild, H. F., Johnson, C. A., Luepker, R. V., & Murray, D. M. The Minnesota Smoking Prevention Program: A seventh-grade health curriculum supplement. *Journal of School Health,* 1981, **51,** 611–616.

Bandura, A. Self-efficacy mechanism in human agency. *American Psychologist,* 1982, **37,** 122–147.

Belloc, N. B. Relationship of health practices and mortality. *Preventive Medicine,* 1973, **2,** 67–81.

Belloc, N. B., & Breslow, L. Relationship of physical health status and health practices. *Preventive Medicine,* 1972, **1,** 409–421.

Belloc, N. B., Breslow, L., & Hochstim, J. R. Measurement of physical health in a general population survey. *American Journal of Epidemiology,* 1971, **93,** 328–336.

Botvin, G. J., Eng, A., & Williams, C. L. Preventing the onset of cigarette smoking through lifeskills training. *Preventive Medicine,* 1980, **9,** 135–143.

Breslow, L. Prospects for improving health through reducing risk factors. *Preventive Medicine,* 1978, **7,** 449–458. (a)

Breslow, L. Risk factor intervention for health maintenance. *Science,* 1978, **200,** 908–912. (b)

Breslow, L., & Enstrom, J. E. Persistence of health habits and their relationship to mortality. *Preventive Medicine,* 1980, **9,** 469–483.

Breslow, L., & Somers, A. R. The lifetime health-monitoring program: A practical approach to preventive medicine. *New England Journal of Medicine,* 1977, **296,** 601–610.

Califano, J. A., Jr. *Healthy people: The Surgeon General's report on health promotion and disease prevention.* Washington, D.C.: U.S. Government Printing Office, (Stock No. 017–001–00416–2), 1979. (a)

Califano, J. A., Jr. *Healthy people: Background papers.* Washington D.C.: U.S. Government Printing Office (Stock No. 017–001–00417–1), 1979. (b)

Carmody, T. P., Fey, S. G., Pierce, D. K., Connor, W. E., & Matarazzo, J. D. Behavioral treatment of hyperlipidemia: Techniques, results and future directions. *Journal of Behavioral Medicine,* 1982, **5,** 91–116.

Carmody, T. P., Matarazzo, J. D., Fey, S. G., & Connor, W. E. Reported Cornell Medical Index symptoms and silent biomedical coronary risk factors. *Health Psychology,* 1982, **1,** 201–216.

Christianson, R. E. The relationship between maternal smoking and the incidence of congenital anomalies. *American Journal of Epidemiology,* 1980, **112,** 684–695.

Collins, R. L., & Marlatt, G. A. Social modeling as a determinant of drinking behavior: Implications for prevention and treatment. *Addictive Behaviors,* 1981, **6,** 233–239.

Cushner, I. M. Maternal behavior and perinatal risks: Alcohol, smoking, and drugs. *Annual Review of Public Health,* 1981, **2,** 201–218.

DeLeon, P. H., & Pallak, M. S. Public health and psychology: An important, expanding interaction. *American Psychologist,* 1982, **37,** 934–965.

Donovan, J. E., Jessor, R., & Jessor, L. Problem drinking in adolescence and young adulthood: A follow-up study. *Journal of Studies on Alcohol,* 1983, in press.

Dwore, R. B., & Matarazzo, J. D. The behavioral sciences and health education: Disciplines with a compatible interest? *Health Education,* May/June, 1981, 4–7.

Epstein, S. The stability of behavior: I. On predicting most of the people much of the time. *Journal of Personality and Social Psychology,* 1979, **37,** 1097–1126.

Evans, R. I. Training social psychologists in behavioral medicine research. In J. R. Eiser (Ed.), *Social psychology and behavioral medicine.* New York: John Wiley & Sons, 1982.

Evans, R. I., & Raines, B. E. Control and prevention of smoking in adolescents: A psychosocial perspective. In T. J. Coates, A. Peterson, & C. Perry (Eds.), *Promoting adolescent health: A dialogue of research and practice.* New York: Academic Press, 1982.

Evans, R., Rozelle, R., Mittlemark, M., Hansen, W., Bane, A., & Havis, J. Deterring the onset of smoking in children: Knowledge of immediate physiological effects and coping with peer pressure, media pressure, and parent modeling. *Journal of Applied Social Psychology,* 1978, **8,** 126–135.

Evans, R. I., Rozelle, R. M., Maxwell, S. E., Raines, B. E., Dill, C. A., Guthrie, T. J., Henderson, A. H., & Hill, P. C. Social modelling films to deter smoking in adolescents: Results of a three-year field investigation. *Journal of Applied Psychology,* 1981, **66,** 399–414.

Flanagan, J. C. A research approach to improving our quality of life. *American Psychologist,* 1978, **33,** 138–147.

Flanagan, J. C. *New insights to improve the quality of life at age 70* (Tech. Report, Grant No. 1–RO1–AGO2453–01). Palo Alto: American Institutes for Research in the Behavioral Sciences, 1982.

Flay, B. R., d'Avernas, J. R., Best, J. A., Kersell, M. W., & Ryan, K. B. Cigarette smoking: Why young people do it and ways of preventing it. In P. Firestone & P. McGrath (Eds.), *Pediatric behavioral medicine.* New York: Springer Verlag, in press.

Folkins, C. E., & Sime, W. E. Physical fitness training and mental health. *American Psychologist,* 1981, **36**, 373–389.

Gibson, R. M., & Waldo, D. R. National health expenditures, 1980. *Health Care Financing Review,* 1981, **3**, No. 1, 1–53.

Green, L. W., Heit, P., Iverson, D. C., Kolbe, L. J., & Kreuter, M. The school health curriculum project: Its theory, practice, and measurement experience. *Health Education Quarterly,* 1980, **7**, 14–34.

Green, L. W., Kreuter, M. W., Deeds, S. G., & Partridge, K. B. *Health education planning: A diagnostic approach.* Palo Alto: Mayfield, 1980.

Hamburg, D. A., Elliott, G. R., & Parron, D. L. *Health and behavior: Frontiers of research in the biobehavioral sciences.* Washington, D.C.: National Academy Press, 1982.

Harris, L. & Associates, Inc. *Health maintenance.* Newport Beach, Calif.: Pacific Mutual Life Insurance Co., 1978.

Harris, P. R. *Promoting health—preventing disease: Objectives for the nation.* Washington, D.C.: U.S. Government Printing Office, 1980.

Harris, P. R. *Health United States 1980: With prevention profile.* DHHS Pub. No. (PHS)81–1232. Washington, D.C.: U.S. Government Printing Office, 1981.

Hollis, J. F., Connor, W. E., & Matarazzo, J. D. Lifestyle, behavioral health and heart disease. In R. J. Gatchel, A. Baum, & J. E. Singer (Eds.), *Behavioral medicine and clinical psychology: Overlapping disciplines.* Hillsdale, N.J.: Lawrence Erlbaum & Associates, 1982.

Hunt, S. M., & McEwen, J. The development of a subjective health indicator. *Sociology of Health and Illness,* 1980, **2**, 231–246.

Hurd, P. D., Johnson, C. A., Pechacek, T., Bast, L. P., Jacobs, D. R., & Luepker, R. V. Prevention of cigarette smoking in seventh grade students. *Journal of Behavioral Medicine,* 1980, **3**, 15–28.

Jessor, R., & Jessor, S. L. *Problem behavior and psychosocial development: A longitudinal study of youth.* New York: Academic Press, 1977.

Jessor, R., & Jessor, S. L. Adolescence to young adulthood: A twelve-year prospective study of problem behavior and psychosocial development. In S. A. Mednick & M. Harway (Eds.), *Longitudinal research in the United States.* Boston: Martinus Nijhoff, 1982.

Johnston, C. Cigarette smoking and the outcome of human pregnancies: A status report on the consequences. *Clinical Toxicology,* 1981, **18**, 189–209.

Jonah, B. A., Dawson, N. E., & Smith, G. A. Effects of a selective traffic enforcement program on seat belt usage. *Journal of Applied Psychology,* 1982, **67**, 89–96.

Kaplan, R. M., & Bush, J. W. Health-related quality of life measurement for evaluation research and policy analysis. *Health Psychology,* 1982, **1**, 61–80.

Kass, L. R. Regarding the end of medicine and the pursuit of health. *The Public Interest,* 1975, No. 40, 11–42.

Knowles, J. H. The responsibility of the individual. In J. H. Knowles (Ed.), *Doing better and feeling worse: Health in the United States.* New York: Norton, 1977.

Kolata, G. Heart study produces a surprise result. *Science,* 1982, **218**, 31–32.

Lalonde, M. *A new perspective on the health of Canadians—A working document.* Ottawa: Information Canada, 1974.

Levy, R. I., & Moskowitz, J. Cardiovascular research: Decades of progress, a decade of promise. *Science,* 1982, **217**, 121–129.

Lunde, A. S. Health in the United States. *Annals of the American Academy of Political and Social Science,* 1981, **453**, 28–69.

Maiman, L. A., & Becker, M. H. The health belief model: Origins and correlates in psychological theory. *Health Education Monographs,* 1974, **2**, 336–353.

Matarazzo, J. D. Behavioral health and behavioral medicine: Frontiers for a new health psychology. *American Psychologist,* 1980, **35,** 807–817.

Matarazzo, J. D. Behavioral health's challenge to academic, scientific and professional psychology. *American Psychologist,* 1982, **37,** 1–14.

Matarazzo, J. D. Education and training in health psychology: Boulder or bolder? *Health Psychology,* 1983, **2,** 73–113.

Matarazzo, J. D., Connor, W. E., Fey, S. G., Carmody, T. P., Pierce, D. K., Brischetto, C. S., Baker, L. H., Connor, S. L., & Sexton, G. Behavioral cardiology with emphasis on the family heart study: Fertile ground for psychological and biomedical research. In T. Millon, C. J. Green, & R. B. Meagher (Eds.), *Handbook of health care psychology.* New York: Plenum, 1982.

Matarazzo, J. D., & Saslow, G. Psychological and related characteristics of smokers and nonsmokers. *Psychological Bulletin,* 1960, **57,** 493–513.

McAlister, A. L., Perry, C., & Maccoby, N. Adolescent smoking: Onset and prevention. *Pediatrics,* 1979, **63,** 650–658.

McAlister, A. L., Perry, C., Killen, J., Slinkard, L. A., & Maccoby, N. Pilot study of smoking, alcohol and drug abuse prevention. *American Journal of Public Health,* 1980, **70,** 719–721.

Mechanic, D. The stability of health and illness behavior: Results from a 16-year follow-up. *American Journal of Public Health,* 1979, **69,** 1142–1145.

Mechanic, D., & Cleary, P. D. Factors associated with the maintenance of positive health behavior. *Preventive Medicine,* 1980, **9,** 805–814.

Miller, H. L., Fowler, R. D., & Bridges, W. F. The public health psychologist: An ounce of prevention is not enough. *American Psychologist,* 1982, **37,** 945–948.

Mills, K. C., Pfaffenberger, B., & McCarthy, D. Guidelines for alcohol abuse prevention on the college campus. *Journal of Higher Education,* 1981, **52,** 399–414.

MRFIT Research Group. Multiple risk factor intervention trial: Risk factor changes and mortality results. *Journal of the American Medical Association,* 1982, **248,** 1465–1477.

Neubuerger, O. W., Miller, S. I., Schmitz, R. E., Matarazzo, J. D., Pratt, H. H., & Hasha, N. Replicable abstinence rates in an alcoholism treatment program. *Journal of the American Medical Association,* 1982, **248,** 960–963.

Parkinson, R. S. & Associates. *Managing health promotion in the workplace: Guidelines for implementation and evaluation.* Palo Alto: Mayfield, 1982.

Rahe, R. H., & Gunderson, E. K. E. *Life stress and illness.* Springfield, Ill.: Charles C Thomas, 1974.

Remington, R. D. Smoking: U.S. data base and trends. *Atherosclerosis Reviews,* 1980, **7,** 285–296.

Rosenstock, I. Historical origins of the health belief model. *Education Monographs,* 1974, **2,** 328–335.

Schachter, S. Recidivism and self-cure of smoking and obesity. *American Psychologist,* 1982, **37,** 436–444.

Schwartz, G. E., & Weiss, S. M. Yale Conference on Behavioral Medicine: A proposed definition and statement of goals. *Journal of Behavioral Medicine,* 1978, **1,** 3–12. (a)

Schwartz, G. E., & Weiss, S. M. Behavioral medicine revisited: An amended definition. *Journal of Behavioral Medicine,* 1978, **1,** 249–251. (b)

Schweiker, R. S. Disease prevention and health promotion. *Journal of Medical Education,* 1982, **57,** 15–19.

Stone, G. C. A specialized doctoral program in health psychology: Considerations in its evolution. *Professional Psychology,* 1979, **10,** 596–604.

Streissguth, A. P., Landesman-Dwyer, S., Martin, J. C., & Smith, D. W. Teratogenic effects of alcohol in humans and laboratory animals. *Science,* 1980, **209,** 353–361.

Sulik, K. K., Johnston, M. C., & Webb, M. A. Fetal alcohol syndrome: Embryogenesis in a mouse model. *Science,* 1981, **214,** 936–938.

Sunday Oregonian, January 25, 1981.

Telch, M. J., Killen, J. D., McAlister, A. L., Perry, C. L., & Maccoby, N. Long-term follow-up of a pilot project on smoking prevention with adolescents. *Journal of Behavioral Medicine,* 1982, **5,** 1–8.

Thom, T. J., & Kannel, W. B. Downward trend in cardiovascular mortality. *Annual Review of Medicine,* 1981, **32,** 427–434.

Waldo, D. R. National health expenditures and related measures. *Health Care Financing Trends,* 1982, **2,** No. 5, 1–34.

Williams, C. L., Carter, B. J., Arnold, C. B., & Wynder, E. L. Chronic disease risk factors among children: The know your body study. *Journal of Chronic Diseases,* 1979, **32,** 505–513.

Wilson, J. The fetal alcohol syndrome. *Public Health, London,* 1981, **85,** 129–132.

Yankelovitch, Skelly, & White: *The General Mills American Family Report, 1978–79: Family health in an era of stress.* Minneapolis: General Mills, Inc., 1979.

CHAPTER 2

PRENATAL AND NEONATAL INFLUENCES ON BEHAVIORAL HEALTH DEVELOPMENT

RICHARD C. LABARBA

University of South Florida

There is a very large body of literature dealing with prenatal and neonatal factors and influences that might place the prenatal organism and the newborn infant at some biological risk, thereby potentially threatening normal health development. Historically, intrauterine influences on prenatal and neonatal development have been presented in the general context of diagnosis, treatment, and rehabilitation; that is, the usual treatment of such information has been oriented toward considerations of the etiology and course of abnormal patterns of health development. For the most part, prevention and intervention have been implicit or restricted to post hoc procedures designed to mitigate various developmental defects.

During the past few years, however, there have been some clear signs of a shift in emphasis in the direction of prevention and intervention. Much of this redirection rests on the foundation of empirical findings in the area of developmental psychology, embryology, obstetrics, and perinatal medicine. The interdisciplinary research efforts of psychologists, biologists, and physicians in these areas show renewed vigor, with improvements in methodology and control leading to increasingly robust findings. It seems natural, therefore, that the trend toward prevention and intervention should emerge as we learn more about etiology in the developmental sciences, particularly etiological events in reproductive and developmental casualties leading to an arrest or decrement in behavioral health development.

The emergence of health psychology and behavioral health as a new discipline in psychology is paralleled by developments in obstetrics and prenatal and perinatal medicine (Hobel, 1980; Matarazzo, 1980; Comptroller General, Note 1; Committee on Labor and Human Resources, Note 2). Both individual and government efforts have brought to light concerted calls for improving pregnancy outcomes and perinatal health through intervention and prevention strategies. This recent surge of interest in preventive medicine is born of the disillusionment with primary treatment approaches and their diminishing returns in cost-benefit. In psychology we face the same set of problems. Many of the reproductive developmental casualties we observe may be attributable to individual failures in, and ignorance of, behaviors known to promote and maintain health and prevent illness and dysfunction. The task before us, it seems, is to present convincingly the data available to us in the hope that the concept of individual responsibility for health development and maintenance will be accepted by everyone. The time has come to seize the opportunity to apply current knowledge to an area of health psychology that is critically significant to health development.

In many respects, the uterine environment is a marvelously designed protective system for the prenatal organism. This support system—the maternal-fetal complex—isolates and protects the developing individual from potentially hazardous maternal states and intrauter-ine conditions, but it is far from perfect in doing so. The dynamic nature of the human intrauterine environment suggests an interesting paradox. The developing human in utero is better protected from the dangers of the external environment than it will ever be again. Simultaneously, however, at no other time during development will the individual be so critically sensitive and vulnerable to alterations in its immediate environment (Joffe, 1969).

The National Center for Health Statistics reports that of the 3.2 million infants born alive annually in the United States, 250,000 are born with a birth defect that impairs health development along a continuum of severity. Congenital birth defects account annually for the deaths of approximately 20,000 infants under the age of 1 year. Those who live beyond the age of 1 year succumb at a mortality rate of 60,000 per year. It is estimated that about 500,000 fetuses a year are aborted, either spontaneously or therapeutically, because of developmental abnormality, and that another 33,000 fetal deaths occur before or at birth. In 1979, the infant mortality rate for the total population in this country was 13 per 1,000 live births, the lowest ever recorded in U.S. history, but still leaving us with a world ranking of 12th in infant mortality rate.

The major determinant in infant mortality and morbidity rates is low birth weight (less than 2,500 grams or 5.5 pounds), accounting for almost two-thirds of our reproductive casualties. The second major threat to infant survival and health development is birth defects, which include congenital physical anomalies, mental retardation, and genetic dis-eases. Birth defects are responsible for approximately 17% of all infant mortality and morbid-ity. These statistics are alarming and worrisome, particularly since 75% of mortality and morbidity rates are attributed to environmental factors or agents. Increased awareness of these environmental influences, along with the adoption of appropriate preventive health behaviors, can significantly improve pregnancy outcomes and promote health development in infants who might otherwise be doomed to lives of illness and dysfunction. I believe we now have a sound enough data base in the developmental sciences to arouse the individual responsibility required to apply this knowledge to enhancing prenatal and neonatal health development. Science has clearly established that pregnant women can enhance the health of their fetuses and newborn infants by self-initiated behaviors over which the mother has complete control—for example, by avoiding unnecessary X rays; by not smoking, drinking, or taking drugs while pregnant; by being inoculated against measles (rubella). We will now examine these dangers and the behaviors necessary to ameliorate or avoid them.

TERATOGENIC AGENTS

Teratogens are environmental agents that produce structural and functional abnormalities in prenatal organisms. Often, teratogens produce characteristic and predictable patterns of defects—a phenomenon described by Wilson (1973) as "agent specificity." These character-istic patterns of abnormal embryogenesis occur because teratogenic agents initiate biochemi-cal sequences of abnormal developmental events by their specific access to certain developing cells and tissues. The relationship between teratogenic mechanisms and metabolic pathogen-esis is complex. Fetal outcomes following exposure to teratogenic agents depend on genetic susceptibility of the prenatal organism, the pregnancy stage, the nature of the agent, the dosage level of the agent, and the duration of exposure. Four categories of teratogens contain agents of known teratogenicity in humans: ionizing radiation, chemicals or drugs, infectious diseases, and metabolic-endocrine disturbances.

Ionizing Radiation Effects

Although exposure to therapeutic and nuclear radiation accounts for less than 1% of reported cases of teratogenesis, it nevertheless seems appropriate to discuss this category briefly, inasmuch as radiological procedures are common diagnostic and therapeutic practice in modern societies and may present hazardous conditions for pregnant women. Ionizing radiation takes a number of forms, and various sources of radiation may generate alpha, beta, gamma, and X rays, or a combination of these. Since ionizing radiation can change the atomic structure of genes and chromosomes, the developmental consequences for the prenatal organism may be severe. Exposure to ionizing radiation can accelerate the frequency of genetic mutations, the large majority of which are deleterious.

Data from both the experimental and the clinical-medical literature strongly indicate that the fetal consequences of early prenatal exposure to ionizing radiation may range from lethal effects to functional deficits. The most commonly reported radiation effects include central nervous system (CNS) defects, with accompanying intellectual retardation, structural and behavioral anomalies, various forms of cancer, retarded growth, spontaneous abortion, and stillbirth (Dekeban, 1968; Joffe, 1969; Rush & Shettles, 1971; Sternberg, 1970). Therefore, diagnostic or therapeutic radiation procedures involving the pelvic area in pregnant women require a critical decision and generally are inadvisable. In medical emergencies, such decisions must be based on careful evaluations of the health needs of the expectant mother, the stage of pregnancy, and the degree of maternal accumulated radiation exposure. When radiation dosage and gestation age exceed minimal safe threshold levels of 8.8 rads during the first 12 weeks of pregnancy, therapeutic abortion may be the wisest decision. Such sources of radiation as dental X rays are relatively weak and are not considered dangerous when proper abdominal shielding is used. Nevertheless, total avoidance of such otherwise routine exposure should be the rule among pregnant women, particularly since it is impossible to determine differential fetal sensitivity to even low, presumably safe radiation levels. This is a simple preventive behavior to follow and one that has potentially high benefits in prenatal health development.

Drugs and Chemical Effects

Reports describing the prevalence and magnitude of drug use and drug abuse by pregnant women are nothing short of alarming. Various surveys over the past decade consistently indicate that as many as 90% of pregnant women take one or more drugs (excluding vitamin and iron supplements) during the course of their pregnancies. In at least 80% of all pregnancies, various drugs are prescribed by physicians, while approximately 65% of pregnant women take self-administered drugs without medical advice or supervision (Howard & Hill, 1979). These prescribed and nonprescribed drugs range from aspirin to narcotics, and reports suggest that the typical expectant mother may take an average of four to five different drugs on a more or less regular basis.

These data are especially disquieting to those of us who are interested in health psychology and healthy human development because virtually all pharmacological substances can cross the placental barrier and enter the fetal circulatory system. The maternal-fetal response to drugs and chemicals is a differential one, and the absence of maternal ill effects from a drug has no implications whatsoever for its potentially toxic effects on the unborn child. The thalidomide disaster 20 years ago—in which the drug affected the fetus but not the mother—bears painful testimony to the differential maternal-fetus sensitivity to pharmacological substances. Fetal responses to drugs and chemicals typically include greater toxicity and metabolic disruption because of increased fetal blood-brain permeability and immature liver function. In human prenatal development, the period of greatest sensitivity to environmental influences is between 20 and 60 days of gestation. The probability of embryopathy, both structural and functional, is highest during this active period of organogenesis. Maternal ingestion of a teratogenic drug beyond safe threshold dosages during this sensitive period in the first trimester of pregnancy may result in embryonic cellular death, agenesis, or dysgenesis. Before and after this sensitive period, the probabilities of teratogenic insult decrease as a function of the absence of organogenic processes.

To date, only three drugs have been positively identified as teratogenic for humans:

thalidomide, steroid hormones, and folic acid antagonists (Wilson, 1973). Data on drug teratogenicity are complex and contradictory, however, and this is compounded by the fact that results from experimental teratology have no necessary implications for human embryogenesis. Although problems in methodology and control preclude definitive conclusions on the teratogenic status of a large number of other suspected drugs, the standard warning is "Safety for use in pregnancy has not been established." The sensible expectant mother will refrain from the use of any drugs or medication during the first trimester of pregnancy, especially without the approval and supervision of her obstetrician.

Thalidomide is the best known human teratogen in the drug category. It was removed long ago in Europe, of course, where it had been developed as a therapeutic drug for nausea and vomiting in early pregnancy, but not before some 5,000 to 10,000 infants were affected. In the early 1960s, thalidomide was prescribed as an ideal antiemetic and sedative because of its apparently total lack of toxicity, as demonstrated in animal studies. Its effect on the human embryo was disastrous, however, with almost 100% teratogenicity among women who took the drug between 20 and 40 days following conception. Infants exposed to thalidomide were born with severe limb defects (phocomelia), in which arm and leg development were arrested or incomplete. CNS involvement was rare, and intelligence appeared to be normally distributed among thalidomide infants reared in normal home environments.

Steroid hormones such as androgen and estrogen have also been identified as teratogenic drugs. Sex steroid exposure during the first 12 to 14 weeks of pregnancy may result in a variety of structural malformations. Virilization of female fetuses has been reported in cases of androgen or progestogen therapy with expectant mothers during the first trimester (Goodner, 1975; Yaffe & Stern, 1976). The various anomalies attributed to prenatal exposure to sex steroids have been collectively described as the "VACTERL" syndrome (Nora & Nora, 1974), referring to the commonly observed vertebral, anal, cardiac, tracheal, esophageal, renal, and limb malformations.

Steroid hormones are often used in clinical obstetrics for prevention of abortion, for diagnostic purposes, and for the treatment of various chronic diseases in pregnant women. The data implicating steroids as a teratogen argue strongly against their use during pregnancy (Howard & Hill, 1979; Yaffe & Stern, 1976). Since oral contraceptives contain sex steroids, continued use of the pill when contraceptive failure is suspected could be extremely hazardous to the embryonic organism. Women whose menstrual cycle has stopped should have an obstetric examination for pregnancy before continuing to take oral contraceptives.

Folic acid is one of the B-group vitamins required for proper formation of blood in the body. A deficiency of this vitamin typically results in anemia. Folic acid antagonists are chemical compounds that neutralize the action of folic acid, resulting in folic acid deficiency. These antagonists are often used therapeutically to treat various leukemias and Hodgkin's disease. The administration of folic acid antagonists to women in the first trimester of pregnancy, however, has been found to be teratogenic. Such treatment in the early months of pregnancy may result in abortion, multiple fetal malformations, and varied symptomotology.

Risks Versus Benefits in Drug Therapy

Although only three drug groups have been clearly identified as human teratogens, many other drugs have been implicated as suspected or potential teratogens. Drug teratogenicity is difficult to establish, both experimentally and clinically. Therefore, drug use in pregnancy must be approached with extreme caution, particularly since deleterious effects arising from teratogens represent a continuous range of reproductive casualties, rather than discrete outcomes. It is probably true that no drug can be considered absolutely safe when taken during pregnancy. Increasing public and government awareness of the dangers of drugs in pregnancy, real or potential, has resulted in the general condemnation by some individuals and groups of all drug therapy during pregnancy.

Although the loss of fetal health potential and development to drug exposure is of great concern, the withdrawal of all medication during pregnancy may not be a feasible alternative. Howard & Hill (1979) argue for an approach to drug therapy in pregnancy that attempts to balance the maternal benefits of needed drugs with a careful evaluation of fetal risks. The evaluative outcome of relative risks versus benefits should lead to the best possible medical decision about drug therapy. Howard & Hill (1979) provide such a categorization of first trimester drug effects. They list commonly prescribed drugs whose use in pregnancy is indicated or contraindicated on the basis of data describing the relative balance of fetal risks and maternal benefits. Drugs of suspected teratogenicity whose risks outweigh maternal benefits include streptomycin, tetracycline, amphetamines, diethylstilbestrol (DES), alcohol, certain antinauseant drugs, sodium warfarin (an anticoagulant), methotrexate (used in the treatment of psoriasis), quinine, iodide, anticonvulsants, and some drugs used in the treatment of diabetes and cancer.

In a recent study, Jick, Holmes, Hunter, Madsen, and Stergachis (1981) observed the incidence of birth defects among the infants of 6,837 women who used a wide variety of commonly prescribed drugs during the first trimester of pregnancy. Since the patients in this study were members of a group health cooperative medical program, all maternal and infant data concerning filled prescriptions, obstetric status and procedures, and diagnosis at birth were computerized. This procedure provided detailed patient information on drug use, dates, course of pregnancy, and neonatal status in machine printout form. Of the approximately 40 drugs recorded in the prescription records, no increases in congenital disorders were found among infants of mothers who had used the drugs as compared with those in the control group. The controls were infants of mothers from the same patient population who had used no drugs during pregnancy. Meprobamate was found to be a suspected drug of possible implication in congenital defects, but its status as a teratogen is far from clear.

Perhaps of major interest in this study were the data on the use of Bendectin, a drug commonly prescribed for nausea and vomiting during pregnancy. One-third of the women in the Jick et al. (1981) study filled prescriptions for Bendectin just before or during the first trimester of pregnancy. The incidence of any congenital disorders among the Bendectin users was 1.1%, compared to a 1.2% incidence among nonusers. Huff (1980) also concludes that there is little evidence to indicate that Bendectin is associated with congenital abnormalities. Howard & Hill (1979) also categorize Bendectin as a drug whose maternal benefits outweigh fetal risks. I mention Bendectin here because it has been widely prescribed as an antiemetic for symptomatic relief of "morning sickness" in early pregnancy, and it has been the subject of recent controversy. The intent of this entire discussion is to bring a realistically cautious, balanced perspective to drug use and pregnancy and to avoid unnecessarily alarmist responses that have no scientific basis.

In summary, the practical, safe use of prescribed drug therapy during pregnancy is a difficult and at times controversial issue at best. The delicate balance between maternal and fetal health may require painfully uncomfortable decisions by both physicians and expectant mothers. The wisest decisions will always be made with awareness by all concerned parties of the risks and benefits of drug therapy in pregnancy, as established by research. Clearly, expectant mothers should avoid over-the-counter drugs or prescription drugs obtained from friends without the approval of their obstetricians. Any medication, no matter how innocuous it may seem, should be taken only with medical approval. The adoption by expectant mothers of this behavioral health practice alone will contribute to prenatal and neonatal health development.

SMOKING, PREGNANCY, AND HEALTH DEVELOPMENT

Recent surveys indicate that between 20% and 50% of pregnant women smoke (Abel, 1980b). Smoking frequency among women of childbearing age is estimated to be approximately one-half pack per day, but it is reasonable to assume that smoking probably increases during pregnancy. The general increase of smoking among females in this country has been the cause of much concern and alarm in the medical and scientific communities. This increase has been accompanied by dramatic increases in lung cancer, cardiovascular disease, and respiratory diseases among women during the past 25 years.

Concerns about the effects of tobacco on adult health and on healthy development in children began to develop shortly after the introduction of tobacco into Europe in 1558 (Surgeon General, 1979). Although clinical impressions and suspicions about smoking and fetal development were expressed in the 19th century, it was the work by Simpson (1957) that primarily stimulated the large number of studies to appear in the 25 years following her report. Simpson demonstrated that maternal smoking during pregnancy led to higher rates of premature births than were found among nonsmoking mothers. Furthermore, her data suggested that the effects were dose-related and were independent of such variables as maternal age, parity, and weight gain. Since then, a great number of reports have appeared in the scientific literature documenting the deleterious effects of maternal smoking on fetal health and development (for recent reports and reviews, see Abel, 1980b; Christianson, 1980; Jenson & Foss, 1981; Johnson, 1981; Surgeon General, 1979, 1981; Young, 1981).

The major, consistent finding in these investigations is that maternal smoking during pregnancy leads to increased rates of prematurity and low birth weight. Various investigators have also reported that the effects of maternal smoking include increases in (a) pregnancy complications, (b) fetal distress, (c) spontaneous abortion, (d) neonatal morbidity, (e) perinatal mortality, (f) growth retardation, and (g) behavioral abnormalities (Abel, 1980b). Research in this area is very difficult, however, and unfortunately is plagued by problems in methodology and control. Therefore, although there is abundant evidence to strongly implicate maternal smoking during pregnancy as a potentially threatening factor in prenatal and neonatal health and development, interpretations of mechanisms and etiology remain unclear and controversial (Lefkowitz, 1981). Although it is true that nicotine has long been a drug suspected as a human teratogen, its teratogenicity has not yet been established. These contradictory findings and lack of clarity with regard to maternal smoking during pregnanc, introduce some balance into the picture, and they should not be interpreted as an exoneration of such self-initiated behavior. Indeed, even the inconclusive evidence should be a compelling enough reason to avoid smoking during pregnancy when one considers that potential fetal risks far outweigh maternal benefits. It remains very clear and unequivocal that smoking is the most easily preventable cause of low birth weight and prematurity, two major determinants of infant mortality and morbidity.

Pharmacology of Smoking

Nicotine is the primary particulate in cigarette smoke that is responsible for the pharmacological effects of smoking. Since nicotine is both water-soluble and lipid-soluble, it is rapidly absorbed and distributed throughout the body. Nicotine is metabolized by the liver, kidney, and lungs and then fairly rapidly eliminated from the body, primarily by the kidneys. It has a pharmacological effect on both the autonomic and central nervous systems, producing a broad spectrum of physiological responses in the smoker (Abel, 1980b). Nicotine easily crosses the placental barrier, but fetal nicotine levels remain low relative to maternal tissue levels, except perhaps in the early stages of pregnancy (Abel, 1980b). The major hypothesis that attempts to account for the mechanism by which maternal smoking affects fetal development, however, is intrauterine hypoxia. Fetal hypoxia results from increased levels of maternal blood carboxyhemoglobin—the bonding of carbon monoxide from cigarette smoke with blood hemoglobin. Since carbon monoxide has a stronger bonding affinity for hemoglobin than oxygen does, blood oxygen unloading in fetal tissue becomes impaired. The result is reduced fetal oxygenation. In addition, smoking is believed to produce uterine vasoconstriction, which reduces placental blood flow. The combined effect of these physiological responses to smoking is hypothesized to increase the probability of fetal hypoxia to dangerous levels.

Smoking Cessation and Prevention Programs

The variable success of smoking cessation programs and the problems of smokers' dependence are well documented (Surgeon General, 1979, 1981; Krasnegor, Note 3; Shiffman, Note 4). Some reports of preliminary or exploratory studies of cessation programs for pregnant women have begun to appear in the literature (Danaher, Shisslak, Thompson, & Ford, 1978). Limited sample sizes and questions of maintenance of smoking abstinence prevent any evaluations of these programs beyond a demonstration of promise. It appears that intervention programs designed to prevent the initiation of smoking will prove to be much more effective. A number of such intervention programs are currently under way (McAlister, Perry, Killen, Slinkard, & Maccoby, 1980; Perry, Killen, Telch, Slinkard, & Danaher, 1980). Most of these programs are directed at adolescent and preadolescent populations in elementary and secondary schools (Surgeon General, 1981). Data from these programs and other surveys strongly suggest that primary prevention programs in smoking education should begin in the early school years. Only through increasing public education and awareness of the hazards of smoking in pregnancy may we expect to stimulate individual responsibility in the prevention and cessation of such behavior.

ALCOHOL, PREGNANCY, AND HEALTH DEVELOPMENT: THE FETAL ALCOHOL SYNDROME

Concern about the effects of alcohol on the developing fetus can be traced back to antiquity. Clinical descriptions of birth defects among infants born to mothers who drank alcohol during pregnancy were reported during the Greek and Roman periods (Finnegan, 1981). Various reports of similar observations appeared during the 18th, 19th, and early 20th centuries, but it was not until 1973 that professional and scientific communities in this country became seriously concerned about alcohol use during pregnancy. Jones and Smith (1973) reported a pattern of malformations in infants born to chronically alcoholic mothers, which they labeled fetal alcohol syndrome (FAS). Following their report, several subsequent studies have been published (for recent reviews, see Abel, 1980a; Finnegan, 1981; NIAAA, Note 5).

The majority of these studies suggest that prenatal exposure to alcohol has teratogenic or embryotoxic effects. Although many of these studies have limitations due to methodological problems of control over a number of maternal conditions associated with excessive drinking or alcoholism, we must nevertheless recognize alcohol as a potentially serious threat to fetal health development. The evidence strongly suggests that FAS and symptom severity are dose-related. The clearest evidence of FAS has been found among heavy drinkers and chronic alcoholics. Since the etiologic mechanisms underlying FAS remain unclear, the status of alcohol as a human teratogen has not been definitely established. Abel (1980a) reports that mental retardation is recognized as the most serious defect and the most frequent manifestation of maternal alcohol use and FAS. For these reasons, he refers to alcohol as a behavioral teratogen.

The major features of FAS have been grouped into four categories (Clarren & Smith, 1978):

1. Central nervous system: mental retardation, poor motor coordination, hypotonia, irritability, hyperactivity.
2. Growth deficiency: prenatal and postnatal reduction in size, weight, and head circumference.
3. Craniofacial abnormalities: short palpebral fissures, short and upturned nose, sunken nasal bridge, epicanthal folds, malformation of midface and jaws.
4. Other major and minor malformations: cardiac, urogenital, and skeletal defects.

Several hundred cases of FAS have been reported since 1973, but the syndrome has not yet been observed in children of nonalcoholic women. Estimates of the incidence of FAS range between 4,000 and 5,000 births per year in the United States. This represents one to two live births with FAS per 1,000 live births overall. Sex differences in the consumption of alcohol are slowly disappearing. Some investigators report that women between 18 and 34 years of age may be overrepresented among heavy drinkers (Abel, 1980a). A heavy drinker is usually defined as one who consumes five to six drinks per day, every day (approximately 3 oz. or 60 ml of ethanol or absolute alcohol daily). In his review of female consumption patterns, Abel (1980a) reports that about 2% of middle-class pregnant women consume two drinks per day, with much higher rates of drinking occurring among pregnant women in low socioeconomic status (SES) groups. Chronically alcoholic women are at much greater risk of giving birth to children with FAS. Although some data suggest that moderate drinking may also result in the syndrome, this evidence is not nearly so compelling (Abel, 1980a; Kolata, 1981). Safe limits of alcohol consumption during pregnancy have not been established. The National Institute on Alcohol Abuse and Alcoholism (NIAAA, Note 5) has a simple message for women: "For baby's sake . . . and yours, don't drink during pregnancy." Major media campaigns by the NIAAA to publicize the dangers of alcohol and pregnancy are controversial (Kolata, 1981) and are considered alarmist by many scientists and professionals in the field.

Since many pregnant women consume alcohol socially in small to moderate quantities, what can such women be told about the potential dangers of such drinking? The NIAAA has published the following recommendations (FDA, 1977):

1. Safe levels of drinking are unknown.
2. Consumption of 3 ounces of absolute alcohol daily places the fetus at risk.
3. Prenatal risk associated with smaller amounts of alcohol is unknown, but caution is advised.
4. Teratogenicity is critically related to peak blood levels of alcohol concentration.
5. Pregnant women are advised not to exceed two drinks per day (1 oz.).

Several alcohol prevention and demonstration projects are currently under way that are designed to minimize alcohol-related problems during pregnancy (NIAAA, Note 5). These include FAS prevention programs that, through media campaigns and print material, issue warnings to women about the dangers of drinking during pregnancy. For women with histories of excessive drinking and chronic alcoholism, it would appear that pregnancy should be avoided through birth control techniques until successful treatment and rehabilitation are established. Although many questions about alcohol and pregnancy remain unanswered, there is little doubt that moderate to heavy alcohol consumption during pregnancy must be avoided for normal fetal and postnatal health development.

MATERNAL DISEASES

The final category of human teratogens comprises maternal diseases and conditions during pregnancy. The major considerations of these teratogen groups are infectious diseases and metabolic disturbances. Infectious diseases, particularly those involving viruses, can be transmitted prenatally either by placental diffusion or by infection of the female genital tract. Viral invasion of the embryo or fetus may result in cellular destruction and congenital malformations. Maternal metabolic disturbances exert their prenatal effects by disrupting or impairing fetal requirements necessary for normal development. Altered physiological states associated with such maternal conditions result in an inadequate or abnormal intrauterine environment.

Three infectious viral diseases have been positively identified as teratogenic for the human prenatal organism: rubella (German measles), cytomegalovirus, and herpes simplex (Langman, 1975). We will discuss only rubella, since data on the other two diseases are sorely lacking and difficult to obtain. The teratogenicity of rubella among pregnant women was first reported in 1941 (Gregg, 1941). It is now well established that rubella contracted during the first trimester of pregnancy results in a syndrome of varied malformations. Depending on the stage of embryonic development at which rubella infection occurs, these malformations may include congenital cardiovascular defects, blindness, deafness, microcephaly, mental retardation, and intrauterine growth retardation. The risk of congenital defects is related to time of maternal infection. If rubella is contracted during the first four weeks of pregnancy, its effects occur in approximately 50% of the newborns; if infection takes place in the fifth to eighth weeks, 22% are affected; and if infection occurs during the ninth to sixteenth weeks of pregnancy, 6% to 7%. After the fourth month of pregnancy, the risk of malformation drops to near zero (Langman, 1975).

Tests are now available to determine maternal antibody levels and immunity to rubella. Effective vaccines have also been developed to protect all individuals from rubella infection, and inoculation should be a high behavioral health priority for everyone. The administration of live virus vaccines is not suggested during pregnancy, however, since such vaccines can infect the fetus. Routine vaccination of all infants and immunity tests for women prior to pregnancy should end rubella as a pregnancy risk and as a hazard to prenatal and postnatal health development.

MATERNAL METABOLIC CONDITIONS

The three maternal metabolic conditions that have been most studied for their teratogenicity are hypothyroidism, hyperthyroidism, and diabetes mellitus. Maternal hypothyroidism may result in iodine deficiencies in the fetus, leading to congenital cretinism, retardation, and structural malformations. Maternal hyperthyroidism may sometimes result in fetal exophthalmos. There is no clear evidence that pharmacological treatment of these maternal conditions has teratogenic effects on the fetus (Takano, 1969).

Disturbances in carbohydrate metabolism associated with maternal diabetes during pregnancy result in a higher incidence of birth defects, stillbirths, neonatal mortality, and abnormally large infants. The frequency of neonatal mortality and morbidity among diabetic mothers approaches 80%. The most commonly observed anomaly among affected infants is the caudal regression syndrome—the absence of one or more sacral and/or lumbar vertebrae and abnormalities of the lower extremities. Obstetric management of diabetic pregnant women is complicated by suspected teratogenicity of some of the drugs used to treat the condition (i.e., insulin, tolbutamide). Teratogenicity of these pharmacological agents has not been established, however.

AGE, PREGNANCY, AND HEALTH DEVELOPMENT

Parental Maturity

It has been recognized for some time that maternal age, particularly over 35 years, may be an influencing factor in prenatal health development. More recent evidence suggests that age as a high-risk factor in pregnancy may also involve women under the age of 17 (Gunter & LaBarba, 1979; Scott, Field, & Robertson, 1981; Comptroller General, Note 1; Committee on Labor and Human Resources, Note 2). In women over 35 years of age, ova stored in the body from birth may be adversely affected by exposure to biological/biochemical changes associated with aging or to various other potentially harmful environmental agents. The incidence of Down's syndrome, or trisomy-21, is known to be strongly related to maternal age. The etiology of this condition has been traced to meiotic nondisjunction on the 21st pair of chromosomes. Approximately 56% of the infants with Down's syndrome are born to mothers aged 35 and older; between the ages of 30 and 34, the incidence drops to about 17% (Smith & Berg, 1976). Down's syndrome is relatively common, occurring in 1 of every 500 to 600 births. Clinical symptoms include severe mental retardation, flattened facial features, and a variety of other birth defects.

The conclusions of early researchers attributed the etiology of trisomy-21 to female meiotic nondisjunction. More recent research efforts, however, using new technological discoveries in cytogenetics, such as chromosomal staining procedures that permit individual parental chromosomal banding, have revealed that 20% to 25% of Down's syndrome results from paternal nondisjunction during spermatogenesis (Mikkeisen, 1981; Roberts & Callows, 1980). Although most recent work shows weak or no paternal age effects in Down's syndrome, there are some data to suggest such effects. Stene, Fisher, Stene, Mikkeisen, & Peterson (1977) and Erickson & Bjerkedal (1981), have reported a significant paternal age effect in Down's syndrome. Fathers aged 50 years or older were found to have an increased risk, 20% to 30%, of contributing to the birth of an infant with Down's syndrome. The evidence for a maternal age effect in Down's syndrome is strongly supported, but attempts to clarify paternal age effects continue. At present, the data point to a weak, independent paternal age effect, but when it begins is unclear. Furthermore, the paternal age effect is found to be much smaller than the increase in risk associated with maternal age.

Thus, the message here for the prevention and reduction of Down's syndrome is, when feasible, for women to complete their childbearing before the age of 35 or so and for men to become fathers before the age of 50. Furthermore, women in their mid-thirties who become pregnant may wish to consider amniocentesis to determine any prenatal abnormalities and to consider abortion if such abnormalities are detected. It should be reemphasized that half of the cases of infants born with Down's syndrome could be prevented by use of birth control procedures by women aged 35 and older. The number of cases may be further decreased by awareness of the potential paternal age effects recently reported in the literature.

Adolescent Childbearing

Epidemiology of Adolescent Pregnancy

Whereas increasing maternal age has long been recognized as a potential hazard to fetal development, only during the last 15 years has adolescence been implicated as a risk factor in prenatal and neonatal health development. Early reports of adverse maternal and neonatal consequences of adolescent childbearing suggested that both teenage mothers and their infants are a high-risk group (Blum & Goldhagen, 1981; Gunter & LaBarba, 1980; Scott et al., 1981; Comptroller General, Note 1). During the past decade, there has been increasing public and scientific attention to, and concern about, adolescent pregnancy in the United States as a serious national, medical, and social problem. Reports from the National Center for Health Statistics between 1976 and 1978 indicated that birthrates among adolescents remained high despite a steady decline for all other maternal age groups. Public and professional awareness of this situation reached acute levels when Lincoln, Joffe, & Ambrose (1976) described adolescent pregnancy as reaching "epidemic" proportions in this country.

Recent reanalyses of the epidemiologic data on adolescent pregnancy have placed this problem in a more balanced perspective (Blum & Goldhagen, 1981; Scott, 1981). An epidemic is defined as a condition or situation that is prevalent and spreading rapidly among people in a community at the same time. Scott (1981) has critically evaluated the claims of the epidemic proportions of adolescent pregnancy. When one considers the rate of teenage births per 1,000 women in an age group rather than the misleading data on the incidence of teenage pregnancy as a proportion of all births, a different picture emerges. Available statistics from 1970 indicate that the birthrate for all but the youngest age group (10–14 years) has declined. Birthrates among the 10- to 14-year-old group have remained stable at 1.2 per 1,000 women. Scott's analysis of the absolute number of births to teenagers from 1966 to 1977 shows a decline in the 18- to 19-year-old group and only slight increases among the 15- to 17-year-old and 10- to 14-year-old groups. Scott correctly concludes, therefore, that epidemic conditions of adolescent childbearing, in terms of both absolute and relative rates, do not currently exist in the United States.

Adolescence as a Prenatal Risk Factor in Health Development

Although it is clear that birthrates among adolescents are declining, the rate of decline is slower than that for the general childbearing population. Furthermore, the proportion of adolescents giving birth in the United States is high relative to most other Western countries. Twenty-five percent of the total annual births in the United States are to adolescent mothers. Well over half a million infants are delivered annually to mothers between 10 and 19 years of age (Blum & Goldhagen, 1981). The rates for black adolescent mothers in different age groups are considerably higher than those for whites, ranging from two to seven times greater, depending on the age group. These figures, plus data suggesting an increase in sexual activity among American teenagers, do present cause for concern in view of the possible implication of adolescence as a risk factor in maternal, prenatal, and postnatal health development.

A large body of scientific literature describing the maternal, perinatal, and developmental consequences of adolescent childbearing has accumulated over the past 20 years (for reviews and summaries, see Blum & Goldhagen, 1981; Gunter & LaBarba, 1980; Lawrence & Merritt, 1981; Scott et al., 1981). Early reports of the consequences of adolescent pregnancy described higher incidences of (a) pregnancy and birth complications, (b) neonatal mortality and morbidity, and (c) deficiencies and/or retardation in intellectual, physical, motor, neurological, social, and emotional development among infants of adolescent mothers relative to those of adult mothers. Many of these studies have methodological limitations that seriously weaken conclusions of adverse maternal and neonatal effects. More recent studies, which control for such factors as socioeconomic status, nutrition, age, prenatal care, and race, reveal good obstetric outcomes among adolescents if they receive adequate prenatal care. The exception in these general findings is the very young adolescent under 14 to 15 years of age, especially when pregnancy occurs within 24 months of menarche (Monkus & Bancalari, 1981). In a recent study, Gunter and LaBarba (1981) found no differences in the incidence of maternal and infant complications between adolescents and adult controls. Multiple regression analysis of the data revealed that an adolescent under the age of 17 is more likely to have an infant with low birth weight if the mother has a low prepregnancy weight, a below-average weight gain during pregnancy, and low delivery hemoglobin, and if she had no prenatal care until late in pregnancy.

Although adolescent pregnancy as a biological variable may not represent as great a risk factor as was previously supposed, the data do point to the psychosocial and economic risks that such conditions impose on the newborn infant. Because of the socioeconomic characteristics of adolescent mothers, the outlook for the postnatal development of their infants is dismal. The intellectual and educational achievements of such children have been lower than those of children of older mothers. The generally inadequate environmental opportunities and advantages often found among adolescent mothers reduce the probabilities of normal patterns of development.

It must be stressed that the question of biological or postnatal social factors in adolescent pregnancy outcome is not completely answered at this time. The data strongly suggest that adolescents under 14 years of age are at greatest risk in terms of infant health development. It also seems quite clear that adequate self-initiated or sponsored prenatal care is an absolute requirement for the pregnant adolescent.

Intervention Programs for Pregnant Adolescents

Regardless of the uncertainty of its consequences or etiology, adolescent pregnancy represents a problem of concern in child health development. This concern has been a major factor in the development of intervention programs for pregnant adolescents that are designed to enhance health and prevent disease. Two approaches have been taken in the development of such programs: (a) primary prevention of adolescent pregnancy and childrearing and (b) secondary prevention, which involves attempts to minimize the potentially adverse consequences of adolescent pregnancy (see Klerman, 1981, for a review of the development and assessment of these programs). Primary prevention programs are designed to encourage behaviors that prevent or reduce the frequency of adolescent pregnancy and childbearing through sex education, provision of contraceptives, abortion, and adoption. Secondary prevention programs attempt to aid pregnant adolescents who have decided to complete their pregnancies and raise their children by providing prenatal care, continuing educational opportunities for the mothers, day care support for the children, and counseling services. Since many of these programs are new, only limited reports of program evaluation are available. Though encouraging, the reports are mixed with regard to the success of the programs (Klerman, 1981; Sandler, Vietze, & O'Connor, 1981). Positive, direct steps at both the federal and state levels seem to show great promise of reducing the behavioral health toll attending the complex problem of adolescent pregnancy.

NUTRITION, PREGNANCY, AND BEHAVIORAL HEALTH DEVELOPMENT

There is little question that prolonged nutritional deficiencies during pregnancy may adversely affect prenatal development, and that maternal malnutrition can contribute to pregnancy complications that threaten both fetal and maternal health (Worthington-Roberts, Vermeersch, & Williams, 1981). It has also been suggested that a history of prepregnancy malnutrition may have implications for the quality of future childbearing (Drillien, 1964). With the exception of folic acid antagonists, no prenatal nutritional deficiencies have been clearly determined to be teratogenic in humans, but a number of studies appear to implicate maternal nutritional deficiency in fetal CNS impairment and subsequent functional impairment (Winick, 1969). Although the difficulty and complexity of isolating maternal dietary factors and deficiencies from other conditions associated with maternal malnutrition have contributed to contradictory reports, most physicians and researchers generally agree that poor nutrition may represent a risk factor during pregnancy, to both mother and fetus.

Malnutrition during pregnancy may result in physiological anemia of pregnancy and inadequate weight gain. Maternal nutritional anemia is more health-threatening to the mother than to the fetus and may lead to birth complications and impaired maternal health (i.e., severe anemia). Inadequate maternal weight gain, defined as less than 2 pounds per month during the second and third trimesters, has been associated with low fetal birth weight, fetal growth retardation, and increased neonatal risk. Maternal-fetal competition for energy sources and nutrients requires increased general caloric intake generally and particular increases in protein, iron, and folic acid. The use of broad-spectrum vitamin and mineral supplements during pregnancy, though common, is somewhat controversial and is seen by some physicians as an unnecessary expense. The promotion and maintenance of maternal and fetal behavioral health development during pregnancy require professional nutritional guidance. Furthermore, it is vital that expectant mothers, especially high-risk mothers such as adolescents, assume the individual responsibility to maintain and ensure the dietary practices that will contribute to maternal and fetal health development.

SUMMARY

From this survey of the major prenatal and neonatal influences on behavioral health development, it is clear that many of the potential threats to maternal and fetal integrity are preventable by self-initiation of a few sensible behaviors on the part of the mother. Through increasing awareness and recognition of potential health-threatening factors and by redirection of the individual health behavior of women in their childbearing years, we can anticipate changes in these hazardous conditions for the pregnant woman and her unborn infant. The emergence of the new fields of health psychology and behavioral health (Matarazzo, 1980, 1982) presents exciting new challenges to our national scientific and professional resources to apply our knowledge to the prevention of wastage of our number one resource—children.

REFERENCE NOTES

1. Comptroller General. *Better management and more resources needed to strengthen federal efforts to improve pregnancy outcomes.* GAO, HRD-80-24, 1981.
2. Committee on Labor and Human Resources (Subcommittee on Child and Human Development). *Oversight on efforts to reduce infant mortality and improve pregnancy outcomes.* June 30, 1980.
3. Krasnegor, N. A. (Ed.) *Cigarette smoking as a dependence process.* DHEW Pub. No. (ADN) 79-800. Rockville, Md.: Alcohol, Drug Abuse, and Mental Health Administration, 1979.
4. Shiffman, S. M. Diminished smoking, withdrawal symptoms, and cessation. In *A safe cigarette?* Banbury Report 3, 1980.
5. National Institute on Alcohol Abuse and Alcoholism (NIAAA). *Alcohol and health.* U.S. Department of Health and Human Services, January 1981.

REFERENCES

Abel, E. L. Fetal alcohol syndrome: Behavioral teratology. *Psychological Bulletin,* 1980, **87,** 29–50. (a)

Abel, E. L. Smoking during pregnancy: A review of the effects on growth and development of offspring. *Human Biology,* 1980, **52,** 593–625. (b)

Blum, R. W., & Goldhagen, J. Teenage pregnancy in perspective. *Clinical Pediatrics,* 1981, **20,** 335–340.

Christianson, R. E. The relationship between maternal smoking and the incidence of congenital anomalies. *American Journal of Epidemiology,* 1980, **112,** 684–695.

Clarren, S. K., & Smith, D. W. The fetal alcohol syndrome. *New England Journal of Medicine,* 1978, **298,** 1063–1067.

Danaher, B. G., Shisslak, C. M., Thompson, C. B., & Ford, J. D. A smoking cessation program for pregnant women: An exploratory study. *American Journal of Public Health,* 1978, **68,** 896–898.

Dekaban, A. Abnormalities in children exposed to x-irradiation during various stages of gestation: Tentative timetable of radiation injury to the human fetus. Part I. *Journal of Nuclear Medicine,* 1968, **9,** 471–485.

Drillien, C. M. *The growth and development of the prematurely born infant.* Baltimore: Williams & Wilkins, 1964.

Erickson, J. D., & Bjerkedal, T. Down's syndrome associated with father's age in Norway. *Journal of Medical Genetics,* 1981, **18,** 22–28.

Finnegan, L. P. The effects of alcohol and narcotics on pregnancy and the newborn. In R. B. Millman, R. Cushman, Jr., & J. H. Lowinson (Eds.), Research developments in drug and alcohol abuse. *Annals of the New York Academy of Science,* 1981, **362,** 1–244.

Food and Drug Administration (FDA). Fetal alcohol syndrome. *FDA Drug Bulletin,* 1977, **7.**

Goodner, D. M. Teratology for the obstetrician. *Clinical Obstetrics and Gynecology,* 1975, **18,** 245–253.

Gregg, N. R. Congenital cataract following German measles in mothers. *Transactions of the Ophthalmology Society,* 1941, **3,** 35–40.

Gunter, N., & LaBarba, R. C. The consequences of adolescent childbearing on postnatal development. *International Journal of Behavioral Development,* 1980, **3,** 191–214.

Gunter, N., & LaBarba, R. C. Perinatal and neonatal consequences of adolescent pregnancy. *International Journal of Behavioral Development,* 1979, **4,** 333–357.

Hobel, C. J. Better perinatal health. *Lancet,* 1980, **1,** 31–33.

Howard, F. M., & Hill, J. M. Drugs in pregnancy. *Obstetrical and Gynecological Survey,* 1979, **34,** 643–653.

Huff, P. S. Safety of drug therapy for nausea and vomiting in pregnancy. *Journal of Family Practice,* 1980, **11,** 969–970.

Jenson, O. H., & Foss, O. P. Smoking in pregnancy: Effects on the birth weight and on thiocyanate concentration in mother and baby. *Acta Obstetrica et Gynecologica Scandinavica,* 1981, **60,** 177–181.

Jick, H., Holmes, L. D., Hunter, J. P., Madsen, S., & Stergachis, A. First-trimester drug use and congenital disorders. *Journal of the American Medical Association,* 1981, **246,** 343–346.

Joffe, J. M. *Prenatal determinants of behavior.* London: Oxford University Press, 1969.

Johnson, C. Cigarette smoking and the outcome of human pregnancies. A status report on the consequences. *Clinical Toxicology,* 1981, **18,** 189–209.

Jones, J. S., & Smith, D. W. Recognition of the fetal alcohol syndrome in early infancy. *Lancet,* 1973, **2,** 999–1001.

Klerman, L. V. Programs for pregnant adolescents and young patients: Their development and assessment. In K. G. Scott, T. Field, & E. Robertson (Eds.), *Teenage parents and their offspring.* New York: Grune & Stratton, 1981.

Kolata, G. B. Fetal alcohol advisory debated. *Science,* 1981, **214,** 642–645.

Langman, J. *Medical embryology* (3rd ed.). Baltimore: Williams & Wilkins, 1975.

Lawrence, R. A., & Merritt, T. A. Infants of adolescent mothers: Perinatal, neonatal, and infancy outcome. *Seminars in Perinatology,* 1981, **5** 19–31.

Lefkowitz, M. M. Smoking during pregnancy: Long-term effects on offspring. *Developmental psychology,* 1981, **17,** 192–194.

Lincoln, R., Joffe, F., & Ambrose, L. *11 million teenagers: What can be done about the epidemic of adolescent pregnancies in the United States.* New York: Allan Guttmacher Institute, 1976.

Matarazzo, J. D. Behavioral health and behavioral medicine: Frontier for a new health psychology. *American Psychologist,* 1980, **35,** 807–817.

Matarazzo, J. D. Behavioral health's challenge to academic, scientific, and professional psychology. *American Psychologist,* 1982, **37,** 1–14.

McAlister, A., Perry, C., Killen, J., Slinkard, L. A., & Maccoby, N. Pilot study of smoking, alcohol and drug abuse prevention. *American Journal of Public Health,* 1980, **70,** 719–721.

Mikkeisen, M. New aspects of a well-known syndrome (Down's syndrome—mongolism). *European Journal of Pediatrics,* 1981, **136,** 15–17.

Monkus, E., & Bancalari, E. Neonatal outcome. In K. G. Scott, T. Field, & E. Robertson (Eds.), *Teenage parents and their offspring.* New York: Grune & Stratton, 1981.

Nora, J. J., & Nora, A. H. Can the pill cause birth defects? *New England Journal of Medicine,* 1974, **291,** 731–740.

Perry, C., Killen, J., Telch, M., Slinkard, L. A., & Danaher, B. G. Modifying smoking behavior of teenagers: A school-based intervention. *American Journal of Public Health,* 1980, **70,** 722–725.

Roberts, D. F., & Callows, M. H. Origin of the additional chromosome in Down's syndrome: A study of 20 families. *Journal of Medical Genetics,* 1980, **17,** 363–367.

Rush, R., & Shettles, L. B. *From conception to birth.* New York: Harper & Row, 1971.

Sandler, H. M., Vietze, P. M., & O'Connor, S. Obstetric and neonatal outcomes following intervention with pregnant teenagers. In K. G. Scott, T. Field, E. Robertson (Eds.), *Teenage parents and their offspring.* New York: Grune & Stratton, 1981.

Scott, K. G. Epidemiologic aspects of teenage pregnancy. In K. G. Scott, T. Field, & E. Robertson (Eds.), *Teenage parents and their offspring.* New York: Grune & Stratton, 1981.

Scott, K. G., Field, T., & Robertson, E. (Eds.). *Teenage parents and their offspring.* New York: Grune & Stratton, 1981.

Simpson, W. J. A preliminary report of cigarette smoking and the incidence of prematurity. *American Journal of Obstetrics and Gynecology,* 1957, **73,** 808–815.

Smith, G. E., & Berg, J. M. *Down's Anomaly* (2nd ed.). London: Churchill, 1976.

Stene, J., Fisher, G., Stene, M., Mikkeisen, M., & Peterson, E. Paternal age effects in Down's syndrome. *Annals of Human Genetics,* 1977, **40,** 299–306.

Sternberg, J. Irradiation and radiocontamination during pregnancy. *Journal of Obstetrics and Gynecology,* 1970, **108,** 490–495.

Surgeon General. Smoking and Health. U.S. Department of H.E.W., Washington, D.C.: U.S. Government Printing Office, 1979.

Surgeon General. Smoking and Health. U.S. Department of H.E.W., Washington, D.C.: U.S. Government Printing Office, 1981.

Takano, K. Comparative teratological effects of metabolic diseases of the mother. In H. Nishimura & J. R. Miller (Eds.), *Methods for teratological studies in experimental animals and man.* Tokyo: Igaku Shoin, 1969.

Wilson, J. G. *Environment and birth defects.* New York: Academic Press, 1973.

Winick, M. Malnutrition and brain development. *Journal of Pediatrics,* 1969, **74,** 667–679.

Worthington-Roberts, B. S., Vermeersch, J., & Williams, S. R. *Nutrition in pregnancy and lactation.* St. Louis: C. V. Mosby, 1981.

Yaffe, S. J., & Stern, L. Clinical implications of perinatal pharmacology. In B. L. Mirkin (Ed.), *Perinatal pharmacology and therapeutics.* New York: Academic Press, 1976.

Young, K. R. Smoking in pregnancy. *British Medical Journal,* 1981, **282,** 2057–2059.

CHAPTER 3

DEVELOPMENTAL PERSPECTIVES IN BEHAVIORAL HEALTH

MICHAEL C. ROBERTS

The University of Alabama

JAMES E. MADDUX

Texas Tech University

LOGAN WRIGHT

Institute of Health Psychology for Children, Oklahoma City

INTRODUCTION

Overview

Behavioral health is a developing concept and field of practice and research with particular importance for children and youth. Essential components of this concept include the promotion of health and the prevention of illness and accidents. The developmental perspective, as an underlying element of behavioral health, assumes a critical role for both promotion and prevention with children (as it should for all ages). This chapter provides an overview to behavioral health as related to children and examines the importance of the developmental perspective. There are developmental differences in the nature of children's health needs and in the characteristics of the approaches used to meet these needs. This chapter provides an orientation to the developmental perspective that is essential for later discussions of the wide variety of specific health problems that affect both children and adults. Numerous existing and recent phenomena relate to the birth of pediatric behavioral health, including pediatric psychology, health psychology, clinical developmental psychology, pediatric medicine, behavioral pediatrics, and preventive medicine. Distinctions and emphases need to be made for this newer development of pediatric behavioral health, particularly in relationship to pediatric psychology and behavioral health in general. The merging of issues and topics of concern to pediatric psychology and behavioral health results in the field of pediatric behavioral health, which can be distinguished from both larger fields.

Relationship to Pediatric Psychology

Pediatric psychology as a field of research and practice has been concerned with a wide variety of topics in the relationship between the psychological and physical well-being of children, including behavioral and emotional concomitants of disease and illness, the role of psychology in pediatric medicine, and the promotion of health and prevention of illness among healthy children (Roberts, Maddux, Wurtele, & Wright, 1982; Roberts & Wright, 1982; Tuma, 1982; Wright, Schaefer, & Solomons, 1979). Because of the force of critical needs in pediatric settings, pediatric psychology has typically emphasized physical, psychological, and behavioral pathology, often at the expense of the relationship between normal psychological processes in children and their physical health. Thus, the promotion of health and prevention of illness in children has received less attention than it deserves, although certainly this aspect has been recognized by both pediatricians and pediatric psychologists (Wright, 1979). The inequity of attention may be corrected with a new emphasis on pediatric behavioral health within pediatric psychology and behavioral health.

Relationship to Behavior Health

Similarly, pediatric behavioral health can be seen as different in important ways from mainstream behavioral health (as represented by the contents of this volume). At present, behavioral health appears more concerned with *adult* health and illness (Matarazzo, 1982). Children certainly are not ignored, but they seem to be viewed largely in terms of the ramifications of child health behavior for later adult health. Such a perspective is valuable in its own right for recognizing the developmental implications related to health. An exclusive focus on it, however, ignores the fact that childhood health problems are very different from adulthood health problems and cannot be fully understood solely in the context of later adult health. The leading cause of death and disability among adults, for example, is cardiovascular disease, accounting for a third of adult deaths (Califano, 1979). If we judge the importance of childhood health-related behavior merely by its potential effect on later adult health, then prevention of cardiovascular disease becomes a major focus (if not *the* major focus) of child health efforts. This leads to programs to change the attitudes and behavior of children regarding smoking, nutrition, alcohol consumption, exercise, and other demonstrated cardiovascular risk factors (e.g., Albino, in press).

These areas of intervention are extremely important, and research in these areas needs to be vigorously pursued. Yet this focus on prevention of adult problems through lifestyle change in childhood should not be allowed to obscure the fact that the leading causes of death and disability among children are accidents, accounting for 45% of all deaths for children between the ages of 1 and 14 years (Califano, 1979). Thus, prevention of accidents or injury control is more crucial for improving the well-being of children while they are children (Harris, 1981; Roberts, Elkins, & Royal, in press). Only by extricating child health behavior from the context of its importance for adult health, such as through the concept of pediatric behavioral health, can critical issues be examined that are of greater importance for children than for adults.

THE DEVELOPMENTAL PERSPECTIVE

Overview

The term *development* refers to orderly changes over time. In relating the developmental process particularly to children's health beliefs, attitudes, and behavior, we are referring to changes that are relatively orderly, predictable, measurable, and understandable. Development and change occur across the life span—from the prenatal period through life to death. In the childhood period, changes occur rapidly, particularly changes in children's abilities to think, reason, understand, and, consequently, make thoughtful decisions about their behavior. The rapidity and extensiveness of such changes make an understanding of them imperative to anyone wishing to understand any child at any age. In contrast, similar changes in adults occur more slowly and with different behavioral content. Understanding the health behavior of adults also depends on developmental considerations. Particular emphasis will be given here, however, to child development and change as related to the type of health problem encountered and the type of intervention that will be effective in preventing the problem.

One rough indicator of developmental change is chronological age. Thus, comparisons often may be based on number of years of life. We caution, however, that age is a gross indicator, at best, of developmental processes (e.g., physiological changes, experiences). Nonetheless, differences associated with age are important to pediatric behavioral health. Comparisons of the stark statistics on children's deaths versus those of adults, for example, demonstrate the major differences related to development and their implications for programming of health promotion and disorder prevention directed to children or to adults. As noted earlier, the leading cause of death among children aged 1 to 14 years is accidents. In 1977, accidents killed 10,000 American children in this age range; this figure is three times that for cancer, the next leading cause (Califano, 1979). In contrast, the leading cause of death among American adults is cardiovascular disease, accounting for over one-third of adult deaths (Califano, 1979). For children, therefore, the chief cause of death (and many thousands more injuries) is environmental circumstances (e.g., motor vehicles). Adults, however, tend to kill themselves by means of a series of independent, autonomous choices concerning what and how much to eat, smoke, and drink; whether or not to exercise; and how to handle problems of living. Obviously, these differences point to differences in needs and in types of intervention in health promotion and problem prevention.

The promotion and prevention needs of children differ from the needs of adults not only because the health problems of children are different, but also because children differ from adults in their capacity to understand health issues, to understand the relationships between behavior and health, and to assume personal responsibility for their health. Additionally, the rapid changes that occur during childhood call for continual changes in interventions. The differences between the adult at 35 years and the adult at 40 are insignificant in comparison to the tremendous differences between a child of 5 years and a child of 10 in the ability to understand causal relationships, to make decisions with deliberation, to plan ahead, to appreciate the consequences of one's actions, and to act autonomously in one's behalf or to one's detriment. Interventions must reflect such changes.

The utility of the developmental perspective may be demonstrated through its application in deciding via research (a) when during the life span certain prevention and health promotion services are most needed and for what kinds of problems, (b) when these services should be offered to maximize their efficacy and their acceptance by the child and those responsible for the child (e.g., parents, teachers), and (c) what types of services might be most effective.

When Services Are Needed

Developmental and epidemiologic information can help determine the points during the life span when certain problems occur and, thus, when services are particularly needed for such at-risk ages or groups of children. Since the data base or norms have not been established for developmental health psychology, we must rely on knowledge of child development to begin building this structure. Child development indicates, for example, that the young child (0–3 years) lacks both the motoric control necessary to ensure even minimum safety when riding in an automobile (e.g., balance, coordination, strength) and the cognitive capacity necessary for making a decision about his or her own safety. Additionally, physical development is such that infants are more susceptible to brain injury because of softer brain consistency and skull construction and that the greater proportion of body weight centered in the head pulls the head forward in collisions for primary contact with obstacles (Alcoff, 1982). Because of these developmental vulnerabilities, it becomes particularly critical that prevention measures be taken for restraining infants and young children in car seats (Baker, 1980; Williams, 1981). (This does not dispute the need for seat belts for all ages.) Similarly, motoric developmental changes suggest that different aged children have different abilities and behaviors. Consequently, different precautions are required when these changes occur.

Pediatric medicine has recognized the importance to child development of prevention efforts through physician counseling. Such anticipatory guidance informs parents of the normal behavioral characteristics of children at different ages while noting the typical accidents and advisory precautions (Brazelton, 1975; Nelson, Vaughan, & McKay, 1975; Roberts & Wright, 1982). Furthermore, examination of morbidity and mortality rates for different ages suggests when particular interventions may be necessary. Most preschoolers, for example, are not covered by laws making immunization mandatory for school attendance. Consequently, preschoolers have lower rates of inoculation compliance and are at greater risk for preventable diseases (Peterson, Note 1). Children aged 1 to 4 years have higher rates of accidental poisoning (Nelson et al., 1975), children aged 5 to 9 years have higher rates of pedestrian accidents (Yeaton & Bailey, 1978), and older children and adolescents have higher rates of accidents on recreational equipment (Califano, 1979; Werner, 1982). Thus, different types of accidents are associated with different developmental levels, and these developmental differences indicate when services are needed.

When Services Are Most Effective

Developmental studies can also indicate the points at which prevention or promotion services are most likely to be utilized optimally. Kanthor (1976), for example, suggests that attempts to increase the acquisition of child car safety seats are best directed at parents during the prenatal period. Other health promotion attempts (e.g., for neonatal and infant nutrition) might be made by the health professional during the intensive series of well-child visits typically scheduled in the first two years of childhood (i.e., anticipatory guidance). These efforts should have maximal effect because parents have the most intense contact with health personnel and are probably the most keenly aware of health issues during this time. This aspect of the developmental perspective suggests the point in life at which certain types of prevention and promotion are most likely to have substantive effects.

What Services Are Effective

Developmentally related research has revealed several examples of the types of services that might be most effective for particular ages or groups experiencing particular problems. Some research indicates, for instance, that antismoking programs for adolescents should be present-oriented rather than future-oriented (Evans, Rozelle, Mittelmark, Hansen, Bane, & Havis, 1978). Gallagher and Moody (1981) suggest that oral hygiene programs for adolescents should focus on benefits to personal appearance, since this age group demonstrates greater concern for physical attractiveness. Other programs can utilize components also shown to be effective for increasing behavior change to positive health habits. For example, active participation of children during their training (e.g., role-playing, guide-practice) appears to enhance their performance of toothbrushing and flossing (Claerhout & Lutzker, 1981), emergency fire recognition and safety behavior (Jones, Kazdin, & Haney, 1981), and pedestrian safety skills (Yeaton & Bailey, 1978). Such techniques appear especially useful for children who need action to maintain attention and practice to ensure skill acquisition and adequate performance.

Summary

These examples demonstrate the utility of the developmental perspective for determining when services are needed, what services are needed, and when they will be most effective. Research is needed to explore further the aspects of the developmental perspective emphasized here in relation to health promotion and preventive services.

IMPORTANCE OF CHILD DEVELOPMENT

Overview

Other chapters in this section apply the developmental perspective to other life periods. The focus of this chapter is on childhood. Fortunately, child development is an established component of life span development. As noted earlier, innumerable changes occur between infancy and adolescence. Perhaps more than at any other period of life, developmental changes in biological make-up, cognitive ability, and psychosocial behavior need to be considered in order to understand and modify the health behavior of the individual.

   Biological-physical changes primarily affect the child's ability to interact with his or her physical environment, the likelihood of encountering certain health hazards in the environment (e.g., reaching the top of the stove or striking a match), and the ability to enact environmental changes to ensure his or her own safety (e.g., buckling seat belts, brushing and flossing teeth). *Cognitive* and *intellectual* changes are crucial to the child's ability to understand health and illness, to understand the relationships between behavior and health and illness, and to make decisions about his or her own health behavior. *Psychosocial* development may be viewed as most important in addressing the issue of individual responsibility in health behavior—or the child's ability to assume responsibility for his or her own behavior. In the first year or two of life, the individual is almost totally dependent on others for health care. This same individual, however, steps into adolescence capable of more autonomous functioning in the care of his or her physical well-being. A child of 12 is not only vastly more capable than a child of 2 not only of understanding relationships between behavior and health but also of independently deciding to perform the behaviors that either enhance health or contribute to its deterioration (e.g., smoking, nutrition, dental hygiene).

   During childhood, attitudes are formed and behavioral patterns and styles are developed that become increasingly more difficult to modify as the child enters adolescence. Thus, the health attitudes and behaviors formed during childhood have a high probability of becoming, for good or ill, lifelong habits. If prevention and health promotion are to succeed, intervention must begin at the time during which the individual is developing an understanding of health and behavior; forming attitudes and behavior patterns regarding such matters as diet, exercise, and hygiene; and developing the psychological autonomy and cognitive capacity necessary for decision making and action taking (Stachnik, 1980). Many children exhibit one or more of the risk factors commonly associated with cardiovascular disease or atherosclerosis: hypertension, obesity, hyperglycemia, high cholesterol, cigarette smoking, and insufficient exercise (Voller & Strong, 1981). This finding suggests that some preventive measures need to be taken long before adulthood.

   Achenbach (1982) asserts that the developmental approach considers behavior in the context of human growth—its developmental tasks and processes. This assertion applies as much to children's physical health problems as to their psychological and behavioral problems (indeed, many health problems *are* behavioral problems). Child development, in particular, provides the empirical foundation for the study and application of behavioral approaches to child health care, health promotion, and disease prevention.

   Many developmental theorists postulate a series of stages or crises to be resolved as the child progresses in life (see summaries by Crain, 1980; Simeonsson, in press). Piaget focused on children's cognitive development through stages; Freud and Erikson considered personality and psychosocial development; Kohlberg and Piaget outlined moral development; and Gesell discussed normative development, particularly of maturation and motor-related abilities. Social learning theory has important implications for developmental theory but relies less on stage formulations. Instead, such theorists as Bandura postulate that the principles of learning are the same across all ages, whereas the specific content or behavior changes over time. As will be exemplified in later sections, these developmental theories and developmental phenomena have direct relationships with health behavior. For economy of presentation, we will examine two particular examples—motoric development and cognitive development in relation to health.

Children's Motoric Development and Health

The child's developmental progress results in changes in both exposure to health hazards and ability to safeguard personal health. Children's motoric and physical maturation and growth, advancements in mobility, and capacity for interaction with the physical environment place them at increasing risk for such environmental hazards as accidents and exposure to sources of disease. Although the restrictions of the crib-bound infant ensure relative safety and security—assuming the presence of a benevolent caretaker—the relative freedom of the crawling toddler virtually assures exposure to numerous preventable home health hazards, such as electrical cords that may be chewed, electrical sockets that invite the insertion of objects, cupboards containing bottles and boxes of toxic substances, and a variety of objects that may be placed in the mouth with adverse results. Standing and walking widens the child's horizon by exposure to the new dangers that come from a greatly accelerated mobility and greatly increased reach: hot stove tops, objects on table tops, steps and stairways, kitchen and bathroom cabinets, and such hazards of the outdoors as motor vehicles, broken glass, and unfriendly dogs. As the child advances in physical size and muscular strength and coordination, he or she begins to engage in increasingly more complex and hazardous recreational activities, including bicycling, riding skateboards, and participation in team sports that involve potentially deadly projectiles and potentially crippling bodily contact. This discussion demonstrates the rather simple, but obviously important, relationship of one type of child development, motoric/physical, to health hazards. Recognition of these developmental changes reveals changing needs and intervention.

Children's Cognitive Development and Health Beliefs

Since children continually are either afflicted themselves or exposed to peers with disorders, their understanding or perceptions of health are important for behavioral health. This importance becomes evident when we examine some of the misconceptions and misperceptions children may have about matters of illness and health. Some children perceive their illnesses as punishment for misbehavior or for harboring bad thoughts. Younger children may believe that it is possible to bleed to death from blood tests. Other misconceptions of behavior and health may include the belief that eating too much sugar can cause diabetes and that playing too hard can cause heart trouble. Such conceptions differ from those of adults. Across the age span, however, health beliefs show relationships with health behavior. Thus, a child's understanding may affect how he or she receives or complies with health regimens and actions (Roberts, Beidleman, & Wurtele, 1981). Furthermore, a child without apparent health problems can interact with afflicted peers either to enhance or impede adjustment. Several aspects of this have been studied, including children's perceptions of illness, conceptions of positive health, and perceived vulnerability or susceptibility to illness. Gochman (1970, 1972), for example, found that children's perceived vulnerability to health problems increases until about age 14 and then decreases with additional interactions deriving from gender and socioeconomic status. Developmental researchers have also found developmental relationships tied to children's cognitive abilities, since development affects their capacity to understand health and illness concepts.

Bibace and Walsh (1979) have proposed and offer support for a stage or phase model of the developmental changes in children's health conceptions. This model is based on Piaget's theory of the development of general cognitive abilities, but it elaborates on the Piagetian model through specific application to ideas concerning health and illness. Each of their six stages represents an increase over the previous stage in the sophistication of the child's thinking regarding the causes of good and poor health and in the child's capacity to assume control of health-related behavior. The sequence of stages follows the Piagetian stages of preoperational, concept operational, and formal operational thought: (a) phenomenism, (b) contagion, (c) contamination, (d) internalization, (e) physiological, and (f) psychophysiological. Some selected examples will illustrate these stages. In the phenomenistic stage, the child explains illness in magical terms; in the contamination stage, the child views illness as transmitted through physical contact with a source; in the physiological stage, the child recognizes multiple causes and cures, with an increased sense of personal behavior as a contributor to health and illness; and in the psychophysiological stage, the child advances to an increased sense of autonomy and personal control and responsibility for more preventive health behaviors. Other researchers have similarly used the Piagetian framework of cognitive development for conceptualizing children's perceptions of illness causality (Simeonsson, Buckley, & Monson, 1979), acceptance of chronically ill children (Potter & Roberts, in press), understanding of contagion (Kister & Patterson, 1980) and general health/illness perceptions (Perrin & Gerrity, 1981; Steward & Regalbuto, 1975; Whitt, Dykstra, & Taylor, 1979). One major developmental trend in these studies is that perceptions progress from the global to the abstract; this pattern corresponds to the development of cognitive abilities.

The relationship of cognitive abilities and health beliefs further relates to health behavior. The developmental changes in children's perceptions of health, illness, causality, and cure should therefore correspond to developmental changes in health behavior. Using the Bibace and Walsh (1979) framework, for example, in the internalization stage children develop the capacity to perceive themselves as actively behaving to promote good health rather than just avoiding illness, and this capacity increases with successive stages. This knowledge can be used in formulating programs. Thus, efforts at educating children about health and prevention should take into consideration the level of cognitive development of the target child. Education efforts that are too sophisticated may serve to confuse and, consequently, may meet with little success. Likewise, presentations that are too simplistic are likely to be ignored and discounted by older children. With young children in particular, the goals of educational programs should probably be modest. Parcel, Tiernan, Nader, and Gottlob (1979), for example, emphasized simple, but important, goals in a health education program for kindergarten children, such as learning to communicate feelings of wellness and illness to adults. An educational effort aimed at older children, the "know your body" program (Williams, Carter, Arnold, & Wynder, 1979), is more sophisticated in its approach and aims at more complex and specific goals (reducing chronic disease risk factors through fostering healthful lifestyles).

Other Developmental Aspects and Health

Some of the other developmental theories noted earlier have relevance for children's health. Erikson, for example, presented the first psychosocial stage of life (0–1½ years) as trust versus mistrust. If an infant's psychological needs are not met in this stage, health problems may occur—namely, failure to thrive, wherein the infant fails to physically grow in health and weight but no physical cause is involved (Roberts & Maddux, in press). A later Erikson stage, industry versus inferiority (6–12 years), involves the child's need to acquire skills and develop competence through personal industry and mastery. Health promotion programs can be oriented to this focus through training in particular skills (e.g., dental hygiene, water or pedestrian safety, children's safety at home without adult supervision).

Similarly, applications can be made of Kohlberg's research on moral principles. The conventional moral stage (age 9–15 years) describes children whose orientation is to follow the rules of society and conformity in order to receive rewards from others. This type of moral development can be utilized in conceptualizing health education. Health standards may be described for children in this stage for oral hygiene, for example, in order to instill societal expectation of daily dental self-care (Rose, Rogers, Kleinman, Shory, Meehan, &

Zumbro, 1979). In addition, programs that provide distinct rules of health behavior and systematic mechanisms for obtaining rewards might have particular success with such conventional stage children—for example, for nutrition management (Morasky & Lilly, 1980) or for general health promotion (Williams et al., 1979). These examples demonstrate the relevance and applicability of the developmental stage theories to health promotion and disease prevention. Social learning theory and research can also be used, as noted, through the use of learning principles that are applicable to all ages. Programs have implemented reward systems for dental hygiene (Claerhout & Lutzker, 1981), pedestrian safety (Yeaton & Bailey, 1978), personal safety (Jones et al., 1981; Poche, Brouwer, & Swearingen, 1981; Peterson, Note 2), and physical exercise compliance (Rushall & Siedentop, 1972). Social learning programs also rely on modeling components, for example, for toothbrushing (Murray & Epstein, 1981) and antismoking (Evans et al., 1978). Other program elements may include reminders or stimulus cues for health behavior such as reminders to parents to acquire dental checkups or disease immunization for their children (Reiss, Piotrowski, & Bailey, 1976; Peterson, Note 1) and reminders to children to use flouride mouth rinse (Lund & Kegeles, 1982).

It is evident that theory and research in developmental psychology, specifically in child development and related fields, have relationships and applications that are relevant to health behavior. The extended discussions of motor development and cognitive development combine with the brief examples just noted to support the utility of this perspective for health promotion and disorder prevention.

Children's Health Behavior and Adult Health

We have deliberately focused our attention in this chapter on child health behavior with implications during the childhood period. Health professionals have repeatedly articulated, and we readily acknowledge, that childhood has important effects on adult health. Attitudes and behavior formulated at an early age carry through life. Other authors in this volume detail this relationship for specific health components—stress management, physical exercise, proper nutrition, weight control, smoking and drug prevention, and cardiovascular considerations, among others. Precursors of all these components of adult health are found in child behavior. Thus, in examining the other chapters, the reader will find that most discuss the child's status primarily as an influence on later adult status. Only a few will emphasize the child for the child's sake (e.g., the chapters by Christophersen, Rivara, and Dershewitz). We will not duplicate these chapters' points here, but we encourage the reader to remember the perspective that programming geared to the child level can and should have implications for the child as well as for his or her adult life.

IMPLICATIONS OF DEVELOPMENT FOR HEALTH PROMOTION AND DISEASE PREVENTION

Overview

Human development has numerous implications for behavioral health. As noted, programming for health promotion and disease prevention needs to account for the developmental process in its design, implementation, and evaluation. Two additional aspects should also be considered. First, children have been thought of as highly dependent on adult caregivers for health-related actions. Second, programming is becoming more oriented to increasing the child's responsibility for his or her health. Both of these aspects relate to the major emphasis in behavioral health articulated by Matarazzo (1980): "individual responsibility in the application of behavioral and biomedical knowledge and techniques to the maintenance of health and prevention of illness and dysfunction" (p. 813). It is the concept of individual responsibility, however, that is the most troublesome in extending the goals of adult behavioral health to pediatric behavioral health. The problems in extrapolation stem mainly from important developmental differences between children and adults in their ability to assume behavioral responsibility for their own health and well-being. Child health problems are largely the result of the behavioral excesses and deficits of adults, of which the child is the victim. Automobiles, for example, are driven by adults, and accidents involving automobiles account for many child deaths. Accidents in the home are similarly the product of adults' ignorance and negligence rather than child irresponsibility. The issue of individual responsibility for health actions is thus a developmental one.

Children's Dependence on Adult Caregivers

The most important advances in child health in the past century have been accomplished primarily through efforts aimed at changing the behavior of adults rather than that of children. Immunization benefits, for example, were achieved by convincing adults of the dangers of childhood disease and of the necessity of immunization for their children. At present, diseases account for a relatively small number of childhood deaths, whereas accidents have become the major threat to the health of children (Haddon & Baker, 1981). In this regard, little may be accomplished without changes in adult behavior, since adults not only control aspects of their own behavior but also determine much of children's environment and behavior. These caregivers are obvious targets for behavioral health programming to benefit children. Roberts et al. (in press), for example, note that promotion and prevention can first target the caregiver's own unsafe behavior that relates to child health (e.g., control vehicle speed, decrease drunk driving, decrease alcohol consumption during pregnancy, not smoke around children). This approach produces benefits to both caregiver and dependent child. A second target can be changing the caregiver's behavior on behalf of the child (e.g., making the home safer, properly supervising play, acquiring car safety seats, acquiring immunizations and health checkups). This approach primarily benefits the child. The third targeting approach requires that the caregiver actively change the child's behavior to be safer and healthier (e.g., train the child in dental hygiene, proper nutrition, recreational safety, self-protection skills). The key element here is to target the caregiver to assume responsibility in changing the child's behavior. This last caregiver target also relates to effects of increasing the child's responsibility for his or her own behavior. The important point here is that children are dependent on adult caregivers for attaining their own level of responsibility. Because of their developmental status, children rely heavily on adults for health promotion and disease prevention; as a consequence, adults as caregivers will remain a major target of programs to benefit children's health (Roberts et al., in press).

Increasing the Child's Responsibility for Health

Consonant with the goals of mainstream behavioral health are attempts to increase the child's individual responsibility for health maintenance and problem prevention. Behavioral change by children will be necessary for significant gain to be achieved in some areas. Programs targeting the child can increase children's responsibility for their own health and well-being and can teach them to make interventions in their own self-interest in the absence of further adult supervision or despite adult apathy and ignorance. Levy, Lodish, & Pawlack-Floyd (1982), for example, designed a program to increase children's responsibility for their own dental treatment.

   The increases in the number of single-parent families and families in which both parents work also mean that children are already being forced, by default, to assume greater responsibility for their own health and safety. In an ever-growing number of households, children are assuming responsibility for their own nutrition, personal hygiene, and leisure activities (e.g., exercise)—areas that have important implications for present and later health. Thus, programs have targeted child training for self-protection (Poche et al., 1981), emergency behavior (Jones et al., 1981), and nutritionally sound food selections (Feshbach, Dillman, & Jordan, 1979). In addition, training programs for the health and safety of at-risk children can be provided for children who are left unsupervised (Peterson, Note 2).

Given appropriate programming, the evidence is that children are able to take over some aspects of their own health care. In addition to the research studies already noted, children have been successfully taught pedestrian safety skills to decrease risk of pedestrian accidents (Yeaton & Bailey, 1978) and to increase their participation in exercise (Rushall & Siedentop, 1972). Tooth-brushing skills have also been effectively taught to children of various ages (Claerhout & Lutzker, 1981). Not all such efforts are effective in increasing children's responsibility for health behavior (e.g., Levy et al., 1982). Nonetheless, the important point remains that, despite major developmental limitations, children can become capable of individual responsibility for their own health and safety (see Roberts et al., in press, for other such programs). To accomplish this goal, health education can be improved beyond what is typically provided in schools. Developmental considerations can be combined with currently known psychological principles to enhance effects. Perhaps the greatest challenge and potential for advancement in pediatric behavior health will come from the efforts to increase children's responsibility for their own health and safety. Underlying the entire approach, however, is the continued reliance on adults in the child's world for making available such growth opportunities and for maintaining a healthy and safe environment— in addition to the adults' changing their own behavior to benefit the child. These adults in the child's world must include parents, teachers, and behavioral health professionals.

SUMMARY

Regulations

Despite the optimistic outlook for behavioral health, it appears that substantial gains for children's health and safety will come only from changes in the environment and institutional make-up. This approach will necessarily include some regulation of industry and individual behavior. Major progress in disease prevention through immunization was not totally realized until inoculation was made mandatory for school attendance (Califano, 1981). The Poison Prevention Packaging Act of 1970, requiring child-proof caps, reduced poison ingestions and deaths (Walton, 1982). Other regulated standards also have had beneficial effects (e.g., regulations for crib safety, children's sleepwear, and the 55 mph speed limit). More regulations may become necessary to produce a condition of health and safety for children (e.g., requirements for airbags in cars). Pediatric behavioral health is necessarily involved in this approach to prevention, although the behavioral components are less direct (Roberts et al., in press).

Research

Further research will be the key to the development of pediatric behavioral health. The developmental perspective applies as well to research as it does to the applied, practical aspects of this emerging area. Developmental research should be expanded to determine how certain health attitudes and behaviors change as the child ages. One developmental research strategy, cross-sectional research, assesses different sets of children at different ages at the same time. White and Albanese (1981), for example, used four age groups in a cross-sectional study of developmental changes in cardiovascular health knowledge. Feshbach et al. (1979) compared children's abilities at different ages to understand nutrition information. The second developmental research strategy, longitudinal research, assesses the same children at different points in their lives. The length of time may be relatively short (e.g., 6 months to a year) or longer (e.g., through childhood and adolescence, a 15-year span). Williams et al. (1979), for example, are following school children over a 3-

year period to assess effects of a chronic disease risk-screening program combined with behaviorally oriented health education. Both types of developmental research, cross-sectional and longitudinal, can contribute to an understanding of the components of behavioral health and the relationship of developmental processes to those components. The developmental perspective, as manifested in these research strategies, can also aid in evaluating the effectiveness of promotion and prevention programs.

Conclusion

The developmental perspective adds much to the prospect of behavioral health. In particular, developmental processes must be taken into account when considering health promotion and disease prevention for children, whether the professional is oriented to improving the health status of the later adult or to improving the well-being of the child. Other chapters detail programs and research for behavioral health, and this chapter has outlined the necessity for considering the developmental perspective in each of these programs.

REFERENCE NOTES

1. Peterson, L. *Increasing immunization levels in high risk preschool children.* Paper presented at the meeting of the Midwestern Psychological Association, St. Louis, Mo., May 1980.

2. Peterson, L. *The "safe at home" game: Training comprehensive prevention skills in latch-key children.* Manuscript submitted for publication, University of Missouri.

REFERENCES

Achenbach, T. M. *Developmental psychopathology* (2nd ed.). New York: John Wiley & Sons, 1982.

Albino, J. Prevention by acquiring health enhancing habits. In M. C. Roberts & L. Peterson (Eds.), *Prevention of problems in childhood: Psychological research and applications.* New York: Wiley-Interscience, in press.

Alcoff, J. M. Car seats for children. *American Family Physician,* 1982, **25,** 167–171.

Baker, S. P. Prevention of childhood injuries. *Medical Journal of Australia,* 1980, **1,** 466–470.

Bibace, R., & Walsh, M. E. Developmental stages in children's conceptions of illness. In G. C. Stone, F. Cohen, & N. E. Adler (Eds.), *Health psychology.* San Francisco: Jossey-Bass, 1979.

Brazelton, T. B. Anticipatory guidance. *Pediatric Clinics of North America,* 1975, **22,** 132.

Califano, J. A., Jr. *Healthy people: The Surgeon General's report on health promotion and disease prevention.* Washington, D.C.: U.S. Government Printing Office, 1979.

Califano, J. A., Jr. *Governing America: An insider's report from the White House and the Cabinet.* New York: Simon & Schuster, 1981.

Claerhout, S., & Lutzker, J. R. Increasing children's self-initiated compliance to dental regimens. *Behavior Therapy,* 1981, **12,** 165–176.

Crain, W. C. *Theories of development: Concepts and applications.* Englewood Cliffs, N.J.: Prentice-Hall, 1980.

Evans, R. I., Rozelle, R. M., Mittlemark, M. B., Hansen, W. B., Bane, A. L., & Havis, J. Deterring the onset of smoking in children: Knowledge of immediate physiological effects and coping with peer pressure, media pressure and parent modeling. *Journal of Applied Social Psychology,* 1978, **8,** 126–135.

Feshbach, N. D., Dillman, A. S., & Jordan, T. S. Children and television advertising: Some research and some perspectives. *Journal of Clinical Child Psychology,* 1979, **8,** 26–30.

Gallagher, E. B., & Moody, P. M. Dentists and the oral health behavior of patients: A sociological perspective. *Journal of Behavioral Medicine,* 1981, **4,** 283–295.

Gochman, D. S. Children's perceptions of vulnerability to illness and accidents. *Public Health Reports,* 1970, **85,** 69–73.

Gochman, D. S. The development of health beliefs. *Psychological Reports,* 1972, **31,** 259–266.

Haddon, W., & Baker, S. P. Injury control. In D. Clark & B. McMahon (Eds.), *Preventive and community medicine.* Boston: Little, Brown, 1981.

Harris, P. *Better health for our children: A national strategy. The report of the select panel for the promotion of child health.* Washington, D.C.: U.S. Government Printing Office, 1981.

Jones, R. T., Kazdin, A. E., & Haney, J. I. Social validation and training of emergency fire safety skills for potential injury prevention and life saving. *Journal of Applied Behavior Analysis,* 1981, **14,** 249–260.

Kanthor, H. A. Car safety for infants: Effectiveness of prenatal counseling. *Pediatrics,* 1976, **58,** 320–328.

Kister, M. C., & Patterson, C. J. Children's conceptions of the cases of illness: Understanding of contagion and use of immanent justice. *Child Development,* 1980, **51,** 839–846.

Levy, R. L., Lodish, D., & Pawlack-Floyd, C. Teaching children to take more responsibility for their own dental treatment. *Social Work in Health Care,* 1982, **7,** 69–76.

Lund, A. K., & Kegeles, S. S. Increasing adolescents' acceptance of long-term personal health behavior. *Health Psychology,* 1982, **1,** 27–43.

Matarazzo, J. D. Behavioral health and behavioral medicine: Frontiers for a new health psychology. *American Psychologist,* 1980, **35,** 807–817.

Matarazzo, J. D. Behavioral health's challenge to academic, scientific, and professional psychology. *American Psychologist,* 1982, **37,** 1–14.

Morasky, R. C., & Lilly, L. P. Nutrition management for dental health: A behavioral approach. *Clinical Preventive Dentistry,* 1980, **2,** 7–9.

Murray, J. A., & Epstein, L. H. Improving oral hygiene with videotape modeling. *Behavior Modification,* 1981, **5,** 360–371.

Nelson, W. E., Vaughan, V. C., & McKay, R. J. *Textbook of pediatrics.* Philadelphia: Saunders, 1975.

Parcel, G. S., Tiernan, K., Nader, P. R., & Gottlob, D. Health education for kindergarten children. *Journal of School Health,* 1979, **49,** 129–131.

Perrin, E. C., & Gerity, P. S. There's a demon in your belly: Children's understanding of illness. *Pediatrics,* 1981, **67,** 841–849.

Poche, C., Brouwer, R., & Swearingen, M. Teaching self-protection to young children. *Journal of Applied Behavior Analysis,* 1981, **14,** 169–176.

Potter, P. C., & Roberts, M. C. Children's perceptions of chronic disease: The roles of disease symptoms, cognitive development, and information. *Journal of Pediatric Psychology,* in press.

Reiss, M. D., Piotrowski, W. D., & Bailey, J. S. Behavioral community psychology: Encouraging low-income parents to seek dental care for their children. *Journal of Applied Behavior Analysis,* 1976, **9,** 387–397.

Roberts, M. C., Beidleman, W. B., & Wurtele, S. K. Children's perceptions of medical and psychological disorders in their peers. *Journal of Clinical Child Psychology,* 1981, **10,** 76–78.

Roberts, M. C., Elkins, P. D., & Royal, G. P. Psychological applications to the prevention of accidents and illness. In M. C. Roberts & L. Peterson (Eds.), *Prevention of problems in childhood: Psychological research and applications.* New York: Wiley-Interscience, in press.

Roberts, M. C., & Maddux, J. E. A psychosocial conceptualization of failure to thrive. *Journal of Clinical Child Psychology,* in press.

Roberts, M. C., Maddux, J. E., Wurtele, S. K., & Wright, L. Pediatric psychology: Health care psychology for children. In T. Millon, C. J. Green, & R. B. Meagher (Eds.), *Handbook of clinical health psychology.* New York: Plenum Press, 1982.

Roberts, M. C., & Wright, L. Role of the pediatric psychologist as consultant to pediatricians. In J. M. Tuma (Ed.), *Handbook for the practice of pediatric psychology.* New York: Wiley-Interscience, 1982.

Rose, C., Rogers, E. W., Kleinman, P. R., Shory, N. L., Meehan, J. T., & Zumbro, P. E. An assessment of the Alabama smile keeper school dental health education program. *Journal of the American Dental Association* 1979, **98,** 51–54.

Rushall, B. S., & Siedentop, D. *The development and control of behavior in sport and physical education.* Philadelphia: Lea & Febiger, 1972.

Simeonsson, R. J. Theories of child development. In C. E. Walker & M. C. Roberts (Eds.), *Handbook of clinical child psychology.* New York: Wiley-Interscience, in press.

Simeonsson, R. J., Buckley, L., & Monson, L. Conceptions of illness causality in hospitalized children. *Journal of Pediatric Psychology,* 1979, **4,** 77–84.

Stachnik, T. J. Priorities for psychology in medical education and health care delivery. *American Psychologist,* 1980, **35,** 8–15.

Steward, M., & Regalbuto, G. Do doctors know what children know? *American Journal of Orthopsychiatry,* 1975, **45,** 146–149.

Tuma, J. M. (Ed.). *Handbook for the practice of pediatric psychology.* New York: Wiley-Interscience, 1982.

Voller, R. D., & Strong, W. B. Pediatric aspects of atherosclerosis. *American Heart Journal,* 1981, **101,** 815–836.

Walton, W. W. An evaluation of the poison prevention packaging act. *Pediatrics,* 1982, **69,** 363–370.

Werner, P. Playground injuries and voluntary product standards for home and public playgrounds. *Pediatrics,* 1982, **69,** 18–20.

White, C. W., & Albanese, M. A. Changes in cardiovascular health knowledge occurring from childhood to adulthood. *Circulation,* 1981, **63,** 1110–1115.

Whitt, J. K., Dykstra, W., & Taylor, C. A. Children's conceptions of illness and cognitive development. *Clinical Pediatrics,* 1979, **18,** 327–339.

Williams, A. F. Children killed in falls from motor vehicles. *Pediatrics,* 1981, **68,** 576–578.

Williams, C. L., Carter, B. J., Arnolds, C. B., & Wynder, E. L. Chronic disease risk factors among children: The "know your body" study. *Journal of Chronic Diseases,* 1979, **32,** 505–513.

Wright, L. Health care psychology: Prospects for the well-being of children. *American Psychologist,* 1979, **34,** 1001–1006.

Wright, L., Schaefer, A. B., & Solomons, G. *Encyclopedia of pediatric psychology.* Baltimore: University Park Press, 1979.

Yeaton, W. H., & Bailey, J. S. Teaching pedestrian safety skills to young children: An analysis and one-year followup. *Journal of Applied Behavior Analysis,* 1978, **11,** 315–329.

CHAPTER 4

ADOLESCENT DEVELOPMENT AND BEHAVIORAL HEALTH

RICHARD JESSOR

University of Colorado

Unbroken in continuity and seamless as time, the life course has nevertheless been subject throughout history to differentiation and partitioning of one sort or another. The divisions have reflected literary fancy, biological regularities, arrangements of the social order, and even the phenomenology of subjective awareness. Whatever the number of stages or periods described, however, their nature has always been somewhat problematic and their boundaries ambiguous and uncertain. Adolescence, as a relatively new emergent in the history of ideas about developmental stages, exemplifies all the difficulties associated with attempts to segment the trajectory of lives. Dissatisfaction with it as a single stage, for example, continues to be expressed in proposals to differentiate it further into early and late adolescence or to create yet another life stage, youth, to lie between adolescence and adulthood.

It has become quite clear by now that no absolute or univocal criteria can be invoked to demarcate periods of the life course—including the adolescent period. The criteria employed usually stem from the discipline or the interest of the developmentalist: an interest in physical growth might direct attention to the calcification of the bony epiphyses, the onset of the menses, or the volume of the testicles; an interest in social growth might focus on the shift toward peer orientation, the initiation of dating, or the assumption of certain role obligations; and a concern with organizing educational arrangements might give prominence to certain characteristics of the thought processes, especially the attainment of formal operational thinking. In short, the criteria that can be used to bracket the adolescent period will vary according to a number of considerations, including the population of young people being dealt with, the social and cultural setting in which they are located, the aim, purpose, or interest of the inquiry, and the time in history in which the inquiry takes place. Obviously, multiple and converging criteria are required for conviction that adolescence as a life stage has in fact been specified.

Despite such cavils about varying criteria and uncertain boundaries, it is apparent that adolescence is widely perceived in contemporary society as a period in the life span that is of key developmental significance. Accompanying this perception is a steadily growing awareness that the time of adolescence has special relevance for health. Not only is it

This chapter was prepared during the tenure of the author's Faculty Fellowship Award from the Council on Research and Creative Work, University of Colorado. Support for the longitudinal research described in the chapter was provided by Grant No. AA03745 from the National Institute on Alcohol Abuse and Alcoholism. I am grateful to Drs. Lee Jessor and John Donovan for their longtime collaboration in that work. I am also indebted to Dr. Cheryl Perry for enlarging my understanding of the field of health-related behavior.

distinctive in itself as a period of relatively high risk for compromising health, but, equally important, it is a developmental period that has long-range implications and reverberating consequences—both positive and negative—for health at later stages of the life span.

ADOLESCENCE IN THE LIFE SPAN

The adolescent period has experienced a major renewal of interest over the last decade or two, and there has been a burgeoning of research focused on it. Some of the impetus for greater attention to adolescence seems to have come from societal concern about the new patterns of behavior, especially those involving drug use and sexual activity, that were embedded in the youth movement of the 1960s and 1970s and that constituted an unanticipated and disconcerting challenge to established norms. Some of the impetus derives from an entirely different quarter—the enhanced awareness within the developmental sciences that plasticity and change are not confined to the earliest years alone and that the course of subsequent development is not already set by the events of infancy and early childhood. Indeed, the emergence of the life span perspective in developmental psychology (Baltes, Reese, & Lipsitt, 1980) and the elaboration of the life course emphasis in sociology (Elder, 1975; Riley, Johnson, & Foner, 1972) were based in large part on the premise that significant developmental change occurs throughout the entire life span. The characteristic pervasiveness and rapidity of change in adolescence has made that period an especially relevant stage for life span or life course research. Finally, recent years have seen the formulation of various theoretical positions (e.g., the problem-behavior theory of Jessor and Jessor, 1977) in which the adolescent period is allocated a pivotal role in the shaping of personality and behavior; this, too, has provided impetus for greater attention to adolescence.

As noted earlier, the absence of clear-cut boundaries around the adolescent period makes it difficult to segregate it from the stages that precede and follow it. When chronological age is relied on to delimit adolescence, the range usually extends from a rough lower bound of 10 to 12 years old to a rough upper bound of 18 to 20 and even beyond. Although it is helpful in locating adolescence as a segment along the life trajectory, chronological age remains a very unsatisfactory criterion for several reasons. First, there is enormous interindividual variation in the relation of age to the various other criteria—biological, psychological, social, and institutional—that must be invoked to bracket the adolescent stage more precisely. Furthermore, there have been long-term, secular changes in the relationship of several of these other criteria to age: the increasingly earlier age of menarche; the earlier age of entry into the secondary school system; and the initiation of sexual activity at increasingly younger ages. Finally, the timing of appearance of the various indicators of adolescence is likely to be asynchronous for a given child; thus, the onset of puberty as an indicator may occur at an earlier age than other indicators, for example, before entrance into junior high or before the assumption of autonomy in personal decision making.

The difficulties that arise from relying on chronological age have led to efforts to focus on alternative criteria on which to map developmental age. Anatomical and physical criteria, such as those used in Tanner staging, can be helpful in specifying a biological age, but children equated in those terms will vary enormously, not only in chronological age, but also on a large number of psychosocial and educational indicators whose convergence is required to implicate adolescence as a full-fledged stage. An additional limitation of reliance on any sort of biological age notion is that there are really no biological criteria that can be used to denote the upper bound of adolescence in a way that parallels their use in establishing the lower bound. Social norms and institutional regularities need to be invoked for that purpose—for example, completion of secondary schooling; entry into the full-time work force; attaining an age that is legally defined as adult, such as the age to vote or drink; living in a committed relationship with a partner; or deciding to start a family. These indicators reflect a social rather than biological definition of the end of adolescence or the beginning of young adulthood.

There are two further problems in dealing with adolescence as a single, delimited life stage. One of these is that adolescence entails a long period of time, an age range that covers at its conclusion nearly half the life span to that point. Over such an extended period of time, the events, experiences, and processes that characterize the earlier portion of adolescence are almost necessarily different from those that characterize the later portion. It is this fact that has prompted proposals to differentiate adolescence into more than a single stage in an effort to capture better the developmental variation that it encompasses. Given the sheer length of the adolescent period and the growth that takes place over those years, accounting for development, transition, and change within adolescence remains as much of a challenge as accounting for development into and out of that period.

Another problem in considering adolescence as a delimited life stage lies in the abundant evidence for continuity rather than discontinuity between adolescence and the stages that precede and follow it. Continuity on the antecedent side has been demonstrated in Kellam's work, for one example: classroom shyness and aggressiveness among first-grade black children was linked to their involvement with drugs a decade later during adolescence (Kellam, Brown, & Fleming, 1982). Continuity on the consequent side has been demonstrated in our own work in the Young Adult Follow-Up Study (Jessor & Jessor, in press), which provides evidence of how adolescent personality, social, and behavioral attributes predict variation in those same domains later in young adulthood. Such continuity between life stages argues against any sharp separation and disjunction of developmental stages, including the stage of adolescence.

Adolescence is best treated, therefore, as a stage that is internally heterogeneous and only roughly delimited, with the criteria of its onset—especially pubertal change—being more consensual than the criteria for its termination. For its full specification as a life stage, multiple and diverse criteria are required. In the final analysis, adolescence can be seen as a biologically marked, socially organized, and personally defined time in the life span. Encompassing nearly all the teenage years, and certainly the years in junior and senior high school, adolescence serves as a bridging period between childhood and young adulthood, and it functions as something of a crucible for the shaping of later life.

ADOLESCENCE AND CHANGE

The hallmark of the adolescent years is change. Extending from the transitions that are organized around the passage out of childhood to those that are concerned with the entry into adulthood, change tends to be pervasive across a wide variety of domains and to take place rapidly relative to its rate in nearly all other life stages. Beyond the more obvious changes in physical size and shape associated with the adolescent growth spurt and the onset of puberty, there are social and psychological changes that are equally transformative in magnitude. Some of these are rather direct reverberations and reflections of the physical changes—for example, elaboration of a new body image, attainment of greater athletic skill, or arrival at a sexually attractive appearance; and some are consequences of entry into new socially defined roles—exposure to new models and opportunities and the exploration of new self-definition and social identity occasioned by the social organization of adolescent life itself.

The developmental changes that are characteristic during adolescence can be approached in different ways. The focus can be on the major directions of overall growth or, alternatively, it can be on the acquisition of specific behaviors or the assumption of specific roles. The former approach has been exemplified by White's (1975) attempt to codify the main developmental trends he discerned in his case studies of late adolescence and early adulthood: the stabilizing of ego identity; the freeing of personal relationships; the deepening of interests; the humanizing of values; and the expansion of caring. Without having to assume that such trends are developmental invariants over history and across societies, we can still appreciate them as illuminating some familiar directions of adolescent psychosocial growth.

In a somewhat similar vein, Havighurst (1972) has proposed the concept of "developmental task." He lists a number of tasks or objectives the socially organized pursuit of which tends to structure change and transition in the adolescent period. These include such objectives as establishing autonomy and separation from family, completing one's education, choosing an occupation, establishing a sense of self, and developing a personal value system. Erikson (1963) has also pointed out several trends that are central to the adolescent stage, including the coming to terms with physical intimacy and the establishment of identity. Finally, our own work suggests additional directions of developmental growth—for example, the trend toward nonconventionality during adolescence and the opposite trend toward greater conventionality and conformity during young adulthood (Jessor, 1983b). Our work also suggests other developmental tasks that nearly all contemporary American adolescents are now having to deal with, such as coming to terms with the use of alcohol and other drugs (Jessor, 1983a).

When change at a more specific level is considered, the emphasis shifts to those key behaviors and nodal experiences that occur for the first time in adolescence—starting to drink or to use other drugs, beginning to work, moving away from home, becoming a nonvirgin—specific events that can have far-reaching effects on the young persons involved and on how they see themselves and come to be seen by others. A focus on specific behavioral changes calls attention to the major role that peers play in adolescence as models and as sources of information and reinforcement.

These comments about change during the adolescent stage in the life course are meant to serve as general background for the elaboration of theoretical issues and findings more closely related to our concern with behavioral health. Before concluding this section, it is worth bringing together several implications for health that seem to be inherent in the adolescent life stage.

First, it is apparent that adolescence is a period in which a variety of behaviors relevant to health are initially learned and tried out—both those that are potentially health-compromising, such as drug use or precocious sexual activity, and those that are likely to be health-enhancing, such as regular schedules of exercise or limiting the intake of calories in the diet. Second, many of the psychosocial attributes that influence and regulate the occurrence of health-related behaviors—values, beliefs, attitudes, motivations, personal controls, self-concept, general lifestyle—are also acquired or consolidated during adolescence. These first two points emphasize the key significance of adolescence as a pivotal time for health-related learning and socialization. Third, the changing environment of adolescence has its own implications for health in several important ways. Peers come to play a greater role at this stage relative to the role of parents or other adults, thus increasing the likelihood of nonconventional and health-compromising behavior; there is greater access at this stage to potentially health-compromising materials—drugs, alcohol, automobiles, and motorcycles—and to opportunities to use them; and the environment of adolescence is itself changing and developing, which results in major shifts in norms, in prevalence of behavior models, and even in legislative regulations, all of which can create uncertainty about appropriate behavior and can impose new demands for adaptation. Fourth, the sheer pervasiveness and rapidity of the personal and social changes that take place during adolescence may be a source of adaptation pressure—especially if multiple changes are under way simultaneously—and may require coping with feelings of inadequacy and expectations of failure. Fifth, the asynchrony of changes during adolescence is also likely to be stressful and problematic for health—for example, the asynchrony between the attainment of reproductive maturity and sexual interest, on the one hand, and societal relaxation of its norms and controls proscribing sexual activity, on the other.

The organization of adolescence around the accomplishment of temporally ordered developmental tasks and the key role that adolescence appears to play in the learning of health-relevant behaviors and orientations suggest one more implication for health. Adolescence may well be a critical period for a particularly significant health-promoting intervention, one involving the societal definition of a new developmental task for all adolescents to master—namely, the assumption and management of personal responsibility for their own health and social responsibility for the health of others.

ADOLESCENCE AS A RELATIVELY HIGH-RISK STAGE OF LIFE

Although it may seem to be obvious, the concept of health risk, in adolescence as elsewhere, is complex. Its employment requires the articulation of a number of different dimensions and qualifications. The prior concept of health, itself problematic, also remains refractory to any simple specification, whether it be the absence of disease on the physical level, the sense of competence and self-actualization at the psychological level, the minimal involvement in nonnormative activities at the behavioral level, or the successful enactment of role requirements at the social level. The complexity of the health risk notion can readily be seen in the elaboration of some of the dimensions along which it varies.

Health risk in adolescence can refer to risk that is immediately consequential within adolescence (e.g., the risk from driving after consuming alcoholic beverages); to risk that has consequences for the postadolescent period—that is, for adulthood and later life (e.g., the risk from obesity, or from a diet high in saturated fats); or to risks that include both present and remote consequences (e.g., the risk from becoming pregnant). It can refer to risk deriving from behavior (e.g., from cigarette smoking or from not using seat belts); to risk deriving from personality characteristics (e.g., risk from the sense of powerlessness or from having a strong need for independence and rebelliousness); to risk related to aspects of the environment (e.g., risk from access to automobiles, from exposure to peer models for drinking, or from opportunities for sex); or to the interactions of all of these kinds of risks. Health risk can refer to risks that are relatively universal and invariant in their consequences for health (e.g., the risk from contracting a sexually transmitted disease or from having adolescent hypertension) or to variable risks that depend for their consequences on the presence of certain situational factors (e.g., the risk from using marijuana just before driving), on gender (e.g., the risk from heavy drinking when pregnant), on body size and weight (e.g., the risk from a high rate of alcohol intake), or on age (e.g., the risk from insufficient hours of sleep in early adolescence). Finally, health risk can also refer to a particular threshold level of intensity of involvement with a behavior or activity; lesser involvement in that behavior need not be risky and, in some instances, may even be health-enhancing (e.g., the risk from overeating, whereas eating lesser amounts of food is actually health-enhancing; or the risk from drinking alcohol, whereas intake of moderate amounts may be health-protective, while both abstinence and heavier drinking may be health-compromising).

When used to characterize an individual's life as a whole, the concept of health risk should reflect the balance that obtains between the health-compromising and the health-enhancing activities in which the person engages. Thus, the risk to health of engaging in health-compromising behaviors should probably be seen as variable; its magnitude will often depend on the extent, the variety, and the intensity of the health-enhancing behavior engaged in by the adolescent at the same time.

In documenting that adolescence is, indeed, a relatively high-risk stage of life for health, it would be entirely appropriate to consider such distal and macro health risks for adolescents as the impending possibility of nuclear devastation or the malignant consequences of poverty and unemployment. My focus here, however, will remain more proximal. I will refer briefly to a few of the major risks that characterize this particular stage of the life span and that can be consequential for the approximately 40 million adolescents in the American population.

It turns out that the primary causes of death and disability at this life stage are behavioral in origin. Most sobering is the fact that some form of violence—traffic accidents, suicides, and homicides—constitutes the leading cause of death among adolescents and youth in the 15 to 24 age range (NCHS, 1982). From 1950 to 1979, the number of deaths per 100,000 from motor vehicle accidents in this age group rose from about 34 to about 47. For white males between age 15 and 24, automobile accidents showed a death rate of 77 per 100,000, accounting for more than 40% of the deaths among this segment of the population. Such figures are even more compelling when we consider that they refer only to mortality and that the prevalence of motor vehicle-related morbidity and disability still has to be taken into account. Furthermore, in any appraisal of the risk associated with accidents, especially motor vehicle accidents, it is essential to recognize the important role played by alcohol and drug use—other key adolescent risk behaviors. Suicide, the third leading cause of death for young white people and fourth for young black people in this age group, implicates a whole other set of risk factors—the psychosocial processes of stress, depression, and coping failure that may surround the developmental tasks confronting young people.

Exposure to and involvement with alcohol, marijuana, and other drugs can be considered another facet of health risk during the adolescent period, with potential consequences for later stages of the life course as well. The fact is that some involvement with alcohol, tobacco, and marijuana is now statistically normative by late adolescence in American society, with 9 out of 10 high school seniors having tried alcohol, 7 out of 10 having tried smoking, and 6 out of 10 having used marijuana.

The most widely used drug, of course, is alcohol, with 71% of a national sample of graduating high school seniors—the class of 1981—reporting use in the preceding month and 6% reporting daily use during that same period (Johnston, Bachman, & O'Malley, 1982). Of considerably more health risk concern than the frequency of use, however, is the evidence about quantity of use per drinking occasion. Johnston et al.'s (1982) same Monitoring the Future report on the class of 1981 indicates that fully 41% of the 17,500 respondents had consumed five or more drinks on at least one occasion during the preceding 2-week interval (an increase, incidentally, from the 37% figure reported by the class of 1975). The consumption of five or more drinks at a single occasion is a level of intake that often leads to drunkenness, loss of control, deficit in perceptual-motor coordination, and accident proneness, the mortality and morbidity potential of which was noted earlier. In addition to the prevalence of such heavy use of alcohol in adolescence, its risk is probably compounded by the fact that most adolescents have their initial experience with alcohol before reaching tenth grade—that is, before age 15. Analyses of the data from another national sample study, this one involving nearly 13,000 junior and senior high school students in 1974 (Rachal, Williams, Brehm, Cavanaugh, Moore, & Eckerman, 1975), found that nearly a third of the adolescents in that sample who drank could be classified as problem drinkers, based on the frequency of reported drunkenness and the negative social and personal consequences associated with their use of alcohol (Donovan & Jessor, 1978).

With respect to marijuana, the most widely used illicit drug among adolescents, 32% of the class of 1981 reported some use in the preceding month, and 7% reported daily use in that period; the latter figure is still substantial, even though reported daily use has been declining from its peak of 11% in the class of 1978. Of particular interest from a health risk perspective is the evidence for significantly earlier onset of marijuana use over the last seven annual measurements made by the Monitoring the Future project. Using retrospective reports by the graduating seniors regarding the school grade in which they first used marijuana, Johnston et al. (1982) show a significant increase in earliness of onset; for the class of 1975, only 17% reported marijuana use prior to tenth grade, whereas for the class of 1981, that percentage had doubled, with 34% reporting some use before tenth grade. When experience with any illicit drug is considered, the data show that 37% of the class of 1975 had used some illicit drug prior to tenth grade, whereas the comparable figure for the class of 1981 was 51%, fully half of the more recent graduating seniors having already had experience with an illicit drug by about the age of 15. The association of marijuana use with traffic crashes has been increasingly noted, as has the tendency to combine marijuana use with alcohol use, both facts pointing to further aspects of the risk potential of marijuana use.

The health risk associated with cigarette smoking is probably best established in relation to cancer and cardiovascular disease, issues that are of greater concern for later stages in the life span than for adolescence. It is in adolescence, however, that initiation to smoking generally takes place, and once there is a commitment to it in adolescence, smoking turns out to be an exceedingly difficult behavior pattern to abandon (however, for a very provocative report about voluntary cessation, see Schachter, 1982). Referring again to the most recent Monitoring the Future report, we find that, in the class of 1981, 20% have smoked one or more cigarettes per day in the preceding month and 13.5% have smoked half a pack or more per day over that same period. In terms of time of onset, nearly two-thirds of those who ever smoked on a regular daily basis began smoking by ninth grade or earlier. Although the data from this project indicate that daily use of half a pack of cigarettes or more declined from 19.4% to 13.5% between 1977 and 1981, the encouragement to be taken from that trend should be mitigated by the fact that the 1981 figure remains substantial and by our awareness of the tenacity of the smoking habit once it is established.

Sexuality is another behaviorally mediated area of potential health risk for adolescents— risk deriving largely from the unintended and often unanticipated consequences of becoming sexually active, primarily pregnancy and contracting a sexually transmitted disease. Recent information about sexual activity among teenagers residing in metropolitan areas is available from a 1979 national survey (Zelnik & Kantner, 1980). Among women aged 15 to 19 who have never married, 46% reported having had intercourse; the comparable figure for a 1976 survey was 39%, and for a 1971 survey it was 28%. The mean age of first intercourse remained stable between 1976 and 1979 at 16.2 years. Chilman's (1978) extensive review of the literature on adolescent sexuality indicates that the major increase in incidence of sexual intercourse among teenagers has occurred among females, making the prevalence of adolescent nonvirginity much more similar for both sexes in recent years than it ever was before.

In the Zelnik and Kantner (1980) survey, over 25% of the sexually active women aged 15 to 19 reported never using contraception. Among all the sexually active women in this age range, the proportion who became pregnant rose from about 28% in 1971 to 30% in 1976 and to 32.5% in 1979. With regard to the total population of women aged 15 to 19, the 1979 data indicate that over 16% of them became pregnant, with an increasing rate of pregnancy at the younger adolescent ages. Pregnancy implicates health risk related to both abortion and child bearing and, of course, to the long-term consequences of adolescent motherhood. On the latter issue, Hardy's (1982) longitudinal studies indicate: "Adolescent mothers experienced high risks of family instability, low educational attainment, inadequate work experience, lower income, greater welfare dependency, and higher fertility than older women" (p. 263). With regard to the other major area of risk associated with sexual activity, 75% of those who have a sexually transmitted disease fall into the 15 to 24 age range, and the rate of rise in incidence of venereal disease, particularly gonorrhea, is highest in the adolescent age range.

Other areas of health-compromising behavior among adolescents involve the potential risk for cardiovascular disease in later life. Among the behaviorally mediated risk factors that have been implicated—aside from smoking—are obesity or overweight; dietary consumption of saturated fat, salt, and sugar; lack of regular aerobic exercise; stress; and certain coping styles referred to as Type A behavior. Although such behaviors are widely prevalent in adolescence, considerable research is still needed to establish just how characteristic they are and whether their initiation and consolidation take place in adolescence or earlier in childhood.

The data cited thus far are intended to make a case for adolescence as a relatively high-risk life stage for health. The risk areas selected for mention are illustrative rather than exhaustive, with the emphasis placed on behaviors that are usually initiated in adolescence and are seen as central to the process of development during that period. Recent trends in several of the behaviors mentioned portend an exacerbation of their risk potential. One trend is the sheer increase in prevalence of potentially health-compromising behavior (e.g., driving after heavy alcohol use); another trend is toward earlier onset or a younger average age of initiation of such behaviors (e.g., marijuana use); and a third trend is the growing homogenization of the sexes, with young women showing an increased prevalence of experience (e.g., in sexual intercourse and especially in cigarette smoking) and thereby "catching up" with the rates for young men. Each of these trends implies greater future health risk for the adolescent age period.

A real lacuna in evaluating overall health risk in adolescence is, of course, the lack of information about health-enhancing behaviors, behaviors that may serve to balance the negative consequences of at least some of the health-compromising behaviors so widely prevalent at this stage. Data are needed concerning such behaviors as seat belt and helmet use, adequate hours of sleep, following a weight control regimen, engaging in regularly scheduled aerobic exercise, nutrition monitoring, stress minimization, cultivation of enduring life interests, and elaboration of a general sense of competence, if a more adequate appraisal of risk in adolescence is ultimately to be achieved.

THE INTERRELATEDNESS OF HEALTH RISK BEHAVIORS IN ADOLESCENCE

A further consideration about the risk behaviors just reviewed warrants attention. A large body of research has shown that many of the behaviors are interrelated and tend to covary systematically. Indeed, the intraindividual linkages among them—their tendency to co-occur within the same adolescent—are such as to suggest that they may constitute a *syndrome*, an organized constellation of behavior, rather than being a collection of independent, discrete activities. Insofar as this is the case, it has important implications for understanding the origin and nature of such behavior as well as for planning intervention and change programs.

The kind of evidence that can be brought to bear in support of this generalization can be illustrated by using the example of adolescent drug use behavior. First, research on adolescent drug use shows that involvement with any drug, such as alcohol, is associated with a higher likelihood of involvement with other drugs, such as marijuana or tobacco. Analyses of the 1978 Research Triangle national survey data (Rachal, Guess, Hubbard, Maisto, Cavanaugh, Waddell, & Benrud, 1980) indicated that frequency of drunkenness was positively correlated with marijuana involvement ($r > .60$) and cigarette smoking ($r > .40$ for males and $r > .30$ for females) among more than 5,000 senior high school youth (Jessor, Donovan, & Widmer, 1980). Second, the use of drugs is associated with a higher likelihood of involvement in other types of risk behavior, such as precocious sexual activity, aggression, and delinquency. Thus, in our longitudinal sample of high school youth (Jessor & Jessor, 1977), 61% of the marijuana users were sexually experienced—that is, nonvirgins—by the end of their senior year as compared to only 18% of the nonusers. With respect to alcohol, 41% of those who drank were sexually experienced, as compared to only 4% of those who were still abstainers. These figures represent major differences in rates of involvement in other health-related behaviors, in this case precocious sexual activity—differences that are linked to involvement with drugs.

Third, the greater or the heavier the involvement with drugs, the greater the likelihood of involvement with other problem behaviors; thus, heavy marijuana users or problem drinkers have higher rates of nonvirginity than do lighter marijuana users or nonproblem drinkers. Fourth, it is clear that various health risk behaviors can be engaged in simultaneously. Thus, continuing with our drug use illustration, 29% of the senior high school students in the 1978 Research Triangle survey reported that they sometimes used marijuana and alcohol together (Rachal et al., 1980). A fifth kind of evidence in favor of a risk-behavior syndrome is the negative relationship that obtains between various health-compromising behaviors, on the one hand, and what we have called conventional or conforming behaviors, on the other. In that same 1978 Research Triangle survey, marijuana use was negatively correlated with church attendance ($r = -.29$ for females and $r = -.24$ for males); the greater the involvement was with marijuana, the less was the involvement with church. Sixth, and finally, there is substantial evidence that the pattern of psychosocial correlates associated with a number of the different risk behaviors—both personality and social environmental correlates—is essentially the very same pattern. This similarity in psychosocial correlates has been shown to apply to alcohol use, marijuana use, cigarette smoking, and sexual intercourse experience for adolescents (Bachman, Johnston, & O'Malley, 1981; Jessor, Chase, & Donovan, 1980; Jessor, Costa, Jessor, & Donovan, 1983; Jessor, Donovan, & Widmer, 1980).

Interrelatedness among risk behaviors for adolescents has also been reported in research outside the United States. In a study of senior high school adolescents in Israel, significant relations were found between cigarette smoking, alcohol use, marijuana use, and sexual experience (Tamir, Wolff, & Epstein, 1982). Also, in a longitudinal study of Finnish adolescents, Pulkkinen (Note 1) reports a correlation of .64 between regular smoking and the use of alcohol at age 14.

The evidence cited thus far has dealt primarily with a subset of adolescent risk behaviors that can be termed problem behaviors (Jessor & Jessor, 1977), behaviors that depart from the regulatory norms of the adult society. A key question that has yet to be addressed systematically in research is the linkage between such behaviors and other health risk behaviors, such as insufficient sleep, lack of exercise, inadequate nutrition, or excess calorie intake—behaviors that, though not involving transgression of societal norms, may nevertheless be risk factors for health during adolescence or later. In short, what is important to establish empirically is how broadly the perimeter needs to be drawn in order to circumscribe the syndrome of risk behaviors among adolescents.

Research bearing on this issue is exceedingly limited. In a follow-up study of adults, Mechanic (1979) has shown significant negative correlations (about $-.20$) between smoking and both engaging in physical exercise and using seat belts when driving. Within a senior high school sample of 15- to 18-year-olds, Hays, Stacy, and DiMatteo (Note 2) report a significant negative correlation between meal regularity (eating breakfast and not skipping other meals) and drug use and a significant positive correlation between meal regularity and greater hours of sleep for both men and women. Rimpelä (Note 3, cited in Pulkkinen, Note 4) found smoking to be related to lack of physical activity, heavy use of sugar, and coffee drinking among Finnish youth. Although they are suggestive and intriguing, these studies only make clearer the need for systematic research into the degree to which the larger set of health risk behaviors tends to covary in adolescence.

The evidence in support of the syndromal nature of adolescent risk behavior is important to note for several reasons. First, it suggests that the various risk behaviors may already be linked in the social ecology of youth, with socially organized opportunities to learn and to practice them together. Second, it suggests that the different behaviors may be serving similar psychological functions and, despite their diverse topography, may have common social and personal meanings. Third, it raises a serious question about whether intervention and change efforts should remain focused on specific behaviors, as they generally are, or should be oriented, instead, toward the syndrome as a whole. Finally, it alerts us to the potential utility of the concept of lifestyle, a notion given wide currency in the health field. The key meaning of lifestyle pertains to an organized pattern of interrelated behaviors, and that is exactly what the evidence for a risk-behavior syndrome suggests is the case. It may be useful, therefore, to conceive of adolescence as a developmental period in which choices are being made among various alternative lifestyles rather than just among behaviors, and in which subsequent development involves the consolidation and integration of the health-related behaviors that the particular lifestyle happens to encompass. Such an emphasis on lifestyle choice is not at all alien to ideas about identity formation in adolescence, such as those elaborated by both White (1975) and Erikson (1963).

THE PSYCHOLOGICAL MEANINGS OF HEALTH RISK BEHAVIORS IN ADOLESCENCE

If the behaviors discussed here constitute risk factors for health and, in at least several instances, can elicit negative sanctions from society (e.g., for illicit drug use), criticism from parents and friends (e.g., for drunkenness or for precocious sexuality), and even self-rejection (e.g., for obesity or for excessive smoking), what accounts for their occurrence and their wide prevalence during adolescence? A comprehensive reply to such a query requires presentation of a social-psychological theory relevant to risk behavior, a task that will be postponed until the following section of this chapter. For present purposes, however, a beginning answer can come from an understanding of the important personal meanings, symbolic significance, and psychological functions that such behaviors can serve for adolescents. Rather than being arbitrary or fortuitous or reflecting some kind of youthful perversity, risk behaviors—like all learned behavior—are purposive, goal-directed, and capable of fulfilling multiple goals that are central to adolescent life. The goals these behaviors can attain and the meanings they may represent are not, of course, intrinsic to the behaviors but depend on larger processes of sociocultural definition and on an adolescent's unique learning and socialization experience.

A listing of some of the major functions, purposes, or goals of engaging in risk behavior can help clarify their likely importance to adolescents and can also illustrate the fact that such goals are not really different from those associated with other kinds of behavior. Engaging in certain risk behaviors in adolescence can serve the following functions:

1. An instrumental effort to attain goals that are blocked or seem otherwise unattainable. Thus, engaging in precocious sexual intercourse and becoming pregnant can be a way of attaining independence from parental control and regulation and taking personal control of one's life.

2. A means of expressing opposition to adult authority and the conventional society whose norms and values are not shared by the younger generation. Much of young people's drug use during the Vietnam era was a symbolic way of repudiating the war by engaging in precisely the behavior that the larger society was trying to proscribe.

3. A coping mechanism for dealing with anxiety, frustration, inadequacy, and failure or with the anticipation that failure is likely—whether in relation to school performance, the expectations of peers, or the high standards of parents. Heavy involvement with alcohol, for example, or even overeating, can be a way of dealing with poor academic achievement, with a sense of social rejection, or with the perception of parental disappointment.

4. A way of gaining admission to the peer group, of expressing solidarity with peers, or of demonstrating identification with the youth subculture. Cigarette smoking or the sharing of a "joint" are well-established and widely recognized marks of membership in the peer group.

5. A confirmation of important attributes of personal identity. Drinking and smoking, and driving after drinking, are readily learned as ways of showing that one is "macho," "cool," or "experienced" or has some other characteristic that is valued in adolescent culture.

6. A transition marker—that is, a symbol of having made a developmental transition, of having gone from a less mature to a more mature status, or of placing a claim

on a more mature status. This function of risk behavior is an especially important one for adolescents. It derives from the fact that certain adolescent behaviors tend to be age-graded—that is, considered by society as appropriate only for those who have reached a certain age or age-related status. The use of alcohol is a good example, since it is proscribed for those below the legal age but permitted for those beyond it. When behaviors are age-graded, engaging in them earlier than is defined as appropriate can be a way of affirming maturity or of marking a developmental transition from adolescence to young adulthood.

This listing is admittedly a partial one; for example, a function frequently emphasized by young people is pleasure or fun, and it is clear that many of the risk behaviors can be seen as providing intrinsic enjoyment and excitement or as serving as a counterpoint to boredom and routine. The aim of the listing has been to show that the motivations for adolescent risk behavior are not only broad-ranging and salient but are, for the most part, the very same motivations that are involved in so much of the rest of adolescent behavior. Clearly, a great deal of additional information is needed about the psychological functions of health-compromising behaviors, especially those, such as overeating or sedentariness, that do not involve transgression of societal norms or of age-graded appropriateness. An understanding of the functional nature of health-compromising behaviors not only helps explain their prevalence but is crucial for yet another reason. If we want to design intervention programs that make available to young people alternative or substitute behaviors that are less health-compromising, we will need to be sure that the alternatives proposed are capable of fulfilling the same or similar functions as the risk behaviors that they are intended to displace.

A THEORETICAL FRAMEWORK FOR HEALTH RISK BEHAVIORS IN ADOLESCENCE

The unsatisfactory state of theory in the field of adolescent health may well be the most serious obstacle to progress in understanding the nature of adolescent risk behavior and in devising effective approaches to reducing risk and enhancing adolescent health. Theoretical contributions such as Bandura's (1977) ideas about modeling and Fishbein and Ajzen's (1975) notions about attitudes and behavioral intentions have been significant and useful. Yet a more general and comprehensive theory—one that can encompass the broad range of health-related behaviors, can specify the psychosocial factors that instigate and sustain them, and can illuminate their role in the process of adolescent development—is still to be achieved. Because the issue of theory is deemed so crucial to progress in the health field, it is worth giving brief attention to a framework that, though obviously limited, has already demonstrated its relevance for at least some of the risk behaviors that have been discussed thus far.

The social-psychological framework is one we have called "problem-behavior theory" (Jessor & Jessor, 1977). It was initially formulated, almost 25 years ago, to guide a study of deviance—especially excessive alcohol use—in a tri-ethnic community in the southwestern United States (Jessor, Graves, Hanson, & Jessor, 1968). Over the years, it has been modified and extended to accommodate a cross-cultural study of drinking behavior among Italian and Italian-American youth (Jessor, Young, Young, & Tesi, 1970), to provide the theory for two national sample surveys of alcohol and drug use among junior and senior high school students (Donovan & Jessor, 1978, 1983; Jessor, Chase, & Donovan, 1980; Jessor, Donovan, & Widmer, 1980), and, most fundamentally, to constitute the framework for a longitudinal study of problem behavior—alcohol use, problem drinking, drug use, sexual activity, aggression, delinquency—in cohorts of adolescents being followed from junior high school through young adulthood (Jessor & Jessor, 1977). The concepts and measures developed in problem-behavior theory have now been used in a large number of studies by other researchers in the United States and elsewhere (e.g., DiTecco & Schlegel, 1982) and have been applied to other risk behavior areas, such as cigarette smoking (e.g., Chassin, Presson, Bensenberg, Corty, Olshavsky, & Sherman, 1981; Rooney & Wright, 1982).

Although the theory has focused primarily on problem behaviors—behaviors that constitute transgressions of societal and/or legal norms and that tend to elicit some sort of social control response—its potential relevance to adolescent health risk behavior derives from several considerations. First, a number of the so-called problem behaviors that have been dealt with by the theory are the very same behaviors that have been referred to as health risk behaviors in this chapter—for example, alcohol use, marijuana use, precocious sexual intercourse, and driving after drinking. Thus, there is at least an area of overlap where the two domains of problem behavior and health risk behavior intersect. Second, some of the health risk behaviors that do not constitute transgressions of societal or legal norms, such as overeating or sedentariness, may nevertheless represent departures from more informal social norms, such as those of the peer group, or even from an individual's personal norms about what is appropriate behavior in these areas. Insofar as departure from any norm may be involved, the formulations of problem-behavior theory would remain apposite. Third, problem-behavior theory has maintained the perspective that to account for variation in problem behavior is to account simultaneously for variation in conventional behavior. Thus, the theory has also attempted to explain—with the same set of concepts—behavior that conforms to the norms and expectations of the larger society and of its institutions, such as school and church involvement. In this sense, the theory may well have relevance not only for health risk behavior, but simultaneously for variation in health-enhancing behavior as well, at least to the extent that the latter can usefully be conceptualized as conventional. Finally, the potential relevance of problem-behavior theory derives from the fact that it includes a developmental formulation about the role of problem behavior (or health risk behavior) in the process of adolescent transition and change, a role already alluded to in the preceding section.

Problem-behavior theory rests on the social-psychological relationships that obtain within and between each of three major systems: the personality system, the perceived environment system, and the behavior system. Within each of the systems, the structures of the variables they encompass are interrelated and organized so as to generate a theoretical resultant, a dynamic state called *proneness,* that summarizes the likelihood of occurrence of problem behavior (or, in the present case, health risk behavior). Thus, it is theoretically possible to speak of personality proneness, environmental proneness, and behavioral proneness, and of their combination as psychosocial proneness toward problem behavior. The sovereign concept of psychosocial proneness is the key theoretical basis for predicting and explaining variations in youthful behavior.

The conceptual structure of problem-behavior theory is schematized in Figure 4.1. Since the rationale for each variable in the figure has been elaborated in detail in Jessor and Jessor (1977), only a brief description will be presented here; attention will be restricted to the three boxes of variables labeled A, B, and C: the personality system, the perceived environment system, and the behavior system, respectively. In the personality system, the main characteristics of theoretical proneness to problem behavior include lower value on academic achievement, higher value on independence, greater value on independence relative to value on achievement, lower expectations for academic achievement, greater social criticism and alienation, lower self-esteem, orientation to an external locus of control, greater attitudinal tolerance of deviance, lesser religiosity, and more importance attached to positive, functions of problem behavior relative to negative functions. The more these personality characteristics obtain for a person at a given time—that is, the more they constitute a coherent pattern or constellation—the more they theoretically convey personality proneness to problem behavior.

Within the perceived environment, an important distinction is drawn between regions or structures in terms of their proximal, versus distal, relation to behavior. Proximal variables

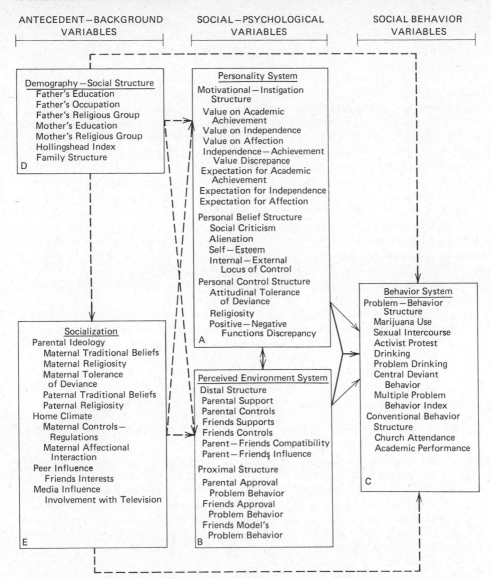

ANTECEDENT—BACKGROUND
VARIABLES

SOCIAL—PSYCHOLOGICAL
VARIABLES

SOCIAL BEHAVIOR
VARIABLES

Demography—Social Structure
Father's Education
Father's Occupation
Father's Religious Group
Mother's Education
Mother's Religious Group
Hollingshead Index
Family Structure

D

Personality System
Motivational—Instigation
Structure
Value on Academic
Achievement
Value on Independence
Value on Affection
Independence—Achievement
Value Discrepance
Expectation for Academic
Achievement
Expectation for Independence
Expectation for Affection

Personal Belief Structure
Social Criticism
Alienation
Self—Esteem
Internal—External
Locus of Control
Personal Control Structure
Attitudinal Tolerance
of Deviance
Religiosity
Positive—Negative
Functions Discrepancy

A

Socialization
Parental Ideology
Maternal Traditional Beliefs
Maternal Religiosity
Maternal Tolerance
of Deviance
Paternal Traditional Beliefs
Paternal Religiosity
Home Climate
Maternal Controls—
Regulations
Maternal Affectional
Interaction
Peer Influence
Friends Interests
Media Influence
Involvement with Television

E

Perceived Environment System
Distal Structure
Parental Support
Parental Controls
Friends Supports
Friends Controls
Parent—Friends Compatibility
Parent—Friends Influence

Proximal Structure
Parental Approval
Problem Behavior
Friends Approval
Problem Behavior
Friends Model's
Problem Behavior

B

Behavior System
Problem—Behavior
Structure
Marijuana Use
Sexual Intercourse
Activist Protest
Drinking
Problem Drinking
Central Deviant
Behavior
Multiple Problem
Behavior Index
Conventional Behavior
Structure
Church Attendance
Academic Performance

C

Figure 4.1 The conceptual structure of problem-behavior theory. (Reprinted with permission from Jessor, R., & Jessor, S. L. *Problem behavior and psychosocial development: A longitudinal study of youth.* New York: Academic Press, 1977. Copyright © 1977 by Academic Press, Inc.)

(e.g., peer models for marijuana use) directly implicate a particular behavior, whereas distal variables (e.g., the degree of normative consensus between parents and peers) are more remote in the causal chain and therefore require theoretical linkage to behavior. Problem-behavior proneness in the distal structure of the perceived environment system consists of low parental support and controls, low peer controls, low compatibility between parent and peer expectations, and low parent influence relative to peer influence. In the proximal structure, problem-behavior proneness includes low parental disapproval of problem behavior and high friends models for, as well as high friends approval of, engaging in problem behavior.

The behavior system is differentiated into a problem-behavior structure and a conventional-behavior structure. The possibility that phenotypically very different problem behaviors (e.g., smoking marijuana or engaging in sexual intercourse) may serve the same social-psychological function (e.g., overt repudiation of conventional norms or expression of independence from parental control) is what underlies the notion of a structure of problem behavior. The conventional-behavior structure is concerned with behavior that is socially approved, normatively expected, and codified and institutionalized as appropriate for adolescents—for example, involvement with school work and with religious activities. Problem-behavior proneness in the behavior system directly reflects the degree of involvement in both the problem-behavior and the conventional-behavior structures and also reflects the balance that obtains between those involvements.

The usefulness of problem-behavior theory has been demonstrated and repeatedly replicated in relation to a variety of adolescent risk behaviors and to a specially constructed composite multiple problem-behavior index. Multiple correlations of the variables in the three systems reach beyond .70 for male and female adolescents in relation to the composite index and to such separate risk behaviors as marijuana use and delinquent-type behavior. The multiple correlations are somewhat lower for problem drinking and for sexual intercourse experience. Thus, the theory has been able to account for between a third and a half of the variance in adolescent problem behavior, providing reasonable evidence for its explanatory relevance.

Nevertheless, even accounting for half the variance in problem behavior means that half remains to be explained. It seems clear by now that other variables, not yet encompassed by the theory, will need to be brought to bear, and this is especially true if the theory is to be extended to deal with health risk behaviors more generally. Variables such as the value of health and fitness, the sense of competence and control in health-related activities, the repertoire of skills for health maintenance and risk avoidance—if measured well—might enlarge the scope of application of the theory as well as increasing its effectiveness.

PROBLEM-BEHAVIOR THEORY AND ADOLESCENT DEVELOPMENT

The discussion of problem-behavior theory to this point has emphasized its usefulness in accounting for variations in cross-sectional data on risk behavior. There are also logical implications in the theory for adolescent development and for behavior change over time. Much of what has been discussed as problem behavior is, of course, only a "problem" relative to age-graded norms; that is, the behavior may be permitted or even prescribed for those who are older while being proscribed only for those who are younger. Drinking, as one example, is a behavior that is proscribed for those under legal age but permitted and even institutionally encouraged for those who are beyond that age; sexual intercourse, a normatively acceptable behavior for adults and even for older adolescents, is a normative departure for a young adolescent, one that is likely to elicit social controls. Awareness among youth of the age-graded norms for such behaviors carries with it the knowledge that occupancy of a more mature status is characterized by engaging in those very behaviors. Thus, engaging in age-graded behaviors for the first time can serve to mark a transition in status from "less mature" to "more mature," from "younger" to "older," or from "adolescent" to "youth" or "adult."

Many of the important transitions that mark the course of adolescent development do involve behaviors, such as precocious sexual intercourse, that depart from the regulatory age norms that define appropriate or expected behavior for that age or stage in life. Since behavior that departs from regulatory norms is precisely what problem-behavior theory is meant to account for, this provides the rationale for systematic application of the theory to developmental change in adolescence. By mapping a new developmental concept, *transition proneness,* onto the already available theoretical concept of problem-behavior proneness, it becomes possible to use problem-behavior theory to specify the likelihood of occurrence of developmental change—change that takes place through engaging in age-graded, norm-departing, transition-marking behaviors such as beginning to drink, becoming sexually active, and the like.

The usefulness of the concept of transition proneness has been tested in relation to the onset of drinking (Jessor, Collins, & Jessor, 1972; Jessor, & Jessor, 1975), the onset of marijuana use (Jessor, 1976), and the initiation of sexual intercourse (Jessor, & Jessor, 1975; Jessor, Costa, Jessor, & Donovan, 1983) among samples of adolescents who had had no prior experience with those behaviors. In each case, multivariate analyses have demonstrated that there is, indeed, a psychosocial pattern that obtains prior to engagement in the behavior and that is predictive of its later occurrence and of variation in the time of its subsequent onset. With regard to predicting the time of first intercourse, as one illustration, it was possible to establish that 142 boys and 204 girls in our junior high school cohorts were still virgins as of the 1970 testing year. Since these adolescents were followed into young adulthood, it was also possible to determine from the follow-up data just when, in the subsequent time period between 1970 and 1979, initial sexual intercourse occurred and the transition to nonvirginity was made. The findings show that variation in time of onset of sexual intercourse across this 9-year interval was already signalled by the prior pattern of problem-behavior theory measures in 1970, when all the participants were still virgins. The multiple correlations ($R = .55$ for males and $R = .53$ for females) are significant and provide support for the predictive role of the concept of transition proneness.

Proneness toward transition, in this case to nonvirginity, was apparent on measures in each of the three systems of problem-behavior theory. Virgins who were to engage in sexual intercourse earlier, relative to those virgins whose onset took place later, were already higher in value on and expectation for independence, lower in value on and expectation for academic achievement, more socially critical in their beliefs about society, more tolerant of deviance, and lower in religiosity. They also perceived less compatibility between the expectations their parents held for them and those their friends held, less influence of their parents relative to that of their friends, and more social approval for and models of problem behavior, including sexual behavior. Finally, they were more involved in other (non-sex-related) problem behavior and less involved in conventional behavior, such as church attendance (Jessor, Costa, Jessor, & Donovan, 1983).

The importance of such findings does not lie only in the support they provide for problem-behavior theory and for its developmental implications. The findings also make clear that the onset of adolescent risk behaviors is neither arbitrary nor fortuitous but is, rather, a systematic outcome of characteristics of the adolescent and of the adolescent's perceived environment that precede onset. These characteristics represent a pattern of psychosocial risk factors—a pattern we have termed transition proneness—conveying differential readiness to engage in health-compromising, problem, or risk behavior. The fact that such a pattern exists in advance of the onset of risk behaviors and is also predictive of onset makes it possible to think of early identification of adolescents at risk and of the feasibility of early intervention to promote health-enhancing alternatives.

The pattern of transition proneness that has emerged in our studies of the onset of problem behavior is very much the same in psychosocial content as the pattern of problem-behavior proneness we have found in our cross-sectional studies; the factors that are effective cross-sectionally are the same or similar to those that are effective longitudinally. The term that best captures the content of the dimension underlying psychosocial proneness is *conventionality-unconventionality*, and that dimension is equally appropriate for characterizing the three explanatory systems in problem-behavior theory. Indeed, it is possible to conceive of personality unconventionality (e.g., high value on independence, greater social criticism, more tolerance of deviance), perceived environment unconventionality (e.g., lower parent and friends controls, more approval, models, and opportunities for risk behavior), and behavioral unconventionality (e.g., greater involvement in risk behavior and lesser involvement in conforming behavior). One of the main generalizations that can be drawn from the research on problem-behavior theory is that the conventionality-unconventionality dimension is central in accounting for variation in problem or risk behavior in adolescence. Achieving an understanding of the role that dimension plays in regulating adolescent health turns out to be an objective of primary importance to the field of behavioral health.

THE CONTINUITY OF HEALTH RISK BETWEEN ADOLESCENCE AND YOUNG ADULTHOOD

Achieving an understanding of the conventionality-unconventionality dimension in adolescence gains even greater importance when the linkage and continuity between adolescence and later life stages, especially young adulthood, are taken into consideration. Insofar as the characteristics referred to as psychosocial proneness to risk behavior in adolescence carry over to or are consequential for postadolescence, it would mean that the degree of risk that obtains in adolescence needs to be multiplied or weighted to take that into account.

Two kinds of data are germane to the issue of continuity or carry-over of health risk from adolescence to young adulthood. One type of data involves the degree to which the components of psychosocial proneness in adolescence are in fact stable over time and do track into young adulthood. Since we were able to measure many of the variables in problem-behavior theory in both adolescence and young adulthood, it was possible to examine their stability directly by correlational analysis. Table 4.1, adapted from Jessor (1983b), presents the stability coefficients for a number of measures between 1972, when our participants were adolescents in the 10th, 11th, and 12th grades, and 1979, when they had reached young adulthood and were 23, 24, and 25 years old.

The data in Table 4.1 are raw Pearson correlations between the 1972 measure and the 1979 measure of each variable. Such correlations are obviously attenuated by the unreliability of the measures and are therefore conservative estimates of stability over time. Correcting for attenuation yields the correlations shown in parentheses for the multi-item scales whose internal reliability can be determined.

Although change has clearly taken place, it has been systematic, and the overriding impression to be gained from the data in the table is that there is a considerable degree of stability across time for nearly all of the measures drawn from problem-behavior theory. In nearly all cases, the correlations are statistically significant; in a number of instances, they are substantial in magnitude. When it is kept in mind that the time interval involved—7 years—is a very long one, that this portion of the life trajectory is considered to be one of major growth and transformation, that the environmental context of life during this period is itself likely to have changed markedly, and that the general social and historical background has also shifted, the stability represented by these correlations is even more impressive. It is worth emphasizing, also, that there is significant stability on measures from all three of the systems of problem-behavior theory—personality, the perceived environment, and behavior. These coefficients, taken together, would therefore seem to suggest some stability of individuality across this segment of the life span. They would also suggest it follows, that there should be continuity and carry-over of health risk between adolescence and young adulthood.

The second type of data that bears on this issue involves the degree to which psychosocial proneness in adolescence is predictive of engagement in risk behavior later in young adulthood. Again, the issue could be examined empirically because of the availability of psychosocial proneness measures in adolescence and of problem-behavior measures in young adulthood within our longitudinal follow-up study. For the example of problem drinking, the findings show that variation in psychosocial proneness in adolescence is modestly predictive of whether a participant is classified as a problem drinker or as a nonproblem drinker 7 years later, in young adulthood. The multiple correlations reach .53 for the males and .45 for the females, with both correlations being statistically significant at the .001 level. Problem drinker status in young adulthood was shown to be significantly linked to a number of

Table 4.1   Stability Coefficients between 1972 and 1979 Psychosocial Measures, Young Adult Follow-Up Study

Measure	High School Sample	
	Males ($N = 172$)	Females ($N = 231$)
Personality System		
Value on achievement	.08 (.12)	.10* (.15)
Value on independence	.22*** (.59)	.23****(.74)
Value on affection	.25****(.42)	.22****(.36)
Expectation for achievement	.24****(.32)	.12** (.15)
Expectation for independence	.22*** (.43)	.10* (.29)
Expectation for affection	.29****(.46)	.22****(.32)
Self-esteem	.46****(.66)	.42****(.60)
Internal-external control—political	.32****(.68)	.25****(.46)
Internal-external control—general	.15** (.38)	.02 (.05)
Social criticism	.24****(.47)	.29****(.52)
Alienation	.37****(.57)	.42****(.62)
Tolerance of deviance	.33****(.41)	.37****(.47)
Religiosity	.53****(.61)	.45****(.51)
Perceived Environment System		
Relative parent vs. peer influence	.12* (.17)	.23****(.32)
Parental approval of drug use	.20***	.27****
Friends' approval of drug use	.27****	.21****
Friends models for drug use	.28****	.20****
Behavior System		
Deviant behavior/past year	.30****(.47)	.29****(.45)
Church attendance/past year	.40****	.42****

Source: Jessor, R. The stability of change: Psychosocial development from adolescence to young adulthood. In D. Magnusson & V. Allen (Eds.), Human development: An interactional perspective. New York: Academic Press, 1983b.
Note: Correlations in parentheses have been corrected for attenuation for those multiple-item scales whose reliability can be ascertained.
* $p \leq .10$.
** $p \leq .05$.
*** $p \leq .01$.
**** $p \leq .001$, two-tailed test.

problem-behavior theory variables in adolescence: lower value on academic achievement, higher value on independence relative to value on achievement, lower expectations for academic achievement, greater tolerance of deviance, lower religiosity, greater perceived approval for and models of problem behavior, greater actual involvement in problem behaviors such as use of marijuana, and less involvement with conventional behavior related to church and school (Donovan, Jessor, & Jessor, 1983). This pattern of psychosocial proneness once again reveals the underlying dimension of adolescent unconventionality, and the pattern is also predictive of other risk behaviors in young adulthood, such as involvement with smoking and with marijuana use.

Taken together, these two types of time-extended data make clear that there is continuity of adolescent health risk beyond the adolescent stage of life. Although evidence for continuity and carry-over is sobering in regard to the relatively enduring consequences of adolescent health risk, there is some consolation, at least, in the obvious corollary of such findings—that there should also be continuity and carry-over of health-enhancing dispositions and behaviors from adolescence to later life.

SOME IMPLICATIONS FOR HEALTH PROMOTION AND RISK REDUCTION IN ADOLESCENCE

It has been stressed throughout this chapter that adolescence is a life stage of relatively high risk for health and that in some areas, such as motor vehicle accidents, and for some groups, such as women, risk seems to be on the increase. Risk has been considered in terms not only of behavior but also of personality attributes and environmental supports. What singles out adolescence as a time of relatively high risk is that it is a key stage in which risk-related learning takes place—learning of new risk behaviors, of risk-prone personality dispositions, and of risk-enhancing opportunities in the environment. Recognition of this fact focuses attention on adolescence as a potentially critical period for the implementation of strategies to reduce health risk and to enhance health. In this final section, some considerations that may be relevant to those topics are briefly touched upon.

Although explanatory, analytic, or theoretically oriented research—research of the sort just reviewed—can be very useful for devising intervention strategies or for guiding change-oriented efforts, it should be kept in mind that it is not research that tells us how best to change things. Thus, what follows is simply an attempt to draw out some general and tentative implications from the perspective and content of the preceding discussion about adolescence and health.

The research showing that psychosocial proneness to risk behavior consists of a coherent pattern of personality, environmental, and behavioral attributes suggests one important implication—namely, that efforts at prevention, risk reduction, or health promotion should not be limited to a focus on behavior alone. Health risk clearly derives from personality proneness and environmental proneness, and attention to attributes in those two systems should logically influence the occurrence of health-related behavior, both health-compromising and health-enhancing. The point here is that intervention efforts might well assume a broader purview than has been characteristic of such efforts, whether the aim has been cessation of cigarette smoking or improvement of nutritional choices. Since any behavior is influenced by all three of the systems comprising problem-behavior theory, advantage should accrue to those programs that intervene simultaneously in all three systems.

The linkage of personality to health-related behavior warrants even further emphasis. Beyond our own focus on the relevance of the conventionality-unconventionality dimension, other attributes of personality have already received special attention in relation to health, such as the sense of personal autonomy or control (Seeman & Seeman, 1983; Wallston & Wallston, 1982). Others should merit special attention in the future, such as personal value on well-being and health or concept of self as competent and fit. Personality attributes of this sort, being central and general, carry relevance for a large variety of behavior choices and lifestyle alternatives; interventions that influence or shape them, therefore, should have broad and reverberating consequences for health as a whole.

Where the focus still needs to remain on behavior, as in cessation or inoculation programs, I have stressed here the necessity to understand the meanings, purposes, functions, or goals the behavior can represent or serve. Such understanding is crucial to any strategy that seeks to provide and reinforce alternative behaviors—lower in risk or even health-promoting—as substitutes for adolescent risk behaviors. Nonproblem or health-promoting behaviors are likely to be successful as substitutes or alternatives only if they serve functions similar to or more highly valued than those served by the original risk behaviors. Although that seems entirely feasible to accomplish in relation to many of the functions listed earlier for risk behaviors—such as demonstrating peer group identity, affirming independence from adults, or coping with failure—certain of the functions—such as establishing a claim on a more mature status or marking the transition out of adolescence—may be more refractory to substitution. To the extent that health-promoting behaviors—e.g., taking personal responsibility for one's health or following a regular schedule of exercise—could become institutionalized as representing or symbolizing adult status, adolescent transition-marking behavior could become more benign than it is at present, when beginning to drink or engaging in sexual intercourse precociously are what seem to be required.

The research findings in support of the syndromal nature of adolescent problem behavior also have implications for health-related change efforts. With a few exceptions, intervention programs with adolescents have tended to be behavior-specific. Prevention programs, especially those based in schools, are usually designed as separate units—for example, programs on drinking as a problem, or on drug use, or for sexually active adolescents—as if these behaviors occurred in isolation from one another. In fact, not only are they associated, but they often occur at the same occasion. Given this knowledge, intervention programs could consider enlarging their scope to accommodate multiple risk behaviors simultaneously and to deal with their common functions and the linkages between them. This implies interventions that, in addition to specific, behavior-relevant information, attitudes, and skills, would orient toward the lifestyle organization of the separate risk behaviors and, therefore, toward alternative lifestyle choice. The general emphasis of such programs would be on health-promoting lifestyles that are relatively incompatible with the syndrome of risk behavior.

Whatever the success of programs for substituting health-enhancing behaviors for health-compromising behaviors and healthy lifestyles for those that incorporate health risk, it seems obvious that most adolescents will sooner or later engage in some behaviors that constitute a risk to health. The prevalence figures for drinking, smoking, marijuana use, and sexual experience among contemporary American adolescents describe an epidemiologic context of almost inexorable insistence. The psychological goals involved are generally central to adolescent life; the representation of such behaviors in adult models and in the media enhances their attractiveness; and since they are, for the most part, age-graded behaviors, it is recognized that they ultimately will be permitted once a particular age or status has been reached. From this perspective, the rhetoric of prevention seems no longer to be entirely apposite. Efforts to promote or enhance health will have to adopt alternative strategies that have somewhat different objectives—objectives that assume that experimentation and exploration of risk behavior are going to occur as part of normal adolescent development.

One such alternative strategy might be called *minimization*. The objective of such a strategy would be not to prevent but to limit or confine involvement in risk behavior to exploration or to a controlled, moderate, or "responsible" level. Indeed, moderation and responsibility may well be the touchstone for minimizing risk to health, since, for most of the behaviors of concern, risk derives largely from heavy, frequent, and chronic involvement.

A second alternative strategy might be called *insulation*. Here the focus would be on insulating the exploration of risk behavior from serious, irreversible, or long-term negative consequences. Strategies that protect a drunken teenager from driving a car or that lessen the likelihood of pregnancy or venereal disease among sexually active adolescents are examples of insulating interventions.

A third alternative strategy to prevention, finally, would be *delay of onset*. The object of this strategy is postponement of the initiation of risk behavior. Postponement for even a year during adolescence can mean greater maturity and skill for dealing more responsibly with risk behavior. There is even some evidence to suggest that the later the onset, the less intense the involvement, at least for drinking, cigarette smoking, and marijuana use (Jessor, 1982).

It has been argued that adolescence is a pivotal stage in the life span for the development of health-related behavior. Not only is it a period of heightened health risk, but what happens in adolescence is consequential for health in later life. The major aim of this chapter has been to show that health risk in adolescence is a systematic outcome of personality, environmental, and behavioral factors that account for variation in prevalence and in time of onset. Such factors can also have relevance for the design of intervention efforts to reduce risk and to enhance health. If the discussion here has increased awareness of the potential contribution of theory to such efforts, then the result for the field of behavioral health should be—in the literal sense—salutary.

REFERENCE NOTES

1. Pulkkinen, L. *Youthful smoking and drinking in a longitudinal perspective.* Unpublished manuscript, University of Jyväskylä, Finland, Department of Psychology, 1982.
2. Hays, R., Stacy, A., & DiMatteo, M. R. *The covariation and factor structure of substance use and other health related behaviors in two samples.* Paper presented at American Psychological Association Annual Meeting, Anaheim, California, 1983.
3. Rimpelä, M. *Incidence of smoking among Finnish youth—A follow-up study.* Unpublished manuscript, University of Tampare, Helsinki, 1980. (Cited in Pulkkinen, Note 4.)
4. Pulkkinen, L. *Social-behavioral precursors of youthful smoking and drinking in a longitudinal perspective.* Unpublished manuscript, University of Jyväskylä, Finland, Department of Psychology, 1982.

REFERENCES

Bachman, J. G., Johnston, L. D., & O'Malley, P. M. Smoking, drinking, and drug use among American high school students: Correlates and trends, 1975–1979. *American Journal of Public Health,* 1981, **71,** 59–69.

Baltes, P. B., Reese, H. W., & Lipsitt, L. P. Life-span developmental psychology. *Annual Review of Psychology,* 1980, **31,** 65–110.

Bandura, A. *Social learning theory.* Englewood Cliffs, N.J.: Prentice-Hall, 1977.

Chassin, L., Presson, C. C., Bensenberg, M., Corty, E., Olshavsky, R. W., & Sherman, S. J. Predicting adolescents' intentions to smoke cigarettes. *Journal of Health and Social Behavior,* 1981, **22,** 445–455.

Chilman, C. S. *Adolescent sexuality in a changing American society: Social and psychological perspectives.* Washington, D.C.: U.S. Government Printing Office, 1978.

DiTecco, D., & Schlegel, R. P. Alcohol use among young adult males: An application of problem behavior theory. In J. R. Eiser (Ed.), *Social psychology and behavioral medicine.* New York: Wiley, 1982.

Donovan, J. E., & Jessor, R. Adolescent problem drinking: Psychosocial correlates in a national sample study. *Journal of Studies on Alcohol,* 1978, **39,** 1506–1524.

Donovan, J. E., & Jessor, R. Problem drinking and the dimension of involvement with drugs: A Guttman scalogram analysis of adolescent drug use. *American Journal of Public Health,* 1983, **73,** 543–552.

Donovan, J. E., Jessor, R., & Jessor, L. Problem drinking in adolescence and young adulthood: A follow-up study. *Journal of Studies on Alcohol,* 1983, **44,** 109–137.

Elder, G. H., Jr. Age differentiation and the life course. *Annual Review of Sociology,* 1975, **1,** 91–123.

Erikson, E. H. *Childhood and society* (Rev. ed.). New York: Norton, 1963.

Fishbein, M., & Ajzen, I. *Belief, attitude, intention, and behavior: An introduction to theory and research.* Reading, Mass.: Addison-Wesley, 1975.

Hardy, J. B. Adolescents as parents: Possible long-range implications. In T. J. Coates, A. C. Petersen, & C. L. Perry (Eds.), *Promoting adolescent health: A dialog on research and practice.* New York: Academic Press, 1982.

Havighurst, R. J. *Developmental tasks and education* (3rd ed.). New York: McKay, 1972.

Jessor, R. Predicting time of onset of marijuana use: A developmental study of high school youth. *Journal of Consulting and Clinical Psychology,* 1976, **44,** 125–134.

Jessor, R. Critical issues in research on adolescent health promotion. In T. J. Coates, A. C. Petersen, & C. L. Perry (Eds.), *Promoting adolescent health: A dialog on research and practice.* New York: Academic Press, 1982.

Jessor, R. A psychosocial perspective on adolescent substance use. In I. F. Litt (Ed.), *Adolescent substance abuse: Report of the Fourteenth Ross Roundtable.* Columbus, Ohio: Ross Laboratories, 1983. Pp. 21–28. (a)

Jessor, R. The stability of change: Psychosocial development from adolescence to young adulthood. In D. Magnusson & V. Allen (Eds.), *Human development: An interactional perspective.* New York: Academic Press, 1983. Pp. 321–341. (b)

Jessor, R., Chase, J. A., & Donovan, J. E. Psychosocial correlates of marijuana use and problem drinking in a national sample of adolescents. *American Journal of Public Health,* 1980, **70,** 604–613.

Jessor, R., Collins, M. I., & Jessor, S. L. On becoming a drinker: Social-psychological aspects of an adolescent transition. In F. A. Seixas (Ed.), *Nature and nurture in alcoholism. Annals of the New York Academy of Sciences,* 1972, **197,** 199–213.

Jessor, R., Costa, F., Jessor, L., & Donovan, J. E. Time of first intercourse: A prospective study. *Journal of Personality and Social Psychology,* 1983, **44,** 608–626.

Jessor, R., Donovan, J. E., & Widmer, K. *Psychosocial factors in adolescent alcohol and drug use: The 1978 national sample study, and the 1974–78 panel study.* Boulder, Colo.: Institute of Behavioral Science, 1980.

Jessor, R., Graves, T. D., Hanson, R. C., & Jessor, S. L. *Society, personality, and deviant behavior: A study of a tri-ethnic community.* New York: Holt, Rinehart & Winston, 1968.

Jessor, R., & Jessor, S. L. Adolescent development and the onset of drinking: A longitudinal study. *Journal of Studies on Alcohol,* 1975, **36,** 27–51.

Jessor, R., & Jessor, S. L. *Problem behavior and psychosocial development: A longitudinal study of youth.* New York: Academic Press, 1977.

Jessor, R., & Jessor, S. L. Adolescence to young adulthood: A twelve-year prospective study of problem behavior and psychosocial development. In S. A. Mednick & M. Harway (Eds.), *Longitudinal research in the United States.* New York: Praeger, in press.

Jessor, R., Young, H. B., Young, E. B., & Tesi, G. Perceived opportunity, alienation, and drinking behavior among Italian and American youth. *Journal of Personality and Social Psychology,* 1970, **15,** 215–222.

Jessor, S. L., & Jessor, R. Transition from virginity to nonvirginity among youth: A social-psychological study over time. *Developmental Psychology,* 1975, **11,** 473–484.

Johnston, L. D., Bachman, J. G., & O'Malley, P. M. *Student drug use in America, 1975–1981.* DHHS Pub. No. (ADM)82–1221. Rockville, Md.: U.S. Department of Health and Human Services, 1982.

Kellam, S. G., Brown, C. H., & Fleming, J. P. The prevention of teenage substance use: Longitudinal research and strategy. In T. J. Coates, A. C. Petersen, & C. L. Perry (Eds.), *Promoting adolescent health: A dialog on research and practice.* New York: Academic Press, 1982.

Mechanic, D. The stability of health and illness behavior: Results from a 16-year follow-up. *American Journal of Public Health,* 1979, **69,** 1142–1145.

National Center for Health Statistics (NCHS). *Health, United States, 1982.* DHHS Pub. No. (PHS)83–1232. Washington, D.C.: U.S. Government Printing Office, 1982.

Rachal, J. V., Guess, L. L., Hubbard, R. L., Maisto, S. A., Cavanaugh, E. R., Waddell, R., & Benrud, C. H. *Adolescent drinking behavior: Volume 1. The extent and nature of adolescent alcohol and drug use: The 1974 and 1978 national sample studies.* Research Triangle Park, N.C.: Research Triangle Institute, 1980.

Rachal, J. V., Williams, J. R., Brehm, M. L., Cavanaugh, B., Moore, R. P., & Eckerman, W. C. *A national study of adolescent drinking behavior, attitudes, and correlates.* Report No. PB–246–002; NIAAA/NCALI–75/27. Springfield, Va.: U.S. National Technical Information Service, 1975.

Riley, M. W., Johnson, M. E., & Foner, A. *Aging and society: A sociology of age stratification.* New York: Russell Sage Foundation, 1972.

Rooney, J. F., & Wright, T. L. An extension of Jessor and Jessor's problem behavior theory from marijuana to cigarette use. *International Journal of the Addictions,* 1982, **17,** 1273–1287.

Schachter, S. Recidivism and self-cure of smoking and obesity. *American Psychologist,* 1982, **37,** 436–444.

Seeman, M., & Seeman, T. E. Health behavior and personal autonomy: A longitudinal study of the sense of control in illness. *Journal of Health and Social Behavior,* 1983, **24,** 144–160.

Tamir, A., Wolff, H., & Epstein, L. Health-related behavior in Israel adolescents. *Journal of Adolescent Health Care,* 1982, **2,** 261–265.

Wallston, K. A., & Wallston, B. S. Who is responsible for your health?: The construct of health locus of control. In G. Sanders & J. Suls (Eds.), *Social psychology of health and illness.* Hillsdale, N.J.: Erlbaum, 1982.

White, R. W. *Lives in progress: A study of the natural growth of personality* (3rd ed.). New York: Holt, Rinehart & Winston, 1975.

Zelnik, M., & Kantner, J. F. Sexual activity, contraceptive use, and pregnancy among metropolitan-area teenagers: 1971–1979. *Family Planning Perspectives,* 1980, **12,** 230–237.

CHAPTER 5

LATE ADULTHOOD AND AGING

ANITA M. WOODS

Texas Research Institute of Mental Sciences, Houston, Texas

JAMES E. BIRREN

Andrus Gerontology Center, University of Southern California

Large-scale longitudinal research on the interactions of health, behavior, and aging have yet to be undertaken, but what evidence there is suggests that, over the life span, our behavior influences the kinds of diseases we will become susceptible to, their outcomes, and very likely the way we age. There is little doubt, in view of the massive evidence, that the aging process and health are intimately related. Not only does the probability of dying increase with age over the adult life span, but the incidence of many chronic diseases and disabilities also increases with age. Despite the fact that the history of humankind has been marked by interest in how lifestyle affects health, we are still groping to understand the principles involved in health maintenance and aging.

Earlier in this century there was a more pervasive, fatalistic view about human aging than we now have. In particular, it was thought that heredity played the dominant role in the course of human life; therefore, the contribution of behavior to how long we lived, how well we lived, and the diseases to which we became susceptible was minimized. The early studies of Raymond Pearl (1922, 1931, 1934) indicated that our longevity was related to the longevity of our grandparents. Clearly, our phylogenetic heritage in evolution gives a characteristic length of life to the human species and also defines the susceptibility to disease. In addition, individual differences in our heredity contribute to individual differences in life expectancy and disease susceptibility. Behavior is thus conceived of as a variable interacting with species predisposition, individual differences in heredity, and environmental circumstance in determining both quantity and quality of life.

Today, popular beliefs about certain health behaviors appear to reflect what the research has described as the basis of a healthy lifestyle—balanced dietary habits, moderate consumption of alcohol, no smoking, adequate bedrest, promotion of relaxation, and regular physical activity. The fact is, however, that the scientific evidence for the etiologic contributions of these factors to disease prevention, though strongly suggestive, is modest (Naughton, 1982).

In the area of cardiovascular disease, the role of behavior is strongly believed to be a causal factor in mortality rates. Clearly, one of the more important changes in the health of our middle-aged and older populations is the notable decline in the mortality rate from cardiovascular disease that has occurred over the last 10 to 15 years. Since our species' characteristics and individual heredity have not changed very much during this period, this change must result either from some behavioral influence or from environmental influence on the occurrence of cardiovascular disease (Levy & Moskowitz, 1982). At the time that the now-famous Framingham studies of heart disease were initiated, the pendulum had not swung toward accepting behavioral variables as risk factors. At that time the only "real" factors in the genesis of cardiovascular disease were thought to be such risk factors as blood pressure, serum lipid levels, and disturbances of the electrophysiology of cardiac muscle. Now the pendulum has swung to recognize that behavioral variables have equal status as risk factors. Indeed, although the risk factors of hypertension, ECG changes, and serum chemistry are perhaps indices of cardiovascular disease, they may or may not be regarded properly as causes. On the other hand, behavior patterns such as those identified in Type A personality characteristics may indeed be considered causal in a chain of events resulting in cardiovascular disease.

The major focus of this chapter will be on one of the newest areas of research in behavior and aging—the effect of physical activity on the aging process. The epidemiologic, physiological, and psychological findings that relate physical activity to health status in middle-aged and older people will be discussed.

PHYSICAL ACTIVITY

There is a regrettable lack of information bearing directly on the effect of physical activity on longevity. The few studies on the effect of an activity program on the length of life in laboratory animals are complicated by the ages at which the exercise was begun (Bloor & Lean, 1968; Edington, Cosmas, & McCafferty, 1972) and by the type of exercise (voluntary versus forced) that was used (Goodrick, 1974; Retzlaff, Fontaine, & Futura, 1966). A recent study by Goodrick (1980) offers more clear-cut results. He found that an exercised group of female rats lived 11.5% longer than the nonexercised controls and that exercised male rats lived 19.3% longer than their nonexercised controls.

Reports linking physical exercise to human longevity are also scarce. Leaf (1973) observed the high level of physical activity in three population groups that were notable for their long lives. A large-scale longitudinal study in Alameda, California, showed that pattern of physical activity was one of the principal correlates of human longevity (Belloc & Breslow, 1972).

It is likely that public health interest in physical activity began with early investigations into the incidence of certain cardiovascular events. Research reported by Hedley (1939) confirmed that the incidence of myocardial infarction and sudden death was lower in subjects engaged in physically active occupations as compared with those engaged in sedentary jobs.

Subsequent epidemiologic studies have supported Hedley's early findings. Some research from England (Morris & Crawford, 1958) also reported reduced rates of cardiac mortality in occupationally active subjects when comparing bus drivers to bus conductors and mail clerks to mail carriers. Here, the issue of occupational selection must be kept in mind, for it is possible that healthier individuals select more physically active jobs. Morris, Chave, Adam, Sirey, Epstein, and Sheehan (1973) later reported that even casual weekend activity was related to some benefits in cardiac function that were not evident in totally sedentary populations.

The large-scale Framingham studies of heart disease also yielded information on the relationship of physical activity to cardiovascular status. Kannel and Sorbe (1979) reported that physical inactivity is a risk factor for the development of ischemic heart disease in men across all ages. They noted:

> While the data fall short of either proving or disproving that an increased level of habitual physical exercise is beneficial, with the number of sedentary persons in the general population growing . . . the need to regain more rigorous exercise habits seems urgent for well being.

Physiological Findings

Exercise physiologists have studied various population groups throughout this century. The designs of these studies have been diverse. Most studies have been cross-sectional, but some are longitudinal. Some research focused on chronically physically active groups, and others studied the effects of physical conditioning on previously sedentary subjects. (Tredway, 1978; Woods, 1981). The literature has been marked by the inconsistent and nonstandardized usage of physical activity and physical fitness measures, however, and by the underutilization of older subject groups.

Regardless of the type of study, some findings have been consistent enough as to serve as generalizations: when compared to sedentary subjects, physically active subjects possess a higher level of work capacity, a lower resting heart rate, lower systolic blood pressure and heart rate at submaximal effort, and a lower myocardial oxygen requirement at rest and at submaximal effort. Other differences in these two groups include findings of greater lean body mass, improved glucose tolerance, and improved insulin tolerance in the physically active subjects.

Many investigations have examined the effects of physical activity on serum lipid levels, especially cholesterol, triglycerides, and high-density lipoprotein cholesterol (HDL-C) (LaRosa, Cleary, & Muesing, 1981; Wood, Haskell, & Williams, 1981). In general, physical activity per se does not influence serum cholesterol levels; instead, loss of substantial amounts of body weight in tandem with an activity program is related to decreased cholesterol level. Triglyceride levels are also found to decrease when body fat is reduced and lean body mass is increased.

Earlier reports that physical activity influenced HDL-C levels have recently been brought into question. Apparently, marathon runners do have higher HDL-C levels than sedentary subjects (Froelicher, Bahler, & McKirnan, 1980), but neither healthy (Wood et al., 1981) nor cardiac patients (LaRosa, Cleary, & Muesing 1981) engaged in physical activity programs evidence significant changes in HDL-C levels. Thus, subject selection biases must be considered influential in the earlier reported studies.

The influence of age on physical fitness levels in healthy subjects has been studied by numerous investigators, including deVries (1970, 1971a, 1971b), Dell (1963), Andersen (1963), Taylor and Montoye (1974), and has been reviewed by Wiswell (1980). Their work has consistently found that level of physical fitness, characterized by a host of measures, decreases with advancing age.

Alexander (1974) operationalized physical fitness in relation to body weight and reported a decrease in cardiovascular fitness ranging from 0.93 to 1.04 ml oxygen per kilogram body weight per minute with each passing year. In other words, oxygen utilization decreased with advancing age. When the decrease was analyzed in relation to habitual physical activity status, however, the decline associated with the aging process was significantly steeper for the sedentary subjects than for the physically active subjects.

Taylor and Rowell (1980) summarized the effects of physical conditioning programs in 12 reported studies. Six of the studies involved young subjects between the ages of 18 and 30, and six studied older subjects with mean ages ranging from 41 to 55 years. Each study reported significant increases in fitness levels, ranging from 10% to 32.5%. These studies indicate that individuals through middle age have a capacity for gains in physical fitness through a program of conditioning.

Cardiovascular and Respiratory Effects

Specifically, exercise has been found to influence the following cardiovascular disease risk factors: blood lipid levels, obesity, hypertension, and blood glucose levels (Pollock, 1979; Simonelli, 1978; Thomas, 1979). Of the many different criteria that may be used to determine overall fitness (e.g., resting heart rate, cardiac output, vital lung capacity, stroke volume of the heart), the best method is to measure the maximum oxygen uptake (also called aerobic capacity or maximum volume of oxygen uptake, VO_2 max) of the individual (Pollock, 1978; Tredway, 1978).

Maximum oxygen uptake is attained when an individual exerts himself or herself to a point at which further increments of work do not significantly increase the rate of oxygen taken up by the lungs. To determine maximum oxygen uptake for a normal, healthy person, a test is given by having the subject work to his or her maximal ability (usually on a treadmill or bicycle ergometer) and measuring the amount of oxygen used by means of a spirometer. When working with elderly subjects, however, this procedure is usually modified so that a submaximal test is used.

It is well established that maximum oxygen uptake of an individual decreases in a linear fashion with age (Dressendorfer & Barstow, 1978; Kent, 1978; Wiswell, 1980). The inevitability of the loss in aerobic capacity is clear, but the extent of the loss is uncertain. At present, it seems that proper physical training can lessen the loss of maximal oxygen uptake with age (American College of Sports Medicine, 1978; Hodgson & Buskirk, 1977). This specific fitness variable, maximum oxygen uptake, has been shown to improve in elderly male and female individuals undergoing a variety of training methods (Adams & deVries, 1973; Buccola & Stone, 1975; deVries, 1970; Hodgson, 1977; Pollock & Dawson, 1976). In deVries's (1970) study, for example, a 30% increase in mean VO_2 max values was found for a group of elderly men (average age, 69.5 years) following a 42-week exercise program.

Another important aspect of cardiovascular-respiratory fitness for an elderly individual is an increase of physical work capacity. This fitness variable is a measure of the amount of work an individual can do before reaching a predetermined heart rate (e.g., 85% of maximum heart rate). The more efficient an individual's cardiovascular-respiratory system becomes, the more work he or she can do before reaching a high heart rate. For elderly individuals engaged in exercise programs, a significant increase in physical work capacity has been found (Adams & deVries, 1973; American College of Sports Medicine, 1978; Sidney & Shepherd, 1978). This means that an older exerciser can engage in more activities than a nonexercising peer without becoming as tired or uncomfortable.

Another role that physical fitness may play in reducing the risk of cardiovascular disease is evidenced in a recent study by Williams, Logue, Lewis, Barton, Stead, Wallace, and Pizzo (1980). This investigation found that fibrinolytic mechanisms that lead to clot dissolution (i.e., a decrease in thrombus formation) in the vascular system are enhanced by physical conditioning. This beneficial fibrinolytic activity was especially augmented in persons with low initial physical fitness levels. In other words, physical conditioning appears to enhance a protective effect against the development of vascular disease. This may be one example of a metabolic consequence of regular exercise that serves to mediate the reduction in risk of cardiovascular disease found in physically active individuals.

Body Composition

Cross-sectional studies have shown a decrease in lean body tissue with age, but not a decrease in total body weight (Sidney, Shepherd, & Harrison, 1977; Wiswell, 1980). In general, this decrease in lean tissue is accompanied by an accumulation of fat in older persons, particularly in the lower part of the trunk. It seems that some loss of lean body tissue is inevitable with age, but that an increase in fat is not necessary.

A major step that can be taken to minimize the loss of lean tissue is participation in a regular exercise program. Numerous studies have reported a reduction in fat and an increase in lean tissue in elderly persons who have participated in exercise programs (Buccola & Stone, 1975; deVries, 1970; Sidney & Shepherd, 1978; Sidney, Shepherd, & Harrison, 1977). In a study by Harris (1981), it was found that older runners weighed more than younger runners but were proportionately less "fatty" than their same-age nonactive peers. The increase in lean muscle tissue is a direct result of hypertrophy of muscle tissues when they are worked, and the decrease in fat is related to an increase in energy expenditure.

There is ample evidence that strength and flexibility (lack of joint stiffness) also decrease with advancing age (see review in Wiswell, 1980), but that elderly persons can counteract or retard these processes through regular exercise (Buccola & Stone, 1975; Chapman, deVries, & Swezey, 1972; deVries, 1970; Sidney, Shephard, & Harrison, 1977).

Metabolic Effects

The effect of exercise on levels of cholesterol in the blood is complex and controversial. It has been reported that one form of cholesterol (alpha cholesterol), which is carried by high-density lipoproteins (HDLs) has a protective effect against cardiovascular disease (Berger, 1978; Chapman, deVries, & Swezey, 1972; Kent, 1978; Tall & Small, 1978). Other studies have reported that some forms of cholesterol are carried in the blood by low-density lipoproteins (LDLs) and very-low-density lipoproteins (VLDLs) and actually promote cardiovascular disease (Adams & deVries, 1973).

Exercise has been shown to relate to increases in levels of HDLs and decreases in levels of LDLs and VLDLs in humans (Adams & deVries, 1973; Wyndham, 1979). Women tend to have higher levels of HDLs and lower levels of LDLs and VLDLs than do men throughout most of their lives (Berger, 1978), which may help account for their lower rates of cardiovascular disease.

The levels of lipoproteins are thought to be tied to estrogen production, however, which begins to decrease at menopause. By the time a woman reaches age 65, she has lipoprotein levels similar to those of an elderly man. She also has similar rates of cardiovascular disease at this age. Thus, elderly men and especially elderly women should be aware of the possible benefits an exercise program can have on blood lipoprotein levels.

The loss of calcium from the bones, or osteoporosis, is considered to be a normal age-related process. Such problems as vertebral compression, bone porosity or brittleness, and the greater probability of bone fractures are related to this decrease in bone calcium levels. Postmenopausal women are again the most vulnerable population for these problems. Exercise has been shown to reduce this calcium loss from bones and even to increase bone calcium levels (Erickson, 1978; Sidney et al., 1977).

Psychosocial Aspects of Exercise

Reviews of the literature relating physical activity to mental status (Tredway, 1978; Woods, 1981) have noted that older exercisers tend to feel less anxious, less tense, and less depressed and to experience enhanced feelings of well-being when compared to older nonexercisers. Other studies have reported that active older people have more positive attitudes toward work, feel in better health, report increased stamina and a greater ability to cope with stress and tension, and have a more positive self-image overall than inactive older people (Heinzelman & Bagley, 1970; Sidney & Shepherd, 1976).

Other studies have found that elderly subjects improved on some gross motor tasks and noncognitive psychological tasks after a 3-month exercise program (Barry, Steinmetz, Page, & Rodahl, 1966). An increasing number of studies, however, are showing some relationship between physical fitness or activity level and psychomotor performance in the aged (Ohlsson, 1976; Spirduso, 1975; Spirduso & Clifford, 1978; Woods, 1981). Since behavioral slowing has long been considered one of the irreversible concomitants of aging in the central nervous system, the findings that psychomotor speed can be modified by physical activity in older persons raises new interest in exercise as a behavioral intervention in the aging process.

This increasing interest in the roles of both physical fitness and exercise-induced arousal for performance of a wide variety of tasks in older persons raises questions related to the mechanisms responsible for improving performance. Physical fitness implies a greater effectiveness of physiological processes in adapting to environmental demands. In regard to aging, it has been proposed in Selye's (1974) stress theory of aging that physiological deficits accumulate over the life span in response to demands of the environment for adaptation. This cumulative wear and tear gradually lessens the individual's ability to adapt to further stresses. Selye (1974) has suggested that exercise, or physical conditioning, may protect an organism from the full brunt of environmental stresses.

In the past, loss of neurons, with an accompanying reduction in synapses, has been considered a relevant factor in slowness of behavior with age. If we view structural changes as adaptive to the activity level of the nervous system, some of what now appears as a pattern of aging could, in fact, be a reflection of the diminished physical activity level of older organisms. In old age, as throughout development, not only may function follow structure, but structure may follow function. Attempts to modify age-related behavioral slowing by means of exercise are potentially viable interventions.

The mechanism by which physical activity affects an older person's performance of a centrally mediated task is open to debate. Certainly, one must consider the possible contribution that physical conditioning makes to circulatory status. It may be that physical conditioning helps ensure the integrity of the vasculature, which in turn assures an adequate supply of oxygen to the brain.

One must also consider a neural mechanism; indeed, neuromuscular activation during physical exercise is extensive. The central nervous system, like other tissues, is characterized by an adaptive plasticity in its structural, biochemical, and functional properties into advanced age. Eccles (1964), for example, has suggested that repeated "exercise" of a neural junction may influence function by enhancing the manufacture and availability of transmitter substances.

A study by Woods (1981) used induced neuromuscular activation via postural changes and physical activity to examine psychomotor performance in both fit and unfit young and elderly subjects. Although the younger groups were always faster than the older groups, fitness level and activation conditions had significant effects on psychomotor speed in the elderly. The older, fit subjects were faster than their unfit peers; in fact, their response times were more similar to those of the young, unfit subjects. All older subjects performed better at some level of physical activation than at rest, with the effect of postural change being particularly significant. Older persons performed fastest while standing up, as compared to sitting and lying down. In other words, the older subjects benefited more than the younger ones from the induced neuromuscular activation of the postural changes and physical activity. Thus, behavioral slowing with age was seen to vary with physical fitness level and to be modified by induced neuromuscular activation.

Much attention had been focused in recent years on the relationship of behavior to the amount and function of transmitter substances and their precursors (Samorajski, 1977). In a comprehensive review of the literature on physical fitness, aging, and psychomotor speed, Spirduso (1980) proposes that psychomotor performance may be influenced by some aspects of activation in the central nervous system that have been shown to be related to acetylcholine neurotransmitter concentration in the ascending reticular system. She suggests that future research may reveal that adaptation effects of chronic exercise training include optimum levels and turnover rate of catecholamines and an optimum balance between transmitter systems that regulate brain function. It may very well be that these effects become ever more important with advancing age.

There has also been evidence that dendritic branching at an active site could be the device for developing increased synaptic action that may persist throughout a lifetime. The great advantage of fit older persons in speed of behavior over unfit older persons may reflect the denser network of neural processes the fit have by virtue of their chronic central nervous system activation via neuromuscular feedback from physical activity.

NUTRITION

There has been little detailed scientific inquiry in the field of metabolism and nutrition in older adults. Of the approximately 50 essential nutrients in human nutrition, few have received investigation with special reference to their metabolism and requirements during advancing old age in humans (Young, 1982).

In relation to human nutrition, it is generally thought that the effects of various environmental, physiological, psychological, and pathological influences are of greater importance in determining variability in nutritional needs among individuals than is age per se. At this point, it is uncertain whether the requirements for essential nutrients change in the healthy individual with advancing age—other than the need for energy, for which the daily requirement declines because of lowered physical activity (Young, 1978, 1982).

Thus, on the basis of quite limited knowledge, the nutrient needs in healthy aged subjects do not appear to differ significantly from those of young adults. It is necessary to keep in mind, however, that a characteristic of aging is increased disease incidence and morbidity, and these are conditions that may be far more important than age per se in determining practical differences between young adults and elderly people in their need for nutrients.

Another factor of particular importance in consideration of diet and nutrient needs during old age is the effect of stressful events, such as those arising from infection or physical trauma, or even those of psychological origin. The net metabolic result in response to stress is a depletion of body nutrients, followed by a physiological increase in the need for nutrients to promote recovery and to compensate for earlier losses. Unfortunately, there are inadequate data to help determine how much nutrient intake should be increased to meet the additional demands created by such stressful conditions as infections, anxiety, pain, or physical trauma, which may be frequent in elderly people.

Various drugs also may have profound effects on nutrient requirements by decreasing nutrient absorption or by altering the utilization of nutrients. Of particular concern in older people is their use of multiple drugs that may have synergistic effects, resulting in the additional loss of essential nutrients.

Finally, one must consider that a broad range of conditions that accompany advancing age may have important effects on the nutritional status of the elderly. In addition to factors previously mentioned, (disease, infections, medication), Exton-Smith (1978) suggested a host of other factors that might lead to inadequate nutrition in the elderly, including depression, loneliness, poor vision, poverty, mental impairment, inadequate knowledge of dietetic principles, and alcoholism.

Clearly, physical and mental disabilities affect quality of life and may lead to changes in dietary patterns and a deterioration of nutritional status. These problems may be compounded by the decrease in taste sensitivity that occurs with old age (Engen, 1977; Young, 1982) and the poor health of the oral tissue, which may restrict the selection of foods. Although many older individuals may never experience nutritional deficiencies, those who are vulnerable to nutritional inadequacies need to be identified.

HEALTH ATTITUDES

Popular belief maintains that older people complain more about their physical health than do younger persons, but a recent study by Costa and McCrea (1980) did not substantiate this. These investigators conducted a longitudinal analysis of somatic complaints in males as a function of age and neuroticism. Their results showed that neuroticism was a better predictor of complaints than was age, and that although it was more likely for an older person to have a somatic complaint, there was no significant increase in such complaints with age.

Health professionals should never dismiss the complaints of older persons with the thought that such complaining is simply a "normal" concomitant of aging that is undeserving of much attention. One study found that older patients often sought medical help much later in the course of an illness (e.g., myocardial infarction) than did younger persons (Gentry & Williams, 1979). This tendency obviously reduces the opportunity for effective treatment of the illness in an older person. It is much more likely that there is actually an underreporting of symptoms and disease by older persons (Besdine, 1981).

Older adults tend not to seek professional help related to either their mental or their physical health status. It is known that a disproportionately small percentage of the aged population is served by community mental health centers. In the area of suicide prevention, for example, Farberow and Moriwaki (1975) indicated that 2.6% of all calls to a suicide prevention center were from older adults, yet suicides by this age group account for 17% of total suicides.

Nuttbrock and Kosberg (1980) recently reported that individuals over age 60 were less likely than younger adults to seek medical help. This finding conflicts somewhat with the stereotyped view of older adults as being hypochondriacal and seeking physician care to an excessive degree. This lack of health-seeking behavior in older adults may reflect their attitudes of pessimism concerning the extent of care available from health professionals. Kleiman and Clemente (1976) showed that confidence in the medical profession is lower in older adults than in younger adults.

Clearly, educational interventions need to be initiated that encourage health-seeking behaviors. Many people—and particularly elderly persons—hold negative attitudes toward the role of exercise in health maintenance. Wiswell (1980) notes that there are three main reasons that older people do not exercise:

1. They tend to underestimate their physical capabilities.
2. They tend to overestimate the conditioning value of the little exercise they do get.
3. They tend to exaggerate the danger that physical exertion may pose to their health.

Many older people are probably embarrassed by what they may consider age-inappropriate behavior in the form of exercise. These attitudes point to the importance of educating persons of all ages about factors included in a healthy lifestyle, with a major focus being on continuous practice of health-maintaining behaviors throughout development.

The future success of psychological and educational interventions designed to improve the health of older adults will depend heavily on the ease with which older adults present themselves for specialized information and follow prescribed regimens. Influencing the successful programs will be the attitudes of the prospective clients, the attitudes of the professionals providing the services, and the characteristics of the institutional systems in which the interventions are embedded.

It seems apparent that physical activity must be promoted throughout the life span to minimize the effects of the aging process on physical performance and to modify the impact of chronic disease. Physical activity must be part of an overall preventive health program that emphasizes not only cardiovascular status but also overall nutrition, musculoskeletal status, and positive lifestyle factors.

REFERENCES

Adams, G. M. & de Vries, H. A. Physiological effects of an exercise training regimen upon women aged 52 to 79. *Journal of Gerontology,* 1973, **28,** 50–55.

Alexander, R. Physical fitness, cardiovascular function and age-discussants: Perspective in epidemiology of aging. DHEW Publication No. (NIH) 75–711, 1974, 243–247.

American College of Sports Medicine. Position statement on the recommended quantity and quality of exercise for developing and maintaining fitness in healthy adults. *Medicine and Science in Sports,* 1978, **10,** 7–10.

Andersen K. L. Physical fitness: Studies of healthy men and women in Norway. In G. Joel & E. Simon (Eds.), *International Research in Sport and Physical Education,* 1963, Springfield, Illinois: Charles C. Thomas Co.

Barry, A. J., Steinmetz, M., Page, H. F. & Rodahl, K. The effects of physical conditioning on older individuals. II. Motor performance and cognitive function. *Journal of Gerontology*, 1966, **21**, 192–199.

Belloc, N. & Breslow, L. Relationship of physical health status and health practices. *Preventive Medicine*, 1972, **1**, 409.

Berger, G. M. B. High-density lipoproteins in the prevention of atherosclerotic disease. *South African Medical Journal*, 1978, **54**, 689–697.

Bloor, C. & Lean, A. Vigorous exercise damages heart muscle in old rats. *Journal of the American Medical Association*, 1968, **204**, 1.

Buccola, V. A. & Stone, W. J. Effects of jogging and cycling programs on physiological and personality variables in aged men. *Research Quarterly*, 1975, **46**, 134–139.

Chapman, E. A., de Vries, H. A. & Swezey, R. Joint stiffness: Effects of exercise on young and old men. *Journal of Gerontology*, 1972, **27**, 218–221.

Dill, D. B. The influence of age on performance as shown by exercise tests. *Pediatrics*, 1963, **32**, 737.

de Vries, H. A. Exercise intensity threshold for improvement of cardiovascular-respiratory function in older men. *Geriatrics*, 1971a, **26**, 94–101.

de Vries, H. A. Prescription of exercise for older men from telemetered exercise heart rate data. *Geriatrics*, 1971b, **26**, 102–111.

de Vries, H. A. Physiological effects of an exercise training regimen upon men aged 52–88. *Journal of Gerontology*, 1970, **25**, 325–336.

Dressendorfer, R. H. & Barstow, T. J. Exercise for sedentary adults. *Primary Cardiology*, 1978, **4**, 40–43.

Eccles, J. C. *The physiology of synapses.* New York: Academic Press, 1964.

Edington, D., Cosmas, A. & McCafferty, W. Exercise and longevity: Evidence for a threshold age. *Journal of Gerontology*, 1972, **27**, 341.

Engen, T. Taste and smell. In J. E. Birren & K. W. Schaie (Eds.), *Handbook of the psychology of aging.* New York: Van Nostrand Reinhold Company, 1977.

Erickson, D. J. Exercise for the older adult. *Physician and Sports Medicine*, 1978, **6**, 99–107.

Froelicher, V., Battler, A. & McKirnan, M. D. Physical activity and coronary heart disease. *Cardiology*, 1980, **65**, 153–190.

Goodrick, C. The effects of exercise on longevity and behavior of hybrid mice which differ in coat color. *Journal of Gerontology*, 1974, **29**, 129–134.

Harris, M. B. Runners' perceptions of the benefits of running. *Perceptual and Motor Skills*, 1981, **52**, 153–154.

Hedley, O. F. Analysis of 5116 deaths reported as due to acute coronary occlusions in Philadelphia, 1933–1937. *Public Health Report*, 1939, **54**, 972.

Heinzelman, F. & Bagley, R. W. Response to physical activity programs and their effects on health behavior. *Public Health Report*, 1970, **85**, 905–911.

Hodgson, J. L. & Buskirk, E. R. Physical fitness and age, with emphasis on cardiovascular function in the elderly. *Journal of the American Geriatrics Society*, 1977, **25**, 385–392.

Kannel, W. B. & Sorlio, P. Some health benefits of physical activity—The Framingham study. *Archives of Internal Medicine*, 1979, **139**, 975–861.

Kent, S. Does exercise prevent heart attacks? *Geriatrics*, 1978, **33**, 95–104.

La Rosa, J., Cleary, P., Meusing, R. A., et al (for Project Staff). The national exercise and heart disease project: Effect of long term moderate physical exercise on serum lipoproteins. *Archives of Internal Medicine*, 1981.

Leaf, A. Unusual longevity, the common denominator. *Hospital Practice*, 1973, **8**, 75.

Morris, J. N., Chave, S. P., Adam, C., Sirey, C., Epstein, L. & Sheehan, D. J. Vigorous exercise in leisure-time and the incidence of coronary heart-disease. *Lancet*, 1973, **1**, 333–339.

Naughton, J. Physical activity and aging. *Primary Care*, 1982, **9**, 231–238.

Ohlsson, M. *Information processing related to physical fitness in elderly people.* Report No. 71. Stockholm: Institute of Applied Psychology, University of Stockholm, 1976.

Pearl, R. *The biology of death.* Philadelphia: Lippincott & Co., 1922.

Pearl, R. The inheritance of longevity. *Human Biology,* 1931, **3,** 245–269.

Pearl, R. & Pearl, R. D. W. *The ancestry of the long-lived.* Baltimore: Johns Hopkins Press, 1934.

Pollock, M. L. Exercise—a preventive prescription. *Journal of School Health,* 1979, **49,** 215–219.

Pollock, M. L. How much exercise is enough? *Physician and Sports Medicine,* 1978, **6,** 50–64.

Pollock, M. L., Dawson, G. A. & Miller, H. S. Physiologic responses of men 49 to 65 years of age to endurance training. *Journal of the American Geriatrics Society,* 1976, **24,** 97–104.

Samorajski, T. Central neurotransmitter substances and aging: A review. *Journal of the American Geriatrics Association,* 1977, **25,** 337–348.

Retzlaff, E., Fontaine, J. & Futura, W. Effect of daily exercise in life-span of albino rats. *Geriatrics,* 1966, **21,** 171.

Selye, H. *Stress and distress.* New York: McGraw-Hill, 1974.

Sidney, K. H. & Shephard, R. J. Frequency and intensity of exercise training for elderly subjects. *Medicine and Science in Sports,* 1978, **10,** 125–131.

Sidney, K. H. & Shephard, R. J. Attitudes toward health and physical activity in the elderly: Effects of a physical training program. *Medicine and Science in Sports,* 1976, **8,** 246–252.

Sidney, K. H., Shephard, R. J. & Harrison, J. E. Endurance training and body composition of the elderly. *American Journal of Clinical Nutrition,* 1977, **30,** 326–333.

Simonelli, C. Cardiovascular and metabolic effects of exercise. *Postgraduate Medicine,* 1978, **63,** 71–77.

Spirduso, W. W. Reaction and movement time as a function of age and physical activity level. *Journal of Gerontology,* 1975, **30,** 435–440.

Spirduso, W. W. & Clifford, P. Replication of age and physical activity effects on reaction and movement time. *Journal of Gerontology,* 1978, **33,** 26–30.

Spirduso, W. W. Physical fitness, aging, and psychomotor speed: A review. *Journal of Gerontology,* 1980, **35,** 850–865.

Tall, A. R. & Small, D. M. Current concepts: Plasma high density lipoproteins. *New England Journal of Medicine,* 1978, **299,** 1232–1236.

Taylor, H. L. & Rowell, L. B. Exercise and metabolism. In W. R. Johnson & E. R. Buskirk (Eds.), *Structural and physiological aspects of exercise and sports.* Princeton, New Jersey: Princeton Book Co., 1980, 84–111.

Taylor, H. L. & Montoye, H. J. Physical fitness, cardiovascular function, and age in epidemiology of aging, 1974. DHEW Pub. No. 75–711, 223–241.

Thomas, G. S. Physical activity and health: Epidemiologic and clinical evidence and policy implications. *Preventive Medicine,* 1979, **8,** 89–103.

Tredway, V. A. Mood effects of exercise program for older adults. Unpublished doctoral dissertation. University of Southern California, 1978.

Williams, R. S., Logue, E. E., Lewis, J. L., Barton, T., Stead, N. W., Wallace, A. G. & Pizzo, S. V. Physical conditioning augments the fibrinolytic response to venous occlusion in healthy adults. *New England Journal of Medicine,* 1980, **302,** 987–991.

Wiswell, R. A. Relaxation, exercise, and aging. In J. E. Birren and R. B. Sloane (Eds.), *Handbook of mental health and aging.* Englewood Cliffs, N.J.: Prentice Hall, 1980, 943–958.

Wood, P. D., Haskell, W. L. & Williams, P. T. Exercise and plasma lipoproteins: A one year randomized controlled trial. Abstract presented at 24th Annual Conference on Cardiovascular Disease Epidemiology, March, 1981, Washington, D.C.

Woods, A. M. Age differences in the effect of physical activity and postural changes on information processing speed. Unpublished doctoral dissertation. University of Southern California, 1981.

Wyndham, C. H. The role of physical activity in the prevention of ischaemic heart disease: A review. *South African Medical Journal,* 1979, **56,** 6–13.

Young, R. Nutrition. In J. W. Rowe & R. W. Besdine (Eds.), *Health and disease in old age.* Boston: Little, Brown and Company, 1982.

Young, V. R. Diet and nutrient needs in old age. In J. A. Behnke, C. E. Finch & G. B. Moment (Eds.), *The biology of aging.* New York: Plenum Press, 1978.

CHAPTER 6

LEVELS OF HEALTH ENHANCEMENT: INDIVIDUAL ATTRIBUTES

BONNIE R. STRICKLAND

University of Massachusetts, Amherst

Washington—I woke up suddenly feeling very wide awake, pulled the light cord, and sat straight up in bed.

"We'll be stopping in Baltimore," I announced loudly, in an authoritative voice. I looked around me. A private car, evidently. Good of the railroad people to supply those fruits, and all those flowers. The furniture looked a bit shoddy, but what can one expect these days? My wife was no doubt in the next stateroom. Where was the connecting door? I got up to explore.

The car was swaying heavily—the roadbed must be a disgrace. I supported myself on a table, and then a desk. Then there was a space of empty floor. I was halfway across it when the car gave a lurch, and I fell down. I sat on the floor for a bit, getting my bearings, then scrambled to my feet again, and opened a narrow green door. A locker, with my own clothes in it. I opened another door—a small bathroom.

Then I came to a much bigger door, and opened it, and leaned against the doorjamb. The swaying had stopped—the train, apparently, had halted. Outside was what I assumed was the Baltimore station—wide platform, dim lights, green tile. A whimpering noise, then silence, and no one to be seen. There was something hellishly grim about the place. Suddenly I was quite sure I didn't want to stop in Baltimore.

"We won't stop here," I said, again in a firm, authoritative voice. "Start up the train, and carry on."

I turned back toward my bed, and the big door closed behind me. I fell down twice on the way back—the crew must be pouring on the power, I thought—and getting into bed was like mounting a bucking horse. Safe in bed, I turned off the light, and was asleep in an instant. (Alsop, 1974, p. 92)

The incident described by Stewart Alsop, a political commentator and journalist, took place not on a private railroad car but in his room in the solid-tumor ward of the cancer clinic of the National Institutes of Health (NIH). The falling down was real enough, however, with bruises the next morning to prove it. The leukemia with which he had been stricken was also real and had brought him to NIH with a number of infections. Four days before he decided he "didn't want to stop in Baltimore," Alsop had undergone a major operation to remove for biopsy a piece of lung tissue so that his physicians could identify a lethal infiltrate that had not responded to drugs and had led them to note his prognosis as grim.

The day after the "train ride," Alsop's doctor remarked that the X rays of his lungs looked a bit better—certainly no worse. The following day, the physicians said there was no doubt about it—the infiltrate was receding. Some days later, the battered old lungs were close to normal. Stewart Alsop did die many months later, but he had guessed that his decision not to "stop at Baltimore" had helped clear his lungs and had given him additional health and time. As he said: "In a kind of fuzzy, hallucinated way, I knew when I announced the decision that it was a decision not to die" (Alsop, 1974, p. 92).

Alsop's story is one of many that suggest that some consolidation and focus of internal attributes can lead to the remission of disease and the improvement of health. We are familiar with tales of the "will to live," the positive impact of hope, and individuals' influencing their bodily states through ideation. Both the scientist and the layperson have special interest in mind–body interactions when we consider that health and life itself may be contingent in some fashion on what we believe and how we think. This chapter will note some of the emotional states and internal cognitions and expectancies that appear to be related to health, at least for some individuals. We are still far from a complete understanding of the intricacies of the relationship of thought to behavior, but evidence is accumulating that documents the sometimes powerful effects of mind–body interactions. Specifically, to show the relevance of a person's internal cognition to his or her health, we will examine altered states of consciousness (hypnotic states and imagery), emotions, and expectations and their relationship to health and physiological functioning.

EFFECTS OF HYPNOSIS

One of the most fascinating mind–body phenomena with which most of us are acquainted is hypnosis. The stage hypnotist is still with us, claiming remarkable physical and psychological feats as a function of hypnosis. Just recently, a hypnotist at an open meeting attempted to hypnotize the entire population of one community who wished to quit smoking. Advertisements about hypnosis abound in every metropolitan area, and an increasing number of health professionals have begun to incorporate hypnotic techniques into their practices. Dentists, psychologists, psychiatrists, and others use hypnosis to aid relaxation, to reduce pain, and to change maladaptive habits. Police officers also have incorporated hypnosis as a tool to help victims and bystanders recall and remember detailed events surrounding criminal activity or to identify alleged criminals. As the use of hypnosis has grown, theories and research on hypnosis have likewise increased. We know a great deal more about the effects of hypnosis than we did just a few years ago. Theoretical explanations for hypnosis and hypnotic trances still conflict, however, and the detailed mechanisms whereby response to hypnotic suggestion influences bodily processes are still largely unknown. Like Mesmer, who first used hypnosis to effect cures for patients suffering from physical symptoms, we still are searching for a scientific understanding of the effects of hypnosis and suggestion on health and physical well-being.

Friedrich Anton Mesmer (1734–1815) was an Austrian physician who believed that by balancing bodily "magnetic" fluids for patients suffering from a number of different ailments and disorders, disabling symptoms could be relieved and health could be restored. Mesmer was most successful in his practice in Paris during the last quarter of the 18th century, as he gathered groups of patients around large vats of chemicals and magnets for purposes of realigning bodily fluids. Mesmer would pass his hands and/or magnets over the afflicted parts of the body, and he believed that the curative powers of his own animal magnetism would affect the patient. Mesmer was convinced of a scientific basis for his successes but could give no clear explanation that could account for his cures. In fact, the French government offered him a large sum of money in exchange for his "secret," which he refused to disclose because he didn't know it (Udolf, 1981). As his fame spread, a number of professionals in the Paris community were increasingly distressed about Mesmer's treatment methods, which resembled seances more than legitimate medicine. In 1784, a commission sponsored by the French Academy of Science was appointed to investigate Mesmer. Distinguished scientists, such as the chemist Lavoisier, Benjamin Franklin, and the man who invented the guillotine, were appointed to this investigative body, which found that the effects that Mesmer described could be best understood as a function of Mesmer's "suggestions" and the patients' imagination. They then pronounced Mesmer's methods worthless and denounced him as someone who could be potentially harmful to patients. The commission noted that people were only helped when they knew they were being "magnetized" and concluded that Mesmer's cures were effected through "the excitement of the imagination." Following these findings, Mesmer ended his controversial treatment, left Paris, and eventually died penniless in Switzerland in 1815. One of Mesmer's pupils still asked, however: "If Mesmer had no other secret than that he was able to make the imagination exert an effective influence upon health, would he still not be a wonder worker?" (Janet, 1925, p. 161). Mesmer's influence continued to be richly felt by a number of physicians who began to use hypnosis to reduce the pain of surgery. The French neurologists Bernheim and Charcot also demonstrated that hysterical symptoms, such as blindness, paralysis, and epileptic-type "fits," could be produced and relieved by hypnosis. During visits to France, Freud studied under both of these men, and his interest in hypnosis marked the beginning of his lifelong search for an understanding of unconscious processes.

After more than 200 years of the clinical practice of hypnosis, controversy still surrounds the experience and use of hypnosis. Explanations of hypnosis range from claims that it extends ordinary imaginative processes to theories regarding altered states of consciousness. The full understanding of the effects of hypnosis and/or suggestion on health and physical well-being remains to be documented, but a number of reviews of hypnosis and psychophysical outcomes indicate that the imagination and responses to suggestion can sometimes produce impressive physiological effects (Barber, 1961, 1965; Crasilneck & Hall, 1959; Gorton, 1949a, 1949b; Levitt & Brady, 1963; Sarbin, 1956; Sarbin & Slagle, 1979; West, 1960).

Very briefly, research suggests that a hypnotic state does not in and of itself represent any special physiological process. Respiration and heart rate, for example, may increase or decrease according to the suggestions of the hypnotist. When subjects are hypnotized and asked to experience certain emotional states, such as fear or happiness, the expected physiological responses occur. It is interesting that few investigators report a difference between the responses of hypnotized subjects and those of control subjects who are given the emotional suggestions but are not hypnotized.

Hypnotic influence on blood flow and body temperature appears to be relatively well supported by research literature. In one study, for example, deeply hypnotized subjects were able to achieve simultaneous alteration of skin temperature in opposite directions in their two hands, whereas unhypnotized control subjects could not. The hypnotized subjects altered their skin temperature, sometimes as much as 4°C. They reported that they used assorted imagery, such as imagining one hand in a bucket of ice water and the other under a heat lamp, to achieve the changes (Maslach, Marshall, & Zimbardo, 1972). In other studies, a variety of skin conditions, including cold sores, blisters, allergic dermatitis, and warts, appear to be susceptible to influence under hypnosis, although methodological limitations raise questions about some of the reported results. Evidently, in attempts to respond to suggestions, hypnotic subjects have sometimes injured themselves to produce wheals or raise blisters.

Physiological outcomes as a function of hypnosis or suggestion have obvious implications for health and for the relief of physical symptoms and disease. None, perhaps, have been of such dramatic interest as those having to do with analgesias and pain reduction. A rather remarkable account of cosmetic breast surgery under hypnosis without drugs is reported by Mason (1955). A patient was hypnotized and told that the chest wall from thyroid notch to xiphisternum, including both breasts, and inward to the ribs would become numb and insensitive to pain. Throughout excision of scars, skin, and a wedge of breast tissue and fat and complete reshaping of the breasts, the patient displayed no distress or signs of pain. After the operation, she remarked that she had felt nothing and remembered nothing. According to Mason, if there was any fear or apprehension, it was felt by the surgeons rather than by the patient.

Although clinical anecdotes routinely note the relief of pain via hypnosis, the research literature is not nearly so straightforward. The experience of pain is a complex phenomenon, and it is highly subjective. Objective indices are difficult to obtain, and individuals are quite varied in their tolerance and reporting of pain. Generally, pain is described as having at least two components: pain sensation, which involves the physiological reactions to pain receptors and their afferent pathways terminating in the brain, and suffering, which is the subjective experience of pain (Kerr, 1981; Udolf, 1981). Some researchers suggest that hypnosis or suggestion involves only the relief of suffering, without significant changes in the physiological component of pain, whereas others believe that hypnosis influences both components of pain, including physiological sensations. In an intriguing series of experiments, Ernest Hilgard (1979) has demonstrated that hypnotized subjects who appear to be oblivious to pain or to sound are, via some cognitive apparatus, processing incoming information in a split-off or dissociated manner. Using what he calls the "hidden observer" technique, Hilgard suggests that a parallel processing of information is occurring, in that information is both accepted and rejected simultaneously. Thus, a few deeply hypnotized subjects report that some part of themselves is fully oriented to reality and is observing the experience of analgesia or deafness. This raises questions, of course, about altered states of consciousness or the degree to which hypnotic states for some individuals are similar to amnesias, fugue states, or multiple personalities.

Although questions remain about the pathways by which hypnosis or suggestion affect physiological responses, a number of myths and misunderstandings about hypnosis have been dispelled. For purposes of health, one of the most significant findings emerging from the hypnosis literature is that many people do use imagination and do respond to appropriate suggestion with resulting beneficial effects.

Entering a state of hypnotic susceptibility is not merely responding to the influence of a Svengali-like character who directs easily influenced, passive people to perform in ways that differ from their ordinary actions. Rather, the ability to suspend judgment and to allow oneself to experience new or different sensations or to experience them more sensitively than usual is an individual attribute that can be used as an adaptive and coping strategy. Most individuals who have the capacity to be hypnotized are also likely to be imaginative and able to become affectively involved in events around them. Hypnosis-susceptible individuals may lose themselves in the experience of direct sensory stimulation, such as the enjoyment of feeling the sun on one's face or walking through a soft rain. They may also easily assume the feelings of characters they read about or see on a screen or stage. Their imaginative involvements may aid in creativity or spur them to action. Imagination and rehearsal can also be used maladaptively, of course. Persons who regularly envision themselves as weak and dependent, subject to the whims of others, may assume that posture in real life. Individuals who fulfill themselves through fantasy that substitutes for reality can become socially withdrawn and inept. When used adaptively, however, the ability to engage in imaginative involvement may represent areas of substantial ego strength. As Josephine Hilgard (1979) writes: "Amid the increasing pressures of adult life, people can experience [sensory-affective and imaginative involvements] . . . as oases of tranquility, of conflict-free participation, and of effortless gratification" (p. 516). Moreover, hypnosis may serve as a form of adaptive regression, whereby the "ego initiates, controls, and terminates regression by temporarily losing contact with reality for the purpose of gaining improved mastery over inner experiences" (Gruenwald, Fromm, & Oberlander, 1979, p. 618). Hypnosis has become an adjunct tool for some of the traditional psychotherapies, and Bowers (1982) argues that some of the therapeutic effectiveness of such nonhypnotic therapies as biofeedback and cognitive behavior modification may be due to individual differences in hypnotic ability and response to suggestion.

When we describe imagination as both a suspension of participation and involvement in the world around us as well as an active, cognitive coping mechanism, such as rehearsal or role-play, we are talking about an active versus passive orientation toward the environment and toward our own internal processes. Within psychoanalytic theory, the ego is active or autonomous when the individual makes a choice or engages in voluntary action. The extreme of passivity occurs when one is overcome by one's instinctual pressures or by the influence of the environment. According to Fromm (1979), *ego receptivity* allows an openness to experience whereby the individual allows events to occur and things to happen. Sensory input dominates formal conceptual thought, alpha waves predominate, attention is diffused, and there is decreased boundary perception. Barriers to the unconscious are lowered, leading to a greater availability of unconscious material. *Ego activity,* in contrast, involves a readiness to manipulate the environment and includes attention, sharp perceptual boundaries, reality orientation, effort, rationality, and logic. Fromm suggests that as one moves from a waking state to such altered states of consciousness as daydreaming, hypnosis, or nocturnal dreams, reality orientation gradually loosens, and the ego may be both active and passive or may alternate these modes. Various meditative states and psychedelic drug reactions also fall along a continuum of attention and consciousness. In general, the more the state of consciousness is altered, the more the individual responds to unconscious prompting and primary process thinking. Since hypnosis is one of these altered states, according to Fromm, one can use it to receive messages from one's inner promptings. In the case of a vivid dream, such as the one described by Alsop, this same kind of theorizing suggests that the individual is actively focused on the events of greatest personal importance, such as his or her health, and is responding to messages from the storehouse of unconscious and preconscious material about the body.

Thus, the study and practice of hypnosis have taken us a long way from the early consideration of hypnotism as an expression of some outside influence, such as magnetic forces or the power of a hypnotist, to an exploration of individual altered states of consciousness and the ability to respond to inner promptings that may lie outside the individual's usual attentional and perceptual modes. An enduring theme that runs throughout the literature on hypnosis is the range of individual differences in responsivity to suggestion and use of imagination. Another is that the ability to engage in focused suggestion or imagination can be used adaptively to promote health and well-being.

IMAGERY

The ego activity/receptivity dimension is also related to imagery across various states of consciousness (Fromm, 1979). In the waking state, one may decide to visualize a scene or a face. In meditation or dreams, images may appear unbidden from some internal processing. Thus, imagery may also be a kind of understanding or guidance toward becoming aware of thoughts that have not been fully in awareness. Fromm (1979) is among those who believe that being able to use imagination, suggestion, hypnosis, autohypnosis, and the like, can allow one not only freedom from a solidly fixed perception of reality but also an opportunity to bring a fresh and creative understanding to one's personal awareness and activity in the world.

The use of imagery is one of the major components of hypnosis and, like hypnosis, has been used as a cognitive manipulation to reduce pain. Individuals may be asked to ignore pain through imaginative inattention, whereby they engage in pleasant imagery and try not to think about pain (Turk, 1978). Somatization is another imagery technique, which entails focusing on the existence, production, or inhibition of sensations. In this strategy, one might be asked to distance oneself from pain by observing and then writing a scientific or biological report analyzing the various components of one's experience of pain. Another strategic use of imagery would be to transform the pain imaginatively by interpreting sensations as something other than discomforting. One might imagine a sharp pain as the rush of cold fresh air across one's face or body on a crisp, snowy morning. This imagery might also involve a transformation of context, so that one imagines using an injured body part, such as a strained shoulder, in the game-winning catch of a touchdown pass. As Turk (1978) notes, everyone has experienced pain and so can fall back on already rehearsed cognitive strategies which they may have used in the past. It should also be noted that individuals appear to use imagery most effectively when they have some choice of the image or cognitive manipulation, rather than having to respond to an experimenter's or clinician's suggested descriptions.

In addition to the use of imagery for elaborating healthy behaviors, it has also been used, with reported success, as an adjunct to the traditional treatments of cancer. The Simontons (1975) noted that patients' responses to cancer are influenced by their attitudes and, in some cases, by their own meditative efforts (Pelletier, 1977). One woman, who had uterine cancer accompanied by infection, told her physicians that she had been drinking four glasses of grape juice a day and that she thought this might account for the 50% reduction in the size of her tumor over a period of 4 weeks. On further questioning, she admitted that she had been reading the work of Edgar Cayce and had been meditating to effect a cure. She was afraid that the physicians would scoff at this "unscientific" approach and so had invented the grape juice story. In light of these reports, plus observation of cancer patients under traditional treatment such as chemotherapy and radiation, the Simontons (1975) combined a technique of autogenic training (self-induced relaxation) and imagery to use as an adjunct therapeutic regimen for selected cancer patients. Using this technique, patients are invited to involve their families and friends in their treatment, and the psychosomatic aspects of cancer, especially the influence of attitudes on the immune system, are discussed. Through group or individual psychotherapy, patients are encouraged to resolve or alter conflictual life problems, and they are taught relaxation and visualization techniques. The visualization consists of having the patients picture their cancer and treatment according to any images that come to them. For example, the patient might envision the energy of radiation as a large army of soldiers marching successfully upon the tumor, destroying it, and triumphantly carrying the remains through the circulatory system for disposal. Cancer drugs might be seen as poisons that are being injected into the tumor, which is then visualized as shrinking or dying. The Simontons (1975) report that a substantial proportion of patients who have positive attitudes and who remain in treatment improve beyond the expected rates.

Some success has also been demonstrated for the use of relaxation accompanied by guided imagery for relief of the aversive effects of chemotherapy in treating cancer (Lyles, Burish, Krozely, & Oldham, 1982). Cancer patients receiving chemotherapy engaged in one of three situations. Some patients were trained in progressive muscle relaxation, which included guided fantasy. (Patients were asked to visualize pleasant and relaxing scenes.) To consider the effect of the presence of therapist support, a second group was accompanied by a clinic staff member, who provided encouragement and the opportunity to engage in conversation. A third control group received chemotherapy in the traditional manner, without relaxation imagery or the presence of a therapist. Patients in the relaxation/imagery group, in contrast to patients in each of the other groups, reported feeling significantly less anxiety and nausea, both during and following chemotherapy. They also showed significantly less physiological arousal (pulse rate, systolic blood pressure) in response to chemotherapy.

It should be noted again that these relaxation and imagery techniques accompanied normal medical treatment, so one cannot say that the adjunct methods work alone nor can causality be demonstrated. It is reasonable to expect, however, that occurrences of some kinds of cancer are related to the immune system and that efforts to improve immune system functioning, perhaps through relaxation and reduction of stress, might be helpful in cancer remediation. Successful attempts to reduce the aversiveness of cancer chemotherapy can also improve the quality of life for cancer patients.

EMOTIONAL STATES AND BEHAVIOR

The fact that some individuals respond more easily to suggestion and can use imagery to affect physical well-being suggests that certain personality types may be related to health maintenance and resistance to the onset of disease. The linkage of emotional reactions and personality to health and illness is, of course, a widely held and long-standing belief. Early Greeks described four humors within the body, which were hypothesized to correspond with physical states. Efforts were directed toward maintaining a balance of humors so that individuals might remain healthy and resist illness. Freud is the major modern figure who developed theories and clinical techniques for understanding the influence of emotion on individual well-being and on physical symptoms. Freud demonstrated that personal attributes and behavioral events in one's life shape responses that influence bodily processes. He considered hysterical neurosis to result from "strangulated affect" (Freud, 1920). Emotions that could not be accepted or expressed were changed through defensive maneuvers, such as repression, into physical symptoms. Catharsis, or the reliving of the traumatic emotional event, could then lead to symptom reduction. Freud used hypnotic techniques in his early work but shifted to a process of free association whereby unconscious impulses could come to light, rather like the ego-receptive states described by Fromm (1979). Freud also considered dreams "the royal road to the unconscious."

Alexander (1950) is perhaps the most influential psychoanalytic theorist to develop a theory of psychosomatic functioning. Alexander and his colleagues attempted to link physical symptoms with constellations of personality traits and to show that certain illnesses could be treated by psychological means as well as by physical intervention. Asthma, for example, was thought to represent a repressed cry. Peptic ulcers were thought to occur as a function of the oral dependency needs of hard-driven executives who could not admit their desires to be "fed" or nourished by others. Although this approach appeared to be promising, symptom patterns and specific diseases simply could not be matched with special personality types. Many overstriving individuals who might be assumed to be beset by dependency needs do not develop ulcers, but they may succumb to heart disease or, indeed, have no symptoms at all. Groups of patients suffering from asthma, ulcerative colitis, arthritis, Raynaud's disease, or any other of the disorders characterized as psychosomatic sometimes have personal characteristics that are more overlapping than not. Moreover, personality psychologists have had difficulty in identifying or describing stable personality types. Considerable debate is found in contemporary literature about whether personal characteristics are enduring and to what degree personality traits remain constant in relation to social and cultural change.

Other theoretical approaches also began to be developed in attempts to understand and treat the disorders that were initially considered to be psychosomatic. Stress was implicated in the development of life-threatening disorders, such as heart disease, as well as infectious and viral illnesses. Behavioral psychology developed relaxation and biofeedback techniques, along with cognitive change strategies, and established a new field of behavioral medicine. The treatment of chronic pain and such lifestyle disorders as heart disease, obesity, and substance abuse is increasingly couched within a behavioral framework, which serves as an adjunct to traditional medicine. Exciting work is under way relating responses of the immune systems to social and personal influences, with implications not only for the autoimmune disorders, such as arthritis, but for other serious disorders, such as multiple sclerosis. We have also made major advances in the discovery of the endogenous opiate systems, which can be selectively activated by environmental manipulations (Watkins & Mayer, 1982). Many of these newer approaches are discussed in detail in other sections of this *Handbook* and so will not be covered here. For purposes of this chapter, I will simply note that the assumed relationships between emotional states and physical health or disease are not at all obvious and clear. Reality may impact on each of us through unexpected personal trauma, social upheaval, and changing cultural influences. At present, the intricate interplay of individual reactions, including physiological concomitants, can only be under-stood through several different conceptual frameworks, including physical, psychological, and social paradigms.

EXPECTATIONS AND ATTRIBUTIONS

Although enduring personality traits have not been linked definitively with constellations of symptoms, psychologists have had some success in relating certain cognitive styles to health. Generally, people who embrace adaptive cognitive interpretations of the events that befall them seem to be better prepared to endure adversity and to improve their physical and emotional well-being than individuals who do not hold these attitudes. These cognitive mediating strategies can be roughly divided into two categories: attributions about causation and expectations about future events. To some degree, both of these categories can be subsumed under the general rubric of personal responsibility and control (Averill, 1973).

Psychologists have been interested in aspects of free will and motivation since the begin-ning of the discipline. Research on perceived control, however, seems to have, as a major impetus, the research arising from Rotter's (1954) social learning theory. Basically, Rotter and his students found that the traditional performance acquisition and extinction curves depend on the expectations of the individuals who are engaged in learning tasks. Persons who believe that their performance is linked to their own skills and abilities show different extinction patterns than individuals who perceive the task as one of chance or luck. These results, as well as clinical intuition regarding responses of patients who feel powerless over life events, in contrast to those who believe themselves to be in control of their destiny, led Rotter to develop the expectancy dimension of internal versus external (I-E) control of reinforcement (Lefcourt, 1976; Phares, 1976; Rotter, 1966, 1975; Rotter, Chance, & Phares, 1972; Strickland, 1977). Simply stated, I-E expectancy refers to the degree to which individuals perceive the events that happen to them as dependent on their behavior or as a result of luck, chance, fate, or powers beyond their personal control and understanding.

As early as 1962, Seeman and Evans found evidence that hospitalized patients with tuberculosis who were internal, as assessed by an early I-E assessment instrument with intelligence controlled, knew more about their disease than matched external counterparts did. The medical staff rated internal patients as higher than externals in objective knowledge about tuberculosis. In wards where information was difficult to obtain, internal patients were significantly less satisfied than externals with the flow of information. Strickland (1978) reviewed the literature on I-E expectancies and health-related behaviors and generally found that internals were more likely than externals to engage in adaptive health responses. For example, internals were more likely than matched externals to engage in preventive and precautionary health behaviors, such as engaging in exercise and wearing seat belts. Internals seem to be able to complete smoking cessation programs somewhat more successfully than externals. Strickland goes on to note, however, that congruence of I-E expectancies and health situations may lead to the most effective functioning.

Cromwell, Butterfield, Brayfield, and Curry (1977) manipulated nursing care, participa-tion in various activities, and information about heart attack for 229 coronary patients. Eighty medical patients with illnesses that were comparable in severity but without cardiac involvement served as controls. Overall, coronary patients were found to be more external than medical controls. Of most interest, however, was the finding that I-E expectancies and congruence of nursing care predicted further illness. No patients who were involved in congruent combinations of I-E beliefs and participation in self-treatment (internals with high participation and externals with low participation) returned to the hospital or died within 12 weeks following their hospitalization. The patients who returned to the hospital ($n = 12$) or who died ($n = 5$) had all been involved in incongruent conditions. Other research also suggests that health care should be tailored to the expectancies of the patient for most effective treatment.

The I-E dimension seems to be an especially promising expectancy variable in relation to health behavior. Special assessment instruments specific to health have been developed (Wallston & Wallston, 1981), and a number of researchers continue this avenue of investigation.

At the same time that researchers have considered the interaction of individual expectancies about control of reinforcement and health-related behaviors, considerable attention has also been directed toward other aspects of perceived and actual control. Subjects in conditions of uncontrollable aversive noise showed deteriorated performance in relation to subjects who could actually control the noise or who were told that they could terminate the noise if they wished (Glass & Singer, 1972). Other experimenters have found that subjects who choose to remain in experiments, in contrast to those who have no choice, report less physical discomfort, such as feeling pain from electric shock or thirst after eating salty crackers doused with hot sauce (Zimbardo, 1969).

One of the most dramatic examples of the role of personal responsibility and health behavior is reported by Langer and Rodin (1976). A group of nursing home residents was told by the hospital staff that their personal care, the arrangement of their rooms, and decisions about how to spend their time were up to them: "It's your life and you can make of it whatever you want" (p. 194). These residents were also encouraged to make suggestions about how the institution might be improved and were given the opportunity to select a small plant to keep and to care for (all members of this group did choose plants). A similar group of residents at the same nursing home was told that the staff was available to help them and would attempt to provide a pleasant environment: "We feel that it's our responsibility to make this a home you can be proud of and happy in, and we want to do all we can to help you" (p. 194). Each of these residents was also handed a plant but was told that the nursing staff would water and take care of it. No differences were noted in health status or indices of personal responsibility prior to the experimental manipulation. Three weeks following the staff communications, 93% of the group that was encouraged in personal responsibility reported themselves and were reported by the nursing staff to be happier and more active. Behavioral measures, such as attending movies, also indicated greater involvement and activity on the part of this group. In startling contrast, 73% of the comparison group became more debilitated. Eighteen months later, Rodin and Langer (1977) conducted a follow-up study and found that residents in the responsibility-induced group were still judged to be significantly more actively interested in their environment, more sociable and self-initiating, and more vigorous and healthy than residents in the comparison group. Of most importance, however, was the finding that only 7 of the 47 residents (15%) in the responsibility-induced group had died during the intervening year and a half, whereas 13 of the 44 residents (30%) of the comparison group had died.

The demonstration of such powerful effects of relatively simple cognitive manipulations remind us of how much is left for us to learn about mind–body interactions. Furthermore, conducting such research and possibly changing treatment regimens as a function of these findings raises ethical concerns as well. In another study of nursing home patients, Shulz and Hanusa (1978) found long-term negative effects following college student visits to residents. Students visited some residents at either expected or unexpected times. Initially, residents benefited from the positive, predictable visits, but across time they exhibited precipitous declines after the visits were terminated.

In considering adaptive responses to personal responsibility, choice, and control, one must also consider the contrasting effect of helplessness or powerlessness that may occur when one is or perceives oneself to be powerless in effecting change in one's life. As examples of this, Bettelheim (1960) and Frankl (1963) have documented the devastating effects of the concentration camps on the inmates, and Seligman (1975) has eloquently communicated the effects of "learned helplessness" on both humans and animals.

Other individual attitudes and cognitive characteristics have also been related to physical health. A perception of oneself as effective and competent not only improves typical performance activities but can influence basic physiological processes (Bandura, 1982; Bandura, Reese, & Adams, 1982). Working within an existential framework, Kobasa emphasizes a characteristic of hardiness which involves commitment, control, and response to challenge (Kobasa & Maddi, 1977; Maddi, 1975). Kobasa (1979) compared middle-management male executives under high stress who reported few illnesses to a matched group who had had a higher number of illnesses over a period of some years. She found that the executives who did not fall ill, even under considerable stress, appeared to have a clear sense of values, goals, and capabilities, with a commitment to, rather than an alienation from, self. These hardy executives also showed a strong tendency toward active involvement with their environment, an unshakable sense of meaningfulness, and an internal sense of control. In a prospective study across 5 years, Kobasa, Maddi, and Kahn (1982) found that hardiness functions as a resistance-to-illness resource and has the greatest health-preserving effect when stressful life events mount.

In considering the responses of victims to accident, disease, and violent trauma, Janoff-Bulman has looked at how patterns of self-blame influence adaptation and recovery. She found that young adults who had been paralyzed as a result of seemingly freak accidents and who blamed themselves for the accidents coped better with their disability than victims who blamed others (Bulman & Wortman, 1977). In trying to explain this seemingly dissonant attribution, Janoff-Bulman noted that most victims and survivors of disaster do, indeed, blame themselves for events that most of us would consider well beyond our personal control. Within these self-blame attributions, she suggests that there are at least two aspects of self-blame, which she categorizes as behavioral or characterological (Janoff-Bulman, 1979; Janoff-Bulman & Lang-Gunn, in press). Victims who engage in behavioral self-blame ("I shouldn't have been on the street at that time of night") in contrast to characterological self-blame ("I'm the kind of person who attracts trouble") feel that they could have had some control over the traumatic event. Thus, a feeling of responsibility for past events may lead persons to believe that they may influence events so that future trauma can be avoided.

Generally, then, research indicates that individuals who believe that they can exercise some control over the events that happen to them are more likely to take steps to maintain their health, improve their physical functioning, and respond more adaptively when stricken with an illness or disorder. It also appears that the congruence of expectancies and health care facilitates recovery from disease or illness. One must be very cautious, however, in assuming a point-for-point correspondence of control and health. In some instances, it may be quite maladaptive for an individual to strive excessively to control his or her life situation in an attempt to remain healthy when an illness may be exacerbated by increased activity or by subsequent disappointment when one does not improve. It would also seem painfully cruel to lead people to expect that they have in some way been responsible for the development of a life-threatening situation or to encourage personal responsibility when the patient needs the support of others and when there is no indication that the patient's efforts can be successful in leading to recovery or alleviation of suffering. This is a very difficult area of judgment, however; we do hear of hopeless cases, with critical prognoses, in which patients recover in spite of the predictions of health care personnel. Obviously, we want patients to maintain hope and optimism if these attributes influence physical well-being or recovery, and we have every indication that, for some patients at least, recovery does seem highly dependent on the patient's beliefs. Norman Cousins writes in *Anatomy of an Illness* (1979):

> It all began, I said, when I decided that some experts don't know enough to make a pronouncement of doom on a human being. And I said I hoped they would be careful about what they said to others; they might be believed and that could be the beginning of the end.

Cousins goes on to discuss his own personal efforts, such as watching Groucho Marx movies and ingesting large amounts of Vitamin C, in conjunction with traditional medical treatment to recover from a progressive disease that is usually fatal.

CONCLUSION

After all the clinical anecdotes, the reported results of carefully controlled research, and the various conceptual systems that describe relationships between beliefs and health, what do we really know about how a person's thought influences his or her physical well-being? How can the scholars and the scientists explain Cousins's return to health or Alsop's dream and subsequent healing? Did Alsop's recovery result from his vivid ideation about deciding not to die or was his dream a reflection of a physical improvement? We must confess that our knowledge is still quite limited. Certain personal characteristics—such as responsivity to appropriate suggestion, ability to use imagination and imagery, a cognitive orientation of perceived efficacy and control, a spirit of hardiness, commitment, and response to challenge—all seem to be helpful for some persons in their attempts to maintain and improve health. Moreover, these characteristics may be helpful when an individual is faced with a physical disorder or illness and attempts to influence bodily states. These are very general notions, however, and they must be weighed against the reality of the effects of trauma and disease. An individual will not likely be able to staunch the arterial gushing of blood from an open wound simply by imagining an impenetrable wall across the wound or by attempting to divert the blood via visualization to other parts of the body. Nevertheless, the ability to relax and to respond to stress as a challenge, the attempts to mobilize the body's inherent strengths in combating the onset of disease, the use of internal promptings, and the role of hope and cognitive adaptation to physical disorder all play a part in health maintenance.

REFERENCES

Alexander, F. *Psychosomatic medicine: Its principles and applications.* New York: Norton, 1950.

Alsop, S. I didn't stop in Baltimore. *Newsweek,* March 4, 1974, p. 92.

Averill, J. R. Personal control over aversive stimuli and its relationship to stress. *Psychological Bulletin,* 1973, **80,** 286–303.

Bandura, A. Self-efficacy mechanism in human agency. *American Psychologist,* 1982, **37,** 122–147.

Bandura, A., Reese, L., & Adams, N. E. Microanalysis of action and fear arousal as a function of differential levels of perceived self-efficacy. *Journal of Personality and Social Psychology,* 1982, **43,** 5–21.

Bettelheim, B. *The informed heart—Autonomy in a mass age.* New York: Free Press, 1960.

Barber, T. X. Physiological effects of "hypnosis." *Psychological Bulletin,* 1961, **58,** 390–419.

Barber, T. X. Physiological effects of "hypnotic suggestions": A critical review of recent research (1960–64). *Psychological Bulletin,* 1965, **63,** 201–222.

Bowers, K. S. The relevance of hypnosis for cognitive-behavioral therapy. *Clinical Psychology Review,* 1982, **2,** 67–78.

Bulman, R. J., & Wortman, C. Attributions of blame and coping in the "real world": Severe accident victims react to their lot. *Journal of Personality and Social Psychology,* 1977, **35,** 351–363.

Cousins, N. *The anatomy of an illness.* New York: Norton, 1979.

Crasilneck, H. B., & Hall, J. A. Physiological changes associated with hypnosis: A review of the literature since 1948. *International Journal of Clinical and Experimental Hypnosis,* 1959, **7,** 9–50.

Cromwell, R. L., Butterfield, E. C., Brayfield, F. M., & Curry, J. L. *Acute myocardial infarction: Reaction and recovery.* St. Louis: Mosby, 1977.

Freud, S. A general introduction to psychoanalysis. New York: Liveright, 1920.

Frankl, V. E. *Man's search for meaning: An introduction to logotherapy.* New York: Washington Square Press, 1963.

Fromm, E. The nature of hypnosis and other altered states of consciousness: An ego-psychological theory. In E. Fromm & R. E. Shor (Eds.), *Hypnosis: Developments in research and new perspectives.* New York: Aldine, 1979.

Glass, D. C., & Singer, J. E. *Urban stress: Experiments on noise and social stressors.* New York: Academic Press, 1972.

Gorton, B. E. The physiology of hypnosis, I. *Psychiatric Quarterly,* 1949, **23,** 317–343. (a)

Gorton, B. E. The physiology of hypnosis, II. *Psychiatric Quarterly,* 1949, **23,** 457–485. (b)

Gruenewald, D., Fromm, E., & Oberlander, M. I. Hypnosis and adaptive progression: An ego-psychological inquiry. In E. Fromm & R. E. Shor (Eds.), *Hypnosis: Developments in research and new perspectives.* New York: Aldine, 1979.

Hilgard, E. R. Divided consciousness in hypnosis: The implications of the hidden observer. In E. Fromm & R. E. Shor (Eds.), *Hypnosis: Developments in research and new perspectives.* New York: Aldine, 1979.

Hilgard, J. R. Imaginative and sensory-affective involvements in everyday life and in hypnosis. In E. Fromm & R. E. Shor (Eds.), *Hypnosis: Developments in research and new perspectives.* New York: Aldine, 1979.

Janet, P. *Psychological healing, a historical and clinical study* (Vol. 1) (E. Paul & C. Paul, trans.). London: George Allen & Unwin, 1925.

Janoff-Bulman, R. Characterological versus behavioral self-blame: Inquiries into depression and rape. *Journal of Personality and Social Psychology,* 1979, **37,** 1798–1809.

Janoff-Bulman, R., & Lang-Gunn, L. Coping with disease and accidents: The role of self-blame attributions. In L. Y. Abramson (Ed.), *Social-personal inference in clinical psychology.* New York: Guilford Press, in press.

Kerr, F. W. L. *The pain book.* Englewood Cliffs, N.J.: Prentice-Hall, 1981.

Kobasa, S. C. Stressful life events, personality, and health: An inquiry into hardiness. *Journal of Personality and Social Psychology,* 1979, **37,** 1–11.

Kobasa, S. C., & Maddi, S. R. Existential personality theory. In R. Corsini (Ed.), *Current personality theories.* Itasca, Ill.: Peacock, 1977.

Kobasa, S. C., Maddi, S. R., & Kahn, S. Hardiness and health: A prospective study. *Journal of Personality and Social Psychology,* 1982, **42,** 168–177.

Langer, E. J,, & Rodin, J. The effects of choice and enhanced personal responsibility for the aged: A field experiment in an institutional setting. *Journal of Personality and Social Psychology,* 1976, **34,** 191–198.

Lefcourt, H. M. *Locus of control: Current trends in theory and research.* Hillsdale, N.J.: Lawrence Erlbaum Associates, 1976.

Levitt, E. E., & Brady, J. P. Psychophysiology of hypnosis. In J. M. Scheneck (Ed.), *Hypnosis in modern medicine* (3rd ed.). Springfield, Ill.: Charles C Thomas, 1963.

Lyles, J. N., Burish, T. G., Krozely, M. G., & Oldham, R. K. Efficacy of relaxation training and guided imagery in reducing the aversiveness of cancer chemotherapy. *Journal of Consulting and Clinical Psychology,* 1982, **50,** 509–524.

Maddi, S. R. The strenuousness of the creative life. In I. A. Taylor & J. W. Getzels (Eds.), *Perspectives in creativity.* Chicago: Aldine, 1975.

Maslach, C., Marshall, G., & Zimbardo, P. G. Hypnosis control of peripheral skin temperature: A case report. *Psychophysiology,* 1972, **9,** 600–605.

Mason, A. A. Surgery under hypnosis. *Anaesthesia,* 1955, **10,** 295–299.

Pelletier, K. R. *Mind as healer, mind as slayer.* London: George Allen & Unwin, 1977.

Phares, E. J. *Locus of control in personality.* Morristown, N.J.: General Learning Press, 1976.

Rodin, J., & Langer, E. J. Long term effects of a control-relevant intervention with the institutionalized aged. *Journal of Personality and Social Psychology,* 1977, **35,** 897–902.

Rotter, J. B. *Social learning and clinical psychology.* Englewood Cliffs, N.J.: Prentice-Hall, 1954.

Rotter, J. B. Generalized expectancies for internal versus external control of reinforcement. *Psychological Monographs,* 1966, **80**(1, Whole No. 609).

Rotter, J. B. Some problems and misconceptions related to the construct of internal versus external control of reinforcement. *Journal of Consulting and Clinical Psychology,* 1975, **43,** 56–67.

Rotter, J. B., Chance, J. E., & Phares, E. J. *Applications of a social learning theory of personality.* New York: Holt, Rinehart & Winston, 1972.

Sarbin, T. R. Physiological effects of hypnotic stimulation. In R. M. Dorcus (Ed.), *Hypnosis and its therapeutic applications.* New York: McGraw-Hill, 1956.

Sarbin, T. R., & Slagle, R. W. Hypnosis and psychophysiological outcomes. In E. Fromm & R. E. Shor (Eds.), *Hypnosis: Developments in research and new perspectives.* New York: Aldine, 1979.

Schulz, R., & Hanusa, B. H. Long-term effects of control and predictability-enhancing interventions: Findings and ethical issues. *Journal of Personality and Social Psychology,* 1978, **36,** 1194–1201.

Seeman, M., & Evans, J. W. Alienation and learning in a hospital setting. *American Sociological Review,* 1962, **27,** 772–783.

Seligman, M. E. P. *Helplessness.* San Francisco: W. H. Freeman, 1975.

Simonton, O. C., & Simonton, S. Belief systems and management of the emotional aspects of malignancy. *Journal of Transpersonal Psychology,* 1975, **7,** 29–48.

Strickland, B. R. Internal-external control of reinforcement. In T. Blass (Ed.), *Personality variables and social behavior.* Hillsdale, N.J.: Lawrence Erlbaum Associates, 1977.

Strickland, B. R. Internal-external expectancies and health-related behaviors. *Journal of Consulting and Clinical Psychology,* 1978, **46,** 1192–1211.

Turk, D. C. Cognitive behavioral techniques in the management of pain. In J. P. Foreyt & D. P. Pathjen (Eds.), *Cognitive behavior therapy: Research and applications.* New York: Plenum Press, 1978.

Udolf, R. *Handbook of hypnosis for professionals.* New York: Van Nostrand Reinhold, 1981.

Wallston, K. A., & Wallston, B. S. Health locus of control scales. In H. M. Lefcourt (Ed.), *Research with the locus of control construct I: Assessment methods.* New York: Academic Press, 1981.

Watkins, L. R., & Mayer, D. J. Organization of endogenous opiate and nonopiate pain control systems. *Science,* 1982, **216,** 1185–1192.

West, L. J. Psychophysiology of hypnosis. *Journal of the American Medical Association,* 1960, **172,** 672–675.

Zimbardo, P. G. *The cognitive control of motivation: The consequences of choice and dissonance.* Glenview, Ill.: Scott, Foresman, 1969.

CHAPTER 7

THE SENSE OF COHERENCE AS A DETERMINANT OF HEALTH

AARON ANTONOVSKY

Ben-Gurion University of the Negev, Beer-Sheba, Israel

Readers of this Handbook surely need not be persuaded of the inadequacy of the traditional medical model in understanding health problems.[1] Most will be familiar with Engel's (1977) biopsychosocial model.[2] His approach, indeed, marks a significant change. Yet the opening thesis of this chapter is that not only the medical model but also Engel's model and ways of thinking that are compatible with it remain caught in the bind of a pathogenic paradigm. Unless they are freed from this bind by the additional adoption of a salutogenic paradigm, major advances in behavioral health will be impeded.

Explication of this thesis will lead us to a discussion of the "sense of coherence" (henceforth, SOC), which is proposed as a key theoretical construct in understanding and dealing with health issues. A later section of the chapter will consider the sources and dynamics of the SOC. Finally, we will turn to some examples of possible practical implications of this approach.

PATHOGENIC THINKING AND ITS CONSEQUENCES

The fundamental assumption of the pathogenic paradigm, from Cannon if not from Bernard, until this very day is that the normal state of affairs of the human organism is one of homeostasis and order. As Knowles (1977) puts it: "Over 99 per cent of us are born healthy and made sick as a result of personal misbehavior and environmental conditions." Homeostasis is occasionally disrupted by microbiological, physical, chemical, and/or psychosocial stressors, vectors, or agents. Regulatory mechanisms—neuropsychological, immunological, endocrinological—come into play in the organism's effort to restore homeostasis. Sometimes these mechanisms are inadequate and disease results. Therapy then seeks to reinforce, enhance, or replace the regulatory mechanisms.

What have been the consequences of the dominance of this paradigm in thinking, research, and action—consequences that remain even when it is expanded to include psychosocial variables? Six phenomena can be noted:

---

[1] Although the major purpose of this chapter is to consider the contribution of the "sense of coherence" concept to the field of behavioral health, this cannot be achieved without an understanding of the intellectual context in which the concept was developed. Since it cannot be assumed that all readers will be familiar with the book in which the thesis was first stated (Antonovsky, 1979) it is necessary to devote the first section of the chapter to a brief summary of the approach that led to the development of the concept.

[2] An even more powerful statement of the new approach—one more appropriate to the concept of behavioral medicine—is found in Noack and Müller (1980).

1. We have come to think dichotomously about people, classifying them as either healthy or diseased. Those in the healthy category, assumed to contain most people, at least in industrial societies, are normal. Their homeostasis is undisturbed. Those in the diseased category are deviant. In many countries, different professions and separate institutional structures are allocated responsibility for the two qualitively different conditions. At best, epidemiologists' warnings about the "iceberg" phenomenon are heeded somewhat, or an organization such as Kaiser sets up a track for the "worried well" (Garfield, Collen, Feldman, Soghikian, Richart, & Duncan, 1976). We become confused by chronically ill but functioning persons, by the handicapped. Moreover, the separation is not separate but equal. The sick, patently suffering and in more immediate danger, clearly have a more direct claim on resources. It is not accidental that public health physicians are lowest on the medical status totem pole, or that research budgets for seeking cures are infinitely greater than those that focus on prevention.

2. Thinking pathogenically, we have almost inevitably taken as our focus of concern a specific pathologic entity: heart disease, or cancer, or schizophrenia. Even those concerned with prevention are channeled, intellectually and institutionally, into prevention of disease X, Y, or Z. We formulate hypotheses related to the specific dependent variable. We seek specific immunities and specific cures. The advantages of such specialization are considerable; the disadvantages are disregarded. The very concept of "disease," as noted a decade ago (Antonovsky, 1972), suggests that there are common factors, both etiologic and symptomatic, to all the specific entities we subsume under the label. Specialization leads to disregard of these common factors; we do not even search for them. We speak of disease, not dis-ease. Our theories become fixated: a Type A behavior pattern is related to coronary heart disease; learned helplessness to depression; internalization of hostility to cancer. We ignore even the possibility of making headway in the development of a theory and practice relating to dis-ease and its prevention. Researchers and practitioners, social scientists and physicians, working on the same disease may come to work together and talk to each other, but they become structurally and psychologically separate from those who are working on other diseases, even if they have had shared training in behavioral medicine.

3. In parallel fashion, the pathogenic paradigm has constrained us to search for the cause or, if enlightened by the concept of multifactorial causation, the causes of disease X. After all, since the organism is naturally homeostatic, we have come to ask about those factors that disturb homeostasis, but always in terms of the specific disease. We have concerned ourselves little with general etiologic factors in dis-ease. More significantly, however, we tend to be surprised by the existence of pathogens and devote our energies to their study. An example is the overwhelming attention given to the Holmes-Rahe scale in the field of stress research. The notion that stressors are ubiquitous, that pathogens are endemic in human existence (see Dubos, 1965) is an alien notion. In other words, prime attention is given to the bugs—as noted earlier, to the specific bugs related to disease X—and not to generalized capacities for coping with bugs.

4. Particularly in the field of stress research, which is a central concern of behavioral health but not unrelated to the "cleanliness is godliness" precept, the pathogenic orientation has led us to assume that stressors are bad. Our goal has become the creation of a sterile environment. Many stressors and pathogens are indeed toxic; but others are neutral in their health consequences; still others may be tonic and salutary; and still others may have both negative and positive consequences. We have disregarded the likelihood that a sterile environment not only is unattainable but also can be literally quite deadly.

5. The pathogenic paradigm underlies the ambience that Dubos (1960) has so cogently warned against, "the mirage of health." Wars against diseases X, Y, and Z are mounted, with confidence and, it must be granted, with some evidence—though less than the generals claim—that many past wars have been won, that in time, with enough resources, diseases X, Y, and Z will be vanquished. This ambience is inhospitable to the relevance of behavioral factors even in prevention, not to mention disease. Toughminded scientists, concerned with

the "magic bullet," are little attracted to the soft pleasantries of what the behavioral scientists have to offer. Moreover, they control the resources, for it is they who, in the general image, have pulled off the miracles. So, presumably, we move closer and closer to utopia.

6. Finally, pathogenesis has given overwhelming priority to the case or, in considering prevention, to the high-risk group. It tends to ignore what methodologists call deviant cases. Thus, for example, we link alcoholism to traffic accidents, smoking to lung cancer, and so on. The data are clear and most valuable, but the risk factor always accounts for only part of the variance. We do not ask about the smokers who do not get lung cancer, the drinkers who stay out of accidents, the type A's who do not have coronaries. Much more important, we do not study, as Brown (1981) puts it, "the symptoms of wellness." Children of schizophrenic parents who do not become schizophrenic do not interest us, because we are tuned in to the specific disease. They may all have been killed in traffic accidents, but that is not our turf. Because we do not study the deviants, however, we generate neither hypotheses nor methodologies to help us understand the full gamut of human health.

THINKING SALUTOGENICALLY

What are the consequences of adopting what I have proposed to be called a salutogenic paradigm, which suggests that the normal state of affairs of the human organism is one of entropy, of disorder, and of disruption of homeostasis? What are the consequences of positing that the great mystery to be studied is that of health, of assuming that human existence obeys the second law of thermodynamics—the immanent tendency to increasing entropy—although, as an open system, it leaves room for negative entropy?

First, salutogenesis opens the way for a continuum conceptualization of what I have called health ease–dis-ease. The total population becomes the focus of concern, since none of us are categorized as healthy or diseased. Rather, we are all somewhere between the imaginary poles of total wellness and total illness. Even the fully robust, energetic, symptom-free, richly functioning person has the mark of mortality: he or she wears glasses, has moments of depression, comes down with the flu, and may well have as yet nondetectable malignant cells. Even the terminal patient's brain and emotions may be fully functional. The great majority of us are somewhere between the two poles. Priority in service might still justly be given to those toward the sicker end of the continuum, but it will be subject to the criterion suggested by Cochrane (1972): "finding the point(s) on the distribution curve where treatment begins to do more good than harm." In thinking and research, we come to ask: "Why does this person—wherever he or she is located on the continuum—move toward the healthy pole?" We do not have to make a choice between being in behavioral health or in behavioral disease (if this is what it should be called).

Second, seeking the mystery of health, we are freed from the isolation of being limited to a particular disease entity. We come to communicate with all others working on the mystery. We begin to deal with the generalized factors involved in movement along the continuum, not just the factors specific to this or that disease entity. Those who are trained in behavioral medicine continue to work in the field as such, not in one of its subspecialties.

Third, assuming that stressors are ubiquitous, we turn our attention away from the potential pathogen and from the specific answer to a given pathogen and become concerned, in research and in practice, with the resources that are valuable in coping with a wide range of pathogens and stressors. In doing so, we anticipate the emergence of new pathogens.

Fourth, we avoid hysteria about stressors and the gimmicks and instant cures that often accompany such hysteria. The question becomes not "How can we eradicate this or that stressor?" but "How can we learn to live, and live well, with stressors, and possibly even turn their existence to our advantage?" Child psychologists will surely see the analogy to the functional role of deprivation and frustration in development. Students of sensory deprivation will quickly grasp the dangers of a sterile environment.

Fifth, recognition of the limited utility of wars against diseases X, Y, and Z, of the search for utopia, leads us to focus on the overall problem of adaptation, of the perpetual struggle for sources of adaptation, negative entropy—of input into the social system, the physical environment, the organism and lower-order systems, down to the cellular level to counteract the immanent trend to entropy. This paradigm not only serves as a countervailing force to biological scientists working on diseases; it opens the way for real cooperation between all scientists and practioners. We behavioral scientists become not the graciously accepted assistants of the biological scientists but their true colleagues, as expert in our system domain as they are in theirs, jointly seeking the theories and practices of negative entropy.

Sixth, the salutogenic paradigm continually focuses on the deviants, on those who make it against the high odds that human existence poses. It posits that we all, by virtue of being human, are in a high-risk group. We come to ask questions at all points of the continuum. In my own work, I have focused on concentration camp survivors, poor people, and blacks in the United States and have slowly begun to ask what it is that enables some of them, even though fewer than in control groups, to do well. Only with the full development of the salutogenic mode of thinking, however, did it become clear that the question is germane to all of us.

It is essential at this point that a misunderstanding be avoided. I am not proposing that the pathogenic paradigm be abandoned, theoretically or institutionally. It has immense achievement and power for good to its credit. I have attempted to point to its limitations, to the blinders involved in any paradigm. Many individuals have not totally submitted to these blinders, even when working under their constraints. My concern has been to stress these constraints and their dangers. Given the reality that it is the overwhelmingly dominant paradigm, a dominance very much expressed in allocation of resources, there seems little danger in presenting a picture that may be exaggerated with regard to the vices of pathogenesis and the virtues of salutogenesis. Since I am involved in a community-oriented medical school, the not irrelevant analogy of primary versus secondary and tertiary care comes to mind. There is little danger in strong criticism of hospital subspecialties and strong support of family medicine. The former is very much here to stay; the crucial question is whether the latter will achieve the place it deserves.

THE SENSE OF COHERENCE

The very core of the salutogenic paradigm is the focus on successful coping, on what may well be called behavioral immunology. Once one adopts the paradigm, one begins to seek those forces and characteristics that are negentropic, that successfully screen out or do battle with the entropic forces.[3]

The question is no longer "What keeps one from getting sicker?" but "What facilitates one's becoming healthier?" wherever one is at any given time on the health ease–dis-ease continuum. This question can be dealt with on varying levels of generality. I contend that the time has come when we are in a position to go beyond limited empirical findings and hypotheses and to formulate a first approximation of a theory that will have the power to subsume many specificities.

Considerable attention has been given in the literature to a wide variety of coping variables. They have largely been conceptualized as buffers, mitigating the effects of stressors and muting the damaging effects on health. The list of these coping variables is long, ranging from money through knowledge to certain coping styles. The current vogue is social supports. What characterizes most of these studies is not only their failure to relate the coping variables

---

[3] As a concrete example of what was meant about the relations between behavioral and other scientists, I might note that, in the brief experience of the past few years, I have discovered psychoneurologists, a membrane biologist, an ophthalmologist, and even a physicist to be asking the same fundamental question: How is disorder turned into order?

under consideration to other coping variables—or, as I have called them, generalized resistance resources—but also their failure to translate the variables to a higher order of abstraction, which would provide a theoretical explanation of how the organism copes successfully to reinforce health.

Perhaps the first serious attempt to move to this level is found in the work of George Engel and his Rochester team. They have made considerable progress in developing the concept of the giving-up–given-up process (Engel & Schmale, 1972). Vaillant's (1976) "hierarchy of ego mechanisms" is also on this broad level of generality. Most recently, Kobasa and her colleagues (Kobasa, Maddi, & Courington, 1981) have proposed the concept of "hardiness" as an overall theoretical construct in explaining health.

These approaches have been mentioned (though space limitations prevent more than a mention) to locate the general context of my own thinking that led to the sense of coherence (SOC) construct, whose original formulation appeared in Antonovsky (1979). This formulation was based on the assumption that, by late early adulthood (about age 30), individuals develop a generalized way of looking at the world, a way of perceiving the stimuli that bombard them. One might use the word *ideology,* were it not for the cognitive, intellectual overtones of the word. The original definition was stated as follows:

> *The* sense of coherence *is a global orientation that expresses the extent to which one has a pervasive, enduring though dynamic feeling of confidence that one's internal and external environments are predictable and that there is a high probability that things will work out as well as can reasonably be expected. (Antonovsky, 1979, p. 123)*

Subsequently, in the course of work designed to develop an operational index representing the SOC, considerable refinement was introduced.[4] The initial definition, it will be noted, essentially referred to two components—predictability and expectation of a reasonable outcome—both of which suggest a generalized expectancy for the future. Subsequent clarification has led me to see the SOC as indeed a generalized orientation, referring to a great variety of stimuli, in the past as well as in the future. Furthermore, I now see it as including three components, which I have come to call comprehensibility, manageability, and meaningfulness.

Components of the Sense of Coherence

The *comprehensibility* component is indeed closest to the original formulation. It refers to the extent to which individuals perceive the stimuli that confront them as making cognitive sense, as information that is ordered, consistent, structured, and clear—and, hence, regarding the future, as predictable—rather than as noisy, chaotic, disordered, random, accidental, and unpredictable. No implication is made as to the desirability of stimuli. When people see the world as comprehensible, it does not mean that they are Panglossian, but only that they see it as understandable. It does not mean that they are unwilling to enter open-ended situations, but that when they do so, they have confidence that sense and order can be made of the situations.

The *manageability* component refers to the extent to which people perceive that resources are at their disposal that are adequate to meet the demands posed by stimuli. There is some similarity to White's (1963) concept of the sense of competence, which he defines as the sense in the living organism of "its fitness or ability to carry on those transactions with the environment which result in maintaining itself, growing, and flourishing." At first glance, it seems related to Kobasa's control component (Kobasa et al., 1981)—people's

---

[4] The 29-item scale that emerged has been submitted to initial testing in a large-scale field study and is available from the author on request.

belief in their ability to influence the course of events—and to the obverse of Seeman's concept of powerlessness (Seeman & Anderson, Note 1). Both these concepts, however, directly derive from Rotter's (1966) internal locus of control measure, and in this they differ from my understanding of manageability. "At one's disposal" may refer to resources under one's own control—the Kobasa, Seeman, and Rotter understanding—but it may also refer to resources controlled by legitimate others—friends, colleagues, God, history—upon whom one can count. No implication exists that untoward things do not happen in life. They do; but when people are high on manageability, they have the sense that, aided by their own resources or by those of legitimate others, they will be able to cope and not grieve endlessly. Moreover, there will be no sense of being victimized by events or of being treated unfairly by life.[5]

The *meaningfulness* component of the SOC is, in a sense, the emotional counterpart to comprehensibility. When people say that something "makes sense," in cognitive terms they mean that it is ordered; in emotional terms, however, they mean that they care. People who are high on meaningfulness feel that life makes sense emotionally, that at least some of the problems and demands posed by living are worth investing energy in, are worthy of commitment and engagement, and are challenges that are welcome rather than burdens that they would much rather do without.

Possible Misinterpretations

Does a person with a strong SOC feel and think that all of life is comprehensible, manageable, and meaningful? This question raises two issues. First, I would call attention to the possibility of a fake strong SOC. Surely, someone who is very extreme on the three components, particularly on the first two, is more likely to be psychotic than not. The claim that everything is comprehensible and that all problems can be managed suggests a profound underlying anxiety that this is not at all the case, a fragile covering that might easily be rent apart.

The second issue is of far greater significance. I call it the issue of boundaries. In much of our exploratory work, we found over and over again persons whom we intuitively classified as having a strong SOC who did not see their entire objective world as coherent. It became clear that all of us set boundaries. What goes on outside these boundaries, whether comprehensible and manageable or not, simply does not matter much, does not trouble us. For one person, the scope may be very wide; for another, it may be relatively narrow. The two crucial questions then become: first, is there at least some part of my life that does matter very much, which I care about? Second, within these boundaries, are stimuli meaningful, comprehensible, and manageable?

Putting it in these terms raises another issue. In another context (Antonovsky & Antonovsky, 1974), Seeman's failure to distinguish between "man's relation to the larger social order" and "expectancies for control in more intimate need areas" in his discussion of alienation was criticized. The boundary notion suggests that one need not necessarily feel that all of life is highly comprehensible, manageable, and meaningful in order to have a strong SOC. Quite conceivably, people might feel that they have little interest in national government or international politics, little competence in manual (or cognitive or aesthetic) skills, little concern for local volunteer groups or trade union activity, and so on, and yet have a strong SOC. Of course, the real world represented by these spheres will objectively influence a person's life—the most apolitical person may be drafted, be sent to war, and be killed—but being apolitical does not obviate a strong SOC. On the other hand, it is inconceivable that people would put beyond the pale their own immediate life, their own feelings, their direct interpersonal relations, their own major sphere of activity. Feelings

---

[5] Scrutiny of the I-E Locus of Control items used by Kobasa and Seeman shows that most items do focus on these negative elements. Again, the salutogenic orientation leads individuals to focus largely on resources, their own and others', the latter being strikingly absent from items formulated by those who think pathogenically.

and beliefs, family and friends, work (paid or not), and existential issues can never be put beyond the pale. If they are, then by definition the person is low on meaningfulness. If people grant that these issues are important in their life, then the question arises whether they are also meaningful—that is, whether they are challenges worthy of investment of energy. It should be noted that, with respect to work, the question is not necessarily one of intrinsic satisfaction. People may find little joy in their work, but if they feel that the work has a meaning because it is how they support their family and keep it functioning smoothly and happily, they can still have a strong SOC.

It can be seen, then, that the three components are inextricably intertwined and can really only be separated for analytic purposes. Theoretically, an individual can be high on one component and low on others, but this is inherently unstable. The person who is high on manageability but low on the other two is like a punch-drunk fighter who will soon give up. People who are high on comprehensibility and meaningfulness but low on manageability are strongly motivated to search for resources that will enable them to think that they can manage. It would be premature at this early stage of development of the construct, theoretically and empirically, to push the discussion much further, although the step is essential.

One final point must be made here. Those of us who study health, which we value, confront a strong temptation. It would be so nice if the characteristics that we personally value and find pleasing were also good for health. It is not at all accidental that a theme runs through the literature that mature, autonomous, creative, warm, and so on, people are also healthy. I would urgently warn against such a misinterpretation of the SOC. To put it bluntly, a person with a strong SOC might well be a terrible person in terms of my (or your) values. Such a person might well be a Nazi or, to bring it closer to home, a highly manipulative, unscrupulous academic, or a member of an extreme religious sect. True believers—keeping in mind the warning about the fake SOC—are likely to have a strong SOC. The true intellectual, however, for substantive and social structural reasons, is not likely to have a strong SOC.

THE SOC AND HEALTH: AVOIDANCE, APPRAISAL, AND ACTIVE COPING

Wherever people are located at any time on the health ease–dis-ease continuum, the theory presented here hypothesizes that the stronger their SOC, the more likely they are to maintain that location or improve it. There is a distinct analogy (in due time it may become more than an analogy) to Burnet's (1971) concept of immunological surveillance, "perpetually patrolling the body, as it were, for evildoers" (p. 157). The research evidence suggesting that this hypothesis is plausible is summarized in Chapter 6 of Antonovsky (1979). Two relatively minor ways and one major way can be suggested to explain how this works.

First, the stronger their SOC, the more people can *avoid* threat or danger. They are more likely to engage in activities that are health-promoting and to avoid those that are health-endangering. People's belief that life is meaningful (which, not incidentally, gives them a good reason for wanting to be healthy in order to be able to function optimally), that they have the resources to manage, and that life is ordered and predictable provides a sound basis for such behaviors. It is worth investing in smoking cessation efforts, exercise, good nutrition, and the like, because they believe that these efforts will pay off. They are less tempted by the "it can't happen to me" mode of thought. Of course, some people become faddists, but this tendency is held in check by the pragmatic criterion of whether a behavior pays off. People with a weak SOC, however, have neither the motivational nor the cognitive basis for the active coping, positive or negative, that the avoidance of threat requires.[6]

---

[6] Bandura's (1977) concept of self-efficacy, which hypothesizes about the conditions under which "coping behavior will be initiated, how much effort will be expended, and how long it will be sustained," is most relevant to this and subsequent sections.

Second, the stronger their SOC, the more likely it is that, confronted by the innumerable stimuli that cannot be avoided, people will appraise the stimuli (see Lazarus & Launier, 1978) not as threats or dangers that paralyze and lead to negative self-fulfilling prophecies, but as opportunities that offer meaningful rewards, as challenges worthy of investment of energy, and as situations that can be managed well. The woman who concludes that, given the specific life conditions under which she lives, she cannot go out to work and must continue being a housewife, will seek, if she has a strong SOC, to focus her energies on childrearing. The recent widower who has had a happy marriage will, together with the pain and sadness, be able to "give up," as Parkes (1971) puts it, and restructure his life. The 30-year-old woman who, for eminently good reasons in her terms, has not wished to commit herself to marriage, may decide to become a single parent. These examples have been chosen in light of the data indicating that accepting the sad inevitability of the stimuli as stressors has deleterious health consequences. To put it in other words, people with a strong SOC, confronted with a potentially noxious situation, will be more able to define or redefine the situation as one to which they need not succumb, one that is not necessarily noxious.

Whatever the possibility of avoiding threat, however, or of redefining situations as nonnoxious, life inevitably confronts us with noxious stimuli, with threats, with stressors. How does a strong SOC function negentropically? I suggest that this is the heart of the matter. It is here that we must turn to the concept of generalized and specific resistance resources, a concept that will be more fully discussed in the later section on the sources of the SOC. For present purposes, the crucial point is that resistance resources—defined as agencies that facilitate coping with pathogens—are potentials. They must be transformed kinetically before they can function to combat and overcome pathogens. In talking of resistance resources, we face the danger of reification. The antibiotic is of no use unless it is taken appropriately. The friend is of no use unless there is communication. Clear cultural norms are of no use until they are applied to the concrete situation. Money is of no use until it is spent.[7] Surely, people differ in the potential resources available to them. Beyond this, however, they differ significantly in the readiness and willingness to exploit the resources that they have at their potential disposal. This is what distinguishes between people with a stronger and a weaker SOC. The former will search very hard for the coping resources that are potentially available; the latter are more likely to "give up" (this time in Engel's sense), and say "Neither God, nor I myself, nor anyone else can help me."

Let us consider the 54-year old man who has had a myocardial infarction. With a strong SOC, he is much more likely to believe and act on the belief that his employers or his trade union will do all in their power to facilitate his return to his job, or to an appropriate one if change is necessitated, than would someone in the same situation with a weak SOC. The person with the strong SOC will reject entering the category of the permanent invalid and thereby, as at least some data indicate, be at less risk of a second infarct. A young person whose involvement in a traffic accident has led to a leg amputation is more likely, if he or she has a strong SOC, to adopt a self-perception (and seek for social reinforcement of this self-perception) as a multifaceted person, one of whose facets is a handicap that is more serious than needing a hearing aid or wearing glasses but less serious than many other handicaps. The person with a weak SOC is more likely to accept the definition, by self and others, of a one-legged person. (For this distinction, see Scott, 1969.) Again, it seems reasonable to make differential health predictions for the two.[8]

I could go on with many other examples. Unfortunately, because our research has been so predominantly pathogenically oriented, the supportive data at this stage can at best be

---

[7] The difference between physical agents and activities and resources, such as friends or norms or money, is that by just thinking about them, we can gain confidence in our ability to cope, much as in the case of the placebo effect.

[8] This discussion of avoiding, appraising, and functioning negentropically is decidedly compatible, though not identical, with that taken by Pearlin and Schooler (1978).

inferential. If we consider, however, such health-consequential matters as self-help groups, active participation in transforming environmental conditions, faith (call it placebos if you wish), or self-definition and the self-fulfilling prophecy, surely it seems reasonable to hypothesize that the person who sees life as comprehensible, manageable, and meaningful is more likely to optimally exploit potential resistance sources. This approach, incidentally, can help explain theoretically why some stress management programs work well for some people but not so well for others.

The final point I would make in this section will necessarily be no more than a statement of need, since it takes me far beyond my field of competence. In the last analysis, if our concern is the relationship between psychological, social, and cultural variables and the health of the organism, a full theory would have to include an understanding of the neuro-physiological, endocrinological, and immunological pathways through which this relationship is mediated. In this respect, I find considerable encouragement for the model advanced here in recent work in these fields. Thus, Henry (1982; see also Schwartz, 1979) concludes a highly sophisticated paper with the following:

> The enormous complexity of human society and man's capacity through his symbol system to identify with more powerful beings—gods or chosen leaders or institutions— give him certain invulnerability to limbic system arousal as long as he perceives himself to be socially supported here or in the hereafter. (p. 378)

SOURCES OF THE SOC

In my original formulation, I characterized the SOC as "enduring though dynamic." It was envisaged as an orientation that emerges out of childhood, adolescence, and early adulthood, at the end of which the individual has become located at some point of the SOC continuum. The two questions to be dealt with in this section are, first, what factors shape a person's location and, second, what *dynamic* means. This discussion will, in turn, lead us to a consideration of meaningful implications for behavioral health.

The SOC construct emerged from a search for a parsimonious answer to the question "*How* do resistance resources seem to eventuate in good health?" as shown by substantial data. Rather, the data, gathered largely in answer to the pathogenic question, show that the absence of resistance resources eventuates in poor health—as seen, for example, in my own work on poverty and social class (Antonovsky, 1967). This search led to a specification of the commonalities of resistance resources—that is, the characteristics that are shared by the different phenomena that are labeled resistance resources. The definition of such a resource had to be such that it would not lead to tautology—that is, defining a resistance resource as something that is empirically found to be related to health. Such findings do not answer the fundamental theoretical question of *how*.

The proposed answer to what resistance resources have in common is that they repeatedly provide life experiences that have three characteristics: consistency, an underload-overload balance, and participation in decision making. It is argued that having money or belonging to the upper class, having a clear ego identity, living in a stable society, having a clear religious stance, having social supports, and so on, all provide such life experiences.

Consistency refers to the extent to which a given life experience fits other previous or contemporary life experiences. Does a given behavior result in the same consequence as it did the last time the person manifested such behavior? Can the person make accurate predictions about what is likely to take place? Do social responses to the person in life area A contradict social responses in life area B? Do people relate to the person in one way today and in a different way tomorrow? Do significant others interact with the person in complementary or similar fashion? From our earliest childhood through the end of our lives, all our life experiences can be characterized as being to some degree consistent with one another. The core of this notion is the extent to which a person's life is laden with surprises for which there is no reasonable explanation. The greater the consistency of our life experiences, the more our lives are predictable. Note, here, the close link to the compre-hensibility component of the SOC.

The *underload-overload balance* refers to the extent to which the life experiences we undergo—which always involve some demand—are appropriate to our capacities. I have found Lipowski's (1975) theory of sensory and information overload, which he links to the phenomena of sensory deprivation, the most profound discussion of this issue. His concept of a "critical tolerance load," applied to both ends of the load spectrum, is crucial here. Again, from birth, we are confronted by demands, emerging from both the internal and the external environments, to which we are called upon to measure up. Over and over again, we experience a greater or lesser degree of success. We can be bored or we can be overwhelmed; or we can repeatedly confront tasks that call on us to exert our energies, skills, knowledge, abilities, and potentials so that the tasks can be coped with successfully.

Much of the literature stresses the significance of overload. Underload is just as significant, however. When we are not called upon, or do not call upon ourselves, to do anything—when we have nothing to manage—our personal and role identities wither. Emptiness is no less dangerous than overload. When our life experiences are just about right in making demands on us, however—even, perhaps, with a slight leaning in the direction of overload, leading to the discovery of hitherto untapped energies and talents—our SOC is thereby strengthened. Note, here, the close link to the manageability component of the SOC.

Life experiences can be seen as having a third major dimension, one that I intuitively included in my original discussion but only began to understand later. Many life experiences can be consistent and balanced but not of our own making or choosing in any way. The question arises whether, with respect to any life experience, we have taken part in choosing to undergo that experience, in judging whether the rules of the game are legitimate, and in solving the problems and tasks posed by the experience. When others decide everything for us—when they set the task, formulate the rules, and manage the outcome—the experience inevitably remains alien and vicarious to us. It is important to stress that the dimension is not control but *participation in decision-making*. What is crucial is that people approve of the tasks set before them; that they have considerable performance responsibility; and that what they do or not do has an effect on the outcome of the experience. This formulation thus has room not only for the largely autonomous person but also for the loyal party member, the religious believer, the work group participant, and the child in a certain kind of family. Repeated experience of this kind of participation provides the basis for the meaning-fulness component of the SOC.

For the developmental psychologist, it will be clear that growing up in certain kinds of subcultures, with their particular childrearing patterns and resources, is likely to provide these kinds of experience. As a sociologist, my focus has been on the historical, social-structural, and cultural aspects of the world of the young adult as being finally decisive in providing, to a greater or lesser extent, the experiences that shape a person's SOC. This approach does not deny the significance of childhood. Surely, the issue warrants much research. For present purposes, however, our central concern is with the thesis that life experiences in these three dimensions shape a person's SOC.[9]

THE POSSIBILITY OF CHANGE

This brings us to another question—namely, how malleable the SOC is from adulthood on. My original commitment was not only to seeing the SOC as a very fundamental part

[9] After this paper was written, my attention was brought to a slim but major contribution to the salutogenic literature. Werner and Smith (1982), using the concept of resilience, report a 17-year followup study of children who, against many odds, do well. I was, of course, pleased that their conclusion links their findings with the sense of coherence.

of a person's makeup, but to seeing the person's location on the SOC continuum as enduring, subject to modification only by very radical and long-lasting changes in the person's life experiences. I must now grant that I gave little attention to the possibility of minor modification, in both directions—changes that, though undramatic, make considerable differences in the health fate of people. Seeking to avoid facile, utopian solutions, I erred in the opposite direction by disregarding the possibility of slight changes that lead to a bit less (or a bit more) suffering. For such changes, people bless (and curse).

In other words, I now see it as possible for movement to occur on the SOC continuum even after early adulthood, within limits that may be fairly narrow but nonetheless with some margin. Those who are concerned not only with understanding the world but with changing it must live with the tension between, on the one hand, not relinquishing the effort for macrosocial change—which, in the long run, is the only hope for substantial change in the SOC of most people—and, on the other hand, searching for the changes in everyday life that make some difference. To the extent that the theoretical model presented here is powerful in explaining reality, the way is open to consideration of actions that can eventuate in improving people's health.

PRACTICAL IMPLICATIONS OF THE SALUTOGENIC MODEL

The purpose of this section is not to assay a full-fledged program for behavioral health. Rather, I have selected some significant human situations and have sought to apply the model to these situations. Once we adopt this mode of thought, many more ideas worthy of testing can surely be developed. The point is that these will not be bright ideas that make (or do not make) intuitive sense to us, but inferences that flow systematically from a theory. The crucial question to be asked, always, is whether the specific proposal is likely to provide, for people involved in the situation, life experiences that are characterized by consistency, an underload-overload balance, and participation in decision making, thereby strengthening the SOC and hence leading to improved health. It will be noted that, rejecting the healthy-sick dichotomy, the discussion deals with persons located at all points of the health ease–dis-ease continuum.

Individual and Social Responsibility

One further issue is appropriate at this point, particularly since this chapter appears in a book whose very conception is based on the spirit of individual and moral responsibility for one's own health, a spirit that has increasingly taken hold in the United States in the last decade. I cannot take exception to this spirit, but major qualifications must be made to put it in proper perspective.

First, the concept of individual responsibility can come dangerously close to blaming the victim. It is surely not wise for a woman to stroll through a park after dark, but blame, should rape occur, must be placed on the rapist and on the society that allows its parks to be unsafe. Given the frequent pronouncements of judges and police, particularly in the ambience of the moral majority, this danger cannot be overstressed.

Second, it is well and good to talk about individual responsibility for the six or seven well-known and important health practices. It is disingenuous, however, to talk about getting enough sleep while disregarding the economic pressures on tens of millions of people, which compel them to moonlight or work extra shifts; to talk about eating well but say nothing about the powerful advertising industry; to talk of not smoking or of drinking moderately yet be blind to the manifold social stressors that lead people to use smoking and drinking as maladaptive coping responses.

Third, although individual behaviors undoubtedly affect health fate considerably, my reading of the epidemiologic data (see Winkelstein, 1972) leads me to conclude that environmental and social conditions—industrial hazards, air pollution, poverty, patterns of work organization, lack of access to health care, social-structural stressors, and so forth—have no fewer and possibly more adverse health consequences.

In sum, it is one thing to say that there is much each of us can do, by modifying our behaviors, to maintain and improve health. This need not and should not, however, become an ideological doctrine that disregards both the powerful sociocultural pressures that shape individual behavior and the sociophysical realities that affect health. It is with this approach in mind that, in the following discussion, primary attention has been given to micro and macro environmental changes that can have health consequences by affecting the SOC.

Hospitalized Patients

In any given year in developed countries, close to 10% of the population will be hospitalized for a mean of 6 to 9 days. Cassell (1976) has described well the loss by the hospitalized patient of the feeling of omnipotence, of connectedness, of personal indestructibility, of the power of rational reasoning, and of the sense of control. Thus, whatever the level of the person's SOC prior to hospitalization, entry into the patient role inherently structures a life experience that threatens it. The crucial question then becomes whether the definition of the patient role by those who hold power in the situation—the hospital staff—maximizes or minimizes the threat. There is, I suggest, considerable margin.

Moos's (1979, Note 2) concept of the environmental system, including physical, organizational, human aggregate, and social climate factors, provides a systematic framework for answering this question. The issue is not one of dehumanization, which we all rightly abhor. Rather, we must ask whether, at each of these levels, the patient's experience can be transformed maximally into an experience that is consistent and balanced and allows for participation in decision making. This comes down to very concrete questions. Is the patient's bed adjustable to a familiar height? Is there one clearly identified source from whom the patient can acquire information? Has the physician been trained to take a history that includes what the patient thinks is relevant? Is the information provided appropriate to what the patient wishes to know? Are the patient's beliefs about the causes of the illness, and the reasons why he or she does not wish to take medicine as prescribed, listened to? Is the inevitably bureaucratic structuring of time amenable to patient and family needs?

Strauss, Fagerhaugh, Suczek, & Wiener (1982) recently called to our attention a most germane notion—the work that the hospitalized and chronic patient does. We have become accustomed to seeing the hospital situation as one in which the patient is passive and others do all the hard work. Others do, indeed, work very hard, but, as the authors note, so do patients. The difference is that the work of the patients is not socially acknowledged. If this were done—if the message were clearly conveyed to the patient that his or her contribution to the process of health care is legitimate, valued, and important; that there can be considerable discretion and leeway in the extent to which the patient makes decisions about treatment—the chances for enhancing the consistency, balance, and participation in the hospital experience, as seen by the patient, would be considerable.

The Paid Worker

The literature on the health consequences of paid work has burgeoned in recent years. Two limiting characteristics, however, are found in much, though not all, of it. First, it is largely pathogenically oriented, focusing on the stressors. Second, it is ergonometric in spirit, asking how persons and technology can be adapted to each other, but in fact taking existent social organization and technology as givens, subject only to minor modification. The salutogenic approach suggests an alternative point of departure—namely, given the desirable health consequences posited to emerge from experiences of consistency, balance, and participation, how work can be organized so that the SOC is strengthened.

In a recent paper, Frankenhaeuser (1981), one of the major contributors to this literature, has come very close to the position I propose, putting it more adequately than I can in a few lines: "On the basis of empirical results, it is argued that a moderately varied flow of stimuli and events, opportunities to engage in psychologically meaningful work, and to exercise personal control over situational factors, may be considered key components in the quality-of-life concept" (p. 491). We need not (though I tend to) accept her "assumption that joy and pride in work are fundamental human needs." It is enough to say that joy and pride are related to meaningfulness; the more this need is fulfilled, the more salutary the health consequences.

I view participation in decision making with regard to the work process as crucial. Not only does it lead to meaningfulness, it also opens the way to structuring the work process so that manageability and consistency will also be experienced. There are and always will be considerable routine drudgery, incompatible workmates, and unpleasant elements in every job. Those of us who are academics know this well. If there is a sense of participation in decision making, however, the opportunity arises to consider how the negative elements can be reduced, and it becomes easier to live with them than when this is not possible.

Meaningfulness at work can be considered at two levels. First, there is the question of the product. When it is perceived as socially valued, those engaged in its production will find meaning in their work. It is the worker, however, who must be able to see clearly how his or her part in the production process is related to the product. Furthermore, it is the worker, not the outside observer, who may have a different set of values, who must be persuaded that the product is indeed valued.

This brings us to the second level, the process of work. In "Modern Times," Charlie Chaplin not only had no idea of what he was producing, he had no voice in the pace of work—and he also was paid badly. To have an idea of what one is doing has a social as well as a technological implication. When people know how their work relates to the work of others—whether it be the scientist attending a conference or the garbage truck driver whose rhythm fits that of his co-workers because he has also worked at picking up cans— the ambience is one of consistency. Having job security means predictability in life. Working in a compatible social group, with shared values and a sense of identification, means that one knows where one is.

Regarding the issue of underload-overload balance, the literature has stressed the overload problem, and there is little to be added. The problem of underload, however, is no less crucial, in my view. How many of us work in jobs in which our potentials are called upon fully? How well is the educational system in our society geared to discover those things that each of us do well? The negative answers to these questions are most painful when we think of minority groups, women, and those whom we call handicapped, mentally and physically. There is reason to think, however, that they apply to many more of us. With respect to overload, I would note that "balance" can be interpreted broadly. Franken- haueuser (1981) is right when she expresses concern about overarousal of the central nervous system and resultant "feelings of excitement and tension" (p. 493), but these feelings can be salutary. If we consider soldiers in battle, surgeons operating, or scientists at research, we can see how the best in us can be brought out at occasions of overload. Of course, the human organism requires rest and relaxation. Thus, the issue is not to avoid tension but to prevent tension from being transformed into stress.

Working at Home

At first glance, the life experiences of the person who bears a major responsibility for running a home (for simplicity's sake, let us call such a person the housewife, for in the great majority of cases that is who it is, though it could be a man or an unmarried person) are largely characterized by consistency and participation in decision making. The problem she generally confronts is overload, particularly if she also engages in paid work. After all, we say, "She runs the house"—that is, she makes the decisions. The routine of cleaning, getting the kids off to school, preparing meals, or whatever the cultural prescriptions for the role may be, makes life consistent and predictable, and there surely seems to be no underload. A much closer analysis of the role as it is defined in at least Western cultures, even in 1984, raises a number of questions, however.

By and large, there is consistency and predictability in the life experiences of the housewife, allowing, of course, for the mysterious illnesses of children and the perpetual anxiety about accidents. Perhaps the major source of unpredictability for the housewife comes from extensive mobility—moving to new neighborhoods and communities (see Weissman & Paykel, 1972) that have few institutional mechanisms for integrating the newcomer. This problem is intensified by the fact that, frequently, the decision to move is not related to the housewife's wishes. Nonetheless, I would judge that consistency in life experiences is a source of strength for most housewives and is less available to those whose waking hours are largely spent away from home.

I do not wish to underestimate the significance of overload in any way. I would only call attention to the fact that the real burden is on poor and working-class women, who have few amenities and little assistance, in a cultural setting in which men do not share the burden, and who engage in paid work as well as housework. In a very fundamental sense, however, the life experiences of the housewife, paradoxically, also involve underload. The earlier discussion used the phrase "tasks that call on us to exert our energies, skills, knowledge, abilities, and potentials." The issue of overload calls attention to the first three words; underload applies to the last two. There is little doubt that childrearing, above all, but also community activity, cooking, emotional integration, and so on, open up possibilities for exploitation of abilities and potentials more than many jobs in the labor market do. Although there are structural pressures in the labor market for discovery and activation of potential, however, the housewife must almost always first solve the problem of overwork and then be internally motivated for such discovery. Only when family structure and values become sufficiently changed to resolve problems of overload, and only when the broader social structure is changed in such matters as provision for child care, flexible working hours, and the end of sex discrimination in the labor market, can serious inroads be made into the problem of underload.

Until such historical changes occur, and, it seems reasonable to predict, even when they do occur, there remains a more fundamental problem with respect to the third dimension of life experiences that is crucial to the strengthening of the SOC: participation in decision making as the source of meaningfulness. If such participation is to lead to meaningfulness, it must be in activity that is socially valued in the individual's culture. The housewife's role is central to her ego identity; she cannot push it beyond the boundaries of what matters in life. Even when she has chosen to enter the role (and often it is *not* a matter of choice), the message is clearly conveyed to her that what she does is not particularly important. In a work-oriented society, she does not "work." In an instrumentally oriented society, the sociologists disregard her instrumental functions and talk vaguely of integrative functions. The tax structure makes it clear that her activities are worth little. In a society that evaluates people in terms of how much they have been socially mobile, the housewife starts and ends her career on the same rung of the ladder. In sum, she has decision-making power with respect to process and product in a sphere that, in Western societies, is not held to be of much account. Unless and until there is a considerable change in our dominant values and their institutional expressions, I can see little potential for restructuring the life experiences of the housewife to provide a basis for the meaningfulness component of the SOC.

SUMMARY

This chapter has presented the thesis that by adopting a salutogenic orientation, we are guided and pressured to confront a central problem of behavioral health—namely, fostering a way of looking at and interacting with the world, which can be intractably difficult and stressful—that will promote our movement toward the health pole of the health ease–disease continuum. This outlook, called the sense of coherence, is a construct that purports to give meaning to the many empirical findings linking generalized and specific resistance resources to health. The nature of the life experiences that foster the strengthening of the SOC has been considered in detail, at the abstract level and then as applied to three major life situations. The construct, it is claimed, gives us a parsimonious and powerful way of analyzing many life situations and—by confronting the issues of consistency, underload-overload balance, and participation in decision making—possibly making programmatic advance. It offers no easy answers, particularly because it raises issues relating to the basic social structures and value systems of Western societies.

The model may seem cogent, and it is, I believe, compatible with much that we know from many empirical studies. I would be the first to stress the necessity for considerable testing and development and much caution in its application. It does, however, give us a fresh way of thinking about the problems of behavioral health.

REFERENCE NOTES

1. Seeman, M., & Anderson, C. *Alienation and alcohol: The role of work, mastery and community in drinking behavior.* Unpublished manuscript, University of California at Los Angeles, Department of Sociology, 1981.

2. Moos, R. *Creating healthy human contexts: Environmental and individual strategies.* Speech presented at the American Psychological Association Convention, Los Angeles, August 1981.

REFERENCES

Antonovsky, A. Social class, life expectancy and overall mortality. *Milbank Memorial Fund Quarterly,* 1967, **45,** 31–73.

Antonovsky, A. Breakdown: A needed fourth step in the conceptual armamentarium of modern medicine. *Social Science and Medicine,* 1972, **6,** 537–544.

Antonovsky, A. *Health, stress and coping.* San Francisco: Jossey-Bass, 1979.

Antonovsky, H., & Antonovsky, A. Commitment in an Israeli kibbutz. *Human Relations,* 1974, **27,** 303–319.

Bandura, A. Self-efficacy: Toward a unifying theory of behavioral change. *Psychological Review,* 1977, **84,** 191–215.

Brown, V. A. From sickness to health: An altered focus for health care research. *Social Science and Medicine,* 1981, **15A,** 195–202.

Burnet, M. *Genes, dreams and realities.* New York: Basic Books, 1971.

Cassell, E. J. *The healer's art.* New York: Penguin, 1976.

Cochrane, A. L. The history of the measurement of ill health. *International Journal of Epidemiology,* 1972, **1,** 89–92.

Dubos, R. J. *The mirage of health.* London: Allen & Unwin, 1960.

Dubos, R. J. The evolution of microbial diseases. In R. J. Dubos & J. G. Hirsch (Eds.), *Bacterial and mycotic infections of man* (4th ed.). Philadelphia: Lippincott, 1965.

Engel, G. L. The need for a new medical model: A challenge for biomedicine. *Science,* 1977, **196,** 129–136.

Engel, G. L., & Schmale, A. H. Conservation-withdrawal: A primary regulatory process for organismic homeostasis. In Ciba Foundation, *Physiology, emotion and psychosomatic illness.* Symposium 8. Amsterdam: Elsevier, 1972.

Frankenhaeuser, M. Coping with stress at work. *International Journal of Health Services,* 1981, **11,** 491–510.

Garfield, S. R., Collen, M.S., Feldman, R., Soghikian, K., Richart, R.H., & Duncan, J.H. Evaluation of a new ambulatory medical care delivery system. *New England Journal of Medicine,* 1976, **294,** 426–431.

Henry, J. P. The relation of social to biological processes in disease. *Social Science and Medicine,* 1982, **16,** 369–380.

Knowles, J. H. The responsibility of the individual. *Daedalus,* 1977, **106**(1), 57–80.

Kobasa, S. C., Maddi, S. R., & Courington, S. Personality and constitution as mediators in the stress-illness relationship. *Journal of Health and Social Behavior,* 1981, **22,** 368–378.

Lazarus, R. S., & Launier, R. Stress-related transactions between person and environment. In L. A. Pervin & M. Lewis (Eds.), *Perspectives in interactional psychology.* New York: Plenum, 1978.

Lipowski, Z. J. Sensory and information inputs overload: Behavioral effects. *Comprehensive Psychiatry,* 1975, **16**(3), 199–221.

Moos, R. Social-ecological perspectives on health. In G. C. Stone, F. Cohen, & N. E. Adler (Eds.), *Health psychology: A handbook.* San Francisco: Jossey-Bass, 1979.

Noack, H., & Müller, H. R. M. Morbidity, illness behaviour and the medical model. In H. Noack (Ed.), *Medical education and primary health care.* London: Croom Helm, 1980.

Parkes, C. M. Psychosocial transitions: A field for study. *Social Science and Medicine,* 1971, **5,** 101–115.

Pearlin, L. I., & Schooler, C. The structure of coping. *Journal of Health and Social Behavior,* 1978, **19,** 2–21.

Rotter, J. B. Generalized expectancies for internal versus external control of reinforcement, *Psychological Monographs,* 1966, No. 80.

Schwartz, G. The brain as a health care system. In G. C. Stone, F. Cohen, & N. E. Adler (Eds.), *Health psychology: A handbook.* San Francisco: Jossey-Bass, 1979.

Scott, R. A. *The making of blind men: A study of adult socialization.* New York: Russell Sage Foundation, 1969.

Strauss, A. L., Fagerhaugh, S., Suczek, B., Wiener, C. The work of hospitalized patients. *Social Science and Medicine,* 1982, **16,** 977–986.

Vaillant, G. E. Natural history of male psychological health: V. The relation of choice of ego mechanisms of defense to adult adjustment. *Archives of General Psychiatry,* 1976, **33,** 535–545.

Weissman, M. M., & Paykel, E. S. Moving and depression in women. *Transaction (Society),* 1972, **9**(9), 24–28.

Werner, E. E., & Smith, R. S. *Vulnerable but invincible: A longitudinal study of resilient children and youth.* New York: McGraw-Hill, 1982.

White, R. W. Sense of interpersonal competence: Two case studies and some reflections on origins. In R. W. White (Ed.), *The study of lives.* Chicago: Aldine, 1963.

Winkelstein, W. Epidemiological considerations underlying the allocation of health and disease care resources. *International Journal of Epidemiology,* 1972, **1,** 69–74.

CHAPTER 8

PROMOTING HEALTH STRENGTHENING AND WELLNESS THROUGH ENVIRONMENTAL VARIABLES

CALVIN W. TAYLOR

University of Utah

My awakening and emerging interest in the health-strengthening field probably occurred quite differently from the entry experiences of almost anyone else now working in the field. My earliest memories of the subject come from some meetings I had nearly a quarter of a century ago when I was working at the National Academy of Sciences/National Research Council in Washington, D.C. During a few sessions with a career statistician in the Public Health Service, he used the term *wellness* repeatedly. He was the first person I had heard use the term—and perhaps one of the first in history to use it. Although I can't remember the man's name, his concept of wellness has stayed with me ever since. In fact, all my research and other professional activities could be described as involving some aspect of the various realms of wellness. As a participant in two relevant national symposiums, for example, I pointed out the need for new types of health professionals, such as health-strengthening psychologists (Taylor, Notes 1 and 2).

The term *wellness,* allows us to develop a beautiful concept of a bipolar dimension, ranging from the lowest depths of illness to the greatest heights of wellness, and wellness and illness each have several subcategories. Traditionally, an illness-focused team is concerned with the depth and span of illness, whereas a health-focused team would be concerned with the height and breadth of wellness. Things that are well designed for people tend to foster wellness, whereas things that are ill designed tend to frustrate people and thereby foster illness. A crucial area, too, is the borderline between wellness-producing and illness-producing features.

The more I considered this concept, the more I realized that the huge numbers of human efforts in the broad field of medicine and in all its companion fields are primarily in the illness area. From that perspective, it appears that the health field, as currently constituted and functioning, is misnamed. It could more accurately be called the "illness industry." Its counterpart, therefore, could strategically be billed as the "wellness industry" (including health-strengthening as a main force for wellness).

An example of this dimension of wellness and illness comes from a recent report by Michael (1982), in which he asks a basic question regarding environmental health crises: "What are the real facts about the health effects of environmental pollution?" He continues by saying that "now people refuse to accept an environment that menaces their health and lowers their enjoyment of life. People are embracing a new public expectation that includes environmental consciousness, a broader vision of reality, and a more profound sense of place in nature." Michael's approach is basically a protection approach—people in society need to be protected against a possibly dangerous environment. Any benefits to people would come as a by-product of this environmental prevention approach.

Rather then focusing primarily on such issues as the potential negative importance of the environment and the restoration of the environment to its more natural state, however, it would be better to focus our efforts directly on the human being, not indirectly through the environment. In other words, a more positive focus is to find variables in the environment that will bring out the best in people, including people who are already healthy. Thus, we seek positive approaches that could be effective in all the possible realms of inquiry in the wellness field. The challenge is to move people upward toward greater heights and wider spans of wellness and thereby farther away from any areas of illness. The approaches described in this chapter emphasize and focus on enlarging human capabilities in order to strengthen health and improve wellness.

One such approach is architectural psychology. The prime justification for constructed environments is that they are designed and built for people. Until very recently, however, the huge design and construction industry, with annual expenditures about 50% larger than the total education costs for the nation, has done practically no basic research concerning people and the environmental designs underlying its practices. Increasing research insights will facilitate design and construction of environments that will bring out the best in people and thereby strengthen their health.

Another program with both direct and indirect implications for increasing wellness through health-strengthening approaches involves research and implementation of techniques for identifying and selecting persons who will become excellent as professionals in such high-level careers as scientists, engineers, physicians, and nurses. In each profession, such improved identification will increase the attributes of excellence and raise the levels of excellence. Physicians so identified, for example, can be better adjusted to and satisfied with their careers and can provide better products and professional services to those whom they serve. Through their improved satisfaction and capabilities, they can counteract somewhat the currently overburdened state of the "illness industry." This overburdening can also be reduced by identifying and developing new professional types for the "wellness industry." In addition, other involved people and organizational, social, and physical environmental features can become more effective, if modified in appropriate ways, in strengthening health generally and thereby noticeably decreasing the present flow of people as clients and patients into the illness industry.

A third research program involves setting up classroom situations and stimulating environmental structures that will systematically activate and develop multiple creative talents and attributes in people of all ages. Activating more and more of the total brainpower through the development and utilization of multiple-talent teaching approaches can produce more effectively functioning people. The activation, development, and utilization of these valuable inner resources will generally strengthen the health and improve the wellness of both mind and body. The strengthening of health by learning to function more fully and effectively in educational, working, and living activities is a good goal for all people.

The broad theme encompassing all these programs is "designing for people" or, more precisely, designing better and better environments and situational programs for more and more people. In the largest sense, all buildings, organizations, and programs are part of our environment and can play a part in weakening, maintaining, or strengthening health.

Enormous research is needed on all environmental features that potentially have various effects and consequences in people, either moving them upward toward greater total wellness or downward toward and even into the illness industry. New professionals can learn to design for positive consequences, leading toward wellness. It will also be important, however, to learn how to decrease the environmental variables that have negative consequences in order to alleviate their health-weakening effects.

All buildings, organizations, and programs for people can and should be designed to be more a part of a capability-enlarging, health-strengthening system and less a part of an illness-producing, illness-recruiting system of a nation. The wellness field is in its early infancy. What is known through research and experience and what is currently sensed, however, provide bases for some degree of soundness in ideas and in the positive theoretical views presented herein.

ENLARGING THE SCOPE OF THE WELLNESS INDUSTRY

One reason for renaming the existing health-related industry the illness industry is that it opens the door to the huge and as yet largely untapped field that can appropriately and deservedly be called the wellness industry. Some physicians and nurses do not like the term *illness industry*. Nonetheless, since they usually are not delivering health but are diagnosing and treating illnesses and trying to restore people up to or just barely above the borderline between illness and health, their work can be considered illness-treating and health-restoring, but not health-increasing. With so much illness in our society, the task in hospitals is to get patients at least barely out of the illness category so that they can be released to go home or to other facilities. Then beds can be freed for more seriously ill patients.

Even so-called preventive programs and health maintenance organizations are primarily designed to keep people from sinking into illness rather than to help them rise higher into wellness. To a great extent, such programs keep people out of hospitals but do not necessarily strengthen their total health. Thus, we actually have, in sequence upward, an illness industry, a preventive maintenance industry, and a wellness industry.

Health strengthening does not merely mean maintaining health just above the borderline of illness. Rather, the task is to increase people's health so that they will be far above the illness borderline and will have a long way to go downward before they would become ill.

Applying the wellness/illness dimension across the various physical and psychological aspects, a person would probably have a health profile of ups and downs. On a given day the individual profiles could be entirely above the borderline for many people; for some others, the profiles might hover above the borderline, dipping barely below the borderline in only one or two types of illness.

Successful, sound health-strengthening efforts by new types of health professionals in all kinds of living and working environments could reduce considerably the number of people who are ill each day, thereby helping to reduce the work load of professionals within the illness industry. Several years ago a very critical report on the nation's health care system stated that quality illness-treating service, especially to nonwhites, was still in very short supply despite the billions of dollars spent. Also, from 1961 to 1969, only about 4% of personal health care expenditures were devoted to disease prevention and to the promotion of health.

This 4% estimate has not increased very much recently, so that physicians and other allied professionals are still greatly overburdened (along with many patients who have become overburdened from the costs of previous illness). Furthermore, the costs and efforts for illness treatment are approximately 20 times the costs and efforts collectively for disease prevention, preventive maintenance, and health strengthening—the only truly positive, upward health offensive in the total illness-and-health effort. In the past, the smallest percentage of all has probably been that which represents health strengthening. This is true even though health strengthening may have the greatest potential for relieving the overburdened illness industry by raising the wellness level of many people to points considerably above the crucial borderline between illness and wellness.

The positive upward movement of health strengthening into the wellness regions has been described variously as health strengthening, health enhancing, health cultivating, health nurturing, health producing, health creating, health developing, health actualizing, health broadening, health expanding, health enlarging, and health spreading (since certain wellnesses may prove to be contagious, just as certain illnesses are).

EARLY WORK IN ARCHITECTURAL PSYCHOLOGY

Now in its third decade of path creating, the University of Utah program in architectural psychology has been training its students to function effectively in practically all areas in the new field. Strength through diversity is featured in the selection of graduate students and in individualizing their educational experiences. The main emphasis is work on real projects, through a broad, problem-focused, interprofessional approach. Such interprofessional approaches are often largely missing in universities, because they are usually against the organizational grain (Steinhart & Cherniack, 1969).

Many discussions in this chapter are based on the pioneering research, training, and experiences in architectural psychology at the University of Utah. Early in 1961, the First International Research Conference on Architectural Psychology and Psychiatry was held (see Bailey, Branch, & Taylor, 1964), and later that year we launched the world's first graduate training program in architectural psychology. For each of these initial steps, a small but invaluable amount of financial support came from the National Institute of Mental Health.

In 1962, one year after the first conference, another stimulating architectural psychology workshop-conference was held. Its topic was the design of mental illness facilities, and one of its important outcomes was the cleverly titled book, *Therapy by Design* (Good, Seigel, & Bay, 1965).

The Second International Research Conference on Architectural Psychology was held in 1966 (Taylor, Bailey, Branch, 1966). It was attended by some 85 researchers and experts from the United States, Canada, Scotland, and England. As the meetings were ending, a participant stated that the conference firmly established the existence of the new field. Little doubt was left regarding the importance of combining the disciplines of architecture and the behavioral sciences and the valuable research that could emerge from that combination.

DESIGNING BETTER ENVIRONMENTS FOR PEOPLE

Considerably more research needs to be done on the environmental features that potentially have various effects and consequences for people, either moving them upward toward greater total wellness or downward toward the wellness/illness borderline and even into illness.

The physical environment in which medical care is provided can do much to facilitate the interaction between the providers of illness treatments and the patients. Architectural psychology applied to the design of health care facilities stresses the total complex environment. This total approach to the architectural environment can also be applied to the organizational, social, and psychological climates.

All effects of environment on people—how people adjust to their environments, how environments can be designed to be adjustable to people, and how people can adjust their environments to themselves—must be considered. A medical building, for example, should be designed to facilitate and support therapy—that is, to provide therapy by design. Its interior and other environmental features should not give any antitherapy messages, such as signs of hopelessness or negative, intimidating effects. The environment to which a patient in an intensive care unit awakens can have a strong effect on the mental state of that patient—the will to live. Effective lobby and waiting room design can reduce anxieties for the family and friends of patients being brought in for emergency treatment.

Attention to human factors engineering in the design of medical facilities can enable both health care professionals and their physically or mentally handicapped patients to increase control and mastery of their own environment. Nursing stations should be designed to provide good visual access and direct visual monitoring of patients. Architectural barriers should be designed out of buildings, to provide for easy access to various areas by the handicapped. All medical facilities should be designed so that they are an effective part of the therapeutic process.

The architect who is designing a new medical building should keep the illness-treatment professionals and especially the patients foremost in mind during the design and construction process. Building characteristics should be reviewed by an architectural psychologist throughout the design process to assure compliance to such requirements.

The physical settings and features of the working environments in businesses and industries sometimes need to be altered in order to strengthen rather than weaken health (Taylor, 1972b). A recent newspaper article listed 15 ways people could develop illness symptoms from 15 different physical and other features of work-day offices—all hazards from working in ill-designed offices. The quality of the air provided by some poor ventilation systems, for example, can deteriorate so gradually that people may fail to notice it. A person who sits most of the day in an ill-designed chair may develop various symptoms and not feel well. If the chair facilitates bad posture and poor breathing, the person may not be taking in enough oxygen and, without being aware of the reasons, may feel drowsy and generally lethargic. Some other potentially damaging environmental features are poor lighting or glaring light, visual displays that cause eyestrain, odors or odorless fumes, and noise, which can affect performance and hearing capabilities.

Some designers of environments and some organization executives expect people to adjust to their environments and climates. Where people have the obligation or requirement to fit the system, however, mismatches can occur, which often are frustrating and illness-enhancing in those people. Our opposite point of view is that man-made environments and organizational programs should be designed so that they fit the people. The best environments are those that fit the greatest variety of people.

ARCHITECTS AND NATURE: ON THE PRIMACY OF MAN

In organizing the Engineering Foundation conference "The Quality of Constructed Environments with Man as the Measure" (Taylor, 1976), we recruited the late Eric Hoffer (longshoreman and author of *The True Believer*) to give a speech. The conference topic fit his thinking at that time regarding whether man's architectural environment was a friend or a foe. Hoffer (1976) chose as his topic what I have used as the title of this section. It gives strong emphasis to the concept that the primacy of humans must be patent, that people are even more important than nature or than architects' ideas of how to design buildings.

Hoffer argued that the harmony with nature of architects' designs must be achieved primarily on human terms. He quoted Pascal: "All the bodies, the firmament, the stars, the earth, are not equal in value to the lowest human being. From all these bodies together, not the slightest thought and not a single impulse of charity can be obtained." Hoffer also pointed out that the men who tamed our savage continent did not side with the fearful forces of nature against man, but they subdued the earth, instead. In their way, they emphasized that the primacy of humans must be defended.

Comparing all of this with the words of Bertrand Russell, that "the sea, the stars, the wind in waste places, mean more to me than even those [human beings] I love best," Hoffer said that he could understand what Russell must have felt when he listened to "the wind in waste places." Russell was lifted out of the paltriness and transitoriness of an individual existence by feeling at one with the eternal reoccurrence in nature and the timeless sea and stars. Yet Hoffer surmised that it would not fare well for mankind if power fell into the hands of the Bertrand Russells. Nor would he give power to a Thoreau, who, when he saw a clump of trees of all sizes, exclaimed, "How much more noble a family of trees is than the family of man."

In closing, Hoffer stated vehemently that power should therefore not be given to people who do not really care for the human species first and foremost, over all other species and features on earth.

PEOPLE IMPACT STATEMENTS

Many people involved in the design and construction business are coming to realize that their work is ultimately for the purpose of building for people. Environmental impact statements have relatively quickly become an integral part of the design and construction processes, and the innovation needed now is what we might call "people impact statements." Such an approach would not merely provide protection against "being damaged," which is the primary effect of environmental impact statements. Rather, it should become a very positive approach bringing out the best in people, including facilitating cultivation of their many high potentials—a splendid thought, indeed!

I have led many different groups in productive thinking sessions about people impact statements versus environmental impact statements. The former are more directly focused on people, whereas the latter affect people only very indirectly. In other words, people impact statements are not concerned with effects on the environment but rather with the environmental effects of either built or natural environments on people.

DESIGNING FOR SUNSHINING

A few years ago, I was asked to speak on the human side of a National Academy of Sciences conference, "Solar Effects on Building Design." The result was a lengthy mimeographed paper (Taylor, Note 3), which has been generally well received as a provocative think piece. Much of what follows in this section has been extracted from that paper.

The task of designing for sunshining calls for a combination of arts and sciences. It involves drawing upon what is known and dealing as effectively as possible with the unknowns. In preparing this paper and in reviewing both my students' thoughts and the available literature on this topic, I sense, however, that it consists of far more unknowns than knowns.

The Sun Serves Man in Many Ways

The importance of sunshine in the lives of people is expressed in many ways—in figures of speech, in familiar quotations, in poems, and in song lyrics. Sunshine and darkness are contrasted many times and also appear in many ways in literature. All humans experience daylight and darkness, not only with their eyes, but also in other psychological and figurative ways.

Some of the most exciting events of nature are the occasional moments of sunshine during a rainstorm or the rays of sunshine that sometimes emerge briefly during a snowstorm. A sunny, springlike day in winter, even though temporary, is most welcome to keep alive the hope of spring. Colorful rainbows created by the sun are always delightful. In seeking variety in colors and lighting within buildings, therefore, I have pondered whether appropriate designing could turn the sun's rays into rainbow rays, with varying color effects throughout the indoors as the sun changes its angle of entrance. Reflected sunlight, too, could be a full topic in itself. The reflection from snow, from white clouds, from lakes, from buildings, and from the moon at night are all intriguing variations in sunlight experiences.

Some architects use the phrase "designing for visual release." Physiologically, our eye muscles relax if we are looking at a far-distant view, and this effect can lead to a more generally relaxed state of the person. The physiological release or relaxation of the eye muscles often has a concomitant mental release, which can free the mind to think. If we are hemmed in by walls or forests or such, however, we may not easily or naturally get this visual release or the accompanying relaxed physiological and psychological condition. The question arises whether only those in high-level jobs that emphasize thinking—such as scientists, planners, and the like—need this visual release. Perhaps all workers in a building, especially clerical and other workers who use their eyes at close range and may become bored with their work, sorely need this physiological and psychological release several times a day, by having distant views within buildings and outside the buildings through windows.

Sunlight can be constant for many hours, as on a summer day, or it can be highly variable, with changing effects on people, throughout some, if not most, days. Consequently, if inside lighting is to be somewhat parallel to outside lighting, the interior lighting should not be continually static but should have changing effects, as does the outdoor lighting. Some of this effect will occur automatically if the building is designed to use the changing outdoor daylight as part of the total indoor lighting system.

Another question is whether the natural environment and existing manufactured environments are friends or foes to humans. The challenge, then, is to design and construct future environments that are almost entirely friendly to humans by minimizing or eliminating any features that are our foes.

Designers could be challenged to counteract such trends as the high suicide rate around the beginning of spring, especially after a long dismal season of cold, snow, ice, and cloudiness, which is not good for man, plant, or beast. (The emphasis here might have been somewhat different if it had been written after a long, hot, cloudless summer rather than after an almost endless, sunless winter.)

In small, dark, solitary dungeons, the peep holes through which light beams enter and sunbeams dance are highly important to the confined person, being his only view and contact with the world outside. There, as elsewhere, a ray of sunshine can be a ray of hope.

People find comfort by lying in the sun's rays. They can be energized by the sun, which is considered a source of power and warmth. Sunroofs on the tops of buildings and porches and private backyards enable people to relax and enjoy sunbathing. The effects of sunshine have been variously described as relaxing, calming, soothing, and harmonious, and as producing serenity and happier, healthier people.

Sunlight and Human Functioning

The many changes in sunlight, daily and yearly, create variety for people: the break of dawn and sunrise, the sun appearing in and behind clouds, shafts of light with different angles, rainbows, twilights, sunsets, eclipses, and various combinations of these, as well as weather changes. In windowless buildings, these daily changes are largely designed out of the experience of those who must remain indoors most of the day. Well-designed "think centers" could be placed in the great outdoors, making use of its stimulating changes in lighting conditions.

Schools are typically not well designed. In one school, for example, although the windows let in the daylight, they were too high for the kids. They could look up and see the sky, but they could not look either directly out or down at the earth, and there was no effective way to change these erroneous height relationships.

A chemist, who had worked for 15 years at a large chemical corporation, told me that he had done his best chemistry work not in his lab or when working at his desk, but when he had turned away from his desk, put his feet on the windowsill, and gazed outside through his office window.

A current challenge is to think about the environment to which patients might awaken in an intensive care unit after a major operation or during a severe illness. Waking in a complex mechanical setup with sterile walls and ceiling would give them no impression of being back on this earth, which consists of dirt, rocks, plants, forest, clouds, streams, rain, snow, mountains and so on. If patients awaken to find a strange room full of strange equipment, they may even vaguely wonder, in their weak and confused state, what planet they have arrived on and whether they want to come back to life wherever they may be. Effective sunshine and daylighting may be essential elements in such settings, and other tangible features could be used to help awakening patients realize that they are surrounded to some degree by good earth and Mother Nature.

One approach is to design so that the natural processes of people (both psychological and physiological) grow and function naturally. If the sun is no longer of concern to life, then there is no living. The task, then, is to design so that sunshining is central to living. There are times, of course, when sunshine is welcome and other times when it is unwelcome; when shading from the sun is welcome or unwelcome; and when nighttime (or absence of daylight) is welcome or unwelcome.

Natural indoor lighting gives a feeling of informality, rather than the feeling of a formal space where people cannot quite relax. One feeling many people would like, though indoors, is the sense that they are near nature and close to earth.

An effective approach, requiring top-notch planning of a building site and layout, is to capture daylight, but not direct sunlight, in order to minimize problems of heating, lighting, comfort, and glare. At the same time, the best views would be possible through all windows that let in the daylight.

Lighting can reduce or increase the complexity and ambiguity of a situation, depending on the effects desired for people. Henry Dreyfuss (1967), for example, proposed that the lighting for an evening party should be so designed that matrons look and feel like young debutantes.

A slide presentation by architect Richard Neutra showed how a house he designed took on different characteristics, indoors and outdoors, throughout the day from sunrise to sunset, according to the successive angles at which the sunlight hit and entered the house. Curtains or drapes that could be completely closed or opened added to the possible variations of daily experiences for people inside the house. Research on how certain animals can change their colors could enable us to design walls that somehow change the "color of their skin," giving us greater variation in the inside coloring of constructed environments.

A belief that the mood of a person can be affected by the presence or absence of sunlight and daylight led to the concept (and now the reality) of a house that rotates on a pivot, allowing different rooms to be in the sunlight, as the tenants desire. This led, in turn, to the concept of a "room of moods," in which people could modify the room by some sort of controls to exaggerate a given mood or to bring about a change in mood. Such a room would be designed to increase the options and the freedom of choice of the users, thus allowing them to react creatively by being in control of the environment, regulating it as they see fit so that it will be a supportive environment for them. Sunlight, daylight, rainbows, and other color changes could be very important variables in this room of moods. People could then be "masters of their moods" by being masters of their environment, adjusting the environment to be best for their desired moods at any time.

Having a manipulable environment is very different from having a bureaucratically controlled built environment, totally designed by others and not under control of the users, so that the users have to adjust themselves to their environment rather than being able to adjust their environment to themselves.

The effectiveness of indoor lighting depends on the illumination level, the brightness contrast, the sparkle of the light, the reflections, the specific qualities of the lighting, the room luminance, the specific glare, and the distribution of lights. On some large design and construction projects, an accompanying research and development program could be established by allocating a small portion of the costs (even 1%) to ensure the primacy of humans in the final design and construction considerations of the building. Thus, the building will truly be designed and built for people. It is necessary to break into the habit patterns of the design and construction professions in order to see that buildings become better designed and provide well for their users.

Radio and television signals can now be reflected from space satellites back to earth—reaching any place on earth, outside or inside any building—and the initial sound and picture are so effectively transmitted that they approximate the full experience at the original source. Similar techniques should be found to pierce the barriers that prevent daily sunlight, daylight, and solar energy from reaching people down on earth, both outside and inside buildings. Except for the two polar regions, the sun shines above every place on earth every day, but this sunshine does not necessarily get down to earth. If you want sunshine during the daytime, however, you need only go high enough to be above the clouds or other barriers.

Energy experts say that the unmet challenge is to convert energy without much loss and to store energy, neither of which man yet does very well. To perfect this concept, inventors could remove or pierce the barriers directly or convert sunlight to some other energy forms in order to pierce the barriers and then reconvert the energy back to natural sunlight to be "piped in" to the desired destination. Creative minds of our generation can hasten the day that such miraculous feats—making the sunlight and daylight available when and where desired at the turn of the switch—can be performed. The main challenge is to get the sun down to earth every day, whenever it is wanted.

REDUCING THE BURDEN IN THE ILLNESS INDUSTRY

Another major area of research and implementation efforts has involved systems for selecting, developing, and improving the performance of professional people. Our initial major studies of professions included measurement of performances, contributions, and attributes of scientists, engineers, and nurses (Ellison, James, Fox, & McDonald, 1969; Taylor & Ellison, 1964, 1967, 1972; Taylor, Smith, & Ghiselin, 1963; Taylor, Ghiselin, Wolfer, Loy, & Bourne, Note 4). The opportunity then arose to do parallel studies on the performances, contributions, and attributes of practicing physicians ("Attributes of Excellence," 1982; Price, 1969; Price, Taylor, Richards, & Jacobsen, 1964; Taylor, Nelson, & Price, 1974; Price, Taylor, Nelson, Lewis, Loughmeller, Mathieson, Murray, and Maxwell, Note 5).

The intent was to have an impact on the selection and educational programs in order to increase the percentage of medical school graduates who would become excellent physicians in practice. Patients would then have more effective physicians, who would get the patients out of the illness industry and back to health more rapidly and soundly. The heavy demands and burdens on physicians, nurses, and allied medical staff would thereby be reduced. Nationally, the same numbers of patients could be handled better and would be restored to health more rapidly by the same total number of illness treatment professionals who have a higher degree of excellence.

Still another approach to reducing the overburdened load on the medical staffs and facilities would be study the flow of patients into the illness industry. Environmentally, where did they come from and why did they become the ill persons out of the total public? What were the "recruiting features" in the total environment affecting those who sought out or were brought into the illness industry's facilities? The challenge is to identify those most important environmental factors and influences that "recruited" these people into the illness industry as clients and patients.

One striking example of this search for the environmental variables that influence people to feel not too well, even ill, was the experience of a former doctoral student of mine. Months after he had begun his first professional job, he told me that he had studied why people took sick leave in his new organization. He had been surprised to discover that the employees took sick leave because they were sick. What these people were sick of, however, seemed to be mainly getting up and going to work! The nature of their jobs and all they entailed, including an unattractive, unexciting total situation and unappealing work activities, made them feel more like avoiding their jobs than facing the job situation any given morning.

In sharp contrast, when Andrew Kay (1970) invited us to tour his organization, an employee was asked how he liked to work there. He answered, "Well, . . . it's heaven!"— and then explained his answer. It is likely that few people in few organizations and few students in few schools would give such an answer.

It soon becomes evident that people of all ages and from all walks of life can encounter some things that lead to their entering the illness industry as clients or patients. They have fallen enough below the wellness/illness borderline in one or another aspect of mind or body to enter the illness industry, willingly or otherwise, and become an additional burden there.

The challenge is, first, to identify all the environmental features that cause people to move downward into the illness industry and then to develop ways and means for counteracting these negative environmental effects. In some cases, it might be possible to greatly reduce the stream of clients flowing into the illness industry. In other cases, it may be extremely difficult to have much impact until further insights are attained.

Several reports from our laboratory involve the climate for creativity, including the organizational climate, the classroom climate, and the physical (architectural) environments for creativity (Ellison, McDonald, James, Fox, & Taylor, 1967; Smith, 1959; Taylor, 1968a, 1972c; Taylor, Smith, & Ghiselin, Note 6).

Secrist (Note 7) conducted a study using a sample of about 1,000 Air Force scientists and engineers. His 600 items on environmental variables included *personal-psychological* conditions, such as life history, personality, and motivation; *organizational-sociological* conditions, such as leadership and organizational climate; and *physical-architectural* conditions, such as the adaquacy of facilities and the extent of freedom to modify, adapt, and personalize the immediate physical-architectural environment. His measures included indices of scientific-engineering productivity and performance, together with measures of need and satisfaction and overall job satisfaction.

Computerized, multivariate data analyses were undertaken to thoroughly analyze a total of 59 variables. Descriptive and distributive analysis, item analysis with double cross-validation, correlational analysis, and multiple correlation/regression analysis were conducted on individual scientist-engineer variables. In addition, 127 team or group variables were analyzed in several appropriate ways on nearly 50 research and development teams and on 5 major research and development field locations. One subset (organizational-sociological and physical-architectural variables) had the highest predictive weights for job satisfaction, and quite a different subset (personal-psychological variables) had the highest predictive weights for productivity.

His findings suggest that, with sound insights, it is possible to design a total set of environmental variables that will bring about both effectiveness and job satisfaction in workers.

Organizational climate was measured in another large scientific research organization by a well-constructed climate questionnaire of more than 200 items (Ellison, McDonald, James, Fox, & Taylor, 1968). A special scoring key was developed through item analysis for each of the 25 criterion target measures of performance, productivity, and other accomplishments of each scientist. On a second sample, the cross-validity correlations for each key against its criterion target were found to be remarkably high, with the upper half ranging from a median of .57 to the highest validity of .73. Thus, from detailed knowledge of organizational characteristics, the many features of organizational climates can be well designed to facilitate the productivity and effective functioning of scientists.

Recent news articles have claimed that a large proportion of causes of deaths can be traced to bad habits and lifestyles. A sound, healthful lifestyle, therefore, can lead to a higher level of total wellness and a greater avoidance of these causes of illness or death.

One possible counteractive approach, of course, is prevention—that is, not cultivating any of these bad habits in the first place.

We hear a great deal recently about stress—about coping effectively with stress, about stress management at work and in other environments, and about how to handle too much total stress, which can deteriorate both the psychological and the physiological functioning of the body. At the other extreme, too little stress might yield such illness tendencies as laziness, apathy, boredom, lethargy, and physical, physiological, and mental atrophy—all resulting from decreased liveliness. In such activities as performing on the stage, giving speeches, and participating in athletics, both too much anxiety and too little can result in lowering the quality of performance.

Some teachers and supervisors provide environments sufficiently stressful to produce frustrations—perhaps severe enough to cause long-lasting scars and even illnesses—in some of their students and employees. Such teachers and supervisors may also be under considerable stress. Likewise, some family stress situations could move some family members toward illness of various kinds and degrees. Political stress, social stress, cultural stress, group stress, highway stress, and the frustrations produced by both manufactured and natural environments (such as unforeseen damaging acts of nature) can move some people in the direction of illness. The occupations and environments of business and government could be major recruiters or contributors to illnesses in some of their workers at all levels.

Stress is one of the largest and most central issues in the huge illness industry, and it can soon become even more important in the wellness industry. The subject of stress is included in various organized programs for promoting and strengthening health in people of all ages and stages in life. In fact, a huge burst of information on the many types of stress and on coping with stress has recently become available to the public through all kinds of media. Many of the various stressful occupations, activities, and environments could be made health-strengthening and wellness-delivering, however, rather than illness-producing. In general, an analysis of the features that recruit persons toward the illness industry suggests that practically all psychologists and human scientists, who have never explicitly thought of themselves as part of either the wellness or the illness industry, could have an important positive effect on everyone they contact. The same could be true of all people, as they influence themselves and others, leading either positively, toward health strengthening, or negatively, toward illness producing. Those who are far removed from the traditional health or illness fields in their professional efforts may be able to have the greatest positive influence on others, especially at the time of the earliest signs, moving them in the direction of wellness and health strengthening and thereby away from the illness industry.

Many programs now promote wellness, along with human potentials, feelings, removing barriers to wellness through self-mastery and personal power, the power of imagery, and programming of neurolinguistic processes. Some programs aim at optimizing health (which may really mean maximizing health) in mind and body. The entire health-strengthening, wellness field is reaching practically all people in our nation through reports of all kinds through many channels. It is heartening to see the rapid increase of awareness throughout the land; it shows the potential speed and power of the media in this scientific age. If people are willing to "go for wellness," they can hope for many improvements in such areas as job satisfaction, personal relations, energy level, self-concepts, greater zest for living, and even living longer. Meaningful attempts at self-directed improvement can also be made if people are aware of their wellness-illness profiles.

Many studies have been done on the origins of mental and physical illnesses. Parallel studies need to be done on the origins and development of health strengthening and total wellness. A major approach in the illness field is to treat the whole person; parallel approaches are needed for the strengthening of total health and wellness.

Typically, people who seek wellness have an above-average tendency to resist overdependency on doctors or hospitals. It is important, however, that people learn to discern symptoms that could lead to dangerous illnesses; then they will not be too independent and will know when to respond to symptoms and not ignore them, especially if they are life-threatening.

Laughter therapy is being tried in relation to both illness and wellness. A person with a good sense of humor or a catching laugh can be a spreader of laughter and wellness (i.e., a carrier of health strengthening through laughter). A vibrant, beaming smile may have a positive and disarming effect—reducing tensions in others and increasing their feelings of well-being. A smiling person thus may be a carrier and a spreader of good humor.

Whatever external factors make people's inner-body and mind processes function more naturally and more fully can also increase their total well-being. The more these inner conditions and natural processes can be sustained by the outer environment, the more people strengthen their total health and move a greater distance from any illness conditions or possibilities.

Our bodies are capable of magically healing and restoring health within us. With proper environmental surroundings and stimulations, they may also be capable of the less-noticed magic of strengthening health and increasing total wellness. People can learn to use their inner energies in rewarding ways with help from an outer environment that is designed to utilize and draw those energies out in wholesome ways. Then their inner bodies will be functioning in a healthful, wellness-oriented way, and their feelings about themselves and their environment will be good and health strengthening. If these energies are being thwarted, stifled, or turned inwardly and negatively, they may have destructive bodily effects, such as ulcers. It has been argued that once people are convinced that it is time to become really well, the challenge is to find ways to get started and to keep going, with full resolve, toward increasing their wellness.

A similar approach is to try to teach people to relax their minds and bodies, to reduce the external and internal stresses on the body, and to increase their peace of mind. The emphasis is on bringing about muscle relaxation and moving away from anxiety, thus returning the body to conditions within its healthy natural limits.

Just as emotional distress may be part of the multifactor causes of disease, the reverse—managing to "keep one's cool"—may be part of the multifactor causes of wellness. Other positive characteristics of people, such as hardiness, may be strengthened through greater insights into environmental effects. Parents, teachers, and supervisors of difficult work can learn how to strengthen the hardiness of people through environmental effects. Some people, for example, show a remarkable and unexpected degree of hardiness when they are faced with survival training and experiences. Thus, at least in some persons, adversity can have the effect of eliciting strong inner resources and heretofore unlocked talents. Studies are needed to determine how parents, teachers, or supervisors of difficult work can strengthen hardiness in the people they influence.

Another important attribute is personal soundness. Studies are needed to determine how others can set the stage and help a person develop so that he or she can be recognized as a very sound person under practically all environmental situations and predicaments. Programs designed to enhance a person's self-concept may also have a spreading effect, both laterally and upward on that person's total wellness.

In the future, new types of psychologists and health-strengtheners will be able to contribute most to health care by taking a positive, health-enhancing approach, rather than by pursuing an illness-focused model. Generally they will be in only minimal conflict with the medical profession.

DESIGNING CLIMATES FOR CREATIVE TALENTS

One of the major research efforts on creativity and other high-level talents has led to an innovative approach to teaching for multiple creative talents. This type of teaching yields more effectively functioning, multitalented people and more effective approaches (Taylor,

1982). One challenge for classrooms is determining how many different kinds of talents or giftedness a program can tolerate (Taylor, 1978). The greater the number of different talents that can be activated, the better it is for all students. This type of education focuses on positive assets rather than on deficiencies.

The use of additional talents is often considered to be the prerogative of adults; children are rarely allowed such opportunities. When teachers deliberately involve students in adult activities, such as planning and decision making, the students feel good about being so treated. Consequently, not only are their talents being developed but their self-concept and self-esteem also improve—a noteworthy secondary gain.

Our continuing work in broadening the base of educational assessments is aimed at measuring more of the whole person and is focused on finding potential assets as well as functioning assets in people. It also involves broadening the base of educational planning and implementation in order to develop and capitalize on these assets. This is at least a small move toward expanding the views of the potentials in people.

There are at least two main types of ignorance—ignorance of knowledge and ignorance of functioning effectively. It is believed that the greater ignorance is ignorance of functioning effectively. The greatest gain, therefore, can be obtained by overcoming this type of ignorance in people, with an almost automatic effect of spreading out to overcome some of the ignorance in knowledge areas.

Barbara Wheeler's research (Note 8) on creativity in social work focused on the idea that the creativeness of the exchange between the professional and the client is at the heart of the effectiveness of all social workers, clinicians, counselors, interviewers, and so on. Ideally, most of the creativeness should come from the client, and this can occur if a catalytic approach is used effectively by the professional person.

The Form U Biographical Inventory (Note 19), which seeks multiple talent assets in people also yields a dropout score. It indicates whether individuals are oriented to stay in the educational system as far as possible versus whether they have a strong tendency to drop out soon because of mismatch features. A challenge for the health-strengthening, illness-resisting field is to counteract, in all ways possible, such a prediction (expected outcomes) that a person will soon drop out. The assumption is that a sizable percentage of those who are predicted to be dropouts will repeatedly prove to be liabilities rather than assets to their society and to themselves. The nature of their educational program could be changed and counselors could be specially trained and used, particularly at elementary schools, to aid in spotting this trend early and reversing it in many potentially valuable human beings.

The recommendation to schools and parents and supervisors is to be talent developers as well as knowledge dispensers (Taylor, 1968a). An effective approach in classrooms is a double curriculum—teaching for multiple creative talents while concurrently covering all of the knowledge in the present curriculum. Such an approach will develop people who are both multitalented and well versed in many knowledge areas (Bobowski, 1978). It also makes it possible to produce talent report cards as well as knowledge report cards and to have students work on their talent strengths, their weaknesses, or both. In theory, all people can be good at something if they have a chance to try enough different talents (Note 10). Basic research shows that there are many different talents available in the total brainpower (Guilford, 1978; Taylor, 1968a). Thus, practically all of us have some talent assets with which we can learn to function quite effectively in one or more areas of human endeavor. This is a heartening finding, which can be most valuable in forming a large health-strengthening, wellness field. Focusing on multiple talents is health-fostering and reduces the number of psychological scars, intimidating effects, and brainpower barriers that are built into many students' minds.

Some training in life is designed to help people adjust to their environment and its features, to learn to conform themselves to situations. There are some clues that such training relates positively to IQ scores and to high grades. It may not always be health-delivering, however; at one extreme, it can cause a person to be merely a "teacher-pleaser." It can also perpetuate bad features in organizations and in other personal-environmental relations. Creative people, in contrast, will show more of a tendency to adjust the environment to themselves; they will thus improve their surroundings in ways that facilitate rather than frustrate them. They thereby become masters of their environment rather than passively becoming by-products of it.

Although many personal characteristics of creative people have been identified, few deliberate attempts have yet been made to focus on and develop these characteristics in anyone at any age. One main characteristic of creative people is a broad striving for and display of independence, autonomy, and self-sufficiency, and the desire to try to do things on their own. In contemplating attempts to train people or to set the stage for such characteristics to emerge, a difficulty may arise because some trainers, knowingly or unknowingly, really want people to become more dependent on them rather than more independent of them. Creative people also tend to resist pressures of their peers to answer or to behave in unsound ways. They also do not hesitate as much as others to ask questions or to report accurately by telling the truth even when outer pressures or punishments are likely for doing so (Taylor, 1963–1964).

These attributes of creative people suggest that it is healthful for them to have programs that support their tendencies to become more fully self-educating. It is suspected also that it would be a health-delivering approach to teach all people to become more self-educating. A basic assumption here is that whatever parents, teachers, or supervisors do for those under their jurisdiction, they will have deprived their children, students, or workers of the opportunites to learn how to do those things themselves (Taylor, 1972a).

New approaches in education attempt to increase the humanizing and individualizing of classrooms and expand the opportunities and the participatory development of students, rather than keeping them in delimited and delimiting situations. In this way, the students can learn to function more fully, more naturally, and more effectively. In many ways, schools could give a greater focus and priority to people by designing better and better for more and more people (Taylor, Note 11). Schools could also foster the teaching, supervising, or parenting art of catalyzing subtly, thereby actualizing many different types of positive potentials in people. This asset-focused approach can replace the usual medical approach in schools of diagnosing and prescribing treatments or otherwise creating an imposed or even coercive type of education on people. The better approach is to develop an incentive environment in which people feel that they can learn how to motivate themselves, manage themselves, and move toward becoming more self-educating (Note 12). Then students might feel better about schooling because they will feel that their time is being well spent in school.

Goals and plans in school are sometimes so completely spelled out that teachers and students do not have much free, unscheduled time to sense and respond to new opportunities—potentially exciting opportunities that can arise unexpectedly. Taking advantage of such opportunities could make an educational program much more fascinating and realistic. Students could learn to sense and respond to opportunities such as those that will arise throughout their lifetime, and they could even learn how to create new opportunities that are needed for their own growth and progress. They need freedom to roam, freedom to search and look around, freedom to think, freedom for serendipity, freedom for time-out periods, freedom to learn to relax creatively, and freedom to become more creative through leisure moments. An important meaning of the word *recreation* is "re-creation"—a time to revitalize or even to create anew during recreational activities or as a later consequence of them. Sometimes, however, people are trained to be almost completely programmed; they have a great loss of freedom by being almost completely instrumentalized. Instead of being overly organized and overdosed with structure and learning chores, students should have the time and freedom to be open to opportunities that are already around them or that could appear unexpectedly.

Teaching for multiple talents involves teaching students to sense and respond effectively to many different types of opportunities and thereby have a lifelong effect of strengthening their total wellness.

A mind—or any part of a mind—is a terrible thing to waste (Proctor, 1978). There is great potential in a person's total brainpower, especially compared to the small and less powerful part of the brain whose use is being rewarded in many classrooms. This continued delimitation of the use of the brain in educational systems is a paradox when we consider that potential human resources are the greatest resources of all. Any program designed to develop people is poorly designed if it leads primarily to very passive participation or nonparticipation. A sit-and-listen, passive role in classrooms is not well-designed to help students learn what is presumedly being taught. Time has been spent but not necessarily well spent in such situations.

Emotionally disturbed children have been taught by the multiple-talent approach in two important efforts, the latest one by the Talents Unlimited Project in Mobile (Nielsen, 1972; Bobowski, 1978; personal communication from Sara Waldrop, Talents Unlimited Project director). The results clearly indicate that if such children were exposed to several different types of thinking along with several active and productive output channels for their daily inner energies, they became less emotionally disturbed and learned to function more effectively. They were also able to acquire and work with higher levels of knowledge— well beyond what the established curriculum experts were sure they could never learn. Their emotional disturbances and disruptive effects were decreased, while their effectiveness in learning and in functioning as persons was increased.

In ten projects across the nation (plus replications) about 450 comparisons were made between multiple-talent classrooms and others (averaging more than 40 comparisons per project). Practically all results were positive for the multiple-talents approach, and the large majority were statistically significant. Across these studies, the multiple-talent teaching approach yielded what may be the longest string of essentially positive comparisons ever demonstrated by any teaching approach (Taylor, 1980). These positive results were found across different measures of knowledge and of talents, including in some cases special measures designed specifically for the control (competitive) classrooms. Therefore, the activation of more of the potential talent resources in the total brainpower of students has produced a spread of positive effects in students. Yet few if any studies listing the needs of students have come up with the need for students to learn to use all aspects of their full brainpower. Teachers should adopt the higher concept of students as thinkers, with unlimited talents, rather than merely as learners. Then students not only would learn to think but would simultaneously acquire more knowledge, more effectively, by using thinking ways of learning.

The "original kids" were seen in seven talent dimensions by Beverly Lloyd, as illustrated in Figure 8.1. Her teaching for these multiple talents also ignited and displayed other attributes in each of these students, so she concluded that she definitely taught "more of the whole person" in her class. Recently we have called our teaching method a *simultaneous double curriculum approach*. We have students use each of their multiple talents in working with and thereby acquiring each type of subject matter in the knowledge curriculum as the ways to work with, process, and thereby acquire the multiple knowledge curriculum.

From all these results comes the recommendation that the natural talent resources in every person should be activated and growing and developing and functioning as naturally and fully as possible. Broadening the band of talents functioning in schools can increase human capabilities, thereby strengthening the total health of students of all ages. Education then would become part of the health-enlarging and health-strengthening systems of the nation.

NEEDED: A HUMAN ENVIRONMENTAL RESEARCH COUNCIL

As a representative of my profession to the several design professions that form the Interprofessional Council on Environmental Design (ICED), I joined a human science subcommittee

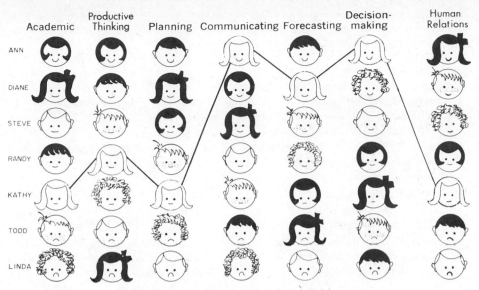

Figure 8.1 Taylor's Talent Totem Poles

of ICED that was organized by a leading engineer, William Hedley. Eventually, this led to Hedley's forming the Environmental Impact Analysis Research Council as part of the American Society of Civil Engineers. People from several professions are members of the council, including several from the social-behavioral professional fields. What is now needed is a parallel organization, drawing upon the highest level of scientists and professional people, to function as a "People Impact Analysis Research Council." Such a council would study positive and negative environmental effects on people, especially on the vital wellness/illness dimension. A systematic, effective movement is needed to learn more, through research, about which environmental features strengthen health and which features fail to do so or even lead toward frustration and illness. The need is for a quasi-governmental research council, formed and located in the Washington, D.C., area, near the existing four learned councils: the National Academy of Sciences/National Research Council, the Social Science Research Council, the American Council on Education, and the American Council of Learned Societies. This new learned council could or should be created by an act of Congress. It should have strong representation and voting powers from the citizenry at large and from human sciences professionals. It would give advice to the public, as well as to federal and state governments, regarding how different environmental features affect people. Such a research council would provide the balance needed between the existing environmental impact statements and the proposed people impact statements. It would help move environmental problems from a largely political arena toward a more scientific and professional arena, functioning for the wellness of all people. Since total health costs are our nation's greatest expenditure and have the highest rate of increased expenditures per year, the entire health field could support this proposal for a fifth learned council. It could go a long way to reduce total health costs per year.

Botanists in their greenhouse labs try to provide the best total climate for the growth of plants. The plants cultivated in such ideal atmospheres can grow so fully and beautifully that they might be described as almost completely happy in their total situation. Ideally, classrooms and organizations should provide comparable greenhouse-like atmospheres for students and for workers, so that they will also grow and function fully and naturally and project radiant waves of wellness.

In summary, the long-range challenge is to determine what effects we want people to receive from their environments—troubled minds and hearts from the ill-designed, or, as a widely-reprinted article discusses, peace of mind and heart from the well-designed. (Peace of mind, 1977).

REFERENCE NOTES

1. Taylor, C. W. *New manpower selection and educational programs for more effective health care performances.* Paper presented at the Annual Meeting of the American Psychological Association, Honolulu, September 1972.

2. Taylor, C. W. *Architectural psychology: Design in teamwork with health professionals.* Paper presented at the Annual Meeting of the American Psychological Association, Montreal, September 1980.

3. Taylor, C. W. Designing for sunshining. In *Solar radiation considerations in building planning and design.* Washington, D.C.: National Academy of Sciences, Building Research Advisory Board, 1976. (Mimeographed)

4. Taylor, C. W., Ghiselin, B., Wolfer, J. A., Loy, L., & Bourne, L. E., Jr. *Development of a theory of education from psychological and other basic research findings.* Final report to Cooperative Research Project No. 621, U.S. Office of Education, 1964.

5. Price, P. B., Taylor, C. W., Richards, J. M., Jr., & Jacobsen, T. L. *Measurement and predictors of physician performance.* Salt Lake City, Utah: L.L.R. Press, 1971. (Available from C. W. Taylor.)

6. Taylor, C. W., Smith, W. R., & Ghiselin, B. *Factors which scientists in one research center consider hindrances to their publishing.* Unpublished manuscript, University of Utah, 1960. (Mimeographed)

7. Secrist, G. E. *A total environmental approach to occupational performance and satisfaction.* Unpublished doctoral dissertation, University of Utah, 1974.

8. Wheeler, B. R. *Creativity in social work: An education experiment.* Unpublished doctoral dissertation, University of Utah, 1978.

9. *Biographical Inventory—Form U.* Salt Lake City: Institute for Behavioral Research in Creativity (IBRIC), 1981. (Available from IBRIC, 1570 S. 11th East, Salt Lake City, UT 84105.)

10. Taylor, C. W. *Potentially all people are gifted.* Paper presented at Interactive Session on Education Programme, 20th International Congress of Applied Psychology, Edinburgh, July 28, 1982.

11. Taylor, C. W. *Teaching for talents and gifts: 1978 status.* Final report (No. NIE-PO-77-0075) to the National Institute of Education, 1978.

12. Taylor, C. W. *Creativity and self-education.* Unpublished manuscript, University of Utah, 1982. (Mimeographed)

REFERENCES

Attributes of excellence, *Scientific American,* May 1982, 98–99.

Bailey, R., Branch, H., & Taylor, C. (Eds.). *Architectural psychology and psychiatry: An exploratory international research conference.* Salt Lake City: University of Utah, 1964.

Bobowski, R. C. The care and feeding of talent. *American Education,* October 1978, 43–48.

Dreyfuss, H. *Designing for people.* New York: Paragraphic Books, 1967.

Ellison, R. L., James, L. R., Fox, D. C., McDonald, B. W., & Taylor, C. *The development and validation of a biographical inventory for the identification of high level nursing talent.* Salt Lake City: University of Utah, 1969.

Ellison, R., McDonald, B., James, L., Fox, D., & Taylor, C. *An investigation of organizational climate.* Greensboro, N.C.: Creativity Research Institute of the Smith-Richardson Foundation, 1967.

Ellison, R., McDonald, B., James, L., Fox, D., & Taylor, C. *An investigation of organizational climate.* Greensboro, N.C.: Creative Research Institute of the Smith-Richardson Foundation, 1968.

Good, L., Siegel, S., & Bay, C. *Therapy by design.* Springfield, Ill.: Charles C Thomas, 1965.

Guilford, J. P. *Way beyond the I.Q.* Buffalo: Creative Education Foundation, 1977.

Hoffer, E. Architects and nature: On the primacy of man. In *The quality of constructed environments with man as the measure.* Proceedings of 1974 Engineering Foundation Conference at Asicomar Conference Center. New York: American Society of Civil Engineers, 1976.

Kay, A. Making organizational changes toward creativity. In C. Taylor (Ed.), *Climate for creativity.* New York: Pergamon Press, 1972.

Michael, J. M. The second revolution in health: Health promotion and its environmental base. *American Psychologist,* 1982, **37,** 936–941.

Nielsen, C. Required project paper for Masters Degree, College of Education, University of Utah, Salt Lake City, June 1972.

Peace of mind from the well designed—the architectural psychologist's goal. *University of Utah Review,* February, 1977.

Price, P. B. A search for excellence. *The American Journal of Surgery,* 1969, **118,** 815–821.

Price, P. B., Taylor, C. W., Richards, J. M., Jr., & Jacobson, T. L. Measurement of physician performance. *Journal of Medical Education,* 1964, **39**(2), 8. (Also final mimeographed report to the Cooperative Research Program, U.S. Office of Education, U.S. Department of Health, Education and Welfare, Contract No. OE–2–10–093.)

Proctor, S. D. A mind is a terrible thing to waste. *Phi Delta Kappan,* November 1978, 201–203.

Smith, W. R. Favorable and unfavorable working conditions reported by scientists at two research centers. In C. W. Taylor (Ed.), *The Third (1959) Research Conference on the Identification of Creative Scientific Talent.* Salt Lake City: University of Utah Press, 1959.

Steinhart, J. S., & Cherniack, S. *The universities and environmental quality: Commitment to problem-focused education.* Office of Science and Technology, Executive Office of the President. Washington, D.C.: U.S. Government Printing Office, 1969.

Taylor, C. W. Clues to creative teaching (10 articles). *Instructor,* September 1963–May 1964.

Taylor, C. W. Be talent developers as well as knowledge dispensers. *Today's Education—NEA Journal,* December 1968, 67–69. (a)

Taylor, C. W. Improving the environment for creativity. In D. V. DeSimone (Ed.), *Education for innovation.* New York: Pergamon Press, 1968. (b)

Taylor, C. W. All students are now educationally deprived. In *Proceedings of the 17th International Congress of Applied Psychology* (Vol. 2). Brussels: Editest, 1972. (a)

Taylor, C. W. Architectural psychology: Production of a new type of man-power. In *Proceedings of the 17th International Congress of Applied Psychology* (Vol. 2). Brussels: Editest, 1972. (b)

Taylor, C. W. (Ed.). *Climate for creativity.* Report of the Seventh National Research Conference on Creativity, Greensboro, North Carolina. New York: Pergamon Press, 1972. (c)

Taylor, C. W. Developing effectively functioning people: The accountable goal of multiple talent teaching. *Education,* November/December 1973, 99–110.

Taylor, C. W. New building measures needed in order to design for people. In *The Quality of Constructed Environments with Man as the Measure.* Proceedings of the 1974 Engineering Foundation Conference at Asilomar Conference Center, California. New York: American Society of Civil Engineers, 1976.

Taylor, C. W. How many types of giftedness can your program tolerate? *Journal of Creative Behavior,* 1978, **12**(1), 39–51.

Taylor, C. W. Multiple talent teaching results. *Congressional Record—Senate,* S12407–S12411. Washington, D.C.: U.S. Government Printing Office, 1980.

Taylor, C. W., Bailey, R., & Branch, H. (Eds.). *Second International Conference on Architectural Psychology.* Salt Lake City: University of Utah, 1966.

Taylor, C. W., & Ellison, R. L. Predicting creative performances from multiple measures. In C. W. Taylor (Ed.), *Widening horizons in creativity.* New York: Wiley, 1964.

Taylor, C. W., & Ellison, R. Biographical predictors of scientific performance: Criteria of scientific performance can be predicted from biographical information. *Science,* 1967, **155**, 1075–1080.

Taylor, C. W., & Ellison, R. L. Selection of scientists who will be productive in their careers. In *Proceedings of the 17th International Congress of Applied Psychology* (Vol. 1). Brussels: Editest, 1972.

Taylor, C. W., Nelson, D. E., & Price, P. B. *Comprehensive analysis of physician and physician-in-training performance* (Vols. 1 & 2). Photocopied reports to the Public Health Service, Contract HSM no. 71171 (NTIS accession nos. PB-248 541/5GI, PB-248 542/3GI), 1974.

Taylor, C. W., Smith, W. R., & Ghiselin, B. The creative and other contributions of one sample of research scientists. In C. W. Taylor & F. Barron (Eds.), *Scientive creativity: Its recognition and development.* New York: Wiley, 1963.

APPENDIX: THE ARTIFICIAL HEART PERIOD IN DR. BARNEY CLARK'S LIFE*

William C. DeVries, Calvin W. Taylor, Lyle D. Joyce, and Wm. Lawrence Hastings, University of Utah

Graphical presentations of Dr. Barney Clark's preoperative and postoperative condition from a wellness-illness perspective are presented in the three charts in Figure 8.2. An intermediate borderline at level zero (0) is used to designate the division between wellness (good health) and illness. Five gradual steps of improving wellness proceed upward from the transition borderline, and five graduated levels of increasing illness proceed downward.

The five (upward) wellness steps in order of improving health are: not quite ill, fairly well, well, very well, and greatest wellness. A listing in the illness category generally indicates a need for hospitalization. The five illness categories (downward) somewhat follow patient classifications used by hospital administrators: satisfactory (but hospitalized), fair, serious, critical, and very critical. Physiological (lungs, central nervous system, kidney, vascular bed, heart, etc.) and psychological (sensitivity awareness, listen-response, talk, etc.) states of wellness-illness are evaluated using these parameters.

The artificial heart operation of Dr. Barney Clark began on December 1, 1982, at 10:30 P.M., which was well ahead of schedule. The operation was started early because his rapid deterioration created a fear that he might die before the operation could be completed. His own bad heart, which was the most critically ill part of his system, was leading and pulling his total body downward to *a point of no return.* It was clear immediately after the implantation that the preoperative condition of Dr. Clark's kidneys and especially the chronic emphysema in his lungs were much worse than previously medically indicated. Marvelously, though, he became the first person in history in whom an artificial heart was implanted. His otherwise inevitable and rapid trend toward death was stopped and reversed by having his artificial heart take over, not only to keep him alive, but afterwards also to pull him upward and improve his condition.

The solid line in *Chart A in Figure 8.2* represents the relative position of each system on the illness-wellness scale prior to and immediately after the total artificial heart implantation. Changes to the systems after the artificial heart implantation are indicated by the length and direction of the broken lines in this and later charts. The cardiac output of the new transplanted heart was cautiously and carefully raised in successive small steps through the first three days after the operation.

Chart B in Figure 8.2 is the intermediate graph of the highest health status attained separately by each of the different systems throughout the postoperative course. Improvements (upward) from Chart A to Chart B can be recognized in nearly every system. Despite overall improvements, several systems (lungs, mobility, exercise, and kidneys) remained in

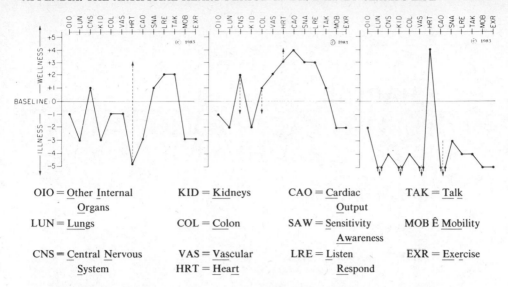

OIO = Other Internal   KID = Kidneys   CAO = Cardiac   TAK = Talk
        Organs   Output

LUN = Lungs   COL = Colon   SAW = Sensitivity   MOB Ê Mobility
                                              Awareness

CNS = Central Nervous   VAS = Vascular   LRE = Listen   EXR = Exercise
        System   HRT = Heart   Respond

Figure 8.2   Three Wellness-Illness Charts of Dr. Barney Clark with an artificial heart

the illness region below the borderline throughout the postoperative period. Only significant changes in Dr. Clark's condition are represented by broken-line arrows. Temporary changes of short duration are not indicated. In Chart B, all setbacks, significant or temporary, include the second operation on the 2nd day to discover and repair the hole in the chronically diseased lungs; the 5th day appearance and treatment of seizures (reflected in the central nervous system); the third operation on the 12th day to replace the broken valve in the artificial heart; the fourth operation of the 45th day to stop a recurring nosebleed; and the later flareup of a colon problem.

Once again, 112 days later on March 23, 1983, Dr. Barney Clark was rapidly reaching *another point of no return.* But this time there was no new technique available in humankind's state of the art to rescue him. Chart C in Figure 8.2 shows the last four hours, during which four prime forces pulled him irreversibly downward, leading to his demise at 10:02 P.M..

By the start of this four-hour period, virtually all systems had already dropped dramatically into the illness categories. The major malfunctioning of the kidneys together with the diseased lungs put an increasing overload of fluids into the circulatory system. The cardiac output of blood through the blood vessels also dropped rapidly because of the dilation and eventual collapse of the vascular part of the circulatory system. The great exception to these downward trends was the artificial heart, which continued to function at top capabilities, even through death.

Dr. Chase Peterson, who had earlier orchestrated the worldwide news releases about Barney Clark, was told recently that this final chart showed the heart being a Mt. Fuji–like peak of wellness against the widespread illness of the rest of the body. This feature of the last chart stirred further thought and discussion among us. The fact that the artificial heart was a high peak of wellness, way above all of the other ill conditions of his body, led to our final conclusion. Ideally, this is exactly the way the graphical picture should be for the artificial heart.

CHAPTER 9

PUBLIC HEALTH POLICY AND BEHAVIORAL HEALTH

PATRICK H. DELEON

U.S. Senate Staff

GARY R. VANDENBOS

American Psychological Association

The health care policies of our nation are in a continual state of flux. This is far more true and far more dramatic than most health care professionals realize. Far from being stagnant (or ideological), our national health policies actively reflect the collective judgment of those currently in elected public office. These elected representatives are quite responsive to the expressed concerns and interests of individuals and organizations in their constituency who have made the effort to become personally involved in the development of health policy. Policymakers must deal with the day-to-day practicalities of such public concerns and constituent pressures.

This is not to suggest that all one need do to effect radical change is to express one's views. Yet, if those who are seriously interested in behavioral health (health enhancement and disease-prevention) are willing to become personally involved in the relevant public policy debate, we have no doubt that the behavioral health gestalt will be successful in revolutionizing our current medical care system within this decade.

One should never lose sight of the fact that health care in our nation—whether at the federal, state, or local level—is intimately involved with the political process. It is our nation's politicians (and indirectly, through their collective judgment, the public at large) who set health care priorities, not the health community. To be successful, the politician must reflect the interests of his or her constituents, including the professionals and the consumers.

State legislatures have enacted complex health codes including licensure or certification provisions that, among other things, define the educational requirements for entry into professions and delineate the appropriate scope of practice for nearly every health care practitioner. In a recent interview for *American Psychologist,* Stuart Eizenstat, former chief domestic policy advisor to President Carter, stated:

> *The health industry is, in my estimation, the most complex and difficult of any industry in the United States. I realize that this is a fairly strong statement, but the reason I say that is because it is the only industry that I am aware of in which the government is so deeply involved, both in terms of direct services and in the reimbursement of private providers and institutions. There really are very few other, if any, industries in which we have so much federal involvement . . . the health industry is also unique in that it is the only industry in which the immediate buyer and seller do not enter*

*into an 'arms length' relationship. You have, instead, a situation in which a patient
and the doctor are in a personal-professional relationship in which cost becomes a
secondary factor. Moreover, it is also unique in that the actual payment of the charge
by the hospital or physician rarely comes directly out of the patient's or buyer's pocket.
(Bevan, 1982)*

Many health care professionals do not realize the extent to which the government is
involved in establishing health care policies nor the extent to which the federal government
has actually become a major purchaser of health care. The federal government is responsible
for paying nearly 40% of all health care costs incurred in our nation (DeLeon and VandenBos,
1980). Not only did health care account for approximately 9.4% of our gross national
product in 1980, or $247 billion, but it has been estimated that in fiscal year 1981 the
federal government alone spent $80.3 billion on health-related expenditures. As a nation,
we spend more on health care than any other country in the world, and health care is
now our third largest industry.

HEALTH PROMOTION AND DISEASE PREVENTION

In April 1974, Marc Lalonde, Minister of National Health and Welfare for Canada, released
his far-reaching and amazingly prophetic report, *A New Perspective on the Health of Canadians.* Since its release, the truly landmark nature of this provocative document has become
even more apparent. It represented the first time that the national government of an advanced
industrial country had articulated to its citizenry the importance of disease prevention and
health promotion (expressly mentioning lifestyle and individual behavior) in the context
of a national health plan. High priority was to be given to developing "*A Health Prevention
Strategy* aimed at informing, influencing and assisting both individuals and organizations
so that they will accept more responsibility and be more active in matters affecting mental
and physical health" (Lalonde, 1974, p. 66).

In releasing this report, the government of Canada brought into the public policy forum
(thus subjecting them to close scrutiny) many of the fundamental assumptions that still
significantly shape our American illness-oriented health care system. Specifically, the report
stated:

*The traditional or generally-accepted view of the health field is that the art or
science of medicine has been the fount from which all improvements in health have
flowed, and popular belief equates the level of health with the quality of medicine.*

*Public health and individual care, provided by the public health physician, the
medical practitioner, the nurse and the acute treatment hospital, have been widely-
regarded as responsible for improvements in health status. Individual health care, in
particular, has had a dominant position, and expenditures have generally been directed
at improving its quality and accessibility. . . .*

*In most minds the health field and the personal medical care system are synonymous.
This has been due in large part to the powerful image projected by medicine of its
role in the control of infective and parasitic diseases, the advances in surgery, the
lowered infant mortality rate and the development of new drugs. This image is reinforced
by drug advertising, by television series with the physician as hero, and by the faith
bordering on awe by which many Canadians relate to their physicians. . . .*

*One finds that close to seven billion dollars a year are spent on a personal health
care system which is mainly oriented to treating existing illness. (Lalonde, 1974, pp.
11–12)*

Minister Lalonde also noted, however:

At the same time as improvements have been made in health care, in the general standard of living, in public health protection and in medical science, ominous counter-forces have been at work to undo progress in raising the health status of Canadians. . . .

For these environmental and behavioral threats to health, the organized health care system can do little more than serve as a catchment net for the victims. Physicians, surgeons, nurses and hospitals together spend much of their time in treating ills caused by adverse environmental factors and behavioural risks. . . .

While it is easy to convince a person in pain to see a physician, it is not easy to get someone not in pain to moderate insidious habits in the interests of future well-being. . . .

It is therefore necessary for Canadians themselves to be concerned with the gravity of environmental and behavioural risks before any real progress can be made. . . .

The Government of Canada now intends to give to human biology, the environment and lifestyle as much attention as it has to the financing of the health care organization so that all four avenues to improved health are pursued with equal vigour. Its goal will continue to be not only to add years to our life but life to our years, so that all can enjoy the opportunities offered by increased economic and social justice. (pp. 5–6)

Five years later, in July 1979, President Carter heralded the announcement of another far-reaching governmental health policy document, *Healthy People: The Surgeon General's Report on Health Promotion and Disease Prevention.* The president stated in his introductory message:

It sets out a national program for improving the health of our people—a program that relies on prevention along with cure. This program is ambitious but achievable. It can substantially reduce both the suffering of our people and the burden on our expensive system of medical care.

Government, business, labor, schools, and health professions must all contribute to the prevention of injury and disease. And all of these efforts must ultimately rely on the individual decisions of millions of Americans—decisions to protect and promote their own good health. (*DHEW, 1979, p. v*)

The U.S. Surgeon General's report was very similar in its orientation and its recommendations to that of the Canadian government:

Prevention is an idea whose time has come. We have the scientific knowledge to begin to formulate recommendations for improved health. . . .

Using that framework [one designed expressly from the Lalonde report] a group of American experts developed a method for assessing the relative contributions of each of the elements to many health problems. Analysis in which the method was applied to the 10 leading causes of death in 1976 suggests that perhaps as much as half of U.S. mortality in 1976 was due to unhealthy behavior or lifestyle. . . .

Personal habits play critical roles in the development of many serious diseases and in injuries. . . .

In fact, of the 10 leading causes of death in the United States, at least seven could be substantially reduced if persons at risk improved just five habits: diet, smoking, lack of exercise, alcohol abuse, and use of antihypertensive medication. (pp. 7–14)

Within the overall health community, there is a steadily increasing awareness of the effectiveness of behavioral health. Dr. Edward N. Brandt, Jr., Assistant Secretary for Health under President Reagan, recently lavishly commended his predecessor for developing *Healthy*

People. Dr. Brandt further expressed a personal commitment to implementing its recommendations during his own tenure. He elaborated:

> *We should not suppose, however, that we can continue to improve the health status of our people solely, or even primarily, by allocating so much of our time and treasure to the development of ever more sophisticated medical equipment and services. In the years ahead, we have come to recognize, the greatest advances in health status, the most meaningful improvements in our national quality of life are likely to accrue from efforts that we, as individuals and as a society, make to improve our health habits and the environment in which we live and work. (Brandt, 1982)*

Unfortunately, there are still signs within the health community of considerable interdisciplinary friction, especially surrounding such basic issues as who should be entitled to provide certain types of care and under what conditions, as well as how these services should be reimbursed. Nonetheless, a number of truly exciting interdisciplinary advances have been made. Perhaps the most significant, from a public policy perspective, is the recent release by the Institute of Medicine of its report *Health and Behavior: Frontiers of Research in the Biobehavioral Sciences* (Hamburg, Elliott, & Parron, 1982). This report was the outgrowth of two and a half years of work by a broadly interdisciplinary steering committee, which assembled the informed assessments of more than 400 leaders in the biomedical and behavioral sciences. It pointed out: "As much as 50 percent of mortality from the 10 leading causes of death in the United States can be traced to life style" (Hamburg et al., 1982, p. 3).

The report stressed the need for considerably more research in these new areas and noted that collaboration between the biomedical and behavioral sciences would be essential to any comprehensive approach to improving our nation's health:

> *Much remains to be learned, but the existing research base provides strong evidence that the biobehavioral sciences can make substantial and unique contributions to dealing with much of the disease that now constitutes the main burden of illness in this country. . . . (p. 16)*
>
> *In the foreseeable future, it should be possible to construct a reasonably unified biobehavioral science pertinent to health and disease, with major applications in all the health professions and by the public at large. (p. 320)*

It is hoped that these recommendations made by the prestigious Institute of Medicine will serve as a catalyst for the clinical and scientific health communities, so that their leadership will begin to testify more frequently on Capitol Hill on behalf of the behavioral sciences—and behavioral health in particular.

The Senate Appropriations Committee, in its deliberations on the fiscal year 1982 supplemental funding bill, specifically cited the Institute of Medicine report in urging the National Institutes of Health (NIH) and the Alcohol, Drug Abuse and Mental Health Administration (ADAMHA) to "study the potential benefit of giving greater priority to prevention research activities that will address 'bad habits'/lifestyle which are so costly to our society" (U.S. Senate, Note 1, p. 129).

POLICY ISSUES AND THE POLITICAL PROCESS

The fundamental health policy question that should be confronting our nation today is "How can the demonstrated merits of behavioral health be given greater priority?" rather than the more common "How can we afford to add new health benefits?" How, we must ask, can we increase the current proportion of the federal health dollar spent on *prevention* from between 2% to 4% to a more realistic and ultimately cost-effective figure? How can we insure that those practitioners who are trained in behavioral health will be compensated by our reimbursment system for practicing such skills? How, as a national strategy, can we facilitate the consumer's selection of healthy behaviors? The answers to these questions lie in the political process.

Despite the fact that in the 1981–1982 election cycle, the American Medical Association and two of its state affiliates comprised three of the top four business and professional political action committees (PACs), the typical health care professional possesses only a very rudimentary, if not downright naive, understanding of the political process. Politics seems to be something alien. Like most Americans, health professionals probably will never seriously consider participating in the political process in order to obtain a professional or personal goal. This lack of personal involvement is not limited to health care professionals, however. Only 53.6% of our voting-age population exercised their voting privilege during our 1980 presidential election. If pressed to explain the reasons for their lack of involvement, the vast majority of health care practitioners and scientists would probably indicate either that they felt powerless to influence the political process or that there was little need to become involved (i.e., they could not see any direct relevance to their own personal or professional lives). They expect, instead, that their professional associations alone should speak and act for them. Unfortunately, these views demonstrate a fundamental misunderstanding of the political process.

Those skilled in the political process are, above all else, accomplished in the art of evolving "reasonable compromises." In attempting to establish priorities for federal funding, for example, one soon becomes aware of the many compelling but unfortunately conflicting interests involved. In the mental health arena, the vast majority of our expenditures (currently around 70%) are for hospital or inpatient care (Kiesler, 1982). This has been true for many years, and it has resulted in the development of considerable vested interests, both professional and economic. No matter how philosophically attractive various alternatives to inpatient care—such as crisis intervention teams or day care programs—may appear, history has demonstrated that it has been most difficult to change the basic thrust of mental health care delivery in our nation. In a recent policy report issued by the University Health Policy Consortium, which is the first Health Care Financing Administration (HCFA) designated Center for Health Policy Analysis and Research, it was pointed out:

> These mental hospitals, in many cases, are powerful institutions in their states, with a solid place in the state bureaucracy backed up by powerful labor unions representing employees. . . with access to their own deep pocket at the state level. (Dorris & McGuire, 1981, p. 97)

Furthermore, as our nation's health care costs continue to escalate (faster than almost any other segment of our economy), the finite nature of our health care dollar will become even more evident. Change is always unsettling, but, as the available financial resources become more constrained, it will become significantly more difficult for those who are economically vested in the status quo not to actively oppose new or experimental approaches. There is a definite comfort in being able to rely on that which one knows will have some tangible effect. The unknown (unsubstantiated promises of theoretically significant improvement) is too abstract for most politicians to deal with, especially in a hostile environment.

Successful politicians are professionals. They are accomplished in the art of developing acceptable consensus and in the process of getting reelected. Unlike most health care professionals, politicians cannot afford the luxury of becoming too narrow in their focus, unless they have been in office for many, many years. Each of us, on some level, expects our elected officials to possess in-depth knowledge of those issues about which we are most concerned—such as behavioral health. We forget or, probably more accurately, never realize the extent to which this is true for everyone in the elected official's constituency. The end result is that, to be successful, all elected officials must acquire a broad appreciation for a great number of highly complex and often pressing issues. They must be able to converse with the media, with their constituents, and with other legislators. Elected officials' most precious commodity soon becomes their time. They simply do not have the time to meet with all who want to meet with them, to read all the background materials that they would like to review, and to attend all the hearings that their committees have scheduled.

A primary objective, therefore, for those who wish to utilize the political process to enhance society's acceptance of behavioral health should be to personally become a catalyst in assisting our nation's politicians in forging health policy. This need not be an all-consuming task, but it must be a regular activity—attended to from time to time in one way or another.

For a reasonable compromise to evolve, there must first exist distinct interests that are perceived to be in conflict. Currently, in the political forum, we have the status quo and a general feeling of dissatisfaction with ever-escalating health care costs. Any perceived conflict is about cost, not about alternative service possibilities. Little, if any, serious attention is being given to behavioral health. Policymakers need to be educated about health care in general and health promotion/disease prevention in particular.

The vast majority of our nation's politicians do not have a personal background in health care. In the 97th Congress (1980–1982), for example, 45% of the 435 members in the House of Representatives possessed a background in law; in the Senate, 59% were lawyers. In marked contrast, only seven members of either the House or Senate had a background in medicine—slightly over 1%.

Taking another perspective, if one reviews the tenure of those individuals who work on the personal staffs of members of Congress as legislative assistants (LAs) specializing in health matters, one finds that, during the 5-year period from 1977 to 1981, the turnover rate was approximately 90%. If one analyzes the tenure of the LAs for those members of Congress who serve the six key subcommittees (or committees) that deal with most health legislation, one finds a turnover rate of approximately 95% (Grupenhoff, Note 2). Furthermore, this is the first postcollege employment for nearly 70% of these legislative assistants.

For our nation's health care professionals to assume that their elected officials, or even their staffs, have the professional background and expertise to appreciate the many intricacies of our health delivery system is simply unreasonable. Because our nation's health care system is such a highly complex entity, however, it provides our elected officials with considerable opportunity, when approached creatively, to be helpful to their constituents—assuming, of course, that the constituents have made their interests known.

Let us consider the mechanisms for forming health policy. During the 97th Congress, the U.S. Senate was organized into 20 committees, 106 subcommittees, and 4 additional joint House–Senate committees. Although three of the health subcommittees—Appropriations, Finance, and Labor and Human Resources—are commonly thought to be the prime health-related forums, six other full committees—Aging, Armed Services, Budget, Governmental Affairs, Veterans Affairs, and Indian Affairs—also possess direct legislative or oversight responsibility for sizable components of our nation's health care system. In addition, the Foreign Relations Committee has jurisdiction over the State Department's international health endeavors, and the Judiciary Committee has jurisdiction over the entire federal judicial system, including the precedent-setting Federal Criminal Code. The business aspects of health care are addressed by both the Small Business Committee and the Commerce, Science, and Transportation Committee, with the latter having jurisdiction over the Federal Trade Commission, which has publicly expressed concern over possible antitrust aspects of current medical practice. Finally, considering all parameters of preventive health care, the Agriculture, Nutrition, and Forestry Committee is significant because of its jurisdiction over the food stamp program and other federal nutritional initiatives.

As must be expected, each of these committees has developed its own personality and priorities over the years. These priorities are based primarily on the composition of the committees' memberships and the pressures brought to bear on them by affected interests. Accordingly, it should be no surprise that experts in health policy who have studied the political process in depth have noted: "No planned intentional national health policy exists. National policy is an ad hoc aggregate of uncoordinated laws, historical accidents, and normative practices that almost defies discussion" (Kiesler, 1980).

To those who appreciate the art of politics (and especially to those who have committed themselves to becoming personally involved in the political process), the very complexity of the legislative arena allows for creative opportunity. If those who believe in the benefits of behavioral health eventually become successful in encouraging their elected officials to provide a higher priority for these endeavors, there will be ample opportunity to do so. Opportunity for impact is inherent in the process of politics. If an individual member of a committee or subcommittee expresses a personal interest in a particular item or type of program, it becomes incumbent on the committee chairperson to be responsive. A reasonable approach must evolve; a committee member's interest may not be simply ignored. Perhaps the committee will hold a special hearing at the chairperson's request to explore the question in more detail. Perhaps the administration will be directed to provide detailed reports or to conduct appropriate pilot projects. In any case, the underlying process will have begun, and those involved will be responsive. It is important to realize, however, that this collegial courtesy does not necessarily extend to other members of the legislative body who do not serve on that particular committee or subcommittee. So long as any member of the committee remains vocally concerned, however, the committee and its chairperson will also be attentive. This is true regardless of whether they are from the same political party or represent similar political ideologies.

The content or subject matter that is being focused on becomes secondary to the process of focusing attention. This is one of the cardinal rules of the political process, and its importance is not fully appreciated by most health care professionals. In preparing for deliberations on the fiscal year 1983 appropriations bill for the Departments of Labor, Health and Human Services, Education, and related agencies, for example, the Senate Appropriations Subcommittee with formal jurisdiction in these areas held approximately 29 public hearings, during which the relevant administration officials formally presented testimony in support of their budgetary requests. The subcommittee also formally heard from approximately 160 public witnesses and received numerous written recommendations from the public at large (also made part of the formal hearing record). The budget document from which the subcommittee members worked eventually will be reprinted in the Senate report accompanying the bill. This budget sheet is essentially composed of line-by-line dollar-item requests. The fiscal year 1982 document was 37 pages long; summarized on *one page* were the dollar requests for the Alcohol, Drug Abuse, and Mental Health Administration (ADAMHA) and the National Institutes of Health (NIH). The budget request for fiscal year 1983 for these programs exceeded $4.1 billion, and the Department of Health and Human Services' budget justification for just this segment of the budget was 719 pages long. Is it any wonder that the personal interest of a U.S. Senator in any given program is important?

Of course, if any member of the subcommittee decided to openly challenge the chairperson's recommendations during the subcommittee's deliberations, his or her arguments could be summarily dismissed by presenting the overwhelming statistical and budgetary evidence readily available in support of the chairperson's recommendation (which frequently reflects that of the administration). As a practical matter, however, this scenario rarely occurs unless the member proposing the modification refuses to accept the compromise offered by the chair. When this does occur, it is usually because the primary purpose of the offeror was not to modify the chair's proposed figure but to posture, for political reasons, on behalf of some particular cause.

As indicated earlier, numerous committees have jurisdiction over the various components of our nation's health care industry. The U.S. Senate has adopted rules prescribing that each senator may serve on only two of the so-called major standing committees—such as Appropriations, Labor and Human Resources, and Finance—and on one of the minor committees—such as Budget, Indian Affairs, and Veterans Affairs. The Senate rules further limit subcommittee membership to three in the first category of committees and two in the latter. Thus, the very structure of the Senate organization provides that, on a subject as complex as health care, any given member may have a significant impact. At the same time, however, a member cannot be totally domineering. In essence, even within the U.S. Senate, we have a system of checks and balances. This is important to understand, because it means that every one of our elected officials can have a significant impact, and, further, that no single senator or representative is the exclusive vehicle for change.

Perhaps the most difficult concept for most health care professionals to appreciate is that it is the support of individual constituents (and not, for example, national professional organizations) that is of paramount importance to the elected official. Elected officials are very sensitive, especially to interpersonal cues. They simply would not survive otherwise. No matter how important their committee assignments may appear or how much national publicity they may receive, senators and representatives only remain in political office as long as a plurality of their local constituents supports them. A politician soon learns that interpersonal slights or perceived indifference to constituents' requests are never forgotten. Politicians do not have to solve every problem, but they must at least listen and convey the impression that they are trying.

Behavioral health has not yet really entered into the public policy forum. We are convinced, however, that if a sufficient number of health care professionals concerned about behavioral health are willing to become personally involved in the political process, this will form the necessary critical mass for our nation to enter into what Michael (1982) has termed the "second public health revolution."

FIVE STEPS FOR CONSTRUCTIVE ACTION

1. Maximize Personal Contact with Your Elected Officials

The single most valuable political effort that those concerned with behavioral health can make is to develop, over time, a personal relationship with their state's elected officials and their staffs. Behavioral health advocates should seek to develop the type of relationship with their representatives that is built on mutual trust and respect. As this relationship develops, behavioral scientists will find themselves able to talk about a wide range of health care policy issues that concern them. The politicians then will be able to utilize their political expertise to resolve whatever problems exist.

Given the extent to which many behavioral scientists are described by their professional colleagues as "behavioral change experts," it is amazing how seldom these behavioral researchers apply their research findings to their own behavior. When urged to visit their elected officials during business or vacation trips to the nation's capitol (so as to develop personal relationships with these national leaders), behavioral health professionals often reply, in good faith, either that they are too busy themselves or that they do not want to burden their senators and representatives with trivia. Instead, they say that they want to wait until they have something "really important" to request, and they promise that they will follow through then.

If taken at face value, their explanations might be reasonable. It is our judgment, however, that they are merely afraid that they might look foolish if they called on their elected representatives for what would be essentially a social visit. As we indicated earlier, such an avoidance response is dysfunctional at best and reflects a significant lack of understanding of the political process. It is the elected officials' responsibility to make them feel at home. In addition, visits and letters from behavioral health advocates *before* a crisis occurs will assure that there never will be that one "critical vote"; instead, all of the important issues will be satisfactorily resolved at the subcommittee level.

As those concerned with behavioral health begin to interact regularly with their elected officials on a person-to-person basis, they will soon come to appreciate that health issues are merely one item on the elected officials' agenda. That elected officials really have minimal (and generally transient) interest in the views of a national professional association will also become clear. Politicians are continually interested, however, in the views of *individuals* from their legislative district who may happen to belong to a professional association. When elected officials desire recommendations or a position statement from a national association in order to further one of their own political priorities, they know very well how to obtain them.

National professional associations can and do perform an excellent service to their membership by arranging initial meetings with elected officials. (After the first visit, it is hoped that one will arrange his or her own subsequent meetings through the elected official's staff.) The national associations also alert health care professionals to pending health care legislative issues and the associations' priorities. The crucial element, however, is the individual constituent's involvement, not the concerns of the national associations. (The corollary conclusion is that a behavioral health expert can have little impact on those elected officials who do not directly represent him or her—for example, those from another state or district). In the best of all worlds, your elected officials would ask you to serve as their liaison to your professional association. We suggest that the aforementioned fundamentally symbiotic relationship between elected officials and individual health care professionals is probably considerably different from what most health care professionals would have anticipated.

2. Involve Your Natural Allies: There Is Strength in Numbers

It has been our experience that most of the fundamental policy issues of prime importance to those who believe in behavioral health are of equal significance to consumers, nonphysician health care providers, and those who pay for our nation's health care services. Yet potentially powerful coalitions with shared interests have unfortunately never materialized. From a public policy perspective, some of the essence of behavioral health involves requirements for accountability and the use of cost-benefit analyses, establishment of health priorities and maintenance of a balanced portfolio of health initiatives, and targeting of limited resources. This is an agenda that many can support.

As we have indicated, however, these logical coalitions have not evolved. Certified nurse-midwives and clinical psychologists, for example, both seek hospital admitting privileges so that they may practice to the full extent allowed by their respective state practice acts. Each profession has pursued this goal independently on both state and national levels, and each profession cites impressive data suggesting that, in their respective specialities, they are cost-effective and preferred by consumers. Yet they have not acted as a unified force. Similarly, coalitions have not developed between our nation's optometrists and physical therapists to eliminate various Veterans Administration policies requiring that their professional services ultimately be under the responsibility of a physician, even though physicians do not have formal training in either optometry or physical therapy. Both the legal profession and the mental health community are intimately involved in issues surrounding mental competency and disability determinations, yet their respective national associations rarely testify together.

A concrete example of the extent to which our nation's health care professionals do not intuitively think of interdisciplinary cooperation was illustrated by Overcast and Sales (1981). After surveying all of the relevant state statutes, they reported that only in California (and perhaps, by a liberal statutory interpretation, in Nebraska) have state psychology statutes been modified to allow establishment of interdisciplinary health care corporations.

Similarly, health promotion and disease prevention specialists should find natural partners among administrators. Those who oversee the purchase of services—such as state social services programs, workers' compensation programs, industrial employee health benefit plans, and so forth—should know that it is in their economic interest to insure or purchase only cost-effective and efficacious therapies. Accordingly, to the extent that preventive efforts (or mental health services, or care provided by alternative providers) can objectively reduce overall health care costs, these services should logically be given priority. With limited resources, it makes good business sense to attempt to maximize the health care benefits of one's beneficiaries or employees.

If only psychologists (or only optometrists) approach unions or chambers of commerce, their concerns can be (and historically have been) dismissed as being parochial or guild-specific. If the more basic issues of accountability and cost-effectiveness are raised by a coalition of concerned alternative health care providers and consumers, however, a critical mass should evolve, and these key issues will be addressed seriously. Once this dialogue begins, those who are interested in behavioral health should be in good stead.

3. Cultivate the Media: They Are Potentially Your Best Allies

If we take the time to reflect on how we as individual members of society learn about developments in our local community (or, for another example, about foreign affairs), we will quickly conclude that it is through the media—both print and electronic. Syndicated columnists and news anchorpersons attempt to shape our views. The very process of selecting topics for discussion ultimately shapes what we think about collectively. The media, in a very real sense, creates the social/political agendas of our era and gives them credibility. Stuart Eizenstat described how the media play a major role in shaping and defining political "crises." In discussing the enactment of Medicaid and the kidney dialysis program in particular, for example, he responded to a question regarding the allocation of financial resources by stating:

> They get made without considering priorities . . . and are often made in response to direct pressure on the Congress. That is the frustration of dealing with the public policy issues. Medicaid . . . was not created with the sort of careful review and analysis that ought to have been done. The dialysis program was created in a similar fashion. . . . There were some news reports about people who were dying because they could not afford dialysis. The problem was crying out for a solution, and, of course, the solution was "let the federal government pay for it." . . . There were some sensational cases. . . . There was a felt need, so a dialysis program was created. I do not think anybody sat down and said "where else should we put this billion dollars." That's not how the system works. Without the public stimulus, that billion dollars would not have been spent. (Bevan, 1982)

For the health care professional who is interested in behavioral health, the media are especially important. Most Americans do not really think about health care until they are clinically ill. There is a clear interest among the public at large in remaining healthy, however, as evidenced by the popularity of numerous diet fads and jogging extravaganzas. In fact, Secretary of Health and Human Services Richard Schweiker recently pointed out:

> Americans are spending $5 billion on health foods and vitamins, $50 million on diet and exercise books, $5 billion on health and fitness clubs, and $8 billion on sporting gear. And that's just the start—the list goes on from $6 billion spent for diet drinks to $1 billion for bicycling equipment. Obviously Americans want desperately to be fit. They'll work and pay for it. (Schweiker, Note 3)

If the clinical techniques of behavioral health are even nearly as effective as we expect, one must assume that the American public will respond enthusiastically, as long as behavioral health is presented in a credible and fashionable light by the media.

If one considers why there is not more media coverage of the advancements developed by behavioral scientists, one should not be surprised to learn that "behavioral science issues or topics are, in fact, covered more than 'hard science.' The nature of behavioral science is such that it frequently is not covered by science writers per se and appears more as feature articles or human interest stories concerning common social problems" (Russell, Note 4).

Furthermore, science and health writers are (somewhat surprisingly) frustrated by the fact that behavioral science findings frequently are not made available to them—and when they are, the potential implications for real world issues often are not made clear. News releases should point out potential implications and indicate how they relate to current public issues. Science seminars should be held at which members of the media can hear first-hand about ongoing research endeavors and expected findings. There are only a finite number of science and health reporters, and these individuals can be identified readily.

When Russell (Note 4) was asked how behavioral health professionals might be more effective in influencing the media, her message was clearly "reach out"—telephone them, visit them, make sure that your national scientific/professional associations inform them of recent important research findings. What a tremendous opportunity for our university departments (and perhaps state associations of all disciplines)! These institutions and organizations should take the lead in developing targeted seminars or public policy meetings at which media representatives and behavioral health professionals have an orchestrated opportunity to interact and exchange ideas. Again, our underlying message should be clear: those who wish to influence the public policy process must take the lead and develop personal contacts. From these contacts, mutually beneficial creative exchanges will evolve (McCall, 1984).

We have every reason to believe that media representatives would welcome such opportunities. Although there never seems to be sufficient time available, the media are always interested in new ideas, interesting developments, and the like. One should never forget that everyone (including our nation's elected and appointed public policy leaders as well as our behavioral health professionals) is personally influenced by what is reported by the media. The health care agenda that the media collectively places before us is a significant part of our nation's health care agenda.

4. Write for an Audience Wider Than Your Own Profession

This fourth step may seem somewhat redundant, since the underlying message is essentially the same (i.e., educate the public and do not limit yourself to addressing only your professional colleagues). We have learned, however, especially with behavioral scientists, that there seems to be an almost unconscious belief that "if I can only survive all of the hurdles in having an article published, then the entire world will read it." We are being facetious to some extent, but less than one might imagine. It is amazing, for example, how slowly we have taught psychologists (who are sincerely interested in public policy development) that having someone from their own profession address a dinner meeting of psychologists is simply not the same as inviting the chairperson of the health committee in the state legislature.

The skills required to write for professional peers may or may not be different from those required to write for lay audiences. There can be no question, however, that the terminology used and the actual scope of the subject matter in articles addressed to these two types of audiences should be drastically different.

It has been our observation that there is no shortage of potential readership markets. One could write for the newsletters or journals of other professions, such as the *Barrister* of the Young Lawyers, for one's local newspapers, or even for *Harper's* magazine. The most important element is to write and share one's experiences and views with the nonconverted. Health care professionals in general (and those interested in behavioral health in particular) should stop naively assuming that the rest of the world possesses their educational background or is in any way even remotely aware of their aspirations to modify our currently illness-oriented health care system. If we hope ultimately to make consumers responsible for their own health habits, we must provide them with sufficient information to make reasoned decisions. As a first step, they must begin to appreciate that decisions are being made.

5. Demonstrate the Clinical and Societal Value of Behavioral Health

No matter how much effort those interested in behavioral health may ultimately exert in developing grass roots support for their approach, if behavioral health does not have demonstrable clinical benefit to consumers, it will not fare well in the resulting public policy examination. The various approaches to public policy or political process that we have described in this chapter are all predicated on the assumption that behavioral health does have something unique to offer. No matter how sincere or well intended they may be, enthusiasm and rhetoric can only accomplish so much. They can insure that our nation's health policy leaders will give behavioral health a close and thorough examination, but the results of that examination will depend largely (if not entirely) on the substantive clinical value of behavioral health. This is as it should be, and we are confident that our nation's behavioral health scientists and practitioners will succeed eventually.

Historically, our collective professions have demonstrated a clear willingness to experiment with, modify, and ultimately adopt creative approaches to health care. Our weakness has been not in the substantive aspects of health care but in taking the step of sharing with others (including both the public at large and our nation's health care leadership) what we have learned.

There are no one or two particular changes in our laws, regulations, or customs that would in themselves bring us into our second public health revolution. This is an evolutionary process. However, effective participation in the political process by those supportive of behavioral health could accelerate the outcome.

In many ways, it may appear that our nation does not yet really have a national health care policy, except that we consciously allow individual consumers and practitioners to select the type of care that they feel is appropriate. As a nation, we possess tremendous diversity, and we pride ourselves on this. Those who are interested in behavioral health are not proposing, nor could we propose, that only our approach should be made available to the public. We are proposing, instead, that behavioral health be granted its due accord, based on its demonstrated clinical value.

CONCLUSION

The development of behavioral health activities has been an evolutionary process that has now brought our nation to the threshold of our second public health revolution. During the current and immediately preceding administrations, the highest levels of our nation's health leadership in the executive branch have spoken out forcefully in favor of prevention and various behavioral health initiatives. There are also significant indications that these innovative efforts are beginning to receive considerable and enthusiastic support within our broad health community.

It is also our impression, however, that our nation is simultaneously continuing on a qualitatively different evolutionary course—one that ultimately will result in the enactment by the Congress of a national health insurance (NHI) program. The driving force behind this movement is primarily economic pressure: our nation's health care costs are continuing to rise faster than nearly any other segment of our economy, and there does not appear to be any solution in sight. Furthermore, it is our judgment that a careful review of the political and economic pressures on the various national legislatures of the other industrialized nations of the world that existed when they enacted their own NHI programs would suggest that our nation is rapidly approaching a similar situation. It is important for our nation's health care professionals to realize that the ultimate decision of whether or not to enact a comprehensive NHI program will be made by the Congress and not by the health community or the executive branch.

Throughout this chapter, we have tried to provide the reader with an appreciation for how our nation's elected officials respond to the various pressures on them, and specifically for how those scientists and practitioners who are interested in behavioral health could contribute personally to the Congress' understanding and appreciation of the long-term importance of behavioral health initiatives. We do not feel that the Congress has yet begun to appreciate the importance of behavioral health. Accordingly, if those who support behavioral health do not become personally involved in the political process, then we must predict that as health care costs continue to escalate, the status quo will become even more firmly entrenched—that is, it will become even more difficult to modify definitions of who should be deemed independent providers and what types of services should ultimately be reimbursed. Eventually, we expect behavioral health to flourish because of its clinical importance. In the meantime, however, unless our nation's politicians are educated as to its effectiveness, we must expect the political process to impede the acceptance at the policy level of behavioral health initiatives, as the finite nature of our nation's health care resources becomes more evident.

The alternative (and what we hope will evolve) is that those who are interested in behavioral health will become actively involved in the political process and, by so doing, will make behavioral health an integral component in the Congress' health care agenda. To accomplish this objective, behavioral health advocates will have to develop personal relationships with their elected officials and with the media. Health care professionals have for too long shunned their societal responsibility to become active participants in the political process. We should never forget that it is our nation's politicians at both the state and federal levels (and indirectly, through their collective judgment, the public at large) who ultimately establish health care policy in our nation, not the health community or our respective professional associations.

REFERENCE NOTES

1. U.S. Senate, Report No. 97–516, accompanying the Supplemental Appropriations Bill, 1982. H.R. 6863, August 3, 1982.
2. Grupenhoff, J. T. *The Congress: Turnover rates of members and staff who deal with medicine/health/biomedical research issues.* Communication No. 1, Science and Health Communications Group, Fall 1982.
3. Schweiker, R. S. Remarks before the American Nurses Association, March 23, 1982.
4. Russell, C. Remarks before APA Division 38/12 Public Policy Committee, April 22, 1982.

REFERENCES

Bevan, W. National policy and human welfare: A conversation with Stuart Eizenstat. *American Psychologist,* 1982, **37.**

Brandt, E. N. Prevention policy and practice in the 1980s. *American Psychologist,* 1982, **37.**

DeLeon, P. H., & VandenBos, G. R. Psychotherapy reimbursement in federal programs: Political factors. In G. R. VandenBos (Ed.), *Psychotherapy: Practice, research, policy.* Beverly Hills: Sage, 1980.

Department of Health, Education and Welfare (DHEW). *Healthy people: The Surgeon General's report on health promotion and disease prevention.* DHEW Pub. No. (PHS) 79–55071. Washington, D.C.: U.S. Government Printing Office, 1979.

Dorris, W. L., & McGuire, T. G. Federal involvement with mental-health services: An evaluation of the community mental health center program. In S. H. Altman & H. M. Sapolsky (Eds.), *Federal health programs: Problems and prospects,* Lexington, Mass.: Lexington Books, D. C. Heath, 1981.

Hamburg, D. A., Elliott, G. R., & Parron, D. L. (Eds.). *Health and behavior: Frontiers of research in the biobehavioral sciences.* Washington, D.C.: National Academy Press, 1982.

Kiesler, C. A. Mental health policy as a field of inquiry for psychology. *American Psychologist,* 1980, **35,** 1066–1080.

Kiesler, C. A. Mental hospitals and alternative care: Noninstitutionalization as potential public policy for mental patients. *American Psychologist,* 1982, **37,** 349–360.

Lalonde, M. *A new perspective on the health of Canadians: A working document.* Ottawa: Government of Canada, 1974.

McCall, R. B., Gregory, T. G., & Murray, J. P. Communicating developmental research results to the general public through television. *Developmental Psychology,* 1984, **20,** 45–54.

Michael, J. M. The second revolution in health: Health promotion and its environmental base. *American Psychologist,* 1982, **37,** 936–941.

Overcast, T. D., & Sales, B. D. Psychological and multidisciplinary corporations. *Professional Psychology,* 1981, **12,** 749–760.

CHAPTER 10

BEHAVIORAL HEALTH ACROSS CULTURES

ROGELIO DIAZ-GUERRERO

National University of Mexico

In Salvat's *Spanish Encyclopedia*, health (*salud*) is defined as "the state in which the organic being exercises normally all of its natural functions." I was amused to find the following definition for health in the *Encyclopedia Britannica:* "a condition of physical soundness or well being in which an organism discharges its functions efficiently." Either the concept of health is the same in cultures as dissimilar as the Spanish and the English, or encyclopedia writers tend to copy from each other. The question underlying this apparently trivial finding is quite serious, however. Is there a universal conception of health, or should we have multiple envisionings of what is denoted and connoted by the idea of health? In Spanish, *salud* is the root of the verb *saludar* and the substantive *saludos,* which translate "to greet" and "greetings." It is as though, in the Spanish tradition, everybody should be wishing good health to everybody else whenever they meet. Although this might be merely another example of what cross-cultural psychologists have demonstrated (that affiliation has greater importance in traditional than in industrialized societies), the behavior of wishing health to others, though Greco-Roman in origin (as the Greeks and Romans drank originally to the health of the gods) using *salud* or "to your health" in toasting, as is done in Anglo-American and other European societies, may show a Western concern with the health of others, even if it is done at the cost of the drinker's health.

At any rate, if, as we shall see later, the concept of health has been found by research procedures to be fairly universal and consistently positive, the concept of behavioral health, as recently defined by Matarazzo (1980) and as used fundamentally in this book, is certainly unique and indicates definite progress over our earlier notions of mental health, public health, and even medical psychology. Medical psychology has made striking progress in several Latin American countries, including Peru, Mexico, and particularly Cuba. Bustamante (1968) describes the very large extent to which psychology has influenced medical studies and physicians. Every graduate physician has undergone psychological diagnosis and guidance or has participated in what Bustamante calls working groups, experiencing psychological group therapy. Psychology in Cuba, under Bustamante, has been fully integrated with the training for and practice of medicine. Even such an impressive accomplishment is not what behavioral health propounds, however. One has to conclude that, up to the present, behavioral health in most underdeveloped and developing countries—and to some extent in the developed countries—has remained in the province of medical folklore and medical tradition. It is also quite likely that, given the differential nature of individuality and the self, as we shall discuss, behavioral health that stresses individual responsibility for the prevention, maintenance, and furtherance of good health in otherwise healthy people will have to undergo a mutation, particularly in the more traditional societies.

The pre-Hispanic codices dealing with the divinities give the impression that it was hard to separate one divinity from another, that there was a close relationship between them and an important participation of certain attributes. Also, pre-Columbian societies give a strong impression of what in biology is called syncytium—that is, a mass of protoplasm with a large number of nuclei. One or more nuclei may be destroyed, but the mass of protoplasm will continue to live. Tanaka Matsumi and Marsella (1976), who studied the experience of depression in Japanese nationals, found that this condition was associated with external references, such as rain and clouds, and with somatic references, such as headache and fatigue. In contrast, Caucasian-Americans and Japanese-Americans associated the concept predominantly with internal mood states, such as sadness and loneliness. They attributed these differences to variations in the self-structure that mediates subjective experience. The Japanese self-structure was considered to be essentially unindividuated, whereas the American self-structure was considered to be fundamentally individuated. In a recent study (Diaz-Guerrero, 1982), focusing on the Mexican sense of self as compared with that of people from 19 different cultural-linguistic groups with the semantic differential, shows that the Mexican subjects scored lowest in evaluation and were among the lowest in potency. However, if the sense of self-worth were to be evaluated in the context of family, parents, older brothers, ceremonial events, and large monuments, we would expect much higher scores on evaluation and potency. These findings, in a developing society and in a developed but also traditional society such as Japan, illustrate that although developing behavioral health worldwide has to be an individual effort, Americans may individually search actively for information of this type, whereas Mexicans and persons in other traditional cultures may initially have to be introduced to behavioral health in groups, by teachers, parents, the church, the state, and so on. Actually, a good idea for marketing this Handbook internationally is to make parents aware that, by reading it, they can help the development of behavioral health in their children.

CROSS-CULTURAL PSYCHOLOGY AND BEHAVIORAL HEALTH

For our present purposes, it is unfortunate that the *International Journal of Social Psychiatry,* inaugurated in 1954, and the *British Journal of Social Psychiatry,* which emerged in 1966, dedicate themselves fundamentally to pathology rather than to health. As I prepared this chapter, having scanned the first of these journals for many years, I vividly recalled Marmor's (1966) paper on nationalism, internationalism, and emotional maturity. He wrote that for an individual to reach emotional maturity (mental health at its best), an open internationalism, with a recognition of the relativistic nature of our own frame of reference, should be an important goal of an otherwise harmonious and developed personality.

The *Journal of Cross-Cultural Psychology* has completed 13 years of publication, but its subject matter has seldom been the study of health and never behavioral health across cultures. These two subjects deserve special attention, however. The journal has the goal of being international and interdisciplinary, and despite these early omissions in its content, the quality is high. I am certain, therefore, that it will accept papers dealing with behavioral health across cultures.

Korten (1971) published a content-analytical study of survival strategies in Ethiopian folktales. He found that the survival strategies in Ethiopia are based on self-protection, deception, and revenge, aimed either at maintaining the status quo or advancing oneself at the expense of others. He also reports that perceived opportunities for initiative and cooperation in service to the community are limited and that personal efficacy (one's personal effectiveness in imagined, future situations) is perceived on the basis of interpersonal exchanges rather than in exchanges with the impersonal and the environment. A curious and relevant study on the sleep–wakefulness cycle in Mexican adults was contributed by Taub (1971), who used a questionnaire to study the sleep–wakefulness patterns of 257 Mexican males and females, ranging in age from the twenties to the eighties. He found that the average duration of sleep exceeded that prescribed in other Western cultures, which is 8 hours out of 24. Amount of sleep varied significantly with age, decreasing some from the twenties to the fifties and then increasing. In all the groups, the duration and frequency of daytime naps, sometimes lasting up to one hour and a half and occurring up to four times a week, revealed a pattern of sleep–wakefulness that the author considers not to be present in other Western cultures. What is the significance to behavioral health of greater or lesser amounts of sleep? According to Kleitman (1939, 1952) and others, it appears that lesser amounts of sleep than those reported by the Mexican population studied would be healthier, both physically and in providing the time necessary for individuals to undertake the care and maintenance of their individual health.

From my travels abroad—and recalling the statement provided by the seven savants of Greece for the Oracle of Delphos, "everything with moderation"—it appears that the behavioral prescription of moderation may be closest to what popular wisdom has advanced regarding behavioral health. Draguns (1973) in his "Comparisons of Psychopathology across Cultures," arrives at the notion that there is cultural plasticity of psychopathology and that cross-cultural studies converge in suggesting that psychopathology represents a caricature and an exaggeration of cultural norms and adaptive patterns of behavior. This may be a confirmation that moderation is one of the goals of behavioral health across cultures.

Tanaka Matsumi and Marsella (1976) and Marsella, Shizura, Brennan, and Kameoka (1981) provide interesting insights across cultures of a methodologically valid approach to the study of one of the archenemies of behavioral health—depression. In the first study, they found that depression is a different phenomenological experience for Americans and Japanese. In the second study by Marsella et al., on depression and body image satisfaction, they hypothesized, when comparing depressed and nondepressed males and females from Caucasian-American, Chinese-American, and Japanese-American college samples, that there would be higher levels of body image dissatisfaction in the depressed than the nondepressed respondents, regardless of ethnicity and gender. The results with 256 subjects supported their hypothesis. There were, however, clear cultural differences in dissatisfactions with specific body parts. Chinese-American males were more dissatisfied with height, hips, body hair, shoulders, and waist under the depression condition. Chinese-American females were particularly concerned with face and general physique, and Japanese-American males with waist, weight, hips, and height. For Japanese-American females, the preoccupation was with posture, hair, face, and nose. For the Caucasian-American males, neck, lips, complexion, and nose were primary concerns, whereas for the American females it was complexion, eyes, hair, and lips. Although the causal relationship, if any, seems to go from depression to body image, these results give an idea of the sources of satisfaction with the body that might lead to occasional depressive reactions. To improve one's behavioral health, therefore, physical exercise and some other techniques might be utilized.

Knight and Kagan (1977) reported on acculturation of prosocial and competitive behaviors among second- and third-generation Mexican-American children. The question is raised by these multicultural and often interdisciplinary studies of whether a cooperative or a competitive model is best for a person's behavioral health. In this study, it was found that the longer the acculturation process of the Mexican-American is to what appears to be the Anglo-American value system, the greater the decrease is in frequency of altruism, group enhancement, and equality choices and the greater the increase is in frequency of rivalry/superiority choices. This led the authors to the conclusion that the longer the Mexican-American remains in the Anglo-American culture, the more prominent becomes the acculturation to the majority (American) model rather than to the barrio (Mexican) model.

Sue, Zane, and Ito (1979) studied alcohol-drinking patterns among Asian and Caucasian-American students. Among other results, they found that Asians reported more moderate drinking; that amount of acculturation to the Angloamerican culture was positively related to drinking; that attitudes toward drinking were correlated to reported drinking and were more negative toward drinking in the case of Asians and their parents; and that Caucasian-

Americans reported more extensive use of cues in the regulation of their drinking. These results suggest the importance of cultural factors in regard to drinking patterns. Fliegel, Sofranko, Williams, and Sharma (1979) studied the relationship between technology and cultural convergence. They address themselves to the idea that basic changes currently taking place in modernizing societies are in most respects similar outcomes. They believe that the final effect will be a gradual erosion of differences among societies. In a critical effort, they studied 336 adult workers from oil-refining and cigarette-manufacturing industries, from a tobacco-growing concern, and from conventional farms. Selected workers performing the same tasks in these technologies in Ghana, Brazil, and India were the subjects. The Tucker and Messick (1963) "Points-of-View" technique, a cross-product form of analysis, was chosen to obtain individual scores on several perceptual dimensions. Fliegel et al. point out that the technique permits data from all the subjects ($n = 336$) on all 22 items to be considered jointly. Next, they used discriminant analysis to investigate how the prespecified groups were arrayed in terms of the perceptual spaces. Their findings did not provide support for the convergence hypothesis. They did not find any greater cross-national similarity in values among workers in the far more modern, capital-intensive technological settings than among workers in the less modern, labor-intensive settings.

In their longitudinal life span study of personality development in two cultures, covering 900 children in age groups between grades 1 and 12, Holtzman, Diaz-Guerrero, and Swartz (1975), after equating their groups and standardizing their measurement and sampling procedures, arrived at a number of findings relevant to a comprehensive behavioral health approach. Their study, along with later work by Diaz-Guerrero (1977, 1979, 1981), illustrated that the higher the alliance was to the traditional Mexican culture, the lower the cognitive intellectual development was. Associative learning is encouraged in Mexican children by the educational system, and in this ability they outdid their North American counterparts. In addition, these authors reported a number of mean differences in several personality variables and a very different response to many variables assessed by the Holtzman Inkblot Test. In a test of time perception, they asked each of their subjects to estimate when one minute had elapsed. They found that 1 minute and 38 seconds (1.64 minutes) passed before Mexicans felt that a minute passed and that 1 minute 16 seconds (1.27 minutes) passed before the North American children responded that a minute had passed. It was also found that time is perceived as passing more slowly (requiring more seconds) in younger children. Lower-class children, particularly females—who are the carriers of the traditional culture in Mexico—experienced the slowest time passing, whereas the lower class in the United States—which presumably carries the traditional American culture—experienced the fastest time passing of all groups. It would be very interesting to find out the relationship of behavioral health, as defined and illustrated in this Handbook, to the perception of time across cultures.

Noteworthy work on the worldwide phenomenon of anxiety has been done by Spielberger (1975), particularly his operationalization of trait and state anxiety and the efforts for its cross-cultural extension and validation (Spielberger & Diaz-Guerrero, 1976, in press).

After this review of a few relevant studies from cross-cultural psychology, it is appropriate to quote from an earlier, wise book edited by Paul (1955):

> If you wish to help a community improve its health you must learn to think like the people of that community. Before asking a group of people to assume new health habits, it is wise to ascertain the existing habits, how these habits are linked to one another, what functions they perform and what they mean to those who practice them. (p. 1)

Paul's book presents more than a dozen case studies, ranging from a comprehensive health program among South African Zulus to a nutritional research program in Guatemala, describing a large number of applications of health programs throughout the world, and ending with a scholarly review of concepts and contents. This book is must reading for any individual or group planning to develop or implement a behavioral health program. Although the book can be of much help to individual readers in the highly developed countries, it will probably help even more individuals and officials in other cultures, particularly those in the developing and underdeveloped countries, who have the responsibility to institute programs for groups and communities to carry out.

THE MEANING OF HEALTH—PROFESSIONALLY AND ACROSS CULTURES

A good description of four perspectives of normality is given by Offer and Sabshin (1974). The first concept, "normality as health," is the one used in clinical psychiatry. It merely refers to the absence of classifiable pathology. The second concept, "normality as utopia," dates from Freud's conception of normality as an ideal fiction. It is considered to be the view not only of psychodynamicists but of humanists, as when Rogers explains his paradigm of the fully functioning person or Goldstein and Maslow speak of self-actualization of potential. The third approach to normality, as average, is closely connected with the notion of normalcy as reflected in the bell-shaped curve of statistics. Here, both extremes of the curve are deviant. Finally, the authors discuss the concept of normality as a transactional system. Here, they refer to interdisciplinarity, to the concepts of process and development; and they quote Erikson's concept of the epigenesis of personality development, including the individual's successful mastery of Erikson's seven stages as essential to the achievement of normal adult functioning and maturity. Although these four concepts and one by Wendell Johnson (whose view postulates that it is normal to produce and create the maximum you can produce within the limitations of your body and personality and the circumstances that surround you) are all valuable in the understanding of what is normal, each of them is clearly lacking when we compare them with the interdisciplinary and multimodal concept of behavioral health.

For the purposes of this chapter, it probably will be of greater interest to the reader for me to report the results of a study regarding the meaning of health across 29 different language-cultures. Osgood (1971) and Osgood, May, and Myron (1975) fully describe the cross-cultural study and their measurement scales, on which the following discussion is based.[1]

Osgood, with Suci and Tannenbaum (1957) and using the Semantic Differential Scales procedure (Snider & Osgood, 1969) he developed, demonstrated that the subjective meaning of everyday concepts (such as big, car, health nurse, etc.) has three fundamental factorial dimensions: evaluation, potency, and activity. Later, with the help of the principal investigators and their colleagues and students in different countries (see Diaz-Guerrero & Salas, 1975; Osgood et al., 1975), he developed local semantic differentials—that is, an instrument to measure the three dimensions of meaning in the concepts or substantives that individuals use to describe their own psychological processes or any entity in the physical world.

The semantic differential (SD) is a measurement tool composed of 13 adjectival scales, such as:

Good . . . . Bad
Strong . . . . Weak
Fast . . . . Slow

Above the scales there is a concept, such as HEALTH. The participants place a cross in the space between the adjectives that express their best guess about the significance of the

---

[1] I am grateful to Osgood for his permission to use the results of the research and to May for his computer study.

concept for them. The scales were derived by factor analyses from 10,000 original adjectives. Four adjectival scales provide the score for the factor of evaluation and four each for potency and activity. The thirteenth scale, Familiar—Unfamiliar, provides a measure of how well the concept is known to the individual. As Osgood (1971) says:

> Successful demonstration of the universality of evaluation, potency and activity, as common dimensions along which all humans differentiate concept meanings provides at least a minimal basis for rigorous cross-cultural comparison. (p. 39)

It is this kind of comparison for the concept of health—its subjective meaning, synonymity, and antonymity—that we are going to undertake, using the printouts for the larger Atlas of Meanings in this study. To better understand these data, it is important to know that from 400 to 500 male adolescent high school students in groups of 40, from each of 30 cultures, judged some of the 600 concepts against 13 semantic differential adjectival scales. These scales were the result of a prior pancultural factor analysis. There were more than 9,000 bits of raw data for each locality as a result.

Table 10.1 gives the affective meaning of the concept of health in 30 language-locations for the standard evaluation (E-Z), the standard potency (P-Z), the standard activity (A-Z), and the standard degree of conflict produced by the concept (CI-Z). The interpretation of the numerical values shown in the table is as follows: 1 is good, potent, and active; 2 is very good, potent, and active; and 3 is extremely good, potent, and active. The negative values −1, −2, and −3 go from bad, weak, and passive to extremely bad, weak, and passive; and 0 is neutral. The conflict index, CI-Z, also goes from −3 to 3, where 3 represents the maximum of disagreement among subjects in a sample about the subjective meaning of a concept and −3 is the least possible disagreement or lowest conflict index.

It can be seen that the concept of health is positively evaluated throughout this sample of the nations and languages in the world, with the only exception being the Greek subjects. This unexpected result may be due to a bad translation of the word *health* or to some very specific meaning of the concept of health in modern Greece. It would be hard to accept that the descendants of the culture that promoted the beautiful platonic concept of health and the concept of the healthy body, healthy mind would now consider that health is bad. The researchers at the Central Station in Illinois, with the help of the Greek principal investigator who studied the seemingly deviant Greek subjects, helped us understand this contrary result. It is immediately observable in the first row of Table 10.1 that for the French subjects, health is highly evaluated, reasonably potent, and very active. The consistent view that health is good, potent, and active is found only in the Magyar from Hungary, in Italians in Italy, and in Serbo-Croatians in Yugoslavia. It would appear that only where there are socialistic and communistic parties in action is the concept of health considered good, potent, and active. The American subjects and the subjects in Calcutta join this group, however, with consistently positive evaluation, potency, and activity and also with low to very low conflict index, indicating that the subjects in all these nations were agreed that this was the proper subjective meaning of the concept of health among their citizens. We have to discount the Spanish-speaking subjects from Yucatan, since they were adults, and health appears more important to these adults of Mayan descent than to the adolescents in Mexico City.

There is also a trend that the better off a country is economically, the higher the evaluation of the concept of health, but there are some exceptions, such as that in the Dari language of Afghanistan. (The study was carried out in the 1960s, but the Dari-speaking subjects of Persian descent were supposedly better off economically than the Pashtu Hindi-Moslem speakers). Although the Delhi Hindi group evaluates health as moderately good, neutral in potency, and quite active, it joins the Mysore Kannada-speakers in showing significant conflict about the concept of health. India, with its large population and many nutritional problems appears not to take easily to the idea of health. The Hungarian Magyar subjects

Table 10.1　The Subjective Meaning of Health Across Cultures

Location	Language	E-Z	P-Z	A-Z	CI-Z
France	French	1.8	0.8	2.0	−0.3
Belgium	Flemish	1.1	0.0	−0.2	−1.6
Netherlands	Dutch	1.7	0.2	0.2	−0.3
Germany	German	1.2	0.1	0.1	0.0
Sweden	Swedish	1.4	0.3	0.5	−1.5
Finland	Finnish	1.3	0.3	0.9	−1.3
U.S. (white)	English	1.2	1.4	1.5	−1.6
U.S. (black)	English	1.0	0.2	−0.4	−0.5
Yucatan (Mexico)	Spanish	1.2	1.3	1.3	−0.7
Mexico	Spanish	1.1	1.1	0.5	−0.9
Costa Rica	Spanish	0.9	0.5	0.8	−1.5
Brazil	Portuguese	0.9	0.3	0.1	−0.4
Hungary	Magyar	1.3	2.0	1.1	−0.9
Rumania	Rumanian				
Yugoslavia	Serbo-Croatian	1.3	1.1	1.3	−0.9
Italy	Italian	1.5	1.3	1.2	−1.7
Greece	Greek	−1.7	0.2	−0.1	−0.8
Israel	Hebrew	1.3	0.3	0.5	−1.0
Turkey	Turkish	0.6	−0.2	1.1	−0.4
Lebanon	Arabic	0.8	0.9	0.0	−1.0
Iran	Farsi	1.2	0.8	0.8	−1.7
Afghanistan	Dari	1.5	0.2	0.3	−0.9
Afghanistan	Pashtu	0.7	0.5	0.5	−0.4
Delhi (India)	Hindi	1.1	0.1	1.6	0.8
Calcutta (India)	Bengali	0.9	1.4	1.3	−0.9
Mysore (India)	Kannada	0.1	1.1	0.1	1.8
Malaysia	Malay	0.9	0.2	0.8	−0.6
Thailand	Thai	1.1	0.6	0.1	−1.2
Hong Kong	Cantonese	1.4	1.6	0.9	−1.1
Japan	Japanese	1.9	−0.4	1.5	−1.2
Mean		1.1	0.6	0.7	−0.8
Standard deviation		0.6	0.6	0.6	0.8

Key: E-Z = standardized evaluation; P-Z = standardized potency; A-Z = standardized activity; CI-Z = standardized conflict index.

stick out from the entire multinational group in the significantly higher potency of their citizens' subjective perception of health. For the Mexican subjects, health is moderately good and potent but not sufficiently active—a call to their health authorities.

In the Osgood et al. (1975) study, the following 24 concepts were classified in the health-sickness category, and semantic differential responses were collated for the 30 language-locations. In alphabetical order, the concepts were ACCIDENT, BATH, CANCER, CLEANLINESS, DEATH, DISEASE, DOCTOR, DRUNKENNESS, FAT, FILTH, GROWING UP, HEALTH, HOSPITAL, HUNGER, INSANE (PATIENT), LIFE MEDICINE, NEUROTIC (PATIENT), NURSE, PAIN, PATIENT, POISON, SICKNESS, and SUICIDE. Although not shown in Table 10.1, it is reassuring that in evaluation, the multiple correlation for these concepts across the 30 language-locations was .89 and highly significant. There is large variation, however, regarding the subjective meaning for their potency across cultures. The mean correlation is only .38 and does not reach significance. The correlation of activity for the health-sickness category is .42, just above the .05 level of significance.

For potency in the subjective meaning of the health-sickness category, the correlations between nations, as expected, are very often low and sometimes negative. Although not shown in Table 10.1, the subjects from Thailand have the most negative correlations including correlations of −.22 with Yugoslavia and −.23 with the Afghanistan Pashtu language. What the correlation of −.22 means is that in assigning subjective meaning on the dimension of potency to the category (health-sickness), the citizens of Thailand and Yugoslavia rated the same list of concepts in opposite directions. Generally, the amount of power that is attributed to the concept of HEALTH across these language-locations varies greatly, probably indicative of the different concern that governments and communities throughout the world place on the importance of health. There is much that this Handbook, government institutions, and communities can do in this area.

Regarding the activity attributed to the concepts in the health-sickness category, the white American English group correlates in the plus eighties with the French, the Italian, and, surprisingly, the Iranian Farsi groups. It correlates in the seventies with the Mexican Spanish, Costa Rican Spanish, Hungarian, Israeli, Turkish, Afghanistan Pashtu, and Calcutta Bengali groups. In the low end, the same health-sickness concepts as rated by white American English-speakers correlate at zero with the Brazilian Portuguese, −.07 with the Lebanese Arabic, only .23 with the Delhi Hindi, and −.35 with the black Americans. The black American English sample, however, must have had some difficulty with the activity dimension of the health-sickness category, for its correlations are negative with 20 of the 30 countries— its highest negative correlation, −.61, being with the Afghanistan Pashtu group. Equal in number, although with less magnitude, are the 20 negative correlations of the Lebanese Arabic group against all other national groups—the largest, −.39, being with the Malaysians and with the Hong Kong Chinese.

It is interesting to observe the ranking in evaluation of the 24 health-sickness category concepts across the world. With an average ranking of 3.2 on a scale from 1 to 24, HEALTH is the first and most universally high-ranked concept in these 30 culture-language locations. In the second and third ranks out of 24, and also universally, we find the concepts of CLEANLINESS and BATH, followed by a high and universally evaluated concept of NURSE. CANCER is the most negatively ranked concept of the 24 (ranking 22.6). Next lowest was the concept SUICIDE, which ranked an average of 20.7. Immediately above these lowest evaluated concepts are the concepts POISON and FILTH, which, however, are not so ranked universally. ACCIDENT and SICKNESS follow as universally low-ranked concepts in evaluation. It is surprising that somewhat far above these (in 16th average rank) we universally find the concepts of DEATH, INSANITY, and HUNGER.

In potency the concept of HEALTH is in the 4th rank, preceded by HOSPITAL, CANCER, and DOCTOR, in that order. When HEALTH or HEALTH BEHAVIOR occupies the first rank in potency, it may finally be above DOCTOR and HOSPITAL across the world.

In the subjective meaning of activity, the concept of HEALTH occupies the second place among all the concepts, preceded only by NURSE. It is important to point out that in amount of conflict—that is, in the extent of disagreement across nations about the concept—HEALTH occupies the lowest rank among all the concepts across nations (i.e., there was least variation around this concept). Thus, HEALTH is a significantly universal concept; that is, on the average, it tends to be lowest in conflict across all the samples in the world. One may conclude that humans do have a highly evaluated, quite potent and active, and well agreed-upon concept of health across cultures.

Concerning the distance in the semantic space of these concepts—that is, how synonymic or antonymic in subjective meaning they are—we find that whereas for the white American English group the closest (most related) concepts among the 24 of the health-sickness category are LIFE and HEALTH and also PAIN and DRUNKENNESS, the farthest (least related) are SICKNESS and HEALTH as well as SICKNESS and LIFE. This differs in the synonymic and antonymic perceptions of the black American English group, for which the three closest concepts are HEALTH and DOCTOR and HUNGER and the two farthest are POISON and MEDICINE. Additionally, for the Mexican Spanish group, MEDICINE and HEALTH and also GROWING and DOCTOR are closest, and the farthest are NURSE and CANCER plus NURSE and DISEASE. An important finding in this research is that, across the world, the subjective synonyms of HEALTH are, first, LIFE and then GROWTH, DOCTOR, and NURSE, in that order. The strongest antonyms of HEALTH are FILTH, followed by CANCER and SUICIDE.

HISTORICAL, ANTHROPOLOGICAL, AND SOCIOLOGICAL VIEWS OF HEALTH

Behavioral health is a new concept (Matarazzo, 1980), but some idea about being healthy and remaining healthy must have existed even in Neolithic times, since circular holes have been found in skulls, apparently used in the process of healing as practiced by early healers. In the 26th century B.C., the Chinese thought that illness resulted from alienation from the natural order of the universe and that health resulted from being in harmony with it. In Greece, the dialogues of Plato set the stage for many views—that health consists in complete inner harmony and the achievement of the highest moral behavior and philosophical knowledge. Possibly Democritus came closest to the conception of behavioral health when he said: "Men pray to their Gods for health; they do not realize that they have control of it themselves."

As many historians of medicine point out, from the time of Galen, the search for localized illness, rather than the generalized concepts of health and disease, took precedence, until psychosomatic medicine, as a modern specialty, stressed the importance of psychological processes in health and disease. It is with a holistic view of health and disease that health science has made its greatest strides. This type of thinking has led to more universally agreed-upon definitions of health, such as the one adopted in 1946 by the World Health Organization (WHO): "Health is a state of complete physical, mental and social well being and is not merely the absence of disease or infirmity."

The enthusiasm engendered in the last few years by the holistic approach, by the discoveries of biofeedback, and by the impact on health from learning and other psychological processes, has led not only to a greater interest in medical psychology but to new disciplines, such as behavioral medicine and health psychology. Matarazzo (1980) points out that these terms have become synonymous with *behavioral health,* but he characterizes them as quite different disciplines. Behavioral medicine focuses its major interest on intervention, or treating illness and dysfunction, whereas behavioral health is concerned with the opposite end of the illness-health continuum in helping to keep currently healthy children and adults healthy. That each of these disciplines is rapidly progressing is shown in such recent publications as Melamed and Siegel's *Behavioral Medicine* (1980) and Stone, Cohen, and Adler's *Health Psychology: A Handbook* (1980). Offer and Sabshin (1974) and Stone, Cohen, and Adler (1980) dedicate large sections to historical, anthropological, and sociological approaches to the concepts of normality and health and should be consulted by readers who are interested in more detail.

In this chapter on behavioral health cross-culturally, I have given some of the main characteristics of the conceptualization of health by anthropologists and sociologists. As Offer and Sabshin (1974) point out, most anthropologists and sociologists shy away from defining "normal." They apparently wish to avoid such a value-laden and "moral" subject. Anthropology has the older cultural relativity position, which considers all behavior as relative to its particular cultural context and stresses that no form of behavior is abnormal in all cultures. Benedict (1934, 1964), however, and Linton (1939, 1959) and Kardiner (1945) tended to combine a culturally relativistic concept with universalistic elements. Munroe and Munroe (1980) state that the expectation that Western psychological findings would frequently be valid at the cross-cultural level was strongly supported by their review. They add, however, that enough exceptions have appeared such that no claim can be made for a simple translation of Western research or universal applicability of its findings across cultures but conclude that the generalizability of much of Western research has proved sufficiently robust that the idea of a "radical cultural relativism" appears outmoded. Wegrocki (1939) tried early to resolve the dilemma of the cultural relativity of abnormal behavior. He believed that if abnormality is considered to be the tendency to choose a type of reaction that leads to escape from a conflict-producing situation instead of facing the problem, much behavior that is considered abnormal is not such if it is the culturally valid response to that specific situation. He mentions the running-amok behavior of the Malaysians and the *defense de toucher* of the Polynesians as examples of behavior that most cultures define as abnormal but that are perfectly normal in these two cultures. Thus, the only way to classify a behavior as abnormal or normal is by delving into its individual and cultural meaning.

Sociologists, among them Merton and Parsons, appear far more interested in assessing the social structures and environmental contexts that elicit behavior than they are in evaluating individual behavior. Thus, Parsons (1958) indicates that we must examine the social structures to determine their significance in promoting the individual's optimum social capacity. Health, therefore, is seen in terms of the structures in society that will promote or hinder it. A truly meaningful concept of behavioral health will thus have to take into account some aspect of cultural relativity.

CULTURAL VERSUS SCIENTIFIC BELIEFS IN DETERMINING HEALTH BEHAVIOR

Almost all people in a traditional society are influenced by their mothers' and grandmothers' experiences and beliefs about disease. Nevertheless, the words *cold* in English and *enfriamiento* in Spanish testify to a very generalized belief that catarrh and flu will be contracted only if we are exposed to winds or cold temperatures. Most physicians that I know still hold to the somewhat more systematized belief that a long exposure to a very cold temperature will diminish the immune response of the individual to flu viruses. Despite the universality of the belief that coldness produces flu, I know of no systematic experimental study, not even with rats or other animals that would be susceptible to the flu virus, in which both experimental and control animals were exposed to the virus but only the experimentals were exposed for variable periods of time to cold temperatures.

While preparing this chapter, I came across Ringler's (1981) *Dictionary of Medical Folklore*. It is interesting that the author not only lists the traditional sociocultural medical beliefs but also tries to find out from reliable medical sources the extent to which these beliefs are or are not based on truth. Thus, we find in the list such oldies as "cleanliness is next to Godliness." The author goes on to point out, however, that cleanliness may in fact lead to itchiness and declares that daily baths may be too drying for certain skins, particularly in cold weather. She fails to mention the number of allergic reactions to many advertised brands of soaps and does not mention that nonallergenic and neutral soaps may be required in a number of cases. This author also analyzes the comment "She died of a broken heart," referring to the belief that a person might die soon after the death of a loved one. She states definitely that the heart pulse has nothing to do with such a death following bereavement, as the heart does not break. She reports a study published in *Lancet* in which the researchers studied 26 persons whose husband or wife had recently died. All the subjects showed suppression of various aspects of their immune system as well as an alteration in hormone levels. The researchers concluded that grief affects some persons so strongly that it makes them susceptible to death from infections or other physical malfunctions, but not heart dysfunction. This is pertinent to the studies on the accumulation of life changes reported by Holmes and Rahe (1967, unpublished), their Schedule of Recent

Experiences, and each person's score in life change units. This study, and many modern efforts to understand stress and the development of physical illness are treated exhaustively by Cohen (1979).

Another traditional belief cited in Rinzler's (1981) dictionary involves the strange food cravings considered normal during pregnancy. The author points out that such cravings are common, but whether they are normal is still a matter of great discussion. She reports that the desire of poor southern mothers to eat clay during pregnancy has been attributed to an iron deficiency, whereas a craving for ice cream or milk may represent a calcium deficiency. She reports that modern psychologists and such writers as Simon de Beauvoir do not subscribe to these beliefs in biological causes but believe in the psychological origin of such cravings, with the idea of inconveniencing the male as the female is inconvenienced by the pregnancy.

Thus, from a cross-cultural prespective, behavioral health must be aware of the presence of a strong medical folklore, particularly in cultures where the average education of the citizens is low. Behavioral health scientists should take it upon themselves to write a dictionary of behavioral health actions that would effectively substitute for these folkloric beliefs. Meanwhile, this Handbook may provide some of the necessary information.

COPING STYLE AND HEALTH BEHAVIOR ACROSS CULTURES

Offer and Sabshin (1974) and Cohen and Lazarus (1979) have contributed works dealing with the concept of coping. Offer and Sabshin (1974) deal with the concepts and work of Robert White, David Hamburg, J. E. Adams, Richard Lazarus, Roy Grinker, George Coelho, and Lois Murphy. Brewster Smith's contention that we need a clear concept of normality if we want to judge abnormality justifiably is also amply entertained by Offer and Sabshin, but they also present fundamental concepts and definitions of coping and discuss the great need for adequate operationalization of the concept. Five years later, Cohen and Lazarus (1979) made us aware that operationalizing coping is in itself a difficult problem. These authors exhaustively review the literature regarding the assessment of coping, starting with the dispositional versus the process approaches. They believe that coping is not a single act but a constellation of behaviors—a number of acts and thoughts that are triggered by a complex set of demands, which, in turn, change with time. They make it clear that many other variables interact with the behavior of coping, among them age, sex, the sociocultural background of the individual, and types of situations. They also report many studies that have successfully related diverse ways of measuring coping behavior with outcomes. They report, for instance, their own work (Cohen & Lazarus, 1973), in which they found that patients who avoided or denied information about a forthcoming elective surgical operation showed faster and less complicated recovery from surgery than patients who sought information about their operation. They also report, however, Layne and Yudofsky's (1971) findings that in serious operations such as open heart surgery, a preoperative denial can result in increased postoperative psychotic reactions. It is interesting that, when dealing with patients' taking an active, involved role versus becoming depressed, they refer to a study using the Holtzman Inkblot Test, in which women who are independent and autonomous (as defined by a body image measure from their responses to the Holtzman Inkblot Test) show greater delay in seeking treatment for symptoms of breast or cervical cancer (Fisher, 1967; Hammerschlag, Fisher, DeCosse, & Kapland, 1964).

In an early paper, Diaz-Guerrero (1967) propounded what apparently was to be the first cross-cultural conception of coping. It was postulated that coping with the stress of life is a universal phenomenon, but that different cultures propagate dissimilar styles of coping. It was believed that traditional societies (the paradigm was the Mexican traditional culture) would stress a passive-affiliative form of coping with problems and the stresses of life, whereas highly industrialized countries (the paradigm being the U.S. culture) would stress an active, external modifier style of coping. Individuals were considered to be using a passive-affiliative coping style if, when dealing with the stresses of life, they would modify their own selves in order to solve the problem, while they would have an active coping style if, in order to face the stress, they would modify the environment—the interpersonal, the social, and the physical environment. Although this conception stimulated more research, several early hypotheses were promulgated regarding the relationship of coping style to physical and psychiatric health. Unfortunately, it was not until very recently that psychologists of the National University of Mexico became interested in testing some of these hypotheses. It had been predicted, for instance, that the active style of coping could lead to hypertension, stomach ulcers, and coronaries and that passive coping could lead to hypochondriasis, neurasthenia, and hysteria. It was considered important to establish the relationship of active coping to an excessive alarm reaction and passive coping to an insufficient alarm reaction in Selye's terminology.

Diaz-Guerrero (1973, 1977) has developed an instrument called the *Filosofia de Vida* (philosophy of life), with the goal of measuring active versus passive coping style in four dimensions. It is probable that a more useful instrument with which to measure coping style cross-culturally will be the Holtzman Inkblot Technique (HIT) (Hill, 1972; Holtzman, Thorpe, Swartz, & Herron, 1961). Not only is this technique an improvement on the Rorschach, with reliabilities for most important variables above .90, but clearly presents each examinee a task that must be coped with. It has been demonstrated in a number of replications (Diaz-Guerrero, 1981; Holtzman et al., 1975) that the HIT clearly differentiates the style of coping of Mexican nationals as compared to that of American nationals. Furthermore, there are low but significant correlations in both these national groups between the passive and the active style of coping, as measured by the Filosofia de Vida and the cultures differentiating HIT variables.

Full and continuing behavioral health can only be secured in any culture if, besides adhering to some of the principles enunciated in this book and carefully taking into account genetic variables, the ratio of successful to unsuccessful coping with all the problems set by life, day in and day out, turns out to be on the positive side—that is, if we more often than not experience success in solving problems, no matter what the culture in which we live. It would be interesting to see what proportion of successful coping versus failures would result in optimal and continuing behavioral health. The problem, however, is probably more complex, especially if our interest is in assessing the individual behavioral health of the citizens within our own cultural or national group.

Unless we also obtain an index of physical health, plus an index of psychological health that assesses the psychological processes and the efficiency of the coping style, plus a measure of sociocultural conformity or deviance, plus an index measuring the extent to which an individual follows the health behavior recommendations in this book (e.g., sleep, diet, exercise), we will hardly have a comprehensive assessment of the total health of the individual. Such a comprehensive measure could resolve such perennial questions as the extent to which individuals can be deviant from their socioculture and still be physically and mentally very healthy.

CONCLUSION

I conclude this chapter with a sobering but important statement by Hamburg (1982), which contains considerable cross-cultural validity:

> *Half of the mortality from the ten leading causes of death in the United States is strongly influenced by lifestyle. Known behavioral risk factors include cigarette smoking, excessive consumption of alcoholic beverages, use of illicit drugs, certain dietary habits, insufficient exercise, reckless driving, nonadherence to medication regimens, and maladaptive responses to social pressures.*

It would appear that his prescription that Americans can materially influence their own individual health by paying attention to these 10 causes of poor health probably applies to the citizens of every other country of the world. At the very least, social scientists in these other countries might wish to study whether or not such is true, and I hope that I have also strengthened the case in the conceptions of health and illness across different cultures.

REFERENCES

Benedict, R. F. *Patterns of culture.* Boston: Houghton-Mifflin, 1934.

Benedict, R. F. Foreword. In J. Henry, *Jungle people.* New York: Random House, 1964.

Bustamante, J. A. *La psicologia medica en la ensenaza de la medicina.* Havana: Academia de Ciencias de Cuba, 1968.

Cohen, F. Personality, stress and the development of physical illness. In G. C. Stone, F. Cohen, & N. E. Adler (Eds.), *Health psychology: A handbook.* San Francisco: Jossey-Bass, 1979.

Cohen, F., & Lazarus, R. S. Active coping processes, coping dispositions and recovery from surgery. *Psychosomatic Medicine,* 1973, **35,** 375–389.

Cohen, F., & Lazarus, R. S. Coping with the stresses of illness. In G. C. Stone, F. Cohen, & N. E. Adler (Eds.), *Health psychology: A handbook.* San Francisco: Jossey-Bass, 1979.

Diaz-Guerrero, R. Sociocultural premises, attitudes and cross-cultural research. *International Journal of Psychology,* 1967, **2**(2), 79–87.

Diaz-Guerrero, R. A Mexican psychology. *American Psychologist,* 1977, **32,** 934–944.

Diaz-Guerrero, R. Interpreting coping styles across nations from sex and social class differences. *International Journal of Psychology,* 1973, **8**(3), 193–203.

Diaz-Guerrero, R. Origines de la personnalite humaine et des systemes sociaux. *Review de Psychologie Appliquee,* 1979, **2,** 139–152.

Diaz-Guerrero, R. El enfoque cultura-contracultural del desarrollo humano y social: El caso de las madres en cuatro sub-culturas mexicanas. *Revista de la Asociacion Latinoamerica de Psicologia Social,* 1981, **1,** 75–92.

Diaz-Guerrero, R. *Psicologia del Mexicano.* Mexico City: Trillas, 1982, pp. 195–241.

Diaz-Guerrero, R. & Salas, M. *El diferencial semantico del idioma Espanol.* Mexico City: Trillas, 1975.

Draguns, J. G. Comparisons of psychopathology across cultures. *Journal of Cross-Cultural Psychology,* 1973, **4**(1), 9–47.

Fisher, S. Motivation for patient delay. *Archives of General Psychiatry,* 1967, **16,** 676–678.

Fliegel, F., Sofranko, A. J., Williams, J. D., & Sharma, N. C. Technology and cultural convergence: A limited empirical test. *Journal of Cross-Cultural Psychology,* 1979, **10**(1), 3–22.

Hamburg, D. A. Health and behavior (Editorial). *Science,* 1982, **217,** 399.

Hammerschlag, C. A., Fisher, S., DeCosse, J., & Kapland, E. Breast symptoms and patient delay: Psychological variables involved. *Cancer,* 1964, **17,** 1480–1485.

Hill, E. F. *The Holtzman Inkblot Technique.* San Francisco: Jossey-Bass, 1972.

Holmes, T. H., & Rahe, R. H. The social readjustment rating scale. *Journal of Psychosomatic Research,* 1967, **11,** 213–218.

Holmes, T. H., & Rahe, R. H. Life crisis and disease onset: II. Unpublished manuscript, University of Washington.

Holtzman, W. H., Diaz-Guerrero, R., & Swartz, J. D. *Personality development in two cultures.* Austin: University of Texas Press, 1975.

Holtzman, W. H., Thorpe, J. S., Swartz, J. D., & Herron, E. W. *Inkblot perception and personality: Holtzman Inkblot Technique.* Austin: University of Texas Press, 1961.

Kardiner, A. *The psychological frontiers of society.* New York: Columbia University Press, 1945.

Kleitman, N. *Sleep and wakefulness.* Chicago: University of Chicago Press, 1939.

Kleitman, N. Sleep. *Scientific American,* November 1952.

Knight, G. P., & Kagan, S. Acculturation of prosocial and competitive behaviors among second and third generation Mexican-American children. *Journal of Cross-Cultural Psychology*, 1977, **8**(3), 273–284.

Korten, D. C. The life game: Survival strategies in Ethiopian folk tales. *Journal of Cross-Cultural Psychology*, 1971, **2**(3), 209–224.

Layne, O. L., Jr., & Yudofsky, S. C. Postoperative psychosis in cardiotomy patients. *New England Journal of Medicine* 1971, **284**, 518–520.

Linton, R. Marquesan culture. In A. Kardiner (Ed.), *The individual and his society*. New York: Columbia University Press, 1939.

Linton, R. *The tree of culture*. New York: Vintage Books, 1959.

Marmor, J. Nationalism, internationalism and emotional maturity. *International Journal of Social Psychiatry*, 1966, **12**(3), 217–220.

Marsella, A. J., Shizura, L., Brennan, J., & Kameoka, V. Depression and body image satisfaction. *Journal of Cross-Cultural Psychology*, 1981, **12**(3), 360–371.

Matarazzo, J. D. Behavioral health and behavioral medicine: Frontiers for a new health psychology. *American Psychologist*, 1980, **35**, 807–817.

Melamed, G. G., & Siegel, L. J. *Behavioral medicine: Practical applications in health care*. New York: Springer, 1980.

Munroe, R. L., & Munroe, R. H. Perspectives suggested by anthropological data. In H. C. Triandis & W. W. Lambert (Eds.), *Handbook of cross-cultural psychology: Vol. 1. Perspectives*. Boston: Allyn & Bacon, 1980.

Offer, D., & Sabshin, M. *Normality: Theoretical and clinical concepts of mental health*. New York: Basic Books, 1974.

Osgood, C. E. Explorations in semantic space: A personal diary. *Journal of Social Issues*, 1971, **27**(4), 5–64.

Osgood, C. E., May, W. H., & Myron, M. S. *Cross-cultural universals of affective meaning*. Urbana: University of Illinois Press, 1975.

Osgood, C. E., Suci, G. J., & Tannenbaum, P. *The measurement of meaning*. Urbana, Ill.: University of Illinois Press, 1957.

Parsons, T. Definitions of health and illness in the light of American values and social structure. In E. G. Jaco (Ed.), *Patients, physicians and illness*. Glencoe, Ill.: Free Press, 1958.

Paul, B. D. (Ed.). *Health, culture and community: Case studies of public reactions to health programs*. New York: Russell Sage Foundation, 1955.

Rinzler, C. A. *The Dictionary of Medical Folklore*. London: Magnum Books, 1979.

Smith, M. B. Normality: For an abnormal age. In D. Offer & D. X. Freedman (Eds.), *Modern psychiatry and clinical research*. New York: Basic Books, 1972.

Snider, J. G., & Osgood, C. E. (Eds.), *Semantic differential technique: A sourcebook*. Chicago: Aldine, 1969.

Spielberger, C. D. The measurement of state and trait anxiety: Conceptual and methodological issues. In L. Levi (Ed.), *Emotions—Their parameters and measurement*. New York: Raven Press, 1975.

Spielberger, C. D., & Diaz-Guerrero, R. *Cross-cultural anxiety*. New York: Hemisphere, 1976.

Spielberger, C. D., & Diaz-Guerrero, R. *Cross-cultural anxiety* (Vol. 2). New York: Hemisphere, in press.

Stone, G. C. Health and the health system: A historical overview and conceptual framework. In G. C. Stone, F. Cohen, & N. E. Adler (Eds.), *Health psychology: A handbook*. San Francisco: Jossey-Bass, 1979.

Stone, G. C., Cohen, F., & Adler, N. E. *Health psychology: A handbook*. San Francisco: Jossey-Bass, 1980.

Sue, S., Zane, N., & Ito, J. Alcohol drinking patterns among Asians and Caucasian-Americans. *Journal of Cross-Cultural Psychology*, 1979, **10**(1), 41–56.

Tanaka Matsumi, J., & Marsella, A. J. Cross-cultural variations in the phenomenological experience of depression. *Journal of Cross-Cultural Psychology*, 1976, **7**(4), 379–396.

Taub, J. M. The sleep-wakefulness cycle in Mexican adults. *Journal of Cross-Cultural Psychology,* 1971, **2**(4), 353–362.

Tucker, L. R., & Messick, S. An individual differences model for multidimensional scaling. *Psychometrika,* 1963, **28**, 333–367.

Wegrocki, H. J. A critique of cultural and statistical concepts of abnormality. *Journal of Abnormal and Social Psychology,* 1939, **34**, 166–178.

SECTION 2
HEALTH ENHANCEMENT MODELS

CHAPTER 11

HEALTH EDUCATION MODELS

LAWRENCE W. GREEN

Center for Health Promotion Research and Development
University of Texas Health Science Center at Houston

Other chapters in this section of the Handbook describe specific models from the behavioral sciences that have application in health education and health promotion. As an enterprise that seeks to apply the best of the models from these various sources, health education spawns a second order of models that synthesize or reconcile elements from various administrative, behavioral, and epidemiologic models. This chapter will attempt to characterize the evolution of some of the predominant models in health education, although in most instances these have not been formally articulated as models by their authors or sponsors. They represent, rather, schools of thought that guide practice for large segments of the health education profession. Each grows out of a tradition of teaching and practice identified with specific settings for health education and their dominant graduate schools of education and public health or health science.

Because most of the models to be described in this chapter emerged informally from experience in practice and from discursive bodies of theoretical and empirical literature, the research and theory building in relation to these predominant models has not been cumulative or cohesive. As a student in this field in the 1960s, I found myself clutching at strands and recurring themes rather than finding a common body of research and theory (Green, 1976a). I was particularly steeped in one of the several traditions of health education and was made only vaguely aware of the others. To reconstruct the development of models in health education in this chapter, I will first outline the major professional branches or subspecialties of health education as a profession. Then I will attempt to trace the major concepts and assumptions underlying the predominant models that have emerged in some of these subspecialties. Finally, I will suggest some directions in which these models need to be further elaborated and consolidated in order to address the current and future challenges of complex lifestyle development. This latter-day challenge to health education has emerged under the rubric of health promotion, by which most people refer to a narrower range of behavior than health education has been concerned with in the past but a more complex type of behavior—sometimes called lifestyle—that requires strategies for support that go beyond the traditional definitions of health education.

THE BRANCHES OF HEALTH EDUCATION

Historically, health education can be traced to three traditions whose distinctions were mainly in the settings or circumstances in which they were practiced rather than the problems or objectives to which they were addressed. By setting, these traditions could be identified as school health education, community health education, and patient education. The last type has been conducted primarily in medical care settings where the learner is already diagnosed and under treatment, which puts it largely outside the purview of this book. I will therefore leave the reader to refer to other major analyses of patient education models (Bartlett, 1980; Deeds & Mullen, 1981–82; Green & Kansler, 1980; Haynes, Taylor, & Sackett, 1979; Mullen & Zapka, 1982; Squyres, 1980).

Further branching on the tree of health education has occurred not only from professional specialization, but as much from merging of common interests among professional groups and the initiatives of voluntary and lay groups. Some of the specializations within school and community health education, for example, have included nutrition education, family planning communications, physical education, continuing education, alcohol and drug education, sex education, and a variety of other subspecialties focused on specific diseases, behavioral problems, and chronic conditions. A few of these have developed more extensive bodies of research literature and theoretical modeling as a result of federal and international priorities supporting research and development. This is most notable with immunization studies in the 1950s and early 1960s (D'Onofrio, Note 1), family planning studies in the 1960s (Cernada, 1982; Kar, 1977; Rogers, 1973; WHO, Note 2; Young, 1973), and hypertension research in the 1970s (Glanz & Scholl, 1982; Haynes, Mattson, & Engebretson, 1980). Research on alcohol and drug education has been extensive over all three decades (Blane & Chafetz, 1979; Bukowski, 1983), as has smoking education research (Danaher, 1982; McAlister, 1979; Schwartz, 1978; Thompson, 1978). These areas of federal priorities have both benefited and suffered from the variety of disciplines seizing upon federal and international research support. They have benefited from the enrichment of perspective that numerous disciplines have brought to bear. They have suffered, however, from a lack of continuity and cohesiveness in the research. It is not uncommon for a number of sociologists engaged in smoking research, for example, to be oblivious to the parallel work of psychologists and health educators. This is probably inevitable in applied research, as distinct from discipline-bounded research, but an applied field "must order its knowledge around the phenomena with which its practice is concerned" (WHO, Note 3).

THE EARLY MODELS OF HEALTH EDUCATION

In school health education, the early models were primarily pedagogical, and professors devoted themselves to preparing teachers and writing textbooks for children and for teacher-training programs. School health education struggled for a professional identity separate from physical education, but most schools could afford only one of the two. The physical education curriculum was more likely to have a mandate in state law, so that physical educators had to be employed and ended up teaching much of the health education. The professors of physical education consequently dominated the academic departments in which many health education training programs were located (Sliepcevich, 1961; Joint WHO/UNESCO Expert Committee, Note 4). Under these circumstances, research and theory building suffered. The strongest conceptual modeling in school health education in the United States began to take place with a national study designed to develop a model curriculum (Veenker, 1963).

Active involvement of the learner has been a consistent principle throughout models and curricula of school health education. This principle will be seen to have a parallel in community health education with the principle of community participation in planning. Involving school administrators and parents also recurs as a theme in school health curriculum models.

Although school health education is centered in schools and colleges, it is not necessarily limited to classrooms or to didactic methods, nor to children or students as the only audience, nor to the health problems of childhood and adolescence (Charlton, 1981; Kolbe & Iverson, 1983). Because classrooms are the primary locus, and because children or adolescents are the major target groups, however, the methods are largely pedagogical and the concentration is on the concerns of children and youth (Bartlett, 1981; Kolbe, 1979). The more fundamentally distinguishing characteristic of school health education from the standpoint of theoretical models is the peculiar functional orientation it has toward behavioral and health outcomes:

> *By what criteria, then, shall schools be held accountable for their expenditures on health education and their consumption of precious curriculum time for health teaching? It would be naive and irresponsible today to settle for improvements in knowledge as the only answer to this question. That answer is now insufficient for virtually all subjects and was never acceptable for reading, writing, and arithmetic. In the age of competency-based instruction and criterion-referenced testing, the educational system has committed itself to assuring at each grade that children are prepared to achieve that level of performance on some test of comprehension and skill that is considered necessary to cope with the demands of school and society at the next age or grade, and in the future.*
>
> *It is taken as a task of school health education, following this logic, that children at each age or grade should be helped to master those health maintenance skills necessary to cope with potential threats to their health in the coming age or grade, and those additional foundation skills necessary to benefit from the instruction next year in relation to the potential health problems of the year after that (Green, Heit, Iverson, Kolbe, & Kreuter, 1980, p. 32).*

THE CAUSAL ASSUMPTIONS OF SCHOOL HEALTH EDUCATION

In the earliest practice of school health education, the health outcomes of concern were infectious diseases, particularly the communicable diseases of childhood. The behaviors required of children and youth were largely assumed to be personal hygienic practices (Means, 1962). Such practices were equated with good manners and moral development (Green & Anderson, 1982; Rosen, 1958). By associating personal hygiene with socially acceptable behavior, an implied causal link was also invoked between personal responsibility for the social good and the communicable nature of the diseases spread by contact (Green & Iverson, 1982). Personal responsibility for the common good is still emphasized in school subjects more tangential to health, such as population education, energy education, and environmental education.

As the communicable diseases were replaced increasingly with chronic, degenerative, developmental, and violent or accidental causes of death and disability, contagion no longer served as the underlying causal theme or assumption for school health education. Today, "proper" health behavior no longer can be morally prescribed on the basis of the common good; unhealthy behavior must be proscribed in relation to increasingly' personal, distant, improbable, or seemingly inevitable morbid events in the future. Simple cause-and-effect relationships between behavior and the inexorable spread of disease are no longer convincing in the face of the stochastic and multivariate conditional probabilities and processes of health maintenance and health improvement in today's comparatively symptom-free children and youth. In contrast to the few major killers and cripplers of concern in the past, current generations are told that virtually every substance they may consume and every pleasure they may seek has some small or large chance of harming them. In short, probabilities have replaced precept, data have replaced dictum, and decision-making skills have replaced prescriptions of proper health practices. School health education has shifted its models from social control through moral education to personal control through values clarification and analytical skills (Kolbe, Iverson, Kreuter, Hochbaum, & Christianson, 1981).

The behavioral sciences have influenced the understanding of the forces affecting behavior, so that educators today are concerned with more than the knowledge and attitudes of their students (Kreuter, Christianson, & Kolbe, 1984). They are expected to design their curricula and lesson plans with cognitive, affective, and psychomotor domains of learning as well as with methods and materials that take into account the contingencies of behavior and that provide for rewards that will reinforce the desired behavior (e.g., Hay 1982; Sleet & Stadsklev, 1977). The latter are understood to be especially important in health education, where the behaviors of increasing concern are so heavily imbedded in lifestyle and social learning. Dietary patterns, for example, will not yield to simplistic lesson plans that drill students on food groups, nor will smoking be prevented by decreasing the small percentage of students who do not know that it may cause cancer.

With these shifts in the problems and the prevalent practices in school health education, the assumptions concerning cause-and-effect relationships between teaching and potential health benefits have become more elaborate and more controversial (Iverson & Kolbe, 1982; Kolbe & Iverson, 1981; Kreuter, 1981). Some teachers and educational evaluators have continued to emphasize content, and the content itself has changed (Popham, 1982). One critique of college health education textbooks found no consistent content that would suggest consensus among health educators (Goldstein, 1975). The majority of health educators have come to grips with the value-laden and socially charged issues of teenage pregnancy, drug abuse, and smoking by placing greater emphasis on factors beyond factual knowledge (Iverson, 1981; McAlister & Gordon, 1980; Mullen, 1981).

THE SCOPE OF SCHOOL HEALTH EDUCATION MODELS

The intermediate variables implied by modern practices of school health education can be divided broadly into three types of factors that are assumed to influence health behavior and to be modifiable by educational intervention. The three sets of factors, classified according to the types of interventions or methods required to modify them, are predisposing factors, enabling factors, and reinforcing factors (Green, 1976b; Green, Kreuter, Deeds & Partridge, 1980). Predisposing factors include the traditional targets of education—including awareness, interest, understanding, attitudes, and beliefs—which are modifiable by means of direct communication of information. Some variables in this category, such as values and perceptions, require more interactive communication to clarify and to adjust inconsistencies in values or misperceptions of reality. The defining characteristic of predisposing factors is their motivational force prior to the decision to take a given health action. Some models in school health education lay the primary, if not exclusive, emphasis here (Case, 1978; Emery, 1980; Lockwood, 1978; Simon & Clark, 1975).

The second class of factors assumed to influence health behavior and to be modifiable through educational processes are enabling factors, including the skills and other resources required by students to carry out an action, whether they are motivated to do so or not. This class calls for educational methods that are more commonly associated with training or drilling to build a repertoire of skills and an automatic recall of information or recognition of symptoms as required to act on specific occasions in response to specific motives or stimuli. Self-care skills and the confidence to use them are emphasized in some models. Ability to recognize cancer warning signs, recall of cardiopulmonary resuscitation (CPR) and other first-aid methods, and skill in estimating relative risks of flossing teeth correctly are examples (Bonk-Luetkins, 1983; Lewis & Lewis, 1980; Robertson, 1980). In broader models, the enabling factors may call for some community health education, parent education, or staff education and organizational development within the school to assure that the resources needed by students to carry out the prescribed actions are accessible (Blackeway & Knickrehn, 1978; Coates & Thoresen, 1978; Anderson, Note 5). The availability of disclosing tablets to detect residual plaque after brushing and flossing or fluoride rinses, of healthful foods in the cafeteria and in school vending machines, and of telephone hot lines for immediate help with crises is of increasing concern to school health educators, who find themselves recommending in the classroom health practices that are blocked by circumstances outside the classroom. When the forces required to change these circumstances or to mobilize the needed resources go beyond education, the health educator must collaborate with others in broader enterprises in health promotion, health services, or health protection, including politics (Freudenberg, 1978; Green, 1980a; Green & Johnson, 1983; Mullen, 1981).

A third set of factors, becoming more prevalent in health education models where the assumed causes of the behavior are largely social or peer influence, is reinforcing factors. These may include token or tangible rewards for successful trials or test performance, but the more significant reinforcing factors of concern are those associated with social learning. One of the most fruitful lines of theory and research in recent health education efforts directed at the problems of smoking, drug abuse, and adolescent sexuality has been with concepts of inoculation against peer pressure, whereby students are reinforced for demonstrating skills in declining or resisting the offer of a cigarette or pressure to engage in sexual activity against their better judgment (Botvin & McAlister, 1981; Evans, 1976; McAlister & Gordon, 1980; McAlister, Perry, Killian, Slinkard, & Maccoby, 1980; Nilson-Giebel, 1980).

The most effective health education programs are those that combine learning experiences directed at all three sets of factors influencing behavior, based on an educational diagnosis of the predominant variables in each category (Bruhn, Parcel & Conference Participants, 1982; Stainbrook & Green, 1982). A behavior that is highly motivated and reinforced will be frustrated if it is not also enabled (Parcel, 1976). A motivated and enabled behavior that meets with social punishment or ridicule rather than reinforcement will not persist. Models of contemporary health education can be organized around various combinations of the three sets of factors influencing health behavior (Green, 1980c). Their utility in practice depends on their adequate coverage of all three sets of factors or their combination with other models that cover the missing elements (Cummins, Becker, & Maille, 1980).

There is also a strong sentiment and prevailing philosophy among school health educators (yet to be formalized in theory) that comprehensive rather than categorical health education should be supported in schools. In concept, a more comprehensive approach to health education would be consistent with the function of schools to build a foundation for living and more generic, adaptable skills. The crisis orientation of programs supported by government because of social problems such as alcohol and teenage pregnancy tends to generate more active community support and antagonism—that is, controversy. This orientation does permit more concentrated efforts on specific health issues or behavioral problems, but to expect the schools to solve these problems through health education alone is to ignore large areas of social reality for students, whose behavior is influenced more powerfully by circumstances in the community.

MODELS OF COMMUNITY HEALTH EDUCATION

In community health education, there were two major American traditions apart from the unsystematic practice of health education "campaigns" by people with little or no training in health education. The two most notable professional traditions were associated with graduate programs in schools of public health. The largest and most influential of these programs were at the University of North Carolina (Morgan & Horning, 1940) and the University of California at Berkeley (Nyswander, 1967).

The models of these dominant schools had in common a commitment to community participation in health planning and self-determination. This was also consistent with international health education (WHO, Note 6). Both traditions also were suspicious of new technology and the mass media on the grounds that they tended to bypass this essential participatory element of education (see, e.g., Griffiths & Knutson, 1960). There were other strands of theory in the field of community health education in those early days. Some health educators were from neither of the two schools of public health dominating the scene professionally, but they shared a common bond of commitment to the principle of participation. Some operated from the perspectives of John Dewey, Clair Turner, Mabel Rugan, and others in school health education, some from the perspectives of Cyril Houle and Malcolm Knowles in adult education, and some from the group dynamics perspective of Kurt Lewin, Dorothy Nyswander, and the National Training Laboratories at Bethel, Maine. These latter models are summarized in their application to community health education by Mico and Ross (1975) and Ross and Mico (1980).

The commitment of health educators to maximum feasible participation in the dominant models of community health education in the United States put them at the forefront of the New Frontier and New Society initiatives in the 1960s. Many of them assumed the executive director positions in comprehensive health planning agencies and health systems agencies before health planning emerged as a distinct professional specialty in health administration. In the Third World, health educators gave leadership to the community development movement (Gunaratne, 1980; Tonon, 1980; Acuna, Note 7). At the same time, the aversion of health educators to mass media and other educational technologies caused them to appear to be lagging behind modern innovations in communication. This appearance was strengthened by the inability of health educators to defend their position with new data (Wallack, 1981) and their tendency to defend it instead with polemic and philosophy. By the early 1970s, health educators had begun to catch up in the application of new media and technologies, including games, computer-assisted instruction, and audiovisual technology (Green, 1978). At the same time, their research began to take on a more cumulative quality, with the publication in *Health Education Monographs* (now *Health Education Quarterly,* the journal of the Society for Public Health Education; see Mico, 1982) of extensive reviews of the literature, pulling together the several strands of theory and research.

THE EMERGENCE OF NEW MODELS IN HEALTH EDUCATION

If we understand the common element of the various schools of health education to be a commitment to participation and self-determination in matters of health behavior, then we must incorporate these elements in any model that attempts to synthesize the best elements of these traditions. We can then finesse the controversy over methods by defining health education as "any combination of learning methods designed to facilitate voluntary adaptations of behavior conducive to health." This definition leaves open the question of which methods or which combination of methods are appropriate under different circumstances and for different people, and the teleological question of whether there is such a thing as free will. Deterministic and mechanistic schools of human behavior will be uncomfortable with this definition. Such views are, in the final analysis, hostile to the philosophy, theoretical assumptions, and even the methodology of much of health education.

Yet the applied methods from these more deterministic fields of psychology can be incorporated in a health education model under this definition so long as the subjects or audience consent to the procedures in pursuit of their own goals. Informed consent, however perfunctory, satisfies the definitional element of voluntary adaptation of behavior (Faden, 1977; Mahoney & Thoresen, 1974; Stainbrook & Green, 1982; Watson & Thorp, 1972). By insisting that health education be limited to those situations in which the subjects or audience are in pursuit of their own goals, we adhere to the principle of participation and distinguish health education from propaganda, marketing, and other forms of communication (Green, 1978).

The other element of this definition that relates it to earlier models of health education, yet opens the door to new technology, is the provision for "any combination of learning experiences." Health education professional training institutions, regardless of their attitude toward the behavioral sciences or their loyalty to one of the dominant schools, have always emphasized the importance of multiple approaches in populations and have inveighed against simplistic notions of health education directed at complex behavior with single interventions. This, indeed, was one source of the knee-jerk reaction against mass media among health educators. The more balanced use of mass media in health education has been demonstrated in the Stanford and North Kerelia projects (Farquhar, Maccoby, & Solomon, 1983; Puska, Koskela, McAlister, 1979; Puska, McAlister, Pekkola, & Koskela, 1981).

It was also never suggested in health education that the learning experiences should be limited to the people whose behavior was in question. Indeed, both the North Carolina model and the Berkeley model of health education, as well as the WHO model, emphasized the importance of educating decision makers, opinion leaders, and "gatekeepers." School health education models have always placed emphasis on teacher training and the involvement of parents and school administrators (e.g., Jensen, 1981; Nyswander, 1942; Young, 1969). The application of health education methods at these levels placed the whole enterprise on a different footing than health education in medical care settings, where, until recently, health education was directed exclusively at patients. Indeed, when professionally trained health educators began to take on direction of some of the patient education programs in place of nurses, the nature of the enterprise shifted noticeably from "patient teaching" to hospital-wide health education, including staff development, family involvement, and community outreach activities (e.g. Simonds, 1976). At the same time, health education objectives shifted from compliance to self-care capacities and self-help groups (Green, Werlin, Schauffler, & Avery, 1977; Levin, 1977, 1981).

The relative emphasis placed on different methods by different types of health educators was partly a function of their setting but was even more a function of their assumptions about the critical determinants of or barriers to behavior conducive to health. The most simplistic health education programs were those that concentrated entirely on information transfer. These programs assumed that the major barrier to good health behavior was lack of knowledge. Such programs had cognitive objectives to increase the recognition of symptoms, the recall of factual information, and the comprehension of health concepts. This simplistic approach to health education was abandoned by professional health educators long ago, even in schools, where the major function of the institution is knowledge transfer. It was replaced, largely, by a professional assumption that the major determinant of health behavior was a combination of knowledge and attitude, which together made up the motivation and skills necessary to predispose and enable behavior conducive to health. Attitude-change strategies included role playing, a variety of other group dynamics methods adapted from Kurt Lewin's work on resolving social conflicts and nutrition education (Lewin, 1943, 1951, 1973), and a variety of persuasive appeals built into health messages and channels of communication based on social psychological research on persuasive communication (Cartwright, 1949; Houland, Janis, & Kelley, 1953; Klapper, 1962).

The most thoroughly evaluated motivational construct added to knowledge and attitudes was health beliefs. The health belief model was introduced from research within the United States Public Health Service on why people sought x-ray examination for tuberculosis (Hochbaum, 1958) and other preventive health services, such as immunizations (Rosenstock, 1966, 1974), in the late 1950s and early 1960s. The model has been applied subsequently to family planning (e.g., Katatsky, 1977; cf. Fisher, 1977), chronic diseases (e.g., Kasl, 1967; Levine, Green, Deeds, Chwalow, & Russell, 1979), and a variety of other health-related behaviors (Becker, 1974). The health belief model has been most influential in providing health educators with a structured set of criteria for health message content and motivational outcomes (Green, 1976a). It continues to be taught in most graduate programs in health education and is currently an organizing theme of research and teaching in the University of Michigan School of Public Health's program in health behavior and health education.

The health beliefs found to be most highly correlated with health behavior in the early research included (a) a belief in personal susceptibility to the disease in question, (b) a belief in the possibility that one could have that disease and not know it, and (c) a belief that early detection of the disease could lead to effective treatment or prevention of more severe consequences (Hochbaum, 1958). The second belief was the most powerful of the three, but it had to be dropped when the model was taken from secondary prevention of tuberculosis to primary prevention in relation to immunization (Leventhal, Hochbaum, & Rosenstock, 1960). Here, the second belief became a belief in the severity of consequences. The third belief, through considerable research, has been elaborated to represent a more generalized belief in the trade-offs between costs and benefits of the action (Maiman & Becker, 1974).

The most recent motivational construct to gain widespread translation in health education practice has been that of values. Although the health belief model grows out of value-expectancy theory, values are also assumed to motivate health behavior by providing a reason or rationale for behavior that transcends one's own short-term beliefs about comfort or gain. Values are the more basic beliefs related to motherhood, personal responsibility, productivity, loyalty, and other such standards for human conduct. They provide people with a meaning for their behavior that relates to some larger meaning for their lives (Cernada, 1975; Rokeach, 1975). Health educators do not assume that they can influence people's more deep-seated values in the short run, and most would find an attempt to influence such values inconsistent with the self-determination precept of health education. It has been found helpful to many, however—particularly young people, whose behavior is buffeted by competing social and economic forces—to go through an exercise of "values clarification" (Osman, 1974; Simon, Howe, & Kirschenbaum, 1972). If young people are helped to sort out what is most important to them, they can find better guiding principles for their behavior in matters of health, even if the ultimate decisions and behavioral outcomes are contrary to the objectives of a health program (Lockwood, 1978).

One other predisposing factor that has appealed to many health educators in evaluating, if not developing, programs, is the construct of health locus of control. This motivational construct is difficult to place among attitudes, beliefs, and values; it tends to generalize enough to qualify as values, yet it has been found to be subject to educational intervention and modification, much like an attitude or a belief (Wallston & Wallston, 1978). The way most health educators apply this construct in health education is to assume that an increase in the internal locus of control—that is, an increase in one's perception that locus of control or reinforcement of behavior exists within oneself rather than with others—increases the probability of taking positive health actions. Unfortunately, this simple application of the construct has not fit the data (Rotter, 1975). The failure to control for values, knowledge, and degree of social support has made it appear that some health behaviors are associated with an internal locus of control, whereas others are correlated with an external locus of control. It appears that health actions that involve the prescribed behavior from a physician or other health professional, for example, are more likely to be followed if the individual has a higher *external* locus of control, unless he or she also has assistance at home (Lewis, Morisky, & Flynn, 1978).

School health educators and patient educators have paid considerable attention to most of the foregoing motivational constructs. Community health educators, however, have tended to discount the importance of these factors in favor of their assumption that the critical determinants of health behavior are in the social and economic environment (Cernada 1982; Faden & Faden, 1978; Green, 1970; Kar, 1977; Levin, 1981; Mico & Ross, 1975; Minkler, Frantz & Wichsler, 1982–83; Mullen, 1981; Nyswander, 1967; Wang, 1977; Young, 1973). The main attention some have given to these predisposing factors is to accuse those who place exclusive educational emphasis on them of "blaming the victim" (Freudenberg, 1978; cf. Allegrante & Green, 1981). Both the North Carolina model and the Berkeley model of community health education have placed greater emphasis on health education methods that would *enable* behavior through community organization and community development strategies to influence the flow of resources. The editorial policy of one of the major journals in community health education states: "Environmental and structural changes will be emphasized and *victim blaming* approaches will be closely examined" (Cernada, 1982–83).

School health educators and patient health educators also have given major attention to a set of enabling factors that fall broadly under the rubric of skills. Some of these skills are cognitive, such as decision-making skills or the ability to estimate probabilities; some are social skills, such as the ability to resist peer pressure; and some are manual dexterity skills, such as the ability to floss and brush teeth effectively (Kolbe, Iverson, Kreuter, Hochbaum, & Christianson, 1981).

With the shift in morbidity and mortality patterns from communicable diseases and acute conditions to an increase in chronic and degenerative diseases and other conditions associated with lifestyle has come a commensurate shift in the focus of community health education. The earlier emphasis on predisposing and enabling factors was successful with behavior that was required only once or occasionally, such as immunizations and screening examinations. The new morbidities and their associated complex lifestyles require increasing attention to the factors that reinforce behavior. Even if the behavior is adequately motivated and enabled, it will not persist unless it is reinforced (Green, Kreuter, Deeds, & Partridge, 1980).

Health educators have borrowed heavily from psychologists to locate and modify environmental stimuli that motivate or reinforce individual behavior (Stainbrook & Green, 1982), and from sociologists to identify the organizational, institutional, and social network factors, including peer and family dynamics, that reinforce behavior (Minkler, Frantz, & Wechsler, 1982–83; Pilisuk, Chandler, & D'Onofrio, 1982–83). They have also looked increasingly to economics to understand the ways in which wages, prices, bonuses, tax credits or exemptions, and other incentives can be used to reinforce behavior through employee arrangements, insurance mechanisms, and market forces (Green, 1978, 1980a, 1980b; Green & Johnson, 1983; Minkler, 1976; Mullen, 1981).

Most of these strategies are still in the exploratory phases and are complicated in the early 1980s by a change in federal administrations that has brought momentous changes in the rules of the game. For example, some of the strategies health educators were developing in the Office of the Assistant Secretary for Health under the Carter Administration are no longer viable options under the Reagan administration (Green, 1980a & b; Iverson & Kolbe, 1982; Mullen, 1981). On the other hand, new opportunities are suggested by President Reagan in his incentives for private sector initiatives (Brennen, 1982; Parkinson, Green, McGill, Pearson, Eriksen, Ware, Beck, & Collings, 1982).

The question that faces health educators as the new phase of environmental and social engineering for health behavior takes hold is whether this approach continues to be consistent with the basic tenet of health education concerning voluntary behavior change.

FROM HEALTH EDUCATION TO HEALTH PROMOTION

The dilemma of health education models that are limited philosophically to voluntary behavior change is that they may not be sufficient in the short run to achieve the changes in behavior demanded by an increasingly impatient legislative and administrative process. The U.S. Objectives for the Nation in Disease Prevention and Health Promotion (Office of the Assistant Secretary for Health, 1981), for example, called for realistic reductions in morbidity and mortality that should be possible by 1990 if we apply what we know today. Unfortunately, many of the actions that we might take today to reduce our major risk factors and improve our health status as a nation are intricately interwoven with the value systems, economics, and social fabric of our communities, our families, our social institutions, and our ethnic and religious tenets. Abortion is only the most dramatic of several examples that challenge the tolerance and political maturity of a pluralistic society (Faden & Faden, 1978). The social uses of alcohol are far more pervasive and take a far greater toll in human life and suffering. The ways we prepare and consume food are even more pervasive in the number of lives they touch and the frequency with which they touch our lives, and they therefore are more resistant to change. The same can be said of exercise and the management of stress in everyday life. Together, in some unknown combination, these three factors make up a large part of the cause of heart disease—the leading cause of death—and contribute heavily to many of the other 10 leading causes of death (Office of the Assistant Secretary for Health, 1979, 1981).

Health education cannot abandon the philosophical commitment to voluntary behavior change (participation in setting the goals for change) without taking the very foundation from beneath the structure and practice of the profession. The complexity of the behavioral change processes now presenting themselves for intervention, however, dwarfs and even trivializes health education as the singular intervention. The more sweeping organizational, economic, and environmental changes necessary to support these behaviors conducive to health call for a return to the principles of community organization and community development, in which education is applied as much to the decision makers, opinion leaders, and gatekeepers as to the people whose behavior is in question (Griffiths, 1965; Nyswander, 1967; Wang, 1977).

Experience in a few short years has taught us, however, that even this level of education is insufficient where there are powerful economic interests at stake, as with the tobacco industry and the advertising of harmful products on children's television programs. Aggressive political advocacy and action is required to dislodge the behavior of these "manufacturers of illness" (McKinley, 1975).

This does not require that the fundamental nature of health education should change from a science-based profession to a political party. Clearly, a stand must be taken on the evidence, the public must be informed of that evidence, and political action is necessary. Although I assert that every professional has an individual responsibility and every profession has a collective responsibility to contribute to political debate, I cannot see the fundamental purpose of a profession as political action. At that point it would cease to be a profession and would become a political party, with all the role encumbrances and opportunities that that presents. A particular health education program can have political action of a specified population as its behavioral objective, but that still does not make politics the raison d'être of the profession. Educated political action is a form of voluntary behavior conducive to health, so it qualifies as *one* of the goals of health education.

The approach that reconciles these positions is one that separates health education and health promotion as two different but complementary enterprises. Health promotion is not a profession any more than health is a profession. Health and health promotion are broader goals or social enterprises in which a variety of professionals, laypersons, institutions, and political action groups can make a contribution. Just as medicine is the central profession in medical care as a social enterprise and law is the central profession in justice as a social goal, health education is a logical choice as the central profession in health promotion. Unlike the cognate behavioral sciences, each of which also has a contribution to make, health education is a service profession first and a scientific discipline secondarily (Steuart, 1965). Health educators start with a problem or a social goal and draw upon the behavioral sciences to try to solve it. Behavioral scientists, on the other hand, start with a theory or a scientific hypothesis and seek a social problem or goal on which to test it. Many behavioral scientists have stepped into the health promotion or problem-solving role and have left theory building behind as their primary purpose. At that point they become health educators, health administrators, or health planners, even though they may continue legitimately to claim their identities as psychologists, sociologists, or anthropologists on the basis of their academic credentials.

Following this logic for the relationship between health education and health promotion models required in our time, health promotion has been defined as "any combination of health education and related organizational, economic, and environmental supports for behavior conducive to health." The main intent of this definition in the context of the federal initiative in disease prevention and health promotion was to assure that health gave first consideration to an educational approach to health behavior but at the same time acknowledged the other supports necessary for such behavior. The priority accorded to health education in this definition is consistent with the Jeffersonian doctrine that "that government is best that governs least." It also recognizes, however, that some behavior—such as drunk driving and child abuse—is harmful not only to the individual's health but to the health of others. In those instances, health education is insufficient as a solution, even in the long run, and more aggressive and even coercive means may be required to control the behavior.

We cannot equate health education and health promotion, because some aspects of health behavior require interventions that are not entirely consistent with the educational philosophy and methodology. There are complex organizational, economic, and environmental issues to be sorted out, and these require more skill and authority than the health educator can claim or mobilize. Just as health care is too large an enterprise to be left entirely to physicians, so is health promotion too large an enterprise to be left entirely to health educators. Just as the physician must depend on biological scientists to provide the scientific foundation of his or her practice, so too does the health educator depend on behavioral scientists to provide the scientific foundations of the health education process. A practicing profession should be one that has more than a scientific body of knowledge to draw upon. It should have a code of ethics, a self-regulating mechanism for quality control, and a primary service function.

Many of us in the behavioral sciences and the health professions, especially the authors of chapters in this book, have tried to maintain positions in both camps. The reality, however, is that we are generally planted more firmly in one camp than in the other, depending on the nature of our training and the course of our careers. Some physicians and health educators among us, for example, have devoted our careers primarily to research and evaluation of issues that would strengthen the practice of medicine or public health. Our primary training in a practical profession gives us a somewhat different orientation to issues in behavioral medicine and behavioral health than that of the authors whose primary training was in one of the behavioral sciences. Among the behavioral scientists, on the other hand, are some whose careers have been more firmly embedded in program administration, planning, or policy. With these various patterns of blending qualifications touching on a relatively new field of endeavor, it is perhaps premature to argue for centering health promotion delivery in one profession. My experience with the history of health education, however, has cautioned me that without a profession devoted exclusively to the subject, there would have been no continuity and no systematic developments in the delivery of programs and services.

Having argued thus for some degree of professionalization in health promotion, I would also acknowledge the dangers of overprofessionalizing and especially overmedicalizing this particular enterprise. Health promotion, by its very nature, is necessarily an activity that depends on individual and family initiatives and continuous effort as much as on professional services and advice. Many of the sources of professional services and advice will be commercial enterprises rather than those of governmental or private-practice professionals. Many of the products for health promotion will come from private sector enterprises, with all the concomitant vagaries of manufacturing, distribution, marketing, and advertising. Rather than striving for increasing control of these products and services by one or more professions, it is surely sensible, and probably more cost-effective in the long run, to strive instead for an informed public through consumer education in health promotion. This, then, is another major argument for a central, if not dominant, role for health education as the lead profession in health promotion.

Finally, I would acknowledge the relative weakness of health education among the health professions, both in numbers of professionals and in prestige. The dominant health professions by these criteria would be nursing in numbers and medicine in prestige. I would argue, however, that these professions have their hands full staying abreast of the knowledge explosion in biomedical sciences. A revolution would be necessary in the curriculum of medical schools and, to a lesser extent, in nursing schools for either of these professions to assume a primary role in health promotion. We have seen little evidence that medical schools are prepared to reorient the education of physicians to include a primary emphasis on disease prevention, much less health promotion. Nor should they be expected to do so before medical faculties are heavily engaged in research on health behavior, insofar as the teaching follows the research.

For reasons, then, of the centrality of health education to health promotion, the professional tradition and training of health educators in applying a variety of social and behavioral models to health behavior, and the unlikely conversion of other health professions (or, more precisely, paramedical professions) to a primary commitment to health promotion, health education appears to be the most dependable professional identity to deliver health promotion programs. Other disciplines will provide the critical scientific base for policy and practice in health promotion; other professions will deliver most of the "official" health education messages and will provide the critical backup of specialized services; other enterprises—both commercial and nonprofit—will provide the investment capital, the products, and the marketing of health promotion. Government agencies must provide the support for research and development, organizational, economic, and environmental regulation in support of behavior conducive to health, and incentives to reinforce healthy behavior.

If behavioral health is to become a force parallel, if not comparable, to the medical system, however, it deserves and needs the nurturance of a profession whose primary purpose is health promotion. Health education is the only formally organized, established, and trained profession that meets this criterion. Health education models reflect the synthesis of various behavioral and social science models with some irreducible principles or tenets of practice— namely, the need for informed consent or participation of clients or consumers in setting the goals for their behavior.

SUMMARY

This review has characterized health education models as having a synthetic rather than a basic theoretical cast. They are derivative and practical rather than original and theoretical. They combine elements of psychology, sociology, economics, cultural anthropology, educational and administrative science, epidemiology, and philosophy. This eclectic character makes them unsuitable for formal testing in the direct and comprehensive way that more refined or specific behavioral models, such as the health belief model, can be tested. But this eclectic character also makes them more robust for purposes of guiding practice in complex institutions and communities where health behavior is embedded. Such practice must be guided by experience, principles, and ethics as much as by theory. This adds to my consideration in this chapter of a concern for the professional traditions, socialization, and status of health education. These factors influence the ways in which models will be selected and applied. I conclude that health education as a profession, on the strength of its experience with its models and the absence of another practicing profession with a *primary* commitment to health promotion, should assume a central role in consolidating and applying the models from other disciplines and testing them in practice. This can be done most objectively with the active collaboration of behavioral scientists and consumers.

REFERENCE NOTES

1. D'Onofrio, C. *Reaching our hard to reach: The unimmunized.* Berkeley: California State Department of Public Health, 1963.

2. World Health Organization (WHO). *Health education in health aspects of family planning: Report of a WHO study group.* Geneva: World Health Organization Technical Report Series No. 483, 1971.

3. World Health Organization (WHO). *Research in health education: Report of a WHO scientific group.* Geneva: World Health Organization Technical Report Series No. 432, 1969.

4. Joint WHO/UNESCO Expert Committee. *Teacher preparation for health education.* Geneva: World Health Organization Technical Report Series No. 193, 1960.

5. Anderson, D. C. Combined influences of nutrition education and school lunch program on dietary behavior of junior high school students. In *Summary of projects approved January 1974.* Ottawa: National Health Research and Development Program, Health and Welfare Canada, 1978.

6. World Health Organization (WHO). *Planning and evaluation of health education services: Report of a WHO expert committee.* Geneva: World Health Organization Technical Report Series No. 409, 1969.

7. Acuna, H. *Community participation in the development of primary health services.* Keynote address to the Ninth International Conference on Health Education. Summarized in *Health education and health policy in the dynamics of development: Summary proceedings.* Geneva: International Journal of Health Education, 1977.

REFERENCES

Allegrante, J., & Green, L. W. When health promotion policy becomes victim-blaming. *New England Journal of Medicine,* 1981, **305,** 1528–1529.

Bartlett, E. E. The contribution of consumer health education to primary care practice: A review. *Medical Care,* 1980, **18,** 862–871.

Bartlett, E. E. The contribution of school health education to community health promotion: What can we reasonably expect? *American Journal of Public Health,* 1981, **71,** 1384–1391.

Becker, M. H. (Ed.). The health belief model and personal health behavior. *Health Education Monographs,* 1974, **2,** (Whole No. 4).

Blackeway, S. F., & Knickrehn, M. E. Nutrition education in the Little Rock school lunch program. *Journal of the American Dietetic Association,* 1978, **72,** 389–391.

Blane, H. T., & Chafetz, M. E. (Eds.). *Youth, alcohol and social policy.* New York: Plenum Press, 1979.

Bonk-Luetkens, M. An overview of simulation games on health subjects. In A. Kaplun & R. Erban (Eds.), *Innovative processes in health policies and their impact on health education.* Cologne: Federal Centre for Health Education, 1983.

Botvin, G., & McAlister, A. L. Cigarette smoking among children and adolescents. In C. Arnold, L. Kuller, & M. Greenlick (Eds.), *Advances in disease prevention* (Vol. 1). New York: Springer, 1981.

Brennen, J. J. (Ed.). Worksite health promotion. *Health Education Quarterly,* 1982, **9** (Fall suppl.).

Bruhn, J. G., Parcel, G. S., & Conference Participants. Current knowledge about the health behavior of young children: A conference summary. *Health Education Quarterly,* 1982, **9,** 142–166.

Bukowski, W. (Ed.). *NIDA drug abuse prevention monograph.* Washington, D.C.: U.S. Government Printing Office, 1983.

Cartwright, D. Some principles of mass persuasion: Selected findings of research on the sale of United States War Bonds. *Human Relations,* 1949, **11,** 253–267.

Case, R. A developmentally based theory and technology of instruction. *Review of Educational Research,* 1978, **48,** 439–463.

Cernada, G. P. *Basic beliefs about human life relating to ethical judgments family planning field workers make about induced abortion: Taiwan, 1973.* Unpublished doctoral dissertation, University of California at Berkeley, 1975.

Cernada, G. P. *Knowledge into action.* New York: Baywood, 1982.

Cernada, G. P. Improving practice through updating. *International Quarterly of Community Health Education,* 1982–83, **3**(inside front cover).

Charlton, A. Health education and the teacher's role. *International Journal of Health Education* 1981, **24,** 102–112.

Coates, T. J., & Thoresen, C. E. Treating obesity in children and adolescents: A public health problem. *American Journal of Public Health,* 1978, **68,** 1143–1157.

Cummins, K. M., Becker, M. H., & Maille, M. C. Bringing the models together: An empirical approach to combining variables used to explain health actions. *Journal of Behavioral Medicine,* 1980, **3,** 123–145.

Danaher, B. G. Smoking cessation programs in occupational settings. In Parkinson, R., Green, L. W., McGill, A. M., Pearson, C. E., Eriksen, M., Ware, B. G., Beck, R. N., & Collings, G. H. (Eds.), *Managing health promotion in the workplace: Guidelines for implementation and evaluation.* Palo Alto: Mayfield, 1982.

Deeds, S. G., & Mullen, P. D. (Eds.) Managing health education in HMOs. *Health Education Quarterly,* 1981–82, **8**(Whole No. 4), **9**(Whole No. 1).

Emery, M. The theory and practice of behavior change in the school context. *International Journal of Health Education,* 1980, **23,** 116–125.

Evans, R. I. Smoking in children: Developing a social psychological strategy of deterrence. *Journal of Preventive Medicine,* 1976, **5,** 122–127.

Faden, R. R. Disclosure and informed-consent: Does it matter how we tell it? *Health Education Monographs,* 1977, **5,** 198–214.

Faden, R. R., & Faden, A. I. (Eds.). Ethical issues in public health policy: Health education and lifestyle interventions. *Health Education Monographs,* 1978, **6**(Whole No. 2).

Farquhar, J., Maccoby, N., & Solomon, D. S. Community applications of behavioral medicine. In W. D. Gentry (Ed.), *Handbook of Behavioral Medicine.* New York: Guilford Press, 1983.

Fisher, A. A. The health belief model and contraceptive behavior: Limits to the application of a conceptual framework. *Health Education Monographs,* 1977, **5,** 244–248.

Freudenberg, N. Shaping the future of health education. *Health Education Monographs,* 1978, **6,** 372–377.

Glanz, K., & Scholl, T. O. Intervention strategies to improve adherence among hypertensives: Review and recommendations. *Patient Counselling and Health Education,* 1982, **4,** 14–28.

Green, L. W. Should health education abandon attitude-change strategies? Perspectives from recent research. *Health Education Monographs,* 1970, **1**(30), 24–48.

Green, L. W. Change-process models in health education. *Public Health Reviews,* 1976, **5,** 5–33. (a)

Green, L. W. Methods available to evaluate the health education components of preventive health programs. In *Preventive Medicine USA: Health Promotion and Consumer Health Education.* New York: Prodist, 1976. (b)

Green, L. W. Determining the impact and effectiveness of health education as it relates to federal policy. *Health Education Monographs,* 1978, **6**(Suppl. 1), 28–66.

Green, L. W. *Emerging federal perspectives on health promotion.* In J. Allegrante (Ed.), *Health promotion monographs,* 1980, **1**(Whole No. 1). (a)

Green, L. W. Healthy people: The Surgeon General's report and the prospects. In W. J. McNerny (Ed.), *Working for a healthier America.* Cambridge: Ballinger, 1980. (b)

Green, L. W. To educate or not to educate: Is that the question? *American Journal of Public Health,* 1980, **70,** 625–626. (c)

Green, L. W., & Anderson, C. *Community health* (4th ed.). St. Louis: C. V. Mosby, 1982.

Green, L. W., Heit, P., Iverson, D. C., Kolbe, L. J., & Kreuter, M. W. The school health curriculum project: Its theory, practice and measurement experience. *Health Education Quarterly,* 1980, **7,** 14–34.

Green, L. W., & Iverson, D. C. School health education. *Annual Review of Public Health,* 1982, **3,** 321–338.

Green, L. W., & Johnson, K. W. Health education and health promotion. In D. Mechanic (Ed.), *Handbook of health, health care and the health professions.* New York: Wiley, 1983.

Green, L. W., & Kansler, C. C. *The professional and scientific literature in patient education: A guide to information sources* (Vol. 5 in the Health Affairs Information Guide Series.). Detroit: Gale Research, 1980.

Green, L. W., Kreuter, M. W., Deeds, S. G., & Partridge, K. B. *Health education planning: A diagnostic approach.* Palo Alto: Mayfield, 1980.

Green, L. W., Werlin, S. H., Schauffler, H. H., & Avery, C. H. Research and demonstration issues in self-care: Measuring the decline of medicocentrism. *Health Education Monographs,* 1977, **5,** 161–189.

Griffiths, W. Achieving change in health practices. *Health Education Monographs,* 1965, **1**(20), 27–42.

Griffiths, W., & Knutson, A. L. The role of the mass media in public health. *American Journal of Public Health,* 1960, **50,** 515–523.

Goldstein, M. Defining and studying health at the college level: An empirical examination of US textbooks followed by reactor comments. *International Journal of Health Education,* 1975, **18,** 241–253.

Gunaratne, V. T. H. Health for all by the year 2000: The role of health education. *International Journal of Health Education,* 1980, **23**(Suppl. to No. 1).

Hay, C. Games and simulations in health education. *Simulation/Games for Learning,* 1982, **11,** 68–74.

Haynes, R. B., Mattson, M. E., & Engebretson, T. O. (Eds.). *Patient compliance to antihypertensive medication regimens: A report to the National Heart, Lung and Blood Institute.* DHHS/PHS, Pub. No. (NIH) 81–2102. Washington, D.C.: U.S. Government Printing Office, 1980.

Haynes, R. B., Taylor, D. W., & Sackett, D. L. (Eds.). *Compliance in health care.* Baltimore: Johns Hopkins University Press, 1979.

Hochbaum, G. M. *Public participation in medical screening programs.* Public Health Service Pub. No. 572. Washington, D.C.: U.S. Government Printing Office, 1958.

Hovland, C., Janis, I. L., & Kelley, H. H. *Communication and persuasion.* New Haven: Yale University Press, 1953.

Iverson, D. C. (Ed.). Promoting health through the schools: A challenge for the 80s. *Health Education Quarterly,* 1981, **8**(Whole No. 1).

Iverson, D. C., & Kolbe, L. J. What can we expect from school health education? *Journal of School Health,* 1982, **52,** 145–150.

Jensen, K. Involvement of gatekeepers in school health education. *International Journal of Health Education,* 1981, **24**(Suppl. to No. 1).

Kar, S. B. *Management and utilization of population communication research.* A Synthesis of Population Communication Experience, Paper 5. Honolulu: East-West Communication Institute, 1977.

Kasl, S. V. The health belief model and behavior related to chronic illness. *Health Education Monographs,* 1974, **2,** 433–454.

Katatsky, M. E. The Health Belief Model as a conceptual framework for explaining contraceptive compliance. *Health Education Monographs,* 1977, **5,** 232–243.

Klapper, J. T. The effects of mass communication. New York: Free Press, 1962.

Kolbe, L. J. Evaluating effectiveness—the problems of behavioral criteria. *Health Education,* 1979, **10,** 12–16.

Kolbe, L. & Iverson, D.C. Implementing comprehensive health education: Educational innovations and social change. *Health Education Quarterly,* 1981, **8,** 57–80.

Kolbe, L. J. & Iverson, D. C. Integrating school and community efforts to promote health: Strategies, policies and methods. *Hygie: International Journal of Health Education,* 1983, **2,** 40–47.

Kolbe, L. J., Iverson, D. C., Kreuter, M. W., Hochbaum, G., & Christianson, G. Propositions for an alternate and complementary health education paradigm. *Health Education,* 1981, **12,** 24–30.

Kreuter, M. W. School health education: Does it cause an effect? *Health Education Quarterly,* 1981, **8,** 43–56.

Kreuter, M. W., Christianson, G., & Kolbe, L. J. *Theoretical foundations of health education.* Palo Alto: Mayfield, 1984.

Leventhal, H., Hochbaum, G., & Rosenstock, I. *The impact of Asian influenza on community life: A study in five cities.* Public Health Service Pub. No. 766. Washington, D.C.: U.S. Government Printing Office, 1960.

Levin, L. S. Forces and issues in the revival of interest in self-care: Impetus for redirection in health. *Health Education Monographs,* 1977, **5,** 115–120.

Levin, L. S. Self-care: Towards fundamental changes in national strategies. *International Journal of Health Education,* 1981, **24,** 219–228.

Levine, D. M., Green, L. W., Deeds, S. G., Chwalow, A. J., & Russell, R. P. Health education for hypertensive patients. *Journal of the American Medical Association,* 1979, **241,** 1700–1703.

Lewin, K. Forces behind food habits and methods of change. *Bulletin of the National Research Council,* 1943, **108,** 35–65.

Lewin, K. *Field theory in social science.* New York: Harper & Row, 1951.

Lewin, K. *Resolving social conflicts.* London: Souvenir Press, 1973.

Lewis, C. E., & Lewis, M. A. Child-initiated health care. *Journal of School Health,* 1980, **50,** 144–148.

Lewis, F. M., Morisky, D. E., & Flynn, B. S. A test of the construct validity of Health Locus of Control: Effects on self-reported compliance for hypertensive patients. *Health Education Monographs,* 1978, **6,** 138–148.

Lockwood, A. L. The effects of values clarification and moral development curricula on school-age subjects: A critical review of recent research. *Review of Educational Research,* 1978, **48,** 325–365.

Mahoney, M. J., & Thoresen, C. E. *Self-control: Power to the person.* Monterey: Brooks-Cole, 1974.

Maiman, L. A., & Becker, M. H. The Health Belief Model: Origins and correlates in psychological theory. *Health Education Monographs,* 1974, **2,** 336–353.

McAlister, A. Smoking. In National Institute of Medicine, *Healthy people: The Surgeon General's report on health promotion and disease prevention. Background papers* (Vol. 2). DHEW Pub. No. (PHS) 79–55071A. Washington, D.C.: U.S. Government Printing Office, 1979.

McAlister, A. L., & Gordon, N. Prevention during early adolescence. In W. Bukowski (Ed.), *Prevention evaluation* (National Institute on Drug Abuse). Washington, D.C.: U.S. Government Printing Office, 1980.

McAlister, A., Perry, C., Killian, J., Slinkard, L. A., & Maccoby, N. Pilot study of smoking, alcohol and drug abuse prevention. *American Journal of Public Health,* 1980, **70,** 719–721.

McAlister, A., Puska, P., Koskela, K., Pallonen, V., Maccoby, N. Psychology in action: Mass communication and community organization for public health education. *American Psychologist,* 1980, **35,** 375–379.

McKinlay, J. B. A case for refocusing upstream: The political economy of illness. In A. Enelow & J. Henderson (Eds.) *Applying Behavioral Science to Cardiovascular Risk.* New York: American Heart Association, 1975.

Means, R. K. *A history of health education in the United States.* Philadelphia: Lea & Febiger, 1962.

Mico, P. R. (Ed.) *The Heritage Collection of Health Education Monographs.* (4 vols.). Oakland: Third Party Associates, 1982.

Mico, P. R., & Ross, H. S. *Health education and behavioral science.* Oakland: Third Party Associates, 1975.

Minkler, M. The use of incentives in family planning programs. *International Journal of Health Education,* 1976, **19**(Suppl. to no. 3).

Minkler, M., Frantz, S., & Wechsler, R. Social support and social action organizing in a "grey ghetto": The Tenderloin experience. *International Quarterly of Community Health Education,* 1982–83, **3,** 3–15.

Morgan, L. S., & Horning, B. G. The community health education program. *American Journal of Public Health,* 1940, **30,** 1323–1330.

Mullen, P. D. Behavioral aspects of maternal and child health: Natural influences and educational intervention. In Report of the Select Panel for the Promotion of Child Health, *Better health for our children: A national strategy* (Vol. 4). DHHS Pub. No. (PHS) 79–55071. Washington, D.C.: U.S. Government Printing Office, 1981.

Mullen, P. D., & Zapka, J. (Eds.). *Guidelines for health promotion and education services in HMOs.* Washington, D.C.: U.S. Government Printing Office, 1982.

Nilson-Giebel, M. Peer groups help prevent dependence among youth in the Federal Republic of Germany. *International Journal of Health Education,* 1980, **23,** 20–24.

Nyswander, D. B. *Solving school health problems.* New York: Oxford University Press, 1942.

Nyswander, D. B. The open society: Its implications for health educators. *Health Education Monographs,* 1967, **1**(22), 3–15.

Office of the Assistant Secretary for Health. *Healthy people: The Surgeon General's report on health promotion and disease prevention.* Washington, D.C.: U.S. Government Printing Office, 1979.

Office of the Assistant Secretary for Health. *Promoting health, preventing disease: Objectives for the nation.* Washington, D.C.: U.S. Government Printing Office, 1981.

Osman, J. The use of selected value clarifying strategies in health education. *Journal of School Health,* 1974, **54**, 21–25.

Parcel, G. S. Skills approach to health education: A framework for integrating cognitive and affective learning. *Journal of School Health,* 1976, **46**, 403–406.

Parkinson, R., Green, L. W., McGill, A. M., Pearson, C. E., Eriksen, M., Ware, B. G., Beck, R. N., & Collings, G. H. *Managing health promotion in the workplace: Guidelines for implementation and evaluation.* Palo Alto: Mayfield, 1982.

Pilisuk, M., Chandler, S., & D'Onofrio, C. Reweaving the social fabric: Antecedents of social support facilitation. *International Quarterly of Community Health Education,* 1982–83, **3**, 45–55.

Popham, W. J. Appropriate measuring instruments for health education investigations. *Health Education,* 1982, **13**, 23–26.

Puska, P., Koskela, K., McAlister, A., Pallonen, V., Vartiainen, E., & Homan, K. A comprehensive television smoking cessation programme in Finland. *International Journal of Health Education,* 1979, **22**(Suppl.).

Puska, P., McAlister, A., Pekkola, J., & Koskela, K. Television in health promotion: Evaluation of a national programme in Finland. *International Journal of Health Education,* 1981, **24**, 1–14.

Robertson, L. S. Crash involvement of teenaged drivers when driver education is eliminated from high school. *American Journal of Public Health,* 1980, **70**, 599–603.

Rogers, E. M. *Communication strategies for family planning.* New York: Free Press, 1973.

Rokeach, M. *The nature of human values.* New York: Free Press, 1975.

Rosen, G. *A history of public health.* New York: MD Publications, 1958.

Rosenstock, I. M. Why people use health services. *Milbank Memorial Fund Quarterly,* 1966, **44**, 94–127.

Rosenstock, I. M. Historical origins of the Health Belief Model. *Health Education Monographs,* 1974, **2**, 328–335.

Ross, H. S., & Mico, P. R. *Theory and practice in health education.* Palo Alto: Mayfield, 1980.

Rotter, J. B. Some problems and misconceptions related to the construct of internal versus external control of reinforcement. *Journal of Consulting and Clinical Psychology,* 1975, **43**, 56–67.

Schwartz, J. L. *Progress in smoking cessation.* New York: American Cancer Society, 1978.

Simon, S. B., & Clark, J. *Moral values clarification.* San Diego: Penant Press, 1975.

Simon, S., Howe, L., & Kirschenbaum, H. *Values clarification: A handbook of practical strategies for teachers and students.* New York: Hart, 1972.

Simonds, S. K. (Ed.). Health education manpower. *Health Education Monographs,* 1976, **4**, 204–284.

Sleet, D. A., & Stadsklev, R. Annotated bibliography of simulations and games in health education. *Health Education Monographs,* 1977, **5**(Suppl.), 74–90.

Sliepcevich, E. M. The responsibility of the physical educator for health instruction. *Journal of Health, Physical Education, and Recreation,* 1961, **32**, 32–33.

Squyres, W. D. (Ed.). *Patient education: An inquiry into the state of the art.* New York: Springer, 1980.

Stainbrook, G., & Green, L. W. Behavior and behaviorism in health education. *Health Education,* 1982, **13**, 14–19.

Steuart, G. W. Health, behavior and planned change: An approach to the professional preparation of the health education specialist. *Health Education Monographs,* 1965, **1**(20), 3–26.

Thompson, E. J. Smoking education programs, 1960–1976. *American Journal of Public Health,* 1978, **68**, 250–257.

Tonon, M. A. Concepts in community participation: A case of sanitary change in a Guatemalan village. *International Journal of Health Education,* 1980, **23**(Suppl. to No. 4).

Veenker, H. C. (Ed.). *Synthesis of research in selected areas of health instruction* (School Health Education Research Monograph). Washington, D.C.: The School Health Education Study, National Education Association, 1963.

Wallack, L. M. Mass media campaigns: The odds against finding behavior change. *Health Education Quarterly,* 1981, **1**(8), 209–260.

Wallston, K. A., & Wallston, B. S. (Eds.). Health Locus of Control. *Health Education Monographs,* 1978, **6**(Whole No. 2).

Wang, V. L. Social goals, health policy and the dynamics of development as bases for health education. *International Journal of Health Education,* 1977, **20,** 13–18.

Watson, D. L., & Thorp, R. G. *Self-directed behavior: Self-modification for personal adjustment.* Monterey, CA: Brooks-Cole, 1972.

Young, M. A. C. Review of research and studies related to health education practice (1961–1966): School health education. *Health Education Monographs,* 1969, **1**(Whole No. 28).

Young, M. A. C. Review of research and studies on the health education and related aspects of family planning (1967–1971): Behavioral and cultural factors. *Health Education Monographs,* 1973, **1**(Whole No. 34).

CHAPTER 12

LEARNING: SOME FACTS AND NEEDED RESEARCH RELEVANT TO MAINTAINING HEALTH

NEAL E. MILLER

The Rockefeller University

Homo sapiens has an unusually rich and varied innate endowment of motivations, memory, intellectual processes, linguistic abilities, and mechanisms for analyzing sensory information and for producing different patterns of responses. Because of these attributes and the snowballing store of culturally transmitted knowledge that they have allowed civilization to accumulate, learning plays an immensely important role in shaping the details of human behavior, including habits that are healthy or unhealthy. This chapter will attempt to describe certain empirically established facts about learning that are significant for attempts to establish the types of behavior that preserve health and prevent disease. It will emphasize some key facts and general empirical laws without becoming involved in admittedly important controversies about theories of learning and accompanying new developments that certainly will lead to significant additional practical applications to health (e.g., Dickinson, 1980; Estes, 1975; Locurto, Terrace, & Gibbon, 1981; Solomon, 1980). As a brief introductory account, the chapter will concentrate on some key factors believed to be useful for health professionals.

Because learning is of little value unless it is used, this chapter will emphasize motivation and performance. The final section will describe recent evidence that learning plays a role in a wider range of health-related phenomena than previously had been recognized, such as responses of visceral organs, responses to drugs, and homeostasis.

REINFORCEMENT AND MOTIVATION

Certain consequences of a response are much more important than others in determining whether it will be performed and learned. The consequences that are important are called reinforcements: positive reinforcements (or rewards) when they increase the probability that the response will occur subsequently, and negative reinforcements (or punishments) when they decrease that probability. Negative reinforcements—for example, pain—are also called aversive stimuli; their removal serves as a positive reinforcement and, conversely, the removal of positive reinforcements serves as a punishment.

Conditions, such as hunger, that determine whether or not a consequence, such as getting food, will serve as a reward, are called drives or motivations. After a response has been learned, its performance tends to vary with the nature and intensity of the drive responsible for the rewarding effectiveness of its outcome. Thus, other things being equal, a person who has learned how to get to a restaurant is much more likely to go there when hungry than after having consumed a large Thanksgiving dinner. Similarly, if, in order to pass an examination, a student has learned all the facts about the relationship of cigarette smoking to lung cancer but at the moment does not care about that remote event but does care about pleasing peers who are urging him or her to smoke, the student is likely to light a cigarette.

Most experiments indicating that learning can occur without any obvious drive or reinforcement use conditions of virtual sensory deprivation except for the presentation of two otherwise isolated perspicuous stimuli. Under normal conditions of life, however, when a variety of responses, including paying attention to a variety of stimuli, are in competition, it is unwise to assume that a desired type of learning will occur effectively, if at all, in the absence of any drive or reinforcement. A student who is not interested in a lecture, for example, and is daydreaming about something else or surreptitiously reading a mystery story will not learn much about what is being said.

Furthermore, if a response is repeated without a suitable reward, it tends to cease being performed, a process that is called extinction. Thus, anyone who is interested in producing the learning and continued performance of healthful habits must pay attention to how they can be rewarded, not only during learning but also thereafter.

Sometimes, whatever habit is started—for example, eating either a healthy or an unhealthy type of food when hungry—will continue to be rewarded. In such cases, it is important to intervene early in order to establish the desirable response first.

The Large, Varied Repertoire of Human Drives and Reinforcements

Hunger, thirst, and pain are basic biological drives, the potential strength of which is often underestimated because the function of a successful society is to protect its individuals from high levels of such needs. For a person with an appropriate drive, acquisition of food and water and escape from pain are powerful rewards. Even such a basic motivation as the hunger-food relationship, however, is modifiable by learning. Thus, a Frenchman may find snails appetizing and corn on the cob repulsive, whereas a farmer in the Midwest may have the opposite reactions. It is believed that feeding infants an excess of salt or sugar may establish a craving for salt or sweets that can result in an unhealthy excess intake of these substances in later life. The acquisition of food habits and preferences will be discussed in detail in chapter 38. Although a considerable amount is known, however, the way in which a drive such as hunger can be modified by learning merits further research.

Fear—or anxiety, as it is called when its source is vague or ubiquitous—can serve as a drive and a sudden reduction in fear can serve as a reward. Fear can be modified by learning; previously neutral stimuli associated with strong pain acquire the ability to elicit fear. It is much easier, however, to condition fear in this way to some stimuli, such as pictures of snakes, than to others, such as pictures of houses (Öhman, Eriksson, & Olofsson, 1975). There probably are many stimulus situations—such as strangeness, the perception of danger, and threats of loss of love, approval, money, or power—that have an innate capacity to elicit fear that can be further increased by learning. Other situations, such as a child clinging to its mother, have an innate capacity to reduce fear (Miller, 1980). Fears can also be reduced by learning. Behavior therapy has had considerable success in reducing specific phobias, such as fears of hypodermic needles and dentists (Pomerleau & Brady, 1979).

Because fear often can be readily aroused—for example, by pictures of the horrible effects of bad health habits—there is a temptation to misuse it. Fear can motivate, however, and a reduction in fear can reward—avoiding a fear-reducing stimulus and suppressing retrieval of fear-inducing memories. Thus, the use of fear can defeat its intended purpose unless a desired type of action can be elicited to reduce it promptly (Janis, 1982; Miller & Dollard, 1941).

Human sex drive is another drive that certainly has an innate basis but can be channeled by learning. There are many other human drives, whose innate bases and learned modifications have not been sorted out, so that they necessarily must be described loosely and with some overlapping. Some of these drives are curiosity and the needs for approval, affection, attention by significant others, acceptance by a group (especially the peer group in adolescence), success in achieving a goal, self-respect, independence, imitation of a prestigious model, power, money, aesthetics, understanding and knowledge, a certain amount of variety, and a certain amount of familiar surroundings. Absence of these factors can serve as drives; achievement of them can serve as rewards (Miller, 1959).

Because of the modifiability of these and other human social motivations, they may vary greatly in different cultures, regions, social classes, occupations, age groups, and with individual personalities. Thus, when one is dealing with people who are different in any of the foregoing characteristics from oneself or from others with whom one has had considerable experience, it is unsafe to assume that one can predict their drives and reinforcements. Also, if the behavior of a particular individual is important, it is unsafe to make important decisions without verifying assumptions about his or her dominant drives and reinforcements. Often, the effective drives and reinforcements in specific situations must be determined by empirical observations of which outcomes do reward behavior. Using a variety of rewards for a given type of behavior can provide a margin of safety and perhaps even a stronger effect, although there has been little study of the way that different drives and rewards summate.

There is a great need to learn more about how to measure, channel, enhance, and decrease social drives. For the purposes of health, for example, it would be valuable to know more about how to modify peer group pressures in the direction of good health habits and away from bad ones and how best to develop a lasting interest in sports or in other activities that can provide an appropriate amount of exercise. We need to know more about how to foster intrinsic interest in activities, so that their maintenance is independent of extrinsic rewards, and how to prevent forced overperformance that is elicited by extrinsic drives and rewards from killing intrinsic interests.

The Gradient of Reinforcement

Immediate rewards or punishments are more effective than delayed ones. The same is true of the effects of anticipated outcomes. This empirical generalization is responsible for the fact that programs of prevention of disease and maintenance of health do not receive nearly the emphasis and financial support that is rationally justified by their cost-effectiveness. The immediate consequences of current illnesses are much more motivating for patients and for legislators than are the remote consequences of preventing future illnesses.

One of the difficulties of learning and continuing to perform healthy habits such as flossing the teeth, exercising, not eating too much food, not drinking too much alcohol, and not smoking is that they involve immediate effort or renunciation of gratification in the here and now in order to achieve greater rewards or to avoid worse punishment in a remote future. Thus, efforts to promote the learning and maintenance of good habits should concentrate on trying to discover and use as many immediate reinforcements as possible. To a considerable extent, as described by Evans in Chapter 48 of this Handbook, successful campaigns to immunize children against the habit of smoking and to encourage people who do smoke to stop have done this by deemphasizing heart disease and lung cancer in adulthood and by emphasizing, instead, the immediate effects of bad taste, bad breath, messiness, increased heart rate, and the decreased ability to taste and smell that result from smoking and the more immediate gains that can be achieved by stopping. Where support of a friend, spouse, or peer group can be mobilized, it can provide relatively immediate rewards for performing behavior that maintains health and stopping behavior that damages it.

From the point of view of immediate reward, it should be worthwhile to investigate the degree to which young people can be induced to pay attention to the various immediate pleasant sensations from a healthy body and from healthy activities such as an appropriate amount of exercise in sports. From the point of view of continuing rewards, emphasis should be on the types of sports and other healthy activities that will continue to be rewarding throughout the longest possible portion of one's life span. Many other ideas will suggest themselves to the resourceful and observant health professional.

Secondary Reinforcement

There are various ways that the gap between an action and a reinforcement can be bridged. One of these is secondary reinforcement. The stimulus regularly and immediately associated with a reward acquires the ability to serve as a reward. In this way a continuous chain of stimulus-response sequences over a reasonable length of time can be built up. It is more difficult to build up longer than shorter chains. Similarly, money, token rewards, or points earned that can later be exchanged for a positive reinforcement may serve as immediate rewards for the responses that produced them. The effectiveness of these arrangements depends on the lack of opportunities to obtain rewards in quicker, easier ways.

Gradients of Stimulus and Response Generalization

When a response is rewarded in one stimulus context, it is more likely to recur in that context. The probability of recurrence is increased also in other similar stimulus contexts, but the increase is progressively less to less similar stimuli. One must not assume that a health-promoting habit will necessarily transfer to other stimulus contexts—for example, from the school or clinic to the rest of life. The probability of such transfer can be increased by trying to attach it to perspicuous cues that are present in both contexts and by rewarding it under a variety of circumstances that are as similar as possible to those in which one hopes that it will be used. Role-playing is one way to facilitate such transfer (see Chapter 48 by Evans).

If such a generalized response is rewarded, the tendency to perform it is strengthened; in this way, the range of cues that can elicit the response is widened. If a generalized response is not rewarded, however, it will be extinguished, and a discrimination will be learned. One advantage of learning is that it can be made quite precise. If a drug such as alcohol, is used, for example, to reduce an unrealistic fear that prevents participation in lively conversation and other activities at a party, it may also reduce the realistic fear of driving too fast on the way home. A person can be taught, however, to discriminate between what is dangerous and what is safe (Miller, 1980).

When a specific response is rewarded, the tendency to perform other similar responses is also increased, but the increase is progressively less the less similar the responses are. This is the basis for a procedure that has been described by Skinner (1938) as "shaping." At first, any response that is at all similar to, or contains any element of, the desired response is rewarded. As responses more similar to the desired behavior occur, they are rewarded, and the reward for the less similar responses is dropped out. In this way, a precise response discrimination can be learned. In many cases, the specific dimensions of stimulus similarity—especially those of response similarity—have not been precisely worked out. In such cases, the details of shaping may be a mixture of science and art.

Intermittent Reinforcement

In many cases in the complex life situation, the relationship between a response and a reward may not be a perfect one but only a probable one. Intermittent reward can maintain the performance of a response, however. Indeed, a response that has been maintained by intermittent reward is more resistant to extinction by nonreward than is one that has been rewarded 100% of the time (Skinner, 1938), although 100% reward is more effective in establishing a response. Therefore, when it is desirable to have a response persist with intermittent reward, it is most efficient to start out with 100% reward and gradually shift to unpredictably intermittent ones. One should bear in mind, however, that if there is competition between two responses, other things being equal, the one receiving more reward will be the one performed.

The Power of Words, Thoughts, and Beliefs

In human behavior, words, thoughts, and beliefs can be enormously important. Their power, however, is complexly dependent on prior learning. A verbal threat, for example, can serve as a powerful motivation, but if one's previous experience has been only with threats that were never reinforced, such a threat is likely to have little motivating power. The same is true of promises. Thus, health care professionals should be wary of using exaggerated threats or promises. Similarly, thoughts can arouse drives; they can also serve as secondary rewards to help bridge the gap between an action and a more remote consequence. These capacities also are dependent on prior learning, however; for example, lower-class children who have not had the opportunity to be rewarded for planning and acting in longer-range terms seem to be less motivated to do so. Some people may say, "I know exactly what I should do and why I should do it, but I don't seem to be able to do it." Thus, we need more research on how self-control is learned.

Words can also serve as cues to elicit correct responses, as when people receive a set of directions or tell themselves the various things they have to do to succeed. Again, this power of words is dependent on previous learning. Thus, saying "You are not brushing your teeth enough" to a person who has not learned how to brush the teeth correctly will not achieve the desired result. One may need to demonstrate exactly how to brush the teeth and also to observe the behavior, correct errors, and reward correct responses by saying "That's right."

Imitation: The Prestige of Models

Demonstration—the use of a person's ability to imitate—depends on the person having the skills required to copy the demonstrated response. Thus, a single demonstration of a simple sequence of standard figures will be adequate to a skilled figure skater, but when shown to a person who knows nothing about ice skating, it cannot be copied. Similarly, sequences of steps that may seem simple to the skilled health professional may seem confusing and complex to the person who has not already learned the different unit skills that are involved.

Both experiments and general observations of social behavior have shown that the tendency to imitate a model is increased when such imitation is rewarded and is decreased when it is not. Thus, a discrimination can be learned between models to imitate and those not to imitate. Furthermore, the perception of similarity to a prestigious model can become rewarding and hence can reinforce imitation of that model (Miller & Dollard, 1941). There is reason to believe that similar principles apply to the establishment of motivation to follow the advice of a prestigious person, such as a health professional, and to be rewarded by his or her approval. In human social life, of course, the types of learning situations and the steps in the foregoing processes and phenomena may be quite complex. Additional factors may be involved, such as the generalization of learned and, perhaps, even innate patterns of reactions toward parents and other dominant figures.

Following the foregoing line of reasoning, it seems plausible that people generally are more likely to be rewarded for following the advice of somebody who gives evidence of really caring about them than for following the advice of someone who may be exploiting them. Janis (1982) describes a number of specific types of behavior that ingenious field studies have shown can enhance the prestige and increase the social power of the health care professional to influence patients. He presents evidence that it is important for the health care professional to have a relationship with the patients that is warm and affectionate and that bolsters their self-confidence. It seems reasonable that imitation of, approval from, and the thought of pleasing such a health care professional can provide immediate reinforcement for healthful habits.

THE WIDE RANGE OF EFFECTS OF LEARNING ON HEALTH

Learning has long been recognized as the process by which knowledge and special skills in the use of the skeletal muscles are acquired. Emotional adjustments, social skills, coping responses, and maladaptive behavior also can be learned (Dollard & Miller, 1950; Levine & Ursin, 1980; Pomerleau & Brady, 1979). The range of phenomena relevant to health in which learning is found to play a significant role is progressively increasing (Miller, 1983).

Classical Conditioning

In classical conditioning, a previously neutral stimulus—for example, a bell—is followed promptly by an unconditioned stimulus (such as food to a hungry subject) that innately elicits an unconditioned response—in this case, salivation. After a number of pairings, the previously neutral bell becomes a conditioned stimulus, with the newly acquired ability to elicit salivation as a conditioned response. In such learning, the unconditioned stimulus (food) is a reinforcement for learning the conditioned response, salivation to the bell. Classical conditioning shows the characteristics that already have been described: a gradient of reinforcement, a gradient of stimulus generalization, experimental extinction, and discrimination (Pavlov, 1927).

A wide range of visceral responses have been found to be modifiable by classical conditioning (Ádám, 1967; Bykov, 1957). In the alimentary tract alone, secretion of saliva, stomach acid, pancreatic juice, and bile, as well as contractions of the stomach, small and large intestines, and gall bladder, have all been found to be subject to classical conditioning—that is, they can be elicited by previously neutral stimuli that frequently have preceded them. It seems reasonable that capacities for such conditioning would not have evolved had they not served some adaptive function, and a plausible function is to prepare the successive stages of the alimentary tract for their activities in digestion and elimination. This hypothesis should be investigated by appropriate experiments. If it is true, it could be one of the reasons why regular regimes of eating and defecating seem to be more healthy than irregular ones (Miller & Dworkin, 1980).

Booth, Lee, and McAleavey (1976) have performed experiments on animals and people showing that the conditioning of satiation to a specific flavor plays an important role in adjusting the amount of intake to the caloric density of the type of food eaten. Without such learning, a person would have to wait until the food was digested before sensing, via some effects of absorption, whether too much or too little had been consumed. These results suggest that the introduction into the diet of too great a variety of new flavors and foods of different caloric densities may interfere with the process of weight regulation—a deduction that should be profitable to test.

Conditioned Compensatory Responses, Addiction, and Relapse

In most cases of classical conditioning, the response (e.g., salivation) that the previously neutral conditioned stimulus (e.g., bell) acquires is similar to that originally elicited by the unconditioned stimulus (e.g., food). In other cases, however, the conditioned response (CR) is opposite to the unconditioned response (UCR). The UCR to epinephrine, for example, is decreased gastric secretion, but the CR is increased gastric secretion; the UCR to atropine is a dry mouth, but the CR is excessive salivation; the UCR to mild doses of insulin is hypoglycemia, but the CR is hyperglycemia. These paradoxical responses seem to be anticipatory, compensatory responses that reduce the disturbance in homeostasis that would be produced by the unconditioned response.

Furthermore, Siegel (1982), who has summarized these and other results, has shown that the UCR to mild doses of morphine is hyperthermia and analgesia, whereas the CR to such stimuli as the injection procedure preceding the action of the drug is hypothermia and hyperalgesia. He and his colleagues have also shown that these learned compensatory responses to morphine (rather than purely pharmacological effects) are involved in the tolerance produced by the repeated administration of this drug. This learned effect is strong enough that animals that have been habituated by progressively increasing doses of morphine in one stimulus situation, until a large dose is relatively ineffective in that situation, will be killed if they are given exactly the same dose in a radically different stimulus situation (Siegel, Hinson, Krank, & McCully, 1982). Such a result is what one would expect from the gradient of stimulus generalization of a learned response; one would not expect it from a purely pharmacological effect.

Finally, Siegel (1982) and Wikler (1980) have pointed out that the conditioned compensatory responses to morphine play a significant role in withdrawal symptoms, which explains why people who have been addicted in one situation and detoxified in a radically different one are prone to relapse when returned to the situation in which they were addicted. People who have been addicted and detoxified in one situation and then returned to a different one are less likely to relapse, however. It should be profitable to conduct research determining the value of applying the foregoing findings to programs aimed at reducing the high rate of relapse of people who have given up drug addiction, excessive drinking, or smoking.

Visceral Learning, Biofeedback, Relaxation, and Homeostasis

We have already seen that visceral responses can be modified by classical conditioning, which has been considered a primitive type of learning and is limited by the fact that the reinforcement must elicit the type of response to be learned or an opposite compensatory response. In instrumental learning (also called trial-and-error learning or operant conditioning), primarily dealt with in the first part of this chapter, the reward reinforces virtually any immediately preceding response. Thus, instrumental learning is more flexible; the same reward may reinforce a variety of responses, or a given response may be reinforced by a variety of rewards.

One firmly held dogma had been that the more flexible instrumental learning could modify the autonomic nervous system controlling the viscera, if at all, only in a way that was considered to be trivial—namely, via the mediation of a skeletal response, such as running, that affects a visceral one, such as heart rate. More recent work has shown that instrumental learning can produce changes in a variety of visceral responses, such as salivation, heart rate, blood pressure, vasomotor responses in a specific area of the skin, and the galvanic skin response. When increases in these responses are rewarded, they are learned; when decreases are rewarded, they are learned. Although it is difficult to prove that these effects produced by rewarding the change in the visceral response are not mediated indirectly via skeletal responses, the results have been found to be far from trivial from the point of view of preventing, causing, or treating disease (Basmajian, 1979; Miller, 1978).

In visceral learning, a variety of rewards have been used. In order to reward a visceral change, however, it must be observed. In biofeedback, easy moment-to-moment observation of otherwise obscure visceral responses is made possible by the use of special measuring devices. In experiments on people, the reward has been either a signal, such as a tone, or direct observation of a measuring instrument indicating when the subject is succeeding in achieving his or her goal. Such information has been called feedback; when it comes from the performance of a biologically significant response, the procedure is called biofeedback.

The roles of motivation and reward in biofeedback are demonstrated clearly by the fact that, given exactly the same feedback, subjects who are motivated (usually by instructions) to learn to increase a response, so that feedback indicating an increase signals success and hence serves as a reward, learn to increase it, whereas subjects who are motivated to decrease a response learn to decrease it (Miller, 1982). The information from the measuring instruments is also useful in other ways. It helps to guide the responses of the patient and the therapist. It can help people to learn the connections between their emotional responses and their symptoms and to be more aware of their emotions and bodies. Rather than having something done to them or for them, biofeedback can teach them how to do something for themselves—to be in better control. Finally, by locating common sources of undue stress in the social and physical environment, it can point the way toward changes that will reduce these stresses and produce a healthier environment. Biofeedback will be dealt with in more detail in Chapter 20, by Schwartz and Chapter 54, by Patel.

The type of biofeedback that provides information from measurement of the electrical activity of muscles has been found to be useful in helping certain patients learn to relax. Its use in the prevention of headaches and attacks of Raynaud's disease, for example, has been one of the factors encouraging increased use of other older and simpler methods of learning relaxation. Often these are equally or more effective. These other methods will be discussed in Chapter 21, by Benson, Chapter 54, by Patel, and Chapter 76, by Collings. Information from measurement of electrical activity of muscles also has been found useful in helping patients with neuromuscular disorders to learn better control over their muscles and thus prevent a lifetime of disability. (Basmajian, 1979).

Homeostasis—the complex pattern of regulations that maintain body conditions at an optimal level—plays a vital role in maintaining health. We have already seen how anticipatory and compensatory conditioned responses can contribute to homeostasis. Instrumentally learned skeletal responses, such as going into the sun when one is too cold and into the shade when one is too hot, also contribute to homeostasis. What about instrumentally learned visceral responses?

Brucke (1977) has worked with patients with high spinal lesions who had suffered for more than 2 years from the homeostatic defect of orthostatic hypotension, so that, whenever they were helped into a more upright position, their blood pressure fell so low that they fainted. He found that biofeedback could be used to teach these patients to produce large increases in blood pressure. They also learned to perceive these large increases so that they could practice by themselves without the measuring instrument. Eventually, they could maintain an appropriately elevated blood pressure virtually automatically while sitting up without fainting, something that greatly increased their range of activity.

Because of the special circumstances of these cases, it was clear that visceral learning had corrected a serious homeostatic defect. One wonders in how many other ways such learning may help maintain homeostatis or correct defects in it—ways that have not yet been noticed because no one has looked for them or because the learning has occurred relatively automatically, motivated by the distress of a departure from acceptable limits and rewarded by the relief of return to these limits (Miller & Dworkin, 1980; Miller, 1981).

Finally, the opportunities for instrumental visceral learning to contribute to homeostasis and, hence, to health will be greater if such learning can occur directly, without requiring the mediation of a skeletal response. In investigating patients paralyzed from the neck down, Miller and Brucker (1979) found that large increases in the tension of nonparalyzed muscles, combined with self-commands to contract all paralyzed muscles, changes in breathing, and a Valsalva maneuver (tested after the 1979 publication), produced modest increases in blood pressure. When requested to use their learned response, however, the patients produced much larger increases in blood pressure without producing any changes in muscle tension or breathing. Furthermore, their heart rates did not change. Therefore, it seems highly probable that these patients had learned direct control over the visceral response of blood pressure.

Learning has been found to have a wider range of effects on health than anyone had previously realized. We may expect future research to discover even more ways in which learning can be used to maintain health and prevent illness.

REFERENCES

Ádám, G. *Interoception and behaviour*. Budapest: Akadémiai Kiadó, 1967.

Basmajian, J. V. *Biofeedback: Principles and practice for clinicians*. Baltimore: Williams & Wilkins, 1979.

Booth, D. A., Lee, M., & McAleavey, C. Acquired sensory control of satiation in man. *British Journal of Psychology*, 1976, **67**, 137–147.

Brucker, B. S. Learned voluntary control of systolic blood pressure by spinal cord injury patients. Unpublished doctoral dissertation, New York University, 1977.

Bykov, K. M. *The cerebral cortex and the internal organs* (W. H. Gantt, trans. and ed.). New York: Chemical Publishing Co., 1957.

Dickinson, A. *Contemporary animal learning theory*. Cambridge, England: Cambridge University Press, 1980.

Dollard, J., & Miller, N. E. *Personality and psychotherapy*. New York: McGraw-Hill, 1950.

Estes, W. K. *Handbook of learning and cognitive processes* (Vols. 1–4). Hillsdale, N.J.: Erlbaum Associates, 1975.

Janis, I. (Ed.). *Counseling on personal decisions*. New Haven: Yale University Press, 1982.

Levine, S., & Ursin, H. (Eds.). *Coping and health* (NATO Conference Series). New York: Plenum Press, 1980.

Locurto, C. M., Terrace, H. S., & Gibbon, J. (Eds.). *Autoshaping and conditioning theory*. New York: Academic Press, 1981.

Miller, N. E. Liberalization of basic S-R concepts: Extensions to conflict behavior, motivation and social learning. In S. Koch (Ed.), *Psychology: A study of a science* (Study 1, Vol. 2). New York: McGraw-Hill, 1959.

Miller, N. E. Biofeedback and visceral learning. *Annual Review of Psychology*, 1978, **29**, 373–404.

Miller, N. E. Applications of learning and biofeedback to psychiatry and medicine. In H. I. Kaplan, A. M. Freedman, & B. J. Sadock (Eds.), *Comprehensive textbook of psychiatry/III*. Baltimore: Williams & Wilkins, 1980.

Miller, N. E. Learning in the homeostatic regulation of visceral processes. In G. Ádám, I. Méscáros, & É. I. Bányai (Eds.), *Advances in physiological science: Vol. 17. Brain and behaviour*. Budapest: Akadémiai Kiadó, 1981.

Miller, N. E. Some directions for clinical and experimental research on biofeedback. In L. White & B. Tursky (Eds.), *Clinical biofeedback: Efficacy and mechanisms*. New York: Guilford Press, 1982.

Miller, N. E. Behavioral medicine: Symbiosis between laboratory and clinic. *Annual Review of Psychology*, 1983, **34**, 1–31.

Miller, N. E., & Brucker, B. S. Learned large increases in blood pressure apparently independent of skeletal responses in patients paralyzed by spinal lesions. In N. Birbaumer & H. D. Kimmel (Eds.), *Biofeedback and self-regulation*. Hillsdale, N.J.: Erlbaum Associates, 1979.

Miller, N. E., & Dollard, J. *Social learning and imitation*. New Haven: Yale University Press, 1941.

Miller, N. E., & Dworkin, B. R. Different ways in which learning is involved in homeostasis. In R. F. Thompson, L. H. Hicks, & V. B. Shvyrkov (Eds.), *Neural mechanisms of goal-directed behavior and learning*. New York: Academic Press, 1980.

Öhman, A., Eriksson, A., & Olofsson, C. One-trial learning and superior resistance to extinction of autonomic responses conditioned to potentially phobic stimuli. *Journal of Comparative and Physiological Psychology*, 1975, **88**, 619–627.

Pavlov, I. P. *Conditioned reflexes* (G. V. Anrep, trans.). London: Oxford University Press, 1927.

Pomerleau, O., & Brady, J. P. (Eds.). *Behavioral medicine: Theory and practice*. Baltimore: Williams & Wilkins, 1979.

Siegel, S. Extensions of principles of learning to effects of drugs. In E. Richter-Heinrich & N. E. Miller (Eds.), *Biofeedback—Basic problems and clinical applications.* Berlin: VEB Deutscher Verlag der Wissenschaften, 1982.

Siegel, S., Hinson, R. E., Krank, M. D., & McCully, J. Heroin "overdose" death: Contribution of drug-associated environmental cues. *Science,* 1982, **216,** 436–437.

Skinner, B. F. *The behavior of organisms.* New York: Appleton-Century, 1938.

Solomon, R. L. The opponent process theory of acquired motivation: The costs of pleasure and the benefits of pain. *American Psychologist,* 1980, **35,** 691–712.

Wikler, A. *Opioid dependence: mechanisms and treatment.* New York: Plenum Press, 1980.

CHAPTER 13

COMMUNICATION AS A MODEL FOR HEALTH ENHANCEMENT

DOUGLAS S. SOLOMON
NATHAN MACCOBY

Stanford Heart Disease Prevention Program, Stanford University

Communication is a relatively young behavioral discipline that came into being in the 1940s and 1950s in response to critical concerns about the impact of the mass media. One of the main areas of interest concerned the impact on society of propaganda disseminated through the mass media. This interest in propaganda's effects led to studies describing the audiences of mass media and to an understanding of the processes of mass media influence. From these beginnings by scholars such as Lasswell, Lazarsfeld, Hovland, and Schramm, the field of communication began to study such concepts as opinion leadership, the two-step flow of information, persuasion processes, and so on.

The field of communication uses a wide variety of theoretical frameworks and methods. Communication is considered to be a process without beginning or end; therefore, it is both difficult to understand and subject to a wide variety of research approaches (Berlo, Note 1).

Communication as a discipline is concerned with interactions at both the individual and the community levels. The communication approach, particularly in health promotion and disease prevention, has been applied at a community level because of the great reach of the mass media and the resulting potential for large-scale behavior change at low per-unit cost. The literature on the impact of mass communication, however, warns one not to ignore interpersonal communication processes. Therefore, this chapter will discuss communication as applied to large-scale health change efforts that incorporate both mass media and interpersonal communication.

Communication has had a relatively long association with the health disciplines. For many years, however, communication, particularly mass media, was considered not very powerful in changing behavior or otherwise influencing individuals toward a more healthful lifestyle (Klapper, 1960). More recently, a more optimistic approach has emerged, as influences of health communication on behavior have been demonstrated (Atkin, 1979; Rice & Paisley, 1981; Roberts & Bachen, 1981; Roberts & Maccoby, in press; Solomon, in press), reinforced by the results of studies such as the Stanford Three Community Study (Farquhar, Maccoby, Wood, Alexander, Breitrose, Brown, Haskell, McAlister, Meyer, Nash, & Stern, 1977; Maccoby, Farquhar, Wood, & Alexander, 1977).

The work reported herein was supported in part by NHLBI Grants No. HL-14174 and HL-21906.

THE ROLE OF THEORY IN THE COMMUNICATION APPROACH TO HEALTH ENHANCEMENT

Kurt Lewin said: "There is nothing so practical as a good theory" (Marrow, 1969). Theory helps focus efforts in achieving health behavior change and is quite useful in pointing out key variables, strategies, and important processes of change. Finally, of course, theory provides a framework for the planning of research and the planning of change and a baseline for the revision of one's beliefs about the importance and efficacy of various health and education program components.

There is no single unified theory of communication related to health enhancement at this time. Nor is it likely that such a theory will emerge in the near future. At this point, an eclectic approach is necessary, since the available theories apply to different variables, various levels of abstraction, and different types of communications.

The Cartwright (1949) model of communication campaigns, for example, applies primarily at the macro level and deals with the availability of certain critical elements of a campaign in a society. Bandura's 1977(a) self-efficacy model, as one component of social learning theory, deals mainly with individuals. Many examples of health campaigns (Solomon, 1982) used a single or a limited theoretical approach and therefore failed because they neglected to take into account key variables that were not within the scope of that particular framework.

Many health enhancement programs in the past have been more or less theory-free. The seatbelt-wearing campaign of Robertson, Kelley, O'Neill, Wixom, Eiswirth, and Haddon (1974) for example, had no apparent theoretical basis. Hence, when it failed, it could not provide an explanation for its lack of success, since the research was not based on a theory of the process of change. In summary, the role of theory at this stage of development in a communication approach to health enhancement is to point the way and to provide a foundation for research rather than (as may be possible in a more developed discipline) actually to provide concrete implications for program design, implementation, and evaluation. Theory, here, is in the making. As theory develops in this field, its usefulness will increase greatly. Theories derived from communication and other related disciplines that have been applied to health enhancement programs will be discussed briefly in the next section.

THREE FRAMEWORKS FOR HEALTH ENHANCEMENT

Three major theoretical frameworks seem to be highly applicable to health enhancement and are currently being applied in research on disease prevention at Stanford University: communication-behavior change, community organization, and social marketing. All three approaches are useful in planning health enhancement in a community setting, since they deal with different variables at differing levels of abstraction in a complementary fashion. Each will be discussed briefly here; since this chapter deals mainly with communication, however, communication-behavior change will be emphasized.

The Communication-Behavior Change Approach

Communication-behavior change is an approach consisting of theories of communication, behavior change, and influence that provide useful perspectives on how individuals and groups change knowledge, attitudes, and behavior. The most widely used approach within this overall framework is that of social learning theory (Bandura, 1977b). Social learning theory is particularly useful because it is concerned not only with the individual, but also with the individual's environment and the reciprocal deterministic factors linking an individual with his or her environment.

Three critical elements of social learning theory have particular relevance for communication and health enhancement: self-efficacy, modeling, and maintenance or self-management. Self-efficacy is a recent modification of social learning theory. It refers to the cognitive and behavioral factors related to an individual's perception of his or her own ability to make lifestyle changes. Self-efficacy appears to be an important mediator between knowledge, attitudes, skills, and subsequent behavior change. It is particularly relevant to health enhancement because it is not only a mediator but seems to be modifiable through particular behavior management strategies (Bandura, 1977a, 1982; Bandura, Adams, & Beyer, 1977; Bandura & Schunk, 1981; Borkovec, 1978). Several recent studies on smoking cessation, for example, suggest that self-efficacy is an important mediator of success in quitting smoking and especially in the maintenance of cessation (Candiotte & Lichtenstein, 1981; DiClemente, 1981).

Modeling—that is, learning through observation of the behavior of others—is another of the major elements of social learning theory. It is important in health enhancement programs for learning, motivation, and enactment of health behaviors. Therefore, the relevance of modeling provides many implications for the use of models in small group programs, in the family setting, in the community setting, and through mass media, which are potentially quite powerful for modeling new behaviors. An important modification of modeling has been employed in smoking prevention programs among youth. What is to be modeled by learners becomes the *invention* as well as the practice of counterarguments to efforts to persuade young people to smoke.

A third element of social learning theory that is particularly relevant to health behavior is self-management and maintenance of behavior change. Self-management generally involves the gradual withdrawal of external reinforcers for behavior, changing the reinforcement to internal cues for eliciting previously learned behavior. Internal cues are essential because they must come into play at the particular time and place when behavior changes must be maintained, which only the involved individual knows. Self-management is crucial both in learning needed skills and in the actual performance of the skills when they are needed. Social learning theory, and research derived from it, deals at great length with strategies for providing maintenance and self-management, since without such strategies it is highly unlikely that behavior change will persist for any length of time.

Another theory relevant to communication is the model created by Dorwin Cartwright (1949) on the role of motivational, cognitive, and particularly action structures in planning and executing mass communication programs. Cartwright's analysis of communication campaigns derived from an assessment of the World War II War Bond sales efforts and particularly emphasized the need for creating "action structures"—mechanisms in society to facilitate behavior changes—arguing that motivation and knowledge are necessary but not sufficient for achieving widespread behavior change.

The diffusion of innovations theory (Rogers with Shoemaker, 1971) also offers an important perspective in the communication-behavior change approach. It looks at the individual change process as well as at the interactions among individuals in society as they affect the adoption of new ideas, practices, and products. Currently, a partial synthesis of social learning theory and diffusion theory appears to be in the making by Bandura and Rogers (Note 2).

Hierarchies of learning such as those proposed by Ray (1973) and McGuire (1969)—generally described as K (knowledge), A (attitudes), B (behavior) approaches—usually begin with knowledge, proceed through attitude change, and move toward behavior change and maintenance of the new behaviors. Both McGuire and Ray caution that individuals do not necessarily proceed in this order, and that the effects of a campaign on one level of a hierarchy may have confounding or even negative effects on other levels of the hierarchy. Some programs may be able to create high levels of knowledge, for example, but at the same time may actually reduce motivation or even create negative attitudes toward change. Therefore, it is important that health promoters be aware of where various subgroups in the audience are currently located on a hierarchy. It is also important that the techniques and messages used in a campaign be pretested and studied as they apply to each level of the hierarchy. It is not safe to assume that effects on one level will positively influence other levels. Finally, both Ray and McGuire suggest that it is important to consider developing an intervention based on where key audience groups currently are located on a hierarchy of change. In a smoking cessation campaign, for example, if most smokers already know about the health consequences and believe they should quit smoking, it is foolish to concentrate messages on these themes. Formative evaluation might reveal that many smokers do not persist in quitting because they think the psychological price of quitting is too high. The education program must then address itself to this problem. It may emphasize, for example, that although withdrawal symptoms persist, they rapidly become less severe and therefore easier to deal with. The education effort could then provide advice on how to deal with urges to smoke before they become too strong, such as by the use of distractors or rehearsed counterarguments—for example, that the urges are relatively infrequent, relatively weak, and of shorter duration after several weeks compared to when first quitting smoking.

Attitude change theories such as those by Fishbein (Ajzen & Fishbein, 1980) are also important in health enhancement, since there is much in the literature that is applicable to the creation and execution of enhancement programs. Fishbein's characterization of attitudes as behavioral intentions is especially useful here because of their psychological proximity to behavior.

It should be clear at this point that all these theories provide information on many variables and processes at different levels of abstraction that are important to consider in health enhancement programs.

THE SOCIAL MARKETING APPROACH

Social marketing concerns the applicability of marketing concepts to problems other than those in the private, for-profit sector. Novelli (Note 3) summarized four basic problems in social campaigns: low visibility, lamentable budget, little research, and lack of continuity. These problems, he and others suggest, can be overcome through the use of a social marketing perspective. Kotler (1975) has described social marketing as:

> . . . the design, implementation, and control of programs seeking to increase the acceptability of a social idea or practice in a target group(s). It utilizes concepts of market segmentations, consumer research, idea configuration, communication, facilitation, incentives, and exchange theory, to maximize target groups' response.

According to Kotler (1972), marketing is a generic exchange process whereby something of value is exchanged among two or more parties because they feel the exchange will best meet their individual needs. The entity of value can be a product, an idea, or a practice. The marketing philosophy says that the goal of an organization should be to meet consumer needs and wants. Therefore, the consumer should be at the top of the organizational pyramid, directing the plans and products. This consumer-based approach is relatively rare in the health field. In health promotion, what is being promoted is often not particularly attractive to consumers, but the social marketing approach dictates that, wherever possible, consumers' wants and needs should be satisfied in some way by the product, practice, or idea being promoted.

A very useful concept of marketing with wide applicability to social campaigns is the so-called four P's: *product, price, place,* and *promotion.* A *product* can have a physical reality or can be an idea, practice, or service. According to the marketing framework, organizations should strive to define their core generic product. If this is defined appropriately, it can lead to many new opportunities for an organization. Many organizations define their generic product too narrowly, however. Many health programs, for example, define their core generic product as the provision of treatment services. It may be interesting to consider which broad generic products for health promotion and enhancement are possible, and what their potential benefits to various target groups could be.

The *price* of a product or service consists of more than just the monetary cost. Other factors need to be considered, including the time spent by the individual engaging in a particular health behavior and the psychological and social costs of engaging in a new and perhaps unpopular health behavior. It is obvious from the many health services that are underutilized, particularly in Third World countries, that even offering free services does not necessarily encourage their use. This is because of the nonmonetary costs involved in new ideas and practices. Such factors need to be considered in the design and implementation of health enhancement programs.

Place means the distribution channels that are used to make a product, service, or idea easily available to a target audience. Many social programs, particularly health programs, have failed because they did not have adequate distribution systems, thus creating barriers to utilization.

Promotion is a broad concept that encompasses publicity about a program, the mass media message design and dissemination, interpersonal communication, and the campaign's monitoring and modification procedures. These considerations obviously involve a great deal of theory and experimental literature that cannot be described here but have great relevance to successful health programs (see McGuire, 1981).

In summary, the four P's remind us that each of these elements is important in health promotion and that none of them can be ignored without jeopardizing the overall results of a program.

COMMUNITY ORGANIZATION MODEL

There is no single theory from the community organization literature that applies adequately to health promotion work. One must borrow from the diffusion of innovations theory (Rogers with Shoemaker, 1971), network analysis theory (Rogers & Kincaid, 1981), social support theory (Antonovsky, 1979; Berkman & Syme, 1979), and community development and organization theories (Rothman, 1979; Spergel, Vorwaller, & Switzer, 1972; Warren, 1965).

Rothman (1979) proposes three elements of community organization: social planning, locality development, and social action. Social planning is an approach that attempts to solve community problems rationally within existing power structures. Social action, on the other hand, is an activist approach that attempts to shift power structures in a community through various methods of coercion. Locality developing is an orientation aimed at developing the potential of a community through self-help techniques and programs within the constraints of the power structure.

Spergel et al. (1972) identify three interrelated tactics derived from community organization frameworks: organizing, intraorganizing, and interorganizing. Organizing is defined as "the process of stimulating, focusing and mobilizing both citizen, elite leadership or agency concern and effort in relation to a community problem or condition" (p. 42). The techniques of organizing include: "establishing commitment, developing leadership, articulating issues, educating and persuading, protest, bargaining, providing support, facilitating self-determination, developing political power, and exercising control" (p. 43).

Intraorganizing focuses on the internal aspects of the change agency itself. This tactic suggests the development of appropriate administrative structures and styles of operation to maximize organization efficiency.

Interorganizing (Davidson, 1976; Groves, 1964) is the most complex community organization tactic. It focuses on the development and improvement of intergroup and interorganizational activities, with the objective of facilitating joint community problem solving. This is the most often discussed type of community organization in the literature and offers many implications and suggestions for action.

If the goal for a health enhancement program is to enable local community organizations and individuals to take over health promotion efforts—which is desirable both from the point of view of achieving long-term effects and from a cost standpoint—then such theories need to be actively considered from the onset of program planning.

APPLICATIONS OF COMMUNICATION AND BEHAVIORAL HEALTH ENHANCEMENT—STANFORD COMMUNITY STUDIES

The Stanford Heart Disease Prevention Program (SHDPP) began in 1970 with the formation of an interdisciplinary group of medical and behavioral scientists, in conjunction with creative media professionals, to explore the potential of cardiovascular risk reduction through the education of entire communities. The goal was to create a model of education that could be administered primarily through the mass media to provide policymakers with a means of education for risk reduction that was potentially widely usable and relatively inexpensive per person.

The Stanford Three Community Study began in 1972. It was a quasi-experimental field study in three Northern California communities. Two of them had extensive mass media campaigns over a 2-year period; in one of these communities, the mass media campaigns were supplemented by intensive face-to-face instruction of a sample subset of individuals in the highest quartile of risk. This treatment, though too expensive to be applied generally, would serve as a "gold standard" against which to compare the uncertain success of the mass-media-only treatment. A third community served as a control and received no treatment. Individuals randomly selected from each community were surveyed and examined for cardiovascular risk factors before the campaign began and at yearly intervals for 3 years afterward. The community with both a mass media campaign and intensive instruction had an initial decrease in risk, as measured by a multiple logistic risk function (Truett, Cornfield, & Kannel, 1967) that was greater in the first year. By the second year, however, the mass-media-only community had equaled it. Risk in the control community increased over the 2 years of the program. The results suggest that mass media educational campaigns directed at entire communities can be effective in reducing the risk of heart attack and stroke, at least temporarily. These results have been published elsewhere (Farquhar et al., 1977; Maccoby et al., 1977).

The theoretical framework for the Three Community Study was based largely on communication-behavior theory, as described earlier; in particular, the framework developed by Cartwright (1949) and social learning theory (Bandura, 1977b) played major conceptual roles.

Maccoby and Alexander (1979) cited several key features of the Three Community Study that might have contributed to its success: (a) the establishment of specific objectives for each component of the campaign over time; (b) clearly defined audience segments; (c) the creation of clear, useful, and salient messages through formative research and pretesting; (d) utilization of creative media scheduling to reach the audience with adequate frequency; (e) stimulation of interpersonal communication to encourage a synergistic effect of multiple channels; (f) advocacy of clear and well-paced behavioral changes in messages; (g) the use of feedback to evaluate the campaign's progress over time; and (h) the use of a long-term campaign to avoid failure to reach changes large enough to be measurable.

The Three Community Study prompted the design of a larger-scale study that could implement more recently developed behavior change strategies and that would include a more extensive process evaluation. This study, initiated in the summer of 1978 as the Five City Project, is currently under way (Maccoby & Solomon, 1981), with a goal of reducing overall risk by about 20% in the treatment versus the control communities. The Five City Project includes many of the successful elements of the previous study, but it has been enlarged and modified: the new communities are much larger than the previous ones; the project will run from 5 to 8 years; through the participation of community groups, community education is being encouraged to continue indefinitely; and the sample of community participants is broadened from ages 35 to 59 to include all people from ages 12 to 74. The larger populations in the communities and the longer time span of the project will make possible not only the measurement of heart disease risk but also detection of differences in cardiovascular morbidity and mortality rates. The Five City Project uses both mass media and face-to-face interactions, conducted largely by community groups in both of the treatment communities. It is based on the theoretical foundations described earlier in this chapter, utilizing recent developments in social learning and other theories that were not available at the time the Three Community Study was planned.

Several other projects similar to the Five City Project are currently under way, including the Minnesota Heart Health Project, the Pennsylvania and Rhode Island projects, and others in countries such as Finland, Australia, Switzerland, West Germany, the Soviet Union, and South Africa. When one or more of these projects provides a successful model, the outcome will be quite useful, because it will have implemented the results of clinic-based trials on the efficacy of various methods to reduce risk, and it will provide public health policymakers with relevant data.

PROCESS AND METHODS OF APPLYING COMMUNICATION TO HEALTH ENHANCEMENT

This section will present an overall framework for applying communication to health enhancement programs. This framework is utilized extensively in the SHDPP and may provide a useful perspective for other health enhancement programs. There are four major areas in this process: problem analysis, media analysis, message/community program design, and evaluation.

Problem Analysis

The first phase of the process—problem analysis and audience analysis—is related to refining the overall goals of the health enhancement program after considerable thinking and at least a minimal level of research. Generally, health programs start with vague, overall objectives that need to be refined according to an understanding of several factors, including the root causes of the problem; the types of people, called audience segments, that are the prospects for a particular problem; and audience needs, attitudes, knowledge levels, and current behaviors. In this process, it is important to understand the existing obstacles to change and to know where individuals currently are located on a hypothesized hierarchy of change. In looking at the population of smokers, for example, it is possible to differentiate various subgroups that differ substantially in behaviors, demographics, attitudes, and knowledge levels. Pregnant smokers, for instance, are quite different in their motivation, and obviously in many other characteristics, from middle-aged male smokers. Similarly, teenagers are quite different from the preceding two groups. Smokers also vary in their degree of motivation to quit. Evaluations by the SHDPP have shown that some materials, such as television programs, can be used successfully to encourage smokers who are highly motivated to quit to do so, whereas more intensive efforts are necessary for smokers who are less motivated to stop smoking.

The problem analysis process also allows one to look for non-communication-related obstacles to change. In the area of nutrition, for example, one may find through a problem analysis that nutritious foods are simply not available to a given target group or are not available in a way that promotes effective utilization. They may be too costly or not available in the usual shopping places. Therefore, communication alone can not influence this group and perhaps some infrastructure or distribution system change needs to be made before initiating communication. Once a problem has been defined and the audience has been divided into various subgroups that can receive different kinds of programs, the process goes on to create refined campaign goals and objectives that must be specific, measurable, and achievable.

Media Analysis and Communication Program Analysis

The second phase of the process involves looking at the channels that can be used to reach individuals and groups with the kinds of programs they most need and desire. In some cases, mass media may be the most appropriate method. This is particularly true when little infrastructure is available and when programs are necessary that involve little cost per person to be educated and minimal labor inputs. In other cases, when labor is available and when a program may require elements of social support, group modeling, and so on, community programs may be preferrable. In most cases, however, some combination of community programs and media programs will provide the most effective intervention through a synergistic effect. Therefore, at this stage in the process, one must look at the "fit" between the media available, including community programs, and the needs and objectives of a particular health enhancement program. One must consider the availability of community groups, their eagerness to participate, and the particular match between the groups' objectives and the program's objectives. In the media area, one should look at the match between the objectives of a media program and the medium used. This area has been overlooked in many cases, and decisions have often been made on the basis of personal preferences for film, videotape, or print, without further consideration. Many questions must be asked in a media analysis, including distribution costs, facilities for distributing media products in the community, the needed level of media sophistication, and the optimal information density of a message. Is it better, for example, to use a high-density information message, such as a printed booklet that can be used at the discretion of the receiver, rather than a low-density information message, such as a TV spot, which cannot be reviewed and repeated at will? Once the media have been chosen, whether they are mass media or interpersonal media, the next phase involves designing the message component.

Message Design

Message design describes the process of setting specific objectives for each message, generating alternative messages, pretesting them, and revising them so that they meet their original objectives. This process applies equally as well to mass media messages and to community programs. Formative research, which will be described in the next section, should be utilized as much as possible in this process. The research need not be expensive or complex but should use the best information available to determine which messages will be received, understood, and acted upon by particular audience segments. It should be remembered that different audience segments may require different messages. Messages to teenagers, which may be disseminated through such channels as radio, should be very different from messages to older adults, which may be disseminated through printed material, such as a newspaper. The sources used, the methods of presenting the information, and even the language of a message should differ for each target group. There is a great deal of research on message variables, which should not be ignored by health enhancement program planners (e.g., McGuire, 1969; Schramm, 1972; Zimbardo, Ebbeson, & Maslach, 1977).

Evaluation

Two main aspects of evaluation need to be considered. The first is formative evaluation—evaluation oriented toward the planning and process analysis of a health enhancement program. The second is summative evaluation—evaluation on the outcomes or effects of a program.

Although most programs incorporate some summative evaluation, few health programs involve formative evaluation. This leads to two serious problems. First, messages and programs that have not been pretested may be seriously flawed. Second, without process analysis, if a program engenders no measured effects at the conclusion, it is difficult to understand why this was the case. Similarly, many programs that have had significant effects but no process evaluation leave little for subsequent researchers and practitioners to draw upon, since the mechanisms of change are not clearly understood and therefore cannot be repeated. The implication of the problem of a lack of process analysis is for health enhancement planners to create a process model for a specific program that defines some particular guideposts that need to be assessed over time in order to understand whether the program is meeting its goals. An exercise promotion program, for example, might hypothesize that mass media messages will set the agenda for exercise in the community and might encourage individuals to call a hotline number to learn about exercise alternatives, such as aerobic dance classes. This could then lead to exercise changes in the community. On the basis of this model, an evaluation can be established to monitor exposure to the mass media messages, attitude changes as a result of the messages, knowledge changes about where to go for help, actual usage of the hotline, enrollment in classes, and resulting behavior changes due to the classes. If any element in this chain breaks down, the evaluation can pinpoint it and can suggest alternatives for the future. Therefore, both *process evaluation* and traditional summative evaluation should be part of behavioral health enhancement programs. These evaluations need not be expensive or complex. At a minimum, they should provide the information necessary to provide a management information system.

Although the process of applying communication to health enhancement as presented here is obviously not new, it has rarely been applied in the practice of behavioral health enhancement. Therefore, it is suggested that these ideas be considered at least in applying the current state of the art in future programs. Without the careful documentation and planning that is part of this recommended planning process, the state of the art will be difficult to improve.

THE ROLE OF FORMATIVE RESEARCH

This section describes in greater detail the role of formative research, since it is an area of great potential for improving health enhancement programs (Palmer, 1981; Rossi, Freeman, & Wright, 1979; Bertrand, Note 4). Indeed, formative research is an essential component of communication programs. Formative research provides the empirical direction for communication efforts. Although many theories in the area of communication, marketing, psychology, and education relate to health enhancement strategies, it has been noted that they provide, at most, only situation-specific implications for action. Therefore, formative research is needed to move from hypotheses derived from theory toward concrete messages, message strategies, and complete communication programs.

Formative research can be defined as research that is oriented toward the planning, implementation, and evaluation processes within a program. It is research aimed at providing guidance for educational planners in facilitating the development of appropriate, attractive, and effective media and community programs. It can be distinguished from summative research in that summative research looks for ultimate outcomes of a program, whereas formative research looks at the planning aspects and the processes of change within a program. Formative research takes the explicit hypotheses created in the planning process for particular educational programs and media and tests them prior to their implementation. Therefore, it has great relevance and importance in creating high-quality educational programs that maximize their potential for success as well as in preventing large-scale errors in community education programs, which can backfire and cause serious problems. Thus, formative research has a proactive as well as a preventive purpose.

A simple framework for the use of formative research within a health promotion program such as the SHDPP would include five basic purposes for formative research. Each purpose will be described here briefly.

Collection of Baseline Data for Developing Audience Profiles and for Defining Specific Subaudience Segments

Collected baseline data contribute to a more detailed understanding of the kinds of people in the audience, their attitudes, their health needs, their desires for change, their lifestyles, and potential points for lifestyle interventions. Within the SHDPP Five City Project, such research has considered the demographics, knowledge, attitudes, risk behaviors, mass media use, and community organization memberships of people in the education communities. In this project, questions were asked regarding the salience of heart disease prevention topics; individuals' past experience with risk reduction; resources they have used for risk reduction, such as schools and community colleges; preferences for ideal weight loss, smoking cessation, and exercise programs; information needs relating to heart disease prevention; and even the semantics of how best to communicate risk reduction information to individuals.

Information for Specific Program Planning

A community program has many different attributes—its price, its location, the types of people involved in it, the educational methods used in it, the time requirements, and so on. By conducting formative research on program design, which is analogous to product design in marketing, one can create optimal and attractive community programs. The SHDPP, for example, has identified various subgroups of smokers and has conducted research on the kinds of programs most attractive to each subgroup. Based on this research, do-it-yourself quit kits were designed for certain segments, television shows for other segments, TV spots for others, and intensive classes for other groups of smokers.

Information for Developing Specific Media Products

This research is analogous to the preceding type but is directed toward media products. It includes many variables that require consideration in designing media products, including the proper sources to use to gain audience attention and to establish credibility, the methods to use in presenting the message to maximize understanding and to stimulate motivation, the best strategies to use for creating knowledge, and so on.

A general approach to message design research is, first, to utilize the existing behavioral theories and specific research undertaken on audience attitudes, knowledge, and so on, to create inexpensive prototype messages that are similar to the form the final messages will take but that can be changed before final production. These messages are then tested on individuals or in groups that are similar to those in the target audience. Once tested, the messages are revised and often retested before finally being implemented. The key consideration is that these messages are assigned specific objectives and are tested against these objectives to determine whether they can be potentially effective in the community setting. Within the SHDPP, such research has been enormously helpful in avoiding the tremendous problems of misunderstanding and misinformation that can occur as a result of poorly designed messages. We have often found, for example, that small changes in the order of presentation in the message can have a great impact on audience understanding and on resulting motivations to change. Although there is no guarantee that messages that are tested and refined in this process will be effective in a community setting, it is almost certain that messages that are ineffective in a pretest will also be ineffective in the community setting. Therefore, there is much to be gained from this kind of formative research.

Process Evaluation of Media Events

This fourth type of formative research is designed to monitor the process of media programs in the community. It is designed to look at the impact of media within a hypothesized process model created for a particular program, as has been described earlier. In the process analysis of a direct mail brochure on nutrition, for example, it is important to determine how many people received the brochure, how many of them read it, what they learned from it, and what they say they will do in terms of changing their future behavior. Although success at any of these guideposts does not necessarily assure behavior change, lack of success indicates probable lack of effectiveness. Sometimes process evaluation of media events involves not just one media program but an entire media campaign. The SHDPP, for example, recently evaluated a month-long blood pressure campaign that included a variety of media programs.

Process Evaluation of Community Events

The final type of formative research for health promotion programs is process evaluation of community events and programs. This evaluation is analogous to process evaluation of media events and considers the same types of variables as they relate to community programs such as races, classes, lectures, exercise groups, and so on. If done on a timely basis, this research allows one to fine-tune programs in order to improve their success for the future.

The methods used for formative research do not differ significantly from the methods used for summative research. They include surveys, individual interviews, focus-group discussions, questionnaires, and virtually all other kinds of research methods. The crucial factors distinguishing formative from summative research methods are the intentions of the researcher and the information that is desired as a result of the research. The emphasis on the process of change and on the reasons for change or lack of change is an important characteristic of formative research methods. Finally, formative research may be quite important in causal analysis of community-based health enhancement programs that are difficult to disentangle. Although formative research cannot provide information on the definitive reasons or processes of change, it can help test hypotheses about the change processes and rule out alternative rival hypotheses. In this way, formative process analysis can help unravel the complex nature of community health enhancement efforts.

SUMMARY

This chapter has considered the role of communication in health enhancement, emphasizing theories of communication and frameworks for these theories as well as pointing to some specific applications of communication in health enhancement. The process model proposed for planning communication is a simple one, with many implications for health enhancement efforts, particularly if the formative research component is utilized in designing and directing the program. It has potential for creating effective programs and, at the same time, furthering the depth and breadth of the theoretical literature in communication for health enhancement, which may be useful in the development of consistent and qualitatively better programs in the future.

REFERENCE NOTES

1. Berlo, D. K. *An empirical test of a general construct of credibility.* Paper presented to the Speech Association of America, New York, 1961.
2. Bandura, A., & Rogers, E. M. Personal communication, 1982.
3. Novelli, W. *Confessions of a social marketer.* Paper presented at the Marketing Educators Conference of the American Marketing Association, August 5, 1980.
4. Bertrand, J. T. *Communications pretesting.* Media Monograph No. 6, University of Chicago, 1978.

REFERENCES

Ajzen, I., & Fishbein, M. *Understanding attitudes and predicting social behavior,* Englewood Cliffs, N.J.: Prentice-Hall, 1980.

Antonovsky, A. *Health, stress, and coping.* San Francisco: Jossey-Bass, 1979.

Atkin, C. K. Research evidence on mass mediated health communication campaigns. *Communication Yearbook 3,* 1979. Transaction Books, New Brunswick, N.J., 665–668.

Bandura, A. Self-efficacy: Toward a unifying theory of behavioral change. *Psychological Review,* 1977, **89,** 191–215. (a)

Bandura, A. *Social learning theory.* Englewood Cliffs, N.J.: Prentice-Hall, 1977. (b)

Bandura, A. The self and mechanisms of agency. In J. Suls (Ed.), *Psychological perspectives on the self* (Vol. 1). Hillsdale, N.J.: Erlbaum Associates, 1982.

Bandura, A., Adams, N. E., & Beyer, J. Cognitive processes mediating behavioral change. *Journal of Personality and Social Psychology,* 1977, **35,** 125–139.

Bandura, A., & Schunk, D. H. Cultivating competence, self-efficacy, and intrinsic interest through proximal self-motivation. *Journal of Personality and Social Psychology,* 1981, **41,** 586–598.

Berkman, L. F., & Syme, L. Social networks, host resistance, and mortality: A nine-year follow-up study of Alameda County residents. *American Journal of Epidemiology,* 1979, **109,** 186–204.

Berkovec, T. D. Self-efficacy: Cause or reflection of behavioral change? *Advances in Behavior Research and Therapy,* 1978, **1,** 163–170.

Candiotte, M. M., & Lichtenstein, E. Self-efficacy and relapse in smoking cessation programs. *Journal of Consulting and Clinical Psychology,* 1981.

Cartwright, D. Some principles of mass persuasion: Selected findings of research on the sale of U.S. War Bonds. *Human Relations,* 1949, **2,** 253–267.

Davidson, S. Planning and coordination of social services in multi-organizational contexts. *Social Service Review,* 1976, **50,** 117–137.

DiClemente, C. C. Self-efficacy and smoking cessation maintenance: A preliminary report. *Journal of Cognitive Therapy and Research,* 1981, **5,** 175–187.

Farquhar, J. W., Maccoby, N., Wood, P. D., Alexander, J. K., Breitrose, H. S., Brown, B. W., Haskell, W. L., McAlister, A. L., Meyer, A. J., Nash, J. D., & Stern, M. P. Community education for cardiovascular health. *Lancet,* 1977, **1,** 1192–1195.

Groves, W. B. *American intergovernmental relations.* New York: Scribner's, 1964.

Klapper, J. T. *The effects of mass communication.* New York: Free Press, 1960.

Kotler, P. The five C's: Cause, change agency, change target, channel, and change strategy: A general discussion. In G. Zaltman, P. Kotler, & I. Kaufman (Eds.), *Creating social change.* San Francisco: Holt, Rinehart & Winston, 1972.

Kotler, P. *"Social marketing" in marketing for nonprofit organizations.* Englewood Cliffs, N.J.: Prentice-Hall, 1975.

Maccoby, N., & Alexander, J. Field experimentation in community intervention. In R. F. Munoz, L. R. Snowden, & J. G. Kelly (Eds.), *Social and psychological research in community settings.* San Francisco, Jossey-Bass, 1979.

Maccoby, N., Farquhar, J. W., Wood, P. D., & Alexander, J. Reducing the risk of cardiovascular disease. *Journal of Community Health,* 1977, **3,** 100–114.

Maccoby, N., & Solomon, D. Heart disease: Community studies. In R. Rice & W. Paisley (Eds.), *Public communication campaigns.* Beverly Hills: Sage, 1981.

Marrow, A. J. *The practical theorist.* New York: Basic Books, 1969.

McGuire, W. J. The nature of attitudes and attitude change. In G. Lindzey & E. Aronson (Eds.), *The handbook of social psychology* (2nd ed., Vol. 3). Reading, Mass.: Addison-Wesley, 1969.

McGuire, W. J. Theoretical foundations of campaigns. In R. Rice & W. Paisley (Eds.), *Public communication campaigns.* Beverly Hills: Sage, 1981.

Palmer, E. Shaping persuasive messages with formative research. In R. Rice & W. Paisley (Eds.), *Public communication campaigns.* Beverly Hills: Sage, 1981.

Ray, M. L. The present and potential linkages between the micro-theoretical notions of behavioral science and the problems of advertising: A proposal for a research system. In H. L. Davis & A. J. Silk (Eds.), *Behavorial and management science in marketing.* New York: John Wiley & Sons, 1972.

Ray, M. L. Marketing communication and the hierarchy of effects. In P. Clarke (Ed.), *New models for mass communication research.* Beverly Hills: Sage, 1973.

Rice, R., & Paisley, W. (Eds.). *Public communication campaigns.* Beverly Hills: Sage, 1981.

Roberts, D. F., & Bachen, C. M. Mass communication. *Annual Review of Psychology,* 1981, **32,** 307–356.

Roberts, D. F., & Maccoby, N. Effects of mass communication. In G. Lindzey & E. Aronson (Eds.), *Handbook of social psychology* (3rd ed.). Reading, Mass.: Addison-Wesley, in press.

Robertson, L. S., Kelley, A. B., O'Neill, B., Wixom, C. W., Eiswirth, R. S., & Haddon, W. A controlled study of the effect of television messages on safety belt use. *American Journal of Public Health,* 1974, **64,** 1071–1080.

Rogers, E. M., & Kincaid, D. L. *Communication networks: Toward a new paradigm for research.* New York: Free Press, 1981.

Rogers, E. M., with Shoemaker, F. F. *Communication innovations: A cross cultural approach* (2nd ed.). New York: Free Press, 1971.

Rossi, P. H., Freeman, H. E., & Wright, S. R. *Evaluation: A systematic approach.* Beverly Hills: Sage, 1979.

Rothman, J. Three models of community organization practice, their mixing and phasing. In F. M. Cox, J. L. Erlich, J. Rothman, & J. E. Tropman (Eds), *Strategies of community organization.* Illinois: Peacock Publishers.

Schramm, W. What the research says. In W. Schramm (Ed.), *Quality in instructional television.* Honolulu: University Press of Hawaii, 1972.

Solomon, D. Health campaigns on television. In D. Pearl, L. Bouthilet, & J. Lazar (Eds.), *Television and behavior: Ten years of scientific progress and implications for the eighties. Vol. 2—Technical Reviews.* Washington, D.C.: National Institute of Mental Health, U.S. Department of Health and Human Services, 1982.

Spergel, I., Vorwaller, D., & Switzer, E. Community organization from a perspective of social work. In L. Wittmer (Ed.), *Issues in community organization.* Chicago: UC Center for the Study of Religion, 1972.

Stern, M. P., Farquhar, J. W., Maccoby, N., & Russell, S. Results of a two-year health education campaign on dietary behavior. *Circulation,* 1976, **54,** 826–833.

Truett, J., Cornfield, J., & Kannel, W. Multivariate analysis of the risk of coronary heart disease in Framingham. *Journal of Chronic Diseases,* 1967, **20,** 511–524.

Warren, R. L. *Types of purposive change at the community level* (Papers in Social Welfare, No. 11). Waltham, Mass.: Brandeis University, 1965.

Zimbardo, P., Ebbesen, E., & Maslach, C. *Influencing attitudes and changing behavior.* Reading, Mass.: Addison-Wesley, 1977.

CHAPTER 14

SOCIAL AND CULTURAL FACTORS IN HEALTH PROMOTION

SOL LEVINE
JAMES R. SORENSON

Boston University School of Public Health

Disease prevention and health promotion activities are neither novel nor unique to this culture or the present time. Whether we look backward at the Greek, biblical, or Islamic civilizations or at literate and nonliterate societies throughout the world today, we learn that most, if not all, societies have provisions or recommendations for promoting the health of their members.

To understand the major mechanism used by a society to enhance the health of its members, we must understand the concept of culture—the total social heritage that is learned and transmitted from generation to generation. Culture embraces values, beliefs, and judgments about what is good, what is desirable, and how people should behave. Culture defines standards of morality, beauty, taste, and health. Societies vary in their conceptions of what constitutes health and their prescriptions for achieving and maintaining health and for combating illness. The culture will prescribe which foods to eat and which to avoid in order to be healthy, and many have varying prescriptions for men and for women, for puberty, for pregnancy and for old age. In sum, the values, practices, and beliefs held by the members of a society affect their health status and behavior and influence the effectiveness and efficiency of professional health promotion efforts.

THE FALLACY OF THE EMPTY VESSEL

In attempting to promote people's health, health professionals must be aware of the "fallacy of the empty vessel." As Polgar (1963) states:

> *Health workers who desire to pour out "new wine" of information—to follow the biblical parallel—often see it spilled on the ground because they disregard the fact that clients already have established health customs. . . . People have very definite ideas, for example, about the proper post-partum behavior for mothers and infants. To ignore these or to dismiss them scornfully as superstition will often result in fewer women coming to the hospital for deliveries.*

Some changes in health behavior may be easy to effect, but others may be more difficult to promote because they run up against established practices that are deeply embedded in the life and values of the society. Professional health workers must know and respect the culture of the population with which they are working, must be aware of their own values and beliefs, and, to the extent possible, must make recommendations that are compatible in form and content with the values and beliefs of the recipient population.

SUBCULTURES

Although we may be aware of broad cultural differences between one large society and another (e.g., American, French, Brazilian, Egyptian), we are less likely to appreciate how much cultural diversity may exist among various subgroups in our own society. Considerable variations in health beliefs and practices are found among people from different socioeconomic, regional, ethnic, and religious backgrounds. Some Hispanics, for example, subscribe to the notion of maintaining a balance between "hot" and "cold" components in order to remain healthy and believe that illness results when this balance is disrupted.

Some foods are deemed to be "hot," such as onions and chile, and some are believed to be "cold," such as cucumbers and pork. The hot-cold distinction in Hispanic culture serves as a guide for enhancing health as well as for treating illness. Clearly, any effort to modify dietary behavior would have to consider the prevailing health beliefs of the particular social, ethnic, or occupational group whose behavior is the target of change (Wellin, 1955).

At the same time, it is important to recognize that health promoters bring not only their personal cultural heritage to health promotion but also a professional culture; that is, they possess a set of professional values, attitudes, and beliefs that may or may not be consistent with the culture of their target populations (Levine, Scotch, & Vlasak, 1969). Many laypersons do not place the same value on health, on healthy environments, or on the promotion of health as do the professional experts. Although health promotion may be the most salient concern of health professionals, it is less frequently the salient issue in the lives of their clients, except when they experience illness or conditions that stop them from performing their major social roles.

In addition, even when laypersons place a high value on health promotion activities, the conception they have of what constitutes health may differ from that of health promoters. At least three major groups are involved in health promotion efforts today: employers, health professionals, and the state. Each may bring to the health promotion situation somewhat varying conceptions of what constitutes health or what ought to be promoted.

CONCEPTIONS OF HEALTH

Until very recently, many health professionals tended to define health largely in terms of a medical model. Health was viewed as the absence of disease or its signs and symptoms and was defined most often in terms of biological and occasionally psychological functioning. Such a formulation necessarily reflects the knowledge base, technology, and perspective of the medical professionals who provide the definitions. This orientation to health has had profound effects on the focus of many health promotion programs and on the criteria and methods used to evaluate the effectiveness of health promotion programs.

A medical orientation to health and health promotion activities is reflected in many of the objectives stated in the DHHS publication *Promoting Health, Preventing Disease* (Note 1). Targeted 10-year goals in this national effort include, for example, (a) reducing infant mortality from 13.8 to 9.0 per 1,000 live births; (b) reducing maternal mortality from 9.6 to 5.0 per 100,000 live births; (c) reducing reported gonorrhea cases from 457 to 280 per 100,000; and (d) reducing the proportion of 9-year-olds who have experienced dental caries from 71% to 60%.

This document also lists many objectives that are aimed at reducing specific health risk behaviors, such as smoking, obesity, poor nutrition, and exposure to toxic chemicals. By and large, these behaviors or conditions are targeted because of their known or suspected role in the etiology of major diseases. Although these objectives are manifestly important, health providers should recognize that lay conceptions of health may vary from those of the professional. A study of conceptions of health among medical students and a group of patients, for example, found that, for both groups, health entailed a consideration of at least three parameters: a general feeling of well-being, an absence of general or specific symptoms (or signs) of illness, and the capacity to do "what a person who is in good physical condition should be able to do" (performance capacity) (Baumann, 1961). These or similar conceptions of health have been documented among various cultural groups in the United States, even among significant minority-ethnic populations. A study of health conceptions among residents of Spanish-speaking villages in northern New Mexico and Southern Colorado, for example, found that "good" or "normal" health was seen as entailing adequate performance for one's age-sex role. This included (a) a high or appropriate level of physical activity; (b) a "well-fleshed body"; and (c) the absence of physical signs or symptoms or, more commonly, the absence of pain (Schulman & Smith, 1963).

Thus, although lay conceptions of health may vary culturally as well as socioeconomically, they tend to cover a broad spectrum of criteria, encompassing biological status, a feeling state, and the capacity to perform major sex and age roles that are important to the individual. Moreover, lay conceptions of health tend to focus on the present more than on the distant future. The design and implementation of disease prevention and health promotion programs must consider these conceptions of health. It may be very difficult to convince people who can function "well enough" and who are not obviously "sick" to change their lifestyles, especially if the change entails not just temporary but permanent alteration of culturally embedded and reinforced behaviors.

THE LAY HEALTH NETWORK

Our discussion of conceptions of health illustrates the degree to which social membership may influence health beliefs and health behavior. The family is the main agency of health promotion, and it is in the family context that many health decisions are made (Litman, 1979). It is from the family that most individuals obtain their dietary habits and food preferences, for example, as well as modes of daily living that will affect their health status. The family also serves to shape the specific values and attitudes an individual has about health—whether health is viewed as the result of luck or individual effort, and what should be done to achieve it. Such early acquired values, behaviors, and beliefs are likely to have a lasting effect on the individual.

Family members, particularly spouses, often serve as a first avenue of information and advice when an individual is confronted with a particular health symptom or problem. Moreover, in taking health actions, individuals often rely on their larger social network of friends and relatives. Studies have examined the relationship between selected family and group memberships and health behavior. In addition to noting that the family and its members serve as one of the most frequent sources of illness and health information and attitudes (Litman, 1971), these studies have also shown that traditional, authoritarian families are more likely than nontraditional families to have "popular" health views and orientations and, accordingly, are less likely to follow the advice of physicians concerning preventive health behavior. Moreover, membership in a social group characterized by ethnic exclusivity, friendship solidarity, or traditional authoritarian relationships has also been found to be associated with such health orientations and behaviors. Pratt (1976) came to this conclusion in an examination of traditional and nontraditional marriages. The latter were characterized by more professionally sanctioned preventive health behaviors. Likewise, Langlie (1977), in a study of social networks, health beliefs, and preventive health behavior, found that social membership was an important predictor of an individual's likelihood to engage in such behaviors as seat belt use, exercise, medical checkups, and immunizations. More specifically, membership in kinship groups characterized by high socioeconomic charac- teristics as well as frequent interaction with non-kin—that is, nontraditional types of family arrangements—was associated with adoption of professionally accepted preventive health behaviors.

Health promotion efforts must take cognizance of the degree to which the individual is involved in social relationships and is influenced by others in his or her health behavior. Efforts to influence the individual will be more effective if other components of the network are involved and support the desired change. Thus, for example, a health promotion effort that tries to encourage eating more fruits and vegetables and less meat, eggs, and dairy products will have little effect if it is not reinforced by other members of the network, particularly the family. Any change in the diet of a manual worker whose spouse is a homemaker would have to involve the spouse. Moreover, people are more likely to change their behavior if they are approved and rewarded by their significant others—that is, people who are important to them. In fact (as we have indicated regarding dietary change), in some cases the target individuals may not be able to modify their behavior without the active involvement of others.

HEALTH-ENHANCING BEHAVIOR

An analysis of our society and its concerns with health-related issues suggests that, as a culture, we are perhaps more interested in and committed to illness and the delivery of medical care to the sick than we are to health and the provision of services to enhance health. Vast sums of money are spent in providing medical care to those who are sick, whereas only a very small percentage of current health dollars is in fact designated for the provision of disease prevention and health enhancement efforts (Hingson, Scotch, Sorenson, & Swazey, 1981).

In addition, our society has developed certain broad conceptions of the "sick role"; that is, there are varying but fairly clear sets of expectations about how someone who is sick or impaired should behave (Levine & Kozloff, 1978). Conversely, it is difficult to delineate an analogous "health role"—that is, a consistent and culturally prescribed set of practices that individuals are expected to engage in to maintain or enhance their health status. In fact, in the recent past, individuals who very purposively sought to enhance their health by eating a highly selective diet, engaging in strenuous exercise, and frequenting "health" stores were considered somewhat unusual, if not deviant. Although it is clear that, for many Americans, some health-enhancing activities, such as exercise, have become important and valued behaviors, it is not infrequent that an intense involvement in health promotion activities—one that involves an entire lifestyle for example—can still bring about social approbation and the label of "health nut."

Perhaps the most systematic and theoretically focused efforts to understand preventive health behavior have grown up about what social scientists have come to call the health belief model (HBM). In its basic form, this perspective argues that much preventive health behavior can be understood as a function of an individual's (a) general concern about health matters; (b) perceived susceptibility of acquiring a particular disease or disorder; (c) perceived seriousness of a risked disease or disorder; (d) perceived benefits to be realized by engaging in particular preventive behavior, as opposed to the costs of such behavior or actions; and (e) cues to action—that is, information or advice that focuses the attention of the individual on specific preventive behavior (Becker, 1979).

A substantial body of research is employing the HBM, much of it providing empirical support for the general model as well as suggesting useful strategies for designing health prevention programs. The health belief model has provided considerable understanding of the use of such preventive medical services as immunizations and screening programs. It is not yet clear, however, how useful this model will be in providing insight into such health-promoting behaviors as dietary and nutrition habits, stress reduction activities, and weight control.

In a recent study, Langlie (1977) examined 11 different preventive health behaviors, including not only use of preventive medical services but also health-promoting behaviors. She found that such behaviors fell into two sets: indirect preventive health behaviors, such as seat belt use, nutrition habits, and medical checkups and immunizations; and direct preventive health behaviors, such as driving and pedestrian behavior, personal hygiene, and nonsmoking. She reports that people who engage in one set of preventive health behaviors are not necessarily likely to engage in the other. Moreover, there are somewhat different predictors for each type of behavior. A strong sense of control over one's health status, perceptions that preventive actions are worthwhile, and membership in a higher socioeconomic group, for example, tend to predict indirect preventive health behavior. Conversely, women and older people are more likely to exhibit direct risk preventive health behavior. In a more recent study, Harris and Guten (1979) explored what they called "health-protective behavior." By this term, they refer to any behavior engaged in by people to promote, protect, or maintain their health, regardless of their health status. This conceptualization goes beyond much previous work on preventive health behavior in that it is not limited to behavior engaged in by healthy people, as is the classic formulation of health behavior (Kasl & Cobb, 1966). Nor do Harris and Guten limit their conceptualization to behaviors that have been shown through research to be health-promoting. They report that people engage in a broad spectrum of behaviors, including eating sensibly, getting enough sleep, seeing a dentist, and so on, with the average respondent reporting that he or she regularly practiced between 5 and 19 specific behaviors aimed at health promotion. They identified five specific types of health promoting activities: (a) health practices—that is, personal daily health routines; (b) safety practices—activities aimed at avoiding or coping with accidents; (c) preventive health care—physical and dental checkups; (d) environmental hazard avoidance—avoiding high crime or pollution areas; and (e) substance avoidance—not smoking, not drinking, and so on.

These authors, like Langlie, found that health-protective behavior is not unidimensional. People who sought preventive examinations or who practiced certain nutritional habits, for example, were generally not much more likely to engage in other preventive practices than were individuals who did not.

These studies provide important information for the design and implementation of disease prevention and health promotion programs. First, they tell us that health promotion behavior in our society is complex and multifaceted. Accordingly, it is unrealistic to expect that people will exhibit consistent behavior with respect to health promotion. In other words, although they may be strongly committed to a strict dietary regime to promote their health, they may not exercise regularly nor seek ways to reduce the major sources of stress in their lives. Second, such studies highlight the fact that, at present, different segments of the population are committed to different health practices. In developing health promotion programs, it will be necessary to provide considerable new and powerful justifications to encourage particular changes in health behavior.

CHANGE STRATEGIES

In promoting health, we are seeking to modify not bizarre or idiosyncratic modes of behavior but normal, everyday practices that are deeply embedded in the social life of people and are reinforced by powerful mechanisms. Drinking alcohol, for example, is encouraged for all kinds of occasions: promotions, loss of job, marriages, divorces, and reconciliation. Airlines provide alcoholic beverages early in the day, and hotels open their cocktail lounges in the mornings. Similarly, the health professional who is trying to get people to stop smoking is confronting a massive and powerful media effort that promotes tobacco consumption in many ways.

Moreover, as we have indicated, the behavioral calculus individuals use to guide their lives may differ significantly from the logic that a health promoter would apply. The increase in life span to be gained from a reduction in culturally and socially approved and reinforced activities may appear substantial to the professional but may be quite insignificant to the layperson. In addition, individuals may adopt satisficing strategies for their disease prevention and health promotion activities, whereas health professionals might be more likely to assume a maximizing approach. Because many harmful health practices are so inveterate and deeply embedded in the normal life of people, it is necessary to consider the role of the health professional as change agent and the types of general strategies that are available.

A change agent is one who tries to modify the attitudes, beliefs, behavior, or conditions of a target population or human system. The target may be an individual, a group, an organization, or a society. Although many examples of change strategies in this Handbook involve efforts to change individuals or groups, it is important to realize that change efforts may be more encompassing, to include larger units such as organizations and communities.

Chin and Benne (1969) have outlined three basic types of purposive intervention or planned change strategies: (a) empirical-rational, (b) normative-reeducative, and (c) power-coercive. The empirical-rational strategies rest on the assumption that people are rational and will act in accordance with their interest once it is known to them. This strategy is highly popular in the United States and has characterized many historical health education efforts. The strategy has some value if the knowledge or information is consonant with the explicit goals or motives of the individuals involved. If the information is not in accord with existing values or goals, however, the individuals may not expose themselves to the message, may not learn it, may forget it, or may distort it.

The normative-reeducative strategies do not deny rationality and intelligence as forces for change but are based mainly on the fact that individuals are social beings and are influenced by values and beliefs, their relationships with others, and the social norms that guide their conduct. Accordingly, change may require relinquishing previous orientations and relationships, learning new skills, attitudes, and beliefs, and developing new perspectives and relationships. One typical type of strategy in this general class is psychotherapy, which attempts to reorient the individual, not just to impart information.

The third type of planned change strategy is based on the use of power to obtain compliance or conformity. These strategies include nonviolent forms of resistance, boycotts, strikes, and the varied uses of the law. Power-coercive strategies are not as legitimate and available in the United States as they may be in China, for example, where not only social ostracism but deprivation of financial allowances may be used to discourage a married couple from giving birth to more than one child. Although legal inducements and fiscal policies may also be involved in the United States, our value system tends to favor individual freedom in health decision making.

Those who are seeking to enhance people's health should be aware, however, of the distinctive advantages of the legal strategy in some cases. Perhaps the most efficient types of intervention are one-shot methods, such as chlorination and fluoridation of the water supplies, which are much more efficient and effectual than placing the responsibility on each individual.

ANTISMOKING CAMPAIGN: LESSONS

The role of social and cultural factors in health promotion may become clearer if we consider in some detail the recent national campaign to discourage cigarette smoking. Despite the recent increase in smoking among women and teenagers, the campaign has been very successful in getting many millions of smokers to stop. What factors explain the success of the campaign?

First, the antismoking campaign was led by people who enjoyed trust and credibility, such as the Surgeon General of the United States, leading scientists, physicians, and dentists, and leaders of various voluntary health agencies. Second, the campaign was not a one-shot information campaign but was conducted in a sustained manner, with constant reinforcement over a long period of time. Third, health messages frequently invoked powerful social values, such as children and family. One television advertisement depicted a child admiring and imitating her father's gait, gestures, and behavior. At one point, the father lit a cigarette and the child looked on. The message was clear and strong and appealed to a most powerful social value—the health of children.

Fourth, the campaign was not restricted to the dissemination of information through the popular media but was reinforced constantly by a wide series of changes in the social environment and in people's daily experience. Airplanes, restaurants, and various public waiting rooms introduced no-smoking sections; prohibitions against smoking were instituted in many public buildings and offices; nonsmokers became more righteous and vocal in their opposition to the contamination of the air by smokers; and various legislative proposals were introduced and public ordinances passed.

Fifth, significant others—family members, relatives, friends, and co-workers—rewarded the smoker for stopping. Children exposed to antismoking education in school pressured their parents to stop and rewarded them for doing so. The role of significant others in the form of self-help or mutual-aid groups supported the smoker who tried to stop. Professionals who seek to promote people's health should establish links with these self-help groups, for they not only may help change behavior but they may translate and reinforce other more complex messages from the popular media. Face-to-face interaction is often more effective in the short run than popular media, which can be effective over the long run. People often have more trust in other people than in the media; face-to-face contact is more flexible, and the person who adheres to the message is rewarded for doing so.

Our consideration of the relative success of the antismoking campaign should alert us to some of the larger social and experiential factors that are important in health promotion. Professionals involved in health promotion must be aware of the realistic factors that may limit their effectiveness. Even if people are convinced of the need to adopt appropriate health habits, it is often difficult for individuals to control their own health behavior. Attention must be paid to the settings in which people work, travel, or live. Work settings, where people spend half of their waking hours, may be noisy and stressful or relatively pleasant and comfortable; they may make it easy for workers to take exercise breaks or they may make it impossible to do so. According to Levine (1981):

> Communities may provide safe, convenient jogging trails or confront residents with potholes, air pollution, and dangerous automobile traffic. People are encouraged to avoid cigarettes, to live "clean" lives, and to avoid accidents, but they are exposed to extreme dangers in the workplaces, on the highways, and in the communities where they live.

Health education, if properly conceived, could be an important factor in promoting health-enhancing behavior. Physicians, nurses, social workers, and other health care personnel could play a crucial role in providing patients with information and in involving significant others, such as spouses and co-workers. Unfortunately, the health insurance system does not pay much attention to health education or to mechanisms that encourage appropriate health behavior. Physicians are reimbursed for surgical procedures and for various forms of diagnosis and treatment but not for health education. Indeed, physicians lose time and money if they attempt to educate their patients. Health personnel should have better incentives to educate their clients.

Our discussion of health promotion has been confined largely to changing health behavior. We cannot stress too strongly, however, that if we are sincere about the importance of health promotion, we must also address more basic social and economic conditions. We could make very great strides in health promotion if we could decrease poverty, make safer automobiles, and remove some of the dangerous pollutants in the environment. Although emphasis on lifestyle and health behavior is important, we must not ignore the many aspects of health promotion that are outside the province of the individual. We must not confine our health promotion efforts only to those that permit us to use our professional skills.

REFERENCE NOTE

1. *Promoting health, preventing disease: Objectives for the nation.* Washington, D.C.: U.S. Department of Health and Human Services, Public Health Service, Fall 1980.

REFERENCES

Baumann, B. Diversities in conceptions of health and physical fitness. *Journal of Health and Human Behavior,* 1961, **2,** 39–46.

Becker, M. Psychosocial aspects of health related behavior. In H. Freeman, S. Levine, & L. Reeder (Eds.), *Handbook of medical sociology* (3rd ed.). Englewood Cliffs, N.J.: Prentice-Hall, 1979.

Chin, R., & Benne, K. General strategies for effecting change in human systems. In W. Bennis, K. Benne, & R. Chin (Eds.), *The planning of change* (2nd ed.). New York: Holt, Rinehart & Winston, 1969.

Harris, D., & Guten, S. Health protective behavior: An exploratory study. *Journal of Health and Social Behavior,* 1979, **20,** 17–29.

Hingson, R., Scotch, N., Sorenson, J., & Swazey, J. *In sickness and in health.* St. Louis: C. V. Mosby, 1981.

Kasl, S., & Cobb, S. Health behavior, illness behavior and sick role behavior: I. Health and illness behavior. *Archives of Environmental Health,* 1966, **12,** 246–266.

Langlie, J. K. Social network, health beliefs, and preventive health behavior. *Journal of Health and Social Behavior,* 1977, **18,** 244–60.

Levine, S. Preventive health behavior. In R. Lamont-Havers & G. Cahill, Jr. (Eds.), *The social context of medical research.* Cambridge, Mass.: Ballinger, 1981.

Levine, S., & Kozloff, M., The sick role: Assessment and overview. *Annual Review of Sociology,* 1978, **4,** 317.

Levine, S., Scotch, N. A., & Vlasak, G. Unraveling technology and culture in public health. *American Journal of Public Health,* 1969, **59,** 237–244.

Litman, T. Health care and the family: A three generational analysis. *Medical Care,* 1971, **9,** 67.

Litman, T. The family in health and health care: A social-behavioral overview. In E. G. Jaco (Ed.), *Patients, physicians, and illness* (3rd ed.). New York: Free Press, 1979.

Polgar, S. Health behavior in cross cultural perspective. In H. Freeman, S. Levine, & L. Reeder (Eds.), *Handbook of medical sociology* (2nd ed.). Englewood Cliffs, N.J.: Prentice-Hall, 1963.

Pratt, L. *Family structure and effective health behavior.* Boston: Houghton Mifflin, 1976.

Schulman, S., & Smith, A. The concept of "health" among Spanish-speaking villagers of New Mexico and Colorado. *Journal of Health and Social Behavior,* 1963, **4,** 226–234.

Wellin, E. Water boiling in a Peruvian town. In P. Benjamin (Ed.), *Health, culture, and community.* New York: Russell Sage Foundation, 1955.

CHAPTER 15

SELF-EFFICACY MODELS

DALE H. SCHUNK

University of Houston

JOSEPH P. CARBONARI

University of Houston and Baylor College of Medicine

Theories of behavior generally focus on two distinct components: acquisition of knowledge and performance of behaviors. Although knowledge is an important influence on behavior, knowledge alone cannot explain the full range of human actions. Persons often consciously act in ways that are not in their best interests, especially in the area of personal health. People continue to smoke cigarettes even though they are cognizant of the many dangers. Overweight individuals do not restrict their diets despite medical warnings on the perils of obesity. Persons make little effort to alter their hurried lifestyles in the face of evidence on the deleterious effects of stress. Such actions suggest that additional variables must be included in any model that seeks to explain behavior.

The central thesis of this chapter is that self-referent thoughts mediate the relationship between knowledge and action. Many behavior theories assign a prominent role to self-referent thoughts as influences on psychological functioning (DeCharms, 1968; Lefcourt, 1976; Rotter, Chance, & Phares, 1972; Seligman, 1975). This chapter focuses on the role of one phenomenon that is central to self-referent thinking: individuals' perceptions of their *self-efficacy* (Bandura, 1977a, 1981)—that is, the sense of "I can do."

The role of self-efficacy in psychological functioning may be viewed more generally within the framework of social learning theory (Bandura, 1977b). Unlike conditioning and reinforcement theories, social learning theory emphasizes vicarious processes, symbolic functioning, and self-regulation in explanations of behavior. Although social learning theory acknowledges that much learning occurs through direct experience, a large body of research across different contexts and subject populations has supported the idea that observation of others influences individuals' self-referent thoughts and actions (Bandura, 1971; Rosenthal & Bandura, 1978). The capacity of people to process and store symbolic information allows them to perform complex cognitive operations, such as anticipating consequences of actions, representing goals in thought and planning the necessary steps to accomplish them, and weighing evidence from different sources to arrive at capability self-appraisals.

Inherent in the social learning conception is the idea that people self-regulate their environments and actions. Although people are acted upon by their environments, they also help create their surroundings. The causal model being advanced in this chapter to explain self-functioning is one in which environmental factors, self-referent thoughts, and behaviors interact continuously and influence one another (Bandura, 1978b, 1982a). Although a full discussion of this system of triadic reciprocality is beyond the scope of this chapter, the operation of self-regulatory processes clearly exemplifies these reciprocal influences. Environments affect how persons think and behave, but individuals who view some aspect of their behavior as personally dissatisfying and who believe that their environment is sustaining the behavior may change the environment. In turn, this change may allow them to act in ways that are consistent with intentions and therefore promote healthier psychological functioning.

SELF-EFFICACY OPERATION IN HUMAN FUNCTIONING

Self-efficacy refers to personal judgments of how well one can organize and implement patterns of behavior in situations that may contain novel, unpredictable, and stressful elements (Bandura, 1981). Perceptions of self-efficacy can have diverse effects on behaviors, thought patterns, and emotional reactions. Perceived efficacy can affect one's choice of activities and environments. Individuals who hold a low sense of efficacy for being able to cope with a prospective situation are apt to avoid it. Persons who have only recently quit smoking might be reluctant to enter cocktail lounges, which may contain numerous cues associated with smoking. Such persons might restrict their environments to those in which they believe they can resist smoking. As such individuals perceive that they are becoming more skillful in maintaining their goal of not smoking, however, they should be more likely to engage in a wider range of activities. In turn, successful active engagement helps strengthen their sense of efficacy. Persons who continue to shun activities out of self-doubts preclude opportunities for skill development and thereby remain inefficacious.

Perceptions of efficacy also influence how much effort people will expend and how long they will persist at a task, especially in the face of difficulties. The stronger the sense of efficacy, the more vigorous are the efforts directed toward succeeding. When confronted with obstacles, persons who hold a higher sense of efficacy persist longer in their efforts, whereas those who harbor self-doubts are apt to slacken their efforts or quit altogether (Bandura & Schunk, 1981; Brown & Inouye, 1978; Schunk, 1981). Individuals who feel efficacious for maintaining their proper weight, for example, and who are exposed to persistent offers for rich desserts are apt to resist the offers successfully. Those who doubt their capability for maintaining weight control may easily succumb.

Perceived efficacy also affects thought patterns and emotional reactions (Bandura, 1982b). Persons who feel inefficacious for successfully interacting in a given situation are apt to ruminate about it excessively, and in the process may experience a high degree of stress (Beck, 1976). Excessive self-doubts and adverse emotional reactions can easily thwart the efforts that would cope with the situation successfully. On the other hand, those who believe that they can handle situational demands are better able to attend to them and cope with problems that may occur.

Feelings of efficacy also help one avoid spending excessive time and energy evaluating potential situations or interactions. Individuals who hold a strong sense of efficacy for behaving in ways conducive to their health are not apt to appraise their capabilities on every occasion when health habits may be challenged. Persons who routinely limit their consumption of alcoholic beverages to two drinks are not likely to wonder before social occasions whether they are capable of sticking to their limit. Conscious self-evaluations of perceived efficacy are more prominent during modification of habits or in response to a drastic change in situational circumstances. Thus, individuals who feel they have been consuming too much alcohol and who wish to cut their consumption may cognitively appraise their capabilities prior to events and take appropriate precautions, such as arriving late or limiting their time in attendance. In related fashion, persons who feel a high sense of efficacy for driving safely on familiar highways may not assess their driving capabilities unless they realize they will have to negotiate unfamiliar terrain and interchanges.

The preceding discussion is not meant to imply that perceptions of efficacy are the only type of self-referent thought to influence behavior. Perceived incentives also affect the activities people engage in and the length of time they persist at them. People are not apt to spend much time on activities if the anticipated rewards seem minimal or nonexistent. Thus, even individuals who feel highly efficacious about their capability to jog 2 miles a day may not do it if they believe that they are deriving few benefits and that their time could be better spent. Personal standards of performance are another, and often related, influence. Unrealistically high or excessively rigid standards concerning what constitutes an acceptable level of performance can prevent persons from engaging in an activity, even though they might otherwise believe that they could succeed. Individuals who feel efficacious about losing weight, for example, but also believe that the only reasonable approach is through a crash diet may not attempt dieting because the concomitant hardship appears too great. Given adequate incentives and standards of performance, perceptions of efficacy are hypothesized to exert an important influence on the health-related activities persons engage in, the amount of effort they expend, the length of time they persevere, and their attendant thoughts and emotional reactions.

RELATED SELF-PHENOMENA

Before discussing how efficacy information is acquired and cognitively processed, it may be helpful to compare self-efficacy with related self-referent processes that have been incorporated into other views of human behavior. The nature of these processes, however, differs in substantive ways from that of self-efficacy.

Self-Concept

Self-referent thoughts have frequently been discussed in terms of the self-concept (Wylie, 1974, 1979). The self-concept is generally viewed as one's composite self-perception, formed through environmental interactions and heavily influenced by reinforcements, interactions with significant others, and self-perceptions of the causes of one's behavior (Shavelson & Bolus, 1982; Shavelson, Hubner, & Stanton, 1976). Although self-concept has traditionally been defined as a global self-image, more recent theories hypothesize that it is hierarchical and multifaceted and that it includes self-perceptions in specific subareas, such as peers, significant others, and physical ability (Shavelson & Bolus, 1982; Shavelson et al., 1976; Shepard, 1979; Wylie, 1979). The self-concept is presumably an important influence on general behavior, which in turn can modify or sustain self-perceptions (Shavelson et al., 1976).

Self-efficacy is concerned with one's capabilities to perform given behaviors in particular situations. The more global notion of self-concept has difficulty in accounting for the variability in behavior that people typically show during different activities, for different occasions, and at different times. A hypothesized internal mediator of behavior cannot be less complex than the diversity of actions it presumably causes (Bandura, 1978b, 1981). Although it is probably fair to say that individuals with more positive self-concepts generally approach situations in a more efficacious fashion than do those who hold lower self-images, there is no automatic relationship between the self-concept and how people cognitively process efficacy information as they engage in a task. Even persons with high self-concepts will be reluctant to persist at a task if they lack a sense of efficacy.

Outcome Expectations

Outcome expectations are personal beliefs that given behaviors will lead to particular outcomes (Bandura, 1977a, 1978a). One might believe, for example, "If I quit smoking I will feel better." Outcome expectations have occupied a prominent position in many theories of behavior that assign mediating roles to self-referent thoughts (Bolles, 1975; Rotter, 1966; Tolman, 1932). Action-outcome beliefs are also central to the learned helplessness phenomenon, which refers to a generally lowered state of functioning because of a perceived lack of covariation between behaviors and results (Maier & Seligman, 1976; Seligman, 1975). People who feel that their personal actions do not alter the environment much are apt to quit trying, and may even manifest symptoms of depression (Seligman, 1975).

Outcome expectations are conceptually distinct from perceptions of efficacy. Persons may believe that a given behavior will result in a certain outcome, but this knowledge will not influence their behavior if they simultaneously doubt their capability to perform the behavior. Those who believe that quitting smoking will lead to better health, for example, will nonetheless continue to smoke if they have serious self-doubts about their ability to quit. The problem is not an unresponsive environment but rather a perceived inability to perform the behavior prerequisite to the outcome.

Ability Attributions

Attributions are the perceived causes of behavior (Heider, 1958). Research has shown that individuals tend to attribute their successes and failures at activities to one or more perceived causes, such as ability, effort, task difficulty, and luck (Weiner, 1977, 1979; Weiner, Frieze, Kukla, Reed, Rest, & Rosenbaum, 1971). Thus, persons who succeed at a task may attribute it to high ability, sufficient effort, low difficulty, or good luck, whereas those who fail may believe their failure was due to low ability, insufficient effort, high difficulty, or bad luck.

In the attributional framework, the factor conceptually most similar to self-efficacy is the ability attribution. Although those who view themselves as having high ability at a task are also apt to feel efficacious for performing it, simply possessing the ability to perform a task does not guarantee a high sense of efficacy. In the self-efficacy model, attributions are a source of efficacy information (Bandura, 1977a). Perceived efficacy is influenced by both ability and nonability factors. Among the latter, the amount of effort required for success is highly prominent. Persons who view themselves as possessing the ability to succeed in some area may nevertheless not feel efficacious if they believe that a great deal of effort is required. Many diets are broken not because individuals lack the ability to restrict their caloric intake but because they no longer wish to exert the requisite effort.

Intentions

What one intends to do should be related to how efficacious one feels about doing it. People normally increase their intention to act in a personally desirable way when they feel that they possess the necessary capabilities. One would expect behavioral intentions to be accompanied by at least a moderate degree of efficacy.

Behavioral intentions constitute the central construct in the theory of reasoned action (Ajzen & Fishbein, 1970, 1977, 1980). According to this theory, intentions are proximal antecedents of behavior and are influenced by attitudes toward the behavior and subjective norms. In turn, one's attitude is a function of beliefs concerning action-outcome sequences as well as a self-evaluation of the outcomes, whereas subjective norms are influenced by beliefs about how significant others view the behavior and the person's motivation to comply. The theory predicts a high correspondence between intentions and behaviors, assuming that the measure of intention specifically corresponds to the behavioral act.

Intentions and perceived efficacy must be distinguished, because the behavioral manifestations of intentions depend in part on the person's level of efficacy for performing them. Inefficacious individuals may not act in accordance with their intentions. Thus, many smokers who intend to quit fail to relinquish their habit because they are beset with strong self-doubts about their capability to do so. Assuming that intentions do manifest themselves behaviorally, their form can be affected by perceived efficacy. To lose weight, for example, one might diet, exercise, or do both. A low sense of efficacy for maintaining a regular exercise program might lead one to focus entirely on dietary restrictions.

SOURCES OF EFFICACY INFORMATION

People do not acquire perceptions of efficacy in a vacuum. Self-knowledge of capabilities is acquired through direct environmental interactions or through socially mediated experiences (Bandura, 1981). There are four sources of efficacy information: actual performance attainments, socially comparative vicarious experiences, social persuasion, and indices of physiological arousal (Bandura, 1981).

Performance Attainments

What we do constitutes the most reliable source of efficacy information; the best way of knowing what we are capable of achieving is to actually attempt it. Repeated successes at an activity will raise perceptions of efficacy for performing it, whereas failures will lower them. Once a strong sense of efficacy is inculcated, an occasional failure should not have adverse effects, particularly if it is attributed to insufficient effort or unusual situational demands. Following a failure, sustained effort that leads to success should strengthen perceived efficacy, since the outcome demonstrates that obstacles can be overcome (Bandura, 1977a).

In behavioral health, people gain much efficacy information through their daily activities. Individuals who hold doubts about their capability to exercise regularly are apt to feel a stronger sense of efficacy after they have been participating regularly for some time. Ex-smokers who once believed that they could never quit smoking will experience a heightened sense of self-assuredness after they have gone several weeks without a cigarette. Persons who consistently maintain a normal weight are apt to possess a strong sense of efficacy for being able to continue their dietary habits.

At the same time, maintaining health requires that humans identify what they are not capable of doing. Entertainers who follow too hectic a schedule are often hospitalized from exhaustion; executives who work long hours may experience debilitating fatigue; and regular consumption of high-calorie desserts often leads to weight escalation and feelings of discomfort. Although social learning theory contends that action-outcome sequences can be learned vicariously and that people need not actually suffer negative consequences to learn their limitations, in fact this commonly occurs.

Vicarious Experiences

Much of our capability self-knowledge is acquired in the absence of actual self-performance. Individuals routinely observe the activities of others and gain a certain amount of efficacy information in the process. A vast literature on the effects of modeling supports the idea that it is similar others who offer the most valid basis of comparison (Bandura, 1971; Rosenthal & Bandura, 1978). Observing others teaches skills and conveys a sense of efficacy for being able to perform likewise. The thinking among observers is that if others are capable, they, too, should be. A person is likely to experience a heightened sense of efficacy for maintaining a regular exercise program if a friend of comparable ability has been able to maintain one for months. At the same time, failures by similar others tend to decrease perceived efficacy in observers.

Vicarious experiences constitute a weaker source of efficacy information than actual performances, because the effects of observations on perceived efficacy can be negated by one's subsequent efforts. Persons who observe several friends quitting smoking have no guarantee that they, too, will be successful, and any increases in efficacy resulting from observation can be negated by personal failures later on.

Children and adolescents gain much health-related information through observation of peers. The role of social comparison as an influence on self-efficacy assumes increasing importance as a result of close interaction in school. The likelihood of students not engaging in addictive habits should depend in part on the observed habits of their closest peers. Observing similar others maintaining healthy lifestyles conveys a sense of efficacy for doing likewise. In turn, this sense of efficacy is validated by actually avoiding addictive substances.

People also gain efficacy information vicariously through activities such as reading or watching television. Reading that millions of people have given up cigarettes is apt to instill a sense of efficacy for quitting. Television would seem to offer a particularly effective means of visually conveying techniques for healthy living and a sense of efficacy for practicing them. To date, however, its effectiveness in these areas has not been adequately explored.

Social Persuasion

Persuasion has been studied extensively in psychological research as a means of promoting attitude change (Fishbein & Ajzen, 1972, 1975). Persuasive techniques can also induce a change in perceived efficacy (Bandura, 1981). People often receive information through suggestion or exhortation that they possess certain capabilities. Doctors, for example, may advise their patients to lose weight, stop smoking, or temper drinking. Such suggestions convey indirectly that patients possess the requisite efficacy to do so and that they can actualize these behaviors through sustained effort.

As with vicarious knowledge, the beneficial effects of persuasive information on perceived efficacy can be negated by actual performance experiences. The illusory boost in perceived competence resulting from persuasion will not be sustained in the face of repeated failure. On the other hand, persuasion can lead people to make a more concerted effort than they might otherwise make, which might help them overcome difficulties. Thus, the sense of efficacy instilled by persuasion is validated by actual performance successes.

Physiological Indices

To some extent, people gain self-knowledge of their capabilities to practice health-related behaviors from physiological indices. A lack of withdrawal symptoms signifies that one is successfully coping with not smoking. Signs of emotional arousal in a given situation indicate that one is not highly capable of handling its demands. Symptoms of stress, such as trembling or sweating, often hinder performance in a given situation; individuals thereby come to expect that such situations will present further difficulties. In turn, thinking about engaging in a stressful situation can further promote self-doubts and can bring about the same types of emotional reactions. Conversely, people who notice that they are reacting in a less agitated fashion to a given situation experience a heightened sense of efficacy for coping with it and are likely to perform more productively.

COGNITIVE PROCESSING OF EFFICACY INFORMATION

Efficacy information derived from various sources does not influence perceived efficacy automatically. People integrate and weigh information, but how they do this is not well understood (Bandura, 1981). An additional factor involved in the self-efficacy judgmental process is that, because people are judging themselves, they may not be entirely objective. This can result in faulty self-appraisals. People may focus on the positive aspects of their performances and overlook the negative ones. Such overestimation can have negative consequences, because individuals may attempt tasks beyond their means. Conversely, those who dwell on their failures underestimate what they can do. They may be reluctant to engage in activities, thereby precluding opportunities for skill and efficacy development.

Successful actual or vicarious performances do not guarantee a stronger sense of efficacy.

Similarly, failures will not necessarily have a negative impact. Much research shows that, although judgments of self-efficacy are influenced by past performances, they are not mere reflections of those performances (Bandura & Adams, 1977; Bandura, Adams, & Beyer, 1977; Bandura & Schunk, 1981; Schunk, 1981, in press). In processing efficacy information from different sources, people take into account cues associated with the sources. These cues can influence efficacy appraisals beyond the effects that are due to performance outcome. Influential cues include perceived task difficulty, effort expenditure, situational circumstances, outcome patterns, model characteristics, and persuader credibility.

Perceived Task Difficulty

The effects on self-efficacy of performance outcomes are tempered by the perceived difficulty of the task. Success at a task that is thought to be easy will raise perceptions of efficacy less than success at a more difficult task. In the same vein, failure at a task that is viewed as difficult is apt to have less of a negative impact on self-efficacy than failure at a task that is considered easy.

People acquire task difficulty information primarily from two sources: social norms and objective task demands. A task at which many persons succeed is judged as easier than one in which the failure rate is high. Many people do not drink alcoholic beverages at social affairs. Persons who wish to stop drinking would not be expected to develop a strong sense of efficacy for doing so by passing up alcohol at a party. On the other hand, the high recidivism rate suggests that continual abstinence is difficult. Thus, a person who is able to quit for a prolonged period should develop a high sense of efficacy for not drinking in a variety of situations.

Tasks also differ in the demands they make on people's time, skills, and cognitive abilities. Success at a task perceived as demanding should instill a stronger sense of efficacy than success at a lesser task. Even among beginners, driving an automobile short distances in uncrowded conditions is apt to have less of an effect on a person's sense of driving efficacy than will successfully negotiating rush-hour freeways over several miles.

Effort Expenditure

Attributional theories stress the role of effort, partly because—unlike ability, task difficulty, and luck—effort is under volitional control and is amenable to change (Weiner, 1977; Weiner et al., 1971). Attributional change programs often focus on training individuals to attribute past failures to insufficient effort rather than to lack of ability, with the idea that greater future effort can lead to success (Andrews & Debus, 1978; Dweck, 1975).

Self-efficacy theory postulates that the amount of effort necessary to succeed at a task affects efficacy appraisals (Bandura, 1981). Assuming that a task is perceived as moderately difficult, success achieved through great effort should have less of an impact on perceived efficacy than if minimal effort were required, since it implies that skills are lacking. At the same time, failure despite great effort should be more likely to convey that capabilities are lacking than failure following minimal effort. Individuals who find that they can maintain exercise programs without suffering undue fatigue should feel more efficacious for sustaining regular participation than those who find exercise laborious. Efficacy for regular exercising should also suffer less among the former individuals if they skip a session occasionally.

Situational Circumstances

In their early stages, many efforts aimed at health improvement are aided by external supports. Many people attend weight loss clinics, engage in alcohol treatment therapies, and participate in smoking cessation programs. Extensive supports are helpful in initiating changes in habits, but they do little to promote perceptions of efficacy if people attribute the changes to external factors, such as the therapist, the program, or other participants. It is imperative that the responsibility for change be shifted gradually onto individual clients to foster ascription to personal capabilities. The same may be said for health-maintaining actions. Adolescents will not gain a high sense of efficacy for maintaining their dental health if their daily dental hygiene and trips to the dentist are orchestrated by concerned parents. A sense of efficacy develops when personal responsibility is assumed.

Persons who hold a high sense of efficacy should not be beset with self-doubts if an occasional failure can be attributed to unusual situational circumstances or physical illness. Normal-weight individuals overeat on festive occasions, husbands drive haphazardly to hospitals with expectant wives, people do not exercise when they are sick, and most of us experience stress when confronted with life-threatening situations. Under such conditions, one would not expect subsequent decrements in perceived efficacy for controlling weight, driving safely, exercising, or handling anxieties.

Outcome Patterns

An occasional failure should not lower perceived efficacy if it is attributed to insufficient effort, demanding circumstances, or temporary physical debilitation. At the same time, one success after many failures will not yield a high sense of efficacy. Several successes are generally required to instill a sense of efficacy.

The pattern of successes and failures plays an influential role in the development of perceived efficacy. Any new behavioral pattern is apt to be fraught with initial failures; "slips" are often the rule rather than the exception. The perception of improvement over time should result in a sense of efficacy for maintenance and further improvement. Thus, persons who notice that they are overeating, smoking, drinking, or worrying less often are apt to be motivated toward further improvement. Perceived efficacy will not be aided much if individuals believe that these behaviors have stabilized at undesirable levels.

Model Characteristics

The perceived similarity of models influences perceptions of efficacy. Seeing similar others improving or maintaining their health conveys the idea that we ought to be able to as well, whereas observed failures cast doubt on our capability to succeed.

Model similarity can be based on two criteria: shared experiences or personal attributes (Bandura, 1981). The behaviors of persons whose lives are similar to ours, such as friends and colleagues, can serve as models for our actions. Close contact provides us with frequent views of their habits. By noting the covariation between their health-related behaviors and their actual health, we gain information on which behaviors to engage in and which to avoid. Models can also convey skills for coping with challenging and problematic situations. Research has demonstrated the effectiveness of coping models in promoting performance among observers (Meichenbaum & Goodman, 1971; Sarason, 1975). Coping models, who initially demonstrate fears but gradually gain self-confidence, have been shown to be more effective than mastery models, who begin with faultless performance (Kazdin, 1973, 1974b; Meichenbaum, 1971).

Attribute similarity also can increase the potency of models, even when the similar attributes have no bearing on the modeled behaviors (Bandura, 1981). The accomplishments of persons who are similar in such attributes as sex, age, ethnic background, and socioeconomic or educational level are often viewed as indicators of one's personal capabilities (Kazdin, 1974a; Kornhaber & Schroeder, 1975; Rosenthal & Bandura, 1978; Thelen, Dollinger, & Roberts, 1975). The importance of these model attributes derives, in part, from cultural stereotypes, even though there is much variability in behavior within any reference group. Modeling based on attribute similarity can have both positive and negative effects. More men than women die from premature heart attacks, for example, and this fact may cause some men to take stock of their health habits and modify those that are linked to coronary heart disease. At the same time, individuals may be reluctant to change unhealthy habits if they feel the need to conform to the stereotype of their reference group. It is probably fair to say that unhealthy food preferences among children, adolescents, and adults derive, in part, from stereotyped preferences of their peer group, such as adolescents being expected to eat fries and drink colas.

Persuader Credibility

A vast amount of social-psychological research shows that the expertise and trustworthiness of a communicator influences the degree of attitude change (Himmelfarb & Eagly, 1973; Jaccard, 1981; McGuire, 1969; Triandis, 1971). These factors can also affect perceptions of efficacy. Individuals should experience some feelings of efficacy if they are persuaded that they are capable by a credible source, whereas they will easily discount the advice of less credible sources.

Credibility can also arise from perceived similarity to the persuader in experiences or attributes. Individuals often discount the advice of an otherwise credible source, however, if they believe that the source does not fully understand the nature of the task demands or the situational circumstances. Advice to quit smoking, for example, may be viewed as less credible if it comes from a source who has never smoked than if it comes from one who quit smoking after many years. Similarly, parents' warnings about their children's eating habits may be discounted if the youngsters believe that their parents do not understand how socially difficult it is to eat foods different from those typically consumed by the peer group.

THE MEDIATING ROLE OF SELF-EFFICACY

Perceived efficacy is hypothesized to form a mediating link between knowledge and behavior (Bandura, 1977a). Demonstration of covariation between knowledge and behavior does not substantiate the presence of a self-efficacy mediator. A stringent test of the theory is provided by obtaining a behavioral measure of the mediator, demonstrating that external information is linked to this measure, and linking the mediator measure to ensuing behavior (Bandura, 1982b).

In testing hypotheses derived from the self-efficacy model, a commonly applied methodology initially orders a series of tasks according to some dimension, such as difficulty, skills required, or stress. Subjects then indicate which tasks they feel capable of performing and their degree of certainty for performing them. Following this assessment, the subjects are given the opportunity to perform each task in the hierarchy. Efficacy judgments and behaviors are then related at the level of individual tasks by comparing each judgment to its comparable behavior to determine degree of correspondence—that is, whether persons indicate that they are capable of performing the task and subsequently do so or judge that they cannot execute the behavior and fail at the task. There is now evidence that judgments of perceived efficacy accurately predict subsequent performances across a variety of domains, including phobias (Bandura & Adams, 1977; Bandura et al., 1977), school achievement (Bandura & Schunk, 1981; Schunk, 1981, 1982), smoking cessation (Condiotte & Lichtenstein, 1981; DiClemente, 1981), physical stamina (Weinberg, Gould, & Jackson, 1979; Weinberg, Yukelson, & Jackson, 1980), and career choices (Betz & Hackett, 1981; Hackett & Betz, 1981).

The idea that judgments of self-efficacy do not simply reflect past accomplishments is best supported by studies in which subjects judge their efficacy for executing behaviors that they have not performed previously. Bandura et al. (1977) worked with people with severe snake phobias who on a pretest judged themselves inefficacious and were unable to perform most tasks on a hierarchy of increasingly threatening interactions with snakes. Some subjects then did not perform the tasks but were merely exposed to a therapist who modeled them. On the posttest, these subjects showed a significant gain in both efficacy and number of tasks performed. Their overall efficacy-behavior correspondence rate was 86%.

METHODS OF BEHAVIOR CHANGE

Experimental studies testing the premises of self-efficacy theory are beginning to emerge. Initial efforts in health promotion and maintenance have been aimed at smoking cessation. Some of this research is summarized here. Other studies attempting to convey efficacy-type information about capabilities to practice healthy behaviors successfully are also reviewed. Although measures of personal efficacy were not collected in these studies, and they therefore provide no direct evidence concerning the mediational role of perceived efficacy, they should be useful to researchers who are interested in exploring the self-efficacy mechanism in health promotion activities.

Condiotte and Lichtenstein (1981) studied the relationship of perceived self-efficacy instilled during smoking cessation programs to subsequent smoking relapse. Prior to receiving treatment on smoking control, cigarette smokers' baseline smoking rates were established and their self-efficacy judgments were collected. For the efficacy measure, subjects were provided with a list of smoking situations, such as finishing a meal, feeling anxious, and drinking coffee or tea. On separate 10-unit efficacy scales, subjects designated the probability that they would be able to resist the urge to smoke in each situation, assuming that they attempted to quit smoking then. Measures of actual smoking and perceived efficacy were collected following treatment and during a 3-month follow-up period.

Results showed that subjects judged their perceived efficacy for resisting smoking higher as a result of treatment. Regression analyses demonstrated that the higher the posttreatment level of perceived efficacy, the more likely subjects were to remain abstinent throughout the entire experimental period and the longer they remained abstinent following treatment. Results of a more fine-grained analysis showed that subjects who relapsed did so in situations for which they made the lowest efficacy judgments following treatment. Furthermore, subjects who smoked at least one cigarette following treatment but did not totally relapse judged their posttreatment efficacy significantly higher than subjects who made no effort to control their posttreatment smoking.

DiClemente (1981) also investigated the relationship between self-efficacy and maintenance of nonsmoking. Individuals who had recently quit smoking judged their efficacy to avoid smoking in 12 situations along a range of stress levels. Subjects were surveyed some months later to determine maintenance. Results showed that maintainers had judged efficacy significantly higher than recidivists and that self-efficacy was a better predictor of future smoking behavior than was smoking history or demographic variables. The efficacy measure was also significantly and positively correlated with weeks of abstinence.

These results support predictions from self-efficacy theory and are also consistent with the position of Marlatt and Gordon (1980) concerning the relapse process. These authors maintain that perceived inability to sustain control over addictive behaviors is a contributory factor in relapse, which in turn results in an expectancy for continued failure. In the self-efficacy framework, persons who possess a strong sense of efficacy to cope with high-risk situations are apt to mobilize their efforts when needed. In contrast, those who hold self-doubts do not organize their efforts. They fail, thereby precluding the opportunity for developing coping skills.

An important means of developing self-efficacy is through goal setting (Bandura, 1977b). A perceived negative discrepancy between present performance level and some desired standard can prompt individuals into action. The anticipated self-satisfaction of goal attainment sustains task involvement and helps develop skills. Goals themselves, however, are less important than their properties: specificity, difficulty level, and temporal proximity. When these properties are internalized as conscious intentions, they serve as incentives for actions

(Latham & Yukl, 1975; Locke, 1968; Locke, Shaw, Saari, & Latham, 1981; Schunk & Gaa, 1981).

Goals that specify actions to be taken and the amount of effort required for success result in a higher level of performance than more general goals, such as "Do your best" (Locke, 1968). People also tend to expend greater effort to attain a more difficult but attainable goal than they do for an easier one. Assuming that the task is under voluntary control, the higher the goal, the greater the performance is (Locke, 1968).

Goals can also be distinguished by how far into the future they project. Goals that are close at hand and that can be achieved rather quickly result in greater motivation directed toward attainment than more distant goals (Bandura, 1977b; Bandura & Schunk, 1981). Because distal goals are subject to more interference by influences occurring prior to their attainment, people may delay action or abandon them. Pursuing proximal goals should develop a higher sense of efficacy than pursuing distal goals. An attainable goal conveys a sense of efficacy for success that can be actualized through effort. Heightened efficacy is subsequently validated as individuals observe their progress toward the goal. It is easier to determine that one is making progress toward a proximal goal than toward a more remote one.

Bandura and Simon (1977) compared the effectiveness of proximal and distal goals in promoting weight loss. Overweight individuals either monitored their eating, pursued goals for reducing the amount of food intake, or received no treatment. Within the goal-pursuing condition, half of the subjects were given distal weekly food-intake goals, whereas the other half received proximal food-intake goals for several daily time periods. Monitoring subjects merely recorded how much food they ate to determine whether weight loss occurred as a result of self-observation. Following the 4-week treatment, subjects were weighed and were administered questionnaires to assess their perceptions of weight-loss strategies.

Although pursuit of proximal and distal goals led to significantly greater weight loss than monitoring, the two conditions did not differ significantly from each other. The questionnaires revealed that about half of the subjects with distal goals set proximal food-intake goals per meal or per day; these subjects lost a significant amount of weight. Those who adhered to the distal goals, however, experienced no change. The results suggest that proximal goals, whether externally supplied or internally generated, are highly effective in promoting behavioral change. Future goal research should incorporate efficacy measures and determine their relationship to behavioral change and maintenance.

In one of the most extensive research programs aimed at enhancing general well-being, Maccoby and Farquhar (1975) sought to reduce cardiovascular disease risk in two communities. Television, radio, newspapers, mail, and billboards were employed to convey information and to promote healthier attitudes and behaviors regarding diet, exercise, and smoking. High-risk subsamples of the populations were also identified according to blood pressure, weight, age, heredity, cholesterol level, and smoking. Some of these persons learned and applied healthier behaviors through a combination of modeling and guided practice. In diet, for example, subjects and instructors participated jointly in simulated market shopping, menu planning, and food preparation. Subjects received feedback on their efforts from encouragement by others, weekly weigh-ins, and progress reports.

Surveys and physical examinations revealed that, compared with a control community that was not exposed to the media campaign, experimental communities adopted more healthy behaviors. It was also found that high-risk individuals receiving intensive instruction changed more in a positive direction than those exposed only to the media campaign.

The procedures used in this study would be expected to boost participants' sense of efficacy for adopting healthier practices. Live and televised modeling conveys new skills to observers as well as a sense of efficacy for being capable of applying them. Vicarious sources of efficacy information are aided by guided practice, since performance attainments validate perceived efficacy inculcated by observing models. Guided practice should be especially beneficial for high-risk individuals. Initially, they probably possess a low sense of efficacy for altering long-standing unhealthy behavior patterns. Their implementation of healthier habits conveys the idea that they are capable of doing so. As they become more efficacious for maintaining new ways, performance aids can be withdrawn gradually.

The effects of television on health awareness and healthier living have only recently been explored. Mikulas (1976) broadcast seven 1-hour programs on self-control over educational television. Viewers were instructed in such topics as how to relax, removing cues associated with undesirable behaviors, restricting behaviors, and removing fears. A nonrandom sample of viewers reported that they profited most from procedures that could be quickly and easily implemented, such as relaxing, removing cues, and observing behavior objectively.

Television is being combined with classroom instruction and parental involvement as part of an ongoing smoking cessation and prevention program sponsored by the University of Southern California, the American Lung Association of Los Angeles County, and television station KABC (Kurz, 1982). More than 50,000 adolescents are receiving the 2-week program, which focuses on the social pressures to smoke, the development of social skills to meet these pressures, and the immediate physical consequences of smoking. Classroom activities include discussions and role playing by peer models. Students and parents watch an evening news segment on healthy living and jointly complete homework assignments. Students will be tested over a 2-year period on social skills to resist smoking and on their actual smoking habits.

Peer models have also been portrayed in smoking prevention films (Evans, Rozelle, Maxwell, Raines, Dill, Guthrie, Henderson, & Hill, 1981). Junior high school students observed filmed models resisting social pressures to smoke. Compared with control subjects who were not shown the films, experimental students subsequently smoked less often and intended to smoke less frequently in the future.

Peer models can constitute a powerful source of vicarious efficacy information. Adolescents who observe other students resisting pressures to smoke not only learn skills for resisting but also experience a heightened sense of efficacy for being able to apply those skills should the need arise. Perceived control over high-risk situations should foster mobilization of skills in such situations.

HEALTHY LIVING THROUGH SELF-REGULATION

Many techniques and strategies are aimed at helping those who wish to change their behavior. Reinforcement comes from seeing personal change occur. More commonly, however, people are attempting to maintain behavior rather than to change it. From a social learning perspective, self-efficacy plays an important role in maintenance and self-regulation. Health-related actions both influence and are affected by self-referent thoughts concerning those actions. As people observe themselves acting in ways that are conducive to their health, their sense of efficacy for continuing is strengthened. A strong sense of efficacy contributes to maintaining healthy actions, especially in high-risk situations. Thus, persons who do not wish to smoke feel efficacious enough to employ numerous behaviors to thwart the urge to smoke, such as refusing offers of cigarettes, avoiding smoke-filled enclosures, and asking others nearby not to smoke.

Whereas some people rely on external supports—such as self-help groups—to enhance or maintain their physical and psychological well-being, others do not. In either case, we propose that an important process involved in healthy living is self-regulation. Individuals can use their cognitive capabilities to plan, create, orchestrate, and modify their behaviors and environments.

The self-regulation process consists of three components: self-monitoring, self-evaluation, and self-reinforcement (Kanfer, 1970, 1971, 1980). Self-monitoring involves deliberate attention to some aspect of one's behavior and often includes recording of its frequency or intensity. During self-evaluation, individuals compare their level of attainment to a desired performance standard. Depending on the outcome of the evaluation, some form of self-reinforcement may be administered.

Self-regulation is not synonymous with will power (Bandura, 1982a). People's wants or intentions will not exert much control over their behaviors if they lack self-regulatory skills. To influence their actions, people must first know what they do. Self-monitoring requires attention to diverse aspects of their behaviors, such as rate, quantity, quality, and situations in which they occur. Because individuals experience many events in the course of daily activities and their memories are often distorted by distinctive events, it is helpful to record relevant aspects of behavior as they occur. Smokers, for example, might use a notebook to record the number of cigarettes they smoke, situations in which smoking occurs, and their thoughts preceding smoking.

There is some evidence that self-monitoring in the absence of overt self-imposed standards or reinforcement contingencies promotes behavioral change (Broden, Hall, & Mitts, 1971; Kazdin, 1974a, 1974b; Sagotsky, Patterson, & Lepper, 1978). Since the chances of altering behaviors are best while they are ongoing, postbehavioral monitoring is not as effective as proximal observation. Intermittent self-monitoring also leads to less effective self-regulation than monitoring that occurs continuously (Mahoney, Moore, Wade, & Moura, 1973).

Once behaviors are known, judgments can be made on their desirability. Personal standards are often employed in this judgmental process. Actions that match standards give rise to feelings of self-satisfaction and perceived efficacy, whereas those that fall short motivate further efforts toward improvement. A person who achieves a goal of exercising four times a week is apt to feel more efficacious about continuing regular exercise than one who sets the same goal but participates only twice.

Other influences on self-evaluation include personal values, attributions, and social comparison (Bandura, 1982a). Different activities are not held in equally high regard. Performances that fall short of goals on low-value activities are apt to produce less negative self-reactions than will deficient performances on activities that are deemed important. How people attribute their performance outcomes can lead to differential affective reactions (Weiner, Russell, & Lerman, 1978). Feelings of pride result when individuals ascribe successes to personal attributes, whereas a sense of shame may be felt when they hold themselves responsible for failures.

Self-evaluation also depends on comparing one's actions with those of others. For much social behavior there is no absolute standard of action; rather, evaluative standards derive from social norms. People most commonly compare themselves against similar others. Self-evaluation should become increasingly negative as individuals deviate from their perceived social norms. Thus, overweight individuals may feel less concern about their weight when most of their associates are overweight than when a majority are not.

People can reinforce themselves in tangible ways and through their affective reactions. Individuals often create self-inducements and make them contingent on certain outcomes. Persons who diet to lose 10 pounds may postpone buying new clothes until they have lost the weight, whereas those who exercise regularly may reward themselves with a new piece of equipment. Research in a variety of contexts demonstrates that contingent self-rewards lead to better performances than noncontingent rewards and no rewards (Bandura & Perloff, 1967; Jeffrey, 1974; Mahoney, 1974). Self-rewards are also often accompanied by external reinforcements. Ex-smokers may receive discounts on life insurance premiums, former heavy drinkers may earn promotions because of increased productivity, and dieters tend to be complimented on their appearances.

Persons often reward themselves through affective self-reactions that are contingent on desired outcomes. People feel happy, praise themselves, and offer self-congratulations when they do something well, whereas they may feel angry or censure themselves when their actions fall short of their goals. Both types of emotional responses can have beneficial effects. Negative reactions can motivate further efforts toward improvement, and self-praise validates perceived efficacy for practicing healthy habits.

Although self-regulation is important for individuals who are attempting to alter unhealthy habits and for those who are striving to maintain healthy patterns, its role will vary somewhat depending on the individual's goals. Persons may become motivated to engage in behavioral change for a variety of physical, psychological, and social-environmental reasons. Heavy smokers who experience frequent coughing and shortness of breath may fear that they are prone to lung cancer or cardiovascular disease. They may also dislike spending the amount of money they do on cigarettes, and they are often pressured by family, friends, and doctors. Changing any kind of habitual behavior is not easy, especially when it is long-standing and addictive. People often fear that they are incapable of changing and that, if they try, they will only suffer anguish and eventually resume their old ways.

Self-regulation can motivate individuals to discard unhealthy habits and simultaneously can convey a sense of efficacy for practicing new ways. A low sense of efficacy requires strong sources of efficacy information if attempts to change stand any hope of succeeding. Through modeling, people can be taught new skills, but actual performance successes early on are necessary. Perceived efficacy develops as individuals self-monitor their behavior and observe that they are capable of practicing healthier habits.

In its early stages, behavioral change often requires severe environmental restrictions to insure success. High-risk situations may have to be avoided temporarily, since people often hold a low sense of efficacy for coping with them; participation may spell failure. Early failures have an especially severe negative effect on a fragile sense of efficacy (Bandura, 1977b). Dieters, for example, may need to avoid favorite bakeries, people who are attempting to quit smoking might feel uneasy in smoke-filled lounges, and individuals who are attempting to control their drinking might be better off not entering establishments that serve liquor.

Restricting environments, though initially helpful, is impractical in the long run. Environmental cues associated with unhealthy habits cannot be avoided completely. Furthermore, abstinence from high-risk situations does not promote a sense of efficacy for coping with them, which is necessary for long-term behavioral maintenance. The goal should be to strengthen perceived efficacy gradually through mastery of progressively more threatening situations. Successful coping with lower-level threats teaches skills and promotes self-efficacy, which are required for conquering more taxing situations.

Changing habits can be a painful process at first. Giving up old ways may be accompanied by withdrawal symptoms, irritability, and agitation. At the same time, people who are attempting such changes can experience physical and psychological benefits—they cough less, suffer less indigestion, feel more energetic, and generally view themselves more favorably. With time, however, these benefits lose their force since they become habitual. Once strong perceptions of efficacy are developed for habitually practicing healthy ways, they are not apt to be foremost in the person's thoughts. What occurs, if the person is successful, is that the self-regulatory system becomes internalized and a negative behavior—such as smoking—does not emerge as a possible alternative in situations that earlier would have strongly called it forth. When this stage is attained, behavior is truly changed.

We contend that overt self-regulation is important in maintaining healthy behaviors because it helps sustain motivation for increasing healthy ways and the sense of efficacy for doing so. People should not simply stop noticing that they feel and look good. Self-recognition that healthy living allows one to derive greater enjoyment from life is a powerful inducement to continue and expand one's healthy ways.

No one is totally immune, however, from behavioral change in an unhealthy direction. People can lose health motivation for different reasons. Stress accompanying personal adversity can lead to the reemergence of compulsive smoking, drinking, or overeating. Daily repetition of the same exercises may become boring and eventually be discontinued. People may also become careless—postponing routine trips to the dentist in the absence of symptoms, and skipping meals in the face of a heavy work load.

Self-regulation can sustain health motivation because it helps identify problems before they become insurmountable. People who self-monitor their actions recognize early warning signs that they are feeling or behaving differently. When individuals actually act in antithetical fashion to long-standing habits, self-monitoring may invoke negative self-evaluation that can prompt restoration of healthier ways. Depending on the situation, people may realize that they need to develop new skills. Persons who are no longer motivated to jog may decide to take lessons in another sport. Individuals who recognize that unhealthy behaviors do not solve personal adversities may engage the services of a psychotherapist.

A strong sense of efficacy is not easily destroyed by a brief failure (Bandura, 1977a). Those who take responsibility for their actions and perceive themselves as capable are apt to alter their behaviors and environments to maintain healthy self-functioning. Furthermore, the public is generally educated about the health hazards of stress, poor diet, smoking, drinking, and sedentary ways. Efficacious individuals who find themselves engaging in what they know to be unhealthy activities will perceive the knowledge-behavior discrepancy. When knowledge of health risks is combined with a strong sense of efficacy for avoiding them, long-term maintenance of healthy lifestyles results.

SUMMARY

What we have defined here is a two-stage model for behavior change and maintenance. Coping skills, restricted environments, and positive models are crucial as a person starts to change. When the person reaches a level of efficacy at which the unwanted behavior no longer emerges as a possibility, self-regulatory behaviors remain central. Their role is to prevent slippage and, more important, to provide motivation for further enhancement of positive health behaviors. None of us leads the perfectly healthy life, and a strong sense of self-efficacy can motivate us even if the apparent rewards become smaller and more distant.

Recent research shows that, as individuals age, they can postpone or prevent many health problems by exerting a measure of control over their lives (Wolinsky, 1982). Besides prolonging life, healthier habits enhance its overall quality. A strong sense of efficacy for behaving in a healthy fashion is central to self-regulation of one's life.

REFERENCES

Ajzen, I., & Fishbein, M. The prediction of behavior from attitudinal and normative variables. *Journal of Experimental Social Psychology,* 1970, **6,** 466–487.

Ajzen, I., & Fishbein, M. Attitude-behavior relations: A theoretical analysis and review of empirical research. *Psychological Bulletin,* 1977, **84,** 888–918.

Ajzen, I., & Fishbein, M. *Understanding attitudes and predicting social behavior.* Englewood Cliffs, N.J.: Prentice-Hall, 1980.

Andrews, G. R., & Debus, R. L. Persistence and the causal perception of failure: Modifying cognitive attributions. *Journal of Educational Psychology,* 1978, **70,** 154–166.

Bandura, A. Analysis of modeling processes. In A. Bandura (Ed.), *Psychological modeling.* Chicago: Aldine-Atherton, 1971.

Bandura, A. Self-efficacy: Toward a unifying theory of behavioral change. *Psychological Review,* 1977, **84,** 191–215. (a)

Bandura, A. *Social learning theory.* Englewood Cliffs, N.J.: Prentice-Hall, 1977. (b)

Bandura, A. Reflections on self-efficacy. In S. Rachman (Ed.), *Advances in behaviour research and therapy* (Vol. 1). Oxford: Pergamon Press, 1978. (a)

Bandura, A. The self system in reciprocal determinism. *American Psychologist,* 1978, **33,** 344–358. (b)

Bandura, A. Self-referent thought: A developmental analysis of self-efficacy. In J. H. Flavell & L. Ross (Eds.), *Social cognitive development: Frontiers and possible futures.* Cambridge, England: Cambridge University Press, 1981.

Bandura, A. The self and mechanisms of agency. In J. Suls (Ed.), *Psychological perspectives on the self* (Vol. 1). Hillsdale, N.J.: Erlbaum, 1982.(a)

Bandura, A. Self-efficacy mechanism in human agency. *American Psychologist*, 1982, **37**, 122–147.(b)

Bandura, A., & Adams, N. E. Analysis of self-efficacy theory of behavioral change. *Cognitive Therapy and Research*, 1977, **1**, 287–308.

Bandura, A., Adams, N. E., & Beyer, J. Cognitive processes mediating behavioral change. *Journal of Personality and Social Psychology*, 1977, **35**, 125–139.

Bandura, A., & Perloff, B. Relative efficacy of self-monitored and externally-imposed reinforcement systems. *Journal of Personality and Social Psychology*, 1967, **7**, 111–116.

Bandura, A., & Schunk, D. H. Cultivating competence, self-efficacy, and intrinsic interest through proximal self-motivation. *Journal of Personality and Social Psychology*, 1981, **41**, 586–598.

Bandura, A., & Simon, K. M. The role of proximal intentions in self-regulation of refractory behavior. *Cognitive Therapy and Research*, 1977, **1**, 177–193.

Beck, A. T. *Cognitive therapy and the emotional disorders.* New York: International Universities Press, 1976.

Betz, N. E., & Hackett, G. The relationships of career-related self-efficacy expectations to perceived career options in college women and men. *Journal of Counseling Psychology*, 1981, **28**, 399–410.

Bolles, R. C. *Learning theory.* New York: Holt, Rinehart & Winston, 1975.

Broden, M., Hall, R. V., & Mitts, B. The effect of self-recording on the classroom behavior of two eighth-grade students. *Journal of Applied Behavior Analysis*, 1971, **4**, 191–199.

Brown, I., Jr., & Inouye, D. K. Learned helplessness through modeling: The role of perceived similarity in competence. *Journal of Personality and Social Psychology*, 1978, **36**, 900–908.

Condiotte, M. M., & Lichtenstein, E. Self-efficacy and relapse in smoking cessation programs. *Journal of Consulting and Clinical Psychology*, 1981, **49**, 648–658.

DeCharms, R. *Personal causation: The internal affective determinants of behavior.* New York: Academic Press, 1968.

DiClemente, C. C. Self-efficacy and smoking cessation maintenance: A preliminary report. *Cognitive Therapy and Research*, 1981, **5**, 175–187.

Dweck, C. S. The role of expectations and attributions in the alleviation of learned helplessness. *Journal of Personality and Social Psychology*, 1975, **31**, 674–685.

Evans, R. I., Rozelle, R. W., Maxwell, S. E., Raines, B. E., Dill, C. A., Guthrie, T. J., Henderson, A. H., and Hill, P. C. Social modeling films to deter smoking in adolescents: Results of a three year field investigation. *Journal of Applied Psychology*, 1981, **66**, 399–414.

Fishbein, M., & Ajzen, I. Attitudes and opinions. *Annual Review of Psychology*, 1972, **23**, 487–544.

Fishbein, M., & Ajzen, I. *Belief, attitude, intention and behavior: An introduction to theory and research.* Reading, Mass.: Addison-Wesley, 1975.

Hackett, G., & Betz, N. E. A self-efficacy approach to the career development of women. *Journal of Vocational Behavior*, 1981, **18**, 326–339.

Heider, F. *The psychology of interpersonal relations.* New York: Wiley, 1958.

Himmelfarb, S., & Eagly, A. H. *Readings in attitude change.* New York: Wiley, 1973.

Jaccard, J. Toward theories of persuasion and belief change. *Journal of Personality and Social Psychology*, 1981, **40**, 260–269.

Jeffrey, D. B. A comparison of the effects of external control and self-control on the modification and maintenance of weight. *Journal of Abnormal Psychology*, 1974, **83**, 404–410.

Kanfer, F. H. Self-regulation: Research, issues, and speculations. In C. Neuringer & J. L. Michael (Eds.), *Behavior modification in clinical psychology.* New York: Appleton-Century-Crofts, 1970.

Kanfer, F. H. The maintenance of behavior by self-generated stimuli and reinforcement. In A. Jacobs & L. B. Sachs (Eds.), *The psychology of private events.* New York: Academic Press, 1971.

Kanfer, F. H. Self-management methods. In F. H. Kanfer & A. P. Goldstein (Eds.), *Helping people change: A textbook of methods* (2nd ed.). Elmsford, N.Y.: Pergamon Press, 1980.

Kazdin, A. E. Covert modeling and the reduction of avoidance behavior. *Journal of Abnormal Psychology*, 1973, **81**, 87–95.

Kazdin, A. E. Reactive self-monitoring: The effects of response desirability, goal setting, and feedback. *Journal of Consulting and Clinical Psychology,* 1974, **42**, 704–714. (a)

Kazdin, A. E. Self-monitoring and behavior change. In M. J. Mahoney & C. E. Thoresen (Eds.), *Self-control: Power to the person.* Monterey: Brooks/Cole, 1974. (b)

Kornhaber, R. C., & Schroeder, H. E. Importance of model similarity on extinction of avoidance behavior in children. *Journal of Consulting and Clinical Psychology,* 1975, **43**, 601–607.

Kurz, C. TV, parents, students linked in novel anti-smoking effort. *Education Week,* March 3, 1982, 7, 16.

Latham, G. P., & Yukl, G. A. A review of research on the application of goal setting in organizations. *Academy of Management Journal,* 1975, **18**, 824–845.

Lefcourt, H. M. *Locus of control: Current trends in theory and research.* Hillsdale, N.J.: Erlbaum, 1976.

Locke, E. A. Toward a theory of task motivation and incentives. *Organizational Behavior and Human Performance,* 1968, **3**, 157–189.

Locke, E. A., Shaw, K. N., Saari, L. M., & Latham, G. P. Goal setting and task performance: 1969–1980. *Psychological Bulletin,* 1981, **90**, 125–152.

Maccoby, N., & Farquhar, J. W. Communication for health: Unselling heart disease. *Journal of Communication,* 1975, **25**(3), 114–126.

Mahoney, M. J. Self-reward and self-monitoring techniques for weight control. *Behavior Therapy,* 1974, **5**, 48–57.

Mahoney, M. J., Moore, B. S., Wade, T. C., & Moura, N. G. M. The effects of continuous and intermittent self-monitoring on academic behavior. *Journal of Consulting and Clinical Psychology,* 1973, **41**, 65–69.

Maier, S. F., & Seligman, M. E. Learned helplessness: Theory and evidence. *Journal of Experimental Psychology,* 1976, **105**, 3–46.

Marlatt, G. A., & Gordon, J. R. Determinants of relapse: Implications for the maintenance of behavior change. In P. O. Davidson & S. M. Davidson (Eds.), *Behavioral medicine: Changing health lifestyles.* New York: Brunner/Mazel, 1980.

McGuire, W. J. The nature of attitudes and attitude change. In G. Lindzey & E. Aronson (Eds.), *Handbook of social psychology.* Reading, Mass.: Addison-Wesley, 1969.

Meichenbaum, D. Examination of model characteristics in reducing avoidance behavior. *Journal of Personality and Social Psychology,* 1971, **17**, 298–307.

Meichenbaum, D., & Goodman, J. Training impulsive children to talk to themselves: A means of developing self-control. *Journal of Abnormal Psychology,* 1971, **77**, 115–126.

Mikulas, W. L. A televised self-control clinic. *Behavior Therapy,* 1976, 7, 564–566.

Rosenthal, T. L., & Bandura, A. Psychological modeling: Theory and practice. In S. L. Garfield & A. E. Bergin (Eds.), *Handbook of psychotherapy and behavior change: An empirical analysis* (2nd ed.). New York: Wiley, 1978.

Rotter, J. B. Generalized expectancies for internal versus external control of reinforcement. *Psychological Monographs,* 1966, **80**(1, Whole No. 609).

Rotter, J. B., Chance, J. E., & Phares, E. J. *Applications of a social learning theory of personality.* New York: Holt, Rinehart & Winston, 1972.

Sagotsky, G., Patterson, C. J., & Lepper, M. R. Training children's self-control: A field experiment in self-monitoring and goal-setting in the classroom. *Journal of Experimental Child Psychology,* 1978, **25**, 242–253.

Sarason, I. G. Anxiety and self-preoccupation. In I. G. Sarason & C. D. Spielberger (Eds.), *Stress and anxiety* (Vol. 2). Washington, D.C.: Hemisphere, 1975.

Schunk, D. H. Modeling and attributional effects on children's achievement: A self-efficacy analysis. *Journal of Educational Psychology,* 1981, **73**, 93–105.

Schunk, D. H. Effects of effort attributional feedback on children's perceived self-efficacy and achievement. *Journal of Educational Psychology,* 1982, **74**, 548–556.

Schunk, D. H., & Gaa, J. P. Goal-setting influence on learning and self-evaluation. *Journal of Classroom Interaction,* 1981, **16**(2), 38–44.

Seligman, M. E. P. *Helplessness: On depression, development, and death.* San Francisco: Freeman, 1975.

Shavelson, R. J., & Bolus, R. Self-concept: The interplay of theory and methods. *Journal of Educational Psychology,* 1982, **74,** 3–17.

Shavelson, R. J., Hubner, J. J., & Stanton, G. C. Self-concept: Validation of construct interpretations. *Review of Educational Research,* 1976, **46,** 407–441.

Shepard, L. A. Self-acceptance: The evaluation components of the self-concept construct. *American Educational Research Journal,* 1979, **16,** 139–160.

Thelen, M. H., Dollinger, S. J., & Roberts, M. C. On being imitated: Its effects on attraction and reciprocal imitation. *Journal of Personality and Social Psychology,* 1975, **31,** 467–472.

Tolman, E. C. *Purposive behavior in animals and men.* New York: Century, 1932.

Triandis, H. C. *Attitudes and attitude change.* New York: Wiley, 1971.

Weinberg, R. S., Gould, D., & Jackson, A. Expectations and performance: An empirical test of Bandura's self-efficacy theory. *Journal of Sport Psychology,* 1979, **1,** 320–331.

Weinberg, R. S., Yukelson, D., & Jackson, A. Effect of public and private efficacy expectations on competitive performance. *Journal of Sport Psychology,* 1980, **2,** 340–349.

Weiner, B. An attributional approach for educational psychology. In L. Shulman (Ed.), *Review of research in education* (Vol. 4). Itasca, Ill.: Peacock, 1977.

Weiner, B. A theory of motivation for some classroom experiences. *Journal of Educational Psychology,* 1979, **71,** 3–25.

Weiner, B., Frieze, I., Kukla, A., Reed, L., Rest, S., & Rosenbaum, R. M. Perceiving the causes of success and failure. In E. E. Jones et al. (Eds.), *Attribution: Perceiving the causes of behavior.* Morristown, N.J.: General Learning Press, 1971.

Weiner, B., Russell, D., & Lerman, D. Affective consequences of causal ascriptions. In J. H. Harvey, W. J. Ickes, & R. F. Kidd (Eds.), *New directions in attribution research* (Vol. 2). Hillsdale, N.J.: Erlbaum, 1978.

Wolinsky, J. Responsibility can delay aging. *American Psychological Association Monitor,* March 1982, 14, 41.

Wylie, R. C. *The self-concept: A review of methodological considerations and measuring instruments* (Rev. ed.). Lincoln: University of Nebraska Press, 1974.

Wylie, R. C. *The self-concept: Vol. 2. Theory and research on selected topics.* Lincoln: University of Nebraska Press, 1979.

CHAPTER 16

STRESS, COPING, AND THE IMMUNE SYSTEM

JOAN BORYSENKO

Beth Israel Hospital, Boston

MODULATION OF DISEASE EXPRESSION BY BEHAVIORAL FACTORS

Keeping well usually involves care of the body through appropriate nutrition and exercise, avoidance of tobacco, moderation of alcohol consumption, immunization against disease, and adequate medical advice or treatment. This approach, though entirely valid, may not be complete. A growing body of evidence, comprising epidemiologic studies of humans as well as laboratory experiments with animals, indicates that psychological factors can often cause disease or modulate the expression of disease caused by other factors.

The premise that the immune system can be compromised behaviorally, leading to a transient acquired immunodeficiency, underlies the rapidly expanding field of psychoneuroimmunology. The nomenclature reflects an interest in exploring the causal connection between psychological events, endocrine secretion, and modulation of immunity. Early animal studies in this area fit under the more general rubric of psychosomatics, paralleling human research. Once the effect of behavioral factors on disease susceptibility was substantiated, the search for intermediary mechanisms began. These mechanisms currently comprise two categories: an indirect pathway whereby behavioral parameters affect immunity through hormonal changes and a putative direct pathway involving bidirectional communication between the central nervous system and the lymphoid organs.

Interaction of Behavioral and Environmental Risk Factors: An Example

There is no doubt that cigarette smoking is a direct cause of lung cancer. Although the majority of those who develop lung cancer are cigarette smokers, however, most cigarette smokers do not develop lung cancer. Kissen (1963, 1967) studied more than 1,000 men with undiagnosed pulmonary disease and concluded that those found to have cancer displayed an inability to express emotions that differentiated them statistically from men with other types of lung disease. Such studies are not conclusive, however, since bodily effects of cancer can cause personality changes, as can emotional reactions to a suspected cancer diagnosis. In other words, it is hard to distinguish whether personality changes are a cause or an effect of the disease. More recently, psychosocial risk factors in lung cancer were evaluated on the basis of a composite scale assessing childhood stability, stability of marriage and job, plans for the future, and recent significant loss (Horne & Picard, 1979). The psychosocial scale accurately predicted diagnosis of benign or malignant disease 73% of the time ($p < .0001$). A multiple regression analysis, with actual diagnosis as the dependent variable and psychosocial scale and smoking history as the independent variables, indicated that psychosocial factors were one to two times as important as smoking history in predicting cancer. This does not imply that cigarette smoking is harmless. Rather, it emphasizes the interaction between physical and psychological determinants of disease.

A Model of Hereditary, Environmental, and Behavioral Factors in Disease Susceptibility

The role of personality and psychosocial factors in determining health was a foremost consideration before development of the current mind-body dualism during the time of Descartes. As medical knowledge increased, however, the direct causes of many diseases were traced to external agents, such as bacteria, viruses, chemicals, and vitamin deficiencies. These discoveries helped extricate science from superstition, but they also led to the premature conclusion that mind and body were entirely separate. Only within the past decade has new research in health psychology and behavioral medicine begun to bridge the gap between mental and physical events.

As Figure 16.1 indicates, there are two main *biological* causes of disease: hereditary predispositions and environmental factors. Hereditary predispositions include inherited weaknesses in certain body tissues or organs that increase susceptibility to disease. Environmental factors include bacteria and viruses, chemical pollutants in the air or water, and even some natural ingredients in the food we eat, such as saturated fats. Some diseases are caused by hereditary or environmental factors alone, whereas others occur only when there is both a hereditary predisposition and subsequent exposure to an environmental agent. As seen in the figure, behavioral factors can also contribute to the disease process. Psychological reactions are sometimes the primary determinants of disease—as in certain types of headaches and gastrointestinal disturbances. In other cases, psychological factors interact with biological factors in producing disease; that is, states of mind can sometimes determine whether processes that are initiated by hereditary or environmental factors will, in fact, cause disease. The interaction of psychological factors and smoking-related cellular changes in the development of lung cancer is a case in point.

In recent years, several comprehensive reviews have evaluated the extensive literature concerning the effects of both physical and psychological stress on the immune system and on host resistance to disease (Ader, 1981; Borysenko & Borysenko, 1982; Rogers,

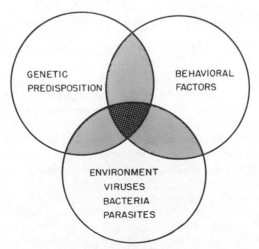

Figure 16.1 A model of hereditary, environmental, and behavioral factors in disease susceptibility.

Dubey, & Reich, 1979). Most studies have demonstrated that a variety of stresses predispose to diseases associated with immunologic responses. Where mechanisms have been explored, there is frequently an association between endocrine changes and inhibition of certain immune parameters. Some studies, however, have found no change and some have even found an enhancement of outcome measures as a function of stress. Inconsistent experimental use of stress and the timing of the stress relative to the measurement are obviously important variables. Furthermore, stress cannot be used generically for any environmental demand that challenges adaptation. Biological effects vary not only with type and chronicity of the stress but also with the degree of control available to the organism.

Behavioral Epidemiology

The publication of the Social Readjustment Rating Scale by Holmes and Rahe (1967) inaugurated a period of intense interest in the effects of stressful life change on disease susceptibility. Such research is methodologically complex. Stress is difficult to define, and situations that are stressful to one person do not necessarily provoke similar responses in others (Lazarus, 1970; Mason, 1975). Both inborn psychobiological differences and the differing fabric of past experience ensure a divergence of psychological and physiological reactions to similar challenges, a point we will return to later. Nonetheless, large studies show that, in general, the more life stresses a person experiences, the higher the probability is that the person will develop physical disorders, including cardiovascular symptoms, infections, allergy, and even cancer (Dohrenwend & Dohrenwend, 1974; Jenkins, 1976). Psychiatric symptoms also increase as life stress mounts. As the ability to cope diminishes, both mental and physical health suffer, often in unison. In a large prospective study, Vaillant (1979) found that poor mental health predicted subsequent poor physical health, even when the obvious variables of alcohol, tobacco, and obesity were statistically controlled.

One of the most powerful stresses is the death of a spouse. We often read or hear accounts of people who die within weeks or even minutes after the death of a loved one. In the 18 months following such a loss, people have a greater risk of death from a variety of illnesses, including infections, heart attacks, and cancer, than do others of the same age and sex (Kraus & Lillienfeld, 1959). Some of the more immediate deaths may involve changes in the autonomic nervous system that can lead to heart attack and stroke (Engel, 1971). Others, such as infectious disease and cancer, are more directly associated with impairment of immune function. Recent studies have shown definitively that lymphocytes from bereaved people have a diminished ability to divide in response to mitogens—agents that cause lymphocytes to multiply in number (Bartrop, Luckhurst, Lazarus, Kiloh, & Penny, 1977; Schleifer, Keller, Camerino, Thornton, & Stein, 1983).

MODULATION OF IMMUNITY AND DISEASE SUSCEPTIBILITY

The immune system is subject to complex regulation. The immune response genes affect collaborative cell-to-cell interactions and control the magnitude and specificity of immune reactions. These genes are located within the major histocompatibility complex; their products are thought to be expressed as specific glycoprotein markers on the lymphocyte surface. Mice's susceptibility to some diseases, particularly viral neoplasms, has been shown to depend on genes of the major histocompatibility complex. Likewise, certain human histocompatibility types are associated with increased incidence of specific diseases, particularly those with an autoimmune component.

Given a particular genetic composition, a number of environmental factors can modify the basic immunocompetence of the host to produce a temporary acquired immunodeficiency. Some cases of immunodeficiency may lead to overt disease, whereas other cases pass with no apparent sequelae. Physical factors leading to acquired immunodeficiency, which have been well studied, include trauma, malnutrition, infection, neoplasia, irradiation, and a variety of drugs used to depress the immune system following organ transplantation. Aging itself is associated with involution of the thymus and a concomitant decline in both cellular and humoral immunity. Perhaps the most prevalent and least well appreciated of the environmental modulators of immune competence, however, are behavioral factors.

Overview of Immunity

To understand how behavioral events might influence the susceptibility to or the course of disease, it is necessary to understand how the immune system functions normally (Eisen, 1980). Immune mechanisms underly resistance to all diseases in which the body must recognize and spare components of "self" while identifying and destroying foreign or "nonself" elements or antigens. The immune system develops in late fetal and neonatal life and diversifies into several distinct populations of immune effector cells, the lymphocytes.

Stem cells arise from the yolk sac islets and later from the bone marrow (Figure 16.2). Some of these cells travel through the bloodstream to establish temporary residence in the thymus. Secretory cells within the thymus produce a hormone that induces maturation of the lymphocytes. These cells acquire unique surface markers that distinguish T-cells (thymus-derived cells) from other lymphocyte types. Other lymphocytes mature in the microenvironment of the fetal liver and the bone marrow itself and are termed B-cells, since they were originally discovered in birds, where maturation occurs in an outpouching of the gut called the bursa of Fabricius. B-cells are distinguished by the presence of immunoglobulins on their surfaces that function as receptors. These two lymphocyte types are for the most part responsible for two basic types of immune reactions: cell-mediated (T-cell) and humoral (B-cell) immunity. In addition to T-cells and B-cells, there is another immune effector cell, the null lymphocyte. This cell lacks the distinctive surface features of T-cells or B-cells, but it participates in a special form of cell-mediated, natural killer-cell activity. Macrophages, large scavenger cells, also play an important role in immunity by ingesting and degrading antigenic material, by aiding lymphocytes in their specific functions, and by performing direct effector-cell functions.

In classical cell-mediated immunity, T-cells that are "sensitized" to an antigen undergo proliferation and form a clone of cells that carry receptors specific to the sensitizing antigen on their cell surface. Sensitized T-cells then migrate to the antigenic source—for instance,

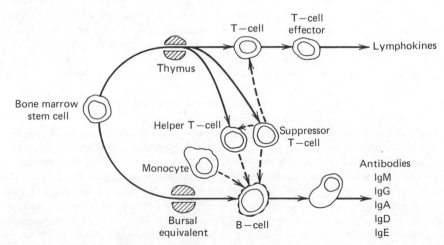

Figure 16.2 The development and basic functions of the immune system. Source: Broder, S., & Waldmann, T. A. The suppressor-cell network in cancer (first of 2 parts). *New England Journal of Medicine,* 1978, **299**, 1281–1284.

an incompatible skin graft—where they release a number of soluble chemicals known as lymphokines. Among the lymphokines are factors that are toxic to the foreign tissue. Other lymphokines attract and activate macrophages and other white blood cells. These, in turn, release more chemicals, which perpetuate the immune response.

In humoral immunity, neutralization of the antigen is accomplished by the production and release of specific antibodies. Sensitized B-cells proliferate into special antibody-producing cells, plasma cells. The plasma cells then produce and secrete the specific antibody required. The blood-borne antibodies act in several ways: they combine with and neutralize soluble antigens, and they coat particulate antigens (e.g., bacteria) to enhance their ingestion by macrophages. Other types of leukocytes perform ancillary roles: control of blood vessel permeability, manufacture of agents that bring effector cells to the site of the tissue reaction, ingestion of bacteria and cellular debris, and removal of antigen-antibody complexes.

T-cells collaborate with B-cells in some immune responses. Humoral antibody production is also regulated by subpopulations of T-cells (see Figure 16.2). Helper T-cells are sometimes required to induce B-cells to proliferate into antibody-producing plasma cells. Suppressor T-cells, on the other hand, inhibit antibody formation. Immune regulation is further determined by a number of genetic factors. Immune response (IR) genes affect collaborative cell-to-cell interactions and help control the magnitude and specificity of immune reactions. In addition to genetic control, recent evidence suggests that the immune system is further modulated both by direct central nervous system activity and by hypothalamic regulation of the pituitary and the autonomic nervous system. These neuroendocrine events can either enhance or depress immune function, and they are altered significantly by stress.

Stress, Endocrine Response, and Immunity

The psychological and concomitant physiological changes accompanying readjustment to a life event comprise stress (Gutmann & Benson, 1971). Mason (1975) has emphasized the specificity of hormonal responses to different types of stress. Furthermore, Frankenhaueser has shown that a person's ability or perceived ability to master (cope with) a stress is a potent modulator of physiological response (Frankenhaueser & Rissler, 1970). Stress comprises a variety of different bodily responses, arising to various stimuli and modulated by the individual's ability to adapt. The specific nature of the stress and its controllability are crucial issues in psychoneuroimmunology. Fear, for example, is easily conditioned. If rats are signaled before a shock is given, they show fear only when the danger signal is on. In rats receiving the same total amount of shock, those that are signaled prior to its occurrence, and thus can discriminate safe from unsafe conditions, have lower levels of the stress hormone corticosterone and a reduced incidence of stomach ulcers compared to those in a state of chronic fear (Weiss, 1971).

Given the variability of stressful stimuli, the learned component of control or coping, and the chronicity of the stress, bodily response is not stereotyped. There is, however, a basic core of integrated hormonal changes induced by stress that support the "fight-or-flight" response, originally described by Cannon (1914).

A potentially stressful stimulus is processed by the cortex of the brain, and the emotional impact is determined by past experience. The limbic system is responsible for relaying emotional information to the hypothalamus, which is concerned with the regulation of homeostasis. Neurosecretory cells in the hypothalamus are stimulated by the perception of stress, releasing small neuropeptides, which then travel to the pituitary gland and to other parts of the brain as well. These messages modulate the release of several hormones, including adrenocorticotropic hormone (ACTH) (see Figure 16.3). ACTH, in turn, amplifies the distress signal by causing release of potent, systemically active corticosteroids from the cortex of the adrenal gland. Hypothalamic neurons in lower brain centers simultaneously increase activity of the sympathetic, or activating, branch of the autonomic nervous system. Increased sympathetic tone causes secretion of catecholamines (epinephrine and norepineph-

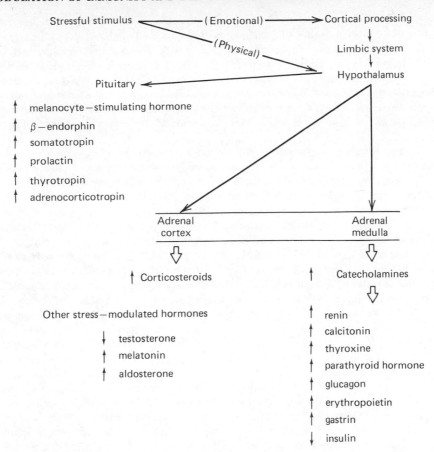

Figure 16.3 Neuroendocrine sequelae of stress—the stereotypic response to stimuli arousing the need for "fight-or-flight."

rine) from the adrenal medulla. The outpouring of catecholamines is then responsible for a secondary cascade of release, liberating an additional eight hormones. It has been hypothesized that the catecholamines have a major role in the integration of endocrine secretion and that their release during stress allows an *anticipatory* change in hormonal milieu initiated by the central nervous system (Landsberg, 1977). The primary effect of this coordinated hormonal symphony is to heighten alertness and provide energy for a fast response. The anticipation of an imagined stress, however, provokes the same widespread hormonal changes.

Recent advances have led to a rudimentary understanding of how emotional factors leading to hormonal changes can sometimes decrease the efficiency of the immune system and consequently increase susceptibility to disease. The corticosteroids and catecholamines are key elements in this regard (Borysenko & Borysenko, 1982). Corticosteroids inhibit the function of both macrophages and lymphocytes as well as inhibiting lymphocyte proliferation. Sufficient exposure to corticosteroids can thus cause atrophy, or withering away, of critical lymphoid tissues. This basic response to chronic stress was originally described by Selye (1936). Whereas lymphoid tissues atrophy, the adrenal glands hypertrophy, or enlarge, in response to constant stimulation. Selye called these stress-induced changes the general adaptation syndrome. The effect of adrenal corticosteroids on the lymphoid tissue of common laboratory animals and man has been well reviewed (Claman, 1977). Corticosteroids actually destroy lymphocytes in the thymic cortex of sensitive species, such as the mouse, rat, rabbit, and hamster, as well as inhibiting the metabolism of other lymphocytes. In corticosteroid-resistant species, including humans and monkeys, corticosteroids inhibit lymphocyte metabolism, interfering with their ability to multiply. Thus, with chronic stress, lymphoid organs progressively wither because cell multiplication is retarded. In the test tube, steroid hormones inhibit the multiplication of human peripheral blood lymphocytes after stimulation with agents known as mitogens. In addition to decreasing the total number of lymphocytes, several specific immunological functions are also impaired by physiological doses of corticosteroids.

The release of catecholamines by the adrenal medulla also affects immune function. Epinephrine binds to specific receptor sites on mature lymphocytes and other leukocytes, usually inhibiting their function. In recent years, lymphocytes have been demonstrated to have membrane surface receptors for a number of different hormones. These include the catecholamines, E-type prostaglandins, somatotropin, histamine, insulin, endorphins, antidiuretic hormone, and parathyroid hormone, among others. All these hormones stimulate cell membrane adenylate cyclase and generate cyclic adenosine monophosphate (cAMP) as a second messenger. Elevation in cAMP increases metabolism in immature cells, stimulating maturation. Although such hormones stimulate proliferation and differentiation of immature cells, they have a distinct inhibitory effect on mature, immunocompetent cells (Bourne, Lichtenstein, Melmon, Henney, Weinstein, & Shearer, 1974). Both human and mouse lymphocyte reactivity to mitogens is depressed by agents that raise intracellular cAMP. Similarly, elevated cAMP inhibits killing of bacteria and cancer cells, interferon production by human lymphocytes, histamine release by human basophils, and antibody formation (Bourne et al., 1974). Cyclic guanosine monophosphate (cGMP), which is liberated as a second messenger by parasympathetic stimulation or cholinergic agonists, generally enhances the immune response, opposing the specific actions of cAMP (for a review, see Borysenko, 1982b). Recent work from our laboratory has investigated the effect of a small, physiological dose of epinephrine injected into normal human volunteers (Crary, Borysenko, Sutherland, Kutz, Borysenko, & Benson, 1983). Fifteen minutes after injection, different subsets of lymphocytes are released into the bloodstream at two to four times their normal numbers. Suppressor lymphocytes, which function to inhibit the activity of other white blood cells, are released in the greatest number and are actively immunosuppressive. Helper cells, which, in contrast, help amplify some aspects of immune function, are reduced in number. These changes may be an important part of stress-induced immunosuppression. It is important to realize, however, that the immune system is an extremely complex system of cells, with a variety of checks and balances. Chronic stress, in which epinephrine is released at a high level over time, may produce different changes from those seen after a single injection.

These data suggest that the autonomic nervous system has immunomodulatory effects and that sympathetic stimulation, with its attendant release of catecholamines and corticosteroids, has an overall inhibitory effect on the function of immunocompetent effector cells. Following prolonged stress, there are fewer circulating lymphocytes, suggesting that the inhibitory effect of corticosteroids on lymphocyte proliferation outweighs the promoting effect of the catecholamines. Furthermore, the function of the existing pool of mature cells is subject to inhibition by both circulating epinephrine and corticosteroids. In addition to effects on lymphocytes, both agents also inhibit functions of macrophages, basophils, mast cells, neutrophils, and eosinophils, which all interact in immune mechanisms.

ANIMAL MODELS

We can get a fuller appreciation of the mechanisms linking stress with disease susceptibility by focusing on experiments with animals, in which key factors can be systematically manipulated in ways that would be impossible with human subjects. Locke (1982) has recently reviewed the entire literature on stress and immunity in humans, most of which relies on opportunistic stress because of the ethical constraints on such studies. Even in animal studies, however, diverse effects have been observed. Although stress generally increases disease susceptibility, it sometimes serves as a protection against infection or neoplasia. The nature and chronicity of the stress, the time at which the infective agent is introduced relative to the stress, the housing and social conditions of the animals, and the nature of the cellular interactions involved in the immune response to the pathogen under investigation are crucial to the outcome. Overall, cause-and-effect relationships between stress and susceptibility to infection are reproducibly demonstrable in adequately controlled animal experiments.

Behavioral Epidemiology in Animal Models

Exposure to experimental stress generally decreases host resistance to infection. A variety of stressors have been evaluated in early behavioral epidemiologic studies. No direct measures of immune function were performed (for a review, see Ader, 1981; Borysenko & Borysenko, 1982; Rogers et al., 1979). Mice subjected to experimental stress by avoidance conditioning in a shuttle box or by physical restraint are more susceptible to infections with herpes simplex virus, poliomyelitis virus, Coxsackie B virus, and polyoma virus. Similarly, the stress of crowding markedly increases susceptibility to Salmonella typhimurium and trichinosis infection. Predator-induced stress (cat versus mouse) increases infectivity with the parasite Hymenolepis nana in animals that have been previously immunized. More recently, we reported that the stress of crowding and exposure to inescapable shock increases both the incidence and the severity of dental caries in rats infected intraorally with streptococcus mutans and maintained on a high sugar diet (Borysenko, Turesky, Borysenko, Quimby, & Benson, 1980). In a few cases, however, stress has been demonstrated to protect against infection.

Stress and Immunity in Animal Models

In animal studies designed to evaluate specific immune functions following stress, deficiencies in both cell-mediated and humoral responses have been demonstrated (for a review, see Ader, 1981; Borysenko & Borysenko, 1982; Rogers et al., 1979). Decreased responsivity to mitogen stimulation, antigen stimulation, and reduced lymphocyte cytotoxicity have been observed following stress. Prolongation in time to rejection of skin allografts, reduced graft-versus-host responsiveness, and diminished delayed hypersensitivity reactions indicate suppression of cell-mediated immunity following stress in animals. When animals are stressed prior to or directly after immunization, there is also reduced antibody titer to flagellin, a bacterial antigen, reflecting suppression of humoral immunity.

Experimental Design in Animal Models

Although stress is most frequently associated with immunosuppression, it can sometimes have an augmenting effect on the immune system (Folch & Waksman, 1974; Mettrop & Visser, 1969). Some of these contradictory findings can be explained by differences in experimental design. The nature of the stress, its duration, and the interval between the stress and the immune measurements are extremely important. Mice subjected to chronic auditory stress, for example, show a biphasic response. During the first two weeks, there is a 50% decrease in lymphocyte cytotoxicity and mitogen responsivity, followed by a significant increase (above baseline) in the same immune functions for two weeks thereafter (Monjan & Collector, 1977). This is an example of rebound overshoot, indicating the importance of timing the stress relative to the measurement.

The comprehensive investigations of Riley (1981) have clarified some of the seemingly contradictory effects of stress on immunity and disease in animals. In his study, rodents living in standard animal quarters were subjected to noise, pheromones, and ultrasound distress signals from other animals undergoing capture or manipulation. The corticosterone levels of such animals were *10 to 20 times* higher than those of rodents housed in a protected, low-stress environment (Riley, 1981). Variables such as population density and proximity of males and females, which are usually uncontrolled, are capable of modulating impressive changes in corticosterone levels. When apparently baseline endocrine parameters are actually already highly elevated, the effects of additional experimental stress cannot be adequately assessed. It is thus of utmost importance to keep animals in a low-stress, well-controlled environment.

In extensive, meticulously controlled experiments employing either virally induced or transplanted tumors, Riley (1981) has shown that stress (either in a standard animal facility or with exposure to a mild, anxiety-provoking rotation) consistently increases tumor growth. These effects can be mimicked by injection of natural or synthetic corticosteroids into the animals. The apparently contradictory results of some early animal experiments showing inhibition of tumor growth by stress become understandable in view of the timing of the stress relative ·to the tumor implant. Both tumor suppression and tumor enhancement can be demonstrated in the same system as a function of such timing. Steroid injection into mice 7 days after implantation of a tumor promotes growth; injection 7 days before implantation retards tumor growth. These differences probably reflect an initial, hormonally sustained immune inhibition followed by a rebound recovery and overshoot of cell-mediated immunity (Monjan & Collector, 1977).

Riley (1975) also explored the interaction between heredity, environmental factors, and psychological factors in cancer etiology. He studied a strain of mice infected with a virus that causes mammary gland cancer in about 80% of females by 400 days of age. One group of these mice was housed in standard animal quarters, where the animals were exposed to the moderate stress that is characteristic of such facilities. Another group was housed in a special, low-stress facility, where the animals were protected from pheromones and ultrasound distress signals. At 400 days of age, over 90% of the moderate stress group, compared to less than 10% of the low-stress group, had developed cancer. By 600 days, when the mice reached old age, the incidence of cancer rose to expected levels in the low-stress group, presumably because of the decreased immunity that normally accompanies aging. Although genetic and environmental (virus) factors were the same in both groups, stress had a highly significant effect on latency period—the time in the animals' lives that the cancers appeared.

Additional experiments with animals have shown that control is an important modulator of outcome in stress experiments. In one study, Sklar and Anisman (1979) first injected three groups of mice with the same number of cancer cells. One group was then exposed to an electric shock that they could learn to escape by jumping over a barrier to safety. A second group, the yoked controls, was exposed to the same duration of shock as the first group, but they had no means of actively coping with the stress. Instead, their shock terminated noncontingently when a mouse from the first group jumped over the barrier. A third group was never shocked. Cancers grew fastest and led to earliest death among the yoked controls, which had no means of coping with their stress. In contrast, the animals in the first group, which received the same amount of shock but could mount an adaptive escape response, did not differ significantly in tumor growth from the animals that had never been shocked at all.

In a series of differential housing experiments, social isolation enhanced tumor growth in mice (Sklar & Anisman, 1980). It was the abrupt change in social conditions, rather than isolation per se, however, that was responsible for increased tumor growth. In mice that were reared in isolation and then switched to group housing following tumor implant, behavior modulated tumorigenesis. Specifically, some mice remained passive after the transfer, whereas others engaged in fighting. The fighters had significantly smaller tumors than the nonfighters. Sklar and Anisman (1980) hypothesized that fighting may comprise an adaptive coping response. Indeed, fighting is known to prevent some of the neurochemical changes induced by stress and to ameliorate the ulcerogenic effects of shock stress. These data parallel human studies. Stress alone apparently does not lead to increased tumor growth; rather, the inability to cope with stress seems most important (for a review, see Borysenko, 1982a).

INTERACTION BETWEEN THE CENTRAL NERVOUS SYSTEM AND THE IMMUNE SYSTEM

Studies involving specific hypothalamic lesions or electrical stimulation of hypothalamic regions suggest that the central nervous system influences immune responses directly (for a review, see Stein, Keller & Schleifer, 1981). Both humoral and cell-mediated immunity are depressed following lesioning of the dorsal hypothalamus in rabbits. Furthermore, such effects are specific to particular hypothalamic regions. Anterior hypothalamic lesions protect against lethal anaphylaxis in guinea pigs, whereas posterior hypothalamic lesions do not. Anterior hypothalamic lesions also inhibit both humoral and cell-mediated immunity in guinea pigs. Although they are reproducible, lesioning studies may be confounded by unintentional damage to nearby feeding and thermoregulatory centers. Alterations of dietary intake and thermoregulation per se are associated with immunologic deficits. Experiments involving electrical stimulation of the central nervous system, however, safeguard against this problem. Stimulation of the mesencephalon enhances the humoral immune response (Korneva & Khai, 1967). When the lateral hypothalamus is stimulated in rats, serum gamma globulins are doubled without further antigenic challenge (Fessel & Forsyth, 1963). Thus, there is a body of evidence suggesting that the central nervous system can modulate immunity. Recent studies further suggest that information from the immune system feeds back directly to the central nervous system. For example, an increase in the firing rate of neurons in the ventromedial nuclei can be recorded in rats following specific immunization (Besodovsky & Sorkin, 1977).

Mediating mechanisms underlying a potential reciprocal communication of the central nervous system and immune system are currently under intense investigation. Sympathetic and parasympathetic neurons arising from the hypothalamus that directly innervate both the thymus and the spleen have been traced using the retrograde transport of horseradish peroxidase (Bullock & Moore, 1980; Williams, Peterson, Shea, Schmedtje, Bauer, & Felten, 1981). The mast cell, located at the periphery of small blood vessels, may be an intermediary that transduces the nerve impulse into a chemical signal read locally by thymic or splenic lymphocytes (Locke, 1982). As in the case of hormonal modulation of immunity, sympathetic stimulation has immunoinhibitory effects. Chemical sympathectomy, for example, enhances the immune response to sheep erythrocytes in mice (Williams et al., 1981). Such studies provide evidence for a direct functional link between the nervous and immune systems.

Further evidence for a direct communication between the central nervous system and the immune system derives from Ader's well-replicated finding that immunosuppression can be conditioned behaviorally in the rat (Ader, 1981; Ader & Cohen, 1975; Rogers, Reich, Strom, & Carpenter, 1976). Using a Pavlovian paradigm, taste aversion is conditioned by pairing a novel taste (saccharin water) with injection of cyclophosphamide, an immunosuppressive cytotoxic drug that produces gastrointestinal upset. Subsequently, conditioned animals that are exposed to saccharin alone, following antigen injection, are significantly immunosuppressed compared to well-conceived control groups. When lithium chloride, a nonimmunosuppressive illness-inducing agent, is substituted for cyclophosphamide, no immunosuppression ensues. Thus, the immunosuppression appears to be truly conditioned and cannot be accounted for indirectly by the stress of conditioned gastrointestinal upset.

THE CHALLENGE FOR BEHAVIORAL HEALTH

The notion that behavioral factors can alter immunity and disease susceptibility through direct central nervous system mechanisms or through endocrinological intermediaries has been adequately demonstrated. Immunologists and physiologists are defining the parameters of these interactions, but they are limited by the dearth of knowledge concerning the relationships between individual differences, psychological response, and endocrine change. McClelland and his colleagues have recently studied the relationships between a specific personality trait, the inhibited power motive syndrome, and urinary epinephrine excretion, salivary secretory immunoglobulin A (IgA) levels, and severity of upper respiratory tract infection (McClelland, Floor, Davidson, & Saron, 1980). The inhibited power motive syndrome consists of a high need for power (higher than the need for affiliation) in combination with high activity inhibition, as reliably and reproducibly measured by the Thematic Apperception Test. Individuals who are high in activity inhibition stringently control the expression of the power motive. Such individuals have a lower concentration of salivary secretory IgA than do controls, report more severe episodes of upper respiratory tract infection, and excrete more epinephrine in urine (McClelland et al., 1980). Recent longitudinal research in our laboratory and McClelland's, conducted on a sample of 64 first-year dental students, confirmed and extended these findings (Jemmott, Borysenko, Borysenko, McClelland, Chapman, Meyer, & Benson, 1983).

The prognosis of cancer has also been related to individual differences, but endocrinological and immunologic correlates have not yet been reported. Women who can express hostility, for example, survive metastatic breast cancer longer than nonassertive, compliant women (Abeloff & Derogatis, 1977). In a similar vein, 5-year outcome after mastectomy for early-stage breast cancer correlates with psychological reaction at diagnosis. Women who either have "a fighting spirit" or are absolute deniers have a statistically significant advantage in both disease-free interval and mortality compared to those who are helpless/hopeless or stoic acceptors (Greer, Morris, & Pettingale, 1979). These recent prospective studies corroborate older retrospective studies showing that the inhibition of anger is associated with poor prognosis in both men and women with a variety of different cancers (Blumberg, West, & Ellis, 1954; Stavraky, Buck, Loh, et al., 1968). Knowledge of the mechanisms by which personality influences physiology may lead to the design of interventions that both preserve health and lead to a better prognosis in the diseased individual.

REFERENCES

Abeloff, M. D., & Derogatis, L. R. Psychologic aspects of the management of primary and metastatic breast cancer. *Progress in Clinical and Biological Research,* 1977, **12,** 505–516.

Ader, R. (Ed.). *Psychoneuroimmunology.* New York: Academic Press, 1981.

Ader, R., & Cohen, N. Behaviorally conditioned immunosuppression. *Psychosomatic Medicine,* 1975, **37,** 333–340.

Bartrop, R. W., Luckhurst, E., Lazarus, L., Kiloh, L. G., & Penny, R. Depressed lymphocyte function after bereavement. *Lancet,* 1977, **1,** 834–836.

Besodovsky, H., & Sorkin, E. Network of immunoneuroendocrine interactions. *Clinical and Experimental Immunology,* 1977, **27,** 1–12.

Blumberg, E. M., West, P. M., & Ellis, F. W. A possible relationship between psychological factors and human cancer. *Psychosomatic Medicine,* 1954, **16,** 276–286.

Borysenko, J. Z. Behavioral-physiological factors in the development and management of cancer. *General Hospital Psychiatry,* 1982, **4,** 69–74. (a)

Borysenko, J. Z. Higher cortical function and neoplasia: Psychoneuroimmunology. In S. Levy (Ed.), *Biological mediators of behavioral disease: Neoplasia,* New York: Elsevier, 1982. (b)

Borysenko, M., & Borysenko, J. Stress, behavior and immunity: Animal models and mediating mechanisms. *General Hospital Psychiatry,* 1982, **40,** 59–67.

Borysenko, M., Turesky, S., Borysenko, J., Quimby, F., & Benson, H. Stress and dental caries in the rat. *Journal of Behavioral Medicine,* 1980, **3,** 233–243.

Bourne, H. R., Lichtenstein, L. M., Melmon, R. L., Henney, C. S., Weinstein, Y., & Shearer, G. M. Modulation of inflammation and immunity by cyclic AMP. *Science,* 1974, **184,** 19–28.

Bullock, K., & Moore, R. Y. Nucleus ambiguus projections to the thymus gland: Possible pathways for regulation of the immune response and the neuroendocrine network. *Anatomical Record,* 1980, **196,** 25.

Cannon, W. B. The emergency function of the adrenal medulla in pain and the major emotions. *American Journal of Physiology,* 1914, **33,** 356–372.

Claman, H. N. Corticosteroids and lymphoid cells. *New England Journal of Medicine,* 1977, **287,** 388–397.

Crary, B., Borysenko, M., Sutherland, D. C., Kutz, I., Borysenko, J. Z., & Benson, H. Decrease in mitogen responsiveness of mononuclear cells from peripheral blood following epinephrine administration. *Journal of Immunology,* 1983, **130,** 694–697.

Dohrenwend, B. S., & Dohrenwend, B. P. (Eds.). *Stressful life events: Their nature and effects,* New York: Wiley, 1974.

Eisen, H. *Immunology* (3rd ed.). New York: Harper & Row, 1980.

Engel, G. Sudden and rapid death during psychological stress. *Annals of Internal Medicine,* 1971, **74,** 771–782.

Fessel, N. J., & Forsyth, R. P. Hypothalamic role in control of gamma globulin levels. *Arthritis and Rheumatism,* 1963, **6,** 771–772.

Folch, H., & Waksman, B. H. The splenic suppressor cell: Activity of thymus dependent adherent cells: Changes with age and stress. *Journal of Immunology,* 1974, **113,** 127–139.

Frankenhaueser, M., & Rissler, A. Effects of punishment on catecholamine release and efficiency of performance. *Psychopharmacologia,* 1970, **17,** 378–390.

Greer, S., Morris, T., & Pettingale, K. W. Psychological response to breast cancer: Effect on outcome. *Lancet,* 1979, **13,** 785–787.

Gutmann, M. C., & Benson, H. Interaction of environmental factors and systemic arterial blood pressure: A review. *Medicine,* 1971, **50,** 543–553.

Holmes, T. H., & Rahe, R. M. The social readjustment rating scale. *Journal of Psychosomatic Research,* 1967, **11,** 213–218.

Horne, R. L., & Picard, R. S. Psychosocial risk factors for lung cancer. *Psychosomatic Medicine,* 1979, **41,** 503–514.

Jemmott, J. B., Borysenko, J. Z., Borysenko, M., McClelland, D. C., Chapman, R., Meyer, D., & Benson, H. Academic stress, power motivation, and decrease in secretion rate of salivary secretory immunoglobulin A. *The Lancet,* 1983, June 25, 1400–1402.

Jenkins, C. D. Recent evidence supporting psychologic and social risk factors for coronary disease. *New England Journal of Medicine,* 1976, **294,** 987–994.

Kissen, D. Personality characteristics in males conducive to lung cancer. *British Journal of Medical Psychology,* 1963, **34,** 27–36.

Kissen, D. Psychosocial factors, personality and lung cancer in men aged 55–64. *British Journal of Medical Psychology,* 1967, **40,** 29–43.

Korneva, E. A., & Khai, L. M. Effect of stimulating different mesencephalic structures on protective immune response patterns. *Fiziologicheskii Zhurnal SSSR Imeni I. M. Sechenova,* 1967, **53,** 42–47.

Kraus, A. S., & Lillienfeld, A. M. Some epidemiological aspects of the high mortality rate in the young widowed group. *Journal of Chronic Diseases,* 1959, **10,** 207–217.

Landsberg, L. The sympathoadrenal system. In S. H. Ingbar (Ed.), *The year in endocrinology.* New York: Plenum Press, 1977.

Lazarus, R. S. Cognitive and personality factors underlying stress and coping. In S. Levine & N. Scotch (Eds.), *Social stress.* Chicago: Aldine, 1970.

Locke, S. E. Stress, adaptation, and immunity: Studies in humans. *General Hospital Psychiatry,* 1982, **4,** 49–58.

Mason, J. W. Emotions as reflected in patterns of endocrine integration. In L. Levy (Ed.), *Emotions: Their parameters and measurement.* New York: McGraw-Hill, 1975.

McClelland, D. C., Floor, E., Davidson, R. J., & Saron, C. Stressed power motivation, sympathetic activation, immune function, and illness. *Journal of Human Stress,* 1980, **6,** 11–19.

Mettrop, P. J., & Visser, P. Exteroceptive stimulation as a contingent factor in the induction and elicitation of delayed-type hypersensitivity reactions to 1-chloro-2 and 4-dinitrobenzene reactions in guinea pigs. *Psychophysiology,* 1969, **5,** 385–388.

Monjan, A. A., & Collector, M. I. Stress-induced modulation of the immune response. *Science,* 1977, **196,** 307–308.

Riley, V. Mouse mammary tumors: Alteration of incidence as an apparent function of stress. *Science,* 1975, **189,** 465–467.

Riley, V. Neuroendocrine influences on immunocompetence and neoplasia. *Science,* 1981, **211,** 1100–1109.

Rogers, M. P., Reich, P., Strom, T. B., & Carpenter, C. B. Behaviorally conditioned immunosuppression: Replication of a recent study. *Psychosomatic Medicine,* 1976, **38,** 447–451.

Rogers, M. P., Dubey, D., & Reich, P. The influence of the psyche and the brain on immunity and disease susceptibility: A critical review. *Psychosomatic Medicine,* 1979, **41,** 147–164.

Schleifer, S. J., Keller, S. E., Camerino, M., Thornton, J. C. & Stein, M. Suppression of lymphocyte stimulation following bereavement. *Journal of the American Medical Association,* 1983, **250,** 374–377.

Selye, H. A syndrome produced by diverse nocuous agents. *Nature,* 1936, **138,** 32.

Sklar, L. S., & Anisman, H. Stress and coping factors influence tumor growth. *Science,* 1979, **205,** 513–515.

Sklar, L. S., & Anisman, H. Social stress influences tumor growth. *Psychosomatic Medicine,* 1980, **42,** 347–465.

Stavraky, K. M., Buck, C. W., Loh, S. S., et al. Psychological factors in the outcome of human cancer. *Journal of Psychosomatic Research,* 1968, **12,** 251–259.

Stein, M., Keller, S. E., & Schleifer, S. J. The hypothalamus and the immune response. In H. Weiner, M. Hofer, & S. Stunkard (Eds.), *Brain, behavior and bodily disease.* New York: Raven Press, 1981.

Vaillant, G. E. Natural history of male psychologic health: Effects of mental health on physical health. *New England Journal of Medicine,* 1979, **301,** 1249–1254.

Weiss, J. M. Effects of coping behavior in different warning signal conditions on stress pathology in rats. *Journal of Comparative and Physiological Psychology,* 1971, **77,** 1–13.

Williams, J. M., Peterson, R. G., Shea, P. A., Schmedtje, J. F., Bauer, D. C., & Felten, D. L. Sympathetic innervation of murine thymus and spleen: Evidence for a functional link between the nervous and immune systems. *Brain Research Bulletin,* 1981, **6,** 83–94.

CHAPTER 17
COPING

FRANCES COHEN

University of California, San Francisco

The aim of this chapter is to discuss the role of coping in the enhancement of health and the prevention of disease. First, a theoretical overview of the stress and coping perspective will outline what coping is and will highlight important issues that deepen our understanding of the coping process. The chapter will then address the following general questions:

1. What role does coping play in the enhancement of health and the prevention of disease?
2. Are certain modes of coping more adaptive than others?
3. What value issues are central in our evaluation of the adaptiveness of coping behaviors?

THEORETICAL FRAMEWORK

Cognitive Appraisal

Lazarus's theoretical framework suggests that the ways individuals appraise a situation affect how they cope and their emotional, physiological, and behavioral reactions to stressful experiences (Lazarus, 1966; Lazarus, Averill, & Opton, 1970, 1974; Lazarus & Launier, 1978). The process of cognitive appraisal mediates psychologically between the person and the environment. There are two types of appraisal: primary appraisal and secondary appraisal. Primary appraisal is an evaluation of the significance of an event—as stressful, benign, positive, or irrelevant. This evaluation, which may be conscious or unconscious, takes into account the person's understanding of the power of the situation to produce harm and the resources the person has to bring to bear against the harm. Such stress appraisals can be one of three types: harm-loss (damage that has already occurred); threat (anticipated harm); or challenge (focusing on the potential gain or mastery rather than on the risks). Secondary appraisal is an evaluation of the person's coping resources and options. Both primary and secondary appraisals may change continuously from moment to moment, a process that has been called reappraisal (Lazarus, 1966).

The type of appraisal that is made is influenced by both situational and person factors (Lazarus, 1966). The strength of the external demand, the imminence of the confrontation, and ambiguity are important situational factors that influence primary appraisals. Person factors include motivational characteristics, belief systems, and intellectual resources and skills. People who believe that they have a high potential for mastery, for example, may be more likely to appraise a situation as challenging rather than threatening. Secondary appraisals are influenced by the type of harm, viability of alternative actions to prevent harm, situational constraints, and environmental resources (situational factors), as well as by motivational patterns, ego resources, coping dispositions, and general beliefs about the environment (person factors). People who believe in letting fate take its course, for example, are less likely to take preventive actions in the face of a tornado and thus are more likely to die as a result (Sims & Baumann, 1972). Individuals' tendencies to believe that they can control outcomes by virtue of their own efforts—an internal locus of control (Rotter, 1966)—is associated with greater use of vigilant rather than avoidant coping strategies in coping with surgery (George, Scott, Turner, & Gregg, 1980; La Montagne, 1982).

Coping Processes

Definition of Coping

Coping is defined as "efforts, both action-oriented and intrapsychic, to manage (that is, master, tolerate, reduce, minimize) environmental and internal demands, and conflicts among them, which tax or exceed a person's resources" (Cohen & Lazarus, 1979, p. 219). Thus, one needs to take into account both the demands on the organism and the resources available for dealing with those demands. This definition does not make a sharp distinction between "coping" and "defensive" processes (cf. Haan, 1977). This distinction involves a value judgment made on the basis of the coping mode utilized, without consideration of the nature of the situation or the total psychological economy of the person (Lazarus, 1966, 1981). Furthermore, defensive and coping processes often interweave in responding to stressful situations, and it is difficult to separate the two (Murphy, 1974; White, 1974). Thus, in this chapter, "coping" and "coping processes" refer to any efforts to manage demands, including processes that others might label as defenses.

Coping can occur prior to a stressful event—anticipatory coping—or in response to a confrontation with harm. Considerable attention has been paid to how people cope in situations of illness and surgery and to the relationship between coping and recovery (for reviews, see Cohen & Lazarus, 1979, 1983). Less attention has been paid to anticipatory coping—that is, the way individuals engage in the active regulation of emotional reactions, selecting their environment, planning, choosing, avoiding, tolerating, and so on. The importance of anticipatory coping activities has been heavily emphasized recently (Folkman, Schaefer, & Lazarus, 1979; Lazarus, 1975; Lazarus & Cohen, 1977; Lazarus & Launier, 1978). Some cognitive behavioral approaches also focus on trying to prevent the occurrence of stressful transactions, rather than just improving the ways individuals deal with those transactions once they have occurred (Cameron & Meichenbaum, 1982).

Functions of Coping

Coping may serve one of two functions: problem-solving or emotion-regulating (Hamburg, Coelho, & Adams, 1974; Lazarus, 1975; Lazarus et al., 1974). Problem-solving functions involve dealing with the environmental or internal demands that create threat. Thus, rehearsing an important speech, leaving an unfriendly group, or studying for an exam all represent efforts to change demands or remove obstacles. Emotion-regulating functions involve efforts to modify the distress that accompanies threat—for example, by denying that the threat exists, by drinking or taking tranquilizers, or by seeking support from others. Emotion-regulating functions are often thought to be maladaptive; there is increasing evidence, however, that these may be important functions, especially in dealing with serious illness (for a review, see Lazarus, 1983). Lazarus (1983), Mechanic (1974), and White (1974) have discussed the importance of illusion and avoidance in confronting serious life events. Mechanic (1974) for example, argues:

This brings me to consideration of a serious misconception that appears to run through the stress literature—the notion that successful adaptation requires an accurate perception of reality. There is perhaps no thought so stifling as to see ourselves in proper perspective. We all maintain our sense of self-respect and energy for action through perceptions that enhance our self-importance and self-esteem, and we maintain our sanity by suppressing the tremendous vulnerability we all experience in relation to the crises of the real world. (pp. 37–38)

People use emotion-focused and problem-focused coping simultaneously. Folkman and Lazarus (1980) found in a sample of middle-aged men and women that both modes were used in 98% of the episodes.

Modes of Coping

Five modes of coping can be identified: information seeking, direct action, inhibition of action, intrapsychic processes, and turning to others for support (Cohen & Lazarus, 1979). Information seeking involves trying to learn more about the situation or problem and about what can be done to deal with it. Direct actions include any concrete act, such as confronting a troublesome neighbor, building a fence, or drinking alcohol. Inhibition of action is also an important strategy, since avoiding impulsive action may often be beneficial. Intrapsychic processes involve ways of reappraising the situation—for example, by minimizing the threat, by refocusing one's attention, or by seeking gratification through other means. This category includes those processes that traditionally are called defenses. Turning to others for support also serves as a mode of coping (Mages & Mendelsohn, 1979) that may enhance one's feelings of well-being or one's efforts to deal with unexpected events (e.g., Cobb, 1976; Schaefer, Coyne, & Lazarus, 1981).

Measurement of Coping

There are two ways of assessing coping: as a disposition (or trait) or as a process (Averill & Opton, 1968; Cohen & Lazarus, 1979). A coping disposition is the tendency of an individual to use a particular mode of coping in a variety of stressful situations. Coping process measures study the modes of coping individuals actually use in dealing with a particular stressful situation.

Overviews of the types of measures used to assess coping are provided in other sources (e.g., Haan, 1982; Lazarus et al., 1974; Moos, 1974; Moos & Billings, 1982). Many of these measures have unknown validity and reliability, however, or assess only certain subcategories of coping behaviors. There is no consensus in the field regarding which measure has the greatest validity or which dimensions of coping are most important. The trait approaches make unwarranted assumptions about consistency in coping behavior; also, research studies show low or nonsignificant correlations among trait measures assessing similar traits (Cohen & Lazarus, 1973; Levine & Spivack, 1964). There are also difficulties in trying to assess coping as a process in naturalistic settings (Cohen & Lazarus, 1979). Much conceptual thinking needs to be done to improve our present systems of classification of coping processes (see, e.g., Moos & Billings, 1982).

Outcomes of Coping

Coping can have effects on psychological, social, and physiological outcomes. Psychologically, coping could affect one's emotional reactions (e.g., how depressed or anxious one is), general sense of well-being, or performance on tasks. Social outcomes include the effect on interpersonal relationships, the fulfillment of social roles, and the ability to function effectively in the work environment. Physiological outcomes include short-term physiological reactions (such as autonomic nervous system, hormonal, immunological, and neuroregulator changes). One must be cautious, however, about assuming that acute physiological changes are necessarily linked to long-term disease outcomes. Behavioral stimuli can result in increases in heart rate, blood pressure, or increased hormonal levels, but we still do not know how or whether acute physiological responses can lead to permanent changes in a person's health (see Elliott & Eisdorfer, 1982). Several physiological models have been proposed recently, however, and are reviewed by Borysenko in Chapter 16 of this handbook.

Adaptiveness of Coping

Every health practitioner wants to know whether or not certain coping strategies are adaptive, but such an apparently simple question cannot be answered easily. The adaptiveness of coping depends on three factors: (a) the domain of outcome examined, (b) the point in time, and (c) the context (Cohen & Lazarus, 1979). As described earlier, adaptiveness can be assessed in physiological, psychological, or social domains, and it may differ according to the domain being considered. Although Type A behavior may be linked to increased risk of coronary heart disease, for example (e.g., Rosenman, Brand, Jenkins, Friedman, Strauss, & Wurm, 1975), it may also be associated with greater satisfaction and more achievement in the workplace (e.g., Burke & Weir, 1980). Which of these outcomes is most important? Clearly, a value judgment is involved. The stress literature is filled with numerous cases in which a particular coping mode may have a positive influence on outcomes in one domain of functioning and a negative influence in another (e.g., Gal & Lazarus, 1975; Singer, 1974). Even within a domain, relationships may vary. Heart attack patients who use denial, for example, are less likely to comply with medical regimens (Croog, Shapiro, & Levine, 1971) but more likely to return to work and show less anxiety and depression than are those who do not deny (Stern, Pascale, & Ackerman, 1977; Stern, Pascale, & McLoone, 1976).

It is also important to distinguish short-run from long-run outcomes. Denial defenses, for example, have been found to be associated with decreased mortality in the coronary care unit (Hackett, Cassem, & Wishnie, 1968) but also with decreased compliance with medical treatment a year later (Croog et al., 1971). Denial defenses appeared to be useful for parents whose child was dying of leukemia before the child died (Wolff, Friedman, Hofer, & Mason, 1964) but seemed to cause increased psychological problems (Chodoff, Friedman, & Hamburg, 1964) and increased hydrocortisone levels after the child died (Hofer, Wolff, Friedman, & Mason, 1972a, 1972b). Thus, long-term and short-term effects may be quite different.

Finally, the context must be taken into account. A particular strategy may be adaptive in one situation but not in another. Cohen and Lazarus (1973), for example, suggest that denial-like forms of coping may be effective mechanisms for patients facing elective surgery, such as for a hernia or a gall bladder operation, but may be maladaptive for patients facing life-threatening open-heart surgery, where this form of coping is associated with increased risk of postoperative delirium (Layne & Yudofsky, 1971; cf. Morse & Litin, 1969). Furthermore, different coping strategies may be effective for dealing with acute as compared to chronic stressors.

THE ROLE OF COPING IN HEALTH PROMOTION AND DISEASE PREVENTION

In recent years, much attention has been given to the role of stress in the etiology of physical disease (for reviews, see Cohen, 1979, 1981; Elliott & Eisdorfer, 1982). There is growing recognition, however, that there is not a simple link between stress and disease outcomes and that how individuals cope with stress is an important modifier of the stress-disease relationship (e.g., Antonovsky, 1979; Jenkins, 1979; Lazarus, 1981; Rahe & Arthur, 1978).

Numerous factors besides coping can also modify the relationship between stress and illness. These include person factors (e.g., personality, past history, genetic variables), process factors (e.g., cognitive appraisal), and environmental factors (e.g., social support, social climate, cultural factors). An examination of the research on other modifiers of stress is beyond the scope of this chapter (see Cohen, 1979; Cohen, Horowitz, Lazarus, Moos, Robins, Rose, & Rutter, 1982). It should be mentioned, however, that modifiers other than coping may interact with coping. Thus, both using a particular coping strategy *and* having a biological predisposition may be necessary before a disease outcome results (Weiner, 1977; and see Borysenko, Chapter 16 of this Handbook).

Mechanisms

What are the mechanisms by which coping can affect the etiology of and recovery from disease? Several pathways might be involved (Cohen & Lazarus, 1979). First, coping may increase hormonal levels, causing direct tissue damage or influencing bodily resistance to illness. The adrenal-cortical hormones, for example, have been thought to lower immunological response (however, see Cohen, 1979; Solomon, 1969), and the adrenal-medullary hormones have been thought to have direct pathological effects on the cardiovascular system (Eliot, 1979). These relationships are more complex, however, than originally had been thought. Furthermore several hormones respond to stressors and could be influenced by coping (Rose, 1980). We need to learn more about the patterns of neuroendocrine response that can be influenced by coping (Mason, 1974) and about how they influence disease outcomes.

Second, coping may involve habits that interfere directly with health, such as smoking or excessive alcohol consumption, or that enhance health, such as following an exercise regimen or doing preventive breast examinations. Smoking cigarettes, for example, increases the risk of numerous diseases, including coronary heart disease and several types of cancers; and smoking postoperatively can interfere with lung functions during recovery.

Third, coping strategies can interfere with adaptive behavior that could lessen the severity of illness (such as seeking treatment early for potentially serious symptoms) or could enhance recovery from illness—as when denial of illness prevents a person from making the necessary effort in physical rehabilitation tasks. Denial may also interfere with the amount of information assimilated from health education programs—for example, during cardiac rehabilitation programs after a myocardial infarction (Shaw, Cohen, Doyle, and Palesky, Note 1).

Fourth, interpersonal styles may affect transactions with health professionals, thereby influencing the type of treatment the patient receives. Demanding, complaining patients, for example, may have their symptoms monitored more closely, allowing treatments to be initiated without delay. This may be one reason why cancer patients who complain and express high negative affect show the longest survival rates (e.g., Blumberg, West, & Ellis, 1954; Derogatis, Abeloff, & Melisaratos, 1979; Klopfer, 1957; Rogentine, van Kammen, Fox, Docherty, Rosenblatt, Boyd, & Bunney, 1979; Stavraky et al., 1968; cf. Krasnoff, 1959).

Finally, others have suggested that positive morale and the will to live may have positive physiological consequences (Cousins, 1976; Mason, Clark, Reeves, & Wagner, 1969). It is possible that a positive mood may trigger production of beta-endorphins, which can reduce pain and may speed healing. Positive emotions may also have beneficial effects on recovery in ways we do not yet understand (Lazarus, Cohen, Folkman, Kanner, & Schaefer, 1980).

The Relationship of Coping to Disease Etiology

Many studies have shown that the way an individual copes may reduce the physiological response to stressors (for a review, see Rose, 1980). "Successful" defenses have been associated with lower levels of 17-hydroxycorticosteroios in patients awaiting breast surgery (Katz, Weiner, Gallagher, & Hellman, 1970; cf. Gorzynski, Holland, Katz, Weiner, Zumoff, Fukushima, & Levin, 1980) and in soldiers facing combat (Bourne, Rose, & Mason, 1967). People who are actively engaged in situations of threat show increased cardiovascular and endocrine reactivity (Gal & Lazarus, 1975; Singer, 1974). Animals' inability to cope with an environmental stressor is related to changes in immunologic response (Sklar & Anisman, 1979).

From a theoretical standpoint, Engel and Schmale (Engel, 1968; Engel & Schmale, 1967; Schmale, 1972) suggest that people who are unable to cope may give up. This giving-up is thought to increase susceptibility to disease in those who are biologically predisposed (see also Seligman, 1975). Animal studies tend to support the hypothesized relationships, but there are serious methodological problems with the human studies, including retrospective confounding, lack of control groups, ignoring of the lag-time issue in cancer, and other alternative explanations (Cohen, 1979). Further research is needed in this area.

Kobasa (1979; Kobasa, Maddi, & Kahn, 1982) has suggested that people who have a strong sense of meaningfulness and commitment to self, a vigorous attitude to life, and an internal locus of control—a constellation she calls "hardiness"—are less likely to report being ill after undergoing many stressful life events. These relationships were found in a study of middle- and upper-level managers but did not hold in a study of lawyers. In that study (Kobasa, 1982), lawyers who were high on commitment and who avoided forms of coping judged to be inauthentic from an existential perspective (such as getting angry, drinking, withdrawing, taking time off) did not show psychophysiological symptoms after undergoing many stressful life events. (In this study, there was no correlation between stressful life events and self-reported illness.) These studies, though thought-provoking, do have considerable methodological problems, including retrospective design (except in Kobasa, Maddi, & Kahn, 1982), use of self-report measures of illness (which may assess only illness behavior, not illness), social desirability confounding, and conceptual unclarity of the personality/coping measures employed. Nonetheless, this work suggests the need to design methodologically sound research studies focusing on positive personality and coping qualities that may protect individuals who are undergoing stressful life events. Antonovsky (1979) also has called for a study of "resistance resources." It would also be useful to investigate further Hinkle's (1974) observation that people who remain healthy while undergoing stressful life experiences may be those who are emotionally insulated and less involved with other people.

Type A Behavior Pattern

Of all the coping variables examined in etiological studies, the strongest findings from methodologically sound studies are those involving Type A behavior. There is considerable evidence that Type A behavior is associated with increased risk of coronary heart disease (e.g., Rosenman et al., 1975), and there is fairly consistent evidence that it may be associated with the process of coronary atherosclerosis (Blumenthal, Williams, Kong, Schanberg, and Thompson, 1978; Frank, Heller, Kornfeld, Sporn, & Weiss, 1978; Williams, Haney, Lee, Kong, Blumenthal, & Whalen, 1980; Zyzanski, Jenkins, Ryan, Flessas, & Everist, 1976; cf. Dimsdale, Hackett, Hutter, Block, & Catanzano, 1978; Dimsdale, Hackett, Hutter, Block, Catanzano, & White, 1979; Krantz, Sanmarco, Selvester, & Matthews, 1979). Type A is a behavior pattern or coping style that includes the following characteristics: a sense of time urgency, aggressiveness, competitiveness, impatience, and underlying hostility (Friedman & Rosenman, 1974). The psychological components that underlie Type A behavior are still poorly understood. Some suggest that the need for control is a primary component of Type A behavior (Glass, 1977; cf. Lovallo & Pishkin, 1980). Others cite the Type A person's hostility as the most damaging component (Williams et al., 1980). It has also been reported that Type A persons use excessive denial and suppression (Pittner & Houston,

1980) which may result in their denying subjective distress and feelings of fatigue and to endure stresses longer than Type B's (Carver, Coleman, & Glass, 1976; Pittner & Houston, 1980).

Further work is needed to pinpoint the central components of Type A behavior that are linked to increased coronary heart disease risk. Before efforts are made to change Type A behavior to reduce risk of disease, evaluation must also be made of whether negative consequences would be found in other areas of life functioning (e.g., Burke & Weir, 1980). Recent studies suggest that Type A behavior may interact with another modifier of stress—cardiovascular reactivity—in influencing cardiovascular outcomes and that cardiovascular reactivity may, indeed, be a better predictor of coronary heart disease than Type A behavior (Dembroski, MacDougall, Eliot, & Buell, 1983).

THE RELATIONSHIP OF COPING TO RECOVERY FROM ILLNESS

In a previous paper, Cohen and Lazarus (1979) have reviewed research addressing the relationship between coping and recovery from illness and surgery. They concluded that many studies reported inconsistent results, which made it impossible to offer simple generalizations about which coping strategies were most adaptive. The nature of the disease, the type of outcome variable employed, and whether trait or process measures of coping were used all influenced the findings. Rather than reviewing this material again, the discussion here will focus on some consistent findings that relate coping to recovery outcomes. The variables to be discussed include (a) active versus avoidant coping strategies and (b) expression versus inhibition of emotion.

Active Versus Avoidant Coping Strategies

There has been considerable controversy in the stress and coping field about the adaptiveness of avoidant or denial-like forms of coping. Janis and Mann (1977) argue that avoidant strategies are maladaptive in decision-making situations (as is hypervigilance, the extreme opposite of avoidance) and in health situations where pain and other physical discomforts must be endured in the short run so that future benefits will be received (Janis & Rodin, 1979). Haan (1977) suggests that avoidant strategies that function as defenses are inherently less adaptive because they do not acknowledge reality.

The review of the literature by Cohen and Lazarus (1979) suggests that avoidance strategies may be quite adaptive in particular health situations, such as while awaiting general surgery or during the initial adjustment to severe illness or injury. Lazarus (1983) reviews literature showing that denial-like processes may be adaptive or maladaptive, depending on the nature of the situation.

Cohen and Lazarus (1983) have recently argued that active participant coping strategies are associated with better long-term rehabilitation after serious illnesses but are also associated with more difficulties in adjustment during the hospital stay. Andreasen, Noyes, and Hartford (1972), for example, found that the burn patients who had the smoothest psychological and physiological course of recovery were those who took an active, involved coping role. Andreasen and his colleagues originally had predicted the opposite, reasoning that the independence and aggressiveness associated with active coping would cause difficulties in adjusting to the dependency and passivity that accompanies prolonged patienthood. Another study found that tuberculosis patients who are active make the best community adjustment after hospital discharge, although they have more problems during their hospital stay (Vernier, Barrell, Cummings, Dickerson, & Hooper, 1961). Furthermore, autonomous women delay longer than passive women in seeking treatment for symptoms of breast or cervical cancer (Fisher, 1967; Hammerschlag, Fisher, DeCosse, & Kaplan, 1964).

Similar results have been found with respect to recovery from surgery. Kornfeld, Heller, Frank, and Moskowitz (1974) report that dominant, self-assured patients had a higher incidence of delirium after open-heart surgery. Cohen and Lazarus (1973) found that vigilant patients had the slowest and most complicated recovery after elective surgery (see also Cohen, 1976; cf. Hitchcock, 1983). George et al. (1980) found that vigilant copers had an overall slower healing rate after dental surgery, and that vigilance was the strongest negative predictor of overall healing after controlling for the degree of physical trauma of the surgery itself.

A recent paper conducted a meta-analysis of 26 studies that examined avoidant versus vigilant coping strategies in relation to measures of physical adaptation and drew similar conclusions to those already mentioned here (Mullen & Suls, 1982). The results of this analysis suggested that avoidant strategies resulted in better adaptation when short-run outcomes were examined, whereas vigilant strategies were related to better outcomes when long-run outcomes were studied. These studies illustrate the importance of taking situations into account when making judgments about whether coping processes are adaptive. They also show that qualities of independence and active, involved coping may result in more difficulties, not less, during short-term hospitalization or when medical treatment is needed.

Expression versus Inhibition of Emotion

If we examine the illness literature, we find that the adaptiveness of being emotionally expressive varies with the type of illness and the outcome measure used. The expression of hostility and other negative affects is associated with longer survival from cancer (e.g., Derogatis et al., 1979; Rogentine et al., 1979; Stavraky et al., 1968). Calden, Dupertuis, Hokanson, and Lewis (1970) found that difficult, nonconforming patients had a faster recovery from tuberculosis than patients who were rated as cooperative (cf. Cuadra, 1953).

In patients suffering from irreversible diffuse obstructive pulmonary syndrome, however, emotional expressiveness was associated with increased respiratory symptoms and physiological decompensation (Dudley, Verhey, Masuda, Martin, & Holmes, 1969). Furthermore, asthma and tuberculosis patients who were emotionally labile required longer hospitalization and (for the asthma patients) more steroid drugs after hospital discharge (Dirks, Jones, & Kinsman, 1977; Dirks, Kinsman, Jones, Spector, Davidson, & Evans, 1977). Among the asthma patients, however, those who were either high or low on this dimension were hospitalized more often than those in the middle (Dirks, Kinsman, Horton, Fross, & Jones, 1978). The authors felt that those who are high on this dimension may exaggerate their symptoms, resulting in greater chance of hospitalization, whereas those who are low on the dimension might allow symptoms to develop unchecked, to the point where rehospitalization would be necessary.

Thus, in some cases the expression of emotion leads to physiological decompensation, whereas in other situations it may draw attention to symptoms that might increase survival rate but might also result in more frequent hospitalization and increased drug treatment.

CONCLUSIONS

This chapter has reviewed only a small segment of the literature on coping and adaptive outcomes, yet the conclusions that can be drawn from this review have broad applicability. Whether one is talking about how individuals cope with the stresses of illness or about how they cope with other life dilemmas and problems, the conclusions seem to be the same: we should not expect a one-to-one relationship between any form of coping and good adaptational outcomes. The same coping process will be associated with positive outcomes under one set of circumstances but with negative outcomes under another. Three important factors must be considered, as has been discussed: the point in time, the context, and the domain of outcome examined.

The domain factor cannot be overemphasized. Those who are interested in behavioral health must consider health in its social, psychological, and physiological domains. An evaluation of values becomes necessary, with one value often being chosen at the expense of another. The Type A behavior literature illustrates this clearly. Type A behavior increases the risk of developing coronary heart disease, but it also involves behaviors that are socially valued and personally rewarding for the person. If intervention efforts are used to change Type A behavior in order to reduce the physical risk, the side effects may be psychologically and socially destructive unless special efforts are made to try to change the physical functions without impairing the psychological and social functions (cf. Roskies, 1980). All three domains of functioning must be studied if we are to understand the effects our interventions have on the total health of the individual.

Furthermore, our focus in coping research may need to be redirected. The key question may not be *which* coping strategies an individual uses but rather *how many* are in his or her repertoire or how flexible the person is in employing different strategies. We may be able to help people to cope better, but to do so requires taking into account the types of persons who might benefit from a strategy and the types of situations in which that strategy might be useful.

People can be offered training in coping skills and can learn more effective means of coping (e.g., Bowers & Kelly, 1979; Cameron & Meichenbaum, 1982; Janis, 1982; Roskies & Lazarus, 1980). Efforts may need to be focused, however, on strategies that help people cope with particular situations (e.g., teaching people how to stop smoking and how to resist smoking), rather than trying to inculcate certain coping strategies on the assumption that they will produce better psychological, social, and physical health for all individuals.

Coping is important in the enhancement of health and the prevention of disease, but there is still much to be understood about which coping strategies are most beneficial, for whom, and under what conditions. As research continues in this area, we will learn more about the positive effects of coping in enhancing the quality of life and in protecting the individual from the potentially deleterious effects of stressful life experiences.

REFERENCE NOTE

1. Shaw, R. E., Cohen, F., Doyle, B., & Palesky, J. *The impact of denial and repressive style on information gain and rehabilitational outcome in myocardial infarction patients.* Manuscript submitted for publication, 1984.

REFERENCES

Andreasen, N. J. C., Noyes, R., Jr., & Hartford, C. E. Factors influencing adjustment of burn patients during hospitalization. *Psychosomatic Medicine,* 1972, **34,** 517–525.

Antonovsky, A. *Health, stress, and coping.* San Francisco: Jossey-Bass, 1979.

Averill, J. R., & Opton, E. M., Jr. Psychophysiological assessment: Rationale and problems. In P. McReynolds (Ed.), *Advances in psychological assessment* (Vol. 1). Palo Alto: Science and Behavior Books, 1968.

Blumberg, E. M., West, P. M., & Ellis, F. W. A possible relationship between psychological factors and human cancer. *Psychosomatic Medicine,* 1954, **16,** 277–286.

Blumenthal, J. A., Williams, R. B., Kong, Y., Schanberg, S. M., & Thompson, L. W. Type A behavior pattern and coronary atherosclerosis. *Circulation,* 1978, **58,** 634–639.

Bourne, P. G., Rose, R. M., & Mason, J. W. Urinary 17-OHCS levels. *Archives of General Psychiatry,* 1967, **17,** 104–110.

Bowers, K. S., & Kelly, P. Stress, distress, psychotherapy, and hypnosis. *Journal of Abnormal Psychology,* 1979, **88,** 490–505.

Burke, R. J., & Weir, T. The Type A experience: Occupational and life demands, satisfaction and well-being. *Journal of Human Stress,* 1980, **6**(4), 28–38.

Calden, G., Dupertuis, C. W., Hokanson, J. E., & Lewis, W. C. Psychosomatic factors in the rate of recovery from tuberculosis. *Psychosomatic Medicine,* 1960, **22,** 345–355.

Cameron, R., & Meichenbaum, D. The nature of effective coping and the treatment of stress related problems: A cognitive-behavioral perspective. In L. Goldberger & S. Breznitz (Eds.), *Handbook of stress: Theoretical and clinical aspects.* New York: Free Press, 1982.

Carver, C. S., Coleman, A. E., & Glass, D. C. The coronary-prone behavior pattern and the suppression of fatigue on a treadmill test. *Journal of Personality and Social Psychology,* 1976, **33,** 460–466.

Chodoff, P., Friedman, S. F., & Hamburg, D. A. Stress, defenses, and coping behavior: Observations in parents of children with malignant disease. *American Journal of Psychiatry,* 1964, **120,** 743–749.

Cobb, S. Social support as a moderator of life stress. *Psychosomatic Medicine,* 1976, **38,** 300–314.

Cohen, F. Psychological preparation, coping, and recovery from surgery (Doctoral dissertation, University of California, Berkeley, 1975). *Dissertation Abstracts International,* 1976, **37,** 454B. (University Microfilms No. 76–15, 145)

Cohen, F. Personality, stress, and the development of physical illness. In G. C. Stone, F. Cohen, N. E. Adler, & Associates, *Health psychology—A handbook.* San Francisco: Jossey-Bass, 1979.

Cohen, F. Stress and bodily disease. *Psychiatric Clinics of North America,* 1981, **4**(2), 269–286.

Cohen, F., Horowitz, M. J., Lazarus, R. S., Moos, R. H., Robins, L. N., Rose, R. M., & Rutter, M. Panel report on psychosocial assets and modifiers of stress. In G. R. Elliott & C. Eisdorfer (Eds.), *Stress and human health.* New York: Springer, 1982.

Cohen, F., & Lazarus, R. S. Active coping processes, coping dispositions, and recovery from surgery. *Psychosomatic Medicine,* 1973, **35,** 375–389.

Cohen, F., & Lazarus, R. S. Coping with the stresses of illness. In G. C. Stone, F. Cohen, N. E. Adler, & Associates, *Health psychology—A handbook.* San Francisco: Jossey-Bass, 1979.

Cohen, F., & Lazarus, R. S. Coping and adaptation in health and illness. In D. Mechanic (Ed.), *Handbook of health, health care, and the health professions.* New York: Free Press, 1983.

Cousins, N. Anatomy of an illness (as perceived by the patient). *New England Journal of Medicine,* 1976, **295,** 1458–1463.

Croog, S. H., Shapiro, D. S., & Levine, S. Denial among male heart patients: An empirical study. *Psychosomatic Medicine,* 1971, **33,** 385–397.

Cuadra, C. A. *A psychometric investigation of control factors in psychological adjustment.* Unpublished doctoral dissertation, University of California, Berkeley, 1953.

Dembroski, T. M., MacDougall, J. M., Eliot, R. S., & Buell, J. C. Stress, emotions, behavior, and cardiovascular disease. In L. Temoshok, C. Van Dyke & L. S. Zegans (Eds.), *Emotions in health and illness: Theoretical and research foundations.* New York: Grune & Stratton, 1983.

Derogatis, L. R., Abeloff, M. D., & Melisaratos, N. Psychological coping mechanisms and survival time in metastatic breast cancer. *Journal of the American Medical Association,* 1979, **242,** 1504–1508.

Dimsdale, J. E., Hackett, T. P., Hutter, A. M., Block, P. C., & Catanzano, D. Type A personality and extent of coronary atherosclerosis. *American Journal of Cardiology,* 1978, **42,** 583–584.

Dimsdale, J. E., Hackett, T. P., Hutter, A. M., Block, P. C., Catanzano, D., & White, P. J. Type A behavior and angiographic findings. *Journal of Psychosomatic Research,* 1979, **23,** 273–276.

Dirks, J. F., Jones, N. F., & Kinsman, R. A. Panic-fear: A personality dimension related to intractability in asthma. *Psychosomatic Medicine,* 1977, **39,** 120–126.

Dirks, J. F., Kinsman, R. A., Horton, D. J., Fross, K. H., & Jones, N. F. Panic-fear in asthma: Rehospitalization following intensive long-term treatment. *Psychosomatic Medicine,* 1978, **40,** 5–13.

Dirks, J. F., Kinsman, R. A., Jones, N. F., Spector, S. L., Davidson, P. T., & Evans, N. W. Panic-fear: A personality dimension related to length of hospitalization in respiratory illness. *Journal of Asthma Research,* 1977, **14,** 61–71.

Dudley, D. L., Verhey, J. W., Masuda, M., Martin, C. J., & Holmes, T. H. Long-term adjustment, prognosis, and death in irreversible diffuse obstructive pulmonary syndromes. *Psychosomatic Medicine,* 1969, **31,** 310–325.

Eliot, R. S. *Stress and the major cardiovascular disorders.* Mount Kisco, N.Y.: Futura, 1979.

Elliott, G. R., & Eisdorfer, C. (Eds.). *Stress and human health.* New York: Springer, 1982.

Engel, G. L. A life setting conducive to illness: The giving up–given up complex. *Bulletin of the Menninger Clinic,* 1968, **32,** 355–365.

Engel, G. L., & Schmale, A. H. Psychoanalytic theory of somatic disorder. *Journal of the American Psychoanalytic Association,* 1967, **15,** 344–363.

Fisher, S. Motivation for patient delay. *Archives of General Psychiatry,* 1967, **16,** 676–678.

Folkman, S., & Lazarus, R. S. An analysis of coping in a middle-aged community sample. *Journal of Health and Social Behavior,* 1980, **21,** 219–239.

Folkman, S., Schaefer, C., & Lazarus, R. S. Cognitive processes as mediators of stress and coping. In V. Hamilton & D. M. Warburton (Eds.), *Human stress and cognition: An information-processing approach.* New York: Wiley, 1979.

Frank, K. A., Heller, S. S., Kornfeld, D. S., Sporn, A. A., & Weiss, M.D. Type A behavior pattern and coronary angiographic findings. *Journal of the American Medical Association,* 1978, **240,** 761–763.

Friedman, M., & Rosenman, R. H. *Type A behavior and your heart.* New York: Knopf, 1974.

Gal, R., & Lazarus, R. S. The role of activity in anticipating and confronting stressful situations. *Journal of Human Stress,* 1975, **1**(4), 4–20.

George, J. M., Scott, D. S., Turner, S. P., & Gregg, J. M. The effects of psychological factors and physical trauma on recovery from oral surgery. *Journal of Behavioral Medicine,* 1980, **3,** 291–310.

Glass, D. C. *Behavior patterns, stress, and coronary disease.* Hillsdale, N.J.: Erlbaum, 1977.

Gorzynski, J. G., Holland, J., Katz, J. L., Weiner, H., Zumoff, B., Fukushima, D., & Levin, J. Stability of ego defenses and endocrine responses in women prior to breast biopsy and ten years later. *Psychosomatic Medicine,* 1980, **42,** 323–328.

Haan, N. *Coping and defending: Processes of self-environment organization.* New York: Academic Press, 1977.

Haan, N. The assessment of coping, defenses, and stress. In L. Goldberger & S. Breznitz (Eds.), *Handbook of stress: Theoretical and clinical aspects.* New York: Free Press, 1982.

Hackett, T. P., Cassem, N. H., & Wishnie, H. A. The coronary-care unit: An appraisal of its psychologic hazards. *New England Journal of Medicine,* 1968, **279,** 1365–1370.

Hamburg, D. A., Coelho, G. V., & Adams, J. E. Coping and adaptation: Steps toward a synthesis of biological and social perspectives. In G. V. Coelho, D. A. Hamburg, & J. E. Adams (Eds.), *Coping and adaptation.* New York: Basic Books, 1974.

Hammerschlag, C. S., Fisher, S., DeCosse, J., & Kaplan, E. Breast symptoms and patient delay: Psychological variables involved. *Cancer,* 1964, **17,** 1480–1485.

Hinkle, L. E., Jr. The effect of exposure to culture change, social change, and changes in interpersonal relationships on health. In B. S. Dohrenwend & B. P. Dohrenwend (Eds.), *Stressful life events: Their nature and effects.* New York: Wiley, 1974.

Hitchcock, L. Improving recovery from surgery: The interaction of preoperative interventions, coping processes, and personality variables (Doctoral dissertation, University of Texas, Austin, 1982). *Dissertation Abstracts International,* 1983, **43,** 2339B (University Microfilms No. DA8227665).

Hofer, M. A., Wolff, C. T., Friedman, S. B., & Mason, J. W. A psychoendocrine study of bereavement: Part 1. 17-hydroxycorticosteroid excretion rates of parents following death of their children from leukemia. *Psychosomatic Medicine,* 1972, **34,** 481–491. (a)

Hofer, M. A., Wolff, C. T., Friedman, S. B., & Mason, J. W. A psychoendocrine study of bereavement: Part 2. Observations on the process of mourning in relation to adrenocortical function. *Psychosomatic Medicine,* 1972, **34,** 492–504. (b)

Janis, I. L. Decision making under stress. In L. Goldberger & S. Breznitz (Eds.), *Handbook of stress: Theoretical and clinical aspects.* New York: Free Press, 1982.

Janis, I. L., & Mann, L. *Decision making: Psychological analysis of conflict, choice and commitment.* New York: Free Press, 1977.

Janis, I. L., & Rodin, J. Attribution, control, and decision making: Social psychology and health care. In G. C. Stone, F. Cohen, N. E. Adler, & Associates, *Health psychology—A handbook.* San Francisco: Jossey-Bass, 1979.

Jenkins, C. D. Psychosocial modifiers of response to stress. *Journal of Human Stress*, 1979, **5**(4), 3–15.

Katz, J. L., Weiner, H., Gallagher, T. G., & Hellman, L. Stress, distress, and ego defenses. *Archives of General Psychiatry*, 1970, **23**, 131–142.

Klopfer, B. Psychological variables in human cancer. *Journal of Projective Techniques*, 1957, **21**, 331–340.

Kobasa, S. C. Stressful life events, personality, and health: An inquiry into hardiness. *Journal of Personality and Social Psychology*, 1979, **37**, 1–11.

Kobasa, S. C. Commitment and coping in stress resistance among lawyers. *Journal of Personality and Social Psychology*, 1982, **42**, 707–717.

Kobasa, S. C., Maddi, S. R., & Kahn, S. Hardiness and health: A prospective study. *Journal of Personality and Social Psychology*, 1982, **42**, 168–177.

Kornfeld, D. S., Heller, S. S., Frank, K. A., & Moskowitz, R. Personality and psychological factors in postcardiotomy delirium. *Archives of General Psychiatry*, 1974, **31**, 249–253.

Krantz, D. S., Sanmarco, M. I., Selvester, R. H., & Matthews, K. A. Psychological correlates of progression of atherosclerosis in men. *Psychosomatic Medicine*, 1979, **41**, 467–475.

Krasnoff, A. Psychological variables and human cancer: A cross-validational study. *Psychosomatic Medicine*, 1959, **21**, 291–295.

La Montagne, L. L. Children's locus of control beliefs as predictors of their preoperative coping behavior (Doctoral dissertation, University of California, San Francisco, 1982). *Dissertation Abstracts International*, 1982, **43**, 679B (University Microfilms No. DA8216803).

Layne, O. L., Jr., & Yudofsky, S. C. Postoperative psychosis in cardiotomy patients. *New England Journal of Medicine*, 1971, **284**, 518–520.

Lazarus, R. S. *Psychological stress and the coping process*. New York: McGraw-Hill, 1966.

Lazarus, R. S. The self-regulation of emotion. In L. Levi (Ed.), *Emotions—Their parameters and measurement*. New York: Raven Press, 1975.

Lazarus, R. S. The stress and coping paradigm. In C. Eisdorfer, D. Cohen, & A. Kleinman (Eds.), *Theoretical bases for psychopathology*. New York: Spectrum, 1981.

Lazarus, R. S. The costs and benefits of denial. In S. Breznitz (Ed.), *Denial of stress*. New York: International Universities Press, in press.

Lazarus, R. S., Averill, J. R., & Opton, E. M. Towards a cognitive theory of emotion. In M. B. Arnold (Ed.), *Feelings and emotions*. New York: Academic Press, 1970.

Lazarus, R. S., Averill, J. R., & Opton, E. M. The psychology of coping: Issues of research and assessment. In G. V. Coelho, D. A. Hamburg, & J. E. Adams (Eds.), *Coping and adaptation*. New York: Basic Books, 1974.

Lazarus, R. S., & Cohen, J. B. Environmental stress. In I. Altman & J. F. Wohlwill (Eds.), *Human behavior and the environment: Current theory and research*. New York: Plenum Press, 1977.

Lazarus, R. S., Cohen, J. B., Folkman, S., Kanner, A., & Schaefer, C. Psychological stress and adaptation: Some unresolved issues. In H. Selye (Ed.), *Selye's guide to stress research* (Vol. 1). New York: Van Nostrand, 1980.

Lazarus, R. S., & Launier, R. Stress-related transactions between person and environment. In L. A. Pervin and M. Lewis (Eds.), *Perspectives in interactional psychology*. New York: Plenum Press, 1978.

Levine, M., & Spivack, G. *The Rorschach index of repressive style*. Springfield, Ill.: Thomas, 1964.

Lovallo, W. R., & Pishkin, V. Performance of Type A (coronary-prone) men during and after exposure to uncontrollable noise and task failure. *Journal of Personality and Social Psychology*, 1980, **38**, 963–971.

Mages, N. L., & Mendelsohn, G. A. Effects of cancer on patients' lives: A personological approach. In G. C. Stone, F. Cohen, N. E. Adler, & Associates, *Health psychology—A handbook*. San Francisco: Jossey-Bass, 1979.

Mason, J. W. Specificity in the organization of neuroendocrine response profiles. In P. Seeman & G. M. Brown (Eds.), *Frontiers in neurology and neuroscience research* (First International Symposium of the Neuroscience Institute). Toronto: University of Toronto, 1974.

Mason, R. C., Clark, G., Reeves, R. B., & Wagner, B. Acceptance and healing. *Journal of Religion and Health,* 1969, **8,** 123–142.

Mechanic, D. Social structure and personal adaptation: Some neglected dimensions. In G. V. Coelho, D. A. Hamburg, & J. E. Adams (Eds.), *Coping and adaptation.* New York: Basic Books, 1974.

Moos, R. H., Psychological techniques in the assessment of adaptive behavior. In G. V. Coelho, D. A. Hamburg, and J. E. Adams (Eds.), *Coping and adaptation.* New York: Basic Books, 1974.

Moos, R. H., & Billings, A. G. Conceptualizing and measuring coping resources and processes. In L. Goldberger & S. Breznitz (Eds.), *Handbook of stress: Theoretical and clinical aspects.* New York: Free Press, 1982.

Morse, R. M., & Litin, E. M. Postoperative delirium: A study of etiologic factors. *American Journal of Psychiatry,* 1969, **126,** 388–395.

Mullen, B., & Suls, J. The effectiveness of attention and rejection as coping styles: A meta-analysis of temporal differences. *Journal of Psychosomatic Research,* 1982, **26,** 43–49.

Murphy, L. B. Coping, vulnerability, and resilience in childhood. In G. V. Coelho, D. A. Hamburg, & J. E. Adams (Eds.), *Coping and adaptation.* New York: Basic Books, 1974.

Pittner, M. S., & Houston, B. K. Response to stress, cognitive coping strategies, and the Type A behavior pattern. *Journal of Personality and Social Psychology,* 1980, **39,** 147–157.

Rahe, R. H., & Arthur, R. H. Life change and illness studies. *Journal of Human Stress,* 1978, **4**(1), 3–15.

Rogentine, G. N., van Kammen, D. P., Fox, B. H., Docherty, J. P., Rosenblatt, J. E., Boyd, S. C., & Bunney, W. E. Psychological factors in the prognosis of malignant melanoma: A prospective study. *Psychosomatic Medicine,* 1979, **41,** 647–655.

Rose, R. M. Endocrine responses to stressful psychological events. *Psychiatric Clinics of North America,* 1980, **3**(2), 251–276.

Rosenman, R. H., Brand, R. J., Jenkins, C. D., Friedman, M., Strauss, R., & Wurm, M. Coronary heart disease in the western collaborative group study: Final follow-up experience of 8½ years. *Journal of the American Medical Association,* 1975, **233,** 872–877.

Roskies, E. Considerations in developing a treatment program for the coronary-prone (Type A) behavior pattern. In P. O. Davidson & S. M. Davidson (Eds.), *Behavioral medicine: Changing health life styles.* New York: Brunner/Mazel, 1980.

Roskies, E., & Lazarus, R. S. Coping theory and the teaching of coping skills. In P. O. Davidson & S. M. Davidson (Eds.), *Behavioral medicine: Changing health life styles.* New York: Brunner/ Mazel, 1980.

Rotter, J. B. Generalized expectancies for internal versus external control of reinforcement. *Psychological Monographs,* 1966, **80**(1, Whole No. 609).

Schaefer, C., Coyne, J. C., & Lazarus, R. S. The health-related functions of social support. *Journal of Behavioral Medicine,* 1981, **4,** 381–406.

Schmale, A. H., Jr. Giving up as a final common pathway to changes in health. *Advances in Psychosomatic Medicine,* 1972, **8,** 20–40.

Seligman, M. E. *Helplessness.* San Francisco: Freeman, 1975.

Sims, J. H., & Baumann, D. D. The tornado threat: Coping styles of the north and south. *Science,* 1972, **176,** 1386–1392.

Singer, M. T. Engagement-involvement: A central phenomenon in psychophysiological research. *Psychosomatic Medicine,* 1974, **36,** 1–17.

Sklar, L. S., & Anisman, H. Stress and coping factors influence tumor growth. *Science,* 1979, **205,** 513–515.

Solomon, G. F. Discussion: Emotions and immunity. *Annals of the New York Academy of Sciences,* 1969, **164,** 461–462.

Stavraky, K. M., and others. Psychological factors in the outcome of human cancer. *Journal of Psychosomatic Research,* 1968, **12,** 251–259.

Stern, M. J., Pascale, L., & Ackerman, A. Life adjustment post myocardial infarction: Determining predictive variables. *Archives of Internal Medicine,* 1977, **137,** 1680–1685.

Stern, M. J., Pascale, L., & McLoone, J. G. Psychological adaptation following an acute myocardial infarction. *Journal of Chronic Diseases,* 1976, **29,** 513–526.

Vernier, C. M., Barrell, R. P. Cummings, J. W., Dickerson, J. H., & Hooper, H. D. Psychosocial study of the patient with pulmonary tuberculosis: A cooperative research approach. *Psychological Monographs,* 1961, **75**(6), 1–32.

Weiner, H. *Psychobiology and human disease.* New York: American Elsevier, 1977.

White, R. W. Strategies of adaptation: An attempt at systematic description. In G. V. Coelho, D. A. Hamburg, & J. E. Adams (Eds.), *Coping and adaptation.* New York: Basic Books, 1974.

Williams, R. B., Haney, T. L., Lee, K. L., Kong, Y., Blumenthal, J. A., & Whalen, R. E. Type A behavior, hostility, and coronary atherosclerosis. *Psychosomatic Medicine,* 1980, **42,** 539–549.

Wolff, C. T., Friedman, S. G., Hofer, M. A., & Mason, J. W. Relationship between psychological defenses and mean urinary 17-hydroxycorticosteroid excretion rates: I. A predictive study of parents of fatally ill children. *Psychosomatic Medicine,* 1964, **26,** 576–591.

Zyzanski, S. J., Jenkins, C. D., Ryan, T. J., Flessas, A., & Everist, M. Psychological correlates of coronary angiographic findings. *Archives of Internal Medicine,* 1976, **136,** 1234–1237.

CHAPTER 18

HEALTH HAZARD/HEALTH RISK APPRAISALS

SHARLENE M. WEISS

Healthy People, Inc., Silver Spring, Maryland

One of the most promising approaches to lifestyle and health behavior change has been the development of health hazard/health risk appraisal (HHA/HRA) instruments. These instruments range from simple self-test, self-scored questionnaires with do-it-yourself suggestions to elaborate multimedia productions, computer-scored and analyzed reports with extensive data presentations, and complex actuarial predictions. All of the instruments feature questions about an individual's health-related behaviors and characteristics. The answers to these questions are then compared to mortality statistics and epidemiologic data in order to estimate the individual's risk (or probability) of dying by some specified future time. The instruments often also calculate the amount of risk that could be eliminated by making appropriate behavioral changes. These measurements of risk and of the potential benefits of behavioral changes are then presented to the individuals to stimulate their participation in activities aimed at changing their lifestyles and improving their health.

OVERVIEW OF HHA/HRA INSTRUMENTS

The instruments used to collect information about clients, to provide feedback to the clients on risks of dying, and to recommend risk reduction strategies are the key elements in the HHA/HRA process. The appendix to this chapter provides descriptions of the various appraisal instruments that are available.

Each HHA/HRA questionnaire has a core of questions to collect client data about age; sex; height and weight; race; blood pressure; whether either parent died before age 60 and of what disease; activity or exercise level; smoking habits and history; alcohol habits and history; family history of diabetes and suicide; driving habits (miles per year); seat belt use; arrest record; whether or not the client carries a weapon; personal history of depression, rectal bleeding, bacterial pneumonia, tuberculosis, emphysema, rheumatic fever, heart murmur; whether or not the client receives an annual sigmoidoscopy; and, for women, sexual intercourse history; history of vaginal bleeding; history of cervical, ovarian, or uterian cancer; frequency of breast self-examination; and frequency and results of pap smears.

The author wishes to acknowledge the work of W. Beery, V. J. Schoenbach, E. H. Wagner, R. M. Graham, J. M. Karon, and S. Pezzullo in the report *Description, Analysis and Assessment of Health Hazards/Health Risk Appraisal Programs*. Chapel Hill: University of North Carolina at Chapel Hill, Health Services Research Center, March 1981. (NTIS No. PD-81–239063)

In addition to these core questions, the questionnaire may ask many others, depending on the purpose for which it was designed. One of Medical Datamation's questionnaires, for example, is an eight-page, multipurpose instrument designed to collect more extensive medical history information and to be used for medical screening. The University of Wisconsin at Stevens Point 14-page Lifestyle Assessment Questionnaire has, in addition to the HHA/HRA's Risk of Death Section, a Wellness Inventory Section, an Alert Section, and a section in which the client indicates preferences for the receipt of further health information. The Personal Health Profile marketed by General Health includes questions related to stress, social supports, coping, and Type A behavior. Most often, these additional data do not figure in the computation of mortality risks but are used as the basis for risk reduction recommendations in the area of stress management and relaxation techniques.

Feedback, or the vehicle by which the results of the appraisal are presented to the client, is an important feature of HHA/HRA. Many risk assessment questionnaires, self-scoring and otherwise, provide individuals with feedback about their health outlook but do not quantify the benefits of behavioral improvement in terms of reduced probability of death. These questionnaires do not use quantified risk factors based on mortality statistics and epidemiologic studies to calculate the individual's chance of dying and reduced chances of death if lifestyle habits are changed.

Some of the more sophisticated and more complete HHA/HRA questionnaires give feedback to the individual on his or her current "risk age," which is based on the average tenure risk of death per 100,000 according to the answers to the questionnaire, and his or her "achievable age," which is based on the achievable tenure risk of death per 100,000, assuming appropriate behavioral changes. In addition, most of the feedback forms list the contributing weights to the risk age of the person's modifiable and unmodifiable risk characteristics and suggest lifestyle changes to reduce those risks that are modifiable.

The differences seen in HHA/HRA feedback modes reflect the purpose for which the instrument was designed and the program context. Certain instruments and feedback mechanisms, for example, were designed to be administered and returned by mail, and thus may rely extensively on printed health education information and explanations of the feedback itself. Others may be more concise in the printed format, because they are designed to be interpreted by a trained health counselor. Feedback reports vary from a single page to a 50-page, illustrated, multicolored book. All of the feedback instruments are designed to make the results understandable to the particular client population.

HISTORICAL DEVELOPMENT OF HHA/HRA

The development of the concept of HHA/HRA is most often associated with the career of Dr. Lewis C. Robbins, formerly of the U.S. Public Health Service. Dr. Robbins and his network of associates developed and refined the ideas and mobilized the resources that resulted in the formulation of the first HHA/HRA publication, entitled *How to Practice Prospective Medicine,* in 1970, with the support of a grant from the Indiana State Board of Health. This manual was written for practicing physicians and was used in calculations of risks. The manual explicitly defined the necessary techniques, including data-gathering instruments, risk computations, and feedback strategy, for the first time. Efforts toward computerization led to several foci of interest in HHA/HRA in the public and private sectors. Of major importance was the interest of the Canadian government, given impetus by the health promotion orientation of the Lalonde (1975) report. Canadian governmental interests in the mortality statistics used in HHA/HRA appeared to be the initiating focus for the involvement of the Centers for Disease Control (CDC) in HHA/HRA. The CDC interest brought the U.S. government into direct involvement in the HHA/HRA—first, through the development of a program for CDC employees; second, through constructing its own questionnaire and computer computation, available to public health agencies; and third, through the development of a research and evaluation contract program. In concert with the CDC, other areas of the federal government—most notably, the National Center for Health Services Research, the National Heart, Lung and Blood Institute, and the Office of Health Information and Health Promotion—have recently sponsored research and/or demonstration projects involving or related to HHA/HRA. Quite independently, the W. K. Kellogg Foundation has funded three HHA/HRA programs.

Initial involvement of the private sector was characterized by marketing of HHA/HRA services—primarily to industry and university health programs—by a series of small firms. More recently, large corporations—notably, in the computer, health products, and insurance industries—have entered or are planning to enter the marketplace. The impact of these large corporations on the dissemination and technology of health promotion is only beginning to be felt.

The major intended audience for Dr. Robbins's original manual was practicing physicians, who could use it as a tool to identify risk variables and to screen their patients. Since 1970, the audience has expanded to include nonmedical personnel, health educators, fitness personnel, employee groups, and community organizations. The growing interest in health promotion in the United States is probably a result, in part, of the widely held concept that further advances in the health status of the American population will not accrue from costly medical technological innovations alone. Also, there is mounting evidence that health is determined by a number of factors that are beyond the purview and control of medical care. Concerns about the costs and limitations of medical care have led planners and consumer groups to consider health promotion activities a less expensive and possibly more effective alternative for reducing morbidity and mortality. The rising costs of health insurance benefits have also stimulated many employers to explore the possibility of reducing costs by promoting health, thereby creating an enormous potential market for HHA/HRA and related programs. This market has attracted the attention of many organizations in the private sector, which have now come to play the dominant role in the continuing development and promotion of HHA/HRA. Extensive marketing of HHA/HRA is only in the beginning phases and will intensify as larger firms enter the marketplace. This prospect, along with the continuing expansion and visibility of the federal involvement in promoting the technique, lends urgency to the need to examine critically the risks and benefits of HHA/HRA.

THE CONTEXT OF HHA/HRA PROGRAMS

It is important to consider the context in which HHA/HRA programs are carried out and the range of activities that are mounted in conjunction with these programs.

Expectations for HHA/HRA Impact

Although HHA/HRA is frequently promulgated as a motivational technique for stimulating health behavior change in clients, the expectations of many of the HHA/HRA programs are often much less ambitious. Occasionally, programs using HHA/HRA view the instrument as a convenient way to collect, organize, and present client health data in order to remind and assist the health provider in addressing preventive health needs. In other instances, programs use HHA/HRA principally as a marketing strategy or "attention grabber" to stimulate participation in risk reduction programs. HHA/HRA is also used by some programs as a means for collecting and summarizing epidemiologic data on populations for health promotion planning. Thus, although probably all HHA/HRA programs are developed with some hope that participation in HHA/HRA will directly stimulate health behavior change, program directors and staff vary widely in their views regarding the salience of this expectation or the likelihood of its fulfillment. Recent anecdotal reports indicate that HHA/HRA programs used in conjunction with other health risk reduction classes appear to facilitate more behavior change than HHA/HRA used independently. Evaluation of the HHA/HRA programs is currently under way in many settings, but published results are unavailable at this time. Anecdotal evidence also indicates that health promotion activities appear to be most effective when they are conducted in an important social context of the client, such as school, workplace, or doctor's office, because of the additional pressures such environments can provide. Such settings also can achieve higher participation rates and have the potential for reaching reluctant high-risk subjects in the populations.

Intensity of Interaction with Clients

At one extreme, HHA/HRA has been used as the exclusive approach to health promotion, with the written feedback serving as the sole communication with the client. At the other extreme, HHA/HRA serves as a data-collection and organization tool in support of intensive involvement with the client in one-on-one and/or small group encounters. In the latter circumstance, the written feedback is interpreted, explained, tailored, and so on, by the program staff for the individual client. In addition to variations in the extent to which the results are discussed with the clients, programs vary widely in the extent to which they directly provide health education and promotion services to clients and maintain contact with them over time.

Remoteness from Health Care

Current HHA/HRA programs range from being part of the family doctor's personal routine to community-based applications in which the client's source of medical care plays no role and is often ignorant of the individual's involvement with such a program. An intermediate situation would be workplace programs in which the employer bears medical responsibility for employees while they are on the job. HHA/HRA has been used as a substitute for or supplement to routine physical examinations and has been included as an integral part of the medical record. Conversely, HHA/HRA conducted at health fairs, shopping centers, or through media applications only sporadically provide systematic information to the client's source of medical care.

THE SCIENTIFIC BASIS FOR RISK ESTIMATION IN HHA/HRA

Space limitations preclude complete discussion here of the scientific basis for risk estimation. Further information on this topic is provided in several reviews (Beery, Schoenbach, Wagner, Graham, Karon, & Pezzullo, 1981, Sec. 3; Davies, 1978; Fullarton, 1977; Hall & Zwemer, 1979; Imrey & Williams, 1977; Brown & Nabert, Note 1).

EFFICACY OF HHA/HRA

An assessment of the efficacy and potential of HHA/HRA is best carried out in terms of the purposes for which the appraisal might be employed. Purposes would include stimulating the interest and participation in health risk reduction programs, communicating health risk information, inducing behavioral change, and several other miscellaneous uses.

Promotion and Recruitment

A number of factors have been suggested as contributing to the apparent attention-getting ability of HHA/HRA. Aspects of HHA/HRA that pertain to the individual include the following:

1. The use of studies, statistical measures, and computer-generated reports makes HHA/HRA appear "scientific" and thus attractive to many individuals.

2. It helps the individual better understand the concept of personal health risk and the role of individual health practices in the etiology of disease.

3. It demonstrates the quantitative nature of risk-taking behavior and the synergistic potential of individual risks added together.

4. It quantifies the relative importance of health practices, so that the individual can choose which ones to work on and where to start.

5. It provides a measure of improved risk if some of the health practices are improved.

Benefits of HHA/HRA on the organizational level include the following:

1. It provides a structure with which to focus discussions of health and behavior.

2. It relies on self-administered questionnaires, physiological measurements, and computer-assisted calculations, making its application to large groups feasible, efficient, and relatively inexpensive.

3. It enhances development of a data base for epidemiologic research and health planning.

4. The data-gathering devices, computer software, and other aspects of the program can be marketed as a package, which stimulates the involvement of commercial firms.

Hsu and Milsum (1975) report many instances of acceptance and enjoyment of HHA/HRA by client groups. In contrast, a study by Johns (1976) reported that only 15% of a random sample ($n = 1186$) of active patients at a multispecialty clinic in northern Utah completed and returned an HHA/HRA instrument they had received in the mail. Low participation rates are not uncommon in many of the programs. Programs differ considerably in the prominence given to HHA/HRA in promotional material. Most HHA/HRA programs collect data on participation, but participation rates can be obtained only for programs with a definite target population. To assess HHA/HRA's effectiveness as a promotional tool, it is necessary to have comparative data from similar promotional efforts that did not include HHA/HRA.

Communication of Health Risk Information and Concepts

Health education, in the sense of communicating information about health and health-related behaviors, is an important ingredient in the health behavior change process. In regard to HHA/HRA, health education would include both general concepts, such as helping people appreciate that their behavior affects their long-term health, and specific factual knowledge concerning characteristics that increase risk, risk behaviors, and the relative importance of these behaviors. Other characteristics of HHA/HRA that may contribute to its usefulness for health education include organizing health concepts and information around a central theme; personalizing the information presented, thereby enhancing the perceived relevance to the client; encouraging active involvement of the learner, since the client supplies the information that is the basis for risk feedback; and structuring an opportunity for discussion of health-related behavioral recommendations by stimulating interest in the health impact of behaviors in general. Considerable variation in educational effectiveness exists across HHA/HRA instruments and settings.

Aspects of HHA/HRA that may limit its effectiveness as a health education aid include its complexity and quantitative emphasis; the inherent difficulty of probabilistic concepts; juxtaposition of nonhomogeneous behaviors; medical history and physiological measures that may be difficult to absorb; the discomfort that many clients experience in discussing one or more of the prognostic characteristics, which may diminish their receptivity to the entire message; and the framework based on risk of dying, which may be less conducive to learning than a more positive framework.

Induction of Behavioral Change

Induction of meaningful, long-term behavioral change is a complex and challenging undertaking (Kasl, 1980). Many reviewers have remarked on the difficulty of such attempts and on the inadequacy of approaches that rely solely on provisions of health information (Breslow, 1977; Cohen & Cohen, 1978; Green, 1978). Several uncontrolled studies, however (Dunton & Rasmussen, 1977; Fultz, 1977; Ladou, Sherwood, & Hughes, 1975), have strengthened the belief in HHA/HRA's effectiveness. But methodological problems in studying behavioral change—including volunteer bias, secular change in the public at large, the absence of a comparison group, and measurement unreliability—severely limit the scientific validity of these studies. Of three randomized control studies that have been reported, one (Cioffi, 1979) found no impact on change in attitudes toward disease susceptibility. A second study (Hancock, Lees, Binhammer, & McDonald, Note 2) found no impact on health-related behaviors. The third, and most elaborate study (Lauzon, 1977) found numerous behavior changes in HHA/HRA groups as compared to the control group, but the study was carried out in such a way that its findings can be viewed only as suggestive. Several programs are currently completing controlled experimental studies designed to determine, among other things, the efficacy of HHA/HRA as a behavior change technique. These current programs include Well Aware About Health, Tucson, Arizona; Michigan Blue Cross/Blue Shield; Rhode Island Group Health Association; Johnson & Johnson; Control Data Corporation; and the U.S. Air Force Heart Program. In addition to the question of HHA/HRA's efficacy in reducing behavioral change among participants in a health risk reduction program, Winkelstein (1979) has raised the broader question of the effectiveness of such a strategy for personal risk factor modification in an entire population. For an intervention to be appropriate for reducing risk in a clinical context, the intervention must have been shown to produce a clinically important reduction in risk without unreasonable disadvantages. Intervention in a population, however, requires not only demonstrated clinical efficacy but also logistic feasibility. Referring to a more detailed exposition of these ideas, Marmot and Winkelstein (1975) observed that, under the very optimistic assumption of complete effectiveness of intervention and full participation in a program, a 45% reduction in coronary heart disease incidents in the U.S. male population aged 35 to 64 would require screening of 28 million men and intervention for the 10.6 million estimated to have two or more of the following risk factors: smoking, elevated serum cholesterol, and hypertension. The percentage reduction in incidence rapidly declines with more realistic assumptions for participation and risk reduction. Given the very large number of people who must be screened and treated, it is questionable whether an approach of this sort is a perfect strategy for risk reduction in an entire population.

Structuring Interaction between Client and Counselor

Structured interaction has been perceived as a considerable benefit of HHA/HRA and may explain some of the technique's rapid dissemination among health risk reduction programs. HHA/HRA provides, in one package, a rationale, a framework in which to present health information, a task in which to involve the client, and personalized feedback that serves both as a gift from the counselor and as a printed summary of the information to improve client recall. It brings nonmodifiable risk characteristics to the health practitioner's awareness and displays risk behaviors as a cluster, so that the practitioner and client can set priorities and work on common underlying factors. Lauzon (1977) has suggested that HHA/HRA facilitates the discussion of potentially emotional or embarrassing issues within the context of the general health behavior assessment. Milsum (1980) has suggested that

HHA/HRA's primary importance is in creating a "teachable moment," when a health professional as counselor and a patient as client come together to discuss comprehensibly the client's health condition and the risk to which he or she is exposed, with a view to developing a contract for lifestyle change.

Training Physicians for Reorienting Medical Practices Toward Prevention

Medical education was one of the original uses of HHA/HRA. As a summary of health-related behaviors and characteristics, HHA/HRA provides an interesting illustrative topic for teaching preventive medicine. HHA/HRA gives the clinician a logical technique for including health-related behaviors in a periodic "review of system" and a client record for assessment and follow-up. Clinicians who are oriented toward preventive medicine may find the technique useful for instruction or interaction with the client, since the inclusion of meaningful data on morbidity and the avoidance of the illusion of precision make the technique suitable for preventive medicine. Fenger (1978) reported on the use of HHA/HRA in the training of first-year medical students. Responses on an evaluation questionnaire near the end of the course indicated that 43% of the students rated the procedure a worthwhile learning experience that gave them a better perception of the risks or benefits of particular health behaviors.

Other suggested potential uses for the HHA/HRA include screening asymptomatic patients for medical problems, identifying high-risk individuals for targeting of surveillance to detect early signs and symptoms, developing a data base for epidemiologic research and health planning, and providing an index of health risk and health-related behaviors.

APPLICABILITY OF HHA/HRA TO POPULATION SUBGROUPS

Anecdotal evidence suggests several problems in the use of HHA/HRA for minority and/or disadvantaged clients. Most of the problems are by no means restricted to HHA/HRA but are encountered by most behavioral risk reduction strategies. First, such clients have a low tendency to volunteer for health promotion efforts in general (Berkanovic, 1976). A second problem is that most questionnaires and feedback forms present substantial barriers in understandability and cultural congruity. Efforts are under way by many groups to simplify the questionnaires and feedback forms. Some of these considerations relate to cultural considerations, and others reflect socioeconomic realities (Milio, 1976). For poor people, the urgency of immediate needs for physical and economic security relegates lifestyle behaviors and health habits to lower priority, and limitations in personal and societal resources constrain behavioral change opportunities.

There is also a concern that occupational health programs emphasizing health behaviors for blue-collar workers have the potential for deflecting the pressure for control of workplace hazards (Bell, Note 3). Since programs that deal with hypertension, smoking, and other personal health characteristics may be much less expensive than efforts to reduce exposure to dust, chemicals, and dangerous equipment, the danger that occupational health will become concerned largely with personal behaviors of workers rather than with elimination of hazards in the workplace environment must be taken into consideration in introducing HHA/HRA programs for blue-collar workers.

Epidemiologic data for blacks and other minority populations are sparse. In appraising black clients, HHA/HRA uses risk factor values that were derived for whites. Although it is generally believed that the same characteristics that increase coronary heart disease (CHD) risk in whites also increase coronary heart disease risk in blacks, there is much less assurance about quantitative equivalence, so that HHA/HRA is more susceptible to inaccuracies. Moreover, since the prevalence of risk characteristics most certainly varies between racial groups, even if the characteristics have the same quantitative impact on CHD risk, HHA/HRA risk factor values need to be different. The inadequacy of epidemiologic data is even more severe for small minority groups than it is for blacks. Concerns have also been expressed about the usefulness of the HHA/HRA approach for persons outside the 30 to 55 age range. Lauzon (1977) asserts that HHA/HRA is not particularly useful for subjects younger than 30 and that subjects older than 55 are difficult to recruit. The risk-based approach, especially when based on mortality, is at a disadvantage with young adults, whose risk of death is relatively low anyway. In addition, longevity and risk of death are generally not considered seriously by teenagers, so that an approach based on enhancing life expectancy and reducing risk would not be expected to have much impact on that group. Some programs working with younger individuals have rewritten their HHA/HRA instruments to yield a health score rather than a risk age, and that appears to be a more fruitful approach with the younger age groups.

For the elderly, risk is so high and life expectancy so low that having these factors explicitly stated can be discouraging and depressing. A death- and fear-oriented approach would appear to be particularly inappropriate in an age group in which there is already considerable fear about dying and in which acceptance of the inevitability of death may be as important as postponing its occurrence. Health risk change efforts among the elderly could have an entirely different thrust—for example, maintenance of fitness, flexibility, and independence. If HHA/HRA continues to be used with clients over age 55, it will be important to determine whether ancedotal evidence for such adverse reactions can be substantiated through further research.

POSSIBLE ADVERSE EFFECTS OF HHA/HRA

The risk of HHA/HRA to clients has received little systematic attention. One study (Lauzon, 1977) found no difference in state or trait anxiety scores between groups that received HHA/HRA feedback and a group that did not. Anecdotal reports of depressive response to life expectancy predictions among older clients have been reported, however. Many other possible disadvantages—such as anxiety, depression, hypochondriasis, unnecessary medical expenses, and confusion or even harm from the information—could result from health promotion programs, including those using HHA/HRA. Overemphasis on personal health habits and the responsibility of the individual may foster a compulsive and distorted understanding of health and disease, leading to guilt, intolerance, and mistakes. Investigation of possible disadvantages of programs aimed at overall lifestyle change is an important issue to be considered in planning further research.

MAJOR AREAS INVOLVING HHA/HRA THAT NEED FURTHER RESEARCH

Further research is needed in the following areas:

1. The determination of health-related behaviors and the factors that sustain them.
2. Strategies for motivating and supporting health-related behavior change, with special attention to those with a positive orientation.
3. The attitudes and beliefs of minority groups toward health risk reduction and the barriers to their participation.
4. The role and impact of the medical practitioner in health risk reduction.
5. Possible harmful effects of behavioral interventions, particularly those using personalized risk information.
6. The source of errors in data collection and their impact on the message given to clients of HHA/HRA programs.
7. The perceptions and knowledge of HHA/HRA clients regarding the information collected from them and returned to them.

8. The efficacy of HHA/HRA, as compared to other approaches, in stimulating participation in risk reduction activities and producing health-related behavior change.

CONCLUSION

Health promotion and disease prevention requires innovative programming and cautious interpretation of results. HHA/HRA is an interesting approach—an appealing technique that has potential as a tool in these efforts. Caution is indicated in the use of HHA/HRA, however, because of its potential for promulgating lifestyles that might be inadequately supported by existing scientific evidence or inconsistent with the values and traditions of specific population groups. There are also concerns that such programs may constitute "blaming the victim" or may pay insufficient attention to the influence of environmental and social factors on health and health-related behaviors. HHA/HRA appears to be a useful adjunct to health education and health counseling, but additional research in a number of different areas is urgently needed to adequately evaluate the effects of this new technique.

APPENDIX: A DIRECTORY OF HEALTH RISK APPRAISAL INSTRUMENTS

This sample listing of health risk appraisal instruments was prepared by the National Health Information Clearinghouse (P.O. Box 1133, Washington, D.C. 20013). The purpose of this list is to identify the range of assessments available. No attempt has been made to evaluate the appraisals, and their appearance on this list does not signify endorsement by the National Health Information Clearinghouse or the U.S. Department of Health and Human Services.

Prices are not quoted, because they are always subject to change. A general rule of thumb, however, is that self-scoring instruments range in price from free to $1.00; prices decrease for bulk orders. Computer-scored instruments range in price from $5.00 to $60.00; prices decrease for bulk orders. Addresses and phone numbers are listed for convenience in obtaining additional information and price lists.

Confidential Health Profile for Adults/Teenagers

Description: The Confidential Health Profile comes in a version for adults and one specifically designed for teenagers (ages 12 to 18). Both versions contain 92 questions for men and women, and both include a section for women only. Section 1 asks the client to rank, on a scale of 1 to 10, his or her personal values (e.g., freedom, happiness). Section 2 asks questions on health attitudes, and Section 3 elicits the information used to derive a health risk score (drinking and smoking habits, family history, mental well-being, and others). The computer printouts for both versions are also similar, varying in length from 6 to 10 pages. Results appearing on the printout are designed to be self-explanatory and are given in a narrative format addressed directly to the reader. The profiles are intended to be used in a group setting, and a group profile is returned with the results for individual clients. A reader's guide is provided for assistance in administering the tests and interpreting the results.

Source: University of Florida
3041 McCarty Hall
Gainesville, FL 32611
(904)392-2202

General Well-Being Questionnaire

Description: The General Well-Being Questionnaire is a second-generation appraisal instrument that asks clients to respond to 137 statements, such as "People who never get sick are just plain lucky." Hand scoring of the questionnaires is possible, and there is a master scoring key. Programs are also available for computer scoring, which provides the following numerical scores (on a scale of 1 to 5) for a group and for each individual: an overall index of well-being; specific scores for physical, emotional, mental, ideological, behavioral, environmental, and experimental areas of well-being; and 30 comprehensive factors that underlie well-being. A shorter version of the questionnaire, which is self-scoring, is also available.

Source: St. Louis University Medical Center
            Department of Health Promotion
            1325 South Grand Boulevard
            St. Louis, MO 63104
            (314)771-7601, Ext. 3633

Go to Health

Description: The health risk appraisal contained in this pamphlet, which is entitled "Your Lifestyle Profile," was adapted from a test produced by the Canadian government. It asks 35 questions on personal health; nutrition; exercise; drug, tobacco, and alcohol use; safety; and general habits. Based on the answers, a rating is made of the client's lifestyle, as excellent, good, risky, or hazardous. Information is also provided on the topics covered by the test, including ways to cope with stress, to change nutritional habits, to embark on an exercise program, and to deal with drinking or smoking problems. The pamphlet concludes with the "Go to Health Lifestyle Contract," which asks the client to record several behavioral changes (e.g., trying to lose weight) that he or she is willing to undertake.

Source: Public Relations Department
            Blue Cross/Blue Shield of Michigan
            600 East Lafayette Boulevard
            Detroit, MI 48226

Health Action Plan

Description: The Health Action Plan provides the client with information to help prevent cancer, heart disease, and stroke, and includes a do-it-yourself personal health record. Nine major health topics are covered—skin and lymph nodes, head and neck, respiratory system, cardiovascular system, urinary tract, gastrointestinal tract, male reproductive system, female reproductive systems, and breast cancer. For each topic, there are four categories of questions, covering present symptoms, family history, personal medical history, and preventive measures that can be taken. The client does not receive a numerical score after filling out the Plan. Instead, he or she should record all questions answered "yes" on the personal health record. Yes answers signal areas for concern. In addition to the questions, there is information on risk factors and possible preventive behaviors for each of the topics.

Source: Preventive Medicine Institute—Strang Clinic
            55 East 34th Street
            New York, NY 10016
            (212)683-1000

Health Education Action Plan

Description: The Health Education Action Plan was adapted from several existing health risk appraisals. It asks 74 questions that can be answered "yes," or "no," or "sometimes" in the following areas: personal health, exercise, diet, safety, dental health, and tobacco, drug, and alcohol use. The Plan also includes a chart that asks clients to repeat the test in 6 months and at intervals thereafter in order to note improvements in the score.

Source: Erie County Health Education Council
           P.O. Box 872
           Erie, PA 16512
           (814)459-4000

Health 80's Questionnaire

Description: The Health 80's Questionnaire is designed for use in group settings: colleges and universities, hospitals, and industry. A fourth point of emphasis is the physician in private practice or other helping professional. The Questionnaire is available in eight-, four-, three-, and two-page versions and asks questions on illnesses and medical problems, feelings, nutritional and exercise habits, family medical history, smoking, self-care, and other topics (depending on the length of the questionnaire). A Quality of Life Assessment is included with the longer versions. In addition, a newly created Life Style Index, available in several questionnaire lengths, uses the information on nutrition and exercise to compare the client's caloric intake to caloric expenditure. The questionnaires are the same for all four categories mentioned but are packaged in different catalogs specifically geared to the particular category of users.

Source: Medical Datamation
           Southwest and Harrison
           Bellevue, OH 44811
           (419)483-6060

Health Graph

Description: The Health Graph is used by the University of Rhode Island to help students evaluate the impact of their lifestyles on their health and to teach them preventive behaviors. It includes 50 questions covering many of the standard topics of appraisals, but it also asks questions on environmental awareness and health fads. Health tips follow each section. Upon completion of the Graph, the client does not receive a numerical score, but rather learns the areas where his or her greatest strengths and weaknesses lie.

Source: University of Rhode Island Health Services
           Health Education Department
           4th Floor, Roosevelt
           Kingston, RI 02881
           (401)792-2392

Health Hazard Appraisal: Automated Personal Risk Registry

Description: The Health Hazard Appraisal was developed in the early sixties by two physicians who pioneered in the field of prospective medicine. It includes 55 questions, with a special section for women only and a section on stress. Questions cover family medical history; alcohol, drug, and tobacco use; exercise; blood pressure and cholesterol levels; transportation habits; and other physical symptoms. A personalized risk analysis is prepared by the computer, giving the client's appraisal age, methods to reduce the appraisal age, and evaluation of the level of stress, and a bar graph showing risks to health in descending order of priority and actions needed to reduce appraisal age to achievable age.

Source: Methodist Hospital of Indiana
            Prospective Medicine Department
            1604 North Capitol
            Indianapolis, In 46202
            (317)924-8494

Health Hazard Appraisal: Clues for a Healthier Lifestyle

Description: This pamphlet gives a great deal of information on the concept and history of the health risk appraisal. It includes a short appraisal adapted from "Your Lifestyle Profile," which is widely used in Canada. Thirty-five questions are posed on exercise; nutrition; alcohol, tobacco, and drug use; road and water safety; personal health; and general habits. Information is also included on the major causes of death for men and women of various ages and on limitations of the health risk appraisal, and a short bibliography is also included.

Source: Public Affairs Pamphlets
            381 Park Avenue South
            New York, NY 10016

Health Hazard Questionnaire

Description: The Questionnaire was designed by Well Aware About Health as part of an overall program of health promotion and education. It contains 99 questions covering general health, feelings, use of health services, family medical history, current medical conditions, living habits, eating habits, women's health concerns, and personal information. The Questionnaire also asks for specific laboratory tests (such as blood chemistry and urinalysis). Based on answers to the written portion and the laboratory tests, the computer printout provides the following kinds of information: present, risk, and achievable ages; a ranked listing of the most likely causes of death within the next 10 years; laboratory test results; physical measurements; new evidence about risks applicable to the client; and a summary.

Source: Well Aware About Health
            University of Arizona
            P.O. Box 43338
            Tucson, AZ 85733
            (602)626-3055

Health Risk Appraisal

Description: The Health Risk Appraisal is similar to the Canadian government's appraisal and is being developed for internal use, for research projects, and for use by state and local health departments. It consists of 37 questions on personal and family health history, alcohol and cigarette use, seat belt use, exercise, and other topics. It also calls for specific test results, such as blood pressure and serum cholesterol. Computer analysis of these data yields a comparison of the client's chronological age to his or her appraised age (estimated probability of dying within the next 10 years) and achievable age. The 12 leading causes of death for individuals of the same age, sex, and race as the client are presented on the same comparative basis. Also included is information on the client's weight (comparison to desirable weight) and on factors requiring modification to attain achievable age. Information on how to interpret the results is provided to the client.

Source: Charles A. Althafer
            Director, Special Projects
            Center for Health Promotion

Centers for Disease Control
Atlanta, GA 30333
(404)329-3415

Health Risk Appraisal Questionnaire

Description: The Health Risk Appraisal Questionnaire asks 41 questions, including 9 for women only. Information on height, weight, blood pressure, and cholesterol is also required. Based on the client's answers and on the findings of the limited physical examination, the computer printout provides a list of the 12 leading causes of death in the next 10 years, an assessment of the client's risk of dying based on precursor characteristics, and recommendations for a personal health management program of risk reduction. If the client is under 30, the computer automatically generates a second printout, which reflects a projected risk profile at age 45. Group profiles are provided at no extra charge.

Source: St. Louis County Health Department
504 East Second Street
Duluth, MN 55805
(218)727-8661

Health Risk Assessment

Description: The Health Risk Assessment asks 43 questions on such topics as medication currently taken, smoking and drinking habits, and family medical history. An additional 15 questions for women only concern family history of breast cancer, vaginal bleeding, pap smear results, and other topics. Computer analysis based on answers to these questions compares the individual to others with similar demographic attributes and offers recommendations to decrease risks. Suggestions include altering lifestyle practices and taking advantage of medical screening procedures. Risk assessment is given in terms of a 10-year projection.

Source: Department of Epidemiology and International Health
University of California at San Francisco
Room 1699 HSW
San Francisco, CA 94143

Health Risk Assessment Questionnaire

Description: The Health Risk Assessment Questionnaire asks 58 questions, 8 of which are for women only. Topics covered include physical measurements (four required), family history, personal health habits, and history of illnesses. Computer analysis yields a two-page printout, which gives the most likely causes of death over the next 10 years for persons of the same age, sex, and race as the client, as well as information on risk factors that the client can and cannot control. In addition, a detailed statistical analysis is available for an additional fee, giving the average, the client's, and the minimum values for all risk factors covered by the Questionnaire. The Center can also supply (again, for an additional fee) consultation on program planning and evaluation, training of staff in the interpretation and counseling of clients, and periodic statistical analysis of the group.

Source: Wisconsin Center for Health Risk Research
University of Wisconsin Center for Health Sciences
600 Highland Avenue
Madison, WI 53792
(608)263-2602

Healthstyle

Description: Healthstyle, produced by the U.S. Department of Health and Human Services, Public Health Service, comes in the form of a brochure. It consists of 24 questions in the following areas: cigarette smoking, alcohol and drugs, eating habits, exercise and fitness, stress control, and safety. Each question is posed as a statement that can be answered "Almost always," "Sometimes," or "Almost never." Scores are calculated separately for each section, so that the client is made aware of the areas of his or her lifestyle that need the most improvement. Following the test are suggestions on how risks can be reduced in each area. Finally, a form is provided for obtaining additional information.

Source: National Health Information Clearinghouse
P.O. Box 1133
Washington, D.C. 20013

Healthwise

Description: Healthwise is a comprehensive health risk profile, with 192 questions covering lifestyle factors, fitness, drinking behavior, stress, eating habits, blood test results, and other topics. From these data, a Health Age and Longevity Appraisal is determined, which provides a comprehensive profile of major risk factors, including personal test results and recommended values. The 10 to 12 leading causes of death (age- and sex-specific) are listed, along with individualized recommendations for risk reduction, based on test results and health history. Also included is a comprehensive Risk Reduction Handbook, which explains how to deal with specific health problems.

A number of other appraisal instruments are also available from this source. Some are short and were designed for use at such events as a health fair; results can be generated immediately. Instruments in this category include, among others, a nutrition profile, a stress profile, and a cancer profile. Also available are longer profiles covering nutrition, coronary risk, and physical fitness, which require laboratory measurements.

Source: Computerized Health Appraisals
Health Services Department
Upper Columbia Conference
P.O. Box 19039
Spokane, WA 99219

Life Score for Your Health

Description: Life Score for Your Health incorporates questions on various risk factors, including exercise, weight, diet, smoking, alcohol use, seat belt use, stress, personal history, family history, and medical care. A numerical score—positive or negative—is awarded for each question. The larger the positive score, the more that factor contributes to a healthy life, and the reverse. If you smoke 50 or more cigarettes a day, for example, you lose 28 points for this one activity alone. The Holmes Scale is used to measure stress. After the test is completed, the client totals his or her points and uses a chart to evaluate level of health and life expectancy.

Source: The Center for Consumer Health Education
380 West Maple Avenue
Vienna, VA 22180
(703)281-5893

Lifestyle Assessment Questionnaire

Description: The Lifestyle Assessment Questionnaire is an extensive appraisal instrument consisting of 286 questions divided into four major sections: wellness inventory, opportunities for learning, risk of death, and medical/behavioral/emotional alert. The computer analysis received by the client indicates the percentage of points scored in each topic area of the wellness inventory (e.g., exercise, nutrition) as well as the average score for all persons who have taken the test. In addition, the printout lists resources available for gaining information on up to six topics requested in the second section. The Risk of Death Section yields a printout listing probable number of years remaining, leading causes of death, and behaviors the client can change to improve his or her chances of survival. The final section provides information that can be used to generate a problem list for the client's home health record.

Source: Institute for Lifestyle Improvement
University of Wisconsin—Stevens Point Foundation
2100 Main Street
Stevens Point, WI 54481
(715)346-3811

The Longevity Game

Description: The Longevity Game, as its name implies, is presented in the form of a game board, with questions and scores based on medical underwriting policies of Northwestern Mutual Life. To start the game, a token is placed at age 74. The token is moved forward (indicating increased longevity) or backward, depending on the client's answers to questions on exercise, family history, smoking, stress, age, and other topics. The final score gives the client an idea of how long he or she can expect to live. Information and tips are also provided for each of the question areas. The Game is also available as a set of posters and score cards for use with larger groups; the information and questions are identical to those in the basic game.

Source: Northwestern Mutual Life
Advertising and Corporate Information
720 East Wisconsin Avenue
Milwaukee, WI 53202
(414)271-1444

Nutrition, Health and Activity Profile

Description: The Nutrition, Health and Activity Profile was designed to uncover shortcomings in nutritional and health habits that could adversely affect health and lead to the risk of cancer and heart disease. It consists of a four-page questionnaire divided into sections on important nutritional factors, food consumption, vitamin and mineral supplements, health factors, and physical activities. The most extensive part of the Profile asks clients to list their daily, weekly, and monthly consumption of 151 different foods and beverages. Based on the answers, a 9- to 13-page computer printout is returned, which gives intake of fats, carbohydrates, proteins, and so on; compares them to established requirements; and discusses their implications. The printout also discusses other crucial health factors, the importance of exercise (including an analysis of the client's current program), and a suggested weight loss program (if appropriate).

Source: Pacific Research Systems
P.O. Box 64218
Los Angeles, CA 90064
(213)478-1718

Personal Health Appraisal Questionnaire

Description: The Personal Health Appraisal Questionnaire (second-generation, updated version) contains 280 questions in the following areas: personal information, attitudes toward health, emotional well-being, life events, personal character traits, past and present health, and a section for women only. The Health Attitudes Section is quite extensive, asking the client to respond to 56 statements or questions, such as "In order to keep illness from happening, there is a lot I can do." Computer analysis of the questionnaire yields a 45-page printout, giving the client's health age, attainable health age, and life expectancy. The right-hand pages provide a personal analysis, describing the client's risk factors and actions that can be taken to reduce risk; the corresponding left-hand pages give general information on the topic. The end of the report gives a summary of mental well-being, risks, accomplishments, and opportunities to reduce risk. Also listed are action options and resources for dealing with such risk areas as stress and high blood pressure.

Source: The Institute for Personal Health
2100 M Street NW, Suite 316
Washington, D.C. 20063
(202)872-5379

Personal Health Profile

Description: The Personal Health Profile consists of 247 questions in the following areas: personal information, attitudes toward health, behavior and health, recent life events, general well-being, coping with stress, past and present health, and women's health. The section on health attitudes was included because the developers of the Profile felt that an individual's attitudes and beliefs about health influenced the likelihood that he or she would take action to protect his or her health. Computer analysis of the Profile yields a 48-page report. The right-hand pages provide a personalized health analysis, while the corresponding left-hand pages contain background information on a particular health area—including a description of the health factor, its importance to health, and what can be done to reduce risk. Some of the specific areas covered include stress, sociability, hypertension, exercise, cholesterol, Type A personality, risk of cancer, and health age.

Source: General Health
1046 Potomac Street NW
Washington, D.C. 20007
(202)965-4881 or
(800)424-2275 (toll-free)   •

Personal Medical History, Female/Male

Description: The Personal Medical History comes in two versions, one for males and one for females. It is designed primarily for use by physicians as a patient medical history and includes questions on personal and family medical history as well as a detailed review of all bodily systems (e.g., pulmonary, cardiovascular). It also contains questions on topics relevant to health risk assessment—for example, emotional factors, exercise, consumption of alcohol, leisure activities, and seat belt use. These are not, however, in a separate section. The computer printout gives two types of information: first, a quick "system review," highlighting relevant information provided by the client (e.g., family history of renal disease) and, second, a health risk profile, giving risk age, achievable age, and other information. (For more information, see the entry on "Your Health Risk Profile," a questionnaire prepared by the same company.)

Source: Life Extension Institute
2970 Fifth Avenue
San Diego, CA 92103
(714)291-9490

Personal Stress Assessment Test

Description: The Personal Stress Assessment Test provides an evaluation of physical, chemical, emotional, and social factors related to health. Points are accrued for various behaviors, such as sugar consumption, caffeine consumption, score on the Holmes-Rahe Scale (Social Readjustment Rating Scale), weight, and marital status. The larger the point value for a particular item, the greater the risk to health. When administered at the Center, this test is used in conjunction with the Cornell Medical Index.

Source: The Pain and Health Rehabilitation Center
Route 2—Welsh Coulee
La Crosse, WI 54601
(608)786-0611

SHAPE Life-Style Questionnaire

Description: The Life-Style Questionnaire covers five factors that affect quality of health: weight, fat content of food consumed, exercise, resting pulse rate, and smoking. The Questionnaire asks clients to record what they ate the day before the test, how much they weigh, how much they smoke, how much and what kind of exercise they get, and what their resting pulse rate is. Based on these answers, a Health Quality Profile is calculated. A maximum of 100 points is awarded, with a 20-point maximum for each of the five health quality factors. A total score of 86 to 100 is rated excellent. The specified target population is general, but the program is primarily targeted to employee groups and is sold through employers.

Source: SHAPE
10700 Meridian Avenue North
Seattle, WA 98133
(206)545-6060

Wellness Inventory

Description: The Wellness Inventory is used to help the client assess his or her position on an "illness-wellness continuum." At one end of the continuum is premature death; at the other is high-level wellness. A total of 100 questions are asked in the following areas (10 questions in each area): productivity, personal care, nutrition, environmental awareness, physical activity, expression of emotions, community involvement, creativity, automobile safety, and parenting. A number of footnotes are also given to provide further information on some of the items in the questions. The client computes his or her score for each section and adds up the totals. Average scores for the test are given, but no other interpretation of results is provided.

Source: Wellness Associates
42 Miller Avenue
Mill Valley, CA 94941
(415)383-3806

Your Health Profile

Description: Your Health Profile evaluates the client's level of health on the basis of questions on exercise; nutrition; alcohol, drug, and tobacco use; personal health; and transportation habits. The Profile has been adapted for use with specific populations, including teenagers and senior adults (in a large-type version). It can also be used with the general adult population.

Source: Health Education Center
200 Ross Street
Pittsburgh, PA 15219
(412)392-3160

Your Health Risk Profile

Description: Your Health Risk Profile, which can be used by individuals alone or in a group setting, contains 70 questions, 11 of which are for women only. It also asks the client to supply as much information as possible on medical characteristics, including blood pressure and cholesterol level. Questions cover such topics as education, medication taken, smoking and drinking habits, feelings, diagnostic procedures undergone, and others. The computer printout reveals current and achievable 10-year risk of death, factors that may offer the greatest reduction in risk, and an explanation of the client's greatest risks, in descending order of importance. For each identified risk, average, current, and achievable risks are provided, as well as the importance of various risk-contributing and risk-reducing factors. Information on the interpretation of the printout and on the various risk factors is also provided. In addition, a Group Risk Profile is available for groups with more than 100 participants.

Source: Life Extension Institute
2970 Fifth Avenue
San Diego, CA 92103
(714)291-9490

Your Lifestyle Profile

Description: Your Lifestyle Profile, which was developed by the Canadian government, provides 35 questions on exercise; nutrition; alcohol, drug, and tobacco use; personal health; road and water safety; and general habits. It is contained in a workbook that provides additional short tests and information on topics covered in the Profile. The workbook includes, for example, tips on losing weight and learning to relax, information on dental health, a questionnaire on alcoholism, a section on the special hazards of being a man, and one on the hazards of being a woman. The workbook was designed for use in the Kansas Program to Lower Utilization of Services (P.L.U.S.), which is geared toward business and industry.

Source: Bureau of Health Education
Kansas Department of Health and Environment
Building 321
Forbes Field
Topeka, KS 66620
(913)862-9360, Ext. 496

REFERENCE NOTES

1.   Brown, K. S., & Nabert, W. *Evaluation of the existing method for calculating health hazard appraisal age.* Final report on the service contract between Non-Medical Use

of Drugs Directorate, Health Protection Branch, Health and Welfare Canada, and the University of Waterloo, Ontario, August 31, 1977.

2. Hancock, J. R., Lees, R. E. M., Binhammer, H. E., & McDonald, I. *Patient compliance with health hazard appraisal recommendations.* Kingston, Ontario: Queen's University, Department of Community Health and Epidemiology, June 1978. (First reported as *Health hazard appraisal as a vehicle for health education and mortality risk reduction.* Paper presented at the Annual Conference of the Canadian Public Health Association, Vancouver, June 29, 1977.)

3. Bell, C. *Health promotion and disease prevention for minorities in the workplace.* Paper presented at the Fifth Annual Minority Health Conference, School of Public Health, University of North Carolina, Chapel Hill, February 20, 1981.

REFERENCES

Beery, W., Schoenbach, V. J., Wagner, E. H., Graham, R. M., Karon, J. M., & Pezzullo, S. *Description, analysis and assessment of health hazards/health risk appraisal programs.* Chapel Hill: University of North Carolina at Chapel Hill, Health Services Research Center, March 1981. (NTIS No. PB-81-239063).

Berkanovic, E. Behavioral science and prevention. *Preventive Medicine,* 1976, **5,** 92–105.

Breslow, L. A policy assessment of preventive health practice. *Preventive Medicine,* 1977, **6,** 242–251.

Cioffi, J. P. The effect of health status feedback on health beliefs: An inquiry into the prebehavioral outcomes of health hazard appraisal. In *Proceedings of the 15th Annual Meeting on Prospective Medicine and Health Hazard Appraisal.* Bethesda: Health and Education Resources, 1979.

Cohen, C. I., & Cohen, E. J. Health education: Panacea, pernicious or pointless? *New England Journal of Medicine,* 1978, **13,** 718–720.

Davies, D. F. Report from the standards committee. In *Proceedings of the 14th Annual Meeting on Prospective Medicine and Health Hazard Appraisal.* Bethesda: Health and Education Resources, 1978.

Dunton, S., & Rasmussen, W. Comparative data on risk reduction, 1975–1977. In *Proceedings of the 13th Annual Meeting of the Society of Prospective Medicine.* Bethesda: Health and Education Resources, 1977.

Fenger, T. A. The role of prospective medicine in medical education. In *Proceedings of the 14th Annual Meeting on Prospective Medicine and Health Hazard Appraisal.* Bethesda: Health and Education Resources, 1978.

Fullarton, J. E. Health hazard appraisal: Its limitations and new directions for risk assessment. In *Proceedings of the 13th Annual Meeting of the Society of Prospective Medicine.* Bethesda: Health and Education Resources, 1977.

Fultz, F. G. Effects of an experimental personal health education course and HHA on selected college students in Illinois. In *Proceedings of the 13th Annual Meeting of the Society of Prospective Medicine.* Bethesda: Health and Education Resources, 1977.

Green, L. W. Determining the impact and effectiveness of health education as it relates to federal policy. *Health Education Monographs,* 1978, **6**(1), 28–66.

Hall, J. H., & Zwemer, J. D. *Prospective medicine.* Indianapolis: Methodist Hospital of Indiana, 1979.

Hsu, D. S. H., & Milsum, J. H. Implementation of HHA and its impediments. *Canadian Journal of Public Health,* 1975, **69,** 227–232.

Imrey, P. B., & Williams, B. T. Statistical hazards of health hazard appraisal. In *Proceedings of the 13th Annual Meeting of the Society of Prospective Medicine.* Bethesda: Health and Education Resources, 1977.

Johns, R. E. Health hazard appraisal—A useful tool in health education? In *Proceedings of the 12th Annual Meeting of the Society of Prospective Medicine.* Bethesda: Health and Education Resources, 1976.

Kasl, S. V. Cardiovascular risk reduction in a community setting: Some comments. *Journal of Consulting and Clinical Psychology,* 1980, **48,** 143–149.

Ladou, J., Sherwood, J. N., & Hughes, L. Health hazard appraisal in patient counseling. *Western Journal of Medicine*, 1975, **122**(2), 177–180.

Lalonde, M. *A new perspective on the health of Canadians: A working document.* Ottawa: Information Canada, 1975.

Lauzon, R. R. J. A randomized controlled trial on the ability of health hazard appraisal to stimulate appropriate risk-reduction behavior. Unpublished doctoral dissertation, University of Oregon, 1977.

Marmot, M., & Winkelstein, W., Jr. Epidemiologic observations on intervention trials for prevention of coronary heart disease. *American Journal of Epidemiology*, 1975, **101**, 177–181.

Milio, N. A framework for prevention: Changing health-damaging to health-generating life patterns. *American Journal of Public Health*, 1976, **66**, 435–439.

Milsum, J. H. Lifestyle changes for the whole person: Stimulation through health hazard appraisal. P. O. Davidson & S. M. Davidson (Eds.). *Behavioral Medicine*, New York: Brunner/Mazel, 1980, 116–150.

Robbins, L. C., & Hall, J. H. *How to practice prospective medicine.* Indianapolis: Methodist Hospital of Indiana, 1970.

Winkelstein, W. An epidemiological look at the methodology of the health hazard appraisal. In *Proceedings of the 15th Annual Meeting on Prospective Medicine and Health Hazard Appraisal.* Bethesda: Health and Education Resources, 1979.

SECTION 3
STRATEGIES FOR HEALTH ENHANCEMENT

CHAPTER 19
OVERVIEW

CARL E. THORESEN

Stanford University

The level of abstraction becomes a key issue in considering ways of promoting or enhancing health. One can think of health enhancement in terms of type of *problem,* such as smoking or exercise, or type of *setting,* such as home, work, or community, or *level* of focus, from intraindividual or interpersonal to family, subculture, or international mass culture. *Models* for health enhancement also exist, such as sociological, educational, and psychological learning models. The organization of this Handbook illustrates the different ways that health enhancement can be considered.

In introducing several chapters on general strategies for enhancing health, I focus primarily on some of the presuppositions or premises underlying theory, research, and clinical practice in health promotion and disease prevention. I do so because there are many problems of premise in the general field of health—that is, presuppositions about what is assumed to be true or valid, what is taken for granted, that serve as the starting points for various recommendations and suggestions for health enhancement. One might think of these presuppositions as logical limits underlying the various conceptual, methodological, and therapeutic strategies. I believe it is crucial to be as clear and as careful as possible about what one presumes to be true in presenting a rationale for a particular strategy for health enhancement. Too often, the logic for a strategy falls apart when its questionable premises are openly examined.

Health as a theoretical concept is discussed briefly, along with two related themes: the need to consider alternative or nontraditional approaches to health enhancement and the need to acknowledge the central role of personal responsibility or self-managed change in almost all approaches to health promotion. Following this discussion, some methodological presuppositions are mentioned, including the need to consider the limits of traditional scientific models based on dichotomous logic (subjective versus objective), unidirectional causality, and the overreliance on null-hypothesis statistical significance testing. The need for more ecologically valid designs is suggested, along with multimethod, multimodal strategies, particularly those using intensive time series protocols spanning longer time periods. Finally, an approach to change strategies for enhancing health is offered, based in part on a proposed synthesis of what appear to be the principal characteristics of most effective change strategies. An expanded cognitive social learning model is offered as an example of a guiding framework for conceptualizing intervention programs for health.

I am most appreciative to my colleague, Jean Eagleston, who commented thoughtfully on earlier drafts of this chapter, and to Ruth Bergman who retyped draft after draft.

CONCEPTUAL PREMISES

Perhaps the many conceptual problems surrounding the concept of health are best highlighted by asking the question, "Are you healthy?" On what basis does one answer such a question, especially if the question is recognized as deserving something more than a yes or no response? Even if the answer is yes, one is still faced with determining what criteria are used in reaching an answer. The most common way of thinking about health, strongly influenced by the pathologically focused medical model, is to view health as the absence of the signs or symptoms of physical disease (setting aside the related concepts of illness and sickness). However, relying on the absence of observable physical disease symptoms as a way of conceptualizing health has been recognized as reductionistic and, at times, extremely misleading (cf. Antonovsky, 1979; Dubos, 1968; Engel, 1977; Knowles, 1977). Furthermore, from a conceptual if not scientific viewpoint, defining a phenomenon by the absence of another phenomenon is confusing at best, since the phenomenon itself is not susceptible to direct assessment and evaluation. Most would find fault, for example, with defining wisdom as the absence of stupidity or wealth as the absence of poverty. Health might exist in the presence of current physical symptomatology; health may also involve factors that transcend pathology.

The inclusive definition offered by the World Health Organization, defining health as a state of complete physical, mental, and social well-being, not merely as the absence of disease and infirmity, sought to remedy the exclusive definition of health strictly in terms of physical symptoms. This conceptual definition has been criticized, however, as being far too inclusive, equating health with all human experience. Antonovsky (1979) adopted an intermediate position of viewing health as a dynamic, continuous phenomenon (rather than a static, dichotomous state) that is very much a function of the particular context or setting in which the person lives; thus, social and cultural factors are introduced. Health is seen as an ongoing process resulting from the interaction of physiological processes, including constitutional and genetic characteristics in concert with mental, emotional, and behavioral habits or patterns of living. In effect, the question "Are you healthy?" becomes "Are you healthy to do what for how long in which context?"

Ahmed, Koeker, and Coelho (1979) offer a viewpoint that emphasizes the social and cultural context of the person in conceptualizing health:

> Our definition of wellness and illness takes into account the specific roles the individual is expected to play in this cultural milieu, as well as the judgments that the individual himself and significant others in his social network, make about the adequacy of his performance. In particular, effective functioning in two social roles, the familial and the occupational, tends to be recorded as crucial to the well-being of the individual and his community. Health, then, must be viewed not merely as a state desirable in itself but it is a means towards the fulfillment of strategic role obligations, and illness as an obstacle to such fulfillment. (p. 13) [emphasis added]

This definition highlights health as the ways a person acts or a means to accomplish certain ends or tasks that are perceived by that person to be worthwhile and desirable, if not essential.

This perspective is closely aligned with the ancient Hippocratic conception of medicine, with its emphasis on maintaining balance and harmony in lifestyle at home and at work. We are confronted, then, with a conception of health as something that goes well beyond hospitals, physicians, surgery, and drugs. Indeed, from this perspective, health becomes a very complex notion, involving a number of interacting systems that affect a person's capacity to adapt to the demands (often self-generated) that are perceived as important in living. From this perspective, diseases are not so much physiological abnormalities to be cured as they are chronic responses to the circumstances of living. Furthermore, symptoms are not to be suppressed with drugs or even equated with disease; instead, they are to be analyzed for their personal meaning and alleviated by personal action. Symptoms say something, they offer an opportunity to learn and to change.

Antonovsky (1979 and Chapter 7 of this Handbook), mindful of the severe limitations of the pathogenic medical model in understanding health, offers a view of health based on a person's capability to handle demands by drawing upon a variety of sources (termed "generalized resistance resources"). From time to time, a "breakdown" is experienced; that is, maladaptive or inadequate actions occur that disrupt performance ("dis-ease"). This perspective has much in common with the general systems orientation advocated by Schwartz (Chapter 20 in this section), particularly in the possibility of homeostasis (self-regulation) at one level of functioning and yet disregulation at another level.

What is particularly interesting in Antonovsky's view of health is the central role of cognitive processes in understanding health, a position recognized by Kendall and Turk (Chapter 27 in this section). Antonovsky concludes that the primary factor mediating health may be the person's outlook about the future—that future events seem generally predictable and that future consequences will be as good as can reasonably be expected. He labels this philosophy a "sense of coherence." His concept of coherence is congruent with Kobasa's (Kobasa, Maddi, & Kahn, 1982) notion of "hardiness," with its themes of control, commitment, and challenge, as well as Bandura's (1982) formulation of personal self-efficacy theory—that is, the conviction that one can successfully perform certain actions needed to accomplish desired goals. More generally, the emphasis on cognitive processes in conceptualizing health—recognizing that cognitive processes are not restricted to conscious awareness and rationality (cf. Lazarus, 1982)—is also represented in the brain-behavior (Weiner, 1981; Wolf, 1981) and biopsychosocial (Engel, 1977) orientations toward health and disease.

Nontraditional Concepts

If one is going to enhance health, it becomes important to have a clear picture in mind of what constitutes health, if not well-being. So long as health is viewed exclusively as the absence of physical disease signs and symptoms, then the prevailing treatment models based on information giving from an authoritative source, along with medication and surgery and, sometimes, placebo effects (Shapiro & Shapiro, Chapter 25 in this section) may seem sufficient. If this perspective is deemed inadequate, however, then the dynamic and more holistic or systems perspectives would appear to deserve consideration—to be thoughtfully examined and carefully evaluated rather than peremptorily dismissed as unorthodox and therefore "unscientific." (Unquestionably, doing science with more dynamic models provides countless problems for traditional scientific methods, an issue to be mentioned shortly.) From various Eastern philosophical perspectives, for example, health is viewed as a web of circumstances—a circular system of actions and reactions—rather than as a specific linear condition in which causality can be pinpointed in a sequence of antecedents and consequences (cf. Bresler, 1980; Kaptchuk, 1982; Palos, 1971; Vithoulkas, 1972).

In many ways, Schwartz (1982) in discussing the different levels of interpretation of biofeedback, offers an alternative model closely akin to nontraditional perspectives. Citing the work of Pepper (1947), Schwartz suggests that the conceptual thinking in theory and research in medicine and health has been going through four developmental stages: from the *categorical* labeling and classification stage, through the *mechanistic* stage, where the focus is on trying to identify specific causal mechanisms, to more recent and complex stages that emphasize the *contextual* understanding (e.g., how main effects are inevitably moderated by complex interactions), to the *organistic* stage, where multidimensional causality and reciprocal influences are commonly recognized.

It seems necessary at this time to consider theoretical perspectives on health and wellness that may not fit comfortably with the background and training of many health professionals. The common practice of rejecting out-of-hand different ways of thinking about health without allowing experiences (empirical data) to be considered needs to be discontinued. A rich array of perspectives of health enhancement, including acupuncture, acupressure, bioenergetics, and transpersonal psychology, to name a few, deserve thoughtful scrutiny.

Personal Responsibility

Permeating the traditional as well as the alternative approaches to health enhancement is a premise that is seldom acknowledged—namely, that people have the means of bringing about meaningful changes in their ways of living that will persist over time. The self-care literature in health and medicine, for example, commonly assumes that if people are informed and encouraged about how to care more effectively for their own health, they will be able to do so (e.g., Levin, Katz, & Holst, 1979). Everly (Chapter 24 in this section), for example, points out that informing people about better methods of time management assumes that they are skilled in self-management—that is, in acting in more personally responsible ways. Typically, it is not recognized that behaving in personally responsible ways—that is, exercising effective self-management—requires a number of skills that are not necessarily inherent in everyone's repertoire (Mahoney & Thoresen, 1974). People need to be taught how to be more caring and more responsible for their own health and well-being, especially when the social environment commonly promotes irresponsible or nonhealthy behavior. Too often, strategies for health enhancement are limited conceptually and fail to acknowledge this need to teach people how to better manage their actions, their thoughts, their emotions, and their social and physical environments.

Reminiscent of the caricature of the physician imploring the patient to "slow down, get more rest, take better care of yourself . . . and don't forget the medication three times a day," it is not enough to inform or admonish people about what they should do. It is also not enough to focus on one or two self-management techniques. A recent critical review of several clinical research projects in childhood asthma (Thoresen & Kirmil-Gray, 1983) illustrates the tendency to equate self-management with one or two techniques (e.g., self-monitoring and relaxation). Similarly Thoresen, Telch, and Eagleston (1981) also found extremely limited approaches to self-managed change being used to alter the Type A behavior pattern.

If health is conceived of as something more complex than the absence of physical disease symptoms, then models of health enhancement must include a broad spectrum of factors that conceptually represent the phenomenon of health and well-being. Thus, a comprehensive program of health enhancement would do more than encourage patients to adhere to medication or to have a medical examination by a physician every few years. In a comprehensive program, primary attention would be given to a person's ability and skills to perform certain tasks with adequate levels of energy and enthusiasm to accomplish those tasks successfully. A crucial focus would be people's perception of demands, of resources to meet those demands, and of responses to demands (coping as well as miscoping responses). Openness to examining a number of nonconventional models or frameworks of health and well-being seems indicated. At the conceptual level, recognizing the need for skills training in personal responsibility (self-management) seems particularly crucial if people are to have the means to promote their health, to prevent premature disease, to avoid the experience of illness, and to reduce the need to assume sick roles in their lives.

METHODOLOGICAL PREMISES

Part of the health problem stems from a sometimes myopic view of what constitutes rigorous scientific research. Clearly, when health is viewed as something more than the absence of specific diseases or infirmities, it becomes a relative term, making for difficult measurement and assessment problems. Health is related to many factors—especially cognitive, social, environmental, genetic, and behavioral factors—and is linked intimately to how the person lives day by day. No one is simply healthy; rather, our degree of health depends on the ongoing interaction of demands, resources, and habitual response patterns in our lives.

In a very provocative critique of methods used in the behavioral sciences, especially psychology, Meehl (1977) argues that method must match theory in offering procedures sufficiently complex to evaluate as well as enhance theory. Too often, the method (e.g., experimental design or statistical analysis) is ill-suited to answer the theory-based questions that are being asked (Suppe, 1977). Is it reasonable, for example, to expect a simple two- or three-group factorial design using pretest-posttest measures to answer questions raised by systems theory, in which multiple response patterns are characterized by strong contextual influences over time? Just as our conceptual models of health enhancement need to be comprehensive enough to capture the full range of experience and meaning associated with health, so do the models of scientific inquiry need to be sufficiently comprehensive to capture the phenomenon and allow for its controlled study.

The controlled artificiality of the laboratory is an exquisite setting to study some health-related processes—but not all. No one denies the robust power of a well-conducted double-blind experiment conducted in the laboratory. Yet power always has its price. Sometimes, particularly if the concern is with discovering and exploring hypotheses rather than discon-firming them, the field setting using participant or nonparticipant observers is well suited, for example, to trying to document observable patterns of social behavior of chronic insomni-acs in their home and work environments (Clark, Thoresen, Kashima, 1983). Regarding health enhancement, we are often interested in helping people behave differently in terms of attitudes and beliefs as well as observable actions in the work setting or the home environment. Therefore, at times we need to use methodologies that allow for the controlled study of the experiences of people in their everyday settings. Mead (1976) referred to this more intensive study of persons over time, using multiple methods and modes of assessment, as developing better "macroscopes" to complement the more microscopic methods of the laboratory setting. Too often, what is observed in laboratory analog studies using undergraduate college students as subjects does not readily generalize to the experience of people in their everyday life settings.

Some have called for more ecologically valid designs, ones in which the mix of real-life variables is amply represented in the study (Cook & Campbell, 1979; Snow, 1974). Bronfenbrenner (1977), for example, in describing the research on child development, la-mented that far too many studies have used time-limited laboratory designs, resulting in data based on the "strange behavior of children in strange situations with strange adults for the briefest possible periods of time" (p. 513). If we seek to understand health enhance-ment, we need to study a broader range of contexts, including familiar people in familiar settings for longer periods of time.

In addition to studying health enhancement in more naturalistic settings, there is a need to go beyond the traditional factorial group experiment, with its pretest, posttest, and occasionally follow-up. Such designs rely on measures of central tendency that may fail to provide information on what the person is experiencing in important settings over time. There are marked limitations in relying on two or three data points based on numerical averages (cf. Rogosa, Brandt, & Zimowski, 1982). More frequent use of intensive time-series experimental designs, allowing for a more controlled study of multiple measures and how they interact over time, seems warranted (cf. Kratochwill, 1978).

The issue is one of developing research methods to fit conceptual models and, more important, exploring the salient questions raised by those models. Frankly, the concern is that the developing models of health and its enhancement, given their complexity, will not be studied because popularly used scientific methods do not lend themselves well to such inquiry. We should not limit inquiry to existing methods; rather, we should expand methods to better fit the phenomenon in question. Schwartz (Chapter 20 in this section) presents a case in point. A systems theory perspective presents a host of methodological obstacles for generally accepted methods. Perhaps serious empirical attention will not be given to this perspective because existing methodology does not comfortably accommodate that way of conceptualizing. Similarly, nontraditional models, such as, Eastern perspectives, question the validity of standard experimental designs that are often based on assumptions of unidirectional causality and the existence of a single causal agent. Indeed, Eastern perspectives recognize that observed mechanisms are commonly confused for causal factors, rather than being identified as parts of a complex process.

A final concern about methodological premises has to do with taking our human subjects more seriously. If we are to consider cognitive factors—particularly how people perceive reality and the meanings they ascribe to events—then we must in some way actively involve subjects in our methods of inquiry, rather than treating them as detached objects of study (Rogers, 1973; Tart, 1972). Doing this disrupts prevailing views of objectivity, but perhaps no more so than classical objectivity has been disrupted by quantum mechanics as compared to traditional Newtonian physics (Bernstein, 1976; Toulmin, 1981). The discussion by Kendall and Turk (Chapter 27 in this section) highlights the issue of subjects as active participants, implying that we must develop valid and reliable methods for gathering cognitive and affective data directly (Kendall & Hollon, 1981). Real dangers exist in inferring thoughts and feelings from the exclusive use of observed actions or characteristics, because any externally observed behavior can be related logically to a variety of cognitive and affective states (Ericsson & Simon, 1980; Mahoney, 1976).

We are quickly reaching the point at which our technical capability is outstripping our understanding of how to use technology in imaginative and productive ways. The technology of ambulatory monitoring, given tremendous impetus by the NASA space program over the last two decades, coupled with the rapid developments in the miniaturization of computers, offers an example. Currently, physiological data such as heart rate, body movement, and basal temperature can be gathered continuously over several days, using microcomputers that store data for processing and graphic and numerical display (Miles & Rule, 1982). The possibility exists that people could be trained to report their subjective experiences, such as feeling state, mood, or selected thoughts (self-statements) over substantial time periods using similar equipment. Furthermore such instrumentation allows concurrent examination of physiological, behavioral, and cognitive variables gathered systematically across different settings. The potential for gathering in vivo cognitive data in relatively unobtrusive ways is particularly intriguing. Besides gathering data, ambulatory methods could also provide types of biological and behavioral feedback to the subject in the natural setting (Schwartz, Chapter 20 in this section).

Care and consideration are needed to prevent current conventions of science from becoming rigid methodological habits, holding us back from developing and expanding methods of inquiry. The strengths and the limitations of any method or procedure must be recognized. The exclusive use of the laboratory setting or the dogmatic reliance on factorial group designs to the exclusion of all others seems antithetical to the spirit of science. As we experience growth and development in our theories and models of health, we also need to cultivate methodological growth. It is too easy to reject a perspective on health prematurely because its complexity does not lend itself immediately to scientific study using traditional methods. Although science, by definition, is very conservative, it need not be reactionary.

STRATEGIES OF CHANGE

What is the best way to help people enhance their health? The answer, of course, depends on how you define health, but it also depends on the level of abstraction involved. One could argue on various abstract theoretical grounds that a particular model or theory of behavior change would be most effective. Alternatively, one could describe a particular technique at a very concrete level of abstraction—for example, Benson's discussion of the relaxation response (Chapter 21 in this section) or Everly's presentation of time-management training (Chapter 24 in this section).

Goldfried (1980) offers an interesting discussion of what he believes are effective common strategies that cut across the more than 130 counseling and psychotherapeutic theories currently identified (Parloff, 1976). His argument is straightforward: at the abstract level of theory there is a vast, if not confusing, array of different concepts and terms; at the level of specific technique or method, there are also many different procedures; but at the intermediate level, that of strategies, there may be only a few that account for most of the successful outcomes of various theories and different techniques. It is this level of abstraction (i.e., strategies or what might be called principles of effective change) that may prove useful in considering how to enhance health optimally.

Goldfried's (1980) review suggests two basic strategies that appear to be effective across many theories: promoting corrective action and providing direct feedback. Corrective action refers to methods or techniques that essentially prompt the client to behave or act differently. Role playing, or behavioral rehearsal, as well as homework assignments in which the person is asked to perform certain actions in home or work settings are examples of corrective action (Chesney, Chapter 22 in this section). Other examples include tasks that require the person to reconceptualize a problem and think about it from a different frame of reference and methods that help the person alter "self-talk." The common thread of this change strategy involves the person taking action, doing something differently to be consistent with specific goals or objectives of treatment. Thus, the procedures suggested by Sensenig and Cialdini (Chapter 26 in this section) for building commitment to change by having people do things that are active, public, and effortful; Eisler's (Chapter 23 in this section) focus on practicing social behaviors and interpersonal skills; and Schwartz's (Chapter 20 in this section) suggestion of having younger persons practice "relaxed self-attention" all exemplify this general strategy of corrective action.

The second common strategy, direct feedback, involves providing specific and immediate information to people about their performance—to facilitate improvement as well as to serve as a source of encouragement. Feedback may be particularly useful when the person feels anxious or self-conscious about trying to act in a different manner. Direct feedback can consist of biological, cognitive, or social information provided to the person.

To these two strategies for effective change, I would add a third: social modeling or observational learning. Observing someone demonstrate a desired behavior in a systematic fashion is a powerful and efficient strategy. A number of different modes can be used, ranging from live demonstration and videotape to booklets and other written material. When considerable ambiguity and anxiety exist about how to behave, the power of a vicarious observational experience, like the proverbial picture, can be worth thousands of words of admonition and advice. Social modeling can, of course, offer various levels of performance competence, including the opportunity to observe someone who is far from perfect (a coping model) and someone who performs at a mastery level.

These three strategies—corrective action, direct feedback, and social modeling—are combined in a procedure termed *participant modeling* (Bandura, 1977). In this strategy, a client observes a demonstration of some facet of a desired performance, coupled with an opportunity to practice what is observed immediately while receiving guidance and support. Various kinds of feedback are provided on the adequacy of the performance, along with suggestions and additional aids to improve performance as needed. For example, many of the risk factor behaviors identified by Matarazzo (Chapter 1 of this Handbook)—such as cigarette smoking, physical exercise, use of seat belts, and chronic stress—lend themselves very well to change by means of a participant modeling strategy. A major requirement for this powerful and efficient strategy, however, is that the goal or objective of treatment must be clearly defined in terms of observable performance, and stating crisp objectives in performance terms depends in part on theoretical models that suggest such goals.

A promising concomitant of a strategy based on participant modeling is its impact not only on behavior but also on self-referent cognitive processes—that is, a person's perceptions and beliefs about himself or herself in relation to the environment. A key self-referent process is personal self-efficacy, or the person's level of conviction that he or she is capable of doing certain things successfully, such as practicing relaxation daily for 20 minutes or refraining from cigarette smoking in certain social situations (Schunk & Carbonari, Chapter 15 in this Handbook). Bandura (1982) discusses a broad range of studies suggesting that self-efficacy is a powerful predictor of what people will do in future situations—at times even more powerful than the person's previous behavior in those situations.

Using strategies, such as participant modeling, that affect self-efficacy may be a key to promoting the kinds of changes needed for optimal health. Self-efficacy seems to influence a variety of human actions, particularly those concerned with acting in a more personally responsible way. Taking responsibility for behavior fosters self-control. What people believe themselves capable of doing (their sense of self-efficacy) strongly influences their decisions and choices about what they do. Self-efficacy also appears to influence how much effort people will make in trying to change. Altering habitual patterns of living requires substantial effort, particularly in the beginning phases of change. Persistence—that is, how long people will sustain their efforts at tasks, particularly in the face of obstacles or unpleasant consequences—is also influenced by self-efficacy.

Furthermore, self-efficacy has been shown to affect other thought processes, such as self-talk and self-instruction, as well as to influence emotional responses. Kendall and Turk (Chapter 27 in this section) recognize that cognitive processes have been virtually ignored until recently in considering health and disease problems. A participant modeling strategy, with its potential impact on enhancing personal self-efficacy, would seem to be an ideal strategy for guiding efforts at enhancing health.

Finally, a model that highlights the reciprocity of factors that influence health is an important perspective when considering strategies for changing health behavior. One such model, the expanded cognitive social learning model (see Figure 19.1), encourages developing intervention programs to consider the multiple reciprocal influences of cognitive, behavioral, environmental, and physiological processes. Based on cognitive social learning theory (Bandura, 1977), the model is useful for designing and evaluating health programs. The model was recently used, for example, to evaluate several childhood asthma programs in their efforts to foster personal responsibility for self-care and treatment (Thoresen & Kirmil-Gray, 1983). Another application of the expanded cognitive social learning model was the design of an intervention program to promote improved health status of postcoronary patients (Thoresen, Friedman, Gill, & Ulmer, 1982).

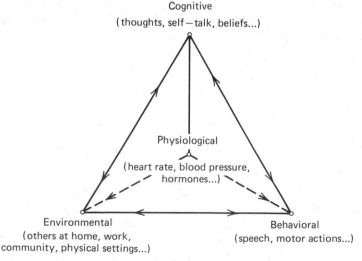

Figure 19.1 Expanded cognitive social learning model.

CONCLUDING COMMENTS

Health is clearly more than the absence of the signs and symptoms of physical disease. Viewed as an ongoing process rather than as a static condition, health is influenced by a number of factors, ranging from processes at the intracellular level to processes concerning subcultural, national, and international factors. Viewed as the ongoing adaptive capability of people to perform tasks in response to their perceived demands and desired goals, health in effect represents people living their lives in home, work, and community settings. Many processes and events at many levels of complexity interact and thus affect this adaptive capability to perform. Perhaps the least examined area involves cognitive and perceptual processes—for example, what people believe themselves capable of doing, how people perceive their environment, and whether people have expectations that life for them is and will be as good as can reasonably be hoped for. In a recent summary of research on the intricate connections between brain, behavior, and health/disease status, Weiner (1981) highlights the vital and complex role played by cognitive processes in health and disease:

> In recent years it has, however, become apparent that the psychological response to experiences is a complex and individual matter. Different persons perceive and appraise an experience in personal ways. The meaning of an event to each person differs: to one it is trivial, while for another it may be portentous. The meaning of the event may also be processed differently by each person and may arouse qualitatively and quantitatively different emotional responses. (pp. 362–363)

We need to be open at this point to a broad spectrum of conceptual models of health and ways to enhance it. At the same time, we need to expand the range of our scientific procedures to capture more fully the richness of health, a richness not to be understood by an exclusive reliance on any one type of research method or data analysis procedure. A major conceptual concern about health enhancement is the need to recognize the primacy of personal responsibility or self-management. The essential question is how we can understand more fully the ways to help people help themselves, often in the face of powerful personal, social, and cultural obstacles. It is not enough to hold people responsible for their health or to admonish them for their personal misbehavior. We must find the means of teaching responsibility, cognizant that it does not develop without high levels of commitment, persistence, and effort.

Methodologically, research on strategies for enhancing health needs to focus on ecologically valid designs that examine experience in everyday settings. Contrived environments typically fail to capture the pattern of subtle cues and consequences that influence health-related behavior in natural settings. There is also much to be learned from controlled, intensive time-series experiments using multiple methods and modes of assessment. Too often, researchers prematurely seek confirmation of a theoretical perspective before a valid and reliable data base has been established. Controlled documentation of the experiences of health deserves high priority.

Intervention strategies can benefit substantially from the use of principles that seem to have generalized across a number of theoretical orientations and therapeutic techniques. Participant modeling, a combination of observational learning with guided practice and corrective feedback, offers a powerful strategy for the field of health promotion. An expanded cognitive social learning model, focused on the reciprocity of cognitive, behavioral, environmental, and physiological factors, also seems useful in designing and evaluating intervention programs to promote health.

Personal health is markedly influenced by "good" habits—adequate exercise, sufficient sleep, nutritious eating—and "bad" habits—cigarette smoking, excessive alcohol consumption, inadequate relaxation. Professionally, when it comes to health enhancement, we may also suffer from questionable habits at the level of theory, research, and practice. Because habit patterns require little conscious attention and focused effort, breaking them is often resisted. Yet the premises and presuppositions underlying our professional patterns—our ways of conceptualizing health, conducting research, and implementing strategies for change—deserve thoughtful scrutiny if we are to make major advances in understanding health and encouraging its enhancement.

As a final thought, perhaps in rethinking what we mean by health, we can adapt Sir William Osler's famous dictum to medical students: "Ask not what kind of disease the person has, ask what kind of person has the disease." Our task, to rephrase his advice, is to "ask not what kind of health the person has, ask what kind of person is healthy."

REFERENCES

Ahmed, P. I., Koeker, A., & Coelho, G. V. Toward a new definition of health: An overview. In P. Ahmed & G. V. Coelho (Eds.), *Toward a new definition of health.* New York: Plenum Press, 1979.

Antonovsky, A. *Health, stress and coping.* San Francisco: Jossey-Bass, 1979.

Bandura, A. *Social learning theory.* Englewood Cliffs, N.J.: Prentice-Hall, 1977.

Bandura, A. Self-efficacy mechanism in human agency. *American Psychologist,* 1982, **37,** 122–147.

Bernstein, P. J. *The restructuring of social and political theory.* Philadelphia: University of Pennsylvania Press, 1976.

Bresler, D. E. Chinese medicine and holistic health. In A. Hastings, J. Fadiman, & J. Gordon (Eds.), *Health for the whole person.* Boulder, Colo.: Westview Press, 1980.

Bronfenbrenner, U. Toward an experimental ecology of human development. *American Psychologist,* 1977, **32:** 7, 513–531.

Clark, J. R., Thoresen, C. E., & Kashima, K. Diurnal experiences of normal and disturbed sleepers: An observation study. Unpublished manuscript, Stanford University, 1983.

Cook, T. D., & Campbell, D. T. *Quasi-experimentation design and analysis for field settings.* Chicago: Rand McNally, 1979.

Dubos, R. *Man, medicine and environment.* New York: Praeger, 1968.

Engel, G. L. The need for a new medical model: A challenge for biomedicine. *Science,* 1977, **196,** 129–136.

Ericsson, K. A., & Simon, H. A. Verbal aspects of data. *Psychological Review,* 1980, **87,** 215–251.

Goldfried, M. R. Toward the delineation of therapeutic change principles. *American Psychologist,* 1980, **35,** 991–999.

Kaptchuk, T. *Web that has no weaver.* New York: St. Martin's Press, 1982.

Kendall, P. C., & Hollon, S. D. (Eds.). *Assessment strategies for cognitive-behavioral interventions.* New York: Academic Press, 1981.

Knowles, J. H. The responsibility of the individual. In J. H. Knowles (Ed.), *Doing better and feeling worse.* New York: Norton, 1977.

Kobasa, S. C., Maddi, S. R., & Kahn, S. Hardiness and health: A prospective study. *Journal of Personality and Social Psychology,* 1982, **42,** 168–177.

Kratochwill, T. R. (Ed.). *Single subject research: Strategies for evaluating change.* New York: Academic Press, 1978.

Lazarus, R. Thoughts on the relations between emotion and cognition. *American Psychologist,* 1982, **37,** 1019–1024.

Levin, L. S., Katz, A., & Holst, E. *Self-care: Lay initiatives in health.* New York: Prodist, 1979.

Mahoney, M. J. *Scientist as subject: The psychological imperative.* Cambridge, Mass.: Ballinger, 1976.

Mahoney, M. J., & Thoresen, C. E. *Self-control: Power to the person.* Monterey: Brooks-Cole, 1974.

Mead, M. Towards a human science. *Science,* 1976, **191,** 903–909.

Meehl, P. E. Theoretical risks and tabular asterisks: Sir Karl, Sir Ronald, and the slow progress of soft psychology. *Journal of Consulting and Clinical Psychology,* 1977, **46,** 806–834.

Miles, L. E., & Rule, R. B. Long-term monitoring of multiple physiological parameters using a programmable microcomputer. In F. D. Stott, E. B. Rafferty, D. L. Clement, & S. L. Wright (Eds.), *Proceedings of the Fourth International Symposium on Ambulatory Monitoring and the Second Gent Workshop on Blood Pressure Variability*. London: Academic Press, 1982.

Palos, S. *The Chinese art of healing*. New York: McGraw-Hill, 1971.

Parloff, M. B. Shopping for the right therapy. *Saturday Review*, February 21, 1976, pp. 14–16.

Pepper, S. C. *World hypotheses*. Berkeley: University of California Press, 1942.

Rogers, C. R. Some new challenges. *American Psychologist*, 1973, **28**, 379–387.

Rogosa, D. R., Brandt, D., & Zimowski, M. A growth curve approach to the measurement of change. *Psychological Bulletin*, 1982, **92**, 726–748.

Schwartz, G. E. Testing the biopsychosocial model: the ultimate challenge facing behavioral medicine. *Journal of Counsulting and Clinical Psychology*, 1982, **50**, 1040–1053.

Snow, R. E. Representative and quasi-representative designs for research in teaching. *Review of Educational Research*, 1974, **44**, 265–291.

Suppe, F. (Ed.). *The structure of scientific theories*. Champaign: University of Illinois Press, 1977.

Tart, C. States of consciousness and state-specific sciences. *Science*, 1972, **176**, 1203–1210.

Thoresen, C. E., Friedman, M., Gill, J. J., & Ulmer, D. K. The Recurrent Coronary Prevention Project. Some preliminary findings. *Acta Medica Scandinavica [Suppl]*, 1982, **660**, 172–192.

Thoresen, C. E., & Kirmil-Gray, K. Self-management psychology in the treatment of childhood asthma. *Journal of Allergy and Clinical Immunology*, 1983, **72**, 596–606.

Thoresen, C. E., Telch, M. J., & Eagleston, J. R. Approaches to altering the Type A behavior pattern. *Psychosomatics*, 1981, **22**, 472–482.

Toulmin, S. Concluding comments. In R. A. Kasschan & C. N. Cofer (Eds.), *Houston Symposium II: Enduring issues in psychology's second century*. New York: Praeger, 1981.

Vithoulkas, G. *Homeopathy: Medicine of the new man*. New York: Avon, 1972.

Weiner, H. Brain, behavior and bodily disease: A summary. In H. Weiner, M. A. Hofer, & A. J. Stunkard (Eds.), *Brain, behavior, and bodily disease* (Vol. 59). New York: Raven Press, 1981.

Wolf, S. Introduction: The role of the brain in bodily disease. In H. Weiner, M. A. Hofer, & A. J. Stunkard (Eds.), *Brain, behavior and bodily disease* (Vol. 59). New York: Raven Press, 1981.

CHAPTER 20

BIOFEEDBACK AS A PARADIGM FOR HEALTH ENHANCEMENT AND DISEASE PREVENTION: A SYSTEMS PERSPECTIVE

GARY E. SCHWARTZ

Yale University

The purpose of this chapter is to consider some of the *potential* roles that biofeedback *may* play in health enhancement and disease prevention. I emphasize the words *potential* and *may* because, at the time this chapter was written, I knew of no empirical data that specifically demonstrated the clinical value of biofeedback in preventing (or delaying) the occurrence of new diseases and promoting general health and well-being. As will be proposed here, however, I believe it is wise to hypothesize that future research will document significant roles for biofeedback in health enhancement and disease prevention.

To understand these potential roles, it is essential to view biofeedback from a comprehensive, multitheoretical, multidisciplinary, and multilevel framework. Systems theory (Miller, 1978; von Bertalanffy, 1968) provides a powerful conceptual framework, not only for understanding biofeedback (e.g., Schwartz, 1979) but also for understanding health enhancement and disease prevention. After briefly reviewing some basic concepts of systems theory as they relate to biofeedback, I will use these systems concepts to describe the nine major approaches to biofeedback (summarized in Table 20.1). When the nine approaches and the associated research in biofeedback are synthesized in this fashion, the overlapping yet unique contributions of each approach to biofeedback become clearer, and some novel and far-reaching applications for the use of biofeedback in promoting health become self-evident.[1]

A SYSTEMS APPROACH TO BIOFEEDBACK

A few general remarks concerning the systems approach to biofeedback must be made before we can consider specific theories and findings as they apply to health enhancement and disease prevention. First, it is important to understand that feedback is a systems

---

The systems synthesis of the nine major biofeedback theories presented in this chapter was inspired by the creative work of Jeanne L. Schwartz in the Yale Behavioral Medicine Clinic and was constructively criticized by graduate students in my course, "Clinical Health Psychology in Psychiatry and Medicine." The synthesis took place coincidental with the occurrence of my father's illness. It is dedicated to the memory of Howard Schwartz, with love.

[1] For readers unfamiliar with systems theory as it applies to bodies of knowledge, scientific disciplines, and behavioral medicine, a brief summary of these concepts and issues is included in the appendix to this chapter.

**Table 20.1   Nine Major Theories of Biofeed-
back and Their Clinical Applications**

9. Social interaction training
8. Motivation and attitude change
7. Education and insight
6. Cognitive-affective-behavioral-environmental
   self-control strategies
5. Discrimination training
4. Motor skills learning
3. Operant-instrumental conditioning
2. Classical conditioning
1. Homeostatic-cybernetic self-regulation

Note: The theories are synthesized using a systems
perspective. They are organized from micro to macro
levels. Each higher-numbered theory incorporates processes described by the lower-numbered theories (see
text for details).

theory concept that applies to any system at any level. There are two types of feedback—
negative and positive. Both types of feedback promote self-regulation in the sense that
when the feedback is connected, the system will regulate itself in particular ways. Negative
feedback leads to "regression to the mean," whereas positive feedback leads to "progression
to the extreme." Negative feedback therefore involves self-regulated moderation, whereas
positive feedback involves self-regulated maximization. Typically, a complex living system
contains various combinations of negative and positive feedback loops (Miller, 1978). As
a result, living systems have the potential to behave in very dynamic and optimally self-
regulated ways.

It directly follows from the foregoing that self-regulation in a system can only occur
to the extent that the feedback is connected and that the information is processed appropriately. If the feedback connections are delayed, diminished, distorted, or, in extreme cases,
disconnected, for whatever reason, the self-regulation will be impaired to various degrees,
including being eliminated altogether in extreme cases. In other words, to the extent that
feedback connections promote order in a system (i.e., make the system behave in a more
orderly and therefore predictable fashion), feedback disconnections will promote disorder
in a system (i.e., make the system behave in a more disorderly and therefore less predictable
fashion). I have proposed that the term *disregulation* be used to refer to the process whereby
distortions and, in extreme cases, disconnections lead to disorder in systems (Schwartz,
1977, 1979, 1983).

Note that the word *regulation* includes the root *regular,* which implies order over time.
In essence, therefore, we can say that regulation is to order as disregulation is to disorder
(see Schwartz, 1983).

It follows that all disease processes, to the extent that they reflect disordered functioning,
involve disregulatory processes occurring somewhere in the system. Biofeedback has the
potential to counteract, if not help correct, internal disregulatory processes that are maladaptive and hence unhealthy.

A highly oversimplified but nonetheless useful diagram of biofeedback is depicted in
Figure 20.1. The diagram illustrates how normal homeostasis (Cannon, 1932), the process
whereby the brain and body maintain states of self-regulated moderation in the face of
environmental challenge and stress, involves intact connections and appropriate information
processing between Stages 2 and 4. Biofeedback becomes a new Stage 5 feedback loop,
parallel to the Stage 4 biological feedback loops within the body.

Biofeedback is unusual in that it interconnects some unique combinations of levels of

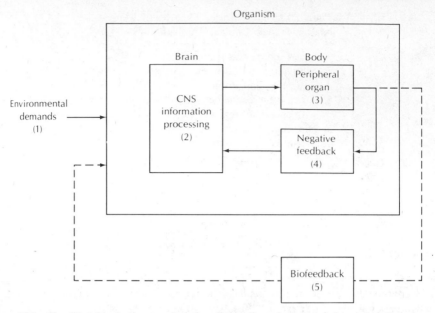

Figure 20.1 Simplified block diagram depicting (Stage 1) environmental demands influencing—via exteroceptors, not shown—(Stage 2) the brain's regulation of its (Stage 3) peripheral organs and (Stage 4) negative feedback from the periphery back to the brain. Biofeedback (Stage 5) is a feedback loop parallel to Stage 4, detecting the activity of the peripheral organs (Stage 3) and converting it into environmental input (Stage 1) that can be used by the brain (Stage 2) to increase self-regulation. (Reprinted by permission from Schwartz, G. E. Psychosomatic disorders and biofeedback: A psychobiological model of disregulation. In J. D. Maser & M. E. P. Seligman (Eds.), *Psychopathology: Experimental models.* San Francisco: Freeman, 1977.)

processes. Physiological information is fed back to the brain in such a way that the brain is able to experience the information in visual, auditory, or other exteroceptive sensory modes. Biofeedback might more aptly be called "biobehavioral feedback" in the sense that, once connected in this fashion, the biological feedback acquires some inherent and immediate psychological qualities that are essential to the feedback's potential to alter the relationship between Stages 2 and 4.

It follows that if it were possible to provide biofeedback for chemical processes directly (something that is difficult to do noninvasively at present), new connections would be made between chemical levels and psychological levels of functioning. Figure 20.1 helps remind us that learned control of skin temperature, for example, with biofeedback actually involves the interconnecting of many different levels—from physical to psychological to neurological to neurohumoral and neurochemical to biochemical and physiological and back to physical. Theoretically, if appropriate measurements could be made, it would be possible to document that changes in all these levels occurred in correct, exquisitively timed sequences of self-regulatory functioning.

The reader should note that Stages 2 through 4 include many different levels within the biomedical sciences, from micro to macro (the levels mentioned earlier, when organized hierarchically, include physical, physical-chemical, chemical, biochemical, cellular, organ, and organism). The same approach to levels of organization can be applied to the behavioral sciences. It is possible to describe many different levels of behavioral processes, organized from micro to macro. Examples include basic sensory and perceptual processes, through higher order cognitive and affective processes, to complex behavioral skills and social interactions.

The concept of micro to macro parallels the concept of subsystem to suprasystem; the concept is relative, and can be applied to any system at any level. I will use the concept of micro to macro to organize and synthesize nine theories of biofeedback broadly within the discipline of psychology.

It should be clear that self-regulation and disregulation can occur within and between various levels of functioning. It follows that, in complex systems, patterns of self-regulation and disregulation within and across levels become complex indeed. Self-regulation at one level can lead to disregulation at another level, and vice versa.

Systems theory helps us make sense of this tremendous complexity. It provides us with an organizing structure to help us tease apart complex interactions that can occur at multiple levels within complex systems. It also follows that biofeedback can be employed to help make connections between various levels, not only at biological and psychological levels but also at social and environmental levels. It is this multilevel nature of biofeedback that makes it a potentially powerful tool in health promotion and disease prevention.

MICRO TO MACRO THEORIES OF BIOFEEDBACK

There are nine major categories of theories of biofeedback that can be organized generally from the micro to the macro (see Table 20.1). Although certain theorists might choose to divide the theoretical pie differently, the present structure does clarify key confusions in the field and can stimulate more refined categories in the future.

At the outset, I should emphasize that these nine theories are not mutually exclusive; rather, the different theories focus on different processes occurring at different levels. Hence, it is even possible for changes in all nine levels to occur in a given individual as a result of the comprehensive use of biofeedback.

Furthermore, we can hypothesize that those patients who experience changes in multiple levels are probably the patients who most likely also maintain the gains they have achieved with biofeedback. Theoretically, the use of biofeedback in health enhancement and disease prevention may profit from changing a person's behavior at each of these levels.

Theory 1: Homeostatic-Cybernetic Self-Regulation

It is curious that this micro-level theoretical orientation (through obviously fundamental to biofeedback, as discussed earlier) has had remarkably little impact on the field as a whole. Only one researcher has focused efforts on investigating cybernetic self-regulatory effects of biofeedback (see Mulholland, 1979, 1982). Mulholland has for 20 years pursued research on the ability of visual stimuli to stabilize and regularize the electroencephalogram (EEG) when the stimuli are connected to the EEG in a negative feedback loop. Mulholland has shown that when visual stimuli are presented to subjects as a function of their EEGs in a negative loop, the EEG becomes more stable and regular and hence ordered. Conversely, he has shown that when the same visual stimuli are connected to the EEG in a positive feedback loop, the EEG becomes more extremistic, showing the wide swings in activity that are characteristic of positive feedback self-regulation.

Mulholland has further shown that the more the subjects attend to the visual stimuli when the visual stimuli are connected in a negative feedback fashion, the more the EEG stabilizes. Recently, he has applied disregulation theory to this EEG-feedback paradigm and has shown that distraction leads to disregulation in the EEG (Mulholland, Note 1).

It is important to appreciate the fact that the self-regulatory (and disregulatory) effects observed by Mulholland occurred automatically; that is, not only were the subjects in these studies uninstructed about controlling their EEG, but no learning was required of them. In fact, the subjects were not even told that the visual stimuli were connected to their EEG activity. The EEG self-regulation occurred automatically, purely as a function of the connections that were made between the external visual stimuli and the internal visual cortex. It follows that intentional effects involving instructions to exert conscious, voluntary control over feedback loops of this sort must occur above and beyond these inherent, automatic, cybernetic feedback effects.

London and Schwartz (1980) have recently demonstrated this fundamental distinction for heart rate control. When the biofeedback was connected to heart rate in a negative feedback (i.e., moderation-producing) manner, the feedback actually interfered with subjects' ability to increase their heart rate when they were instructed to do so intentionally. In fact, subjects who were given false biofeedback were more effective in consciously raising their heart rates when instructed to do so than were subjects who were actually given true feedback that was connected in a negative feedback fashion. When biofeedback was connected to heart rate in a positive feedback fashion, however, subjects who were given true biofeedback did better at raising their heart rate intentionally than did subjects who were given the same instructions but received false biofeedback. Hence, cybernetic self-regulatory feedback effects can interact with intentional, goal-directed learning effects. The cybernetic feedback effects represent fundamental, micro-level, self-regulatory processes that have for all practical purposes been ignored by most biofeedback research to date.

Like the EEG effects obtained by Mulholland, the cybernetic heart rate effects obtained by London and Schwartz occur in the absence of apparent conscious awareness in the subjects. London and Schwartz (1980) found, for example, that subjects' ratings of their perception of the role that the biofeedback played in helping them control their heart rate was consistently associated with the instructions given them but not with whether the biofeedback was actually true or false. Hence, automatic biofeedback cybernetic effects, like homeostasis of bodily processes, can occur in the relative absence of conscious intent. It follows that higher order cognitive processes can influence these cybernetic effects and modulate their basic functioning, even if the subjects are not consciously aware of these changes.

A striking example of how cognitive processes can influence cybernetic self-regulatory effects automatically and unintentionally is illustrated by the recent findings of Schwartz and Rennert (Note 2). Briefly, these authors hypothesized that self-attention to bodily processes per se can strengthen Stage 2 to Stage 4 feedback connections (Figure 20.1) and thereby enhance the inherent automatic homeostatic stabilization. Self-attention was achieved by (a) instructing subjects to attend to specific bodily processes and (b) requesting that subjects touch their hands to parts of their bodies to increase their awareness of specific physiological changes (i.e., tactile biofeedback). The findings were quite dramatic. Self-attention to breathing resulted in automatic breathing stabilization plus enhanced sinus rhythm (heart rate homeostasis in synchrony with breathing). Self-attention to heart rate resulted in automatic heart rate stabilization, especially when subjects were sensing their pulse tactilely. These selective self-regulatory effects occurred in the absence of any instructions for subjects to produce these physiological changes voluntarily. Furthermore, the effects occurred even though subjects reported that they were unaware of having changed their bodies in this fashion. Thus, these organ-specific self-regulatory effects occurred automatically, simply through the process of passive self-attention.

We can hypothesize that these cybernetic self-regulatory effects may be a fundamental mechanism by which guided imagery leads to enhanced physiological regulation and thereby promotes healing and health. We can further hypothesize that when this cybernetic self-regulatory mechanism is distorted (e.g., when patients inappropriately worry about their bodies, they may convert a natural negative feedback process into a positive feedback process), the feedback information distortion may contribute to physical disease. To the extent that future research validates these hypotheses, such research could provide a framework for hypothesizing that meditation and self-awareness training initiated at an early age can facilitate learned homeostasis (see Theory 2) and thereby help prevent future disease and promote health. It is possible that young children may be particularly malleable and responsive to such learning. This self-attention/cybernetic mechanism may help explain the recent findings of Mullen and Suls (1982), which indicate that increased private consciousness, as measured by the Self-Consciousness Scale, helps moderate physical responses to life stress and thereby helps prevent disease under high-stress conditions.

The important point to remember here is that, according to systems theory, homeostatic-cybernetic self-regulatory effects should occur to various degrees in all feedback situations. Furthermore, the cybernetic effects should interact with all of the other higher level processes involved in biofeedback learning (Theories 2–9). The hypothesis that self-attention can promote self-healing is obviously controversial and has important implications for the role of self-awareness and attitudes in health promotion. The hypothesis of attitude change through biofeedback, which is important for disease prevention and health promotion, is discussed later as Theory 8. It is mentioned here, however, to illustrate how the demonstration of attentional cybernetic effects to patients can result in attitude change, which is particularly important to long-term behavioral and lifestyle changes.

Theory 2: Classical Conditioning

Like homeostatic-cybernetic theory, classical conditioning theory has had little impact on biofeedback research and applications. Part of the reason is a result of the history of biofeedback research. Biofeedback research began in an attempt to demonstrate operant-instrumental conditioning (Theory 3, described later) of physiological responses that were previously thought to evidence learning only through classical conditioning (e.g., Kimmel, 1968; Miller, 1969). Another part of the reason probably has to do with the fact that early researchers tended to view all biofeedback theories as being mutually exclusive rather than complementary and interactive. Current animal research on basic theories of learning, however, has moved toward examining classical and operant conditioning interactions. We can hypothesize that classical and operant conditioning interactions probably occur in biofeedback as well.

Schwartz (1974) proposed that the nature of the biofeedback stimulus itself could have classical conditioning effects (via unconditional stimuli) and thereby could influence learned physiological control with biofeedback. He further suggested that certain biofeedback stimuli might be more effective in training one response system than others. This hypothesis followed from research on biological preparedness in classical conditioning (Seligman, 1970), in which certain types of conditioned stimuli were found more likely to be associated with certain types of unconditioned stimuli. Schwartz (1974) proposed, for example, that temperature warming itself might be a potent biofeedback stimulus for teaching subjects to warm their hands. Other authors (e.g., Furedy, 1979; Garcia & Rusiniak, 1977; Tursky, 1982) have extended these ideas and have made important suggestions for improving the efficacy of biofeedback training by taking advantage of these inherent classical conditioning effects.

Classical conditioning theory can be thought of as a logical extension of homeostatic-cybernetic theory. When so-called unconditioned stimuli are paired with physiological responses, this must, by definition, establish a feedback loop that will have negative and/or positive feedback self-regulatory effects. The difference here is that if the feedback system has the potential for conditioning, learning may be added to the cybernetic loop. In other words, the behavior of certain self-regulating systems (e.g., living systems) can change as a function of experience. This means that homeostatic and classical conditioning interactions conceivably can occur (see Dworkin, 1982).

The hypothesis that classical conditioning can occur in the context of a cybernetic feedback loop has important implications for health enhancement and disease prevention. Drawing on Schwartz's (1979) concept of the brain as a health care system, for example, it follows that when an individual experiences pain as a result of some physical injury or disease, the adaptive brain not only will detect the pain and make appropriate regulatory responses to remove the pain, but it will learn to anticipate via aversive classical conditioning (Theory 2), producing certain responses, and it will avoid, via operant conditioning (Theory 3), behaving in certain ways so as to promote healing.

When someone breaks a bone, for example, the adaptive person will quickly learn what movements he or she should not make in order to avoid pain. This presumably facilitates healing. The operant avoidance responses (Theory 3) are prompted by classically conditioned anticipatory aversive reactions (Theory 2). It follows that once the injury has healed, the individual must then unlearn (i.e., extinguish) the aversive reactions and avoidance responses so as to return to normal functioning. Some individuals readily learn and unlearn these responses; others do not.

It is conceivable that biofeedback can help promote this learning and unlearning process. In other words, not only can biofeedback training itself potentially be improved by selecting appropriate feedback to match the physiological responses—for example, providing pressure biofeedback in a blood pressure cuff as feedback for learning to control blood pressure (Tursky, 1982)—but biofeedback may be used to help teach individuals how to develop appropriate classical conditioned responses to physiological responses associated with specific risk factors, so as to improve the development of stable, long-term health behaviors. The important point to realize here is that by drawing distinctions between homeostatic-cybernetic (Theory 1), classical conditioning (Theory 2), and operant-instrumental conditioning (Theory 3) theories, sources of confusion are potentially resolved, and new ideas for research and application are suggested.

Theory 3: Operant-Instrumental Conditioning Theory

Operant-instrumental learning theory provided the primary impetus for early biofeedback research and applications (Kimmel, 1968; Miller, 1969). The most systematic, paradigmatic, and comprehensive research on biofeedback was stimulated by the basic theoretical question of determining whether physiological responses innervated by the autonomic nervous system could show operant-instrumental learning. This research sought to demonstrate selective control over specific responses, using various shaping procedures and schedules of reinforcement. Because this research was directed toward testing a fundamental learning theory question, the goal for the research was to document that the specific learned control of autonomic responses was due to the contingency of reinforcement and not to instructions to subjects. Instructions regarding voluntary control could encourage the learning of cognitive, affective, and skeletal muscle strategies rather than promoting direct control over autonomic responses (Crider, Schwartz, & Shnidman, 1969; Katkin & Murray, 1967).

Space limitations preclude a thorough review of this early research. The important points to recognize here are threefold: (a) operant-instrumental conditioning, by definition, involves connecting a binary (yes/no) cybernetic feedback loop (Theory 1) that has the inherent potential for promoting intrinsic classical conditioning (Theory 2); (b) operant-instrumental learning of any response often takes place in a virtual sea of cognitive, affective, and skeletal muscle processes, and these processes can play an important role in learning (see Theories 4–8); and (c) operant-instrumental conditioning is a fundamental phenomenon and can play an important role in biofeedback learning.

Considering the third point, a number of early studies (e.g., Schwartz & Johnson, 1969) showed that subjects could be taught to increase or decrease spontaneous galvanic skin response (GSR) activity (in the absence of associated changes in other responses such as heart rate) selectively, without having been instructed (a) that the reinforcers were related to their physiological activity (in Schwartz and Johnson, 1969, the reinforcers were pictures from *Playboy* magazine) and (b) that their task was to control their GSRs. These early studies found that specificity of autonomic learning occurred quickly in subjects receiving contingent reinforcement and not in subjects receiving noncontingent reinforcement. Furthermore, this learning occurred in the apparent absence of conscious awareness on the part of the subjects (a) that the stimuli were related to their psychological or physiological state and (b) that they had changed their GSRs in particular ways. The reader will recall that self-regulatory effects can occur without awareness (e.g., the Mulholland studies mentioned in the discussion of Theory 1, in which the subjects were not aware that attending to the visual stimuli led to increased stabilization of their EEG). As will be discussed later (Theories 4–6), when subjects are specifically instructed (a) that the feedback is related to their physiology and (b) that their task is to control their physiology, this alters the learning situation dramatically, adding higher order (higher level) learning processes to the situation.

Since most clinical applications involve instructing subjects about the nature of the task and the desired goals, and provide feedback that is continuous rather than binary (see Theory 4 discussion), operant-instrumental conditioning, in its relatively pure form, is not widely employed today. There are two instances, however, in which operant-instrumental conditioning theory provides an important framework for research and clinical work. One instance involves research on visceral learning in lower animals, in which verbal instructions obviously play little role. The second instance concerns clinical applications in infants and young children. It is possible to shape autonomic responses in infants and young children using operant conditioning procedures. These procedures potentially can be used with a disease prevention and health promotion orientation.

At the time this chapter was being written, Jeanne L. Schwartz, in the Yale Behavioral Medicine Clinic, was teaching a 3-year-old boy with serious migraine headaches how to relax his muscles and warm his hands. Operant conditioning was an important component of the boy's treatment; for example, the child was given "cheese doodles" contingently for decreasing his electromyogram (EMG) levels and warming his hands. The boy showed rapid learning of both these responses, which was accompanied by an 80% decrease in his headaches. The boy then learned to prevent headaches by detecting the subjective precursors of a headache and practicing hand warming before the headache occurred (see discussion of Theory 5).

It is possible that parents can be educated to reinforce their children for certain health-oriented autonomic control (e.g., hand warming), which in turn could set the stage for more health-oriented behavior to occur in adolescence and adulthood. Future research may justify the conclusion that the regular practice of certain autonomic regulation exercises should be as much a part of health promotion as learning to brush one's teeth or exercise one's skeletal muscles regularly.

Theory 4: Motor Skills Learning

Theories 1 through 3, and their interactions—although each of them can become quite complex in its own right—are relatively micro in their complexity compared to Theory 4 and the subsequent theories to be discussed here. Motor skills theory implicitly assumes that cybernetic, classical, and operant conditioning processes occur but that the learning of complex motor skills involves higher order combinations of these underlying processes. Lang (1970) was the first biofeedback researcher to emphasize a motor skills approach to biofeedback, and other researchers quickly moved up conceptual levels and adopted motor skills theory (e.g., Brener, 1974; Schwartz, 1974).

Motor skills theory tends to emphasize the importance of providing detailed information (feedback) regarding performance and places special emphasis on building complex skills from more basic skills (see Bilodeau, 1966). Research by Lang and colleagues has documented some basic similarities between autonomic skill learning and skeletal muscle skill learning by manipulating parameters that relate speed of learning to the amount of feedback provided. Research by Schwartz, Young, and Vogler (1976) has documented that specificity of heart rate skill learning can occur, which is similar to specificity of motor skill learning. Learning a strength and endurance heart rate skill, for example, does not necessarily transfer to learning a heart rate reaction time skill, and vice versa. Nonetheless, despite the important parallels that can be drawn between motor skills and autonomic skills, there has been relatively little systematic research to establish the degree of similarity across response systems parametrically.

Unfortunately, many motor skills researchers in biofeedback have treated operant-instrumental theory as if it were a contrasting theory rather than a micro theory. It is not widely appreciated that motor skills training includes cybernetic, classical, and operant components and then adds such components as instructions, complexity of information and reinforcement, and complexity of the response manipulations practiced.

Experienced biofeedback clinicians often recognize the importance of having patients practice various ways of controlling a given physiological response and having them practice this control in different situations. This is especially true in clinical work involving muscular rehabilitation, in which the connection between biofeedback learning and motor skills training is most obvious.

If biofeedback is used preventively, it seems prudent to hypothesize that greater self-regulatory effects will be obtained if people are educated to think about learning autonomic skills as being similar to learning skills that they are already familiar with, such as learning to play a sport or a musical instrument, rather than thinking about biofeedback only in terms of Theories 1 through 3. In fact, if people can be educated to think that autonomic skill learning is a healthy and enjoyable challenge, their attitude regarding health promotion and self-control may be improved (see discussion of Theory 8). A major lesson that motor skills theory teaches us is that learning complex skills takes practice, and that once the skills have been learned, the skills can be maintained with regular practice and reinforcement. As Lang (1970) wrote (only partially tongue in cheek), "learning to play the internal organs" provides a conceptual framework that can help parents and children develop more comprehensive self-control.

Theory 5: Discrimination Learning

Drawing on William James's (1880) ideomotor theory of voluntary control, Brener (1974) proposes that an essential component of biofeedback learning involves the subject's ability to learn to detect interoceptive feedback of physiological activity. Brener proposed that exteroceptive feedback (biofeedback, Stage 5) made it possible for subjects to learn to detect interoceptive feedback (Stage 4) from specific physiological responses (Stage 3, see Figure 20.1). Brener further hypothesized that the learned physiological awareness made it possible for subjects to control these responses subsequently without requiring the continued presence of the exteroceptive biofeedback.

Discrimination theory implicitly combines elements of Theories 1 through 4 and then adds the component of enhanced visceral awareness as a precursor to achieving learned voluntary control that no longer requires biofeedback. The theory predicts that successful biofeedback training should lead to enhanced visceral awareness (measured by various discrimination paradigms). The theory also predicts that direct training in visceral awareness (using discriminating training techniques) should lead to more rapid learning of visceral skills with biofeedback.

Some evidence supporting both of these hypotheses has been obtained (reviewed in Brener, 1982). It appears, however, that biofeedback learning can occur in the absence of corresponding increases in visceral awareness per se. Typically, what does seem to increase is subjects' awareness of various cognitive, affective, and somatic processes that are correlated with the physiological desired changes (see Brener, 1982; Schwartz, 1982a). In other words, recent research shows a progression from Theory 5 to Theory 6 (see later discussion).

Discrimination training has important clinical utility. If subjects can be trained to detect the small changes in muscle tension that are precursors to the muscular pains (e.g., tension headaches), for example, they can then learn to use these cues to prevent actual occurrence of the pain. Also, subjects can learn to detect what kinds of situations trigger the physiological responses that act as precursors to the pain, and they can then engage in anticipatory activities that can prevent the occurrence of the symptoms.

At this point, we can only speculate on the potential preventive value of teaching young children to become more aware of normal changes in breathing, muscle tension, skin temperature, sweat gland activity, and so forth. The goal here would be to teach the children to become better at detecting and interpreting physiological feedback, so as to facilitate more adaptive, health-oriented behavior.

When individuals ignore physiological feedback as a result of repression, Type A behavior, or other disattention mechanisms, they may short-circuit (disregulate) the fundamental mechanisms underlying homeostasis, thereby potentially contributing to the development of stress-related physical disorders (Schwartz, 1977, 1979, 1983). Early discrimination training (with appropriate caution not to teach excessive, hypochondriacal interpretation of physiological feedback) has the potential to help prevent the development of disregulation and disease.

Theory 6: Cognitive-Affective-Behavioral-Environmental Self-Control

It will be recalled that a major impetus for biofeedback was basic research designed to determine whether operant conditioning of visceral and glandular responses was possible (Theory 3). The primary alternative theory to the theory of direct operant conditioning of autonomic responses was what could be called the theory of indirect operant conditioning of autonomic responses. From the very beginning, controversy raged regarding the possibility that operant autonomic conditioning was actually operant skeletal muscle conditioning or operant conditioning of cognitive and affective processes. Basic researchers disagreed about whether the autonomic changes were merely secondary changes accompanying skeletal muscle or cognitive learning (Crider et al., 1969; Katkin & Murray, 1967). Today, basic researchers are coming to recognize that mediated learning of this sort is interesting in its own right (e.g., Roberts & Martin, 1979) and has important implications for understanding the relationship between psychological and physiological levels of functioning.

Whereas the mediation issue was considered to be a problem by basic researchers concerned with testing operant conditioning theory (Theory 3), it was considered to be a solution by clinicians concerned with using biofeedback to help patients deal with practical problems. As Schwartz (1973) noted, the goal of a responsible clinician is to help the patient discover any and every mediating variable (mechanism) that contributes to his or her physical problem. This broad goal can help the patient learn more varied and flexible means of reducing the causes of his or her problems, thereby preventing continued occurrence of the disease. From this perspective, the patient ideally should learn better control over all types of variables that potentially contribute to his or her physical health. Using the language of prevention, we can hypothesize that biofeedback can be used to help patients learn to recognize and control key risk factors that contribute to physical health and illness.

Schwartz (1973) further noted that biofeedback could be used to help therapist and patient select the most effective clinical strategies for reducing excessive physiological responding. Biofeedback can be used, for example, to help the therapist and patient discover which relaxation technique or combination of relaxation techniques is effective in reducing the patient's physiological signs of stress. It follows that biofeedback can be used to help the therapist guide a patient through cognitive behavioral therapy techniques such as desensitization. It also follows that biofeedback can be used by the therapist to help a patient learn to exercise more effectively or even to select foods and drugs more effectively to promote health.

From this perspective, we see that biofeedback can be used to help guide patients in learning to control thoughts, feelings, and/or behaviors that directly or indirectly contribute to their physiological disregulations. It follows that future preventive research can address the issue of using biofeedback to aid the learning of certain relaxation techniques and interpersonal skills that may help people deal more effectively with everyday stresses (see discussion of Theory 9). It also follows that future preventive research can address the issue of using biofeedback to facilitate exercise programs and even food and drug usage programs. This is not meant to imply that people should become their own diagnosticians and take full responsibility for treating themselves. Rather, within certain limits, teaching people to develop self-regulatory skills may be useful in helping them live more healthy and productive lives.

This broad orientation to the use of biofeedback implies a fundamental and far-reaching shift in the way we view self-regulation and health. As we will see in the discussion of Theory 8, biofeedback can be used to help change our fundamental attitudes regarding self-regulation. Furthermore, these attitude changes can occur in the health providers as well as in the people they serve.

Theory 7: Education and Insight

This approach to biofeedback incorporates processes outlined in all the previous theories and adds the potential role of physiological feedback in facilitating general education and personal insight. Personal insight is typically a goal of psychotherapy. Although some writers have talked about the use of biofeedback to help educate students about general mind/body relationships—for example, as part of a high school course on health and behavior (e.g., Peper, 1979)—and to facilitate the process of psychotherapy (e.g., Rickles, Oranda, & Doyle, 1982), there has been little systematic research in evaluating these beliefs.

My personal experience using biofeedback demonstrations in undergraduate psychology courses has reinforced the conclusion that such demonstrations can provide a powerful educational experience. My clinical experience using biofeedback in psychotherapy has also reinforced the conclusion that, under the right circumstances, such demonstrations can be a powerful tool for promoting insight and reducing defenses in patients. I place education and insight in one general theoretical category because they both involve higher order cognitive/affective learning that can be related to specific physical diseases or symptoms.

Weinberger, Schwartz, and Davidson (1979) have demonstrated that among subjects who report low anxiety on standard paper and pencil scales, only a subset of these subjects are "true low anxious"—that is, accurate in their self-monitoring and in the conclusions they draw about their anxiety levels. Another subset of subjects who also report low anxiety are actually defensive and "repressive"; that is, this subset of subjects are inaccurate in their self-monitoring and are self-deceptive about their anxiety levels. Using a second paper and pencil scale (the Marlow-Crowne scale) to divide subjects who report low anxiety into true low anxious and repressive subgroups, we found that true low anxious subjects showed less behavioral and physiological evidence of anxiety reactions to a laboratory stressor (a sentence completion task) than did a third group of subjects reporting high anxiety, whereas repressors (who turned out to report even less anxiety than the true low anxious subjects), showed equal or greater behavioral and physiological evidence of anxiety reactions than the high anxious subjects.

Drawing on predictions from general disregulation theory, I have proposed that repression involves a disattention process (i.e., disattention to negative emotional experiences and associated physiological cues). The disattentation involves underlying neuropsychological disconnections (between the left and the right hemispheres) that can promote disregulation. This disregulation results in disordered homeostasis (expressed as increased physiological reactivity and poor recovery), which potentially can contribute to disease. Hence, disattention can involve disconnections that can promote disregulation and thereby contribute to disorder and disease. It follows that teaching patients to attend to these processes and correctly interpret the feedback in a healthy fashion (i.e., a negative feedback fashion) should facilitate neuropsychological reconnections, leading to enhanced self-regulation, which in turn should facilitate ordered control of the physiological processes and increase health ("ease"). Data bearing on each of these components are reviewed elsewhere (see Schwartz, 1983).

Biofeedback can play a fundamental role in helping therapists and patients discover particular issues that trigger negative emotional reactions. When a patient experiences the immediate external biofeedback representing physiological changes that he or she may be misperceiving or disregarding altogether, this feedback provides an important source of data that can help change the patient's mind about his or her interpretations. Also, the patient can come to discover how, by resolving certain conflicts (for example, by expressing the negative emotions freely to the therapist), this can be accompanied by decreased physiological activity.

Implications for potential use of biofeedback to promote education and insight in health enhancement and disease prevention should be self-evident. Biofeedback can help persons discover which key situations trigger their physiological reactions and which cognitions and behaviors (e.g., Type A behavior) contribute to excessive and unnecessary reactivity in stressful situations. Viewing biofeedback as a tool for promoting self-education and insight can help health professionals and the lay public think more integratively about mind/body/behavior/environment connections.

Theory 8: Motivation and Attitude Change

It follows from Theory 7 (education and insight) that biofeedback can have effects on a person's motivation and can lead to fundamental changes in self-concept and attitudes. Clearly, changing a person's motivation and attitudes involves complex cognitive and affective learning. This is why motivation and attitude change is listed hierarchically as high as Theory 8. Furthermore, motivation and attitude change is listed as a separate, higher order theory because it emphasizes changes in perception and belief that go beyond whatever specific physiological responses are being controlled. These motivational and attitudinal changes can be quite broad and can have wide-ranging effects on a person's lifestyle.

As mentioned earlier, even when biofeedback is used primarily for micro-level learning (e.g., basic skills training), it is possible that more macro-level learning may be taking place simultaneously. Macro-level learning can occur whether or not the therapist is aware of these changes and whether or not the therapist is deliberately trying to promote this learning. Many patients spontaneously report that as they gain self-control over specific physiological responses, their self-perception changes. Not only do patients discover certain cognitive or other strategies that facilitate bodily control (Theory 6) and basic aspects of themselves that relate to their ability to maintain self-control (Theory 7), some patients also develop an increased sense of self-efficacy (Bandura, 1977)—that is, a general sense of control that makes them feel happy, hopeful, and more energized.

Some clinicians have been sensitive to the fact that this level of general attitude change can and does take place. As a result, these clinicians may prescribe biofeedback training even for certain patients whose primary goal is a change in their general emotional state and belief system.

Motivation and attitude change is sometimes the rationale for recommending that biofeedback be used in the treatment of certain cases of alcholism, drug addiction, weight control, and depression. For this purpose, the specific physiological responses selected for control may have no direct physiological or biochemical bearing on the particular disorder. Instead, those physiological responses that can be learned relatively rapidly (e.g., EMG responses) are selected so as to help the patients have a relatively rapid success.

Biofeedback treatment may be employed primarily, however, to help change patients' motivation and attitudes from a minimal sense of self-control and self-efficacy to a more active sense of self-control and self-efficacy. Armed with these new beliefs, patients can then become more responsive to those behavioral, psychotherapeutic, counseling, and pharmacological treatment programs that are focused more specifically on the patients' particular problems.

It is interesting that, in the past, the use of biofeedback for this macro level of cognitive/affective change was viewed negatively by some investigators. In the same way that early investigators interested in operant conditioning theory (Theory 3) viewed cognitive mediation as a negative alternative theory (Theory 6), early investigators focusing on operant conditioning theory or other relatively specific theories (Theories 1–5), also considered general attitude change to be a negative alternative theory (Theory 8).

Some investigators suggested that attitude changes were merely suggestion effects (pun intended) and hence placebo effects. Furthermore, some investigators hypothesized that biofeedback was nothing more than an instruction or suggestion effect (e.g., Stroebel & Gluck, 1973).

It should be clear that the macro theory proposed in this chapter strongly resists the temptation to view biofeedback in such an either-or fashion. Instead, even in the example cited earlier concerning the use of EMG biofeedback to facilitate attitude change, the systems approach leads to the hypothesis that, depending on how the EMG biofeedback is used, many of the lower order theories (and hence processes) will simultaneously be involved in the treatment as well. For example, EMG biofeedback can have specific cybernetic (Theory 1), classical conditioning (Theory 2), and operant conditioning (Theory 3) effects on localized muscle control, and can promote more generalized changes in muscle activity as a result of instructions involving specific strategies for relaxation (Theory 6) that may be used by the therapist in conjunction with the biofeedback.

There has been a paucity of empirical research measuring attitude changes that spontaneously occur in different types of biofeedback studies (e.g., London & Schwartz, 1980). Furthermore, there has been virtually no research on the use of clinical biofeedback for the primary purpose of producing motivation and attitude change. It should be clear, however, that this level of change not only is important clinically but has fundamental paradigmatic implications for health enhancement and disease prevention.

If parents, teachers, physicians, and other professionals can change their beliefs and attitudes concerning the fundamental role that the brain plays in physiological self-regulation (and, hence, behavior) and can come to realize that the capacity for conscious, voluntary control over bodily processes is substantially greater than previously believed, this change in attitude can encourage adults to teach young children to practice bodily self-control using biofeedback as an aid. A major goal here would be to change children's general attitudes concerning their ability and responsibility, in conjunction with health professionals, to self-regulate (take care of) their bodies. The potential for conducting research on the use of biofeedback as a means of promoting a generally health-oriented attitude change is clearly indicated.

Theory 9: Social Interaction Training

Theories 1 through 8 explicitly focus on the individual, even when the individual is implicitly learning self-regulation in a social context (Theories 6–9). Social interaction training is listed as an upper level macro theory to highlight its explicitly personal nature. Biofeedback has the potential to be used as a means of helping individuals learn more adaptive and psychophysiologically healthy strategies of social interaction. The integration of social, psychological, and physiological levels of analysis is termed social psychophysiology.

An example of applied social psychophysiology is social communication training. Recent research by Ewart (1982) has documented that when hypertensive patients are taught less aggressive communication styles with their spouses (using biofeedback to show the patients and their spouses how their communication styles produce large increases in blood pressure), blood pressure responses during social communication are reduced. In fact, it can be demonstrated to patients and spouses that if they interact using their "old" style again, the large blood pressure increases will return.

Lynch, Thomas, Paskewitz, Malinow, and Long (1982) have written an important article illustrating how social interaction styles can be assessed psychophysiologically and how biofeedback can be used to help persons learn healthier social styles. This is clearly a potentially important and pioneering area for biofeedback, and it deserves serious research attention in the future.

At this time, we can only speculate about how the behavior and attitudes of children might change if they were taught at an early age to understand and appreciate how their styles of social interaction affect not only their physiology but the physiology of the people with whom they interact. It is becoming feasible for patients, and even the lay public, to monitor physiological processes out of the laboratory in everyday situations, using cost-effective portable biofeedback equipment. A high-quality temperature ring, for example, is now commercially available, making it possible for people to monitor their skin temperature responses in various social situations.

As the technology improves for 24-hour psychophysiological monitoring, it will become feasible to conduct research designed to determine whether in vitro biofeedback-based social interaction training (in the laboratory or the clinic) is facilitated by in vivo biofeedback monitoring and practice (in everyday situations), and vice versa. It should also be noted that future research may support the hypothesis that certain pediatric diseases should be reinterpreted from a social psychophysiological perspective as reflecting excessive stress upon (or within) the family (possibly caused by faulty social interactions within the family itself), and that family therapy with the aid of biofeedback can be used to help resolve these problems.

SUMMARY AND CONCLUSIONS: CHANGING PARADIGMS

As noted by various writers (e.g., Capra, 1982; deRosnay, 1979), it appears that we are in the midst of a major paradigm change (Kuhn, 1962) concerning integrative ways of thinking about science and nature. I agree with these writers that the emergence of systems theory is a fundamental example of this paradigm shift. As I have discussed in detail elsewhere (Schwartz, 1982b), the shift from single-cause–single-effect thinking to multicause–multieffect thinking, employing systems principles of hierarchy of levels and emergent properties, is having major effects on scientific thinking and research in all disciplines. I further believe that the emergence of behavioral medicine is itself a sign of this broad shift in paradigm.

Systems theory has the potential to help organize and synthesize information across various levels and disciplines, from the micro to the macro. As I have illustrated in this chapter, the systems perspective helps us see the interacting and complex ways that biofeedback can be used to facilitate psychobiological change from micro to macro levels. From a systems perspective, biofeedback has paradigmatic implications for health care, and particularly for health promotion. The systems perspective suggests that people can use biological feedback to help them gain control over various aspects of their lives, from specific physiological strategies involving relatively direct and simple learning (Theories 1–3) through more complex strategies of self-regulation involving cognitive, affective, behavioral, and environmental self-control, including pharmacological self-control (Theories 4–7, see Table 20.1).

Probably the most far-reaching and controversial implication of biofeedback for the emerging areas of health promotion and disease prevention concerns our fundamental attitudes about treatment and self-efficacy (Theory 8). As we shift our perceptions from viewing treatment as something that is always done to us by someone else (the serial feedback model of treatment) to viewing treatment as something that we can do directly to ourselves with the aid of the advice and specialized skills of others (the parallel feedback model of treatment), it becomes easier to view our personal responsibility for promoting our health and helping prevent (or delay) disease in ourselves and others. From this perspective, a person who has high blood pressure (or has a genetic predisposition to high blood pressure), can reconceptualize exercise or the taking of drugs as self-administered treatments that are selected and followed with the parallel feedback advice and guidance of appropriately trained health providers, rather than viewing them as other-administered treatments that are determined and controlled solely by the health provider in a purely serial feedback fashion. Future research will ultimately determine how biofeedback, at its various levels (Theories 1–9), can contribute to these more comprehensive approaches to health care.

APPENDIX: INTRODUCTION TO SYSTEMS THEORY AND BEHAVIORAL MEDICINE

Systems theory is concerned with general principles that apply to any system, regardless of the system's level (deRosnay, 1979; von Bertalanffy, 1968). The concept of level, with its intimate relationship to the concept of hierarchy of information and structure, is fundamental to the concept of a system. Briefly, a system is hypothesized to be a whole composed of a set of interacting parts. The unique behaviors of a given system are hypothesized to be an emergent property of the dynamic interactions that occur among the system's parts as the system interacts with its environment.

The concept of emergent property is a key concept of systems theory. It is often stated simplistically in terms of the whole being more than the sum of its parts. More precisely, the whole is hypothesized to be determined by the unique interactions that occur among the system's parts as the system interacts with its environment. Emergent phenomena are ubiquitous; they have been observed at every level and in every discipline. In fact, the emergent property principle provides the framework for understanding why different scientific disciplines have evolved to classify and understand phenomena occurring at different levels in nature.

Table 20.2 illustrates the relationship between levels of systems, bodies of knowledge, and their associated basic science disciplines. It can be seen that, as we move up hierarchically from fundamental particles through complex groups of organisms to ecological levels and beyond, the system, by definition, becomes more complex and therefore more difficult to study. This progression presumably reflects evolution, from physical through biological to psychological and social levels. Table 20.2 illustrates how important it is to keep levels of measurement and analysis straight. Because many scientists have had little training in systems thinking, they often combine information from different levels in haphazard, if not confusing, ways (see Weinberg, 1975).

As I have discussed in detail elsewhere (Schwartz, 1982b), it appears that we are approaching a point in the history of science at which concern with synthesis (across levels) is becoming more the rule than the exception. Numerous new disciplines or, more appropriately, "interdisciplines," have emerged in order to study interactions that occur across different levels. Moving up hierarchically, examples include physical chemistry, biochemistry, neurophysiology, psychophysiology, social psychology, and social ecology. Some recent interdisciplines have attempted to embrace and describe interactions that occur across three or more levels, such as sociobiology, psychoneuroimmunology, and social psychophysiology. It is within this broad scientific movement toward synthesis that behavioral medicine has emerged.

Various writers have proposed that the hallmark of behavioral medicine is its focus on evaluating interactions that occur across biological, psychological, and social levels (e.g., Leigh and Reiser, 1980). According to systems theory, it follows that psychology is the "middle" discipline, whereas medicine is a biopsychosocial profession (Schwartz, 1982b). This is not to say that people who are formally trained in psychology (psychologists) cannot make important contributions to medicine (in terms of theory, research, practice, and teaching), or that people who are formally trained in medicine (physicians) cannot make important contributions to psychology (also in terms of theory, research, practice, and teaching). From systems theory, however, it does follow that if a comprehensive biopsychosocial approach to patient evaluation and treatment is desired, a team approach to comprehensive assessment and care is called for, and an appropriately trained physician is needed to integrate and coordinate the team (i.e., a physician trained not only in the biological sciences but also in core aspects of the behavioral sciences).

This conclusion regarding who should integrate and coordinate a biopsychosocial/behav-

Table 20.2   Levels of Complexity in Systems and Associated
Academic Disciplines

Level and Complexity of the System	Academic Field Associated with the Level of the System
Beyond earth	Astronomy
Supranational	Ecology
National	Government, political science, economics
Organizations	Organizational science
Groups	Sociology
Organism	Psychology, ethology, zoology
Organs	organ physiology (e.g., neurology, cardiology)
Cells	Cellular biology
Biochemicals	Biochemistry
Chemicals	Chemistry, physical chemistry
Atoms	Physics
Subatomic particles	Subatomic physics
Abstract systems	Mathematics, philosophy

Source: Schwartz, G. E. Testing the biopsychosocial model: The ultimate challenge facing behavioral medicine? In E. Blanchard (Ed.), Special issue on behavioral medicine, *Journal of Consulting and Clinical Psychology,* 1982, **50,** 1040–1053.
Note: According to systems theory, in order to understand the behavior of an open system at any one level, it is essential to have some training in the academic disciplines below that level plus some training in the relevant discipline at the next highest level.

ioral medicine team is admittedly controversial, since it proposes that psychologists are by definition "disciplinists" and therefore should be satisfied to work as part of a biopsychosocial assessment and treatment team. Important, too, is that the biopsychosocial model (when interpreted from a systems perspective) also illustrates the contexts in which psychology as a discipline should take more of a leadership role.

One example concerns psychological education and research in medical schools. Since it is hypothesized that psychology as the middle discipline needs to be part of the training of all physicians (not just psychiatrists), it follows that persons who are formally trained in the basic science of psychology typically will be the best qualified to teach this information to medical students and to direct discipline-oriented research. This conclusion provides strong support for the idea that separate psychology departments within medical schools should be formed alongside other existing basic science departments (e.g., physiology).

A second example concerns health enhancement and disease prevention, which is the primary concern of this Handbook. Disease prevention and health enhancement are intimately involved with human behavior. Since psychologists are specifically trained to help change human behavior, as broadly defined, it follows that they should play a leading role in helping healthy individuals remain healthy. As discussed in this chapter, biofeedback can influence learning in many ways. Extensive training in psychology therefore becomes important for understanding and using biofeedback comprehensively and effectively to reach these goals.

REFERENCE NOTES

1. Mulholland, T. *Regulation and disregulation of parietal and occipital EEG.* Unpublished manuscript, 1983.

2. Schwartz, G. E. & Rennert, K. *Effects of attention and sensory feedback on automatic self-regulation of heart rate versus respiration.* Manuscript in preparation, 1983.

REFERENCES

Bandura, A. Self-efficacy: Toward a unifying theory of behavioral change. *Psychological Review,* 1977, **84,** 191–215.

Bilodeau, E. A. *Acquisition of skill.* New York: Academic Press, 1966.

Brener, J. M. A general model of voluntary control applied to the phenomena of learned cardiovascular change. In P. A. Obrist, A. H. Black, J. Brener, & L. V. DiCara (Eds.), *Cardiovascular psychophysiology.* Chicago: Aldine, 1974.

Brener, J. M. Psychobiological mechanisms in biofeedback. In L. White & B. Tursky (Eds.), *Clinical biofeedback: Efficacy and mechanisms.* New York: Guilford Press, 1982.

Capra, F. *The turning point.* New York: Simon & Schuster, 1982.

Cannon, W. B. *The wisdom of the body.* New York: Norton, 1932.

Crider, A., Schwartz, G. E., & Shnidman, S. On the criteria for instrumental autonomic conditioning: A reply to Katkin and Murray. *Psychological Bulletin,* 1969, **71,** 455–457.

deRosnay, J. *The macroscope.* New York: Harper & Row, 1979.

Dworkin, B. R. Clinical innovation: Instrumental learning for the treatment of disease. *Health Psychology,* 1982, **1,** 45–59.

Ewart, C. A couple's approach to stress reduction: Applications in hypertension. In T. Coates (Ed.), *A handbook of behavioral medicine.* Champaign, Ill.: Research Press, 1982.

Furedy, J. Teaching self-regulation of cardiac function through imaginational Pavlovian and biofeedback conditioning: Remember the response. In N. Birbaumer & H. D. Kimmel (Eds.), *Biofeedback and self-regulation.* Hillsdale, N.J.: Erlbaum, 1979.

Garcia, J., & Rusiniak, K. W. Visceral feedback and the taste signal. In J. Beatty & H. Legewie (Eds.), *Biofeedback and behavior.* New York: Plenum Press, 1977.

James, W. *The principles of psychology.* New York: Holt, 1880.

Katkin, E. S., & Murray, E. N. Instrumental conditioning of autonomically mediated behavior. *Psychological Bulletin,* 1969, **71,** 462–466.

Kimmel, H. D. Instrumental conditioning of autonomically mediated behaviors. *Psychological Bulletin,* 1968, **67,** 337–345.

Kuhn, T. S. *The structure of scientific revolutions.* Chicago: University of Chicago Press: 1962.

Lang, P. J. Autonomic control or learning to play the internal organs. *Psychology Today,* 1970, October, 37–41.

Lang, P. J. Learned control of human heart rate in a computer directed environment. In P. A. Obrist, A. H. Black, J. Brener, & L. V. DiCara (Eds.), *Cardiovascular psychophysiology.* Chicago: Aldine, 1974.

Leigh, H., & Reiser, M. F. *The patient: Biological, psychological and social dimensions of medical practice.* New York: Plenum Press, 1980.

London, M. D., & Schwartz, G. E. The interaction of instruction components with cybernetic feedback effects in the voluntary control of human heart rate. *Psychophysiology,* 1980, **17,** 437–443.

Lynch, J. J., Thomas, S. A., Paskewitz, D. A., Malinow, K. L., & Long, J. M. Interpersonal aspects of blood pressure control. *Journal of Nervous and Mental Disease,* 1982, **170**(3), 143–153.

Miller, J. G. *Living systems.* New York: McGraw-Hill, 1978.

Miller, N. E. Learning of visceral and glandular responses. *Science,* 1969, **163,** 434–445.

Mulholland, T. Experiments and control systems: An analogy. In N. Birbaumer & H. D. Kimmel (Eds.), *Biofeedback and self-regulation.* Hillsdale, N.J.: Erlbaum, 1979.

Mulholland, T. Comments on the chapter by Furedy, Riley & Tursky. In L. White & B. Tursky (Eds.), *Clinical biofeedback: Efficacy and mechanisms.* New York: Guilford Press, 1982.

Mullen, B., & Suls, J. Know thyself: Stressful life changes and ameliorative affect of private self-consciousness. *Journal of Experimental Social Psychology,* 1982, **18,** 43–55.

Peper, E. Biofeedback in education. In E. Peper, S. Ancoli, & M. Quinn (Eds.), *Mind/body integration.* New York: Plenum Press, 1979.

Rickles, W. H., Oranda, L., & Doyle, C. C. Task force study section report: Biofeedback as an adjunct to psychotherapy. *Biofeedback and Self-Regulation,* 1982, **7,** 1–33.

Roberts, L. E., & Martin, R. G. Some comments on the self-description of visceral response states. In N. Birbaumer & H. D. Kimmel (Eds.), *Biofeedback and self-regulation.* Hillsdale, N.J.: Erlbaum, 1979.

Schwartz, G. E. Biofeedback as therapy: Some theoretical and clinical issues. *American Psychologist,* 1973, **29,** 666–673.

Schwartz, G. E. Toward a theory of voluntary control of response patterns in the cardiovascular system. In P. A. Obrist, A. H. Black, J. Brener, & L. V. DiCara (Eds.), *Cardiovascular psychophysiology.* Chicago: Aldine, 1974.

Schwartz, G. E. Psychosomatic disorders and biofeedback: A psychobiological model of disregulation. In J. D. Maser & M. E. P. Seligman (Eds.), *Psychopathology: Experimental models.* San Francisco: Freeman, 1977.

Schwartz, G. E. The brain as a health care system: A psychobiological framework for biofeedback and health psychology. In G. Stone, N. Adler, & F. Cohen (Eds.), *Health psychology.* San Francisco: Jossey-Bass, 1979.

Schwartz, G. E. Comments on the chapters by Brener and Shapiro. In L. White & B. Tursky (Eds.), *Clinical biofeedback: Efficacy and mechanisms.* New York: Guilford Press, 1982. (a)

Schwartz, G. E. Testing the biopsychosocial model: The ultimate challenge facing behavioral medicine? In E. Blanchard (Ed.), Special issue on behavioral medicine, *Journal of Consulting and Clinical Psychology,* 1982, **50,** 1040–1053. (b)

Schwartz, G. E. Disregulation theory and disease: Applications to the repression/cerebral disconnection/ cardiovascular disorder hypothesis. In J. Matarazzo, N. Miller, & S. Weiss (Eds.), Special issue on behavioral medicine, *International Review of Applied Psychology,* 1983, **32,** 95–118.

Schwartz, G. E., & Johnson, H. J. Affective visceral stimuli as operant reinforcers of the GSR. *Journal of Experimental Psychology,* 1969, **80,** 28–32.

Schwartz, G. E., Young, L. D., & Vogler, J. Heart rate regulation as skill learning: Strength-endurance versus cardiac reaction time. *Psychophysiology,* 1976, **13,** 472–478.

Seligman, M. E. P. On the generality of the laws of learning. *Psychological Review,* 1970, **77,** 406–418.

Stroebel, C. F., & Gluck, B. C. Biofeedback treatment in medicine and psychiatry: An ultimate placebo? In L. Birk (Ed.), *Biofeedback: Behavioral medicine.* New York: Grune & Stratton, 1973.

Tursky, B. An engineering approach to biofeedback. In L. White & B. Tursky (Eds.), *Clinical biofeedback: Efficacy and mechanisms.* New York: Guilford Press, 1982.

von Bertalanffy, L. *General systems theory.* New York: Braziller, 1968.

Weinberg, G. M. *An introduction to general systems thinking.* New York: Wiley, 1975.

Weinberger, D. A., Schwartz, G. E., & Davidson, R. J. Low anxious, high anxious, and repressive coping styles: Psychometric patterns and behavioral and physiological responses to stress. *Journal of Abnormal Psychology,* 1979, **88,** 369–380.

CHAPTER 21

THE RELAXATION RESPONSE AND STRESS

HERBERT BENSON

Beth Israel Hospital and Harvard Medical School, Boston

Stress results from behavioral adjustments (Gutmann & Benson, 1971) and is associated with a series of physiological reactions, the most prominent being the so-called emergency reaction or fight-or-flight response (Cannon, 1914) or, as it is alternatively named, the ergotrophic reaction (Hess, 1957) or the defense reaction (Abrahams, Hilton, & Zbrozyna, 1960; Hess & Brugger, 1943). The fight-or-flight response is mediated by the sympathetic nervous system. When a specific hypothalamic area is electrically stimulated, dilation of the pupils, increased blood pressure, increased respiratory rate, and heightened motor excitability are consistently produced. Cannon (1914) reasoned that this integrated response prepared the animal for "fight or flight" when faced with a threatening environmental situation. Humans also respond to threatening environmental conditions or to environmental situations that require behavioral adjustment by a coordinated physiological response that mimics that of the increased sympathetic nervous system activity in the fight-or-flight response (Gutmann & Benson, 1971).

Individuals possess an opposite, alternative response—the relaxation response—that counteracts the effects of stress. The relaxation response is believed to be an integrated hypothalamic response that results in generalized decreased sympathetic nervous system activity (Benson, 1975; Benson, Beary, & Carol, 1974) and consists of changes counter to those of the fight-or-flight response (Allison, 1970; Wallace, 1970; Wallace & Benson, 1972; Wallace, Benson, & Wilson, 1971). This response, termed the "trophotropic response," was first described by Hess (1957) in the cat. Electrical stimulation of hypothalamic areas results in hypodynamia or adynamia of skeletal musculature, decreased blood pressure, decreased respiratory rate, and pupil constriction. Hess (1957) states:

> Let us repeat at this point that we are actually dealing with a protective mechanism against overstress belonging to the trophotropic-endophylactic system and promoting restorative processes. We emphasize that these adynamic effects are opposed to ergotrophic reactions which are oriented toward increased oxidative metabolism and utilization of energy. (p. 40)

The major physiological elements of the relaxation response were first defined in humans during the practice of Transcendental Meditation (Wallace, 1970; Wallace et al., 1971): decreased oxygen consumption, carbon dioxide elimination, and changes in heart rate, respi-

---

Work reported herein was supported in part by Grants HL-22727 and HL-07374 from the National Institutes of Health, U.S. Public Health Service.

ratory rate, minute ventilation, and arterial blood lactate. Systolic, diastolic, and mean blood pressures remained unchanged compared to control levels. Rectal temperature also remained unchanged, whereas skin resistance markedly increased and skeletal muscle blood flow slightly increased (Levander, Benson, Wheeler, & Wallace, 1972). The electroencephalogram demonstrated an increase in the intensity of slow alpha waves and occasional theta wave activity. These changes are consistent with generalized decreased sympathetic nervous system activity and are distinctly different from the physiological changes noted during quiet sitting or sleep. The changes occur simultaneously and are consistent with those noted by Hess (1957).

THE TECHNIQUE OF ELICITING THE RELAXATION RESPONSE

Four basic elements are usually necessary to elicit the relaxation response in humans:

1. *Mental device:* There should be a constant stimulus—for example, a sound, word, or phrase repeated silently or audibly, or fixed gazing at an object. The purpose of these procedures is to shift from logical, externally oriented thought.

2. *Passive attitude:* If distracting thoughts do occur during the repetition or gazing, they should be disregarded and the subject's attention should be redirected to the technique. The subject should not worry about how well he or she is performing the technique.

3. *Decreased muscle tonus:* The subject should be in a comfortable posture so that minimal muscular work is required.

4. *Quiet environment:* A quiet environment should be chosen, with decreased environmental stimuli. Most techniques instruct the practitioner to close his or her eyes. A place of worship is often suitable, as is a quiet room.

HISTORICAL SUBJECTIVE WRITING SUPPORTING THE EXISTENCE OF THE RELAXATION RESPONSE

Techniques have existed for centuries, usually within a religious context, for allowing an individual to experience the relaxation response. In the West, for example, a 14th-century Christian treatise entitled *The Cloud of Unknowing* discusses how to attain an altered state of consciousness, which is required to attain alleged union with God (Progoff, 1969). The anonymous author of this treatise states that this goal cannot be reached in the ordinary levels of human consciousness but rather by use of "lower" levels. These levels are reached by eliminating all distractions and physical activity, all worldly things, including all thoughts. As a means of "beating down thought," the use of a single-syllable word, such as "god" or "love," should be repeated:

> *Choose whichever one you prefer, or, if you like, choose another that suits your taste, provided that it is of one syllable. And clasp this word tightly in your heart so that it never leaves it no matter what may happen. This word shall be your shield and your spear. . . . With this word you shall strike down thoughts of every kind and drive them beneath the cloud of forgetting. After that, if any thoughts should press upon you . . . answer him with this word and with no other words. (Progoff, 1969, pp. 76–77)*

There will be moments when "every created thing may suddenly and completely be forgotten. But immediately after each stirring, because of the corruption of the flesh, it [the soul] drops down again to some thought or some deed" (Progoff, 1969, p. 68). An important instruction for success is ". . . do not by another means work in it with your mind or with your imagination" (Progoff, 1969, p. 69).

Another Christian work, *The Third Spiritual Alphabet,* written in the 10th century by Fray Francisco de Osuna, deals with an altered state of consciousness (Osuna, 1931). He wrote that "contemplation requires us to blind ourselves to all that is not God" (p. viii), and that one should be deaf and dumb to all else and must "quit all obstacles, keeping your eyes bent on the ground" (pp. 293–294). The method can be either a short, self-composed prayer, repeated over and over, or may involve simply saying no to thoughts when they occur. This exercise should be performed for one hour in the morning and evening and should be taught by a qualified teacher. Fray Francisco wrote that such an exercise would help in all endeavors, making us more efficient in our tasks and the tasks more enjoyable. He stated that all persons, especially the busy, secular people as well as the religious, should be taught this meditation, for it is a refuge to which one can retreat when faced with stressful situations.

The famous 15th-century Christian mystics Saint John and Saint Terese described the major steps required to achieve the mystical state (Anonymous, 1954; Saint Terese, 1901), which include ignoring distractions, usually by repetitive prayer. Christian meditation and mysticism was well developed within the Byzantine church and was known as Hesychasm (Norwich & Sitwell, 1966). This method of repetitive prayer, described in the 14th century at Mount Athos in Greece by Gregory of Sinai, is called "The Prayer of the Heart" or "The Prayer of Jesus." It dates back to the beginnings of the Christian era. The prayer itself was called secret meditation and was transmitted from older to younger monks through an initiation rite. Emphasis was placed on having a skilled instructor. The method of prayer recommended by these monks was as follows:

Sit down alone and in silence. Lower your head, shut your eyes, breathe out gently, and imagine yourself looking into your own heart. Carry your mind, i.e., your thoughts, from your head to your heart. As you breathe out, say "Lord Jesus Christ, have mercy on me." Say it moving your lips gently, or simply say it in your mind. Try to put all other thoughts aside. Be calm, be patient and repeat the process very frequently. (French, 1968, p. 10)

To reach such a state, a tranquil environment is necessary. "It may happen that a man who has been busy all day gives himself to prayer for an hour . . . so that during that time the thoughts of his earthly preoccupations are forgotten" (Ross, 1965, p. 87).

In Judaism, similar practices leading to this altered state of consciousness date back to the time of the second temple in the second century B.C. and are found in one of the earliest forms of Jewish mysticism, Merkabalism (Scholem, 1967). In this practice of meditation, the subject sat with his head between his knees, whispered hymns and songs, and repeated a name of a magic seal. In the 13th century A.D., the works of Rabbi Abulafia were published and his ideas became a major part of Jewish cabalistic mysticism (Scholem, 1967). Rabbi Abulafia felt that the normal life of the soul is kept within limits by our sensory perceptions and emotions and that since these perceptions and emotions are concerned with the finite, the soul's life is finite. Man therefore needs a higher form of perception, which, instead of blocking the soul's deeper regions, opens them up. An "absolute" object upon which to meditate is required. Rabbi Abulafia found this in the Hebrew alphabet. He developed a mystical system of contemplating the letters of God's name. Bokser (1954) describes Rabbi Abulafia's prayer:

. . . immersed in prayer and meditation, uttering the divine name with special modulations of the voice and with special gestures, he induced in himself a state of ecstasy in which he believed the soul had shed its material bonds, and, unimpeded, returned to its divine source. (p. 9)

The purpose of this prayer and methodical meditation is to experience a new state of consciousness, described as harmonious movement of pure thought, which has severed all relation to the senses. This is compared by Scholem (1967) to music and yoga:

[Rabbi Abulafia's] teachings represent but a Judaized version of that ancient spiritual technique which has found its classical expression in the practices of the Indian mystics who follow the system known as Yoga. *To cite only one instance out of many, an important part in Abulafia's system is played by the technique of breathing; now this technique has found its highest development in the Indian* Yoga, *where it is commonly regarded as the most important instrument of mental discipline. Again, Abulafia lays down certain rules of body posture, certain corresponding combinations of consonants and vowels, and certain forms of recitation, and in particular some passages of his book "The Light of the Intellect" give the impression of a Judaized treatise on* Yoga. *The similarity even extends to some aspects of the doctrine of ecstatic vision, as preceded and brought about by these practices. (p. 139)*

The basic elements that elicit the relaxation response in certain practices of Christianity and Judaism are also found in Islamic mysticism, or Sufism (Trimingham, 1971). Sufism developed as a reaction against the external rationalization of Islam and made use of intuitive and emotional faculties that are claimed to be dormant until they are utilized through training under the guidance of a teacher. The method of employing these faculties is known as Dhikr. It is a means of excluding distractions and drawing nearer to God by the constant repetition of His name, either silently or aloud, and by rhythmic breathing. Music, musical poems, and dance are also employed in the ritual of Dhikr, for it was noticed that they could help induce states of ecstasy. Originally, Dhikr was practiced only by members of the society who made a deliberate choice to redirect their lives to God as the preliminary step in the surrender of the will. Upon initiation to his order, the initiate received the *wird,* a secret, holy sound. The old Masters felt that the true encounter with God could not be attained by all, for most men are born deaf to mystical sensitivity. By the 12th century, however, this attitude had changed. It was realized that this ecstasy could be induced in the ordinary man in a relatively short time by rhythmic exercises involing posture, control of breath, coordinated movements, and oral repetitions (Trimingham, 1971).

In the Western world, the relaxation response elicited by religious practices was not part of the routine practice of religions, but rather was within the mystical tradition. In the East, however, meditation that elicited the relaxation response was developed much earlier and became a major element in religion and in everyday life. Writings from Indian scriptures, the Upanishads, dated sixth century B.C., note that individuals might attain "a unified state with the Brahman [the Deity] by means of restraint of breath, withdrawal of senses, meditation, concentration, contemplation and absorption" (Organ, 1970, p. 303).

A multitude of Eastern religions and ways of life, including Zen and Yoga with their many variants, can elicit the relaxation response. They employ mental and physical methods, including the repetition of a word or sound, the exclusion of meaningful thoughts, a quiet environment, and a comfortable position, and they stress the importance of a trained teacher. One of the meditative practices of Zen Buddhism, Zazen, employs a Yoga-like technique of coupling respiration and counting to 10—that is, 1 on inhaling, 2 on exhaling, and so on to 10. With time, one stops counting and simply "follows the breath" (Johnston, 1971, p. 78) in order to achieve a state of no thought, no feeling, and to be completely in nothing (Ishiguro, 1964).

Shintoism and Taoism are important religions of Japan and China. In Shintoism, one method of prayer consists of sitting quietly, inspiring through the nose, holding inspiration for a short time, and expiring through the mouth, with eyes directed toward a mirror at their level. Throughout the exercise, the priest repeats 10 numbers, or sacred words, pronounced according to the traditional religious teachings (Herbert, 1967). Fujisawa (1959) noted: "It is interesting that this grand ritual characteristic of Shintoism is doubtlessly the same process as *Yoga*" (p. 23). Taoism, one of the traditional religions of China, employs, in addition to methods similar to those of Shintoism, concentration on nothingness to achieve absolute tranquility (Chang, 1963).

Similar meditational practices are found in practically every culture of man. Shamanism, a form of mysticism associated with feelings of ecstasy, is practiced in conjunction with tribal religions in North and South America, Indonesia, Oceania, Africa, Siberia, and Japan. Each shaman has a song or chant to bring on trances, usually entering into solitude to do so. Music, especially the drum, plays an important part in shamanistic trances (Johnson, 1959).

Many less traditional religious practices are prevalent in the United States. One aim of the practices is achievement of an altered state of consciousness, which is induced by techniques similar to those that elicit the relaxation response. Subub, Nichiren Sho Shu, Hare Krishna, Scientology, Black Muslimism, Meher Baba, and the Association for Research and Enlightenment are but a few examples of such practices (Needleman, 1970).

In addition to techniques that elicit the relaxation response within a religious context, secular techniques also exist. One method often used involves gazing upon an object and keeping attention focused on that object to the exclusion of all else (Lowell, 1892; Underhill, 1957). Some people, the so-called nature mystics, have been able to elicit the relaxation response by immersing themselves in quiet—often in the quiet of nature. Wordsworth believed "that when his mind was freed from preoccupation with disturbing objects, petty cares, 'little enmities and low desires,' that he could then reach a condition of equilibrium, which he describes as a 'wise passiveness' or 'a happy stillness of the mind' " (Spurgeon, 1970, p. 61). Wordsworth believed that anyone could deliberately induce this condition in himself by a kind of relaxation of the will. Thoreau (1971) made many references to such feelings attained by sitting for hours alone with nature; indeed, Thoreau compared himself to a Yogi (Sanborn, 1894). William James (1920) described similar experiences. A treatise on other such experiences may be found in Johnson's (1959) *Watcher on the Hill.*

OBJECTIVE DATA SUPPORTING THE WIDESPREAD EXISTENCE OF THE RELAXATION RESPONSE

Physiological changes occur during the practice of various techniques that elicit the relaxation response. These changes include decreased oxygen consumption, respiratory rate, heart rate, and muscle tension, and increases in skin resistance and EEG alpha wave activity.

Autogenic training is a technique of medical therapy that is said to elicit the trophotropic response of Hess (1957) or the relaxation response. Autogenic therapy is defined as "a self-induced modification of corticodiencephalic interrelationships" that enables the lower brain centers to activate "trophotropic activity" (Luthe, 1969). The method of autogenic training is based on six psychophysiological exercises devised by a German neurologist, H. H. Shultz, which are practiced several times a day until the subject is able to shift voluntarily to a wakeful low-arousal (trophotropic) state. The "standard exercises" are practiced in a quiet environment, in a horizontal position, and with closed eyes (Luthe, 1969). Exercise 1 focuses on the feeling of heaviness in the limbs, Exercise 2 on the cultivation of the sensation of warmth in the limbs. Exercise 3 deals with cardiac regulation, while Exercise 4 consists of passive concentration on breathing. In Exercise 5, the subject cultivates the sensation of warmth in his or her upper abdomen, and Exercise 6 is the cultivation of feelings of coolness in the forehead. Exercises 1 through 4 most effectively elicit the trophotropic response, whereas Exercises 5 and 6 are reported to have different effects (Luthe, 1969). The subject's attitude toward the exercise must not be intense and compulsive but rather of a quiet, "let it happen" nature. This is referred to as *passive concentration* and is considered absolutely essential (Luthe, 1972).

Progressive relaxation (Jacobson, 1938) is a technique that seeks to achieve increased discriminative control over skeletal muscle until the subject is able to induce very low levels of tonus in the major muscle groups. Jacobson (1938), who devised the technique, states that anxiety and muscular relaxation produce opposite physiological states and therefore cannot exist together. Progressive relaxation is practiced in a supine position in a quiet room; a passive attitude is essential because mental images induce slight, measurable tensions in muscles, especially those of the eyes and face. The subject is taught to recognize even slight contractions of the muscles so that he or she can avoid them and achieve the deepest degree of relaxation possible.

Hypnosis is an artificially induced state characterized by increased suggestibility. A subject is judged to be in the hypnotic state if he or she manifests a high level of response to test suggestions such as muscle rigidity, amnesia, hallucination, anesthesia, and posthypnotic suggestion, which are used in standard scales such as that of Weitzenhoffer and Hilgard (1959). The hypnotic induction procedure usually includes suggestion (autosuggestion for self-hypnosis) of relaxation and drowsiness, closed eyes, and a recumbent or semisupine position (Barber, 1971).

Procedures for self-hypnotic and heterohypnotic induction and for elicitation of the relaxation response appear to be similar. Furthermore, before experiencing hypnotic phenomena, during either a traditional or an active induction, a physiological state exists that is comparable to the relaxation response. This state is characterized, in part, by decreased heart rate, respiratory rate, and blood pressure. After the physiological changes of the relaxation response occur, the individual proceeds to experience other exclusively hypnotic phenomena, such as perceptual distortions, age regression, posthypnotic suggestion, and amnesia (Benson, Arns, & Hoffman, 1981).

Yoga has been an important part of Indian culture for thousands of years. It is claimed to be the culmination of the efforts of ancient Hindu thinkers to "give man the fullest possible control over his mind" (Hoenig, 1968). Yoga consists of meditation practices and physical techniques, usually performed in a quiet environment, and it has many variant forms. Yoga began as Raja Yoga, which sought "union with the absolute" by meditation. Later, there was an emphasis on physical methods in attempts to achieve an altered state of consciousness; this form is termed Hatha Yoga. It has developed into a physical culture and is claimed to prevent and cure certain diseases. Essential to the practice of Hatha Yoga are appropriate posture and control of respiration (Ramamurthi, 1967). The most common posture is called the Lotus (seated on the ground with legs crossed). This posture helps the spine stay erect without strain, and it is claimed to enhance concentration. The respiratory training promotes control of the duration of inspiration and expiration and the pause between breaths, so that one eventually achieves voluntary control of respiration. Bagchi and Wenger (1957), in studies of Yoga practitioners, reported that Yoga could produce a 70% increase in skin resistance, a decreased heart rate, and increased EEG alpha wave activity. Others have included decreased oxygen consumption (Anand, Chhing, & Sinch, 1961; Sugi & Akutsu, 1968) and decreased respiratory rate (Onda, 1965). These observations led them to suggest that Yoga is "deep relaxation of a certain aspect of the autonomic nervous system without drowsiness or sleep" (Onda, 1965).

Transcendental Meditation is a form of Yoga. The technique, as taught by Maharishi Mahesh Yogi (1966), comes from the Vedic tradition of India. Instruction is given individually, and the technique is allegedly easily learned at the first instruction session. It is said to require no physical or mental control. The individual is taught a systematic method of repeating a word or sound, the mantra, without attempting to concentrate on it specifically.

Zen is very similar to Yoga, from which it developed, and is associated with the Buddhist religion (Onda, 1965). In Zen meditation, the subject is said to achieve a "controlled psychophysiologic decrease of the cerebral excitatory state" by a crossed-leg posture, closed eyes, regulation of respiration, and concentration on the Koan (an alogical problem—e.g., "What is the sound of one hand clapping?"), or by prayer and chanting. Respiration is adjusted by taking several slow, deep breaths, then inspiring briefly and forcelessly and expiring long and forcefully, with subsequent natural breathing. Any sensory perceptions or mental images are allowed to appear and leave passively. A quiet, comfortable environment is essential. Experienced Zen meditators elicit the relaxation response more efficiently than novices (Sugi & Akutsu, 1968).

A SIMPLE, NONCULTIC TECHNIQUE

Incorporating the four elements common to many historical techniques, a simple noncultic technique was developed in our laboratory (Beary & Benson, 1974). Use of the technique results in the same physiological changes that our laboratory first noted using Transcendental Meditation as a model. The instructions for this noncultic technique are as follows:

1. Sit quietly in a comfortable position and close your eyes.
2. Deeply relax all your muscles, beginning at your feet and progressing up to your face. Keep them deeply relaxed.
3. Breathe through your nose. Become aware of your breathing. As you breathe out, say the word *one* silently to yourself; for example, breathe in . . . out, *one;* in . . . out, *one;* and so forth. Continue for 20 minutes. You may open your eyes to check the time, but do not use an alarm. When you finish, sit quietly for several minutes, at first with closed eyes and later with opened eyes.
4. Do not worry about whether you are successful in achieving a deep level of relaxation. Maintain a passive attitude and permit relaxation to occur at its own pace. Expect other thoughts. When these distracting thoughts occur, ignore them by thinking "Oh well" and continue repeating "one." With practice, the response should come with little effort. Practice the technique once or twice daily, but not within two hours after any meal, since the digestive processes seem to interfere with the subjective changes.

CLINICAL USEFULNESS OF THE RELAXATION RESPONSE

The continual stresses of contemporary living have led to excessive elicitation of the fight-or-flight response (Gutmann & Benson, 1971). Within the constructs of our society, the behavioral features of this response, running or fighting, are often inappropriate. Indeed, excessive and inappropriate arousal of the fight-or-flight response, with its corresponding sympathetic nervous system activation, may have a role in the pathogenesis and exacerbation of several disorders. Regular elicitation of the relaxation response may be of preventive and therapeutic value in diseases in which increased sympathetic nervous system activity is implicated.

   Several longitudinal investigations have demonstrated that regular elicitation of the relaxation response lowers blood pressure in both pharmacologically treated and untreated hypertensive patients (Benson, Marzetta, & Rosner, 1974a, 1974b; Datey, Deshmukh, Dalvi, & Vinekar, 1969; Patel 1973, 1975; Stone & DeLeo 1976). In an early investigation done by our laboratory, would-be initiates of Transcendental Meditation who were also hypertensive volunteered to participate in the study (Benson et al., 1974a, 1974b). Baseline measurements of blood pressure were taken weekly for approximately 6 weeks, after which the subjects were taught to bring forth the relaxation response through the practice of Transcendental Meditation. Of the 36 patients included in the study, 22 received no medication during the investigation and 14 remained on unaltered antihypertensive medications during both the baseline and the experimental periods. In the 22 nonmedicated subjects, control blood pressures averaging 146.5 mmHg systolic and 94.6 mmHg diastolic decreased significantly to 139.5 mmHg systolic ($p < 0.001$) and 90.8 mmHg diastolic ($p < 0.002$) after regular elicitation of the relaxation response through the practice of Transcendental Meditation. In the 14 patients who maintained constant antihypertensive medications, mean control blood pressures of 145.6 mmHg systolic and 91.9 mmHg diastolic dropped significantly to 135.0 mmHg systolic ($p < 0.01$) and 87.0 mmHg diastolic ($p < 0.05$) postintervention.

   Several other researchers report similar findings. Datey and co-workers (1969) noted decreases in both systolic and diastolic blood pressures in 47 hypertensive patients who evoked the relaxation response through the practice of another Yogic technique, called Shavasan. In this study, subjects served as their own controls. Information was not reported, however, regarding the length of the preintervention control period and the number of control blood pressure measurements made.

In several well-controlled longitudinal investigations, Patel (1973, 1975; Patel & Carruthers, 1977; Patel, Marmot, & Terry, 1981) combined Yogic relaxation with biofeedback techniques in the treatment of 20 hypertensive patients on antihypertensive medication. In one study, the average systolic blood pressure in these subjects was reduced by 20.4 ± 11.4 mmHg, while mean diastolic pressure was reduced by 14.2 ± 7.5 mmHg ($p < 0.001$). A hypertensive control group matched for age and sex was employed. Length of testing sessions, number of attendances, and the procedure for measuring the blood pressure of the control group were identical to those of the treatment group. Control patients were not given instruction in the relaxation technique, however, but simply were asked to rest on a couch. No significant changes in blood pressure occurred in the control group. (Also see Patel, Chapter 54 of this Handbook.)

Further substantiation of the usefulness of the relaxation response in the treatment of hypertension has come from Stone and DeLeo (1976), who obtained significant decreases in systolic and diastolic blood pressures using a Buddhist meditation exercise. The control group, which received no psychotherapeutic intervention, was matched for blood pressure, age, and race, and exhibited virtually no change in systolic and diastolic pressures.

Another example of the clinical usefulness of the relaxation response is that it reduces the number of premature ventricular contractions (PVCs) (Benson, Alexander, & Feldman, 1975). Participating in a study were 11 nonmedicated ambulatory patients who had proven ischemic heart disease of at least 1 year's duration, with documented relatively stable PVCs. Frequent PVCs are correlated with an increased mortality in such patients (Desai, Hershberg, & Alexander, 1973; Tominaga, Blackburn, & Coronary Drug Project Research Group, 1973). The frequency of the PVCs was measured over 48 consecutive hours, after which the subjects were taught to elicit the relaxation response by using the noncultic technique described earlier. After 4 weeks of regularly practicing the relaxation technique and recording their frequency of practice, the patients returned to repeat the 2 days of monitoring.

A reduced frequency of PVCs was observed in 8 of the 11 patients. Before the intervention, the PVCs per hour per patient for the total group had averaged 151.5 for the entire monitoring session. Four weeks after the intervention was instituted, the average PVCs per hour per patient dropped to 131.7. The reduction of PVCs was even more marked during sleep. Initially, the number of PVCs per hour per patient during sleeping hours averaged 125.5, whereas after 4 weeks of regular elicitation of the relaxation response, the PVCs during sleep decreased to 87.9 ($p < 0.05$). When the PVCs were expressed per 1,000 heartbeats per patient for the entire group, there was a significant decrease during sleeping hours from 29.0 to 21.1 ($p < 0.05$).

The results suggest that regular elicitation of the relaxation response, with its hypothesized accompanying decreased sympathetic nervous system activity, may have been the mechanism by which PVCs were reduced. This finding is consistent with that of Lown, Temte, Reich, et al. (1976), who reported in a recent case study that a patient was able to abolish his arrhythmias by meditation. These results were attributed to lessened sympathetic tone (Lown, Tykocinski, Garfein, 1973), although others (Weiss, Lattin, & Engelman, 1975) implicate increased parasympathetic activity as a mechanism for the reduction of PVCs.

USEFULNESS OF THE RELAXATION RESPONSE IN PREVENTION OF DISEASE

An experiment conducted at the corporate offices of a manufacturing firm investigated the effects of daily relaxation breaks on five self-reported measures of health, performance, and well-being (Peters, Benson, & Porter, 1977). For 12 weeks, 126 volunteers filled out daily records and reported biweekly for additional measurements. After 4 weeks of baseline monitoring, they were divided randomly into three groups. Group A was taught a technique for producing the relaxation response; Group B was instructed to sit quietly; and Group C received no instructions. Groups A and B were asked to take two 15-minute relaxation breaks daily. After an 8-week experimental period, the greatest mean improvements on every index occurred in Group A; the least improvements occurred in Group C; and Group B was intermediate. Differences between the mean changes in Groups A versus C reached statistical significance ($p < 0.05$) on four of five indices: Symptoms, Illness Days, Performance, and Sociability-Satisfaction. Improvements on a Happiness-Unhappiness index were not significantly different among the three groups. The relationship between amount of change and rate of practicing the relaxation response was different for the different indices. Although fewer than three practice periods per week produced little change on any index, two daily sessions appeared to be more practice than was necessary for many individuals to achieve positive changes. Somatic symptoms and performance responded with less practice of the relaxation response than did behavioral symptoms and measures of well-being.

During the baseline period, mean systolic blood pressures were 119.7, 118.4, and 114.2 mmHg for Groups A, B, and C, respectively; mean diastolic pressures were 78.7, 76.8, and 75.7 (Peters, Benson, & Peters, 1977). Between the first and the last measurements, mean changes in systolic blood pressure were −11.6, −6.5, and +0.4 mmHg in Groups A, B, and C; and mean diastolic blood pressure decreased by 7.9, 3.1, and 0.3. Between the 4-week baseline period and the last 4 weeks of the experimental period, mean systolic blood pressure decreased by 6.7, 2.6, and 0.5, while mean diastolic blood pressure decreased by 5.2, 2.0, and 1.2. For both systolic blood pressure and diastolic blood pressure, mean changes in Group A were significantly greater than those in Group B ($p < 0.05$) and those in Group C ($p < 0.001$). The same pattern of changes among the three groups was exhibited by both sexes, by all ages, and at all initial levels of blood pressure. In general, however, within Group A, the higher the initial blood pressure was, the greater was the decrease. Thus, blood pressure within the "normal" range was significantly lowered after regular elicitation of the relaxation response. This finding may have significant implications for primary prevention of hypertension.

RECENT FINDINGS

Although the physiological changes of the relaxation response are consistent with decreased sympathetic nervous system activity, direct measurement of plasma norepinephrine during elicitation of the response did not reveal significant decreases in the concentration of this hormone (Michaels, Haber, & McCann, 1976). Indeed, some researchers have found increased levels of plasma norepinephrine in subjects who regularly elicit the relaxation response (Lang, Dehof, Meurer, & Kaufmann, 1979).

Recent physiological data resolve the apparent paradox of unchanged or increased plasma norepinephrine levels associated with elicitation of the relaxation response (Hoffman, Benson, Arns, Stainbrook, Landsberg, Young, & Gill, 1982). Sympathetic nervous system reactivity was assessed in 10 experimental and 9 control subjects who were exposed to graded orthostatic and isometric stress on monthly hospital visits. Between visits, experimental subjects practiced a technique that elicited the relaxation response, whereas control subjects sat quietly for an equivalent time. Heart rate and blood pressure reactions to the graded stresses did not differ between visits in either group. In the experimental group, however, the levels of plasma norepinephrine corresponding to graded stresses were significantly augmented after elicitation of the relaxation response. No changes in plasma norepinephrine levels were noted in the control group. After completion of this phase, these results were then replicated in the control group in a crossover experiment; that is, heart rate and blood pressure responses were unchanged but plasma norepinephrine levels were significantly higher after this group crossed over and elicited the relaxation response. Hence, repeated elicitation of the relaxation response resulted in enhanced sympathetic nervous system reactivity to orthostatic and isometric stress that was not reflected in larger heart rate and blood pressure responses. These observations are most consistent with reduced norepinephrine end-organ responsivity.

CONCLUSIONS

Although emphasis has been placed on the processes by which stress may lead to disease states through elicitation of the fight-or-flight response, we should be aware of the beneficial, healthful aspects of an alternative response—the relaxation response. The relaxation response is a valuable adjunct to our current therapies, and it may also be useful as a preventive measure. This response can be elicited by nonreligious or noncultic techniques or by other methods that patients may prefer. A religious patient, for example, might select meditative prayer as the most appropriate method for bringing forth the relaxation response. The freedom to choose a technique that conforms to a patient's personal beliefs should enhance compliance. Elicitation of the relaxation response is a simple and natural phenomenon to use in counteracting the harmful effects of stress. It does not require complex equipment for monitoring of physiological events, and it does not involve the expense and side effects of drugs. The implications for disease prevention and health enhancement are clearly worthy of further study.

REFERENCES

Abrahams, V. C., Hilton, S. M., Zbrozyna, A. W. Active muscle vasodilatation produced by stimulation of the brain stem: Its significance in the defense reaction. *Journal of Physiology,* 1960, **154,** 491–513.

Allison, J. Respiration changes during Transcendental Meditation. *Lancet,* 1970, **1,** 833–834.

Anand, B. K., Chhing, G. S., & Singh, B. Studies on Shri Ramananda Yogi during his stay in an air-tight box. *Indian Journal of Medical Research,* 1961, **49,** 82–89.

Anonymous. *A Benedictine of Stanbrook Abbey: Mediaeval mystical tradition and Saint John of the Cross.* London: Burns and Oates, 1954.

Bagchi, B. K., & Wenger, M. A. Electrophysiological correlations of some Yoga exercises. *Electroencephalography and Clinical Neurophysiology,* 1957, 7(Suppl.), 132–149.

Barber, T. X. Physiological effects of hypnosis and suggestion. In *Biofeedback and self-control 1970.* New York: Aldine-Atherton, 1971.

Beary, J. F., & Benson, H. A simple psychophysiologic technique which elicits the hypometabolic changes of the relaxation response. *Psychosomatic Medicine,* 1974, **36,** 115–120.

Benson, H. *The relaxation response.* New York: Morrow, 1975.

Benson, H., Alexander, S., & Feldman, C. L. Decreased premature ventricular contractions through use of the relaxation response in patients with stable ischemic heart disease. *Lancet,* 1975, **2,** 380–382.

Benson, H., Arns, P. A., & Hoffman, J. W. The relaxation response and hypnosis. *International Journal of Clinical and Experimental Hypnosis,* 1981, **29,** 259–270.

Benson, H., Beary, J. F., & Carol, M. P. The relaxation response. *Psychiatry,* 1974, **37,** 37–46.

Benson, H., Marzetta, B. R., & Rosner, B. A. Decreased blood pressure in borderline hypertensive subjects who practiced meditation. *Journal of Chronic Diseases,* 1974, **27,** 163–169. (a)

Benson, H., Marzetta, B. R., & Rosner, B. A. Decreased blood pressure in pharmacologically treated hypertensive patients who regularly elicited the relaxation response. *Lancet,* 1974, **1,** 289–291.

Bokser, R. B. Z. *From the world of the cabbalah.* New York: Philosophical Library, 1954.

Cannon, W. B. The emergency function of the adrenal medulla in pain and the major emotions. *American Journal of Physiology,* 1914, **33,** 356–372.

Chang, C-Y. *Creativity and Taoism.* New York: Julian Press, 1963.

Datey, K. K., Deshmukh, S. N., Dalvi, C. P., & Vinekav, S. L. "Shavasan": A Yogic exercise in the management of hypertension. *Angiology,* 1969, **20,** 325–333.

Desai, D., Hershberg, P. I., & Alexander, S. Clinical significance of ventricular premature beats in an out-patient population. *Chest,* 1973, **64,** 564.

French, R. M. (Trans.). *The way of a pilgrim.* New York: Seabury Press, 1968.

Fujisawa, C. *Zen and Shinto.* New York: Philosophical Library, 1959.

Gellhorn, E. *Principles of automatic-somatic interactions.* Minneapolis: University of Minnesota Press, 1967.

Gutmann, M. C., & Benson, H. Interaction of environmental factors and systemic arterial blood pressure: A review. *Medicine,* 1971, **50,** 543–553.

Herbert, J. *Shinto: At the fountain-head of Japan.* London: Allen and Unwin, 1967.

Hess, W. R. *Functional organization of the diencephalon.* New York: Grune & Stratton, 1957.

Hess, W. R., & Brugger, M. Das subkortikale Zentrum der afferktiven Abwehrreaktion. *Helvetica Physiolica Acta,* 1943, **1,** 33–52.

Hoenig, J. Medical research on Yoga. *Confinia Psychiatrica,* 1968, **11,** 69–89.

Hoffman, J. W., Benson, H., Arns, P. A., Stainbrook, G. L., Landsberg, L., Young, J. B., & Gill, A. Reduced sympathetic nervous system responsivity associated with the relaxation response. *Science,* 1982, **215,** 190–192.

Ishiguro, H. *The scientific truth of Zen.* Tokyo: Zenrigaku Society, 1964.

Jacobson, E. *Progressive relaxation.* Chicago: University of Chicago Press, 1938.

James, W. *Letters.* Boston: Atlantic Monthly Press, 1920.

Johnson, R. C. *Watcher on the hill.* New York: Harper and Brothers, 1959.

Johnston, W. *Christian Zen.* New York: Harper & Row, 1971.

Lang, R., Dehof, K., Meurer, K. A., & Kaufmann, W. Sympathetic activity and Transcendental Meditation. *Journal of Neural Transmission,* 1979, **44,** 117–135.

Levander, V. L., Benson, H., Wheeler, R. C., & Wallace, R. K. Increased forearm blood flow during a wakeful hypometabolic state. *Federal Proceedings,* 1972, **31,** 405.

Lowell, P. *The soul of the Far East.* Boston: Houghton Mifflin, 1892.

Lown, B., Temte, J. V., Reich, P., et al. Basis for recurring ventricular fibrillation in the absence of coronary heart disease and its management. *New England Journal of Medicine,* 1976, **294,** 623–629.

Lown, B., Tykocinski, M., Garfein, A., et al. Sleep and ventricular premature beats. *Circulation,* 1973, **48,** 691.

Luthe, W. (Ed.). *Autogenic therapy* (Vols. 1–5). New York: Grune & Stratton, 1969.

Luthe, W. Autogenic therapy: Excerpts on applications to cardiovascular disorders and hypercholesterolemia. In *Biofeedback and Self-Control 1971.* New York: Aldine-Atherton, 1972.

Maharishi Mahesh Yogi. *The science of being and art of living.* London: International SRM Publications, 1966.

Michaels, R. R., Haber, M. J., & McCann, D. S. Evaluation of transcendental meditation as a method of reducing stress. *Science,* 1976, **192,** 1242–1244.

Needleman, J. *The new religions.* Garden City, N.Y.: Doubleday, 1970.

Norwich, J. J., & Sitwell, R. *Mount Athos.* New York: Harper & Row, 1966.

Onda, A. Autogenic training and Zen. In W. Luthe (Ed.), *Autogenic training* (International ed.). New York: Grune & Stratton, 1965.

Organ, T. W. *The Hindu quest for the perfection of man.* Athens: Ohio University Press, 1970.

Osuna, Fray Francisco de. *The third spiritual alphabet.* London: Benziger, 1931.

Patel, C. H. Yoga and biofeedback in the management of hypertension. *Lancet,* 1973, **2,** 1053–1055.

Patel, C. H. Twelve-month follow-up of Yoga and biofeedback in the management of hypertension. *Lancet,* 1975, **1,** 62–64.

Patel, C., & Carruthers, M. Coronary risk factor reduction through biofeedback-aided relaxation and meditation. *Journal of the Royal College of General Practitioners,* 1977, **27,** 401–405.

Patel, C., Marmot, M. G., & Terry, D. J. Controlled trial of biofeedback-aided behavioral methods in reducing mild hypertension. *British Medical Journal,* 1981, **282,** 2005–2008.

Peters, R. K., Benson, H., & Peters, J. M. Daily relaxation response breaks in a working population: II. Effects on blood pressure. *American Journal of Public Health,* 1977, **67,** 954–959.

Peters, R. K., Benson, H., & Porter, D. Daily relaxation response breaks in a working population: I. Effects on self-reported measures of health, performance, and well-being. *American Journal of Public Health,* 1977, **67,** 946–953.

Progoff, I. (Ed. & Trans.). *The cloud of unknowing.* New York: Julian Press, 1969.

Ramamurthi, B. Yoga: An explanation and probable neurophysiology, *Journal of the Indian Medical Association,* 1967, **48,** 167–170.

Ross, F. H. *Shinto: The way of Japan,* Boston: Beacon Press, 1965.

Saint Terese of Avila. *The way of perfection* (A. R. Waller, Ed.). London: J. M. Dent, 1901.

Sanborn, F. B. *Familiar letters of Henry David Thoreau.* Boston: Houghton, Mifflin, 1894.

Scholem, G. G. *Jewish mysticism.* New York: Schocken Books, 1967.

Spurgeon, C. F. E. *Mysticism in English literature.* Port Washington, N.Y.: Kennikat Press, 1970.

Stone, R. A., & DeLeo, J. Psychotherapeutic control of hypertension. *New England Journal of Medicine,* 1976, **294,** 80–84.

Sugi, Y., & Akutsu, K. Studies on respiration and energy-metabolism during sitting in Zazen. *Research Journal of Physical Education,* 1968, **12,** 190–206.

Thoreau, H. D. *Walden.* Princeton: Princeton University Press, 1971.

Tominaga, S., Blackburn, H., & Coronary Drug Project Research Group. Prognostic importance of premature beats following myocardial infarction. *Journal of the American Medical Association,* 1973, **223,** 1116.

Trimingham, J. S. *Sufi orders in Islam.* Oxford: Clarendon Press, 1971.

Underhill, E. *Mysticism.* London: Methuen, 1957.

Wallace, R. K. Physiological effects of Transcendental Meditation. *Science,* 1970, **167,** 1751–1754.

Wallace, R. K., & Benson, H. The physiology of meditation. *Scientific American,* 1972, **226,** 85–90.

Wallace, R. K., Benson, H., & Wilson, A. F. A wakeful hypometabolic state. *American Journal of Physiology,* 1971, **221,** 795–799.

Weiss, T., Lattin, G. W., & Engelman, K. Vagally mediated suppression of premature ventricular contractions in man. *American Heart Journal,* 1975, **89,** 700.

Weitzenhoffer, A. M., & Hilgard, E. *Stanford Hypnotic Suggestibility Scale.* Palo Alto: Consulting Psychologists Press, 1959.

CHAPTER 22

BEHAVIOR MODIFICATION AND HEALTH ENHANCEMENT

MARGARET A. CHESNEY

SRI International, Menlo Park, California

Behavior modification is a cornerstone of behavioral health. They share the heritage of behavioral science, which in the last several decades has sought to identify principles that could be used to explain and influence human behavior. Behavior modification attempts to apply these principles by manipulating the relationships between behavior and environmental events so that desirable behaviors increase and undesirable ones decrease. Early in its development, behavior modification was applied to such important health behaviors as weight control and cigarette-smoking cessation. Now, as the field of behavioral health is burgeoning, the potential application of behavior modification to health enhancement is enormous. This chapter will introduce behavior modification by providing a brief history of its development. Following this introductory section, the major principles upon which behavior modification is based will be described. In the final section, the procedures by which behavior modification is applied to health enhancement will be illustrated by examples drawn from the behavioral health literature.

HISTORICAL PERSPECTIVE

Behavior modification is based on the extensive learning and conditioning research that views behavior as a result of interactions between organisms and the environment. Historically, two orientations to this interaction resulted in a division of the field into two schools of thought with regard to the processes underlying learning: operant conditioning and respondent conditioning.

Thorndike (1898, 1913) laid the foundation for one of these orientations with his assertion that behavior can be strengthened or weakened by its consequences. Subsequently, an impressive line of theorists and researchers, including Tolman (1932), Hull (1943), and Dollard and Miller (1950), contributed to this formulation of the organism–environment interaction. It was the research of Skinner, however, and most notably his book *Science and Human Behavior* (1953), that established the concept that behaviors are emitted by the organism in relation to certain environmental factors that either reinforce the behaviors or fail to do so. Thus, what a person does—his or her response—is central to obtaining reinforcement. Skinner labeled a behavior that operates on the environment to produce a reinforcing effect an *operant*. Hence, operant conditioning focuses on responses or operants and argues that responses followed by reinforcers are likely to be manifested again; that is, the more we reinforce these operants, the more they will be manifested. Influenced by Skinner's innovative theories and confirmatory laboratory demonstrations of operant learning and conditioning, such collaborators as Ayllon and Azrin (1964), Ferster (1966), and Lindsley (1966) took his principles to the clinic and began modifying behavior by changing environmental contingencies of reinforcement. Since these initial behavior modification efforts, the application of behavior modification and operant techniques in treatment, rehabilitation, and education has proliferated. This proliferation is demonstrated by the numerous journals, compendia, and annual reviews of behavior modification that cite recent advances in techniques and document an increase in the application of operant conditioning technology in diverse disciplines, including education, business, psychology, psychiatry, and medicine.

An alternative perspective of the interaction between the organism and the environment is reflected in respondent conditioning. Pavlov (1927) and Sherrington (1906) were respondent conditioning's counterparts to Thorndike and Skinner. Rather than focusing on the environmental events following behavioral responses, Pavlov and others attended to the environmental events that regularly precede and elicit reflexive or relatively fixed and stereotyped responses in the organism, such as the salivation response to food or the knee-jerk response to patellar tap. These researchers demonstrated how new stimuli would acquire the ability to elicit responses after being paired with the initial eliciting environmental event. Wolpe (1958), influenced by the work of Sherrington, conducted laboratory studies eliciting emotional fear responses in cats to neutral stimuli by pairing the neutral stimuli with innately feared stimuli. In his book *Psychotherapy by Reciprocal Inhibition,* Wolpe described the transition from the laboratory to the clinic setting and the application of conditioning principles to the understanding and treatment of neurotic anxiety responses, which would be considered behavioral disorders. Therapeutic approaches such as Wolpe's, which are based on respondent or classical conditioning, including desensitization, are forerunners of the relaxation strategies applied in behavioral medicine, discussed in Chapters 21 and 54.

The immense advance in behavior modification over the past 25 years precludes a complete review of principles, strategies, and applications in a single chapter. Instead, because behavior modification draws the majority of its techniques and methodology from operant conditioning, this chapter will provide an outline of those operant conditioning principles and methods that are most likely to be of use to the health professional.

PRINCIPLES OF BEHAVIOR MODIFICATION

Over the past several decades, an impressive body of knowledge from animal laboratory and human experimental investigations has provided insights into the principles that determine the acquisition, maintenance, and modification of behavior. The principles that apply to the addition of new behaviors as well as to the elimination of undesired behaviors will be described in this section.

The Acquisition of New Behavior

Reinforcement is the central factor in the acquisition of new behavior. Three requirements are necessary for reinforcement strategies to be effective (Bandura, 1969): (a) the reinforcer must have incentive value; (b) the reinforcing events must be contingent on the desired behavior; and (c) the desired behavior must be elicited or emitted for it to be reinforced. Reinforcers, by definition, always increase the frequency of a behavior. Conversely, if a behavior occurs frequently, it can be assumed that the behavior is being reinforced in some way. A *positive* reinforcer is an event, behavior, or object that will increase the frequency of any behavior on which it is contingent. A *negative* reinforcer is not a punishment; rather, it is an event whose contingent withdrawal increases the rate of behavior. A few events or items, such as food, rest, and shelter, are primary positive reinforcers. Similarly, a few events, such as pain and discomfort, are primary negative reinforcers; the cessation of pain will increase the frequency of the behavior that was associated with the elimination of pain. The majority of reinforcers are acquired secondarily—that is, by a history of association with primary reinforcers or with items or events that already function as reinforcers. It is through this association that such events as praise, smiling, and the very presence of certain individuals come to be reinforcing. As a result of our different learning histories, events that are reinforcing for one person are not necessarily reinforcing for another. Each of us has a unique inventory of reinforcers. Perhaps because of these individual differences, extensive use has been made of Premack's (1965) differential probability principle in selecting reinforcers. This principle refers to the phenomenon that preferred activities occurring with a high probability, such as eating, can be used as reinforcers by making their performance contingent on the performance of the less preferred activity. This is actually the age-honored principle that underlies many parental rules—for example, "You can have dessert after you eat your vegetables."

Contingencies must be arranged between performance of the desired behavior and the reinforcement. Finding appropriate reinforcers with sufficient incentive value will not ensure their effectiveness. Reinforcement must be perceived as contingent on a behavior for the reinforcement to have an effect. It has been clearly demonstrated that noncontingent reinforcement fails to increase the desired behavior, whereas contingent application of the same reinforcer will exert control. Thus, if the feedback of a good dental checkup is not made contingent on good dental hygiene, individuals are less likely to improve their dental hygiene than they are if they are given positive feedback on the health status associated with their performance of good health habits.

Not only must the reinforcement be perceived as contingent on behavior, but temporal aspects are also important in determining the impact of reinforcement. In general, the degree of control exerted by reinforcement decreases with increased delay following the target behavior. Delays permit irrelevant or even detrimental behaviors to intervene between the performance of the desired behavior and its reinforcement. In such cases, the reinforcement can be inaccurately perceived as contingent on an intervening behavior, which may result in strengthening of a form of behavior that is undesirable.

The desired behavior must be produced before it can be reinforced. Selection of powerful incentives and skillful application of contingencies will be of little consequence unless the desired behavior is emitted by the individual. For many health behaviors, such as exercise and management of dietary intake, the individual already has the skills required for health enhancement, and all that is needed is contingent application of incentives to increase and maintain the desired response pattern. If the existing level of frequency of the desired behavior, such as exercise, is low, however, it is important not to make reinforcement contingent on a high level of performance. If the criterion is set too high, most, if not all, of the individual's efforts will go unrewarded and will gradually fade. Instead, a procedure referred to as *shaping,* or *successive approximation,* is advocated. This strategy involves initially adopting a low criterion for reinforcement, so that responses to be rewarded are within the person's capabilities but may represent only a fraction of the final desired behavior. As aspects of the desired behavior are performed, the criterion for reinforcement is successively increased, so that closer and closer approximations of the final desired behavior are being reinforced. Individuals who have an ultimate goal of exercising 40 minutes three times each week, for example, may begin by reinforcing themselves for exercising 10 minutes three times each week and successively lengthen the time required for reinforcement each week until 40 minutes is achieved.

Graduated modeling provides an effective alternative for teaching new, complex behaviors. When the behavior to be learned is complex, shaping or successive approximation alone can be very time-consuming. Consider the steps involved in learning surgical skills or playing a musical instrument. For tasks such as these, and for many others, learning occurs by observing someone else, a model, performing the task. In modeling, complex patterns of behavior are conveyed as integrated sequences. There is an extensive body of literature on modeling (Bandura, 1969; Rosenthal & Bandura, 1978), to which the interested reader is referred. Of the procedures that have been developed, graduated and participant modeling have considerable applicability to health enhancement. Graduated modeling is a strategy incorporating the concept of shaping, in that models graduate or order the behaviors performed so that the subject or patient is led to practice and to be reinforced for behaviors that are progressively more and more similar to the final target behavior. In participant modeling, the model is present, demonstrating and either verbally or physically guiding the patient or subject in performing the desired behaviors.

The Elimination of Undesired Behavior

Behaviors that are considered undesirable or detrimental can be eliminated or their frequency or intensity can be reduced through the use of punishing consequences. Punishment may consist of the removal of positive reinforcers or the presentation of aversive events (Azrin & Holz, 1966). Laboratory and field research indicate that withholding positive reinforcers may be a more effective strategy for behavior change than the use of aversive events, because aversive events more often make the recipient of the punishment anxious, resentful, or angry, whereas withdrawal of positive reinforcement usually does not have these negative results. Research on punishment has also demonstrated that elimination of detrimental behavior is most effectively achieved by punishment when competing response patterns are rewarded simultaneously. Thus, if reduction of dietary sodium is desired, a person might withhold praise from the cook for a dish with a salty sauce while reinforcing the family chef with praise for using more herbs for seasoning.

Applied Behavior Analysis

Aside from the foregoing principles and related techniques, the operant approach has given behavior modification specific methodological characteristics, including the focus on individual subjects; the assessment of clearly defined, overt target behaviors; and the focus on antecedents and consequences in understanding and modifying behavior. The strategy that encompasses these characteristics is known as applied behavior analysis (Baer, Wolf, & Risley, 1968; Kazdin, 1978). This strategy involves identifying a specific target behavior to be modified (e.g., increasing physical activity) and observation of the current behavior, its antecedents, and its consequences. Following the observation period, strategies are imposed to modify the behavior by changing the environmental antecedents and consequences.

Antecedent events influence behavior in a manner similar to consequences. Antecedent events promote or cue behavior by identifying the conditions under which a behavior will be reinforced or not reinforced. Cues of this kind are called discriminative stimuli, because they help to discriminate the appropriate conditions for particular behaviors. Thus, finishing a meal and having a cup of coffee is an antecedent or cue for many smokers to light cigarettes, whereas taking a shower is not such a cue. Much of our behavior comes under the control of antecedent stimuli, and one strategy for modifying behavior is stimulus control, whereby antecedent stimuli or cues are manipulated to increase desirable behaviors and to decrease undesirable behaviors. Many people salt food before tasting it, for example, because they see the salt shaker on the table. A stimulus control strategy to reduce sodium intake would be to remove the cue—the salt shaker—from the table.

In applied behavioral analysis, the consequences that maintain existing behaviors receive emphasis. As mentioned previously, behaviors that occur with some frequency, even behaviors associated with health risk, are being reinforced. Hypertensive individuals, for example, may skip their prescribed blood pressure medication because taking the medication is associated with negative side effects. In this instance, nonadherence is negatively reinforced by the absence of side effects. Similarly, cigarette smoking is often maintained by the reinforcing effects of nicotine for nicotine addiction, as well as by the lower weight associated with cigarette consumption. It is essential to identify the consequences that maintain existing behavior patterns in order to devise effective contingency management systems that will modify the behavior.

Maintenance of Behavior Change

The principles and related strategies outlined earlier have been shown to be effective in changing behavior; however, maintaining behavior after the initial reinforcement program is withdrawn has been found to be a problem. Typically, behaviors revert back to or approach preintervention levels (for review, see Kazdin, 1975, 1977; Stokes & Baer, 1977). Perhaps the most straightforward strategy for maintaining behavior change is continuing the reinforcement. In this regard, intermittent schedules of reinforcement—that is, when less than every occurrence of a behavior is reinforced—should be used. Such schedules repeatedly have been shown to be superior to continuous schedules in maintaining new behaviors (Ferster & Skinner, 1957). An alternative strategy that is particularly relevant to health enhancement is the use of self-control techniques. Self-reinforcement programs have received increasing attention in recent years, particularly in the realm of such health behaviors as weight reduction and smoking cessation. Individuals can be trained in self-monitoring and self-management so that when they observe their health behaviors lapsing to preintervention levels, they can perform a self-behavior analysis and reinstitute their behavior change strategies to reestablish health-enhancing behaviors. Such self-control strategies are described thoroughly by Thoresen and Mahoney (1974) in their book *Behavioral Self-Control* and in the Self-Management Psychology Series, edited by Carl Thoresen of Stanford University (Thoresen, Note 1).

Self-Efficacy

The various behavioral treatment and maintenance strategies discussed in this chapter have shown mixed success. In some cases, certain behavioral approaches are superior to others; in other cases, behavioral approaches with remarkably good track records fail to produce effects. Bandura (1977) has proposed a theory to account for this variability in therapeutic effectiveness. This theory asserts that behavioral treatments create and strengthen a person's expectation of personal effectiveness. Expectations of efficacy influence people's choices of activities, how hard they will strive to accomplish a task, and how long they will persist despite difficulties. Expectations of self-efficacy are based on four primary sources of information: personal performance accomplishments, observing others' accomplishments, verbal persuasion or other types of social influence, and states of physiological arousal from which individuals judge their anxiety, health, and vulnerability.

Empirical tests of this theory (Bandura, Adams, & Beyer, 1977) have confirmed that treatments are more effective when they provide dependable sources of information about personal efficacy, thus increasing self-efficacy. Treatments that allow people to engage in graduated participant modeling and experience personal accomplishment, for example, have been shown to produce greater improvement in the self-efficacy of overcoming a fear than treatments that involve observing a model performing the feared activity or undertaking a relaxation-based fear reduction approach (systematic desensitization). In these studies, self-efficacy has been found to predict accurately the extent of change resulting from various behavior modification treatments, suggesting that self-efficacy is a common cognitive mechanism that regulates overt behavior. Thus, it appears that health behavior modification programs that incorporate elements for increasing self-efficacy will be more successful in enhancing health.

BEHAVIOR MODIFICATION PROGRAMS FOR HEALTH ENHANCEMENT

The application of behavior modification to health enhancement can best be illustrated by describing actual programs that are designed to promote health through behavioral strategies. Several such programs will be described in this section, with an emphasis on features that rely on behavior modification principles.

Behavioral Control of Obesity

In 1979, Albert Stunkard wrote: "Obesity occupies a central position in the concerns of behavioral medicine" (p. 279). As Stunkard points out, behavioral approaches to obesity predate behavioral medicine as a field. In 1962, Ferster, Nurnberger, and Levitt wrote their classic paper, "Behavioral Control of Eating," applying operant conditioning principles to eating behavior. It was a report by Stuart in 1967, however, that triggered widespread interest in the topic. This report describes the best results obtained to that time in the outpatient treatment of obesity, and it constitutes a landmark in our understanding of this disorder. The operant principles Stuart applied now form the foundation of commercial programs to treat obesity. Each week, 4 million people receive behavior modification for obesity under lay auspices (Stunkard, 1979), and thousands more receive similar treatment from health professionals. Comprehensive descriptions of behavioral approaches to the treatment of obesity and weight management are beyond the scope of this chapter; the interested reader is referred to detailed descriptions by Mahoney and Mahoney (1976) and to the manuals by Stuart (1972) and Ferguson (1975). Recent programs have evolved to incorporate increased physical activity, restructuring of cognitions, and systematic nutrition education. These additions have not substantively enhanced the effectiveness of the treatment as initially described by Stuart according to operant principles.

One program that is representative of those based on Stuart's approach was developed at the University of Pennsylvania (Penick, Filion, Fox, & Stunkard, 1971). This program consists of four stages that represent the applied behavioral analysis strategy described earlier in this chapter:

1. Description of target behavior
2. Control of the environmental antecedents
3. Development of new eating behavior
4. Manipulation of the environmental consequences

In the first stage, description of target behavior, patients are instructed to keep detailed records of their eating. Each time they eat, they are to write down the food, the time of day, the location, the people they were with, and the feelings they were experiencing.

In the second stage, control of the environmental antecedents, an analysis of the dietary records identifies stimuli or events that precede and may cue the eating. Examples of such stimuli acting as cues are high-calorie foods in sight or present in the pantry and behaviors that are associated with eating, such as watching television. Based on an examination of the individual's dietary record, stimulus control procedures would be agreed upon to reduce the number and salience of the stimuli that control eating. Families are encouraged, for example, not to have high-calorie foods on hand, and eating is restricted to one place, such as the dining room.

In the third stage, development of new eating behavior, patients are instructed, through modeling and behavioral description, to modify their actual eating behavior. They are taught to reduce the speed of their eating, to focus on their food, and to stop combining eating with other activities, such as reading or watching television, that interfere with focusing on the food.

The fourth stage of the program is manipulation of environmental consequences. In the University of Pennsylvania program, separate reinforcements are used for weight loss and for behavior changes. Patients give themselves points for carrying out such new eating behaviors as putting utensils down between bites or eating in one location. These points serve as immediate reinforcement for healthy behaviors and are later converted into tangible rewards. In addition, patients establish contracts in which rewards are to be earned with loss of weight per se.

Long-term follow-up of weight losses achieved with behavioral treatments revealed that, following treatment, obese patients tend to regain the weight they lose during treatment (Stunkard & Penick, 1979). The explanation for this phenomenon proposed by Kingsley and Wilson (1977)—namely, that continued self-regulation of any behavior, including eating, requires social support or reinforcement—has been most widely accepted. A number of studies have since supported this hypothesis by demonstrating that training spouses of over-weight individuals to model, monitor, and reinforce appropriate eating behaviors and to refrain from criticizing their partners' weight loss efforts has led to maintenance of weight at 6-month (Brownell, Heckerman, Westlake, Hayes, & Monti, 1978) and 12-month follow-up assessment (Pearce, LeBow, & Orchard, 1981).

Early treatment of obesity has received attention recently as studies have documented the relationship of obesity in childhood to adult obesity (Abraham, Collins, & Nordsieck, 1971; Hawk & Brook, 1979). Efforts to explain childhood obesity have noted family relation-ships for obesity (Hartz, Giefer, & Rimm, 1976) and have led some researchers to suggest that childhood eating and exercise patterns are modeled after parental behavior (Garn & Clark, 1976). Thus, it is not surprising that some of the programs for weight reduction in children are family-based. In one such study (Epstein, Wing, Koeske, Andrasik, & Ossip, 1981), overweight preadolescents and parents participated as families in a behavioral weight loss program. Strong positive relationships between parent and child weight losses were observed during treatment, suggesting that family-based changes in health habits were initi-ated. Follow-up data indicated, however, that the children were more successful than their parents in maintaining weight losses. This finding underscores the potential benefits of initiat-ing behavioral change programs for health enhancement in the young.

Smoking Prevention in Adolescents

In recent years, a number of programs have focused on prevention of smoking behavior among adolescents. Smoking rates among young people escalate sharply, beginning in junior high school and continuing to rise until early adulthood. The National Survey of Drug Abuse (Abelson, Fishburne, & Cisin, 1977) estimated the following prevalence of regular smokers among teenagers: age 12–13 years, 10%; 14–15 years, 22%; 16–17 years, 35%. The prevalence of young smokers, coupled with the established health risk associated with smoking, spurred efforts to prevent adolescents from making the transition from experiment-ing with cigarettes to habitual smoking.

The Counseling Leadership About Smoking Pressures (CLASP) program developed by McAlister and his colleagues is an example of a smoking prevention program based on behavior modification principles (McAlister, Perry, & Maccoby, 1979). The CLASP program was based on the evidence that initial attitudes and peer group pressures influence the decisions young people make about smoking. The purpose of this program was to teach adolescents skills for handling peer group pressures. Given that a complex behavior was to be elicited, peer modeling was the central feature of the CLASP program. Eighth- and ninth-grade student leaders led small groups of younger students in discussions that empha-sized modeling, guided practice, and positive reinforcement of statements resisting the social pressure to smoke made by the students in role-playing situations.

The program consisted of seven sessions and was given in groups to the entire seventh-grade class at one school. Self-reported smoking by students in the seventh grade at the intervention school was compared to self-reported smoking by seventh-grade students at two control schools. In the first reported results of this program (McAlister et al., 1979), approximately 2% of the students at all three schools reported "smoking during the past week" at the beginning of the school year, before the program began. By the end of the school year, 5.3% of the students in the school that had the CLASP program reported smoking during the past week, whereas the comparable figure for the control schools was 9.9%.

During the second year, the students in the treatment school received two follow-up interventions focused on demonstrating the adverse or punishing psychological effects that occur immediately with smoking. When surveyed at the end of the second year, 7.1% of the students in the treatment school, 18.8% of the students in one control school, and 21.9% of the students in the second control school reported smoking in the past week.

A third follow-up assessment of the treatment school and one of the control schools revealed that the students in the treatment school were continuing to smoke less than students in the control school (Telch, Killen, McAlister, Perry, & Maccoby, 1982). The proportion of weekly smokers among the treatment school students had dropped to 5.1%, whereas the proportion of weekly smokers among students of the control school, though less than the percentage at the end of the second year, was 14.8%.

The CLASP program appears to have been successful in preventing habitual use of cigarettes among a substantial number of adolescents. The percentage of the students in the intervention school at the 33-month follow-up is notably lower than the national figure of 12.2% for weekly smokers among adolescents in the same age group (U.S. DHEW, 1979). The investigators who conducted the program attribute the result to the students having learned new skills to resist the social pressure to smoke (Telch et al., 1982). The vehicles for this learning were strategies from behavior modification modeling, guided practice, and positive reinforcement.

Behavioral Approaches to Physical Activity

Accumulating evidence suggests that physical inactivity is associated with an increased probability of heart disease (Pickering, 1981). Longitudinal studies have associated physically active lifestyles with less frequent and less severe cardiovascular pathology (Morris, Chave, Adam, Sirey, Epstein, & Sheehan, 1973; Paffenbarger, Wing, & Hyde, 1978; Salonen, Puska, & Tuomilehto, 1982). Recent laboratory animal studies (Kramsch, Aspen, Abramowitz, Kreinmendahl, & Hood, 1981) have attempted to identify the protective mechanism for exercise and have indicated that moderate exercise may prevent atherosclerosis. Aside from its cardiovascular effects, popular surveys (Pickering, 1981) reveal that people who exercise regularly are much more likely to perceive themselves as healthy, not subject to depression, relaxed, energetic, and disciplined than people who do not exercise. Despite the evidence supporting the benefits of exercise and despite the existence of several national campaigns (President's Council on Physical Fitness, 1962, 1965), there is a general lack of physical activity in our population. This low prevalence can be ascribed to the fact that exercise, like other health behaviors, though associated with long-term reinforcing consequences, is more likely to evoke negative or punishing consequences in the short term.

Several programs have incorporated behavior modification principles to increase and maintain exercise behavior. Wysocki, Hall, Iwata, and Riordan (1979) instituted the concept of "earned aerobic points" to deliver positive reinforcement closer in time to actual exercising. A dozen undergraduate and graduate university students signed "contracts" with the investigators, committing themselves to earning a self-selected number of aerobic points by performing certain exercises. To give the points some meaning, each subject deposited a number of personal items with the experimenters. By fulfilling their contracts and carrying out other program activities, the students could "earn" back their personal items. Of the 12 students offered the program, 4 students withdrew during the baseline observation period, and 1 student withdrew halfway through the program. The 7 remaining students increased their physical activity substantially and earned back their personal items by the end of the program. Moreover, at 1-year follow-up, each of these 7 subjects reported a level of continued physical activity that was greater than their baseline level.

Katell, Martin, Webster, and Zegman (Note 2) examined several reinforcement strategies for improving adherence to increased physical activity—namely, jogging. Half of the 33 program enrollees were given standard feedback and praise for attendance, jogging style, and fitness level. The other half of the enrollees received feedback and praise more frequently and in a way that was tailored to each enrollee's strengths and weaknesses. In addition, each of the two groups was subdivided so that half received time-based goals and half received distance-based goals for jogging. No differences were observed between the two types of goal-setting procedures. The personalized praise group, however, showed a clear superiority over the standard feedback and praise group for attendance at training sessions, adherence to jogging assignments outside the training sessions, fitness level during a 12-minute test, and maintenance of jogging at 3-month follow-up. This illustrates the importance of the relevance of reinforcement, discussed earlier in this chapter. The more personal feedback was more personally relevant and had a greater impact on modifying behavior and enhancing health, both during the program and at follow-up.

FUTURE DIRECTIONS

The behavior modification programs described in the preceding section demonstrate the central role that behavior modification is capable of playing in health enhancement. In addition to these exemplary programs, there are several arenas in which behavior modification principles could be applied to make a greater, more comprehensive contribution to health enhancement.

Media Health Behavior Modification

The principles used to modify health behavior in the programs described in the preceding section are applicable to enhancing health in larger groups, but intervention strategies need to be translated into more cost-effective approaches to be feasible. It is most likely that among these approaches will be use of the media. The media have been effective in providing health education to large groups, as shown by the Stanford Heart Disease Prevention Program (Farquhar, Maccoby, & Solomon, 1981), which provided health education to communities for reducing coronary heart disease risk, and by the Swedish Diet and Exercise Program (Stunkard, 1979), in which all segments of the society, including government, industry, and schools, became mobilized in the interest of health enhancement. Health education does not necessarily produce behavior change, however. This has been amply demonstrated by the current health behavior of our population. Consider, for example, the vast numbers of young people who smoke despite extensive education about the risks associated with smoking. Education must be bolstered by applying such behavior modification principles as reinforcement and by enhancing self-efficacy expectations. The German Federal Republic and the Max Planck Institute of Psychiatry in Munich (Ferstl, Henrich, Richter, Buhringer, & Brengelmann, 1977; Stunkard, 1979) conducted a television weight reduction program that reached 7.8 million people. Of these, 2.8 million were overweight. The program consisted of seven units, each covering 1 month, with a major 45-minute show aired one Sunday in the month and 3-minute shows aired on the other Sunday evenings. In addition to the traditional health education information regarding the risks of being overweight and the importance of nutrition and counting calories, the program included elements from standard behavioral programs, such as self-monitoring of eating behaviors, self-reinforcement and other self-management strategies, and stimulus control. Modeling was also incorporated into the televised program by following five obese men and five obese women who were applying behavioral strategies. An evaluation of the program's effectiveness indicated that it produced weight losses that were significantly greater than those achieved with no treatment. The television program was less effective than a well-established bibliotherapy program, however, and when used in conjunction with the bibliotherapy program, it added little. Stunkard (1979) attributed the program's minimal results to its schedule, which spaced the major 45-minute programs 1 month apart, noting that behavioral weight management programs typically utilize face-to-face hour-long sessions at weekly intervals and that lengthening the intersession intervals results in lowered treatment effectiveness. Despite the minimal results, as Stunkard points out, the German televised weight reduction program demonstrates the feasibility of media-based health behavior modification efforts for groups as large as the medium's audience.

Industry-based Programs

The occupational setting, like schools, is an ideal setting for health behavior modification. The majority of adults between ages 20 and 65 can be reached through the work setting. Thus, health programs can be made convenient for the providers as well as for the consumers. This is exemplified in the Belgian Heart Disease Prevention Project (DeBacker,Kornitzer, Thilly, & Depoorter, 1977), in which 7,398 male workers in 30 factories were screened for risk, and those found to be at high risk ($n = 1,597$) were given individual health counseling. In addition to convenience, the work setting offers numerous advantages for programs in health behavior modification (Chesney & Feuerstein, 1979), including stability of samples for longitudinal studies, opportunities for behavior observation in a natural environment, and existing organizational and social structures that can be utilized in the design of behavioral interventions.

Behavior modification programs in the occupational setting have dealt with a wide array of health behaviors, including cardiovascular fitness, hypertension control, stress management, weight reduction, and smoking cessation. A prime example of health behavior modification in industry was the smoking cessation program sponsored by the Dow Chemical Company in Freeport, Texas, and the Texas chapter of the American Cancer Society (described by Chesney & Feuerstein, 1979). The program package included both health education through company newsletters and bulletins and reinforcement of nonsmoking behavior. Smokers were given a one-dollar wage increase for each week of abstinence. For each month ex-smoking employees reported abstinence, they earned a lottery ticket for a chance to win a quarterly prize of fifty dollars and a grand prize of a boat and motor. In order to extend the program to all employees, former smokers and nonsmokers were used to recruit smokers into the program. For each recruit, the recruiter won a chance in a separate lottery for a boat and motor. The program enrolled 395 smokers; at the end of the year, 74% reported continued abstinence. This program, with its incentives and mobilization of social support and reinforcement from co-workers, demonstrates how characteristics unique to the industrial setting can be used to facilitate health enhancement through behavior modification.

Behavioral Additions to Existing Programs

Large numbers of people seek health enhancement through existing behaviorally oriented programs, such as Weight Watchers and the SmokEnders and American Cancer Society smoking cessation clinics. Other health-related programs, such as Alcoholics Anonymous and the YMCA Cardiac Therapy Program, serve large numbers of motivated people but do not systematically incorporate principles of behavior modification, which might increase their effectiveness. Levitz and Stunkard (1974) investigated this issue with TOPS (Take Off Pounds Sensibly), a self-help group that in 1970 enrolled 300,000 members in 12,000 chapters nationwide (Stunkard, Levine, & Fox, 1970). In a controlled investigation, TOPS chapters led by professional or lay leaders who were trained in behavior modification were compared with TOPS chapters led by lay leaders who were trained in nutrition and with TOPS chapters that followed the standard self-help format. At 1-year follow-up, the behavior modification TOPS chapters showed significantly greater weight losses than either the nutrition or the standard TOPS chapters. Unfortunately, TOPS chapters that participated in the study have not continued to use behavioral strategies in their programs (Stunkard, 1979). To maintain their behavior modification focus, the TOPS chapters might have needed reinforcement by periodic feedback and support from weight reduction experts or training in self-monitoring and self-reinforcement. The TOPS experience indicates the feasibility of introducing behavior modification into large groups through existing organizations.

Prevention in an Entire Population

Health enhancement of a population through behavior modification may at first sound utopian. There are specific ways, however, in which contingencies can be established to reinforce healthy behavior. Lower life insurance premiums for nonsmokers and lower auto insurance premiums for individuals who do not have accidents are examples of positive reinforcement for positive health behavior. Reinforcement contingencies and other behavioral strategies could be applied to increase the frequency of other health behaviors. Actors could be shown modeling the use of seat belts; low-income mothers could receive payment in the form of baby care products for obtaining prenatal care; people of normal weight could receive bonus credits toward health insurance premiums.

Self-management perhaps has the greatest potential for use of the principles and strategies discussed in this chapter in the populace at large. Use of the media, social models, and reinforcement can be focused on teaching self-efficacy in self-management of health behaviors. Rather than a regimen of abstinence and strict adherence, the most appropriate goal for the majority may be to learn to control and maintain cigarette smoking and alcohol consumption at reduced moderate levels and to achieve a balance between food consumption and energy expended through physical activity in order to maintain weight that is close to the average for people of the same age and sex.

CONCLUSIONS

This chapter began by describing the historical foundation of behavior modification. The operant learning and conditioning research by early behavioral scientists not only gave behavior modification such concepts as contingencies of positive and negative reinforcement, punishment, shaping, and modeling, but it provided methodological characteristics that provide a framework for understanding and changing behavior. These principles are illustrated by their application in the health enhancement programs described in this chapter. In time perspective, behavior modification is relatively young, and its application to health is even younger. The recent programs described here not only demonstrate the feasibility of health behavior modification but also suggest the potential benefits to be accrued from such modification in the future.

REFERENCE NOTES

1. Thoresen, C. E. (Ed.), *The Self-management psychology series.* Englewood Cliffs, N.J.: Prentice-Hall.

2. Katell, A. D., Martin, J. E., Webster, J. S., & Zegman, M. A. *Exercise adherence: Impact of feedback, praise and goal-setting procedures.* Paper presented at the Annual Meeting of the Association for the Advancement of Behavior Therapy, New York, 1980.

REFERENCES

Abelson, H. I., Fishburne, P. N., & Cisin, I. *National survey on drug abuse: 1977.* DHEW Pub. No. (ADM)78–618. Washington, D.C.: U.S. Government Printing Office, 1977.

Abraham, S., Collins, G., & Nordsieck, M. Relationship of childhood weight status to morbidity in adults. *HSMHA Health Reports,* 1971, **86,** 273–284.

Ayllon, T., & Azrin, N. H. Reinforcement and instructions with mental patients. *Journal of the Experimental Analysis of Behavior,* 1964, **7,** 327–332.

Azrin, N. H., & Holz, W. C. Punishment. In W. K. Honig (Ed.), *Operant behavior: Areas of research and application.* New York: Appleton-Century-Crofts, 1966.

Baer, D. M., Wolf, M. M., & Risley, T. R. Some current dimensions of applied behavior analysis. *Journal of Applied Behavior Analysis,* 1968, **1,** 91–97.

Bandura, A. *Principles of behavior modification.* New York: Holt, Rinehart & Winston, 1969.

Bandura, A. Self-efficacy: Towards a unifying theory of behavioral change. *Psychological Review,* 1977, **84,** 191–215.

Bandura, A., Adams, N. E., & Beyer, J. Cognitive processes mediating behavioral change. *Journal of Personality and Social Psychology,* 1977, **35,** 125–139.

Brownell, K. D., Heckerman, C. L., Westlake, R. J., Hayes, S. C., & Monti, P. M. The effect of couples training and partner cooperativeness in the behavioral treatment of obesity. *Behaviour Research and Therapy,* 1978, **16,** 323–333.

Chesney, M. A., & Feuerstein, M. Behavioral medicine in the occupational setting. In J. R. McNamara (Ed.), *Behavioral approaches to medicine: Application and analysis.* New York: Plenum Press, 1979.

DeBacker, G., Kornitzer, M., Thilly, C., & Depoorter, A. M. The Belgian multifactor preventive trial in CVD: Design and methodology. *Heart Bulletin,* 1977, **8,** 143.

Dollard, J., & Miller, N. E. *Personality and psychotherapy.* New York: McGraw-Hill, 1950.

Epstein, L. H., Wing, R. R., Koeske, R., Andrasik, F., & Ossip, D. J. Child and parent weight loss in family-based behavior modification programs. *Journal of Clinical and Consulting Psychology,* 1981, **49,** 674–685.

Farquhar, J., Maccoby, N., & Solomon, D. Community applications of behavioral medicine. In D. Gentry (Ed.), *Handbook of behavioral medicine.* New York: Guilford Press, 1981.

Ferguson, J. M. *Learning to eat: Behavior modification for weight control.* Palo Alto: Bull, 1975.

Ferster, C. B. Animal behavior and mental illness, *Psychological Record,* 1966, **16,** 345–356.

Ferster, C. B., Nurnberger, J., & Levitt, E. B. Behavioral control of eating. *Journal of Mathetics,* 1962, **1,** 87–109.

Ferster, C. B., & Skinner, B. F. *Schedules of reinforcement.* New York: Appleton-Century-Crofts, 1957.

Ferstl, R., Henrich, G., Richter, M., Buhringer, G., & Brengelmann, J. C. Die Beeinflussung des Überge-wichts. In *Abschlussbericht* (Proceedings). Munich: Max Planck Institute for Psychiatry, 1977.

Garn, S. M., & Clark, D. C. Trends in fatness and origins of obesity. *Pediatrics,* 1976, **57,** 433–456.

Hartz, A., Giefer, E., & Rimm, A. A. Relative importance of the effect of family environment and heredity on obesity. *Annals of Human Genetics,* 1977, **41,** 188–193.

Hawk, L. J., & Brook, C. G. D. Influence of body fat in childhood on fatness in adult life. *British Medical Journal,* 1979, **1,** 151–152.

Hull, C. L. *Principles of behavior.* New York: Appleton-Century-Crofts, 1943.

Kazdin, A. E. *Behavior modification in applied settings.* Homewood, Ill.: Dorsey, 1975.

Kazdin, A. E. *The token economy: A review and evaluation.* New York: Plenum Press, 1977.

Kazdin, A. E. The application of operant techniques in treatment, rehabilitation, and education. In S. L. Garfield & A. E. Bergin (Eds.), *Handbook of psychotherapy and behavior change: An empirical analysis* (2nd ed.). New York: Wiley, 1978.

Kingsley, R. B., & Wilson, G. T. Behavior therapy for obesity: A comparative investigation of long-term efficacy. *Journal of Consulting and Clinical Psychology,* 1977, **45,** 288–298.

Kramsch, D. M., Aspen, A. J., Abramowitz, B. M., Kreimendahl, T., & Hood, W. B. Reduction of coronary atherosclerosis by moderate conditioning exercise in monkeys on an atherogenic diet. *New England Journal of Medicine,* 1981, **305,** 1483–1489.

Levitz, L., & Stunkard, A. J. A therapeutic coalition for obesity: Behavior modification and patient self-help. *American Journal of Psychiatry,* 1974, **131,** 423–427.

Lindsley, O. R. An experiment with parents handling behavior at home. *Johnstone Bulletin,* 1966, **9,** 27–36.

Mahoney, M. J., & Mahoney, K. *Permanent weight control: A total solution to the dieter's dilemma.* New York: Norton, 1976.

McAlister, A. L., Perry, C. L., & Maccoby, M. Adolescent smoking: Onset and prevention. *Pediatrics,* 1979, **63,** 650–657.

Morris, J. N., Chave, S. P., Adam, C., Sirey, C., Epstein, L., & Sheehan, D. J. Vigorous exercise in leisure time and the incidence of coronary heart disease. *Lancet,* 1973, **1,** no. 7799, 333–339.

Paffenbarger, R. S., Jr., Wing, A. L., & Hyde, R. T. Physical activity as an index of heart attack risk in college alumni. *American Journal of Epidemiology,* 1978, **108,** 161–175.

Pavlov, I. P. *Conditioned reflexes.* New York: Dover, 1927.

Pearce, J. W., LeBow, M. D., & Orchard, J. Role of spouse involvement in the behavioral treatment of overweight women. *Journal of Consulting and Clinical Psychology,* 1981, **49,** 236–244.

Penick, S. B., Filion, R., Fox, S., & Stunkard, A. J. Behavior modification in the treatment of obesity. *Psychosomatic Medicine,* 1971, **33,** 49–55.

Pickering, T. G. Exercise and the prevention of coronary heart disease. *Cardiovascular Reviews and Reports,* 1981, **2,** 227–229.

Premack, D. Reinforcement theory. In D. Levine (Ed.), *Nebraska Symposium on Motivation: 1965.* Lincoln: University of Nebraska Press, 1965.

President's Council on Physical Fitness. *Physical fitness elements in recreation: Suggestions for community programs.* Washington, D.C.: U.S. Government Printing Office, 1962.

President's Council on Physical Fitness. *Adult physical fitness: A program for men and women.* Washington, D.C.: U.S. Government Printing Office, 1965.

Rosenthal, T. L., & Bandura, A. Psychological modeling: Theory and practice. In S. L. Garfield & A. E. Bergin (Eds.), *Handbook of psychotherapy and behavior change: An empirical analysis* (2nd ed.). New York: Wiley, 1978.

Salonen, J. T., Puska, P., & Tuomilehto, J. Physical activity and risk of myocardial infarction, cerebral stroke and death: A longitudinal study of Eastern Finland. *American Journal of Epidemiology,* 1982, **115,** 526–537.

Sherrington, C. S. *The integrative action of the nervous system.* New Haven: Yale University Press, 1906.

Skinner, B. F. *Science and human behavior.* New York: Macmillan, 1953.

Stokes, T. G., & Baer, D. M. An implicit technology of generalization. *Journal of Applied Behavior Analysis,* 1977, **10,** 349–367.

Stuart, R. B. Behavioral control of overeating. *Behaviour Research and Therapy,* 1967, **5,** 357–365.

Stuart, R. B. *Slim chance in a fat world: Behavioral control of obesity.* Champaign, Ill.: Research Press, 1972.

Stunkard, A. J. Behavioral medicine and beyond: The example of obesity. In O. F. Pomerleau & J. P. Brady (Eds.), *Behavioral medicine: Theory and practice.* Baltimore: Williams and Wilkins, 1979.

Stunkard, A. J., Levine, H., & Fox, S. The management of obesity: Patient self-help and medical treatment. *Archives of Internal Medicine,* 1970, **125,** 1067–1072.

Stunkard, A. J., & Penick, S. B. Behavior modification in the treatment of obesity: The problem of maintaining weight loss. *Archives of General Psychiatry,* 1979, **36,** 801–806.

Telch, M. J., Killen, J. D., McAlister, A. L., Perry, C. L., & Maccoby, N. Long-term follow-up of a pilot project on smoking prevention with adolescents. *Journal of Behavioral Medicine,* 1982, **5,** 1–8.

Thoresen, C. E., & Mahoney, M. J. *Behavioral self-control.* New York: Holt, Rinehart & Winston, 1974.

Thorndike, E. L. Animal intelligence: An experimental study of the associative processes in animals. *Psychological Review Monograph,* 1898, **2** (Suppl).

Thorndike, E. L. *The psychology of learning* (Educational Psychology, II). New York: Teachers College, 1913.

Tolman, E. C. *Purposive behavior in animals and men.* New York: Appleton-Century-Crofts, 1932 (Reprinted, University of California Press, 1949).

U.S. Department of Health, Education, and Welfare (U.S. DHEW). Cigarette smoking among teenagers and young women. DHEW Pub. No. (NIH)77–1203. Washington, D.C.: U.S. Government Printing Office, 1979.

Wolpe, J. *Psychotherapy by reciprocal inhibition.* Stanford, Calif.: Stanford University Press, 1958.

Wysocki, T., Hall, G., Iwata, B., & Riordan, M. Behavioral management of exercise: Contracting for aerobic points. *Journal of Applied Behavior Analysis,* 1979, **12,** 55–64.

CHAPTER 23

PROMOTING HEALTH THROUGH INTERPERSONAL SKILLS DEVELOPMENT

RICHARD M. EISLER

Virginia Polytechnic Institute and State University

Consistent with the health enhancement themes evident throughout this handbook, this chapter will discuss the important implications of interpersonal skills development for the maintenance of psychological and physical health and the prevention of somatic or mental dysfunction. Throughout history, the ability of individuals to promote and maintain mutually rewarding relationships with their fellows has been regarded as crucial to their success and perhaps even to their survival in increasingly complex social environments. The family, tribe, kinship network, and nation have all been organized for the growth and security of the species. Although some individuals have clearly benefited more than others from these social networks, no individual could survive completely outside all of them.

In contemporary society, social skills are required to obtain mutual satisfaction from one's family and friends, to promote oneself successfully in a chosen vocation or career, and to develop a position of influence in the larger community. Although a precise definition of social skill that is comprehensive enough to encompass all social interactions has eluded researchers, some common characteristics of basic interpersonal processes appear to be available to increase our understanding of what is involved in a useful conceptualization of social skills. Included among these processes would be acquisition of a repertoire of verbal and nonverbal behavior patterns that are pertinent to social interaction. Examples of such patterns are the ability to select the most effective responses to fit the occasion from alternative possibilities, the ability to perceive accurately the wishes and intentions of others, awareness of the impact of one's own behavior on others, and the ability to elicit the behavior one desires from others. In pragmatic terms, this means that socially skilled individuals must display appropriate verbal and emotional behaviors in a wide range of social situations. They must know how to express opinions effectively and how to negotiate and compromise for mutually beneficial outcomes to solve conflict. They must know how and when to express a gamut of emotions, from anger to sadness, and how to display or respond to humor. In addition, socially adept individuals must know how to listen effectively in order to respond appropriately to the wishes and feelings of others.

THE PSYCHOSOMATIC PERSPECTIVE

The notion of significant interrelationships between successful interpersonal behavior and resistance to psychological and somatic dysfunction is not entirely new. Early psychodynamic formulations of psychosomatic illness during the 1940s and 1950s stressed the role of the individual's predominant response style (personality) and his or her conflicts over emotional expression as significant factors in the etiology of stress-induced disease (Alexander, 1950; Grace & Graham, 1952; Mahl, 1950). Unfortunately, the environmental stresses and emotional conflicts were cast in terms of intrapsychic dynamics rather than interpersonal transactions. Thus, the zeitgeist of the times focused on internal psychopathology rather than interpersonal competence in dealing with the stresses of social interaction. Alexander, French, and Pollock (1968), for example, have described the early psychodynamic position with respect to the etiology of essential hypertension:

> *In cases of essential hypertension the central findings are the patient's continuous struggle against expressing hostile, aggressive feelings and his difficulty in asserting himself. These patients fear losing the affection of others and so control the expression of their hostility. . . . The characteristic onset situation consists in life circumstances that mobilize hostility and the urge for self-assertion and at the same time prohibit their free expression. (pp. 13–14)*

Although this description comes close to viewing emotional behavior, with its deleterious effects, from an interpersonal perspective, the intrapsychic struggles over aggressive impulses and loss of love are emphasized to the neglect of the social transactions eliciting anger, and the ability of the individual to express emotions effectively tends to be ignored.

Although the early psychosomatic hypotheses generated a good deal of interest and research, attempts to link specific personality characteristics and emotional response patterns to particular types of psychosomatic disorders failed to receive empirical support. On the other hand, the idea that habitual reactions to interpersonal stressors may adversely affect normal physiological processes—for example, increased gastric motility, tachycardia, vascular contraction, and muscle tension—to the point of producing somatic illness is still viable. In fact, as we shall see, newer formulations that attempt to deal with the interplay of biological, social-environmental, and psychological coping response systems may provide new insights into the nature of healthy functioning from the perspective of competent social interaction.

THE MENTAL HEALTH PERSPECTIVE

Mental health professionals have probably always known, to some extent, that psychologically disturbed individuals are less competent in dealing with their social environments than their less troubled fellows. Whether the diagnosis was neurosis, personality disorder, or psychosis, psychiatric patients appeared to have more than their share of difficulties in transactions with family, spouses, employers, and members of the community.

These clinical assumptions were substantiated in a series of studies by Edward Zigler and Leslie Phillips during the 1960s. These investigators compared psychiatric patients with normal individuals on broad indicators of educational and vocational attainment as well as marital and personal adjustment. The evidence showed that the psychologically disturbed individuals were lower in social adjustment than the normal people and that high levels of disturbance were related to lower levels of competence (Phillips & Zigler, 1961, 1964; Zigler & Phillips, 1960). In studying the outcome of treatment, Zigler and Phillips found that level of interpersonal competence prior to onset of symptoms predicted satisfactory life adjustment following hospital release better than any form of treatment received. As with the psychosomatic illnesses discussed earlier, the intrapsychic zeitgeist focused undue attention on the role of mental illness in producing the poor social adjustment. The alternative possibility, that ineffectual social relationships played a role in producing psychological symptomatology, was largely ignored. If the latter possibility had been more seriously considered, there might have been greater attempts to help patients deal more competently with problematic relationships, with less focus on symptoms.

It remained for two clinical researchers to attempt to improve the behavioral interactions of patients suffering from anxiety in interpersonal situations. Joseph Wolpe and Arnold Lazarus (1966) were among the first to articulate a training paradigm for teaching an important group of social skills that they referred to as *assertiveness*. In their initial efforts, training was focused on showing clients how to express their feelings appropriately and how to "stand up for their rights" when confronted with the unreasonable expectations of others. In these encounters, according to the theory, assertiveness would inhibit anxiety, and more effective interpersonal behaviors would eventuate. Assertiveness training, originally designed to "countercondition" anxiety, has been applied to a wide range of clinical problems, including sexual deviation (Edwards, 1972), depression (Libet & Lewinsohn, 1973), marital difficulties (Eisler, Miller, Hersen, & Alford, 1974; Fensterheim, 1972), and alcoholism (Foy, Miller, Eisler, & O'Toole, 1976).

In contrast to the anxiety inhibition model of social anxiety proposed by Wolpe and Lazarus (1966), a number of researchers expressed the view that in many cases of psychological impairment, the requisite social skills had never been learned (Eisler & Frederiksen, 1980; Gutride, Goldstein, & Hunter, 1973; McFall & Twentyman, 1973). This revised conceptualization of the relationship between social adequacy and diverse symptomatology came to be known as the social skill deficit hypothesis (Eisler & Frederiksen, 1980). Briefly, this model required a broader view of assertiveness to include a greater range of social skills. Furthermore, the goals of treatment were expanded from anxiety reduction to teaching the client a repertoire of socially effective coping responses to be employed in a variety of problematic social situations. Depressed persons for example, were taught how to elicit a greater density of positively reinforcing consequences from others (Lewinsohn, 1975; Lewinsohn & Shaffer, 1971). Couples in conflict were taught how to negotiate and compromise for their mutual benefit (Eisler & Frederiksen, 1980). Aggressive and violence-prone individuals were taught how to obtain what they needed without verbal and physical abusiveness toward others (Frederiksen, Jenkins, Foy, & Eisler, 1976; Matson & Stephans, 1978). Alcoholics were taught how to resist social pressure from peers to resume drinking (Foy et al., 1976). Also, hospitalized psychiatric patients were taught the rudimentary social skills necessary for life adjustment following discharge from the hospital (Eisler, Blanchard, Fitts, & Williams, 1978; Goldsmith & McFall, 1975).

HEALTH MAINTENANCE AND COPING SKILLS

There is a growing belief among medical practitioners and mental health workers that a person's ability to cope with everyday stress is more important to overall morale, social adjustment, and somatic health than is the frequency or severity of the stress episodes themselves (Roskies & Lazarus, 1980). Stress, once defined in terms of environmental pressure and heightened or prolonged physiological response of the organism (Selye, 1956), is currently viewed as the failure of the individual to cope successfully with the demands of the environment. Thus, the individual who copes with marital difficulties or job dissatisfaction by excessive drinking, smoking, or overeating or by continually taking tranquilizers not only risks his or her somatic health but also damages potential sources of social support. This, in turn, often triggers greater dependence on alcohol, drugs, and so on, with deleterious effects on mental and physical health. From this perspective, coping skills are viewed not only as a response to unavoidable stressors but also as an active process operating to prevent person–environment transactions from becoming too stressful in the first place.

With increasing emphasis on active coping as a continuous process, it is possible to think more in terms of preventing somatic and psychological dysfunction. Therefore, it is no longer fruitful to view certain kinds of medical illness solely in terms of the adequacy of the individual's biological response systems. Similarly, behavioral disorders cannot be viewed only in terms of the individual's psyche. Medical researchers seeking to understand the multicausal factors in coronary heart disease have had to look beyond genetics, blood chemistry, and diet toward behavioral patterns of coping with stress and issues of lifestyle. Nowhere is this interactionist view quite so compelling as in the mounting evidence linking the Type A behavior pattern to a predisposition to coronary heart disease (Friedman & Rosenman, 1974; Rosenman & Friedman, 1978). A similar case can be made for psychological researchers studying maladaptive behavior patterns. Those investigators looking at the maintenance of cigarette smoking in smokers who acknowledge the habit's harmful effects must be aware of the biologically addicting effects of nicotine, of how the nicotine-altered blood chemistry interacts with emotional (physiological) arousal, of external stress, and of the smoker's ability to cope with life stresses.

Thus, we are witnessing a novel weaving of old threads, linking, in some cases, similar antecedent factors to both somatic and psychological health. One common thread appears to be the individual's ability to cope with a diversity of life's challenges. If the person has the necessary skills and resources to do so successfully, health is likely to be maintained. On the other hand, if the individual's abilities and resources are taxed beyond his or her ability to cope successfully, breakdown and vulnerability to dysfunction in biological, behavioral, and psychological systems may occur.

SOCIAL SKILLS IN COPING WITH INTERPERSONAL STRESS

It is only beginning to be recognized that much of the symptom-producing stress faced by most individuals frequently involves problematic interpersonal transactions. Thus, moving to a new community, dealing with a difficult supervisor at work, handling adolescent turmoil in the family, dealing with the stresses of a dysfunctional marriage, and making the social adjustment following divorce, all involve a degree of proficiency in interpersonal coping skills. Presumably, these social skills have been learned throughout a person's life, either by observing relevant models or by having the fortitude and ability to learn from past experiences. To the extent that people employ maladaptive coping patterns or emulate unsuccessful models in seeking solutions through withdrawal, excessive aggression, or personal rigidity, they do not learn adequate social skills. Not only does this exacerbate the stressful nature of the particular problem, but it alienates individuals in the natural environment who could help facilitate satisfactory solutions.

The classical symptom reduction focus of the traditional medical and mental health professions provides, at best, only palliative assistance in dealing with social stress and does little to prevent the recurrence of symptoms. The result is that individuals tend to be labeled as patients of one kind or another and become chronically dependent on professional services, rather than learning how to reduce sources of their stress.

It is probably becoming obvious at this point that I am advocating teaching distressed individuals social coping skills as an alternative to treating the symptoms that result from excessive stress. I am suggesting social skills training for those individuals who are, to varying degrees, stressed by their inability to deal effectively with others in their social environments. This approach would apply to those individuals who have never learned social skills, those who have learned maladaptive social behaviors, and those whose life experiences have not prepared them to deal with new or more complex social situations.

SOCIAL SKILLS TRAINING

Social skills training programs have been developed under a variety of rubrics, including "problem solving" (D'Zurilla & Goldfried, 1971), "structured learning therapy" (Goldstein, 1973), "behavioral training" (McFall & Twentyman, 1973), and "stress inoculation training" (Novaco, 1975). Although interpersonal training programs differ with respect to their emphasis on the client's cognitive coping responses, emotional responses, and overt behavioral performance, they share some common rationales and training methods. One is the belief that socially competent responses can be learned according to the same social learning principles that govern the acquisition of other learned behaviors. A second belief is that training techniques should be empirically verifiable. Third is the notion that training should produce demonstrable improvements in the individual's interactions with others in the natural environment, in contrast to the "insight" criterion typically employed in the psychodynamic therapies. In other words, training should result in improvements in the ways in which the individual appraises and responds to stressful situations. Fourth, all training approaches require a fairly detailed assessment of specific social skills deficits, including irrational or maladaptive thoughts, inappropriate emotional reactions, and unskilled behavioral performances. Self-report assessment measures are typically bolstered by observer evaluations of the client's social performances in natural environment situations whenever possible and through in vivo role playing.

A typically agreed-upon goal of most social skills training programs is to improve social interaction patterns successively during training sessions, combined with practice in the natural environment between sessions. Clinicians who specialize in social skills training agree that another major objective of training is to ensure generalization of socially skilled performances from an agreed-upon criterion during training to anticipated stressful situations that the client will encounter in the future. The latter objective requires continued practice or "homework" during training sessions and mutual feedback between client and trainer regarding how well the newly acquired social behavior is working in novel situations.

Training can be done with individual clients, with groups of people who have similar skill deficits, such as in assertiveness, or with naturally occurring social networks, such as dysfunctional families with poor problem-solving capacities. Most practitioners report that treatment requirements are briefer than would be the case with traditional psychotherapeutic approaches, ranging from five to twelve sessions. At present, however, there is little empirical evidence regarding how much training, with what kinds of clients, is either desirable or necessary. There is some evidence, however, to suggest that social skills training is superior to traditional psychotherapeutic approaches (Goldsmith & McFall, 1975; Gutride et al., 1973; Martinson & Zerface, 1970).

Skills Training Techniques

In general, most social skills paradigms include a number of integrated training components that are utilized for different aspects of training. For purposes of discussion, these components may be categorized as follows: (a) cognitive restructuring, (b) response acquisition, and (c) response practice.

Cognitive Restructuring

A good deal of the initial training is directed toward assessment and modification of the individual's cognitions about what is appropriate or inappropriate behavior in social situations. One of the leading proponents of cognitive restructuring has been Donald Meichenbaum (1977), who has noted that most skills training programs have overemphasized the importance of environmental stressors and have underemphasized how the client perceives and appraises those events.

Evidence from several research programs has suggested that teaching people to reevaluate their thoughts about themselves in a more positive and confident manner during social encounters tends to reduce anxiety and facilitate transfer of learned skills (Meichenbaum, 1977; Spivack & Shure, 1974). Also, a study by Eisler, Frederiksen, and Peterson (1978), which compared behaviorally assertive with behaviorally nonassertive individuals, found that the assertive people chose descriptions of socially effective responses more frequently than the nonassertive people did; the assertive people also expected that more favorable or reinforcing consequences would result from their social behavior than did the nonassertive people. These results highlight the importance of expanding the client's range of knowledge of socially appropriate alternatives during training.

Some individuals fail to demonstrate socially adequate behavior during certain encounters because they hold faulty or erroneous beliefs about what kinds of behavior are appropriate or effective. Ellis (1962) has noted that irrational or self-defeating beliefs may restrict the client's range of effective social responses and may lead to inappropriate emotional states. Some people believe, for example, that "it is not polite" *ever* to express anger or displeasure toward anyone under any circumstances. Thus, in anger-engendering situations, these individuals might feel stressed and might experience severe anxiety and possible depression.

Another cognitive process relevant to social skills training involves the ability to accurately perceive the intentions of others in social encounters. Some unskilled individuals are not sensitive to the cues or signals displayed in their interpersonal encounters; for example, when the host yawns several times and becomes more silent, it might be time for the guest to think about going home. On the other hand, some individuals are predisposed to hypervigilance during encounters; every gesture or word may be perceived as a threat. Another major cognitive factor regulating social interactions is the individual's expectations of the probable consequences resulting from engaging in certain social behaviors. In most social situations, individuals behave in ways that they hope will produce consequences they desire and that will minimize the probability of negative consequences they hope to avoid. Very often, socially unskilled individuals have difficulty in correctly anticipating the consequences of their behavior, and they are taken by surprise by other people's reactions. In general, cognitive restructuring helps clients accept more realistic beliefs about the nature of their relationships with others during social interaction. To the extent that training provides more accurate appraisals of the consequences of the individual's actions, social behavior can become more effective. Finally, revised conceptions about the self and others tends to promote transfer of training to a greater diversity of social situations.

Response Acquisition

As previously noted, the bulk of social skills training requires utilization of behavioral techniques based on social learning principles. Two procedures frequently employed during the response acquisition portion of training are *coaching* and *modeling*. Coaching is used to instruct clients in the expression of relevant social response patterns. When the clients describe particular stressful aspects of social interactions, they are coached in specific response alternatives that might reduce stress. Coaching includes discussions of relevant nonverbal behaviors, such as tone of voice, eye contact, and posture, that accompany and often emphasize various portions of the verbal communication.

Studies have shown that social response acquisition is often facilitated by modeling displays (Eisler et al., 1978). It is usually convenient for the trainer to model the response to be learned, just as a baseball coach shows a hitter how to stand and swing the bat. When training is done in groups, however, it may be more efficient to use models recorded on videotape. Research has shown that modeling is most useful when the intricate nuances of the behavior cannot easily be explained through simple coaching or when the trainees are very deficient in social skills (Hersen, Eisler, Miller, Johnson, & Pinkston, 1973). A combination of coaching and modeling has proved to be effective in demonstrating social behavior patterns to be learned and in ensuring that the clients can perform the required behaviors. These elements cannot be accomplished with cognitive restructuring techniques alone.

Response Practice

Response practice, sometimes called behavior rehearsal, is an integral component in virtually all social skills training programs. During response practice, clients' new social behavior is strengthened to the point at which they feel comfortable with the new behavior patterns and can utilize them in real-life encounters almost without thinking about them. Behavior rehearsal of novel social responses in simulated interpersonal interactions (role playing) has the advantage of minimal risk to the clients before they are ready to test the responses under the stress of actual encounters. Successive rehearsals also give individuals feelings of mastery and confidence in deployment of the responses. In addition, the trainer can provide corrective feedback during rehearsal to ensure that the individuals are delivering the most effective responses they are capable of performing.

A variation of rehearsal procedures has been advocated by Kazdin (1975). Rather than actually performing the new social responses, the clients covertly rehearse performing them in imagination. The obvious advantage of the covert rehearsal procedure is that individuals can practice the social responses wherever and whenever they please, often just prior to their use. The major disadvantage of covert rehearsal is that the trainer has no direct way of assessing the adequacy of the imagined response.

During response practice, corrective feedback and reinforcement techniques are sometimes employed to refine the social behaviors and to enhance the probability of their transfer to a variety of natural environment situations. Feedback informs the clients how close their performance is to the desired criterion and what additions or deletions might make the responses appear more effective. Reinforcement, in the form of trainer-administered praise or group approval, helps motivate the clients during training and encourages the use of the learned responses in the natural environment. It is hoped that socially skilled behavior will be maintained through reinforcement in the natural environment because it meets with the acceptance and approval of the individuals' real-life partners.

SOME NEW APPLICATIONS OF SOCIAL SKILLS TRAINING

It has been pointed out in earlier sections of this chapter that social skills training has been employed successfully for people with diverse clinical problems, including hospitalized psychotics, dysfunctional couples, antisocial aggressive individuals, and those who individually suffer from clinically significant anxiety or depression. No professional who has worked with any of these clinical syndromes would allege that social skills training can cure schizophrenia, eliminate marital discord, or change antisocial individuals into models of interpersonal effectiveness. Nor has it been advocated that social competence training should be used for every case of anxiety or depression. Instead, social skills training has been conceptualized as a means of attaining requisite skills for coping with a variety of stressors that foster symptom formation. From our theoretical perspective, strengthening a person's interpersonal coping abilities should help break the cycle between external stressors and symptoms forming out of inadequate coping resources. Thus, social skills improvements can help prevent ordinary (as well as extraordinary) interpersonal difficulties from becoming sources of stress. Second, interpersonally effective people tend to obtain more of what they need from the environment in a socially sanctioned manner. Finally, socially adept individuals are likely to develop and maintain vitally important social support networks, which previous research has shown to reduce the effects of other stressors (Roskies & Lazarus, 1980).

Anger and Type A Behavior

Anger is a commonly experienced emotional state that often appears as a clinical problem singularly or in combination with other maladaptive behavior patterns. Despite the prevalence of anger in many clinical problems, research on anger control has not been studied systematically independent of aggressive behavior. Part of the reason for this may be that aggression is conceptualized as an overt, more easily quantified response, with more obvious destructive effects, especially on the social environment. On the other hand, anger is an inferred construct, with less obvious deleterious effects, especially to others. Anger has been presumed to be a precursor to much of human aggression, and most research paradigms have attempted to induce anger for the purpose of studying aggression (Bandura, 1973; Edmunds, 1981).

Anger typically has been defined as a covert response to certain kinds of stressors, known as provocations, which in turn lead to various adaptive or maladaptive coping behaviors to reduce anger arousal (Bandura, 1973). Examples of maladaptive behaviors are excessive smoking, alcohol, and drug abuse, as well as aggressive interactions that provoke retaliation. Most investigators would agree that anger is composed of both cognitive and physiological components, although some would say that the individual is not always aware of the cognitive component—that is, repressed anger. The cognitive component consists of emotionally charged self-statements about a situation or about recall of a situation (Meichenbaum, 1977), or labels applied to an arousal state—for example, "That person is making a fool of me, I'm getting angry." The physiological components of anger include increased blood pressure, increased levels of free fatty acids, increased facial and neck muscle tonus, peripheral vasodilation, and others (Stearns, 1972). Thus, it would appear that sustained levels of anger arousal would have important negative implications for maintenance of health.

Chronic anger arousal as a serious stress factor and health risk has recently been brought into much sharper focus with Friedman and Rosenman's (1974) revelations concerning what they called the Type A behavior pattern in relation to the risk of developing coronary heart disease. Although numerous behavioral components have been associated with the Type A pattern, Rosenman (1978) has suggested that the core elements involve extreme interpersonal competitiveness, aggression, and chronic hostility. In a review of recent research on the Type A behavior pattern, Matthews (1982) indicated that the Type A pattern is not a trait but a set of behaviors elicited from the susceptible individual by a (perceived) challenging environment.

There appears to be little doubt at this point that some of the core elements associated with the Type A behavior pattern—which Friedman and Rosenman (1974) have defined as "an action-emotion complex that can be observed in any person who is aggressively involved in a chronic, incessant struggle to achieve more and more in less and less time, and if required to do so, against the opposing efforts of other things and other persons" (p. 67)—constitute a major risk factor in the development of coronary atherosclerosis (Blumenthal, Williams, Kong, Schonberg, & Thomson, 1978). Furthermore, it appears that chronic anger arousal and competitiveness are central to the coping behavior of persons identified as Type A, coronary-prone individuals.

We may speculate that extreme competitiveness and the tendency to dominate others in social interactions constitute a maladaptive coping pattern used by Type A individuals to deal with all kinds of interpersonal threats. Although many aggressive Type A individuals appear successful, particularly in their work, continual deployment of anger in excess of environmental necessity may have many undesirable effects on their cardiovascular systems. In addition, there is a high probability that continuous interpersonal conflict and turmoil may adversely affect their social networks and support systems. If this formulation is correct, then effective treatment strategies need to be designed to teach the Type A individual effective coping strategies without relying on chronic anger arousal.

Cognitive and Social Skills Training

A number of treatment strategies are currently being developed for individuals who experience high levels of anger and/or behave aggressively toward others. Although these interventions have not been specifically tailored for people who have been identified as Type A individuals, there is every reason to believe that remedial strategies focusing on improved interpersonal coping behavior and reduction of anger may be of value in the amelioration of some critical aspects of Type A behavior.

Novaco (1975) has pioneered a cognitive-behavioral anger reduction strategy based on a form of Meichenbaum's (1975) stress inoculation training. The essence of the treatment is (a) that subjects are provided with a sharper conceptualization of their anger, consisting of a combination of excessive emotional arousal and cognitive labeling of the situation, and (b) that they are typically given self-instructional training, whereby they are asked to prepare cognitively for provocations with more neutral self-statements about the situations and to rehearse more rational means for coping with the provocations. The results assessed on physiological and self-report measures of anger, as well as on imaginal, role-played, and contrived laboratory-based provocations, strongly support the use of cognitive training.

Social skills training, a somewhat different approach to anger reduction, has employed assertiveness training and teaching of alternatives to aggressive behavior during stressful encounters (Eisler & Frederiksen, 1980). The rationale for this approach, which has been researched primarily on psychiatric patients, is outlined by Bandura (1973):

> Socially and verbally unskilled persons having limited means for handling discord are likely to become physically aggressive on slight provocation. . . . Assaultive people can therefore benefit greatly from a treatment program that teaches them nonviolent techniques for handling interpersonal conflicts. (pp. 255–256)

Eisler and his colleagues, in a series of studies of "explosive" psychiatric patients, have demonstrated the effectiveness of direct behavioral training in social skills for verbally abusive and behaviorally assaultive psychiatric patients (Foy, Eisler, & Pinkston, 1975; Frederiksen & Eisler, 1977; Frederiksen et al., 1976).

Although Novaco's (1975) approach to anger reduction focuses more on cognitive coping strategies than on the social skills training approach advocated by Eisler and Frederiksen (1980), which focuses on training behavioral alternatives to socially inappropriate behavior, there are some similarities. Both techniques are expected to reduce inappropriate anger in social situations; both approaches teach the individual alternative methods of coping with interpersonal stress; and both techniques have received some experimental verification of their efficacy on diverse outcome measures. Additional research may show that a combination of behavioral and cognitive training approaches produces more useful effects than would result from either training approach alone. The utility of coping skills training in individuals who exhibit the coronary-prone Type A behavior pattern shows promise. At this point it would appear that Type A individuals, who tend to stress themselves through misperceptions of their social environments and to exhibit antagonistic social behavior patterns, might benefit from interpersonal skills training.

Social Skills and Children

Over the past 30 years, there appears to be a growing body of evidence that relates the poor social functioning of children to serious personal adjustment problems faced by these individuals in their adult life. At one end of the spectrum, a notable proportion of school-age children appears to experience excessive shyness, passivity, and fear in social relationships with peers and adults. This problem has been documented by Gronlund (1959), who reported that 18% of third- through sixth-grade children had no friends or only one friend in their classes. At the other end of the spectrum of childhood social dysfunction is a group of aggressive children whose behavior may involve throwing temper tantrums when frustrated, ignoring the rights and feelings of other children, making excessive demands on teachers, and physically assaulting peers to settle conflicts. The evidence is clear that both aggressive and withdrawn children continue such maladaptive social behavior patterns into later life (Kagan & Moss, 1962), at great cost to themselves and society.

Most experts would agree that children require the security of positive reciprocal relationships with their peers, parents, and teachers for maximal growth and development. Social behavior to facilitate these relationships is learned by children through observing and modeling their behavior from their parents, peers, siblings, teachers, and even fictional characters portrayed in the media (Bandura & Walters, 1963). Necessary social skills for these relationships involve learning how to initiate friendly contacts, how to communicate their needs effectively, how to share possessions and engage in cooperative play, and how to seek help and advice appropriately when needed. These are all examples of prosocial skills in children, which facilitate positive interactions between them and their social environment. To the extent that children do not master these skills, they do not receive the social support necessary for their well-being.

It would appear, then, that social skills training programs designed to remediate social deficiencies should be employed to prevent a variety of psychological and emotional problems in adolescence and later life. It is obvious from what we now know that children who become isolated from or who alienate their social environment receive less of an opportunity to learn functional patterns of coping with stress. Socially maladaptive patterns that begin in childhood clearly continue into adult life, establishing a vicious cycle that is difficult to reverse.

Research in the area of social skills training with children has just begun and is building momentum (Combs & Slaby; 1977; Rinn & Markle, 1979). Investigators are discovering that definitions of social skills, assessment methods, and intervention strategies developed for adults will probably have to be revised for application to children. On the other hand, it may be easier to devise and implement social skills training with children through parent and teacher training programs. Children tend to learn quickly and are not so handicapped by ingrained patterns of social behavior. Also, with children, it should be possible to study the natural acquisition of social skills from a developmental perspective, so that we can have a better idea of age-appropriate norms and of how to capitalize on natural reward systems.

REFERENCES

Alexander, F. *Psychosomatic medicine: Its principles and applications.* New York: Norton, 1950.

Alexander, F., French, T. M., & Pollock, G. *Psychosomatic specificity: Experimental study and results* (Vol. 1). Chicago: University of Chicago Press, 1968.

Bandura, A. *Aggression: A social learning analysis.* Englewood Cliffs, N.J.: Prentice-Hall, 1973.

Bandura, A., & Walters, R. H. *Social learning and personality development.* New York: Holt, Rinehart & Winston, 1963.

Blumenthal, J. A., Williams, R. B., Kong, Y., Schonberg, S. M., & Thomson, L. W. Type A behavior pattern and coronary atherosclerosis. *Circulation,* 1978, **58**, 634–639.

Combs, M. L., & Slaby, D. A. Social skills training with children. In B. B. Lahey & A. E. Kazdin (Eds.), *Advances in clinical child psychology* (Vol. 1). New York: Plenum Press, 1977.

D'Zurila, T., & Goldfried, M. Problem solving and behavior modification. *Journal of Abnormal Psychology,* 1971, **32**, 47–51.

Edmunds, G. Aggression (psychological). In R. H. Woody (Ed.), *Encyclopedia of clinical assessment* (Vol. 1). San Francisco: Jossey-Bass, 1981.

Edwards, N. B. Case conference: Assertive training in a case of homosexual pedophilia. *Journal of Behavior Therapy and Experimental Psychiatry,* 1972, **3**, 55–63.

Eisler, R. M., Blanchard, E. B., Fitts, H., & Williams, J. G. Social skill training with and without modeling for schizophrenic and nonpsychotic hospitalized psychiatric patients. *Behavior Modification,* 1978, **2**, 147–171.

Eisler, R. M., & Frederiksen, L. W. *Perfecting social skills: A guide to interpersonal behavior development.* New York: Plenum Press, 1980.

Eisler, R. M., Frederiksen, L. W., & Peterson, G. L. The relationship of cognitive variables to the expression of assertiveness. *Behavior Therapy,* 1978, **9**, 419–427.

Eisler, R. M., Miller, P. M., Hersen, M., & Alford, H. Effects of assertive training on marital interaction. *Archives of General Psychiatry,* 1974, **30**, 643–649.

Ellis, A. *Reason and emotion in psychotherapy.* New York: Lyle Stuart, 1962.

Fensterheim, H. Assertive methods and marital problems. In R. D. Rubin, H. Fensterheim, J. D. Henderson, & L. P. Ualman (Eds.), *Advances in behavior therapy.* New York: Academic Press, 1972.

Foy, D. W., Eisler, R. M., & Pinkston, S. Modeled assertion in a case of explosive rages. *Journal of Behavior Therapy and Experimental Psychiatry,* 1975, **6**, 135–137.

Foy, D. W., Miller, P. M., Eisler, R. M., & O'Toole, D. H. Social skills training to teach alcoholics to refuse drinks effectively. *Journal of Studies on Alcohol,* 1976, **37**, 1340–3145.

Frederiksen, L. W., & Eisler, R. M. The control of explosive behavior: A skill development approach. In D. Upper (Ed.), *Perspectives in behavior therapy.* Kalamazoo, Mich.: Behaviordelia, 1977.

Frederiksen, L. W., Jenkins, J. O., Foy, D. W., & Eisler, R. M. Social skills training in the modification of abusive verbal outbursts in adults. *Journal of Applied Behavior Analysis,* 1976, **9**, 119–125.

Friedman, M., & Rosenman, R. H. *Type A behavior and your heart.* Greenwich, Conn.: Fawcett, 1974.

Goldsmith, J. B., & McFall, R. M. Development and evaluation of an interpersonal skill training program for psychiatric inpatients. *Journal of Abnormal Psychology,* 1975, **84**, 51–58.

Goldstein, A. P. *Structured learning theory: Toward a psychotherapy for the poor.* New York: Academic Press, 1973.

Grace, W. J., & Graham, D. T. Relationships of specific attitudes and emotions to certain bodily diseases. *Psychosomatic Medicine,* 1952, **14**, 243–251.

Gronlund, N. E. *Sociometry in the classroom.* New York: Harper, 1959.

Gutride, M. E., Goldstein, A. P., & Hunter, G. F. The use of modeling and role-playing to increase social interaction among social psychiatric patients. *Journal of Consulting and Clinical Psychology,* 1973, **40**, 408–415.

Hersen, M., Eisler, R. M., Miller, P. M., Johnson, M. B., & Pinkston, S. G. Effects of practice, instructions, and modeling on components of assertive behavior. *Behaviour Research and Therapy,* 1973, **11**, 443–451.

Kagan, S., & Moss, H. A. *Birth to maturity: A study in psychological development.* New York: Wiley, 1962.

Kazdin, A. E. Covert modeling, imagery assessment, and assertive behavior. *Journal of Consulting and Clinical Psychology,* 1975, **43**, 716–724.

Lewinsohn, P. M. The behavioral study and treatment of depression. In M. Hersen, R. M. Eisler, & P. M. Miller (Eds.), *Progress in behavior modification* (Vol. 1). New York: Academic Press, 1975.

Lewinsohn, P. M., & Shaffer, M. Use of home observations as an integral part of the treatment of depression. *Journal of Consulting and Clinical Psychology,* 1971, **37**, 87–94.

Libet, J., & Lewinsohn, P. M. The concept of social skill with special references to the behavior of depressed persons. *Journal of Consulting and Clinical Psychology,* 1973, **40**, 304–312.

Mahl, G. F. Anxiety, HCL secretion and peptic ulcer etiology. *Psychosomatic Medicine,* 1950, **12**, 158–169.

Martinson, W. D., & Zerface, J. P. Comparison of individual counseling and a social program with nondaters. *Journal of Counseling Psychology,* 1970, **17**, 36–40.

Matson, J. L., & Stephans, R. M. Increasing appropriate behavior of explosive chronic psychiatric patients with a social skills training package. *Behavior Modification,* 1978, **2**, 61–76.

Matthews, K. A. Psychological perspectives on the Type A behavior patterns. *Psychological Bulletin,* 1982, **91**, 293–323.

McFall, R. M., & Twentyman, C. T. Four experiments on the relative contribution of rehearsal, modeling, and coaching to assertion training. *Journal of Abnormal Psychology,* 1973, **81**, 199–218.

Meichenbaum, D. A. Self-instructional approach to stress management: A proposal for stress inoculation training. In C. D. Spielberger & I. G. Sarason (Eds.), *Stress and anxiety* (Vol. 2). New York: Wiley, 1975.

Meichenbaum, D. A. *Cognitive behavior modification: An integrative approach.* New York: Plenum Press, 1977.

Novaco, R. W. *Anger control.* Lexington, Mass.: Lexington Books, 1975.

Phillips, L., & Zigler, E. Social competence: The action-thought parameter and vicariousness in normal and pathological behaviors. *Journal of Abnormal and Social Psychology,* 1961, **63**, 137–146.

Phillips, L., & Zigler, E. Role orientation, the action-thought dimension, and outcome in psychiatric disorder. *Journal of Abnormal and Social Psychology,* 1964, **68**, 381–389.

Rinn, R. C., & Markle, A. Modification of skills deficits in children. In A. S. Bellack & M. Hersen (Eds.), *Research and practice in social skills training.* New York: Plenum Press, 1979.

Rosenman, R. The interview method of assessment of the coronary prone behavior pattern. In T. M. Dembroski, S. M. Weiss, J. L. Shields, S. G. Haynes, & M. Feinlieb (Eds.), *Coronary-prone behavior.* New York: Springer-Verlag, 1978.

Rosenman, R. H., & Friedman, M. Modifying Type A behaviour pattern. *Journal of Psychosomatic Research,* 1978, **21,** 323–333.

Roskies, E., & Lazarus, R. S. Coping theory and the teaching of coping skills. In P. O. Davidson & S. M. Davidson (Eds.), *Behavioral medicine: Changing health life-styles.* New York: Brunner/ Mazel, 1980.

Selye, H. *The stress of life.* New York: McGraw-Hill, 1956.

Spivack, G., & Shure, M. B. *Social adjustment of young children: A cognitive approach to solving real-life problems.* San Francisco: Jossey-Bass, 1974.

Stearns, F. R. *Anger: Psychology, physiology, pathology.* Springfield, Ill.: Charles C Thomas, 1972.

Wolpe, J., & Lazarus, A. A. *Behavior therapy techniques: A guide to the neurosis.* New York: Pergamon Press, 1966.

Zigler, E., & Phillips, L. Social effectiveness and symptomatic behaviors. *Journal of Abnormal and Social Psychology,* 1960, **61,** 231–238.

CHAPTER 24

TIME MANAGEMENT: A BEHAVIORAL STRATEGY FOR DISEASE PREVENTION AND HEALTH ENHANCEMENT

GEORGE S. EVERLY, JR.

Loyola College of Maryland and Psychological Sciences Institute, Baltimore

The more a person is able to direct his life consciously, the more he can use time for constructive benefits.—Rollo May

Other chapters in this Handbook describe self-control and self-management strategies as they apply to disease prevention and health enhancement. This chapter will examine the role of time management in fostering the development of such strategies for reducing risk and developing a health-enhancing lifestyle.

TIME: A HISTORICAL PERSPECTIVE

Our society appears to be virtually obsessed with a concern for time. Impatience and feelings of time urgency seem to characterize many aspects of present society. Where does this obsession with time come from?

Anthropologists tell us that humans have expressed a concern for the passage of time for thousands of years. The ancient Egyptians were apparently the first to leave a written record of the passage of time. This record appears in the form of the Palermo Stone. As an artifact, the Palermo Stone represents a chronicle of the major events that transpired in Egypt around 2500 B.C. (Grant, 1980). Perhaps the earliest evidence of human attempts at the actual measurement of time itself is found in the megaliths of Stonehenge. These stone structures date back to 1900 B.C. and are thought to be an early form of chronograph (Grant, 1980). They can be found on England's Salisbury Plain. Humankind seemed simply to accept the passage of time as an unalterable constant up until the fifth century B.C. (deRomilly, 1968). It was at this point, as evidenced in the extant Greek tragedies, that the notion of time urgency began to appear in civilized society.

Thus, we see that humankind's interest in time urgency dates back thousands of years. It was not until the religious urgings of the Puritan ethic, however, combined with the capitalistic incentives of the industrial revolutions of France and England, that a large-

The author is grateful to Eileen C. Newman, University of Miami Department of Psychology, for her assistance in the preparation of this chapter.

scale push for efficient time utilization emerged in 18th-century Europe. These industrial revolutions prompted the first known attempts to analyze time utilization by factory workers. In effect, these movements gave birth to the first time-efficiency studies (Minge-Klevana, 1980).

The process of analyzing work-related time appeared in the United States some years later. The best known time analysis projects were the time and motion studies of Frank Gilbreth (1911), who separated production-level tasks into component parts and analyzed each task while searching for "wasted" time and effort.

The 1950s and 1960s represented an era, both in Europe and the United States, when effective time utilization was considered to be not only the key to economic success but the "sine qua non" of business enterprise. Peter Drucker's (1954) influential text on management practices suggested that time was man's most perishable resource and that effective time utilization was the key to effective management. This was also an era of indictment, however. In the 1960s, influential studies emerged (Sayles, 1963; Stewart, 1967) indicating that most managers failed to use their time efficiently. Not coincidentally, the 1960s and 1970s were the temporal stage for a plethora of time management training programs and textbooks that seem to be gaining popularity in the 1980s.

Thus, we see that the psychological stage was set for our society's quest to capture time. It is certainly a quest fueled by external forces—for example, our growing dependence on high-technology data acquisition and effector systems, as predicted in Alvin Toffler's (1970) *Future Shock*. This concern for efficient time utilization apparently has carried over from work to home and even leisure activities. This suggests that our apparent obsession with efficient time utilization may be as much self-imposed as environmentally dictated.

TIME AND HEALTH

Historically, we have seen our society's concern for time and time management focused on business and industrial considerations. But what of the effects of time factors on health? No data currently exist to demonstrate that time factors are indeed major determinants of human health. On the other hand, it may be suggested that one's perception of the availability of time is associated with certain health-related risk factors and with the practice of a health-enhancing lifestyle.

One of the more interesting cases in point is that of the relationship between impatience and time urgency, on the one hand, and the increased risk of heart disease, on the other. As early as 1910, evidence was mounting that there was a relationship between impatience and time urgency and heart disease or dysfunction. Sir William Osler lectured in London before the Royal College of Physicians on the topic of angina pectoris. In his lectures, he noted that the majority of his 268 angina patients were individuals who tended to be highly ambitious, and hard-driving, and seemed to possess a chronic sense of time urgency (Osler, 1910).

Subsequent research initiated by cardiologists Meyer Friedman and Ray Rosenman went even further to link impatience and chronic time urgency with heart disease. In their studies of behavioral predictors of coronary heart disease, Friedman, Rosenman, and their colleagues identified the Type A coronary-prone behavior pattern. Based on a critical review of evidence relating the Type A behavior pattern to coronary heart disease, the Review Panel on Coronary-Prone Behavior and Coronary Heart Disease, convened by the National Heart, Lung and Blood Institute (Note 1), has generally accepted the Type A behavior pattern as being associated with an increased risk of coronary heart disease. Relevant to the discussion here, one of the core components of this coronary-prone behavior pattern is a chronic sense of impatience and time urgency. The extreme Type A individual is often plagued by "a lack of time to do everything each day *he* thinks he should get done" (Rosenman, 1978, p. 60). In further describing the extreme Type A individual, Rosenman (1978) notes:

He is obstructed by a dearth of time. *And so, he begins his never ending struggle with time. Rarely, does he attempt to defeat his adversary by lightening his load. No, he tries to* accelerate *the usual rate of doing things and thus he believes he can accomplish more in a given time.* (*p. 61*)

It is important to note that the time urgency that plagues the Type A individual is self-imposed. Thus, the Type A individual has been identified as suffering from a self-imposed "hurry sickness" (Friedman & Rosenman, 1974).

Research into the assessment of Type A behavior yielded data supporting the pathogenic role of impatience in coronary heart disease. Efforts aimed at identifying the internal structure of the structured interview (an interview designed to assess Type A behavior patterns) revealed the existence of two factors that correlated with the subsequent emergence of coronary heart disease: competitive drive and impatience (Matthews, Glass, Rosenman, & Bortner, 1977).

Studies examining physiological reactions to social conditions indicate that stress arousal is associated with social conditions containing a time pressure/urgency condition. Studies by Dembroski and his colleagues (Dembroski, MacDougall, & Shields, 1977; Dembroski, MacDougall, Shields, Pettito, & Lushene, 1978) found that social challenges with time pressure conditions imposed on them resulted in activation of the sympathetic nervous system. These studies support the earlier observations of Friedman, Rosenman, and Carroll (1958) that accountants experienced elevated serum cholesterol levels as their sense of time urgency increased prior to the April 15 income tax deadline. There is suggestive evidence that, under certain conditions, these physiological reactions may be related to the development of coronary heart disease (Gilmore, 1974; Herd, 1981).

Having examined the relationship between impatience and time urgency and the subsequent risk of coronary heart disease, there is suggestive evidence that impatience and time urgency may also be related to the more overt practice of health risk behaviors and even to the avoidance of health-enhancing behavior. Friedman and Rosenman (1974) suggest that the time-pressured Type A individual smokes more cigarettes and tends to exercise less than non-Type A individuals. In a preliminary study of the relationship between time pressure and health-related behavior patterns, Everly (Note 2) found that subjective reports of time pressure were positively correlated with generally accepted biobehavioral risk factors, such as caffeine consumption and smoking, among 64 clerical personnel working in a high-technology multinational corporation. In this same study, the author found that the subjective feeling of time pressure was inversely correlated with the practice of health-enhancing behavior, such as exercise and relaxation breaks. These data support earlier findings. Everly and Rosenfeld (1981) reported that their patients with psychophysiological disorders were hesitant to practice relaxation techniques because of a lack of perceived time available. Furthermore, Carrington, Collings, Benson, Robinson, Wood, Leher, Woolfolk, and Cole (1980) found lack of time to be the major reason for lack of compliance in a meditation program. Finally, although no studies directly indicate that time urgency is a major causal factor, impatience and time urgency have been implicated as risk factors for industrial and vehicular accidents. According to Brody (1963):

At the root of any *accident will be found human factors of one kind or another. . . . Essentially, the overall problem of accidents appears to be a matter of functional disharmony or imbalance between man and environment, resulting in a stressful situation.* (*p. 659*)

Anton (1979) notes that pressure creates "ergonomic stress," which appears to be a risk factor for accidents. Schulzinger (1956) implicates time pressure and haste as contributing factors to the generic accident syndrome in his review of this area. It should be noted that accidents rank among the five leading causes of death in the United States.

In summarizing this section on time and health, no direct evidence has been found to demonstrate that our society's concern for time and time urgency represents a major determinant of health. On the other hand, there is intriguing indirect support for the notion that time factors may indeed interact with other intrapersonal and environmental variables and may be related to more generally accepted health-related factors. Thus, methodologically, we would expect time factors to demonstrate interaction effects rather than "main" effects when assessing behavioral determinants of health.

Having traced the historical development of our society's concern with time and having noted its potential association with certain health risk factors, let us examine the notion of managing time.

TIME MANAGEMENT, SELF-RESPONSIBILITY AND BEHAVIORAL HEALTH

The term *time management* is a misnomer and may indeed lead to an inappropriate conclusion regarding the nature of this health enhancement strategy. The leading technique-oriented texts in the field agree that successful time management is based not on *managing time* per se but on *managing oneself* in relation to how one utilizes time. MacKenzie (1968), in defining time management, notes: "Time passes at a predetermined rate no matter what we do. It is a question not of managing the clock but of managing ourselves with respect to the clock" (p.3). Douglass and Douglass (1980) write: "Managing time really refers to managing ourselves in such a way as to optimize the time we have. It means conducting our affairs within the time available so that we achieve gratifying results" (p.2). Finally, Jongeward (1976) concludes that "managing time means investing your time to get what you want out of life" (p.77). These prescriptive definitions are congruent with my empirical observations (Everly, 1980a, 1980b) in the design and implementation of health-related time management programs. Thus, we see that literal management of time is an exercise in futility, for time does not lend itself to control. Therefore, time management really represents the management of self—the employment of self-responsibility and self-management skills for the utilization of time as a resource.

Recalling the quotation from Rollo May that opened this chapter, it seems reasonable to suggest that time management techniques can be employed to better enable persons to consciously direct their lives and to avail themselves of the time to pursue health via a health-enhancing lifestyle. Matarazzo (1982) has delineated some of the behavioral health challenges awaiting us. He lists among them helping currently healthy citizens learn to exercise regularly, establish proper sleeping and rest habits, employ basic safety behaviors, use dental floss, and affect a more healthful diet. It seems a tenable notion that, in the final analysis, successfully meeting any and all of these challenges will depend, in part, on individuals' perceptions that they have the time available to devote to such activities.

Thus, we see that the emphasis in time management is on self-responsibility, because individual responsibility and self-initiated behavior form the foundation of behavioral health (see Matarazzo, 1980). It may be argued that time management is a fundamental behavioral health-enhancing strategy, because even the potentially most effective behavioral risk reduction and health-enhancing strategies will be impotent unless individuals perceive that they have the time to employ them.

A MODEL FOR TIME MANAGEMENT

It was suggested earlier in this chapter that time management is a particularly important behavioral health strategy because it potentiates a general availability of time for the specific practices of disease prevention and health enhancement. Unfortunately, no studies have been done (to my knowledge) that have isolated time management techniques and tested their effects on risk factors such as Type A behavior, stress, and accidents, nor on the frequency of health-enhancing behavior. Suinn (1978, 1980) and Gentry (1978), however, have reviewed behavioral interventions that contained varying degrees of time management strategies. These reviews are supportive of the notion that programs containing some time management strategies may reduce coronary risk factors. Bhalla (1980) implemented a stress management program that contained a time management component. He found that such a program was able to reduce cardiovascular and electromyographic indices of stress arousal. In none of the reports cited, however, is it possible to determine to what degree the time management techniques themselves were effective in effecting a positive health outcome. Intuitively, it seems that time management interventions play an *interactional* role with other health-promoting strategies to account for the positive health outcomes reported in the aforementioned studies. Perhaps time management techniques provide individuals with the temporal opportunities to practice health-enhancing behaviors. This hypothesis is supported by the study conducted by Rader and Schabacker (1980), which found that generic time management techniques did, indeed, increase the amount of time available to subjects practicing such time management behaviors.

To fully understand the concept of time management, the question must be raised of what time management really does. As noted in the preceding section, time management is a generic term applying to the employment of techniques that allow individuals to become more effective in their utilization of time. More specifically, however, it becomes useful to identify the active mechanisms that underlie the process of time management:

1. Attending to the highest priority activities with a limited amount of time, thus potentially reducing demand while maximizing effort expenditure.
2. Increasing the amount of functional time available to attend to high priority activities.
3. Reducing the perception of time-urgent conditions.

The following model is intended to provide a generic form of time management. Because time management techniques tend to be most effective when they are tailored specifically to the idiosyncratic needs and environment of the individual, this generic model may be used as a basis from which more specific models can be developed. This model is not designed solely to increase the productivity of the individuals employing the model, as is often the case in business-oriented models. Rather, as noted earlier in this chapter, generic time management is designed to allow individuals to manage their lives relative to the resource of time. From a behavioral health perspective, this approach includes providing time for the practice of health-enhancing behaviors and for potentially reducing certain risk factors associated with time urgency and impatience, such as stress and Type A behavior patterns. The generic model presented here is a time management model integrating the work of Lakein (1973), Gentry (1978), Suinn (1978), Girdano and Everly (1979), Douglass and Douglass (1980), Porat (1980), and Radar and Schabacker (1980).

I. Setting Priorities

Modern society is often characterized by its tendency to place a multitude of time-consuming demands on individuals' limited supply of time and energy. In such conditions, when time demand exceeds supply, time management strategies may assist individuals by increasing their ability to determine and attend to the perceived highest priority demands, given a limited supply of time. This result may be achieved as follows:

A. Review/establish important personal (including health-related) objectives or goals. These can be short-term goals (less than 1 year) or long-term goals (1, 5, or 10 years).

B. Establish goal-path clarity by listing the subgoals or steps that are necessary for achieving each major personal goal. In other words, determine what needs to be done to achieve the goals enumerated in step A.

C. Analyze current time-consuming activities; that is, determine how current daily and weekly time is regularly spent. Ideally, current activities should support and lead to the ultimate achievement of personal goals or objectives. If such is not the case, either step A or step C will probably need to be altered. (Time analysis may be achieved through the use of daily time logs to chart daily time utilization.)

D. Once steps A and C are congruent, it becomes necessary to prioritize current time-consuming activities. Prioritization primarily involves attending only to those current activities that yield the most significant payoff relative to the major personal goals or objectives stated in Step A.

II. Increasing Functional Time

Once the determination of high-priority current activities has been made, it becomes desirable to allocate sufficient time to attend to such tasks. This is done by harnessing and increasing the functional time available, as follows:

A. Identify/reduce sources of "wasted" time—that is, current time-consuming activities that in no way or only minimally contribute to the achievement of important goals or objectives. The effect of reducing time-wasting activities is to increase the functional amount of time available for high-priority activities.

B. Delegation of time-consuming activities to others will functionally increase the amount of time an individual has to spend on high-priority items. In order to delegate, support groups must be identified. Spouses, children, friends, relatives, and co-workers (peers and subordinates) are all potential sources of support to whom lower priority activities may be delegated. If applicable, an individual might even hire others or barter for work to be performed.

C. Schedule high-priority activities. It seems to be commonly accepted in the time management literature that what doesn't get scheduled doesn't get done. The time analysis log mentioned earlier may assist in effective scheduling.

III. Reducing Perceptions of Time Urgency

Having determined high-priority activities and allocated time for attending to them, the final step in this generic time management model involves reducing the perception of time pressure and time urgency. This result is accomplished as follows:

A. Analyze and minimize perceived sources of time pressure and time urgency. Not all perceptions of time urgency are warranted; some are arbitrary and needlessly self-imposed. Therefore, the following steps are necessary:

1. Determine which sources of time urgency are environmentally dictated with valid reason.
2. Determine which sources of time urgency are environmentally dictated needlessly.
3. Determine which sources of time urgency are constructively self-imposed.
4. Determine which sources of time urgency are needlessly self-imposed.
5. Minimize needless time urgency.

B. Overcome procrastination. Procrastination appears to be an attitudinal barrier to effective time management. It can frequently be traced to two major sources: the reluctance to make a mistake and the inability to know how to start or initiate action. Success in overcoming procrastination may be increased once the individual accepts the notion that few decisions are, in reality, irrevocable and that making mistakes is actually nothing more than a part of trial-and-error learning. Similarly, learning to break a seemingly large or overwhelmingly complex task down into its smallest functional task units may prove to be extremely valuable in helping people start projects on which they might have been procrastinating because of their size or complexity. Lakein (1973) calls this strategy "swiss-cheesing."

This generic time management model has potential for three obvious health-related applications: (a) as a general model for increasing the availability of time that potentially could be used for the practice of health-enhancing strategies; (b) as a model for reducing health-related risk factors that may be related to time urgency; and (c) as a specific model for implementing any given health-enhancing or risk-reducing behavior.

SUMMARY

In this chapter, time management has been presented as a fundamental practice within the field of behavioral health. Our society's preoccupation with time urgency and time pressure has been implicated as being involved in health-related risk factors. Time management techniques appear to have the potential to reduce time pressure. Furthermore, from a behavioral health perspective, time management techniques may potentiate the availability of time for the practice of health-enhancing behaviors. In the final analysis, the practice of a health-enhancing lifestyle will most likely be predicated on the perception of available time to do so. Finally, and perhaps most fundamentally, time management and behavioral health share the same basic core. Just as self-responsibility and self-management form the core of time management, so, too, do they form the core of the practice of behavioral health.

REFERENCE NOTES

1. National Heart, Lung and Blood Institute. *Proceedings of the National Heart, Lung and Blood Institute Panel on Coronary Prone Behavior and Coronary Heart Disease,* Amelia Island, Florida, 1978.

2. Everly, G. *Time urgency and health-related coping behavior.* Unpublished research report, Loyola College, Baltimore, 1982.

REFERENCES

Anton, T. *Occupational safety and health management.* New York: McGraw-Hill, 1979.

Bhalla, V. *Neuroendocrine, cardiovascular, and musculoskeletal analyses of a holistic approach to stress reduction.* Unpublished doctoral dissertation, University of Maryland, 1980.

Brody, L. Methodology and patterns of research in industrial accidents. *Annals of the New York Academy of Sciences,* 1963, **107,** 659–663.

Carrington, P., Collings, G., Benson, H., Robinson, H., Wood, L., Leher, P., Woolfolk, R., & Cole, J. The use of meditation-relaxation techniques for the management of stress in a working population. *Journal of Occupational Medicine,* 1980, **22,** 221–231.

Dembroski, T., MacDougall, J., & Shields, J. Physiologic reactions to social challenge in persons evidencing the Type A coronary-prone behavior pattern. *Journal of Human Stress,* 1977, **3,** 2-10.

Dembroski, T., MacDougall, J., Shields, J., Petitto, J., & Lushene, R. Components of the Type A coronary-prone behavior pattern and cardiovascular response to psychomotor performance challenge. *Journal of Behavioral Medicine,* 1978, **1,** 159–176.

deRomilly, J. *Time in Greek tragedy.* Ithaca: Cornell University Press, 1968.

Douglass, M., & Douglass, D. *Manage your time, manage your work, manage yourself.* New York: AMACOM, 1980.

Drucker, P. *The practice of management.* New York: Harper, 1954.

Everly, G. The development of less stressful personality traits in adult learners: Preliminary findings. In *Proceedings of the Lifelong Learning Research Conference.* College Park: U.S. Adult Education Association and the University of Maryland, 1980. (a)

Everly, G. The development of less stressful personality traits in adults through educational intervention. *Maryland Adult Educator,* 1980, **2**, 63–66. (b)

Everly, G., & Rosenfeld, R. *The nature and treatment of the stress response: A practical guide for clinicians.* New York: Plenum Press, 1981.

Friedman, M., & Rosenman, R. *Type A behavior and your heart.* New York: Knopf, 1974.

Friedman, M., Rosenman, R., & Carroll, V. Changes in the serum cholesterol and blood clotting time in men subjected to cyclic variation of environmental stress. *Circulation,* 1958, **117**, 825–861.

Gentry, W. D. Behavior modification of the coronary-prone behavior pattern. In T. M. Dembroski, S. M. Weiss, J. L. Shields, S. G. Haynes, & M. Feinlieb (Eds.), *Coronary-prone behavior.* New York: Springer-Verlag, 1978.

Gilbreth, F. *Motion study.* New York: Van Nostrand, 1911.

Gilmore, J. P. Physiology of stress. In R. Eliot (Ed.), *Stress and the heart.* Mt. Kisco, N.Y.: Futura, 1974.

Girdano, D., & Everly, G. *Controlling stress and tension.* Englewood Cliffs, N.J.: Prentice-Hall, 1979.

Grant, J. *The book of time.* Westbridge Books, 1980.

Herd, J. Behavioral factors in physiologic mechanisms of cardiovascular disease. In S. Weiss, J. Herd, & B. Fox (Eds.), *Perspectives on behavioral medicine.* New York: Academic Press, 1981.

Jongeward, D. *Everybody wins: Transactional analysis applied to organizations.* Reading, Mass: Addison-Wesley, 1976.

Lakein, A. *How to get control of your time and your life.* New York: Wyden, 1973.

MacKenzie, R. A. *Time trap.* New York: AMACOM, 1968.

Matarazzo, J. D. Behavioral health and behavioral medicine: Frontiers for a new health psychology. *American Psychologist,* 1980, **35**, 807–817.

Matarazzo, J. Behavioral health's challenge to academic, scientific, and professional psychology. *American Psychologist,* 1982, **37**, 1–14.

Matthews, K., Glass, D., Rosenman, R., & Bortner, R. Competitive drive, pattern A and coronary heart disease: A further analysis of some data from the Western Collaborative Group Study. *Journal of Chronic Diseases,* 1977, **30**, 489–498.

Minge-Klevana, W. Does labor time decrease with industrialization? *Current Anthropology,* 1980, **21**, 279–298.

Osler, W. The Lumleian Lectures on angina pectoris. *Lancet,* 1910, **1**, 696–700; 839–844; 974–977.

Porat, F. *Creative procrastination.* San Francisco: Harper & Row, 1980.

Rader, M., & Schabacker, J. The effectiveness of time management training. *Arizona Business,* 1980, **27**, 3–7.

Rosenman, R. The interview method of assessment of the coronary-prone behavior pattern. In T. M. Dembroski, S. M. Weiss, J. L. Shields, S. G. Haynes, & M. Feinlieb (Eds.), *Coronary-prone behavior.* New York: Springer-Verlag, 1978.

Sayles, L. *Managerial behavior administration in complex organizations.* New York: McGraw-Hill, 1963.

Schulzinger, M. *The accident syndrome.* Springfield, Ill.: Charles C Thomas, 1956.

Stewart, R. *Managers and their jobs: A study of the similarities and differences in the ways managers spend their time.* London: Macmillan, 1967.

Suinn, R. The coronary-prone behavior pattern: A behavioral approach to intervention. In T. M. Dembroski, S. M. Weiss, J. L. Shields, S. G. Haynes, & M. Feinlieb (Eds.), *Coronary-prone behavior.* New York: Springer-Verlag, 1978.

Suinn, R. Pattern A behaviors and heart disease: Intervention approaches. In J. Ferguson & C. B. Taylor (Eds.), *The comprehensive handbook of behavioral medicine* (Vol.1). New York: Spectrum, 1980.

Toffler, A. *Future shock.* New York: Random House, 1970.

CHAPTER 25

PATIENT–PROVIDER RELATIONSHIPS AND THE PLACEBO EFFECT

ARTHUR K. SHAPIRO
ELAINE SHAPIRO

Mount Sinai School of Medicine, New York

The literature on the placebo effect includes general discussions of the phenomenon and reports of laboratory and clinical studies. Many authors have attempted to review this literature, which consists of more than 2,000 papers. These reviews can be characterized as a catalogue of studies describing different samples, measures, procedures, findings, interpretations, and conclusions (Brody, 1980; Frank, 1973; Hass, Fink, & Hartflider, 1963; Honigfeld, 1964a, 1964b; Jospe, 1978; Kissel & Barrucand, 1964; Shapiro, 1959, 1960, 1971, 1978; Shapiro & Morris, 1978; Turner, Gallimore, & Fox-Henning, 1980). In this chapter, uncontrolled clinical studies and philosophical, speculative, and general discussions of the placebo effect are not reviewed. The extensive literature on laboratory studies of the placebo effect are also omitted because of poor methodology, small samples, post hoc analyses, use of measures with unknown or low reliability, absence of demonstrated validity or generalized relationship to clinical phenomena, and, above all, absence of consensual validation among studies. This literature includes studies using laboratory tests of suggestibility, persuadability, and other presumed measures of the placebo effect and employing experimenters and volunteers rather than clinical patients and healers (Shapiro, 1978; Shapiro & Morris, 1978; Shapiro, Struening, & Shapiro, 1980). In these studies, the relationships among tests of suggestibility are frequently trivial and inconsistent, and their relationship to clinical measures of the placebo effect have not been empirically demonstrated (Shapiro, Struening, & Shapiro, 1980). In addition, they pose the problem of whether the results of laboratory experiments can be generalized to clinical conditions. For example, behavioral techniques reduce tics and the symptoms of Tourette syndrome in the laboratory or during therapeutic sessions, but the treatment effects do not generalize to other life situations (Shapiro, Shapiro, Bruun, & Sweet, 1978). Similarly, although blood pressure was significantly reduced by placebos during clinic visits in one study, ambulatory monitoring at other times showed no effect of placebos on blood pressure (Gould, Mann, Davies, Altman, & Raftery, 1981). The literature on communication and persuasion (Hovland, Janis, & Kelley, 1953) also fails to demonstrate transfer of results to life outside the laboratory (Lepper, 1981; Petty, Ostrom, & Brock, 1981). Moreover, in our opinion, the clinical utility of laboratory procedures such as biofeedback, Transcendental Meditation, and others to treat physical illnesses is not supported by data-oriented studies.

This chapter focuses on clinical studies of the placebo effect. When reviewed critically, however, the literature in this area reveals an absence of a systematic approach. Conclusions about the determinants and strengths of the placebo effect are frequently based on post hoc analyses and have a tendency to interpret positive results and ignore negative results. Most measures of placebo reaction vary from study to study and have unknown or low reliability and validity. Other methodological limitations include the use of small and heterogeneous clinical samples, independent and dependent variables without documented reliability, inadequate controls for spontaneous change, retrospective analyses leading to Type I errors, and other shortcomings. In our opinion, the results of studies of personality, psychodynamics, learned contingencies, cognitive dissonance, misattribution, sociocultural factors, and patient, healer, and situational factors fail to explain the power of the placebo, do not support a specific or clinically important effect of the placebo on physical illness, and do not identify specific personality characteristics or placebo reactors or specify independent variables that will predict placebo response (Shapiro & Morris, 1978; Shapiro & Shapiro, 1982).

Our discussion of the patient–provider relationship and the placebo effect will be more meaningful if we first define several frequently used terms and concepts (see Dorland, 1981; Shapiro, 1964a, 1964b, 1968, 1976; Shapiro & Morris, 1978).

DEFINITIONS

A *patient* is a person who seeks information about or treatment for maintenance of health, prevention of disease, or management of an illness. A *provider* is a source of information about health and disease, including physicians, psychologists, social workers, public health workers, educators, lecturers, and any medium that disseminates the beliefs, fads, or superstitions that become part of the zeitgeist for a culture or a cultural subgroup.

Therapy or *treatment* is "the management and care of a patient for the purpose of combating disease or disorder" (Dorland, 1981) by a professional who is sanctioned by society or a nonprofessional who is used by members of subcultures in a society. Therapies can also be self-administered—for example, a patient's use of organic foods to avoid toxic substances, exercise to promote general health, aspirin to minimize heart attacks, and Transcendental Meditation to reduce stress.

The definitions of *placebo* and *placebo effect* used in this chapter are restricted ones, although extensive definitions, including hypothesized mechanisms to explain their action, have been provided by other authors (Brody, 1980; Frank, 1973; Grünbaum, 1981; Shapiro, 1964a, 1964b, 1968, 1971; Shapiro & Morris, 1978). Our discussion and proposed definitions, which we believe fulfill historical and heuristic criteria, are extracted from previous papers (Shapiro, 1964a, 1964b, 1968, 1971; Shapiro & Morris, 1978): A *placebo* is defined as any therapy or component of therapy that is deliberately used for its nonspecific, psychological, or psychophysiological effect, or that is used for its presumed specific effect but is without specific activity for the condition being treated. When used as a control in experimental studies, a placebo is defined as a substance or procedure that is without specific activity for the condition being evaluated. The *placebo effect* is defined as the psychological or psychophysiological effect produced by placebos.

The definition of placebo has several important features. No assumptions are made about the intent of the therapist to issue placebo therapy. The therapist may knowingly give placebo treatment, or, conversely, may administer a treatment that is thought to be effective but by *objective evaluation* has no specific activity for the condition being treated. Furthermore, no assumptions are made about the effects of therapy. Placebos may have positive, negative, or no effects. They may or may not induce side effects.

Implicit in this definition is the assumption that active treatments may have placebo components. Even specific therapies can include both placebo and nonplacebo effects. Treatments that are devoid of active, specific components are known as pure placebos, whereas therapies that include nonplacebo components are called impure placebos. Treatments with specific components that exert their effects primarily through nonspecific mechanisms are considered placebo therapies. The placebo component of therapies is likely to decrease as knowledge about the causes and cures of illnesses increases and as therapies affect illness more directly and specifically.

The key concept in defining placebo is "specific activity." In somatic therapies, specific activity is often equated with nonpsychological factors. Separating specific from nonspecific activity, however, is inappropriate for psychological therapies. Therefore, a more general definition is proposed. *Specific activity* is defined as the therapeutic influence attributable solely to the contents or processes of the therapies rendered. The criteria for specific activity and for the placebo effect should be based on scientifically controlled studies.

The definition of placebo does not include the mechanism of placebo action, because placebogenic factors are not yet sufficiently understood or well documented, but it implies that psychological factors are important determinants. The placebo effect is a multideter-mined phenomenon that is influenced by many different factors and processes. Some of these factors are considered in subsequent sections of this chapter.

Although this definition may prove to be too inclusive, for heuristic reasons it would be premature to make specific exclusions at this time. It is likely that placebogenic factors will be isolated in the future. When we know enough about the placebo effect so that we can predict it, the definition will no longer be needed and will appear only in lexicons of obsolete terms. Narrowing the definition is something to consider for the future.

The terms *placebo reactor, responder, response,* and *action* will be used interchangeably.

THE PLACEBO EFFECT IN THE HISTORY OF MEDICAL TREATMENT

Despite the tendency of medical historians—who usually are not scientists, experimenters, or clinicians—to glamorize and romanticize the history of medicine, medical treatment until recently, with rare exceptions, has rested on placebo foundations. The history of medical treatment is testimony to the power of the placebo effect (Frank, 1973; Garrison, 1921; Houston, 1938; Pepper, 1945; Shapiro, 1959, 1960, 1968, 1976, 1978). This history is charac-terized by the introduction by physicians and quacks of new placebos when older ones failed, often accompanied by vehement and vituperative denunciation of other physicians who, without scientific justification, preferred other placebos (Shapiro & Struening, 1973a, 1973b, 1974). We have shown that physicians who held such strong beliefs and feelings without objective evidence of a therapy's effectiveness were defensive about their treatment and were more likely to recognize another provider's treatment as a placebo than to so identify their own (Shapiro & Struening, 1973a). Despite the occasional insights of astute clinicians, most physicians, including the gifted, were astonishingly and abysmally wrong about treatment. Intelligence, professional status, clinical insights, and elaborate theories were no protection against the development of placebo therapies. Indeed, they resulted in elaborately ineffective and expensive placebo remedies, often with potential for harming and killing patients. Untrained healers who unwittingly relied on placebo effects rather than on elaborate theory were occasionally more correct about treatment than physicians were. When a treatment is a placebo, it is easy to imitate, and counterfeit therapies and quackery flourish. Whenever many different remedies are used to treat a disease, or when a single remedy is used to treat many diseases, it can be assumed that little is known about how to treat the disease and that the remedies are likely to be placebos (Garrison, 1921). The expensiveness of a treatment, its acceptance by professionals and society, and its popularity are not guarantees of its efficacy. Theoretical proof is an ineffective weapon against the emotions generated by a strong belief in therapeutic efficacy. A review of medical history indicates that concentration on the process of therapy, to the exclusion or minimiza-tion of the study of effectiveness, is a major theme in the history of the placebo effect. The study of efficacy should precede or occur concomitantly with the study of process.

THE PLACEBO EFFECT AS AN ADAPTIVE MECHANISM[1]

What is this powerful placebo effect? Explanatory concepts derived from the history of medical treatment include the mechanisms of suggestion, mobilization of hope, and catharsis. Catharsis can include physical methods, such as the use of emetics, purges, evacuation, depletion, and dehydration, as well as the use of psychological methods such as psychotherapy. Such mechanisms may act independently, may be additive, or may potentiate one another. The placebo effect may be an adaptive mechanism that helps ensure survival. In the prescientific era, survival could have been impaired if individuals reacted realistically to their overwhelming and unpredictable environment. The ability to explain the unknown by projection of internal fantasy onto the environment could have provided adaptive psychological outlets in the form of externalization of fantasy, catharsis, control over the internal and external environment, and other psychological mechanisms. Thus, anxiety, depression, despair, and hopelessness could decrease, releasing the optimism and energy required for realistic adaptation to economic and psychosocial problems. People have always reacted to unknown stressful stimuli with unrealistic fantasies of optimism, pessimism, or a combination of the two (Wilson, 1978). This was reflected in primitive society by elaborate mythologies, in which the world was populated by benevolent and malevolent forces, by devils and gods, and by a belief in magic. In such a setting, an optimistic fantasy might provide an adaptive denial of an otherwise unmanageable world, a pessimistic fantasy would prepare for adversity, a capacity for reality testing would modify unrealistic fantasy, and the propitious combination of these factors would be useful for survival, adaptation, and increased control of the environment.

As knowledge about the physical world increased, diffuse fantasy and projection were less necessary. Today, scientific methodology is used increasingly to explain the unknown; religion has become institutionalized and increasingly restricted to vague spiritual aspects of existence. In medicine, however, despite advances in the understanding and treatment of disease, illness still provokes fantasy because of its importance to the individual. Society's greater success in conquering the physical environment than in furthering psychological understanding has led to a preoccupation with psychological problems, whereas previously the physical environment was inexplicably intertwined with psychological problems and their resolution. With increasing control of the physical environment, somatic displacement and projection of psychological problems became a less adequate and less necessary outlet, and psychological problems could be approached directly. Comprehension of impulses, conflicts, and relationship with others and psychological insight into self are still inadequate, however. With the failure of traditional religious explanations, individual fantasy and projection has focused on self-understanding, and psychotherapy has become the institutionalized outlet for the expression and resolution of conflict. Placebo effects, primarily associated with physical treatment, can be expressed and experienced through psychological treatment in the form of psychotherapy or even psychochemotherapy. This development is exemplified in the massive overpsychologizing of our society in the last 75 years and the birth of more than 250 types of psychotherapy (Herink, 1980; Parloff, 1982). As our society becomes more intricate, technological, and understandable, however, knowledge becomes more specialized. In reaction to this development, there has been a movement toward individual responsibility and an increasing desire to determine and control one's destiny. Recent therapeutic trends include psychotherapeutic treatment by clergy, nurses, laypersons, gurus, a multitude of self-help modalities, and, most recently, the interest in holistic medicine and behavioral health, as exemplified by increasing involvement in jogging, natural foods, vitamins, stress reduction, and speculative beliefs about how the mind affects the body. The evidence necessary to substantiate the effectiveness of these methods does not yet exist.

---

[1] This section is adapted from a previously published paper (Shapiro, 1971).

Nevertheless, the enthusiasm with which they have gained recognition leads us to paraphrase a maxim: *Those who forget the history of the placebo effect are destined to repeat it.* In our opinion, there is only one protection against this recurrent history of the placebo effect— namely, the use of established classical scientific principles applied to the controlled study of the evaluation of therapies, which includes the use of double-blind procedures, adequate sampling, control groups, reliable and valid independent and dependent variables, predictive hypotheses, replication of findings, appropriate statistics and other well-known methodological principles. Despite the enthusiasm with which these new therapies have been received, they must be scientifically evaluated, not only to demonstrate effectiveness but also to elucidate the mechanisms of action.

PLACEBO EFFECTS IN MODERN MEDICINE

Modern medicine, perhaps only 30 to 40 years old, no longer relies chiefly on placebo effects. Although placebo effects are more prominent in some therapies than in others, and although the availability of specific therapies has increased, the importance of the placebo effect continues even in modern medicine. Psychological or placebo effects can be minimized or excluded if the dosage of a drug is high enough to cause physiological toxicity or death. Therapeutic drug dosages, however, are usually within a range in which placebo effects are important. Placebos have been reported to induce addiction and to mimic, be more powerful than, and reverse the action of some active drugs. The use of placebos has been reported in dentistry, podiatry, optometry, biofeedback, acupuncture, oncology, surgery, electroconvulsive therapy, and in every medical specialty and for every treatment (Shapiro & Morris, 1978). A testimony to the power of the placebo is that it is the only drug approved by the Food and Drug Administration without fulfilling the criterion required for all other drugs—that its effectiveness be proved by several double-blind studies.

According to our definition of the placebo effect, active treatment may induce placebo effects that are more powerful than the specific effects of the active drug. For example, the major effect of diazepam (Valium) and other so-called antianxiety drugs, whose clinical pharmacological effects are similar to the sedative-hypnotic drugs, may be a placebo effect (Shapiro, 1976, 1978; Shapiro, Struening, & Shapiro, 1980; Shapiro, Struening, Shapiro, & Milcarek, 1983). We recently completed a well-controlled, double-blind study of 224 neurotic, anxious outpatients, who were treated with either diazepam or placebo and 10 to 15 minutes of minimal, brief psychotherapy (Shapiro et al., 1983). Diazepam was effective for only the first week of treatment and contributed only 1.4% to the improvement variance, compared to 11% to 22% contributed by placebo and other nonspecific variables. Diazepam was not more effective than placebo and did not contribute to improvement, whereas placebo and nonspecific variables accounted for 20% to 26% of the improvement variance at the end of the study. Despite this meager effect, diazepam is the most successful drug ever marketed by a pharmaceutical firm, grossing more than a million dollars daily. Diazepam and the burgeoning number of benzodiazepines, when used as antianxiety agents, may be the major placebos of our time.

THE PLACEBO EFFECT OF THE PLACEBO

Placebo effects become associated with any successful therapy, whether it is a specific, active, or placebo therapy. With the growing appreciation of the healing power of the placebo, its therapeutic power has been exaggerated. A recent best-seller, for example, extolled the placebo as a cure for the author's serious illness (Cousins, 1979), and a newly introduced therapy was cited as the ultimate placebo. Current beliefs about megavitamins, nutrition and organic foods (Armaroli, 1982; Stave, 1982), stress reduction, jogging, holistic medicine, and even the concept of behavioral health may be examples of recent popular placebos, since there is little substantive evidence to demonstrate that these techniques are clinically useful or effective. In our opinion, the belief that placebos and psychological factors have a specific and clinically meaningful effect on physical illness is not supported by a critical, data-oriented review of the literature. Thus, the effectiveness of the placebo may be largely a placebo effect.

STUDIES OF THE PLACEBO EFFECT

The published literature on the placebo effect is quite extensive, with at least 1,000 references (Turner et al., 1980), and has been reviewed extensively in previous publications (Brody, 1980; Frank, 1973; Hass et al., 1963; Honigfeld, 1964a; 1964b; Jospe, 1978; Kissel & Barrucand, 1964; Shapiro, 1959, 1960, 1971, 1978; Shapiro & Morris, 1978; Turner et al., 1980). The reader is referred to these papers for the extensive bibliography that will not be cited in this review. Selected results will be summarized here from previously published studies by the authors (Chassen, Janulis, & Shapiro, 1975; Morris & Shapiro, 1973, 1974; Shapiro, Frick, Morris, Chassen, & Shapiro, 1974; Shapiro, Mike, Barten, & Shapiro, 1973; Shapiro & Struening, 1973a, 1973b, 1974; Shapiro, Struening, Barten, & Shapiro, 1975, 1976, 1980; Shapiro, Struening, & Shapiro, 1980; Shapiro, Wilensky, & Struening, 1968) and from seven as yet unpublished studies of more than 1,000 psychiatric outpatients (Shapiro et al., in press).

Frequency and Types of Placebo Reaction

Placebo effects are ubiquitous and always occur in treatment. Popular mass health beliefs are particularly prone to placebo effects. Frequency ranges up to 100% in some studies and varies according to the type of illness, the sample of patients, and the methods, measurements, and procedures of the study.

Although positive placebo effects are described more frequently than other types of placebo reactions, we consistently identified four types of placebo reactions in six studies: (a) positive placebo reactors, or patients who report decreased symptoms; (b) negative placebo reactors, or those who describe exacerbation of their symptoms; (c) neutral or nonplacebo reactors, or patients without change of symptoms; and (d) a fourth group of patients who report new symptoms or side effects, referred to as placebo-induced side effects. Patients who react negatively or positively to a placebo tend to develop placebo-induced side effects more frequently than do neutral placebo reactors. In these studies, which used a standardized 1-hour placebo test at initial evaluation, the range was 40% to 54% for positive placebo reaction, 30% to 41% for neutral placebo reaction, 10% to 21% for negative placebo reaction, and 44% to 71% for placebo-induced side effects. Our studies indicate that it is important that these types of placebo reactions be identified, since each of them may be associated with a different origin, significance, and findings.

Placebo-induced side effects are similar in range and complexity to those reported with drug treatment, and they have contributed to the mystique and power of placebos. One study reported that 23% of 3,549 patients who participated in 67 studies had at least one side effect following treatment with placebos (Pogge, 1963). In one controlled study, we found that patients who were given placebos in the form of a drug tablet reported significantly more somatic side effects, in contrast to the cognitive and affective side effects reported by those who were given a psychotherapeutic-type placebo stimulus or patients in the control condition (Shapiro et al., 1974). Neutral and negative placebo reactors and placebo reactors with placebo-induced side effects are less extensively discussed in the literature than positive placebo reactors.

Consistency of Placebo Reaction

Five types of placebo reactors can be hypothesized: (a) general traits that predispose to placebo reactions in various environments or (b) in only specific situations, (c) specific traits that predispose to placebo reactions in various environments or (d) only in certain situations, and (e) placebo reactions as state, situational, or environmental variables.

The failure to demonstrate consistency of placebo reactions to similar placebos or to repeated administration of different types of placebo stimuli does not support the concept of a consistent placebo reactor or trait. A prevailing heuristic view, however, is that certain placebo traits, in combination with state, situational, and other factors, may predispose some individuals to placebo reactions (Calestro, 1972; Evans, 1967; Frank, 1973; Shapiro & Morris, 1978).

Demographic Variables

There are no consistent data relating demographic variables, such as age, sex, intelligence, race, social class, and ethnic or religious background, to placebo reaction.

Personality Variables

The most extensively investigated personality factor is the concept of suggestion. Tests of suggestion—most frequently a laboratory test such as the sway test—correlated with the placebo effect in four studies but not in seven others. Three of six studies, however, reported a relationship between suggestibility and clinical course. Even better results were obtained when a clinically relevant placebo test was used to predict clinical course. Five of seven studies by other investigators and seven of our studies describe a weak but significant and consistent relationship between placebo reaction and clinical course. The amount of improvement variance in our studies accounted for by initial placebo reaction varied from 2% to 16%. This relationship tended to be associated with brief and not extensive treatment. These results imply a common or overlapping mechanism for tests of suggestibility and a placebo effect that is more apparent in the clinical patient–provider relationship than in the subject–experimenter situation.

There is no evidence of a relationship between placebo reaction and such personality variables as field independence or dependence, dependency, dominance, compliance, social desirability, introversion, and extraversion. There is weak but inconsistent support for some measures of acquiescence.

Psychopathology and Symptomatology

Anxiety has been related to the placebo effect in ten studies by other investigators and in all seven studies conducted by us. Other symptoms, such as fatigue and depression, are more variable. Symptoms unrelated to placebo reaction in our studies include somatization, hyperchondriasis, obsessive-compulsiveness, anger-hostility, bewilderment-confusion, and performance difficulties. Twenty-three psychopathology variables derived from the Minnesota Multiphasic Personality Inventory (MMPI) essentially fail to identify consistent factors across samples in six of our studies.

Patient Attitude to Provider

In our seven studies of more than 1,000 psychiatric outpatients treated with placebos, psycho-chemotherapy, and psychotherapy for 6 weeks to 1 year, two variables significantly predicted improvement. The patient's positive attitude to the treatment, measured on a 7-point Likert scale, significantly correlated with improvement in all studies, accounting for 4% to 9% of the improvement variance. Even more consistently and strongly, the patient's attitude to the provider, measured by ratings of the provider's likability, physical attractiveness, and competence, accounted for 9% to 36% of the improvement variance. Since the four variables were measured at the same time, however, interpretation is limited by halo effects and by the inability to determine whether patient attitudes or attributes lead to or are produced by improvement. We were interested in assessing the objectivity of patient ratings. We asked the 13 providers in one study to rate one another's likability, physical attractiveness, and competence. Their ratings did not correlate with patient ratings, suggesting that patients do not view the provider objectively (Chassen, Janulis, Shapiro, Shapiro, Adelson, Brown, Crain, & Pinney, 1980; Shapiro, Struening, Barten, & Shapiro, 1975, 1976, 1980).

Provider Variables

Provider Attitude to Patient

The importance of the relationship between the provider and the patient has long been considered an important determinant of response to treatment. Independent variables or attributes that reflect the provider's attitude to the patient are associated with placebo effects. These attributes include warmth, friendliness, liking, interest, sympathy, and empathy, or neutrality, lack of interest, rejection, or hostility. These variables also tend to be associated with the patient's acceptance of therapy, with the number of patient dropouts and complaints, and with response to therapy.

In seven of our studies, there was a significant correlation between the physician's attitude to the patient (measured by the rating of the patient as likable, physically attractive, and a good patient for treatment) and improvement, accounting for about 25% of the improvement variance across studies. Although interpretation is limited by the previously cited halo effects, the results suggest that provider attitudes to the patient are important, not only for placebo effects but also for active or specific treatment.

Provider Attitude to Treatment

The provider's attitude to treatment is consistently reported as a nonspecific factor in placebo effects and in most treatment. Attitudes that influence outcome include faith, belief, enthusiasm, conviction, commitment, neutrality or skepticism, positive or negative expectations, and disbelief and pessimism. These factors may be independent of or may interact with the provider's attitude to the patient.

Provider Attitude to Results

The provider's attitude to results refers to data distortion caused by random observer effects and by intentional or unintentional observer bias (Rosenthal, 1966; Rosenthal & Halas, 1962). Sources of experimenter or provider bias that influence the results of the study or treatment include the provider's hypotheses, motivation, and prestige, as well as such variables as cheating, the influence of early data returns, nonspecific factors in pre-data-gathering interaction, verbal conditioning, visual and verbal cues, and experimenter and subject physical, demographic, and personality characteristics.

Status of Provider

The prestige of the investigator, provider, or healer influences clinical and experimental results and has always been one of the common denominators in "bandwagon effects" in science (Kety, 1961) and in the success of quacks (Frank, 1973), shamans (Eliode, 1964), and other healing techniques. Several studies have demonstrated that students simulating high status obtained more positive results than students simulating low status (Goldstein, 1962). On the other hand, several studies report that younger or less experienced providers obtain better results than older, more experienced providers. Younger providers may be more interested and enthusiastic than older, more experienced providers.

Indirect Iatroplacebogenics

The provider's interest in treatment and in the patient has synergistic effects and is a necessary component of most therapies. When the interest is expressed directly and induces placebo or therapeutic effects, the mechanism is referred to as direct iatroplacebogenesis. Another mechanism, probably more subtle and extensive, is referred to as indirect iatroplacebogenesis. Indirect iatroplacebogenesis occurs when patients displace the provider's interest in the therapy to themselves and experience the interest in treatment as a personal one. The provider may, in fact, be neutral or only minimally interested in the patient. However, the provider's commitment to a treatment modality may produce an intense interest in the results of therapy and may be interpreted by patients as an interest in themselves. Moreover, the provider's interest in treatment may enable the provider to be more tolerant of the patient's idiosyncracies and to accept the patient without criticism or rejection. The patient interprets this as warmth and interest. In other words, in some cases, treatment, though ostensibly directed at the patient, may unknowingly affect the provider and then mediate psychological change in the patient. The effectiveness of such treatments would be primarily due to the process of indirect iatroplacebogenesis. Support for this notion is discussed extensively elsewhere (Shapiro, 1969, 1971; Shapiro & Morris, 1978).

Situational Variables

The setting in which placebo or nonplacebo therapy is administered is an important determinant of its effectiveness. Situational variables include the effect of the setting, such as differences in reaction to wounds or pain, depending on whether they occurred as a result of surgery or in battle (Beecher, 1956); interpretation of subjective reactions by means of situational cues (Schachter & Singer, 1962); the general therapeutic milieu of treatment, such as staff attitudes, expectations, biases, conflicts, and harmony among staff; "Hawthorne effects"; whether the treatment is primarily in an institution or in a private office; whether it is part of a research protocol; whether the sample comprises volunteers, experimental subjects, or clinical patients; group pressures and reactions to other patients; intercurrent significant life events; the process of filling out questionnaires; the type of referral; the cost of treatment; the type and size of the practice; the reputation of the therapist; the atmosphere of the office (informal or intermittent, busy or unhurried, supporting or rejecting, etc.); the use of therapeutic adjuncts, such as nurses or aides, to administer treatments; reinforced directions by means of written information or audiovisual aids that describe treatment and potential side effects; and so on.

THEORIES OF PLACEBOGENESIS

Many theories have been proposed to explain placebo effects. Although there is no experimental verification for most of these theories, they may be important heuristically in organizing and integrating the relationships and predisposing factors associated with the placebo effect. These theories, described elsewhere (Jospe, 1978; Shapiro & Morris, 1978), can be grouped into three categories: social influence effects (suggestion, persuasion, transference, role demands, operant conditioning, and guilt reduction); expectance effects (cognitive dissonance, classical conditioning, internal standards, and mobilization of hope); and evaluation effects (response artifacts, labeling, and misattribution).

SUMMARY AND CONCLUSIONS

We are still far from understanding the placebo effect, although many studies have attempted to do so. Studies of personality, psychodynamics, learned contingencies, cognitive dissonance, and demographic, sociocultural, and other factors have not succeeded in explaining the power of the placebo. We have also concluded that, on the whole, these studies do not support a specific or important effect of the placebo on physical illness.

In six of our studies of the placebo effect and subsequent psychiatric treatment, we have demonstrated a consistent association between positive placebo reaction and the patient's desire for drug treatment if the placebo is a drug; a trusting attitude toward the doctor, reflected by the patient's desire to leave the choice of treatment to the doctor; the presence of symptoms of anxiety or fatigue; a positive attitude to the physician, reflected by rating the doctor high on likability, physical attractiveness, and competence; and faith in the physician and treatment, reflected by the patient's assumption that the placebo stimulus is an active and specific drug for the patient's problems, rather than an inappropriate, inactive, or nonspecific drug. Less frequently, positive placebo reactions have been associated with previous treatment, the tendency to admit to symptoms, prior use of over-the-counter medications, and some but not all measures of acquiescence. Patients with minor, acute, or subacute illness (especially those with a spontaneous waxing and waning of symptomatology)—such as anxiety, fatigue, depression, rheumatoid arthritis, pain, and irritable colon—are more likely to respond with positive placebo reactions than are patients with severe, chronic, and unremitting illness, such as malignancies, severe congestive heart failure, heart block, chronic obsessive-compulsive illness, or schizophrenia.

We have been unable to account for individual variation in placebo responsivity. Why do some patients have the capacity to be optimistic or positive placebo reactors, while others have little or no capacity for the development of optimism and are not placebo reactors, and still others—the negative placebo reactors—remain depressed, symptomatic, and impaired? Possibly, part of the answer is genetic. Positive placebo reactors may have an evolutionary advantage, since positive attitudes may lead to the maintenance of health and the prevention of illness and may ensure survival and procreation, whereas negative attitudes may increase illness and hasten death.

Perhaps we should search for a genetic placebo hormone that stimulates the hope, optimism, and motivation required to deal with a difficult world. Although one study cited endogenous, self-induced opiates as a possible candidate for an analgesic placebo hormone in dental pain (Levine, Gordon, & Fields, 1978), the findings have not yet been replicated (Watkins & Mayer, 1982).

Although the issue of how to use the placebo effect in provider–patient relationships is largely unsolved (despite widespread interest throughout medical history), a few simple and obvious suggestions are possible. The positive relationship between improvement and the patient's faith in the provider's treatment and competence can be enhanced if the provider relies on scientific evidence and medical data about how to treat most effectively. This factor assumes greater importance today, as medicine has become more technologically sophisticated and specific.

At the same time, nonspecific factors involved in the art of medicine—the provider–patient relationship and the placebo effect of treatment—can be used to improve therapy in largely unknown, nonspecific, and unpredictable ways. Certain factors in the provider–patient relationship have been identified that augment placebo effects. These factors include the patient's perception of the provider as warm, empathic, reliable, stable, physically attractive, likable, and competent, and the patient's belief in the provider and the treatment. Whether they are fantasied or real, these attitudes will tend to maximize the nonspecific or placebo effects of treatment. Other factors that influence the interactions between the two participants play complicated roles in the placebo effect of treatment. Providers who are sensitive to these factors and who use them, knowingly or unknowingly, may be most successful in maintaining the patient's health, which ultimately is the art of medicine.

Traditionally, the provider has been concerned with health maintenance and treatment of the disease process; thus, the provider was the healer and the sick person was the patient. The development of new technologies and the broadening scope of medicine to include the concept of prevention may alter the traditional relationship between the provider and the patient. The new technologies—such as biofeedback, behavioral techniques, and reliance on physical exercise and diet—have increased individual responsibility by assigning an active, independent role to the patient.

Although this development is probably multidetermined, the placebo effect may be its most important determinant. Implicit in the placebo effect is the recognition that the patient brings attitudes and belief systems to the therapeutic situation that can be more powerful than the specific action of a drug. Self-help therapies—those that maximize individual responsibility—have, perhaps unknowingly, taken advantage of this factor. The provider now provides a milieu that maximizes the patient's contribution by changing his or her role from passive to active. Reliance on individual responsibility may maximize placebo effects in our culture. Although substantative evidence that these methods can reverse the course of an illness or influence health is lacking, the health-promoting principles implicit in the concepts of self-help methods, holistic medicine, and behavioral health have an obvious face validity. Precise methods and the extent to which they influence the prevention of disease and the maintenance and promotion of health are empirical issues that will require carefully controlled study by epidemiologists, social and learning psychologists, sociologists, and professionals in other relevant disciplines.

REFERENCES

Armaroli, B. Rx for good health—Nutrition. *Medicine on the Midway,* 1982, **36,** 3.

Beecher, H. K. Relationship of significance of wound to pain experienced. *Journal of the American Medical Association,* 1956, **161,** 1609–1613.

Brody, H. *Placebos and the philosophy of medicine.* Chicago: University of Chicago Press, 1980.

Calestro, K. M. Psychotherapy, faith healing and suggestion. *International Psychiatry,* 1972, **10,** 83.

Chassen, J., Janulis, P. T., & Shapiro, A. K. An application of intensive design to psychotherapy. *Journal of Psychosynthesis,* 1975, **7,** 32–35.

Chassen, J., Janulis, P. T., Shapiro, A. K., Shapiro, E., Adelson, E. T., Brown, J. W., Crain, P., & Pinney, E., Jr. Preliminary study of intensive design in psychotherapy. *Comprehensive Psychotherapy,* 1980, **1,** 111–125.

Cousins, N. *Anatomy of an illness.* New York: Norton, 1979.

Dorland, W. A. N. *The American illustrated medical dictionary.* Philadelphia: Saunders, 1981.

Eliode, M. *Shamanism.* New York: Random House, 1964.

Evans, F. S. Suggestibility in the normal waking state. *Psychological Bulletin,* 1967, **67,** 114–129.

Frank, J. D. *Persuasion and healing.* Baltimore: Johns Hopkins University Press, 1973.

Garrison, F. H. *An introduction to the history of medicine.* Philadelphia: Saunders, 1921.

Goldstein, A. P. *Therapist-patient expectancies in psychotherapy.* New York: Pergamon Press, 1962.

Gould, B. A., Mann, S., Davies, A. B., Altman, D. G., & Raftery, E. B. Does placebo lower blood pressure? *Lancet,* 1981, **2,** 1377–1381.

Grünbaum, A. The placebo concept. *Behaviour Research and Therapy,* 1981, **19,** 157–167.

Hass, J., Fink, H., & Hartflider, G. Das placebo problem . . . Translation of selected parts. *Psychopharmacology Service Center Bulletin,* 1963, **2,** 1–65.

Herink, R. *The psychotherapy handbook.* New York: New American Library, 1980.

Honigfeld, G. Non-specific factors in treatment: I. Review of placebo reactions and placebo reactors. *Diseases of the Nervous System,* 1964, **25,** 145–156. (a)

Honigfeld, G. Non-specific factors in treatment: II. Review of social-psychological factors. *Diseases of the Nervous System,* 1964, **25,** 225–239. (b)

Houston, W. R. The doctor himself as a therapeutic agent. *Annals of Internal Medicine,* 1938, **8,** 1416–1425.

Hovland, C. E., Janis, I. L., & Kelley, H. H. *Communication and persuasion: Psychological studies of opinion change.* New Haven: Yale University Press, 1953.

Jospe, M. *The placebo effect in healing.* Lexington, Mass.: Lexington Books, 1978.

Kety, S. The academic lecture, the heuristic aspect of psychiatry. *American Journal of Psychiatry,* 1961, **118**, 363–397.

Kissel, P., & Barrucand, O. *Placebos et effet placebo en médecine.* Paris: Mason e Cie, 1964.

Lepper, M. R. The effects of persuasion. Review of: *Cognitive responses in persuasion,* edited by R. E. Petty, T. M. Ostrom, and T. C. Brock. *Science,* 1981, **214**, 326.

Levine, J. D., Gordon, N. C., & Fields, H. L. The mechanism of placebo analgesia. *Lancet,* 1978, **11**, 654.

Morris, L. A., & Shapiro, A. K. Performance of psychiatric patients on the rod-and-frame test. *Journal of Clinical Psychology,* 1973, **29**, 180–181.

Morris, L. A., & Shapiro, A. K. MMPI scores for FD and FI psychiatric outpatients. *Journal of Consulting and Clinical Psychology,* 1974, **42**, 364–369.

Parloff, M. B. Psychotherapy research evidence and reimbursement decisions: Bambi meets Godzilla. *American Journal of Psychiatry,* 1982, **139**, 718.

Pepper, O. H. P. A note on the placebo. *American Journal of Pharmacy,* 1945, **117**, 409.

Petty, R. E., Ostrom, T. M., & Brock, T. C. (Eds.). *Cognitive responses in persuasion.* Hillsdale, N.J.: Erlbaum, 1981.

Pogge, R. The toxic placebo. *Medical Times,* 1963, **91**, 773–778.

Rosenthal, R. *Experimenter effects in behavioral research.* New York: Appleton-Century-Crofts, 1966.

Rosenthal, R., & Halas, E. S. Experimenter effect in the study of invertebrate behavior. *Psychological Reports,* 1962, **11**, 251–256.

Schachter, S., & Singer, J. E. Cognitive, social and physiological determinants of emotional state. *Psychological Review,* 1962, **69**, 379–399.

Shapiro, A. K. The placebo effect in the history of medical treatment: Implications for psychiatry. *American Journal of Psychiatry,* 1959, **116**, 298–304.

Shapiro, A. K. A contribution to a history of the placebo effect. *Behavioral Science,* 1960, **5**, 109–135.

Shapiro, A. K. A historic and heuristic definition of the placebo. *Psychiatry,* 1964, **27**, 52–58. (a)

Shapiro, A. K. Rejoinder. *Psychiatry,* 1964, **27**, 178–181. (b)

Shapiro, A. K. Semantics of the placebo. *Psychiatric Quarterly,* 1968, **42**, 653–695.

Shapiro, A. K. Iatroplacebogenics. *International Pharmacopsychiatry,* 1969, **2**, 215–248.

Shapiro, A. K. Placebo effects in psychotherapy and psychoanalysis. In A. E. Bergin & S. L. Garfield (Eds.), *Handbook of psychotherapy and behavior change.* New York: Aldine, 1971.

Shapiro, A. K. Psychochemotherapy. In R. G. Grenell & S. Gabay (Eds.), *Biological foundations of psychiatry.* New York: Raven Press, 1976.

Shapiro, A. K. The placebo effect. In W. G. Clark & J. Del Guidice (Eds.), *Principles of psychopharmacology.* New York: Academic Press, 1978.

Shapiro, A. K., Frick, R., Morris, L., Chassen, J., & Shapiro, E. Placebo induced side effects. *Journal of Operant Psychiatry,* 1974, **6**, 43–46.

Shapiro, A. K., Mike, B., Barten, H., & Shapiro, E. Study of the placebo effect with a test of placebo reactivity. *Comprehensive Psychiatry,* 1973, **14**, 535–548.

Shapiro, A. K., & Morris, L. The placebo effect in healing. In S. L. Garfield & A. E. Bergin (Eds.), *Handbook of psychotherapy and behavior change.* New York: Aldine, 1978.

Shapiro, A. K., & Shapiro, E. The placebo effect: Art or science? *Medical Times,* 1982, **110**, 45s; 46s; 50s; 52s.

Shapiro, A. K., Shapiro, E., Bruun, R. D., & Sweet, R. D. *Gilles de la Tourette syndrome.* New York: Raven Press, 1978.

Shapiro, A. K., & Struening, E. L. Defensiveness in the definition of placebo. *Comprehensive Psychiatry,* 1973, **14**, 107–120. (a)

Shapiro, A. K., & Struening, E. L. The use of placebos: A study of ethics and physicians' attitudes. *Psychiatry in Medicine,* 1973, **4**, 17–29. (b)

Shapiro, A. K., & Struening, E. L. Attributing the use of placebos or nonspecific treatment to other physicians. *Journal of Psychiatric Research,* 1974, **10**, 217–229.

Shapiro, A. K., Struening, E. L., Barten, H., & Shapiro, E. Correlates of placebo reaction in an outpatient population. *Psychological Medicine,* 1975, **5,** 389–396.

Shapiro, A. K., Struening, E. L., Barten, H., & Shapiro, E. Prognostic correlates of psychotherapy. *American Journal of Psychiatry,* 1976, **113,** 802–808.

Shapiro, A. K., Struening, E. L., Barten, H., & Shapiro, E. Predictors of treatment outcome in psychiatric outpatients. *Comprehensive Psychotherapy,* 1980, **1,** 126–176.

Shapiro, A. K., Struening, E. L., & Shapiro, E. Reliability and validity of a placebo test. *Journal of Psychiatric Research,* 1980, **15,** 253–290.

Shapiro, A. K., Struening, E. L., Shapiro, E., & Milcarek, B. I. Diazepam: How much better than placebo? *Journal of Psychiatric Research,* 1983, **17,** 51–73.

Shapiro, A. K., Wilensky, H., & Struening, E. L. Study of the placebo effect with a placebo test. *Comprehensive Psychiatry,* 1968, **9,** 118–137.

Stave, F. J. Of myths and megavitamins. *Medicine on the Midway,* 1982, **36,** 3.

Turner, J. L., Gallimore, R., & Fox-Henning, C. *An annotated bibliography of placebo research* (Journal Supplement Abstract Service). Washington, D.C.: American Psychological Association, 1980.

Watkins, L. R., & Mayer, D. J. Organization of endogenous opiate and nonopiate pain control systems. *Science,* 1982, **216,** 1185.

Wilson, E. O. *On human nature.* Cambridge, Mass.: Harvard University Press, 1978.

CHAPTER 26

SOCIAL-PSYCHOLOGICAL INFLUENCES ON THE COMPLIANCE PROCESS: IMPLICATIONS FOR BEHAVIORAL HEALTH

PHYLLIS E. SENSENIG
ROBERT B. CIALDINI

Arizona State University

There certainly has been no shortage of comprehensive reviews of the distressingly large problem of patient noncompliance and of methods to reduce the problem (e.g., Blackwell, 1973, 1976; Cohen, 1979; Haynes, Taylor, & Sackett, 1979; Masur, 1981; Sackett & Haynes, 1976; Svarstad, 1976; Withersty, Stevenson, & Waldman, 1980). Therefore, this chapter will not provide another examination of the same work. Rather, the chapter is designed to complement the earlier reviews by offering a somewhat different orientation to the overall topic.

The major point of departure of our approach lies in its nearly exclusive focus on psychological *principles* in the determination of *general* compliance action. Although much of value has been learned from research into specific procedures—many of them nonpsychological (e.g., telephone reminders, written instructions, mobile clinics, enhanced supervision)—that are likely to increase adherence to health regimens, we believed that a more conceptual and social-psychological analysis would also be of benefit. An understanding of the compliance process based on basic social-psychological principles would enable a health practitioner to tailor potentially useful compliance procedures more successfully to the features of a specific health program.

The psychological principles that determine general compliance action often generate well-learned, automatic behavior patterns. These behavior patterns are adaptive to the individual (most of the time) because they reduce the number of decisions that must be made in dealing with the environment on a daily basis. The act of driving an automobile, for example, is frequently guided by overlearned, automatic behavior patterns. The patterns that guide compliance behaviors may also be overlearned ways of reacting to certain crucial cues in the environment.

Cues in the structure of the environmental setting can determine whether a particular automatic behavior pattern is enacted. Knowledgeable compliance professionals can structure a setting in such a way that naturally occurring behavior tendencies are maximized, resulting in the desired compliance behavior.

In order to identify the social-psychological principles that underlie the general compliance process, Cialdini (1984) undertook an extensive program of systematic observation into the workings of naturally existing compliance settings, particularly those of a commercial nature. This insight into the ecological potency of a principle or variable is not one that is typically afforded by controlled, experimental research. The experimental paradigm, in which naturally occurring and potentially overwhelming or interacting sources of extraneous variance are eliminated, is better suited to answering the question of whether an effect is reliable rather than whether it is meaningfully-sized. For a more complete discussion of the respective roles of experimentation and cross-situational natural observation in the study of compliance, the reader may wish to refer to Cialdini (1980). Cialdini's (1984) decision to focus on compliance contexts involving merchandising, bargaining, and fund raising was based on a highly valuable property of these contexts for an observer—the success or failure of a technique within them tends to be money-based. Because the livelihoods of compliance professionals in such areas depend on the effectiveness of the tactics they use, procedures that are powerful and work well will necessarily rise to prominence. A logic akin to that governing the law of natural selection assures it. Professionals who employ practices that produce compliance will flourish; those who do not will fail and consequently will not pass their practices on to succeeding generations.

Wherever the success of compliance strategies is linked directly to professional survival, a body of adaptive strategies will develop and proliferate. This is not so true, however, in contexts such as patient compliance, in which an ineffective compliance device does not so inexorably or so ruthlessly affect the welfare of the practitioner. The consequence of the survival-of-the-fittest character of commercial compliance techniques is that, as a group, they offer richly instructive information regarding the most potent influences on the compliance process. This is especially so when systematic observation reveals which of these influences appear consistently within and across a range of compliance settings. If, for example, such observation determined that a variety of compliance professionals constructed their techniques so as to engage the action of a certain psychological principle when it existed naturally in a situation, to amplify it when it existed only minimally, or, most tellingly, to manufacture it when it did not exist normally in the situation, all those interested in the compliance process should take note. It would be highly likely that the principle represented a forceful and pervasive motivator of compliance.

Of course, the specific techniques used by commercial compliance professionals are not directly transferable to patient compliance and promotive health settings. In many instances, these tactics are neither ethically nor practically appropriate for the medical context. Examples of specific techniques will be used here, however, to illustrate the operation of the underlying social-psychological principle that provides a technique's power. An understanding of the underlying principle will allow the health practitioner to apply it to specific health programs.

A small number of basic social-psychological principles account for the great majority of specific compliance tactics employed in commercial settings (Cialdini, 1984). The remainder of this chapter will describe the four principles we deem to be most prevalent in the range of compliance practices surveyed and, simultaneously, most applicable to health settings. This group of four principles is by no means an exhaustive list. Other compliance-related principles exist that enjoy much use and success (e.g., scarcity, liking, dependency). It is our belief, however, that the four principles treated fully in this chapter offer the best prospects for programs designed to enhance patient compliance. In addition to brief conceptual treatments of the principles and illustrations of how they are frequently employed in standard compliance contexts, we will offer suggestions regarding how the principles can be used to reduce the problem of patient nonadherence to promotive health care regimens.

COMMITMENT AND CONSISTENCY

Social scientists have noted a strong pressure for people to be and to appear consistent in their words and actions (Festinger, 1957; Heider, 1958; Tedeschi, Schlenker, & Bonoma,

1971). This pressure for consistency is engaged in a given situation through the act of commitment. Once a position is taken, there is a resultant tendency to behave in ways that are congruent with that position.

The ability of even minimal commitments to generate relatively large-scale and long-term behavioral consistency has been demonstrated experimentally in research on the foot-in-the-door compliance technique (Freedman & Fraser, 1966). A requester using this technique first asks a target person for a small favor that is virtually certain to be granted. After making this sort of commitment, the target person becomes more likely to comply with much larger, related requests.

Freedman and Fraser (1966) suggested that the foot-in-the-door technique is so effective because it influences the target person's self-perception. After agreeing to some small request—for example, signing a petition in favor of safe driving—the target person comes to view himself or herself as the sort of person who supports road safety and who generally takes public service action. Later, larger public service requests are more likely to be granted because they are consistent with this revised self-image. Thus, the key to an initial commitment's overall capacity to induce compliance is its effect on relevant self-perceptions.

For maximal impact on self-perception, a commitment should possess at least four properties. It should be active (Bem, 1967), public (Deutsch & Gerard, 1955), effortful (Aronson & Mills, 1959), and viewed as internally motivated—that is, uncoerced (Freedman, 1965). In addition to its immediate impact on an individual's self-image, a commitment incorporating these four features is likely to maintain consistent behavior for another reason: the individual will be motivated to seek and generate new reasons to support the commitment (Erlich, Guttman, Schonbach, & Mills, 1957).

The way compliance professionals employ a small commitment strategy to greatly enhance compliance is illustrated by the reaction of certain door-to-door sales operators to the enactment of "cooling-off" laws in many states. These laws allow customers several days to reconsider any major purchase and, if they wish, to cancel the purchase agreement without penalty. Because they typically use tactics designed to push customers into a hasty, ill-considered decision, many door-to-door sales operations were hurt by legislation giving customers a chance to reconsider after the salesperson had left. The companies' solution to the problem was elemental: they now have the customer, rather than the salesperson, fill out all the details of the bill of sale and contract. According to the report of one prominent encyclopedia sales company, that personal commitment alone has proved to be a very important psychological aid in preventing customers from backing out of their contracts.

Even though the commitment procedure employed by the hard-sell companies is quite simple, it embodies all four of the features that lead to lasting compliance. Personally writing down the specifics of an agreement is an active, public, relatively effortful behavior that requires little coercion. The result, apparently, is that customers live up to what they have written down.

Health practitioners may wish to take into account the experimental and marketplace evidence for the effectiveness of commitment in designing procedures to improve adherence to promotive health care programs among their patients. Such procedures should incorporate the components of action, publicness, effort, and perceived internal motivation. To reduce missed appointments for annual checkups, for example, patients might be asked to write out their own appointment reminders. Similarly, during annual checkups, patients might be requested to generate and write down their own health goals, in the form of a contract with the health professional and significant others (Steckel & Swain, 1977; Swain & Steckel, 1981). Recent research indicates that these goals will be more effective if they are proximate rather than long-term (Bandura & Schunk, 1981). If patients are allowed to determine their own health goals and to select from an array of sound diet and exercise regimens, contracting will have all four properties of a commitment that can have maximal impact on the patients' self-perceptions: it is active, public, effortful, and internally motivated.

Contracting also induces a more active patient orientation to lifestyle change and to the prevention of health problems.

Contracting also may be useful in prenatal care. Pregnant women could be encouraged to contract with their spouses and family members to abstain from drugs and alcohol for the duration of their pregnancies, and to follow the diet and exercise recommendations of their physicians. Such a procedure also may be useful in encouraging dental hygiene; dental patients may contract with the dental hygienist and their spouses or parents to brush and floss their teeth regularly.

Commitment may also be used to improve adherence to promotive health regimens in other, less traditional health care settings. Wearing a printed T-shirt that advocates exercise or advertises a health spa will strengthen one's commitment to exercise by increasing its publicness.

As individuals continue to comply with their chosen promotive health regimens, they will seek to strengthen existing reasons for this compliance and to generate new ones (Erlich et al., 1957). Therefore, it is important that the health practitioner make available materials or information that can provide such reasons (feeling healthier, looking better, living longer, etc.) throughout the promotive health program, rather than only at its outset, as is typical.

SOCIAL VALIDATION

One of the most important sources of information about the correctness of our beliefs and actions in a situation is how others in the situation are believing and acting (Festinger, 1954; Kelley, 1952). For this reason, compliance professionals of various kinds use *social evidence*—sometimes real, sometimes manufactured—to convince target persons to behave in desired ways. The tip jars of bartenders and the collection baskets of church ushers, for example, are often "salted" from the outset, usually with dollar bills, to give the impression that others believe folding money to be the appropriate contribution. Charity telethons feature the incessant reading of pledges from donors of all types, suggesting wide-ranging social support for a positive attitude and a helpful stance toward the cause. Door-to-door charity solicitors show potential donors long lists of other contributors; this device has been experimentally demonstrated to be effective by Reingen (1982), who found that the longer the list of prior contributors shown a prospect, the more likely was a donation.

As a compliance technique, social evidence is most powerful under two circumstances: when the situation is ambiguous and when the comparison others are similar to the target person. Regarding ambiguity, for example, research on bystander intervention has shown that the helping responses of witnesses to an emergency are strongly influenced by the actions of others only when the nature of the situation is unclear (e.g., Clark & Word, 1972, 1974). Additional evidence from the literature documents the importance of similarity. Hornstein, Fisch, and Holmes (1968), for instance, showed that New Yorkers' decisions to return a lost wallet were affected by the prior experience of a model only when the model was depicted as similar to themselves.

Health professionals who are concerned with patient compliance may wish to commission the power inherent in social evidence through the use of such procedures as (a) publicizing increases in exercising and other promotive health behaviors among the general population, (b) displaying before and after pictures of other patients who have been successful in reaching their health and exercise goals, and (c) obtaining written testimonials to the beneficial effects of promotive health programs from successful patients. Health practitioners should keep a variety of such pictures and testimonials on hand so that all patients can view models who are similar to themselves.

Community health organizations may also encourage environmental and city planners to develop exercise facilities in popular public parks and recreation areas. Seeing a variety of people working through a Par course at a popular park can provide social validation for this type of behavior to other members of the population. The marketing activities of a variety of health clubs and weight loss services also provide social validation for healthful behaviors. The health practitioner may wish to discuss with patients programs that are deemed acceptable and beneficial, to improve the credibility of such programs and to enhance the power of the social evidence they provide.

CREDIBILITY

It is hardly surprising that recommendations that come from a prestigious and credible source will be more influential than those from a less respected communicator (Aronson, Turner, & Carlsmith, 1963). Nonetheless, credibility's potency as a mediator of compliance should not be minimized, as witnessed by the frequent appeals to credibility embedded in advertising messages of various sorts. Manufacturers strive to enhance the perceived value of their products through their claims as specialists ("Babies are our business, our only business") or long-standing experts ("Since 1841") and through links to trustworthy spokespersons or organizations ("The breakfast drink selected by NASA for the astronauts").

The dual components of credibility—expertise and trustworthiness—are nicely represented in the standard health setting, typically within the physician, whose occupation is traditionally accorded much status and respect by our culture. Many times, however, those health practitioners who are charged with stimulating and monitoring patient adherence to prescribed regimens have positions with less built-in credibility (e.g., physician's assistant, physical therapist, nurse). All other things being equal, they are less likely to generate compliance with the suggested regimen.

One way to reduce this problem would be to have physicians play a more active, personal role in promoting adherence. Where this is unfeasible, the physician may lend his or her credibility to the assistant by attesting at the outset of the treatment program to the assistant's experience with the medical problems at hand, by noting any special training received, and by citing examples of the assistant's past successful treatment of persons similar to the patient (thereby also bringing to bear the influence of social validation). Messages of this kind may be enhanced by display of diplomas received by the entire staff on the walls of the examining room or wherever patients receive instruction. Of course, the assistants can also bolster their own credibility by maintaining a professional demeanor and by sharing information relevant to their personal training and competence.

Health practitioners' personal physical fitness can have a great impact on their credibility when they are recommending lifestyle changes to patients. If the health professionals smoke, are overweight, or do not exercise regularly, their credibility in the eyes of the patients will suffer, regardless of the excellence of their training. A "do as I say, not as I do" stance on promotive health behavior by health professionals can be extremely detrimental to the success of any promotive health program. Those who are involved in health-related fields must look closely at their own health behavior before recommending lifestyle changes to others.

RECIPROCATION

It is a well-documented social-psychological phenomenon that a person who receives a favor from an individual will be more likely to provide a favor to that individual in the future (e.g., Regan, 1971). This phenomenon occurs because there is a social norm in our society that says "you should give benefits to those who give you benefits" (Gouldner, 1960).

Many sales and fund-raising techniques make use of this social pressure. The salesperson initially gives something to the potential customer, thereby causing the consumer to be more likely to give something in return. Of course, this "something in return" is what the salesperson had in mind from the outset. An unsolicited gift, accompanied by a request for a donation, is a commonly used technique that utilizes the norm for reciprocation.

One example, experienced by many people, is the Hare Krishna solicitor who gives the unwary passerby a book or a flower and then asks for a donation. Other organizations send gifts through the mail and count on the fact that most recipients will not go to the trouble of returning the gift, but will feel uncomfortable about keeping it without reciprocating in some way. Such organizations also count on the willingness of people to send a contribution that is larger than the cost of the gift they received.

A variation of the norm for reciprocation of favors is the reciprocation of concessions. The reciprocal concessions procedure for inducing compliance has been documented by Cialdini, Vincent, Lewis, Catalan, Wheeler, and Darby (1975). When one bargaining party retreats from an initial demand to a second, smaller one, social conventions require the other party to reciprocate that concession. If the first party starts out, however, by making a request much greater than that which is actually desired, he or she may make concessions down from the original demand, eventually "settling" for what was really wanted in the first place.

This reciprocal concessions procedure makes use of both the social pressure for reciprocation and a perceptual contrast effect. After comparison to the larger request, the smaller request appears even smaller. In combination, the influences of reciprocity pressures and perceptual contrast produce a very powerful effect.

In a health-related setting, Cialdini and Ascani (1976) used the reciprocal concessions technique to solicit blood donors. They first requested a person's involvement in a long-term donor program. When that request was refused, the solicitor made a smaller request for a one-time donation. Fifty percent of these subjects volunteered to donate once, whereas significantly fewer (32%) of the control subjects, who were asked only for the smaller request (the one-time donation), agreed to do so. Furthermore, when the subjects subsequently arrived at the donation center, those who had been exposed to the reciprocal concessions technique were much more likely to maintain their compliance by volunteering for future donations than were the control subjects who had come to donate (84% vs. 43%).

The powerful social pressure for reciprocation may be applied in other health settings to improve patient compliance. The health practitioner may be able to give the patient free books outlining selected diet and exercise regimens or, where possible, one of a limited number of free placements in a health organization's fitness program. If the health practitioner stresses the importance of adhering to the prescribed regimen and makes it clear that the free materials are scarce and that providing them is a favor, the patient should feel more inclined to reciprocate the favor by following the regimen faithfully. It must be made clear that it is important to the health practitioner that the patient comply with the prescribed regimen. It is also important that the same health practitioner whom the patient perceives as most interested in his or her compliance should be the one to whom the favor is owed.

The reciprocal concessions technique also may be used to increase patient adherence to promotive health regimens. The health practitioner may make use of this technique by first recommending the most beneficial (even if most difficult) regimen. If the patient adheres to this regimen, there is no compliance problem, and maximal benefit can be achieved. If the patient fails to adhere to this difficult regimen, as may well occur, the health practitioner may retreat to an easier but still adequate regimen. The health practitioner should emphasize that this is a concession on his or her part. In contrast to the first regimen, the second will appear much more practicable. Combined with a socialized desire to reciprocate the concession, the perceptual contrast effect should induce the patient to adhere to this new regimen.

The reciprocal concessions technique may have a variety of health-related uses, from improving appointment keeping to improving adherence to a lifestyle change regimen. Each situation is different, so each health practitioner must adapt the technique to his or her own needs. The important point to remember is that it is most advisable to start the patient on a rigorous regimen rather than on the one the health practitioner believes is most likely to be complied with. The health practitioner may wish to use the other compliance pressures (consistency, credibility, social validation, and so on) to induce the patient to adhere to the most beneficial and rigorous regimens. If these pressures fail to maintain compliance, the physician can then use the retreat procedure of reciprocal concessions.

This approach, as compared to recommending a less difficult and less effective regimen from the outset, will allow compliance with the most beneficial program among those patients who are willing to follow it and should also enhance compliance with the still adequate program among those patients who do not find the more difficult program feasible. Two warnings are necessary, however. First, the health practitioner should avoid characterizing noncompliance with the initial regimen as a failure on the part of the patient; a perception of failure could discourage the patient to the point of being unable to comply with the second regimen as well. Instead, the health practitioner should indicate that the first regimen was simply ill-suited for that patient and should then use the retreat procedure. Second, such a sequencing of recommended treatment programs is advisable only when patient noncompliance is detectable. If the patient's failure to adhere to the first, more rigorous regimen cannot be assessed, the technique would, of course, be inapplicable. In the many health settings where detection of noncompliance is not a great problem (such as weight loss or dental hygiene), however, the practitioner may wish to consider the usefulness of the reciprocal concessions procedure.

DISCUSSION

Health professionals may become more successful in inducing their patients to comply with therapeutic regimens by broadening their perspectives on compliance to include the compliance literature developed outside the medical field. Of particular interest are the compliance tactics devised by professionals who depend on the efficacy of their techniques for their livelihoods. Of course, the specific compliance techniques devised by salespeople and other compliance professionals generally are not appropriate for use by health professionals, for they often are high-pressure tactics that would be unethical in a medical context. The social psychological principles that underlie the specific compliance tactics, however, may be applied to the medical context in an ethical manner.

It is to our minds wholly ethical, for instance, for health practitioners to enhance their credibility—and consequent persuasiveness regarding promotive health—by displaying legitimately earned health care credentials (diplomas, certifications, etc.). This is entirely different from the unethical credibility-enhancing tactics of certain sales operators, who employ bogus information concerning their backgrounds. In both cases, the force of a powerful influence on compliance is employed, but the specific tactics that engage that influence are importantly different. Therefore, we advise learning not specific compliance tactics but, rather, the principles governing human decision-making and compliance behavior and then applying these principles ethically to the context of health behavior.

Our focus to this point has been on the individual principles and their effect on compliance with promotive health regimens. It is our view, however, that such principles will be maximally effective when they are combined in a systems approach (Varela, 1971, 1977). By combining these principles in an integrated program that is designed to increase adherence, the health practitioner can generate a powerful and multiply-based intervention that is likely to be effective for a wider range of individuals than would be an approach based on any single principle. In addition, the action of one principle in such a system can increase the power of the other principles involved.

A health professional whose credibility has been enhanced, for example, would be more persuasive in suggesting actions that could produce health behavior commitments from the patient. A patient so persuaded to make a commitment to joining an exercise group, for example, would then receive social validation for this commitment from the other members of the group. This social validation would, in turn, increase the patient's commitment to the chosen health behaviors.

Combining several principles into a systems approach could also be helpful in deterring children from smoking cigarettes. A person who is credible to a group of teenagers, such as a popular teacher, could encourage the group to contract among themselves not to start smoking (or to quit if they have already started). The first member of the group to smoke might, for example, have to perform a small chore for every other member of the group. This type of intervention would engage the principles of credibility, commitment, and social validation as the teenagers observe one another behaving in the agreed-upon manner. The group members might also feel inclined to reciprocate the attention and interest shown by the credible adult by engaging in the desired behavior.

Organizations whose primary focus is not health behavior can also encourage people to engage in healthy activities. The walk-a-thons promoted by a variety of charity organizations as fund-raisers, for example, combine the principles of commitment and social validation to encourage people to engage in healthful behaviors and, at the same time, to raise funds for a worthy cause. Participants commit themselves to the walk-a-thons through the act of obtaining sponsors for their performance; seeing a large number of similar others also participating provides social validation for the behavior. Health professionals may wish to encourage their patients to participate in such activities, and work to encourage charity organizations to imbue their fund-raising activities with this type of commitment to healthy activity.

It would seem to be more cost-effective to make changes in behavior settings that influence the compliance behavior of the majority of people who encounter them, rather than trying to change the behavior of the individual from the outset. People who are resistant to social-psychological compliance influences may then be treated more intensively on an individual basis. For any compliance approach to have maximal impact, however, it is necessary that patients take an active orientation to their own health. Health professionals must stress individuals' responsibility for their own health behavior; only the patients can ensure that the health regimens are followed.

Health care practitioners can structure professional encounters in such a way that the principles that naturally induce compliance are present and add to other inducements already present in the environment. Each health care setting is different, so health professionals must adapt their use of the principles to fit the needs of their individual situations. Therefore, it is important that health professionals themselves understand the nature of the principles.

REFERENCES

Aronson, E., & Mills, J. The effect of severity of initiation on liking for a group. *Journal of Abnormal and Social Psychology,* 1959, **59,** 177–181.

Aronson, E., Turner, J., & Carlsmith, J. Communicator credibility and communication discrepancy as determinants of opinion change. *Journal of Abnormal and Social Psychology,* 1963, **67,** 31–36.

Bandura, A., & Schunk, D. H. Cultivating competence, self-efficacy, and intrinsic interest through proximal self-motivation. *Journal of Personality and Social Psychology,* 1981, **41,** 586–598.

Bem, D. J. Self-perception: An alternative interpretation of cognitive dissonance phenomena. *Psychological Review,* 1967, **74,** 182–200.

Blackwell, B. Patient compliance. *New England Journal of Medicine,* 1973, **289,** 249–253.

Blackwell, B. Treatment adherence. *British Journal of Psychiatry,* 1976, **129,** 513–531.

Cialdini, R. B. Full cycle social psychology. In L. Bickman (Ed.), *Applied social psychology annual* (Vol. 1). Beverly Hills: Sage, 1980.

Cialdini, R. B. *Influence.* New York: Morrow, 1984.

Cialdini, R. B., & Ascani, R. Test of a concession procedure for inducing verbal, behavioral and further compliance with a request to give blood. *Journal of Applied Psychology,* 1976, **3,** 295–300.

Cialdini, R. B., Vincent, J., Lewis, S., Catalan, J., Wheeler, D., & Darby, B. Reciprocal concessions procedure for inducing compliance: The door-in-the-face technique. *Journal of Personality and Social Psychology*, 1975, **31**, 206–215.

Clark, R. D., III, & Word, L. E. Why don't bystanders help? Because of ambiguity? *Journal of Personality and Social Psychology*, 1972, **24**, 392–400.

Clark, R. D., III, & Word, L. E. Where is the apathetic bystander? Situational characteristics of the emergency. *Journal of Personality and Social Psychology*, 1974, **29**, 279–287.

Cohen, S. (Ed.). *New directions in patient compliance*. Lexington, Mass.: Lexington Books, 1979.

Deutsch, M., & Gerard, H. B. A study of normative and informational social influences upon individual judgment. *Journal of Abnormal and Social Psychology*, 1955, **51**, 629–636.

Erlich, D., Guttman, I., Schonbach, P., & Mills, J. Postdecision exposure to relevant information. *Journal of Abnormal and Social Psychology*, 1957, **54**, 98–102.

Festinger, L. A theory of social comparison processes. *Human Relations*, 1954, **7**, 117–140.

Festinger, L. *A theory of cognitive dissonance*. Evanston, Ill.: Row and Peterson, 1957.

Freedman, J. L. Long-term behavioral effects of cognitive dissonance. *Journal of Experimental Social Psychology*, 1965, **1**, 145–155.

Freedman, J., & Fraser, S. Compliance without pressure: The foot-in-the-door technique. *Journal of Personality and Social Psychology*, 1966, **4**, 195–202.

Gouldner, A. W. The norm of reciprocity: A preliminary statement. *American Sociological Review*, 1960, **25**, 161–178.

Haynes, R. B., Taylor, D. W., & Sackett, D. L. *Compliance in health care*. Baltimore: Johns Hopkins University Press, 1979.

Heider, F. *The psychology of interpersonal relationships*. New York: Wiley, 1958.

Hornstein, H. A., Fisch, E., & Holmes, M. Influence of a model's feeling about his behavior and his relevance as a comparison other on observer's helping behavior. *Journal of Personality and Social Psychology*, 1968, **10**, 222–226.

Kelley, H. The two functions of reference groups. In G. Swanson, T. Newcomb, & E. Hartley (Eds.), *Readings in social psychology* (2nd ed.). New York: Holt, 1952.

Masur, F. T. Adherence to health care regimens. In C. Prokop & L. A. Bradley (Eds.), *Medical psychology: Contributions to behavioral medicine*. New York: Academic Press, 1981.

Regan, D. Effects of a favor and liking on compliance. *Journal of Experimental Social Psychology*, 1971, **7**, 627–639.

Reingen, P. Test of a list procedure for inducing compliance with a request to donate money. *Journal of Applied Psychology*, 1982, **67**, 110–118.

Sackett, D. L., & Haynes, R. B. *Compliance with therapeutic regimens*. Baltimore: Johns Hopkins University Press, 1976.

Steckel, S. B., & Swain, M. A. Contracting with patients to improve compliance. *Hospitals*, 1977, **51**, 81–84.

Svarstad, B. Physician-patient communication and patient conformity with medical advice. In D. Mechanic (Ed.), *The growth of bureaucratic medicine*. New York: Wiley, 1976.

Swain, M. A., & Steckel, S. B. Influencing adherence among hypertensives. *Research in Nursing and Health*, 1981, **4**, 213–222.

Tedeschi, T., Schlenker, B., & Bonoma, T. Cognitive dissonance: Private ratiocination or public spectacle. *American Psychologist*, 1971, **26**, 685–695.

Varela, J. A. *Psychological solutions to social problems: An introduction to social technology*. New York: Academic Press, 1971.

Varela, J. A. Social technology. *American Psychologist*, 1977, **32**, 914–923.

Withersty, D., Stevenson, J., & Waldman, R. (Eds.). *Communication and compliance in a hospital setting*. Springfield, Ill.: Charles C Thomas, 1980.

CHAPTER 27

COGNITIVE-BEHAVIORAL STRATEGIES AND HEALTH ENHANCEMENT

Philip C. Kendall

University of Minnesota

Dennis C. Turk

Yale University

The history of the cognitive-behavioral perspective can be traced to the Stoic philosopher Epictetus and his now-famous dictum: "Men are disturbed not by things which happen, but the opinions about the things." Although the importance of cognitive factors has been noted since the time of Epictetus (e.g., Kant's *Critique of Pure Reason,* 1781), only within the last century—and more strongly within the last decade—have psychological theorists emphasized the role of cognitive factors in mental illness and focused on alteration of the client's cognitions (e.g., Beck, 1976; Ellis, 1962; Goldfried & Davison, 1976; Kelly, 1955; Mahoney, 1974; Meichenbaum, 1977). Much of this recent upsurge of interest in cognitive factors can be viewed as a reaction against the perceived inadequacies of psychoanalytic and radical behavioral thinking and the limitations of these approaches to treatments in terms of efficacy, generalization, and durability of results.

As a general rubric, the cognitive-behavioral perspective encompasses a number of strategies. The theoretical foundation upon which cognitive-behavioral intervention strategies are based, however, is not fully established (Turk & Speers, 1983). It is not that there is a complete absence of theory, nor have preliminary postulates been falsified; rather, there are several guiding principles (as opposed to one grand theory) that appear to characterize the cognitive-behavioral perspective. The following list parsimoniously captures these guiding principles (adapted from Kendall & Bemis, 1983; Mahoney, 1977; Mahoney & Arnkoff, 1978):

1. Rather than responding directly to the environment, humans respond primarily to cognitive representations of the environment.
2. A large portion of human learning is cognitively mediated.
3. Cognitions (thoughts), emotions (feelings), and behaviors (actions) are causally inter-related.
4. The prediction and understanding of maladaptive psychopathological states and the beneficial effects of psychotherapy or counseling are enhanced by attention to the cognitive activities of the client (e.g., expectancies, beliefs, self-statements, attributions).

5. It is possible and desirable to combine and integrate cognitive approaches to treatment with performance-based (enactive) techniques and behavioral contingency management.

6. The cognitive-behavioral intervener assesses maladaptive cognition and behavioral skills deficits and works with the client in designing and implementing learning experiences to remediate dysfunctional thought and action.

Although they are guided by these fundamental principles, there are variations in the actual implementation of cognitive-behavioral interventions. For instance, the *target* of change varies. Whereas rational restructuring (Goldfried, 1979), stress inoculation training (Meichenbaum, 1977), self-instructional procedures (Kendall, 1977, 1981; Meichenbaum, 1975, 1977), and cognitive therapy of depression (Beck, Rush, Shaw, & Emery, 1979) seek to change cognitions and behaviors directly, rational-emotive therapy (RET) (Ellis, 1962) targets philosophical change. In terms of the therapeutic relationship, the other approaches take a more collaborative stance in which client and therapist cooperation is by design, whereas RET is more didactic and confrontational. Finally, the various interventions place differing degrees of emphasis on the need for empirical evidence on which to base cognitive reappraisals. The RET approach is less empirical (more rational) than the approaches that rely to a greater degree on client data as the source of reappraisals.

The RET approach emerges as somewhat distinct from other cognitive-behavioral approaches (Kendall & Kriss, 1983). This may be surprising, for RET has provided the cognitive-behavioral approach with the single most influential theory: that beliefs mediate the emotional and behavioral consequences of activating events. Theoretical developments continue, with RET's seminal theoretical perspective remaining a part of the guiding principles of cognitive-behavioral interventions.

Cognitive-behavioral interventions are typically active, time-limited, and fairly structured. Interventions are designed to assist clients in identifying, reality-testing, and correcting maladaptive conceptualizations, problematic patterns of thinking, and dysfunctional beliefs. Clients are helped to recognize connections among cognition, affect, and behavior, along with their joint consequences, and are encouraged to become aware of and monitor the role of inappropriate, negative, or maladaptive thoughts and beliefs in the maintenance of their dysfunctional behaviors.

In general, cognitive-behavioral interventions employ environmental manipulations, as do behavior therapies, but for the former, such manipulations represent informational feedback trials, which provide an opportunity for the individual to question, reappraise, and acquire self-control over maladaptive cognitions (e.g., beliefs, appraisals, attributions, schemata), feelings, and behaviors. Cognitive-behavioral interventions focus on skills deficiencies (e.g., inadequate coping repertoires, deficient problem-solving skills) and on production deficiencies (i.e., factors that inhibit the implementation of adaptive responses when the situation warrants).

Although cognitive-behavioral interventions originally were developed and applied to emotionally based disorders (e.g., depression, phobias, impulse control, evaluation anxiety), several trends in medicine have suggested that cognitive factors likely play an important role in all areas along the health–disease continuum. Cognitive-behavioral strategies have been useful beyond their initial focus. Before describing some of the applications of cognitive-behavioral interventions in behavioral health, several developing trends in medicine that support the applicability of these interventions will be considered briefly.

COGNITIVE FACTORS IN HEALTH, DISEASE, AND ILLNESS

Historically, the suggestion that psychological factors can influence physiological symptoms and overt behaviors can be dated from the classical Greek philosophers and physicians. The role attributed to psychological factors in health and disease, however, has waxed and waned over time. During the past century, disease has been viewed as the result of a single pathogenic agent (e.g., toxin, virus), a nutritional deficiency (e.g., inadequate vitamin C in the etiology of scurvy, insufficient iron in the development of goiters), or some physiological aberration (e.g., endocrine imbalance, autoimmune disease). Consideration of psychological factors in health and disease has been relegated to the peripheral areas of the health sciences (e.g., psychosomatics, public health, medical sociology). Only recently, with the increased recognition that the etiology of disease is multidetermined, has the role of psychological factors received broader attention.

Recent Trends

One of the impetuses for the resurgence of interest in psychological factors has been the distinctions made between disease, illness, and health behavior (Kasl & Cobb, 1966a, 1966b; Mechanic, 1968). Mechanic (1968) noted that, in contrast to disease, illness involves three components: (a) the patient's attentiveness to symptoms, (b) the processes affecting how symptoms are defined, and (c) the patients' help-seeking behavior, alterations of life routines, and so forth. Thus, "illness" refers to the patient's *subjective experience* of the *objective disease.*

Kasl and Cobb (1966a) define health behavior as "any activity undertaken by a person believing himself to be healthy, for the purpose of preventing disease or detecting it in an asymptomatic state" (p. 246). Recently, Harris and Guten (1979) have expanded on this definition to broaden the concept of health behavior to include individuals who are symptomatic or asymptomatic and to incorporate health-promoting and health-maintaining behaviors as well as disease-preventing behaviors. Harris and Guten have labeled this expanded category "health-protective behaviors" and have suggested that the objective effectiveness of the behavior need not be established.

Attempts to predict the performance of health behaviors or health-protective behaviors have largely relied on the health beliefs model originally formulated by Rosenstock (1966). The original health beliefs model predicted that preventive health actions would more likely be performed by individuals who (a) feel threatened by a disease (perceive the consequences of the disease as serious), (b) perceive the benefits of the preventive action to outweigh the costs of such actions, and (c) are exposed to some behavioral cues to action—all of these being modified by (d) a set of demographic, structural, and social factors. This model has been modified by Becker and his colleagues (Becker, 1974; Becker & Maiman, 1975) to account for more types of health-related behaviors than merely recommended preventive health actions (e.g., adherence to therapeutic regimens). Current conceptualizations of illness behavior, health behavior, and health-protective behavior place a heavy emphasis on cognitive factors.

Individuals develop elaborate conceptualizations of health and disease—causes, cures, self-responsibility, control, and so forth. These idiosyncratic conceptualizations have been shaped by a variety of sources, including prior experiences, friends and relatives who frequently have given advice and imparted information, mass media reports, and many other sources of accurate and erroneous information. Individuals' conceptualizations will, in turn, affect their health-protective behaviors, their illness behavior, their symptom perception and appraisal, how they feel, and how long and in what ways they will behave.

A second trend that has instigated interest in psychological factors has been the recognition that learned, maladaptive behavior patterns, consisting of substance abuse (i.e., alcohol, tobacco, and psychoactive drugs), excessive caloric intake, sedentary activity patterns, and maladaptive modes of responding to stress contribute directly to poor health and to some of the major causes of death (Lalonde, 1974; U.S. Surgeon General, 1979). The recognition that individuals engage in such detrimental, health risk-related behaviors has resulted in a proliferation of psychological approaches to modifying these maladaptive behaviors directly.

A final trend that has fostered the resurgence of interest in psychological factors has been the dramatic advances in medical technology and pharmacology. These advances have created, paradoxically, a host of aversive diagnostic (e.g., gastrointestinal endoscopic examination, cardiac catheterization) and therapeutic treatments (e.g., chemotherapy and radiation therapy for cancer victims, renal dialysis for patients with kidney failure, laser photocoagulation for retinopathy) that many patients find themselves subject to and that require coping and adjustment. Moreover, therapeutic advances have prolonged the lives of many individuals with chronic diseases that in earlier times would have been fatal (e.g., diabetes, renal failure, spinal cord injuries). Prolongation of life despite debilitating diseases and conditions has resulted in a need for patients to cope with their conditions for extended periods of time.

From this abbreviated review, it is apparent that cognitive factors—individuals' beliefs, appraisals, attributions, and conceptualizations—play a role in all aspects of health, disease, and illness and can therefore no longer be divorced from medical practice.

Recent Evidence

Increasing amounts of evidence have been accumulating that support the important role of cognitive factors at all points along the health–disease (illness) continuum. An extensive review of this literature is beyond the scope of this chapter; however, several diverse examples will underscore this point (for more detail, see Turk, Meichenbaum, & Genest, 1983).

Recently, Leventhal and his associates (Leventhal, Meyer, & Nerenz, 1981; Leventhal & Nerenz, Note 1) have suggested that disease conceptions (or cognitive organizations about disease, such as disease schemata) consist of four components: (a) a disease identity (usually consisting of symptoms), (b) causes of the disease, (c) consequences of the disease, and (d) a time line (expected course of the disease—acute, chronic, or episodic). Leventhal et al. (1981) examined the association between hypertensive patients' conceptions of their disease and continuation in treatment and adherence to therapeutic regimens. They found that 42% of hypertensives who believed that high blood pressure is an acute illness dropped out of treatment, whereas 83% of the hypertensives remained in treatment when their model of hypertension was chronic. These authors also found that the monitoring of symptoms was related to treatment adherence. Seventy percent of the hypertensives took their medication because they believed that the treatment helped the "symptoms." In addition, many patients used symptoms as an indication of the existence of hypertension, despite the fact that hypertension is asymptomatic. Moreover, 94% of those who dropped out of treatment reported that awareness of a symptom instigated their return to treatment.

The importance of hypertensive patients' conceptualizations of their disease and treatment in treatment adherence was noted in Davis's (1967) observational study. Davis reported that farmers suffering from cardiac disease who did not adhere to treatment held some of the following beliefs: "If you wait long enough, you can get over any illness"; "Some of the old fashioned remedies are still better than things you get at the drug store"; "You need to give your body some rest from medicine once in a while; otherwise your body becomes dependent on it or immune to it."

Despite the fact that many studies have employed behavioral techniques to alter such health risk behaviors as obesity, smoking, and excessive use of alcohol, long-term maintenance of preliminary gains is often disheartening, with relapses as high as 90% (Armor, Polich, & Stambul, 1976; Stunkard, 1977). Dissatisfaction with the long-term efficacy of behavioral approaches to these risk-related behaviors has led a number of investigators to examine potential causes of relapse.

Sjoberg and Persson (1979) examined the conditions under which thoughts and feelings lead to deviations from weight control regimens. They reported that, in the majority of cases, episodes of overeating were preceded by maladaptive and distorted thinking—for example, "An extra sandwich now will help me to eat less later" or "I've already lost a lot of weight, so I can indulge myself this once." Sjoberg and Persson report that such thoughts often had a domino effect, with one episode of relapse leading to increasingly more episodes.

In an examination of relapse of abstinent smokers, Sjoberg and Johnson (1978) noted the presence of both positive and negative moods preceding relapse and of distorted reasoning similar to that observed among the obese relapsers: "I've been doing so well, I'll treat myself to just one cigarette." Relapsed smokers also reported fatalistic attitudes about the results of treatment and a low sense of self-efficacy related to their repeated failure to quit: "Once a smoker, always a smoker" (Blittner, Goldberg, & Merbaum, 1978). Finally, the importance of cognitive and affective factors in relapse among successful completers of alcohol treatments has been identified and described by Marlatt (1978, 1979).

Several reviews (e.g., Klein, 1975; Krantz, 1980) indicate that the ways coronary patients cope with hospitalization and recuperation may influence their chances of survival. Turk (1979) and Weisman and Sobel (1979) have also reported the effects of coping on the adjustment of patients with chronic illnesses. What our selective review suggests is that psychological factors, particularly cognitive factors, play an important role that spans the entire health–disease continuum.

COGNITIVE-BEHAVIORAL INTERVENTIONS

Cognitive-behavioral interventions have been employed with a host of populations and problems that fit under the general headings of behavioral medicine and behavioral health. Some of these applications include treatment of alcohol abuse (Chaney, O'Leary, & Marlatt, 1978), modification of Type A coronary-prone behavior (Jenni & Wollersheim, 1979), weight reduction (Mahoney & Mahoney, 1976), smoking cessation (Pechacek & Danaher, 1979), prevention of maladaptive responses to job-related stress (Sarason, Johnson, Berberich, & Siegel, 1979), preparation for noxious medical diagnostic examination (Kendall, Williams, Pechacek, Graham, Shisslak, & Herzoff, 1979), treatment of psychophysiological disorders (Brooks & Richardson, 1980; Holroyd, Andrasik, & Westbrook, 1977), treatment of acute pain (Wernick, Jaremko, & Taylor, 1981), treatment of chronic pain (Herman & Baptiste, 1981; Randich, 1982), and enhancing coping skills for chronic illness (Weisman, Worden, & Sobel, 1980). Although the list of applications is extensive and growing, the efficacy of various cognitive-behavioral interventions must still be treated as preliminary, and some conclusions remain tentative. The results to date are encouraging, however.

As noted earlier, the range of techniques encompassed under the cognitive-behavioral rubric is quite broad, and space does not permit a detailed examination and description of each (for more extensive coverage, see Foreyt & Rathjen, 1978; Kendall, 1982; Kendall & Hollon, 1979; Turk et al., 1983). We will describe here a few select examples of the application of specific cognitive-behavioral interventions.

Preparation for Stressful Medical Procedures

Recent advances in medical technology have led to the development of a number of diagnostic and therapeutic procedures that assist in the prolongation of life; however, these procedures often are aversive and frequently are stressful (e.g., cardiac catheterization, gastrointestinal endoscopic examination, renal dialysis, radiation, and chemotherapy). Typically, the patient who is scheduled to undergo such procedures does not suffer from any serious psychological dysfunctions, nor are disastrous medical complications the inevitable outcome. In short, patients must collect themselves for confrontation with the stress created by a medical procedure that is designed to be of benefit to them. In some cases, paradoxically, the treatment may create symptoms that are more aversive than the medical problem that is being addressed (e.g., "tubbing" in the treatment of burns; chemotherapy and radiation therapy in the treatment of cancer). Psychological preparation of patients for coping with such aversive procedures fits directly within the definition of behavioral health (Matarazzo, 1980).

To illustrate the utility of the cognitive-behavioral approach in preparation for aversive medical procedures, one comprehensive treatment regimen that has received attention, stress inoculation (Meichenbaum, 1975; Meichenbaum & Turk, 1976), will be described in some detail.

Stress inoculation training is a cognitive-behavioral intervention that focuses on altering a person's conceptualization and processing of information about a stressful situation and focuses on cognitive and behavioral coping skills to modify maladaptive ways of reacting in stressful situations. Stress inoculation training has been outlined as having three stages: (a) preparation, (b) skills training, and (c) application training (Meichenbaum & Cameron, Note 2). In the preparation stage, the therapist helps the patient identify the relationship among maladaptive cognitions (e.g., thoughts, self-statements, beliefs) and maladaptive patterns of emotional response and behavior. This preparatory stage is primarily educational (although the entire program can be viewed as educational), with the therapist presenting the patient with a rationale for the profound effects of cognitive factors in the interpretation of both bodily states and situational cues. The goal of the preparation stage is assisting patients in reconceptualizing stress from "overwhelming" to "controllable" and altering their view of themselves to "efficacious" rather than "helpless." The reconceptualization is accomplished through a collaborative examination of the patients' perceptions of the environment, behavioral actions, and internal dialogue about whether and how they can cope with the situation.

The second stage of stress inoculation training focuses directly on skills training. The focus of this stage may be on eliciting and adapting coping strategies already within the patients' repertoires to confront the stress or on teaching them specific coping techniques that are especially relevant to the nature of the stress they will confront. A variety of procedures have been employed, including mental and physical relaxation, cognitive restructuring, self-instructional training, and the presentation of a "cafeteria-style" array of techniques from which patients can select techniques that have the most face validity and are congruent with the patients' coping styles (e.g., Turk et al., 1983). Cognitive restructuring and self-instructional training focus on the patients' reexamination of the aversive situation and their own emotional reactions, and on their learning to implement various cognitive and behavioral coping strategies.

The final stage of stress inoculation training involves the patients' application and practice of the newly acquired skills in stressful situations. Although the amount of necessary practice will vary, it is essential that patients have an opportunity actually to engage in the use of the skills, either imaginally or in reality. The stressful situation may be presented as a set of small units, each of which can be presented as a manageable problem that the patient has appropriate skills for confronting. The application phase enables the patient to consolidate the skills covered in the earlier stages and to identify any problems, which the therapist can then address.

The stress inoculation regimen described has been employed successfully with a number of different populations, including patients hospitalized for severe stress reactions (Holcomb, 1979), laboratory pain (Horan, Hackett, Buchanan, Stone, & Demchik-Stone, 1977), chronic pain patients (Randich, 1982), cancer (Moore & Altmaier, 1981), surgery (Langer, Janis, & Wolfer, 1975), burns (Wernick et al., 1981), and patients who had to undergo aversive diagnostic medical procedures (Kendall et al., 1979).

To illustrate the use of stress inoculation training in behavioral health, we will consider the recent study by Kendall and his colleagues (1979), in which they compared the effectiveness of their cognitive-behavioral treatment (an adaptation of stress inoculation) and a patient education treatment in reducing the stress of patients undergoing cardiac catheterization. To control for the effects of the increased attention given to treated patients, an attention placebo control group was employed. A second control group completed the assessment measures but received only typical current hospital experiences (i.e., current conditions control). Patients in the cognitive-behavioral treatment group received individual training in the identification of those aspects of the hospitalization that aroused distress in them and in the application of their own cognitive coping strategies to lessen that anxiety. The identifying of subjects' own coping strategies was conducted as follows. The therapist explained to the patients that stress is typical and that people cope in various ways. The therapist served as a coping model by self-disclosing a source of personal stress and discussing the strategy used to cope. The patients then discussed prior sources of stress and how they were addressed. The therapist next illustrated ways in which the patients' strategies could be used in the current situation. The therapist then helped the patients rehearse the use of such cognitive and behavioral coping in response to the stress cues.

A closer look at examples of this procedure is enlightening. Two cues that were identified as stressful by cardiac catheterization patients were the medical machinery and the young physicians. In reexamining the stressful nature of the machinery, the therapist might say, "A room full of machinery sure is foreign-looking, sort of science fiction. They're especially odd if you don't know what the machines do. What do the machines make you think of?" The patient might reply, "Oh, something will go wrong with one of them." The therapist works with the patient to recognize that when thoughts about the machines—that something is going to go wrong—start to run through the patient's head, it's the cue to seek information about what the machines are for, how they work, and what happens if something goes awry. Another possibility is to use the machines as cues to think about the advances in technology and medical science. The therapist might say, "As soon as you start thinking about the machines, remember how far technology has come to be able to even perform this test. Your health is in better hands now than before the machines were available. Technology has come a long way to be able to check you out so thoroughly."

To patients in their later years, the physicians may look very young: "These young doctors make me worry; they're just out of diapers and green all over. What do they know?" Physicians may wear beards or longer hair and may appear nonprofessional to older patients. The therapist might point out, "You know, those young doctors just finished their medical training. They're not bothered by middle age crisis, they're not thinking about their teenage children, and they're not set in their ways. They are trying to show that they're experts; they have a positive view of their abilities, and, most important, they are up on the latest advances in medicine. They're not performing the procedure for the first time, and they're not doing it out of routine either." In these illustrations of the intervention provided by Kendall et al. (1979), the therapist guides the patient to recognize the stress cues and to use them as reminders to engage in cognitive coping (see also Kendall, 1983).

Subjects in the patient education group received individual teaching related to heart disease and the catheterization procedures to which they were to be exposed. Sample catheters and a heart model were used to display the procedures, and a pamphlet with additional information was provided. Subjects in the attention placebo control group received a nondirective discussion with the therapist, who listened and reflected feelings.

The results of the Kendall et al. (1979) study indicated that patients' self-reported anxiety was significantly lower for the cognitive-behavioral, patient education, and attention placebo groups than for the current hospital conditions control group after the intervention. Self-reported anxiety levels *during* the catheterization, however, were significantly lower only for the cognitive-behavioral and patient education groups. Physicians and technicians independently rated the patients' behaviors during catheterization, and these ratings indicated that the patients receiving the cognitive-behavioral treatment were best adjusted—that is, least tense, least anxious, most comfortable (see Table 27.1). The patient education group was rated as better adjusted than the two control groups but significantly less well adjusted than the cognitive-behavioral group.

Kendall et al. (1979) also examined the thoughts that patients reported having during the catheterization procedure. The authors developed a 20-item self-statement inventory that required patients to indicate on a 5-point scale how frequently each self-statement characterized their thoughts during the catheterization procedure. There were 10 positive self-statements (e.g., "I was thinking that the procedure could save my life") and 10 negative

Table 27.1 Anxiety Scores and Ratings of Adjustment for Four Groups

Group	Anxiety Score			Rating of adjustment	
	Assessment period				
	1	2	3	Physician	Technician
Current hospital conditions control					
Mean	8.72	8.54	8.18	18.82	18.36
Standard deviation	4.26	2.58	3.03	2.23	3.29
Attention placebo control					
Mean	7.27	6.45	7.54	18.09	18.64
Standard deviation	2.49	1.69	2.29	2.26	2.77
Patient education intervention					
Mean	6.82	4.91	5.64	19.91	20.00
Standard deviation	2.36	1.51	2.11	3.53	3.03
Cognitive-behavioral intervention					
Mean	7.00	5.64	4.91	22.00	21.83
Standard deviation	2.20	1.43	1.04	1.84	2.32

Source: Adapted from Kendall, P. C., Williams, L., Pechacek, T., Graham, L., Shisslak, K., & Herzoff, N. Cognitive-behavioral and patient education interventions in cardiac catheterization: The Palo Alto medical psychology project. *Journal of Consulting and Clinical Psychology,* 1979, **47**, 49–58. Copyright 1979 by the American Psychological Association. Reprinted by permission.
Note: For each group, $n = 11$. Assessment period 1 = preintervention; 2 = postintervention; 3 = retrospective reports of catheterization taken just after catheterization.

self-statements (e.g., "I was listening and expecting them to say something bad about my health") on the inventory. Patients' negative self-statement scores were found to be significantly and negatively correlated with both the physicians' ratings of adjustment ($r = -.34$), and the technicians' ratings of adjustment ($r = -.37$). Positive self-statement scores were not significantly related to adjustment. The data indicate that a negative internal dialogue is related to poor adjustment (see also "The power of non-negative thinking" in Kendall & Hollon, 1981).

Cognitive-Behavioral Interventions with Type A Coronary-Prone Clients

It is now widely acknowledged that many factors combine to produce stress (Rabkin & Struening, 1976). Recognition of the environmental, cognitive, affective, and behavioral factors that contribute to the appraisal of threat and stress leads to a multidimensional conceptualization of the stressor and, consequently, to comprehensive stress management programs (Meichenbaum & Turk, 1982). The cognitive-behavioral approach to stress management is designed to take into account both the objective environment and the individual's appraisal that may lead to emotional arousal and stress responses.

Since the pioneering work of Friedman and Rosenman (1959), growing evidence has pointed to a relationship between coronary heart disease (CHD) and a pattern of behavior (Type A coronary-prone behavior) characterized by intense ambition, constant preoccupation with occupational deadlines, a sense of time urgency, and competitive drive (Friedman & Rosenman, 1959; Rosenman, Brand, Schultz, & Friedman, 1976).

Glass (1977) suggests that Type A behavior is elicited, in susceptible individuals, by stressful situations that are perceived to be uncontrollable. Dembroski, MacDougall, and

Shields (1977) and Glass (1977) have also indicated that Type A individuals may create much of their own distress by perceiving challenges where others do not.

Suinn and Bloom (1978) based a cognitive-behavioral intervention on the possible interaction among stress, Type A behavior, and coronary heart disease. Their treatment was designed to teach new ways of coping with stress to substitute for the less adaptive, Type A behaviors. The stress management program developed by Suinn and Bloom (1978) was conducted with volunteer subjects who considered themselves as having Type A characteristics. The training program included use of imagery to precipitate stress. The imaginal stress served to facilitate the identification of muscular signs of stress onset. Finally, training in stress reduction through relaxation was conducted. Additional emphasis was placed on practicing stress management in response to feelings of time urgency. These subjects were compared with a control group who only discussed factors related to stress. Suinn and Bloom reported that the stress management training group reported comparatively less anxiety following the training. Cholesterol levels, triglycerides, and blood pressure, however, were not significantly reduced. No follow-up was reported, nor was the credibility of the attention placebo group established. Thus, the Suinn and Bloom data must be interpreted with caution.

Jenni and Wollersheim (1979) conducted a study in which they contrasted Suinn and Bloom's stress management program with a cognitive-behavioral therapy that was based on modifying stressful appraisals of events. In addition, "irrational beliefs " (Ellis, 1962) believed to be relevant for Type A individuals (e.g., "I must be perfect, thoroughly competent and achieving in everything I do") were presented, with the goal of having subjects become aware of how maladaptive such ideas might be. Finally, subjects were taught to reinterpret situations associated with time pressure, competitiveness, and hostility.

Subjects in the Jenni and Wollersheim (1979) study either were referred by physicians or responded to a newspaper advertisement. All subjects received six weekly 90-minute sessions. Compared to the stress management group, the cognitive-behavioral therapy group self-reported reduced Type A behavior and anxiety but failed to demonstrate reductions in cholesterol levels or blood pressure. These results were evident at a 6-week follow-up as well.

Roskies and her colleagues (Roskies, Kearney, Spevack, Surkis, Cohen, & Gilman, 1979; Roskies, Spevack, Surkis, Cohen, & Gilman, 1978) contrasted two treatments for Type A behaviors: (a) a psychodynamically oriented approach, focused on resolving the behavior pattern by elucidating unconscious conflicts, and (b) a cognitive-behavioral approach focused on increasing awareness of control over behavior, relaxation training, and self-monitoring. These treatments included 14 therapy sessions spread over a period of 5 months. The two groups of subjects were composed of healthy volunteers (no CHD); a third group consisted of subjects who already had signs of CHD. This third group received the cognitive-behavioral treatment.

All three groups showed significant reductions of anxiety and other psychological symptoms, as well as reductions of serum cholesterol levels (psychodynamic group: 237.1 mg/ml to 221.0 mg/ml; cognitive-behavioral groups: 238.2 mg/ml to 197.5 mg/ml) and blood pressure (psychodynamic group: systolic 127.9 mmHg to 122.6 mmHg, diastolic 83.2 mmHg to 83.4 mmHg; cognitive-behavioral groups: systolic 122.5 mmHg to 117.9 mmHg, diastolic 83.4 mmHg to 81.4 mmHg) following treatment. The two cognitive-behavioral treatment groups showed greater, but not significantly different, reduction in serum cholesterol levels than the psychodynamically oriented group did. At 6-month follow-up, all three groups showed good maintenance of treatment effects; the cognitive-behavioral treatment groups tended to demonstrate better maintenance than the psychotherapy group. It is interesting that these changes occurred without modification of diet, exercise, smoking, or work load. Thus, it appears that psychological interventions without modification of some risk factors can result in desired gains.

Some preliminary findings from the Recurrent Coronary Prevention Project (Thoresen, Friedman, Gill & Ulmer, 1982) offer encouragement to the cognitive-behavior therapist working with Type A clients. These researchers designed their project to answer two questions: (a) Can a behavior change program reduce the recurrence rate of postcoronary subjects? and (b) Can the Type A behavior pattern be changed, and do such changes correspond to reductions in coronary heart disease? Thoresen et al. (1982) studied 1,035 subjects and conducted a comparison of a behavior change program, a cardiologist program (with medications, diet, and exercise), and a routine treatment control. Within the behavior change program, a cognitive-behavioral strategy (cognitive social learning) was employed. The multifaceted intervention included self-control training, behavioral contracting, and cognitive as well as environmental restructuring. Within the cognitive area, perceptions, beliefs, and self-statements were targeted, and specific intervention techniques were included. During the first year, group sessions of 8 to 10 subjects were held weekly and then twice monthly for 90 minutes each. After the first year, sessions are to be held monthly. The preliminary findings are after 1 year of treatment.

For those in the behavior change group, compared to the other groups of subjects, there was a significant reduction in the recurrence rate. Moreover, the data suggested that subjects in the behavior change program had altered their Type A behavior pattern. These findings are of interest not only because of the degree of meaningful change achieved, but also because of the authors' impression that cognitive factors, such as the personal meaning and individual beliefs associated with Type A behaviors, were of primary importance. The findings reported by Thoresen et al. (1982) were described as preliminary, leading us to await with anticipation the appearance of further reports.

The studies cited thus far indicate the potential of cognitive-behavioral techniques for modifying Type A behavior, but they must be regarded as somewhat tentative, since they have not yet reported extended follow-up morbidity and mortality data. Obviously, modifying subjects' self-reports and even Type A behaviors is not sufficient, and there is a need for additional demonstrations of physiological effects (see also Roskies, 1983, for a discussion of these issues).

CLOSING COMMENT

Our message in this chapter is straightforward: individuals' cognitive activities (e.g., appraisals, attributions, beliefs, expectations, self-statements) play an important role in behavioral health, and some recent data endorse this focus on cognition. Cognitive-behavioral programs designed to assist psychologically nondisturbed persons in developing and maintaining more healthy patterns of behavior and in coping with unavoidable aversive situations have been reasonably successful and merit further attention. In addition, there is much to be learned from the study of the cognitions of persons who, of their own determination, engage in health-maintaining behaviors, as well as those who persist in health-threatening behaviors.

REFERENCE NOTES

1. Leventhal, H., & Nerenz, D. R. *Illness cognitions as a source of distress in treatment.* Paper presented at the Annual Meeting of the American Psychological Association, Los Angeles, September 1981.
2. Meichenbaum, D., & Cameron, R. *Stress inoculation: A skills training approach to anxiety management.* Unpublished manuscript, University of Waterloo, 1973.

REFERENCES

Armor, D. J., Polich, J. M., & Stambul, H. B. *Alcoholism and treatment* (R-1739-NIAAA). Santa Monica: The Rand Corporation, 1976.

Beck, A. T. *Cognitive therapy of the emotional disorders.* New York: International Universities Press, 1976.

Beck, A. T., Rush, A. J., Shaw, B. F., & Emery, G. *Cognitive therapy of depression.* New York: Guilford Press, 1979.

Becker, M. H. (Ed.). The health belief model and personal health behavior. *Health Education Monographs,* 1974, **2**, 236–473.

Becker, M. H., & Maiman, L. A. Sociobehavioral determinants of compliance with health and medical care recommendations. *Medical Care,* 1975, **13**, 10–24.

Elittner, M., Goldberg, J., & Merbaum, M. Cognitive self-control factors in the reduction of smoking behavior. *Behavior Therapy,* 1978, **9**, 553–561.

Brooks, G. R., & Richardson, F. C. Emotional skills training: A treatment program for duodenal ulcer. *Behavior Therapy,* 1980, **11**, 198–207.

Chaney, E., O'Leary, M., & Marlatt, G. A. Skill training with alcoholics. *Journal of Consulting and Clinical Psychology,* 1978, **46**, 1092–1104.

Davis, M. S. Predicting non-compliant behavior. *Journal of Health and Social Behavior,* 1967, **8**, 265–271.

Dembroski, T. M., McDougall, J. M., & Shields, J. L. Physiologic reactions to social challenge in persons evidencing the Type A coronary-prone behavior pattern. *Journal of Human Stress,* 1977, **3**, 2–9.

Ellis, A. *Reason and emotion in psychotherapy.* New York: Stuart, 1962.

Foreyt, J. P., & Rathjen, D. P. *Cognitive behavior therapy: Research and application.* New York: Plenum Press, 1978.

Friedman, M., & Rosenman, R. H. Association of specific overt behavior pattern with blood and cardiovascular findings: Blood cholesterol level, blood clotting time, incidence of arcus senilis, and clinical coronary artery disease. *Journal of the American Medical Association,* 1959, **169**, 1286–1296.

Glass, D. C. *Behavior patterns, stress, and coronary disease.* Hillsdale, N.J.: Erlbaum, 1977.

Goldfried, M. R. Anxiety reduction through cognitive-behavioral intervention. In P. C. Kendall & S. D. Hollon (Eds.), *Cognitive-behavioral interventions: Theory, research, and procedures.* New York: Academic Press, 1979.

Goldfried, M. R., & Davison, G. C. *Clinical behavior therapy.* New York: Holt, Rinehart & Winston, 1976.

Harris, D. M., & Guten, S. Health-protective behavior: An explanatory study. *Journal of Health and Social Behavior,* 1979, **20**, 17–29.

Herman, E., & Baptiste, S. Pain control: Mastery through group experience. *Pain,* 1981, **10**, 79–86.

Holcomb, W. *Coping with severe stress: A clinical application of stress inoculation therapy.* Unpublished doctoral dissertation, University of Missouri–Columbia, 1979.

Holroyd, K. A., Andrasik, F., & Westbrook, T. Cognitive control of tension headache. *Cognitive Therapy and Research,* 1977, **1**, 121–133.

Horan, J., Hackett, G., Buchanan, J., Stone, C., & Demchik-Stone, D. Coping with pain: A component analysis. *Cognitive Therapy and Research,* 1977, **1**, 211–221.

Jenni, M. A., & Wollersheim, J. P. Cognitive therapy, stress management training, and the Type A behavior pattern. *Cognitive Therapy and Research,* 1979, **3**, 61–74.

Kasl, S. V., & Cobb, S. Health behavior, illness behavior, and sick-role behavior: I. Health and illness behavior. *Archives of Environmental Health,* 1966, **12**, 246–266. (a)

Kasl, S. V., & Cobb, S. Health behavior, illness behavior, and sick-role behavior: II. Sick-role behavior. *Archives of Environmental Health,* 1966, **12**, 531–541. (b)

Kelly, G. A. *The psychology of personal constructs.* New York: Norton, 1955.

Kendall, P. C. On the efficacious use of self-instructional procedures with children. *Cognitive Therapy and Research,* 1977, **1**, 331–341.

Kendall, P. C. Cognitive-behavioral interventions with children. In B. B. Lahey & A. E. Kazdin (Eds.), *Advances in clinical child psychology* (Vol. 4). New York: Plenum Press, 1981.

Kendall, P. C. Cognitive processes and procedures in behavior therapy. In C. M. Franks, G. T. Wilson, P. C. Kendall, & K. Brownell, *Annual review of behavior therapy.* New York: Guilford Press, 1982.

Kendall, P. C. Stressful medical procedures: cognitive-behavioral strategies for stress management and prevention. In D. Meichenbaum & M. E. Jarinco (Eds.), *Stress Reduction and Prevention.* New York: Plenum, 1983.

Kendall, P. C., & Bemis, K. M. Thought and action in psychotherapy: The cognitive-behavioral approaches. In M. Hersen, A. E. Kazdin, & A. S. Bellack (Eds.), *The clinical psychology handbook.* New York: Pergamon Press, 1983.

Kendall, P. C., & Hollon, S. D. (Eds.). *Cognitive-behavioral interventions: Theory, research, and procedures.* New York: Academic Press, 1979.

Kendall, P. C., & Hollon, S. D. Assessing self-referent speech: Methods in the measurement of self-statements. In P. C. Kendall & S. D. Hollon (Eds.), *Assessment strategies for cognitive-behavioral interventions.* New York: Academic Press, 1981.

Kendall, P. C., & Kriss, M. R. Cognitive-behavioral interventions. In C. E. Walker (Ed.), *Handbook of clinical psychology.* Homewood, Ill.: Dow Jones–Irwin, 1983.

Kendall, P. C., Williams, L., Pechacek, T. F., Graham, L., Shisslak, C., & Herzoff, N. Cognitive-behavioral and patient education interventions in cardiac catheterization procedures: The Palo Alto medical psychology project. *Journal of Consulting and Clinical Psychology,* 1979, **47,** 49–58.

Klein, R. F. Relationship between psychological and physiological stress in the coronary care unit. In W. D. Gentry & R. B. Williams, Jr. (Eds.), *Psychological aspects of myocardial infarction and coronary care.* St. Louis: Mosby, 1975.

Krantz, D. S. Cognitive processes and recovery from heart attack: A review and theoretical analysis. *Journal of Human Stress,* 1980, **6,** 27–38.

Langer, E. J., Janis, I. L., & Wolfer, J. Reduction of psychological stress in surgical patients. *Journal of Experimental Social Psychology,* 1975, **11,** 155–165.

Lalonde, M. *A new perspective on the health of Canadians.* Ottawa: Ministry of National Health and Welfare, 1974.

Leventhal, H., Meyer, D., & Nerenz, D. R. The common sense representation of illness danger. In S. Rachman (Ed.), *Contributions to medical psychology* (Vol. 2). Oxford, England: Pergamon Press, 1980.

Mahoney, M. J. *Cognition and behavior modification.* Cambridge, Mass.: Ballinger, 1974.

Mahoney, M. J. Reflections on the cognitive-learning trend in psychotherapy. *American Psychologist,* 1977, **32,** 5–13.

Mahoney, M. J., & Arnkoff, D. B. Cognitive and self-control therapies. In S. L. Garfield & A. E. Bergin (Eds.), *Handbook of psychotherapy and behavior change* (2nd ed.). New York: Wiley, 1978.

Mahoney, M. J., & Mahoney, K. *Permanent weight control.* New York: Norton, 1976.

Marlatt, G. A. Craving for alcohol, loss of control, and relapse: A cognitive behavioral analysis. In P. E. Nathan, G. A. Marlatt, & T. Loberg (Eds.), *Alcoholism: New directions in behavioral research and treatment.* New York: Plenum Press, 1978.

Marlatt, G. A. Alcohol use and problem drinking: A cognitive-behavioral analysis. In P. C. Kendall & S. D. Hollon (Eds.), *Cognitive-behavioral interventions: Theory, research, and procedures.* New York: Academic Press, 1979.

Matarazzo, J. D. Behavioral health and behavioral medicine: Frontiers for a new health psychology. *American Psychologist,* 1980, **35,** 807–817.

Mechanic, D. *Medical sociology.* New York: Free Press, 1968.

Meichenbaum, D. Self-instructional methods. In F. Kanfer & A. Goldstein (Eds.), *Helping people change.* New York: Pergamon Press, 1975.

Meichenbaum, D. *Cognitive-behavior modification: An integrative approach.* New York: Plenum Press, 1977.

Meichenbaum, D., & Turk, D. The cognitive-behavioral management of anxiety, anger and pain. In P. Davidson (Ed.), *Behavioral management of anxiety, depression and pain.* New York: Brunner/Mazel, 1976.

Meichenbaum, D. H., & Turk, D. C. Stress, coping, and disease: A cognitive-behavioral perspective. In R. W. J. Neufeld (Ed.), *Psychological stress and psychopathology.* New York: McGraw-Hill, 1982.

Moore, K., & Altmaier, E. Stress inoculation training with cancer patients. *Cancer Nursing,* 1981, **4,** 389–393.

Pechacek, T. F., & Danaher, B. G. How and why people quit smoking. In P. C. Kendall & S. D. Hollon (Eds.), *Cognitive-behavioral interventions: Theory, research, and procedures.* New York: Academic Press, 1979.

Rabkin, J. G., & Struening, E. L. Life events, stress and illness. *Science,* 1976, **194,** 1013–1020.

Randich, S. R. *Evaluation of stress inoculation as a pain management program for rheumatoid arthritis.* Unpublished doctoral dissertation, Washington University, St. Louis, 1982.

Rosenman, R. H., Brand, R. J., Shultz, R. I., & Friedman, M. Multivariate prediction of coronary heart disease during 8.5 year follow-up in the Western Collaborative Group Study. *American Journal of Cardiology,* 1976, **37,** 903–910.

Rosenstock, I. M. Why people use health services. *Milbank Memorial Quarterly,* 1966, **12,** 246–266.

Roskies, E. Stress management for Type A individuals. In D. H. Meichenbaum & M. E. Jaremko (Eds.), *Stress prevention and management: A cognitive-behavioral approach.* New York: Plenum Press, 1983.

Roskies, E., Kearney, H., Spevack, M., Surkis, A., Cohen, C., & Gilman, S. Generalizability and durability of treatment effects in an intervention program for coronary-prone (Type A) managers. *Journal of Behavioral Medicine,* 1979, **2,** 195–207.

Roskies, E., Spevack, M., Surkis, A., Cohen, C., & Gilman, S. Changing the coronary-prone (Type A) behavior pattern in a nonclinical population. *Journal of Behavioral Medicine,* 1978, **1,** 201–215.

Sarason, I. G., Johnson, J. H., Berberich, J. P., & Siegel, J. M. Helping police officers to cope with stress: A cognitive-behavioral approach. *American Journal of Community Psychology,* 1979, **7,** 593–603.

Sjoberg, L., & Johnson, T. Trying to give up smoking: A study of volitional breakdowns. *Addictive Behaviors,* 1978, **3,** 139–164.

Sjoberg, L., & Persson, L-O. A study of attempts by obese patients to regulate eating. *Addictive Behaviors,* 1979, **4,** 349–359.

Stunkard, A. J. Behavioral treatment of obesity: Failure to maintain weight loss. In R. B. Stuart (Ed.), *Behavioral self-management: Strategies, techniques, and outcomes.* New York: Brunner/ Mazel, 1977.

Suinn, R. M., & Bloom, L. J. Anxiety management training for pattern A behavior. *Journal of Behavioral Medicine,* 1978, **1,** 25–37.

Thoresen, C. E., Friedman, M., Gill, J. K., & Ulmer, D. K. The Recurrent Coronary Prevention Project: Some preliminary findings. *Acta Medica Scandinavica,* 1982, **660,** 172–192.

Turk, D. C. Factors influencing the adaptive process with chronic illness. In I. Sarason & C. Spielberger (Eds.), *Stress and anxiety* (Vol. 6). Washington, D.C.: Hemisphere, 1979.

Turk, D. C., Meichenbaum, D. H., & Genest, M. *Pain and behavioral medicine: Theory, research, and a clinical guide.* New York: Guilford Press, 1983.

Turk, D. C., & Speers, M. A. Cognitive schemata and cognitive processes in cognitive-behavioral interventions: Going beyond the information given. In P. C. Kendall (Ed.) *Advances in cognitive-behavioral research and therapy* (Vol. 2). New York: Academic Press, 1983.

U.S. Surgeon General. *Healthy people: The Surgeon General's report on health promotion and disease prevention.* DHEW Pub. No. (PHS) 79–55071). Washington, D.C.: U.S. Government Printing Office, 1979.

Weisman, A. D., & Sobel, H. J. Coping with cancer through self-instruction: A hypothesis. *Journal of Human Stress,* 1979, **5,** 2–8.

Weisman, A. D., Worden, J. W., & Sobel, H. J. *Psychosocial screening and intervention with cancer patients: Research report.* Cambridge, Mass.: Shea Press, 1980.

Wernick, R. L., Jaremko, M. E., & Taylor, P. W. Pain management in severely burned adults: A test of stress inoculation. *Journal of Behavioral Medicine,* 1981, **4,** 103–109.

SECTION 4

EXERCISE

CHAPTER 28

OVERVIEW: HEALTH BENEFITS OF EXERCISE

WILLIAM L. HASKELL

Stanford University School of Medicine

Regular participation in physical activity is frequently cited by the general public as a very important habit in maintaining good health but one that many individuals tend not to perform (Pacific Mutual, Note 1). This belief in the health benefits of exercise increased substantially in the United States during the 1970s as a result of a general increase in its promotion by various health organizations, a greater interest in medical self-help among the public, an increase in the social acceptability of being physically active, and a growing interest in performing vigorous exercise for its own enjoyment among middle-aged and older men and women. During the past decade, it has become very popular to look, dress, and act as if you are either on your way to or from participating in vigorous exercise. If there are such strong interests and beliefs in the personal and social value of regular exercise, then why has it been so difficult to achieve long-term adherence in many of the health-oriented exercise programs offered (Oldridge, 1982)?

The major objectives of this section are to provide (a) the scientific background for why we believe exercise should be included as one component of a comprehensive program of health promotion or disease prevention; (b) practical procedures that can be used to assess exercise habits of health promotion program participants as well as their level of physical fitness; (c) techniques used to design and implement a health-oriented exercise program; and (d) strategies to improve adherence to a recommended activity plan. Special attention has been paid to the psychological benefits of exercise, the role of exercise in weight control, and the implementation of exercise programs for older adults. Some theoretical discussion will be found in each chapter, but the primary emphasis is on background information, operational guidelines, and resource material. No attempt has been made to develop a "party line" regarding the role of exercise in health or preferred strategies for its implementation, but technical terminology has been applied consistently throughout the section.

This chapter is intended to provide a brief review of the body's response to exercise and a general overview of available data that address the potential health benefits and risks of exercise by adults. Although many people exercise regularly to improve their performance capacity or their appearance, these issues will not be specifically addressed. Also, the use of exercise in the detection, diagnosis, or prognosis of disease is not considered, nor is the role of exercise in therapy or rehabilitation, except where such information will shed light on the use of exercise in primary prevention. For additional information, the reader is referred to the selected references at the end of this chapter and the succeeding chapters and to the resource materials listed in them.

THE BODY'S RESPONSE TO EXERCISE

Dynamic Exercise

When an individual begins to walk, run, swim, cycle, or perform other similar large-muscle, *dynamic exercise,* the contraction of skeletal muscles that produces movement requires an immediate increase in energy. To supply that energy, the muscle cells begin to increase their rate of metabolism through the use of available metabolic substrates, including muscle glycogen and fat, blood glucose, and fats (free fatty acids) that are transported in the blood from fat stores to the working muscles. To maintain this increase in metabolic activity, oxygen also has to be provided to the working muscles or fatigue will rapidly develop. This increase in metabolic rate by the skeletal muscles, the need to transport substrates and oxygen to this muscle tissue, and the need to rapidly remove the metabolic waste products all produce a variety of adaptive responses by the body (Table 28.1).

The central nervous system initiates a number of changes to meet these demands; there is a general reduction in parasympathetic tone and a rapid rise in sympathetic nervous system drive. The magnitude of these responses is proportional to the intensity of the exercise expressed in relation to the aerobic capacity of the individual.

To facilitate oxygen delivery and carbon dioxide removal, breathing rate and depth are increased and ventilation volume can increase from a resting average of 10 to 12 liters per minute to more than 120 liters per minute during strenuous exercise. However, the rate of ventilation and the body's ability to diffuse oxygen and carbon dioxide across lung membranes do not limit the exercise capacity of a healthy person. Only in a person with chronic obstructive lung disease would the ability to move oxygen into the arterial blood

Table 28.1 Responses to Large-Muscle, Dynamic Exercise

Measurement	Resting	Submaximal Exercise	Maximal Exercise
Heart rate (beats/min)	72	150	180
Stroke volume (ml)	72	90	92
Cardiac output (L/min)	5.2	13.5	16.6
a-Vo_2 differential (vol %)	5.0	11.0	16.2
O_2 uptake (ml/kg/min)	3.5	19.8	35.8
Blood flow (ml/min)			
Coronary	260	600	900
Brain	740	740	740
Viscera	2,700	900	500
Inactive muscle	550	500	300
Active muscle	550	10,360	13,760
Skin	400	400	400
Total	5,200	13,500	16,600
Blood pressure (mmHg)			
Systemic arterial SBP	120	156	200
Systemic arterial DBP	74	76	76
Pulmonary ventilation (L/min)	10.2	44.8	129
Respiratory rate (breaths/min)	12	30	43
Tidal volume (L)	.850	1.5	3.0
Blood lactic acid (mM/L)	0.7	3.9	11.0
Blood pH	7.43	7.41	7.33

Note: Typical responses estimated for a healthy man, aged 45 years, weighing 75 kg.

be a limiting factor for how much exercise he or she can perform. The feelings that healthy persons get when they are "short of breath" during exercise have nothing to do with lung function but are due to the inability of the heart and blood vessels to transport sufficient oxygen to the working muscles.

During vigorous dynamic exercise, metabolic demands rise rapidly, and blood flow to the working skeletal muscle must rise to meet these needs. To insure adequate perfusion of the exercising muscle, a finely integrated series of events takes place, including a large increase in cardiac performance and marked differential changes in regional blood flow. Increased blood flow to the working muscle is achieved by several changes. First, when the muscles begin to contract, there is a release of metabolites into the surrounding tissues and bloodstream that causes an instantaneous massive vasodilation of the resistance vessels of the exercising muscle group, thereby enhancing blood flow. Along with the marked decrease in resistance to arterial blood flow, there is a drop in venous resistance, which results in an increased venous return and contributes to an exercise-induced increase in cardiac stroke volume. These same metabolites also act on the central nervous system, particularly the sympathetic portion, to cause a very rapid and dramatic vasoconstriction that shuts down blood flow to nonexercising tissues and redirects it to the working muscle. This vasoconstriction affects not only nonexercising muscle but especially the viscera.

At the beginning of exercise, there is a general decrease in blood flow to the skin, so that the immediate cooling of the skin is a normal response. As the body's heat load accumulates during vigorous and prolonged exercise, however, vascular resistance in skin vessels drops and blood flow increases to as much as 15% of the total cardiac output in an attempt to dissipate this heat through sweating.

Systolic blood pressure also rises during exercise, and this results in a greater driving or perfusion pressure. Thus, the vasodilated exercising muscle bed receives an enormous increase in its blood flow—as much as 15 to 20 times its resting flow—due to the local decrease in vascular resistance and the increase in systemic perfusion pressure. In addition, during exercise there is a substantial increase in the amount of oxygen extracted from the arterial blood as it goes through the muscle. This results in a greater arterial-venous oxygen difference. With the body at rest, the difference between the oxygen saturation of arterial and venous blood may be about 50 or 60 ml of oxygen per liter of blood. At maximum exercise, the difference may be as high as 150 to 180 ml.

Another way the body keeps up with the oxygen demands of exercising muscle is by augmenting cardiac output. When the central nervous system is stimulated by exercise, there is an immediate increase in heart rate and stroke volume, and the increased venous return from the exercising muscle supplies more blood to be pumped. If sustained, this increased cardiac output will permit dynamic exercise to persist for long periods of time. Cardiac output generally increases linearly with increasing oxygen consumption and exercise intensity, but it may drop during prolonged exhaustive exercise because of a late drop in stroke volume.

Heart rate more or less directly reflects the amount of effort being expended in exercise; the linear relationship is close enough for it to be used as a guide to exercise intensity. Heart rate may increase two- to threefold over resting values during vigorous exercise. The heart rate of a 45-year-old man at rest is usually about 72 beats per minute. During moderate exercise, it will increase to about 145 beats per minute, and at maximum exercise it may be about 170 to 175 beats per minute. Stroke volume, which at rest may be approximately 70 ml of blood per heartbeat, will increase to as much as 120 or 130 ml during large-muscle dynamic exercise. Thus, an individual who has a cardiac output of about 5 liters at rest will increase cardiac output during moderate exercise to about 12 or 13 liters per minute and during heavy exercise to about 18 or 20 liters.

There are several important changes in blood pressure during aerobic exercise. Systolic blood pressure rises promptly with large-muscle dynamic exercise, and its rise is roughly proportional to the work intensity. A healthy man with a resting systolic blood pressure of 120 mmHg may have a blood pressure of 150 to 160 during moderately intense exercise and up to 180 or 200 during high-intensity exercise. Diastolic blood pressure normally does not increase with aerobic exercise. It may go up or down a few millimeters during exercise, but the normal response is for diastolic pressure not to change.

Exercise also places an increased demand on the heart muscle, or myocardium. This muscle normally extracts most of the oxygen carried in the arterial blood and thus is unable to increase its oxygen extraction during exercise, which means that blood flow to the myocardium must increase. During near-maximal exercise, this blood flow has been found to increase three- or fourfold in healthy individuals. One can think of the demands being made on the heart during exercise in terms of the incremental rise in heart rate and blood pressure. In fact, an excellent index for determining how much work the heart is doing during exercise is heart rate times systolic blood pressure, or the rate-pressure product.

The increase in substrate availability to the working muscle is made possible by an increase in glucose production by the liver (from its own glycogen stores and from the conversion of selected fats, proteins, and carbohydrates in the blood) and a release of free fatty acids from fat stores throughout the body. Although at rest most of the energy produced by skeletal muscles is from glucose, during moderate-intensity exercise, of the sort most frequently used in health promotion programs, up to 50% of energy is provided by fat.

Static or Heavy-Resistance Exercise

The responses to low-resistance dynamic exercise are usually considered to place a high-volume load (large increase in cardiac output) on the heart and vascular system, whereas static (isometric) or heavy-resistance dynamic exercise (for example, lifting objects) places a pressure load with a relatively small increase in cardiac output but a large rise in blood pressure (Asmussen, 1981). Especially during static exercise, there is a rapid rise in both systolic and diastolic blood pressure as the blood flow through the contracting muscle is impeded by the constant increase in intramuscular pressure. When the blood flow to the working muscle is cut off, tissue hypoxia develops, and this stimulates the rise in blood pressure, primarily due to an increase in constriction of vascular beds in other tissues. The body acts as if it is trying to force blood through the blood vessels that are occluded by the contracting muscle. This type of exercise will increase the strength of the muscle being contracted but has very few, if any, other health-related benefits; thus, it is usually not included in health-oriented exercise programs.

THE POTENTIAL HEALTH BENEFITS OF EXERCISE

The biological and psychological changes reportedly produced by frequent exercise are extremely diverse and vary substantially with regard to scientific documentation of a cause-effect relationship. Certain health-related benefits ascribed to exercise are well established and, it can be correctly assumed, are achievable by anyone who exercises appropriately; other benefits frequently promoted by exercise advocates usually do not occur, however. At times, it is very difficult to determine to what degree of scientific certainty a particular benefit has been demonstrated to exist. As with many other areas of health promotion, enthusiasm to do good can easily outstrip the scientific basis for such actions. Even if the health professional assumes a relatively conservative posture regarding the health benefits of exercise, however, there still are many very important reasons why exercise should be included in a comprehensive program of health promotion. This action is especially valid if the concept of prudent behavior is accepted; that is, if some action is reasonably likely to provide some health benefit and if the costs or risks involved are minimal, then it would seem a prudent behavior to perform.

There should be no doubt that if an increase in exercise capacity or physical fitness is desired, the only way to achieve this goal is through a systematic increase in habitual activity (exercise training). The increase in capacity is an adaptive response to the increase in stress placed on tissues and biological functions by the exercise. If the appropriate exercise is performed at the proper intensity, duration, and frequency, sedentary individuals of all ages can achieve significant improvements in physical capacity, including endurance, strength, and flexibility (Wilmore, 1982). Such increases in physical fitness often are equated with improvement in health status or disease prevention, but it should be recognized that even patients with significant diseases, such as coronary heart disease, diabetes, hypertension, or chronic obstructive lung disease, can significantly increase their fitness through exercise yet not be healthy by the usual definition. That is not to say that they might not be more healthy when they are active, but just that being healthy and being physically fit are not synonymous and that one characteristic might change without necessarily influencing the other.

The type of exercise that appears to provide the greatest health benefits is that which requires the use of large muscles and consists of moving the body weight against gravity or over a distance using rhythmic or dynamic movements. Such exercise frequently is referred to as endurance or aerobic exercise, since if it is performed at an intensity that is moderate relative to the participant's capacity, then most of the energy required for muscle contractions is produced in the presence of oxygen. It is during this type of exercise—walking, jogging, running, hiking, cycling, swimming, active games or sports, and selected around-home or at-work activities—that we can expend the most energy (calories) with the least muscle fatigue and in the shortest period of time. This increase in energy expenditure seems to be the necessary stimulus for producing many health-related changes attributed to exercise.

Of the various claims made regarding the health benefits of exercise, those with the most substantial scientific basis appear to be the maintenance of optimal body weight or composition, the prevention of coronary heart disease, and the normalization of carbohydrate metabolism. Other areas in which benefits are likely but persuasive data are not so available include the prevention of elevated blood pressure or hypertension, the maintenance of bone density (the loss of which occurs with aging), the prevention of the lower back pain syndrome, and improved psychological status. There are a number of other areas in which if patients with an established disease exercise, they tend to show clinical improvement, but there is no evidence that exercise prevents these disorders. Diseases included in this category include chronic obstructive lung disease (emphysema or bronchitis), kidney failure, and arthritis. There is little if any data supporting the notion that exercise prevents any infectious disease, and, on the average, more active people have a greater mortality from accidents than would be expected if they remained sedentary.

Separate chapters in this section review information on the relationship of exercise to weight control, psychological status, and aging. Also included in this section are brief reviews of the potential benefits of exercise in the prevention of coronary heart disease, elevated blood pressure, and abnormal carbohydrate metabolism. For each of these areas, information is included on the potential mechanism of benefit and the characteristics of the exercise needed to achieve the effect.

Prevention of Coronary Heart Disease

Men who select a physically active lifestyle on their own generally demonstrate fewer clinical manifestations of coronary heart disease (CHD) than their sedentary counterparts; when events do occur, they tend to be less severe and to appear at an older age (Costas, Garcia-Palmieri, Nazario, & Sorlie, 1978; Morris, Pollard, Everitt, & Chave, 1980; Paffenbarger, Wing, & Hyde, 1978). A recent report from Finland provides evidence of a similar relationship for women (Salonen, Puska, & Tuomilehto, 1982). A majority of the published observational or population studies tend to support this conclusion, with some reporting significantly lower disease rates for the more active, some showing only a favorable trend, and some finding no difference (Froelicher & Oberman, 1972). It is important to point out that no study has found that more active individuals have a significantly *higher* rate of CHD. These results demonstrate an association between level of exercise and a reduced risk of CHD but do not establish a cause-and-effect relationship, which is yet to be demonstrated by an adequately designed randomized clinical trial.

No specific study characteristics can be identified that explain the differences in results among the various studies, but in some cases the measurement of physical activity is not very accurate and the activity gradient among the population is quite small (Shapiro, Weinblatt, Frank, & Sager, 1969). Also, in populations where CHD mortality is exceptionally high and major risk factors such as hypercholesterolemia, hypertension, and cigarette smoking are prevalent, even very high levels of physical activity do not appear to exert a major protective effect. Finnish lumberjacks are an example of physically active individuals in whom CHD risk remains high (Karvonen, Rautaharju, & Orma, 1961). Such results strongly argue for a multifactor approach to CHD prevention.

A major criticism of the observational studies that demonstrate a protective effect of exercise is that the differences in CHD rates between active and inactive individuals may be because less healthy people select a less active lifestyle, not because increased activity prevents disease. Such self-selection may account for some of the differences reported, but in several reports the investigators have considered this problem in their data analyses and have still found exercise to be of significant benefit (Kahn, 1963; Paffenbarger & Hale, 1975).

A striking feature of many studies demonstrating a reduced CHD risk for more active individuals is that the greatest difference in risk is between people who do almost nothing and those who do a moderate amount of exercise on a regular basis. Much smaller differentials in risk are observed when moderately active individuals are compared to the most active participants. This relationship appears to be true for both job-related and non-job-related activity, but only for recent activity, as compared to activity performed in years past.

Both the intensity and the duration of activity that is associated with a decrease in CHD clinical manifestations vary substantially among the various studies. Several investigators have observed significant differences in CHD indicators with quite small increases in habitual activity level at a relatively low intensity (Rose, 1969; Shapiro et al., 1969), whereas other authors interpret their data to indicate that a threshold of higher intensity or amount of activity is needed in order to obtain a benefit (Cassel, Heyden, Bartel, Kaplan, Tyroler, Cornoni, & Hames, 1971; Paffenbarger et al., 1978). The types of activity performed by the more active groups include brisk walking on the level or up stairs, lifting and carrying of light objects, lifting of heavy objects, operation of machinery or appliances, light and heavy gardening and home maintenance or repairs, and participation in active games and sports. Participation in physical fitness or athletic conditioning programs appears to contribute very little to the more active classification in most observational studies.

As can be seen in Table 28.2, the amount of activity per day (above that performed by the least active group) associated with a decreased risk of CHD is in the range of 100 to 500 kilocalories per day for non-job-related activity and 300 to 800 kilocalories per day for job-related activity. This difference for nonjob or leisure-time activity, which averages out to about 300 kilocalories per day, is an amount of activity achievable by most healthy adults within 30 to 60 minutes of moderate-intensity exercise. This level of energy expenditure (3 to 12 kilocalories per minute) can be achieved most easily by performing large-muscle, dynamic exercise, and it is one of the scientific cornerstones on which the exercise prescription for health promotion is based.

How Exercise Might Provide Protection Against CHD

A variety of biological changes or mechanisms have been proposed to explain how physical activity might prevent the development of CHD manifestations (Table 28.3). Most of these

Table 28.2 Amount of Physical Activity Associated with Less Coronary Heart Disease

Study	Kilocalories		Type of Activity
	Rate[a]	Total/Day[b]	
Job-related activity			
North Dakota—U.S. (Zukel et al., 1959)	5–8	300–600	Farming, laboring
Evans Country—U.S. (Cassel et al., 1971)	3–7.5	400–500	Farming, laboring
Railroad—U.S. (Taylor & Parlin, Note 2)	5–8	350–600	Walking, climbing, hanging
HIP, New York—U.S. (Shapiro et al., 1969)	4–8	300–500	Walking, lifting, carrying
Longshoremen—U.S. (Paffenbarger & Hale, 1975)	5.2–7.5	810	Cargo handling
Non-job-related activity			
Civil servants—England (Rose, 1969)	4–7	100–140	Walking 5 days/ week
HIP, New York—U.S. (Shapiro et al., 1969)	4–12	250–500	Walking, recreation, home activity
College graduates—U.S. (Paffenbarger et al., 1978)	3–12	250–350	Walking, stair climbing, sports
Civil servants—England (Morris et al., 1980)	7.5	225	Recreation, home activity

[a] Estimated kilocalorie per minute expenditure for 70 kg man.
[b] Estimated difference in total kilocalorie per day expenditure between the least active and more active subjects.

mechanisms act in some way to decrease the likelihood that the oxygen demands of the myocardium will exceed the oxygen delivery capacity of the coronary arteries and prevent the development of myocardial ischemia. Thus, mechanisms can be classified as either those that contribute to the maintenance or increase of oxygen supply to the myocardium or those that contribute to a decrease in myocardial work and oxygen demands. These are the very same mechanisms through which most preventive and therapeutic measures for reducing clinical manifestations of CHD are considered to operate.

Since the primary cause of symptoms resulting from coronary atherosclerosis is a reduction in the supply of oxygen to the myocardium, the most direct beneficial effect of physical training might be to maintain or increase myocardial oxygen delivery. Enhanced oxygen availability to the myocardium could be achieved by the regression or delayed progression of coronary atherosclerosis, by an increase in lumen diameter of major coronary arteries, or by coronary collateral vascularization. A major factor limiting our ability to directly collect information about these possibilities is the difficulty in obtaining the necessary invasive measurements before and after training in both an exercise training group and a comparable control group.

Delay of Atherosclerosis. One way that exercise training could maintain or enhance myocardial oxygen supply would be by retarding the progression of coronary atherosclerosis or even by stimulating regression of existing plaques. The concept of coronary atherosclerosis prevention or reversibility as observed in primates (Kramsch, Aspen, Abramowitz, Kreimendahl, & Hood, 1981) is very attractive, but only limited human experimental data are available to support the isolated animal and epidemiologic observations that lend support

Table 28.3 Biological Mechanisms by Which Exercise Might Contribute to the Primary Prevention of Coronary Heart Disease

---

Maintain or increase myocardial oxygen supply
Delay progression of coronary atherosclerosis [possible]
   Improve lipoprotein profile (increase HDL-C/LDL-C ratio) [probable]
   Improve carbohydrate metabolism (increase insulin sensitivity) [probable]
   Decrease platelet aggregation and increase fibrinolysis [probable]
Increase coronary collateral vascularization [unlikely]
Increase coronary blood flow (myocardial perfusion) or distribution [unlikely]

Decrease myocardial work and oxygen demand
Decrease heart rate at rest and during submaximal exercise [usually]
Decrease systolic and mean systemic arterial pressure during submaximal exercise [usually]
   and at rest [possible]
Decrease cardiac output during submaximal exercise [probable]
Decrease circulating plasma catecholamine levels (decrease sympathetic tone) at rest [probable] and during submaximal exercise [usually]
Decrease adiposity [usually]

Increase myocardial function
Increase stroke volume at rest and during submaximal and maximal exercise [likely]
Increase ejection fraction at rest and during exercise [possible]
Increase intrinsic myocardial contractility [unlikely]
Increase myocardial function due to decreased afterload [probable]
Increase myocardial hypertrophy but may not reduce CHD risk [probable]

Increase electrical stability of myocardium
Decrease regional ischemia at rest or during submaximal exercise [possible]
Decrease catecholamines in myocardium at rest and during submaximal exercise [probable]
Increase ventricular fibrillation threshold due to reduction of cycle AMP [possible]

Note: The expression of likelihood that the effect will occur for an individual participating in endurance-type training program for 16 weeks or longer at 65% to 80% of functional capacity for 25 minutes or longer per session (300 kilocalories) for three or more sessions per week ranges from unlikely, possible, likely, probable, to usually.

to such a possibility. No study has been reported in which the progression of coronary atherosclerosis in relation to exercise status has been measured in asymptomatic individuals, and only a few studies have reported any such data on cardiac patients (Selvester, Camp, & Sanmarcos, 1977). Recently, a few investigators have attempted to study myocardial perfusion changes using thallium 201 radionuclide imaging, but reproducibility and precision problems with the measurement technique have contributed to inconclusive results (Verani, Hartung, Hoepfel-Harris, Welton, Pratt, & Miller, 1981).

Indirect evidence that vigorous exercise might beneficially influence the rate of atherosclerosis is suggested by the relationship of exercise to several established CHD risk factors. In healthy adults, exercise training has been shown to alter the blood lipoprotein profile in a direction thought to be less atherogenic; high-density lipoprotein cholesterol (HDL-C) is increased, while low-density lipoprotein cholesterol (LDL-C), very low density lipoprotein cholesterol (VLDL-C), total cholesterol, and triglycerides are sometimes lower (Wood & Haskell, 1979). Of particular recent interest is the apparent antiatherogenic effect of increased HDL-C and the elevating effect on it of both endurance exercise and weight loss.

If occlusion of narrowed coronary arteries resulting from blood clots significantly contributes to the increased incidence of CHD, then exercise might exert a beneficial influence by delaying clotting or by increasing fibrinolysis. Moderate-intensity exercise (70% of functional capacity for 30 minutes) significantly increases fibrinolytic activity (Astrup, 1973).

Coronary Collateral Vascularization.   The intriguing hypothesis that exercise training might be an adequate stimulus for the development of coronary collateral vessels has been supported by some early animal studies (Eckstein, 1957). Such encouraging results, however, have not been obtained systematically in any human study using coronary arteriography (Ferguson, Petitclerc, Choquette, Chaniotis, Gauthier, Huot, Allard, Jankowski, & Campean, 1974) nor has there been any evidence of an increase in coronary blood flow as a result of exercise training by cardiac patients (Ferguson, Cote, Gauthier, & Bourassa, 1978). This discrepancy is probably due to a species difference, although the insensitivity of the measurement technique in detecting small changes in coronary anatomy and coronary flow should not be overlooked. Also, it would be of interest to observe subjects before and after exercise training of greater intensity than that used in the studies reported so far. The necessary stimulus for enhancing coronary collateral vascularization appears to be myocardial hypoxia induced by the atherosclerotic disease process itself, and increases in myocardial work, coronary blood flow, or coronary perfusion pressure produced during exercise do not significantly alter the size of the functional vascular bed.

Decreases in Myocardial Oxygen Demand.   A reduction in the frequency or severity of the clinical manifestations of CHD may occur with physical training as a result of a decrease in myocardial oxygen requirement at rest and during exercise. Following exercise training, a substantial percentage of angina patients increase the exercise intensity necessary to provoke ischemia; in some patients, exertional ischemia is eliminated altogether (Ehsani, Heath, Hagberg, Sobel, & Holloszy, 1981). The primary reason for this increase in ischemia-free working capacity is a decrease in myocardial oxygen demand due to a systematic decrease in exercise heart rate with less of a reduction in systolic blood pressure. The decrease in heart rate at a given work load or oxygen uptake appears to be the key to improving the clinical status of many CHD patients with angina pectoris, as it is the major factor in the exercise-related decrease in indexes of myocardial work. The precise mechanism by which training produces exercise bradycardia is still not fully understood. It currently appears that the training-induced decrease in exercise heart rate is due to changes in the skeletal muscle used for training and to some other more central change, such as increased blood volume, myocardial hypertrophy, increased myocardial contractility, or altered central nervous system regulation.

Antidysrhythmic Effect of Exercise.   The lower rate of sudden deaths reported for the more active subjects in several of the observational studies could result from an antidysrhythmic effect of exercise. This idea is still highly speculative, however, since very few data on which to evaluate this question have been published. The concept is plausible because of the known effects that training has on the nervous regulation of the heart, on the reduction of myocardial oxygen demand, and in lowering circulating plasma catecholamines (Cousineau, Ferguson, de Champlain, Gauthier, Cote, & Bourassa, 1977). Because of the rather low test-retest reproducibility of cardiac dysrhythmias during 24-hour ambulatory monitoring and exercise testing, measurement problems associated with answering this question are substantial.

In one study, when subjects who were classified as compliers to an exercise training program (greater than 75% attendance) were compared to the inactive controls, the number of premature ventricular contractions (PVCs) per person in those subjects displaying ventricular ectopic activity was significantly less in the exercise group ($p = 0.04$), but the percentage of subjects manifesting PVCs was not different (Blackburn, Taylor, Hamrell, Buskirk, Nicholas, & Thorsen, 1973). Although they are inconclusive, these data do suggest that exercise training may have an antidysrhythmic potential for some individuals.

Exercise and Blood Pressure Control

Exercise should not be considered as a first-line therapy for the control of high blood pressure, even though as a general preventive measure an active lifestyle probably is of some benefit. It is well established that individuals can have a high level of physical fitness and yet be hypertensive, but that in the general population, more active individuals tend to have lower systolic and diastolic pressures (Cooper, Pollock, Marin, White, Linnerud, & Jackson, 1976). Several studies have found that endurance-type exercise training by border-line or essential hypertensive patients results in a lower blood pressure, with the decline usually greater in systolic than in diastolic pressure (Choquette & Ferguson, 1973; Roman, Camuzzi, Villalon, & Klenner, 1981). The results of many such studies are difficult to interpret because nonexercising control groups were not included, and there is a reasonable likelihood that some of the blood pressure reduction observed can be accounted for by increased familiarization with the research personnel and environment or regression toward the mean in studies of hypertensive patients.

A very consistent finding is that systolic blood pressure during submaximal exercise is significantly lowered as a result of exercise training (Choquette & Ferguson, 1973). This reduction in pressure may have important health consequences if ambulatory or operational blood pressure, as well as resting pressure, is important in the negative health consequences of hypertension (coronary heart disease, hypertensive heart disease, stroke, renal failure, and so on). This decrease in exercise systolic pressure has been observed in numerous studies, even when no change in resting blood pressure was reported.

The biological mechanisms responsible for the reductions in blood pressure as a result of exercise training are not well established. The major hypothesis considered to date is a decrease in sympathetic nervous system activity reflected by a decrease in circulating plasma catecholamine levels. A decrease in sympathetic tone at rest has not been observed by all investigators, whereas the decrease at submaximal exercise of a set intensity is more consistently reported and tends to be of a greater magnitude (Cousineau et al., 1977). Also, in some circumstances there appears to be a small reduction in cardiac output at rest and during submaximal exercise following training, which may contribute to a lower systemic arterial pressure. There is some indication that the lower blood pressure values reported for more active individuals are due, at least in part, to their tendency to be leaner than their sedentary peers. Even when statistical adjustments are made for these differences in obesity, however, the more active individuals still have lower pressures (Cooper et al., 1976).

Large-muscle, dynamic exercise is by far the type of exercise most frequently performed by people with lower pressures and most frequently used in the training studies reported in this section. Moderate-intensity exercise appears to be of value, but no greater effects are reported with higher intensity exercise (Roman et al., 1981).

Normalization of Carbohydrate Metabolism

It has been recognized repeatedly throughout the history of medical care that exercise decreases the symptoms of hyperglycemia in many diabetic patients. Almost as frequent, however, has been the expression of caution regarding vigorous exercise by diabetic patients because of its detrimental effects on the brittle or uncontrolled patient. Allen, Stillman, and Fritz (1919) demonstrated that the rate of glucose uptake from the blood in diabetic patients was significantly increased during exercise as compared to rest. Such results generally were ignored, and little attention was given to the potential role of exercise in the prevention or treatment of adult-onset or Type II diabetes. The idea that exercise had little if any role in normalizing glucose metabolism was due, at least in part, to the findings that there is no consistent difference in the fasting plasma glucose levels between healthy sedentary and active adults. The difference in glucose metabolism becomes apparent when the rate of glucose uptake from the blood and the plasma insulin levels are measured in response to an oral glucose challenge (Leon, Conrad, Hunninglake, & Serfass, 1979) or during infusion of glucose into the bloodstream. In these situations, the rate of glucose removal tends to be more rapid in physically active individuals, and the amount of insulin required during this enhanced glucose uptake is significantly less (Soman, Veikko, Deibert, Felig, & De-Fronzo, 1979). In the physically active state, the sensitivity of insulin receptors in skeletal muscle and adipose tissue increases, with a lower insulin production being required for the body to use a given amount of glucose. This difference in insulin sensitivity can be seen most dramatically when plasma insulin levels are measured during the course of a glucose tolerance test before and after an endurance-type training program (Leon et al., 1979).

During large-muscle, dynamic exercise of moderate intensity, the glycogen stored in skeletal muscle is used for the production of energy and becomes partly depleted. For the next 24 to 72 hours after such exercise, this glycogen is replaced by the uptake of glucose from the blood. In addition to this immediate or acute effect of increased glucose removal, there also appears to be a chronic training effect that increases the rate of glucose removal at any given level of plasma insulin. These insulin-sparing effects of exercise probably reduce the long-term insulin production requirements of the beta cells in the pancreas and may reduce the risk of insulin deficiency developing with increasing age.

Carbohydrate metabolism seems to be improved with endurance exercise of moderate intensity or duration, with even greater changes occurring with more vigorous exercise. Rate of glucose uptake from the plasma is enhanced in sedentary adults undertaking a 30 to 40 minute per day, 3 day per week program for 6 weeks (Soman et al., 1979), and reduced insulin levels were observed during an oral glucose tolerance test in sedentary obese male college students following 16 weeks of vigorous walking (3.2 mph at 10%), 90 minutes per day, 5 days per week (1100 kilocalories per session) (Leon et al., 1979). In men with impaired glucose tolerance, an exercise training program (60% to 90% $\dot{V}O_2$ two times a week for 45 min) lasting 6 months significantly increased glucose uptake during a glucose tolerance test, with no further improvements at 12 and 18 months of training (Saltin, Lindgarde, Houston, Horlin, Nygaard, & Gad, 1979). Thus, the regular performance of endurance-type exercise, especially when coupled with maintenance of optimal body composition, significantly contributes to the normalization of carbohydrate metabolism and may reduce the frequency or delay the onset of Type II diabetes.

HEALTH RISKS OF EXERCISE

The promotion of exercise for health reasons has the potential of being a two-edged sword: it surely can be of benefit when carried out properly, but it literally can present dangers to life and limb. The most commonly encountered problems are orthopedic discomfort or disability produced by overuse (tennis elbow, shin splints, and the like) or injury due to a collision with the ground, an object, or another person (Koplan, Powell, Sikes, Shirley, & Campbell, 1982). Although they are not life-threatening in most cases, these problems are a major deterrent to many middle-aged or older adults who are either initiating or maintaining a program of vigorous exercise. Of more severe consequence, but much less frequent, is the precipitation of a major cardiac event, either cardiac arrest or myocardial infarction, during exercise. Over the past 30 years, the risk of a heart attack during exercise in an apparently healthy adult has been one of the key determinants in the design of adult exercise recommendations. It has significantly influenced the need for a preexercise medical examination, medical supervision during exercise, and an actual exercise plan (especially regarding the type and intensity of exercise). There are many other health risks of exercise, but these are usually limited to individuals with established disease (i.e., diabetes, asthma, or kidney failure) or occur only with very extended or competitive exercise. The most important of these risks is probably the development of severe heat injury (England, Fraser, Hightower, Tirinnanzi, Greenberg, Powell, Slovis, & Varsha, 1982).

Orthopedic injuries most often occur during health-oriented exercise programs as a result of the added weight-bearing stress on feet, ankles, legs, knees, and lower back associated with jogging, running, and racket sports. Most of these injuries are caused by irritations of bones, tendons, ligaments, and sometimes muscles. There is a wide range of susceptibility to such injuries, and it is difficult to predict who will have problems and who will not as the intensity and amount of exercise they perform increases. Risk becomes greater with advancing age, history of previous injury, and substantial obesity. Preventive procedures include the use of non-weight-bearing activities, such as swimming, riding a stationary cycle or rowing machine, and substituting brisk walking or hiking in the hills instead of jogging. Exercise should be performed on soft surfaces, such as padded rugs or grass, instead of on asphalt or cement wherever possible, and jumping-type activities, including aerobic dancing, on hard floors may need to be avoided or approached with caution. Good athletic or running shoes, with thick, shock-absorbing soles, raised heels, and arch supports, are valuable; model and brand selection depends on individual preference. It is important to begin a new program of exercise very slowly to allow the support structures time to accommodate to the new stress being placed on them. When problems do develop, it is important to relieve the stress by decreasing the amount or intensity of activity, switching to an alternative exercise, or resting and applying appropriate therapy.

Whenever someone has a heart attack or dies suddenly while exercising vigorously, the event receives much more publicity than if the same individual had died at home or work. Because of this publicity, the percentage of all sudden cardiac deaths in apparently healthy adults that occur during vigorous exercise probably is lower than it would seem to be according to casual observation. Even though it is well established that the increase in work and oxygen demand placed on the heart by intense dynamic or static exercise can precipitate sudden cardiac arrest or myocardial infarction, such events occur only when the heart's function has been impaired by some disease of its arteries, valves, or muscle. The risk of a major cardiac event being produced by an appropriate program of health-oriented exercise is very small and should not be a deterrent to exercise for the sedentary person. The risk obviously is greater for individuals who have a higher risk of developing coronary heart disease; thus, risk increases for men, aged over 35 years, with a family history of premature heart disease and the major modifiable risk factors (cigarette smoking, elevated blood pressure, and hypercholesterolemia). The absolute risk is difficult to determine because of the problem of documenting the circumstances surrounding all major cardiac events. In a recent retrospective survey of 40 exercise facilities over 5 years, the fatality rate during exercise was estimated to be one death in every 887,526 man-hours of exercise, or about 1% per year, nearly the same as the annual mortality rate in the United States (Vander, Franklin, & Rubenfire, 1982). In 33,726,000 man-hours of exercise, a total of 38 fatal cardiac complications were reported, which means that one could expect one death per year among 3,400 adults who each exercise 5 hours per week. Most of the reported deaths occurred during court games, jogging, and swimming, which were the vigorous exercises performed most frequently. In adults who have been cleared for exercise by a recent medical examination, the risk of a cardiac event appears even lower (Gibbons, Cooper, Meyer, & Ellison, 1980).

The prevention of all cardiac events during exercise cannot be achieved, since some victims are asymptomatic until the fatal event, or else the cardiac anomaly that was the cause could have been detected only by an elaborate, and in some cases dangerous, invasive evaluation procedure. Most events can be prevented if individuals remain under good general medical care (periodic evaluations and appropriate treatment when needed), control major cardiac risk factors, learn the proper skills for health-oriented exercise, use this knowledge in carrying out a program of regular exercise, and take heed of body signals that indicate when the exercise plan should be modified or medical attention should be sought. Proper medical clearance, individualized program planning and implementation, and personal monitoring are the keys to safe exercise.

SUMMARY

Results from animal, experimental, observational, and clinical research support the general contention that physical activity can help delay—if not prevent—the onset or reduce the severity of several of the major chronic degenerative diseases responsible for much of the premature disability that occurs in Western industrialized cultures. Areas in which particular benefit is achieved with appropriate exercise appear to be weight control, prevention of coronary heart disease, normalization of lipid and carbohydrate metabolism, and delay of bone strength and skeletal muscle function degeneration associated with aging. Intriguing data exist on the psychological benefits of exercise, but definitive data demonstrating a cause-and-effect relationship are still missing. The type, intensity, and amount of exercise needed to achieve many of the health benefits are well within the capacity of most healthy adults at all ages. Large-muscle, dynamic exercise appears to contribute the most to improved health status, with the primary stimulus for beneficial changes being a sustained increase in energy expenditure. An energy expenditure of 300 to 400 kilocalories per day at moderate intensity should be the goal for health-oriented exercise.

The greatest success in initiating and maintaining exercise is achieved with individually designed programs that take into account not only the person's goals and exercise capacity but also his or her interests, skills, and exercise opportunities. Clients should be given instructions to set aside 30 to 60 minutes at least every other day for exercise and to fill it with any number of activities, rather than selecting a single activity as the sole basis for increasing exercise for health purposes. The activity plan should be convenient to perform, should fit within the general lifestyle of the client, and should be considered fun or at least enjoyable. Success at exercise is increased when the client has acquired the *knowledge* of what is to be done and why, the *confidence* that he or she can be successful at it, and the *patience* to wait for the benefits to accrue.

REFERENCE NOTES

1. Pacific Mutual Life Insurance Company. Exercise. In *Health maintenance: A nation-wide survey of the barriers towards better health and ways of overcoming them.* Oakland, Calif.: Pacific Mutual Life Insurance Company, 1978.
2. Taylor, H. L., & Parlin, R. W. *The physical activity of railroad clerks and switchmen: Estimation of on-the-job calorie expenditure by time and task measurements and classification of recreational activity by a questionnaire.* Written presentation at "Three Days of Cardiology," Seattle, June 1966.

REFERENCES

Allen, F. M., Stillman, E., & Fritz, R. Total dietary regulation in the treatment of diabetes. In *Exercise*, (Monograph #11). New York: Rockefeller Institute of Medical Research, 1919.

Asmussen, E. Similarities and dissimilarities between static and dynamic exercise. *Circulation Research,* 1981, **48**(II), 1–3.

Astrup, T. The effects of physical activity on blood coagulation and fibrinolysis. In J. P. Naughton & H. R. Hellerstein (eds.), *Exercise testing and training in coronary heart disease.* New York: Academic Press, 1973.

Blackburn, H., Taylor, H. L., Hamrell, B., Buskirk, E., Nicholas, V. C., & Thorsen, R. Premature ventricular complexes induced by stress testing: Their frequency and response to physical conditioning. *American Journal of Cardiology,* 1973, **31**, 441–449.

Cassel, J., Heyden, S., Bartel, A. G., Kaplan, B., Tyroler, A., Cornoni, J., & Hames, C. Occupation and physical activity and coronary heart disease. *Archives of Internal Medicine,* 1971, **128**, 920–928.

Choquette, G., & Ferguson, R. J. Blood pressure reduction in "borderline" hypertensives following physical training. *Canadian Medical Journal,* 1973, **108**, 699–703.

Cooper, K. H., Pollock, M., Marin, R., White, S., Linnerud, A., & Jackson, A. Physical fitness levels vs. selected coronary risk factors. *Journal of the American Medical Association,* 1976, **236**, 166–169.

Costas, R., Garcia-Palmieri, M. R., Nazario, E., & Sorlie, P. Relation of lipids, weight and physical activity to incidence of coronary heart disease: The Puerto Rico Heart Study. *American Journal of Cardiology,* 1978, **42**, 653–658.

Cousineau, D., Ferguson, R., de Champlain, J., Gauthier, P., Cote, P., & Bourassa, M. Catecholamines in coronary sinus during exercise in man before and after training. *Journal of Applied Physiology,* 1977, **43**, 801–806.

Eckstein, R. W. Effect of exercise and coronary artery narrowing on coronary collateral circulation. *Circulation Research,* 1957, **5**, 230–235.

Ehsani, A., Heath, G., Hagberg, J., Sobel, B., & Holloszy, J. Effects of 12 months of intense exercise training on ischemic ST-segment depression in patients with coronary artery disease. *Circulation,* 1981, **64**, 1116–1124.

England, A. C., Fraser, D. W., Hightower, A. W., Tirinnanzi, R., Greenberg, D. J., Powell, K., Slovis, C. M., & Varsha, R. A. Preventing severe heat injury in runners: Suggestion from the 1979 Peachtree Road Race experience. *Annals of Internal Medicine,* 1982, **97**, 196–201.

Ferguson, R. J., Cote, P., Gauthier, P., & Bourassa, M. G. Changes in exercise coronary sinus blood flow with training in patients with angina pectoris. *Circulation,* 1978, **58**, 41–47.

Ferguson, R. J., Petitclerc, R., Choquette, G., Chaniotis, P., Gauthier, R., Huot, R., Allard, C., Jankowski, L., & Campeau, L. Effect of exercise capacity, collateral circulation, and progression of coronary disease. *American Journal of Cardiology,* 1974, **34**, 764–769.

Froelicher, V. F., & Oberman, A. Analysis of epidemiologic studies of physical inactivity as risk factors for coronary artery disease. *Progress in Cardiovascular Disease,* 1972, **15**, 209–227.

Gibbons, L. W., Cooper, K. H., Meyer, B. M., & Ellison, R. C. The acute cardiac risk of strenuous exercise. *Journal of the American Medical Association,* 1980, **244**, 1799–1801.

Kahn, H. A. The relationship of reported coronary heart disease mortality to physical activity of work. *American Journal of Public Health,* 1963, **53**.

Karvonen, M. J., Rautaharju, P. M., & Orma, E. Heart disease and employment: Cardiovascular studies on lumberjacks. *Journal of Occupational Medicine,* 1961, **3**, 49–53.

Koplan, J. P., Powell, K. E., Sikes, R. K., Shirley, R. W., & Campbell, C. C. An epidemiologic study of the benefits and risks of running. *Journal of the American Medical Association,* 1982, **248**, 3118–3121.

Kramsch, D. M., Aspen, A., Abramowitz, B., Kreimendahl, T., & Hood, W. B. Reduction of coronary atherosclerosis by moderate conditioning exercise in monkeys on an atherogenic diet. *New England Journal of Medicine,* 1981, **305**, 1483–1489.

Leon, A., Conrad, J., Hunninglake, D., & Serfass, R. Effects of a vigorous walking program on body composition, and carbohydrate and lipid metabolism of obese young men. *American Journal of Clinical Nutrition,* 1979, **32**, 1776–1787.

Morris, J. N., Pollard, R., Everitt, M. G., & Chave, S. P. W. Vigorous exercise in leisure time: Protection against coronary heart disease. *Lancet,* 1980, **8206**, 1207–1210.

Oldridge, N. B. Compliance and exercise in primary and secondary prevention of coronary heart disease: A review. *Preventive Medicine,* 1982, **11**, 56–70.

Paffenbarger, R. S., & Hale, W. E. Work activity and coronary heart disease mortality. *New England Journal of Medicine,* 1975, **292**, 545–550.

Paffenbarger, R. S., Wing, A. L., & Hyde, R. T. Physical activity as an index of heart attack in college alumni. *American Journal of Epidemiology,* 1978, **108**, 161–175.

Roman, O., Camuzzi, A. L., Villalon, E., & Klenner, C. Physical training program in arterial hypertension: A long-term prospective follow-up. *Cardiology,* 1981, **67**, 230–243.

Rose, G. Physical activity and coronary heart disease. *Proceedings of the Royal Society of Medicine,* 1969, **62**, 1183–1186.

Salonen, J. T., Puska, P., & Tuomilehto, J. Physical activity and risk of myocardial infarction, cerebral stroke and death: A longitudinal study in Eastern Finland. *American Journal of Epidemiology,* 1982, **115**, 526–537.

Saltin, B., Lindgarde, F., Houston, M., Horlin, R., Nygaard, E., & Gad, P. Physical training and glucose tolerance in middle-aged men with chemical diabetes. *Diabetes,* 1979, **28**(Suppl. 1), 30–32.

Selvester, R., Camp, J., & Sanmarcos, M. Effects of exercise training on progression of documented coronary atherosclerosis. In P. Milvey (ed.), *The marathon: Physiological, medical, epidemiological, and psychological studies.* New York: New York Academy of Sciences, 1977.

Shapiro, S., Weinblatt, E., Frank, C. W., & Sager, R. V. Incidence of coronary heart disease in a population insured for medical care (HIP). *American Journal of Public Health,* 1969, **59**(Suppl.), 1–101.

Soman, V. R., Veikko, A. K., Deibert, D., Felig, P., & DeFronzo, R. A. Increased insulin sensitivity and insulin binding to monocytes after physical training. *New England Journal of Medicine,* 1979, **301**, 200–204.

Vander, L., Franklin, B., & Rubenfire, M. Cardiovascular complications of recreational physical activity. *Physician and Sports Medicine,* 1982, **10**, 89–95.

Verani, M., Hartung, H., Hoepfel-Harris, J., Welton, D., Pratt, C., & Miller, R. Effects of exercise training on left ventricular performance and myocardial perfusion in patients with coronary artery disease. *American Journal of Cardiology,* 1981, **47**, 797–802.

Wilmore, J. H. *Training for sport and activity* (2nd ed.). Boston: Allyn & Bacon, 1982.

Wood, P. D., & Haskell, W. L. The effect of exercise on plasma high-density lipoprotein. *Lipids,* 1979, **14**, 417–427.

Zukel, W. J., Lewis, R. N., & Enterline, P. E. A short-term community study of the epidemiology of coronary heart disease. *American Journal of Public Health,* 1959, **49**, 1630–1639.

CHAPTER 29

HOW TO ASSESS EXERCISE
HABITS AND PHYSICAL FITNESS

STEVEN N. BLAIR

University of South Carolina and Institute for Aerobics Research, Dallas

The purpose of this chapter is to present techniques and methods for measurement of exercise patterns and levels of physical fitness. A brief review of previous research and methods is presented, followed by a more thorough discussion of an interview method for assessing exercise habits and a physical fitness test that has been used in several health screening applications.

Researchers and clinicians in behavioral health programs may wish to monitor both exercise participation and physiological status. It is reasonable to assume that exercise is the important factor in disease prevention and health promotion, not the absolute level of physical fitness. Although physical fitness is extensively influenced by exercise habits, it also has a significant genetic component. The assessment of physical fitness, however, is probably a more objective procedure than the assessment of exercise habits. Fitness improvement undoubtedly reflects an increase in exercise and is an adequate marker for behavioral change. Therefore, the individual scientist or clinician may elect to measure either exercise or fitness, or both, depending on program requirements.

ASSESSMENT OF EXERCISE PATTERNS

Measuring an individual's habitual exercise pattern is difficult. Validation of methods is complicated by the fact that it probably is impossible to obtain a "gold standard" measurement. This difficulty has also been referred to in dietary assessment (Block, 1982). If we cannot ascertain the truth about an individual's exercise habits, how can we validate an instrument or method that purports to estimate the truth? Although this question is probably the central issue in assessment of exercise in free-living individuals, and although it can not be answered with complete satisfaction, methods are presented in this section that provide reasonable estimates of true exercise patterns.

Problems and Issues

There are several important issues related to exercise assessment. What is the importance, for example, of the relative accuracy of estimating group data versus accurate measurement

I thank Drs. William Haskell, Peter Wood, and J. W. Farquhar of the Stanford Heart Disease Prevention Program where much of the developmental work was done on the 7-day recall and the submaximal bicycle ergometer test. Ping Ho deserves special thanks for conducting many of the first recall interviews, for assisting in the development of the interviewer instructions, and for helping to train the field interviewees. June Lambert, Angie Meadows, and Karen Robertshaw were especially helpful during the preparation of the manuscript. I thank Dr. Russell Pate for his comments on an early draft.

for a single individual? For research purposes, it may be adequate for group means to be determined reliably and for the method to be sensitive enough to detect change in group exercise patterns. Methods that meet these criteria obviously would be useful in community or worksite intervention studies. In a clinical setting, however, where assessment of exercise pattern, exercise prescription, and follow-up are needed for a behavioral health program involving exercise, accurate individual assessment is needed.

What type of exercise must be measured? Is it necessary to obtain estimates of total energy output, or should we concentrate on measuring only high-intensity activities? Morris, Pollard, Everitt, and Chave (1980) and Paffenbarger, Wing, and Hyde (1978) have shown that relatively vigorous activity (requiring at least 7.5 kcal/min) seems to offer protection against heart disease. For weight control, stress management, or other presumed benefits of physical activity, however, increasing total energy expenditure by more moderate everyday activities may also be beneficial. If only vigorous activities are measured, assessment becomes simpler, since most individuals in our society engage in relatively little vigorous exercise, and these bouts are easy to remember, observe, count, and measure.

Should assessment emphasis be on leisure activities, occupational activities, or both? The vast majority of individuals have relatively sedentary jobs. Few occupational tasks require energy output above the moderate level. In many settings, occupational activity may be ignored with little effect on the data. In some studies, in which entire communities or worksites are surveyed, it may be wise to include occupational activities in the assessment. If a community survey includes an area with many field agricultural workers ("stoop labor"), for example, occupational activity probably should be included. Surveys of universities or white-collar industries, such as insurance companies, can focus only on leisure time physical activity.

Is it important that a method provide a quantitatively accurate measure of physical activity, or is classification of individuals into activity categories adequate? It is intrinsically satisfying to obtain a quantitative measure of physical activity, such as caloric expenditure, and this may also be of value when communicating results to participants or clients. Participants in a weight control program, for example, might benefit from self-monitoring of both caloric intake and caloric expenditure, using the same units (kcal/day). Graphing these values (perhaps red lines for intake and green for expenditure) might be a useful exercise and might aid in an intervention program. There remains the question, however, of whether available methods warrant the appearance of such accuracy. Calculation of daily caloric expenditure may give false security and too much confidence in methods that are too imprecise. Classifying individuals into categories is probably easier than attempting precise quantification. It is not clear, however, that classification methods are sensitive enough to detect moderate change in activity patterns. The usefulness of classification methods in clinical settings is also questionable.

An additional issue that makes assessment difficult is sampling. It is well established that the health benefits of physical activity result from regular participation over several weeks, or perhaps months (ACSM, 1978). The logistics of assessment preclude continuous measurement over extended time periods; therefore, the researcher or practitioner must select a sample of no more than a few days in which to obtain data. It is difficult and sometimes impossible to select these days at random. Measurements usually will be made when a participant comes to a survey center or clinic. It is obviously not feasible to randomly sample a few days extending back over the past several months and expect to obtain a valid recall of actual physical activity. Therefore, if any of the recall procedures are used, activity may be assessed only for the few days immediately preceding the visit. It has been observed that several days are necessary to obtain stable estimates of dietary intake (Liu, Stamler, Dyer, McKeever, & McKeever, 1978), and the same is probably true for physical activity. One way to avoid the sampling issue is to use an activity pattern questionnaire. With this approach, the participant is asked to report general or typical patterns of activity, rather than to recall specific activities. One such technique will be discussed in detail later (Taylor, Jacobs, Schucker, Knudsen, Leon, & Debacker, 1978). This typical pattern method has been used successfully for dietary surveys (Burke & Stuart, 1938) and is viewed as a valid method by nutritionists (Block, 1982).

Another problem with measurement of physical activity is intrusion or respondent burden. In some cases, the burden may be great enough that the participants will not comply with the measurement protocol. In other situations, they may attempt to comply, but the effort required may cause them to alter their normal activities. This problem is particularly relevant to record-keeping methods and physiological monitoring.

The foregoing problems and issues notwithstanding, numerous attempts have been made to develop and test methods of physical activity assessment. As stated earlier, a gold standard method is not available, so validation generally has been attempted by face validity and logical argument. If a method is valid in identifying more active individuals, the more active persons would be expected to be leaner and to have higher levels of physical fitness. If several methods appear to be valid by face validity, then there should be relatively high agreement among the several techniques.

Physiological Monitoring

Participation in physical activity produces certain known physiological adjustments. To provide for the increased energy demand of the working muscles, circulatory and respiratory parameters increase to supply the needed oxygen (O_2) and fuel for metabolic processes. Metabolic by-products—notably, carbon dioxide (CO_2)—are also transported by the circulo-respiratory system. The primary changes required by increased metabolic rates are greater blood flow and increased ventilation of the lungs. Increased blood flow or cardiac output is accomplished by an increased stroke volume (amount of blood pumped with each heart beat) and increased heart rate (number of beats per minute). Measuring stroke volume is a relatively complicated laboratory procedure and is not feasible for field application. Fortunately, cardiac output, and therefore delivery of O_2 to the tissues for increased metabolism, is linearly related to heart rate. This linear association applies over the range of heart rates from rest to near-maximal activity. Although emotion can also effect heart rate, this effect is generally overridden by metabolic demands at moderate or higher work levels. Thus, at work loads from slow walking to running, heart rate is an accurate indicator of total body energy expenditure. Unfortunately, this association is highly individualized because of genetic variation and physical fitness level. If two individuals are both working at a heart rate of 140 beats/minute, for example, their energy expenditures are considerably higher than when their heart rates are 100 beats/minute, but interindividual comparisons are not possible from these data alone. A heart rate of 140 beats/minute may be achieved by moderate walking in a sedentary and deconditioned individual. Another person of the same age and sex who exercises regularly and is quite fit may have a heart rate of 140 beats/minute when running at an 8 minute/mile pace. Heart rate monitoring is therefore useful in comparing the relative strenuousness of activity within an individual but not for accurately estimating actual energy output for interindividual comparisons. The latter goal can be achieved if individual heart rate–energy expenditure calibration curves are established in the laboratory. If an individual has a heart rate of 130 beats/minute and an energy expenditure of 7.5 kcal/minute while walking on a treadmill in the physiology laboratory, one can assume an equivalent energy expenditure while walking down the street at a heart rate of 130 beats/minute. There are some technical problems, such as different heart rate responses to arm versus leg work or for isometric work, but the approach described is generally valid.

Using the foregoing approach to assess physical activity in free-living individuals requires establishing the individual heart rate–energy expenditure relationship and then recording heart rates during daily activities. Detailed methods for carrying out these measurements are given by Andersen, Masironi, Rutenfranz, Seliger, Degre, Trygg, and Orgim (1978) and in several papers in a special issue of the *American Journal of Clinical Nutrition* (Bradfield, 1971). If one is interested in intraindividual comparisons and changes only, quantification of energy output would not be necessary. Relative intensity would be indicated by heart rate alone, and the calibration curve would not need to be developed.

Another approach to physiological monitoring is to measure body movement. Greater body movements presumably would be related to increased energy expenditure. These methods also have some artifact—for example, sitting with legs crossed and swinging the crossed leg would be registered as leg movement by an attached sensor. The energy cost of that activity, however, would be far less than that for leg movements due to walking. Nonetheless, body movement recording appears to have some validity. Recent papers by LaPorte, Kuller, Kupfer, McPartland, Matthews, and Caspersen (1979) and Wong, Webster, Montoye, and Washburn (1981) indicate that these methods discriminate between activity levels and are correlated with direct measurement of O_2 uptake in the laboratory. How well body movement recorders estimate energy output in activities other than walking, running, or cycling has not been firmly established. The present electronic movement sensors (LaPorte et al., 1978; Wong et al., 1981) are a clear improvement over mechanical pedometers, which are of very limited value (Washburn, Chin, & Montoye, 1980). Instruments with multiple recording channels, which monitor heart rate and movement in one or more planes, may ultimately prove to have advantages over the current generation of recording devices.

Monitoring activity by instruments such as those just discussed is somewhat intrusive. Subjects must visit a laboratory or clinic to have electrodes or devices attached or to have the recorder "dumped" into a computer for analysis. Measurement of certain activities, such as swimming, may be prohibited.

The cost of these instruments and the associated costs of collecting, processing, and analyzing the data are relatively high. This approach to physical activity assessment probably has greater application in the clinical setting than for collecting data in large-scale epidemiologic surveys. Further developmental work is needed.

Questionnaires

Most attempts at assessing physical activity have used interviewer- or self-administered questionnaires. Problems of sampling, recall, and intrusion have already been discussed here. Nonetheless, questionnaire estimates of physical activity have predicted development of coronary heart disease (CHD) (Morris et al., 1980; Paffenbarger et al., 1978) and have been associated with body composition (Buskirk, Harris, Mendez, & Skinner, 1971; Montoye, 1975) and caloric intake (Blair & Haskell, Note 1).

Yasin, Alderson, Marr, Pattison, and Morris (1967) described an interview procedure for assessing physical activity in British civil servants. Participants were interviewed on Monday and questioned about their activities on the preceding Friday and Saturday or were queried on Tuesday about the preceding Sunday and Monday. The participants were asked to recall and describe every activity on the days under consideration. Activities of at least 5 minutes' duration were recorded and coded into five categories, based on intensity. Total activity scores for the day were calculated; they were found to be relatively stable in a group of men who were interviewed repeatedly. Validation of the procedure was attempted by comparing caloric intake and body composition in groups of men with different activity scores. Active men had higher caloric intake and thinner skin fold measurements.

Another interviewer-administered questionnaire was developed for the Tecumseh community study (Reiff, Montoye, Remington, Napier, Metzner, & Epstein, 1967) and was later simplified by Taylor et al. (1978). This questionnaire asks participants to recall their physical activity over the past year. (This is probably more accurately termed a physical activity history than a recall procedure.) Participants are asked to read an extensive list of leisure time pursuits, including sports, recreation, and home maintenance activities. They check the months in which the activity was performed, the average number of times per month, and the duration of each session. A sample section of the questionnaire is shown in Figure 29.1. Intensity of the various activities is graded by multiples of resting metabolism (METS),

Leisure Time Physical Activities

Listed below are a series of Leisure Time activities. Related activities are grouped under general headings. Please read the list and check "yes" in column 2 for those activities which you have performed in the last 12 months, and "no" in column 1 for those you have not. Do not complete any of the other columns.

Name _____

I.D. # _____

Date _____

	Did you perform this activity?		Month of Activity												For clinic Personnel Use Only			
	No (1)	Yes (2)	Jan	Feb	Mar	Apr	May	June	July	Aug	Sept	Oct	Nov	Dec	Average number of times per month	Time per occasion		
																Hours	Min.	
SECTION A: Walking and Miscellaneous																		
Walking for pleasure																		010
Walking to and from work																		015
Walking during work breaks																		020
Using stairs when elevator is available																		030
Cross country hiking																		040
Back packing																		050
Mountain climbing																		060

Activity																	
Bicycling to work and/or for pleasure																	115
Dancing—Ballroom and/or square																	125
SECTION B: Conditioning Exercise																	
Home exercise																	150
Health club																	210

Figure 29.1 Sample section of the Minnesota Leisure Time Physical Activities Questionnaire. (Reprinted with permission from the *Journal of Chronic Diseases*, **31**; H. L. Taylor, D. R. Jacobs, B. Schucker, J. Knudsen, A. S. Leon, & G. Debacker, A questionnaire for the assessment of leisure time physical activities. Copyright 1978, Pergamon Press, Ltd.)

where the work metabolic rate (WMR) is divided by the rest metabolic rate (RMR). Thus, walking at 3.5 mph requires 3.5 times as much energy (or O_2) as rest, and WMR/RMR = 3.5. Activity intensity codes are given in Table 29.1. A total activity score is calculated by multiplying the times per month by the number of months by the time per occasion to obtain the total time per year spent in an activity. This value is multiplied by the activity code (Table 29.1) for that activity to obtain a total energy expenditure for that activity for a year. Scores for all activities are summed to give a total leisure time physical activity index. Scores may also be summed in light, moderate, and heavy categories to yield a partition of the total score.

The Minnesota leisure time activities (LTA) questionnaire (Taylor et al., 1978) was validated by comparison with physical work capacity determined by treadmill testing in 175 middle-aged men. Significant multiple correlations (with adjustment for several clinical and demographic variables) between the LTA score and various measures of treadmill performance were generally in the 0.4 to 0.5 range. Not surprisingly, the heavy activities component of the total LTA score contributed most to the relationship with physical work capacity.

The Tecumseh and Minnesota questionnaires are valid, but they involve rather formidable procedures. The Tecumseh version takes 1.0 to 1.5 hours to complete and the Minnesota interview takes 15 to 20 minutes. The list of activities is long, and recall for all activities, including number of months, times per month, and duration, is tedious and difficult. Since relatively recent activity (the last several weeks) is more closely associated with health status than more distant activity, it may not be necessary to obtain a recall over an entire year.

7-Day Recall

A 7-day physical activity recall procedure was developed for use in a community health survey as part of a study on community prevention of CHD. The method was designed to have a relatively short recall period for increased accuracy, to be simple and easy to administer, to be applicable to both sexes across a wide age spectrum, and to assess both occupational and leisure activity. The questionnaire is interviewer-administered and takes about 10 to 15 minutes to complete. One of the major advantages of this method is that most people spend most of their waking hours in light activity. Since light activity is ignored during the interview and is obtained by subtraction, most individuals actually have to account only for relatively small blocks of time in which they engage in moderate, hard, and very hard activities. For most individuals, such activities are rare enough that they are easy to remember and specify.

Interviewer Instructions

Instructions for interviewers for the 7-day recall interview are given in the Appendix to this chapter, along with the list of activities shown to the participants and the interview questions.

Several interviewers in four community health survey centers have been trained to use the 7-day recall procedure. A few hours of training, some role playing and guided interviews, and follow-up support and supervision have made the method relatively easy to implement. The most common problems or questions arise over how to classify some unfamiliar activity. Use of energy cost tables in standard physiology textbooks (e.g., Katch & McArdle, 1977) can usually help determine to which category an activity should be assigned.

Application and Calculations

Raw data from the questionnaire (hours in the various categories) are used to calculate energy expenditure. The basis of these calculations is that resting metabolism (one MET

Table 29.1 Intensity Codes from the Minnesota Leisure Time Physical Activities Questionnaire

Code	Activity	Intensity Code	Code	Activity	Intensity Code
010	Walking for pleasure	3.5	295	Swimming at the beach	6.0
015	Walking to and from work	4.0	310	Scuba diving	7.0
020	Walking during work break	3.5	320	Snorkeling	5.0
030	Using stairs when elevator is available	8.0	340	Snow skiing, downhill	7.0
040	Cross-country hiking	6.0	350	Snow skiing, cross country	8.0
050	Back packing	7.0	360	Ice (or roller) skating	7.0
060	Mountain climbing	8.0	370	Sledging or tobogganing	7.0
115	Bicycling to work and/or for pleasure	4.0	390	Bowling	3.0
125	Dancing—Ballroom and/or square	5.5	400	Volley ball	4.0
150	Home exercise	4.5	410	Table tennis	4.0
160	Health club	6.0	420	Tennis, singles	8.0
180	Jogging and walking	6.0	430	Tennis, doubles	6.0
200	Running	8.0	440	Softball	5.0
210	Weight lifting	3.0	450	Badminton	7.0
220	Water skiing	6.0	460	Paddle ball	6.0
235	Sailing	3.0	470	Racket ball	7.0
250	Canoeing or rowing for pleasure	3.5	480	Basketball; non-game	6.0
260	Canoeing or rowing in competition	12.0	490	Basketball; game play	8.0
270	Canoeing on a camping trip	4.0	500	Basketball; officiating	7.0
280	Swimming (at least 50 ft) at a pool	6.0	510	Touch football	8.0
			520	Handball	12.0
			530	Squash	12.0
			540	Soccer	7.0
			070	Golf: riding a power cart	3.5
			080	Golf: walking, pulling clubs on cart	5.0

Table 29.1 (*Continued*)

Code	Activity	Intensity Code	Code	Activity	Intensity Code
090	Golf: walking and carrying clubs	5.5	620	Carpentry in workshop	3.0
550	Mowing lawn with riding mower	2.5	630	Painting inside of house, includes paper hanging	4.5
560	Mowing lawn walking behind power mower	4.5	640	Carpentry outside	6.0
570	Mowing lawn pushing hand mower	6.0	650	Painting outside of house	5.0
580	Weeding and cultivating garden	4.5	660	Fishing from river bank	3.5
590	Spading, digging, filling in garden	5.0	670	Fishing in stream with wading boots	6.0
600	Raking lawn	4.0	680	Hunting pheasants or grouse	6.0
610	Snow shoveling by hand	6.0	690	Hunting rabbits, prairie chickens, squirrels,raccoon	5.0
			710	Hunting large game; deer, elk, bear	6.0

Source: Reprinted with permission from *Journal of Chronic Diseases,* **31**; H. L. Taylor, D. R. Jacobs, B. Schucker, J. Knudsen, A. S. Leon & G. Debacker, A questionnaire for the assessment of leisure time physical activities. Copyright 1978, Pergamon Press, Ltd.

or RMR) requires 3.5 ml of O_2 per kilogram of body weight per minute. This is equal to approximately one kilocalorie (kcal) per kilogram per hour (kcal·kg^{-1}·hour^{-1}). Thus, activities requiring three METS (WMR/RMR = 3) would expend 3 kcal·kg^{-1}·hour^{-1}. The activity categories and associated MET values for the 7-day recall are as follows

Sleep	= 1 MET
Light activity	= 1.1–2.9 METS
Moderate activity	= 3.0–4.9 METS
Hard Activity	= 5.0–6.9 METS
Very hard activity	= >7.0 METS

In making the energy cost calculations, consider light activities to average 1.5 METS, moderate activities to average 4 METS, hard activities to average 6 METS, and very hard activities to average 10 METS. To calculate energy cost in kcal·kg^{-1}·day^{-1}, simply multiply the hours spent in an activity category by the average MET value for that category and sum over all categories. Table 29.2 gives examples for these calculations from the raw data for both an active and an inactive person. Note that the hours in each activity category are on a per day basis; this requires calculating an average value from the response to the recall questions. It is easier to do the recall if participants recall weekend and weekday activities separately and if you obtain total time for each category for the weekdays and weekend days, but calculations are done on an average day. Early on, we asked participants if the last week's activity was more, less, or about the same compared to their usual activity. Adjustments based on their responses did not prove to be useful, and we now recommend no adjustment. As noted in the instructions, if the last week was highly atypical, the previous week can be used for the recall. The calculations demonstrated in Table 29.2 can easily be done by computer. It may also be useful to sum energy output for hard and very hard activities as an index of vigorous activity.

The recall procedure can also be used in clinical work as a daily record. Participants

Table 29.2 Calculation Examples for 7-Day Recall Data

Activity	Raw Data (hours)[a]	MET Value for Activity	Total (kcal · kg^{-1} · day^{-1})
Active Person			
Sleep	8.0	1.0	8.0
Light activity[b]	12.5	1.5	18.75
Moderate activity	2.0	4.0	8.0
Hard activity	0.5	6.0	3.0
Very hard activity	1.0	10.0	10.0
Total	24.0		47.75[c]
Inactive Person			
Sleep	9.0	1.0	9.0
Light activity[b]	14.0	1.5	21.0
Moderate activity	1.0	4.0	4.0
Hard activity	0.0	6.0	0.0
Very hard activity	0.0	10.0	0.0
Total	24.0		34.0[c]

[a] Data from 7-day physical activity recall interview.
[b] Obtained by subtraction (24 hours minus sleep and moderate, hard, and very hard activity).
[c] Total energy output per day.

can record their activity each day in an activity log and can make their own calculations with a calculator. The worksheet presented in Table 29.3 gives a step-by-step approach to the calculations. The average values presented in the worksheet are based on random samples of more than 2,000 men and women from four California towns (data courtesy of the Stanford Heart Disease Prevention Program, Dr. J. Farquhar, Director). We find that individuals who have relatively active lifestyles have energy expenditures of 40 kcal·kg·$^{-1}$·day^{-1} or greater; persons with values in the mid to high 30s are inactive; and those with scores in the low 30s are very inactive. These standards are relatively constant for men and women across the age range. Although fitness levels and ability to do high-intensity work are less in women and decline with age, the total amount of exercise needed for good health is relatively constant (ACSM, 1978).

Self-Administered 7-Day Recall

The 7-day interview procedure has been simplified and adapted to a self-administered format (Table 29.4). Energy expenditure calculations can be based on an average 8 hours of sleep,

Table 29.3   Worksheet for Calculating Daily Energy Expenditure

1. Add up all the hours of sleep and naps you had. _____
2. Multiply the total number hours of sleep and naps (line 1) by 1. $\times 1 =$ _____
3. Add up the total number of hours spent in moderate activity. _____
4. Multiply the hours spent in moderate activity (line 3) by 4. $\times 4 =$ _____
5. Add up the total number of hours spent in hard activity. _____
6. Multiply the hours spend in hard activity (line 5) by 6. $\times 6 =$ _____
7. Add up the total number of hours spent in very hard activity. _____
8. Multiply the hours spent in very hard activity (line 7) by 10. $\times 10 =$ _____
9. Add up the figures in lines 1, 3, 5, and 7.
    $(1 + 3 + 5 + 7) =$ _____
10. Hours spent in light activity is equal to 24 hours minus the hours in lines 1, 3, 5, and 7.
    $24 - (1 + 3 + 5 + 7) =$ _____
11. Multiply the figure in line 10 by 1.5. $\times 1.5 =$ _____
12. Add up the figures in lines 2, 4, 6, 8, and 11.
    $(2 + 4 + 6 + 8 + 11) =$ _____
13. The figure you arrived at in line 12 is the total kilocalories per kilogram of body weight expended per day.
    $(\text{kcal} \cdot \text{kg}^{-1} \cdot \text{day}^{-1}) =$ _____
14. To calculate the total number of calories you expended in one day, multiply your total body weight in kilograms (weight in pounds $\div$ 2.2046 = kilograms) by the figure in line 13. Body weight (kg) $\times$ kcal·kg^{-1}·day^{-1} = total calories expended = _____

The following are some average kcal · kg^{-1}· day^{-1} for individuals of different ages:

	17–19 years	*20–29 years*	*30–39 years*
male	= 44	= 40	= 38
female	= 35	= 35	= 33

	40–49 years	*50–59 years*	*60–69 years*
male	= 37	= 36	= 34
female	= 31	= 30	= 29

Table 29.4 Self-Administered 7-Day Physical Activity Recall Questionnaire

During the last seven days, how much total time did you spend doing VIGOROUS physical activity and MODERATE physical activity? Record only time actually engaged in the activity (ignore breaks, rest periods, etc.). Please do not record any LIGHT physical activity (office work, light housework, very light sports such as bowling, or any activities involving sitting).

	Total hours for last 7 days to nearest .5 hours
VIGOROUS ACTIVITY (jogging or running, swimming, strenuous sports such as singles tennis or racquetball, digging in the garden, chopping wood, brisk walking, etc.)	_____
MODERATE ACTIVITY (sports such as golf or doubles tennis, yard work, heavy housecleaning, bicycling on level ground, brisk walking, etc.)	_____

and light activity again can be obtained by subtraction. In the self-administered version, the hard and very hard categories are combined, since calculations assume a MET value of 8 for the vigorous activity category. The simplified version has been field-tested, and preliminary results are promising. It may be adequate for assessing exercise pattern changes in a large group, but its clinical usefulness for individuals has not been tested. Much more work is needed, and it should be used with caution.

ASSESSMENT OF PHYSICAL FITNESS

Diagnostic versus Fitness Testing

Several authors have debated the value of exercise stress testing (Diamond & Forrester, 1979; Epstein, 1978; Morris & McHenry, 1978). This controversy has centered on the predictive accuracy of exercise test findings. Stated simply, calculations show that unacceptably high false-positive rates are obtained when ECG-monitored exercise testing is used as a screening examination in an asymptomatic population with a low prevalence of coronary heart disease. Although this controversy has important implications for clinical medicine, it has no relevance to the topic of this chapter. The purpose here is to discuss physical fitness testing in health promotion programs, and a clear distinction is drawn between that purpose and the issues just mentioned. Physical fitness testing makes three important contributions to the physical activity component of a health promotion program. First, it apparently has a motivating effect and helps participants make changes in their exercise habits (Bruce, DeRouen, & Hossack, 1980). Second, assessment of physical fitness is useful in developing an individual's exercise prescription (Pollock & Blair, 1981). Finally, physical fitness testing is also used to monitor changes resulting from an exercise program.

Laboratory Assessments

Maximum oxygen uptake ($\dot{V}O_{2\ max}$) is a widely accepted standard measure of physical fitness (Larson, 1974). It represents the maximum functional capability of the integrated performance of the heart, lungs, vascular system, and muscle tissue. Oxygen is transported from the atmosphere to the working muscles and combined with an energy source to release energy for muscular work. Direct measurement of maximum energy release in human beings requires a large calorimeter and is an expensive and difficult laboratory procedure (Consolazio, Johnson, & Pecora, 1963). Indirect calorimetry (measuring oxygen uptake) provides a highly reliable and valid substitute for the direct procedure, since oxygen uptake is linearly related to energy expenditure. Measurement of oxygen uptake involves determining pulmonary ventilation and the concentration of O_2 and CO_2 in the expired air. Since the composition of inspired air from the atmosphere is known, it is a simple matter to calculate how much O_2 was extracted during metabolic processes (Consolazio et al., 1963). The laboratory test for $\dot{V}O_{2\ max}$ involves having subjects perform work on some kind of ergometer (bicycle, treadmill, or step), with progressively harder work loads until they reach exhaustion. At this point, there is a plateau in O_2 uptake, and the highest value attained is $\dot{V}O_{2\ max}$.

Although $\dot{V}O_{2\ max}$ is routinely measured in exercise physiology laboratories, it is a relatively time-consuming procedure, and the cost of analytical instruments can amount to more than $10,000. Fortunately, simpler and less costly options are available for behavioral health programs. Estimates of O_2 uptake are reliable and valid, are simple to obtain, and require limited equipment. The theory underlying these estimates is relatively simple. One of the major limiting factors in an individual's ability to work at high levels and consume large volumes of O_2 is the ability of the circulatory system to move large volumes of O_2-saturated arterial blood from the lungs to the muscles. When a person begins to perform muscular work, the demand of muscle tissue is met by increasing blood flow to the area. As work increases, higher and higher volumes of blood (cardiac output) are required. This increase in cardiac output results from increases in heart rate and amount of blood pumped with each beat (stroke volume of the heart).

The increase in heart rate is linearly related to increases in cardiac output and therefore to increases in O_2 uptake. This heart rate–O_2 uptake relationship is depicted diagramatically in Figure 29.2. Note that maximum heart rate is about the same for trained and untrained individuals; however, at any given submaximal work load, the trained individual will have a lower heart rate. As any individual becomes more physically fit, the heart rate for a submaximal work load decreases. Thus, heart rates obtained during submaximal work (or immediately after, within 15 seconds) can be used to monitor changes in fitness resulting from an exercise program. The practical application is that virtually any standard exercise bout lasting at least 3 to 4 minutes can be used to monitor changes in fitness. This can be accomplished in the laboratory on a treadmill (or other ergometer), with heart rate measured by ECG or heart rate meter. Alternatively, walking around the block or climbing

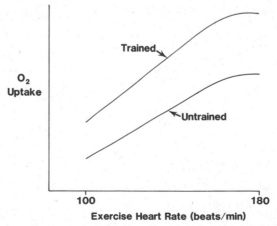

Figure 29.2 Relationship between exercise heart rate and oxygen uptake in trained and untrained individuals.

several flights of stairs at a controlled speed, with heart rate determined by palpating the pulse, can also provide a valid indication of changes in physical fitness. This means that simple fitness self-testing protocols can be devised and implemented in the natural environment and can be made part of a health behavior regimen.

If estimates of $\dot{V}O_2$ max are desired in order to compare an individual's fitness level to some criterion, additional information and calculations are needed. The amount of energy necessary to accomplish a given amount of work is known (1 kcal = 427 kilogram meters of work). Since the O_2-kilocalorie relationship is also known, if we further assume that the human body is 22% to 23% efficient in performing measurable work, we can calculate and estimate how much O_2 is needed for a given work load. Formulas for estimating O_2 uptake for climbing stairs, for working on a bicycle ergometer, and for walking and running are given in Table 5. Thus, if a standard work test is applied, estimates can be made of the O_2 an individual will have to consume in order to perform the task. If progressively harder work loads are applied to a subject during a physical fitness test, the highest tolerated work load can provide an estimate of the subject's $\dot{V}O_2$ max. If the maximum bicycle ergometer work load a person can perform, for example, is 900 kilogram meters·minute^{-1}, the $\dot{V}O_2$ max is 2,100 ml, or (900 × 2) + 300. Since it is customary to adjust $\dot{V}O_2$ max for body size, in this example for a 70 kg person, the $\dot{V}O_2$ max is 30 ml·kg^{-1}·min^{-1}.

Although more assumptions are needed and the calculations are more complicated, the foregoing techniques can be extended to estimate $\dot{V}O_2$ max from submaximal exercise tests. As was shown in Figure 29.2 maximum heart rates do not vary by level of physical fitness. They do vary by age, however. A general guideline is that maximum heart rate (max HR) can be estimated as follows: max HR = 220 − age in years. Thus, the predicted max HR for a 40-year-old is 180(220−40). If heart rate is measured at two or more known submaximal work loads, the regression of heart rate on O_2 can be extrapolated to the predicted age-adjusted max HR and $\dot{V}O_2$ max can be estimated. An example of this approach is shown in Figure 29.3. In this example, the estimated $\dot{V}O_2$ max is 2,700 ml; adjusting for body weight in an 80 kg individual, the estimated $\dot{V}O_2$ max is 33.7 ml·kg^{-1}·min^{-1}.

Estimated $\dot{V}O_2$ max may be used to compare an individual's fitness level to some criterion or to develop an exercise prescription. Further information on fitness standards and exercise prescription are given in other chapters in this section of the Handbook (see, especially, Ribisl's chapter).

Table 29.5 Formulas for Estimating Oxygen Uptake for Walking, Running, Climbing Stairs, and Bicycle Ergometry

Horizontal walking (50–100 meters/minute)
VO_2 (ml · kg^{-1} · min^{-1}) = (speed in meters/minute × 0.1) + 3.5

Horizontal running (speeds greater than 134 meters/minute, or 5 mph)
VO_2 (ml · kg^{-1} · min^{-1}) = (speed in meters/minute × 0.2) + 3.5

Climbing stairs
VO_2(ml · kg^{-1} · min^{-1}) = (height of step in meters × stepping rate per minute × 2.39) + (stepping rate ÷ 2.86)

Bicycle ergometery
VO_2 (ml) = (work load in kilogram meters × 2) + 300

Source: Formulas are adapted from American College of Sports Medicine, *Guidelines for graded exercise testing and exercise prescription* (2nd ed.). Philadelphia: Lea & Febiger, 1980.

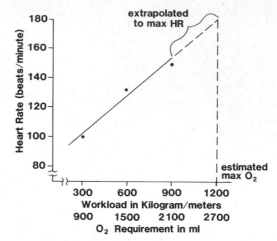

Figure 29.3 Submaximal exercise heart rates and workload. Heart rate may be extrapolated to maximum heart rate and can be used to estimate maximum oxygen uptake. The oxygen requirement for each work load is also shown on the horizontal axis.

Field Testing

12-Minute Test

The most widely recognized field test for $\dot{V}O_{2 \text{ max}}$ is the 12-minute walk-run popularized by Cooper (1968a). Quite simply, the objective of the test is to cover the greatest possible distance in 12 minutes. The test can be performed on any measured course, indoors or outside. If participants are motivated to give a maximal effort, the distance covered is highly correlated ($r = 0.897$) with $\dot{V}O_{2 \text{ max}}$ (Cooper, 1968b). Reliability coefficients of 0.80 to 0.90 have been reported (Blair & Gatch, 1969). Cooper (1968b) found that a performance of 1.0 miles in 12 minutes was equivalent to a $\dot{V}O_{2 \text{ max}}$ of 25 $ml \cdot kg^{-1} \cdot min^{-1}$. Increments of .25 mile were associated with an increase in $\dot{V}O_{2 \text{ max}}$ of approximately 9 $ml \cdot kg^{-1} \cdot min^{-1}$.

Bicycle Ergometer Testing

The bicycle ergometer has frequently been used for fitness assessment in field settings as well as in the laboratory. Field testing has typically been submaximal, especially when older or less fit participants have been tested. Astrand and Ryhming (1954) demonstrated the validity of estimating $\dot{V}O_{2 \text{ max}}$ by submaximal testing 30 years ago. A modification of their technique has recently been published (Siconolfi, Cullinane, Carleton, & Thompson, 1982). Regression equations were developed for men and women aged 20 to 70 years who were given the submaximal test as well as a directly measured $\dot{V}O_{2 \text{ max}}$ test. $\dot{V}O_{2 \text{ max}}$ was predicted from estimates of O_2 uptake from the original Astrand and Ryhming (1954) nomogram and age. The regression equations were cross-validated in a second study of 63 men and women who were similar to the original test group. The correlation between measured and estimated $\dot{V}O_{2 \text{ max}}$ in this second group was $R = 0.94$. The standard error in predicting $\dot{V}O_{2 \text{ max}}$ was 248 $ml \cdot min^{-1}$. This study clearly indicates the acceptability of submaximal testing to estimate $\dot{V}O_{2 \text{ max}}$ in field studies in adult men and women.

A similar submaximal bicycle ergometer test was developed for field use in a community health survey. It has since been used in an employee health program in an insurance company and, with slight modification, in a health screening in several companies of a large corporation. The test was designed to provide an index of fitness based on submaximal exercise heart rates. The objective of this test is to assess physical fitness quickly, easily, and safely in field settings. The test is expected to discriminate among individuals' physical fitness levels and to be a valid indicator of change. A description of the low-level bicycle physical fitness test (BIKE TEST) is presented in Table 29.6.

Bicycle ergometry is a non-weight-bearing activity, and bigger individuals with a large muscle mass have an inherent performance advantage. To account for this factor, and also to consider the individual's probable level of fitness, different test protocols were established (see Table 29.6). Different protocols based on individual characteristics help ensure that the initial work load will be neither too high nor too low; that test increments can be managed with relative comfort; and that the test will be relatively the same duration for all individuals, while at the same time increasing the probability that most individuals will complete at least two stages. In a health screening in an occupational health promotion program, more than 90% of approximately 1,500 men and women were able to complete two stages of the test successfully (Blair, Note 2).

One of the three BIKE TEST protocols is selected (Table 29.6). Activity status is determined subjectively by the test administrator from a review of questionnaire data provided by the participant or by direct oral query. Basically, individuals who have been regularly participating (the last 3 months) in vigorous activities, such as jogging, singles tennis, or heavy labor, for at least 15 minutes at a time for a minimum of three times per week are classified as very active. Thus, a 175-pound individual who plays squash 5 days a week for an hour at a time would be tested with protocol B.

Exercise heart rates are monitored during the test. This can be done by palpation of the carotid or radial artery and counting the pulse for 10 seconds or by electronic monitoring. Heart rate is to be checked during the last 15 seconds of each test stage. The test is terminated when the heart rate reaches 70% of the predicted age-adjusted maximum (see Table 29.7). If participants' heart rate reaches the target during a stage, they are allowed to complete the stage unless the heart rate exceeds the target by 6 beats/minute. Heart rates recorded at the end of each completed work load are used to estimate $\dot{V}O_{2\ max}$, as illustrated in Figure 29.3 and discussed earlier.

Table 29.6   BIKE TEST Protocols and Criteria for Protocol Selection

	Protocol Selection Criteria		
		Very Active[a]	
Body Weight (lbs)	No		Yes
< 160	A[b]		A
160–199	A		B
200 or more	B		C

	Work Load[c] for Test Protocols		
	Test Stages (minutes)		
Protocol	I (1–2)	II (3–4)	III (5–6)	IV (7–8)
A	150	300	450	600
B	150	300	600	900
C	300	600	900	1200

[a] Activity status determined by questionnaire.
[b] Test protocol to be used, see bottom part of table.
[c] Work load in kilogram meters.

Table 29.8 Scale for Ratings of Perceived Exertion

6	
7	Very, very light
8	
9	Very light
10	
11	Fairly light
12	
13	Somewhat hard
14	
15	Hard
16	
17	Very hard
18	
19	Very, very hard
20	

Table 29.7 Target Heart Rates for the BIKE TEST

Age (years)	Heart Rate (beats/minute)
< 20	140
20–29	135
30–39	130
40–49	120
50–59	115
60–65	110

In addition to exercise heart rate, the participants' subjective feelings of fatigue are used as second check on exercise intensity. Participants are asked to provide a rating of perceived exertion (RPE) at the end of each test stage, according to the scale shown in Table 29.8 (Borg, 1973). They are asked to rate how hard they are working during that stage, compared to the hardest they have ever worked (20 on the scale in Table 29.8). The test is terminated if the participant gives an RPE of 15 or greater.

Additional criteria for stopping the test before the target heart rate is achieved include any extreme fatigue or pain, observable extreme pallor or other indications of distress, inability to respond when questioned, or the participant's wanting to stop for any reason. These criteria are rarely used, as indicated by the high percentage (>90%) of subjects who successfully complete the test.

When the test is terminated, the resistance on the bicycle ergometer is reduced to the lowest setting. The participant is instructed to continue pedaling slowly (30–40 rpm) for approximately one minute. This allows for gradual readjustment of circulation and respiration to resting levels and helps prevent venous pooling in the legs, which might cause lightheadedness or fainting.

Safety

The BIKE TEST has been administered in a field setting without direct medical supervision to more than 5,000 males and females from 12 to 65 years of age. No serious complications have developed. For most individuals, the test is no more strenuous than brisk walking or other common everyday activities. Therefore, the vast majority of individuals whose activity is not limited by their physicians should be able to complete the test without undue hazard. Conservative criteria are used for stopping the test. Finally, careful screening for eligibility to take the test eliminates most individuals who are likely to develop problems. Individuals are excluded from the test for any of the reasons given in Table 29.9.

These eligibility criteria were adapted from the physical activity readiness questionnaire (PAR-Q), developed by the Department of National Health and Welfare, Canada (Chisholm, Collis, Kulak, Davenport, Gruber, & Stewart, Note 3). An extensive validation of the PAR-Q confirmed its usefulness as a screening device for the Canadian home fitness test (Bailey,

Table 29.9 Exclusion Criteria for the BIKE TEST

1. History of heart disease, including heart attack, cardiac arrest, valvular disease, congestive heart failure, myocarditis, or any other heart disease treated by a doctor
2. Any history of chest pain diagnosed by a physician as angina pectoris
3. Any known cardiac dysrhythmias or conduction defects
4. History of stroke
5. Use of medications for the heart or blood vessels during the last 3 months, including medicine for chest pain, dysrhythmias, congestive heart failure, or hypertension; specific medications warranting exclusion:
    a. Beta blockers (propranolol)
    b. Digitalis
    c. Quinidine or procainamide
    d. Nitroglycerin
    If there is any question about a drug, the test should be postponed pending clearance by the participant's physician.
6. Any acute infectious disease (colds, flu, virus, etc.)
7. Neuromuscular, musculoskeletal, or orthopedic disorders that would make the test uncomfortable or dangerous
8. Renal, hepatic, or other metabolic insufficiency
9. Resting blood pressure greater than 160 mmHg systolic or 100 mmHg diastolic
10. The participant does not want to take the test for any reason
11. The test supervisor can also exclude based on clinical judgment

Shephard, & Mirwald, 1976). PAR-Q and the home fitness test have been used in Canada for the past several years by an estimated 500,000 participants without a single serious accident (Shephard, 1980).

The BIKE TEST and other submaximal fitness tests appear to have an acceptably low risk for the apparently healthy adult, particularly with prescreening by the PAR-Q. Shephard (1980) estimated that if 5 million middle-aged men and women took a 6-minute submaximal fitness test each year, 33 to 66 years would pass before the first fatal event. Administration of a fitness test such as the BIKE TEST by a nurse or exercise test technologist would almost certainly reduce the risk further. If it were required that these tests be physician-monitored, and if the physician had an 80% chance of resuscitating the victim, the cost of saving a single life would exceed $40 billion. Therefore, it appears reasonable to recommend the BIKE TEST for use in field studies or in behavioral health programs involving exercise.

SUMMARY

Assessing exercise habits and physical fitness is a difficult but not impossible task. The methods presented in this chapter and others cited in the discussion can provide meaningful data for behavioral health programs. These methods can be applied in large-scale surveys to make population estimates or in clinical settings for individual health counseling.

REFERENCE NOTES

1. Blair, S. N., & Haskell, W. L. *Stanford Heart Disease Prevention Program, Community Health Survey* (Dr. J. Farquhar, director).
2. Blair, S. N. *Johnson and Johnson Live for Life Program* (Dr. C. Wilbur, director).
3. Chisholm, D. M., Collis, M. C., Kulak, L. L., Davenport, W., Gruber, N., & Stewart, G. Par-Q validation report: The evaluation of a self-administered pre-exercise screening questionnaire for adults. Ottawa: Department of National Health and Welfare, Health Services and Promotion Branch, Promotion and Prevention Directorate, 1978.

REFERENCES

American College of Sports Medicine (ACSM). Position statement on the recommended quantity and quality of exercise for developing and maintaining fitness in healthy adults. *Medicine and Science in Sports and Exercise*, 1978, **10**, vii–x.

Andersen, K. L., Rutenfranz, J., Masironi, R., Seliger, V., Degre, S., Trygg, K., & Orgim, M. *Habitual physical activity and health.* Copenhagen: World Health Organization, Regional Office for Europe, 1978.

Astrand, P. O., & Ryhming, I. A nomogram for calculation of aerobic capacity (physical fitness) from pulse rate during submaximal work. *Journal of Applied Physiology*, 1954, **7**, 218–221.

Bailey, D. A., Shephard, R. J., & Mirwald, R. L. Validation of a self-administered home test of cardio-respiratory fitness. *Canadian Journal of Applied Sport Sciences*, 1976, **1**, 67–78.

Blair, S., & Gatch, W. Reliability of the "12-minute" test. *Journal of Health, Physical Education, and Recreation*, 1969, **1**, 11.

Block, G. A review of validations of dietary assessment methods. *American Journal of Epidemiology*, 1982, **115**, 492–505.

Borg, G. A. V. Perceived exertion: A note on "history" and methods. *Medicine and Science in Sports*, 1973, **5**, 90–93.

Bradfield, R. B. (Ed.). Assessment of typical daily energy expenditure. *American Journal of Clinical Nutrition*, 1971, **24**(September & December).

Bruce, R. A., DeRouen, T. A., & Hossack, K. F. Pilot study examining the motivational effects of maximal exercise testing to modify risk factors and health habits. *Cardiology*, 1980, **66**, 111–119.

Burke, B. S., & Stuart, H. C. A method of diet analysis. *Journal of Pediatrics*, 1938, **12**, 493–503.

Buskirk, E. R., Harris, D., Mendez, J., & Skinner, J. Comparison of two assessments of physical activity and a survey method for calorie intake. *American Journal of Clinical Nutrition*, 1971, **24**, 1119–1125.

Consolazio, C. F., Johnson, R. E., & Pecora, L. J. Physiological measurements of metabolic functions in man. New York: McGraw-Hill, 1963.

Cooper, K. H. *Aerobics.* New York: Bantam, 1968. (a)

Cooper, K. H. A means of assessing maximal oxygen intake. *Journal of the American Medical Association*, 1968, **203**, 201–204. (b)

Diamond, G. A., & Forrester, J. S. Analysis of probability as an aid in the clinical diagnosis of coronary artery disease. *New England Journal of Medicine*, 1979, **300**, 1350–1357.

Epstein, S. E. Value and limitations of the electrocardiographic response to exercise in the assessment of patients with coronary heart disease. *American Journal of Cardiology*, 1978, **42**, 667–674.

Katch, F. I., & McArdle, W. D. *Nutrition, weight control and exercise.* Boston: Houghton Mifflin, 1977.

LaPorte, R. E., Kuller, L. H., Kupfer, D. J., McPartland, R. J., Matthews, G., & Caspersen, C. An objective of physical activity for epidemiological research. *American Journal of Epidemiology*, 1979, **109**, 158–168.

Liu, K., Stamler, J., Dyer, A., McKeever, J., & McKeever, P. Statistical methods to assess and minimize the role of intra-individual variability in obscuring the relationship between dietary lipids and serum cholesterol. *Journal of Chronic Disease,* 1978, **31,** 399–418.

Montoye, H. J. *Physical activity and health: An epidemiologic study of an entire community.* Englewood Cliffs, N.J.: Prentice-Hall, 1975.

Morris, J. N., Pollard, R., Everitt, M. G., & Chave, S. P. W. Vigorous exercise in leisure-time: Protection against coronary heart disease. *Lancet,* 1980, **2,** 1207–1210.

Morris, S. N., & McHenry, P. L. Role of exercise stress testing in healthy subjects and patients with coronary heart disease. *American Journal of Cardiology,* 1978, **42,** 659–666.

Paffenbarger, R. S., Wing, A. L., & Hyde, R. T. Physical activity as an index of heart attack risk in college alumni. *American Journal of Epidemiology,* 1978, **108,** 161–175.

Reiff, G. G., Montoye, H. J., Remington, R. D., Napier, J. A., Metzner, H. L., & Epstein, F. H. Assessment of physical activity by questionnaire and interview. *Journal of Sports Medicine and Physical Fitness,* 1967, **7,** 135–142.

Shephard, R. J. The current status of the Canadian home fitness test. *British Journal of Sports Medicine,* 1980, **14,** 114–125.

Siconolfi, S. F., Cullinane, E. M., Carleton, R. A., & Thompson, P. D. Assessing $VO_{2\ max}$ in epidemiologic studies: Modification of the Astrand-Ryhming test. *Medicine and Science in Sports and Exercise,* 1982, **14,** 335–338.

Taylor, H. L., Jacobs, D. R., Schucker, B., Knudsen, J., Leon, A. S., & Debacker, G. A questionnaire for the assessment of leisure time physical activities. *Journal of Chronic Diseases,* 1978, **31,** 741–755.

Washburn, R., Chin, M. K., & Montoye, H. J. Accuracy of pedometer in walking and running. *Research Quarterly for Exercise and Sport,* 1980, **51,** 695–702.

Wong, T. C., Webster, J. G., Montoye, H. J., & Washburn, R. Portable accelerometer device for measuring human energy expenditure. *IEEE Transactions on Biomedical Engineering,* 1981, **BME-28,** 467–471.

Yasin, S., Alderson, M. R., Marr, J. W., Pattison, D. C., & Morris, J. N. Assessment of habitual physical activity apart from occupation. *British Journal of Preventive Social Medicine,* 1967, **21,** 163–169.

APPENDIX: INTERVIEWER INSTRUCTIONS FOR THE 7-DAY RECALL INTERVIEW[1]

Interviewing Technique

Your technique should limit bias, and you should try to keep the interview from becoming tedious. It may be difficult for participants to remember their past week's activity. Some may not try very hard, and others may get bogged down in details. You should strive to achieve a happy medium. You should control the pace of the interview; extraneous talk should be avoided. If participants are going into excessive detail, you should remind them that they need not account for every minute but that an average or estimate is expected. You might ask, "How much time in general?"

It is important to remember that most of the participants you see will spend the vast majority of their waking hours in light activity. Many tiring and unpleasant household or occupational tasks do not have a very high energy cost. Clerks in a store, for example, may be on their feet all day and may feel fatigued, but the energy cost is in the light category. An exception to this example would be time spent in stocking shelves, which probably would be moderate activity. Also, for most occupational tasks that require at

[1] The interviewer instructions are adapted from Taylor, H. L., Jacobs, D. R., Schucker, B., Knudsen, J., Leon, A. S., & Debacker, G. A questionnaire for the assessment of leisure time physical activities. *Journal of Chronic Diseases,* 1978, **31,** 741–755.

least moderate energy expenditure, it is important to accurately determine the time spent in the activity. In the stock clerking example, even though a person might do that activity for an entire shift, it probably would not equal 8 hours. You should try to subtract time spent on lunch, breaks, and the like.

Interviewing Suggestions

You will be handing people lists of moderate, hard, and very hard activities (Table 29.A1). We have found it easier to give them all three lists to look at at once, before we ask them any questions about their activity level in the past 7 days.

Explain the following things before you hand them the list of activities (otherwise, they may not attend to what you are saying because they'll be too busy looking at the list):

1. They are to think of the past 7 days. Stress that this is a recall of actual activities for the past week, not a history of what they usually do.
2. Weekdays and weekends will be treated separately. You may even help them figure out which days to include; for example, Monday through Thursday this week and Friday of last week would comprise the past 5 weekdays.
3. Weekdays include evenings as well.
4. We are not considering light activities, such as deskwork, standing, slow walking, light housework, softball, archery, bowling, and the like.
5. They should also consider types of activities that are not included on the lists but are similar in strenuousness.

Mention the following things before you ask them questions about their activity level:

1. You will ask them questions about each category of activities separately (because people tend to give stream-of-consciousness reports of their week).
2. You may ask them if the amount of activity they report is more, less, or about the same as usual (because people tend to be defensive, exaggerate the numbers, or offer rationales for low activity levels). This may enable the participants to give more accurate estimates of their activity level.

While they are reporting the frequency with which they engage in various activities, be aware of the following:

1. Don't let them sidetrack you.
2. You may wish to ask them about their weekends first. This enables them to practice giving you the information you need in a smaller block of time.
3. Check if the amount of time they are reporting is per weekend, per week, or per day. Someone may say, for example, "I did one hour of digging this past weekend," when what is really meant is, "I did one hour of digging each of the two days this past weekend."
4. Some people have trouble recalling or pinpointing the moderate to very hard activities they have engaged in in the past 7 days. In such cases, try to cue them by asking, for example, "How about any housework that made you work up a sweat; do you take stairs at work; do you walk briskly to work; did you participate in any sports, any vigorous family activities; did you do any vigorous home repair or gardening?"
5. Some people have trouble quantifying the amount of time they spent doing moderate, hard, or very hard activities. In such cases, break down all of their activities into

specific events and ask them how long they did each activity. Then sum up the amount of time relevant to each category. Finally, ask them if they agree with your calculations.

6. If you are unsure of the strenuousness of an activity that they may have participated in, ask them to describe the physical effort involved—for example, what does the activity entail, what other activity is it comparable to, do they work up a sweat? We have found that walking and running provide good frames of reference for classifying other activities. Everyone should be familiar with the relative intensity of brisk walking, which is at about the midpoint of the moderate activity category. Therefore, if some other activity subjectively seems to be about as strenuous to the individual as walking briskly, then the activity should be coded as moderate. Running at any speed falls into the very hard category. If some activity seems about as strenuous to the individual as running, classify the activity as very hard. If the activity in question seems harder than walking but not as strenuous as running, place it in the hard category. Be careful to be certain that the activity in question is performed continuously for at least 5 minutes. Some activities may be quite strenuous, but if they are performed intermittently, the overall energy cost may place them in the moderate category. A good example of this is weight lifting.

7. If the last week was totally atypical—for example, in the hospital or in bed, or involving a family crisis, a work crisis, or travel—it is permissible to go to the previous week for the survey. Do not take this action lightly; use it only in unusual circumstances.

8. If a person has weekdays instead of weekends off from work (for example, Tuesday and Wednesday instead of Saturday and Sunday), count the days off as weekends for purposes of the survey.

9. Be sure that the time reported for an activity was actually spent doing the activity. Being at the pool for 2 hours but only swimming for 15 minutes, for example, should be recorded as 15 minutes, not 2 hours. Working in the garden all day Saturday (8 hours) should mean actually working for 8 hours. Do not count the time on breaks, rest periods, meals, and the like.

10. For most activities, the rate at which they are performed can make a huge difference in the energy cost. It is possible to play singles tennis, for example, so as not to move around very much and not spend much energy. The rate of digging, for another example, could make the MET cost range from 3 to 12. Try to get some indication of how hard they are working at a particular task.

The actual questions to be asked during the interview are presented in Table 29.A2.

Table 29.A1 7-Day Physical Activity Recall Interview Questionnaire

Now we would like to know about your physical activity during the past 7 days. But first, let me ask you about your sleep habits.

1. On the average, how many hours did you sleep each night during the last 5 weekday nights (Sunday–Thursday)? (Record to nearest quarter-hour.)

   ☐☐ ☐☐ HOURS

2. On the average, how many hours did you sleep each night last Friday and Saturday nights?

   ☐☐ ☐☐ HOURS

Table 29.A1 *(Continued)*

Now I am going to ask you about your physical activity during the past 7 days; that is, the last 5 weekdays and last weekend, Saturday and Sunday. We are not going to talk about light activities, such as slow walking, light housework, or nonstrenuous sports such as bowling, archery, or softball. Please look at this list (Table 29.A2), which shows some examples of what we consider moderate, hard, and very hard activities. (Interviewer: Hand subject list and allow time for the subject to read it over.) People engage in many other types of activities, and if you are not sure where one of your activities fits, please ask me about it.

3. First, let's consider moderate activities. What activities did you do and how many total hours did you spend during the last 5 weekdays doing these moderate activities or others like them? Please tell me to the nearest half-hour.

    ⬚⬚ ⬚   HOURS

4. Last Saturday and Sunday, how many hours did you spend on moderate activities and what did you do? (Probe: Can you think of any other sport, job, or household activities that would fit into this category?)

    ⬚⬚ ⬚   HOURS

5. Now let's look at hard activities. What activities did you do and how many total hours did you spend during the last 5 weekdays doing these hard activities or others like them? Please tell me to the nearest half-hour.

    ⬚⬚ ⬚   HOURS

6. Last Saturday and Sunday, how many hours did you spend on hard activities and what did you do? (Probe: Can you think of any other sport, job, or household activities that would fit into this category?)

    ⬚⬚ ⬚   HOURS

7. Now let's look at very hard activities. What activities did you do and how many total hours did you spend during the last 5 weekdays doing these very hard activities or others like them? Please tell me to the nearest half-hour.

    ⬚⬚ ⬚   HOURS

8. Last Saturday and Sunday, how many hours did you spend on very hard activities and what did you do? (Probe: Can you think of any other sport, job or household activities that would fit into this category?)

    ⬚⬚ ⬚   HOURS

Table 29.A2   List of Activities Shown to Participants During 7-day Physical Recall Interview

Moderate Activities

Occupational Tasks:
1. Delivering mail or patrolling on foot
2. House painting
3. Truck driving (making deliveries—lifting and carrying light objects)

Household Activities:
1. Raking the lawn
2. Sweeping and mopping
3. Mowing the lawn with a power mower
4. Cleaning windows

Sports Activities (*actual playing time*):
1. Volleyball
2. Ping Pong
3. Brisk walking for pleasure or to work (3 mph or 20 min/mile)
4. Golf—walking and pulling or carrying clubs
5. Calisthenic exercises

Hard Activities

Occupational Tasks:
1. Heavy carpentry
2. Construction work—doing physical labor

Household Tasks:
1. Scrubbing floors

Sports Activities (*actual playing time*):
1. Doubles tennis
2. Disco, Square, or Folk dancing

Very Hard Activities

Occupational Tasks:
1. Very hard physical labor—digging or chopping with heavy tools
2. Carrying heavy loads, such as bricks or lumber

Sports Activities (*actual playing time*):
1. Jogging or swimming
2. Singles tennis
3. Racquetball
4. Soccer

CHAPTER 30

DEVELOPING AN EXERCISE PRESCRIPTION FOR HEALTH

PAUL M. RIBISL

Wake Forest University

In a recent nationwide survey (Pacific Mutual, Note 1), the respondents were asked to identify what they considered to be the most important things in their lives. The overwhelming first choice was good health, and this choice far outdistanced other items, such as having a good job, living in a good neighborhood, and maintaining a high standard of living. These same individuals also agreed that they would be much healthier if they improved their lifestyles by eating a more nutritious diet, stopping smoking, controlling the stress in their lives, and taking more regular exercise. Unfortunately, of those who recognized that they needed more exercise, the majority (75%) had never been advised of this by their doctor. Although we all desire to be physically fit, many of us are unsure of how to go about it ourselves or how to counsel others in this pursuit. The main focus of this chapter is the development of physical fitness. It is directed toward the allied health professional with a basic science background and knowledge of physiological function who needs sound guidance on a safe and effective approach to developing an exercise prescription for health.

BRIEF HISTORY OF EXERCISE AND FITNESS PROGRAMS

Although exercise and sport have played a significant role in society for centuries, the recently increased interest in fitness was stimulated by the results of the Kraus-Weber test in 1954, which revealed the physical unfitness of our American youth. Shortly thereafter, in 1956, the President's Fitness Council was appointed by Dwight D. Eisenhower; this council has been maintained to this day by succeeding administrations. Over the past quarter-century, the scientific aspects of exercise and health have been carefully studied and promoted by specialists in three major professional organizations: the Young Men's Christian Association (YMCA), the American Alliance for Health, Physical Education, Recreation and Dance (AAHPERD), and the American College of Sports Medicine (ACSM). Each of these organizations has developed special programs and guidelines that are currently being used in both the evaluation and the enhancement of health and fitness in populations with varied age, sex, and disease status.

Special programs also have been successfully developed and promoted by select individuals, and some of these have received substantial attention from the media and a reasonable degree of support from the American public. Two of the more popular programs today are the aerobics system, developed by Kenneth H. Cooper, M.D., and aerobic dancing, developed by dancer/choreographer Jackie Sorensen. Both approaches are based on the concept of aerobics, which literally means "with oxygen." Aerobics includes vigorous physical activities, such as running, cycling, swimming, and dancing, that stimulate the cardiovascular system and can be maintained for an extended session of approximately 30 minutes or more. These programs, along with others, will be explored in greater detail later in this chapter.

Exercise and fitness programs are being widely promoted today in popular books, magazine articles, and special television shows dealing with exercise. This interest has also stimulated the proliferation of commercial health clubs and spas and the development of public facilities for exercise, such as the Parcours. The fitness movement has also reached business and industry; many companies are now offering "wellness" programs for their employees. These programs utilize a multidimensional approach to achieving a healthful lifestyle, which includes regular physical activity, smoking cessation, proper diet, and stress management. As a consequence, a new organization, the American Association of Fitness Directors in Business and Industry (AAFDBI), has emerged whose expressed purpose is the promotion of health and fitness through wellness programs offered throughout business and industry.

The benefits of exercise have been addressed in Haskell's chapter in this section of the Handbook, and the issue of compliance will be more closely examined in the next chapter by Oldridge. Although the benefits to be accrued from exercise are directly dependent on the quality and the accuracy of the prescription, there must be continued compliance to this prescription for improvement and change to be realized and maintained. Unfortunately, we are more fully aware today of the scientific and technical aspects of the physiological response of the body to exercise than we are about the appropriate means to motivate individuals to commence or maintain an exercise program.

MOTIVATION FOR EXERCISE

The knowledge we have gained by studying the physiological and biochemical response to exercise may enable us to accurately prescribe an exercise program for virtually everyone. This knowledge has very limited application, however, if we do not learn how to properly motivate individuals to develop an exercise program for life. It appears that two goals or reasons are most commonly given by people who continue to exercise regularly: they want to feel good, and they want to look better. If these are important reasons why active people maintain their exercise habit, then we should try to capitalize on this information and use it in the development of an exercise prescription. It is also important that the exercise program reinforce these goals and that there are no negative aspects of the program that might become counterproductive to the attainment of these goals.

IMPORTANCE OF GOALS AND OBJECTIVES

Before a fitness program can be designed and before a prescription can be written, some direction must be given to the program by deciding what is most important to the individual. The needs of an athlete differ considerably from those of the average person, and each person must identify the qualities that are to be developed. The preceding chapter in this section, by Blair, explains how to evaluate exercise habits and physical fitness; this evaluation must take place before the exercise program can be designed. The emphasis in this chapter will be on the development of physical fitness (as measured by muscular strength, muscular endurance, body composition, flexibility, and cardiovascular endurance) rather than motor fitness (as measured by agility, balance, coordination, kinesthetic perception, power, reaction time, and speed). Physical fitness characteristics are essential to maintenance of good health, whereas motor fitness is more appropriate for the athlete and his or her success in sport.

MEDICAL EVALUATION

It is generally agreed that healthy individuals of any age can increase their level of physical activity significantly if there are no contraindications to exercise and if they follow a sensible program. Vigorous exercise may be dangerous for some individuals with known disease (cardiovascular, pulmonary, diabetes), however. The guidelines established by the American College of Sports Medicine (1980) provide specific recommendations for the extent of medical evaluation and supervision that is recommended for individuals who fall into different classifications based on age and health status.

GENERAL PRINCIPLES OF TRAINING

As a result of years of research and experience with training, several important principles have been developed that provide guidance in the design of programs for most individuals and under most conditions to be encountered. These principles include *overload, progression,* and *specificity,* which must be considered together rather than separately.

Principle of Overload

The most important principle of training is the overload principle—that for an adaptive response to occur, a system must be subjected to a load significantly greater than the load to which it is accustomed. At the beginning of an exercise program, when an individual is perhaps deconditioned from years of a sedentary life, a small amount of work may represent a significant overload. As the individual's fitness level improves, greater amounts of work must be used as an overload in order to stimulate change. This point is illustrated in Figure 30.1, where the daily energy cost of exercise for a cardiac patient is compared to that of a normal individual over a 24-month period of training. Both individuals are starting their programs in an unconditioned state at a relatively low level of fitness. The cardiac patient is starting at only 100 kilocalories per workout, which is comparable to a slow walk for 30 minutes at 2.5 mph. In contrast, a normal individual of comparable body weight may alternately walk and jog, at an average speed of 5 mph, for only 20 minutes in order to obtain a 200 kilocalorie workout.

For both individuals to improve their level of cardiovascular fitness, they must increase the amount of work they are doing by applying an overload. In this example, both individuals continue to increase their daily energy expenditure until a desirable maintenance level is reached. At this point, the exercise level may be maintained indefinitely to retain the desired benefits.

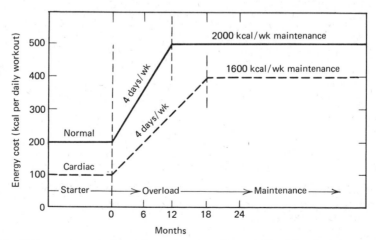

Figure 30.1 Daily energy cost of exercise sessions over 2 years of training for normal persons and cardiac patients. (*Source:* After Pollock, M. L., Ward, A., & Foster, C. Exercise prescription for rehabilitation of the cardiac patient. In M. L. Pollock & D. H. Schmidt (Eds.), *Heart disease and rehabilitation.* Boston: Houghton Mifflin, 1979.)

It is apparent from the figure that the rate of overload is not applied equally to the normal person and the cardiac patient. This may also be true for other categories of individuals, such as younger versus older individuals or even males versus females. The rate at which overload is applied is referred to as the principle of progression.

Principle of Progression

The overload during an exercise program should be applied in a gradual, progressive manner, in accordance with the level of fitness. Initially, the rate of progression should be relatively slow for all individuals; this is referred to as a *starter program*. The starter program may last from one to several weeks, but its importance cannot be overemphasized. Individuals who have been sedentary are much more prone to muscle soreness and injury at the start of a new program. Their muscles are unaccustomed to the stress and strain of vigorous exercise, since they have been in relative disuse. The starter program should include a great deal of stretching and low-level activity to gradually condition the muscles, tendons, ligaments, and joints for increasing levels of work. It is particularly important to minimize the discomfort and soreness at the early stage of a training program to maintain a positive attitude toward the training. Musculoskeletal injuries are sometimes slow to heal, and they can significantly reduce the enthusiasm of a person who has decided to start an exercise program. Although this enthusiasm is usually beneficial, it must also be tempered to prevent the individual from doing too much, too soon. This is a common problem faced by exercise leaders who direct beginning exercise classes; most participants want to make significant gains as soon as possible.

The rate of progression also should be slower for older, more unfit individuals, and the overload must be applied at a rate that allows progressive adaptation to take place. Without sufficient adaptation to one load, no additional overload can be applied. As shown in Figure 30.1, the rate of improvement (and overload) is more rapid for the normal individual than for the cardiac patient; this rate is reflected by the slope of the line, where it can be seen that the expected rate of improvement for the cardiac patient is slower and more gradual and that the cardiac patient is starting at a much lower level of initial fitness.

Principle of Specificity

The principle of specificity is based on the fact that the body adapts to an overload stimulus in a manner that is specific to the type of training (aerobic or anaerobic) as well as to the muscles involved in the training. Recent research has revealed that there is little transfer of training effects, either from one type of training to another or from one muscle group to another (Fox, 1980). In one study (Magel, Foglia, McArdle, Gutin, Pechar, & Katch, 1975), in which swimming was used as the primary mode of training, there was little or no change in the capacity of the legs for work on a treadmill. The adaptation to training occurred primarily in the muscles of the arm and trunk, since these were the muscles used in swimming, whereas no overload was placed upon the legs. In another study of run training (McArdle, Magel, Delio, Toner, & Chase, 1978), the reverse was also found to be true, and the running produced only minor improvement in the physiological response to swimming.

The results are similar when types of training are compared (Holloszy & Booth, 1976). Different types of exercise place different demands on the mechanisms for energy production. The immediate energy source, the high-energy phosphagens (ATP-PC), is called upon for brief work of a power nature during such activities as weight lifting, sprints, and field events such as the high jump and shot put. The short-term energy source, glycolysis, is used for intense work of intermediate duration, lasting 2 to 3 minutes, such as the 400-meter dash, 100-meter swim, and boxing and wrestling. The long-term energy source, the aerobic or oxidative mechanism, is utilized during activities of extended duration, such as the distance events in running, cycling, and swimming. Since the mechanism of energy production differs for each of these types of activity, there is little, if any, transfer from one type of exercise to another. The weight lifter would not benefit from training the oxidative mechanisms, and the marathon runner does not depend on development of the immediate energy sources for successful performance.

DEVELOPING THE PRESCRIPTION

The previous section dealt with three basic principles that must be applied in the development of an exercise prescription. In this section, the exercise prescription will be developed through specific guidelines based on these broad principles.

Establishing Goals and Objectives

As mentioned earlier, specific goals and objectives must be established before a suitable program can be developed. Since this section will deal with the development of physical fitness, rather than motor fitness or fitness for sport, the goals and objectives to be focused upon include flexibility, muscular strength and endurance, cardiovascular endurance, and body composition.

Norms and Standards

The goals and objectives of an exercise program can be based partly on already developed norms or standards. In the area of body composition, for example, certain standards have been developed for acceptable percentage of body fat. It may be, however, that a certain individual will desire to be either above or below that standard, according to personal preference. Therefore, a standard may be used as a guide, but the individual must ultimately determine his or her own goals and objectives for each component of physical fitness.

Desirable levels of physical fitness may also be determined from norms that have been developed from large numbers of individuals of a comparable age and sex. Norms for each component of physical fitness (flexibility, muscular strength and endurance, cardiovascular endurance and body composition) have recently been developed by the YMCA (Golding, Myers, & Sinning, 1982), and these could be used to identify individual weaknesses or deficiencies. Similar norms are also available from a number of other sources, but the needs and interests of the individual must be kept in mind in setting any goals for physical fitness.

Personal Preference

Although norms and standards are useful in establishing goals and objectives, they may not provide as much incentive or motivation for adherence to a program as personal preference does. It is important to recognize this fact and to try to match the goals and objectives to the desires and interests of the individual. It makes little sense, for example, to establish a weight goal of 165 pounds for an individual (that is, estimated ideal weight for age, height, and body frame) when that individual believes that it is unrealistic to go below 175 pounds. Each person may choose to be either more or less ambitious when establishing goals, and this preference must be respected if we are to facilitate compliance to a program.

Planning the Program

Once the goals and objectives have been established, an appropriate program can be planned. The specific recommendations in this plan are called the *exercise prescription*. The exercise prescription incorporates activities into a program that develops each component of physical fitness. This program can be divided into daily training sessions and a long-range plan for training. The daily training sessions are the acute training phase, and the long-range plan is the longitudinal phase of the training, which is modified by continued application of the daily stimulus. The long-range plan is illustrated in Figure 30.1, which shows that the longitudinal application is characterized by a *starter* program, an *overload* phase and, finally, a *maintenance* program. In contrast, the daily training sessions are characterized by the *warm-up*, the *stimulus* phase, and the *cool-down*.

DAILY TRAINING SESSIONS

Each of the components of physical fitness (flexibility, muscular strength and endurance, cardiorespiratory endurance, and body composition) should be developed by the activities utilized in the daily training sessions. The flexibility and muscular strength and endurance exercises are incorporated in the warm-up and cool-down exercises, whereas the cardiorespiratory endurance and body composition activities are incorporated in the aerobic stimulus phase. These phases are illustrated in Figure 30.2, which shows the transition that occurs as a person progresses from a starter program through progressive overload to a maintenance program.

The Warm-up Phase

Vigorous physical activity should always be preceded by a warm-up; the more strenuous the activity, the greater the need for warm-up. There is more than adequate scientific support for the benefits of warm-up. The following are some of the reasons why warm-up exercises, which increase total body and muscle temperature, are beneficial to performance as well as to safety:

1. Warm-up facilitates enzymatic activity.
2. It increases rate of metabolic activity.
3. It improves vasodilation and decreases peripheral resistance.
4. It improves perfusion of the muscles with blood.
5. It improves delivery of oxygen and removal of carbon dioxide.
6. It increases speed of nerve conduction and speed of contraction.
7. It decreases muscle viscosity and improves rate of contraction and relaxation.

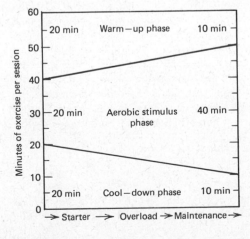

Figure 30.2 Suggested time allotment during progressive overload from a starter program to a maintenance program.

The types of exercises used in warm-up include stretching and flexibility exercises as well as exercises to improve muscular strength and endurance. In Figure 30.2, it can be seen that, initially, one-third of the total exercise session (20 of 60 minutes) is devoted to warm-up activities. The following is an example of what might be included in the warm-up phase of an exercise session:

1. 10 minutes of stretching and flexibility exercises of the major muscle groups, such as the neck, back, shoulders, hips, abdomen, groin, quadriceps, hamstrings, and ankles.
2. 5 minutes of muscular strength and endurance exercises, such as push-ups, pull-ups, sit-ups, toe raises, and squat thrusts.
3. 5 minutes of general gross muscle activity, such as walking, jogging, bicycling, or swimming at a gradually increasing intensity into the stimulus phase.

These activities will provide a safe and effective 20-minute warm-up in preparation for the stimulus phase. In the starter program, there is an increased emphasis on the warm-up, since the individual is not conditioned for vigorous activity and the warm-up activities will lessen the likelihood of strain and injury. It will also prepare the body adequately for the more vigorous activity of the aerobic stimulus phase.

As a person progresses from the starter program to the progressive overload phase, decreasing emphasis is placed on the warm-up. This is because the muscles should have become more flexible from several weeks of stretching; therefore, less time is required to obtain the same degree of flexibility in a given session. In addition, as training progresses, more time should be devoted to the aerobic stimulus phase because of its beneficial effects on the cardiorespiratory system.

The Aerobic Stimulus Phase

The aerobic stimulus phase deserves the most attention in the development of an exercise prescription for several reasons. First, the major causes of disease and death in the United States are related to disorders of the heart and circulation and are complicated by excess weight and obesity. The aerobic stimulus phase can exert its greatest influence on cardiovascular condition and body composition. It has the potential for preventing, delaying, and even reversing the deleterious effects of a sedentary lifestyle. Second, if this phase is not prescribed correctly, it also has the potential for creating significant problems for the individual. These problems can range from very minor complications, such as muscle soreness or fatigue, to serious injury and death. Third, the aerobic stimulus phase may play a major role in the individual's compliance to an exercise program. If the activity is not prescribed correctly, taking into account both effectiveness and enjoyment or reinforcement, then continued adherence to the program is in jeopardy. For these reasons, careful consideration must be given to the development and implementation of this phase.

Although the principles of overload and progression are also applied in the warm-up and cool-down phases of an exercise session, the aerobic stimulus phase requires a more careful manipulation and coordination of the following factors in order to produce the desired results: type, intensity, duration, and frequency of activity. It will be seen that all these factors must be taken into consideration simultaneously to produce a safe and effective overload.

Type of Activity

For a type of activity to be considered satisfactory as an aerobic stimulus, several criteria must be met: it must involve *vigorous* activity of *large muscle groups,* which is *rhythmic* in nature and is performed *aerobically*. If an activity cannot meet all these criteria, it will be unsatisfactory. Some of the better activities that meet these criteria are as follows:

Aerobic dancing	Kayaking
Badminton	Racquetball
Basketball	Rope skipping
Bicycling	Soccer
Canoeing	Squash
Cross-country skiing	Swimming
Fencing	Tennis
Handball	Walking/jogging/running

There are other activities that could be used to complement the foregoing activities since they are also rhythmic and aerobic and involve large muscle groups; however, they are usually not vigorous enough to provide an adequate stimulus. Some of these other activities are as follows: backpacking, gardening activities, golf (walking—no cart), hiking, nature walking, skiing (downhill), and skin diving.

It is important to realize that all activities in the first list can be excellent activities for providing an aerobic stimulus only if they are performed properly—that is, at the proper intensity, duration, and frequency.

Another important point is that the individual should give serious thought to selecting the activity or activities that will be most conducive to compliance. (These factors are covered in detail in the following chapter, by Oldridge.) The activities must be enjoyable to the individual and they must be convenient enough to permit frequent participation. There is a wide range of activities that could be included, and no rule exists. What should be stressed is regular participation (compliance). If a person can maintain a program with only a single aerobic activity, such as walking, jogging, swimming, cycling or aerobic dancing, then this is entirely acceptable. Since variety is a factor that influences both enjoyment and compliance, however, it is desirable that the person choose to engage in several activities (depending on availability, weather, seasonal preference, and the like). It is obvious that there is no rigid, inflexible approach to this decision; what is right is what works for that individual.

It was pointed out earlier that the activity must be vigorous to produce an effective stimulus; the next factor, intensity, regulates this aspect of an activity.

Intensity of Activity

The intensity of activity refers to the percentage of the person's maximum capacity that is achieved during the exercise stimulus. It is very important that this factor be determined carefully, because exercise at too low an intensity will fail to provide an adequate stimulus or overload, and little or no adaptation will occur. Exercise at a stimulus that is too great is a potential hazard, however, since it may result in musculoskeletal injury (soreness or muscle/connective tissue tear) or cardiac complications (ischemia and lethal dysrhythmias). It is obvious that a safe and effective range must be carefully determined. The upper part of the range is influenced by the safety factor, and the lower part of the range is influenced by effectiveness.

The lower limit of effectiveness has not been determined with any degree of precision, but it appears to be approximately 60% of the individual's maximal capacity (ACSM, 1978) after the initial starter program has been completed. The starter program would require that individuals start at as low as 40% to 50% of capacity and gradually increase this to 60% and above after several weeks of training. The starter program assures that musculoskeletal problems will be minimized and that there will be a gradual adaptation of the muscles, tendons, ligaments, and joints to the work. The upper limit of safety also has not yet been determined for all groups of individuals, but it appears to be approximately 80% of the person's capacity.

The relationship between intensity of activity and both safety and effectiveness is clearly illustrated in Figure 30.3, which shows that the improvement in functional capacity (gain in maximal oxygen uptake) is closely tied to the level of intensity of activity. As the intensity level increases, greater improvement in functional capacity is realized. As the intensity exceeds a given range, however, the risk of cardiovascular complications increases somewhat exponentially. It should be emphasized that these cardiovascular complications are found primarily in individuals with known or suspected heart disease and that they are related to the potential ischemic manifestations of a compromised coronary circulation, such as angina pectoris and lethal dysrhythmias. For the young and healthy individual, the most likely complication of exceeding the upper limit would be fatigue. Nevertheless, there seems to be an optimal range of intensity of activity between 60% and 80% of the $\dot{V}O_{2\ max}$ (that is, functional capacity).

From a practical standpoint, how does a person determine this range and apply it to his or her own exercise prescription? The answer to this question depends on how much information is available, since the most accurate determination depends on knowledge of the true resting and maximal heart rates. These rates are usually determined from a graded exercise test, which is administered on a treadmill or bicycle ergometer (or other ergometer). The physiological response (heart rate, ECG reading, blood pressure, oxygen uptake, and so on) of the individual is monitored through a progressive range from a low level of activity through maximum effort. From these results, the proper range of intensity is prescribed for the individual. It should be pointed out that this is indeed an individualized prescription, since every individual has a different physiological response to work, and the resting and maximal heart rates will differ widely among individuals.

There are several approaches to this determination of the target heart rate, and their details will not be presented here. (The interested reader is referred to Davis and Convertino, 1975, which explains these methods in more detail.) The approach in this chapter will be to recommend a simplified method based on the use of heart rates that are either accurately measured during a graded exercise test or estimated from a formula based on age. This method also takes into consideration the influence of resting heart rate in the calculation,

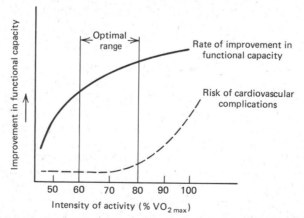

Figure 30.3 Relationship between intensity of activity and gains in functional capacity versus risk of cardiovascular complications. (*Source:* After Dehn, M., & Mullins, C. Physiologic effects and importance of exercise in patients with coronary heart disease. *Cardiovascular Medicine,* 1977, **2,** 365.)

since the use of the HR reserve ($HR_{max} - HR_{rest}$) provides a more accurate determination of intensity than using HR_{max} alone (Davis & Convertino, 1975). This approach is presented in Table 30.1, which lists the recommended training heart rate ranges for the aerobic stimulus phase, when the resting and maximum heart rates are either known or estimated. To use the table, locate the resting heart rate in the left column (which ranges from 50 to 80 beats per minute) and the maximum heart rate in the top row (which ranges from 120 to 200 beats per minute) and determine the recommended training heart rate at the intersection of these two values. For example, an individual with a resting heart rate of 75 beats per minute and a maximum heart rate of 182 beats per minute would have a training heart rate range of 136 to 158 beats per minute. The values in parentheses in the table are training heart rates expressed as 10-second counts made during the first few seconds after exercise. These values make it convenient for the individual to count his or her own pulse for only 10 seconds at various times during the workout and to use this value, rather than continuing to multiply the 10-second pulse rate by 6 in order to obtain the per-minute value.

The exercise heart rates may be obtained by palpating the radial (wrist) or carotid (neck) pulse or by holding the hand over the chest at the apex of the heart. People should be cautioned not to massage or press too hard on the carotid region to avoid inducing the carotid sinus reflex, which may cause either bradycardia (slow heart rate) or dysrhythmias (irregular rate); this could result in dizziness from impaired circulation or complications from the irregular rate.

In addition to using the heart rate range as a means of controlling intensity, individuals may also regulate their intensity level by how they feel. If there are any symptoms of light-headedness, confusion, nausea, dyspnea, chest pain, or other significant pain or discomfort, the exercise should be terminated, since these symptoms could reflect an inadequate cardiovascular response to the work. If the symptoms persist, medical attention should be sought.

Another approach to controlling the exercise intensity is the use of the rating of perceived exertion (RPE). This method, developed by Borg (1973), is finding increasing applications in the prescription of exercise (Noble, 1982). This approach is based on the knowledge that an individual's perception of effort is closely correlated with physiological measures of effort and that, under most conditions, individuals can accurately regulate the intensity of their activity by following their perceptual cues. As intensity of work increases, certain physiological changes occur (increased heart rate, blood pressure, pulmonary ventilation, oxygen uptake, body temperature, sweating, lactic acid production, and so on), and a roughly linear association exists between these physiological parameters and the RPE (Pandolf, 1977). For this reason, the Borg RPE scale is often used during graded exercise tests to provide a perceptual measure of physiological strain. The Borg scale is presented in Table 30.2. The scale ranges numerically from 6 to 20, with verbal anchors for the odd numbers that describe the individual's perception of the level of effort.

Although the precise relationship between RPE and intensity of effort has not been determined for all populations (based on age, sex, level of training, disease status) and under all conditions (altitude, temperature, humidity, anxiety, psychological status), it appears that the training range for RPE should probably be between 11 and 15 units on the Borg scale. The effort should probably exceed "fairly light" (RPE = 11) as the lower threshold, but it should not exceed "hard" (RPE = 15) as the upper limit. Confirmation of this recommendation awaits further research.

Duration of Activity

Duration of activity refers to the length of time that the individual trains at the specified intensity. Any discussion of the optimal duration of activity recommended for training the cardiovascular system, however, must include intensity as well as frequency of activity.

Table 30.1 **Training Heart Rate Ranges for Individuals with Different Resting and Maximum Heart Rates**

Resting Heart Rate (beats/min)		Maximum Heart Rate (beats/min)[a]								
		120	130	140	150	160	170	180	190	200
50	Lo-Hi[b]	92–106	98–114	104–122	110–130	116–138	122–146	128–154	134–162	140–170
	(10 sec)[c]	(15–18)	(16–19)	(17–20)	(18–22)	(19–23)	(20–24)	(21–26)	(22–27)	(23–28)
60	Lo-Hi	96–108	102–116	108–124	114–132	120–140	126–148	132–156	138–164	144–172
	(10 sec)	(16–18)	(17–19)	(18–21)	(19–22)	(20–23)	(21–25)	(22–26)	(23–27)	(24–29)
70	Lo-Hi	100–110	106–118	112–126	118–134	124–142	130–150	136–158	142–166	148–174
	(10 sec)	(17–18)	(18–20)	(19–21)	(20–22)	(21–24)	(22–25)	(23–26)	(24–28)	(25–29)
80	Lo-Hi	104–112	110–120	116–128	122–136	128–144	134–152	140–160	146–168	152–176
	(10 sec)	(17–19)	(18–20)	(19–21)	(20–23)	(21–24)	(22–25)	(23–27)	(24–28)	(25–29)

Source: Adapted from Haskell, W. L. Design and implementation of cardiac conditioning programs. In N. K. Wenger & H. K. Hellerstein (Eds.), *Rehabilitation of the coronary patient.* New York: Wiley, 1978.

[a] Maximum heart rate should be determined from a graded exercise test; however, a less accurate method is to estimate it according to age—that is, $HR_{max} = 220 - age$.

[b] Lo-Hi refers to the lower (60%) and higher (80%) target heart rate values during exercise, expressed in beats per minute.

[c] (10 sec) refers to the lower and higher heart rates, expressed as counts per 10 seconds.

Table 30.2   Borg's RPE Scale for Ratings of Perceived Exertion

6	
7	Very, very light
8	
9	Very light
10	
11	Fairly light
12	
13	Somewhat hard
14	
15	Hard
16	
17	Very hard
18	
19	Very, very hard
20	

Intensity and duration of activity are inversely related, and maintenance of a very high intensity is only possible for a short duration of effort. If the duration of effort is to be extended, then the intensity must be reduced accordingly.

As with intensity, duration of effort is an important component of the exercise prescription, since too short a duration will fail to provide an adequate stimulus for cardiovascular adaptation and too long a duration has the potential for creating orthopedic complications for the individual. Although some improvement in cardiovascular function can be measured after only a few sessions as short as 5 to 10 minutes per day at an optimal intensity, these changes are minimal, and continued improvement is unlikely to be sustained without the stimulus of an adequate duration. In general, the gains in functional capacity are roughly proportional to the duration of effort if all other factors (type, intensity, and frequency of activity) remain constant.

This point is clearly illustrated in Figure 30.4, which shows that the rate of improvement in functional capacity increases with greater duration of exercise at a fixed intensity (75% $\dot{V}O_{2\ max}$). As the duration of the session exceeds 30 minutes, however, the risk of orthopedic complications increases disproportionately (Pollock, Gettman, Milesis, Bah, Durstine, & Johnson, 1977). The optimal range, at least for those beginning an exercise program, appears to be between 20 and 30 minutes per session. It should be emphasized at this point that this relationship would not hold true as individuals become better trained and as their muscles, joints, and tendons become adapted to the exercise. As a person goes through the starter and overload phases of training (see Figure 30.1), the duration of the aerobic stimulus phase can be gradually increased, without complication, beyond the 20- to 30-minute range.

Although the trend in the literature is to find a progressive improvement in functional capacity with greater duration of effort, it should be reemphasized that there is a strong interdependence of intensity and duration of effort in the production of a significant training effect. The combined effect of intensity and duration can be expressed as *total work output*, and this product can be equivalent with differing combinations of intensity and duration of effort. In other words, work at a lower intensity would require a longer duration, whereas work at a higher intensity would require a shorter duration to produce equivalent work outputs. The goal should be to determine the correct blend of intensity and duration that will produce the desired work load. This concept is illustrated in Figure 30.5, which presents

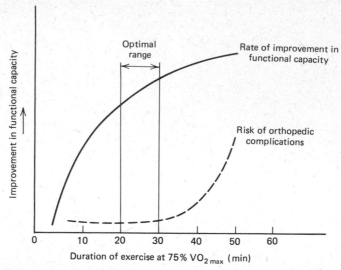

Figure 30.4 Relationship between duration of activity and gains in functional capacity versus risk of orthopedic complications. (*Source:* After Dehn, M., & Mullins, C. Physiologic effects and importance of exercise in patients with coronary heart disease. *Cardiovascular Medicine,* 1977, **2,** 365.)

the theoretical relationship between intensity and duration of effort for individuals with differing functional capacity. Individuals with a low functional capacity, for example, would be expected to work at only 60% of their capacity for a 30-minute session, whereas a moderately trained individual should be able to sustain work at approximately 75% of capacity for the same duration. In this example, it should be obvious that the moderately trained individual would be producing more total work than the individual with a low functional capacity and that the latter individual would have to work either for a longer duration or with greater frequency to achieve a comparable work output.

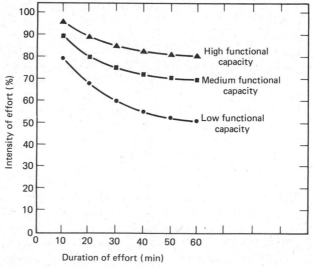

Figure 30.5 Theoretical relationship between intensity and duration of effort in individuals of differing functional capacity. (*Source:* After Ribisl, P. M. Guidelines and principles of cardiovascular conditioning and exercise prescription. In G. A. Stull & T. K. Cureton (Eds.), *Encyclopedia of physical education, fitness, and sports.* Salt Lake City: Brighton, 1980.)

Frequency of Activity

Frequency of activity refers to the number of exercise sessions completed per week. Consideration of this factor must also include both intensity and duration and the interaction of all three factors in the production of a total work output. For example, an individual who worked at 80% intensity for 90 minutes' duration only two times per week would have provided a greater training stimulus than another individual who worked at 60% intensity for 20 minutes' duration four times per week. For this reason, all three factors must be considered together in the discussion of frequency of activity. In fact, any legitimate comparison of the effectiveness of different training frequencies should hold all other factors constant in order to isolate the frequency variable. When this is done, it becomes apparent that the improvements in functional capacity are roughly proportional to the frequency of training, since a greater frequency results in a proportionally greater total work output (Gettman, Pollock, Durstine, Ward, Ayers, & Linnerud, 1976).

The relationship between rate of improvement in functional capacity and frequency of exercise is illustrated in Figure 30.6, which shows that there is a progressive increase in functional capacity with increasing frequency of training. It can also be seen, however, that with increasing frequency, the risk of orthopedic complications also increases. Again, it should be emphasized that these data are based on studies with beginners, who are more susceptible to injuries than individuals who have been training for several months or more and whose muscles, joints, and tendons have become adapted to the stress of the activity. Therefore, caution must be exerted in the prescription of exercise for the beginner. It appears that exercise on alternate days (that is, 3 to 4 days/week) is the most prudent recommendation for obtaining optimal cardiovascular benefits with the lowest risk of orthopedic complications.

Regularity of Training

Regularity of training is often mentioned in conjunction with frequency of training, and the usual recommendation is that the training days be evenly spaced, with a day of rest between training sessions. At this point, little research data are available to support this recommendation. In fact, one study (Moffatt, Stamford, & Neill, 1977) revealed that there

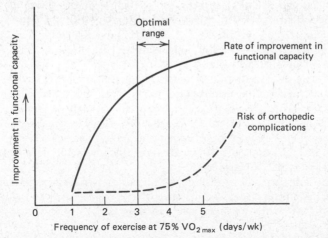

Figure 30.6 Relationship between frequency of activity and gains in functional capacity versus risk of orthopedic complications. (*Source:* After Dehn, M., & Mullins, C. Physiologic effects and importance of exercise in patients with coronary heart disease. *Cardiovascular Medicine,* 1977, **2**, 365.)

were no differences in improvement between groups who trained on consecutive days (Monday, Tuesday, Wednesday) versus alternate days (Monday, Wednesday, Friday). Until further research is available to support another position, the recommendation should still be to provide an evenly spaced stimulus, such as training on alternate days, rather than to allow a substantial lapse during which detraining could potentially occur.

The Cool-down Phase

Just as the warm-up period physiologically prepares the individual for the aerobic stimulus phase of the exercise session, so does the cool-down phase allow for proper recovery from an exercise bout. The need for a cool-down period after exercise will vary according to the intensity of the exercise and the degree of heat load that has been generated by the work.

Several reasons are offered as a rationale for the cool-down period after exercise, but the most immediate concern is to maintain the venous return. When exercise has been maintained at a high level during the stimulus phase, cardiac output is maintained by the heart rate and stroke volume. There is also considerable vasodilation (both muscular and cutaneous), which lowers the peripheral resistance to accommodate the cardiac output and to allow perfusion of the muscles and skin. If exercise stops abruptly, the vasodilation will cause considerable pooling of the blood, especially in the active muscles of the lower extremities, unless the individual keeps moving. By continuous movement, the venous return is enhanced by the pumping action of the muscles, which compress the veins and force the blood only in the direction of the heart, since the valves in the veins prevent any backflow of the blood. Failure to maintain continuous movement in recovery would reduce venous return because of venous pooling, and hypotension could result. Since the myocardial oxygen demand immediately after vigorous exercise is still high, a low level of venous return could create an ischemic condition in the heart, with resultant complications (angina and dysrhythmias).

When the intensity of exercise exceeds 50% to 60% of $\dot{V}O_{2\ max}$ in the untrained individual, the steady state of aerobic metabolism can no longer be maintained. The result is accumulation of lactic acid and eventual fatigue. After exercise, the removal of lactic acid is facilitated by an active rather than a passive recovery (Hermansen & Stensvold, 1972). The nature of this recovery has not been firmly established, but it is clear that the greater the intensity of the work bout, the higher the activity level must be in the recovery period to facilitate the removal of lactate. The mechanism is unclear, but this faster rate may be associated with greater perfusion of the tissues that are responsible for lactate removal, such as the heart and skeletal muscle and the liver. It is interesting that other research (Bonen & Belcastro, 1976) has revealed that when individuals are left to their own choice, they voluntarily select the optimal intensity during active recovery.

Finally, the cool-down period after exercise is often necessary in order to dissipate a heat load that has been built up as a result of an imbalance between the heat gain through exercise or environmental conditions and the heat loss through the conventional, avenues of radiation, conduction, convection, and evaporation. For effective cooling to take place, conditions must exist to permit adequate evaporation from the skin. These conditions include a large surface area of exposure, low relative humidity, and sufficient air movement over the skin to facilitate the convective loss.

The types of activities to be used during the cool-down phase are very similar to those used in the warm-up phase. The only difference is that these activities would be performed in a reverse order from the warm-up progression to allow a gradual tapering off of the activity toward a lower level.

SPECIAL EXERCISE PROGRAMS

The preceding section of this chapter presented the principles of training that govern the development of an exercise prescription for health and outlined guidelines for the safe and effective implementation of this prescription so that an individual could develop either a personal exercise prescription or plan a program for others. This section will deal with several other approaches and resources that can be used to supplement the principles and guidelines.

YMCA Programs

For years, the YMCA has been involved with the development and implementation of exercise programs across the United States. Many of these programs have been developed or upgraded recently. The following standardized health enhancement programs are currently available:

Activetics	A program of health and fitness for adults
Feelin' Good	A similar program to Activetics, designed for children
Slim Living	A program for weight control
Healthy Back	A program for prevention of and rehabilitation for back problems
YMCArdiac Therapy	A program of cardiac rehabilitation
Risk Factor Education	A program for the management of coronary risk factors

Additional information can be obtained by calling (312) 823-2973 or writing The YMCA of the USA, Program Resources, 6400 Shafer Court, Rosemont, IL 60018. In addition, the interested reader is referred to a recent YMCA publication (Golding, et al., 1982), which provides guidelines for the development of physical fitness programs and includes a wealth of resource materials.

Aerobics

In 1968, Kenneth H. Cooper, M.D., published his first book on aerobics, which explained a program for the development and maintenance of cardiovascular fitness through aerobic-type activity. This program has been updated with his new book, *The Aerobics Way* (1977). Cooper has developed a program that includes an evaluation of fitness through a graded exercise test with ECG (for deconditioned individuals over 35 years of age) or through a 12-minute run for conditioned individuals under 35 years of age. Individuals are then placed into fitness categories on the basis of these results, and programs are recommended for each fitness category.

The fitness programs consist of starter programs (first 12 weeks) and maintenance programs (12 weeks and beyond) for the following activities: walking, running, cycling, swimming, stationary running, stationary cycling, stair climbing, rope skipping, and such sport activities as handball, racquetball, squash, basketball, lacrosse, soccer, and hockey. These activities are assigned "aerobic points" on the basis of their estimated energy cost (1 point = 7 ml/kg/min of oxygen consumption), and greater intensities and durations are awarded proportionally more points. Cooper recommends a minimum of 30 points per week for males and 24 points per week for females for optimal fitness.

Cooper estimates that each aerobic point is equivalent to 20 kilocalories, which works out to be approximately 600 kcal/wk (that is, 30 points/wk × 20 kcal/point). Although the system that Cooper recommends is basically sound and is based on established principles of training, the 30 point/week standard is probably too low a goal and should be revised upward. The recommendation for optimal fitness, based on the majority of previous research, should be closer to 800 kcal/wk as a starter program and approximately 2,000 kcal/wk for an optimal maintenance program (see Figure 30.1).

Aerobic Dancing

The development of aerobic dancing is usually credited to Jackie Sorensen, the dancer and entrepreneur who directs the highly successful franchises of Aerobic Dancing, Inc. Enrollment in the classes of Aerobics Dancing, Inc., has grown fivefold since 1978 (Legwold, 1982) and now involves 150,000 participants in each of the four yearly sessions held throughout the United States and in a few foreign countries.

Little published research is available to document the physiological benefits to be accrued from a program of aerobic dancing, but the energy cost has been measured to be between 250 and 500 kcal/hr (Legwold, 1982) during the aerobic stimulus phase of dancing. Since the typical sessions are preceded by a warm-up and followed by a cool-down, the total dancing time during an hour session may be only 30 to 40 minutes, which would reduce the total energy cost per workout accordingly. Nevertheless, aerobic dancing has a number of positive features. The exercise has the potential for meeting the standards for a good cardiovascular activity: it is a rhythmic activity of the large muscle groups that is vigorous enough to be within the 60% to 80% intensity range; the duration usually exceeds 30 minutes per session; and classes are usually offered two to four times per week. In addition, participants find the classes to be enjoyable and, subjectively, they believe that they look and feel better as a result of participation. These latter reasons are especially important, because they have a positive effect on compliance to the activity.

Special Populations

The previous guidelines for exercise prescription have been developed for the normal, healthy individual who is starting an exercise program. It is recognized, however, that there are unique populations that deserve special consideration and modification of the prescription, based on their individual needs. Although it is beyond the scope of this chapter to address this issue in detail, the interested reader is referred to key references that deal with each of these populations:

1. For persons with coronary heart disease: Wenger, N. K., & Hellerstein, H. K. (Eds.), *Rehabilitation of the coronary patient* (New York: Wiley, 1978); and Pollock, M. L., & Schmidt, D. L. (Eds.), *Heart disease and rehabilitation* (Boston: Houghton Mifflin, 1979).

2. For persons with chronic obstructive pulmonary disease (COPD): American College of Sports Medicine, *Guidelines for exercise testing and exercise prescription for patients with pulmonary disease* (Madison: Author, 1982); and Shephard, R. J. Exercise and chronic obstructive lung disease, in J. Keogh & R. S. Hutton (Eds.), *Exercise and sport science reviews* (Vol. 4) (Santa Barbara: Journal Publishing Affiliates, 1976).

3. For persons with diabetes: Proceedings of a conference on diabetes and exercise, *Diabetes,* 1979, **28,**(Suppl. 1), 1–113; and Cunningham, L. N., The adult diabetic and exercise, in R. C. Cantu (Ed.), *The exercising adult* (Lexington, Mass.: Collamore Press, 1982).

4. For obese persons: Dempsey, J. A., Exercise and obesity, in A. J. Ryan & F. L. Allman (Eds.), *Sports medicine* (New York: Academic Press, 1974); and Stuart, R. B., & Davis, B., *Slim chance in a fat world* (Champaign, Ill.: Research Press, 1972).

Within each of the special populations cited, there are also subpopulations that deserve attention. In coronary heart disease, for example, there are distinct categories of patients, such as those with angina pectoris or intermittent claudication or those who have undergone surgery for coronary artery bypass grafts. Under chronic obstructive pulmonary disease, there are patients with asthma, emphysema, and bronchitis. In diabetes, the juvenile diabetic differs from the adult-onset diabetic. The foregoing references should be viewed only as a starting point; each reference has an extensive bibliography, which should be consulted for more in-depth information.

The American Association of Fitness Directors in Business and Industry

The American Association of Fitness Directors in Business and Industry (AAFDBI) has been in existence for less than 10 years (incorporated in 1977), but it has become the major organization for individuals who are involved in the planning and implementation of programs of health enhancement in business and industry. The AAFDBI publishes a quarterly newsletter and holds national and regional meetings each year. This organization is a good source of information for those who are interested in developing fitness programs in business or industry.

Membership and organizational materials are available from American Association of Fitness Directors in Business and Industry, 700 Anderson Hill Road, Purchase, NY 10577. An additional relevant source is McGill (1979), which is available from the Superintendent of Documents, U.S. Government Printing Office, Washington, DC 20402.

REFERENCE NOTE

1. Pacific Mutual Insurance Company. *Health maintenance.* Nationwide survey by Louis Harris and Associates, Inc., November 1978.

REFERENCES

American College of Sports Medicine (ACSM). The recommended quantity and quality of exercise for developing and maintaining fitness in healthy adults. *Medicine and Science in Sports,* 1978, **10**(3), vii–ix.

American College of Sports Medicine (ACSM). *Guidelines for graded exercise testing and exercise prescription* (2nd ed.). Philadelphia: Lea & Febiger, 1980.

Bonen, A., & Belcastro, A. N. Comparison of self-selected recovery methods on lactic acid removal rates. *Medicine and Science in Sports,* 1976, **8**(3), 176–178.

Borg, G. A. Perceived exertion: A note on "history" and methods. *Medicine and Science in Sports,* 1973, **5**(2), 90–93.

Cooper, K. H. *The aerobics way.* New York: Bantam, 1977.

Davis, J. A., & Convertino, V. A. A comparison of heart rate methods for predicting endurance training intensity. *Medicine and Science in Sports,* 1975, **7**(4), 295–298.

Fox, E. L. Physiological effects of training. In G. A. Stull & T. K. Cureton (Eds.), *Encyclopedia of physical education, fitness, and sports.* Salt Lake City: Brighton, 1980.

Gettman, L. R., Pollock, M. L., Durstine, J. L., Ward, A., Ayers, J., & Linnerud, A. C. Physiological responses of men to 1, 3 and 5 day per week training programs. *Research Quarterly,* 1976, **47**(4), 638–646.

Golding, L. A., Myers, C. R., & Sinning, W. E. (Eds.). *The Y's way to physical fitness.* Chicago: YMCA, 1982.

Hermansen, L., & Stensvold, I. Production and removal of lactate during exercise in man. *Acta Physiologica Scandinavica,* 1972, **86**, 191–201.

Holloszy, J. O., & Booth, F. W. Biochemical adaptations to endurance exercise in muscle. *Annual Reviews of Physiology,* 1976, **38**, 273–291.

Legwold, G. Does aerobic dance offer more fun than fitness? *Physician and Sportsmedicine,* 1982, **10**(9), 147–151.

McArdle, W. D., Magel, J. R., Delio, D. J., Toner, M., & Chase, J. M. Specificity of run training on $\dot{V}O_{2\ max}$ and heart rate changes during running and swimming. *Medicine and Science in Sports,* 1978, **10**(1), 16–20.

Magel, J. R., Foglia, F., McArdle, W. D., Gutin, B., Pechar, G. S., & Katch, F. I. Specificity of swim training on maximum oxygen uptake. *Journal of Applied Physiology,* 1975, **38**(1), 151–155.

McGill, A. M. (Ed.). *Proceedings of the National Conference on Health Promotion Programs in Occupational Settings.* Washington, D.C.: U.S. Government Printing Office, 1979.

Moffatt, R. J., Stamford, B. A., & Neill, R. D. Placement of tri-weekly training sessions: Importance regarding enhancement of aerobic capacity. *Research Quarterly,* 1977, **48**(4), 583–591.

Noble, B. Preface to the symposium on recent advances in the study and clinical use of perceived exertion. *Medicine and Science in Sports and Exercise,* 1982, **14**(5), 376.

Pandolf, K. B. Psychological and physiological factors influencing perceived exertion. In G. Borg (Ed.), *Physical work and effort.* Oxford: Pergamon Press, 1977.

Pollock, M. L., Gettman, L. R., Milesis, C. A., Bah, M. D., Durstine, L., & Johnson, R. B. Effects of frequency and duration of training on attritition and incidence of injury. *Medicine and Science in Sports,* 1977, **9**(1), 31–36.

CHAPTER 31

ADHERENCE TO ADULT EXERCISE FITNESS PROGRAMS

N. B. OLDRIDGE

McMaster University

Adults, healthy or otherwise, are generally neither attracted to join nor motivated to adhere to health-oriented exercise programs. Although adults who have been surveyed apparently believe in the health value of exercise, the majority do not turn their beliefs into action; even among those who do, as many as 50% drop out of the programs after 6 months. Therefore, a central issue confronting professionals in behavioral health—"a new inter-disciplinary sub-specialty within behavioral medicine specifically concerned with the maintenance of health and prevention of illness and dysfunction in currently healthy persons" (Matarazzo, 1980)—is to motivate adults to join and continue in regular health-oriented exercise programs.

A majority of healthy American adults in 1973 (President's Council, Note 1) and 1978 (Harris, Note 2) and Canadian adults in 1982 (Canada Fitness Survey, Note 3) agreed with the statement: "Exercise is important for good health." Those who exercise also stated that regular physical activity results in feeling better, looking better, and doing better, but they make up a small proportion of the population (Harris, Note 2). The most recent survey (Harris, Note 2) examining and evaluating the American public's attitudes toward and participation in physical fitness and exercise programs reported that approximately 15% of U.S. adults participate regularly in recreational physical activity in which the level of energy expenditure is in excess of 1,500 kcal per week (Table 31.1). An energy expenditure of 1,500 to 2,000 kcal per week translates into an hour of walking daily at 3.0 to 3.5 mph, a daily 20- to 30-minute run at 6.0 mph, or 1 hour's swim at 1 mph on 5 days a week for a 70 to 80 kg person. Aerobic exercise carried out 3 to 5 days a week for 15 to 60 minutes per session at more than 60% of maximum heart rate may be the most appropriate exercise for developing and maintaining cardiorespiratory fitness and body composition in the healthy adult (ACSM, 1978). So-called recreationally low-active or nonactive individuals, who may be farmers or homemakers, for example, may in fact be expending more than 1,500 kcal per week in work bouts of more than 15 minutes at more than 60% maximum heart rate on more than 3 days a week. Evidence from Israel (Epstein, Keren, Udassin, & Shapiro, 1981) describes significantly higher oxygen uptakes among agricultural communal settlement members than among urbanites between the ages of 22 and 40 years; this occupa-

Particular thanks are extended to Drs. J. Martin, C. Jago, R. Rempel, and P. Donnelly for their thoughtful and constructive criticism from both a professional and an exercisers' points of view. Special thanks go to Laura Diskin for assistance in preparation of the manuscript. Participaction provided the originals of their promotional slogans.

Table 31.1 Recreational Activity Classification in the U.S. Population

Classification	Approximate Energy Expenditure (kcal/week)	Activity Equivalent (Walk or Jog) for 70 kg Person[a]	Percentage of the U.S. Population
High-active	>1,500	@ 3 mph = 18.0 mi/week @ 6 mph = 13.5 mi/week	15
Moderate-active	1,500–1,000	@ 3 mph = 15.0 mi/week @ 6 mph = 11.0 mi/week	16
Low-active	1,000–500	@ 3 mph = 9.0 mi/week	28
Nonactive	<500	@ 3 mph = <6.0 mi/week	41

Source: From definitions and data in Harris, L., & Associates. *The Perrier Study: Fitness in America.* Vital and Health Statistics of the National Center on Health Statistics. Washington, D.C., 1978.

[a] 3 mph = 1.2 kcal·kg^{-1}·mile^{-1}; 6 mph = 1.6 kcal·kg^{-1}·mile^{-1}

tional relationship is confounded by the report that the urbanites were less likely to participate in sports. There is no evidence, however, that these individuals report feeling better, looking better, and doing better because of their occupational energy expenditure; these factors apparently are related to recreational energy expenditure.

The belief that regular physical activity habits are positively associated with good health is confirmed by recent clinical observations. Morris, Everitt, Pollard, Chave, and Semmence (1980) reported a reduced incidence of coronary heart disease and fatal heart attack with regular exercise of approximately 1,500 to 2,000 kcal per week. They state that the "activities which make up vigorous exercise . . . are by no means extreme—our men are no athletes. Indeed, the remarkable ordinariness . . . is further encouragement" (Morris et al., 1980). The reduced incidence of heart disease and heart attack is substantiated by Paffenbarger and associates in both occupational activity (Paffenbarger, Hale, Brand, & Hyde, 1977) and recreational activity (Paffenbarger, Wing, & Hyde, 1978). This may be explained in part by the higher fitness in individuals whose lifestyle and daily activities demand at least a minimum level of energy expenditure (Morris et al., 1980; Paffenbarger et al., 1977; Paffenbarger et al., 1978), but this protective threshold for first heart attack apparently is not seen in trials of exercise and recurrent myocardial infarction (Rechnitzer, Cunningham, Andrew, Buck, Jones, Kavenagh, Oldridge, Parker, Shephard, Sutton, & Donner, 1983). Other benefits of regular exercise, discussed in the Haskell, Weltman, and Smith chapters in this section of the Handbook, can be summarized as including, among other more specific factors, (a) a reduced body weight, (b) increased functional capacity, (c) a reduced work of the heart at rest and during submaximal work, and (d) an improved psychological outlook.

Compliance, defined as the extent to which a protocol is adhered to, is a major problem in medical management (Sackett & Snow, 1979) and extends to rehabilitation, including exercise programs (Oldridge, 1982). The term *compliance* is essentially synonymous with *adherence,* except that *compliance* is probably more appropriate in the context of medical management, when the behavior is prescribed for the patient being treated. *Adherence* is best used in the context of voluntary behavior prompted either by a personal decision or by advice from some other person or persons.

To achieve the end of involving people in exercise programs that are beneficial to their health, professionals in behavioral health should attempt to reinforce the concept of self-responsibility. As a recent editorial suggests: "Perhaps the most promising potential for improving public health resides in what people can be motivated to do for themselves" (Aring, 1978). It is a matter of not "I am my brother's keeper" but "I am my own keeper." Thus, an important public health task is to motivate as many as possible of the approximately 70% of the U.S. population (and other nationals, as will be shown later) who are presently low-active or nonactive (Table 31.1) to become more physically active. This should be done without overevangelizing the potential health benefits. In addition, the need for tremendous energy expenditures, an obvious requirement in marathon running, should be deemphasized, and the importance of moderate levels of enjoyable habitual exercise should be emphasized.

The focus of this chapter is on how to recruit healthy adults into enjoyable, moderate-intensity exercise and how to ensure their adherence to these habits. It is important to keep in mind that dropping out of an exercise program does not automatically mean dropping out of exercise (Oldridge, 1982). Individuals may simply be turned off by a particular program or may not be able to meet the scheduling demands; they may in fact join another program or continue to exercise on their own.

PHYSICAL ACTIVITY PATTERNS

Given the considerable social and cultural differences, physical activity pattern data from various countries are surprisingly consistent.

Surveys

Nonactive adults over 18 years (Table 31.1) made up approximately 41% of the U.S. population in 1978 (Harris, Note 2), 45% in 1973 (President's Council, Note 1), and 75% in 1961 (Harris, Note 2). The 1978 U.S. proportion is similar to the 1982 proportion for adult Canadians over 20 years reported to be nonactive (Canada Fitness Survey, Note 3). The continuing decrease in nonactive individuals appears to be promising, but it must be kept in perspective and contrasted with the disappointingly low 15% of the U.S. population that exercises at an energy level in excess of 1,500 kcal per week (Table 31.1). This 15% high-active proportion is approximated in general populations in such countries as Australia (Wankel, 1980), Canada (Jette, 1980), and Belgium (DeBacker, Kornitzer, Sobolski, Dramaix, Degre, de Marneffe, & Denolin,1981); the proportion is lower (approximately 3%) in Ireland (Hickey, Mulcahy, Bourk, Graham, & Wilson-Davis, 1975) and is considerably higher (approximately 40%) in specific populations such as Harvard alumni (Paffenbarger et al., 1978).

Exercise Program Follow-up

Clearly, the 15% high-active proportion of the U.S. population (and other nationals) can be classified as exercise diehards. The 16% moderate actives are probably going to continue exercising at that intensity on a regular basis, and some may be persuaded to increase the intensity of their exercise. What is the probability, however, of getting the 41% nonactives and 28% low-actives to initiate an exercise program and to become and remain regularly active at least at moderate intensities (1,000–1,500 kcal/week)?

In Australia (Sedgwick, Brotherhood, Harris-Davidson, Taplin, & Thomas, 1980), of 673 males aged 25 to 65 years who started a 12-week exercise program, 34% were still regularly active on retesting 4 to 6 years later. Assuming that 30% of those who were not retested were also active, then only 20% of the original 673 could be classified as active. In Finland, 28% of those retested 3 years after completing an 18-month program (Ilmarinen & Fardy, 1977) were classified as equally active, but 43% were less active. In the United States, adherence (defined as continued participation) was 80% at the end of a 15-week starter program, 61% a year later, and 25% at 5 years (Bjurstrom & Alexiou, 1978). In another U.S. study (Mann, Garrett, Farhi, Murray, & Billings, 1969), adherence dropped from 59% in the supervised 6-month program to 29% after 6 months of unsupervised exercise.

Summary

The data suggest that only 15% of the general U.S. population is high-active and that this is probably true in other countries. As much as 70% of the U.S. population may be categorized as low-active or nonactive, and the 41% U.S. nonactive figure is closely approximated in Canada. Moreover, studies show that less than 30% of those volunteering to engage in exercise programs continued to be active over a mean of 3.5 years.

RECRUITMENT

Characteristics of Volunteers

Recruitment is usually discussed as a minor aspect of most large studies of exercise, but identification of volunteer bias might give insight into strategies for motivating adults to exercise. One study of volunteer behavior stresses that exercise volunteers cannot be assumed to be representative of the general population (Remington, Taylor, & Buskirk, 1978).

In general, the recruitment of employees into exercise programs is not encouraging.

Approximately 30% or less of the potential population actually volunteer (Bjurstrom & Alexiou, 1978; Cox, Shephard, & Corey, 1981; Durbeck, Heinzelmann, Schechter, Haskell, Payne, Moxley, Nemiroff, Limoncelli, Arnoldi, & Fox, 1972; Faulkner & Stewart, 1978; Shephard, Morgan, Finncane, & Schimmelfing, 1980; Teraslinna, Partainen, Oja, & Koskela, 1970), with as many as 25% of these volunteers reporting themselves to be regularly active at the time of volunteering (Shephard et al., 1980). Reasons frequently given for nonparticipation include high work loads, travel problems, and conflicts between job and exercise program scheduling (Bjurstrom & Alexiou, 1978; Durbeck et al., 1972; Mann et al., 1969; Teraslinna, Partainen, Koskela, & Oja, 1969; Teraslinna et al., 1970).

There is some agreement that volunteers in employee exercise programs live or work near the exercise facility (Durbeck et al., 1972; Teraslinna et al., 1969, 1970) and that they tend to be white-collar workers (Durbeck et al., 1972; Cox et al., 1981; Faulkner & Stewart, 1978; Pollock, Foster, Salisbury, & Smith, 1982; Shephard et al., 1980), who have been reported to be much more likely to exercise than blue-collar workers (Alison & Coburn, Note 4). Volunteer behavior is not consistently associated with either activity status (Durbeck et al., 1972; Remington et al., 1978; Shephard et al., 1980; Terraslinna et al., 1969, 1970) or with smoking habits (Remington et al., 1978; Shephard et al., 1980; Terraslinna, et al., 1969, 1970).

Certain characteristics are associated with individuals who have patterns of activity that can be broadly defined as active or nonactive, but again, these people may not be typical of the general population. Large-scale surveys in the United States (Harris, Note 2) and in Canada (Canada Fitness Survey, Note 3), however, suggest that active individuals, both males and females, tend to be younger and to have higher incomes. They also tend to live in the suburbs (Harris, Note 2) and are most likely to be professionals/managers and to have completed at least a secondary school education, with those who have university degrees being the most active (Canada Fitness Survey, Note 3). The active individuals are also likely to be more confident in their outlook on life and themselves (Canada Fitness Survey, Note 3). The nonactives in the United States tend to be female, older, and with lower incomes (Harris, Note 2), whereas in Canada they tend to be older blue-collar workers, with lower incomes and with a low educational level—that is, elementary school or less (Canada Fitness Survey, Note 3).

Improving Recruitment Strategies

As in smoking cessation programs, the major problem with poor exercise adherence rates may stem from poor recruitment, marketing, and motivational strategies (Morgan, Note 5). Persons in higher social class and socioeconomic groups are more likely to be aware of and to make use of health care facilities and services (Morris, 1979). It may be that education—frequently a covariant of socioeconomic status—is the crucial factor in the utilization or nonutilization of services (Morris, 1979). Higher social class and socioeconomic status have been associated with more active exercise behaviors in North America (Harris, Note 2; Canada Fitness Survey, Note 3). An argument can be made that those in lower social classes and socioeconomic status groups participate in less recreational exercise because they may perceive themselves to be sufficiently active, they may believe that they lack control over time available for exercise or that exercise is frivolous, they may have less working flexibility, and they may generally perceive a lack of control over health threats. If we accept the value of regular recreation or sports activity, then the role of improved public education regarding exercise and good health cannot be overemphasized, particularly for those groups who have disproportionately low exercise rates.

In Canada, more than 75% of the population are aware of Participaction (Wankel, 1980), an independent nonprofit corporation that uses a light but provocative advertising and marketing approach to the promotion of increased physical activity and physical fitness (see Figure 31.1). Reported awareness in similar promotional programs was 90% in West

OK Canada
it's time to
pull up
your socks.

(If you can bend over that far.)

PARTICIPACTION
The Canadian movement for personal fitness

Fitness. In your heart you know it's right.

You can't get into
swimming if you can't
get into your
swimsuit.

PARTICIPACTION®

Figure 31.1 Slogans used by Participaction to market physical activity and physical fitness.

Germany and 79% in Australia (Wankel, 1980). The disappointing feature is that these programs have stimulated only a small number of people to become regularly active—10% in West Germany, 12% in Australia, and 17% in Canada (Wankel, 1980). These figures illustrate the discrepancy previously reported in a U.S. Public Health Service study (Taylor, Buskirk, & Remington, 1973) between initial attitudes to exercise and subsequent decreasing exercise behavior (Heinzelmann, 1973). This apparent short-term ineffectiveness can also be positively interpreted, however, in that there is often a slow take-off period followed by an exponential increase; 17% in the first 10 years of a promotional program may mean a further 35% in the next 5 years. Mass media efforts have had positive effects on cardiovascular health behaviors in communities receiving specific attention, particularly when the efforts are coordinated in such a way as to stimulate and attract people to programs of interpersonal instruction (Farquhar, Maccoby, Wood, Alexander, Breitrose, Brown, Haskell, McAlister, Meyer, Nash, & Stern, 1977). It may be that workplace-based exercise programs have the greatest potential for increasing participation in physical activity among adults (Task Force #3, 1981; Haskell & Blair, 1980), and the strategic use of newsletters, posters, and other media techniques may prove useful in drawing attention to exercise programs in the workplace and elsewhere (Farquhar et al., 1977; Faulkner & Stewart, 1978).

The limited data available on recruiting strategies in exercise programs suggest using small group discussion that includes the spouse in the proceedings (Heinzelmann, 1973) as well as small group discussion plus a fitness evaluation (Faulkner & Stewart, 1978). One consistent observation is that attitudes toward the health value of exercise do not have a major impact on participation in programs; rather, participation in the program has an impact on attitudes (Bjurstrom & Alexiou, 1978; Heinzelmann, 1973; Henizelmann & Bagley, 1970; Shephard et al., 1980; Wankel, 1980). It seems, therefore, that social marketing techniques may be successfully applied to exercise recruitment strategies. The focus of marketing health promotion—that is, exercise—is to emphasize the process whereby something of perceived value is attained by participating in one alternative rather than in another (see later discussion of research strategies). Given the opportunity for social interaction, fun, enjoyment, and increased fitness, particularly when supervised by good exercise leaders (Oldridge, 1977; Stoedefalke, 1973), the participant may eventually become aware of a number of physiological and behavioral changes, including an increased work capacity, greater efficiency in daily activities, a greater sense of stamina, less stress and tension, weight reduction, an improved job attitude and performance, and an increased level of physical activity outside the program. All these factors are associated with better health (Bjurstrom & Alexiou, 1978; Faulkner & Stewart, 1978; Heinzelmann, 1973; Heinzelmann & Bagley, 1970; Shephard et al., 1980; Wankel, 1980).

Summary

The task for the behavioral health professional is to find methods of persuading individuals who frequently are inactive, may be smokers, and may be blue-collar workers who are not convinced that exercise is of any value to them to become physically active. An emphasis on individualizing the exercise and making it enjoyable enough to compete successfully with alternative activities may be the key to success in motivating many of the nonactives to become active. This is a complex issue involving some knowledge of the prospective exerciser's expectations as well as the social and exercise background. This knowledge needs to be considered in the context of the motivational factors, which might include challenge, social approval, boredom, pleasure, or improved health. Only when individuals are motivated to begin exercise does the issue of adherence need to be considered.

ADHERENCE

If we accept that most adults are not strongly motivated to initiate an exercise program, what is the actual adherence rate in those who start exercising? There is considerable anecdotal evidence that adherence is high in community programs designed for healthy adults. Since dropouts are easily forgotten and adherers are easily remembered, however, anecdotal adherence evidence is considerably biased. Reported compliance rates in prescribed exercise programs for patients with coronary heart disease suggest that approximately 40% to 50% of those who enter programs drop out within 6 to 12 months (Oldridge, 1982). Available evidence for healthy adults in fitness programs that last at least 6 months is summarized in Table 31.2. The data suggest an adherence rate (also variously defined as compliance,

Table 31.2 Summary of Adherence in Adult Exercise Fitness Programs

Study Author	Eligible (n)	Start (n)	Active ÷ Start (%)	Duration	Active ÷ Eligible (%)
Mann et al. (1969)	136	105	59	6 months	46
		25	12[a]		
		80	76[b]		
Massie & Shephard (1971)	40	38	48[c]	7 months	45
	12	11	82[d]		75
Durbeck et al. (1972)	998	259	25	12 months	6
Oja et al. (1974)		89	86	18 months	
Taylor et al. (1973)		209	50	6 months	
Sime et al. (1976)		41	24	38 months	
Ilmarinen & Fardy (1977)	178	160	49	36 months	44
Pollock et al. (1977)		58	76[e]	20 weeks	
		69	65		
Bjurstorm & Alexiou (1978)	847	431	81	15 weeks	68 (male + female)
		288	78 (female)		
	847	431	66	12 months	52 (male + female)
		288	54 (female)		
		251	52	36 months	
		182	11 (female)		
		47	42	60 months	
		63	11 (female)		

Study				
Reid & Morgan (1979)		38	26	6 months
		74	32	
Owen et al. (1980)	441	248	81	120 months 45
Sedgwick et al. (1980)	673	339	34	60 months 17
Dishman & Ickes (1981)		66	65	20 weeks
Cox et al. (1981)	1125 (male + female)	161	37	6 months
		231	40 (female)	

Note: Studies are not strictly comparable because of differences in methodology of reporting adherence. Data pertain to males except where specified.
[a] Firemen
[b] Other subjects
[c] Individual program
[d] Group program
[e] Frequency/week controlled
[f] Duration/session controlled
[g] Physician consult only
[h] Physician consult plus health education program plus self-monitoring

retention, attendance, or participation rate) of approximately 50% to 60% (range = 13% to 87%) by 6 months, dropping to about 35% to 40% after 2 or more years (Bjurstrom & Alexiou, 1978; Cox et al., 1981; Dishman & Ickes, 1981; Dishman, Ickes, & Morgan, 1980; Durbeck et al., 1972; Ilmarinen & Fardy, 1977; Mann et al., 1969; Massie & Shephard, 1971; Oja, Teraslinna, Partainen, & Karava, 1974; Owen, Beard, Jackson, & Prior, 1980; Pollock, Gettman, Milesis, Bali, Durstine, & Johnson, 1977; Reid & Morgan, 1979; Sedgwick et al., 1980; Sime, Whipple, Stamler, & Berkson, 1976; Taylor et al., 1973; Wysocki, Hall, Iwata, & Riordan, 1978).

One possible approach to reducing this dropout rate in volunteers (a self-selected group in the first place) is to identify the potential dropouts so that individual intensive efforts can be made to persuade them to adhere. The limited data available on characteristics of the individual dropout are inconsistent, however, and prediction therefore becomes difficult (Dishman, 1982; Oldridge, 1982). A potentially more effective approach is to incorporate strategies designed to improve compliance on entry into the program as well as throughout the duration of the program (Martin & Dubbert, 1982; Oldridge, 1982). This approach has been the focus of recent investigations in clinical populations (Oldridge & Jones, 1983) and in healthy populations (Epstein, Wing, Thompson, & Griffin, 1980; Martin & Dubbert, 1982; Thompson & Wankel, 1980; Wankel & Thompson, 1977; Wysocki et al., 1978).

Characteristics of Dropouts

Recent reviews of exercise adherence in healthy and clinical populations by Dishman (1982), Martin and Dubbert (1982), and Oldridge (1982) have critically examined the phenomenon of dropping out. Information on the characteristics of healthy adult adherers in exercise programs is limited and inconsistent. The only consistent biological characteristic associated with subsequent dropout from adult fitness programs has been overweight (Dishman, 1981; Massie & Shephard, 1971; Owen et al., 1980; Pollock et al., 1982). When this is combined with self-motivation in a psychobiological model, Dishman and colleagues report 80% accuracy in predicting adherence or dropout (Dishman et al., 1980; Dishman & Ickes, 1981). Health beliefs at entry into a program apparently are not associated with subsequent exercise behavior (Dishman et al., 1980; Morgan, Note 5). Attitudes toward exercise, unless extreme (Dishman & Ickes, 1981), also are apparently not associated with adherence or dropout (Taylor et al., 1973; Morgan, Note 5).

Strategies to Improve Adherence

Behavior management strategies may be a considerably more viable approach to improving adherence than prediction and targeting of what appears to be a somewhat unpredictable dropout profile. Although various behavior management techniques have been successful in improving adherence in a number of situations (Epstein & Wing, 1979, 1980; Thoresen & Coates, 1976), dropouts will always occur. Even among Texas prison inmates there was a 25% dropout rate from an exercise program (Pollock et al., 1977)—presumably not because the inmates ran away.

Behavioral self-management clearly has exciting potential for modifying exercise behaviors. Self-management promotes self-motivation and self-responsibility and may ultimately result in achievement of the desired behavior. The intent of behavioral self-management is to increase self-control, which can be defined as "learnable cognitive processes used in generating controlling responses which in turn, alter factors modifying behavior over time" (Thoresen & Coates, 1976, p. 312). Behavioral self-management techniques that have been investigated in exercise studies include reinforcement, stimulus control, self-contracting and goal setting, and other cognitive techniques.

A small but steadily increasing body of knowledge in the behavioral medicine literature deals with exercise compliance in subjects with various conditions, such as coronary heart disease (Oldridge & Jones, 1983) and obesity (Epstein & Martin, 1977; Mullen & Culjat,

1980; Stalonas, Johnson, & Christ, 1978). In the behavioral health field, strategies designed to improve adherence to exercise programs have not been extensively investigated, but here, also, the number of studies is increasing. Martin and Dubbert (1982) have recently reviewed the topic of self-management in exercise promotion and adherence in behavioral medicine, with particular emphasis on recommendations for future research.

Strategies for improving adherence to exercise programs can be considered for use on entry into the program, during the program, and after completion or even dropout from the program. With respect to dropouts, it is important to bear in mind that dropout from one exercise program does not necessarily mean dropout from exercise per se (Oldridge, 1982).

Entry into a Program

Goal setting, whether in the form of an agreement or contract with a second party or as a self-contract, has been shown to have some success in altering exercise behavior. Martin and Dubbert (1982) suggest that the most effective goal-setting strategy for improving exercise adherence appears to be one that is flexible and self-set rather than instructor-fixed. Wanzel (1978), however, reported that 92% of the subjects did not achieve their goal and dropped out of the exercise program within 6 months; there was also a disappointingly high 60% dropout rate among those who had achieved their broad and nonspecific goals, such as improving general conditioning. When the goal is set up as an agreement or contract (Epstein & Wing, 1979; Thoresen & Coates, 1976), there is evidence that adherence is likely to be improved.

Wysocki et al. (1978) contracted with college students for achievement of aerobic points to earn back items of personal value; the strategy appeared to be successful in both short-term adherence (10 weeks) and long-term maintenance (1 year) of exercise habits. Contracting and lottery procedures have been used successfully by Epstein and colleagues (1980) to improve short-term exercise attendance among female college students. We have recently reported (Oldridge & Jones, 1983) that 80% of cardiac patients who did not sign an agreement to comply actually dropped out, whereas only 35% of those who signed the agreement dropped out. We now use the agreement strategy regularly in our rehabilitation program and have observed considerable improvement in compliance. This success tends to provide indirect support for the self-motivation component of Dishman's psychobiological model (Dishman et al., 1980) and also provides some substantiation for the observation that simply asking people about their expected health behavior may be the best single predictor of adherence (Haynes, Sackett, Gibson, Taylor, Hackett, Roberts, & Johnson, 1976). Reid and Morgan (1979) have reported that a health education program, in addition to a brief physician consultation and written directions, has significantly improved exercise adherence at 3 months but not at 6 months. This suggests that education efforts are short-lived and do not necessarily result in increased self-motivation.

One clear implication of the available data is that general and distant goals such as "to improve health" or "to feel better" do not have significant immediate motivational value. Realistic goals need to be set by the individual (with some direction from the exercise leader to keep the exercise intensity at an appropriate level), they need to be intermediate in time expectation (changes will not occur overnight, but do not set the goal for too distant a target), and they should be flexible. It is therefore important that the participant set short-term goals that are realistic and flexible, but specific. Experience also suggests that in addition to a public commitment, a time of day at which to exercise goal has a greater chance of long term success.

During the Program

Both social reinforcement in the program and the type of program chosen apparently have an effect on exercise adherence. Heinzelmann and Bagley (1970) reported that, whereas social aspects of exercise were unimportant factors on entry, the same factors were reported to be among the best-liked features at the end of the program and apparently had influenced the participants' adherence; furthermore, almost 90% of 195 respondents stated they preferred doing their exercise with a group. Massie and Shephard (1971) have reported an 82% adherence rate with a YMCA-type group program, as compared to a 47% adherence rate in an individual exercise group. The need for group participation is not universal, however; Perrin (1979) has reported that as many as 35% of the active exercisers surveyed prefer to exercise on their own. This highlights the need for a variety of alternatives within programs and at least some freedom to choose the preferred one. Martin and Dubbert (1982) have suggested that exercise packaging and individual tailoring may have a considerable impact on long-term motivation and adherence to exercise programs.

Cognitive, rather than behavioristic, strategies, have also been associated with increased adherence. Wankel and Thompson (1977), using a balance-sheet technique found by Hoyt and Janis (1975) to be effective in improving attendance, have shown that as a result of telephone conversations in which only positive outcomes were discussed, exercise behavior was enhanced among female health club members. Furthermore, Thompson and Wankel (1980) have shown that female health club members who were led to believe that their activity preferences were considered in their exercise program had higher adherence rates than control subjects in the same exercise program. The fact that even perceived choice had a significant positive effect on adherence suggests that further improvements in adherence are likely if it is possible to consider the participant's exercise preference.

The support of the spouse and family is important in maintaining exercise adherence in healthy populations (Bjurstrom & Alexiou, 1978; Mann et al., 1969; Taylor et al., 1973; Morgan, Note 5) and in cardiac patients (Andrew, Oldridge, Parker, Cunningham, Rechnitzer, Jones, Buck, Kavanagh, Shephard, Sutton, & McDonald, 1981). Inconvenience has been implicated in dropouts (Andrew et al., 1981; Bjurstrom & Alexiou, 1978; Martin et al., 1982), but a positive spouse and family attitude suggests a certain willingness to accept inconvenience, as well as providing moral and social support (Andrew et al., 1981; Epstein et al., 1980; Wankel, 1980). Spouses can be involved by including them in the recruitment process, the original assessment of the participant, the reassessment, and the educational and social programs.

Orthopedic injuries have been implicated in exercise dropouts, particularly early in the program and when the exercise intensity is too high (Franklin, 1978a; Mann et al., 1969; Pollock et al., 1977). In reviewing this aspect of exercise, Franklin (1978a) points out that the potential for injury is greatest in sprint-type activities and is further compounded by a high frequency of exercising. Therefore, careful control of exercise intensity and frequency should reduce this potential cause of dropout to a minimum.

Reinforcement is an important strategy for providing feedback to the participant about both the daily exercise sessions and long-term changes in such variables as weight and fitness. Martin and Dubbert (1982) have shown that adding a lottery to the reinforcement given during the exercise sessions does not provide any added incentive for increasing adherence. Perhaps the most important person in providing feedback is the exercise leader, who is the essential cog in maintaining adherence in any group program and in individual programs that are run from an exercise facility (Franklin, 1978b; Heinzelmann & Bagley, 1970; Oldridge, 1977; Stoedefalke, 1973; Taylor et al., 1973). The most important qualities for excellence in exercise leadership include knowledge, competence, an outgoing personality and ability to communicate and to be aware of individual needs and concerns (Franklin, 1978; Oldridge, 1977; Stoedefalke, 1973).

After the Program

Long-term commitment to the maintenance of exercise habits developed during supervised programs was discussed earlier in this chapter. The data are disappointing, with recidivism rates reported to be as high as 70% or more over 5 years. No data are available on strategies designed to help maintain regular exercise habits when the individual has left the program for one reason or another. Intuition suggests that follow-up procedures may be useful, at least for some people. An introduction to another exercise program or to individual exercises might be useful if the individual has to move. Invitations to have regular exercise testing, to join the social events put on by the exercise program, to return on a regular, infrequent basis, or to participate in fun-runs may prove to be of value in maintaining exercise habits if the individual has to give up the organized sessions. In cardiac rehabilitation programs, Kavanagh and Shephard (1980) have reported that although a personal activity prescription reinforced by one supervised session every 8 weeks proved to be safe, the therapeutic effectiveness—that is, gain in aerobic power—was doubtful. These investigators suggest that the group setting provides additional motivational stimuli to continue exercising. It may be that certain subgroups of healthy adults are more likely to become exercise diehards and are quite prepared to exercise on their own, whereas others will always need some degree of continued support to maintain regular exercise habits. There is evidence that people can be persuaded to change their daily activity habits by stimulus control (Brownell, Stunkand, & Albaum, 1980). Perhaps similar strategies can be used to help people maintain exercise habits that they developed while in supervised programs; this may be particularly useful in business and industry fitness programs.

The Potential Cost-Benefit Impact of Exercise Adherence

The potential benefits of exercise, generally presented as either physiological or behavioral, are summarized in Table 31.3. It is generally accepted that these benefits do not become apparent immediately upon entry into a program. To gain benefits requires a certain commitment to continued adherence, with increased habitual levels of physical activity. Furthermore, the level of exercise required need not be particularly intense, as evidenced by data from studies in Great Britain (Morris et al., 1980), the United States (Paffenbarger et al., 1978), Israel (Epstein et al., 1981), and elsewhere.

The physiological benefits are perhaps the best established—for example, increased strength, changes in blood lipids, reduction in heart rate at submaximal work loads, increasing oxygen utilization by the working muscles, increased functional capacity, and maximal oxygen consumption. The behavioral changes reported—such as enhanced confidence, prevention and alleviation of anxiety and depression, and increased sense of independence—

Table 31.3   Summary of Potential Benefits of Regular Exercise

Physiological benefits:
Increased physical work efficiency and capacity, associated with
1.   Improved cardiorespiratory performance
2.   Increased ability to deliver and utilize oxygen
3.   Other changes, including muscular, neurological, hormonal, metabolic, and hemodynamic functions

Behavioral benefits:
Enhanced independence, associated with
1.   Prevention or alleviation of anxiety and depression
2.   Improved confidence and self-esteem

Source: Adapted from A. H. A. Committee Report, Statement on Exercise, Subcommittee on Exercise/Cardiac Rehabilitation (Carlton, R. A., Chairman, Blomquist, C. G., Mitchell, J. H., Hartley, L. H., James, F., McHenry, P. L., Oliviero, M., Pollock, M. L., Selvester, R. H., Yauowitz, F. G., & Brinkley, S. B.). *Circulation,* 1981, **64,** 1327A–1329A.

are perhaps less well established, but this does not mean that they are any less important. In cardiac rehabilitation, practical experience and experimental evidence suggest that the behavioral benefits of group programs are as important as, for example, an increase in maximal oxygen consumption (Oldridge & Jones, 1983; Stern & Cleary, 1981). Although the physiological benefits, cardiorespiratory and muscular, are frequently extolled as the beneficial outcomes of adult fitness programs—probably because of the available experimental evidence—there should be a more concerted effort to emphasize the potential behavioral benefits, which in turn need more scientific validation. It is also conceivable that the mechanisms for these behavioral benefits may be physiological—for example, hormonal.

Of considerable interest is the introduction of adult fitness programs at the worksite (Eliot et al., 1981; Everett, 1979; Haskell & Blair, 1980; Shephard, in press), where employer-employee health promotion programs have been introduced in an attempt to improve cardiovascular health, to reduce the incidence and prevalence of cardiovascular disease, to increase productivity, to decrease absenteeism, and to reduce medical costs. Everett (1979) has suggested that the time and effort costs of physical fitness programs may exceed the economic benefits of such programs.

A recent series of articles (Cox, et al., 1981; Shephard, Corey, Renzland, & Cox, 1982; Shephard, Cox, & Corey, 1981) may challenge this concept of the value of employee fitness programs suggested by Everett (1979). The potential of employee exercise programs in reducing health care costs has been investigated in two life insurance companies—one as the experimental group, the other as the control group. Approximately 20% of the experimental company employees were enrolled in the program, but only about 45% were described as high adherents at 6 months. Employee absenteeism and turnover was lowest among the high adherents in the experimental company, with no reported difference in productivity between the two companies. Based on these data, the investigators have argued that there is a potential for a 1% reduction of company payroll costs from reduced turnover and absenteeism, given 20% employee participation in the program (Cox et al., 1981). Furthermore, the test company employees tended to have fewer hospital days and fewer medical claims after the exercise program had been instituted, and the investigators calculated that the health care savings would average $84.50 (Canadian) per employee per year (Shephard et al., 1982). Whether these savings were a specific consequence of the exercise program or resulted from some other factors, such as improved lifestyle or working conditions, is not known. Both the experimental and control populations showed a significant increase in physical fitness, although, as expected, the improvement was greatest in the high adherers, who were less than 10% of the company employees, a figure slightly less than that reported for high-actives in the general population (Table 31.1). Whether these observations can be replicated in other employee fitness settings requires continued investigation. Only then can the hypothesized economic benefit of a program regularly attended by 10% of the population be established.

From these and other reports (Bjurstrom & Alexiou, 1978; Durbeck et al., 1972; Heinzelmann, 1973; Linden, 1969; Owen et al., 1980), it appears that it may be worthwhile to consider incorporating an exercise program option into the basic health benefit scheme (Haskell & Blair, 1980). It appears, however, that in-house, on-work-time exercise programs for all employees probably do not result in economic benefits, despite the very large health costs incurred by many employers (Everett, 1979). It may be economically more feasible to provide health education programs as part of the basic employee benefit scheme and to provide access to facilities and to sports and exercise programs outside regular working hours (Everett, 1979; Haskell & Blair, 1980; Shephard et al., 1982). However the exercise package is developed, those employees who are most committed to regular physical activity habits appear to show the greatest gains in physical fitness and to have the lowest absenteeism and turnover rates, and these employees also appear to be regular exercisers in the first place—perhaps the "diehards"? Once again, the areas where the emphasis needs to be concentrated are (a) the development of techniques to promote the value of regular patterns of physical activity as a lifestyle and (b) the development of strategies to motivate people to consider exercising and to adhere to the new behaviors.

Summary

Much research is still needed in the attempt to improve adherence. The available data, both empirical and experimental, suggest that certain basic approaches will help to maintain, and perhaps increase, exercise adherence. As has been pointed out, some 15% of the American public are exercise diehards, who would probably continue to exercise despite almost any negative experience; another 15% are exercise moderates. Accepting the value of regular physical activity habits, therefore, it is the low-actives and the nonactives, approximately 70% of the population, who should be the major target of practicing and research-oriented health behavior professionals. To reduce this proportion of the population to a minimum, research should be directed toward developing various recruiting and adherence strategies.

RESEARCH IMPLICATIONS AND PRACTICAL APPLICATION

Recruitment

Canadian, West German, and Australian mass media promotional programs designed to improve physical activity patterns have reached a high proportion of their respective populations, but their persuasive power seems to be somewhat limited (Wankel, 1980). When appropriately designed, however, mass media education programs have had some success (Farquhar et al., 1977) and, when directed specifically at the targeted population, may result in increased awareness and utilization of a specific health behavior (Morris, 1979). The degree to which the nonactive and low-active proportion of the population responds is related to the degree of persuasion, which is in turn determined by the perceived value of exercise. If we accept the health benefits of exercise, the rationale for the degree of desirable persuasion obviously ranges from acceptable and valid—that is, exercise means better health—to nonacceptable and invalid—that is, exercise means running marathons.

Research

Motivational strategies to persuade nonactive and low-active healthy adults to exercise regularly have not been investigated extensively. There is an increasing awareness of the value of marketing concepts and strategies in providing more effective designs and delivery of exercise. The central concept in marketing is that the consumer must exchange something for the product (Brehony, 1979). The cost to the exercisers is their time, their convenience, or even their discomfort in exchange for the benefits—fitness, fun, and health. Questions such as the following need to be answered: What are we marketing—health, fitness, fun, competition, or satisfaction in overcoming obstacles? To whom are we marketing exercise—individuals, groups, or communities, the diehards or the low-actives and nonactives? When are we marketing exercise—in childhood or in adulthood? How are we marketing exercise? The last question may be the most important in terms of motivation and adherence-improving strategies once the question of what, who, and when have been answered. Determining the relative effectiveness of educational and informational measures, such as mass media promotion, newsletters, posters, signs, lectures, seminars, and demonstrations, further evaluation of their use as motivational tools by various agencies, such as employees, private enterprise, community agencies, the health care system, and the schools, colleges, and universities is needed. Adults participate voluntarily in exercise for a variety of real and imagined reasons. Appropriate strategies must be investigated in order to optimize the likelihood of exercise behavior in particular subgroups, including males/females, older/younger, competitive/noncompetitive, white-collar/blue-collar, and previously active/inactive.

Practical Application

The current state of the art suggests that the practitioner has some valid exercise recruitment strategies to consider. The objectives of an exercise program should be set by the exerciser and should be positive, clearly stated, and unambiguous; they should be immediate and specific (to run a mile today, to swim a length, to get fit for skiing, to have fun, to lose 3 pounds) rather than distant and general (to become healthier, to become fitter, to look better, to do better), although all the benefits may be health-related. Promotion of the program should utilize various mass media aspects but should emphasize intensive interpersonal instruction and counseling, with small group sessions and exercise testing. The promotional program should reinforce the opportunity for individualized attention, even in group programs, and the opportunity for spouse and family involvement in the exercise program or in associated social activities should be promoted.

The issue of motivating the nonactive and low-active 70% of the North American population to become regularly active precedes the issue of maintaining activity in those who have become active. This is not to say that the problem of persuasion to exercise supersedes the problem of maintenance of exercise; they are equally important, but motivation comes earlier. Before adherence can become a problem, people need to be motivated to start exercising.

Adherence

The data available on adherence to adult fitness programs show that the majority of people who start exercising will give up or will leave the program within 2 years. If we accept the concept that a lifestyle that includes regular exercise is beneficial to long-term well-being, then the adherence issue demands attention from health behavior professionals.

Research

Provision of information is not likely to lead to major changes in behavior; it may make individuals more supportive of exercise but it is not likely to get them more active or even to keep them active. There is a need to develop appropriate counseling strategies; although there appear to be certain subgroups who may need special counseling and others who do not, this needs substantiation. There is also a need to examine existing strategies designed to improve adherence and then to design other alternatives if necessary. Behavior management techniques have been used successfully, including stimulus control, reinforcement control, and self-control, but the temporal sequencing of different strategies and their appropriateness needs investigation. These strategies should be investigated and replicated in different subgroups, in particular settings, in combination, and alone. Subgroups and subgroup strategies need further definition; it may be that certain strategies will be more effective when applied to a particular individual or to a subgroup with peculiar demographies, lifestyles, or biological and psychological traits. Packaging of exercises that are suitable for individual tailoring may have much impact on long-term adherence; this, too, needs extensive investigation.

In many of the adherence studies, the definition of adherence is unclear; consequently, comparison of dropout rates in different studies is difficult. Dishman (1982) has suggested that the investigation of the adherence or dropout phenomenon has been largely atheoretical and unsystematic. Admittedly, in many studies the critical behavioral mechanisms cannot be assessed; nevertheless, the practitioner has been provided with data regarding the clinical practical effectiveness (or lack of it) of various strategies and a description of subgroups who appear likely to need special attention. Investigators have been and are testing models that include participant and setting characteristics with the evaluation of specific interventions (Dishman et al., 1980; Epstein et al., 1980; Martin & Dubbert, 1982; Oldridge & Jones,

1983; Shephard et al., 1980; Thompson & Wankel, 1980; Wankel & Thompson, 1977). Their findings are providing a more definitive understanding of the dropout phenomenon and should in the future identify the most appropriate intervention strategies for specific subgroups.

Practical Application

Health behavior professionals and exercise practitioners have evidence of the success of certain strategies in reducing dropouts and increasing adherence to exercise programs. Factors influencing adherence to exercise are different from those influencing recruitment. Adherence is likely to be affected by convenience of the exercise facility, scheduling and work conflicts, type and choice of activity, intensity of the exercise, the manner in which the goals are set up, the degree of social interaction generated, and the organization and leadership of the program. Characteristics of dropouts are not consistent, although overweight, smoking, and low self-motivation frequently have been associated with dropouts. Health beliefs do not appear to affect exercise behavior; rather, exercise behavior apparently is related to participants' improved attitudes about physical activity and about themselves.

Exercise programs should be designed with these factors in mind. Programs should meet the needs and interests of the participants; there should be flexibility in scheduling, but keeping the time consistent, and in choice of activity. Goals should be self-set (perhaps in conjunction with an exercise leader) rather than instructor-set, and they should be short-term rather than long-term, with a public statement of commitment or intent. There should be opportunity for group interaction and involvement of the spouse and family in family evenings or other social activities. In the same way, flexible planning should be considered to meet the needs and interests of loners. Reinforcement should be provided not only at regular intervals through exercise testing, but also regularly during each session; additional reinforcement can be provided by participation or achievement awards. The success or failure of an exercise program is primarily affected by the leadership, even when a variety of exercise types is available and when the facility is totally adequate. The exercise leader's ability to communicate, to inform, to assist, to motivate, to organize, to reinforce, and to be spontaneously creative in encouraging fun and enjoyment—in other words, to provide effective leadership—is essential for program success.

Finally, and perhaps most important, exercisers must take responsibility for their own exercise behaviors. No matter how well exercise programs are promoted, organized, and directed, intervention or management strategies will not make programs successful. The success of promotional programs in motivating people to become active ultimately depends on the central issue of self-responsibility—will I or won't I? The objective of adherence-improving strategies is to reduce the potential participation barriers to a minimum and to provide optimal opportunities to enhance adherence. An adequate awareness of access to the appropriate information and a sensible application of that information are necessary for the development of self-responsibility for exercise and health. Self-responsibility underlies adherence, and adherence to a regular exercise program optimizes the potential health benefits of exercise.

REFERENCE NOTES

1. President's Council on Physical Fitness and Sports. *National adult physical fitness survey.* Washington, D.C., 1973.
2. Harris, L., & Associates. *The Perrier Study: Fitness in America.* Vital and Health Statistics of the National Center on Health Statistics, 1978.
3. Canada Fitness Survey. *Canada's fitness.* Ottawa, 1982.
4. Alison, K., & Coburn, D. *Blue collar workers and physical activity.* Toronto: Fitness Ontario, 1981.

5. Morgan, W. P. Involvement in vigorous physical activity with special reference to adherence. In L. I. Gedvilas & M. E. Knees (Eds.), *National College of Physical Education proceedings.* Chicago: University of Illinois at Chicago, Office of Public Service, 1977.

REFERENCES

American College of Sports Medicine (ACSM). Position statement: The recommended quality and quantity of exercise for developing and maintaining fitness in healthy adults. *Medicine and Science in Sports,* 1978, **10,** vii-ix.

Andrew, G. M., Oldridge, N. B., Parker, J. O., Cunningham, D. S., Rechnitzer, P. A., Jones, N. L., Buck, Kavanagh, Shephard, Sutton, & McDonald. Reasons for dropout from exercise programs in post-coronary patients. *Medicine and Science in Sports and Exercise.* 1981, **13,** 164–168.

Aring, C. D. On improving public health. *Journal of the American Medical Association,* 1978, **239,** 2557–2558.

Bjurstrom, L. A., & Alexiou, N. G. A program of heart disease intervention for public employees. *Journal of Occupational Medicine,* 1978, **20,** 521–531.

Brehony, K. A. Marketing and behavioral medicine: A provocative marriage. *Behavioral Medicine Advances,* 1979, **2,** 9–10.

Brownell, K., Stunkard, A., & Albaum, J. Evaluation and modification of exercise patterns in the natural environment. *American Journal of Psychiatry,* 1980, **137,** 1540–1545.

Cox, M., Shephard, R. J., & Corey, P. Influence of an employee fitness programme upon fitness, productivity and absenteeism. *Ergonomics,* 1981, **24,** 795–806.

DeBacker, G., Kornitzer, M., Sobolski, J., Dramaix, M., Degre, S., deMarneffe, M., & Denolin, H. Physical activity and physical fitness levels of Belgian males aged 40–55 years. *Cardiology,* 1981, **67,** 110–128.

Dishman, R. K. Biologic influences on exercise adherence. *Research Quarterly for Exercise and Sport,* 1981, **52,** 143–159.

Dishman, R. K. Compliance/adherence in health-related exercise. *Health Psychology,* 1982, **1,** 237–267.

Dishman, R. K., & Ickes, W. Self-motivation and adherence to therapeutic exercise. *Journal of Behavioral Medicine,* 1981, **4,** 421–438.

Dishman, R. K., Ickes, W., & Morgan, W. P. Self-motivation and adherence to habitual physical activity. *Journal of Applied Social Psychology,* 1980, **2,** 115–132.

Durbeck, D. C., Heinzelmann, F., Schecter, J., Haskell, W. L., Payne, G., Moxley, R. T., Nemiroff, Limoncelli, Arnoldi, & Fox. The National Aeronautics and Space Administration–U.S. Public Health Service evaluation and enhancement program. *American Journal of Cardiology,* 1972, **30,** 784–790.

Epstein, L. H., & Martin, J. E. Compliance and side-effects of weight regulation groups. *Behavior Modification,* 1977, **1,** 551–558.

Epstein, L. H., & Wing, R. R. Behavioral contracting: Health behaviors. *Clinical Behavior Therapy Review,* 1979, **1,** 2–22.

Epstein, L. H., & Wing, R. R. Behavioral approaches to exercise habits and athletic performance. In J. Ferguson & C. B. Taylor (Eds.), *Advances in behavioral medicine.* Hollinswood, N.Y.: Spectrum, 1980.

Epstein, L. H., Wing, R. R., Thompson, J. K., & Griffin, W. Attendance and fitness in aerobics exercise: The effects of contract and lottery procedures. *Behavior Modification,* 1980, **4,** 465–479.

Epstein, Y., Keren, G., Udassin, R., & Shapiro, Y. Way of life as a determinant of physical fitness. *European Journal of Applied Physiology,* 1981, **47,** 1–5.

Everett, M. D. Strategies for increasing employees' level of exercise and physical fitness. *Journal of Occupational Medicine,* 1979, **21,** 463–467.

Farquhar, J. W., Maccoby, N., Wood, P. D., Alexander, J. K., Breitrose, H., Brown, B. W., Haskell, McAlister, Meyer, Nash, & Stern. Community education for cardiovascular health. *Lancet,* 1977, **2,** 1192–1195.

Faulkner, R. A., & Stewart, G. W. Exercise programmes—Recruitment/retention of participants. *Recreation Canada*, 1978, **36**, 21–27.

Franklin, B. Exercise testing and prescription. In H. K. Hellerstein & N. Wenger (Eds.), *Rehabilitation of the coronary patient*. New York: Wiley, 1978. (a)

Franklin, B. Motivating and educating adults to exercise. *Journal of Physical and Health Education and Recreation*, 1978, **49**, 13–17. (b)

Haskell, W. L., & Blair, S. N. The physical activity component of health promotion in occupational settings. *Public Health Reports*, 1980, **95**, 109–118.

Haynes, R. B., Sackett, D. L., Gibson, E. S., Taylor, D. W., Hackett, B. C., Roberts, R. S., & Johnson. Improvement of medication compliance in uncontrolled hypertension. *Lancet*, 1976, *i*, 1265–1268.

Heinzelmann, F. Social and psychological factors that influence effectiveness of exercise programs. In J. P. Naughton & H. K. Helenstein (Eds.), *Exercise testing and exercise training in coronary heart disease*. New York: Academic Press, 1973.

Heinzelmann, F., & Bagley, R. W. Response to physical activity programs and their effects on health behavior. *Public Health Reports*, 1970, **85**, 905–911.

Hickey, N., Mulcahy, R., Bourk, G. J., Graham, I., & Wilson-Davis, K. Study of coronary risk factors related to physical activity in 15,171 men. *British Medical Journal*, 1975, **3**, 507–509.

Hoyt, M. F., & Janis, I. L. Increased adherence to a stressful decision via a motivational balance-sheet procedure: A field experiment. *Journal of Personality and Social Psychology*, 1975, **31**, 833–839.

Ilmarinen, J., & Fardy, P. S. Physical activity intervention for males with high risk of coronary heart disease: A three-year follow-up. *Preventive Medicine*, 1977, **6**, 416–425.

Jette, M. The participation of Canadian employees in physical activity. *Canadian Journal of Public Health*, 1980, **71**, 109–111.

Kavanagh, T., & Shephard, R. J. Exercise for postcoronary patients: An assessment of infrequent supervision. *Archives of Physical Medicine and Rehabilitation*, 1980, **61**, 114–118.

Linden, V. Absence from work and physical fitness. *British Journal of Industrial Medicine*, 1969, **26**, 47–53.

Mann, G. V., Garrett, H. L., Farhi, A., Murray, H., & Billings, F. T. Exercise to prevent coronary heart disease. *American Journal of Medicine*, 1969, **46**, 12–27.

Martin, J. E., & Dubbert, P. M. Exercise applications and promotion in behavioral medicine: Current status and future directions. *Journal of Consulting and Clinical Psychology*, 1982, **50**, 1004–1017.

Massie, J. F., & Shephard, R. J. Physiological and psychological effects of training—A comparison of individual and gymnasium programs, with a characterization of the exercise "dropout." *Medicine and Science in Sports*, 1971, **3**, 110–117.

Matarazzo, J. D. Behavioral health and behavioral medicine: Frontiers for a new health psychology. *American Psychologist*, 1980, **35**, 807–817.

Morris, J. N. Social inequalities undiminished. *Lancet*, 1979, **1**, 87–90.

Morris, J. N., Everitt, M. G., Pollard, R., Chave, S. P. W., & Semmence, D. M. Vigorous exercise in leisure-time: Protection against coronary heart disease. *Lancet*, 1980, **2**, 1207–1210.

Mullen, P. D., & Culjat, D. Improving attendance in weight-control programs. *Health Education Quarterly*, 1980, **7**, 4–13.

Oja, P., Teraslinna, P., Partainen, T., & Karava, R. Feasibility of an 18 months' physical training program for middle-aged men and its effect on physical fitness. *American Journal of Public Health*, 1974, **64**, 459–465.

Oldridge, N. B. What to look for in an exercise class leader. *Physician and Sports Medicine*, 1977, **5**, 85–88.

Oldridge, N. B. Compliance and exercise in primary and secondary prevention of coronary heart disease: A review. *Preventive Medicine*, 1982, **11**, 56–70.

Oldridge, N. B., & Jones, N. L. Improving patient compliance in cardiac exercise rehabilitation: Effects of written agreement and self-monitoring. *Journal of Cardiac Rehabilitation*, 1983, **3**, 257–262.

Owen, C. A., Beard, E. F., Jackson, A. S., & Prior, B. W. Longitudinal evaluation of an exercise prescription intervention program with periodic ergometric testing: A ten-year appraisal. *Journal of Occupational Medicine*, 1980, **22**, 235–240.

Paffenbarger, R. S., Hale, W. E., Brand, R. J., & Hyde, R. T. Work-energy level, personal characteristics and fatal heart attack: A birth-control effect. *American Journal of Epidemiology*, 1977, **105**, 200–213.

Paffenbarger, R. S., Wing, D. L., & Hyde, R. T. Physical activity as an index of heart attack risk in college alumni. *American Journal of Epidemiology*, 1978, **108**, 161–175.

Perrin, B. Survey of physical activity in the Regional Municipality of Waterloo. *Recreation Research Review*, 1979, **6**, 48–52.

Pollock, M. L., Foster, C., Salisbury, R., & Smith, R. Effects of a YMCA starter fitness program. *Physician and Sports Medicine*, 1982, **10**, 89–91; 95–99; 101.

Pollock, M. L., Gettman, L. R., Milesis, C. A., Bali, M. D., Durstine, L., & Johnson, R. B. Effects of frequency and duration of training on attrition and incidence of injury. *Medicine and Science in Sports*, 1977, **9**, 31–36.

Rechnitzer, P. A., Cunningham, D. A., Andrew, G. M., Buck, C. W., Jones, N. L., Kavanagh, T., et al. Relationship of exercise to the recurrence rate of myocardial infarction in men—Ontario Exercise Heart Collaborative Study. *American Journal of Cardiology*, 1983, **51**, 65–69.

Reid, E. L., & Morgan, R. W. Exercise prescription: A clinical trial. *American Journal of Public Health*, 1979, **69**, 591–595.

Remington, R. D., Taylor, H. L., & Buskirk, E. R. A method of assessing volunteer bias and its application to a cardiovascular disease prevention programme involving physical activity. *Journal of Epidemiology and Community Health*, 1978, **32**, 250–255.

Sackett, D. L., & Snow, J. C. The magnitude of compliance and non-compliance. In R. B. Haynes, D. W. Taylor, & D. L. Sackett (Eds.), *Compliance in health care*, Baltimore: John's Hopkins University Press, 1979.

Sedgwick, A. W., Brotherhood, J. R., Harris-Davidson, A., Taplin, R. E., & Thomas, D. W. Long-term effects of physical training programme on risk factors for coronary heart disease in otherwise sedentary men. *British Medical Journal*, 1980, **2**, 7–10.

Shephard, R. J., Corey, P., Renzland, P., & Cox, M. The influence of an employee fitness and lifestyle modification upon medical care costs. *Canadian Journal of Public Health*, 1982, **73**, 259–263.

Shephard, R. J., Cox, M., & Corey, P. Fitness program participation: Its effect on worker performance. *Journal of Occupational Medicine*, 1981, **23**, 359–363.

Shephard, R. J., Morgan, P., Finncane, R., & Schimmelfing, L. Factors influencing recruitment to an occupational fitness program. *Journal of Occupational Medicine*, 1980, **22**, 389–398.

Sime, W. E., Whipple, I. T., Stamler, J., & Berkson, D. M. Effects of long-term (38 months) training on middle-aged sedentary men: Adherence and specificity of training. In *Proceedings of the International Congress of Physical Activity Sciences: Physical Activity and Human Well-Being*. Quebec City: CISAP, 1976.

Stalonas, P. M., Johnson, W. G., & Christ, M. Behavior modification for obesity: The evaluation of exercise, contingency management, and program adherence. *Journal of Consulting and Clinical Psychology*, 1978, **3**, 463–469.

Stern, M. J., & Cleary, P. National Exercise and Health Disease Project: Psychosocial changes observed during a low-level exercise program. *Archives of Internal Medicine*, 1981, **141**, 1463–1467.

Stoedefalke, K. G. Principles of conducting exercise programs. In J. P. Naughton & H. K. Hellerstein (Eds.), *Exercise testing and exercise training in coronary heart disease*. New York: Academic Press, 1973.

Task Force #3. The physician in the work setting (Elliot, R. S., chairman). *American Journal of Cardiology*, 1981, **47**, 751–766.

Taylor, H. L., Buskirk, E. R., & Remington, R. D. Exercise in controlled trials of the prevention of coronary heart disease. *Federation Proceedings*, 1973, **32**, 1623–1627.

Teraslinna, P., Partainen, T., Koskela, A., & Oja, P. Characteristics affecting willingness of executives to participate in an activity program aimed at coronary heart disease prevention. *Journal of Sports Medicine and Physical Fitness*, 1969, **9**, 224–229.

Teraslinna, P., Partainen, T., Oja, P., & Koskela, S. Some social characteristics and living habits associated with willingness to participate in a physical activity intervention study. *Journal of Sports Medicine and Physical Fitness*, 1970, **10**, 138–144.

Thompson, C. E., & Wankel, L. M. The effects of perceived anxiety choice upon frequency of exercise behavior. *Journal of Applied Social Psychology,* 1980, **10,** 436–443.

Thoresen, C. E., & Coates, T. J. Behavioral self-control: Some clinical concerns. In M. Hersen, R. M. Eisler, & P. M. Miller (Eds.), *Progress in behavior modification* (Vol. 2). New York: Academic Press, 1976.

Wankel, L. M. Involvement in vigorous physical activity: Considerations for enhancing self-motivation. In R. R. Danielson & K. F. Danielson (Eds.), *Fitness motivation.* Toronto: Orcol Publications, 1980.

Wankel, L. M., & Thompson, C. E. Motivating people to be physically active: Self-persuasion versus balanced-decision making. *Journal of Applied Social Psychology,* 1977, **7,** 332–340.

Wanzel, R. Toward preventing dropouts in industrial and other fitness programmes. *Recreation Canada,* 1978, **36,** 39–42.

Wysocki, T., Hall, G., Iwata, B., & Riordan, M. Behavioral management of exercise: Contracting for aerobic points. *Journal of Applied Behavioral Analysis,* 1978, **12,** 55–64.

CHAPTER 32

PSYCHOLOGICAL BENEFITS OF EXERCISE TRAINING IN THE HEALTHY INDIVIDUAL

WESLEY E. SIME

University of Nebraska–Lincoln

Much historical and empirical evidence suggests that physical exertion is associated with an enhanced state of mind. The ancient Greeks wrote of the relationship, *mens sana in corpore sano*—which translates "a healthy mind in a healthy body." Throughout this century, as mechanization has eliminated the inherent physical demands of the occupational and home environments, average population fitness levels have decreased dramatically. Concurrently, the incidence of documented anxiety and depression appears to have increased, although the greater availability of clinical treatment centers has probably inflated the number of reported cases. In contrast, there has been a dramatic upsurge of interest in this country in leisure activities, particularly such endurance activities as running. Because of this, there is a much wider variety of fitness levels in the adult population. With more sophisticated tools for psychological assessment and with the wide dispersion of activity levels, there have been numerous opportunities to document the association between exercise habits and psychological states. In addition, as individuals initially engage in exercise programs, it is possible to study changes within individuals (contrasted with nonexercising controls) resulting from their exercise programs.

More important, and more explicitly, the growing population of avid exercisers continues to report exaltingly positive cognitive experiences during and after exercise, including: feeling good, feeling very relaxed, elation, detached consciousness, improved quality of life, euphoria, and a sense of accomplishment, worth, and well-being. For some, these experiences are so intense that they result in an apparent need (referred to affectionately as an addiction) whenever the interval between exercise bouts is extended longer than a day or so. By contrast, some others who engage in vigorous activity find it to cause an allergic-like reaction, but fortunately these are rare cases. Ironically, it is apparent that the individuals who have the greatest need for exercise from a psychological, cardiovascular, or weight loss standpoint are the least likely to participate on their own initiative.

The psychological benefits associated with exercise are usually classified under the heading of mental health. The topics to be discussed herein include anxiety, depression, mood, temperament, self-concept, muscle tension, and emotional stress tolerance.

ANXIETY

Anxiety caused by real or imagined threats is characterized by high levels of sympathetic nervous system activity and numerous psychosomatic complaints, such as fear, nervousness, irritability, nausea, fatigue, headache, and muscular pain. The impact of even minor, subclinical symptoms is associated with decreased work effectiveness and absenteeism (Ganster, Mayes, Sime, & Tharp, 1982; Mackay & Cox, 1974) as well as increased health care costs and personal unhappiness (Petrich & Holmes, 1977).

State Anxiety versus Trait Anxiety

There is a distinction between state anxiety and trait anxiety that differentiates the immediate from the long-term experience of anxiety (Spielberger, Gorsuch, & Lushene, 1970). It is state anxiety that has been shown most convincingly to decrease in response to physical exercise. Another distinction must be made between the acute effects of a single bout of exercise, observed immediately postexercise, and the chronic effects of an extended program of exercise of moderate intensity (70% to 85% of maximum capacity), duration (20 to 60 minutes), and frequency (3 to 5 days/week) (Mihevic, 1982). Chronic effects must be observed in circumstances separate and distinct from the actual exercise session—that is, no less than 1 hour before and perhaps 4 to 8 hours after a daily exercise bout. By these standards, one study has shown a significant decrease in self-reported state anxiety and tension following 6 weeks of basic training (Kowal, Patton, & Vogel, 1978). These results, however, were significant only for the subpopulation of males, not for female participants. Another study on college students showed females to be less responsive than males to anxiety reduction following exercise (Wood, 1977). These results are particularly meaningful, since anxiety is more common among females than among males (Biaggio & Nielsen, 1976; Justice & McBee, 1978). Fortunately, the results from other more definitive studies have shown clearly that the psychological responses to exercise are similar among men and women (Dienstbier, Crabbe, Johnson, Thorland, Jorgensen, Sadar, & LaVelle, 1981; Wilson, Berger, & Bird, 1981; Young, 1979).

Cognitive versus Somatic Anxiety

In addition to the temporal aspects of anxiety, another contrast of characteristics for anxiety must be distinguished. There appears to be a dichotomous relationship among symptoms of anxiety into cognitive versus somatic processes (Schwartz, Davidson, & Goleman, 1978). Not surprisingly, it also appears that a 2×2 double dichotomy exists between predominant manifestations of anxiety (cognitive versus somatic) and sources of relief (physical exercise versus relaxation). Individuals involved in a program of vigorous exercise reported relatively less somatic and more cognitive anxiety than individuals involved in a program of mental training focused on relaxation (Davidson & Schwartz, 1976; Schwartz et al., 1978). Whether this relationship holds up in a prospective study with individuals reporting comparable levels of anxiety (cognitive versus somatic) who are also randomly assigned to exercise versus relaxation treatment groups is not yet known.

Some of the cognitive elements of anxiety include worry, lack of concentration, and insomnia, whereas the contrasted somatic elements include nervousness, tension, nausea, headache, palmar sweating, and rapid pulse rate at rest.

Effect of Exercise on Anxiety

The most recent review articles addressing the issue of exercise and anxiety have summarized a large body of evidence which strongly supports the notion that exercise of an appropriate level, duration and frequency has an anxiolytic effect (anxiety reducing) during the postexercise period lasting anywhere from 30 minutes to several hours (Berger, in press; Folkins & Sime, 1981; Mihevic, 1982; Morgan, 1981). The general consensus among all reviewers, however, is that the evidence (see Table 32.1) is suggestive but inconclusive because of methodological and design problems. Only one of the studies listed in Table 32.1 used a

Table 32.1 Effects of Physical Fitness Training on Affect

Study	Primary Focus	Subjects	Demonstrated Fitness Effects?	Psychological Measures and Tasks	Outcome
Brown et al. (1978, Phase 1)[a]	Depression	High school and university athletes	No (10 wks, jogging)	Zung Self-Rating Depression Scale	Improved
deVries (1968)[a]	Tension	Middle-aged males	Yes	Electromyogram	Improved
Folkins (1976)[a]	Moods	Middle-aged males at risk of CHD	Yes[b]	Multiple Affect Adjective Check List (MAACL)	Improved (anxiety)
Folkins et al. (1972)[a]	Personality, moods, work, sleep	College males and females	Yes[b]	MAACL, rating scales	Improved (females)
Hanson (1971)[c]	Anxiety	4-year-olds	No (10 wks, 30 min movement training, 5 × wk)	Holtzman Inkblot Test, teacher rating	Improved
Karbe (1966)[d]	Anxiety	College females	No (15 wks, 40 min swimming, 2 × wk)	Institute for Personality and Ability Testing (IPAT) Anxiety Scale, Swimming Anxiety and Fear Check List	Improved
Kowal et al. (1978)[a]	Moods, self-concept, personality	Male and female recruits	Yes[b] (males only)	Spielberger State–Trait Anxiety Inventory (STAI), Profile of Mood States, Eysenck Personality Inventory	Mood improved (males)
Lynch et al. (Note 2)[a]	Moods	Middle-aged males	No (university exercise class, jogging)	MAACL	Improved
McPherson et al. (1967)[a]	Moods	Postinfarct and normal adult males	No (24 wks, graduated exercise, 2 × wk)	Semantic differentials (moods)	Improved
Morgan et al. (1970)[a]	Depression	Adult males	No	Self-Rating Depression Scale	No change

Morris & Husman (1978)[a]	Well-being	College students	Yes	Pflaum Life Quality Inventory	Improved
Popejoy (1968)[a]	Anxiety	Adult females	No (20 wks, 4 × wk, fitness training)	IPAT Anxiety Scale, Neuroticism Scale Questionnaire	Improved
Tredway (Note 3)[d]	Moods	Older adults	No	STAI, Self-Rating Depression Scale, Mood State Inventory	Improved
Young (1979)[d]	Well-being, anxiety	Male and female adults	Yes[b]	Life Satisfaction and Health Rating Scales, MAACL	Improved

Source: Reprinted by permission from Folkins, C. H., & Sime, W. E. Physical fitness and mental health. *American Psychologist,* 1981, **36**, 373–389.

Note: CHD = coronary heart disease.

[a] Approximates nonequivalent control group quasi-experimental design, but random assignment assumption is not met; McPherson et al. (1967) used matching procedures.
[b] Cardiovascular fitness.
[c] Experimental design.
[d] Preexperimental design.

true experimental design, and it was conducted on 4-year-olds with no objective measure of fitness change concurrent with reduced anxiety. In the final analysis, it will be necessary to establish such concurrence in order to present a convincing argument for the anxiolytic effect of exercise. The scarcity of experimental research is perhaps not surprising, given the logistical problems in conducting a carefully designed experimental study with two elements, one so cumbersomely intrusive as exercise and the other so nebulous and elusive as anxiety.

Attempts to Improve Research Design in Exercise/Anxiety Studies

Three exercise/anxiety studies characterized by somewhat better experimental design have been reported recently. All have control groups, but none utilized random assignment to treatment. The first study was conducted on a group of 128 elderly females, 65 to 90 years of age (Reiter, 1981). Exercise participants reported significantly lower state anxiety, better sleep patterns, and less tension than a comparable group that participated in nonvigorous arts and crafts activities. Two other studies were conducted on a younger population (18 to 27 years) utilizing a variety of exercise modes. The first of these focused on running and an exercise class, in comparison with a control group that met socially for lunch at the same regular intervals (Wilson et al., 1981). The control group was notably higher in anxiety before treatment, illustrating the selection bias problem and the fact that those in greatest need are least likely to choose exercise voluntarily. Posttreatment anxiety levels were significantly lower for all groups, suggesting in this case that diversionary or social activities are effective and may account for some of the benefits of exercise programs. The most recent study on exercise and anxiety utilized a college swimming class (40 minutes, twice weekly for 14 weeks) for the experimental group and a lecture class (50 minutes, three times weekly for 14 weeks) for the control group (Berger & Owen, Note 1). The results showed that swimming produced significant decreases in tension, anxiety, depression, anger, and confusion as well as an increase in vigor. Although very little other research has dealt with swimming, the fact that it incorporates large muscle mass activity, usually with much vigor, seems to make its results comparable to the outcomes of numerous studies on running.

Morgan and Pollock (1977) analyzed the psychological characteristics of the elite distance runner. They concluded that the general affect of the elite runner was comparable to other athletes and clearly superior to the general population. Furthermore, since these runners were comparable to the general population, it was theorized that the distinct difference in positive affect was a consequence of exercise, not an antecedent (selection) factor.

Relationship of Exercise to Other Nondrug Anxiolytic Techniques

Anxiety is one of the basic symptoms of an emotional stress reaction in which both cognitive and somatic symptoms are manifest. Exercise is but one of many techniques aimed at controlling anxiety and other stress-related symptoms (see later sections of this chapter). A comparison of exercise with some of the other techniques in carefully controlled studies is of interest here. The importance of this comparison stems from the issue of cognitive versus somatic aspects of anxiety (Davidson & Schwartz, 1976). If these two aspects exist separately and distinctly in a large portion of the population, then exercise may deserve equal stature with other behavioral intervention (relaxation) strategies. In addition, studies comparing exercise and relaxation might provide further support for a causal relationship between exercise and anxiety reduction, rather than merely an associative relationship.

Comparison of Exercise and Relaxation Strategies

Remarkably few studies have focused on the comparison of exercise and relaxation. Studies by Morgan and colleagues have yielded the most detailed information. In the first of these

(Morgan, Horstman, Cymerman, & Stokes, 1979), a series of five substudies was conducted systematically to determine how variation in intensity and mode of exercise would affect level of anxiety during exercise and at various time intervals following exercise. Consummate results indicated that state anxiety rose significantly during bouts of exercise up to maximal aerobic power but dropped dramatically to levels lower than preexercise baseline within less than 5 minutes after terminating exercise and remained low for at least 20 to 30 minutes postexercise. The final aspect of this study was a comparison of a meditation procedure with a placebo treatment during the actual exercise bout. Whereas the control group exhibited typical exercise-induced anxiety, both the placebo and the meditation groups showed greatly reduced anxiety during exercise, indicating an ironic reciprocal effect—that is, that anxiety induced by exercise (ordinarily thought to be anxiolytic) can be controlled cognitively. Morgan and another colleague, Bahrke, extended this line of research with a different approach, this time comparing exercise and meditation as separate and distinct treatment procedures (Bahrke & Morgan, 1979). They observed highly significant decreases in anxiety with both vigorous exercise and meditation, confirming much of the empirical and clinical data that preceded their work. Surprisingly, however, the control group exhibited similar decreases in anxiety, indicating that mere diversional activity or a time-out effect might be equally as effective as other more active (somatic or cognitive) procedures. The important point is not that exercise failed to outdo the control anxiolytically but that the list of effective interventions is growing and that individuals who find exercise aversive might get therapeutic benefit from a seemingly forced time-out experience.

Effect of Exercise Combined with Cognitive Strategies

Two other studies have contrasted the effects of a combination of exercise and a cognitive strategy. Both have utilized an additional hybrid treatment group, consisting of both an exercise and a cognitive relaxation strategy, and have focused on subjects with a specific anxiety problem—test anxiety. Driscoll (1976) compared the effects of (a) exercise, (b) mental imagery (positive thinking), (c) combined imagery and exercise, and (d) a wait-list control group. Significant decreases in anxiety were observed for both the exercise and the imagery groups, but the combined exercise and imagery group had even greater reductions. The exercise component in this study was running in place, and anxiety was measured during simultaneous presentation of exercise and visual scenes of test-related activities. Contradictory results appeared in a parallel study by Sime (1977), in which test-anxious subjects took a final exam for a university course immediately after one of five experimental treatments. The treatments included (a) exercise on a treadmill for 12 minutes at a heart rate of 110 beats/min; (b) meditation and relaxation response, according to Benson (1975); (c) a combination of exercise and the relaxation response; (d) a placebo pill purported to be a tranquilizer; and (e) a control experience of sitting quietly. The results indicated that all three active intervention groups showed significant reductions in muscle tension, and state anxiety was reduced, though nonsignificantly.

Physiological Considerations in Exercise, Relaxation, and Anxiety

Recently, researchers and clinicians have recognized the practical potential of interaction between exercise and relaxation. Benson and colleagues have demonstrated remarkable cardiorespiratory changes when exercising subjects simultaneously invoke a relaxation response (Benson, Dryer, & Hartley, 1978; Cadarette, Hoffman, Kutz, Levin, Benson, & Goleman, 1982). In their initial research effort, oxygen consumption during a fixed-intensity bout of exercise was significantly reduced when experienced meditators were instructed to elicit a relaxation response during exercise (Benson et al., 1978). In a follow-up study with similar design, however, they found a significant decrease in respiration rate with a compensatory increase in tidal volume but no significant change in oxygen consumption (Cadarette et al., 1982). The difference between the two studies that probably accounts for this discrepancy is that the first study utilized only one group, which served as its own control. In the more recent study, which had better experimental conditions and separate treatment and control groups, the remarkable oxygen consumption results were negated.

In another unique approach, heart rate biofeedback was utilized in a treadmill training study (Goldstein, Ross, & Brady, 1977). After 5 weeks of training, the biofeedback group showed significantly lower heart rate and blood pressure than the control group, with both exercising at the same work load (2.5 mph, 6% grade). These results have great potential in exercise training studies with postinfarct patients, in whom cardiovascular efficiency is crucial.

Muscle Tension

In the search for physiological mechanisms to account for the anxiolytic effect of exercise, deVries (1968, 1981; deVries & Adams, 1972) has conducted a long series of studies documenting the fact that exercise decreases skeletal muscle (forearm) tension. With electromyographic measures of tension, deVries (1968; deVries & Adams, 1972) showed clearly that exercise of appropriate type, intensity, and duration can bring about a significant tranquilizer effect. More recently, deVries (1981) has corroborated those findings using two additional physiological measures—the Hoffman reflex activation and the spinal reflex activation level measured by mechanical stimulation of the Achilles tendon reflex. Parallel studies have produced mixed findings. Utilizing frontalis area electromyography as the criteria, one study found no significant decrease following exertion (Farmer, Olewine, Comer, Edwards, Coleman, Thomas, & Hanes, 1978). Sime (1977), however, utilized a procedure similar to that of deVries and found that relatively light-intensity exercise was sufficient to reduce tension. The studies by deVries (1968, 1981; deVries & Adams, 1972) did not report on state anxiety responses, and Sime (1977) did not observe significant reductions following exercise. It is quite possible that exercise of the low intensity discussed here is sufficient to reduce muscle tension but may not reach the threshold necessary to reduce anxiety.

Beta-Endorphins

The most exciting physiological research affecting the exercise/relaxation/anxiety question is that dealing with beta-endorphin levels. Recent evidence indicates that the wide variation in subjective perception of a standardized noxious stimulus (pain) is due, in part, to the level of endorphin in the bloodstream (Lewis, Cannon, & Liebeskind, 1980; Willer, Dehen, & Cambier, 1981). Extrapolation of these findings to exercise and more specific research with trained long distance runners yielded very interesting results. The level of beta-endorphins in the blood was clearly shown to be higher following exercise; furthermore, endorphin levels were linearly related to the intensity of the exercise (Colt, Wardlow, & Frantz, 1981). These results have been corroborated by another research team, which extended knowledge in this area another step. In a study with sedentary females, the acute effect of exercise was to increase endorphin levels; more important, 2 months of training (running and bicycle ergometer) for 1 hour per day, 6 days per week, at 85% of maximal capacity was shown to augment the acute effect of exercise (Carr, Buller, Skrinar, Arnold, Rosenblatt, Beitens, Martin, & McArthur, 1981). The classic method of confirming the role of beta-endorphins in pain control or stress analgesia is to demonstrate reversal of the effect with injection of the drug naloxone (known to deactivate endorphin) (Willer et al., 1981). Thus it seemed very appropriate when researchers used the same model in an exercise study. Markoff, Ryan, and Young (1982) injected naloxone (double-blind and counterbalanced to avoid order effects) after 1 hour of exercise in 16 subjects who served as their own controls. State anxiety and other measures of affect were recorded using the profile of mood states (McNair, Lorr, & Droppleman, 1971), but no actual measures of endorphin levels were obtained. Anxiety and other mood levels were significantly reduced following exercise, but there was no significant difference between control and naloxone conditions.

Markoff et al. (1982) argue that these results show that mood change is not endorphin-mediated. In analyzing their procedures closely, however, it is noted that they used only 0.8 mg of naloxone. In pain research, Willer et al. (1981) observed that low doses of naloxone (0.8 to 2.0 mg) do not have any effect in normal and relaxed subjects. Dosages of up to 20 mg have been utilized in the past. Thus, it is apparent that beta-endorphins may yet prove to be a strong mediating force in the composite physiological mechanism that accounts for the apparent anxiolytic effect of exercise. Furthermore, Appenzeller (1981) has noted that the presence of endorphin following very prolonged intense exercise (46 km mountain race) lasts at least 2 hours. These results are in keeping with the empirical observations of regular exercisers; that is, anxiety levels following exercise are decreased for 30 minutes to several hours, after which there is a progressive increase until the next bout of exercise.

Exercise Prescription for Anxiety Reduction

Berger (in press) suggests that "frequent and strenuous exercise is most effective in anxiety reduction." Interpreting this more specifically, it appears (a) that intensity must be sufficient to elicit sustained heavy breathing without going to exhaustion; (b) that duration should be at least 20 minutes and up to 1 to 2 hours, in accordance with individual tolerance and compensatory reduction of intensity; and (c) that frequency should be at least three times per week and more often as indicated by symptoms. Harper (in press) has projected additional recommendations based on clinical experience, including (a) choosing to exercise at midday or later, whenever peak anxiety levels occur; (b) exercising in an environment conducive to achieving some serenity and relaxation; and (c) maintaining moderate intensity of exercise, never pushing to maximum for extended periods, which would incur an exhausted state. These recommendations are based on clinical judgement and empirical wisdom; the authors do not report specific documentation of a titration process that yields such conclusions. Other research reviewed herein, however, lends support to these postulates. Morgan et al. (1979) demonstrated that maximal exercise produced an increase in anxiety rather than a decrease, at least during and immediately after exercise. At the other extreme, Sime (1977) showed that very light exercise at a heart rate of 110 beats/minute for 12 minutes was insufficient to reduce state anxiety, even though it was adequate to significantly reduce one of the somatic manifestations of anxiety—muscle tension. The general conclusion from deVries's research (1968, 1981; deVries & Adams, 1972) would suggest that light to moderate exercise was sufficient, although that research did not monitor state anxiety per se. Dienstbier et al. (1981), however, showed that both light (6 miles) and marathon distance runs resulted in decreased anxiety for women and men who were well trained for distance efforts. Obviously, the definition of light, moderate, and heavy work in each of the prescriptive criteria (intensity, duration, and frequency) will differ greatly among subjects in accordance with ability and training level. For the final statement on prescription for anxiety, it is advisable to consider incorporating a cognitive relaxation strategy during and/or after the exercise bout. The available research indicates it is effective in reducing both anxiety and its physiological concomitants during and after exercise (Bahrke & Morgan, 1979; Benson, 1975; Benson et al., 1978; Cadarette et al., 1982; Driscoll, 1976; Goldstein et al., 1977; Morgan et al., 1979; Sime, 1977). Specific techniques to achieve this paradoxical relaxed/exertional status range from a running meditation procedure as an adjunct to psychotherapy (Soloman & Bunpus, 1978) to an associative versus dissociative strategy characteristic of elite runners (Morgan & Pollock, 1977). Tibetan monks, who frequently run distances of 300 miles in less than 30 hours on rough terrain at very cold temperatures and high altitude, are known to repeat a mantra, keeping their respiration and pace in time with it (Broad, 1979). In consideration of this extraordinary phenomenon and of the laboratory research described here, Sime (1982) proposed a pace-assisted dissociation/association procedure that could be used by novice runners, who often have a tendency to overexert, causing respiratory discomfort and muscular strain. Synchronizing breath and stride frequency seems to modulate pace and effort toward a comfortable level and is also a diversionary tactic for the unavoidable aversive sensations in running.

DEPRESSION

Clinical depression is characterized by feelings of despair, sadness, hopelessness, low self-esteem, and pessimism, sometimes associated with a significant loss (Klerman, 1979). The range of symptoms extends from the very minor fatigue, irritability, indecisiveness, and social withdrawal to the most severe and ultimate expression of depression—suicide (Akiskal & McKinney, 1975). More women than men (two to six times more) suffer from depression (Penfold, 1981). This disproportionate burden upon women may be due to hormonal differences or to social influence, whereby women are generally more dependent and have a stronger need for approval (Scarf, 1979).

The role of exercise in the prevention or treatment of clinical depression is very viable because of its active nature, which provides side benefits in the form of enhanced body image (weight loss, increased strength and fitness), with an apparent increase in feelings of self-worth. These additional outcomes of exercise would seem to facilitate the antidepressant response, particularly among individuals who value strength, fitness, and weight control.

Effect of Exercise on Depression

Several recent review articles have summarized the research on the antidepressant effect of exercise (Berger, in press; Folkins & Sime, 1981; Mihevic, 1982). The most comprehensive of these reviews (Folkins & Sime, 1981) compared eight studies dealing with exercise and depression (see Table 32.1). All of these studies showed significant improvements in subjects' moods state, particularly when level of depression was higher than normal prior to training (Davidson & Schwartz, 1976; Folkins, 1976; Folkins, Lynch, & Gardner, 1972; Kowal et al., 1978; Morgan Roberts, Brand, & Feinerman, 1970; Lynch, Folkins, & Wilmore, Note 2; Tredway, Note 3). Only four of these, however, showed documented evidence of simultaneous increase in fitness level attendant to the antidepressant effect (Davidson & Schwartz, 1976; Folkins, 1976; Folkins et al., 1972; Kowal et al., 1978). Furthermore, as with the research on anxiety, the aforementioned studies are quite encouraging but are fraught with experimental design problems, thus precluding any definitive statement.

Attempts to Improve Research Design in Exercise/Depression Studies

More recent research since the cited reviews has yielded a series of studies with somewhat better experimental control (Blue, 1979; Buffore, 1980; Joesting, 1981a, 1981b; Wilson, Berger, & Bird, 1981; Wilson, Morley, & Bird, 1980; Rueter, & Harris, Note 4). Two of these studies showed that exercise therapy was an effective treatment for depression (Blue, 1979; Rueter & Harris, Note 4), particularly when used simultaneously with traditional psychotherapy (Rueter & Harris, Note 4). Experimental control was still lacking, but Joesting (1981a, 1981b) demonstrated in two cross-sectional studies that level of depression was lower in populations self-selected into vigorous activity. The studies involved runners versus sailors (Joesting, 1981a) and distance runners (Joesting, 1981b). These results are flawed, of course, by self-selecting bias. The counterarguments are that some depressed individuals seek out vigorous activity and, at the other extreme, that exercise may be considered one of a number of treatments, all of which are differentially effective among various subgroups. The results thus indicate a need for a more sensitive diagnostic process and a selective prescriptive process, assigning patients to therapy according to success-oriented criteria. Two other studies have provided data suggesting that the relative degree of distance/intensity and adherence is related to mood enhancement. Among three groups ranked according to intensity of exercise habits, there was a negative linear relationship between distance covered (versus a no-exercise control) and level of depression (Wilson et al., 1981). Similarly, compliance was clearly associated (negatively) with level of depression in a long-term follow-up study over 4 years in cardiac patients (Kavanagh, Shephard, Tuck, & Qureshi, 1977). One of the most likely reasons for a negative correlation between depression and extent of exercise in essentially correlational research is that one of the major symptoms or products of depression is a feeling of lassitude or even antipathy toward exercise of any sort.

Clinical Research on Exercise and Depression

The most well-controlled clinical treatment research regarding exercise and depression has been performed by Griest, Klein, Eischens, Faris, Gurman, and Morgan (1978, 1979). They conducted a series of studies utilizing clinically depressed patients who, most important, were randomly assigned to treatment groups. In the first and most dramatic phase, they observed that exercise was equally as effective in reducing depression as time-limited psychotherapy (Greist et al., 1978). Subsequent studies aimed at comparing exercise to meditation and group psychotherapy were less impressive because of methodological problems that disrupted compliance (Greist, 1981). The success that Griest continues to have with depressed patients is apparently due to the very slow, graduated exercise program. Apparently, it fosters a sense of mastery, a new, positive self-image, and perhaps some cathartic relief, while minimizing strain and injury that would hamper compliance, particularly among a patient population.

Although the clinical efficacy of antidepressant exercise awaits conclusive, definitive support, there is enough evidence of the association to pursue preventive strategies and to seek experimental data to support it. Brown, Ramirez, and Taub (1978) embarked upon a very large study regarding the effect of antidepressant exercise on a normal population. In a two-phase project, they worked with more than 600 students who self-selected an activity, varying according to aerobic work demands and according to frequency per week. Acknowledging the limitations associated with self-selection, it was still apparent that the reductions in depression were a function of intensity, duration, and frequency of exercise.

Psychophysiological Outcomes of Exercise That Account for Antidepressant Effect

Cortical Blood Flow

From a physiological or biochemical standpoint, there are several possible mechanisms to link exercise outcome with decreased depression. One practicing clinician in the field (Kostrubala, 1977) has suggested that increased blood flow and oxygenation might have a significant influence on the central nervous system, thus causing mood changes. Laboratory research supporting this hypothesis comes from Oleson (1971), who showed a regional increase in cerebral blood flow in the area of the motor cortex of the hemisphere contralateral to the isolated hand that was exercised.

Catecholamines (Epinephrine and Norepinephrine)

Another theory suggests that since exercise increases norepinephrine level (Howley, 1976) and since norepinephrine is known to be low in depressed persons (Schildkraut, 1965), perhaps it is the norepinephrine that accounts for the antidepressant effect of exercise. In contrast, however, those increased levels of catecholamines (norepinephrine and epinephrine) both at rest and during exercise are associated with higher levels of trait anxiety (Peronnet, Blier, Brisson, Ladoux, Volle, & deCarufel, 1982), particularly in persons with type A coronary-prone behavior patterns (Olewine, Thomas, Simpson, Ramsey, Clark, & Hames, 1981). Thus, high levels of both epinephrine and norepinephrine have been shown to correspond to elevations in both positive and negative emotions and moods, suggesting some support for those approaches to emotion that suggest the importance of the cognitive interpretation made by the individual in the context of arousal.

Self-Concept

Several researchers have suggested that it is the sense of mastery and self-control that leads many exercising patients out of their depression (Buffone, in press; Greist, et al., 1978). Improved body image and increased feelings of self-concept and self-worth would also play a major role in the prevention of depression (Folkins & Sime, 1981). Table 32.2 summarizes eight studies on self-concept. Six of these studies showed significant improvement, with concomitant increases in fitness level to substantiate the relationship. Distinctly different from anxiety and depression research, the studies on self-concept demonstrate much better experimental controls (presumably because they tend to focus on normal populations).

Subsequent to the review by Folkins and Sime (1981), two additional studies (both randomized and controlled) have come forth that show equally positive results. Collingwood (1972) showed significant increases in physical fitness, body attitude, and self-acceptance in a clinical rehabilitation setting after 4 weeks of training. Further self-concept research by Jasnoski, Holmes, Solomon, and Agular (1981) demonstrated increased fitness and self-perception following a 10-week aerobic exercise class with randomized assignment to treatment versus wait-list control. They failed, however, to show a correlation between fitness changes and perceptual changes. They concluded that group participation and expectancies played a major role in the elevated self-concept. Fortunately, exercise, by its very nature, carries a strong expectancy factor (more so than most other behavioral or drug interventions), which should be considered a complimentary aspect of the treatment. Self-concept has been treated as a factor that is somewhat related to depression, although it is generally considered to be a component of personality. Other dimensions of personality are reviewed in the next section.

Exercise Prescription for Control of Depression

The state of the art in exercise therapy has not advanced to the sophistication of prescribing specific exercises according to diagnostic criteria or narrowly defined psychological problems. Some basic guidelines do apply to depression, however, as indicated by the successes observed in some clinical programs. These guidelines are outlined in great detail by Eischens and Greist (in press) and Berger (in press).

Clinical Efficacy of Exercise Prescription for Depression

From the perspective of a very successful clinical practice and a clinical research program, Eischens and Greist (in press) make several recommendations. They suggest that the therapist provide a leadership program with a slow, progressively increasing exercise plan. Patients will have greater likelihood of symptom abatement when they (a) have developed a regularly scheduled routine, allowing much patience for results; (b) have a specific goal and intend to accomplish something other than just symptom relief while appreciating the process as much as or more than the outcome—that is, enjoyment; and (c) have developed a consciousness about physical and psychological responses, striving toward a feeling of self-mastery yet knowing when to use distractions and fantasies. They further suggest that the therapist will be more effective by (a) ensuring that treatment never does more harm than good—acknowledging that exercise, like many therapies, is a double-edged sword; (b) ensuring that the treatment is, in fact, appropriate for each patient—acknowledging the contraindications for exercise based on watchful concern for endogenous psychotic depressives as well

Table 32.2 Effects of Physical Fitness Training on Personality and Self-Concept

Study	Primary Focus	Subjects	Demonstrated Fitness Effects?	Psychological Measures and Tasks	Outcome
Personality					
Folkins et al. (1972)[a]	Personality (present adjustment)	College males and females	Yes	ACL (self-confidence and personal adjustment)	Improved (for females)
Ismail & Young (1973)[b]	Personality	Middle-aged males	Yes[c]	16PF	Some improved?
Ismail & Young (1977)[b]	Personality	Middle-aged males	Yes[c]	16PF, Eysenck Personality Inventory, MAACL (anxiety)	No change
Kowal et al. (1978)[a]	Moods, self-concept, personality	Male and female recruits	Yes[c] (males only)	STAI, Profile of Mood States, Eysenck Personality Inventory	Mood improved (males)
Mayo (1975)[a]	Personality	Seventh- and eighth-grade females	Yes[c]	Cattell Junior-Senior High School Questionnaire	No change
Naughton et al. (1968)[a]	Clinical scales	Postinfarct males	Yes[c]	MMPI	No change
Tillman (1965)[a]	Personality	High school males	Yes	16PF, Kuder Preference Record-Form C	No change
Werner & Gottheil (1966)[b]	Personality	College males	No (4-yr athletic program)	16PF	No change
Young & Ismail (1976)[b]	Personality	Middle-aged males	Yes[c]	16PF, Eysenck Personality Inventory, MAACL (anxiety)	Some improved
Self-Concept					
Bruya (1977)[a]	Self-concept	Fourth-graders	No (4 wks, 30 min movement session, 2 × wk)	Piers-Harris Children's Self Concept Scale	No change

Table 32.2 (*Continued*)

Study	Primary Focus	Subjects	Demonstrated Fitness Effects?	Psychological Measures and Tasks	Outcome
Collingwood (1972)[a]	Body and self attitudes	Adult male rehabilitation clients	Yes[c]	Body Attitude Scale, semantic differentials, Bills Index of Adjustment and Values	Improved
Collingwood & Willett (1971)[b]	Body and self attitudes	Obese male teenagers	Yes[c]	Same as Collingwood (1972)	Improved
Hanson & Nedde (1974)[b]	Self-concept	Adult females	Yes[c]	Tennessee Self-Concept Scale (TSCS)	Improved

Note: 16PF = Cattell's (1972) Sixteen Personality Factor Questionnaire; ACL = Adjective Check List; MAACL = Multiple Affect Adjective Check List; STAI = State–Trait Anxiety Inventory; MMPI = Minnesota Multiphasic Personality Inventory.

[a] Approximates nonequivalent control group quasi-experimental design, but random assignment assumption is not met; Mayo (1975) and Collingwood (1972) used matching procedures.

[b] Preexperimental design.

[c] Cardiovascular fitness.

[d] Quasi-experimental design (separate-sample pretest-posttest).

as patients with significant cardiovascular risk; and (c) ensuring that the dosage is correct at the outset and throughout a preplanned program of graduated exercise instruction.

Physiological Considerations in Exercise Prescription for Depression

Berger (in press) has reviewed a larger volume of research relevant to antidepressant exercise therapy. She recommends a prescription specifying a minimum of three times per week (frequency), 20 minutes per session (duration), at 70% to 85% of maximal aerobic capacity (intensity), which is typical of a standard aerobic exercise program for development of cardiovascular fitness. Brown et al. (1978), however, have shown that a frequency of five sessions per week is more effective than three sessions for reducing depression. Furthermore, regarding duration of exercise, 40 to 60 minutes per session has been shown to be more effective in reducing depression than 20 minutes (Carmack & Martens, 1979). At the other extreme, Dienstbier et al. (1981) have shown that a moderate intensity (distance of 6 miles) is more effective in reducing depression than a full marathon, even in well-trained runners. They also suggested that the exercise therapy should follow a scheduled routine that does not disrupt normal lifestyle, occupation, or domestic patterns. Further practical considerations put forth by Berger (in press) include having the patient (a) begin slowly and run with a companion; (b) select good quality running shoes, use short, comfortable leg stride, and avoid hard, uneven surfaces; (c) keep moving, even if fatigue precludes running and necessitates slow walking; (d) monitor intensity with the talk test (never exerting beyond capacity to maintain conversation if it is desired) and decrease subsequent session intensity or duration if recovery from a single exercise bout exceeds 1 hour; (e) keep a log of activity for motivation, for immediate reinforcement, and for chronicling progress; and (f) make a behavioral contract, with a substantial bonus for success and a meaningful penalty for failure.

Psychotherapy Combined with Exercise Therapy

The likelihood of success with antidepressant exercise therapy is greater if the therapist includes traditional counseling or psychotherapy during or in conjunction with exercise and if the therapist ensures that the patient always views the running experience in a positive light (Rueter & Harris, Note 4). Heaps (1978) showed that patients who ran with a faster confederate who made derogatory comments had lower self-acceptance and more negative feelings about their fitness and body functioning than patients who ran with a confederate who was complimentary regardless of the patient's actual fitness level. These findings seem obvious, but they have great importance in the overall success of a program. Dienstbier (1978) made some additional insightful comments, noting that novice runners need more extrinsic rewards at the outset of an exercise program. His observation was that novice runners do not experience the same immediate pleasures from running that habitual runners encounter. They might not experience mood elevation, stress reduction, peak experiences, and sense of accomplishment, for example, until after 2 to 3 months of exercise at progressively increasing duration and intensity. Thus, the novice runner must be instructed to notice the short-term pleasures (tension relief, scenic outdoors, and the like) and to anticipate the long-term benefits to be derived in the near future. Finally, the patient should be fully cognizant of the fact that exercise is a very aggressive, active therapy for depression and that it will lead to a feeling of self-responsibility.

Although much of the preceding discussion has dealt with clinical therapy, the principles are as appropriate for prevention as for treatment. In an era when prevention, wellness, and health promotion are emphasized, any treatment that shifts the burden of responsibility from the health care treatment institution back to the patient is commendable and worth the additional efforts needed to foster it.

OTHER PERSONALITY DIMENSIONS

Research relating physical activity to personality has been abundant and very encouraging, but few studies have had good experimental control. Folkins and Sime (1981) concluded that there was no consensus, primarily because most research has been either cross-sectional or quasi-experimental. Their review (see Table 2) shows that about as many studies found that exercise effected no change in personality as found improvements. Furthermore, of the nine reviewed studies, three were reports of identical data from a single population study (Ismail & Young, 1973, 1977; Young & Ismail, 1976). In contrast, however, Dienstbier (in press) reviewed the literature more recently and documented more support for the benefits of exercise. He acknowledged the weakness of many previous studies and listed several criteria that personality/exercise research should meet: (a) assessment of personality changes over time, with careful pretesting and posttesting; (b) adjustment for background factors that might confound the interpretation of results—that is, using matched control groups; (c) adjustment for changes in self-esteem, social contacts, and other lifestyle factors; and (d) control for expectancy effects—perhaps the most difficult problem. Dienstbier's (in press) review of five major studies utilizing Cattell's (1972) Sixteen Personality Factor (16PF) Questionnaire revealed a consistent observation that exercise was associated with more emotional stability, trust, liberalness, relaxation, self-sufficiency, and imaginativeness, as well as with less shyness and in some cases with less apprehension. These results are particularly remarkable given the fact that personality traits are often quite rigid and are not likely to change much over time or as a result of intervention.

One additional remark should be made about exercise and personality as related to other behavioral interventions. Large, Hartung, and Borland (1979) compared runners and meditators on the Cattell 16PF test, with surprising results. The meditators were significantly more assertive and enthusiastic than the runners. They were also less conscientious and controlled, as well as more experimenting and suspicious. Measurement of these dimensions before and after training in a controlled study could be quite enlightening with regard to the differential effectiveness of various behavioral strategies in treating or preventing depression.

EMOTIONAL STRESS RESPONSES

The underlying psychological benefit associated with exercise often is reflected secondarily in the adaptation to emotional stress. Many of the psychological manifestations discussed earlier are loosely grouped together among the stress-related disorders. If stress is defined in the traditional fight-or-flight terminology, then exercise is a classic method of stress management through its active, dynamic release of physiological preparedness. Numerous studies have documented the psychophysiological responses to stress, and particularly those that exercise tends to ameliorate. Specific physiological changes that respond to exercise include muscle tension (deVries, 1968, 1981; deVries & Adams, 1972; Sime, 1977), peripheral blood flow and galvanic skin response (Wilson et al., 1981), heart rate and blood pressure (Bell, 1977; Cantor, Zillman, & Day, 1978), and catecholamines (Peronnet, Cleroux, Perrault, Cousineau, deChamplain, & Nadeau, 1981).

PSYCHOLOGICAL INSTRUMENTS TO ASSESS ANXIETY, DEPRESSION, AND OTHER PERSONALITY VARIABLES

Personality

The Minnesota Multiphasic Personality Inventory (MMPI) is the most valid, reliable, and prominently utilized inventory for assessment of long-term stress on the personality structure of the patient (Hathaway & McKinley, 1967). Its chief drawback is its length (550 items).

Another measure of personality is the Sixteen Personality Factor (16PF) Questionnaire by Cattell (1972), which is considerably shorter (187 items).

Anxiety

Two useful measures of anxiety are (a) the Taylor (1953) Manifest Anxiety Scale (TAS), which measures the prevalence of anxiety in the patient, utilizing 50 items; and (b) the State–Trait Anxiety Inventory (STAI), which has 20 items for trait anxiety and another 20 items just for acute situational state anxiety (Spielberger et al., 1970).

Depression

Three psychological instruments commonly used to assess clinical depression are (a) the Zung (1965) Depression Scale, (b) the Depression Adjective Check List (Lubin, 1967), and (c) the Beck Depression Inventory (Beck, Ward, Mendelson, Mock, & Erbaugh, 1961).

There are also two subjective self-report measures of affect and mood. The first is the Multiple Affect Adjective Check List (MAACL) by Zuckerman and Lubin (1965), which is used to assess how the patient feels either at a given moment or in general. The other self-report measure is the Profile of Mood States by McNair et al. (1981), which is becoming widely used because it is relatively short. It provides an assessment of six mood states: tension–anxiety, depression–dejection, anger–hostility, vigor–activity, fatigue–inertia, and confusion–bewilderment.

CONCLUSION

Empirical and clinical evidence suggests that exercise produces a greatly improved state of mind. Hundreds of research studies have focused on some aspect of the psychological benefits of exercise. The largest portion of these studies have dealt with anxiety and depression. Other personality dimensions of interest include self-concept, emotional stability, and creativity. The problems inherent in providing experimental controls for exercise studies are almost overwhelming. It is nearly impossible, for example, to administer an exercise program so that it is either single-blind or double-blind. Furthermore, there is considerable popular opinion in favor of the benefits of exercise. Thus, the expectancy and demand characteristics associated with exercise intervention are extremely powerful and sometimes confounding. It is also obvious that individuals who volunteer for an exercise program vary in expectancy and response characteristics. Since exercise is always time-consuming and sometimes painfully uncomfortable, it is not programmatically feasible to assign subjects randomly to exercise or nonexercise regimes. With all these obstacles, it is not surprising that most research on exercise and mental health has usually violated traditional experimental controls. Given the logistical constraints, however, it appears that the available data, though mostly quasi-experimental, provide very strong support for an associative (not causative) relationship between exercise and an improved state of mind.

REFERENCE NOTES

1. Berger, B., & Owen, D. *The positive effects of swimming on mood: Swimmers really do feel better.* Paper presented at the Annual Conference of the North American Society for the Psychology of Sport and Physical Activity, University Park, Maryland, May 1982.
2. Lynch, S., Folkins, C. H., & Wilmore, J. H. *Relationship between three mood variables and physical exercise.* Unpublished manuscript, 1978.
3. Tredway, V. A. *Mood effects of exercise programs for older adults.* Paper presented at the meeting of the American Psychological Association, Toronto, August 1978.

4. Rueter, M., & Harris, D. *Effects of running on individuals who are clinically depressed.* Paper presented at the American Psychological Associates Convention, Montreal, September 1980.

REFERENCES

Akiskal, H. S., & McKinney, W. T. Overview of recent research in depression. *Archives of General Psychiatry,* 1975, **32,** 285–305.

Appenzeller, O. What makes us run. *New England Journal of Medicine,* 1981, **305,** 578–580.

Bahrke, M., & Morgan, W. Anxiety reduction following exercise and meditation. *American Corrective Therapy Journal,* 1979, **33,** 41–44.

Beck, A. T., Ward, C. H., Mendelson, M., Mock, J., & Erbaugh, J. An inventory for measuring depression. *Archives of General Psychiatry,* 1961, **4,** 561–571.

Bell, F. *The effect of exercise status on the response of selected biochemical physiological, emotional and task-related variables to noise in adult men.* Unpublished doctoral dissertation, Purdue University, 1977.

Benson, H. *The relaxation response.* New York: Avon, 1975.

Benson, H., Dryer, T., & Hartley, L. Decreased Vo_2 consumption during exercise with elicitation of the relaxation response. *Journal of Human Stress,* 1978, **4**(2), 28–42.

Berger, B. Running away from anxiety and depression: A female as well as male race. In M. Sachs & G. Buffone (Eds.), *Running as therapy: An integrated approach.* Lincoln: University of Nebraska Press, in press.

Biaggio, M. K., & Nielsen, E. C. Anxiety correlates of sex-role identity. *Journal of Clinical Psychology,* 1976, **32,** 619–623.

Blue, R. Aerobic running as a treatment for moderate depression. *Perceptual and Motor Skills,* 1979, **48,** 228.

Broad, W. Focus or fantasy: Techniques produce differing results. *Science Digest,* April 1979, 57–61.

Brown, R. S., Ramirez, D. E., & Taub, J. M. The prescription of exercise for depression. *Physician and Sports Medicine,* 1978, **6,** 34–49.

Bruya, L. D. Effect of selected movement skills on positive self-concept. *Perceptual and Motor Skills,* 1977, **45,** 252–254.

Buffone, G. Exercise as therapy: A closer look. *Journal of Counseling and Psychotherapy,* 1980, **3**(2), 101–115.

Buffone, G. Running and depression. In M. Sachs & G. Buffone (Eds.), *Running as therapy: An integrated approach.* Lincoln: University of Nebraska Press, in press.

Cadarette, B., Hoffman, J., Kutz, L., Levin, L., Benson, H., & Goleman, R. Effects of relaxation response on selected cardiorespiratory responses during physical exercise. *Medicine and Science in Sport and Exercise,* 1982, **14,** 17. (Abstract)

Cantor, J., Zillman, D., & Day, K. Relationship between cardiovascular fitness and physiological responses to films. *Perceptual and Motor Skills,* 1978, **46,** 1123–1130.

Carmack, M., & Martens, R. Measuring commitment to running: A survey of runners' attitudes and mental states. *Journal of Sport Psychology,* 1979, **1,** 25–42.

Carr, D., Buller, B., Skrinar, G., Arnold, M., Rosenblatt, M., Beitens, I., Martin, J., & McArthur, J. Physical conditioning facilitates the exercise-induced secretion of beta-endorphin and beta-lipotropin in women. *New England Journal of Medicine,* 1981, **305,** 560–563.

Cattell, R. *The Sixteen Personality Factor Questionnaire.* Champaign, Ill.: Institute for Personality and Ability Testing, 1972.

Collingwood, T. The effects of physical training upon behavior and self-attitudes. *Journal of Clinical Psychology,* 1972, **28,** 583–585.

Collingwood, T. R., & Willett, L. The effects of physical training upon self-concept and body attitudes. *Journal of Clinical Psychology,* 1971, **27,** 411–412.

Colt, E., Wardlow, S., & Frantz, A. The effect of running on plasma β-endorphin. *Life Sciences,* 1981, **28,** 1637–1640.

Davidson, F. J., & Schwartz, G. E. The psychobiology of relaxation and related states: A multi-process theory. In D. I. Mostofsky (Ed.), *Behavior control and modification of physiological activity.* Englewood Cliffs, N.J.: Prentice-Hall, 1976.

deVries, H. Immediate and long term effects of exercise upon resting muscle action potential level. *Journal of Sports Medicine and Physical Fitness,* 1968, **8,** 1–11.

deVries, H. Tranquilizer effect of exercise: A critical review. *American Journal of Physical Medicine,* 1981, **60,** 57–66.

deVries, H., & Adams, G. Electromyographic comparison of single doses of exercise and meprobamate as to effects on muscular relaxation. *American Journal of Physical Medicine,* 1972, **51,** 130–141.

Dienstbier, R. A. Running and personality change. *Today's Jogger,* 1978, **2,** 30–33; 48–49.

Dienstbier, R. The impact of exercise on personality. In M. Sachs & G. Buffone (Eds.), *Running as therapy: An integrated approach.* Lincoln: University of Nebraska Press, in press.

Dienstbier, R. A., Crabbe, J., Johnson, G. O., Thorland, W., Jorgensen, J. A., Sadar, M. M., & LaVelle, D. C. Exercise and stress tolerance. In M. Sachs & M. Sachs (Eds.), *Psychology of running.* Champaign, Ill.: Human Kinetics Publishers, 1981.

Driscoll, R. Anxiety reduction using physical exertion and positive images. *Psychological Record,* 1976, **26,** 89–94.

Eischens, R., & Greist, J. Beginning and continuing running: Steps to psychological well-being. In M. Sachs & G. Buffone (Eds.), *Running as therapy: An integrated approach.* Lincoln: University of Nebraska Press, in press.

Farmer, P. K., Olewine, D. A., Comer, D. W., Edwards, M. E., Coleman, T. M., Thomas, G., & Hanes, C. G. Frontalis muscle tension and occipital alpha production in young males with coronary prone (Type A) and coronary resistant (Type B) behavior patterns. *Medicine and Science in Sports,* 1978, **10,** 51.

Folkins, C. H. Effects of physical training on mood. *Journal of Clinical Psychology,* 1976, **32,** 385–388.

Folkins, C. H., Lynch, S., & Gardner, M. M. Psychological fitness as a function of physical fitness. *Archives of Physical Medicine and Rehabilitation,* 1972, **53,** 503–508.

Folkins, C., & Sime, W. Physical fitness training and mental health. *American Psychologist,* 1981, **36,** 373–389.

Ganster, D., Mayes, B., Sime, W., & Tharp, G. Managing organizational stress: A field experiment. *Journal of Applied Psychology,* 1982, **67,** 533–542.

Goldstein, D., Ross, R., & Brady, J. Biofeedback heart rate training during exercise. *Biofeedback and Self-Regulation,* 1977, **2,** 107–125.

Greist, J. H. Addendum to "Running through your mind." In M. Sacks & M. Sachs (Eds.), *Psychology of running.* Champaign, Ill.: Human Kinetics Publishers, 1981.

Greist, J. H., Klein, M. H., Eischens, R. R., Faris, J., Gurman, A. S., & Morgan, W. P. Running through your mind. *Journal of Psychosomatic Research,* 1978, **22,** 259–294.

Greist, J. H., Klein, M. H., Eischens, R. R., Faris, J., Gurman, A. S., & Morgan, W. P. Running as treatment for depression. *Comprehensive Psychiatry,* 1979, **20,** 41–54.

Hanson, D. S. The effect of a concentrated program in movement behavior on the affective behavior of four year old children at university elementary school (Doctoral dissertation, University of California, Los Angeles, 1970). *Dissertation Abstracts International,* 1971, **31,** 3319A. (University Microfilms No. 71–00629)

Hanson, J. S., & Nedde, W. H. Long term physical training effect in sedentary females. *Journal of Applied Physiology,* 1974, **37,** 112–116.

Harper, F. Jogotherapy: Jogging as psychotherapy. In M. Sachs & G. Buffone (Eds.), *Running as therapy: An integrated approach.* Lincoln: University of Nebraska Press, in press.

Hathaway, S., & McKinley, J. *Manual for the MMPI.* New York: The Psychological Corporation, 1967.

Heaps, R. Relating physical and psychological fitness: A psychological point of view. *Journal of Sports Medicine and Physical Fitness,* 1978, **18,** 399–408.

Howley, E. The effect of different intensities of exercise on the excretion of epinephrine and norepinephrine. *Medicine and Science in Sports,* 1976, **8,** 219–222.

Ismail, A. H., & Young, R. J. The effect of chronic exercise on the personality of middle-aged men by univariate and multivariate approaches. *Journal of Human Ergology*, 1973, **2**, 47–57.

Ismail, A. H., & Young, R. J. Effect of chronic exercise on the personality of adults. *Annals of the New York Academy of Sciences*, 1977, **301**, 958–969.

Jasnoski, M., Holmes, D., Solomon, S., & Agular, C. Exercise, changes in aerobic capacity and changes in self-perceptions: An experimental investigation. *Journal of Research in Personality*, 1981, **15**, 460–466.

Joesting, J. Comparison of personalities of athletes who sail with those who run. *Perceptual and Motor Skills*, 1981, **52**, 514. (a)

Joesting, J. Running and depression. *Perceptual and Motor Skills*, 1981, **52**, 442. (b)

Justice, B., & McBee, G. W. Sex differences in psychological distress and social functioning. *Psychological Reports*, 1978, **43**, 659–662.

Karbe, W. W. The relationship of general anxiety and specific anxiety concerning the learning of swimming (Doctoral dissertation, New York University, 1966). *Dissertation Abstracts*, 1966, **28**, 3489A. (University Microfilms No. 66–90459)

Kavanagh, T., Shephard, R. J., Tuck, J. A., & Qureshi, S. Depression following myocardial infarction: The effects of distance running. In P. Milvy (Ed.), *The marathon: Physiological, medical, epidemiological, and psychological studies. Annals of the New York Academy of Sciences*, 1977, **301**.

Klerman, G. L. The age of melancholy. *Psychology Today*, April 1979, 36–42; 88.

Kostrubala, T. Jogging and personality change. *Todays Jogger*, 1977, **1**(2), 14–15.

Kowal, D., Patton, J., & Vogel, J. Psychological states and aerobic fitness of male and female recruits before and after basic training. *Aviation, Space and Environmental Medicine*, 1978, **49**, 603–606.

Large, E., Hartung, G., & Borland, C. Runners and meditators: A comparison of personality profiles. *Journal of Personality Assessment*, 1979, **43**, 501–502.

Lewis, J., Cannon, J., & Liebeskind, J. Opioid and nonopioid mechanisms of stress analgesis. *Science*, 1980, **208**, 623–625.

Lubin, B. Manual for the Depression Adjective Check List. San Diego: Educational and Industrial Testing Service, 1967.

Mackay, C., & Cox, T. Stress at work. In T. Cox (Ed.), *Stress*. Baltimore: University Park Press, 1974.

Markoff, R., Ryan, P., & Young, T. Endorphins and mood changes in long-distance running. *Medicine and Science in Sports and Exercise*, 1982, **14**, 11–15.

Mayo, F. M. The effects of aerobics conditioning exercises on selected personality characteristics of seventh- and eighth-grade girls (Doctoral dissertation, North Texas State University, 1974). *Dissertation Abstracts International*, 1975, **35**, 4163A. (University Microfilms No. 75–00890)

McNair, D. M., Lorr, M., & Droppleman, L. F. *Profile of Mood States manual*. San Diego: Educational and Industrial Testing Service, 1971.

McPherson, B. D., Paivio, A., Yuhasz, M. S., Rechnitzer, R. A., Pickard, H. A., & Defcoe, N. B. Psychological effects of an exercise program for postinfarct and normal adult men. *Journal of Sports Medicine and Physical Fitness*, 1967, **7**, 95–102.

Mihevic, P. Anxiety, depression and exercise. *Quest*, 1982, **32**(2), 140–153.

Morgan, W. P. Alterations in anxiety following acute physical activity. In S. Fuenning, K. Rose, F. Strider, & W. Sime (Eds.), *Proceedings of the Research Seminar on Physical Fitness and Mental Health*. Lincoln: University of Nebraska Foundation, 1981.

Morgan, W., Horstman, D., Cymerman, A., & Stokes, A. Use of exercise as a relaxation technique. In G. Hendrix (Ed.), *Proceedings of the Second National Conference on Emotional Stress and Heart Disease. Journal of South Carolina Medical Association*, 1979, **75**(11), 596–601.

Morgan, W., & Pollock, M. Psychological characterization of the elite distance runner. In P. Milvy (Ed.), *The marathon: Physiological, medical, epidemiological, and psychological studies. Annals of the New York Academy of Sciences*, 1977, **301**.

Morgan, W., Roberts, J., Brand, F., & Feinerman, A. Psychological effect of chronic physical activity. *Medicine and Science in Sports*, 1970, **2**, 213–217.

Morris, A. F., & Husman, B. F. Life quality changes following an endurance conditioning program. *American Corrective Therapy Journal*, 1978, **32**, 3–6.

Naughton, J., Bruhn, J. G., & Lategola, M. T. Effects of physical training on physiologic and behavioral characteristics of cardiac patients. *Archives of Physical Medicine and Rehabilitation,* 1968, **49,** 131–137.

Oleson, J. Contralateral focal increase of cerebral blood flow in man during arm work. *Brain,* 1971, **94,** 635–646.

Olewine, D., Thomas, G., Simpson, M., Ramsey, F., Clark, F., & Hames, C. Exercise response of plasma and urinary catecholamines in young males with type A and B behavior patterns. *Medicine and Science in Sport and Exercise,* 1981, **13,** 80.

Penfold, S. General papers: Women and depression. *Canadian Journal of Psychiatry,* 1981, **26,** 24–31.

Peronnet, F., Blier, P., Brisson, G., Ladoux, M., Volle, M., & deCarufel, D. Relationship between trait anxiety and plasma catecholamine concentration at rest and during exercise. *Medicine and Science in Sport and Exercise,* 1982, **14,** 172–173.

Peronnet, F., Cleroux, J., Perrault, H., Cousineau, D., deChamplain, J., & Nadeau, R. Plasma norepinephrine response to exercise before and after training in humans. *Journal of Applied Physiology,* 1981, **51,** 812–815.

Petrich, J., & Holmes, T. H. Life changes and onset of illness. *Medical Clinics of North America,* 1977, **61,** 835–838.

Popejoy, D. I. The effects of a physical fitness program on selected psychological and physiological measures of anxiety (Doctoral dissertation, University of Illinois, 1967). *Dissertation Abstracts,* 1968, **29,** 4900A. (University Microfilms No. 68–08196)

Reiter, M. Effects of a physical exercise program on selected mood states in a group of women over age 65 (Doctoral dissertation, Columbia University, 1981). *Dissertation Abstracts International,* 1981, **42.** (University Microfilms No. 81–23283)

Scarf, M. The more sorrowful sex. *Psychology Today,* April 1979, 45–52; 89–90.

Schildkraut, J. The catecholamine hypothesis of affective disorders: A review of supporting evidence. *American Journal of Psychiatry,* 1965, **122,** 509–522.

Schwartz, G. E., Davidson, R. J., & Goleman, D. J. Patterning of cognitive and somatic processes in the self-regulation of anxiety: Effects of medication versus exercise. *Psychosomatic Medicine,* 1978, **40,** 321–328.

Sime, W. A comparison of exercise and meditation in reducing physiological response to stress. *Medicine and Science in Sport,* 1977, **9,** 55. (Abstract)

Sime, W. A new look at association/dissociation in long distance running. *Running Psychologist,* May 1982, 5–6.

Soloman, E., & Bunpus, A. Running meditation response: An adjunct to psychotherapy. *American Journal of Psychotherapy,* 1978, **32,** 583–592.

Spielberger, C. D., Gorsuch, R. L., & Lushene, R. *State–trait Anxiety Inventory manual.* Palo Alto: Consulting Psychologists Press, 1970.

Taylor, J. A scale for manifest anxiety. *Journal of Abnormal and Social Psychology,* 1953, **48,** 285–290.

Tillman, K. Relationship between physical fitness and selected personality traits. *Research Quarterly,* 1965, **36,** 483–489.

Werner, A. C., & Gottheil, E. Personality development and participation in college athletics. *Research Quarterly,* 1966, **37,** 126–131.

Willer, J., Dehen, H., & Cambier, J. Stress induced analgesia in humans: Endogenous opioids and naloxone reversible depression of pain reflexes. *Science,* 1981, **212,** 689–691.

Wilson, V. E., Berger, B. G., & Bird, E. I. Effects of running and of an exercise class on anxiety. *Perceptual and Motor Skills,* 1981, **53,** 472–474.

Wilson, V. E., Morley, N. C., & Bird, E. I. Mood profiles of marathon runners, joggers, and non-exercisers. *Perceptual and Motor Skills,* 1980, **50,** 117–118.

Wood, D. The relationship between state anxiety and acute physical activity. *American Corrective Therapy Journal,* 1977, **31,** 67–69.

Young, R. J. The effect of regular exercise on cognitive functioning and personality. *British Journal of Sports Medicine,* 1979, **13,** 110–117.

Young, R. J., & Ismail, A. H. Personality differences of adult men before and after a physical fitness program. *Research Quarterly,* 1976, **47,** 513–519.

Zuckerman, M., & Lubin, B. *Manual for the Multiple Affect Adjective Check List.* San Diego: Educational and Industrial Testing Service, 1965.

Zung, W. W. K. A self-rating depression scale. *Archives of General Psychiatry,* 1965, **11,** 63–70.

CHAPTER 33

EXERCISE AND DIET TO OPTIMIZE BODY COMPOSITION

ARTHUR WELTMAN

University of Colorado
Center for Sports Medicine and Health Fitness
St. Francis Medical Center
Peoria, Illinois

OBESITY

One of the most common health concerns among Americans today is body fat. The numerous fad diets and weight-reduction devices available are evidence of our widespread preoccupation with body fat. Each year, millions of individuals undertake weight loss programs for a variety of reasons.

Associated Medical Problems

It is well known that obesity is associated with a number of health problems (Angel, 1972; Angel & Roncari, 1978). These problems include impairment of cardiac function due to an increase in the work of the heart (Alexander & Peterson, 1972); left ventricular dysfunction (Alexander & Pettigrove, 1967; Gordon & Kannel, 1973); hypertension (Bachman, Freschuss, Hallberg, & Melcher, 1972; Chaing, Perlman, & Epstein, 1969; Stamler, Stamler, Riedlinger, Algera, & Roberts, 1978); diabetes (Stein & Hirsch, 1972; West, 1978); renal disease (Weisinger, Seeman, Herrera, Assal, Soeldner, & Gleason, 1974); gall bladder disease (Mabee, Meyer, DenBesten, & Mason, 1978; Rimm, Werner, Bernstein, & Van Yserloo, 1972); respiratory dysfunction (Burwell, Robin, Whaley, & Bickelmann, 1956); joint diseases and gout (Thorn, Wintrobe, Adams, Braunwald, Isselbacher, & Petersdorf, 1977); endometrial cancer (Blitzer, Blitzer, & Rimm, 1976); abnormal plasma lipid and lipoprotein concentrations (Matter, Weltman, & Stamford, 1980; Rossner & Hallberg, 1978; Weltman, 1983); problems in the administration of anesthetics during surgery (Warner & Garrett, 1968); and impairment of physical work capacity (Katch & McArdle, 1977). As a result, weight reduction is frequently advised by physicians for medical reasons. In addition, a vast number of individuals are on weight reduction programs for aesthetic reasons.

Incidence of Obesity

It is estimated that about 50 million men and 60 million women between the ages of 18 and 79 and 10 million teenagers are overly fat and need to reduce excess weight (Abraham & Johnson, 1980; McArdle, Katch, & Katch, 1981). We all have some fat, and we should; fat becomes a problem only when we have too much. But how much is too much? To have a better understanding of what is involved in a proper weight loss program, one must have some knowledge of the composition of the human body.

BODY COMPOSITION COMPONENTS

Two-Component System: Lean Weight and Fat Weight

The weight of the body can be viewed as a two-component system—lean weight and fat weight. Lean body weight includes the weight of bones, muscles, organs, body water, and other fat-free tissue. Fat is also divided into two components—essential fat and storage fat.

Essential Fat

Essential fat is fat that is thought to be essential for life and normal physiological functioning. It includes the fat in cell membranes and the fat stored in the marrow of the bones as well as in the heart, lungs, liver, kidneys, spleen, intestines, skeletal muscles, and central nervous system. In men, essential fat accounts for approximately 3% of the body weight (Behnke & Wilmore, 1974). In women, essential fat is higher—approximately 12% of the body weight. The difference between sexes is believed to be a result of the fact that although women have the same 3% essential fat as men, they also have an additional 9% essential fat, termed *sex-specific fat*. When prepubescent boys and girls are evaluated for percentage body fat, few differences exist. During the pubescent period, however, girls develop a layer of fat that boys do not. When one compartmentalizes this additional fat, it seems as though it is located in the mammary glands and in the pelvic region. As such, it has been suggested that this sex-specific fat is related to child-bearing and other hormone-related functions and is included as part of the essential fat component in women (McArdle et al., 1981).

Storage Fat

The other major fat deposit, the storage fat, consists of fat located in the adipose tissue. The storage fat includes the fatty tissues that protect the internal organs as well as the layer of subcutaneous fat located beneath the skin surface.

Whereas essential fat is believed to remain constant, storage fat has been shown to increase in humans with age. College-age males have approximately 15% body fat, 3% essential fat, and 12% storage fat, whereas college-age females have approximately 25% to 27% body fat, 12% essential fat, and 13% to 15% storage fat. Older men, however, carry approximately 22% of their body weight as fat, whereas the body fat level of older women is approximately 32% (McArdle et al., 1981). The most likely reasons for this increase in fat with age are a reduction in physical activity, an increase in caloric intake, and a reduction in basal metabolic rate. In addition, aging causes the skeleton to become demineralized, increasing body fat percentage at any given body weight because of a reduction in bone density. The observed increase in percentage body fat with aging, however, can be ascribed primarily to lifestyle, as studies have shown that older individuals involved in fitness programs have body fat levels that are significantly lower than their sedentary counterparts (Kasch & Wallace, 1976).

Assessing body fat is not as simple, however, as stepping on a scale. It is possible to be heavy—and even overweight, according to height-weight charts—without having too much fat. This is often the case in professional athletes, especially professional football players. Conversely, it is possible to be termed normal according to height-weight tables and still have too much fat. What matters is the percentage of the body weight that is fat.

TECHNIQUES FOR DETERMINING BODY FAT

Direct Measurement by Chemical Analysis

Direct measurement of body composition involves chemical analysis. This technique also provides the basis for many indirect techniques. Although this technique has been widely applied to various species of animals, it has had limited application in human cadavers. Such analyses are time-consuming and tedious, require specialized laboratory equipment, and involve ethical and legal problems in obtaining cadavers. The data from animal studies and human studies are clear, however, with respect to the fact that the weight of the dry, fat-free skeleton remains remarkably constant, even when large variations exist in the percentage of total body fat. Thus, the most variable component of the body is fat (Katch & McArdle, 1977; Pitts, 1963). The fact that the skeleton and the percentage of water in fat-free tissue remain constant in both lean and fat individuals, coupled with the fact that fat tissue and lean tissue have distinctly different density values, has allowed for the development of accurate mathematical equations to estimate the percentage of body fat from body density (Brozek, 1963; Garrett, 1968).

Indirect Techniques: Use of Body Density

The basis for many indirect techniques used to estimate body composition is the fact that fat tissue and nonfat tissue have different densities. Fat is less dense than water, so that fat floats; lean tissue is more dense than water, so that lean tissue sinks. If you view the body weight as a two-component system (lean weight or fat weight), then percentage of body fat can be estimated from body density. The basic equation for density for a two-component system is as follows:

$$D = \frac{F + L}{(F/f) + (L/l)}$$

where D = body density
F = fat component of the body
L = lean component of the body
f = density of fat tissue
l = density of lean tissue

Since the body is viewed as a two-component system and the whole system equals the sum of its parts, $F + L = 1$:

$$D = \frac{1}{(F/f) + (L/l)}$$

This equation can then be solved for F and written as follows:

$$F = \frac{1}{D} \times \frac{f \times l}{l - f} - \frac{f}{l - f}$$

Since the density of fat and lean tissue can be estimated from tissue extracted from the human body (Brozek, Grande, Anderson, & Keys, 1963; Siri, 1956), the equation can be solved for percentage body fat. The two most common equations are those of Brozek et al. (1963):

$$\text{Percentage body fat} = \frac{4.57}{\text{body density}} - 4.142 \times 100$$

and Siri (1956):

$$\text{Percentage fat} = \frac{4.95}{\text{body density}} - 4.50 \times 100.$$

These equations differ slightly because of different estimations of the densities of fat and lean tissue, but comparison of calculations of percentage fat using either equation shows less than a 1% difference.

Carefully conducted experiments with different species of animals (guinea pigs, cattle, sheep, and rats) have indicated a nearly perfect linear relationship between percentage body fat estimated from body density determination and percentage body fat measured by carcass chemical analysis (Garrett, 1968). Thus, the body density technique for percentage body fat determination has been widely applied in humans.

Body Density Determination in Humans

Density is defined as weight per unit volume. Weight can be determined easily and accurately by using a precision scale. Body volume is more difficult to measure. Furthermore, body volume must be measured accurately, because small variations in volume can affect the calculation of body density and the conversion from body density to percentage body fat. In the laboratory, body volume can be measured by water displacement or underwater weighing.

Water Displacement and Underwater Weighing Techniques

The volume of an object submerged in water can be measured by water displacement—the rise in the level of water within a calibrated body volume tank. With this technique, the subject enters a tank with a known volume of water. As the subject is submerged, the level of the water will rise. Since the initial level of the water and the dimensions of the tank are known, volume can be calculated from the rise in the water level.

The underwater weighing technique is the most common laboratory measurement of body volume in humans. This technique is based on a principle discovered by the Greek mathematician Archimedes. Archimedes discovered that the weight of an object in air minus its weight underwater is equal to the volume that the object displaces. Thus, the body volume is equal to the loss of weight in water with the appropriate temperature correction for the density of water.

With the underwater weighing technique, the subject's body weight is first determined in air on an accurately calibrated scale (beam balance scales are usually accurate to ±50 g). The subject is then weighed underwater. This requires a tank of water, an accurate scale (sensitive to ±10 g), and a lightweight chair system that is suspended from the scale. Often, a weight belt is necessary to insure that fatter subjects stay submerged during the underwater weighing procedure (the underwater weight of the belt and chair must be subtracted from the subject's total underwater weight score) (Katch, Michael, & Horvath, 1967).

With both the water displacement technique and the underwater weighing technique for the determination of body volume, the volume of air in the lungs must be calculated. Since air in the lungs tends to help keep one buoyant, it will register as fat on the scale. Therefore, unless the lung volume is accounted for, an overestimation of percentage body fat will result.

Most underwater weighing procedures involve weighing at the point of residual volume. This requires that the subject make a forced expiration as the head is lowered underwater. This procedure is usually repeated eight to twelve times, because subjects learn to expel more air from their lungs with each additional underwater weighing trial (Katch, 1969).

Usually, the average of the last two or three trials is used as an estimate of the true underwater weight score (Katch, 1969). With this technique, a correction must be made for residual lung volume.

Recently, the underwater weighing technique at residual volume (UWW-RV) was compared with underwater weighing at total lung capacity (UWW-TLC) (Weltman & Katch, 1981). With UWW-TLC, subjects take a maximal inspiration and submerge their heads underwater while holding their breath. This technique has two advantages: (a) it appears to be more comfortable for subjects than UWW-RV, and (b) since UWW-TLC does not have the same learning effect as UWW-RV, only three or four trials are necessary. Furthermore, the accuracy of estimation of body density of the two UWW techniques appears to be comparable (Weltman & Katch, 1981).

As mentioned, lung volumes must be corrected for in all body volume determinations. Vital capacity can be determined using standard pulmonary function techniques, and residual volume can be measured using an oxygen dilution technique (Wilmore, 1969). Total lung capacity equals vital capacity plus residual volume. The formula for calculating the density of the body (D_b) is as follows:

$$D_b = \frac{\text{mass}}{\text{volume}} = \frac{M_a}{(M_a - M_w)/D_w} - LV$$

where M_a = weight in air
M_w = the underwater weight score (corrected for tare weight)
D_w = the correction for water density at a given temperature
LV = lung volume (residual volume, total lung capacity)

Skin Fold Measurements

Although underwater weighing and water displacement are two of the most accurate methods of measurement of body density, they require laboratory facilities and sophisticated equipment. Since laboratory procedures are complicated, expensive, and beyond the reach of many people, alternative simple procedures have been devised for predicting percentage body fat. One of the most common simple predictive techniques is the measurement of skin folds.

The rationale for use of skin fold measurements to predict body fat is based on the fact that approximately half of the body's total fat content is located in fat deposits directly beneath the skin. Therefore, the more fat you can grasp when you pinch a fold of skin, the more likely it is that the person is fat. The procedure for measuring skin folds is to grasp a fold of skin between the thumb and forefinger. If this is done properly, the subcutaneous fat is pulled away from the underlying muscular tissue. The most common areas for taking skin fold measurements are at the triceps, subscapula, suprailliac, abdomen, and upper thigh.

Numerous regression equations have been devised to predict percentage body fat. Essentially, a scientist measures percentage body fat using a laboratory procedure such as underwater weighing and also takes a series of skin fold measurements. The skin fold measures are then used to predict percentage fat from underwater weighing, and an equation is developed.

There are problems, however, in predicting body fat from skin fold measurements. One problem is the skinfold measure itself. It takes practice to learn where the fat ends and where the muscle begins. If you pinch too hard, you will pinch muscle as well as fat and hence overestimate percentage body fat. If you do not pinch hard enough, you will not pinch all the fat, and an underestimation of percentage body fat will result.

A second problem is that the equations are population-specific. A given equation reflects the characteristics of the people on whom laboratory tests were used to derive the equation. The equation will not work well for a group of people with different characteristics; that is, equations for men will not work for women, equations for young individuals will not work for older individuals, and so on. Recent research has indicated that the accuracy of the use of skin fold measurements to predict body fat can range from very accurate (when a skilled evaluator uses the appropriate prediction equation) to a prediction error of ±200% in percentage body fat (when an unskilled evaluator uses an inappropriate prediction equation) (Katch & Katch, 1980).

Ideal Body Weight

Once an accurate determination of percentage body fat is made, the following equation can be used to estimate ideal body weight:

$$X = \frac{A - WY}{.85 - Y}$$

where X = number of pounds of body weight the person needs to lose
A = current pounds of body fat
W = present weight (pounds)
Y = desired percent body fat (decimal form).

This equation is based on the assumption that if a sound weight loss program is followed, approximately 85% of the weight loss will be fat and only 15% of the weight loss will be water and lean tissue.

Although any values for desired percentage fat can be used, it is suggested that 15% body fat for men and 24% body fat for women are reasonable values.

Considerations for Weight Loss

From the discussion of body composition, we see that health professionals must have two concerns when making weight loss recommendations for an individual: (a) that the ideal body weight be based on fat weight loss and favorable alterations in body composition rather than loss of body weight alone; and (b) to provide a patient with a good estimate of ideal body weight, that an accurate body composition assessment should be performed.

Once desired body composition and ideal body weight levels are determined, one must consider approaches to achieving these goals. The next section focuses on different approaches to weight loss and how they affect body composition.

WEIGHT LOSS AND BODY COMPOSITION CHANGES

This section will deal with desirable and undesirable weight loss programs.[1] Desirable weight loss programs are defined as those that are nutritionally sound and result in maximal losses in fat weight and minimal losses of fat-free tissue. Undesirable weight loss programs are defined as those that are not nutritionally sound, that result in large losses of fat-free tissue, that pose potential serious medical complications, and that cannot be followed for long-term weight maintenance.

Fasting and Severe Caloric Restriction

Since the early work of Keys, Brozek, Henschel, Mickelson, and Taylor (1950) and Bloom (1959), which indicated that marked reduction in caloric intake or fasting (starvation or

[1] This material was prepared in part by the author for the American College of Sports Medicine (ACSM) *Position Stand on Proper and Improper Weight Loss Programs.*

semistarvation) rapidly reduces body weight, numerous fasting, modified fasting, fad diet, and weight loss programs have emerged. Although such programs promise and generally cause rapid weight loss, they often are associated with significant medical risks.

The medical risks associated with these types of diet and weight loss programs are numerous. Blood glucose concentrations have been shown to be markedly reduced in obese subjects who undergo fasting (Bray, Davidson, & Drenick, 1972; Drenick, Swenseid, Blahd, & Tuttle, 1964; Rooth & Carlstrom, 1970; Stewart & Fleming, 1973). Furthermore, in obese, nondiabetic subjects, fasting may result in impairment of glucose tolerance (Beck, Koumans, Winterling, Stein, Daughaday, & Kipnis, 1964). Ketonuria begins within a few hours after fasting or low-carbohydrate diets are begun (Lawlor & Wells, 1969). Hyperuricemia is also common among subjects who fast to reduce body weight (Bray et al., 1972; Runcie & Thomson, 1969). Fasting results in high serum uric acid levels, with decreased urinary output (Murphy & Shipman, 1963). Fasting and very low caloric diets also result in urinary nitrogen loss and a significant decrease in lean tissue (Ball, Canary, & Kyle, 1967; Benoit, Martin, & Watten, 1965; Grande, 1968; Yang & Van Itallie, 1976). In comparison to ingestion of a normal diet, fasting substantially elevates urinary excretion of potassium (Drenick et al., 1964; Grande, 1968; Lawlor & Wells, 1969; Runcie & Thomson, 1970). This, coupled with the aforementioned nitrogen loss, suggests that the potassium loss is due to loss of lean tissue (Runcie & Thomson, 1970). Other electrolytes, including sodium (Drenick et al., 1964; Lawlor & Wells, 1969), calcium (Drenick, Hunt, & Swenseid, 1969; Stewart & Fleming, 1973), magnesium (Drenick et al., 1969; Stewart & Fleming, 1973), and phosphate (Stewart & Fleming, 1973), have been shown to be elevated in the urine during prolonged fasting. Reductions in blood volume and body fluids are also common with fasting and fad diets (Bray et al., 1972) and can be associated with weakness and fainting (Drenick et al., 1964). Congestive heart failure and sudden death have also been reported in fasting subjects (Kahan, 1968; Sours, Frattali, Brand, Feldman, Forbes, Swanson, & Paris, 1981; Spencer, 1968) or during marked caloric restriction (Sours et al., 1981). Myocardial atrophy appears to contribute to sudden death (Sours et al., 1981). Sudden death may also occur during refeeding (Sours et al., 1981). Untreated fasting has also been reported to reduce serum iron-binding capacity, resulting in anemia (Jagenburg & Svanborg, 1968; Rooth & Carlstrom, 1970; Thomson, Runcie, & Miller, 1966). Liver glycogen levels are depleted with fasting (Garrow, 1974; Nilsson & Hultman, 1973; Oyama, Thomas, & Grant, 1963), and liver function (Drenick, 1968; Drenick, Simmons, & Murphy, 1970; Garnett, Barnard, Ford, Goodbody, & Woodehouse, 1969; Rozental, Biava, Spencer, & Zimmerman, 1967; Verdy, 1966) as well as gastrointestinal tract abnormalities (Billich, Bray, Gallagher, Hoffbrand, & Levitan, 1972; Drenick et al., 1964; Lawlor & Wells, 1969; Pitman, 1966; Stewart, Pollock, Hoffbrand, Mollin, & Booth, 1967) are associated with fasting. Although fasting and calorically restricted diets have been shown to lower serum cholesterol levels, a large portion of the cholesterol reduction is a result of lowered HDL-cholesterol levels (Thompson, Jeffrey, Wing, & Wood, 1979; Weltman, Matter, & Stamford, 1980). Other risks associated with fasting and very low calorie diets include lactic acidosis (Berger, 1967; Cubberly, Polster, & Schulman, 1965), hair loss (Rooth & Carlstrom, 1970), hypoalonemia (Felig, Owen, Wahren, & Cahill, 1969), edema (Collison, 1967; Runcie & Thomson, 1970), anuria (Yang & Van Itallie, 1976), hypotension (Bray et al., 1972; Drenick et al., 1970; Runcie & Thomson, 1970), elevated serum bilirubin (Barrett, 1971a, 1971b), nausea and vomiting (Lawlor & Wells, 1969), alterations in thyroxine metabolism (Portnay, O'Brian, Bush, Vagenakis, Azizi, Arky, Ingbar, & Braverman, 1974; Vagenakis, Burger, Portnay, Rudolph, O'Brian, Azizi, Arky, Nicod, Ingbar, & Braverman, 1975), impaired serum triglyceride removal and production (Streja, Marliss, & Steiner, 1977), and death (Garnett et al., 1969; Kahan, 1963; Norbury, 1964; Sours et al., 1981; Spencer, 1968).

The major objective of any weight reduction program is to lose body fat while maintaining lean tissue. The vast majority of research in the area reveals that starvation and low-calorie diets result in large losses of water, electrolytes, and lean tissue. One of the best controlled experiments in this area was conducted from 1944 to 1946 at the Laboratory of Physiological

Hygiene at the University of Minnesota (Keys et al., 1950). In this study, subjects had their baseline caloric intake cut by 45% and body weight and body composition changes were followed for 24 weeks. During the first 12 weeks of semistarvation, body weight declined by 25.4 lbs (11.5 kg), with only an 11.6 lb (5.3 kg) decline in body fat. During the second 12-week period, body weight declined an additional 9.1 lbs (4.1 kg), with only a 6.1 lb (2.8 kg) decrease in body fat. These data clearly demonstrate that lean tissue and water significantly contribute to weight loss from semistarvation. Similar results have been reported by several other investigators. Buskirk, Thompson, Lutwak, and Whedon (1963) reported that the 13.5 kg weight loss in six subjects on a low-calorie mixed diet averaged 76% fat and 24% water and lean tissue. Passmore, Strong, and Ritchie (1958) reported similar results of 78% weight loss (15.3 kg) as fat and 22% as water and lean tissue in seven women who consumed a 400 kcal/day diet for 45 days. Yang and Van Itallie (1976) followed weight loss and body composition changes for the first 5 days of a weight loss program with subjects either consuming an 800 kcal mixed diet or an 800 kcal ketogenic diet or undergoing starvation. On the mixed diet, subjects lost 1.3 kg of weight (59% fat loss, 3.4% protein loss, 37.6% water loss); on the ketogenic diet, subjects lost 2.3 kg of weight (33.2% fat, 3.8% protein, 63% water); and on starvation, subjects lost 3.8 kg of weight (32.3% fat, 6.5% protein, 61.2% water). Grande (1961) and Grande, Taylor, Anderson, Buskirk, and Keys (1958) reported similar findings with a 1000 kcal carbohydrate diet. It was further reported that water restriction combined with 1000 kcal/day of carbohydrate resulted in greater water loss and less fat loss.

Recently, there has been renewed speculation about the efficacy of the very low calorie diet (VLCD). Krotkiewski, Toss, Bjorntorp, and Holm (1981) studied the effects on body weight and body composition of 3 weeks on the so-called Cambridge diet. Two groups of middle-aged women were studied. One group had a VLCD only, while the second group had a VLCD combined with a 55 min/day, 3-day/week exercise program. The VLCD-only group lost 6.2 kg in 3 weeks, of which only 2.6 kg was fat loss, whereas the VLCD-plus-exercise group lost 6.8 kg in 3 weeks, with only a 1.8 kg body fat loss. Thus, it can be seen that VLCD results in undesirable losses of body weight and that the addition to VLCD of the normally protective effect of chronic exercise does not reduce the catabolism of fat-free tissue. Furthermore, with VLCD, a large and unfavorable reduction (29%) in HDL-cholesterol is also seen (Wechsler, Hutt, Wenzel, Klor, & Ditschuneit, 1981).

Thus, it can be seen that both fasting and severe caloric restriction fall under the category of undesirable weight loss programs.

Caloric Restriction

Even mild caloric restriction (reduction of 500–1000 kcal/day from baseline caloric intake), when used alone as a tool for weight loss, results in the loss of moderate amounts of water and lean tissue. In a study by Goldman, Bullen, and Seltzer (1963), 15 female subjects consumed a low-calorie mixed diet for 7 to 8 weeks. Weight loss during this period averaged 6.43 kg (0.85 kg per week), with 88.6% of the weight loss as fat. The remaining 11.4% represented water and lean tissue. Zuti and Golding (1976) examined the effect of 500 kcal/day caloric restriction on body composition changes in adult females. Over a 16-week period, the women lost approximately 5.2 kg of body weight. However, 1.1 kg of the weight loss (21%) was due to a loss of water and lean tissue. More recently, Weltman et al. (1980) examined the effects of 500 kcal/day caloric restriction (from baseline levels) on body composition changes in sedentary middle-aged males. Over a 10-week period, subjects lost 5.95 kg, of which 4.03 kg (68%) was due to fat loss and 1.92 kg (32%) was loss of water and lean tissue. Furthermore, with caloric restriction only, these subjects exhibited a large decrease in HDL-cholesterol. In the same study, two other groups who exercised or combined dieting with exercise were able to maintain their HDL-cholesterol levels. Similar results for females have also been presented by Thompson et al. (1979). It should be noted that the decrease seen in HDL-C levels with weight loss may be an acute effect. There are data indicating that stable weight loss has a beneficial effect on HDL-cholesterol (Cagguila, Christakis, Farrand, Hulley, Johnson, Lasser, Stamler, & Widdowson, 1981; Contaldo, Strazullo, Postiglione, Riccardi, Palti, DiBiase, & Mancini, 1980; Thompson et al., 1979).

An additional problem associated with the use of caloric restriction alone for effective weight loss is the fact that it is associated with a reduction in basal metabolic rate (Appelbaum, Bostsarron, & Lacatis, 1971). Apparently, caloric restriction combined with exercise can counter this response (Bjorntorp, Sjostrom, & Sullivan, 1979). Thus, although mild caloric restriction appears to lead to more favorable body composition changes than fasting or severe caloric restriction, larger than desired amounts of fat-free tissue are lost with a program of caloric restriction only.

Exercise

Several studies have indicated that exercise helps maintain lean tissue while promoting fat loss. Total body weight and fat weight are generally reduced with endurance training programs (Pollock & Jackson, 1977), whereas lean body weight remains constant (Franklin, Buskirk, Hodgson, Gahagan, Kollias, & Mendez, 1979; Leon, Conrad, Hunninghake, & Serfass, 1979; Pollock, 1973; Pollock & Jackson, 1977) or increases slightly (O'Hara, Allen, & Shephard, 1977; Weltman et al., 1980; Zuti & Golding, 1976). Programs conducted at least 3 days per week (Pollock, 1973; Pollock, Broida, Kendrick, Miller, Janeway, & Linnerud, 1972; Pollock, Cureton, & Greninger, 1969; Pollock, Tiffany, Gettman, Janeway, & Lofland, 1969; Wilmore, Royce, Girandola, Katch, & Katch, 1970), for at least 20 min duration (Milesis, Pollock, Bah, Ayres, Ward, & Linnerud, 1976; Pollock, 1973; Wilmore et al., 1970), and of sufficient intensity and duration to expend at least 300 kcal per exercise session have been suggested as providing a threshold level for total body mass and fat weight reduction (Cureton, 1969; Gwinup, 1975; Pollock, 1973; Pollock & Jackson, 1977). Increasing caloric expenditure above 300 kcal per exercise session and increasing the frequency of exercise sessions will enhance fat weight loss while sparing lean tissue (Leon et al., 1979; Zuti and Golding, 1976). Leon et al. (1979) had six obese male subjects walk vigorously for 90 minutes, 5 days/week, for 16 weeks. Work output was increased weekly to an energy expenditure of 1000–1200 kcal/session. At the end of 16 weeks, subjects averaged 5.7 kg of weight loss, with a 5.9 kg loss of fat weight and a 0.2 kg gain in lean tissue. Similarly, Zuti and Golding (1976) followed adult women who expended 500 kcal/ exercise session 5 days per week for 16 weeks of exercise. At the end of 16 weeks, the women had lost 5.8 kg of fat and had gained .9 kg of lean tissue.

For an exercise to be calorically expensive (as well as cardiovascularly productive), it must be a big-muscle exercise, it must be prolonged, and it must elevate the heart rate (see Ribisl, Chapter 30 in this Handbook). Table 33.1 provides the caloric cost of some common activities.

Several areas must be considered when beginning an exercise program. If the individual is overweight, it would be advisable to begin with activities that are non-weight-bearing (i.e., swimming, cycling). This should help to avoid orthopedic problems. If the individual has any known symptoms or is sedentary, asymptomatic, and over age 35, a complete fitness evaluation should be performed (see Ribisl, Chapter 30 in this Handbook).

Although exercise obviously falls under the category of desirable weight loss programs, it should be noted that the rate of weight (fat) loss with exercise alone may be slower than most patients desire. If a combination of caloric restriction with exercise is too difficult to adhere to all at once, however, it is recommended that the exercise program be developed first. After the exercise program becomes part of the individual's lifestyle, a dietary intervention plan can be instituted. Developing the exercise program initially should help to avoid the large losses of lean tissue associated with diet alone.

Table 33.1   Energy Expenditure in Various Activities (kcal/min)

Activity	Weight (lbs)		
	110	150	190
Basketball	6.9	9.4	11.9
Circuit training	9.3	12.6	15.9
Climbing hills			
With no load	6.1	8.2	10.4
With 22-pound pack	7.0	9.5	12.0
Cycling			
Leisure	5.9	8.0	10.1
Racing	8.5	11.5	14.5
Dancing			
Ballroom	2.6	3.5	4.4
Choreographed	8.4	11.4	14.4
Football	6.6	9.0	11.4
Golf	4.3	5.8	7.3
Running			
9 min/mile	9.7	13.1	16.6
8 min/mile	10.8	14.2	17.7
7 min/mile	12.2	15.6	19.1
6 min/mile	13.9	17.3	20.8
Swimming			
Crawl, fast	7.8	11.0	13.9
Crawl, slow	6.4	10.6	13.4
Tennis	5.5	7.4	9.4
Walking	4.0	5.4	6.9

Note: For a more complete listing, see Katch and McArdle (1977) or McArdle, Katch, and Katch (1981).

Caloric Restriction Combined with Exercise

A review of the literature cited here strongly indicates that optimal body composition changes occur with a combination of caloric restriction (while on a well-balanced diet) plus exercise. This combination promotes loss of fat weight while sparing lean tissue. The data of Zuti and Golding (1976) and Weltman et al. (1980) support this contention. Caloric restriction of 500 kcal/day (from baseline levels) combined with 3 to 5 days of exercise requiring 300–500 kcal per exercise session results in favorable changes in body composition. The optimal rate of weight loss appears to be from 1 to 2 pounds per week. The optimal diet appears to be one that contains greater than 50% of the daily caloric consumption as carbohydrate (primarily starches and naturally occurring sugars), less than 30% of the daily caloric consumption as fat, and 10% to 12% of the daily caloric consumption as protein.

SUMMARY

The primary problem with losing weight is that although many individuals succeed in doing so, they invariably put the weight on again (Hafen, 1981). Thus, the goal of an effective weight loss regimen is not merely to lose weight. Weight control requires a lifelong commitment, an understanding of one's eating habits, and a willingness to change them.

To institute a desirable pattern of caloric restriction plus exercise, behavior modification techniques should be incorporated to identify and eliminate habits contributing to obesity (Dahlkoetter, Callahan, & Linton, 1979; Ferguson, 1975; Stalonas, Johnson, & Christ, 1978; Stuart & Davis, 1972; Wilson, 1980; Wooley, Wooley, & Dyrenforth, 1979). Frequent exercise is necessary, and accomplishment must be reinforced to sustain motivation. Crash dieting and other promised weight loss "cures" are ineffective (Hafen, 1981).

Based on the existing body of knowledge, the following recommendations are made to aid in the initiation of a desirable weight loss program. A desirable weight loss program is one that:

1. Provides a caloric intake not lower than 1200 kcal/day for adults, in order to get a proper blend of foods to meet nutritional requirements (this requirement may differ for children, pregnant and lactating women, older individuals, athletes, and so on).

2. Includes foods acceptable to the dieter from the various viewpoints of sociocultural background, usual habits, taste, cost, and ease of acquisition and preparation.

3. Provides a negative caloric balance (not to exceed 500–1000 kcal/day lower than baseline), resulting in gradual weight loss without metabolic dearrangements; maximal weight loss should be 1 kg/week.

4. Includes the use of behavior modification techniques to identify and eliminate dieting habits that contribute to improper nutrition.

5. Includes an endurance exercise program of at least 3 days/week, 20 to 30 minutes in duration, at a minimum intensity of 60% maximum heart rate (see ACSM, 1978).

6. Provides new eating and physical activity habits that can be continued for life in order to maintain the achieved lower body weight.

REFERENCES

Abraham, S., & Johnson, C. L. Prevalence of severe obesity in adults in the United States. *American Journal of Clinical Nutrition,* 1980, **33,** 364–370.

Alexander, J. K., & Peterson, K. L. Cardiovascular effects of weight reduction. *Circulation,* 1972, **45,** 310–318.

Alexander, J. K., & Pettigrove, J. R. Obesity and congestive heart failure. *Geriatrics,* 1967, **22,** 101–108.

American College of Sports Medicine (ACSM). Position statement on the recommended quantity and quality of exercise for developing and maintaining fitness in healthy adults. *Medicine and Science in Sports,* 1978, **10,** vi.

Angel, A. Pathophysiologic changes in obesity. *Canadian Medical Association Journal,* 1978, **119,** 1401–1406.

Angel, A., & Roncari, D. A. K. Medical complications of obesity. *Canadian Medical Association Journal,* 1978, **119,** 1408–1411.

Appelbaum, M., Bostsarron, J., & Lacatis, D. Effect of caloric restriction and excessive caloric intake on energy expenditure. *American Journal of Clinical Nutrition,* 1971, **24,** 1405–1409.

Bachman, L., Freschuss, V., Hallberg, D., & Melcher, A. Cardiovascular function in extreme obesity. *Acta Medica Scandinavica,* 1972, **193,** 437–445.

Ball, M. F., Canary, J. J., & Kyle, L. H. Comparative effects of caloric restrictions and total starvation on body composition in obesity. *Annals of Internal Medicine,* 1967, **67,** 60–67.

Barrett, P. V. D. The effect of diet and fasting on the serum bilirubin concentration in the rat. *Gastroenterology,* 1971, **60,** 572–576. (a)

Barrett, P. V. D. Hyperbilirubinemia of fasting. *Journal of the American Medical Association,* 1971, **217,** 1349–1353. (b)

Beck, P., Koumans, J. J. T., Winterling, C. A., Stein, M. F., Daughaday, W. H., & Kipnis, D. M. Studies of insulin and growth hormone secretion in human obesity. *Journal of Laboratory and Clinical Medicine,* 1964, **64,** 654–667.

Behnke, A. R., & Wilmore, J. H. *Evaluation and regulation of body build and composition.* Englewood Cliffs, N.J.: Prentice-Hall, 1974.

Benoit, F. L., Martin, R. L., & Watten, R. H. Changes in body composition during weight reduction in obesity. *Annals of Internal Medicine,* 1965, **63,** 604–612.

Berger, H. Fatal lactic acidosis during "crash" reducing diet. *New York State Journal of Medicine,* 1967, **67,** 2258–2263.

Billich, C., Bray, G., Gallagher, T. F., Hoffbrand, A. V., & Levitan, R. Absorptive capacity of the jejunum of obese and lean subjects: Effect of fasting. *Archives of Internal Medicine,* 1972, **130,** 377–387.

Bjorntorp, P., Sjostrom, L., & Sullivan, L. The role of physical exercise in the management of obesity. In J. F. Munro (ed.), *The treatment of obesity.* Lancaster, England: MTP Press, 1979.

Blitzer, P. H., Blitzer, E. C., & Rimm, A. A. Association between teenage obesity and cancer in 56,111 women. *Preventive Medicine,* 1976, **5,** 20–31.

Bloom, W. L. Fasting as an introduction to the treatment of obesity. *Metabolism,* 1959, **8,** 214–220.

Bray, G. A., Davidson, M. B., & Drenick, E. J. Obesity: A serious symptom. *Annals of Internal Medicine,* 1972, **77,** 797–805.

Brozek, J. (ed.). Body composition: Parts 1 and 2. *Annals of the New York Academy of Sciences,* 1963, **110.**

Brozek, J., Grande, F., Anderson, J. T., & Keys, A. Densiometric analysis of body composition: Revision of some quantitative assumptions. *Annals of the New York Academy of Sciences,* 1963, **110**(Part I), 113–140.

Burwell, C. S., Robin, D., Whaley, R. O., & Bickelmann, A. G. Extreme obesity associated with alveolar hypoventilation—A Pickwickian syndrome. *American Journal of Medicine,* 1956, **21,** 811–818.

Buskirk, E. R., Thompson, R. H., Lutwak, L., & Whedon, G. D. Energy balance of obese patients during weight reduction: Influence of diet restriction and exercise. *Annals of the New York Academy of Sciences,* 1963, **110,** 918–940.

Cagguila, A. W., Christakis, G., Farrand, M., Hulley, S. B., Johnson, R., Lasser, N. L., Stamler, J., & Widdowson, G. The multiple risk factor intervention trial: IV. Intervention on blood lipids. *Preventive Medicine,* 1981, **10,** 443–475.

Chaing, B. M., Perlman, L. V., & Epstein, F. H. Overweight and hypertension: A review. *Circulation,* 1969, **39,** 403–421.

Collison, D. R. Total fasting for up to 249 days. *Lancet,* 1967, **1,** 112.

Contaldo, F., Strazullo, P., Postiglione, A., Riccardi, G., Palti, L., DiBiase, G., & Mancini, M. Plasma high density lipoprotein in severe obesity after stable weight loss. *Atherosclerosis,* 1980, **37,** 163–167.

Cubberley, P. T., Polster, S. A., & Schulman, C. L. Lactic acidosis and death after the treatment of obesity by fasting. *New England Journal of Medicine,* 1965, **272,** 628–633.

Cureton, T. K. *The physiological effects of exercise programs upon adults.* Springfield, Ill.: Charles C Thomas, 1969.

Dahlkoetter, J., Callahan, E. J., & Linton, J. Obesity and the unbalanced energy equation: Exercise versus eating habit change. *Journal of Consulting and Clinical Psychology,* 1979, **47,** 898–905.

Drenick, E. J. The relation of BSP retention during prolonged fasts to changes in plasma volume. *Metabolism,* 1968, **17,** 522–527.

Drenick, E. J., Hunt, I. F., & Swenseid, M. E. Magnesium depletion during prolonged fasting of obese males. *Journal of Clinical Endocrinology and Metabolism,* 1969, **29,** 1341–1348.

Drenick, E. J., Simmons, F., & Murphy, J. F. Effect on hepatic morphology of treatment of obesity by fasting, reducing diets and small-bowel bypass. *New England Journal of Medicine,* 1970, **282,** 829–834.

Drenick, E. J., Swenseid, M. E., Blahd, W. H., & Tuttle, S. G. Prolonged starvation as treatment for severe obesity. *Journal of the American Medical Association,* 1964, **187,** 100–105.

Felig, P., Owen, D. E., Wahren, J., & Cahill, G. F., Jr. Amino acid metabolism during prolonged starvation. *Journal of Clinical Investigation,* 1969, **48,** 584–594.

Ferguson, J. *Learning to eat: Behavior modification for weight control.* Palo Alto: Bull Publishing, 1975.

Franklin, B., Buskirk, E., Hodgson, J., Gahagan, H., Kollias, J., & Mendez, J. Effects of physical conditioning on cardiorespiratory function, body composition and serum lipids in relatively normal-weight and obese middle-aged women. *International Journal of Obesity,* 1979, **3,** 97–109.

Garnett, E. S., Barnard, D. L., Ford, J., Goodbody, R. A., & Woodehouse, M. A. Gross fragmentation of cardiac myofibrils after therapeutic starvation for obesity. *Lancet,* 1969, **1,** 914.

Garrett, W. N. Experiences in the use of body density as an estimator of body composition of animals. In *Body Composition in Animals and Man* (Pub. No. 1958). Washington, D.C.: National Academy of Sciences, 1968.

Garrow, J. S. *Energy balance and obesity in man.* New York: American Elsevier, 1974.

Goldman, R. F., Bullen, B., & Seltzer, C. Changes in specific gravity and body fat in overweight female adolescents as a result of weight reduction. *Annals of the New York Academy of Sciences,* 1963, **110,** 913–917.

Gordon, T., & Kannel, W. B. The effects of overweight on cardiovascular diseases. *Geriatrics,* 1973, **28,** 80–88.

Grande, F. Nutrition and energy balance in body composition studies. In J. Brozek & A. Henschel (eds.), *Techniques for measuring body composition.* Washington, D.C.: National Academy of Sciences—National Research Council, 1961 (Reprinted by the Office of Technical Services, U.S. Department of Commerce, Washington, D.C., as U.S. Government Research Report AD286, 1963).

Grande, F. Energy balance and body composition changes. *Annals of Internal Medicine,* 1968, **68,** 467–480.

Grande, F., Taylor, H. L., Anderson, J. T., Buskirk, E., & Keys, A. Water exchange in men on a restricted water intake and a low calorie carbohydrate diet accompanied by physical work. *Journal of Applied Physiology,* 1958, **12,** 202–210.

Gwinup, G. Effect of exercise alone on the weight of obese women. *Archives of Internal Medicine,* 1975, **135,** 676–680.

Hafen, B. A. *Nutrition, food and weight control.* Boston: Allyn & Bacon, 1981.

Jagenburg, R., & Svanborg, A. Self-induced protein-calorie malnutrition in a healthy adult male. *Acta Medica Scandinavica,* 1968, **183,** 67–71.

Kahan, A. Death during therapeutic starvation. *Lancet,* 1968, **1,** 1378–1379.

Kasch, F. W., & Wallace, J. P. Physiological variables during 10 years of endurance exercise. *Medicine and Science in Sports,* 1976, **8,** 5–8.

Katch, F. I. Practice curves and errors of measurement in estimating underwater weight by hydrostatic weighing. *Medicine and Science in Sports,* 1969, **1,** 212–216.

Katch, F. I., & Katch, V. L. Measurement and prediction errors in body composition assessment and the search for the perfect prediction equation. *Research Quarterly for Exercise and Sport,* 1980, **51,** 249–260.

Katch, F. I., & McArdle, W. D. *Nutrition, weight control and exercise.* Boston: Houghton Mifflin, 1977.

Katch, F. I., Michael, E. D., & Horvath, S. M. Estimation of body density from underwater weighing: Description of a simple method. *Journal of Applied Physiology,* 1967, **23,** 811–813.

Keys, A., Brozek, J., Henschel, A., Mickelson, O., & Taylor, H. L. *The biology of human starvation.* Minneapolis: University of Minnesota Press, 1950.

Krotkiewski, M., Toss, L., Bjorntorp, P., & Holm, G. The effect of a very-low-calorie diet with and without chronic exercise on thyroid and sex hormones, plasma proteins, oxygen uptake, insulin and c peptide concentrations in obese women. *International Journal of Obesity,* 1981, **5,** 287–293.

Lawlor, T., & Wells, D. G. Metabolic hazards of fasting. *American Journal of Clinical Nutrition,* 1969, **22,** 1142–1149.

Leon, A. S., Conrad, J., Hunninghake, D. M., & Serfass, R. Effects of a vigorous walking program on body composition and carbohydrate and lipid metabolism of obese young men. *American Journal of Clinical Nutrition,* 1979, **32**, 1776–1787.

Mabee, F. M., Meyer, P., DenBesten, L., & Mason, E. E. The mechanisms of increased gallstone formation on obese human subjects. *Surgery,* 1978, **79**, 460–468.

Matter, S., Weltman, A., & Stamford, B. A. Body fat content and serum lipid levels. *Journal of the American Dietetic Association,* 1980, **77**, 149–152.

McArdle, W. D., Katch, F. I., & Katch, V. L. *Exercise physiology: Energy, nutrition and human performance.* Philadelphia: Lea & Febiger, 1981.

Milesis, C. A., Pollock, M. L., Bah, M. D., Ayres, J. J., Ward, A., & Linnerud, A. C. Effects of different durations of training on cardiorespiratory function, body composition and serum lipids. *Research Quarterly,* 1976, **47**, 716–725.

Murphy, R., & Shipman, K. H. Hyperuricemia during total fasting. *Archives of Internal Medicine,* 1963, **112**, 954–959.

Nilsson, L. H., & Hultman, E. Total starvation or a carbohydrate-poor diet followed by carbohydrate refeeding. *Scandinavian Journal of Clinical and Laboratory Investigation,* 1973, **32**, 325–330.

Norbury, F. B. Contraindication of long term fasting. *Journal of the American Medical Association,* 1964, **188**, 88.

O'Hara, W., Allen, C., & Shephard, R. L. Loss of body weight and fat during exercise in a cold chamber. *European Journal of Applied Physiology,* 1977, **37**, 205–218.

Oyama, J., Thomas, J. A., & Grant, R. L. Effect of starvation on glucose tolerance and serum insulin-like activity of Osborne-Mendel rats. *Diabetes,* 1963, **12**, 332–334.

Passmore, R., Strong, J. A., & Ritchie, F. J. The chemical composition of the tissue lost by obese patients on a reducing regimen. *British Journal of Nutrition,* 1958, **12**, 113–122.

Pitman, F. E. Primary malabsorption following extreme attempts to lose weight. *Gut,* 1966, **7**, 154–158.

Pitts, G. C. Studies of body composition by direct dissection. *Annals of the New York Academy of Sciences,* 1963, **110**, 11–22.

Pollock, M. L. The quantification of endurance training programs. In J. Wilmore (ed.), *Exercise and sports sciences reviews.* New York: Academic Press, 1973.

Pollock, M. L., Broida, J., Kendrick, Z., Miller, H. S., Jr., Janeway, R., & Linnerud, A. C. Effects of training two days per week at different intensities on middle aged men. *Medicine and Science in Sports,* 1972, **4**, 192–197.

Pollock, M. L., Cureton, T. K., & Greninger, L. Effects of frequency of training on working capacity, cardiovascular function and body composition of adult men. *Medicine and Science in Sports,* 1969, **1**, 70–74.

Pollock, M. L., & Jackson, A. Body composition: Measurement and changes resulting from physical training. In *Proceedings of the National College Physical Education Association for Men and Women,* Orlando, Fla., 1977.

Pollock, M. L., Tiffany, J., Gettman, L., Janeway, R., & Lofland, H. Effects of training on serum lipids, cardiovascular function and body composition. In B. D. Franks (ed.), *Exercise and fitness.* Chicago: Athletic Institute, 1969.

Portnay, G. I., O'Brian, J. T., Bush, J., Vagenakis, A. G., Azizi, F., Arky, R. A., Ingbar, S. H., & Braverman, L. E. The effect of starvation on the concentration and binding of thyroxine and triiodothyronine in serum and on the response to TRH. *Journal of Clinical Endocrinology and Metabolism,* 1974, **39**, 191–194.

Rimm, A. A., Werner, L. H., Bernstein, R., & Van Yserloo, B. Disease and obesity in 73,532 women. *Obesity and Bariatric Medicine,* 1972, **1**, 77–84.

Rooth, G., & Carlstrom, S. Therapeutic fasting. *Acta Medica Scandinavica,* 1970, **187**, 455–463.

Rossner, S., & Hallberg, D. Serum lipoproteins in massive obesity. *Acta Medica Scandinavica,* 1978, **204**, 103–110.

Rozental, P., Biava, C., Spencer, H., & Zimmerman, H. J. Liver morphology and function tests in obesity and during total starvation. *American Journal of Digestive Diseases,* 1967, **12**, 198–208.

Runcie, J., & Thomson, T. J. Total fasting, hyperuricemia and gout. *Postgraduate Medical Journal,* 1969, **45**, 251–254.

Runcie, J., & Thomson, T. J. Prolonged starvation—A dangerous procedure? *British Medical Journal,* 1970, **3,** 432–435.

Siri, W. E. Gross composition of the body. In J. H. Lawrence & C. A. Tobias (eds.), *Advances in biological and medical physica* (Vol. IV). New York: Academic Press, 1956.

Sours, H. E., Frattali, V. P., Brand, C. D., Feldman, R. A., Forbes, A. L., Swanson, R. C., & Paris, A. L. Sudden death associated with very low calorie weight reduction regimens. *American Journal of Clinical Nutrition,* 1981, **34,** 453–461.

Spencer, I. O. B. Death during therapeutic starvation for obesity. *Lancet,* 1968, **2,** 679–680.

Stalonas, P. M., Johnson, W. G., & Christ, M. Behavior modification for obesity: The evaluation of exercise, contingency, management, and program behavior. *Journal of Consulting and Clinical Psychology,* 1978, **46,** 463–467.

Stamler, R., Stamler, J., Riedlinger, W. F., Algera, G., & Roberts, R. H. Weight and blood pressure. Findings in hypertension screening of 1 million Americans. *Journal of the American Medical Association,* 1978, **240,** 1607–1610.

Stein, J. S., & Hirsch, J. Obesity and pancreatic function. In D. Steener & N. Frankel (eds.), *Handbook of physiology:* Section 1. Endocrinology. (Vol. 1). Washington, D.C.: American Physiological Society, 1972.

Stewart, J. S., Pollock, D. L., Hoffbrand, A. V., Mollin, D. L., & Booth, C. C. A study of proximal and distal intestinal structure and absorptive function in idiopathic steatorrhea. *Quarterly Journal of Medicine,* 1967, **36,** 425–444.

Stewart, W. K., & Fleming, L. W. Features of a successful therapeutic fast of 382 days duration. *Postgraduate Medical Journal,* 1973, **49,** 203–209.

Streja, D. A., Marliss, E. B., & Steiner, G. The effects of prolonged fasting on plasma triglyceride kinetics in man. *Metabolism,* 1977, **26,** 505–516.

Stuart, R. B., & Davis, B. *Slim chance in a fat world: Behavioral control of obesity.* Champaign, Ill.: Research Press, 1972.

Thompson, P. D., Jeffrey, R. W., Wing, R. R., & Wood, P. D. Unexpected decrease in plasma high density lipoprotein cholesterol with weight loss. *American Journal of Clinical Nutrition,* 1979, **32,** 2016–2021.

Thomson, T. J., Runcie, J., & Miller, V. Treatment of obesity by total fasting up to 249 days. *Lancet,* 1966, **2,** 992–996.

Thorn, G. W., Wintrobe, A., Adams, M. M., Braunwald, E., Isselbacher, K. J., & Petersdorf, R. G. *Harrison's principles of internal medicine* (8th ed.). New York: McGraw-Hill, 1977.

Vagenakis, A. G., Burger, A., Portnay, G. I., Rudolph, M., O'Brian, J. R., Azizi, F., Arky, R. A., Nicod, P., Ingbar, S. H., & Braverman, L. E. Diversion of peripheral thyroxine metabolism from activating to inactivating pathways during complete fasting. *Journal of Clinical Endocrinology and Metabolism,* 1975, **41,** 191–194.

Verdy, M. B.S.P. retention during total fasting. *Metabolism,* 1966, **15,** 769.

Warner, W. A., & Garrett, L. P. The obese patient and anesthesia. *Journal of the American Medical Association,* 1968, **205,** 102–103.

Wechsler, J. G., Hutt, W., Wenzel, H., Klor, H., & Ditschuneit, H. Lipids and lipoproteins during a very-low-calorie diet. *International Journal of Obesity,* 1981, **5,** 325–331.

Weisinger, J. R., Seeman, A., Herrera, M. G., Assal, J. P., Soeldner, J. S., & Gleason, R. E. The nephrotic syndrome: A complication of massive obesity. *Annals of Internal Medicine,* 1974, **80,** 332–341.

Weltman, A. Unfavorable serum lipid profiles in extremely overfat women. *International Journal of Obesity,* 1983, **7,** 109–114.

Weltman, A., & Katch, V. Comparison of hydrostatic weighing at residual volume and total lung capacity. *Medicine and Science in Sports and Exercise,* 1981, **13,** 210–213.

Weltman, A., Matter, S., & Stamford, B. A. Caloric restriction and/or mild exercise: Effects on serum lipids and body composition. *American Journal of Clinical Nutrition,* 1980, **33,** 1002–1009.

West, K. *Epidemiology of diabetes and its vascular lesions.* New York: Elsevier, 1978.

Wilmore, J. H. A simplified method for determination of residual lung volume. *Journal of Applied Physiology,* 1969, **27,** 96–100.

Wilmore, J. J., Royce, J., Girandola, R. N., Katch, F. I., & Katch, V. L. Body composition changes with a 10 week jogging program. *Medicine and Science in Sports,* 1970, **2,** 113–117.

Wilson, G. T. Behavior modification and treatment of obesity. In A. J. Stunkard (ed.), *Obesity.* Philadelphia: W. B. Saunders, 1980.

Wooley, S. C., Wooley, O. W., & Dyrenforth, S. R. Theoretical, practical and social issues in behavioral treatments of obesity. *Journal of Applied Behavior Analysis,* 1979, **12,** 3–25.

Yang, M., & Van Itallie, T. B. Metabolic responses of obese subjects to starvation and low calorie ketogenic and nonketogenic diets. *Journal of Clinical Investigation,* 1976, **58,** 722–730.

Zuti, W. B., & Golding, L. B. Comparing diet and exercise as weight reduction tools. *Physician and Sports Medicine,* 1976, **4,** 49–57.

CHAPTER 34

SPECIAL CONSIDERATIONS IN DEVELOPING EXERCISE PROGRAMS FOR THE OLDER ADULT

EVERETT L. SMITH

University of Wisconsin

Physical activity programming for any population, whether young or old, requires an understanding of the needs and limitations of the group for which it is designed. Knowledge of these needs and limitations allows the population to be educated, trained, and motivated in moving their bodies through time and space. The duration, frequency, and intensity of physical activity must be appropriate to the physiological and mental capabilities of the participants. Activities that enhance endurance, strength, flexibility, balance, and coordination must be included to produce total fitness.

Age should not be a limiting factor for anyone wishing to participate in physical activity. On the contrary, physical activity is important for older adults in maintaining independence in their own environment. It is often difficult, however, to program for older adults, because knowledge of their needs and limitations is sparse and because their physical capabilities cover a wide spectrum. The wheelchair-bound older adult or the 75-year-old marathoner is more frequently spotlighted than the vast majority of older adults who fall between these extremes. Lack of understanding and fear of injuring the aging population makes the design of physical fitness and quality-of-life programs difficult. Although there is a large physiological variation in the older adult population, there are certain general characteristics that apply to most older adults.

Human aging may be defined chronologically or physiologically. The older adult population may be divided into three groups: the young old, the old old, and the athletic old. The young old are generally 55 to 75 years of age, have a fitness level (6–7 mets) that does not severely restrict their lifelong activities, and maintain homes of their own in the community. The old old are generally over 75 years of age, have limited physical capacity (2–3 mets) because of a variety of age-related disorders, and may not be able to live independently, (see Table 34.1). The athletic old are those who have maintained a high level of physical fitness (9–10 mets) and are still competing in sports (Morse & Smith, 1981).

Categorization of the older adult population by chronological age is convenient, but physiological age is more expressive of a specific individual's capability. Physiological aging may be defined as the loss of ability to adapt to one's environment. In general, peak physiological function is reached at age 30. After that age, physiological capabilities decline in sedentary persons.

The loss of ability to exercise is the first obvious functional decline with age. There

Table 34.1 Maximal Volitional Treadmill Exercise Test Results in Older Adults

Groups	N	Age		$\dot{V}O_2$ (ml/kg·min)		Heart Rate	
		Mean	S.D.	Mean	S.D.	Mean	S.D.
Young old							
Male	13	72.15	4.26	20.12	2.82	130.69	8.69
Female	42	70.23	5.71	18.90	3.88	135.17	12.38
Old old	24	84.54	6.15	9.51	2.52	114.79	13.20

Source: Reprinted with permission of the publisher from Morse, C. E., & Smith, E. L., Physical activity programming for the aged. In E. L. Smith & R. C. Serfass (eds.), *Exercise and aging: The scientific basis.* Hillside, N.J.: Enslow Publishers, 1981, p. 113.

are also changes with age in work capacity, cardiac output, heart rate, blood pressure, respiration, basal metabolic rate, muscular and nerve contraction, sensory acuity, flexibility, bone, and total body water (see Table 34.2).

PHYSIOLOGICAL DECLINES WITH AGE

Between the ages of 30 and 70, maximal work capacity decreases 25% to 30% (see Table 34.2). This loss is related to declines in several body functions.

Cardiovascular Declines

Cardiac output decreases during this period because of declines in both maximum stroke volume and maximum heart rate (see Table 34.2). The stroke volume decline is related to decreases in muscle mass of the heart and muscle contractility. During mild exercise, stroke volume is adequate, but it cannot increase in response to more severe exercise, as it does in the young. The heart rate must then increase to maintain adequate blood flow to the tissues. The maximum heart rate declines by approximately 6–8 beats/decade. Therefore, the limited heart rate and stroke volume account for a 30% decrease in maximal cardiac output and result in the lessened maximal work capacity.

Parallel to decreased cardiac output is an increase in resistance to blood flow. Shephard (1978) states that an elderly person sustains a 20% higher systemic pressure than a younger person at half the cardiac output. The resting systolic pressure increases by 10–40 mmHg and the diastolic pressure by 5–10 mmHg, and systolic pressures may rise above 200 mmHg during exercise.

Lung Declines

Vital capacity declines 40% to 50% by age 70, and residual volume increases 30% to 50% (see Table 34.2). As a result, maximal air movement during exercise is limited and is reached at a low level of work. The breathing rate is increased, and thus resistance to air movement increases and the respiratory musculature must work harder.

Physiological parameters of the lung also change. Total surface area declines by 25% to 30%, or about 20 m², between the ages of 30 and 70. In the aging lung, there are three common changes that affect alveoli, ventilation, and blood perfusion: (a) a reduction or cessation of capillary bloodflow to some alveoli; (b) gas exchange reduced by early closure of alveoli; and (c) some alveoli not ventilated at all or only during forced resistance, such as pursed-lips expiration. Thus, blood oxygen levels are lowered as a result of decreased lung surface area and decreased alveoli ventilation and blood perfusion.

Table 34.2 Biological Functional Changes Between the Ages of 30 and 70

Biological Function	Change	References
Work capacity	↓25%–30%	Astrand (1967); Shock (1962); Sidney (1981)
Cardiac output	↓30%	Becklake et al. (1965); Brandfonbrener et al. (1955); Harris (1970); Kilbom & Astrand (1971); Shaw et al. (1973); Shephard (1978, 1981)
Maximum heart rate	↓24 beats	Astrand (1960); Robinson (1965)
Blood pressure		Harris (1968, 1970); Miall & Lovell (1967)
Systolic	↑10–40 mmHg	
Diastolic	↑5–10 mmHg	
Respiration		Jones et al. (1978); Morris et al. (1971);
Vital capacity	↓40%–50%	Murray (1976); Needham et al. (1954);
Residual volume	↑30%–50%	Neufeld et al. (1973); Niinimaa & Shephard (1978)
Basal metabolic rate	↓ 8%–12%	Shock (1961, 1962); Tzankoff & Norris (1977)
Musculature		Aniansson et al. (1978); Drinkwater et
Muscle mass	↓25%–30%	al. (1975); Fitts (1981); Gutmann &
Hand grip strength	↓25%–30%	Hanzlikova (1976); Moritani (1981); Robinson et al. (1975)
Nerve conduction		Kemble (1967); Shock (1977)
velocity	↓10%–15%	
Flexibility	↓20%–30%	Adrian (1981); Boone & Azen (1979); Chapman et al. (1972); Clarke (1975); Greey (1955); Jervey (1961); Munns (1981)
Bone		Garn et al. (1967); Mazess & Cameron
Female	↓25%–30%	(1973); Smith et al. (1976)
Male	↓15%–20%	
Total body water	↓10%–15%	Edelman et al. (1952); Fryer (1962); Keys & Brozek (1953); Rossman (1977)
Renal function	↓30%–50%	Griffiths et al. (1976); Lindeman (1975); Rowe et al. (1976)
Liver function	↓40%	Bhanthumnavin & Schuster (1977); Hyams (1973)
Response to heat and cold	20%–30% less able to give off heat	Henschel et al. (1968); Pickering (1936); Robinson et al. (1965); Shock (1977)

Basal Metabolic Rate Declines

Basal metabolic rate declines by 8% to 12% between the ages of 30 and 70 (see Table 34.2). This decline, though relatively small, results in two major problems: (a) body weight and body fat increase if youthful eating patterns are maintained; and (b) the individual is uncomfortable except in a very narrow temperature range. The decline in basal metabolism is directly related to the decline in lean body mass or total muscle mass, not to changes in cell metabolism (Tzankoff & Norris, 1977).

Neuromuscular Declines

Decreases in both the number and size of muscle fibers result in a 25% to 30% decline in muscle mass, which is reflected by a 25% to 30% decline in strength (see Table 34.2). Burke, Tuttle, Thompson, Janney, and Weber (1953) studied 311 normal males between the ages of 12 and 79. Both grip strength and grip strength endurance peaked in the 20 to 24 age group. Grip strength endurance declined continually after this age, whereas the rate of decline of grip strength sharpened after age 60. The grip strength and grip strength endurance of 75-to 79-year-olds were comparable to those of 12-to 15-year-olds.

Campbell, McComas, and Petito (1973) demonstrated decreased muscle mass and muscle strength of the extensor digitorum brevis in 28 healthy subjects aged 60 to 69. The changes resulted from the loss of functional motor units and slowed muscle twitch response in the surviving motor units. No motor unit decline was observed in 66 control subjects aged 3 to 58 years. After age 60, however, a continual loss of functional units was found.

There are three basic fiber types in skeletal musculature: Type I (slow twitch, high oxidative), Type IIA (fast twitch, high oxidative), and Type IIB (fast twitch, low oxidative). With age there is a preferred loss of Type IIA and IIB fibers, resulting in an increased percentage of Type I fibers. Larsson, Sjodin, and Karlsson (1978) found Type I fibers of the quadriceps increased by 15% between the ages of 20 to 25 and 60 to 65 in men. Larsson, Grimby, and Karlsson (1979) showed that strength decline with age was significantly correlated with the loss of Type II fibers. The fiber type change may affect both the endurance and the coordination of the older adult.

Nerve conduction velocity declines by 10% to 15% in the older adult. This may be due to metabolic and synaptic changes that slow the transfer of impulses from one nerve ending to the next. Synaptic changes at the neuromuscular junction in the aged include decreased surface of the neuromuscular junction, reduced numbers of junctional folds, increased width of the synaptic cleft, and decreased availability of acetylcholine packets (D. O. Smith, 1982). The result is slowed transmission of impulses from the nerve to the muscle cell membrane and thereby slowed muscle contraction response. Where the central nervous system and the peripheral nervous system interact in psychomotor speed, additional effects may occur.

Spirduso (1980) defines psychomotor speed as "a rubric describing the speed with which an individual can perform a task which involves reacting motorically to an environmental stimulus." Reaction time is influenced by both central and peripheral components. Slowed reaction time in the older adult is probably due more to central than to peripheral nervous system factors (Spirduso, 1975). Simple reaction time and movement time have been demonstrated to decline with age. Birren, Carden, and Phillips (1963) reported that the time needed to press a key in response to a musical note was .18 seconds for young adults and .22 seconds in adults over 65, an increase of 22%. Welford (1965) reported that simple sensory motor tasks may take 50% longer for 65-year-olds than for 20-year-olds.

Sensory Declines

Both neurological and mechanical changes occur in the older adult's auditory system. Mechanical changes consist of a thickening and loss of elasticity of the tympanic membrane (eardrum) and reduced efficiency of articulation in the bones of the middle ear. This restricts peripheral conduction of sound. Neurological changes occur in the cochlea and temporal lobe of the cerebral cortex, resulting in decreased sound discrimination and greater time-related processing. Because of these changes, both auditory acuity and interpretation are inhibited in the older adult. The older adult also is often unable to hear high-frequency sounds and may have great difficulty communicating with a speaker who has a high voice (Shephard, 1978).

Three general changes occur in the visual system of the older adult:

1. The lens thickens, yellows, and becomes less elastic.
2. The photochemistry of the retina changes, and the number of rods and cones is reduced.
3. The iris cannot open as widely as it can in younger adults.

Because of these changes, better conditions are necessary for adequate vision. Light intensity must be high enough to overcome the reduced opening of the iris, but glare must be minimized because of the distortion caused by the yellowing of the lens. With these requirements and the reduced number of rods and cones, night vision is restricted in the older adult. Other functional changes include difficulty in distinguishing between dark red and blue shades, reduced accommodation, and reduced depth perception.

Flexibility Declines

Flexibility declines by 20% to 30% in the older adult (see Table 34.2). Research in flexibility change is sparse. Anatomical changes occur in muscle, tendon, and joint capsules, all of which affect flexibility. The major cause of declining flexibility is lack of movement, and joints not normally used in the activities of daily living are most affected. Inokuchi, Ishikawa, Iwamoto, and Kimura (1975) reported increased connective tissue and fat on muscle. Balazs (1977) reported decreased responsiveness of connective tissue to mechanical stress and movement. This decline is reflective of the increased cross-linking of the collagen fibers, resulting in tendons and connective tissues in general becoming stiffer and less flexible. Allman (1974) reports that the aging joint is less flexible and less mobile. Connective tissue changes in muscles, ligaments, joint capsules, and tendons are responsible for 98% of the lost flexibility in the aged (Johns & Wright, 1962).

Bone Declines

Bone loss is a significant problem for both women and men (see Table 34.2). The problem is more severe for women, who lose 1% to 1.3% of their bone each year after the age of 30 to 35. As much as 2% to 3% per year may be lost during the climacteric period. Thus, many women lose 30% of their bone by age 70. The decreased strength of the bone results in approximately 150,000 hip fractures per year, with approximately 30% of women who fracture their hips dying within 1 year. Men begin to lose bone at about age 55 at the rate of .4% per year and generally do not have a significant bone problem until age 80.

Other Declines

Shock (1961) reports that renal function declines approximately 30% to 50% between the ages of 30 and 70 (see Table 34.2). The kidney plays a vital role in the clearance of toxic and waste products created by the body and drugs and other chemicals taken into the system. As a result of kidney function decline, the acid-base balance control, glucose tolerance, and clearance of drugs are decreased. Since drug clearance is slowed, dosages must be adjusted to avoid toxicity while maintaining physiological function. For example, digitoxin, which is used to assist heart contractility, is easily misadjusted, resulting in arrhythmias and myocardial complications.

Total body water declines by 10% to 15% because of the decline in total cellular water (see Table 34.2). As a result, the older adult dehydrates more rapidly when faced with a hot environment, burns, or dysentery. Water loss from evaporation and perspiration needs to be considered in exercising older adults. In conjunction with decreased body water, increased body fat, and decreased integrity of the cardiovascular system, there is a delayed onset of sweating in the unfit older adult.

The older adult is 20% to 30% less able to dissipate heat because of the 15% to 20% increase in fat content and is therefore more susceptible to heat stroke. Physical activity programs should be scheduled at times when the older adult will not be exposed to direct sunlight. Cold environments also endanger the older adult. The cold causes vasoconstriction, which, combined with higher blood pressure, may overtax the heart and result in ischemia and possible infarct during physical activity such as snow shoveling.

BENEFITS OF PHYSICAL ACTIVITY

In constructing an exercise program, the total physiological status of the person must be considered. Many of the physiological changes can be reversed, however, with physical activity. There are indications that as much as 50% of physiological decline is related to disuse and that a high level of physiological function can be maintained into the seventh and eighth decades with regular physical activity (deVries & Adams, 1972; Heath, Hagberg, Ehsani, & Holloszy, 1981).

Cardiovascular Benefits

The benefits of physical activity in the younger adult have been clearly documented over the past 20 years. There are few longitudinal studies, however, that demonstrate the benefits of physical activity in slowing the rate of the aging process. Kasch and Wallace (1976) are among the few researchers who have demonstrated the benefits of physical activity in the aging adult over a 10-to 15-year period. Their study shows that the 1% per year loss of cardiovascular function may be prevented through regular physical activity. Sidney and Shephard (1978) demonstrated that the older adult who exercises 2 to 4 times per week improves in $\dot{V}O_2$ max and general cardiovascular fitness. deVries (1970) also demonstrated that cardiovascular improvement could be accomplished through physical activity of the older adult. Barry, Daly, Pruett, Steinmetz, Page, Birkhead, and Rodahl (1966) found improvements in the maximal oxygen consumption of institutionalized individuals who completed a 3-month conditioning program. Their initial fitness level was quite low, however, and the gain may have been due to attitudinal as well as physiological improvement. deVries (1970), Barry et al. (1966), and Sidney and Shephard (1977) all reported that resting systolic and diastolic blood pressures declined significantly in the exercising older adult. Sidney and Shephard (1977) also reported declines in exercise systolic and diastolic blood pressures.

Stamford (1972) compared the physical work capacity and trainability of geriatric mental patients, including seven chronically institutionalized patients, five recently institutionalized patients, and seven chronically institutionalized patients assigned to a control group. The mean ages of the groups were 66.7, 58.2, and 70.0 years, respectively. The two experimental groups participated in a treadmill-walking program for 18 weeks. The chronically institutionalized patients were significantly lower in fitness capacity than were the recently hospitalized patients. Stamford reported improved fitness and blood pressure reduction in the exercise subjects and no change in the control group.

The wide variation in fitness and environmental conditions of older adults, who range from the institutionalized to the average community dweller to the athlete, make interpretation of research data complex. For all three groups, however, cardiovascular fitness improves in response to physical activity.

Morse and Smith (1981) demonstrated the benefits of a fitness trail for older adults. Three groups participated: 17 in an exercise group (mean age, 70.8), 10 in a control group (mean age, 69.5), and 4 in a test-retest group (mean age, 69.5). The test-retest group took the initial work capacity test and repeated it 3 weeks later to determine the effects of acclimation. The experimental group participated in a 3-month walking program, which consisted of a 1 mile fitness trail separated into quarter-mile loops. This provided a way to progressively increment the distance walked up to 3 miles per day. In each of the quarter-mile loops was an exercise station, where subjects did three to four exercises. Three to four subjects of similar fitness walked together, providing social reinforcement as well as safety precautions. At the end of the 3-month study, the work capacity (maximal $\dot{V}O_2 \cdot kg^{-1} \cdot min^{-1}$) of the exercise group had increased by 32% and that of the control group by 27%. These values were not significantly different from one another but were significantly better than those of the test-retest group.

In regions with variable climate, such as the midwest, an exercise maintenance program for the older adult must include facilities for exercise in the winter, such as in gymnasiums and shopping malls, to prevent physiological decline due to long periods of inactivity.

Neuromuscular Benefits

Most research on the effects of physical activity on aging muscle involves animals rather than humans. McCafferty and Edington (1970) postulated that there may be an age threshold beyond which training may not affect either the heart or skeletal muscles. Gutmann and Hanzlikova (1966), however, observed that the diaphragm degenerates minimally compared to other body muscles. This may be reflective of the continual motor impulses and activity of the diaphragm muscle in respiratory function. Jennekens, Tomlinson, and Walton (1971) reported that a 78-year-old well-trained male had limb musculature and fiber size comparable to that of young subjects and that Type II fibers were larger than Type I fibers. No conclusions may be generalized from this one study, however.

Petrofsky and Lind (1975) found no changes in muscular endurance or muscular strength in men between age 22 and 65 employed in an aircraft corporation machine shop and performing similar work activities. Ikai and Fukunaga (1961) hypothesized that there are two primary mechanisms for possible strength gain: (a) an increase in the rate of discharge of the motor unit (neural activity) acting on the muscle, and (b) morphological changes in the contractile tissue, resulting in hypertrophy. Moritani (1981) observed increased muscular strength through physical activity in both young and old subjects. Seven young males between 18 and 26 years and five older subjects between 67 and 72 (mean age, 69.6) participated in an 8-week regimen of isotonic strength training. At the end of the study, there was a significant increase in strength. The young participants exhibited both increased neural activity and muscle hypertrophy, whereas the aged subjects increased in neural function only. Further research is needed to clarify whether muscle hypertrophy in the aged can result from physical activity.

The decline observed in reaction time with advancing age may be not age-induced but disuse-induced. Older adults who are active in racket sports react to visual stimuli about as quickly as young college men, whereas sedentary older men reveal the classic aging effect of slowed simple and choice reaction times (Spirduso, 1975). This is not entirely due to a preference for athletic activity by those with quicker reaction time. Spirduso and Farrar (1981) studied both young and old rats who were exercised aerobically for 6 months on a rodent treadmill. Although there was no difference between the control and exercise animals prior to the exercise program, after 6 months the exercise animals had significantly quicker reaction time than the controls of the same age group.

Flexibility Benefits

The decline in flexibility with age is readily observed but seldom quantitated. Chapman, deVries, and Swezey (1972) sought to quantitate the increased stiffness in the aging population. They selected 20 subjects between the ages of 63 and 88 and 20 subjects between 15 and 19. The index finger was used in a flexibility model to compare the two groups. There was significantly greater joint stiffness (30%) in the older subjects than in the younger subjects. This was determined by the criteria of torque and energy requirement in passive oscillation of the index finger. After a 6-week training program, the older and younger subjects both demonstrated improved flexibility and a significant reduction in torque requirement in flexibility movements. No greater gains were noted in the younger group than in the older group. Lesser (1978) studied the effects of rhythmic exercises on range of motion in 60 elderly subjects aged 61 to 79 (mean age, 75). Pretests and posttests of flexion and extension at the shoulder, elbow, wrist, hip, and knee were measured with a goniometer. Thirty subjects participated in a 10-week physical activity program consisting of half-hour sessions two times per week. Significant improvements were observed in 66% of the sites measured. Munns (1981) developed a physical activity program in which 40 subjects ranging in age from 65 to 88 (mean age, 72) participated in a 12-week program, 3 days per week. This physical activity program was a movement and dance program designed to enhance total fitness and range of motion. Twenty subjects were randomly assigned to the exercise group and twenty to a control group. The participation rate of the exercise group was 92%, with the majority of the subjects missing fewer than three classes. There were no dropouts. All subjects were pretested and posttested using the Leighton flexometer. The sites measured were neck, shoulder, wrist, hip/back, knee, and ankle. No significant difference was observed between the control and experimental groups on any of the parameters at the pretest. After 12 weeks of participation in the physical activity, significant improvements were observed in the experimental group at all sites. The improvement in the experimental group and the decline in the control group are presented in Table 34.3.

Bone Benefits

Although the cause of bone loss with age is multifactorial, physical activity or inactivity is an important parameter in bone maintenance. The two primary mechanical forces acting on bone are gravity or weight bearing and muscle contraction. If either of these factors is eliminated, reduced, or increased, bone mineral content is changed, as evidenced by studies of immobilization of a limb through casting, denervation, weightlessness, or loss of muscle function. Donaldson, Halley, Voge, Hattner, Bayers, and MacMillan (1970) completed a 6-month bed-rest study in which three young men lost 39% of their calcaneus. After 6 months of ambulation, bone mass had returned to normal. Mack, LaChance, Vose, and

Table 34.3   Change in the Range of Joint Motion Following a 12-Week Exercise and Dance Program

Site Measured	Experimental Group	Control Group
Neck (flexion/extension)	↑27.8%	↓3.6%
Shoulder (abduction/adduction)	↑ 8.3%	↓5.1%
Wrist (flexion/extension)	↑12.8%	↓2.3%
Hip/back (flexion/extension)	↑26.9%	↓3.7%
Knee (flexion/extension)	↑11.6%	↓2.7%
Ankle (flexion/extension)	↑48.3%	↓5.1%

Source: Reprinted with the permission of the publisher from Munns, K. Effects of exercise on the range of joint motion in elderly subjects. In E. L. Smith & R. C. Serfass (eds.), *Exercise and aging: The scientific basis.* Hillside, N.J.: Enslow Publishers, 1981, p. 175.

Vogt (1967) reported bone mineral loss in the Gemini-Titan IV, V, and VII astronauts. The loss was attributed to the decreased effects of gravity and muscular pull in the weightless condition. It is hypothesized that the decreased activity levels of the aged play a significant role in the decline of bone mineral mass.

Bone is a dynamic tissue, and it responds directly to the forces acting upon it. Bassett (1971) reported that bone responds like a piezoelectric crystal to stress and strain, and that the charges produced function as a primary control of the bone. Numerous research studies have reported on the effects of unilateral exercise such as tennis. Jones, Priest, Hayes, Tichenor, and Nagel (1977) found a 34.9% hypertrophy in the dominant humerus (compared to the nondominant humerus) of male tennis players ($n = 44$) and a 28.4% hypertrophy in female tennis players ($n = 28$). Montoye, Smith, Fardon, and Howley (1980) measured the dominant and nondominant arms of 61 male tennis players with a mean age of 64. They reported a 13% humeral bone mineral mass increase in the playing arm compared to the nonplaying arm and a 7.9% hypertrophy in the radius. Smith, Reddan, and Smith (1981) reported on a group of 30 elderly women (mean age, 81) studied for 3 years. Twelve subjects participated in an exercise program for 40 to 45 minutes, 3 days per week, for 3 years. Eighteen subjects served as controls, with no modification of their physical activity lifestyle during the course of the 3 years. The physical activity group participated in a series of chair exercises at a 1.5–3.5 met range. Bone mineral of the radius midshaft, measured by the photon absorptiometry technique, decreased by 3.28% in the control group and increased by 2.29% in the physical activity group over the 3-year period. Although the mechanisms controlling bone response to physical activity have yet to be delineated, it would appear that bone loss is reduced in the older adult through exercise (see Table 34.4).

EVALUATION AND WORK CAPACITY TESTING

It is important to identify older adults who would be at high risk during moderately strenuous physical activity by evaluation prior to their participation in a physical activity program. Evaluations may range from a minimal examination to an extensive work capacity test. Every older adult entering a physical activity program should have had a medical physical examination within 2 years so that contraindications to physical activity (whether orthopedic, muscular, neurological, or cardiovascular) may be considered. Many older adults have not seen a family physician recently and are unaware of limitations of heart function, blood pressure, or physical capability. At the minimum, a pre-physical-activity evaluation should include a general physical and resting blood pressure and 12-lead electrocardiogram. A work capacity test is mandatory if the resting blood pressure or electrocardiogram is abnormal. This provides protection for both the participant and the physical activity designer or leader.

Table 34.4 Bone Mineral Content (BMC) and Bone Mineral/
Width (BMC/W) Changes of the Radius over 36 Months

	Control	Physical Activity	t-Ratio
BMC	−3.28	+2.29	<.005
BMC/W	−2.59	+1.71	<.01

Source: Reprinted with permission of the publisher from Smith, E. L., Exercise for the Prevention of Osteoporosis: A review, *The Physician and Sportsmedicine*, 10(3), March, 1982, p. 79.
Note: The percentage change and comparison of the groups were done by regression analysis using indicator variables.

Both laboratory and field work capacity evaluations have been adapted for the older adult. The most prevalent evaluation methods are treadmill, bicycle ergometer, and step tests, or walking outdoors at a set speed. Regardless of the evaluation method, adaptations to safeguard the older adult from injury and a gradually incremented work load are necessary. For maximal safety, all work capacity tests should be conducted by trained staff under medical supervision. If at all possible, exercise ECG should be monitored continually, with blood pressure monitored at frequent intervals.

Treadmill Testing

A modified Balke protocol (Balke & Ware, 1959) is recommended for the elderly person. The treadmill should be set at 2 mph, with a grade increment of 2% every 2 minutes, resulting in about a .55 met increment in work load (see Table 34.5). This work load increment reduces the probability of overstressing the subject. A low profile treadmill that begins at 0 mph is preferable for the older adult who lacks the coordination to step onto a moving belt. Increasing the speed from 0 to 2 mph to start the testing procedure provides easier acclimation. Although walking is a natural mode of locomotion, some older adults have difficulty because of orthopedic or balance problems. Fear of falling is a limiting factor in treadmill testing for some older individuals.

Bicycle Ergometer Testing

Bicycle testing is non-weight-bearing, and the handlebars and seat provide greater stability than is found with the treadmill. Many older adults find the seat uncomfortable, however, or are unable to coordinate the pedal revolutions. Quadriceps fatigue may intervene before the cardiovascular system is maximally stressed. For older adults, the bicycle ergometer protocol should be modified to start at a lower work load and to increase in smaller increments than are used for the young adult. The usual exercise protocol, starting at 300 kg/min (ACSM, 1980), may exceed the maximal capacity of older subjects. A suggested protocol, starting at approximately 2 mets and increasing by about .55 mets each 2 minutes, is shown in Table 34.6.

Chair Step Test

The chair step test (Smith & Gilligan, in press) is performed with the subject sitting in a straight-backed kitchen chair. Steps of varying heights (6 in., 12 in., 18 in.) are placed in front of the subject. At 1-second intervals, the subject alternately places the arch of each foot to the front edge of the step and returns it to the floor. The chair step test has a different time sequence than the treadmill test, as at each level of the test the subject works first 2 minutes and then 5 minutes if no limiting symptoms occur. Heart rate is monitored; if it is less than 75% predicted maximum after 5 minutes, the subject is tested with the next step height. After completing the 18-inch step, the final level requires the subject to extend the corresponding arm at shoulder height when the foot raises to the 18-inch step and to return the arm to the knee when the foot returns to the floor. The met increments are similar to those of the modified Balke treadmill test (see Table 34.5).

Walking Speed Tests

Tests of walking speed generally involve walking as fast as possible for a period of 12 minutes. It is necessary that the speed of walking be constant for evaluation of peak met level and estimation of maximum capacity to be accurate. Regulated speed requires practice, and monitoring of blood pressure is difficult during the test. Frequently, only one level of stress is observed.

Table 34.5 Comparison of the 3 mph Balke Treadmill Test, the Modified Balke Test, and the Chair Step Test

3 mph Balke Treadmill Test[a]			2 mph Modified Balke Test[a]			Chair Step Test[b]		
Grade	$\dot{V}o_2$/kg	Met	Grade	$\dot{V}o_2$/kg	Met	Step HT	$\dot{V}o_2$/kg	Met
0.0%	10.5	3.0	0.0%	7.0	2.0	6"	8.0	2.3
2.5%	14.0	4.0	2.0%	8.9	2.5	12"	10.0	2.9
5.0%	17.5	5.0	4.0%	10.8	3.1	18"	12.3	3.5
7.5%	21.0	6.0	6.0%	12.7	3.6	18"	13.7	3.9
						w/arms		
10.0%	24.5	7.0	8.0%	14.6	4.2			
			10.0%	16.5	4.7			

Source: Reprinted with the permission of the publisher from Smith, E. L., & Gilligan, C. Physical activity prescription for the older adult. *Physician and Sports Medicine*, 1983, **11**, 91–101.
[a] Energy costs calculated from formulas provided in B. Balke and R. W. Ware, An experimental study of physical fitness of Air Force personnel, *US Armed Forces Medical Journal*. 1959, **10**, 675.
[b] Energy costs obtained from unpublished data from our laboratory testing oxygen consumption during the chair step test.

Table 34.6   Suggested Bicycle Ergometer Protocol for Older Adults

Weight		Initial Load[a]		Load Increment[a]	
Kg	Lb	Kg/min	Watts	Kg/min	Watts
50	110	25	4.25	50	8.5
60	132	50	8.5	50	8.5
70	154	100	16.6	75	12.5
80	176	125	21	75	12.5
90	198	175	27	75	12.5
100	220	200	33.3	100	16.6

[a] Values for the met levels, based on weight and load, were determined by the formula V_{O_2} (1/min) = kg/min × 2 + 300 (ACSM, 1980, p. 146). The initial load is approximately 2 mets and the load increment is approximately .55 mets. Values of kg/min are rounded to the nearest 25 because of the limitations of dial settings on bicycle ergometers.

PHYSICAL ACTIVITY PRESCRIPTION

An individual's work capacity, regardless of the testing procedure used in evaluation, is an important parameter in the design of a physical activity program. The maximum work capacity fixes the intensity range at which an individual should exercise. Once the intensity is set, the duration and frequency may be determined. Like any other person who exercises, the older adult reaps benefits proportional to the consistency and stress level of participation. The older adult should exercise at between 40% and 70% of maximal work capacity. If a work capacity evaluation (modified Balke treadmill test, modified bicycle ergometer test, chair step test) has not been performed, the maximal work capacity can be estimated using the average work capacities for the young old and old old given in Table 34.1.

The intensity of specific activities can be determined in two ways:

1. Look up the met level of the activities involved, if this information is available (some examples are given in Table 34.7). Note, however, that these met levels are averages and may be affected by the amount of vigor the individual invests in the activity.

2. Monitor the heart rate of the participant and use this to determine the met level of the activity, based on the heart rates and met levels in the work capacity test.

To determine exercise intensity using exercise heart rate (EXHR), first determine (on a maximal work capacity test) or estimate (220 − age) the individual's maximum heart rate (MAXHR). Then calculate the percentage heart rate (%HR) at which an individual participates, as follows:

$$\%HR = (EXHR - RESTHR)/(MAXHR - RESTHR) \times 100 \qquad (34.1)$$

Although the actual maximum heartrate of an individual may vary 10% to 15% from the formula (220 − age) (Shephard, 1978, 1981), an individual's heart rate response to exercise is generally linear within the range of maximum work capacity.

Using the maximum met level (MAXMET) and %HR, the exercise met level (EXMET) can be determined as follows:

$$EXMET = \%HR/100 \times MAXMET \qquad (34.2)$$

Table 34.7 Met Levels of Walking and Recreational Activities

A. Walking[a]

Mph	Met Level
2	2.0
2.5	2.5
3.0	3.0
3.5	3.5
3.75	4.0
4.0	4.6
4.5	5.7
5.0	6.9

B. Recreational Activities[b]

Met Level	Activities
1.5–2.0	Knitting, sewing, playing cards, model ship building
2.0–2.5	Darts, billiards, bowling, light woodworking, playing piano, fishing from a boat, on the bank, or on the ice, croquet, power boating, shuffleboard
2.5–3.0	Cycling (5 mph), canoeing (2.5 mph), horseshoe pitching, car washing
3.5	Sailing small boat (handling boat), flyfishing, archery, badminton, raking leaves
4.0	Table tennis (recreational), golf (no cart), mowing lawn with a power mower, recreational volleyball, cycling (6.5 mph), canoeing (3 mph), gardening, carpentry
5.0	Cycling (8 mph), dancing, recreational softball, shoveling
6.0	Cycling (9 mph), fishing (wading in stream), hiking cross country, square dancing, rhumba, hunting

Source: Reprinted with the permission of the publisher from Smith, E. L., & Gilligan, C. Physical activity prescription for the older adult. *Physician and Sports Medicine,* in press.
[a] Energy costs from Pollock, M. L., Wilmore, J. H., & Fox, S. M. *Health and fitness through physical activity.* New York: Wiley, 1978.
[b] Energy costs from Skinner, J. S. *Body Energy.* Mountain View, Calif.: Anderson World, 1981.

For example, if an individual had a maximum met level of 5 mets on a treadmill test and was exercising at 70% heart rate, his exercise level would be

$$\text{EXMET} = 70/100 \times 5 \text{ mets} = 3.5 \text{ mets} \qquad (34.3)$$

The maximum met level can be estimated from individual submaximal work capacity tests by using a %HR at the maximal load attained and the predicted maximum heart rate:

$$\text{MAXMET} = \text{mets} \times 100/\%\text{HR} \qquad (34.4)$$

It has been suggested that 10% of daily maintenance caloric intake should be expended in vigorous exercise (Astrand & Rodahl, 1970). The maintenance caloric intake of older adults is generally lower than that of the younger population. This is because of reductions in both metabolic rate and activity level. Surveys have found that the average daily caloric intake is 1400 kcal for older women and 1700 kcal for older men (Sempos, 1979). Other studies have estimated that the average metabolic rate of older adults is approximately 1.1 mets/hour (Astrand & Rodahl 1970). Calories may be determined from mets by the following formula:

$$\text{Calories (kcal)} = \text{mets} \times \text{WT(kg)} \times 1.05 \times \text{hours} \qquad (34.5)$$

where the 1.05 was determined by

$$\frac{5 \text{ kcal}}{\text{liter } O_2} \times \frac{3.5 \text{ ml } O_2}{\text{met} \cdot \text{kg} \cdot \text{min}} \times \frac{1 \text{ liter}}{1000 \text{ ml}} \times \frac{60 \text{ min}}{\text{hour}} = 1.05 \frac{\text{kcal}}{\text{met} \cdot \text{kg} \cdot \text{hour}}$$

with 5 kcal/liter O_2 from Astrand and Rodahl (1970). Using Astrand and Rodahl's (1970) average met level of 1.1, daily caloric intake (KCAL/DAY) for an older adult would then be

$$\text{KCAL/DAY} = \text{WT(kg)} \times 1.05 \times 1.1 \times 24(\text{hours}) \qquad (34.6)$$

If food records are available for the individual, the average caloric intake can be obtained more accurately.

For calories expended during exercise, what should be considered are the calories over the calories consumed at rest (1 met). For our calculations of exercise calories (EXKCAL), formula 34.5 is modified to reflect this:

$$\text{EXKCAL} = \text{WT(kg)} \times (\text{EXMET} - 1) \times 1.05 \times \text{hours} \qquad (34.7)$$

Using the criteria that EXKCAL should be 10% of KCAL/DAY and substituting the intensity and duration parameters (equation 34.7) for exercise calories, we obtain

$$\text{WT(kg)} \times (\text{EXMET} - 1) \times 1.05 \times \text{hours} = 0.1 \times \text{KCAL/DAY} \qquad (34.8)$$

or

$$(\text{EXMET} - 1) \times \text{hours} = \frac{0.1 \times \text{KCAL/DAY}}{\text{WT(kg)} \times 1.05}$$

One may use a figure for KCAL/DAY from dietary analysis or one of the estimates given here. Using formula 34.6 for caloric use, the intensity and duration requirements simplify to

$$(\text{EXMET} - 1) \times \text{hours} = \frac{0.1 \times \text{WT(kg)} \times 1.05 \times 1.1 \times 24}{\text{WT(kg)} \times 1.05} = 2.64 \qquad (34.9)$$

Once the intensity of an exercise program is set, the duration formula is Hours = 2.64/(EXMET − 1).

As we can see, the required duration and intensity of an exercise program are interdependent. The intensity should always be between 40% and 70% of the person's maximum, but the exact level used can depend on the individual's limitations and interests. The duration should be at least 30 minutes and should satisfy the formula Hours = 2.64/(EXMET − 1). Older adults initially may have difficulty in exercising long enough to meet this requirement because of low work capacity. If this is the case, exercise may be divided into 30-minute sessions. Working at 40% to 70% of maximum for 30 minutes each day will increase the individual's work capacity, and this will allow the person to increase the met level of the program and decrease its recommended duration.

The intensity of exercise should not exceed the level obtained in an exercise work capacity test. The physiological responses to exercise have been monitored at these levels, and thus it is safer for the subject. Exercising at higher levels may provoke symptoms not seen on a submaximal test.

Example 1

A 70-year-old woman has been tested using the chair step test. Her resting heart rate is 60 and her predicted maximum heart rate is $(220 - 70) = 150$. She had heart rates of 101 (41%), 106 (52%), 116 (63%), and 123 (70%) on the four levels of the step test. Using the heart rate and met level of the final level completed, her maximal work capacity is $100/\%HR \times mets = 100/70 \times 3.9 = 5.6$ mets. If she exercises at an intensity of 50% (met level of 2.8, heart rate 105), the duration of her exercise should be $2.64/(EXMET - 1) = 2.64/1.8 = 1.55$ hours, or 93 minutes. If she exercises at 70% (met level 3.9, heart rate 123), her duration is $2.64/2.9 = .91$ hours, or 55 minutes.

Example 2

An 80-year-old with a resting heart rate of 80 has been tested using the modified Balke test; he reached his maximum heart rate $(220 - 80 = 140)$ at 8% grade. His maximum met level is thus 4.2 mets (see Table 34.5). No abnormalities appeared on the ECG, and blood pressure readings were not excessive. At a recommended exercise intensity of 70%, he should exercise at 2.9 mets, or a heart rate of 122. The duration is $2.64/1.9 = 1.4$ hours, or 83 minutes.

Example 3

A 60-year-old woman, weight 70 kg, resting heart rate 65, is tested using the bicycle ergometer. The protocol starts at 100 kg/min and increases by 75 kg/min. At a load of 400 kg/min, her heart rate is 122 (60%), but she is unable to continue the test because of leg pain. Based on a .55 increment of the bicycle ergometer test, she stopped at 4.2 mets, and her estimated maximum met level is $100/60 \times 4.2 = 7$ mets. As she has not been monitored past a 60% load, the exercise program intensity should be 60% or less. At 60% (met level 4.2, heart rate 122), the duration is $2.64/3.2 = .83$ hours, or 50 minutes.

Example 4

You have determined that the average daily intake of a 50 kg woman is 1200 calories per day and that her maximum met level is 5 mets. Using formula 34.8, the intensity and duration of her exercise program should satisfy the following formula:

$$(EXMET - 1) \times hours = \frac{0.1 \times 1200}{50 \times 1.05} = 2.29$$

Setting her exercise intensity at 70%, or 3.5 mets, she should exercise $2.29/2.5 = .92$ hours, or 55 minutes.

PHYSICAL ACTIVITY PROGRAMS

Limitations of the cardiovascular system, musculoskeletal systems, or joints are more common in older adults than in the young, and this may require modification of physical activity programs. For persons with these limitations, low-intensity exercises 5 to 6 days per week are needed to stimulate their cardiovascular systems and enhance or maintain their fitness. Walking, hiking, swimming, various aerobic games, and dancing are beneficial aerobic activities for older adults. Although activities such as jogging, skating, cross-country skiing, bicycle riding, or other aerobic sports are not precluded, they stress the cardiovascular system and joints more strenuously. Activities of lower intensity and with lower joint stress should be programmed until fitness and muscular strength are sufficient for these more vigorous activities.

The primary purpose of physical activity programming for older adults is to enhance the physical quality of life, aiding them in the activities of daily living and in maintaining their independence. Physical activity for the older adult must be geared to the individual's capability and must contain the necessary components for total fitness. Programming should stress all muscle groups and joints. Chair exercises, water-support activities, and fitness trails are programs that are encouraged for older adults. Using a chair for support, an increased range of motion of all joints and stimulus to all muscle groups may be accomplished with greater stability. Chair and water-support exercises are well suited for individuals with orthopedic limitations. Fitness trails can be set up in shopping malls or in local parks for groups of older adults. If muscular tone is adequate, recreational activities such as biking, hiking, jogging, or games adapted for the older adult can be pursued as part of a total fitness program.

Chair Exercises

Chair exercises range in intensity from approximately 1.5 to 4.5 mets. Movements generally take place at a rate of one per second. The participant sits with the spine firmly against the back of a kitchen chair. Some examples are as follows (examples are taken from Smith & Stoedefalke, 1978):

1. *Toe-heel rise* (1.5 mets): The participant raises the toes of both feet from the floor on the count of 1. On the count of 2, the toes return to the floor and the heels are lifted.

2. *Sideward arm and leg spread* (4 mets): The legs are extended parallel to the floor, with the arms parallel over them. The legs are then spread apart approximately 2 feet and returned to the center with the arms following the same pattern. This activity stimulates the musculature of both the upper and the lower body.

In other activities, the individual stands behind the chair with hands resting gently on the back of the chair. Examples are as follows:

1. *Half-knee bends* (2.6 mets): The person bends his or her knees one-third to one-half of the way down and returns to the erect standing position. This exercise stimulates the quadriceps and knee joints.

2. *Heel lift* (2.1 mets): The participant goes up onto the toes, lifting heels as high as possible, and returns heels to the floor.

Chair exercises provide a stimulus to the cardiovascular system as well as stability. The number of repetitions can be built up from about 15 to 60 each as muscle tone and endurance improve.

Water-Support Activities

It is important to realize that older adults have decreased muscle mass and a lower metabolic rate, and that they rapidly become chilled in a 79° swimming pool. Therefore, a temperature of 83° to 84° is recommended. Activities in the swimming pool should be monitored by heart rate like any other activities. In the water, however, the heart rate of the older adult is approximately 20 beats below that in land activities at the same met level (Claremont, Reddan, & Smith, 1981). The recommended exercise heart rate should be adjusted downward for water activities in order to maintain the fitness of older adults without stressing them beyond their capabilities.

Example

The 70-year-old woman in Example 1 wants to use water-support exercises for her program. She has been exercising at 70% (met level, 3.9) on land, with a heart rate of 123. For swimming activities, her heart rate should be set at 103 rather than 123. This will keep her met level at 3.9; were she to exercise in the water at a heart rate of 123, she would be exercising at $(123 + 20 - 60)/(150 - 60) = 92\%$, rather than at 70%.

Water-support activities may include circle games, walking forward or backward at various depths (thighs, waist, midchest), and bobbing. Equipment such as flutterboards or inflated balls may be used. In addition, those who have the capability may swim laps. Some examples using flutterboards are as follows:

1. The flutterboard may be held in front of the body for support while the participant propels himself or herself forward by fluttering the feet.
2. The flutterboard is held in front of the body parallel to the body plane. While walking through the water, the participant moves the board in a circle perpendicular to the plane of the body, so that it is sometimes immersed and sometimes out of the water.

Fitness Trails

Fitness trails (Morse & Smith, 1981) combine walking with chair exercises. The trail is 1 mile long, with exercise stations at quarter-mile intervals. Different areas of the body are exercised at each station. The first station, for example, works with the quadriceps, biceps, and triceps. First, the individual sits on a bench and raises one leg or the other to the top of a vertical post and returns it to the ground. The post ensures that the leg will be raised to a consistent height. After a certain number of repetitions, the participant turns to rubber tubing, attached to a pole with a screw eye, and alternately stretches and releases the tubing to strengthen biceps and triceps musculature. Which specific exercises are done at each station is not important, but all segments of the body should be stimulated over the course.

When fitness trails are developed outdoors, emergency procedures should be developed. A small hand-held siren has been used to signal emergencies in our program. The program staff should be trained to call paramedical personnel and rush to the site of emergency upon hearing the siren. Walkie-talkies have also proved adequate for this task. Specific plans and details for individual sites should be outlined and tested for maximal protection of the participant. Terrain and weather conditions should be monitored continually in outdoor programs so that injuries due to falls may be reduced to the minimum. Where the trail crosses hilly terrain, the additional energy requirement and changes in heart rate should be determined by the staff. All participants should be educated as to the specific requirements and stresses of the trail and the emergency procedures to follow if an accident occurs to them or to a partner.

Fun

The importance of fun in programming exercise for the older adult cannot be overemphasized. If the program is not enjoyable, the older adult will not be enticed to join or continue in it. Many older adults have been taught that recreational activity and the benefits of physical activity are only for the young and that the prerogative of growing old is inactivity. The interests of the participant should be considered in any program. Group programs should provide opportunities for socialization and interaction among the class members. Continued regular participation is thus encouraged by other participants as well as by the instructor. The names of the individual participants should be repeated often to acquaint class members with one another.

LEADING AN OLDER ADULT EXERCISE PROGRAM

Because of the low physical capability of many older adults, 60-minute class periods of low intensity are probably the most beneficial. Class activities should be carried out 5 days a week rather than the 3 days a week that is typical for younger individuals. This will ensure continued muscle tone, range of motion, and cardiovascular benefits. It is of paramount importance that the participants be educated and that a program for total fitness, through the components of endurance, strength, range of motion, coordination, and balance, be provided. Adaptation and modification of low-organized games, team sports, and recreational outings should be provided to maintain the interest of the participants. The older adult, despite decreased capability of movement, responds to program variety and to the programmer's interest. Physical activity programs and exercises for the older adult are available in a variety of books (Cooper, 1970; Frankel & Richard, 1977; Smith, Stoedefalke, & Gilligan, Note 1).

Physical activity programming for the older adult, though a rewarding and exciting task, requires special attention to the needs of the total person. Care must be taken in selecting facilities, providing an accessible program, and being prepared for emergencies.

Emergency Preparedness

Some older adults are at higher risk than younger individuals for cardiovascular accidents (heart or stroke). Staff members should be trained and certified in cardiopulmonary resuscitation (CPR). Emergency procedures should be developed carefully and the staff should be trained and periodically rehearsed in their use. Telephone numbers of the closest paramedic team should be placed on the phones, with directions for the most rapid access to the building. Although we have not yet needed to implement such procedures, the possibility of accidents is inherent in dealing with older adults, and it is important to be prepared.

Facilities

Special attention should be paid to the exercise facility. Visual changes in the older adults should be considered. It is particularly difficult for older adults to maneuver where light is poor, so hallways, stairwells, and gymnasium should be well lit. Stairways should have handrails on both sides. As reduced depth perception makes it difficult to distinguish between a floor and stairs of the same color, landings and top and bottom steps should be colored different from the other steps to indicate the change at these points. This will reduce the possibility of stumbling. Shower room floors should be dry and should have nonslip surfaces so that the older adults, whose reaction times are slowed, can avoid slipping. Whenever possible, the gymnasium should be reserved exclusively for the older adult exercise period, so that noise from other groups will not interfere. Under quiet conditions, an older adult can hear and interpret speech very clearly. With a noisy background, poor acoustics, or distortion of voices by reverberation, words are frequently misinterpreted. Articulation of some consonants and vowels reaches the high-frequency loss area of the older adult, which results in these sounds being heard poorly or not at all. Therefore, it takes longer for words to be processed by the brain. Slower speech allows greater time to discriminate sounds. When sound discrimination is a problem, increased volume may only irritate the older adult, rather than making speech more understandable. The instructor should speak slowly and clearly, and a schedule of activities should be provided on a blackboard. When new exercises or materials are introduced, a smaller room, which reduces reverberations and distance from the leader, should be used. This assists the older adult to see and hear the material presented more easily.

REFERENCE NOTE

1. Smith, E. L., Stoedefalke, K. G., & Gilligan, C. *Aging and exercise: Freedom through fitness.* Book in preparation, 1983.

REFERENCES

Adrian, M. J. Flexibility in the aging adult. In E. L. Smith & R. C. Serfass (eds.), *Exercises and aging: The scientific basis.* Hillside, N.J.: Enslow Publishers, 1981.

Allman, F. L. Conditioning for sports. In A. J. Ryan & F. L. Allman (eds.), *Sports medicine.* New York: Academic Press, 1974.

American College of Sports Medicine (ACSM). *Guidelines for graded exercise testing and exercise prescription.* Philadelphia: Lea & Febiger, 1980.

Aniansson, A., Grimby, G., Hedberg, M., Rundgren, A., & Sperling, L. Muscle function in old age. *Scandinavian Journal of Rehabilitative Medicine,* 1978, **6,** 43–49.

Astrand, I. Aerobic work capacity in men and women with special reference to age. *Acta Physiologica Scandinavica,* 1960, **49**(Suppl. 169), 1–92.

Astrand, I. *Aerobic work capacity: Its relation to age, sex and other factors.* Monograph No. 15. New York: American Heart Association 1967.

Astrand, P.-O., & Rodahl, K. *Textbook of work physiology.* New York: McGraw-Hill, 1970.

Balazs, E. A. Intercellular matrix of connective tissue. In C. Finch & L. Hayflick (eds.), *Handbook of the biology of aging.* New York: Van Nostrand Reinhold, 1977.

Balke, B., & Ware, R. W. An experimental study of physical fitness of Air Force personnel. *U.S. Armed Forces Medical Journal,* 1959, **10,** 675.

Barry, A. J., Daly, J. W., Pruett, E. D. R., Steinmetz, J. R., Page, H. F., Birkhead, N. C., & Rodahl, K. The effects of physical conditioning on older individuals: I. Work capacity, circulatory-respiratory function and electrocardiogram. *Journal of Gerontology,* 1966, **21,** 182–191.

Bassett, C. A. L. Biophysical principles affecting bone structure. In G. H. Bourne (ed.), *The biochemistry and physiology of bone.* New York: Academic Press, 1971.

Becklake, M. R., Frank, H., Dagenais, G. R., Ostiguy, G. L., & Guzman, G. A. Influence of age and sex on exercise cardiac output. *Journal of Applied Physiology,* 1965, **20,** 938–947.

Bhanthumnavin, K., & Schuster, M. M. Aging and gastrointestinal function. In C. E. Finch & L. Hayflick (eds.), *Handbook of the biology of aging.* New York: Van Nostrand Reinhold, 1977.

Birren, J. E., Carden, P. V., & Phillips, S. L. Reaction time as a function of the cardiac cycle in young adults. *Science,* 1963, **140,** 195–196.

Boone, D. C., & Azen, S. P. Normal range of motion of joints in male subjects. *Journal of Bone and Joint Surgery,* 1979, **61A,** 756–759.

Brandfonbrener, M., Landowne, M., & Shock, N. W. Changes in cardiac output with age. *Circulation,* 1955, **12,** 557–566.

Burke, W. E., Tuttle, W. W., Thompson, C. W., Janney, C. D., & Weber, R. J. The relation of grip strength and grip-strength endurance to age. *Journal of Applied Physiology,* 1953, **5,** 629–630.

Campbell, M. J., McComas, A. J., & Petito, F. Physiological changes in aging muscles. *Journal of Neurology, Neurosurgery and Psychiatry,* 1973, **36,** 174–182.

Chapman, E. A., deVries, H. A., & Swezey, R. Joint stiffness: Effects of exercise on young and old men. *Journal of Gerontology,* 1972, **27,** 218–221.

Claremont, A. D., Reddan, W. G., & Smith, E. L. Metabolic costs and feasibility of water support exercises for the elderly. In F. J. Nagle & H. J. Montoye (eds.), *Exercise in health and disease.* Springfield, Ill.: Charles C Thomas, 1981.

Clarke, H. H. Joint and body range of movement. *Physical Fitness Research Digest,* Series 5, 1975.

Cooper, K. *The new aerobics.* New York: Lippincott, 1970.

deVries, H. A. Physiological effects of an exercise training regimen upon men aged 52–88. *Journal of Gerontology,* 1970, **25,** 325–336.

deVries, H. A., & Adams, G. M. Comparison of exercise responses in old and young men: II. Ventilatory mechanics. *Journal of Gerontology,* 1972, **27,** 349–352.

Donaldson, C., Halley, S. B., Voge, J. M., Hattner, R. S., Bayers, J. H., & MacMillan, D. E. Effect of prolonged bedrest on bone mineral. *Metabolism,* 1970, **19,** 1071–1084.

Drinkwater, B. L., Horvath, S. M., & Wells, C. L. Aerobic power of females ages 10 to 68. *Journal of Gerontology,* 1975, **30,** 385–394.

Edelman, I. S., Haley, H. B., Schloerb, P. R., Sheldon, D. B., Friis-Hanson, B. J., Stoll, G., & Moore, F. D. Further observations on total body water: I. Normal values throughout the life span. *Surgery, Gynecology and Obstetrics,* 1952, **95,** 1–12.

Fitts, R. H. Aging and skeletal muscle. In E. L. Smith & R. C. Serfass (eds.), *Exercise and aging: The scientific basis.* Hillside, N.J.: Enslow Publishers, 1981.

Frankel, L. J., & Richard, B. B. Be alive as long as you live. Charleston, W. Va.: Preventicare, 1977.

Fryer, J. H. Studies of body composition in men aged 60 and over. In N. W. Shock (ed.), *Biological aspects of aging.* New York: Columbia University Press, 1962.

Garn, S. W., Rohmann, C. G., & Wagner, B. Bone loss as a general phenomenon in man. *Federal Proceedings,* 1967, **26,** 1729–1736.

Greey, G. W. *A study of flexibility in selected joints of adult males age 18–72.* Unpublished doctoral dissertation, University of Michigan, 1955.

Griffiths, G. J., Robinson, K. B., Cartwright, G. O., & McLachlan, M. S. F. Loss of renal tissue in the elderly. *British Journal of Radiology,* 1976, **49,** 111–117.

Gutmann, E., & Hanzlikova, V. Motor unit in old age. *Nature,* 1966, **209**(5026), 921–922.

Gutmann, E., & Hanzlikova, V. Fast and slow motor units in aging. *Gerontology,* 1976, **22,** 280–300.

Harris, R. E. Long-term studies of blood pressure recorded annually, with implications for the factors underlying essential hypertension. *Transactions of the Association of Life Insurance Medical Directors,* 1968, **51,** 30.

Harris, R. *The management of geriatric cardiovascular disease.* Philadelphia: Lippincott, 1970.

Hayflick, L. The cellular basis for biological aging. In C. E. Finch & L. Hayflick (eds.), *Handbook of the biology of aging.* New York: Van Nostrand Reinhold, 1977.

Heath, G. W., Hagberg, J. M., Ehsani, A. E., & Holloszy, J. O. A physiological comparison of young and older endurance athletes. *Journal of Applied Physiology: Respiratory, Environmental and Exercise Physiology,* 1981, **51**(3), 634–640.

Henschel, A., Cole, M. B., & Lyczkowskyj, O. Heat tolerance of elderly persons living in a subtropical climate. *Journal of Gerontology,* 1968, **23,** 17–22.

Hyams, D. E. The liver and biliary system. In J. C. Brocklehurst (ed.), *Textbook of geriatric medicine and gerontology.* London: Churchill Livingstone, 1973.

Ikai, M., & Fukunaga, T. A study on training effect on strength per cross-sectional area of muscle by means of ultrasonic measurement. *Int. Z. Angew. Physiol.,* 1961, **28,** 173–180.

Inokuchi, S., Ishikawa, H., Iwamoto, S., & Kimura, T. Age related changes in the histological composition of the rectus abdominis muscle of the adult human. *Human Biology,* 1975, **47,** 231–249.

Jennekens, F. G., Tomlinson, B. E., & Walton, J. W. Histochemical aspects of five limb muscles in old age: An autopsy study. *Journal of Neurological Science,* 1971, **14,** 259–276.

Jervey, A. *A study of flexibility of selected joints in specified groups of adult females.* Unpublished doctoral dissertation, University of Michigan, 1961.

Johns, R. J., & Wright, U. Relative importance of various tissues in joint stiffness. *Journal of Applied Physiology,* 1962, **17,** 824–828.

Jones, H. H., Priest, J. D., Hayes, W. C., Tichenor, C. C., & Nagel, D. A. Humeral hypertrophy in response to exercise. *Journal of Bone and Joint Surgery,* 1977, **59A,** 204–208.

Jones, R. L., Overton, T., Hammerlindel, D., & Sproule, B. J. Effects of age in regional residual volume. *Journal of Applied Physiology: Respiratory, Environmental and Exercise Physiology,* 1978, **44,** 195–199.

Kasch, F. W., & Wallace, J. P. Physiological variables during 10 years of endurance exercisse. *Medicine and Science in Sports and Exercise,* 1976, **8**(1), 5–8.

Kemble, F. Conduction in the normal adult median nerve: The different effect of aging in men and women. *Electromyography,* 1967, **7,** 275–289.

Keys, A., & Brozek, J. Body fat in adult man. *Physiology Review,* 1953, **33,** 245–325.

Kilbom, A., & Astrand, I. Physical training with submaximal intensities in women: II. Effect on cardiac output. *Scandinavian Journal of Clinical and Laboratory Investigation,* 1971, **28,** 163–175.

Larsson, L., Grimby, G., & Karlsson, J. Muscle strength and speed of movement in relation to age and muscle morphology. *Journal of Applied Physiology: Respiratory, Environmental and Exercise Physiology,* 1979, **46,** 451–456.

Larsson, L., Sjodin, B., & Karlsson, J. Histochemical and biochemical changes in human skeletal muscle with age in sedentary males, age 22–65 years. *Acta Physiologica Scandinavica,* 1978, **103,** 31–39.

Lesser, M. The effects of rhythmic exercise on the range of motion in older adults. *American Corrective Therapy Journal,* 1978, **32**(4), 118–122.

Lindeman, R. D. Age changes in renal function. In R. Goldman & M. Rockstein (eds.), *The physiology and pathology of human aging.* New York: Academic Press, 1975.

Mack, P., LaChance, P., Vose, G., & Vogt, F. Bone demineralization of foot and hand of Gemini-Titan IV, V, and VII astronauts during orbital flight. *American Journal of Roentgenology,* 1967, **100,** 503–511.

Mazess, R. B., & Cameron, J. R. Bone mineral content in normal U.S. whites. *International Conference on Bone Mineral Measurements,* 1973, 228–238.

McCafferty, W. B., & Edington, D. W. Skeletal muscle and organ weights of aged and trained male rats. *Gerontology,* 1970, **20,** 44–50.

Miall, W. E., & Lovell, H. G. Relation between change of blood pressure and age. *British Medical Journal,* 1967, **2,** 660–664.

Montoye, H. J., Smith, E. L., Fardon, D. F., & Howley, E. T. Bone mineral in senior tennis players. *Scandinavian Journal of Sports Science,* 1980, **2**(1), 26–32.

Moritani, T. Training adaptations in the muscles of older men. In E. L. Smith & R. C. Serfass (eds.), *Exercise and aging: The scientific basis.* Hillside, N.J.: Enslow Publishers, 1981.

Morris, J. F., Koski, A., & Johnson, L. C. Spirometric standards for healthy non-smoking adults. *American Review of Respiratory Disease,* 1971, **103,** 57–67.

Morse, C. E., & Smith, E. L. Physical activity programming for the aged. In E. L. Smith & R. C. Serfass (eds.), *Exercise and aging: The scientific basis.* Hillside, N.J.: Enslow Publishers, 1981.

Munns, K. Effects of exercise on the range of joint motion. In E. L. Smith & R. C. Serfass (eds.), *Exercise and aging: The scientific basis.* Hillside, N.J.: Enslow Publishers, 1981.

Murray, J. F. *The normal lung.* Philadelphia: Saunders, 1976.

Needham, C. D., Rogan, M. C., & McDonald, I. Normal standards for lung volumes, intra-pulmonary gas mixing and maximum breathing capacity. *Thorax,* 1954, **9,** 313–325.

Neufeld, O., Smith, J., & Goldman, S. Arterial oxygen tension in relation to age in hospital subjects. *Journal of the American Geriatrics Society,* 1973, **21,** 4–9.

Niinimaa, V., & Shephard, R. J. Training and oxygen conductance in the elderly: I. The respiratory system. *Journal of Gerontology,* 1978, **33,** 354–361.

Petrofsky, J. S., & Lind, A. R. Aging, isometric strength and endurance, and cardiovascular responses to static effort. *Journal of Applied Physiology,* 1975, **39,** 91–95.

Pickering, G. W. The peripheral resistance in persistent hypertension. *Clinical Science,* 1936, **2,** 209–235.

Pollock, M. L., Wilmore, J. H., & Fox, S. M. *Health and fitness through physical activity.* New York: Wiley, 1978.

Robinson, S., Belding, H. S., Consolazio, F. C., Horvath, S. M., & Turrell, E. S. Acclimitization of older men to work in heat. *Journal of Applied Physiology,* 1965, **20,** 583–586.

Robinson, S., Dell, D. B., Tzankoff, S. P., Wagner, J. A., & Robinson, R. D. Longitudinal studies of aging in 37 men. *Journal of Applied Physiology,* 1975, **38,** 263–267.

Rossman, I. Anatomic and body composition changes with aging. In C. E. Finch & L. Hayflick (eds.), *Handbook of the biology of aging.* New York: Van Nostrand Reinhold, 1977.

Rowe, J. W., Shock, N. W., & DeFronzo, R. A. The influence of age on the renal response to water deprivation in man. *Nephron,* 1976, **17,** 270–278.

Sempos, C. T. *Evaluation of quality of diets of elderly people residing in fourteen nursing homes in Wisconsin.* Unpublished master's thesis, University of Wisconsin, 1979.

Shaw, D. J., Rothbaum, D. A., Angell, C. S., & Shock, N. W. The effects of age and blood pressure upon the systolic time intervals in males aged 20–89 years. *Journal of Gerontology,* 1973, **28,** 133–139.

Shephard, R. J. *Physical activity and aging.* Chicago: Year Book Medical Publishers, 1978.

Shephard, R. J. Cardiovascular limitations in the aged. In E. L. Smith & R. C. Serfass (eds.), *Exercise and aging: The scientific basis.* Hillside, N.J.: Enslow Publishers, 1981.

Shock, N. Physiological aspects of aging in man. *Annual Review of Physiology,* 1961, **23,** 97–122.

Shock, N. W. The physiology of aging. *Scientific American,* 1962, **206**(1), 100–108.

Shock, N. W. Systems integration. In C. E. Finch & L. Hayflick (eds.), *Handbook of the biology of aging.* New York: Van Nostrand Reinhold, 1977.

Sidney, K. H. Cardiovascular benefits of physical activity in the exercising aged. In E. L. Smith & R. C. Serfass (eds.), *Exercise and aging: The scientific basis.* Hillside, N.J.: Enslow Publishers, 1981.

Sidney, K. H., & Shephard, R. J. Perceptions of exertion in the elderly: Effects of aging, mode of exercise and physical training. *Perceptual and Motor Skills,* 1977, **44,** 999–1010.

Sidney, K. H., & Shephard, R. J. Frequency and intensity of exercise training for elderly subjects. *Medicine and Science in Sports and Exercise,* 1978, **10,** 125–131.

Skinner, J. S. Body energy. Mountain View, Calif.: Anderson World, 1981.

Smith, D. M., Khairi, M. R. A., Norton, J., & Johnston, C. C. Age and activity effects on rate of bone mineral loss. *Journal of Clinical Investigation,* 1976, **58,** 716–721.

Smith, D. O. Physiological and structural changes at the neuromuscular junction during aging. In E. Giacobini, C. Filogamo, G. Giarobini, & A. Vernadakis (eds.), *The aging brain: Cellular and molecular mechanisms of aging in the nervous system.* New York: Raven Press, 1982.

Smith, E. L. Exercise for prevention of osteoporosis: A review. *Physician and Sports Medicine,* 1982, **10**(3), 72–83.

Smith, E. L., & Gilligan, C. Physical activity prescription for the older adult. *Physician and Sports Medicine,* in press.

Smith, E. L., Reddan, W., & Smith, P. E. Physical activity and calcium modalities for bone mineral increase in aged women. *Medicine and Science in Sports and Exercise,* 1981, **13**(1), 60–64.

Smith, E. L., & Serfass, R. C. (eds.). *Exercise and aging: The scientific basis.* Hillside, N.J.: Enslow Publishers, 1981.

Smith, E. L., & Stoedefalke, K. G. *"Aging and exercise."* Mimeo, 1978. Copyright by the authors.

Spirduso, W. W. Reaction and movement time as a function of age and physical activity level. *Journal of Gerontology,* 1975, **30,** 435–440.

Spirduso, W. W. Physical fitness, aging, and psychomotor speed: A review. *Journal of Gerontology,* 1980, **35,** 850–865.

Spirduso, W. W., & Farrar, R. P. Effects of aerobic training on reactive capacity: An animal model. *Journal of Gerontology,* 1981, **36,** 654–662.

Stamford, B. A. Physiological effects of training upon institutionalized geriatric men. *Journal of Gerontology,* 1972, **27,** 451–455.

Tzankoff, S. P., & Norris, A. H. Effect of muscle mass decrease on age-related BMR changes. *Journal of Applied Physiology,* 1977, **43,** 1001–1006.

Welford, A. T. Performance, biological mechanisms and age: A theoretical sketch. In A. T. Welford & J. E. Birren (eds.), *Behaviour, aging and the nervous system.* Springfield, Ill.: Charles C Thomas, 1965.

SECTION 5
HEALTHFUL DIET

CHAPTER 35

OVERVIEW: HEALTHFUL DIET

JUDITH RODIN

Yale University

There is little doubt that one of the most significant of all health-relevant behaviors is food intake. Like sleep, it represents a basic biological need, for without food and sleep the organism could not survive. What makes the study of food intake so interesting is that, unlike sleep, the effects of cognition, environment, and culture, all extrinsic to biological state, are nonetheless its major determinants. People eat what they like, at times and in ways that are most convenient or socially mandated; they tend to eat what others whom they perceive as similar to them eat; and frequently they eat too much or too little, depending on the influence of environmental cues and social pressure.

Food intake that is no longer responsive even in a limited way to the energy expenditure needs of the individual may result in obesity, at one extreme, or emaciation, at the other. Except in illness-induced anorexia or genetic obesity conditions such as the Prader Willi syndrome, much of the problem in anorexia and obesity arises when the normal tendency to respond to cognitive and sociocultural factors goes awry. In most cases, the extreme states of anorexia and obesity result only in high-risk individuals (through genetic, psychological, or morphological predisposition), but early identification of individuals who are vulnerable to food-related disorders has as yet eluded scientists working in this area. There are some promising leads, both in genetic and early environmental experience factors, and the next decade should provide the answer to this question. In the short run, however, our prevention efforts are hampered by incomplete knowledge.

What complicates this complex area even further is that the behaviors of over- and undereating and the physical conditions of obesity and anorexia are in turn related to the onset and maintenance of physical disease and ill health. Thus, their prevention has added importance for health enhancement and disease prevention. Here, too, the final word has yet to be said. As is evident in the chapters in this section, there is still a fair amount of controversy regarding the role of the specifics of food intake and level of body weight in relation to health. What does seem clear is that many identified diseases are controlled, ameliorated, or cured by weight loss or by the intake of specific nutrients. What is controversial is whether these diseases can be prevented by the same food- or weight-relevant behavioral changes that are influential in controlling or curing them. The controversy centers on how one interprets current data regarding historical changes in patterns of disease and death and how one relates them to changes in weight and dietary intake over the same time periods. The safest assumption is that these dietary and body weight factors surely play a role in disease prevention but that this role is subtle and is different for different individuals as a function of their genetic background and environmental circumstances. Until the specific predisposing factors can be clearly identified, we simply are unable to tell how much of the variance is accounted for by nutrition and body weight.

Less controversial is the assumption that good health and feeling well depend on an appropriate intake of nutrients and calories and on maintaining a level of body weight that is appropriate for one's age, sex, body build, and daily energy expenditure. Nutritional guidelines and body weight norms allow identification of what is appropriate, at least for the average individual. The specific needs of any particular person may deviate markedly from these norms, however, and here issues of self-monitoring and self-regulation of behavior become especially crucial. People must learn how to examine and modify their own food-relevant behaviors in line with the observed effects and in light of desired outcomes. This has led to an effort to identify not only individuals who are at high risk because of biological predisposition but also high-risk behavior patterns, such as skipping breakfast, overconsuming refined sugar, or binging and purging. This section reviews the literature on current strategies for modifying problem behaviors and their relative efficacy. Since the majority of the public never seeks professional help on these matters, the most recent efforts at intervention target the school, the workplace, or the local community at large, where significant numbers of people may be influenced to change their dietary habits. Not only are these procedures important because they reach greater numbers of people, but there appears to be an increment in the ability to change individual food intake practices when intervention occurs in the context of a group. Presumably, the group provides some combination of models for appropriate behavior, peer pressure, and social support. Food intake habits may be especially responsive to such intervention efforts since they are so strongly influenced by social and environmental factors.

Although this section focuses solely on the relationship of dietary intake and weight to physical health, I must note also their strong relationship to mental health. Anorexia is often a concomitant of severe depression, and the relationship between dysphoria and the extremes of both overeating and undereating is well known. Anorexia nervosa is a clearly psychopathological condition, linked to family structure, need for achievement, and sense of control.

Bulimia nervosa, a recently documented disorder that alarmingly is reaching almost epidemic proportions among college-age females in particular, is a pattern of binging and purging whose etiology is presently unknown. The whole cycle of behavior is a psychologically destructive and unhappy one, often leaving its victims with little time or energy for any sort of life beyond the binges and purges. The syndrome taxes the person's emotional and physical resources, leading to severe guilt and shame as well as, in some cases, antisocial behavior such as stealing money or food to enable a binge. This represents the closest thing to addictive behavior that we have seen in the food intake area. Finally, obesity has also been linked with emotional distress and, in some extreme cases, with frank psychopathology.

Although the correlations between food intake problems and mental health are clear, their causal relationship is not. In a society where thinness is highly valued, as in most Western cultures, excessive efforts to reach a body weight consistent with that norm may be psychologically and biologically stressful and disregulatory for a great number of individuals. In a society such as ours, obese people may be unhappy because they are fat rather than fat because they are unhappy. Unfortunately, norms regarding beauty have thus far proved to be far more influential in determining type and level of food intake and feelings of well-being than information regarding health-promoting dietary practices. For thousands of years, people have been willing to damage their bodies in order to look good to members of their particular social group. Efforts at intervention must continuously be aware that the desire to be healthy is not the only or even the most important determinant of a person's behavior.

In addition, many have argued that mood and even some personality disturbances may be the result of specific nutrient deficits, again suggesting that mental health follows from rather than causes food intake problems. Many interesting questions remain regarding the relationship of mental health, diet, and body weight, and they should be of great concern for practitioners of health enhancement.

In conclusion, we know that there is a strong and important relationship between food intake and body weight, on the one hand, and physical and mental health, on the other. The chapters in this section explore some of these relationships and raise important public health questions. The first group of chapters considers what kinds of diets are most healthful and for whom, what the determinants of people's food choices are, and how these dietary practices may be modified. The second group of chapters examines obesity—the most common food intake/energy expenditure problem in modern society—and considers the health-relevant consequences of obesity and the success of techniques to treat it. The final chapter challenges us to view the effects of changing one health-relevant behavior—cigarette smoking—on another—body weight—noting that we must always be aware of possible interactive effects in our health promotion efforts.

CHAPTER 36

WHAT IS A HEALTHFUL DIET?

D. M. HEGSTED

Harvard School of Public Health and New England
Regional Primate Center, Harvard Medical School

A healthful diet is a diet that minimizes the risk of all nutrition-related diseases. This means that the diet must provide adequate amounts of all essential nutrients (energy, protein, vitamins, and essential minerals) and, at the same time, must minimize the risk of diseases associated with overconsumption. To some degree, these are conflicting objectives. It should also be recognized that a recommended diet will not be very useful unless it is reasonably acceptable to the population that is expected to consume it and can be provided by the available food supply. Dietary recommendations that are overly restrictive—too monotonous, too expensive, too difficult to find or prepare, and the like—are likely to turn off the consumers. They may decide that the treatment is worse than the disease, and little will be accomplished, particularly since we strive for a diet that will be consumed throughout a lifetime. Thus, in developing dietary recommendations, the food habits of the population must be considered; our judgment must be based not only on nutritional knowledge but also on practical considerations. People who are responsible for developing such recommendations for a Japanese population, for example, might reach considerably different conclusions from those of people who are responsible for the U.S. population, even though there is no reason to believe that the nutrient needs of the two population are different. It is also worthwhile to emphasize the word *minimize*. Some nutrition-related problems can be eliminated by currently feasible diets; for others, we can probably hope only to limit their impact. Again, a judgment must be made between what one may think is optimal and what is feasible. Finally, whatever the dietary recommendations may be, they need to be presented in ways that are understandable and that can be put into practice by the consumer in order to have a favorable impact on food practices.

The complexity of the problem can be appreciated if we realize that the requirements and tolerances for various materials vary substantially from one individual to another; that there are over 50 nutrients and food constituents of nutritional importance, not including natural toxicants, food additives, and contaminants which may be important; and that the consumer may have over 10,000 items available in a supermarket from which he must select his food. Many of these may be relatively new foods of unknown composition to the consumer. Clearly, the opportunities for selection of a less than optimal diet are enormous.

Probably the most surprising thing is that in such a complex system, most people do maintain a reasonably satisfactory nutritional state. Health statistics reveal that a reasonably good, if not optimal, state of health can be maintained upon a wide variety of diets. The

Reprinted with permission from Hegsted, D. M. What is a healthful diet? *Primary Care,* 1982, **9,** 445–473.

conventional wisdom of the body must be substantial, and the human body must be able to adapt to a wide range of foods. An ideal diet cannot be defined. Thus the nutritionist, in advising the general public on diet, must guard against being too specific, developing diets which will not be acceptable to the general public, and also guard against making recommendations that are so general that they are not useful to the consumer.

This chapter does not deal with therapeutic diets. When the risk is high, rigid dietary instruction may be justified and required. Under these circumstances, the most effective approach is for a well-trained dietitian or nutritionist to attempt to develop a diet which, to the degree possible, fits the dietary prescription for the food preferences of the individual. Some authors have suggested that in an ideal world, such advice would be available to all individuals. This is clearly impossible, of course, but even if we had that capability, it would probably not be an effective solution to nutritional problems. We have abundant evidence that although most obese people know that they either have to eat less or exercise more, the advice is often not effective. It is easy to understand that for a person to modify his diet when everyone around him is eating foods forbidden to him, requires a degree of self-control that is often impossible. The temptations and opportunities are usually too great unless motivation is extremely high. We now have many examples which demonstrate that effective reduction in risk factors related to coronary heart disease is most easily accomplished by modification of the family diet or that of the community. It is not difficult to understand why this is true.

Furthermore, a healthful diet must have long-range objectives. Chronic diseases, such as coronary heart disease, are not of immediate concern to children, adolescents, or young adults, but the antecedents begin at an early age. We have only limited capacity to determine who will eventually be at risk, but most Americans will be at risk for a chronic disease at some point. Our objective must be not only to meet immediate nutritional needs but to establish food habits that will be protective throughout a lifetime. Thus, the target should be the entire family or the community in which the individual lives rather than each individual.

CURRENT DIETARY PRACTICE

Nutrient requirements depend on body size, rates of growth, sex, and so forth, and dietary standards have emphasized the nutrient needs of different age and sex groups. However, as is shown in Table 36.1, and as previously emphasized (Windham, Wyse, Hurst, et al., 1981), the food that the different age and sex groups actually eat is remarkably similar in nutrient density (nutrient per 1000 kcal). This is not unexpected and reflects how people are fed and eat. Whoever is responsible for the purchase and preparation of food prepares a meal and places it on the table. All members of the family select portions of the foods available and, as Table 36.1 demonstrates, tend to select more or less proportionate amounts of each food available. This reinforces the conclusion already reached that if one wants to modify the diet, the appropriate target is the family or the group with which the individual eats.

Current survey data indicate that although lower income households (income less than 6000 dollars per year) appear to consume somewhat less total food, the nutrient density of that food is not greatly different from that of higher income households. This can be achieved since lower cost foods are not necessarily of lower nutrient content. The data are probably skewed by those at the very low end of the economic scale who may not only have difficulty in getting enough food, but make less satisfactory food choices. Still, the data emphasize that the majority of Americans have sufficient food and that access to essential nutrients is not markedly dependent on income. Undoubtedly, this is primarily the result of the rather extensive food and nutrition programs currently provided which have certainly increased the availability of food. Whether such programs will remain available is, of course, now in some doubt.

Table 36.1 Average Concentration of Nutrients in the Diets Consumed by Americans

Sex and Age (yrs)	Individuals (number)	Food Energy in Total Diet (kcal)	Protein (gm)	Fat (gm)	Carbohydrate (gm)	Calcium (mg)	Iron (mg)	Magnesium (mg)	Phosphorus (mg)	Vitamin A Value (I.U.)	Thiamin (mg)	Riboflavin (mg)	Preformed Niacin (mg)	Vitamin B6 (mg)	Vitamin B12 (µg)	Vitamin C (mg)
			Nutrient per 1000 kcal													
Males and females																
Under 1	78[a]	794	37.0	39.0	118.5	1,008	22.1	161	838	4,601	1.13	1.96	11.4	0.80	2.96	101
1-2	264[b]	1,164	40.3	41.4	118.9	633	7.0	137	732	2,895	0.77	1.25	8.7	0.79	2.66	65
3-5	437	1,435	38.9	41.8	119.6	503	6.8	125	657	2,638	0.75	1.11	9.5	0.79	2.64	50
6-8	469	1,711	39.0	41.8	119.4	511	6.6	126	669	2,790	0.77	1.10	9.6	0.80	2.57	50
Males																
9-11	216	2,000	39.4	43.1	115.3	458	6.8	122	631	2,299	0.77	1.06	10.1	0.80	2.48	43
12-14	313	2,366	38.7	44.3	113.7	458	6.5	121	624	2,395	0.74	1.03	9.6	0.77	2.22	40
15-18	400	2,698	40.0	45.1	110.0	440	6.5	118	629	2,274	0.69	0.96	9.4	0.74	2.19	42
19-22	287	2,569	41.2	45.3	102.6	390	6.3	121	623	1,934	0.62	0.86	9.9	0.75	2.10	35
23-34	770	2,449	40.5	45.7	101.2	347	6.6	129	604	2,258	0.64	0.82	10.0	0.74	2.25	41
35-50	784	2,314	42.5	46.4	97.3	341	7.0	140	617	2,701	0.64	0.84	10.7	0.76	2.51	41
51-64	634	2,148	43.1	46.5	98.5	342	7.4	148	617	3,438	0.69	0.91	11.0	0.83	3.73	49
65-74	295	1,970	41.6	46.7	105.5	376	7.6	152	644	3,625	0.74	0.98	10.9	0.83	3.10	54
75 and over	127	1,808	42.2	46.5	104.3	387	7.6	154	646	3,833	0.81	0.98	10.9	0.86	2.52	54
Females																
9-11	241	1,865	38.4	41.6	120.7	462	6.6	129	630	2,451	0.76	1.04	9.7	0.80	2.15	49
12-14	309	1,903	38.8	43.7	114.9	459	6.2	118	637	2,189	0.69	0.97	9.1	0.72	2.17	45
15-18	402	1,791	40.2	44.0	111.9	436	6.3	122	626	2,361	0.67	0.93	9.7	0.73	2.11	47
19-22	337	1,621	41.9	45.7	105.6	403	6.7	134	653	2,426	0.65	0.88	9.5	0.76	2.42	52
23-34	949	1,616	42.6	44.6	104.0	384	6.9	143	634	2,920	0.65	0.86	10.3	0.79	2.37	52
35-50	942	1,514	43.4	45.9	100.4	353	7.6	183	638	3,080	0.69	0.87	12.2	0.81	2.67	57
51-64	792	1,522	43.9	45.9	102.7	360	7.7	163	638	4,120	0.71	0.94	11.7	0.87	3.29	67
64-74	377	1,444	41.9	44.2	110.6	406	7.5	164	652	4,659	0.76	1.01	11.1	0.87	3.11	70
75 and over	197	1,367	40.3	42.6	115.6	443	7.6	160	658	4,683	0.77	1.07	10.4	0.86	3.45	68
All individuals	9,620[c]	1,865	41.4	44.7	106.9	409	7.1	142	638	2,966	0.70	0.95	10.4	0.79	2.64	51

Source: Based on a 24-hour dietary recall of the day preceding the interview, spring 1977. The survey included individuals from 48 states, all urbanizations, and all income groups. [From USDA Nationwide Food Consumption Survey 1977–78, 48 conterminous states, spring 1977 (preliminary).]
[a] Excludes 36 breast-fed infants.
[b] Excludes 4 breast-fed infants.
[c] Excludes 40 breast-fed infants.

Although the data are admittedly inadequate, current information indicates that nutritional deficiency diseases in the United States are relatively rare and mild. This simply has to mean that the average American diet provides a reasonably adequate intake of essential nutrients for most Americans. Since the nutrient density of the diet is approximately the same for people of varying age and the two sexes, this must also mean that the difference in total food intake (and thus a difference in nutrient intake) is adequate to account for the difference in nutrient needs that do change with body, size, age, and sex.

Quite obviously half the population consumes levels of food and nutrients below the average amount. Nutrient deficiencies are most likely to be found in those with lower than average intake either because of a lower total food intake or poorer than average food selection. This must mean that even the average intake provides some barrier against deficiency or is above the minimal need of most people. Otherwise, much of the population would demonstrate nutritional deficiency. We cannot argue, of course, that the nutrient content of the average American diet is ideal or optimal, but without contrary evidence it does provide a reasonable basis for establishing the nutrient content of a healthful diet. It is a diet currently attainable by the majority of Americans. Unless there is evidence that the average American diet is unnecessarily high in a nutrient, our first objective with respect to nutrient consumption should be to elevate the nutrient consumption of disadvantaged groups to that of the average, thus ensuring that discrimination on a nutritional basis does not occur.

THE RECOMMENDED DIETARY ALLOWANCES

The nutrient standards in the United States have long been the Recommended Dietary Allowances (RDA) (Food and Nutrition Board, 1980). Although these have evolved over the years and have been modified frequently, the basic philosophy has remained the same. It is understood that individuals of similar age, sex, and activity level may have different nutrient needs. Both genetic and environmental factors are presumably involved. The needs of an individual, however, are rarely known. Thus, if an adequate intake of a nutrient is to be assured for all or most individuals, the nutrient standard must be established at the upper end of the range of requirements of the group; the RDA represent a relatively generous estimate of need, thought to be adequate for the great majority of individuals. This standard, however, is not without difficulty since it also means that the RDA—if they are correctly established—also represent levels which are actually above the need of most individuals. The principle is valid, but there is some obvious confusion about the conclusions to be drawn when consumption levels fall below the RDA.

Recognizing that nutrient needs do depend upon such factors as age, sex, and activity level, the RDA provide specific recommendations for 17 age and sex groups (Tables 36.2 and 36.3). As knowledge about nutrient needs has improved, the number of nutrients included has increased. In 1958, 10 nutrients were included, but in the most recent publication of the RDA there are 30 nutrients, including energy (Food and Nutrition Board, 1980). This results in a table of nearly 500 age-sex-nutrient recommendations ($17 \times 30 = 510$). Although one can appreciate why this has occurred, it is nevertheless true that the table is now so complicated that the RDA are of limited utility as a practical guide to nutrition. Even well-qualified nutritionists equipped with appropriate computer facilities have difficulty knowing what to do with the RDA or how to utilize the values in developing recommended food patterns.

Another difficult problem is that in the attempt to assure an adequate intake of essential nutrients for all, some of the RDA have been placed so high that they are either impossible or difficult to achieve. Since the nutrient intake tends to parallel energy intake, that is, the nutrient density is about the same for various age and sex groups (see Table 36.1), those groups with relatively low energy intakes—teenage girls, adult women, and the elderly—are usually those with the most difficulty in achieving the recommended levels of intake. As shown in Table 36.4 (pages 560–561), which compares average intakes with

Table 36.2 Recommended Daily Dietary Allowances

	Age (yrs)	Weight (kg)	Weight (lb)	Height (cm)	Height (in)	Protein (gm)	Fat-Soluble Vitamins: Vitamin A (μg RE)[a]	Vitamin D (μg)[b]	Vitamin E (mg α-TE)[c]	Water-Soluble Vitamins: Vitamin C (mg)	Thiamin (mg)	Riboflavin (mg)	Niacin (mg NE)[d]	Vitamin B-6 (mg)	Folacin (μg)[e]	Vitamin B-12 (μg)	Minerals: Calcium (mg)	Phosphorus (mg)	Magnesium (mg)	Iron (mg)	Zinc (mg)	Iodine (μg)
Infants	0.0-0.5	6	13	60	24	kg × 2.2	420	10	3	35	0.3	0.4	6	0.3	30	0.5[f]	360	240	50	10	3	40
	0.5-1.0	9	20	71	28	kg × 2.0	400	10	4	35	0.5	0.6	8	0.6	45	1.5	540	360	70	15	5	50
Children	1-3	13	29	90	35	23	400	10	5	45	0.7	0.8	9	0.9	100	2.0	800	800	150	15	10	70
	4-6	20	44	112	44	30	500	10	6	45	0.9	1.0	11	1.3	200	2.5	800	800	200	10	10	90
	7-10	28	62	132	52	34	700	10	7	45	1.2	1.4	16	1.6	300	3.0	800	800	250	10	10	120
Males	11-14	45	99	157	62	45	1000	10	8	50	1.4	1.6	18	1.8	400	3.0	1200	1200	350	18	15	150
	15-18	66	145	176	69	56	1000	10	10	60	1.4	1.7	18	2.0	400	3.0	1200	1200	400	18	15	150
	19-22	70	154	177	70	56	1000	7.5	10	60	1.5	1.7	19	2.2	400	3.0	800	800	350	10	15	150
	23-50	70	154	178	70	56	1000	5	10	60	1.4	1.6	18	2.2	400	3.0	800	800	350	10	15	150
	51+	70	154	178	70	56	1000	5	10	60	1.2	1.4	16	2.2	400	3.0	800	800	350	10	15	150
Females	11-14	46	101	157	62	46	800	10	8	50	1.1	1.3	15	1.8	400	3.0	1200	1200	300	18	15	150
	15-18	55	120	163	64	46	800	10	8	60	1.1	1.3	14	2.0	400	3.0	1200	1200	300	18	15	150
	19-22	55	120	163	64	44	800	7.5	8	60	1.1	1.3	14	2.0	400	3.0	800	800	300	18	15	150
	23-50	55	120	163	64	44	800	5	8	60	1.0	1.2	13	2.0	400	3.0	800	800	300	18	15	150
	51+	55	120	163	64	44	800	5	8	60	1.0	1.2	13	2.0	400	3.0	800	800	300	10	15	150
Pregnant						+30	+200	+5	+2	+20	+0.4	+0.3	+2	+0.6	+400	+1.0	+400	+400	+150	—[g]	+5	+25
Lactating						+20	+400	+5	+3	+40	+0.5	+0.5	+5	+0.5	+100	+1.0	+400	+400	+150	—[g]	+10	+50

Source: From the National Research Council: Recommended Dietary Allowances. Edition 9. Food and Nutrition Board National Academy of Sciences, 1980. The allowances are intended to provide for individual variations among most normal persons as they live in the United States under usual environmental stresses. Diets should be based on a variety of common foods in order to provide other nutrients for which human requirements have been less well defined.

[a] Retinol equivalents. 1 retinol equivalent = 1 μg retinol or 6 μg β carotene.
[b] As cholecalciferol. 10 μg cholecalciferol = 400 I.U. of vitamin D.
[c] α-Tocopherol equivalents. 1 mg d-α tocopherol = α-TE.
[d] 1 NE (niacin equivalent) is equal to 1 mg of niacin or 60 mg of dietary tryptophan.
[e] The folacin allowances refer to dietary sources as determined by Lactobacillus casei assay after treatment with enzymes (conjugases) to make polyglutamyl forms of the vitamin available to the test organism.
[f] The recommended dietary allowance for vitamin B-12 in infants is based on average concentration of the vitamin in human milk. The allowances after weaning are based on energy intake (as recommended by the American Academy of Pediatrics) and consideration of other factors, such as intestinal absorption.
[g] The increased requirement during pregnancy cannot be met by the iron content of habitual American diets nor by the existing iron stores of many women; therefore the use of 30 to 60 mg of supplemental iron is recommended. Iron needs during lactation are not substantially different from those of nonpregnant women, but continued supplementation of the mother for 2 to 3 months after parturition is advisable in order to replenish stores depleted by pregnancy.

Table 36.3 Estimated Safe and Adequate Daily Dietary Intakes of Selected Vitamins and Minerals

	Vitamins			Trace Elements[a]						Electrolytes		
Age (yrs)	Vitamin K (μg)	Biotin (μg)	Pantothenic Acid (mg)	Copper (mg)	Manganese (mg)	Fluoride (mg)	Chromium (mg)	Selenium (mg)	Molybdenum (mg)	Sodium (mg)	Potassium (mg)	Chloride (mg)
Infants												
0–0.5	12	35	2	0.5–0.7	0.5–0.7	0.1–0.5	0.01–0.04	0.01–0.04	0.03–0.06	115–350	350–925	275–700
0.5–1	10–20	50	3	0.7–1.0	0.7–1.0	0.2–1.0	0.02–0.06	0.02–0.06	0.04–0.08	250–750	400–1200	425–1275
Children and adolescents												
1–3	15–30	65	3	1.0–1.5	1.0–1.5	0.5–1.5	0.02–0.08	0.02–0.08	0.05–0.1	325–975	550–1650	500–1500
4–6	20–40	85	3–4	1.5–2.0	1.5–2.0	1.0–2.5	0.03–0.12	0.03–0.12	0.06–0.15	450–1350	775–2325	700–2100
7–10	30–60	120	4–5	2.0–2.5	2.0–3.0	1.5–2.5	0.05–0.2	0.05–0.2	0.10–0.3	600–1800	1000–3000	925–2775
11+	50–100	100–200	4–7	2.0–3.0	2.5–5.0	1.5–2.5	0.05–0.2	0.05–0.2	0.15–0.5	900–2700	1525–4575	1400–4200
Adults	70–140	100–200	4–7	2.0–3.0	2.5–5.0	1.5–4.0	0.05–0.2	0.05–0.2	0.15–0.5	1100–3300	1875–5625	1700–5100

Note: Because there is less information on which to base allowances, these figures are not given in the main table of Recommended Dietary Allowances and are provided here in the form of ranges of recommended intakes.

[a] Since the toxic levels for many trace elements may be only several times usual intakes, the upper levels for the trace elements given in this table should not be habitually exceeded.

the RDA, there are "problem nutrients"—calcium, iron, magnesium, and vitamin B_6—which are generally not consumed in recommended amounts by these groups. Zinc, folic acid, and some other trace minerals also fall below RDA levels, although data on food composition (and hence interpretation of the consumption data) are less adequate than for other nutrients.

Thus, several issues relative to the RDA need consideration. One is whether it is useful to provide such detailed standards. I do not attempt to appraise all uses of the RDA here, but I do conclude that they are not an appropriate base for developing dietary instructions. More general standards aimed at the diet of the total family are needed.

The second issue is whether the RDA, particularly for the nutrients discussed above which are generally not consumed in recommended amounts, are too high. Since deficiencies of most of these nutrients appear not to be common or have not yet been identified as such, I conclude that they are too high or at least that the evidence is insufficient to justify these levels.

It should be clearly recognized, however, that the establishment of nutritional standards represents a judgment and should be based upon all information available. The fact that some of the RDA are substantially above average consumption levels obviously means that there are data and expert opinion to support such recommendations, and this cannot be ignored. I believe the issue must be addressed by considering the strength of the evidence and also considering how difficult it is to reach higher levels in the diet—how much disruption of the usual diet will result if higher levels of intake are actually consumed? Generous levels of most nutrients can be defended if they are readily provided by the available food supply. Much stronger evidence, particularly epidemiologic and clinical, is required for recommendations that will cause a marked change in dietary practice.

For example, rather generous levels of vitamin C, well above absolute nutrient needs, are readily available in our food supply. Current evidence demonstrates that high levels of intake assist in iron absorption and may protect against formation of nitrosamine. Thus, a relatively high intake can be easily defended. Similarly, amounts of fruits and vegetables capable of providing generous amounts of vitamin A are readily available. High levels of intake of fruits and vegetables can be defended on other grounds and generous intakes may provide some protection against certain forms of cancer. There appears to be no argument for recommending minimal intakes. In contrast, the recommended levels of iron and zinc and some other nutrients are for all practical purposes not achievable by adult women from ordinary foods. The only obvious method of reaching the RDA levels of the so-called "problem nutrients" is either through fortification of foods or by the consumption of supplements. Such recommendations require much greater evidence of need and benefit.

Given the current evidence that deficiencies of essential nutrients are not widespread public health problems, I conclude that while we should encourage consumption patterns that will raise the intakes of the "problem nutrients," the evidence of need is not sufficient to justify a change in fortification policy or the general consumption of supplements. Our primary objective should be to assist and encourage disadvantaged groups to reach average consumption levels.

EXCESS CONSUMPTION

In contrast to the limited evidence indicating insufficient consumption of essential nutrients, there is an abundance of evidence that the great majority of Americans suffer from overconsumption. This not only refers to sugar, salt, and alcohol, but relates to the major health problems of our population, the so-called "chronic" diseases. Their importance can scarcely be overemphasized. Obesity affects about 20% of the population; atherosclerotic heart disease accounts for approximately 40% of deaths and cancer for approximately 20% of deaths; about 20% of the total population has clinical hypertension and the prevalence reaches 60% or more in black elderly women; probably over 5% of the population has diabetes and the prevalence is thought to be rising. Altogether, these conditions affect the great majority of all Americans. A general improvement in the health of Americans depends primarily on better control of these diseases.

It should be noted that these diseases have multiple causes and may not be as directly related to nutrition as scurvy and pellagra. Yet several—atherosclerosis, hypertension, and certain cancers—are practically nonexistent in some populations with dietary habits that differ from our own. Undoubtedly the genetic makeup of the individual plays a major role, but we must not make the mistake of assuming that genetics is an "all or none" affair, that is, that either you are or are not susceptible. Rather, our genetic makeup determines our susceptibility under any particular set of circumstances. For example, there is considerable evidence that salt consumption is related to hypertension and as salt consumption rises, an increased number of hypertensives are found in the population. Those who develop hypertension *may* be those who consume more salt than the average individual in the population, but they are also those who are susceptible at the average level of salt consumption. Similarly, hypercholesterolemic individuals in our population may be those who consume above average levels of fat and cholesterol but are more likely to be those who are susceptible while consuming the average diet. The situation is the same as in women who become iron deficient. They may be those whose iron intake is exceptionally low, but they are more likely to be those whose menstrual blood losses are excessive. Thus, a case control study may fail to demonstrate that iron intake is related to iron deficiency even though it is certain that insufficient iron causes iron deficiency anemia. Case control studies usually fail to identify excessive caloric intake as a cause of obesity. The point to be emphasized is that in a relatively homogenous population, case control studies may fail to demonstrate the causal dietary factor and thus lead to unfortunate conclusions.

Diseases such as coronary heart disease, hypertension, and cancer, require public health approaches (Blackburn, 1979). This is true not only because of the extent of the problem, but because our ability to identify susceptible individuals is limited, treatment is expensive and may be relatively ineffective, and they are indeed chronic diseases that develop over a prolonged period of time. To some degree, intervention is already too late when the disease becomes manifest. The development of public health approaches does not, of course, diminish the need for clinical methods of detection and treatment. When susceptible individuals can be identified, they deserve and require such care as can be provided. However, it should be self-evident that individual treatment cannot control these diseases and, as I have already argued, individual dietary advice is unlikely to be effective. Our audience should be the family and the community.

It is pertinent to note that absolute prevention of some, or perhaps all, chronic diseases is probably not possible. The eventual death rate is 100%. Some have even argued that we should not attempt to prevent coronary heart disease since this will mean that we will die of another disease. Such an argument is sterile since it is clear that any successful intervention does indeed increase our statistical chances of dying of something else. Undoubtedly the prevalence of the chronic diseases in our society is primarily the result of the successful interventions related to infectious and deficiency diseases. Only when the treatment or control of one disease results in direct causation of another malady is the issue relevant. There is no evidence that a more moderate diet, recommended for the amelioration of the chronic diseases, increases susceptibility to others.

Ordinarily, however, "prevention" of the chronic diseases means a delay in the onset of the disease—shifting of the age-mortality or age-morbidity curve to the right. The prevalence of coronary heart disease, cancer, hypertension, and stroke is so large that even modest shifts in the curve to older age groups represents a major accomplishment in public health.

In considering the nutritional issues we should also recognize that most Americans consume enough food, or an excess, and cannot tolerate more. An increase in total consumption of food is not a reasonable expectation. Thus, increased sales or intakes of practically any product can be expected to require a decrease in consumption of some other product.

Table 36.4 Nutritive Value of Food Consumed by Americans (Expressed as a Percentage of the RDA)

Sex and Age (yrs)	Individuals (number)	Food Energy	Protein	Calcium	Iron	Magnesium	Phosphorus	Vitamin A Value	Thiamin	Riboflavin	Preformed Niacin[a]	Vitamin B6	Vitamin B12	Vitamin C
Males and females														
Under 1	78[b]	100	189	171	147	208	209	188	218	302	133	129	251	219
1–2	264[c]	97	210	100	53	125	125	159	145	204	112	113	160	162
3–5	437	92	197	89	79	97	116	152	133	175	136	93	148	155
6–8	469	81	206	108	111	94	142	140	118	155	116	90	143	184
Males														
9–11	216	80	205	97	102	85	133	111	117	140	117	92	162	176
12–14	313	87	195	90	85	80	122	109	122	149	122	99	175	176
15–18	400	96	190	99	95	79	141	115	130	151	137	98	192	183
19–22	287	89	188	123	160	88	200	100	104	129	134	88	176	140
23–34	770	91	175	104	159	86	183	100	111	124	134	82	165	149
35–50	784	86	171	96	158	89	175	109	103	117	132	79	165	143
51–64	634	87	161	88	155	87	161	118	122	134	144	79	156	164
65–74	295	82	145	91	145	82	156	124	117	132	130	72	155	167
75 and over	127	88	133	85	134	76	142	128	117	124	117	68	128	161

Females

9–11	241	80	181	89	92	88	122	115	114	134	110	84	129	186
12–14	309	87	159	72	64	73	99	102	117	139	114	75	134	159
15–18	402	85	152	64	62	71	92	105	107	126	120	65	121	132
19–22	337	76	148	77	58	65	123	95	93	104	106	60	112	129
23–34	949	80	145	72	59	70	120	103	98	109	120	60	107	123
35–50	942	76	144	64	60	74	115	104	101	105	124	59	110	131
51–64	792	83	148	67	114	78	119	121	105	113	132	65	111	155
65–74	377	80	137	71	106	76	116	137	107	117	120	62	108	154
75 and over	197	85	123	74	101	71	110	136	101	117	106	58	97	150
All individuals	9620[d]	85	165	85	104	83	136	116	112	130	126	76	139	152

Source: Percentage of 1980 Recommended Dietary Allowances in a day, spring 1977. Based on a 24-hour dietary recall of the day preceding the interview. The survey included individuals from 48 states, all urbanizations, and all income groups. [From USDA Nationwide Food Consumption Survey 1977–78, 48 conterminous states, spring 1977 (preliminary).]

[a] Based on Recommended Dietary Allowance values as milligrams preformed niacin rather than niacin equivalents.
[b] Excludes 36 breast-fed infants.
[c] Excludes 4 breast-fed infants.
[d] Excludes 40 breast-fed infants.

Although the extensive data relating diet to chronic disease cannot be covered here the most pertinent facts are as follows:

Obesity.   It is readily apparent that many Americans have difficulty controlling their energy intake relative to their energy expenditure. A diet high in fat makes this more difficult since fat contains approximately twice as many calories per gram as carbohydrate and protein. The most successful reducing regimens include diets with increased bulk but lower in fat.

Atherosclerotic heart disease.   There is abundant evidence that the most important risk factors of coronary heart disease are elevated serum cholesterol levels (Food and Nutrition Board, 1980) and elevated blood pressure. Indeed, in the extensive studies of Keys (1980), some risk factors identified in the United States, such as obesity, cigarette smoking, and sedentary lifestyle, could not be shown to be related to coronary heart disease. Atherosclerosis does not develop in populations with low cholesterol levels, and thus it appears that an elevated cholesterol level is a necessary causal factor. Other risk factors apparently become important in atherosclerotic populations. Epidemiologic, clinical, and experimental animal studies are consistent in demonstrating that the kind and amount of fat and the amount of cholesterol in the diet are primary determinants of serum cholesterol. Saturated fat and dietary cholesterol elevate serum cholesterol levels; polyunsaturated fat lowers serum cholesterol levels. Some forms of dietary fiber assist in maintaining lower cholesterol levels.

Long-range studies such as the Framingham studies demonstrate that there is a near linear relationship between serum cholesterol level and risk of coronary disease (Dawber, 1980). Very low or risk-free levels appear to be below 180 mg per 100 ml. The average American male has a serum cholesterol level of about 220 mg per 100 ml, and thus the average American is at some risk for the development of coronary disease.

Cancer.   Epidemiologic data indicate that a large proportion of cancer is caused by environmental factors, especially diet. The dietary factors most implicated are high levels of fat consumption and a relative lack of dietary fiber. This evidence is consistent with extensive data from animal studies which demonstrate that diets high in fat or relatively purified diets increase the susceptibility of animals to both spontaneous tumors and a variety of carcinogenic agents. Since we have practically no ability to identify individuals susceptible to cancer nor to determine directly the relative importance of carcinogenic agents in man, it is generally recognized that we must rely heavily on animal data for the identification and control of carcinogenic agents. The high-fat American diet is thus heavily implicated.

Diets low in fiber are also implicated, especially in cancer of the lower bowel. Much of the epidemiologic data are not helpful in distinguishing the role of high-fat and low-fiber diets since high-fat diets are usually associated with a low consumption of fiber. Recent data from Finland, where fat consumption is high and coronary disease excessive, and the incidence of cancer of the colon is relatively low, suggest that the latter may be due to the consumption of dark bread, a good source of dietary fiber (Reddy, Hedges, Laakso, et al., 1978). The Finnish data would indicate that neither physical activity nor the consumption of dietary fiber are very protective against coronary disease.

Hypertension.   The major evidence indicts high consumption of salt in the etiology of hypertension. This includes still limited epidemiologic data indicating a rough parallelism between salt consumption and prevalence of hypertension, the favorable response of many hypertensive individuals to low salt intakes, and the production of hypertension in animals with diets high in salt. Populations with low salt intakes demonstrate practically no increase in blood pressure with aging and a near zero incidence of hypertension. Modest increases in blood pressure are now acknowledged to constitute a health risk and are of concern.

There is increasing evidence that blood pressure in both experimental animals and in man can be lowered by diets that are lower in fat and that provide an increased proportion of unsaturated fatty acids. The hypertensive effects of high-salt diets in animals can be almost abolished by modifying the dietary fat (Smith-Barbaro, Fisher, Quinn, et al., 1980). Thus, diets high in fat are also implicated in hypertension.

Diabetes. Modern recommendations emphasize diets that are lower in fat and higher in complex carbohydrate sources, perhaps dietary fiber. The recommendations are consistent with the well-known susceptibility of diabetics to heart attacks and atherosclerosis.

Dental caries. It is generally recognized that diets high in sugar favor the development of dental caries, a near universal and expensive disease in Americans. It is also agreed, however, that the frequency of sugar consumption and the kind of sugar sources consumed are more important than the absolute amount of sugar consumed, since sugar provides the substrate for cariogenic organisms. The provision of adequate fluoride intake through fluoridation of water supplies is the primary public health method available for the control of dental caries.

An etiologic role of sugar in diabetes and other chronic diseases is not yet accepted. No advantage, however, has yet been demonstrated for diets high in sugar and, at the very least, sugar acts as a diluent that limits the intake of essential nutrients. A recommendation to reduce sugar consumption is entirely consistent with good dietary practice. Although the consumption of white sugar (sucrose) has remained relatively constant at approximately 100 lb per capita per year, the consumption of other caloric sweeteners has increased rapidly in recent years. Since total energy intakes have fallen, the proportion of sugars in the diet has increased.

DISEASE AND DIETARY FIBER

As already noted, there is reason to believe that a low consumption of dietary fiber is etiologically related to cancer of the lower bowel and also to constipation and diverticulosis. A recommendation to increase consumption of dietary fiber by increased consumption of fruits, vegetables, and whole grains is reasonable but, since dietary fiber is not well-defined and different sources have different effects, it is impossible to establish quantitative estimates of desirable levels.

A healthful diet should be protective against all nutrition-related disease. It is theoretically possible that a diet protective against one disease could be causally related to another. Fortunately, when one reviews the entire spectrum of the major diseases, it is apparent that the evidence uniformly indicts the high fat, energy concentrated diet. Such a diet is generally high in saturated fat and cholesterol and low in fruits, vegetables, and whole grain cereals. Cholesterol, sugar, and salt are also, but less uniformly, indicted. No advantage has been claimed or demonstrated for diets that are high in fat, saturated fat, cholesterol, sugar, or salt. The direction that dietary recommendations should take is thus quite clear.

PROVISION OF DIETARY ADVICE TO THE PUBLIC

Given the diversity in our food supply and the variability in the composition of foods, it is obviously difficult to develop simplified instructions for the public. Presumably this requires the classification of foods into groups which have similarities in composition and make some sense to people who must buy foods and prepare meals. The Basic Four Food Groups have been used in this country for many years:

1. Fruits and vegetables: 4 servings per day
2. Breads and cereals: 4 servings per day
3. Dairy products: 2 to 4 servings per day
4. Meats, poultry, fish, and beans: 2 servings per day

These are obviously simple and understandable, but it has been argued that they represent an oversimplification and are too commonplace to attract the interest of consumers. They provide no assistance in avoiding excessive consumption of fats, cholesterol, sugar, and salt.

The provision of a fifth group—fats, sweets, and alcohol—with advice to limit consumption of this group (Science and Education Administration, 1980, 1981) represents some advance but is only a partial solution to this problem.

A recent publication (see Appendix) from the Departments of Agriculture and Health and Human Services provides substantial, useful information on how to avoid excessive amounts of fat, saturated fat, cholesterol, sugar, and salt. This publication fails to deal adequately with the provision of essential nutrients and also fails to provide the quantitative information (how much is too much or what levels are excessive?) needed for the best dietary planning.

It is apparent that the issue of how to convey dietary information to the public requires re-examination and that new approaches must be developed not only with a primary emphasis on the chronic diseases, which are the major nutrition-related problems of our population, but also with better information on how the message is received, what it achieves in dietary practice, and how the message can be most efficiently and effectively transmitted. Several activities are now underway, and we can expect developments in the near future.

CONCLUSION

I have argued that (1) after infancy all members of the family tend to eat about the same proportions of the foods available—the nutrient densities of the diets of different age and sex groups tend to be about the same; (2) that this average American diet is reasonably successful in preventing nutrient deficiencies even though absolute nutrient needs vary with age, sex, and level of activity; (3) that this diet results in a large proportion of the American public being at risk for one of the chronic diseases; (4) that modification of the diet of an individual is difficult and usually not successful; and (5) that a healthful diet must not only meet the immediate needs of the individual but be protective against nutrition-related diseases over a lifetime. All these considerations lead to the conclusion that the primary problems are the chronic diseases and that the primary target for nutritional education must be the family or group within which the individual lives.

I do not interpret this to mean that the advice to all ages and sexes should necessarily be *exactly* the same. One may encourage men to consume more bread or encourage children to consume more milk as long as these kinds of departures from the usual diet have a reasonable relationship to the way we eat. Bread and milk, for example, are usually consumed as individual items, but we cannot expect the individual to consume a diet which differs markedly from that of the family.

The principle to be followed in establishing dietary recommendations for the general public, whether they relate to essential nutrients or to excessive consumption, is the same— to recommend a diet that will be protective of the most vulnerable groups. For essential nutrients such groups will be those who consume relatively small amounts of food—adolescent girls, adult women, and the elderly. The nutrient content should thus attempt to provide adequate amounts for these groups and will necessarily provide more than is probably required by most children, adolescent boys, and adult men. With regard to excessive consumption, the vulnerable groups are more difficult to identify since most Americans are at some risk. With regard to coronary heart disease these groups include adolescent boys (who begin to develop atherosclerosis at this age) and young and adult men, but those at risk for cancer, hypertension, obesity, and diabetes can probably not be identified. It is well understood that attempting to reduce risk in this great majority, whoever they may be, will impose some unnecessary limitations on those who are not vulnerable. In either case, the recommendations will not be effective if they impose too onerous a burden or do not provide a pleasurable food pattern. Whatever decisions are made, they represent a

CONCLUSION 565

judgment upon how significant the health issue is considered to be and what a reasonable proportion of the public may accept. These judgments are always subject to change as new information develops and, if one considers what has happened to the American diet in the past few decades, it is apparent that what may be reasonable or unreasonable now may be quite different in the future.

As a first step in developing standards for all Americans—with the exception of very high-risk individuals—I suggest the standards outlined in Table 36.5. I consider them "reasonable" at this time, although not all are equally defensible.

Table 36.5 Suggested Nutritional Standards for the American Family Diet

Nutrient	Amount (per 1000 kcal)	Comments
Protein	40 gm	Approximately average consumption levels. This will provide amounts substantially above the RDA or actual need for many individuals, but acceptable diets in the United States will rarely be at lower levels. They can be justified in terms of iron, zinc, and some other nutrients in protein sources. There is some concern about excessive protein consumption in the United States, but the data are insufficient to recommend a reduction in the average protein consumption level.
Calcium	400 mg	Somewhat above average consumption levels but less than the RDA for several groups. It is easily achieved with our food supply. A differential consumption for some age and sex groups may be recommended since milk consumption does not depend on the general family diet.
Iron	7.5 mg	Somewhat above the average consumption level. Much below the RDA for women but probably about the maximal level that can be achieved with ordinary foods. Current consumption data include the consumption of some heavily fortified foods, such as breakfast cereals. Iron utilization will be assisted by high intakes of ascorbic acid and generous protein intakes. Adult women should be encouraged to find out whether they would benefit from iron supplements, which probably should be provided to all pregnant women.
Magnesium	170 mg	Somewhat above current consumption levels but appears achievable with good dietary practice. The RDA for several groups is substantially higher.
Zinc	6.5 mg	Substantially above current consumption levels but probably achievable with good dietary practice. RDA for several groups well above this level.

Table 36.5   (*Continued*)

Nutrient	Amount (per 1000 kcal)	Comments
Phosphorus	700 mg	Slightly less than current consumption levels. There is some concern about excessive phosphate consu..ption, but the significance of the prol·lem is not well defined. Lower limits in a reasonable diet are not known.
Vitamin A	3500 I.U.	Above current consumption levels but readily achievable and consistent with recommendations to increase consumption of fruits and vegetables.
Thiamin	0.8 mg	Current consumption level.
Riboflavin	1.0 mg	Current consumption level.
Niacin	10 rng	Current consumption level.
Vitamin B$_6$	0.9 mg	Above the current consumption level and may, in fact, not be readily achievable but substantially below the RDA for several groups.
Vitamin B$_{12}$	2.0 μg	Data on food consumption inadequate, but this value is thought to approximate the average consumption level, which appears to be adequate.
Folic acid	200 μg	Data on food composition inadequate, but this value is probably substantially above current consumption levels. It is consistent with the recommendation for increased consumption of fruits and vegetables.
Vitamin C	50 mg	This value is approximately the current consumption level but is substantially above the RDA for most groups. It is consistent with the recommendation to increase consumption of fruits and vegetables and also justified by effects of ascorbic acid on iron absorption and inhibition of nitrosamine formation.
Fat	30–35 gm	Various expert groups have recommended 25 to 35% of calories. A 30 gm level would represent about a 25% reduction from current consumption levels but is achievable with good dietary planning. We may expect the introduction of new products to make diets lower in fat more accessible. One third of the total fat as saturated fat and one third as polyunsaturated fat should be the goal.
Cholesterol	150 mg	Most expert groups have recommended 300 mg/day or less. For family planning this needs expression in terms of calories.

Table 36.5   (*Continued*)

Nutrient	Amount (per 1000 kcal)	Comments
Sugar	?	Some groups have recommended 10% of calories. Data on sugar content of foods is inadequate nor do we have sufficient experience on the acceptability of diets low in sugar. Probably best handled as in the Dietary Guidelines, that is, moderation in sugar use, particularly of high sugar snacks and drinks between meals.
Salt	?	As with sugar, a recommended level is difficult to establish since the salt content of many foods is unknown and highly variable and we have relatively little information on the acceptable levels of salt in various foods. The best advice at this time is probably the avoidance of foods high in salt and restriction of table use. Labeling of foods in the future can be expected to assist the consumer in limiting salt intake.

REFERENCES

Blackburn, H.: Diet and mass hyperlipidemia: A public health view. *In* Levy, R., Rifkind, B., Dennis, B., et al. (eds.): Nutrition, Lipids and Coronary Heart Disease. New York, Raven Press, 1979.

Dawber, T. R.: The Framingham Study: The Epidemiology of Atherosclerotic Disease. Cambridge, Massachusetts, Harvard University Press, 1980.

Food and Nutrition Board: Recommended Dietary Allowances. Edition 9, revised. Washington, D.C., National Research Council, National Academy of Sciences, 1980.

Keys, A.: Seven Countries: A Multivariate Analysis of Death and Coronary Heart Disease. Cambridge, Massachusetts, Harvard University Press, 1980.

Reddy, B. S., Hedges, A. R., Laakso, K., et al.: Metabolic epidemiology of large bowel cancer, fecal bulk and constituents of high-risk North Americans and low-risk Finnish population. Cancer, *42*:2832, 1978.

Science and Education Administration: Food. Home and Garden Bulletin No. 228. Washington, D.C., United States Department of Agriculture, 1980. For sale by Superintendent of Documents, United States Government Printing Office, Washington, D.C. 20402.

Science and Education Administration/Human Nutrition: Ideas for Better Eating. Washington, D.C., United States Department of Agriculture, 1981. For sale by Superintendent of Documents, United States Government Printing Office, Washington, D.C. 20402.

Smith-Barbaro, P., Fisher, H., Quinn, M. R., et al.: The effect of varying polyunsaturated fat rations on salt induced hypertension in rats. Nutr. Rep. Int., *22*:759, 1980.

Windham, C. T., Wyse, B., Hurst, R. L., et al.: Consistency of nutrient consumption patterns in the United States. J. Am. Diet. Assoc., *78*:587, 1981.

APPENDIX: NUTRITION AND YOUR HEALTH—DIETARY GUIDELINES FOR AMERICANS*

What should you eat to stay healthy?

Hardly a day goes by without someone trying to answer that question. Newspapers, magazines, books, radio, and television give us a lot of advice about what foods we should or should not eat. Unfortunately, much of this advice is confusing.

Some of this confusion exists because we don't know enough about nutrition to identify an "ideal diet" for each individual. People differ—and their food needs vary depending on age, sex, body size, physical activity, and other conditions such as pregnancy or illness.

In those chronic conditions where diet may be important—heart attacks, high blood pressure, strokes, dental caries, diabetes, and some forms of cancer—the roles of specific nutrients have not been defined.

Research does seek to find more precise nutritional requirements and to show better the connections between diet and certain chronic diseases.

But today, what advice should you follow in choosing and preparing the best foods for you and your family?

The guidelines below are suggested for most Americans. They do not apply to people who need special diets because of diseases or conditions that interfere with normal nutrition. These people may require special instruction from trained dietitians, in consultation with their own physicians.

These guidelines are intended for people who are already healthy. No guidelines can guarantee health or well-being. Health depends on many things, including heredity, lifestyle, personality traits, mental health and attitudes, and environment, in addition to diet.

Food alone cannot make you healthy. But good eating habits based on moderation and variety can help keep you healthy and even improve your health.

Dietary Guidelines for Americans

Eat a variety of foods

Maintain ideal weight

Avoid too much fat, saturated fat, and cholesterol

Eat foods with adequate starch and fiber

Avoid too much sugar

Avoid too much sodium

If you drink alcohol, do so in moderation

Eat a Variety of Foods

You need about 40 different nutrients to stay healthy. These include vitamins and minerals, as well as amino acids (from proteins), essential fatty acids (from vegetable oils and animal fats), and sources of energy (calories from carbohydrates, proteins, and fats). These nutrients are in the foods you normally eat.

Most foods contain more than one nutrient. Milk, for example, provides proteins, fats, sugars, riboflavin and other B-vitamins, vitamin A, calcium, and phosphorus—among other nutrients.

No single food item supplies all the essential nutrients in the amounts that you need. Milk, for instance, contains very little iron or vitamin C. You should, therefore, eat a variety of foods to assure an adequate diet.

*U.S. Department of Agriculture. *Nutrition and Your Health—Dietary Guidelines for Americans,* Home and Garden Bulletin No. 232. Washington, D.C.: U.S. Government Printing Office, February 1980.

The greater the variety, the less likely you are to develop either a deficiency or an excess of any single nutrient. Variety also reduces your likelihood of being exposed to excessive amounts of contaminants in any single food item.

One way to assure variety and, with it, a well-balanced diet is to select foods each day from each of several major groups: for example, fruits and vegetables; cereals, breads, and grains; meats, poultry, eggs, and fish; dry peas and beans, such as soybeans, kidney beans, lima beans, and black-eyed peas, which are good vegetable sources of protein; and milk, cheese, and yogurt.

Fruits and vegetables are excellent sources of vitamins, especially vitamins C and A. Whole grain and enriched breads, cereals, and grain products provide B-vitamins, iron, and energy. Meats supply protein, fat, iron and other minerals, as well as several vitamins, including thiamine and vitamin B_{12}. Dairy products are major sources of calcium and other nutrients.

To Assure Yourself an Adequate Diet
Eat a variety of foods daily, including selections of

Fruits

Vegetables

Whole grain and enriched breads, cereals, and grain products

Milk, cheese, and yogurt

Meats, poultry, fish, eggs

Legumes (dry peas and beans)

There are no known advantages to consuming excess amounts of any nutrient. You will rarely need to take vitamin or mineral supplements if you eat a wide variety of foods. There are a few important exceptions to this general statement:

Women in their childbearing years may need to take iron supplements to replace the iron they lose with menstrual bleeding. Women who are no longer menstruating should not take iron supplements routinely.

Women who are pregnant or who are breastfeeding need more of many nutrients, especially iron, folic acid, vitamin A, calcium, and sources of energy (calories from carbohydrates, proteins, and fats). Detailed advice should come from their physicians or from dietitians.

Elderly or very inactive people may eat relatively little food. Thus, they should pay special attention to avoiding foods that are high in calories but low in other essential nutrients—for example, fat, oils, alcohol, and sugars.

Infants also have special nutritional needs. Healthy full-term infants should be breastfed unless there are special problems. The nutrients in human breast milk tend to be digested and absorbed more easily than those in cow's milk. In addition, breast milk may serve to transfer immunity to some diseases from the mother to the infant.

Normally, most babies do not need solid foods until they are 3 to 6 months old. At that time, other foods can be introduced gradually. Prolonged breast or bottlefeeding— without solid foods or supplemental iron—can result in iron deficiency.

You should not add salt or sugar to the baby's foods. Infants do not need these "encouragements"—if they are really hungry. The foods themselves contain enough salt and sugar; extra is not necessary.

To Assure Your Baby an Adequate Diet

Breastfeed unless there are special problems

Delay other foods until baby is 3 to 6 months old

Do not add salt or sugar to baby's food

Maintain Ideal Weight

If you are too fat, your chances of developing some chronic disorders are increased. Obesity is associated with high blood pressure, increased levels of blood fats (triglycerides) and cholesterol, and the most common type of diabetes. All of these, in turn, are associated with increased risks of heart attacks and strokes. Thus, you should try to maintain "ideal" weight.

But, how do you determine what the ideal weight is for you?

There is no absolute answer. The table [below] shows "acceptable" ranges for most adults. If you have been obese since childhood, you may find it difficult to reach or to maintain your weight within the acceptable range. For most people, their weight should not be more than it was when they were young adults (20 to 25 years old).

It is not well understood why some people can eat much more than others and still maintain normal weight. However, one thing is definite: to lose weight, you must take in fewer calories than you burn. This means that you must either select foods containing fewer calories or you must increase your activity—or both.

To Improve Eating Habits

Eat slowly

Prepare smaller portions

Avoid "seconds"

Suggested Body Weights

Range of Acceptable Weight		
Height (feet-inches)	Men (Pounds)	Women (Pounds)
4'10"		92–119
4'11"		94–122
5'0"		96–125
5'1"		99–128
5'2"	112–141	102–131
5'3"	115–144	105–134
5'4"	118–148	108–138
5'5"	121–152	111–142
5'6"	124–156	114–146
5'7"	128–161	118–150
5'8"	132–166	122–154
5'9"	136–170	126–158
5'10"	140–174	130–163
5'11"	144–179	134–168
6'0"	148–184	138–173
6'1"	152–189	
6'2"	156–194	
6'3"	160–199	
6'4"	164–204	

Note: Height without shoes; weight without clothes.
Source: HEW conference on obesity, 1973.

If you need to lose weight, do so gradually. Steady loss of 1 to 2 pounds a week— until you reach your goal—is relatively safe and more likely to be maintained. Long-term success depends upon acquiring new and better habits of eating and exercise. That is perhaps why "crash" diets usually fail in the long run.

Do not try to lose weight too rapidly. Avoid crash diets that are severely restricted in the variety of foods they allow. Diets containing fewer than 800 calories may be hazardous. Some people have developed kidney stones, disturbing psychological changes, and other complications while following such diets. A few people have died suddenly and without warning.

To Lose Weight

Increase physical activity

Eat less fat and fatty foods

Eat less sugar and sweets

Avoid too much alcohol

Gradual increase of everyday physical activities like walking or climbing stairs can be very helpful. The chart below gives the calories used per hour in different activities.

A pound of body fat contains 3500 calories. To lose 1 pound of fat, you will need to burn 3500 calories more than you consume. If you burn 500 calories more a day than you consume, you will lose 1 pound of fat a week. Thus, if you normally burn 1700 calories

Approximate Energy Expenditure by a 150 Pound Person in Various Activities

Activity	Calories per hour
Lying down or sleeping	80
Sitting	100
Driving an automobile	120
Standing	140
Domestic work	180
Walking, 2-½ mph	210
Bicycling, 5-½ mph	210
Gardening	220
Golf; lawn mowing, power mowing	250
Bowling	270
Walking, 3-¾ mph	300
Swimming, ¼ mph	300
Square dancing, volleyball; roller skating	350
Wood chopping or sawing	400
Tennis	420
Skiing, 10 mph	600
Squash and handball	600
Bicycling, 13 mph	660
Running, 10 mph	900

Source: Based on material prepared by Robert E. Johnson, M.D., Ph.D., and colleagues, University of Illinois.

a day, you can theoretically expect to lose a pound of fat each week if you adhere to a 1200-calorie-per-day diet.

Do not attempt to reduce your weight below the acceptable range. Severe weight loss may be associated with nutrient deficiencies, menstrual irregularities, infertility, hair loss, skin changes, cold intolerance, severe constipation, psychiatric disturbances, and other complications.

If you lose weight suddenly or for unknown reasons, see a physician. Unexplained weight loss may be an early clue to an unsuspected underlying disorder.

Avoid Too Much Fat, Saturated Fat, and Cholesterol

If you have a high blood cholesterol level, you have a greater chance of having a heart attack. Other factors can also increase your risk of heart attack—high blood pressure and cigarette smoking, for example—but high blood cholesterol is clearly a major dietary risk indicator.

Populations like ours with diets high in saturated fats and cholesterol tend to have high blood cholesterol levels. Individuals within these populations usually have greater risks of having heart attacks than people eating low-fat, low-cholesterol diets.

Eating extra saturated fat and cholesterol will increase blood cholesterol levels in most people. However, there are wide variations among people—related to heredity and the way each person's body uses cholesterol.

Some people can consume diets high in saturated fats and cholesterol and still keep normal blood cholesterol levels. Other people, unfortunately, have high blood cholesterol levels even if they eat low-fat, low-cholesterol diets.

There is controversy about what recommendations are appropriate for healthy Americans. But for the U.S. population as a whole, reduction in our current intake of total fat, saturated fat, and cholesterol is sensible. This suggestion is especially appropriate for people who have high blood pressure or who smoke.

The recommendations are not meant to prohibit the use of any specific food item or to prevent you from eating a variety of foods. For example, eggs and organ meats (such as liver) contain cholesterol, but they also contain many essential vitamins and minerals, as well as protein. Such items can be eaten in moderation, as long as your overall cholesterol intake is not excessive. If you prefer whole milk to skim milk, you can reduce your intake of fats from foods other than milk.

To Avoid Too Much Fat, Saturated Fat, and Cholesterol

Choose lean meat, fish, poultry, dry beans and peas as your protein sources

Moderate your use of eggs and organ meats (such as liver)

Limit your intake of butter, cream, hydrogenated margarines, shortenings and coconut oil, and foods made from such products

Trim excess fat off meats

Broil, bake, or boil rather than fry

Read labels carefully to determine both amount and types of fat contained in foods

Eat Foods with Adequate Starch and Fiber

The major sources of energy in the average U.S. diet are carbohydrates and fats. (Proteins and alcohol also supply energy, but to a lesser extent.) If you limit your fat intake, you should increase your calories from carbohydrates to supply your body's energy needs.

In trying to reduce your weight to "ideal" levels, carbohydrates have an advantage over fats: carbohydrates contain less than half the number of calories per ounce than fats.

Complex carbohydrate foods are better than *simple* carbohydrates in this regard. Simple carbohydrates—such as sugars—provide calories but little else in the way of nutrients. Complex carbohydrate foods—such as beans, peas, nuts, seeds, fruits and vegetables, and whole grain breads, cereals, and products—contain many essential nutrients in addition to calories.

Increasing your consumption of certain complex carbohydrates can also help increase dietary fiber. The average American diet is relatively low in fiber. Eating more foods high in fiber tends to reduce the symptoms of chronic constipation, diverticulosis, and some types of "irritable bowel." There is also concern that low fiber diets might increase the risk of developing cancer of the colon, but whether this is true is not yet known.

To make sure you get enough fiber in your diet, you should eat fruits and vegetables, whole grain breads and cereals. There is no reason to add fiber to foods that do not already contain it.

To Eat More Complex Carbohydrates Daily

Substitute starches for fats and sugars

Select foods which are good sources of fiber and starch, such as whole grain breads and cereals, fruits and vegetables, beans, peas, and nuts

Avoid Too Much Sugar

The major health hazard from eating too much sugar is tooth decay (dental caries). The risk of caries is not simply a matter of how much sugar you eat. The risk increases the more frequently you eat sugar and sweets, especially if you eat between meals, and if you eat foods that stick to the teeth. For example, frequent snacks of sticky candy, or dates, or daylong use of soft drinks may be more harmful than adding sugar to your morning cup of coffee—at least as far as your teeth are concerned.

Obviously, there is more to healthy teeth than avoiding sugars. Careful dental hygiene and exposure to adequate amounts of fluoride in the water are especially important.

Contrary to widespread opinion, too much sugar in your diet does not seem to cause diabetes. The most common type of diabetes is seen in obese adults, and avoiding sugar, without correcting the overweight, will not solve the problem. There is also no convincing evidence that sugar causes heart attacks or blood vessel diseases.

Estimates indicate that Americans use on the average more than 130 pounds of sugars and sweeteners a year. This means the risk of tooth decay is increased not only by the sugar in the sugar bowl but by the sugars and syrups in jams, jellies, candies, cookies, soft drinks, cakes, and pies, as well as sugars found in products such as breakfast cereals, catsup, flavored milks, and ice cream. Frequently, the ingredient label will provide a clue to the amount of sugars in a product.

To Avoid Excessive Sugars

Use less of all sugars, including white sugar, brown sugar, raw sugar, honey, and syrups

Eat less of foods containing these sugars, such as candy, soft drinks, ice cream, cakes, cookies

Select fresh fruits or fruits canned without sugar or light syrup rather than heavy syrup

Read food labels for clues on sugar content—if the names sucrose, glucose, maltose, dextrose, lactose, fructose, or syrups appear first, then there is a large amount of sugar

Remember, how often you eat sugar is as important as how much sugar you eat

Avoid Too Much Sodium

Table salt contains sodium and chloride—both are essential elements.

Sodium is also present in many beverages and foods that we eat, especially in certain processed foods, condiments, sauces, pickled foods, salty snacks, and sandwich meats. Baking soda, baking powder, monosodium glutamate (MSG), soft drinks, and even many medications (many antacids, for instance) contain sodium.

It is not surprising that adults in the United States take in much more sodium than they need.

The major hazard of excessive sodium is for persons who have high blood pressure. Not everyone is equally susceptible. In the United States, approximately 17 percent of adults have high blood pressure. Sodium intake is but one of the factors known to affect blood pressure. Obesity, in particular, seems to play a major role.

In populations with low-sodium intakes, high blood pressure is rare. In contrast, in populations with high-sodium intakes, high blood pressure is common. If people with high blood pressure severely restrict their sodium intakes, their blood pressures will *usually* fall—although not always to normal levels.

At present, there is no good way to predict who will develop high blood pressure, though certain groups, such as blacks, have a higher incidence. Low-sodium diets might help some of these people avoid high blood pressure if they could be identified before they develop the condition.

Since most Americans eat more sodium than is needed, consider reducing your sodium intake. Use less table salt. Eat sparingly those foods to which large amounts of sodium have been added. Remember that up to half of sodium intake may be "hidden," either as part of the naturally occurring food or, more often, as part of a preservative or flavoring agent that has been added.

To Avoid Too Much Sodium

Learn to enjoy the unsalted flavors of foods

Cook with only small amounts of added salt

Add little or no salt to food at the table

Limit your intake of salty foods, such as potato chips, pretzels, salted nuts and popcorn, condiments (soy sauce, steak sauce, garlic salt), cheese, pickled foods, cured meats

Read food labels carefully to determine the amounts of sodium in processed foods and snack items

If You Drink Alcohol, Do So in Moderation

Alcoholic beverages tend to be high in calories and low in other nutrients. Even moderate drinkers may need to drink less if they wish to achieve ideal weight.

On the other hand, heavy drinkers may lose their appetites for foods containing essential nutrients. Vitamin and mineral deficiencies occur commonly in heavy drinkers—in part, because of poor intake, but also because alcohol alters the absorption and use of some essential nutrients.

Sustained or excessive alcohol consumption by pregnant women has caused birth defects. Pregnant women should limit alcohol intake to 2 ounces or less on any single day.

Heavy drinking may also cause a variety of serious conditions, such as cirrhosis of the liver and some neurological disorders. Cancer of the throat and neck is much more common in people who drink and smoke than in people who don't.

One or two drinks daily appear to cause no harm in adults. If you drink you should do so in moderation.

Remember, if you drink alcohol, do so in moderation

CHAPTER 37

A HEALTHFUL DIET AND ITS IMPLICATIONS FOR DISEASE PREVENTION

ALFRED E. HARPER

University of Wisconsin–Madison

Sound nutrition is not a panacea. Good food that provides appropriate proportions of nutrients should not be regarded as a poison, a medicine, or a talisman. It should be eaten and enjoyed. (NAS/NRC, 1980a)

Knowledge about human needs for sources of energy and some 45 essential nutrients, gained through the science of nutrition, has provided us with the information needed to prevent nutritional deficiency diseases and to develop guidelines for nutritionally adequate and healthful diets. Despite these accomplishments, many nutritional questions remain unanswered. Can we devise better dietary guidelines? Are there diets with unique properties for disease prevention or for slowing the deterioration of physiological functions that occurs with aging? There is much speculation and debate about these subjects. This has helped identify questions for research that is needed to provide the body of conclusive scientific evidence on which new dietary guidelines that will ensure further improvement of health must be based. The vigor of the debate on this subject, in itself, attests to the inadequacy of present knowledge as the basis for highly specific dietary guidelines for disease prevention.

My objective in this chapter will be to examine the state of health in the United States in relation to diet; to outline those dietary guidelines that are generally accepted as having a sound scientific basis; and then to raise some critical questions about proposals for additional guidelines.

Consumption of an adequate amount of nutritious food is a basic human need. Failure to satisfy this need leads to deterioration of health. The effects are seen most vividly under extreme conditions—emaciation and death during famines or as the result of neglect of the food needs of young children and the aged; debilitating and even fatal diseases, such as beri-beri, scurvy, pellagra, and rickets, resulting from diets that are deficient in specific essential nutrients. Effects of marginally inadequate intakes of nutrients are less obvious. They may be as mild as nondebilitating impairment of some physiological function, such as mild anemia resulting from marginally inadequate iron intake—a common finding in nutrition surveys, even in the United States. The consequences of this anemia are unlikely to be debilitating except during periods of severe physical exertion. Nevertheless, such observations emphasize that the ability of the body to respond effectively to stresses such as prolonged physical activity and infection may be impaired by consumption of a diet that does not meet the full requirements for essential nutrients (NAS/NRC, 1980b).

Besides being nutritious, a healthful diet must also be safe. The greatest potential health hazard from diet is contamination of foods with microorganisms that cause human diseases. A second but generally much less serious potential hazard is the presence of toxic substances in foods. Advances in knowledge of the microbiology and toxicology of foods have provided us with an understanding of the more obvious potential hazards from foods and, thereby, with the knowledge required to develop guidelines for a diet that is safe (Chou, 1979).

Standards have been established by governmental agencies for sanitation and for ensuring the microbiological and chemical safety of the food supply. Regulations and guidelines based on these standards assure that, within the limits of human error, food available in the marketplace is safe. The major threat to health from food-borne diseases is not from the food supply itself but from inappropriate handling or storage of foods by caterers or in the home. To illustrate the microbiological safety of the food supply, it might be noted that 95% of reported instances of food poisoning have been traced to improper food handling. Between 1940 and 1977, for example, 700 of the 705 deaths from botulism resulted from improper preparation or storage of food in the home (Chou, 1979).

Foods do contain substances that are potentially toxic, many of which are naturally occurring substances. Claims that the presence of such chemicals makes food unsafe are usually based on a lack of understanding of the difference between potential toxicity and hazard. Nutrients such as vitamin A and selenium are toxic when ingested in large amounts, yet small amounts are essential for survival. Thus, despite their potential toxicity, they become hazardous only when they are ingested in amounts that exceed the capacity of the body to degrade or eliminate them. Additives included in foods to improve their sensory or storage properties must undergo extensive testing before their use is approved. The effectiveness of the program in protecting the public is attested to by the fact that no documented cases of human illness or death have been attributed to them (Benarde, 1981).

In recent years, the assumption has become widespread that the nutritional quality of the U.S. food supply has deteriorated. Chronic and degenerative diseases are presently the major causes of death in the United States among people over 45 years of age (Omran, 1977; U.S. DHEW 1979), and claims have been made that the incidence of these diseases has increased owing to changes that have occurred in the American diet (Senate Select Committee on Nutrition and Human Needs, 1977). Widespread dissemination of these claims has led to pressures for extending guidelines for healthful diets to include guidelines for disease prevention. It is therefore important to establish whether there is a body of convincing scientific evidence to support proposals for extending guidelines for healthful diets beyond those presently accepted as assuring a safe and nutritious diet, and, if so, what implications any proposed additional guidelines might have for disease prevention (Harper 1981a; NAS/NRC, 1979; Olson, 1981).

Conclusions about diet in relation to health and disease prevention can be viewed only in relation to our knowledge of current health status, so we should first briefly examine the current state of health in the United States.

CURRENT HEALTH STATUS—PERCEPTIONS AND REALITIES

According to Lewis Thomas (1977), president of Memorial Sloan-Kettering Cancer Center in New York, the public's perception of its own health has changed during the past 25 years. He states that the general belief "seems to be that the body is fundamentally flawed" and is "subject to disintegration at any moment." The "public preoccupation with disease," he continues, "is . . . assuming the dimensions of a national obsession." This public perception is not in accord with the opening statement of the Surgeon General's report (U.S. DHEW, 1979): "The health of the American people has never been better." These contrasting views would suggest that there is a discrepancy between public perceptions and realities in relation to health status.

If we look at the changes that have occurred in health status throughout this century, it is not difficult to find support for the conclusion reached by the Surgeon General. Life expectancy at birth has increased from 47 years in 1900 to 73 years in this decade (70 years for males and 76 years for females). The proportion of infants who can be expected to survive to or beyond age 65 has increased from about 37% to over 75% during this century (Fries, 1980). This has come about through steady and sharp reductions in infant, childhood, and maternal mortality and modest declines in death rates among adults of all ages (Omran, 1977; U.S. DHEW, 1979). These achievements have been attributed in large measure to improvements in sanitation, housing, and nutrition (U.S. DHEW, 1979) and also to improved medical and preventive health care, including immunization against several infectious diseases. There can be no doubt that health has improved during this century in association with whatever changes have occurred in the U.S. food supply and diet.

These improvements in health have resulted in a vast increase in the number of elderly people in the population (Butler, 1977). The proportion of the population 65 years of age or older has increased from 4% in 1900 to almost 12% at present. This shift in the percentage of people in different age groups—a lower proportion of children and a higher proportion of elderly—has been accompanied by a shift in the major causes of death in the United States. In the early 1900s, cardiovascular diseases (CVD)—heart disease and stroke—were the leading cause of death, although they accounted for only 14% of total deaths. Then, most deaths resulted from a variety of infectious diseases. Today CVDs remain the major cause of death but now account for almost 50% of all deaths (Omran, 1977; U.S. DHEW, 1979). Various cancers account for another 20% (American Cancer Society, 1979; Omran, 1977; U.S. DHEW, 1979). It is clear that most deaths are now attributable to chronic and degenerative diseases.

If this trend is to be kept in proper perspective, it is necessary to recognize that violence (accidents, suicide, and homicide), not disease, is the major cause of death among those between the ages of 1 and 45 years and to remember that more than 75% of all infants born can expect to live to 65 years of age or older (about 70% of males and 84% of females) (National Research Council, 1982). High mortality rates from cardiovascular diseases and cancer are associated with an aging population. In fact, death rates from most diseases increase exponentially with increasing age beyond 35 years, as is shown for heart disease and cancer in Figure 37.1.

Another question in connection with perceptions and realities about current health status is how life expectancy in the United States compares with that in other countries. Despite the substantial increases in life expectancy (the average age of death for a population) that have occurred in many countries during this century (Fries, 1980), there is no evidence

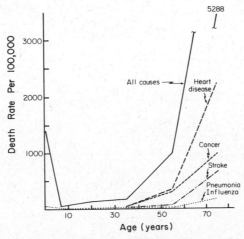

Figure 37.1 Changes in mortality from some major diseases with increasing age.

that the human life span (the greatest fully documented age at death of any individual) has been lengthened. Also, differences in longevity among the populations of the 15 countries with the greatest life expectancies are small (United Nations, 1979). Nevertheless, differences in the major causes of death are great, as is evident from a comparison of life expectancies in countries with very high and very low mortality from heart disease or cancer (Table 37.1). Sweden, the Netherlands, and Japan have similar life expectancies but vastly different death rates from heart disease (Kritchevsky, 1979; Stamler, 1979) and cancer (American Cancer Society, 1979); the same is true for the United States, Italy, and France. It is also noteworthy that women outlive men by at least 5 years in all of these countries, regardless of the differences in the major causes of death.

It would seem, therefore, that although environmental factors may substantially influence average age at death, which differs greatly from country to country, and the diseases that are the major causes of death, which also differ greatly among countries, genetic factors are the major determinant of life span. This raises a question that deserves serious consideration. If we do discover how environmental factors influence disease patterns, will it be possible to modify these factors in such a way as to reduce disability and death rates generally, or will such modifications merely result in reciprocal changes in mortality rates from various causes?

It is also important, in considering the implications of dietary guidance in relation to health and disease prevention, to realize that age at death is a biological variable. Like other biological variables, it has a standard deviation and a range (Kohn, 1977). If, as with most other biological variables, the coefficient of variation is 10% to 15%—say, 12.5%— we would expect the range of age at death to follow a normal distribution such that when average age at death is 72, as for men in Sweden, the anticipated range would be 45 to 99 years. With average age at death of 77, as for women in several countries, the anticipated range would be 49 to 107 years. The upper ends of these ranges approach a human life span of 116 years. If the coefficient of variation were slightly greater than 12.5%, the anticipated upper end of the range would be even closer to the observed maximum length of life. It is biologically unrealistic to assume that deaths occurring before some specified age are premature deaths.

It is striking that life expectancy at age 65 has increased little during this century, despite medical and technological advances (U.S. DHEW, 1979). It thus seems doubtful

Table 37.1 Life Expectancy at Birth and at Age 65 in Relation to Mortality from Heart Disease and Cancer for Selected Countries among the 15 Countries with the Greatest Life Expectancies

Country	Life Expectancy (yrs)[a]		At Age 65 (Male)	Age-adjusted Mortality (per 100,000 persons)	
	At Birth			Heart Disease[b]	Cancer[c]
	Male	Female		(Males, 35–74 yrs.)	(Males)
Sweden	72	77	14	588	115
Japan	71	76	13	115	141
Netherlands	71	77	14	506	187
Switzerland	70	76	13	279	179
United States	69	76	14	793	157
France	69	77	13	205	187
Italy	69	75	13	309	173

[a] United Nations (1979).
[b] Stamler (1979).
[c] American Cancer Society (1979).

that any substantial increase in life expectancy at age 65 can be anticipated unless some way is discovered of delaying the gradual but steady declines in physiological functions that accompany aging. The question that then arises is whether health can be improved within the fixed life span of the race so that the incidence of debilitating chronic diseases will be reduced or the onset of these diseases will be delayed and so that quality of life, at least for a substantial portion of the population, will be better.

There have been many such accomplishments over time. Among the most outstanding are medical advances—such as control of diabetes through the discovery of insulin, control of infections by antibiotics, and improvements of many types in surgical rehabilitation—and advances in preventive medicine, such as control of several infectious diseases through the development of vaccines and prevention of dietary deficiencies following the discoveries of essential nutrients. It would seem that a major focus of both medical and preventive health care programs should be on research to identify the reasons for early deaths and to develop ways of relieving the disabilities associated with deteriorating physiological function and the onset of chronic and degenerative diseases.

GUIDELINES FOR A HEALTHFUL DIET

In approaching the concept of a healthful diet and its implications for disease prevention, we should look first at the dietary guidelines that have prevailed as we have progressed over the years to our current basically satisfactory state of health. Then we should look at the proposals that have been made for modifying these guidelines, the basis for them, and their implications for disease prevention and improvement of the quality of life.

Prior to the 20th century, such dietary guidelines as there were, were a mixture of myth, magic, folk wisdom, and common sense. Only after the discoveries of the major vitamins and recognition of the nutritional essentiality of several amino acids and minerals in the 1920s and 1930s did it become possible to develop guidelines for a healthful diet on a sound scientific basis.

Pellagra—niacin-tryptophan deficiency—was a serious public health problem well into the 1930s, with from 3,000 to 6,000 people dying yearly from this dietary deficiency disease. It remained a public health problem even after an effective method of treating the disease was discovered. Only after a public policy of fortifying cereal grains with niacin was instituted in the early 1940s did the incidence of the disease decline to the point at which it ceased to be a public health problem. This is an example of how application of knowledge of nutrition gained through basic scientific research has contributed to disease prevention (Goldsmith, 1964; Sandstead, 1973).

During this time Recommended Dietary Allowances (RDA) were developed by the Food and Nutrition Board of the National Research Council/National Academy of Sciences (NAS/NRC, 1980b). These were dietary standards for levels of intake of essential nutrients considered by the Board to be adequate to meet the known nutritional needs of practically all healthy persons. They were technical guidelines for use by health professionals. They were not designed for use by the public generally. Guidelines for nutritionally adequate diets that could be used readily by the population as a whole were developed initially during the early 1940s (Hayes, Trulson, & Stare, 1955; Page & Phipard, 1957). The purpose of the guidelines was to provide easily understood information on how to meet requirements for essential nutrients from the food supply by consuming sufficient quantities of various protective foods—foods that are rich in proteins, vitamins, and minerals.

The USDA (Page & Phipard, 1957) developed a food guide in which foods were grouped into four categories based on the nutrients they contributed to the diet (Table 37.2). The four groups were milk and milk products, breads and cereals, fruits and vegetables, meats and legumes. By selecting appropriate numbers of servings daily from each of these groups (Health and Welfare Canada, 1979), it was possible for adults to obtain from 80% to 120% of the amounts of nutrients recommended in the RDA from about 1,200 to 1,800

Table 37.2 Pattern of Nutrients Provided by the Four Food Groups

Milk and Milk Products	Breads and Cereals	Fruits and Vegetables	Meat and Legumes
Vitamin A		Vitamin A	Vitamin A
	Thiamin		Thiamin
Riboflavin	Riboflavin		Riboflavin
	Niacin		Niacin
		Folic Acid	Folic Acid
		Vitamin C	
Vitamin D			
Calcium			
	Iron	Iron	Iron
Protein	Protein		Protein
Number of Servings (adults)			
2[a]	3–5	4–5	2

Source: Adapted from Health and Welfare Canada (1979).
[a] Two to four servings for children, depending on age, and for pregnant and lactating women to meet the higher needs of these groups for calcium.

kilocalories of food, depending on body size (American Medical Association, 1979; King, Cohenour, Corruccini, & Schneeman, 1978). This provided the basis for a nutritionally adequate diet. The rest of the required calories could then be obtained, together with additional quantities of essential nutrients, from additional servings of foods within or outside the food groups.

The food group system is a guideline for prevention of nutritional inadequacy through variety in the selection of foods. It continues to be the primary guideline for a healthful diet. Many countries have adopted some modification of such a food guide. Scientific evidence supporting the reliability of the basic four food guide has been obtained from studies of the amounts of nutrients provided by the appropriate number of servings of foods (Table 37.2) selected according to the recommendations (American Medical Association, 1978; King, Cohenour, Corrucini, & Schneeman, 1978).

A guideline for variety in food selection is sound for two other reasons. First, nutritional deficiencies occur primarily when food selection is restricted to a relatively few choices. The occurrence of beri-beri, for example, is associated with a high intake of polished rice—a food that is deficient in thiamin. The occurrence of pellegra is associated with a high intake of corn and a low intake of foods of animal origin, resulting in a diet low in both niacin and tryptophan. Nutritional deficiencies still are occasionally encountered in the United States among individuals who, for various reasons (alcoholism, neglect, poverty, ignorance), consume diets that are restricted to a narrow selection of foods. Second, foods may contain potentially toxic substances, either naturally occurring or through contamination. Such substances are occasionally ingested in hazardous amounts in some of the poor countries of the world, usually because food shortages cause the population to depend for survival on consumption of a product containing such a substance. The body has a substantial capacity for detoxification or elimination of many chemical compounds, but if a large quantity of a potentially toxic substance is consumed, this capacity may be exceeded. In some parts of India, for example, one of the serious health problems is a high incidence of permanent paralysis of the lower limbs caused by consumption of the seeds of a vetch (*Lathyrus satiuum*). This plant is drought-resistant, so the seeds, which contain a neurotoxin, may make up a substantial part of the diet when other foods are in short supply. When the food supply is highly varied, the probability of consuming a hazardous amount of a naturally occurring toxic substance or of a contaminant present in a food is greatly reduced.

The second guideline for a healthful diet is for moderation in food consumption—maintaining appropriate body weight for height by consuming an amount of food sources of energy (calories) that just balances the amount of energy expended. The question of control of energy intake and obesity is discussed in another chapter, so it is sufficient to say here that appropriate body weight cannot be defined rigidly. Body weight about 20% above the commonly used standards for appropriate body weight is not associated with any demonstrable increase in risk to health (Andres, 1980; Bray, 1978; Keys, 1981). Excessive overweight—obesity—is associated with an increased risk of developing hypertension, diabetes, biliary disease, and certain cancers and, through diabetes and hypertension, with increased risk of developing heart disease. There is a strong genetic component that predisposes many people toward diseases associated with excessive body weight. Diabetes and hypertension, in particular, are known to occur as the result of genetic predisposition (Craighead, 1978; Langford, 1979; U.S. DHEW, 1979). Increased health risk from obesity is greatest among young adults. There are also increased health risks from excessive underweight.

Quite apart from the evidence that obesity is associated, in a proportion of the population, with increased risk of developing several diseases, excessive food consumption increases the work load of many metabolic and organ systems, and excessive body weight makes physical activity difficult and often has undesirable social consequences. This is sufficient reason in itself for including moderation in food consumption as a major guideline for ensuring health.

If energy expenditure is low, as it is in most industrialized societies, the amount of food required to maintain body weight will be low. Low total food intake increases the risk of consuming inadequate amounts of some of the essential nutrients. The American Medical Association (1979) and the Food and Nutrition Board (NAS/NRC, 1980a, 1980b), therefore, recommend maintaining at least a moderate degree of physical activity, which increases caloric expenditure—an important part of any program for weight control—rather than depending solely on downward adjustment of food intake.

If food intake is low because of inactivity, dieting, or illness, it is advisable to curtail intake of fats and oils, sugar, alcohol, and high-carbohydrate foods that contain low quantities of essential nutrients and to substitute highly nutritious foods. If food intake falls below 1200 kcal, as it does in many weight reduction programs, supplementary quantities of essential nutrients may be desirable. A supplement that provides a balanced pattern of essential nutrients between 50% and 100% of the quantities recommended in the RDA (NAS/NRC, 1980b) is the appropriate way to accomplish this. There is no scientifically established health benefit from consumption of large quantities of essential nutrients—that is, in excess of the RDA.

A guideline for moderation in food consumption should extend beyond concern for only total calories. It should also include moderation in the consumption of individual foods and nutrients. Fat-soluble vitamins A and D, essential minerals such as copper, selenium, and iron, and even the water-soluble vitamin niacin can be toxic when ingested in excessive amounts (Harper, 1979). Consumption of excessive amounts of individual essential nutrients other than sodium will occur only from excessive use of nutritional supplements. If the guideline for variety in food consumption is followed, and if food intake is not impaired because of ill health, dieting, or some other reason, nutrient needs can be met readily from the food supply (Gortner, 1975); there is no need for dietary supplements.

Sodium is probably the nutrient consumed in greatest excess in the United States in relation to the requirement. The Food and Nutrition Board, in the most recent edition of the RDA (NAS/NRC, 1980b), proposed that appropriate intakes of sodium chloride (salt), the main dietary source of sodium, range between 3 and 8 gm daily. Most of the population, about 85%, tolerates salt well and can safely consume 10 gm or more of salt daily. Therefore, hypertension—high blood pressure—is unlikely to occur in this segment of the population unless their intake of salt is highly excessive. About 15% of the population is susceptible to hypertension at some time during life, probably mainly through heredity (U.S. DHEW, 1979). In many of this group, the condition is aggravated by a high salt intake; in others who are susceptible, salt restriction helps reduce the severity of the hypertension and may prevent it. Unfortunately, those who are susceptible are not readily identified, and it is doubtful that hypertension can be prevented in those who are susceptible to it unless intake of salt is reduced below 3 gm/day, a therapeutic recommendation. This is difficult to achieve from the usual food supply. Nevertheless, for those who do develop hypertension, restriction of salt intake may help them reduce the dosage of drugs required to control the condition (U.S. DHEW, 1979). For the rest, the upper limit proposed should be more than adequate even for those who may have high salt loss from working in a hot environment.

Although guidelines for healthful diets developed in the early 1940s did not include a specific recommendation for fiber—a diet component that is receiving much emphasis today—the guidelines for fruit, vegetable, and cereal consumption represented recommendations for a moderate intake of fiber. This intake can contribute to the health of the gastrointestinal tract by helping to maintain intestinal muscle tone and by easing evacuation of wastes. Claims that fiber intake, especially a high intake, has unique disease preventive action are tantalizing but not convincing (NAS/NRC, 1980a; National Research Council, 1982). Also, large intakes of fiber can have adverse effects, both by creating intestinal distress and by increasing fecal losses of nutrients. The available scientific evidence supports a guideline for moderate fiber intake—amounts that can be obtained by consuming appropriate numbers of servings (Table 37.2) of foods of plant origin (Health and Welfare Canada, 1979; NAS/NRC, 1980b; Page & Phipard, 1957).

These were essentially the guidelines for a healthful diet during the period when life expectancy increased so greatly in this country. The improved health during this century, which has been documented extensively, obviously did not occur solely because of improvements in diet. There were many other reasons, including improved sanitation, housing, and control of infectious diseases, but it is doubtful that the current satisfactory state of health could have been achieved or maintained without improvement in diet and nutritional status.

A diet that provides adequate quantities of essential nutrients without providing a surplus of calories is absolutely essential for maintenance of health. It is also important for maintaining vigorous defense mechanisms against diseases. It will prevent diseases that are caused by nutritional deficiencies and will ensure that diseases from other causes will not be complicated by the occurrence of such deficiencies. It cannot be assumed, however, that a nutritious diet will protect against the gradual deterioration of physiological function that occurs with aging or against chronic and degenerative diseases. This leads us to the question of relationships between diet and diseases other than the nutritional deficiency diseases that are assumed to be linked in some way to diet.

DIET IN RELATION TO PREVENTION OF CHRONIC AND DEGENERATIVE DISEASES

The virtual elimination of nutritional deficiency diseases, together with control of many infectious diseases that were major causes of death during the early part of this century, has led to a shift in emphasis in medicine and public health toward treatment and control of chronic and degenerative diseases, especially heart disease, stroke, and cancer, which together now account for close to 70% of all deaths (U.S. DHEW, 1979).

Although death rates from these diseases are higher than they were during the early part of the century, the shift in the age distribution within the population toward a larger proportion of elderly must be taken into account in assessing the significance of changes in mortality rates over time. The population pyramids in Figure 37.2 illustrate the problem.

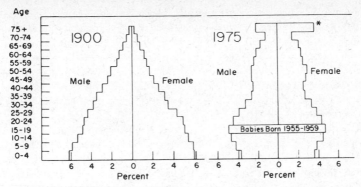

*The final band, representing people 75 years and over on the pyramids

Figure 37.2 Population pyramids showing the change in the distribution of age groups within the U.S. population, 1900 vs. 1975. (Courtesy of the Population Reference Bureau, Washington, D.C.)

Early in the century, most of the population was young. As life expectancy has increased, the proportion of people in the older age groups has increased. Therefore, in determining changes in mortality rates over time, it is important to compare the rates for each age group and to take into account changes in the numbers of people in each age group. The National Center for Health Statistics reports age-adjusted mortality rates calculated in this way so that comparisons over time can be made on a standard basis.

The age-adjusted death rate from cardiovascular diseases, which was high in the 1920s, began to decline between 1930 and 1940 (Grove & Hetzel, 1968) and has continued to do so since then (U.S. DHEW, 1978). The decline started earlier for women and has been greater for them than for men. For the most part, age-adjusted death rates from cancer have remained quite constant; mortality from cancer of the lung, associated with cigarette smoking, has increased substantially—more for men than for women—but mortality rates from gastric and uterine cancers have declined steadily (American Cancer Society, 1979). Overall, death rates at every age have declined and life expectancy has lengthened, indicating that deaths from these diseases are occurring later in life than they did previously. Clearly, there has been no epidemic of chronic and degenerative diseases (U.S. DHEW, 1979), which in itself invalidates claims that the high incidence of these diseases is the result of changes that have occurred in the U.S. diet (Senate Select Committee, 1977). It also casts doubt on proposals for dietary goals and guidelines designed to reverse the assumed trend (Grundy, Bilheimer, Blackburn, Brown, Kwiterovich, Mattson, Schorfeld, & Weidman, 1982; National Research Council, 1982; U.S. Department of Agriculture, 1980) as has been emphasized by skeptics of this view (Ahrens, 1979; American Medical Association, 1979; Harper, 1981a, 1981b; NAS/NRC, 1980a; Oliver, 1978; Olson, 1979).

What changes have occurred in the composition of the food supply? For most essential nutrients, the amounts available per person have increased during this century despite a modest decrease in total calories (Gortner, 1975). The proportion of energy (calories) available from starches has fallen by about 10%, and the proportion from fat has increased by about 10%. The proportion of energy from saturated fat has not changed significantly, nor has the cholesterol content of the food supply. The fiber content of the diet has declined somewhat, and the unsaturated fat content has increased (Page & Friend, 1978). There is no evidence from either measurements of food composition or surveys of the health status of the population that the nutritional quality of the food supply has deteriorated, despite many claims that it has.

Most of the proposals for new guidelines call for decreased consumption of saturated fat and cholesterol, increased consumption of polyunsaturated fat, decreased consumption of sugar, and increased consumption of starch as measures for reducing the incidence of chronic and degenerative diseases, especially heart disease (Grundy et al., 1982; Senate Select Committee, 1977). More recently, decreased total fat consumption has been proposed as a measure for decreasing the risk of cancer (National Research Council, 1982). There has also been concern with the possible adverse effects of food additives, food contaminants, and processed foods, particularly smoked and salt-cured foods (National Research Council, 1982; Senate Select Committee, 1977; U.S. DHEW, 1979), but these claims have not been substantiated, even according to advocates of dietary guidelines for disease prevention (National Research Council, 1982).

All these proposals are controversial (Ahrens, 1979; American Medical Association, 1979; Blackburn, 1979; Doll & Peto, 1981; Harper, 1981a, 1981b; McNamara, 1982; NAS/NRC, 1980a; Oliver, 1978; Olson, 1979, 1981; Stamler, 1979)—for many reasons. First, and foremost, the causes of the chronic and degenerative diseases for which they are proposed as control measures are not known. For persons considered to be at high risk of developing heart disease—especially for those with greatly elevated serum cholesterol concentration—reductions in total fat, saturated fat, and cholesterol and increased polyunsaturated fat in the diet have been recommended for many years. This is not controversial, but it certainly is controversial whether similar recommendations are appropriate for those who are not known to be at risk. Second, the major evidence supporting the proposed new guidelines is from epidemiologic studies in which correlations have been observed between the incidence of heart disease or cancer and environmental factors in different countries. Such studies provide evidence only of associations, not of cause and effect relationships, which have been the basis in the past for instituting public health measures for disease control. Third, the overall body of evidence assembled to support such proposals is not consistent. In some countries with similar diets, the incidence of chronic and degenerative diseases is quite different. Even a single exception to a hypothesis is evidence that the hypothesis is inadequate (Harper, 1981b). Fourth, the basic assumption underlying these proposals—that in the United States an increased incidence of chronic and degenerative diseases has been associated with changes that have occurred in the food supply—is not true. As indicated earlier, the incidence of these diseases in the United States has not increased. Finally, the scientific knowledge needed to devise dietary regimens for prevention of chronic and degenerative diseases is not available. In tests designed to demonstrate the effectiveness of the proposed dietary modifications, positive results have not been obtained consistently, and the beneficial effects observed have been disappointingly small, even when the population studied has been identified as being at high risk (Ahrens, 1979; McNamara, 1982; Oliver, 1978). It is not surprising, then, that there is controversy between those who believe that associations suggestive of links between diet and the incidence of such diseases provide an adequate basis for initiating proposals for general diet modification for the entire population (Blackburn, 1979; Grundy et al., 1982; National Research Council, 1982; Senate Select Committee, 1977; Stamler, 1979) and those who are unwilling to support dietary proposals for prevention of disease unless the scientific evidence that they will be effective is indisputable and compelling (Ahrens, 1979; American Medical Association, 1979; Doll & Peto, 1981; Harper, 1981a; McNamara, 1982; NAS/NRC, 1980a; Oliver, 1978; Olson, 1979).

Although it is not possible to review here the immense literature on associations between diet and chronic and degenerative diseases and to elaborate on the controversy it has generated, some aspects of this subject should be mentioned in order to indicate further why proposals for diet modification as a measure for disease prevention are so controversial.

The debate over diet and prevention of chronic and degenerative diseases is a debate about the most appropriate proportions of major energy sources in the diet. It centers mainly on the assumption that populations (not specific individuals) who consume less than 30% of the calories they need from fat, especially saturated fat, will have a lower risk of developing chronic and degenerative diseases such as heart disease (Grundy et al., 1982) and some forms of cancer (National Research Council, 1982) than will those who consume higher fat diets.

The sources of energy (calories) in diets—fats and carbohydrates, and to a lesser extent proteins—can be substituted for each other within limits. Some minimal quantity of fat (about 10% of calories) is needed to provide the required quantity of essential fatty acids, and some minimal quantity of protein (about 10% of calories) is necessary to meet the requirements for essential amino acids. After these specific needs have been satisfied, the remaining energy needs can be met from a wide range of proportions of carbohydrate, fat, and protein. Nevertheless, there is evidence from both human and animal studies of an upper limit of tolerance for fat and protein in apparently healthy individuals. Insofar as can be established, the upper limit of tolerance for various energy sources in a generally healthy population is beyond the range encountered in routinely consumed human diets. This is probably due, in large measure, to the adaptive capacity of the mammalian body. Enzymatic responses occur in higher organisms that consume disproportionately large amounts of these energy sources, which increase the ability of the body to metabolize them. Within a population, however, there are individuals whose ability to tolerate large quantities of fat, carbohydrate, or protein is limited.

Diabetes impairs the ability to use carbohydrates as a source of energy; certain inherited hyperlipoproteinemias limit the tolerance for either fat or carbohydrate as sources of energy; and renal failure impairs the ability to tolerate protein. Metabolic defects that cause such impairment may be hereditary or may be induced by disease or by overeating. The effects of these metabolic limitations can be relieved to varying degrees by modification of the proportions of energy sources in the diet. A low protein intake reduces the load of waste products that must be handled by an impaired kidney, for example. Modifications of the proportion, type, or quantity of fat or carbohydrate are commonly used in the management of diabetes and hyperlipoproteinemias. Diet modification is accepted generally as therapy for such conditions, even when, as in hyperlipoproteinemias, the underlying cause of the problem may be unknown and the value of the treatment has not been clearly established (McNamara, 1982; Oliver 1978; Olson 1979).

It is frequently assumed, however, that if diet modification is an appropriate treatment for those who have such conditions, it should also be an appropriate preventive measure for those who do not have the condition. The fallacy of such reasoning is that, unless the treatment is based on removing the cause of the metabolic impairment, as with nutritional deficiency diseases, diet modification is being used merely to treat the signs and symptoms, not the disease. Effective prevention programs must be based on identifying and eliminating the causes of disease and on identifying those who are susceptible and require special and usually comprehensive treatment.

Both animal studies and epidemiologic studies indicate that wide ranges in the dietary content of carbohydrates, proteins, and fats are tolerated well. In fact, it is doubtful that any diet containing certain specific proportions of these nutrients is associated with unique health benefits. This is emphasized by examining the caloric sources of two populations with close to the maximum known life expectancy (Table 37.2): the Swedish population has a diet high in fat and sugar and low in starch, and the Japanese population has one high in starch and low in fat and sugar. The patterns of major diseases in these two countries are distinctly different, but life expectancy is the same. The extent to which the difference in disease patterns is determined by the difference in the dietary patterns is not known, but it seems clear that disease patterns are influenced by environmental factors. The fact that life expectancy is the same in these different environments indicates that modification of the environment, including diet, is likely to have both beneficial and detrimental effects that are not predictable with our present knowledge. This alone should make us highly skeptical that we know enough to be able to predict the effects of modification of the proportions of energy sources in diets on health and disease, except in relation to deficiencies of essential nutrients and in dealing symptomatically with metabolic problems.

Where, then, does this leave us? We have a scientifically sound basis for recommending variety in food consumption to meet essential nutrient needs, and an equally sound basis for recommending that at least 10% of calories should be from protein and 10% from fat, both from a variety of sources. We have a good basis for recommending that at least 20% of calories should be from carbohydrate, for its ability both to spare the body's need to convert protein to carbohydrate and to prevent ketosis, which could occur, especially during periods of physical activity, from excessive consumption of fat (Harper, 1978). This still leaves some 60% of calories to be distributed among these three nutrients.

The American Heart Association (Grundy et al., 1982) has recommended that the proportion of energy derived from fat should not exceed 35%, with one-quarter to one-third of this proportion coming from polyunsaturated fatty acids. They also recommend that cholesterol consumption should be reduced from current values of 450–500 mg/day to about 300 mg/day. The National Research Council (1982) Committee on Diet, Nutrition and Cancer proposed in its interim recommendations that fat intake should not exceed 30% of total calories. These recommendations have been given specifically as measures for prevention of coronary heart disease and certain types of cancers. The Committee on Dietary Allowances of the Food and Nutrition Board of the National Research Council (NAS/NRC, 1980b) "does not believe that it is desirable to make a blanket recommendation for dietary change for the entire population" but does acknowledge that for persons in the high-risk category for certain diseases, dietary modifications are an appropriate part of a comprehensive program of health care. This is also essentially the view of the American Medical Association (1979). The bases for differences of opinion about general dietary recommendations for disease prevention, cited earlier, have been outlined particularly well in a recent report on diet and cancer (Council for Agricultural Science and Technology, 1982). Resolution of these differences will require much more knowledge—knowledge that can be gained only through further research on relationships between diet and the development of chronic and degenerative diseases.

We need to keep in mind that for infants, young children, the elderly, and pregnant women, consumption of a low-fat, high-carbohydrate diet is often associated with the occurrence of nutritional inadequacy; that for those who are sedentary, many high-fat or high-carbohydrate foods provide disproportionately high amounts of calories and disproportionately low amounts of essential nutrients; and that for active children and young people, energy expenditure is high, so that they need high caloric intakes. With our present state of knowledge, we cannot specify, on a sound scientific basis, exact proportions of the various energy sources. We can recommend only ranges, although for certain population groups we may be able to narrow the ranges somewhat. This then leaves us with recommendations for healthful diets in which protein may range from 10% to 15% of calories, fat from 20% to 40%, and carbohydrate from 45% to 70%—all provided from a variety of sources, using as a general guideline the four food group approach (Harper, 1978). Unfortunately, we have no sound basis for assuring that any specific proportions of these nutrients will be effective measures for prevention of chronic and degenerative diseases.

It is important to emphasize that the controversy over extending dietary guidelines to include recommendations for appropriate proportions of the major nutrients has little to do with the nature of the guidelines themselves. The aforementioned ranges for the proportions of major nutrients that may be present in healthful diets would include most of the proposed guidelines. The controversy has to do with the implied promises that such modifications are effective measures for disease prevention and improved health. There is a danger in diverting resources into programs that represent premature application based on excessive claims. We should promote prevention only when "we know what can be delivered and how to deliver it" (Eisenberg, 1977). Unless we heed this advice, we run the risk of undermining science and public health programs.

There obviously is no single uniquely healthful diet; rather, there are many healthful diets. The populations of Sweden, the Netherlands, France, Italy, Japan, and northern North America all consume healthful diets, yet the assumed national diets of these countries are quite different. Also, within each national diet there undoubtedly is wide variety in food selection. Yet the populations of these countries generally have enviable health records by world standards, even though there are people in each country who fall below the national average. It is important not to succumb to the frequently repeated claims that diet has deteriorated and that, because of this, health is continuously at risk. Scientific evidence to support such claims is lacking. Fear of food and fear for health create apprehension and can lead to acceptance of unsound and even bizarre dietary practices.

From time immemorial, food has served functions other than nutritional ones. Food was viewed by most tribal societies as the gift of the gods; for example, the Mayan word for corn, *ixim,* means "the grace of god." Foods were frequently endowed with symbolic values. Myths developed about the transfer of characteristics of the food source to the eater, such as the myth that warriors would acquire courage from eating the heart of the lion but timidity from eating chicken. Such beliefs are based on mythical thinking, a type of thinking that has enabled people with little knowledge of nature to deal with many types of fears. Unlike science, myths do not give people power over the environment, but they do, according to Levi-Strauss (1978), "give them the illusion that they can understand the universe." Myths about food gave people the illusion that they understood the nature of health and disease and that they could exert control over both by selecting foods according to their various symbolic values. This provided a set of beliefs that, though illusionary, enabled people to deal with fear of the unknown in relation to health and disease.

The current prevalence of this type of thinking, albeit frequently presented in pseudoscientific garb, should not be underestimated. One need only recognize the widespread acceptance of the unending succession of pseudoscientific and sometimes dangerous articles and books on diets for weight reduction and health promotion, and the extensive use of the worthless and potentially toxic cyanogenic glycoside from apricot pits as a cure for cancer, to realize the willingness of many people today to base their actions regarding promotion of health and prevention of disease on mythical thinking. It is this type of thinking, as a substitute for scientific thinking, that makes so many people so highly susceptible to the blandishments of amateur nutritionists, charlatans, and politicians who promise simplistic methods for prevention and cure of the diseases they fear.

As Phillip Handler (Note 1) has stated: "The necessity for scientific rigor is even greater when scientific evidence is being offered as the basis for formulation of public policy than when it is simply expected to find its way in the market place of accepted scientific understanding." It is crucial that this principle be followed in devising dietary guidelines for disease prevention. Unless we can assure the public that such guidelines will be both effective and safe on the basis of scientifically acceptable tests, we are following practices that would not meet the Food and Drug Administration's standards for claims regarding the health benefits of commercial products. Unless we maintain the same standards that we would impose on the producers who claim that their products provide health benefits, we are in danger of undermining the credibility of the science of nutrition and of science generally. The effectiveness of dietary proposals for prevention of chronic and degenerative diseases remains to be established.

SUMMARY

We can devise guidelines for healthful diets. A nutritious diet that provides adequate quantities of all the essential nutrients and sources of energy from a variety of foods, in amounts needed to achieve and maintain desirable body weight, is necessary for general health and for vigorous defense mechanisms against diseases. We cannot devise diets for disease prevention, however, even though we know how to modify diets to relieve some of the effects of metabolic impairments associated with certain diseases. Guidelines for a nutritionally adequate and healthful diet, based on variety and moderation in the selection of foods, have a sound scientific basis. There is no sound scientific evidence, however, that consumption of large quantities of individual nutrients has any unique health benefit.

There is evidence that the patterns of diseases that are major causes of death are different in different countries, but proposals that diet modification can be used as a public health measure for altering disease incidence remain unproved and controversial.

REFERENCE NOTE

1. Handler, P. Dedication address, Northwestern University Cancer Center, May 18, 1979.

REFERENCES

Ahrens, E. H., Jr. Dietary fats and coronary heart disease: Unfinished business. *Lancet,* 1979, **2,** 1345–1348.

American Cancer Society. *Cancer facts and figures, 1979.* New York: American Cancer Society, 1979.

American Medical Association. Concepts of nutrition and health. *Journal of the American Medical Association,* 1979, **242,** 2335–2338.

Andres, R. *Overview of the aging process.* Symposium of the Food and Nutrition Board. Washington, D.C.: NAS/NRC, 1980.

Benarde, M. A. *The food additives dictionary.* New York: Simon & Schuster, 1981.

Blackburn, H. Diet and mass hyperlipidemia: Public health considerations—A point of view. In R. I. Levy, B. M. Rifkind, B. H. Dennis, & N. D. Ernst (Eds.), *Nutrition, lipids and coronary heart disease.* New York: Raven Press, 1979.

Bray, G. A. To treat or not to treat—that is the question? In G. A. Bray (Ed.), *Recent advances in obesity research 2.* London: Newman, 1978.

Butler, R. N. Nutrition: Aging and the elderly. In *Diet Related to Killer Diseases, 7.* Hearing before the Select Committee on Nutrition and Human Needs of the U.S. Senate, September 23, 1977. Washington, D.C.: U.S. Government Printing Office, 1977.

Chou, M. The preoccupation with food safety. In M. Chou & D. P. Harmon, Jr. (Eds.), *Critical food issues of the eighties.* New York: Pergamon Press, 1979.

Council for Agricultural Science and Technology. *Diet, nutrition and cancer: A critique.* Special Publication No. 13. Ames, Iowa: Council for Agricultural Science and Technology, 1982.

Craighead, J. E. Current views on the etiology of insulin-dependent diabetes mellitus. *New England Journal of Medicine,* 1978, **299,** 1439–1445.

Doll, R., & Peto, R. The causes of cancer: Quantitative estimates of avoidable risks of cancer in the United States today. *Journal of the National Cancer Institute,* 1981, **66,** 1191–1308.

Eisenberg, L. The perils of prevention: A cautionary note. *New England Journal of Medicine,* 1977, **297,** 1230–2.

Fries, J. F. Aging, natural death and the compression of morbidity. *New England Journal of Medicine,* 1980, **303,** 130–135.

Goldsmith, G. A. The B vitamins: Thiamine, riboflavin, niacin. In G. H. Beaton & E. W. McHenry (Eds.), *Nutrition—A comprehensive treatise (Vol. II).* New York: Academic Press, 1964.

Gortner, W. A. Nutrition in the United States, 1900 to 1974. *Cancer Research,* 1975, **35,** 3246.

Grove, R. D., & Hetzel, A. M. *Statistics rates in the United States, 1940 to 1960.* Washington, D.C.: National Center for Health Statistics, DHEW, 1968.

Grundy, S. M., Bilheimer, D., Blackburn, H., Brown, W. V., Kwiterovitch, P. O., Jr., Mattson, F., Schonfeld, G., & Weidman, W. H. Rationale of the diet-heart statement of the American Heart Association. *Circulation, 1982, 839A–854A.*

Harper, A. E. What are appropriate dietary guidelines? *Food Technology,* 1978, **32,** 48–53.

Harper, A. E. Vitamins and megavitamins: Fact and fancy. *Urban Health,* 1979, **8,** 22–26.

Harper, A. E. Dietary goals. In L. Ellenbogen (Ed.), *Controversies in nutrition.* New York: Churchill Livingstone, 1981.(a)

Harper, A. E. Human nutrition: Its scientific basis. In N. Selvey & P. L. White (Eds.), *Nutrition in the 1980s: Constraints on our knowledge (Progress in Clinical and Biological Research,* **67).** New York: Alan R. Liss, 1981.(b)

Hayes, O., Trulson, M. F., & Stare, F. J. Suggested revisions of the basic 7. *Journal of the American Dietetic Association,* 1955, **31,** 1103–1107.

Health and Welfare Canada. *Canada's food guide.* Ottawa: Minister of Supply and Services Canada, 1979.

Keys, A. Overweight, obesity, coronary heart disease and mortality. In N. Selvey & P. L. White (Eds.) *Nutrition in the 1980s: Constraints in our knowledge (Progress in Clinical and Biological Research, 67).* 1981.

King, J. C. Cohenour, S. H., Corruccini, C. G., & Schneeman, P. Evaluation and modification of the basic four food guide. *Journal of Nutrition Education,* 1978, **10,** 27–32.

Kohn, R. R. *Principles of mammalian aging.* Englewood Cliffs, N.J.: Prentice-Hall, 1977.

Kritchevsky, D. Dietary Interactions. In R. I. Levy, B. M. Rifkind, B. H. Dennis, & N. D. Ernst (Eds.), *Nutrition, lipids and coronary heart disease.* New York: Raven Press, 1979.

Langford, H. G. Dietary sodium and hypertension. In *Proceedings of the Lillian Fountain Smith Conference for Nutrition Educators.* Fort Collins: University of Colorado, 1979.

Levi-Strauss, C. *Myth and meaning.* Toronto: University of Toronto Press, 1978.

McNamara, D. J. Diet and hyperlipidemia: A justifiable debate. *Archives of Internal Medicine,* 1982, **142,** 1121–1124.

National Academy of Sciences/National Research Council (NAS/NRC(, Food and Nutrition Board. *Research needs for establishing dietary guidelines for the U.S. population.* Washington, D.C.: NAS/ NRC, 1979.

National Academy of Sciences/National Research Council (NAS/NRC), Food and Nutrition Board. *Toward Healthful Diets.* Washington, D.C.: NAS/NRC, 1980(a).

National Academy of Sciences/National Research Council (NAS/NRC), Food and Nutrition Board. *Recommended Dietary Allowances* (9th ed.). Washington, D.C.: NAS/NRC, 1980(b).

National Research Council. *Diet, nutrition and cancer.* Washington, D.C.: National Academy Press, 1982.

National Research Council. On some major human diseases. In *Outlook for science and technology: The next five years.* San Francisco: W. H. Freeman, 1982.

Oliver, M. F. Diet and coronary heart disease. In J. Yudkin (Ed.), *Diet of man: Needs and wants.* London: Applied Science Publishers, 1978.

Olson, R. E. Is there an optimum diet for the prevention of coronary heart disease? In R. I. Levy, B. M. Rifkind, B. M. Dennis, & N. Ernst (Eds.), *Nutrition, lipids and coronary heart disease—A global view. Nutrition in health and disease.* (Vol. 1). New York: Raven Press, 1979.

Olson, R. E. New horizons for meat and nutrition policy. In *Meat in nutrition and health.* Danville, Ill.: National Livestock and Meat Board, 1981.

Omran, A. R. Epidemiologic transition in the U.S.: The health factor in population change. *Population Bulletin 32* (No. 2). Washington, D.C.: Population Reference Bureau, 1977.

Page, L., & Friend, B. The changing United States diet. *Biological Science,* 1978, **28,** 192.

Page, L., & Phipard, E. F. Essentials of an adequate diet. *Home Economics Research Report No. 3,* Washington, D.C.: U.S. Government Printing Office, 1957.

Sandstead, H. H. Clinical manifestations of certain vitamin deficiencies. In R. S. Goodhart & M. E. Shils (Eds.), *Modern nutrition in health and disease* (5th ed.). Philadelphia: Lea & Febiger, 1973.

Senate Select Committee on Nutrition and Human Needs. *Dietary goals for the United States—& supplemental views.* Washington, D.C.: U.S. Government Printing Office, 1977.

Stamler, J. Population studies. In R. I. Levy, B. M. Rifkind, B. H. Dennis, & N. D. Ernst (Eds.), *Nutrition, lipids and coronary heart disease.* New York: Raven Press, 1979.

Thomas, L. On the science and technology of medicine. *Daedalus,* Winter 1977, 35–46.

United Nations. *Demographic yearbook, historical supplement 1.* New York: United Nations, 1979.

U.S. Department of Agriculture, U.S. DHEW: *Nutrition and your health.* Washington, D.C.: U.S. Government Printing Office, 1980.

U.S. Department of Health, Education and Welfare (U.S. DHEW). *Facts of life and death.* DHEW Pub. No. (HRA)74–122. Washington, D.C.: U.S. Government Printing Office, 1978.

U.S. Department of Health, Education and Welfare (U.S. DHEW). *Healthy people—The Surgeon General's report on health promotion and disease prevention.* DHEW Pub. No. 79–55071. Washington, D.C.: U.S. Government Printing Office, 1979.

CHAPTER 38

THE ACQUISITION OF FOOD HABITS AND PREFERENCES

PAUL ROZIN

University of Pennsylvania

Food is at one and the same time *the* source of nutrition, a vector for harmful microorganisms, a potential source of toxins, a great source of pleasure and satisfaction, and a vehicle for the expression of social relations and values. It is not surprising, therefore, that human beings spend a great deal of time working to obtain food, to select it, to prepare it, and to eat it. It is surprising that we know so little about the origin of people's preferences, likes, and attitudes. This lack of knowledge is due in large part to the fact that psychology, the science most appropriate to explore these issues, has been fascinated with the issue of what determines how much people (and animals) eat, rather than what they eat. The greater appeal of this admittedly important problem as a subject for scientific study results from (a) the availability of a physiological model of energy regulation as a solid base for theory, observation, and experiment; (b) the belief that hunger might be accounted for in terms of a single basic underlying process, in contrast to the transparently multivariate causation of food preferences; (c) the prevalence of obesity, a highly visible, possibly harmful, and (in the United States) socially undesirable condition, linked to the study of hunger and regulation of food intake; and (d) the belief that hunger, unlike food selection, could be studied outside a sociocultural context. Whatever the merit of these arguments, the result is that this chapter, centering on the acquisition of food preferences and attitudes, will be filled with unanswered questions and suggestive, as opposed to definitive, findings.

A GUIDE TO THE LITERATURE

Food selection is not a well-defined scholarly domain within psychology, biology, or anthropology. As a result, very few journals have a high density of articles in this area. The journals *Appetite* and *Ecology of Food and Nutrition* are the most likely sources for papers that represent the research done in these three disciplines. The *Journal of the American Dietetic Association* and the *Journal of Nutrition Education* have frequent articles on this subject from the perspective of nutrition. The broadest collection of papers representing many perspectives is in Barker's (1982) *Psychobiology of Human Food Selection;* see also *Criteria of Food Acceptance* (Solms & Hall, 1981). The role of the chemical senses in food choice is emphasized in two collections of papers, *Preference Behavior and Chemoreception* (Kroeze, 1979) and *The Chemical Senses and Nutrition* (Kare & Maller, 1977). There is

Preparation of this chapter was supported by National Institutes of Health Grant HD 12674. Thanks go to Patricia Pliner for her helpful comments on the manuscript.

also a useful annotated bibliography of the subject (Wilson, 1973) and a text (Lowenberg, Todhunter, Wilson, Savage, & Lubawski, 1974) that covers the topic primarily from the perspective of nutrition. More specialized sources include a comprehensive review of sensory approaches (Amerine, Pangborn, & Roessler, 1965) and a collection of papers examining food use and choice from the folklore perspective (Fenton & Owen, 1981).

SOURCES OF VARIANCE IN FOOD SELECTION

The aim of this chapter will be to review what is known about why humans eat what they eat, with an emphasis on psychological factors. Both universal aspects of human food choice and individual differences will be considered. In either case, the major determinant of what is eaten is probably availability, a factor that is largely independent of individual behavior. Until this century, for most people almost all the food available for choice was the food raised in the region. Food choice was highly constrained by geographic-climatic factors, and it still is to a notable extent. Economic factors also severely constrain food choice. Though acknowledging these potent factors, the focus of this chapter will be more on the interaction of people with food, assuming the accessibility of the food.

All other determinants of food choice can be conveniently, if somewhat simplemindedly, categorized as biological, cultural, or individual (psychological). Biological explanations are more likely for universal features of food choice, whereas cultural or psychological explanations are more likely for individual differences. There are rather few universals and a great many individual and cultural differences, and here is where our ignorance begins to show. If one were interested in determining as much as possible about adults' food preferences and attitudes and could ask them only one question, the question undoubtedly should be: What is your culture or ethnic group? I know of no hard evidence on this point, but it is, nonetheless, obviously true. In the process of enculturation, the exposure to particular foods is controlled and food values and attitudes are conveyed. There are many differences, however, in preferences and attitudes among members of the same culture. What is responsible for these differences? Surprisingly, we don't know. There is no very informative second question to ask our hypothetical persons. Sex differences (AuCoin, Haley, Rae, & Cole, 1972; Rozin, Fallon & Mandell, 1984) and such biological factors as differences in taste sensitivity (Bartoshuk, 1979; Cowart, 1981; Pangborn, 1981) account for very little variance. The obvious second question would relate to family factors: What are the preferences and attitudes of the parents? Surprisingly, when culture is factored out, studies have found either no relation or a very small one (correlations usually below .3) between preferences of children and those of their parents (Birch, 1980b; Pliner, 1984; Rozin et al., 1984). The only substantial within-culture parent-child resemblance that we know of has to do with a particular food attitude—disgust sensitivity (degree of concern for cleanliness of foods and the possibility that they have contacted offensive substances) (Rozin et al., 1984). Although family resemblance can be caused by genetic factors or experience, we are inclined to attribute most of the reported resemblances to experience. The only significant parent-child correlations have been found when the children were of college age (more than 17 years of exposure to parents) (Pliner, 1984; Rozin et al., 1984), and almost all of the negative findings are with young children (2 to 7 years of exposure) (e.g., Birch, 1979b; and see Birch, 1980b, or Pliner, 1984, for reviews of other studies). Furthermore, mother-father correlations in preferences or attitudes are equal to or higher than parent-child correlations (Rozin et al., 1984), and these correlations tend to increase with number of years married, indicating an effect of mutual exposure and influence (Price & Vandenberg, 1980). A relatively small role for genetic factors is also indicated by very low heritabilities for taste preferences (Greene, Desor, & Maller, 1975). There are indications, however, of possible genetic effects, including the fact that, although mothers have much more contact with their children than fathers do, especially in feeding situations, the correlation in food preferences or attitudes between father and child is no smaller than the correlation between mother and child (Burt & Hertzler, 1978; Pliner, 1984; Rozin et al., 1984).

In this chapter, I will suggest some causes of some of the unexplained variation by examining the processes through which individuals acquire preferences for foods.

BIOLOGICAL FACTORS IN FOOD SELECTION

Humans are quintessential omnivores. They have general-purpose dentition and digestive systems and are inclined to exploit a wide variety of nutrient sources. Since it is not possible to specify in advance what sensory properties will characterize sources of nutrition (or toxins) in any particular environment, the omnivore must discover what is edible (Rozin, 1976); that is, it is a fundamental part of omnivore biology to have few biological constraints or predispositions about foods. There are, of course, many powerful biological determinants in the background, such as the nutritional needs of the organism and the particular classes of chemicals that the chemical senses can detect. With specific reference to food choice, the well-documented biological constraints are an innate (present at birth) preference for sweet tastes and avoidance of bitter tastes and irritation of the oropharyngeal surface (as produced by irritant spices or tobacco) (Cowart, 1981; Steiner, 1977); an interest in new foods, coupled with a fear of them (Rozin, 1976); and some special abilities to learn about the delayed postingestional consequences of foods (Booth, 1982; Rozin, 1976). It is also possible that there is a biological bias toward a preference for meat.

These abilities or constraints, and some yet undiscovered ones, could conceivably guide a hypothetical human child who is uninfluenced by culture to choose wisely among foods. Such a claim for wisdom of the body was supported with a great deal of evidence for the laboratory rat by Curt Richter (1943) and for humans by Clara Davis (1928). In a well-known study, for a period of months to years immediately after weaning, Davis offered three infants an array of about a dozen foods to choose from at each meal. She reported that the children showed normal growth, even though what they ate was completely under their own control. These are important and fascinating findings, but they do not establish a case for a biological wisdom of the body. All the foods offered to the children were of good nutritional value, so that random choice among them probably would have led to normal growth. No refined products (e.g., sugar) or flavorings were added to the foods. Most critically, the preferred foods of the infants were milk and fruit, the two sweetest choices available. We do not know what they would have done had sweet desserts been on the menu.

The biologically based responses to basic tastes, especially sweetness, have been studied extensively (see Weiffenbach, 1977, for a review; Desor, Maller, & Greene, 1977; Moskowitz, 1977; Pfaffman, 1977). There seems to be a universal attraction to sugar, which is even used as a supplement to infant foods in many cultures (Jerome, 1977). There are characteristic hedonic functions (plotted as degree of liking against concentration) for the basic tastes (sweet, sour, salty, bitter), but there is also wide variation in these functions within cultures (Moskowitz, 1977; Pangborn, 1970, 1981) and between cultures (Moskowitz, Kumaraiah, Sharma, Jacobs, & Sharma, 1975).

Biological factors can explain some individual differences in food choice (see Pangborn, 1981, for a full discussion of variability in sensory and affective responses to tastes and odors). There are well-documented genetically based differences in sensitivity to some bitter compounds in humans (Fischer, Griffin, England, & Garn, 1961), which show some weak relations to preferences for bitter foods. Changes in taste and smell sensitivity with age (Cowart, 1981; Murphy, 1979; Schiffman, 1979; Schiffman, Orlandi, & Erickson, 1979) may account for small changes in preferences with age. One gets the impression on reading this literature, however, that the rather extensive biological changes with aging (e.g., loss of taste or smell receptor cells) produce less of a deficit in detection or other responses to stimuli than one might expect. Measurable psychophysical changes with age also seem to have less effect on food selection and appreciation than we would expect them to have. These disparities between biological, psychophysical, and food selection measures may result from heavy reliance on detection thresholds in the psychophysics. A number of investigators in the field have suggested that more attention be paid to the suprathreshold growth of sensation and to hedonic (affective) measures in psychophysical studies (Bartoshuk, 1979; Pangborn, 1981; Schiffman, 1979).

Metabolic differences among individuals and among ethnic groups may account for different preferences in some individuals and for some differences in cultural practices (Katz, 1982; Simoons, 1982). A case in point is lactose intolerance. Most humans today cannot digest lactose (milk sugar) as adults (Simoons, 1978, 1979). Moderate amounts of milk produce gas, bloating, and diarrhea, and the substantial carbohydrate component of milk is not absorbed. Lactose is digestible by adults who come from cattle-herding, milk-drinking traditions, such as Northern Europeans. The evidence is strong that lactose tolerance in adulthood is an inherited trait, and that, across cultures, the use and acceptance of milk is related to the degree of lactose tolerance in the population (Simoons, 1979).

There is one other major domain for biological factors. The physiological or metabolic state of a person is a potent determinant of food choice. The clearest case is the state of satiety. It is common knowledge that people choose different foods when hungry or sated. They learn to consume more calorically rich foods when they are hungry than when they are sated (Booth, 1982; Booth, Lee, & McAleavey, 1976). In addition, the pleasantness of sweet tastes varies with state of repletion (Cabanac, 1971). The effect of other metabolic variables on preference is less well documented, but there is some evidence for enhancement of the taste of sodium in people with sodium deficiency (Wilkins & Richter, 1940). Food cravings during pregnancy (Trethowan & Dickens, 1972) may also result from changes in internal (hormonal) state.

CULTURAL FACTORS IN FOOD SELECTION

The impact of culture on food selection is varied and immense (de Garine, 1971; Katz, 1982; Simoons, 1982). Cultural traditions and technologies have unlinked the search for food from the ingestion of food and have greatly extended the availability of food through agriculture and importation. The agricultural revolution, and to a lesser extent the domestication of animals, has considerably reduced the number of different species consumed (currently, 45% of the food consumed in the world is rice or wheat) and has greatly increased the amount of processing and combinations of the smaller number of foods. The quality of food and the social setting and significance of eating have been regulated and constrained, but we do not yet have an adequate formal way to describe these cultural constraints and predispositions, which we might call cuisine. With attention to the foods and the way they are prepared, cuisines have been categorized into three elements (E. Rozin, 1982): staple foods, processing methods, and added flavorings. There remains the sequencing of foods in the meal (Douglas & Nicod, 1974) as well as the etiquette and significance of eating. These factors are substantial in all cultures but perhaps are clearest in India, where the personal history of a particular food (who cooked or touched it) imbues the food with social qualities that make it desirable for some and undesirable for others (Appadurai, 1981). Food is a medium of social expression in the Indian home, a way of establishing or confirming the social relations and importance of individuals in the family (Appadurai, 1981). This review can only acknowledge these powerful influences, which are certainly present though less salient in American culture.

BIOLOGY AND CULTURE AS INTERACTING CONSTRAINTS

We can view biological and cultural factors as establishing constraints or predispositions within which any individual develops a unique set of preferences and attitudes. The biological, cultural, and psychological domains interact in complex ways, however. In particular, biological factors are expressed in individuals, and culture is created by individuals. One might reasonably expect biological features of human food selection to be represented in cultures, and they are. Indeed, some anthropologists (Harris, 1974; Katz, 1982) and cultural geographers (Simoons, 1982) have attempted to explain specific cultural practices in terms of their adaptive value and adaptive fit with specific biological characteristics of members of the culture. In general, the best examples show adaptations of culture to nutritional needs; for example, to the extent that American cultures rely on corn, they process it in such a way as to improve its quality as a source of minerals, vitamins, and protein through the tortilla-making tradition (Katz, Hediger, & Valleroy, 1974). The question remains, however, whether biologically based behavioral aspects of selection are represented in culture. Here there are rather few examples (Rozin, 1982), largely because there are very few biological biases. Clearly, however, the widespread use of sweets, the domestication of plants that produce sweet edibles, sugar refining, and the development of artificial sweeteners are all instances of cultural institutions prompted by our basic urge for sweets (Mintz, 1979; P. Rozin, 1982). There are many counterinstances, however, such as the widespread ingestion by humans of foods that innately taste bad (coffee, tobacco, alcohol, chili pepper, etc.). Here, sociocultural forces arrange for a pattern of exposure to these initially undesirable items that ultimately induces a preference for them and reverses a biological bias (P. Rozin, 1982). In addition, the culture-biology influence works both ways. The adult inability to digest milk has prompted some cultures to develop technologies for digesting the lactose externally in such products as cheese and yogurt. This instance of biology influencing culture is countered by the opposite process with respect to the same food, milk. It was the establishment of the cultural traditions of dairying and milk drinking that established the selection pressure for adult ability to digest lactose—a case in which culture affects human biology (P. Rozin, 1982; Simoons, 1978).

A TAXONOMY OF PREFERENCES AND AVOIDANCES

In this section, the psychological structure of preference and avoidance will be discussed. This should precede analysis of the mechanisms that account for preference. We must first distinguish among three very different terms—*use, preference,* and *liking* (Rozin, 1979)—which are often confused with one another. *Use* refers to whether a person or group consumes a particular food and how much of it. *Preference* assumes a choice situation, referring to which of two or more foods is chosen. A person might prefer lobster over potatoes but might eat more potatoes because of price or availability. *Liking,* usually measured with verbal scales, refers to an affective response to foods; it is one determinant of preference. A dieter might prefer (choose) cottage cheese over ice cream but might like ice cream better. There is some relation among these terms; all other things being equal (which they rarely are), we eat (use) what we prefer and we prefer what we like. Correlations among these measures often run in the .4 to .8 range (Birch, 1979b; Pilgrim, 1961). Availability, price, and convenience, however, are critical determinants of use but not of preference or liking; and the perceived health value of a food, though a potent determinant of preference and use (Krondl & Lau, 1982), may have little to do with liking. Indeed, in accounting for results of attempts to increase acceptance of soya products in cafeterias, Woodward (1945) suggests that emphasis on the nutritive value of new foods implies that they do not taste good.

Such distinctions require that we look systematically at what motivates people to consume or reject foods. By early adulthood, every human in every culture comes to adopt a culturally based set of beliefs and attitudes about the edibility of objects in the world. We (Fallon & Rozin, 1983; Rozin & Fallon, 1980, 1981) have explored this psychological categorization of substances in American culture through interviews and questionnaire studies. We have concluded that there are three basic types of reasons for acceptance or rejection of potential food objects (see Table 38.1). Each of these reasons in one form motivates acceptance

Table 38.1 **Psychological Categories of Acceptance and Rejection**

Dimensions	Rejections				Acceptances			
	Distaste	Danger	Inappropriate	Disgust	Good Taste	Beneficial	Appropriate	Transvalued
Sensory-affective	−			−	+			+
Anticipated consequences		−				+		
Ideational		?	−	−		?	+	+
Contaminant				−				+
Examples	Beer, chili, spinach	Allergy foods, carcinogens	Grass, sand	Feces, insects	Saccharine	Medicines	Ritual foods	Leavings of heroes or deities

Source: Fallon, A. E., & Rozin, P. The psychological bases of food rejections by humans. Ecology of Food and Nutrition.

and in the opposite form motivates rejection. This simplified system emphasizes the principal feature motivating acceptance or rejection. We will now briefly consider each of the three basic reasons.

Sensory-Affective Factors

Some items are rejected or accepted as food primarily because of their sensory effects in the mouth (or sometimes their odor or appearance). We call such accepted items "good tastes" and those that are rejected "distastes." Good tastes and distastes, by definition, produce appropriate positive and negative affect (like or dislike). Sensory-affective reactions can be innately attached to certain objects (acceptance of sweet tastes, rejection of bitter) or acquired. Substances that fall into the sensory-affective category for any individual are almost always acceptable foods in that person's culture. Individual differences on sensory-affective grounds (e.g., liking or disliking lima beans) probably account for most variation in food preferences within a culture.

Anticipated Consequences

Some substances are accepted or rejected as food primarily because of anticipated consequences of ingestion. These consequences could be rapid effects, such as nausea or cramps or the pleasant feeling of satiation. More delayed effects involve beliefs and attitudes about the health value of substances (such as vitamins or low-fat foods on the positive side and potential carcinogens on the negative side). Anticipated consequences may be social, such as an expected change in social status as a consequence of eating a particular food. We place all acceptances based on anticipated consequences in the beneficial category and all rejections for similar reasons in the dangerous category. I must emphasize again that there may or may not be a liking for the taste of these items. If a liking (disliking) is present, it would be considered a secondary cause of acceptance (rejection).

Ideational Factors

Some substances are rejected or accepted as food primarily because of our knowledge of what they are and where they come from. Ideational factors predominate in many food rejections but are less common in acceptances. Two clearly distinct subcategories of food rejection can be identified primarily on ideational grounds.

A large group of items can be classified as *inappropriate*. These items are considered inedible within the culture and are refused simply on this basis. Grass and sand are examples. In such cases, there is not typically a presumption that these items taste bad, and the items are usually affectively neutral; they are inoffensive.

In contrast, the category of *disgust* carries a strong negative affective loading. By our analysis, disgusting items reliably elicit nausea and are thought to have unpleasant tastes, although in most instances they have never been tasted. There is also a negative affective response to their odor and appearance and to skin contact or the presence of the offending substance in the body. Items viewed as disgusting are contaminants or pollutants. The possibility of their presence in a food, even in the tiniest amounts, makes the food unacceptable. A few substances, such as feces, seem to be universally disgusting. Within American culture, the category includes insects, dogs, and many other types of animals.

Other Taxonomies

This taxonomy differs from other food taxonomies in that it includes all substances—edible and inedible, acceptable and not acceptable within the culture in question. A number of other useful taxonomies or multivariate analysis of food choice provide a finer grained analysis within the framework of culturally acceptable foods (e.g., Bell, Stewart, Radford, & Cairney, 1981; Krondl & Law, 1982; Schutz, Rucker, & Russell, 1975; Worsley, 1980). In general, flavor emerges as a central determinant of food use, classification, and liking (Krondl & Lau, 1982; Worsley, 1980; Yoshida, 1981), with health-nutrition effects also prominent (Bell et al., 1981; Krondl & Lau, 1982). Most of the factors (other than sensory properties) extracted in these and other studies would fall in the category of anticipated consequences, including nutritive and health effects and social effects (prestige). The studies of Bell et al. (1981) and Worsley (1980) use a technique that elicits the dimensions that differentiate foods from each subject and allows the creation of individualized food taxonomies.

ACQUISITION OF LIKES AND DISLIKES FOR FOODS

We will now consider what is known about the circumstances in which objects come to have good or bad tastes, in contrast to those in which they are simply accepted or rejected on the basis of anticipated consequences or ideational factors (the inappropriate category). The acquisition of liking or disliking is of special interest in the study of food selection for two reasons. First, it is particularly puzzling. We can understand that people might avoid a food because they have been told it will make them sick, but what would make them come to dislike its taste? Second, from the point of view of public health, it would be highly desirable for people to like what was good for them and to dislike what was bad for them. Acceptance of a food based on liking is particularly stable, because the food is then eaten for itself, rather than for some extrinsic reason.

We will consider three contrasting pairs of categories (from Table 38.1). In each case, the first member of the pair involves an affective (taste like or dislike) response and the second does not. The contrasts will be (a) distasteful versus dangerous foods, (b) good tasting versus beneficial items, and (c) disgusting versus inappropriate items.

Distaste versus Danger

There is an innate aversion to bitter foods. Many items that are initially acceptable, however, come to be rejected—some because they come to taste bad, others because we learn that they are dangerous.

When ingestion of a food is followed by nausea or vomiting, humans (and rats) develop a strong aversion to it (Bernstein, 1978; Garb & Stunkard, 1974; Garcia, Hankins, & Rusiniak, 1974; Logue, Ophir, & Strauss, 1981; Rozin & Kalat, 1971). This acquired bad taste can occur after a single negative experience, with a delay of some hours between ingestion and its consequences, and there is a tendency to associate novel tastes with the illness. Taste aversions will occur even if the persons know that the food they have eaten did not cause the illness.

Nausea and vomiting are particularly potent in causing an acquired distaste (Pelchat & Rozin, 1982). Other negative events, such as hives, respiratory distress, headache, or cramps following eating, usually induce avoidance motivated by danger rather than by distaste. This contrast can be illustrated by examples of two individuals who avoid shrimp. One has an allergy to shrimp and gets skin symptoms or respiratory distress after eating shrimp. Such a person will avoid shrimp as dangerous but likes the taste of shrimp. If the allergy could be treated, this person would be delighted to consume shrimp. The other person originally liked shrimp but became sick and vomited after eating shrimp. Such a person typically will dislike the taste of shrimp and will avoid them, even though realizing that they in fact are not dangerous and perhaps were not even the cause of the sickness.

There are limits to the explanatory power of the distaste–nausea linkage. It seems very unlikely that most acquired distastes have a history of association with nausea. Somewhat less than half of the people surveyed (Garb & Stunkard, 1974; Logue et al., 1981; Pelchat

& Rozin, 1982) could remember even one instance of a food-nausea experience, and these same people had a great many distastes. We must presume, therefore, that the many people who dislike lima beans, fish, broccoli, and so on, do so for reasons as yet undiscovered; unfortunately, there are no sound theories regarding what other paths to distaste might be.

Good Tastes versus Beneficial Substances:

The puzzle in this area is not why people ingest things that are good for them (beneficial substances) but why some substances come to be liked. There is much more research and information about acquired likes than about dislikes, but no single factor (as potent as nausea for dislikes) has been identified (see Beauchamp & Maller, 1977, for a review). The overriding empirical relation in the study of acquired likes in all domains is that exposure tends to increase liking. Zajonc (1968) has suggested that exposure is a sufficient condition for liking (the mere exposure theory). The demonstration of this principle with food involves repeated ingestion of a new food in neutral circumstances. The most straightforward study with food in the laboratory setting (Pliner, 1982) reported that liking for the flavor of exotic fruit juices increased with number of exposures (ranging from 0 to 20). In a study on development of liking for evaporated milk (Hollinger & Roberts, 1929), it was concluded that just trying it—becoming familiar with it—was the critical variable. The mere exposure effect has its limits. It does not always work (Peryam, 1963), and the reverse can occur with overexposure to the same food (Stang, 1975). Judging from the literature on exposure in domains other than food (Berlyne, 1970; Harrison, 1977; Zajonc, 1968), mere exposure should be most effective with moderate levels of exposure to novel and complex foods. The fundamental question that remains for understanding mechanisms of acquired likes is whether mere exposure is ever sufficient, or whether exposure simply allows some other process to occur. In either event, it is clear that other factors contribute to the acquisition of likes. I shall list and evaluate some possibilities and consider what underlies the distinction between good tastes and beneficial items.

The simplest explanation of increased liking with exposure is that exposure allows fear of a new food to dissipate; the person learns that the food is safe (Rozin, 1979). This has been shown to occur. Torrance (1958), for example, found that liking for a buffalo meat (pemmican) ration increased markedly from first to second exposure, even for subjects who found it unpleasant on the first exposure. It is not clear, however, how gradual dissipation of fear would in itself produce a liking as opposed to neutrality.

The most straightforward explanation parallel to the creation of distastes would be that some physiological consequence of ingestion, most appropriately an upper gastrointestinal effect (parallel to the nausea–distaste linkage), induces liking. Booth (1982) and Booth, Mather, and Fuller (1982) have demonstrated a clear effect of rapid satiety. Hungry subjects come to prefer (and increase their liking for) the flavor of a high-starch (high-calorie) food to the flavor of a low-calorie food. This change in liking occurs after only a few pairings. They also demonstrate that a flavor associated with a high-calorie food will become less preferred than a low-calorie food flavor if it is consumed when satiated. Unlike the nausea-produced decreases in liking, these changes in liking and preference seem to be state-dependent; that is, flavor A paired with high calories in a hungry person is preferred only when the person is in the same (hungry) state. This type of liking may be somewhat different from what we would call stable likes; that is, there is an important sense in which lobster is more preferred than tomatoes whether the person is hungry or not. In any event, rapid satiety (which could be thought of as an upper gastrointestinal sensation or as a consequence of rapid entry of nutrients into the blood supply) seems to be an effective way to produce at least a state-dependent liking. As with the taste aversion–nausea linkage, the domain of positive physiological effects that is effective is quite limited. Oral medicines with distinctive tastes, for example, produce positive consequences, such as relief of headache, respiratory distress, and heartburn, but these medicines, as a group, are not highly favored as good tastes. There is no particular advantage of any particular medicinal consequences, even the upper gastrointestinal pain relief produced by antacids (Pliner, Rozin, Cooper, & Woody, Note 1).

It seems entirely reasonable that association of a neutral or disliked food (flavor) A with an already liked food B would enhance the liking for A. The simplest form of association would be to offer A and B together or to follow ingestion of A by B. This Pavlovian type of procedure has been effective with rats (Holman, 1975), with sugar as the unconditioned stimulus. There have been a few positive studies with humans using this paradigm with items other than foods (see review by Martin & Levey, 1978). Gauger (1929) reported an enhancement of preference to the point of mild liking for some disliked items (e.g., egg white, vinegar) when presentation of these items to young children was followed by chocolate. (Incidentally, positive reactions to chocolate decreased during the same study!) Positive results with the Pavlovian design can also be interpreted as mere exposure effects, since the target food is presented repeatedly. Proper exposure controls must be run to distinguish such effects, and it is possible that Gauger's results, obtained without such controls, can be explained in terms of exposure. In a recent laboratory study, flavor A was served to young adults in a sweet (palatable) beverage, while flavor B was served equally frequently in an unsweetened, less palatable form. With exposure thus controlled, there was still an enhanced liking for flavor A, even when both flavors were served in the unsweetened form (Zellner, Rozin, Aron, & Kulish, 1983). At present, we do not know the set of conditions, particularly in the real world, in which this type of conditioning would operate. There would certainly be cultural constraints; for example, it is unlikely that a new meat could be made more acceptable to Americans by sweetening it with chocolate syrup.

In the animal literature on preferences, a consistent finding is that it is much harder to establish preferences than aversions (Rozin & Kalat, 1971; Zahorik, 1979). Whereas a rat's innate sweet preference can be reversed with one pairing with nausea, it is extremely difficult to produce preferences for innately unpalatable (e.g., bitter or irritant spicy) foods (Rozin, Gruss, & Berk, 1979). Booth (1982) and Booth, Stoloff, and Nicholls (1974) have reported substantial preference shifts for rather neutral tastes using rapid satiation, but in general such changes have been hard to come by. The relative weakness of acquired preferences in animals and the great strength of these preferences in humans suggests that some important factors operate only in humans. Sociocultural influence is an obvious candidate.

We believe that social factors operate at two levels. First, social pressure (custom, the behavior of elders, the foods made available to the child) essentially forces exposure, and, as has been pointed out, exposure fosters liking. Second, the perception that a food is valued by respected others (such as parents) may itself be a mechanism for establishment of liking.

Children increase their preferences for foods that are presented (in a story context) as preferred by elders or heroes, and this enhanced preference is not transient (Duncker, 1938; Marinho, 1942). Birch (1980a) has recently extended these findings in a rigorous and convincing way. She has shown that nursery school children show stable preference enhancements in the direction of foods chosen by their peers (the children sitting at a lunch table with them). She has also shown that preference for a snack is enhanced if the snack is given to the child in a positive social context or, better yet, is used by the teacher as a reward (Birch, Zimmerman, & Hind, 1980). It is the teacher's indication that he or she values the food (using it as a reward) that seems to be critical. If the same food is given to other children with the same frequency in a nonsocial context (e.g., left in their locker), there is no enhancement of preference (Birch et al., 1980).

The importance of the perception of social value in acquired liking is emphasized by the converse phenomenon. What types of experience can reverse liking for a food or object, or, as this problem is described in the literature, how can an object of intrinsic value (which we call a liked object) lose some of this value? The answer, from research by Lepper (1980) and by Birch and her colleagues (Birch, Birch, Marlin, & Kramer, 1982), is that the perception by the child that others do not value the food *per se,* and that they must be bribed into eating it (e.g., rewarded, told how healthy it is), seems to reduce the child's liking for the food. This has been demonstrated in a study in which preschool children were rewarded for eating a particular food (Birch et al., 1982). This manipulation increased ingestion while the reward was in effect but produced a slightly negative effect on later preference.

These results are compatible with self-perception theory in social psychology (Bem, 1967). The basic idea is that people infer their attitudes (e.g., liking a food) from their own behavior (e.g., choosing a food). If ingestion occurs without clear extrinsic motivation, there is a tendency to justify the behavior by increasing the value of the object. This relation would not hold, however, if the people interpret their behavior as externally constrained (e.g., if they were forced to eat a food or if there was nothing else to eat). The decline in value of an object when extrinsic reward is employed is called the "overjustification effect" (Lepper, 1980).

A well-known study on adults put these principles to a test by comparing the effectiveness of different techniques in inducing an increased liking for grasshoppers. The most effective technique used the smallest financial reward and a communicator (person encouraging the ingestion) who was relatively cool and not especially likable. According to the theory, having ingested the grasshopper, the subjects would be more likely to consider their own behavior as internally motivated (since external causes were absent) and to increase their liking.

The notion that reward decreases or perhaps blocks liking is consistent with the fact that people are less likely to come to increase their liking of oral medicines than of foods, since medicine ingestion is clearly motivated by anticipated beneficial consequences (Pliner et al., Note 1).

We have listed a set of possible mechanisms for acquired food likes. The list can be extended further by including the development of liking for innately aversive substances, such as various forms of alcohol, tobacco, coffee, and the irritant spices. These are among the more popular items consumed by humans around the world. Many of these substances have positive postingestional effects, although, as has been pointed out, there is no evidence for the effectiveness of such effects (other than satiety) in enhancing liking. The spices are usually eaten with rather bland nutritive foods, allowing for satiety. Coffee is often consumed with sugar, allowing for pairing with a hedonically positive taste.

We have been investigating how people come to like the initially distasteful burn of chili pepper. This happens by age 5 to 8 years in many chili-eating cultures (Rozin & Schiller, 1980). As in the cases described earlier, there is no obvious physiological effect of chili pepper that can explain this liking (Rozin, 1978). Capsaicin, the active agent in chili pepper, does stimulate the gastrointestinal system, causing salivation, increased gastric secretion, and gut motility. Also, the salivation does enhance the flavor of the frequently bland and mealy diets that are eaten in association with chili pepper. In addition to this possibility, I am inclined to emphasize the potency of social factors. A study of the acquisition of liking for chili pepper in a Mexican village suggests that chili eating is not explicitly rewarded but is acquired as an imitation of the behavior of respected adults and peers (Rozin & Schiller, 1980).

Ironically, initial dislike may be a critical element in some processes of acquired liking. I will present here two possible explanations of the acquired liking for chili (and perhaps other innately unpalatable substances) that depend on the initial negativity.

The mouth pain produced by chili may become pleasant as people realize that it is not really harmful. This puts the pleasure of eating chili pepper in the category of thrill seeking (or "benign masochism"), in the same sense that the initial terror of a roller coaster ride or parachute jumping is replaced by pleasure. People may come to enjoy the fact that their bodies are signaling danger when their minds know that there really is no danger (Rozin & Schiller, 1980).

Alternatively, the many painful mouth experiences produced by chili may cause the brain to attempt to modulate the pain by secreting endogenous opiates—morphine-like substances produced in the brain. There is evidence that, like morphine, these brain opiates reduce pain; at high levels, they might produce pleasure. Hundreds of experiences of chili-based mouth pain may cause larger and larger brain opiate responses, resulting in a net pleasure response after many trials (Rozin, Ebert, & Schull, 1982). See Solomon (1980) for a statement of opponent process theory, which could account for the hypothesized effect.

We are very far from an understanding of the development of liking for foods. The issue is complicated by two factors. First, many substances are consumed for multiple reasons (Shutz, Rucker, & Russell, 1975). People may drink coffee or smoke for the pleasant oral sensations, for the positive pharmacological effects of the drugs, to avoid withdrawal after they are addicted to the drugs, to be social, to avoid eating, or out of habit (Russell, 1974). Individuals have multiple motivations, and the pattern of motives also varies from one individual to another. In this respect, an acquired liking for chili pepper is simpler to understand than one for coffee or tobacco, since the motivation for consuming chili is predominantly oral pleasure (P. Rozin, 1982; Rozin & Schiller, 1980). Second, our experience in trying to understand the liking for chili pepper convinces us that there are multiple routes to liking. We can find convincing arguments against every single mechanism we have been able to suggest. This does not indicate that these mechanisms play no role in acquisition, but it implies that there may be more than one way of producing an acquired like.

Disgusting versus Inappropriate Items

Disgusting items are almost invariably animal products (Angyal, 1941; Rozin & Fallon, 1980) and hence potential foods. Most inappropriate items, however, are inorganic and of minimal nutritive value. The question is why some items (by and large, the animal products) come to be offensive, charged with negative affect, while other inedibles, such as paper, are treated as neutral objects. Three features of disgust seem to be universal: a characteristic facial expression, the inclusion of feces in the disgust category, and the fact that disgusting items serve as psychological contaminants (rendering otherwise good food undesirable after the slightest contact with the disgusting item) (Angyal, 1941; Rozin & Fallon, 1981). There is no evidence of an innate basis for disgust; that is, infants do not innately avoid feces, and decay odor does not seem to be innately aversive (Petó, 1936). Similarly, children in the United States do not develop the contamination response until the first years of elementary school (Fallon, Rozin, & Pliner, 1984). We presume that the offensiveness of disgusting items is somehow conveyed to children by their parents, perhaps through facial and other forms of emotional expression. It seems reasonable that feces disgust is developmentally the first disgust and that it arises through the process of toilet training, but there is no firm evidence on this point (Rozin & Fallon, 1981), nor on the general issue of how ideas about the nature or origin of a substance become affectively charged.

VARIETY AND FAMILIARITY

A very important aspect of human food selection, with implications for public health, is receptivity to new foods. Interest in and simultaneous fear of new foods are presumably part of our omnivorous heritage. They appear as a desire for variety and, at the same time, a preference for familiar foods. A number of studies have documented that, in American culture, highly monotonous diets decline in palatability (Kamen & Peryam, 1961; Siegel & Pilgrim, 1958). In these studies, the monotony was in the cycle of feeding (alternating two meals or 3- versus 6-day meal cycles). There is also a more localized effect, known as sensory specific satiety (LeMagnen, 1967; Pliner, Polivy, Herman, & Zakalusny, 1980; Rolls, Rolls, & Rowe, 1982). The palatability of a given food drops within one meal with respect to other, similar items that have not been consumed in that meal. Presumably as a consequence of this, when people are offered a variety of items (e.g., different sandwiches or different desserts), they eat more in one meal than they do of the single most favored item when it is served alone.

Another feature of human food selection that is as salient as the avoidance of monotony is the way most people narrowly circumscribe the range of acceptable foods. Even in a society as ethnically varied as ours, without its own well-defined cuisine, many foreign cuisines (e.g., the food of India) have failed to be accepted, even as occasional curiosities. Meanwhile, the fast-food chains, which provide a highly predictable, invariable, and narrow range of foods, prosper—at least partly because people like the fact that they know exactly what they are getting. The desire for comfort and familiarity in eating is not surprising; eating involves putting things into the body—a very personal act—and one surely does not want the emotional importance and pleasure of eating to be marred by fears and uncertainties.

There are wide individual differences in the importance of familiarity and receptivity to new foods. This is seen strikingly in the United States in the development by many young children (particularly those in the 2- to 4-year age range) of rejections of almost all foods (Bakwin & Bakwin, 1972). Although the few foods consumed by such children may form an adequate diet, the behavior is very disturbing to parents. We do not know the role of constitutional factors and early experience in this common syndrome. We also do not know what causes some adults with many food choice opportunities to eat a tuna sandwich or chocolate ice cream every day.

The basic desire for familiar food is seen at the level of culture and can be described as the conservatism of cuisine (Rozin, 1976). Most of the world's major cuisines have retained their identities for hundreds or thousands of years with rather little change. New foods, flavorings, or forms of cooking are usually resisted. Historically, the major exception to this is in the "Columbian exchange" (Crosby, 1972)—the mixing of Western and Eastern hemisphere foods (and diseases, ideas, etc.) following the discoveries of Columbus. Tomatos, chili peppers, corn, cassava, chocolate, peanuts, potatoes, and other American products clearly had an impact on the Old World, as did cows, pigs, and other Eastern Hemisphere products on the West. In general, cuisines seem to have a certain completeness and integrity. One can see in them the forces for both variety and familiarity. Most of the world's cuisines have characteristic flavor combinations (flavor principles) (E. Rozin, 1983) added to all their staple foods. The potential monotony generated by continued use of the same flavorings is tempered, however, by subtle variation of these flavors from dish to dish, as in the variation in the amounts and identity of the more than ten spices and herbs used in any part of India to form a curry. These culinary themes and variations (Rozin & Rozin, 1981) seem to represent, at the level of culture, the same processes that we see at work in individuals.

Attempts to change cuisines, often in the direction of providing a more balanced or economical dietary, have met with failure more than success because of the basic conservatism of cuisine. This conservatism is clearly seen within our own culture in the fact that the ethnic origins of Americans are more clearly revealed in their kitchens and on their dining room tables than in other aspects of their behavior. Third-generation Italian-Americans, for example, who are well integrated in many ways into the mainline of American culture, still eat a great deal of Italian food, especially on holidays (Goode, Theophano, & Curtis, 1981). The problem of changing food habits has been and remains an important part of public health. A group of excellent researchers in areas related to this problem focused their interests on it during World War II under the leadership of Margaret Mead (1943). This group appreciated the importance of the context of eating, and therefore the importance of understanding a cuisine and the role of food in a culture, as a prerequisite to planning dietary change. The message from this group is one that everyone interested in food must always keep in mind: people eat food, not nutrients. Food is an aspect of culture and has implications far beyond the act of eating. The involvement of food in the social matrix is more elaborate in some cultures than in others (Appadurai, 1981; Meigs, 1978). It is perhaps less embedded in American values and the American social system than it is in many other cultures. There may be some justification in playing down these features when we try to do food selection research in our own culture, but a world perspective on food preference and food attitudes cannot ignore them.

CONCLUSION

At present, we are not able to explain why Cynthia likes lima beans but Alfred does not. We surely would not have predicted that, despite the well-publicized dangers of cigarette smoking, the number of cigarettes smoked in the United States has not decreased over the last few decades. We have no clear evidence regarding whether food experiences early in life have a special effect in shaping lifelong food attitudes and preferences (Beauchamp & Maller, 1977). We do have some promising starts, however, and a set of problems that we hope will attract a generation of talented researchers.

REFERENCE NOTE

1. Pliner, P., Rozin, P., Cooper, M., & Woody, G. *Role of Medicinal context and specific post-ingestional effects in the acquisition of liking for tastes.* Unpublished manuscript, 1983.

REFERENCES

Amerine, M., Pangborn, R. M., & Roessler, E. B. *Principles of sensory evaluation of food.* New York: Academic Press, 1965.

Angyal, A. Disgust and related aversions. *Journal of Abnormal and Social Psychology,* 1941, **36**, 393–412.

Appadurai, A. Gastropolitics in Hindu South Asia. *American Ethnologist,* 1981, **8**, 494–511.

AuCoin, D., Haley, M., Rae, J., & Cole, M. A comparative study of food habits: Influence of age, sex and selected family characteristics. *Canadian Journal of Public Health,* 1972, **63**, 143–151.

Bakwin, H., & Bakwin, R. M. *Behavior disorders in children.* Philadelphia: Saunders, 1972.

Barker, L. M. (Ed.). *Psychobiology of human food selection.* Westport, Conn.: AVI, 1982.

Bartoshuk, L. M. Preference changes: Sensory versus hedonic explanations. In J. H. A. Kroeze (Ed.), *Preference behaviour and chemoreception.* London: Information Retrieval, 1979.

Beauchamp, G. K., & Maller, O. The development of flavor preferences in humans: A review. In M. R. Kare & O. Maller (Eds.), *The chemical senses and nutrition.* New York: Academic Press, 1977.

Bell, A. C., Stewart, A. M., Radford, A. J., & Cairney, P. T. A method for describing food beliefs which may predict personal food choice. *Journal of Nutrition Education,* 1981, **13**, 22–26.

Bem, D. Self-perception: An alternative interpretation of cognitive dissonance phenomena. *Psychological Review,* 1967, **74**, 183–200.

Berlyne, D. E. Novelty, complexity and hedonic value. *Perception and Psychophysics,* 1970, **8**, 279–286.

Bernstein, I. L. Learned taste aversions in children receiving chemotherapy. *Science,* 1978, **200**, 1302–1303.

Birch, L. L. Dimensions of preschool children's food preferences. *Journal of Nutrition Education,* 1979, **11**, 77–80. (a)

Birch, L. L. Preschool children's food preferences and consumption patterns. *Journal of Nutrition Education,* 1979, **11,** 189–192. (b)

Birch, L. L. Effects of peer models' food choices and eating behaviors on preschooler's food preferences. *Child Development,* 1980, **51,** 489–496. (a)

Birch, L. L. The relationship between children's food preferences and those of their parents. *Journal of Nutrition Education,* 1980, **12,** 14–18. (b)

Birch, L. L., Birch, D., Marlin, D. W., & Kramer, L. Effects of instrumental consumption on children's food preference. *Appetite,* 1982, **3,** 125–134.

Birch, L. L., Zimmerman, S. I., & Hind, H. The influence of social-affective context on the formation of children's food preferences. *Child Development,* 1980, **51,** 856–861.

Booth, D. A. Normal control of omnivore intake by taste and smell. In J. Steiner (Ed.), *The determination of behavior by chemical stimuli.* ECRO Symposium, Jerusalem, 1982.

Booth, D. A., Lee, M., & McAleavey, C. Acquired sensory control of satiation in man. *British Journal of Psychology,* 1976, **67,** 137–147.

Booth, D. A., Mather, P., & Fuller, J. Starch content of ordinary foods associatively conditions human appetite and satiation, indexed by intake and eating pleasantness of starch-paired flavors. *Appetite,* 1982, **3,** 163–184.

Booth, D. A., Stoloff, R., & Nicholls, J. Dietary flavor acceptance in infant rats established by association with effects of nutrient composition. *Physiological Psychology,* 1974, **2,** 313–319.

Burt, J. V., & Hertzler, A. A. Parental influence on the child's food preference. *Journal of Nutrition Education,* 1978, **10,** 127–128.

Cabanac, M. Physiological role of pleasure. *Science,* 1971, **173,** 1103–1107.

Cowart, B. J. Development of taste perception in humans: Sensitivity and preference throughout the life span. *Psychological Bulletin,* 1981, **90,** 43–73.

Crosby, A. W. *The Columbian exchange: Biological and cultural consequences of 1492.* Westport, Conn.: Greenwood Press, 1972.

Davis, C. Self-selection of diets by newly-weaned infants. *American Journal of Diseases of Children,* 1928, **36,** 651–679.

de Garine, I. The socio-cultural aspects of nutrition. *Ecology of Food and Nutrition,* 1971, **1,** 143–163.

Desor, J. A., Maller, O., & Greene, L. S. Preference for sweet in humans: Infants, children and adults. In J. M. Weiffenbach (Ed.), *Taste and development: The genesis of sweet preference* DHEW Pub. No. (NIH) 77–1068. Washington, D.C.: U.S. Government Printing Office, 1977.

Douglas, M., & Nicod, M. Taking the biscuit: The structure of British meals. *New Society,* 1974, 19 December, 744–747.

Duncker, K. Experimental modification of children's food preferences through social suggestion. *Journal of Abnormal and Social Psychology,* 1938, **33,** 489–507.

Fallon, A. E., & Rozin, P. The psychological bases of food rejections by humans. *Ecology of Food and Nutrition,* 1983, **13,** 15–26.

Fallon, A. E., Rozin, P., Pliner, P. The child's conception of food. The development of food rejections, with special reference to disgust and contamination sensitivity. *Child Development,* in press.

Fenton, A., & Owen, T. M. (Eds.). *Food in perspective.* Edinburgh: John Donald, 1981.

Fischer, R., Griffin, F., England, S., & Garn, S. M. Taste thresholds and food dislikes. *Nature,* 1961, **191,** 1328.

Garb, J. L., & Stunkard, A. Taste aversions in man. *American Journal of Psychiatry,* 1974, **131,** 1204–1207.

Garcia, J., Hankins, W. G., & Rusiniak, K. W. Behavioral regulation of the milieu interne in man and rat. *Science,* 1974, **185,** 824–831.

Gauger, M. E. The modifiability of response to taste stimuli in the preschool child. *Teacher's College, Columbia University, Contributions to Education,* No. 348. New York: Bureau of Publications, Teacher's College, Columbia University, 1929.

Goode, J., Theophano, J., & Curtis, K. Group-shared food patterns as a unit of analysis. In S. A. Miller (Ed.), *Nutrition and behavior.* Philadelphia: Franklin Institute Press, 1981.

Greene, L. S., Desor, J. A., & Maller, O. Heredity and experience: Their relative importance in the development of taste preference in man. *Journal of Comparative and Physiological Psychology,* 1975, **89,** 279–284.

Harris, M. *Cows, pigs, wars and witches: The riddles of culture.* New York: Random House, 1974.

Harrison, A. A. Mere exposure. In L. Berkowitz (Ed.), *Advances in experimental social psychology* (Vol. 10). New York: Academic Press, 1977.

Hollinger, M., & Roberts, J. L. Overcoming food dislikes: A study with evaporated milk. *Journal of Home Economics,* 1929, **21,** 923–932.

Holman, E. Immediate and delayed reinforcers for flavor preferences in rats. *Learning and Motivation,* 1975, **6,** 91–100.

Jerome, N. Taste experience and the development of a dietary preference for sweet in humans: Ethnic and cultural variations in early taste experience. In J. M. Weiffenbach (Ed.), *Taste and development: The genesis of sweet preference.* DHEW Pub. No. (NIH) 77–1068. Washington, D.C.: U.S. Government Printing Office, 1977.

Kamen, J. M., & Peryam, D. R. Acceptability of repetitive diets. *Food Technology,* 1961, **15,** 173–177.

Kare, M. R., & Maller, O. (Eds.). *The chemical senses and nutrition.* New York: Academic Press, 1977.

Katz, S. Food, behavior and biocultural evolution. In L. M. Barker (Ed.), *Psychobiology of human food selection.* Westport, Conn.: AVI, 1982.

Katz, S. Hediger, M. L., & Valleroy, L. A. Traditional maize processing techniques in the new world. *Science,* 1974, **184,** 765–773.

Kroeze, J. A. H. (Ed.). *Preference behavior and chemoreception.* London: Information Retrieval, 1979.

Krondl, M., & Lau, D. Social determinants in human food selection. In L. M. Barker (Ed.), *Psychobiology of human food selection.* Westport, Conn.: AVI, 1982.

LeMagnen, J. Habits and food intake. In C. F. Code (Ed.), *Handbook of physiology, Section 6, Alimentary Canal. Vol. 1: Control of Food and Water Intake.* Washington, D.C.: American Physiological Society, 1967.

Lepper, M. R. Intrinsic and extrinsic motivation in children: Detrimental effects of superfluous social controls. In W. A. Collins (Ed.), *Minnesota Symposium on Child Psychology* (Vol. 14). Hillsdale, N.J.: Lawrence Erlbaum Associates, 1980.

Logue, A. W., Ophir, I., & Strauss, K. E. The acquisition of taste aversions in humans. *Behavior Research and Therapy,* 1981, **19,** 319–333.

Lowenberg, M. E., Todhunter, E. N., Wilson, E. D., Savage, J. R., & Lubawski, J. L. *Food and man* (2nd ed.). New York: Wiley, 1974.

Marinho, H. Social influence in the formation of enduring preferences. *Journal of Abnormal and Social Psychology,* 1942, **37,** 448–468.

Martin, I., & Levey, A. B. Evaluative conditioning. *Advances in Behavior Research and Therapy,* 1978, **1,** 57–102.

Mead, M. (Ed.). The problem of changing food habits. *National Research Council Bulletin,* 1943, **108**(October), 1–77. (Whole volume)

Meigs, A. S. A Papuan perspective on pollution. *Man,* 1978, **13,** 304–318.

Mintz, S. Time, sugar, and sweetness. *Marxist Perspectives,* 1979, **2,** 56–73.

Moskowitz, H. R. Sensations, measurement and pleasantness: Confessions of a latent introspectionist. In J. Weiffenbach (Ed.), *Taste and development: The genesis of sweet preference.* DHEW Pub. No. (NIH)77–1068. Washington, D.C.: U.S. Government Printing Office, 1977.

Moskowitz, H. R., Kumaraiah, V., Sharma, K. N., Jacobs, H. L., & Sharma, S. D. Cross-cultural differences in simple taste preferences. *Science,* 1975, **190,** 1217–1218.

Murphy, C. The effect of age on taste sensitivity. In S. S. Han & D. H. Coons (Eds.), *Special senses in aging.* Ann Arbor, Mich.: Institute of Gerontology, 1979.

Pangborn, R. M. Individual variation in affective responses to taste stimuli. *Psychonomic Science,* 1970, **21,** 125–126.

Pangborn, R. M. Individuality in response to sensory stimuli. In J. Solms & R. L. Hall (Eds.), *Criteria of food acceptance: How man chooses what he eats.* Zurich: Forster Verlag, 1981.

Pelchat, M. L., & Rozin, P. The special role of nausea in the acquisition of food dislikes by humans. *Appetite,* 1982, **3**, 341–351.

Peryam, D. R. The acceptance of novel foods. *Food Technology,* 1963, **17**, 33–39.

Petó, E. Contribution to the development of smell feeling. *British Journal of Medical Psychology,* 1936, **15**, 314–320.

Pfaffman, C. Biological and behavioral substrates of the sweet tooth. In J. M. Weiffenbach (Ed.), *Taste and development: The genesis of sweet preference.* DHEW Pub. No. (NIH)77–1068). Washington, D.C.: U.S. Government Printing Office, 1977.

Pilgrim, F. J. What foods do people accept or reject? *Journal of the American Dietetic Association,* 1961, **38**, 439–443.

Pliner, P. The effects of mere exposure on liking for edible substances. *Appetite,* 1982, **3**, 283–290.

Pliner, P. Family resemblance in food preferences. *Journal of Nutrition Education,* 1984.

Pliner, P., Polivy, J., Herman, C. P., & Zakalusny, I. Short-term intake of overweight individuals and normal weight dieters and non-dieters with and without choice among a variety of foods. *Appetite,* 1980, **1**, 203–213.

Price, R. A., & Vandenberg, S. G. Spouse similarity in American and Swedish couples. *Behavior Genetics,* 1980, **10**, 59–71.

Richter, C. P. Total self regulatory functions in animals and human beings. *Harvey Lecture Series,* 1943, **38**, 63–103.

Rolls, B. J., Rolls, E. T., & Rowe, E. A. The influence of variety on human food selection and intake. In L. M. Barker (Ed.), *The psychobiology of human food selection.* Westport, Conn.: AVI, 1982.

Rozin, E. *Ethnic cuisine: The flavor principle cookbook.* Brattleboro, Vt.: Stephen Greene Press, 1983.

Rozin, E. The structure of cuisine. In L. M. Barker (Ed.), *The psychobiology of human food selection.* Westport, Conn.: AVI, 1982.

Rozin, E., & Rozin, P. Culinary themes and variations. *Natural History,* 1981, **90**(2), 6–14.

Rozin, P. The selection of food by rats, humans and other animals. In J. Rosenblatt, R. A. Hinde, C. Beer, & E. Shaw (Eds.), *Advances in the study of behavior* (Vol. 6). New York: Academic Press, 1976.

Rozin, P. The use of characteristic flavorings in human culinary practice. In C. M. Apt (Ed.), *Flavor: Its chemical, behavioral and commercial aspects.* Boulder, Colo.: Westview, 1978.

Rozin, P. Preference and affect in food selection. In J. H. A. Kroeze (Ed.), *Preference behavior and chemoreception.* London: Information Retrieval, 1979.

Rozin, P. Human food selection: The interaction of biology, culture and individual experience. In L. M. Barker (Ed.), *Psychobiology of human food selection.* Westport, Conn.: AVI, 1982.

Rozin, P., Ebert, L., & Schull, J. Some like it hot: A temporal analysis of hedonic responses to chili pepper. *Appetite,* 1982, **3**, 13–22.

Rozin, P., & Fallon, A. E. The psychological categorization of foods and non-foods: A preliminary taxonomy of food rejections. *Appetite,* 1980, **1**, 193–201.

Rozin, P., & Fallon, A. E. The acquisition of likes and dislikes for foods. In J. Solms & R. L. Hall (Eds.), *Criteria of food acceptance: How man chooses what he eats.* Zurich: Forster Verlag, 1981.

Rozin, P., Fallon, A. E., & Mandell, R. Family resemblances in attitudes to foods. *Developmental Psychology,* 1984.

Rozin, P., Gruss, L., & Berk, G. The reversal of innate aversions: Attempts to induce a preference for chili pepper in rats. *Journal of Comparative and Physiological Psychology,* 1979, **93**, 1001–1014.

Rozin, P., & Kalat, J. W. Specific hungers and poison avoidance as adaptive specializations of learning. *Psychological Review,* 1971, **78**, 459–486.

Rozin, P., & Schiller, D. The nature and acquisition of a preference for chili pepper by humans. *Motivation and Emotion,* 1980, **4**, 77–101.

Russell, M. A. H. The smoking habit and its classification. *Practitioner,* 1974, **212**, 791–800.

Schiffman, S. Changes in taste and smell with age: Psychophysical aspects. In J. M. Ordy & K. Brizzee

(Eds.), *Sensory systems and communication in the elderly. Vol. 10: Aging.* New York: Raven Press, 1979.

Schiffman, S., Orlandi, M., & Erickson, R. P. Changes in taste and smell with age: Biological aspects. In J. M. Ordy & K. Brizzee (Eds.), *Sensory systems and communication in the elderly. Vol. 10: Aging.* New York: Raven Press, 1979, pp. 247–268.

Schutz, H. G., Rucker, M. H., & Russell, G. F. Food and food-use classification systems. *Food Technology,* 1975, **29,** 50–64.

Siegel, P. S., & Pilgrim, F. J. The effect of monotony on the acceptance of food. *American Journal of Psychology,* 1958, **71,** 756–759.

Simoons, F. J. The geographic hypothesis and lactose malabsorption: A weighing of the evidence. *Digestive Diseases,* 1978, **23,** 963–980.

Simoons, F. J. Dairying, milk use, and lactose malabsorption in Eurasia: A problem in culture history. *Anthropos,* 1979, **74,** 61–80.

Simoons, F. J. Geography and genetics as factors in the psychobiology of human food selection. In L. M. Barker (Ed.), *The psychobiology of human food selection.* Westport, Conn.: AVI, 1982.

Solms, J., & Hall, R. L. (Eds). *Criteria of food acceptance: How man chooses what he eats.* Zurich: Forster, 1981.

Solomon, R. L. The opponent-process theory of acquired motivation. *American Psychologist,* 1980, **35,** 691–712.

Stang, D. J. When familiarity breeds contempt, absence makes the heart grow fonder: Effects of exposure and delay on taste pleasantness ratings. *Bulletin of the Psychonomic Society,* 1975, **6,** 273–275.

Steiner, J. E. Facial expressions of the neonate infant indicating the hedonics of food-related chemical stimuli. In J. M. Weiffenbach (Ed.), *Taste and development: The genesis of sweet preference.* DHEW No. (NIH)77–1068. Washington, D.C.: U.S. Government Printing Office, 1977.

Torrance, E. P. Sensitization versus adaptation in preparation for emergencies: Prior experience with an emergency ration and its acceptability in a simulated survival situation. *Journal of Applied Psychology,* 1958, **42,** 63–67.

Trethowan, W. H., & Dickens, G. Cravings, aversions and pica of pregnancy. In J. S. Howells (Ed.), *Modern perspectives in psycho-obstetrics.* New York: Brunner/Mazel, 1972.

Weiffenbach, J. M. (Ed.). *Taste and development: The genesis of sweet preference.* DHEW Pub. No. (NIH)77–1068. Washington, D.C.: U.S. Government Printing Office, 1977.

Wilkins, L., & Richter, C. P. A great craving for salt by a child with cortico-adrenal insufficiency. *Journal of the American Medical Association,* 1940, **114,** 866–868.

Wilson, C. S. Food habits: A selected annotated bibliography. *Journal of Nutrition Education,* 1973, **5**(Suppl 1), 38–72.

Woodward, P. The relative effectiveness of various combinations of appeal in presenting a new food: Soya. *American Journal of Psychology,* 1945, **58,** 301–323.

Worsley, A. Thought for food: Investigations of cognitive aspects of food. *Ecology of Food and Nutrition,* 1980, **9,** 65–80.

Yoshida, M. Trends in international and Japanese food consumption and desirable attributes of foods as assessed by Japanese consumers. In J. Solms & R. L. Hall (Eds.), *Criteria of food acceptance: How man chooses what he eats.* Zurich: Forster Verlag, 1981.

Zahorik, D. Learned changes in preferences for chemical stimuli: Asymmetrical effects of positive and negative consequences, and species differences in learning. In J. H. A. Kroeze (Ed.), *Preference behavior and chemoreception.* London: Information Retrieval, 1979.

Zajonc, R. B. Attitudinal effects of mere exposure. *Journal of Personality and Social Psychology,* 1968, **9**(Part 2), 1–27.

Zellner, D. A., Rozin, P., Aron, M., & Kulish, C. Conditional enhancement of human's liking for flavor by pairing with sweetness. *Learning Motivation,* in press.

CHAPTER 39

THE DEVELOPMENT AND MODIFICATION OF DIETARY PRACTICES IN INDIVIDUALS, GROUPS, AND LARGE POPULATIONS

THOMAS A. WADDEN
KELLY D. BROWNELL

University of Pennsylvania School of Medicine

We must acknowledge and recognize that the public is confused about what to eat to maximize health. If we as a government want to reduce health costs and maximize the quality of life for all Americans, we have our obligation to provide practical guidelines to individual consumers as well as set national dietary goals for the country as a whole. . . . Such an effort is long overdue. Hopefully, this study will be a major step in that direction.   —Senate Select Committee (1977b, p.v.)

With this foreword, Senator George McGovern introduced *Dietary Goals of the United States,* a report prepared by the Senate Select Committee on Nutrition and Human Needs in December 1977. The report represented the first comprehensive statement by the federal government on risk factors associated with the American diet. In addition, it made specific recommendations concerning the types and quantities of foods that Americans should consume (Figure 39.1) and extended the concept of the Recommended Dietary Allowances (RDA) to include carbohydrates, fats, cholesterol, and sodium. In making these recommendations, the Senate Select Committee took another step toward providing the country with something it desperately needs—a national nutrition policy.

The Senate Select Committee's report enjoyed a receptive audience. Most American consumers are "very concerned about nutrition" (Gallup, 1980; *Woman's Day,* 1978), although less than 25% believe that they are very well informed on the topic. Their dietary beliefs generally reflect current scientific knowledge. Six of ten respondents, for example, are concerned about cholesterol (*Woman's Day,* 1980), and 85% avoid serving certain foods that are high in fat content (General Mills, 1981). Nearly 95% realize that excessive salt use may contribute to hypertension (Marketing Science Institute, 1980), and 75% try to avoid foods that are high in salt content (General Mills, 1981).

Consumers report the *increased* use of fruits, whole grains, vegetables, fish, and poultry and the *decreased* use of fried foods, sugar, salt, and salty snacks (General Mills, 1981). The U.S. Department of Agriculture (1979) statistics generally confirm these self-reports

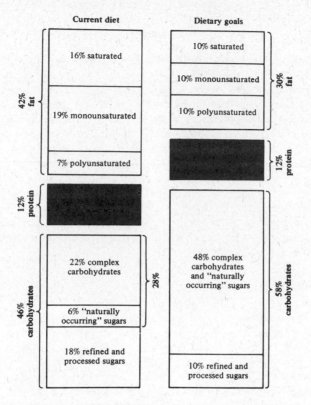

Percent of Calories from Different Nutrients

Source: Dietary Goals for the United States, 1977; prepared by the Senate Select Committee on Nutrition and Human Needs.

Figure 39.1 National dietary goals recommended by the U.S. Senate Select Committee on Nutrition and Human Needs, 1977.

of dietary change. Thus, consumers appear to be interested in improving the quality of their diets, and many have already taken steps to do so.

IMPEDIMENTS TO CHANGING DIETARY BEHAVIOR

Several policy factors are likely to impede consumers' attempts to change dietary habits, including (a) a divided scientific community, (b) an inadequate food labeling policy, and (c) the overprocessed and rapidly changing nature of the food supply.

Divided Scientific Community

It is not surprising that consumers are confused by conflicting statements concerning food and nutrition (General Mills, 1981). The Senate Select Committee's report drew sharp rebuttals from several commodities industries (dairy, egg, and cattle), whose sales would decline if Americans adopted the *Dietary Goals*. The report was also criticized by some members of the nutrition community (Harper, 1978), as well as by the American Medical Association (1977). As expressed in *Toward Healthful Diets*, published by the Food and Nutrition Board of the National Academy of Sciences (NAS/NRC, 1980), the dissenting view supports the use of dietary interventions on an individual basis with patients who clearly have diet-related diseases. It opposes, however, the prescription of dietary practices for the population at large, contending that the benefits of such practice have not been demonstrated conclusively. As Hitt (1982) has remarked, the Food and Nutrition Board "fell back to the medical intervention strategy of prescribing dietary modification where appropriate for each individual who comes into contact with the medical care system" (p.15). This approach downplays attempts at disease prevention, instead dealing with consumers only when they have become patients.

There is merit to both sides of this issue. From a strict scientific perspective, evidence is needed from long-term, large-scale prospective studies in which dietary manipulations can be measured and carefully studied. A single study of this nature is extremely costly, and dozens of studies are needed. Furthermore, these studies can only evaluate changes in populations of individuals. The prediction of change in individual persons, based on population data, may prove inaccurate. The possibility exists that dietary changes may aid the majority of individuals but may hurt others. If needed studies could be completed, they would be open to criticism because of weaknesses in available methods of evaluation. Therefore, it is unlikely that definitive studies can or will be done in the foreseeable future. This leaves two options: to avoid policy decisions until the evidence is complete, or to advocate widespread dietary change in the belief that its adoption presents little risk and offers substantial benefit to some.

Inadequate Labeling Policy

To change their dietary habits, consumers need information about the foods they are eating—particularly if they are processed foods. It is difficult, for example, for hypertensive patients to adhere to a low-salt diet, given the large amounts of sodium hidden in everyday foods such as canned soups, cereals, and frozen vegetables.

Despite repeated legislative efforts to enact a comprehensive labeling policy, labeling remains a voluntary practice, and one that is opposed by many in the food industry. Mayer (1973b) has summarized the food industry's public defense against labeling:

> Opposition to the comprehensive scheme is usually based on male commiseration for the poor women who, faced with a dozen numbers on the label, are supposed to fall completely apart. (p. 152)

A comprehensive labeling scheme should be adopted that lists not only a product's ingredients but also its calorie content and amounts of fat (saturated and polyunsaturated), cholesterol, salt, sugar, protein, vitamins, and minerals. Similar information should be made available in supermarkets for unpackaged commodities such as fruits, meats, and vegetables. The use of simplified codes (color schemes, 10-point scales) would help consumers identify products that are high or low in certain substances. Polls indicate that consumers would be willing to pay the small additional costs of comprehensive labeling (Better Homes and Gardens, 1979; Marketing Science Institute, 1980).

Overprocessed and Changing Nature of the Food Supply

Approximately 50% of the 20,000 food items now available to consumers are processed (Hegsted, 1979). Most of these foods contain hidden amounts of salt and/or sugar (the two most frequently used substances in processing), and many are nutritionally unrecognizable from the standpoint of the basic four food groups. (Just how should one classify a frozen pizza with cheese, green peppers, and sausage—as a bread, vegetable, meat, or dairy serving, or perhaps as a sodium and saturated fat nightmare?) This problem is compounded by the fact that the food supply is changing so rapidly that even the most sophisticated consumers will lack information about what they are eating 10 years from now (Brody, 1981).

The food industry will have to be responsive to the nation's needs for dietary change. Otherwise, consumer efforts will be weakened by industry policies. Of the annual 93 pounds per capita consumption of sugar in this country, for example, only 22 pounds are purchased directly by consumers. The remainder is directly contained in the foods that shoppers purchase. The biggest culprits are soft drinks. The 295 twelve-ounce sodas quaffed down by the average American each year account for about 30% of total sugar consumption, including sucrose and high-fructose corn syrup (USDA, 1980).

Food industry executives argue that they do not create food preferences but merely respond to them. The validity of this argument is open to debate, particularly when the industry's pattern of media advertising is analyzed. It is true, however, that consumers have some distinctive, and perhaps innate, food preferences.

DETERMINANTS OF FOOD SELECTION

Attempts to alter nutritional practices depend on knowledge of the degree to which people will eat less of foods they prefer and more of foods they do not prefer. This knowledge requires an understanding of the process by which food preferences and aversions are acquired and maintained. Only recently has the complexity of food selection been appreciated. In this section of the chapter, we will present information on physiological and cultural determinants of food preferences. The purpose is not to specify why an individual eats particular foods; the state of our knowledge does not permit such specification. Rather, we would like to convey our appreciation for the strength of the habits we seek to alter.

The array of foods humans find acceptable is striking. People in various cultures enjoy foods ranging from reindeer milk to cow's milk, whale blubber to ground beef, and seaweed to Brussels sprouts. Infants can be encouraged by their parents to try almost any food, indicating great malleability in human food preferences. Once these early preferences are established, however, they persist with remarkable strength. Preferences for native foods in immigrants can resist change more than many other cultural patterns. Foreign travel often creates longings for preferred foods that are unavailable, and dieters complain of strong cravings and even dreams of foods they resist. People do not forgo preferred foods easily.

Food aversions can be even more powerful than food preferences. Consider the affective and physiological responses engendered by the mere thought of eating an insect (say, a cockroach); yet the same "food" is accepted in some cultures. Few of those who are repulsed by such items have had experience on which to base their strong reactions. In cases where a substance produces an adverse response, aversion may be permanent. Research with both humans and animals indicates that ingestion of food followed by nausea and other gastrointestinal distress can create a lifelong aversion to the food (Garb & Stunkard, 1974; Garcia, Hankins, & Rusiniak, 1974; Rozin & Kalat, 1971).

Biological Predisposition

Humans and animals are born with the ability to discriminate tastes. Studies using facial expression and movement as indices of taste sensation have found that newborn infants respond positively to sweet solution and negatively to quinine, salt, and other substances (Crook, 1978; Desor, Maller, & Turner, 1973; Engen, Lipsitt, & Peck, 1974; Lipsitt, 1977; Peiper, 1963; Steiner, 1974). Taste also influences physiological responses such as heart rate (Crook & Lipsitt, 1976). This ability to discriminate tastes has adaptive value, because sweet substances are often the source of nutrients, and bitter tastes often belong to toxic substances (Rozin & Fallon, 1980a; Shallenberger & Acree, 1971).

Humans and animals may also be predisposed to the consumption of a high-fat diet.

This possibility is suggested by Sclafani and Springer's (1976) work with a "supermarket" diet, consisting of milk chocolate, peanut butter, salami, chocolate chip cookies, bananas, marshmallows, sweetened condensed milk, cheese, and a fat ration. These authors found normal energy intake and body weight in adult rats that were given *ad libitum* access to laboratory chow. The rats were then allowed *ad libitum* access to both the laboratory food and the supermarket diet, in which the meals were changed frequently and at least seven foods were given at any one time. In the 2-month experiment, the animals showed a very strong preference for the supermarket diet and gained 269% more weight than the control animals on the standard chow.

This preference for high-fat foods can be explained in evolutionary terms. Since fat contains twice the energy (calories) per unit weight than either protein or carbohydrate, an uncertain food supply would foster the most efficient means of storing energy. The tendency toward excessive intake would be expressed only when calorically dense foods were available chronically, as is the case in industrialized countries. This seems to be a case in which culture has created a situation for which biology has not yet adapted.

Cultural/Psychological Determinants

Many environmental factors influence the type and amount of food eaten. These factors have been viewed from several perspectives, underscoring the anthropological and geographical reasons for acceptance and rejection of certain foods (Simoons, 1980), the psychological and social mechanisms by which cultures transfer preferences and aversions to their people (Rozin, 1980), and the environmental factors that trigger eating (Rodin, 1980).

Rozin and his colleagues have developed a scheme for classifying food choices and have traced the ontogeny of food classification (Rozin, 1980; Rozin & Fallon, 1980b). They describe three broad reasons why substances are either accepted or rejected. The first category deals with sensory-affective factors—that is, whether a food tastes good. These factors may have biological origins but are shaped by culture. Anticipated consequences are the second reason for acceptance or rejection. These consequences include the long- and short-term physiological reactions to a food and the social advantages or disadvantages of eating a substance that may or may not be accepted by a culture. Ideational factors form the third category. This category includes the rejection of substances considered inappropriate (wood or sand), disgusting (insects), or degrading (foods associated with the lower class). Learning in each of these three categories is influenced by family, peers, the media, and other sources. The following is one example of such preference learning.

Television Advertising

The average American child watches television nearly 4 hours each day and over the course of a year devotes more time to television than to the classroom (FTC, 1978). Much of television advertising is designed to influence food preferences in children; before most children can even talk, they recognize and reach for advertised products from their seats in the shopping cart. The food industry recognizes that food preferences can be shaped early in life; nearly half of the $1.2 billion spent on food advertisements each year is targeted for children (Senate Select Committee, 1977a, 1977b).

Each year the average child sees 20,000 commercials, 10,000 of which are for food (FTC, 1978). Most of the commercials are for certain types of foods. One review examined food advertisements during the first 9 months of 1975 for the Saturday and Sunday daytime viewing hours on the three commercial networks (Choate, 1977). Of the 7,515 food commercials, 51% were for cereals, 22% were for candy and gum, and 11% were for cookies and crackers. Only 4.3% of the commercials were for nonsugared products; there was one commercial for vegetables. The most frequently advertised foods, sugared cereals, are approximately 40% sugar, and some are as high as 70% sugar. There is little doubt that these commercials influence what children want and what they eat.

The television commercial is one of the most powerful teaching devices yet invented for placing a relatively simple message in a child's mind (FTC, 1978). Children under 8 years of age rarely recognize that commercials are designed to promote products, and they distinguish programs from commercials only by saying that the commercials are "funnier" or "shorter" (FTC, 1978). Younger children believe that there is someone inside the television talking to them, and the commercial has the quality of an order rather than a suggestion (Lesser, 1977).

This learning translates to actual behavior. In one study, 516 families were observed making cereal selections in the supermarket. In two-thirds of the cases, children initiated the selection by demanding or requesting a specific brand (Atkin, Note 1). Of 591 mothers interviewed in another study, 75% who purchased sugared products acknowledged being influenced by their children's request (Reilly Group, 1973). Children successfully influence 85% of mothers for cereal selection, 58% for snack foods, and 40% for candy (Gussow, 1972; Ward & Wackman, 1972). Parents are twice as likely to comply with a child's demand as to deny it (Atkin, Note 1).

The television commercial is a powerful medium for influencing food preferences and food selections. Current advertising by the food industry overwhelms what few attempts there are to teach proper nutritional practices. The harnessing of this teaching method may be one means of promoting large-scale changes in eating practices.

ASSESSMENT OF NUTRITIONAL PRACTICES

The ability to identify biological and cultural determinants of food preferences, or to track changes in dietary habits, is highly dependent on our ability to measure food intake accurately. Perhaps because this assessment is deceptively difficult, the issue has been given little attention in the scientific literature. For example, the sixth edition of the classic *Modern Nutrition in Health and Disease* (Goodhart & Shils, 1980) contains no discussion of the reliability or validity of assessment methods. It is important to consider this issue because our conclusions about nutrition and health are only as strong as our assessment procedures.

The use of imprecise methods of nutritional assessment has important implications. Two examples illustrate this point. First, the diet-heart hypothesis maintains that consumption of cholesterol and saturated fat is related to the occurrence of atherosclerosis. Part of the evidence for this theory comes from epidemiologic studies relating dietary practices in individuals to morbidity and mortality. Self-reports of food intake are used to assess nutritional practices, and there is some question about the validity of these reports. Another example is the increasing emphasis on exercise in the treatment of obese persons. This is based in part on the theory that obese persons eat no more than thin persons but that they exercise far less. The speculation about consumption in obese and thin persons is no stronger than the questionable self-report measures of food intake used in most studies.

Our purpose here is to note some of the strengths and weaknesses of the most frequently used methods of nutritional assessment. In addition, we would like to underscore the risk in drawing firm conclusions based on weak measures.

Self-Report Measures

Self-report measures are the most frequently used indices of food intake. Two basic instruments are used: a continuous diary of all food eaten, and both short- and long-term retrospective recalls of consumption. There are problems inherent in both approaches. With the continuous diary, subjects must first remember to complete the records. Little is known about how much food escapes the attention of such diaries. Subjects who are capable of completing these records accurately may differ from one another in important respects (e.g., concern about nutrition) (Rush & Kristal, 1982). The accuracy of the records also depends on the subject's ability to estimate portion sizes and to identify foods (Lansky & Brownell, 1982). Finally, the act of recording one's food consumption may have reactive effects and may influence intake. The recall methods are subject to the same problems and are weakened by reliance on memory of food eaten at least 24 hours before the assessment is done.

Twenty-four-Hour Dietary Recall

This measure is the most frequently used method of assessing food intake. The 24-hour recall requires that a person state types and amounts of foods eaten in the previous 24 hours, either unaided or with the use of a food list. This approach has been popular in clinical studies, nutrition surveys, and epidemiologic investigations (Beaton, Milner, & Corey, 1979; McGandy, 1982).

Validity is the first concern with any self-report measure, and several approaches have been used to assess this factor. The most comprehensive approach is to compare reported intake with observed intake. Stunkard and Waxman (1981), for example, observed six obese and nonobese boys in their homes and then asked them to recall what they had eaten. They found a high correlation (.96) between reported and observed intake. Similar findings have been reported for lactating women in a hospital (Linusson, Sanjur, & Erikson, 1975), elderly persons in a lunch program (Madden, Goodman, & Guthrie, 1976), morbidly obese patients (Bray, Zachary, Dahms, Atkinson, & Oddie, 1978), a rural population in Scandinavia (Samuelson, 1970), and various populations of children and adolescents (Bransby, Daubney, & King, 1948; Greger & Etnyre, 1978; Samuelson, 1970). Several studies have shown poor validity, however, particularly in children (Carter, Sharbaugh, & Stapell, 1981; Emmons & Hayes, 1973). In addition, the studies showing good validity may be biased because direct observation may both increase awareness of eating and alter what is eaten. One consistent finding in these studies is overestimation of low caloric intake and underestimation of high intake.

One additional way of assessing the validity of the 24-hour recall is to use corrobroative reports from family members (Kolonel & Lee, 1981). Although there is usually high correspondence between records, the family records may have the same weaknesses as the patient records. Also, if patients systematically delete or forget eating done in private, the family records would appear to agree with self-reports even though both are in error.

The reliability of the 24-hour recall varies widely among studies (Balogh, Kahn, & Medalie, 1971; Beaton et al., 1979; Rush & Kristal, 1982). Reliability depends on the population, the sex and age of the subjects, and other factors. Recent studies suggest that the 24-hour recall has greatest utility when readministered two to four times with each individual (Rush & Kristal, 1982).

The 24-hour recall is probably the best measure we have for evaluating food intake cost-efficiently. Validity is the biggest problem, and although many studies report favorable results, we must consider that the 24-hour recall has been (and can only be) compared with measures of questionable accuracy. This is an important issue, and it provides fertile ground for further research. In the meantime, research on nutrition and health must continue, but we must consider that public health policies based on imperfect measures may be imperfect.

Physiological Measures

Diet influences health through its effects on the body's acquisition and utilization of many nutrients. It may be possible to work in a reverse direction to measure food intake by using physiological status as an estimate of eating practices. Serum albumin concentrations (supplemented by transferrin measurements), for example, may be a useful index of general malnutrition (Harper & Simopoulos, 1982). Other measures can indicate more specific conditions, thus raising the possibility that dietary excesses and deficits will reveal themselves in physiological status. An issue of the *American Journal of Clinical Nutrition* (1982) covered some of these possibilities. As yet, this is only a developing science in a very complicated area. We must await studies to relate specific tests to nutritional status, to relate nutritional status to dietary patterns, and to account somehow for the individual variability in the ways food intake influences physiological functioning.

Naturalistic Observations

Many studies have been done on measuring food intake and eating patterns in public settings. Much of this work has stemmed from an interest in the eating styles of obese and nonobese persons (Stunkard & Kaplan, 1977). Studies have been done in restaurants, cafeterias, fast-food establishments, and other public locations (Brownell, 1981; Stunkard & Kaplan, 1977). The weaknesses in this approach are that individuals are not studied over time and that private eating cannot be measured. Therefore, this method may be useful in cross-sectional analyses of a narrow range of eating behaviors, but it lacks the specificity needed for a study of nutrition and health.

Controlled Environments

In rare cases, the food intake of groups of humans can be carefully controlled and measured. Such cases would include persons in hospitals, institutions, prisons, and so forth. Since the food in such settings is generally provided by the institution, great control of the available food can be achieved. Eating itself can be observed or measured in nonobtrusive ways, and nutritional status of individuals can then be determined. In some settings, individuals can be followed over many years, thus permitting longitudinal studies. This approach holds great promise, but it has several drawbacks. First, there are difficult ethical problems inherent in manipulating and measuring the behavior of confined populations. Second, the diets in institutions may not reflect what the general population consumes. Third, living in the institution may influence physiology in many ways. This, combined with the special characteristics of a population of prisoners or institutionalized individuals, raises the possibility that the results might be biased. Fourth, large-scale epidemiologic studies would be difficult to perform because of the limited numbers of subjects. In summary, this approach may be useful in preliminary investigations of diet and nutritional status but may not tell us enough about how people really eat in the long run.

MODIFICATION OF ADULT DIETARY HABITS

Attempts to modify the dietary habits of the general American public have begun only recently. Thus, this area is ripe for both research and clinical opportunities because so little has been done. The most fruitful approach to dietary change will probably be an interdisciplinary one, involving (a) dieticians and nutritionists, who bring a wealth of experience in treating diet-related diseases; (b) psychologists and similar professionals who are skilled in behavior modification; (c) physicians and nurses who are knowledgeable about the physiology of disease; and (d) communications and media experts, who can convey information effectively. There are three different sectors in which dietary modification has been attempted: (a) individual and family interventions; (b) worksite, supermarket, and restaurant programs; and (c) public health campaigns.

Individual and Family Interventions

Two excellent books are available for those attempting dietary change: Farquhar's (1978) *The American Way of Life Need Not Be Hazardous to Your Health* and Ferguson, Taylor, and Ullman's (1978) *A Change of Heart: Your Family and the Food You Eat.* Each of these books can be used by practitioners working with individuals or groups or by lay persons seeking a self-help approach.

This approach to dietary change borrows heavily from behavioral techniques for weight control. In the first stage, individuals take an inventory of the foods in their household and keep records of their daily food intake. During the baseline period of 1 to 2 weeks, they are also taught to identify "artery blockers" and "heart-healthy foods"—foods that are high and low in cholesterol, saturated fat, salt, and sugar (see Figure 39.2). Examination of self-monitoring data reveals the scope of the individual's dietary modification needs.

In the second stage, individuals make small changes in their diets by substituting healthy

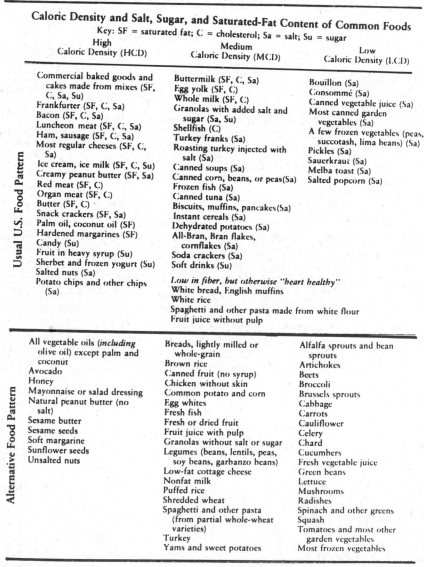

Caloric Density and Salt, Sugar, and Saturated-Fat Content of Common Foods

Key: SF = saturated fat; C = cholesterol; Sa = salt; Su = sugar

	High Caloric Density (HCD)	Medium Caloric Density (MCD)	Low Caloric Density (LCD)
Usual U.S. Food Pattern	Commercial baked goods and cakes made from mixes (SF, C, Sa, Su) Frankfurter (SF, C, Sa) Bacon (SF, C, Sa) Luncheon meat (SF, C, Sa) Ham, sausage (SF, C, Sa) Most regular cheeses (SF, C, Sa) Ice cream, ice milk (SF, C, Su) Creamy peanut butter (SF, Sa) Red meat (SF, C) Organ meat (SF, C) Butter (SF, C) Snack crackers (SF, Sa) Palm oil, coconut oil (SF) Hardened margarines (SF) Candy (Su) Fruit in heavy syrup (Su) Sherbet and frozen yogurt (Su) Salted nuts (Sa) Potato chips and other chips (Sa)	Buttermilk (SF, C, Sa) Egg yolk (SF, C) Whole milk (SF, C) Granolas with added salt and sugar (Sa, Su) Shellfish (C) Turkey franks (Sa) Roasting turkey injected with salt (Sa) Canned soups (Sa) Canned corn, beans, or peas(Sa) Frozen fish (Sa) Canned tuna (Sa) Biscuits, muffins, pancakes(Sa) Instant cereals (Sa) Dehydrated potatoes (Sa) All-Bran, Bran flakes, cornflakes (Sa) Soda crackers (Sa) Soft drinks (Su) *Low in fiber, but otherwise "heart healthy"* White bread, English muffins White rice Spaghetti and other pasta made from white flour Fruit juice without pulp	Bouillon (Sa) Consommé (Sa) Canned vegetable juice (Sa) Most canned garden vegetables (Sa) A few frozen vegetables (peas, succotash, lima beans) (Sa) Pickles (Sa) Sauerkraut (Sa) Melba toast (Sa) Salted popcorn (Sa)
Alternative Food Pattern	All vegetable oils (*including* olive oil) except palm and coconut Avocado Honey Mayonnaise or salad dressing Natural peanut butter (no salt) Sesame butter Sesame seeds Soft margarine Sunflower seeds Unsalted nuts	Breads, lightly milled or whole-grain Brown rice Canned fruit (no syrup) Chicken without skin Common potato and corn Egg whites Fresh fish Fresh or dried fruit Fruit juice with pulp Granolas without salt or sugar Legumes (beans, lentils, peas, soy beans, garbanzo beans) Low-fat cottage cheese Nonfat milk Puffed rice Shredded wheat Spaghetti and other pasta (from partial whole-wheat varieties) Turkey Yams and sweet potatoes	Alfalfa sprouts and bean sprouts Artichokes Beets Broccoli Brussels sprouts Cabbage Carrots Cauliflower Celery Chard Cucumbers Fresh vegetable juice Green beans Lettuce Mushrooms Radishes Spinach and other greens Squash Tomatoes and most other garden vegetables Most frozen vegetables

Figure 39.2 Calorie density and salt, sugar, and saturated fat content of commonly consumed foods and of recommended alternative foods. (Reprinted by permission from Farquhar, J. W. *The American way of life need not be hazardous to your health.* Stanford, Calif.: The Portable Stanford, 1978.)

foods for a few unhealthy ones. These changes are facilitated by the use of self-monitoring forms, as shown in Figure 39.3, and by concentrating on the modification of only one food group at a time (shaping). Cholesterol and saturated fat could be targeted for the first three months, for example, salt and caffeine for the second three, followed by reductions in sugar and alcohol usage and the increased use of complex carbohydrates. This gradually paced 1-year program should prevent clients from feeling overwhelmed.

In addition to contracting and shaping, other components of the behavioral program for obesity may be helpful. Clients should be encouraged to shop from a heart-healthy list and to beware of impulse buying, since most impulse items are both expensive and nutritionally unsound (Bloom, 1973). If undesirable foods are purchased, their use in the home could be minimized by cue control techniques (Brownell, Note 2). Cooperation and mutual support among family members may also be an important ingredient of dietary change (Brownell, 1980). Family members can both monitor and reward food choices through praise or other incentives. Given the relationship of food and family, the modification of dietary habits undoubtedly will be a family affair to some extent. This belief is supported by the fact that spouses of patients participated in both the national Multiple Risk Factor Intervention Trial (Farrand & Mojonnier, 1980) and the Stanford Three Community Study (Farquhar, Maccoby, Wood, Alexander, Breitrose, Brown, Haskel, McAlister, Meyers, Nash, & Stern, 1977).

Other Individual Approaches

Several other helpful books are available, including *The American Heart Association Cookbook* (AHA, 1977), *The Alternative Diet Book* (Connor, Connor, Fry, & Warner, 1976), *The Fat and Sodium Control Cookbook* (Payne & Callahan, 1975), and *Jane Brody's Nutrition Book* (Brody, 1981). Each of these books provides valuable nutrition information and recipe suggestions. In addition, studies describing successful interventions with hyperlipidemia, myocardial infarction, and atherosclerosis provide clinical techniques that can be adapted to dietary programs (Farrand & Mojonnier, 1980; Karvetti, 1981; Keys, Anderson, & Grande, 1965; Mojonnier, Hall, Berkson, Robinson, Wethers, Pannbacker, Moss, Pardo, Stamler, Shekelle, & Raynor, 1980; National Diet–Heart Study Report, 1968; Olendzki, Tolpin, & Buckley, 1981). Food models (Karvetti, 1981), slide-tape presentations (Mojonnier et al., 1980), discussion groups (Farrand & Mojonnier, 1980), and special materials such as the *Brand Name Shopper's Guide* (Gotto, Scott, Foreyt, & Reeves, 1975) may be useful. Similar materials are available for those needing sodium restriction (Gillum, Elmer, & Prineas, 1981; Morgan, Adam, Gillies, Wilson, Morgan, & Carney, 1978; Stamler, Farinaro, Mojonnier, Hall, Moss, & Stamler, 1980).

Reinforcement of Dietary Change

Maintaining motivation for dietary change may be difficult. This task is probably easiest for people in whom dietary modification may alleviate physical problems; for example, sodium restriction in the hypertensive person may reduce the need for medication, and weight loss in the diabetic may reduce the need for insulin. In such cases, dietary change carries major rewards.

Prevention of illness may be a powerful incentive for healthy individuals, but more immediate rewards are usually more important. The financial rewards for changing dietary behavior should be emphasized by examining grocery bills before and after modification and by identifying the inordinate price of many unhealthy foods (Gussow, 1979). Although we are all outraged by gasoline prices of $1.50 per gallon, we think nothing of spending almost $3.00 per gallon for brand name soft drinks, not to mention $15.00 per gallon for gourmet ice creams. A portion of the money saved by eliminating unhealthy foods could be used by consumers to reward themselves for improved behavior.

DINNER FOOD CHECKLIST

Day of the Week _Friday_   _June 2nd_ Date

Group	Column 4	Column 3	Column 2	Column 1
Milk	whole milk			non-fat or skim
Cheese	all firm or cheddar	partly skim	mozzarella or ricotta	cottage cheese / skim milk cheese
Cream	whole cream, half and half	powdered cream substitutes	liquid cream substitutes	non-fat milk
Eggs	1 per person	1/2 per person	1/4 per person	none, or substitute
Meats and Organ Meats	liver, kidneys, brains, sweetbreads or fatty meats, or tongue or cold cuts	choice steak, other fat meats	meat trimmed of fat (beef, lamb, pork or ham)	very lean meat or veal, baby beef, calf, lean ground round or fillet or flank, or sirloin tip
Shellfish & Fish	shrimp, or deep-fat fried fish		shellfish other than shrimp	all non-deep-fat fried fish
Poultry	domestic duck, goose, or deep-fat fried chicken		chicken, turkey or game hens	skinned chicken, turkey or game hens or wild game
Spreads	butter, lard or margarine made with palm oil	margarines with hydrogenated oil	soft cube margarine	polyunsaturated tub margarines
Oils and Shortenings	lard or coconut or palm oil	hydrogenated oil shortenings	peanut oil or olive oil	safflower or corn oil or soybean, cottonseed, sesame or sunflower oil
Other	meat substitutes or extenders			cooked dried beans or textured protein
Total:	3 x3= 9	0 x2= 0	2 x1= 2	0 x0= 0

Grand Total: _11_ cholesterol points

Figure 39.3 Example of self-monitoring form for reducing cholesterol intake. Foods are rated for their cholesterol content, ranging from 0 for foods in column 1 to 3 for those in column 4. Total cholesterol points are determined by multiplying the number of entries in each column by the corresponding rating and summing the columns. The lower the grand total, the lower the cholesterol intake. (Reprinted by permission from Ferguson, J. M., Taylor, C. B., & Ullman, P. *A change of heart: Your family and the food you eat.* Palo Alto, Calif.: Bull Publishing Co, 1978.)

618

In addition, the use of behavioral and subjective measures might reveal to people that they feel better physically and psychologically, work more efficiently, or fall asleep at night more easily as a result of dietary change, thus providing immediate reinforcement for behavior change. Such reports are common among people who are reducing their alcohol, sugar, and caffeine intake. These measures should be accompanied by periodic (every 3 to 6 months) blood tests to monitor levels of cholesterol, saturated fat, sodium, and other substances. Positive results sustain motivation and provide needed feedback about dietary choices. Other measures, such as frequent blood pressure readings, may be helpful for some.

Worksite, Restaurant, and Supermarket Programs

Americans spend 35 cents of every food dollar eating outside the home (Brody, 1981). This money is spent at restaurants, worksite cafeterias, hot dog stands, and increasingly at fast-food franchises. Nutrition education conceivably could take place in all of these situations.

Worksite Programs

Industry has become increasingly active in promoting employee health by offering programs for smoking cessation (Danaher, 1982; Orleans & Shipley, 1982), exercise (Haskell & Blair, 1982), and stress reduction (Peters, Benson, & Porter, 1977; Schwartz, 1982). Weight reduction efforts have been offered by many companies, and a majority of these programs have included some nutrition education (Foreyt, Scott, & Gotto, 1982; Stunkard & Brownell, 1980). With a few exceptions, however, such as the Campbell Soup Company (Cox & Wear, 1972), industry has yet to develop comprehensive dietary modification programs that include not only nutrition counseling, but the measurement of such factors as plasma lipids, triglycerides, and sodium.

In the Campbell program, employees' annual physicals include an assessment of weight, blood pressure, serum cholesterol, and triglycerides (Cox & Wear, 1972). Individuals needing dietary modification for weight loss or hyperlipidemia are seen individually by a nurse and are provided a low-fat diet. Assessment is repeated periodically to determine whether dietary goals have been achieved. About 90% of the employees successfully reduce their weight and serum triglycerides on a short-term basis. By 1-year follow-up, however, only about 10% are dieting adequately—a fact that underscores the need to make maintenance a part of every program.

A second approach for the worksite involves offering alternative, healthier foods in the company cafeteria. The ARA Food Service Company was a pioneer in this area with its development in 1978 of the Rainbow Nutrition Program for the approximately 60,000 employees of Boeing in Seattle (Farnon, 1981). The program offered low-calorie, low-fat foods (including salads, sandwiches, fruits, vegetables, and skim milk) on a daily basis as alternatives to the conventional menu. These foods were identified by tags bearing a rainbow and a statement of caloric content. Approximately 12% of the cafeteria's clientele regularly used the Rainbow foods.

At present, ARA Services, under contract to companies such as Xerox, Sun Oil, Boeing, and Smith-Kline, offers a special line called Physfoods, which meets the dietary goals of the Senate Select Committee on Nutrition and Human Needs (Farnon, 1981). The name Physfoods was chosen to emphasize the importance of physical activity in addition to prudent dietary habits. The program uses colorful posters to introduce the seven dietary goals and features recipe contests and special foods each month. The program can be administered independently by ARA, but its impact is strengthened when it is conducted in conjunction with a company's medical service, as at a Xerox facility in Leesburg, Virginia (Marshall, Note 3). A similar alternative food program is offered by Stouffer's Food Service (Farnon,

1981). Comprehensive evaluation of such programs would be very useful but is lacking at present.

Zifferblatt, Wilbur, and Pinsky (1980) provide an excellent example of the measurement and modification of food choices in a cafeteria. These authors monitored food selection for 15 consecutive months in a National Institutes of Health cafeteria equipped with an inventory control cash register system, which recorded the categories of the food items purchased. A colorful "Food for Thought" nutrition program was then introduced. With each meal purchased, employees were given one of 52 playing cards that contained nutrition information on a food product served in the cafeteria. Using the playing card motif, employees traded in their "poker hands" for small prizes at various times during the 8-week program.

Employees significantly decreased their average daily caloric intake (from 459 to 433 Kcal) and their consumption of bread and dessert servings during the program. Skim milk purchases increased significantly, but no significant changes were observed in the other food categories (fish, fowl, meat, starches, vegetables, etc.). Although the program was successful, the results also highlighted a well-known fact—that it is difficult to change food preferences. Zifferblatt et al. (1980) concluded that "employees were willing to forgo some items (i.e., eat less bread and fewer desserts) but were unwilling to substitute new foods for old preferences" (p. 19).

This finding has important implications, for although consumers can forgo foods such as soft drinks and chocolate candies with impunity, protein losses from reducing the consumption of meat and eggs must be replaced by other sources.

Restaurants

The proliferation of vegetarian and health food restaurants is another indication of public interest in modifying dietary habits. It would also be helpful if traditional restaurants provided nutrition education on the foods they served.

Scott, Foreyt, Manis, O'Malley, and Gotto (1979) developed a "Help Your Heart" menu for a steak house in Houston. The menu provided caloric values for all foods listed and offered low-calorie appetizers, desserts, and entrees that were reduced in cholesterol and saturated fat. Although the monthly percentage of sales from the special menu was relatively small (averaging 3.4%), the program was deemed sufficiently successful by the restaurant owners to be adopted permanently.

Another example is the restaurant Chez Eddy, run by the Institute of Preventive Medicine of the Baylor College of Medicine (Foreyt, Note 4). The restaurant serves gourmet French foods that are greatly reduced in saturated fat, cholesterol, salt, and sugar. These healthy dishes (see Figure 39.4) are made with no butter or cream, little salt and sugar, and increased amounts of polyunsaturated fat and carbohydrates. The restaurant has been acclaimed by food critics, proving that healthy foods can be delicious.

Supermarkets

Education programs in supermarkets would appear to be a potent, economical means of modifying shoppers' knowledge and consumption of certain foods, since approximately 50% of all food purchase decisions are made while consumers are in the store (Point of Purchase Advertising Institute, 1978). Several monetary factors, however, may discourage retail stores from promoting nutrition education on a wide-scale basis.

Supermarket retailers depend on a large volume of business to make even marginal profits, because such basic commodities as fruits, vegetables, bread, and milk are sold at cost or at only pennies above cost (Bloom, 1973). The retailers' largest profits are made on purchases of impulse items, which are marked up 10%, 20%, 30%, or more (Bloom, 1973). These are the items most likely to be high in salt, sugar, and fat (e.g., cookies, crackers, chips, pies).

HOUSTON CITY revisits:

Chez Eddy. Forget all that boring stuff about virtue being its own reward. Chez Eddy is so handsome, and its food so interesting, that you can almost forget it's good for you—low in salt and fats, not to mention calories, the nasty things. Some of the kitchen's innovative dishes could pass muster even with confirmed hedonists: plump, garlicky mussels *bourguignon*; lobster medallions on a curly nest of Belgian endive, tossed in a mustardy blueberry-vinegar dressing; a tart leek-and-watercress soup, or one of mushrooms, garlic, and chives. House wine is excellent and modestly priced. Desserts are indecently good, particularly those made with the restaurant's iced yogurt—spiked with brandied apple-and-raisin sauce, say, or layered with kiwi and strawberries in a *coupe maison.* Quibbles? Oh, a few. Trout Nova Scotia stuffed with a subtle salmon mousse could have done with more of its winy sauce. A quail-like roast game bird called a chukar in a darkly delicious wine sauce was too dry. And light, fresh-tasting fish and tofu salad needed a shot of that fresh dill the menu promised (surely there's a fresh herb supplier out there somewhere). Still and all, this nonprofit Med Center operation attached to the Sid Richardson Institute for Preventive Medicine is something of a tour de force. *(6560 Fannin. 790-6474. Mon–Sat lunch 11:30–2, dinner 6–10, closed Sun. Reservations recommended. Jackets required for dinner. MC, V, AE. Expensive.)*

Figure 39.4 Summary of a review of the Chez Eddy Restaurant in Houston, Texas. (Reprinted with permission from *Houston Magazine,* November 1978.)

Nutrition education programs also run the risk of offending the food industry, which could take economic sanctions against individual retailers. In addition, such campaigns require floor space, which is at a premium in stores and is used by retailers to secure special deals from distributors in return for high product visibility.

These problems notwithstanding, large chain stores in Washington, D.C. (Farnon, 1981), and Chicago (Soltan, 1979) have begun consumer education programs of their own. The Washington, D.C., project is being conducted by Giant Food, Inc., in conjunction with the National Heart, Lung, and Blood Institute (NHLBI). The Foods for Health program stresses the relationship of diet and heart disease in a series of biweekly pamphlets developed by NHLBI experts. The effects of the program will be determined by comparing food sales in Giant's Washington stores with those in their Baltimore stores, where the nutrition program has not been introduced (Farnon, 1981).

Jeffery, Pirie, Rosenthal, Gerber, and Murray (in press) conducted a preliminary study involving eight stores in Minneapolis. First, a nutrition survey was administered to shoppers to assess their knowledge of cholesterol and fat. Then, an education program, targeted at promoting the consumption of low-fat dairy products, was instituted in four stores. The intervention lasted 6 months and consisted of posters, tear-off recipes, and brochures strategically placed on the dairy shelves.

Unfortunately, the results of the study were not definitive. It was found that nutrition knowledge increased equally among consumers in both the control and the experimental stores. Both conditions showed a high level of understanding of foods that would reduce risk of cardiovascular disease. Sales data for 25 dairy products that had been tracked for a 10-month baseline period showed no clear-cut changes as a result of the intervention. Some encouraging trends were observed in the increased proportion of low-fat frozen desserts and low-fat cottage cheese purchased by consumers, but they either were of small magnitude or were not clearly attributable to the education campaign.

Although the Jeffery et al. (in press) study did not yield robust results, it did provide a useful methodology for further investigations. The authors noted that more intensive—perhaps face-to-face—interventions may be needed, as well as a focus on the family's total eating patterns (rather than just consumption of dairy products). Although the use of objective sales data would appear desirable, seasonal variability and distributor-retailer sales agreements will complicate interpretation of the results.

Public Health Media Campaigns

Newspapers, magazines, television, and radio appear to be ideally suited for teaching the public about dietary modification because of their large audiences. In addition, community leaders and agencies can assist in this effort (McAlister, Puska, Koskela, Pallonen, & Maccoby, 1980). Mass media and community interventions have been employed effectively in several health campaigns directed at smoking cessation (McAlister et al., 1980; Brownell, Note 5) and dietary modification (Cerqueira, Casanueva, Ferrer, Fontanot, Chavez, & Flores, 1979; Foreyt, Scott, & Gotto, 1976; Higgins, 1982). Three large multiple-risk intervention programs are currently being conducted in the United States and one in Finland, all of which make extensive use of the mass media: (a) the Community Health Improvement Program (CHIP), in Williamsport, Pennsylvania (Stunkard, 1979); the Minnesota Heart Health Program (Luepker, Note 6); the Pawtucket Heart Health Program in Rhode Island (Abrams, Elder, Lasater, & Carlton, Note 7); and the North Karelia project in Finland (Puska, Note 8). Only preliminary results are available from these studies. Findings are available, however, from an earlier program, the ambitious Stanford Three Community Study, upon which these later programs have been heavily modeled.

The Stanford Three Community Study

The interested reader should consult the original descriptions of this project (Farquhar et al., 1977; Maccoby, Farquhar, Wood, & Alexander, 1977; Stern, Farquhar, Maccoby, & Russell, 1976). To summarize briefly its dietary components, residents of three Northern California communities were randomly sampled and asked to complete a dietary questionnaire, which measured consumption of cholesterol, saturated and polyunsaturated fats, refined sugar, alcohol, and salt. Blood specimens were obtained to determine plasma cholesterol, and subjects were assessed on their knowledge of dietary risk factors.

Residents of two communities, Watsonville and Gilroy, were then exposed for 2 years to a multimedia campaign consisting of television programs, public service announcements on radio and television, newspaper columns by a physician and a dietician, and advertisements on posters and billboards. The objectives of the campaign were to teach and persuade people to adopt the skills needed to alter their nutrition. In addition to receiving this intervention, a random sample of residents of Watsonville who were at high risk of coronary heart disease attended nine intensive instruction sessions, which amplified topics covered by the media. Residents of a third community, Tracy, served as a no-treatment control group.

All assessment inventories were readministered at 1 and 2 years postbaseline. It was found that residents of Gilroy and Watsonville had a significantly lower self-reported consumption of cholesterol and saturated fat (at both 1 and 2 years) than did residents of Tracy, as well as significantly greater reductions in plasma cholesterol. Residents of the first two communities also showed significantly greater increases in their knowledge of dietary risk factors. The significant reduction in systolic blood pressure observed in the two experimental communities may also have been diet related (decreased salt intake).

Residents of Watsonville who participated in the face-to-face intensive instruction groups scored significantly better on some measures (consumption of cholesterol and saturated fat for males) than did the Watsonville and Gilroy residents who were exposed only to the media campaign. At the end of two years, however, differences between the media-only and intensive instruction conditions had generally disappeared as a result of continued improvements in the former condition and slight slippage in the latter. This is an extremely important finding, suggesting that media interventions are as effective over the long term in modifying dietary behavior as traditional and more expensive face-to-face programs. These results have been supported by those from a similar study conducted in Mexico (Cerqueria et al., 1979).

Results of the four current public health media campaigns are eagerly anticipated. In addition to determining whether the Stanford study can be replicated, these projects will provide important information concerning the relationship of dietary change to morbidity and mortality.

MODIFICATION OF CHILDREN'S DIETARY HABITS

A significant proportion (5% to 20%) of school-age children have elevated blood lipids and blood pressure, which, if left unchecked, predispose them to the development of cardio-vascular disease (Berenson, 1980; Frerichs, Srinivasan, Webber, & Berenson, 1976; Lauer & Shekelle, 1980; Miller & Shekelle, 1976). Increased risk among children may be the result of imprudent dietary behavior. Like his or her parents, the average American child consumes over 40% of the day's calories in fat (15% to 18% of which are saturated fat) and ingests approximately 300 mg of cholesterol per day (Frank, Voors, Schilling, & Berenson, 1972; Glueck, Mattson, & Bierman, 1978). Sugar consumption among children is extremely high—about 100 pounds per year. In addition, obesity in children is a serious problem (Brownell & Stunkard, 1980).

Childhood may be the ideal time to establish preventive dietary habits. This belief has led educators to incorporate some form of nutrition education in school curricula. Such programs may be offered by the school's dietician, physical education instructor, nurse, science teacher, or parents' group. A recent review of school-based nutrition programs is available (Levy, Iverson, & Walberg, 1980). We will briefly examine some of its conclusions and then consider two programs designed specifically for reduction of cardiovascular risk among children.

Enhancement of Knowledge versus Behavior

A host of studies has shown that children and adolescents show increased knowledge of nutrition as a result of exposure to education programs (Boysen & Ahrens, 1972; Cosper, Hayslip, & Foree, 1977; Lovett, Barker, & Marcus, 1970; Mangham & Vickery, 1981; Smith & James, 1980; Smith & Justice, 1979). Interventions usually focus on increasing students' knowledge of the basic four food groups (over a 4- to 8-week period) through the use of food models and pictures, written materials, and/or students' examination of their own lunches. The success of these interventions is measured using pre- and postquestion-naires; in some cases, control groups are also included (Cosper et al., 1977; Smith & Justice, 1979).

The obvious question is whether enhanced knowledge improves dietary behavior. Studies using self-reports and parental reports of children's dietary habits have yielded both positive (Boysen & Ahrens, 1972; Lovett et al., 1970) and negative findings (Bell & Lamb, 1973; Cosper et al., 1977; Picardi & Porter, 1976). Studies measuring actual food consumption have yielded some positive findings, in the form of increased use of milk (Boysen & Ahrens, 1972; Smith & James, 1980), but otherwise have yielded inconclusive findings. Levy et al. (1980) have thus concluded that "education does have the potential to affect and change nutrition behavior" (p. 119) but that this potential has not been fully realized at present.

A less obvious question concerns whether the basic four food groups, the cornerstone of most school education programs, represent a practical and sound approach to nutrition. Mayer (1973b) believes that the four food groups are outdated, since over 50% of the foods currently consumed are highly processed and defy simple categorization. Mayer laments nutrition educators' nostalgia for the "old foods" and believes that contemporary nutrition education must be based on an understanding of a food's nutrient content, including amount of calories, protein, fat, and carbohydrate. An adequate food-labeling policy will have to be enacted before this approach can be adopted.

Gussow (1979) believes that reliance on the four food groups may be nutritionally unsound. The four food groups, which were shaped in large part by the lobbying efforts of commodities groups, overemphasize the consumption of meat, eggs, and dairy products, to the detriment of fruits, vegetables, grains, and beans. Thus, as shown in Figure 39.5, the average American child growing up in Kansas will think that he or she should have

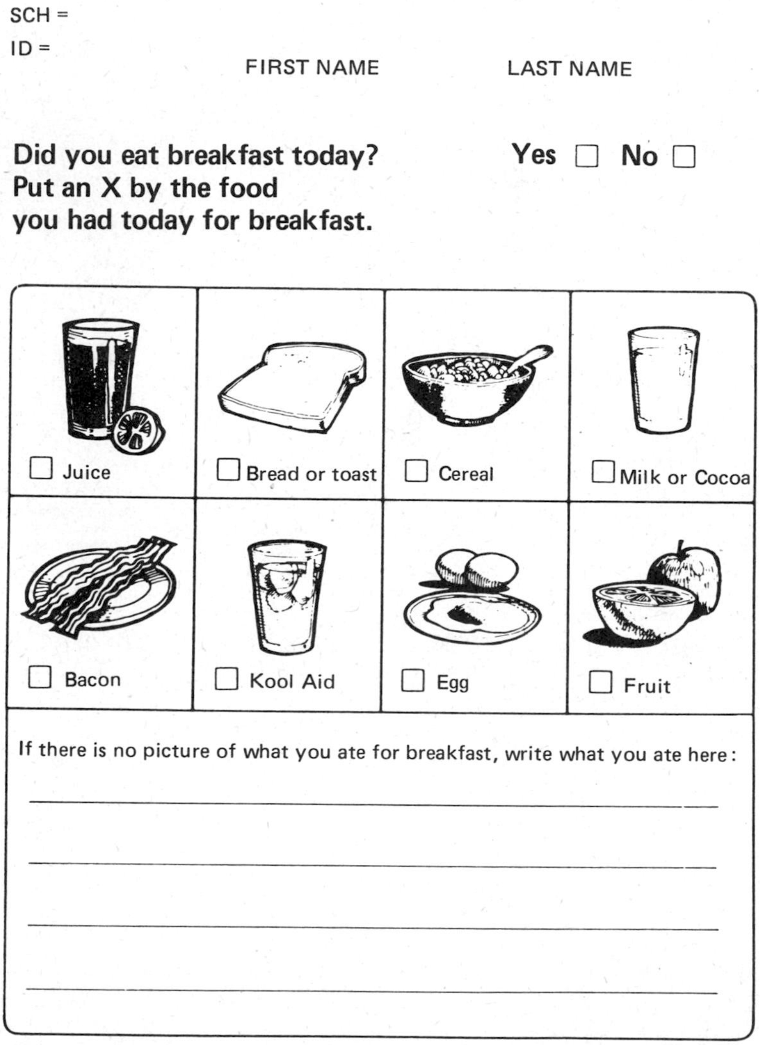
SCH =
ID =
FIRST NAME LAST NAME

Did you eat breakfast today? **Yes** ☐ **No** ☐
Put an X by the food
you had today for breakfast.

☐ Juice
☐ Bread or toast
☐ Cereal
☐ Milk or Cocoa
☐ Bacon
☐ Kool Aid
☐ Egg
☐ Fruit

If there is no picture of what you ate for breakfast, write what you ate here:

Figure 39.5 Example of elementary school teaching materials for the Four Food Groups, which inadvertently promote the overconsumption of high-cholesterol (eggs) and high-fat (bacon) foods. (Reprinted by permission from Lovett, R., Barker, E., & Marcus, B. The effect of a nutrition education program at the second grade level. *Journal of Nutrition Education,* 1970, **2,** 81–95.)

eggs or bacon for breakfast every morning—even though these foods are extremely high in cholesterol and saturated fat. Lifetime adherence to such a diet clearly could increase the individual's risk of developing coronary heart disease.

Heart-Healthy Programs

Recognizing the problems inherent in the four food groups, several investigators have refocused school nutrition programs toward heart-healthy eating (Coates, Jeffery, & Slinkard, 1981; Podell, Keller, Mulvihill, Berger, & Kent, 1978). Podell et al. (1978) introduced a Heart Disease Awareness program to 357 high school students who previously had been screened for cholesterol and triglyceride levels and knowledge of cardiovascular nutrition. The 3-week intervention included a cardiovascular education program, presentation of low-cholesterol diets, and the use of movies and reading materials from the American Heart Association. Students kept a 2-day food diary and calculated their consumption of cholesterol and fat (both saturated and polyunsaturated).

Results showed a significant increase in knowledge of cardiovascular nutrition and a significant improvement in self-reported eating patterns, as reflected in decreased consumption of fat and cholesterol. Students with initial baseline cholesterol values in the upper quartile reported making significantly greater efforts at adhering to a low-cholesterol diet than did those with initial readings in the lower quartile. As measured at 1-year-postbaseline, however, students' cholesterol values had actually increased significantly (from 159 to 171), as had those of students in a control school. The incongruity between the self-report and objective measures may reflect the fact that the students' average cholesterol values were low to begin with and that the dietary modifications they undertook were not sufficiently potent to affect these levels. Alternatively, the incongruity may reflect the unreliability of self-reports of eating behavior (Lansky & Brownell, 1982).

A similar study by Coates et al. (1981) corrected for this shortcoming by using objective measures of food consumption. Participants in their program were 72 fourth-graders and 89 fifth-graders. During the baseline period, children's lunch boxes were examined to determine the number of heart-healthy foods they contained, and trash receptacles were examined for the amount of such foods thrown away. A nutrition education program, occupying three 45-minute periods per week for 2 weeks, was then instituted as part of the school science curriculum. The program emphasized (a) using fruits and vegetables for snacks; (b) eating heart-healthy meals, reduced in cholesterol, saturated fat, salt, and sugar; and (c) learning to read food labels in order to make heart-healthy selections while shopping. Training in physical activity was also included but is not reported here.

Results revealed that the fourth- and fifth-graders' lunch boxes contained significantly greater amounts of heart-healthy foods by 39% and 38%, respectively, as compared to baseline. The percentage of heart-healthy food items in the trash decreased from baseline to posttreatment for both groups of children (averaging about 6%), indicating that lunches were not thrown away at higher rates during the intervention period. Analysis of children's lunch boxes 4 months later, following summer vacation, showed that students were still consuming a significantly greater number of heart-healthy foods. Both fourth- and fifth-graders increased in their knowledge of heart-healthy nutritional concepts from pre- to posttreatment, and these gains were maintained at follow-up.

The Coates et al. (1981) study represents a major advancement in nutrition education studies, in both its research methodology and its attention to cardiovascular fitness. The use of physiological measures such as weight, blood pressure, cholesterol, and triglycerides, would have made this very good study even better. Other innovative behavioral approaches to modifying children's eating habits can be found in the work of Brownell & Kaye (1982); Epstein, Masek, and Marshall (1978); Herbert-Jackson and Risley (1977); and Madsen, Madsen, and Thompson (1974).

CONCLUSION

Modification of dietary habits in healthy children and adults is a new and exciting area, offering both research and clinical opportunities. We hope this review has underscored the complexity of the behavior to be changed and has provided an overview of intervention strategies. It should be clear that wide-scale modification of dietary habits will necessitate a cooperative effort among health professionals, food industry executives, retailers, and government officials. Federal and state governments, in particular, must make a long-term commitment to improving the nutrition of all Americans by embracing the goals of the McGovern report and continuing to fund special nutrition programs for the poor and elderly and for women, infants, and children. Behavioral scientists can play a major role in this developing field, in such areas as public policy formation, program development and evaluation, basic research, and clinical practice.

REFERENCE NOTES

1. Atkin, A. *Effect of television advertising on children: Parent-child communication in supermarket breakfast cereal selection.* Report No. 7. Unpublished manuscript, Michigan State University, 1975.
2. Brownell, K. D. *Behavior therapy for weight control: A treatment manual.* Unpublished manuscript, University of Pennsylvania, 1979.
3. Marshall, J. Personal communication, June 29, 1982.
4. Foreyt, J. Personal communication, July 28, 1982.
5. Brownell, K. D. *Quit with the Q.* Radio program for smoking cessation, developed by Community Health Improvement Program (CHIP), Williamsport, Pennsylvania, July 1982.
6. Luepker, R. Personal communication, August 3, 1982.
7. Abrams, D. B., Elder, J., Lasater, S., & Carlton, R. *Social learning theory principles: An integration across levels of intervention.* Paper presented at the AABT convention, Los Angeles, 1982.
8. Puska, P. *North Karelia project: A programme for community control of cardiovascular diseases.* Community Health Series A, No. 1. Publication of the University of Kuoppio, Finland, 1974.

REFERENCES

American Heart Association (AHA). *The American Heart Association cookbook.* New York: Ballantine, 1977.

American Journal of Clinical Nutrition. Assessment of nutritional status: Selected papers: Conference on the assessment of nutritional status. *American Journal of Clinical Nutrition,* 1982, **35**, 1089–1325.

American Medical Association (AMA). Statement of the American Medical Association on dietary goals for the United States. In Senate Select Committee on Nutrition and Human Needs, *Dietary goals for the United States: Supplemental views.* Washington, D.C.: U.S. Government Printing Office, 1977.

Balough, M., Kahn, H. A., & Medalie, J. H. Random repeat 24-hour dietary recalls. *American Journal of Clinical Nutrition,* 1971, **24**, 304–310.

Beaton, G. H., Milner, J., & Corey, P. Sources of variance in 24-hour dietary recall data: Implications for nutrition study design and interpretation. *American Journal of Clinical Nutrition,* 1979, **32**, 2456–2459.

Bell, C. G., & Lamb, M. W. Nutrition education and dietary behavior of fifth graders. *Journal of Nutrition Education,* 1973, **5**, 196–199.

Berenson, G. S. *Cardiovascular risk factors in children*. New York: Oxford University Press, 1980.

Better Homes and Gardens. Food—A comparison of attitudes on food: Rounds I & II. The *Better Homes and Gardens* consumer panel report. Des Moines: *Better Homes and Gardens*, 1979.

Bloom, G. F. Distribution of food, In J. Mayer (Ed.), *U.S. nutrition policies in the seventies*. San Francisco: Freeman, 1973.

Boysen, S. C., & Ahrens, R. A. Nutrition introduction and lunch surveys with second graders. *Journal of Nutrition Education*, 1972, **4**, 172–175.

Bransby, E. R., Daubney, C. G., & King, J. Comparison of results obtained by different methods of individual dietary survey. *British Journal of Nutrition*, 1948, **2**, 89–94.

Bray, G. A., Zachary, B., Dahms, W. T., Atkinson, R. L., & Oddie, T. H. Eating patterns of massively obese individuals: Direct vs. indirect measurements. *Journal of the American Dietetic Association*, 1978, **72**, 24–28.

Brody, J. E. *Jane Brody's nutrition book*. New York: Norton, 1981.

Brownell, K. D. *The partnership diet program*. New York: Rawson Wade, 1980.

Brownell, K. D. Assessment of eating disorders. In D. H. Barlow (Ed.), *Behavioral assessment of adult disorders*. New York: Guilford, 1981.

Brownell, K. D., & Kaye, F. S. A school-based behavior modification, nutrition education and physical activity program for obese children. *American Journal of Clinical Nutrition*, 1982, **35**, 277–283.

Brownell, K. D., & Stunkard, A. J. Behavioral treatment for obese children and adolescents. In A. J. Stunkard (Ed.), *Obesity*. Philadelphia: Saunders, 1980.

Carter, R. L., Sharbaugh, C. O., & Stapell, C. A. Reliability and validity of the 24-hour recall. *Journal of the American Dietetic Association*, 1981, **79**, 542–547.

Cerqueiera, M. T., Casanueva, E., Ferrer, A. M., Fontanot G., Chavez, A., & Flores, R. A comparison of mass media techniques and a direct method for nutrition education in rural Mexico. *Journal of Nutrition Education*, 1979, **11**, 133–137.

Choate, R. B. *Edible television, your child, and food commercials*. Testimony before Federal Trade Commission. Washington, D.C.: U.S. Government Printing Office, 1977.

Coates, T. J., Jeffery, R. W., & Slinkard, L. A. Heart healthy eating and exercise: Introducing and maintaining changes in health behaviors. *American Journal of Public Health*, 1981, **71**, 15–23.

Connor, W. E., Connor, S. L., Fry, M. M., & Warner, S. L. *The alternative diet book*. Iowa City: University of Iowa Press, 1976.

Cosper, B. A., Hayslip, D. E., & Foree, S. B. The effect of nutrition education on dietary habits of fifth-graders. *Journal of School Health*, 1977, **47**, 475–477.

Cox, M., & Wear, R. F. Campbell Soup's program to prevent atherosclerosis. *American Journal of Nursing*, 1972, **72**, 253–259.

Crook, C. K. Taste perception in the newborn infant. *Infant Behavior and Development*, 1978, **1**, 52–69.

Crook, C. K., & Lipsitt, L. P. Neonatal nutritive sucking: Effects of taste stimulation upon sucking rhythm and heart rate. *Child Development*, 1976, **47**, 518–522.

Danaher, B. G. Smoking cessation programs in occupational settings. In R. S. Parkinson (Ed.), *Managing health promotion in the workplace: Guidelines for implementation and evaluation*. Palo Alto: Mayfield, 1982.

Desor, J. A., Maller, O., & Turner, R. E. Taste in acceptance of sugars by human infants. *Journal of Comparative and Physiological Psychology*, 1973, **84**, 496–501.

Emmons, L., & Hayes, M. Accuracy of 24-hour recalls of young children. *Journal of the American Dietetic Association*, 1973, **62**, 409–412.

Engen, T., Lipsitt, L. P., & Peck, M. B. Ability of newborn infants to discriminate sapid substances. *Developmental Psychology*, 1974, **10**, 741–744.

Epstein, L. H., Masek, B. J., & Marshall, W. R. A nutritionally based school program for control of eating in obese children. *Behavior Therapy*, 1978, **9**, 766–778.

Farnon, C. Let's offer employees a healthier diet. *Journal of Occupational Medicine*, 1981, **23**, 273–276.

Farquhar, J. W. *The American way of life need not be hazardous to your health*. Stanford, Calif.: The Portable Stanford, 1978.

Farquhar, J. W., Maccoby, N., Wood, P. D., Alexander, J. K., Breitrose, H., Brown, B. W., Haskel, W. L., McAlister, A. L., Meyer, A. J., Nash, J. D., & Stern, M. P. Community education for cardiovascular health. *Lancet,* 1977, **2,** 1192–1195.

Farrand, M. E., & Mojonnier, L. Nutrition in the Multiple Risk Factor Intervention Trial (MRFIT). *Journal of the American Dietetic Association,* 1980, **76,** 347–352.

Federal Trade Commission (FTC). *FTC Stass report on television advertising to children.* Washington, D.C.: Federal Trade Commission, February 1978.

Ferguson, J. M., Taylor, C. B., & Ullman, P. *A change of heart: Your family and the food you eat.* Palo Alto: Bull, 1978.

Foreyt, J. P., Scott, L. W., & Gotto, A. M. Diet modification in the community. In B. J. Williams, S. Martin, & J. P. Foreyt (Eds.), *Obesity: Behavioral approaches to dietary management.* New York: Brunner/Mazel, 1976.

Foreyt, J. P., Scott, L. W., & Gotto, A. M. Weight control and nutrition education programs in occupational settings. In R. S. Parkinson (Ed.), *Managing health promotion in the workplace: Guidelines for implementation and evaluation.* Palo Alto: Mayfield, 1982.

Frank, G. C., Voors, A. W., Schilling, P. E., & Berenson, G. S. Dietary studies of rural school children in a cardiovascular survey. *Journal of the American Dietetic Association,* 1977, **72,** 31–35.

Frerichs, R. R., Srinivasan, R. R., Webber, L. S., & Berenson, G. S. Serum cholesterol and triglyceride levels in 3,446 children from a biracial community: The Bogalusa Heart Study. *Circulation,* 1976, **54,** 302–308.

Gallup Organization, Inc. Changing food preparation and eating habits. Princeton: The Gallup Organization, 1980.

Garb, J., & Stunkard, A. J. Taste aversion in man. *American Journal of Psychiatry,* 1974, **131,** 1204–1207.

Garcia, J., Hankins, W. G., & Rusiniak, K. W. Behavioral regulations of the milieu interne in man and rat. *Science,* 1974, **185,** 824–831.

General Mills, Inc. A summary report on U.S. consumers' knowledge, attitudes, and practices about nutrition—1980. Minneapolis: General Mills, Inc., 1981.

Gillum, R. F., Elmer, P. J., & Prineas, R. J. Changing sodium intake in children: The Minneapolis children's blood pressure study. *Hypertension,* 1981, **3,** 698–703.

Glueck, C. J. Mattson, F., & Bierman, E. L. Diet and coronary heart disease: Another view. *New England Journal of Medicine,* 1978, **298,** 1471–1474.

Goodhart, R. S., & Shils, M. E. *Modern nutrition in health and disease* (6th ed.). Philadelphia: Lea & Febiger, 1980.

Gotto, A. M., Scott, L. W., Foreyt, J. P., & Reeves, R. *Brand name shopper's guide.* Houston: 1975.

Greger, J. L., & Etnyre, G. M. Validity of 24-hour dietary results by adolescent females. *American Journal of Public Health,* 1978, **68,** 70–75.

Gussow, D. Counternutritional messages of TV ads aimed at children. *Journal of Nutrition Education,* 1972, **8,** 52–57.

Gussow, J. D. Why we need nutrition guidelines. In *Nutrition guidelines: Toward a national strategy.* Proceedings of the Third Conference on Nutrition and the American Food System. Washington, D.C.: Community Nutrition Institute, 1979.

Harper, A. E. Dietary goals—A skeptical view. *American Journal of Clinical Nutrition,* 1978, **31,** 310–321.

Harper, A. E., & Simopoulos, A. P. Proceedings of the conference on assessment of nutritional status: Summary, conclusions and recommendations. *American Journal of Clinical Nutrition,* 1982, **35,** 1098–1107.

Haskell, W. L., & Blair, S. N. The physical activity component of health promotion in occupational settings. In R. S. Parkinson (Ed.), *Managing health promotion in the workplace: Guidelines for implementation and evaluation.* Palo Alto: Mayfield, 1982.

Hegsted, D. M. What Americans are eating now. In *Nutrition guidelines: Toward a national strategy.* Proceedings of the Third Conference on Nutrition and the American Food System. Washington, D.C.: Community Nutrition Institute, 1979.

Herbert-Jackson, E., & Risley, T. R. Behavioral nutrition: Consumption of foods of the future by toddlers. *Journal of Applied Behavior Analysis,* 1977, **10,** 407–413.

Higgins, J. Nutrition education through the mass media in Korea. *Journal of Nutrition Education*, 1972, **4**, 58–64.

Hitt, C. Risk reduction: A community strategy. *Community Nutritionist*, 1982, January–February, 12–17.

Jeffery, R. W., Pirie, P. L., Rosenthal, B., Gerber, W. M., & Murray, D. Nutrition education in supermarkets: Effects on knowledge and product sales. *Behavior Therapy*, in press.

Karvetti, R. L. Changes in the diet of myocardial infarction patients: Effects of nutrition education. *Journal of the American Dietetic Association*, 1981, **79**, 660–667.

Keys, A., Anderson, J. T., & Grande, F. Serum cholesterol response to changes in the diet: II. The effect of cholesterol in the diet. *Metabolism*, 1965, **14**, 759–765.

Kolonel, L. N., & Lee, J. Husband-wife correspondence in smoking, drinking and dietary habits. *American Journal of Public Health*, 1981, **34**, 99–104.

Lansky, D., & Brownell, K. D. Estimates of food quantity and calories: Errors in self-report among obese patients. *American Journal of Clinical Nutrition*, 1982, **35**, 727–732.

Lauer, R. M., & Shekelle, R. B. (Eds.). *Childhood prevention of atherosclerosis and hypertension*. New York: Raven Press, 1980.

Lesser, H. *Television and the preschool child*. New York: Academic Press, 1977.

Levy, S. R., Iverson, B. K., & Walberg, H. J. Nutrition education research: An interdisciplinary evaluation and review. *Health Education Quarterly*, 1980, **7**, 107–126.

Linusson, E. E. I., Sanjur, D., & Erikson, E. C. Validating the 24-hour recall method as a dietary survey tool. *Archives of Latin American Nutrition*, 1975, **24**, 277–282.

Lipsitt, L. P. Tastes in human neonates: Its effects on sucking and heart rate. In J. M. Weiffenbach (Ed.), *Taste and development: The genesis of sweet preference*. DHEW Pub. No. (NIH)77–1068. Washington, D.C.: U.S. Government Printing Office, 1977.

Lovett, R., Barker, E., & Marcus, B. The effect of a nutrition education program at the second grade level. *Journal of Nutrition Education*, 1970, **2**, 81–95.

Maccoby, N., Farquhar, J. W., Wood, P. D., & Alexander, J. Reducing the risk of cardiovascular disease: Effects of a community-based campaign on knowledge and behavior. *Journal of Community Health*, 1977, **3**, 100–114.

Madden, J. P., Goodman, S. J., & Guthrie, H. A. Validity of the 24-hour recall: Analysis of data obtained from elderly subjects. *Journal of the American Dietetic Association*, 1976, **68**, 143–148.

Madsen, C. H., Madsen, C. K., & Thompson, F. Increasing rural Head Start children's consumption of middle-class meals. *Journal of Applied Behavior Analysis*, 1974, **7**, 257–262.

Mangham, D. B., & Vickery, C. E. Introducing nutrition education. *Journal of School Health*, 1981, **51**, 110–112.

Marketing Science Institute. Determinants of food usage behavior: A market segmentation approach. Cambridge, Mass.: Marketing Science Institute, 1980.

Mayer, J. Introduction: Toward a national nutrition policy. In J. Mayer (Ed.), *U.S. nutrition policies in the seventies*. San Francisco: Freeman, 1973. (a)

Mayer, J. Labeling. In J. Mayer (Ed.), *U.S. nutrition policies in the seventies*. San Francisco: Freeman, 1973. (b)

Mayer, J. USDA: Built-in conflicts. In J. Mayer (Ed.), *U.S. nutrition policies in the seventies*. San Francisco: Freeman, 1973. (c)

McAlister, A., Puska, P., Koskela, K., Pallonen, U. & Maccoby, N. Mass communication and community organization for public health education. *American Psychologist*, 1980, **35**, 375–379.

McGandy, R. B. Methodological aspects of nutritional surveys of young and middle-aged adults. *American Journal of Clinical Nutrition*, 1982, **35**, 1269–1272.

Miller, R. A., & Shekelle, R. B. Blood pressure in tenth grade students. *Circulation*, 1976, **54**, 993–1000.

Mojonnier, M. L., Hall, Y., Berkson, D. M., Robinson, E., Wethers, B., Pannbacker, B., Moss, D., Pardo, E., Stamler, J., Shekelle, R. B., & Raynor, W. Experience in changing food habits of hyperlipidemic men and women. *Journal of the American Dietetic Association*, 1980, **77**, 140–148.

Morgan, T., Adam, W., Gillies, A., Wilson, M., Morgan, G. & Carney, S. Hypertension treated by salt restriction. *Lancet*, 1978, **1**, 227–230.

National Academy of Sciences, National Research Council (NAS/NRC), Food and Nutrition Board. *Toward healthful diets.* Washington, D.C.: NAS/NRC, 1980.

National Diet–Heart Study Report. Serum cholesterol response. *Circulation,* 1968, **37,** I-181–I-223.

Olendzki, M. C., Tolpin, H. G., & Buckley, E. L. Evaluating nutrition intervention in atherosclerosis: Some theoretical and practical considerations. *Journal of the American Dietetic Association,* 1981, **79,** 9–16.

Orleans, C. S., & Shipley, R. H. Worksite smoking cessation initiatives: Review and recommendations. *Addictive Behaviors,* 1982, **7,** 1–16.

Payne, A., & Callahan, D. *The fat and sodium control cookbook.* Boston: Little, Brown, 1975.

Peiper, A. *Cerebral function in infancy and childhood.* New York: Consultant's Bureau, 1963.

Peters, R. K., Benson, H., & Porter, D. Daily relaxation response breaks in a working population: I. Effects on self-reported measures of health, performance, and well-being. *American Journal of Public Health,* 1977, **67,** 946–953.

Picardi, S. M., & Porter, D. Multidimensional evaluation of food and nutrition minicourse. *Journal of Nutrition Education,* 1976, **8,** 162–168.

Podell, R. N., Keller, K., Mulvihill, M. N., Berger, G., & Kent, D. F. Evaluation of the effectiveness of a high school course in cardiovascular nutrition. *American Journal of Public Health,* 1978, **68,** 573–576.

Point of Purchase Advertising Institute. *Dupont consumer buying habits study.* New York: Point of Purchase Advertising Institute, 1978.

Reilly Group, Inc. Meals and snacking: The child and what he eats. *Child,* 1973, **2,** 98–106.

Rodin, J. Social and immediate environmental influences on food selection. *International Journal of Obesity,* 1980, **4,** 364–370.

Rozin, P. Acquisition of food preferences and attitudes to food. *International Journal of Obesity,* 1980, **4,** 356–363.

Rozin, P., & Fallon, A. E. The acquisition of likes and dislikes for foods. In J. Solms & R. L. Hall (Eds.), *Criteria of food selection: How man chooses what he eats.* Zurich: Forster Verlag, 1980. (a)

Rozin, P., & Fallon, A. The psychological categorization of foods and non-foods: A preliminary taxonomy of food rejections. *Appetite,* 1980, **1,** 193–201. (b)

Rozin, P., & Kalat, J. W. Specific hungers and poison avoidance as adaptive specializations of learning. *Psychological Review,* 1971, **78,** 459–486.

Rush, D., & Kristal, A. R. Methodologic studies during pregnancy: The reliability of the 24-hour dietary recall. *American Journal of Clinical Nutrition,* 1982, **35,** 1259–1268.

Samuelson, G. An epidemiological study of child health and nutrition in a northern Swedish country: II. Methodological study of the recall technique. *Nutrition and Metabolism,* 1970, **12,** 321–333.

Schwartz, G. E. Stress management in occupational settings. In R. S. Parkinson (Ed.), *Managing health promotion in the workplace: Guidelines for implementation and evaluation.* Palo Alto: Mayfield, 1982.

Sclafani, A., & Springer, D. Dietary obesity in adult rats: Similarities to hypothalamic and human obesity syndromes. *Physiology and Behavior,* 1976, **17,** 461–471.

Scott, L. W., Foreyt, J. P., Manis, E., O'Malley, M. P., & Gotto, A. M. A low-cholesterol menu in a steak restaurant. *Journal of the American Dietetic Association,* 1979, **74,** 54–56.

Senate Select Committee on Nutrition and Human Needs. *Dietary goals for the United States.* Washington, D.C.: U.S. Government Printing Office, February 1977. (a)

Senate Select Committee on Nutrition and Human Needs. *Dietary goals for the United States* (2nd ed.). Washington, D.C.: U.S. Government Printing Office, December 1977. (b)

Shallenberger, R., & Acree, T. E. Chemical structures of compounds and their sweet and bitter tastes. In L. Beidler (Ed.), *Handbook of sensory physiology: IV. Chemical senses, 2: Taste.* New York: Springer Verlag, 1971.

Simoons, F. Effects of culture of food selection: Geographical and historical approaches. *International Journal of Obesity,* 1980, **4,** 387–394.

Smith, H. M., & Justice, C. L. Effects of nutrition programs on third grade students. *Journal of Nutrition Education,* 1979, **11,** 92–95.

Smith, S. F., & James, M. A. School lunch as a nutrition education resource for fourth graders. *Journal of Nutrition Education,* 1980, **12,** 46–49.

Soltan, F. Jewel stores scene of study on nutrition education. *Minneapolis Tribune,* June 18, 1979.

Stamler, J., Farinaro, E., Mojonnier, L. M., Hall, Y., Moss, D., & Stamler, R. Prevention and control of hypertension by nutritional-hygienic means. *Journal of the American Medical Association,* 1980, **243,** 1819–1823.

Steiner, J. The human gustofacial response. In J. F. Bosma (Ed.), *Fourth symposium on oral sensation and perception: Development in the fetus and infant.* Washington, D.C.: U.S. Government Printing Office, 1974.

Stern, M. P., Farquhar, J. W., Maccoby, N., & Russell, S. H. Results of a two-year health education campaign on dietary behavior: The Stanford Three Community Study. *Circulation,* 1976, **54,** 826–832.

Stunkard, A. J. Statement on the Pennsylvania Community Health Intervention Project. *Congressional Record* 96–4: 32–45, March 21, 1979.

Stunkard, A. J., & Brownell, K. D. Work-site treatment of obesity. *American Journal of Psychiatry,* 1980, **137,** 252–253.

Stunkard, A. J., & Kaplan, D. Eating in public places: A review of reports of direct observation of eating behavior. *International Journal of Obesity,* 1977, **1,** 89–101.

Stunkard, A. J., & Waxman, M. Accuracy of self-reports of food intake. *Journal of the American Dietetic Association,* 1981, **79,** 547–551.

U.S. Department of Agriculture (USDA). *Agricultural Statistics—1979.* Washington, D.C.: U.S. Government Printing Office, 1979.

U.S. Department of Agriculture (USDA). *Sugar and sweetener report.* SSR-Vol. 5, No. 2. Washington, D.C.: U.S. Department of Agriculture, 1980.

Ward, B., & Wackman, K. Children's purchase influence attempts and parental yielding. *Journal of Marketing Research,* 1972, **9,** 316–319.

Woman's Day Magazine. *Nutrition: A study of consumers' attitudes and behaviors towards eating at home and out of the home.* Greenwich, Conn.: *Woman's Day,* 1978.

Woman's Day Magazine/Food Marketing Institute. *Nutrition vs. inflation: The battle of the eighties.* Greenwich, Conn.: *Woman's Day,* 1980.

Zifferblatt, S. M., Wilbur, C. S., & Pinsky, J. Changing cafeteria eating habits. *Journal of the American Dietetic Association,* 1980, **76,** 15–20.

CHAPTER 40

THE ROLE OF WEIGHT CONTROL IN HEALTH PROMOTION AND DISEASE PREVENTION

GEORGE A. BRAY

University of Southern California

The disadvantages of increased body fat can be expressed in many ways. Overweight might decrease longevity; it might aggravate the onset and clinical progression of other diseases; and it might modify the social or economic quality of life. Weight loss, however, can reverse all or most of these disadvantages. I shall review here some of the data relating overweight and, where possible, obesity, to lifestyle in an effort to put the risks of obesity into proper prospective. It must be kept clearly in mind that almost all the data I shall review were collected and analyzed in terms of overweight, which refers to deviations in body weight from some standard weight related to height. Overweight does not necessarily imply obesity. This distinction is most obvious in athletes but may also apply to other groups. The correlation between measures of body weight such as relative weight, percentage overweight, ponderal index $[ht/(wt)^{1/3} = ht/\sqrt[3]{wt}]$ or body mass index (wt/ht^2), and skin folds or body density is 0.8 or less. Until better methods of measuring obesity are available, the results of epidemiologic studies using only body weight must be interpreted carefully.

BODY WEIGHT AND LIFE EXPECTANCY

Two kinds of studies have evaluated the effects of overweight on longevity. The most widely quoted and most extensive studies are the retrospective analyses on the effects of relative weight (i.e., weight in relation to height) on individuals with life insurance policies who were followed up in collaborative studies by the insurance industry's Society of Actuaries. The most recent study utilizing such data, *Build and Blood Pressure Study, 1979,* was published in 1979 by the Society of Actuaries. The second kind of data involves prospective studies of carefully controlled populations. Several of these studies have been analyzed recently (Andres, 1980; Keys, 1980a).

Retrospective Studies on Overweight and Longevity

In most cases, an applicant for life insurance must undergo a medical examination. Among the data that are routinely recorded are height, weight, and blood pressure, although in many cases height and weight may be obtained only from verbal reports by the patient and may not actually be measured. Analysis of such data, with all its limitations, (Keys, 1975; Seltzer, 1966) has provided us with the major retrospective studies on the effects of overweight on mortality and morbidity. In evaluating these studies, it is important to recognize that the population under study is selected. The subjects are generally of above-average economic circumstances, Caucasian, free of serious medical diseases, and usually engaged in safe occupations. Such a group represents a special segment of the population. Results from analysis of these data may thus not be applicable to the entire population. That this is so is suggested by the fact that mortality among insured individuals is less than the mortality rate for the entire population at all ages between 15 and 70 years (Mann, 1974). This might have been expected, however, since the insured subjects under study were in safe occupations and were free from major diseases at the time the insurance policy was obtained. Figure 40.1 summarizes the effect on excess mortality of deviations from normal body weight (Bray, 1976). For this figure the overall mortality rate was taken as 100, and the groups were subdivided into various percentage deviations from the mean for the entire age group. The death rate in each of these subgroups was compared to the population as a whole and is expressed as a percentage deviation from 100. The minimum death rate is slightly less than the average weight for the entire population. As body weight increases above the average, there is a progressive increase in excess mortality. Similarly, there is a small increase in excess mortality with very low body weight. This increase is more pronounced in the younger age group than in the older one and may reflect a higher number of smokers.

The factors involved in this excess mortality are summarized in Table 40.1. Diabetes mellitus, digestive diseases, hypertension, cardiovascular diseases, and neoplasms were the major causes of excess mortality. The degree of excess mortality associated with overweight rises with the degree of excess weight and is greater among males than among females.

The hazards to life of gross obesity have been dramatized by Drenick Gurunanjappa, Seltzer, and Johnson (1980), who reviewed a group of 200 morbidly obese men with average weight of 143.5 kilograms at age 23 years who were admitted for a weight control program and followed for 7.5 years. Of these men, 185 were followed until death or termination of the study. The age range was 23 years to 70 years, with a mean of 42.7 years. Markedly higher mortality was found for all ages in the study group as compared with the mortality expected for the general population of U.S. males. Of particular interest was that in men aged 25 to 34, the excess mortality was 1200%. In the group aged 35 to 44, the excess mortality had declined to 550%. In the men aged 45 to 54, it was still 300%. In men

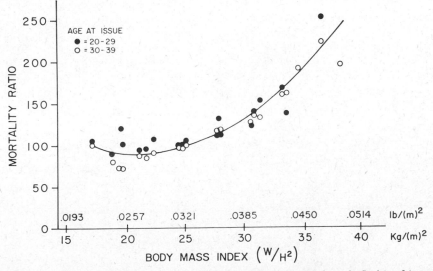

Figure 40.1 Relationship of body mass index to excess mortality. The data from the Society of Actuaries *Build and Blood Pressure Study, 1979,* have been replotted from the calculations of Seltzer (1966).

Table 40.1   Causes of Death Associated with Overweight

Diagnosis	Degree Overweight (%)	Mortality Ratio (%)
Diabetes mellitus	5–15	125
	15–25	200
	>25	500
Heart and circulatory disease	15–25	130
	25–45	150
	45–65	200
Coronary artery disease	15–25	130
	25–55	160
	>60	180
Hypertensive heart disease	5–15	170
	>15	250
Digestive diseases	15–35	140
	>25	250

Source: Data for males from Society of Actuaries (1979).

aged 55 to 64, the excess mortality was only double that of the normal U.S. population.

If significant degrees of overweight are hazardous to health, does weight reduction improve longevity? Few data are available to help answer this question, except for data from the life insurance industry (Marks, 1960; Society of Actuaries, 1979). The individuals in this subgroup came from a group of people who initially had received substandard insurance because they were overweight but who subsequently were issued other policies when they reached a lower weight. Among policyholders who lost weight and maintained the loss, life expectancy improved to that of insured people with standard risk (see Table 40.2).

Prospective Studies of Overweight and Longevity

Several prospective studies have also examined the importance of overweight and obesity in the development of cardiovascular disease. I will review several of them in detail here, including the Framingham Study (Gordon & Kannel, 1973; Kannel & Gordon, 1979), the International Cooperative Study of Cardiovascular Epidemiology (Keys, 1970; Keys, Aravanis, Blackburn, VanBuchem, Buzina, Djordjevic, Fidanza, Karvonen, Menotti, Puddu, & Taylor, 1972), the Los Angeles Heart Study (Chapman, Coulson, Clark, & Borun, 1971), and the Gothenberg Study (Larsson, Bjorntorp, & Tibblin, 1981).

Table 40.2   Effect of Weight Reduction on Excess Mortality

	Mortality Ratio (%)	
Source	All Men	Men 25% Overweight
Build and Blood Pressure Study, 1959	102	—
Build and Blood Pressure Study, 1979	71	110

The Framingham Study

One of the most widely quoted studies of the risk factors related to coronary artery disease was conducted with 5,209 men and women living in Framingham, Massachusetts. Initial examinations of this population were conducted between 1948 and 1950 (Kannel & Gordon, 1979) and participants were examined at 2-year intervals thereafter. The incidence of various forms of heart disease, including angina pectoris, sudden death, myocardial infarction, and cerebral vascular disease, was related to relative body weight. Two criteria have been used to define relative body weight. The first, Framingham relative weight, is based on the median body weights for heights obtained from the initial examinations carried out between 1948 and 1950. The median body weights of subjects in the Framingham Study were almost identical to the upper limits for individuals with heavy frames given in the tables provided by the Metropolitan Life Insurance Company. To make the Framingham data more comparable with other data in the literature, they have been compared to the median weights of the Metropolitan Life Insurance tables. Using these comparisons as desirable weights, approximately 15% of the men and 20% of the women were at least 35% overweight, and 3% of the men and 9% of the women were more than 50% overweight.

In the Framingham Study, weight gain was associated with a rise in serum lipids, an increase in blood pressure, an impairment in glucose tolerance, and a slight rise in uric acid (Kannel & Gordon, 1979). Overall mortality in the overweight participants of both sexes was lower than for those of normal body weight, but mortality from coronary artery disease, and especially sudden death, was substantially higher in the overweight subjects. There was a higher incidence of coronary attacks, coronary insufficiency, cerebrovascular infarction, and congestive heart failure in the overweight, but excess weight had no effect on the frequency of intermittent claudication. By using multivariate analysis, a relative risk was assigned to each factor associated with cardiovascular disease. In women, the net effect of overweight or obesity was small for all cardiovascular events except congestive heart failure. In men, there was a significant relationship between overweight and cardiovascular mortality, even when such atherogenic factors as hypertension, smoking, and family history were taken into account. Both angina pectoris and coronary attacks were significantly related to overweight in the men. The attack rate of myocardial infarction, however, had a less striking relation to overweight. This relatively small effect of excess body weight on the likelihood of developing a myocardial infarction has been observed in most of the prospective studies. As Kannel and Gordon (1979) summarized:

> Although there is some unique effect, obesity (overweight) is clearly not a major independent predictor of cardiovascular incidence (disease) given knowledge of the major risk factors. This is not to say that overweight is an unimportant consideration in prophylaxis against cardiovascular disease, but rather that it is not particularly helpful in estimating risks.

In general, other risk factors, such as sex, age, hypertension, elevated cholesterol, and smoking, are better discriminators for coronary artery disease than obesity is. From the data collected in the Framingham Study, however, it is estimated that "if everyone were at optimal weight, there would be 25% less coronary heart disease, and 35% less congestive heart failure and brain infarction" (Kannel & Gordon, 1979).

The International Cooperative Study of Cardiovascular Epidemiology

This prospective study involved an international collaborative examination of coronary heart disease involving 14 cohorts of men in Holland and Finland (2,349 men, the Northern European group), Italy, Greece, and Yugoslavia (6,519 men, the Southern European group), and railway workers in the United States (2,442 men) (Keys, 1980b). The men were between

40 and 59 years old at entry into the study. The assessment of body weight and fatness was based on the body mass index (wt/ht^2). Those considered obese were individuals with a body mass index greater than 27. Measurements of the tricep and subscapular skin folds were also used, and obesity was defined as a sum of skin folds greater than 37 mm. Using these criteria, more than half (52.3%) of the United States railway men were considered obese. This was substantially higher than the proportion of obese men in the Northern European group but was comparable to that in the Southern European group. Coronary events were divided into two subgroups: the "hard" events, meaning that death was from coronary heart disease or definite myocardial infarction, and the "soft" events, including classical angina pectoris and clinical judgment of possible heart disease. An examination of the data reveals the similarity between body mass index for U.S. railway workers and for the population in Southern Europe and a sharp difference from that observed in the men from Northern European countries. Among the men from the United States and Southern Europe, there were few, if any, significant relationships of body weight when hard events were the measure of coronary heart disease. There were statistically significant correlations, however, between overweight and the soft criteria for coronary artery disease. Among the men from Northern Europe, the relationship was nearly reversed. There were statistically significant correlations between all measures of body weight and hard criteria for coronary artery disease among the males from Northern Europe but no significant association between body weight and soft diagnostic criteria for coronary artery disease.

To explore these data further, a multivariate analysis was performed in which relative risk could be assigned to each factor investigated. A high correlation was observed between relative weight and blood pressure. This finding has been observed in almost all studies in which body weight and blood pressure have been measured. From this multivariate analysis, Keys et al. (1972) concluded that in none of the relationships did the measures of relative weight or fatness have any independent value in predicting the risk of developing coronary heart disease. Thus, as an independent predictor of developing coronary heart disease, body weight has little value. Excess body weight is important, however, because of its association with high blood pressure. It should be noted that the data of Keys et al. (1972) were obtained from a study of men aged 40 to 59 at the time of entry into the study. The effects of overweight diminished as the age at which life insurance was issued increased and in the follow-up of overweight men by Drenick et al. (1980). This suggests that overweight may have its major influences on mortality in men under age 40 and explains why it might not have been detected in the seven-country study of older men (Keys, 1975; Keys et al., 1972).

Los Angeles Heart Study

A group of 1,859 male (1,552 white, 302 black, 5 oriental) civil servants were periodically reexamined for up to 15 years. During this time there were 242 new cases of heart disease among the 1,503 men at risk, giving an annual rate of 10.7 per 1,000 men. In this study, the body weight and height were related using the ponderal index [ht/(wt)$^{1/3}$]. Men with a ponderal index of less than 12 were considered obese. Although there was a trend for myocardial infarction to occur more frequently in the overweight men, this change was neither consistent nor statistically significant. Chapman et al. (1971) showed that body weight was associated with the development of coronary artery disease in men who were between 30 and 39 years old at the beginning of the study. In men over age 40 at entry, there was a significant relationship of body weight to the development of angina pectoris but not to myocardial infarction; and in men over age 50, body weight added no predictive value for discriminating the likelihood of developing coronary artery disease. In this study, the principal effect of body weight on heart disease was in younger men aged 30 to 39, in whom it was predictive for developing myocardial infarction, and in men aged 40 to 49 for predicting angina pectoris. The lack of association of overweight and heart disease in older men is similar to the conclusions of the first two cited prospective studies.

The Gothenburg Study

A recent prospective study from Gothenburg, Sweden, provided additional information about the health consequences of moderate obesity (Larsson et al., 1981). A sample of 855 men (88% of those invited) were randomly selected from the general population in 1963, and an evaluation was made of their initial degree of obesity and various health indicators. Of these men, 787 (84%) were reexamined at age 60, or 10 years following the initial examination. A second group of 226 50-year-old men was examined at the same time. Obesity was determined from anthropometric measures and from total body fat, as determined by the quantity of the naturally occurring isotope of potassium (^{40}K) in the body. About one-third of the study population were using prescribed drugs, which were used more frequently among the obese individuals then among those of normal weight. The main reason for this higher drug use was for treatment of hypertension in the overweight men. Subjective indicators of illness, however, were not related to the degree of fatness. In the longitudinal analysis of men followed for the 10- to 12.5-year period, those who developed kidney stones, gallstones, and diabetes were significantly more obese in the initial examination than those who did not develop these problems. An increase in body mass index or body fatness was also weakly associated with an increased risk for developing strokes. Those who developed angina pectoris, intermittant claudication, or peptic ulcer did not differ significantly in their initial weight status. Obesity was also not a risk factor for the development of myocardial infarction or death. Larsson and his colleagues (1981) concluded "that even moderate obesity increases the risk for hypertension, diabetes mellitus, gallstone disease, kidney-stone disease and cerebrovascular disease."

The extensive literature on the relationship between overweight or obesity and the likelihood of developing atherosclerosis or other medical complications can be depicted in two ways (Figure 40.2). There might be a causal relationship, in which obesity is directly related to the onset of these other conditions as a cause-and-effect phenomenon (panel A). This is the conclusion that might be reached from the various retrospective studies. The several prospective studies make any simple relationship unlikely, however. For this reason, the diagram depicted in panel B seems more likely. With this model, obesity and the various medical conditions with which it is frequently associated are not causally related to one

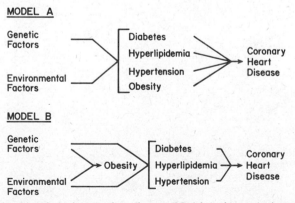

Figure 40.2 Relationship of obesity to other diseases. Model A shows obesity as a causative effect and Model B shows obesity as a phenomenon that is not directly related to the major risks of coronary artery disease. (From Rimm et al 1972).

another. Under these circumstances, obesity could serve as a useful marker for the possible presence of these medical conditions but could also occur in their absence.

The effects of excess weight may well be of more importance in younger people than when overweight develops in later life. Alternatively, in men who are overweight early in life, the extra mortality may have been dissipated by the time they reach age 40. In men under 40 years of age, those whose weight increased by 10% or more had a significantly greater risk of hypertension than men who gained less weight. The most convincing evidence for the proposition that obesity early in life is more hazardous is that of Drenick et al. (1980) and Abraham, Collins, and Nordsieck (1971). The data of Abraham et al. (1971) relate the changes in weight status between childhood and adulthood to the incidence of hypertensive and cardiovascular renal disease among 715 males (Figure 40.3). Childhood weight status was determined from school records obtained between ages 9 and 13. Follow-up was at an average age of 48. The highest prevalence for both conditions occurred in the men with the lowest childhood weight who became overweight as adults. It may well be that changing weight categories during adolescence and early adult years has more influence on the development of subsequent diseases than maintaining a higher weight category throughout life. Such a hypothesis awaits further research.

OVERWEIGHT AND MORBIDITY

Overweight and Blood Pressure

Hypertension can be defined as a sustained blood pressure with a systolic reading above 160 mmHg and a diastolic reading above 95 mmHg. The range of diastolic pressures from 90 to 95 mmHg is considered borderline, and only those below 90 mmHg are considered normal. For systolic pressure, 140 to 160 mmHg is borderline, and less than 140 mmHg is considered normal. Technical problems in the measurement of blood pressure in obese subjects have proved troublesome and must be considered in evaluating the importance of any epidemiologic studies on this problem. It is widely taught that the indirect auscultatory

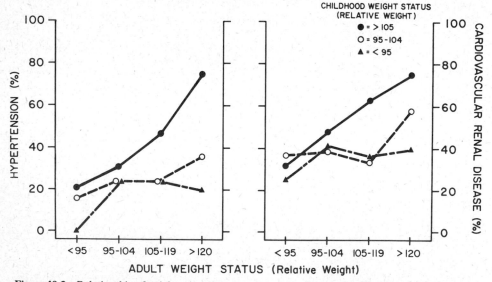

Figure 40.3 Relationship of weight gain to hypertension and cardiovascular renal disease. The individuals who gained weight in adult life and who had a normal (95–104) or low (<95) weight status as children showed the highest incidence of both diseases as adults. (Adapted from Abraham et al 1971).

method of obtaining blood pressure with an inflatable cuff tends to give higher readings in obese individuals than those obtained by direct intraarterial measurement. This widely held belief has come in for critical reevaluation. In a careful study of the various factors involved in the measurement of arterial blood pressure, King (1967) found that the length of the cuff bladder for the manometer was of prime importance. When the cuff was short, there were great differences between systolic and diastolic pressures measured by intraarterial methods as compared to indirect measurements. The more nearly the inflatable bladder of the pressure cuff surrounds the arm, however, the more reliable the indirect measurements will become. Maxwell, Waks, Schroth, Karam, and Dornfeld (1982) compared 84,000 measurements of blood pressure in 1,240 obese subjects using three commercially available cuffs. They observed a greater difference in both systolic and diastolic pressures in comparing the regular and large cuffs. On the basis of their observations, using data from subjects with arm circumferences of 33 to 41 cm (large arms), they estimated that nearly 37% of those found to be hypertensive may actually be normotensive. In spite of these problems, most population studies show a rise in blood pressure with an increase in body weight or other indices of body fatness (Garn, 1982; Stamler, Farinaro, Mojonnier, Hall, Moss, & Stamler, 1980).

A comprehensive review of the relationship between overweight and hypertension has been published by Chiang, Perlman, and Epstein (1969). It will suffice here to emphasize only a few points. Robinson and Brucer (1940) examined the relationship between blood pressure and modified ponderal index, which included chest circumference (wt/ht × 100/ chest circumference). Two points emerged. First, overweight had a striking correlation with a lateral body build; that is, individuals with a large chest circumference relative to their height and weight had a higher blood pressure than slender individuals. Hypertension was present in 37% of the broad-chested men but only in 3% of the slender men. Body build exerted an almost proportionate effect on systolic and diastolic blood pressure. Second, when blood pressure was compared in groups with constant body build, there was no significant correlation between obesity and hypertension. The greatest correlation of blood pressure with obesity was observed in the men with slender builds. A much smaller correlation was found in the broad-chested men. From these data, it would appear that body build is more important than obesity per se in the positive correlation between blood pressure and body weight.

Even with the limitations in the techniques of measuring blood pressure by indirect auscultation, the available data almost uniformly indicate the important relationship between body weight and blood pressure. The increased blood pressure in heavier persons probably results from increased peripheral arterial resistance. The increase in peripheral resistance may in turn be due to the increased secretion of catecholamines from a hyperactive sympathetic nervous system (Young & Landsberg, 1980).

The beneficial effect of weight loss on blood pressure frequently follows successful weight reduction. Epidemiologic data obtained during World War II revealed that during periods of caloric deprivation, hypertension was almost nonexistent. A number of clinical studies correlating changes in blood pressure with weight reduction have been summarized by Chiang et al. (1969). Fletcher (1954) studied the effect of weight reduction on blood pressure of 38 women who were more than 20% overweight. The mean weight loss in 6 months was 32 pounds (14.5 kg), and the drop in diastolic blood pressure was 16.6 mmHg in the subgroup with initial diastolic pressures above 100 mmHg. Adlersberg, Coler, and Laval (1946) had similar results, with 72% of 54 patients showing a significant drop in blood pressure. Martin (1952), however, had a lower success rate. Heyden, Walker, and Hames (1971) have also noted a drop in systolic and diastolic blood pressure in the patients that they observed. Reisin, Abel, Modan, Silverberg, Eliahou, and Modan (1978) and Tuck, Sowers, Dornfeld, Kledzik, and Maxwell (1981) showed that this reduction in blood pressure occurred even when salt intake was held constant. The beneficial effects of weight loss on blood pressure, cholesterol, blood glucose, and uric acid are shown in Table 40.3, from

Table 40.3 Effects of Weight Loss on Athero-genic Traits

Atherogenic Trait	Mean Decrease[a]
Cholesterol	11 mg/dl
Blood pressure, systolic	5 mmHg
Blood glucose	2 mg/dl
Uric acid	0.4 mg/dl

Source: Adapted from Kannel and Gordon (1979)
[a] Mean decrease with 10% reduction in body weight in males.

the Framingham Study. It should be noted that weight reduction is more effective in lowering systolic blood pressure than in lowering diastolic pressure. Whether the therapeutic effect of weight reduction is related to the magnitude of the decline in body weight or to other environmental factors is unclear; however, weight reduction can produce a significant reduction in blood pressure in more than half of the hypertensive patients.

Overweight and Cardiovascular Function

The relationship between overweight and cardiovascular disease has been studied extensively (Vaughan, Conahan, 1980). The obese individual shows an increase in intra- and extracellular fluid volume. Blood volume also increases with excess weight (Alexander, Amad, & Cole, 1976), but when expressed in terms of ideal weight it is normal. Cardiac output is increased in relation to the oxygen consumption associated with obesity (Alexander, Amad, & Cole 1976). The increased cardiac output is in turn produced primarily by increasing the stroke volume of the heart, since resting heart rate usually remains in the normal range in the overweight patient. A major reason for the increased cardiac output is the increased blood flow to adipose tissue. When the blood volume and cardiac output are expressed per kilogram of body weight, they are only about 60% of the predicted value. The use of gross weight, however, does not allow correction for differences in the composition of the extra weight. Surface area probably provides a more appropriate basis for this comparison. Estimates of blood flow through various peripheral tissues of obese patients indicate that they are essentially normal, although renal blood flow tends to be high. Studies of the heart itself have shown that the transverse diameter, as measured on routine chest X ray, shows a positive correlation with body weight. These radiographic data are supported by the fact that the weight of the heart increases with increasing body weight. This is mainly the result of myocardial hypertrophy (Kannel & Gordon, 1979). Because the circulation is overtaxed as body weight increases, congestive heart failure may occur in grossly obese individuals (Vaughan, & Conahan, 1980).

Essentially all of the abnormalities in vascular and cardiac function return toward normal with weight loss (Alexander & Peterson, 1972). The heart rate, stroke volume, cardiac work, and oxygen uptake are all reduced. Table 40.4 shows the cardiovascular findings before and after weight loss in nine grossly obese patients. Note that every parameter improved. It thus appears that most of the cardiovascular changes observed in obese patients are a consequence of the obesity and, like hypertension, are ameliorated by weight reduction.

Overweight and Pulmonary Function

Measurement of pulmonary function in obese individuals shows a number of abnormalities (Luce, 1980; Rochester & Enson, 1974). At one extreme are patients with the Pickwickian syndrome—named by Burwell, Robin, Whaley, and Bickelman (1956) after Joe, the fat

Table 40.4   Effect of Weight Loss on Cardiovascular Function

Measurement	Before Weight Loss	After Weight Loss
Weight (kg)	112–218	−53 kg
Heart rate (min^{-1})	73 ± 10	68 ± 8
Stroke volume (ml)	107 ± 15	92 ± 17
Left ventricular stroke work (g-m)	150 ± 29	110 ± 29
Left ventricular work (kg-m/min)	11.1 ± 3.9	7.4 ± 2
Vo_2(ml/min)	360 ± 82	247 ± 43
Cardiac output (l/min)	7.9 ± 1.8	6.2 ± 1.2
Systemic arterial pressure (mmHg)	102 ± 16	87 ± 12
Blood volume (l)	7.8 ± 1.5	6.1 ± 1.4

Source: Adapted from Alexander and Peterson (1972) by permission of the American Heart Association, Inc.

boy in Dicken's *Pickwick Papers*—characterized by somnolence, obesity, and hypoventilation. At the other extreme are patients with impairments in work capacity caused by the increased mass of fat. Obese patients show a fairly uniform decrease in expiratory reserve volume—the volume of air that can be blown out after normal ventilation (Bray, 1976). They also have a low maximum rate of voluntary ventilation as well as a tendency toward a general reduction in lung volumes. Studies on airway resistance, on the compliance of the lung, and on the oxygen cost of breathing have also revealed abnormalities in the obese. Lung compliance appears to be normal, but studies on the mechanics of breathing indicate that there is an increase in oxygen consumption associated with breathing, since more work is required to move the mass of the obese chest. Finally, there appears to be some element of venous admixture—that is, segments of the lung that are not well perfused but are ventilated and other regions that are perfused but not adequately ventilated, leading to a fairly consistent finding of modest degrees of decreased arterial oxygenation without corresponding increases in arterial carbon dioxide content (Douglas & Chang, 1972). Some obese patients show a diminished sensitivity of the respiratory center to the stimulatory effects of carbon dioxide. When breathing 5% CO_2, these patients do not show the usual and expected increase in rate of respiration. This may play a role in the development of pulmonary abnormalities observed with the Pickwickian syndrome (Rochester & Enson, 1974). Lourenco (1969) proposed one explanation for some of the pulmonary difficulties associated with obesity. He measured the activity of the diaphragm when the obese patient breathed increasing amounts of CO_2. The patients with hypoventilation showed less diaphragmatic activity, suggesting that the inability of this muscle to function normally may play an important role in the pulmonary abnormality observed in obesity. The supine position is another factor that impairs pulmonary function in obesity (Vaughan, Bauer, & Wise, 1976). With weight loss, all these abnormalities return to normal.

Overweight and Gallbladder Disease

Association of obesity or overweight with gallbladder disease has been suggested in several studies. In an autopsy study in which 612 gallbladder specimens were examined, 377 had gross disease, with 44 of the diseased gallbladders coming from subjects weighing over 210 pounds (Bray, 1976). A second source for this association is insurance company statistics (Society of Actuaries, 1979). In a detailed study of just over 73,000 respondents to a questionnaire issued by the TOPS club (Take Off Pounds Sensibly, Milwaukee), Rimm, Werner, Bernstein, and van Yserloo (1975) found that the incidence of gallbladder disease increases with each decade from age 25 to over age 55. They also showed that, within any age group, the frequency of gallbladder disease increases with the level of body weight. Among women aged 25 to 34 years who were 100% or more overweight, 18% had gallbladder disease. Nearly 35% of the women aged 45 to 55 who were 100% or more overweight had gallbladder disease. A third study demonstrating the relationship between weight and gallbladder disease was conducted by Sturdevant, Pearce, and Dayton (1973). The body weight of their subjects who did not have gallstones was significantly lower than that of the men with gallstones. The incidence of gallstones at autopsy in men who were more than 9.1 kg overweight was 43% (12/28); in men who were less than 9.1 kg overweight, there was an incidence of only 16% (25/156).

Overweight and Diabetes

Life insurance data show the association of diabetes mellitus with increased mortality (Society of Actuaries, 1979) but the relationship is complex (Bray, 1976). Rimm et al. (1975) investigated this relationship among more than 73,000 respondents to the TOPS club questionnaire and found that increasing body weight and age were both associated with a rising frequency of diabetes mellitus. Less than 1% of normal-weight women aged 25 to 44 had diabetes mellitus, whereas 7% of those of the same age who were 100% overweight had this complication.

The percentage increase in body weight for males and females between the ages of 25 and 60 in four different countries is related to the frequency of diabetes (Table 40.5). The mortality from diabetes mellitus was highest among females who had the greatest gain in weight between ages 25 and 60. Canada and United States, whose populations had the greatest percentage increase in body weight between ages 25 and 60, had the highest mortality from diabetes.

The stress to the pancreas imposed by obesity is shown in data presented by Keen (Note 1). The siblings of diabetic patients were examined for the presence of diabetes, and the results were related to the prevalence of obesity (Table 40.6). When the initial subject with diabetes mellitus was overweight, the frequency of diabetes in the sibling was somewhat lower than when the subject was not overweight. Moreover, diabetes mellitus was present two to four times as often in the obese siblings of the diabetic family member who originally reported with diabetes as when the siblings were not obese. These data lend credence to the concept that in the presence of obesity, diabetes develops more readily in individuals with pancreatic injury, whether of genetic, chemical, or viral origin, than in similar individuals who are not obese.

Table 40.5 Relationship of Mortality from Diabetes to Weight Gain After Age 25

| Country | Percentage Increase in Weight Between Ages 25 and 60 | | Mortality From Diabetes (%) | | | |
| | | | Over Age 45 | | All Ages | |
	M	F	M	F	M	F
Japan	0.4	0.4	—	—	2.4	2.0
England	3.6	15.5	14.0	25.2	5.3	10.1
Canada	4.6	19.3	55.6	91.5	16.2	24.5
United States	8.1	15.0	67.7	111.6	20.7	34.0

Source: Adapted from Hundley (1956).
[a] Mortality rates per 100,000 population in 1948.

Table 40.6 Frequency of Diabetes Mellitus Among Siblings of Diabetics

Weight Status of Initial Diabetic Subject	Frequency of Diabetes among Siblings in Two Weight Groups (%)	
	Obese	Nonobese
Obese	10.8	4.8
Nonobese	27.3	7.3

Source: Adapted from Keen (Note 1).

Obesity and Skin Problems

Two abnormalities in the skin have been associated with obesity. The first is a condition known as fragilitas cutis inguinalis. Ganor and Even-Paz (1967) examined the resistance to stretching of the inguinal skin in 200 patients who were divided into three subgroups: lean, normal, and fat. In 63 of the 200 patients, the inguinal skin ruptured linearly at right angles to the applied force. This phenomenon was restricted to the groin and was unrelated to the sex or age of the patient, but it was clearly associated with obesity. Nearly 70% of the fat patients, as compared to 20% to 25% of the medium-weight patients, showed this phenomenon. These authors also noted a positive relationship between the presence of stria and obesity, but not between the presence of stria and the tendency of the inguinal skin to rupture under stretching. The meaning of the sensitivity of the inguinal skin in obese subjects to rupture during stretching is unclear.

Acanthosis nigricans is a second dermal abnormality that has a significant association with obesity. Darkening of the skin in the creases of the neck and in the axillary regions is important because it is sometimes associated with highly malignant cancers, usually an intraabdominal adenocarcinoma occurring in middle-aged and elderly patients. In the study of 90 patients by Brown and Winkleman (1968), 17 had the malignant form and 73 the benign form of acanthosis nigricans. In the patients with obesity and the benign acanthosis nigricans, most had stigmata of other endocrine diseases, including hirsutism, acne, amenorrhea, abdominal striae, and moon facies.

Renal Function and Obesity

Description of the nephrotic syndrome in four patients with massive obesity has reawakened interest in the interrelationship between obesity and renal function (Weisinger, Kempson, Eldridge, & Swenson, 1974). The four patients in this report had proteinuria ranging from 3.1 to 19.2 grams per day. Hematuria was absent, however, and X rays of the kidney in three of these patients showed a normal pattern in two and a horseshoe kidney in one. Renal biopsies obtained in two patients showed only minimal abnormalities and no definable pathological cause for the nephrotic syndrome. Of particular importance was the relationship between the proteinuria and body weight. In all four patients, there was a significant decline in protein excretion as the patients lost weight.

Obstetrics and the Overweight Patient

For the present discussion, I will focus on the relationship between prepregnancy weight and factors related to labor and the weight of the infant. Peckham and Christianson (1971) performed a careful analysis of women in the Oakland clinic of the Kaiser-Permanente

Medical Care Plan for whom prepregnancy weights were available. In this group were 3,939 white women who delivered babies between 1963 and 1965. At each height, the women with the lowest 10%, the middle 10%, and the highest 10% in body weight were selected for review. This technique provides the same distribution of heights in each of the three weight groups. Among the heavy women, body weight averaged 169 pounds. These women were older, averaging 29 years of age as compared to 25 years for the lightest women. Nearly 22% of the heavy women were over 35, but only 7.4% of the light women had attained this age. Moreover, 40% of the women in the light weight group were having their first pregnancies, but this percentage was much smaller in the heavy group. Menarche occurred at a younger age in the heavy women and was somewhat delayed in the light weight women; 27.5% of the heavy women had begun menstruating by age 11, but only 16.5% of the light ones had. In contrast, menstruation began after age 14 in 28% of the light women but in only 13.7% of the heavy women. Among the heavy women, the frequencies of toxemia of pregnancy and hypertension were significantly increased. In addition, the duration of labor was longer. In over 7% of the heavy women, labor lasted more than 24 hours. This occurred in only 0.8% of the light women. Cesarean section was performed in 5.5% of the heavy patients but in only 0.7% of the light ones. Thus, more obstetrical complications were present in the heavy group than in the light one.

The weights of infants born to the heavy women were significantly higher than the weights of babies born to the light women. Garn (1982) also noted this relationship in analyzing data from the National Collaborative Perinatal Project. Of particular interest in his studies were the relationships between placental weight, birth weight, and weights at 7 years of age. He demonstrated a direct relationship between placental weight and prepregnancy body weight. Birth weight and maternal prepregnancy weight were also significantly related. If infants born to mothers with comparable placental weights were compared at age 7, approximately 50% of the incremental weight status difference could be accounted for by the differences in placental weight at birth. The remaining 50% of the difference is accounted for by the postnatal nutritional environment. Similar observations have been made by McKeown and Record (1957). In their studies; the mean birth weight of the infants increased with maternal height and increasing maternal weight. They failed, however, to observe any relationship between the duration of labor and the effect of body weight or body build.

The risk associated with operating on obese women with adenocarcinoma of the uterus has been examined by Prem, Mensheha, and McKelvey (1965). The mortality rate following treatment of malignancy of the uterus was higher in obese women. Women weighing over 300 pounds had a 20% mortality, compared to 5% (1/18) for women weighing 250 to 299 pounds and only 2% (1/65) for women weighing between 200 and 249 pounds. This finding thus bears out a long-held clinical impression that marked obesity is associated with some enhanced risks of surgical mortality. Anesthesia also involves more risk in obese patients (Vaughan et al., 1976).

METABOLIC EFFECTS OF OBESITY

A relationship between body surface area and resting energy expenditure or total metabolism has been demonstrated in all studies of obesity in which this measurement has been reported. The heavier individuals are, the higher their total energy requirements are (Garrow, 1978; James, Bailes, Davies, & Dauncey, 1978). For any weight range, however, there is a variability of approximately 20% from high to low levels of energy expenditure. Part of this variance may be due to intrinsic differences in metabolism between individuals, but part of it may also be due to adaptive responses to the quantity of food that is eaten. When caloric intake is reduced below levels required for maintenance of body weight, there is an adaptive reduction in energy expenditure in both obese and lean subjects (Bray, 1976). This reduction occurs during total starvation and is also observed with caloric intakes up to 800 calories per day. The adaptive reduction in energy expenditure may well be one basis for the difficulty many people claim to have when trying to lose weight.

The thermic effects of food—that is, the increased heat production, measured as higher oxygen consumption, or heat loss associated with eating a meal—have been demonstrated in both obese and lean subjects (Bray, 1983). The best available evidence would suggest that obese subjects, particularly those who are diabetic, have reduced thermic responses to a meal as compared to lean subjects (Bray, 1983).

The mechanism for the thermic responses to food has been of considerable interest for many years. Recent experimental work has suggested that it may be related to increased metabolism of a specialized heat-producing tissue known as brown adipose tissue (Glick, Teague, & Bray, 1981). Brown adipose tissue, so named because of its color, clusters in the intrascapular region, around parts of the heart, and along the great vessels and adjacent structures. Its function is primarily to heat the blood that flows through it. Brown fat is particularly prominent in newborn animals and in animals exposed to the cold or during hibernation. It has recently been proposed that this tissue may also represent a final common pathway for heat production during periods of overfeeding. One way of testing the responsiveness of brown adipose tissue is to measure the response of overall metabolism (i.e., oxygen consumption or total heat production) during the infusion of norepinephrine. One recent study has suggested that obese subjects show a smaller response than lean subjects to an infusion of norepinephrine (Jung, Shetty, & James, 1979), but another study did not find this to be so (Daniels, Katzeff, Ravussin, Garrow, & Danforth, 1982). This defect may persist even after weight reduction, suggesting that there may be differences between normal and overweight subjects in the metabolism of brown adipose tissue. The role of brown adipose tissue in obesity is currently a strongly debated issue.

The energy requirement for physical activity is related to the mass being moved. Thus, the heavier an individual is, the greater are the energy requirements needed for movement. When the resting energy requirements are taken into consideration, the overall efficiency for oxidation of metabolic fuels used in muscular activity is approximately 30%. Since overweight and normal individuals have the same efficiency for metabolism during exercise, this implies that the processes for generation of adenosine triphosphate (ATP) are similar in the two groups (Whipp, Bray, Koyal, & Wasserman, 1975).

The idea that differences in the efficiency of metabolic processes might contribute to the development of obesity has been revived by recent suggestions that the rate at which sodium is pumped across the cell membranes may be altered in obesity (Bray & York, 1979; DeLuise, Blackburn, & Flier, 1980). The activity of the sodium-pumping enzyme (sodium, potassium-dependent ATPase) is abnormal in some kinds of experimental obesity but not in others. In red cells from obese human beings, the sodium pumping enzymes are reduced or unchanged. In contrast, measurements of this activity in liver from obese human has shown its concentration to be increased. These divergent data in obese humans provide an arena in which further studies are needed.

Lipids and Obesity

There is a consistent correlation between the concentration of very low density lipoproteins (VLDL) and obesity (Vaughan et al., 1980). Moreover, it is well recognized that weight reduction is the best treatment for hypertriglyceridemia resulting from increased levels of VLDL. This increase probably reflects increased hepatic synthesis of VLDL, since peripheral removal of triglyceride is normal.

The turnover of total body cholesterol has a highly significant correlation with obesity. Garn (1982) used the data from the National Collaborative Perinatal Project to assess the effects of weight status on lipid parameters. By using z-scores for cholesterol and triglycerides, they were able to show a significant correlation between the degree of fatness and each of these variables (Figure 40.4). They were also able to confirm numerous previous

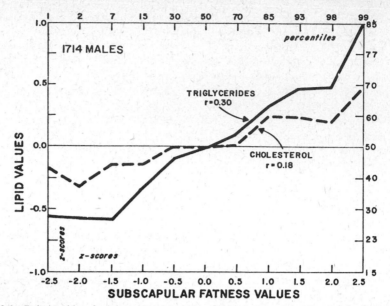

Figure 40.4 Relationship of triglyceride and cholesterol to body weight. Deviations in lipid values from the medial values are shown using z scores (left and bottom) and percentiles (right and top). Both cholesterol and triglycerides showed a positive and significant correlation with weight, but the slope and the degree of correlation for the triglycerides were greater than those for cholesterol. (Reprinted by permission from Garn, 1982.)

studies that have documented the relationships between blood pressure and body weight. For each kilogram of additional triglyceride, the body synthesizes about 20 mg of cholesterol per day. This is partly a reflection of increased dietary intake of lipids but may also result from de novo synthesis of cholesterol in the liver (Angel & Bray, 1979). The cholesterol associated with high-density lipoproteins (HDL cholesterol) is consistently reduced in obese males and females. There is a growing body of evidence to suggest that the concentration of HDL cholesterol may bear an inverse relationship to the risk of developing coronary artery disease; that is, people with high levels of HDL cholesterol are at lower risk than people with low concentrations of HDL. This may be one of the mechanisms by which obesity is associated with an increased risk of developing cardiovascular disease (Albrink, Krauss, Lindgren, Von der Groeben, Pan, & Wood, 1980).

The concentration and turnover of free fatty acids are both increased in obese subjects as a result of the enhanced basal lipolysis by large fat cells (Bray, 1982). It is the increased release of free fatty acids and glycerol from the enlarged fat cells that is responsible for the supply of free fatty acids to the liver, which may be used for the synthesis of VLDL and which enter the circulation to produce hypertriglyceridemia. The increased lipolysis of large fat cells may also provide a mechanism for limiting the size to which the fat cell grows.

The Adipocyte and Obesity

A consistent body of literature has shown that obese subjects have enlarged fat cells (Bjorntorp, 1974; Hirsch & Batchelor, 1976). Indeed, many of the metabolic changes in insulin and triglycerides appear to be related to the size of the adipocyte itself (Bjorntorp, 1974). There is a direct correlation between the size of fat cells and the basal rate of triglyceride breakdown from the storage droplet of the fat cell; that is, big fat cells have a higher rate of glycerol and free fatty acid release than small fat cells.

Many obese individuals and essentially all persons whose body weight is more than 175% above the desirable level show an increased number of fat cells (Hirsch & Batchelor, 1976). This results partly because fat cells appear to have an upper limit of size at approximately 0.7 to 0.8 μg of lipid per cell. Above that size, fat cells tend to increase in number in order to store additional fat (Knittle, Timmers, Ginsberg-Fellner, Brown, & Katz, 1979). Recent evidence in experimental animals indicates that an increase in number of fat cells can be produced at any age in certain deposits when animals overeat high-fat diets (Faust, 1980). This is not surprising if the animal must continue to store increased quantities of fat.

Two other changes in obesity may also be related to the size of the fat cells. First, there is an increased concentration of lipoprotein lipase (LPL). The regulation of LPL in fat cells from obese subjects may also be impaired. In one report, LPL remained elevated even when obese individuals lost weight, implying that the metabolic abnormality had not returned to normal (Schwartz & Brunzell, 1978).

With weight gain in normal subjects, there is a small but significant increase in plasma glucose and an easily discernible rise in the concentration of insulin (Sims, Danforth, Horton, Bray, Glennon, & Salans, 1972). Not only is there an increased basal level of insulin, but there is an increased release of insulin in response to the administration of glucose, arginine, glucagon, l-leucine, and tolbutamide (Bray, 1976). Similarly, in obese subjects there is a reduced response to the infusion of exogenous insulin, indicating the presence of insulin resistance. One mechanism for the resistance to insulin may be a reduction in the number of receptor sites on fat cells and other tissue cells (Archer, Gorden, & Roth, 1975). A second mechanism that exists in some obese people is a postreceptor disturbance whose nature has yet to be clearly defined (Kolterman, Insel, Saekow, & Olefsky, 1980). The mechanism for hyperinsulinemia in obesity is incompletely understood; either humoral or neural mechanisms may play a role. In contrast to insulin, neither the basal nor stress-induced rise in glucagon appears to be abnormal in obese individuals who are free of diabetes (Glass, Burman, Dahms, & Boehm, 1980). The third pancreatic hormone, pancreatic polypeptide, is increased after a test meal in obese individuals who have had a jejuno-ileal bypass operation and may be depressed in the Prader-Willi syndrome.

Pituitary Hormones

It has been recognized for 20 years that the release of growth hormone is impaired in obese subjects. The expected rise in growth hormones with sleep or 4 to 5 hours after a meal is blunted in obesity, as is the rise after administering arginine or levodopa or inducing hypoglycemia with insulin. This impairment is reversible after weight loss (Sims et al., 1972). Moreover, normal subjects who overeat show a reduction in their responsiveness of growth hormone release to a variety of stimuli, indicating the adaptive nature of this response (Sims et al., 1972). In contrast to growth hormone, somatomedin C, a peptide that is thought to mediate the effects of growth hormone at cellular level, is usually normal in obesity. Prolactin secretion in obese humans appears to be normal in both the basal and the stimulated state (Glass, Buvman, Dahms, & Boehm, 1981).

Thyroid Hormones

Nutrition is more important than body weight in determining the circulating concentration of thyroid (T4) hormones. Regardless of initial body weight, predictable changes in the pathways of T4 metabolism will occur if calorie or carbohydrate intake changes. Both total calories and the relative proportion of carbohydrate, protein, and fat are important parameters in the thyroidal adaptation to food.

During fasting, total thyroxine levels are normal; but during 4 weeks of fasting, serum concentration of total triiodothyronine (T3) is reduced and the concentration of reverse triiodothyronine (rT3) are increased (Portnay, O'Brien, Bush, Vagenakis, Azizi, Arky, Ingbar, & Braverman, 1974; Vagenakis, Burger, Portnay, Rudolph, O'Brien, Azizi, Arky, Nicod, Ingbar, & Braverman, 1975). Fasting also changes the responsiveness of pituitary thyrotrophs to release thyrotropin (TSH) after injection of thyrotropin-releasing hormones (TRH) (Alexander & Bray, in press, Croxson, Hall, Kletzky, Jaramillo, & Nicoloff, 1977).

In contrast to starvation, overnutrition is associated with a rise in serum T3 and a fall in rT3 values. Bray (1982) showed that T3 levels increased in both obese and lean subjects during overfeeding. Danforth, Horton, O'Connell, Sims, Burger, Ingbar, Braverman, and Vagenakis (1979) studied both short- and long-term overfeeding and found a significant increase in serum T3 concentration from 136 ng/dl prior to overfeeding to 152 ng/dl after 7 months of increased caloric intake. Short-term overfeeding also resulted in an increase in T3 levels (Danforth et al., 1979). Davidson and Chopra (1979) noted a similar increase in triiodothyronine in their subjects who were given more than 4,000 calories per day for 1 week. During overfeeding, reverse triiodothyronine levels decline in many studies, but the differences between the reverse triiodothyronine before and after overfeeding do not always attain statistical significance. During long-term overfeeding, Danforth et al. (1979) did not find any difference in rT3 levels before and after 7 months of overfeeding. Both the metabolic clearance and the production rate of radiolabeled T3 were increased during short-term overfeeding. In contrast, there were no changes in the clearance or production rates for thyroxine. In summary, changes in thyroid hormone levels in overfeeding tend to be in an opposite direction to those seen in fasting. Triiodothyronine values increase in overfeeding but decrease in fasting. Reverse T3 goes in the opposite direction, falling with overfeeding and rising with fasting. The release of TSH after injection of TRH falls in fasting subjects but has differing responses in lean and obese subjects who are overfed. Metabolic clearance for both T3 and T4 are higher in overfed subjects, whether they are lean or obese.

The Adrenal Gland

In obese subjects at their usual weight, the plasma level of cortisol and the urinary concentration of free cortisol are normal (Glass et al., 1981). The circadian rhythm of cortisol (high in the morning and low in the evening) in plasma or urine is normal. The adrenal secretion of cortisol, however, and the excretion of urinary metabolites of cortisol are significantly increased. The release of adrenocorticotropic hormone (ACTH) from the pituitary after hypoglycemia is induced with insulin, and the rise in plasma or urinary 11-deoxycorticosteroids after administration of metyrapone, a drug that blocks 11-β-hydroxylase, appear to be normal whether they are measured as changes in plasma concentrations of the appropriate steroid or as urinary concentrations of these substances (Bray, 1982).

The Testis and Obesity

There is a consistent reduction in the concentration of total serum testosterone in obesity (Glass et al., 1981). This is probably the result of a reduction in the concentration of sex hormone binding globulin (SHBG), which transports testosterone in the serum. The mechanism for the reduction in SHBG is presently unknown. The concentration of free testosterone remains essentially normal, suggesting that the pituitary gonadal dynamics are intact. Testicular size and the basal concentration of the pituitary gonadotropins follicle-stimulating hormone (FSH) and luteinizing hormone (LH) are normal. Similarly, the pituitary release of LH and FSH in response to an injection of luteinizing hormone-releasing hormone (LHRH) is normal, as is the concentration of these pituitary peptides during treatment with clomiphene. Some reports indicate that there is an increase in the correlating concentration of estrone and estradiol in males. This may be related to the reduction in the concentration of SHBG and the circulating level of total testosterone.

The Ovary and Obesity

In contrast to the normal anatomy of the testis in obese males, the ovary in obese women shows an increase in hyalinization and an increased frequency of atretic follicles (Glass et al., 1981). In obese women, there is a reduction in the concentration of SHBG just as there is for males. The turnover of androstenedione, with the formation of estrone in peripheral tissues, is related to the degree of obesity. Similarly, secretion of the adrenal androgen dehydroepiandrosterone (DHEA) and its metabolism to and excretion as urinary-17-ketosteroid (17-KS) are increased in many obese women. The basal concentrations of LH and FSH, however, are normal in obese women. The response of these circulating pituitary gonadotropins to the administration of LHRH is also normal. In contrast to the increased secretion of adrenal androgens and enhanced conversion of androstenedione to estrone in fibroblasts from adipose tissue of obese subjects, the turnover of estradiol in obese women appears to be reduced. These defects might enhance the risk of developing endometrial cancer and might reduce fertility.

Miscellaneous Hormones

Gastrin, a peptide that stimulates hydrogen release by the stomach, is normal in obese subjects. (Glass et al., 1981) Gastric inhibitory polypeptide of GIP (also called glucose insulin polypeptide) is known to stimulate the release of insulin. Release of this hormone in response to an oral glucose load appears to be normal in obese subjects. Endorphin and lipotropin, two components of the larger proopiomelanocortin molecule present in the anterior pituitary have been measured and are increased in obesity. Vasopressin, a posterior pituitary hormone, however, is normal. The renal hormone renin is also normal. The concentrations of parathyroid hormone may be significantly increased and are reduced following intestinal bypass surgery (Atkinson, Dahms, Bray, & Schwartz, 1979).

This brief review of metabolic and hormonal changes in obesity indicates a wide-ranging series of alterations (Glass et al., 1981, Vaughan et al., 1980). Some of these alterations, such as hyperinsulinemia, impaired growth hormone response, reduction in sex hormone binding globulin, and enhanced conversion of androstenedione to estrone by adipose tissue, are reversed with weight loss. Other alterations, however, specifically those associated with an increased number of adipocytes, such as lipoprotein lipase, overall metabolism, the function of brown adipose tissue, and the function of the adrenal or thyroid system, may not be improved by weight loss.

SOCIAL DISADVANTAGES OF OBESITY

Social Attitudes toward the Obese

Obesity carries a social stigma (Allon, 1975; Cahnman, 1968). This was clearly shown by studies with children and adults who were asked to express a preference for various forms of disability, including obesity (Richardson, Hastorf, Goodman, & Dornbusch, 1961). These children and adults were shown six pictures, including (a) a child with no disability; (b) a child with crutches and a brace on his left leg; (c) a child in a wheelchair with a blanket over his legs; (d) a child with a left hand missing; (e) a child who is disfigured around the left side of the mouth; and (f) an obese child. The sex of the child in the drawings corresponded with that of the person being shown the pictures. In the first study, groups of boys and girls aged 10 to 11 from New York City, from a school in Montana, and from Northern California were asked to rate the pictures by selecting the child they would find most easy to like. The chosen picture was removed and the subjects were then asked to select the child they would find next most easy to like, until all six pictures had been rated. The order of the rating was the same for all groups of children, regardless of sex, socioeconomic status, racial background, and whether they came from rural or urban communities. In all cases, the obese child was liked least. The numbers of children used in the original study by Richardson et al. (1961) was such as to leave little doubt about the social stigma attached to being an obese child. In an extension of this study, Goodman, Richardson, Dornbusch, & Hastorf (1963) showed that a group of adults, including physical therapists, occupational therapists, nurses, physicians, and social workers, gave an identical rating to the same six pictures as had the children from rural and urban United States. Maddox, Back, and Liederman (1968) provided confirmation of this data. They used the same group of pictures with patients from an outpatient clinic. The clinic population as a whole gave almost the same rank-order to the six pictures as had the children and adults. Disabled adults and children did not like the obese child. These authors were surprised by the observation that black females, who often value obesity, rated the obese child as fourth from the top—not much improvement. When asked why the obese child was ranked at the bottom, many indicated that the other disabled children were the unfortunate victims of the environment. By implication, the obese child was frequently thought to be responsible for his plight. In addition, many obese patients disliked the drawing of the obese child because it reminded them of themselves.

The potential disadvantages of obesity have also been emphasized in studies on social mobility and dating behavior. Elder (1969) indicated that physical appearance was the most important factor for women in attracting upwardly mobile men for marriage. Physical attractiveness was again the single most important factor in dating behavior among college-age students (Walster, Aronson, Abrahams, & Rottmann, 1966). Because of the importance of attitudes about physical attractiveness in our society and the relatively unattractive view of obesity by many children and adults, it is easy to understand the relative social positions and feelings of many obese individuals. This has been emphasized by Monello and Mayer (1963) in a study of the attitudes of obese adolescent girls. They observed that these girls showed excessive concern with status, acceptance of dominant values in the culture, and passivity, with a tendency toward withdrawal. These authors noted that all of these reactions are characteristics of minority groups, and they suggested that the obese adolescent girls may behave as a minority group in their responses toward the dominant culture.

Obesity as a social disability has been examined further by Maddox and his collaborators (Maddox, Anderson, & Bogdonoff, 1966; Maddox & Liederman, 1969). In a study in the outpatient clinic at Duke University, the concordance between entries in the physician's chart concerning overweight and the actual degrees of overweight in the sample were compared. There was only about one chance in four that a patient who was more than 20% overweight would encounter a physician who would note in the medical record that the patient's body weight was significantly increased and who would also propose a program for management of this problem. The average weight of those who received no mention was 193 pounds; the average weight of those whose weight was mentioned in the chart but for whom no proposal for management was made was 202 pounds. Those patients for whom a program of management was suggested weighed, on average, 212 pounds. An elevation in blood pressure or the presence of hypertension or coronary artery disease made it more likely that the weight problem would be noted and that a proposal for action would be initiated. To explore the problem further, Maddox and Liederman (1969) submitted a questionnaire to 197 senior physicians, house officers, and medical student clerks who were working in an outpatient clinic. Only 51% of the questionnaires were returned. Among the responding physicians, 93% said that their major source of knowledge about obesity was from personal experience; 66% indicated that personal research had contributed to their understanding of obesity; 50% had learned about obesity in medical conferences; and a bare 22% stated that their sources of information included medical school lectures. More than half of the physicians admitted that they were usually unsuccessful in treating obesity, but 40% indicated that careful management was the preferred approach, despite its relatively low success rate. Nevertheless, less than half of the physicians actually made proposals for treatment of patients who were more than 20% overweight, indicating that the physicians' awareness had not been activated by this degree of overweight. A number of personal characteristics were assessed by severely obese persons and by the physicians. There were sharp differences in the overall assessment. In general, *active, strong, successful,* and *fast* were descriptive adjectives applied by physicians to only 3% to 14% of the severely overweight persons. In contrast, self-description by overweight persons used these adjectives from 31% to 45% of the time. Thus, overweight individuals tended to assess themselves more positively than did the physicians caring for them. Moreover, there was a strong negative reaction to the obese patient on the part of many physicians. The intense negative judgment of obese patients was characterized by descriptions of their weakness and unattractive features. The overweight patients were frequently described as awkward and weak-willed. These negative value judgments on the part of medical professionals working in an outpatient clinic are similar to those of the professionals working with disabled children who assessed likable characteristics of the disabled individuals.

Educational Disadvantages of Obesity

The low value with which the obese are viewed in the eyes of many might prejudice their educational opportunities. This has been suggested by Canning and Mayer (1966, 1967), who assessed obesity by measuring the thickness of the triceps of skin fold. Among the high school students studied were 81 obese males and 96 obese females. Obesity and intelligence were not correlated. The mean IQs for the group of obese and nonobese students ranged between 112 and 114. The college Scholastic Aptitude Test (SAT) scores were also similar for both groups. There were significantly fewer obese males in the top third of the high school class, however, than there were lean males (21% versus 26%, $p < .01$). Suggestive differences were also present for females, but they were not statistically significant (41% versus 32% for nonobese versus obese). Finally, the mean range of high school marks was lower for the obese than for the nonobese, but this was also not statistically significant. In this study, there were no differences in school attendance records or in plans for jobs and education following graduation from high school. Yet when Canning and Mayer (1966) examined the frequency of obese and nonobese individuals in Ivy League colleges, they found a significantly lower number of obese females than of nonobese females. These data suggested that there might be a prejudicial admission policy toward obese high school students. These authors noted that the obese and nonobese students were equally interested in attending high-ranking colleges and that evaluation of their capacities by objective data such as high school standing and intelligence quotient showed no significant differences. Louderback (1970) has explored this question more thoroughly in the book *Fat Power*. In it, he suggests the need for more tolerance toward the obese members of our society (Allon 1975).

Obesity and Employment

In a survey of opinion in Southern California, television station KNXT found that nearly two-thirds of the 500 respondents believed that employers were reluctant to hire fat people. Documentation of this, is difficult to obtain, however (Henschel, 1967). One study suggests that fat bosses get lower salaries than their lean counterparts (Roe & Eickwort, Note 2). This study was conducted among 15,000 men who were known to an employment agency. Among the men who were more than 10% overweight, only 9% were earning $25,000 to $40,000 per year. Of the men earning between $10,000 and $20,000 per year, however, 40% were more than 10% overweight. This employment agency had had only one job request for an obese man, and that was to fill a job as an executive for a clothing company that made clothes for overweight men. In this study on obesity and unemployment, Roe and Eickwort (Note 2) observed that unemployment was associated with obesity mainly through the presence of such defects as arthritis, varicose veins, diabetes, hypertension, and a history of gallbladder disease.

Further observations on the economic difficulties associated with overweight have appeared in newspaper articles. A federal judge recently ordered a major airline to pay back salary and interest to stewardesses who were dismissed because of overweight. This ended the dismissal of stewardesses because they did not meet weight limits. In another case, a candidate scoring near the top in her civil service examination was fired for being 50 pounds overweight. This patent discrimination in employment practices is being ended by action in the federal courts, but these instances illustrate the significant economic and social hurdles that the obese must overcome in American society today.

CONCLUDING REMARKS

The focus of this chapter has been on the role of weight control in promoting good health. Several types of evidence have been marshaled to show that excess weight is detrimental to longevity, to health while living, and to some social interactions. Equally important, most of these detrimental effects can be reversed by weight reduction. In conclusion, the motto of this chapter might appropriately be: "Overweight is risking fate."

REFERENCE NOTES

1. Keen, H. *Obesity and diabetes.* Paper presented at the First International Congress of Obesity, London, 1974.
2. Roe, D., & Eickwort, J. L. Unpublished data.

REFERENCES

Abraham, S., Collins, G., & Nordsieck, M. Relationship of childhood weight status to morbidity in adults. *HSMHA Health Reports,* 1971, **86,**273–384.

Adlersberg, D., Coler, H. R., & Laval, J. Effect of weight reduction on course of arterial hypertension. *Journal of Mt. Sinai Hospital, New York,* 1946, **12,** 984–992.

Albrink, M. J., Krauss, R. M., Lindgren, F. F., von der Groeben, J., Pan, S., & Wood, P. D. Intercorrelations among plasma high density lipoprotein, obesity and triglycerides in a normal population. *Lipids,* 1980, **15,** 668–676.

Alexander, C., & Bray, G. A. *Thyroid and obesity.* In S. H. Ingbar & L. Braverman (Eds.), *The Thyroid.* New York: Hoeber, 1983.

Alexander, J. K., Amad, K. H., & Cole, V. W. Chapter, In G. A. Bray (Ed.), *Obesity in perspective.* Fogarty International Center Series on Preventive Medicine, Vol. 2, Parts 1 and 2. DHEW Pub. No. (NIH) 75–708. Washington, D.C.: U.S. Government Printing Office, 1976.

Alexander, J. K., & Peterson, K. L. Cardiovascular effects of weight reduction. *Circulation,* 1972, **45,** 310–318.

Allon, N. The stigma of overweight in everyday life. In G. A. Bray (Ed.), *Obesity in perspective.* Fogarty International Center Series on Preventive Medicine, Vol. 2, Parts 1 and 2. DHEW Pub. No. (NIH) 75–708. Washington, D.C.: U.S. Government Printing Office, 1975.

Andres, R. Effect of obesity on total mortality. *International Journal of Obesity,* 1980, **4,** 381–386.

Angel, A., & Bray, G. A. Synthesis of fatty acids and cholesterol by liver, adipose tissue and intestinal mucosa from obese and control patients. *European Journal of Clinical Investigation,* 1979, **9,** 355–362.

Archer, J. A., Gorden, P., & Roth, J. Defect in insulin binding to receptors in obese man: Amelioration with calorie restriction. *Journal of Clinical Investigation,* 1975, **55,** 166–174.

Atkinson, R. L., Dahms, W. T., Bray, G. A., & Schwartz, A. Parathyroid hormone levels in obesity: Effects of intestinal bypass surgery. *Mineral and Electrolyte Metabolism,* 1978, **1,** 315–320.

Azizi, F. Effect of dietary composition on fasting induced changes in serum thyroid hormones and thyrotropin. *Metabolism,* 1978, **27,** 935–942.

Bjorntorp, P. Effects of age, sex and clinical conditions on adipose tissue cellularity in man. *Metabolism,* 1974, **23,** 1091–1102.

Bray, G. A. *The obese patient.* Major Problems in Internal Medicine, Vol. 9. Philadelphia: Saunders, 1976.

Bray, G. A. Obesity. In *Current Concepts, A Scope Publication.* Kalamazoo: The UpJohn Co., 1982.

Bray, G. A. The energetics of obesity. *Medicine and Science in Sports and Exercise,* 1983, **15,** 32–40.

Bray, G. A., & York, D. A. Hypothalamic and genetic obesity in experimental animals: An autonomic and endocrine hypothesis. *Physiological Reviews,* 1979, **59**(7), 719–809.

Brown, J., & Winkelman, R. K. Acanthosis nigricans: A study of 90 cases. *Medicine,* 1968, **47,** 33–51.

Burwell, C. S., Robin, E. D., Whaley, R. D., & Bickelman, A. G. Extreme obesity associated with alveolar hypoventilation: A Pickwickian syndrome. *American Journal of Medicine,* 1956, **21,** 811–818.

Cahnman, W. J. The stigma of obesity. *Sociological Quarterly,* 1968, **9,** 283–299.

Canning, H., & Mayer, J. Obesity: Its possible effect on college acceptance. *New England Journal of Medicine,* 1966,**275,** 1172–1174.

Canning, H., & Mayer, J. Obesity: An influence on high school performance. *American Journal of Clinical Nutrition,* 1967, **20,** 352–354.

Chapman, J. M., Coulson, A. H., Clark, V. A., & Borun, E. R. The differential effect of serum cholesterol blood pressure and weight on the incidence of myocardial infarction and angina pectoris. *Journal of Chronic Diseases,* 1971, **23,** 631–647.

Chiang, B. N., Perlman, L. V., & Epstein, F. H. Overweight and hypertension: A review. *Circulation,* 1969, **39,** 403–421.

Croxson, M. S., Hall, T. D., Kletzky, D. A., Jaramillo, J. E., & Nicoloff, J. T. Decreased serum thyrotropin induced by fasting. *Journal of Clinical Endocrinology and Metabolism,* 1977, **45,** 560–568.

Daniels, R. J., Katzeff, H. L., Ravussin, E., Garrow, J. S., & Danforth, E., Jr. Obesity in the Pima Indians: Is there a thrifty gene? *American Journal of Clinical Nutrition,* 1982, **35,** 835. (Abstract)

Danforth, E., Horton, E. S., O'Connell, M., Sims, E. A. H., Burger, A. G., Ingbar, S. H., Braverman, L., & Vagenakis, A. G. Dietary-induced alterations in thyroid hormone metabolism during overnutrition. *Journal of Clinical Investigation,* 1979, **64,** 1336–1347.

Davidson, M. B., & Chopra, I. J. Effect of carbohydrate and noncarbohydrate sources on plasma 3,5,3′ triiodothyroninine concentrations in man. *Journal of Clinical Endocrinology and Metabolism,* 1979, **48,** 577–581.

DeLusie, M., Blackburn, G. L., & Flier, J. S. Reduced activity of the red-cell sodium potassium pump in human obesity. *New England Journal of Medicine,* 1980, **303,** 1017–1022.

Douglas, F. G., & Chang, P. Y. Influence of obesity on peripheral airways patency. *Journal of Applied Physiology,* 1972, **33,** 559–563.

Drenick, E. J., Gurunanjappa, S. B., Seltzer, F. S. A., & Johnson, D. G. Excessive mortality and causes of death in morbidly obese men. *Journal of the American Medical Association,* 1980, **243,** 443–445.

Elder, G. H., Jr. Appearance and education in marriage mobility. *American Sociological Review,* 1969, **34,** 519–533.

Fletcher, A. P. Effect of weight reduction upon blood pressure of obese hypertensive women. *Quarterly Journal of Medicine,* 1954, **23,** 331–345.

Ganor, S., & Even-Paz, Z. Fragilitas cutis inguinalis: A phenomenon associated with obesity. *Dermatologic ,* 1967, **134,** 113–124.

Garn, S. M. Some consequences of being obese. In M. R. C. Greenwald (Ed.), *Health and obesity.* New York: Raven Press, 1982.

Garrow, J. S. *Energy balance and obesity in man* (2nd ed.). Amsterdam: Elsevier North Holland Biomedical Press, 1978.

Glass, A. R., Burman, K. D., Dahms, W. T., & Boehm, T. M. Endocrine function in human obesity. *Metabolism,* 1981, **30,** 89–103.

Glick, Z., Teague, R. J., & Bray, G. A. Brown adipose tissue: Thermic response increased by a single low protein meal. *Science*, 1981, **213**, 1125–1127.

Goodman, N., Richardson, S. A., Dornbusch, S. M., & Hastorf, A. H. Variant reactions to physical disabilities. *American Sociological Review*, 1963, **28**, 429–435.

Gordon, T., & Kannel, W. B. The effects of overweight on cardiovascular diseases. *Geriatrics*, 1973, **28**, 80–88.

Grundy, A. M., Mok, H. Y. I., Zech, L., Steinberg, D., & Berman, M. Transport of very low density lipoprotein triglycerides in varying degrees of obesity and hypertriglyceridemia. *Journal of Clinical Investigation*, 1979, **63**, 1274–1283.

Henschel, A. Obesity as an occupational hazard. *Canadian Journal of Public Health*, 1967, **58**, 491–493.

Heyden, S., Walker, L., & Hames, C. G. Decrease of serum cholesterol level and blood pressure in the community. Seven to nine years of observation in the Evans County Study. *Archives of Internal Medicine*, 1971, **128**, 982–986.

Hirsch, J., & Batchelor, B. Adipose tissue cellularity in human obesity. *Journal of Clinical Endocrinology and Metabolism*, 1976, **5**, 299–311.

Hundley, J. M. Diabetes: Overweight; U.S. problems. *Journal of the American Dietetic Association*, 1956, **32**, 417–422.

James, W. P. T., Bailes, J., Davies, H. L., & Dauncey, M. J. Elevated metabolic rates in obesity. *Lancet*, 1978, **1**, 1122–1125.

Jung, R. T., Shetty, P. S., & James, W. P. T. Reduced thermogenesis in obesity. *Nature*, 1979, **279**, 322–323.

Kannel, W. B., & Gordon, T. Physiological and medical concomitants of obesity: The Framingham Study. In G. A. Bray (Ed.), *Obesity in America*. DHEW Pub. No. (NIH) 79–359. Washington, D.C.: U.S. Government Printing Office, 1979, pp. 125–153.

Keys, A. (Ed.). Coronary heart disease in seven countries. *Circulation* 1970, **41**(Suppl), 1–53.

Keys, A. Overweight and the risk of heart attack and sudden death. In G. A. Bray (Ed.), *Obesity in perspective*. Fogarty International Center Series on Preventive Medicine, Vol. 2, Parts 1 and 2. DHEW Pub. No. (NIH) 75–708. Washington, D.C.: U.S. Government Printing Office, 1975.

Keys, A. Overweight, obesity, coronary heart disease and mortality. *Nutrition Reviews*, 1980, **38**, 297–307. (a)

Keys, A. *Seven countries: A multivariate analysis of death and coronary heart disease*. Cambridge, Mass.: Harvard University Press, 1980. (b)

Keys, A., Aravanis, C., Blackburn, H., Van Buchem, F. S. P., Buzina, R., Djordjevic, B. S., Fidanza, F., Karvonen, M. J., Menotti, A., Puddu, V., & Taylor, H. J. Coronary heart disease: Overweight and obesity as risk factors. *Annals of Internal Medicine*, 1972, **77**, 15–27.

King, G. E. Errors in clinical measurement of blood pressure in obesity. *Clinical Science*, 1967, **32**, 223–237.

Knittle, J. L., Timmers, K., Ginsberg-Fellner, F., Brown, R. E., & Katz, D. D. The growth of adipose tissue in children and adolescents: Cross-sectional and longitudinal studies of adipose cell number and size. *Journal of Clinical Investigation*, 1979, **63**, 239–246.

Kolterman, O. G., Insel, J., Saekow, M., & Olefsky, J. M. Mechanisms of insulin resistance in human obesity: Evidence for receptor and postreceptor defects. *Journal of Clinical Investigation*, 1980, **65**, 1272–1284.

Larsson, B. Bjorntorp, P., & Tibblin, G. The health consequences of moderate obesity. *International Journal of Obesity*, 1981, **5**, 97–116.

Louderback, L. *Fat power: Whatever you weigh is right*. New York: Hawthorn Books, 1970.

Lourenco, R. V. Diaphragm activity in obesity. *Journal of Clinical Investigation*, 1969, **48**, 1609–1614.

Luce, J. M. Respiratory complications of obesity. *Chest*, 1980, **78**, 626–631.

Maddox, G. L., Anderson, C. F., & Bogdonoff, M. D. Overweight as a problem of medical management in a public outpatient clinic. *American Journal of Medical Science*, 1966, **252**, 394–402.

Maddox, G. L., Back, K. W., & Liederman, V. R. Overweight as social deviance and disability. *Journal of Health and Social Behavior*, 1968, **9**, 287–298.

Maddox, G. L., & Liederman, V. Overweight as a social disability with medical implications. *Journal of Medical Education,* 1969, **44,** 214–220.

Mann, G. V. Obesity, the nutritional spook. *American Journal of Public Health,* 1974, **61,** 1491–1498.

Marks, H. H. Influence of obesity in morbidity and mortality. *Bulletin of the New York Academy of Science,* 1960, **36,** 296–312.

Martin, L. Effect of weight reduction on normal and raised blood pressures in obesity. *Lancet,* 1952, **2,** 1051–1053.

Maxwell, M. H. Waks, A. U., Schroth, P. C., Karam, M., & Dornfeld, L. P. Error in blood pressure due to incorrect cuff size in obese patients. *Lancet,* 1982, **2,** 33–36.

McKeown, T., & Record, R. G. The influence of body weight on reproductive function in women. *Journal of Endocrinology,* 1957, **15,** 410–422.

Monello, L. F., & Mayer, J. Obese adolescent girls: Unrecognized minority group. *American Journal of Clinical Nutrition,* 1963, **13,** 35–38.

Peckham, C. H., & Christianson, R. E. The relationship between prepregnancy weight and certain obstetric factors. *American Journal of Obstetrics and Gynecology,* 1971, **111,** 1–7.

Portnay, G. I., O'Brien, J. T., Bush, J., Vagenakis, A. G., Azizi, F., Arky, R. A., Ingbar, S. H., & Braverman, L. E. The effect of starvation on the concentration and binding of thyroxine and triiodothyronine in serum and on response to TRH. *Journal of Clinical Endocrinology and Metabolism,* 1974, **39,** 191–194.

Prem, K. A. Mensheha, N. M., & McKelvey, J. L. Operative treatment of adenocarcinoma of the endometrium in obese women. *American Journal of Obstetrics and Gynecology,* 1965, **92,** 16–21.

Reisin, E., Abel, R., Modan, M., Silverberg, D., Eliahou, H. E., & Modan, B. Effect of weight loss without salt restriction on the reduction of blood pressure in overweight hypertensive patients. *New England Journal of Medicine,* 1978, **298,** 1–6.

Richardson, S. A., Hastorf, A. H., Goodman, N., & Dornbusch, S. M. Cultural uniformity in reaction to physical disabilities. *American Sociological Review,* 1961, **26,** 241–247.

Rimm, A. A., & White, P. L. Obesity: Its risks and hazards. In G. A. Bray (Ed.), *Obesity in America.* DHEW Pub. No. (NIH) 79–359. Washington, D.C.: U.S. Government Printing Office, 1979.

Robinson, S. C., & Brucer, M. Hypertension: Body build and obesity. *American Journal of Medical Science,* 1940, **199,** 819–829.

Rochester, D. F., & Enson, Y. Current concepts in the pathogenesis of the obesity-hypoventilation syndrome: Mechanical and circulatory factors. *American Journal of Medicine,* 1974, **57,** 402–420.

Schwartz, R. S., & Brunzell, J. D. Increased adipose-tissue lipoprotein-lipase activity in moderately obese men after weight reduction. *Lancet,* 1978, **1,** 1230–1231.

Seltzer, C. C. Some reevaluations of the build and blood pressure study, 1959, as related to ponderal index, somatotype and mortality. *New England Journal of Medicine,* 1966, **274,** 254–259.

Sims, E. A. H., Danforth, E., Jr., Horton, E. S., Bray, G. A., Glennon, J. A., & Salans, L. B. Endocrine and metabolic effects of experimental obesity in *Recent Progress in Hormone Research,* 1972, **29,** 457–487.

Society of Actuaries. Build and blood pressure study, 1979. Chicago: Society of Actuaries, 1979.

Stamler, J., Farinaro, E., Mojonnier, L. M., Hall, Y., Moss, D., & Stamler, R. Prevention and control of hypertension by nutritional-hygienic means. *Journal of the American Medical Association,* 1980, **243,** 1819–1823.

Sturdevant, R. A. L., Pearce, M. L., & Dayton, S. Increased prevalence of cholelithiasis in men ingesting a serum cholesterol lowering diet. *New England Journal of Medicine,* 1973, **288,** 24–27.

Tuck, M. L., Sowers, J., Dornfeld, L., Kledzik, G., & Maxwell, M. The effect of weight reduction on blood pressure, plasma renin activity, and plasma aldosterone levels in obese patients. *New England Journal of Medicine,* 1981, **304,** 930–933.

Vagenakis, A. G., Burger, A., Portnay, G. I., Rudolph, M., O'Brien, J. T., Azizi, F., Arky, R. A., Nicod, P., Ingbar, S. H., & Braverman, L. E. Diversion of peripheral thyroxine metabolism from activating to inactivating pathways during complete fasting. *Journal of Clinical Endocrinology and Metabolism,* 1975, **41,** 191–194.

Vaughan, R. W., Bauer, S., & Wise, L. Effect of position (semi-recumbent versus supine) on post-operative oxygenation in markedly obese subjects. *Anesthesia and Analgesia,* 1976, **55,** 37–41.

Vaughan, R. W., & Conahan, T. J., III. Minireview: Part I. Cardiopulmonary consequences of morbid obesity. *Life Sciences,* 1980, **26,** 2119–2127.

Vaughan, R. W., Gandolfi, A. J., & Bentley, J. B. Minireview: Part II. Biochemical considerations of morbid obesity. *Life Sciences,* 1980, **26,** 2215–2221.

Walster, E., Aronson, V., Abrahams, D., & Rottmann, L. Importance of physical attractiveness in dating behavior. *Journal of Personality and Social Psychology,* 1966, **4,** 508–516.

Weisinger, J. R., Kempson, R. L., Eldridge, F. L., & Swenson, R. S. The nephrotic syndrome: A complication of massive obesity. *Annals of Internal Medicine,* 1974, **81,** 440–447.

Whipp, B. J., Bray, G. A., Koyal, S. N., & Wasserman, K. Exercise energetics and respiratory control in man following acute and chronic elevation of caloric intake. In G. A. Bray (Ed.), *Obesity in perspective.* Fogarty International Center Series on Preventive Medicine, Vol. 2, Parts 1 and 2. DHEW Pub. No. (NIH) 75–708. Washington, D.C.: U.S. Government Printing Office, 1975.

Wilens, S. L. Bearing of general nutritional state on atherosclerosis. *Archives of Internal Medicine,* 1947, **79,** 129–147.

Young, J. B., & Landsberg, L. Impaired suppression of sympathetic activity during fasting in the gold-thioglucose-treated mouse. *Journal of Clinical Investigation,* 1980, **65,** 1086–1094.

Zwillich, C. W., Sutton, F. D., Pierson, D. J., Creagh, E. M., & Weil, J. V. Decreased hypoxic ventilatory drive in the obesity hypoventilation syndrome. *American Journal of Medicine,* 1975, **59,** 343–348.

CHAPTER 41

WEIGHT CONTROL TREATMENTS

G. TERENCE WILSON

Rutgers University

OBESITY, DISEASE, AND IMPROVED HEALTH

Obesity is a widespread condition in the United States, with estimates of prevalence ranging from 15% to 50% (Bray, 1976). Prevalence is inversely related to socioeconomic status, and it increases with age (Stunkard, 1975). These prevalence rates are disturbing, because obesity entails serious medical and psychological consequences. Studies have clearly shown relationships between obesity and hypertension, hyperlipidemia, diabetes, pulmonary and renal problems, osteoarthritis, and recovery from surgery (Bray, 1976; Van Itallie, 1979).

The most commonly used norms for determining ideal body weight are from the Build and Blood Pressure Study of 1959 (Metropolitan Life, 1960). These norms provide a range of ideal weights rated by sex, height, and body frame. The data from this study were widely interpreted as establishing a positive relationship between increasing weight and mortality. Subsequent epidemiologic studies have produced conflicting findings, however, and whether obesity increases risk for cardiovascular disease is currently a subject of some controversy. Keys (1979) conducted a prospective study of coronary heart disease in seven countries and found that both gross obesity and marked leanness were related to increased risk. There was no relationship between body weight and heart disease for all other weight categories. Data from the Framingham Study indicate that the lowest mortality is at the average rather than the ideal weight, although that risk increases with increases in body weight (Kannel & Gordon, 1979). Lew and Garfinkel (1979) investigated the association between weight and mortality in 750,000 men and women as part of the American Cancer Society Study from 1959 to 1972. They found that the lowest mortality was shown in people who were roughly 10% to 20% below average weight. Mortality increased 50% in people who were 30% to 40% above average weight, and 90% in those who were 50% above average weight. Coronary heart disease was the main contributor to mortality, but rates of cancer were higher for those who were 40% or more above average weight. Andres (1980), however, reanalyzed the data from several of the major epidemiologic studies and reported no clear relationship between weight and mortality for people who were less than 30% overweight.

To summarize the evidence, severely overweight people are clearly at greater risk for disease than their normal-weight counterparts, and weight reduction is a priority for improved health. This increased threat to health has not been established for individuals who are 10% to 30% overweight. Nevertheless, as Brownell (1982b) points out, even if these moderately overweight people are not at greater risk relative to thin people, they may still be part of the population at high risk for chronic disease related to lifestyle. Since weight loss can result in lowered blood pressure, reduced cholesterol, and increased physical activity that has its own health benefits, these mildly to moderately overweight people may be able to influence their individual risk factors. Significantly, as noted later in this chapter, it is this group that seems most successful in achieving weight loss.

The psychological and social consequences of obesity may be as important as its physical hazards. Society seems biased against overweight people, and obese children, adolescents, and adults all suffer the secondary social sequelae of the condition, such as rejection, isolation, and job discrimination. Obese people not only are stigmatized by society, but also are blamed for their physical condition. They are commonly viewed as lazy, lacking willpower, and gluttonous. Yet the obese do not seem to eat more than their leaner counterparts, and the causes of obesity remain to be identified. It is not surprising that many obese individuals experience depression and loss of self-esteem and become preoccupied with weight in a manner that is damaging to their emotional well-being. Despite the health benefits of weight loss, the women who consistently comprise the majority of participants in weight reduction programs are motivated primarily by cosmetic reasons. They want to look better. In their study of people who joined Weight Watchers in North America, Stuart and Jacobson (1979) found:

> 85% of the men and 91% of the women saw improved appearance as an objective . . . while 48% of the men and only 20% of the women were primarily motivated to lose weight by the goal of achieving better health. Clearly, then, the desire to meet social rather than health challenges is differentially reflected in the structure of decisions reached by men and women. (p. 249)

Psychosocial benefits that may indirectly help to promote improved personal health usually accompany successful weight loss. The well-being of those obese individuals who fail to lose weight, however, despite repeated struggles, will be helped only to the extent that society and the professionals who treat them adopt a more informed and humane view of this refractory condition (Wooley, Wooley, & Dyrenforth, 1979).

METHODS FOR WEIGHT CONTROL

The most extensively studied and widely used psychological methods for weight control are those that fall under the broad rubric of behavior therapy. Accordingly, this chapter focuses predominantly on the description and evaluation of behavioral procedures. Alternative methods, including psychotherapy, self-help groups, and pharmacotherapy, are referred to only briefly in comparison with the effects of behavioral programs.

Behavioral Principles and Procedures

Behavioral treatment departs fundamentally from alternative forms of treatment, such as traditional psychotherapy, special diets, drugs, or surgery, in that the goal is to alter the person's eating and activity habits. The emphasis is on changing behavior in order to restrict caloric consumption and increase caloric expenditure through physical exercise, thereby producing a negative energy balance and consequent weight loss. The emphasis has been on gradual weight loss (1 to 2 pounds per week), on the assumption that this reduces the likelihood of increased hunger and enables the person to integrate behavioral changes into his or her lifestyle without undue disruption. Beginning in the late 1960s, behavioral treatment for weight control was originally based on the assumption that obesity is a learned habit disorder that is the direct function of overeating. Corollary beliefs were that there are important differences in the eating style of obese and nonobese persons and that training an obese person to behave like an nonobese one would result in weight loss. Subsequent research has shown that the early behavioral assumptions about obesity were largely unfounded or incomplete. Today there is greater recognition that, aside from the person's individual social learning history, various genetic, metabolic, and physiological factors also influence weight control. Nevertheless, although the etiology and regulation of obesity are more complex than originally envisaged, behavioral methods can still be recommended as the preferred form of treatment for mild and moderate cases of obesity (Wilson & Brownell, 1980).

Restricting Caloric Intake

The core of most behavioral treatments, derived from Stuart and Davis's (1972) program, consists of four main elements: self-monitoring and goal setting; stimulus control for restricting the external cues that set the occasion for eating; changing the topography of eating patterns; and reinforcement of this altered behavior. Record keeping, or self-monitoring of specific behavior, thoughts, or feelings in relation to eating and exercise, is a vitally important component of a successful treatment program. Not only is self-monitoring the mainstay of behavioral assessment of obesity (Brownell, 1981), but it is also part of the behavioral change process. Self-monitoring of daily caloric intake, not merely of the occurrence of eating or its surrounding circumstances, is reactive in that it alone can result in significant weight loss. This reactivity results from people evaluating their performance against the specific goals, or consumption limits, they set for themselves. Failure to remain within the prescribed limits creates dissatisfaction, which motivates efforts to reduce subsequent intake. Some performance goals are more effective than others in increasing motivation for change. Goals that are too general, too difficult, or set too far in the future function poorly as incentives. Simple, short-term subgoals are significantly more effective in producing weight loss than more long-term goals (Bandura & Simon, 1977).

There is no direct evidence that restricting food cues or decreasing their salience, as exemplified by stimulus control procedures (e.g., eating only in one place or doing nothing else, such as reading or watching TV, while eating), actually results in weight change. Although programs based on the general principle of stimulus control have yielded success, Loro, Fisher, and Levenkron (1979) have pointed out that stimulus control has always been evaluated in conjunction with other procedures and that their own data on stimulus control as a single treatment modality indicate that it is "relatively ineffective." Similarly, the data do not reliably link modification of eating topography to weight loss. Whereas some studies have shown that changes in eating habits are related to weight loss (e.g., Ost & Gotestam, 1976), others have failed to find such a relation (Brownell, Heckerman, Westlake, Hayes, & Monti, 1978; Stalonas, Johnson, & Christ, 1978). Rosenthal and Marx (1978) found that after participation in a standard behavioral treatment program, overweight subjects did alter their eating patterns in the prescribed manner (e.g., they ate more slowly); however, both subjects who were successful and those who were unsuccessful in losing weight showed this altered eating topography to the same degree.

Several forms of reinforcement procedures have been used to modify eating habits. In contingency contracting, the therapist arranges a contract in which a specified outcome, such as a habit change or a designated amount of weight loss, is rewarded by the return to the client of portions of a refundable money deposit. Alternatively, failure to meet predetermined goals may result in the client forfeiting a sum of money to his or her most disliked organization or political group. One potential problem with contingency contracting for weight loss is that it may lead to unhealthy dietary practices. Mann (1972) obtained significant weight loss with contingency contracting but only at the cost of subjects' resorting to a variety of undesirable procedures (e.g., diuretics, vomiting, and starvation). Jeffery, Thompson, and Wing (1978), however, obtained impressive short-term weight losses without any of the negative dietary practices reported by Mann (1972), and Wing, Epstein, Marcus, and Shapira (1981) found that the prolonged use of strong monetary contracts may also facilitate maintenance of weight loss.

Broadening the Treatment Base

Contemporary behavioral programs rely on multifaceted interventions that go well beyond the aforementioned procedures. Among these strategies are cognitive and behavioral skills training for coping with interpersonal situations and emotional states that often trigger eating; cognitive self-control methods; a focus on the interpersonal context of the problem; and increased emphasis on physical activity. Social skills training may assist obese individuals in coping constructively with interpersonal situations that trigger inappropriate eating. Social skills training has been useful with diverse patient populations, including alcoholics (Chaney, O'Leary, & Marlatt, 1978). Many of the interpersonal difficulties faced by problem drinkers are shared by the obese. Declining a cocktail when dining at a restaurant is no different from refusing dessert. The obese person needs the assertive skills to say no without feeling guilt, shame, or rejection. If a behavioral assessment reveals that eating occurs in response to anxiety, anger, or depression, a comprehensive treatment program should include techniques to combat these feelings (e.g., Beck, Rush, Shaw, & Emery, 1979; Novaco, 1976).

Cognitive factors influence food intake, and there is reason to believe that combining cognitive with behavioral methods might enhance therapeutic efficacy. Dunkel and Glaros (1978) demonstrated that the addition of self-instructional training to the standard behavioral program significantly improved the short-term outcome. In self-instructional training (Meichenbaum, 1977), clients are taught to identify negative thoughts (e.g., "I really *need* to eat something"); to dispute such thoughts and replace them with more constructive alternatives that stress personal adequacy and counteract worry over failure (e.g., "I *want* to eat now, but I really don't *need* to; I can cope with this situation"); and to praise themselves for successful self-control. Rodin's (Note 1) results from a multifaceted treatment program that emphasized cognitive reappraisal and coping strategies such as self-instructional training are particularly promising, although some negative findings have also been reported (Wilson & Brownell, 1980).

Increasing Physical Activity

There are several reasons for emphasizing increased physical activity in attempts to control weight. Perhaps least important is the increase in energy expenditure. Possibly more significant is the potential of increased physical activity for increasing basal metabolism. The body reacts to caloric deprivation by reducing metabolic rate, an adaptation that can become permanent with repeated attempts at dieting (Wooley, et al., 1979). Some evidence suggests that this homeostatic reduction in metabolic rate may be offset by the effects of exercise. Physical exercise minimizes the amount of lean tissue involved in weight loss and has favorable effects on problems associated with obesity (e.g., high blood pressure and lipid levels), even in the absence of weight loss (Weltman, Matter, & Stamford, 1980).

The beneficial effects of exercise have been demonstrated in several studies. Harris and Hallbauer (1973) compared a behavioral program designed to change eating habits to the same program combined with exercise instructions. Weight losses for the two groups did not differ after 12 weeks of treatment, but the exercise group showed greater weight losses at 4-month follow-up. Stalonas et al. (1978) found that a structured program contributed to the maintenance of weight loss at 1-year follow-up, although the addition of exercise was no more beneficial than the addition of contingency contracting procedures. Other studies have similarly shown that exercise improved the short-term efficacy of behavioral treatments (e.g., Dahlkoeter, Callahan, & Linton, 1979). Moreover, Miller and Sims (1981) found that exercise was one of the few factors that predicted long-term maintenance of the relatively large weight losses they obtained in their residential treatment program. Compliance with instructions to increase physical activity is a major problem in treatment programs. Rather than prescribing specialized exercise programs, Brownell and Stunkard (1980) have recommended that weight reduction treatments focus on routine activities, such as walking or climbing stairs, that are more easily integrated within existing lifestyles.

Maintenance Strategies

Maintenance of the effects of any program of treatment can be ensured only to the extent that strategies explicitly designed to accomplish this objective are an integral part of the overall intervention.

Booster Sessions

Booster sessions, scheduled at various points after the end of treatment, have been the most commonly used maintenance strategy, yet the results have been largely disappointing. Booster sessions that are prearranged to occur at fixed intervals may be insufficient to ensure implementation of the self-regulatory strategies the individual acquires during therapy. According to the social learning approach, clients need to monitor problem behaviors and to reinstate self-corrective procedures at the first signs of erosion of the treatment-produced improvement. In a maintenance strategy described by Bandura and Simon (1977), clients monitored their weight and used a specific weight level as a cue to reinstate self-regulatory strategies. Stuart and Guire (1978) found that the perception of being overweight at no more than 3 pounds above goal weight was a key correlate of long-term maintenance in the Weight Watchers program. Although this correlational study precludes definitive conclusions, it is consistent with the view that successful maintenance requires constant vigilance and willingness to prevent problems by the timely reinstatement of self-regulatory procedures.

Successful maintenance of therapeutic change also involves arranging incentives that sustain the reinstatement of self-regulatory measures. Booster sessions may have periodic utility if they happen to occur at the appropriate times and serve as incentives for reinstating waning self-control activities. In other cases, prearranged booster sessions may be too little and too late to shape up deteriorating self-regulatory capacities. In these instances, sources of external support probably need to be tailored to the obese person's particular needs.

Social Support Systems

Eating and exercise are responsive to social influence, and support from family, friends, and fellow workers may help the obese person adhere to the rigors of a behavioral treatment program. This possibility has been studied in both home and work settings.

Initial studies found that including the spouses of obese individuals in behavioral programs resulted in superior weight loss. Brownell et al. (1978), for example, demonstrated that the inclusion of spouses in the standard behavioral treatment program produced significantly greater weight loss at 3- and 6-month follow-up evaluations than treatments in which spouses did not participate. In their couples training program, spouses learned to monitor their partners' behavior, to model prescribed eating habits and set a good example, and to assist their obese partners in coping with high-risk situations by engaging them in activities that were incompatible with eating. Subjects in the couples training (spouse-present) treatment showed an average weight loss of nearly 30 pounds 8.5 months after the beginning of treatment. Pearce, LeBow, and Orchard (1981) compared a couples training group with a behavioral program for wives alone, an alternative nonbehavioral treatment, and a delayed-treatment control group. As in the Brownell et al. (1978) study, results at posttreatment indicated that the behavioral groups were more effective than the control groups but that they did not differ significantly from each other. At 3-, 6-, 9-, and 12-month follow-ups, however, the couples training group was significantly superior to the wives-alone group in weight loss. Women in the couples training group not only maintained weight loss but even improved on their status at posttreatment.

Other studies have failed to replicate these promising findings, however (Brownell & Stunkard, 1981a; Dubbert & Wilson, in press). The Brownell and Stunkard (1981a) investigation, with treatment conditions carefully modeled after those used by Brownell et al. (1978), indicated that couples training did little to facilitate maintenance of weight loss at 1-year follow-up. The inconsistency in outcome among similar studies using the same interventions—an all-too-common occurrence in clinical research on the treatment of obesity—remains to be explained.

The potential social support and physical convenience of the workplace are being explored as a means of facilitating both treatment of obesity and subsequent maintenance of weight loss (Abrams, Follick, & Thompson, in press; Foreyt, Scott, & Gotto, 1980; Stunkard & Brownell, 1980). Behavioral programs have been implemented with union members in urban department stores, with hospital employees, and with members of the armed services. Brownell (1982a) has summarized the available evidence as follows:

> Two findings stand out from these studies: Weight losses are somewhat less than those obtained in clinical settings, and 50% or more of program participants tend to drop out of treatment within six months or less. Both may result from several factors. First, the lack of a program fee in most instances, and the ease with which patients receive treatment, might attract participants who are less motivated than persons who seek out a clinical program. Second, the potential benefits of social support need to be weighed against the potential drawbacks. For instance, Stunkard and Brownell (1980) assumed that employees in their program would encourage each other to attend sessions, so that any partnerships and friends would be as strong as their stronger members. However, employees may influence each other to drop out, so that some partnerships may be only as strong as their weakest member. (p. 195)

Relapse Prevention Strategies

Cognitive-behavioral strategies for preventing relapse in the addictive disorders have been incorporated into weight control treatments (Marlatt, in press). Inevitably, even people who have successfully lost weight will begin to deviate from therapeutic prescriptions after termination of the treatment. At this point, whether or not persons revert to previous patterns of overeating (and failure to exercise sufficiently), reestablish control, or reenter treatment for this purpose will be influenced in part by the way in which they interprets the violation of posttreatment adherence to a program for control of weight gain. It may be not the violations per se that will determine subsequent behavior but the meaning that the persons attach to them. The typical negative reaction is for the person to consider the failure to adhere to the requirements of the weight control program an affirmation of his or her personal inability to regulate weight. Previous treatment success is discounted as insignificant. Among the adverse consequences of such an attribution is a sense of helplessness. Other self-defeating cognitions involve rationalization. Obese persons who occasionally eat too much might decide that since they have "blown" the treatment program for that day, they might as well overindulge for the remainder of the day and return to the treatment program the next day. Some never return.

The degree to which the client will be able to resist these negative cognitive reactions to posttreatment setbacks in adhering to a controlled behavioral routine will depend on treatment-induced expectations of self-efficacy. As proposed by Bandura (1977), efficacy expectations are the convictions that one can cope successfully with given situations. Self-efficacy theory holds that efficacy expectations will determine whether coping behavior will be initiated, what effort will be expended, and how resolute one will be in continuing to cope in the face of the inevitable pressures and problems that are encountered by the individual who is struggling to control weight. The client who, as a result of treatment, has strong efficacy expectations about coping with high-risk situations is more likely to overcome the potentially destructive consequences of a posttreatment transgression.

A number of specific treatment and maintenance strategies derive from these cognitive-behavioral formulations of the maintenance of treatment effects. It is important to anticipate possible or probable setbacks or transgressions during treatment and to equip the client with cognitive and behavioral coping strategies for negotiating such setbacks. Teaching the client the appropriate cognitive reappraisal and coping strategies involves role-playing and imaginal rehearsal of high-risk situations. Specific difficulties are confronted, and the client's self-statements, self-evaluation, and labeling of the situation are carefully monitored.

The importance of patients' attributions of behavior change and weight loss is illustrated by Craighead, Stunkard, and O'Brien's (1981) study. A combined pharmacotherapy (fenfluramine) and behavior modification treatment produced substantial weight loss at posttreatment (32 pounds). Where behavior modification treatment alone produced further weight loss at 6-month follow-up, however, the combined treatment group regained 10 pounds. This maintenance failure is probably due to subjects' attributing their weight loss to the drug rather than to their own efforts. A heightened sense of self-efficacy based on self-attribution of behavior change must be the target of obesity control programs.

EVALUATION OF TREATMENT EFFECTS

The outcome of weight control treatments is best determined by evaluating what method was administered, by whom, for what problem, in which person, with what effects on what measure, for how long, and at what cost (Wilson & Brownell, 1980).

What Methods Are Most Effective?

In general, controlled-outcome studies have shown that behavioral treatments produce greater weight losses than a number of alternative methods *in the short-term*. The alternatives have included equally credible attention-placebo treatments, emphasizing social pressure and group cohesiveness (Kingsley & Wilson, 1977); nutrition education (Levitz & Stunkard, 1974); relaxation training (Hall, Hall, Hanson, & Borden, 1974); traditional medical treatment; and group psychotherapy (Penick, Filion, Fox, & Stunkard, 1971). The absence of controlled studies of the effects of psychodynamic therapies makes it impossible to evaluate the efficacy of these methods. Stunkard (1980) has reported that psychoanalysis may produce significant, long-lasting weight reduction, but methodological flaws in the studies on which this assessment was based (e.g., the absence of suitable controls) renders them largely uninterpretable.

A noteworthy exception to the superiority of behavioral treatments in producing short-term weight loss has been pharmacotherapy. Craighead et al. (1981) compared four treatment conditions: (a) routine doctor's office treatment with fenfluramine; (b) behavior therapy in groups; (c) fenfluramine combined with Rogerian nondirective therapy in groups; and (d) fenfluramine combined with group behavior therapy. After 25 weekly sessions, the average weight losses for the four conditions were 14.1, 24, 29.9, and 31.9 pounds, respectively. These data suggest that medication can lead to substantial weight loss if used in the context of group therapy. Addition of behavior therapy improved weight loss somewhat, and the drug (with or without behavior therapy) was more effective than behavior therapy alone. A 1-year follow-up, however, revealed a high relapse rate in those individuals who had received fenfluramine. In contrast, the behavioral treatment produced good long-term maintenance of weight loss. Brownell and Stunkard (1981a) have replicated these findings.

What Qualifications Are Necessary for Administering Weight Control Programs?

Behavioral treatments have been carried out by a variety of people, ranging from experienced therapists to graduate students and dieticians with uneven expertise. There is, however, no definitive evidence regarding the level of experience or professional expertise that is necessary to obtain the optimal treatment effects. Jeffery, Wing, and Stunkard (1978) found that experienced therapists produced greater weight loss than novice therapists. Similarly, Levitz and Stunkard (1974) demonstrated that professional therapists obtained significantly better results than lay therapists. Results obtained with a relatively impersonal self-prescription program manual have been comparable, however, to those obtained with a therapist-administered program in some studies (Hagen, 1974), suggesting that, for the most part, the therapist's contribution to successful weight control program may be quite limited.

Which People Are the Best Candidates for Treatment?

A consistent finding from behavioral studies is that a few people achieve clinically significant weight reduction, some achieve only modest weight loss, and others achieve little or no weight loss during treatment. A serious shortcoming is that reliable predictors of treatment have yet to be identified. The only variable that emerges from the literature is that behavior therapy is most appropriate for the mild to moderately obese. The morbidly obese, those above 300 pounds, appear to be poor risks for behavioral and other treatments (Van Itallie & Kral, 1981). Within the mild to moderate range of obesity, the evidence indicates that demographic, personality, and behavioral variables have not been reliably related to outcome.

In a study of who succeeds and who fails in a behavioral weight control treatment, Dubbert and Wilson (in press) found that percentage body fat (derived from skin fold measures) at pretreatment was the best predictor. A combination of the best six predictive measures available early in treatment (pretreatment percentage body fat, initial weight, age, spouse percentage overweight, reported caloric intake during week 2, and weight loss during the first 3 weeks) accounted for 59% of the variance in total weight loss throughout the 19-week program. Jeffery et al. (1978) found that a combination of six similar subject-characteristic variables accounted for about 25% of the variance in outcome for clients in their program. To the clinician, this reduction in unexplained variance is not particularly encouraging, since the six predictor variables Dubbert and Wilson used, like the Jeffery et al. (1978) subject characteristics, may be less responsive to treatment.

What Effects Does Behavioral Treatment Have on Which Measures?

Attrition

In contrast to other forms of treatment, behavior therapy has dramatically decreased attrition from treatment programs. The average attrition in traditional treatments has been as high as 80% (Stunkard, 1975), and in self-help groups the figure is at least 50% (Stunkard & Brownell, 1979). By contrast, the attrition rate in studies of behavioral treatment has been approximately 12%. Making refunds of money deposits contingent on continuing participation in treatment is associated with significantly reduced attrition rates.

Body Weight

The average weight loss in behavioral treatments is 10 to 11 pounds. This figure is remarkably consistent across different studies, despite different client populations, therapists of varying expertise, and treatment programs of different durations (a range of roughly 8 to 16 weeks). Since the average length of treatment programs is 12 weeks, this mean weight loss is consistent with the usual goal of a gradual weight loss of 1 to 2 pounds each week. The extent to which these results can be improved upon is still unclear. In an intensive, multifaceted program lasting 19 weeks, which was designed to remedy some of the shortcomings of previous behavioral treatments (e.g., combining standard group treatment with individual treatment sessions), Dubbert and Wilson (in press) obtained an average weight loss of 17 pounds. Using a sophisticated cognitive-behavioral treatment over a 20-week period, Rodin (Note 1) has reported some of the best results yet—a loss of 24.4 pounds, or 41% of excess weight. It is obvious, however, that the vast majority of participants in behavioral treatment programs do not reach their goal weights.

Any weight control treatment faces the challenge of producing lasting, long-term results. Many people can lose weight, but few can keep it off. Unacceptably high rates of relapse characterize virtually all treatments. Pharmacotherapy is a case in point. Both Craighead et al. (1981) and Brownell and Stunkard (1981a) found that fenfluramine produced substantial weight loss at posttreatment, roughly 60% of which had been regained at 1-year follow-up. In contrast to most approaches, behavioral treatments show good maintenance of weight loss at 1-year follow-up (Foreyt, Mitchell, Garner, Gee, Scott, & Gotto, 1982; Wilson & Brownell, 1980). Although weight loss is maintained for at least a year in most behavioral programs, most participants do not continue to lose weight during this follow-up period. Finally, there is no evidence of successful maintenance of weight loss beyond a 1-year period. The available evidence—which is very meager—is not encouraging (Stunkard & Penick, 1979).

Psychological Effects

The results of nonbehavioral treatments indicate that depression, anxiety, fatigue, irritability, or similar symptoms occur in at least 50% of all dieters (Stunkard & Rush, 1974). No study, however, has shown any adverse emotional effects of behavioral treatment, despite careful assessment of the psychological concomitants and sequelae of weight control. Rather, the psychological consequences of behavioral programs have been positive, including reliable decreases in depression (Craighead et al., 1981; Taylor, Ferguson, & Reading, 1978) and improvement in body image (Dubbert & Wilson, in press). Behavior therapy is a safe form of treatment for weight control.

Measures of Cardiovascular Functioning

Weight control treatments have had demonstrable health benefits. Among these are clinically significant reductions in blood pressure (Dubbert & Wilson, 1983) and favorable changes in the balance of serum lipids (Brownell & Stunkard, 1981b; Thompson, Jeffery, Wing, & Wood, 1979). Using behavioral treatment plus nutrition education, Brownell and Stunkard (1981b) found that, in men, a 10.7 kg weight loss was associated with a 5% increase in the HDL cholesterol level, a 15.8% decrease in the LDL cholesterol level, and a 30.1% increase in the HDL/LDL ratio. In contrast, obese women showed an 8.9 kg weight loss, a 3.3% decrease in the HDL cholesterol level, a 4.7% decrease in the LDL cholesterol level, and no significant change in the HDL/LDL ratio. These changes in serum lipids in men seemed directly attributable to weight loss and not to correlated changes in alcohol consumption, cigarette smoking, nutrition, or exercise. Whether or not the beneficial changes in lipids that follow weight control treatments are limited primarily to men requires further investigation.

COST-EFFECTIVENESS OF TREATMENT

The cost-effectiveness of any treatment depends on the efficacy of each program component, the cost of each component, and the effectiveness of the delivery system (Yates, 1978). Nothing definitive can be concluded about the efficacy and cost of specific program components, even in behavioral treatments, which have been most intensively studied. More is known about how efficiently behavioral treatments can be delivered. These methods have almost always been implemented on a standardized group basis. Moreover, they seem to have a robust effect that can be achieved by inexperienced therapists under supervision.

In addition to their efficiency, behavioral treatment methods can be disseminated because they are well-defined and replicable across settings. An instructive example of the cost-effectiveness of behavioral treatment comes from their incorporation by self-help groups. The most prominent of the low-cost self-help groups is Weight Watchers, evaluations of which have generally shown results comparable to those obtained by medical practice (Stuart & Mitchell, 1978). The addition of behavioral methods to the fundamental elements of Weight Watchers—the positive group environment and carefully structured nutrition—may have enhanced their general efficacy. Based on a 12-week study of more than 7,000 Weight Watchers members, Stuart (1977) showed that the addition of behavioral methods to the traditional Weight Watchers program resulted in greater weight loss. A further idea of the effects of the revamped Weight Watchers program can be gleaned from Stuart and Guire's (1978) correlational analysis of long-term outcome. Fifteen months after members reached their goal weights, 24.6% were below goal at the time of follow-up; 28.9% were within 5% of their goal weights; 17.5% were between 6% and 10% above their goal weights; and 17.5% were 11% or more above their goal weights.

Evaluation of any treatment will ultimately depend on what outcome criteria are considered and how heavily they are weighed. In many instances, somewhat reduced effectiveness may be acceptable if the treatment is widely applicable and easily disseminated. The fact that a particular treatment has a moderate impact on a large number of people at relatively minimal cost may be more important in the overall picture of a health delivery system than a highly effective treatment that is limited to a select population. Weight control treatment can be viewed in this manner.

COMBINING BEHAVIORAL TREATMENT WITH OTHER METHODS

The likely advantages of emphasizing the cost-effectiveness of standardized behavioral treatment programs—namely, a modest weight loss in a large number of people at relatively low cost—should not detract from efforts to develop more effective but more expensive methods. This raises the question of combining behavioral programs with other treatment modalities.

The typical pattern of weight loss in behavioral treatment is a decelerating one in which weight loss that is most marked in the early stages of treatment gradually tapers off and often ceases completely when treatment is discontinued. A likely cause of this phenomenon is the body's homeostatic reaction to caloric deprivation, whereby basal metabolism is slowed (Wooley et al., 1979). Another factor might be that initial weight loss is facilitated by the early enthusiasm and optimism of participants in a new treatment program. Inevitably, this enthusiasm wears off, and adherence to treatment demands becomes more taxing. Many individuals become frustrated with weight losses that are too slow, too small, and too variable. Dissatisfaction with the lack of rapid success might contribute to the inconsistent results of behavioral programs. This raises the possibility of combining behavior therapy with other methods that produce rapid weight loss—namely, drugs and specialized diets.

As noted earlier, pharmacotherapy promotes rapid and substantial weight loss but is contraindicated because of its high relapse rate. Combining pharmacotherapy with behavioral treatment has not remedied this problem with relapse (Brownell & Stunkard, 1981a; Craighead et al., 1981); however, there are different ways to sequence a combination of behavioral and drug treatment (Lasagna, 1980), and research is only beginning to address these possibilities (Craighead, Note 2).

Another promising means of producing rapid and large weight loss is the very-low-calorie diet, or the protein-sparing modified fast (PSMF). Although concerns about its safety have been voiced, the diet is safe if used properly by individuals who are carefully screened and monitored medically on a regular basis (Howard & Bray, 1981; Wadden, Stunkard, & Brownell, Note 3). Extended average weight losses of approximately 4 pounds per week can be expected, with positive effects on blood pressure and lipid levels. Adherence to this diet of 400 to 800 calories per day is better than that obtained with the caloric restriction goals (1,000 to 1,500 calories per day) of standard behavioral weight control programs. Evidence on long-term efficacy is lacking, although major problems with relapse can be predicted confidently. Combining this very-low-calorie diet with behavioral procedures designed to facilitate transition to a conventional diet while maintaining weight loss may help overcome the relapse problem. An illustration of how this might be accomplished can be seen in Katell, Callahan, Fremouw, and Zitter's (1979) use of behavioral treatment in combination with the PSMF. They reported a carefully documented case in which the client, finding that weight loss was too slow and too variable under the conventional behavioral program, resorted to PSMF under medical supervision. Following rapid weight loss during the 8 weeks she received this diet, the client returned to the behavioral program, with successful maintenance of weight loss at 6 months. Other uncontrolled clinical trials have reported impressive results using a combination of behavioral treatment and the PSMF (Bistrian, 1978; Lindner & Blackburn, 1976). The procedure of beginning with a behavioral program, introducing a drug or a diet after behavior change has taken place and weight loss has reached a plateau, and following with continued behavioral treatment as the drug or diet is withdrawn, needs to be evaluated. Such treatment must also be geared to helping the participants attribute their weight loss to their own efforts, rather than to the external and necessarily temporary agency of drug or diet. It is possible that unresolved problems with these attributional processes were responsible for the failure of the combined treatment conditions in the Brownell and Stunkard (1981a) and Craighead et al. (1981) studies.

WHEN TREATMENT FAILS

To reiterate, obesity has remained resistant to most treatment methods, and even the most effective procedures have produced relatively modest successes. The failure to maintain weight loss remains the major obstacle to improved treatment. Far too many obese individuals are trapped in a recurring cycle of losing and regaining weight. This off-again, on-again pattern can have deleterious consequences for the person's physical health and psychological well-being. In a comprehensive behavioral weight control program emphasizing slow weight loss through caloric restriction and increased exercise, the health risks incurred by treatment failure are probably minimal. There is evidence, however, showing that the more typical pattern of failure to achieve weight reduction—repeated periods of severe caloric restriction and rapid weight loss followed by excessive overeating and equally rapid weight gain— may result in recovery of metabolic rate to prediet level taking longer and metabolic rate falling more rapidly with return to caloric restriction than it did originally (Wooley et al., 1979). Exercise is an important part of treatment programs, because it may help to reverse this metabolic adaptation.

Some of the psychological effects of failure (dropping out of treatment, inability to lose weight, or relatively rapid regaining of weight that was lost in treatment) have already been touched upon in the discussion of Marlatt (in press) cognitive-behavioral model of the relapse process. Unsuccessful participants may feel guilty or depressed, may develop a sense of helplessness or hopelessness about controlling their weight, may engage in self-blame, and may experience a diminished sense of self-efficacy. To the extent that persons who have treatment failures suffer these emotional reactions, they are less likely to succeed in subsequent weight control efforts. It is clear, however, that failure to lose weight in one sort of treatment does little to deter a great number of obese people from trying the same program at later times or shopping around for alternative forms of treatment. Many obese individuals who seek behavioral treatment following previous failures can be helped to lose weight and even to maintain this weight loss. Dubbert and Wilson (in press), for example, found that none of their measures of previous dieting or unsuccessful weight loss history correlated significantly with weight loss at posttreatment. It would seem, therefore, that treatment failure in either behavioral or nonbehavioral programs does not doom the person who would be slimmer to inevitable or recurring lack of success in subsequent behavioral programs.

REFERENCE NOTES

1. Rodin J. *The Yale weight control program.* Unpublished manuscript. Yale University, 1980.
2. Craighead, L. W. *Sequencing of behavior therapy and pharmacotherapy for obesity.* Paper presented at the Annual Convention of the Association for Advancement of Behavior Therapy, Los Angeles, November 17, 1982.
3. Wadden, T. A., Stunkard, A. J., & Brownell, K. D. *Very-low-calorie diets: Efficacy, safety, and future.* Unpublished manuscript, University of Pennsylvania, 1982.

REFERENCES

Abrams, D., Follick, M., & Thompson, C. Work site weight loss intervention. *Journal of Consulting and Clinical Psychology,* in press.

Andres, R. Influence of obesity on longevity in the aged. In C. Borek, C. M. Fenoglio, & D. W. King (Eds.), *Aging, cancer, and cell membranes.* Stuttgart: Thieme Verlag, 1980.

Bandura, A. *Social learning theory.* Englewood Cliffs, N.J.: Prentice-Hall, 1977.

Bandura, A., & Simon, K. M. The role of proximal intentions in self-regulation of refractory behavior. *Cognitive Therapy and Research,* 1977, **1,** 177–193.

Beck, A. T., Rush, A. J., Shaw, F. B., & Emery, G. *Cognitive therapy of depression.* New York: Guilford Press, 1979.

Bistrian, B. Clinical use of a protein sparing modified fast. *Journal of the American Medical Association,* 1978, **240,** 2299–2302.

Bray, G. A. *The obese patient.* Philadelphia: Saunders, 1976.

Brownell, K. D. Assessment of eating disorders. In D. H. Barlow (Ed.), *Behavioral assessment.* New York: Guilford Press, 1981.

Brownell, K. D. The addictive disorders. In C. M. Franks, G. T. Wilson, P. Kendall, & K. D. Brownell (Eds.), *Annual review of behavior therapy: Theory and practice* (Vol. 8). New York: Guilford Press, 1982. (a)

Brownell, K. D. Obesity: Understanding and treating a serious, prevalent, and refractory disorder. *Journal of Consulting and Clinical Psychology,* 1982, **50,** 820–840.(b)

Brownell, K. D., Heckerman, C. L., Westlake, R. J., Hayes, S. C., & Monti, P. M. The effect of couples training and partner co-operativeness in the behavioral treatment of obesity. *Behaviour Research and Therapy,* 1978, **16,** 323–334.

Brownell, K. D., & Stunkard, A. J. Exercise in the development and control of obesity. In A. J. Stunkard (Ed.), *Obesity.* Philadelphia: Saunders, 1980.

Brownell, K. D., & Stunkard, A. J. Couples therapy, pharmacotherapy, and behavior therapy in the treatment of obesity. *Archives of General Psychiatry,* 1981, **38,** 1224–1229. (a)

Brownell, K. D., & Stunkard, A. J. Differential changes in plasma high-density lipoprotein-cholesterol levels in obese men and women during weight reduction. *Archives of Internal Medicine,* 1981, **141,** 1142–1146. (b)

Chaney, E. F., O'Leary, M. R., & Marlatt, G. A. Skill training with alcoholics. *Journal of Consulting and Clinical Psychology,* 1978, **46,** 1092–1104.

Craighead, L., Stunkard, A. J., & O'Brien, R. Behavior therapy and pharmacotherapy for obesity. *Archives of General Psychiatry,* 1981, **38,** 763–768.

Dahlkoeter, J., Callahan, E., & Linton, J. Obesity and the unbalanced energy equation: Exercise vs. eating habit change. *Journal of Consulting and Clinical Psychology,* 1979, **47,** 898–905.

Dubbert, P., & Wilson, G. T. Treatment failures in behavior therapy for obesity: Causes, correlates, and consequences. In E. Foa & P. M. G. Emmelkamp (Eds.), *Treatment failure in behavior therapy.* New York: Wiley, 1983.

Dubbert, P., & Wilson, G. T. Goal setting and spouse involvement in the treatment of obesity. *Behavior Research and Therapy,* in press.

Dunkel, L. D., & Glaros, A. Comparison of self-instructional and stimulus control treatments for obesity. *Cognitive Therapy and Research,* 1978, **2,** 75–78.

Foreyt, J., Goodrick, K., & Gotto, A. M. Limitations of behavioral treatment of obesity: Review and analysis. *Journal of Behavioral Medicine,* in press.

Foreyt, J., Mitchell, R. E., Garner, D. T., Gee, M., Scott, L. W., & Gotto, A. M. Behavioral treatment of obesity: Results and limitations. *Behavior Therapy,* 1982, **13,** 153–161.

Foreyt, J., Scott, L., & Gotto, A. Weight control and nutrition education programs in occupational settings. *Public Health Reports,* 1980, **95,** 127–136.

Hagen, R. L. Group therapy versus bibliotherapy in weight reduction. *Behaviour Therapy,* 1974, **5,** 222–234.

Hall, S. M., Hall, R. G., Hanson, R. W., & Borden, B. L. Permanence of two self-managed treatments of overweight. *Journal of Consulting and Clinical Psychology,* 1974, **42,** 781–786.

Harris, M. B., & Hallbauer, E. S. Self-directed weight control through eating and exercise. *Behaviour Research and Therapy,* 1973, **11,** 523–529.

Howard, A. N., & Bray, G. A. (Eds.). Proceedings of a symposium on evaluation of very-low-calorie diets. *International Journal of Obesity,* 1981, **5,** 193–352.

Jeffery, R. W., Thompson, P. D., & Wing, R. R. Effects on weight reduction of strong monetary contracts for calorie restriction or weight loss. *Behaviour Research and Therapy,* 1978, **16,** 363–369.

Jeffery, R. W., Wing, R. R., & Stunkard, A. J. Behavioral treatment of obesity: The state of the art. *Behavior Therapy,* 1978, **9,** 189–199.

Kannel, W. B., & Gordon, T. Physiological and medical concomitants of obesity: The Framingham Study. In G. A. Bray (Ed.), *Obesity in America.* DHEW Pub. No. (NIH)79-359. Washington, D.C.: U.S. Government Printing Office, 1979.

Katell, A., Callahan, E., Fremouw, W., & Zitter, R. The effects of behavioral treatment and fasting on eating behaviors and weight loss: A case study. *Behavior Therapy,* 1979, **10,** 579–587.

Keys, A. Is overweight a risk factor for coronary heart disease? *Cardiovascular Medicine,* 1979, **4,** 1233–1242.

Kingsley, R. G., & Wilson, G. T. Behavior therapy for obesity: A comparative investigation of long-term efficacy. *Journal of Consulting and Clinical Psychology,* 1977, **45,** 288–298.

Lasagna, L. Drugs in the treatment of obesity. In A. J. Stunkard (Ed.), *Obesity.* Philadelphia: Saunders, 1980.

Levitz, L. S., & Stunkard, A. J. A therapeutic coalition for obesity: Behavior modification and patient self-help. *American Journal of Psychiatry,* 1974, **131,** 423–427.

Lew, E. A., & Garfinkel, L. Variations in mortality by weight among 750,000 men and women. *Journal of Chronic Diseases,* 1979, **32,** 563–576.

Lindner, P. G., & Blackburn, G. L. An interdisciplinary approach to obesity utilizing fasting modified by protein-sparing therapy. *Obesity and Bariatric Medicine,* 1976, **5,** 198–216.

Loro, A. D., Jr., Fisher, E. B., Jr., & Levenkron, J. C. Comparison of established and innovative weight-reduction treatment procedures. *Journal of Applied Behavior Analysis,* 1979, **12,** 141–155.

Mann, R. A. The behavior-therapeutic use of contingency contracting to control an adult behavior problem: Weight control. *Journal of Applied Behavior Analysis,* 1972, **5,** 99–109.

Marlatt, G. A. *Relapse prevention.* New York: Guilford Press, in press.

Meichenbaum, D. *Cognitive behavior modification.* New York: Plenum, 1977.

Metropolitan Life Insurance. Frequency of overweight and underweight. *Statistical Bulletin,* 1960, **41,** 4–7.

Miller, P. M., & Sims, K. L. Evaluation and component analysis of a comprehensive weight control program. *International Journal of Obesity,* 1981, **5,** 57–66.

Novaco, R. W. Treatment of chronic anger through cognitive and relaxation controls. *Journal of Consulting and Clinical Psychology,* 1976, **44,** 681.

Ost, L., & Gotestam, K. Behavioral and pharmacological treatments for obesity: An experimental comparison. *Addictive Behaviors,* 1976, **1,** 331–338.

Pearce, J. W., LeBow, M., & Orchard, J. Role of spouse involvement in the behavioral treatment of overweight women. *Journal of Consulting and Clinical Psychology*, 1981, **49**, 236–244.

Penick, S., Filion, R., Fox, S., & Stunkard, A. J. Behavior modification in the treatment of obesity. *Psychosomatic Medicine*, 1971, **33**, 49–55.

Rosenthal, B. S., & Marx, R. D. Differences in eating patterns of successful and unsuccessful dieters, untreated overweight and normal weight individuals. *Addictive Behaviors*, 1978, **3**, 129–134.

Stalonas, P. M., Johnson, W. G., & Christ, M. Behavior modification for obesity: The evaluation of exercise, contingency management and program adherence. *Journal of Consulting and Clinical Psychology*, 1978, **46**, 463–469.

Stuart, R. B. (Ed.). *Behavioral self-management.* New York: Brunner/Mazel, 1977.

Stuart, R. B., & Davis, B. *Slim chance in a fat world.* Champaign, Ill.: Research Press, 1972.

Stuart, R. B., & Guire, K. Some correlates of the maintenance of weight loss through behavior modification. *International Journal of Obesity*, 1978, **2**, 225–235.

Stuart, R. B., & Jacobson, B. Sex differences in obesity. In E. S. Gomberg & V. Franks (Eds.), *Gender and disordered behavior: Sex differences in psychopathology.* New York: Brunner/Mazel, 1979.

Stuart, R. B., & Mitchell, C. A professional and a consumer perspective on self-help weight control programs. In A. J. Stunkard (Ed.), *The Psychiatric Clinics of North America Symposium on Obesity.* Philadelphia: Saunders, 1978.

Stunkard, A. J. From explanation to action in psychosomatic medicine: The case of obesity. *Psychosomatic Medicine*, 1975, **37**, 195–236.

Stunkard, A. J. (Ed.). *Obesity.* Philadelphia: Saunders, 1980.

Stunkard, A. J., & Brownell, K. D. Behavior therapy and self-help programmes for obesity. In J. F. Munno (Ed.), *Treatment of obesity.* Lancaster, England: MTP Press, 1979.

Stunkard, A. J., & Brownell, K. D. Work site treatment for obesity. *American Journal of Psychiatry*, 1980, **137**, 252–253.

Stunkard, A. J., & Penick, S. Behavior modification in the treatment of obesity: The problem of maintaining weight loss. *Archives of General Psychiatry*, 1979, **36**, 801–806.

Stunkard, A. J., & Rush, J. Dieting and depression re-examined: A critical review of reports of untoward responses during weight reduction for obesity. *Annals of Internal Medicine*, 1974, **81**, 526–533.

Taylor, C. B., Ferguson, J. M., & Reading, J. C. Gradual weight loss and depression. *Behavior Therapy*, 1978, **9**, 622–625.

Thompson, P. D., Jeffery, R. W., Wing, R., & Wood, P. D. Unexpected decrease in plasma high-density lipoprotein cholesterol with weight loss. *American Journal of Clinical Nutrition*, 1979, **32**, 2016.

Van Itallie, T. B. Obesity: Adverse effects on health and longevity. *American Journal of Clinical Nutrition*, 1979, **32**, 2723–2733.

Van Itallie, T., & Kral, J. G. The dilemma of morbid obesity. *Journal of the American Medical Association*, 1981, **246**, 999–1003.

Weltman, A., Matter, S., & Stamford, B. A. Caloric restriction and/or mild exercise: Effects on serum lipids and body composition. *American Journal of Clinical Nutrition*, 1980, **33**, 1002–1009.

Wilson, G. T., & Brownell, K. Behavior therapy for obesity: An evaluation of treatment outcome. *Advances in Behaviour Research and Therapy*, 1980, **3**, 49–86.

Wing, R., Epstein, L., Marcus, M., & Shapira, B. Strong monetary contingencies for weight loss during treatment and maintenance. *Behavior Therapy*, 1981, **12**, 702–710.

Wooley, S. C., Wooley, O. W., & Dyrenforth, S. R. Theoretical, practical, and social issues in behavioral treatments of obesity. *Journal of Applied Behavior Analysis*, 1979, **12**, 3–25.

Yates, B. Improving the cost-effectiveness of obesity programs: Three basic strategies for reducing the cost per pound. *International Journal of Obesity*, 1978, **2**, 249–266.

CHAPTER 42

THE RELATIONSHIP BETWEEN CIGARETTE SMOKING AND BODY WEIGHT: A HEALTH PROMOTION DILEMMA?

JUDITH RODIN
JEFFERY T. WACK

Yale University

Evidence accumulated during the last 20 years indicates that many of the most serious modern diseases are the result of detrimental behaviors that have accompanied change in our society, such as smoking, overeating, and a lack of exercise (Gori & Richter, 1978). It is interesting, however, that smoking and excess weight are themselves inversely related; smokers tend to weigh less than nonsmokers, on the average, and weight gain typically follows smoking cessation.

Numerous epidemiologic studies have compared the body weights of smokers and nonsmokers, and nearly all have suggested that smokers as a group, regardless of sex, socioeconomic status, or culture, weigh consistently less than persons who have never smoked. Keys, Aravanis, and Blackburn (1966), for example, studied 15 populations of males in seven countries and found that, on the average, smokers weighed less than nonsmokers in all 15. Among the largest studies bearing on this issue is that of Khosla and Lowe (1971, 1972, 1973) who obtained data on the height, weight, and smoking history of 10,482 steelworkers in South Wales. This study found that smokers weighed significantly less than nonsmokers, with the weight differences being greatest among the older cohorts. The average difference was about 10 pounds, a magnitude similar to that in many other studies reporting that smokers weighed less than nonsmokers (Ashford, Brown, Duffield, Smith, & Fay, 1961; Holcomb & Meigs, 1972; Huston & Stenson, 1974; Karvonen, Keys, Orma, Fidanzo, & Brozek, 1959; Kopczynski, 1972; Lincoln, 1969, 1970).

The Framingham Study (Gordon, Kannel, Dawber, & McGee, 1975) is one of the largest studies providing data regarding longitudinal changes associated with stopping cigarette smoking. The study cohort of 5,209 men and women ranged in age from 29 to 62 years old when it came under study in 1948. Members of that cohort have undergone extensive physical examinations and have provided information regarding smoking and other health-related habits every 2 years since the beginning of the study. At entry into the study, the difference in weight between cigarette smokers and nonsmokers was about 8 pounds—a magnitude of difference similar to those studies cited previously. At subsequent evaluations, those who had quit smoking at some point in the 2-year interim had gained, on the average,

This chapter is adapted from Wack, J. T., & Rodin, J. Smoking and its effects on body weight and the systems of caloric regulation. *American Journal of Clinical Nutrition*, 1982, **35**, 366–380.

5 pounds. This figure may be somewhat low because of selection artifacts inherent in such longitudinal designs; some persons may have stopped smoking because of poor health, a factor that would be correlated with weight loss.

The first report of a longitudinal study of the effect of the cessation of smoking on body weight appears to have been that of Brozek and Keys (1957), who compared the weights of a small cohort of business and professional men who had quit smoking with the weights of a control cohort of men who had continued to smoke. Comparisons of each group's weights 2 years before the experimental group stopped smoking and 2 years after the experimental group stopped smoking (i.e., a 4-year period), revealed that the experimental cohort showed a uniform and significant weight gain averaging 8.2 pounds, whereas the control group had lost an average 1.1 pounds during this time.

Comstock and Stone (1972) reported a study of weight gain after cessation of smoking in 501 male telephone workers aged 40 to 59 in which body weight as well as subscapular and triceps skin fold thickness (indices of overweight) were obtained twice on each subject, 5 years apart. Forty-six men were found to have quit smoking during this study period, and their weight changes were compared with those of the 244 men who continued to smoke. The men who quit smoking were found to have gained an average 11.2 pounds, 8.8 pounds more than their peers who continued to smoke. These body weight changes were also found to be significantly correlated to increases in the measure of subscapular skin fold thickness, suggesting that increases in the amount of adipose tissue were the source of weight gain. On the basis of these and comparable studies documenting weight gain after smoking cessation, the average gain across all studies appears to be about 10 pounds (e.g., Bjelke, 1973; Blitzer, Rimm, & Giefer, 1977; Bosse, Garvey, & Costa, 1980; Fletcher & Doll, 1969; Garvey, Bosse, & Seltzer, 1974; Hammond & Percy, 1958; Howell, 1971; Swineford, 1958).

This relationship between smoking and weight presents a dilemma for those who wish to recommend both maintenance of moderate weight and cessation of smoking as important health-promoting behaviors. Indeed, the general public is aware of this inverse relationship (U.S. DHEW, 1979), and, as a consequence, many smokers indicate that one reason they have difficulty stopping smoking, or have never tried at all, is that they would rather continue smoking than gain weight. Indeed, some who have successfully given up smoking have begun to smoke again because they have gained weight (U.S. DHEW, 1976).

EFFECTS OF SMOKING ON FOOD CONSUMPTION

The popular wisdom assumes that the weight gain that follows smoking cessation derives from overeating. Given the evidence that smokers weigh, on the average, 10 pounds less than nonsmokers, it would also be reasonable to suppose that smokers weigh less because they consume fewer calories. Actually, there are a variety of reasons why increased consumption might be expected to occur following smoking cessation. Psychodynamic theories most often hypothesize oral gratification as the underlying cause of smoking behavior (Jacobs, Knapp, Anderson, Karnsh, Meissner, & Richman, 1965; Jacobs & Spilken, 1971; Veldman & Brown, 1966); persons with oral tendencies might eat more to substitute for the absence of cigarettes. A second line of reasoning, which focuses on commonalities among substance uses, might argue for the interchangeability of food for cigarettes at some level (Solomon & Corbit 1974; Ternes, 1977). Both theories predict increased frequency of consumption after smoking cessation. At present, support for these assertions is largely anecdotal. Several other possible factors affecting the relationship between food intake and smoking have received empirical consideration, however.

Palatability

Since the amount one consumes at a meal is strongly affected by the perceived palatability of the food (Rodin, 1975; Spitzer & Rodin, 1981; Young, 1967), several investigators have considered whether smoking affects the senses of taste and olfaction. Although former smokers often report that they experience an improvement in their senses of smell and taste upon quitting (Elgerot, 1978), experimental evidence regarding whether smoking or nicotine actually alters the smoker's sense of taste or smell is inconclusive. Pangborn and Trabue (1973) review 11 studies reported between 1937 and 1970 investigating the effects of smoking on the gustatory senses, many of which, however, are lacking in experimental and analytic rigor. Most of these studies attempted to assess differences between smokers and nonsmokers in their sensory thresholds for the four primary tastes or acuity of smell. A majority of these studies did not find that cigarette smoking generally affects taste thresholds (Fergensen, Moss, Dzendolet, Sawyer, & Moore, 1975; Laird, 1939; McBarney & Moskat, 1975; Pangborn & Trabue, 1973; Pangborn, Trabue, & Pikielna, 1967; Sinnott & Rauth, 1937). At least two studies using larger sample sizes (Kaplan, Glanville, & Fisher, 1964; Krut, Perrin, & Bronte-Stewart, 1961), however, have reported differential taste sensitivity to the taste of bitter, with thresholds being higher among smokers compared to nonsmokers. In addition, the data obtained by Pursell, Sanders, and Haude (1973) suggests that smokers may be more sensitive to the taste of sweet. The conflicting results of these studies may well be due to the variety of procedures, numbers of subjects, test methods, and stimulus concentrations used. The findings, therefore, do not appear sufficiently consistent to conclude whether or not smoking affects taste thresholds.

The purpose of most of the previously cited studies was to assess the effects of smoking on sensory thresholds, but they did not test the question of what effect smoking has on the hedonic properties of taste stimuli. Changes in taste preferences, but not perceived intensities, have frequently been demonstrated to occur with changes in hunger and satiety (Booth, 1976; Cabanac, 1971) and after weight reduction (Rodin, Moskowitz, & Bray, 1976). Consequently, how smoking or stopping smoking might affect perceptions of palatability would be important to know. Pangborn and Trabue (1973) obtained ratings of liking of varying concentrations of sucrose and NaCl solutions from smokers and nonsmokers. No significant differences were observed between the two groups in hedonic response to either of the two tastes. If differences between groups of smokers and nonsmokers were found, however, it would be unclear whether such differences were caused by smoking or whether persons with certain hedonic responsiveness are predisposed to begin or continue smoking. To determine whether the cessation of smoking results in alterations in perceptions of palatability that might result in changes in calorie intake, it would be necessary to compare the same individuals before and after they stopped smoking.

The mechanism by which smoking or nicotine may affect taste preference is speculative at this time. There is evidence, however, that smoking results in both physical (King, 1971) and chemical (Radsel & Kambic, 1978) changes in the oropharyngeal cavity that could affect perceptions of palatability. Russell (1976) has posited the existence of a salivo-gastric nicotine recirculation cycle that seems to concentrate nicotine in the salivary glands (Russell, 1978). A study of whole-body autoradiography of mice injected intravenously with C-labeled nicotine clearly showed that the radioactivity was concentrated in the salivary glands and the fundas of the stomach (Schmiterlow, Hansson, Andersson, Applegren, & Hoffman). This prompted Russell and Feyerabend (Note 1) to measure the nicotine concentration in saliva following smoking. The levels they obtained were many times higher than is ever found in blood; these levels were not simply due to nicotine deposited directly in the mouth during smoking, because similar levels were obtained after an intravenous injection of nicotine.

Eating Habits

After smoking cessation, factors affecting meal termination might also be altered. Many smokers report that they crave a cigarette upon completion of a meal; casual observations tend to confirm the immediacy with which many smokers light up after eating. It may be that, for the smoker, this cigarette is an unambiguous marker of the termination of the meal. Upon cessation of smoking, the individual loses this marker and may be more inclined to take second helpings or the high-calorie desserts that are often consumed at the end of a meal.

Studies investigating changes in eating habits following the cessation of smoking have relied primarily on retrospective interviews. Wynder, Kaufman, and Lesser (1967) found that among 224 subjects, all of whom had quit smoking from 3 months to 10 years earlier, 67% reported that their actual food intake, especially their consumption of sweets, had increased when they stopped smoking. In a similar study, however, Gaudet and Hugli (1969) found no significant changes in the consumption of sweet foods, leading them to conclude that the commonly accepted belief that the cessation of smoking leads to increased consumption of sweets does not appear to be true. Retrospective studies of this type are problematic, however; considerably increased or different patterns of food intake may not have actually occurred, but rather may have been invoked by the subjects as a post hoc explanation of the weight gain they knew they had experienced (Nisbett & Wilson, 1977).

Clearly, increases in the frequency and duration of meals, increases in the amount of food consumed at a meal, or changes in the types of food eaten (e.g., the proportions of protein, carbohydrate, and fat) could contribute to the weight gain persons experience upon stopping smoking. Four laboratory studies have attempted to test the effects of smoking cessation on amount or type of food eaten. It is difficult to know, however, whether the behaviors observed while subjects are abstaining from smoking for the short period of time encompassed by a laboratory study are representative of changes associated with the long-term cessation of smoking. Nonetheless, the following studies suggest some intriguing hypotheses.

Schachter and Nesbitt (Note 2) provided a variety of foods to habitual smokers during two 8-hour sessions. In one of these sessions, subjects were not allowed to smoke. The data indicated that subjects ate proportionately more sweet and salty foods during the no-smoking condition, but it is unclear whether this indicates that abstinence from smoking leads to increased consumption of snack foods that happen to be sweet and salty or reflects a general increase in food consumption.

Perlick (Note 3) studied habitual smokers who were either deprived of cigarettes for about 2 hours or allowed to smoke low-nicotine cigarettes or high-nicotine cigarettes. While completing a questionnaire, the deprived and low-nicotine groups ate twice as many gumdrops as did the high-nicotine group, who ate the same amount as a control group of nonsmokers. Again, however, it is unclear whether short-term abstinence from smoking leads to overall increases in caloric consumption or to increased consumption of certain types of foods.

Finally, a decreased preference for sweet foods associated with smoking and nicotine was observed recently in two studies by Grunberg (1980). In the first study, three groups of subjects—nonsmokers, smokers, and smokers asked to abstain from smoking for the short period of the experiment—were presented with nine foods, three of which were sweet, three bland, and three salty. Subjects were unaware that the quantity of each of these foods they consumed while completing scales and questionnaires was the dependent measure. It was found that smokers, whether allowed to smoke or not, consumed less of the sweet foods than did nonsmokers. Smokers who were allowed to smoke consumed somewhat less than those who were deprived, although the difference was not statistically significant. There were no differences among the three groups in the consumption of salty or bland foods. In a complementary study investigating the effects of nicotine on caloric intake in rats, three concentrations of sucrose solutions were made available in addition to the rats' normal chow diet over a period of 2 weeks. Groups of these rats were then continuously infused with nicotine or saline for a second period of about 2 weeks. This was followed by a third period during which the rats were no longer being infused with nicotine. The data indicated that administration of nicotine resulted in a decrease in caloric intake, but the reduction in caloric intake came solely from a reduced consumption of the sweetest solutions, not the chow. After cessation of nicotine administration, rats who had received the highest dose of nicotine increased consumption of sweet solutions. A similar increase in the preference for these sweeter tastes may mediate the weight gain observed upon cessation of smoking in humans.

Taken together, these four studies suggest a selective suppression of sweet, and perhaps salty, food intake during nicotine ingestion and a selective increased intake of these same substances upon cessation of smoking. The increased consumption could contribute to the weight gain experienced by smokers following smoking cessation. Yet correlations between smoking and *higher* daily sucrose intake (Burns-Cox, Doll, & Ball, 1969; Elwood, Moore, Waters, & Sweetnam, 1970; Paul, MacMillan, McKean, & Park, 1968), alcohol consumption (Gordon et al., 1975), and carbohydrate consumption (King, 1971) have also been reported. Moreover, several field studies suggest that, when one examines overall consumption, smokers actually may be consuming a greater number of calories prior to cessation than nonsmokers do.

Lincoln (1969) evaluated a national sample of 885 middle-aged men who completed questionnaires concerning their food and beverage consumption over a period of 24 hours. Analyses revealed that the smokers reported consuming, on average, about 350 calories more than the nonsmokers, with the heaviest smokers consuming about 575 calories more than the nonsmokers. Nonetheless, these smokers weighed about 6.5 pounds less than the nonsmokers. Data for a few recent abstainers were also available and indicated that within a few months of stopping smoking, these ex-smokers had gained an average of about 8 pounds, despite a reported decrease in daily food intake of 200 calories. A correlation between higher daily sucrose intake and tobacco smoking has also been reported in epidemiologic studies conducted primarily to identify factors contributing to heart disease (Burns-Cox et al., 1969; Elwood et al., 1970; Paul et al., 1968). Gordon et al. (1975) also observed that persons who never smoked used less alcohol than smokers and that, among smokers, the amount of alcohol consumed was correlated with the number of cigarettes smoked. Although the consumption of both sucrose and alcohol involves the intake of calories, the consumption of all other calorie sources was not assessed in these studies. Consequently, it is not possible to conclude whether the findings actually reflect a greater number of total daily calories consumed by nonsmokers.

King (1971) telephoned a sample of adolescent male smokers and nonsmokers at the end of each day to determine the types of food they had consumed during the day. He found that the smokers consumed somewhat more beverages and fruits and vegetables than the nonsmokers. Exact proportions of food consumed were not reported, however; consequently, it is unclear whether the smokers actually consumed more calories daily than the nonsmokers, or whether the data reflect different food preferences among smokers.

Additional evidence suggesting that smoking is associated with consumption of more rather than less calories comes from data regarding the food intakes of smokers and nonsmokers during pregnancy. In view of the wide-ranging endocrine changes that accompany a pregnancy, however, inferences from the pregnant to the nonpregnant state must be made with caution. Picone, Allen, Schramm, and Ferris (Note 4) monitored the weight gains of a matched group of smokers and nonsmokers over the course of their pregnancies. At each clinic visit, a dietary assessment by 24-hour recall was obtained, resulting in the collection of two to six recalls for each of the 60 subjects. Overall, despite lower weight gains during pregnancy, the smoking mothers reported consuming significantly more (310) calories per day than did the nonsmoking mothers. These results are highly consistent with those of another study (Higgins, 1973), in which it was found that the average daily intake of expectant mothers who smoked was 294 calories and 10 grams of protein per day greater than for pregnant nonsmokers.

At present, based on the studies cited here, it is difficult to determine with certainty whether smokers consume more or fewer calories prior to cessation than nonsmokers. The studies that yield conflicting evidence differ in setting (laboratory vs. field), methods of data collection, length of observation period, and types of food available for consumption. It will be impossible to reconcile the two types of findings without additional studies that investigate smoker versus nonsmoker differences in ingestive behaviors and diet, and especially changes that occur following cessation of smoking. We propose, however, that smoking, in addition to affecting ingestive behavior, has a variety of physiological effects that may play a more important role than amount of calories consumed in accounting for lower body weights among smokers and weight gain after cessation of smoking. Let us next consider the physiological consequences of smoking, and of nicotine in particular, for caloric regulation and body weight.

PROPOSED CENTRAL EFFECTS OF NICOTINE

Although nicotine might be expected to modify central mechanisms involved in the processes of body weight maintenance, no studies bear directly on this issue. It has been difficult to determine the direct action of nicotine on localized regions of the central nervous system because nicotine has so many pharmacological actions that its effects are easily confounded, reinforced, and obscured (Domino, 1967). Given nicotine's role as a cholinergic agonist, however, and the fact that it readily crosses the blood-brain barrier, it is possible to speculate about the effects smoking may have on processes of ingestion.

Intracerebral administration of other cholinergic agonists has been demonstrated to stimulate the regions of the brain that are involved in consummatory behaviors. Carbachol, for example, elicits drinking behavior in satiated rats when it is applied to many sites within the hypothalamus, thalamus, preoptic region, medial septum, cingulate gyrus, and hippocampus (Fisher & Coury, 1962; Grossman, 1960, 1962, 1964; Krikstone & Levitt, 1970; Levitt, White, & Sander, 1970; Miller, 1965; Miller, Gottesman, & Emory, 1964; Quartermain & Miller, 1966). Thus, as a consequence of nicotine's effect on central drinking systems, smokers might ingest more calories than nonsmokers because they drink more calorie-containing beverages—coffee, sodas, or alcohol, for example. The involvement of the cholinergic system in feeding behavior is less clear, however. Intrahypothalamic carbachol has been demonstrated to elicit feeding behavior in rabbits (Sommer, Novin, & Levine, 1967), but has not been demonstrated to have effects in cats (Myers, 1964) or rats. Booth (1968) concluded that, at least in the rat, it is the adrenergic rather than the cholinergic system that is involved in the control of food intake.

The extent to which the effects of carbachol or other cholinergic agonists administered intracerebrally to animals can be inferred to be analogous to those of nicotine absorbed via the lungs in the human is unclear, however. The inference of a stimulating effect by nicotine is especially problematic, given that nicotine appears to have a dual physiological effect, at least peripherally. At moderate levels, nicotine stimulates autonomic ganglia. In larger quantities, however, nicotine paralyzes the ganglia by depolarization, resulting in the ganglia becoming insensitive to acetylcholine (Paton, 1954). Should nicotine have dual effects centrally, it would be critical not only to know what regions of the brain are affected by nicotine but, as important, to know the concentrations of nicotine to which the neural synapses are exposed (Silvette, Hoff, Larson, & Haag, 1962).

A second mechanism may exist by which nicotine could influence the probability of consummatory behavior. Low doses of d-amphetamine (Glick & Muller, 1971) and mild tail pinch (Antelman, Rowland, & Fisher, 1975) have been shown reliably to induce eating in sated rats. Both d-amphetamine and mild tail pinch seem to activate the catecholaminergic pathways that compose the brain arousal mechanisms. As a cholinergic agonist, nicotine could have a similar effect in people. Antelman and his colleagues (1975) proposed that the observed increase in feeding is due to the facilitation of brain catecholaminergic function, which leads to a heightened sensitivity and responsivity to survival-oriented or prepotent environmental stimuli. This means that eating would be more probable when the animal is aroused and in an environment where food is available. This proposal, of course, is subject to some of the same limitations of inference as the first, but there are many more data to support the existence of such an operative mechanism in the smoker.

The stimulating effect of nicotine and smoking on the brain-stem activating system has been well documented by electroencephalography (Domino, 1973; Hauser, Schwartz, Roth, & Bickford, 1958). That smoking has some effect on information processing and cognitive functioning is suggested by many smokers' claims that their concentration and efficiency are improved after smoking a cigarette. More concrete evidence comes from a number of studies. Frankenhauser, Myrsten, Post, and Johansson (1971) found that cigarettes spaced 20 minutes apart prevented the increase in reaction time that would normally occur with visual tasks during 80 minutes of testing under monotonous conditions. In the vigilance tasks of a simulated driving situation, the performance and reaction times of smokers were maintained at a higher level while smoking than when deprived of smoking (Heimstra, Bancroft, & DeKock, 1967). Other evidence that nicotine may alter information-processing capacity comes from a signal detection task in which subjects were required to detect pauses in the sweep second hand of a clock. It was found that detection performance was improved by smoking and that there was less deterioration in detection over the test period compared with controls (Warburton, 1975).

These cognitive tasks are similar to those that have been used to validate the construct of external responsiveness (Rodin, 1973; Rodin, Herman, & Schachter, 1974; Rodin & Slochower, 1976), a construct of interest in relation to the development of obesity. Indeed, heightened sensitivity to and processing of external stimuli have been demonstrated to predict subjects who would gain weight while attending a summer camp where food and food cues were abundant (Rodin & Slochower, 1976). The weight gain experienced by the more externally stimulated subjects was attributable to their increased food consumption. Hence, the nicotine ingested by the smoker may activate brain arousal mechanisms, thereby heightening sensitivity to environmental cues and increasing the probability that the smoker would eat if there were stimulating food cues in the environment.

Although the inferences are considerable, if nicotine has any effects on central mechanisms involved in consummatory behavior, these effects may be biasing smokers toward greater caloric intake than that of nonsmokers. Whereas the central effects of nicotine on food intake are quite speculative, its effects on peripheral processes involved in the metabolism of calories are more readily understood. Let us next consider the effects of smoking on calorie utilization.

PERIPHERAL EFFECTS OF NICOTINE

To assess the direct physiological effects of nicotine, Schnecter and Cook (1976) administered 0.4 or 0.8 mg/kg of nicotine intraperitoneally to rats two or three times per day for 5 weeks. During this period, the animals lost weight, compared to saline-injected controls, but without a decrease in food consumption or change in activity levels. This finding is consistent with other evidence from dogs (Kershbaum, Bellet, & Khorsandrian, 1965), guinea pigs (Evans, Hughes, & Jones, 1967; Hughes, Jones, & Nicholas, 1970), and hamsters, mice, and rats (Passey, 1957, 1958), showing a depression of body weight or growth induced by cigarette smoke or nicotine, despite no decrease in food consumption or decreases insufficient to explain the amount of weight loss. This observation of weight loss without parallel decreases in food consumption suggests two further possible effects of smoking. The nicotine ingested by habitual smokers may result in less efficient storage of calories by changing the physiology of the gut, thereby disrupting absorption, or by biasing particular metabolic processes away from storage. A second effect of nicotine may be that of altering the processes of metabolism in a manner that facilitates calorie expenditure. Activation of either or both of these mechanisms could account for body weight being lower among smokers than among nonsmokers, even if calorie ingestion is equal or greater among smokers.

EFFECTS OF SMOKING ON THE GASTROINTESTINAL TRACT

Only 5% of the nicotine taken in during smoking enters the gastrointestinal tract directly—for example, by the swallowing of nicotine-containing saliva (Radsel & Kambic, 1978). There it is quickly absorbed and delivered via the portal system directly to the liver, where it is metabolized to psychopharmacologically inert derivatives of nicotine. The remaining 95% of the nicotine absorbed is inhaled and enters general circulation in the bloodstream through lung alveoli (Radsel & Kambic, 1978). Consequently, many effects of smoking on the physiology of the gastrointestinal tract are indirect, mediated by the autonomic nervous system through the innervation of organs involved in calorie intake and through the release of hormones that affect metabolism.

If nicotine does have a stimulating effect on the gut, one effect that would be predicted is an alteration in the rate of gastric secretion. Evidence on this point is conflicting, however. Most studies of the effect of smoking on the alimentary tract have been conducted in relation to smoking's etiologic role in ulcers of the stomach and duodenum. Cooper and Knight (1956) were unable to demonstrate any change in volume, pH, free acid, or pepsin output of gastric juice in response to smoking two to three cigarettes. Debas, Cohen, Holubitsky, and Harrison (1971) also observed no significant overall difference in rate of pentagastrin-stimulated acid secretion in response to smoking three cigarettes. By contrast, Steigmann, Dolehide, and Kaminski (1954) found a definite increase in gastric acidity following the smoking of one cigarette in a major proportion of their subjects, and Wilkinson and Johnson (1971) found that smoking inhibited pentagastrin-stimulated gastric secretion. Murthy, Dinoso, Clearfield, and Chey (1977) found that smoking induced a transient rise of basal acid output, followed by a slight decrease. It is interesting that a strong correlation across time was also observed between plasma concentrations of nicotine and the inhibition of fluid and bicarbonate secretion by the pancreas. Finally, Novis, Marks, Banks, and Sloan (1973) observed a significant correlation between basal acid output and the number of cigarettes smoked per day in a population of 176 students, evidence that suggests that smoking over a long period stimulates either the vagus or basal gastrin secretion.

In addition to altering the chemistry of the gut, smoking may also alter gastric motility and emptying. Schnedorf and Ivy (1938) conducted an interesting series of studies in the 1920s to assess just such effects. They observed that "hunger contractions" of the stomach ceased after the first few puffs of smoke and did not recur for 15 to 60 minutes after cessation of smoking. After demonstrating that inhibition did not occur in three dogs whose vagus was sectioned above the diaphragm, they concluded that the tobacco smoke inhibited the contractions through a reflex mechanisms, the vagus being the motor side of the reflex arc. They subsequently studied whether such an inhibition by smoking would have a delaying effect on the emptying time of a test meal. The smoking of three to four cigarettes, as compared to not smoking in the hour after consuming a liquid test meal, did not have an effect on the rate at which the stomach of chronic smokers emptied. This conclusion is in disagreement with a more recent, more technically sophisticated experiment by Grimes and Goddard (1978).

In the Grimes and Goddard (1978) study, 10 habitual smokers ate two test meals 1 week apart, each consisting of a radioactive-labeled solid and liquid component. Subjects smoked two cigarettes immediately after one of the two meals. A smaller group of nonsmokers was also given one test meal. Then, for 1 hour after each meal, the upper abdomen of the recumbent subject was viewed by a gamma-camera. From the data obtained, the investigators concluded that smoking a cigarette increased the rate at which the liquid, but not the solid, phase of the meal was cleared. The smokers did not differ from the nonsmokers when they were not smoking, but the variability of the smokers' rate of gastric emptying was striking, suggesting that smoking may have acute effects on gastric motility in some persons.

Schnedorf and Ivy (1938) conducted the only study in which the effect of smoking on clearance through the entire alimentary tract was compared between smokers and nonsmokers. The dietary histories of one group of 10 habitual smokers and a second group of 10 nonsmokers were obtained, and a 2-week dietary regime was prescribed so as to keep quantity and quality of food intake constant. With the noon meal on each day of the 2 weeks, subjects consumed knotted, colored strings to serve as markers. In the first week, both groups continued smoking or not smoking; in the second week, the habitual smokers stopped smoking, whereas the nonsmokers smoked a minimum of six cigarettes per day. The time at which the colored strings were passed in the stools was the measure and tended to confirm the currently accepted impression that smoking tends to increase the propulsive activity of the colon. If consumed foodstuffs are moved through the alimentary tract more quickly in the smoker than in the nonsmoker, then the gut of the smoker may be wasting more of the calories that are consumed, thereby permitting increased caloric consumption and equal or lowered body weight.

Unfortunately, neither Schnedorf and Ivy (1938) nor others have attempted to assess the relative efficiency with which the alimentary tract of smokers, as compared to nonsmokers or former smokers, absorbs calories. Evidence exists to suggest that in rats, nicotine pretreatment results in greater absorption of glucose by the intestine (Bhagat, van Beaumont, & Ellert, 1974). Given a known calorie intake, the proportion of calories expelled in waste would provide such a measure.

EFFECTS OF SMOKING ON THE DYNAMICS OF CALORIE STORAGE

The lower body weights observed among smokers may also be explained by alterations in metabolic pathways caused by smoking, resulting in fewer of these calories being stored or in their being stored via less energy-conserving enzymatic pathways (Newsholme, 1980; Newsholme & Crabtree, 1976; Stirling & Stock, 1973). In normal metabolism, two antagonistic pancreatic hormones—insulin and glucagon—provide coordinated control over enzymes in the liver and adipose tissue that direct the storage mobilization of the different metabolic fuels (Randle, Garland, Hales, Newshalme, Denton, & Pogson, 1966; Unger, 1974). Calories in the form of glucose and amino acids, crossing the intestinal wall into the blood of the hepatic-portal system, stimulate the secretion of insulin, which in turn promotes the formation of fat and glycogen while inhibiting their mobilization. In the postabsoptive period, however, insulin secretion declines and glucagon secretion increases the edge, promoting caloric expenditure by mobilizing liver glycogen (Marliss, Aoki, Unger, Soeldner, & Cahill, 1970). The utilization of calories stored as fat is additionally stimulated by the elevated levels of growth hormone, adrenal corticoids, and the catecholamines (i.e., epinephrine and norepinephrine) that are observed during fasting (Exton, 1972). Furthermore, hormones that promote storage and expenditure bear an antagonistic relationship with one another; the output of catecholamines, for example, has been demonstrated to inhibit the secretion of insulin (Porte, Graber, Kuzuya, & Williams, 1966). A differing balance among the metabolic hormones that facilitate storage and those that facilitate expenditure would introduce pathway bias into the system.

Since the pharmacological effect of moderate amounts of nicotine on the autonomic nervous system is stimulation, one would predict greater secretion of catecholamines as a consequence of smoking. Indeed, numerous acute and long-term studies have demonstrated that smoking results in increased output of both adrenaline and noradrenaline, as measured in plasma (Cryer, Haymond, Santiago, & Shah, 1976) and in urine (Frankenhauser, Myrsten, Waszak, Nerie, & Post, 1968; Kershbaum, Bellet, Jimenez, & Feinberg, 1966).

Winternitz and Quillen (1977) assessed the effects of smoking on other metabolically important hormones. Their basic design involved sampling blood from smokers for cortisol, growth hormone, follicle-stimulating hormone (FSH), luteinizing hormone (LH), and insulin every 20 minutes over a period of 4 hours. Baseline readings were obtained during the first hour of the session. During the experimental period, each subject was required to smoke two high-nicotine cigarettes in the first 20 minutes and then six more cigarettes over the next 90 minutes—that is, one every 15 minutes. Both cortisol and growth hormone were found to be elevated, beginning with the first blood draw after smoking the first two cigarettes. No consistent changes were observed in insulin, LH, or FSH. The researchers concluded that the experiment provided evidence for stimulation of the adrenals by nicotine. These results should be interpreted with caution, however, since elevations in both cortisol and growth hormone are often observed in response to psychological stress (Mason, 1975), and the rate of smoking required in the study—an average of more than four cigarettes per hour—is almost double the hourly rate of most smokers (Frederiksen & Frazier, 1977). Nonetheless, the endocrine picture is a bias of pathways away from storage and toward energy mobilization.

Three other studies suggest that, in the smoker, calories consumed are less likely to be stored. In a study using a within-subject design to compare metabolic differences between a period of smoking and one of not smoking, Glauser, Glauser, Reidenberg, Rusy, and Tallarida (1970) compared the fasting blood glucose level of subjects before and 1 month after they had stopped smoking. No differences were found in mean fasting blood glucose levels at the two times. The mean 30-minute postprandial blood glucose level, however, was 137 mg/100 ml before cessation of smoking, whereas after smoking this value had dropped significantly to 123 mg/100 ml. This suggests that while the subjects were smoking, the anabolic pathways were less efficient in moving glucose out of the bloodstream and into storage. Again, a word of caution is in order in interpreting these results, given the lack of appropriate controls. The weight gain that occurred in the subjects between the two sessions, and either an increase in physical activity or ingestion of more carbohydrates, could have led to the same metabolic results.

A second line of evidence supports the hypothesis that smokers do not clear calories from general circulation and into storage as efficiently as nonsmokers do. Arginine is an amino acid that stimulates the release of insulin (Floyd, Fajans, Conn, Knopf, & Rull, 1966). Taminato, Seino, Goto, Inone, Matsukura, and Imura (1978) infused a known quantity of arginine into subjects intravenously and monitored plasma insulin, glucagon, and glucose. The same subjects also smoked three cigarettes in the half-hour prior to a second arginine pulse. It was found that whereas glucagon was unaffected, the peak insulin response was attenuated by about 40%. Thus, smoking was having an inhibitory effect on the secretion of insulin, an effect that was probably mediated by the catecholamine increase caused by smoking, although catecholamines were not measured in this study.

The bias away from the deposition of ingested calories into storage and their maintenance in the general circulation appears to be one of the major effects of smoking. The Taminato et al. (1978) study found not only that insulin levels were lower in the smoking condition, but that glucose levels also remained higher for a longer period of time. Acute smoking has also been demonstrated to increase the level of free fatty acids in the bloodstream (Kershbaum et al., 1966). Since fatty acids are the primary precursor of cholesterol, this observation is in agreement with the epidemiologic data (Hjermann, Helgeland, Holme, Lung-Larsen, & Leren, 1976; Silvers, Stern, & Wood, 1972), which indicate that serum cholesterol levels are correlated with number of cigarettes smoked per day and that these levels return to near normal within 5 years of not smoking. One consequence of these free fatty acids remaining in the bloodstream is that they become an available source of energy for protein formation. Indeed, oral administration of nicotine to pigs increased the proportion of protein in muscle compared to fat deposits (Cunningham & Friend, 1964). Storing calories in the form of protein, however, is far more energy costly than storing the same calories as fat. Thus, a major effect of smoking appears to be that of biasing metabolic pathways such that more calories, either ingested or mobilized from fat stores, remain in the bloodstream longer, where they are more readily available for utilization or excretion as waste. The calorie storage that does occur may favor more energy-expending pathways, such as protein synthesis, over fat storage.

This bias away from storage of calories in adipose tissue among those who smoke provides a key for explaining why smokers could actually weigh less than nonsmokers while eating as much or more. The lipostatic hypothesis of body weight regulation has a long tradition in physiology. The original formulation of this hypothesis posited that food intake is adjusted appropriately so as to regulate body fat reserves around some predetermined set point (Kennedy, 1953; Mayer, 1955). Although set point explanations of body weight regulation are currently regarded as too mechanistic by many investigators (e.g., Mrosovsky & Powley, 1977), there is substantial evidence suggesting that an optimal amount of fat reserves is maintained through the complex short- and long-term interplay of genetic, neural, hormonal, and behavioral factors (Davis & Levine, 1977; Friedman & Stricker, 1976; Mrosovsky & Powley, 1977; Van Itallie, Smith, & Quartermain, 1977). Most relevant in this context are studies of rats in which adipose tissue was excised. In response to the excision, the animals increased their food intake and stored more fatty acids in the adipose cells that remained (Faust, Johnson, & Hirsch, 1977a, 1977b; Kennedy, 1953; Leibel, 1976; Liebelt, Ichinoe, & Nicholson, 1965; Mayer, 1955; Mrosovsky & Powley, 1977; Van Itallie et al., 1977). Apparently, some mechanism exists for signaling the need for food intake when a depletion of an optimal energy reserve in adipose tissue is sensed. Nicotine's effect on metabolic pathways may be that a desired level of adipose reserve is not attained and one hunger signal in the smoker is left on more often.

EFFECT OF SMOKING ON METABOLIC RATE AND THERMOGENESIS

Thus far, we have focused primarily on the mechanisms of caloric intake and storage that may be altered by smoking and that may return to normal upon smoking cessation, leading to weight gain. Recalling the operation of the model of body weight maintenance presented earlier, the weight gain upon cessation of smoking may also occur without a change in caloric intake, as a result of lessened caloric expenditure. We are unaware, however, of any data indicating that persons who stop smoking also reduce their physical activity. Indeed, our own unpublished observations suggest quite the opposite; even former smokers who have begun exercise programs upon cessation of smoking have sometimes gained weight. Consequently, there may be a general reduction in thermogenic efficiency after stopping smoking, leading to the storage of more calories.

Newsholme (1980; Newsholme & Crabtree, 1976; Newsholme & Underwood, 1966) has suggested the importance of substrate or "futile" cycles in the dissipation of chemical energy as heat (hence their role in regulation of body weight) and has posited the importance of elevated catecholamines in modulating the action of enzymes involved in increasing the activity of these cycles. This suggests a plausible thermogenic mechanism by which smoking affects weight. Smoking, which results in greater sympathetic tone and, hence, higher catecholamine levels, increases the activity of energy-expending substrate cycles, thereby burning calories at the expense of storage and leading to lower body weights. Stopping smoking presumably would return catecholamine levels to nearer normal levels, thereby facilitating more efficient energy utilization and consequent weight gain.

Were smoking, in fact, to cause an increase in thermogenic efficiency, the effect would be reflected in higher resting metabolic rates, higher body temperatures, and an increase in respiratory quotients (Goldman, Haisman, Bynum, Salans, Danforth, Horton, & Sims, 1976). At least in the short term, the evidence is quite clear that, for most subjects, smoking results in a detectable increase in metabolic rate. Dill, Edwards, and Forbes (1934) had eight smokers rest for a period of 90 minutes prior to smoking one cigarette over a period of 5 to 10 minutes. Oxygen consumption was observed to increase on the average of about 10% in the 45 minutes after smoking, a change consistent with the 90% increase in metabolic rate observed by Kiestand, Ramsey, and Hale (1940). Long-term studies directly investigating whether changes in thermogenic efficiency occur as a result of the cessation of smoking would appear to be difficult and expensive to conduct, however. Smoker versus nonsmoker between-group designs would likely require prohibitively large numbers of subjects in order to identify and attain significant differences because of the great intrasubject variability in relevant measures. Therefore, longitudinal within-subject designs would be preferable but would require that subjects be willing and able to stop smoking during the study. In addition, because they also affect the variables of interest with respect to thermogenesis, both the quantity and composition of the subjects' diets, as well as the extent of their physical activity, would have to be rigorously controlled over a substantial number of weeks. How many weeks would be necessary in order to detect which changes is a matter of speculation given our current knowledge. Finally, even if intake and gross activity were controlled, if thermogenic changes were to be found, their metabolic correlates would likely be confounded by concomitant changes in weight. For many of these reasons, the findings of the two studies bearing most directly on this issue are difficult to interpret; unfortunately, they also conflict.

In the metabolic study conducted by Glauser et al. (1970), noted earlier, protein-bound iodine levels and rates of oxygen consumption, both indicators of metabolic rate, were found to be lower after cessation of smoking, suggesting that a decrease in metabolic rate might account for the energy conservation leading to weight gain. As noted earlier, however, neither changes in dietary intake nor changes in physical activity (known to have changed in one subject) were controlled.

Burse, Bynum, Pandolf, Goldman, Sims, and Danforth (1975) studied the effects of smoking on metabolic events and thermogenesis. In their study, one-pack-a-day smokers participated in a study using a smoking/no-smoking design in periods of 3 weeks each. The dietary intake of the subjects was regulated by giving them constant diets composed of TV dinners. The extent to which the researchers had control over subjects' physical activity and the potential for their continuing to smoke or eat without the investigators' knowledge is unclear. They report, however, that during the period of presumed abstinence from smoking, there was no change in body weight, resting metabolic rate, thermic response to exercise or meals, or body temperature. They also found none of the increases in serum triiodothyronine or thyroxine that would be expected to accompany increased thermogenesis. Given that subjects did report an increase in their appetites during the nonsmoking period, the investigators concluded that increased consumption must account for the tendency of reformed smokers to gain weight. Hence, more direct attempts to assess whether smoking is associated with a change in metabolic rate have proved inconclusive. Pharmacological studies provide another way to study this same issue, however.

Clinical studies in smokers have shown decreased pharmacological effects of many drugs, including pentazocine (Keeri-Szanto & Pomeroy, 1971), propoxyphene (Jick, 1974), and benzodiazepine (Jick, 1974), suggesting that smoking increases the rate of drug metabolism. Two studies have provided more direct evidence that smoking stimulates drug metabolism by showing an increased clearance rate in smokers of antipyrine, a marker for several liver microsomal drug-metabolism systems (Brodie & Axelrod, 1950; Soberman, Brodie, Levy, Axelrod, Hollander, & Steele, 1949). In one of these studies the half-life of antipyrine was assessed in 307 male subjects aged 18 to 92. The subjects' age, smoking habits, and caffeine and alcohol consumption were entered as predictors in a multiple regression analysis to relate these variables to the metabolic clearance rates observed. The analyses indicated that smoking explained 12% of the variance in metabolic clearance rate, whereas no other predictor accounted for more than 3% of the remaining variance.

Vestal, Norris, Tobin, Cohen, Shock, and Andres (1975) studied antipyrine disappearance rate experimentally as an index of hepatic drug metabolism in 17 nonsmokers and 25 smokers. Eight smokers were also restudied about 2 months after they had stopped smoking. Results indicated that the antipyrine half-life was significantly lower in smokers than in nonsmokers, providing further evidence that smoking accelerates at least some metabolic mechanism of the liver. Furthermore, among smokers who stopped smoking, the antipyrine half-life increased 23% between the first and the last studies. Unfortunately, weight, diet, and physical activity were not controlled, making interpretation of these data somewhat ambiguous.

Admittedly, different drugs are metabolized by different enzymatic pathways. If the rate of clearance of these drugs is also an indication of the general effects of smoking on pathways involved in the expenditure of calories, however, one is tempted to speculate that this is an important mechanism that would enable smokers to weigh less while eating as much or more than nonsmokers. The decelerating rate of metabolism that would follow cessation of smoking suggests a mechanism by which former smokers would gain weight.

CONCLUSIONS

The factors that are directly involved in the normal processes of calorie regulation are multifarious and complex, as are the effects of smoking. This chapter has reviewed studies bearing on smoking's effects on the system of calorie regulation in an attempt to assess the current state of knowledge about the interrelationships between the two.

Evidence is substantial that smokers as a group weigh less than nonsmokers and that former smokers gain weight to a new plateau that is indistinguishable from that of people who have never smoked. The popular wisdom is that this weight difference is a result of differences in calorie intake—that smokers weigh less because they consume less and that they gain weight upon stopping smoking as a consequence of consuming more. The laboratory studies showing that smokers consume fewer sweets than nonsmokers and increase their sweet consumption when abstaining from cigarettes are consistent with this hypothesis. Nonetheless, other data suggest that smokers may consume more calories than nonsmokers. Even if this were the case, smokers could, of course, increase their consumption further when they stop smoking. Whatever the final verdict on these issues of differences in food intake, our review of the literature suggests the importance of understanding the metabolic consequences of smoking in order to explain the lower body weights of smokers and their weight gain upon cessation of smoking.

There is substantial evidence to suggest that smoking and nicotine function to lower the efficiency of calorie storage and/or to increase the rate of metabolism, each of which would be expected to lead to lower body weight in smokers. Such a mechanism would help explain the body of cross-sectional data suggesting that the total daily calorie intake of smokers is greater, rather than equal to or less than, that of nonsmokers; that is, an increased rate of expenditure and a less efficient use of calories that are consumed might be hypothesized to motivate the smoker to compensate by eating more. Weight gain after stopping smoking, therefore, could result from the regained efficiency and reduced expenditures of metabolic processes.

Although the metabolic explanation is not inconsistent with a hypothesis explaining weight gain following smoking cessation on the basis of increased calorie intake, the evidence reviewed here suggests that weight gain following smoking cessation would be possible even without increased consumption, given a hypothesized combination of mechanisms influenced by the physiological effects of nicotine. If newly abstinent smokers notice their weight gain, as they undoubtedly must, they may reduce their food intake in an effort to curb the weight gain. Against the background of a newly sluggish metabolism, however, greatly reduced food consumption may be precisely the wrong strategy, since too few calories tend to make metabolic processes slow down even further (Rodin, 1978, 1981; and see Bray, Chapter 40 of this Handbook). It is likely that aerobic exercise, which speeds up metabolism, would reverse the metabolically induced weight gain, although no systematic study with newly abstinent smokers has tested this hypothesis.

At a more general level, this chapter is intended to emphasize that many of the behaviors that are important for health promotion and disease prevention may bear complex relations to one another at the physiological, behavioral, and even sociocultural levels. Thus, recommending changes in one domain may provoke reverberating effects in several others. Good research and practice in the health promotion area must continue to take account of this fact.

REFERENCE NOTES

1. Russell, M. A. H., & Feyerabend, R. Personal communication, 1980.
2. Schachter, S., & Nesbitt, P. Unpublished observations.
3. Perlick, D. Unpublished observations.
4. Picone, T. A., Allen, L. H., Schramm, M., & Ferris, M. *Maternal pregnancy weight gains and smoking: Effects on human placental development and neonatal behavior.* Paper presented at the Federation of American Societies for Experimental Biology, Anaheim, California, April 17, 1980.
5. Rodin, J. *Obesity: Why the losing battle?* Master Series Lecture, American Psychological Association Convention, San Francisco, 1977.

REFERENCES

Antelman, S. M., Rowland, N. E., & Fisher, A. E. Stimulation bound ingestive behavior: A view from the tail. *Physiology and Behavior,* 1975, **17**, 743–748.

Ashford, J. R., Brown, S., Duffield, D. P., Smith, C. S., & Fay, J. W. J. The relation between smoking habits and physique, respiratory symptoms, ventilatory function, and radiological pneumoconiosis amongst coal workers at three Scottish collieries. *British Journal of Preventive and Social Medicine,* 1961, **15**, 106.

Bhagat, B. van Beaumont, W., & Ellert, M. S. Effect of chronic administration of nicotine on metabolic responses and intestinal glucose transport. In J. M. Singh & H. Lal (Eds.), *Proceedings of the Second International Symposium on Drug Addiction.* New York, Thieme-Stratton, 1974.

Bjelke, E. Variation in height and weight in the Norwegian population. *British Journal of Preventive and Social Medicine,* 1973, **14**, 344–346.

Blitzer, P. H., Rimm, A. A., & Giefer, E. E. The effect of cessation of smoking on body weight in 57,032 women: Cross-sectional and longitudinal analysis. *Journal of Chronic Diseases,* 1977, **30**, 415–429.

Booth, D. A. Effects of intrahypothalamic glucose injection on eating and drinking elicited by a single injection of insulin. *Journal of Comparative and Physiological Psychology,* 1968, **65**, 13–16.

Booth, D. A. Approaches to feeding control. In T. Silverstone (Ed.), *Appetite and food intake.* Braunschweig: Pergamon Press, 1976.

Bosse, R., Garvey, A. J., & Costa, P. T. Predictors of weight change following smoking cessation. *International Journal of Addictive Behavior,* 1980, **15**, 969–991.

Bray, G. A., & Campfield, L. A. Metabolic factors in the control of energy stores. *Metabolism,* 1975, **24**, 99–117.

Brodie, B. B., & Axelrod, J. The fate of antipyrine in man. *Journal of Pharmacology and Experimental Therapeutics,* 1950, **98**, 97–104.

Brozek, J., & Keys, A. Changes of body weight in normal men who stop smoking cigarettes. *Science,* 1957, **125**, 1203.

Burns-Cox, C. J., Doll, R., & Ball, K. Sugar intake and myocardial infarction. *British Heart Journal,* 1969, **31**, 485–490.

Burse, R. L., Bynum, G. D., Pandolf, K. B., Goldman, R. F., Sims, E. A. H., & Danforth, E. Increased appetite and unchanged metabolism upon cessation of smoking with diet held constant. *Physiologist,* 1975, **18**, 157.

Cabanac, M. Physiological role of pleasure. *Science,* 1971, **173**, 1103–1107.

Comstock, G. W., & Stone, R. W. Changes in body weight and subcutaneous fatness related to smoking habits. *Archives of Environmental Health,* 1972, **24**, 271–276.

Cooper, P., & Knight, B. Effects of cigarette smoking on gastric secretion of patients with duodenal ulcer. *New England Journal of Medicine,* 1956, **255**, 17–21.

Cryer, P. E., Haymond, M. W., Santiago, J. V., & Shah, S. D. Norepinephrine and epinephrine release and adrenergic mediation of smoking associated with hemodynamic and metabolic events. *New England Journal of Medicine,* 1976, **295**, 573.

Cunningham, H. M., & Friend, D. W. Effect of nicotine on nitrogen retention and fat deposition in pigs. *Canadian Journal of Animal Sciences,* 1964, **23,** 717.

Davis, J. O., & Levine, M. W. A model for the control of ingestion. *Psychological Review,* 1977, **84,** 379–412.

Debas, H. F., Cohen, M. M., Holubitsky, I. B., & Harrison, R. C. Effect of cigarette smoking on human gastric secretory responses. *Gut,* 1971, **12,** 93–96.

Dill, D. B., Edwards, H. T., & Forbes, W. H. Tobacco smoking in relation to blood sugar, blood lactic acid and metabolism. *American Journal of Physiology,* 1934, **109,** 118–122.

Domino, E. F. Electroencephalographic and behavioral arousal effects of small doses of nicotine: A neuropsychopharmacological study. *Annals of the New York Academy of Sciences,* 1967, **142,** 216–244.

Domino, E. F. Neuropsychopharmacology of nicotine and tobacco smoking. In W. L. Dunn (Ed.), *Smoking behavior: Motives and incentives.* Washington, D.C.: Winston, 1973.

Elgerot, A. Psychological and physiological changes during tobacco abstinence in habitual smokers. *Journal of Clinical Psychology,* 1978, **34,** 759–764.

Elwood, P. C., Moore, S., Waters, W. E., & Sweetnam, R. Sucrose consumption and ischaemic heart disease in the community. *Lancet,* 1970, **1,** 1014–1016.

Evans, J. R., Hughes, R. E., & Jones, P. R. Some effects of cigarette smoke in guinea pigs. *Proceedings of the Nutrition Society,* 1967, **26,** xxxvi.

Exton, J. H. Gluconeogenesis. *Metabolism,* 1972, **21,** 945–990.

Faust, I. M., Johnson, P. R., & Hirsch, J. Adipose tissue regeneration following lipectomy. *Science,* 1977, **197,** 391–393. (a)

Faust, I. M., Johnson, P. R., & Hirsch, J. Surgical removal of adipose tissue alters feeding behavior and the development of obesity in rats. *Science,* 1977, **197,** 393–396. (b)

Fergenson, P. E., Moss, S., Dzendolet, E., Sawyer, F. M., & Moore, J. W. The effect of signal probability, food intake, sex and smoking on gustation as measured by the theory of signal detection. *Journal of General Psychology,* 1975, **92,** 109–127.

Fisher, A. E., & Coury, J. N. Cholinergic tracing of a central neural circuit underlying the thirst drive. *Science,* 1962, **138,** 691–693.

Fletcher, C., & Doll, R. A survey of doctors' attitudes to smoking. *British Journal of Preventive and Social Medicine,* 1969, **23,** 145–153.

Floyd, J. C., Jr., Fajans, S. S., Conn, J. W., Knopf, R. F., & Rull, J. Stimulation of insulin secretion by amino acids. *Journal of Clinical Investigation,* 1966, **45,** 1487–1502.

Frankenhauser, M., Myrsten, A. L., Post, B., & Johannson, G. Behavioral and physiological effects of cigarette smoking in monotonous situations. *Psychopharmacology,* 1971, **22,** 1–7.

Frankenhauser, M., Myrsten, A., Waszak, M., Nerie, A., & Post, B. Dosage and time effects of cigarette smoking. *Psychopharmacology,* 1968, **13,** 311–319.

Frederiksen, L. W., & Frazier, M. Temporal distribution of smoking. *Addictive Behaviors,* 1977, **2,** 187–192.

Friedman, M. I., & Stricker, E. M. The physiological psychology of hunger: A physiological perspective. *Psychological Review,* 1976, **83,** 409–431.

Garvey, A. J., Bosse, R., & Seltzer, C. C. Smoking, weight change and age: A longitudinal analysis. *Archives of Environmental Health,* 1974, **28,** 327–329.

Gaudet, F. J., & Hugli, W. C., Jr. Concomitant habit changes associated with changes in smoking habits. *Medical Times,* 1969, **97,** 195–205.

Glauser, S. C., Glauser, E. M., Reidenberg, M. M., Rusy, B. E., & Tallarida, R. J. Metabolic changes associated with the cessation of cigarette smoking. *Archives of Environmental Health,* 1970, **20,** 377–381.

Glick, S. D., & Muller, R. U. Paradoxical effects of low doses of d-amphetamine in rats. *Psychopharmacology,* 1971, **22,** 396–402.

Goldman, R. D., Haisman, M. F., Bynum, G., Salans, L. B., Danforth, E., Jr., Horton, E. S., & Sims, E. A. H. Experimental obesity in man: VII. Metabolic rate in relation to dietary intake.

In G. A. Bray (Ed.), *Obesity in perspective.* Washington, D.C.: U.S. Government Printing Office, 1976.

Gordon, T., Kannel, W. B., Dawber, T. R., & McGee, D. Changes associated with cigarette smoking: The Framingham Study. *American Heart Journal,* 1975, **90,** 322–328.

Gori, G., & Richter, B. J. Macroeconomics of disease prevention in the United States. *Science,* 1978, **200,** 1124–1130.

Grimes, D. S., & Goddard, L. Effect of cigarette smoking on gastric emptying. *British Medical Journal,* 1978, **2,** 460–461.

Grossman, S. P. Eating or drinking elicited by direct adrenergic or cholinergic stimulation of hypothalamus. *Science,* 1960, **132,** 301–302.

Grossman, S. P. Direct adrenergic and cholinergic stimulation of hypothalamic mechanisms. *American Journal of Physiology,* 1962, **202,** 872–882.

Grossman, S. P. Behavioral effects of chemical stimulation on the ventral amygdala. *Journal of Comparative and Physiological Psychology,* 1964, **57,** 29–36.

Grunberg, N. The effects of nicotine on food consumption and taste preferences (Doctoral dissertation, Columbia University, 1980). *Dissertation Abstracts International,* 1980, **41,** 728B.

Hammond, E. C., & Percy, C. Ex-smokers. *New York State Journal of Medicine,* 1958, **58,** 2956–2959.

Hart, P., Farrell, G. C., Cooksley, W. G. E., & Powell, L. W. Enhanced drug metabolism in cigarette smokers. *British Medical Journal,* 1976, **2,** 147–149.

Hauser, H., Schwartz, B. E., Roth, G., & Bickford, R. G. Electroencephalographic changes related to smoking. *Electroencephalography and Clinical Neurophysiology,* 1958, **10,** 576.

Heimstra, N. W., Bancroft, N. R., & DeKock, A. R. Effects of smoking upon sustained performance in a simulated driving task. *Annals of the New York Academy of Sciences,* 1967, **142,** 295–307.

Higgins, A. C. Nutritional supplements and the outcome of pregnancy. In *Proceedings of the NAS Workshop,* Sagamere Beach, Massachusetts, November 3–5, 1971. Washington, D.C.: National Academy of Sciences Press, 1973.

Hjermann, I., Helgeland, A., Holme, I., Lung-Larsen, G., & Leren, P. The intercorrelation of serum cholesterol, cigarette smoking and body weight: The Oslo Study. *Acta Medica Scandinavica,* 1976, **200,** 479–485.

Holcomb, H. S., & Meigs, J. W. Medical absenteeism among cigarette and cigar and pipe smokers. *Archives of Environmental Health,* 1972, **25,** 295–300.

Howell, R. W. Obesity and smoking habits. *British Medical Journal,* 1971, **47,** 625.

Hughes, R. E., Jones, P. R., & Nicholas, P. Some effects of experimentally produced cigarette smoke on the growth, vitamin C metabolism and organ weights of guinea pigs. *Journal of Pharmacy and Pharmacology,* 1970, **22,** 823–827.

Huston, J. J., & Stenson, K. The development of obesity in fit young men: A regimental study. *Practitioner,* 1974, **212,** 700–705.

Jacobs, M. A., Knapp, P. H., Anderson, L. S., Karnsh, N., Meissner, R., & Richman, S. J. Relationship of oral frustration factors with heavy cigarette smoking in male college students. *Journal of Nervous and Mental Disease,* 1965, **141,** 161–171.

Jacobs, M. A., & Spilken, A. Z. Personality patterns associated with heavy cigarette smoking in male college students. *Journal of Consulting and Clinical Psychology,* 1971, **37,** 428–532.

Jick, H. Smoking and clinical drug effects. *Medical Clinics of North America,* 1974, **58,** 1143.

Kaplan, A. R., Glanville, E. V., & Fisher, R. Taste thresholds for bitterness and cigarette smoking. *Nature,* 1964, **202,** 1366.

Karvonen, M., Keys, A., Orma, E., Fidanzo, F., & Brozek, J. Cigarette smoking, serum cholesterol, blood pressure and body fatness: Observations in Finland. *Lancet,* 1959, **1,** 452–464.

Keeri-Szanto, M., & Pomeroy, J. R. Atmospheric pollution and pentazocine metabolism. *Lancet,* 1971, **1,** 947–949.

Kennedy, G. C. The role of depot fat in the hypothalamic control of food intake in the rat. *Proceedings of the Royal Society of London,* 1953, **137,** 535–549.

Kershbaum, A., Bellet, S., Jimenez, J., & Feinberg, L. J. Differences in effects of cigar and cigarette smoking on free fatty acid mobilization and catecholamine excretion. *Journal of the American Medical Association,* 1966, **195,** 1095–1098.

Kershbaum, A., Bellet, S., & Khorsandrian, R. Elevation of serum cholesterol after administration of nicotine. *American Heart Journal,* 1965, **69,** 206–210.

Keys, A., Aravanis, C., & Blackburn, H. W. Epidemiologic studies related to coronary heart disease: Characteristics of men aged 40–59 in seven countries. *Acta Medica Scandinavica [Suppl.],* 1966, **460,** 1–75.

Khosla, T., & Lowe, C. R. Obesity and smoking habits. *British Medical Journal,* 1971, **4,** 10–13.

Khosla, T., & Lowe, C. R. Obesity and smoking habits by social class. *British Journal of Preventive and Social Medicine,* 1972, **26,** 249–256.

Khosla, T., & Lowe, C. R. Relative risks of obesity and smoking. *British Medical Journal,* 1973, **4,** 106.

Kiestand, W. A., Ramsey, H. J., & Hale, D. M. The effects of cigarette smoking on metabolic rate, heart rate, oxygen, pulse and breathing rate. *Journal of Laboratory and Clinical Medicine,* 1940, **25,** 1013–1017.

King, A. J. Stress, cigarette smoking and smoking behavior in adolescent males. *Canadian Journal of Public Health,* 1971, **62,** 297–302.

Kopczynski, J. Height and weight in adults in Cracow. *Epidemiology Review,* 1972, **26,** 452–464.

Krikstone, B. J., & Levitt, R. A. Interactions between water deprivation and chemical brain stimulation. *Journal of Comparative and Physiological Psychology,* 1970, **71,** 334–340.

Krut, L. H., Perrin, M. J., & Bronte-Stewart, B. Taste perception in smokers and nonsmokers. *British Medical Journal,* 1961, **1,** 384–387.

Laird, D. The effect of smoking on taste preferences. *Medical Record,* 1939, **149,** 404.

Leibel, R. L., A biologic radar system for the assessment of body mass. *Journal of Theoretical Biology,* 1977, **66,** 297–306.

Levitt, R. A., White, C. S., & Sander, D. M. Dose-response analysis of carbachol elicited drinking in the rat limbic system. *Journal of Comparative and Physiological Psychology,* 1970, **72,** 345–350.

Liebelt, R. A., Ichinoe, S., & Nicholson, N. Regulatory influences of adipose tissue on food intake and body weight. *Annals of the New York Academy of Sciences,* 1965, **131,** 559.

Lincoln, J. E. Weight gain after cessation of smoking. *Journal of the American Medical Association,* 1969, **210,** 1965.

Lincoln, J. E. Relation of income to body weight in cigarette smokers and nonsmokers. *Journal of the American Medical Association,* 1970, **214,** 1121.

Marliss, E. B., Aoki, T. T., Unger, R. H., Soeldner, J. S., & Cahill, G. F. Glucagon levels and metabolic effects in fasting man. *Journal of Clinical Investigation,* 1970, **49,** 2256–2270.

Mason, J. W. Emotion as reflected in patterns of endocrine integration. In L. Levi (Ed.), *Emotions: Their parameters and measurement.* New York: Raven Press, 1975.

Mayer, J. Regulation of energy intake and body weight: The glucostatic and the lipostatic hypothesis. *Annals of the New York Academy of Sciences,* 1955, **63,** 15–42.

McBarney, D. H., & Moskat, L. J. Taste thresholds in college-age smokers and nonsmokers. *Perception and Psychophysics,* 1975, **18,** 71–73.

Miller, N. E. Chemical coding of behavior in the brain. *Science,* 1965, **148,** 328–338.

Miller, N. E., Gottesman, K. S., & Emory, N. Dose response to carbachol and norepinephrine in rat hypothalamus. *American Journal of Physiology,* 1964, **206,** 1384–1388.

Mrosovsky, N., & Powley, T. L. Set points of body weight and fat. *Behavioral Biology,* 1977, **20,** 205–223.

Murthy, S. N. S., Dinoso, V. P., Clearfield, H. R., & Chey, W. Y. Simultaneous measurement of basal pancreatic, gastric acid secretion, plasma gastrin and secretin during smoking. *Gastroenterology,* 1977, **73,** 758–761.

Myers, R. D. Emotional and autonomic responses following hypothalamic chemical stimulation. *Canadian Journal of Psychology,* 1964, **18,** 6–14.

Newsholme, E. A. A possible metabolic basis for the control of body weight. *New England Journal of Medicine,* 1980, **302,** 400–405.

Newsholme, E. A., & Crabtree, B. Metabolic aspects of enzyme activity regulation. *Symposia of the Society for Experimental Biology,* 1976, **41,** 61–110.

Newsholme, E. A., & Underwood, A. H. The control of glycolysis and gluconeogenesis in the kidney cortex. *Biochemical Journal,* 1966, **99,** 24C–26C.

Nisbett, R. E., & Wilson, T. Telling more than we can know: Verbal reports on mental processes. *Psychological Review,* 1977, **84,** 231–259.

Novis, B. H., Marks, I. N., Banks, S., & Sloan, A. W. The relation between gastric acid secretion and body habitus, blood groups, smoking and the subsequent development of dyspepsia and duodenal ulcer. *Gut,* 1973, **14,** 107–112.

Pangborn, R. M., & Trabue, I. M. Gustatory responses during periods of controlled and ad lib cigarette smoking. *Perception and Psychophysics,* 1973, **14,** 139–144.

Pangborn, R. M., Trabue, I. M., & Pikielna, N. B. Taste, odor, and tactile discrimination before and after smoking. *Perception and Psychophysics,* 1967, **2,** 529–532.

Passey, R. D. Cavedrogenity of cigarette tars. *British Empire Cancer Campaign Annual Report,* 1957, **35,** 65–66.

Passey, R. D. Cigarette smoke and cancer of the lung. *British Empire Cancer Campaign Annual Report,* 1958, **36,** 48–49.

Paton, W. D. M. Transmission and block in autonomic ganglia. *Pharmacology,* 1954, **6,** 59–67.

Paul, O., MacMillan, A., McKean, H., & Park, H. Sucrose intake and coronary heart disease. *Lancet,* 1968, **2,** 1049–1051.

Pincherle, G. Obesity and smoking habits. *British Medical Journal,* 1971, **4,** 298.

Porte, D., Graber, A. L., Kuzuya, T., & Williams, R. D. The effect of epinephrine on immunoreactive insulin levels in man. *Journal of Clinical Investigation,* 1966, **45,** 228–236.

Pursell, E. D., Sanders, R. E., & Haude, R. H. Sensitivity to sucrose in smokers and nonsmokers: A comparison of TSD and percent correct measures. *Perception and Psychophysics,* 1973, **14,** 34–36.

Quartermain, D., & Miller, N. E. Sensory feedback in time response of drinking elicited by carbachol in pre-optic area of the rat. *Journal of Comparative and Physiological Psychology,* 1966, **62,** 350–353.

Radsel, Z., & Kambic, V. The influence of cigarette smoke on the pharyngeal mucosa. *Acta Oto-Laryngologica,* 1978, **85,** 128–134.

Randle, P. J., Garland, P. B., Hales, C. N., Newsholme, E. A., Denton, R. M., & Pogson, C. I. Interactions of metabolism and the physiological role of insulin. *Recent Progress in Hormone Research,* 1966, **22,** 1–44.

Rodin, J. Effects of distraction on the performance of obese and normal subjects. *Journal of Comparative and Physiological Psychology,* 1973, **83,** 68–78.

Rodin, J. The effects of obesity and set point on taste responsiveness and intake in humans. *Journal of Comparative and Physiological Psychology,* 1975, **89,** 1003–1009.

Rodin, J., Herman, C. P., & Schachter, S. Obesity and various tests of external sensitivity. In S. Schachter & J. Rodin (Eds.), *Obese humans and rats.* Washington, D.C.: Erlbaum, 1974.

Rodin, J., Moskowitz, H. R., & Bray, G. A. Relationship between obesity, weight loss, and taste responsiveness. *Physiology and Behavior,* 1976, **17,** 591–597.

Rodin, J., & Slochower, J. Externality in the nonobese: The effects of environmental responsiveness on weight. *Journal of Personality and Social Psychology,* 1976, **29,** 557–565.

Rodin, J. Has the internal versus external distinction outlived its usefulness? In G. A. Bray (Ed.), *Recent advances in obesity research* (Vol. II). London: Newman, 1978.

Rodin, L. The current status of the internal-external obesity hypothesis: What went wrong. *American Psychologist,* 1981, **36,** 361–372.

Ruch, T. C., & Patton, H. D. (Eds.). *Physiology and biophysics* (19th ed.). Philadelphia: Saunders, 1965.

Russell, M. A. H. Tobacco smoking and nicotine dependence. In *Research advances in alcohol and drug problems.* New York: Wiley, 1976.

Schmiterlow, C. G., Hansson, E., Andersson, G., Applegren, L. E., & Hoffman, P. C. Distribution of nicotine in central nervous system. *Annals of the New York Academy of Sciences,* 1967, **142,** 2–14.

Schnecter, M. D., & Cook, P. Nicotine induced weight loss in rats without an effect on appetite. *European Journal of Pharmacology,* 1976, **38,** 63–69.

Schnedorf, J. C., & Ivy, A. C. The effect of tobacco smoking on the alimentary canal. *Journal of the American Medical Association,* 1938, **112,** 898–903.

Silvers, A., Stern, M., & Wood, P. Plasma cholesterol and glyceride levels in relation to smoking, ponderal index and physical activity in Central Valley, California. *Clinical Research,* 1972, **20,** 175.

Silvette, H., Hoff, E. C., Larson, P. S. J., & Haag, H. B. The actions of nicotine on central nervous system functions. *Pharmacology Review,* 1962, **14,** 137–173.

Sinnot, J., & Rauth, J. E. Effect of smoking on taste thresholds. *Journal of General Psychology,* 1937, **17,** 151–153.

Soberman, R., Brodie, B. B., Levy, B. B., Axelrod, J., Hollander, V., & Steele, J. M. The use of antipyrine in the measurement of total body water in man. *Journal of Biological Chemistry,* 1949, **179,** 31–42.

Solomon, R. L., & Corbit, J. D. An opponent-process theory of motivation: The temporal diagnosis of affect. *Psychological Review,* 1974, **81,** 119–145.

Sommer, S., Novin, D., & Levine, M. Food and water intake following intrahypothalamic injections of carbachol in the rabbit. *Science,* 1967, **56,** 983–984.

Spitzer, L., & Rodin, J. Studies of human ingestive behaviors: A critical review. *Appetite,* 1981, **2,** 293–329.

Steigmann, F., Dolehide, H., & Kaminski, L. Effects of smoking tobacco on gastric acidity and motility of hospital controls and patients with peptic ulcer. *American Journal of Gastroenterology,* 1954, **22,** 399–409.

Stirling, J. L., & Stock, M. J. Non-conservative mechanisms of energy metabolism in thermogenesis. In M. Apfelbaum (Ed.), *Energy balance in man.* Paris: Masson, 1973.

Swineford, O., & Ochota, L. Smoking and chronic respiratory disorders: Results of abstinence. *Annals of Allergy,* 1958, **16,** 455–458.

Taminato, T., Seino, Y., Goto, Y., Inoue, Y., Matsukura, S., & Imura, H. Cigarette smoking inhibits arginine-induced insulin release in man. *Hormone and Metabolic Research,* 1978, **10,** 78–79.

Ternes, J. W. An opponent-process theory of habitual behavior with special reference to smoking. In M. E. Jarvik, J. W. Cullen, E. R. Gritz, T. N. Vogt, & L. J. West (Eds.), *Research on smoking behavior.* NIDA Research Monograph 17. Washington, D.C.: U.S. Government Printing Office, 1977.

Unger, R. H. Alpha- and beta-cell interrelationships in health and disease. *Metabolism,* 1974, **23,** 581–593.

U.S. Department of Health, Education and Welfare (U.S. DHEW). *Adult use of tobacco.* Washington, D.C.: U.S. Government Printing Office, 1976.

U.S. Department of Health, Education and Welfare (U.S. DHEW). *Healthy people: The Surgeon General's report on health promotion and disease prevention.* Washington, D.C.: U.S. Government Printing Office, 1979.

Van Itallie, T. B., Smith, N. S., & Quartermain, D. Short-term and long-term components in the regulation of food intake: Evidence for a modulatory role of carbohydrate status. *American Journal of Clinical Nutrition,* 1977, **30,** 742–757.

Veldman, D. J., & Brown, O. H. Personality and performance characteristics associated with cigarette smoking among college freshmen. *Journal of Consulting and Clinical Psychology,* 1966, **33,** 109–119.

Vestal, R. E., Norris, A. H., Tobin, J. D., Cohen, B. H., Shock, N. W., & Andres, R. Antipyrine metabolism in man: Influence of age, alcohol, caffeine and smoking. *Clinical Pharmacology and Therapeutics,* 1975, **18,** 425–443.

Warburton, D. M. *Brain, behavior and drugs.* New York: Wiley, 1975.

Wilkinson, A. R., & Johnson, D. Inhibitory effect of cigarette smoking on gastric secretion stimulated by pentagastrin in man. *Lancet,* 1971, **2**, 628–632.

Winternitz, W., & Quillen, D. Acute hormonal response to cigarette smoking. *Journal of Clinical Pharmacology,* 1977, **17**, 389–392.

Wynder, E. L., Kaufman, P. L., & Lesser, R. L. A short-term follow-up study on ex-cigarette smokers with special emphasis on persistent cough and weight gain. *American Review of Respiratory Disease,* 1967, **96**, 645–655.

Young, P. T. Palatability: The hedonic response to foodstuffs. *Handbook of Physiology,* 1967, **1**, 353–366.

SECTION 6
SMOKING PREVENTION

CHAPTER 43

OVERVIEW

RICHARD I. EVANS

University of Houston

As we began to plan the section of this Handbook dealing with smoking, it became evident that among the various health behaviors that would be addressed in the Handbook, smoking would perhaps have to be considered the most critical. It is not necessary here to review the vast amount of evidence that links smoking, both by itself and in conjunction with other risk factors, to almost every major disease. Since the focus of this Handbook is disease prevention and health promotion, it is evident that both smoking prevention and smoking treatment or cessation are components of the primary prevention of disease, thus justifying their inclusion in this smoking section. In order to present to the reader a sophisticated view of progress in the control of smoking, we decided to include six chapters with distinctively different foci.

Chapter 44, by Lichtenstein and Mermelstein, is a review of the state of the art in nonpharmacological behavioral techniques for the control of smoking. As can be easily determined from this chapter, even though many nonpharmacological techniques have short-term success in controlling smoking, the general problem of overcoming regression or back-sliding has hardly been mastered, regardless of the techniques that have been employed. After some years of coping with this long-term compliance problem with increasing sophistication in both treatment content and evaluation methodology, however, researchers now know a good deal more about what might constitute a truly effective strategy to control smoking indefinitely, whether the technique employed is solely self-initiated or is initiated in conjunction with an external program of some sort.

Another aspect of the smoking problem is the rapid development of pharmacological approaches to smoking control. This has been documented in Chapter 45, by Kozlowski. In reviewing the various pharmacological techniques that have been introduced, Kozlowski concludes that no short-term program developed so far would necessarily be effective in the long-run, but he does suggest that some promising directions have been taken by investigators employing pharmacological smoking treatment techniques.

The next chapter in this section, Chapter 46, has to do with the important area of the measurement of smoking frequency. This chapter, by Pechacek, Fox, Murray, and Luepker, shows clearly that great strides have been made in increasing the validity of measures of smoking frequency. With this increasing sophistication in such measurements, one can have some confidence that evaluations of any smoking control program now can be implemented more effectively in terms of the really critical outcome measures, frequency and pattern of smoking.

Two other chapters in this section deal with specific techniques in smoking control: one in the area of treatment or cessation and the other in prevention. Suedfeld's chapter on restricted environmental stimulation therapy (REST) discusses a unique application of environmental control techniques, previously used in other areas of behavioral research, to the treatment of smoking. Although this technique has not been exposed to truly long-term evaluations, it appears to be so nonaversive, yet effective, that it could prove to be a particularly significant procedure when employed either by itself or in conjunction with other methods. It certainly justifies some large-scale prospective evaluations.

My chapter, which describes a social inoculation strategy to prevent smoking in adolescents, represents the other specific technique. This approach, which was based on various principles in social learning and communication theory, suggests an encouraging direction for the deterrence of cigarette smoking. The prevention of smoking could, because of the promise of such behavioral interventions, become an increasingly effective area of primary disease prevention.

These five chapters collectively suggest that there are considerable grounds for optimism for an increasingly effective attack on the smoking problem. If, as indicated in my chapter, very little smoking is now initiated after an individual leaves high school, the evidence that suggests modest to dramatic impact of behavioral smoking prevention programs in the schools provides grounds for considerable optimism for the value of attacking the smoking problem with programs to prevent smoking in children and adolescents. In addition to prevention of smoking, so much more is known about both pharmacological and nonpharmacological smoking treatment programs that smokers can now choose from among several approaches, according to the temperament of the smoker.

The fact that some areas of success are reported in smoking control efforts, at both prevention and treatment levels, plus the generally reinforcing nature of the rapidly expanding nonsmoking social climate, suggest that our culture may well be on the way toward significantly reducing this destructive behavior. This optimism is supported in a final chapter in this section, by Bell and Levy, that deals with public policy and smoking prevention. Bell and Levy suggest that in the area of public policy, there is an increasing awareness of progress in the smoking control area. Resources in government are rapidly beginning to support an even greater effort to deal with this behavior, which is now clearly recognized as a serious threat to the personal and economic well-being of members of our society.

CHAPTER 44

REVIEW OF APPROACHES TO SMOKING TREATMENT: BEHAVIOR MODIFICATION STRATEGIES

EDWARD LICHTENSTEIN

University of Oregon and Oregon Research Institute

ROBIN J. MERMELSTEIN

University of Oregon

Cigarette smoking is one of the relatively easiest behavioral problems to assess. It is also one of the most resistant problems to modify permanently. There is as yet no dependable behavioral technology for the treatment of dependent cigarette smokers. Behavioral approaches have shown promise, however, and they are certainly the most explicit and carefully evaluated programs on the smoking treatment scene.

Behavior modification approaches apply respondent, operant, and cognitive-behavioral principles to the treatment of cigarette smoking. Behavioral treatments work on modifying both the antecedents and consequences of smoking and teach smokers thought management and coping techniques. Early behavioral work tended to view smoking as a learned habit that would be amenable to operant or respondent strategies borrowed from treatments for other behavioral problems. Initial naiveté about smoking has given way to the recognition of smoking as a complex, multidimensional behavior involving behavioral, pharmacological, and cognitive mechanisms (Lichtenstein, 1982; Pomerleau, 1981). Interventions, however, are still guided more by general behavioral principles than by a valid, specific model of smoking, although developing knowledge about smokers—for example, the pharmacological effects of nicotine—is being incorporated into some treatment programs (e.g., Foxx & Brown, 1979).

Behavioral interventions have shifted in response to both empirical and theoretical developments. Single-strategy treatment programs (e.g., Levinson, Shapiro, Schwartz, & Tursky, 1971), for example, have given way to multicomponent programs. In addition, increasing attention is being paid to the maintenance of nonsmoking in response to the growing awareness of the recidivism problem. Cognitive processes in smoking cessation are similarly receiv-

Preparation of this chapter was facilitated by Grant No. 1 RO1 HL29547 from the National Heart, Lung, and Blood Institute.

ing increasing attention, reflecting a more general turn toward mediation processes in behavior therapy (Bandura, 1977).

Because cigarette smoking lends itself to a variety of behavioral strategies and tactics, there is no single behavioral treatment program. Some features characterize most programs, however, and may be said to impart a behavioral essence. These features include (a) the use of systematic self-monitoring or personal record keeping for both treatment and evaluation purposes; (b) the explicit use of self-management or self-control strategies, whereby participants are taught coping skills for their smoking; and (c) the use of homework assignments to practice skills presented during treatment sessions.

In this chapter, we will first discuss issues in evaluating the effectiveness of behavioral treatments. Following this discussion, the bulk of the chapter will review intervention methods. It is convenient to construe treatment programs as having three interdependent phases: preparation for quitting, quitting, and maintenance of nonsmoking. Principles and methods for each of these phases will be reviewed and recommendations will be offered.

ISSUES IN EVALUATING EFFECTIVENESS

Outcome measures, length of follow-up, attrition, and replicability of results are critical points to note when evaluating the effectiveness of treatment programs. It is no longer acceptable, for example, to rely solely on self-reports of smoking status, no matter how these data are collected. The developing technology for biochemical detection of smoking (see Chapter 46 of this Handbook) provides investigators and practitioners with several options for confirming self-reported smoking status. The use of significant others to corroborate self-reports of abstinence is inexpensive and can be useful.

Another issue to consider in evaluating treatment effectiveness is the length of follow-up. Results of studies by Hunt, Barnett, and Branch (1971) and by Hunt and Bespalec (1974) indicate that almost all treatments show large and rapid relapse, with most relapses occurring within the first 3 months after treatment. Even after 6 months, relapses continue to occur (Lichtenstein & Rodrigues, 1977). Long-term follow-up, through at least 6 months and preferably 1 year posttreatment, is thus imperative for adequately assessing treatment effectiveness.

Attrition may also affect a study's overall success rate. Obviously, some attrition will almost always occur. Participants may move, become ill, or fail to complete the program for a variety of reasons. We do not know, however, what the average attrition rate is. Treatment programs with very low attrition rates are noteworthy, because one assumes that a treatment will be more effective if subjects participate and because success rates are more impressive if the program can appeal to more subjects. For completeness and evaluation of data, researchers should report attrition rates and note whether data on dropouts were excluded from the data analyses or were included as treatment failures. The latter procedure is clearly the more conservative one.

Finally, there is the problem of the replicability of results. The most impressive treatment programs are the ones that have potential for widespread dissemination and are effective across a variety of populations. Yet the small numbers, different recruitment procedures, and different populations in the smoking treatment studies, and the possibility of group effects, limit the conclusions that can be drawn about the generalizability of treatment programs. In any controlled-outcome study, the within-group variability is likely to be large. Some subjects in both treatment and control groups will be abstinent, while some will return to baseline levels. A large sample size is likely to be needed to detect a significant effect.

Because of differences in recruitment procedures and sample compositions, it is often difficult to compare results across studies. Results based on college student samples are likely to be less impressive than a comparable abstinence rates among older, more dependent smokers. Thus, recruitment procedures and sample composition should be explicitly described.

Many programs provide group treatment, and a given condition or treatment in a design is sometimes represented by only one group. The possibility of group effects—results produced by idiosyncratic group processes—has not been adequately recognized. Although practical constraints may preclude using groups as the unit of analysis, each condition or treatment should be represented by a minimum of two groups, and preferably more.

In summary, a valid and useful outcome report would include biochemical verification of self-reports; 6-month and/or 1-year follow-up; explicit information about attrition, recruitment procedures, and sample compositions; and replication across groups and across settings.

INTERVENTION METHODS

Various strategies and tactics have been derived from the behavioral or social learning perspective. For the most part, these strategies can be grouped into three main types of intervention methods: aversive strategies, nicotine fading and controlled smoking strategies, and self-control strategies. The primary focus of both the aversive and nicotine fading methods is on helping the smoker to achieve abstinence. The self-control methods, in contrast, may run through all phases of the quitting process, from preparing to quit, to quitting, to maintaining abstinence. Although the different methods initially were used independently, investigators recently have been combining these methods in hope of maximizing treatment effectiveness. Before discussing the resulting broad-spectrum or multicomponent programs, however, we will examine each of the three intervention methods individually. The evaluations and recommendations given here are based on the literature in combination with clinical experience.

Aversive Strategies

Aversive strategies have been used frequently for cigarette smoking problems, as for other intrinsically rewarding behavior problems, and they are perhaps the single most widely used technique. Three major kinds of aversive stimuli have been used: electric shock, imaginal stimuli (covert sensitization), and cigarette smoke itself.

Electrical Aversion

The research literature on the use of contingent electric shock paired with smoking has been consistently negative (e.g., Russell, Armstrong, & Patel, 1976). Comprehensive reviews of the literature concur on the uniformly negative results of laboratory contingent shock (Lichtenstein & Danaher, 1976; Pechacek, 1979). A more promising technique involves pairing shock with the thoughts, images, or covert speech that smokers are assumed to produce during smoking, but the data on this technique are only suggestive (Berecz, 1972, 1976). Although shock is reasonably convenient and safe, it cannot be recommended in light of the research evidence.

Covert Sensitization

In covert sensitization, both the aversive stimuli and the target behavior are presented imaginally by instructing the smoker to visualize getting ready to smoke and then to imagine becoming nauseated and vomiting. An escape dimension is included by suggesting that the smoker will feel better as soon as the imaginary cigarette is rejected. The procedure is safe, requires no apparatus, can be self-administered, and reflects current interest in cognitive behavior therapy. The research evidence, however, is consistently negative (e.g.,

Barbarin, 1978). Programmatic use of covert sensitization is not recommended, but clinicians who are skillful in its use may still wish to apply it selectively with clients who have good imagery skills.

Cigarette Smoke Aversion

The initial use of cigarette smoke as an aversive stimulus involved a cumbersome apparatus that blew smoke into the subjects' faces (Wilde, 1964). The smoke machine gave way to two more convenient procedures: rapid smoking and satiation. These procedurally distinct methods are sometimes confused. Satiation is a take-home procedure whereby the subject doubles or triples the baseline smoking rate in the natural environment. It is very convenient but difficult to monitor or control. Rapid smoking is essentially a clinic or laboratory procedure whereby subjects smoke continually, inhaling every 6 to 8 seconds, until tolerance is reached.

Satiation.   Following two encouraging reports on the effectiveness of satiation (Resnick, 1968a, 1968b), there was a series of negative results (e.g., Sushinsky, 1972). In most of the satiation studies, there was minimal treatment time or experimenter contact. More recent work with satiation has been in the context of more intensive, multicomponent programs. The research programs headed by Best (Best, Owens, & Trentadue, 1978) and Lando (1977) have had impressive outcomes using satiation in multicomponent programs. Delahunt and Curran (1976) obtained similarly positive results.

Rapid smoking.   Rapid smoking is the most widely researched aversion method, having spawned three sets of studies: (a) a sizable outcome literature on its effectiveness, (b) a controversial literature concerning side effects and health risks, and (c) a search for nonrisky alternative procedures that still involve the use of cigarette smoke.

   Effectiveness of rapid smoking. Danaher (1977b) reviewed 22 studies employing rapid smoking. Of the 14 studies that permitted a comparison with placebo control or alternative treatment, rapid smoking was more effective in producing long-term abstinence in 10, but in no case were these differences statistically significant. In 11 comparison studies reporting smoking rate data, rapid smoking was superior in 8 and the difference reached statistical significance in 3. A long-term follow-up, 2 to 6 years posttreatment, of subjects in the original series of rapid smoking studies by Lichtenstein and his colleagues revealed a moderate degree of relapse. Thirty-four percent of the subjects were now abstinent, down from 54 percent at 3- or 6-month follow-up (Lichtenstein & Rodrigues, 1977).

   More recent rapid smoking studies have continued to show both positive results (e.g., Best et al., 1978; Hall, Sachs, & Hall, 1979) and negative findings (e.g., Gordon, 1978; Raw & Russell, 1980). The positive findings tend to outnumber the negative, but this could reflect publication contingencies that work against negative results. Evaluation of rapid smoking studies is further complicated in that recent work often includes rapid smoking as part of a multicomponent package (e.g. Best et al., 1978), and the specific contribution of rapid smoking is not assessed (Tongas, 1979; Younggren & Parker, 1977). Rapid smoking still appears to be an effective procedure, but its use will be constrained by how workers view the risks involved and the costs of necessary screening procedures.

   Side effects of rapid smoking. It is clear that, compared to regular smoking, rapid smoking produces significant increases in heart rate, carboxyhemoglobin, other blood gases, and blood nicotine levels (Hall et al., 1979; Russell, Raw, Taylor, Feyerabend, & Saloojee, 1978; Sachs, Hall, & Hall, 1978). The clinical and practical significance of these findings remains controversial in that investigators differ in their interpretations of the risks involved.

   Cardiovascular complications remain the major concern, and cardiovascular irregularities, as measured by electrocardiographic (ECG) readings, have been reported in several studies (e.g., Hall et al., 1979; Horan, Hackett, Nicholas, Linberg, Stone, & Lukoski, 1977), but these have not led to any significant clinical symptoms. Sachs, Hall, Pechacek, and Fitzgerald (1979) concluded that rapid smoking is safe and beneficial in healthy individuals, but they used extensive and expensive screening procedures that would be out of the reach of most investigators. In contrast, the screening procedures suggested by Lichtenstein and Glasgow (1977) are less costly and rigorous. Rapid smoking seems safe for nonsymptomatic, relatively young adults. A risk-benefit assessment is a trickier judgment to make, since it depends in part on the availability and the effectiveness of less risky alternatives (Sachs et al., 1979). The screening and selection considerations of rapid smoking limit its applicability. Rapid smoking seems primarily useful for the individual practitioner and in certain medical settings where screening and/or medical consultation is readily available.

  Alternatives to rapid smoking. Investigators have sought variations of rapid smoking that would avoid or minimize its riskiness while retaining its therapeutic effectiveness. One alternative is focused smoking (Hackett & Horan, 1978), whereby subjects smoke at a normal rate while instructed to concentrate attention on their negative sensations.

  A more recent alternative is smoke holding, whereby subjects hold smoke in their mouths for a specified period of time without inhaling. Initial work indicates that this procedure produced minimum physiological stress and has led to a 33% abstinence rate at 6-month follow-up (Kopel, Suckerman, & Baksht, Note 1). Several alternatives to rapid smoking were compared on measures of physiological risk and subjective unpleasantness (Orleans, White, & Nagey, Note 2). Smoke holding emerged as the most promising alternative; it was rated high in subjective unpleasantness and had minimal impact on the physiological risk measures. Although these nonrisky alternatives to rapid smoking do not yet have a substantial track record, they seem worthy of use.

Nicotine Fading and Controlled Smoking

Evidence strongly suggests that nicotine is a major factor in cigarette smoking (Jarvik, 1979; Russell, 1976; Schachter, 1978). Nicotine fading is a behavioral treatment strategy that addresses both pharmacological (i.e., the role of nicotine) and psychological factors. Clients work toward a target quitting date by switching brands to progressively lower nicotine/tar content cigarettes (Foxx & Brown, 1979). Clients may also calculate and plot estimated nicotine intake. The procedure involves minimal effort and virtually assures initial success and positive feedback. Clients are told that the brand switching will minimize withdrawal symptoms at quitting time.

  In the initial study (Foxx & Brown, 1979), monitored nicotine fading was superior to its two component procedures, nicotine fading alone and self-monitoring (of nicotine and tar intake) alone, and to an American Cancer Society stop-smoking program, although the differences were not significant. A set of studies at the University of Oregon further explored monitored nicotine fading. Beaver, Brown, and Lichtenstein (1981) found that monitored nicotine fading produced less long-term abstinence than was found by Foxx and Brown (1979). Brown, Lichtenstein, McIntyre, and Harrington-Koster (in press) combined monitored nicotine fading with self-management and a cognitive-behavioral relapse-prevention program designed to improve maintenance. A clinical trials evaluation of this multicomponent package yielded 46% abstinence (11 of 24) at 6-month follow-up. A subsequent controlled study (Brown et al., in press), however, resulted in much lower abstinence rates at 3- and 6-month follow-up, and the nicotine fading condition was not superior to that of a control group. The evidence for the efficacy of nicotine fading is not impressive thus far. It is a relatively convenient procedure, however, and clinical experience indicates that it has much apparent validity. Clients seem quite willing to try it when they are given a choice.

  The nicotine fading procedure may have yet another benefit, however. In all the aforementioned nicotine fading studies, the most nonabstinent nicotine fading subjects continued to smoke a lower tar/nicotine cigarette than their baseline brand and did not increase their rate. These data suggest the possibility of a controlled smoking effect, although compensation (e.g., more puffs, deeper inhalation) was not evaluated with biochemical or topographic measures (e.g., puff duration, puff volume, puff frequency). Prue, Krapfl, and Martin (1981) administered nicotine fading (termed brand switching) to nine subjects, who stabilized on the lower tar/nicotine brands. All showed reduced biochemical exposure (carbon monoxide and saliva thiocyanate) posttreatment.

The logic of the controlled smoking approach is pragmatic. The traditional goal of abstinence has not proved feasible for all smokers, and thus we should consider less hazardous smoking as a more realistic alternative for some smokers (Russell, 1974). In addition to those who are unable to quit, there may be many who are unwilling to quit but would attempt less hazardous smoking. Controlled smoking may also be achieved by training smokers to alter their smoking topography. Frederiksen and Simon (1978a, 1978b) employed single-subject designs by which they demonstrated that smoking topography could be effectively modified using simple verbal instructions ("Take shorter puffs" or "Take six puffs or less on each cigarette") and frequent practice. Concurrently, reductions were demonstrated in carbon monoxide levels and percentage of tobacco burned.

Taken together with the nicotine fading work, these studies provide preliminary evidence that controlled smoking is feasible and that biochemical risk factors may thereby be reduced. Abstinence remains the preferred goal, but the extension of controlled smoking to larger and more diverse populations seems warranted.

Self-Control Strategies

Self-control approaches to smoking cessation view smoking as a learned habit that is associated with many distinctly identifiable situations. Theoretically, smokers' urges to smoke are not random occurrences but are associated with specific environmental cues, cognitions, or feelings. Because smoking has become a learned response to certain situations, smokers can similarly learn how to not smoke in those situations. Social learning programs thus tend to include techniques for modifying both environmental determinants of smoking and cognitive influences. Essentially, most programs consist of a preparation phase, a target quitting date, and some combination of three main components: self-monitoring, contingency contracting, and self-management.

Preparation Phase

The preparation phase involves strengthening the participant's motivation to quit and commitment to the program, setting a target quitting date, and self-monitoring to establish baselines and to increase self-awareness of individual smoking patterns. The simplest and most powerful way to enhance cooperation with the treatment program is by means of some contingency deposit. After the details of the program have been explained, the smoker is asked to agree to deposit a certain amount of money, which will be returned contingent upon satisfactory compliance. Compliance typically involves attendance, record keeping, and homework assignments. The deposit refund is contingent not upon quitting smoking, but upon carrying out program activities that are believed to be relevant for a successful outcome. Details of how much money is forfeited for which kinds of transgressions can be worked out according to program structure. Commitment may also be enhanced by the judicious use of health information, but strong fear-arousal messages are probably best avoided (Leventhal, 1968). Participants also can list specific reasons for quitting and the benefits they hope to realize from quitting. Perceived benefits of quitting may be more important than fear of the health consequences of continued smoking (Mausner, 1973).

Target Quitting Date

All programs must decide whether to have clients quit cold turkey or to go through a gradual reduction. Unfortunately, there is no clear empirical evidence of which choice is better. There is suggestive evidence, however, that cold turkey quitting is more effective (Flaxman, 1978) and appears to produce fewer withdrawal symptoms (Shiffman, 1979). Based on these data and clinical experience, the establishment of a target quitting date at the very beginning of a program is recommended. The exact timing of the quitting date will vary according to the schedule of meetings and the nature of the program. The crucial point is to have a clearly established quitting time toward which the participants can work. The target quitting date should allow time for clients to learn some maintenance skills beforehand. It is possible to build in some degree of reduction of smoking before the quitting date, but this reduction generally should not be lower than 50% of baseline or about 12 cigarettes a day, whichever is lower. Reductions below this point are likely to be counterproductive (Levinson, et al., 1971).

Self-Monitoring

Self-monitoring is a fundamental element in the behavioral assessment of smoking as well as an important treatment component for tracking progress. A small index card or sheet of paper that can be attached to or wrapped around the cigarette pack can facilitate recording. Smokers record the number of cigarettes smoked, the time of day, and, importantly, a brief notation about the situations in which smoking occurs (e.g., with coffee, after a meal, worrying about work). The situational information is crucial for a functional analysis of smoking and often highlights the environmental influences that trigger smoking.

Undoubtedly, self-monitoring is reactive. McFall and Hammen (1971) and Rozensky (1974) have noted that self-monitored smoking rates tend to be several cigarettes per day less than the actual baseline. The reactivity may be somewhat beneficial, however, although self-monitoring alone has rarely produced long-term abstinence (McFall, 1970; Pechacek, 1979). In general, the specific effects of self-monitoring are transitory, but self-monitoring is an important tool to be combined with other procedures.

Contingency Contracting

Contingency contracting—the simple procedure of arranging monetary consequences for smoking or not smoking—has been fairly effective. Elliot and Tighe (1968), for example, collected a deposit from a client that was forfeited if the client smoked. At the end of treatment, 84% of their sample were abstinent, but this figure dropped substantially to 38% at follow-up. Since Elliot and Tighe's treatment included other techniques as well, the results cannot definitely be attributed to contingency contracting. Winett (1973) found that an impressive 50% of the subjects in a contingency contracting condition were abstinent at 6-month follow-up, as compared to only 23.5% abstinent in a non-contingent-repayment group. Lando (1976), too, found that a response-cost condition was more effective initially than a non-response-cost condition, but the differences were nonsignificant at follow-up.

Contingency contracting may thus help to initiate short-term behavioral changes. The technique's long-term effectiveness in preventing relapse is less certain, however.

Self-Management

Self-management procedures bring the treatment and the responsibility for change under the client's control. Treatment actually takes place not in the clinic but in the smoker's natural environment, with the smoker modifying either the antecedents or the consequences of a given smoking-related situation. As noted earlier, according to social learning theory, specific situations will trigger the urge to smoke. Self-management strategies aim to break up the situation → urge → smoke chain by modifying either the antecedent condition or the consequent response.

Stimulus-control procedures are aimed at restricting or altering the antecedent conditions that are associated with smoking. One strategy—restricting or avoiding the situations in which smoking occurs—is based on the assumption that the fewer situations in which smoking occurs, the easier it will be for smokers to attain total abstinence (Bernstein & Glasgow, 1979). In some of the first versions of stimulus-control procedures, clients gradually reduced their smoking in the presence of smoking cues. Usually, clients constructed a hierarchy of situations in which they were likely to smoke, at first refraining from smoking in the easy situations and then gradually eliminating smoking in the more difficult situations (Marston & McFall, 1971; Sachs, Bean, & Morrow, 1970; Winett, 1973).

More recent programs have also taught clients to reduce the strength of the smoking cues by having them alter the antecedent situation (Lichtenstein & Brown, 1980). Many smokers have a favorite chair, for example, in which they read and smoke. Simply switching chairs to read in or changing positions—such as lying down on a couch while reading— changes the strength of the smoking cue and may make smoking less automatic or desired. Similarly, altering the availability of cigarettes or ashtrays may help inhibit the smoking response.

The evidence on the effectiveness of stimulus control alone is only moderately encouraging (Bernstein & Glasgow, 1979; Harris & Rothberg, 1972; McGrath & Hall, 1976; Nelson, 1977). Best and Bloch (1979) suggest that one reason stimulus-control procedures may be relatively ineffective is that they require a gradual reduction in smoking. As noted earlier, there is some evidence that abrupt quitting is more successful than a more gradual tapering-off (Flaxman, 1978). Although the evidence for the efficacy of stimulus-control procedures alone is not impressive, the technique is nevertheless useful when used in combination with other procedures. Clinically, stimulus-control procedures provide clients with a sense of control over their smoking, thus perhaps acting to increase their expectations about their ability to quit. Because stimulus-control procedures are simple to learn and easy to administer, and seem to have some subjective clinical utility, we recommend their inclusion in smoking cessation programs.

One particular subset of antecedent conditions that has been singled out for study includes stress or anxiety situations. Smoking and anxiety or tension have been linked anecdotally for years, with tension being a strong smoking signal. Investigators have thus attempted to use anxiety management techniques, including relaxation training, as a means of decreasing or eliminating smoking. Most attempts at this approach, however, have been relatively ineffective. Systematic desensitization, for example, whereby smoking situations are paired with relaxation, has not been successful in eliminating smoking (e.g., Gerson & Lanyon, 1972; Levenberg & Wagner, 1976). Similarly, relaxation training in general, which aims to lower the individual's tension level and hence to lower the desire to smoke, has not produced encouraging results in helping smokers to quit (Lichtenstein & Brown, 1980). Relaxation training does have a great deal of apparent validity for smokers, however, many of whom assume that they smoke more under stress than at other times and would therefore like to relieve some of their tension. Quitting smoking may be somewhat stressful in itself, and relaxation training might help to relieve this additional tension, easing the quitting smoker's task of remaining abstinent. Thus, although relaxation training seems to do little in helping smokers to quit, it may be a useful procedure to recommend to clients who seem particularly tense as a result of quitting.

Self-management procedures are also designed to disrupt the smoking chain at the point of the smoking response by developing nonsmoking alternative behaviors. Best and Bloch (1979) distinguish between two types of alternative responses to smoking: functional responses and nonfunctional responses. Functional responses serve essentially the same purpose as smoking. If a smoker smokes to relax or to cope with boredom, for example, a functional alternative would involve finding other ways to relax or to keep busy. Nonfunctional responses, in contrast, simply decrease the probability of smoking (e.g., taking a walk after a meal instead of smoking). Although the distinction between these two types of responses is plausible, there are no data on their relative efficacy in curbing smoking.

Several smoking cessation programs include response-substitution techniques (e.g., Best et al., 1978; Chapman, Smith, & Layden, 1971; Lichtenstein & Brown, 1980), although the specific contribution of this technique has rarely been examined. One of the initially more interesting procedures for developing alternative behaviors has involved reinforcing coverants, or thoughts, that are incompatible with smoking (e.g., "Smoking is dangerous to my health"). The majority of investigations using coverant control, however, have found it to be no more successful in the long run than other treatments (Danaher, 1976; Keutzer, 1968; Lawson & May, 1970).

Brockway, Kleinmann, Edelson, and Gruenewald (1977) provide some evidence for the effectiveness of reinforcing more overt alternative behaviors to smoking. These investigators trained smokers to use alternative responses to situations that cue smoking. Some of these alternative responses involved simple motor behaviors, such as bending a paperclip, and the use of assertive no-smoking requests. Compared to a control group, the positive reinforcement group showed significantly greater reductions in smoking at the end of treatment and through the 6-month follow-up. Differences between the two groups were not significant at the 12-month follow-up.

Like the other program components described, the evidence for the effectiveness of reinforcement techniques is mixed, yet there are glimmers of encouragement. Reinforcing incompatible behaviors that are in themselves nonproblematic and socially acceptable, as well as training clients in the use of self-reinforcement, is a promising technique but, again, probably works best when used in combination with other procedures.

MAINTENANCE STRATEGIES

Most smoking-control program participants either quit or greatly reduce their smoking by the end of the program. Within three months of program termination, however, the bulk of these participants will have resumed smoking or will have increased their smoking to near pretreatment levels. Recognition of these high resumption rates has led to an increasing focus on maintenance or relapse prevention in smoking cessation research. Most maintenance strategies have not been guided by any coherent theoretical framework. Rather, they have tended to consist of some combination of extending contact beyond the end of the program, enhancing social support, or teaching coping skills. Both behavioral and cognitive coping strategies have been used. Behaviorally based programs have tended to emphasize training in coping skills (Lichtenstein, 1979), such as stress management, anticipating and coping with potential relapse situations, and learning substitute behaviors. Cognitive maintenance strategies, in contrast, assume that some change must occur "within the head" for behavior change to endure. Such changes might involve attitudes, self-perceptions, or covert verbalizations. Applications of attribution theory (e.g., Colletti & Kopel, 1979) or self-efficacy theory (Bandura, 1977; Condiotte & Lichtenstein, 1981) are examples of cognitive maintenance strategies.

Extended Contacts

Maintenance strategies and tactics are often taught during the course of a program. Alternatively, some workers have utilized posttreatment interventions. The most obvious of these is the booster session, consisting of a follow-up contact either in person or by telephone to provide the client with additional information, skill training, or possibly social support. Overall, the literature on booster sessions is consistently negative, but one innovative and potentially cost-effective procedure deserves mention. Dubren (1977) provided recent ex-smokers with pretaped telephone messages aimed at providing reinforcement for the ex-smoker during the first 4 weeks after quitting. An evaluation indicated that the messages were utilized, and subjects with access to the messages had a higher abstinence rate as a group (19/32) at 1-month follow-up than did subjects in a control condition (11/32).

Social Support

Maintaining abstinence requires self-control. Wilson and Brownell (1980) have argued that "continued self-regulatory behavior requires social support; like any other behavior, it will extinguish in the absence of the appropriate reinforcement" (p. 76). Besides reinforcing maintenance efforts, social support may facilitate coping with the changes brought about by quitting smoking (Ockene, Nuttall, Benfari, Hurwitz, & Ockene, 1981). Quitting smoking is somewhat stressful, and several studies have found that smoking increases with stress (e.g., Caplan, Cobb, & French, 1975; Ockene, Benfari, Hurwitz, & Nuttall, in press). Social support may play a role in protecting people from the effects of stressful events (see Heller, 1979; Kaplan, Cassel, & Gore, 1977) and in helping to buffer against the impact of relapse-provoking stressors.

Despite the appealing nature of arguments promoting the benefits of social support for maintenance, researchers have conducted little systematic work on social support for smokers. An early study by Janis and Hoffman (1970) is one exception. They found that individuals who had daily phone contact with a designated "buddy" had a lower mean smoking rate at 1-year posttreatment as compared to a control group.

Although the use of buddy systems may encourage support, such systems are somewhat artificial and therefore may not remain intact for an extended time period. A more stable and important source of support is the smoker's family. Mermelstein, Lichtenstein, and McIntyre (1982) developed an instrument to measure the support a smoker received during treatment from a spouse or living partner. They found that successful abstainers 6 months posttreatment had reported receiving significantly more support from their partners during treatment than either those who never quit or those who quit and relapsed. More specifically, partners of successful abstainers were more reinforcing, participated more actively and cooperatively in the smoker's quitting efforts, and were less punishing than were those of unsuccessful abstainers. Ockene, Benfari, Hurwitz, & Nuttall (1982) also found support for the notion of the facilitative effects of social support; successful abstainers in their study received significantly more social support during treatment (as measured by attendance at group sessions by a subject's significant other) than did those smokers who were unable to quit.

Besides the specific support for quitting smoking received from a treatment buddy or from one's family, social support in general may enhance maintenance. Other social support systems, such as at the workplace or in the community at large, may also provide opportunities for promoting maintenance. Environmental changes, such as restricting smoking areas, or attitudinal influences, such as using the local media to promote the health benefits of quitting smoking, may have an impact on maintenance. Clearly, there are a number of ways to capitalize on the support systems that already exist in the natural environment, and future research should focus on innovative ways to facilitate maintenance through social support.

Coping Skills

Cognitive and behavioral skills for coping with situations or emotional states that often trigger smoking have received the most attention in behavioral work. Although many investigators have developed and evaluated multicomponent programs that include coping skills maintenance procedures (e.g., Best, Bass, & Owens, 1977; Danaher, 1977a; Glasgow, 1978; Lando, 1977; Pechacek, 1977; Pomerleau, Adkins, & Pertshuk, 1978), most have not specifically examined the incremental effect of these maintenance components. Given the inconsistent results across these studies, however, with some yielding very successful results (e.g., Lando, 1977) and others yielding relatively unimpressive ones (e.g., Pechacek, 1977), the ability to draw conclusions about coping skills in general is quite restricted.

Lichtenstein (1982) has argued that more knowledge about the maintenance and relapse processes is needed before effective programs of coping skills training can be designed.

Nevertheless, support is growing for the notion of using coping skills to aid maintenance and to prevent relapse. In a situational analysis of relapse crises, Shiffman (1982) found that ex-smokers who performed *any* coping response in a relapse crisis were more successful in forestalling relapse than those who did not attempt to cope. It may well be that the key element in self-management or coping skills training is to instill, by whatever means, an active, problem-solving orientation so that clients produce any coping response in their natural environment.

Marlatt's recent formulation of the phenomenon of relapse and strategies for forestalling relapse (Marlatt, 1978; Marlatt & Gordon, 1980) shows promise for facilitating the maintenance of treatment effects. Both cognitive and behavioral strategies are included in Marlatt's model. The initial focus is on teaching participants how to identify high-risk situations—in which they would be strongly tempted to smoke—and on training them to cope with these situations using behavioral and cognitive strategies. The focus then shifts to the consequences of slips or momentary failures in self-control, resulting in a smoking episode. According to Marlatt, whether the individual fully relapses or regains control depends, in part, on how he or she interprets this abstinence violation. Negative self-attributions about a slip are likely to lead to a full-blown relapse. Equally important to an individual's ability to resist these negative cognitions and further smoking, however, are his or her self-efficacy expectations. Self-efficacy expectations, according to Bandura (1977), determine both whether one attempts to cope initially and whether one continues to cope in the face of a struggle to regain control over smoking. Treatments that teach individuals to deal with slips and that also enhance their efficacy expectations about coping with high-risk situations are likely to have positive results.

Marlatt's model is interesting, but it has not yet received empirical validation in the smoking field. Brown et al. (in press) designed a maintenance program based on some of the strategies suggested by Marlatt and Gordon (1980) and found supportive evidence for its effectiveness in a pilot study. A controlled-outcome study comparing the relapse prevention program to a discussion control group did not, however, find any significant differences between the two conditions at follow-up (Brown & Lichtenstein, Note 3). It is possible, though, that relatively low initial abstinence rates in this study may have reduced the likelihood of finding a significant effect for relapse prevention. Providing participants with a programmed relapse is another strategy of the model, but this procedure has also yielded negative results (Cooney, Kopel, & McKeon, Note 4). Despite the current lack of empirical support for Marlatt's model, its framework provides investigators with a number of cognitive and behavioral strategies to implement and to test, and it undoubtedly will receive more attention.

BROAD-SPECTRUM APPROACHES

It is clear from the foregoing review that no single intervention method has been very effective in the long run for all smokers. Given the complex, multidetermined nature of smoking, however, it is not surprising that there is no single magical intervention. As a result, most programs are now best described as broad-spectrum or multicomponent, including a variety of strategies and tactics that are combined in some rational manner. Broad-spectrum programs typically include self-monitoring, stimulus-control procedures, development of substitute behaviors, and self-rewards. Coping skills training of some sort is also usually incorporated. Many programs include a manual, which not only provides the client with an overview of the program and instructions for the implementation of procedures but also guides the client through homework assignments. A study by Glasgow (1978) highlights the potential benefits of self-help manuals.

Broad-spectrum programs often have two stages. Initially, the programs focus on helping participants to quit; then the explicit focus is on maintenance strategies. Lando and his associates (Lando, 1977; Lando & McCullough, 1978), for example, have developed a multicomponent program that appears to be effective and dependable. The program consists of five daily group meetings, usually including an aversive strategy such as satiation or rapid smoking, that aim at achieving abstinence. Following these sessions, the groups meet for seven maintenance sessions, the frequency of which is gradually reduced. Powell and McCann (1981) report a successful broad-spectrum approach, although it has not yet been replicated. Their program has the advantage of not requiring any risky aversive methods. Another relatively successful broad-spectrum approach, based on a manual by Pomerleau and Pomerleau (1977), emphasizes nonaversive techniques such as relaxation and covert conditioning. Pomerleau (1980) reports that of 100 subjects in the program, 32% were abstinent at 1-year follow-up and 29% at 2 years. Hamilton and Bornstein (1979) also report a fairly successful broad-spectrum approach that emphasizes a social support maintenance package and paraprofessional training.

The largest multicomponent program subjected to careful evaluation is worth noting, although its methods were not exclusively behavioral. In the multiple risk factor intervention trial (MRFIT), several thousand middle-aged men who were at risk for cardiovascular disease were randomly assigned to either special intervention or "usual care" groups (Hughes, Hymowitz, Ockene, Simon, & Vogt, 1981). Interventions varied across study sites, utilized behavioral and educational strategies, and included maintenance visits for abstainers and repeated programs for recidivists. The special intervention subjects ($N = 4,103$) achieved a 46% confirmed (by biochemical measures) quit rate after 4 years. This is probably state-of-the-art effectiveness for high-risk individuals.

We must emphasize that most of the successful broad-spectrum programs have not yet been replicated. They appear to be the best that the field now has to offer, however, and the reader is referred to them for more detailed descriptions of methods and procedures. It should be noted that the components of these programs have not been selected because of their empirical track record. Rather, the selection of the components typically is guided by some combination of research, clinical experience, and clinical lore. The various components that might go into a broad-spectrum behavioral program are listed in Table 44.1, organized around the preparation, quitting, and maintenance phases.

SUMMARY

Despite their extensive development and evaluation, the empirical success record of behavioral or social learning programs admittedly is not strong. The most effective single method to date is rapid smoking. Yet the health risks involved in this procedure preclude its widespread and automatic use for all smokers. Some multicomponent programs have been effective, but they have not always been dependably replicated. Clearly, the major goal of future behavioral programs is the same as it was almost two decades ago: to produce high initial abstinence rates and to identify strategies that will maintain abstinence.

In a recent study of self-quitters, Schachter (1982) suggests that achieving abstinence may take several attempts, that quitting smoking may take practice. Thus, the major goal of a cessation program may be not necessarily to have all clients leave the program abstinent but perhaps, more pragmatically, to have all clients leave the program with the skills and the knowledge of how to quit. Emphasizing to clients that quitting is under their control, that quitting is a skill that can be learned, and that, like any other skill, quitting takes practice may help engender a willingness on the client's part to keep trying to quit by continuing to use the techniques taught in the program. Behavioral techniques of self-monitoring, stimulus control, response substitution, and coping skills are most suitable for such an approach. A program's success, then, may be measured not only in terms of the number of clients who are abstinent at the end of treatment or at follow-up but also in terms of the number of clients who continue to use the techniques to try to quit and who set new target quitting dates.

Behavior modification strategies have the potential advantage of being readily adapted

Table 44.1   Options for a Multicomponent Program

Preparation
Mobilizing client motivation and commitment
—Deposits contingent on following through with program
   requirements
—Review of reasons for quitting and benefits of stopping
Self-monitoring to increase client's awareness of smoking
   patterns
Setting target quitting date
Self-management training
—Stimulus control for modifying antecedents of smoking
—Stress management training; relaxation
—Use of substitutes and alternative nonsmoking behaviors

Quitting
Aversive strategies
—Electric shock
—Covert (sensitization) aversion
—Rapid smoking and satiation
—Focused smoking and smoke holding
Nonaversive strategies
—Nicotine fading
—Target quitting date contract

Maintenance
Booster sessions
Coping skills training
—Transfer of self-management skills to maintenance
—Cognitive and behavioral coping (anticipating high-risk
   situations and planning for coping with them)
—Avoiding the abstinence violation effect
Social Support

for both public service group programs and self-help programs. They can also be disseminated by mass media (e.g., Best, 1980) and used by health professionals (Lichtenstein & Danaher, 1978). Behavioral strategies can also be combined with pharmacological and other strategies described elsewhere in this Handbook. It is likely that such multicomponent programs will be most effective.

REFERENCE NOTES

1. Kopel, S. A., Suckerman, K. R., & Baksht, A. *Smokeholding: An evaluation of physiological effects and treatment efficacy of a new nonhazardous aversive smoking procedure.* Paper presented at the 13th Annual Meeting of the Association for Advancement of Behavior Therapy, San Francisco, December 1979.

2. Orleans, C. T., White, M. L., & Nagey, D. A. *Comparative physiological effects and aversiveness of four nonhazardous aversive smoking procedures: Alternatives for the pregnant woman.* Paper presented at the Annual Meeting of the Association for Advancement of Behavior Therapy, Toronto, November 1981.

3. Brown, R. A., & Lichtenstein, E. *Effects of a cognitive-behavioral relapse prevention program for smokers.* Paper presented at the 88th Annual Meeting of the American Psychological Association, Montreal, September 1980.

4. Cooney, N. L., Kopel, S. A., & McKeon, P. *Controlled relapse training and self-efficacy in exsmokers.* Paper presented at the Annual Meeting of the American Psychological Association, Washington, D.C., 1982.

REFERENCES

Bandura, A. Self-efficacy: Toward a unifying theory of behavioral change. *Psychological Review,* 1977, **84,** 191–215.

Barbarin, O. A. Comparison of symbolic and overt aversion in the self-control of smoking. *Journal of Consulting and Clinical Psychology,* 1978, **46,** 1569–1571.

Beaver, C., Brown, R. A., & Lichtenstein, E. Effects of monitored nicotine fading and anxiety management training on smoking reduction. *Addictive Behaviors,* 1981, **6,** 301–305.

Berecz, J. M. Modification of smoking behavior through self-administered punishment of imagined behavior: A new approach to aversion therapy. *Journal of Consulting and Clinical Psychology,* 1972, **38,** 244–250.

Berecz, J. Treatment of smoking with cognitive conditioning therapy: A self-administered aversion therapy. *Behavior Therapy,* 1976, **7,** 641–648.

Bernstein, D., & Glasgow, R. The modification of smoking behavior. In O. F. Pomerleau & J. P. Brady (Eds.), *Behavioral medicine: Theory and practice.* Baltimore: Williams & Wilkins, 1979.

Best, J. A. Mass media, self-management, and smoking modification methods. In P. O. Davidson & S. M. Davidson (Eds.), *Behavioral medicine: Changing health lifestyles.* New York: Brunner/Mazel, 1980.

Best, J. A., Bass, F., & Owens, L. E. Mode of service delivery in a smoking cessation program for public health. *Canadian Journal of Public Health,* 1977, **68,** 469–473.

Best, J. A., & Bloch, M. Compliance in the control of cigarette smoking. In R. B. Haynes, D. W. Taylor, & D. L. Sackett (Eds.), *Compliance in health care.* Baltimore: Johns Hopkins University Press, 1979.

Best, J. A., Owens, L. E., & Trentadue, L. Comparison of satiation and rapid smoking in self-managed smoking cessation. *Addictive Behaviors,* 1978, **3,** 71–78.

Brockway, B. S., Kleinmann, G., Edelson, J., & Gruenewald, K. Non-aversive procedures and their effects on cigarette smoking: A clinical group study. *Addictive Behaviors,* 1977, **2,** 121–128.

Brown, R. A., Lichtenstein, E., McIntyre, K. O., & Harrington-Kostur, J. Effects of nicotine fading and cognitive relapse prevention in smoking treatment. *Journal of Consulting and Clinical Psychology,* in press.

Caplan, R. D., Cobb, S., & French, J. R. P., Jr. Relationships of cessation of smoking with job stress, personality, and social support. *Journal of Applied Psychology,* 1975, **60,** 211–219.

Chapman, R. F., Smith, J. W., & Layden, T. A. Elimination of cigarette smoking by punishment and self-management training. *Behaviour Research and Therapy,* 1971, **9,** 255–264.

Colletti, G., & Kopel, S. A. Maintaining behavior change: An investigation of three maintenance strategies and the relationship of self-attribution to the long-term reduction of cigarette smoking. *Journal of Consulting and Clinical Psychology,* 1979, **47,** 614–617.

Condiotte, M. M., & Lichtenstein, E. Self-efficacy and relapse in smoking cessation programs. *Journal of Consulting and Clinical Psychology,* 1981, **49,** 648–658.

Danaher, B. G. Coverant control of cigarette smoking. In J. D. Krumboltz & C. E. Thoresen (Eds.), *Counseling methods.* New York: Holt, Rinehart & Winston, 1976.

Danaher, B. G. Rapid smoking and self-control in the modification of smoking behavior. *Journal of Consulting and Clinical Psychology,* 1977, **45,** 1068–1075. (a)

Danaher, B. G. Research on rapid smoking: Interim summary and recommendations. *Addictive Behaviors,* 1977, **2,** 155–166. (b)

Delahunt, J., & Curran, J. P. Effectiveness of negative practice and self-control techniques in the reduction of smoking behavior. *Journal of Consulting and Clinical Psychology,* 1976, **44,** 1002–1007.

Dubren, R. Self-reinforcement by recorded telephone messages to maintain nonsmoking behavior. *Journal of Consulting and Clinical Psychology,* 1977, **45,** 358–360.

Elliott, R., & Tighe, T. Breaking the cigarette habit: Effects of a technique involving loss of money. *Psychological Record,* 1968, **18,** 503–513.

Flaxman, J. Quitting smoking now or later: Gradual, abrupt, immediate, and delayed quitting. *Behavior Therapy,* 1978, **9,** 260–270.

Foxx, R. M., & Brown, R. A. Nicotine fading and self-monitoring for cigarette abstinence or controlled smoking. *Journal of Applied Behavior Analysis,* 1979, **12,** 111–125.

Frederiksen, L. W., & Simon, S. J. Modification of smoking topography: A preliminary analysis. *Behavior Therapy,* 1978, **9,** 946–949. (a)

Frederiksen, L. W., & Simon, S. J. Modifying how people smoke: Instructional control and generalization. *Journal of Applied Behavior Analysis,* 1978, **11,** 431–432. (b)

Gerson, P., & Lanyon, R. I. Modification of smoking behavior with an aversion-desensitization procedure. *Journal of Consulting and Clinical Psychology,* 1972, **38,** 399–402.

Glasgow, R. E. Effects of a self-control manual, rapid smoking, and amount of therapist contact on smoking reduction. *Journal of Consulting and Clinical Psychology,* 1978, **46,** 1439–1447.

Gordon, J. R. The use of rapid smoking and group support to induce and maintain abstinence from cigarette smoking (Doctoral dissertation, University of Washington, 1978). *Dissertation Abstracts International,* 1978, **39,** 2831. (University Microfilms No. 78–20,725)

Hackett, G., & Horan, J. J. Focused smoking: An unequivocally safe alternative to rapid smoking. *Journal of Drug Education,* 1978, **8,** 261–265.

Hall, R. G., Sachs, D. P. L., & Hall, S. M. Medical risk and therapeutic effectiveness of rapid smoking. *Behavior Therapy,* 1979, **10,** 249–259.

Hamilton, S. B., & Bornstein, P. H. Broad-spectrum behavioral approach to smoking cessation: Effects of social support and paraprofessional training on the maintenance of treatment effects. *Journal of Consulting and Clinical Psychology,* 1979, **47,** 598–600.

Heller, K. The effects of social support: Prevention and treatment implications. In A. P. Goldstein & F. H. Kaufos (Eds.), *Maximizing treatment gains.* New York: Academic Press, 1979.

Harris, M. B., & Rothberg, C. A self-control approach to reducing smoking. *Psychological Reports,* 1972, **31,** 165–166.

Horan, J. J., Hackett, G., Nicholas, W. C., Linberg, S. E., Stone, C. I., & Lukoski, H. C. Rapid smoking: A cautionary note. *Journal of Consulting and Clinical Psychology,* 1977, **45,** 341–343.

Hughes, G. H., Hymowitz, N., Ockene, J. K., Simon, N., & Vogt, T. H. The multiple risk factor intervention trial (MRFIT): Intervention on smoking. *Preventive Medicine,* 1981, **10,** 476–500.

Hunt, W. A., Barnett, L. W., & Branch, L. G. Relapse rates in addiction programs. *Journal of Clinical Psychology,* 1971, **27,** 455–456.

Hunt, W. A., & Bespalec, D. A. An evaluation of current methods of modifying smoking behavior. *Journal of Clinical Psychology,* 1974, **30,** 431–438.

Janis, I. L., & Hoffman, D. Facilitating effects of daily contact between partners who make a decision to cut down on smoking. *Journal of Personality and Social Psychology,* 1970, **17,** 25–35.

Jarvik, M. E. Tolerance to the effects of tobacco. In N. A. Krasnegor (Ed.), *Cigarette smoking as a dependence process.* NIDA Research Monograph 23, DHEW Pub. No. (ADM)79–800. Washington, D.C.: U.S. Government Printing Office, 1979.

Kaplan, B. H., Cassell, J. C., & Gore, S. Social support and health. *Medical Care,* 1977, **15,** 47–58.

Keutzer, C. S. Behavior modification of smoking: The experimental investigation of diverse techniques. *Behaviour Research and Therapy,* 1968, **6,** 137–157.

Lando, H. A. Aversive conditioning and contingency management in the treatment of smoking. *Journal of Consulting and Clinical Psychology,* 1976, **44,** 312.

Lando, H. A. Successful treatment of smokers with a broad-spectrum behavioral approach. *Journal of Consulting and Clinical Psychology,* 1977, **45,** 361–366.

Lando, H. A., & McCullough, J. H. Clinical application of a broad-spectrum behavioral approach to chronic smokers. *Journal of Consulting and Clinical Psychology,* 1978, **46,** 1381–1385.

Lawson, D. M., & May, R. M. Three procedures for the extinction of smoking behavior. *Psychological Record,* 1970, **20,** 151–157.

Levenberg, S. B., & Wagner, M. K. Smoking cessation: Long-term irrelevance of mode of treatment. *Journal of Behavior Therapy and Experimental Psychiatry,* 1976, **7,** 93–95.

Leventhal, H. Experimental studies of anti-smoking communications. In E. F. Borgatta & R. R. Evans (Eds.), *Smoking, health, and behavior.* Chicago: Aldine, 1968.

Levinson, B. L., Shapiro, D., Schwartz, G. E., & Tursky, B. Smoking elimination by gradual reduction. *Behavior Therapy,* 1971, **2,** 477–487.

Lichtenstein, E. Social learning, smoking, and substance abuse. In N. A. Krasnegor (Ed.), *Behavioral analysis and treatment of substance abuse.* NIDA Research Monograph 25, DHEW Pub. No. (ADM)79–839. Washington, D.C.: U.S. Government Printing Office, 1979.

Lichtenstein, E. The smoking problem: A behavioral perspective. *Journal of Consulting and Clinical Psychology,* 1982, **50,** 804–819.

Lichtenstein, E., & Brown, R. A. Smoking cessation methods: Review and recommendations. In W. R. Miller (Ed.), *The addictive behaviors: Treatment of alcoholism, drug abuse, smoking, and obesity.* Oxford: Pergamon Press, 1980.

Lichtenstein, E., & Danaher, B. G. Modification of smoking behavior: A critical analysis of theory, research and practice. In M. Hersen, R. M. Eisler, & P. M. Miller (Eds.), *Progress in behavior modification.* New York: Academic Press, 1976.

Lichtenstein, E., & Danaher, B. G. What can the physician do to assist the patient to stop smoking? In R. E. Brashear & M. L. Rhodes (Eds.), *Chronic obstructive lung disease: Clinical treatment and management.* St. Louis: C. V. Mosby, 1978.

Lichtenstein, E., & Glasgow, R. E. Rapid smoking: Side effects and safeguards. *Journal of Consulting and Clinical Psychology,* 1977, **45,** 815–821.

Lichtenstein, E., & Rodrigues, M-R. P. Long-term effects of rapid smoking treatment for dependent cigarette smokers. *Addictive Behaviors,* 1977, **2,** 109–112.

Marlatt, G. A. Craving for alcohol, loss of control, and relapse: A cognitive-behavioral analysis. In P. E. Nathan, G. A. Marlatt, & T. Loberg (Eds.), *Alcoholism: New directions in behavioral research and treatment.* New York: Plenum Press, 1978.

Marlatt, G. A., & Gordon, J. R. Determinants of relapse: Implications for the maintenance of behavior change. In P. O. Davidson & S. M. Davidson (Eds.), *Behavioral medicine: Changing health lifestyles.* New York: Brunner/Mazel, 1980.

Marston, A. R., & McFall, R. M. A comparison of behavior modification approaches to smoking reduction. *Journal of Consulting and Clinical Psychology,* 1971, **36,** 153–162.

Mausner, B. An ecological view of cigarette smoking behavior. *Journal of Abnormal Psychology,* 1973, **81,** 115–126.

McFall, R. M. Effects of self-monitoring on normal smoking behavior. *Journal of Consulting and Clinical Psychology,* 1970, **35,** 135–142.

McFall, R. M., & Hammen, C. L. Motivation, structure, and self-monitoring: Role of nonspecific factors in smoking reduction. *Journal of Consulting and Clinical Psychology,* 1971, **37,** 80–86.

McGrath, M. J., & Hall, S. M. Self-management treatment of smoking behavior. *Addictive Behaviors,* 1976, **1,** 287–292.

Mermelstein, R. J., Lichtenstein, E., & McIntyre, K. O. Partner support and relapse in smoking cessation programs. *Journal of Consulting and Clinical Psychology,* 1982, **51,** 465–466.

Nelson, S. K. Behavioral control of smoking with combined procedures. *Psychological Reports,* 1977, **40,** 191–196.

Ockene, J. K., Benfari, R. C., Hurwitz, I., & Nuttall, R. L. Relationship of psychosocial factors to smoking behavior change in an intervention program. *Preventive Medicine,* 1982, **11,** 13–28.

Ockene, J. K., Nuttall, R., Benfari, R. C., Hurwitz, I., & Ockene, I. S. A psychosocial model of smoking cessation and maintenance of cessation. *Preventive Medicine,* 1981, **10,** 623–638.

Pechacek, T. F. An evaluation of cessation and maintenance strategies in the modification of smoking behavior (Doctoral dissertation, University of Texas at Austin, 1977.) *Dissertation Abstracts International,* 1977, **38,** 2380. (University Microfilms No. 77–23,013)

Pechacek, T. F. Modification of smoking behavior. In *Smoking and health: A report of the Surgeon General.* DHEW Pub. No. (PHS)79–50066. Washington, D.C.: U.S. Government Printing Office, 1979.

Pomerleau, O. F. Why people smoke: Current psychological models. In P. O. Davidson & S. M. Davidson (Eds.), *Behavioral medicine: Changing health lifestyles.* New York: Brunner/Mazel, 1980.

Pomerleau, O. F. Underlying mechanisms in substance abuse. *Addictive Behaviors,* 1981, **6,** 187–196.

Pomerleau, O. F., Adkins, D., & Pertschuk, M. Predictors of outcome and recidivism in smoking cessation treatment. *Addictive Behaviors,* 1978, **3,** 65–70.

Pomerleau, O. F., & Pomerleau, C. S. *Break the smoking habit: A behavioral program for giving up cigarettes.* Champaign, Ill.: Research Press, 1977.

Powell, D. R., & McCann, B. S. The effect of multiple treatment and multiple maintenance procedures on smoking cessation. *Preventive Medicine,* 1981, **10,** 94–104.

Prue, D. M., Krapfl, J. E., & Martin, J. E. Brand fading: The effects of gradual changes to low tar and nicotine cigarettes on smoking rate, carbon monoxide, and thiocyanate levels. *Behavior Therapy,* 1981, **12,** 400–416.

Raw, M., & Russell, M. A. H. Rapid smoking, cue exposure and support in the modification of smoking. *Behaviour Research and Therapy,* 1980, **18,** 363–372.

Resnick, J. H. The control of smoking behavior by stimulus satiation. *Behaviour Research and Therapy,* 1968, **6,** 113–114. (a)

Resnick, J. H. Effects of stimulus satiation on the overlearned maladaptive response of cigarette smoking. *Journal of Consulting and Clinical Psychology,* 1968, **32,** 501–505. (b)

Rozensky, R. H. The effect of timing of self-monitoring on reducing cigarette consumption. *Journal of Behavior Therapy and Experimental Psychiatry,* 1974, **5,** 301–303.

Russell, M. A. H. Realistic goals for smoking and health: A case for safer smoking. *Lancet,* 1974, **1,** 254–258.

Russell, M. A. H. Tobacco smoking and nicotine dependence. In R. J. Gibbons, Y. Israel, H. Kalent, R. E. Popham, W. Schmidt, & R. G. Smart (Eds.), *Research advances in alcohol and drug problems* (Vol. 3). New York: Wiley, 1976.

Russell, M. A. H., Armstrong, E., & Patel, U. A. The role of temporal contiguity in electrical aversion therapy for cigarette smoking: Analysis of behavior changes. *Behaviour Research and Therapy,* 1976, **14,** 103–123.

Russell, M. A. H., Raw, M., Taylor, C., Feyerabend, C., & Saloojee, Y. Blood nicotine and carboxyhemoglobin levels after rapid-smoking aversion therapy. *Journal of Consulting and Clinical Psychology, 1978,* **46,** 1423–1431.

Sachs, D. P. L., Hall, R. G. & Hall, S. M. Effects of rapid smoking: Physiologic evaluation of a smoking cessation therapy. *Annals of Internal Medicine,* 1978, **88,** 639–641.

Sachs, D. P. L., Hall, R. G., Pechacek, T. F., & Fitzgerald, J. Clarification of risk-benefit issues in rapid smoking. *Journal of Consulting and Clinical Psychology,* 1979, **47,** 1053–1060.

Sachs, L. B., Bean, H., & Morrow, J. E. Comparison of smoking treatments. *Behavior Therapy,* 1970, **1,** 465–472.

Schachter, S. Pharmacological and psychological determinants of smoking. *Annals of Internal Medicine,* 1978, **88,** 104–114.

Schachter, S. Recidivism and self-cure of smoking and obesity. *American Psychologist,* 1982, **37,** 436–444.

Shiffman, S. M. The tobacco withdrawal syndrome. In N. A. Krasnegor (Ed.), *Cigarette smoking as a dependence process.* NIDA Research Monograph 23, DHEW Pub. No. (ADM)79–800. Washington, D.C.: U.S. Government Printing Office, 1979.

Shiffman, S. Relapse following smoking cessation: A situational analysis. *Journal of Consulting and Clinical Psychology,* 1982, **50,** 71–86.

Sushinsky, L. W. Expectation of future treatment, stimulus satiation, and smoking. *Journal of Consulting and Clinical Psychology,* 1972, **39,** 343.

Tongas, P. N. The Kaiser-Permanente smoking control program: Its purpose and implications for an HMO. *Professional Psychology,* 1979, **10,** 409–418.

Wilde, G. J. S. Behaviour therapy for addicted cigarette smokers: A preliminary investigation. *Behaviour Research and Therapy,* 1964, **2,** 107–109.

Wilson, G. T., & Brownell, K. D. Behavior therapy for obesity: An evaluation of treatment outcome. *Advances in Behavior Research and Therapy,* 1980, **3,** 79–86.

Winett, R. A. Parameters of deposit contracts in the modification of smoking. *Psychological Record,* 1973, **23,** 49–60.

Younggren, J. N., & Parker, R. A. The smoking control clinic: A behavioral approach to quitting smoking. *Professional Psychology,* 1977, **8,** 81–87.

CHAPTER 45

PHARMACOLOGICAL APPROACHES TO SMOKING MODIFICATION

LYNN T. KOZLOWSKI

Addiction Research Foundation and University of Toronto

Quackeries abound in the history of the pharmacological modification of cigarette smoking. One striking early remedy for smoking caused diarrhea, sweating, and the passing of green urine (Van Proosdy, 1960); these effects were meant to demonstrate that poisons were being flushed from the body. Some of the early patent medicines undoubtedly flushed money and health rather than habits and toxins from the user. This chapter reviews modern pharmacological treatments. Since some so-called less hazardous tobacco products (i.e., smokeless tobaccos, pipes, cigars) depend partly on pharmacological effects for their continued use, and since they are employed to treat the problem of cigarette smoking, they are reviewed along with the pharmaceuticals. Low-yield cigarettes (Kozlowski, 1981b) will not be considered, because they are more a placebo than a drug therapy. The secret of the ultra-low-*tar* cigarette (< 4 mg tar) is an ultra-low-*smoke* cigarette (Kozlowski, 1981c): 79% of each puff of a 1 mg tar cigarette may be diluted with air. Compensatory smoking can turn even the lowest-yield cigarettes into medium- or high-yield cigarettes (Kozlowski, Rickert, Pope, Robinson, & Frecker, 1982).

Given the time, care, and skill required to conduct a successful behavioral treatment program, the grass might easily appear greener on the pharmacotherapeutic side of the fence. A drug problem might seem a particularly ideal object for a drug therapy. Unfortunately, most pharmacotherapies offer only partial solutions. At best, these therapies provide adjunctive support for programs that will succeed or fail largely because of a host of non-drug-specific factors. At worst, failed drug therapy might convince an unsuccessful abstainer that his or her smoking habit is intractable. Drug therapies that have the most drug-specific effects on smoking are somewhat dissatisfying in that they usually involve the continued use of tobacco in some form.

KEY ISSUES

Pharmacology as a Determinant of Cigarette Use

Cigarette smoking is controlled by many determinants, some having more to do with consumer psychology than with behavioral pharmacology (Kozlowski, 1982). No pharmacother-

The author's thanks go to N. Grunberg, L. Jelinek, M. Pope, L. Nonis, R. Frecker, and K. Wagner for their assistance.

apy—even those that include nicotine—provides a "magic bullet" to kill cigarette smoking. Both biological and psychosocial factors control cigarette use, and any treatment that denies one class of factors courts failure (Kozlowski & Herman, note 1). The high-nicotine bolus hypothesis (Russell & Feyerabend, 1978) argues that cigarettes are especially addictive because inhaled smoke causes high-concentration hits of nicotine to be delivered rapidly to the brain. Even if this hypothesis is correct, these high-nicotine boli are embedded in a matrix of tastes, smells, and behaviors that contribute to the overall rewarding nature of cigarettes (Kozlowski, 1982).

Motivation

Where there is no will, there is no way that any of the drug therapies has much to offer the would-be nonsmoker. The problem of motivation is at issue with all smoking treatment programs, of course, but it is especially problematical for the pharmacotherapies. Drug therapy is the type of treatment most preferred by smokers (Brengelmann & Sedlmayr, 1975). Many persons believe (a) that drugs, especially prescription drugs, can solve problems that can not be solved by individual effort and (b) that drugs can do so easily—that is, with little trouble for the user. It is further assumed that pharmacotherapies can be tried casually. Someone faced with a drug therapy might reason, "What have I got to lose? If it helps me, I'll know it right away; if I don't like it, I can stop." In contrast, a behavioral program that requires weeks of involvement before results can be expected will not attract half-hearted dabblers.

Some less hazardous forms of tobacco use (smokeless tobaccos, pipes, cigars) are pharmacotherapies that can be self-applied easily by those who are poorly motivated to modify their smoking. These therapies can be tried casually, with no appreciation of the monitoring and attention that their careful use demands. Over-the-counter smoking deterrents and less hazardous tobacco products can be sampled with no public commitment, and hence they often lack the benefits of the social supports that can increase compliance to other therapeutic approaches.

Although drug therapies may be approached casually, a skilled therapist should try to use any drug treatment as an occasion for instigating a serious cessation attempt. The drug therapy can be seen to offer a new way for those who have tried other techniques. The therapist should instill enthusiasm and confidence in the benefits of the treatment without overselling it. The drug should be described as an aid to cessation, and it should be stressed that the user will be ultimately responsible for the success of the treatment.

Use of the Placebo Effect

Placebo-controlled studies in this area show that the active preparations usually have little effect beyond the placebo effect (e.g., Ross, 1967). Therapists who wish to use drug therapy should learn to employ the placebo effect. (See the discussion of the placebo effect in Chapter 25 of this Handbook.) Just as drug therapies can be used casually by poorly motivated patients, they can be used casually and unproductively by poorly informed (or poorly motivated) health care providers. The therapist's belief in the drug, authority in giving the drug, and rapport with the patient will alter drug effectiveness. Therapists should avoid drug therapies about which they have misgivings or doubts.

Nonspecific treatment effects should influence the successful transition to smokeless tobaccos, pipes, or cigars. These options need to be sold to the appropriate patients as skillfully as any drug therapy is sold; appropriate patients are those who cannot or will not abstain from tobacco entirely.

Duration of Treatment Effect

None of the short-term pharmacotherapies (less than 1 month) have been shown persuasively to have any long-term (1 year or more) therapeutic benefit. Given the usual standards for evaluating smoking treatment programs, this long-term failure is damning criticism. Nonetheless, short-term benefits may be valuable in themselves (easing discomfort is beneficial) and may have some secondary benefits. A less traumatic withdrawal experience, for example, might lead to a greater willingness to give abstinence another try in the future. Evidence indicates that several attempts to give up smoking over a few years may succeed whereas a single cessation attempt has failed (Schachter, 1982).

Cost-effectiveness

One argument for the use of pharmacotherapies is that the few long-term cessations are accomplished at little cost (Raw, 1978; Schwartz & Dubitsky, 1968), especially compared to the costs of other types of treatment.

Methodological Concerns

Pharmacological aids to smoking cessation require the cooperation of the smoker. Some researchers have designed their studies to test the influence of drug X on smokers who are not trying to quit or modify their cigarette intake (e.g., Whitehead & Davies, 1964). Such a procedure, it is argued, eliminates the factor of will power, but it also reduces the chances of discovering a pharmacological cessation aid (see Kozlowski & Herman, Note 1, for a discussion). If a drug did aid in cessation because it reduced withdrawal symptoms, for example, it might have no effect on a smoker who is not trying to reduce consumption and therefore is not experiencing any withdrawal symptoms. Studies that have tested smoking deterrents without the cooperation of the smoker, in effect, make a very limited assumption about how a drug might be able to alter smoking.

Theoretically, one type of drug might reduce intake because it reduces tolerance for tobacco and another very different type of drug might reduce intake because it reduces withdrawal effects (Kozlowski & Herman, in press). Studies of pharmacological modifiers of smoking should test the drugs in the psychosocial circumstances in which they would actually be employed.

Few studies meet the criteria for adequate research on smoking treatment. Sample sizes are small; measures are unreliable; results are incompletely reported. (See also, the later discussion of double-blind procedures.) Only some of the studies on nicotine-containing gum and less hazardous tobacco products employ objective measures of smoke exposure and cigarette abstinence; otherwise, self-reports of cigarette intake have been taken at face value (Kozlowski, Herman, & Frecker, 1980). One study, for example, would have concluded from unvalidated self-reports that the drug was effective, but validated self-reports revealed that the drug had no advantage over a placebo (Malcolm, Sillett, Turner, & Ball, 1980).)

PHARMACEUTICALS

Over-the-Counter Smoking Deterrents

An expert panel of the U.S. Food and Drug Administration (FDA) recently proposed labeling standards for over-the-counter (OTC) smoking deterrent drug products (Federal Register, 1982). A smoking deterrent is a substance that helps one stop smoking cigarettes. Purportedly, OTC smoking deterrents either (a) spoil the taste of tobacco, so that smoking is less rewarding; (b) substitute lobeline (a drug with some similarities to nicotine) to prevent tobacco withdrawal and craving for cigarettes; or (c) use tasty lozenges, candies, or gums to provide substitute oral activities (these nonpharmacological smoking deterrents will not be considered here).

The labeling recommendations of the FDA panel highlight some of the issues that have been discussed here. They proposed that labels on OTC smoking deterrents should include one or more of the following statements: "A temporary aid to those who want to stop smoking cigarettes"; "Helps you stop the cigarette urge temporarily"; "Helps you stop cigarettes temporarily"; "A temporary aid to breaking the cigarette habit." The panel also recommended another statement for all labels: "This product's effectiveness is directly related to the user's motivation to stop smoking cigarettes." Consistent with the emphasis on temporary effectiveness, the panel judged that adequate studies of OTC smoking deterrents need only last 4 weeks (1 week baseline, 3 weeks study period).

The panel concluded that there were no established active ingredients; that is, no OTC pharmacological ingredient has been demonstrated to their satisfaction to be an effective cessation aid. The following ingredients were judged to be ineffective: quinine ascorbate; licorice root extract, ground coriander, ground ginger, ground cloves, lemon oil, and orange oil in combination; methyl salicylate; eucalyptus oil; menthol; and thymol. The panel decided that insufficient data were available for judging the efficacy of lobeline and silver acetate.

Lobeline

Lobeline, an alkaloid found in *Lobelia inflata,* has been used formally as a smoking deterrent since 1936 (Dorsey, 1936). Pharmacologically, lobeline is similar to nicotine and has some of the same physiological effects, especially on the autonomic ganglia. Lobeline is generally recognized as safe when as much as 2 mg are taken three times a day. The FDA panel suggests that the drug should not be used for longer than 6 weeks, because no long-term toxicity studies have been performed. Lobeline is the active ingredient in such products as Bantron and Nikoban. (Despite the belief of some consumers, no OTC pharmaceuticals in the United States, the United Kingdom, or Canada contain nicotine.) The large majority of placebo-controlled studies show that lobeline has no effect beyond a placebo effect (e.g., Edwards, 1964; Scott, Cox, Maclean, Price, & Southwell, 1962; "Smoking-Deterrent Study," 1963). Davison and Rosen (1972) found that results from the lobeline and placebo groups in their study did not differ. (See Davison & Rosen, 1972, for an interesting critical review of the previous research on lobeline. The FDA panel apparently did not consider this article.)

Four of the 12 placebo-controlled studies considered by the FDA panel indicated a lobeline-specific treatment effect, but none is particularly convincing (London, 1963; Perlstein, 1964; Rapp, Dusza, & Blanchet, 1959; Rapp & Olen, 1955). All four of these studies show almost no placebo effect for their placebo preparations; placebo successes ranged from 0% (in two instances) to 6%. Such small placebo effects are rare and raise questions about the success of blinding procedures (Provost, 1964). Rapp & Olen (1955) conducted a 4-week (28-day) experiment on 200 subjects and apparently had not a single dropout. They found that 83% of the group abstained from cigarettes when given the lobeline preparation. Subjects in this experiment were not selected because they wanted to abstain; they were told, however, that the drug was designed to curb the desire to smoke. Such remarkable results (see also Rapp et al., 1959) have not been replicated by independent laboratories (e.g., Bartlett & Whitehead, 1957).

In a series of laboratory studies on pharmacological manipulation of cigarette smoking, lobeline was found to have no effect on smoking, whereas nicotine did have a small effect (Schuster, Lucchesi, & Emley, 1979). This finding undermines the rationale for employing lobeline as a substitute for nicotine.

Despite the FDA panel's decision to reserve judgment on lobeline, the preponderance of evidence indicates that lobeline has no drug-specific smoking deterrent actions (Raw, 1978).

Silver Acetate and Other Taste Spoilers

Since their first appearance in the late 1850s, a number of pharmacological products that spoil the taste of tobacco have been tried. Local anesthetics have been used to block the taste of cigarettes, and silver nitrate, copper sulphate, and permanganate of potash have been reported to yield a nauseating, sweetish taste when combined with tobacco smoke (Van Proosdy, 1960).

The use of silver acetate (e.g., Tabmint) purportedly influences the mucous membranes of the mouth to produce a "nasty metallic sweet taste" when a cigarette is smoked (Federal Register, 1982). The FDA panel found only three placebo-controlled studies of silver acetate. One reported a significant short-term treatment effect (Rosenberg, 1977); one reported no abstinence data (see Arvidsson in Federal Register, 1982); and one found a marginally significant abstinence effect ($p = .09$) in a large sample that had lost over 20% of the overall group to attrition before the completion of the study (Schmidt, 1977). The placebo effect again appears to be a major component of the efficacy of taste-spoilers.

The FDA panel recommended that 6 mg of silver acetate every 4 hours (not more than 6 doses per 24 hours) was probably a safe dosage, but that this product should not be used for more than 3 weeks. Heavy use of silver salts can cause argyrism—a permanent bluish staining of the mouth or skin (East, Boddy, Williams, MacIntyre, & McLay, 1980). Although this staining carries no known physical risks, it could cause cosmetic and psychological problems.

From one perspective, this type of self-administered aversion therapy makes little behavioral sense. Taking the medicine is as voluntary as the act of not smoking. The decision to take the medicine can be considered a second-order decision not to smoke. To enjoy cigarettes again, the patient needs only to stop taking the drug, since the silver acetate effect lasts for only about 4 hours per dose.

More research is needed on the use of taste-spoiling drugs in behavioral treatment programs. Perhaps such drugs might be useful as an aid to relapse prevention in high-risk settings (e.g., at parties). Because of the possibility of argyrism, however, prolonged use of silver acetate should be discouraged.

The Sodium Bicarbonate or Urinary pH Cure

Although they are not marketed as smoking deterrents, urinary alkalinizers (e.g., sodium bicarbonate) have received attention as a treatment for smoking (e.g., Ogle, 1981). Manipulations of urinary pH alter the excretion rate of nicotine (Beckett, Rowland, & Triggs, 1965): More nicotine is excreted in an acidic urine than in an alkaline urine. Schachter, Kozlowski, and Silverstein (1977) have demonstrated that more cigarettes are smoked when the urine has been acidified than when it has been alkalinized. Note that pH influences excretion rate; if the body contains no nicotine, no excretion rate remains to be influenced by urinary pH. Theoretically, then, manipulations of urinary pH should affect only short-term abstinence from cigarettes.

The only scientific account of empirical research on the usefulness of sodium bicarbonate as a cessation aid has found no significant effects on cessation (Fix, Daughton, Kass, Smith, Wickiser, & Golden, in press). Earlier popular accounts of this research announced a positive treatment effect ("Acid Test," 1979; Garfield, 1979); at present, however, neither evidence nor theory supports the use of urinary alkalinizers as a cessation aid.

Prescription Smoking Deterrents

Only one prescription product (in the United Kingdom, Canada, and Sweden, and perhaps soon in the United States) has been created especially to treat smoking—nicotine-containing chewing gum (Nicorett®). (It is an OTC product in Switzerland.) Otherwise, prescription drugs that were developed to treat the symptoms of a number of conditions have been used in the symptomatic treatment of smoking. Tranquilizers (i.e., diazepam, meprobamate, hydroxyzine) have been given on the grounds that they either (a) substitute for the apparent tranquilizing effects of tobacco or (b) treat the anxiety and irritability of tobacco withdrawal.

Stimulants (i.e., methylphenidate, amphetamines, and their close relative, fenfluramine) have been given to substitute for the apparent stimulation provided by cigarettes. Methodologically, much of the research in this area is so preliminary that no conclusion should be drawn (e.g., diazepam, $n = 5$; methylphenidate, $n = 6$; control, $n = 5$; see Whitehead & Davies, 1964). Some of the research on meprobamate is inconclusive because subjects were not trying to reduce cigarette intake (Bartlett & Whitehead, 1957).

Tranquilizers

If they have any effect, tranquilizers such as meprobamate and hydroxyzine appear to inhibit smoking cessation. Schwartz and Dubitzky (1967) found that meprobamate patients were less successful than placebo patients. Unfortunately, abstinence data are not reported; the successes are those who reduced consumption by 85% or more. No objective validation checks were performed. At 1-year follow-up, the placebo was still found superior to the tranquilizer (Schwartz & Dubitzky, 1968).

Hydroxyzine was examined in one study of 50 smokers who were motivated to quit (Turle, 1958). Despite the lack of placebo control, it appears that this antihistamine was a dismal failure as a cessation aid. Only 23 of the 50 subjects completed the 4-week treatment, and only 1 of the 23 (4%) gave up smoking even for the short run.

Benzodiazepines (e.g., diazepam) have not been tested adequately as smoking deterrents (Whitehead & Davies, 1964).

Though not strictly a tranquilizer, propranolol (a beta-adrenergic blocker) has been tested in a double-blind, placebo-controlled experiment (Farebrother, Pearce, Turner, & Appleton, 1980), because it has been found to relieve some of the somatic symptoms of anxiety. Only 26% of the original group ($N = 73$) completed the study. Of those completing the study, 32% quit smoking. Propranolol and placebo abstinence rates did not differ.

Stimulants

Ross (1967) performed a complicated study of 11 different drug treatments (including placebo conditions) on samples of from 15 to 210 persons attending cessation clinics ($N = 728$). Unfortunately, it is not clear which between-group comparisons are justified. A number of drugs (amphetamine, amphetamine-lobeline, methamphetamine, and methamphetamine-pentobarbital) were more effective than placebos in promoting immediate cessation, but long-term follow-up (10 to 56 weeks, depending on the group) showed no effect of the medication.

One double-blind, placebo-controlled study on fenfluramine (a mild stimulant used as an anorexiant) showed no drug-specific effect (Evans, 1971). Methylphenidate has not been tested adequately (Whitehead & Davies, 1964).

Nicotine-Containing Chewing Gum

Nicotine-containing gum (Nicorette) releases nicotine into the mouth as it is chewed. Plasma levels of nicotine rise more gradually after chewing the gum (15–20 minutes to reach appreciable levels) than after smoking a cigarette (1–5 minutes); nevertheless, steady intake of the gum (1 piece of 4 mg gum every hour) produces similar plasma levels to a steady intake of cigarettes (Russell, Feyerabend, & Cole, 1976).

The gum is intended to provide (a) substitute oral activity and (b) a direct means to prevent nicotine withdrawal symptoms. With this approach, cigarette dependence is dealt with in two stages. In stage one, the smoker learns to live without the cigarette habit, while nicotine withdrawal is managed. In stage two, all nicotine use is stopped. Because of the lack of bolus doses of nicotine, the abuse potential is said to be low (see Kozlowski, 1982, for a criticism of this argument).

Optimum use of the gum requires attention to nonspecific treatment factors and to particular challenges to acquisition of this new style of nicotine use. Russell, Raw, and Jarvis (1980) give explicit advice about clinical use of the gum. If Nicorette is chewed as a candy gum (i.e., rapidly to extract flavor), it will quickly become irritating to the mouth and generally unpleasant. The user must learn to chew the gum slowly and to stop chewing temporarily if the gum irritates. Also, since the gum takes longer than cigarettes to deliver substantial plasma levels of nicotine, it may be important that the user learn to plan for times of high need by chewing the gum well in advance of actual cravings.

The gum reduces ad-lib smoking slightly (Kozlowski, Jarvik, & Gritz, 1975; Russell, Wilson, Feyerabend, & Cole, 1976) and decreases tobacco withdrawal symptoms (Jarvis, Raw, Russell, & Feyerabend, 1982; Fagerström, Note 2). Only one (Malcolm et al., 1980) of the five placebo-controlled trials with abstinence as a goal (Fee & Stewart, 1982; Jarvis et al., 1982; Puska, Bjorkqvist, & Koskela, 1979; Fagerström, Note 2) has failed to find short-term success for the active gum. Table 45.1 shows the long-term success rates in these studies for those who started treatment. (Ball, 1979, reports additional data from the Malcolm et al., 1980, study.) Using the Mantel-Haensel chi-square technique to combine the results across studies (Fleiss, 1981), one finds that nicotine gum is more effective overall than placebo ($\chi^2 = 13.19$, df $= 1$, $p < .001$). The three most successful studies employed carbon monoxide tests to confirm abstinence. To date, Nicorette stands alone among pharmacological cessation aids in that it gives evidence of long-term effectiveness; some questions remain, however, about the adequacy and generalizability of the published studies.

Table 45.1 Summary of Placebo-Controlled Double-Blind Clinical Trials of Nicotine-Containing Chewing Gum

Study and Sample Size	Percentage Abstinent[a]	Significance Level	Dosing Information
1. Puska et al. (1979)			
Active 116	25	N.S.	4 mg; as needed, for as long
Placebo 113	19		as desired
2. Fee & Stewart (1982)			
Active 180	13	N.S.	2 mg; up to 20 pieces daily;
Placebo 172	9		long-term availability not reported
3. Malcolm et al. (1980) & Ball (1979)			
Active 73	11	$p < .10$	2 mg; at least 10 pieces daily; encouraged 3 months
Placebo 63	2		of use
4. Fagerström (Note 1)			
Active 50	60	$p < .05$	probably 2 mg; duration or
Placebo 50	44		daily rate not reported
5. Jarvis et al. (1982)			
Active 58	47	$p < .05$	2 mg; as needed, for at least 3 months; 22% of active and 17% of placebo abstainers used gum at 1 year
Placebo 58	21		

[a] Percentage abstinent of those who started treatment at 6-month (studies 1, 3, 4) or 12-month (studies 2, 5) follow-up. Most follow-ups are from start not end of treatment (see text). For study 4, four subjects dropped out after one session, and the author omits them fom his percentages; the calculation here assumes that two dropped out of each group.

Adequacy of the double-blind procedure. Unfortunately, it is rarely checked whether an experimenter has remained blind to treatment condition, and a trial that starts out double-blind is simply assumed to remain so until the code is broken. All the gum trials involved repeated sessions of psychological counseling. The three most successful studies (see Table 45.1, Studies 3, 4, 5) offered the greatest opportunity for a sensitive therapist to detect treatment condition and unwittingly influence success rates. Studies 1 and 2 employed several therapists for their adjunctive counseling groups, and gums were randomly assigned within groups. In studies 3 and 4, the principal investigator was the sole provider of the individual counseling; in Study 5, two therapists saw three treatment and three control groups, and gums were randomized between groups. Despite various attempts, no study has successfully made a placebo gum that cannot be discriminated from the active gum in 20 minutes of chewing. After the first session, subjects easily could have given cues to therapists (e.g., complaints or praise for the gum) that might have allowed a better-than-chance prediction of treatment condition—and hence, the gift of at least partial sight to the blind experimenter. As a methodological precaution, it would be best (a) to employ therapists who are blind to the purposes of the study and (b) to ask all therapists to guess the treatment condition of the subjects at key study points. To the extent that therapist-patient rapport has led to insight or accurate hunches about treatment condition, the double-blind procedure has failed.

Duration of use. Long-term use of the gum (>3 months) is correlated with high success rates (67% in Raw, Jarvis, Feyerabend, & Russell, 1980; 68% in Wilhelmson & Hjalmarsson, 1980; 75% in Jarvis et al., 1982). These findings have led to advice that the gum should be used for 4 months, even if the patient feels able to do without it (Russell, Raw, & Jarvis, 1980). Self-selected persistent gum users may be highly dependent on nicotine, and Fagerström (Note 2) has shown that nicotine gum is most effective on the most dependent smokers.

Temporary cessation aid or ongoing substitute. The processes underlying the correlation between long-term gum use and abstinence may offer a key to understanding the effective use of nicotine gum. A distinction needs to be made between the use of nicotine gum as (a) a transitional aid to cessation and (b) an ongoing substitute for the nicotine in cigarettes. The marketers of Nicorette have been careful to advise against long-term substitution of the gum for cigarettes; nevertheless, Nicorette is probably the least hazardous of any tobacco/nicotine product, and its long-term use is preferable to long-term cigarette smoking (Kozlowski, Appel, Frecker, & Khouw, 1982). The published reports on Nicorette do not preserve the distinction between the gum as substitute versus the gum as transitional device, and they have not been analyzed in a way that permits unequivocal evaluation of these processes.

Assuming that all subjects who still use the gum at any given follow-up point are abstainers from cigarettes, it can be estimated in the Raw et al. (1980) study (a) that of the 67% of the long-term users who abstained from cigarettes, 60% were still using the gum at one year (and 20% of the 67% were unable to give up the gum), and (b) that of all abstainers at one year, 23% were still chewing gum at follow-up. Jarvis et al. (1982) report that 22% of their abstainers at one year were still chewing the active gum. Unfortunately, in both these studies follow-up is reported from start of treatment rather than from end of treatment). To evaluate the gum as a transitional cessation aid, it is necessary to know abstinence rates at a follow-up one year from the end of treatment (i.e., from the end of gum use). An advantage of the gum is the ease of extending the treatment phase well beyond the time periods usually practical for behavioral treatment programs. The Raw et al. (1980) comparison of Nicorette use versus psychological treatments is marred by a failure to employ comparable end-of-treatment follow-up for both groups.

Smokeless Tobaccos

Oral smokeless tobaccos (wet snuff, chewing tobacco) are nonprescription sources of nicotine that have pharmacokinetics similar to nicotine gum. For some patients, these products might be used as cessation aids, using nicotine gum as a model (cf. Kozlowski, Appel, Frecker, & Khouw, 1982). Some of the disadvantages of oral smokeless tobaccos compared to Nicorette are (a) that the tobacco contains more carcinogens and (b) that the tobacco product may be less convenient and less socially acceptable (Kozlowski, 1982). Some of the advantages are (a) that the tobacco products are cheaper, (b) that they do not require a prescription, and (c) that they may be more pleasurable and, hence, a better substitute for cigarettes. If the tobacco products are more rewarding a disadvantage could be created by a greater abuse potential. Nasal (dry) snuff might also be tried as a cessation aid (Fletcher, 1977).

Less Hazardous Tobacco Products

Pharmacological less-hazardous tobacco therapies try to supply rewarding levels of nicotine while minimizing, if not eliminating, exposure to other toxic smoke products—notably, "tar" and carbon monoxide. Constituents of tar can cause cancer, and carbon monoxide is implicated in cardiovascular disease (U.S. Department of Health, Education and Welfare, 1979; U.S. Department of Health and Human Services, 1982). Nicotine itself has not been shown to cause any major smoking-related disease (except possibly addiction to tobacco), although there are many plausible physiological mechanisms for explaining a causative link if it were found. Even if one is concerned about the risks of nicotine, it is very likely that nicotine is the least of the three main evils in cigarette smoking (Russell, Jarvis, & Feyerabend, 1980).

There has been essentially no experimental research on getting cigarette smokers to switch to less-hazardous products other than low-yield cigarettes. Standard low-yield cigarettes are ostensibly placebo rather than drug cigarettes. As such, they are not pharmacological treatments for the smoking and health problem, even though they may have slight toxicological benefits for some smokers (Kozlowski, Frecker, & Lei, 1982). This section will not be able to consider success rates or placebo-controlled trials, but will focus on reasonable precautions that should be taken when smokers try to switch to less-hazardous tobacco products.

A Last Resort

First, an attempt should be made to prevent or stop all tobacco use (especially cigarette use). Failing that, the health risks should be ameliorated as much as possible. Less-hazardous tobacco therapy is at best a compromise. None of the products are without risk (U.S. DHEW, 1979), but if they are properly used, their ill effects are probably less life-threatening than those from cigarettes. A detailed discussion of the overall merits of less-hazardous tobacco products is beyond the scope of this section (see Kozlowski, in press-a, for a discussion). Suffice it to say here that, if one decides to employ these products, caution should be taken. The health care provider who simply tells a patient to try a less-hazardous tobacco product is like one who simply tells an anxious patient that he needs to relax. We can do better than that, and it is dangerous with less-hazardous tobacco products not to do better than that.

Minimize Use

No tobacco product is safe. No matter what type of tobacco product is being used, the user should be encouraged to minimize exposure. Most tobacco products have shown clear dose–effect relationships with disease; that is, disease increases as use increases (U.S. DHEW, 1979). Users should know that reduced exposures are still their responsibility—even if they have selected a so-called less-hazardous product. Apart from the elimination of fire hazards when smokeless tobaccos are used, risk reduction depends more on the user than on the particular product.

Excessive use of any tobacco product is to be avoided. Users should actively try to limit their intake. They should be encouraged to use the product only when they cannot comfortably forgo its use. Obviously, the terms *excess* and *comfort* are subjective. Nonetheless, it should be worthwhile to bias the user toward minimization of exposure, rather than to permit the assumption that unlimited intake is acceptable.

Acute excess (too much tobacco per hour or minute) may be as important to avoid as chronic excess (too much per day or week) (Kozlowski & Herman, Note 1). Users who limit their use during the day but expose themselves to intense bouts of tobacco use in the evening should be warned of the need to restrain their consumption of tobacco throughout the day.

An advantage of smokeless tobaccos is easy monitoring of the dose taken by the user. One pinch or wad of tobacco every few hours should provide a predictable dose of tobacco. Pipes and cigars, however, present at least as many problems in perceiving dose as do cigarettes (Kozlowski, 1981a; in press-b). Four cigars or pipes per day might sound like a small number compared to 20 cigarettes per day, but it should be noted that 5 cigarettes can be smoked in the hour it takes to smoke a pipe or cigar and that rate and volume of inhalation are subject to wide variation.

Convenience and Social Acceptability

Ortiz (1947) described pipes as suited to the sedentary, cigars to the ambulatory, and cigarettes to the impatient. Different tobacco products are indeed best suited to particular people or to particular situations. Since excessive use is to be avoided, social and situational constraints can assist in the effort to limit intake. A change in tobacco products can be impractical, however, because of a lack of acceptance by associates or surroundings. Not every spouse would warm to a shift from the "elegance" of smoking to the "disgusting spectacle" of chewing tobacco. Even among confirmed tobacco users, there has been a charming jingoism, such that individuals who enjoy dry snuff in the nose are amazed at the repugnant practice of using wet snuff in the mouth, and vice versa (Kozlowski, 1982).

Symbolic Value

Being a pipe smoker or a snuff user presents a different image to the world than being a cigarette smoker. If this image is intolerable or even uncomfortable for the switcher, it will likely prevent the successful switch from cigarettes.

Regular Oral Examinations

Ideally, the use of pipes, cigars, and smokeless tobaccos limits exposure to toxins to the oral cavity. Oral cancers are less likely to be lethal and are more easily detected than are lung cancers (U.S. DHHS, 1982). To aid in early detection of oral problems, users should be taught to inspect their mouths before they switch, so that they can report to a physician any noticeable changes in the oral mucosa. Any changes (irritations, thickenings, lumps, bumps, ulcers) should be discussed with a physician. In addition to regular self-inspections, the patient's physician and dentist should be advised to watch for early signs of oral cancers.

A Note on Medium-Nicotine, Low-Tar Cigarettes

Russell (1974) has proposed that medium-nicotine, low-tar cigarettes could provide the nicotine needed by smokers while exposing the smokers to less tar. Unfortunately, the ratio of tar to nicotine, as measured by standard smoking-machine assay, is a poor predictor of tar/nicotine ratios attained by smokers (Stepney, 1981). Manipulations of butt length or puff number can alter the tar/nicotine ratio (Kozlowski, Rickert, Robinson, & Grunberg, 1980; Young, Robinson, & Rickert, 1981), and behavioral blocking of filter ventilation holes can decrease the tar/nicotine ratio be 25% (Kozlowski, Frecker, Khouw, & Pope, 1980). Medium-nicotine, low-tar cigarettes can be constructed in a number of different ways (e.g., by adding nicotine to low-tar tobacco); such cigarettes are still being developed and as yet remain largely untested. If genuine medium-nicotine, low-tar cigarettes can be produced, they may be less-hazardous cigarettes, but they would still be riskier than not smoking.

Pipes and Cigars

Epidemiologic studies (see U.S. DHEW, 1979, for review) have found that pipe or cigar smokers are generally at lower risk of disease than are cigarette smokers. Assuming that these self-selected pipe or cigar smokers are not constitutionally or otherwise different from self-selected cigarette smokers, it has been suggested that pipes and cigars are less hazardous than cigarettes. Unfortunately, the epidemiologic research is based for the most part on individuals who have never smoked cigarettes. These so-called primary cigar and pipe smokers appear not to inhale (i.e., take smoke into the lungs), whereas former cigarette smokers who became secondary pipe or cigar smokers give evidence of inhaling (Castledon & Cole, 1973; Turner, Sillett, & McNicol, 1977, 1981). It is currently being debated whether uninhaled cigar or pipe smoke causes significant amounts of nicotine to be absorbed (McNicol & Turner, 1982; Turner et al., 1977; Wald, Idle, Boreham, Bailey, & Van Vunakis, 1981); and there is some evidence that inhalation by secondary pipe smokers may not be prevalent (see McCusker, McNabb, & Bone, 1982; Wald et al., 1981).

Even if secondary pipe or cigar smokers do inhale, recent epidemiologic evidence indicates that although these smokers are at greater risk of dying than primary cigar or pipe smokers, they are still at lower risk than continuing cigarette smokers (Doll & Peto, 1976).

Indicators of carboxyhemoglobin levels provide measures of inhalation and can be used to assess whether a pipe or cigar smoker is inhaling. It is not known whether secondary pipe or cigar smokers can be taught to avoid or minimize inhalation.

Pipes versus cigars. Seltzer (1972) has criticized the failure to distinguish between pipe and cigar smokers. Although these products are alike in delivering alkaline smoke (cigarette smoke is usually acidic), there are differences in the socioeconomic status and constitutions of pipe and cigar smokers. In general, pipes are less strongly associated with mortality than are cigars (U.S. DHEW, 1979; Wald et al., 1981). On the basis of this limited evidence, it appears better to direct cigarette smokers to pipes than to cigars.

Great care must be taken in the selection of pipes and pipe tobaccos. The user should be taught how to maintain and clean the pipe and how to store tobacco. Books on pipe smoking can be helpful in teaching the cigarette smoker how to smoke a pipe (e.g., Ehwa, 1974; Herment, 1955). The cut of the tobacco affects burn rate; some supposedly mild tobaccos, if cut too fine, can produce a harsh, hot smoke when used by a novice smoker. Smokers should be advised that it may take several weeks of experimenting (and acclimatizing) before a rewarding pipe habit can be acquired. They also should be warned against unrestrained use of the pipe.

Smokeless Tobacco

Nasal (dry) snuff, oral (wet) snuff, and chewing tobacco are all capable of delivering nicotine to the user (Gritz, Baer-Weiss, Benowitz, Van Vunakis, & Jarvik, 1981; Russell, Jarvis, Devitt & Feyerabend, 1981), although some users of oral smokeless tobaccos appear to receive negligible amounts of nicotine (Gritz et al., 1981). The use of smokeless tobaccos is not associated with lung cancer, chronic obstructive lung disease, or bronchitis. Oral smokeless tobaccos are associated with oral cancers (U.S. DHHS, 1982), however, and manufactured nasal snuff may cause nasopharyngeal cancer, although direct evidence is lacking for such an effect (Russell et al., 1981). Oral smokeless tobaccos are also associated with leukoplakia (in about 5% of cases, a precancerous lesion), gingival recession, and dental problems (Christen, Armstrong, & McDaniel, 1979; Hsu, Pollack, Hsu, & Going, 1980). The swallowing of tobacco juice or tobacco quids can cause nicotine poisoning and can be fatal (Harrison, 1964), and the licorice in chewing tobacco has been associated with hypokalemia, or pseudoaldosteronism (Blackley & Knochel, 1980).

There is no experimental data on switching from cigarettes to smokeless tobaccos. Anecdotally, it is known that occupational limitations on smoking (e.g., miners, baseball players, defense-plant workers) can increase the use of smokeless products (see Kozlowski, 1982). As with pipes, cigars, or even cigarettes, smokeless tobacco is an acquired taste, and users should not expect to enjoy it at first. Some wet snuffs are packaged in individual-serving gauze pouches (pouch and tobacco are placed in the mouth). This product may prove more convenient and less messy for some users.

Given the growing debate on the use of smokeless tobaccos to treat the smoking and health problem (e.g., Blum, 1980; Harrison, 1964; Kirkland, 1980; Russell, Jarvis, & Feyerabend, 1980), it is important that these products be proposed only for those who are unwilling or unable to abstain from tobacco.

Smokeless tobaccos not only act to eliminate the possible problems of passive smoking, they also eliminate the definite problems of passive fire-starting. Cigarettes and smoking materials are major causes of fires (McLoughlin, 1982). In California in 1975, 26% of all institutional fires were caused by smoking materials (National Fire Data Center, Note 3); and 44% of 463 fire fatalities in Maryland between 1972 and 1977 were caused by cigarettes (Berl & Halpin, Note 4). Since smoking materials are an important cause of nursing home, hospital, and residential fires (National Fire Data Center, Note 3), infirm, disabled, or alcoholic smokers might be urged to switch to smokeless tobaccos, especially when their mishaps might endanger others.

SUMMARY

No current pharmacotherapy offers an easy solution to the problem of cigarette smoking; each approach depends on non-drug-specific (placebo) factors and on the cooperation and motivation of the smoker. Overall, there is little evidence of long-term benefits from short-term drug therapies. At the present, primitive stage of empirical knowledge on this topic, nicotine-containing products (chewing gum, noncigarette tobacco products) appear most likely to offer drug-specific treatment benefits; however, these products may succeed mainly as continuing substitutes for cigarettes (i.e., as ongoing less-hazardous tobacco use) rather than as transitional aids to cessation of all nicotine and tobacco use. If anything, tranquilizers are counterproductive as smoking deterrents. Some stimulants may be helpful in the short term but give no evidence of long-term benefits. Lobeline seems to be no more helpful than placebo, and research on taste-spoiling drugs is inconclusive. Some so-called less-hazardous tobacco products (i.e., pipes, cigars, smokeless tobaccos) can be a last resort for those who are unable or unwilling to quit cigarette smoking, but exposure to these products should be minimized and monitored. Except for the lack of fire hazards from smokeless tobaccos, reduced risk will be related to the level of use and therefore can be determined more by the user than by the product. Although most of the current pharmacological treatments may not owe their successes to pharmacology, they are about as successful as many behavioral treatment programs, and they are not as expensive.

REFERENCE NOTES

1. Kozlowski, L. T., & Herman, C. P. Controlled tobacco use. In W. Harding & N. Zinberg (Eds.), *Control of intoxicant use,* in press.
2. Fagerström, K.-O. *Tobacco smoking, nicotine dependence, and smoking cessation.* Uppsala, Sweden: Repro-C, HSC, Uppsala University, 1981.
3. National Fire Data Center. *Fire in the United States.* December 1978.
4. Berl, W. G., & Halpin, B. M. *Human fatalities from unwanted fires.* Baltimore: Johns Hopkins University, Applied Physics Laboratory, December 1978.

REFERENCES

Acid test: A way to quit smoking? *Science News,* 1979, **115**(15), 244.

Ball, K. P. How to stop smoking. In L. M. Ramstrom (Ed.), *The smoking epidemic: A matter of worldwide concern.* Proceedings of the Fourth World Conference on Smoking and Health. Stockholm: Almqvist & Wiksell, 1979.

Bartlett, W. A., & Whitehead, R. W. The effectiveness of meprobamate and lobeline as smoking deterrents. *Journal of Laboratory and Clinical Medicine,* 1957, **50,** 278–281.

Beckett, A. H., Rowland, M., & Triggs, E. G. Significance of smoking in investigations of urinary excretion rates of amines in man. *Nature,* 1965, **207,** 200–201.

Blackley, J. D., & Knochel, J. P. Tobacco chewer's hypokalemia: Licorice revisited. *New England Journal of Medicine,* 1980, **302,** 784–785.

Blum, A. Smokeless tobacco. *Journal of the American Medical Association,* 1980, **244,** 192–193.

Brengelmann, J. C., & Sedlmayr, E. Therapy for smoking. In J. C. Brengelmann, J. T. Quinn, P. J. Graham, J. J. Harrison, & H. McAllister (Eds.), *Progress in behavior therapy,* New York: Springer-Verlag, 1975.

Castledon, C. M., & Cole, P. V. Inhalation of tobacco smoke by pipe and cigar smokers. *Lancet,* 1973, **2,** 21–22.

Christen, A. G., Armstrong, W. R., & McDaniel, R. K. Intraoral leukoplakia, periodontal breakdown, and tooth loss in a snuff dipper. *Journal of the American Dental Association,* 1979, **98,** 584–586.

Davison, G. G., & Rosen, R. C. Lobeline and reduction of cigarette smoking. *Psychological Reports,* 1972, **31,** 443–456.

Doll, R., & Peto, R. Mortality in relation to smoking: 20 years' observation on male British doctors. *British Medical Journal,* 1976, **2,** 1525–1536.

Dorsey, J. L. Control of the tobacco habit. *Annals of Internal Medicine,* 1936, **10,** 628–631.

East, B. W., Boddy, K., Williams, E. D., MacIntyre, D., & McLay, A. L. C. Silver retention, total body silver and tissue silver concentrations in argyria associated with exposure to an anti-smoking remedy containing silver acetate. *Clinical and Experimental Dermatology,* 1980, **5,** 305–311.

Edwards, G. Double-blind trial of lobeline in an antismoking clinic. *Medical Officer,* 1964, **112,** 158–160.

Ehwa, C., Jr. *The book of pipes & tobacco.* New York: Random House, 1974.

Evans, J. W. Double-blind trial of fenfluramine as an aid to stopping smoking. In *Seminar on fenfluramine and obesity,* Nassau, Bahamas, February 22–26, 1971. *South African Medical Journal* (Supplement), June 19, 1971, pp. 33–34.

Farebrother, M. J. B., Pearce, S. J., Turner, P., & Appleton, D. R. Propranolol and giving up smoking. *British Journal of Diseases of the Chest,* 1980, **74,** 95–96.

Federal Register, U.S. Department of Health and Human Services (Food and Drug Administration). Smoking deterrent drug prospects for over-the-counter human use: Establishment of a monograph. *Federal Register,* 1982, **47**(2).

Fee, W. M., & Stewart, M. J. A controlled trial of nicotine chewing gum in a smoking withdrawal clinic. *Practitioner,* 1982, **226,** 148; 151.

Fix, A. J., Daughton, D., Kass, I., Smith, J. L., Wickiser, A., & Golden, C. J. Urinary alkalinization and smoking cessation. *Journal of Clinical Psychology,* in press.

Fleiss, J. L., *Statistical methods for rates and proportions.* New York: Wiley, 1981.

Fletcher, C. Snuff to give up smoking. *Practitioner,* 1977, **218,** 338–341.

Garfield, E. Nicotine addiction is a major medical problem: Why so much government inertia? *Current Contents,* July 30, 1979, 5–13.

Gritz, E. R., Baer-Weiss, V., Benowitz, N. L., Van Vunakis, H., & Jarvik, M. E. Plasma nicotine and continine concentrations in habitual smokeless tobacco users. *Clinical Pharmacology and Therapeutics,* August 1981, **30,** 201–209.

Harrison, D. F. N. Snuff—Its use and abuse. *British Medical Journal,* 1964, **2,** 1649–1651.

Herment, G. *The pipe.* New York: Simon and Schuster, 1955.

Hsu, S. C., Pollack, R. L., Hsu, A.-F. C., & Going, R. E. Sugars present in tobacco extracts. *Journal of the American Dental Association,* 1980, **101,** 915–918.

Jarvis, M. J., Raw, M., Russell, M. A. H., & Feyerabend, C. Randomised controlled trial of nicotine chewing-gum. *British Medical Journal,* 1982, **285,** 537–540.

Kirkland, L. R. The nonsmoking uses of tobacco. *New England Journal of Medicine,* 1980, **303,** 165.

Kozlowski, L. T. Application of some physical indicators of cigarette smoking. *Addictive Behaviors,* 1981, **6,** 213–219.(a)

Kozlowski, L. T. The changing cigarette: Behavioral aspects. In *The health consequences of smoking: The changing cigarette.* U.S. Surgeon-General's Report, U.S. Public Health Service. Washington, D.C.: U.S. Government Printing Office, 1981.(b)

Kozlowski, L. T. Smokers, non-smokers, and low-tar smoke. *Lancet,* 1981, **1,** 508.(c)

Kozlowski, L. T. The determinants of tobacco use: Cigarettes in the context of other forms of tobacco use. *Canadian Journal of Public Health,* 1982, **73,** 236–241.

Kozlowski, L. T. Less hazardous tobacco use as treatment for the smoking and health problem. In Y. Israel, F. Glaser, H. Kalant, R. E. Popham, W. Schmidt, & G. R. Smart (Eds.), *Research advances in alcohol and drug problems* (Vol. 8). New York: Plenum Press, in press. (a)

Kozlowski, L. T. Perceiving the risks of low-yield ventilated-filter cigarettes: The problem of hole-blocking. In V. Colvello, W. G. Flamm, J. Rodericks, & R. Tardiff (Eds.), *Proceedings of the international workshop on the analysis of actual vs. perceived risks,* New York: Plenum Press, in press. (b)

Kozlowski, L. T., Appel, C. P., Frecker, R. C., & Khouw, V. Nicotine, a prescribable drug available without prescription. *Lancet,* 1982, **1,** 334.

Kozlowski, L. T., Frecker, R. C., Khouw, V., & Pope, M. The misuse of "less-hazardous" cigarettes and its detection: Hole-blocking of ventilated filters. *American Journal of Public Health,* 1980, **70,** 1202–1203.

Kozlowski, L. T., Frecker, R. C., & Lei, H. Nicotine yields of cigarettes, plasma nicotine in smokers and public health. *Preventive Medicine,* 1982, **11,** 240–244.

Kozlowski, L. T., Herman, C. P., & Frecker, R. C. What researchers make of what cigarette smokers say: Filtering smoker's hot air. *Lancet,* 1980, **1,** 699–700.

Kozlowski, L. T., Jarvik, M., & Gritz, E. Nicotine regulation and cigarette smoking. *Clinical Pharmacology and Therapeutics,* 1975, **17,** 93–97.

Kozlowski, L. T., Rickert, W. S., Pope, M. A., Robinson, J. C., & Frecker, R. C. Estimating the yield to smokers of tar, nicotine, and carbon monoxide from the "lowest-yield" ventilated-filter cigarettes. *British Journal of Addiction,* 1982, **77,** 159–165.

Kozlowski, L. T., Rickert, W., Robinson, J., & Grunberg, N. E. Have tar and nicotine yields of cigarettes changed? *Science,* 1980, **209,** 1550–1551.

London, S. J. Clinical evaluation of a new lobeline smoking deterrent. *Current Therapeutic Research,* 1963, **5**(4), 167–175.

Malcolm, R. E., Sillett, R. W., Turner, J. A. McM., & Ball, K. P. The use of nicotine chewing gum as an aid to stopping smoking. *Psychopharmacology,* 1980, **70,** 295–296.

McCusker, K., McNabb, E., & Bone, R. Plasma nicotine levels in pipe smokers. *Journal of the American Medical Association*, 1982, **248**, 577–578.

McLoughlin, E. The cigarette safety act. *Journal of Public Health Policy*, 1982, **3**, 226–228.

McNicol, M. W., & Turner, J. A. McM. Nicotine, carbon monoxide and heart disease. *Lancet*, 1982, **1**, 40–41.

Ogle, J. *The stop smoking diet.* New York: Evans, 1981.

Ortiz, F. *Cuban counterpoint: Tobacco and sugar.* New York: Knopf, 1947.

Perlstein, I. B. Smoking deterrent therapy in private practice. In *The first annual M. R. Thompson symposium on recent advances in the medical aspects of smoking.* New York: Matthew, 1964.

Provost, G. P. Of doubtful value: Drugs to curb the tobacco habit. *Journal of the American Pharmaceutical Association*, 1964, **NS4**(7), 339; 342–343.

Puska, P., Bjorkqvist, S., & Koskela, K. Nicotine-containing chewing gum in smoking cessation: A double blind trial with half year follow-up. *Addictive Behaviors*, 1979, **4**, 141–146.

Rapp, G. W., Dusza, B. T., & Blanchet, L. Absorption and utility of lobeline as a smoking deterrent. *American Journal of the Medical Sciences*, 1959, **237**, 287–292.

Rapp, G. W., & Olen, A. A. A critical evaluation of a lobeline based smoking deterrent. *American Journal of the Medical Sciences*, 1955, **230**, 9–14.

Raw, M. The treatment of cigarette dependence. In Y. Israel, F. Glaser, H. Kalant, R. Popham, W. Schmidt, & R. Smart (Eds.), *Research advances in alcohol and drug problems* (Vol. 4). New York: Plenum Press, 1978.

Raw, M., Jarvis, M. J., Feyerabend, C., & Russell, M. A. H. Comparison of nicotine chewing-gum and psychological treatments for dependent smokers. *British Medical Journal*, 1980, **281**, 481–482.

Rosenberg, A. An investigation into the effect on cigarette smoking of a new antismoking chewing gum. *Journal of International Medical Research*, 1977, **5**, 68–70.

Ross, C. A. Smoking withdrawal research clinics. *American Journal of Public Health*, 1967, **57**, 677–681.

Russell, M. A. H. Realistic goals for smoking and health: A case for safer smoking. *Lancet*, 1974, **1**, 254–258.

Russell, M. A. H., & Feyerabend, C. Cigarette smoking: A dependence on high-nicotine boli. *Drug Metabolism Reviews*, 1978, **8**, 29–57.

Russell, M. A. H., Feyerabend, C., & Cole, P. V. Plasma nicotine levels after cigarette smoking and chewing nicotine gum. *British Medical Journal*, 1976, **1**, 1043–1046.

Russell, M. A. H., Jarvis, M. J., Devitt, G., & Feyerabend, C. Nicotine intake by snuff users. *British Medical Journal*, 1981, **283**, 814–817.

Russell, M. A. H., Jarvis, M. J., & Feyerabend, C. A new age for snuff? *Lancet*, 1980, **1**, 474–475.

Russell, M. A. H., Raw, M., & Jarvis, M. J. Clinical use of nicotine chewing gum. *British Medical Journal*, 1980, **280**, 1599–1602.

Russell, M. A. H., Wilson, C., Feyerabend, C., & Cole, P. V. Effect of nicotine chewing gum on smoking behavior and as an aid to cigarette withdrawal. *British Medical Journal*, 1976, **2**, 391–393.

Schachter, S. Recidivism and self-cure of smoking and obesity. *American Psychologist*, 1982, **37**, 436–444.

Schachter, S., Kozlowski, L. T., & Silverstein, B. Effect of urinary pH on cigarette smoking. *Journal of Experimental Psychology: General*, 1977, **106**, 13–19.

Schmidt, F. Raucherentwöhnung durch anti-raucherkaugummi-dragées. *Muenchener Medizinische Wochenschrift*, 1977, **119**, 1343–1344.

Schuster, C. R., Lucchesi, B. R., & Emley, G. S. The effects of d-amphetamine, meprobamate, and lobeline on the cigarette smoking behavior of normal human subjects. In N. A. Krasnegor (Ed.), *Cigarette smoking as a dependence process.* NIDA Research Monograph No. 23, DHEW Pub. No. (ADM) 79–800. Washington, D.C.: U.S. Government Printing Office, 1979.

Schwartz, J. L., & Dubitzky, M. The smoking control research project: Purpose, design, and initial results. *Psychological Reports*, 1967, **20**, 367–376.

Schwartz, J. L., & Dubitzky, M. One-year follow-up results of a smoking cessation program. *Canadian Journal of Public Health,* 1968, **59,** 161–165.

Scott, G. W., Cox, A. G. C., Maclean, K. S., Price, T. M. L., & Southwell, N. Buffered lobeline as a smoking deterrent. *Lancet,* 1962, **1,** 54–55.

Seltzer, C. C. Differences between cigar and pipe smokers in healthy white veterans. *Archives of Environmental Health,* 1972, **25,** 187–191.

Smoking-deterrent study: A report from the research committee of the British Tuberculosis Association. *British Medical Journal,* 1963, **2,** 486–487.

Stepney, R. Would a medium-nicotine, low-tar cigarette be less hazardous to health? *British Medical Journal,* 1981, **283,** 1292–1296.

Turle, G. C. An investigation into the therapeutic action of hydroxyzine (Atarax) in the treatment of nervous diseases and the control of the tobacco habit. *British Journal of Psychiatry,* 1958, **104,** 826–833.

Turner, J. A. McM., Sillett, R. W., & McNichol, M. W. Effect of cigar smoking on carboxyhaemoglobin and plasma nicotine concentrations in primary pipe and cigar smokers and ex-cigarette smokers. *British Medical Journal,* 1977, **2,** 1387–1389.

Turner, J. A. McM., Sillett, R. W., & McNicol, M. W. The inhaling habits of pipe smokers. *British Journal of Diseases of the Chest,* 1981, **75,** 71–76.

U.S. Department of Health, Education and Welfare (Public Health Service). *Smoking and health: A report of the surgeon general.* DHEW Pub. No. (PHS)79–50066. Washington, D.C.: U.S. Government Printing Office, 1979.

U.S. Department of Health and Human Services (Public Health Service, Office on Smoking and Health). *The health consequences of smoking: Cancer, a report of the surgeon general.* DHEW Pub. No. (PHS)82–50179. Washington, D.C.: U.S. Government Printing Office, 1982.

Van Proosdy, C. *Smoking: Its influence on the individual and its role in social medicine,* New York: Elsevier, 1960.

Wald, N. J., Idle, M., Boreham, J., Bailey, A., & Van Vunakis, H. Serum cotinine levels in pipe smokers: Evidence against nicotine as a cause of coronary heart disease. *Lancet,* 1981, **2,** 775–777.

Whitehead, R. W., & Davies, J. M. A study of methylphenidate and diazepam as possible smoking deterrents. *Current Therapeutic Research,* 1964, **6**(5), 363–367.

Wilhelmsen, L., & Hjalmarsson, A. Smoking cessation experience in Sweden. *Canadian Family Physician,* 1980, **26,** 737–743.

Young, J. C., Robinson, J. C., & Rickert, W. S. A study of chemical deliveries as a function of cigarette butt length. *Beiträge zur Tabakforschung International,* 1981, **11**(2), 87–95.

CHAPTER 46

REVIEW OF TECHNIQUES FOR MEASUREMENT OF SMOKING BEHAVIOR

TERRY F. PECHACEK

University of Minnesota

BERNARD H. FOX

National Cancer Institute

DAVID M. MURRAY

University of Minnesota

RUSSELL V. LUEPKER

University of Minnesota

Until recently, the measurement of smoking behavior in surveys has been relatively straightforward. Prior to the 1960s, when most of the classic studies on smoking and health were initiated, the brand smoked was of minor importance and exposure was primarily a function of the number of cigarettes smoked. Smoking and disease relationships were based on a dose measure described by cigarettes smoked per day (U.S. PHS, 1964). Recent dramatic changes in types of cigarettes and patterns of smoking have changed those relationships (U.S. PHS, 1981). Although cigarette smoking may appear relatively simple on the surface, it is now recognized as a very complex behavior pattern (Griffiths & Henningfield, 1982; Kozlowski, 1981a; Thornton, 1978). Also, although this common behavior has been the subject of extensive study by behavioral researchers, there has been little rigorous evaluation of its complex components (Frederiksen, Martin, & Webster, 1979; Griffiths & Henningfield, 1982).

This chapter will describe some of the complexities of smoking in order to define the potential sources of variance in the measurement of smoking behavior. Methods of cigarette smoking measurement will be discussed and contrasted, including self-reported behavior, direct observations, mechanical measurements, physiological measures of smoke exposure, physical indicators of exposure, and chemical measures. Finally, the varying needs for measurement with differing populations will be considered, including adolescents, those involved in smoking reduction and cessation, and the general population.

Many of these topics in the measurement of smoking have been separately reviewed (Frederiksen & Martin, 1979; Frederiksen et al., 1979; Larson and Silvette, 1961, 1968,

1971, 1975; Moss & Prue, 1982; Pechacek, Murray, Luepker, Mittelmark, Johnson, & Schultz, in press; Prue, Martin, & Hume, 1980; Vesey, 1981). In addition, a comprehensive review has been published recently (Orleans & Shipley, 1982). This chapter will summarize the issues of measurement without dwelling unnecessarily on details already well described.

THE CHANGING NATURE OF SMOKING

Changes in Smoking Across the Life Span

Little is known about the changes in the act of smoking between the time an adolescent first experiments with cigarettes until he or she either quits smoking or dies. As with any complex human behavior, the varied rituals of cigarette smoking take time to develop (Baugh, Hunter, Webber, & Berenson, 1982). It may take months if not years before an adolescent experimenting with cigarettes develops an adultlike pattern of inhalation and cigarette usage (Baugh et al., 1982; Hunter, Webber, & Berenson, 1980; Pechacek et al., in press). The majority of adolescents who experiment with cigarettes do not progress to regular smoking (Bachman, Johnston, & O'Malley, 1981; Green, 1979). This transitory nature of adolescent smoking complicates the formation of consistent definitions of adolescent smoking (Schinke & Gilchrist, in press).

Smoking during early adolescence is infrequent and episodic. By late adolescence, however, more adultlike patterns of daily smoking become the norm (Bachman et al., 1981; Pechacek et al., in press). Although information is available on the relative frequency of smoking (Green, 1979), almost no data are available on actual exposure among adolescents to the components in cigarette smoke (Hunter et al., 1980; Pechacek et al., in press).

Adult patterns of cigarette usage are almost exclusively characterized by regular, daily smoking (Moss, 1979). It is generally assumed that these patterns remain relatively stable until the smoker begins to make efforts to quit. At this point, the smoker may try to reduce his or her level of smoking, change the type of cigarette smoked, or discontinue smoking for periods of time. Smoking cessation researchers show little agreement in their definitions and measures of this changing state (Shipley, Rosen, & Williams, 1982).

Across this total life span of smoking, the individual smoker may experience considerable variance in actual exposure. This dynamic and varied individual history of smoking is seldom addressed (Ashton and Stepney, 1982; Stepney, 1980). Instead, almost all studies of smoking capture smoking behavior in a cross-sectional assessment that usually cannot detect this exposure history.

The Changing Nature of Adult Smoking

The American smoking public has displayed dramatic reductions in smoking during the last two decades (Harris, 1979), yet more than 54 million Americans still smoke (Moss, 1979). As smokers have become aware of the health risk of smoking but have been unable to quit, they have made changes in the type of cigarette they smoke (Harris, 1979). Filter cigarettes now dominate the tobacco market in this country, and the sales-weighted average "tar" level per cigarette smoked in this country has declined steadily since the 1960s (U.S. PHS, 1981). The market share of cigarettes that can be classified as low in tar (15 mg or less of tar per cigarette) has steadily risen during the 1970s and is now approaching 50% (Myers, Iscoe, Jennings, Lenox, Minsky, & Sacks, Note 1).

Although it was originally assumed that smoking the lower tar and nicotine cigarettes would directly reduce a smoker's exposure to toxins, it is now recognized that actual exposure is based on many other factors (see Table 46.1), including how the cigarette is smoked and inhalation characteristics (Ashton & Stepney, 1982; Frederiksen et al., 1979; Kozlowski, 1981b, 1981c). Hence, even if the number of cigarettes smoked per day does not change when a smoker changes to a lower yield cigarette, there are behaviors that the smoker

Table 46.1 Factors Affecting the Composition of Tobacco Smoke and Exposure to Smoke Constituents

Factor		Sources of Variance
I.	The tobacco product	A. Plant strain
		B. Soil and climate conditions
		C. Time of harvest
		D. Portion of leaf used
		E. Method of curing, aging, and fermentation
		F. Storage
		G. Use of additives or reconstituted sheets
II.	Cigarette design	A. Amount of tobacco used
		B. Moisture content
		C. Length of tobacco rod
		D. Draw resistance
		E. Nature and efficiency of the filter used
		F. Paper porosity and ventilation
		G. Use of additives and substitutes
III.	How cigarette is smoked	A. Puffs per cigarette
		B. Duration of each puff
		C. Volume of each puff
		D. Draw rate of each puff
		E. Unsmoked butt length
		F. Obstruction of filter ventilation
IV.	Inhalation	A. Volume of each inhalation
		B. Depth of each inhalation
		C. Duration of each inhalation

Source: adapted from Ashton, H., & Stepney, R. *Smoking: Psychology and pharmacology.* London: Tavistock Publications, 1982, Fig. 30.

Factors I and II determine *standard delivery* established by smoking machine.
Factors I, II, and III determine *mouth-level exposure.*
Factors I, II, III, and IV determine *actual dose* available to the smoker.

can employ to increase the nicotine yield of a cigarette well beyond the yield estimated by Federal Trade Commission (FTC) testing (Kozlowski, 1981b).

Rickert, Robinson, Young, Collishaw, and Bray (1983) demonstrated that varying the puffing parameters on a smoking machine testing 36 brands of low-tar cigarettes could more than double the delivery of tar, nicotine, and carbon monoxide in comparison with standard testing. Cigarette could produce as wide a range of specific gases and tars as has been found in their testing of all Canadian cigarettes under standard conditions. Since the standard smoking machine profile (35 ml puffs of 2-second duration every 60 seconds until the cigarette is smoked to a length of 23 mm or to the length of the filter and overwrap plus 3 mm, if in excess of 23 mm) differs significantly from the pattern of puffing and inhaling employed by smokers with many lower yield cigarettes today (Kozlowski, 1981b; Kozlowski, Rickert, Pope, Robinson, Frecker, 1982; Thornton, 1978), FTC-estimated yields probably do not estimate actual exposures (Jaffe, Kanzler, Friedman, Stunkard, & Verebey, 1981; Rickert & Robinson, 1981; Russell, Jarvis, Iyer, & Feyerabend, 1980).

The need for more objective measures of smoke exposure is widely recognized in almost all phases of smoking research (Kozlowski, Herman, & Frecker, 1980; Moss & Prue, 1982; Orleans & Shipley, 1982; Pechacek et al., in press; Thornton, 1978). Although self-reported number of cigarettes smoked per day continues to have validity as a global measure of exposure, the validity of individual reports of smoking (Brockway, 1978; Isacsson & Janzon, 1976; Kozlowski et al., 1980; Neaton, Broate, Cohen, Fishman, Kjelsberg, & Schoenberger, 1981; Ohlin, Lundh, & Westling, 1976; Ronan, Ruane, Graham, Hickey, & Mulcahy, 1981; Sillett, Wilson, Malcolm, & Ball, 1978), relative exposure estimates based on FTC testing data (Jaffe et al., 1981; Rickert & Robinson, 1981; Rickert, Robinson, Young, Collishaw, & Bray, 1983; Russell et al., 1980), and self-reports of inhalation depth (Stepney, 1982; Wald, Idle, & Bailey, 1978; Wald, Idle, Boreham, & Bailey, 1981) are questionable.

AVAILABLE MEASURES OF SMOKING

Behavioral Measures

Behavioral scientists have been intrigued by the act of smoking for many years. It occurs with high frequency in a wide variety of situations and is amenable to direct observation (Frederiksen et al., 1979). A wide variety of studies have been undertaken; unfortunately, almost all of these have used self-reported rate as the sole dependent measure (Frederiksen et al., 1979; McFall, 1978; Orleans & Shipley, 1982). Frederiksen et al. (1979) and Orleans and Shipley (1982) have reviewed the behavioral methods available to assess smoking, including self-report, direct observation, and laboratory measurement. Each of these techniques has advantages and disadvantages, depending on the needs of the researcher.

As measures of smoking, self-reports by questionnaire and self-monitoring are by far the most popular, probably because they are inexpensive and easy to use and provide discrete data. Questionnaires are dependent on retrospective assessment of one's own behavior, however, and are thus subject to distortions in accuracy (McFall, 1978; Orleans & Shipley, 1982).

Retrospective estimates of smoking rate show a very strong digit bias (e.g., about 70% of all smokers report rates in units of ten) and often underestimate actual consumption (Warner, 1978). Self-monitoring of smoking involves the recording of smoking information on a more continuous basis. Orleans and Shipley (1982) reviewed the studies that have examined the effects of the nature of recorded information, the recording device, and the timing of the recording (Abrams & Wilson, 1979; Frederiksen, Epstein, & Kosevsky, 1975; Rozensky, 1974). The act of self-monitoring decreases the smoking rate (Frederiksen et al., 1975), and it is generally agreed that self-reported records need to be validated (McFall, 1978; Orleans & Shipley, 1982).

Direct observation of smoking behavior has obvious advantages but presents several practical problems (Frederiksen et al., 1979; Orleans & Shipley, 1982). Observers are not able to record a subject's behavior 24 hours per day consistently, and even if they could, the cost of such data gathering could be prohibitive. Such direct observational data have typically been used as probes to verify self-report measures (Lichtenstein, 1982; McFall, 1978) or in controlled laboratory sessions (Frederiksen & Simon, 1978), which limits the generality of the data.

Other, indirect measurement and validation procedures include collection and counting of cigarette butts (Robinson & Young, 1980), supplying and counting of returned cigarettes (Jaffe, Kanzler, Cohen, & Kaplan, 1978; Jaffe, Kanzler, Friedman, & Kaplan, 1982), and weighing or measuring of cigarettes before and after smoking to determine weight or length of tobacco smoked (Young, Robinson, & Rickert, 1981).

Measurement of Smoking Topography

Measurement of smoking pattern can give potentially useful information regarding an individual's smoke exposure (Frederiksen et al., 1979), but these measures have been relatively difficult to obtain, and their use has been limited almost entirely to the laboratory (Comer & Creighton, 1978; Creighton, Noble, & Whewell, 1978; Frederiksen, Miller, & Peterson, 1979; Gust, Pickens, & Pechacek, 1983a, 1983b; Herning, Jones, Bachman, & Mines, 1981). Nevertheless, laboratory procedures give the potential for precise measurement of smoking behavior in a controlled environment, provided that care is taken to avoid disruption of normal smoking (Gust & Pickens, 1982). Smoking in the laboratory may be different from smoking in the natural environment, however (Russell, Sutton, Iyer, & Feyerabend, 1982). In order to analyze smoking behavior comprehensively, the topographical components (i.e., the pattern, duration, and volume of puffing) should be recorded both in the laboratory and in the smokers' natural environment, using techniques that give valid and reliable measurements without disrupting normal smoking behavior (Gust et al., 1983a, 1983b; Ossip-Klein, Martin, Lomax, Prue, & Davis, in press).

Portable units have been developed to measure inhalation characteristics in the natural environment (Creighton et al., 1978; Henningfield, Stitzer, & Griffiths, 1980; Henningfield, Yingling, Griffiths, & Pickens, 1979; Pickens, in press). The unit developed by Pickens can measure all frequency and durational aspects of smoking topography for more than 200 individual cigarettes before it must be brought to the laboratory for data removal (Pickens, 1983). Portable units have difficulty measuring volume, however (Creighton et al., 1978).

Puff volume measurement has also proved to be difficult in the laboratory. Several methods have been reported: (a) graphical integration of the area under the respiration curve (Kumar, Cooke, Lader, & Russell, 1977; Gritz, Note 2); (b) measurement of the vacuum produced in a cigarette holder during puffing (Dunn & Freiesleben, 1978; Herning et al., 1981); and (c) continuous integration of flow rate, as measured by pressure drop during a puff (Adams, 1978; Creighton et al., 1978; Guillerm & Radziszewski, 1978; Rawbone, Murphy, Tate, & Kane, 1978). Each of these methods may be less than accurate because of the accumulation of particulate matter during the smoking of a single cigarette and/or the nonlinear relationships between flow rate and pressure drop. Also, a possible bias arises because an inhalation resistance is placed between the cigarette and the smoker. Gust, Pickens, and Pechacek (1983), have described a method of measuring puff volume that avoids some of these problems. It involves the use of a pneumotachograph placed before the cigarette in the airflow sequence.

Inhalation volume, depth, and duration all need to be assessed to characterize tobacco smoke exposure accurately (Ashton & Stepney, 1982). Chest wall and diaphragm movement during smoking can be monitored and quantified relatively easily (Gust et al., 1983; Gritz, Note 2). Inhalation can be measured more accurately by respiratory inductive plethysmography, a technique that does not interfere with normal body movements or breathing patterns during smoking, as does spirometry (Tobin & Sackner, 1982). Inhalation measures are primarily limited to the laboratory (Gust et al., 1983; Gritz, Note 2), but portable units are being tested (Creighton et al., 1978).

Physiological Reactions to Cigarette Exposure

A variety of acute and chronic physiological consequences of smoking can be used to track smoke exposure. Primarily because of the strong pharmacological effects of nicotine, any tobacco exposure that permits the uptake of nicotine will produce measurable but transitory changes in heart rate, blood pressure, hand tremor, and skin temperature (Battig, 1978; Goodman & Gilman, 1975; Larson & Silvette, 1975; Russell & Feyerabend, 1978). These measures may be useful in the study of tobacco abstinence phenomena among smokers and in tracking nicotine tolerance (Krasnegor, Note 3). Unfortunately, each measure has wide variability under normal conditions, and careful baselines are needed in order to study within-subject change.

Chronic exposure to tobacco smoke also affects pulmonary function and blood lipid levels. That smokers experience a relatively more rapid decline in various measures of pulmonary function is widely documented (U.S. PHS, 1979). As with the aforementioned acute measures, however, the various measures of pulmonary function are subject to fairly large individual differences in assessment and can have substantial measurement error (Hepper, Drage, LaMothe, Schoenfelder, Davis, Rupp, & Munson, 1980). Here, also, careful baselines would be needed to study within-subject change, and even if established, they could rarely be used to discriminate between individual smokers and nonsmokers (Hepper et al., 1980).

High-density lipoprotein levels (HDL) as a measure of tobacco smoke exposure suffer from similar measurement difficulties. Chronic tobacco smoke exposure depresses serum HDL levels (Garrison, Kannel, Feinleib, Castelli, McNamara, & Padgett, 1978; Hulley, Cohen, & Widdowson, 1977; Pooling Project Research Group, 1978), and smoking cessation has been shown to reverse this effect (Stubbe, Eskilsson, & Nilsson-Ehle, 1982). Unfortunately, the magnitude of difference in HDL level between smoking and nonsmoking is very close to the measurement error of the HDL level itself. Therefore, care needs to be taken in using HDL levels as a measure of change in smoking behavior.

Physical Measures of Exposure

Estimated mouth-level nicotine intake can provide another measure of tobacco smoke exposure. The amount of nicotine puffed into the smoker's mouth can be calculated from the butt nicotine content and the efficiency of the filter (Forbes, Robinson, Hanley, & Colburn, 1976; Robinson & Young, 1980). This procedure is nonintrusive and can be performed on cigarette filters collected in the natural environment. Butt nicotine content can produce a good estimate of the actual yield of the smoked cigarette (Forbes et al., 1976; Robinson & Young, 1980), but the manner in which the smoke is actually inhaled (length, depth, and duration of lung inhalation) can still produce fairly wide variability in smoke exposure.

An innovative measure of smoke exposure involves color-matching the stain pattern on a smoker's cigarette filter in order to estimate actual mouth exposure level to tar and nicotine (Kozlowski, 1981a; Kozlowski et al., 1982). Preliminary data on this technique suggest that the stain pattern is highly related to the number of puffs taken and is probably a very accurate estimate of mouth-level delivery of nicotine (Kozlowski et al., 1982). This procedure shares some of the same problems that butt nicotine assays have (particularly the assumption of constant filter retention-efficiency), but it has wide potential as a relatively unobtrusive measure of smoke yield to the individual subject, and it is a mechanism for providing direct feedback to the smoker who is attempting to reduce exposure.

Selection of Biochemical Measures

Cigarette smoke is a complex mixture of chemicals, many of which are not present in the native tobacco leaf but are formed by chemical reactions during the curing process and by pyrolysis or incomplete combustion during smoking (U.S. PHS, 1979, 1981). The yield of an individual cigarette is normally reported as the "tars" (defined as the total particulate matter minus water and the nicotine alkaloids, or nicotine level) and specific gas-phase compounds, such as carbon monoxide and hydrogen cyanide gases (Jenkins, Quincy, & Guerin, Note 5). More than 4,000 compounds have been identified in the particulate phase, nearly all in very low concentrations (U.S. PHS, 1979). The gas phase, which makes up more than 90% of the tobacco smoke, contains a much smaller number of compounds, but these are present in larger quantities (Wynder & Hoffman, 1979).

Only a small percentage of the total number of compounds present in smoke are known to be harmful (U.S. PHS, 1979). Therefore, efforts to monitor smoke exposure chemically should focus on specific chemical by-products that are suspected as major toxic agents but are sufficiently stable and specific to tobacco smoke exposure to permit accurate measurement.

Three chemical measures of smoking will be evaluated in detail: carbon monoxide, thiocyanate, and cotinine levels. The metabolism, sensitivity, specificity, and technical aspects of their use will be individually considered. Each of the three measures has strengths and weaknesses, but all have been found useful in certain applications.

Carbon Monoxide

Metabolism. Carbon monoxide (CO) is a major measurable toxin present in cigarette smoke (Ashton, Stepney, & Thompson, 1981; Frederiksen & Martin, 1979; Jarvis, Russell, & Saloojee, 1980; U.S. PHS, 1979). Carbon monoxide is present in high concentrations in tobacco (2–20 mg per cigarette) and cannot be selectively removed from cigarettes by common filters (Wynder & Hoffman, 1979). Carbon monoxide is rapidly absorbed into the bloodstream during smoke inhalation and diffuses across alveolar membranes to bind with hemoglobin and form carboxyhemoglobin (COHb) (Stewart, 1975). Since CO is not readily absorbed outside the alveoli, depth of inhalation and pulmonary dynamics influence CO absorption more than other factors (Stewart, 1975; Coburn, 1979).

Alveolar ventilation rate is the major factor in the rate of CO elimination (Coburn, 1979; Stewart, 1975). Most CO is eliminated unchanged, with less than 1% of the gas being oxidized within the body to carbon dioxide (Stewart, 1975). The biological half-life of the gas in healthy, sedentary adults at sea level is 4 to 5 hours (Ringold, Goldsmith, Helwig, Finn and Schuette, 1962; Stewart, 1975). Increased respiratory rates (as during exercise) can decrease the half-life markedly (Coburn, Forster, and Kane, 1965; Hawkins, 1976). Levels can be measured directly in venous blood samples or estimated with a high degree of precision in an expired-air sample collected under controlled conditions (Jones, Ellicott, Cardigan, & Gaensler 1958; Ringold et al., 1962). In subjects with normal lung functions, expired-air CO and COHb percent are highly correlated ($r = 0.9$) (Jarvis et al., 1980; Stewart, Steward, Stamm, & Seelen, 1976; Wald, Idle, Boreham, and Bailey, 1981).

Sensitivity. Given the high concentrations of CO in tobacco smoke, it is not surprising that both COHb% and expired-air CO levels are strongly related to cigarette smoke exposure (Cohen, Perkins, Ury, & Goldsmith, 1971; Goldsmith & Aronow, 1975; Hawkins, 1976; Janzon, Lindell, Trell, & Larme, 1981; Kahn, Rutledge, Davis, Altes, Gantner, Thornton, & Wallace, 1974; Meade & Wald, 1977; Rea, Tyrer, Kasap, & Beresfort, 1973; Ringold et al., 1962; Stewart, Baretta, Platte, Stewart, Kalbfleisch, Van Yserloo, & Rimm, 1974; Vesey, Saloojee, Cole, & Russell, 1982; Wald, Howard, Smith, & Bailey, 1975; Wald et al., 1978; Wald, Idle, Boreham, & Bailey, 1981). Because of the short half-life of CO, however, levels show marked diurnal variability (Collins & Epstein, 1978; Meade & Wald, 1977) and are significantly influenced by time since last cigarette (Horan, Hackett, & Linberg, 1978; Hughes, Frederiksen, & Frazier, 1978; Rickert & Robinson, 1981; Vogt, Selvin, Widdowson, & Hulley, 1977). An assessment late in the day, standardized for time since last cigarette, is recommended to give the best estimate of CO level (Frederiksen & Martin, 1979; Henningfield, Stitzer, & Griffiths, 1980; Horan et al., 1978; Hughes et al., 1978).

If adult smokers are assessed late in the day and have no forewarning of the test, the sensitivity of either COHb% or expired-air CO is very good (Frederiksen & Martin, 1979; Wald, Idle, Boreham, & Bailey, 1981). Even when assessments are made earlier in the day, there is a very high probability that smokers will be detected (Janzon et al., 1981; Kahn et al., 1974). Atypical smokers (e.g., those who smoke fewer than eight cigarettes per day or deny inhaling) have been difficult to identify, however (Vogt et al., 1977). Similarly, few regular but nondaily adolescent smokers can be detected by expired-air CO levels (Pechacek et al., in press).

Specificity. Carbon monoxide is widely distributed in the environment as a result of industrial and auto pollution (Frederiksen & Martin, 1979; Stewart, 1975). The uptake of ambient CO is proportional to ambient concentration and duration of exposure (Coburn, 1979; Godin & Shephard, 1972; Stewart, 1975; Wallace, Davis, Rutledge, & Kahn, 1974). Thus, long-term, low-level exposures to metropolitan pollution can produce COHb% levels in nonsmokers equivalent to those for light smokers (Kahn et al., 1974; Stewart, 1975; Wallace et al., 1974) and can confound the interpretation of levels in light smokers. This is particularly a problem in the assessment of infrequent or episodic smokers (Vogt et al., 1977) and adolescents (Pechacek et al., in press). The inhalation of smoke from open fires (e.g., by firemen) or from other organic products (e.g., marijuana) can also elevate the CO level in the body (Frederiksen & Martin, 1979; Stewart et al., 1976). The presence of CO in marijuana smoke (Aronow & Cassidy, 1974) detracts from the utility of CO as a measure of adolescent smoking and appears to produce higher rates of false positives for cigarette smoking among older adolescents (Pechacek et al., in press). Nevertheless, in general populations, only 2% to 5% of nonsmokers will exceed 1% COHb (Janzon et al., 1981; Kahn et al., 1974).

Technical issues. Since CO can be reliably assessed in expired air (Commins, 1975; Jarvis et al., 1980; Jones et al., 1958; Rea et al., 1973; Stewart et al., 1976; Wald, Idle, Boreham, & Bailey, 1981), the measurement can be carried out simply and, once the necessary equipment is obtained, inexpensively.[1] Care needs to be taken to collect alveolar breath samples (Jones et al., 1958; Ringold et al., 1962) and filter out ethanol contamination (Rea et al., 1973). Expired-air samples from individuals with pulmonary disease or impaired lung function will estimate COHb% less accurately (Jarvis et al., 1980; Rea et al., 1973), and spectrophotometric estimates of COHb% may need to be used on these individuals (Commins, 1975; Rickert & Robinson, 1981; Wigfield, Hollebone, MacKeen, & Selwin, 1981). Although the short half-life of CO limits its sensitivity, it also permits the measure to be used to track recent changes in smoking rate or inhalation style (Frederiksen & Martin, 1979; Herning et al., 1981; Martin & Frederiksen, 1980; Wald et al., 1978). The numerous sources of variance in both CO and tobacco exposure, however, make the detection of small rate changes difficult (Henningfield et al., 1980; Vogt, Selvin, & Billings, 1979).

Hydrogen Cyanide

Metabolism. Hydrogen cyanide gas is another toxic agent present in high concentration (30–200 μg per cigarette) in the gas phase of cigarette smoke (Wynder & Hoffman, 1979). Since hydrogen cyanide is very active chemically and biologically and is rapidly detoxified by the liver (Boxer & Rickards, 1952; Langer & Greer, 1977; Vesey, 1981), cyanide concentration alone is of little value. Rather, thiocyanate (SCN), a product of cyanide detoxification, accumulates in body fluids and provides an estimate of exposure to hydrogen cyanide in tobacco smoke (Butts, Kuehneman, & Widdowson, 1974; Pettigrew & Fell, 1974; Prue et al., 1980; Rickert and Robinson, 1981; Vesey, 1981). Thiocyanate is distributed in all extracellular fluid (including serum, saliva, gastric juices, and cerebrospinal fluid) and eliminated at a slow rate, primarily through the kidneys and to a small extent through perspiration (Langer & Greer, 1977). The biological half-life of the stable SCN by-product is between 10 and 14 days (Langer & Greer, 1977; Vesey, 1981).

Factors that influence extracellular volume also affect SCN concentration. Diuresis (from exercise or antihypertensive agents) can elevate the SCN concentration (Neaton et al., 1981; Vesey, 1981), as can pregnancy, menstrual cycle, or differences in renal functions (Vesey,

---

[1] More detailed information on CO monitors is available from the authors. Newer solid state units can be purchased for less than $1,000.

1981). SCN concentrations in saliva and gastric juices are much higher than in plasma; therefore, vomiting will lower plasma concentration.

SCN is found in the fluids of all anion-concentrating tissues, including thyroid, salivary glands, gastric mucosa, and mammary glands (Langer & Greer, 1977). As is true for many inorganic compounds, salivary SCN levels are most reliably measured in parotid gland secretions (Shannon, Suddick, & Dowd, 1974). Parotid gland secretions show some seasonal and diurnal variability, however (Dogon, Amdur, & Bell, 1971; Shannon et al., 1974). Secretion rate of the parotid gland can also markedly influence saliva concentrations (Dogon et al., 1971). At low flow rates, concentrations are dramatically increased, but they asymptote beyond 0.3 ml/min/gland of secretion. Hence, fresh saliva from a well-stimulated parotid gland should be used to estimate SCN level (Dogon et al., 1971; Shannon et al., 1974).

Sensitivity. It has been recognized for many years that smokers have elevated SCN levels that can be reliably detected in serum, saliva, or urine (Lawson, Sweeney, & Dudley, 1943; Maliszewski & Bass, 1955). Cross-sectional surveys have been able to define reasonable cutpoints to discriminate between smokers and nonsmokers (Benfari, McIntyre, Benfari, Baldwin, & Ockene, 1977; Borgers & Junge, 1979; Butts et al., 1974; Vesey et al., 1982; Vogt et al., 1977), but detection of light or infrequent smokers remains a problem (Hunter et al., 1980; Luepker, Pechacek, Murray, Johnson, Hund, & Jacobs, 1981; Pechacek et al., in press; Vogt et al., 1977). Among adult daily smokers, over 90% can be correctly classified on the basis of a single SCN assessment (Benfari et al., 1977; Borgers & Junge, 1979; Butts et al., 1974; Cohen & Bartsch, 1980; Vesey et al., 1982; Vogt et al., 1977), but among younger adolescents, only a third or less could be identified reliably on a single assessment (Hunter et al., 1980; Luepker et al., 1981; Pechacek et al., in press).

Serum SCN has been used as a measure of smoking cessation (Brockway, 1978; Neaton et al., 1981) and as a more objective measure of tobacco exposure in epidemiologic studies (Heliovaara, Karvonen, Punsar, Rautanen, & Haarakoski, 1981; Koskela, 1981; Neaton et al., 1981). Comparative analyses between serum and saliva samples indicate that SCN levels are 15 to 20 times higher in saliva than in serum (Barylko-Pikielna & Pangborn, 1968; Densen, Davidow, Bass, & Jones, 1967; Langer & Greer, 1977; Pechacek, Luepker, Jacobs, Fraser, & Blackburn, 1979; Vesey, 1981), but that saliva levels are more variable (Pechacek et al., 1979). Intercorrelations between serum (or plasma) and saliva SCN have been found to range from $r = 0.58$ to $r = 0.89$ (Pechacek et al., 1979; Vesey, 1981). Urinary SCN levels are altered by urinary flow and other factors affecting excretion, making urine a less reliable monitoring fluid (Densen et al., 1967).

Specificity. Although nonsmoking exposures to hydrogen cyanide gases or cyanogens can occur occupationally (Lawson et al., 1943; NIOSH, Note 5) or as a by-product of the drug sodium nitroprusside (Page, Corcoran, Dustan, & Koppanyi, 1955), the most common nonsmoking source of cyanogens and thiocyanate is diet (Boxer & Rickards, 1952; Langer & Greer, 1977). Plant foods high in either cyanogenic glycosides (fruit pits like almonds, bamboo shoots, cassava, sugar cane, and certain beans) or naturally occurring SCN (especially the *Brassica* genus of cabbage, kale, cauliflower, broccoli, and brussel sprouts, and in beer (Greer, 1950; Langer & Greer, 1977) have been shown experimentally to produce levels of SCN in serum or saliva equivalent to the average levels of smokers, even in known nonsmokers (Langer & Greer, 1977; Pechacek et al., 1979). The hops used to make beer and ale also contain SCN (Langer & Greer, 1977), and regular drinkers can have increased SCN levels (Neaton et al., 1981). There are other minor sources of SCN, including normal metabolism (Boxer & Rickards, 1952; Funderburk & Middlesworth, 1971; Langer & Greer, 1977), passive smoke exposure (Pekkanen, Elo, & Hanninen, 1976), and bacterial infections (Vesey, 1981), but alone these produce small increases in body correlations.

Table 46.2 provides a summary of known sources of SCN in body fluids and the relative influence of each source. It should be noted that very large variances in nonsmoker SCN

Table 46.2   Sources of SCN in Body Fluids

Source	Relative Effects
I. Tobacco smoke	Rapid elevation of SCN level; major source among daily smokers
II. Diet (*Brassica* genus, cyanogenic glycosides, beer)	Can be large but is commonly seasonal; can produce SCN levels in nonsmokers equivalent to those in light smokers
III. Industrially produced cyanogens (electroplating, insecticides, fungicides, nitriles, air pollution)	Low-level exposure common in urban settings; can be a primary source among exposed smokers
IV. Marijuana	Smoke contains concentrations of hydrogen cyanide gas as large or larger than tobacco smoke
V. Metabolism	Minor influence
VI. Cyanogenic Drugs	Sodium nitroprusside can produce extremely high SCN levels but is rarely used outside acute care

levels are commonly shown (Benfari et al., 1977; Borgers & Junge, 1979; Butts et al., 1974; Neaton et al., 1981; Vesey et al., 1982) and that the distributions of light smokers and nonsmokers significantly overlap (Borgers & Junge, 1979; Neaton et al., 1981; Vesey et al., 1982). Given the sources of nonsmoking SCN (Langer & Greer, 1977; Pechacek et al., 1979), variability in these exposures can easily mask tobacco smoke exposure (Vogt et al., 1977). Among heavier smokers, however, discrimination between smokers and nonsmokers can be easily determined (Benfari et al., 1977; Borgers & Junge, 1979; Neaton et al., 1981; Vesey et al., 1982).

Among adolescents, SCN has been shown to have a lower intercorrelation with smoking rate than that of carbon monoxide, largely because of the greater variance in nonsmoker SCN levels (Pechacek et al., in press). The relationship between smoking level and SCN improves among older adolescents (Pechacek et al., in press; Hunter et al., 1980), but the specificity declines (Pechacek et al., in press). Since marijuana smoke also contains high concentrations of hydrogen cyanide gas (Brunnemann, Yu, & Hoffmann, 1977), it is difficult to determine if the increased rate of potentially false positives among older adolescents is due to nontobacco sources of SCN (including marijuana and diet) or false reporting of smoking (Pechacek et al., in press).

Technical issues.   Thiocyanate is a stable compound (Langer & Greer, 1977), detected simply by colorimetric procedures (Bowler, 1944; Butts et al., 1974; Densen et al., 1967; Hund, Pechacek, Luepker, & Neibling, Note 6) or with greater accuracy by gas chromatography (DeBrabander & Verbeke, 1977; Lundquist, Martensson, Sorbo, & Ohman, 1979). Although the most common colorimetric procedures (Butts et al., 1974; Densen et al., 1967) may be somewhat nonspecific (Lundquist et al., 1979), they are very inexpensive and easily automated (Butts et al., 1974; Hund et al., Note 6). Research in our own laboratory and elsewhere (Prue et al., 1980; Prue, Martin, Hume, & Davis, 1981) indicates that SCN concentrations in saliva samples are very stable and store well, as long as evaporation and bacterial growth are prevented. Less is known about the shelf life of serum or plasma SCN, but cyanide can be produced if whole blood is not kept adequately refrigerated (Ballantyne, 1977a, 1977b).

As noted earlier, if saliva is used for analysis, an adequate parotid gland sample must be stimulated. We have recommended the use of dental rolls for stimulation and collection

(Luepker et al., 1981; Hund et al., Note 6), but other forms of stimulation are available, including chewing paraffin wax or rubber objects, lozenges, or citric acid drops (Shannon et al., 1974). A more detailed discussion of collection methods is available upon request (Pechacek, Murray, & Luepker, Note 7).

Nicotine and Cotinine

Metabolism. Nicotine and its metabolic by-product, cotinine, are important estimators of the particulate phase of tobacco smoke (Hill & Marquardt, 1980). Nicotine has been well studied, since it is frequently cited as the addictive component in cigarette smoke (U.S. PHS, 1981).

The metabolism and pharmacokinetics of nicotine have been discussed extensively elsewhere (Russell, 1976; Russell & Feyerabend, 1978) and will be only briefly reviewed here. Nicotine, one of the few natural liquid alkaloids, is lipid-soluble and readily penetrates cell membranes in a free-base state (Russell, 1976; Russell & Feyerabend, 1978). This being so, it is rapidly absorbed through the skin or mucosa (oral, bucal, nasal, or gastrointestinal). Nicotine volatilized in burning tobacco suspends on minute droplets of tar that can be carried to the alveoli, where nicotine is readily absorbed. Absorption by the mucosa is highly pH-dependent (Russell, 1976; Feyerabend & Russell, 1978), so that high-pH cigar smoke is more readily absorbed by the mucosa, whereas more acidic burley tobacco smoke (as found in most cigarettes) is more easily inhaled and absorbed in the lungs (Russell, 1976).

Nicotine is a biologically active alkaloid and is rapidly metabolized by the liver. The half-life of nicotine is estimated to be between 20 and 60 minutes (Isaac & Rand, 1972; Russell, 1976; Russell & Feyerabend, 1978).

Based on estimated yields, 0.05 to 2.0 mg of nicotine are delivered to the mouth by each cigarette (Jenkins et al., Note 4). Plasma nicotine levels increase rapidly after smoking each cigarette (Armitage, Dollery, George, Houseman, Lewis, & Turner, 1975; Russell, 1976; Russell et al., 1980) but also decay quickly as nicotine is metabolized into cotinine and nicotine-N-oxide by the liver and excreted unchanged by the kidneys, especially in the presence of acidic urine (Feyerabend & Russell, 1978). Individual differences in rate of nicotine metabolism have been discussed (Russell & Feyerabend, 1978), but few studies have been done to determine how much smokers vary in rate of metabolism (Benowitz, 1983).

It has been estimated that about 90% of ingested nicotine is metabolized into cotinine (Benowitz, 1983; Langone, Gjika, & Van Vunakis, 1973). Cotinine is distributed throughout extracellular fluid and excreted through the kidneys and salivary gland; however, it is primarily eliminated by metabolism rather than by direct excretion (Benowitz, 1983).

Since the issue of individual differences in rate of cotinine metabolism is still being studied (Benowitz, 1983), care should be taken in estimating between-subject differences in dose exposure from a single cotinine assessment. Cotinine generally has been estimated to have an approximately 30-hour-half-life (Langone et al., 1973; Zeidenberg, Jaffe, Kanzler, Levitt, Langone, & Van Vunakis, 1977), but recent data suggest that the half-life may be shorter (Benowitz, 1983). Cotinine levels are elevated shortly after each cigarette (Armitage et al., 1975), but because of cotinine's moderately long half-life, mean blood levels are only weakly related to time since last cigarette (Rickert & Robinson, 1981). Cotinine concentrations do increase during waking (and smoking) hours, however, so average cotinine concentrations should be assessed later in the day (Benowitz, 1983).

Sensitivity. Because nicotine is unique to tobacco, not only cigarette smokers (Haley, Axelrod, & Tilton, 1983; Rickert & Robinson, 1981; Russell et al., 1980; Zeidenberg et al., 1977) but also cigar and pipe smokers (McCusker, McNabb, & Bone, 1982; Wald, Idle, Boreham, Bailey, & Van Vunakis, 1981) and smokeless tobacco users (Gritz, Baer-

Weiss, Benowitz, Van Vunakis, & Jarvik, 1981; Russell, Jarvis, Devitt, & Feyerabend, 1981) can be readily detected by blood nicotine and cotinine levels. Even nonsmokers smoking a single cigarette show detectable levels of nicotine (Armitage et al., 1975; Haines, Mahajan, Miljkovic, Miljkovic, & Vessell, 1974).

Since cotinine has a more stable and enduring blood level, it, rather than nicotine, is recommended as a measure of tobacco exposure (Langone et al., 1973). Regular smokers are detected, almost without exception, by urinary, blood, or saliva cotinine analyses (Benowitz, 1983; Haley et al., 1983; Hill, Haley, & Wynders, 1983; Paxton & Bernacca, 1979; Rickert & Robinson, 1981; Wilcox, Hughes, & Roland, 1979; Zeidenberg et al., 1977). The most dramatic demonstration of the sensitivity of plasma cotinine levels was that 95% of even adolescent smokers were detected by the test (Williams et al., 1979).

Both nicotine and cotinine levels have been recommended in studies of nicotine regulation (Moss & Prue, 1982). Both plasma nicotine levels (Herning, Jones, Benowitz, & Mines, 1983; Russell et al., 1980) and cotinine levels (Hill & Marquart, 1980; Hill et al., 1983; Rickert & Robinson, 1981) have been measured to evaluate the nicotine titration hypothesis (Russell, 1976). As noted earlier, until individual differences in rate of nicotine and continine metabolism are better defined, estimations of individual exposure based on a single nicotine or cotinine level should be made with caution (Benowitz, 1983).

Specificity. Smokers commonly have blood cotinine levels of 200–400 ng/ml, and even light smokers rarely have blood levels below 40–50 ng/ml (Benowitz, 1983; Haley et al., 1983; Hill & Marquardt, 1980; Rickert & Robinson, 1981; Zeidenberg et al., 1977; Hill et al., 1983). In contrast, when known nonsmokers have been tested, they rarely have any detectable cotinine (Benowitz, 1983; Haley et al., 1983; Wilcox et al., 1979; Zeidenberg et al., 1977), and cotinine levels when detected in plasma are usually below 10 ng/ml, except in recent ex-smokers (whose self-reports can be questioned) or in users of other tobacco products (Benowitz, 1983; Haley et al., 1983; Gritz et al., 1981; Zeidenberg et al., 1977). Ambient exposure to nicotine from second-hand smoke does occur (Horning, Horning, Carroll, Stillwell, & Dzidic, 1973), but the magnitude of this type of exposure has not been carefully studied because the level seen in most exposed nonsmokers is almost too low to be detected (Haley et al., 1983; Horning, Horning, Carroll, Stillwell, & Dzidic, 1973).

Among adolescents, the sensitivity and specificity of plasma cotinine was well demonstrated by Williams et al. (1979). Only 2% of claimed nonsmoking adolescents were found to have detectable cotinine levels. Studies of the relative sensitivity and specificity of plasma cotinine levels among infrequent and episodic adolescent smokers is continuing, and results appear favorable (Haley, et al., 1983).

Technical issues. Methods are available for measuring nicotine and cotinine in urine, blood, and saliva (Beckett & Triggs, 1966; Castro, Monji, Malkus, Eisenhart, McKennis, & Bowman, 1979; Dow & Hall, 1978; Feyerabend & Russell, 1979; Gruenke, Beelen, Craig, & Petrakis, 1979; Haines et al., 1974; Hengen & Hengen, 1978; Horning, Horning, Carroll, Dzidic, & Stillwell, 1973; Horning, Horning, Carroll, Stillwell, & Dzidic, 1973; Isaac & Rand, 1972; Jacobs, Wilson, & Benowitz, 1981; Langone et al., 1973; Langone, Van Vunakis, & Hill, 1975; Maskarinec, Harvey, & Caton, 1978; Matsukura, Sakamoto, Seino, Tamada, Matsuyama, & Muranaka, 1979; Matsukura, Sakamoto, Takahashi, Matsuyama, & Muranaka, 1979; Paxton & Bernacca, 1979; Rickert & Robinson, 1981; Saunders & Blume, 1981; Watson, 1977). Urine has been used for assays (e.g., Paxton & Bernacca, 1979; Wilcox et al., 1979), but the effects of urinary pH and flow rates suggest that urinary levels are too variable (Feyerabend & Russell, 1978; Matsukura, Sakamoto, Seino, Tamada, Matsuyama, & Muranaka, 1979; Matsukura, Sakamoto, Takahashi, Matsuyama, & Muranaka, 1979). Plasma or serum cotinine levels appear to be the most stable and are recommended (Benowitz, 1983; Langone et al., 1973; Rickert & Robinson, 1981).

Nicotine and cotinine are also excreted in the saliva, but in regular smokers, excreted salivary nicotine cannot be discriminated from unabsorbed nicotine deposited in the oral cavity. Therefore, only salivary cotinine levels are being studied. Preliminary data suggest that salivary cotinine levels are somewhat higher than blood levels and may be feasible for general use (Haley, et al., 1983; Best, Rickert, & Robinson, Note 8; Pechacek & Luepker, Note 9).

All methods available for the quantification of nicotine and/or cotinine are relatively complicated and expensive. Radioimmunoassay (Langone et al., 1973; Langone et al., 1975) and gas-chromatographic methods (Feyerabend & Russell, 1979; Jacobs et al., 1981; Rickert & Robinson, 1981) are well established and available.

Summary

Although there are thousands of compounds in tobacco smoke, carbon monoxide, thiocyanate, and cotinine permit an estimation of exposure from both gas phase and particulate phase in the individual subject. Carbon monoxide, thiocyanate, and cotinine measures have sufficiently good sensitivity and specificity to permit reliable estimates of tobacco exposure. Care must be taken with the carbon monoxide measure, because of its short half-life, to insure that results are not overly influenced by recent smoke exposure (Frederiksen & Martin, 1979). Similarly, cotinine, with a somewhat longer half-life, can still be influenced by recent exposure (Zeidenberg et al., 1977). Thiocyanate is a measure with a much longer half-life (Prue et al., 1980), and it is easy to analyze (Butts et al., 1974), which makes it more suitable for epidemiologic surveys (Heliovaara et al., 1981; Neaton et al., 1981; Vesey et al., 1982); however, nonsmoking sources of thiocyanate limit its specificity (Langer & Greer, 1977; Vesey, 1981). Others have suggested and used carbon monoxide level, either alone (Ashton et al., 1981; Frederiksen & Martin, 1979; Jarvis et al., 1980) or in conjunction with thiocyanate (Cohen & Bartsch, 1980; Vesey et al., 1982; Vogt et al., 1977). Cotinine is used less often, partly because of its analytic complexity and cost (Rickert & Robinson, 1981). As procedures improve, however, the superior sensitivity and specificity of this measure should encourage wider use (Haley et al., 1983).

Rickert and Robinson (1981) utilized a wide range of chemical measures—levels of carboxyhemoglobin (COHb), breath CO, plasma cotinine, plasma thiocyanate (SCN), and saliva thiocyanate—in a survey of 240 smokers to study the possible relationship between brand yield and exposure. Subjects' cigarette consumption varied from 2 to 60 per day. All chemical measures were significantly correlated with consumption level. Various brands' nominal yields of specific compounds—carbon monoxide (CO), nicotine, hydrogen cyanide (HCN)—were unrelated, however, to the corresponding chemical measures adjusted for consumption levels ($r = 0.10$ between CO delivery and COHb level; $r = 0.01$ between HCN delivery and plasma SCN level; $r = 0.08$ between nicotine delivery and plasma cotinine level). Although this study demonstrated that from 5% to 40% of the variance in the chemical measures could be accounted for by level of consumption, Rickett and Robinson (1981) did not attempt to measure inhalation style or variables other than brand that might account for the bulk of the variance in the chemical measures.

Herning et al. (in press) have recently attempted to account for as much of the variance in acute nicotine uptake as possible by measuring inhalation variables during the act of smoking different yield cigarettes. When individual differences in smoking behavior were taken into account, almost all of the variance in the blood nicotine level boosts was explained (multiple $R = 0.93$).

All of the chemical measures (COHb%, breath CO, serum or plasma SCN, and cotinine) display large variability among subjects with similar consumption levels. Within the multiple risk factor intervention trial (MRFIT), the 1,693 subjects self-reporting a daily consumption of 16 to 25 cigarettes per day (almost all reported about 20 per day) had a mean serum SCN of 153.7 μmol/L, with a standard deviation of 53.0 μmol/L (Neaton et al., 1981).

Similarly, 4,754 smoking nonindustrial workers had a mean COHb% of 4.44%, with a standard deviation of 2.6% (Kahn et al., 1974).

Cotinine has not been so widely studied, but in one survey of 450 smokers, a mean plasma cotinine level of 259 ng/ml, with a standard deviation of 135.8 ng/ml, was found (Hill et al., 1983). Based on the results from Herning et al. (in press), it is assumed that most of the variance in chemical measures is due to differences in inhalation parameters. Individual differences in metabolism and excretion rates (e.g., exercise-shortened half-life of CO, more rapid metabolism of cotinine) could also account for the variabilities, however, even among smokers self-reporting similar consumption levels.

The validation of all chemical measures has been hampered by the lack of a criterion for actual exposure. Daily cigarette consumption has been used either alone (e.g., Butts et al., 1974) or along with nominal yield of cigarette (e.g., Rickert & Robinson, 1981) to estimate exposure, but this approach explains only a small portion of the variance in the chemical measures. The individual smoker's inhalation style also needs to be assessed. This can be done directly in a laboratory setting (e.g., Gust et al., 1983; Herning et al., 1983), or by a somewhat less direct method, estimating mouth-level nicotine intake (Robinson & Young, 1980).

MEASUREMENT PROBLEMS IN SPECIAL POPULATIONS: ADOLESCENTS

In many ways, researchers studying adolescent smoking have led the field in exposing the need for objective measures of smoking (Evans, Hansen, & Mittelmark, 1977). It generally has been held that adolescents are likely to misreport their use of tobacco (Evans et al., 1977; Kozlowski et al., 1980; Luepker et al., 1981).

Traditionally, adolescent smoking had been assessed simply by asking, "How much do you smoke?" We recently reported data indicating that evidence of a national decline in adolescent smoking (Bachman et al., 1981; Green, 1979) may reflect a decline more in the validity of the self-reports than in actual smoking rates (Mittelmark, Murray, Luepker, & Pechacek, 1983).

Two strategies have been suggested to resolve the problem of underreporting: (a) procedures can be introduced to improve the validity of self-reports (Evans et al., 1977); and (b) objective measures can be employed (Luepker et al., 1981; Pechacek et al., in press). The sensitive nature of adolescent smoking led Evans and his colleagues (1977) to adapt the "bogus pipeline" procedure (Jones & Sigal, 1971) for use in smoking research. Jones and Sigal (1971) found greater disclosure of psychologically sensitive attitudes when subjects were led to believe that the experimenters had an independent, physiological method of verifying responses. Evans et al. (1977) showed students a film demonstrating how smoking could be detected through analysis of a saliva specimen for nicotine. Saliva samples were then collected from each student prior to obtaining self-reports. Compared to those who were not exposed to this pipeline procedure, twice the number of students reported weekly use of cigarettes. These data have since been replicated by Luepker et al. (1981) and by Bauman and Dent (1982). These results have led to the widespread use of the pipeline method to enhance the validity of self-report data (Botvin, Eng, & Williams, 1981; Lauer, Akers, Massey, & Clarke, 1982; McAlister, Perry, & Maccoby, 1979; Perry, Killen, Telch, Slinkard, & Danaher, 1980). It is important to note, however, that because most smoking prevention researchers have used true biological measures for smoking, the label "pipeline" rather than "bogus pipeline" can be more appropriately applied to these procedures (Pechacek et al., in press).

The pipeline procedure to encourage more valid self-reports is now widely accepted, but a recent retest of it conducted by Akers, Massey, Clarke, and Lauer (in press) did not detect any pipeline effect. Akers et al. (in press) concluded that valid reports of smoking can be obtained from adolescents if a good and trusting relationship has been formed between the researchers and the students. This issue and questions regarding how anonymity is assured (Harlin, 1972; McAlister, Note 12) require additional study.

Our own data (Mittelmark et al., 1982) clearly indicate that in an initial, cross-sectional survey (when there has been no opportunity to establish a good and trusting relationship), strategies to increase the validity of adolescent self-reporting (Pechacek et al., in press) are still highly recommended. The use of the validity-enhancing protocol appears to be responsible for the much higher rates of smoking prevalence documented in our population (Mittelmark et al., 1982) in comparison to United States statistics (Bachman et al., 1981; Green, 1979). Prevalence rates in our study for self-reported smoking in the previous week were 11.9% for 11- to 14-year-old males, 24.1% for 15- to 16-year-old males, 13.5% for 11- to 14-year-old females, and 39.6% for 15- to 16-year-old females (Mittelmark et al., 1982). These rates are 1.5 to 4 times higher than those reported in recent surveys using self-report methods without the influence of the pipeline effect (Green, 1979).

In addition to the pipeline effect that can be engendered by the use of chemical measures, these measures can provide a more objective estimate of exposure (Pechacek et al., in press) and an additional dependent measure (Hurd, Johnson, Pechacek, Bast, Jacobs, & Luepker, 1980; Luepker et al., 1981). All three of the primary measures—carbon monoxide (CO), thiocyanate (SCN), and cotinine—have been used with adolescents. Expired-air CO levels correlate well with self-reported smoking rates ($r = .69$ for weekly smoking among 11- to 17-year-olds), but among younger adolescents, where most smoking is episodic, fewer than half of even daily smokers can be detected (Pechacek et al., in press; Pederson, Sidney, & Lefcoe, 1977).

The specificity of saliva SCN is limited by marijuana and diet, a problem that results in rather low intercorrelations (e.g., $r = .20$ for weekly smoking among 11- to 13-year-olds), but the longer half-life of the measure is reflected in higher sensitivity (e.g., over 90% of 16- to 17-year-old daily smokers can be detected with saliva SCN) (Luepker et al., 1981; Pechacek et al., in press). Plasma SCN results (Hunter et al., 1980) are comparable with saliva SCN levels (Pechacek et al., in press). With both saliva and plasma SCN tests, there is difficulty in detecting younger and infrequent smokers.

Plasma cotinine data are very encouraging (Williams et al., 1979), and saliva cotinine assessments seem to be practical (Best et al., Note 9; Haley et al., 1983; Pechacek & Luepker, Note 12). Williams et al. (1979) detected 95% of daily adolescent smokers and found only 2% of reported nonsmokers to have detectable levels. The higher specificity of cotinine may enable its use to detect even the younger, infrequent smokers with whom CO and SCN measures offer difficulties. Unfortunately, smokeless tobacco use can confound the measurement of cigarette smoking (Gritz et al., 1981).

Despite the advances that have been made in developing chemical measures to detect adolescent smoking, self-reports must still be the primary dependent variables, especially among younger adolescents (Pechacek et al., in press). Therefore, issues related to the enhancement of adolescent self-report validity (Akers et al., in press; Bauman & Dent, 1982; Evans et al., 1977; Mittelmark et al., 1983; Pechacek et al., in press) still require additional study.

MEASURING SMOKING IN GENERAL POPULATIONS

Warner (1978) and Vogt et al. (1977) present data suggesting that self-reports in general surveys of smoking behavior may be decreasing in validity. The need for measures to validate adult self-reports after smoking cessation intervention is clear. Data indicate that up to 40% of reported quitters can be detected as likely smokers using chemical measures (Brockway, 1978; Isacsson & Janzon, 1976; Kozlowski et al., 1980; Neaton et al., 1981; Ohlin et al., 1976; Sillett et al., 1978). The need for such measures in general population surveys is still questioned, however (Petitti, Friedman, & Kahn, 1981).

Although smokers are unlikely to report abstinence falsely on general surveys, self-reports of smoking exposure and inhalation style have been shown to have limited validity (Jaffe et al., 1981; Rickert & Robinson, 1981; Russell et al., 1980; Stepney, 1982; Wald et al., 1978; Wald, Idle, Boreham, & Bailey, 1981), and strength of cigarette smoked does not account for much variance in actual exposure (Rickert & Robinson, 1981; Russell, et al., 1980). Therefore, some form of chemical assessment is now recommended for surveys of smoking (Jarvis, Raw, Russell, & Feyerabend, 1982; Vogt, 1982). In addition, chemical measures are needed to discriminate between inhaling and noninhaling pipe and cigar smokers (Castleden & Cole, 1973; Cowie, Sillett, & Ball, 1973; Goldman, 1976, 1977; Turner, Sillett, & McNicol, 1977, 1981; Wald, Idle, Boreham, Bailey, & Van Vunakis, 1981).

Tracking Changes in Smoking

Moss and Prue (1982), Orleans and Shipley (1982), and Frederiksen et al. (1979) have reviewed the problems of measuring reductions in smoking rate or brand changes among continuing smokers. In addition to the chemical measures, innovative measures, including butt nicotine assays (Robinson & Young, 1980; Robinson, Young, & Rickert, in press) and filter stain patterns (Kozlowski et al., 1982), offer relatively inexpensive measures of actual exposure. When nicotine manipulations are being undertaken, dose exposure to nicotine needs to be estimated along with relative toxic exposure (Moss & Prue, 1982; Russell et al., 1982). Since CO and SCN levels are elevated by gas phase exposure and cotinine by particulate phase exposure, a combination of CO and/or SCN with cotinine may be the optimal strategy for monitoring changes in exposure.

Self-reported reductions in smoking rate have been commonly reported in the evaluation of smoking modification studies (Leventhal & Cleary, 1980; Lichtenstein, 1982; McFall, 1978; Pechacek, 1979). Unfortunately, such self-reported changes have not been validated by chemical assessments (Ockene, Hymowitz, Sexton, & Brostes, 1982; Vogt et al., 1979). Similarly, reductions in exposure produced by changes to a lower yield brand have also been questioned (Jaffe et al., 1981; Rickert & Robinson, 1981). Hence, chemical measures are almost essential for any evaluation of smoking reduction (Orleans & Shipley, 1982).

Evaluating Smoking Cessation

It has become obvious that smokers will falsely report abstinence following a cessation program at surprisingly high rates (Brockway, 1978; Isacsson & Janzon, 1976; Kozlowski et al., 1980; Neaton et al., 1981; Ockene et al., 1982; Ohlin et al., 1976; Paxton & Bernacca, 1979; Sillett et al., 1978; Wilcox et al., 1979). It is generally agreed that some form of validation of self-reports is necessary (Lichtenstein, 1982; McFall, 1978; Orleans & Shipley, 1982; Pechacek, 1979).

Expired-air CO and COHb% (Isaccson & Janzon, 1976; Lando, 1975; Ohlin et al., 1976; Sillett et al., 1978), urinary nicotine (Paxton & Bernacca, 1979; Russell et al., 1980; Wilcox et al., 1979), and serum SCN (Brockway, 1978; Neaton et al., 1981; Ockene et al., 1982) have all been used to document abstinence following smoking cessation interventions. Other validation procedures can be employed, including informant reports, butt counts, and cigarette purchasing behaviors (Lichtenstein, 1982; McFall, 1978; Orleans & Shipley, 1982). Unfortunately, the alternatives to chemical measures do not provide any valid assessments of changes in dose. As noted earlier, data from the MRFIT have shown that self-reported reductions in amount smoked by those who fail to quit have not been validated when CO and SCN measures are used (Neaton et al., 1981; Ockene et al., 1982; Vogt et al., 1979). Since no chemical measure has perfect sensitivity, the use of comparisons between baseline (smoking) and follow-up CO, SCN, or cotinine levels can increase the accuracy of decisions about follow-up smoking status or amount smoked. Based on existing data, unvalidated self-reported smoking rate data should *not* be used as a parametric measure of exposure. Rather, changes in CO, SCN, or cotinine levels may provide a parametric measure of change.

Several additional variables have been suggested by Orleans and Shipley (1982) for assessment after smoking cessation treatment. These variables include measures of side effects, factors influencing abstinence and relapse, and health benefits needed for adequate cost/ benefit analyses. These are all important areas requiring attention. Orleans and Shipley (1982) have discussed these variables in detail, and they also have discussed the lack of consensus among researchers regarding what is defined as abstinence following treatment. Many smokers briefly relapse but return to abstinence at a subsequent follow-up. Shipley, Rosen, and Williams (1982) surveyed published smoking research and found great disagreement regarding the length of abstinence needed to be classed a success, how to deal with brief relapses, and how to classify pipe, cigar, and nontobacco smoking behavior. Measurement and reporting conventions are clearly needed. Orleans and Shipley (1982) provide useful guidelines and sample follow-up forms.

SUMMARY

Self-reported smoking rates collected by retrospective questionnaires or self-monitoring have been the primary dependent variable in almost all behavioral studies of adolescent and adult smoking (Ashton and Stepney, 1982; Green, 1979; Leventhal & Cleary, 1980; Lichtenstein, 1982; McFall, 1978; Orleans & Shipley, 1982). Traditionally, it had been assumed that such self-reports were relatively valid estimates of rate and that they provided an adequate and approximate parametric measure. Recent data have raised serious questions about that assumption (e.g., Evans et al., 1977; Neaton et al., 1981; Sillett et al., 1978; Vogt et al., 1979; Warner, 1978). Given the strong digit bias present in smoking reports, questions about underreporting of daily rate, even among adults (Warner, 1978), and questionable validity of reports of reduction in rates after intervention (e.g., Sillett et al., 1978; Vogt et al., 1979), self-reported rate of smoking may be more an ordinal than a continuous measure of cigarette usage.

Significant advances have been made in recent years in the development of chemical measures to validate adolescent and adult self-reports. Carbon monoxide and thiocyanate measures are relatively inexpensive and easy to use (Fredericksen & Martin, 1979; Orleans & Shipley, 1982; Prue et al., 1980). Cotinine is a much more specific measure of tobacco exposure, but it is more difficult to measure.

Other measures of exposure that are especially appropriate for objective assessments of dose reduction have also been developed, including butt nicotine assays (Robinson & Young, 1980) and filter stain-pattern matching (Kozlowski et al., 1982), as well as direct measures of puffing profiles (Comer & Creighton, 1978; Creighton et al., 1978; Gust et al., 1983; Henningfield et al., 1980; Herning et al., 1983; Rawbone et al., 1978; Tobin & Sackner, 1982; Gritz, Note 2). These recent advances in measurement have documented the surprisingly large variability in smoke exposure that occurs among individuals smoking the same number of cigarettes of similar strength.

Whether the target population is adolescents, general populations, or smokers trying to reduce or quit, advances in the measurement of smoking are improving rapidly. Asking the straightforward question, "How many cigarettes do you smoke in an average day?" should and will remain important (Petitti et al., 1981), but its usefulness as a valid research tool has changed dramatically (Evans et al., 1977; Kozlowski et al., 1980; Vogt, 1982). It is hoped that this chapter will provide researchers with information about the alternatives that are available, so that research on smoking behavior can continue with greater precision.

REFERENCE NOTES

1. Myers, M., Iscoe, C., Jennings, C., Lenox, W., Minsky, E., & Sacks, A. *Federal Trade Commission staff report on the cigarette advertising investigation.* Washington, D.C.: Federal Trade Commission, May 1981.

2. Gritz, E. Patterns of puffing in cigarette smokers. In N. A. Krasnegor (Ed.), *Self-administration of abused substances: Methods for study.* National Institute on Drug Abuse, Research 20 Monograph Series, No. 200. Washington, D.C.: DHEW, ADA/ MHA, 1978.

3. Krasnegor, N. A. (Ed.). *Cigarette smoking as a dependence process.* NIDA Research Monograph No. 23. Washington, D.C.: National Institute on Drug Abuse, 1979.

4. Jenkins, R., Quincy, R., & Guerin, M. *Selected constituents in the smokers of U.S. commercial cigarettes: "Tar," nicotine, carbon monoxide and carbon dioxide.* Oak Ridge National Laboratory Pub. No. ORNL/PM-6870, May 1979.

5. National Institute for Occupational Safety and Health (NIOSH). *Occupational exposure to hydrogen cyanide and cyanide salts.* DHEW Pub. No. (NIOSH)77–108. Washington, D.C.: DHEW, NIOSH, 1976.

6. Hund, F. W., Pechacek, T. F., Luepker, R. V., & Neibling, M. J. *Determination of saliva thiocyanate to measure tobacco smoking activity: An automated method.* Manuscript submitted for publication, 1983.

7. Pechacek, T. F., Murray, D. M., & Luepker, R. V. *Saliva sample collection manual: Version II.* Minneapolis: University of Minnesota, School of Public Health, Health Behaviors Measurement Laboratory, July 1980.

8. Best, J. A., Rickert, W. S., & Robinson, J. C. Unpublished data from the University of Waterloo Smoking Prevention Study. University of Waterloo, Ontario, Canada, 1982.

9. Pechacek, T. F., & Luepker, R. V. Unpublished data. University of Minnesota, 1982.

10. McAlister, A. C. Tobacco, alcohol and drug abuse: Onset and prevention. In D. A. Hamburg, E. O. Nightingale, & U. Kalmar (Eds.), *Healthy people: The Surgeon General's report on health promotion and disease prevention: Background papers.* DHEW Pub. No. (PHS)79–55071A. Washington, D.C.: U.S. Public Health Service, 1979.

REFERENCES

Abrams, D. B., & Wilson, G. T. Self-monitoring and reactivity in the modification of cigarette smoking. *Journal of Consulting and Clinical Psychology,* 1979, **47,** 243–251.

Adams, P. I. The influence of cigarette smoke yields on smoking habits. In R. E. Thornton (Ed.), *Smoking behavior: Physiological and psychological influences.* New York: Churchill Livingstone, 1978.

Akers, R. L., Massey, J., Clarke, W., & Lauer, R. Are self-reports of adolescent deviance valid? Biochemical measures, randomized response, and the bogus pipeline in smoking behavior. *Social Forces,* in press.

Armitage, A., Dollery, C., George, C., Houseman, T., Lewis, P., & Turner, D. Absorption and metabolism of nicotine from cigarettes. *British Medical Journal,* 1975, **4,** 413–416.

Aronow, W. S., & Cassidy, J. Effect of marijuana and placebo-marijuana smoking on angina pectoris. *New England Journal of Medicine,* 1974, **291,** 65–67.

Ashton, H., & Stepney, R. *Smoking: Psychology and pharmacology.* London: Tavistock Publications, 1982.

Ashton, H., Stepney, R., & Thompson, J. W. Should intake of carbon monoxide be used as a guide to intake of other smoke constituents? *British Medical Journal,* 1981, **282,** 10–13.

Bachman, J. G., Johnston, L. D., & O'Malley, P. M. Smoking, drinking, and drug use among American high school students: Correlates and trends, 1975–1979. *American Journal of Public Health*, 1981, **71**, 59–69.

Ballantyne, B. Factors in the analysis of whole blood thiocyanate. *Clinical Toxicology*, 1977, **11**, 195–210. (a)

Ballantyne, B. In vitro production of cyanide in normal human blood and the influence of thiocyanate and storage temperature. *Clinical Toxicology*, 1977, **11**, 173–193. (b)

Barylko-Pikielna, N., & Pangborn, R. M. Effect of cigarette smoking on urinary and salivary thiocyanates. *Archives of Environmental Health*, 1968, **17**, 739–745.

Battig, K. (Ed.). *Behavioral effects of nicotine: International workshop on behavioral effects of nicotine.* New York: S. Karger, 1978.

Baugh, J. G., Hunter, S. M., Webber, L. S., & Berenson, G. S. Development trends of first cigarette smoking experience of children: The Bogalusa Heart Study. *American Journal of Public Health*, 1982, **72**, 1161–1164.

Bauman, K. E., & Dent, C. W. Influence of an objective measure on self-reports of behavior. *Journal of Applied Psychology*, 1982, **67**, 623–628.

Beckett, A., & Trigg, E. Determination of nicotine and its metabolite, cotinine, in urine by gas chromatography. *Nature*, 1966, **211**, 1415–1417.

Benfari, R. C., McIntyre, K., Benfari, M. J. F., Baldwin, A., & Ockene, J. The use of thiocyanate determination for indication of cigarette smoking status. *Evaluation Quarterly*, 1977, **1**, 629–638.

Benowitz, N. Biochemical measures of tobacco smoke consumption. In J. Grabowski & C. Bell (Eds.), *Measurement of smoking behavior.* Nida Research Monograph 48. Washington, D.C.: National Institute on Drug Abuse, 1983.

Borgers, D., & Junge, B. Thiocyanate as an indicator of tobacco smoking. *Preventive Medicine*, 1979, **8**, 351–357.

Botvin, G. J., Eng, A., & Williams, C. L. Preventing the onset of cigarette smoking through life skills training. *Preventive Medicine*, 1981, **9**, 135–143.

Bowler, R. G. The determination of thiocyanate in blood serum. *Journal of Biochemistry*, 1944, **38**, 385–388.

Boxer, G. E., & Rickards, J. C. Studies on the metabolism of the carbon of cyanide and thiocyanate. *Archives of Biochemistry*, 1952, **39**, 7–26.

Brockway, B. S. Chemical validation of self-reported smoking rates. *Behavior Therapy*, 1978, **9**, 685–686.

Brunnemann, K., Yu, L., & Hoffmann, D. Chemical studies on tobacco smoke: XLIX. Gas chromatographic determination of hydrogen cyanide and cyanogen in tobacco smoke. *Journal of Analytical Toxicology*, 1977, **1**, 1–56.

Butts, W. C., Kuehneman, J., & Widdowson, G. M. Automated method for determining serum thiocyanate to distinguish smokers from nonsmokers. *Clinical Chemistry*, 1974, **20**, 1344–1348.

Castleden, C. M., & Cole, P. V. Inhalation of tobacco smoke by pipe and cigar smokers. *Lancet*, 1973, **2**, 21–22.

Castro, A., Monji, N., Malkus, H., Eisenhart, W., McKennis, H., Jr., & Bowman, E. R. Automated radioimmunoassay of nicotine. *Clinical Chimica Acta*, 1979, **95**, 473–481.

Coburn, R. Mechanism of carbon monoxide toxicity. *Preventive Medicine*, 1979, **8**, 310–322.

Coburn, R., Forster, R., & Kane, P. Considerations of the physiological variables that determine the blood carboxyhemoglobin concentration in man. *Journal of Clinical Investigation*, 1965, **44**, 1899–1910.

Cohen, J., & Bartsch, G. A comparison between carboxyhemoglobin and serum thiocyanate determinations as indicators of cigarette smoking. *American Journal of Public Health*, 1980, **70**, 284–286.

Cohen, S. I., Perkins, N. M., Ury, H. K., & Goldsmith, J. R. Carbon monoxide uptake in cigarette smoking. *Archives of Environmental Health*, 1971, **22**, 55–60.

Collins, F. L., Jr., & Epstein, L. H. Temporal analysis of cigarette smoking, *Addictive Behaviors*, 1978, **3**, 93–97.

Comer, A., & Creighton, D. The effect of experimental conditions on smoking behavior. In R. E.

Thornton (Ed.), *Smoking behavior: Physiological and psychological influences.* New York: Churchill Livingston, 1978.

Commins, B. T. Measurement of carbon monoxide in the blood: Review of available methods. *Annals of Occupational Hygiene,* 1975, **18,** 69–77.

Cowie, J., Sillett, R. W., & Ball, K. P. Carbon monoxide absorption by cigarette smokers who change to smoking cigars. *Lancet,* 1973, **1,** 1033–1035.

Creighton, D. E., Noble, M. J., & Whewell, R. T. Instruments to measure, record and duplicate human smoking patterns. In R. E. Thornton (Ed.), *Smoking behavior: Physiological and psychological influences.* New York: Churchill Livingstone, 1978.

DeBrabander, H. F., & Verbeke, R. Determination of thiocyanate in tissues and body fluids of animals by gas chromatography with electron-capture detection. *Journal of Chromatography,* 1977, **138,** 131–142.

Densen, P. M., Davidow, B., Bass, H. E., & Jones, E. W. A chemical test for smoking exposure. *Archives of Environmental Health,* 1967, **14,** 865–874.

Dogon, I. L., Amdur, B. H., & Bell, K. Observations on the diurnal variation of inorganic constituents of human parotid saliva in smokers and nonsmokers. *Archives of Oral Biology,* 1971, **16,** 95–105.

Dow, J., & Hall, K. Capillary-column combined gas chromatography–mass spectrometry method for the estimation of nicotine in plasma by selective ion monitoring. *Journal of Chromatography,* 1978, **153,** 521–525.

Dunn, P., & Freiesleben, E. The effects of nicotine-enhanced cigarettes on human smoking parameters and alveolar carbon monoxide levels. In R. E. Thornton (Ed.), *Smoking behavior: Physiological and psychological influences.* New York: Churchill Livingstone, 1978.

Evans, R. I., Hansen, W. B., & Mittelmark, M. B. Increasing the validity of self-reports of smoking behavior in children. *Journal of Applied Psychology,* 1977, **62,** 521–523.

Feyerabend, C., & Russell, M. A. H. Effect of urinary pH and nicotine excretion rate on plasma nicotine during cigarette smoking and chewing nicotine gum. *British Journal of Clinical Pharmacology,* 1978, **5,** 293–297.

Feyerabend, C., & Russell, M. A. H. Improved gas-chromatographic method and microextraction technique for the measurement of nicotine in biological fluids. *Journal of Pharmacy and Parmacology,* 1979, **31,** 73–76.

Forbes, W., Robinson, J., Hanley, J., & Colburn, H. Studies on the nicotine exposure of individual smokers: I. Changes in mouth-level exposure to nicotine on switching to lower nicotine cigarettes. *International Journal of the Addictions,* 1976, **11,** 933–950.

Frederiksen, L. W., Epstein, L. H., & Kosevsky, B. P. Reliability and controlling effects of three procedures for self-monitoring smoking. *Psychological Record,* 1975, **25,** 255–263.

Frederiksen, L. W., & Martin, J. E. Carbon monoxide and smoking behavior. *Addictive Behaviors,* 1979, **4,** 21–30.

Frederiksen, L. W., Martin, J. E., & Webster, J. S. Assessment of smoking behavior. *Journal of Applied Behavior Analysis,* 1979, **12,** 653–664.

Frederiksen, L. W., & Simon, S. J. Modification of smoking topography: A preliminary analysis. *Behavior Therapy,* 1978, **9,** 946–949.

Funderburk, C., & Middlesworth, L. V. The effect of thiocyanate concentration on thiocyanate distribution and excretion. *Society for Experimental Biology and Medical Procedures,* 1971, **136,** 1249–1252.

Garrison, R. J., Kannel, W. B., Feinleib, M., Castelli, W. P., McNamara, P. M., & Padgett, S. J. Cigarette smoking and HDL cholesterol. The Framingham Offspring Study. *Atherosclerosis,* 1978, **30,** 17–25.

Godin, G., & Shephard, R. On the course of carbon monoxide uptake and release. *Respiration,* 1972, **29,** 317–329.

Goldman, A. L. Cigar inhaling. *American Review of Respiratory Disease,* 1976, **113,** 87–89.

Goldman, A. L. Carboxyhemoglobin levels in primary and secondary cigar and pipe smokers. *Chest,* 1977, **72,** 33–35.

Goldsmith, J. R., & Aronow, W. S. Carbon monoxide and coronary heart disease: A review. *Environmental Research,* 1975, **10,** 236–248.

Goodman, A. G., & Gilman, A. (Eds.). *The pharmacological basis of therapeutics.* New York: Macmillan, 1975.

Green, D. E. *Teenage smoking: Immediate and long-term patterns.* Washington, D.C.: National Institute of Education, 1979.

Greer, M. Nutrition & goiter. *Physiology Reviews,* 1950, **30,** 513–548.

Griffiths, R., & Henningfield, J. Experimental analysis of human cigarette smoking behavior. *Federation Proceedings,* 1982, **41,** 234–240.

Gritz, E., Baer-Weiss, V., Benowitz, N., Van Vunakis, H., & Jarvik, M. Plasma nicotine and cotinine concentrations in habitual smokeless tobacco users. *Clinical Pharmacology and Therapeutics,* 1981, **30,** 201–209.

Gruenke, L., Beelen, T., Craig, J., & Petrakis, N. The determination of nicotine in biological fluids at picogram levels by selective ion recording. *Analytical Biochemistry,* 1979, **94,** 411–416.

Guillerm, R., & Radziszewski, E. Analysis of smoking pattern including intake of carbon monoxide and influence of changes in cigarette design. In R. E. Thornton (Ed.), *Smoking behavior: Physiological and psychological influences.* New York: Churchill Livingstone, 1978.

Gust, S., & Pickens, R. Does cigarette nicotine yield affect puff volume? *Clinical Pharmacology and Therapeutics,* 1982, **32,** 418–422.

Gust, S., Pickens, R., & Pechacek, T. Relation of puff volume to other topographical measures of smoking. *Addictive Behaviors,* 1983, **8,** 115–119. (a)

Gust, S., Pickens, R., & Pechacek, T. A methodology for the recording of smoking topography. *Behavior Research Methods and Instrumentation,* 1983, **15,** 341–343. (b)

Haines, C., Jr., Mahajan, D., Miljkovic, D., Miljkovic, M., & Vessell, E. Radioimmunoassay of plasma nicotine in habituated and naive smokers. *Clinical Pharmacology and Therapeutics,* 1974, **16,** 1083–1089.

Haley, N., Axelrod, C., & Tilton, K. Validation of self-reported smoking behavior: biochemical analysis of cotinine and thiocyonate. *American Journal of Public Health,* 1983, **73,** 1204–1207.

Harlin, V. The influences of obvious anonymity on the response of school children to a questionnaire about smoking. *American Journal of Public Health,* 1972, **62,** 566–574.

Harris, P. E. Cigarette smoking in the United States, 1950–1978. In U.S. PHS, *Smoking and health: A report of the Surgeon General.* Washington, D.C.: U.S. Government Printing Office, 1979.

Hawkins, L. Blood carbon monoxide levels as a function of daily cigarette consumption and physical activity. *British Journal of Industrial Medicine,* 1976, **33,** 123–125.

Heliovaara, M., Karvonen, M., Punsar, S., Rautanen, Y., & Haarakoski, J. Serum thiocyanate concentration and cigarette smoking in relation to overall mortality and to deaths from coronary heart disease and lung cancer. *Journal of Chronic Diseases,* 1981, **10,** 353–363.

Hengen, N., & Hengen, M. Gas-liquid chromatographic determination of nicotine and cotinine in plasma. *Clinical Chemistry,* 1978, **24,** 50–53.

Henningfield, J., Stitzer, M. & Griffiths, R. Expired air carbon monoxide accumulation and elimination as a function of number of cigarettes smoked. *Addictive Behaviors,* 1980, **5,** 265–272.

Henningfield, J., Yingling, J., Griffiths, R. R., & Pickens, R. W. An inexpensive portable device for measuring puffing behavior by cigarette smokers. *Pharmacology, Biochemistry and Behavior,* 1979, **12,** 811–813.

Hepper, N., Drage, C., Davies, S., Rupp, W., La Mothe, J., Schoenfeldor, P., Munson, P. Chronic obstructive pulmonary disease: a community-oriented program including professional education and screening by volunteer health agency. *American Review of Respiratory Disease,* 1980, **121,** 97–104.

Herning, R. I., Jones, R. T., Benowitz, N. L., & Mines, A. H. How a cigarette is smoked determines nicotine blood levels. *Clinical Pharmacology and Therapeutics,* 1983, **33,** 84–90.

Herning, R., Jones, R., Bachman, J., & Mines, A. Puff volume increases when low-nicotine cigarettes are smoked. *British Medical Journal,* 1981, **283,** 1255–1259.

Hill, P., & Marquardt, H. Plasma and urine changes after smoking different brands of cigarettes. *Clinical Pharmacology and Therapeutics,* 1980, **27,** 652–658.

Hill, P., Haley, N., & Wynder, E. Cigarette smoking: carboxyhemoglobin, plasma nicotine, cotinine, and thiocyanate versus self-reported smoking data and cardiovascular disease. *Journal of Chronic Diseases,* 1983, **36,** 439–449.

Horan, J., Hackett, G., & Linberg, S. Factors to consider when using expired air carbon monoxide in smoking assessment. *Addictive Behaviors*, 1978, **3**, 25–28.

Horning, E., Horning, M., Carroll, D., Dzidic, I., & Stillwell, R. New picogram detection system based on a mass spectrometer with an external ionization source at atmospheric pressure. *Analytical Chemistry*, 1973, **45**, 936–943.

Horning, E., Horning, M., Carroll, D., Stillwell, R., & Dzidic, I. Nicotine in smokers, nonsmokers, and room air. *Life Sciences*, 1973, **13**, 1331.

Hughes, J., Frederiksen, L., & Frazier, M. A carbon monoxide analyzer for measurement of smoking behavior. *Behavior Therapy*, 1978, **9**, 293–296.

Hulley, S. B., Cohen, R., & Widdowson, G. Plasma high-density lipoprotein cholesterol level: Influence of risk factor intervention. *Journal of the American Medical Association*, 1977, **238**, 2269–2271.

Hunter, S. M., Webber, L. S., & Berenson, G. Cigarette smoking and tobacco usage behavior in children and adolescent: Bogalusa Heart Study. *Preventive Medicine*, 1980, **9**, 701–712.

Hurd, P., Johnson, C., Pechacek, T., Bast, L., Jacobs, D., & Luepker, R. Prevention of cigarette smoking in seventh grade students. *Journal of Behavioral Medicine*, 1980, **8**, 15–28.

Isaac, P. F., & Rand, M. J. Cigarette smoking and plasma levels of nicotine. *Nature*, 1972, **236**, 308–310.

Isacsson, S. O., & Janzon, L. Results of a quit-smoking research project in a randomly selected population. *Scandinavian Journal of Social Medicine*, 1976, **4**, 25–29.

Jacobs, P., III, Wilson, M., & Benowitz, N. L. Improved gas chromatographic method for the determination of nicotine and cotinine in biologic fluids. *Journal of Chromatography*, 1981, **222**, 61–70.

Jaffe, J., Kanzler, M., Cohen, M., & Kaplan, T. Inducing low tar/nicotine cigarette smoking in women. *British Journal of Addiction*, 1978, **73**, 271–281.

Jaffe, J., Kanzler, M., Friedman, L., & Kaplan, T. Money and health messages as incentives for smoking low tar/nicotine cigarettes: Changes in consumption and exhaled carbon monoxide. *British Journal of Addiction*, 1982, **77**, 21–34.

Jaffe, J., Kanzler, M., Friedman, L., Stunkard, A., & Verebey, K. Carbon monoxide and thiocyanate levels in low tar/nicotine smokers. *Addictive Behaviors*, 1981, **6**, 337–343.

Janzon, L., Lindell, S., Trell, E., & Larme, A. Smoking habits and carboxyhaemoglobin. *Journal of Epidemiology and Community Health*, 1981, **35**, 271–173.

Jarvis, M. J., Raw, M., Russell, M., & Feyerabend, C. Randomized control trial of nicotine chewing gum. *British Medical Journal*, 1982, **285**, 537–540.

Jarvis, M., Russell, M., & Saloojee, Y. Expired air carbon monoxide: A simple breath test of tobacco smoke intake. *British Medical Journal*, 1980, 484–485.

Jones, E. E., & Sigal, H. The bogus pipeline: A new paradigm for measuring affect and attitude. *Psychology Bulletin*, 1971, **76**, 349–364.

Jones, R. H., Ellicott, M. F., Cardigan, J. B., & Gaensler, E. A. The relationship between alveolar and blood carbon monoxide concentrations during breath-holding. *Journal of Laboratory and Clinical Medicine*, 1958, **51**, 553–564.

Kahn, A., Rutledge, R., Davis, G., Altes, J., Gantner, G., Thornton, C., & Wallace, D. Carboxyhemoglobin sources in the metropolitan St. Louis population. *Archives of Environmental Health*, 1974, **29**, 127–135.

Koskela, K. *A community-based anti-smoking programme as a part of a comprehensive cardiovascular programme* (*The North Karelia Project*). Kuopio, Finland: University of Kuopio, Research Institute of Public Health, 1981.

Kozlowski, L. Applications of some physical indicators of cigarette smoking. *Addictive Behaviors*, 1981, **6**, 213–220. (a)

Kozlowski, L. The changing cigarette: Behavioral aspects. In U.S. PHS, *The Health consequences of smoking: The changing cigarette. U.S. Surgeon General's report*. Washington, D.C.: U.S. Government Printing Office, 1981. (b)

Kozlowski, L. Tar and nicotine delivery of cigarettes. *Journal of the American Medical Association*, 1981, **245**, 158–159. (c)

Kozlowski, L., Herman, C., & Frecker, R. What researchers make of what cigarette smokers say: Filtering smokers' hot air. *Lancet*, 1980, **1**, 699–700.

Kozlowski, L., Rickert, W., Pope, M., & Robinson, J. A color-matching technique for monitoring tar/nicotine yields to smokers. *American Journal of Public Health,* 1982, **72,** 597–599.

Kumar, R., Cooke, E., Lader, M., & Russell, M. Is nicotine important in tobacco smoking? *Clinical Pharmacology and Therapeutics,* 1977, **21,** 520–529.

Lando, H. A. An objective check upon self-reported smoking levels: A preliminary report. *Behavior Therapy,* 1975, **6,** 547–549.

Langer, P., & Greer, M. A. *Antithyroid substances and naturally occurring goitrogens.* Basel and New York: S. Karger, 1977.

Langone, J. J., Gjika, H. B., & Van Vunakis, H. Nicotine and its metabolites: Radioimmunoassays for nicotine and cotinine. *Biochemistry,* 1973, **12,** 5025–5030.

Langone, J. J., Van Vunakis, H., & Hill, P. Quantitation of cotinine in sera of smokers. *Research Communication in Chemical Pathological and Pharmacology,* 1975, **10,** 21–28.

Larson, P. S., & Silvette, H. *Tobacco: Experimental and clinical studies, Supplement I, II, III.* Baltimore: Williams & Wilkins, 1961, 1968, 1971, 1975.

Lauer, R. M., Akers, R., Massey, J., & Clarke, W. Evaluation of cigarette smoking among adolescents: The Muscatine Study. *Preventive Medicine,* 1982, **11,** 417–428.

Lawson, A. H., Sweeney, T. R., Dudley, H. C. Toxicology of acrylonitrile (vinyl cyanide): III. Determination of thiocyanates in blood and urine. *Journal of Industrial Hygiene and Toxicology,* 1943, **25,** 13–19.

Leventhal, H., & Cleary, P. D. The smoking problem: A review of the research and theory in behavioral risk modification. *Psychological Bulletin,* 1980, **88,** 370–405.

Lichtenstein, E. The smoking problem: A behavioral perspective. *Journal of Consulting and Clinical Psychology,* 1982, **5,** 804–819.

Luepker, R. V., Pechacek, T. F., Murray, D. M., Johnson, C. A., Hund, F., & Jacobs, D. R. Saliva thiocyanate: A chemical indicator of cigarette smoking in adolescents. *American Journal of Public Health,* 1981, **12,** 1320–1324.

Lundquist, P., Martensson, J., Sorbo, B., & Ohman, S. Method for determining thiocyanate in serum and urine. *Clinical Chemistry,* 1979, **25,** 678–681.

Martin, J. E., & Frederiksen, L. W. Self-tracking of carbon monoxide levels of smokers. *Behavior Therapy,* 1980, **11,** 577–587.

Maliszewski, T. F., & Bass, D. E. True and "apparent" thiocyanate in body fluids of smokers and nonsmokers. *Journal of Applied Physiology,* 1955, **8,** 289–291.

Maskarinec, M., Harvey, R., & Caton, J. A novel method for the isolation and quantitative analysis of nicotine and cotinine in biological fluids. *Journal of Analytical Toxicology,* 1978, **2,** 124–126.

Matsukura, S., Sakamoto, N., Seino, Y., Tamada, T., Matsuyama, H., & Muranaka, H. Cotinine excretion and daily cigarette smoking in habituated smokers. *Clinical Pharmacology and Therapeutics,* 1979, **25,** 555–561.

Matsukura, S., Sakamoto, N., Takahashi, K., Matsuyama, H., & Muranaka, H. Effect of pH and urine on urinary nicotine excretion after smoking cigarettes. *Clinical Pharmacology and Therapeutics,* 1979, **25,** 549–554.

McAlister, A., Perry, C. L., & Maccoby, N. Adolescent smoking: Onset and prevention. *Pediatrics,* 1979, **63,** 650–658.

McCusker, K., McNabb, E., & Bone, R. Plasma nicotine levels in pipe smokers. *Journal of the American Medical Association,* 1982, **248,** 577–578.

McFall, R. M. Smoking cessation research. *Journal of Consulting and Clinical Psychology,* 1978, **76,** 703–712.

Meade, R. W., & Walde, N. J. Cigarette smoking patterns during the working day. *British Journal of Preventive Social Medicine,* 1977, **31,** 25–29.

Mittelmark, M. B., Murray, D. M., Luepker, R. V., & Pechacek, T. F. Cigarette smoking among adolescents: Is the rate declining? *Preventive Medicine,* 1982, **11,** 708–712.

Moss, A. J. Changes in cigarette smoking and current smoking practices among adults: United States, 1978. *Advance Data from NCHS,* 1979, **52,** 1–19.

Moss, R., & Prue, D. Research on nicotine regulation. *Behavior Therapy,* 1982, **13,** 31–46.

Neaton, J., Broate, S., Cohen, L., Fishman, E., Kjelsberg, M., & Schoenberger, J. The multiple risk factor intervention trial (MRFIT): VII. A comparison of risk factor changes between the two study groups. *Preventive Medicine,* 1981, **10,** 519–543.

Ockene, J. K., Hymowitz, N., Sexton, M., & Brostes, S. Comparison of patterns of smoking behavior change among smokers in the multiple risk factor intervention trial (MRFIT). *Preventive Medicine,* 1982, **11,** 621–638.

Ohlin, P., Lundh, B., & Westling, H. Carbon monoxide blood levels and reported cessation of smoking. *Psychopharmacology,* 1976, **49,** 263–265.

Orleans, C. S., & Shipley, R. H. Assessment in smoking cessation research: Some practical guidelines. In F. J. Keefe & J. A. Blumenthal (Eds.), *Assessment strategies in behavioral medicine.* New York: Grune and Stratton, 1982.

Ossip-Klein, D. J., Martin, J. E., Lomax, D., Prue, D. M., & Davis, C. J. Assessment of smoking topography generalization across laboratory, clinical, and naturalistic settings. *Addictive Behaviors,* in press.

Page, I. H., Corcoran, A. C., Dustan, H. P., & Koppanyi, T. Cardiovascular actions of sodium nitroprusside in animals and hypertensive patients. *Circulation,* 1955, **11,** 188–198.

Paxton, R., & Bernacca, G. Urinary nicotine concentration as a function of time since last cigarette: Implications for detecting faking in smoking clinics. *Behavior Therapy,* 1979, **10,** 523–528.

Pechacek, T. F. Modification of smoking behavior. In U.S. PHS, *Surgeon General's report on smoking and health.* DHEW Pub. No. 79–50066. Washington, D.C.: U.S. Government Printing Office, 1979.

Pechacek, T. F., Luepker, R., Jacobs, D., Fraser, G., & Blackburn, H. Effect of diet and smoking on serum and saliva thiocyanates. *Cardiovascular Disease Epidemiology Newsletter,* 1979, **27,** 96.

Pechacek, T., Murray, D., Luepker, R., Mittelmark, M., Johnson, C., & Shultz, J. Measurement of adolescent smoking behavior: Rationale and methods. *Journal of Behavioral Medicine,* in press.

Pederson, L., Sidney, K., & Lefcoe, N. M. An objective measure of the validity of children's responses to a questionnaire on health and smoking. *Canadian Journal of Public Health,* 1977, **68,** 497–498.

Pekkanen, T. J., Elo, O., & Hanninen, M. L. Changes in nonsmokers' saliva thiocyanate levels after being in a tobacco smoke-filled room. *World Smoking and Health,* 1976, **1,** 37–39.

Perry, C. L., Killen, J., Telch, M., Slinkard, L. A., & Danaher, B. G. Modifying smoking behavior of teenagers: A school-based intervention. *American Journal of Public Health,* 1980, **66,** 399–414.

Petitti, D., Friedman, G., & Kahn, W. Accuracy of information on smoking habits provided on self-administered research questionnaires. *American Journal of Public Health,* 1981, **71,** 308–311.

Pettigrew, A. R., & Fell, G. S. Simplified colorimetric determinations of thiocyanate in biological fluids, and its application to investigation of toxic amblyopias. *Clinical Chemistry,* 1974, **18,** 966–1000.

Pickens, R. Measurement of source factors of cigarette smoking topography in the natural environment. In J. Grabowski & C. Bell (Eds.), *Measurement in the analysis and treatment of smoking behavior: NIDA Research Monograph 48.* Washington, D.C.: National Institute of Drug Abuse, 1983.

Pooling Project Research Group. Relationship of blood pressure, serum cholesterol, smoking habit, relative weight and ECG abnormalities to incidence of major coronary events: Final report of the Pooling Project. *Journal of Chronic Disease,* 1979, **31,** 201–306.

Prue, D., Martin, J., & Hume, A. A critical evaluation of thiocyanate as a biochemical index of smoking exposure. *Behavior Therapy,* 1980, **11,** 368–379.

Prue, D., Martin, J., Hume, A., & Davis, N. The reliability of thiocyanate measurement of smoking exposure. *Addictive Behaviors,* 1981, **6,** 99–105.

Rawbone, R., Murphy, K., Tate, M., & Kane, S. The analysis of smoking parameters: Inhalation and absorption of tobacco smoke in studies of human smoking behavior. In R. E. Thornton (Ed.), *Smoking behavior: Physiological and psychological influences.* New York: Churchill Livingstone, 1978.

Rea, J., Tyrer, P., Kasap, H., & Beresfort, Expired air carbon monoxide, and other variables: A community study. *British Journal of Preventive Social Medicine,* 1973, **27,** 114–120.

Rickert, W., & Robinson J. Estimating the hazards of less hazardous cigarettes: II. Study of cigarette yields of nicotine, carbon monoxide, and hydrogen cyanide in relation to levels of cotinine, carboxy-hemoglobin, and thiocyanate in smokers. *Journal of Toxicology and Environmental Health,* 1981, **7**, 391–403.

Rickert, W., Robinson, J., Young, I., Collishaw, N., & Bray, D. A comparison of tar, nicotine, and carbon monoxide of 36 brands of Canadian cigarettes tested under three conditions. *Preventive Medicine,* 1983, **12**, 682–694.

Ringold, A., Goldsmith, J., Helwig, H., Finn, R., & Schuette, F. Estimating recent carbon monoxide exposures. *Archives of Environmental Health,* 1962, **5**, 308–318.

Robinson, J., & Young, J. Temporal patterns in smoking rate and mouth-level nicotine exposure. *Addictive Behaviors,* 1980, **5**, 91–95.

Robinson, J., Young, J., & Rickert, W. A comparative study of the amount of smoke absorbed from low-yield cigarettes; Part I: non invasive measures. *British Journal of Addictions,* in press.

Ronan, G., Ruane, P., Graham, M., Hickey, N., & Mulcahy, R. The reliability of smoking history amongst survivors of myocardial infarction. *British Journal of Addiction,* 1981, **76**, 425–428.

Rozensky, R. H. The effect of timing of self-monitoring behavior on reducing cigarette consumption. *Journal of Behavior Therapy and Experimental Psychiatry,* 1974, **5**, 301–303.

Russell, M. A. H. Tobacco smoking and nicotine dependence. In R. J. Gibbins, Y. Israel, H. Kalant, R. E. Popham, W. Schmidt, & R. G. Smart (Eds.), *Research advances in alcohol and drug problems* (Vol. 3). New York: Wiley, 1976.

Russell, M. A. H., & Feyerabend, C. Cigarette smoking: A dependence on high-nicotine boli. *Drug Metabolism Reviews,* 1978, **8**, 29–57.

Russell, M., Jarvis, M., Devitt, G., & Feyerabend, C. Nicotine intake by snuff users. *British Medical Journal,* 1981, **283**, 814–817.

Russell, M., Jarvis, M., Iyer, R., & Feyerabend, C. Relation of nicotine yield of cigarettes to blood nicotine concentrations in smokers. *British Medical Journal,* 1980, **280**, 972–976.

Russell, M. A. H., Sutton, S. R., Iyer, R., Feyerabend, C., & Vesey, C. J. Long-term switching to low-tar, low-nicotine cigarettes. *British Journal of Addictions,* 1982, **77**, 145–158.

Saunders, J., & Blume, D. Quantitation of major tobacco alkaloids by high-performance liquid chroma-tography. *Journal of Chromatography,* 1981, **205**, 147–154.

Schinke, S. P., & Gilchrist, L. D. Survey and evaluation methods: Smoking prevention among children and adolescents. In J. Grabowski & C. Bell (Eds.), *Measurement in the analysis & treatment of smoking behavior: NIDA Research Monograph 48.* Washington, D.C.: National Institute on Drug Abuse, 1983.

Shannon, I., Suddick, R., & Dowd, F., Jr. Saliva: Composition and secretion. In H. Myers (Ed.), *Monographs in oral science* (Vol. 2). New York: S. Karger, 1974.

Shipley, R. H., Rosen, T. S., & Williams, C. Measurement of smoking: Surveys and some recommenda-tions. *Addictive Behaviors,* 1982, **7**, 299–302.

Sillett, R., Wilson, M., Malcolm, R., & Ball, K. Deception among smokers. *British Medical Journal,* 1978, **2**, 1185–1186.

Stepney, R. Smoking behaviour: A psychology of the cigarette habit. *British Journal of Diseases of the Chest,* 1980, **74**, 325–344.

Stepney, R. Are smokers' self-reports of inhalation a useful measure of smoke exposure? *Journal of Epidemiology and Community Health,* 1982, **36**, 109–112.

Stewart, R. D. The effect of carbon monoxide on humans. *Annual Review of Pharmacology,* 1975, **15**, 409–425.

Stewart, R. D., Baretta, E. D., Platte, L. R., Stewart, E. B., Kalbfleisch, J. H., Van Yserloo, B., & Rimm, A. A. Carboxyhemoglobin levels in American blood donors. *Journal of the American Medical Association,* 1974, **229**, 1187–1195.

Stewart, R. D., Steward, R. S., Stamm, W., & Seelen, R. P. Rapid estimation of carboxyhemoglobin level in fire fighters. *Journal of the American Medical Association,* 1976, **235**, 390–392.

Stubbe, I., Eskilsson, J., & Nilsson-Ehle, P. High density lipoprotein concentration increases after stopping smoking. *British Medical Journal,* 1982, **285**, 537–540.

Thornton, R. E. (Ed.). *Smoking behavior: Physiological and psychological influences.* New York: Churchill Livingstone, 1978.

Tobin, M. J., and Sackner, M. A. Monitoring smoking patterns of low and high tar cigarettes with inductive plethysmography. *American Review of Respiratory Diseases,* 1982, **126,** 258–264.

Turner, J., Sillett, R., & McNicol, M. Effect of cigar smoking on carboxyhaemoglobin and plasma nicotine concentrations in primary pipe and cigar smokers and ex-cigarette smokers. *British Medical Journal,* 1977, **2,** 1387–1389.

Turner, J., Sillett, R., & McNicol, M. The inhaling habits of pipe smokers. *British Journal of Diseases of the Chest,* 1981, **75,** 71–76.

U.S. Public Health Service (PHS). *Smoking and health.* PHS Pub. No. 1103. Washington, D.C.: U.S. Government Printing Office, 1964.

U.S. Public Health Service (PHS). *Smoking and health: A report of the Surgeon General.* DHEW Pub. No. 79–50066. Washington, D.C.: U.S. Government Printing Office, 1979.

U.S. Public Health Service (PHS). *The health consequences of smoking: The changing cigarette.* DHHS Pub. No. 81–50156. Washington, D.C.: U.S. Government Printing Office, 1981.

Vesey, C. Thiocyanates and cigarette consumption. In R. M. Greenlaugh (Ed.), *Smoking and arterial disease.* London: Pitman Press, 1981.

Vesey, C., Saloojee, Y., Cole, P. V., & Russell, M. Blood carboxyhemoglobin, plasma thiocyanate, and cigarette consumption: Implications for epidemiology studies in smokers. *British Medical Journal,* 1982, **284,** 1511–1513.

Vogt, T. M. Questionnaires vs. biochemical measures of smoking exposure. *American Journal of Public Health,* 1982, **72,** 93.

Vogt, T., Selvin, S., & Billings, J. Smoking cessation program: Baseline carbon monoxide and serum thiocyanate levels as predictors of outcome. *American Journal of Public Health,* 1979, **69,** 1156–1159.

Vogt, T. M., Selvin, S., Widdowson, G., & Hulley, S. B. Expired air carbon monoxide and serum thiocyanate as objective measures of cigarette exposure. *American Journal of Public Health,* 1977, **67,** 545–549.

Wald, N., Howard, S., Smith, P. G., & Bailey, A. Use of carboxyhaemoglobin levels to predict the development of diseases associated with cigarette smoking. *Thorax,* 1975, **30,** 133–140.

Wald, N., Idle, M., & Bailey, A. Carboxyhaemoglobin levels and inhaling habits in cigarette smokers. *Thorax,* 1978, **33,** 201–206.

Wald, N., Idle, M., Boreham, J., & Bailey, A. Carbon monoxide in breath in relation to smoking and carboxyhaemoglobin levels. *Thorax,* 1981, **36,** 366–369.

Wald, N., Idle, M., Boreham, J., Bailey, A., & Van Vunakis, H. Serum cotinine levels in pipe smokers: Evidence against nicotine as cause of coronary heart disease. *Lancet,* 1981, **2,** 775–777.

Wallace, N., Davis, G., Rutledge, R., & Kahn, A. Smoking and carboxyhemoglobin in the St. Louis metropolitan population. *Archives of Environmental Health,* 1974, 136–142.

Warner, K. Possible increases in the underreporting of cigarette consumption. *Journal of the American Statistical Association,* 1978, **73,** 314–318.

Watson, I. D. Rapid analysis of nicotine and cotinine in the urine of smokers by isocratic high-performance liquid chromatography. *Journal of Chromatology,* 1977, **143,** 203–206.

Wigfield, D., Hollebone, B., MacKeen, J., & Selwin, J. Assessment of the methods available for the determination of carbon monoxide in blood. *Journal of Analytical Toxicology,* 1981, **5,** 122–125.

Wilcox, R., Hughes, J., & Roland, J. Verification of smoking history in patients after infarction using urinary nicotine and cotinine measurements. *British Medical Journal,* 1979, **2,** 1026–1028.

Williams, C., Eng, A., Botvin, G., Hill, P., & Wynder, E. Validation of students' self-reported cigarette smoking status with plasma cotinine levels. *American Journal of Public Health,* 1979, **69,** 1272–1274.

Wynder, E., & Hoffman, D. Tobacco and health, a societal challenge. *New England Journal of Medicine,* 1979, **300,** 894–903.

Young, J., Robinson, J., & Rickert, W. A study of chemical deliveries as a function of cigarette butt length. *Beitraege zur Tabakforschung International,* 1981, **11,** 87–95.

Zeidenberg, P., Jaffe, J. H., Kanzler, M., Levitt, M. D., Langone, J. J., & Van Vunakis, H. Nicotine:cotinine levels in blood during cessation of smoking. *Comprehensive Psychiatry,* 1977, **18,** 93–101.

CHAPTER 47

RESTRICTED ENVIRONMENTAL STIMULATION THERAPY (REST)

PETER SUEDFELD

University of British Columbia

Restricted environmental stimulation therapy (REST) is a third-generation offspring of experimental perceptual isolation, which was first used with human subjects in the early 1950s. The first generation of that research, lasting until the early 1960s, saw the development of three major methodologies: monotonous stimulation, achieved by constant diffused light and noise; and two types of reduced stimulation, in dark and soundproof chambers or in water immersion. There were also some minor variants. A rapidly growing literature showed multiple, complex, and inconsistent effects and procedures (Solomon, Kubzansky, Leiderman, Mendelson, Trumbull, & Wexler, 1961). The second generation, which drew to a close in the late 1960s, was characterized by programmatic research projects focusing on the basic effects of stimulus reduction—for example, on cognition, perception, and motivation (Zubek, 1969).

In the third and current stage, research has explored the use of REST in lifestyle modification. Two modified versions of earlier procedures are used. Both versions use darkness and silence; in one, the participant spends up to 24 hours on a bed, whereas in the other he or she floats in a body-temperature salt and water solution for about an hour. The former technique has been used in most of the systematic research efforts, whereas the latter has become popular as a recreational and relaxation experience available in commercial facilities or in one's own home (Suedfeld, 1980).

Studies have used REST successfully to treat psychiatric symptoms (Adams, 1980), childhood dysfunction (see Suedfeld, 1980), and problems properly coming under the rubric of health psychology, such as essential hypertension, obesity, neurological training, and excessive alcohol use (see Suedfeld, 1980; Suedfeld & Kristeller, 1982). The most thoroughly explored application of the technique in the area of health-related habit modification, however, has been in the realm of smoking cessation.

THEORETICAL BASES

When we look at the rationale for using REST in habit modification, several theoretical and empirical bases become apparent. Some of these are relevant to the effects of REST per se; others explain why the technique should potentiate the effects of other interventions.

The author is grateful for the financial support of the National Institutes of Health Biomedical Sciences Support Program and the National Heart, Lung and Blood Institute. The collaboration of research assistants and colleagues, particularly E. J. Ballard, J. A. Best, R. A. Borrie, P. B. Landon, and the late F. F. Ikard, has been instrumental in the design and completion of the research.

Although the evidence for various explanatory constructs differs widely, the REST phenomena to which they are related seem fairly well established.

The Regulatory Effects of REST

One can look at smoking and other health-dysfunctional behaviors as failures of self-regulation (Carver & Scheier, 1981; Schwartz 1979). The usual feedback from adverse conditions, which in turn modifies the response in order to ameliorate the problem, is somehow attenuated so that no problem-solving response occurs. REST may act as a re-regulating mechanism in several possible ways.

Reverse Quarantine

Reverse quarantine originates in medicine. Individuals who are highly susceptible to infection are kept in strictly isolated, controlled environments for a prolonged period. The term *reverse* is used because the standard concept of quarantine involves isolating the individual disease carrier from the general public.

In applying this construct to REST, we view the normal environment as a possible source of "infection," whereby environmental cues may trigger disregulated and self-damaging behaviors such as smoking. There are two such cues: the overall level of stimulus bombardment, which may result in stress that leads to smoking, and specific events that, through either association or reinforcement, have become conditioned stimuli for smoking. These events may include such things as a cup of coffee, the end of a meal, conversation with friends, or tension at work. In REST, the general level of environmental stimulation is drastically lowered, and the specific stimuli to which smoking has become a learned response are removed.

The abstinence from smoking that is enforced during REST differs from abstinence in the everyday environment. In the latter, when the learned stimulus-response association is broken, the individual feels stressed and frustrated because of the prohibition against smoking. The craving for a cigarette becomes even stronger. This leads to a cyclical increment in tension and subsequent craving that sooner or later is very likely to result in relapse. In REST, because the original stimulus is absent, the link is not just interrupted, it is prevented from ever becoming activated. As a result, even heavy smokers do not experience severe cigarette craving during REST—a phenomenon that appears to carry over into the post-REST period. In many cases it has been reported to persist throughout follow-up. The realization that one can go for 24 hours without either smoking or suffering may be sufficient to initiate a cognitive/affective reorganization and break the cycle.

Internal Focusing

Survival pressures throughout the history of the human species and of the individual human being and the high level of stimulation in modern environments lead to information-processing strategies that tend to process exogenous inputs as signal. Endogenous messages tend to be dismissed as noise unless they reach a very high level of intensity. As a result, important information frequently is ignored or at least inefficiently processed—a major component of disregulation (Schwartz, 1979). Biofeedback attempts to re-regulate the system by amplifying endogenous stimuli or by transforming such stimuli from their original modality into one that is more easily monitored.

REST achieves the same goal by the opposite approach: instead of amplifying the internal message, it greatly attenuates the external message, to some extent reversing the normal categorization of signal and noise. In REST, the participant pays a great deal of attention to bodily feedback, which may include such factors as a cough or sore throat from smoking, as well as to the cognitive, emotional, memory, imagery, and similar components of continued smoking. Thus, both the adverse effects of smoking and its psychological aspects are attended to more intensely and with fewer interruptions than would normally be the case. This spontaneous focusing on internal signals can result in a greater concern with one's health. The consequent adoption of a health-enhancing lifestyle that generalizes beyond the focal problem being treated (such as smoking) to a variety of beneficial side effects is a phenomenon frequently noted by REST participants.

De-automation of Behavior

As has been pointed out by many theorists, overlearned behaviors eventually come to demand and get very little attention (see Carver & Scheier, 1981). For many habitual smokers, the sequence of taking out, lighting, and smoking a cigarette acquires this nature. Many such individuals report that they frequently find themselves with cigarettes in their mouths without any clear recollection of the acts leading up to that realization. REST disrupts this well-organized pattern (Tomkins, 1968), forcing smokers to redirect conscious attention to the smoking sequence. As a result, the behavior is brought under better volitional control. Attention may also make the behavior more disjointed, providing a greater number of points at which the sequence can be terminated (Blumenthal, 1977).

The Potentiating Role of REST

Another relevant aspect of REST is its ability to increase the potency of other intervention techniques. Some of these techniques have been used primarily in conjunction with REST (e.g., messages specifically designed to be used in REST); others can be adapted from the literature on behavioral interventions. So far, these approaches have included satiation smoking, covert aversive conditioning, self-monitoring followed by functional analysis, and counseling. Why should REST interact synergistically with these treatments?

Increased Openness to Information

REST participants become more attentive and open to new information in general and to information going against their established beliefs and attitudes in particular (Suedfeld, 1969a; Myers, Murphy, Smith, & Goffard, Note 1). One reason for this may be that REST impairs complex cognitive performance. The individual may experience some difficulty in clearly perceiving the exact relationships among various arguments, facts, beliefs, and opinions (Tetlock & Suedfeld, 1976), increasing the likelihood that a message presenting a contrary opinion will appear more believable. In this sense, REST acts as an agent of the unfreezing stage, which has been postulated as the first necessary condition for attitude change to occur (Lewin, 1952).

Stimulus Hunger

One of the oldest established effects of REST is the subject's desire for additional stimulation while in the chamber (e.g., Jones, 1969). Participants eagerly seek out and attend to whatever stimulation is available. Information that may normally be ignored or warded off because of its anxiety-arousing nature is not so easy to discard when no obvious and more attractive alternatives are available. Thus, once the unfreezing stage of attitude change has been initiated by the REST condition itself, the changing phase (Lewin, 1952) is facilitated because stimulus hunger increases the impact of the message. The sequence of increased openness and increased acceptance has been proposed as a general two-stage process of persuasibility in REST, and it is clearly applicable to messages related to health and behavior (Suedfeld, Note 2).

Arousal and Twilight State

Almost since the beginning of research with the REST technique, it has been theorized that this environment induces a state of low arousal (Solomon et al., 1961). Thus, it may be in the same family of therapeutic approaches as meditation, hypnosis, and systematic relaxation (Suedfeld, 1980; Wickramasekera, Note 3). According to one theorist (Budzynski, 1976), the low-arousal, or twilight, state changes mental processes. The hemispheres of the brain have different deactivation thresholds, so that as the twilight state deepens, the dominant hemisphere becomes less active while the nondominant one continues functioning without impairment. As a result, processes that are centered in the nondominant hemisphere become more salient, leading to a greater predominance of theta waves, more creativity, a freer flow of imagination and a state of alert relaxation. This state would logically be the neurophysiological substrate for deeper introspection, improved attention, and more openness to new information.

Nonspecific Factors

It has been argued by some critics that the powerful effects of REST may be due to nonspecific factors. Like other medical and behavioral treatments, REST does have nonspecific components. There may be a strong positive expectation of success. The REST experience may appear to be a rite of passage, demarcating previous behavior patterns and self-concepts from new and improved ones. One might also argue that the experience is so impressive and unusual, and requires so much commitment, that to maintain one's previous unhealthy activities afterward would arouse cognitive dissonance, which is an aversive state. This might be particularly true if, like most participants, one had made a public commitment about the REST experience.

In response to this hypothesis, several points can be made. One is that the investment in REST is considerably smaller than that involved in many other treatment procedures that may take much more time, call for more effort, cost more money, and possibly involve experiences and activities that are equally unusual and certainly more stressful (e.g., rapid smoking). Second, the degree to which REST effects are influenced by expectancy has not been settled, despite a large number of relevant studies (Suedfeld, 1969b). Thus, there are no grounds for concluding that cognitive dissonance, public commitment, expectancy, and so on, are any more important to the effects of REST than they are to other treatment approaches. REST groups have shown significantly higher success rates in smoking cessation and weight reduction than placebo groups. A study currently being conducted has introduced what we are calling the subtractive expectancy placebo procedure. In this study, participants undergoing REST and another active behavioral treatment are informed that one of the two techniques is the actual treatment and the other is a tangential procedure that is not expected to have any impact on their smoking (Suedfeld, Note 4). The results of this study should demonstrate the extent to which REST affects smoking cessation rate in the absence of any expectancy that it will do so.

EMPIRICAL STUDIES

The applications of REST procedures to smoking cessation represent the single largest body of literature on the use of this technique in health psychology (Suedfeld & Kristeller, 1982). Even so, there has been only one long-term program in the area, with a few single studies contributed by various research teams. The data are quite positive, but much more needs to be done both in exploration and in replication.

After Patrick's (1965) unsuccessful attempt to reduce smoking among psychiatric patients by showing them an antismoking film after an hour of REST, subsequent studies have generally followed the design described in Suedfeld, Landon, Pargament, and Epstein (1972).

REST in a dark, silent chamber for 24 hours is varied independently with some other procedure (in the case of Suedfeld et al., 1972, a brief taped antismoking message).

Although the majority of the studies, in common with most of the literature until very recently, rely on self-reported smoking rates, the accuracy of the rates has been borne out both by the reports of third parties (Suedfeld & Ikard, 1973, 1974) and by studies in which biochemical measures were used to supplement verbal reports (saliva thiocyanate in Christensen & DiGiusto, 1982, and exhaled carbon monoxide in Suedfeld, Note 4, and Suedfeld, Ballard, & Landon, Note 5). This is compatible, of course, with previous findings that show high correlations between chemical and self-reported measures of smoking. The manipulated independent variables have included the number and content of messages, the combination of REST with other treatment procedures, the duration of the session, and the degree to which stimulus and response restriction were imposed. I will briefly describe here the manipulations used in smoking studies.

REST Treatments

Complete REST

Complete REST is defined as 24 hours of confinement in a dark, soundproof chamber. Usually, there are also reductions in other modalities (e.g., the use of a liquid diet food that eliminates biting and chewing and provides only a bland taste). Participants are requested to remain lying on the bed during the entire session, except when using the chemical toilet, which is located in the chamber. As in all REST studies, a monitor is on duty during the entire treatment session and has audio communication with the chamber to be able to answer questions, fulfill requests (e.g., for more food or water), or intervene if the participant appears to be violating the rules by excessive movement or noise (Suedfeld & Ikard, 1973, 1974; Suedfeld et al., 1972; Suedfeld, Note 4; Suedfeld et al., Note 5).

Brief REST

Any treatment that involves total REST, as just defined, for periods significantly under 24 hours is classified as brief REST (Suedfeld et al., Note 5, 12 hours; Ovadia, Note 6, 6 and 12 hours).

Partial REST

In the studies on smoking cessation, partial REST conditions have included REST with movement permitted in the chamber (Ovadia, Note 6); visual deprivation and/or social isolation in the chamber, in some cases with smoking permitted during the session (Christensen & DiGiusto, 1982; Hennessy, Note 7); and lying on the bed in a dark room with continuous diffuse noise (Christensen & DiGiusto, 1982; Barnes, Note 8).

REST and Messages

Partial or complete REST may be interrupted briefly by periodic presentation of one or more relevant messages (Suedfeld & Ikard, 1973, 1974; Suedfeld et al., 1972; Suedfeld, Note 4; Suedfeld et al., Note 5; Barnes, Note 8; Best & Suedfeld, Note 9). Messages have dealt with health hazards, self-protection and self-respect, relaxation, substitute activities, and coping with relapse.

REST Combinations

In this category are studies in which complete or partial REST has been combined with active treatments that have been established in the literature. So far, these treatments have

been satiation smoking (Best & Suedfeld, Note 9), aversive conditioning, and covert sensitization (Suedfeld, Note 4; Ovadia, Note 6). Other components of standard techniques, such
as self-monitoring, tallying, functional analysis, and counseling, have also been used (Suedfeld, Note 4; Ovadia, Note 6; Hennessy, Note 7; Best & Suedfeld, Note 9).

Control Treatments

Three types of control groups have been used in smoking cessation studies involving REST:
active treatment control, placebo control, and untreated control.

Active Treatment

Active treatment controls have been used in the five-day plan (Barnes, Note 8) and in
behavior modification packages including satiation smoking (Best & Suedfeld, Note 9) and
covert aversive conditioning (Suedfeld, Note 4).

Placebo Control

Placebo treatments have primarily involved presenting messages to one group in REST
and to another (control) group in a normal environment (Suedfeld & Ikard, 1974; Suedfeld
et al., 1972); a more elaborate subtractive expectancy treatment, described previously, is
included in Suedfeld (Note 4).

Untreated Control

In these studies, one group of subjects either is put on a waiting list or is given only
repeated measures of smoking rate without intervening treatment (Suedfeld & Ikard, 1974;
Suedfeld et al., 1972; Ovadia, Note 6).

COMPARATIVE EFFECTIVENESS AND COST-EFFECTIVENESS

In every study comparing REST with a placebo group or an untreated group, the former
showed significantly higher success at the end of follow-up. Comparisons among a variety
of partial REST treatments show no differential effects (Christensen & DiGiusto, 1982;
Ovadia, Note 6; Hennessy, Note 7), but the 24-hour period appears to be more effective
than shorter durations (Christensen & DiGiusto, 1982; Suedfeld et al., Note 5). There
were no significant differences between REST and two standard smoking treatment methods
(Barnes, Note 8; Best & Suedfeld, Note 9), but REST plus such a standard treatment
was significantly better than either REST itself or the standard treatment itself (Best &
Suedfeld, Note 9).

Table 47.1 shows a comparison between the effects of REST and REST combinations
and results summarized from review articles evaluating the entire field of smoking intervention. Only data from 1-year follow-ups are cited, in view of the known instability of shorter
periods. Unfortunately, this criterion eliminates the partial and brief REST studies (see
Suedfeld & Kristeller, 1982, for a summary). Other techniques that, according to the reviewers, have not been shown to be effective in controlled designs with at least 1-year follow-
ups include hypnosis, acupuncture, relaxation, systematic desensitization, punishment, stimulus control, reinforcement of nonsmoking, drugs, and psychoanalysis.

REST compares favorably with the methods that are currently standard in smoking
clinics, and it potentiates the effect of other techniques. From studies that compare REST
with another active treatment, it becomes apparent that the advantage of the sensory reduction technique does not lie in its greater initial success. It, too, follows the pattern described
by Hunt and Bespalec (1974), which shows that success rates at the end of treatment are

Table 47.1 Mean Abstinence Rates at 1-Year Follow-up

Review Source	Method	Percentage Abstinence
This chapter	Complete REST	26[a]
	Complete REST with messages	38[a]
	REST combination	53
Hunt, Barnett, & Branch (1971)	Overview	22
Keutzer, Lichtenstein, & Mees (1968)	Five-day plan	15–20
	Multimodal	20
	Group discussion	26 (18-month follow-up)
	Group therapy	10–18
Bernstein & McAlister (1976)	Rapid smoking and warm air	19
	Rapid smoking	15–20
	Multimodal	Up to 55–65
Raw (1978)	Group therapy and drugs	19
	Nicotine gum	23
	Rapid smoking	20
	Multiple techniques	12

[a] Includes early data from Suedfeld et al. (Note 5).

approximately equal regardless of the intervention procedure (although end of treatment comes considerably faster with REST). The relatively high level of efficacy of REST appears to stem from the greater ability of REST participants to maintain gains over the posttreatment period. If, as reviews of the literature seem to indicate, maintenance is the primary problem in lifestyle change, this characteristic of REST speaks strongly in favor of adopting the technique; the results of Best and Suedfeld (Note 9) imply that adding REST to a self-management procedure results in a doubling of the long-term success rate of the self-management procedure.

Cost-effectiveness is another issue. Unfortunately, to date, very few evaluations of this variable have been made in the smoking cessation literature, and there is only one, seriously flawed, evaluation of REST. Barnes (Note 8) compared the cost-effectiveness of partial REST (constant diffuse noise) and messages with that of the five-day plan. The effectiveness of the two programs was evaluated as being approximately the same at the end of 6 months. The cost was estimated at $28 per subject and $33.25 per successful subject for the REST treatment and at $6.79 and $8.06 for the five-day plan. The calculated cost of REST, however, included the purchase of four chemical toilets ($128), which of course could be amortized across any number of participants, thereby greatly reducing the cost per client. In addition, the five-day plan was conducted by volunteers from the Seventh Day Adventist Church, which developed and disseminated the program and also supplied audiovisual and printed materials without charge to the research project. In contrast, staff salaries of $300 were charged against the cost of administering the REST treatment. Obviously, then, the comparisons were not very valid.

This leaves us with essentially no hard data concerning comparative cost-effectiveness. The initial outlay may deter some potential users; however, a recent examination of this issue (Borrie, 1980) indicated that an adequate facility could be developed for under $1000. This would involve putting in a reasonable amount of soundproofing in a small room, away from heavy traffic and noise. Furnishing the experimental chamber and the control room would cost less than $500 each. REST requires a much lower time commitment than most clinical techniques, and premature dropout from treatment is relatively low (85% to 90% of REST participants complete the 24 hours). Operating costs (liquid diet food, disinfectant and toilet paper for the chemical toilet, laundering of bed linens) are about $5 per session. Monitors can be employees who have not had much special training; university students have been employed at the rate of $30 to $40 a day. It should be remembered that the monitor has very little to do; the major tasks are to respond to questions or emergencies and, in some treatment conditions, to turn the tape recorder on and off (the latter task can be automated). The rest of the time, the monitor may sleep or engage in whatever activity he or she desires, thus justifying the relatively low rate of pay.

CONCLUSION

It is difficult to know why the REST procedure is not being more widely adopted in clinical settings. It is safe, nonaversive, economical, and, above all, effective. It is clear that research still needs to be done on such issues as the optimal content of messages (e.g., messages explicitly designed to take advantage of such general effects of REST as stimulus hunger, vivid imagery, and improved learning ability) and the best techniques to be applied in combination with REST. Although it is also desirable to conduct more applications and more long-term follow-ups, some of the parameters of optimal use are beginning to take shape. A 24-hour period of absolute darkness, silence, reduced mobility, and minimal stimulation in other modalities, with appropriate messages presented throughout the session, is the most reliably powerful technique (Suedfeld et al., Note 5). The prospects for even greater therapeutic success with a combination of this particular REST package and other, more standard behavioral methods appear to be good. The time seems right to move away from pilot, demonstration, and experimental research toward large-scale clinical trials and the inclusion of the technique as a standard component of smoking cessation programs.

REFERENCE NOTES

1. Myers, T. I., Murphy, D. B., Smith, S., & Goffard, S. J. *Experimental studies of sensory deprivation and social isolation.* HumRRO Tech. Rep. 66–8. Washington, D.C.: George Washington University, 1966.

2. Suedfeld, P. *Attitude manipulation in restricted environments: V. Theory and research.* Paper presented at the 20th International Congress of Psychology, Tokyo, August 1972.

3. Wickramasekera, I. *Psychophysiological stress reduction procedures and a suggestion hypothesis: Sensory restriction and low arousal training.* Paper presented at the meeting of the American Association for the Advancement of Tension Control, 1977.

4. Suedfeld, P. *The subtractive expectancy placebo procedure: A measure of nonspecific factors in behavioral interventions.* Manuscript submitted for publication, 1982.

5. Suedfeld, P., Ballard, E. J., & Landon, P. B. *Restricted environmental stimulation therapy in smoking cessation: The roles of session duration and message scheduling.* Manuscript in preparation, 1982.

6. Ovadia, F. T. *Twenty four hour sensory deprivation: Its effects on smoking and eating behaviours.* Master's thesis, University of New South Wales, 1979.

7. Hennessy, T. D. *Visual deprivation as a therapeutic tool in the treatment of smoking behavior.* Master's thesis, University of Manitoba, 1975.

8. Barnes, L. J. *Comparative effectiveness of a five-day plan and a sensory deprivation program on reduction and abstinence from cigarette smoking.* Master's thesis, Dalhousie University, 1976.

9. Best, J. A., & Suedfeld, P. *Restricted environmental stimulation therapy and behavioural self-management in smoking cessation.* Manuscript submitted for publication, 1982.

REFERENCES

Adams, H. B. Effects of reduced stimulation on institutionalized adult patients. In P. Suedfeld, *Restricted environmental stimulation: Research and clinical applications.* New York: Wiley, 1980.

Bernstein, D. A., & McAlister, A. The modification of smoking behavior: Progress and problems. *Addictive Behaviors,* 1976, **1,** 89–102.

Blumenthal, A. L. *The process of cognition.* Englewood Cliffs, N.J.: Prentice-Hall, 1977.

Borrie, R. A. A practical guide to clinical REST. In P. Suedfeld, *Restricted environmental stimulation: Research and clinical applications.* New York: Wiley, 1980.

Budzynski, T. H. Biofeedback and the twilight states of consciousness. In G. E. Schwartz & D. Shapiro (Eds.), *Consciousness and self-regulation: Advances in research* (Vol. 1). New York: Plenum Press, 1976.

Carver, C. S., & Scheier, M. F. *Attention and self-regulation: A control-theory approach to human behavior.* New York: Springer-Verlag, 1981.

Christensen, H., & DiGiusto, E. The effect of sensory deprivation on cigarette craving and smoking behaviour. *Addictive Behaviors,* 1982, **7,** 281–284.

Hunt, W. A., & Bespalec, D. A. An evaluation of current methods of modifying smoking behavior. *Journal of Clinical Psychology,* 1974, **30,** 431–438.

Hunt, W. A., Barnett, L. W., & Branch, L. G. Relapse rate in addiction programs. *Journal of Clinical Psychology,* 1971, **27,** 455–456.

Jones, A. *Stimulus-seeking behavior.* In J. P. Zubek (Ed.), *Sensory deprivation: Fifteen years of research.* New York: Appleton-Century-Crofts, 1969.

Keutzer, C. S., Lichtenstein, E., & Mees, H. L. Modification of smoking behavior: A review. *Psychological Bulletin,* 1968, **6,** 520–533.

Lewin, K. Group decision and social change. In G. E. Swanson, T. M. Newcomb, & E. L. Hartley (Eds.), *Readings in social psychology* (Rev. ed.). New York: Holt, 1952.

Patrick, R. O. Partial sensory depatterning and propaganda assimilation. *Dissertation Abstracts,* 1965, **26,** 3488–3489.

Raw, M. The treatment of cigarette dependence. In Y. Israel, F. B. Glaser, H. Kalant, R. E. Popham, W. Schmidt, & R. G. Smart (Eds.), *Research advances in alcohol and drug problems* (Vol. 4). New York: Plenum Press, 1978.

Schwartz, G. E. Disregulation and systems theory: A biobehavioral framework for biofeedback and behavioral medicine. In N. Birbaumer & H. D. Kimmel (Eds.), *Biofeedback and self-regulation.* Hillsdale, N.J.: Lawrence Erlbaum Associates, 1979.

Solomon, P., Kubzansky, P. E., Leiderman, P. H., Mendelson, J. H., Trumbull, R., & Wexler, D. (Eds.), *Sensory deprivation.* Cambridge, Mass.: Harvard University Press, 1961.

Suedfeld, P. Changes in intellectual performance and in susceptibility to influence. In J. P. Zubek (Ed.), *Sensory deprivation: Fifteen years of research.* New York: Appleton-Century-Crofts, 1969.(a)

Suedfeld, P. Theoretical formulations: II. In J. P. Zubek (Ed.), *Sensory deprivation: Fifteen years of research.* New York: Appleton-Century-Crofts, 1969.(b)

Suedfeld, P. *Restricted environmental stimulation: Research and clinical applications.* New York: Wiley, 1980.

Suedfeld, P., & Ikard, F. F. Attitude manipulation in restricted environments: IV. Psychologically addicted smokers treated in sensory deprivation. *British Journal of the Addictions,* 1973, **68,** 117–176.

Suedfeld, P., & Ikard, F. F. The use of sensory deprivation in facilitating the reduction of cigarette smoking. *Journal of Consulting and Clinical Psychology,* 1974, **42,** 888–895.

Suedfeld, P., & Kristeller, J. L. Stimulus reduction as a technique in health psychology. *Health Psychology,* 1982, **1,** 337–357.

Suedfeld, P., Landon, P. B., Pargament, R., & Epstein, Y. M. An experimental attack on smoking: Attitude manipulation in restricted environments, III. *International Journal of the Addictions,* 1972, **7,** 721–733.

Tetlock, P. E., & Suedfeld, P. Inducing belief instability without a persuasive message: The roles of attitude centrality, individual cognitive differences, and sensory deprivation. *Canadian Journal of Behavioural Science,* 1976, **8,** 324–333.

Tomkins, S. S. A modified model of smoking behavior. In E. F. Borgatta & R. R. Evans (Eds.), *Smoking, health, and behavior.* Chicago: Aldine, 1968.

Zubek, J. P. (Ed.). *Sensory deprivation: Fifteen years of research.* New York: Appleton-Century-Crofts, 1969.

CHAPTER 48

A SOCIAL INOCULATION STRATEGY TO DETER SMOKING IN ADOLESCENTS

RICHARD I. EVANS

University of Houston

As indicated in my introduction to this section on smoking prevention, it is obvious that an increasing focus of public policy—and a major stimulus for this Handbook—is primary prevention of disease (e.g., U.S. DHEW, 1979). In the areas of behavioral health that relate to such primary prevention, cigarette smoking has been linked both separately and synergistically to probably the greatest and most serious incidence of morbidity and mortality. In 1973, our social psychology research group was invited to address this problem, as the Baylor College of Medicine was preparing an application to the National Heart, Lung, and Blood Institute for what was to become the nation's first National Heart and Blood Vessel Research and Demonstration Center.

Because smoking cessation efforts have a history of poor long-term effectiveness (e.g., Evans, Henderson, Hill, & Raines, 1979a; Leventhal & Cleary, 1980), and because cessation may, in fact, present a problem that is more clinical than social-psychological, we decided to focus on prevention. We therefore prepared a proposal, which was funded by the National Heart, Lung, and Blood Institute within the overall Baylor Heart Center, to develop, implement, and evaluate social-psychological strategies to prevent the onset of cigarette smoking in adolescents.

The complex multidimensional nature of smoking, incorporating biological, social, and social-psychological variables, has now become even more specifically documented (Evans et al., 1979a, 1979b; Evans & Raines, 1982; Leventhal & Cleary, 1980; Reeder, Note 1) than when we began this work. Identifying and coping with the factors involved in the initiation of smoking among adolescents is an endeavor that may require diverse conceptualizations and strategies. Various conceptions in social and developmental psychology appear to be useful in generating hypotheses to account for the initiation of smoking and in providing conceptual bases for prevention programs.

In this chapter, I will briefly review some of these general conceptions that influenced the development of our intervention strategy, then describe the specific rationale for what might be described as our social inoculation approach, and, finally, summarize some of our prospective investigations utilizing this intervention strategy.

SOME PSYCHOLOGICAL CONCEPTS RELATED TO SMOKING INITIATION

Many of the general conceptions in social and developmental psychology that might have relevance to the initiation of smoking and that guided the general formulation of our social inoculation intervention strategy were described in some detail in earlier publications (e.g., Evans, 1976, 1982; Evans & Raines, 1982; Evans, Smith, & Raines, in press). These conceptualizations included the cognitive developmental theory of Piaget (Evans, 1973), which is concerned with the nature and origin of knowledge. Piaget's view of the development of knowledge appears to offer some applications to understanding the informational and decisional aspects of the initiation of smoking in the developing child.

Piaget views knowledge as developing out of the individual's adaptive interaction with the environment through the processes of assimilation (incorporation of concepts into existing cognitive structures) and accommodation (modification of cognitive structures). Four major, qualitatively distinct stages of intellectual development are posited (Evans, 1981b; Piaget, 1960). The adolescent has generally reached the formal operational period (11–15 years) during which it is recognized that reality is but one set of all possibilities. Thinking is characterized by hypothetical-deductive reasoning, propositional and rule-governed logic, combinational analysis (i.e., the consideration of multiple factors), and a futuristic perspective. The formal operational period is further divided into two stages (Inhelder & Piaget, 1958), with the first stage (11–13 years) described as a transition from the concrete operational period (7–11 years) to the later, true formal operational period. This first transitional stage is characterized by experimentation, hypothesis making, and analysis of cognitive materials. Piaget's theory thus predicts the child's shift from an unquestioning acceptance of health beliefs proposed by authority figures to a more critical assessment of the probabilities of personal dangers of smoking.

Piaget's ideas involving adaptation to the social environment have not been systematically explored, and the initiation of smoking, apparently an age-related behavior, appears most often to occur within the context of social interactions. Yet smoking does involve an important decisional component requiring the utilization of cognitive or knowledge structures. By the time they reach the seventh grade, the vast majority of children believe that smoking is dangerous to one's health (Evans, 1976; Evans, Rozelle, Mittelmark, Hansen, Bane, & Havis, 1978). Despite this knowledge, however, many adolescents aged 12 to 14 will experiment with smoking, and roughly 4% to 5% will smoke regularly. This situation suggests that social adaptation may override intellectual adaptation or knowledge.

One contemporary psychoanalytic developmental model that might be relevant to smoking initiation and our prevention strategy is Erikson's stage theory of psychosocial development (Erikson, 1963; Evans, 1981a), which identifies eight psychosocial crises. Of particular interest with reference to the initiation of smoking are Erikson's fourth and fifth psychosocial stage crises—industry versus inferiority (6–11 years) and identity versus role diffusion (12–18 years).

Both the struggle to overcome inferiority and the effort to establish a self-identity have been cited in one form or another by numerous researchers interested in interpreting the initiation of smoking in adolescents. Erikson's "identity-crisis" in adolescence (being torn between the roles of child and adult), for example, might be an interesting basis for explaining the apparent influence of peer pressure in the initiation of smoking, particularly if this notion were explored empirically in some depth.

Newman and Newman's (1979) developmental model, based on Erikson's theory, might provide testable hypotheses for further research emanating from the utilization of the social inoculation strategy. Useful stages from this model include middle school age (8–12 years), with a stage crisis of industry versus inferiority, and early adolescence (13–17 years), with a stage crisis of group identity versus alienation. Central processes are specified for the stages as education and peer pressure, respectively. Middle school age is described as a period during which children become increasingly vulnerable to personal, social, and environmental influences, some of which, such as smoking, may have deleterious effects. Generally, as children reach the age of 10 or 11, they have more free, unstructured time and less supervision. Thus, at that age, children have more opportunities to experiment with such behaviors as smoking and are more susceptible to social and environmental pressures to engage in such activities. As children reach early adolescence, they experience greatly increased vulnerability, greater mobility, and greater freedom from adult authority figures. Experimentation with potential lifestyles, which marks this period of development, could include smoking, and conflicting expectations could override both personal beliefs and parental or family values. This model predicts the initiation of smoking for children as young as 10 or 11 and identifies smoking both as a form of rebellion against authority and as part of a new and different lifestyle for adolescents during the early teenage years.

Other conceptual areas in psychology could well be explored as they relate to our prevention strategy directed at initiation and prevention of smoking. Festinger's (1957) theory of cognitive dissonance should be useful in explorations of conflict between health beliefs and the initiation of health-threatening behaviors such as smoking. Jessor and Jessor's (1977) multideterminant conceptual structure of problem behavior, which has been successful in predicting age-graded problem behaviors—those behaviors acceptable in adults but not in adolescents and children—might well be relevant to smoking in adolescents. This model has, in fact, been incorporated into a longitudinal design (Sherman, Presson, Chassin, Bensenberg, Corty, & Olschavshky, 1982; Sherman, Chassin, & Presson, Note 2). These investigators attempt to explain the onset of smoking and the transition from nonsmoker to smoker. Ajzen and Fishbein (1970; Fishbein & Ajzen, 1975) have proposed a framework for predicting behavioral intentions, which are assumed to mediate and thus predict subsequent overt behavior. This rather elegant model, which has been applied with some success in studies of alcohol use in adolescents (Schlegel, Crawford, & Sanford, 1977), lends itself to empirically testable hypotheses that could tease out important components of the development of smoking behavior. Henderson's (Note 3) small-scale study of smoking in a population of ninth-grade students, based on Fishbein and Ajzen's model, provides a provocative basis for more elaborate investigations. Other theoretical models that appeared relevant to our intervention strategy include Kohlberg's (1964) theory of moral development, impression formation (Tedeschi, Schlenker, & Bonoma, 1971), attribution theory (Jones & Davis, 1965; Kelley, 1971), decision making in children (Bruner, 1973), and the concept of risk-taking (Dion, Baron, & Miller, 1970).

DEVELOPMENT OF AN INTERVENTION STRATEGY

In order to apply any concept or rationale to the problem of smoking prevention, it should be noted that smoking initiation reflects an upward trend from elementary grades and most significantly junior high school into high school (NIH, 1976; Johnson, Backman, & O'Malley, Notes 4, 5). This trend has been reported consistently in the literature (Evans et al., 1979b; Thompson, 1978; Creswell, Huffman, & Stone, Note 6). Within this estimate of smoking frequency, and as indicated earlier, it was determined that the most effective way to attack the problem would be to influence entering junior high school students not to initiate smoking.

A survey of junior high school programs dealing with prevention of smoking (Evans & Raines, 1982) revealed that more traditional efforts (a) generally were focused perhaps too intensely on fear arousal; (b) largely emphasized the future consequences of smoking, such as heart disease or cancer, and failed to recognize that teenagers tend to care more about the present than the future; (c) in using films and other media of communication, failed to utilize previous research on effective use of media; and (d) evoked responses that might even be counterproductive. In light of these findings, we decided to undertake a long-term study in the Houston Independent School District (Evans, 1976; Evans, Rozelle, Maxwell, Raines, Dill, Guthrie, Henderson, & Hill, 1981; Evans et al., 1978), perhaps one of the largest school districts in the United States.

Interviews conducted before both a pilot study (Evans, 1976) and a 3-year study (Evans et al., 1978) with a large population of seventh-graders suggested that peer pressure, models of smoking parents, and smoking models or messages in the mass media, such as cigarette advertising, may individually or collectively outweigh the belief of adolescents that smoking is dangerous. By the time they had reached seventh grade, all the children believed smoking was dangerous. Some of them between the ages of 4 and 11 had even spent time trying to persuade their parents to give up smoking. As they grew older, social pressures to smoke became superimposed on the fear of this behavior, and the fear and knowledge of the dangers of smoking became insufficient to prevent the onset of smoking.

From among the various available conceptions in psychology that generally might have related to our intervention strategy, Bandura's (1977) social learning theory offered particularly relevant insights. As applied to the initiation of smoking (Evans et al., in press), this theory suggests that children acquire expectations and learned behaviors with regard to smoking through observation. Children can learn vicariously, for example, that cigarette smoking relieves tension or anxiety. Thus, they might come to expect that if they feel tense, smoking will have a relaxing effect. In addition, when a model engages in an apparently enjoyable behavior that the observer expects to be socially prohibited, but negative consequences do not follow, disinhibition results. Thus, the children's learned expectation of negative consequences is weakened, possibly to the point where they will engage in the same behavior as the model. Vicariously learned expectations of the positive and negative consequences of cigarette smoking would therefore appear to be important factors in the ultimate decision regarding smoking. As also presented earlier (Evans et al., in press), Figure 48.1 shows the array of possible influences to smoke.

The model that emerged from our investigations postulates that both social-environmental and personality determinants contribute to the complex of psychological predispositions related to smoking. These psychological predispositions tend to produce an intention either to smoke or not smoke. Nevertheless, the actual decision to smoke (or not smoke) on a particular occasion may depend on the impact of situational social influences. Teaching adolescents to cope with such influences might decrease the probability that they would initiate smoking. Also, such an approach could logically be incorporated within existing school health education programs. Examining the other components of smoking initiation, as reflected in Figure 48.1, we believed that, within the constraints of the school system with which we would be working, we would not be able to design significant interventions to modify the social environment. Likewise, although other investigators (e.g., Botvin, Eng, & Williams, 1980; Hurd, Johnson, Pechacek, Bast, Jacobs, & Leupker, 1980) subsequently developed interventions directed toward altering some of the intrapersonal determinants of smoking, we also believed that, within the constraints of the institutions with which we would be working, such an alteration attempt would require too complex an array of commitments. Therefore, inoculation against social influences to smoke became the primary focus of our intervention.

To guide the development of our interventions, we found McGuire's (1968) communication-persuasion model both relevant and provocative. It analyzes the impact of communications according to five components: attention, comprehension, yielding, retention, and action. It is obvious that, to be effective, a communication must hold the person's attention and be understandable to that person. In addition, the communication must elicit yielding (or agreement) on the part of the person exposed to the message. Induced agreement must be maintained (retention) over time for it to be translated into action in appropriate situations.

Various elements of the filmed messages we produced address problems of attention, comprehension, and yielding (Evans et al., in press). First, instead of adults, adolescent narrators, selected for their poise and appearance, take the role of information brokers. Using language that is specifically geared to the audience's level of comprehension, the narrators present scientific information. In keeping with their role as information brokers, however, these student narrators make no claim to having scientific expertise of their own. Thus, such phrases as "the researchers asked me to tell you . . ." and "the researchers found that . . ." are included at appropriate points.

Second, much of the content of the films and discussions dealing with psychosocial

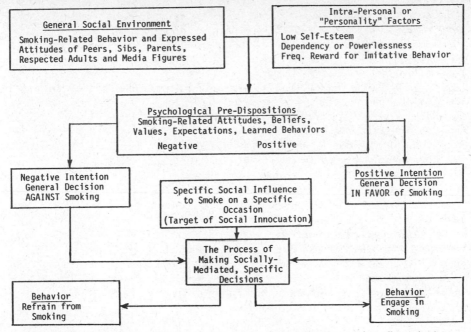

Figure 48.1 A model of smoking-related social psychological processes that affect behavior.

influences to smoke and with strategies for coping with these influences are based on data obtained from students who are similar to those in the audience. Most of the footage in the films shows students acting out situations that their peers have described to us in preintervention surveys and focused group interviews. Our process evaluation suggests that these scenes and situations are perceived by the student audience as realistic.

Third, the messages in the films and discussions are presented in a manner directed toward reinforcing self-attributions or the ability of the members of the audience to self-determine their decision whether or not to smoke. The student narrators repeatedly tell the audience, "You can decide for yourself," "Knowing these facts might help you to decide," and "Here's something you might want to think about." Process evaluations have indicated that the student audiences are favorably impressed by this self-attributional aspect of the films and discussions.

In addition to tailoring our intervention to the model, as suggested earlier, we also employ a behavioral variation of McGuire's (1961) inoculation approach to attitude change. McGuire suggests that existing attitudes may be strengthened by inoculating individuals against counterarguments to which they might be exposed. By explicating the nature of various social influences to smoke, our intervention program attempts to inoculate the audience against these influences. Further, we suggest to the students specific strategies that they might use to cope with these social influences when they encounter them.

To increase the probability of impact of the social inoculation interventions, information is presented that is intended to motivate the student to develop a negative smoking intention—an intention *not* to smoke. Information presented includes the immediate health effects of smoking, the negative social consequences of smoking, and the cost of smoking. A film depicting immediate health effects includes statements of commonly held beliefs about smoking followed by demonstrations that either confirm or refute the accuracy of these beliefs. Another message attempts to increase students' awareness of the dangers of experimental smoking.

Prior to the presentation of the social inoculation messages, various messages familiarized the students with various social influences to smoke. Three social influences were defined in our pilot study (Evans et al., 1978)—modeling, peer pressure, and cigarette advertising—and scenes representing examples of each of these influences are presented. Our current investigation has incorporated adult nagging, since responses in a preintervention survey indicated that this was a more frequently cited factor in smoking than had previously been apparent. In the case of cigarette advertising, content analyses of ads are used to reveal to students the techniques employed by advertisers. When students subsequently encounter a situation in which a social influence to smoke is present, they will be better able to recognize that social influence consciously and to understand how it operates. This recognition and understanding might well enable the students to make a specific decision that is based more on personal intention than on the demands of the particular situation. As indicated earlier, in the various filmed messages and group discussions, the students are encouraged to make a *conscious* decision about smoking, rather than to be influenced by external influences without being sufficiently vigilant concerning the effects of such external influences.

The social inoculation consists of the presentation of strategies and skills for coping with social influences to smoke that the students may encounter in the future. Various films depict specific strategies that the nonsmoking students themselves indicate they use for coping with peer pressure to smoke. During discussions following the films, students are given the opportunity to role-play peer pressure situations that they might encounter and to rehearse ways of coping with them.

EVALUATION OF THE SOCIAL INOCULATION STRATEGY

As we proceeded to evaluate this social inoculation strategy, we concluded that school systems appeared to be the most promising agencies for the delivery of such smoking prevention programs to large groups of adolescents. No other agency in our culture has the school's capability to reach adolescents from all racial, ethnic, religious, and socioeconomic groups. Within the context of the educational institution, however, an intervention program developer must consider the following constraints:

1. The amount of class time that the school is willing to allocate to smoking prevention
2. The amount of time required for school personnel to be trained adequately to implement the program.

Guided by these considerations, we decided to develop a system for delivering interventions that would require a minimum of class time, would not require prior training of school personnel or students, and would be relatively immune to the unique characteristics of the presenter. This delivery system involves four interrelated modes. First, a set of films or videotapes presents a number of messages. Second, discussions and role plays are used to reinforce, clarify, and personalize these messages. Third, posters assist students in retaining information. Fourth, as the intervention program progresses, feedback is provided concerning retention of knowledge and frequency of smoking.

The time of each intervention session and the frequency of intervention are negotiated with school system officials. The central core of our intervention is designed to require one class period on each of four occasions. There appears to be a point of diminishing returns in terms of amount of classroom time devoted to the intervention because of possible habituation or "nag" effects.

Although the sequence of presentation of the components of the intervention was more concentrated in the pilot study, the essence of the intervention procedure remained essentially the same. Films presented on the first day included information about the dangers of smoking to health and, most prominently, a section describing and illustrating peer pressure and its effect on smoking behavior. Other films recapped the first film and presented information about parental influences on smoking behavior, including a depiction of parental pressure to smoke and not to smoke and children's modeling of parents' smoking behavior. Still other films recapped the earlier films and presented information dealing with mass media pressures to smoke. These films included a pictorial analysis of such advertising techniques as artistically hiding the Surgeon General's warning on cigarette packages and appeals based on implied sexual attractiveness and popularity. The final films were a general recap of earlier films. The various treatment films of the pilot were either presented in their entirety (all four films presented) or absent (no treatment presented) in various experimental and control groups.

Following the films, students were asked for written and oral responses to questions. The experimenter distributed brief questionnaires for subjects' written responses. Four sets of questions were prepared and presented in conjunction with each film. The questions, which incorporated a quasi-role-playing device of allowing the respondent to make decisions concerning whether or not to respond to social pressure to smoke, were formulated so that they attributed motivation to resist pressures to smoke to persons who had seen the films and attributed ability to decide whether or not to smoke to persons subjected to smoking pressure.

Each film presentation was followed by a discussion designed to reinforce the messages in the films. To reinforce these messages further, posters representing scenes from the films were displayed in the classrooms. The posters thus served as continuous reminders of the film messages.

The five dependent measures included smoking information, smoking attitudes, intention to smoke, and reported smoking behavior, as well as the nicotine-in-saliva analysis of Horning and his collaborators (Horning, Horning, Carrol, Stillwell, & Dzidic, 1973), which was used as an objective measure of the presence or absence of smoking. In the earlier investigations, the Horning test determined the amount of nicotine present in saliva samples by a mass-spectrometric analysis. In later investigations, thiocyanate analyses were employed. These analyses provided the basis for inferences about the degree of smoking behavior of the subjects. The cost of these chemical analyses precluded analysis for each subject on each occasion. Therefore, a sampling of saliva specimens from each group was analyzed both as an indicator of smoking frequency and as part of a technique to increase the validity of self-reports of smoking. Earlier studies (e.g., Evans, Hansen, & Mittelmark, 1977) found that when subjects learned from a short film that in some instances their saliva would be analyzed to determine smoking behavior and how this analysis was done, self-reports of smoking frequency increased.

In a 10-week pilot study (Evans et al., 1978), rates of onset of smoking in the treatment schools were significantly lower than the onset rates in the pretest, single posttest control groups. More than 18% of the subjects in the control groups had begun smoking, whereas less than 10% of those in the experimental groups had begun smoking. (The small number of subjects already smoking in the various experimental groups precluded a statistical comparison of onset rates among the experimental groups and the control group.) In a follow-up 3-year study (Evans et al., 1981) involving 13 junior high schools, utilizing a complex multiple experimental–control group design, results indicate that those who gained information from films were smoking less than those who did not gain information. Using the criterion of smoking two cigarettes a day or more, 7% fewer subjects in the treatment schools were smoking that frequently than those in the control schools. Using the criterion of not smoking at all, 8% fewer subjects in the control schools were smoking than in the treatment schools. Both of these differences were statistically significant. Furthermore, significant interactions were found among information presented in the films and discussions, intention to smoke, and smoking. These results indicate that such interventions may prove more useful in deterring smoking among junior high school students than would merely instructing them in more traditional health education programs. Perhaps of most importance is the indication from these findings that various kinds of interventions may be effective if they have a reasonable social-psychological conceptual base framed in terms of data from the target audience about its perceptions of the influences to smoke and the ways to cope with them (Evans et al., 1979a, 1979b; Evans & Raines, 1982). Other investigators (e.g., Hurd et al., 1980; McAlister, Perry, & Maccoby, 1979), using variations of our conceptual and developmental approaches that have also reported promising results, appear to support this contention.

SUMMARY AND CONCLUSIONS

This chapter first presented various psychological concepts that might relate to the initiation of smoking, then traced the development of our social inoculation strategy and summarized some prospective investigations that implemented and evaluated this strategy. By focusing on the development and evaluation of this primary prevention program involving a strategy of social inoculation to deter smoking in adolescents, it is hoped that insight was provided concerning the general problem of how early modifications of health lifestyles might be approached in primary prevention of disease efforts in general. Clearly, the less well-established a health lifestyle is, the greater may be the probability of its modification. In the case of behaviors such as smoking that possess addictive characteristics, it is almost mandatory that deterrence of these behaviors, before they become addictive, become a major focus of health education in the future.

A word of caution might be introduced, however. The results of this social-psychologically derived primary prevention program—this social inoculation strategy—surely demonstrates some promise. It must be remembered, however, that the bottom line for prevention of smoking is not that which is demonstrated in a program's relatively short-term effectiveness— that is, reducing smoking through the early adolescent years. Rather, we must determine whether, as these adolescents move through high school, such a strategy actually reduces the incidence of addictive smoking. This cannot be determined until the individuals reach the end of their high school years, since very little cigarette smoking is initiated after students leave high school, and the incidence of smoking addiction among high school seniors approaches the level of the general adult population (Evans & Raines, 1982). It is important, therefore, to continue to evaluate such interventions and their impact or to introduce additional interventions through later adolescent years. A similar caution must be considered in the evaluation of any program directed at the primary prevention of disease that involves children and/or adolescents, particularly when the end points of such programs involve not only influencing a behavior (as in the case of our social inoculation approach) but ultimately influencing the incidence of morbidity and/or mortality.

REFERENCE NOTES

1. Reeder, L. G. Sociocultural factors in the etiology of smoking behavior: An assessment. In M. E. Jarvik, J. W. Cullen, E. R. Gritz, T. M. Mogt, & L. J. West (Eds.), *Research on smoking behavior.* NIDA Research Monograph No. 17 (U.S. DHEW, PHS, ADA/ MHA, NIDA). DHEW Pub. No. (ADM)78–581, December 1977.

2. Sherman, S. J., Chassin, L., & Presson, C. C. *Social psychological factors in adolescent cigarette smoking.* Paper presented at the meeting of the American Psychological Association, New York, September 1979.

3. Henderson, A. H. *Adolescent smoking decisions: Role of health beliefs and social-psychological perceptions.* Paper presented at the meeting of the American Psychological Association, New York, September 1979.

4. Johnson, L. D., Backman, J. G., & O'Malley, P. M. *Drugs and the class of '78: Behaviors, attitudes and recent national trends.* U.S. DHEW, Public Health Service, Pub. No. (ADM)79–877, 1979.

5. Johnson, L. D., Backman, J. G., & O'Malley, P. M. *1979 highlights: Drugs and the nation's high school students. Five-year national trends.* U.S. DHEW, Public Health Service, Pub. No. (ADM)80–930, 1979.

6. Creswell, W. H., Jr., Huffman, W. J., & Stone, D. B. *Youth smoking behavior characteristics and their educational implications.* A report of the University of Illinois Anti-Smoking Education Study. Champaign: University of Illinois, June 30, 1970.

REFERENCES

Ajzen, I., & Fishbein, M. The prediction of behavior from attitudinal and normative variables. *Journal of Experimental Social Psychology,* 1970, **6,** 466–487.

Bandura, A. *Social learning theory.* Englewood Cliffs, N.J.: Prentice-Hall, 1977.

Botvin, G. J., Eng, A., & Williams, C. L. Preventing the onset of cigarette smoking through life skills training. *Preventive Medicine,* 1980, **9,** 135–143.

Bruner, J. S. *Beyond the information given.* New York: Norton, 1973.

Dion, K. L., Baron, R. S., & Miller, N. Why do groups make riskier decisions than individuals? In L. Berkowitz (Ed.), *Advances in experimental social psychology* (Vol. 5). New York: Academic Press, 1970.

Erikson, E. H. *Childhood and society.* New York: Norton, 1963.

Evans, R. I. *Jean Piaget: The man and his ideas.* New York: Dutton, 1973.

Evans, R. I. Smoking in children: Developing a social psychological strategy of deterrence. *Journal of Preventive Medicine,* 1976, **5,** 122–127.

Evans, R. I. *Dialogue with Erik Erikson.* New York: Praeger, 1981.(a)

Evans, R. I. *Dialogue with Jean Piaget.* New York: Praeger, 1981.(b)

Evans, R. I. Modifying health lifestyles in children and adolescents: Development and evaluation of a social psychological intervention. In A. Baum & J. E. Singer (Eds.), *Handbook of psychology and health: Issues in child health and adolescent health* (Vol. 2). Hillsdale, N.J.: Lawrence Erlbaum Associates, 1982.

Evans, R. I., Hansen, W. B., & Mittelmark, M. B. Increasing the validity of self-reports of smoking behavior in children. *Journal of Applied Psychology,* 1977, **62,** 521–523.

Evans, R. I., Henderson, A. H., Hill, P. C., & Raines, B. E. Current psychological, social and educational programs in control and prevention of smoking: A critical methodological review. In A. M. Gotto & R. Paoletti (Eds.), *Atherosclerosis reviews* (Vol. 6). New York: Raven Press, 1979.(a)

Evans, R. I., Henderson, A. H., Hill, P. C., & Raines, B. E. Smoking in children and adolescents: Psychosocial determinants and prevention strategies. In *Smoking and health: A report of the Surgeon General.* DHEW Pub. No. (PHS)79–50066. Washington, D.C.: U.S. Government Printing Office, 1979.(b)

Evans, R. I., & Raines, B. E. Control and prevention of smoking in adolescents: A psychosocial perspective. In T. J. Coates, A. C. Petersen, and C. Perry (Eds.), *Promoting adolescent health: A dialog on research and practice.* New York: Academic Press, 1982.

Evans, R. I., Rozelle, R. M., Maxwell, S. E., Raines, B. E., Dill, C. A., Guthrie, T. J., Henderson, A. H., & Hill, P. C. Social modeling films to deter smoking in adolescents: Results of a three-year field investigation. *Journal of Applied Psychology,* 1981, **66,** 399–414.

Evans, R. I., Rozelle, R. M., Mittelmark, M. B., Hansen, W. B., Bane, A. L., & Havis, J. Deterring the onset of smoking in children: Knowledge of immediate physiological effects and coping with peer pressures, media pressure, and parent modeling. *Journal of Applied Social Psychology,* 1978, **8,** 126–135.

Evans, R. I., Smith, C. K., & Raines, B. E. Deterring cigarette smoking in adolescents: A psycho-social-behavioral analysis of an intervention strategy. In A. Baum, J. Singer, & S. Taylor (Eds.), *Social psychological aspects of health.* Hillsdale, N.J.: Lawrence Erlbaum Associates, in press.

Festinger, L. *A theory of cognitive dissonance.* Stanford, Calif.: Stanford University Press, 1957.

Fishbein, M., & Ajzen, I. *Belief, attitude, intention, and behavior: An introduction to theory and research.* Reading, Mass.: Addison-Wesley, 1975.

Horning, E. C., Horning, M. G., Carrol, D. I., Stillwell, R. N., & Dzidic, I. Nicotine in smokers, non-smokers and room air. *Life Science,* 1973, **13**, 1331–1346.

Hurd, P. D., Johnson, C. A., Pechacek, T., Bast, L. P., Jacobs, D. R., & Leupker, R. V. Prevention of cigarette smoking in seventh grade students. *Journal of Behavioral Medicine,* 1980, **3**, 15–28.

Inhelder, B., & Piaget, J. *The growth of logical thinking from childhood to adolescence.* New York: Basic Books, 1958.

Jessor, R., & Jessor, S. I. *Problem behavior and psychosocial development: A longitudinal study of youth.* New York: Academic Press, 1977.

Jones, E. E., & Davis, K. E. From acts to dispositions: The attribution process in person perception. In L. Berkowitz (Ed.), *Advances in experimental social psychology* (Vol. 2). New York: Academic Press, 1965.

Kelley, H. H. *Attribution in social interaction.* Morristown, N.J.: General Learning Press, 1971.

Kohlberg, L. Development of moral character and moral ideology. In M. L. Hoffman & L. W. Hoffman (Eds.), *Review of child development research* (Vol. 1). New York: Russell Sage Foundation, 1964.

Leventhal, H., & Cleary P. D. The smoking problem: A review of the research and theory in behavioral risk modification. *Psychological Bulletin,* 1980, **88**, 370–405.

McAlister, A. L., Perry, C., & Maccoby, N. Adolescent smoking: Onset and prevention. *Pediatrics,* 1979, **63**, 650–658.

McGuire, W. J. The effectiveness or supportive refutational defenses in immunizing and restoring beliefs against persuasion. *Sociometry,* 1961, **24**, 184–197.

McGuire, W. J. The nature of attitudes and attitude change. In G. Lindzey & E. Aronson (Eds.), *Handbook of social psychology* (Vol. 3): *The individual in a social context.* Reading, Mass.: Addison-Wesley, 1968.

National Institutes of Health (NIH). *Teenage smoking: National patterns of cigarette smoking, ages 12 through 18, in 1972 and 1974.* U.S. DHEW, Public Health Service, Pub. No. (NIH)76–391. Washington, D.C.: U.S. Government Printing Office, 1976.

Newman, B. M., & Newman, P. R. *Development through life: A psychosocial approach.* Homewood, Ill.: The Dorsey Press, 1979.

Piaget, J. *The psychology of intelligence.* London: Routledge and Kegan Paul, 1960.

Schlegel, R. P., Crawford, C. A., & Sanford, M. D. Correspondence and mediational properties of the Fishbein model: An application to adolescent alcohol use. *Journal of Experimental Social Psychology,* 1977, **13**, 421–430.

Sherman, S. J., Presson, C. C., Chassin, L., Bensenberg, M., Corty, E., & Olshaveshky, R. W. Smoking intentions in adolescents: Direct experience and predictability. *Personality and Social Psychology Bulletin,* 1982, **8**, 376–383.

Tedeschi, J. T., Schlenker, B. R., & Bonoma, T. V. Cognitive dissonance: Private ratiocination or public spectacle? *American Psychologist,* 1971, **26**, 685–695.

Thompson, E. I. Smoking education programs 1960–1976. *American Journal of Public Health,* 1978, **68**, 250–257.

U.S. Department of Health, Education and Welfare (DHEW). *Disease prevention and health promotion: Federal programs and prospects.* Report of the department task force on prevention. U.S. DHEW Pub. No. (PHS)79–55071B. Washington, D.C.: U.S. Government Printing Office, 1979.

CHAPTER 49

PUBLIC POLICY AND SMOKING PREVENTION: IMPLICATIONS FOR RESEARCH

CATHERINE S. BELL

U.S. Department of Health and Human Services

SANDRA M. LEVY

National Cancer Institute

A custom lothsome to the eye,
hatefull to the nose, harmfull to the
braine, dangerous to the lungs . . .

—*King James I of England,*
"A Counter Blaste to Tobacco," 1604

Essential to democracy is the idea of personal freedom. Often the goals of the government appear to conflict with the individual's desire to express these freedoms. Nowhere is this more apparent than in the controversy over the health consequences of cigarette smoking.

It is well recognized by society that the decision to smoke is essentially a personal one. The consequences of smoking extend far beyond the individual, however. The economic and health care costs associated with the maintenance of this habit make it a matter of concern to the general public, as well as to government agencies responsible for maintaining the public welfare.

Translation of societal concerns into legislation that would provide the means of reducing the incidence of disease associated with cigarette smoking has created controversy within the federal bureaucracy. When does government action conflict with personal health behaviors? Does the government have the right to protect the individual from self-injury? If such authority exists, what role should the government play? Where should the government focus its legislative and regulatory attention—on the tobacco industry or on the smoker? These questions call for ethical as well as legal responses.

To date, the federal government's philosophy has been primarily one of education and information dissemination regarding the health consequences of cigarette smoking, with only peripheral attempts to sponsor intervention research. In general, two factors have led to a disproportionately low level of government-sponsored intervention research in the area of smoking and health: (a) limited congressional appropriations specifically designated for such research and (b) the low-priority status of smoking research at the departmental level.

So that government activity can be viewed in the proper context, this chapter provides a historical perspective on the development of tobacco, smoking, and health policy within the federal sector. Included are discussions of the social and economic forces that influence policy formation and an assessment of the implications of governmental policy on research funding in the area of behavioral health.

MAJOR INFLUENCES ON THE FORMATION OF PUBLIC POLICY

The Tobacco Industry

Despite early attempts by various segments of society to halt the spread of the smoking habit, its popularity expanded rapidly. A key factor in this expansion has been the economic value tobacco has had for governments, which have benefited from enormous tax revenues, and for entrepreneurs, who have profited from the farming, production, and distribution of tobacco.

Today, the most powerful influence on the formation and implementation of smoking-related public policy is the tobacco lobby. This group consists of manufacturers, farmers, and allied industries, ranging from advertising to transportation.

Because of its impressive economic and political power, the tobacco industry has played a significant role in influencing the maintenance of tobacco as an unregulated consumer product, as well as in influencing the level and direction of federally sponsored policy in the area of smoking and health research.

A recent issue of *Tobacco Outlook and Situation* (USDA, Note 1) noted that tobacco-related activities provide 2 million jobs annually, representing over $30 billion in wages and earnings. Furthermore, the tobacco industry commits more than $15 billion in capital investments annually and returns to the government, through tax provisions, more than $22 billion per year (USDA, Note 1). A 1979 study by the Wharton Applied Research Center of the University of Pennsylvania (Note 2) amplified these statements by noting that the contribution of tobacco to the gross national product exceeds $57 billion annually.

The Grower

In 1980, tobacco was ranked by the U.S. Department of Agriculture (USDA) as the sixth largest cash crop in the United States, with an estimated value of $2.7 billion (The Tobacco Institute, Note 3). Tobacco farming is located almost entirely in the southeastern section of the country, with over 90% of the total crop destined for cigarette production. Crop yields during 1981 are estimated at over 5 billion pounds of domestic leaf, representing a 5% increase over 1980. The majority of the tobacco-producing farms are small and are maintained with family labor and rudimentary agricultural technology (USDA, Note 1; The Tobacco Institute, Note 3). Currently, more than 500,000 farm families grow tobacco in the United States and its protectorates.

Thus, three factors are the key to understanding the political influence of the tobacco grower: the economic value of tobacco as a cash crop; concentration of tobacco farming within a restricted geopolitical area; and the relatively large number of farmers and their employees. Collectively, these factors have had a significant impact on the development of a powerful constituency that is capable of influencing legislators and thus public policy.

Recognizing that restrictions on smoking behavior would create severe economic hardship, the tobacco grower has developed a highly effective political forum. Together with the tobacco manufacturers, growers represent one of the most influential congressional lobbying efforts in the nation.

The skill of the growers in affecting major legislation is demonstrated by their success in influencing and maintaining a congressionally mandated price-support program under the Agricultural Adjustment Act. Articles included under this act require that the USDA support activities that include research aimed at enhancing both the tobacco plant and the farming process, as well as the development and dissemination of tobacco marketing news.

The Manufacturer

Much like the farming community, tobacco manufacturing is located within a geographically concentrated area—essentially in the southeast and mid-Atlantic states. During 1981, the tobacco industry cigarette output was estimated at a record 736 billion cigarettes (USDA, Note 1; The Tobacco Institute, Note 3). This represents a 3% increase over figures reported in 1980. Some 69,000 persons are directly involved in the production of cigarettes, with another 8,300 persons employed in the production of cigars (USDA, Note 1; Wharton Applied Research Center, Note 2). In addition, warehousing and the manufacture of cigarette papers, filter materials, and tubes provide employment for thousands of persons (USDA, Note 1; The Tobacco Institute, Note 3). Retailing, wholesaling, advertising, and shipping, though indirectly related to tobacco manufacturing, employ millions of persons whose incomes are tied to the tobacco economy. During 1980, the tobacco industry reported that exports of leaf and manufactured tobacco totaled nearly $2.5 billion (USDA, Note 1; Wharton Applied Research Center, Note 2; The Tobacco Institute, Note 3). When balanced with imports, this figure represents a $1.9 billion contribution to the U.S. balance of payments (The Tobacco Institute, Note 3).

The strength and influence of the tobacco manufacturing community is attributed both to its economic contribution to the national economy and to the economic dependence of large numbers of persons whose income is tied to tobacco production and sales. Both profits and personal interests have served the tobacco manufacturer by developing and maintaining a tobacco interest group within Congress.

Friedman (1976) noted that the tobacco grower and manufacturer "possess three of the basic resources useful in obtaining political influence: votes, money and information." In combination, these factors allow the presentation of an impressive argument for limited government control (Friedman, 1976). An example of the impact of this cohesive lobbying effort is demonstrated by the congressional restrictions placed on the Food and Drug Administration and the Consumer Products Safety Commission. Their regulatory functions have been stymied by the tobacco industry. Although approximately 20 federal offices, agencies, and departments are charged with the responsibility for monitoring various aspects of the smoking and health problem, their activities have remained remarkably limited. Furthermore, when action has been initiated, the results are often viewed by both the public and the health community as protobacco.

Although the political power of the tobacco industry has been felt on Capitol Hill, its effect on biomedical research is less well recognized. The tobacco lobby demands, for example, that rigorous standards of certainty be applied to statistical evidence linking smoking and the development of disease. Without a demonstrable biological model identifying the actual causal relationship between smoking and disease, the industry has managed to stand firm in supporting its product in the face of overwhelming biomedical evidence to the contrary.

The Smoker

Central to the success of the tobacco economy is the consumer. Although 33 million adults are reported to have given up the smoking habit, approximately 54 million adults continue to smoke cigarettes (U.S. PHS, 1981). In a recent statement, USDA economist Robert Miller (Note 4) noted that the 1981 consumption of cigarettes by persons aged 18 years and over totaled 3,840 cigarettes (192 packs) per year. This figure represents a gradual upward trend in total cigarette consumption, which can be partially explained by an expanding smoking-age population. Furthermore, it is anticipated by the research community that a significant proportion of the adolescent population will develop the smoking habit during the next decade, thus providing a continued consumer population.

Although it is important to recognize that many of these people are aware of the health hazards involved in initiating or continuing smoking, termination of these behaviors is unlikely to occur without major intervention. Although it has been suggested numerous times that smoker behavior be regulated by federal or state mandate, it is unlikely that such an action would be desirable, workable, or even enforceable in all situations.

Although the influence of the individual smoker as a voter should be recognized, it may be more important to identify those who smoke. Many influential legislators, federal officials, lobbyists, educators, and industrialists are included in the ranks of the smokers. It should be recognized that the individual and collective political power of these smokers may influence public policy formation and implementation and, subsequently, the funding of research. In addition, even nonsmokers are likely to lobby against any attempt by the government to regulate personal behavior, however costly or offensive that behavior may be. It can be anticipated that legislation of this type would run counter to the personal philosophy of many Americans.

THE FEDERAL SECTOR

The Legislative Branch

Through the legislative process, Congress can modify the behavior of smokers, alter the character of the cigarettes themselves, or change the economic climate within which cigarettes are sold. In general, congressional hearings have been held in response to agency rule-making, as was the case with the Federal Trade Commission's decision to seek a ban on cigarette advertising. Hearings have also been generated in response to new or emerging scientific evidence, as is obvious from the congressional response following release of the report of the Surgeon General's Advisory Committee on Smoking and Health in 1964. Such actions directly affect agency activity by shifting research priorities, allocations, and mandated activities.

Historical Perspective

Early legislation excluded tobacco products from the jurisdiction of the Food and Drug Administration by declassifying tobacco as an addictive substance. Furthermore, protobacco legislation was included in the Agricultural Adjustments Acts of 1938 and 1949, which provided for a yearly system of price support for the tobacco grower.

The tobacco industry remained the dominant influence on the formation of public policy in this area until the late 1950s, when congressional hearings first addressed the question of smoking and health. These hearings were held in response to mounting medical evidence linking cigarette smoking with increased incidence of disease. Health-related legislation and regulatory activity were effectively forestalled, however, through the efforts of the tobacco industry until 1964, when two key actions by the executive branch brought the smoking issue to national attention. In the spring of that year, the Federal Trade Commission (FTC) issued trade regulations intended to prevent deceptive advertising of cigarettes and requiring that all cigarette packages carry a version of the now-famous Surgeon General's warning (Fritschler, 1975). In addition, the Surgeon General's Advisory Committee on Smoking and Health issued its report, which stated that cigarette "smoking is of sufficient hazard to health to warrant remedial action."

Congressional response to the smoking controversy peaked in 1965 with the signing of the Federal Cigarette Labeling and Advertising Act. This law mandated the establishment of the Office on Smoking and Health (formerly the National Clearinghouse for Smoking and Health) and required placement of the warning label both on cigarette packages and in print advertising. The Federal Communication Commission's response came in 1967 with application of the fairness doctrine to cigarette advertising. Subsequent congressional legislation resulted in the termination of cigarette advertising on radio and television.

Numerous hearings and rule-making activities have occurred since the late 1960s. One of the most recent of these activities was the introduction of amendments to the Public Service Act of 1969. The proposed amendments include the permanent establishment of the Office on Smoking and Health as the central focus for smoking and health information and research coordination. A second component would provide a system of rotational warnings aimed at strengthening present labeling practices. These actions are anticipated to have an impact on the level and direction of administrative policy, including the allocation of funds specifically targeted for research in the area of smoking intervention. A summary of legislative policy and regulatory activities is provided in Table 49.1.

The Executive Branch

Agencies of the federal government are organizationally placed within the executive branch and derive their power from acts of Congress. This power is dispensed by the individual agencies through two distinct means: rule-making and adjudicatory authority. In addition, each agency has been given a specific mandate, a budgetary allocation, and a reporting requirement by the Congress. Agency response to the smoking and health issue must therefore be viewed within this network of influence.

Table 49.1   A Summary of Smoking and Health Legislation, Policy, and Regulation

Year	Activity
1906	Food and Drug Act: Tobacco is removed from jurisdiction of the FDA
1938 & 1949	Agricultural Adjustment Act and amendments provide price supports for tobacco growers
1957	Congressional hearings on smoking and health
1965	FTC publishes trade regulations on cigarette labeling and advertising
	Public Health Service restricts distribution of free cigarettes in PHS and Indian hospitals
	Federal Cigarette Labeling Act passes into law
	Establishment of the National Clearinghouse on Smoking and Health (currently the Office on Smoking and Health)
1966	FTC institutes testing procedures for reporting tar and nicotine levels
1967	FCC expands fairness doctrine to include cigarette advertising
1969	FCC proposes rule to ban cigarette advertising from electronic media
	FTC issues notice of rule-making requiring warnings on cigarette packages and extends warning requirements on all advertising
	Congress holds hearings on cigarette labeling and advertising legislation.
1970	Passage of Public Health Cigarette Smoking Act of 1969
	FTC sets aside regulations on required tar and nicotine disclosures in response to industry's voluntary action to include such information in all advertising
1971	Legislation introduced to restrict smoking on airliners, buses, and trains
	Bill introduced in Congress to prohibit mailing of unsolicited cigarettes
	Cigarette manufacturers comply with FTC consent order to include health warnings on all advertising
	Civil Aeronautics Board proposes separate smoking sections on airliners
	Department of Health, Education and Welfare prohibits smoking in designated areas in the federal workplace
	Supreme Court upholds legislative ban on cigarette commercials
1973	Congress considers legislation banning "little cigar" commercials
1974	Adult Education Act includes education on health consequences of smoking
1979	Public Health Service Act provides a Health Education Risk Reduction Grant Program
1981	Comprehensive Smoking Prevention Act proposes strengthening of cigarette warning labels
	Agriculture and Food Act proposes reduction of taxpayer burden for tobacco price-support program

Department of Health and Human Services

The bulk of smoking and health research activity is found within this department, successor to the Department of Health, Education and Welfare. Until the late 1970s, funded research focused on investigations of the physiological and biological mechanisms of disease as they relate to cigarette smoking.

Epidemiologic research established the statistical linkages between cigarette smoking and the increased incidence of such conditions as cancer and cardiovascular disease. During this period, behavioral research generally focused on pharmacological studies of nicotine use, and little research attention was directed at understanding or altering smoker behavior. It was not until 1978, with the release of Secretary Califano's initiative to combat smoking, that behavioral science received the appropriations necessary to fund large-scale biobehavioral and social intervention programs. Table 49.2 displays the dollar expenditures, by institute, for smoking and health-related research during fiscal year 1981.

The goal of the initiative was the coordination of departmental efforts on smoking and health and the development of a research strategy for behavioral and biomedical studies. Agency response to this and subsequent initiatives directed at smoking and health included the development of institute-specific research agendas. The major thrust of these research activities is summarized in Table 49.3.

Prevention and health risk reduction are key initiatives of the current administration. Research leading to a reduction in cigarette smoking and a subsequent reduction in the incidence and mortality associated with this behavior is anticipated to have priority status for the next several years.

Federal Communications Commission

In 1967, the Federal Communications Commission (FCC) extended its jurisdiction by applying the fairness doctrine to cigarette advertising. This action required broadcasters to provide sufficient time for public service announcements (PSAs) warning of the health hazards of cigarette smoking. By 1971, the FCC had obtained congressional approval to restrict advertising of cigarettes on any medium of electronic communication. This action resulted in the elimination of the fairness doctrine and thus effectively ended requirements to air PSAs.

Recent research on the impact of these actions and related activities shows the importance

Table 49.2   U.S. Public Health Service Smoking and Health Budget

Institute	FY 81 (est.) ($000)	FY 82 (est.) ($000)
National Institute of Drug Abuse	2.1	2.1
National Cancer Institute	10.1	10.9
National Institute of Child Health and Development	1.7	1.7
National Heart, Lung and Blood Institute	9.1	9.2
National Institute of Environmental Health Science	1.3	1.3
Centers for Disease Control	11.5	0.4
Office on Smoking and Health	2.0	1.9
TOTAL	37.8	27.5

Source: Office on Smoking and Health. Statement prepared for inclusion in *DHHS 1990 Research Objectives,* April 22, 1982.

Table 49.3 Department of Health and Human Services, 1978 Smoking and Health Research Initiatives

National Institute of Drug Abuse
The application of behavioral and pharmacological principles to studies of nicotine/tobacco dependence and treatment

National Institute of Occupational Safety and Health
Investigations directed at understanding the potentially synergistic nature of smoking and occupational exposures and the contributions of smoking to increased workplace accidents

National Institute of Child Health and Human Development
Research aimed toward understanding antecedent factors that lead to smoking, identifying factors that may deter the onset of smoking, and identifying risk factors for smoking mothers and offspring

National Institute of Allergic and Infectious Diseases
Studies directed at understanding the effects of tobacco on the immune system

National Cancer Institute
Biobehavioral, toxicological, biological, and epidemiologic research aimed at understanding factors that contribute to increased incidence of cancer due to cigarette smoking or tobacco use, including studies addressing prevention and cessation of smoking

National Heart, Lung and Blood Institute
Research activities focused on understanding the effects of tobacco smoking on cardiovascular and respiratory systems and the hemostatic properties of the blood, including development of intervention strategies

National Institute on Aging
Development of longitudinal surveys to examine smoking habits in adult populations

Food and Drug Administration
Studies directed at understanding the potential synergistic effects of combined smoking and alcohol use

Institute of Environmental Health Science
Research focusing on the effects of smoking as a co-factor of environmental pollution

Centers for Disease Control
Support for intervention projects aimed at preventing smoking and alcohol use by children and adolescents in schools and community settings

Office on Smoking and Health
Responsible for monitoring all Public Health Service smoking and health-related programs to insure compliance with departmental policies and goals, as well as serving as a clearing-house for scientific and technical information

National Center for Health Statistics
Survey research on smoking prevalence and preferences

National Center for Health Services Research
Research aimed at understanding public policy and economic factors related to cigarette smoking

of the media as effective means of providing health education. Further research in this area is needed before future policy regarding the use of PSAs or direct media advertising can be formulated and implemented.

Department of Agriculture

The USDA is administratively responsible for maintaining a tobacco program, which is comprised of two interrelated activities: price supports and marketing restrictions. The Agricultural Adjustment Act of 1938, as amended in 1949, authorizes the Secretary of USDA to establish yearly quotas and assigns a share for individual growers, based on production history. The support is provided through loans to growers' cooperative associations, whose job it is to purchase tobacco from growers who cannot sell their crops on the open market at approved support-price levels. As a condition of eligibility for support, growers must meet marketing restrictions established by the USDA.

The primary cost of the USDA tobacco program is the financial loss that occurs when sales proceeds from a crop are insufficient to fully repay the price-support loan made to an association. USDA figures indicate that as of December 1981, the outstanding loan principle on uncommitted stocks totaled $54 million. In an attempt to reduce the burden on the taxpayer, Congress passed the Agricultural and Food Act of 1981, which includes legislation intended to eliminate costs traditionally borne by the general public (USDA, Note 5).

Federal Trade Commission

The authority to monitor the advertising practices of the tobacco industry falls to the Federal Trade Commission (FTC). Regulatory actions taken by this agency have focused on misleading and false advertising, especially as it related to the early health claims made by cigarette manufacturers. Although it was 1972 before warning labels actually appeared on both cigarette packages and advertising, the FTC had established itself as the major federal watchdog of the tobacco industry. In 1967, the FTC announced that it would test cigarettes for tar and nicotine content and subsequently for carbon monoxide levels. Unfortunately, the tobacco industry has turned the FTC scoring into a promotional boon by producing and promoting the lower tar, lower nicotine cigarette as the "less hazardous cigarette."

Since 1967, the FTC has reported to Congress on the effectiveness of health warnings and current cigarette advertising practices, as well as on studies directed at assessing the state of consumer knowledge regarding the hazards associated with cigarette smoking. The 1981 FTC recommendations included increased consumer education, self-regulation by the tobacco industry, systems of mandatory rotational warning labels, and disclosure of carbon monoxide levels. The current legislative response may have a significant impact on the level of regulatory authority of the FTC, as well as on allocations for future research by agencies of the Executive Branch (FTC, Note 6).

Other Federal Agencies

Several agencies that have played a lesser role in the smoking and health controversy include the Civil Aeronautics Board, the Departments of Education, Labor, Defense, and Commerce, and the Office of Personnel Management. The role of these federal entities, with few exceptions, has been limited to consultation, liaison, and the development of internal policies directed at curtailing smoker behavior within the federal workplace.

STATE GOVERNMENT

In partial response to federal activity, more than 30 states have passed some form of legislation restricting cigarette smoking in public places—primarily, "clean indoor air" laws (U.S.

PHS, Note 7). Although the intent of these regulations is to protect the nonsmoker, such laws may have the secondary effect of deterring smoking by limiting the places and occasions where such behavior can occur. In addition, such legislative actions may reinforce the idea that smoking is a socially unacceptable behavior. During the past decade, more than 20 state governments have increased the cigarette excise tax, with the intention of reducing smoking through a policy of economic deterrence. Studies currently being conducted to measure the impact of these legislative activities may result in shifts in public policy and may indicate new directions for behavioral research.

THE VOLUNTARY SECTOR

During the early 1960s, the burgeoning interest of the voluntary sector in cigarette smoking and health effects resulted in sufficient pressure to interest congressional leaders in the problem. An example of this influence is the successful separation of smokers from nonsmokers on airplanes. In addition to its lobbying efforts, the voluntary sector traditionally has provided a forum for presentation of research results that serve as a basis for public policy development at the state and national levels (American Cancer Society, Note 8).

Agencies such as the American Cancer Society, the American Lung Association, and the American Heart Association have been sources of research funding for investigators as well as developing and delivering smoking intervention programs on a national basis.

Historically, the voluntary sector has approached the problem of smoking and health from independent and sometimes conflicting philosophical viewpoints. A recent effort has been made, however, to develop a national policy group to represent the major voluntary health organizations: the Coalition on Smoking *or* Health (American Cancer Society, Note 9). Such a group would bring issues of related importance to the attention of legislators and federal officials and would maintain a concentrated lobbying effort aimed at increasing support for federally sponsored smoking research.

MAJOR ISSUES

Health Care Costs

Although health care expenditures have risen dramatically during the past decade, only marginal improvements have been made in overall health levels. This fact has contributed to a movement toward a preventive orientation within medicine and the encouragement of individuals to alter unhealthy lifestyles. Because of the scientific and medical attention given to the health hazards of smoking, this behavior is an obvious target for elimination.

The economic implications of smoking are enormous. Luce and Schweitzer (1978) stated that the "total direct health-care cost of smoking is . . . estimated to be $8.2 billion, which is approximately 7.8 percent of the total direct health-care cost to the nation." When indirect costs, defined as loss of earnings, are calculated into the formula, the economic burden of smoking-induced illness, in terms of 1976 economics, is $27.5 billion.

Using figures supplied by the Health Care Finance Administration, including the effects of inflation from 1976 to 1980, the total health care cost of persons suffering from or disabled by smoking-related disease was estimated to be $43 billion in 1980 (Social Security Administration, 1980, 1981, Note 10).

Other Indirect Costs

Generally not included in economic analyses of costs are considerations of the indirect factors that result from the act of smoking. Some of these factors include auto accidents and fires, increases in insurance premiums and janitorial services, reduced work efficiency, and potentially negative health effects on nonsmokers. Inclusion of these costs would increase the overall economic burden significantly. Furthermore, inflation and escalating health care costs are likely to increase smoking- and illness-related cost figures dramatically over the next decade.

Scientific Evidence

Cigarette smoking has long been recognized as one of the nation's leading preventable causes of disease and disability and as a major cause of cancer. The 1964 Surgeon General's report established the causal link between cigarette smoking and lung cancer and connected smoking with other serious, often fatal, health problems such as coronary heart disease, arteriosclerosis, and peripheral vascular disease. Since then, the evidence linking chronic disease to smoking has been overwhelming (U.S. PHS, 1982).

Epidemiologic data clearly documented that, in 1977, smoking was a major factor in 220,000 deaths from heart disease, 78,000 deaths from lung cancer, and 22,000 deaths from other cancers, including cancer of the larynx, esophagus, and oral cavity, and that it may be associated with an additional 15,000 deaths due to cancer of the bladder, kidney, and pancreas (U.S. PHS, 1982). The 1982 Surgeon General's report, *The Health Consequences of Smoking: Cancer,* noted that 30% of all cancer deaths are attributed to tobacco use. Furthermore, certain subgroups of the population who are exposed to toxic substances in the workplace (e.g., asbestos, radon, coal, and chemical) have had their risk of disease exacerbated by cigarette smoking. In addition to the effects of active tobacco smoking, there is increased concern about the effects of side-stream and passive smoke on the health of the nonsmoker.

Experimental and epidemiologic data suggest that thousands of children and adolescents become smokers every day (U.S. PHS, 1981). Children are starting to smoke at an earlier age, and the percentage of girls who smoke has increased eightfold since 1968. Data published by the National Center for Health Statistics indicate that there are more than 6 million regular smokers among adolescents between 13 and 19 years of age (U.S. PHS, 1982).

Smoking-related research has advanced the investigators' understanding of the biobehavioral mechanisms underlying smoking, especially among children, adolescents, and those self-selected individuals who wish to terminate their smoking behavior through participation in formal cessation programs (U.S. PHS, 1079). Further research into behavioral factors leading to recruitment to or maintenance of smoking or tobacco use is likely to have a positive impact on reducing the "single most preventable cause of premature illness and death in United States" (Brandt, Note 11).

SUMMARY

Scientific and medical evidence linked cigarette smoking with the increased incidence of disease early in the 1930s. The federal government was slow to respond, however, to both the need to fund biomedical research for defining the hazardous potential of this substance and the need to notify cigarette users of this potential health hazard. In this chapter, we have reviewed the economic and ideological bases of this reluctance.

As discussed earlier, the Department of Health and Human Services is the principal federal agency that funds tobacco smoking and health research. The National Institutes of Health and the Alcohol, Drug Abuse and Mental Health Administration are mandated to promote and carry out research in the interest of the public welfare.

The development of science policy and research priorities is a complex process, with multiple sources of input. Often, new scientific knowledge generates new questions to be answered. In turn, these questions must be perceived as important by those in a policy-making role. Members of Congress make their views known through hearings and inquiries, which have a major impact on the development and implementation of science research policy. Ultimately, congressional decisions are influenced by constituencies and by special interest lobbies. Given the rising costs of health care, the current trend toward preventive medicine, the collective concern of the research community, and a growing awareness within the Congress, the shaping of federal policy and subsequent research priorities in the area of smoking and health should continue to be a lively process in the next decade.

REFERENCE NOTES

1. U.S. Department of Agriculture (USDA). *Tobacco outlook and situation.* TS178, December 1981.

2. Wharton Applied Research Center, University of Pennsylvania. *A study of the U.S. tobacco industry's economic contribution to the nation, its 50 states, and the District of Columbia.* Philadelphia: Wharton Applied Research Center and Wharton Econometric Forecasting Associates, August 1979.

3. The Tobacco Institute. *Tobacco industry profile, 1981.* Washington, D.C.: The Tobacco Institute, 1981.

4. Miller, R. H. Statement, in Tobacco consumption patterns and prospects, *Agricultural Economist.* Washington, D.C.: U.S. Department of Agriculture, National Economics Division, March 9, 1982.

5. U.S. Department of Agriculture (USDA). *Tobacco in the United States.* Agricultural Marketing Services, Miscellaneous Pub. No. 2, 1979.

6. Federal Trade Commission (FTC). Report to Congress pursuant to the Federal Cigarette Labeling and Advertising Act, 1981.

7. U.S. Public Health Service (U.S. PHS). *State legislation on smoking and health.* DHHS, U.S. PHS, Pub. No. (CDC)80–8386, 1980.

8. American Cancer Society. *A national dilemma: Cigarette smoking or the health of Americans.* Report of the National Commission on Smoking and Public Policy to the Board of Directors, American Cancer Society, 1978.

9. American Cancer Society. *Developing a blueprint for action.* Report of the National Conference on Smoking or Health, American Cancer Society, New York, November 18–20, 1981.

10. Social Security Administration (SSA). *Characteristics of Social Security Disability Insurance beneficiaries, 1975.* SSA Pub. No. 13–11947, December 1979.

11. Brandt, E. N., Jr. Statement prepared for the Subcommittee on Health and the Environment, Committee on Energy and Commerce, U.S. Congress, March 11, 1982.

REFERENCES

Friedman, K. M. *Public policy and the smoking-health controversy: A comprehensive study.* Lexington, Mass.: Lexington Books, D. C. Heath, 1976.

Fritschler, A. L. *Smoking and politics: Policy making and the federal bureaucracy.* Englewood Cliffs, N.J.: Prentice-Hall, 1975.

Luce, B. R., & Schweitzer, S. O. Smoking and alcohol abuse: A comparison of their economic consequences. *New England Journal of Medicine,* 1978, **298,** 569–571.

Social Security Administration (SSA). *Health Care Financing Review,* Summer 1980.

Social Security Administration (SSA). *Social Security Bulletin,* 1981, **44**(6).

U.S. Public Health Service (U.S. PHS). *Smoking and health: A report of the Surgeon General.* DHEW Pub. No. (PHS)79–50066. Washington, D.C.: U.S. Government Printing Office, 1979.

U.S. Public Health Service (U.S. PHS). *The health consequences of smoking: The changing cigarette. A report of the Surgeon General.* DHHS Pub. No. (PHS)81–50156. Washington, D.C.: U.S. Government Printing Office, 1981.

U.S. Public Health Service (U.S. PHS). *The health consequences of smoking: Cancer. A report of the Surgeon General.* DHHS Pub. No. (PHS)82–50179. Washington, D.C.: U.S. Government Printing Office, 1982.

SECTION 7
BLOOD PRESSURE

CHAPTER 50

OVERVIEW OF HYPERTENSION: ITS TREATMENT AND PREVENTION

J. ALAN HERD

Baylor College of Medicine, Houston, Texas

STEPHEN M. WEISS

National Heart, Lung and Blood Institute, Bethesda, MD.

Hypertension is one of America's greatest health problems. By itself, hypertension can lead to stroke, heart failure, renal failure, and blindness. Along with other risk factors, such as cigarette smoking and high levels of serum cholesterol, it can lead to ischemic heart disease, peripheral arterial disease, and sudden death. Although the term *hypertension* connotes cardiovascular disease, it actually identifies one end of the spectrum of arterial blood pressure. Since there is no exact dividing line between high and low levels of blood pressure, the definition of arterial hypertension is a matter of statistical analysis and is more a statement of risk than an identification of disease. Thus, high levels of arterial blood pressure are associated with increased incidence of cardiovascular disease.

The prevalence of hypertension is dependent on levels of arterial pressure identified as increasing risks for cardiovascular disease. The most recent estimate of prevalence in the United States (U.S. DHHS, 1981) indicates that approximately 17% of all Americans have definite hypertension—defined as levels for systolic blood pressure equal to or greater than 160 mmHg and levels for diastolic blood pressure equal to or greater than 95 mmHg. Since the majority of vascular complications of hypertension are observed in patients with even lower levels of blood pressure, the usual definition of hypertension is blood pressure equal to or greater than 140 mmHg systolic and 90 mmHg diastolic. By these lower criteria, approximately 25% of all Americans have borderline or definite hypertension. Thus, to prevent vascular complications by drug treatment, perhaps 25% of the population would have to be treated.

There is increasing evidence that all patients with hypertension should be treated. In the Framingham Study, a population of 5,000 men and women were followed medically for more than 20 years. This study showed a positive, increasing relationship between baseline blood pressure and subsequent risk of cardiovascular disease (Gordon, Sorlie, & Kannel, Note 1). When the mathematical relationships between risks for cardiovascular disease and the occurrence of disease were determined, it was demonstrated that high-density lipoprotein cholesterol (HDL) and low-density lipoprotein cholesterol (LDL) showed the strongest relationships. The level of systolic blood pressure and the presence of left ventricular hypertrophy, however, contributed independently to risk of ischemic heart disease (Walker & Duncan, 1967). When the same statistical approach was taken with risk and occurrence of stroke, the level of systolic blood pressure was the major factor associated with subsequent stroke (Kannel, Wolf, & Dawber, 1978). In general, results from the Framingham Study indicated that men between 45 and 64 years of age with levels of systolic blood pressure greater than 170 mmHg were at least twice as likely to experience complications of ischemic heart disease as those with systolic blood pressures below 130 mmHg.

The total economic cost of illness in fiscal year 1975 (Paringer & Berk, Note 2) included costs of treatment for diseases of the circulatory system that were more than $16 billion, 13.5% of total direct costs. Since hypertension is one of the major contributors to cardiovascular disease, it is responsible for a substantial portion of medical expenditures, and it is a major cause of disability.

The recommendation that patients with hypertension should be treated is based on results from several clinical trials. Major support for aggressive treatment of mild hypertension comes from the Hypertension Detection and Follow-up Program Cooperative Group (1979). Support also comes from results of the Australian National Blood Pressure Study (Management Committee of the Australian Hypertension Trial, 1979; Management Committee of Australian Therapeutic Trial, 1982). In both these clinical trials, patients who received aggressive treatment of mild hypertension had lower mortality from cardiovascular complications than patients in the control group.

The Hypertension Detection and Follow-up Program was a large multicenter trial involving approximately 11,000 patients with diastolic blood pressures above 90 mmHg. The experimental, or stepped-care, group received complete, intensive, and free medical care in special clinics, while the control patients, or referred-care group, received whatever medical care they could find or afford in the community. A major finding of the study was that in borderline and mild hypertension with diastolic blood pressures from 90 to 104 mmHg, mortality from cardiovascular causes was 26% lower in the stepped-care patients than in the referred-care group. In addition, there was a 45% reduction in fatal myocardial infarction found in the stepped-care patients with mild hypertension. Diastolic blood pressure was reduced from an average of 96.3 to 83.4 mmHg in the stepped-care patients, while reductions from 96.4 to 87.8 mmHg occurred in the referred-care patients.

The Australian trial had a similar design, except that diastolic blood pressures on entry ranged between 95 and 109 mmHg only. Approximately 3,500 patients were treated and followed for four years. The difference in trial end points between control and treated patients in the group was most evident in patients with initial diastolic pressures of 100 mmHg or higher. Furthermore, the Australian study found that patients with diastolic pressures averaging less than 95 mmHg during the trial showed no relation between level of diastolic pressure and incidence of cardiovascular complications (Management Committee of Australian Therapeutic Trial, 1982). Since there is a tendency to assume that risk of cardiovascular complications is related to height of blood pressure in untreated patients, it is often assumed that lowering blood pressure by administration of antihypertensive drugs reduces risks in proportion to the effectiveness of lowering the blood pressure. Results of several trials, however (Helgeland, 1980; MRFIT Research Group, 1982), have shown that reduction to a given level by treatment does not confer the same protection observed in untreated patients with the same levels of blood pressure.

Although treatment of hypertensive patients with antihypertensive drugs has been shown to be effective in lowering blood pressure and in reducing cardiovascular complications, the results of treatment with drugs are difficult to interpret. The results of the Veterans Administration controlled trial indicated that benefits of antihypertensive drugs are greater in patients with severe hypertension than patients with mild hypertension (Veterans Administration Cooperative Study Group, 1970). Furthermore, antihypertensive drug treatment is most effective in preventing complications of hypertension, such as stroke, renal failure, heart failure, and aortic dissection. It is least effective in preventing atherosclerotic complications, including coronary heart disease. In the Oslo trial (Heigland, 1980), more myocardial infarction occurred in the treated patients; and in the Multiple Risk Factor Intervention Trial (MRFIT Research Group, 1982), patients with hypertension and abnormal electrocardiograms had a greater mortality in the treated group than in the control or referred-care group. In view of the uncertainties, it may cause more harm than good to administer lifelong drug treatment to patients with borderline or mild hypertension. The way is open to assume that prevention and treatment of hypertension by exercise, weight control, and sodium restriction may be more effective as well as less expensive than treatment with antihypertensive drugs (Kaplan, 1983; McAlister, 1983; Pickering, 1983).

EPIDEMIOLOGY OF HYPERTENSION

Elevated blood pressure is linked to several factors, including demographics, genetic and family history, anthropometrics, and other personal attributes, such as physical activity, alcohol consumption, and use of oral contraceptives. The relationship of blood pressure to these factors in the U.S. population was reported in the National Health and Nutrition Examination Survey of 1971 to 1974 (Vital and Health Statistics, Note 3, Note 4). Mean systolic blood pressure was found to increase with age; mean diastolic blood pressure increased until about age 60 and then remained relatively constant. Differences were found in both blood pressures for sex and age groups; blacks had higher systolic and diastolic blood pressures than whites, and education and family income varied inversely with systolic and diastolic blood pressures. These results are consistent with results reported by other investigators (Johnson, Epstein, & Kjelsberg, 1965).

A specialized sample from the survey of 10,419 adults aged 18 years and over was studied (Stanton, Braitman, Riley, Khoo, & Smith, 1982). This sample consisted of adults who were not being treated for hypertension and who provided dietary intake data indicating that they were not engaging in unusual dietary practices. In this sample, almost all of the explained variation appeared to be a function of age and anthropometric variables such as body mass index (wt/ht²). After controlling for effects of age and body mass index, it was found that diet, physical activity, alcohol consumption, and use of oral contraceptives did not have statistically significant effects on blood pressure. For the total sample, age and body mass index in a linear regression model accounted for 31.1% and 21% of the variance in systolic and diastolic blood pressures. Although effects of other factors cannot be excluded with certainty, it is likely that such variables as family history of hypertension might have an important effect on levels of blood pressure.

The effect of age on blood pressure varies in different societies. In industrialized societies, blood pressure increases with age, and blood pressure at one age is related to blood pressure at an earlier age (Kotchen, McKean, & Kotchen, 1982). A number of primitive societies have been identified, however, in which blood pressure does not increase with age (Page, 1980). Although individuals within those societies consume little salt, a number of other environmental differences may influence levels of blood pressure in selected primitive and industrialized societies. Body weight, for example, does not increase with age in primitive populations that do not show an increase in blood pressure (Mann, Shaffer, Anderson, & Sandstead, 1964; Severs, Gordon, Peart, & Beighton, 1980). Differences in social, psychological, and behavioral factors also may influence levels of blood pressure in both primitive and industrialized societies.

Blood pressure also is closely related to growth and maturation. Furthermore, it has not yet been demonstrated that level of blood pressure in the prepubertal child is predictive of level in the young adult (Katz, Hediger, Schall, Bowers, Barker, Autrand, Eveleth, Gruskin, & Parks, 1980). Adolescents and young adults with relatively high blood pressure, however, are at increased risk for developing hypertension. In an eight-year follow-up of high school students in Kentucky (Kotchen, Kotchen, Guthrie, Cottrill, & McKean, 1980), there were highly significant correlations between repeated measurements of both systolic and diastolic blood pressure. In addition, change in systolic blood pressure over time was positively correlated with change in body mass index. Thus, identification of adolescents and young adults with relatively high blood pressures defines a high-risk group, and preventive strategies may be useful in this group to prevent cardiovascular disease in later years.

Effect of dietary sodium intake also has been related to development of hypertension (Freis, 1976). Population studies suggest that primitive populations who ingest a diet very low in sodium and relatively high in potassium have a much lower prevalence of hypertension, and their blood pressure does not increase with age, as it does in industrialized societies where sodium is ingested in large amounts. Attempts to relate blood pressure to sodium intake within given populations, however, have not been successful. Furthermore, societies often differ vastly in factors other than dietary sodium intake (Pickering, 1980).

An additional explanation is that high sodium intake affects blood pressure of only a susceptible minority within a population. Otherwise, blood pressures of individuals within a given population should be correlated with their sodium intake, and hypertensive subjects should consume and excrete more sodium than normal subjects. Since such correlations are weak (Pickering, 1980; Simpson, 1979), heterogeneity and sensitivity to sodium intake seem more likely. Furthermore, evidence indicates that the relationship between sodium and blood pressure is heritable (Pietinen, Wong, & Altschul, 1979). The relation of 24-hour urinary sodium output to mean blood pressure in normotensive individuals with and without a family history of hypertension among first-degree relatives showed a relationship in normotensive individuals only when there was a history of hypertension among first-degree relatives. A similar relation of weight to mean blood pressure was seen in the same individuals, and weight was related to blood pressure only when there was a family history of hypertension.

GENETIC FACTORS AND FAMILY HISTORY

Numerous studies indicate that genetic factors influence levels of blood pressure. Information concerning familial associations has been obtained from the original Framingham Study (Gordon, Castelli, Hjortland, Kannel, & Dawber, 1977). In addition, a follow-up examination has been carried out with children of the original cohort who themselves are adults of approximately the age their parents were when they first entered the study (Kannel, Feinleib, McNamara, Garrison, & Castelli, 1979). Many of the same factors, such as weight, heart rate, and alcohol consumption, were found to correlate with blood pressure in both generations. The relationship of blood pressure in adult offspring showed correlations similar to those done concurrently in the usual family study, when blood pressures of parents and children are evaluated at the same time (Havlik, Garrison, Feinleib, Kannel, Castelli, & McNamara, 1979). Correlations of about .15 were found in parents and adult offspring whose families had been separated for some years. Recognizing that familial aggregation brings more than heredity, effects of shared environment confound the effect of genetic factors. Since spouses share the same home environment to a major degree, the common environment influences blood pressure. In addition, individuals of the same age, appearance, and habits tend to marry more often. These are likely explanations for correlations between spouse pairs in the Framingham Study cohort and in the offspring (Havlik et al., 1979).

Another approach to the study of genetic factors is the study of twins. This strategy involves a statistical comparison of the similarities between identical and fraternal twins. For systolic and diastolic blood pressure, the correlations for middle-aged twins were much higher for monozygotic than for dizygotic twins (Feinleib, Garrison, Fabsitz, Christian, Hrubec, Borhani, Kannel, Rosenman, Schwarz, & Wagner, 1977). Statistical analysis leads to the conclusion that approximately 60% of the variability can be attributed to heredity. Investigations using college-age twins, involving a sodium-loading and depletion protocol, produced evidence for a genetic influence on physiological factors that help regulate blood pressure (Grim, Luft, Miller, Rose, Christian, & Weinberger, 1980). Ideally, genetic markers would be found that could pinpoint those at higher risk for hypertension. Early and precise identification of high-risk individuals would strengthen preventive measures as well as guide therapeutic interventions.

PHYSIOLOGICAL FACTORS

Arterial blood pressure is regulated by cardiovascular function and renal function. Although there are neurogenic mechanisms, such as baroreceptor reflexes, that tend to keep arterial pressure within a narrow range, the ultimate control of arterial blood pressures resides more in cardiac function, tissue metabolic requirements, and renal function than in neurogenic mechanisms. An increase in tissue metabolic requirements reduces arteriolar resistance, reduces work for the heart, and increases cardiac output. Any increase in arteriolar resistance that increases arterial pressures causes greater work for the heart and a reduction in cardiac output. In addition, elevations in arterial pressure cause an increase in renal excretion of salt and water with a consequent reduction in blood volume and a decrease in venous return to the heart. When less blood is returned to the heart, less is pumped to the periphery, and arterial blood pressure returns toward original values.

Although much is known about local regulation of blood flow and systemic regulation of arterial blood pressure, it is still not entirely known which variables are regulated by what mechanism under normal conditions. Although some patients have hypertension caused by renal or endocrinologic mechanisms, the majority of patients have hypertension in which no specific cause can be identified. Such hypertension of unknown cause is called *essential hypertension*. Intrepretation of results from studies of patients with essential hypertension is complicated by the realization that many pathophysiological mechanisms contribute to elevations of arterial blood pressure. These mechanisms include renal, cardiac, vascular, endocrinologic, metabolic, and neurogenic factors and are influenced by diet, exercise, and psychological state as well as by genetic factors. Since different combinations of these pathophysiological characteristics are evident in patients, it has become apparent that essential hypertension is caused by different pathogenic mechanisms. Evidence also suggests, however, that neurogenic and renal factors contribute to the maintenance of essential hypertension in all patients. Therefore, controlling neurogenic and renal factors that maintain essential hypertension should be somewhat effective in all patients. Particular attention has been focused on neurogenic factors, since renal, cardiac, and vascular mechanisms are influenced by sympathetic nervous system activity.

The influence of neurogenic factors is particularly evident in young patients with labile hypertension or borderline levels of hypertension. Evidence that some patients with mild hypertension had increased neurogenic activity was found using head-up tilt to test for a neural component (Louis, Doyle, & Anavekar, 1973). Patients with mild hypertension had an increase in blood pressure in response to tilt and higher plasma catecholamine levels than patients with higher levels of blood pressure who had orthostatic hypotension in response to tilt. Further studies have shown that hyperdynamic circulation with modest elevation of cardiac output is common in patients with mild hypertension (Ibrahim, Tarazi, Dustan, & Bravo, 1974; Ulrych, Frohlich, Tarazi, Dustan, & Page, 1969). Several investigators (Dustan and Tarazi, 1978; Julius, Esler, & Randall, 1975; Safar, Weiss, London, Frackowiak, & Milliez, 1974; Ulrych et al., 1969) have found a relative increase in cardiopulmonary blood volume. The mechanism by which neural mechanisms may operate in hypertension involves increased adrenergic drive, which diminishes the capacity of venous reservoirs, displacing blood into the central pulmonary circulation and increasing activity of cardiac adrenergic nerves. Thus, increased cardioadrenergic drive can be demonstrated in patients with hypertension, and administration of adrenolytic drugs is often effective in reducing blood pressure to normal levels.

The role of renal function in essential hypertension is even more complex. Some forms of renovascular disease may cause hypertension, and the importance of a renopressor system is recognized in those conditions (Dustan, Tarazi, & Frolich, 1970). It seems likely, however, that the renopressor system has little significance in essential hypertension. Even so, a normal renal blood flow, glomerular filtration rate, and sodium excretion in patients with essential hypertension indicates that renal mechanisms are operating to maintain a high level of blood pressure.

Sodium balance determines body fluid volumes, influences neuroendocrine factors, and affects the activity of the sympathetic nervous system. In addition, a proportion of hypertensive patients are influenced by sodium balance, and some patients with hypertension become normotensive with salt restriction. When patients with essential hypertension were given very low or very high sodium intakes, they could be divided into two distinct groups—a salt-sensitive group and a salt-resistant group (Laragh, Case, Atlas, & Sealey, 1980). The salt-sensitive group retained more sodium on the high-sodium diet and had higher levels of blood pressure. Other studies (Lever, Beretta-Piccoli, Brown, Davies, Fraser, & Robertson, 1981) have shown that total body sodium was positively correlated with blood pressure in hypertensives but not in normal subjects. These correlations were greater for older than for younger patients. Thus, in young hypertensives, blood pressure may be more closely related to neurogenic factors, and a secondary abnormality such as a renal lesion may develop later to cause a susceptibility to high dietary sodium intake. Finally, the sodium excretory capacity and its regulatory mechanisms have been shown to be under genetic influences (Grim et al., 1980; Luft, Fineberg, Miller, Rankin, Grim, & Weinberger, 1980). Since essential hypertension is influenced by genetic factors, it is likely that sensitivity to dietary sodium intake has a genetic component (Luft, Weinberger, & Grim, 1982).

Obesity is also a risk factor for development of hypertension. Although not all obese persons are hypertensive, there is a close association between obesity and hypertension (Mujais, Tarazi, Dustan, Fouad, & Bravo, 1982). Furthermore, measures that reduce obesity also tend to reduce hypertension. The relationship between obesity and hypertension may involve metabolic and neurogenic mechanisms. It has been shown that middle-aged hypertensives tend to have high levels of plasma insulin (Berglund, Larsson, Andersson, Larsson, Svardsudd, Bjorntorp, & Wilhelmsen, 1976), and they also tend to have glucose intolerance. Thus, they have varying degrees of insulin resistance. These metabolic abnormalities are particularly evident in patients with enlargement of fat cells and distribution of fat in the upper trunk (Bjorntorp, Bengtsson, Blohme, Jonsson, Sjostrom, Tibblin, Tibblin & Wilhelmsen, 1971; Kissebah, Vydelingum, Murray, Evans, Hartz, Kalkhoff, & Adams, 1982). In addition, measurements of subscapular skin fold thickness have been found to be the best predictor of both systolic and diastolic blood pressure, whereas triceps skin fold thickness has no significant relation (Vital and Health Statistics; Note 5). The central distribution of body fat acquired in adult years, the diminished glucose tolerance, and the hypertension suggest a disturbance of adrenocorticoid secretion (O'Connell, Danforth, Horton, Salans, & Sims, 1973); however, derangements of pituitary-adrenal function in the obese hypertensive have not been studied intensively.

An additional possibility is that high levels of plasma insulin in overweight hypertensive patients may contribute to sodium retention and hypertension. Insulin can directly affect renal sodium reabsorption in human subjects (DeFronzo, Cooke, Andres, Faloona, & Davis, 1975). When glucose is maintained in blood at a normal level while infusing variable amounts of insulin, reabsorption of sodium was increased by insulin without change in filtration rate or in concentration of aldosterone in the serum. This renal action of insulin may provide an explanation for the natriuresis of fasting and the antinatriuresis of refeeding (DeFronzo, 1981). Another set of mechanisms also may contribute to retention of sodium in obese hypertensive patients. These mechanisms involve synergistic actions of thyroid hormones and catecholamines. Deprivation of food has been shown to reduce rates of turnover for norepinephrine in the hearts of rats (Landsberg & Young, 1981). In the reverse situation, overfeeding increases concentration of thyroid hormones in blood and increases the reactivity of tissues to catecholamines (Danforth, Horton, O'Connell, Sims, Burger,

Ingbar, Braverman, & Vagenakis, 1979). Thus, the catecholamine response to overfeeding may contribute directly to sodium retention and to development of hypertension in susceptible subjects following overfeeding (Landsberg & Young, 1981)

NUTRITIONAL FACTORS

A significant association between relative weight and blood pressure was reported in the Framingham Study (Kannel & Gordon, Note 6) and in the Evans County study (Tyroler, Heyden, & Hames, 1975). In both studies, it was demonstrated that overweight subjects who were normotensive at the beginning of the study were more likely to develop hypertension later on than subjects who were not overweight. Furthermore, subjects in the Framingham Study who spontaneously reduced body weight had a proportional reduction in blood pressure (Ashley & Kannel, 1974). Treatment of hypertension by weight reduction also has been applied successfully, and regaining weight was associated with an increase of the blood pressure to pre-weight-loss levels (Adlersberg, Coler, & Laval, 1946). Since obese patients have an increased risk of developing cardiovascular disease, the most logical treatment appears to be weight reduction.

Caloric intake may be the single most important nutritional consideration in the pathogenesis of hypertension. Although it is possible that increased caloric intake is associated with excessive sodium ingestion, the demonstration that weight reduction without a change in average sodium intake lowers blood pressure suggests an independent effect of total calories on blood pressure control (Reisen, Abel, Modan, Silverberg, Eliahou, & Modan, 1978). Carbohydrate intake has not been shown to differ between patients with hypertension and those with normal levels of blood pressure. Reduction of carbohydrate intake during weight loss, however, has been associated with reductions in plasma insulin levels (Bistrian, Blackburn, Flatt, Sizer, Scrimshaw, & Sherman, 1976) and in sympathetic nervous system activity (Young and Landsberg, 1977) that parallel improvements in blood pressure. Reductions in protein intake also have been associated with lower blood pressures (Muirhead, 1980). Finally, the source and type of lipids in the diet influence levels of blood pressure (Iacono, Dougherty, & Puska, 1982). Thus, the amounts and sources of calories influence levels of blood pressure.

Studies concerning the role of sodium restriction in control of blood pressure are difficult to perform. The dietary program is difficult to formulate, and patient compliance is difficult to document. Clinical trials of sodium restriction in the treatment of essential hypertension have been conducted, however, (MacGregor, Best, Can, Markandic, Elder, Sagnella, & Squires, 1982; Morgan, Gillies, Morgan, Adam, Wilson, & Carney, 1978; Parijs, Joossens, Van der Linden, Verstreken, & Amery, 1977). Each study demonstrated that relatively modest restrictions in sodium intake reduced systolic blood pressure by about 8 mmHg and diastolic blood pressure by about 6 mmHg in patients with mild hypertension. Although decreases in arterial blood pressure were modest, they were sufficient to reduce risk of cardiovascular disease. More dramatic changes in blood pressure were produced by the Kempner diet (Kempner, 1945). The Kempner diet was not just a low sodium diet, however; it was also low in protein, fat, calcium, and phosphorus, and high in potassium, magnesium, and carbohydrate. The contributions of other diet changes to the antihypertensive action of this diet may have been as important as that of reducing the sodium content.

Studies of the relationship between dietary fat and blood pressure also show significant effects (Iacono et al., 1982). When fat was limited to 25% of total energy intake and the ratio of polyunsaturated fat to saturated fat was maintained at about 1.0, blood pressure was significantly lower in healthy males and females in the 40- to 60-year age group. When the subjects resumed their usual diets, their blood pressures reverted to baseline values. Body weights of the subjects remained relatively constant in those studies, and sodium chloride intake averaged 8 to 12 grams per day. Results of these studies suggest that lowering of blood pressure by dietary linoleic acid is mediated through prostaglandins.

BEHAVIORAL FACTORS

Many studies of sympathetic nervous system activity in association with psychological stimuli have been reported in which blood pressure and heart rate are the independent variables measured. The associations between blood pressure, heart rate, and plasma norepinephrine levels have been studied during physical activity in hypertensive men (Watson, Hamilton, Reid, & Littler, 1979). In each subject, a statistically significant linear relationship was observed in the logarithm of plasma norepinephrine and systolic blood pressure. A similar relationship was observed in the logarithm of plasma norephinephrine and heart rate in most subjects. Since heart rate, systolic blood pressure, and diastolic blood pressure are not independent variables, a multiple correlation coefficient was determined, which indicated that 66% of the variance of plasma norepinephrine was associated with changes in blood pressure and heart rate. These observations suggest that plasma norepinephrine levels reflect short-term changes in sympathetic nervous system activity.

Indices of sympathetic nervous system activity in patients with mild high-renin essential hypertension, hypertensive patients with normal plasma renin activity, and normal human subjects have been compared (Esler, Julius, Zweifler, Randall, Gardiner, & DeQuattro, 1977). Plasma norepinephrine concentration was elevated in patients with high-renin hypertension, as compared to normal subjects and to hypertensive patients with normal plasma renin activity. Possible origins of the increased sympathetic nervous system activity also were investigated. These investigations included measurements of psychological factors. Hypertensive patients were found to have normal anxiety levels, as assessed by psychometric instruments. Suppressed hostility was prominent in the hypertensive patients, but only in those with elevated plasma renin activity. As a group, the patients with high-renin essential hypertension were controlled, guilt-prone, and submissive, with a high level of unexpressed anger. Results of these investigations suggest that hypertension in these patients with high-renin activity was neurogenic and possibly caused by psychological factors.

Counteracting effects of increased sympathetic nervous system activity in patients with arterial hypertension may be achieved using relaxation techniques. Several studies have shown significant reductions of blood pressure using relaxation techniques with patients who have borderline hypertension and sustained hypertension (Benson, Rosner, Marzetta, & Klemchuk, 1974; Blackwell, Bloomfield, Gartside, Robinson, Hanenson, Magenheim, Nidich, & Zigler, 1976; Blanchard, Young, & Haynes, 1975; Goldstein, Shapiro, Thanonopavrey, & Samhi, 1982; Green, Green, & Norris, 1979; Patel, 1973, 1975a, 1975b; Patel, Marmot, & Terry, 1981). Relaxation is believed to be associated with decreased sympathetic nervous system activity, and reductions in blood pressure may be the result of decreased sympathetic nervous system activity extending into other periods of the day. As noted in her chapter in this section, in addition to lowered blood pressure levels, Patel also found significant reductions in serum cholesterol and smoking behavior when group biofeedback-assisted relaxation therapy was used. Thus, these techniques may have salutary effects on other cardiovascular risk factors as well.

Behavioral factors also influence use of alcohol and tobacco, which influences levels of blood pressure and risks for cardiovascular disease. The relation of alcohol use to hypertension has become a major question for research, and cigarette smoking is associated with alcohol use. Both alcohol consumption and cigarette smoking carry independent risks for complications of cardiovascular disease. It has been found in many studies that individuals who drink relatively large amounts of alcohol tend to have higher than average levels of blood pressure (Klatsky, Friedman, Siegelaub, & Gerard, 1977; Mitchell, Morgan, Boadle, Batt, Marstrand, McNeil, Middleton, Rayner, & Lickiss, 1980). A study of 87,000 ambulatory adult subscribers to the Kaiser-Permanente Medical Care Program showed a steady rise in blood pressure among both men and women as alcohol consumption increased beyond two drinks per day. In white men and women, the prevalence of hypertension was approximately twice as great in those consuming more than six drinks per day as compared to those consuming two drinks or fewer (Klatsky et al., 1977). Further analysis showed that the alcohol–blood pressure association was not attributable to demographic characteristics, adiposity, reported salt use, cigarette smoking, or coffee consumption. Although population studies have suggested a possibly protective effect of small or intermediate amounts of alcohol against coronary heart disease (Barboriak, Rimm, Anderson, Schmidhoffer, & Tristani, 1977; Hennekens, Rosner, & Cole, 1978; Stason, Neff, Miettinen, & Jick, 1976), heavy drinking is associated with increased incidence of hospitalization for hypertension and stroke. In most studies, cigarette smokers have shown similar or slightly lower blood pressures than nonsmokers (Friedman & Siegelaub, 1980). Stopping cigarette smoking, however, has nearly as great a benefit in reducing cardiovascular risk as lowering blood pressure to normal levels.

A further influence of behavioral factors in hypertension is compliance with antihypertensive treatment. Several features of hypertension make compliance with treatment particularly difficult; the disease is generally asymptomatic, many antihypertensive drugs have unpleasant side effects, treatment is of long duration, and medical regimens are often complex. Average rates of compliance with antihypertensive medication have been reported to be approximately 65% (McKenney, Slining, Anderson, Devins, & Barr, 1973). Even with one-a-day regimens of diuretics, only 62% took at least 80% of their medication. Averaged rates, however, understate the problem of compliance. The majority of patients take almost all or almost none of their medication. Unfortunately, as indicated by medication monitors for dispensing drugs, highly erratic dispensing behavior occurred over periods of several months (Mounding, 1979; Moulding, Onstad, & Sharbaro, 1970; Norell, 1979). In particular, patients were likely to miss midday doses more often than morning or evening doses. Finally, some patients may alternate between taking too much and too little of their prescribed medications. Thus, averaged values for medication-taking behavior understate the complexity of assessing compliance with medical regimens.

Measures of compliance include self-reports (Caron & Roth, 1968), pill counts (Sackett, Haynes, Gibson, Hackett, Taylor, Roberts, & Johnson, 1979), medication monitors (Moulding, 1971), and measurements of drug levels or levels of drug metabolites in urine or blood (Gordis, Markowitz, & Lilienfeld, 1969). Comparisons of alternative compliance measures showed overestimates of compliance by self-report (Caron & Roth, 1968) and failure of pill counts to reveal erratic medication taking (McKenney et al., 1973). Clues to poor compliance include failure to keep appointments (Gordis et al., 1969) and variable effectiveness of medication in achieving desired therapeutic effects. Because of these difficulties, preventing poor compliance is a more effective strategy than correcting poor performances after treatments have begun.

Many behavioral interventions have been tested for their effects in improving compliance with medical regimens in chronic diseases. These include patient education (Haynes, 1979), increased supervision (Blackwell, 1979), self-monitoring (Haynes, Mattson, Chobanian, Dunbar, Engebretson, Garrity, Leventhal, Levine, & Levy, 1982), tailoring to daily routines, regimen simplification, special pill containers (Eshelman & Fitzloff, 1976), and monetary incentives (Dunbar, Marshall, & Hovell, 1979). When patients with poor compliance have been identified, self-monitoring techniques and special counseling have proved effective in improving compliance (Dunbar, Note 7).

Studies of compliance with medical regimens have focused most often on self-administration of medication. Compliance is equally important, however, in maintaining nonpharmacological measures to control hypertension. Although many behavioral, nutritional, and physiological interventions may be effective in controlling hypertension, their effectiveness is dependent on each patient's compliance with the prescribed regimen.

SYMPATHETIC NERVOUS SYSTEM ACTIVITY IN ESSENTIAL HYPERTENSION

The observation that plasma levels of catecholamines reflect sympathetic nervous system activity has lead many investigators to measure plasma levels of epinephrine and norepinephrine in patients with arterial hypertension. Comparative studies of plasma norepinephrine in patients with essential hypertension and in normotensive controls consistently have reported higher resting levels of norepinephrine in the hypertensive groups, but the differences often have been small and frequently have not been statistically significant (Goldstein, 1981a, 1981b). More consistent has been the observation that levels of plasma norepinephrine have increased with age (Franco-Morselli, Elghozi, Joly, DiGiuilio, & Meyer, 1977; Lake, Ziegler, Coleman, & Kopin, 1977; Sever, Osikoroska, Birch, & Tunbridge, 1978). Consequently, plasma norepinephrine concentrations in young hypertensives tend to be higher than concentrations in hypertensives who are over 50 years of age (Franco-Morselli et al., 1977). In contrast, measurements of epinephrine concentrations have given more significant results (Franco-Morselli et al., 1977). In normotensive subjects, plasma epinephrine tended to decrease with age, and concentrations were considerably raised in a significant number of patients with hypertension. Furthermore, the higher plasma epinephrine concentrations were observed in hypertensive subjects over the age of 35. Thus, the more obvious increase in plasma epinephrine levels, as compared with plasma norepinephrine, may reflect an increase in sympathoadrenomedullary activity rather than in general sympathetic nervous system activity. Also, general sympathetic nervous system activity may be more elevated in young patients than in patients over the age of 50.

Difficulties in interpreting results of studies conducted with resting subjects have been overcome by studies of subjects in orthostasis and physical exercise (Goldstein, 1981a, 1981b). Although increments in norepinephrine upon standing were similar in hypertensive and normotensive subjects, hypertensives showed much larger increments in norepinephrine in response to exercise than normotensives. For both standing and isotonic exercise, absolute changes in norepinephrine during orthostasis and exercise correlated with basal norepinephrine in the hypertensive subjects but not in those with normal arterial blood pressure. These results suggest that there exists within the hypertensive population a subgroup of patients with elevated norepinephrine levels at rest and excessive sympathetic nervous system responsiveness to exercise.

A more sophisticated approach to evaluation of sympathetic nervous system activity has been undertaken using analysis of norepinephrine kinetics (Elser, Jackman, Bobik, Leonard, Kelleher, Skews, Jennings, & Korner, 1981). Methods for studying kinetics were developed because plasma concentration of norepinephrine provides a very indirect measure of sympathetic nervous system activity. Only a small proportion of norepinephrine released from nerve terminals escapes into the plasma, because most is subject to local reuptake by the sympathetic nerves (Kopin, 1979; Paton, 1976). Furthermore, the plasma concentration of norepinephrine is affected not only by rate of appearance in plasma after release but also by rate of removal from the circulation (Esler, Jackman, Bobik, Kelleher, Jennings, Leonard, Skews, & Korner, 1979). Rates for spillover of norepinephrine into plasma and clearance from plasma can be determined using radioisotope tracer techniques. In normal subjects, disappearance of radioactively labeled norepinephrine from plasma was governed by two rates of removal. Approximately half was removed with a half-time of 2 minutes, and the remainder was removed with a half-time of approximately 33 minutes. The faster rate of removal was lengthened by a selective inhibitor of neuronal epinephrine uptake and was prolonged in patients with peripheral sympathetic nerve dysfunction. In 8 of 37 hypertensive patients, the initial rate of disappearance was lengthened beyond 2.8 minutes, which was longer than in any normal subject. Presumably, a lower rate of reuptake would expose adrenergic receptors to high local concentrations of norepinephrine. Therefore, a defect in neuronal reuptake of norepinephrine may be important in the pathogenesis of blood pressure elevation in some patients with essential hypertension.

Several experimental interventions have been studied for their effects on norepinephrine spillover rates and plasma concentration values. Administration of the tricyclic antidepressant, desipramine, lowered the norepinephrine spillover rate in normal subjects, but the plasma concentrations of norepinephrine were unchanged because the slow clearance rate was also reduced (Esler, Jackman, Leonard, Skews, Bobik, & Korner, 1981). Changing dietary caloric intake also altered both the rapid and the slow rates of clearance for norepinephrine from plasma. Normal healthy subjects on a high-calorie diet had an 81% increase in norepinephrine spillover rate and an increase in the slow clearance process, with the result that plasma concentrations of norepinephrine rose very little (Esler, 1982). The difficulty in using plasma norepinephrine measurements as an index of sympathetic nervous system activity also was demonstrated in patients treated with antihypertensive drugs (Esler, 1982). Six patients with essential hypertension who were treated for one month with a beta-adrenergic blocking agent, oxprenolol, had a rise in plasma levels of norepinephrine because of a substantial reduction in the slow clearance rate of norepinephrine. In contrast, six patients treated with clonidine, a drug that reduces secretion rates of norepinephrine, also had a rise in plasma levels of norepinephrine without any change in the slow rate for clearance of norepinephrine from plasma. Thus, plasma norepinephrine concentrations do not always follow release rate values for norepinephrine and do not reliably indicate sympathetic nervous system activity.

In general, a subgroup of patients with arterial hypertension apparently has increased sympathetic nervous system activity, but further studies are necessary to determine mechanisms governing plasma levels of epinephrine and norepinephrine. Those patients who have increased sympathetic nervous system activity are more likely to be young people with labile hypertension and with increases in blood pressure evident upon standing and during vigorous physical activity. Although plasma levels of norepinephrine are difficult to interpret as an index of sympathetic nervous system activity, patients with untreated essential hypertension tend to have plasma levels of norepinephrine that are proportional to rates of norepinephrine release from sympathetic nerve terminals (Esler, Jackman, Bobik, Leonard, Kelleher, Skews, Jennings, & Korner, 1981).

RECOMMENDATIONS FOR DIAGNOSIS, TREATMENT, AND PREVENTION OF ARTERIAL HYPERTENSION

General rules for diagnosing, treating, and preventing arterial hypertension are difficult to state, and exceptions are many. Accordingly, medical evaluation and supervision of treatment are extremely important. A review of the chapters in this section, however, will indicate general strategies that can be applied to various subgroups of patients with arterial hypertension.

Diagnosis should include medical evaluation, family history, physical characteristics, and evaluation of risk factors, as well as level of arterial blood pressure. A strong family history of arterial hypertension suggests a greater likelihood that weight control, sodium restriction, exercise, and behavioral interventions might be effective. Physical characteristics, such as age, weight, and history of physical activity, also indicate how effective nonpharmacological interventions might be. Evaluation of risk factors is important, because combinations of hyperlipidemia, cigarette smoking, diabetes mellitus, and obesity with arterial hypertension markedly increase the likelihood that a patient will suffer coronary heart disease or cerebrovascular disease in the future. Finally, the pattern of blood pressure levels and blood pressure responses to standing and vigorous exercise give some indication of contributions from neurogenic factors.

Treatment of arterial blood pressure depends on level of blood pressure at rest and removal of such primary causes as renal disease, hypersecretion of adrenal cortex or adrenal medulla, or other correctable conditions. The approach to medical treatment of patients with a diastolic blood pressure greater than 95 mmHg usually starts with antihypertensive medication. Although drug treatment in the past usually has started with a diuretic, such as chlorothiazide, many physicians now use a beta-blocking agent, such as propranolol, as the first drug administered. When arterial blood pressure has been reduced to normal levels, attempts usually are made to step down therapy in the hopes of reducing side effects and determining a minimum effective dose (Finnerty, 1981). The possibility that step-down therapy will be successful can be increased by addition of nonpharmacological interventions.

Treatment of patients with levels of diastolic blood pressure below 95 mmHg often begin with nonpharmacological interventions. In many patients, reduction of body weight and increase of physical activity will bring blood pressure down to normal values. In addition, a trial of sodium restriction may be successful in lowering blood pressure if salt intake is lowered below 1.5 grams per day. Finally, a trial of relaxation therapy may lower blood pressure to normal levels in patients who are well motivated to practice relaxation under a regular daily schedule. All of these nonpharmacological interventions may be effective in lowering blood pressures to normal levels and may reduce the need for antihypertensive medication. Indeed, the inconvenience, cost, and complications of antihypertensive medication may be undesirable in patients with low levels of arterial hypertension.

Prevention of arterial hypertension focuses on early detection of high blood pressure levels in young people, identification of individuals at high risk for arterial hypertension, and general advice to the population at large. Screening of individuals for high levels of blood pressure should start with young people who have passed puberty, because high levels of arterial blood pressure tend to persist after puberty. In these individuals, nonpharmacological interventions should be established as a way of life in an effort to prevent the necessity for antihypertensive medication. Subjects known to be at high risk for arterial hypertension include those with a strong family history and those with racial origins predisposing to arterial hypertension. Thus, blacks with a family history of hypertension are particularly susceptible to arterial hypertension and its complications. In these individuals, weight control, regular exercise, sodium restriction, and relaxation therapy may be useful interventions in delaying or preventing the necessity for antihypertensive medication. Finally, general education for the population at large should include advice to control weight, increase physical activity, restrict intake of sodium, and adopt stress management strategies. Since all of these measures could be expected to improve health and have little risk, these nonpharmacological approaches to controlling blood pressure make good common sense. There is no current evidence, however, that people will follow such general advice to the extent necessary to meaningfully influence levels of arterial blood pressure. Accordingly, our greatest efforts probably should be directed toward young people with high levels of arterial blood pressure and toward individuals at high risk for arterial hypertension. These appear to be the individuals most likely to benefit from intensive efforts at diagnosis, treatment, and prevention.

REFERENCE NOTES

1. Gordon, T., Sorlie, P., & Kannel, W. B. *Section 27, coronary heart disease atherothrombotic brain infarction. Intermittent claudication. A multivariate analysis of some factors related to their incidence: Framingham Study, 16-year follow-up.* U.S. Department of Health, Education and Welfare, Public Health Service. NIH Pub. No. 1740–0320, 1971.

2. Paringer, L. C., & Berk, A. *Costs of illness and disease, fiscal year 1975.* Report No. B1. Georgetown University, Washington, D.C. Public Services Lab. National Technical Information Service, U.S. Department of Commerce, PB-280–298, 1977.

3. Vital and Health Statistics, Series 1, No. 10b. *Plan and operation of the Health and Nutrition Examination Survey, U.S., 1971–1973.* DHEW Pub. No. (HRA) 77–1310, 1977.

4. Vital and Health Statistics, Series 1, No. 14. *Plan and operation of the Hanes I Augmentation Survey of Adults 25–74 Years, U.S., 1974–1975.* DHEW Pub. No. (PHS)78–1314, 1978.

5. Vital and Health Statistics, Series 11, No. 208. *Blood pressure levels of persons 6–74 years, U.S., 1971–1974.* DHEW Pub. No. (HRA) 78–1648, 1977.

6. Kannel, W. B., & Gordon, T. Physiological and medical concomitants of obesity: The Framingham Study. In G. A. Bray (Ed.), *Obesity in America*. NIH publication, 1979.

7. Dunbar, J. Assessment of medication compliance: A review. In R. B. Haynes, M. E. Mattson, & T. O. Engebretson (Eds.), *Patient compliance to prescribed antihypertensive medication regimens*. DHHS Pub. No. (NIH)81–2101, 1980.

REFERENCES

Adlersberg, D., Coler, H. R., & Laval, J. Effect of weight reduction on course of arterial hypertension. *Journal of the Mount Sinai Hospital,* 1946, **12**, 984–992.

Ashley, F. W., & Kannel, W. B. Relation of weight change to changes in atherogenic traits: The Framingham Study. *Journal of Chronic Diseases,* 1974, **27**, 103–114.

Barboriak, J. J., Rimm, A. A., Anderson, A. J., Schmidhoffer, M., & Tristani, F. E. Coronary artery occlusion and alcohol intake. *British Heart Journal,* 1977, **39**, 289–293.

Benson, H., Rosner, B. A., Marzetta, B. R., & Klemchuk, H. P. Decreased blood pressure in borderline hypertensive subjects who practiced meditation. *Journal of Chronic Disease,* 1974, **27**, 163–169.

Berglund, G., Larsson, B., Andersson, O., Larsson, O., Svardsudd, K., Bjorntorp, P., & Wilhelmsen, L. Body composition and glucose metabolism in hypertensive middle-aged males. *Acta Medica Scandinavica,* 1976, **200**, 163–169.

Bistrian, B. R., Blackburn, G. L., Flatt, J. P., Sizer, J., Scrimshaw, N. S., & Sherman, M. Nitrogen metabolism and insulin requirements in obese diabetic adults on a protein-sparing modified fast. *Diabetes,* 1976, **25**, 494–504.

Bjorntorp, P., Bengtsson, C., Blohme, G., Jonsson, A., Sjostrom, L., Tibblin, E., Tibblin, G., & Wilhelmsen, L. Adipose tissue fat cell size and number in relation to metabolism in randomly selected middle-aged men and women. *Metabolism,* 1971, **20**, 927–935.

Blanchard, E. B., Young, L. D., & Haynes, M. R. A simple feedback system for the treatment of elevated blood pressure. *Behavior Therapy,* 1975, **6**, 241–245.

Green, C. E., Green, A. N., & Norris, P. A. Preliminary observation of the new non-drug method for control of hypertension. *Journal of the South Carolina Medical Association,* 1979, **75**, 575–586.

Kaplan, N. M. Therapy for mild hypertension. *Journal of the American Medical Association,* 1983, **249**, 365–368.

McAlister, N. H. Should we treat mild hypertension? *Journal of the American Medical Association,* 1983, **249**, 379–383.

Patel, C., Marmot, M. G., & Terry, D. J. Controlled trial of biofeedback-aided behavioral methods in reducing mild hypertension. *British Medical Journal,* 1981, **6281**, 2005–2008.

Pickering, T. Treatment of mild hypertension and reduction of cardiovascular mortality: The "of or by" dilemma. *Journal of the American Medical Association,* 1983, **249**, 399–401.

Blackwell, B. The drug regimen and treatment compliance. In R. B. Haynes, D. W. Taylor, & D. L. Sackett (Eds.), *Compliance in health care*. Baltimore: Johns Hopkins University Press, 1979.

Blackwell, B., Bloomfield, S., Gartside, P., Robinson, A., Hanenson, I., Magenheim, H., Nidich, S., & Zigler, R. Transcendental meditation in hypertension: Individual response patterns. *Lancet,* 1976, **1**, 223–226.

Blanchard, E. B., Young, L. D., & Haynes, M. A. A simple feedback system for the treatment of elevated blood pressure. *Behavior Therapy,* 1975, **6**, 241–245.

Caron, H. S., & Roth, H. P. Patients' cooperation with medical regimens. *Journal of the American Medical Association,* 1968, **203**, 922–926.

Danforth, E., Jr., Horton, E. S., O'Connell, M., Sims, E. A. H., Burger, A. G., Ingbar, S. H., Braverman, L., & Vagenakis, A. G. Dietary induced alterations in thyroid hormone metabolism during overnutrition. *Journal of Clinical Investigation,* 1979, **64**, 1336–1347.

DeFronzo, R. A. The effect of insulin on renal sodium metabolism: A review with clinical implications. *Diabetologia,* 1981, **21**, 165–171.

DeFronzo, R. A., Cooke, R. A., Andres, R., Faloona, G. R., & Davis, P. J. The effect of insulin on renal handling of sodium, potassium, calcium and phosphate in man. *Journal of Clinical Investigation,* 1975, **55,** 845–855.

Dunbar, J. M., Marshall, G. D., & Hovell, M. F. Behavioral strategies for improving compliance. In R. B. Haynes, D. W. Taylor, & D. L. Sackett, (Eds.), *Compliance in health care.* Baltimore: Johns Hopkins University Press, 1979.

Dustan, H. P., & Tarazi, R. C. Cardiogenic hypertension. *Annual Reviews of Medicine,* 1978, **29,** 485–493.

Dustan, H. P., Tarazi, R. C., & Frohlich, E. D. Functional correlates of plasma renin activity in hypertensive patients. *Circulation,* 1970, **41,** 555–567.

Eshelman, F. N., & Fitzloff, J. Effect of packaging on patient compliance with antihypertensive medication. *Current Therapeutic Research,* 1976, **20,** 215–219.

Esler, M. Assessment of sympathetic nervous function in humans from noradrenaline plasma kinetics. *Clinical Science,* 1982, **62,** 247–254.

Esler, M., Jackman, G., Bobik, A., Kelleher, D., Jennings, G., Leonard, P., Skews, H., & Korner, P. Determination of norepinephrine apparent release rate and clearance in humans. *Life Sciences,* 1979, **25,** 1461–1470.

Esler, M., Jackman, G., Bobik, A., Leonard, P., Kelleher, D., Skews, H., Jennings, G., & Korner, P. Norepinephrine kinetics in essential hypertension: Defective neuronal uptake of norepinephrine in some patients. *Hypertension,* 1981, **3,** 149–156.

Esler, M., Jackman, G., Leonard, P., Skews, H., Bobik, A., & Korner, P. Effect of norepinephrine uptake blockers on norepinephrine kinetics. *Clinical Pharmacology and Therapeutics,* 1981, **29,** 12–20.

Esler, M., Julius, S., Zweifler, A., Randall, O., Harburg, E., Gardiner, H., & DeQuattro, V. Mild high-renin essential hypertension. *New England Journal of Medicine,* 1977, **296,** 405–411.

Feinleib, M., Garrison, R. J., Fabsitz, R., Christian, J. C., Hrubec, Z., Borhani, N. O., Kannel, W. B., Rosenman, R., Schwarz, J. T., & Wagner, J. O. The NHLBI twin study of cardiovascular disease risk factors: Methodology and summary of results. *American Journal Epidemiology,* 1977, **106,** 284–295.

Finnerty, F. A. Step-down therapy in hypertension: Importance in long-term management. *Journal of the American Medical Association,* 1981, **246,** 2593–2596.

Franco-Morselli, R., Elghozi, J. L., Joly, E., DiGiuilio, S., & Meyer, P. Increased plasma adrenaline concentrations in benign essential hypertension. *British Medical Journal,* 1977, **2,** 1251–1254.

Freis, E. D. Salt, volume and the prevention of hypertension. *Circulation,* 1976, **53,** 589–595.

Friedman, G. D., & Siegelaub, A. B. Changes after quitting cigarette smoking. *Circulation,* 1980, **61,** 716–723.

Goldstein, D. S. Plasma norepinephrine on essential hypertension: A study of the studies. *Hypertension,* 1981, **3,** 48–52. (a)

Goldstein, D. S. Plasma norepinephrine during stress in essential hypertension. *Hypertension,* 1981, **3,** 551–556. (b)

Goldstein, J. B., Shapiro, D., Thanonopavrey, E., & Samhi, M. P. Comparison of drug and behavioral treatments of essential hypertension. *Health Psychology,* 1982, **1,** 7–26.

Gordis, L., Markowitz, M., & Lilienfeld, A. M. Studies in the epidemiology and preventability of rheumatic fever: IV. A quantitative determination of compliance in children on oral penicillin prophylaxis. *Pediatrics,* 1969, **43,** 173–182.

Gordon T., Castelli, W. P., Hjortland, M. C., Kannel, W. B., & Dawber, T. B. Predicting coronary heart disease in middle-aged and older persons: The Framingham Study. *Journal of the American Medical Association,* 1977, **238,** 497–499.

Green, C. E., Green, A. N., & Norris, P. A. Preliminary observation of the new non-drug method for control of hypertension. *Journal of the South Carolina Medical Association,* 1979, **75,** 575–586.

Grim, C. E., Luft, F. C., Miller, J. Z., Rose, R. J., Christian, J. J., & Weinberger, M. H. An approach to the evaluation of genetic influences on factors that regulate blood pressure in man. *Hypertension,* 1980, **2**(Suppl. I), 1–39.

Havlik, R. J., Garrison, R. J., Feinleib, M., Kannel, W. B., Castelli, W. P., & McNamara, P. M. Blood pressure aggregation in families. *American Journal of Epidemiology*, 1979, **110**, 304.

Haynes, R. B. Strategies to improve compliance with referrals, appointments, and prescribed medical regimens. In R. B. Haynes, D. W. Taylor, & D. L. Sackett (Eds.), *Compliance in health care*. Baltimore: Johns Hopkins University Press, 1979.

Haynes, R. N., Mattson, M. E., Chobanian, A. V., Dunbar, H. M., Engebretson, T. O., Garrity, T. F., Leventhal, H., Levine, R. J., & Levy, R. L. Management of patient compliance in the treatment of hypertension: Report of the NHLBI Working Group. *Hypertension*, 1982, **4**, 415–423.

Helgeland, A. Treatment of mild hypertension: A five-year controlled drug trial: The Oslo Study. *American Journal of Medicine*, 1980, **69**, 725–732.

Hennekens, C. H., Rosner, B., & Cole, D. S. Daily alcohol consumption and fatal coronary heart disease. *American Journal of Epidemiology*, 1978, **107**, 196–200.

Hypertension Detection and Follow-up Program Cooperative Group. Five-year findings of the hypertension detection and follow-up program: I. Reduction in mortality of persons with high blood pressure, including mild hypertension. *Journal of the American Medical Association*, 1979, **242**, 2562–2571.

Iacono, J. M., Dougherty, R. M., & Puska, P. Reduction of blood pressure associated with dietary polyunsaturated fat. *Hypertension*, 1982, **3**, 34–42.

Ibrahim, M. M., Tarazi, R. C., Dustan, H. P., & Bravo, E. L. Cardioadrenergic factor in essential hypertension. *American Heart Journal*, 1974, **88**, 724–732.

Johnson, B. C., Epstein, F. H., & Kjelsberg, M. O. Distributions and familial studies of blood pressure and serum cholesterol levels in a total community—Tecumseh, Michigan. *Journal of Chronic Diseases*, 1965, **18**, 147–160.

Julius, S., Esler, M. D., & Randall, O. S. Role of the autonomic nervous system in mild human hypertension. *Clinical Science and Molecular Medicine*, 1975, **48**(Suppl. 2), 243s–252s.

Kannel, W. B., Feinleib, M., McNamara, P. M., Garrison, R. J., & Castelli, W. P. An investigation of coronary heart disease in families: The Framingham Offspring Study. *American Journal of Epidemiology*, 1979, **110**, 281–290.

Kannel, W. B., Wolf, P., & Dawber, T. R. Hypertension and cardiac impairments increase stroke risk. *Geriatrics*, 1978, **33**, 71–83.

Kaplan, N. M. Therapy for mild hypertension. *Journal of the American Medical Association*, 1983, **249**, 365–368.

Katz, S. H., Hediger, M. L., Schall, J. L., Bowers, E. F., Barker, W. F., Autrand, S., Eveleth, P. B., Gruskin, A. B., & Parks, J. S. Blood pressure, growth, and maturation from childhood through adolescence: Mixed longitudinal analysis of the Philadelphia blood pressure project. *Hypertension*, 1980, **2**(Suppl. I), I55–I69.

Kempner, W. Treatment of kidney disease and hypertensive vascular disease with rice diet. *North Carolina Medical Journal*, 1945, **5**, 125–133.

Kissebah, A. H., Vydelingum, N., Murray, R., Evans, D. J., Hartz, A. J., Kalkhoff, R., & Adams, P. W. Relation of body fat distribution to metabolic complications of obesity. *Journal of Clinical Endocrinology and Metabolism*, 1982, **54**, 254–260.

Klatsky, A. L., Friedman, G. D., Siegelaub, A. B., & Gerard, M. J. Alcohol consumption and blood pressure: Kaiser-Permanente Multiphasic Health Examination data. *New England Journal of Medicine*, 1977, **296**, 1194–1200.

Kopin, I. J. Biochemical assessment of peripheral adrenergic activity. In D. M. Paton (Ed.), *The release of catecholamines from adrenergic neurons*. Oxford: Pergamon Press, 1979.

Kotchen, J. M., Kotchen, T. A., Guthrie, G. P., Cottrill, C. M., & McKean, H. E. Correlates of adolescent blood pressure at 5 year follow-up. *Hypertension*, 1980, **2**(Suppl. I), I124–I129.

Kotchen, J. M., McKean, H. E., & Kochen, T. A. Blood pressure effects of aging. *Hypertension*, 1982, **4**(Suppl. III), III128–III134.

Lake, C. R., Ziegler, M. G., Coleman, M. D., & Kopin, I. J. Age-adjusted plasma norepinephrine levels are similar in normotensive and hypertensive subjects. *New England Journal of Medicine*, 1977, **296**, 208–209.

Landsberg, L., & Young, J. B. Diet-induced changes in sympathoadrenal activity: Implications for thermogenesis. *Life Sciences*, 1981, **28**, 1801–1819.

Laragh, J. H., Case, D. B., Atlas, S. A., & Sealey, J. E. Captopril compared with other antirenin system agents in hypertensive patients: Its triphasic effects on blood pressure and its use to identify and treat the renin factor. *Hypertension,* 1980, **2,** 586–593.

Lever, A. F., Beretta-Piccoli, C., Brown, J. J., Davies, D. L., Fraser, R., & Robertson, J. I. S. Sodium and potassium in essential hypertension. *British Medical Journal,* 1981, **283,** 463–468.

Louis, W. J., Doyle, A. E., & Anavekar, S. Plasma norepinephrine levels in essential hypertension. *New England Journal of Medicine,* 1973, **288,** 599–601.

Luft, F. C., Fineberg, N. S., Miller, J. Z., Rankin, L. I., Grim, C. E., & Weinberger, M. H. The effects of age, race and heredity on glomerular filtration rate in normal man. *American Journal of the Medical Sciences,* 1980, **279,** 15–24.

Luft, F. C., Weinberger, M. H., & Grim, C. E. Sodium sensitivity and resistance in normotensive humans. *American Journal of Medicine,* 1982, **72,** 726–736.

MacGregor, G. A., Best, F. E., Can, J. M., Markandic, N. D., Elder, D. M., Sagnella, S. A., & Squires, M. Double-blind randomized cross-over trial of moderate sodium restriction in essential hypertension. *Lancet,* 1982, **1,** 351–354.

Management Committee of the Australian Hypertension Trial. Initial results of the Australian Trial in Mild Hypertension. *Clinical Science,* 1979, **57**(Suppl. 5), 449s–452s.

Management Committee of the Australian Therapeutic Trial in Mild Hypertension. Untreated mild hypertension. *Lancet,* 1982, **1,** 185–191.

Mann, G. V., Shaffer, R. D., Anderson, R. S., & Sandstead, A. H. Cardiovascular disease in the Masai. *Journal of Atherosclerotic Research,* 1964, **4,** 289–312.

McAlister, N. H. Should we treat mild hypertension? *Journal of the American Medical Association,* 1983, **249,** 379–383.

McKenney, J. M., Slining, J. M., Anderson, H. R., Devins, D., & Barr, M. Effect of clinical pharmacy services on patients with essential hypertension. *Circulation,* 1973, **48,** 1104–1111.

Mitchell, P. I., Morgan, M. J., Boadle, D. J., Batt, J. E., Marstrand, J. L., McNeil, H. P., Middleton, C., Rayner, K., & Lickiss, J. N. Role of alcohol in the aetiology of hypertension. *Medical Journal of Australia,* 1980, **2,** 198–200.

Morgan, T., Gillies, A., Morgan, G., Adam, W., Wilson, M., & Carney, S. Hypertension treated by salt restriction. *Lancet,* 1978, **1,** 227–230.

Moulding, T. S. The medication monitor for studying the self-administration of oral contraceptives. *American Journal of Obstetrics and Gynecology,* 1971, **110,** 1143–1144.

Moulding, T. S. The unrealized potential of the medication monitor. *Clinical Pharmacology and Therapeutics,* 1979, **25,** 131–136.

Moulding, T., Onstad, G. D., & Sharbaro, J. Supervision of outpatient drug therapy with the medication monitor. *Annals of Internal Medicine,* 1970, **73,** 559–564.

Muirhead, E. E. Antihypertensive functions of the kidneys. *Hypertension,* 1980, **2,** 444–464.

Mujais, S. K., Tarazi, R. C., Dustan, H. P., Fouad, F. M., & Bravo, E. L. Hypertension in obese patients: Hemodynamics and volume studies. *Hypertension,* 1982, **4,** 84–92.

Multiple Risk Factor Intervention Trial (MRFIT) Research Group. Risk factor changes and mortality results. *Journal of the American Medical Association,* 1982, **248,** 1465–1477.

Norell, S. E. Improving medication compliance: A randomized clinical trial. *British Medical Journal,* 1979, **2,** 1031–1033.

O'Connell, M., Danforth, E., Jr., Horton, E. S., Salans, L., & Sims, E. A. H. Experimental obesity in man: III. Adrenocortical function. *Journal of Clinical Endocrinology and Metabolism,* 1973, **6,** 323–329.

Page, L. B. Dietary sodium and blood pressure: Evidence from human studies. In R. K. Lauer & R. B. Shekelle (Eds.), *Childhood prevention of atherosclerosis and hypertension.* New York: Raven Press, 1980.

Parijs, J., Joossens, J. V., Van der Linden, L., Verstreken, G., & Amery, A. Moderate sodium restriction and diuretics in the treatment of hypertension. *American Heart Journal,* 1977, **85,** 22–34.

Patel, C. Yoga and biofeedback in the management of hypertension. *Lancet,* 1973, **2,** 1053–1055.

Patel, C. 12-month followup of yoga and biofeedback in the management of hypertension. *Lancet,* 1975, **1,** 62–65. (a)

Patel, C. Yoga and biofeedback in the management of hypertension. *Journal of Psychosomatic Research,* 1975, **19,** 355–360. (b)

Patel, C., Marmot, M. G., & Terry, D. J. Controlled trial of biofeedback-aided behavioral methods in reducing mild hypertension. *British Medical Journal,* 1981, **6281,** 2005–2008.

Paton, D. M. *The mechanism of neuronal and extraneuronal transport of catecholamines.* New York: Raven Press, 1976.

Pickering, G. W. Salt intake and essential hypertension. *Cardiovascular Reviews and Reports,* 1980, **1,** 13–17.

Pickering, T. Treatment of mild hypertension and reduction of cardiovascular mortality: The "of or by" dilemma. *Journal of the American Medical Association,* 1983, **249,** 399–401.

Pietinen, P. I., Wong, O., & Altschul, A. M. Electrolyte output, blood pressure, and family history of hypertension. *American Journal of Clinical Nutrition,* 1979, **32,** 997–1005.

Reisen, E., Abel, R., Modan, M., Silverberg, D. S., Eliahou, H. E., & Modan, B. Effect of weight loss without salt restriction on the reduction of blood pressure in overweight hypertensive patients. *New England Journal of Medicine,* 1978, **298,** 1–6.

Sackett, D. L., Haynes, R. B., Gibson, E. S., Hackett, B. C., Taylor, D. W., Roberts, R. S., & Johnson, A. L. Randomized clinical trial of strategies for improving medication compliance in primary hypertension. *Lancet,* 1979, **1,** 1205–1207.

Safar, M., Weiss, Y. A., London, G. M., Frackowiak, R. F., & Milliez, P. L. Cardiopulmonary blood volume in borderline hypertension. *Clinical Science and Molecular Medicine,* 1974, **47,** 153–164.

Severs, P. S., Gordon, D., Peart, W. S., & Beighton, P. Blood pressure and its correlates in urban and tribal Africa. *Lancet,* 1980, **2,** 60–64.

Severs, P. S., Osikowska, B., Birch, M., & Tunbridge, R. D. G. Plasma noradrenaline in essential hypertension. *Lancet,* 1978, **1,** 1078–1081.

Simpson, F. O. Salt and hypertension: A skeptical review of the evidence. *Clinical Science,* 1979, **57**(Suppl. 5), 463s–480s.

Stanton, J. L., Braitman, L. E., Riley, A. M., Khoo, C. S., & Smith, J. Demographic, dietary, life style, and anthropometric correlates of blood pressure. *Hypertension,* 1982, **4**(Suppl. III), III135–III142.

Stason, W. B., Neff, R. K., Miettinen, O. S., & Jick, H. Alcohol consumption and nonfatal myocardial infarction. *American Journal of Epidemiology,* 1976, **104,** 603–608.

Tyroler, H. A., Heyden, S., & Hames, C. G. Weight and hypertension: Evans County studies of blacks and whites. In O. Paul (Ed.), *Epidemiology and control of hypertension.* Stuttgart: Thieme, 1975.

Ulrych, M., Frohlich, E. D., Tarazi, R. C., Dustan, H. P., & Page, I. H. Cardiac output and distribution of blood volume in central and peripheral circulations in hypertensive and normotensive man. *British Heart Journal,* 1969, **31,** 570–574.

U.S. Department of Health and Human Services (DHHS), Public Health Service. *Health United States, 1980, with prevention profile.* DHHS Pub. No. (PHS)81–1232. Washington, D.C.: U.S. Government Printing Office, 1981.

Veterans Administration Cooperative Study Group on Antihypertensive Agents. Effects of treatment on morbidity in hypertension: II. Results in patients with diastolic blood pressure averaging 90 through 114 mmHg. *Journal of the American Medical Association,* 1970, **213,** 1143–1152.

Walker, S., & Duncan, D. B. Estimation of the probability of an event of a function of several independent variables. *Biometrika,* 1967, **54,** 167–179.

Watson, R. D. S., Hamilton, C. A., Reid, J. L., & Littler, W. A. Changes in plasma norepinephrine, blood pressure and heart rate during physical activity in hypertensive men. *Hypertension,* 1979, **1,** 342–346.

Young, J. B., & Landsberg, L. Suppression of sympathetic nervous system during fasting. *Science,* 1977, **196,** 1473–1475.

CHAPTER 51

RATIONALE FOR INTERVENTION ON BLOOD PRESSURE IN CHILDHOOD AND ADOLESCENCE

WILLIAM R. HARLAN

University of Michigan Medical School

Practical importance attends the elaboration of behavioral factors related to blood pressure in childhood and adolescence. Persistent elevation of blood pressure is an important risk factor for the development of cardiovascular, cerebrovascular, and renal diseases, which are the major causes of mortality and morbidity in industrialized societies. Recent intervention trials in adults clearly indicate the value of lowering elevated blood pressure with drug therapy, and there has also been notable success in development of pilot preventive approaches that rely on change in personal behavior rather than on drugs (Veterans Administration, 1970; Hypertension Detection, 1979; Management Committee, 1980). The current conventional strategy for treatment of hypertension in adults is identification and pharmacological therapy. The strategy for the future should be identification of those at risk for hypertension and prevention through hygienic, nonpharmacological means. Hygienic approaches that rely on developing lifelong behaviors would be most effectively introduced early in life and would likely be more efficacious therapeutically. Identification of young individuals at high risk for development of sustained blood pressure elevations (hypertension) carries the potential for early behavioral intervention and prevention of both hypertension and its vascular complications without the use of pharmacological therapy.

Determination of factors that convey or increase risk for high blood pressure have research as well as practical implications. Identification of behavioral factors related to blood pressure may provide new leads and hypotheses regarding the psychological mechanisms that control blood pressure. Persistent hypertension is conceived as resulting from disordered or aberrant control of the interlinking neurological, endocrinologic, and cardiovascular systems that normally regulate blood pressure. In adults and after progression of disease, these mechanisms and their interactions are often perverted by organ damage. Delineation of factors in the early years of life, however, has greater promise of providing new etiologic leads because compensating mechanisms and organ damage have not obscured pathogenetic mechanisms.

This chapter provides a scientific background for evaluating blood pressure in the young and a rationale for behavioral intervention on factors associated with high blood pressure. The natural history of blood pressure in childhood and adolescence is described, and the variables associated with levels of systolic and diastolic blood pressure are identified and evaluated. Although the primary focus is on personal behavioral characteristics, these are placed in the context of genetic and structural determinants of blood pressure, even though

Preparation of this chapter was supported in part by NHLBI Grant HL28094-01.

these latter features cannot be altered. This perspective is used to provide a quantitative assessment of the role of behavioral factors.

Behavioral variables are broadly defined in this review as observable (and potentially measurable) responses by individuals to external situations. Often, the response or behavior can be selected or controlled by the individual—for example, food selection, cigarette usage, physical activity. In many instances, the environment of the individual is not under his or her control but nonetheless calls for a personal behavioral response. Examples include ambient environment (noise and air pollution) and social situations that are necessary but not selected, such as work situations, socioeconomic changes, and geographic mobility. Both types of situations evoke individual behaviors that may have implications for blood pressure.

It should be appreciated that blood pressure itself can be and is defined as a behavioral variable. One of the measurable responses to psychological and physiological stress is a transient increase in blood pressure (and pulse), and this may be the basis for assessment of responsiveness in polygraph tests and physical exercise. Such transient and situational elevations of blood pressure are common and must be differentiated from sustained elevations of pressure, which are defined as high blood pressure or hypertension. To distinguish persistent blood pressure elevations, it is necessary to make multiple measurements over a period of weeks to months unless the levels are extremely high. A single blood pressure, particularly one recorded in a unique and perhaps threatening situation, is subject to considerable variability and may not characterize an individual's usual blood pressure level. This is true of young people and adults. The circumstances of blood pressure recording and the instruments and methodology, which are important, are covered in a report from the American Heart Association (AHA Committee Report, 1980). The standards described in this report should be used in both clinical and investigative situations, and particular attention is directed to its discussion of pediatric blood pressure recording.

In sequence, this chapter's discussion of pediatric blood pressure addresses the following issues: changes in blood pressure with age, longitudinal consistency of blood pressure, and nutritional and psychological factors associated with blood pressure and blood pressure change.

BLOOD PRESSURE CHANGES WITH AGE AND GROWTH

In all societies, whether preindustrial (developing) or industrial, blood pressure increases in the individual from infancy through early childhood. This observation is based on cross-sectional studies, but the universal finding in all populations suggests that the increase is a normal physiological accompaniment to individual growth and development. Systolic and diastolic pressures are essentially the same for boys and girls at each age during infancy and childhood, and the increments in pressures follow similar patterns in societies with very diverse cultural and nutritional habits (Cornoni-Huntley, Harlan, & Leaverton, 1979; Harlan, Cornoni-Huntley, & Leaverton, 1979; NHLBI, 1977; Oliver, Cohen, & Neel, 1975; Szklo, 1979; Beaglehcle, Salmond, & Eyles, 1977). Blood pressure changes are closely related to age and stature, and these variables are, in turn, highly correlated. These age-related blood pressure increments in early childhood have been interpreted as reflecting another, generally unmeasured feature of the cardiovascular system—blood volume and vascular capacity, which expands in response to growth and is directly related to stature. These changes are considered a physiological response to normal growth and development, and blood pressure correlations are more robust with assessments of growth (such as bone age) than with chronological age (Cornoni-Huntley et al., 1979; Harlan et al., 1979).

In infancy, blood pressure increases rapidly in the first 6 weeks following birth and remains relatively constant thereafter until 4 to 6 years of age. The trends in blood pressure are usefully displayed in the blood pressure curves from the report of the NHLBI Task Force on Blood Pressure Control in Children (Figure 51.1). Systolic and diastolic pressures

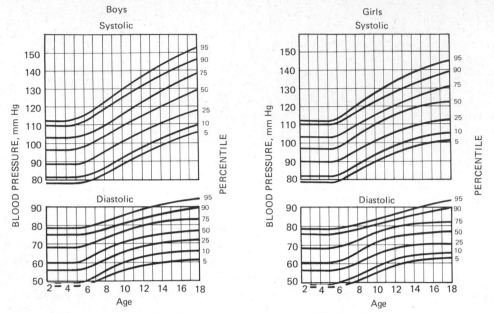

Figure 51.1 Percentiles of blood pressure in the United States. (Reprinted from National Heart, Lung and Blood Institute: Report of the Task Force on Blood Pressure Control in Children. *Pediatrics,* 1977, **59**(Suppl.), 797.)

are plotted by percentiles for each age for boys and girls, ages 2 to 18 years. Similar age trends for blood pressures have been found in other studies, including the National Health Examination Survey (Cornoni-Huntley et al., 1979; Harlan et al., 1979), but the absolute levels differ somewhat because of differences among surveys in recording of blood pressure and in handling of subjects. No important blood pressure differences are found between boys and girls through puberty. During adolescence, however, systolic pressure is higher in males than in females, and this difference persists through adult life until age 50. In the United States, no consistent or significant differences are found between the blood pressures of white and black youths through age 18 years, although black males and females have consistently higher pressures throughout adulthood after 18 years of age. The blood pressure percentiles (Figure 51.1) in late adolescence document that plots of the higher percentiles (75th, 90th, and 95th) continue to increase with the same slope, whereas those of the 50th and lower percentiles have a more gradual increment or plateau between 14 and 18 years of age. The increases that occur in American adolescents when growth and development are complete contrast with findings of no change in adolescents of nonindustrialized countries or traditional societies.

The display of blood pressure percentiles is useful because it permits one to rank a specific individual within his or her peer group with respect to systolic or diastolic pressure. This method of presentation is familiar to those caring for pediatric patients in whom weight, height, and weight by height graphs are used to assess growth and development. Both blood pressure charts and height and weight charts are derived from cross-sectional studies, but there are important differences between the inferences that can be drawn from the two types of charts. For weight and stature, the normal individual has a strong tendency to track over time—that is, remain at the same relative rank within the peer group while undergoing growth-related changes in weight and height. Therefore, a youth at the 75th percentile for height at 12 years would likely be at or near that percentile at 18 years. Correlation coefficients of .80 are common. Blood pressure is considerably more variable, however, both in the short term and the long term, and the prediction of future blood pressures based on current measurements is more limited.

Blood pressure does track; there is a consistent, statistically significant rank-order correlation in blood pressures when groups are followed longitudinally. This correlation is less than .20 before 6 months, is .20 during childhood, and increases in adolescence to .40 and to .60 to .70 in adulthood. Therefore, blood pressure stability over time varies during childhood, adolescence, and adulthood, and the predictions that can be made about future pressures become progressively better as age increases. The implications for intervention should be more conservatively drawn in childhood than in adolescence, and repeated measurements assume greater importance with blood pressure than with weight and height, which have less measurement variability.

In all age ranges, greater correlations are found with systolic pressure and when basal, rather than casual, blood pressures are compared (Harlan, Oberman, Mitchell, & Graybiel, 1973). Basal blood pressures are recorded in the supine position after a period of rest and usually in the fasting state, whereas casual pressures are measured without special preparation of the subject and correspond more closely to those recorded in the usual clinical situation. Basal pressures are lower than casual pressures, and the improved correlation over time relates to minimizing the biological variability attributable to excitement, physical activity preceding measurement, diurnal changes, and other physiological stimuli. Although basal pressures provide better prediction, their use is limited because the practitioner usually cannot control the examining situation.

EVALUATION OF BLOOD PRESSURE IN CHILDHOOD AND ADOLESCENCE

Blood pressure tracking is a useful concept that can identify adolescents in the highest percentiles, who are at higher risk of developing high blood pressure. When percentile ranking is combined with other variables, it is possible to define a group that is more likely to have higher pressures in the future and is likely to benefit from institution of hygiene measures to reduce pressure and to prevent the anticipated increases with age. Care should be taken to avoid incorrect or premature labeling during the assessment of individuals initially found to be in the upper percentiles. Labeling someone as hypertensive might result in psychological, social, and employment harm that can have a lifetime effect (Bloom & Monterossa, 1981; Stenn, Noce, & Buck, 1981). Blood pressure is highly variable, and about 30% to 40% of individuals in the highest quintile on the first examination will be found to be in lower quintiles on subsequent examination. Second, there is no expert consensus and no valid epidemiologic or clinical studies that define hypertensive levels during childhood or adolescence and predict subsequent vascular mortality or morbidity. Studies that link blood pressure levels to subsequent mortality and morbidity are confined to adults, and even in that age group, considerable difference of opinion continues regarding levels that require treatment (140/90 mmHg or 150/100 mmHg) (Fries, 1982).

The diagnosis of high blood pressure at all ages is based on persistent elevation of blood pressure and requires multiple determinations of pressure on several occasions to establish the persistence of elevated pressure. A suggested approach (Figure 51.2) is to record a single pressure initially and then to repeat at annual or biennial intervals. If the pressure is below the 75th percentile for age (Figure 51.1), no further evaluation is needed until the next examination. If it is at or above the 75th percentile, several pressures should be recorded on each of at least three separate visits (preferably over an interval of weeks to months) and the mean blood pressures should be determined for each visit and for all visits. During these evaluations, no actual diagnosis is made. A consistently high pressure is defined as an average pressure at or above the 90th percentile for either systolic or diastolic pressure. Youths evaluated in this manner should not be labeled as hypertensive unless the mean is greater than 150/100 mmHg. During the period of rapid growth and

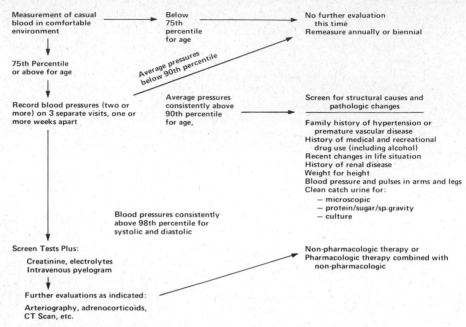

Figure 51.2 A clinical algorithm for evaluating blood pressure in children and adolescents.

maturation (ages 6 to 14 years) stature should be taken into consideration, because rapid growth may be associated with higher pressures than would be inferred from chronological age. In this situation, height can be used to define precocious growth, and tables are available that take height into account (Voors, Webber, Frerichs, & Berenson, 1977). For youths persistently at or above the 90th percentile, an evaluation of contributing factors should be undertaken. This includes hereditary factors, alterable behaviors, environmental influences, and structural abnormalities that may cause secondary hypertension.

Before examining the behavioral factors, two questions should be addressed: What patients require evaluation for the potential presence of pathological, nonbehavioral causes of hypertension, and what is an efficient and effective approach to this evaluation? The evaluation should be guided by the generalization that the younger the patient and the higher the pressure, the more likely one is to find underlying organic pathology. In childhood, perhaps a quarter to a half of children with pressures consistently at or above the 95th percentile will have demonstrable structural, functional pathology (Loggie, 1975). In adolescence, this rate declines, and in late adolescence, the proportion is probably 10% or less (Berenson, Voors, Webber, Frank, Farris, Tobian, & Aristimuno, 1983; Loggie, 1975). Children or adolescents with pressures consistently above the 98th percentile are more likely to have organic pathology that requires extensive laboratory investigation. No absolute rules regarding laboratory investigation can be stated, but the algorithm presented in Figure 51.2 offers a useful approach that is financially and medically conservative. A detailed discussion of these tests and procedures is beyond the scope of this chapter, but one should recognize clues to potential organic etiology for hypertension. Negative findings on the historical items (family history of hypertension, lean habitus, and drug use), for example, may heighten suspicion and persuade one to pursue laboratory and radiological investigation. During these studies and subsequent behavioral therapy, it is perhaps better to label the youth as at risk for high blood pressure rather than as hypertensive. This evaluation is not directed solely toward determination of structural causes for hypertension; a more important and more useful goal is identification of potentially alterable influences on blood pressure, which will be described in subsequent sections. Correction or modification of these factors is preferable to pharmacological therapy, although those who are unresponsive to behavioral therapy may require drugs (Berenson et al., 1983).

FACTORS RELATED TO BLOOD PRESSURE LEVELS

Genetic Influence

To put environmental and behavioral variables into perspective, it is useful first to define and quantify genetic contributions to blood pressure determination. Although genetic factors cannot be altered directly by intervention, there is usually a genetic–environmental interaction, and the genetic influence may be diminished by blunting of the environmental interaction. Studies of population cohorts, families, and monozygotic and dizygotic twins confirm the importance of familial and genetic factors in determining blood pressure (Annest, Sing, Biron, & Mongeau, 1979; Daughterty, Miller, Weinberger, & Grim, 1982; Grim, Luft, Miller, Rose, Christian, & Weinberger, 1980; Havlik & Feinleib, 1982).

In families, both genes and environment are shared, and most evaluations seek to separate the two effects. Such studies may be summarized as demonstrating that genetic factors are more important than the shared environment of the family, although assortive mating (the marriage of individuals possessing similar characteristics) and household environment (food, noise, etc.) also contribute to blood pressure levels. The quantification of the hereditability of blood pressure is difficult, as the genetic model that best explains the experimental observations in humans implicates the influence of several, perhaps many, genes; it is a polygenetic model. Comparisons of monozygotic and dizygotic twins suggest that approximately 60% of blood pressure variability may be attributed to heredity (Havlik & Feinleib, 1982). Estimates using other models indicate that 45% of blood pressure variability may be explained by nonshared environment (Annest et al., 1979). These estimates, which are generally concordant, indicate that approximately half of blood pressure variability is determined by familial influences, with the major factor being genetic.

These genetic factors and the nature of their interaction with the environment remain undefined. Genetically determined response to dietary sodium has been explored most extensively. Studies on twins reveal hormonal differences in response to sodium loading (Daughterty et al., 1982; Grim et al., 1980). The influence of weight on blood pressure may depend on inherited characteristics, and a recently described phenomenon—membrane cotransport of sodium—may represent a genetic marker for the differential responses to sodium loading or obesity (Canessa, Adragna, Solomon, Connolly, & Tosteson, 1980; Woods, Falk, Pittman, Klemmer, Watson, & Namboodiri, 1982). These observations should be considered preliminary, but the search for genetic markers and the elaboration of their interaction with environmental factors have important practical implications for prevention. If individuals could be identified as having a quantitatively different response to common environmental influences, then a specific and individualized intervention strategy could be applied in childhood to the offending factor. In the absence of a genetic marker, one is left with a family history of hypertension in first-degree relatives or a history of premature cardiovascular mortality (< 55 years) as an indicator of genetic influence. All potential environmental factors must be identified and an intervention developed without regard to individual susceptibility. An important goal for developing future preventive strategies will be identification of genetic markers and delineation of the environmental interactions.

Cross-Cultural Comparisons

The relationship of age and sex to blood pressure has been described for industrialized countries. In less developed countries and traditional societies, however, mean blood pressures do not increase after puberty (Page, 1981, 1974) and hypertension is uncommon in adults. Blood pressure increases with age during childhood growth, but thereafter, little increase is evident through adolescent and adult life. The striking difference between adult pressures in industrial and lesser developed countries is evident during adolescence, which suggests that comparison of cultural characteristics and lifestyles in diverse societies might disclose potential preventive approaches.

Epidemiologic studies of traditional societies in geographically separate locations have disclosed many differences from modern, industrial societies and have fostered several hypotheses to explain the contrasts in blood pressure during adolescence and adulthood. Two salient nutritional features contrast the traditional and industrialized cultures and have been related to blood pressure. Weight for height or body mass is greater in industrialized, modern societies at all ages, and the per capita consumption of sodium is usually 150 mEq/day or greater in these countries. Because high caloric intake is usually associated with higher sodium intake, various attempts have been made in an effort to disentangle the confounding effects on blood pressure. The evidence suggests that both factors, body mass and sodium intake, are important and can operate independently (Page, 1981). Cross-sectional comparisons of populations confirm the importance of sodium intake when the levels of consumption of the compared groups are at the extremes (Figure 51.3). If sodium intake is less than 70 mEq/day, mean blood pressure in the population will be low, and little or no increase in blood pressure will be found in older age groups. If sodium intake is above 150 mEq/day, mean pressures are higher; and above 200 mEq/day, there is a direct relationship between intake and blood pressure. Between 100 and 150 mEq/day, however, no direct linear relationship is apparent, and this is the range for many Western industrialized societies. The independence of dietary sodium from body mass has been demonstrated in several populations, characterized by an age-associated rise in blood pressure but no change in body mass. These groups have a sodium intake of 150 mEq/day or greater and maintain a traditional culture (Page, 1981; Baker & Hanna, Note 1).

Conversely, persons in some societies—notably, the Tokelau Islanders—gain weight after attaining adult stature and experience a gradual rise in blood pressure with age but maintain a sodium intake of 30–50 mEq/day (Prior, Hooper, Huntsman, Stanhope, & Salmond, 1977) In general, the effect of obesity and body mass is a linear, direct relationship and is found throughout the entire range of weight/stature. These blood pressure relationships to sodium and obesity are not ethnically determined. Somoans living in three different cultural milieu have been studied, for example; the lowest blood pressures have been found in those with the most traditional cultures (Western Samoa) and the highest pressures in those living in Hawaii, where individual weight is considerably greater (Baker & Hanna, Note 1). There are other examples of ethnically or genetically similar groups who have different blood pressures depending on the cultural environment, but the most relevant to

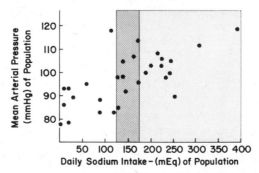

Figure 51.3 Relationship between mean blood pressure and daily sodium intake (estimated from dietary studies) in different populations. Blood pressure for the 50- to 59-year-old group is plotted for each population. (Reprinted from McCarron, D. A., Henry, H. J., & Morris, C. D. Human nutrition and blood pressure regulation: An integrated approach. *Hypertension*, 1982, **4**(Suppl. III), III-2–III-13.)

Americans are blood pressure findings in black groups. Blood pressures are low in rural African populations, but they are higher in urban Africans and in Africans residing in industrialized countries (Severs, Gordon, Peart, & Beighton, 1980).

Traditional and industrialized societies differ in more dimensions than weight gain and sodium intake. Few studies relate blood pressure to social and psychological differences among groups, however, and relatively few have measured social and psychological changes associated with cultural transition. These diversely different cultures are characterized by considerably different social and physical demands on the individual and by social support networks based on family and small group or tribal systems. Expressions of individual personality traits, such as aggressiveness and response to stress, are different among cultures and may well result in modified response when traditional cultures change through modernization or emigration.

Despite the potentially interesting psychosocial lessons that might be learned from cross-cultural comparisons, the most useful information relates to dietary intake. Growth during childhood is associated with a physiological increase in blood pressure. Excessive weight gain during childhood and continued weight gain after growth is complete represent adipose tissue increase and are associated with continued high blood pressure during late adolescence and adulthood and higher pressures generally. Sodium intake is directly and independently related to blood pressure at the extremes of consumption (less than 100 mEq/day and more than 200 mEq/day), but between these levels the relationship is not linear. The high-sodium culture of industrialized nations makes it difficult to reduce sodium intake without major public health measures or intensive educational efforts because of the pervasive use of sodium in the storage, processing, and preparation of food. Serious attempts to prevent high blood pressure will require both educational intervention and technological changes by the food industry, which, in turn, depend on incentives to the industry. Major public health initiatives must be tempered by an appreciation that nutritional improvement in infants and children in industrialized countries is a major reason for improved infant and childhood mortality rates over the last 80 years. Some important questions require answers, however. Can dietary changes be made in adolescence, or does childhood exposure to high sodium intake or caloric excess condition blood pressure-regulating responses that cannot easily be altered by later alteration of diet? If particular care is directed to altering sodium and caloric intake of industrialized societies during childhood, will the growth-related rise in blood pressure occur but the excessive rise in adolescence and early adulthood be aborted? Can specific dietary restrictions be accomplished in free-living families without changing the improved childhood nutrition that differentiates industrialized and developing countries with respect to childhood mortality and childhood and adolescent growth rates? Without clear answers to these questions, no political or regulative action should be taken to change the diet for the entire population, including children. Rather, the best strategy is identification of young individuals who are at risk of developing high blood pressure and institution of changes in lifestyle to prevent or ameliorate development of hypertension.

FACTORS RELATED TO BLOOD PRESSURE IN INDUSTRIALIZED COUNTRIES

Considerable information is available about group and individual characteristics that are related to blood pressure within childhood and adolescent groups in the United States and in comparable westernized populations. Most studies are cross-sectional, but an increasing number of longitudinal observations are available and have generally served to confirm the findings from the cross-sectional studies. In succeeding sections, the identified and potentially alterable variables associated with blood pressure are discussed. Where only cross-sectional observations are available and information has been developed for adults but not for children, this will be noted, and conservative inferences will be made regarding the relationships in childhood.

Nutritional Factors

Weight and Body Mass

Weight and body mass are the most important nutritional factors related to blood pressure. Weight and weight change over time have been consistently related to levels of systolic and diastolic blood pressure and to changes in pressures. In all cross-sectional surveys of populations in industrialized countries, weight or an index of body mass (such as weight/height^2) has been directly related to blood pressure. This relationship holds for all age groups from 5 to 74 years, for both sexes, and for both white and black individuals (Ellison, Sosenko, Harper, Gibbons, Pratter, & Miettinen, 1980; Harlan et al., 1973; Harlan, Hull, Schmauder, Thompson, Larkin, & Landis, in press; Higgins, Keller, Metzner, Moore, & Ostrander, 1980; Kannel, Brand, & Skinner, 1967; Voors, Webber, & Berenson, 1980). In the United States, the correlation between weight and blood pressure is somewhat greater for white persons than for black persons at all ages. In stepwise multiple regression analysis, weight or body mass is usually the first nutritional variable selected (Cornoni-Huntley et al., 1979; Harlan et al., 1979; Harlan et al., in press). Weight change is directly related to blood pressure. Cohort studies of youths and adults followed for 5 to 40 years indicate an incremental increase in systolic and diastolic pressure associated with weight gain and, conversely, stability of blood pressure when there is little or no change in weight over time (Clarke, Schrott, Leaverton, Conner, & Lauer, 1978; Harlan et al., 1973). In longitudinal studies of adolescents and adults, weight change is the major variable selected in analysis. Short-term studies of adults in weight reduction programs confirm that weight loss is accompanied by significant and important increases in blood pressure and, moreover, that blood pressure reduction is not dependent on sodium restriction (Reisen, Abel, Modan, Silverberg, Eliahou, & Modan, 1978).

The influence of weight and weight change on blood pressure can be further discriminated, particularly in children undergoing growth and development. In adults and children, the use of a body mass index that accounts for stature improves the correlation with blood pressure. The most appropriate function of height remains somewhat controversial, but weight/height^2, the Quietelet Index, has a consistent relationship with multiple biological parameters in children and youths and the further advantage of considerable accumulated experience (Killeen, Vanderburg, & Harlan, 1978). The use of an index is preferable to the use of tables of "normal values," whose definition may change over time and, in children, may not accommodate individual differences in growth rate.

Correcting weight for stature also implies judgments about body composition. Correlations have been found between blood pressure and measures of adiposity (skin fold thickness), muscle mass (muscle circumference), and skeletal size (bone maturation) in children (Killeen, et al., 1978). Skin fold measurements correlate with systolic and diastolic pressures in children at about the same level as body mass or weight, and similar correlations are found regardless of the site measured. This finding is consonant with the association between weight gain and blood pressure increase after completion of growth, as such weight gain is usually adipose tissue.

In growing children, weight gain is also related to more rapid growth and maturation. Bone maturation, which directly reflects physiological growth, has a better correlation than chronological age with blood pressure (Cornoni-Huntley et al., 1979; Harlan et al., 1979). Bone age radiographs are not routinely obtained, however, and if growth is to be accounted for, an index of height for age would be favored.

In summary, adiposity has an important relationship to childhood, adolescent, and adult blood pressure in both cross-sectional and longitudinal studies. The implications are obvious for intervention on adiposity to prevent blood pressure increases in adolescence and adulthood. Weight/height^2 serves as a good measure when skin fold measurements are not available. In growing children, the relationship between weight and adiposity is confounded by growth, and height may be useful in accounting for blood pressure differences related primarily to growth (Voors et al., 1977).

Sodium and Potassium

The relationship of sodium intake to blood pressure levels is not as clear in industrialized countries as it is in cross-cultural comparisons. A relationship may be demonstrated between national levels of salt intake and mean blood pressures when countries with widely divergent dietary sodium levels are contrasted (Figure 51.3). Within countries or societies, however, there is not a clear or consistent relationship. In the United States, no significant relationship can be demonstrated (Cooper, Liu, Trevisan, & Stamler, 1983; Ellison et al., 1980; Harlan et al., in press). The lack of association occurs whether dietary intake or urinary sodium excretion (which is considered more accurate) is measured. Therefore, the failure to find a relationship within industrialized populations has been attributed to the concept that the relationship is linear below 100–150 mEq/day and that above this level, the organism is saturated and is unresponsive to small differences in intake. Population studies have demonstrated, however, that the Na/K ratio of dietary intake has a modest relationship to blood pressure (Harlan et al., in press).

Within industrialized countries, the role of sodium intake in blood pressure regulation can be demonstrated regularly in carefully controlled situations when sodium is restricted below 75 mEq/day (Parijs, Joossens, Van der Linden, Vertreken, & Amery, 1977). Moreover, this blood pressure-lowering effect may be augmented by potassium supplementation (Meneely & Battarbee, 1976). The most striking demonstration of this effect was the use of the Kempner rice diet for effective treatment of patients with severe or malignant hypertension (Kempner, 1948). The original diet was low in sodium and moderately high in potassium. Monitoring of compliance was assured by obtaining random urine samples for sodium measurement. Because sodium excretion is nil when the rice diet is followed, the presence of appreciable sodium content indicated that the patient was not adhering to the regimen. The development of effective and relatively safe pharmacological therapy has made this extremely restrictive diet of historical interest. Other, less restrictive diets have been shown to lower blood pressure effectively in hypertensive patients and normal patients (Parijs et al., 1977). Modification of the customary diet to cause reduction in blood pressure requires care in eliminating salt-containing foods and food products, minimizing salt (and monosodium glutamate) added in food preparation and serving, and substituting potassium salts and herbs as flavoring agents. In the current high-salt culture of industrialized countries, it is difficult to achieve the level of sodium restriction necessary for lowering blood pressure without intensive dietary instruction and proscription of many processed foods and of frequent dining out. Moreover, monitoring of dietary adherence is difficult. It is possible to achieve significant blood pressure lowering in motivated individuals when sodium intake is held at or below 75 mEq/day, but this requires training, monitoring of compliance, and feedback to the individual.

Increased potassium intake can increase the efficacy of sodium restriction in lowering blood pressure in hypertensive individuals, and it has this effect even in the absence of salt restriction (Meneely & Battarbee, 1976). The effect of potassium supplementation without sodium restriction is short-term and is not expressed in normotensive persons. Moreover, there is no convincing evidence that chronic administration of potassium has a prolonged pressure-lowering effect. Generally, it would seem reasonable to combine increased potassium intake with decreased sodium intake to maximize blood pressure lowering. Therapeutic intervention on sodium and potassium intake remains controversial and difficult to summarize. Sodium restriction and potassium supplementation are useful in treatment of established hypertension, however, and are complementary to drug therapy. Dietary changes to prevent increases in pressure in adolescents require further study of feasibility and efficacy before general application.

Other Ions

The roles of calcium and magnesium in blood pressure regulation have aroused renewed interest because of recent population studies and improved understanding of their action on vascular tissue to modulate blood vessel tone. Several studies, including the large nutritional survey of the U.S. population (National Health and Nutrition Examination Survey), indicate that dietary calcium and phosphorus content have a direct relationship with blood pressure (Harlan et al., in press). An inverse relationship was found for serum phosphate levels and blood pressure, and a direct relationship was found for serum calcium and serum magnesium. The relationship with serum phosphate is confirmed in the Framingham Study (Havlik & Feinleib, 1982). These relationships are independent of age, race, sex, and body mass effects and have thus far been documented only in adult groups. Dietary calcium may have therapeutic implications. In adults, calcium supplementation in treatment of osteoporosis resulted in blood pressure decrease in those receiving calcium (McCarron, 1982; McCarron, Morris, & Cole, 1982). Moreover, the use of agents to block calcium transport through cell membranes promises to improve our understanding of the role of calcium in maintaining the tone of blood vessels as well as its interactions with sodium and other ions (Blaustein, 1977). Although the evidence at hand regarding dietary intervention is too preliminary to warrant incorporation into therapeutic plans for children and youths, these provocative observations suggest a need to explore dietary supplementation as a preventive measure, particularly since this implies an emphasis on dairy products, which enhances the health of the young.

Alcohol

Alcohol intake is related to blood pressure, but the nature and mechanism of the relationship appear to be complex. In adults, ingestion of large amounts of alcohol (more than 6 drinks/day or more than 5 ounces of absolute alcohol equivalents) is associated with significantly higher mean blood pressures and a greater incidence of hypertension. (Criqui, Wallace, Mishkel, Barrett-Conner, & Heiss, 1981; Harlan et al., in press; Klatsky, Friedman, Siegelaub, & Gerard, 1977). The type of beverage (wine, beer, or spirits) is unrelated to the effect. The relationship to alcohol appears to be curvilinear, with the highest pressures occurring with heavy consumption, the next highest in alcohol abstainers, and the lowest pressures in those consuming small amounts (1–3 drinks/day) of alcohol. The relationship between alcohol and blood pressure is independent of other nutritional variables, such as body mass and salt intake, and of nonnutritional variables, such as race and socioeconomic status. The mechanism is unknown, although a sympathetically medicated withdrawal from the depressant effects of alcohol has been cited as a possibility. In an adult population, alcohol abuse may contribute significantly to the incidence of hypertension, and many clinicians have been impressed with the beneficial effects on blood pressure when alcohol abstinence has been achieved in problem drinkers. The alcohol effect appears to be reversible even after years of abuse. The contribution of alcohol to blood pressure elevation in adolescents is unknown, as this issue is seldom addressed in studies. The increased and rather pervasive use of alcohol by teenagers, however, suggests that this should be an important aspect of interviewing and counseling of youth.

Exercise and Physical Activity

Blood pressure, particularly systolic pressure, rises acutely in response to exercise, and dynamic exercise has been used as a therapeutic mode to lower chronically elevated pressures. The epidemiologic associations are complex. Levels of physical activity are related to body mass and adiposity, and this confounds the relationship of physical activity to blood pressure. Equally important, the difficulty in making reliable and valid estimates of customary activity without physiological testing has blurred these relationships. Careful observations are available, however, regarding the use of physical training to lower risk factors for cardiovascular disease, and blood pressure has been one of the major factors investigated. In adolescents, a greater than usual increase in systolic pressure in response to dynamic exercise has been taken as an indication of a hyperkinetic circulation and a premonitory sign for later hypertension (Schieken, Clarke, & Lauer, 1983). A long-term follow-up is required, however, to prove the assertion that blood pressure response to exercise has predictive validity greater than resting or casual pressures.

The use of dynamic exercise as a therapeutic modality is more clearly established, although the mechanism underlying blood pressure lowering is not clear. Numerous studies have demonstrated decreases in mean systolic and diastolic pressures with programs of increased physical activity when aerobic, rhythmic exercise was used and a conditioning effect was demonstrable. Isometric exercise (weight lifting, dynamic tension), which increases muscle mass but does not afford aerobic conditioning, is associated with increases in blood pressure during the period of muscle training but no subsequent pressure lowering, and it may be hazardous in the hypertensive individual. In the conditioned individual, there is an associated decline in resting heart rate, and this may be physiologically related to the decrease in systolic pressure as the two measures correlate. Physical training may result in an adaptation of the central portion of the sympathetic nervous system and peripheral adrenergic receptors that results in a slower pulse and diminished vascular tone. In addition, exercise conditioning programs generally result in a loss of weight, primarily adipose tissue, and some of the decrease in blood pressure may be attributable to associated weight loss. There are reports, however, of decreases in systolic and diastolic pressures without change in weight and speculation that metabolic changes—specifically, a decline in serum insulin levels—were related to blood pressure decline because the subjects did not lose weight (Bjontrop, 1982). Clarification of the mechanism has practical importance, because exercise might be used to accomplish weight reduction or a different level of conditioning might be sought that achieves metabolic changes without weight changes.

Despite the lack of information about the mechanism, aerobic physical activity is a useful lifestyle change and may favorably alter several cardiovascular risk parameters, although evidence for changes in mortality and morbidity are lacking. The advantage of incorporation of physical activity into programs for adolescents includes the prospect for establishing lifelong health behaviors and the frequently associated weight control. Moreover, there is a relatively low likelihood of severe or fatal complications from an exercise program that is initiated in youth.

Nonnutritional Factors

Sociocultural and Demographic Characteristics

Considerable information is available on demographic, social, and cultural correlates with blood pressure in the United States. Surprisingly, some of these features that have strong relationships in adults have little or no association with blood pressure during childhood and adolescence. The most striking example is race. In surveys of adults in the United States, blood pressures are systematically higher in black persons than in white persons at all ages and in both males and females (Harlan et al., in press). This difference persists even after accounting for weight (or weight/height^2). Blood pressures of white children and adolescents through 18 years, however, are slightly higher than those of black youths (Cornoni-Huntley et al., 1979; Harlan et al., 1979). This slight difference remains after standardizing for weight/height^2 or for sexual and skeletal maturation. The racial relationship of blood pressure changes between 18 and 25 years of age, during the period when secondary school leavers enter the work force or pursue further education or training. It has been suggested in the context of adult observations that the black/white differences in blood pressure result from social pressures and constraints related to the black experience in the United States (Harburg, Erfurt, Hauestein, Chape, Schull, & Schork, 1973). By extension, the findings in childhood might be explained by the relative protection of the individual from these social forces until he or she leaves school and enters the work situation. Alternatively, other subtle factors (e.g., diet, stress) may be operative during childhood but have a long latency period before their expression. Such factors could only be identified and quantified through longitudinal studies that span the adolescent and young adulthood periods of life.

Reviews of other demographic and social factors reveal few characteristics consistently related to blood pressures. In the national surveys of the U.S. population, there are only small differences in blood pressure by geographic region, and none are consistently significant. Likewise, these surveys reveal no urban/rural differences in blood pressure. Small differences are found when income status or educational attainment of parents is examined, but the effect diminishes if pressures are corrected for the influence of weight/height^2. Several studies of particular groups or populations have found urban/rural or socioeconomic differences, with urban life generally being associated with higher pressures. The differences are small, however, and diminish when race and body mass are controlled in analysis.

Social and economic mobility and cultural change have been linked to higher blood pressures in groups and populations experiencing rapid change. The focus for these studies has been populations of lesser developed countries undergoing rapid economic development or, in industrialized countries, individuals experiencing job and economic improvement or degradation. The psychological stress of insecurity and the continued demand for adaptation to a different environment have been used as explanations for these associations, but most of these studies have not measured other important changes in behaviors and lifestyles, such as diet, and the attribution of blood pressure changes to social and cultural factors may be premature (Harlan, 1981). These studies have related primarily to adult groups, and relatively little is known about changes in childhood groups and about whether their responses are concordant with the observations in adults.

Oral Contraceptives and Pregnancy

Oral contraceptive use is associated with an increase in blood pressure in current users, but the blood pressure effect is rapidly reversed after use is stopped. This effect is found in all age groups, including adolescents. For some individuals, this rise in blood pressure will place them in the hypertensive category. Therefore, the blood pressure of persons using oral contraceptives should be monitored, and other, nonhormonal means of contraception should be substituted if the rise in blood pressure results in persistent hypertension. There is insufficient evidence that the new generation of oral contraceptives is associated with lesser increments of pressure, despite a decreased estrogen content.

High blood pressure may occur in pregnancy in three different situations (Chesley, 1980; Wallace, Tamir, Heiss, Rifkind, Christensen, & Glueck, 1979). Preexistent hypertension may be aggravated or initially discovered during pregnancy and is almost always detectable in the first 20 weeks of gestation. Detection and management of high blood pressure before pregnancy have important preventive consequences for the other two forms of pregnancy-associated hypertension. Preeclampsia, which occurs after the first 20 weeks of gestation, is defined as a diastolic pressure over 90 mmHg associated with proteinuria (over 0.3 gm/ 24 hours) and edema. Antecedent hypertension and renal vascular disease are important risk factors for preeclampsia, as is being a young (under 17 years) primigravida. Therefore, identification and management of elevated blood pressure assume particular importance in the adolescent, who is at greater risk for eclamptic complications. In addition, there is suggestive evidence that the offspring of eclamptic mothers are more likely to develop high blood pressure in childhood.

Gestational hypertension is defined as an elevated blood pressure occurring in the latter half of pregnancy or the first day following pregnancy and is not associated with proteinuria or edema. Gestational hypertension usually disappears within 10 days after delivery, but the individual is at greater risk of developing persistent hypertension later in life. The implications for surveillance of women before and during pregnancy are obvious, as is the potential benefit of preventive, nonpharmacological intervention (Kotchen, McKean, & Kotchen, 1982).

Psychological and Neurophysiological Factors

Considerable investigative effort has been devoted to exploration of psychological factors related to high blood pressure and of the neurophysiological mechanisms responsible for blood pressure regulation. Blood pressure rises acutely in response to acute psychological and physiological stress, and this observation has stimulated the hypothesis that recurrent acute stresses or chronic situations may lead to a sustained or persistent elevation in blood pressure. The evidence to support this hypothesis has been elusive. The measurement of environmental stress has proved difficult, as has the evaluation of individual responsiveness to the stress. Moreover, personal knowledge of the existence of hypertension may alter individual perceptions and responses, which diminishes the validity of cross-sectional comparisons of hypertensive and normal individuals. The bias introduced by diagnostic labeling is less in adolescents, but investigation of this group is complicated by the small number of individuals with persistently high blood pressures and the requirement for relatively long follow-up to confirm the development of persistently elevated pressures. The predictive ability of the tests is dependent on these longitudinal observations. In general, however, studies performed on adolescent groups have been consonant with the observations made on adults, and some of the results in these two age groups are compared.

To clarify and unify the observations by investigators from rather diverse disciplines and orientations, it is necessary to describe a scheme that links stress and behavioral and neurophysiological responses. Stress is defined as a stimulus or threat external to the individual that requires a response or adaptation by the individual. The nature and intensity of some stresses can be measured (e.g., noise, cold, and physical exertion), but other stresses are primarily psychological, and assessment of their intensity is subjective and difficult to quantify objectively. Individual response to such stresses can be measured through observable behavior (speech, expressions, cutaneous reactivity, and blood pressure). It has been assumed that this behavioral response could be identified and assessed early in life and would remain relatively consistent within individuals. The underlying neurophysiological state and its responsiveness are considered to be genetically determined and conditioned by experiences and psychological support networks. The response initiated by the stress involves a complex and interacting system of neuronal and neurohormonal changes. Measurements of neurophysiological activity in humans are made difficult by the requirement to sample at a site remote to the focus of activity—for example, serum neurohormonal changes or surface electrical activity. Many segments of neurophysiological responsiveness have been assessed in hypertension, and provocative but often unsubstantiated findings have been uncovered.

Hypertensive adults have been characterized as having more anger and anxiety than normotensive subjects, but they appear to suppress or internalize their behavioral display of these feelings. A Type A personality pattern has been characterized as an aggressive, time-oriented behavior that is reliably determined by speech stylistics during an interview. This behavioral pattern operates as an independent risk factor for coronary heart disease. In the original studies of Rosenman, Brand, Jenkins, Friedman, Straus, and Wurm (1975), no relationship was found between Type A behavior and blood pressure, and this was confirmed in a subsequent study of air traffic controllers, who experience an extremely high incidence of high blood pressure that is assumed to be related to the stressful nature of their work (Rose, Jenkins, & Horst, Note 2). In this latter study, a Type B behavior pattern, the antithesis of Type A, was significantly related to the prevalence of hypertension.

The personality pattern that emerges from studies of adults is of an anxious, fearful person who responds behaviorally with a rapid, placid manner, seemingly not expressing these internal anxieties.

In a study of adolescents, impatience and life dissatisfaction were more commonly associated with those having higher blood pressures, and these relationships were independent of the effect of weight/height[2] (Siegel & Leitch, 1981). In this study, Type A behavior, hostility, and anger were also associated with high blood pressure, but when weight/height[2] was controlled in analysis, these behavioral features were no longer significant. In a separate study of children 8 to 16 years of age, the high blood pressure group scored higher on masculinity-femininity and sleep disturbance (Kron, Laing, Sines, Clarke, & Lauer, 1980). The personality profile inferred from these observations was of a less comfortable, less appropriately assertive, and more over- "controlled behavior" in the high blood pressure group. Notably, in these adolescent studies and others, no independent association between Type A behavior pattern and blood pressure was identified. This is consistent with adult studies and portrays the adolescent with higher blood pressures as displaying a lack of assertiveness and inhibited behavior despite strong internal feelings. Numerous additional psychometric tests have been applied to youths, but no other consistent findings emerge. Thus far, studies of behavior in adolescents have been cross-sectional and have utilized subjects in the higher percentiles of blood pressure. The predictive value of this profile for subsequent high blood pressures remains to be proved.

The preceding observations primarily address the personality dimension of adolescents, but several studies have been directed toward environmental stresses. Two stresses, noise and mental activity, have been studied in adults and adolescents. Environmental noise has been observed to increase blood pressure acutely in adults subjected to 80 dB or greater noise levels, primarily in occupational settings. A concordant rise in plasma catecholamines has suggested activation of the sympathetic nervous system as the probable mechanism. In adults, however, persistent elevation of blood pressure has not been demonstrated after removal of the noise stimuli. In children, a noisy school environment (resulting from location in an aircraft flight corridor) was associated with significantly higher blood pressures than were recorded in a less noisy school (Cohen, Evans, Krantz, & Stokols, 1980). The blood pressures were recorded in a quiet examination environment, and several important factors were controlled in analysis. The apparent effect on blood pressure was greatest for children with the most recent exposure to the high-noise environment (less than 2 years), and pressure differences diminished after 3 to 4 years in the high-noise school. These observations are provocative and deserve further study, as high-noise environments are common in the United States and the implications for public policy are important.

Another common stress for adolescents is performance of a mental task against a deadline. Increased rises in blood pressure and pulse have been reported in adolescents with borderline hypertension when performing mental tasks. Similarly, children with higher resting blood pressures responded with higher systolic blood pressures and heart rates than lower blood pressure children when a word-scrambling test was used (Falkner, Kushner, Onesti, & Angelakos, 1981). These responses are similar to observations of adults with sustained high blood pressure when exposed to mental stress, and the findings suggest that the nature of blood pressure responses is similar in both age groups. In adults, concomitantly measured plasma levels of catecholamines were increased, suggesting an enhanced reaction of the sympathetic nervous system. The inference that altered sympathetic response to mental stress is antecedent to hypertension in either the adolescent or adult, however, requires support from longitudinal studies.

Neurophysiological Status

The scheme relating environmental stress to high blood pressure hypothesizes that an altered sympathetic nervous system responsiveness is the effector mechanism for the higher pressures.

Efforts to assess sympathetic activity have focused on measurement of plasma catecholamines or surrogate measures of sympathetic arousal state. A recent review highlights the ambiguity surrounding catecholamine measurements in hypertension (Goldstein, 1981). Slightly fewer than half (40%) of the studies reviewed reported significantly higher plasma norepinephrine levels in hypertensives when compared with normotensives. It is interesting that the hypertensive–normotensive differences were inversely related to the age of subjects, with younger, consistently hypertensive subjects showing greater differences. Plasma epinephrine levels also tend to be higher, and total catecholamine levels provide the best differentiation between hypertensive and normotensive persons. Further studies of cathecholamine responsiveness during stress in adolescents would appear to be a promising direction for research. The current data support a role for the sympathetic nervous system in determining blood pressure, and it appears likely that this system mediates the stress-behavioral response that may characterize early hypertensives. Further study could yield valuable information and set the stage for early identification of adolescents who have an increased likelihood of developing hypertension.

Pulse rate has been considered a surrogate measure of a hyperkinetic cardiovascular system and of the sympathetic nervous system influence on the heart and blood vessels. In virtually every study of children and adolescents and most studies of adults, there is a significant correlation between resting pulse rate and systolic blood pressure. The relationship to diastolic blood pressure is less consistent, and the correlation tends to be lower. In the few studies in which longitudinal observations are available, however, resting pulse rate does not appear to have predictive value. Therefore, the correlation in cross-sectional studies appears to be related to current physiological events and does not disclose an inherent difference in cardiovascular responsiveness that characterizes the individual as one likely to develop hypertension. Because pulse rate varies with the situation at the time of examination, short-term variability diminishes the reliability and consequently the validity of this assessment in the clinical evaluation of an individual.

Assessments of neurophysiological status provide an intriguing avenue of investigation into the pathogenesis of high blood pressure. The utility of information is currently limited, however. Tests of behavioral patterns and personality do not appear to be helpful in identifying adolescents who are likely to develop hypertension, but linking these measures to catecholamine response may improve prediction. The assessment of plasma catecholamines, either in the resting state or after provocation, is promising, but longitudinal assessments must be made before they can be said to have predictive value. With respect to stressful environments, the cross-sectional study of noise stress provides an interesting approach, but confirmation of the cross-sectional observations and longitudinal follow-up are required to provide a sound scientific basis for intervention. Intervention in the other areas also requires greater study before one could endorse either an individual behavior approach or policy changes.

AN AGENDA FOR HEALTH PROVIDERS

Behavioral intervention on adolescent high blood pressure affords great potential for treatment, and this approach is endorsed by medical providers (Soltero, Tsong, Cooper, Stamler, Stamler, & Garside, 1980). Prevention of high blood pressure in adolescents is not so well accepted. This reflects some uncertainty about precise identification of those who are at risk for development of elevated pressure and an unfamiliarity with the use of nonpharmacological approaches and their efficacy. It is possible to identify youths who are more likely to have persistently high pressures through family history, peer ranking of blood pressure, and body mass (Paffenbarger, Thorne, & Wing, 1968). Intervention through dietary change has a strong scientific rationale, although there is not consensus on the optimal nutritional approach. Several other relevant behaviors are easily identified—for example, alcohol abuse and oral contraceptives—and alteration can beneficially affect blood pressures. Other potentially important aspects of blood pressure regulation, such as stress and personality, require further investigation before a strong rationale can be put forward for intervention. The impact on individual health of early identification and management is so great that the investment of resources will be returned manyfold.

REFERENCE NOTES

1. Baker, P. T., & Hanna, J. M. *Modernization of the biological fitness of Samoans: A progress report on a research program.* Paper presented at the Seminar on Migration and Health, Wellington, New Zealand, 1979.
2. Rose, R. M., Jenkins, C. D., & Horst, M. W. *Air traffic controller health change study.* Report to the Federal Aviation Administration, August 1978.

REFERENCES

AHA Committee Report (Kirkendall, W. M., Feinleib, M., Fries, E. D., & Mark, A. L.). Recommendations for human blood pressure determination by sphygonomarometes. *Circulation,* 1980, **62,** 1145A–1155A.

Annest, J. L., Sing, C. F., Biron, P., & Mongeau, J. G. Familial aggregation of blood pressure and weight in adoptive families: II. Estimation of the relative contributions of genetic and common environment factors to blood pressure correlations between family members. *American Journal of Epidemiology,* 1979, **110,** 205–218.

Beaglehole, R., Salmond, C. E., & Eyles, E. F. A longitudinal study of blood pressure in Polynesian children. *American Journal of Epidemiology,* 1977, **105,** 87.

Berenson, G. S., Voors, A. W., Webber, L. S., Frank, G. C., Farris, R. P., Tobian, L., & Aristimuno, G. G. A model of intervention for prevention of early essential hypertension in the 1980's. *Hypertension,* 1983, **5,** 41–54.

Bjontrop, P. Hypertension and exercise. *Hypertension,* 1982, **4**(Suppl. 3), III56–III59.

Blaustein, M. P. Sodium ions, calcium ions, blood pressure regulation and hypertension: A reassessment and a hypothesis. *American Journal of Physiology,* 1977, **232,** C165.

Bloom, J. R., & Monterossa, S. Hypertension labeling and sense of wellbeing. *American Journal of Public Health,* 1981, **71,** 1228–1232.

Canessa, M., Adragna, N., Solomon, H. S., Connolly, T. M., & Tosteson, D. C. Increased sodium-lithium countertransport in red cells of patients with essential hypertension. *New England Journal of Medicine,* 1980, **302,** 772.

Chesley, L. C. Hypertension in pregnancy: Definitions, factors, and remote prognosis. *Kidney International,* 1980, **18,** 234.

Clarke, W. R., Schrott, H. G., Leaverton, P. E., Conner, W. E., & Lauer, R. M. Tracking of blood lipids and blood pressure in school age children: The Muscatine Study. *Circulation,* 1978, **58,** 626.

Cohen, S., Evans, G. W., Krantz, D. S., & Stokols, D. Physiological, motivational, and cognitive effects of aircraft noise on children: Moving from the laboratory to the field. *American Psychologist,* 1980, **35,** 231–243.

Cooper, R., Liu, K., Trevisan, M., Miller, W., & Stamler, J. Urinary sodium excretion and blood pressure in children: Absence of a reproducible association. *Hypertension,* 1983, **5,** 135–139.

Cornoni-Huntley, J. C., Harlan, W. R., & Leaverton, P. E. Blood pressure in adolescence: The United States Health Examination Survey. *Hypertension,* 1979, **1,** 566.

Criqui, M. H., Wallace, R. B., Mishkel, M., Barrett-Conner, E., & Heiss, G. Alcohol consumption and blood pressure: The Lipid Research Clinics prevalence study. *Hypertension,* 1981, **3,** 557.

Daughterty, S. A., Miller, J. Z., Weinberger, M. G., & Grim, C. E. Blood pressure response to dietary sodium changes in young identical twins and their families. *Circulation,* 1982, **66**(Suppl.), 2–36.

Ellison, R. C., Sosenko, J. M., Harper, G. P., Gibbons, L., Pratter, F. E., & Miettinen, O. S. Obesity, sodium intake and blood pressure in adolescents. *Hypertension,* 1980, **2,** I-78–I-82.

Falkner, B., Kushner, H., Onesti, G., & Angelakos, E. T. Cardiovascular characteristics in adolescents who develop essential hypertension. *Hypertension,* 1981, **3,** 521–527.

Fries, E. D. Should mild hypertension be treated? *New England Journal of Medicine,* 1982, **307,** 306–309.

Goldstein, D. S. Plasma catecholamines and essential hypertension: An analytical review. *Hypertension,* 1981, **3,** 48–52.

Grim, C. E., Luft, F. C., Miller, J. Z., Rose, R. J., Christian, J. C., & Weinberger, M. H. An approach to the evaluation of genetic influences on factors that regulate arterial blood pressure in man. *Hypertension,* 1980, **2**(Suppl. I), I34.

Harburg, E., Erfurt, J. C., Hauestein, L. S., Chape, C., Schull, W. J., & Schork, M. A. Socioecological stress, suppressed hostility, skin color, and black-white male blood pressure: Detroit. *Psychosomatic Medicine,* 1973, **35,** 276–295.

Harlan, W. R. Physical and psychosocial stress. *Circulation,* 1981, **63,** 266A–271A.

Harlan, W. R., Cornoni-Huntley, J. C., & Leaverton, P. E. Blood pressure in childhood: The National Health Examination Survey. *Hypertension,* 1979, **1,** 559.

Harlan, W. R., Hull, A. L., Schmauder, R. P., Thompson, F. E., Larkin, F. A., & Landis, J. R. Relationships among blood pressure, nutritional variables and clinical biochemistries: The National Health and Nutrition Examination Survey. In *Vital and Health Statistics,* Series II. Washington, D.C.: U.S. Public Health Service, in press.

Harlan, W. R., Oberman, A., Mitchell, R. E., & Graybiel, A. A 30-year study of blood pressure in a white male cohort. In G. Onesti, K. E. Kin, & J. H. Moyer (Eds.), *Hypertension, mechanisms and management.* New York: Grune and Stratton, 1973.

Havlik, R. J., & Feinleib, M. Epidemiology and genetics of hypertension. *Hypertension,* 1982, **4**(Suppl. III), III121–III127.

Higgins, M. W., Keller, J. B., Metzner, H. L., Moore, F. E., & Ostrander, L. D. Study of blood pressure in Tecumseh, Michigan: II. Antecedents in childhood of high blood pressure in young adults. *Hypertension,* 1980, **2**(Suppl. I), I117.

Hypertension Detection and Follow-up Program Cooperative Group. Five-year findings of the hypertension detection and follow-up program: I. Reduction in mortality of persons with high blood pressure, including mild hypertension. *Journal of the American Medical Association,* 1979, **242,** 2562–2571.

Kannel, W. B., Brand, N., & Skinner, J. J. The relation of adiposity to blood pressure and development of hypertension: The Framington Study. *Annals of Internal Medicine,* 1967, **67,** 48–59.

Kempner, W. Treatment of hypertensive vascular disease with rice diet. *American Journal of Medicine,* 1948, **4,** 545.

Killeen, J., Vanderburg, D., & Harlan, W. R. Application of weight/height ratios and body indices to a juvenile population: The National Health Examination Survey Data. *Journal of Chronic Diseases,* 1978, **31,** 529–537.

Klatsky, A. L., Friedman, G. D., Siegelaub, A. B., & Gerard, M. J. Alcohol consumption and blood pressure. *New England Journal of Medicine,* 1977, **296,** 1194.

Kotchen, J. M., McKean, H. E., & Kotchen, T. A. Blood pressure trends with aging. *Hypertension,* 1982, **4**(Suppl. III), III-128–III-134.

Kron, J. M., Laing, J. A., Sines, J. O., Clarke, W. R., & Lauer, R. M. Personality and casual blood pressure in school age children. *Journal of Psychosomatic Research,* 1980, **24,** 75–77.

Loggie, J. M. H. Hypertension in children and adolescents. *Hospital Practice,* 1975, **10,** 81.

Management Committee of the Australian Hypertension Trial. The Australian Therapeutic Trial in Mild Hypertension. *Lancet,* 1980, **1,** 1261–1269.

McCarron, D. A. Calcium, magnesium and phosphorus balance in human and experimental hypertension. *Hypertension,* 1982, **4**(Suppl. III), III27–III33.

McCarron, D. A., Morris, C. D., Cole, C. Dietary calcium and human hypertension. *Science,* 1982, **217,** 267–269.

Meneely, G. R. T., & Battarbee, H. D. High sodium–low potassium environment and hypertension. *American Journal of Cardiology,* 1976, **38,** 768.

National Heart, Lung and Blood Institute (NHLBI). Report of the Task Force on Blood Pressure Control in Children. *Pediatrics,* 1977, **59**(Suppl.), 797.

Oliver, W. J., Cohen, E. L., & Neel, J. V. Blood pressure, sodium intake and sodium related hormones in the Yanomamo Indians, a "no-salt" culture. *Circulation,* 1975, **52,** 146.

Paffenbarger, R. S., Thorne, M. C., & Wing, A. L. Chronic disease in former college students: VIII. Characteristics in youths predisposing to hypertension in later years. *American Journal of Epidemiology*, 1968, **88**, 25.

Page, L. B. Nutritional determinants of hypertension. *Current Concepts in Nutrition*, 1981, **10**, 113–116.

Page, L. B., Damon, A., & Moellering, R. C. L. Antecedents of cardiovascular disease in six Solomon Islands societies. *Circulation*, 1974, **46**, 1132.

Parijs, J., Joossens, J. V., Van der Linden, L., Vertreken, G., & Amery, A. Moderate sodium restriction and diuretics in the treatment of hypertension. *American Heart Journal*, 1977, **85**, 22.

Prior, I. A. M., Hooper, A., Huntsman, J., Stanhope, J. M., & Salmond, C. E. The Tokelau Island Migrant Study. In G. A. Harrison (Ed.), *Population structure and human variation.* Cambridge, England: Cambridge University Press, 1977.

Reisen, E., Abel, R., Modan, M., Silverberg, D. S., Eliahou, H. E., & Modan, B. Effect of weight loss without salt restriction on the reduction of blood pressure in overweight hypertensive patients. *New England Journal of Medicine*, 1978, **298**, 1.

Rosenman, R. H., Brand, R. J., Jenkins, C. D., Friedman, M., Straus, R., & Wurm, W. Coronary heart disease in the Western Collaborative Group Study: Final follow-up experience of 8½ years. *Journal of the American Medical Association*, 1975, **233**, 872–877.

Schieken, R. M., Clarke, W. R., & Lauer, R. M. The cardiovascular responses to exercise in children across the blood pressure distribution. *Hypertension*, 1983, **5**, 71–78.

Severs, P. S., Gordon, D., Peart, W. J., & Beighton, P. Blood pressure and its correlates in urban and tribal Africa. *Lancet*, 1980, **2**, 60–64.

Siegel, J. M., & Leitch, C. J. Behavioral factors and blood pressure in adolescence: The Tacoma Study. *American Journal of Epidemiology*, 1981, **113**, 171–181.

Soltero, I., Tsong, Y., Cooper, R., Stamler, J., Stamler, R., & Garside, D. A survey of patterns of nonpharmacologic care for hypertensive patients, including recommendations for their children. *Hypertension*, 1980, **2**, 215–220.

Stenn, P. G., Noce, A., & Buck, C. A study of the labeling phenomenon in school children with elevated blood pressure. *Clinical and Investigative Medicine*, 1981, **4**, 179–181.

Szklo, M. Epidemiologic patterns of blood pressure in children. *Epidemiologic Review*, 1979, **1**, 143.

Veterans Administration Cooperative Study Group on Antihypertensive Agents. Effects of treatment on morbidity in hypertension: II. Results in patients with diastolic blood pressure averaging 90 through 114 mm Hg. *Journal of the American Medical Association*, 1970, **213**, 1143–1152.

Voors, A. W., Webber, L. S., & Berenson, G. S. Time course study of blood pressure in children over a three-year period: Bogalusa Heart Study. *Hypertension*, 1980, 2(Suppl I), I102–I109.

Voors, A. W., Webber, L. S., Frerichs, R. R., & Berenson, G. S. Body height and body mass as determinants of basal blood pressure in children: The Bogalusa Heart Study. *American Journal of Epidemiology*, 1977, **106**, 101–108.

Wallace, R. B., Tamir, I., Heiss, G., Rifkind, B. M., Christensen, B., & Glueck, C. J. Plasma lipids, lipoproteins, and blood pressure in female adolescents using oral contraceptives. *Journal of Pediatrics*, 1979, **95**, 1055–1059.

Woods, J. W., Falk, R. J., Pittman, A. W., Klemmer, P. J., Watson, B. D., & Namboodiri, K. Increased red-cell, sodium-lithium counter-transport in normotensive sons of hypertensive parents. *New England Journal of Medicine*, 1982, **306**, 593.

CHAPTER 52

POTENTIAL FOR CONTROL AND PREVENTION OF ESSENTIAL HYPERTENSION IN THE BLACK COMMUNITY

RICHARD F. GILLUM

BRENDA S. GILLUM

University of Minnesota

Speak the truth to the people
Talk sense to the people
Free them with reason
Free them with honesty
Free the people with Love and Courage and Care for their being . . .
                                        —Mari Evans (Evans, 1970)

BACKGROUND

Prevalence and Incidence of Essential Hypertension in Blacks

Essential hypertension and its sequelae are the leading health problems of black Americans. The prevalence of definite hypertension (blood pressure > 160/95 mmHg) among black adults is approximately twice that among white adults (Figure 52.1) (Apostolides, Cutter, Kraus Oberman, Blaszkowski, Borhani, & Entwisle, 1980; Gillum, 1979; NCHS, 1975; Wassertheil-Smoller, Apostolides, Miller, Oberman, & Thom, 1979). Likewise, mean blood pressure levels at any given age among black adults average 5 to 10 mm higher than those among white adults. Although it is uncertain whether genetic or physiological bases exist for these differences, the lower socioeconomic status and higher socioecological stress levels

The work reported herein was supported by grants from the Minnesota Affiliate, Inc., American Heart Association; Medical Staff Fund, Mt. Sinai Hospital; The Prudential Foundation; the Minnesota Medical Foundation; and Research Career Development Award K04–HL00329 from the National Heart, Lung and Blood Institute. The authors wish to acknowledge the contributions of the following persons to our community demonstration effort: Francine Chakolis, M.S.W.; William Udoka, M.P.H.; Daniel K. Zismer, Ph.D.; the administrators, principals, and health teachers of the Minneapolis Public Schools; Sandra Seibert, R.N.; and Drs. Cheryl Perry and Neil Bracht of the Minnesota Heart Health program. The authors also thank Drs. H. Blackburn, R. Grimm, and S. A. James and Ms. Arlene Hall for their editorial assistance.

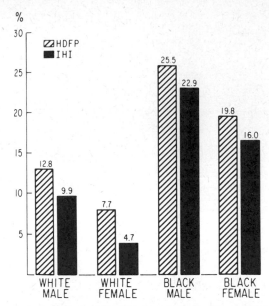

Figure 52.1 Prevalence of elevated diastolic blood pressure (≥ 95 mmHg) in 1973–1974 (HDFP) and 1977–1978 (IHI) among persons aged 30 to 69 years in three U.S. communities: Baltimore, Md.; Birmingham, Ala.; Davis, Calif. (From Apostolides, A. Y., Cutter, G., Kraus, J. F., Oberman, A., Blaszkowski, T., Borhani, N. O., & Entwisle, G. Impact of hypertension information on high blood pressure control between 1973 and 1978. *Hypertension,* 1980, **2,** 708–713. Reproduced by permission of the American Heart Association, Inc.)

of blacks are probably important (Gillum, 1979). Most surveys have found no consistent blood pressure differences between black and white children below the age of 10 (Gillum, Horibe, & Palta, 1980). The blood pressure differences seen in adults first become consistently apparent in adolescence (NCHS, 1977). It is also interesting that blood pressures of blacks in America are consistently higher than even those of urbanized blacks in West Africa (Akinkugbe, 1972). The vascular sequelae of hypertension are the leading killers of blacks in the United States (Gillum, 1982; Gillum & Grant, 1982; Wing & Manton, 1981). For hypertensive disease and stroke (Figure 52.2), the black-to-white mortality ratios are as high as 7 to 1, especially in younger age groups. This mortality is out of proportion to hypertension prevalence and is a reflection of inadequate hypertension detection and treatment. Black men have coronary heart disease rates similar to those of white men, but black women have much higher coronary heart disease rates than white women (Gillum, 1982; Gillum & Grant, 1982). This observation requires intensive investigation.

Hypertension Control in Blacks

Greatly improved hypertension awareness, treatment and control levels since the 1960's may have played a role in accelerating the declines in death rates from stroke (Figure 52.2) and coronary heart disease (Gillum, 1982; Gillum & Grant, 1982; Wing & Manton, 1981). Despite continuing progress, however, surveys from the 1970s indicate that hypertension control levels among blacks remain unacceptably poor, particularly in view of the high prevalence (Figure 52.3) (Apostolides et al., 1980; Wassertheil-Smoller et al., 1979). Of special concern are black men, who have the highest prevalence of any group (Figure 52.1) and also the poorest control rates (Figure 52.3). Control rates in many areas of the country may be even poorer than those shown in the figures.

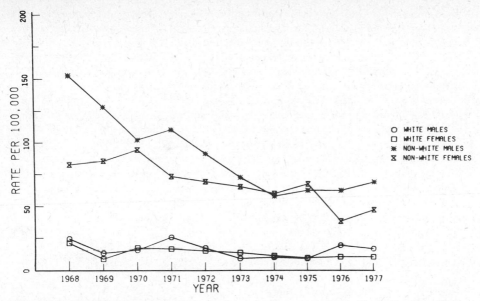

Figure 52.2 Mortality rate for stroke in blacks and whites aged 40–45, North Carolina, 1968 to 1977. (From Wing, S., & Manton, K. G. A multiple cause of death analysis of hypertension-related mortality in North Carolina, 1968–1977. *American Journal of Public Health,* 1981, **71,** 823–830. Reproduced by permission.)

Hypertension Control and Prevention: Potential versus Reality

The Hypertension Detection and Follow-up Program has clearly demonstrated the potential of hypertension control for reducing mortality among blacks (Hypertension Detection, 1979). Mortality was 22.4% lower for blacks in the intensive step-care program compared with

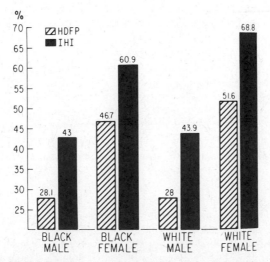

Figure 52.3 Percentage of actual hypertensives (DBP ≥ 95 mmHg or on treatment) treated and under control (DBP < 95 mmHg) in 1973–1974 (HDFP) and 1977–1978 (IHI) among persons aged 30 to 69 years in three U.S. communities: Baltimore, Md.; Birmingham, Ala.; Davis, Calif. (From Apostolides, A. Y., Cutter, G., Kraus, J. F., Oberman, A., Blaszkowski, T., Borhani, N. O., & Entwisle, G. Impact of hypertension information on high blood pressure control between 1973 and 1978. *Hypertension,* 1980, **2,** 708–713. Reproduced by permission of the American Heart Association, Inc.)

those randomized to usual care in the community. The corresponding differential was only 10% for whites. Computations using attributable risk statistics, based on results of screening programs, indicate a similar potential for mortality reduction (Ouellet, Apostolides, Entwisle, & Hebel, 1979). Tyroler, Heyden, and Hames (1975) have also shown that control of obesity in the black community might prevent nearly 30% of the new cases of hypertension. A reduction in sodium intake and an increase in potassium and calcium intakes might also contribute to prevention (Prineas, Gillum, & Blackburn, 1980).

High rates of noncompliance with follow-up and drug therapy, however, seriously compromise the efforts of community-wide programs. Indeed, noncompliance with therapeutic or preventive health advice is now the major barrier to effective hypertension control in the United States. The determinants of noncompliance among blacks have been investigated (Gillum & Barsky, 1974; Gillum, Neutra, Stason, & Solomon, 1979). Several strategies for improving the rates of referral and short-term blood pressure control in black populations have been reported (Gillum, 1974; Gillum, Solomon, Kranz, Boepple, & Creighton, 1976; Gillum, Stason, & Weinstein, 1978; Zismer, Gillum, Johnson, Becerra, & Johnson, 1982), but few communities have implemented them.

AN APPROACH TO HYPERTENSION CONTROL AND PREVENTION

A Community Demonstration Program

Our goal has been to develop and implement a comprehensive and rational plan for hypertension control and prevention in a black urban community (Gillum et al., 1978) and to do this with a minimum of external funding, in the hope that our experience might be broadly applicable, given today's economic realities. With funds available in any given year ranging from only $8,000 to $20,000, an ongoing demonstration program was established.

The first stage of the program consisted of the evaluation and improvement of hypertension management in a large family practice. An audit of hypertension management was conducted, and a system for appointment reminders and patient education was developed and evaluated (Zismer et al., 1982). The patient education component was administered by the clinic nurse and a graduate student. Patient education was associated with a statistically significant difference in blood pressure lowering in the treatment group after 6 months, as compared to a randomized control group (Table 52.1).

Case finding in the family practice continued, and an outreach strategy was planned and implemented (Gillum et al., 1978). A baseline blood pressure screening targeted at black men included a questionnaire survey to identify barriers to hypertension control that were specific to this group. The early findings of this survey were important in developing the community education program, which aimed at improving hypertension prevention and control, especially among younger black men.

A targeted screening program was initiated in the spring of 1981 after consultation with community leaders and health professionals. The targeted group was black men under the age of 60. Two strategies were used to reach this group: door-to-door screening and site screening.

Door-to-door screening was conducted in a census tract where 75% of the residents enumerated in the 1970 census were black. The census tract contained a public housing project, low-income apartments, and some single-family dwellings. Dwelling units were enumerated and listed. A team of community persons was recruited and trained to administer a 30-minute interview and to measure blood pressure in the home using standard technique. Two readings from the right arm were taken, with the subject seated after 5 minutes rest. The readings were averaged. Limited resources prevented conducting the survey in the entire census tract as originally planned. The results, therefore, are not to be considered representative of the entire census tract or the entire Minneapolis black community.

Site screenings were held at prominent community locations: a shopping center, a super-

Table 52.1   Blood Pressure Changes Associated with Intervention in Treatment and Control Groups after 6 Months (in mmHg)

Group	Blood Pressure	Baseline, Mean [a]	Follow-up, Mean [b]	Change, Mean [c]
Treatment	Systolic	143.58(15.16)	130.50(12.46)	−13.08(10.41)
(N = 26)	Diastolic	93.23(10.41)	85.00(8.70)	−8.23(8.46)
Control	Systolic	148.23(16.11)	150.85(18.70)	+2.62(9.84)
(N = 13)	Diastolic	91.54(11.68)	92.00(11.78)	+0.46(6.90)

Source: Reproduced by permission from Zismer, D., Gillum, R. F., Johnson, C. A., Becerra, J., & Johnson, T. H. Improving hypertension control in a private medical practice. Archives of Internal Medicine, 1982, **142**, 297–299.
Note: Numbers in parentheses are standard deviations.
[a] Preintervention comparison of mean blood pressure in treatment and control groups, using a t test for independent samples: systolic, $t(37) = 0.89$, $p > .3$; diastolic, $t(37) = 0.46$, $p > .5$.
[b] Postintervention comparison of mean blood pressure in treatment and control groups, using a t test for independent samples: systolic, $t(37) = 4.05$, $p < .01$; diastolic, $t(37) = 2.10$, $p > .05$.
[c] Comparison of mean blood pressure changes in treatment and control groups, using a t test for independent samples: systolic, $t(37) = 4.52$, $p < .001$; diastolic, $t(37) = 3.20$, $p < .001$.

market, and a youth fair sponsored by a community agency. A short, two-page questionnaire on knowledge, attitudes, and beliefs about hypertension was administered to black men only. Blood pressure was measured as described earlier. Given the limited resources available, the site-screening strategy proved to be much more cost-effective.

Targeted site screenings are being continued in cooperation with the Minneapolis Urban League. All persons screened and found to have elevated blood pressures are referred to their private physicians or clinics, or to a community health facility if they have no family physician. Approximately 4 weeks later, all persons so referred are recontacted by mail to reinforce the advice to see a physician about their blood pressure. Although the program itself has not had resources to establish a communitywide tracking program, it has attempted, with some success, to stimulate health providers of the community to improve follow-up systems for patients served. The tickler file tracking system originally established by the program in the private family practice is still being used there (Zismer et al., 1982). A major county-funded community health center is currently conducting a comprehensive hypertension audit and is establishing a tracking system.

Questionnaire Results

Table 52.2 shows some demographic and personal characteristics of persons interviewed at home and at site screenings. Between 22% and 62% (depending on sex and site) of persons who gave a history of having been told of elevated blood pressure or of having a diastolic blood pressure $\geq$ 95 mmHg at screening claimed to have been on medication at one time. Less than half of these were currently on medication. Among a random sample of 1,038 white men in the Minneapolis–St. Paul metropolitan area in 1980, 59.4% of 281 with a history of hypertension had ever been on medication, and 83% of these were still on medication.

Table 52.3 shows the results of an item analysis of the questionnaire concerning knowledge, attitudes, and beliefs about hypertension given to black men at site screening. Completed questionnaires were obtained from 96 of the 131 black men screened. Responses are reported separately for those with a history of hypertension and for those with no history of hypertension. Only 25% of those with a hypertension history were currently on medication. Most claimed to have had their blood pressure measured within the last 6 months, and the vast majority within the last year. Overall, the level of knowledge about hypertension was low,

Table 52.2   Demographic Characteristics and Hypertension Prevalence among Minneapolis Blacks Screened in 1981

Characteristic	Home Screen (%)		Site Screen (%)	
	BM[a]	BW[b]	BM[c]	BW[d]
History of HBP	28.3	36.0	19.8	51.9
DBP ≥ 95	10.3	7.0	11.0	13.6
History of HBP or DBP ≥ 95	37.9	39.4	25.2	59.1
SPB ≥ 160	1.7	8.3	1.5	0.0
History of HBP and ever on medication	29.4	44.4	38.5	57.1
History of HBP and still on medication	17.6	25.9	3.8	28.6
History of HBP or DBP ≥ 95 and ever on medication	22.7	39.3	31.2	61.5
History of HBP or DBP ≥ 95 and still on medication	13.6	14.3	3.1	30.7
Age < 50	70.0	98.7	86.3	70.4
Height ≤ 69 in.	75.0	96.0	48.1	100.0
Weight > 160 lbs	73.7	9.3	63.4	25.9

Note: BM = black men; BW = black women; HBP = high blood pressure; DBP = diastolic blood pressure; SBP = systolic blood pressure.
[a] Number screened = 60.
[b] Number screened = 75.
[c] Number screened = 131.
[d] Number screened = 27.

and there were important areas of misinformation. Most respondents believed that high blood pressure has symptoms and that they could tell when their blood pressure was high. Although most knew that high blood pressure was related to heart attack and stroke, very few knew its relationship to kidney disease. Many respondents were unaware of the need for combined long-term drug and dietary therapy for high blood pressure. A third of those without a history of hypertension feared sexual and other side effects of medications. Such misinformation, paired with a low perceived susceptibility, poses a significant barrier to hypertension control and prevention. Furthermore, most respondents were suspicious of health programs sponsored by government or voluntary agencies. More than 50% feared government spying. Despite this attitude, most expressed a strong desire for more help with community health problems. Compared to the aforementioned 1980 survey of white men, knowledge levels of black men were lower for the comparable questions asked each group.

Community Education

Since previous experience in this community and the preliminary survey results indicated that lack of information and misinformation about hypertension prevention and control constituted a major barrier to effective control and prevention, a community education effort, the Community Heart Health Program, was undertaken. Program goals were improvement in hypertension control, especially among younger black men, and prevention of hypertension among all community residents. Community leaders, health professionals, and media representatives were involved in the planning. A long-time community resident was selected as program coordinator. Cooperative arrangements and communication lines were estab-

Table 52.3   Knowledge, Attitudes, and Beliefs about High Blood Pressure among Black Men Responding to Questionnaire, Minneapolis, 1981

Respondent Characteristics	History of Hypertension	No History of Hypertension
Number	25	71
Age in years (mean ± SD)	41 ± 16	32 ± 8
Months since diagnosis (mean ± SD)	46 ± 46	—
HBP diagnosed by M.D. office or hospital (%)	91	—
On medication (%)	25	—
Months on medication (mean ± SD)	52 ± 42	—
Questionnaire statements:[a]		
"Hypertension" is same as "HPB"	39	28
HPB is a problem of blacks under 50 years	33	15
Race or age doesn't matter	33	71
HPB is mostly a problem for men	94	92
HPB can be cured by doctor	50	78
HPB has symptoms	77	78
I can tell when by BP is high	70	53
Use own judgment on M.D. advice	32	54
My health is out of control	23	6
HBP changes lifestyle	35	66
HBP affects many of my age and sex	65	56
BP pills cause		
Dizziness	24	23
Sex problems	12	36
Nausea	8	21
Tiredness	28	32
No effects	28	21
Other effects	8	7
Community health programs are used for government spying on people	48	57
My BP is		
High	39	0
Normal	30	74
Low	0	0
Don't know	30	26
HBP symptoms reported (%)		
Headaches	60	55
Dizziness	56	59
Nose bleeds	28	34
Rash	0	7
Seeing stars	16	18
Tiredness	16	18
Nervousness	16	35
No symptoms	40	46

Note: SD = standard deviation; HBP = high blood pressure; BP = blood pressure.
[a] Percentage agreeing with the statement.

lished with other agencies and institutions with an interest in or responsibility for hypertension control, in an attempt to prevent duplication of services or needless competition. The Minneapolis Urban League has been particularly cooperative. An office was established in the community as a base for operations and an information center for residents.

High School Component

In a special effort to reach younger black men, a hypertension and cardiovascular education module was developed for high school seniors (Table 52.4). It seeks to provide adolescents with vital health information for the prevention and control of hypertension. This information may be shared with family members and friends now and will be reinforced by community education efforts in later years, when these young people are at higher risk for the disease. The project coordinator and a medical student taught the 4-hour module in health classes in five senior high schools, where minority enrollments ranged from 16% to 100%. American Heart Association and National High Blood Pressure Education Program materials were used for the course.

The effectiveness of the module was evaluated as follows. Class attendance was taken. Of 682 students enrolled in the module, only 37 students missed two or more of the 4 hours. An additional 74 students missed 1 hour. These absentee rates are at or below those generally observed at these schools. A test consisting of 30 true–false questions was given to the students before and at the conclusion of the module. For the 617 students completing both tests, the average score on the pretest was 17.4 of 30 correct (58%), rising to 26.7 of 30 correct (89%) on the posttest. In addition, students were asked to rate the program on a five-point scale; 81.4% rated it highly favorable or moderately favorable, 14.1% adequate, 3% poor, 0.5% not beneficial.

Community Organization Component

To reach adults in the black community, existing community service, professional, and social organizations were enlisted to assist in providing hypertension information to their

Table 52.4 Four-Day Program for High School Seniors

Day	Activities
Day One	(1) Introduction of the program
	(2) Administration of the pretest
	(3) Film: "Understanding High Blood Pressure"
	(4) Definitions: atherosclerosis, cholesterol, sodium, etc.
	(5) Demonstration of the relationship between hypertension and some identifiable risk factors—e.g., obesity, heredity, salt intake, sex, age, stress
Day Two	(1) Film: "The Hard Way," produced by the National High Blood Pressure Education Program
	(2) Discussion, questions, answers, and review
Day Three	(1) Administration of the posttest
	(2) Review of previous activities from Day One and Day Two
	(3) Film: "Game of Chance," produced by the American Heart Association
	(4) Filmstrip/tape: "Heart Hearty—Low Salt Diet"
	(5) Explanation and demonstration of blood pressure equipment, hands-on practice
Day Four[a]	(1) Return of pretests and posttests to students, review of tests
	(2) Distribution of literature on high blood pressure
	(3) Completion of course evaluations by students and teachers

Note: Classes in the Minneapolis Public Schools are 50 minutes long. Presentations are made to four to five health classes daily for a period of 4 days and are self-contained units; that is, even if one or more days of the program are missed, a student will benefit from any sessions attended.
[a] Day Three and Day Four can be combined, if necessary.

members. Presentations were made and literature distributed at scheduled meetings of these organizations. Some of the same films and educational materials presented to high school students were used. One approach developed by the project coordinator involved presenting information in block clubs that initially had been organized for crime prevention.

Media Coverage

Feature stories, a health column, and advertisements were run intermittently in the three black-oriented community newspapers, together with health message spots and appearances on talk shows on the low-power community radio station. In addition, community service spots were placed on several commercial radio and television stations. These spots were produced by the American Heart Association and National High Blood Pressure Program specifically for black audiences. News coverage of community screening events were obtained from several television stations. Flyers and posters publicizing screening events were distributed, and a telephone information line was set up to provide information on hypertension and cardiovascular health.

DISCUSSION

The current experience in Minneapolis indicates that high blood pressure treatment and control levels remain low, particularly among black men in urban environments. Misinformation on hypertension abounds and deters efforts to improve high blood pressure control. Although the respondents were suspicious of programs conducted by outside agencies, they clearly wanted more help with health problems in their community. The favorable response to the present community demonstration program indicates that it can serve as a model for overcoming these barriers to hypertension and control in the black community. It must be evaluated along with similar local and statewide programs to assess their long-term impact on hypertension prevalence and control in the black community.

From the literature available on barriers to hypertension control in the black community, it is clear that inadequate financial resources, inconvenient locations of health care facilities, and long waiting times are serious problems (Gillum, 1974; Gillum et al., 1979). Information about knowledge, attitudes, and beliefs in a large sample of black respondents is available from two nationwide surveys conducted by the National High Blood Pressure Education Program of the National Institutes of Health (National Heart and Lung Institute, 1973; National Heart, Lung and Blood Institute, 1981). The 1973 survey included 2,829 blacks, with a response rate of 69%. It indicated that, although most blacks perceive hypertension as serious, knowledge about hypertension and its causes, complications, prevention, and treatment was low. Common misconceptions were that high blood pressure is symptomatic and that stress is the major cause. The 1979 follow-up survey included 1,449 blacks, with a 66% response rate. Among those surveyed, hypertension prevalence and treatment status had changed little between 1973 and 1979. In general, there was some improvement in knowledge about hypertension, but major gaps and misconceptions in the areas of definitions, sequelae, and treatment remained. Of black hypertensives who had ever been on medication, 83% said they could tell when their blood pressure was high; 69% of hypertensives never on medication and 51% of normotensives gave this response. These findings were similar to the results of our small Minneapolis survey. Substantial differences in the degree and type of misinformation and lack of information existed between blacks and whites in both surveys. Gains in knowledge were greater in blacks than in whites, indicating that high blood pressure education efforts of the 1970s did have an impact and that continuous vigorous efforts in the black community are likely to be fruitful.

Williams (1979) administered a 50-item questionnaire assessing awareness of coronary heart disease risk factors to 300 adults aged 18 to 65 years in predominantly black neighborhoods of a southern city. Overall, a low level of awareness of coronary risk factors, including hypertension, was found, with a mean score for the entire sample of 12.73 correct. Scores were higher among older people, among those with higher educational levels, and among women. The differences were not large, however. Results for questions about hypertension were not reported separately.

A Chicago study demonstrated a lower baseline level of knowledge about coronary risk among blacks compared to whites but a greater gain in knowledge and a decrease in serum cholesterol with intervention among blacks (Mojonnier, Hall, Berkson, Robinson, Wethers, Pannbacker, Moss, Pardo, Stamler, Shekelle, & Raynor, 1980).

RECOMMENDATIONS FOR FUTURE RESEARCH AND PROGRAMS

Hypertension, through its sequelae, coronary heart disease and stroke, is the leading health problem in the black community. Coronary heart disease is the number one killer of blacks in the United States, whose mortality rates are among the highest in the world. Coronary heart disease mortality rates are higher in black women than in white women. Stroke mortality is also exceedingly great, constituting the second leading cause of death, with rates much higher in blacks of both sexes than in whites.

These diseases are largely preventable through vigorous treatment and prevention of hypertension. There is an urgent need for further research in black communities around the country on the behavioral barriers to adequate hypertension control and prevention among blacks. Data currently available indicate that there are major racial differences in knowledge, attitudes, beliefs, and misconceptions concerning hypertension control.

Limited program resources, including National Heart, Lung and Blood Institute research and demonstration grants, should be targeted to the black community because of the much higher cost-effectiveness in terms of lives saved and reduced mortality and morbidity there, as demonstrated by the Hypertension Detection and Follow-up Program. Program emphasis should be shifted from one-time screening to follow-up of established hypertensives' compliance with medication and to community education for hypertension control and prevention. That patient tracking and education do improve hypertension control has been documented. Tracking and education procedures should be implemented in all health care facilities in black communities. Community education efforts should use the information now available on knowledge gaps and misconceptions to develop effective health messages. Since surveys have shown that, next to physicians' offices, radio and television are the most important sources of health information in the community (National Heart and Lung Institute, 1973; National Heart, Lung and Blood Institute, 1981), they should be used heavily in community education efforts. Relatives and friends are also important sources and motivators, as are community organizations.

Health programs generated from within the black community, administered through existing organizations and networks, and supported by government and private funding sources are most likely to gain acceptance. Such programs can improve control and prevention of hypertension among blacks.

The public health professions must persist in efforts to educate the public and its elected officials on the importance of continued progress in the struggle for social and economic justice in improving the health status and life expectancy of blacks and other minorities (Cooper, Steinhauer, Schatzkin, & Miller, 1981).

REFERENCES

Akinkugbe, O. O. *High blood pressure in the African.* Edinburgh: Churchill Livingstone, 1972.

Apostolides, A. Y., Cutter, G., Kraus, J. F., Oberman, A., Blaszkowski, T., Borhani, N. O., & Entwisle, G. Impact of hypertension information on high blood pressure control between 1973 and 1978. *Hypertension,* 1980, **2**, 708–713.

Cooper, R., Steinhauer, M., Schatzkin, A., & Miller, W. Improved mortality among U.S. blacks, 1968–1978: The role of the antiracist struggle. *International Journal of Health Services,* 1981, **11**, 511–522.

Evans, M. *I am a black woman.* New York: Morrow, 1970.

Gillum, R. F. Patient education. *Journal of the National Medical Association,* 1974, **66,** 156–159.

Gillum, R. F. Pathophysiology of hypertension in blacks and whites: A review of the basis of racial blood pressure differences. *Hypertension,* 1979, **1,** 468–475.

Gillum, R. F. Coronary heart disease in black populations: I. Mortality and morbidity. *American Heart Journal,* 1982, 104, 839–851.

Gillum, R. F., & Barsky, A. Diagnosis and management of patient non-compliance. *Journal of the American Medical Association,* 1974, **228,** 1563–1567.

Gillum, R. F., & Grant, C. T. Coronary heart disease in black populations: II. Risk factors. *American Heart Journal,* 1982, 104, 852–864.

Gillum, R. F., Horibe, H., & Palta, M. Blood pressure and other characteristics of urban Native American school children. *Hypertension,* 1980, **2,** 744–749.

Gillum, R. F., Neutra, R., Stason, W. B., & Solomon, H. S. Determinants of drop-out rate among hypertensive patients in an urban clinic. *Journal of Community Health,* 1979, **5,** 94–100.

Gillum, R. F., Solomon, H. D., Kranz, P., Boepple, P., & Creighton, M. Improving hypertension detection and referral in an ambulatory setting. *Archives of Internal Medicine,* 1976, **138,** 700–703.

Gillum, R. F., Stason, W. B., & Weinstein, M. C. Screening for hypertension: A rational approach. *Journal of Community Health,* 1978, **4,** 67–72.

Hypertension Detection and Follow-up Program. Five-year findings of the Hypertension Detection and Follow-up Program: II. Mortality by race, sex and age. *Journal of the American Medical Association,* 1979, **242,** 2572–2577.

Mojonnier, M. L., Hall, Y., Berkson, D. M., Robinson, E., Wethers, B., Pannbacker, F. B., Moss, D., Pardo, E., Stamler, J., Shekelle, R. B., & Raynor, W. Experiences in changing food habits in hyperlipidemic men and women. *Journal of the American Dietetic Association,* 1980, **77,** 140–148.

National Center for Health Statistics (NCHS). *Blood pressure of persons 18–74 years in the United States, 1971–1972.* Vital and Health Statistics, Series 11, No. 150. Washington, D.C.: U.S. Government Printing Office, 1975.

National Center for Health Statistics (NCHS). *Blood pressure of youths 12–17 years, United States, 1966–70.* Vital and Health Statistics, Series 11, No. 163, DHEW Pub. No. (HRA)77–1645. Washington, D.C.: U.S. Government Printing Office, 1977.

National Heart and Lung Institute. *The public and high blood pressure.* DHEW Pub. No. (NIH)74–356. Washington, D.C.: U.S. Government Printing Office, 1973.

National Heart, Lung and Blood Institute. *The public and high blood pressure: Six-year followup survey of public knowledge and reported behavior.* NIH Pub. No. 81–2118. Washington, D.C.: U.S. Government Printing Office, 1981.

Ouellet, R. P., Apostolides, A., Entwisle, G., & Hebel, J. R. Estimated impact of hypertension control in a high risk population. *American Journal of Epidemiology,* 1979, **109,** 531–538.

Prineas, R. J., Gillum, R. F., & Blackburn, H. Possibilities for primary prevention of hypertension. In R. M. Lauer & R. B. Shekelle (Eds.), *Childhood prevention of atherosclerosis and hypertension.* New York: Raven Press, 1980.

Tyroler, H. A., Heyden, S., & Hames, C. G. Weight and hypertension: Evans County studies of blacks and whites. In O. Paul (Ed.), *Epidemiology and control of hypertension.* New York: Stratton Intercontinental Medicine Books, 1975.

Wassertheil-Smoller, S., Apostolides, A., Miller, M., Oberman, A., & Thom, T. Recent status of detection, treatment and control of hypertension in the community. *Journal of Community Health,* 1979, **5,** 82–93.

Williams, P. B. Assessing awareness of coronary disease risk factors in the black community. *Urban Health,* 1979, **8,** 34–39.

Wing, S., & Manton, K. G. A multiple cause of death analysis of hypertension-related mortality in North Carolina, 1968–1977. *American Journal of Public Health,* 1981, **71,** 823–830.

Zismer, D., Gillum, R. F., Johnson, C. A., Becerra, J., & Johnson, T. H. Improving hypertension control in a private medical practice. *Archives of Internal Medicine,* 1982, **142,** 297–299.

CHAPTER 53

HYPERTENSION AND EXERCISE: THE ROLE OF PHYSICAL CONDITIONING IN TREATMENT AND PREVENTION

J. ALAN HERD

Baylor College of Medicine, Houston, Texas

L. HOWARD HARTLEY

Harvard Medical School, Boston, Massachusetts

Prevention and treatment of hypertension by exercise, weight control, and sodium restriction have been suggested as alternatives to drug treatment for otherwise healthy people. The possibility that regular exercise and physical conditioning might be effective in controlling levels of arterial blood pressure is suggested by two lines of evidence. The first line of evidence is based on the physiological effects of physical conditioning, which result in lower heart rates (Branwell & Ellis, 1929), lower plasma concentrations of plasma catecholamines during exercise (Hartley, Mason, Hogan, Jones, Kotchen, Mougey, Wherry, Pennington, & Ricketts, 1972a, 1972b), and lower rates of uptake and turnover for norepinephrine in hearts of conditioned animals (Ostman, Sjostrand, & Swedin, 1972; Salzman, Hirsch, Hellerstein, & Bruell, 1970). The likelihood that physical conditioning reduces sympathetic nervous system activity, at least during exercise, suggests that physical conditioning might reduce the neurogenic component of hypertension.

A second line of evidence is based on the observation that populations or individuals with high levels of physical activity have a lower prevalence of coronary heart disease and lowered death rates from cardiovascular diseases (Fox, Naughton, & Haskell, 1971; Morris, Pollard, Everitt, & Chave, 1980; Paffenbarger & Hale, 1975). Although arterial hypertension is only one risk factor contributing to coronary heart disease, reduced incidence of arterial hypertension probably contributes to the reduced incidence of morbidity and mortality. Experimental studies of nonhuman primates have demonstrated that regular exercise reduces the severity of coronary artery disease (Kramisch, Aspen, Abramowitz, Kreimendahl, & Hood, 1981). Thus, the cardiovascular response to exercise and physical conditioning apparently has an effect on levels of arterial blood pressure and severity of coronary heart disease.

The type of exercise usually referred to in physical conditioning programs is isotonic exercise of large muscle groups during such activities as walking, running, bicycling, and swimming. When these forms of exercise are performed at an intensity supported by oxygen and metabolic substrates that can be delivered by circulating blood during exercise, they are referred to as aerobic exercise. The concept of aerobic exercise implies that oxygen is supplied in sufficient amounts to meet metabolic requirements during performance of the exercise. The oxygen is delivered by blood flowing intermittently between muscle contractions, which are occurring rhythmically. Other types of exercise that involve lifting, pushing, pulling, or holding with isometric contractions cannot be sustained for long periods of time because blood flow to active skeletal muscles is impeded by their contractions. This muscular work that is not supported by an adequate flow of oxygenated arterial blood is called anaerobic exercise. Vigorous isometric exercise frequently is used to increase muscle mass but has little benefit for increasing the capacity of the cardiopulmonary system to support vigorous physical activity.

Isotonic training with aerobic exercise produces marked cardiovascular adaptations when exercise is carried out in three to four sessions per week for 20 to 45 minutes per session at an intensity level exceeding 60% of the maximal effort possible for short periods of time (Brynteson & Sinning, 1973; Fox, Bartels, Billings, O'Brien, Bason, & Mathews, 1975; Pollock, Cureton, & Greninger, 1969; Sharkey, 1970). As a physical training program proceeds, there is a gradual and progressive increase in cardiovascular fitness over a 5- or 6-week period (Saltin, Blomqvist, Mitchell, Johnson, Wildenthal, & Chapman, 1968). Although the amount of improvement in capacity for physical work varies among individuals, capacity for exercise can be almost doubled after an extended period of regular exercise.

BENEFITS FROM EXERCISE

The effects of regular aerobic exercise on resting blood pressure have been examined in normotensive and healthy subjects as well as in subjects with arterial hypertension. Comparisons between resting blood pressures in athletes and nonathletes have shown lower resting pressures in the athletes (Bevegard, Holmgren, & Jonsson, 1963; Branwell & Ellis, 1929; Mellerowicz, 1966; Saltin & Grimby, 1968). Epidemiologic studies of the relationship between blood pressure and regular exercise have shown variable effects of exercise on blood pressure (Blackburn, 1978; Montoye, Metzner, Keller, Johnson, & Epstein, 1972). Results of longitudinal studies are more persuasive that regular exercise influences resting blood pressures. Lowering of blood pressure with training has been reported in normal subjects by several investigators (Wilmore, Royce, Girandola, Katch, & Katch, 1970). Studies of blood pressure in young people, however, showed little effect of physical conditioning (Ekblom, Astrand, Saltin, Stenberg, & Wallstrom, 1968; Saltin et al., 1968; Tabakin, Hanson, & Levy, 1965). The most consistent reductions in blood pressure following physical conditioning were observed in middle-aged and older subjects (Barry, Daly, Pruett, Steinmetz, Pagett, Birkhead, & Redah, 1966; Hartley, Grimby, Kilbom, Nilsson, Astrand, Bjure, Ekblom, & Saltin, 1969; DeVries, 1970; Terjung, Baldwin, Cooksey, Samson, & Sutter, 1973), suggesting that the benefit of exercise conditioning on blood pressure is better demonstrated in older subjects. The mechanism by which aerobic exercise results in a decrease in arterial blood pressure has been shown to be a decrease in resting cardiac output (Ekblom et al., 1968; Pavlik, Molnar, Farsang, Fenkl, 1980; Saltin et al., 1968; Tabakin et al., 1965). Apparently, little change occurred in peripheral vascular resistance.

Effects of physical conditioning on blood pressure have been better demonstrated in patients with elevated levels of arterial blood pressure. Several investigators have reported results of studies in small groups of subjects (Boyer, Hartley, Hellerstein, Loggie, & Ryan, 1976; Boyer & Kasch, 1970; Choquette & Ferguson, 1973; Hanson & Nedde, 1970; Storer & Ruhling, 1981). Results of these studies suggested that patients with borderline or labile hypertension when cardiac output and heart rate were elevated received greater benefits from physical conditioning than did patients with increased peripheral vascular resistance. Although it is tempting to speculate that physical conditioning reduces sympathetic nervous system activity, the most consistent effects of physical conditioning have been a reduction in resting cardiac output, suggesting a reduction in venous tone and venous return to the heart. In addition, older patients were less likely to have increased sympathetic nervous system activity as a prominent feature of their disorder. Perhaps increased venous tone is a select manifestation of sympathetic nervous system activity in middle-aged and older individuals.

Additional benefits from exercise have been demonstrated in normalizing metabolic disturbances associated with obesity. Effects of physical conditioning on obese subjects seldom influence body weight or body fat composition unless caloric intake is restricted (Bjorntorp, 1976; Bjorntorp, deJounge, Krotkiewski, Sullivan, Sjostrom, & Stenberg, 1973; Bjorntorp, deJounge, Sjostrom, & Sullivan, 1970). Physical training does have pronounced effects, however, on normalizing metabolic disturbances associated with obesity (Bjorntorp, 1976). These metabolic disturbances include decreases of plasma insulin and triglycerides as well as blood glucose. Studies of women with varying degrees of obesity during a physical conditioning program showed that blood pressure decreased consistently after physical training (Krotkiewski, Mandroukas, Sjostrom, Sullivan, Wetterqvist, & Bjorntorp, 1979). Blood pressure elevation was not related to body fat mass, nor was the decrease in blood pressure associated with decrease in body fat content. Instead, correlations were found between decreases in blood pressure and decreases in plasma insulin concentration, levels of triglycerides, and concentrations of blood glucose. These results suggest an association between elevated blood pressure and hyperinsulinemia. The decrease in plasma insulin concentration followed a 6-month period of physical conditioning, but it also has been observed at an earlier stage in a physical training program (Fahlen, Stenberg, & Bjorntorp, 1972). Apparently, physical conditioning may influence metabolic factors as well as cardiac output and sympathetic nervous system activity.

PHYSIOLOGY OF HYPERTENSION

The response of patients with hypertension to vigorous exercise provides additional insight into the pathophysiology of hypertension. Hemodynamic studies of hypertensive patients have shown that heart rate response was greater in the hypertensive patients than in normotensive subjects (Lund-Johansen, 1967). At the same time, there was less of an increase in stroke volume and cardiac output. Total peripheral vascular resistance was higher at all levels of work in the hypertensive individuals, causing a greater increase in blood pressure. The lower cardiac output was balanced by a greater arteriovenous-oxygen difference, and the arteriovenous-oxygen difference increased with age. Both at rest and during exercise, resistance to blood flow through skeletal muscle was increased in hypertensives (Amery, Bossaert, & Verstraete, 1969).

There is also a subgroup of patients with arterial hypertension who have a hyperdynamic circulation (Ulrych, Frohlich, Tarazi, Dustan, & Page, 1969). They have an unusually high cardiac output, heart rate, and cardiopulmonary blood volume (Dustan & Tarazi, 1978; Frohlich, Tarazi, & Dustan, 1969; Ibrahim, Tarazi, Dustan, & Bravo, 1974; Safar, Weiss, London, Frackowiak & Milliez, 1974; Ulrych et al., 1969). During vigorous physical activity, however, peripheral vascular resistance remained higher in the hypertensive subjects than in normotensive subjects, and the left ventricle of those hypertensive subjects performed greater work and was less effective in increasing cardiac output. Thus, the hyperdynamic circulation during rest may be caused by increased sympathetic nervous system activity. A hypertensive response to exercise seems less likely, however, to be caused by abnormal sympathetic nervous system activity.

The physiology of hypertension also includes abnormalities of body composition and glucose metabolism (Berglund, Larsson, Andersson, Larsson, Svardsudd, Bjorntorp, & Wilhelmsen, 1976). Studies of body fat, body cell mass, fasting blood sugar, glucose tolerance, and fasting insulin levels were conducted in both hypertensive and normotensive middle-aged males. The hypertensive subjects were more often obese and more often had an impaired glucose tolerance with a higher fasting insulin level, as compared to normotensive subjects.

These differences were apparent even when hypertensive subjects were matched in body fat composition with normotensive control subjects. Thus, the impaired glucose metabolism demonstrated in the hypertensive subjects may be one of the factors contributing to arterial hypertension. Increased sympathetic nervous system activity may contribute, however, to impairment of glucose metabolism as well as to alterations in hemodynamics of patients with arterial hypertension.

PHYSICAL CONDITIONING

Aerobic exercise training programs involving isotonic exercise of large muscle groups produce a significant increase in capacity for work if the programs continue for at least 4 to 6 weeks, with a schedule of at least 30 minutes per day and three to four sessions per week (Fox et al., 1975; Pollock et al., 1969; Sharkey, 1970). The laboratory procedure used most often to evaluate capacity for physical work is the measurement of maximal possible oxygen uptake when the subject is performing increasing work (Astrand & Rodal, 1970; Rowell, 1974). The principal determinant of oxygen uptake is extraction and consumption of oxygen by tissues, and the principal limitation on delivery of oxygen to tissues is cardiac output. Thus, improvements in capability for physical work cause increases in maximal amount of oxygen consumed, which, in turn, is supported by either an increase in cardiac output or an increase in oxygen extraction by tissues, or by a combination of these two. In normal, healthy subjects, changes in cardiac output are usually proportional to changes in oxygen consumption (Rowell, 1974; Saltin et al., 1968). In addition, enhanced oxygen extraction during exercise accounts for about 50% of the increase in oxygen utilization, an effect that is most prominent in young persons (Rowell, 1974). Thus, the cardiovascular response to physical conditioning includes improvement in cardiac function and improvement in tissue extraction of oxygen.

The effect of physical conditioning on heart rate is usually to lower heart rate at submaximal work loads (Choquette & Ferguson, 1973) with a slight reduction in maximal heart rate (Saltin et al., 1968). Since cardiac output at all levels of work is usually not changed to the extent that heart rate slows following physical conditioning, it follows that stroke volume must be greater both at rest and during exercise. Approximately 50% of the increase in oxygen delivery following physical conditioning is supported by an increase in stroke volume (Rowell, 1974), and the increase in maximum cardiac output is maintained by an increase in stroke volume. Effects of physical conditioning on total peripheral resistance have been variable (Bevegard et al., 1963; Ekblom et al., 1968; Saltin et al., 1968).

Since the cardiovascular system is influenced by endocrine function and sympathetic nervous system activity, it is possible that physical conditioning exerts its effects through endocrine and neurogenic factors. Accordingly, the endocrine response to exercise has been studied in human subjects before and after a physical conditioning program (Hartley et al., 1972a, 1972b). As intensity of physical work was gradually increased, subjects showed increases in plasma concentrations of norepinephrine, epinephrine, growth hormone, and cortisol and a decrease in levels of insulin. Cortisol and epinephrine levels became elevated above resting values only during very heavy work. After 7 weeks of physical conditioning, lower plasma norepinephrine responses to moderate and heavy work and higher insulin levels at all work loads were observed. Since plasma insulin levels were decreased in the presence of increased concentrations of catecholamines (Ellis, 1962), the higher insulin levels at all work loads following physical conditioning may have been caused by lower plasma norepinephrine responses. The lower norepinephrine concentrations and increased insulin levels after training would promote greater utilization of glucose during exercise. No differences in levels of norepinephrine, epinephrine, cortisol, or insulin concentrations at rest were observed following physical conditioning.

In contrast to effects of physical conditioning in subjects of average weight, the effects of physical conditioning in obese subjects included reductions in plasma insulin concentration at rest (Bjorntorp et al., 1970; Bjorntorp, Holm, Jacobsson, Schiller-deJounge, Lundberg, Sjostrom, Smith, & Sullivan, 1977). Even though physical conditioning did not decrease body weight or adipose tissue mass, there was a marked decrease in plasma insulin concentration. Glucose tolerance was not altered, however, and results were interpreted as indicating an increased insulin sensitivity of tissues.

Clinical studies have demonstrated that blood glucose concentrations in patients with diabetes mellitus fall during exercise, and physical conditioning diminishes requirements for exogenous insulin and improves glucose tolerance (Richter, Ruderman, & Schneider, 1981). Physical conditioning also improved glucose tolerance in some noninsulin-treated diabetic subjects (Vranic & Berger, 1979) and markedly decreased the insulin response to glucose administration (Lohman, Liebold, Heilmann, Singer, & Pohl, 1978). These studies also indicated that physical conditioning increased tissue sensitivity to insulin.

The mechanism of augmented insulin sensitivity has been studied through measurements of insulin binding to monocytes in well-trained male athletes and sedentary male control subjects (Koivisto, Soman, Conrad, Hendler, Nadel, & Felig, 1979). The specific binding of radioactive-labeled insulin to monocytes was 69% higher in athletes than in sedentary controls and was correlated with greater physical working capacity. In addition, the concentrations of unlabeled insulin necessary to decrease the specific binding of radioactive-labeled insulin by 50% occurred in monocytes from athletes at a concentration of unlabeled insulin that was lower than in control subjects. These results suggest that physical training increases insulin sensitivity through increased insulin binding to tissue.

SYMPATHETIC NERVOUS SYSTEM ACTIVITY IN HYPERTENSION

The observation that physical conditioning reduces plasma levels of norepinephrine during submaximal work (Hartley et al., 1972a, 1972b) suggests that sympathetic nervous system activity is decreased following physical conditioning. The plasma concentration of norepinephrine, however, provides only a very indirect measure of sympathetic nerve discharge rate. Only a small proportion of the norepinephrine released from sympathetic nerves escapes to plasma (Kopin, 1979; Paton, 1976). In addition, the plasma concentration of norepinephrine is determined not only by the rate of spillover to plasma after release but also by the subsequent rate of removal of norepinephrine from the circulation (Esler, Jackman, Bobik, Kelleher, Jennings, Leonard, Skews, & Korner, 1979). In normal subjects, the disappearance of radioactive-labeled norepinephrine from plasma has been measured after infusion of tracer amounts to a steady-state concentration in plasma. The disappearance of labeled norepinephrine was biexponential, with approximately half of the norepinephrine disappearing with a rapid half-time of approximately 2 minutes and the remainder disappearing with a longer half-time of approximately 33 minutes. The rapid component of removal, which has been attributed to neuronal reuptake of norepinephrine, was prolonged in patients with peripheral sympathetic nerve dysfunction. Hypertensive patients had a prolongation of the rapid early rate of removal to values greater than 2.8 minutes (Esler, Jackman, Bobik, Leonard, Kelleher, Skews, Jennings, & Korner, 1981). This was interpreted as defective neuronal norepinephrine uptake after norepinephrine was released from nerve terminals and greater rates of spillover into plasma. This defect could expose adrenergic receptors to high local norepinephrine concentrations and could contribute to blood pressure elevation in some patients with essential hypertension. Reductions in plasma levels of norepinephrine during work following physical conditioning may represent decreased sympathetic nervous system activity, with either decreased rates of release or increased rates of reuptake. It also is possible that decreased plasma levels represent an increase in the slow removal phase, with increased extractions by active skeletal muscle (Esler, 1982). Unfortunately, results of these studies do not prove that physical conditioning reduces sympathetic nervous system activity either at rest or during exercise.

The possibility that physical conditioning reduces sympathetic nervous system activity directs attention toward the central nervous system mechanisms controlling arterial blood pressure. Many of the antihypertensive drugs that influence sympathetic nervous system activity do so by effects on the central nervous system (Korner & Angus, 1981). Some drugs, such as clonidine and propranolol, have effects on both the central and peripheral components of the sympathetic nervous system. Administration of clonidine to patients with essential hypertension caused marked reductions in plasma norepinephrine concentration by reducing amounts released from nerve terminals and escaping into plasma (Esler, 1982). In contrast, administration of oxprenolol, a beta-adrenergic blocking agent, increased plasma norepinephrine concentrations by reducing the rate at which norepinephrine was removed from plasma (Esler, 1982). If physical conditioning reduces activity in the central component of the sympathetic nervous system, the kinetics of norepinephrine release should be similar to those observed following administration of clonidine. If the lower heart rate following physical conditioning is caused by reduced sensitivity to norepinephrine released from nerve endings, plasma clearance of norepinephrine should be reduced, as is seen in patients treated with beta-adrenergic blocking agents. Since physical conditioning reduces circulating levels of catecholamines, it probably reduces activity in the central components of the nervous system.

Central nervous system control of sympathetic nervous system activity is complex (Korner & Angus, 1981). Catecholamine-containing neurons are located principally in the medullary region of the brain stem and send axons to numerous other regions. Dopamine-containing neurons are located principally in the midbrain and diencephalon and send fibers to the spinal cord. Most antihypertensive drugs that affect the central nervous system influence synthesis, release, or reuptake of catecholamines. Results of recent studies, however, have indicated a role for dopaminergic and serotonergic input in the regulation of sympathetic nervous system activity (Janowsky, Okada, Manier, Applegate, Sulser, & Steranka, 1982; Sowers, Golub, Berger, & Whitfield, 1982; Sowers, Nyby, & Jasberg, 1982; Whitfield, Sowers, Tuck, & Golub, 1980). The relation of dopaminergic activity and control of blood pressure has been uncovered by treatment of patients with bromocriptine, a central and peripheral dopamine agonist (Kaye, Shaw, & Ross, 1976; Kolloch, Kobayaski, & DeQuattro, 1980; Stumpe, Higuchi, Kolloch, Kruck, & Vetter, 1977). This drug has been administered to reduce pituitary secretions of prolactin. It also has been observed to reduce arterial blood pressure in some normotensive subjects (Kolloch, Myers, Kobayaski, & DeQuattro, 1980) and in patients with essential hypertension (Kaye et al., 1976; Stumpe et al., 1977). Bromocriptine reduced arterial blood pressure at rest and during isometric exercise in normotensive subjects and in patients with arterial hypertension (Sowers, Golub, Berger, & Whitfield, 1982). It also decreased the norepinephrine response to upright posture and isometric exercise (Sowers, Golub, Berger, & Whitfield, 1982). Thus, it is apparent that the effects of physical conditioning mimic effects of the dopamine agonist, bromocriptine. Perhaps patients with arterial hypertension have decreased central dopaminergic activity that is partially restored by physical conditioning.

RECOMMENDATIONS FOR TREATMENT AND PREVENTION OF HYPERTENSION

Results of epidemiologic, clinical, and experimental studies of patients with arterial hypertension suggest that many factors contribute to elevations of arterial blood pressure. One subgroup of patients with arterial hypertension may have increased sympathetic nervous system activity, while another group may have metabolic abnormalities marked by increased plasma levels of insulin and reduced insulin sensitivity. Physical conditioning may be effective in both these groups of patients through influences on central activity of the sympathetic nervous system. Young patients with labile and borderline hypertension with increased cardiac output and increased venous tone may be improved by physical conditioning, resulting in reduced heart rate and cardiac output at rest and during submaximal exercise. Although it remains to be proved that physical conditioning reduces sympathetic nervous system activity, the evidence suggests that it does. Accordingly, young patients with high levels of arterial blood pressure and a strong family history of hypertension should be encouraged to undertake vigorous aerobic isotonic exercise under a regular and lifelong schedule.

The effects of physical conditioning on metabolic processes indicate that obese patients with hypertension and reduced glucose tolerance might also be improved by regular aerobic isotonic exercise. Although the relation between obesity and hypertension is still unclear, physical conditioning apparently improves both cardiovascular and metabolic function in these patients.

REFERENCES

Amery, A., Bossaert, H., & Verstraete, M. Muscle blood flow in normal and hypertensive subjects: Influence of age, exercise and body position. *American Heart Journal,* 1969, **78**, 211–216.

Astrand, P. O., & Rodal, K. *Textbook of work physiology.* New York: McGraw-Hill, 1970.

Barry, A. J., Daly, J. W., Pruett, E. D., Steinmetz, J. R., Pagett, F., Birkhead, N. C., & Redah, I. K. The effects of physiological conditioning on older individuals. *Journal of Gerontology,* 1966, **21**, 182–191.

Berglund, G., Larsson, B., Andersson, O., Larsson, O., Svardsudd, K., Bjorntorp, P., & Wilhelmsen, L. Body composition and glucose metabolism in hypertensive middle-aged males. *Acta Medica Scandinavica,* 1976, **200**, 163–169.

Bevegard, B. S., Holmgren, A., & Jonsson, B. Circulatory studies in well trained athletes at rest and during heavy exercise, with special reference to stroke volume and the influence of body position. *Acta Physiologica Scandinavica,* 1963, **57**, 26–50.

Bjorntorp, P. Exercise in the treatment of obesity. *Clinics in Endocrinology and Metabolism (London),* 1976, **5**, 431–453.

Bjorntorp, P., deJounge, K., Krotkiewski, M., Sullivan, L., Sjostrom, L., & Stenberg, J. Physical training in human obesity: III. Effects of long-term physical training on body composition. *Metabolism,* 1973, **22**, 1467–1475.

Bjorntorp, P., deJounge, K., Sjostrom, L., & Sullivan, L. The effect of physical training on insulin production in obesity. *Metabolism,* 1970, **19**, 631–638.

Bjorntorp, P., Holm, G., Jacobsson, B., Schiller-deJounge, K., Lundberg, P., Sjostrom, L., Smith, U., & Sullivan, L. Physical training in human hyperplastic obesity: IV. Effects on the hormonal status. *Metabolism,* 1977, **26**, 319–328.

Blackburn, H. Non-pharmacological treatment of hypertension. *Annals of the New York Academy of Sciences,* 1978, **304**, 236–242.

Boyer, J. L., Hartley, L. H., Hellerstein, H. K., Loggie, J., & Ryan, A. J. Panel discussion: Exploring the effects of exercise on hypertension. *Physician and Sports Medicine,* 1976, **4**, 38–49.

Boyer, J. L., & Kasch, F. W. Exercise therapy in hypertensive men. *Journal of the American Medical Association,* 1970, **211**, 1668–1671.

Branwell, C., & Ellis, R. Clinical observations on Olympic athletes. *Arbeitsphysiologie,* 1929, **2**, 51–60.

Brynteson, P., & Sinning, W. E. The effects of training frequencies on the retention of cardiovascular fitness. *Medicine and Science in Sports,* 1973, **5**, 29–33.

Choquette, C., & Ferguson, R. J. Blood pressure reduction in "borderline" hypertension following physical training. *Canadian Medical Association Journal,* 1973, **108**, 699–708.

DeVries, H. A. Physiological effects of an exercising training regimen upon men aged 52–88. *Journal of Gerontology,* 1970, **25**, 325–336.

Dustan, H. P., & Tarazi, R. C. Cardiogenic hypertension. *Annual Review of Medicine,* 1978, **29**, 485–493.

Ekblom, B., Astrand, P. O., Saltin, B., Stenberg, J., & Wallstrom, B. Effect of training on circulatory response to exercise. *Journal of Applied Physiology,* 1968, **24**, 518–528.

Ellis, S. E. The effects of sympathomimetic amines and adrenergic blocking agents on metabolism. *Physiology and Pharmacology,* 1962, **4,** 179–226.

Esler, M. Assessment of sympathetic nervous function in humans from noradrenaline plasma kinetics. *Clinical Science,* 1982, **62,** 247–254.

Esler, M., Jackman, G., Bobik, A., Kelleher, D., Jennings, G., Leonard, P., Skews, H., & Korner, P. Determination of norepinephrine apparent release rate and clearance in humans. *Life Sciences,* 1979, **25,** 1461–1470.

Esler, M., Jackman, G., Bobik, A., Leonard, P., Kelleher, D., Skews, H., Jennings, G., & Korner, P. Norepinephrine kinetics in essential hypertension: Defective neuronal uptake of norepinephrine in some patients. *Hypertension,* 1981, **43,** 149–156.

Fahlen, M., Stenberg, J., & Bjorntorp, P. Insulin secretion in obesity after exercise. *Diabetologia,* 1972, **8,** 141–144.

Fox, E. L., Bartels, R. L., Billings, C. E., O'Brien, R., Bason, R., & Mathews, D. K. Frequency and duration of interval training programs and changes in aerobic power. *Journal of Applied Physiology,* 1975, **38,** 481–484.

Fox, S. M., III, Naughton, J. P., & Haskell, W. L. Physical activity and the prevention of coronary heart disease. *Annals of Clinical Research,* 1971, **3,** 404–432.

Frohlich, E. D., Tarazi, R. C., & Dustan, H. P. Re-examination of the hemodynamics of hypertension. *American Journal of the Medical Sciences,* 1969, **257,** 9–23.

Hanson, J. S., & Nedde, W. H. Preliminary observations on physical training for hypertensive males. *Circulation Research,* 1970, **27,** 49–53.

Hartley, L. H., Grimby, G., Kilbom, A., Nilsson, N. J., Astrand, I., Bjure, J., Ekblom, B., & Saltin, B. Physical training in sedentary middle-aged and older men: III. Cardiac output and gas exchange at submaximal and maximal exercise. *Scandinavian Journal of Clinical and Laboratory Investigation,* 1969, **24,** 335–344.

Hartley, L. H., Mason, J. W., Hogan, R. P., Jones, L. G., Kotchen, T. A., Mougey, E. H., Wherry, F. E., Pennington, L. L., & Ricketts, P. T. Multiple hormonal responses to graded exercise in relation to physical training. *Journal of Applied Physiology,* 1972, **33,** 602–606.(a)

Hartley, L. H., Mason, J. W., Hogan, R. P., Jones, L. G., Kotchen, T. A., Mougey, E. H., Wherry, F. E., Pennington, L. L., & Ricketts, P. T. Multiple hormonal responses to prolonged exercise in relation to physical training. *Journal of Applied Physiology,* 1972, **33,** 607–610.(b)

Ibrahim, M. M., Tarazi, R. C., Dustan, H. P., & Bravo, E. L. Cardioadrenergic factor in essential hypertension. *American Heart Journal,* 1974, **88,** 724–732.

Janowsky, A., Okada, F., Manier, D. H., Applegate, C. D., Sulser, F., & Steranka, L. R. Role of serotonergic input in the regulation of the β-adrenergic receptor-coupled adenylate cyclase system. *Science,* 1982, **218,** 900–910. (Abstract)

Kaye, S. B., Shaw, E. M., & Ross, E. J. Bromocriptine and hypertension (Letter to the Editor). *Lancet,* 1976, **1,** 1176–1177.

Koivisto, B. A., Soman, V., Conrad, P., Hendler, R., Nadel, E., & Felig, P. Insulin binding to monocytes in trained athletes: Changes in the resting state after exercise. *Journal of Clinical Investigation,* 1979, **64,** 1011–1015.

Kolloch, R., Kobayaski, K., & DeQuattro, V. Dopaminergic control of sympathetic tone and blood pressure: Evidence in primary hypertension. *Hypertension,* 1980, **2,** 390–394.

Kolloch, R., Myers, M., Kobayaski, K., & DeQuattro, V. Evidence for central dopaminergic modulation of sympathetic nerve activity and blood pressure in primary hypertension. *Clinical Research,* 1980, **28,** 37A. (Abstract)

Kopin, I. J. Biochemical assessment of peripheral adrenergic activity. In D. M. Paton (Ed.), *The release of catecholamines from adrenergic neurons.* Oxford: Pergamon Press, 1979.

Korner, P. I., & Angus, J. A. Central nervous control of blood pressure in relation to antihypertensive drug treatment. *Pharmacology and Therapeutics,* 1981, **13,** 321–356.

Kramisch, D. M., Aspen, A. J., Abramowitz, B. M., Kreimendahl, T., & Hood, W. B., Jr. Reduction of coronary atherosclerosis by moderate conditioning exercise in monkeys on an atherogenic diet. *New England Journal of Medicine,* 1981, **305,** 1484–1526.

Krotkiewski, M., Mandroukas, K., Sjostrom, L., Sullivan, L., Wetterqvist, H., & Bjorntorp, P. Effects of long-term physical training on body fat, metabolism, and blood pressure in obesity. *Metabolism,* 1979, **28**, 650–658.

Lohman, D., Liebold, F., Heilmann, W., Singer, H., & Pohl, A. Diminished insulin response in highly trained athletes. *Metabolism, Clinical and Experimental,* 1978, **27**, 521–524.

Lund-Johansen, P. Hemodynamics in early hypertension. *Acta Medica Scandinavica,* 1967, **181**(Suppl. 482), 1–105.

Mellerowicz, H. The effect of training on heart and circulation and its importance in preventive cardiology. In W. Raab (Ed.), *Prevention of ischemic heart disease.* Springfield, Ill.: Charles C Thomas, 1966.

Montoye, H. J., Metzner, H. L., Keller, J. E., Johnson, B. C., & Epstein, F. H. Habitual physical activity and blood pressure. *Medicine and Science in Sports,* 1972, **4**, 175–181.

Morris, N. J., Pollard, R., Everitt, M. G., & Chave, S. P. Vigorous exercise in leisure-time: Protection against coronary heart disease. *Lancet,* 1980, **2**, 1206–1210.

Ostman, I., Sjostrand, N. O., & Swedin, G. Cardiac noradrenaline turnover and urinary catecholamine excretion in trained and untrained rats during rest and exercise. *Acta Physiologica Scandinavica,* 1972, **86**, 299–308.

Paffenbarger, R. S., Jr., & Hale, W. E. Work activity and coronary heart mortality. *New England Journal of Medicine,* 1975, **292**, 545–550.

Paton, D. M. *The mechanism of neuronal and extraneuronal transport of catecholamines.* New York: Raven Press, 1976.

Pavlik, G., Molnar, G., Farsang, C., & Frenkl, R. Cardiac output and total peripheral resistance in athletes and in nonathletes at rest. *Acta Physiologica Academiae Scientiarum Hungaricae,* 1980, **55**, 13–18.

Pollock, M. L., Cureton, T. K., & Greninger, L. Effects of frequency of training on working capacity, cardiovascular function, and body composition of adult men. *Medicine and Science in Sports,* 1969, **1**, 70–74.

Richter, E. A., Ruderman, N. P., & Schneider, S. H. Diabetes and exercise. *American Journal of Medicine,* 1981, **70**, 201–209.

Rowell, L. B. Human cardiovascular adjustments to exercise and thermal stress. *Physiological Reviews,* 1974, **54**, 75–159.

Safar, M. E., Weiss, Y. A., London, G. M., Frackowiak, R. F., & Milliez, P. L. Cardiopulmonary blood volume in borderline hypertension. *Clinical Science and Molecular Medicine,* 1974, **47**, 153–164.

Saltin, B., Blomqvist, G., Mitchell, J. H., Johnson, R. L., Jr., Wildenthal, K., & Chapman, C. B. Response to exercise after bed rest and after training. *Circulation,* 1968, **38**(Suppl. VII), VII-1– VII-78.

Saltin, B., & Grimby, G. Physiological analysis of middle-aged and old former athletes: Comparison with still active athletes of the same ages. *Circulation,* 1968, **38**, 1104–1115.

Salzman, S. H., Hirsch, E. Z., Hellerstein, H. K., & Bruell, J. H. Adaptation to muscular exercise: Myocardial epinephrine-³H uptake. *Journal of Applied Physiology,* 1970, **29**, 92–95.

Sharkey, B. J. Intensity and duration of training and the development of cardiorespiratory endurance. *Medicine and Science in Sports,* 1970, **2**, 197–202.

Sowers, J. R., Golub, M. S., Berger, M. E., & Whitfield, L. A. Dopaminergic modulation of pressor and hormonal responses in essential hypertension. *Hypertension,* 1982, **4**, 424–430.

Sowers, J. R., Nyby, M., & Jasberg, K. Dopaminergic control of prolactin and blood pressure: Altered control in essential hypertension. *Hypertension,* 1982, **4**, 431–438.

Storer, T. W., & Ruhling, R. O. Essential hypertension and exercise. *Physician and Sports Medicine,* 1981, **9**, 58–72.

Stumpe, K. O., Higuchi, M., Kulloch, R., Kruck, F., & Vetter, H. Hyperprolactinemia and antihypertensive effect of bromocriptine in essential hypertension: Identification of abnormal central dopamine control. *Lancet,* 1977, **2**, 211–214.

Tabakin, B. S., Hanson, J. S., & Levy, A. M. Effects of physical training on the cardiovascular and respiratory responses to graded upright exercise in distance runners. *British Heart Journal,* 1965, **27,** 205–210.

Terjung, R. L., Baldwin, K. M., Cooksey, J., Samson, B., & Sutter, R. A. Cardiovascular adaptation to twelve minutes of mild daily exercise in middle-aged sedentary men. *Journal of the American Geriatrics Society,* 1973, **21,** 164–168.

Ulrych, M., Frohlich, E. D., Tarazi, R. C., Dustan, H. P., & Page, I. H. Cardiac output and distribution of blood volume in central and peripheral circulations in hypertensive and normotensive man. *British Heart Journal,* 1969, **31,** 570–574.

Vranic, M., & Berger, M. Exercise and diabetes mellitus. *Diabetes,* 1979, **28,** 147–163.

Whitfield, L., Sowers, J. R., Tuck, M. L., & Golub, M. S. Dopaminergic control of plasma catecholamine and aldosterone responses to acute stimuli in normal man. *Journal of Clinical Endocrinology and Metabolism* 1980, **51,** 724–729.

Wilmore, J. H., Royce, J., Girandola, R. N., Katch, F. I., & Katch, V. L. Physiological alterations resulting from a 10-week program of jogging. *Medicine and Science in Sports,* 1970, **2,** 7–14.

CHAPTER 54

A RELAXATION-CENTERED BEHAVIORAL PACKAGE FOR REDUCING HYPERTENSION

Chandra Patel

London School of Hygiene and Tropical Medicine, University of London,

Hypertension is one of the major risk factors for coronary heart disease (CHD) and other vascular diseases, which together are responsible for more than half of the total deaths in most Western countries (Intersociety Commission, 1970). Although the etiology of essential hypertension is unproven, its empirical treatment with antihypertensive agents has been shown to reduce deaths from strokes, hypertensive heart disease, and renal damage in patients with moderate to severe hypertension but not deaths from CHD (Veterans Administration 1967, 1970). In order to reduce mortality from CHD, patients with mild hypertension are increasingly being treated.

In earlier studies of mild hypertension (DBP 90–104 mmHg), benefit was seen mostly in patients over 50 years of age or in those with renal and cardiovascular abnormalities (Smith, 1977; Veterans Administration, 1972). Some studies reported a significantly higher dropout ratio because of drug side effects (Smith, 1977). Severe side effects were reported in a large-scale international trial with one of the initial beta blockers, Practolol, which was later withdrawn from the market (Multicentre International Study, 1975). One more recent study (Hypertension Detection, 1979), however, has shown that drug treatment of mild hypertension can significantly reduce mortality from CHD.

In reviewing the complexity of design and the results of several mild hypertension studies, the World Health Organization/International Society of Hypertension Liaison Committee (WHO/ISH, 1982) recommended that treatment of mild hypertension be postponed until better evidence is accumulated. Increased concern regarding the hazards of mass medication and the cost of such prophylactic treatment has been expressed by other well-known authorities in the field (Rose, 1981; Stammler, Farinaro, Mojonnier, Hall, Moss, & Stammler, 1980). Hypertension afflicts 20% to 40% of the adult population, and, since mild hypertensives constitute over 70% of all hypertensives (Hypertension Detection, 1979), a reasonable question is being asked: Are there no other alternatives to decades-long administration of antihypertensive drugs? Such thinking has brought to the forefront old beliefs held by many laypeople regarding the role of emotional stress and lifestyle in the etiology of essential hypertension. Reducing sodium intake, decreasing body weight, increasing physical activity, relaxation, and biofeedback may all play some part in lowering blood pressure, either alone or with pharmacological agents. In this chapter, however, the part played by emotional stress and how it can be countered to reduce blood pressure will be discussed. Only by becoming aware of these factors can we develop insight into possible mechanisms leading to hypertension and into what we can do to formulate rational intervention programs.

ENVIRONMENTAL STRESS

Despite medical skepticism, the category "emotional pressure, worry, anxiety" was considered the single most important cause of high blood pressure by the lay public in a national survey in the United States (Harris & Associates, Note 1). No less than 48% of the general public and 53% of the hypertensives surveyed considered it the number one cause. Surprisingly, more whites than blacks, more college graduates than those with less education, and more young than old thought that emotional pressure was the most likely cause. Since the medical profession cannot be blamed for propagating such possible myths, people's own common sense and observations must be the bases of such belief. The same survey also showed that the level of hypertension decreased with increasing income and that more blacks than whites had hypertension, suggesting that the stress of not making it financially, alienation from society, and discrimination were probable contributing factors.

More scientific evidence is provided by epidemiologic studies. Henry and Cassel (1969) arranged 18 worldwide studies into three strata: populations showing no rise in blood pressure with age, those with moderate rise, and those with a steep rise in blood pressure with age. The conclusion was that a man living in a stable society, well-equipped by his cultural background to deal with the familiar world around him, will not show a rise in blood pressure with age, whether he is a modern technocrat who became a fighter pilot early in life or a Stone Age bushman who is a skilled hunter-gatherer living in the Kalahari Desert (Henry & Stephens, 1977). When radical cultural changes disrupt his familiar environment with a new set of demands for which he is not traditionally prepared, however, the emotional strain of continuous behavioral adjustment is reflected in rising blood pressure. This has been amply demonstrated in several studies of migrants (Beaglehole, Salmond, Hooper, Huntsman, Stanhope, Cassel, & Prior, 1977; Cruz-Coke, 1960; Cruz-Coke, Etcheversy, & Nagel, 1964; Hinkle & Wolff, 1957; Maddocks, 1961; Scotch, 1963).

Job-Related Stress

Jobs requiring constant vigilance or extreme responsibility can have an adverse effect on blood pressure. Cobb and Rose (1973) found a higher mean pressure and a higher prevalence and increased incidence of hypertension occurring at a younger age in air traffic controllers, as compared to second-class airmen. Even among the controllers, those working at high-traffic-density towers had a higher incidence than those at low-traffic-density towers. Excessive strain on the nervous system at a relatively younger age was considered responsible for a three times higher incidence of hypertension among workers at the central telephone exchange in the Soviet Union (Miasnikov, 1962). Morris, Kagan, Pattison, Gardner, and Raffle (1966) reported higher levels of blood pressure as well as more ischemic heart disease in London bus drivers, as compared to conductors.

Financial insecurity and loss of pride caused by unemployment can be a factor responsible for elevation of blood pressure. Kasl and Cobb (1970) followed a number of blue-collar workers after a plant shutdown and found that their blood pressure rose and remained higher during the period of unemployment. In those who were fortunate enough to find permanent reemployment, blood pressure began to decrease. Scotland, which has the highest death rate from coronary heart disease, also has the highest rate of unemployment and poor socioeconomic background. In a longitudinal study of 18,000 London civil servants, Marmot, Rose, Shipley, and Hamilton (1978) found that men in lowest socioeconomic grade (messengers) had 3.6 times the coronary heart disease mortality and higher levels of blood pressure, as compared to men in the highest employment grade (administrators).

Personality Factors

Alexander (1939), from his own and other investigators' experience using psychiatric interview, described hypertensive patients as impulsive, hostile, and aggressive. In a prospective study, a number of college women with above-average blood pressure at entry were studied over 4 to 11 years and were described as abrasive, tense, and hostile (Harris, Sokolow, Carpenter, Freedman, & Hunt, 1953; Kalis, Harris, Bennett, & Sokolow, 1961). Studies using more objective standardized interviews and psychological assessment, however, demonstrated more conflicting results (Cochrane, 1969; Ostfeld & Lebovitz, 1959; Robinson, 1964; Sainsbury, 1960; Weiner, 1970). In a study of U.S. Air Force officers, the highest casual pressures were found in those who were dominant, assertive, decisive, task-oriented, and generally effective in leadership qualities but with narrow range of interests; had low thresholds for perceiving threat, challenge, and hostility in others; and were overcontrolling, rigid, stereotyped, and obtuse in social relations (Harris & Forsyth 1972). When typescript interviews were assessed blindly by trained psychoanalysts, however, the hypertensives were found to be having a continuous struggle against expressing hostile aggressive feelings and difficulty in asserting themselves (Harris & Forsyth, 1972).

Friedman and Rosenman (1959) described Type A, "coronary-prone" behavior as characterized by intense ambition, competitive drive, constant preoccupation with occupational deadlines, and a keen sense of time urgency. Such behavior has proved to be an independent risk factor in a prospective Western collaborative group study (Rosenman, Brand, Jenkins, Friedman, Straus, & Wurm, 1975) and in the ongoing Framingham Study (Haynes, Feinleib, & Kannel, 1980). A typical Type A person, according to Rosenman (1974), is an individual engaged in a relatively chronic struggle to obtain an unlimited number of things from his or her environment in the shortest possible time against all the odds. Type A individuals speak louder and faster than non-coronary-prone Type B persons (Schucker & Jacobs, 1977). They are less satisfied with their jobs (Howard, Cunningham, & Rechnitzer, 1977) and, although working closer to their endurance limits on a treadmill, they are rarely likely to express fatigue (Carver, Coleman, & Glass, 1976). Although their resting blood pressures may not be elevated, they are more likely to respond to stressful and challenging stimuli, such as stressful interviews, involvement in competitive videogames, history quizzes, and other egocentric mental or psychomotor activities, with greater increases in systolic blood pressure, heart rate, and catecholamine release (Dembroski & MacDougall, 1978; Dembroski, MacDougall, Herd, & Shields, 1979; Dembroski, MacDougall, & Shields, 1977; Friedman, Byers, Diamant, & Rosenman, 1975; Glass, Krakoff, Contrada, Hilton, Kehoe, Mannucci, Collins, Snow, & Elting, 1980).

Constitutional Factors

It is generally accepted that hypertension results from an interaction between genetic predisposition and environmental factors. The individual responds to stress by a generalized increase in sympathetic activity but consistently shows maximal response in one or two components (Lacey & Lacey, 1962; Malmo, Shagass, & Davis, 1950). Whether from a stressful interview, pain, fear, or an anger-inducing stimulus, hypertensives show a greater rise in blood pressure than normotensives (Innes, Miller, & Valentine, 1959; Schachter, 1957; Shapiro 1961; Wolf & Wolff, 1951). High reactivity of a given response system, whether it is gastrointestinal, respiratory, cardiovascular, or musculoskeletal, if frequently mobilized is likely to lead to malfunction of that system, resulting in peptic ulcer, asthma or chronic bronchitis, hypertension, or headache, respectively. Even though this predilection is probably inherited, it would still be important to identify the idiosyncratic pattern of a particular individual so that appropriate preventive measures can be applied.

Physiological Mechanisms

Whenever an environment is felt to be threatening or overdemanding, the hypothalamic defense alarm, or the "fight-or-flight" response, is mobilized, with its behavioral correlates ranging from alertness, frustration, fear, aggression, and anger to rage and corresponding degrees of physiological correlates, including a rise in blood pressure, tachycardia, erratic breathing, tense muscles, increased blood clotting tendency, increased sweat gland activity, desynchronized electroencephalographic pattern, and other signs of sympathetic nervous system activity. In a person who is susceptible to hypertension, however, the cardiovascular component, particularly a rise in blood pressure, is likely to be most prominent. Mechanisms leading to blood pressure elevations are likely to be direct stimulation of adrenergic and noradrenergic receptors on the heart and blood vessels or indirect stimulation of the hypothalamo-adreno medullary response leading to catecholamine release, mobilization of pituitary-adreno-cortical response leading via adrenocortiotrophic hormone and cortisol to possible sodium and water retention, or mobilization of the renin-angiotensin-aldosterone axis. Angiotensin II is considered to be 40 times more powerful as a vasoconstrictor than catecholamine, whereas aldosterone is likely to raise blood pressure through sodium and water retention.

Most people would accept the concept that mobilization of stress response would temporarily cause a rise in blood pressure. What is disputed, however, is the possibility of such temporary elevations causing permanent hypertension. There is a considerable body of evidence suggesting that repeated and exaggerated elevations of blood pressure in a susceptible individual can lead to resetting of the baroreceptors at a higher level ("Baroceptors," 1979; Kezdi, 1953; Kubicek, Kottke, Laker, & Visscher, 1953; McCubbin, Green, & Page, 1956; Sleight, 1975) structural hypertrophy of the resistant vessels (Folklow, Grimby, & Thulesius, 1958; Folklow, Hallback, Lundgren, Sivertsson, & Weiss, 1973; Sivertsson, 1970), and these factors can maintain high blood pressure even in the absence of initiating stress factors. There is also some evidence that if blood pressure is reduced and effectively maintained at the lower level, some of the factors responsible for maintaining and perpetuating hypertension may reverse, at least partially (Folkow et al., 1973; Vaughan Williams, Hassan, Floras, Sleight, & Jones, 1980). Sympathetic overactivity is also implicated in the observations that blood pressure is lower during sleep (Richardson, Vetrovec, & Williamson, 1972). Most hypotensive drugs reduce sympathetic activity at some level or produce the effects opposite to those of sympathetic activity or stress hormones, and they produce a greater decrease in blood pressure in hypertensives than in normotensives (Doyle & Smirk, 1955).

Summary

In industrialized societies with fast-advancing technology, rapid changes in the environment are likely. With an increase in the complexity of tasks, a comparable increase in vigilance and job responsibility is unavoidable. Rising unemployment and inflation put extra demands on individuals to gain more education and more technical skills to compete for these jobs. With explosion in travel and communication, there is increase in social mobility. People move away from friends and relations and from familiar surroundings and cultures to unknown locations with strange cultures and differing social strata. All these factors are likely to put people under stress. Should we allow the circumstances in which we find ourselves to strain our health, however? Some people do manage to remain healthy in the face of stress, and perhaps we can learn something from them. After all, the power to reflect and the ability to plan our future make human beings unique and versatile. It is the ability of the organism to deal with changing conditions that determines whether it remains alive or dies.

STRESS WITHOUT DISTRESS—PROTECTIVE FACTORS

Personality

In his book *Stress without Distress,* Hans Selye (1967), the father of stress research, pointed out an important contrast. Joyous excitement or pride in excellence, for example, are what give zest to life and are not feelings to be avoided. Unfulfilled need for achievement, perception of personal failure, or deprivation, however, lead to distress or frustration and a lack of purpose. Selye said that people must find jobs they can do, where their fellows appreciate their efforts. Constant censure or lack of reward makes work frustrating and harmful. Wolf and Goodell (1968) stated that circumstances that "a man sees to be dangerous, lonely and hopeless, may drain him not only of hope but also of health." Given "self-esteem, hope, purpose and belief in his fellows, he will endure great burdens and take cruel punishment," however. These authors demonstrated a rise in blood pressure and renal vasoconstriction by stress-inducing interviews. Antonovsky (1974) speaks of homeostatic flexibility, meaning the ability to accept alternatives. A person who sees himself as successfully playing multiple roles of husband, father, singer, gardener, cook, doctor, grandfather, and so on, is likely to be helped in surviving a loss by his increased chances that some role or roles will remain open to him. The capacity to accept conflicting values has a distinct advantage over an inflexible attitude and is more likely to help such a person recover rapidly to the point of going about his affairs normally, without a great deal of emotional strain.

Despite major life changes, there are people who remain free from illness. What are the characteristics that help insulate these people from the environmental changes and demands that increase susceptibility in others? Hinkle (1974) studied 1,300 telephone operators to see the effect of changes in cultural or social milieu or interpersonal relationships on health. The study showed that people who remained healthy liked their work and found it easy and satisfying. They also liked their friends and colleagues and were content and comfortable in their lives. Those who had many illnesses were more likely to find work confining and boring and were more likely to be unhappy with their lot in life and their place in the family. In a corresponding study of Chinese and Hungarian refugees, Hinkle (1974) again showed that those who experienced a greater amount of illness perceived their environment as more threatening, challenging, demanding, and frustrating, whereas the people with healthy personalities could endure social change and personal loss without undue emotional response. He described them as having personalities with "sociopathic flavor," since they lacked the normal intensity of attachment to people, goals, and groups and too readily shifted to other relationships, behaving as if their own well-being was their primary concern.

Kobasa (1982) described a hardy personality that resists stressful life events as having a disposition of commitment, control, and challenge. Such persons have a sense of purpose and find meaningfulness in the events, things, and persons of their environment. They involve themselves in whatever they are doing and recognize their goals and priorities and their ability to make decisions. They are resourceful persons who know where to turn for help in times of need. Susceptible persons, however, are more alienated from themselves and their work. They do not derive support from people at work and often have no one to turn to. Resilient persons also have a tendency to believe that they can exert some control over the course of events. They take responsibility for what happens to them. In contrast, susceptible persons are more likely to blame their luck, other people, or things for their problems. They either believe they have no choice in the matter or they allow themselves to be governed by others. Hardy persons are prepared to accept challenge and turn stressful life events into opportunities for personal growth rather than a simple threats to security. They respond to the unexpected with a sense of interest and exploration. They are much more flexible in their thinking. Kobasa based her evidence on cross-sectional studies of middle- and upper-level management personnel, army officers, and lawyers.

Social Support

Social support has recently been discussed as a moderator of life stresses (Cassel, 1976; Cobb, 1976; LaRocco, House, & French, 1981). This support can come from such sources as spouses, friends, work supervisors, fellow workers, and health care professionals. House (1981) defines social support as a flow between people of one or more of four types of support. The first type leads the subject to believe that he or she is loved and cared for and that someone is prepared to listen, understand, and show concern. The second kind of social support involves material assistance given by friends, relatives, or the state in a welfare society. The third class of support leads to social congruity derived from a shared network of information and easy availability of advice, suggestions, and directions in times of need. The fourth type of support involves appraisal and feedback, which leads a person to self-esteem as a result of public expression of group approval, making it possible to have a favorable position in the social hierarchy. Such support can enhance health and well-being because it directly meets important human needs for security, affiliation, approval, and affection.

The beneficial effects of the traditional social network in close-knit communities with stronger family bonds and group cohesiveness were thought to be responsible for the lower incidence of CHD in German Protestants living in Nazareth, Pennsylvania, as compared to the non-German minority (Bruhn, Wolf, Lynn, Bird, & Chandler, 1968); in Catholic Americans of Italian descent living in Rosetto, Pennsylvania, as compared to those in neighboring communities (Stout, Morrow, Brandt, & Wolf, 1964); and in traditional Japanese-Americans living in California, as compared to Japanese-Americans who had adopted Western culture (Marmot & Syme, 1976). In a study of 10,000 Israeli civil servants, Medalie and Goldbourt (1976) found that the incidence of angina pectoris was only half in those who perceived their wives as loving and supportive. Perhaps the "old boy network" might be a supportive and hence a protective factor in the administrators of the London Whitehall Study, discussed earlier (Marmot et al., 1978), in addition to the highly esteemed, worthwhile, and satisfying jobs they hold.

Problems of Application

It may be possible in highly motivated, intelligent, middle-class individuals to instill some insights regarding health-promoting or stress-buffering personal characteristics, including Type B personality, assertiveness, hardiness disposition, the importance of giving and receiving emotional and social support, and the usefulness of belonging to a self-help group or community network. In a small number of individuals, it may even be possible actually to induce enough behavioral changes that increase their resilience and resourcefulness and minimize the impact of stress.

For a large number of ordinary men and women, however, this is philosophical jargon beyond comprehension or with little personal relevance. To a person who is one of several thousand employees of a large corporation, talking about control and challenge is of doubtful value. To a person with limited skills who is living in poverty, talking about satisfying, esteemed jobs or an interest in arts and music is superficial. We must therefore develop simpler programs that are applicable to most people in the society.

Ethical Considerations

Before recommending therapeutic behavioral modifications, one must also take other considerations into account. As Eliot (1979) pointed out, to produce an individual who is modified to the extent of losing his relevance and his ability to function appropriately in his environment and society is to contribute to the demise of that individual and his society.

Any primary prevention program in a Type A person who is active, energetic, highly productive, and fulfilling his obligations to himself, his family, and his company poses special problems. Being competitive, ambitious, and hard-working may increase a person's chances of dying from coronary heart disease, but it also increases his or her chances of social, economic, and occupational success. Before trying to alter such a person's behavior, we must also find out what it is in the Type A behavior that we are trying to alter (Roskies, 1980). Hard work, job involvement, and achievement concerns, for example, may not be related to coronary heart disease if such attributes lack a competitive hostility component (Matthews, Glass, Rosenman, & Bortner, 1977).

A SIMPLE AND EFFECTIVE BEHAVIORAL PACKAGE

In order to cure disease, prevent illness, and enhance the health and well-being of a human being, all of the person's physical, emotional, and spiritual needs must be considered and their interrelationships acknowledged. The new field of behavioral medicine is exciting because it allows integration of various disciplines into a common framework to provide the totality of human needs. In fulfilling those needs, communications should be brought down to the level of the consumer. The skills or target behaviors taught must necessarily be simple, like breathing or relaxation. To a medical practitioner who has until now assumed a highly technical and authoritarian role, this idea is unfamiliar and may even be uninteresting. If practitioners accept the responsibility for the health of valuable and physiologically complex human lives, however, then they must also accept the requirement that therapeutic behavioral modification, no matter how simple, must remain in the hands of skilled clinicians.

The behavioral program I have used for hypertensive patients involves several subdivisions, which I will discuss in some detail in the following sections.

Health Education

In order to solve a problem logically, we must understand it. From what has been described so far, we can identify two major problem areas. The first consists of external factors, including demands made by a changing environment, work-related stress, lack of social support, financial insecurity, bereavement, and other predictable and unpredictable factors. Most of these factors are beyond individual control, but awareness of them may influence politicians, industrialists, corporations, town planners, and community leaders to be sensitive to the health needs of people. To some extent, understanding of these factors may also help individuals either to avoid them or to prepare themselves to face them more appropriately.

The second problem area encompasses internal factors—how persons perceive, integrate, interpret, and evaluate situations in daily life and how they cope with external demands and their internal needs. These factors are more within the control of the individual and within the scope of health care personnel. A simple yet informative audio-visual program is used to help patients discriminate appropriate and inappropriate appraisals of environmental situations as well as adaptive and maladaptive responses. Attempts are made to alter irrational thinking and distorted inferences. Daily life occurrences are depicted so that the patients begin to identify situations that they evaluate and respond to inappropriately.

An educational 16 mm sound film, *Understanding Stresses and Strains,* produced by Walt Disney, Ltd. (available in many languages), is shown to most patients. This film depicts the primitive fight-and-flight response and shows how it is mobilized inappropriately when the threat is not real but merely imagined and when it is not life that is threatened but our ego, prestige, and position in the society or family. The purpose behind showing this film is to start a dialogue with the patients, which they continue with themselves afterward to decide on the threatening value of each environmental situation to which they are exposed. Through trial and error, they gain insight and learn to control their habitual maladaptive behavior.

Other educational material presented covers pathophysiology, the causes and consequences of essential hypertension, the benefits of lowering high blood pressure, details of treatment available, both behavioral and pharmacological, and the logic of the specific program used. In my opinion, most patients would like to play their part if the physician takes the trouble to explain how they can do so. An increased sense of participation ensures extraordinarily high cooperation and increases the responsibility that patients are prepared to take in the management of the program. Their coping skills are strengthened by learning and regularly practicing a relaxation response, with components opposite to those of the fight-or-flight response, including breathing exercises, deep muscle relaxation, simple meditation as a form of mental relaxation, and, finally, learning to integrate the relaxation response in everyday life.

Breathing Exercises

When persons become excited or angry, their breathing becomes erratic. It may be deep and irregular, or there may be periods of apnea or shallow upper chest breathing interrupted with sighing. With hysterical hyperventilation, the patients may have symptoms that mimic pathology in almost any system of the body, including an abnormal electrocardiographic pattern (Lum, 1981). When persons are calm and composed, however, their breathing is slow and regular. By deliberate, simple, and rhythmic diaphragmatic breathing exercises, a certain amount of physical calmness can be induced. The advantage of this exercise is that it can be performed anywhere, in any position, during most daily activities and without anyone else noticing.

Deep Muscle Relaxation

If mobilization of hypothalamic response leads to an increase in muscle tension in anticipatory preparation for the fight-or-flight response with concomitant increase in blood pressure, one can assume that deliberate relaxation of muscles could lead to a decrease in the intensity of sympathetic responsiveness of the individual and thus allow blood pressure to come down. At the base of this assumption are observations from animal experiments, including an increase in proprioception through passive movements, increased sensitivity of the posterior hypothalamus, and a considerable rise in blood pressure when the hypothalamus was electrically stimulated. The rise was less, however, when muscles were relaxed by curarizing the animal (Bernhaut, Gellhorn, & Rasmussen, 1953; Gellhorn, 1964; Hess, 1957).

It is thought that the intensity of the response is directly proportional to the sensory input to the brain (Gellhorn & Kiely, 1972). If this is correct, it would be easier to explain the higher incidence of hypertension in industrialized countries, where we are constantly bombarded with auditory (noise), visual, emotional, and other sensory stimuli, as compared to primitive countries, where people have a low incidence of essential hypertension and a lack of rise in blood pressure with advancing age. The observations from human experiments further support this assumption. With an increase in isometric muscle contraction during hand-grip or weight-lifting experiments, a sharp rise in blood pressure, out of proportion to the amount of work done, has been noted (Lind, Taylor, Humphreys, Kennelly, & Donald, 1964; Taylor, 1974).

For the purpose of training in deep muscle relaxation, the patient is asked to lie supine on a couch or a reclining chair, with legs slightly apart and rotated externally at the hip joints so that the heels are pointing inward and the toes are pointing outward. This position reduces the tension in the muscles around the knee joints. The arms are kept by the side, a few inches away from the trunk and, if possible, the palms are turned upward and the fingers are kept slightly flexed. The head, neck, and trunk are kept in a straight line. Although the position of the head is elevated to a comfortable level in the beginning, the patient is encouraged to lie flat; within a few days, most patients are able to do so. The eyes are kept closed.

The person is then asked to relax each group of muscles in sequence, starting from the right toes and progressing to include the right heel, ankle, calf, knee, thigh, and hip and then similarly going over the left leg, right arm, left arm, shoulders, neck, jaws, cheeks, forehead, around the eyes, and the scalp. Throughout this process, the patient is asked to become aware of the sensation of relaxation so that he or she would recognize the tension that is inappropriate and be able to relax as soon as it begins to build up in everyday life. Finally, the patient is asked to direct attention to breathing and to relax the muscles of the chest and abdomen.

Meditation

The aim of meditation is to get in touch with oneself, to recuperate the mind, and to bring about spiritual awareness. Frequent frustrations, aggravations, and disappointments—common in our daily life—exhaust us mentally and prevent us from getting the best from our mental capacity. Brain researchers tell us that, at best, we are using only 10% to 15% of our potential brain capacity. In order to exploit more of our mental capacity and to feel happy and fulfilled, we need to achieve a balance among mental exercise, rest, and mental relaxation. There are empirical reasons for believing that a practice incorporating principles of meditation will restore that balance. It is said that, just as an arrow pulled back on a bow gathers more force and momentum, the mind pulled back during the practice of meditation gathers more mental energy and creativeness. Some great poets and writers stumbled on the technique almost by accident, and they were able to go in and out of this state very swiftly. Most of us, however, must go through it step by step.

Before meditation can begin, we must assume a passive attitude, regulate our breathing, and relax physically (as described) in order to achieve a state of sensory withdrawal (Patel, 1983). Then we begin to narrow down the focus of attention so that the mind becomes more at rest and concentrating. By giving voluntary concentration to a subject and by emotionally detaching ourselves from that subject, not only are we able to think about it objectively, but the mind also brings into consciousness all the different ideas in our memory associated with that subject, and we are able to find solutions to any problem because our mind is flooded with all the relevant ideas and facts.

As we reach a deeper state of concentration, the mind becomes sharply focused. The mind has a tendency to wander, however, so techniques are devised to learn to become more steady through concentrating on an object of contemplation. The object can be any one of many—a flower, a blank wall, a vase, a candle flame, our own breathing, or an idea. We may close our eyes and listen to various sounds—for example, a word or phrase, or a mantra, repeated mentally, or a piece of music.

Meditation is an intimate and compelling process. The mind that holds an idea in turn becomes held by it. We know that if persons constantly tell themselves that they are failures or that they are inferior to others, they eventually come to believe it themselves. This power of the subconscious is used to build character and desirable traits and to weed out undesirable characteristics and emotions. As the individuals imagine themselves, again and again, to be in possession of a desired trait, they begin to express the thought in actions; eventually, the new image becomes fixed and becomes a characteristic.

Another more mundane advantage of meditation is that it prevents sleep. Relaxation is very conducive to sleep (Magoun, 1963) and, although sleep may be beneficial in its own right, our aim is to learn a skill by which blood pressure can be kept down during the wakeful period of daily life. The little mental activity involved during the practice of meditation is effective in preventing patients from falling asleep. Meditative practice is also known to change the EEG pattern into a more synchronized one, with the high-amplitude, slow-wave pattern of the relaxed brain that is not passing into sleep (Wallace & Benson, 1972). It is also known to increase coherence between the two cerebral hemispheres and between the anterior and posterior parts of each hemisphere (Banquet, 1973).

Biofeedback

In biofeedback therapy, electronic instruments that measure and display certain physiological functions are used. The person connected to the instruments tries to change those functions in the desired direction by a change in subjective state. A success or failure immediately becomes known to the person. The idea behind this procedure is that knowledge of success reinforces learning. A blood pressure feedback machine would be more logical for hypertensive patients, but there is no satisfactory instrument on the market that can give a continuous display of the blood pressure record without disturbing the patient in any way.

I have found galvanic skin resistance (GSR) feedback quite satisfactory for training patients in a therapeutic behavior. This procedure measures resistance of the skin to a passage of minute electric current, which, among other things, is dependent on the activity of the sweat glands supplied by adrenergic nerves. By convention, the auditory signal is arranged so that as the patient relaxes, the signal becomes fainter and fainter until it stops. When that happens, the frequency is increased and a bigger electric current is passed to give a further signal, and so on. The task of the patient is made more and more difficult as he or she becomes better and better at relaxing. Patients accept this challenge quite enthusiastically.

Although it is the subjective behavioral change that brings about reduction in blood pressure, biofeedback does seem to play an important role in the entire therapy. First, the objective display of the patients ability to control their physiology increases their self-esteem and their motivation to continue with the practice. Second, the procedure disciplines the patients to remain immobile while connected to the instrument (as moving about would cause loud noises), thus allowing the relaxation to deepen fairly quickly. In addition to relaxation feedback, the patients are also given verbal, overall feedback of their blood pressure at the beginning and at the end of each session. In fact, every success the patients have is taken as an opportunity to raise their self-esteem and their motivation to continue with the program on a long-term basis.

In recent work, I have introduced a multicircuit GSR machine for group use that allows a group of up to 10 patients to be trained simultaneously. Each person is connected with a pair of finger electrodes to his or her own GSR circuit and can hear the feedback signal on one side of the stereophonic headphones while listening to the common instruction in relaxation and meditation, given by a cassette tape, delivered through the other side of the headphones.

The number of biofeedback training sessions necessary has varied in different studies, but with standardization of the procedure and experience over a number of years, I have found one session per week for 8 weeks to be adequate. In addition, the patients are asked to practice twice a day for 10 to 20 minutes. If it is difficult to include two home practices, I advocate one in the evening, before a meal. The patients are also loaned instruction cassettes for home practice, but they are advised to wean themselves off the device gradually as they become more experienced.

Stress Management

Finally, the patients are asked to use their coping skills of better cognitive appraisal, breathing exercises, relaxation, and meditation to manage their everyday stress. They are asked to view anxiety-inducing stimuli or symptoms of physiological arousal—such as sweaty palms, racing heart, tense muscles, or such signs of maladaptive behavior as reaching for a cigarette or alcohol—as signals to employ their coping behavior for functioning more efficiently. Instead of feeling helpless, they are encouraged to demonstrate calm competence. Of course, many aggressive or stress-inducing stimuli are common in everyday life, and we are not often aware of their actual or potential arousal effects. For generalization and longer persistence of treatment effect, ringing telephones, red traffic lights while driving, waiting in a doctor's or dentist's office, interviews, speaking in public, or other occasions that patients find stressful are used as opportunities for taking slow breaths and releasing undue tension from the body. The patients also have colored dots stuck to their wristwatch dials so that they are reminded to relax every time they look at their watches. This is an especially appropriate intervention, as time pressure is considered an important component of the Type A behavior pattern.

Evidence of the Efficacy of the Behavioral Package

The behavioral package has been tried in a number of studies involving hypertensive patients. In a pilot study (Patel, 1973, 1975a) involving 20 patients being controlled on antihypertensive drugs, the reduction in mean blood pressure was significant ($p < .001$), amounting to 20 mmHg systolic and 14 mmHg diastolic, in addition to a reduction in drugs in 12 patients, averaging 44% of the total drugs for the group. The control group, who attended the same number of sessions to have their blood pressure checked, did not show a significant reduction in blood pressure, and their drug requirements remained unchanged. At 1-year follow-up, the results were maintained.

In a randomized crossover trial (Patel & North, 1975) involving 34 hypertensive patients, the decrease in blood pressure was 26 mmHg systolic and 15 mmHg diastolic in the treatment group, compared with 8 mmHg and 4 mmHg in the control group, who also attended the same number of sessions but were asked to lie down and relax in a way that they thought was true relaxation. After the crossover, the new treatment group showed similar reduction, whereas the group treated in the first phase (now the control group) maintained the blood pressure reductions. These patients were on hypertensive drugs, their drug regimens were kept constant.

In another trial, 32 hypertensive patients were randomly allocated and subjected to standardized exercise and cold-pressor tests before and after the trial (Patel, 1975b, 1977). The results showed a significant reduction in the magnitude and the duration of pressure rises in the treatment group as compared to the control group in all measures except systolic pressure following the exercise test (two-tailed). In two further pilot studies, not only blood pressure was reduced but also serum cholesterol and cigarette smoking (Patel, 1976; Patel & Carruthers, 1977).

In a recent large-scale, randomized, controlled study in an industry, approximately 200 unselected patients, found by screening examination to be at increased risk of having coronary heart disease and not to be on pharmacological treatment, were treated. The results confirmed the previous observations, with highly significant reductions in blood pressure over an 8-month follow-up. Further supportive evidence of a significant reduction in plasma renin activity and plasma aldosterone levels at 8-week follow-up, but not at 8 months, was found in subgroups (Patel, 1981, 1982; Patel, Marmot, & Terry, 1981). This study has been in progress for over three and a half years; final follow-up, which will look into morbidity data, is being processed, but there are indications that morbidity may also be reduced.

Limitations and Contraindications

Some patients may find the time commitment, personal responsibility, and mystical aspects of meditation less acceptable, although such patients are rare in my experience. In some, despite adherence to instructions, the therapy is either ineffective or inadequate. Other psychological benefits may make its practice worthwhile, however, alongside more effective pharmacological measures. Studies that can predict which patients are most likely to succeed are badly needed. The technique, if practiced as prescribed, is remarkably safe; however, induction of psychosis in individuals practicing meditation for extensive periods, similar to that developing from prolonged sensory deprivation, was reported by Benson, Beary, and Carol (1974); and Wolpe (1958) reported that some patients became depressed with relaxation. Therefore, the therapy is better avoided in psychotic and depressed patients. Patients commonly experience a floating sensation, abnormality of body image, parasthesia, or other strange feelings as a result of altered states of consciousness. These are not in any way indications that the practice should be stopped, and the patients should be reassured.

Resistance and Compliance

Some patients resist the therapy for fear it will make them neglect their responsibilities to their families. This therapy is not an escape from social responsibility or a withdrawal from excitement or enjoyment of life. In fact, patients often develop a deeper appreciation of their family and other interpersonal relationships. Sometimes, people become disappointed because they expect too much from the therapy.

Motivating symptomless hypertensive patients to comply with time-consuming practice is difficult, but it is still relatively easier than making them comply with antihypertensive medication regimens. Providing a sense of mastery, raising self-esteem, offering the therapy as an alternative to medication or to an increase in medication, expressing the therapist's sincere concern about the patient and genuine desire to help, maintaining social interaction with the patient, dispensing health education material in small quantities and in simple language augmented by illustrations—all these factors help ingrain the new habits in the mental scheme of the patient. An occasional reinforcing session and adequate follow-up are then necessary to maintain the therapeutic behavior.

REFERENCE NOTE

1. Harris, L., & Associates, Inc. *The public and high blood pressure.* Survey conducted for the National Heart and Lung Institute. DHEW Pub. No. (NIH)74–356, 1973.

REFERENCES

Alexander, F. Emotional factors in essential hypertension: Presentation of tentative hypothesis. *Psychosomatic Medicine,* 1939, **1**, 173–179.

Antonovsky, A. Conceptual and methodological problems in the study of resistance resources and stressful life events. In B. S. Dohrenwend & B. P. Dohrenwend (Eds.), *Stressful life events: Their nature and effects.* New York: Wiley, 1974.

Banquet, J. P. Spectral analysis of the EEG in meditation. *Electroencephalography and Clinical Neurophysiology,* 1973, **35**, 143.

Baroreceptors and high blood pressure (Editorial). *Lancet,* 1979, **1**, 1277–1279.

Beaglehole, R., Salmond, C. E., Hooper, A., Huntsman, J., Stanhope, J. M., Cassel, J. C., & Prior, I. A. M. Blood pressure and social interaction in Tokelauan nigrants in New Zealand. *Journal of Chronic Disease,* 1977, 30, 803–812.

Benson, H., Beary, J. F., & Carol, M. P. The relaxation response. *Psychiatry,* 1974, **37**, 37–46.

Bernhaut, M., Gellhorn, E., & Rasmussen, A. T. Experimental contributions to problem of consciousness. *Journal of Neurophysiology,* 1953, **16**, 21–35.

Bruhn, J. C., Wolf, S., Lynn, T., Bird, H., & Chandler, B. Social aspects of coronary-heart disease in a Pennsylvania German community. *Social Science and Medicine,* 1968, **2**, 201–212.

Carver, C. S., Coleman, A. E., & Glass, D. C. The coronary-prone behaviour pattern and suppression of fatigue on a treadmill test. *Journal of Personality and Social Psychology,* 1976, **33**, 460–466.

Cassel, J. The contribution of the social environment to host resistance. *American Journal of Epidemiology,* 1976, **102**, 107–123.

Cobb, S. Social support as a moderator of life stress. *Psychosomatic Medicine,* 1976, **38**, 300–314.

Cobb, S., & Rose, E. M. Hypertension, peptic ulcer and diabetes in air traffic controllers. *Journal of the American Medical Association,* 1973, **224**, 489–492.

Cochrane, R. Neuroticism and the discovery of high blood pressure. *Journal of Psychosomatic Research,* 1969, **13**, 21–25.

Cruz-Coke, R. Environmental influences and arterial blood pressure. *Lancet,* 1960, **2**, 885–886.

Cruz-Coke R., Etcheversy, R., & Nagel, R. Influence of migration on blood pressure of Eastern islanders. *Lancet,* 1964, **1**, 697–699.

Dembroski, T., & MacDougall, J. Stress effects on affiliation preference among subjects possessing the Type A coronary-prone behaviour pattern. *Journal of Personality and Social Psychology,* 1978, **36**, 23–33.

Dembroski, T. M., MacDougall, J. M., Herd, J. A., & Shields, J. L. Effect of level of challenge on pressor and heart rate responses in Type A and B subjects. *Journal of Applied Social Psychology,* 1979, **9**, 209–228.

Dembroski, T., MacDougall, J., & Shields, J. Physiologic reactions to social challenge in persons evidencing the Type A coronary-prone behaviour pattern. *Journal of Human Stress,* 1977, **3**, 2–9.

Doyle, A. E., & Smirk, R. H. The neurogenic component in hypertension. *Circulation,* 1955, **12**, 543–552.

Eliot, R. S. *Stress and the major cardiovascular disorders.* New York: Futura, 1979.

Folkow, B., Grimby, G., & Thulesius, O. Adaptive structural changes of the vascular walls in hypertension and their relation to the control of the peripheral resistance. *Acta Physiologica Scandinavica,* 1958, **44**, 255–272.

Folkow, B., Hallback, M., Lundgren, Y., Sivertsson, R., & Weiss, L. Importance of adaptive changes in vascular design for establishment of primary hypertension: Studies in man and in spontaneously hypertensive rats. *Circulation Research,* 1973, **32–33**, (Suppl. 1), 2–16.

Friedman, M., Byers, S. O., Diamant, J., & Rosenman, R. H. Plasma catecholamine response of coronary-prone subjects (type A) to a specific challenge. *Metabolism,* 1975, **24**, 205–210.

Friedman, M., & Rosenman, R. H. Association of specific overt behaviour pattern with blood and cardiovascular findings: Blood cholesterol level, blood clotting time, incidence of arcus senilis and clinical coronary artery disease. *Journal of the American Medical Association,* 1959, **169**, 1286–1296.

Gellhorn, E. Motion and emotion: The role of proprioception in the physiology and pathology of the emotions. *Psychological Review,* 1964, **71**, 457–472.

Gellhorn, E., & Kiely, W. F. Mystical states of consciousness: Neurological and clinical aspects. *Journal of Nervous and Mental Disease,* 1972, **154**, 399.

Glass, D. C., Krakoff, L. R., Contrada, R., Hilton, W. F., Kehoe, K., Mannucci, E. G., Collins, C., Snow, B., & Elting, E. Effect of harassment and competition upon cardiovascular and catecholamines responses in type A and type B individuals. *Psychophysiology,* 1980, **17**, 453–463.

Harris, R. E., & Forsyth, R. P. Personality and man. In G. Onesti, K. E. Kim, & J. H. Moyers (Eds.), *Hypertension: Mechanisms and management.* New York: Grune and Stratton, 1972.

Harris, R. E., Sokolow, M., Carpenter, L. G., Freedman, M., & Hunt, S. P. Response to psychologic stress in persons who are potentially hypertensive. *Circulation,* 1953, **7**, 874–879.

Haynes, S. G., Feinleib, M., & Kannel, W. B. The relationship of psychosocial factors to coronary heart disease in the Framingham Study: III. 8-year incidence of CHD. *American Journal of Epidemiology,* 1980, **211**, 37–58.

Henry, J. P., & Cassel, J. C. Psychosocial factors in essential hypertension: Recent epidemiological and animal experimental evidence. *American Journal of Epidemiology,* 1969, **90**, 171–200.

Henry, J. P., & Stephens, P. M. *Stress, health and the social environment: A sociobiologic approach to medicine.* New York: Springer-Verlag, 1977.

Hess, W. R. Hypothalamus and Vegatative Autonomic Function. In Functional organisation of diencephalon. J. R. Hughes (Ed.) New York: Grune & Stratton, 1957.

Hinkle, L. E., Jr. The effect of exposure to culture change, social change and changes in interpersonal relationships on health. In B. S. Dohrenwend & B. P. Dohrenwend (Eds.), *Stressful life events: Their nature and effects.* New York; Wiley, 1974.

Hinkle, L. E., & Wolff, H. G. The nature of man's adaptation to his total environment and the relation of this to illness. *Archives of Internal Medicine,* 1957, **99**, 442–460.

House, J. S. *Work, stress and social support.* Reading, Mass.: Addison-Wesley, 1981.

Howard, J. H., Cunningham, D. A., & Rechnitzer, P. A. Work patterns associated with Type A behaviour: A managerial population. *Human Relations,* 1977, **30**, 825–836.

Hypertension Detection and Follow-up Program Co-operative Group. Five-year findings of the Hypertension Detection and Follow-up Program: 1. Reduction in mortality of persons with high blood pressure, including mild hypertension. *Journal of the American Medical Association,* 1979, **242**, 2562–2571.

Innes, G., Miller, W. M., & Valentine, M. Emotion and blood pressure. *Journal of the Medical Sciences,* 1959, **105**, 840–851.

Intersociety Commission for Heart Disease. Primary prevention of the atherosclerotic diseases. *Circulation,* 1970, **42** (Suppl. II), A55–A95.

Kalis, B. L., Harris, R. E., Bennett, L. F., & Sokolow, M. Personality and life history factors in persons who are potentially hypertensive. *Journal of Nervous and Mental Disease,* 1961, **132,** 457–468.

Kasl, S. V., & Cobb, S. Blood pressure changes in men undergoing job loss: A preliminary report. *Psychosomatic Medicine,* 1970, **32,** 19–38.

Kezdi, P. Sino aortic regulatory system. Role in pathogenesis of essential hypertension: Their course and prognosis. *American Journal of the Medical Sciences,* 1953, **197,** 332–343.

Kobasa, S. C. The hardy personality: Towards a social psychology of stress and health. In J. Suls & G. Sanders (Eds.), *The social psychology of health and illness.* Hillsdale, N.J.: Lawrence Erlbaum Associates, 1982.

Kubicek, W. G., Kottke, F. J., Laker, D. J., & Visscher, M. B. Adaptation in pressor-receptor reflex mechanisms in experimental neurogenic hypertension. *American Journal of Physiology,* 1953, **175,** 380–382.

Lacey, J. I., & Lacey, B. C. The law of initial value in longitudinal study of autonomic constitution: Reproducibility of autonomic responses and response patterns over a four year interval. *Annals of the New York Academy of Sciences,* 1962, **98,** 1257–1290.

La Rocco, J. M., House, J. S., & French, J. R. P., Jr. Social support, occupational stress and health. *Journal of Health and Social Behaviour,* 1981, **21,** 202–218.

Lind, A. R., Taylor, S. H., Humphreys, P. W., Kennelly, B. M., & Donald, K. W. The circulatory effects of sustained voluntary muscle contraction. *Clinical Science,* 1964, **27,** 229–244.

Lum, L. C. Hyperventilation and anxiety state. *Journal of the Royal Society of Medicine, 1981,* **74,** 1–4.

Maddocks, I. Possible absence of essential hypertension in two complete Pacific Island populations. *Lancet,* 1961, **2,** 396.

Magoun, H. W. *The waking brain* (2nd ed.). Springfield, Ill.: Charles C Thomas, 1963.

Malmo, R. B., Shagass, C., & Davis, F. H. Symptom specificity and bodily reactions during psychiatric interview. *Psychosomatic Medicine,* 1950, **12,** 362–366.

Marmot, M. G., Rose, G., Shipley, M., & Hamilton, P. J. S. Employment grade and coronary heart disease in British civil servants. *Journal of Epidemiology and Community Health,* 1978, **32,** 244–249.

Marmot, M. G., & Syme, S. L. Acculturation and coronary heart disease in Japanese-Americans. *American Journal of Epidemiology,* 1976, **104,** 225–246.

Matthews, K. A., Glass, D. C., Rosenman, R. H., & Bortner, R. Competitive drive, pattern A, and coronary heart disease: A further analysis of some data from the Western Collaborative Group Study. *Journal of Chronic Diseases,* 1977, **30,** 489–498.

McCubbin, J. W., Green, J. H. & Page, I. H. Baroreceptor function in chronic renal hypertension. *Circulation Research,* 1956, **4,** 205–210.

Medalie, J. H., & Goldbourt, W. Angina pectoris among 10,000 men: II. Psychosocial and other risk factors as evidenced by a multivariate analysis of a five year incidence study. *American Journal of Medicine,* 1976, **60,** 910–921.

Miasnikov, A. L. The significance of disturbances of higher nervous activity in the pathogenesis of hypertensive disease. In J. H. Cort, V. Fencl, Z. Hejl, J. Zirka (Eds.), *WHO/Czechoslovak Cardiology Society symposium on the pathogenesis of essential hypertension.* Prague: State Medical Publishing Co., 1961.

Morris, J. N., Kagan, A., Pattison, D. C., Gardner, M. J., & Raffle, P. A. B. Incidence and prediction of ischaemic heart disease in London busmen. *Lancet,* 1966, **2,** 553–559.

Multicentre International Study. Improvement in prognosis of myocardial infarction by long term beta-adrenoreceptor blockade using Practolol. *Britsh Medical Journal,* 1975, **3,** 735–740.

Ostfeld, A. M., & Lebovits, B. Z. Personality factors and pressor mechanisms in renal and essential hypertension. *AMA Archives of Internal Medicine,* 1959, **104,** 43–52.

Patel, C. H. Yoga and biofeedback in the management of hypertension. *Lancet,* 1973, **2,** 1053–1055.

Patel, C. 12-month follow up of yoga and biofeedback in the management of hypertension. *Lancet,* 1975, **1,** 62–65.(a)

Patel, C. Yoga and biofeedback in the management of "stress" in hypertensive patients. In *Proceedings of the Third Symposium of the International Society of Hypertension*, Milan. September 1974. *Clinical Science and Molecular Medicine*, 1975, **48** (Suppl.), 171–174.(b)

Patel, C. Reduction of serum cholesterol and blood pressure in hypertensive patients by behaviour modification. *Journal of the Royal College of General Practitioners*, 1976, **26**, 211–215.

Patel, C. H. Biofeedback-aided relaxation and meditation in the management of hypertension. *Biofeedback and Self-Regulation*, 1977, **2**, 1–41.

Patel, C. H. Yoga and biofeedback in the management of hypertension. In D. Wheatley (Ed.), *Stress and the heart*. New York: Raven Press, 1981.

Patel, C. Primary prevention of coronary heart disease. In Surwit, R. S., Williams, R. B., Steptoe, A., & Biersner R. (Eds.), *Behavioural treatment of disease*. New York: Plenum, 1982.

Patel, C. Yogic therapy. In R. Woolfolk & P. Lahrer (Eds.), *Clinical guide to stress management*. New York: Guildford Press, 1983.

Patel, C., & Carruthers, M. Coronary risk factor reduction through biofeedback-aided relaxation and meditation. *Journal of the Royal College of General Practitioners*, 1977, **27**, 401–405.

Patel, C., Marmot, M. M., & Terry, D. J. Controlled trial of biofeedback-aided behavioural methods in reducing mild hypertension. *British Medical Journal*, 1981, **282**, 2005–2008.

Patel, C., & North, W. R. S. Randomised controlled trial of yoga and biofeedback in the management of hypertension. *Lancet*, 1975, **2**, 93–95.

Richardson, D. W., Vetrovec, G. W., & Williamson, W. C. Effect of sleep on blood pressure in patients with hypertension. In G. Onesti, K. E. Kim, & J. H. Moyer (Eds.), *Hypertension: Mechanisms and management*. New York and London: Grune & Stratton, 1972.

Robinson, J. O. A possible effect of selection on the test scores of a group of hypertensives. *Journal of Psychosomatic Research*, 1964, **8**, 239–243.

Rose, G. Strategy for prevention: Lessons from cardiovascular disease. *British Medical Journal*, 1981, **282**, 1847–1851.

Rosenman, R. H. The role of behaviour patterns and neurogenic factors in the pathogenesis of coronary heart disease. In R. S. Elliott (Ed.), *Stress and the heart*. New York: Futura, 1974.

Rosenman, R. H., Brand, R. J., Jenkins, C. D., Friedman, M., Straus, R., & Wurm, M. Coronary heart disease in the Western Collaborative Group Study: Final follow-up of 8½ years. *Journal of the American Medical Association*, 1975, **233**, 872.

Roskies, E. Consideration in developing a treatment programe for the coronary-prone (type A) behaviour pattern. In P. Davidson & S. M. Davidson (Eds.), Behavioural medicine: Changing health lifestyles. New York: Brunner/Mazel, 1980.

Sainsbury, P. Psychosomatic disorder and neurosis in out patients attending a general hospital. *Journal of Psychosomatic Research*, 1960, **4**, 261–273.

Schachter, J. Pain, fear and anger in hypertensives and normotensives. *Psychosomatic Medicine*, 1957, **19**, 17.

Schucker, B. & Jacobs, D. R. Assessment of behavioural risk for coronary disease by voice characteristics. *Psychosomatic Medicine*, 1977, **39**, 219–228.

Scotch, N. A. Sociocultural factors in the epidemiology of Zulu hypertension. *American Journal of Public Health*, 1963, **55**, 1205–1213.

Selye, H. *Stress without distress.* New York: Lippincott and Crowell, 1967.

Shapiro, A. P. An experimental study of comparative responses of blood pressure to different noxious stimuli. *Journal of Chronic Disease*, 1961, **13**, 293–311.

Sivertsson, R. The haemodynamic importance of structural vascular changes in essential hypertension. *Acta Physiologica Scandinavica* [Suppl.] 1970, **343**, 6–56.

Sleight, P. Baroreceptor function in hypertension. In C. Berglund, L. Hanson, & L. Werke (Eds.), *Pathophysiology and management of arterial hypertension*. Malndan, Sweden: A. Lindgren & Soner, 1975.

Smith, W. M. Treatment of mild hypertension. Results of a ten year intervention trial. *Circulation Research*, 1977, **40** (Suppl. I), 98–105.

Stammler, J., Farinaro, E., Mojonnier, L. M., Hall, Y., Moss D., & Stammler R. Prevention and control of hypertension by nutritional hygienic means. *Journal of the American Medical Association*, 1980, **243**, 1819–1823.

Stout, C., Morrow, J., Brandt, E., & Wolf, S. Unusually low incidence of death from myocardial infarction in an Italian-American community in Pennsylvania. *Journal of the American Medical Association*, 1964, **188**, 845–849.

Taylor, S. H. The circulation in hypertension. In *Hypertension—Its nature and treatment: An international symposium*. Malta, October 1974. Horsham, England: Ciba Laboratories, 1975.

Vaughan-Williams, E. M., Hassan, M. P., Floras, J. S., Sleight, P., & Jones, V. J. Adaptation of hypertensives to treatment with cardioselective and nonselective beta-blockers. Absence of correlation between bradycardia and blood pressure control and reduction in slope of QT/RR relation. *British Heart Journal*, 1980, **44**, 437–487.

Veterans Administration Co-operative Study Group on Antihypertensive Agents. Effects of treatment on morbidity in hypertension: Results in patients with diastolic blood pressures averaging 115 through 129 mmHg. *Journal of the American Medical Association*, 1967, **202**, 1028–1034.

Veterans Administration Co-operative Study Group on Antihypertensive Agents. Effects of treatment on morbidity in hypertension: II. Results in patients with diastolic blood pressure averaging 90 through 114 mmHg. *Journal of the American Medical Association*, 1970, **213**, 1143–1152.

Veterans Administration Co-operative Study Group on Antihypertensive Agents. Effects of treatment on morbidity in hypertension: III. Influence of age, diastolic pressure and cardiovascular disease. *Circulation*, 1972, **45**, 991–1004.

Wallace, R. K., & Benson, H. The physiology of meditation. *Scientific American*, 1972, **226**, 84–90.

Weiner, H. Psychosomatic research in essential hypertension: Retrospect and prospect. In M. Koster, H. Musaph, & P. Visser (Eds.), *Psychosomatics in essential hypertension. Bibliotheca Psychiatrica*, 1970, **144**, 58–116.

WHO/ISH Mild Hypertension Liaison Committee. Trails of the treatment of mild hypertension: An interim analysis. *Lancet*, 1982, **1**, 149–156.

Wolf, S., & Goodell, H. (Eds.) *Harold G. Wolff's Stress and Disease* (2nd ed.). Springfield, Ill.: Charles C Thomas, 1968.

Wolf, S., Wolff, H. G. A summary of experimental evidence relating life stress to the pathogenesis of essential hypertension in man. In E. T. Bell (Ed.), *Hypertension*. Minneapolis: University of Minnesota Press, 1951.

Wolpe, J. Psychotherapy by reciprocal inhibition. Stanford, Calif.: Stanford University Press, 1958.

CHAPTER 55

WORKSITE TREATMENT OF HYPERTENSION

MICHAEL H. ALDERMAN

Cornell University Medical College

Diseases of the heart and blood vessels, or cardiovascular disease, claim the lives of 900,000 Americans annually—700,000 from heart attack and 200,000 from stroke. This represents more than half of the deaths in this country every year. Another million Americans become disabled by these diseases annually. Furthermore, cardiovascular disease is the leading consumer of health dollars. In 1977, for example, the national bill for coronary heart disease was $80 billion—an estimated $54 billion in indirect costs and $26 billion in direct medical care spending—or 10% of the national medical bill.

Although not all causes of cardiovascular disease are completely understood, high blood pressure, or hypertension, is thought to be the single most important risk factor. Recent studies show that individuals with hypertension are three times as likely to develop coronary heart disease, six times as likely to experience congestive heart failure, and seven times as likely to have a stroke as those with normal blood pressure. About 60 million people, or more than one in four adult Americans, have some elevation of blood pressure—35 million with definite hypertension and 25 million with borderline hypertension—and are therefore at greater risk for premature death or disability. This risk is increased and life expectancy is reduced progressively as blood pressure rises (see Table 55.1).

Effective treatment can alleviate the impact of hypertension. In fact, of all known risk factors, high blood pressure is the one that can be most reliably and readily altered. An individual can hardly influence his genetic composition; there is no sure way to break the tobacco habit; and it has not been easy to identify a technique for altering serum cholesterol and other blood lipids that is both safe and acceptable for free-living people. In fact, we do not even know whether lowering cholesterol, minimizing stress, losing weight, or exercising will actually reduce the number of early strokes or heart attacks.

The situation is very different for hypertension. Since the mid-1950s, a variety of effective and well-tolerated drugs have been available for lowering blood pressure. Moreover, it has been convincingly demonstrated that blood pressure reduction saves lives (VA Cooperative Study Group, 1971). In many studies, the treatment of high blood pressure has been shown to reduce the risk of stroke and heart disease by 20% to 50%.

Although there are no clear symptoms of high blood pressure, it emerges principally in middle life. A large proportion of America's workers (almost 70%) are between the ages of 35 and 64, the age group in which the prevalence of hypertension increases rapidly. Furthermore, significant proportions of management and supervisory personnel are between 55 and 64, a period in life when the consequences of high blood pressure—heart attack and stroke—reach a peak of concern.

Although some of the tragedy of worker disability due to stroke or heart attack is

Table 55.1   Life Expectancy and Elevated Blood Pressure

	Male Patients			Female Patients	
Age	Blood Pressure	Loss of Life Expectancy (years)	Age	Blood Pressure	Loss of Life Expectancy (years)
35	Normal	—			
	130/90	4			
	140/95	9			
	150/100	16.5			
45	Normal	—	45	Normal	—
	130/90	3		130/90	1.5
	140/95	6		140/95	5
	150/100	11.5		150/100	8.5
55	Normal	—	55	Normal	—
	130/90	1		130/90	.5
	140/95	4		140/95	3
	150/100	6		150/100	4

Source: Society of Actuaries. Blood Pressure Study 1979 by Society of Actuaries and the Association of Life Insurance Medical Directors of America, November 1980.

unavoidable, much can be avoided by identifying hypertensive employees early and ensuring that they are provided proper care.

At least half of hypertensive Americans are members of the labor force. Although employed persons face specific practical difficulties in obtaining care, they are also a group whose characteristics might actually promote long-term care. Among these characteristics is the sense of urgency provoked by the tremendous economic impact on business and industry of the large number of working hypertensive persons. Recent government figures indicate that cardiovascular disease causes the loss of some 26 million workdays each year and costs more than $16 billion annually.

Moreover, an awareness by both management and labor of the unmet needs in this area of health management is emerging. The traditional responsibility that industry has assumed for reducing industrial hazards and accidents is now being extended to reducing the burden of cardiovascular disease. In the last few years, the workplace itself has become a focus of the overall national effort to control high blood pressure in an effort to contain the epidemic of cardiovascular disease.

COMPLIANCE

A crucial element in antihypertensive therapy is assuring that the patient takes his medication. The rule of thumb that has been traditionally applied is that two-thirds of hypertensives are in treatment but that only half that group achieves controlled blood pressure. Some studies suggest that as few as 20% of people who know themselves to be hypertensive are under good control (Baltz & Shimizu, 1977; Borhani, 1975). Moreover, up to 50% of hypertensives drop out of care within one year (Alderman & Engelland, 1979). The drugs used for control of the disease are effective, but they are prescribed "for life" to a usually asymptomatic patient, and therein lies much of the problem of compliance. It has also been found that the longer patients are under treatment, the less likely they are to comply (Mevyvesta, 1970).

According to the health belief theory, the probability that a person will take a preventive action is a function of the perceived susceptibility to the disease, the perceived severity of the disease, and the perceived benefits and barriers related to the recommended action. According to the theory, compliance may also be influenced by the patient's motivations, patient–provider interactions, characteristics of the therapeutic source and regimen, and social interaction.

Some strategies recommended for use in the treatment of hypertensive patients are as follows (Ackerman, 1977):

1. Accommodation of the environment to meet the patient's needs, not those of the staff.
2. Support of the patient's coping mechanisms as an index of the patient's readiness to learn and become responsible for self-care.
3. Correction of knowledge deficiencies and misconceptions.
4. Support and reinforcement of appropriate beliefs.
5. Application of behavior modification techniques, if appropriate, in areas of smoking and weight reduction.
6. Collaboration with the patient in setting realistic short- and long-term goals.

With these compliance problems and the poor treatment prognosis for hypertensives in mind, a model was created to detect and treat hypertensives at their workplace (Alderman and Schoenbaum, 1975).

WORKSITE TREATMENT

Worksite treatment was seen to have the advantage of minimizing both time lost from work and the travel expense involved in visits to a private doctor or clinic—inconveniences that can present real obstacles to the hypertensive. Worksite treatment also provides psychological support—a solidarity with fellow hypertensive employees who are being treated at the same place for the same problem by a health professional who is familiar to them. Finally, existing programs remove direct financial costs from the patient.

In this model, key elements are provision of all diagnostic and therapeutic services at the worksite, integration of a delivery system with the administration of a labor union, adherence to a rigid protocol, and continuous patient surveillance by nurses and paraprofessionals under physician supervision.

Initially, this hypertension control program began with support from federal, city, and foundation research sources. Subsequently, industry health and security plans (administered by joint boards of union and management representatives) assumed full financial responsibility for implementation of this program. Actual medical direction, however, is entirely the responsibility of the hypertension control group at Cornell University Medical College, Department of Public Health.

The program originated among the employees of Gimbel's and Bloomingdale's department stores in New York City. This program has been replicated and currently serves more than 3,000 patients in 24 sites in the New York metropolitan area. The organization of each treatment site is based on the original program model, which will be described here (see Figure 55.1).

METHODS

An initial educational campaign provides employees with information about high blood pressure, its diagnosis and treatment, and the plan to provide detection and treatment at the worksite. All employees are then invited to be screened during time released from work. Management and union leadership schedule several persons for testing each day, so that each employee is away from work for 10 to 15 minutes. A one-page questionnaire

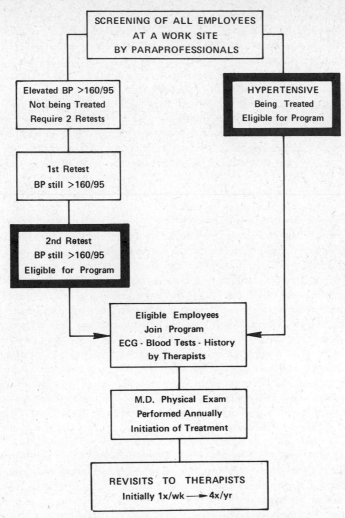

Figure 55.1 Flow chart for hypertensive patients.

providing basic historical, demographic, and anthropometric data is completed before the screening session.

Paraprofessional therapists or nurses measure blood pressure, according to American Heart Association (AHA) guidelines, in the employee cafeteria, lounge, or meeting room. When the average of two recordings at the initial encounter equals or exceeds 160 mmHg systolic and/or 95 mmHg diastolic, the employee is asked to return for a second set of recordings a week later. Employees with sustained elevation are asked to return for a third visit. An employee is considered to have hypertension requiring treatment when blood pressure is ≤ 160 mmHg systolic and/or ≤ 95 mmHg diastolic on each of the three visits or if he or she is already being treated for high blood pressure. The blood pressure levels required to establish need for treatment are modified for employees under age 30 (150/90) or over age 65 (170/100).

All employees are given the results of their blood pressure tests. Hypertensives are advised to initiate treatment and are offered the option of care on site or through regular medical sources. Workers who choose worksite therapy are given a complete medical evaluation before any treatment begins. At the first appointment, the company nurse will obtain a medical history, draw blood for laboratory tests, analyze urine for protein and glucose, and record an electrocardiogram (ECG). A second appointment is scheduled for the following week, when the in-house physician reviews the medical history and laboratory test results and performs a complete physical examination. Based on these findings, the physician will assess the worker's eligibility for the treatment program and, if so indicated, will begin therapy.

Follow-up visits to the worksite treatment clinic begin one week after therapy is initiated. At first, these visits are frequent—as often as once a week while medication is being adjusted to the proper dosage—but they decrease to once every 3 months as blood pressure control is achieved. At each follow-up visit, blood pressure is measured and recorded, medication is maintained or adjusted if necessary, and any side effects or problems of therapy are discussed. All visits, with the exception of the initial medical evaluation and laboratory workup, are brief and can be scheduled on the employee's own time during the workday—during a break, at lunchtime, or immediately before or after work. A nurse or paraprofessional can easily handle the routine revisits.

Hypertensive workers should be counseled about altering their lifestyle if it includes any major cardiovascular risk factors (smoking, overweight, immoderate salt intake, etc.). Some patients actually are able to achieve and maintain blood pressure control through dietary modification. For the vast majority of patients, however, the basis of modern therapy remains antihypertensive drugs. The method of administering the drugs, which is tailored to the needs of a worksite treatment program, is stepped, or sequential, using a protocol. The scheme is designed to ensure that each patient receives the least possible medication consistent with satisfactory blood pressure control.

The protocol enables a nurse to manage the treatment regimen comfortably once the patient has been evaluated and therapy has been started. Such a protocol, which generally uses a diuretic as the first step in treatment, gives detailed instructions for adding additional drugs in a specified sequence if required by blood pressure levels that remain uncontrolled.

Using a protocol makes it possible to employ a physician only part-time. Program physicians are responsible for development of treatment, initial evaluation and determination of eligibility for the worksite program, initiation of therapy, education of the staff, chart review, continuing consultation, annual physical examinations, and overall supervision of care. The nurse performs an expanded function as the key caretaker—interpreting the carefully detailed protocol as well as educating and counseling the patient. This one-to-one interaction is a critical element for the program's success, and the nurses are selected primarily for their ability to relate well to patients. The patient's regular physician is informed of the patient's participation in the program, and information is shared with him or her if requested.

Little is required in the way of equipment. A sphygmomanometer, an ECG machine, a 6-foot folding table covered with an air mattress, a file cabinet, and a desk with a locked drawer for records are the basic equipment needed. Now in its ninth year, this program continues to have only a 6% to 7% annual attrition rate, with more than 80% of the workers maintaining good blood pressure control (see Figure 55.2). These results can be put into perspective by comparing them with experience in treating high blood pressure in the usual way. In hospital clinics and private physicians' offices, for example, it has been found that nearly half of all patients stop therapy within the first year of treatment. Of those remaining under care, only about half achieve satisfactory blood pressure control (see Table 55.2). In worksite-sponsored programs, nearly three times as many hypertensives realize the benefits of treatment. Perhaps the explanation for this difference lies in the nature of the disease itself and the special characteristics of the work environment that make it a unique place in which to approach the problem of hypertension.

The advantage of bringing all screening and therapeutic facilities to the worksite are (a) minimization of time and travel, (b) peer and social support, (c) treatment at low or no cost to the worker, and (d) the cohesiveness of the work environment. The provision

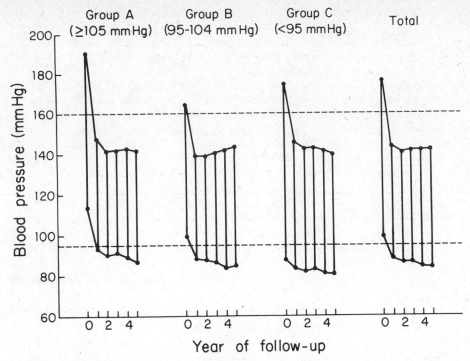

Figure 55.2 Blood pressure levels of patients, by diastolic blood pressure at entry and by year of follow-up. (From Madhavan, S., Davis, T., & Alderman, M. H. Profile of hypertensives as determinant of long term antihypertensive medication needs. *Hypertension,* 1981, **S-3,** 242–244. Reprinted by permission.)

of all services to treat hypertension at the workplace is one of several modalities of worksite-sponsored treatment.

This model of care is suitable for workers with uncomplicated, asymptomatic hypertension. For the rare employee with a serious medical problem requiring frequent visits to a doctor, or with abnormal laboratory findings suggesting a secondary cause of hypertension, worksite treatment is not appropriate. The majority of employees who are diagnosed as being hypertensive, however, have mild, uncomplicated disease and will be well served by a worksite treatment program.

Table 55.2 Treatment Results after 1 Year for Patients with High Blood Pressure

Treatment Site	Dropped Out (%)	Good Blood Pressure Control (%)
Private physician's office (1966–1976)	58	29
Hospital clinic (1964–1971)	48	33
Work site (1973–1976)	12	75

AN ALTERNATIVE WORKSITE-BASED PROGRAM

The formats of other existing programs vary widely. It is clear that efforts to involve detection and unsupervised referral to conventional sources of care existing in the community produce little in the way of improved blood pressure control. By contrast, programs that involve systematic efforts to ensure effective referral and sustained follow-up and to ensure adherence to a therapeutic regimen can produce dramatic improvement over usual approaches. To be effective in a setting where actual treatment is provided in the community, linkage of the worksite to both physicians and patients seems necessary. Such a program has proved effective for the employees at Massachusetts Mutual in Springfield (Alderman & Melcher, 1981), and this has been associated with company savings in excess of the cost of the program. Positive medical results, in terms of blood pressure control, are only slightly less than those achieved through on-site treatment.

Although the existing worksite programs vary in format, all include several components that seem essential to success in blood pressure control:

1. *Education:* Explaining to workers the danger of high blood pressure and what is to be gained from treating it.
2. *Screening:* Taking the blood pressure of all willing employees to identify those with high blood pressure.
3. *Referral:* Explaining the meaning of a high reading and referring the employee to a source of medical care in the community, or offering on-site treatment.
4. *Follow-up:* Optimally, contact with both physician and employee/patient to verify that referral was successful and to monitor his or her progress in therapy. A scheme that links the physicians and pharmacist's billing to follow-up has proved highly effective (Alderman and Melcher, 1981).

A sensitive issue surrounding worksite hypertension control is that of confidentiality and job security. The label "hypertensive" is feared to be grounds for not hiring, denying promotions, forcing early retirement, or even dismissal. This makes the employee's right to privacy in work-setting hypertension control programs a very important consideration.

The attitude of management toward persons with high blood pressure has changed a great deal in recent years. An employee whose high blood pressure is controlled by medication is now unlikely to encounter discrimination by an employer. In fact, most informed employers recognize that an effectively treated hypertensive is a far better investment than an uncontrolled and sometimes secret hypertensive who has a heightened chance of having a stroke or a heart attack. Since many hypertensives nevertheless remain wary that their jobs may be jeopardized if their high blood pressure becomes known through their participation in a worksite hypertension program, however, it is important that they be specifically reassured.

Many worksite programs with high screening participation and good compliance attribute their success partly to steps taken to ensure confidentiality and job security. Such measures can range from excluding management from the premises during screening and treatment to preventing the release of patient records without the written consent of the employee. This guarantees that only program sponsors and health care personnel know which employees are hypertensive and are familiar with their progress in therapy.

More and more, employers are recognizing the benefits that can derive from taking advantage of already existing facilities within the company. Many firms are modifying their occupational health care services to include a hypertension program, using the formal and informal in-house channels of communication in the work setting to encourage workers to seek and maintain treatment.

Because of the magnitude of the problem and the special burden untreated hypertension imposes on business and labor, it makes good sense for industry to improve the treatment of hypertension among employees. The conditions of the workplace—stability, long-term relationships of trust, and peer support—as well as the economic stake employers and unions have in achieving blood pressure control, have already led to the establishment of some highly successful programs.

Public and private institutions have now begun to encourage replication of those programs that have proved to be particularly effective. New programs designed to take advantage of the special assets of the workplace are appearing all the time, and there is a clear trend toward greater use of the worksite as an efficient place to improve blood pressure control.

REFERENCES

Ackerman, A. M. Patient education and its relevance to compliance. In M. H. Alderman (Ed.), *Hypertension—The nurse's role in ambulatory care*. New York: Springer, 1977.

Alderman, M. H., & Engelland, A. Blood pressure control in private practice: A case report. *American Journal of Public Health*, 1979, **69**(1), 25–29.

Alderman, M. H., & Melcher, L. A company-instituted program to improve blood pressure control in primary care. *Israel Journal of Medical Sciences*, 1981, **17**(2–3), 122–128.

Alderman, M. H., & Schoenbaum, E. E. Detection and treatment of hypertension at the worksite. *New England Journal of Medicine*, 1975, **293**(2), 65–68.

Baltz, T., & Shimizu, A.: Blood pressure surveys. *American Family Physician*, 1977, **23**, 70.

Borhani, N. Implementation and evaluation of community hypertension programs. In P. O. Miainy (Ed.), *Epidemiology and control of hypertension*. Chicago: Symposia Specialists, 1975.

Mevyvesta, M. Compliance with medical regimens. *Nursing Research*, 1970, **19**(4), 318.

Veterans Administration Cooperative Study Group on Antihypertensive Agents. Effects of treatment on morbidity in hypertension: II. Results in patients with diastolic blood pressure averaging 90 through 114 mmHg. *Journal of the American Medical Association*, 1971, **213**, 1143–1152.

CHAPTER 56

SODIUM EXCRETION AND BLOOD PRESSURE

GÖRAN BERGLUND

Sahlgrenska Hospital, University of Göteborg, Sweden

Sodium excretion over one or more 24-hour periods is an acceptable reflection of sodium intake (Liu, Cooper, McKeever, McKeever, Byington, Soltero, Stampler, Gosch, Stevens, & Stamler, 1979) and can be used for estimation of salt intake in epidemiologic studies. Blood pressure is a roughly distributed variable known to be statistically associated with the development of cardiovascular diseases, especially cerebrovascular disease and coronary heart disease. The mechanisms responsible for the development of high blood pressure (hypertension) are not known, but genetic and environmental factors, including a high salt intake, have been claimed to be involved (Freis, 1976). Average salt intake varies widely among communities but is usually 8–12 g/day in Europe and the United States. In unacculturated societies, salt intake is often below 2 g/day. Hypertension does not seem to occur in these societies, and blood pressure does not increase with age in the Western world (for a review, see Freis, 1976). Between-population studies seem to indicate that the prevalence of hypertension is positively related to the level of salt intake in the community (Freis, 1976). The relationship between salt intake and blood pressure within a population is more unclear, however; some studies show a positive relationship, whereas others have been unable to verify the relationship (Berglund, 1980). Scientists in the field are divided into believers and nonbelievers, as has become clear at several meetings devoted to the question of whether salt restriction should be recommended at the individual or community level (Berglund, Simpson, 1979). Intervention trials on individuals are few, and several of them are open to criticism (Morgan, Adam, Gillies, Wilson, Morgan, & Carney, 1978; Parijs, Jossens, Van der Linden, Verstreken, & Amery, 1973). Intervention trials at the community level are lacking so far. Despite the obvious lack of hard scientific proof for a beneficial effect of salt restriction on blood pressure level, public health measures have been taken in several countries. In Belgium, for example, legislation has been established to decrease the salt content in bread and other foods. In Canada, the Mustard Committee report to the Minister of National Health and Welfare on diet and cardiovascular disease recommended decreased salt consumption. In 1977, a U.S. Senate committee recommended that salt intake in the United States should be reduced to below 3 g/day. Recently, nationwide educational campaigns aiming at decreasing salt intake have been started in the United States. In response to public health concerns involving salt, sodium, and hypertension, a number of federal agencies, the health industry, and several consumer groups have joined together in a major educational campaign coordinated by the Food and Drug Administration (FDA). In the county of North Karelia in Finland, a community-based intervention study of the feasibility and effects of salt reduction was started in the spring of 1979.

Thus, health professionals planning to start campaigns aimed at preventing the development of hypertension through a decrease in salt intake should be aware that conclusive scientific evidence for a successful outcome of their campaigns does not exist. History, however, is full of examples in which intervention proved successful long before scientific evidence for the intervention measures was at hand. The aim of this chapter is to describe hitherto-presented intervention programs involving salt reduction, to evaluate which factors within the programs seem essential for a successful outcome, to evaluate the available information on how to reduce salt intake in individuals or communities, and to provide practical advice on measures that can be taken to achieve the public health goal—prevention of essential hypertension.

INTERVENTION PROGRAMS INVOLVING SALT RESTRICTION

Programs Directed Toward Hypertensive Subjects

Hypertensive subjects who have mild or moderate hypertension should not be regarded as having a disease. They have a risk factor for future cardiovascular disease, much in the same way as smokers, subjects with high cholesterol values, or obese persons have a risk factor for future disease. Therefore, hypertensive subjects should be reached in any salt reduction campaign aimed at preventing illness, and several trials have been undertaken using salt restriction to lower blood pressure in such patients. Many research groups have used salt reduction as sole or adjunct therapy in the treatment of hypertensive patients, but controlled trials using an untreated control group or a control group that is given other antihypertensive treatment are limited in number (MacGregor, Best, Cam, Markandu, Elder, & Sagnella, 1982; Morgan et al., 1978; Parijs et al., 1973). Parijs et al. (1973) found that advice given by a dietician on how to avoid salt-rich food reduced patients' 24-hour urinary sodium excretion from 200 to 93 mmol/day and also significantly reduced blood pressure measured at home. Studies in both Australia and Japan (Morgan et al., 1978; Shibata & Hatano, 1975) have shown that rather simple instruction programs—for example, one lecture of 2.5 hours combined with pamphlets giving background information on salt content of various foods—resulted in a sustained decrease of blood pressure. Some of these trials did not have an untreated control group, and hence the blood pressure reduction might have been at least partly caused by the participants' getting used to the personnel and to the circumstances surrounding the blood pressure measurement. Findings in an English trial (MacGregor et al., 1982) in which a parallel control group, with usual salt intake, was included do, however, confirm the blood pressure-reducing effect of even moderate salt restriction achieved by verbal and written dietary advice. Together, these trials also confirm that salt intake can be changed for long periods of time with rather simple dietary advice and without an obvious decrease in the quality of life.

Programs Directed Toward Normotensive Subjects: Pilot Studies

Most studies with normotensives were done with medical students who were given diets with various sodium contents prepared in a metabolic ward kitchen (Luft, Grim, Higgins, & Weinberger, 1977; Parfreys, Wright, Holly, Evans, Concon, Wandenburg, Goodwin, & Ledingham, 1981; Sullivan, Ratts, Taylor, Kraus, Barton, Patrick, & Reed, 1980). They were all short-term studies (weeks), and they showed that reduction of sodium intake from normal to lower levels does not decrease blood pressure in young, normal subjects. The design of these studies, however, does not permit one to confirm or refute the hypothesis that the development of hypertension can be prevented by low sodium intake.

Intervention in Total Populations

Large-scale campaigns to decrease salt intake have been launched in only a few countries. The probable reason for this is the lack of evidence for a positive effect on blood pressure level in the population and the lack of an effective means to achieve lower salt intake in the community. Nationwide efforts have been undertaken so far only in Belgium, Canada, Finland, and the United States. In Canada, the efforts have been limited to statements from the health authorities regarding the need to decrease salt intake. In Belgium, a campaign was launched modestly in 1968, slowly increasing in intensity over the next decade, and with the biggest effort during 1978. The salt reduction program was based on a consensus among university specialists that it was desirable to conduct the experiment—a consensus shared also by most general practitioners. The campaign was backed by the Ministry of Health, the National Hypertension Committee, the Iban (a nutrition research and advisory board), and the Cardiological League. The message to decrease salt intake and how to do it was spread by newspapers, magazines, television, radio, and a large number of talks by specialists to practitioners, people in the food industry, and laypeople all over Belgium. The Ministry of Health limited the salt content of bread to 200 mmol/kg, and in 1981 the average salt content of food was even lower, around 170 mmol/kg. Bakers were encouraged to offer salt-free white and brown bread as an alternative. Low-salt cheese and salt-free preserves were manufactured by the food industry after negotiations with the campaign leaders. Restaurants were encouraged to ask their customers whether they wished added salt in the preparation of the food. The results of the campaign showed that average salt consumption had decreased from 250 mmol/24 hours in 1966 to 165 mmol/24 hours in 1979. For its value as proof of the salt hypothesis, stroke mortality decreased faster in Belgium than in any other Common Market country during the time period. (Details of the campaign can be acquired from Professor Jozef Joossens, Division of Epidemiology, School of Public Health, University of Leuven, Belgium.)

In Finland a community-based intervention program to reduce general salt intake was launched in the spring of 1979 in North Karelia, a county with 178,000 inhabitants. North Karelia had a high occurrence of cardiovascular diseases, a previously developed organization for a hypertension intervention program, and epidemiologic registers for cardiovascular diseases. The previous program had not, however, included salt reduction as a major objective; the hypertension control had concentrated on detection, treatment, and follow-up of the hypertensives in the community. The aim of the new study was to assess the feasibility and effects of a community-based intervention program to reduce salt intake among the population of North Karelia. Its special objectives were as follows:

1. To obtain epidemiologic data on salt intake and its association with blood pressure and other cardiovascular risk factors.
2. To assess the feasibility of salt reduction at the community level.
3. To assess whether and to what extent a general reduction of salt intake is associated with changes in the blood pressure level of the population.
4. To assess the feasibility and effects of the program in population subgroups of strategic importance: treated hypertensives, untreated mild hypertensives, family members of hypertensive patients, and children.
5. To assess the effects of salt reduction and the need for and costs of antihypertensive drug treatment in the community.

The intensified community-based salt reduction intervention, which started in the spring of 1979 and continued until the spring of 1982, involved the entire county of North Karelia. The intervention included the following practical elements:

1. General health education directed to the whole population.
2. Promotion of patient health education and nutrition counseling.
3. Training of personnel.
4. Environmental changes (use of a substitute table salt and other low-sodium products).

The intervention strategies included the following:

1. Dissemination of health knowledge about the role of salt in hypertension.
2. Promotion of positive attitudes toward salt reduction.
3. Persuasion for the needed changes.
4. Teaching of the practical skills necessary for salt reduction.
5. Promotion of social support for maintenance of the change.
6. Modification of the environment to facilitate the needed individual measures.
7. Community organization for promotion of the given objectives.

The practical intervention activities were integrated as much as possible into the existing service structure and social organization of the community.

The feasibility evaluation will assess the extent to which it was possible to implement the planned activities of salt reduction. Feasibility evaluation includes the following procedures:

1. Assessing the extent and coverage of the intervention measures concerning reduction of salt intake and lowering of blood pressures in the community.
2. Assessing changes in health knowledge about salt and blood pressure and attempts to reduce salt intake among the population.
3. Assessing treatment and compliance changes in antihypertensive therapy.
4. Assessing environmental changes concerning salt consumption.

The outcome evaluation will concern main objectives (blood pressure level), intermediate objectives (level of salt consumption, compliance), and costs of hypertension control in the community. Indicators of these objectives are measured at the outset and at the end of the program, both in the intervention community and in a matched reference community. Changes in the reference community show the changes in the population that did not have any specific intensive program. The effect of the program is considered to be the change in the intervention community minus the change in the reference community.

Representative population samples were drawn for the program and reference communities and were examined before and after the intervention period. The target population of evaluation was between 14 and 65 years of age. Different cross-sectional samples were used at the beginning and at the end of the program. In addition, a hypertension register, including most of the hypertensive patients in the area, has been operating since 1972 in North Karelia. The register is used in evaluating the feasibility of the program and the changes among the hypertensive patients.

The surveys in 1979 and 1982 included a self-administered questionnaire, completed at home, and supplementary inquiries and physical measurements at the place of examination. Internationally accepted methods and recommendations were followed as closely as possible. The sample size was approximately 2,500 in both surveys.

The questionnaire included such areas as health behavior and dietary habits. A special health knowledge questionnaire was also used. At the examination, height, weight and casual blood pressure were measured, and all participants were asked to collect a 24-hour urine sample to be returned to the examination place. Sodium and potassium content of the urine were then determined.

So far, no results of this important study have been published. (Questions can be addressed to Professor Pekka Puska, National Public Health Laboratory, Epidemiological Research Unit, Mannerheimintie 166, 00280 Helsinki 28, Finland.)

In the United States, in response to public health concerns involving salt intake and hypertension, a number of federal agencies and health, industry, and consumer groups have joined together in a major educational campaign. The Food and Drug Administration (FDA) is coordinating the effort through a continuous exchange of ideas and information among such groups as the American Medical Association, food manufacturers, trade associations, the National High Blood Pressure Education Program, and the U.S. Department of Agriculture (USDA). These groups, especially the FDA, have produced materials that discuss this topic, including several pamphlets for the general public and for hypertensives. Public service announcements from the FDA and the USDA are also components of the campaign, as well as a television program and a slide presentation. The FDA is planning to distribute print materials and the slide set through its 52 regional consumer affairs offices. The staffs of these offices work with local-level consumer groups and schools to inform residents about a variety of consumer issues, including those related to sodium.

The sodium education campaign is an integral part of the United States goverment's effort to encourage the food industry to list sodium content on its product labels voluntarily. Because major food processors, whose products make up over 40% of those on store shelves, stated that they would list sodium content before the end of 1982, Congress postponed action on legislation to make sodium labeling mandatory.

The following materials, generated as part of the education campaign, are available to the general public:

1. *Diet and Hypertension,* a bilingual publication discussing weight and sodium control and potassium intake. Published in English, Cambodian, Laotian, Chinese, and Vietnamese. Available in single copies from May Sung, Asian/Pacific Islander Task Force, 7988 Capwell Drive, Oakland, CA 94621.

2. *Health Is "In" Salt Is "Out",* produced by the Baltimore High Blood Pressure Coordinating Council in cooperation with the Maryland Department of Health and Mental Hygiene and the American Heart Association, Maryland Affiliate. Lists foods by what to eat and what not to eat for reduced sodium diets. Discusses sources of sodium and no-salt ways to season foods. Includes recipes and hints for eating out. *Contact:* Maryland HBP Coordinating Council, 415 N. Charles Street, Baltimore, MD 21201. Single copies free. For bulk orders, contact Earl Sherman (301)539-0821.

3. *Living Without Salt,* by K. B. Baltzell and T. M. Parsley (Elgin, Ill.: The Brethren Press). A cookbook of low-sodium recipes, with discussions of salt's role in history and the role of salt in diet. Many recipes use items found in health food stores. *Contact:* The Brethren Press, 1451 Dundee Avenue, Elgin, IL 60120. Cost: $7.95 plus $.85 postage and handling. For bulk orders, contact the publisher at 800-323-8039.

4. *Sodium Sense,* produced in 1982 by the Washington, D.C., Food Marketing Institute in cooperation with the FDA and NHBPEP. Describes sodium and salt; sources of sodium (food, medications, and drinking water); how to find sodium on a food label; and ways to reduce sodium intake. Lists sodium and potassium content of everyday foods. *Contact:* Food Marketing Institute, 1750 K Street, N.W., Washington, D.C. 20006. 1 to 5 copies free with self-addressed, stamped #10 envelope; 6 to 99 copies, $.10 each; 100 or more, $8.00 per hundred; 1,000 or more, $70.00 per thousand. Reproducible artwork: $25 per set.

5. *Sodium: Think About It,* produced by the U.S. Department of Agriculture. Designed to inform the general public about sodium in the diet. Discusses where sodium is found, gives ranges of sodium content of foods in the 4 major food groups, and gives tips on how to balance high-sodium foods and meals with low-sodium ones. *Contact:* Consumer Information Center, USDA, Pueblo, CO 81900. Single copies available free. For negatives to reproduce multiple copies, contact USDA-FSIS Information, Room 1163 South, Washington, D.C. 20250.

6. *Straight Talk About Salt: What You Should Know About Salt and Sodium in Your Diet,* produced in 1982 by the Salt Institute, Alexandria, Va., in cooperation with the FDA and NHBPEP. A well-referenced discussion of sodium; salt; sodium's effect on hyper-

tensives and persons with kidney, liver, and heart ailments; sodium in food processing; and how sodium is measured. Lists sodium and calorie content of many foods. *Contact:* Salt Institute, 206 N. Washington St., Alexandria, VA 22314. Single copies $.25 or free with self-addressed, stamped #10 envelope. For bulk orders or permission to reproduce, contact Lincoln Harner, Director of Public Relations, (703)549-4648.

In summary, large-scale intervention programs aimed at reducing dietary intake of sodium have been implemented in very few communities. The program of the North Karelia Project in Finland is the only controlled effort so far presented. Nationwide educational campaigns have been started in Belgium and the United States, but without preparations for evaluation of the effects of the campaigns on blood pressure levels and on hypertensive complications.

CORNERSTONES OF INTERVENTION PROGRAMS

The following points should be carefully evaluated by any group planning a program for restriction of sodium intake aimed at prevention of hypertension.

Participants

A program can be directed toward known, treated or untreated hypertensives, relatives of known hypertensives, other subjects known or suspected to have an increased risk of developing hypertension, or the general population, including all ages and both sexes. It should be recognized that methods to achieve the salt restriction probably will differ, depending on what target population is chosen. The total population approach undoubtedly offers the best possibility of achieving the goal of prevention of hypertensive complications in the community.

Intervention Strategies

The strategies should include the following;

1. Increasing knowledge of the role of sodium in the development of hypertension— that is, health education.
2. Building up a positive attitude toward reduction of salt intake and the changes in eating habits that are necessary to achieve this reduction.
3. Teaching the practical efforts necessary to achieve a lower salt intake.
4. Promoting changes in the food industry to diminish the salt content of food and to list salt content on the labels of all prepared food.

Practical Implementations

Depending on the group toward which the intervention is directed and the society in which the program will be implemented, all or some of the following approaches can be chosen:

1. Influencing the way people cook at home toward using less salt.
2. Decreasing the use of salt at the table at home. (Approaches 1 and 2 can be promoted with the help of a table salt containing less sodium and more potassium.
3. Decreasing the content of salt in food prepared in schools, at worksites, and in restaurants.
4. Requiring the food industry to diminish the salt content of prepared food, including bread.
5. Providing intensive information to hypertensive patients and their relatives regarding why and how to decrease salt intake.

In all these activities, primary attention should be paid to subjects who take part in cooking and preparing food.

Duration of the Program

It is well known that changes in basic habits, such as cooking and the use of salt, take a long time to implement. A program duration of several years must therefore be anticipated, even in societies with an abundance of mass media.

Evaluation of the Effects of the Program

The following variables can be measured as indicators of the effects of the program. Ideally, these indicators should also be measured in a reference population in which no intervention has taken place.

1. Sodium excretion as a mirror of salt intake.
2. Blood pressure.
3. Hypertensive complications (e.g., cardiovascular diseases, hypertensive organ manifestations).
4. Quality of life.

These indicators should be measured before intervention starts and again when the full effect of the intervention program is anticipated. An example of such an evaluation was seen in the North Karelia Project in Finland.

REFERENCES

Berglund, G. (Ed.). *Salt and hypertension.* Stockholm: Cederroths.

Berglund, G. Should salt intake be cut down to prevent primary hypertension? *Acta Medica Scandinavica,* 1980, **207**, 241.

Freis, E. D. Salt, volume and the prevention of hypertension. *Circulation,* 1976, **53**, 589.

Liu, K., Cooper, R., McKeever, J., McKeever, P., Byington, R., Soltero, I., Stampler, R., Gosch, F., Stevens, E., & Stamler, J. Assessment of the association between habitual salt intake and high blood pressure: Methodological problems. *American Journal of Epidemiology,* 1979, **119**, 219.

Luft, F. C., Grim, C. E., Higgins, J. T., & Weinberger, M. H. Differences in response to sodium administration in normotensive white and black subjects. *Journal of Laboratory and Clinical Medicine,* 1977, **90**, 555–562.

MacGregor, G. A., Best, F. E., Cam, J. M., Markandu, N. D., Elder, D. M., & Sagnella, G. A. Double-blind randomised crossover trial of moderate sodium restriction in essential hypertension. *Lancet,* 1982, **1**, 351.

Morgan, T., Adam, W., Gillies, A., Wilson, M., Morgan, G., & Carney, S. Hypertension treated by salt restriction. *Lancet,* 1978, **1**, 227.

Parfreys, P. S., Wright, P., Holly, J. M. P., Evans, S. J. W., Concon, K., Wandenburg, M. J., Goodwin, F. C., & Ledingham, J. M. Blood pressure and hormonal changes following alterations in dietary sodium and potassium in young men with and without familial predisposition to hypertension. *Lancet,* 1981, , 113–117.

Parijs, J., Jossens, J. V., Van der Linden, L., Verstreken, G., & Amery, A. K. P. C. Moderate sodium restriction and diuretics in the treatment of hypertension. *American Heart Journal,* 1973, **85**, 22.

Shibata, H., & Hatano, S. A salt restriction trial in Japan. In P. Oglesby (Ed.), *Epidemiology and control of hypertension.* New York: Stratton Intercontinental Medical Books, 1975.

Simpson, F. O. Salt and hypertension: A sceptical review of the evidence. *Clinical Science,* 1979, **57**, 463s–480s.

Sullivan, J. M., Ratts, T. E., Taylor, J. C., Kraus, D. H., Barton B. R., Patrick, D. R., & Reed, S. W. Hemodynamic effects of dietary sodium in man. *Hypertension,* 1980, **2**, 506–514.

CHAPTER 57

BLOOD PRESSURE AND OBESITY

JAMES K. ALEXANDER

Baylor College of Medicine, Houston, Texas

EPIDEMIOLOGY

An association between obesity and systemic hypertension has long been recognized, but attempts to clarify this relationship have been beset by difficulties in characterizing and quantifying obesity. Since the presence of increased weight alone is not a satisfactory criterion for determination of obesity, several indices have been utilized in an attempt to quantitate it involving the relation between height and weight. These indices include the ponderal index (weight in pounds/height in inches), the Quetelet index (weight/height^2 × 100), and the height-weight percent (percent standard weight for given height). Other approaches to the characterization of obesity include measurement of skin fold thickness or body fat. A few studies have involved calculation or measurement of body surface area.

The correlation of body bulk and blood pressure is most prominent in young adults, tending to disappear after middle age (Miall, Bell, & Lovell, 1968; Evans & Rose, 1971; Johnson, Cornoni, Cassell, Tyroler, Hayden, & Hames, 1975). In normotensive young adults, height-weight percent correlates better with systolic than with diastolic blood pressure (Boynton & Todd, 1948). In obese young adults, there is a correlation between blood pressure and skin fold thickness as well as calculated body fat, but the majority of obese young adults are *not* hypertensive, and some of the most obese are normotensive (Court, Hill, Dunlop, & Boulton, 1974). Thus, although the association of obesity and elevated blood pressure is sufficient to result in a significant statistical correlation, the presence of obesity, even when extreme, does not always result in the development of hypertension.

Several studies document an increased prevalence of hypertension in obese adults. In a survey of 2,858 persons who were 6% or more over ideal weight compared to 658 persons at or below ideal weight applying for insurance, it was found that for increments in weight 26% to 42% above the ideal, the incidence of hypertension (systolic blood pressure 150 mmHg or greater, diastolic pressure 90 mmHg or more) was 10% for those over ideal weight versus 3% for those at ideal weight; for diastolic hypertension, the incidence was 15% versus 7%. For those 41% or more above ideal weight, the incidence of systolic hypertension rose to 32% and that of diastolic hypertension rose to 36%. In this study, the differences were greater in the age group 50 to 59 years (Short & Johnson, 1939). Using levels of 160 mmHg or more systolic and 95 mmHg or more diastolic as criteria for hypertension in the Framingham Study, it was found that the prevalence of hypertension in those with relative weights greater than 120 (relative weight = actual weight/average weight for height) was twice that for relative weight of 100 or below for the age group 50 to 59 years, 2 to 3 times for the age group 40 to 49, and in those aged 30 to 39, 5 times for men and 17 times for women (Kannel, Brand, Skinner, Dawber, & McNamara, 1967).

Systolic and diastolic hypertension is more common in obese women than in obese men, with increased incidences ranging from 150% to 300% (Robinson, Bruces, & Mass, 1939). Cross-sectional data from a study of a group of men in the Chicago Peoples Gas, Light and Coke Company aged 40 to 59 years at entry indicated a prevalence rate of diastolic hypertension for persons 15% above ideal weight approximately twice that of those at or below ideal weight. For those who were 25% or more above ideal weight, the proportion was even greater (Stamler, 1967). More recently, in a survey of more than one million persons screened by the Community Hypertension Evaluation Clinic Program across the United States from 1973 to 1975, there is a consistent relationship between overweight and hypertension—in all age groups, for both men and women, and for both whites and blacks—that is independent of family history of hypertension (Stamler, Stamler, Riedlinger, Algera, & Roberts, 1978). The prevalence rate of hypertension is 50% to 300% higher in overweight subjects than in underweight or normal weight subjects, averaging 100% above the normals in the age group 20 to 39 years and 50% above the normals in the age group 40 to 64.

Although epidemiologic studies demonstrate some correlation between relative weight and blood pressure, and a significantly increased prevalence of hypertension among obese subjects, the impact of obesity as a risk factor for hypertension is not great. In surveys of large numbers of hypertensive patients, the relationship between blood pressure elevation and adiposity tends to be modest. In the Seven Countries Study, less than 5% of the variance of blood pressure is explained by relative weight or fatness (Keys, 1970). In another large survey of hypertensive patients, a relationship between blood pressure and adiposity could be established only in male nonsmokers (Ballantyne, Devine, & Fife, 1978). These observations do not deny the importance of obesity as a public health problem, nor the associated increased hazard in relation to hypertension; rather, they highlight our lack of insight into the relationship between hypertension and obesity and the mechanisms involved.

In summary, there is some correlation between body bulk and blood pressure in young adults, which is much less apparent after middle age. The prevalence of frank hypertension is significantly increased in obese children and adults, men and women, and whites and blacks in the United States. Obesity does not always imply hypertension, however, and even in extremely obese individuals, about one-third are normotensive (Alexander, 1963). Although the impact of obesity as a health hazard for hypertension is clear, the correlation of the overall incidence of hypertension with obesity is of a low order (Kannel et al., 1967), suggesting the possibility of separate and distinct mechanisms in the genesis of obesity hypertension.

ETIOPATHOGENETIC CONSIDERATIONS

The mechanisms responsible for the development of hypertension in obese subjects have not yet been identified. Difficulties involved in a satisfactory analysis of such factors are highlighted by two circumstances. First, it has not been possible to invoke volume loading and arteriolar narrowing as important factors, as may be the case in other forms of essential hypertension, because measurements of blood volume in obese subjects do not correlate with the presence or absence of hypertension (Alexander, 1963; Messerli, Christie, DeCarvalho, Aristimuno, Suarez, Dreslinski, & Frohlich, 1981), and calculated systemic vascular resistance in obese hypertensive subjects is less than that in lean hypertensives (Alexander, 1963; Messerli et al., 1981). Although there is a positive correlation between total blood volume and cardiac output in both lean and obese hypertensive individuals (Messerli et al., 1981), the fact that systemic vascular resistance is significantly less in the very obese subjects suggests that the mechanisms of blood pressure elevation are different. This is all the more apparent if diastolic pressures are considered rather than mean arterial blood pressure. Second, even with severe obesity, about one-third of such subjects may be normotensive (Alexander, 1963), and it has not been possible to identify any known factor or factors predisposing to blood pressure elevation that are unique to the hypertensive group. Even the relative significance of body weight versus degree of adiposity in relation to the hypertension of obesity is controversial. Hypertension is better correlated with body weight in one study (Kannel et al., 1967) but with skin fold thickness in another (Palmai, 1962).

Steroid turnover rates are increased with obesity (Schteingart & Conn, 1965). No clear cut evidence that elevated aldosterone levels play a significant role in the genesis of obesity hypertension has been forthcoming, however, on the basis of studies during weight reduction. Although diminished aldosterone levels accompany reduction in blood pressure associated with weight loss in obese hypertensives, there is no correlation between the two (Tuck, Sowers, Dornfeld, Kledzik, & Maxwell, 1981). Similarly, plasma renin activity remains relatively stable during the first 4 weeks of weight reduction, when decrements in blood pressure tend to be the most pronounced (Tuck et al., 1981). Since salt restriction together with reduction in caloric intake may effect lowering of blood pressure in obese hypertensives, it has been suggested that the combination of high salt and caloric intake results in elevated blood pressure (Dahl, Silver, & Christie, 1958). The concept that high salt intake is essential for obesity hypertension has been challenged, however, by the demonstration of substantial decreases in blood pressure in obese hypertensives during weight reduction with diminished caloric intake but normal salt intake (Reisin, Abel, & Modan, 1978).

A potential role for the thyroid in the genesis of obesity hypertension has been suggested (Sims, Phinney, & Vaswani, 1978). Since overfeeding of laboratory animals increases triiodothyronine (T_3), and since the number of cardiac β-adrenergic receptors may increase with elevated T_3 levels, it is possible that an altered receptor response to various pressor agents may play a role in the mechanism of obesity hypertension. There is no evidence directly supporting this at present, however.

Several observations have evoked interest in the concept that hyperinsulinemia may be an important factor in the etiopathogenesis of hypertension with obesity (Sims, 1977; Dustan, 1983). It is well known that obesity, especially when marked, predisposes to glucose intolerance and fat cell insulin resistance with hyperinsulinemia (Porte & Badgade, 1970; Cahill, 1977). With the recognition that insulin augments sodium reabsorption by the kidney (DeFronzo, Codee, Andres, Faloon, & Davis, 1975), and the finding that blood pressure reduction of obese women with exercise training was better correlated with decrements in serum insulin levels than body weight, it was suggested that hyperinsulinemia might be a contributing factor to blood pressure elevation with obesity (Krotkiewski, Mandrokas, Sjostrom, Sullivan, Witterquist, & Bjorntorp, 1979). In addition, insulin icreases the catecholamine turnover rate in sympathetic nervous system synapses experimentally (Bjorntorp, 1982), and augments plasma norepinephine levels together with heart rate blood pressure product in man acutely. (Rowe, Young, Minaker, Stevens, Pallotta, & Landsberg, 1981). However, these are all short term effects. The consequences of chronic hyperinsulinemia in obese subjects with relation to blood pressure have not yet been critically examined.

Another hypothesis worthy of further study relates to the necessity for augmented perfusion pressure to overcome the resistance to blood flow secondary to capillary compression by increased tissue pressure (Simmons, 1981). The concept that large fat cells in adipose tissue depots compress capillaries is supported by the observation that in experimental animals, the density of blood capillaries increases as fat cells become smaller (Tedeschi, 1965). This theory would also explain the magnitude of the early reduction in blood pressure in obese hypertensives following modest degrees of weight loss due to lower tissue pressure in adipose depots.

In summary, it appears that the mechanisms of hypertension and obesity are not the same as those that are operative in other forms of essential hypertension, and further study will be required to identify them. In particular, an explanation must be found for the fact that some obese persons are hypertensive and others are not.

ASSESSMENT OF BLOOD PRESSURE IN OBESE PERSONS

Accurate measurement of blood pressure by the auscultatory method in obese subjects, particularly very obese subjects, has long been fraught with difficulty, and this is no less true today. Of the several factors contributing to this difficulty, it appears that the most important relate to circumference, configuration, and compliance of the upper arm, as well as the size of the inflatable cuff used. Comparison of blood pressure levels obtained by the auscultatory method with those measured directly by intra-arterial needle in obese persons has indicated that, overall, both systolic and diastolic pressures are overestimated (Berliner, Fujiy, Lee, Yildiz, & Garnier, 1961; King, 1967; Kvols, Rohlfing, & Alexander, 1969; Nielsen & Janniche, 1974). With modest or moderate obesity, the discrepancy may not be great, usually less than 10 mmHg (Tedeschi, 1965). In subjects who are very much over-weight, however, differences greater than 20 mmHg and up to 40 or 50 mmHg may be found in a significant percentage of subjects (Kvols et al., 1969; Nielsen & Janniche, 1974; Tedeschi, 1965). The difference between the indirectly measured blood pressure and the directly measured pressure may be reduced by using a large cuff, 14 × 45 cm, instead of the smaller standard cuff, 12 × 23 cm, so that the mean differences between direct and indirect pressures are on the order of 6 to 7 mmHg (Nielsen & Janniche, 1974). In any sizeable series, however, there remain rather gross inaccuracies of both over- and underesti-mation in individual cases. These discrepancies are not predictable on the basis of increased arm circumference or blood pressure level (Nielsen & Janniche, 1974). Attempts to increase the accuracy of the measurement obtained by cuff by utilizing tables to "correct" for arm circumference appear to add little, since the relationship between arm circumference and auscultatory blood pressure level is indirect and is due to the high correlation between arm circumference and weight. Indeed, to correct readings for arm circumference is, in effect, to eliminate the influence of body weight (Khosla & Lowe, 1965). In one small series of six very obese subjects with large flabby arms, there was good agreement between the intra-arterial blood pressure and the auscultatory method utilizing a cuff around the forearm, with auscultation of Korotkoff sounds over the radial artery (Trout, Bertrand, & Williams, 1956). In a later study, however, it was found that measurements of the pressure with the cuff on the forearm and auscultation over the radial artery yielded values that were no more accurate than those obtained on the upper arm when compared with direct intra-arterial measurements, and, unfortunately, Korotkoff sounds frequently are inaudible over the radial artery (Kvols et al., 1969).

In summary, the use of a large cuff (14 × 42 cm) increases the accuracy of indirect blood pressure recordings in obese subjects, and such cuffs should probably be used routinely in this setting. Although the auscultatory method usually overestimates blood pressure levels in obese persons, there may be a great deal of random variation, particularly in very obese subjects, with underestimation as well as overestimation. This variation is not predictable on the basis of arm circumference or level of blood pressure. True systemic hypertension is usually present when cuff readings exceed the normotensive values by 30 mmHg or more (Kvols et al., 1969), but this rule of thumb may be particularly misleading in very obese individuals with unusual arm configurations or difficulty in application of the large cuff. Certainly, in these subjects and in any other obese individuals in whom difficulties are encountered in obtaining consistent values, direct intra-arterial measurement is recommended before prolonged antihypertensive therapy is initiated (Berliner et al., 1961; Kvols et al., 1969; Nielsen & Janniche, 1974).

PREVENTIVE ASPECTS

There is a paucity of data to aid in defining the interrelationships between obesity and hypertension in children or young adults and their implications for development of hyperten-sion in later life by utilizing any index of obesity other than weight. Several studies indicate, however, that weight gain over the long term, rather than initial weight as a young person, constitutes the greatest hazard for the development of hypertension. In a study of 717 boys aged 9 to 13 followed to an average age of 48 years, the highest risk for hypertensive cardiovascular disease was found in individuals who acquired their overweight status as adults (Abraham, Collins, & Nordsieck, 1971). A higher prevalence of hypertension among overweight adults was largely attributed to those who had moved from a below-average weight status as a child to an overweight category as an adult. The moderately or markedly overweight adult who was similarly classified as a child did not appear to be at greater risk than the average-weight adult who had been an average-weight child (Figure 57.1). Similar conclusions were reached in another study of 1,056 normotensive young men followed for 24 years (Oberman, Lane, Harlan, Graybiel, & Mitchell, 1967). At age 24, there was no correlation between systolic blood pressure and the amount of weight gain over the ideal. During the follow-up period, however, there was a very definite correlation between the amount of weight gain and subsequent increments in systolic blood pressure. In another

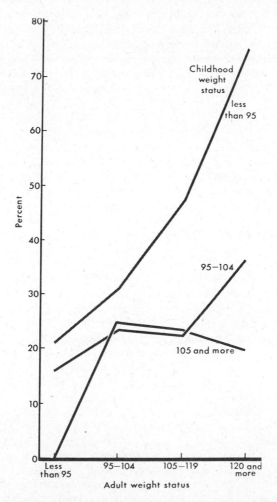

Figure 57.1 Prevalence of hypertensive vascular disease according to childhood and adult weight status. Weight status categories are below average (less than 95 pounds), average (95 to 104), moderately overweight (105 to 119), and markedly overweight (120 or more). (From Abraham, S., Collins, G., & Nordsieck, M. Relationship of childhood weight status to morbidity in adults. *HSMHA Health Reports*, 1971, **86**, 273–284. Reproduced with permission.)

study involving a 7- to 9-year follow-up of 2,530 persons, the increment in weight correlated with both increments in systolic and diastolic blood pressure (Heyden, Hawes, Bartel, Cassel, Tyroler, & Cornoni, 1971). Thus, body build and weight factors play some role in determining blood pressure in young adults but do not appear to be as important as later weight gain in relation to development of hypertension (Miall et al., 1968).

Although the bulk of evidence indicates that change in weight—that is, weight gain— over the long term is more important in the development of sustained hypertension than is initial weight status, initial weight of 9 kg above the "standard" weight appeared to carry an increased risk of about 2.5 times that for below-standard weight in a study of 22,741 U.S. Army officers in World War II followed for an average period of 9.8 years (Levy, White, Stroud, & Hillman, 1946). A similar conclusion was reached in the Framing- ham Study, which involved observations on 5,127 men and women over an 8-year period, with ages 30 to 59 at entry (Kannel et al., 1967). The morbidity ratio for hypertension in those with relative weight 120% or more of standard was 3 times that for those with standard weights at the median or below. Another study with similar implications, involving a follow-up of 7,685 college men from mean age 19 to age 46, indicated that those with the heaviest ponderal index were at one-third increased risk of developing hypertension, as compared with those with a lesser index (Paffenbarger, Thorne, & Wing, 1968).

Thus, from a preventive standpoint, it appears that the most important consideration relative to the risk of developing hypertension in association with obesity is the avoidance of weight gain with advancing age. Of lesser significance is the presence of obesity as a young adult.

A second issue of importance is the impact of weight reduction on elevated blood pressure and its complications in obese individuals with established hypertension. In regard to hyper- tension itself, studies based on relatively small numbers of patients indicate decrements in blood pressure following weight reduction to or toward normal in 40% to 70% of such patients, with little difference in relation to age (Adlersberg, Coler, & Laval, 1946; Fletcher, 1954; Martin, 1952). In one large series of 1,884 men and 2,095 women followed for 8 years, not all of whom were hypertensive, 50% of the men who lost weight had a fall in systolic blood pressure, 28% were unchanged, and 22% had an increase (Johnson, Karunas, & Epstein, 1973). Of the women who lost weight, 40% had a drop in systolic blood pressure, 34% were unchanged, and 26% had an increment in pressure. Thus, although weight reduction provides no guarantee of establishing normotension in subjects with preexisting hypertension, a favorable effect on blood pressure may be expected in about one-half of obese hypertensives, regardless of age or relative weight (Ashley & Kannel, 1974). Further- more, there is no good correlation between the decrement in pressure and the amount of weight lost (Martin, 1952). Modest weight reduction is often associated with considerably lower blood pressure levels (Greminger, Studer, Luscher, Mutter, Grimm, Siegenthaler, & Vetter, 1982). Once weight reduction has taken place, maintenance of the lower weight or continued weight loss is more likely to be associated with stable lowered pressure, whereas regain of weight is likely to be accompanied by return of hypertension (Adlersberg et al., 1946).

Currently, there is virtually no information available regarding the assessment of the effect of weight reduction on the complications of hypertensive cardiovascular disease in obese persons with elevated blood pressure. It has been suggested that obese hypertensives, who have a lower total peripheral vascular resistance than lean hypertensives, may be at a lesser risk for development of systemic vascular disease (Messerli et al., 1981). This stance is supported by the results of two long-term follow-up studies indicating that overall mortality among obese hypertensive subjects is significantly lower than that among nonobese hyperten- sives (Frant & Groen, 1950; Sokolow & Perloff, 1961). Since obesity, particularly when extreme, is assocated with augmented ventricular preload and in some instances systolic dysfunction, however (Alexander, Woodard, Quinones, & Gaasch, 1978), the augmented afterload consequent to hypertension will predispose to earlier development of congestive heart failure (Alexander & Pettigrove, 1967).

An important complication of dietary therapy relating to blood pressure is the development of postural hypotension and dizziness or syncope in patients on fasting or markedly restricted caloric regimens (DeHaven, Sherwin, Hendler, & Felig, 1980; Drenick, 1978; Jung, Shetty, Barrand, Callingham, & James, 1979). During the first several days of severe caloric deprivation, a brisk natriuresis ensues, as well as augmented ketone excretion, obligatory water loss accompanying excretion of solutes, and high catabolism of lean tissue, permitting liberation of three parts of tissue water for every part of protein (Boulter, Spark, & Arky, 1974; DeHaven et al., 1980; Drenick, 1978; Sigler, 1975). The resultant contraction of plasma volume predisposes to hypotension; from a mechanistic standpoint, however, suppression of sympathetic nervous activity appears to be a more significant factor. Inhibition of centrally mediated sympathetic activity indicated by parenchymal norepinephrine turnover rates in association with a fall in blood pressure is well documented in fasted rats (Young & Landsberg, 1977, 1978). That a comparable process takes place in man is supported by several lines of evidence. Following marked reduction of caloric intake, urinary catecholamines, plasma norepinephrine concentrations, and plasma renin activity fall, with enhanced aldosterone secretory rates (Boulter et al., 1974; DeHaven et al., 1980; Jung et al., 1979), and decrease in blood pressure, even though total body sodium is maintained (Jung et al., 1979). If the hypotensive effect was mediated primarily through decrements in plasma volume or body sodium, the opposite effects on catecholamines, renin, and aldosterone would be anticipated.

Furthermore, plasma renin activity and aldosterone levels, with upright posture and isometric exercise (handgrip), are reduced after 8 weeks on a low-caloric protein diet (Sowers, Nyby, Stern, Beck, Baron, Catania, & Vlachis, 1982). Since the sympathetic nervous system plays a major role in the modulation of renin release during these maneuvers, its activity appears reduced. All these observations strongly suggest suppression of sympathetic nervous activity with fasting in humans, consistent with the hypothesis that lowered catecholamines may mediate the hypotensive effect in several ways: (a) direct action on vascular adrenergic receptors, (b) reduction in renin and angiotensin, and (c) natriuretic effect of reduced renin (Jung et al., 1979; Landsberg & Young, 1978).

In summary, whether an individual is obese or not, development of sustained hypertension with advancing age is partially preventable by the maintenance of stable body weight. If hypertension has already supervened in an obese person, weight reduction, even of modest degree, and maintenance of stable body weight thereafter result in a sustained decrement in blood pressure in about one-half of these individuals. If the preexisting degree of obesity is severe, the potential for subsequent development of congestive heart failure is thus minimized. Postural hypotension, largely secondary to suppression of sympathetic nervous activity, is an important complication of fasting or markedly restricted caloric regimens.

REFERENCES

Abraham, S., Collins, G., & Nordsieck, M. Relationship of childhood weight status to morbidity in adults. *HSMHA Health Reports,* 1971, **86,** 273–284.

Adlersberg, D., Coler, H., & Laval, J. Effect of weight reduction on course of arterial hypertension. *Journal of Mt. Sinai Hospital,* 1946, **12,** 984–992.

Alexander, J. K. Obesity and the circulation. *Modern Concepts of Cardiovascular Disease,* 1963, **32,** 799–803.

Alexander, J. K., & Pettigrove, J. R. Obesity and congestive heart failure, *Geriatrics,* 1967, **22**(7), 101–108.

Alexander, J. K., Woodard, C. B., Quinones, M. A., & Gaasch, W. H. Heart failure from obesity. In M. Mancini, B. Lewis, & F. Cartaldo (Eds.), *Medical complications of obesity.* London: Academic Press, 1978.

Ashley, F. W., Jr., & Kannel, W. B. Relation of weight change to changes in atherogenic traits: The Framingham Study. *Journal of Chronic Diseases,* 1974, **27,** 103–114.

Ballantyne, D., Devine, B. L., & Fife, R. Interrelation of age, obesity, cigarette smoking, and blood pressure in hypertensive patients. *British Medical Journal,* 1978, 1(6117), 880–881.

Berliner, K., Fujiy, H., Lee, D. H., Yildiz, M., & Garnier, B. Blood pressure measurements in obese persons: Comparison of intra-arterial and auscultatory measurements. *American Journal of Cardiology,* 1961, **8,** 10–17.

Bjontrop, P. Hypertension and exercise. *Hypertension,* 1982, 4(Suppl. III), 56–59.

Boulter, P. R., Spark, R. F., & Arky, R. A. Dissociation of the renin-aldosterone system and refractoriness to the sodium retaining action of mineralocorticoid during starvation in man. *Journal of Clinical Endocrinology and Metabolism,* 1974, **38,** 248–254.

Boynton, R. E., & Todd, R. L. Relation of body weight and family history of hypertensive disease to blood pressure levels in university students. *American Journal of Medical Science,* 1948, **216,** 397–402.

Cahill, G. F., Jr. Obesity and diabetes. In G. Brey (Ed.), *Recent Advances in Obesity Research, II.* London: Newman, 1977, pp. 101–110.

Court, J. M., Hill, G. J., Dunlop, M., & Boulton, T. J. C. Hypertension in childhood obesity. *Australian Paediatric Journal,* 1974, **10,** 296–300.

Dahl, L., Silver, L., & Christie R. Role of salt in the fall of blood pressure accompanying reduction of obesity. *New England Journal of Medicine,* 1958, **258,** 1186–1192.

DeFronzo, R. A., Codee, R. A., Andres, R., Faloon, G. R., & Davis, P. J. The effect of insulin in renal handling of sodium, potassium, calcium and phosphate in man. *Journal of Clinical Investigation,* 1975, **55,** 845–855.

DeHaven, J., Sherwin, R., Hendler, R., & Felig, P. Nitrogen and sodium balance and sympathetic-nervous-system activity in obese subjects treated with a low calorie protein or mixed diet. *New England Journal of Medicine,* 1980, **302,** 477–482.

Drenick, E. J. Starvation in the management of obesity. In N. L. Wilson (Ed.), *Obesity.* London: Academic Press, 1978.

Dustan, H. P. Mechanisms of hypertension associated with obesity. *Annals of Internal Medicine,* 1983, **98**(5, Supp. pt. 2), 860–864.

Evans, J. G., & Rose, G. Hypertension. *British Medical Bulletin,* 1971, **27,** 37–42.

Fletcher, A. P. The effect of weight reduction on the blood pressure of obese hypertensive women. *Quarterly Journal of Medicine,* 1954, **47,** 331–45.

Frant, R., & Groen, J. Prognosis of vascular hypertension: A nine-year follow-up study of four hundred and eighteen cases. *Archives of Internal Medicine,* 1950, **85,** 727–750.

Greminger, P., Studer, A., Luscher, T., Mutter, B., Grimm, J., Siegenthaler, W., & Vetter, W. Gewichtsreduktion und Blutdruck. *Schweizerische Medizinische Wochenschrift,* 1982, **112,** 120–123.

Heyden, S., Hames, C. G., Bartel, A., Cassel, J. C., Tyroler, H. A., & Cornoni, J. C. Weight and weight history in relation to cerebrovascular and ischemic heart disease. *Archives of Internal Medicine,* 1971, **128,** 956–60.

Johnson A. L., Cornoni, J. C., Cassel, J. C., Tyroler, H. A., Heyden, S., & Hames, C. G. Influence of race, sex and weight on blood pressure behavior in young adults. *American Journal of Cardiology,* 1975, **35,** 523–530.

Johnson, B. C., Karunas, T. M., & Epstein, F. H. Longitudinal change in blood pressure in individuals, families, and social groups. *Clinical Science and Molecular Medicine,* 1973, **45**(Suppl), 35–45.

Jung, R. T., Shetty, P. S., Barrand, M., Callingham, B. A., & James W. P. T. Role of catecholamines in hypotensive response to dieting. *British Medical Journal,* 1979, **1,** 12–13.

Kannel, W., Brand, N., Skinner, J., Dawber, T., & McNamara, P. Relation of adiposity to blood pressure and development of hypertension: The Framingham Study. *Annals of Internal Medicine,* 1967, **67,** 48–59.

Keys, A. Coronary heart disease in seven countries. *Circulation,* 1970, **41**(Suppl 1–211).

Khosla, T., & Lowe, C. R. Arterial pressure and arm circumference. *British Journal of Preventive and Social Medicine,* 1965, **19,** 159–63.

King, G. E. Errors in clinical measurement of blood pressure in obesity. *Clinical Science,* 1967, **32,** 223–237.

Krotkiewski, M., Mandrokas, M., Sjostrom, L. M., Sullivan, H., Witterguist, H., & Bjorntorp, P. Effects of longterm physical training body fat, metabolism and blood pressure in obesity. *Metabolism,* 1979, **28,** 650–658.

Kvols, L. K., Rohlfing, B. M., & Alexander, J. K. A comparison of intra-arterial and cuff blood pressure measurements in very obese subjects. *Cardiovascular Research Center Bulletin,* 1969, **7**(3), 118–123.

Landsberg, L., & Young, J. B. Fasting, feeding and regulation of the sympathetic nervous system. *New England Journal of Medicine,* 1978, **298,** 1295–1301.

Levy, R. L., White, P. D., Stroud, W. D., & Hillman, C. C. Overweight: Its prognostic significance in relation to hypertension and cardiovascular-renal diseases. *Journal of the American Medical Association,* 1946, **131,** 951–953.

Martin, L. Effect of weight-reduction on normal and raised blood pressures in obesity. *Lancet,* 1952, 1051–1053.

Messerli, F. H., Christie, B., DeCarvalho, J. G. R., Aristimuno, G. G., Suarez, D. H., Dreslinski, G. R., & Frohlich, E. D. Obesity and essential hypertension: Hemodynamics, intravascular volume, sodium excretion, and plasma renin activity. *Archives of Internal Medicine,* 1981, **141,** 81–85.

Miall, W. E., Bell, R. A., & Lovell, H. G. Relation between change in blood pressure and weight. *British Journal of Preventive Social Medicine,* 1968, **22,** 73–80.

Nielsen, P. E., & Janniche, H. The accuracy of auscultatory measurement of arm blood pressure in very obese subjects. *Acta Medica Scandinavica,* 1974, **195,** 403–409.

Oberman, A., Lane, N. E., Harlan, W. R., Graybiel, A., & Mitchell, R. E. Trends in systolic blood pressure in the thousand aviator cohort over a twenty-four-year period. Circulation, 1967, **36,** 812–822.

Paffenbarger, R. S., Jr., Thorne, M. C., & Wing, A. L. Chronic disease in former college students: VIII. Characteristics in youth predisposing to hypertension in later years. *American Journal of Epidemiology,* 1968, **88,** 1;25–32.

Palmai, G. Skin-fold thickness in relation to body weight and arterial blood pressure. *Medical Journal of Australia,* 1962, **49**(2), 13–15.

Porte, D., Jr., & Badgade, J. D. Human insulin secretion—an integrated approach. *Annual Review of Medicine,* 1970, **21,** 219–240.

Reisin, E., Abel, R., & Modan, M. Effect of weight loss without salt restriction on the reduction of blood pressure in overweight hypertensive patients. *New England Journal of Medicine,* 1978, **298,** 1–6.

Robinson, S. C., Bruces, M., & Mass, J. Hypertension and obesity. *Journal of Laboratory Clinical Medicine,* 1939, **25,** 807–822.

Rowe, J. W., Young, J. B., Minaker, K. L., Stevens, A. L., Pallotta, J., & Landsberg, L. Effect of insulin and glucose infusion on sympathetic nervous system activity in normal man. *Diabetics,* 1981, **30,** 219–225.

Schteingart, D. E., & Conn, J. W. Characteristics of the increased adrenocortical function observed in many obese patients. *Annals of the New York Academy of Sciences,* 1965, **131,** 388–403.

Short, J. J., & Johnson, H. J. An evaluation of the influence of overweight on blood pressures of healthy men. *American Journal of Medical Science,* 1939, **198,** 220–224.

Sigler, M. H. The mechanism of the natriuresis of fasting. *Journal of Clinical Investigation,* 1975, **55,** 377–387.

Simmons, V. P. Circulatory pathophysiology: I. The role of capillary compression in the etiology of essential (idiopathic) hypertension. *Journal of Insurance Medicine,* 1981, **12**(2), 2–9.

Sims, E. A. Mechanisms of hypertension in the overweight. *Hypertension,* 1977, **4**(Suppl. III), 43–49.

Sims, E. A. H., Phinney, S. D., & Vaswani, A. The management of hypertension associated with obesity. *International Journal of Obesity,* 1978, **3,** 215–223.

Sokolow, M., & Perloff, D. The prognosis of essential hypertension treated conservatively. *Circulation,* 1961, **23,** 697–713.

Sowers, J. R., Nyby, M., Stern, N., Beck, F., Baron, S., Catania, R., & Vlachis, N. Blood pressure and hormone changes associated with weight reduction in the obese. *Hypertension,* 1982, **4,** 686–691.

Stamler, J. *Preventive cardiology.* New York: Grune and Stratton, 1967.

Stamler, R., Stamler, J., Riedlinger, W. F., Algera, G., & Roberts, R. H. Weight and blood pressure: Findings in hypertension screening of one million Americans. *Journal of the American Medical Association,* 1978, **240,** 1607–1610.

Tedeschi, C. G. Pathological anatomy of adipose tissue. In A. E. Renold & G. F. Cahill (Eds.), *Handbook of physiology* (Sec. 525, "Adipose Tissue"). Washington, D.C.: American Physiological Society, 1965.

Trout, K. W., Bertrand, C. A., & Williams, M. H. Measurement of blood pressure in obese persons. *Journal of the American Medical Association,* 1956, **162,** 970–971.

Tuck, M. L., Sowers, J., Dornfeld, L., Kledzik, G., & Maxwell, M. The effect of weight reduction on blood pressure, plasma renin activity, and plasma aldosterone levels in obese patients. *New England Journal of Medicine,* 1981, **304,** 930–933.

Young, J. B., & Landsberg, L. Suppression of sympathetic nervous system during fasting. *Science,* 1977, **196,** 1473–1475.

Young, J. B., & Landsberg, L. Weight loss and reduction in blood pressure. *New England Journal of Medicine,* 1978, **298,** 1033.

SECTION 8
DENTAL HEALTH

CHAPTER 58

OVERVIEW

WILLIAM A. AYER

Bureau of Economic and Behavioral Research, American Dental Association

Dental disease continues to be one of the three most expensive diseases in the United States, resulting in expenditures of over $15.9 billion in 1979 (Gift, Newman, & Loewy, 1981; Ayer, 1981). Such cost data, along with the observations that 10% of the population accounts for 75% of these expenditures and that 3% of the population accounts for over 50% of these expenditures, provide an indication of the magnitude of the problem of oral disease and an idea of the enormous number of individuals who do not regularly avail themselves of dental services (Newman & Anderson, Note 1). Although most dental disease is due to caries and periodontal conditions, other diseases or dysfunctional conditions also play significant roles, such as oral cancer, traumatic injuries, malocclusions, and oral habits. With the exception, perhaps, of malocclusions and craniofacial anomalies, most oral disorders can be prevented, reduced, or eliminated through changes in lifestyle behaviors and modification of certain environmental factors.

DENTAL CARIES

Dental caries are an example of a disease that is modifiable by both changes in behavior and changes in environment. In a recent survey (American Dental Association, Note 2), some 94% of a large national opinion survey sample reported that they brushed their teeth one or more times per day. Most also used a fluoridated dentifrice. Only 38% reported that they used dental floss daily. Although brushing is practiced almost universally among the U.S. population, flossing is practiced considerably less. The addition of fluorides to community water supplies has substantially reduced caries in populations that have access to these water supplies (Glass, 1982; Liss, Evenson, Loewy, & Ayer, 1982). The National Institute of Dental Research (NIDR) survey (Note 3) found that caries have been reduced almost 50% in children aged 5 to 17 years within the last decade, primarily as a result of community water fluoridation. The NIDR study also reported that some 58% of the children aged 5 to 11 years had caries-free permanent teeth. A number of reports have also documented the decline in the prevalence of caries in other western countries that have fluoridated water supplies (Glass, 1982). In developing countries, dental caries have been observed to be increasing, largely as a result of the increased consumption of refined carbohydrates (Davis, 1980; Glass, 1982).

Currently, only about 50% of the U.S. population has access to community fluoridated water supplies. It is not likely that this percentage will increase substantially in the future because of the small size of the unserved communities and the expense of implementing public water fluoridation in them. It is interesting, also, that of some 31 countries reviewed by the World Health Organization in 1972, in only 3 did more than 10% of the population have access to fluoridated community water supplies (Kostlan, Note 4).

Glass and Fleisch (1981) have reported reductions in tooth decay in areas without the benefit of water fluoridation, but these decreases have not been of the same magnitude. They have attributed these decreases to such factors as the use of fluoride-containing dentifrices, fluoride supplements, topical fluorides, and fluoride rinses; widespread use of antibiotics; and possible changes in dietary patterns. Although evidence for the role of dietary change is less strong, it is an important consideration.

PERIODONTAL DISEASE

Whereas caries are the major cause of tooth loss before the age of about 35, periodontal disease is the major cause after that age. Periodontal disease is almost universally prevalent. Although the evidence for reductions in dental caries is clear, evidence for any changes in the prevalence of periodontal disease is more equivocal at this point. With changes in the caries rate and decreased loss of teeth, one might hypothesize that periodontal disease prevalence should decrease also. Using data collected by the National Center for Health Statistics on periodontal disease for the last several decades, some investigators have reported what appears to be a decrease in the prevalence of periodontal disease, although the severity of the disease itself has remained high (Liss et al., 1982). Two other studies, however, have reported increases in the prevalence of periodontal disease (Bonito, Donnelly, & Kleiger, 1978; Bawden & DeFriese, Note 5). Thus, it must be cautioned that the findings of these studies remain controversial at this time.

Although a significant amount of tooth decay can be reduced or eliminated through community water fluoridation, reduction or elimination of periodontal disease seems largely dependent on individual home self-care procedures, such as daily flossing.

The importance of implementing and enhancing compliance with self-care regimens continues to attract a significant amount of research effort as more investigators come to question the cost and efficacy of such "magic bullets" as caries and periodontal disease vaccines (Loe, 1981; Mandel, 1981); not only are they extremely costly, but even if they were available today, their effects would not be seen until after the year 2000. Mandel (1981) has speculated that although caries vaccines might not be practical for mass vaccinations in the United States, they might be appropriate in developing countries, where other resources do not exist or are in extremely short supply. The importance of regular self-care procedures such as brushing and flossing has been pointed out by Davis (1980), among others, as the current best method for controlling or preventing periodontal disease. Thus, the emphasis continues on the development of self-care behaviors.

EDENTULOUSNESS

Edentulousness (total loss of teeth) has also declined for virtually all age groups within the last three decades, probably again reflecting some of the benefits of water fluoridation, changes in dietary patterns, the use of fluoridated dentifrices, and a change in the formerly prevalent attitude that edentulousness is an inevitable accompaniment of old age.

ORAL CANCER

Oral cancer accounts for some 3% to 4% of all cancers and is found primarily in males over the age of 40. It was estimated that in 1982 approximately 26,800 new cases of oral cancer would be detected (American Cancer Society, 1982). This rate appears to have been relatively stable in the United States and throughout the world. Death rates for oral cancer appear to have remained relatively constant since the 1950s. Smoking has been one of the factors implicated in these diseases. It has been suggested that survival rates may increase with improved detection methods, which will place increased responsibility on the patient to seek treatment in the early stage of the disease.

OTHER CONDITIONS

Congenital and acquired craniofacial anomalies, malocclusions, and traumatic facial and dental injuries contribute substantially to dental care costs (Johnson, 1975). Unfortunately, the epidemiologic data on these conditions are very sparse and do not permit development of a perspective regarding frequency of the conditions or any changes in their prevalence. There is some evidence that mouth guards may have helped reduce orofacial injuries in sports activities and that seat and shoulder belts in automobiles have reduced other traumatic facial and head injuries (Huelke & Sherman, 1973). Ayer and his colleagues (Liss et al., 1982) have noted that the increase in the number of participants in sports that do not require protective headgear, such as running, should probably be associated with an increase in orofacial injuries. Currently, however, no data exist regarding such injuries.

Other conditions that are of interest to dentists, and that may affect the oral health of individuals, include such oral habits as thumb and finger sucking, bruxing and grinding behaviors, and myofascial pain dysfunction syndrome. All these conditions appear to be amenable to prevention or modification through behavioral methods.

The focus of this Handbook is on healthy people and on keeping healthy people healthy. Because dentistry and oral health in general are unfamiliar to many health care professionals, it was thought necessary to provide a brief overview of the types of problems encountered in this field. Also, it was believed important to examine certain areas in which significant progress has been made in reducing or eliminating dental disease. Unfortunately, most of the progress in reducing dental disease has occurred in caries prevention within the white population, particularly among children. For the first time, a significant number of children are caries-free. Minority groups continue to exhibit significantly higher levels of dental disease, however, as do semiskilled and blue-collar workers. Even when these individuals are given the advantage of water fluoridation, their failure to engage in regular self-care activities, dietary control, and routine preventive dental visits results in some erosion of the advantage over time. Thus, efforts to continue the health advantage of such individuals in areas that have water fluoridation are urgently needed. The two major reasons individuals give for not engaging in routine preventive dental visit behavior are "no perceived need to go" and "fear and anxiety regarding dentistry." Thus, attempts to increase the relevance of good dental health and to emphasize the necessity of routine preventive visits are required to get the individual into the dental health care and maintenance system. Once in the system, most patients probably engage in reasonably good self-care activities and maintenance behaviors. As noted earlier, however, this segment of the population appears quite small, and the data to support this generalization are minimal.

SECTION SUMMARY

The chapters in this section represent state-of-the-art approaches to the problems of preventing disease and maintaining oral health and are designed to present a broad overview of behavioral and health enhancement activities in dentistry.

Schools have long been viewed as desirable and appropriate places to provide health education in an effort to promote good health practices. As early as 1903, Bell proposed that schools be utilized to instruct students in oral hygiene. Although the logic of such a strategy is readily apparent, it has not been very productive for a variety of reasons (Ayer, 1972, 1979). One reason has been that teachers have not been well prepared to provide effective and accurate oral health education. Goldstein and Freed (1975) examined college health textbooks for information on preventive dentistry and periodontal disease and concluded that where information was provided (about periodontal disease, for example), many professional health educators were not knowledgeable about periodontal disease and, furthermore, did not consider it a significant health problem. An additional reason for the relative ineffectiveness of health education programs in schools has been the tendency for the programs to be one-shot affairs, whose effects, if any, have been very short-lived. As reported by Kegeles and Lund in Chapter 59, more sophisticated attention is being devoted to determining effective approaches to such problems. Health education and promotion programs in the schools have also caused some investigators to consider the worksite as an appropriate setting in which to foster oral health, but no scientific studies using the workplace have actually been conducted in the United States. The advantage of using such arenas is readily apparent—particularly for blue-collar and semiskilled workers, who also happen to be underutilizers of dental services and at high risk for dental disease. Some slight evidence suggests that the effect for these kinds of workers (where dental insurance programs exist) may be more on their families than on the workers themselves (Avnet & Nikias, Note 6). A study to examine health promotion efforts focused primarily on blue-collar workers in workplace settings has been initiated by Ayer and his colleagues in six industrial sites in Maine (Ayer, Davis, Deatrick, & Seffrin, Note 7). Other settings are also potentially useful, such as nursing homes and other institutions that could be used to insure that optimal oral health is maintained throughout the life span. In Chapter 64, Kiyak describes her work with geriatric patients—a group that will become increasingly significant in dentistry as well as in other health areas.

Whereas Chapters 59 and 64 address methods of providing and promoting oral health outside the dental system, the other chapters in this section are primarily concerned with what goes on when the individual gets into the system.

Dental fear and anxiety continue to be the significant reasons many persons avoid dental visits. In Chapter 60, Corah and Gale examine methods currently available for modifying anxiety and fears in patients. It is particularly interesting to speculate on how some of these techniques, such as modeling, might be used in preventive education approaches and might be presented in nontraditional settings, such as schools, PTA meetings, and the like, in an effort to provide naive individuals with information about what goes on in a dental office and what the individual might expect there. It seems enormously important to enable more individuals to enter the health system and to encourage them to take advantage of regular, routine visits to monitor their oral health status. Corah and Gale also briefly discuss the effect of the dentist–patient interaction on whether the individual remains in the system once he or she has gained admittance to it. O'Shea, Corah, and Ayer (1983) have begun to provide evidence that some dentists may exclude individuals from practice and thus deny them the advantage of regular checkups. Health promotion and health maintenance continue to require the services of dentists, and it is important to understand how dentists' perceptions of clients may prevent the achievement of health promotion goals. In Chapter 62, Philip Weinstein documents the effects of dentists' behaviors on children's responses and provides important guidance in how to achieve more cooperation from patients and how to prepare them for lifelong dental encounters.

Malocclusion that requires orthodontic correction is a rather unique condition in relation to the other issues considered in this section. For many individuals, orthodontic treatment is a routine part of adolescence. Also, orthodontic correction is increasingly viewed as something not limited to adolescents; today, more and more adults who did not have the benefit of orthodontics as children are seeking and obtaining such treatment—largely for cosmetic rather than functional reasons. Judith Albino discusses this area in depth in Chapter 61, largely from the perspective of what such treatment means for the concept of quality of life.

Such oral habits as thumb and finger sucking, bruxing and grinding behaviors, and myofascial pain dysfunction syndrome cause problems for many people. Adequate and effective techniques are currently available for preventing or eliminating these problems. In Chapter 63, John Rugh discusses these techniques and their role in health promotion and health maintenance.

The chapters in this section provide an indication of the progress of selected health enhancement efforts in the area of dentistry. As the reader will observe, the problems in dentistry require the same sorts of concerted efforts as other health problems do. Many of the approaches described in other sections of this Handbook—for example, to promote healthy diets, to eliminate smoking, to increase the use of seat and shoulder belts—have potentially significant implications for oral health.

REFERENCE NOTES

1. Newman, J. F., & Anderson, O. W. *Patterns of dental service utilization in the United States: A nationwide social survey.* Center for Health Administration Studies, University of Chicago Research Series No. 30, 1972.

2. American Dental Association (Bureau of Economic and Behavioral Research). *Dental habits and opinions of the public: Results of a 1978 survey.* Chicago: American Dental Association, 1979.

3. National Institute of Dental Research. *Prevalence of dental caries in United States children, 1969–1978.* National Dental Caries Prevalence Survey. Bethesda, Md.: National Institute of Dental Research, 1981.

4. Kostlan, J. Systems of prevention in dental care. In WHO Regional Office for Europe, *Health planning and organization of medical care.* Copenhagen: World Health Organization, 1972.

5. Bawden, J. W., & DeFriese, G. H. (Eds.). *Planning for dental care on a statewide basis.* Published as part of the W. K. Kellogg Foundation series, "Issues in Dental Health Policy." Chapel Hill: Dental Foundation of North Carolina, 1981.

6. Avnet, H. H., & Nikias, M. K. *Insured dental care.* New York: Group Health Dental Insurance, Inc., 1967.

7. Ayer, W. A., Davis, D., Deatrick, D., & Seffrin, S. *Dental health promotion in workplace settings.* Study funded by the American Fund for Dental Health, 1982.

REFERENCES

American Cancer Society. *Cancer facts and figures.* New York: American Cancer Society, 1982.

Ayer, W. A. Efforts to improve oral hygiene practices: A review and critical evaluation. *Journal of the American Dental Hygienist's Association,* 1972, **46,** 437–441.

Ayer, W. A. Motivating people to oral health. *Dental Hygiene,* 1979, **53,** 221–224.

Ayer, W. A. Dental providers and oral health behavior. *Journal of Behavioral Medicine,* 1981, **4,** 273–282.

Bell, V. C. *The necessity of school instruction in dental hygiene.* New York: P. P. Simmons, 1903.

Bonito, A. J., Donnelly, C. J., & Kleiger, W. A. The oral health of adults in the Baltimore SMSA study area. *International Dental Journal,* 1978, **28,** 365–374.

Davis, P. *The social context of dentistry.* London: Croom-Helm, 1980.

Gift, H. C., Newman, J. F., and Loewy, S. B. Attempts to control dental health care costs: The U.S. experience. *Social Science and Medicine,* 1981, **15A,** 767–779.

Glass, R. L. (Ed.). The First International Conference on the Declining Prevalence of Dental Caries. The evidence and the impact on dental education, dental research, and dental practice. *Journal of Dental Research,* 1982, **61** (Special Issue, November).

Glass, R. L., & Fleisch, S. Decreases in caries prevalence. In J. J. Hefferren, H. Koehler, & W. A. Ayer (Eds.), *Foods, Nutrition and Dental Health* (Vol. 3). Park Forest South, Ill.: Pathotox, 1981.

Goldstein, M. S., & Freed, J. R. Periodontal disease information in college health education. *Journal of Preventive Dentistry,* 1975, **2,** 4.

Huelke, D. F., & Sherman, H. W. Automobile injuries—The forgotten area of public health dentistry. *Journal of the American Dental Association,* 1973, **86,** 384–393.

Johnson, J. E. Causes of accidental injuries to the teeth and jaws. *Journal of Public Health Dentistry,* 1975, **135,** 123.

Liss, J., Evenson, P., Loewy, S., & Ayer, W. Changes in the prevalence of dental disease. *Journal of the American Dental Association,* 1982, **105,** 75–79.

Loe, H. Periodontal research. *Journal of the American Dental Association,* 1981, **102,** 622–623.

Mandel, I. Caries research. *Journal of the American Dental Association,* 1981, **102,** 621.

O'Shea, R., Corah, N., & Ayer, W. A. Dentists' perceptions of the good adult patient: An exploratory study. *Journal of the American Dental Association,* 1983, **106,** 813–816.

CHAPTER 59

ADOLESCENTS' ACCEPTANCE OF CARIES-PREVENTIVE PROCEDURES

S. STEPHEN KEGELES

University of Connecticut Health Center

ADRIAN K. LUND

Insurance Institute for Highway Safety, Washington, D.C.

In this chapter, we will discuss findings from a program of research on the initiation and maintenance of preventive health behavior among adolescents. We will also discuss the future research directions suggested by these findings.

The need for such research in dentistry is obvious and is comparable to the need for research in other chronic diseases. Many professionally recommended mechanisms for preventing dental decay and periodontal disease require changes in health behavior over long periods of time. Despite greater than anticipated benefits from fluorides (Loverett, 1982) and despite some very promising microbiological and immunological research on dental disease, reduction and control of dental disease still depends on people's carrying out activities similar to those they have been asked to do in the past. Yet many people have not been willing to take such actions (Kegeles, 1975; Kegeles, Note 1; Silversin and Kornacki, Note 2). A 1975 report to the Minister of Health, British Columbia, and to the president of the College of Dental Surgeons concluded:

> *As long as behavioural scientists are unable to determine a well-developed technology that induces behavioural change, programmes of preventive dentistry that attempt to alter the individual's personal habits and lifestyle appear to have a limited chance of succeeding. (Children's Dental Research Project, Note 3).*

THE RESEARCH

Our efforts to establish an experimental and theoretical foundation for a technology of preventive dental health behavior for adolescents have proceeded in two phases. In the first phase, two intervention strategies drawn from very different psychological traditions were contrasted in two different preventive programs. In the second phase, findings from

The research reported here was supported by PHS (NIDR) Grant No. DEO3868. The authors wish to express their appreciation to Ms. Juliet Miozza for her contributions to the entire series of studies discussed in this chapter.

Phase I were replicated and extended by incorporating new elements in the intervention strategies, based on findings from other psychological research.

Comparison of Attitude Change and Contingency Reinforcement as Means of Eliciting Behavior: Phase I

In 1973, the likelihood of eliciting (or changing) behavior as a result of altering attitudes or beliefs seemed reasonable. The senior author was a major proponent of the health belief model, and a monograph was soon to be published that would subsequently make this model a major conceptual force in the health field (Becker, 1974). As a result, our first intervention was intended to produce adolescent health beliefs consistent with participation in the program. The method chosen for this purpose was peer group discussions.

At the same time, studies that used contingency reinforcement for populations other than delinquent children, institutionalized populations, or alcoholics were just beginning to be reported. It appeared that stimulus control and reinforcement control were concepts that had great power to mold desirable behavior. Thus, our second intervention strategy was to provide contingent, material rewards for children's preventive behavior.

In order to test and compare these two strategies, two successive experiments were carried out, one year apart, in both urban, lower-income schools and suburban, upper-income schools. The first experiment asked seventh-grade children to accept three topical fluoride treatments, applied to their teeth by hygienists at 5½-month intervals within their school health room. In the second experiment, one year later, a new population of seventh-grade children from the same urban and suburban schools were asked to use a fluoridated mouthrinse daily, at home, for 20 weeks. It was expected that the mouthrinsing procedure would be more difficult for children because of the need for daily activity. Both experiments used identical factorial designs: (a) an information-alone condition, which used a slide show and a demonstration, (b) an information plus group discussion condition, and (3) an information plus contingency reward condition, with rewards given subsequent to each successful event. These two experiments modeled two very different ways in which dental preventive agents may be made available to the public: those that are provided by trained professionals and those that require frequent and constant activity from individuals.

In both experiments, children were asked to volunteer for the program and bring back parental permission forms before they were enlisted into the program. In the mouthrinse program, children who obtained parental permission were sent appointment letters telling them where and when to come at school to obtain their first bottle of rinse. Then, they were to return their old bottles and obtain new ones every two weeks, at the same time and day of the week.

Mouthrinse use in both Phase I and Phase II studies was measured in three ways: (a) the proportion of children continuing to obtain new bottles of rinse, (b) the average number of doses used from each mouthrinse bottle, and (c) the average number of days children reported using the rinse during each 2-week period. To increase the validity of these measures, the bottle that dispensed the mouthrinse was designed to deliver one 5 ml dose no more frequently than every 2 hours; as the bottle emptied, this period lengthened to 12 to 15 hours. In addition, the lid of the dispenser was sealed with special tape so that it could not be opened without our knowledge. Children were informed about the nature of the bottle and were told they would not receive rewards if the bottle had been opened. In short, children were constrained to use the rinse at the recommended frequency, and, although all possible forms of cheating on the system were not eliminated, it was nearly as difficult to subvert the system as to comply with the recommendations. The results of these experiments are shown in Figures 59.1 (topical experiment) and 59.2 (first mouthrinse experiment).

In the topical experiment, we found (a) that over 60% of the children offered an opportunity to participate completed all three treatments, (b) that the rewards condition was signifi-

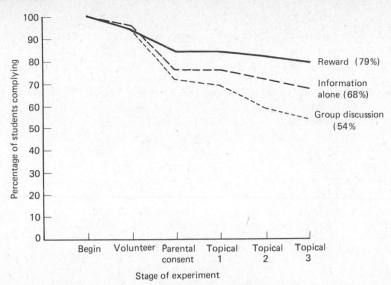

Figure 59.1 Percentages of students in each motivational condition who complied with the topical treatment program at each stage. (From Lund, A. K., & Kegeles, S. S. Children's preventive dental program. In B. D. Ingersoll; R. J. Seine, & W. R. McCurcheon (Eds.), *Behavioral dentistry,* Proceedings of the First National Conference, West Virginia University, 1977.)

cantly better in obtaining parental permission and in obtaining completion of all three treatments than the information control procedure, (c) that the group discussion procedure led to the smallest percentage of students who completed all three treatments, and (d) that there was no difference in the compliance of urban and suburban children (Lund, Kegeles, & Weisenberg, 1977).

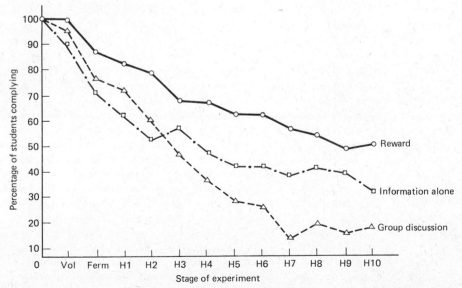

Figure 59.2 Percentages of students in each motivational condition who complied with each stage of the mouth-rinse program. (Copyright by Pergamon Press, Ltd. From Kegeles, S. S., Lund, A. K., & Weisenberg, M. Acceptance by children of a daily home mouthrinse program. *Social Science and Medicine,* 1978, **12,** 206. Reprinted by permission.)

In the second experiment, we found nearly identical results: (a) the rewards condition was significantly superior to the group discussion condition and to the information-demonstration condition, (b) the group discussion condition was significantly inferior to the information condition, and (c) whether a child was from an urban or suburban school did not significantly affect participation in the program (Kegeles, Lund, & Weisenberg, 1978). The evidence was unequivocal that contingent rewards could be used to increase children's practice of recommended dental activities. This conclusion was hardly surprising, given the vast literature showing the relative efficacy of token economies and other contingent reward procedures for controlling a wide range of behavior (Kazdin, 1975; Lepper & Green, 1978a, 1978b). Somewhat more surprising was the discovery that group discussion actually led to lower compliance. Thus, the modification of health beliefs appeared to offer little utility for initiating new dental health habits among adolescents, whereas contingent rewards had been singularly successful. Even the contingent reward system was less effective than often desired in public health programs, however. In the daily home mouthrinse program, for example, 50% of the children had discontinued participation after only 20 weeks, even in the best (contingent rewards) condition. Moreover, it seemed unlikely that public health officials would be morally willing or financially able to maintain complex contingencies of material rewards for the length of time that some behavior must be maintained; fluoride rinsing, for example, is presumably a lifelong activity.

Thus, our research in Phase II focused on the two issues of augmenting the effects of contingent rewards and assessing the problems of long-term compliance.

Augmenting and Extending the Effect of Contingent Rewards: Phase II, Experiment 3

In our third experiment, two procedures for increasing the effects of contingent rewards were examined in the context of the mouthrinsing paradigm: postcard reminders for obtaining new rinse supplies and action instructions for using the rinse. The contingent reward procedure was the same as that found to be effective in the first mouthrinse experiment (Lund & Kegeles, 1982).

Postcard reminders were mailed to children shortly before their appointments to trade old mouthrinse dispensers for new ones. The postcards were intended to serve as cues that would remind the children of the need for preventive dental action (as discussed by proponents of the health belief model (e.g., Becker, 1974) and the availability of contingent rewards for behavior (as discussed by behavioral theorists) (e.g., Sulzer-Azaroff & Mayer, 1977). Thus, the postcard reminders dealt with the potential obstacle of appointment keeping in the mouthrinse program.

Action instructions were detailed instructions given at various stages of the program. They were intended to help each participant develop specific, step-by-step plans for carrying out the recommended procedures. The instructions were modeled after a series of investigations carried out by Leventhal and his colleagues, which had shown that action instructions can increase the effectiveness of communications intended to persuade people to take action in the prevention of health problems. Detailed descriptions of where, when, and how specific actions can be taken, accompanied by information about the health threat to be prevented, have made patient compliance easier and more likely in several different medical interventions (Evans, Rozelle, Lasater, Dembroski, & Allen, 1970; Johnson & Leventhal, 1974; Leventhal, Singer, & Jones, 1965; Leventhal, Watts, & Pagano, 1967). Because, in most cases, action instructions contain no information that is new to the targets of the communication, Leventhal et al. (1965) speak of action instructions as providing an opportunity to rehearse a coherent plan of action. To create such action plans for the mouthrinsing program, children were provided suggestions about obtaining parental permission, getting the rinse to and from school, and using the rinse at home.

Table 59.1   Students Who Obtained Bottles and Used Rinse, Averaged Across Bottle Periods

Locale	Action Instructions	Students Obtaining Any Given Bottle (%)[a]	Average Daily Use of Rinse During Any Given Period (%)[b]
Urban	Yes	78	75
	No	73	67
Suburban	Yes	70	64
	No	71	67

Source: Copyright by Lawrence Erlbaum Associates, Inc.
From Lund, A. K., & Kegeles, S. S. Increasing acceptance of long-term personal health behavior. *Health Psychology,* 1982, **1**, 27–43. Reprinted by permission.
[a] The average number of bottles obtained in each condition can be derived by multiplying the average proportion obtaining rinse by 10 (e.g., .78 × 10 = 7.8 bottles).
[b] Children not obtaining a bottle for any given period received a 0.00 score for rate of use during that period.

In the experiment, one-quarter of the children received action instructions and postcard reminders; another one-quarter received action instructions but no postcards; another one-quarter received postcards but no action instructions; and the other children received neither action instructions nor postcards. All children received contingent rewards for compliance.

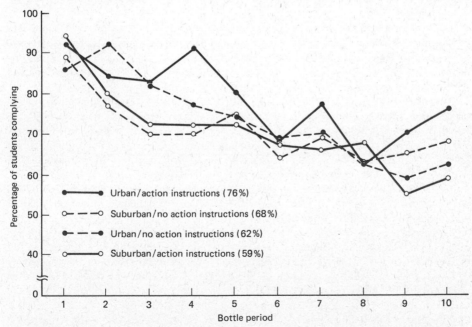

Figure 59.3 Percentages of enrollees who obtained mouthrinse during each period. (Copyright by Lawrence Erlbaum Associates, Inc. From Lund, A. K., & Kegeles, S. S. Increasing acceptance of long-term personal health behavior. *Health Psychology,* 1982, **1**, 27–43. Reprinted by permission.)

Each condition was replicated in one urban and one suburban school. The major results of the experiment are shown in Table 59.1 and Figure 59.3.

Basically, there was no overall effect on behavior of either action instructions or reminders. There was an interaction, however, between locale (central city versus suburban) and action instructions. Among urban volunteers, those who were provided action instructions were more likely to obtain parental consent than those who were not provided such instructions; the opposite was true among suburban volunteers. Among urban children, action instructions resulted in greater participation, whereas among suburban children, they resulted in less participation. Among urban children, participation fell at a lower rate with action instructions than without, whereas the opposite was true among suburban children (Lund & Kegeles, 1982). There were no other effects of the experimental procedures.

These results from Experiment 3 were disappointing but nevertheless important. They confirmed the fact that certain instructional strategies can improve compliance, even among children already receiving substantial rewards for compliance, but that the strategies may have unpredictable effects for some populations of adolescents. At this time, neither action instructions nor postcard reminders can be recommended unequivocally for fostering new health habits. Nevertheless, it was encouraging that the participation of urban children was increased substantially by the provision of action instructions; more than 70% of these children were still participating at the end of 20 weeks. Thus, it seems that it is possible to keep as many as 70% of these children active in a preventive program, such as the mouthrinse program, given a combination of contingent rewards and action instructions.

Assessing Long-Term Compliance: Experiment 4

In our fourth experiment, we sought to determine the long-term carry-over of new health habits learned under contingent reward conditions. For such behavior, we had to consider the possibility of simplifying, thinning, or even eliminating material rewards after the behavior is established.

Thus, we assessed the effect of different reward schedules (Reynolds, 1968) and self-management activities (Kanfer, 1977) on both short- and long-term participation. Both of these variables have been related theoretically to maintenance and generalization of rewards behavior. The 2 × 2 design we used included two schedules of rewards (standard and partial) and the presence or absence of self-management instruction.

The standard reward schedule was a shorter version of the previous contingent reward procedures, whereby children received prizes for every returned bottle and a bonus prize based on overall compliance. The only divergence was that prizes were awarded for only the first seven bottle periods, with the bonus awarded for maximal use of those seven bottles. After the first 14 weeks, no further prizes were given, and postreward participation was monitored for the remaining 6 weeks of the school year. An additional 20 weeks of postreward follow-up were carried out during the following school year. This design allowed us to assess the long-term, postreward effects of a reward schedule known to produce increments in participation while in effect.

The partial reward schedule provided prizes for participation only part of the time and included no bonus prize. Although it was expected that this reward schedule might result in less participation during the period of reward (14 weeks), literature on the psychology of learning suggests that it should be more resistant to the effects of reward termination (Reynolds, 1968). Thus, the partial condition, as compared to the standard condition, could lead to higher levels of program participation in the long run. The partial schedule was operationalized as a fading contract schedule; that is, children were told at the introduction that they would sometimes receive prizes for their performance and that we would always tell them ahead of time what they had to do to earn them. Then, when they picked up the first bottle, they were told that they would get prizes when they returned it. As in the standard condition, the level of prize they could choose depended on the level of rinse they used. When they received the third bottle, however, the children were told that their next prize would be based on their use of that bottle and the fourth. Similarly, when they picked up the fifth bottle, they were told their next and final prize would be based on their use of the fifth, sixth, and seventh bottles.

The two reward schedules were crossed by the presence or absence of specific self-management strategies. Self-management strategies have been suggested both as methods of behavior control in their own right (Kanfer, 1977; Mahoney, 1974) and as mechanisms that can reduce the likelihood of extinction after the withdrawal of other externally controlled rewards (Ford & Foster, 1976). We hoped that self-management strategies would bolster compliance with the mouthrinse procedures, even during the period of reward, by providing additional feedback in the form of self-monitoring, self-evaluation, and self-reinforcement for the rinsing activities that occurred at home. Additionally, we hypothesized that self-management activities would maintain the mouthrinsing activity at a higher level once the external rewards were withdrawn.

The operationalization of the self-management intervention included various self-monitoring activities at home, self-reinforcing activities both at home and at school, and attempts to associate mouthrinsing with other regular home activities. These self-management techniques were introduced at various times during the first 14 weeks; they were continued in force during the whole 2-year period.

Although the results from this experiment were quite complex, the general pattern of the data is shown in Figures 59.4 and 59.5.

The decline in participation over time was gradual and linear over the original reward period. Removal of rewards, however, decreased compliance substantially. Whereas almost 60% obtained the eighth bottle (when the final reward was given), only 40% came back for the ninth bottle (the first bottle after rewards were removed). By the twelfth week of the second-year follow-up, only 10% to 15% were still participating. At that time, rewards were reinstituted, accounting for the slight increase in participation in the final weeks.

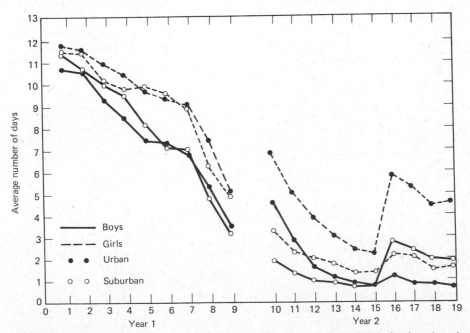

Figure 59.4 Average number of days rinse was used during each 2-week period, by locale and gender. (Adapted from Lund, A. K., & Kegeles, S. S. Rewards and adolescent behavior. Submitted for publication.)

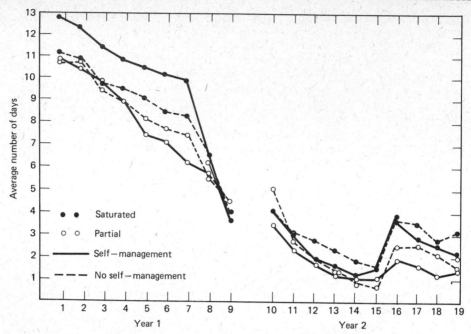

Figure 59.5 Average number of days rinse was used during each two-week period presented by reward schedule and self-management condition. (Adapted from Lund, A. K., & Kegeles, S. S. Rewards and adolescent behavior. Submitted for publication.)

There were some interesting effects of experimental conditions; for example, children in the saturated reward condition generally complied more than those in the partial condition. In addition, girls complied more than boys and urban children more than suburban children. In addition, in a finding reminiscent of the effects of action instructions in Experiment 3, it was found that during the first year, self-management instruction increased urban participation but decreased suburban participation. Despite these variations in pattern, however, most children in all conditions eventually discontinued participation.

This provided the general set of experimental findings from our fourth experiment. (More complete findings are to be found in Lund and Kegeles, in press.) The ramifications of these findings will be discussed more fully subsequent to a discussion of the intraindividual data obtained.

EFFECT OF INTRAINDIVIDUAL CHARACTERISTICS ON BEHAVIOR

As noted, this research was begun with an expectation that adolescents' attitudes could be changed, with resultant changes in and maintenance of new health behavior. As indicated, the first two experiments attempted to do just that, through use of a group discussion paradigm, only to find that the technology fared even less well than the information control procedure.

It was possible, however, that the problem was the group discussion technology, rather than the attitude change conceptualization. Thus, we needed to look to other sets of information that had been collected in order to determine two facts: (a) whether adolescents with appropriate intraindividual characteristics, regardless of experimental condition or in interaction with experimental condition, behaved differently from those with inappropriate characteristics, and (b) whether those adolescents who changed intraindividual characteristics toward a more appropriate level complied more than those whose characteristics failed to change.

The attitudinal model used throughout this research was the health belief model. That model specifies that health-related behavior is more likely among people who feel susceptible to a health problem (perceived susceptibility) that they perceive as serious (perceived seriousness), who feel that the behavior is likely to have beneficial effects (perceived benefits) that outweigh the costs of the behavior (perceived barriers), and who are exposed to cues for the behavior. There is a general notion that there is a multiplicative relationship between these variables and behavior.

We have reviewed elsewhere the literature in regard to the empirical relationship between health beliefs and behavior (Kegeles, 1980; Kegeles & Lund, 1982; Weisenberg, Kegeles, & Lund, 1980). As a brief summary, however, four points stand out. First, the findings have not been uniformly supportive of the model. Second, most studies have been retrospective rather than prospective, with most support for the model occurring in the retrospective studies. Third, even in supportive prospective studies, causality is often difficult to determine because the behavior is usually ongoing (like checkup behavior), and past experience with that kind of behavior has not been controlled for. Finally, very few studies have shown that it is possible to change behavior by changing the beliefs.

In our first experiment, we found that only beliefs in susceptibility were consistently associated with behavior, and these effects were negative; that is, the effects were opposite to the predictions of the model. Generally, beliefs about seriousness and effectiveness were not related to behavior. Only children's beliefs about effectiveness were changed by the intervention, and these changes were not related to behavior. In addition, the findings failed to support the model, whether we used beliefs that were relatively global or those that were relatively specific to the preventive activity, and whether they were measured well in advance or immediately before the behavior was to begin (Weisenberg et al., 1980).

Findings from the second experiment generally replicated those from the first experiment (Kegeles & Lund, 1982). The only belief that changed was effectiveness, and this change did not lead to greater compliance. Again, some significant negative relationships were found between susceptibility and behavior and some significant negative findings between seriousness and behavior, which had been only trends in the first study.

Findings from our third and fourth experiments replicate the findings from the first two experiments (Kegeles & Lund, Note 4). Moreover, we found that beliefs at the end of the study did not account for the previous behavior.

Thus, these analyses indicate no positive relationship between children's health beliefs and their participation in any of our programs. In fact, there may be an unexplainable negative relationship between participation and beliefs in susceptibility and in the seriousness of dental disease. Moreover, we have found that beliefs in neither susceptibility nor the seriousness of dental disease appear alterable, at least by the procedures we have used to attempt to change them. This has raised the question of whether the level of these health beliefs, assumed to be valuable for determination because of their presumed mutability, might instead be comparable to personality variables and thus immutable.

We have also reported data indicating that certain experiences and practices that children report are predictive of their beliefs, whereas other experiences and practices are predictive of their behavior. These data begin to partially substantiate our thesis that beliefs and behavior might arise from different experiences and be related only coincidentally (Weisenberg et al., 1980).

Earlier in our research program, we reported some data indicating that children classified as internal in perceived control were more likely to participate than those classified as external (Lund & Kegeles, Note 5); we have failed to replicate these findings in later research, which raises questions about the earlier findings. In summary, we have not found any personal characteristics of children that consistently predict participation in our research.

CONCLUSIONS AND FUTURE RESEARCH DIRECTIONS

After four experiments carried out over 7 years of research, we are still far from the goal we set for ourselves—to establish a theoretical and experimental foundation for a technology of adolescents' dental health behavior change and behavior maintenance. The task was not so simple as originally envisioned, and much of what was tried did not produce usable findings. We believe our findings are comparable to those found in many efforts to change health behavior; for example, the techniques available from psychological laboratories and clinics are not nearly so effective as was hoped by Weiss (1982) and by Matarazzo (1982).

Nevertheless, these data do contribute significantly to our understanding of adolescent health behavior. First, it is clear that health beliefs and the interventions based on them have little relationship to the health habits of adolescents. Contingent rewards are much more effective for fostering new health habits, at least for brief periods of time. Second, it is clear that some successful interventions, even when coupled with effective rewards, can have negative results for compliance with new preventive habits; in our research, this was particularly true of action instructions and self-management instructions among suburban children. Finally, and disappointingly, the data showed that rewarded health behavior soon ceased when rewards were no longer available.

These conclusions have guided the development of Phase III of our research. Phase III is intended to follow up, first, on the different effects for urban and suburban children of instruction intended to deal with the process of personal health behavior and, second, on the lack of maintenance of long-term behavior following discontinuation of rewards.

Urban-Suburban Differences in Response to Instruction

Action instructions and instruction in self-management techniques had very similar effects in our first two experimental phases. Both action instructions and self-management instructions led to very high levels of compliance among urban children receiving the standard schedule of rewards. Among suburban children in the third experiment, however, action instructions significantly reduced compliance. In the fourth experiment, self-management instructions had a smaller impact among suburban than among urban children; moreover, when the rewards ceased, there was a significant interaction of self-management and locale, with self-management helping the urban children but harming the suburban children. These similar results suggest some important conceptual similarities between action instructions and self-management interventions. Despite their different theoretical roots, the reason for both strategies is that their proponents wish to change behavior that, for the most part, is performed outside their spheres of direct influence. People cannot be directed at each step, nor can their successful completion of the behavior always be reinforced directly. Thus, action instructions help people break a complex behavior sequence into concrete steps and help them recognize the times and situations in which each step might occur. Similarly, self-management instructions teach people to monitor their behavior relative to a standard and to set up reinforcing consequences for satisfactory performance. It is hoped by the practitioners of both strategies that these activities will assure and support the desired behavior in the intervals between direct contacts with the influence agent. Used in this manner, action instructions and self-management interventions are complementary approaches to the overall problem of self-management.

This analysis is consistent with our findings that urban children receiving the standard reward program increased their performance significantly and importantly with each of these strategies. It does not account, however, for the fact that the self-management intervention was not particularly helpful for urban children under the partial reward condition and ultimately had the negative effect of action instructions for the suburban children. We suspect that these unexpected effects are due to a second common aspect of the two strategies—namely, that both action instructions and self-management interventions are instructional procedures. Though targeted differently, both strategies instruct people (such as our adolescents) to perform certain secondary actions (such as keeping the rinse in a safe, obvious place and monitoring rinsing on a calendar) in support of the primary action (using the rinse). The fact that the intended effects of self-management are achieved by instructions to act in certain ways in addition to the desired act has implications from both social-psychological and behavioral perspectives. From the social-psychological perspective, attempts to instruct or influence the behavior of others can lead to the phenomenon of psychological reactance (Brehm, 1966), whereby the targets of influence not only resist the influence attempt but change their attitudes in a negative direction. Such reactance is increased when the influence attempt decreases the target's perception of choice and control (Worchel & Brehm, 1970), when the target population is more competent in the area of influence attempt (Wicklund & Brehm, 1968), when it has higher self-esteem (Grabitz-Gniech, 1971), and when it has attitudes already consonant with those espoused (Snyder & Wicklund, 1976). It is possible that one effect of the action instructions and self-management interventions was to decrease the perception of control and choice; these strategies not only asked the children to perform the desired behavior but also attempted to tell them how to do it. Since our earlier experiments found that the suburban children had higher self-esteem and greater perceptions of control over their lives (Cipes, Kegeles, Lund, and Otradovec, in press), it is possible that they experienced greater reactance to the heavy control of both sets of instructions than the urban children did.

An alternative interpretation is provided by an operant analysis, based not on the overcontrolling aspect of the instructions but on the quantity of additional behavior specified by them. This additional behavior, like the mouthrinsing itself, must be maintained by some set of reinforcement contingencies. The only contingencies provided by the program are the material and verbal rewards available at the end of each 2-week period; these must maintain both the rinsing and the self-management behavior. It seems reasonable to hypothesize that the likelihood of compliance will decrease as the number of specific activities in the behavioral chain increases, given a constant level of reward; such an hypothesis could account for the noneffects, and even negative effects, of self-management interventions under schedules of partial reinforcement. In addition, assuming that the income levels of suburban families make available to their children a greater variety of more valuable rewards for a wider range of activities, then our rewards program experiences greater competition with alternative reinforcement contingencies in the suburban locale than in the urban locales. Hence, the behavioral chain that can be supported by our reward program probably is shorter for suburban children than for urban children; the smaller or negative effects of action instructions and self-management interventions could indicate that these strategies introduced behavior chains that were too long for the suburban children, using our current reward program.

In summary, data from Experiments 3 and 4 are consistent with an interpretation of action instructions and self-management interventions as having intended effects on complementary components of the process of self-management of a personal health activity. Thus, action instructions and self-management interventions should have a beneficial impact on personal health habits when the additional behavior is successfully initiated and maintained. In fact, the two strategies should have additive effects, since they affect different components of the self-management process. With both strategies, however, the effects are achieved by asking for larger changes in personal behavior than are required by the act of rinsing alone; therefore, they have a greater likelihood of generating psychological reactance to the behavioral chain that can be supported by a given reward program.

These are important implications. The data from our urban population indicate the substantial benefits that can accrue from effective action and self-management instruction. If our analysis is correct, the problem is to counteract the increased behavioral cost of compliance and the increased potential for reactance to the influence attempt, which are unintended results of these strategies. Snyder and Wicklund (1976) have reported that psychological reactance was attenuated when targets of an influence attempt were provided the opportunity to exercise some choice in the relevant situation prior to the actual influence attempt. Similarly, Loro, Fisher, and Levenkron (1979) have found that a self-initiated program of self-management of weight loss was more successful than either situational engineering (based on Stuart's program of weight loss) or eating behavior control (based on Mahoney's program of self-control). The self-initiated procedure consisted primarily of allowing the participants to choose from among a variety of self-control procedures, rather than directing them to use certain ones. Thus, a key conceptual variable for greater acceptance of influence attempts seems to be the presence of choice.

It seems very possible that the positive effects of the action instructions and self-management interventions among urban children might be duplicated for suburban children if the variable of choice were manipulated appropriately. If such effective action instruction and self-management packages could be developed, their effects would be expected to be additive, thereby providing a very high level of compliance among both urban and suburban children, at least during the period when rewards are available. The specification of such instructional packages seems imperative for the ultimate development of effective public health programs in the area of personal health behavior. The data from Experiment 4 present a serious challenge to the goal of developing a theory and technology for the establishment of personal dental (or other) health habits. We have found in our earlier experiments, as have other researchers (Greenberg, 1977; Martens, Frazier, Hirt, Meskin, & Proshek, 1973), that contingent rewards seem unsurpassed in obtaining acceptance of recommended dental health behavior. The pattern of behavior we obtained in Experiment 4 following the provision of the final reward, however, is probably best described as extinction. Although urban children maintained a higher rate of compliance after termination of the rewards than did suburban children, their performance was declining and probably would have become as low as that of the suburban children. Had we not reinstituted a reward program, it seems that no more than 10% of the children would have continued to participate.

One direction our new research will take in dealing with this problem is to investigate some of the contextual factors that have been related recently to postreward behavior (Lepper & Green, 1978a, 1978b). It has been shown, for example, that when behavior has been rewarded contingently, the same behavior is more likely to recur in subsequent unrewarded situations if the original rewards are given unexpectedly rather than expectedly (Lepper, Green, & Nisbett, 1973), if the rewards are contingent on the quality of task performance rather than on task engagement alone (Karniol & Ross, 1977), if the rewards are accompanied by information pointing to their implications for personal competence and achievement (Deci & Porac, 1978), and if the rewards are too insufficient or inconsequential to justify performing the behavior (Bem, 1972; Kelley, 1967). Although the process by which these effects are obtained is the subject of much debate, there seems to be some agreement that contingent, tangible rewards are more likely to have a positive effect on postreward behavior when they "are used so that they primarily convey information that a person is competent and self determining and that they aren't intended as controllers of behavior" (Deci & Porac, 1978).

Comparing our current standard reward procedure to the conditions earlier found to enhance the effects of reward on subsequent behavior, it would appear that we have made behavioral control information dominant. Although the reward procedures emphasized the quality of performance as well as task engagement, they also were expected rather than unexpected, they were not described as indicating personal achievement, and they were chosen to be as attractive as possible to increase the likelihood of compliance. In addition, a substantial proportion of children have indicated on questionnaires that the rewards were an important reason for participating. The poor performance of our children following the cessation of rewards may be due to these various characteristics of the reward program. Thus, one direction our new research will take is to examine whether the reward program can be reestimated on these variables in such a way as to increase postreward compliance.

The preceding section discussed potential modification to our mouthrinse program that might maximize long-term compliance with short-term interventions. This effort assumes that preventive health behavior can eventually become "functionally autonomous" (Allport, 1937) of the conditions that initiated it. Indeed, our studies provide some limited evidence for this assumption, as approximately 10% of the children were long-term compliers despite the cessation of rewards. If we wish to reach larger proportions of the public with health behavior programs, however, it may prove necessary to accept the fact that some form of external, tangible incentive or reward will be necessary for the duration of the period in which the behavior is relevant; this is a second direction of our new research on long-term behavior.

In theory, incentives and rewards need not be tangible (e.g., the usefulness of peer interactions and activities as rewards might be explored), but tangible rewards are usually easier to administer and control than such rewards as peer interactions and attractive activities. In addition, the use of tangible rewards provides greater comparability of the results with our current research. Thus, we need to ask what form long-term, tangible reinforcement contingencies might take, and with what effects.

In the development of such a long-term contingency program, the problem becomes one of constructing schedules of reinforcement that are saturated enough to maintain the desired behavior but thin enough and varied enough to avoid satiation of the reward program. Numerous investigations have been made of the behavioral patterns maintained by different schedules of reinforcement (Sulzer-Azaroff & Mayer, 1977). Since the mouthrinse program required regular (daily) behavior, a variable ratio schedule seems most appropriate, as it tends to maintain a constant level of performance in the intervals between reinforcement.

Thus, our new research will continue to have several characteristics:

1. It will be experimental rather than descriptive.
2. It will use intervention techniques that have been shown to be effective in changing behavior in other contexts.
3. It will ask the population studied to carry out specific behaviors on a number of occasions over a long period, for which behaviors the population will be provided with a health service.
4. It will require alternative kinds of behavior from the population in order to assess generalization of intervention techniques.
5. It will assess personal attributes and health experiences of the new population before it is provided the health service and subsequent to each study to determine the effect of these variables on behavior.

We believe that this kind of programmatic research continues to be essential for understanding and changing preventive health behavior.

REFERENCE NOTES

1. Kegeles, S. S. Gaining acceptance of preventive measures. In J. F. Fogarty, *Prevention of oral health.* DHEW Pub. No. (NIH)74–407, 1973.
2. Silversin, J., & Kornacki, M. J. Controlling dental disease through prevention: Individual, institutional, and community dimensions. In L. K. Cohen & P. S. Bryant (Eds.), *Social sciences and dentistry* (Vol. 2). Federation-Dentaire Internationale, in press.
3. Children's Dental Research Project. *Report to the Minister of Health, British Columbia, and the President, College of Dental Surgeons.* Victoria, B.C., Canada: Queen's Printer, 1975.
4. Kegeles, S. S., & Lund, A. K. *Adolescents' health beliefs and acceptance of a novel preventive dental activity: A further note.* Manuscript submitted for publication.

5. Lund, A. K., & Kegeles, S. S. *Social-psychological intervention in children's preventive behavior.* Paper presented at the meeting of the American Psychological Association, Toronto, August 30, 1978.

REFERENCES

Allport, G. W. The functional autonomy of motives. *American Journal of Psychology,* 1937, **50,** 141–156.

Becker, M. H. (Ed.). The health belief model and personal health behavior. *Health Educational Monograph,* 1974, **2,** 236–473.

Bem, D. J. Self-perception theory. In L. Berkowitz (Ed.), *Advances in experimental social psychology* (Vol. 6). New York: Academic Press, 1972.

Brehm, J. W. *A theory of psychological reactance.* New York: Academic Press, 1966.

Cipes, M., Kegeles, S. S., Lund, A. K., & Otradovec, C. Differences in dental experiences, beliefs and compliance with preventive programs of urban and suburban adolescents. *American Journal of Public Health,* in press.

Deci, E. L., & Porac, J. Cognitive evaluation theory and the study of human motivation. In M. R. Lepper & D. Green (Eds.), *The hidden cost of reward.* Hillsdale, N.J.: Lawrence Erlbaum Associates, 1978.

Evans, R. I., Rozelle, R. M., Lasater, T. M., Dembroski, T. M., & Allen, B. P. Fear arousal persuasion and actual versus implied behavioral change: New perspective utilizing a real-life dental hygiene program. *Journal of Personality and Social Psychology,* 1970, **16,** 220–227.

Ford, J. D., & Foster, S. L. Extrinsic incentives and token-based programs: A re-evaluation. *American Psychologist,* 1976, **31,** 87–90.

Grabitz-Gniech, G. Some restrictive conditions for the occurrence of psychological reactance. *Journal of Personality and Social Psychology,* 1971, **19,** 188–196.

Greenberg, J. S. A study of behavior modification applied to dental health. *Journal of School Health,* 1977, **47,** 594–596.

Johnson, J. E., & Leventhal, H. Effects of accurate expectations and behavioral instructions on reactions during a noxious medical examination. *Journal of Personality and Social Psychology,* 1974, **29,** 710–718.

Kanfer, F. H. The many faces of self-control, or behavior modification changes its focus. In E. B. Stuart (Ed.), *Behavioral self-management: Strategies, techniques and outcomes.* New York: Brunner/Mazel, 1977.

Karniol, R., & Ross, M. The effects of performance-relevant and performance-irrelevant rewards on children's intrinsic motivation. *Child Development,* 1977, **48,** 482–487.

Kazdin, A. E. Recent advances in token economy research. In M. Hersen, R. M. Eisler, & P. M. Miller (Eds.), *Progress in behavior modification* (Vol. 1). New York: Academic Press, 1975.

Kegeles, S. S. Public acceptance of dental preventive measures. *Journal of Preventive Dentistry,* 1975, **2,** 10–27.

Kegeles, S. S. The health belief model and personal health behavior. *Social Science and Medicine,* 1980, **14c,** 227–229. (Book review)

Kegeles, S., & Lund, A. Acceptance of a novel preventive dental activity. *Health Educational Quarterly,* 1982, **9** (2 + 3), Summer-Fall 96/192–112–208.

Kegeles, S. S., Lund, A. K., & Weisenberg, M. Acceptance by children of a daily home mouthrinse program. *Social Science and Medicine,* 1978, **12,** 199–210.

Kelley, H. Attribution theory in social psychology. In D. Levine (Ed.), *Nebraska Symposium on Motivation* (Vol. 15). Lincoln: University of Nebraska Press, 1967.

Lepper, M. R., & Greene, D. Overjustification research and beyond: Toward a means-ends analysis of intrinsic and extrinsic motivation. In M. R. Lepper & D. Green (Eds.), *The hidden costs of reward.* Hillsdale, N.J.: Lawrence Erlbaum Associates, 1978(a).

Lepper, M. R., & Green, D. Divergent approaches to the study of rewards. In M. R. Lepper & D. Green (Eds.), *The hidden costs of reward.* Hillsdale, N.J.: Lawrence Erlbaum Associates, 1978(b).

Lepper, M. R., Greene, D., & Nisbett, R. E. Undermining children's intrinsic interest with extrinsic rewards: A test of the "overjustification" hypothesis. *Journal of Personality and Social Psychology,* 1973, **28,** 129–137.

Leventhal, H., Singer, R., & Jones, S. Effects of fear and specificity of recommendation upon attitudes and behavior. *Journal of Personality and Social Psychology,* 1965, **2,** 20–29.

Leventhal, H., Watts, J. C., & Pagano, I. Effects of fear and instructions on how to cope with danger. *Journal of Personality and Social Psychology,* 1967, **6,** 313–321.

Loro, A. D., Fisher, E. B., Jr., & Levenkron, J. C. Comparison of established and innovative weight-reduction treatment procedures. *Journal of Applied Behavior Analysis,* 1979, **12,** 141–155.

Loverett, D. H. Fluorides and the changing prevalence of dental caries. *Science,* 1982, **217,** 26–30.

Lund, A. K. & Kegeles, S. S. Rewards and adolescent health behavior, *Health Psychology,* in press.

Lund, A. K., & Kegeles, S. S. Increasing adolescents' acceptance of long-term personal health behavior. *Health Psychology,* 1982, **1,** 27–43.

Lund, A. K., Kegeles, S. S., & Weisenberg, M. Motivational techniques for increasing acceptance of preventive health measures. *Medical Care,* 1977, **15,** 678–692.

Mahoney, M. J. Self-reward and self monitoring techniques for weight control. *Behavior Therapy,* 1974, **5,** 48–57.

Martens, L. V., Frazier, P. J., Hirt, K. J., Meskin, L. H., & Proshek, J. Developing brushing performance in second graders through behavior modification. *Health Services Reports,* 1973, **88,** 818–823.

Matarazzo, J. D. Behavioral health's challenge to academic, scientific, and professional psychology. *American Psychologist,* 1982, **37,** 1–14.

Reynolds, G. S. *A primer of operant conditioning.* Atlanta: Scott, Foresman, 1968.

Snyder, M. L., & Wicklund, R. A. Prior exercise of freedom and reactance. *Journal of Experimental Social Psychology,* 1976, **12,** 120–130.

Sulzer-Azaroff, B., & Mayer, G. R. *Applying behavior-analysis procedures with children and youth.* New York: Holt, Rinehart & Winston, 1977.

Weisenberg, M., Kegeles, S. S., & Lund, A. K. Children's health beliefs and acceptance of a dental preventive activity. *Journal of Health and Social Behavior,* 1980, **21,** 59–74.

Weiss, S. M. Health psychology: The time is now. *Health Psychology,* 1982, **1,** 81–91.

Wicklund, R. A., & Brehm, J. W. Attitude change as a function of felt competence and threat to attitudinal freedom. *Journal of Experimental Social Psychology,* 1968, **4,** 64–75.

Worchel, S., & Brehm, J. W. Effect of threats to attitudinal freedom as a function of agreement with the communicator. *Journal of Personality and Social Psychology,* 1970, **14,** 18–22.

CHAPTER 60

METHODS OF REDUCING DENTAL FEAR AND ANXIETY

NORMAN L. CORAH
ELLIOT N. GALE

School of Dentistry, State University of New York at Buffalo

The expectation that dental treatment will be painful provides the basis for most dental fears. The extent to which this anticipation, anxiety, or fear keeps patients from visiting the dentist is unclear. Moen (1954) reported that 2.1% of the respondents in his survey said that they had not seen a dentist in the previous year because it was unpleasant and painful. A survey conducted by Freidson and Feldman (1958), however, found that 9% of patients gave "don't like to go, afraid of dentistry, it hurts" as a reason for not seeing the dentist more often; and 21% gave "afraid to go, dread it, it hurts too much" as the reason why the respondent or member of the family did not get needed dental care. A range between 2% and 20% of reported avoidance of dentistry related to fear and anxiety indicates a problem of considerable importance.

Sensitivity to pain or prior painful experiences have been implicated as potential etiologic factors in the development of dental fears. Shoben and Borland (1954) found that high-fear dental patients reported more unfavorable family dental experiences and more unfavorable family attitudes toward dentistry than did low-fear patients. A subsequent reanalysis of their data by Forgione and Clark (1974) suggested that low pain tolerance, traumatic facial experience, and high general anxiety may also be etiologic for dental fears—at least to the extent that patient self-reports can be accepted as a basis for etiology. Research by Kleinknecht and Bernstein (1978) also indicated that fearful dental patients report higher levels of painful dental experience than do nonfearful patients. Thus, a circular process presumably occurs in which pain-sensitive patients become fearful and fearful patients are more susceptible to pain.

Consequently, dental fear and anxiety may not only provide patient discomfort and distress but may also prevent many patients or potential patients from receiving appropriate oral care. It is almost needless to point out that patients who avoid dental care until it is absolutely necessary are those whose subsequent dental experiences are most likely to reinforce their fears and anxieties.

That the dental situation, in fact, can induce and maintain fear-related behavior has been supported by the work of Bernstein, Kleinknecht, and Alexander (1979) and Venham and Quatrocelli (1977). In a retrospective study of subjects with high and low fear of dentistry, factors that appear to differentiate the groups included pain experiences in the dental operatory and dentists' behaviors (Bernstein et al., 1979). It is of interest that fear sensitization in the dental setting is not always a global affair. Venham and Quatrocelli (1977) found that, although children became increasingly sensitized to anesthesia injection over a series of visits, patient responses to the other less threatening parts of the dental procedure decreased in intensity.

It is readily apparent that the reduction of fear and anxiety is important to the maintenance of good oral health. Behavioral procedures directed toward this goal have been investigated in recent years. The techniques are either preventive or involve intervention where dental fears or phobias have developed. In the preventive area, methods derive from patient management behaviors involving the dentist–patient relationship and from technique-oriented methods of anxiety reduction.

Dentist behaviors deriving from the dentist–patient relationship have been the least studied area of patient anxiety reduction. Recently, Weinstein, Getz, Ratener and Domoto (1982a, 1982b) evaluated dentists' responses to children's fear-related behaviors and found that the dentists' responses were often counterproductive. Methods that were used most often to deal with disruptive behavior, such as setting rules, coercion, coaxing, and reassurance, were least effective in reducing fear-related behaviors. Least often used methods, such as giving direction and reinforcement and questioning for feelings, were most effective in reducing children's fear-related behaviors. Touching the patients also tended to reduce fear, whereas stopping treatment to manage the child was not effective. This area appears to be very promising, but a great deal more research is required.

PREPARATORY COGNITIVE-INFORMATIONAL APPROACHES

Preparatory techniques designed to prevent the occurrence of anxiety and stress during dental procedures have been developed primarily for use with young children. The implicit assumption that lack of experience with the dental setting will produce fear and negative behavior in children appears to be a reasonable one. Consequently, several approaches have been developed to prepare the child patient for the new experience.

Two informational approaches have been used with some success. One of these involves providing information concerning the procedures to be experienced. This approach provides some detail about the procedures, sensations, sights, and sounds that comprise the dental experience (Siegel & Peterson, 1980, 1981).

The second preparatory approach stresses the development of coping skills, such as relaxation, regular breathing, positive imagery, calming self-talk, and provides some information about the procedures to be experienced (Machen & Johnson, 1974; Siegel & Peterson, 1980, 1981). Compared to control groups with no preparation, both approaches have resulted in reduced anxiety and less disruptive negative behavior during amalgam restorations.

A large school-based program conducted by Herbertt and Innes (1979) raises some questions about the amount of preparatory information that should be given to children. These investigators studied the use of lessons in general dental health, familiarization with clinic facilities, and explanation of specific dental procedures. No differences were found in the effects of the three types of information, but a curvilinear relationship was found between amount of information and anxiety exhibited during dental procedures. Low and high levels of information both produced higher levels of anxiety than a moderate amount of information. One session of specific information or two sessions of clinic familiarization produced the lowest levels of treatment anxiety. It is difficult to generalize from these findings to other informational approaches that have been used successfully.

The only attempt to use this type of approach with adults in a controlled investigation was that of Auerbach, Kendall, Cuttler, and Levitt (1976). They used two types of information with patients awaiting extractions: (a) a general information approach, describing the facilities and providing details about everything except the extraction procedure itself, and (b) a specific informational approach, describing the extraction process in detail. The effects of type of information interacted with the personality characteristic locus of control. Those patients who perceived themselves as having personal control over the effects of their own behavior (internals) benefited from the specific information, while those patients who perceived their life events as being determined by chance (externals) adjusted better with the general information. These findings suggest that, with a history of increased dental experience, preparatory techniques may not yield simple benefits to patients.

Modeling, another cognitive approach designed to prevent dental fears and anxiety, has been studied extensively with children. Machen and Johnson (1974) studied a group of 3-year-old to 5-year-old children who had never visited the dentist. One group of children was shown an 11-minute videotape of a child exhibiting positive behavior during dental treatment, with the dentist giving verbal reinforcement (praise) for the good behavior. These children showed less fear and more positive behavior than did a control group during a dental restoration.

A series of modeling studies by Melamed and her colleagues also supports the usefulness of this technique (Melamed, Hawes, Heiby, & Glick, 1975; Melamed, Weinstein, Hawes, & Katin-Borland, 1975; Melamed, Yurcheson, Fleece, Hutcherson, & Hawes, 1978). In the initial studies (Melamed et al., 1975a, 1975b), inner-city children of 5–9 and 5–11 years of age were studied. The experimental groups in the two studies viewed a 13-minute videotape that showed a child coping with his anxiety during a dental restoration in a context of verbal reinforcement for cooperative behavior by the dentist. The control group in the first study drew pictures for 13 minutes, and the control group in the second study viewed a videotape unrelated to dental treatment. Following the modeling experience, the experimental group children in both studies showed a greater decrease in disruptive behaviors and a slight decrease in anxiety during a dental restoration than did the control groups.

Although it appears that modeling may be effective in reducing disruptive behavior and anxiety in children, a subsequent study by Melamed et al. (1978) suggests that the effect is not a simple one. Lower socioeconomic status pedodontic patients aged 4 to 11 were assigned to five different groups, and each group saw a different videotape. The videotapes were (a) a 10-minute restoration, using a 7-year-old model who remained cooperative and fearless throughout; (b) a 10-minute demonstration of the restorative procedure, without a model, in which the dentist describes expected patient behavior; (c) a 4-minute model tape showing only anesthesia injection and examination; (d) a 4-minute demonstration like the preceding tape, but without a model; and (e) a 10-minute videotape unrelated to dentistry (control). Children who saw a modeling tape exhibited somewhat fewer disruptive behaviors during a dental restoration than did those who saw a demonstration tape.

A number of complex interactions emerged from this study. An age-related finding suggests that children closest in age to the model (6 to 8 years old) showed the greatest reduction in anxiety. Previous experience also interacted with the experimental conditions. Children who had no previous experience, the 4- to 6-year-olds in particular, benefited most from the long videotape with the model. The demonstration videotapes appeared to sensitize the children who had no previous experience. The more experienced child patients benefited more from a demonstration videotape. Thus, for young children with no previous experience, a long modeling tape should be most effective. This result is consistent with the findings of Machen and Johnson (1974). Older children with prior dental experience appear to benefit from either a modeling tape or a demonstration tape. In all cases of modeling, the findings suggest that the model should be close to the age of the child patient.

The preparatory cognitive-informational approaches all appear to have some beneficial effects, as demonstrated in the studies that have used appropriate control groups. Studies that have compared different approaches have found differences not among the various experimental conditions but only between experimental and control conditions. These findings suggest, perhaps, that almost any technique will have some benefit. An example of a minimal technique—providing a period of time between diagnosis and treatment—has been demonstrated in a study by Baldwin (1966). Baldwin found that the time of recovery from trauma of tooth extraction was reduced for children who had to wait a week or more before the procedure, as compared with children who had an immediate extraction following diagnosis.

At least two major shortcomings of the investigated preparatory techniques are evident. First, they have been restricted to child dental patients. It is reasonable to assume that some variation of these procedures could be used with adult patients, and at least some investigation of this possibility should be conducted. Second, there is no evidence to indicate that there is any long term benefit from their use. In any event, these approaches can be packaged easily and should be relatively cost-effective.

PREVENTIVE TECHNIQUES USED DURING DENTAL PROCEDURES

Recently, attempts have been made to systematically investigate techniques used concurrently with dental procedures. In most cases, these studies have involved adult patients with varying dental histories. None of these patients would be characterized as phobic or extremely fearful. The techniques used were designed to reduce or alleviate the stress that may accompany normal dental procedures. The assumed benefit of these approaches is fewer negative feelings about dental work and a greater likelihood that patients would obtain more regular dental care.

One technique for reducing stress is relaxation. This technique is derived from the techniques presented by Jacobson (1929) as modified by Wolpe (1964). The technique was used primarily in the desensitization of phobic patients. (That usage is discussed in a later section of this chapter.) The procedure has been used primarily in vitro to prepare patients for confronting the objects of their phobias. The present usage has been in vivo, whereby the patient is trained to relax during the dental procedure. The effectiveness of this technique is based on the principle that it is impossible to be relaxed and anxious at the same time. A clinical demonstration of this principle using physiological measures has been provided by Gale, Hyman, and Ayer (1970).

The procedure to be discussed here was studied initially by Corah, Gale, and Illig (1979a, 1979b). The relaxation instructions were tape-recorded and presented through earphones to the patient in the dental chair. The tape-recorded instructions began with a brief statement of their purpose (to help the patient relax) and then proceeded to instruct the patient to relax various parts of the body and eventually the entire body. The instructions specifically exempted the mouth, and the patient was instructed to keep the mouth open wide throughout the dental procedure. The instructions were presented at a slow pace in a calm, quiet voice (Corah, Note 1). Subsequent research has demonstrated that both the instructional content and the style of presentation are important (Corah, Gale, Pace, & Seyrek, 1981a). The relaxation instructions were begun 3 to 5 minutes before the beginning of the dental procedure—that is, prior to anesthesia injection. Comparison of the responses of patients who received this procedure with a control group demonstrated reduced stress during amalgam restorations.

The second behavioral technique used to reduce stress during dental procedures was distraction. Although distraction has often been mentioned as a means of alleviating anxiety and pain, no systematic investigation of its utility in dentistry had been conducted prior to the work of Corah et al. (1979a, 1979b). It was thought that a distraction technique had to engross the patient's attention actively in order to be effective.

A video ping-pong game was selected as the patient distraction method. A television receiver was mounted near the ceiling of the dental operatory at an angle, providing a comfortable view for the patient in the dental chair. The game control was mounted on the arm of the chair appropriate for the patient's preferred hand with a Velcro fastener. A game was played "against the house" so that no other player need be involved. A variety of speeds was provided that would appropriately challenge any player. The patient was invited to play the game beginning 3 to 5 minutes before the beginning of the dental procedure and was encouraged to continue throughout the entire dental procedure. Again, patients who used this technique showed evidence of reduced stress when compared with control patients (Corah et al., 1979a, 1979b).

It is noteworthy that the studies of Corah and his colleagues have found consistently beneficial effects from the relaxation and distraction procedures as compared with an ordinary dental visit (control condition). No significant differences have been found between the two techniques, however. This lack of difference might suggest that, as in the studies with children, almost any feature added to the dental visit will have some benefit. There is some evidence that such a conclusion would be wrong. When various types of musical programming were compared with relaxation, they were no more effective than the ordinary control condition as contrasted with relaxation (Corah, Gale, Pace, & Seyrek, 1981b). When an audio comedy program was compared with the video game distraction, it was not effective in reducing stress (Corah, Gale, Pace, & Seyrek, Note 2). A fast-paced comedy video tape was as effective as the video game, however. Although these procedures are easy to use, they suffer from the same problems as the cognitive-informational approaches. Most noteworthy is the lack of data concerning their long-term effectiveness. On the positive side, they can be reused readily on successive dental visits.

INTERVENTION IN ESTABLISHED DENTAL FEARS

Once the potential or former dental patient has established strong fears or phobic reactions, he or she is unlikely to be available for any of the procedures already discussed. The extremely fearful patient deals with the fears by avoiding their object—in this case dental procedures. Consequently, several therapeutic procedures have been studied in an attempt to alleviate or eliminate these fears.

The most recent work has attempted to use stress inoculation or cognitive strategies for reducing dental avoidance (Kleinknecht & Bernstein, 1979; Klepac, Dowling, Hauge, & McDonald, 1981). These studies have used symbolic modeling as well as a number of other components to reduce fear. The symbolic modeling requires that a patient view a videotape of a person preparing for and going to a dental visit. The therapist also initiates the training of relaxation skills and cognitive and imaginal coping skills. A set of coping skills is tailored for each patient, who must then practice and refine the skills before attempting a dental visit (Klepac et al., 1981).

Although this approach has had some success in the laboratory setting, research has not yet been completed with long-term follow-ups on dental patients. Case studies of patients with a 1-year follow-up have demonstrated that similar procedures have permitted fearful individuals to schedule and maintain dental treatment visits (Kleinknecht & Bernstein, 1979). These cognitive strategies are potentially viable intervention techniques, but more research is required for a clear demonstration of their utility.

The most extensive work in the area of reducing fear in phobic patients has been with systematic desensitization and various modifications of desensitization (Wolpe, 1964). The first reported case of treatment of a dental phobic used standard desensitization (Gale & Ayer, 1969). The therapist developed a hierarchy of feared dental stimuli ranging from least threatening to most fear-provoking. These stimuli were presented gradually in the context of deep relaxation. The patient learned to visualize the dental scenes while he or she was relaxed, thus detracting from their fear-provoking character. After nine sessions, the patient was no longer afraid and was able to complete all needed dental treatment. This fear reduction was maintained after a 1-year period (Gale & Ayer, Note 3; Ayer & Gale, Note 4). The same technique was also evaluated with a group of dental phobics and again was maintained at a 1-year follow-up (Corah, Gale, & Illig, 1978). Klepac (1975) has also demonstrated successful use of systematic desensitization with dental phobics.

Although systematic desensitization has been shown to be an effective intervention technique, it is costly in terms of therapist time and effort. Consequently, attempts have been made to automate the process and eliminate much of the therapist's time. One excellent example of this approach was a study by Carlsson, Linde, and Öhman (1980). The study included 10 patients who had been referred for dental treatment with general anesthesia because of their inordinate fear of dentistry.

After an initial interview, each patient was given tape-recorded relaxation instructions. Relaxation training was reinforced with frontalis muscle tension biofeedback, presented by either audio or visual display to the patient who was seated in a dental chair. Instead of the usual imaginal scenes, this study used videotape-recorded segments from a dental procedure. The patient had a panel of buttons with which to choose any of the scenes at random. Consequently, the patient not only had the visual representation under his or her own control but also was receiving continuous feedback concerning relaxation. At the first sign of impending anxiety, the patient could terminate the visual segment and receive automatic relaxation instructions. The apparatus permitted the patient to initiate a dental scene, terminate it, repeat it, or produce another scene while relaxing. Thus, the patient had control over a self-paced desensitization procedure that did not require much therapist time.

A range of from 4 to 11 one-hour sessions was required for these patients to feel sufficiently comfortable to begin their dental treatment. The patients also showed a significant reduction in dental anxiety on a standard measure. They were able to complete treatment without the use of general anesthesia. The advantage of this approach is its cost-effectiveness. Developmental costs for the procedure are high, but once it is developed and implemented, the cost per patient is significantly lower than the cost of the standard desensitization procedure. Research using this technique has continued in Sweden, and the cost–benefit ratio is reported to be extremely low (Bergman & Carlsson, Note 5).

It should be noted that of all the attempts to reduce severe phobic behaviors, only systematic desensitization has been consistently successful. Reported success rates vary from 80% to 95%. It is not surprising, then, that any attempts to develop other techniques borrow heavily from desensitization. Even the so-called symbolic modeling developed for some of the more recent cognitive approaches involves presentation of a hierarchy of dental stimuli, beginning with the least fearful and moving to the most fearful. One of the most successful approaches to use symbolic modeling found that it was only successful in the context of a relaxed state (Wroblewski, Jacob, & Rehm, 1977). A visual hierarchy presented in the context of relaxation is a variant of desensitization. Presumably, more attempts will be made to find cost-effective adaptations of desensitization to reduce dental fears.

SUMMARY AND CONCLUSIONS

Dental procedures have always evoked fear and anxiety in patients. Indeed, dental anxiety is so common that it is one of the few socially acceptable anxieties in Western culture. Much effort has been expended in the last two decades to develop methods for reducing dental fears and anxieties, and some highly successful methods have been developed. The most successful procedure has been systematic desensitization. Although this approach has permitted many fearful patients to resume and maintain appropriate oral care, it has been an expensive procedure to use. Many current efforts have been directed at developing variations of this procedure that are more cost-effective.

It is likely that the most cost-effective procedures for dealing with dental anxiety are those that prevent its occurrence or reduce its impact before serious phobic tendencies are developed. A number of cognitive-informational techniques have been studied to prepare patients for dental work. Most of these have been restricted to child patients.

The success of cognitive-informational approaches appears to vary with the age and previous dental experience of the patient. For patients with no previous experience, providing an understanding of the dental procedures in a nonthreatening way is probably the most successful approach. Modeling films or videotapes in which a dental procedure is conducted on a child model of similar age, and in which the model successfully copes with the anxiety, appear to be successful preparatory techniques. A similar approach has also been useful with older, more experienced patients. The more experienced patient may also be helped by an informational approach, which acts as a reminder of what will happen and what behaviors are expected by the dentist.

Techniques designed to reduce stress during dental procedures for adult patients have also been successful. Deep-relaxation instructions borrowed from the desensitization procedure and presented throughout the dental procedure have been useful in reducing anxiety. Patient distraction through the use of a video game during the dental procedure has also been effective in reducing stress.

There is reason to believe that the most important approach to reducing patient stress derives from the behavior of the dentist in the dentist–patient interaction. Some research in this area with child patients has indicated some effective dentist behaviors, but much work remains to be done in this important area.

REFERENCE NOTES

1. Corah, N. L. *Patient relaxation during dental procedures.* Audio cassette. State University of New York at Buffalo, Educational Communications Center, 1981.

2. Corah, N. L., Gale, E. N., Pace, L. F., & Seyrek, S. K. *Comparison of three distraction techniques in reducing dental stress.* Paper presented at the 59th general session of the International Association for Dental Research, Chicago, March 19–22, 1981.

3. Gale, E. N., & Ayer, W. A. *Treatment of dental fears by reciprocal inhibition.* Paper presented at the meeting of the International Association for Dental Research, Washington, D.C., March 1969.

4. Ayer, W. A., & Gale, E. N. *Treatment of dental fears by reciprocal inhibition.* Invited presentation to the 110th annual session of the American Dental Association Council on Dental Research, New York, October 1969.

5. Berggren, U., & Carlsson, S. G., University of Goteborg, Sweden. Personal communication, October 1981.

REFERENCES

Auerbach, S. M., Kendall, P. C., Cuttler, H. F., & Levitt, N. R. Anxiety, locus of control, type of preparatory information, and adjustment to dental surgery. *Journal of Consulting and Clinical Psychology,* 1976, **44,** 809–818.

Baldwin, D. C. An investigation of psychological and behavioral responses to dental extraction in children. *Journal of Dental Research,* 1966, **45,** 1637–1651.

Bernstein, D. A., Kleinknecht, R. A., & Alexander, L. D. Antecedents of dental fear. *Journal of Public Health Dentistry,* 1979, **39,** 113–124.

Carlsson, S. G., Linde, A., & Öhman, A. Reduction of tension in fearful dental patients. *Journal of the American Dental Association,* 1980, **101,** 638–641.

Corah, N. L., Gale, E. N., & Illig, S. J. Assessment of a dental anxiety scale. *Journal of the American Dental Association,* 1978, **97,** 816–819.

Corah, N. L., Gale, E. N., & Illig, S. J. Psychological stress reduction during dental procedures. *Journal of Dental Research,* 1979, **58,** 1347–1351. (a)

Corah, N. L., Gale, E. N., & Illig, S. J. Use of relaxation and distraction to reduce psychological stress. *Journal of the American Dental Association,* 1979, **98,** 390–394. (b)

Corah, N. L., Gale, E. N., Pace, L. F., & Seyrek, S. K. Evaluation of content and vocal style in relaxation instructions. *Behaviour Research and Therapy,* 1981, **19,** 458–460. (a)

Corah, N. L., Gale, E. N., Pace, L. F., & Seyrek, S. K. Relaxation and musical programming as means of reducing psychological stress during dental procedures. *Journal of the American Dental Association,* 1981, **103,** 232–234. (b)

Forgione, A. G., & Clark, R. E. Comments on an empirical study of the cause of dental fears. *Journal of Dental Research,* 1974, **53,** 496.

Friedson, E., & Feldman, J. J. Public looks at dental care. *Journal of the American Dental Association,* 1958, **57,** 325–335.

Gale, E. N., & Ayer, W. A. Treatment of dental fears (phobias). *Journal of the American Dental Association,* 1969, **78,** 1304–1307.

Gale, E. N., Hyman, E., & Ayer, W. A. Physiological measures during systematic desensitization: A report of two cases. *Journal of Clinical Psychology,* 1970, **26,** 247–250.

Herbertt, R. M., & Innes, J. M. Familiarization and preparatory information in the reduction of anxiety in child dental patients. *Journal of Dentistry for Children,* 1979, **46,** 319–323.

Jacobson, E. *Progressive relaxation.* Chicago: University of Chicago Press, 1929.

Kleinknecht, R. A., & Bernstein, D. A. The assessment of dental fear. *Behavior Therapy,* 1978, **9,** 626–634.

Kleinknecht, R. A., & Bernstein, D. A. Short term treatment of dental avoidance. *Journal of Behavioral Therapy and Experimental Psychiatry,* 1979, **10,** 311–315.

Klepac, R. K. Successful treatment of avoidance of dentistry by desensitization or by increasing pain tolerance. *Journal of Behavioral Therapy and Experimental Psychiatry,* 1975, **6,** 307–310.

Klepac, R. K., Dowling, J., Hauge, G., & McDonald, M. Direct and generalized effects of three components of stress inoculation for increased pain tolerance. *Behavior Therapy,* 1981, **12,** 417–424.

Machen, J. B., & Johnson, R. Desensitization, model learning, and the dental behavior of children. *Journal of Dental Research,* 1974, **53,** 83–87.

Melamed, B. G., Hawes, R., Heiby, E., & Glick, J. Use of filmed modeling to reduce uncooperative behavior of children during dental treatment. *Journal of Dental Research,* 1975, **54,** 797–801.

Melamed, B. G., Weinstein, D., Hawes, R., & Katin-Borland, M. Reduction of fear-related dental managment problems with use of filmed modeling. *Journal of the American Dental Association,* 1975, **90,** 822–826. (b)

Melamed, B. G., Yurcheson, R., Fleece, E. L., Hutcherson, S., & Hawes, R. Effects of modeling on the reduction of anxiety-related behaviors in individuals varying in level of previous experience in the stress situation. *Journal of Consulting and Clinical Psychology,* 1978, **46,** 1357–1367.

Moen, B. D. Family dental survey: II. Frequency of visits to the dentist; annual dental bill. *Journal of the American Dental Association,* 1954, **48,** 74–77.

Shoben, E. J., & Borland, L. An empirical study of the etiology of dental fears. *Journal of Clinical Psychology,* 1954, **10,** 171–174.

Siegel, L. J., & Peterson, L. Stress reduction in young dental patients through coping skills and sensory information. *Journal of Consulting and Clinical Psychology,* 1980, **48,** 785–787.

Siegel, L. J., & Peterson, L. Maintenance effects of coping skills and sensory information on young children's response to repeated dental procedures. *Behavior Therapy,* 1981, **12,** 530–535.

Venham, L., & Quatrocelli, S. The young child's response to repeated dental procedures. *Journal of Dental Research,* 1977, **56,** 734–738.

Weinstein, P., Getz, T., Ratener, P., & Domoto, P. Dentists' responses to fear-nonfear-related behaviors in children. *Journal of the American Dental Association,* 1982, **104,** 38–40. (a)

Weinstein, P., Getz, T., Ratener, P., & Domoto, P. The effect of dentists on fear-related behaviors in children. *Journal of the American Dental Association,* 1982, **104,** 32–38. (b)

Wolpe, J. Behavior therapy in complex neurotic states. *British Journal of Psychiatry,* 1964, **110,** 28–34.

Wroblewski, P., Jacob, T., & Rehm, L. The contribution of relaxation to symbolic modelling in the modification of dental fears. *Behavior Research and Therapy,* 1977, **15,** 113–117.

CHAPTER 61

PSYCHOSOCIAL ASPECTS OF MALOCCLUSION

JUDITH E. ALBINO

State University of New York at Buffalo

Malocclusion is impairment of the anatomical relations and functioning of the teeth and adjacent craniofacial structures. Even when more severe congenital anomalies, such as cleft lip and cleft palate, are excluded, occlusal malrelations can result in difficulties of speech, swallowing, or mastication; chronic pain; and increased vulnerability to dental caries and periodontal disease. Such problems are rare, however, and for most persons with malocclusion the most salient effects of the condition are esthetic. Although, by conservative estimates, 70% to 75% of the population have some deviation from normal occlusion (Jago, 1974; Kelly & Harvey, 1977), about 80% of those who seek treatment do so for cosmetic reasons (Rosenberg, Note 1). This suggests, of course, that the impact of malocclusion is primarily psychosocial, reflecting attempts to adjust to and cope with impaired appearance. Moreover, there is general agreement among dental and orthodontic professionals that decisions about intercepting or correcting occlusal malrelations should involve consideration of the psychosocial as well as physical effects of the particular malocclusion.

As this discussion may already suggest, issues of behavioral health or primary prevention take on a unique meaning with respect to malocclusion. The variety of physical conditions represented by the term *malocclusion* simply are not preventable in a true sense. The prevention of rampant caries and periodontal disease can minimize the loss of teeth and thereby prevent certain malrelations of occlusion in susceptible individuals, and the prevention of some severe congenital defects might be approached through genetic counseling. For the broad range of frequently occurring deviations from normal occlusion, however, neither of these approaches is relevant. When we speak of behavioral health in relation to malocclusion, therefore, we are concerned primarily with appropriate decisions regarding orthodontic treatment, a procedure that often is essentially cosmetic in its results. It is important to recognize, also, that the decision to obtain treatment is complicated by factors unrelated to the occlusion of the potential orthodontic patient. Treatment is expensive; it is virtually unavailable to the medically indigent and usually is not included in insurance plans. In addition, treatment still is most frequently and appropriately begun during adolescence, a time characterized by disturbed self-image and overreaction to matters of personal appearance. In most cases, parents, rather than their adolescent children, make the final decision about obtaining expensive and probably elective orthodontic treatment. Finally, cultural and societal standards may differentially affect perceptions of malocclusion and the need for its correction.

With respect to behavioral health, then, two questions seem to be crucial in gaining an understanding of the psychosocial aspects of malocclusion: (a) what effects does malocclusion has on psychosocial functioning? and (b) who suffers from these effects and how can individual risk for these problems be assessed? Although answers to these questions are incomplete, research findings have provided substantial information and some highly promising directions.

EFFECTS OF MALOCCLUSION ON PSYCHOSOCIAL FUNCTIONING

The idea that unattractive dental-facial appearance has debilitating social and psychological consequences is widely accepted. There is considerable evidence in the social-psychological literature that general physical attractiveness is related to interpersonal popularity and to others' favorable evaluations of personality, social behaviors, quantity and quality of social interactions, and intellectual expression (Barocas & Daroly, 1972; Berscheid, Dion, Walster, & Walster, 1971; Berscheid & Walster, 1974; Dion, 1972; Dion, Berscheid, & Walster, 1972; Goldman & Lewis, 1977; Reis, Nezlek, & Wheeler, 1980). In his developmental approach to the social psychology of appearance, Adams (1977) extended such findings to predict the responses of attractive and unattractive individuals in social situations. He described four assumptions about the association of inner behavioral processes and outer appearance, which are supported by studies on physical attractiveness such as those already cited:

1. Individuals have differing expectations of attractive and unattractive others.
2. Physically attractive persons more frequently are recipients of positive social exchanges.
3. As a result of different degrees of social exchange, physically attractive and unattractive persons are likely to develop differing social images, self-expectations, and personality styles.
4. As a result of greater degrees of positive social interaction, physically attractive persons are likely to maintain confident interpersonal behavior.

The research on responses to disfiguring handicaps other than malocclusion appears to fit Adams's explanation in at least some respects. Children with repaired cleft lip and palate, as well as those with mild orthopedic impairments or cerebral palsy, have been reported to avoid social behaviors that require responsiveness from others in order to minimize teasing, harassment, or disappointment from inadequate social exchange (Harper & Richman, 1978; Richman & Harper, 1978, 1979). When compared to normal control subjects, children with cleft palate and lip were reported to be less academically successful (Brantley & Clifford, 1979b; Kapp, 1979; Richman & Harper, 1978); to feel less accepted by their parents (Brantley & Clifford, 1979a, 1979b); to be more dissatisfied with their physical appearance (Kapp, 1979); to be more external on locus of control (Brantley & Clifford, 1979b); and to display greater inhibition of impulse (Richman, 1978; Starr, 1978). Measures of self-esteem and self-concept of children with cleft palate and lip in these studies were not significantly different, however, from same-age children without these impairments (Brantley & Clifford, 1979a; Kapp, 1979; Starr, 1978).

In addressing the relationship between malocclusion and social functioning, Rosenberg (Note 1) has argued that cultural or social standards of appearance determine self-concept. Only as we develop ideas about how others perceive us do we adopt consistent views of ourselves and our roles in relation to others. Thus, if one is perceived as unattractive by others because of occlusal malrelations, this view is incorporated into one's self-concept. One then behaves, presumably, as one expects an unattractive person to behave. This view is largely compatible with Adams's (1977) theory of physical attractiveness, particularly in Rosenberg's emphasis on the function of social participation in determining psychological response. Rosenberg further suggested that orthodontic treatment offers a clear way of minimizing the potentially negative effects of occlusal appearance on both self-image and social functioning.

Macgregor's (1951, 1970) work on the effects of facial deformity also began with a view of self-concept as emerging from interactions with others. She suggested, however, that individuals with milder forms of facial disfigurement, such as malocclusion, probably suffer more psychological distress than do individuals with greater deformity. She reasoned that the responses to visible occlusal malrelations are inconsistent and unpredictable, ranging from no response at all to overt ridicule. As a result, the affected individual maintains a constant state of anxiety in social interactions and yet does not have the well-developed protective mechanisms that are usually acquired by those with more severe, visible defects. Macgregor's proposition remains untested, however, and there is only scattered evidence in the research literature for either negative social consequences of malocclusion or positive consequences of its treatment.

The research literature does show clearly that, when other features of appearance are held constant, normal occlusion is perceived as more attractive than malocclusion. This conclusion is based on a number of studies involving various procedures for evaluating the attractiveness of mouths. Most of these studies have used photographs or drawings that are altered to show the effects of various types of dental-facial malrelations (Cohen & Horowitz, 1970; Jenny, Cons, Kohout, & Frazier, 1980; Lucker, Graber, & Pietromonaco, 1981; Prahl-Andersen, 1978; Shaw, 1981; Albino, Note 2). Gochman (1972, 1975) even found that some children preferred straight, evenly spaced teeth with noticeable carious lesions to healthy but poorly aligned and crowded dentition. His studies involving 774 schoolchildren were focused on assessing the relative salience of health and appearance motives. Whereas inner-city children under age 12 chose pictures of healthy teeth more frequently, those over 12 and those not living in the inner city generally viewed appearance of the dentition as more important than health of the teeth, or absence of caries. Across all subjects, only 20% clearly preferred noncarious but crowded teeth to straighter but less healthy dentition.

In a British study of social response to dental-facial appearance, Shaw (1981) used standard photographs of children that were altered to depict either normal occlusion or impaired dental-facial relations of four types. He found that both child and adult raters judged the photographed children with normal dental-facial arrangements to be more attractive, more desirable as friends, more intelligent, and less inclined to aggression than those with prominent incisors, a missing lateral incisor, crowded incisors, or a unilateral cleft lip. Judges in the study were 840 children aged 11 to 13 and 840 men and women aged 20 to 65. When background facial attractiveness was also varied, the more attractive face was always preferred to the less attractive face, regardless of occlusal characteristics. The results indicated that although general attractiveness of the face may be more salient than dental appearance per se, visible aspects of occlusion nevertheless represent a feature that significantly affects assessment of appearance. This is consistent with Lucker, Graber, and Pietromonaco's (1981) explanation of malocclusions as detectable "signals" that affect facial esthetics.

Shaw, Meek, and Jones (1980) reported data indicating that young children with malocclusion are the recipients of teasing, harassment, and unflattering nicknames related to problems of occlusion and dental-facial appearance. These data were derived from confidential interviews with 531 schoolchildren aged 9 to 13 years. Teeth represented the fourth most common target of such teasing, after height, weight, and hair. It is interesting that teasing about the teeth resulted in stronger feelings of upset and a sense of being harassed significantly more often than did other types of teasing. Although only 7% of the total sample reported such teasing, the data certainly suggest that unattractive occlusal appearance can result in negative social interactions.

In a survey research study reported by Linn (1966), only 15% of respondents indicated that dental-facial appearance was not important in the social situations described to them. Dating among young people was the situation for which dental-facial appearance was perceived as most important. Subjects in a study conducted by Samuels and Proshek (1973) reported dental-facial appearance to be especially important in occupations that they had ranked as higher in prestige or visibility.

The effects of malocclusion on psychosocial functioning can also be inferred from studies that examine changes in self-image or other personality constructs as a result of orthodontic treatment. Rutzen (1973) administered personality measures to 250 persons 5 years after completion of orthodontic treatment and compared their responses to those of 67 individuals whose diagnosed malocclusions had not been treated. The treated persons reported significantly more positive assessments of their appearance, more often mentioned oral features as their most attractive characteristics, and had lower levels of anxiety. They did not obtain higher scores on an assessment of self-esteem or on measures of extraversion or neuroticism, however. Using occupational rankings developed by Hollingshead, Rutzen found that those in the treatment group had achieved a slightly but significantly higher level of occupational status, although they did not differ on social class or educational level. Unfortunately, Rutzen's work did not provide for pretreatment measures, and it was impossible to determine whether the effects identified were actually due to treatment or merely resulted from sample differences.

More recently, Dennington and Korabik (1977) found positive changes on Tennessee Self-Concept Scale scores for a group of 77 patients measured before treatment and 7 months after being fitted with orthodontic bands. They had no control group, however, nor have follow-up data been reported that would provide an assessment of the durability of such changes. Klima, Wittemann, and McIver (1979), however, found no significant differences between orthodontic patients in retention, prospective patients, and nonpatients on measures of body image or self-concept. Their study appears somewhat limited by the absence of control for objectively evaluated dental-facial appearance or for other variables that might mediate results.

To summarize the available evidence for the existence of psychosocial responses to malocclusion, it is clear that normal occlusion generally is perceived as more attractive than dental-facial malrelations and that there is probably some negative social feedback associated with highly visible and less attractive forms of dental-facial malrelations. For some persons, this negative feedback may eventually translate into psychological and behavioral responses, including withdrawal, isolation, and even depression.

The complexity of the issue increases, however, when we acknowledge frequent observations that the objective degree of esthetic impairment is not directly related to subjective perceptions of malocclusion (Jenny, 1975; Lewit & Virolainen, 1968; Secord & Backman, 1959; Shaw, 1981; Stricker, Clifford, Cohen, Giddon, Meskin, & Evans, 1979; Albino, Note 3). This is particularly important to a consideration of psychosocial functioning, since only a person who perceives a deficit—whether real or imagined—will respond behaviorally to that problem.

THE ROLE OF SELF-PERCEPTION

Among the more recent studies relating subjectively perceived and objective assessments of dental-facial attractiveness is Shaw's (1981) report indicating that the majority of 200 children tested could neither identify photographs of their own teeth and jaws nor accurately describe their anterior occlusal features. The same was true for a randomly selected subsample of mothers of 50 of these children. Graber and Lucker (1980), however, received fairly accurate evaluations by 481 children aged 10 to 13 who were asked to assess the "straightness" of their teeth. These same children demonstrated a distinctly positive bias when asked to assess their level of satisfaction with the appearance of their teeth, however.

Pitt and Korabik (1977) suggested that perceptions of dental-facial attractiveness are determined by self-satisfaction rather than by objective appearance. They found, among a group of subjects who could not identify their own profiles, that those with high self-esteem judged their profiles to be closer to the ideal than they actually were, while those with low self-esteem judged their profiles to be further from the ideal than they actually were.

Albino and Tedesco (Note 4) found that 113 eighth- and ninth-grade children who were not seeking orthodontic treatment had significantly more positive perceptions of their own occlusal attractiveness than did 50 children who were seeking treatment. In this study, potential effects of the objective degree of malocclusion were controlled statistically. In another study, Albino, Cunat, Fox, Lewis, Slakter, and Tedesco (1981) applied discriminant analysis techniques to distinguish between subjects seeking or not seeking orthodontic treatment on the basis of 10 dental-related and 12 personality, or psychosocial, variables. In addition to the objective measures of malocclusion and dental-facial attractiveness, assessments of a child's self-perception of dental-facial appearance and his or her concern about occlusion and wish for treatment were measures that contributed substantially to a significant discriminant function. These analyses also indicated that groups choosing or not choosing treatment achieved significantly different scores on measures of need for affiliation with parents or peers and need to avoid harm. Neither these nor other personality variables contributed, however, to the discrimination provided by measures directly related to occlusion and appearance.

Although the foregoing discussion may seem to suggest that determining who needs orthodontic treatment is simply a matter of identifying those who perceive their teeth and occlusion as unattractive, there are clearly difficulties with such an approach. Dissatisfaction with the teeth may represent displaced concerns about the self that are unrelated to malocclusion. This phenomenon has been documented in studies of patient response to facial surgery.

In a recent study of 74 patients who had undergone orthognathic surgery as a part of orthodontic treatment, Kiyak, West, Hohl, and McNeill (1982) reported a decline in adaptation 9 months after surgery. This effect followed increases in adaptation at 1 to 2 days, at 3 weeks, and at 4 months postsurgically. The decline occurred for mean scores on the Tennessee Self-Concept Scale and for scores on a facial image scale, although scores on a chin image scale showed improved satisfaction with that particular aspect of facial appearance. Kiyak suggested that by 9 months after surgery, patients could no longer avoid confrontation with any unrealistic expectations they might have had. The fact that facial self-image scores at the 9-month assessment were even lower than presurgical measures suggested that patients were simply transferring a generally negative self-evaluation from one focal point on the face to another.

No data are available that document similar responses to orthodontic treatment that does not involve surgery. Although conventional orthodontics involves more gradual changes, which may allow the individual to adapt with greater ease to changing dental-facial features, there nevertheless is a "moment of truth" when orthodontic bands are finally removed and the result must be faced. It is certainly possible, therefore, that a pattern of responses such as that reported by Kiyak et al. (1982) could occur in orthodontic treatment, with shifts in focus from the alignment of the teeth to other facial features.

As data from a variety of studies are considered, it becomes increasingly clear that what is most important in terms of psychosocial response to malocclusion is not the absolute degree of disfigurement that results from malocclusion but rather how the individual perceives and evaluates the esthetic effects of these dental-facial problems. The construct of greatest interest, then, is self-evaluation of appearance. Self-evaluation can only be accomplished with reference to internalized standards, however; that is, the individual perceives his or her dental-facial characteristics as generally more or less attractive than those perceived in referent others. Social and cultural standards are important here, as are age-peer standards, which are particularly relevant for adolescents, who are extremely peer-oriented in their values.

THE INFLUENCE OF SIGNIFICANT OTHERS

The evidence for peer pressure in the form of teasing and harassment has already been discussed. In considering social influence on the adolescent as he or she is involved in evaluating malocclusion and making a decision about seeking treatment, the role of parents and their attitudes must also be considered. Linn's (1966) research indicated that parents generally consider the dental appearance of their children to be highly important, although their reasons vary. Based on responses to a questionnaire completed by 250 orthodontic patients and their families, Baldwin and Barnes (1965, 1966) suggested that the decision to seek treatment for malocclusion reflects such maternal factors as achievement need, social aspirations, disturbed self-image, identification with the child's malocclusion, and displacement of unresolved family problems. They pointed out that these complex motivational patterns vary in degree and that degree determines whether the decision to seek care for the child is constructive and results in cooperation or is destructive and results in resistance.

Lewit and Virolainen (1968) have reported the only notable attempt to test a complex model of social factors in the perception of malocclusion and need for treatment. They hypothesized a need-press model in which pressures from three sources—parental, peer, and inner-personal—would function additively to predict whether 129 eighth-grade subjects would seek orthodontic treatment. Results indicated that for middle-class adolescents, desire for orthodontic treatment was related to parental pressures when dependency needs were high. When dependency needs were low, however, peer pressures were more likely to be decisive for those with high need for peer approval, whereas objective orthodontic standards most influenced those with low need for peer approval. For independent working-class children, this pattern was not identified, and there was also a generally lower level of conformity to parental standards. Although the study provides an interesting evaluation of several variables that appear to influence the desire for orthodontic treatment, its usefulness is limited by the criterion measures, which were self-reports of intention rather than the actual behavior of seeking orthodontic treatment.

Correlational data reported by Albino (Note 2) also offer substantial support for the general idea that parents' attitudes and values have considerable influence on the decision to seek orthodontic treatment and on a child's evaluation of his or her dental-facial attractiveness. The correlation matrix presented in Table 61.1 summarizes some of the data collected for 151 adolescents. Fifty-one of these subjects were seeking orthodontic treatment through a program funded by New York state. The remainder were a comparison group of age peers who were not seeking treatment, randomly selected from school rosters, and roughly equivalent to the treatment subsample on such variables as race, residence, and socioeconomic status.

The first of the nine variables, Treatment or No Treatment, represents the decision to seek or not seek orthodontic treatment. The correlations of other measures with this categorical variable, therefore, are equivalent to significant mean differences for the two subsamples on each of those measures. The second measure is the Treatment Priority Index (TPI), a standardized index of malocclusion that provides an objective measure of the severity of malocclusion (Grainger, 1967). The Child's Dental-Facial Attractiveness score (Albino, Note 2) is based on attractiveness evaluations of photographs of the subjects' teeth and jaws made by peer raters who had no dental training. The measure utilizes standard photographs, or examples, selected systematically by a second group of raters to anchor the five points on the scale. The measures of Child's Self-Perception of Occlusion and Mother's and Father's Perception of Child's Occlusion involve the rank-ordering for attractiveness of a set of eight line drawings depicting the same child with normal occlusion or with one of eight common types of malocclusion. After all pictures are rank-ordered, the child picks a picture that looks most like him or her, and the parent selects a picture that looks most like the target child. The rank-order score originally assigned to that picture represents the score for self-perception or perception of the child. Finally, the scores on Mother's and Father's Wish and Concern for Treatment reflect responses to a questionnaire that directly addresses issues related to malocclusions and orthodontic treatment.

In examining the pattern of correlations, it should first be noted that all of the correlations are statistically significant at the .05 level. It is especially interesting that mothers' perceptions

Table 61.1 Intercorrelations of Nine Key Variables

Variables	(1)	(2)	(3)	(4)	(5)	(6)	(7)	(8)
(1) Treatment or No Treatment								
(2) Child's Malocclusion (TPI) Score	.57							
(3) Child's Dental-Facial Attractiveness	.44	.47						
(4) Child's Self-Perception of Occlusion	.42	.31	.38					
(5) Child's Wish and Concern for Treatment	.37	.32	.33	.45				
(6) Mother's Perception of Child's Occlusion	.53	.53	.55	.61	.48			
(7) Father's Perception of Child's Occlusion	.32	.35	.48	.45	.39	.43		
(8) Mother's Wish and Concern for Treatment	.51	.49	.40	.33	.37	.48	.34	
(9) Father's Wish and Concern for Treatment	.48	.47	.36	.27	.50	.41	.45	.50

of their children's appearance and their attitudes toward treatment are related to the decision to seek treatment at higher levels than either the child's self-perception scores or the dental-facial attractiveness scores. Mothers' perceptions are also very strongly related to both the child's dental-facial attractiveness and the child's self-perceptions. Although this might suggest that mothers are particularly influential in shaping attitudes and decisions related to orthodontic treatment, it should be noted that the patterns for mothers and fathers are actually quite similar. The lower correlations for fathers may be related to the smaller sample size, since only 111 fathers participated, whereas the mothers of all 151 children were involved. These data are merely descriptive, of course, and are limited to some extent by sampling procedures. Experimental work is needed to adequately identify the actual effects of the variables on children's perceptions of their occlusion and on their decisions to seek treatment.

Finally, in viewing negative self-perception as a primary psychosocial effect of malocclusion, some attention should be given to the potential stability and relative salience of the attitudes and self-images of adolescents or others contemplating orthodontic treatment for the correction of dental-facial malrelations. Negative perceptions of one's dental-facial appearance will not have great impact on psychosocial functioning, nor will the correction of perceived defects, if these problems do not represent relatively strong and clearly focused concerns with some basis in objective assessments, rather than mere reflections of general self-dissatisfaction.

IDENTIFYING THE POPULATION AT RISK

The earlier sections of this chapter lead quite naturally to our second question: Who is most likely to suffer from the psychosocial effects of malocclusion? We might put this somewhat differently: Who is most likely to reap psychosocial benefits—perhaps in addition to benefits that reflect improved physical functioning—from orthodontic treatment? In the dental and orthodontic literature, these questions have been approached most frequently as measurement issues. It may be useful, therefore, to review briefly some of the approaches that have been employed in assessing the need for treatment.

Helm (1977) provided a cogent statement of assessment needs related to malocclusion. Although his approach is from a public health and epidemiologic perspective, the critical issues are also highly applicable to the consideration of individual need for treatment. He perceives the primary problem of assessing treatment need as the gap between the identification of individual morphological traits and the establishment of criteria based on these traits that would reflect treatment need. Since the publication of Angle's classification of occlusal traits in 1970, Helm points out, orthodontists have been developing and refining approaches to measuring these characteristics. Nevertheless, there remains a major discrepancy between such classifications, which are merely descriptors, and the experienced need for treatment.

Prahl-Andersen (1978) has attributed these assessment problems, in part, to the lack of a true normative concept in professional diagnoses of malocclusion. Instead of a norm, orthodontics tends to rely on the concept of ideal occlusion, with malocclusion identified as any deviation from that morphological ideal. The problem with this approach is that there is no evidence that ideal occlusion is actually associated with significantly better dental health, in terms of caries and periodontal disease or in terms of better oral functioning. Furthermore, to return to the original theme of this chapter, there certainly is no clear-cut evidence that individuals with ideal occlusion, as a group, have better psychological health, better social functioning, or even more positive self-images than do those with occlusal characteristics that deviate from the ideal.

Need for treatment, therefore, cannot be equated with deviations from ideal occlusion. Furthermore, it is apparent that social standards, which are so important in evaluating dental-facial appearance, may allow a wide range of different occlusal arrangements.

A number of standardized indices for the assessment of malocclusion have included attempts to consider the effects of occlusal variation on esthetics by weighting more heavily those features that seem to affect appearance. These have included the Draker Labiolingual Deviations Index (Draker, 1960), the Grainger Treatment Priority Index (Grainger, 1967), Salzmann's AAO Handicapping Malocclusion Assessment Record (Salzmann, 1971), Summers' Occlusal Index (Summers, 1971), and the Eastman Esthetic Index (Howitt, Stricker & Henderson, 1967). Despite such efforts, standardized measures continue to be perceived as inadequate because of their lack of grounding in socially defined esthetic standards.

The validity and reliability of standardized measures of malocclusion have been discussed in detail by Carlos (1970), Katz (1978), Helm (1977), and others. The discussion will not be reopened here except to add that there is also evidence suggesting that scores on the Treatment Priority Index, and perhaps on other indices, do overlap to some degree with judgments focused on esthetics. In a study of clinical assessments of malocclusion, Lewis, Albino, Cunat, and Tedesco (1982) found judgments of the need for treatment to be more strongly correlated with judgments of dental-facial attractiveness than with judgments of the impact on dental health and function. The correlations between Treatment Priority Index scores and Child's Dental-Facial Attractiveness scores presented in Table 61.1 suggest that TPI scores overlap considerably with both peer evaluations of appearance and self-evaluations of occlusal appearance. Because the standardized measures are tied conceptually to morphological ideals, however, they do have special utility for describing both population characteristics and treatment requirements. For these reasons, too, any attempt to evaluate treatment need should probably include one of the objective indices of malocclusion. Clearly, what is *not* needed at this point—as has already been pointed out by Albino (Note 3), Carlos (1970), Helm (1977), and Jenny et al. (1980)—is another standardized measure of the severity of malocclusion. Rather, the relationships between available measures and other types of assessment need to be established.

The recent work of Albino and her colleagues (Tedesco, Albino, Cunat, Green, Lewis, & Slakter, 1982; Tedesco, Albino, Cunat, Slakter, & Waltz, 1982; Albino Note 2) and of Jenny and Cons and their colleagues (Jenny et al., 1980; Jenny, Cons, & Kohout, 1982; Cons, Jenny, Freer, Eismann, & Kohout, Note 5) represent a step in this direction. Both groups have developed measures of dental-facial attractiveness that reflect social standards, and they have documented the correlations of these measures with indices of the severity of malocclusion.

In addition to the use of objective measures of the severity of occlusal malrelations and their impact on appearance, attempts to identify individuals at risk for psychosocial problems related to malocclusion should include at least two other types of assessment. The first of these would be some assessment of self-perception of occlusion. Although the picture-ranking technique developed by Albino (Note 2) and described earlier in this chapter represents one approach, it is possible that a technique such as that of Kiyak and her colleagues (1982), combining general and feature-specific assessments of facial self-image, might be more appropriate.

Finally, some assessment is advisable of the social presses and relative concerns of the individual that are directly related to malocclusion and its treatment. The Orthodontic Attitude Survey (Fox, Albino, Green, Farr, & Tedesco, 1982; Albino, Note 2) is one such instrument. It is based, in part, on an earlier measure developed by Lewit and Virolainen (1968) and a critical incident technique described by Linn (1966). This 24-item questionnaire includes five factors presented as subscales, each related to specific aspects in the consideration of malocclusion and its treatment. The subscales are the measures of Wish and Concern for Treatment listed in Table 61.1 and subscales titled Positive Aspects of Treatment, Relative Value of Orthodontic Treatment, and General Importance of Occlusion. A straightforward questionnaire technique such as this also has the advantage of ease in administration and can be used to indicate the consistency of attitudes and motives over time.

In summary, orthodontic treatment for correction of the broad range of normally occurring malocclusions will have its greatest impact on dental-facial esthetics, rather than on health or function. For most individuals, then, the psychosocial impact of malocclusion should be a major factor in the decision to obtain treatment. Although data are sparse, a synthesis of available research suggests that measures of the social acceptability of dental-facial appearance, self-perception of appearance, and strength of social and personal presses will be the most useful adjuncts to professional evaluation of severity of malocclusion.

Although the state of the art does not yet provide sophisticated techniques for predictive combination of the various measures recommended here, a sound understanding of the psychosocial dynamics reflected by these measures can adequately guide their use in decisions regarding orthodontic treatment.

REFERENCE NOTES

1. Rosenberg, M. *Malocclusion and craniofacial malformation: Self-concept implications.* Paper presented at the Workshop on Psychological Aspects of Craniofacial Malformation, Hilton Head, S.C., 1974.

2. Albino, J. E. *Development of methodologies for behavioral measurements related to malocclusion: Final report.* State University of New York at Buffalo and National Institute of Dental Research, Bethesda, Md., 1981.

3. Albino, J. E. Facial esthetics and behavior: Historical review and new directions. In *Chronicle of the 58th IADR General Session.* Osaka, Japan: International Association for Dental Research, 1980.

4. Albino, J. E., & Tedesco, L. A. *Adolescents' self-perceptions of dental-facial appearance and orthodontic treatment.* Paper presented at the annual meeting of the American Psychological Association, Los Angeles, 1981.

5. Cons, N. C., Jenny, J., Freer, T. J., Eismann, D., & Kohout, F. *Perceptions of occlusal conditions in Australia, the German Democratic Republic and the United States of America.* Manuscript submitted for publication, 1982.

REFERENCES

Adams, G. R. Physical attractiveness research: Toward a developmental psychology of beauty. *Human Development,* 1977, **20,** 217–239.

Albino, J. E., Cunat, J. J., Fox, R. A., Lewis, E. A., Slakter, M. J., & Tedesco, L. A. Variables discriminating individuals who seek orthodontic treatment. *Journal of Dental Research,* 1981, **60,** 1661–1667.

Baldwin, D. C., & Barnes, M. L. Psychosocial factors motivating orthodontic treatment. *IADR Abstracts,* 1965, No. 153.

Baldwin, D. C., & Barnes, M. L. Patterns of motivation in families seeking orthodontic treatment. *IADR Abstracts,* 1966, No. 142.

Barocas, R., & Daroly, P. Effects of physical appearance on social responsiveness. *Psychological Reports,* 1972, **31,** 495–500.

Berscheid, E., Dion, K. K., Walster, E., & Walster, G. W. Physical attractiveness and dating choice: A test of the matching hypothesis. *Journal of Experimental Social Psychology,* 1971, **7,** 173–189.

Berscheid, E., & Walster, E. Physical attractiveness. In L. Berkowitz (Ed.), *Advances in experimental social psychology* (Vol. 7). New York: Academic Press, 1974.

Brantley, H. T., & Clifford, E. Cognitive, self-concept and body image measures of normal, cleft palate and obese adolescents. *Cleft Palate Journal,* 1979, **16,** 177–182. (a)

Brantley, H. T., & Clifford, E. Maternal and child locus of control and field-dependence in cleft palate children. *Cleft Palate Journal,* 1979, **16,** 183–187. (b)

Carlos, J. P. Evaluation of indices of malocclusion. *International Dental Journal,* 1970, **20,** 606–617.

Cohen, L. K., & Horowitz, H. S. Occlusal relations in children born and reared in an optimally flouridated community: III. Social-psychological findings. *Angle Orthodontist,* 1970, **40,** 159–169.

Dennington, R. J., & Korabik, K. Self-concept changes in orthodontic patients during initial treatment. *American Journal of Orthodontics,* 1977, **72,** 461–466.

Dion, K. K. Physical attractiveness and evaluations of children's transgressions. *Journal of Personality and Social Psychology,* 1972, **24,** 207–213.

Dion, K. K., Berscheid, E., & Walster, E. What is beautiful is good. *Journal of Personality and Social Psychology,* 1972, **24,** 285–290.

Draker, H. L. Handicapping labiolingual deviations: A proposed index for public health purposes. *American Journal of Orthodontics,* 1960, **46,** 295–305.

Fox, R. N., Albino, J. E., Green, L. J., Farr, S. D., & Tedesco, L. A. Development and validation of a measure of attitudes towards malocclusion. *Journal of Dental Research,* 1982, **61,** 1039–1043.

Gochman, D. S. The organizing role of motivation in health beliefs and intentions. *Journal of Health and Social Behavior,* 1972, **13,** 285–293.

Gochman, D. S. The measurement and development of dentally relevant motives. *Journal of Public Health Dentistry,* 1975, **35,** 160–164.

Goldman, W., & Lewis, P. Beautiful is good: Evidence that the physically attractive are more socially skillful. *Journal of Experimental Social Psychology,* 1977, **13,** 125–130.

Graber, L. W., & Lucker, G. W. Dental esthetic self-evaluation and satisfaction. *American Journal of Orthodontics,* 1980, **77,** 163–173.

Grainger, R. M. *Orthodontic Treatment Priority Index.* Public Health Service Pub. No. 1000, Series 2, No. 25. Washington, D.C.: U.S. Government Printing Office, 1967.

Harper, D. C., & Richman, L. C. Personality profiles of physically impaired adolescents. *Journal of Clinical Psychology,* 1978, **34,** 636–642.

Helm, S. Epidemiology and public health aspects of malocclusion. *Journal of Dental Research,* 1977, **56,** C27–C31.

Howitt, J. W., Stricker, G., & Henderson, R. Eastman Esthetic Index. *New York Dental Journal,* 1967, **33,** 215–220.

Jago, J. D. The epidemiology of dental occlusion: A critical appraisal. *Journal of Public Health Dentistry,* 1974, **34,** 80–93.

Jenny, J. A social perspective on need and demand for orthodontic treatment. *International Dental Journal,* 1975, **25,** 248–256.

Jenny, J., Cons, N. C., & Kohout, F. Assessing severity of malocclusions and need for treatment: Comparisons of SASOC, OJ, TPI, HLD, and Orthodontist Judgment. *IADR Abstracts,* 1982, No. 1324.

Jenny, J., Cons, N. C., Kohout, F., & Frazier, P. J. Test of a method to determine socially acceptable occlusal conditions. *Community Dentistry and Oral Epidemiology,* 1980, **8,** 424–433.

Kapp, K. Self-concept of the cleft lip and/or palate child. *Cleft Palate Journal,* 1979, **16,** 171–176.

Katz, R. V. Relationships between eight orthodontic indices and an oral self-image satisfaction scale. *American Journal of Orthodontics,* 1978, **73,** 328–334.

Kelly, J. E., & Harvey, C. R. *An assessment of the occlusion of the teeth of youths 12–17 years.* Vital and Health Statistics: Series 11, No. 162, DHEW Pub. No. (HRA) 77–1644. Washington, D.C.: U.S. Government Printing Office, 1977.

Kiyak, H. A., West, R. A., Hohl, T., & McNeill, R. W. The psychological impact of orthognathic surgery: A 9-month follow-up. *American Journal of Orthodontics,* 1982, **81,** 404–411.

Klima, R. J., Wittemann, J. K., & McIver, J. E. Body image, self-concept, and the orthodontic patient. *American Journal of Orthodontics,* 1979, **75,** 507–516.

Lewis, E. A., Albino, J. E., Cunat, J. J., & Tedesco, L. A. Reliability and validity of clinical assessments of malocclusion. *American Journal of Orthodontics,* 1982, **81,** 473–477.

Lewit, D. W., & Virolainen, K. Conformity and independence in adolescents' motivation for orthodontic treatment. *Child Development,* 1968, **39,** 1189–1200.

Linn, E. L. Social meanings of dental appearance. *Journal of Health and Human Behavior,* 1966, **7,** 289–295.

Lucker, G. W., Graber, L. W., & Pietromonaco, P. The importance of dentofacial appearance in facial esthetics: A signal detection approach. *Basic and Applied Social Psychology,* 1981, **2,** 261–274.

Macgregor, F. C. Some psychosocial problems associated with facial deformities. *American Sociological Review,* 1951, **16,** 629–638.

Macgregor, F. C. Social and psychological implications of dentofacial disfigurement. *Angle Orthodontist,* 1970, **40,** 231–233.

Pitt, E. J., & Korabik, K. The relationship between self-concept and profile self-perception. *American Journal of Orthodontics,* 1977, **72,** 459–460. (Abstract)

Prahl-Andersen, B. The need for orthodontic treatment. *Angle Orthodontist,* 1978, **48,** 1–9.

Reis, H. T., Nezlek, J., & Wheeler, L. Physical attractiveness in social interaction. *Journal of Personality and Social Psychology,* 1980, **38,** 604–617.

Richman, L. C. Parents and teachers: Differing views of behavior of cleft palate children. *Cleft Palate Journal,* 1978, **15,** 360–364.

Richman, L. C., & Harper, D. C. Personality profiles of physically impaired adolescents. *Journal of Clinical Psychology,* 1978, **38,** 553–568.

Richman, L. C., & Harper, D. C. Self identified personality patterns of children with facial or orthopedic disfigurement. *Cleft Palate Journal,* 1979, **16,** 257–261.

Rutzen, S. R. The social importance of orthodontic rehabilitation: Report of a five year followup study. *Journal of Health and Social Behavior,* 1973, **14,** 233–240.

Salzmann, J. A. Handicapping malocclusion assessment to establish treatment priority. *American Journal of Orthodontics,* 1971, **59,** 552–567.

Samuels, J., & Proshek, J. The importance of dental appearance in a prestige hierarchy of occupation. *IADR Abstracts,* 1973, No. 118.

Secord, P. F., & Backman, C. W. Malocclusion and psychological factors. *Journal of the American Dental Association,* 1959, **59,** 931–938.

Shaw, W. C. The influence of children's dentofacial appearance on their social attractiveness as judged by peers and lay adults. *American Journal of Orthodontics,* 1981, **79,** 399–415.

Shaw, W. C., Meek, S. C., & Jones, D. S. Nicknames, teasing, harassment and the salience of dental features among school children. *British Journal of Orthodontics,* 1980, **7,** 75–80.

Starr, P. Self-esteem and behavioral functioning of teen-agers with oral-facial clefts. *Rehabilitation Literature*, 1978, **39**, 233–235.

Stricker, G., Clifford, E., Cohen, L. K., Giddon, D. B., Meskin, L. H., & Evans, C. A. Psychosocial aspects of craniofacial disfigurement: A "state of the art" assessment conducted by the Craniofacial Anomalies Program Branch, The National Institute of Dental Research. *American Journal of Orthodontics*, 1979, **76**, 410–422.

Summers, C. J. The Occlusal Index: A system for identifying and scoring occlusal disorders. *American Journal of Orthodontics*, 1971, **59**, 552–567.

Tedesco, L. A., Albino, J. E., Cunat, J. J., Green, L. J., Lewis, E. A., & Slakter, M. J. A dental-facial attractiveness scale: Part I, reliability and validity. *American Journal of Orthodontics*, 1983, **83**, 38–43.

Tedesco, L. A., Albino, J. E., Cunat, J. J., Slakter, M. J., & Waltz, K. J. A dental-facial attractiveness scale: Part II, consistency of perception. *American Journal of Orthodontics*, 1983, **83**, 44–46.

CHAPTER 62

INFLUENCE OF DENTIST VARIABLES ON PATIENT BEHAVIOR: MANAGING CHILD BEHAVIOR IN THE OPERATORY

PHILIP WEINSTEIN

University of Washington School of Dentistry, Seattle

There is considerable documentation that patients' encounters with health providers exert a strong influence on patient behavior. A number of disciplines, including psychology, sociology, operatory research, and linguistics, have applied their perspectives to this health-oriented topic. Most of the research has been accomplished in medicine, but studies have been reported in dentistry, nursing, pharmacy, and allied health professions. Patient parameters have also varied; all age groups and most special populations have been studied in the process of receiving health services. Diverse methodologies are apparent, not only between but within disciplines.

This chapter will review a number of studies of dentist encounters with children in the operatory and will focus on my work with the Washington Research Group. Similar studies in ambulatory settings, with the exception of the work of Korsch and associates (Korsch & Aley, 1973; Korsch, Gozzi, & Francis, 1968; Korsch & Negrete, 1974), are largely lacking in medical research, which has focused almost entirely on the management of hospitalized patients. Although there are many reports of dentist–adult interactions, few empirical studies exist, and space limitations preclude a thorough review here. The interested reader is referred to the work of Weinstein, Milgrom, Ratener, Read, and Morrison (1978); Weinstein, Smith, and Bartlett (1973); Weinstein, Smith, and Packer (1972); Nikias (1980); and Moretti, Curtiss, and Hoerman (1982).

BRIEF REVIEW OF THE LITERATURE

The Nature of the Problem

The cooperation of children in the operatory has always been of concern to dentists. For the dentist to complete technical procedures, children must cooperate or at least passively accept treatment in the dental chair. In the past, the terms *child management* and *behavior management* have usually referred to establishing and maintaining compliance. Wright (1975), however, cites McElroy, who noted in 1895 that "although the operative dentistry may be perfect, the appointment is a failure if the child departs in tears." This was the first note in the dental literature of child management being assessed on anything other than a technical basis.

There is now considerable agreement that successful management of the child not only is essential for compliant behavior in the chair and completion of neeessary dental procedures but is even more important for laying a foundation for future acceptance of dental services.

Research on the etiology of dental fear supports the assumption that the process of providing care to children is at least as important as the outcome. Forgione and Clark's (1974) reassessment of Shoben and Borland's (1954) data indicates not only that the attitude of the child's family is important but that negative experience in the operatory is a significant factor. The work of Lautch (1971), Kleinknecht and his research group (Bernstein, Kleinknecht & Alexander, 1979; Kleinknecht, Klepac, & Alexander, 1973), and Molin and Seeman (1979) indicates that patients' traumatic experiences with dentists lead to fear.

Nonpharmacological Approaches to Child Management

Historically, it was not until the 1930s that the profession began to detail children's reactions to dentistry. The early descriptions, however, were for the most part based on asystematic clinical observations. Beginning in the 1960s, a relatively small number of better controlled investigations began to appear in the dental literature. The information that resulted from even these investigations, however, was contradictory and confusing and did not provide the clinician with useful guidelines for the management of children.

The perceptions and opinions of clinicians and academics endure as the mainstay of knowledge in this area. This clinical lore includes a tremendous variety of individual techniques for handling fearful children that have nothing in common other than that they seem to work. Lewis and Law (1958) and Roder, Lewis, and Law (1961), for example, found that polygraph and heart rate measurements of dentist and patient vital signs showed no significant differences when the mother was present or absent from the treatment room during an injection. A survey of 910 Washington dentists showed, however, that 60% of the parents were required to be out of the treatment room. Other researchers have specified a number of other approaches, such as the "hand-over-mouth" and "tell-show-do" techniques (Addelston, 1958; Fisher, 1958, Ireland, 1943; Jenks, 1964; Levitas, 1974; Mayo, 1945). Although these techniques may employ underpinnings from learning theory that explain their apparent clinical success (e.g., aversive conditioning for "hand-over-mouth" and behavioral rehearsal and immediate positive reinforcement for "tell-show-do"), there have been few carefully designed studies to investigate the efficacy of common management techniques. Moreover, there has been no study of the frequency or skill with which these management techniques have been employed.

There has been some attempt, however, to introduce and assess new behavioral techniques of child management. Preappointment letters to parents and desensitizing pretreatment visits have been recommended as preventive measures. A few sophisticated behavioral techniques—systematic desensitization, modeling, and behavioral rehearsal—have begun to be investigated as methods for controlling fearful reactions of children and adults. The majority of these studies, however, describe small numbers of case histories. Melamed and her research group (Melamed, Hawes, Heiby, & Glick, 1975; Melamed, Weinstein, Hawes, & Katin-Borland, 1975) have experimentally assessed the effectiveness of various filmed models and other treatments in reducing incidents of dental fear-related problems during treatment. Recently, using other techniques, Melamed (1979) found, after training dentists in four different child management conditions, that the most effective strategy for promoting child compliance was the neutral control condition, in which the dentist "clearly stated what the child should do, without evaluating the child's behavior." The contingent use of positive reinforcement (praise) or punishment (criticism) and the simultaneous use of positive reinforcement for desirable behavior and punishment for disruptive behavior were surprisingly inferior. Melamed believes that these trends indicate a need for reevaluation of assumptions regarding the efficacy of reinforcement or feedback. After viewing and analyzing a small sample of Melamed's tapes, our research group concluded that pure experimental child management conditions, such as the use of punishment or reinforcement, are difficult if not impossible to present in clinical settings. Although dentists may attempt to follow a particular general strategy, moment-to-moment management styles exert a profound influence. Assumptions that dentists behave as instructed and that the instruction provided is the most important parameter in child treatment may lead to erroneous labeling of treatment and/or erroneous conclusions. The behavior of the dentist must be carefully observed and studied in all investigations of child management.

Pharmacological Approaches to Child Management

Although an extremely wide variety of pharmacological agents has been used to help secure child cooperation, nitrous oxide is dentistry's most basic and most widely used form of sedation. Although data on the utilization of nitrous oxide and other drugs by general practitioners are not available on a national basis, local studies of individual researchers may be suggestive. Our in-depth dentist interviews concerning the pharmacological practices of a random sample of King County, Washington, general practitioners and pedodontists indicated that 32 of 35 dentists contacted (92%) used premedication on child patients, at least in selected cases. Of the 32 premedicating dentists, 26 (81%) used nitrous oxide. No difference was found between general practitioners and pedodontists for use of nitrous oxide or other premedications. It should be noted that the proportion of pedodontists now using nitrous oxide appears to be much greater (35% versus 93%) than that found in a 1971 survey of pedodontic diplomates (American Association of Pedodontic Diplomates, 1972) or in a larger study of pedodontists conducted by Wright and McAuley (1973). The second most frequent drug utilized was Valium (13%). Practitioners reported a wide range in percentages of patients receiving premedication. Whereas 14 of the 32 dentists (43%) used premedication on less than 10% of their patients, 10 dentists (31%) used premedication in more than 80% of their patients. Premedication, especially nitrous oxide, appears to be a routine child management technique.

Effect of Nitrous Oxide Sedation

Although the use of nitrous oxide is perceived as an old and effective method for managing pain and anxiety associated with dental visits, almost all research on the effect of this drug has dealt with its analgesic properties. These effects on children and adults have been clearly defined in a number of clinical and experimental studies conducted by Emmertsen (1965), Hogue, Ternisky, and Iranpour (1971), Berger (1972), and Devine, Adelson, Goldstein, Valins, and Davison (1974). In all these studies, analgesic effects increased in accordance with gas concentration. Individual differences were considerable, however; wide variation from subject to subject was reported at the same concentration of nitrous oxide.

The ability of nitrous oxide to manage patient anxiety has not received as careful attention as the drug's analgesic effect. The few studies that exist are poor, with the exception of the work of Nathan (1982), who compared N_2O, O_2, and an unmasked control group. This is extremely unfortunate, as the present approach in the clinical literature is to deemphasize the analgesic effect of nitrous oxide exceeding 40% and to emphasize the sedative benefits of dilute concentrations less than 40%. It should be noted that the professional literature recognizes that nitrous oxide sedation is only a helpful aid or adjunct. Warnings are often proffered that nitrous oxide sedation is not a substitute for nonpharmacological child management techniques. In other words, there is at least recognition that nonpharmacological considerations influence the effectiveness of premedication in managing children. The specification of the parameters that influence the effectiveness of this and other widely utilized premedication has not yet begun.

Preparation of the Child and Other Provider Variables Influencing the Efficacy of Nitrous Oxide Sedation

As already mentioned, the clinical literature often states explicitly that the psychological preparation of the child is important. Barenie's (1979) suggestions are typical:

> *More important than the physical preparation of the equipment is the psychologic preparation of the child and the introductory technic used. The child must understand that he will not be "put to sleep," but will be awake and aware at all times. The "Tell-Show-Do" approach is most helpful in establishing rapport with the child during this period.*
>
> *It is essential that all procedures and sensations which may be experienced by the child be described in advance. The possible sensations of warmth, tingling in the extremities, auditory changes, and changes in perceived body weight should be described to the child in a very positive manner. The use of good, positive descriptions will make the most of children's susceptibility to suggestion. Using language and concepts which the child can understand, such as comparing the experience to that of pilots and astronauts, simplifies the introduction.*

Moreover, Barenie (1979) notes that the child's reactions should be monitored during introductory administration. The child should be questioned about his or her feelings, and a "continuing description of sensations he/she may become aware of should be related." Sorenson and Roth's (1973) suggestions on how to introduce nitrous oxide to the child also demonstrate an appreciation of the role of psychological preparation of the child. Their first three steps are as follows:

1. *Seat the patient comfortably in the chair.*
2. *Check openings of inspiratory valve and tension of expiratory valve on nasal inhaler for suggested settings. Open tanks and check pressure gauges for adequate levels of gases.*
3. *Predict symptoms the child will feel and tell child he will experience a pleasant sensation, a tingling sensation in toes, fingertips, on the tongue, and on the upper lip. Use a pleasant, controlled tone of voice.*

Other experts, such as Langa (1968) and Simon and Vogelsberg (1975) maintain that the administration of a nitrous oxide and oxygen mixture should be accompanied by supportive dentist behaviors, and the patient should be told about the mixture's beneficial effects. It is not unreasonable to conclude, therefore, that when nitrous oxide sedation is effective in reducing the distress of patients, it may be a result of the behavioral child management technique, with the nitrous oxide sedation contributing very little.

The role of suggestion (describing and predicting future events) in effective patient management is an important but almost totally unresearched topic. Neilburger (1978), in the only reported clinical investigation, compared the effect of suggestion ("When I brush your teeth it will tickle and make you laugh even more. You don't have to laugh too much, but many children do") to no suggestion ("Hello, Billy. How are you? Today we are going to clean your teeth with a magic toothbrush and toothpaste"). Using ratings of resistant, laughing, or silent-cooperative child responses as the dependent measure, his results indicated that suggestion decreased resistant behaviors. The most positive reaction was found among 6- to 8-year-old children. Although this was not a blinded study and it was done without sophisticated measures, the results are suggestive. The results of only one clinical investigation, however, are very far from definitive.

THE WORK OF THE WASHINGTON RESEARCH GROUP

Behavioral research in child management has been based on a tacit assumption—that the child is the problem and that it is his or her behavior that must be altered. This assumption has led to studies attempting to assess interventions designed to modify child behavior. Moreover, although a child control is customary, these studies have not carefully controlled nor attempted to understand how dentist and dental assistant variables influence outcomes. At present, our research is beginning to lead to an understanding of what transpires during dental treatment of the child. Research may indicate that a given management approach, such as nitrous oxide sedation, is more or less effective. Until we understand the variation in application of these approaches, however—that is, what is said and done when the nitrous oxide is administered—the results of even drug studies may not be clinically useful. Such an understanding requires study of the behavior of the dentist, the assistant, and their interaction with child patients.

Pilot Study

As a result of our interest in the process of managing child behavior, we initiated a pilot study to begin to identify communication patterns in pedodontics (Wurster, Weinstein, & Cohen, 1979). This research is based on two assumptions. The first recognizes that the context within which all dentistry is accomplished is determined by the relationship between practitioners and the patient. The quality of this relationship is in turn determined by the interaction that occurs between the practitioner and the patient.

The second assumption is that human relationships are complex and consist of constantly changing processes that defy "first cause" descriptions. As a result, research based on this assumption seeks to identify regular patterns or sequences of behavior that tend to induce structure or place constraints on later sequences. These patterns are best characterized by probability statements, rather than by predictions of direct cause and effect.

The purpose of the pilot study was to identify and define the parameters of the relationship between the practitioner and the child. Interaction analysis techniques were used to review videotapes of dental students providing treatment to their child patients during regular appointments. Dental students' confidence in child management skills was also considered.

Subjects for this research were 16 fourth-year dental students randomly chosen from the senior class at the University of Washington. The 16 child patients who participated were regularly assigned patients. These relatively inexperienced students and their patients were assigned to an operatory equipped with a videotape recorder and camera. The first 30 minutes of a regularly scheduled appointment were then recorded.

Students completed the Confidence in Child Management Scale prior to videotaping. This pretested 20-item scale requires rating of confidence in managing problem behaviors from children of both sexes and a variety of ages on a 10-point, behaviorally anchored scale. Subsequent studies have indicated the reliability and validity of this instrument (Weinstein, Domoto, Getz, & Enger, 1979).

After videotaping was completed, the behaviors of the dentists and the children were coded. The coding system used in this research was based on the work of Szasz and Hollender (1956). Four mutually exclusive and exhaustive categories of dental student communication were developed:

1. *Directive guidance behaviors:* The student provides the child with a straightforward statement of instruction, expectation, or feedback concerning the child's behavior during treatment.
2. *Permissive behaviors:* The student allows problem behaviors to continue unabated and/or tries to persuade the child to cooperate.

3. *Coercive behaviors:* The student attempts to overcome problem behaviors by force, either verbal or nonverbal. Such behaviors include threatening, blaming, ridiculing, humiliating, or using physical restraints.

4. *Other behaviors:* This category includes any behaviors not covered by the first three categories.

Four mutually exclusive and exhaustive categories for child behaviors were also developed:

1. *Cooperative behaviors:* The child shows a positive desire to cooperate with the practitioner and the ability to respond to him or her in a relaxed and nonfearful manner.

2. *Resistant behaviors:* The child reluctantly cooperates while demonstrating that the treatment is barely tolerable for him or her. Although these behaviors indicate that the child experiences stress, they do *not* interfere with delivery of care.

3. *Uncooperative behaviors:* The child resists to the point of interfering with treatment procedures.

4. *Other behaviors:* This category includes any behaviors not covered by the first three categories.

In this pilot study we attempted to generate first-order Markov probabilities. The equipment used to code the dental student-child interaction, the Behavioral Observation and Scoring System (BOSS), involves the use of a microprocessor to maintain the order of events. Behavior was coded at 6-second intervals. The 6-second intervals included one dental student behavior and one child behavior, coded 3 seconds apart.

The results of the pilot study indicate that child behavior appears to be systematically related to the communication style of the student. The probabilities that a given category of child behavior will follow a given category of dentist behavior are presented in Table 62.1. The probability that directive guidance, for example, will be followed by cooperation is .85. The probability of resistance or uncooperative behaviors following directive guidance is about .13. The likelihood that the dental student's permissiveness will be followed by cooperation is .18; the likelihood that either a resistant or uncooperative consequent will follow is .75. Furthermore, the probability that coercive behavior will be followed by cooperation is .03, whereas the likelihood of either resistance or noncooperation is .97.

Table 62.2 presents another perspective—the probabilities that categories of the dentist's behavior follow categories of the child's behavior. When the child behaved uncooperatively, for example, the dental student's consequent response tended to be either permissive or

Table 62.1   Transition Frequencies and Transition Probabilities for Dental Student–Child Interactions

Antecedent States (Student)		Consequent States (Child)				
		Cooperation	Resistance	Noncooperation	Other	Total
Directive guidance	Total f	2,551	328	56	58	2,993
	p	.85	.11	.02	.02	1.00
Permissive behavior	Total f	19	9	66	8	102
	p	.18	.08	.67	.07	1.00
Coercive behavior	Total f	5	61	91	0	157
	p	.03	.39	.58	0	1.00
Other behavior	Total f	177	8	0	153	338
	p	.52	.02	0	.46	1.00

$N = 16.$

Table 62.2 Transition Frequencies and Transition Probabilities for Child–Dental Student Interactions

Antecedent States (Child)		Consequent States (Student)				
		Directive Guidance	Permissive Behavior	Coercive Behavior	Other Behavior	Total
Cooperation	Total f	2,381	7	2	183	2,573
	p	.93	.00	.00	.07	1.00
Resistance	Total f	304	11	61	14	390
	p	.78	.03	.16	.03	1.00
Noncooperation	Total f	47	67	63	2	178
	p	.26	.37	.36	.01	1.00
Other	Total f	59	10	1	171	241
	p	.25	.04	.00	.71	1.00

$N = 16$.

coercive (Markov probability = .73). The probability of the student's directive guidance in such circumstances was only .26. When the child showed resistance, directive guidance was the principal consequent response; the probability for permissive or coercive consequent responses was only .19. When the child showed cooperation, the probability of directive guidance was exceptionally high (.93), and the probability of permissive and coercive consequences approached zero.

Phase analysis indicated that all of the uncooperative behaviors and most of the resistant behavioral interactions occurred during the first three phases. Chi-square one-sample tests showed significantly more permissive behaviors during the preinjection and placing of the rubber dam phases. Student coerciveness during the injection phase led to either resistant or uncooperative behavior from the child in every instance. Permissive behavior during the preinjection phase and the placing of the rubber dam phase led to uncooperative behavior in 73 of 103 occurrences. Relatively more uncooperative and resistant behaviors occurred during injection of the local anesthetic than during any other phase.

Dental students' confidence scores were used to discriminate behavior profiles for the more confident students (i.e., students who scored above the group mean on the Confidence in Child Management Scale) and for the students who scored below the group mean. Less confident students' interactions with children accounted for 86% of the permissive behaviors, 95% of the coercive behaviors, and 87% of the uncooperative behaviors exhibited. These scores were also analyzed using chi-square one-sample tests. The results indicated that less confident students accounted for significantly more permissive and uncooperative behaviors than the more confident students.

The institutional setting of this pilot study and the relative inexperience of the dental students limit generalizations to clinicians in private practice. Moreover, the simple coding scheme and lack of coding behavior in real time were limitations of the study.

Major Field Study

Subjects in this study were 25 volunteer practitioners solicited by mail after selection of a random list of names from the files of the King County Dental Association and the Washington State Academy of Pediatric Dentists. The volunteers included 22 general practitioners and 3 pedodontists. The dentists identified 50 of their regular child patients, aged 3 to 5 years, to participate in the study. These children were then screened by the dentists during their next appointments. At that time, the children's behavior during prophylaxis was observed and their dental health was recorded. Children with a need for treatment requiring two or more sessions in which injections would be required were eligible for participation in the study. In all, each dentist was to provide two or more treatment sessions to two children, leading to 100 appointments.

All participating dentists and assistants completed confidence and experience surveys and a short questionnaire concerning their expectations of the behavior of each child at each session. The dentists also agreed to not use nitrous oxide or any other premedication Aside from this prohibition, they were asked to treat the child as they ordinarily would.

All sessions were videotaped by an experienced technician, who visited the operatory in advance to establish maximal camera positioning and camera angle. Eighty-seven video-tapes from 23 offices have been produced and provide the basis for the data presented in this report.

The Coding Scheme

The researchers—two psychologists, a dentist, and a dental student—independently observed approximately 20 hours of videotapes of dental students and practitioners in an attempt to list important behaviors. These behaviors were then placed on index cards and sorted into dimensions. The dimensions were then used to code behavior from the videotapes and to generate tentative hypotheses.

Interjudge agreement was estimated as the final version of the code was established. Pearson r for major dimensions ranged from .85 to .94; percentage agreement was found to average .89. Although an attempt was made to operationalize each code, we have found that the context of the behavior often must be considered when coding. The final coding scheme is given in Table 62.3.

The behavior of child, dentist, and assistant is coded independently in real time from the videotape. The equipment used for the coding, Microprocessor Operated Recording Equipment (MORE), is a system comprising a microprocessor unit with a small keyboard, a recorder, a computer interface device, and a software package. When the coder identifies an event, he or she presses a series of keys. Events are timed in seconds from the first keystroke of an event to the first keystroke of the next event. Phases of dental treatment are edited into the data set at a later point. Following the coding of all events of a given individual, data are transferred to audiotape for storage and later reloading into the MORE for transmission to the host computer. Such systems, first developed and tested by Sackett and colleagues (Sackett, 1978; Sackett, Holm, Crowley, & Henkins, 1979; Sacket, Stephenson, & Ruppenthel, 1979), have proved invaluable in sequential analyses of observational data.

A major goal of this study was to identify sequences, patterns, and repetitive cycles of behavior (a) within the responses of individual subjects and (b) between pairs or groups of subjects. The study of such dependencies poses the most difficult measurement and analyses problem in observational research. A traditional approach would use Markov chains to identify conditional probabilities among behaviors. Although first-order transition probabilities are easily generated, as they were in our pilot study, higher-order probabilities are costly to generate and result in an enormous amount of difficult-to-interpret data.

An alternative approach, mentioned earlier, is lag sequential analysis. This method is based on the principles of autocorrelation and cross-lag correlation. Lags are defined as the number of events or time units between events. Lag sequential analysis measures the number of times behaviors of interest (criterion categories) follow or precede a selected behavior at various lag steps removed in the ordered data. Included here are analyses of events. A time sequential analysis would proceed in a similar fashion.

Many different types of analyses have been performed to date. Here I will focus on two dentist-related analyses that have been confirmed with a number of subsets of our sample.

Table 62.3   Coding Scheme

Dentists' Behaviors

Guidance
Directs immediate behavior by command
Explains, shows, demonstrates, responds to questions concerning treatment or appointment
Sets rules and limits for future behavior
Provides specific feedback—positive and negative (reinforcement)
Provides nonspecific feedback concerning behavior—positive and negative (reinforcement)
Coerces, finds fault with angrily, threatens, acts gruff
Coaxes, tries to persuade by personal appeal
Raises rhetorical questions (dentist interested not in the question but in the child's response)
No direction

Empathy
Questions for feelings or pain, provides signal mechanism, or acknowledges feelings or
   pain
Reassures, both verbally and nonverbally
Ignores or denies expressed feelings or pain
Puts down, humiliates, belittles
None of the foregoing

Physical contact
Working contact—touches face or mouth as part of normal procedure
Pats, strokes, or tickles
Holds (child not moving or interfering with treatment)
Restrains child in any way—including placement of mouth props (child moving or interfering
   with treatment)
Assists child in entering or leaving chair or assists in positioning
No physical contact

Verbalization
No verbalization (silence)
Dental to child
Nondental to child
Dental to assistant
Nondental to assistant

Child's Behaviors

Movement and physical positioning
Appropriate positioning
Child-initiated appropriate child movement, such as reopening mouth without cue
Dentist-initiated appropriate child movement
Child-initiated minor movement, positioning still appropriate
Child-initiated minor movement, positioning no longer appropriate
Child-initiated major movement, positioning no longer appropriate

Verbal behavior
Silence
Talk or question—uninterpretable
Talk or question—nondental matters
Talk or question—dental matters
Statement of hurt or discomfort—including "ouch!"

Table 62.3 *(Continued)*

Verbal protest or complaining, such as "I don't want . . ." or termination request, "Stop
  it!"
Verbal abuse or threats
Whimpering, sniveling, soft crying
Loud crying and screaming

Comfort
Comfort—pleasantness, lack of tension, smile, laugh, eyelids motionless except for normal
  blinks, no creases in upper lid of closed eye, feet and hands relaxed
Neutral
Discomfort—unpleasantness, tension (both minor and major), grimaces, tension of facial
  muscles, tears in eye, chokes, gags, coughs, vomits, feet and hands tensed
Unobservable

The Effect of Dentist Variables on Child Behavior

The relationships between dentist and child behaviors were determined by cross-lagging
child behavior on dentist behavior and dentist behavior on child behavior. This section
presents the conditional probabilities for fear-related child behaviors following dentist behaviors in each of the four provider dimensions.

To facilitate data analysis, child behaviors were grouped into fear-related and non-fear-
related categories. The following behaviors comprised the fear-related behavior category:
minor and problem movement, crying, screaming, whimpering, protest, hurt, and discomfort.
All these items are found in the Preschool Observation Scale of Anxiety (Glennon & Weisz,
1978). The relationships between this dichotomous measure of fear-related behavior and
variables within the dentist dimensions were specified for the entire appointment and for
each phase of treatment. Only the former are presented here in detail.

Table 62.4 **Conditional Probabilities That a Child Will Respond with Fear-related Behaviors Following a Dentist's Guidance Behaviors**

Lag	Direction	Explanation	Rules	Reinforcement	Coercion	Coaxing	Rhetorical Question
1	.199↓	.300↑	.479↑	.199↓	.824↑	.552↑	.257↓
2	.245↓	.289	.378↑	.258↓	.875↑	.507↑	.299↑
3	.267↓	.278	.381↑	.250↓	.625↑	.516↑	.275
4	.271↓	.292↑	.385↑	.250↓	.600↑	.531↑	.319↑
5	.258↓	.280	.417↑	.261↓	.667↑	.508↑	.289
6	.276	.274	.588↑	.268↓	.600↑	.556↑	.264↓

Note: Unconditional probability is .282.
↓ = Conditional probability of observed behavior significantly lower than expected value ($p \leq .05$).
↑ = Conditional probability of observed behavior significantly higher than expected value ($p \leq .05$).

Results for the guidance dimension, presented in Table 62.4, appear consistent over
six event lags. Direction and reinforcement result in less fear-related behavior. Coercion,
coaxing, and the use of rules result in greater fear-related behavior. Rhetorical questions
are not as effective as direction, and explanation is surprisingly ineffective. In reviewing

the use of explanation during individual phases, it appears that explanation decreases fear during chair placement but increases fear during oral examination, injection, and filling/polishing stages.

Table 62.5 presents the results of the empathy dimension. Ignoring or denying fear-related child behavior is clearly the least successful management approach, appearing to be more ineffective than putdowns. Questioning for feeling was the most successful behavior in this dimension, showing a decrease in fear-related child behaviors at lags 1, 3, and 5. Reassurance was surprisingly ineffective during all phases. In reviewing the effect of questioning for feelings over phases of treatment, the data indicate that this technique is most effective during the injection phase.

The results of the verbalization dimension are presented in Table 62.6. Although they are not as interesting as the foregoing two dimensions, these results indicate that nondental verbalization to the child (distraction) resulted in not less but more fear-related behavior overall. Distraction was least effective during placement of the rubber dam and had mixed results in the other phases. The other behaviors—silence, dental verbalization to child, and dental and nondental verbalization to assistant—were found to result in less fear-related behavior.

Table 62.7 presents the overall results of the physical contact dimension. Although it was a relatively infrequent dentist behavior (84 events coded), patting/stroking was followed by a significant reduction in fear responses for the first five of six event lags. When the dentist was holding or restraining the child, fear-related responses increased, of course.

Table 62.5 Conditional Probabilities That a Child Will Respond with Fear-related Behaviors Following a Dentist's Empathy Behaviors

Lag	Questioning for Feelings	Reassurance	Ignoring/Denying	Putdowns
1	.366↓	.484↑	.678↑	.429
2	.472↑	.543↑	.634↑	.615↑
3	.371↓	.522↑	.608↑	.583↑
4	.485↑	.569↑	.600↑	.600↑
5	.413↓	.517↑	.629↑	.556↑
6	.528↑	.574↑	.576↑	.500↑

Note: Unconditional probability is .452.
↓ = Conditional probability of observed behavior significantly lower than expected value ($p \leq .05$).
↑ = Conditional probability of observed behavior significantly higher than expected value ($p \leq .05$).

Table 62.6 Conditional Probabilities That a Child Will Respond with Fear-related Behaviors Following a Dentist's Verbalization Behaviors

Lag	No Verbalization (Silence)	Dental to Child	Nondental to Child	Dental to Assistant	Nondental to Assistant
1	.275↓	.311↑	.360↑	.269↓	.211↓
2	.290	.294	.319↑	.284	.218↓
3	.268↓	.316↑	.322↑	.272↓	.239↓
4	.278↓	.307↑	.318↑	.264↓	.226↓
5	.267↓	.321↑	.275↓	.269↓	.224↓
6	.278↓	.308↑	.272↓	.280↓	.268↓

Note: Unconditional probability is .295.
↓ = Conditional probability of observed behavior significantly lower than expected value ($p \leq .05$).
↑ = Conditional probability of observed behavior significantly higher than expected value ($p \leq .05$).

Table 62.7 Conditional Probabilities That a Child Will Respond with Fear-related Behaviors Following a Dentist's Physical Contact Behaviors

Lag	Working Contact	Patting/ Stroking	Holding	Restraining	Assisting	No Contact (Apart)
1	.429↑	.295↓	.618↑	.846↑	.278↓	.360↓
2	.401	.333↓	.545↑	.833↑	.329↓	.381
3	.429↑	.286↓	.545↑	.818↑	.218↓	.358↓
4	.399	.298↓	.563↑	.556↑	.333↓	.398
5	.434	.283↓	.484↑	.750↑	.382	.362↓
6	.410↑	.531↑	.613↑	.571↑	.407↑	.389

Note: Unconditional probability is .399.
↓ = Conditional probability of observed behavior significantly lower than expected value ($p \leq .05$).
↑ = Conditional probability of observed behavior significantly higher than expected value ($p \leq .05$).

Child fear responses decreased when the dentist had no physical contact with the child (apart), with the exception of the injection phase and when the dentist assisted the child in physical positioning (assist). Positioning during this phase appears to be repositioning of the child to permit continued treatment after child movement.

An analysis of the guidance dimension shows that, as we hypothesized, fear-related behaviors decrease following the use of direction and reinforcement, for the appointment overall and for each individual phase across six lags. It was not surprising to find that the use of rhetorical questions—such as "Would you like to get into the chair now?"—in place of specific direction was much less effective in decreasing fear-related behaviors.

Although we suspected that explanation was not the most effective technique with young children, we were surprised by its almost total ineffectiveness. As noted previously, only during the low-stress first phase did the use of explanation lead to a significant decrease in fear. This finding is supported by Howitt and Stricker (1965), who determined that clarification was more effective with mildly anxious than with highly anxious children.

Questioning for feelings, which attempts to recognize child feelings, appears to be the most effective empathic behavior. Reassurance, however, may deny or ignore feelings— for example, "Everything will be okay, don't worry." Analysis of dentist empathy responses shows that reassurances were used most frequently in the injection, rubber dam, and drilling phases, with very few occurrences recorded in earlier phases. It appears that reassurances are used most frequently in stressful situations but have little effect in reducing fear.

Distracting children does not appear to be an extremely useful approach for the dentists in our study. It is especially poor during the rubber dam phase. After the injection, children are generally wary. Distraction at that time may be perceived as a cue that another stressful procedure lies ahead.

In examining the other, broader categories of verbalization, one might initially conclude that talking to the child should be avoided. A closer examination reveals that dentist verbalizations to the child increase as fear is exhibited, generally to alleviate fear and to prevent disruption of the appointment. Conversely, dentist silence and verbalizations to the assistant increase when nonfear behaviors are exhibited by the child.

In all, the evidence suggests that giving specific directions and using positive reinforcement are most consistently followed by a reduction in the child's fear-related behaviors or distress. Patting and stroking behaviors also tend to be followed by a lessening of fear behaviors, but they are infrequently utilized by the dentists. Questioning for feelings is a useful technique, but ignoring or denying child feelings does not extinguish fear-related behaviors over the six event lags that were studied. Reassurances were surprisingly ineffectual. Coercion, coaxing, and putdowns tend to be followed by a substantial increase in fear-related responses by the child. The use of explanations, though employed frequently, does not appear to reduce fear responses significantly.

Identifying Responsive and Invariant Dentist Behaviors Under Fear and Nonfear Conditions

The analyses presented in this section attempt to specify the responsiveness of dentists to different child behaviors. In these analyses, the conditional probabilities for dentist behavior in a given coding dimension following fear-related and non-fear-related child behavior were assessed. Although figures were generated both for the entire appointment and for each phase of treatment for every dimension of dentist behavior, only the former are presented and discussed.

Results for the first two lags of the guidance dimension are presented in Table 62.8. For the first lag, immediately after fear-related child behavior, occurrences of direction and reinforcement significantly decrease; following non-fear-related child behaviors, these behaviors significantly increase.

The probability of dentists using rules, force, and coaxing is significantly enhanced immediately after a child shows fear-related behaviors. When fear is not present, force and coercion are much less likely. At two lags the situation alters; although rules, reinforcement, and force following fear and reinforcement following nonfear show similar results, the only significant difference between fear and nonfear conditions occurs for reinforcement.

Table 62.9 presents the results of the empathy dimension. Immediately after fear-related child behavior, the probabilities of reassurance, ignoring/denying, and putdowns are significantly increased, while the probability of questioning for feelings decreases. Following nonfear child behaviors, questioning for feelings increases, while ignoring/denying behaviors decrease. Differences between fear and nonfear conditions are significant for all behaviors except

Table 62.8   Conditional Probabilities of Dentist Guidance Behaviors Following Fear and Nonfear Child Behaviors for Two Lags

Lag	Behavior	Fear	Nonfear	Difference	Standard Score (z)	Significance Level (p)
1	Direction	.171↓	.194↑	−.023	−2.485	<.02
	Explanation	.284	.266	.018	1.717	
	Rules	.010↑	.004	.007	3.559	<.001
	Reinforcement	.107↓	.161↑	−.054	−6.339	<.001
	Force	.006↑	.005↓	.005	4.966	—[a]
	Coaxing	.016↑	.005↓	.011	5.206	<.001
	Rhetorical question	.014	.013	.001	.420	
2	Direction	.189	.188	.001	.122	
	Explanation	.280	268	.013	1.174	
	Rules	.008↑	.005	.002	1.348	
	Reinforcement	.122↓	.156↑	−.034	−3.909	<.001
	Force	.005↑	.001	.004	3.901	—[a]
	Coaxing	.014	.013	.001	.232	
	Rhetorical question	.366	.364↑	.002	.168	

↓ = Conditional probability of observed behavior significantly lower than expected value ($p \leq .05$).
↑ = Conditional probability of observed behavior significantly higher than expected value ($p \leq .05$).
[a] Insufficient number of cases.

Table 62.9 Conditional Probabilities of Dentist Empathy Behaviors Following Fear and Nonfear Child Behaviors for Two Lags

Lag	Behavior	Fear	Nonfear	Difference	Standard Score (z)	Significance Level (p)
1	Questioning for Feelings	.100↓	.134↑	−.034	−3.140	<.01
	Reassurance	.120↑	.116	.004	.451	
	Ignoring/denying	.035↑	.015↓	.020	3.856	<.01
	Putdowns	.007↑	.002	.005	2.339	<.02
2	Questioning for Feelings	.112↑	.118	−.006	−.026	
	Reassurance	.140↑	.101	.039	−3.468	<.001
	Ignoring/denying	.033↑	.021	.012	1.945	<.05
	Putdowns	.007↑	.002	.005	2.357	<.001

↓ = Conditional probability of observed behavior significantly lower than expected value ($p \leq .05$).
↑ = Conditional probability of observed behavior significantly higher than expected value ($p \leq .05$).

reassurance. After two lags the situation again alters. Following child fear, all empathy behaviors, including questioning for feelings, significantly increase; following nonfear, none of the probabilities are significant. Differences between probabilities for fear and nonfear conditions indicate that all behaviors except questioning for feelings are significant.

The results of the verbalization dimension are presented in Table 62.10. Immediately after child fear behavior, silence and talk to the assistant decrease, while talk to the child increases. Under nonfear conditions, there is greater silence, less dental talk to the child, and more dental talk to assistants. All differences between fear and nonfear are significant. After two lags, little has changed under fear conditions; dental talk to the assistant is no longer significantly reduced. With no fear, nondental talk to the child (distraction) decreases and there is more verbalization, both chatting and work-related, to the assistant. Differences between conditions are significant for all behaviors except dental talk to assistant.

Table 62.10 Conditional Probabilities of Dentist Verbalization Behaviors Following Fear and Nonfear Child Behaviors for Two Lags

Lag	Behavior	Fear	Nonfear	Difference	Standard Score (z)	Significance Level (p)
1	Silence	.270↓	.344↑	−.075	−6.10	<.001
	Dental to Child	.521↑	.421↓	.100	7.716	<.001
	Nondental to Child	.080↑	.062	.018	2.707	<.01
	Dental to Assistant	.119↓	.154↑	−.035	−3.825	<.001
	Nondental to Assistant	.009↓	.018	−.009	−2.943	<.01
2	Silence	.304↓	.329	−.025	−2.048	<.05
	Dental to Child	.472↑	.444	.028	2.155	<.05
	Nondental to Child	.079↑	.060↓	.018	2.831	<.01
	Dental to Assistant	.136	.148↑	−.012	−1.279	
	Nondental to Assistant	.008↓	.018↑	−.010	−3.093	

↓ = Conditional probability of observed behavior significantly lower than expected value ($p \leq .05$).
↑ = Conditional probability of observed behavior significantly higher than expected value ($p \leq .05$).

Table 62.11 Conditional Probabilities of Dentist Physical Contact Behaviors Following Fear and Nonfear Child Behaviors for Two Lags

Lag	Behavior	Fear	Nonfear	Difference	Standard Score (z)	Significance Level (p)
1	Contact	.615↑	.582	.033	2.002	<.05
	Patting/stroking	.022	.027	−.005	−.947	
	Holding	.012↑	.008	.005	1.391	
	Restraining	.008↑	.000↓	.008	3.859	<.001
	Assisting	.020↓	.031↑	−.011	−1.990	<.05
	Apart	.321↓	.352	−.031	−1.925	<.05
2	Contact	.596	.605	−.009	−.543	
	Patting/stroking	.023	.026	−.002	−.435	
	Holding	.012↑	.008	.005	1.387	
	Restraining	.008↑	.001	.007	3.290	<.001
	Assisting	.028	.024	.004	.816	
	Apart	.331↓	.336	−.005	−.339	

↑ = Conditional probability of observed behavior significantly higher than expected value ($p \leq .05$).
↓ = Conditional probability of observed behavior significantly lower than expected value ($p \leq .05$).

Table 62.11 presents the results of the physical contact dimension. For the first lag, under the fear conditions, all contact with the child increases except patting and assisting (assisting decreases). Under nonfear conditions, assisting increases, while restraining decreases. Differences between conditions are significant for all behaviors except patting and holding. After two lags, the increase in work-related touching (contact) and the decrease in assisting the child in positioning or repositioning are abated under the fear condition. The increase in assisting and the decrease in restraining are gone in the nonfear condition, as no significant alteration in probability is evident. Only one significant difference pertaining to restraints is now manifest between conditions.

As one would expect, when the child begins to exhibit fear-related behaviors, the dentist interacts more with the child; consequently, silence and conversation with the dental assistant decreases. Of course, physical contact with the child also tends to increase. Patting/stroking, however, a behavior found in our study to decrease fear-related behaviors, does not increase. Similarly, direction and reinforcement, effective guidance behaviors, were found to decrease, while the probability of ineffective and counterproductive behaviors—namely, rules, force, and coaxing—tended to increase. All empathic behaviors, with the exception of questioning for feelings—the most effective behavior—increased in probability. The evidence we have presented elsewhere suggests that these behaviors do not lead to a reduction in fear-related child behavior.

A few behaviors did not change when the fear/nonfear condition was altered. Explanation, rhetorical questions, and patting/stroking were invariant and seemed to be more a function of the style of the dentist than a response to child behavior.

REFERENCES

Addelston, H. K. Child patient training. *Fortnightly Review of the Chicago Dental Society*, 1958, **38**, 7–11.

American Association of Pedodontic Diplomates. Technique for behavior management—A survey. *Journal of Dentistry for Children*, 1972, **39**, 368–372.

Barenie, J. T. Inhalation conscious sedation: Nitrous oxide analgesia. In L. W. Ripa & J. T. Baranie (Eds.), *Management of dental behavior in children*. Littleton, Mass.: PSG, 1979.

Berger, D. E. Assessment of the analgesic effects of nitrous oxide on the primary dentition. *Journal of Dentistry for Children,* 1972, **39,** 265–268.

Bernstein, D. A., Kleinknecht, R. A., & Alexander, L. D. Antecedents of dental fear. *Journal of Public Health Dentistry,* 1979, **39,** 113–124.

Devine, V., Adelson, R., Goldstein, J., Valins, S., & Davison, G. C. Controlled test of the analgesic and relaxant properties of nitrous oxide. *Journal of Dental Research,* 1974, **53,** 486–490.

Emmertsen, E. The treatment of children under general analgesia. *Journal of Dentistry for Children,* 1965, **2,** 123–124.

Fisher, G. C. Management of fear in the child patient. *Journal of the American Dental Association,* 1958, **57,** 792–795.

Forgione, A., & Clark, C. Comments on an empirical study of the cause of dental fears. *Journal of Dental Research,* 1974, **53,** 496.

Glennon, B., & Weisz, J. R. An observational approach to the assessment of anxiety in young children. *Journal of Consulting and Clinical Psychology,* 1978, **46,** 1246–1257.

Hogue, D., Ternisky, M., & Iranpour, B. The responses to nitrous oxide analgesia in children. *Journal of Dentistry for Children,* 1971, **38,** 129–133.

Howitt, J. W., & Stricker, G. Child patient response to various dental procedures. *Journal of the American Dental Association,* 1965, **20,** 70–74.

Ireland, R. L. Introducing the child to dentistry. *Journal of the American Dental Association,* 1943, **30,** 280–286.

Jenks, L. How the dentist's behavior can influence the child's behavior. *Journal of Dentistry for Children,* 1964, **31,** 358–366.

Kleinknecht, R. A., Klepac, R. K., & Alexander, L. D. Origins and characteristics of fear of dentistry. *Journal of the American Dental Association,* 1973, **86,** 842–848.

Korsch, B., & Aley, E. Pediatric interviewing techniques. *Current Problems in Pediatrics,* 1973, **3,** 1–42.

Korsch, B., Gozzi, E. K., & Francis, V. Gaps in doctor-patient communication: Doctor-patient interaction and patient satisfaction. *Pediatrics,* 1968, **42,** 855–871.

Korsch, B., & Negrete, V. F. Doctor-patient communication. *Scientific American,* August 1974, **7,** 66–74.

Langa, H. *Relative analgesia in dental practice.* Philadelphia: Saunders, 1968.

Lautch, H. Dental phobia. *British Journal of Psychiatry,* 1971, **119,** 151–158.

Levitas, T. C. Home hand-over-mouth exercise. *Journal of Dentistry for Children,* 1974, **39,** 178–182.

Lewis, T. M., & Law, D. B. Investigation of certain autonomic responses of children to specific dental stress. *Journal of the American Dental Association,* 1958, **57,** 769–777.

Mayo, R. W. Child management in the dental office. *Journal of Dentistry for Children,* 1945, **12,** 48–49.

Melamed, B. G. Strategies for patient management in pediatric dentistry. In B. D. Ingersoll & W. R. McCutcheon (Eds.), *Clinical research in behavioral dentistry: Proceedings of the Second National Conference on Behavioral Dentistry.* Morgantown: West Virginia University, 1979.

Melamed, B. G., Hawes, R. R., Heiby, E., & Glick, J. Use of filmed modeling to reduce uncooperative behavior of children during dental treatment. *Journal of Dental Research,* 1975, **54,** 797–801.

Melamed, B. G., Weinstein, D., Hawes, R., & Katin-Borland, M. Reduction of fear-related dental management problems with use of filmed modeling. *Journal of the American Dental Association,* 1975, **90,** 822–826.

Molin, C., & Seeman, K. Disproportionate dental anxiety: Clinical and nosological considerations. *Acta Odontologica Scandinavica,* 1979, **28,** 197–212.

Moretti, R. J., Curtiss, G., & Hoerman, K. C. Dentist non-verbal communication skills, patient anxiety and patient treatment satisfaction. *Journal of Dental Research,* 1982, **61,** 264.

Nathan, J. Assessment of anxious pedodontic patients to nitrous oxide. *Journal of Dental Research,* 1982, **61,** 224.

Neilburger, E. J. Child response to suggestion. *Journal of Dentistry for Children,* 1978, **45,** 52–58.

Nikias, M. Compliance with preventive oral home care regimens. *Journal of Dental Research*, 1980, **59**, 2216–2225.

Roder, R. E., Lewis, T. M., & Law, D. B. Physiological responses of dentists to the presence of a parent in the operatory. *Journal of Dentistry for Children*, 1961, **28**, 263–270.

Sackett, G. P. Measurement in observational research. In G. P. Sackett (Eds.), *Observing behavior* (Vol. 2). Baltimore: University Park Press, 1978.

Sackett, G. P., Holm, R., Crowley, C., & Henkins, A. A Fortran program for lag sequential analysis of contingency and cyclicity in behavioral interaction data. *Behavioral Research Methods and Instrumentation*, 1979, **11**, 366–378.

Sackett, G. P., Stephenson, E., & Ruppenthel, G. C. Digital data acquisition systems for observing behavior in laboratory and field settings. *Behavioral Research Methods and Instrumentation*, 1973, **5**, 344–348.

Shoben, E. M., & Borland, L. An empirical study of the etiology of dental fears. *Journal of Clinical Psychology*, 1954, **10**, 171–174.

Simon, J. F., & Vogelsberg, G. M. Use of nitrous oxide-oxygen inhalation sedation for children. In G. Z. Wright (ed.), *Behavior management in dentistry for children*. Philadelphia: Saunders, 1975.

Sorenson, H. W., & Roth, G. I. A case for nitrous oxide–oxygen inhalation sedation: An aid in the elimination of the child's fear of the "needle." *Dental Clinics of North America*, 1973, **17**, 769–781.

Szasz, T. J., & Hollender, M. H. A contribution to the philosophy of medicine—The basic models of the doctor-patient relationship. *Archives of Internal Medicine*, 1956, **97**, 585–592.

Weinstein, P., Domoto, P., Getz, T., & Enger, R. Reliability and validity of a measure of confidence in child management. *Journal of Dental Research*, 1979, **58**(Special Issue A), 408.

Weinstein, P., Milgrom, P., Ratener, P., Read, W., & Morrison, K. Dentists' perceptions of the patients: Relationship to quality of care. *Journal of Public Health Dentistry*, 1978, **38**, 10–21.

Weinstein, P., Smith, T. A., & Bartlett, R. A study of the dental student–patient relationship. *Journal of Dental Research*, 1973, **52**, 1287–1292.

Weinstein, P., Smith, T. A., & Packer, M. A. Method for evaluating patient anxiety and the interpersonal effectiveness of dental personnel: An exploratory study. *Journal of Dental Research*, 1972, **50**, 1324–1326.

Wright, G. Z. *Behavior management in dentistry for children*. Philadelphia: Saunders, 1975.

Wright, G. Z., & McAuley, D. J. Current premedicating trends in pedodontics. *Journal of Dentistry for Children*, 1973, **40**, 185–187.

Wurster, C. A., Weinstein, P., & Cohen, A. J. Communication patterns in pedodontics. *Perceptual and Motor Skills*, 1979, **48**, 159–166.

CHAPTER 63

SIGNIFICANCE OF ORAL HABITS

JOHN D. RUGH

University of Texas Health Science Center, San Antonio, Texas

ROBERT R. LEMKE

Trinity University

Oral habits may have both short-term and long-term effects on oral structures. The muscular pain and stiffness experienced following a night of heavy bruxism is immediate but is usually self-limiting. The long-term consequences of chronic bruxism, however, are often irreversible, resulting in oral conditions that may require extensive dental restorative efforts or even surgical intervention. The pathological consequences of oral habits and self-destructive parafunctional behaviors range from malocclusion to degenerative joint disease (Figure 63.1). The impact of oral habits in terms of financial loss, compromised masticatory function, pain, and suffering is significant but poorly publicized (Glaros & Rao, 1977; Zarb & Carlsson, 1979; Bryant, Gale, & Rugh, Note 1). Recent epidemiologic studies of masticatory pain and dysfunction indicate that about half of persons aged 15 to 44 have at least one symptom

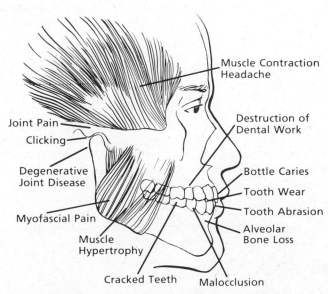

Figure 63.1 Oral consequences of chronic oral habits.

of masticatory pain and dysfunction (Agerberg & Carlsson, 1972; Helkimo, 1976; Solberg, Woo, & Houston, 1979). In children it is not uncommon to find temporomandibular joint clicking and/or masticatory muscle tenderness in 20% to 35% of the population (Egermark-Eriksson, Carlsson, & Ingervall, 1981; Williamson, 1977).

The consequences of oral habits often must be managed by the dentist. This chapter, however, does not deal with the pathological consequences of oral habits; rather, it emphasizes early identification and prevention of oral parafunctional activities such that the long-term destructive consequences of these behaviors may be avoided. The chapter is not intended to serve as a comprehensive literature review; rather, it is a synthesis of clinical impressions and research findings. Several oral habit problems will be discussed in the chapter. For each, we provide a brief description of the oral habit, its etiology, prevalence, and deleterious consequences; then we elaborate on the identification and prevention of the oral habit.

PATIENT PREPARATION AND EDUCATION

Several concerns are common to the prevention of all oral habit disorders. As in most behavioral change programs, patient education and motivation are key factors. Awareness of the consequences of an oral habit is the first step in developing patient interest in a behavioral change program. The long-term deleterious effects of the behavior and the positive aspects of change should be discussed. A portfolio of pictures or diagrams showing the untreated natural course of the oral habit is often useful. A discussion of the cause-and-effect relationships in clear, nontechnical terms is useful to help provide a suitable cognitive set before initiating a behavioral change program. Behavioral change programs for many oral motor behaviors also involve self-monitoring and charting of the target behavior and/or symptoms related to the behavior. Self-monitoring is intended to increase patient awareness of the behavior and to identify situations in which there is a high probability that the behavior will occur. Charting of the changes in target behavior, symptoms, and drug usage provides positive reinforcement and a measure of the efficacy of the behavioral change program.

Some oral parafunctional activities and related pain symptoms have structural or systemic etiologies. A high crown or a denture with increased vertical dimension, for example, may stimulate muscle hyperactivity, masticatory pain, and dysfunction. In such cases the patient can usually relate the onset of symptoms to dental treatment. Before attempting to manage oral habits or functional oral conditions, it is important to rule out dental and medical etiologic factors.

NOCTURNAL BRUXISM

Nocturnal bruxism is the forceful clenching or grinding of the teeth during sleep. It is sometimes accompanied by audible gnashing of the tooth surfaces, but this sound does not serve as a reliable diagnostic aid. Bruxism may involve both rhythmic chewing-like movements and long periods of isotonic maximal contraction of the jaw-closing muscles. These isotonic contractions are often in excess of 90 seconds, sufficiently long to produce muscular pain and fatigue (Christensen, 1981). Although muscle and joint symptoms usually are limited to one side of the face, most nocturnal bruxism episodes involve simultaneous bilateral contractions (Etchison, Rugh, Fisher, & Ware, 1982). Nocturnal bruxism has been related to temporomandibular joint pain and dysfunction, masticatory muscle pain and stiffness, excessive tooth wear, tooth mobility, destruction of dental restorations, denture soreness, and headache (Clark, Beemsterboer, and Rugh, 1981; Glaros & Rao, 1977).

Adult Nocturnal Bruxism

Less than 10% of the adult population report awareness of nocturnal bruxism; however, objective signs and symptoms related to bruxism are found in 21% to 78% of the population

(Frolich, 1966; Solberg et al., 1979). Dental theories of nocturnal bruxism suggest that it is related to premature tooth contacts; however, this theory has not received experimental support. A few cases of bruxism may be related to amphetamine or phenothiazine usage (Ashcroft, Eccleston, & Waddell, 1965; Brandon, 1969; Kamen, 1975). Evidence suggests that nocturnal bruxism in most individuals is related to emotional conditions of the preceding day. High levels of bruxism measured through nightly electromyographic recordings of masseter muscle activity (Figure 63.2) have been correlated with emotionally stressful day-time activities or anticipation of stressful events (Funch & Gale, 1980; Rugh & Solberg, 1976).

Short-Term Management

Contingent nocturnal feedback or avoidance conditioning during sleep has consistently been shown to suppress nocturnal bruxism and is useful for short-term (10–14 days) management (Clarke & Kardachi, 1977; DeRisi, 1970; Funch & Gale, 1980; Heller & Strang, 1973; Johnson & Rugh, 1980; Kardachi, Bailey, & Ash, 1978; Rugh & Solberg, 1975). This treatment protocol involves monitoring nocturnal masseter muscle activity with a portable electromyographic (EMG) instrument in the patient's home. Most studies have found that this method provides only temporary suppression of the bruxism. The results of a study by Beemsterboer, Clark, and Rugh (1978), however, suggest that the suppression may be more lasting if patients are required to awaken fully for a few minutes following each bruxism episode.

Other methods of treating nocturnal bruxism in adults have involved intraoral appliances (night guards or splints), massed practice, muscle exercises, hypnosis, and pharmacological agents such as tranquilizers (Rugh, Jacobs, Taverna, & Johnson, in press). Although each of these methods has been found to suppress the bruxism temporarily for brief periods (10–14 days), none has been demonstrated to provide long-term results. Occlusal adjustment has been found to have no systematic effect on levels of nocturnal bruxism (Bailey & Rugh, 1980; Kardachi et al., 1978).

Long-Term Management

Prevention of nocturnal bruxism may best be accomplished by comprehensive stress control, counseling, and behavioral change programs (Figure 63.3). The relationship between waking

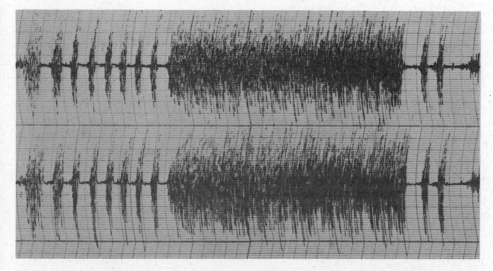

Figure 63.2 Electromyographic activity of masseter muscles during nocturnal bruxism. Bilateral, rhythmic bursts, similar to chewing, are followed by a 20-second period of sustained contraction.

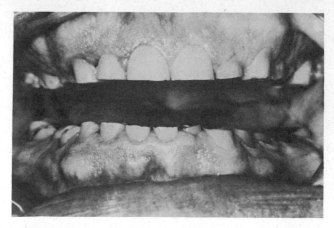

Figure 63.3 Tooth wear in a 27-year-old male nocturnal bruxist. Dental reconstruction for this patient is contraindicated unless bruxism is controlled.

emotional conditions and nocturnal bruxism is fairly well established (Glaros & Rao, 1977; Rugh et al., in press). Clinically, it is commonly observed that a patient's bruxism problem is often resolved coincident with major lifestyle changes (completion of school, divorce, occupational changes, etc.). Specific modes of therapy for the long-term management of nocturnal bruxism depend on the patient's unique psychological problems and lifestyle.

A technique that is useful to any behavioral change program, however, is the nightly monitoring of levels of nocturnal bruxism. Portable electromyographic integrators can provide a nightly measure of bruxist activity (Figure 63.4). Nocturnal bruxism may be monitored over several weeks while daily behavioral patterns are systematically altered until bruxism is eliminated. Graphs of nightly recordings are helpful in identifying emotional problems, maintaining the patient's interest and motivation, and developing concepts of self-control.

Figure 63.4 Bruxism may be evaluated through recording of masseter muscle activity through portable electromyographic integrators. (Photo courtesy of Aaron Laboratories, San Antonio, Texas.)

A 14- to 21-day baseline period is first established. During this baseline and self-monitoring period, graphs are kept of (a) daily activities and events, (b) the patient's subjective emotional responses to the events, and (c) subjective pain symptoms. This material is reviewed with the patient and lists are made of behaviors, cognitions, and life situations that appear to be related to high levels of nocturnal bruxism. These problems are then rank-ordered with respect to their emotional impact and the probability that they could be altered. Problems that rank high may be dealt with through traditional counseling.

Effort is also directed at identifying behavioral patterns, activities, and cognitive conditions preceding nights of very low levels of bruxism. In patients with work-related stress, low levels of bruxism are often observed on Saturday and Sunday nights. These correlations help delineate sources of stress or emotional difficulty. An attempt is made to increase the frequency of behavioral patterns and cognitive conditions that are empirically correlated with low levels of nocturnal bruxism.

It is sometimes useful to demonstrate the relationship between daily stress and nocturnal bruxism and facial pain symptoms. This may be done, after establishing a baseline, by eliminating bruxism for a few nights by pharmacological means (Valium) or through contingent nocturnal feedback (Figure 63.5). A significant drop in bruxism and a relief of symptoms is usually observed. Such a demonstration helps motivate the patient and provides support for the clinical hypothesis regarding the etiology of the bruxism and facial pain symptoms (Figure 63.6).

In some patients it is difficult to identify specific behavioral or cognitive conditions related to the patient's bruxism behavior. In such cases it is useful to begin with a general stress-control program involving masseter EMG feedback, thermal feedback, taped relaxation exercises for home use, and development of coping skills. The typical length of therapy has been 6 to 12 weekly 1-hour visits and a 6-month follow-up visit, at which time levels of nocturnal bruxism are measured for a period of 1 week. If significant bruxism or facial pain symptoms are observed, the patient's lifestyle and behavioral patterns are reexamined and modified to again reduce the bruxism levels, as measured through nightly recordings of masseter EMG levels.

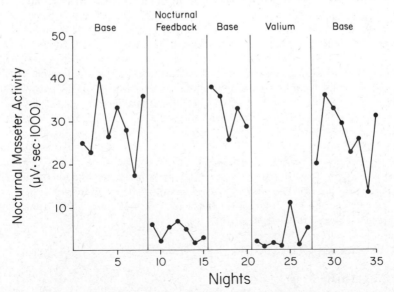

Figure 63.5 Nocturnal bruxism can be reduced for short periods through contingent nocturnal feedback of a tone or by 5 mg of Valium given 30 minutes before bedtime. Long-term management usually requires a comprehensive stress-control program.

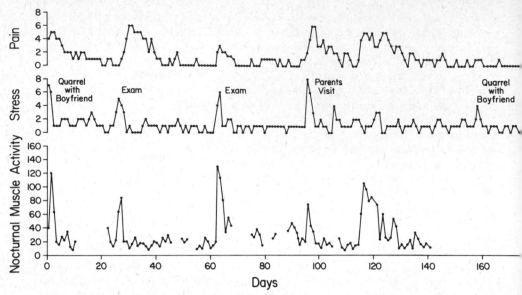

Figure 63.6 Long-term EMG monitoring of nocturnal bruxism in this 23-year-old female demonstrates a relationship between stress and nocturnal bruxism and facial pain symptoms. The cyclic character of the bruxism and facial pain is a common clinical observation.

Childhood Nocturnal Bruxism

Childhood and adult bruxism are often discussed together. Evidence suggests, however, that these are two distinct problems, having different etiologic factors and requiring different methods of management (Kuch, Till, & Messer, 1979; Olkinuora, 1969; Reding, Rubright, & Zimmerman, 1966). Nocturnal bruxism is found in 12% to 15% of children between the ages of 3 and 12 (Lindqvist, 1971; Reding et al., 1966). The problem is usually identified through parental reports of grinding noises during the child's sleep or by an evaluation of tooth wear. The child is usually unaware of nocturnal bruxism and seldom complains of masticatory muscle tenderness, temporomandibular joint pain, or clicking, although these symptoms are common in children (Grosfeld & Czarnecka, 1977; Williamson, 1977).

The etiology of nocturnal bruxism in children is unknown. A genetic predisposition to bruxism has been demonstrated (Lindqvist, 1974). Emotional stress, nutritional deficiencies, allergies, and the eruption of teeth have been proposed as immediate causes, but documentation supporting these factors is weak and therapeutic or preventive methods have not been developed (Rugh et al., in press; Ayer, Note 2). Clinical management usually involves crowning excessively worn or decayed teeth and letting the child "outgrow" the habit. Indeed, it is common for the bruxism to stop before puberty, but the long-term effects of childhood bruxism are not known. In extreme cases, plastic mouthpieces similar to those used in football may be used to protect the child's teeth (Everett, 1982). Screening and control procedures need to be developed.

ORAL HABITS IN CHILDREN

Thumb Sucking and Finger Sucking

Thumb or finger sucking usually occurs in the first few months of life and decreases with age. In a study of 2,650 infants and children, 46% were found to be digit suckers (Traisman

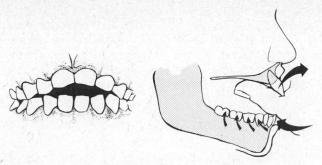

Figure 63.7   Thumb sucking, if continued after age 5, frequently results in an anterior open bite malocclusion.

& Traisman, 1958). If the behavior is stopped before the age of 5, few long-term effects are reported. Continued sucking past the age of 5, however, commonly results in an anterior open bite, requiring orthodontic correction (Figure 63.7). There is evidence that sucking may also be a factor in Class II malocclusion, narrowing of the dental arches, and mucosal trauma (Egermark-Eriksson, 1982; Phelan, Bachara, & Satterly, 1979; Popovich & Thompson, 1973).

Identification of thumb or finger sucking may be accomplished by questioning the parents or siblings. An examination of the hands will often reveal a callous, a clean fingernail, or sometimes a reddish discoloration of the digit involved. The presence of an anterior open bite should also elicit suspicion of a sucking habit (Gellin, 1978). Ayer (Note 2) identified several categories of treatment methods that have been used in the management of thumb and finger sucking.

Restraint or prevention of the habit has been accomplished by making the habit physically impossible through such means as nightgowns without sleeves (Levin, 1958). Benjamin (1967) reported significantly less sucking in a group of neonates who wore mittens during their first few months of life.

Incompatible or substitute behaviors may be employed. The use of a pacifier dramatically reduces the frequency of thumb and finger sucking (Popovich & Thompson, 1973). The pacifier results in less damage because of the reduced mechanical force.

Modification of presleep behavioral patterns may also alter the probability of finger and thumb sucking. In a comparative study of 50 thumb suckers and 50 nonsuckers, Ozturk and Ozturk (1977) found that 96% of the thumb suckers had been left alone or without sucking opportunity while going to sleep. In contrast, all of the nonsuckers were either rocked, lullabied, or fed by breast or bottle prior to sleep.

Positive reinforcement has been attempted in several studies (Baer, 1962; Knight & McKenzie, 1974; Martin, 1975; Skiba, Pettigrew, & Alden, 1971). Each study showed success in decreasing digit sucking through giving attention, praising, reading bedtime stories, or showing cartoons when the child was not sucking. Various methods of positive reinforcement appear to work; they may not be cost-effective, however, as they require the active and constant support of the parents.

Aversive conditioning has also been found to curb digit sucking. This method may involve the use of dental appliances, such as palatal arches or palatal cribs. Overall these techniques are very effective with chronic digit suckers. Haryett, Hansen, Davidson, and Sandilands (1967) compared six types of treatments: counseling, palatal arches, palatal arches and counseling, palatal cribs, palatal cribs and counseling, and a control. In the palatal crib and the palatal crib and counseling groups, all of the patients stopped their habits. The application of a bitter substance on the fingers or thumb (Johnson, 1938) has historically proved useful in some cases, but such material often gets into the child's eyes.

The potential emotional and physical problems caused by aversive techniques such as the appliances are controversial. Haryett et al. (1967) noted that 36% of the children treated with the palatal crib were initially upset. Speech problems were described in 59%, and 41% reported eating difficulties. The problems were only temporary, however, lasting from 1 week to 2 months. No symptom substitution problems have been reported; in fact Haryett and colleagues (1967) reported a reduction in a number of associated habits coincident with a reduction in sucking.

Tongue Thrust Swallowing

A behavior modification technique and exercise program known as myofunctional therapy has been developed to correct certain deviant swallowing patterns that are believed to cause or maintain the anterior open bite. This treatment, though commonly used, has not received research support. A joint committee of representatives from the American Association of Orthodontics and the American Speech and Hearing Association, after reviewing the literature, concluded that there was no evidence to support the claims of significant, stable, or long-term changes in swallowing patterns or occlusal conditions with myofunctional therapy (Joint Committee, 1974). It is generally held that tongue thrust swallowing habits stop with orthodontic therapy that closes the open bite (Mason, Note 3).

Bottle Caries

Modification of children's feeding habits may be necessary for prevention of dental decay on the primary maxillary incisors (Cone, 1981). Rampant decay of the upper front teeth has been linked to parents' habit of putting the child to bed with a baby bottle. The liquid in the bottle, usually milk or sweetened juices, serves as a substrate for cariogenic bacteria to produce acid that leads to dental decay (Hansen, 1978; King & Leimone, 1978). Because dental treatment is difficult in young children, special precaution to prevent caries is warranted.

DIURNAL ORAL HABITS IN ADULTS

Effects, Etiology, and Prevalence

Diurnal oral habits include teeth clenching or grinding, lip or cheek biting, nail biting, unilateral chewing, biting or holding foreign objects in the mouth (finger, pencils, tack, etc.) (Figure 63.8), and a variety of posturing habits that involve holding the mandible in unnatural positions. These habits have been implicated in tooth wear, muscle and joint

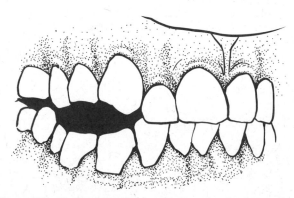

Figure 63.8 Tooth wear and intrusion in a chronic pipe smoker.

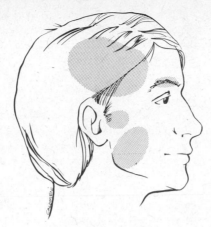

Figure 63.9   Masticatory muscle tenderness and joint pain from oral muscle hyperactivity are commonly confined to one side of the head but may occur at several sites.

pain, headache (Figure 63.9), condylar remodeling, denture soreness, tooth abrasion, and periodontal conditions (DeBoever, 1973; Glaros & Rao, 1977; Bryant et al., Note 1). The most common problems related to adult oral muscle hyperactivity are symptoms of myofascial pain and dysfunction. Epidemiologic studies have found that over half of the adult population have symptoms of masticatory pain and dysfunction. Fortunately, these symptoms are usually mild and self-limiting; Solberg et al. (1979), however, reported that 5% of the young adults examined had symptoms that would qualify them for treatment. Mild, transitory masticatory symptoms are often overlooked; some researchers have suggested, however, that untreated muscular pain and dysfunction may result in degenerative joint disease later in life (Blackwood, 1966; Laskin, 1969; Toller, 1973). Oral habits may also be important because of their frequent relationship to headache, a problem affecting 28% of the female population (Magnusson, 1980; Dupuy, Engel, Devine, Scanlon, & Querec, Note 4).

The conditions that elicit and maintain diurnal oral habits and muscle hyperactivity are varied. Diurnal oral habits may be viewed as operants maintained by internal or external contingencies; clinically, however, it is often difficult to identify the reinforcement contingencies. The patient who has a habit of protruding or chronic forward posturing of the jaw, for example, may do so to compensate for a weak chin (retrognathic mandible). In such cases, the contingencies may involve subtle feedback from peers regarding physical appearance. Some jaw-posturing habits are related to occupational factors. Divers and violinists, for example, have been found to suffer muscular and joint problems believed to result from chronic posturing of the jaw (Pinto, 1966; Rieder, 1976).

Other oral habits may be linked to nonverbal communication. Clenching of the teeth is a common expression of anger or threat in many cultures. Laboratory studies demonstrate that various emotional conditions (frustration, anxiety, fear, etc.) consistently elicit masticatory muscle tension (see reviews by Rao & Glaros, 1979; Rugh & Solberg, 1976; Yemm, 1976) as well as changes in the muscles of facial expression (Schwartz, Ahren, & Brown, 1979).

Oral habits often persist even though the conditions under which the habit originally developed are altered. Unilateral chewing, for example, may result from tooth pain or from a periodontal problem on one side of the mouth, so that the patient chews on the opposite side to avoid pain. After the dental problem is rectified, the patient often continues to chew unilaterally, which may result in condylar remodeling and muscle disuse atrophy. Some oral habits may be viewed as superstitious behavior, which may have been initially reinforced by the chance pairing of a reinforcing event. Chewing on a pencil, for example, may be initially reinforced by finding the solution to a test question. As with other habits, reinforcement principles may help account for the acquisition of oral habits, but associative learning may help maintain the habits. Hunt, Matarazzo, Weiss, and Gentry (1979) have provided an excellent review of the theoretical issues underlying the development and maintenance of habits.

Prevention of Diurnal Oral Habits

The evaluation and prevention of diurnal oral habits involve several techniques and instruments. The procedures will vary for each patient because of the uniqueness of the habits and the conditions of their occurrence. Clinical procedures designed to deal with oral habits involve four aspects:

1. Identification of oral habits and delineation of their significance in terms of oral health.
2. Increasing patient motivation to alter the habit.
3. Modification of the habit and/or stimulus conditions correlated with its occurrence.
4. Establishment of maintenance and follow-up procedures.

Identification of Oral Habits

Identification of diurnal oral habits may involve questionnaires, histories, self-monitoring, pain charting, in-clinic EMG evaluations, and ambulatory monitoring of jaw muscle activity in the patient's natural environment. Questionnaires provide an economical and systematic way to gather information regarding the patient's knowledge of specific oral habits, reaction to the habits, and medical and psychosocial history. During the interview, the clinician should watch for oral habits such as lip, tongue, or cheek biting and clenching or posturing of the mandible.

Pain diaries (hourly, daily, or weekly) are very useful for identifying cycles and stimuli that elicit the habits. Such records frequently provide a demonstration of the relationship between emotional conditions and muscle hyperactivity and pain. Pain and behavioral charting are particularly useful when used with a portable EMG instrument to monitor muscle activity levels.

The patient's oral habits and oral pain symptoms are often only one aspect of a general emotional condition or personality disorder. Gold, Lipton, Marbach, and Gurion (1975) reported that over 50% of the 135 myofascial pain dysfunction (MPD) patients they evaluated were frequent users of psychotropic medication. Furthermore, these patients had a high incidence of ulcers and other stress-related conditions. Evaluation procedures should thus include one of several inventories to help identify personality patterns, emotional conditions, or lifestyles that may underlie the condition. The Life Events Scale has been found useful in our clinic to help identify precipitating conditions that may account for acute episodes. Malow, Olson, and Greene (1981) suggest that the following psychological tests are useful: Self-Rating Depression Scale (Zung, 1965); Multiple Affect Adjective Checklist (Zuckerman & Lubin, 1965); Interpersonal Adjective Checklist (LaForge & Suczek, 1955; Leary, 1957); State-Trait Anxiety Inventory (Spielberger, Gorsuch, & Lushene, 1970); and the Minnesota Multiphasic Personality Inventory (MMPI).

Clinical EMG Evaluations

Many diurnal oral habits fit the description provided by Hunt et al. (1979). They often seem automatic and involuntary. Patients are commonly unaware of a habit, and it is often difficult to identify the reinforcing stimuli that maintain the habit. Fortunately, most oral habits are accompanied by an increase in amplitude or duration of jaw muscle contraction and can thus be detected electromyographically. In the clinic, an EMG instrument may be used to answer the following questions (see Table 63.1):

Table 63.1   Clinical Electromyographic Procedures

Patient _____
Date _____
EMG Unit _____

1) Evaluate the patient's ability to relax jaw and facial muscles. (Procedure) Place the electrodes as shown in the figure. With the patient seated and head upright ask the patient to relax the jaw and facial muscles and record EMG activity level.

        EMG Level _____

2) Evaluate the patient's muscle activity required to maintain a normal upright posture. (Procedure) Record the patient's EMG while sitting comfortably with lips closed (teeth need not touch).

        EMG Level _____

3) Evaluate the patient's muscular activity associated with a manual dexterity task. (Procedure) With the patient sitting comfortably in an upright position, ask the patient to perform a standard manual dexterity task such as separating a chain of paper clips. Observe the EMG meter reading for bursts of activity and note the average EMG level.

        Results _____
        Average EMG _____

4) Evaluate the patient's muscular activity during a time pressure-stress task. (Procedure) Repeat #3, however, put a time limit on the task which the patient will not likely meet.

        Results _____
        Average EMG _____

5) Evaluate the patient's ability to habituate or adapt to a stressful task. (Procedure) Repeat the above procedure (#4) several times. Does the patient progressively decrease muscular activity in the facial muscles as the task is repeated? Note the number of trials required to bring muscular tension levels down to a relaxed level and record the average EMG reading on each trial.

        Trials; avg. EMG _____, _____, _____, _____, _____

6) Evaluate the patient's facial muscular tension while discussing emotional problem areas. (Procedure) Following the above procedures, the clinician may easily direct the patient into a discussion of emotionally difficult areas. Continuously monitor the patient's muscular tension levels and note bursts of activity and the verbal stimuli accompanying the increased EMG activity.

        Results _____
        _____

1. Does the patient have the ability to voluntarily relax the masticatory muscles? Are the muscles currently in a state of continued contraction or spasm? (Procedure 1)

2. Does the patient use excessive muscle tension when maintaining a normal sitting posture? Is the patient posturing the jaw in a strained position? (Procedure 2)

3. Does the patient demonstrate increased masticatory or facial muscle activity when performing manual tasks? (Procedure 3)

4. Does the patient respond with masticatory muscular tension when under mild emotional stress? (Procedure 4)

5. Does the patient demonstrate the usual habituation to stressful stimuli, or does muscular tension increase over time? (Procedure 5)

Answers to these questions facilitate identification of the muscle hyperactivity and oral habits. During the treatment period, these measurements are repeated to provide a measure of treatment effects.

Some experience is necessary to interpret the clinical EMG results. Instrument calibration standards have not been agreed upon, and so comparisons cannot be made of readings obtained using instruments from different manufacturers. Each clinician must evaluate a few healthy subjects to establish normative data.

Ambulatory Monitoring

Identification of oral habits is facilitated by the use of a small, portable EMG instrument worn in the patient's natural environment (Figure 63.10). This instrument helps identify the habit, its frequency, and the conditions of its occurrence. The patient is instructed to keep records of the habit frequency (as indicated by the tone), the nature of the habit, and the situations or thoughts that accompany occurrence of the habit. Periods of muscle hyperactivity are frequently tied to specific stressful life situations. This information is valuable in structuring a treatment program. During the treatment phase, the instrument is used to help increase the patient's awareness of the habit and to assess the results of treatment.

The clinician is often faced with the difficult task of determining the clinical significance of the oral habit or muscle hyperactivity—that is, whether the habit is of sufficient magnitude or frequency to be harmful. This assessment can be made through cumulative monitoring of jaw muscle activity levels in the patient's natural environment using a portable EMG integrator (Burgar & Rugh, 1982). Patients with myofascial pain are reported to have mean waking or sleeping cumulative EMG values more than two standard deviations above the mean of asymptomatic controls (Finlayson, Rugh, & Dolwick, 1982). The timing of the assessment may be critical because of the cyclic nature of myofascial pain and oral muscle hyperactivity problems.

Modification of Diurnal Oral Habits

The management of diurnal oral habits may involve hypnosis, muscular exercises, counseling, contingent aversive reinforcement, pain charting, assertiveness training, massed practice, general relaxation, biofeedback, self-monitoring, habit reversal, and other procedures (Malow et al., 1981; Melamed & Mealiea, 1981; Olson, 1980; Rugh & Robbins, 1981; Bryant et al., Note 1). Clinicians are familiar with the majority of these procedures. Only those procedures that have been developed specifically for oral habits and oral muscle hyperactivity conditions are discussed in detail here. For many adult diurnal oral habits, a simple awareness of the behavior and its long-term consequences are all that are required. Gingival recession and tooth abrasion from the zealous use of toothpicks or a toothbrush, for example, can often be stopped simply by calling attention to the problem.

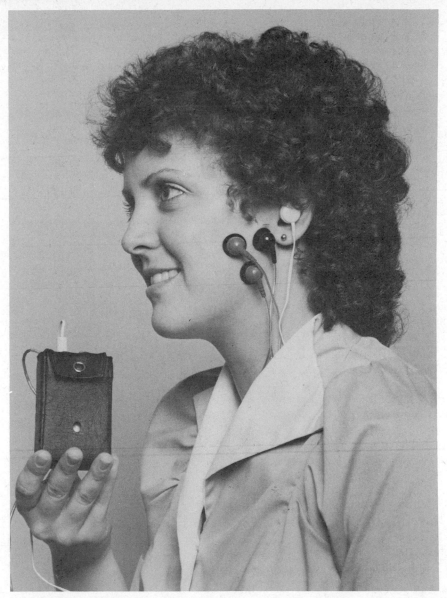

Figure 63.10 A portable EMG unit provides a tone through an earphone when muscle contraction exceeds a preset threshold. The instrument is used to increase the patient's awareness of habits and to help identify stimuli that elicit the habit. (Photo courtesy of Aaron Laboratories, San Antonio, Texas.)

EMG Feedback for Jaw Muscle Relaxation

Jaw and facial muscle relaxation training through EMG biofeedback has been a central feature of several programs designed to manage oral habits and masticatory muscle hyperactivity conditions (Brooke, Stenn, & Mothersill, 1977; Carlsson, Gale, & Ohman, 1975; Dohrmann & Laskin, 1978; Gessel, 1975; Olson, Greene, & Solar, 1980; Rugh, 1977; Stenn,

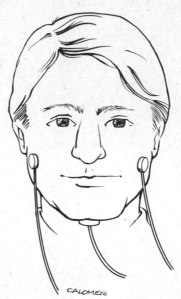

CALOMENI

Figure 63.11 Widely spaced, bilateral active electrode placement provides an EMG signal reflecting the activity of several jaw and facial muscles, including deep muscles such as the lateral and medial pterygoids. This placement is used during assessment and during EMG biofeedback training. The reference electrode is placed symmetrically under the chin.

Mothersill, & Brooke, 1979). The procedures and instrumentation used have varied, but satisfactory results have been reported with each. Jaw and facial muscle relaxation may be accomplished in the clinic through use of auditory or visual feedback provided by one of several good-quality commercial EMG feedback instruments. The instrument should have a short time constant or integration period (less than 2 seconds) such that activity associated with swallowing may be discriminated. Active electrodes may be placed on each side of the face approximately 20 mm anterior to the tragus to provide a signal that reflects the activity of many jaw and facial muscles (Figure 63.11). Electrode impedance should be reduced to less than 10,000 ohms by abrasion of the skin to reduce artifacts and noise. The use of silver/silver chloride electrodes will also reduce noise levels.

The training session should begin with a brief baseline period. Ten 1-second integrator time periods are recorded with the jaw in its usual postural position. Ideally, this measure is taken with the patient's attention distracted from the measure. Next, 10 readings are recorded after asking the patient to relax without the aid of the feedback. These two baseline measurements aid in assessing treatment effects and progress. Feedback is then provided with a visual (analog) display at eye level. The response of the feedback instrument to muscle contraction is demonstrated by having the patient clench, swallow, and then smile. After becoming familiar with the instrument, the patient is asked to relax the facial and jaw muscles, using the visual and auditory feedback to assist in the learning task. Visual imagery and suggestion often help patients relax their jaws. It is helpful when teaching a relaxed vertical mandibular position to tell the patient, "Slowly let your jaw drop open just as if you are opening to take a bite of food." Muscle activity will decrease until a null point is reached; opening further will cause an increase in muscle activity. A relaxed anterior-posterior jaw position is found by asking the subject to move the jaw slightly forward then backward. Again, a null in the EMG reading provides an indication of the most relaxed position. Relaxed midline posture is determined in the same manner by asking the subject to move the mandible slightly left and right while observing the EMG instrument response. Patients are often surprised to learn that the jaw muscles are not relaxed when the teeth are held together.

Once the most relaxed jaw posture is learned, the patient's speed and skill at achieving this posture are developed by clenching then returning to the relaxed mandibular position. This is practiced until the patient achieves a relaxed posture ($< 2 \mu V$) within 3 seconds after a hard clench. The skill is then practiced without the aid of the feedback instrument, with only the therapist observing the visual display. To increase the patient's awareness of jaw muscle tension, it is helpful to periodically ask him or her to estimate the level of jaw muscle contraction, in terms of microvolts, without viewing the feedback display. The relaxation skills are then practiced with different head positions. The patient will observe that a relaxed jaw position will depend on head inclination.

Finally, jaw and facial muscle relaxation is practiced while the patient performs various physical and mental tasks. Chaining paper clips, writing, and wadding paper can be used as manual tasks. Visual imagery of unpleasant events and "serial sevens" are used as cognitive stimuli. The patient learns to engage in these tasks while maintaining relaxed jaw and facial muscles. The patient's progress in these skills is plotted at the end of each session (Figure 63.12).

The response is generalized to the natural environment through the use of a portable EMG instrument worn under the patient's clothing (Figure 63.10). Surface EMG electrodes are placed unilaterally over the masseter or temporalis muscle on the symptomatic side. The instrument's threshold is set such that it provides a beep through an earphone if the patient engages in the oral habit. Various oral habits can be detected by altering electrode placement or the threshold and time constant of the instrument. It is useful for the patient to wear the unit a few hours every other day for a week. Constant use appears to result in habituation to the tone.

Use of the portable EMG instrument in the patient's natural environment without first training the patient to relax the muscles in the clinic is ill-advised. Some patients who have not learned to relax the jaw muscles are frustrated by the instrument's beeping and end up clenching more.

The efficacy of EMG biofeedback training to relax the jaw and facial muscles in the treatment of masticatory pain and dysfunction has been reasonably well established (Berry & Wilmot, 1977; Dohrmann & Laskin, 1978; Gessel, 1975; Olson, 1977; Peck & Kraft, 1977; Stenn et al., 1979). This therapy has been found useful in patients who have been refractory to other forms of therapy (Carlsson & Gale, 1977; Carlsson et al., 1975) and as an adjunct to dental therapy (Berry & Wilmot, 1977). Recently, the American Dental Association Council on Dental Care Programs has listed biofeedback and other behavior modification techniques as recommended initial treatments for symptoms of masticatory pain and dysfunction (Council on Dental Care Programs, 1982).

Training of masticatory muscle relaxation may also be useful in managing pain patients who have degenerative joint disease and occlusal conditions for which no solution can be found. These patients learn to minimize trauma to the joint and oral soft tissue by keeping the jaw muscles relaxed. The self-control programs outlined here for oral habits have not been found useful in clinically depressed patients, patients who are poorly motivated, or patients for whom secondary gain is a factor. Patients who have a history of previous successful attempts at self-control (smoking, weight loss, nail biting, etc.) generally do extremely well.

FUTURE DIRECTIONS

Oral health professionals have been successful with preventive programs. Public awareness and use of oral hygiene methods have reduced the incidence of tooth decay and periodontal disease. In contrast, little attention has been given to early detection and modification of self-destructive oral habits. The insidious nature of these habits in terms of long-term oral

Name_____   Dr. _____

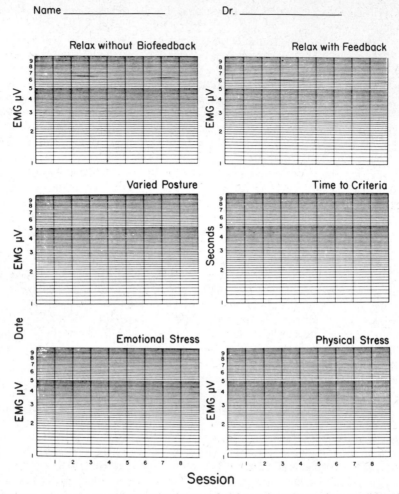

Figure 63.12 The patient's ability to relax jaw and facial muscles under various conditions is plotted each session. Logarithmic scales emphasize changes in low levels of electromyographic activity when progress is more difficult.

health suggests that increased effort should be given to early detection and modification of these relatively common problems. Modification of oral habits and prevention of related oral conditions are relatively new applications of learning principles and behavioral medicine techniques. There are few well-controlled clinical studies, and treatment parameters have not been optimized through parametric clinical trials. As discussed in this chapter, however, many of the principles, procedures, and methods developed for other preventive programs may be used to meet the challenge of managing these conditions.

REFERENCE NOTES

1. Bryant, P., Gale, E., & Rugh, J. (eds.). *Oral motor behavior: Impact on oral conditions and dental treatment.* NIH Pub. No. 79–1845. U.S. Department of Health, Education and Welfare, August 1979.

2. Ayer, W. A. Thumb-, fingersucking and bruxing habits in children. In P. Bryant, E. Gale, & J. Rugh (eds.), *Oral motor behavior: Impact on oral conditions and dental*

treatment. NIH Pub. No. 79–1845. U.S. Department of Health, Education and Welfare, August 1979.

3. Mason, R. M. Tongue thrust. In P. Bryant, E. Gale, & J. Rugh (eds.), *Oral motor behavior: Impact on oral conditions and dental treatment.* NIH Pub. No. 79–1845. U.S. Department of Health, Education and Welfare, August 1979.

4. Dupuy, H. J., Engel, A., Devine, B. K., Scanlon, J., & Querec, L. *Selected symptoms of psychological stress.* U.S. Public Health Service Pub. No. 1000, Series 11, No. 37. National Center for Health Statistics, 1970.

REFERENCES

Agerberg, G., & Carlsson, G. E. Functional disorders of the masticatory system. Distribution of symptoms according to age and sex as judged from investigation by questionnaire. *Acta Odontologica Scandinavica,* 1972, **30,** 597.

Ashcroft, G. W., Eccleston, D., & Waddell, J. L. Recognition of amphetamine addicts. *British Medical Journal,* 1965, **1,** 57.

Baer, D. M. Laboratory control of thumbsucking by withdrawal and re-presentation of reinforcement. *Journal of the Experimental Analysis of Behavior,* 1962, **5,** 525–528.

Bailey, J. O., Jr., & Rugh, J. D. Effect of occlusal adjustment on bruxism as monitored by nocturnal EMG recordings. *Journal of Dental Research,* 1980, **59,** 317. (Abstract)

Beemsterboer, P. L., Clark, G. T., & Rugh, J. D. Treatment of bruxism using nocturnal biofeedback with an arousal task. *Journal of Dental Research,* 1978, **57**(Special Issue A), 366. (Abstract)

Benjamin, L. S. The beginning of thumbsucking. *Child Development,* 1967, **38,** 1065–1078.

Berry, D. C., & Wilmot, G. The use of a biofeedback technique in the treatment of mandibular dysfunction pain. *Journal of Oral Rehabilitation,* 1977, **4,** 255–260.

Blackwood, H. J. J. Adaptive change in the mandibular joint with function. *Dental Clinics of North America,* 1966, **10,** 559–566.

Brandon, S. Unusual effects of fenfluramine. *British Medical Journal,* 1969, **4,** 557.

Brooke, R. I., Stenn, P. G., & Mothersill, K. J. The diagnosis and conservative treatment of myofascial pain dysfunction syndrome. *Oral Surgery,* 1977, **44,** 844–852.

Burgar, C. G., & Rugh, J. D. An EMG integrator for muscle activity studies in ambulatory subjects. *IEEE Transactions on Biomedical Engineering,* 1982, **BME-30**(1), 66–69.

Carlsson, S. G., & Gale, E. N. Biofeedback in the treatment of long-term temporomandibular joint pain: An outcome study. *Biofeedback Self-Regulation,* 1977, **2,** 161–171.

Carlsson, S. G., Gale, E. N., & Ohman, A. Treatment of temporomandibular joint syndrome with biofeedback training. *Journal of the American Dental Association,* 1975, **91,** 602–605.

Christensen, L. V. Jaw muscle fatigue and pains induced by experimental tooth clenching: A review. *Journal of Oral Rehabilitation,* 1981, **8,** 27–36.

Clark, G. T., Beemsterboer, P. L., & Rugh, J. D. Nocturnal masseter muscle activity and the symptoms of masticatory dysfunction. *Journal of Oral Rehabilitation,* 1981, **8,** 279–286.

Clarke, N. G., & Kardachi, B. J. The treatment of myofascial pain-dysfunction syndrome using the biofeedback principle. *Journal of Periodontology,* 1977, **48,** 643–645.

Cone, T. E., Jr. The nursing bottle caries syndrome. *Journal of the American Medical Association,* 1981, **245,** 2334.

Council on Dental Care Programs. Providing benefits for diagnosis and treatment of temporomandibular joint (TMJ) disorders under prepayment programs. American Dental Association, May 1982.

DeBoever, J. Functional disturbances of the temporomandibular joint. *Oral Science Review,* 1973, **2,** 100–117.

DeRisi, W. J. A conditioning approach to the treatment of bruxism (Doctoral dissertation, University of Utah, 1970). *Dissertation Abstracts International,* 1970, **31,** 1532-B. (University Microfilms No. 70-17,275)

Dohrmann, R. J., & Laskin, D. M. An evaluation of electromyographic biofeedback in the treatment of myofascial pain-dysfunction syndrome. *Journal of the American Dental Association,* 1978, **96,** 656–662.

Egermark-Eriksson, I. Malocclusion and some functional recordings of the masticatory system in Swedish schoolchildren. *Swedish Dental Journal,* 1982, **6,** 9–20.

Egermark-Eriksson, I., Carlsson, G. E., & Ingervall, B. Prevalence of mandibular dysfunction and orofacial parafunction in 7-, 11- and 15-year-old Swedish children. *European Journal of Orthodontics,* 1981, **3,** 163–172.

Etchison, P. F., Rugh, J. D., Fisher, J. G., & Ware, J. C. Bilateral activity of the temporal and masseter during nocturnal bruxism. *Journal of Dental Research,* 1982, **61,** 240. (Abstract)

Everett, M. S. Mouth protectors. *Dental Hygiene,* 1982, **56,** 27–33.

Finlayson, R. S., Rugh, J. D., & Dolwick, M. F. Electromyography of myofascial pain patients and controls in the natural environment. *Journal of Dental Research,* 1982, **61,** 277. (Abstract)

Frolich, E. Die Parofunktionen, Symptomatologie, Atiologie und Therapie. *Deutsche Zahnaerztliche Zeitschrift,* 1966, **21,** 536–547.

Funch, D. P., & Gale, E. N. Factors associated with nocturnal bruxism and its treatment. *Journal of Behavioral Medicine,* 1980, **3,** 385–397.

Gellin, M. E. Digital sucking and tongue thrusting in children. *Dental Clinics of North America,* 1978, **22,** 603–619.

Gessel, A. H. Electromyographic biofeedback and tricyclic anti-depressants in myofascial pain-dysfunction syndrome: Psychological predictors of outcome. *Journal of the American Dental Association,* 1975, **91,** 1048–1052.

Glaros, A. G., & Rao, S. M. Effects of bruxism: A review of the literature. *Journal of Prosthetic Dentistry,* 1977, **38,** 149–157.

Gold, S., Lipton, J., Marbach, J., & Gurion, B. Sites of psychophysiological complaints in MPD patients: II. Areas remote from orofacial region. *Journal of Dental Research,* 1975, **54**(Special Issue A), 165. (Abstract)

Grosfeld, O., & Czarnecka, B. Musculo-articular disorders of the stomatognathic system in school children examined according to clinical criteria. *Journal of Oral Rehabilitation,* 1977, **4,** 193–200.

Hansen, M. K. From the president. *Journal of Dentistry for Children,* 1978, **45,** 4.

Haryett, R. D., Hansen, F. C., Davidson, P. O., & Sandilands, M. L. Chronic thumb-sucking: The psychologic effects and the relative effectiveness of various methods of treatment. *American Journal of Orthodontics,* 1967, **53,** 569–585.

Helkimo, M. Epidemiological surveys of dysfunction of the masticatory system. *Oral Science Review,* 1976, **1,** 54–69.

Heller, R. F., & Strang, H. R. Controlling bruxism through automated aversive conditioning. *Behaviour Research and Therapy,* 1973, **11,** 327–329.

Hunt, W. A., Matarazzo, J. D., Weiss, S. M., & Gentry, W. D. Associative learning, habit, and health behavior. *Journal of Behavioral Medicine,* 1979, **2,** 111–124.

Johnson, L. R. Control of habits in treatment of malocclusion. *American Journal of Orthodontics and Oral Surgery,* 1938, **24,** 909–924.

Johnson, R. W., & Rugh, J. D. Temporal analysis of nocturnal bruxism during EMG feedback. *Journal of Dental Research,* 1980, **59,** 481. (Abstract)

Joint Committee on Dentistry and Speech Pathology, American Speech and Hearing Association and American Association of Dental Schools. Positions statement on myofunctional therapy. *Journal of the American Speech and Hearing Association,* 1974, **16,** 347.

Kamen, S. Tardive dyskinesia, a significant syndrome for geriatric dentistry. *Oral Surgery, Oral Medicine, Oral Pathology,* 1975, **39,** 52.

Kardachi, B. J. R., Bailey, J. O., Jr., & Ash, M. M., Jr. A comparison of biofeedback and occlusal adjustment on bruxism. *Journal of Periodontology,* 1978, **49,** 367–372.

King, D. L., & Leimone, C. A. Nursing bottle caries—A preventive dilemma. *Dental Assistant,* September/October 1978, pp. 18–19.

Knight, M. F., & McKenzie, H. S. Elimination of bedtime thumb-sucking in home settings through contingent reading. *Journal of Applied Behavior Analysis,* 1974, **7,** 33–38.

Kuch, E. V., Till, M. J., & Messer, L. B. Bruxing and non-bruxing children: A comparison of their personality traits. *Pediatric Dentistry,* 1979, **1,** 182–187.

LaForge, R., & Suczek, R. F. The interpersonal dimension of personality: An interpersonal check list. *Journal of Personality,* 1955, **24,** 94–112.

Laskin, D. M. Etiology of the pain-dysfunction syndrome. *Journal of the American Dental Association,* 1969, **79,** 147–153.

Leary, T. *Interpersonal diagnosis of personality.* New York: Ronald, 1957.

Levin, B. J. Chronic thumb sucking in older children. *Journal of the Canadian Dental Association,* 1958, **24,** 148–150.

Lindqvist, B. Bruxism in children. *Odontologisk Revy,* 1971, **22,** 413–424.

Lindqvist, B. Bruxism in twins. *Acta Odontologica Scandinavica,* 1974, **32,** 177–187.

Magnusson, T. Changes in recurrent headache and mandibular dysfunction after treatment with new complete dentures. *Journal of Oral Rehabilitation,* 1980, **7,** 1–11.

Malow, R. M., Olson, R. E., & Greene, C. S. Myofascial pain dysfunction syndrome: A psychophysiological disorder. In C. Golden, S. Alcaparras, F. Strider, & B. Graber (eds.), *Applied techniques in behavioral medicine.* New York: Grune and Stratton, 1981.

Martin, D. A six year old "behaviorist" solves her sibling's chronic thumbsucking problem. *Corrective and Social Psychiatry and Journal of Behavioral Technology Methods and Therapy,* 1975, **21,** 19–21.

Melamed, B. G., & Mealiea, W. L. Behavioral intervention in pain related problems in dentistry. In J. Ferguson & C. Taylor (eds.) *The comprehensive handbook of behavioral medicine* (Vol. 2). Jamaica, N.Y.: Spectrum, 1981.

Olkinuora, M. Bruxism: A review of the literature on, and a discussion of studies of bruxism and its psychogenesis and some new psychological hypotheses. *Suomen Hammaslaakariseuran Toimituksia,* 1969, **65,** 312–324.

Olson, R. E. Biofeedback for MPD patients non-responsive to drug and biteplate therapy. *Journal of Dental Research,* 1977, **56**(Special Issue B), B61. (Abstract)

Olson, R. E. Myofascial pain-dysfunction syndrome: Psychological aspects. In B. G. Sarnat & D. M. Laskin (Eds.), *The temporomandibular joint: A biological basis for clinical practice* (3rd ed.). Springfield, Ill.: Charles C Thomas, 1980.

Olson, R. E., Greene, C. S., & Solar, S. Comparison of two relaxation methods for the treatment of MPD syndrome. *Journal of Dental Research,* 1980, **59**(Special Issue A), 518. (Abstract)

Ozturk, M., & Ozturk, O. M. Thumbsucking and falling asleep. *British Journal of Medical Psychology,* 1977, **50,** 95–103.

Peck, C. L., & Kraft, G. Electromyographic biofeedback for pain related to muscle tension. *Archives of Surgery,* 1977, **112,** 889.

Phelan, W. J., III, Bachara, G. H., & Satterly, A. R. Severe hemorrhagic complication from thumb sucking. *Clinical Pediatrics,* 1979, **18,** 769–770.

Pinto, O. F. P. Temporomandibular joint problems in underwater activities. *Journal of Prosthetic Dentistry,* 1966, **16,** 772–781.

Popovich, F., & Thompson, G. W. Thumb- and finger-sucking: Its relation to malocclusion. *American Journal of Orthodontics,* 1973, **63,** 148–155.

Rao, S. M., & Glaros, A. G. Electromyographic correlates of experimentally induced stress in diurnal bruxists and normals. *Journal of Dental Research,* 1979, **58,** 1872–1878.

Reding, G. R., Rubright, W. C., & Zimmerman, S. O. Incidence of bruxism. *Journal of Dental Research,* 1966, **45,** 1198–1204.

Rieder, C. E. Possible premature degenerative temporomandibular joint disease in violinists. *Journal of Prosthetic Dentistry,* 1976, **35,** 662–664.

Rugh, J. D. A behavioral approach to the diagnosis and treatment of functional oral disorders: Biofeedback and self-control techniques. In J. D. Rugh, D. B. Perlis, & R. I. Disraeli (Eds.), *Biofeedback in dentistry: Research and clinical applications.* Phoenix: Semantodontics, 1977.

Rugh, J. D., Jacobs, D. T., Taverna, R. D., & Johnson, R. W. Psychophysiological changes and oral conditions. In L. K. Cohen & P. F. Bryant (Eds.), *Social science in dentistry* (Vol. II). Chicago: International Quintessence Publishing Group, in press.

Rugh, J. D., & Robbins, J. W. Oral habit disorders. In B. Ingersoll (Ed.), *Behavioral aspects in dentistry.* New York: Appleton-Century-Crofts, 1981.

Rugh, J. D., & Solberg, W. K. Electromyographic studies of bruxist behavior before and during treatment. *Journal of the California Dental Association,* 1975, **3**, 56–59.

Rugh, J. D., & Solberg, W. K. Psychological implications in temporomandibular pain and dysfunction. *Oral Science Review,* 1976, **1**, 3–30.

Schwartz, G. E., Ahren, G. L., & Brown, S. L. Lateralized facial muscle response to positive and negative emotional stimuli. *Psychophysiology,* 1979, **16**, 561–571.

Skiba, E. A., Pettigrew, L. E., & Alden, S. E. A behavioral approach to the control of thumbsucking in the classroom. *Journal of Applied Behavior Analysis,* 1971, **4**, 121–125.

Solberg, W. K., Woo, M. W., & Houston, J. B. Prevalence of mandibular dysfunction in young adults. *Journal of the American Dental Association,* 1979, **98**, 25–34.

Spielberger, C. D., Gorsuch, R. L., & Lushene, R. E. *State-Trait Anxiety Inventory* (Manual). Palo Alto: Consulting Psychologists Press, 1970.

Stenn, P. G., Mothersill, K. J., & Brooke, R. I. Biofeedback and a cognitive behavioral approach to treatment of myofascial pain dysfunction syndrome. *Behavioral Therapy,* 1979, **10**, 29–36.

Toller, P. A. Osteoarthrosis of the mandibular condyle. *British Dental Journal,* 1973, **134**, 223–231.

Traisman, A. S., & Traisman, H. S. Thumb- and finger-sucking: A study of 2,650 infants and children. *Journal of Pediatrics,* 1958, **52**, 566–572.

Williamson, E. H. Temporomandibular dysfunction in pretreatment adolescent patients. *American Journal of Orthodontics,* 1977, **72**, 429–433.

Yemm, R. Neurophysiologic studies of temporomandibular joint dysfunction. *Oral Science Review,* 1976, **1**, 31–53.

Zarb, G. A., & Carlsson, G. E. (Eds.), *Temporomandibular joint: Function and dysfunction.* Copenhagen: Munksgaard, 1979.

Zuckerman, M., & Lubin, B. *Manual for the Multiple Affect Adjective Checklist.* San Diego: Educational and Industrial Testing Service, 1965.

Zung, W. W. K. A self-rating depression scale. *Archives of General Psychiatry,* 1965, **12**, 63–70.

CHAPTER 64

ORAL HEALTH PROMOTION FOR THE ELDERLY

H. Asuman Kiyak

University of Washington, Seattle

The concept of oral health promotion or preventive dentistry for the elderly seems anomalous to both dental practitioners and older persons themselves. It is often assumed that dental disease and tooth loss are natural concomitants of aging. Furthermore, these persons ask, once the individual has lost many teeth from poor dental health in the middle years, what is there to prevent? In my own research and community education experience, this attitude of surprise and the accompanying misconceptions have emerged from dental practitioners, professionals and nonprofessionals alike who work with the elderly (including, amazingly, health educators) and especially from older persons. Even in current journal articles and books on health promotion for the elderly, recognition of the need for oral health promotion is lacking. Thus, for example, an excellent new book on this topic (Wells, 1982), which covers a broad spectrum of health issues, includes no references to oral health.

It is the aim of this chapter to introduce the reader to preventive dentistry for the elderly and to recognize its value for the overall health of older persons. It has been argued that health promotion and disease prevention can enhance the quality of life for the individual. It is the premise of this chapter that, because oral health is a critical factor in nutrition, speech, and esthetics, the prevention of oral disease has an even greater impact on the quality of life for older persons.

HEALTH BEHAVIORS IN THE ELDERLY

Interest in the health needs and behaviors of the elderly has increased steadily as the population over age 65 has grown. In 1900, this segment represented only 4% of the total U.S. population. By 1970, their ranks had expanded to 10.5%, with an increase to 11.5% in the latest census (U.S. Department of Commerce, 1982). The trend is expected to continue, with the greatest growth among the population aged 80 and older. This pattern of rapid population increase among older persons has been found throughout the developed and developing nations.

The implications of this burgeoning population for health care are quite evident. With increasing age, there is a greater incidence of disease and its accompanying disabilities. Among the population aged 65 and older, 80% have at least one chronic disease; a significant number have two or more, particularly among institutionalized elderly (NCHS, Note 1). This translates into high medical expenses for the aged person. In 1977, elderly Americans accounted for 22% of physician charges, 28% of hospital costs, and 84% of nursing home expenses. They also used 25% of all prescriptions dispensed in this country (Gibson &

Fisher, 1979). These increased expenses are not only because of higher utilization of medical services (6.7 physician contacts in 1975–1976 among the elderly versus 4.1 among those under 17 years of age, according to the National Center for Health Statistics (Note 2), but because the cost of treating multiple chronic illnesses is much higher than the cost of prevention. This is also true in current dental care of the elderly. Although utilization rates are quite low (for reasons that will be described later), dental treatment of older persons is often more complex and costly than treatment for the young. This is because today's elderly are more likely to seek professional dental care for fabrication and repair of dental prostheses and for oral problems caused by complete or partial dentures, both of which are more expensive than prevention (American Dental Association, 1978). By introducing preventive dentistry to older persons, we can reduce the high financial costs to the patient and to government or private insurers as well as the psychological costs of emergency dental care and the mortality risks of oral cancer. As stated by Stokes (1979), the cost of preventive health care is much lower than the cost of treatment for disease.

ORAL HEALTH BEHAVIOR IN THE ELDERLY

With the growing awareness of preventive dentistry in youth and middle age, tooth loss (edentulism) in the later years has become less prevalent. In 1958, 67% of persons over age 65 were edentulous. This percentage has steadily declined to 60% in 1971 and 51% in 1975 (American Dental Association, 1979). Once the individual has reached old age, however, self-care and professional dental care behaviors appear to decline, as evidenced by the reduced incidence of dental service utilization: 1.3 visits per year on average versus 1.8 for those aged 45 to 64, according to the National Center for Health Statistics (Note 3). Almost half (44%) have received no dental services in more than 5 years. Visits for checkups and/or cleaning are fewest for this age group; emergency treatment is highest.

Worse yet, edentulous elderly perceive even less need for prevention. Home care techniques for dentures are usually based on misinformation, television advertising, and information received 20 to 40 years ago, when the older person first obtained his or her dentures. Dental science has advanced considerably since then, with great strides in our understanding of the construction and care of dental prostheses. Many older persons report that they have not seen a dentist since they first received dentures many years ago, "because the dentures fit just fine, so why should I spend my money on dentists!" Surveys by the National Center for Health Statistics (Note 4) provide evidence for the prevalence of this attitude: 72% of edentulous elderly in a national survey reported that they had not seen a dentist in more than five years; only 5% indicated that they visited a dentist in any given year.

At this point, the reader may well ask why it is important to seek professional dental services as part of oral health promotion. One might argue, after all, that preventive health implies self-care and self-reliance, without relying on professional health care providers. Preventive dentistry, however, requires regular interaction with a professional dental team. The concept of preventive dentistry encompasses periodic examination of the dentition, soft tissue, and supporting structures, as well as professional prophylaxis, fluoride application, and education in appropriate home care behaviors for the individual's particular needs. This becomes especially important in the elderly, who, because of normal physiological changes, multiple chronic illnesses, and a high consumption of medications, often experience changes in the oral cavity and its functions. These include a change in the ridge that supports dentures, dry mouth (xerostomia), inflammation, and diseases of the soft tissue. Furthermore, it is important to provide the older person with up-to-date information on home care that is relevant to his or her current oral status. Hence, regular interaction with the dental team is a critical component of preventive dentistry for the elderly. In my experience, older persons have been found to benefit most from a combined program of periodic oral examination by a dentist and an interactive educational approach to teach them home care techniques.

APPROACHES TO PREVENTIVE DENTISTRY FOR THE ELDERLY

Background

I have recently completed two studies on enhancing self-care in dentistry among the elderly (Price & Kiyak, 1981; Kiyak, Note 5). This research was based on the premise that older persons, whether institutionalized or living independently in the community, can learn techniques of preventive dentistry that will improve oral hygiene, prevent further disease, and have a significant impact on their psychological well-being. By experiencing improved oral health through his or her own efforts, the older person's personal responsibility for health and competence will increase and learned helplessness will decrease, resulting in improved perceptions of general health and increased self-esteem.

It should be noted at the outset that preventive dentistry for the elderly was defined differently for these studies than the traditional concept. In the younger population, prevention implies freedom from disease and maintenance of all adult teeth. For older persons, particularly those who have lost some or all of their natural dentition, preventive dentistry must focus on the prevention of further disease, particularly iatrogenic disease caused by poorly fitting dental prostheses and prescribed regimens for medical conditions. The comfort and maximization of oral functions such as mastication and speech must be the goal of any preventive dentistry program for the elderly.

Both studies utilized techniques from behavioral psychology that have been applied successfully to gerontology. Among the various behavioral change programs, perhaps the most successful are those that have been used with institutionalized elderly. Verbal communication increased significantly among elderly mental hospital patients in two studies that used operant procedures (Hoyer, Kafer, Simpson, & Hoyer, 1974; Mueller & Atlas, 1972). Token economy programs have been successful with the elderly in increasing their exercise behavior (Libb & Clements, 1969), in reducing bizarre and dependent behavior while increasing interactions (Mishara, 1978), and in improving performance on experimental tasks (Swenson, 1971). The use of positive reinforcement in the form of material or verbal rewards has proved successful with diverse elderly persons (Meichenbaum, 1974; Rinke, C. L., Williams, J. J., Lloyd, K. E., & Smith-Scott, W., 1978; Sachs, 1975), but only one other study has attempted to change dental behaviors among older persons.

Description of the Program

One of the disadvantages of many behavioral change programs is their reliance on an external change agent. The researcher or an assistant monitors the individual's behavior and controls the reinforcement. This may be one reason why many behavioral change programs do not produce long-term effects. One of the few studies that utilized a self-management approach with the elderly was conducted by Meichenbaum (1974). The success of this technique suggests that it might be more effective in motivating the elderly, in enhancing their perception of control over their lifespace, and in producing long-term changes. A self-management approach should be particularly effective in improving oral health behavior. The behavior is within the direct control of the individual. It can easily be recorded by the performer, and even minor improvements are clearly detectable. This technique was therefore selected as the behavioral change approach to be tested in our study.

It was hypothesized in both studies that a self-monitoring system based on principles of behavior management (Hoyer, Mishara, & Reidel, 1975; Mishara, 1978; Sachs, 1975; Skinner, 1953; Weinstein & Getz, 1978) would be better than a traditional educational program in oral health. This approach should reduce oral disease conditions and improve the self-sufficiency of the elderly. It was anticipated that this self-sufficiency would spill into other areas of the aged individual's functioning, thereby increasing his or her perception of active mastery. The combined effects of better oral health and increased self-sufficiency should improve the morale, self-esteem, and perceived health status of participants in such a program. The effectiveness of self-monitoring for both immediate and long-term change was compared with an education-only program, and these two approaches were each combined with periodic oral examinations. A control group received no intervention. Both short-term and long-term changes in objectively assessed oral health status, perceived health status, morale, and self-esteem were measured.

Participants

The first study applied this model to a sample of older persons residing in a nursing home. Residents who were free of dementing illness and were physically capable of oral self-maintenance (i.e., their manual dexterity was not seriously impaired) were selected to participate in this study. Even in this skilled care facility, 76 of the 128 residents fulfilled these research criteria. Among the potential list of 76 persons, 68 completed the study. Their mean age was 82.8; the majority were female.

In the second study (Price & Kiyak, 1981), we sought to replicate our findings with elderly persons who were living in the community and to compare ethnic differences in response to the preventive dentistry intervention. The experiment was conducted in two local senior centers; in one the elderly were primarily Caucasians, and in the second they were all Japanese. In the latter setting, the educational program was conducted in Japanese by senior author S. Price. Twenty-seven elderly persons participated in the former, 33 in the latter. As one might expect, the mean age for this sample was lower than the nursing home sample (74.6 versus 82.8). This provided an opportunity to test the efficacy of a dental health promotion program for both "young-old" and "old-old," for both institutionalized and community elderly, and for two ethnic groups.

Research Design

Figure 64.1 illustrates the research design. As shown in the figure, interviews and baseline tooth and denture cleaning were conducted with all participants two weeks before the experimental interventions. Elderly persons who had been randomly assigned to the two experimental conditions were assessed for plaque levels just before the interventions. (For a description of the interview contents and the techniques of plaque assessments, see Kiyak, Note 5, and Price and Kiyak, 1981.) The educational interventions were conducted separately for the two groups during the subsequent three weeks. The content of these two health education programs was identical; techniques of maintenance for dentures and natural teeth, nutritional needs, and procedures for daily and professional oral health care were presented during the six sessions for each group. Modeling of correct behaviors was conducted for both groups. Each session lasted 25 to 30 minutes, with ample time for one-to-one interactions with the course instructor. The lack of published material for oral health education of the elderly made it difficult to provide appropriate handouts, but brief instructions, with diagrams, were given to participants, who were eager for such material to take back with them.[1] It was important to provide participants with appropriate preventive dentistry materials at the start of the intervention, in order to reduce the bias of varied preventive aids. Hence, each older person was provided with a new toothbrush and/or denture brush, toothpaste, floss and floss holders for those with natural teeth, and toothbrushes with special grips for those with grasping difficulties.

[1] The lack of material in this area has prompted me to produce written and audiovisual information specifically for the elderly. With a grant from the Jenny Baker Foundation, two booklets on caring for natural teeth and dentures were developed specifically for the elderly. A subsequent grant from the American Fund for Dental Health has allowed me to produce five slide-tapes and three videotapes on preventive dentistry issues for the elderly. Information about these materials may be obtained from the author.

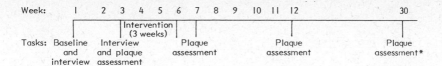

*Conducted in nursing home program only

Figure 64.1 Research design for nursing home and community studies.

Participants in the self-monitoring condition were given charts at the start of each week. Separate charts were designed for denture-wearers and for those with natural teeth. The former group was to note their frequency of washing and brushing dentures each day and whether the dentures had been removed each night before retiring. Those with natural teeth were asked to record frequency of brushing and flossing each day. Sample charts are presented in Figures 64.2 and 64.3.

Participants brought their charts to each session; areas of progress and areas in which no change had occurred were discussed in the group. Positive verbal reinforcement was provided by the instructor and other members when an individual showed improvement from week to week. It was decided that material reinforcements would not be used. In this manner, we could conclude that an effective intervention was clearly attributable to self-monitoring. Furthermore, future applications of this approach in settings for the elderly would probably not include material reinforcers.

WEEK _____

HOME CARE FOR: _____

(PUT AN X EVERYTIME YOU DO ANY OF THE FOLLOWING THINGS)

DAYS	BRUSHED DENTURES OR PARTIALS	CLEANED MOUTH	SOAKED DENTURES OR PARTIALS
MONDAY			
TUESDAY			
WEDNESDAY			
THURSDAY			
FRIDAY			
SATURDAY			
SUNDAY			

Figure 64.2 Self-reporting chart for prosthesis wearers.

WEEK _____

HOME CARE FOR: _____

(PUT AN X EVERYTIME YOU DO ANY OF THE FOLLOWING THINGS)

DAYS	BRUSHED TEETH	CLEANED MOUTH
MONDAY		
TUESDAY		
WEDNESDAY		
THURSDAY		
FRIDAY		
SATURDAY		
SUNDAY		

Figure 64.3 Self-reporting chart for dentulous elderly.

Follow-up

Each participant in the two nursing home experimental groups was assessed for plaque levels immediately after the educational intervention, 5 weeks later, and 4 months later. In the community sample, time constraints precluded a 4-month assessment. The control group was assessed for plaque levels at baseline and again 12 weeks later.

Group comparisons in the nursing home study revealed significant differences at the preintervention, immediate postintervention, and 12-week assessments. Although the self-monitoring group had the highest plaque levels before the intervention, they showed a significant and steady decline to 12 weeks postintervention. Their plaque levels then stabilized in the subsequent 4 months but did not decline further. This was particularly true for denture-wearers. There was no reduction in plaque levels for the education-only and control groups. This supports the need for a self-monitoring program if preventive dentistry education is to reduce plaque levels in the elderly.

A follow-up interview was conducted with all subjects at the 12-week assessment, to determine whether any changes had occurred in self-reports of oral health maintenance, perceived health, morale, and self-esteem. Significantly more elderly in the self-monitoring group reported using the correct procedures for oral hygiene (e.g., soaking dentures, frequent brushing of teeth and dentures) at follow-up than did those in the education-only group. That the self-monitoring group did indeed perform better and more frequent oral hygiene behaviors is supported by their improved plaque scores. Consistent with these findings, that group rated themselves highest on perceived health at the postintervention interview. Although the education-only groups also showed some improvement, the change was nonsignificant. Self-esteem did not change for any group, but persons in the self-monitoring group showed higher morale at the postintervention interview than at preintervention, and theirs was the highest of any group.

In the community study, we found no differences at preintervention between the Japanese and Caucasian elderly persons in plaque levels, self-reports of oral health behavior, and oral hygiene status. The Caucasians, however, held stronger beliefs than the Japanese regarding the importance of oral health. At the immediate postintervention assessment, both the self-monitoring and education-only groups showed significantly lower plaque levels than the control group in both the Japanese and the Caucasian centers. The second follow-up revealed that the plaque levels for those doing self-monitoring remained stable but that they increased for those in the education-only and control groups. This effect was particularly pronounced in the Japanese center. Perceived oral hygiene improved significantly only for the Japanese group at the follow-up interview. Significant improvements in dental beliefs and dental behaviors were found in both self-monitoring groups, but the Caucasian elderly in the lessons-only group also showed improvements in dental beliefs.

IMPLICATIONS FOR ORAL HEALTH PROMOTION FOR THE ELDERLY

These results provide dramatic support for the value of a behavioral approach to preventive dentistry education for the elderly. Long-term improvements are particularly impressive with self-monitoring techniques, although short-term change is possible with an education-only approach for community elderly. It is worth noting that self-monitoring techniques have a powerful impact on many aspects of preventive dentistry: home care, plaque levels, perceived health in general, beliefs about the importance of oral health, and morale. When one considers the role of beliefs in motivating the elderly to seek dental care, the finding that a self-monitoring approach can change beliefs is in itself a strong justification for using this technique in any health promotion program for the elderly. Furthermore, the success of this technique with two very different ethnic groups suggests that it may be a universally superior approach to a program that uses information dissemination alone.

Previous studies in general health education for the elderly (German, 1982; Lewis, Resnick, Schmidt, & Waxman, 1973) suggest that self-care instruction is effective for this population. It should be noted, however, that these studies relied on self-reports of behavioral change, not on objective assessments as in the preventive dentistry program reported here.

Hagebak and Hagebak (1980) cite six attitudinal barriers to effective practitioner–patient relationships. Although their focus is on the mental health worker, their findings may be generalized to all health care providers. The attitudinal barriers are as follows:

1. Older people cannot learn.
2. Older patients arouse one's own awareness of aging and mortality.
3. The "why bother" or "it is too late for them anyway" attitude is common.
4. The older person is forgetful and will quickly forget what is taught.
5. Unresolved parent-child conflicts are projected to the aged patient.
6. Older persons are perceived as experiencing a "second childhood" and should consequently be treated as children.

Research in gerontology has disputed many of these myths of aging, yet many health care providers persist in such beliefs. It is particularly important to overcome these stereotypes if effective health education programs are to be developed for the elderly. Both dental health educators and practitioners must recognize that older persons can in fact learn; that with repeated information presentation and self-monitoring they can assume responsibility for their own oral health; and that it is never too late for preventive dentistry, albeit with a different focus in old age. Finally, interactions between educator or practitioner and older person must always be on an adult level, although many seemingly basic concepts of oral health must be introduced to this age group, which has generally had little experience in oral health education.

In summary, therefore, we must emphasize that oral health promotion is not only possible but extremely effective for the elderly. Both persons living independently in the community and those with multiple chronic illnesses living in nursing homes may benefit from active participation in oral health education. A few principles must be kept in mind, however, when designing oral health promotion programs for the elderly. A detailed discussion of learning ability in the elderly and implications for health education is presented by Whitbourne and Sperbeck (1982).

The following principles grew out of my own experiences with preventive dentistry for the elderly:

1. Learning occurs more slowly in old age, and the rate of recall is slower. Hence, any information presented to the older learner must be repeated several times and reinforced both visually and aurally. Thus, for example, slides and films to describe graphically the information presented in a lecture, as well as booklets, pamphlets, or other handouts should be used.

2. Active learning techniques are generally better than passive learning for all age groups, but particularly for the elderly. Because of changing learning styles with aging, a self-monitoring program in which the individual actively participates in his or her learning progress is more effective than a lecture-only approach.

3. Because of sensory changes with aging, written material must be presented in large print with contrasting figure-ground relations. Photos and charts must be simple and of high visual quality.

4. Because fatigue occurs more rapidly for the elderly, it is important to keep information sessions brief, preferably less than 45 minutes. Frequent and brief sessions are far superior to fewer sessions that each last an hour or longer.

5. A professional dental practitioner or health educator is not necessary in presenting an effective oral health promotion program. A volunteer or paraprofessional can present the necessary information after developing the key concepts and design with a professional.

6. Motivation will be significantly enhanced with regular feedback to participants regarding their success in achieving predetermined oral health goals. To the extent that older persons received individual feedback and praise from the educator in our experimental programs, they were more likely to take an active role in their change program and less likely to drop out.

By keeping in mind these principles of health education and applying them to any oral health promotion program, future program developers will increase the potential of successful outcomes. As we have shown, older persons of diverse functional capacity and different ethnic groups can benefit from a well-designed program to promote individual responsibility and self-care in oral health.

REFERENCE NOTES

1. National Center for Health Statistics (NCHS). *Health characteristics of persons with chronic activity limitation: U.S., 1974*. Vital and Health Statistics, Series 10, No. 112, 1976.

2. National Center for Health Statistics (NCHS). *Physician visits volume and interval since last visit, U.S., 1975*. Vital and Health Statistics, Series 10, No. 125–129, 1978.

3. National Center for Health Statistics (NCHS). *Dental visits volume and interval since last visit, U.S., 1978 & 1979*. Vital and Health Statistics, Series 10, No. 138, 1982.

4. National Center for Health Statistics (NCHS). *Edentulous persons, U.S., 1971.* Vital and Health Statistics, Series 10, No. 89, 1974.

5. Kiyak, H. A. *An experimental preventive dentistry program for institutionalized elderly.* Final report submitted to NIDR (Grant No. 123-De 05235), 1979.

REFERENCES

American Dental Association. *Utilization of dental services by the elderly population.* Chicago: Author, 1978.

German, P. S. Delivery of care to older people: Issues and outlooks. In T. Wells (ed.), *Aging and health promotion.* Rockville, Md.: Aspen Systems Corporation, 1982.

Gibson, R. M., & Fisher, C. R. Age differences in health care spending: Fiscal year 1977. *Social Security Bulletin,* 1979, **42,** 3–16.

Hagebak, J. E., & Hagebak, B. R. Serving the mental health needs of the elderly. *Community Mental Health Journal,* 1980, **16,** 263–275.

Hoyer, W. J., Kafer, R. A., Simpson, S. C., & Hoyer, F. W. Reinstatement of verbal behavior in elderly mental patients using operant procedures. *Gerontologist,* 1974, **14,** 149–152.

Hoyer, W. J., Mishara, B. L., & Riedel, R. G. Problem behaviors as operants: Applications with elderly. *Gerontologist,* 1975, **15,** 452–456.

Lewis, C. E., Resnick, B. A., Schmidt, G., & Waxman, D. Activities, events and outcomes in ambulatory patient care. *New England Journal of Medicine,* 1973, **280,** 645.

Libb, J. W., & Clements, C. B. Token reinforcement in an exercise program for hospitalized geriatric patients. *Perceptual and Motor Skills,* 1969, **28,** 957–958.

Meichenbaum, D. Self-instructional strategy training: A cognitive prosthesis for the aged. *Human Development,* 1974, **17,** 273–280.

Mishara, B. L. Geriatric patients who improve in token economy and general milieu treatment programs: A multivariate analysis. *Journal of Consulting and Clinical Psychology,* 1978, **46,** 1340–1348.

Mueller, D. J., & Atlas, L. Resocialization of regressed elderly residents: A behavioral management approach. *Journal of Gerontology,* 1972, **27,** 390–392.

Price, S., & Kiyak, H. A. A behavioral approach to improving oral health among the elderly. *Special Care in Dentistry,* 1981, **1,** 267–274.

Rinke, C. L., Williams, J. J., Lloyd, K. E., Smith-Scott, W. The effects of prompting and reinforcement on self-bathing by elderly residents of a nursing home. *Behavior Therapy,* 1978, **9,** 873–881.

Sachs, D. A. Behavioral techniques in a residential nursing home facility. *Journal of Behavioral Therapy and Experimental Psychiatry,* 1975, **6,** 123–127.

Skinner, B. F. *Science and human behavior.* New York: Macmillan, 1953.

Stokes, B. Self-care: A nation's best health insurance. *Science,* 1979, **205,** 1.

Swenson, E. W. The effect of instruction and reinforcement on the behavior of geriatric psychiatric patients. In R. D. Rubin, H. Fensterheim, A. A. Lazarus, & C. M. Franks (Eds.), *Advances in behavior therapy.* New York: Academic Press, 1971.

U.S. Department of Commerce (Bureau of the Census). *Population estimates and projections.* Series P-25. Washington, D.C.: U.S. Government Printing Office, 1977, 1982.

Weinstein, P., & Getz, T. *Changing health behavior for dental professionals.* Chicago: Science Research Associates, 1978.

Wells, T. (Ed.). *Aging and health promotion.* Rockville, Md.: Aspen Systems Corporation, 1982.

Whitbourne, S. K., & Sperbeck, D. J. Health care maintenance for the elderly. In T. Wells (Ed.), *Aging and health promotion.* Rockville, Md.: Aspen Systems Corporation, 1982.

SECTION 9
SAFETY

CHAPTER 65

OVERVIEW

EDWARD R. CHRISTOPHERSEN

University of Kansas Medical Center

The maintenance of health can and should be a cost-effective enterprise, an enterprise that attracts young, enthusiastic investigators, an enterprise that attracts more money for research and for services than any kind of treatment program. Ironically, programs that concentrate their efforts on the elimination or reduction of injuries and accidents have attracted relatively little interest from the medical community. Yet injuries and accidents claim more lives, cause more suffering, and cost society more money than any other area covered in this handbook.

Dr. Leon Robertson introduces some provocative thoughts and figures on childhood injuries, using child passenger safety as the main point of departure. He emphasizes the efficacy of passive measures, including actions by the manufacturers of products as well as legislative actions that might affect the production and distribution of products, and reviews the most effective campaigns in the area of childhood safety.

Dr. Edward Christophersen summarizes the research aimed at increasing the safety of the single most dangerous environment for our nation's children—the automobile. Although it sounds complex, his detailing of an ideal child passenger safety program serves as an example of how to analyze and break down a complex program so that no single individual or department is responsible for more than a small piece of the total effort. The fact that such programs are already operational in several places proves that they can be carried from the drawing board to reality without huge expenditures of state or federal monies.

Dr. Frederick Rivara's chapter provides a comprehensive review of the epidemiology of childhood injuries. He carefully details exactly what types of injuries take what kind of toll from society each year. The figures he presents are remarkable—sometimes shocking. His discussion of the threshold theory of injury causation provides a very useful format for summarizing the existing knowledge in the field of injury prevention.

Dr. Robert Dershewitz's chapter builds upon and extends Dr. Rivara's work to include the topic of childhood household safety. He reviews the existing literature on household safety in a way that leaves the reader feeling familiar with and conversant in an area of investigation of which he or she might not even have been aware previously.

No book on health behaviors would be complete without a discussion of injuries and accidents, since every estimate places accidents as the leading cause of death and suffering in the United States. It is ironic that the major third-party payers will pay for the results of accidents but not for the prevention of them; reimbursement programs, too, will pay for management of acute and chronic trauma cases, but they will not pay to prevent the traumas in the first place.

CHAPTER 66

BEHAVIOR AND INJURY PREVENTION: WHOSE BEHAVIOR?

LEON S. ROBERTSON

Yale University

Injuries are the third leading cause of death in the United States, following cardiovascular diseases and cancers. Because of the age distributions of the persons involved, however, injury-related deaths contribute disproportionately to years of life lost. Injuries account for as many preretirement years lost as cardiovascular diseases and cancers combined (Haddon & Baker, 1981). The median age at death is 76 for cardiovascular diseases, 65 for cancers, 27 for motor vehicle injuries, 53 for other unintentional injuries, 32 for homicide, and 50 for suicide.

Half of the deaths due to injuries (excluding intentional injuries) and half of the permanent disabilities associated with traumatic spinal cord damage result from motor vehicle crashes. Because of their prominence, the years of life lost, and the fact that research in injury epidemiology and control has been directed largely at motor vehicle injuries, most of the material in this chapter is drawn from that literature. To a large extent, however, the principles of injury control are applicable not only to all injuries but to environmental hazards generally (Haddon, 1980).

For centuries, the events called accidents were mostly considered to be the consequence of human behavior, luck, or "acts of God." The sudden onset of the events and the lack of intent of those involved were emphasized in such thinking—to the neglect of agents, vehicles, and environmental factors involved. The conceptualization of agents that do harm, vehicles that convey the agents to susceptible human beings, and environmental factors that intensify or diminish exposure was applied successfully to the sudden, unintended events called infectious diseases in the nineteenth century. Up to that time, these events were also attributed to errant behavior, luck, and God. A few critical scholars were aware that more than human error or misbehavior was involved in injuries, but the concepts of epidemiology were not fully considered until the third quarter of the twentieth century (Haddon, Suchman, & Klein, 1964). A perceptive experimental psychologist, James G. Gibson, apparently was the first person to recognize the various forms of energy—mechanical, thermal, electrical, ionizing—as the necessary and specific agents of injury (Gibson, 1961).

The importance of necessary and specific agents for harm cannot be overemphasized. If such agents can be identified and controlled, the harm will not occur. As an illustration, if the mechanical energy associated with motor vehicles, guns, and falls from elevated heights can be controlled so that it does not exceed the injury tolerance of human tissue, injury associated with these vehicles would not occur. Other than the use of motor vehicles, guns,

Preparation of this chapter was supported by a grant from the Henry J. Kaiser Family Foundation.

stairs, and the like, there is no human behavior that is a necessary condition for injury. Relative risk of injury is greater when people behave in certain ways—such as drinking more than one ounce of alcohol per hour—but not all people whose behavior contributes to injury have consumed alcohol. Therefore, it is not a necessary condition.

The behavior of persons present when an injury occurs has been the major focus of injury research and injury control efforts. Largely ignored, however, is the behavior of designers, manufacturers, and suppliers of agents and vehicles of injury. Thus, there are three groups whose behavior is problematic with respect to understanding injuries and injury control: persons at the scene, persons who provide hazardous products and environments, and scientists who focus on the former to the neglect of the latter.

Injury control programs directed at individual behaviors may attempt to change behaviors that contribute to injuries—driving skills, alcohol use, aggression, attentiveness—or behaviors that increase protection, such as seat belt use. Programs aimed at voluntary behavioral change are called by a variety of names—education, rehabilitation, motivation, behavior modification, anticipatory guidance, incentives, social support. These approaches can generally be characterized as persuasion. Sometimes the stated goal is to change cognition, emotions, attitudes, values, and the like, but the fundamental question is whether the relevant behavior is changed and whether that change is sufficient and sustained so that injuries are reduced. Another type of effort involves laws or administrative rules directed at specific behaviors, with sanctions for nonconformity.

PERSUASION

Education is usually directed at training in skills related to handling energy or vehicles and at attitudes, values, and emotions that may affect the exercise of those skills. The assumption that formal educational programs conducted by specially trained instructors are superior to informal training or learning of skills is not supported by studies of driver education. Studies that found lower crash rates among students who had driver education in high school than among those who did not have been discredited (McGuire & Kersh, 1969). The correlation virtually disappeared when miles driven and school achievement were controlled statistically (Conger, Miller, & Rainey, 1966). Recent experiments in which students were assigned to formal driver education and control groups, rather than self-selecting into the course, found no difference in subsequent crashes per licensed driver or per mile driven (Ray, Weaver, Brink, & Stock, 1982; Shaoul, 1975). In the case of motorcyclist education, crashes per licensed driver were higher in the trained group than in the control group in one study, apparently because the training increased confidence without reducing risk (Raymond & Tatum, 1977).

An unanticipated harmful effect of driver education has been found in its resulting earlier licensure of younger drivers. In one of the controlled experiments, the formally trained drivers, who were licensed earlier, had more crashes per person in the follow-up period compared to the control group, who learned on their own or were trained by parents (Shaoul, 1975). A comparison of 27 states revealed about the same fatal crash rate per 10,000 licensed drivers 16 to 17 years old in states where most such drivers had high school driver education and in states where only a small proportion were trained in high school. The proportion of the 16- to 17-year-old population that was licensed was much higher in correlation with the greater numbers taking high school driver education. The net effect was higher death involvement rates per 16- to 17-year-old population by drivers of that age in states that had more high school driver education (Robertson & Zador, 1978).

In Connecticut high schools, driver education was eliminated in nine school districts when state funds for the program were no longer available. The licensure of 16- to 17-year-olds and their crash involvement declined precipitously in those communities, compared to little change in similar districts that retained the course. Only about 25% of 16- to 17-

year-olds who would have been licensed after taking high school driver education did so after home or commercial training; three out of four waited until they were 18 or older (Robertson, 1980).

High school driver education is what economists call a moral hazard. No matter how benevolent the intention, the program makes the injury problem worse. And since 16- to 17-year-old drivers kill two other people for each one of them who dies, the risk increases for everyone in the community, not just for those who choose to take the course. The taxpayers' money is being used for a program that increases the taxpayers' risk.

Among older drivers who have been or would be licensed with or without formal training, the potential for driver education to reduce crashes remains to be demonstrated by adequately designed research. Persons trained in commercial driver training schools (Jones, 1973) or on specially designed training tracks (Council, Roper, & Sadof, Note 1) have no better subsequent records per licensed driver than those trained in high school. The National Safety Council claims that its "Defensive Driving" course reduces crashes, but the research base for the claims is flawed by numerous potential biases (O'Neill, 1974).

The "Defensive Driving" course has been studied in an experiment involving random assignment to training and control groups of drivers convicted of particular offenses. Those given the "Defensive Driving" course had fewer subsequent convictions but no difference in crash records compared to those who received the usual court treatment (Hill & Jamieson, 1978).

Screening of high-risk drivers for training or rehabilitation assumes that the criteria for screening are substantially predictive of subsequent crash records and that the training and rehabilitation will effectively reduce crashes. The search for traits indicative of accident proneness continues in some circles, despite the overwhelming evidence that no such traits exist. Studies dating from the 1930s (Forbes, 1939) have found that most drivers involved in crashes during a period of 1, 2, or 3 years will not be involved in the subsequent period. In a random sample of 17,769 California drivers, for example, 70% of those who crashed in a 3-year period had had no crashes in the prior 3 years (Burg, 1970); and at least some of the repeated crashes could have occurred because of relatively constant exposure to more hazardous driving conditions.

In the California sample, seven different aspects of vision as well as driver age, annual mileage, and prior convictions were not effectively predictive of subsequent crash records. Only 8% of the variation in crash records of males and 6% of that of females was explained by the best predictive equation (Burg, 1971). Studies that include measures of psychological traits as well as measures of exposure find little or no correlation between crashes and standardized measures of psychological traits (Schuster & Guilford, 1964).

The best researched behavioral correlate of serious crashes is blood alcohol concentration. About half the drivers killed have blood alcohol levels of 0.10% by weight or more compared to less than 5% of drivers tested at the same times and places and moving in the same direction as the fatally injured drivers (McCarroll & Haddon, 1962). Screening such drivers from the population, however, is problematic. About 1 in 2,000 drivers with illegal blood alcohol levels is actually arrested. The offense may be reduced to a less serious charge or no conviction obtained, so that very few drivers in fatal crashes have alcohol-related convictions on their prior records.

Using prior violation records to predict severe crash rates results in better predictions than using them to predict all crashes. Nevertheless, the number of false positives and false negatives is very large. About 23% of drivers involved in fatal crashes have more than one conviction for a moving violation in the prior 3 years, compared to 6.5% of a sample of all drivers (Robertson & Baker, 1975). Half of those involved in fatal crashes have no prior convictions (false negatives). Moreover, if 6.5% of licensed drivers were identified as positives, about 9.4 million drivers would have to be treated with absolute success to prevent less than a fourth of fatal crashes. Thus, there would be more than 9 million false positives.

Not only would rehabilitation of drivers so screened not be absolute, but the evidence for any efficacious effect is difficult to find. The alcohol safety action projects, which included increased law enforcement, improved court procedures, and rehabilitation programs in selected cities, produced no statistically significant reduction in fatalities when compared to cities that did not have the projects (Zador, 1976). In a controlled study of persons convicted of driving while intoxicated, those who received court-assigned rehabilitation were compared to those who received the usual court treatment; the rehabilitation group had a worse subsequent crash record than the control group. Drivers in the rehabilitation program were allowed to keep their licenses, but some in the comparison group had their licenses suspended for a time, possibly accounting for the difference (Preusser, Ulmer, & Adams, 1976).

A Texas study assigned drivers with poor records either to a rehabilitation-training program or to a control group. The identified groups were drivers aged 21 years or older who had four or more crashes or convictions and younger drivers who had two or more crashes or convictions. The trained drivers who were 25 to 34 years old showed a slight improvement in subsequent crash records compared to the control group, but among the younger drivers, the control group improved more than the trained group. The net effect for all groups was not presented (Edwards & Ellis, 1976).

In Wisconsin, an individual counseling program for drivers who accumulated demerit points for convictions during a certain period (12 in 12 months, 18 in 24 months, or 24 in 36 months) was compared to a randomly selected control group with the same points but no counseling. During the following year, counseled drivers had fewer convictions but the same number of crashes as the control group (Fuchs, 1980). Apparently, some training and rehabilitation programs change some of the behaviors that increase probability of arrest and conviction for moving violations. The correlation between such convictions and crashes is so low, however, that the effect on crashes is negligible.

It is clear that increasing knowledge or skills does not necessarily reduce risk to the individual, and, to the extent that increased knowledge or skills leads to increased exposure to hazardous agents and vehicles, the net effect is to increase rather than reduce injuries. The use of alcohol and drugs that increases the risk of injury has probably been exacerbated by the proliferation of alcohol and drug education in high schools. A comparison of students assigned to a drug education course (including alcohol) and those in a control group found that use of alcohol, marihuana, and LSD and selling of the latter two drugs increased among those who had taken the course. Apparently, the education, while increasing knowledge, had reduced fear of using the drugs (Stuart, 1974).

Other than the public educational system, the mass media are the primary means available for reaching large numbers of people with a relatively uniform persuasive approach. The media are not as effective at changing consumer behavior as advertising agencies would have us believe, however. Many ad campaigns fail, and even the successful ones usually change buying behavior by only a few percentage points. So-called public service advertising related to health behaviors is seldom researched adequately before it is used widely.

Advertising urging seat belt use in cars was not properly evaluated until the 1970s. In a study in which radio and television advertising developed by private and governmental agencies was used intensively in one community and moderately in another, belt use in these communities was compared to its use in a third community that did not have the advertising. The advertising campaigns had no effect (Fleischer, Note 2).

Television advertising, based on factors correlated with belt use in a prior study (Robertson, O'Neill, & Wixom, 1972) was shown for 9 months on one cable of a two-cable television system in a community used for marketing studies. The ads were shown some 900 times, often in prime time—contrary to most public service ads—and were used on programs appealing to specific audiences for whom the ads were designed. Belt use of drivers was observed before, during, and after the campaign, and license numbers were used to match the households where the cars were garaged to the households on each cable. Belt use was no different among people from households on the two cables or among those not on the cables before, during, or after the campaign (Robertson, Kelley, O'Neill, Wixom, Eis-wirth, & Haddon, 1974). Campaigns said to be effective are based on claimed rather than observed use, and follow-up observations reveal no actual effect (Robertson, 1977a).

Clinically based programs have a small effect on child restraint use but no effect on removal of hazards in the home, as discussed by other authors in this section. Apparently, these more personalized approaches, which are not possible in the mass media, can have an effect, but the discomfort and inconvenience associated with the use of seat belts and child restraints and with rearrangement of the home environment is difficult to counter by persuasion.

Persuasion by irritation has not been effective. In an attempt to avoid a governmental rule for improving the crashworthiness of cars, auto executives persuaded the government to allow a continuous buzzer-light warning system in 1972–1973 model cars and an interlock system in 1974 models that would prevent the cars from starting if belts were not extended from their stowed positions in front outboard seats. Within 6 months of the introduction of the buzzer-light system, a survey of belt use in 1972 cars found no significant difference in use in cars manufactured before the rule went into effect January 1, 1972, and those manufactured afterward (Robertson & Haddon, 1974).

Surveys of belt use in 1974 interlock-equipped cars found that belt use doubled in compari-son to use in 1973 models, but this effect of the interlock system was temporary. Complaints that cars would not start with dogs, groceries, and the like, in the front seat resulted in congressional action to prohibit governmentally required interlock systems (Robertson, 1975).

The use of rewards for belt users results in increased use so long as the rewards continue, but belt use returns to preexperimental rates when the rewards are removed. Drivers who were given a chance to win a prize if they were subsequently observed using seat belts at a parking lot increased their use from 17% to a range of from 34% to 43%, depending on frequency of prizes during the period that prizes were given (Elman & Killebrew, 1978). When such incentives are no longer available, however, belt use returns to the old rate (Geller, Talbott, & Paterson, Note 3).

It has been argued that belt use is a habit that, once established, will continue. This does not appear to be the case when the increased use is a result of rewards. Although the increases found in studies involving rewards encourage the conclusion that protective behavior can be increased, maintenance of those increases for behaviors that must occur frequently to be fully effective remains to be demonstrated.

It may be possible to apply the principles of operant conditioning to optimize the magni-tude and frequency of rewards for substantially increasing protective behaviors. For such a program to be successful for a wide variety of behaviors, however, substantial sums of money and a large contingent of observers would have to be employed indefinitely. The potential for corruption would also pose a major problem.

LAWS

Generally more successful than the persuasive approach are laws and administrative rules applied to publicly observable behaviors. Seat belt use in such countries as Australia and New Zealand has been sustained at about 80% since the enactment of laws requiring belt use in those countries in the early 1970s. A belt use law was found to be less successful in Ontario, Canada, where belt use declined from 70% immediately after the law's enactment to about 50% 6 months later. Belt use by teenagers did not increase at all in Ontario and is lower than belt use by adults in Australia and New Zealand (Robertson, 1978).

Motor vehicle deaths have declined as a result of belt use laws, though not as much as would be expected from the known effectiveness of belts in crashes and the observed use rate. In Australia, deaths were reduced 20% in urban areas and 10% in rural areas in Victoria when the law was enacted, compared to changes in other provinces that did not enact the law at the same time (Foldvary & Lane, 1974). This reduction would have been twice as large if belt use had increased uniformly among groups in the population with differences in fatal crash involvement prior to the law. To the extent that the more crash-involved groups, such as teenagers, do not comply with the law, the potential effect is not realized in fact.

Use of child restraints or seat belts is required by law in the United States only for children 4 years old and younger. Following the lead of Tennessee—the first state to adopt such a law—about 20% of the states had child restraint laws by 1982. The Tennessee law increased restraint use for children up to age 4 from 8% to 29% in the first 2 years (Williams & Wells, 1981). The vast majority of children remain unrestrained in cars, and states have quickly adopted the 4-year-old limit for required use, apparently because of the precedent in the first state to have such a law.

Even when laws directed at individual behavior are effective, political action by persons affected by the laws may result in their repeal. Laws requiring helmet use by motorcyclists were enacted in most states in the 1960s. Surveys found virtually 100% use of helmets in states with such laws, and motorcyclist deaths declined 30% in those states, compared to no change in states without the laws in the same period (Robertson, 1976). Yet in the 1970s, about half the states repealed their helmet laws in response to intense lobbying by a minority of motorcyclists who were opposed to the laws. Public opinion polls found that the majority of the public and even a majority of motorcyclists were in favor of the laws, but the legislatures apparently were convinced by the special pleading of the minority (Baker, 1980).

Laws directed at behaviors that are more difficult to observe are much less effective. To accurately detect an illegal blood alcohol concentration, it is necessary under U.S. law to have probable cause for stopping a driver and requesting a blood or breath sample. Many drivers whose abilities to react in an emergency are severely impaired by alcohol are nevertheless able to operate the vehicle under normal conditions in compliance with other traffic laws (Moskowitz, Note 4). This at least partially explains the fact that only about 1 in 2,000 drivers illegally impaired by alcohol is actually arrested for the offense.

Special crackdowns on drunk driving sometimes create a perception that the probability of arrest has increased. The British Road Safety Act of 1968 initially created that impression, and the death rate was temporarily reduced by 25%. When drivers learned that the probability of arrest was much lower than that claimed by the authorities, however, the death rate returned to the level that would have been expected without the new law (Ross, 1973). The threat of severe penalties for drunk driving, such as jail sentences in the Scandinavian countries, had no discernible effect on death rates coincident with adoption of the penalties (Ross, 1975). Visitors to those countries are often impressed that in a group situation in which drinking occurs, someone abstains and drives the others home. It is likely that most such groups consist of light drinkers rather than those who consume the amounts necessary to produce the blood alcohol concentrations commonly found in fatally injured drivers.

In organizations that have substantial administrative control of their members' behavior, some effect of alcohol control programs has been found. Airmen at an air force base who were involved in alcohol-related crashes were labeled as deviant and were subjected to administrative review and psychiatric referral. Injury rates declined in comparison to those at another base that did not have an alcohol control program (Barmack & Payne, 1961).

THE PASSIVE APPROACH

Historically, the most successful public health programs have been those that modify agents, vehicles, and environments to reduce potential harm without requiring each individual to be protected to take any action. This approach has been appropriately called *passive* (Haddon & Goddard, 1962). Good examples are pasteurization of milk by the processor before it reaches the consumer and treatment of water by the supplier to reduce or eliminate pathogens.

The passive approach has been effective even where behavior is deliberately directed toward self-destruction. In Birmingham, England, marked reductions in suicides involving use of domestic coal-gas were observed when the carbon monoxide content of the gas was reduced. Only a slight increase in suicides using other methods was found among men and no increase was found among women. The net effect was a reduction in suicides without any attempt to change suicidal behavior (Hassel & Trethowan, 1972).

In 1968, new cars manufactured for sale in the United States were required by federal standards to meet performance criteria for crashworthiness and crash avoidance. Steering assemblies that absorb energy in frontal crashes, rather than spearing drivers in the chest, and highly penetration-resistant windshields were important requirements. Reduced light reflection in drivers' eyes and redundant braking systems were required to increase the protection not only of drivers and passengers but of other road users as well. Within 10 years, deaths to car occupants and other road users were about 9,000 fewer per year than would have been expected from the mix of types and ages of vehicles (Robertson, 1981).

Despite the demonstrated success of the modest initial standards, vehicle manufacturers have massively and systematically resisted any further governmental requirements. Occasionally, an executive of one of the manufacturing companies will acknowledge that federal standards are necessary so that all must meet the same criteria to the competitive advantage of none. There has been no single instance, however, in which a specific standard was supported by a manufacturing company in the rule-making process. In a propaganda war against the government, the car companies have used such tactics as accounting tricks to overstate costs (U.S. Department of Transportation, Note 5).

Behavioral scientists have not yet found these behaviors of manufacturers worthy of systematic study. A few have been party to the promotion of a theory claiming that increased crash protection is ineffective because of drivers' adjustments to reduced personal risk. According to this theory, drivers have a level of risk that they are willing to accept, and they drive more "intensively" when that risk is reduced—thus increasing the hazard to other road users (Peltzman, 1975).

Studies of driver behavior and injuries to other road users when crash protection is increased do not support the theory. Comparison of seat belt use by drivers who were the first to stop when traffic lights changed to red and by those who drove through the light found 9% belt use among the former and 1% belt use among the latter (Deutsch, Sameth, & Akinyemi, Note 6). Following distances maintained by drivers on freeways in Ontario, where belt use is required by law, are distributed similarly to those maintained across the river in Michigan, where belt use is less than a third that in Ontario. In both areas, belt users allow a greater gap between their cars and cars in front of them than nonusers do (Evans, Wasielewski, & von Buseck, Note 7). In the aforementioned study of federal safety standards, cars that met the standards had significantly fewer fatal collisions with pedestrians, motorcyclists, and bicyclists per miles driven than other cars and trucks did (Robertson, 1981). Proponents of "danger compensation theory" cite a study that found slightly higher speeds on curves by drivers whose vehicles were equipped with studded tires than by those without such equipment (Rumar, Gerggrund, Jernberg, & Ytterbon, 1976). The tire-gripping capability more than compensated for the higher speeds, however, and the possibility that those who drive faster may more often choose studded tires could account for the difference, rather than choice of speed given the equipment.

Modifications of vehicles and road environments using available technology would reduce motor vehicle deaths by substantially more than half in a decade (Robertson, 1977c). The developer of a research safety vehicle that would provide crash protection far in excess of any proposed standard says that it could be mass-produced and sold at about the same cost to the consumer as currently priced compact cars (Kramer, 1978). Surveys of the public's willingness to pay for increased crash protection repeatedly find that most people desire such protection and are willing to pay for it (Robertson, 1977b). Private marketing studies by General Motors more than a decade ago found that half of new car buyers wanted air bags that inflate automatically in severe frontal crashes and were willing to pay their cost (General Motors Corporation, Note 8). Yet GM offered air bags on only a few luxury models for a couple of years in the mid 1970s, with virtually no advertising of their availability. Potential buyers were discouraged by dealers and often experienced delays in receiving their cars when they persisted (Karr, 1976).

The head rest in recent-model cars is actually intended to cushion the head and neck from so-called whiplash injury in rear-end collisions. Integrated seat backs that do not require adjustment—the passive approach—have long been known to be more effective than those that must be adjusted (O'Neill, Haddon, Kelley, & Sorenson, 1972). Yet the auto companies continue to use the adjustable types in many models. Furthermore, adjustable seat backs cost an average $28 more per car than integrated seat backs (U.S. Department of Transportation, Note 9). Thus, it is not an attempt to save costs, as is often claimed, that explains corporate behavior.

One-third of motor vehicle deaths occur when vehicles crash into trees, utility poles, bridge abutments, and the like. The sites where these are likely to occur have been identified (Wright & Robertson, 1976), and the means are available to remove the hazards or to provide energy-absorbing material in front of them. Yet few dollars for road modification are spent for that purpose. Moreover, in some states, road authorities have a policy of requiring a cost-benefit analysis of each site before it is modified. In some cases, that analysis probably costs more than the work necessary to remove the hazard.

Why do corporate and government officials behave as they do regarding the public's risk of injury? That is a prominent question on the agenda of behavioral health.

REFERENCE NOTES

1. Council, F. M., Roper, R. B., & Sadof, M. G. *An evaluation of North Carolina's multi-vehicle range program in driver education: A comparison of range and non-range students.* Chapel Hill: North Carolina Highway Safety Research Center, 1975.

2. Fleischer, G. A. *An experiment in the use of broadcast media in highway safety.* Los Angeles: University of Southern California, Department of Industrial and Systems Engineering, 1972.

3. Geller, E. S., Talbott, E., & Paterson, L. *A cost-effective incentive strategy for motivating seat belt usage.* Blacksburg: Virginia Polytechnic Institute, 1981. (Mimeographed)

4. Moskowitz, H. A behavioral mechanism of alcohol-related accidents. In *Proceedings of the First Annual Conference of the National Institutes of Alcohol Abuse and Alcoholism.* Washington, D.C.: U.S. Department of Health, Education and Welfare, 1971.

5. U.S. Department of Transportation. *The Secretary's decision concerning motor vehicle occupant protection.* Washington, D.C.: Author, 1976.

6. Deutsch, D., Sameth, S., & Akinyemi, J. Seat belt usage and risk-taking behavior at two major traffic intersections. In *Proceedings of the Annual Meeting of the American Association for Automotive Medicine,* 1980.

7. Evans, L. Wasielewski, P., & von Buseck, C. R. *Compulsory seat belt usage and driver risk-taking behavior.* Warren, Mich.: General Motors Research Laboratories, 1980.

8. General Motors Corporation. *Consumer opinions relative to automotive restraint systems.* Advertising and Merchandising Section, Report No. 71–27p, 1971.

9. U.S. Department of Transportation. *NHTSA report indicates head restraints effective in reducing whiplash injuries.* Washington, D.C.: National Highway Traffic Safety Administration, 1982.

REFERENCES

Baker, S. P. On lobbies, liberty, and the public good. *American Journal of Public Health,* 1980, **70,** 573–575.

Barmack, J. E. & Payne, D. E. The Lackland accident countermeasure experiment. *Highway Research Board Proceedings,* 1961, **40**, 513–522.

Burg, A. The stability of driving record over time. *Accident Analysis and Prevention,* 1970, **2**, 57–65.

Burg, A. Vision and driving: A report on research. *Human Factors,* 1971, **13**, 79–87.

Conger, J. J., Miller, W. C., & Rainey, C. V. Effects of driver education: The role of motivation, intelligence, social class, and exposure. *Traffic Safety Research Review,* 1966, **10**, 67–71.

Edwards, M. L., & Ellis, N. C. An evaluation of the Texas driver improvement training program. *Human Factors,* 1976, **18**, 327–334.

Elman, D., & Killebrew, J. Incentives and seat belts: Changing a resistant behavior through extrinsic motivation. *Journal of Applied Social Psychology,* 1978, **8**, 72–83.

Foldvary, L. A., & Lane, J. C. The effectiveness of compulsory wearing of seat-belts in casualty reduction. *Accident Analysis and Prevention,* 1974, **6**, 59–81.

Forbes, T. W. The normal automobile driver as a traffic problem. *Journal of General Psychology,* 1939, **20**, 471–474.

Fuchs, C. Wisconsin driver improvement program: A treatment-control evaluation. *Journal of Safety Research,* 1980, **12**, 107–114.

Gibson, J. J. The contribution of experimental psychology to the formulation of the problem of safety: A brief for basic research. In *Behavioral approaches to accident research.* New York: Association for the Aid of Crippled Children, 1961.

Haddon, W., Jr. Advances in the epidemiology of injuries as a basis for public policy. *Public Health Reports,* 1980, **95**, 411–421.

Haddon, W., Jr., & Baker, S. P. Injury control. In D. Clark & B. MacMahon (Eds.), *Preventive medicine* (2nd ed.). Boston: Little, Brown, 1981.

Haddon, W., Jr., & Goddard, J. L. An analysis of highway safety strategies. In *Passenger car design and highway safety.* New York: Association for the Aid of Crippled Children and Consumers Union of the United States, 1962.

Haddon, W., Jr., Suchman, E. A., & Klein, D. (Eds.). *Accident research: Methods and approaches.* New York: Harper & Row, 1964.

Hassel, C., & Trethowan, W. H. Suicide in Birmingham. *British Medical Journal,* 1972, **1**, 717.

Hill, P. S., & Jamieson, B. D. Driving offenders and the defensive driving course—An archival study. *Journal of Psychology,* 1978, **98**, 117–127.

Jones, M. H. *California training evaluation study.* Sacramento: California State Department of Motor Vehicles, 1973.

Karr, A. R. Saga of the air bag, or the slow deflation of a car-safety idea. *Wall Street Journal,* November 11, 1976, p. 1.

Kramer, L. Auto makers under pressure to become innovative again. *Washington Post,* November 26, 1978, p. F1.

McCarroll, J. R., & Haddon, W., Jr. A controlled study of fatal motor vehicle crashes in New York City. *Journal of Chronic Diseases,* 1962, **15**, 811.

McGuire, F. L., & Kersh, R. C. *An evaluation of driver education.* Berkeley: University of California Press, 1969.

O'Neill, B. Comments on "An evaluation of the National Safety Council's Defensive Driving course in various states." *Accident Analysis and Prevention,* 1974, **6**, 299–301.

O'Neill, B., Haddon, W., Jr., Kelley, A. B., & Sorenson, W. W. Automobile head restraints: Frequency of neck injury claims in relation to the presence of head restraints. *American Journal of Public Health,* 1972, **62**, 399–406.

Peltzman, S. The effects of automobile safety regulation. *Journal of Political Economy,* 1975, **83**, 677.

Preusser, D. F., Ulmer, R. G., & Adams, J. R. Driver record evaluation of a drinking driver rehabilitation program. *Journal of Safety Research,* 1976, **8**, 98–105.

Ray, H. W., Weaver, J. K., Brink, J. R., & Stock, J. R. *Safe performance secondary school driver education curriculum demonstration project.* Springfield, Va.: National Technical Information Service, 1982.

Raymond, S., & Tatum, S. *An evaluation of the effectiveness of the RAC/ACU motor cycle training scheme—Final report.* Salford: University of Salford, 1977.

Robertson, L. S. Factors associated with safety belt use in 1974 starter-interlock equipped cars. *Journal of Health and Social Behavior,* 1975, **16**, 173–177.

Robertson, L. S. An instance of effective legal regulation: Motorcyclist helmet and daytime headlamp laws. *Law and Society Review,* 1976, **10**, 467–477.

Robertson, L. S. Auto industry belt use campaign fails. In *Background manual on the passive restraint issue.* Washington, D.C.: Insurance Institute for Highway Safety, 1977.(a)

Robertson, L. S. Car crashes: Perceived vulnerability and willingness to pay for crash protection. *Journal of Community Health,* 1977, **3**, 136–141.(b)

Robertson, L. S. Motor vehicle injuries: Causes and amelioration. *Public Health Reviews,* 1977, **6**, 25–35.(c)

Robertson, L. S. Automobile seat belt use in selected countries, states and provinces with and without laws requiring belt use. *Accident Analysis and Prevention,* 1978, **10**, 5–10.

Robertson, L. S. Crash involvement of teenaged drivers when driver education is eliminated from high school. *American Journal of Public Health,* 1980, **70**, 599–603.

Robertson, L. S. Automobile safety regulations and death reductions in the United States. *American Journal of Public Health,* 1981, **71**, 818–822.

Robertson, L. S., & Baker, S. P. Prior violations of 1447 drivers involved in fatal crashes. *Accident Analysis and Prevention,* 1975, **7**, 121–128.

Robertson, L. S., & Haddon, W., Jr. The buzzer-light reminder system and safety belt use. *American Journal of Public Health,* 1974, **64**, 814–815.

Robertson, L. S., O'Neill, B., & Wixom, C. W. Factors associated with observed safety belt use. *Journal of Health and Social Behavior,* 1972, **13**, 18–24.

Robertson, L. S., & Zador, P. L. Driver education and fatal crash involvement of teenaged drivers. *American Journal of Public Health,* 1978, **68**, 959–965.

Robertson, L. S., Kelley, A. B., O'Neill, B., Wixom, C. W., Eiswirth, R. S., & Haddon, W., Jr. A controlled study of the effect of television messages on safety belt use. *American Journal of Public Health,* 1974, **64**, 1071–1080.

Ross, H. L. Law, science, and accidents: The British Road Safety Act of 1967. *Journal of Legal Studies,* 1973, **2**, 1–78.

Ross, H. L. The Scandinavian myth: The effectiveness of drinking-and-driving legislation in Sweden and Norway. *Journal of Legal Studies,* 1975, **4**, 285–310.

Rumar, K., Gerggrund, U., Jernberg, P., & Ytterbon, U. Driver reaction to a technical safety measure— Studded tires. *Human Factors,* 1976, **18**, 443–454.

Schuster, D. H., & Guilford, J. P. The psychometric prediction of problem drivers. *Human Factors,* 1964, **6**, 393–421.

Shaoul, J. *The use of accidents and traffic offenses as criteria for evaluating courses in driver education.* Salford: University of Salford, 1975.

Stuart, R. B. Teaching facts about drugs: Pushing or preventing? *Journal of Educational Psychology,* 1974, **66**, 189–201.

Williams, A. F., & Wells, J. A. K. The Tennessee child restraint law in its third year. *American Journal of Public Health,* 1981, **71**, 163.

Wright, P. H., & Robertson, L. S. Priorities for roadside hazard modification: A study of 300 fatal roadside object crashes. *Traffic Engineering,* 1976, **46**, 24–30.

Zador, P. L. Statistical evaluation of the effectiveness of alcohol safety action projects. *Accident Analysis and Prevention,* 1976, **8**, 51–66.

CHAPTER 67

PREVENTING INJURIES TO CHILDREN: A BEHAVIORAL APPROACH TO CHILD PASSENGER SAFETY

EDWARD R. CHRISTOPHERSEN

University of Kansas Medical Center

Recently, Julius Richmond (1975), a pediatrician and, at the time, U.S. Secretary of Health, Education and Welfare, made the following observation:

> *The contributions of research advances to nutrition, hygiene, metabolism and infectious diseases have resulted in the decline of nutritional disorders and infectious diseases. The striking advances in the development of preventive and therapeutic agents have brought about major reductions in infant mortality and childhood morbidity and mortality. As a consequence, physical and social factors in the form of accidents have now become the leading cause of childhood mortality. (p. 519)*

The discipline of pediatrics has been responsible for significant improvements in the health of children, thereby contributing to the increase in the average life expectancy in the United States. The introduction of routine immunizations has prevented many children from contracting childhood illnesses that, at one time, were life threatening (e.g., smallpox, measles, whooping cough, poliomyelitis, tetanus, and diphtheria). Similarly, the pediatrician's knowledge of nutrition and the development of infant formulas have prevented a great number of the problems associated with malnutrition, both immediate risks and sequelae. Pediatrics has now entered into a new era—an era in which accidents are claiming more lives than any other cause.

The largest single threat to life and limb in the United States is the motor vehicle. More children and teenagers are killed or injured by automobiles than by any pediatric disease. In terms of the total loss to society by person-years (that is, the number of potential years lost from normal life expectancy of 65 years times the number of children killed), the automobile is a greater killer than cancer, coronary heart disease, or strokes (*Morbidity and Mortality,* 1982). One reason for this is that a stroke or heart attack victim who dies at the age of 60 has lived roughly 5 years less than normal life expectancy, whereas a

Preparation of this chapter was supported, in part, by a grant from NICHD (HD 03144) to the Bureau of Child Research, University of Kansas, Lawrence, and by a grant from the National Highway Traffic Safety Administration (7-A02) to the University of Kansas Medical Center, Kansas City.

Table 67.1 Deaths from Automobile Accidents and Potential Years of Life Lost for Children and Adolescents, United States, 1975

Age (years)	Number of Deaths	Potential Years of Life Lost
<1	225	14,400
1–4	1,321	82,563
5–9	1,576	91,408
10–14	1,710	90,630
15–19	8,052	386,496
Total	12,884	665,497

Source: Adapted from Robertson, L. S. Present status of knowledge in childhood injury prevention. In A. B. Bergman (Ed.), *Preventing childhood injuries.* Report of the 12th Ross Roundtable on Critical Approaches to Common Pediatric Problems. Columbus, Ohio: Ross Laboratories, 1982.

2-year-old child killed in an automobile accident has lost roughly 63 years of life expectancy. Thus, as shown in Table 67.1, 12,884 infants, children, and teenagers in the United States in 1975 lost a total of 665,497 person-years from their potential life expectancy as a result of automobile accidents.

The impact of accidents is further elucidated by comparing the estimated annual total of potential years lost before age 65 for various causes of death in the United States for all ages in 1980 (Table 67.2).

The technology for greatly reducing death and injury of infants and children from automobile accidents already exists in the form of infant and child restraint devices, including, of course, the automobile seat belt (and the technology for increasing the use of such lifesaving devices is developing rapidly). As Table 67.3 shows, the likelihood of a child being killed in an automobile accident is reduced tremendously by the use of a child restraint device. A child riding unrestrained in an automobile during an accident has 14 times greater probability of being killed than a child riding in a restraint seat.

Table 67.2 Estimated Annual Total of Potential Years of Life Lost Before Age 65 by Cause of Death, All Ages, United States, 1980

Cause of Death	Potential Years of Life Lost
Accidents and adverse effects	2,684,850
Malignant neoplasms	1,804,120
Diseases of the heart	1,636,510
Suicides, homicides	1,401,880
Chronic liver disease and cirrhosis	301,070
Cerebrovascular diseases	280,430

Source: *Morbidity and Mortality Weekly Report,* 1982, **31** (March 12), 117.

Table 67.3   Fatalities of Children Aged 0–4 Years as Passengers in Motor Vehicles, State of Washington, 1970–1980

	Number of Fatalities	Total Number of Child Passengers	Ratio of Fatalities to Total Passengers
Unrestrained	146	33,200	1/227
Restrained	2	6,300	1/3,150

Source: Scherz, R. G. Auto safety: "The First Ride . . . A Safe Ride" campaign. In A. B. Bergman (Ed.), *Preventing childhood injuries.* Report of the 12th Ross Roundtable on Critical Approaches to Common Pediatric Problems. Columbus, Ohio: Ross Laboratories, 1982.

USAGE OF RESTRAINT DEVICES

A number of factors may influence parents' purchase and usage of child restraint devices: legislation, loaner programs, public education programs, hospital-based programs, restraint seat design, and physician-based programs.

Legislation

Probably the least expensive influence on restraint device usage has been the passage of state legislation that prohibits unsafe transportation of children in automobiles. The pioneering legislation was passed in 1978 in Tennessee. Figure 67.1 shows the dramatic results in Tennessee compared to Kentucky, which has no child passenger safety legislation. The figure indicates usage rates in Nashville and Knoxville and results of a parallel survey in two Kentucky cities. Child restraint seat usage in Tennessee for children under 4 years tripled, from 9% before enactment of the law to 29% in April 1980.

Along with the passage of legislation, Tennessee provided a 3-year grant for development and implementation of a public information and education program. This program included 760,000 brochures, highway billboards, television and radio public service announcements, articles and features in some 200 newspapers, in-service training programs for police, seed monies for loaner programs, and periodic statewide surveys to monitor usage rates.

As of 1982, 12 other states have passed child passenger restraint laws: Florida, Kansas, Maine, Massachusetts, Michigan, Minnesota, Nebraska, New York, North Carolina, Rhode Island, Virginia, and West Virginia; and many other states introduced such legislation during the 1982 legislative session.

The Tennessee program did not rely on strict enforcement of the child passenger safety act. There was, in fact, very little actual enforcement in the sense of ticket writing and traffic fines. Apparently, passage of the law compelled many people in Tennessee to comply with the law without enforcement.

Legislation alone, however, provides encouraging but inadequate increases in correct child restraint seat usage.

Loaner Programs

Where availability of child restraint seats is a problem, loaner programs provide ready and inexpensive access to the devices. The Michigan Highway Safety Office, in conjunction with the Michigan Jaycee Auxiliary, has developed and disseminated the EarlyRider program, which includes much of the technology necessary to establish and maintain a loaner program for child restraint seats (*EarlyRider,* Note 1). Most of the details essential to the conduct and survival of such a program are incorporated in the EarlyRider program, includ-

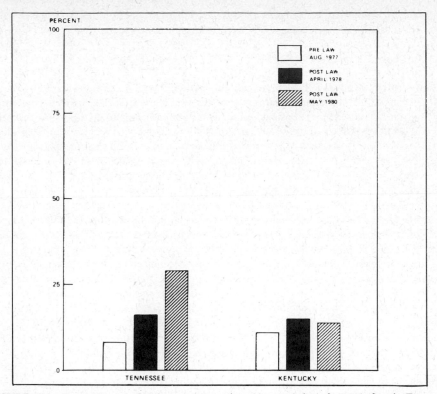

PERCENT
100

75

50

25

0

PRE LAW
AUG 1977

POST LAW
APRIL 1978

POST LAW
MAY 1980

TENNESSEE   KENTUCKY

FIGURE 67.1   Percentage use of child restraints anchored by seat belts before and after the Tennessee law was in force (January 1, 1978). (Reproduced with permission from Sanders, R. S. Legislative approach to auto safety: The Tennessee experience. In A. B. Bergman (Ed.), *Preventing childhood injuries.* Report of the 12th Ross Roundtable on Critical Approaches to Common Pediatric Problems. Columbus, Ohio: Ross Laboratories, 1982.)

ing liability considerations, loaner program paperwork, and written informed-consent statements.

Most current loaner programs rent infant restraint seats for a deposit of about $10 and $1 per month for the first 6 months. In one suburban hospital in the Kansas City metropolitan area, with a total of 400 infant restraint seats in the loaner program, the income generated from the program is almost $400 per month. This income is used to purchase new infant restraint seats for expanding the program and to replace seats that either are worn out or have not been returned. In these days of rapidly escalating hospital costs, a prevention program that makes a small profit for the sponsor is likely to survive the prevalent budgetary cuts.

Public Education Programs

Kelley (1979) described a carefully conducted study by the Insurance Institute for Highway Safety on the effectiveness of a media campaign on adult use of auto seat belts. The study estimated that, if conducted on a national basis, a television advertising campaign would have cost approximately $7 million—the equivalent of a major advertising campaign for a new product. The data indicate that the program was totally ineffective in motivating citizens to use their seat belts when traveling by automobile.

Numerous office-based education programs conducted by pediatricians have been similarly ineffective. A study that used actual observation of parents in their automobiles revealed that only a very small percentage used child restraint seats correctly (Williams, 1976).

Hospital-based Programs

Reisinger and Williams (1978) reported on an innovative hospital-based program for encouraging parents to use an infant restraint seat on the ride home from the hospital's maternity unit and on all subsequent occasions. Of the four groups compared, the most successful was the group that received a *free* infant restraint seat during their hospital stay along with literature on the hazards of unrestrained travel for infants. Almost inexplicably, however, only 40% of these free seats were observed to be present in the passenger compartment of the car, and only 11% were used to restrain the newborn correctly.

In an effort to determine the reason for the lack of correct restraint seat use in the Reisinger and Williams (1978) study, I observed numerous mothers as they were discharged from two different hospital maternity units. A striking finding was that the nurses, nurse's aides, or volunteers who transported the mothers and their newborn infants to their cars at the time of discharge *never* mentioned child passenger safety to them. Typically, the aide would hold the infant while the mother positioned herself in the front passenger seat (the most dangerous place in a car). Then the aide would hand the infant to the mother, wish her the best of luck, and close the car door. Since this practice appeared to be an example of inappropriate modeling (Bandura, 1969), I conducted a study specifically to address this modeling phenomenon. This study (Christophersen and Sullivan, 1982) used two groups of mothers and their newborns, with random assignment in pairs between the groups. The control group mother-infant pairs received no education about auto safety and were discharged from the maternity unit as they normally would be—which meant being placed in the front seat with no mention of child passenger safety. In the experimental group, the mothers were given a free infant restraint seat, as in the Reisinger and Williams (1978) study, but the timing was changed so that the seat was offered at the time the mother was actually being discharged from the hospital's maternity unit. The experimental group mothers were shown, in their hospital rooms, exactly how to position their infants correctly in the infant restraint seats and, at curbside, how to fasten the infant restraint seats correctly with the automobile seat belt.

Table 67.4 provides a comparison of the Reisinger and Williams (1978) data with the Christophersen and Sullivan (1982) data. These comparisons clearly show that (a) a significantly greater percentage of mothers exposed to appropriate modeling correctly restrained their infants at discharge, and (b) a significantly greater percentage of mothers without appropriate modeling held their infants in their arms both at hospital discharge and at 1-month follow-up in the pediatrician's office. However, the percentage of mothers who

Table 67.4   Comparison of Discharge Procedures and Follow-ups

Observation	Reisinger & Williams (1978) Study	Christophersen & Sullivan (1982) Study
Seat fastened at discharge	11%	66%
Seat fastened at follow-up	28%	28%
Child in mother's arms at discharge	87%	20%
Child in mother's arms at follow-up	51%	7%

Source: Christophersen, E. R., & Sullivan, M. A. Increasing the protection of newborn infants in cars. *Pediatrics,* 1982, **70**, pp. 21–25.

were using restraint seats correctly at 1-month follow-up was exactly the same for the two groups (28%). Detailed observer records revealed that in the Christophersen and Sullivan (1982) study, *all* of the mothers who were using restraint seats at discharge but not at follow-up had switched to flimsy, unsafe infant feeding chairs. These chairs, marketed under the trade name Infanseat, frequently are on display next to restraint seat displays in juvenile products departments and are common shower gifts for expectant mothers. Scherz (1976), Williams (1976), and Reisinger and Williams (1978) reported on the number of mothers who used infant feeding chairs but did not report that parents switched from approved restraint seats to feeding chairs.

In a study that is currently in progress, I have replicated the Christophersen and Sullivan (1982) study, with several additions. First, the nurses use a mock-up of a passenger car front seat to model for the mothers and to let the mothers practice correct placement of the infant in the restraint seat and the restraint seat in the seat belt. (The use of such a mock-up was suggested by Toledo, Peck, Burke, and Butler, 1980.) Second, the mothers are warned about the hazards of using infant feeding chairs in lieu of child restraint seats. Third, the mothers are provided with a written set of instructions on how to interact with their infants while the infants are in the infant restraint seats. At hospital discharge, 85% of the experimental group mothers correctly restrained their infants, and 72% correctly restrained their infants at follow-up.

Restraint Seat Design

Weber (1980) showed that parents have a much higher probability of using a restraint seat consistently when the seat design is simple. The more buckles and straps a restraint seat has, the less likely a mother is to use it. Restraint seats that require a top tether strap (a seat belt-type strap that anchors the top of the seat firmly to a rear seat belt or to the structure of the car) are less desirable than seats that do not require a tether strap. *Consumer Reports* ("Child Safety Seats," 1982) also reported that their panel of consumers preferred less complicated seats to more complicated seats. In fact, they down-rated any seats that require a tether strap. It is interesting to note that most of the manufacturers of infant and child restraint seats have introduced models that are simpler to use and do not require the use of a tether strap.

Pediatrician-based Programs

In virtually all of the early literature on restraint seat usage, the responsibility for educating parents was assumed to be primarily with the pediatrician (Kanthor, 1976; Pless, 1978). Basically, the pediatrician tried to acquaint parents with the dangers of automobile travel and encouraged them to purchase an infant or child restraint seat. However vital the role played by pediatricians in motivating parents to purchase and use child restraint seats, several studies have shown that the majority of pediatricians are not informing their patients about the dangers of automobile travel. Pless, Roghmann, and Algranati (1972) found that less than half of the respondents in a telephone survey reported that they had been advised of accident prevention measures. Of those who reported receiving advice, not one spontaneously mentioned physicians as a source of safety information. When asked directly, 96% denied any recollection that their pediatricians had counseled them. Only 21% recalled seeing safety literature in the doctor's office. In a postal survey of area pediatricians, 34% reported that they sometimes advised their patients about car safety, 21% often, and 3% always. Seventy-one percent of the pediatricians in the survey acknowledged the importance of such a discussion.

Reisinger and Bires (1980) indirectly confirmed the figures on pediatricians' safety counseling to parents. They report that, on the average, 4% of a well-child visit (with an average duration of 10 minutes) was devoted to discussion about safety; that comes to an average of less than one-half minute of discussion on child safety (which includes burns, falls, and ingestion hazards).

For those pediatricians who do elect to advise parents about the benefits and risks of auto travel for children, Reisinger, Williams, Wells, John, Roberts, and Podgainy (1981) provide one of the best outcome studies. They used a multicomponent program including (a) in-hospital discussion by the pediatrician, written literature, and a written prescription for the purchase of a restraint seat; (b) an office reminder at the 1-month visit, including having the pediatrician actually demonstrate the correct use of an infant restraint seat using a mock-up of an automobile front seat; and (c) an additional verbal reminder at the 2-month well-child visit. Reisinger et al. (1981) reported initial usage rates of 38%, which gradually increased to 56% by the 15-month well-child visit.

A BEHAVIORAL APPROACH TO ACCIDENT PREVENTION

The majority of approaches to encouraging parents to purchase and use child restraint seats have relied on an *avoidance learning* paradigm; that is, the parents are told that if they follow the pediatrician's advice, they will avoid injury or death to their child. The avoidance learning paradigm, in theory, has several characteristics that argue against its use in the matter of child passenger safety. First, unlike much of the basic laboratory research on avoidance, for automobile dangers the aversive event is highly remote. In a typical laboratory study on avoidance using animals, if the animal does not emit an appropriate operant response, the probability of the aversive event (usually electric shock) is very high—in most cases, certain. The likelihood of a particular child being injured during one car ride without a child restraint seat, however, is extremely remote.

Theoretically, using this avoidance paradigm, any time the parent is reminded of the possible aversive consequences of unrestrained child travel—for example, a reminder by the pediatrician, a television public service announcement, or a newspaper clipping about a child killed in an automobile accident—the parent's motivation increases. Every time a parent transports a child in an automobile with a child restraint seat and accidents do not occur, however, the parent's motivation gradually weakens to the point that almost any excuse is sufficient for the parent to refrain from using the restraint seat "just this one time."

A *reinforcement paradigm* is always maintained much better by the natural environment if naturally occurring reinforcers can be identified. For child restraint seat usage, Christophersen (1977) identified a potentially powerful reinforcer for maintaining parents' use of child restraint seats—that children behave much better when they are transported in restraint seats. Christophersen had observers ride with two groups of parents, one group of parents who regularly used restraint seats and one group who did not use restraint seats. The toddlers who usually rode in restraint seats behaved appropriately during more than 95% of the observation intervals. The toddlers who did not ride in restraint seats behaved appropriately during less than 5% of the observation intervals. Christophersen recommended that pediatricians use the children's improved behavior during car rides as a "selling point" for motivating parents to use restraint seats regularly when traveling by automobile. Theoretically, every time the parent transported the child in a restraint seat and the child behaved well, the parent would be reinforced for using the restraint seat. (For an extensive discussion of reinforcement and avoidance learning, see Bandura, 1969.)

Christophersen and Gyulay (1981) tested this "selling point" by recruiting mothers of toddlers who were not using a restraint seat during automobile trips. Each parent was exposed to one office visit where the advantages of restraint seat travel (i.e., better behaved children) were emphasized without any mention of the safety aspects and the parent was offered a loaner seat. After an average baseline usage of 0%, the parents improved to a rate of 62% immediately after the one office visit. Three months later, 75% were still using the restraint seat correctly. Six months later, 62% were still restrained and, one full year later, 37% were still traveling in a restraint seat.

The parents in the Christophersen and Gyulay (1981) study were told that every time they used the restraint seat, their child would behave well (based on the Christophersen, 1977, study), and, as their data showed, the children in restraints *did* behave much better. Thus, the parents were reinforced by their children's appropriate behavior every time they complied with the physicians' recommendation to use the restraint seats. Conversely, every time the parents elected not to use the restraint seats, the children behaved inappropriately (climbed around the car, turned the radio on and off, jumped from front seat to back seat, etc.). The data indicated that, as in the 1977 study, the unrestrained children behaved inappropriately. In this way, the natural consequence of the children's behavior maintained the parents' motivation to use the restraint seat, with consequences for both restraint seat use and nonuse. Over an extended period of time, the parents were differentially reinforced for their compliance with the providers' recommendation.

There are several additional advantages of restraint seat usage. First, children in restraint seats may be less likely to experience car sickness, since they sit higher, where they can see out and focus on objects farther away from the automobile; thus, the child's visual field is less likely to be subjected to violent up-and-down motions. Second, children usually sleep much better in restraint seats because they are better secured and the support provided by the seat may be more comfortable. Also, there is no danger of the child falling off the seat during routine or emergency maneuvers. Third, children who are transported in restraint seats are much less likely to distract the driver, thereby reducing the likelihood that they will inadvertently cause an accident (Hall, 1980). In Hall's analysis of 236 automobile accidents in which children were present as passengers, 55% were scored as "definitely preventable" if the child had been restrained, with another 11% scored as "probably preventable." Fourth, Agran (1981) presented data showing that children in restraint seats were unlikely to be injured during automobile travel by falling within the vehicle and striking a hard surface in the vehicle interior. Williams (1981) reported that, in 1978 in the United States, 38 children 5 years of age or younger were killed when they fell from the passenger compartments of moving vehicles that were *not* involved in crashes or emergency maneuvers.

Parent-Child Interaction During Automobile Travel

Virtually all of the literature on child passenger safety has been directed at getting parents to purchase and consistently use infant or child restraint seats. Practically nothing has been written for parents to instruct them on how to interact with their children during routine automobile travel while the children are secured in a restraint seat. Christophersen (1979) detailed a brief list, in the form of a written protocol, that describes the practical application of well-established behavioral principles for parents' use in encouraging appropriate travel in restraint seats (Table 67.5). This written protocol includes several procedures that are well supported in the behavioral literature: (a) the child should be reinforced, by parental praise and attention, for appropriate behavior; (b) inappropriate behavior, in the form of crying or begging, should be ignored; (c) dangerous behavior, such as removing the seat belt that secures the restraint seat, should be stopped by the parent; (d) the parent is encouraged to distract the child by carrying soft, safe toys, books, and the like, for the child to play with during automobile travel. This is the written protocol that was used during the single office visit in the Christophersen and Gyulay (1981) study.

The guidelines detailed in Table 67.6 were recently published for use with parents of newborns and infants (Christophersen, 1982). In addition to advice on parents' reinforcement of appropriate behavior and extinction of inappropriate behavior, these guidelines include suggestions on the placement of the infant within the vehicle's interior. Although the recommendation that the infant be placed in the front seat when traveling with just one parent contradicts the recommendations of many safety experts, the reality of the situation is

Table 67.5 *Using an Automobile Car Seat:* **Guidelines for Parents**

Automobile trips can and should be a pleasant time for you and your child. This is an excellent time for pleasant conversation and for teaching your child acceptable and appropriate behavior in the car. It is also the safest mode of travel, even short trips, for your child.

1. Introduce the car seat to your child in a calm, matter-of-fact manner as a learning experience. Allow him to touch it and check it out.

2. Remind the child about the rules of behavior *nicely* before the first ride and between rides.

3. Your first rides with the seat should be short practice rides, perhaps once around the block, to teach him the expected and acceptable behavior. Point out interesting things that he can see. Make it a positive experience for both of you.

4. Praise him often for appropriate behaviors. (Example: "Mike, you are sitting so quietly in your seat. Mommy is proud of you. You are a good boy . . .") This explanation teaches him the expected and appropriate behavior. Young children need specific directions. They cannot make the opposite connection of what is meant by "Quit that!" Catch 'em being good. You cannot praise him too often.

5. Include the child in pleasant conversation. (Example: "That was sure a good lunch . . . you really like hot dogs . . . you were a big help to me in the store . . . it'll be fun visiting grandma . . .")

6. This is also a good time to teach your child about his world. (Example: "Jon, see that *big, red* fire truck? Look at how *fast* it is going. What *do* firemen do? The light on the *top* is *red* . . . what else is red?") This needs to be geared to the age of your child.

7. By your frequent praise, teaching, and pleasant conversation, your child will remain interested and busy and will not spend his time trying to get out of the seat. He will give you his frequent attention.

8. Ignore yelling, screaming, and begging. The instant he is quiet, praise him for being quiet. You also should not yell, scream, and beg. Remember, remain calm and matter-of-fact. Keep your child busy in conversation and observations of his world. Do not give in and let him out. This only teaches him that yelling, screaming, and begging will finally get mom or dad to let him do what he wants. Show who's the boss.

9. Older siblings should also be expected to behave appropriately. If the young child sees an older sibling climbing or hanging out the window, he will want to become a participant. The older sibling(s) should also be included in the conversation, praise, and teaching.

10. Provide one or two toys that your child associates with quiet play, such as books, stuffed animals, dolls, etc. It may help to have special quiet riding toys that are played with only in the car. This decreases boredom. Remember, the young child's attention span is *very* short. Do not expect him to keep occupied for more than a couple of minutes or less, particularly at the beginning and depending upon his age. Anticipating this will prevent throwing toys, temper tantrums, crying, or fussing.

11. Reward him with five to ten minutes of your time in an activity that he likes immediately after the ride, such as reading a story, playing a game, helping prepare lunch, helping put away the groceries, etc. Do not get into the habit of buying your child favors or presents for his good behavior. He enjoys time with you and it's less expensive and more rewarding for both of you. Remember, catch 'em being good and praise him often.

12. If your child even begins to try to release his seat belt or to climb out of the car seat, immediately tell him "No!" in a firm voice. On your first few trips, which should just be around the block, stop the car if you think that is necessary. Also, state the

Table 67.5 (*Continued*)

rule once, clearly, "Do not take off your seat belt." Parental discipline may be necessary if the child attempts to exit the restraint seat.

13. Remember, without the praise and attention for good behavior in the car, your child will learn nothing from the training trips. The combination of praise and attention, with occasional discipline, can and will teach the behavior you want in the car.

Source: Christophersen, E. R. Behavioral emphasis key to car seat use. *Feelings and their medical significance,* 1979, **21**(1), pp. 1–4. Columbus, Ohio: Ross Laboratories. © Jo-Eileen Gyulay and Edward R. Christophersen, 1978.

Table 67.6 *Using an Infant Seat:* **Guidelines for Parents**

Automobile travel can and should be a safe and pleasant time for you and your baby. This is an excellent time for you to talk to your baby and to teach your baby how enjoyable automobile travel can be.

1. If both parents are traveling in the car, one adult and the baby should ride in the back seat. The baby should be in an infant safety seat which is connected to the car with the seat belt so that the baby rides facing backwards.
2. If one parent is traveling alone with the baby, then the baby should be placed in the front seat, next to the parent in an infant safety seat which is connected to the car with the seat belt so that the baby rides facing backwards.
3. Any time that your baby is asleep, don't disturb him; leave him alone. An infant safety seat is the most comfortable place for your baby to sleep and you don't have to worry about his safety.
4. Any time that you baby is awake and behaving nicely (either quiet or jabbering, looking around, etc.) make sure that you interact with your baby. In this way, your baby will learn to enjoy automobile travel because you are fun to ride with. You can try singing or humming songs, talking about what you are doing or where you are going (e.g., "We're going to go see Nana and Papa.") If your baby has a favorite blanket, place it next to or in the safety seat within his reach.
5. Carry one or two soft, stuffed toys that your baby will learn to associate with quiet travel. It may help to have special quiet riding toys that are played with only in the car. This helps decrease boredom. Remember, your baby's attention span is very short. Don't expect him to keep occupied for more than a couple of minutes or less, particularly early in life.
6. Ignore yelling, screaming, and begging. The instant your baby is quiet, begin talking or singing to him again. You should not yell, scream, or nag. Do not take your baby out of his safety seat because he is crying. To do so will only teach him to cry more until you will take him out.
7. Older brothers and sisters should also be expected to behave in the car and to ride with their seat belts fastened correctly. If your baby grows up always riding with a seat belt on, he will not mind having it on at all.
8. By your frequent praise and pleasant conversation, your child will remain interested and busy and will not spend his time crying. He will already have your attention.
9. Many parents like to rest their elbows near the front of the infant safety seat so that they can hold their baby's hand, rearrange his clothing, or generally play with the baby. Babies like this kind of attention and will ride better in the car if you do this some of the time.
10. If you are on a long trip, periodic rest stops will be necessary in order to feed the baby, change his diapers, etc. Do not start the habit of taking him out of his infant

Table 67.6   *(Continued)*

safety seat when he is crying. Instead, when you know he needs your attention (feeding or diaper change), try to stop before he starts to fuss.

11.   If your baby is going to travel in an automobile with other persons (grandparent, aunt, uncle, babysitter, etc.) insist that they use the infant safety seat correctly fastened with the auto seat belt.

12.   REMEMBER. If you are pleasant and talk and interact with your baby during car rides, he will learn to enjoy both his safety seat and the rides in the car. If you allow him to get accustomed to riding in the car without a safety seat, it will probably make it harder to get him to use one correctly when he gets older.

13.   In KANSAS, it is illegal for a child to ride in the front seat of a car without being securely buckled into his safety seat. The reason it is illegal is because it is very, very dangerous. Please do what's best for your baby—use a safety seat during every car ride.

14.   Your baby should continue to use a safety seat until he is about 8 to 10 years old, when he can comfortably see out of the car with just a seat belt on. Sometime around 9 to 12 months of age, you will need to switch either to a toddler safety seat or change the riding position of the infant safety seat if it is the convertible type. Please ask your pediatrician or the nurse when to switch to a toddler safety seat.

Source: Christophersen, R. R. Incorporating behavioral pediatrics into primary care. *Pediatric Clinics of North America,* 1982, **29**, 261–296. © Edward R. Christophersen, 1981.

that both the parent and the infant enjoy the interaction that is made possible by placing the infant in the front seat. Ironically, many of the films prepared for viewing by parents implicitly recommend placement of the child in the front seat by showing the restraint seat in the front seat, which further justifies this recommendation.

AN IDEAL CHILD PASSENGER SAFETY PROGRAM

As indicated by the literature reviewed here, an ideal child passenger safety program should include the following components:

1.   State legislation mandating the use of restraint devices (Sanders, 1982).

2.   Hospital and community loaner programs providing inexpensive access to restraint seats (EarlyRider, Note 1).

3.   Nursing support for loaner programs, including having nurses stress child passenger safety by modeling the appropriate behavior when discharging mothers and infants from maternity units (Christophersen & Sullivan, 1982).

4.   Physician support at four specific times:

   a.   by requesting that the parents receive a demonstration of correct infant restraint seat usage during the mother's stay in the maternity unit (Christophersen & Sullivan, 1982).

   b.   by requesting that the infant be discharged from the maternity unit in an infant restraint seat (Christophersen & Sullivan, 1982);

   c.   by periodically reminding parents, during well-child visits, of the importance of restraint seat usage (Reisinger et al., 1981); and

   d.   by providing the parents with a prescription for the purchase of the restraint seat to make the cost tax-deductible (Christophersen, 1979).

5. Community support from service groups and PTAs to promote the use of infant and child restraint seats.

6. Manufacturers' cooperation in marketing restraint seats that do not have unnecessary tether straps and that are easy to use ("Child Safety Seats," 1982; Weber, 1980).

CONCLUDING REMARKS

The area of auto passenger safety for children clearly exemplifies the advantages of a collaborative effort among physicians, nurses, hospitals, and behavioral scientists. The collective efforts of numerous interdisciplinary studies have, in fact, helped to bring about a dramatic change in the greatest threat to life and limb in the United States. In all probability, these results could not have been achieved by only one discipline, or they would have taken much more time to accomplish.

The conceptualization of restraint seat usage as a problem in compliance, with the search for naturally occurring reinforcers to maintain the parents' behavior, provides a model that may well work in many other areas of health and health-related behavior. Behavioral scientists have repeatedly demonstrated that human behavior is maintained or modified by alterations in the environment (Cataldo, 1982). The search must now begin for naturally occurring reinforcers that can maintain the behavior of individuals engaged in exercise regimens, dietary regimens, and control programs for obesity, hypertension, alcohol, and smoking. Perhaps this one ingredient, reinforcement, can add as much to these other regimens as it has apparently added in the area of child passenger safety. Certainly, health behavior is at least partially controlled by its immediate consequences.

REFERENCE NOTE

1. *EarlyRider,* U.S. Department of Transportation, National Highway Traffic Safety Administration, Washington, D.C., 1979.

REFERENCES

Agran, P. F. Motor vehicle occupant injuries in noncrash events. *Pediatrics,* 1981, **67,** 838–840.

Bandura, A. *Principles of behavior modification.* New York: Holt, Rinehart & Winston, 1969.

Cataldo, M. F. The scientific basis for a behavioral approach to pediatrics. *Pediatric Clinics of North America,* 1982, **29,** 415–423.

Child safety seats. *Consumer Reports,* April 1982, pp. 171–176.

Christophersen, E. R. Children's behavior during automobile rides: Do car seats make a difference? *Pediatrics,* 1977, **60,** 69–74.

Christophersen, E. R. Behavioral emphasis key to car seat use. *Feelings and their medical significance,* 1979, **21**(1), pp. 1–4. Columbus, Ohio: Ross Laboratories.

Christophersen, E. R. Incorporating behavioral pediatrics into primary care. *Pediatric Clinics of North America,* 1982, **29,** 261–296.

Christophersen, E. R., & Gyulay, J. E. Parental compliance with car seat usage: A positive approach with long-term follow-up. *Journal of Pediatric Psychology,* 1981, **6,** 301–312.

Christophersen, E. R., & Sullivan, M. A. Increasing the protection of newborn infants in cars. *Pediatrics,* 1982, **70,** 21–25.

Hall, W. L. Warning: In cars, children may be hazardous to their parents' health: The role of restraints in preventing collisions. In *Proceedings of the 24th Conference of the American Association for Automotive Medicine* (Rochester, New York). Morton Grove, Ill.: American Association for Automotive Medicine, 1980.

Kanthor, H. A. Car safety for infants: Effectiveness of prenatal counseling. *Pediatrics,* 1976, **68,** 320–322.

Kelley, A. B. A media role for public health compliance? In R. B. Haynes, D. W. Taylor, & D. L. Sackett (Eds.), *Compliance in health care*. Baltimore: Johns Hopkins University Press, 1979.

Morbidity and Mortality Weekly Report, 1982, **31**(March 12), 117.

Pless, I. B. Accident prevention and health education: Back to the drawing board? *Pediatrics,* 1978, **62,** 431–435.

Pless, I. B., Roghmann, K., & Algranati, P. The prevention of injuries to children in automobiles. *Pediatrics,* 1972, **49,** 420–427.

Reisinger, K. S., & Bires, J. A. Anticipatory guidance in pediatric practice. *Pediatrics,* 1980, **66,** 889–892.

Reisinger, K. S., & Williams, A. F. Evaluation of programs designed to increase the protection of infants in cars. *Pediatrics,* 1978, **62,** 280–287.

Reisinger, K. S., Williams, A. F., Wells, J. K., John, C. E., Roberts, T. R., & Podgainy, H. J. Effect of pediatricians' counseling on infant restraint use. *Pediatrics,* 1981, **67,** 201–206.

Richmond, J. B. An idea whose time has arrived. *Pediatric Clinics of North America,* 1975, **22,** 517–523.

Robertson, L. S. Present status of knowledge in childhood injury prevention. In A. B. Bergman (Ed.), *Preventing childhood injuries*. Report of the 12th Ross Roundtable on Critical Approaches to Common Pediatric Problems. Columbus, Ohio: Ross Laboratories, 1982.

Sanders, R. S. Legislative approach to auto safety: The Tennessee experience. In A. B. Bergman (Ed.), *Preventing childhood injuries*. Report of the 12th Ross Roundtable on Critical Approaches to Common Pediatric Problems. Columbus, Ohio: Ross Laboratories, 1982.

Scherz, R. G. Restraint systems for the prevention of injury to children in automobile accidents. *American Journal of Public Health,* 1976, **66,** 451–455.

Scherz, R. G. Auto safety: "The First Ride . . . A Safe Ride" campaign. In A. B. Bergman (Ed.), *Preventing childhood injuries*. Report of the 12th Ross Roundtable on Critical Approaches to Common Pediatric Problems. Columbus, Ohio: Ross Laboratories, 1982.

Toledo, J. R., Peck, L. A., Burke, A. J., & Butler, J. R. *Workshop handbook to accompany Automobile Safety for Children Manual for Health Providers*. Denton: North Texas State University, Center for Safety and Accident Prevention Research, 1980.

Weber, K. Survey of infant restraint usability. In *Proceedings of the 24th Conference of the American Association for Automotive Medicine* (Rochester, New York). Morton Grove, Ill.: American Association for Automotive Medicine, 1980.

Williams, A. F. Observed child restraint use in automobiles. *American Journal of Diseases of Children,* 1976, **130,** 1311–1317.

Williams, A. F. Children killed in falls from motor vehicles. *Pediatrics,* 1981, **68,** 576–577.

CHAPTER 68

EPIDEMIOLOGY OF CHILDHOOD INJURIES

FREDERICK P. RIVARA

University of Tennessee Center for the Health Sciences and LeBonheur Children's Medical Center, Memphis

In the United States at present, injuries are the greatest cause of morbidity and mortality between the ages of 1 and 45 years (National Center, Note 1). During childhood, injuries account for more deaths than the next nine leading causes combined. With the advent of immunizations, antibiotics, and effective chemotherapeutic agents for childhood cancers, injuries remain the most important factor in childhood disease, disability, and death. The prevention of this unnecessary toll must be addressed.

The initial task in the prevention of any disease is to gain an understanding of its epidemiology—how the disease varies among persons, places, and times, and why. We need to examine who is injured in the population and who is not, where these injuries occur and where they do not, which vectors are repeatedly involved with producing injuries and which are not. In attempting to answer these questions, this chapter will identify the children at risk for injury and the contribution of behavior and culture to this risk. It will also suggest methods for reducing injuries in childhood.

INJURIES VERSUS ACCIDENTS

Before examining patterns of injury in the population, we should clarify just what it is that we are talking about. Throughout this chapter, the term *injuries* will refer to "damage resulting from acute exposure to physical or chemical agents" (Haddon & Baker, 1981). The term *accident* will not be used; it is an inaccurate anachronism reflecting unscientific attitudes toward injuries. *Accident* connotes randomness—that is, events occurring at random, without pattern or predictability. In fact, however, injuries are for the most part nonrandom in their distribution, as will be shown here.

The term *accident* should also be abandoned because of its moral connotations. In years past, epidemics of plague, cholera, and malaria were depicted as punishment for evil behavior. So, too, accidents have been viewed as rightful punishment for negligent and careless behavior. This attitude is underscored by the fact that prevention of the problem has been approached through deterrence and punishment of those who are "guilty"—an unsuccessful method for decreasing traumatic deaths.

The term *injury*, however, refocuses scientific attention on the problem—the damage to the person. As Doege (1978) succinctly states: "An injury is no accident."

Finally, it is important to distinguish between the event and the injury itself. The latter does not necessarily follow from the former. A motor vehicle crash may occur, but if the occupants are safely packaged, injury will be prevented. Conceptual separation of the event from the injury dramatically broadens the methods available for prevention. Seat belts, safety glass, roll bars, padded dashboards, infant seat-restraint devices, and airbags all can prevent injury, despite occurrence of a crash. Such approaches may be more effective than attempts to prevent the event itself.

THE INJURY TOLL

Perhaps the first level of any epidemiologic investigation is an examination of mortality. Since the purpose here is to discover common etiologic factors in deaths from all types of injuries, all so-called violent deaths will be considered. These include not only nonintentional injuries—the type of injury of primary interest—but also homicides and suicides. The rationale for including all three types involves a number of factors. Some etiologic agents, such as guns, are common to all three. The secular trends in mortality rates for these three problems have been similar, in that although deaths from other causes among teenagers and young adults continue to decrease, fatalities from violent causes have actually increased over the past two decades (Weiss, 1976). Finally, prevention efforts can be targeted to have simultaneous influences on all three types of violent deaths.

The number of fatalities from nonintentional injuries increase throughout childhood, with the highest rates in the late teenage–young adulthood years (Table 68.1). Deaths from motor vehicle injuries represent nearly 60% of the fatalities, making this the most common cause of death in childhood—more than the next nine leading causes combined. In teens as well as in adults, nearly half of the motor vehicle deaths are related to alcohol use.

Drownings are responsible for 2,800 deaths per year to children and adolescents 19 years of age and under. Fire deaths include those resulting both from burns and from smoke inhalation and asphyxiation—the cause of 75% of deaths in residential fires. Largely because of the 1970 Poison Prevention Packaging Act, poisonings have claimed relatively fewer lives in recent years, although these deaths, too, probably were largely preventable (Walton, 1982).

Males have far more deaths from injuries than do females, even in the youngest age group. By the time a male reaches young adulthood, he has nearly four times the risk of dying from a nonintentional injury than does a female. This sex difference in injury mortality

Table 68.1   Violent Deaths in Children and Adolescents, United States, 1977

Cause of Death	Age (years)					Total
	<1	1–4	5–9	10–14	15–19	
All violent deaths	1,281	3,696	3,157	3,834	16,448	28,416
Nonintentional injuries	1,173	3,297	2,967	3,398	12,680	23,515
Motor vehicle injuries	253	1,219	1,485	1,657	9,085	13,699
Drowning	66	631	485	549	1,075	2,806
Fire	159	608	344	206	272	1,589
Poisoning	18	111	30	69	446	674
Falls	54	121	50	72	234	531
Firearms (nonintentional)	1	47	104	240	390	782
Suffocation	275	168	42	37	87	609
Other	347	392	427	568	1,091	2,825
Homicide	108	399	188	248	1,897	2,840
Suicide	—	—	2	188	1,871	2,061

Source: National Center for Health Statistics, *Vital Statistics of the United States, 1977.* DHHS Pub. No. (PHS)81–1101, 1981.

is true in both whites and nonwhites. Although mortality from injuries decreased by 23% from 1950 through 1976, the differential between male and female rates increased from a 2.6- to a 3-fold difference (National Center, Note 2).

One way to better understand the importance of nonintentional injuries is to examine the years of life lost from various causes. Although injuries rank fifth in terms of overall number of deaths in the United States, motor vehicle-related deaths alone account for more potential years of life lost than any other single cause (Centers for Disease Control, 1982). Most trauma deaths occur to adolescents and young adults, as contrasted to cancer, coronary heart disease, and stroke, which are diseases of the elderly. This predominance of young victims accounts for the large number of potential years of life lost. When incidence-based costs of these four diseases are compared, results similar to those of the potential years-of-life-lost-method are found. Motor vehicle injuries alone are the second most expensive medical condition in the United States (Hartunian, Smart, & Thompson, 1980).

Among other violent deaths in children and adolescents, homicides account for nearly 3,000 deaths per year; suicides add another 2,000 to the total. Homicides are second only to motor vehicle crashes as a leading cause of death among all teenagers and are the leading cause of death among nonwhite teenagers. At present, almost 85% of these homicides involve firearms, 75% of which are handguns (Rivara & Stapleton, 1982).

Suicide is the third most common cause of death in teenage males and the fourth for females. As with homicides, firearms have played an important role in the increase in suicide deaths and are now the most common means of suicide in males of all ages (Holinger, 1979).

Survivors of these violent events do not escape unscathed. In 1980, an estimated 68 million persons were injured—21 million of them under 17 years of age. This resulted in 86,879,000 days of restricted activity, more days than for any other single cause (National Center, Note 3). Injuries overall accounted for an incredible 357 days of restricted activity per 100 persons per year—more than 3.5 days for every man, woman, and child in the United States. Nearly one-third of all impairments in function are due to injuries, resulting in more than 12 million people suffering traumatic impairments in 1977 (National Center, Note 4).

Lifestyle, especially alcohol use, and the availability of lethal weapons, most notably motor vehicles and handguns, are clearly involved in the majority of violent deaths among children and adolescents. Any serious effort to halt the rise in mortality of teens and young adults must develop effective methods for dealing with these problems.

INTERNATIONAL COMPARISONS

Injury statistics from other areas of the world illustrate the pervasiveness of the problem (Table 68.2). Unlike its infant mortality showing, the United States has a relatively low rate of traumatic death. Sweden, however, which traditionally has the lowest infant death rate, has one of the higher rates of death due to injuries. Nevertheless, one of the most preventable injuries—handgun fatalities—is more common among North American males than anywhere else in the world (Marcusson & Oehmisch, 1977). There appears to be a direct correlation between ownership laws and fatalities. The rate of handgun ownership in the United States is far above the total firearm ownership rate in most European countries. In England, which has very restrictive laws on handgun use, the homicide rate is 40-fold lower than that of the United States; robberies involving gun use are 60-fold lower (Newton & Zimring, 1969).

AGE AND SEX DIFFERENCES IN INJURY RATES

The most striking epidemiologic findings in the foregoing mortality statistics are the age and sex variations in injury rates. In the United States during 1976, males had a higher

Table 68.2   International Mortality Comparison

Deaths per 100,000 Population[a]

Country	Total	All Accidents	Motor Vehicle Accidents	Infant Mortality Rate[b]
Austria	1,277	99	33	14.7
Belgium	1,210	85	26	11.2
Denmark	1,001	64	17	8.8
Finland	927	88	24	7.7
France	1,047	99	22	10.0
Greece	886	47	17	18.7
Ireland	1,121	52	21	12.4
Italy	984	50	19	15.3
Netherlands	803	52	17	8.7
Norway	1,002	62		8.8
Portugal	1,037	74	35	
Spain	841	40	13	12.7
Sweden	1,075	75	17	7.3
Switzerland	873	73	21	8.5
United Kingdom	1,184	45	12	12.8
West Germany	1,174	77	24	13.5
United States	889	48	22	13.0

Source: National Center for Health Statistics. *Vital Statistics of the United States, 1975.* DHEW Pub. No. (PHS)79–1114, 1979. Wegner, M. E. Annual summary of vital statistics, 1980. *Pediatrics,* 1981, **68**, 755–762. *Euro Health Handbook, 1978.* New York: Robert S. Furst, Inc., 1978.
[a] 1975 data.
[b] Deaths to children less than 1 year of age per 1,000 live births, 1979 data.

total rate of fatal injuries as compared to females for the age groups 1–4 years (50% higher), 5–14 years (112% higher), and 15–24 years (372% higher) (National Center, Note 2). Mortality statistics, however, do not provide the degree of detail necessary to explore these age and sex differences. Perhaps the most detailed national data on injuries are those collected by the National Electronic Injury Surveillance System (NEISS). This system, operated by the Consumer Product Safety Commission (CPSC), is a representative sampling of 130 hospital emergency rooms in the United States and its territories. Data on injuries are abstracted daily from emergency room records, keypunched at the local hospital, and transmitted to the central computer facility in Washington, D.C. Information is gathered only on injuries related to consumer products, which include most things we use everyday. The one important exception is injuries caused by motor vehicles, since these are not under the jurisdiction of the CPSC.

In 1978, 197,000 consumer product-related injuries to children 18 years of age or less were reported through NEISS. This represents 4,646,000 injuries to children treated in hospital emergency rooms in the United States. Only 40% of all medically treated injuries are treated in emergency rooms; the remainder are treated in physicians' offices, clinics, and other outpatient facilities. Among children, the probability of emergency room versus office treatment of an injury does not vary with age or sex, but it does vary with the type and severity of the injury. As expected, the more severe injuries and those involving the head and face are more often treated in emergency rooms than in doctors' offices.

Epidemiologic studies traditionally either group all children together or analyze the data in arbitrary age categories, such as the 0–4, 5–14, and 15–19 age groups used by the National Center for Health Statistics. However, in order to determine different developmental and behavioral patterns in injury rates, analysis logically should proceed along developmental lines. Thus, the age categories used in the study results reported here reflect this concern with the relationship of injuries to developmental stage: infants under 1 year of age, the 1- to 2-year-old toddler, the 3- to 6-year-old preschooler, the 7- to 12-year-old school-aged child, and the 13- to 18-year-old teenager (Rivara, Bergman, LoGerfo, & Weiss, 1982).

As shown in Figure 68.1, males have significantly higher total rates of injuries than females among children over the age of 2 years. Overall, one in ten toddlers is treated in a hospital emergency room each year for trauma or poisoning. This difference becomes progressively more pronounced with age, reaching a rate of 90% more injuries in males in the oldest age group. It should be noted, although it is not shown here, that this increase in the rate of injuries among males as compared to females continues until the seventh decade.

Not only do the overall rates vary with age and sex, but the types of injuries and the parts of the body involved show distinct age and sex patterns. Many types of injuries are possible; NEISS classifies them into 33 different categories. Among children, however, four types of injuries account for 83% of the total: lacerations (35%), skin contusions and abrasions (25%), sprains and strains of muscles and ligaments (12%), and fractures (10%). In Table 68.3, it can be seen that males have higher rates of injuries than females at nearly all ages and for all four types of injuries. More important, these patterns are established

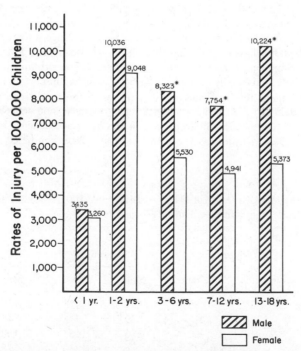

FIGURE 68.1 National estimates of rates of injuries per 100,000 children by age, group, and sex, United States, 1978. The cross-hatched bars represent rates of injury per 100,000 male children; the solid bars are the corresponding female rates. For all age groups beyond 2 years of age, males statistically have a greater rate of injuries than females, as indicated by the asterisk ($p < .05$). (Reproduced with permission from Rivara, F. P., Bergman, A. B., LoGerfo, J. P., and Weiss, N. S. Epidemiology of childhood injuries: II. Sex differences in injury rates. *American Journal of Diseases of Children*, 1982, **136**, 502–506. Copyright 1982, American Medical Association.)

Table 68.3   Types of Injuries per 100,000 Children: National Estimates, United States, 1978

Age Group (years)	Lacerations		Skin Contusions and Abrasions		Sprains and Strains		Fractures	
	Male	Female	Male	Female	Male	Female	Male	Female
<1	1,335	605	1,263	1,268	0	0	84	49
1–2	5,316	3,560	2,007	1,517	23	121	447	424
3–6	4,575	2,667	1,606	1,136	131	260	454	546
7–12	2,650	1,681	1,776	1,178	1,033	650	1,011	622
13–18	2,803	1,153	2,482	1,457	2,120	1,375	1,327	466
All ages	3,240	1,791	1,999	1,308	1,123	766	929	506

at very early ages, by age 1 for lacerations and fractures, by age 2 for contusions and abrasions, and by school age for sprains. It is interesting that no sprains are recorded for infants under 1 year of age. Children in this age group do not have the developmental skills or activity to produce sprains, although fractures are commonly seen. The fractures may represent injuries from falls or may be due to abuse.

In contrast, rates for other less common but high-morbidity injuries, such as poisonings, burns, and foreign-body ingestions, show no significant sex differences (Table 68.4). In burn injuries, the child is more likely to be a passive participant than to be actively involved in the production of the burn, as he or she might be with a laceration or fracture. In the case of poisoning, the behaviors producing the injury—curiosity and fine motor manipulation—are not developmental skills in which sex differences are prominent.

When injuries are analyzed by the part of the body involved, important variations appear, particularly with regard to age (Table 68.5). Injuries to the head, face, mouth, and eye are serious injuries in terms of initial manifestations, treatment, and sequelae. Such injuries are more common in preschool children than in the older age groups. In males under 1 year of age, over 80% of injuries are to the head and face, compared to only 19% of

Table 68.4   National Estimate of Rates of Injury per 100,000 Children by Recorded Injury Diagnosis, Age, and Sex, United States, 1978

Age Group (years)	Foreign-Body Ingestions		Poisonings		Burns, thermal and scald	
	Male	Female	Male	Female	Male	Female
<1	78	85	117	115	238	308
1–2	239	207	839	772	541	437
3–6	84	80	280	155	160	184
7–12	28	25	6	10	78	71
13–18	13	12	6	45	138	119
All ages	54	46	137	158	179	166

Source: Reproduced with permission from Rivara, F. P., Bergman, A. B., LoGerfo, J. P., and Weiss, N. S. Epidemiology of childhood injuries II: Sex differences in injury rates. *American Journal of Diseases of Children,* 1982, **136,** 502–506. Copyright 1982, American Medical Association.

Table 68.5   National Estimates of Rates of Injury per 100,000 Children

Age Group (years)	Head		Face, Mouth, Eye		Extremities	
	Male	Female	Male	Female	Male	Female
<1	1,436	1,268	1,450	873	396	656
1–2	2,224	1,297	4,311	3,256	2,002	1,586
3–4	1,538	1,058	2,378	1,519	3,631	2,343
7–12	814	301	1,208	680	4,828	3,544
13–18	607	312	1,195	388	7,061	3,770
Total	1,028	597	1,710	967	4,959	3,118

Source: Reproduced with permission from Rivara, F. P. Epidemiology of childhood injuries. In A. B. Bergman (Ed.), *Preventing childhood injuries.* Report of the 12th Ross Roundtable on Critical Approaches to Common Pediatric Problems. Columbus, Ohio: Ross Laboratories, 1982, pp 13–18.

injuries in the teenage male. Again, males at all ages have higher rates of head and face injuries than females, even among the youngest age groups.

In contrast to injuries around the head and face, injuries to the extremities are seen primarily in older children. Table 68.5 shows that injuries to the extremities account for 70% of the total injuries to teenage boys and 60% of those to teenage girls. This large number of extremity injuries to males in the older age groups plays a significant part in accounting for the overall male–female difference in injury rates.

EXPOSURE TO RISK

Differences in the rates of injury for particular groups could be due to a number of different factors. One group could be at higher risk for injury simply because of a greater exposure to the vector causing injury—for example, X-ray technicians and radiation injury, football players and knee injuries, construction workers and head injuries.

Another possible reason for differences in rates is that one group may exhibit more risk-taking behavior than another. This same hypothesis can be used to explore the reasons for the age and sex differences in injury rates. Males may use a particular product more than females and therefore may be exposed to risk of injury more frequently than females. If males and females had a similar risk of injury per degree of use, adjusting for exposure should remove the differences in injury rates. Few studies have actually done this adjustment. Routledge, Repett-Wright, and Howarth (1974) examined the difference in exposure to risk of pedestrian injury in children. They found that, at the peak ages for pedestrian injuries (5–8 years), males and females had equal exposure to risk, as measured by the number of roads crossed in the course of a day and the traffic densities on these roads. Males in this age group had higher rates of pedestrian injuries, but not because of increased exposure to risk.

Information provided by the CPSC and NEISS allowed for a similar analysis for a number of different products (Figure 68.2). A separate household survey was performed by the CPSC to determine usage rates of some commonly used products. When these figures were used as denominators for the injury rates, some interesting findings appeared. Males in all age groups had higher rates for bicycle-related injuries. However, correcting for exposure reduced this excess risk of injury in males. This indicates that, for bicycles, males had a higher rate of injury because they used them more frequently or for more hours, not because they had more injuries for the same amount of use. Similar results have been found in studies conducted for the National Safety Council (Chlapecka, Schupack, Planek, et al., 1975).

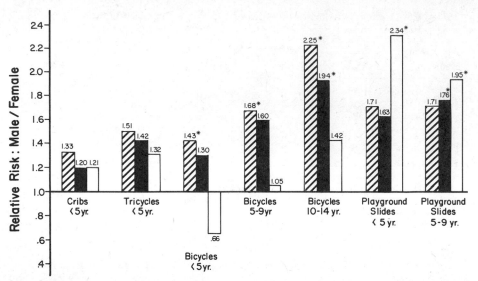

FIGURE 68.2   Rates of injury corrected for degree of product use. The cross-hatched bars represent the relative risk ratio of male/female rates of injury per 100,000 children. The solid bars represent the relative risk ratio of injury rates corrected for the number of users. The open bars represent the relative risk ratio corrected for both number of users and hours of use. The starred numbers indicate relative risk ratios that are significantly different from unity at the $p = .05$ level of significance. (Reproduced with permission from Rivara, F. P., Bergman, A. B., LoGerfo, J. P., and Weiss, N. S. Epidemiology of childhood injuries: II. Sex differences in injury rates. *American Journal of Diseases of Children,* 1982, **136,** 502–506. Copyright 1982, American Medical Association.)

Correcting for product use did not remove the difference between male and female rates for injuries involving playground slides. Although males had higher rates of injury, females had higher rates of product use. Thus, correction for product use in this case actually increased the relative risk of injury for males as compared to females. This is just one example in which the sex differences in injury rates cannot be fully explained by differences in exposure to risk. Other factors must be operating to account for these differences, as in the case of pedestrian injuries.

SEX ROLES AND SOCIALIZATION

Differences in exposure to risk cannot fully account for the increased risk of injury in males. Another possible explanation is sex differences in motor skills. When locomotor skills were correlated with injury rates, children with poorer skills were found to have higher rates of injury (Angle, 1975).

Few studies have explored the sex differences in motor skills in infants and young children. The Bayley Developmental Test (Bayley, 1969), for instance, does not differentiate between males and females below the age of 5 years. At birth, females, on the average, are developmentally more mature than males but no more active. Infant boys seem to show a greater interest in new and complex stimuli than infant girls do, but girls are more vocal and speak at an earlier age. Although girls continue to mature earlier and faster than boys, boys at all ages are more coordinated than girls in gross motor skills. In addition, boys are stronger and have faster reaction times (Maccoby & Jacklin, 1974).

Therefore, boys have, if anything, better motor skills than girls, and these differences become even greater at puberty and during the teenage years. This is the same period in which sex differences in injury rates are greatest. If motor skills were responsible for differences in injury rates, males would be expected to have fewer injuries, not more. The same discrepancy pertains to race. Black children in the United States have higher rates of injury than white children, yet black children are more advanced in gross motor skills than white children (Malina, 1973).

Finally, differences in rates could be due to differences in behavior between the sexes. Sex differences in infant behavior have been observed as early as 1 year of age (Maccoby & Jacklin, 1974). Male infants are more active than female infants, more exploratory, and more vigorous in their play. One-year-old boys have been observed to engage in more "forbidden" play than girls of the same age: they played with wall sockets, pulled curtains, and climbed up on furniture (Smith & Daglish, 1977).

As children mature, males have much more physically aggressive behavior than females. These differences have been found to be present by the age of 3 years. Among school-aged children, boys more often use physical aggression and have an aggressive approach to problem solving (Shope, Hedrick, & Green, 1978). This aggressive behavior in boys is reinforced by self-rewards, by the acceptance of others, and by success in such activities as athletic games.

The difference in injury rates may be related to the sex role behaviors of males and females. Four factors affect the development of sex role behavior in children: genetic factors, the shaping of behavior by parents and other socializing forces, the imitation of sex-appropriate behavior by the child, and the child's cognitive development of masculinity and femininity (Maccoby & Jacklin, 1974).

Although it cannot be ascertained which factor may contribute more to the development of sex roles, the differences in injury rates can be correlated to these differences in behavior. The age at which the sex differences appear—the toddler age group—corresponds to the age at which the sex role-appropriate behaviors develop. The types of injuries that reflect the most marked sex differences are contusions, abrasions, lacerations, fractures, and concussions. These are exactly the types of injuries that result from the more physically active and aggressive style of the male. The injuries that do not exhibit sex differences in rates, particularly poisoning and burns, are different kinds of injuries. These are injuries that are related less to gross motor activity than to fine motor skills and innate curiosity.

The qualitatively different behavior of males, beginning at a very early age and continuing through adulthood, seems to be responsible for their greater risk of injury. As mentioned earlier, this phenomenon is not limited to the United States; it appears to be present in all developed countries of the world. Nor is it surprising, except in the magnitude of the differences in injury rates involved. Can parents and society change their emphasis to behaviors that are less likely to result in injury? Will the feminist movement of the last decade result in increased risk for females, as has occurred in lung cancer and heart disease? Long-term trends in injury rates will reveal the answers.

ACCIDENT PRONENESS, ACCIDENT REPEATERS, AND FAMILY FACTORS

For many years, studies of the host factors involved in childhood injuries have focused on attempts to pinpoint the accident-prone child. Are there innate characteristics of a child that result in a greater frequency of injury? As mentioned earlier, children with impaired locomotor skills do have a greater frequency of injury (Angle, 1975). This may represent a mismatch between the developmental abilities of the child and the skills demanded by the task at hand, but it is not accident proneness. Other studies of children's personality characteristics, behavior, activity, and social adjustment have been inconsistent in their ability to identify such children and predict the risk of injury (Manheimer & Mellinger, 1967; Matheny, Brown, & Wilson, 1972; Padilla, Rohsenaw, & Bergman, 1975).

Most scientists involved with injury research have now discounted the theory of accident proneness. Although some individuals in a group may have higher injury rates than others, the available evidence at present indicates that, over a long period of observation, this is essentially a shifting group of individuals, with new persons constantly entering and leaving the group (Klein, 1980). Moreover, statistical correlations between past and future injuries are low, and a multitude of possible confounding factors, inadequately controlled in previous studies, may account for the high rate of injury in some groups.

The question does arise, however, of why children become members (albeit temporary) of this group of individuals with repeated injuries. A number of sociocultural factors can be identified as clearly playing a role in increasing the risk of injury to a child. As part of a long-term study of newborns, McCormick, Shapiro, and Starfield (1981) identified maternal age as the most important predictor of injury to children in the first year of life. Infants born to teenager mothers had an approximately 50% increase in the risk of injury as compared to infants of older mothers.

Injuries and ingestions can be viewed as pediatric "social diseases," along with child abuse and neglect. Newberger, Reed, Daniel, et al. (1977) studied the stress factors in the environment that lead to these problems in children under 4 years of age. Injuries were found to correlate highly with current stresses in the household, such as recent moves and changes in household composition. Ingestions were more common in families encountering other child-rearing problems or in which there had been mother-child separation. Padilla and colleagues (1975) found very similar results when they compared risk taking in seventh-grade boys. There was a significant correlation between injury over a 5-month period and degree of life change, as measured by the Holmes and Rahe Social Readjustment Rating Questionnaire. There was no correlation of risk-taking behavior and injury during the same period. Other studies have shown that high rates of injury correlate with single-parent families, relatively loose parental supervision, and family stress. Children living in poverty also have higher injury rates, probably because of the social disruption of their lives (MacKay, Halpern, McLoughlin, et al., 1979).

Although these factors associated with higher risk of injury in children can be identified, they are not highly discriminatory. The problem is that high-risk children represent only a small proportion, probably less than 20%, of children injured annually. The predictors cited here can identify most of these but will have a false-positive rate on the order of 75%. Programs aimed at reducing injuries in these high-risk children can be expected to have only a small impact on the total number of injuries occurring in the United States each year.

THE THRESHOLD THEORY OF INJURY CAUSATION

How can the foregoing epidemiologic information be united in a general theory of injury causation? How do the age and sex variations, the differences in socioeconomic factors, and the differences in host skills come together to produce variations in injury rates? Perhaps the best explanation available is the *threshold theory*.

The threshold theory of injuries, first expounded over a decade ago by Waller and Klein (Note 5), rests on the schema, developed by Haddon and Baker (1981) of injuries as damage resulting from the transfer of energy. In an injury, mechanical, thermal, electrical, or radiation energy is transferred to an individual through a vehicle or energy transducer. The energy transfer is the specific and necessary agent for injury; the transducer or vector, however, may assume many forms. This characterization of injury as resulting from energy transfer permits a more rational conceptualization of injury events and allows the development of more effective countermeasures.

The threshold model applies this conceptualization of injury to a schema that explains the epidemiologic variations discussed earlier, the reason for the special vulnerability of children, and the role of behavior and product design in injury prevention.

The essence of the theory is that an injury occurs when the skills demanded in the use of a particular vector exceed the capabilities of human performance (if only for a moment). Individuals using vectors vary enormously in their capabilities. In children, human performance clearly is dependent first and foremost on the developmental stage of the child. The child's motor skills of strength, coordination, balance, dynamic activity, and reaction time increase with age in an almost linear fashion. Cognitive abilities, including assessment and judgment in new situations, are also determined by the developmental stage. Children interpret disease causation according to their stage of development; injury causation as viewed by the child probably follows a similar progression.

In addition to these normal developmental variations in human performance, physical handicaps, chronic illness, emotional disorders, and limited intelligence can have a major impact on children's ability to interact with the vectors of energy transfer in their environment. Finally, changes in performance occur constantly day by day, if not minute by minute.

The demands of dealing with the products in our environment—the energy vectors—also vary widely. Some, such as motor vehicles and guns, may become lethal weapons in the hands of those who use them. The task of using the vector may be simple and easily understandable, requiring no training, little strength, and limited judgment. Conversely, the operation of a vector may demand all of these factors to such an extent that few people can use it without frequent failure and risk of injury.

An additional factor enters into the equation for children—inexperience. Injuries occur more frequently to individuals using a vector for the first time. For children, virtually all vectors are new and unfamiliar, posing an increased risk of injury.

An injury can occur in three different situations. In each case, the energy transfer producing the injury occurs when task demands exceed the child's performance. In the first instance, depicted in Figure 68.3, the level of skill required is not high and is well within the normal capabilities of the child. However, sudden failure in the child's performance results in a decrease in skills to a level below the threshold of task demands, and an injury occurs. An example is a child riding a bicycle who has a seizure, falls, and fractures his arm. This type of cataclysmic failure in human performance is probably an uncommon cause of injury in children, but it may play a much more significant role in the elderly.

The second situation is the scenario most people attach to "accidents"—sudden failure of the product (Figure 68.4). The individual of average abilities is usually well able to carry out the task but is not able to cope with the suddenly increased demands caused by

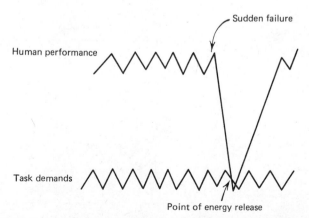

FIGURE 68.3 Sudden human failure in the presence of normal task demands. The upper line represents the normal performance level of the individual. The lower line represents the task demands. Injury occurs when human performance fails. (Reproduced with permission from Waller, J. A. & Klein, D. Society, energy and injury—Inevitable triad? In F. T. Falkner & S. H. Knutti (Eds.), *Research directions toward the reduction of injury in the young and the old.* DHEW Pub. No. (NIH)73–124, 1973.)

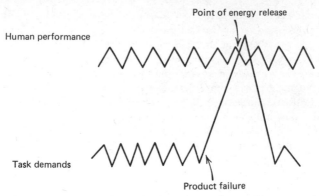

FIGURE 68.4 Sudden environmental failure in the presence of normal human performance. Sudden failure of the product exceeds the capacity of the individual, and injury occurs. (Reproduced with permission from Waller, J. A., & Klein, D. Society, energy and injury—Inevitable triad? In F. T. Falkner & S. H. Knutti (Eds.), *Research directions toward the reduction of injury in the young and the old.* DHEW Pub. No. (NIH)73–124, 1973.)

malfunction of the vector. This type of situation, however, accounts for a relatively small proportion of injury events. In studies of bicycle injuries to children, malfunction of the bicycle accounted for only 18% of injuries (Chlapecka et al., 1975). Vehicular problems similarly account for a small proportion of crashes, although proper packaging of the passenger would prevent many of the injuries resulting from a crash.

The third situation is probably the most common—a relative mismatch between the skills demanded by the task and those available to the individual (Figure 68.5). The vector may be a particularly dangerous one or one that is difficult to use, or the individual may not have the appropriate capabilities, for either developmental, physical, or cognitive reasons. Risk of injury is high, and injury occurs whenever the level of performance dips below the task demands or whenever the threshold rises above the performance level.

Children depend a great deal on parents to choose the products in the environment with which they interact. Proper choices are products that are developmentally appropriate

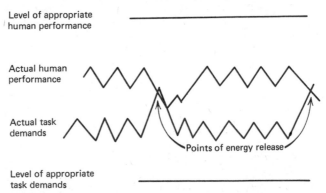

FIGURE 68.5 Mismatch of human performance and an overly demanding task. Injury occurs because of the mismatch of relatively low levels of skill and an overly demanding task. (Reproduced with permission from Waller, J. A. & Klein, D. Society, energy and injury—Inevitable triad? In F. T. Falkner & S. H. Knutti (Eds.), *Research directions toward the reduction of injury in the young and the old.* DHEW Pub. No. (NIH)73–124, 1973.)

for the child. Improper choices place the child in situations for which he is ill prepared developmentally.

The threshold theory explains, I believe, the male–female difference in childhood injury rates. Males are taught by their parents to be action oriented and physical in their play. Parents believe that male children should interact with their environment in a physically challenging manner. Yet, as mentioned earlier, males are not more skilled than females in their motor development. When they are placed on bicycles too early—or on minibikes at age 10—their developmental skills are inadequate to perform the task safely; hence, an injury occurs.

Evidence for the effect of parental expectations on the incidence of childhood injuries is contradictory. One study showed that parents with strong needs for achievement and mastery of their environment may urge their children into precocious interaction with vectors (Waller & Klein, Note 5). Another study showed that most parents have a relatively poor conception and knowledge of child development (Rivara & Howard, 1982). However, no studies have been performed that relate parental knowledge or child-rearing practices to injury rates in their children.

PREVENTION

Methods for reducing the human losses resulting from injuries can be approached within the conceptual schema of the threshold model. Some examples of how the model is useful in developing prevention strategies will be presented here. Many other strategies, not cited, are undoubtedly applicable.

Based on the threshold schema, injury losses can be reduced in one or more of three ways: (a) the demands of the task and the potentially releasable energy can be reduced; (b) the skills of the individual and/or the injury threshold can be raised; and (c) the match between the requirements of the task and the capabilities of the individual can be made more appropriate.

Reduction of Task Demands and High Energy Vectors

Prevention of injury and reduction of human losses can be approached through so-called passive injury control measures, whereby the environment or the energy vector is modified to make interaction less risky. Automatic or passive protection is gaining increasing recognition as a major focus of prevention efforts, because it requires no individual action by those protected and has significant potential for preventing injury morbidity and mortality (Haddon & Baker, 1981). Particularly for children, decreasing the demands necessary for safe interaction with a product is an important method of injury control.

Examples of this type of injury prevention strategy range from elimination of certain hazards from the environment to modification of the product to reduce the potential for injurious energy release. Many of the most successful injury prevention strategies in pediatrics are based on this approach. Since the Poison Prevention Packaging Act was enacted in 1970, ingestions of substances covered by the act have decreased by nearly 50%. Over the past 20 years, the death rate for childhood poisonings has decreased from 2 per 100,000 to 0.5 per 100,000 for children under 5 years of age (Walton, 1982). Behavioral approaches have not been successful. Recent studies of poisoning prevention by using an adversive sticker (Mr. Yuk) have failed to show any effect on poisoning rates and level of household hazard (Fergusson, Harwood, Beautrais, & Shannon, 1982).

Another common source of injury to small children is hot tap water, which can cause serious scald burns after less than 2 seconds of contact. Each year, 4,000 persons require extended hospital care for tap water scalds (Feldman, Schaller, Feldman, et al., 1978). These injuries can be virtually eliminated by simply limiting water heater temperatures to no more than 120°F (48.9°C). Such action could be performed at the factory, thus requiring no effort from the individual homeowner.

As mentioned earlier, drownings are an important cause of death in children. In Honolulu, where legislation requires protective fencing around public and private pools, childhood drowning fatalities associated with swimming pools occur substantially less frequently than in cities without such legislation. Pearn, Wong, Brown et al. (1979) have compared swimming pool fatalities in Honolulu and Brisbane, Australia—cities with similar sizes, climates, life-styles, and ratio of swimming pools to houses. The fatality rate for drownings in Honolulu was 0.9 per 100,000, compared to a rate of 2.6 per 100,000 in Brisbane, which does not have such legislation.

Other energy vectors are inherently unsafe, and the only practical approach to prevention appears to be total removal from the environment. Handguns are probably the most striking example. Handguns account for only approximately 20% of the firearms in use today, yet they are involved in 90% of the criminal and nonintentional firearm misuse (Rivara & Stapleton, 1982). Moreover, they are ineffective as hunting weapons, because of their inaccuracy, or as weapons of protection. A homeowner is six times more likely to have a nonintentional injury in his family because of a handgun than he is to shoot a burgular. Modification of the handgun to make it a safer instrument is not feasible; total elimination of the handgun from the environment is the only practical approach.

Children in low-income families have been shown to have a higher rate of injuries as well as a greater incidence of injury repeaters. (Westfelt, 1982). One of the reasons may be that children in such families are especially likely to encounter vectors that require an inordinately high level of performance if injury is to be avoided. Space heaters, open fireplaces, faulty wiring, fire-trap tenements, and play areas with high traffic density are constant hazards to the inhabitants of such an environment. Combined with the inherent lack of judgment of children and the social disruption in the lives of the poor, this relatively danger-ous environment provides the backdrop for frequent and repeated injury. Behavioral ap-proaches to injury prevention seem to be least successful among such low-income families; modification of the environment appears to be necessary.

Increased Skills or Injury Threshold

Many injuries occur when the skills of the person are decreased either temporarily or permanently. The most common factors that temporarily lower the performance level of the individual are alcohol and drugs. These substances, commonly involved in adult motor vehicle collisions, are also an important contributor to the risk of injury in teenagers. A recent study in Baltimore found that 40% of teenage automobile crash victims and 25% of motorcycle victims had detectable blood alcohol levels at the time of the crash (Soderstrom, DuPriest, Brenner, et al., 1979). Alcohol and drug use may also play a prominent role in non-motor-vehicular injuries. Dietz and Baker (1974) reported that nearly 50% of teenage drowning victims over 14 years of age had positive blood alcohol concentrations at autopsy.

Teenagers have the highest motor vehicle fatality rate, peaking at 18 years of age. Further-more, driver education, by promoting the licensure of 16- and 17-year-olds, increases the number of motor vehicle crashes (Robertson & Zador, 1978). Driver education does not result in safer drivers, but succeeds only in putting more young drivers on the road. As a result, 10% of the motor vehicle fatalities in 1978 involved 16- to 17-year-old drivers.

An approach to the problem would be to reduce the number of young drivers on the road and decrease their access to alcohol. Raising the minimum age of licensure to 18 years would probably decrease by 75% the number of motor vehicle fatalities in 16- and 17-year-olds. Increasing the minimum drinking age has been found to result in a 25% reduction in the number of nighttime fatal crashes, which account for nearly 50% of the total motor vehicle crashes in this age group (Insurance Institute, 1981).

Unfamiliarity with a task also carries an increased risk of injury. Many childhood injuries involving sports and recreational equipment, such as bicycles, skateboards, snow skis, and roller skates, happen to unskilled first-time users. Proper instruction and supervision, combined with appropriate use of the equipment, can prevent many of these injuries.

The injury threshold of the body can be raised through proper physical conditioning. Most adolescent athletes are unaware that it takes up to three weeks for the body to fully acclimatize to the vigorous levels of exercise required in organized athletic activities. Many young athletes arrive at the first day of tryouts without benefit of a gradual acquisition of fitness and try to perform above their level of fitness. Young athletes should be encouraged to achieve a level of cardiopulmonary fitness and strength commensurate with their age and sport.

Appropriate Match of Skills and Task Demands

One of the most fruitful areas of injury prevention, especially from a behavioral point of view, is the appropriate match of a person's level of skill with the task at hand. A mismatch of the two factors is one of the leading causes of injury in children and adolescents.

As mentioned earlier, many parents are not aware of the normal developmental skills of children. Incorporating study of child development in the high school curriculum and developing day care centers at high schools would provide students with an important knowledge base. An additional benefit would be an increase in the number of teenage mothers able to attend school.

Safety education programs should be developmentally oriented. Bass and his colleagues at the Framingham Union Hospital in Massachusetts have designed a screening questionnaire to be used by physicians in their offices (Bass & Mehta, 1980). This developmentally based safety survey, geared to four age groups (infants, preschool, school age, and adolescents) and six areas of prevention (general household and environmental hazards, poisonings, burns, drownings, motor vehicle safety, and toys), assists the physician in assessing the match of risks and skills. Vectors in the environment that are unsuitable for the age group are identified and become topics for physician–parent discussion and counseling.

Among children playing competitive sports, risk of injury can be reduced by matching the players by size and developmental level. Division by age alone often produces inequitable situations and resultant injuries, but most athletic programs still continue to do so, ignoring the differences in development. The Selection Classification Age Maturity Program has been developed to match youngsters of similar maturity and skill. The classification scheme uses five criteria to match athletes: type of sport; level of competition; test for ability, strength, speed, and endurance; level of skill; and physical maturity. Using such a scheme, Hafner (1975) reported that only 3 of 200 children playing football were injured, compared to a national rate of 50% in boys at similar ages.

FUTURE RESEARCH DIRECTIONS

The research needs in the understanding and prevention of childhood injuries are enormous. Further examination of the reasons for male predominance in injuries is essential. Better characterization of the development of behavioral differences in males and females has major implications not only for childhood injuries but probably for many of the diseases of adulthood in which lifestyle plays an etiologic role. These diseases are the subject of many of the other chapters in this handbook: smoking and lung cancer, coronary heart disease, hypertension, alcohol abuse, and intentional and nonintentional injuries. What are the factors in the sociocultural environment that influence the development of an aggressive lifestyle in males? What is the role of the media, especially television, compared to the contribution of the home and the school in this process? Long-term follow-up of injury rates is needed to document any change in the male–female ratio concurrent with the feminist movement of the last decade, as such changes are occurring in other areas, most notably smoking and lung cancer.

The role of differential exposure to risk as a cause of the greater rate of injury in some groups has been mentioned here, but few studies have examined this in sufficient detail. Before the risk associated with a particular product can be accurately assessed and compared to that of other products, however, the denominator for the risk—that is, the number of users and the amount of use—must be known.

Although accident proneness as a cause of injuries to children has been effectively discounted, how do different child-rearing styles contribute to the varying incidence of injury? Can high-risk children be identified better than they are at present? The studies of Newberger et al. (1977) suggest that they can, but much more work is needed.

Further studies of injury using the threshold model as a conceptual framework need to be performed. Evaluation of parents' perception of children's developmental stages and injury risks should be performed and correlated with the incidence of injury in different groups of children.

The identification of different hazards associated with specific socioeconomic groups requires much further research. It is often assumed that the poor are surrounded by a greater number and variety of environmental hazards, yet children of higher socioeconomic levels may encounter totally different types of hazards associated with their more privileged status. Similarly, the effectiveness of different prevention strategies in varying socioeconomic groups must be analyzed. Infant seat-restraint programs, for example, are probably ineffective among indigent families unless they are combined with a loaner program.

McCormick et al. (1981) identified maternal age as an important factor associated with risk of injury in childhood. Why do infants of teenage parents have this higher risk, and how can it be reduced? Is it because the teenage mothers are unaware of the risks in the environment, are unaware of the child's developmental abilities, or fail to supervise their play appropriately? Answers to these questions are currently lacking.

Finally, continued epidemiologic surveillance is essential. Changes in the pattern of injuries and the appearance of new hazards can only be discovered in a timely fashion through continued surveillance of injury losses.

REFERENCE NOTES

1. National Center for Health Statistics. *Vital statistics of the United States, 1977.* DHHS Pub. No. (PHS)81–1101, 1981.

2. National Center for Health Statistics. *Facts of life and death.* DHEW Pub. No. (PHS)79–1222, 1978.

3. National Center for Health Statistics. *Current estimates from the National Health Interview Survey: United States, 1980.* Series 10, No. 139, DHHS Pub. No. (PHS)82–1567, 1981.

4. National Center for Health Statistics. *Prevalence of selected impairments: United States, 1977. Vital and health statistics.* Series 10, No. 139, DHHS Pub. No. (PHS)81–1562, 1981.

5. Waller, J. A., & Klein, D. Society, energy and injury: Inevitable triad? In F. T. Falkner & S. H. Knutti (Eds.), *Research directions toward the reduction of injury in the young and the old.* National Institute of Child Health and Human Development, DHEW Pub. No. (NIH)73–124, 1973.

REFERENCES

Angle, C. R. Locomotor skills and school accidents. *Pediatrics,* 1975, **56**, 819–821.

Bass, J. L., & Mehta, K. A. Developmentally oriented safety surveys. *Clinical Pediatrics,* 1980, **19**, 350–356.

Bayley, N. *Bayley Scales of Infant Development.* New York: The Psychological Corporation, 1969.

Center for Disease Control. Introduction to Table V: Premature deaths, monthly mortality and monthly physician contacts—United States. *Morbidity and Mortality Weekly Report,* 1982, **31**(March 12), 109–110; 117.

Chlapecka, T. W., Schupack, S. A., Planek, T. W., et al. *Bicycle accidents and usage among elementary school children in the United States.* Chicago: National Safety Council, 1975.

Dietz, P. E., & Baker, S. P. Drowning: Epidemiology and prevention. *American Journal of Public Health,* 1974, **64**, 303–312.

Doege, T. C. An injury is no accident. *New England Journal of Medicine,* 1978, **298**, 509–510.

Feldman, K. W., Schaller, R. T., Feldman, J. A., et al. Tap water scalds in children. *Pediatrics,* 1978, **62**, 1–7.

Fergusson, D. M., Harwood, L. J., Beautrais, A. L., & Shannon, F. T. A controlled field trial of a poisoning prevention method. *Pediatrics,* 1982, **69**, 515–520.

Haddon, W., Jr. Advances in the epidemiology of injuries as a basis for public policy. *Public Health Reports,* 1980, **95**, 411–421.

Haddon, W., Jr., & Baker, S. P. Injury control. In D. Clark & B. McMahon (Eds.), *Preventive medicine* (2nd ed.). Boston: Little, Brown, 1981.

Hafner, J. Problems in matching young athletes: Baby fat, peach fuzz, muscle and moustache. *Sports Medicine,* 1975, **3**, 96–98.

Hartunian, N. S., Smart, C. N., & Thompson, M. S. The incidence and economic costs of cancer, motor vehicle injuries, coronary heart disease and stroke: A comparative analysis. *American Journal of Public Health,* 1980, **70**, 1249–1260.

Holinger, P. C. Violent deaths among the young: An epidemiological study of recent trends in suicide, homicide and accidents. *American Journal of Psychiatry,* 1979, **136**, 1144–1147.

Insurance Institute for Highway Safety. Teens and autos: A deadly combination. *Highway Loss Reduction Status Report,* 1981, **16**(14), 1–11.

Klein, D. Societal influences on childhood accidents. *Accident analysis and prevention,* 1980, **12**, 275.

Maccoby, E., & Jacklin, C. *The psychology of sex differences.* Stanford, Calif.: Stanford University Press, 1974.

MacKay, A., Halpern, J., McLoughlin, E., Locke, J., & Crawford, J. D. A comparison of age-specific burn injury rates in five Massachusetts communities. *American Journal of Public Health,* 1979, **69**, 1149–1150.

Malina, R. M. Ethnic and cultural factors in the development of motor abilities and strength in American children. In G. L. Rarrick (Ed.), *Physical activity: Human growth and development.* New York: Academic Press, 1973.

Manheimer, D. I., & Mellinger, G. D. Personality characteristics of the child accident repeater. *Child Development,* 1977, **48**, 250–254.

Marcusson, H., & Oehmisch, W. Accident mortality in childhood in selected countries of different continents, 1950–1971. *World Health Statistics Report,* 1977, **30**, 57–89.

Matheny, A. P., Brown, A. M., & Wilson, R. S. Assessment of children's behavioral characteristics. *Clinical Pediatrics,* 1972, **11**, 437–439.

McCormick, M. C., Shapiro, S., & Starfield, B. H. Injury and its correlates among normal birth weight and low birth weight one-year-old infants. *American Journal of Diseases of Children,* 1981, **135**, 159–163.

Newberger, E. H., Reed, R. B., Daniel, J. H., et al. Pediatric social illness: Toward an etiologic classification. *Pediatrics,* 1977, **60**, 178–185.

Newton, G. D., & Zimring, F. A. *Firearms and violence in American life.* Washington, D.C.: National Commission on the Causes and Prevention of Violence, 1969.

Padilla, E. T., Rohsenaw, J., & Bergman, A. B. Predicting accident frequency in children. *Pediatrics,* 1975, **56**, 819–821.

Pearn, J. A., Wong, R. Y., Brown, J., et al. Drowning and near drowning involving children: A five-year total population study from the city and county of Honolulu. *American Journal of Public Health,* 1979, **69**, 450–454.

Rivara, F. P., Bergman, A. B., LoGefgo, J. P., & Weiss, N. S. Epidemiology of childhood injuries: II. Sex differences in injury rates. *American Journal of Diseases of Children,* 1982, **136**, 502–506.

Rivara, F. P., & Howard, D. Parental knowledge of child development and injury risks. *Journal of Developmental and Behavioral Pediatrics,* 1982, **3,** 103–105.

Rivara, F. P., & Stapleton, F. B. Handguns and children: A dangerous mix. *Journal of Developmental and Behavioral Pediatrics,* 1982, **3,** 35–38.

Robertson, L. S., & Zador, P. L. Driver education and fatal crash involvement of teenage drivers. *American Journal of Public Health,* 1978, **68,** 959–965.

Routledge, D. A., Repett-Wright, R., & Howarth, C. I. The exposure of young children to accident risk on pedestrians. *Ergonomics,* 1974, **17,** 456–480.

Shops, G. L., Hedrick, T. E., & Green, R. G. Physical/verbal aggression: Sex differences in style. *Journal of Personality,* 1978, **46,** 23–42.

Smith, P. K., & Daglish, L. Sex differences in parent and infant behavior in the home. *Child Development,* 1977, **48,** 250–254.

Soderstrom, C. A., DuPriest, R. W., Brenner, C., et al. Alcohol and roadway trauma: Problems of diagnosis and management. *American Surgeon,* 1979, **45,** 129–136.

Walton, W. W. An evaluation of the Poison Prevention Packaging Act. *Pediatrics,* 1982, **69,** 363–370.

Weiss, N. S. Recent trends in violent deaths among young adults in the United States. *American Journal of Epidemiology,* 1976, **102,** 416–422.

Westfelt J. N. Environmental factors in childhood accidents. *Acta Paediatrica Scandinavica, Supplement,* 1982, **291,** 1–75.

CHAPTER 69

CHILDHOOD HOUSEHOLD SAFETY

ROBERT A. DERSHEWITZ

Michael Reese Hospital & Medical Center and
the University of Chicago Pritzker School of Medicine

We are all familiar with the expression "A man's home is his castle." Although the expression is not meant to imply this, it should be noted that some castles are dark, dirty, and dangerous. The characteristics of a home and its environment greatly influence the physical and mental health of its inhabitants. Wilner, Walkley, Pinkerton, and Tayback (1962, chap. 18) have shown that those who live in overcrowded or inadequate housing experience more home accidents, infections, illnesses, family discord, emotional disturbances, and school problems than those who live in better housing. These patterns persist even when such variables as race and income are controlled. With the proper physical and emotional environment, however, homes can provide a nurturing milieu. Since more children are injured in their homes than anywhere else, it is incumbent upon us to minimize the household dangers to which our children are exposed.

Many common household items may not appear dangerous, and ways of preventing them may not be obvious. The first part of this chapter will be an overview of childhood household safety, and the second section will discuss its preventable aspects. I will propose an approach to safety counseling that is different from the usual, and I will provide practical points on safety-proofing, by injury category, to be covered during the health education process. For a more theoretical framework on the prevention of injuries, the reader is referred elsewhere (Baker, 1973, 1975).

OVERVIEW

The Scope of the Problem

Accidents claim more lives of children between the ages of 1 and 14 years than the next six leading causes combined (see Table 69.1). It is estimated that 29,000 accidents must occur to result in 2,800 minor injuries, 97 major injuries, and one death (Kiefer, 1973). Most accidental deaths to children younger than 5 years occur at home. After age 6, most accidents and accidental deaths occur outdoors (Joliet, 1961). Annually, an estimated 3,200 children from infancy to 14 years of age die in home accidents. Deaths related to fires are the leading cause, followed by suffocation and drowning (see Table 69.2 and *Accident Facts*, 1981). The kitchen is the most dangerous room in the home; approximately 18% of all home injuries occur there. Next, in descending order of frequency, the living room, bedroom, yard, and bathrooms are the areas where most injuries occur; together, they account for 67% of all home accidents (Takahata, Colflesh, Digon, et al., 1974, p. 249).

Table 69.1 Causes of Death of Children Aged 1 to 14 Years, 1978

Category	Total Number of Deaths
Accidents	9,622
Motor vehicle	4,417
Drowning	1,640
Fires, burns	1,328
Firearms	348
Cancer	2,099
Congenital anomalies	1,677
Homicide	767
Heart disease	636
Pneumonia	621
Cerebrovascular disease	299

Source: National Center for Health Statistics data, reported in *Accident Facts—1981.* Chicago: National Safety Council, 1981.

Susceptible Children

Every child is at risk of home injury. Thus, as a general preventive strategy, it would not be wise to focus efforts on profiling the at-risk population. Yet special situations warrant special attention. Disruption and strife (either physical or emotional) greatly contribute to the child's susceptibility to home accidents. Family moves, for example, are prime times for children to have accidents, because the physical environment is chaotic and supervision is often compromised. Children who have three or more accidents per year that require medical attention are considered accident-repeaters. The accident-repeater is often a maladjusted child who comes from a disturbed or stressed family (Jones, 1980), and the entire family should be evaluated for possible counseling.

Table 69.2 Principal Causes of Accidental Home Deaths of Children Aged 0 to 14 Years, 1978

Category	Number of Deaths
Fires, burns	1,050
Suffocation—ingested object	570
Drowning	410
Suffocation—mechanical	340
Falls	220
Firearms	210
Poisoning	120
Other	480

Source: Accident Facts—1981. Chicago: National Safety Council, 1981.

Approaches to Reducing Household Injuries

Injury control (used interchangeably with *accident prevention*) strategies consist of two broad types of countermeasures: active and passive. A well-designed home safety program should incorporate both types of interventions. Although the objectives of each type are different, they are often complementary. The underlying premise of the passive approach is that individuals cannot be taught or relied on to safety-proof their homes. Even if initial safety-proofing were accomplished, it is doubtful that such an environment could be maintained. Moreover, children, by nature, are likely to be injured by hazards around the house. If legislation or safety standards could reduce or eliminate risk to the child, however, one would not need to rely on human behavior. Such standards have been established for a variety of conditions and have been effective consistently; for example, 3 years after the promulgation of the 1970 Poison Prevention Packaging Act, use of safety caps reduced accidental ingestion of baby aspirin by 68% (Clarke & Walton, 1979).

Voluntary recall of dangerous items by manufacturers may also achieve passive control without mandated legislation. After a third child died by strangulation while playing with a Creative Playthings Indoor Gym House, the company initiated a nationwide campaign to recall and replace the unsafe ladder component free of charge. At the time of the 15 March 1982 recall, it was estimated that between 137,000 and 239,000 dangerous units were in use.

Because hazards may remain in spite of warnings, recall, or banning and because not every potentially dangerous situation can be resolved by legislation, the active approach to accident prevention has an important role. Essentially, this approach requires health education to teach the parents and children about safety. This will change their preventive behavior (an assumption), which in turn will reduce accidents (another assumption). The onus of responsibility is on the parents, however, which is the major liability of the approach. The greatest advantage of this countermeasure is its flexibility. Safety-proofing can correct most, but not all, potentially dangerous situations. If parents stored medications properly, for example, fewer ingestions would occur; and if matches or lighters were not accessible to children, fewer home fires would start.

Unfortunately, it has been shown repeatedly that not all parents respond to health education. In fact, safety counseling fails more often than it succeeds. People are more likely to learn if the desired action is simple, nonrepetitive, convenient, and short term. Safety practices that require continuous attention or that are inconvenient are not likely to be maintained. Thus, ease is a facilitator but is neither necessary nor sufficient for parents to maintain a safe home. Even providing safety devices free of charge to parents does not assure that they will be used. In one study, mothers were given free Kindergards (plastic locking devices) and electric outlet covers. They all received health education and were shown how to install the devices (Dershewitz, 1979). Results were disappointing, indicating only an increased use of outlet covers, because it was much easier to insert an outlet cover than to install a Kindergard (1 second versus about 15 minutes). The findings are not surprising, but they do highlight the difficulty of successfully translating health education into actual practice.

State of the Art

The current technique in safety counseling is to target the message in each session, rather than delivering a comprehensive diatribe on the many ways of safety-proofing a home. As we shall see in the next section, the most successful health education studies have had narrow goals, attempting to reduce one type of accident. Dershewitz and Williamson (1977) failed in their health education attempt to train middle- and upper-middle-class mothers in comprehensively safety-proofing their homes.

Marketing techniques, ranging from subliminal bombardment to subtle fear tactics, can also have a powerful effect. Following aggressive marketing and widespread recommendations to install smoke detectors, for example, sales skyrocketed. In 1970, fewer than 5% of homes had smoke detectors. In 1980, 46% of all households in the United States had them (Massey & Jones, Note 1).

The Need for Evaluation

Because of a lack of convincing evidence on the effectiveness of health education and safety counseling, many question their role as an important countermeasure. That the state of the art is primitive should provide all the more reason to intensify efforts at improving the effectiveness of our counseling. Because there are very few reported pediatric studies in which health education was used as the sole means to reduce household injuries, conclusions about the efficiency of this approach remain tentative. Also, until more evaluative research is done on innovative programs, most published literature on household safety will continue to be descriptive studies alerting us to the multitude of household hazards that injure children.

Most often a health care provider—e.g., a pediatrician or nurse practitioner—delivers safety counseling. If not totally by design, at least by default, this task is delegated to such people. Too frequently, however, such counseling actually is merely providing health information, since only facts are disseminated, orally or in writing. A wide variety of health care professionals are capable health educators. For example, nurse practitioners, clinical psychologists, school nurses, and dieticians can teach effectively. The settings may be as diverse as individual counseling sessions, group discussions, and PTA meetings, and supplemental instructional media may be as varied as displays, video cassettes, and computerized feedback programs. With multiple modalities and personnel representing many professional disciplines, one can assemble a health education program geared for an office setting or for an entire community. The community approach has the inherent advantage of reaching far more people than individual sessions; its main disadvantage is cost. This strategy has been used in attempts to reduce childhood accidents, but without consistently positive results (Schlesinger, Dickson, Westaby, et al., 1966; Ingraham & Polk, Note 2).

Evaluation must be a component of any health education program. Knowledge, belief, and behavior can be measured, but several studies have shown that acquisition of knowledge does not necessarily lead to a change in behavior and that behavior may change without a gain in knowledge. Indeed, the effectiveness of any program must evaluate outcome, whether it be health status or changes in behavior. Having a control group is methodologically invaluable and is essential for programmatic evaluation. A recent report illustrates the necessity for evaluation. Project Burn Prevention used a community approach to try to reduce the incidence of burns (McLaughlin, Vince, Lee, et al., 1982). Significant resources and a sound approach consisting of community interventions, school health programs, and a variety of media messages were employed. Only those in the school program had a gain in knowledge. More important, there was not a reduction in burn injuries. The authors conclude, and probably the majority of workers in the injury control field concur, that emphasis should be on the passive approach, in which safety standards have had a much better record of reducing injuries.

HAZARDS AND SAFETY RECOMMENDATIONS

This section will emphasize specific types of home accidents, reviewing the pertinent literature and offering practical recommendations to parents on how to reduce those injuries. Generally, only one facet of safety-proofing, such as poison prevention, should be covered at a time in safety counseling. Because most one-on-one safety counseling takes place during well-child visits to the pediatrician, a schedule of topics to be covered at each recommended well-child visit through age 5 is provided in Table 69.3. The topic at each counseling session

Table 69.3 Recommended Safety Counseling During Well-Child Visits to the Pediatrician

Recommended Age at Visit[a]	Suggested Safety Topic
Newborn	Car restraints
2–4 wk.	Crib environment
2 mo.	Baby furniture
4 mo.	Toy safety
6 mo.	Electrical burns and scalds
9 mo.	Ingestions
12 mo.	Falls
15 mo.	Cuts
18 mo.	Repetition of poisonings including dangerous indoor plants
24 mo.	Yard safety
36 mo.	Repetition of appropriateness of toys, e.g. tricycle, big wheels
5 yr.	Fire prevention

[a] From American Academy of Pediatrics. *Manual on standards of child health care* (3rd ed.). Author, 1977. Available from the AAP, P.O. Box 1034, Evanston, Illinois 60204.

should be most relevant to the hazard exposure or danger to the child at his present age and should be attuned to the child's development. To say the least, this opportunity for anticipatory counseling during well-child visits has not been utilized as powerfully as it could or should be: The American Academy of Pediatrics Recommends a conceptually similar approach, and in 1983 implemented its Injury Prevention Program (Tipp). For a practical yet comprehensive guide to safety-proofing a home, I recommend *Unsafe as Houses: A Guide to Home Safety* (Wart, 1981).

Poisonings

Without doubt, the greatest breakthrough in reducing accidental ingestions has been the result of passive measures, i.e., mandatory use of safety caps, establishment of poison control centers, and reduction of the amount of available medication—for example, allowing no more than 36 baby aspirin in each bottle. The ingestion rate for all substances requiring child-resistant closures (see Table 69.4) declined from 5.7 per 1,000 children in 1973 to 3.4 per 1,000 children in 1978. Walton (1982) estimated that child-resistant closures prevented approximately 200,000 accidental ingestions since 1973. Table 69.5 lists the most frequently reported products ingested by children under 5 years of age. As is apparent, the passive approach will never eliminate the need for health education. (See Table 69.6 for poisoning safety tips.)

Social learning theory and the "natural law" that most parents are protective of their offspring would lead one to believe that in the homes of children who have had an accidental poisoning, the poisonous substances available to children would be reduced. That this is not the case vividly highlights major problems with the active approach to injury control. Baltimore and Meyer (1969) and Sobel (1969), in separate but related studies, conducted unannounced visits to homes where toddlers had recently ingested a poison and to homes of a control group. The findings were similar. Mothers of the control group gave themselves credit that their children did not have any ingestions because of how well they safety-proofed their homes. Actually, the home inspection revealed a great many exposed toxic

Table 69.4   Products That Must Be Packaged in Child-Resistant Closures, 1981

Aspirin
Furniture polish
Methyl salicylate
Controlled drugs
Sodium and/or potassium hydroxide
Turpentine
Kindling and/or illuminating preparations
Methyl alcohol
Sulfuric acid
Prescription drugs
Ethylene glycol
Paint solvents
Iron-containing drugs
Dietary supplements
Acetaminophen

substances in homes of both groups. Of the 52 mothers of children who had ingestions, 29 claimed that they changed the way they stored products after the ingestion. A comparison of inspections right after the ingestion and one year later showed that no such change in storage patterns had occurred. It is interesting that all groups had a good knowledge of poisonings.

Mr. Yuk, Officer Ugg, and Serpent stickers are widely recommended and distributed. If for no other reason, these stickers are useful in that they have the telephone number of a poison control center printed on them. Proponents argue that if children can be taught to recognize as dangerous all products having the warning sticker, they will keep away from the poison. Unfortunately, this tactic has been poorly evaluated. One recent study in New Zealand found that Mr. Yuk labels may not be effective (Fergusson, Harwood, Beautrais, & Shannon, 1982). Since the children studied were between 2 and 3 years of age, however, and hence were younger than the usually recommended target population, the results may not be generalizable to children of all ages. If parents put stickers on certain products, will they become complacent about further efforts to reduce exposure to other poisonous substances? If children do not see a poison sticker, will they assume that

Table 69.5   Products Most Frequently Ingested by Children Under 5 Years of Age

Vitamins	Paint
Baby Aspirin	Fertilizer, plant food
Cologne	Gasoline
Perfume	Shampoo
Nail polish remover	Mushrooms
Isopropyl alcohol	Nail polish
Philodendron	Tylenol
Drug Combinations	Hydrogen peroxide
Clorox	Personal deodorant

Source: National Clearing House for Poison Control Centers, 1981, **25**(6).

Table 69.6 Poisonings—Safety Tips

Keep all medicines and dangerous household products out of the reach of children. Lock up all medicines or have the medicine cabinet locked. For highly dangerous cleaning items, such as Drano or Liquid Plummer, buy only when needed, then discard immediately after using.

Do not keep medicines in your pocketbook.

Never call medicine "candy."

Avoid taking medicines in a child's presence, because children imitate adults.

Beware of poisonous house plants.

Handle and store insecticides safely.

Keep cosmetics out of the reach of children.

Have syrup of ipecac at home, and write the poison control center's telephone number on the label. Always get medical advice before using the ipecac.

Use low cabinets to store food, not cleaning products.

Keep all substances, especially cleaning materials, in their original containers, never in pitchers, milk containers, or soda bottles.

Before discarding containers of cleaning products, pour contents down the drain or in the toilet and rinse the containers well. Do not put a container into a receptacle with its contents.

Always read the label before giving or taking medicine.

the product is safe? These questions, which need to be answered, again illustrate the need for programs to be evaluated on a demonstration basis before they are widely implemented.

Two extensive community efforts at reducing poisonings were successful. In Monroe County, New York, a program employing multiple community outreach seminars, school curricular seminars, retail outreach efforts, distribution of informational materials, and the use of mass media decreased poisonings by 66% (Fisher, Van Buren, Nitzken, et al., Note 3). The initial disposal of unwanted medical preparations (DUMP) program in Scotland was unsuccessful. (Thomson & Frame, 1979). Its goal was to have people bring all their old, unused, and unwanted medicines to pharmacies for disposal. The second attempt, which involved a mass-media blitz, yielded over 3,000 kilos of drugs—as opposed to only 51 kilos from the first attempt. It was assumed, but not shown, that there would be a concomitant reduction in accidental poisonings.

Burns

Each year, approximately one out of every 17 homes in the United States has a fire. In fact, the United States has more deaths due to fires annually than any other country. Morbidity and mortality result not only from fire itself but also from hypoxia and the toxic fumes produced by the burning product. Most fires start in the kitchen and fortunately remain relatively minor. In considering strategies for the reduction of burns in children, emphasis should be in four areas: (a) smoke detectors, (b) scalds, (c) sleepware, and (d) overt environmental hazards.

Smoke Detectors

More than 10 million smoke detectors are sold annually in the United States. The industry recently has undergone significant technological advances. There are currently three major types of fire warning systems, each with advantages and disadvantages: heat detectors, photoelectric smoke detectors, and ionization detectors. These systems are all of proven effectiveness. As an incentive for people to install them, many insurance companies are discounting insurance premiums on homes that use smoke or fire detectors. Many cities have building codes requiring this type of warning system. There is no doubt that if codes were more comprehensive (and were enforced), fewer people would perish in fires.

Reisinger (1982) reported on a study in which pediatricians in private practice tried to persuade parents to use smoke detectors. Mothers were given a pamphlet and then discussed fire safety with their pediatricians during well-child visits. After the visits, mothers were offered smoke detectors at cost. There was also a control group. An inspection was made in homes of both groups 4 to 6 weeks after the office visits.

> Of the 120 families in the experimental group, 27 (23%) purchased a detector in the office. Of these 27 families, 19 of 26 surveyed had already installed the detectors at the time of the home visit. Of all households inspected, one or more smoke detectors were present in 64 (61%) of the 108 homes in the experimental group. An unexpected finding was a relatively large number (18%) of detectors that were incorrectly installed or inoperable. A significant variable determining the presence of a smoke detector was that of home ownership; only 18% of rental units contained correctly installed and operable detectors, compared to 55% of those that were occupant-owned. The results of this investigation indicate that pediatricians can be at least partially successful in altering parents' behavior with regard to smoke detector purchase and installation. (Reisinger, 1982).

Scalds

Scald injuries to children result most frequently from spills of a hot beverage, such as coffee or tea, and in bath tubs. (Child abuse is another major cause; because it is a separate problem, however, it will not be covered in this chapter.) Feldman (1978) pioneered work in this area. His conclusion is that most tap water burns to children could be prevented if home water heaters were reduced to a maximum level of 120°F, rather than the usual setting of 130°–140°F. This argument is both an endorsement of the passive approach and a refutation of the active approach, since parents cannot be relied on to keep constant watch over their children. Some states, such as Massachusetts and Florida, have enacted codes that limit the temperature produced by water heaters, but until the current antiregulatory mood of this country changes, widespread implementation of similar standards is unlikely.

The problem of hot water spills and grease burns can be addressed only by health education. Many babies sit on their mothers' laps while the mothers drink hot tea or coffee. The babies frequently knock over the cup, and the spills result in first-, second-, or third-degree burns.

Another problem area is the kitchen. Infants like to be near their mothers, and mothers want to supervise their children. Since the mother (or caretaker) traditionally spends a large part of her day in the kitchen, there is ample opportunity for hot water and grease to spill on the baby. Tips for preventing these avoidable injuries are presented in Table 69.7.

Sleepwear Hazards

As a result of the 1967 Flammable Fabrics Act amendments requiring that children's sleep garments be flame-resistant, there has been a dramatic reduction in flame burns to young children. Shriner Burn Institute in Boston reported that between 1969 and 1976, the distribution of children admitted to their unit for flame burns fell progressively from 61% to 42%, while the percentages of burns from all other categories increased (McLaughlin, Clarke, Stahl, et al., 1977). Certain natural fabrics, such as wool, and synthetics, such as nylon

Table 69.7 Burns—Safety Tips

General
Every household should conduct fire drills regularly (including a fire escape plan).
Every home should have a fire extinguisher.

Smoke Detectors
Read directions for selection of proper site(s) of installation and maintenance instruction.
Check batteries monthly.

Scalds
Set your home water heater regulator no higher than 120°F.
Always test the water before your child gets into a bathtub.
Keep your child out of the kitchen while you are preparing meals.
Make sure your child is far from the coffee pot or hot drinks at the table.
Turn handles of pans toward the back of the stove to prevent your child from grabbing
    the handles and being burned by the pan or its contents.
Purchase cool-air vaporizers rather than steam vaporizers.

Clothing
When buying sleepwear for your child, make sure that the garment is flame-retardant. In
    general, purchase flame-retardant or flame-resistant clothes.

Fires and Burns
Never smoke in bed.
Do not have matches or lighters lying around the house.
Do not overload circuits.
Always unplug the iron and put it out of reach of children, even if you are leaving for
    just a few minutes.
Carefully supervise electrically operated toys.
Repair all worn electrical wires.
Place guards in front of fireplaces, open heaters, and radiators.

Electrical Burns
Do not let infants crawl or play near electrical heaters.
Use snap-in plastic covers on unused wall outlets.
Tightly wrap the ends of extension cords so that the joining wires cannot be pulled apart.

---

and modacrylic, are flame-resistant. Cottons and rayons, which are highly flammable, are
most often used in infant sleepwear, however. Prior to 1977, most of these garments were
treated with the flame-retardant Tris-BP (tris [2,3, dibromopropyl] phosphate). Because
of reports by the National Cancer Institute in 1977 that Tris is mutogenic (and likely
carcinogenic), the Consumer Product Safety Commission (CPSC) banned the use of Tris-
treated children's garments. Since three washings removes as much as 95% of the Tris,
existing Tris-treated garments were not recalled from the marketplace, but the public health
hazard was not perpetuated. Some people questioned the actions of CPSC, however, arguing
that mandatory flame-retardant sleepwear (a passive measure) is known to be highly effective
in reducing flame burns to children, whereas the risk of cancer is speculative (Bergman,
1977).

Since 1977 there has been a relaxation in the manufacturing codes for children's garments.
Unfortunately, other safe flame-retardant chemicals tend to produce effects that are objection-
able to consumers, such as discoloring or stiffening of the fabric. Modacrylics and other
synthetics do not have these problems but tend to be expensive. At present, the role of
health education in this area is twofold: (a) to encourage parents to read labels on childrens

clothing and buy only flame-retardant or flame-resistant garments, especially sleepwear, and (b) to dispel the residual cancer scare that was rampant in 1977–78, since many parents remember (or are confused about) the concern over Tris-treated garments. This is one of the few examples in which safety counseling not only complements but also compensates for weakened legislative efforts to reduce injuries to children.

Overt Environmental Hazards

Most of the foregoing examples are obvious, but in some cases, a dramatic reduction in household burns occurred only after these problems were brought to the forefront. Only a few decades ago an inordinate and disproportionate number of young girls were burned at home. The cause soon became apparent; their nightgowns caught on fire when they snuggled up to an open fireplace. When wire screens were placed around fireplaces, most of these fires were prevented. As another example, the Boston Fire Department reported 159 house fires in the winter of 1959 due to malfunctioning oil-burning space heaters. As a result of a massive citywide campaign to correct this problem, only six space heater fires occurred the following year (Brown, 1961).

Other environmental hazards exist, and constant parental supervision is necessary to reduce their danger. Fire codes play a major role in reducing the start or propagation of fires, but if parents leave matches or lighters around, smoke in bed, overload circuits, don't repair worn-out electrical wires, and so forth, home fires will start. Parents must be reminded of these dangers and must be admonished to eliminate them. (See Table 69.7 for suggestions.)

Falls

In one study of 4,963 injury-related emergency room visits at a children's hospital, 2,079 (42%) were due to falls. In over 40% of these injuries, the falls occurred at home, with injuries caused by playing, bicycling, walking, falls from bed, and roller skating most prevalent (*Morbidity and Mortality,* 1978).

All children fall as they are learning to walk. Obviously, most of these falls do not result in injuries. Adherence to the recommendations found in Table 69.8 can reduce the occurrence of falls. When injuries do result from falls, they are usually minor. Since falls can result in serious morbidity, however, one should not minimize their potential danger. Children frequently fall out of bed, but fortunately they are not usually hurt. Yet skull fractures and injuries to the brain, such as intracranial bleeds, can result from even "minor" falls. Falls through glass doors and out of windows are not common, but when they occur, they often result in serious injury or death. Baby walkers are enormously popular because (a) many parents feel that they will foster gross motor development of their infants (an erroneous belief) and (b) walkers contain the baby and hence prevent the infant from getting into other mischief. This latter reason is, in reality, danger substitution. The CPSC estimated that 23,900 babies received medical attention in 1981 for injuries associated with baby walkers (*Pediatric News,* 1982). The majority of these injuries resulted from falls down stairs while the baby was in a walker. The Juvenile Products Manufacturers Association and CPSC are currently attempting to set standards for walker construction and to design more stable walkers. Most injuries, however, will be prevented only through health education.

Glass Door Hazards

Detached homes often have glass patio doors or walls. Because of the impulsive nature of children and their play, they are the ones who most frequently run into or fall through glass doors. Untreated—i.e., nonsafety—glass breaks into razor-sharp pieces, causing severe lacerations and other major injuries. Fortunately, many states have building codes requiring that only safety glass be used in these high-risk areas. This glass, even if broken, will not

Table 69.8   Falls—Safety Tips

General
Use gates with latches across porches and at tops of stairs.
Use good lighting in all traffic areas, especially stairs.
Never store anything on stairs.
Avoid small scatter rugs and anchor other rugs.
Avoid overwaxing floors.
Keep frequently walked-on areas as free from furniture as possible.
Repair loose boards and floor coverings.
Keep electric cords out of walkways.
Clean up water and grease spills on the floor immediately.
Install a nonskid surface in the bathtub.
Do not leave a baby unattended on a changing table.
Always keep the crib sides up.
Because infant seats tip over easily, use them only on the floor or in the playpen, never
   on a table or counter top.

Glass Doors
Mark glass doors and walls with decals that are visible from both sides.
Use either safety glass or a plastic substitute, instead of regular glass, in doors or walls.

Windows
All windows should have window locks that limit the distance they can be opened, to
   prevent children from falling through.
All screens should be fastened firmly.
Do not allow children to play on windowsills.

---

scatter or pierce. One should install bars across nonsafety glass or place highly visible decorations on it so that the glass will be seen.

Falls from Heights

In 1976, the New York City Board of Health passed an ordinance requiring that multiple-dwelling buildings have window guards on windows of all apartments where children up through 10 years of age live. A herculean campaign, combining active and passive measures, followed, utilizing mass media, community education, and individualized discussions by outreach workers. The result was a dramatic reduction in the number of children falling from windows (Spiegel & Lindaman, 1977).

Strangulation and Asphyxiation

So many objects that are part of a baby's environment—such as rattles, nipples, and pacifiers—can cause death by asphyxiation. Food is another potential danger. In a review of the Maryland medical examiner's records from 1970–1978, it was found that 42 children younger than 10 years died of asphyxiation. Aspiration of hot dogs caused six deaths; asphyxial death from sandwiches occurred in 2 children; and aspiration of a gum drop, cashew nut, potato, piece of hamburger, and candy each resulted in one death (Baker & Fisher, 1980).

Education emphasizing close supervision may prevent some of these fatalities (see Table 69.9). Parents should be told not to offer nuts or popcorn to infants and toddlers, for they are often aspirated. For the same reason, children should be forbidden from running

Table 69.9   Strangulation and Asphyxiation—Safety Tips

General

Enforce a rule prohibiting running with food in the mouth.

Keep all small objects away from infants and toddlers.

Do not allow infants and toddlers to eats nuts and popcorn.

Safely discard plastic bags and wrappings, (e.g., those from the cleaners).

Crib

Be sure the crib mattress fits snugly.

If an old crib is used, make sure that slats are no more than 2⅜ inches apart.

Do not permit any string, or any object that could be used like a string, in the crib,
   because it could cause strangulation.

while chewing food or gum. Parents should learn the Heimlich maneuver, since it can be life-saving in children (or adults) who are choking and are in danger of asphyxiation.

The CPSC issued its "small parts" standard in 1980, intending to prevent children from choking on small objects that become detached from toys. This passive countermeasure can have limited effects, at best, since (a) the regulation is intended only for children less than 3 years old, (b) most homes have many small objects lying about, and (c) omnipresent balloons, which are not regulated, cause more aspiration deaths in children than any other small object.

Cribs cause or contribute to many asphyxial deaths in a variety of ways, including the infant's head being caught between a broken side rail and the mattress or under a poorly fitting mattress, strangulation in the mesh of a portable crib, the infant being trapped between the mattress and spring when the lower side rail is not properly fastened, and the infant hanging himself on a pacifier cord that is hooked around a crib post (Bass, 1977; Smialek, Smialek, & Spitz, 1977). A CPSC regulation in effect for many years stipulates that the crib slats be not more than 2⅜ inches apart in order to prevent the infant's head from becoming trapped, leading to strangulation.

Other Important Preventable Home Accidents

Drowning

The most common accident in this category is bathtub drowning. The only way of prevention by health education is to promote better parental supervision (see Table 69.10). Children should not be left unattended in a bathtub, even if just for a moment to answer the telephone or doorbell.

Each year many infants are victims of pail immersion drownings. Typically, the infant crawls up to the bucket, bends over, and traps his shoulders and head in the bucket. One hospital recently reported its experience with pail immersion drownings; four infants drowned or nearly drowned in pails (Walker & Middlekamp, 1981). Because this danger is not uncommon, and because general awareness of this hazard is minimal, it must be included in safety counseling.

Not everyone is fortunate enough to own a swimming pool, but those who do should fence off the pool area. This simple act effectively prevents most drownings from accidental falls. Of course, no child should be unsupervised while in the pool. All children, especially those who have ready access to swimming pools, should be taught how to swim. Secondary preventive measures, such as training all pool owners in cardiopulmonary resuscitation, is also recommended.

Table 69.10 Miscellaneous Safety Tips

Drowning

Never leave children unattended in a bathtub.

Be aware that infants can drown in buckets, so never permit pails containing liquids to be accessible to infants.

If you have a swimming pool, supervise children at all times when they are in the pool. Pools should be fenced in.

Toys

Keep all small toys and objects away from small children.

Make sure that toys are appropriate for the child. Keep older children's toys away from younger children.

Repair or discard broken toys.

Teach your child to use toys safely.

Supervise your small child's play.

Yards

Supervise and teach your child to have safe play habits around playground equipment, such as swings.

Inspect your yard to remove dangerous items, such as broken glass.

Do not have poisonous outdoor plants or shrubbery.

Make sure all play equipment is safe—e.g., no sharp edges or protruding parts.

The surface under swings and climbing equipment should be absorptive.

Make sure children do not have access to electrical equipment, such as lawn mowers.

Other

Safely store firearms.

If workshops at home have dangerous items, either safety-proof the areas or keep children away.

The single most important point is never to leave a young child alone in the house, not even for a minute.

Toy Hazards

The CPSC plays a key role in monitoring toys that might injure children and in withdrawing dangerous toys from the market. In the first half of the last decade, about 1,500 unsafe toys were banned. Toys with small points and propelled objects can be very dangerous weapons, especially to young children. Toys will always have the potential to injure children, either by faulty design or by not being age-appropriate. Many young children harm themselves while playing with toys that are intended for older children. It is obvious that a 6-month-old child should not play with jacks because of the danger of aspiration. Certain other activities, such as roller skating, even when age-appropriate, result in many injuries. Many of these injuries can be avoided if the child wears protective equipment, such as knee pads and a helmet, particularly before proficiency is achieved. There are countless other toys and baby furniture that usually are not thought of as hazardous but may be so. For example, it was estimated that in 1978, 3,367 children under 5 years old received emergency treatment for injuries caused by toy boxes or toy chests (Singer & Lutner, 1982). Since children, parents, and grandparents cannot be expected to anticipate all the possible ways that toys can harm children, agencies such as the CPSC must play a role in assuring the safety of toys. As always, however, parents should still carefully select toys for their children. (Suggestions for toy safety are offered in Table 69.10.)

Outdoor Hazards

Yards and driveways are extensions of homes. Each year, thousands of children are injured by motor vehicle injuries in their own driveways. In 1978, 63,100 children were injured on home playground equipment (Weiner, 1982). Most of these playground injuries can be prevented either by careful supervision or by environmental control, such as installing protective surfaces on the ground. Health education *should* be the major countermeasure to reduce these types of injuries (see Table 10). To reiterate a grim reality, however, persuading parents to supervise their children more closely or motivating them to resurface their yards is difficult at best. (Consider the problems of persuading parents to use car restraints, theoretically a less formidable task).

Outdoor equipment, such as lawn mowers, can be quite dangerous, and accidents occur all too commonly. It is estimated that 161,000 lawn mower-related injuries occur annually (Madigan & McMahan, 1979). Other outdoor accidents happen perhaps freakishly but certainly tragically and can only point to the need for careful supervision. To cite an example, two children in Minnesota were killed by electrically operated garage doors within one month of each other (Satran, 1981).

A comprehensive list of potential household hazards would be practically endless. Another category that warrants emphasis is firearm injuries, which usually result in mortality or significant morbidity. Because of the limitation of passive measures and the political difficulties in enacting gun control legislation, the best way to prevent these completely avoidable mishaps is by storing firearms safely. If parents are not already cognizant of the danger, safety counseling can be effective.

SUMMARY AND FUTURE DIRECTIONS

Three central themes have been presented in this chapter. First, all injury control programs should combine active measures (health education) and passive measures (legislation to mandate safety requirements). The passive measures will reduce but not eliminate the requirement that parents continuously monitor the safety at home. Second, the all-inclusive approach to safety counseling should be abandoned. A more focused approach is recommended, consisting of selective counseling on the most problematic category of injuries at each developmental stage. For example, when the baby learns to crawl, advice on preventing accidental poisoning should be offered to the parents. This targeted advice, now recommended by many organizations, including the American Academy of Pediatrics, has a greater likelihood of success than approaches that have been tried in the past. Indeed, all but one of the successful programs cited in this chapter concentrated on only one aspect of safety prevention. Finally, all programs need to be evaluated before they are implemented on a grand scale. Demonstration projects are ideal for this purpose.

Safety codes and standards should be extended; they have an impressive record of reducing injuries. Thus far, health education has had a disappointing record. The more focused approach is promising and may restore the potency of health education. Many of the other innovative programs that also have great potential are based on the premise that safety counseling should not be restricted to pediatricians or nurse practitioners. Advice from outreach workers, neighborhood resource agencies, and educated peers may be highly effective. As a corollary, safety counseling should not take place only during well-child visits. Maintaining a general level of awareness requires constant messages from multiple media and from many individuals of varying backgrounds. Posters, displays, popular media, and the like, should be utilized in such diverse settings as school health programs, community health programs, PTA meetings, and church groups, for example. Whenever possible, individual discussions should be tailored to the needs and questions of the parent. This form of health education is probably the most effective, practical, and expeditious.

In summary, a comprehensive accident prevention program should have a three-pronged approach, consisting of technology, legislation, and health education. Technology contributes by developing and improving safety devices, such as smoke detectors, and we can anticipate continued technological advances in our society. Legislative, or passive, measures will survive and probably will even propagate, but this approach is being challenged by our country's current antiregulatory mood. Health education sorely needs intensified and innovative efforts. Unless all three approaches work successfully and in concert, however, accident prevention will be less effective than it should be, resulting in excessive human waste and suffering.

REFERENCE NOTES

1. Massey, J. D., & Jones, V. B. *A detector in every other home.* Summary of a household survey of smoke and fire detector owners conducted for the National Fire Data Center, U.S. Fire Administration (WMW-C-0029).
2. Ingraham, W. R., & Polk, L. D. *Accident control demonstration project.* Philadelphia Department of Public Health, 1964.
3. Fisher, L., Van Buren, J., Nitzken, J. et al. *Highlight results of the Monroe County Poison Prevention Demonstration Project.* Paper presented at the Annual Joint Meeting of the American Association of Poison Control Centers, the American Academy of Clinical Toxicology, and the Canadian Academy of Clinical and Analytical Toxicology, Minneapolis, August 1980.

REFERENCES

Accident Facts—1981. Chicago: National Safety Council, 1981.

Baker, S. P. Injury control: Accident prevention and other approaches to reduction of injury. In P. Sartwell (Ed.), *Preventive medicine and public health* (10th ed.). New York: Appleton-Century-Crofts, 1973.

Baker, S. P. Determinants of injury and opportunities for intervention. *American Journal of Epidemiology,* 1975, **101,** 98–102.

Baker, S. P., & Fisher, R. S. Childhood asphyxiation by choking or suffocation. *JAMA; Journal of the American Medical Association,* 1980, **244,** 1343–1346.

Baltimore, C., Jr., & Meyer, R. J. A study of storage, child behavior traits and mother's knowledge of toxicology in 52 poisoned families and 52 comparison families. *Pediatrics,* 1969, **55**(Suppl.), 816–820.

Bass, M. Asphyxial crib death. *New England Journal of Medicine,* 1977, **296,** 555–556.

Bergman, A. G. Flame-resistant sleepwear: Have the bird-watchers gone ape? *Pediatrics,* 1977, **60,** 652–654.

Brown, E. W. Space-heater hazards. *New England Journal of Medicine,* 1961, **265,** 794–795.

Clarke, A., & Walton, W. W. Effect of safety packaging on aspirin ingestion by children. *Pediatrics,* 1979, **63,** 687–693.

Dershewitz, R. A. Will mothers use free safety devices? *American Journal of Diseases of Children,* 1979, **133,** 61–64.

Dershewitz, R. A., & Williamson, J. W. Prevention of childhood household injuries: A controlled clinical trial. *American Journal of Public Health,* 1977, **67,** 1148–1152.

Feldman, K. W., Schaller, R. T., Feldman, J. A., et al. Tap water scald burns in children. *Pediatrics,* 1978, **62,** 1–7.

Fergusson, D. M., Harwood, L. J., Beautrais, A. L., & Shannon, F. T. A controlled field trial of a poisoning prevention method. *Pediatrics,* 1982, **69,** 515–520.

Joliet, P. V. Home safety. In M. N. Halsey (Ed.), *Accident prevention: The role of physicians and public health workers.* New York: McGraw-Hill, 1961.

Jones, J. G. The child accident repeater: A review. *Clinical Pediatrics,* 1980, **19,** 284–288.

Kiefer, N. C. Accidents—The foremost problem in preventive medicine. *Preventive Medicine,* 1973, **2,** 106–122.

Madigan, R. R., & McMahan, C. J. Power lawn mower injuries. *Journal of the Tennessee Medical Association,* 1979, **72,** 653–655.

McLaughlin, E. Clarke, N., Stahl, K., et al. One pediatric burn unit's experience with sleepwear-related injuries. *Pediatrics,* 1977, **60,** 405–409.

McLaughlin, E., Vince, C. J., Lee, A. M., et al. Project Burn Prevention: Outcome and implications. *American Journal of Public Health,* 1982, **72,** 241–247.

Morbidity and Mortality Weekly Report, 1978, **27,** 197.

Pediatric News, 1982, **16**(4), 8.

Reisinger, K. S. Preventing deaths due to fire. In A. B. Bergman (Ed.), *Preventing childhood injuries.* Report of the 12th Ross Roundtable on Critical Approaches to Pediatric Problems. Columbus, Ohio: Ross Laboratories, 1982.

Satran, L. Fatalities caused by electrically operated garage doors. *Pediatrics,* 1981, **68,** 422–423.

Schlesinger, E. R., Dickson, D. G., Westaby, J., et al. A controlled study of health education in accident prevention: The Rockland County Child Injury Project. *American Journal of Diseases of Children,* 1966, **111,** 490–496.

Singer, W. D., & Lutner, L. Trauma from toy boxes. *Journal of Pediatrics,* 1982, **100,** 242–243.

Smialek, J. E., Smialek, P. Z., & Spitz, W. U. Accidental bed deaths in infants due to unsafe sleeping situations. *Clinical Pediatrics,* 1977, **16,** 1031–1036.

Sobel, R. Traditional safety measures and accidental poisonings in childhood. *Pediatrics,* 1969, **55**(Suppl.), 811–816.

Spiegel, C. N., & Lindaman, F. C. Children can't fly: A program to prevent childhood morbidity and mortality from window falls. *American Journal of Public Health,* 1977, **67,** 1143–1146.

Takahata, G. K., Colflesh, V. G., Digon, E., et al. *Childhood injuries associated with consumer products.* New York: Academic Press, 1974.

Thomson, W., & Frame, W. Prevention of accidental poisoning in children. *Health Bulletin (Edinburgh),* 1979, **37,** 221–224.

Walker, S., & Middlekamp, J. N. Pail immersion accidents. *Clinical Pediatrics,* 1981, **16,** 341–343.

Walton, W. W. An evaluation of the Poison Prevention Packaging Act. *Pediatrics,* 1982, **69,** 363–370.

Wart, N. E. *Unsafe as houses: A guide to home safety.* Poole Dorset, U.K.: Blandford Press, 1981.

Weiner, P. Playground injuries and voluntary product standards for home and public playgrounds. *Pediatrics,* 1982, **69,** 18–20.

Wilner, D. M., Walkley, R. P., Pinkerton, T. C., & Tayback, M. *The housing environment and family life.* Baltimore: Johns Hopkins Press, 1962.

SECTION 10
PREVENTION OF ALCOHOL ABUSE

CHAPTER 70

ALCOHOLISM PREVENTION: INTRODUCTION

SHELDON I. MILLER

Sheppard & Enoch Pratt Hospital, Baltimore, Md.

In a field with as many unanswered questions as alcoholism, the topic of prevention is perhaps as confused as any. Although there generally appears to be no disagreement about the importance of prevention, there also appears to be no agreement about the approaches to the issue, the most effective strategies, the appropriate targets, and the percentage of effort necessary from those working in the field. Perhaps these questions become even more complex when one considers that the causes of alcohol abuse and alcoholism, the object of the prevention effort, have yet to be defined. Indeed, the theories about the etiology of alcoholism are perhaps as varied as the theories about recommended procedures for prevention. The theories that have been promulgated to explain alcoholism and alcohol abuse have included personality theory, psychodynamic approaches, social and economic theories, and, most recently, some good evidence of a strong genetic component (Goodwin, Schulsinger, Moller, Hermansen, Winokur, & Guze, 1974; Vaillant & Milofsky, 1982).

The importance of the effort to understand and to prevent alcoholism cannot be overemphasized. The federal government has recently established a task force to evaluate and recommend ways to curb just one of the major problems associated with alcohol abuse—drunk driving. Many other consequences of this disorder also have extensive personal health and societal consequences. The National Council on Alcoholism and others have estimated that if all of the causes of death resulting from alcoholism are considered, it is one of the top three leading causes of death in the United States, along with heart disease and cancer. In addition, alcohol abuse has been linked prominently to crime (Aarens, Cameron, Roizen, Roizen, Room, Schneberk, & Wingard, Note 1), and other economic losses were estimated to be as high as $43 billion in 1975 (Berry, Boland, Smart & Kanak, Note 2).

Although alcoholism and alcohol abuse are very democratic problems, with virtually no age, sex, or occupational group being totally free of risk, some groups appear to be particularly vulnerable. Included in this category are women, Native Americans, black Americans, the elderly, and others (*Fourth Special Report,* Note 3).

In addition to those individuals who are directly affected by the problems of alcoholism and alcohol abuse are those who are indirectly affected. The family is disrupted in many ways through disturbed and disrupted equilibrium and dynamics and, at times, through direct abuse of a spouse or child by the alcoholic or alcohol abuser (*Fourth Special Report,* Note 3). This, of course, is in addition to the results of the economic pressures that alcoholism can cause in the principal wage earner. Clearly, this is not an exhaustive list of the chaos alcohol abuse produces in family systems, but it serves as a minimal example.

Another example of alcohol abuse affecting a nonabusing individual is the fetal alcohol syndrome (Jones, Smith, Ulleland, & Streissguth, 1973). Although there is some question regarding the amount of alcohol necessary to cause damage (Sokol, Miller, Debanne, Golden, Collins, Kaplan, & Martier, 1981) and other factors that may contribute to the problem (Flynn, Martin, Sokol, Miller, Golden, & Villano, 1981), there is little question of a strong relationship between alcohol use during pregnancy and poor fetal outcome (Sokol, Miller, & Reed, 1980).

The magnitude of the alcohol abuse and alcoholism problems demands the attention of those who are interested in and concerned with helping to keep healthy children and adults healthy. The following two chapters address some of the issues and problems associated with preventing alcohol abuse and alcoholism. Although the authors view the problem from different perspectives (sociological and psychological), there are common themes to be inferred. There seems to be a feeling of dissatisfaction with our current state of knowledge regarding the effectiveness of a variety of prevention approaches. Too often, public policy statements are made as if there were sound data to support what really are beliefs and opinions influenced by personal experience, moral teachings, and other personal and societal pressures. Both chapters advocate the creation of sound prevention programs that are designed to evaluate results objectively. Furthermore, each chapter offers examples of potentially effective approaches to the prevention of alcohol abuse and alcoholism.

REFERENCE NOTES

1. Aarens, M., Cameron, T., Roizen, J., Roizen, R., Room, R., Schneberk, D., & Wingard, D. *Alcohol, casualties and crime*. Special report prepared for the National Institute on Alcohol Abuse and Alcoholism under Contract No. (ADM)281–76–0027. Berkeley: University of California, Social Research Group, 1977

2. Berry, R. E., Jr., Boland, J. P., Smart, C. N., & Kanak, J. R. *The economic costs of alcohol abuse and alcoholism—1975*. Final report to the National Institute on Alcohol Abuse and Alcoholism under Contract No. (ADM)281–76–0016. Boston: Policy Analysis, August 1977

3. *Fourth special report to the U.S. Congress on alcohol and health*. Secretary of Health and Human Services, January 1981.

REFERENCES

Flynn, A., Martier, S. S., Sokol, R. J., Miller, S. I., Golden, N. L., Del Villano, B. C. Zinc status of pregnant alcoholic women: A determinant of fetal outcome. *Lancet*, 1981, **1**, 572–575.

Goodwin, D. W., Schulsinger, F., Moller, N., Hermansen, L., Winokur, G., & Guze, S. B. Drinking problems in adopted and non-adopted sons of alcoholics. *Archives of General Psychiatry*, 1974, **31**, 164–169.

Jones, K. L., Smith, D. W., Ulleland, C. N., & Streissguth, A. P. Pattern of malformation in offspring of chronic alcoholic mothers. *Lancet* 1973, **1**, 1267–1271.

Sokol, R. J., Miller, S. I., Debanne, S., Golden, N., Collins, G., Kaplan, J., & Martier, S. Cleveland NIAAA prospective alcohol-in-pregnancy study: The first year. *Neurobehavioral Toxicology and Teratology*, 1981, **3**(2), 203–209.

Sokol, R. J., Miller, S. I., & Reed, G. Alcohol abuse during pregnancy: An epidemiologic study. *Alcoholism: Clinical and Experimental Research*, 1980, **4**(2).

Vaillant, G. E., & Milofsky, E. S. The etiology of alcoholism: A prospective viewpoint. *American Psychologist*, 1982, **37**(5), 494–503.

CHAPTER 71

SOCIAL MODELS OF PREVENTION IN ALCOHOLISM

BARRY S. TUCHFELD

Sheppard and Enoch Pratt Hospital, Baltimore, Md.

SUSAN H. MARCUS

Texas Christian University

Recently, there has been an accelerating interest in developing prevention strategies for alcohol abuse and alcoholism that are founded on socially based models. This interest appears to stem from an acknowledgement that, from a social model perspective, "treatment and prevention can be seen as complements to one another, rather that competitors" (More & Gerstein, 1981, p. 51). This chapter provides a brief overview of three generic models that predominate socially based prevention strategies: (a) the sociocultural model, (b) the social-structural model, and (c) the public health model. These models are summarized in Table 71.1. At the conclusion of this chapter, we will also present an alternative view to these current approaches to prevention.

These generic types are indicative of a number of different policy actions undertaken by change agents at the local, state, and national levels. It should be understood, however, that there is no generally accepted typology for prevention strategies. Blane (1976), for example, identifies four types of models: social science, public health, distribution of consumption, and proscriptive. The labels we have adopted here, however, provide a simple framework for contrasting fundamentally different assumptions, implementation strategies, and criticisms of the models.

SOCIOCULTURAL MODELS

The major focus of sociocultural models of prevention is on the normative patterns of belief about alcohol use and associated behaviors that characterize different populations. Central to such models is the notion, based on the Ullman/Blacker hypothesis (Blacker, 1966; Ullman, 1958), that if drinking practices are well integrated into a culture and if the rules and contexts for drinking behavior are clearly defined, then the rate of alcoholism should be relatively low. Various studies have indicated, for example, that low rates of alcoholism in Jewish, Chinese-American, and Italian-American populations are a function of a highly circumscribed set of cultural–religious drinking traditions and rituals (Wilkinson, 1970).

Because drinking is considered to be imbedded in the matrix of social and cultural factors, three implications for prevention can be drawn. First, the sociocultural model suggests that manipulating the normative structure of a population (that is, prohibiting excessive drinking, prescribing moderate drinking, and deriving rules for drinking practices) will result in the reduction of excessive alcohol use (Blane, 1976). A contemporary example of

Table 71.1   Summary of Three Social Models of Prevention

	Sociocultural Models	Social-Structural Models	Traditional Public Health Models
Dimension assumptions	Prevention through indirect cultural, normative control	Prevention through direct externally imposed control	Prevention at any point of interaction of host, agent, and environment
Social policy implementation strategies	Education; mass media; persuasion; conciousness raising	Regulation of availability; creation of laws; ecological restructuring	Biomedical research; epidemiologic treatment interventions
Criticisms	Limitations of cross-cultural applications; assumes isomorphism between norms and behavior; assumes intracultural homogenity	No explication of how mechanisms of control are translated into behavior; carries significant social risks (denies freedom of the individual); assumes a unidirectional causal model	Limitations of disease model orientation; overemphasis on secondary prevention; limited empirical and practical utility

this model is the promotion of responsible drinking by civil rights leaders in the black community. This effort is symbolized by Reverend Jesse Jackson's words: "We cannot stagger to freedom" (Jackson, Note 1). Taking the model to its logical extreme would suggest that an abstinent society could be induced through the introduction of a highly proscriptive set of norms.

A second inference of the sociocultural model is that excessive alcohol use can be prevented by encouraging integration of drinking within prescribed social activities, rather than drinking being an activity that is indulged in for its own sake. Such social activities would include family meals, religious rites, or specific occasions. Third, this model implies that the controlled introduction of alcohol to children at an early age encourages the incorporation of the society's or culture's normative drinking practices.

To initiate changes in these values and norms, social policymakers have utilized several strategies, all of which focus on information transfer or persuasion and attitude change. These strategies include educational programs and mass media communications, which are usually transmitted through organized social institutions, such as churches, schools, medical programs, and community organizations. A recent example of this type of prevention approach is the McKenzie Area Prevention Project (MAPP) (Small, Note 2). This effort was designed to encourage community involvement in dealing with alcohol abuse, through (a) education of young people about alternatives to alcohol misuse; (b) provision of workshops, family management programs, and "rap groups"; and (c) establishment of lines of communication to other public and private social institutions.

Although the sociocultural model remains a widely used vehicle for prevention strategies, three major criticisms can be cited that bring into question the efficacy of this approach. First, it seems pragmatically (and empirically) inappropriate to assume that the normative values regulating drinking behavior in one culture or society would be applicable standards to introduce into another society. This would be especially true if the larger social structures of those cultures were incompatible (for example, socialist versus democratic governments) or if the drinking patterns were integrated within different types of traditions (for example, religious rituals versus economic or occupational positions).

Second, this approach to prevention is problematic in that it assumes an isomorphism between norms and behavior. This occurs at two levels. At a definitional level, it is unclear whether *norm* refers to (a) rules of behavior (that is, typical ways of thinking); (b) prescriptive standards (what people think should be done); or (c) model behaviors (what people actually do) (Heath, Note 3). At a theoretical level, this model unduly emphasizes the notion that attitude change through persuasive communication (a social-psychological issue) is a successful means of implementing a normative change (a sociological issue). In other words, there is a gap in the translation of a macro-societal relationship to the micro-individual level.

Finally, this model assumes intracultural homogeneity—that is, that all individuals within the culture share identical views with respect to the propriety of alcohol-related social cues, attitudes, and behaviors. As Gusfield (1976) points out, "Between the 'polite cocktail' and the 'hard belt' there is a great gap between attitudes and functions [of alcohol use]" (p. 279).

SOCIAL-STRUCTURAL MODELS

Social-structural models of prevention focus on policies that "are directed at the conditions, structures, environmental availabilities, [and/or] physical facilities which surround the person" (Gusfield, 1976, p. 272). The critical assumption of this model is that conditions may be manipulated and behavior subsequently affected in ways that are independent of the personal beliefs and values of the alcohol users. The extreme example of this perspective was the enactment of prohibition by means of the 18th amendment to the U.S. Constitution. By attempting to limit the options of individuals through legislation, the goal was to restrict alcohol use, regardless of any individual's values or belief systems.

A useful approach for prevention strategies based on this model has been proposed by Moore and Gerstein (1981). From their perspective, prevention of alcohol abuse can be encouraged through three general strategies: (a) regulation of the availability of alcohol; (b) creation of laws to control alcohol use; and (c) ecological restructuring of the environment.

Regulation of availability does not have to extend to prohibition. Popham, Schmidt, and De Lint (1975), for example, have assessed regulatory control measures ranging from hours of alcohol sales to restrictions on number and type of retail outlets. Their analyses pointed to the importance of taxation policy in the prevention of alcoholism in the general population.

Such findings are consistent with one interpretation of the Ledermann model of the distribution of alcohol consumption. This model proposes that the level of general alcohol consumption in any society is directly related to the extent of alcohol problems found within that society. In other words, the greater the number of alcohol users, the greater the number of people who will have alcohol problems, (see Beauchamp, 1980, pp. 102–111). One interpretation of this model for social policymaking is that alcohol problems within a society can be prevented most effectively by significantly increasing selling prices, thereby reducing the total number of alcohol users.

With the second strategy, numerous legal tactics have been attempted as prevention vehicles. Most exemplary of these efforts are laws directed toward drunken driving and public intoxication. In assessing the apparent effect of drinking laws, Roam (1978) concludes that the actual impact is not clear, given the available research findings. Nevertheless, the legal strategy continues to be viewed as a major deterrent to alcohol abuse. This is evidenced by the continuing state-by-state debates over the appropriate minimum drinking age.

Ecological restructuring refers to efforts to change the drinking environment so as to create a safer world for those who drink to excess or for those who are potential victims of alcohol abusers. This strategy implies an acceptance that some proportion of excessive alcohol users will always exist and that one rational prevention approach is to minimize societal costs. In addition to efforts to emphasize consumer safety through passive highway barriers, this strategy promotes programs to train bartenders as quasi-therapeutic agents and to encourage sober friends to drive intoxicated friends.

Although the social-structural model strategies would appear to have the desirable attribute of minimizing changes in personal belief systems, a common criticism of these strategies is that they carry significant social risks with regard to civil liberties. External manipulations (legal or otherwise) imply the denial of some degree of freedom of choice, since these interventions externally limit the range of available choices of behavior.

Conceptual criticisms emphasize the traditional issue of levels of analysis. In particular, the processes that mediate between structural changes and behavioral responses are rarely actually specified. Changes in drunk driving laws, for example, may work by deterring drivers' alcohol use, but law enforcement officers may choose to enforce the law loosely. In effect, this becomes an individual's choice to circumvent the intent of the law.

These models also tend to connote a unidirectional influence of structure on human behavior. The causal implication of simplistic versions is that individuals' behaviors accommodate structural change but that social structures are relatively insensitive to human action. Hence, reactions by population groups to changes in alcohol distribution practices are presumed to have little impact.

TRADITIONAL PUBLIC HEALTH MODELS

The so-called traditional public health model had its beginnings in the early 1900s (Beauchamp, 1980) with an orientation toward governmental promotion of responsible behavior among citizens. As alcoholism began to be defined a disease, the problem became increasingly subject to the auspices of public health and the logic of control and prevention of infectious diseases. The logic of this "disease model assumes that expression of the disorder depends on an interaction between the individual, the agent of the disease (alcohol), and the environment in which the disease process develops" (Mello, 1976, p. 174).

This apparently all-encompassing approach provides biomedical research of biomedical or genetic causes of alcoholism (Chalmers, Rinsler, MacDermott, Spicer, & Levi, 1981; Ryback, Eckardt, & Pautler, 1980). The prevention strategy would then be based on such alternatives as genetic counseling or the discovery of alcohol blocking agents. This strategy would be a classic example of primary prevention efforts to intervene before a problem manifests itself.

This general model would also promote epidemiologic research directed at the identification of prognostic and diagnostic correlates of high-risk populations. National survey research, for example, has resulted in the beginnings of social and psychological profiles of persons who are active problem drinkers, as well as in some specification of correlates and descriptors of symptomatic problem drinkers (Cahalan, 1974). With such information available, policymakers and change agents might be better able to focus prevention activities on specific target groups.

A crucial implication of the disease model aspect is its legitimation of alcoholism as a treatable disorder. Technically, this implies either secondary or tertiary prevention, since intervention occurs after the problem has begun to manifest itself.

In general, the public health model has been a major positive force in the field of alcoholism. Nevertheless, there are two criticisms that warrant notice. First, even though other important biological research findings about alcohol and the human body have been forthcoming from research efforts, research that supports biological or genetic causes of excessive alcohol use and alcoholism thus far remains inconclusive (Finlay, 1979). Second, some have argued (Blane, 1976) that the public health model has emphasized secondary prevention at the expense of primary prevention, while publicly justifying its value according to the potential that primary prevention efforts could have. In any case, the public health model has been a salient framework and political force in the field of alcoholism.

DISCUSSION

This chapter has presented a brief overview of three generic social models that are the bases for most prevention efforts in the field of alcohol abuse and alcoholism. Each model has a distinctive focus. The sociocultural model directs attention to the values and norms of individuals and their social groups within the larger society. The social-structural model emphasizes the control of options external to the psyche or beliefs of any single individual. The traditional public health model purports to incorporate reciprocal interactions among individuals, the larger society, and the drug alcohol.

These models, however, have certain commonalities that warrant recognition. First, all three are goal-oriented perspectives that seek to control selected variables to produce desired effects. Second, the extent of research support and empirical justification for these models is limited. Moreover, there are few systematic evaluations of the actual impact of various prevention strategies and programs. The limited availability of data is partially because most prevention programs are limited in scope and are conducted in social settings. Few large-scale programs have been undertaken.

Finally, though perhaps most important, these models are founded and currently justified on the basis of conventional wisdoms that are assumed to be indicative of appropriate societal goals. The central domain assumption is that it is legitimate to use external controls in an effort to define and direct, or at least significantly influence, appropriate behavior for the public good. It is this domain assumption that, though usually unspoken, justifies governmental action and intervention by other vested interest groups.

Moreover, one should recognize that there are alternative perspectives, which can be interwoven within the general model. Some have referred to these alternatives as the new public health model (Beauchamp, 1980).

The new public health movement is more a perspective than an explicit model. Though lacking a clear statement of philosophy, it can be characterized by a shift of emphasis from governmental responsibility to balanced responsibilities between the citizenry (or community) and governmental agencies. With regard to prevention efforts, the new approach is best exemplified by a shift from an emphasis on rules and mandatory public safeguards (such as laws and labels) to the development of techniques that do not limit exposure to the potential hazard—that is, beverage alcohol. If biological blocking agents, for example, could be added to beverage alcohol, which would inhibit intoxication, then the new perspective would accomplish its goals of prevention with minimal individual or societal disruption.

Our perspective is that extensions and modifications of the classic view of social models of prevention is best referred to as a trend toward a social-interactional model. Rather than being based exclusively on a cultural, structural, or objective view of public health, this social-interactional approach acknowledges that the final product and result of interventions is actually an emergent, rather than a fixed, process. In addition to acknowledging the benefits of allowing the human agent to participate in defining the prevention process, the interactional approach proposes that the process of prevention strategies in a society or subculture is as important to the prevention of alcohol problems as the goals of the efforts themselves. In conclusion, the promotion of a social conscience and awareness of the problem has an important symbolic dimension that should not remain unrecognized (Gusfield, 1976), nor should its yet-undocumented potential value remain unexplored.

REFERENCE NOTES

1. Jackson, J. Quotation taken from a poster, published by NIAAA Clearinghouse, Rockville, Md., 1978.
2. Small, J. (Ed.). *NIAAA Information and Feature Service (IFS)*. IFS No. 96. Rockville, Md.: National Clearinghouse for Alcohol Information of NIAAA, June 1, 1982.

3. Heath, D. B. A critical review of the socio-cultural model of alcohol use. In T. C. Harford, D. A. Parker, & L. Light (Eds.), *NIAAA Research Monograph 3:* Normative approaches to the prevention of alcohol abuse and alcoholism. DHEW Pub. No. (ADM)79–847, 1980.

REFERENCES

Beauchamp, D. E. *Beyond alcoholism: Alcohol and public health policy.* Philadelphia: Temple University Press, 1980.

Blacker, E. Sociocultural factors in alcoholism. *International Clinical Psychiatry,* 1966, 3(2), 51–80.

Blane, H. T. Issues in preventing alcohol problems. *Preventive Medicine,* 1976, **5,** 176–186.

Cahalan, D. *Problem drinkers.* San Francisco: Jossey-Bass, 1970.

Chalmers, D. M., Rinsler, M. G., MacDermott, S., Spicer, C. C., & Levi, A. J. Biochemical and haematological indicators of excessive alcohol consumption. *Gut,* 1981, **22,** 992–996.

Finlay, D. G. Alcoholism is an illness. Right? Wrong! In D. Robinson (Ed.), *Alcohol problems: Reviews, research and recommendations.* New York: Holmes and Meier, 1979.

Gusfield, J. The prevention of drinking problems. In W. J. Filstead, J. J. Rossi, & M. Keller (Eds.), *Alcohol and alcohol problems: New thinking and new directions.* Cambridge, Mass.: Ballinger, 1976.

Mello, N. K. Some issues in research on the biology of alcoholism. In W. J. Filstead, J. J. Rossi, & M. Keller (Eds.), *Alcohol and alcohol problems: New thinking and new directions.* Cambridge, Mass.: Ballinger, 1976.

Moore, M. H., & Gerstein, D. R. (Eds.). *Alcohol and public policy: Beyond the shadow of prohibition.* Washington D.C.: National Academy Press, 1981.

Popham, R. E., Schmidt, W., & De Lint, J. The prevention of alcoholism: Epidemiological studies of the effects of government control measures. *British Journal of Addiction,* 1975, **70,** 125–144.

Roam, R. Evaluating the effect of drinking laws on drinking. In J. A. Ewing & B. A. Rouse (Eds.), *Drinking: Alcohol in American society—Issues and current research.* Chicago: Nelson-Hall, 1978.

Ryback, R. S., Eckardt, M. J., & Pautler, C. P. Biochemical and hematological correlates of alcoholism. *Research Communications in Chemical Pathology and Pharmacology,* 1980, **27,** 533–550.

Ullman, A. D. Sociocultural backgrounds of alcoholism. *Annals of the American Academy of Political and Social Science,* 1958, **351,** 48–54.

Wilkinson, R. *The prevention of drinking problems.* New York: Oxford University Press, 1970.

CHAPTER 72
A PSYCHOLOGICAL PERSPECTIVE OF PREVENTION IN ALCOHOLISM

DAVID ENGSTROM

University of California, Irvine

Excessive consumption of alcohol has been implicated as a major factor in the development of hazardous lifestyles (Haggerty, 1977). Not only has chronic alcohol abuse been linked with a variety of physical problems, including cirrhosis of the liver and heart dysfunction and disease, but people who consume excessive quantities of alcohol are also much more likely to suffer injury or death from automobile accidents, homicide, and suicide (Berg, 1976). The mortality rate attributable to alcohol and alcoholic disorders has been increasing sharply over the past ten years, and alcohol consumption has often been cited as primarily responsible for both absenteeism from the job and impaired performance in industry. Taken together, all these issues, plus the ever-escalating cost of health care delivery systems to industry and to the individuals involved, have led health researchers and clinicians to pay more attention to the question of whether alcohol-related problems in general can be prevented.

Both social policymakers and helping professionals have tried to adapt the traditional public health model of prevention to the prevention of alcohol-related problems. Currently, this is an area in which scientific data are extremely weak or nonexistent. The conventional model for understanding prevention in general has derived from the standard epidemiologic studies of infectious disease. Within this model, a communicable disease in an individual results from the interaction of three separate factors: (a) a susceptible host or individual; (b) an agent (particularly a parasite, bacteria, or virus); and (c) an appropriate environment. Although some researchers (Blane, 1976) have questioned whether such a model can be applied to a social problem whose etiology is still not specific and whose environmental interrelationships remain unclear, the model still has a profound influence on the structure and classification of preventive programs. Alcoholism is neither an infectious nor a communicable disease, however, but is viewed more as a chronic illness. It apparently is related to the complex interaction of biological, sociocultural, and psychological factors that are inherent in, or impinge upon, the individual. Nevertheless, many well-known researchers, such as Noble (1979), argue that this classic epidemiologic model is applicable to the disease of alcoholism. Within this model, three levels of prevention may be distinguished from one another: *primary prevention,* which refers to the removal or modification of the causes of a disorder to prevent its occurrence; *secondary prevention,* the early identification and treatment of a disorder; and *tertiary prevention,* generally believed to correspond with treatment of the fully developed or developing disorder.

Traditionally, prevention strategies of all three types have focused on educating individuals about alcoholism, with emphasis on the symptoms that are associated with various stages in the progressive development of the disease (Wilkinson, 1970). This orientation offers very few strategies for avoiding or minimizing alcohol problems other than total abstinence. Since we live in a society where many people drink and will continue to drink, the prospect of lifelong abstinence from alcohol is not practicable in all cases.

SECONDARY PREVENTION

Secondary prevention programs focus their efforts on populations judged to be at high risk for alcoholism. Some populations so identified include drinking drivers, children of alcoholics, juvenile delinquents, and employees displaying absenteeism and impaired performance on the job (Blane, 1976). To date, the most common target populations for these efforts have been drinking drivers and drinking employees. With regard to impaired drinking drivers, Selzer, Vinokur, and Wilson (1977) found that impaired drivers fall somewhere between normal drinkers and alcoholics in most measures of consumption and psychological problems. They consume larger amounts of alcohol, drink more frequently, and report higher levels of stress or depression than normal drinkers but less than many hard-core alcoholics. These drivers are seen as very appropriate targets for secondary prevention, since they usually display elevated blood alcohol concentrations upon arrest and are likely to be arrested repeatedly for intoxification while driving.

Generally, alcohol-impaired driver programs follow an educational format. They concentrate on increasing the impaired driver's awareness of alcohol and its relationship to traffic fatalities. The data on whether or not such programs lead to behavior change are very unclear. Controlled studies have found that intervention programs produce no greater changes than the traditional fines imposed on the impaired driver (Blumenthal and Ross, Note 1). They conclude that the decreases in consumption that occur are probably a function of the aversive nature of the arrest process, rather than a positive benefit gained from the diversion program. Scoles and Fine (1977) have further suggested that diversion programs for the impaired driver that are developed in the future should take the form of individually tailored treatment formats, rather than the traditional group educational format.

Another well-known form of secondary prevention is the employee assistance program, often developed by business, union, and certain local, state, and federal government agencies to assist employees who have drinking problems before they reach the later stages of the disease. Although these programs have more frequently concentrated on treating the alcoholic employee than on prevention, they have many characteristics that make them a good route toward secondary prevention. Roman and Trice (1976) estimate that 3% to 5% of all company employees have drinking problems and that few of them seek help through traditional programs. It is likely that alcohol abuse can be detected readily through job impairment fairly early in the course of the problem. It is a well-known fact that alcohol-related problems can cost employers a great deal in terms of job absenteeism, impairment of performance, reduced morale, and sick benefits. The greatest reason that industrial alcoholism programs are an effective method of prevention is that, whereas alcoholism and alcohol-related problems often remain a private issue for many people, as soon as they surface as problems related to job performance (such as absenteeism), they are exposed to legitimate intervention—and the employer has the right to intervene. As opposed to educational formats used with drinking drivers, occupational programs often involve the training of supervisors and managers in recognition of the drinking employee and referral of the employee to an established treatment facility through facilitation and confrontation. There is currently great support for occupational programs and many employers, with the backing of labor leaders, will provide both sick leave benefits and continued job security while the employee seeks treatment. Further leverage is to be gained by making it clear to the employee that the possibility of job termination will be considered if the employee does not seek help.

PRIMARY PREVENTION

Unlike most secondary and tertiary prevention approaches, primary prevention of alcoholism is an area in which scientific data remain extremely weak. It differs from secondary and tertiary prevention in that it aims at preventing alcoholism problems before they begin in any form. This kind of prevention requires a basic understanding of the reasons people begin to drink alcoholic beverages. From this standpoint, the largely educational and disease-oriented preventive methods, although they are superficially well intentioned, may not be best constructed for primary prevention efforts. This is true because these approaches are not based on an understanding of why people begin to drink or why most people who drink do not have alcohol problems; rather, they are focused on resurrected prohibitionistic beliefs that if alcohol were made less available and attractive through institutional intervention, fewer people would become alcohol abusers and alcoholics.

In general, the goal of these programs is to increase knowledge about the effects of alcohol on the body and about the consequences of alcohol abuse, thus producing changes in attitudes toward consumption itself. Most of these educational programs have focused on school systems—high school or university—in attempts to reach young people and their parents and teachers.

One of the major difficulties in primary prevention is that, although professionals often present arguments strongly in favor of alcohol education, so far there have been few well-designed studies to support the effectiveness of such programs. Randall and Wong (1976) reviewed more than 200 articles on prevention and found that only 23 studies reported any systematic evaluation. Of these 23, only 15 involved a pre-post assessment design and control group to allow for a true comparison of the effects of prevention efforts. A number of other problems are apparent from a review of the studies in this area. Not the least of these is the apparent evidence that some adolescents and children demonstrate a more favorable attitude toward drug and alcohol use as their knowledge about these substances increases. One study found no change in alcohol use upon completion of an educational program on alcohol prevention (Tennant, Weaver, & Lewis, 1973). It appears that alcohol education programs are moderately successful in increasing knowledge about alcohol but less successful in producing attitude change and much less successful in producing behavior change when measured in a controlled fashion. Many researchers have come to the conclusion that present alcohol education programs require modification, but they are unwilling or unable to elaborate the changes required.

In summary, large-scale primary preventive strategies have yet to demonstrate a high level of effectiveness. Desired behavior changes, such as reduction in consumption, do not always follow alcohol education and public information programs. Many reviewers of this topic suggest that primary prevention may be premature at our point of knowledge, since we still lack credible information about the causes of alcoholism. Blane (1976) suggests that, because of this scarcity of techniques and information, preventive efforts should more appropriately be directed at secondary programs for the time being. That primary prevention can and does work in the individual case should not be overlooked, however. Evidence abounds that individuals raised in some families (educational environments) either never drink or, if they do, rarely become excessive users or problem drinkers. The best examples are children raised in Moslem, Jewish, Mormon, or Baptist households.

PREVENTION AND BEHAVIORAL PSYCHOLOGY

Although behavioral treatment approaches to alcohol problems are relatively new, several writers have recommended that they be employed in prevention programs (Berg, 1976; Miller & Munoz, 1976). Early findings have been both impressive and positive, and because of their promise in application with alcoholics (Miller, 1976), there is every reason to think that they might work with problem drinkers and might also have measurable success in the areas of primary and secondary prevention. Miller's (1978) work on behavioral self-management seems very applicable to prevention programs. His model proposes teaching problem drinkers how to cope with alcohol and life stresses in a more manageable way.

All modern behavioral approaches operate on one central assumption—that behavior is controlled by events that precede it and follow it. In a careful analysis of events that precipitate and follow drinking in alcoholics, there are some fairly explicit clues regarding the origin of problem drinking in nonalcoholic populations and the beginning of high-risk drinking in adolescents. Since behavioral procedures have been shown to have demonstrable effects in the treatment of the disease of alcoholism, the next logical step is to bring problem drinkers and those at risk for developing alcoholism some of the benefits of methods previously available only to those diagnosed as alcoholic.

Several behavioral treatment techniques can easily be extended to a prevention treatment context. The functional analysis model of drinking, for instance, could easily be adapted for use in prevention. Similarly, self-monitoring, contracting, and environmental restructuring could be extended to prevention approaches. A preventive self-management program could go beyond the traditional educational format and could provide problem drinkers with specific and concrete techniques that they can employ.

One of the major problems in prevention that has been addressed repeatedly by reviewers is the issue of flexibility and tailoring of programs to fit specific group and individual needs. As further knowledge is gained in the areas of assessment and behavioral treatment, and as we know more about the development of alcoholism and the effectiveness of behavioral treatment methods with alcoholics, it is being realized that this knowledge can be used in establishing effective programs for people who otherwise might develop serious drinking problems.

The Alcohol Use Inventory (AUI) developed by Wanberg, Horn, and Foster (1975) represents a major effort to increase precision in alcohol assessment. Based on a differential assessment model of alcoholism, the AUI is a self-administered instrument that yields information about an individual's drinking patterns, associated behavior, and perceived reasons for drinking alcohol. Normative data have been gathered for a number of alcoholic subgroups, allowing alcohol-use profiles to be compared between individuals or across groups.

The development of modern behavioral techniques for alcoholism treatment has evolved from two directions. First, during the 1970s it was found that cognitive factors can play a major role in mediating the impact of alcohol on aggression, sexual arousal, social anxiety, and loss of control (Lang, Goeckner, Adesso, & Marlatt, 1975; Marlatt, Demming, & Reid, 1973; Wilson, 1977). A second major factor in determining the course of behavioral approaches to alcoholism involved the development of what have become known as alternative skills training approaches, fostered by Peter Miller and his colleagues (Miller, 1976).

Marlatt (1976), a pioneer in the behavioral assessment of drinking and relapse of addiction, has developed a drinking profile questionnaire by which individual patterns of causal factors can be established by self-report. His careful and unique studies in this area have stimulated much of the following discussion.

Because it is so apparent that our levels of understanding, applying, and measuring the technology of prevention are still crude, it follows that more basic analysis is needed. Since one of the major criticisms of preventive efforts by reviewers has been lack of specificity, a more accurate analysis of some of the elements involved seems warranted. To this end, my colleagues and I have developed a drinking analysis assessment technique based on responses about drinking and its components collected from various populations.

DRINKING SURVEY

In an attempt to catagorize the basic situational factors involved in drinking, an open-ended survey was developed that asks individuals who already drink (normal drinkers and others) to analyze the components involved in their drinking. For this initial work, there were no specific categories of response, but simply an open-ended question, asking respondents to think about the things in their lives that were most important in leading them to drink. The specific question asked of the respondent was as follows:

> As you think about your life and the part that alcohol has played in it, I want you to give me some idea of the most important things which have led you to drink. These might take the form of private thoughts and feelings about yourself, thoughts and feelings you have had about other people and many different behaviors and situations. I would like you to name as many of these as you can, with the most important ones first.

This survey method was applied to two different groups. The first was a group of hospitalized alcoholics ($N = 20$, mean age $= 38.8$), all patients in an inpatient program, each of whom had been given a primary diagnosis of chronic alcoholism or alcohol dependence. The survey was also given to a group of adolescents with varying histories of alcohol abuse ($N = 20$, mean age $= 15.1$). This group consisted of adolescents currently involved in outpatient treatment, all of whom had been given a diagnosis of alcohol abuse or alcohol dependence.

Raw data from this survey were reduced to 19 separate categories or situational factors. A list of these factors, along with their reported frequencies by both groups, is presented in Table 72.1. Although there is a wide range of reported mean frequencies for the combined groups, from 79% to 34%, it is clear from a comparison of group data that the adult

TABLE 72.1 Reported Frequency of Situational Factors Associated with Drinking by Adult Alcoholics and Alcohol-Abusing Adolescents

Situational Factors	Hospitalized Alcoholics[a] (%)	Alcohol- Abusing Adolescents[b] (%)	Mean (%)
Boredom	77	81	79
Depression	81	64	73
Anxiety	84	60	72
Interpersonal Conflict	71	70	71
Tension Reduction	77	52	65
Anger Out	45	82	64
Mood Change	65	61	63
Frustration	61	63	62
Craving	79	42	61
Social Pressure	43	62	53
Personal Control Challenge	68	31	50
Pain	75	21	48
Anger In	45	42	44
Social Facilitation	53	33	43
Cognitive Change	50	36	43
Physical Change	59	24	42
Imitation	20	56	38
Curiosity	23	44	34
Peer Acceptance	20	47	34

[a] $N = 20$.
[b] $N = 20$.

hospitalized alcoholics responded very differently from the alcohol-abusing adolescents. This is apparent from the differences in the percentage scores between the two groups in Table 72.1 and is particularly true for the factors of Pain, Craving, Personal Control Challenge, and Physical Change, which were reported with much higher frequency by the adult alcoholics and, conversely, for Anger Out and Imitation, reported much more often by the adolescent group.

This survey process shows that many of the factors associated with drinking alcoholic beverages for both adult alcoholics and alcohol-abusing adolescents can be categorized reliably for both individuals and groups. The next step in this assessment procedure is the development of the drinking analysis.

DRINKING ANALYSIS

The broadest categories in which all of the identified situational and contextual factors associated with drinking appear to fit are *antecedents* and *consequences.* The antecedent category is made up of causal sets—situations, states, and behaviors that have led to or lead to drinking alcohol. These antecedents include the following categories: Curiosity, Craving, Boredom, Frustration, Anxiety, Pain, Anger In (internalized anger), Depression, Imitation (modeling), Social Pressure, Interpersonal Conflict, Anger Out (externalized anger), and Personal Control Challenge (testing control over alcohol).

Borrowing from the research on focus of control (see other sections of this Handbook), two other general antecedent categories were added to the analysis, although they were not explicitly stated by respondents: Internal Causation, the perception that forces from within an individual lead to drinking; and External Causation, the perception that forces outside an individual lead to drinking. These are more general categories than the other antecedents and are believed to incorporate them.

Consequences are defined as the perceived or expected results of drinking alcohol. They include Mood Changes, Cognitive Change, Physical Change (including pain), Tension Reduction, Peer Acceptance, and Social Facilitation.

Two other consequence categories were included in this group: Internal Control, the belief or expectation that alcohol consumption will increase the internal control of one's behavior; and External Control, the belief or expectation that alcohol consumption will increase the outside forces controlling one's behavior. These are also general categories and incorporate other reported consequences.

The initial drinking analysis was reworked and organized into a scale based on the 15 antecedents and 8 consequences described. It is a self-report scale, which can be administered either in an individual or group format. Specific inquiries are made regarding each of the 23 factors in one of two ways, depending on the population being assessed. If the assessment is being made on individuals who have consumed or are consuming alcohol, the inquiry regarding each factor is done in the following manner:

Please rate on a scale from 0–10, with 10 being the most and 0 being the least, how much importance (factor) plays in your drinking. In other words, how important is (factor) to you as a reason for consuming alcohol?

If the population consists of individuals who do not consume alcohol, the inquiry is made in the following manner:

Please rate on a scale from 0–10, with 10 being the most and 0 being the least, how important you think (factors) would be in leading you to drink alcohol. In other words, how much do you think you would drink because of (factors)?

ASSESSMENT BY DRINKING ANALYSIS

The drinking analysis was administered to four separate groups: (a) hospitalized alcoholics ($N = 20$; 24–69 years old, mean age $= 38.1$ years); (b) alcohol-abusing adolescents involved in outpatient treatment ($N = 23$; 12–18 years old, mean age $= 15.9$); (c) nondrinking adolescents with a family history of two or more diagnosed alcoholics among blood relatives within two generations (positive family history, $N = 16$; 11–19 years old, mean age $= 16.3$); and (d) nondrinking adolescents with no family history of alcoholism (negative family history, $N = 18$; 14–21 years old, mean age $= 16.8$). The individuals in each of these four groups were administered the drinking analysis in an individualized format.

Table 72.2 shows means and standard deviations of reported scores on each of the factors by the first two groups—hospitalized adult alcoholics and outpatient alcohol-abusing adolescents. Although some of the standard deviations are fairly large, as shown by the

TABLE 72.2 Means and Standard Deviations of Reported Scores on Drinking Factors by Hospitalized Alcoholics and Alcohol-Abusing Adolescents

Factors	Hospitalized Alcoholics[a]		Drinking Adolescents, Mixed Family Histories[b]	
	Mean	Standard Deviation	Mean	Standard Deviation
Curiosity	19.8	6.6	29.4	3.3*
Craving	43.2	10.1	16.9	4.1*
Boredom	53.1	6.1	58.4	9.3
Frustration	39.7	8.4	31.7	9.1
Anxiety	50.4	9.3	42.5	10.6
Pain	38.3	8.1	18.9	6.6**
Anger In	23.5	6.9	32.3	8.1*
Depression	43.1	5.2	19.3	5.0***
Imitation	18.8	5.2	67.4	14.6***
Social Pressure	29.3	9.3	63.8	11.2***
Interpersonal Conflict	38.4	9.8	54.1	10.7*
Anger Out	40.6	7.7	49.6	9.4
Personal Control Challenge	21.8	5.2	11.9	3.2**
Internal Causation	48.5	8.1	23.6	5.1***
External Causation	58.4	9.6	71.6	13.4**
Mood Change	43.0	6.2	58.4	11.6**
Cognitive Change	23.6	5.7	30.5	8.8
Physical Change	31.5	7.1	19.8	6.1**
Tension Reduction	52.0	9.6	40.4	8.3**
Peer Acceptance	9.2	2.4	62.1	9.7***
Social Facilitation	31.9	5.1	37.2	6.2
Internal Control	49.8	11.4	33.2	5.8**
External Control	27.7	8.1	34.6	7.5*

[a] $N = 20$; 24–69 years old, mean age $= 38.1$
[b] $N = 23$; 12–18 years old, mean age $= 15.9$
* $p < .05$
** $p < .01$
*** $p < .005$

probability levels, it is apparent that many of the mean scores are significantly different across the groups. Specifically, the hospitalized adult alcoholics scored significantly higher in the factors of Depression, Internal Causation, Pain, Personal Control Challenge, Physical Change, Tension Reduction, Internal Control, and Craving. The outpatient drinking adolescents scored significantly higher in the areas of Imitation, Social Pressure, Peer Acceptance, External Causation, Mood Change, Curiosity, Anger In, Interpersonal Conflict, and External Control.

When this same group of drinking adolescents is compared with the group of nondrinking adolescents with positive family histories, a larger number of highly significant differences arise. These scores are shown in Table 72.3. The drinking adolescent group scored significantly higher in the categories of Boredom, Imitation, Social Pressure, Peer Acceptance, Social Facilitation, Curiosity, Anger In, Anger Out, Craving, Internal Control, Depression,

TABLE 72.3 Means and Standard Deviations of Reported Scores on Drinking Factors by Alcohol-Abusing Adolescents and Nondrinking Adolescents with Positive Family Histories

Factors	Drinking Adolescents, Mixed Family Histories[a]		Nondrinking Adolescents Positive Family Histories[b]	
	Mean	Standard Deviation	Mean	Standard Deviation
Curiosity	29.4	3.3	15.6	5.9***
Craving	16.9	4.1	11.2	3.3**
Boredom	58.4	9.3	23.2	4.9****
Frustration	31.7	9.1	36.3	6.2
Anxiety	42.5	10.6	37.8	8.4
Pain	18.9	6.6	18.4	4.4
Anger In	32.3	8.1	18.5	4.3***
Depression	19.3	5.0	13.4	3.2*
Imitation	67.4	14.6	18.2	5.1****
Social Pressure	63.8	11.2	13.4	4.0****
Interpersonal Conflict	54.1	10.7	48.1	9.1*
Anger Out	49.6	9.4	29.9	6.2***
Personal Control Challenge	11.9	3.2	23.3	4.7****
Internal Causation	23.6	5.1	26.2	5.1*
External Causation	71.6	13.4	52.7	10.2*
Mood Change	58.4	11.6	62.4	9.0
Cognitive Change	30.5	8.8	23.0	6.1*
Physical Change	19.8	6.1	13.0	3.5*
Tension Reduction	40.4	8.3	48.3	8.6*
Peer Acceptance	62.1	9.7	20.6	4.9****
Social Facilitation	37.2	6.2	12.4	3.6****
Internal Control	33.2	5.8	23.3	5.1**
External Control	34.6	7.5	41.7	21.1*

[a] $N = 23$; 12–18 years old, mean age = 15.9
[b] $N = 16$; 11–19 years old, mean age = 16.3.
* $p < .05$
** $p < .01$
*** $p < .005$
**** $p < .001$

TABLE 72.4 Means and Standard Deviations of Reported Scores on Drinking Factors by Nondrinking Adolescents with Positive Family Histories and Nondrinking Adolescents with Negative Family Histories

Factors	Nondrinking Adolescents, Positive Family Histories[a]		Nondrinking Adolescents, Negative Family Histories[b]	
	Mean	Standard Deviation	Mean	Standard Deviation
Curiosity	15.6	5.9	23.5	7.7*
Craving	11.2	3.3	9.1	2.6
Boredom	23.2	4.9	26.4	5.6
Frustration	36.3	6.2	11.9	4.1****
Anxiety	37.8	8.4	23.6	8.2***
Pain	18.4	4.4	8.9	2.2**
Anger In	18.5	4.3	9.1	2.8**
Depression	13.4	3.2	12.8	3.5
Imitation	18.2	5.1	18.1	6.1
Social Pressure	13.4	4.0	23.5	5.3***
Interpersonal Conflict	48.1	9.1	18.6	3.8****
Anger Out	29.9	6.2	25.1	5.9
Personal Control Challenge	23.3	4.7	14.7	4.6**
Internal Causation	26.2	5.1	15.5	4.8**
External Causation	52.7	10.2	10.9	3.2****
Mood Change	62.4	9.0	36.1	7.2****
Cognitive Change	23.0	6.1	8.1	2.1**
Physical Change	13.0	3.5	16.6	4.3
Tension Reduction	48.3	8.6	10.7	2.3****
Peer Acceptance	20.6	4.9	10.8	2.0*
Social Facilitation	12.4	3.6	16.5	3.8*
Internal Control	23.3	5.1	12.3	3.1**
External Control	41.7	12.2	16.6	5.1****

[a] $N = 16$; 11–19 years old, mean age $= 16.3$
[b] $N = 18$; 14–21 years old, mean age $= 16.8$
* $p < .05$
** $p < .01$
*** $p < .005$
**** $p < .001$

Interpersonal Conflict, External Causation, Cognitive Change, and Physical Change. The nondrinking adolescents with positive family histories scored significantly higher in categories of anticipated Personal Control Challenge, Internal Causation, Tension Reduction, and External Control.

A comparison of nondrinking adolescents from positive versus negative family backgrounds is shown in Table 72.4. The adolescents with positive family histories showed many significantly higher scores than their counterparts with negative family histories in anticipated Frustration, Interpersonal Conflict, External Causation, Mood Change, Tension Reduction, External Control, Anxiety, Pain, Anger In, Personal Control Challenge, Internal Causation, Cognitive Change, Internal Control, and Peer Acceptance. The adolescent group with negative family histories showed significantly higher scores on only three measures, including anticipated Social Pressure, Curiosity, and Social Facilitation.

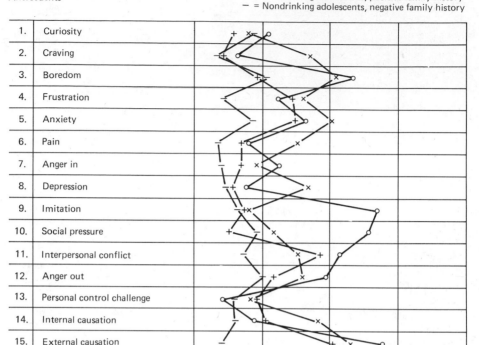

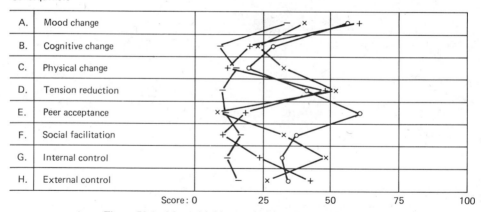

Figure 72.1   Mean drinking analysis profiles of four groups.

The data from the four measured groups show many highly significant differences between groups. The patterns that emerge from these data, if further research shows that they are stable and consistent, could form the basis of a group comparison study to develop profiles relative to risk of alcohol use and behavior for different subgroups of our population. Figure 72.1 summarizes the mean drinking analysis profiles of all four groups. For purposes of more accurate measurement, scores were standardized for the summary from 0–10 to 0–100. This profile comparison graphically shows some of the significant differences that were observed between groups in the foregoing tables.

From this analysis, it could reasonably be expected that extreme differences in profiles of an older group of hospitalized chronic alcoholics versus a younger group of problem drinkers would reflect some of the early signs and symptoms of problem drinking as it develops in youth. Since the most outstanding parts of the alcohol-abusing adolescent profiles are in the areas of External Causation, including Imitation, Social Pressure, and Interpersonal Conflict, and since Peer Acceptance seems to be an important consequence of drinking, treatment programs might well be developed for problem-drinking adolescents that incorporate these factors by using different social modeling and social learning therapies. Also, since the Boredom factor seems to be important for both chronic alcoholics and problem-drinking adolescents, one important part of therapy and prevention should include the substitution of activities that might reduce the frequency and extent of periods of boredom.

When alcohol-abusing adolescents are compared with nondrinking adolescents with positive family histories, the similarities rather than the extreme differences in their profiles could yield some suggestions about possible preventive interventions on a primary level for children of alcoholics and adolescents from alcoholic families. Antecedents in which both groups scored high include Frustration, Anxiety, Interpersonal Conflict, Anger Out, and External Causation. One consequence that was scored high for both groups was Mood Change. These highly correlated, highly scored factors may give more information about the development of alcohol-related problems in high-risk groups, which of course include adolescents with positive family histories, and may allow for more precisely targeted preventive measures. It is apparent from these suggestive data that preventive strategies for children of alcoholics would do well to include quasi-therapeutic, self-educational, or group process measures to help reduce frustration and anxiety, as well as social learning techniques to deal more specifically with interpersonal conflict and management of anger.

When nondrinking adolescents with positive versus negative family histories are compared, the extreme differences in scores may have some implications for the most primary kind of prevention. It must be remembered, however, that both of these profiles of nondrinking adolescent groups are pure measures of expectation of the antecedents and consequences of drinking alcohol, without actual experience of the target behavior itself. It must be assumed, then, that both of these groups are basing their expectations on environmental and social cues and modeling. We noted with considerable interest that the three major factors influencing the expectations of these two adolescent groups were (in descending order of importance) (a) television and movies, (b) observations of the family, and (c) information gained from peers. It follows that, although social pressure may operate to a great extent among adolescents who are already abusing alcohol, the expectations of those who have not yet begun are largely guided by what they observe from the mass media and at home. If both nondrinking adolescent groups are exposed to essentially the same mass media, most of the differences in their profiles originate from observation and modeling that takes place within the family. The wide disparity in profiles in the areas of Anxiety, Frustration, and Interpersonal Conflict suggest that children raised in alcoholic families report the influence of alcohol abuse and dependence on these three measures in very different ways from adolescents raised in nonalcoholic homes.

If differences among target groups are consistently and significantly different from one another, the approach suggested by the drinking analysis might better guide future efforts at prevention. Children and adolescents, especially those at high risk for the development of alcoholism, seldom learn how to relax, to be assertive, or to manage their own behavior in a systematic manner. Preparing children with these skills prior to their exposure to alcohol may decrease the chances that they will become problem drinkers or alcoholics in the future. Although the emphasis here has been on prevention in adolescence of future alcohol abuse, the drinking analysis format could be applied just as easily to other target (risk) groups discussed earlier. It might be used either to gather profile information about persons already diagnosed or categorized or to develop individualized patterns for analysis and prevention intervention.

The major extant techniques in the field of prevention in alcoholism largely consist of nonspecific strategies that are inconsistently applied and poorly measured. At this stage of our knowledge, we should not assume that we know a great deal about the preventive needs of different populations. Our preliminary results suggest that analysis of those populations in terms of the basic causes and expectations of behavior seems to be a good place to start.

REFERENCE NOTE

1. Blumenthal, M., & Ross, H. L. *Two experimental studies of traffic law: Volume I. The effect of legal sanctions on DUI offenders.* DOT Pub. No. HS-800, 825. Washington, D.C.: U.S. National Highway Traffic Safety Administration, 1973.

REFERENCES

Berg, R. L. The high cost of self-deception. *Preventive Medicine,* 1976, **5**, 483–495.

Blane, H. T. Education and the prevention of alcoholism. In B. Kissin & H. Begleiter (Eds.), *The biology of alcoholism,* Vol. IV. New York: Plenum Press, 1976.

Haggerty, R. J. Changing lifestyles to improve health. *Preventive Medicine,* 1977, **6**, 276–289.

Lang, A. R., Goeckner, D. J., Adesso, F. J., & Marlatt, G. A. Effects of alcohol on aggression in male social drinkers. *Journal of Abnormal Psychology,* 1975, **84**, 508–518.

Marlatt, G. A. The drinking profile: A questionnaire for the behavioral assessment of alcoholism. In E. J. Mash & L. G. Terdal (Eds.), *Behavior therapy assessment: Diagnosis, design and evaluation.* New York: Springer, 1976.

Marlatt, G. A., Demming, B. and Reid, J. B. Loss of control drinking in alcoholics; an experimental analogue. *Journal of Abnormal Psychology,* 1973, **81**, 233–241.

Miller, P. M. *Behavioral treatment of alcoholism.* New York: Pergamon Press, 1976.

Miller, W. R. Behavioral treatment of problem drinkers: A comparative outcome study of three controlled drinking therapies. *Journal of Consulting and Clinical Psychology,* 1978, **46**, 74–86.

Miller, W. R., & Munoz, R. F. *How to control your drinking.* Englewood Cliffs, N.J.: Prentice-Hall, 1976.

Noble, E. Prevention of alcoholism: The way of the future, *New York Ayerst Alcoholism Update,* 1979, **2**, 6.

Randall, D., & Wong, M. R. Drug education to date: A review. *Journal of Drug Education,* 1976, **6**, 1–21.

Roman, P. M., & Trice, H. M. Alcohol abuse and work organizations. In B. Kissin & H. Begleiter (Eds.), *The biology of alcoholism,* Vol. IV. New York: Plenum Press, 1976.

Scoles, P., & Fine, E. W. Short-term effects of an educational program for drinking drivers. *Journal of Studies on Alcohol,* 1977, **38**, 633–637.

Selzer, M. L., Vinokur, A., & Wilson, T. D. A psychosocial comparison of drunken drivers and alcoholics. *Journal of Studies on Alcohol,* 1977, **35**, 1294–1312.

Tennant, F. S., Weaver, S. C., & Lewis, C. E. Outcomes of drug education: Four case studies. *Pediatrics,* 1973, **52**, 246–251.

Wanberg, K. W., Horn, J. L., & Foster, M. F. A differential assessment model for alcoholism. *Journal of Studies on Alcohol,* 1977, **38**, 512–543.

Wilkinson, R. *The prevention of drinking problems: Alcohol control and cultural influences.* New York: Oxford University Press, 1970.

Wilson, G. T. Alcohol and human sexual behavior. *Behavior Research and Therapy,* 1977, **15**, 239–252.

SECTION 11
SETTINGS FOR HEALTH PROMOTION

CHAPTER 73

THE WORKSITE AS A SETTING FOR HEALTH PROMOTION AND POSITIVE LIFESTYLE CHANGE

PETER E. NATHAN

Rutgers, The State University of New Jersey

Although no one questions the cost-benefits of disease prevention as compared to treatment, it is legitimate to ask why we should establish disease prevention in the worksite. Workers are generally healthy, and the consequences of disease seem remote to them. Employers may be chary of intruding on employees' rights to privacy with health promotion efforts. Prevention efforts—especially attempts at positive lifestyle change—cost money, and businesspeople do not part readily with funds that do not contribute directly to the production, distribution, or sale of products. Why promote disease prevention in the workplace, then?

In theory, prevention of physical disease at the worksite makes a great deal of sense. In fact, the benefits of prevention in the workplace remain enticing—but essentially unproven. Empirical data confirming the superiority of efforts at prevention—health promotion—in the workplace over other prevention sites have not been easy to gather, both because of design and control problems (Schramm, 1977) and because large-scale tests are necessary for thorough cost-benefit analyses. The benefits of worksite prevention are several, however. They include the advantages of working with persons who are functioning at adequate vocational, emotional, and interpersonal levels or better, who are healthy physically and psychologically, and who possess financial and familial resources. Prevention programs in the workplace also benefit from a captive audience, which will read well-placed notices of programs and activities and heed the advice of enthusiastic co-workers who have taken part in them. Peer enthusiasm is understandably facilitative in worksite prevention settings, although management support is also essential to the success of these programs, as will be noted later. The convenience of worksite programs—that employees do not have to travel a great distance to participate in prevention activities—is also an advantage. Finally, employees' morale—and their consequent willingness to be part of health promotion efforts—is almost certainly heightened when they recognize their employer's willingness to support a voluntary program that is clearly for their benefit (Goldbeck & Koefhaber, 1981; Higgins & Philips, 1979; Institute for Health Planning, 1981).

Foremost among problems posed by prevention programs in the workplace is confidentiality—specifically, fear of disclosure. Every potential client of an in-house alcoholism prevention or treatment program worries that company managers will know that he or she has sought help (DuPont & Basen, 1980), and even participation in a positive lifestyle change program may represent a disclosure threat. Potential participants in company-based, on-site prevention programs for weight control, smoking cessation, or stress management may choose not to attend because of the threat they see from their potential "failed participation" on their future promotional opportunities. Although steps can be taken to minimize the chilling effect of this concern on participation, the effect nonetheless remains a potent one.

Health promotion programs in the workplace rarely offer services to the families of the employees they serve (Cunningham, 1982), making it more difficult for the employee whose spouse or family contributes to his or her lifestyle problem to benefit fully from program involvement. In addition, even in companies whose senior officers wholeheartedly endorse company-sponsored health promotion efforts, some middle managers will see the programs as interfering with productivity, affecting morale, and diminishing their authority. These views obviously affect their willingness to permit or encourage employees to participate.

Many corporations now offer at least some employee smoking, stress, or weight control programs (Keir & Lauzon, 1980; Milsum, 1980; Roskies, 1980); these programs generally supplement more traditional and more widely accepted alcoholism treatment-oriented employee assistance programs (EAPs). Whereas the former programs are designed to help employees with lifestyle problems that have the potential to cause health problems in future years, EAPs confront alcoholic lifestyles, which are usually sources of very real current concern. In contrast to EAPs, whose focus on immediate and definitive treatment demands a comprehensive and coordinated company-wide marketing and service delivery system, smoking, stress, and weight programs are typically uncoordinated. An important reason is that the persons usually responsible for these programs, located most often in personnel or medical departments, see their primary responsibilities as diagnosis and referral or treatment of established disorders (such as alcoholism or work-related injuries) rather than prevention of prospective disorders.

A few forward-looking firms, however, have given sufficiently high funding priority to comprehensive and coordinated positive lifestyle change programs so that they can organize and administer broadly conceived programs (Fitness Systems, 1980; Arthur D. Little, 1982; NHIC, 1981). Justifications for the expenditure of what frequently are substantial funds for these programs include prospects for enhanced employee morale, improved productivity, and greater loyalty to the corporation, as well as savings in health insurance and hospitalization costs.

Both the benefits and the problems of promoting healthy lifestyle changes in the workplace are clearly illustrated by the following three chapters, which describe specific health promotion programs at the worksite.

REFERENCES

Cunningham, R. M., Jr. *Wellness at work: An inquiry book.* Chicago: Blue Cross Association, 1982.

DuPont, R., & Basen, M. Control of alcohol and drug abuse in industry: A literature review. *Public Health Reports,* 1980, **95,** 137–148.

Fitness Systems, Inc. *Corporate fitness programs: Trends and results.* Los Angeles: Fitness Systems, Inc., 1980.

Goldbeck, W. B., & Koefhaber, A. K. Wellness: The new employee benefit. *Group Practice Journal,* 1981, 20–26.

Higgins, C. W., & Philips, B. U. How company sponsored fitness programs keep employees on the job. *Management Review,* 1979, 53–55.

Institute for Health Planning. *Promoting health in the work setting.* Madison, Wis.: Institute for Health Planning, March 1981.

Keir, S., & Lauzon, R. Physical activity in a healthy lifestyle. In P. O. Davidson & S. M. Davidson (Eds.), *Behavioral medicine: Changing health lifestyles.* New York: Brunner/Mazel, 1980.

Little, Arthur D., Inc. *Employee health enhancement: A new corporate challenge.* Cambridge, Mass.: Arthur D. Little, Inc., 1982.

Milsum, J. H. Lifestyle changes for the whole person: Stimulation through health hazard appraisal. In P. O. Davidson & S. M. Davidson (Eds.), *Behavioral medicine: Changing health lifestyles.* New York: Brunner/Mazel, 1980.

National Health Information Clearinghouse (NHIC). *Employee health promotion.* Washington, D.C.: National Health Information Clearinghouse, 1981.

Roskies, E. Considerations in developing a treatment program for the coronary-prone (Type A) behavior pattern. In P. O. Davidson & S. M. Davidson (Eds.), *Behavioral medicine: Changing health lifestyles.* New York: Brunner/Mazel, 1980.

Schramm, C. J. (Ed.). *Alcoholism and its treatment in industry.* Baltimore: Johns Hopkins University Press, 1977.

CHAPTER 74

JOHNSON & JOHNSON'S LIVE FOR LIFE: A COMPREHENSIVE POSITIVE LIFESTYLE CHANGE PROGRAM

PETER E. NATHAN

Rutgers, The State University of New Jersey

Johnson & Johnson's Live for Life, sponsored by the nation's largest health care products company, is the largest, best funded, and perhaps the most effective positive lifestyle program yet developed. In operation for more than 3 years, the program is currently offered to close to 10,000 employees. Employees participating in Live for Life live and work in the central New Jersey–eastern Pennsylvania region, which is also the location of Johnson & Johnson's corporate headquarters. Eventual plans are to offer the program to all 60,000 Johnson & Johnson employees worldwide.

The small core staff of Live for Life are all full-time employees of Johnson & Johnson. The head of Live for Life reports to a corporate vice-president. The approximately 10 core Live for Life staff are supplemented by several outside consultants, including myself, and by a larger number of students, many of whom are graduate students in clinical psychology at Rutgers. The graduate students conduct the action groups (to be described later), which are at the heart of the program. The consultants help set the program's overall goals and methods, select and plan the interventions, set selection and training standards for group and volunteer leaders, and design the epidemiologic study.

From its inception, Live for Life was conceived as a means to make Johnson & Johnson employees the healthiest in the world. This is the explicit aim of the program as envisioned by Johnson & Johnson's chief executive officer, James Burke—the program's principal supporter. To this end, Live for Life is predicated on two assumptions: (a) that employees' daily lifestyle decisions regarding exercise, eating, smoking, and stress management have a direct impact on their present and future health, the quality of their lives, and their job performance; and (b) that a company-sponsored positive lifestyle change program, administered by full-time personnel but voluntary and open to all employees, will motivate employees to make positive lifestyle changes sufficient to affect both health and quality of life. As a Live for Life promotional piece puts it:

> *Our objectives include* measureable, sustained *lifestyle improvements among the greatest number of* employees possible *in regular exercise, smoking cessation, weight control, stress management, health knowledge, and awareness of medical intervention programs.*

Johnson & Johnson is a company whose success derives both from the quality of its products and from its finely wrought marketing efforts. Live for Life has been imbued with both philosophies. Not only must the product—in this case, programs to alter lifestyles—be sustainable and effective, but it must be marketed effectively to the widest possible employee clientele. Marketing of Live for Life rests on three premises:

1. *The positive approach:* Live for Life competes for the attention of employees in a world full of powerful distractors. Hence, it must attract participants by emphasizing the positive, immediate benefits of the program, including better relationships, more energy, and greater productivity, rather than the negative, delayed benefits of avoiding premature death from cardiovascular disorders and cancer.

2. *Focus on health:* Employees who require medical or professional attention are served by the company's medical department and its employee assistance programs. Live for Life serves healthy persons who wish to stay that way.

3. *Practicality:* Participants learn how to lose weight, stop smoking, manage stress, and engage in exercise; the emphasis is on action.

ELEMENTS OF THE PROGRAM

The core elements of Live for Life are reviewed here in the sequence in which employees encounter them.

Health screen.   The current health and lifestyle status of each participating employee are evaluated by questionnaire and by biometric measurement. Items evaluated include health knowledge, nutrition practices, physical activity, efforts at stress management, dental health, blood lipids, blood pressure, body fat, weight, and estimated maximum oxygen uptake.

Lifestyle seminar.   Current health and lifestyle status are fed back to employees in a confidential lifestyle profile at a 3-hour lifestyle seminar, which is also designed to promote the Live for Life program to all interested employees as a means of altering lifestyle practices that negatively affect current and future health and quality of life.

Action groups.   Professionally led action groups (for the most part, led by advanced graduate students in clinical psychology) are multisession, action-oriented, education/intervention/prevention modules, designed to teach employees how to alter lifestyles and then maintain them on a permanent basis. Action groups have been offered on smoking cessation, weight control, exercise, applied stress management, nutrition, yoga, personal power, and alcohol and drug education. The first five areas are most strongly emphasized.

Creation of a healthy environment.   Creation of a work environment that supports and encourages positive health practices is another prime goal of Live for Life. Environmental improvements in key health and lifestyle areas made by company volunteer leaders have included the following: *fitness/exercise* (shower and locker facilities on site, exercise facilities on site or rented from local organizations); *weight control/nutrition* (scales in restrooms, convenient nutrition and calorie information where food is sold, availability of nutritious foods in company cafeterias and vending machines); *stress management* (management training programs to improve employee-manager relations, flexible scheduling of worktime, car pools, self-administered blood pressure equipment); and *smoking cessation* ("Thank You For Not Smoking" signs, no-smoking areas).

Feedback and follow-up.   Each employee receives a quarterly summary of "lifestyle points" earned during the previous quarter. Points accrue for participation in Live for Life programs, for lifestyle improvements, and for fitness achievement. Participants are also contacted at 1, 3, 6, 9, and 12 months after the end of a lifestyle improvement program, either by letter or telephone, for information on their progress and their reactions to the program.

Epidemiologic study. Health and lifestyle changes among employees at four "test" companies, each with an active Live for Life program, will be contrasted over a 2-year period with changes among employees at comparable "control" companies that have not yet begun their Live for Life programs. The Live for Life epidemiologic study, unique among similar studies elsewhere in terms of both goals and comprehensiveness, promises to yield data on both the overall effectiveness of the program in altering lifestyles and changing medical utilization patterns and the determinants of employee participation in a positive lifestyle change program.

HISTORY OF THE PROGRAM: 1978–1982

The Live for Life program in 1982 differs markedly from the program envisioned in 1978. In 1978, most of those responsible for Live for Life believed that it should and could be almost entirely volunteer-organized and volunteer-run, with few professionals and administrators involved and major responsibility for success or failure of the program given over to volunteer leaders at each site who would organize and manage their own company's Live for Life program themselves. Despite some doubts about whether this idealistic plan would work—whether busy Johnson & Johnson employees would find the time to run a complex positive lifestyle change program along with demanding full-time jobs—the plan was implemented. Accordingly, a great deal of time and energy went into development of procedures for volunteer selection, training, and support. Unfortunately, a year's test indicated strongly that the volunteer concept was largely impractical and unworkable, that ultimate responsibility for the program should be in the hands of on-site coordinators hired and trained by Live for Life, and that action groups and other interventions should be led by paid professionals with the expertise to do so.

Original Live for Life plans envisioned an alcohol problems action group with both an intervention mode (for those whose drinking caused them concern) and a prevention component (for those with an interest in alcohol problems but no pressing individual concerns about alcoholism). When this plan was reviewed by a representative of one of the corporation's employee assistance programs (some of the Johnson & Johnson companies have EAPs, while others do not), it was strongly attacked, largely on "turf" issues. The EAPs provide treatment for alcoholism; since Live for Life is supposed to offer prevention services, it cannot provide treatment. As a result, the action group on alcohol problems was transformed into an alcohol education program. As such, it was only marginally interesting to most of the participants in Live for Life. Eventually, it was no longer offered.

A final instructive difference between Live for Life in 1978 and now has to do with differences in the attention paid by Live for Life staff to managers and supervisors during program promotional efforts. When Live for Life was begun, little effort was made to engage managers in Live for Life, either for themselves or for their employees. When the importance of their active cooperation with and enthusiasm for the program was recognized, however— a year into the program—a much greater effort to sell the program to managers and supervisors preceded efforts to market the program to their employees. A lesson learned by earlier generations of employee assistance program facilitators (e.g., Alander & Campbell, 1975)— the central importance of supervisors and managers in encouraging employee involvement in health promotion efforts—was a bit late in coming to Live for Life.

EVALUATION

A management tradition on which Johnson & Johnson has long prided itself is that it is a family of allied companies in partnership, rather than a single, monolithic giant. Although certain corporate functions are centralized at corporate headquarters in New Brunswick, each of Johnson & Johnson's companies, of which there are more than 100 worldwide, is responsible for its own planning, marketing, budgeting—and profit making. Hence, when it came time to offer the Live for Life program beyond its initial test location (a small, local computer facility near New Brunswick), Live for Life staff had to market the program—and justify its cost—to each of the Johnson & Johnson companies to which it was being offered. Because the program's continuing costs had to be met by each company to which it was sold, those costs had to be justified to highly cost-conscious managers.

Accordingly, virtually the first issue Live for Life marketers were asked to address was the question of the program's cost-benefit ratio. Company boards and officers wanted to know whether the program would earn back its costs in a reasonable time and how these costs and the program's benefits would be measured. The same question is asked by virtually all corporate decision makers when they must consider "nonessential" human services programs for employees (Nathan, in press).

Unfortunately, the cost-benefit question, especially the costs and benefits of positive lifestyle change programs, remains impossible to answer at this point in the virtual infancy of human services programs for industry. Although some data can be cited in support of the moderate effectiveness of smoking cessation, weight control, and stress management programs (e.g., Kornitzer, Dramaix, Kittel, & DeBacker, 1980; Schwartz, 1980; Stunkard & Brownell, 1980), the relationship, if any, between successful participation in such a program and enhanced job performance, reduced usage of health or hospitalization insurance, or improved morale (all indices with cost significance to a businessperson) has not been established. In fact, even in the face of strong advocacy by the chief executive officer of Johnson & Johnson, Live for Life could not be marketed successfully to all Johnson & Johnson companies visited because its staff could not provide data, its own or those of others, attesting to its cost-effectiveness.

Johnson & Johnson's manufacturing, marketing, and research philosophy is to achieve the highest quality result, regardless of the level of competitors' product. As a consequence, initial Live for Life planning included a more extensive, more comprehensive evaluation component than any others had attempted. The complexity of the evaluation added substantially to the costs of the program. It also promised to yield the data on the costs and benefits of the program that were necessary for a rational decision on its continuation and, ultimately, its expansion throughout (and possibly beyond) the Johnson & Johnson family of companies.

Preliminary evaluation data of three kinds are reported here. The first are attitudinal data from employees who participated in one of several action groups during the program's first full year. The second data set, though somewhat less subjective, nonetheless relies, like the first, on self-report data; it consists of outcome evaluations of specific action group intervention modes. The evaluation reported here is of a self-help smoking cessation package, a variant of the usual leader-led smoking cessation action group. The all-important cost-benefit analysis of Live for Life will come from detailed analyses of first-year and, especially, second-year data from the multicompany epidemiologic study. Data from that study reported here are preliminary data from the first year. They link health attitudes, objective physiological measures of fitness and health, health knowledge, and health practices to participation in the Live for Life program.

Survey of Attitudes

A four-part questionnaire was sent to a random sample of company employees who participated in smoking cessation, stress management, weight control, and nutrition action groups during the first full year of Live for Life. Employees were drawn from eight Johnson & Johnson companies in central New Jersey and eastern Pennsylvania. Of the employees contacted (who represented fewer than 20% of all employees participating in these action groups), between 80% and 90% answered affirmatively when asked, "Was the program helpful to you in your efforts to make a health or lifestyle improvement?" Most satisfied were the seven employees who agreed unanimously that the nutrition action group had been a success; least satisfied were the 22% of participants in the weight control action group who felt it had not been helpful. To the question "In your opinion, should any additional skills or knowledge have been included in the program?" between 20% and 40% of participants in the four kinds of intervention groups felt they could have been improved. Among their suggestions were that more action group sessions be scheduled beyond the (typically) eight actually programmed, that follow-up booster sessions be offered, and that a broader spectrum of self-help skills be taught in each action group.

The demand characteristics of this questionnaire and the fact that it was almost certainly completed more often by satisfied than by unsatisfied participants reduce its value significantly. Without more information on the extent to which those who completed the questionnaire truly represented all those who participated in Live for Life, modification of the program on the basis of these findings is not justified.

Evaluation of the Smoking Self-Help Module

In an effort to provide employees who could not or would not participate in the standard eight-session action group on smoking cessation another opportunity to stop smoking, a self-paced, self-help smoking cessation package was developed that required minimal involvement with Live for Life staff. Similar modifications in other action group programs have been developed and evaluated, along with—and in comparison with—standard action groups. Hence, this report on this evaluation serves as a sample of evaluations of intervention modifications in Live for Life.

The test (Nepps, 1982) assessed the effectiveness of a self-help smoking cessation program offered to 36 adults (20 women, 16 men) who held white-collar jobs at a single Johnson & Johnson facility in central New Jersey. The program contained nine modules, which prescribed a series of self-control and aversive (smoke-holding) techniques for quitting smoking and avoiding relapse. The modules were dispensed sequentially to participants, contingent upon completion of a progress report on the previous module. Minimal professional contact was maintained with a trained consultant at the worksite, who collected progress reports, dispensed modules, and answered questions as needed. After completion of the last module, participants reported their posttreatment smoking rates to the consultant. Dropouts were contacted by telephone to obtain posttreatment smoking levels. All participants were contacted by telephone at 1-month and 4-month follow-ups.

The program had a high dropout rate, with 47.2% of participants failing to return for the second module. At the end of treatment, 8 of the 36 participants who had received the first module were abstinent from cigarette smoking (22.2%). At the 1-month and 4-month follow-ups, the number of abstinent participants had fallen to five (13.9%), indicating a treatment maintenance rate of 62.5%.

Although abstinence rates were somewhat diluted by the high dropout rate, the treatment appears to have been effective for those who completed all or most of the program. Furthermore, the effects of treatment seemed to be markedly durable for those who did achieve abstinence, a result, perhaps, of the inclusion in the program of specific relapse prevention instructions. It appears that minimal-contact, self-help quitting programs at the worksite hold promise as a means of reaching smokers who are unwilling or unable to attend group or clinic smoking cessation programs.

Data on standard and special Live for Life interventions with weight, stress, and nutrition problems yield similar data, and outcomes are comparable to those reported by investigators in other settings—generally neither superior nor inferior to the efforts of others. The advantage of Live for Life, then, seems to be in the increased access to intervention it provides healthy, well-functioning persons who might not otherwise consider making changes in lifestyle.

Epidemiologic Study

A 2-year broad-spectrum epidemiologic study of Live for Life is now in progress. For this purpose, a quasi-experimental research strategy, employing what Campbell and Stanley (1963) term a "non-equivalent control groups design," has been chosen. The treatment group consists of 2,139 employees from four Johnson & Johnson companies in which Live for Life was implemented between September 1979 and May 1980. The control group includes 2,021 employees from five companies that offered their employees the initial health screen— the source of baseline data for all subsequent evaluation comparisons—but did not then put Live for Life into effect. Three behavioral samples comprise the evaluation. The first sample, at baseline (the initial health screen), was taken between September 1979 and May 1980 for employees of all nine companies; the second sample was taken a year later; and the third will be taken 2 years after the initial health screen at each company.

Of the 2,139 employees of the four treatment group companies eligible for the health screen (and, hence, eligible for Live for Life participation), 1,606 (75.1%) completed the health screen. Of the 2,012 employees of the five control companies, 1,440 (71.5%) chose to complete the health screen.

Variables tapped during the health screen and at the 1-year and 2-year follow-ups include the following: (a) *biometric measures,* such as blood lipids, blood pressure, body fat, weight, and estimated maximum oxygen uptake; (b) *behavioral measures,* such as smoking behavior, alcohol usage, physical activity, nutrition practices, and coronary-prone behavior patterns; and (c) *attitudinal measures,* such as general sense of well-being, ability to handle job strains and stresses, personal relations, organizational commitment, and job involvement.

Preliminary findings for employees who took part in both the baseline and first-year health screens (excluding those from one treatment group company whose 1-year health screen data were not complete) suggest strongly that employees working in treatment group companies experienced greater improvements in the major health and lifestyle areas addressed by Live for Life. Specifically, employees in treatment group companies showed significant improvements (beyond the .01 level of significance) beyond those made by control group company employees in aerobic calories expended per week (a measure of exercise and robust physical activity), weight, general well-being, satisfaction with working conditions, satisfaction with personal relations at work, and ability to handle job strain. Treatment group employees also showed differential improvement (at the .05 level) in smoking behavior, self-reported sick days, and job self-esteem. There was also a nonsignificant reduction in treatment group employees' blood pressure.

These preliminary data, though encouraging, represent only a first—and very preliminary—approximation to the definitive assessment of this most complex undertaking. Full documentation of the total, sustained impact of Live for Life must await reporting of the 2-year epidemiologic study completed in mid-1982. It is important to note that these data do not weigh the program's costs and benefits. That ultimately necessary task is made somewhat easier, however, by the fact that Johnson & Johnson is self-insured, so that any consistent change in number or dollar amount of illness care claims attributable to this positive lifestyle change program would reflect directly on the program's fiscal benefits. Other potential benefits, to be measured at the conclusion of the study, include absenteeism, employee turnover rates, accident rates, and the several employee and management attitudes toward themselves, their work, and one another that constitute morale.

LIVE FOR LIFE IN THE WORKSITE

Despite disappointments, which were inevitable in the wake of the enthusiasm and optimism that accompanied implementation of the Live for Life program at Johnson & Johnson, the program continues to enroll new participants and to facilitate meaningful lifestyle changes. As it unfolds throughout the Johnson & Johnson family of companies—ultimately to the corporation's 60,000 worldwide employees—it will offer behavioral scientists a unique opportunity to test the costs and benefits of a comprehensive health promotion effort that has called on contemporary, state-of-the-art technology and marketing approaches to facilitate positive lifestyle change. Within two years, the story may be told.

REFERENCES

Alander, R., & Campbell, T. An evaluation study of an alcohol and drug recovery program: A case study of the Oldsmobile experience. *Human Resource Management,* 1975, **2,** 15–18.

Campbell, D. T., & Stanley, J. C. *Experimental and quasi-experimental designs for research.* Chicago: Rand McNally, 1963.

Kornitzer, M., Dramaix, M., Kittel, F., & DeBacker, G. The Belgian Heart Disease Prevention Project: Changes in smoking habits after two years of intervention. *Preventive Medicine,* 1980, **9,** 496–503.

Nathan, P. E. Alcoholism prevention in the workplace: Three examples. In P. M. Miller & T. D. Nirenberg (Eds.), *Prevention of alcohol abuse.* New York: Plenum Press, in press.

Nepps, M. M. *An evaluation of the effectiveness of a minimal contact self-help smoking cessation program in an industrial setting.* Unpublished doctoral dissertation, Rutgers, The State University, 1982.

Schwartz, G. Stress management in occupational settings. *Public Health Reports,* 1980, **95,** 99–108.

Stunkard, A., & Brownell, K. Worksite treatment for obesity. *American Journal of Psychiatry,* 1980, **13,** 252–253.

CHAPTER 75

THE STAYWELL PROGRAM

MURRAY P. NADITCH

Control Data Corporation

PROMISE AND OPPORTUNITY

The workplace setting provides a unique opportunity for research into and clinical application of behavioral health psychology. Workplace organizations provide access to large, concentrated, stable populations where people spend a significant proportion of their lives. The workplace provides opportunities to utilize psychosocial aspects of the workplace culture as fundamental program elements. Workplace programs provide opportunities to apply social-psychological and behavioral approaches to health behavior change and to develop empirically based theory and cumulative scientific knowledge in situations that provide an opportunity to implement, evaluate, and modify industrial programs over extended periods of time.

Empirically based workplace efforts committed to the evolution of more effective behavioral risk reduction programs reflect a unique convergence of the needs of organizations to control rapidly escalating health care costs and the needs of public health–oriented scientists to develop more affective programs.

This chapter describes the Control Data STAYWELL program, reports some initial evaluation data, reviews the program's return-on-investment simulation model, and discusses a computer-managed program of health behavior change.

BASIC PROGRAM DESCRIPTION

The STAYWELL program was initiated in 1979 and is currently being delivered to approximately 22,000 Control Data employees and spouses in 14 American cities as well as to a number of other companies. The program is offered as a free corporate benefit to all Control Data employees and spouses.

The program is based on the premise that lifestyle and behavior have an important impact on health, and that people can be helped to understand and modify their health behaviors. Emphasis is on long-term changes in health behavior, facilitated by providing people with awareness, skills, and a workplace environment conducive to the initiation and maintenance of positive lifestyle behaviors. The program focuses on smoking cessation, weight control, fitness behavior, stress management, and nutritional practices related to the reduction of cholesterol, salt, and sugar.

The STAYWELL program consists of orientations for employees and management, a behavioral health screening and health hazard appraisal, behaviorally oriented courses in each program area, and an extensive program utilizing employee volunteers to positively modify and affect aspects of the work environment and workplace norms that are related to health behaviors. The program is offered on the employees' time, except for the orientation and the screening, which are given on company time.

Program implementation in new sites begins with a 2- to 3-month preparation phase that includes an extensive communication program with local management. The objective is not only to inform managers but to enlist active management support, to use managers as role models, and to have the program minimize work disruption and accommodate the unique needs of each facility.

Employee enrollment has ranged from 65% to 95%. Enrollment is higher at worksites where people do less traveling, and among women employees and employees who have more education.

Employees who enroll attend a health screening at which data on health lifestyle, height, weight, and blood pressure are collected. Data from the health screening are used to generate a confidential health risk profile for each employee.

The health risk profile is a computer-generated analysis of each participant's most significant health risks. Participants receive a report comparing their chronological age with their risk age (how old they are in terms of risk) and their achievable age (how old they could be if they decide to make the appropriate changes in their health-related behaviors).

Control Data has a strict confidentiality policy. No one in the company can have access to any individual data. Only aggregate data are used for evaluation purposes. The only exception is in the case of an abnormal blood or blood pressure profile. Abnormal profiles are reviewed by a physician, but that review is not shared with the company, and participants decide when they register for the program whether they would like possible abnormal findings sent to their personal physicians. Follow-up letters encouraging participants to review abnormal profiles with their physicians are sent.

Health risk profiles are interpreted for employees at group interpretation workshops. Workshops help people identify their health risks and provide immediate opportunities for initiation of specific health actions, such as registration in courses or in the employee voluntary participation group program.

The program includes 1-hour introductory courses related to lifestyle and health as well as longer, more comprehensive courses that teach employees the skills required to change health habits. Lifestyle change courses are offered in smoking cessation, stress management, weight control, nutrition, and fitness. The courses are taught by health educators, psychologists, exercise physiologists, and other health professionals trained by Control Data to deliver the program.

Employee volunteer participation groups are the primary vehicle through which the program attempts to initiate and maintain health behavior using sociocultural processes. The purpose of participation groups is to modify the worksite environment in a manner that will effect norms and expectations of positive health-related activities.

During the program-preparation phase, the names of informal leaders are obtained during management interviews. Informal leaders and other employee volunteers are invited to special orientation sessions in which they are encouraged to take an active leadership role in the program and are given direct opportunities to initiate and lead action teams. Action teams focus on changing some aspect of the work environment or on forming support groups in which employees assist one another in changing health-related behaviors.

Action teams focus on such activities as obtaining more nutritious food for vending machines or initiating low-calorie cooking classes, clubs or activities related to running, walking, hiking, bicycling, aerobic dance, or any other activity related to health behavior–promoting activities.

Support groups form during the final phase of each lifestyle change course. Support groups assist members in implementing, continuing, and maintaining the difficult job of changing lifelong habits related to health behaviors. Support group activities include sharing of experiences, innoculation against failure techniques, and other activities whose purpose is to provide a supportive, sympathetic environment in which to continue or initiate health habit changes.

Participation groups give people opportunities to interact socially, extend opportunities for program entry beyond the formal entry phases, and facilitate program momentum. Participation group activities have been positively received by employees, and there tends to be more participation in these activities than in formal courses.

INITIAL EVALUATION DATA

Program evaluation data are used for formative, summative, and program management purposes. Based on these evaluation data, significant changes have been made in the content and process of the program. In addition to the modification of the program process related to middle management support discussed earlier, significant changes have been made in course content, delivery modes, and the processes used for the participation group program. As an example, an initially lower participation rate by blue-collar employees and by employees who spent large portions of their work time outside the office resulted in the introduction of an additional set of courses in each risk area that could be delivered in half-hour lunchtime slots open to blue-collar workers. These sessions focused on a more hands-on, how-to-do-it and a less academic content and enabled people who missed sessions to receive summaries so that missing sessions would not result in increased program dropout. A set of correspondence self-instructional courses was also developed to facilitate more active involvement by employees who either traveled frequently or did not wish to participate in group-based courses. As a result of formative evaluation data, a social incentive system was introduced in some courses to reduce the number of course dropouts. The current weight control course, for example, allows every member of the course to receive a gourmet low-calorie cookbook if the average attendance level is above a certain level.

Two bodies of summative evaluation data are reported in this chapter: (a) the Health Attitude Survey, which contains data on health behavior change, and (b) the Employee Attitude Survey, which contains data related to health behavior norms in the workplace.

The Health Attitude Survey is administered annually to a 10% representative sample ($N = \pm 5,000$) of all domestic Control Data employees. These data enable comparison of responses by employees in STAYWELL sites with employees in matched non-STAYWELL control sites and comparison of responses of employees at varying levels of program participation at the STAYWELL sites. Four levels of STAYWELL participation are differentiated: nonactive employees at STAYWELL sites, participation limited to the health risk profile (HRP), any program activity beyond the HRP, and enrollment in lifestyle change courses.

Health behavior change was defined as whether employees reported significant changes over the past year in relevant health behaviors. The percentages of employees who reported any or substantial improvement in each area of health-related behavior are shown in Table 75.1.

Participants in each of the lifestyle change courses report significantly more improvements in the five relevant health behaviors than either STAYWELL employee groups at lesser levels of participation or employees at non-STAYWELL control sites. The strongest effects are in the area of smoking cessation, for which 58% of respondents indicate some change in habits and 35% indicate a substantial improvement in smoking behavior, as compared to a 15% rate of any improvement and an 8% rate of substantial improvement at control sites. These data are consistent with other data we have collected on a smoking cessation program, which indicated that smokers enrolled in the course smoked an average of 1.6 packs per day and that 12 months after the course 30.3% were not smoking, 43.5% were smoking less than one pack a day, and 24.2% were continuing to smoke one or more packs a day.

The data shown in Table 75.1 include all people who participated in each course, not

Table 75.1 Percentage of Employees Reporting Improvement in Health-Related Behaviors, by Subject Area and Level of Program Participation

| | Level of Program Participation | | | | | |
| | | Staywell Sites | | | | |
Subject Area	Control Sites	Not Active	HRP Only	Any Post-HRP Activity	Course Participation	Significance Level PC
Weight control						
% Improved	30	29	33	39	62	.0001
% Substantially improved	8	11	8	11	18	.05
n	1,688	223	226	169	74	
Smoking cessation						
% Improved	15	15	13	11	58	.0001
% Substantially improved	8	9	6	6	35	.0001
n	1,661	216	218	204	31	
Exercise						
% Improved	40	27	34	53	62	.0001
% Substantially improved	11	9	11	16	29	.01
n	1,678	220	229	200	42	
Stress management						
% Improved	34	28	32	31	62	.0001
% Substantially improved	7	8	5	5	9	n.s.
n	1,676	220	228	149	92	
Nutrition						
% Improved	31	29	33	39	52	.01
% Substantially improved	8	7	7	9	15	n.s.
n	1,684	220	228	197	48	

just course completers. The inclusion of noncompleters and dropouts in these statistics represents a more accurate assessment of the effect of the courses on all people who enrolled and gives a more conservative estimate of effects.

Additional data collected in the 1981 and 1982 Health Attitude Surveys suggest that these results are not the result of self-selection bias. The 1981 Health Attitude Survey results indicate that employees who enroll in lifestyle change courses perceive more difficulty in changing health lifestyle and feel less capable of changing their health lifestyle on their own than do those who do not enroll in lifestyle change courses. The 1982 Health Attitude Survey results indicate course participants are more likely to agree with items indicating that they are more likely to be motivated by co-workers, encouragement from doctors, and opportunities for group activity in changing their health lifestyle than are other employees. Citing reasons why people do not change their behaviors, course participants are also more likely than nonparticipants to identify insufficient individual will power, lack of support from family and friends, and the need for help to make behavior changes. These data suggest that participants were more, not less, likely to depend on social facilitation to initiate health behavior changes, and that they would not have shown as much positive health change without course participation.

An important premise underlying the STAYWELL program is that long-term health behavior change will be facilitated in a normatively conducive environment. The primary focus of the participation group program is to create positive changes in health-related norms. Changes in health-related norms are measured by the STAYWELL Employee Attitude Survey. The survey involves a 10% sample of full-time employees. Normative change is measured by asking respondents the extent to which they perceive that other employees at the worksite are making positive changes in specific health-related behaviors. Table 75.2 shows 3-year trend data reflecting responses to the positive changes on the part of other employees in the areas of physical fitness, overweight, smoking, stress, nutrition, energy level, coffee consumption, and alcohol use. These data indicate that STAYWELL participants observe more change than do nonparticipants at STAYWELL sites or controls. Nonparticipants at STAYWELL sites also consistently observe more normative change than do people at control sites.

These data are interpreted as suggesting that the STAYWELL program has been successful in initiating positive normative change in targeted areas, that these changes are perceived by nonparticipants as well as by participants, and that the change becomes greater during the program's second year.

Two items included to test for positive response bias and Hawthorne effects were perceived changes in coffee consumption and alcohol problems. These are socially desirable areas of change that are not part of the STAYWELL program. There were no significant differences in these areas in either STAYWELL or control sites over the 2 years of this analysis.

RETURN-ON-INVESTMENT MODEL

A major premise underlying workplace health promotion programs is that such programs will be cost-effective for the companies that sponsor them. Control Data is in a unique position to assess cost-effectiveness because the company is not only self-insured but also processes its own health care insurance claims.

The health care claims data base has been included as part of the STAYWELL evaluation process, and the relationships between behavioral health risks and health care costs and between changes in health behaviors and health care costs are being examined. This evaluation is being done in the context of a mathematical simulation model. The model uses data in the STAYWELL evaluation as well as epidemiologic and health economics data to estimate present and future potential cost savings.

The model begins by estimating the percentage of people who smoke, have high cholesterol levels, have high blood pressure, are overweight, and are not physically fit, using demographic data on age, sex, and education and normative data from Control Data's health hazard appraisal results. The extent to which the estimated population of employees at risk can modify their behaviors is calculated by using program participation rates, based on the STAYWELL experience, STAYWELL evaluation data related to behavior change, and other health behavior change results from studies in the behavioral medicine literature. Data on these behavior changes are used to determine estimated changes in chronic degenerative diseases over the long run, using the Framingham Study data and other epidemiologic data, and to estimate short-term changes in health care and employee performance costs. The estimated potential health savings are discounted to current rates and are compared with the cost of the program to estimate potential return on investment.

The model is useful because it makes assumptions explicit, provides a forum for scientists to critique the validity of studies underlying the model and to focus research on the development of more scientifically vigorous studies, allows users to vary assumptions and to examine

Table 75.2   Percentage of Employees Reporting Positive Health-Related Changes at the Worksite, by Subject Area and Level of Program Participation

Subject Area	Control Sites	Level of Program Participation		Significance Level PC
		Staywell Sites		
		Nonparticipants	Participants	
Overweight				
1980–1981	13	20	19	.0005
1981–1982	13	27	32	.0001
Smoking during work				
1980–1981	25	26	32	.015
1981–1982	20	30	32	.0001
Nutritious food availability				
1980–1981	19	26	31	.0001
1981–1982	19	26	32	.0001
Physical fitness				
1980–1981	12	30	44	.0001
1981–1982	13	40	54	.0001
Effective stress management				
1980–1981	11	13	20	.0001
1981–1982	12	20	24	.0001
Energy level at work				
1980–1981	8	12	15	.0001
1981–1982	9	13	18	.0001
Alcohol-related problems				
1980–1981	11	10	10	n.s.
1981–1982	13	16	12	n.s.
Coffee consumption				
1980–1981	7	8	8	n.s.
1981–1982	9	11	8	n.s.
Sample size				
1981	1,436	378	412	
1982	1,464	338	563	

sensitivity of outcomes as a function of the models assumptions, and facilitates use of operations research maximization models for optimal program impact planning by estimating such factors as which potential target populations will yield the maximum return on investment. The model is an organizing force for planning the program and for utilizing evaluation results as they become available.

A COMPUTER-MANAGED PROGRAM OF HEALTH BEHAVIOR CHANGE

Control Data is developing a computer-managed program of health behavior change. The program uses computer technology to address problems that resist solution in traditional clinical approaches. The program is highly individualized; each person is matched with the intervention most likely to be effective for that person. The program is also modified while the person is in it, as a function of behavior change and compliance. The efficiency of matching and reassignment is evaluated by a mathematical model that enables the program to make more decisions as more people complete the program.

Increased recognition of the importance of individual differences in response to health behavior change programs is an often-cited area of needed inquiry in behavioral medicine. Clinically and academically based programs have difficulty in responding to the need for more individually tailored programs because samples are usually too small to perform the complex multivariate analysis required to determine which interventions work with what kinds of people to what effect.

The STAYWELL program has a large enough population to establish the basic parameters required for an individualized program. Program users complete a behavioral profile prior to entry into the program. This behavior profile contains a listing of the major variables that have been hypothesized to relate to individual differences in response to programs in the clinical literature. In the weight control area, for example, such variables as knowledge about nutrition, the degree of social support at home, the degree of overweight, the number of programs a person has participated in previously, sex, and other demographic characteristics are included in the profile.

In the initial iteration of the program, subjects are randomized across a number of intervention approaches. When a sufficient sample of people have run through the program, the individual difference variables are examined to determine their efficacy in predicting outcomes at program end and 12 months after program completion. Individual difference variables that are useful predictors remain in the model, and those that do not account for significant variance are deleted. Variables whose main or interactive effects accounted for significant variance are used to match individuals to program paths in the next intervention. This procedure is repeated with each iteration (approximately whenever 2,500 people have completed the program), so that the system is able to make increasingly accurate predictions about the effects of matching people to program paths.

Each program path includes branches, so that individuals who are not doing well may move to an alternative intervention, may have the current intervention enriched with adjunctive material, or may repeat certain aspects of the current intervention. Each branch point is treated and tested as an alternative experimental intervention. The efficiency of the branch points is evaluated and reconsidered with each new cohort of people, comprising one of the iterations in the evaluation process.

Using this approach, the computer-managed model can be considered a paradigm for the evolution of empirically based theory that could yield cumulative scientific knowledge of this area. This method is consistent with the structural equation modeling paradigm using theory construction proposed by Blalock (1969).

The computer-managed program is individualized further by using a friendly, supportive tone, using the subject's name, remembering statements made by the subject earlier in the program, providing quantifiable and graphic feedback on the user's progress, facilitating comparison of the individual's progress with that of other similar people in the program, and allowing users a wide latitude of choice.

The emphasis of the program is on behavior change, rather than being limited to education. Users receive only the information relevant to their specific problems. Users have opportunities to use new information in computer-managed simulation situations, to set specific goals and objectives for behavior during the week following the session, and to receive individualized, computer-generated feedback on their success or lack of success in applying the techniques between lessons.

Programs for smoking cessation, weight control, stress management, fitness and blood pressure management were implemented during the first half of 1983. A nutrition management program will be available in 1984.

REFERENCE

Blalock, H. M. *Theory construction: From verbal to mathematical formulation.* Englewood Cliffs, N.J.: Prentice-Hall, 1969.

CHAPTER 76

STRESS AND THE WORKPLACE

G. H. COLLINGS, JR.

New York Telephone

It is commonly accepted that stress is a significant part of the modern world. Whether we are subjected to greater stresses than our cavemen forebears or even our grandparents may be a matter of debate. We all have stress in our daily lives, however, and it is only realistic to recognize that these stress levels wax and wane depending on life's circumstances and our responses to them over time.

In today's world, the one constant characteristic is change, and change is inherently stressful to the human organism. We are experiencing vast social changes in the structure and fabric of our society. The increasing number of employed women has resulted in most families having two working members. The changing roles of men and women and our rapidly altering moral and ethical values are striking down traditional sources of security while substituting new and unfamiliar relationships and complexities. Massive changes in technology, communications, and transportation and many other equally significant developments are altering the substance of the average lifestyle. The working world is undergoing revolutionary alterations—such as the change from a predominantly blue-collar to a predominantly white-collar work force—individual performance or craft skills are being replaced by team-oriented demands, whereby relationships with others become more important than physical output. As corporations grow with success or change with failure, there are frequent internal reorganizations and functional realignments, as well as mergers of previously independent companies. These changes have extensive and serious implications for long-term employees. In such a world, the employees have a less secure future, greater anxieties about their abilities to meet yet-unfaced demands, more competitive pressures, and many other real or perceived stresses as a normal part of each day's activity. It should not be surprising, therefore, that we see these influences reflected in employees' performance on the job and also in the body's "performance" as evidenced by the occurrence of illness and disability.

In most industrial medical organizations, it has long been recognized that probably 40% or more of all patients who walk into a medical facility are there either because of psychosomatic symptomatology alone or because of physical disease that has strong emotional or situational overtones. Despite this recognition, industrial medical services have not been very effective in coping with such cases. In fact, the general tendency has been to treat the presenting symptomatology and not to delve into the true cause if it was not obviously organic. This situation is changing as the relationship between life's stressors and the occurrence of organic disease becomes clarified and more widely accepted and as medical programs at the worksite become more preventive in character. Behavioral and attitudinal opportunities for intervention in health maintenance have set the stage for new approaches to health improvement for the work force. The exploration and development of such health improvement methodology by the New York Telephone Company offers the opportunity for a case study in stress management methodology. Specifically, meditation/ relaxation will be used as the example, *although it constitutes but one phase in the overall stress management strategy of the company.*

The company has had a long-standing interest in employee health and has a well-developed medical program aimed at promoting general health, improving coping ability, and reducing the effects of disability. An early interest in meditation was sparked by the work of Dr. Herbert Benson related to the relaxation response. (see Chapter 21 of this Handbook). The company medical department engaged in a few preliminary trials of Dr. Benson's relaxation method (currently referred to as the Respiratory One Method, or ROM), initially in connection with the clinical management of moderate hypertension and among employees in the general working population who expressed an interest in learning about meditation.

In these early trials, the common experience was an initial high interest and enthusiasm on the part of employees, with large numbers responding to the first invitation to join a group on meditation. Over a period of months, however, the dropout rate was very large, and experience indicated that the training methods used were not very successful. By the end of 6 months or so, only a handful of individuals could be found who professed to be continuing in the meditating process. Among those who continued, however, some lives were profoundly improved. It was also observed that those who seemed to benefit were, almost without exception, individuals who had been experiencing high levels of stress at the time they entered the meditation program.

Because it seemed that some good was being achieved—at least for a small number of highly stressed individuals—and because of the observation that the training methods needed substantial improvement, a major study was designed, to be devoted solely to intervention among individuals at higher than average levels of stress. The objectives of the study were as follows:

1. To field-test more effective meditation training methods (preferably by semiautomated means).
2. To study the comparative practical usefulness of various relaxation techniques for individuals at high stress levels in the work setting.

The study (reported in Carrington, Collings, Benson, Robinson, Wood, Lehrer, Wollfolk, & Cole, 1980) explored the foregoing objectives by comparing the effects of three leading meditation/relaxation techniques on symptoms of employee stress, measured over a 5½-month period.

Stress levels were determined by the SCL-90-R questionnaire (Derogatis, 1977)—a well-validated multidimensional measure of distress, developed by Dr. L. Derogatis of Johns Hopkins University—and by the A-C questionnaire (an in-house instrument of New York Telephone)—an instrument developed by the author to evaluate the perceived value of meditation/relaxation to the participant.

For this study, 154 employee volunteers, self-selected on the basis of subjectively perceived stress and screened to eliminate persons with previous experience in meditation/relaxation, were randomly assigned to one of four groups, as follows:

1. Clinically standardized meditation (CSM)—38 subjects
2. Respiratory One Method (ROM) meditation—38 subjects
3. Progressive muscle relaxation (PMR)—38 subjects
4. Control group, receiving no intervention—40 subjects

The results of the study were very revealing. Compliance with meditation/relaxation practice was even higher than had been hoped for. At the end of the study, 81% of the

CSM subjects, 76% of the ROM subjects, and 63% of the PMR subjects were still practicing their respective techniques.

As expected, the participants in the three treatment groups taken as a whole showed symptom reduction, as measured by the SCL-90-R, over the 5½ months of observation. A surprising finding was that controls also showed substantial symptom reduction over that same period, though less than the meditators.

Figure 76.1 shows the symptom improvement for meditation/relaxation practicers and Figure 76.2 shows the results for the control group (nonpracticers). Practicers showed significantly more symptom improvement than the control group (nonpracticers) on every one of the symptom dimensions and on the summary indexes of the SCL-90-R (somatization, depression, anxiety, hostility, interpersonal sensitivity, paranoid ideation, psychoticism, obsessive compulsive, and phobic anxiety). Moreover, stress reduction was observed whether subjects practiced their techniques frequently or infrequently—another unexpected finding.

To assess the clinical importance of these findings, the SCL-90-R scores for all four groups were then compared with the scores of groups previously studied by Derogatis (1977)—a nonpatient normal group ($N = 974$) and a psychiatric outpatient group ($N = 1,002$). Before meditation/relaxation practice was begun, the SCL-90-R scores of participants in the study fell between those of Derogatis's psychiatric outpatients and his nonpatient normal subjects, at a level of stress that might be considered on the borderline of the clinical range (Figure 76.3). This confirmed the presumption that our self-selected target population was indeed living with stress levels considerably above normal. At the end of the study (5½ months later) the scores for those in the meditation/relaxation groups had come down to the middle of the normal range, with scores on one dimension, somatization, now significantly below normal (Figure 76.4). In contrast, scores for the control group at the end of the study were still significantly above those of Derogatis's nonpatient normal group.

When the three meditation/relaxation techniques were examined separately in terms of degree of symptom reduction, the methods were found to differ in their effectiveness.

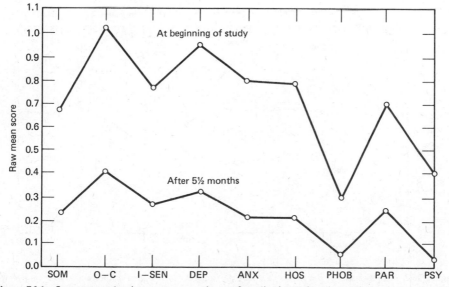

Figure 76.1 Symptom reduction among practicers of meditation/relaxation techniques over the 5½-month study period. (*Key:* SOM = somatization; O-C = Obsessive compulsion; I-SEN = interpersonal sensitivity; DEP = depression; ANX = anxiety; HOS = hostility; PHOB = phobic anxiety; PAR = paranoid ideation; PSY = psychoticism.)

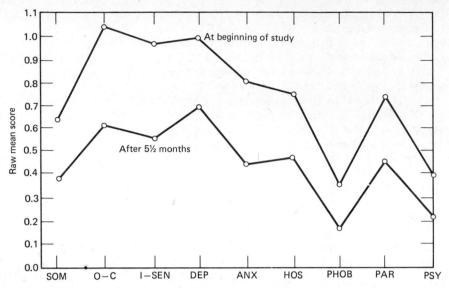

Figure 76.2 Symptom reduction among control group members—nonpracticers of meditation/relaxation techniques—over the 5½-month study period. (*Key:* SOM = somatization; O-C = obsessive compulsion; I-SEN = interpersonal sensitivity; DEP = depression; ANX = anxiety; HOS = hostility; PHOB = phobic anxiety; PAR = paranoid ideation; PSY = psychoticism.)

The progressive muscle relaxation (PMR) group showed no more improvement than controls, but the two meditation groups (CSM and ROM) were substantially and significantly better. Thus, meditation, not muscle relaxation, appeared to be effective as a therapeutic agent for these people.

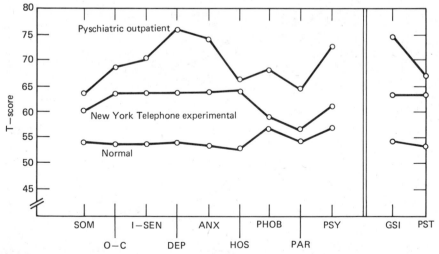

Figure 76.3 Comparison of the scores of study participants before mediation/relaxation practice was begun with the scores of psychiatric outpatients and nonpatient normal subjects in the Derogatis (1977) study. (*Key:* SOM = somatization; O-C = obsessive compulsion; I-SEN = interpersonal sensitivity; DEP = depression; ANX = anxiety; HOS = hostility; PHOB = phobic anxiety; PAR = paranoid ideation; PSY = psychoticism; GSI = general severity index; PST = positive symptom total.)

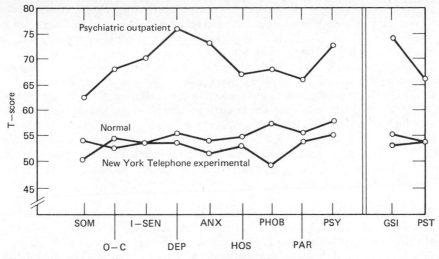

Figure 76.4 Comparison of the scores of study participants at the end of the 5½-month study period with the scores of psychiatric outpatients and nonpatient normal subjects in the Derogatis (1977) study. (*Key:* SOM = somatization; O-C = obsessive compulsion; I-SEN = interpersonal sensitivity; DEP = depression; ANX = anxiety; HOS = hostility; PHOB = phobic anxiety; PAR = paranoid ideation; PSY = psychoticism; GSI = general severity index; PST = positive symptom total.)

As mentioned earlier, a second instrument (the A-C questionnaire) covering benefits perceived by the participant was also used in the study. The results of this questionnaire agreed with those of the SCL-90-R where the two instruments were exploring similar aspects, but the A-C questionnaire provided an opportunity for recording improvements that were not measured by the SCL-90-R. The most frequently reported perceived benefits were improvement in ability to think clearly, increased objectivity, greater alertness, better social functioning, and enhanced enjoyment of life. These findings suggest that benefits of meditation other than stress reduction may include improved efficiency, increased coping ability, and greater satisfaction with life. These benefits may be particularly relevant for programs involving preventive health measures.

Of special interest from the point of view of employee health was the observation that physiological complaints related to psychosomatic disorders showed highly significant reductions following use of the meditation/relaxation techniques. Also, those who practiced these techniques showed markedly lowered hostility and a sharp decrease in moderate symptoms of depression (a clinical condition generally considered difficult to modify by pharmacological or psychotherapeutic means). This lessened irritability appears especially relevant for the use of meditation in the workplace, as well as for the management of such personality disorders as alcoholism, for which hostility scores on the SCL-90-R have frequently been found to be elevated.

The high compliance rates, in the 70% to 80% range, have already been mentioned. It was interesting to note that, with but a single exception, all subjects who stopped practicing did so within the first 3 months. Thereafter, although some subjects switched from frequent to occasional practicing and back again, they did not discontinue their practice. This suggests that meditation/relaxation practice may stabilize within the first 3 months.

The study demonstrated that semi-automated instruction in meditation could be used in an organizational setting with no loss of effectiveness relative to personal instruction in the technique. In addition, the timetable of attrition suggested that, once it is successfully adopted and practiced for a period of several months, meditation might become a permanent coping strategy, which could then be called upon by the trainees when they have need of it—in short, that the strategic use of meditation is not likely to be abandoned. Semi-automated meditation training thus appeared to have considerable potential value for health maintenance programs in organizational settings, a value that is enhanced when the relative safety and inexpensiveness of this training is taken into account.

The study also showed that meditation could be highly effective in reducing stress levels among individuals who started out as distressed people. This was in contrast to the relative ineffectiveness that had been initially experienced in the application of meditation randomly to unselected employee populations. Therefore, it became important to determine the prevalence of distress in the total company employee population—that is, how many distressed people existed at any particular time. To shed light on this subject, a survey was conducted of 4,000 randomly selected employees at all levels of the company, from blue-collar craft workers to top executives. The survey instrument was the SCL-90-R, which was completed and returned by 2,363 employees in the survey sample, for an overall response rate of 59%.

The findings from this survey were as follows. First, a significant proportion of employees (overall, about 25%) revealed stress levels in the clinical range (what will be referred to here as *distress*). This observation was true for all of the stress indicators (dimensions of the SCL-90-R). Second, the employee's level in the company was significantly related to stress, with higher and middle management revealing the lowest percentage of distressed people (less than 20% in the clinical range), followed by lower management with higher scores (23% distressed), and then by nonmanagement employees, who revealed the highest stress levels (27% distressed). These distinctions were evident for both sexes but were particularly dramatic among females. Third, male employees revealed higher proportions of stressed people than female employees when comparisons were made with the gender-keyed norms. It was found that 10% of male managers but only 3% of female managers had scores greater than two standard deviations above the normative mean—with these proportions going to 12% for males versus 4% for females among lower management and to 14% versus 5% among nonmanagement employees. Fourth, male and female employees manifested different characteristic patterns of symptomatic stress. Men had a tendency to show higher levels of obsessive-compulsive and hostility symptoms, whereas women tended to reveal greater symptoms of phobic anxiety. Finally, there was no evidence of substantial alteration in the foregoing observations as a function of age.

The data in this survey were also used to calculate specific local SCL-90-R norms for each employee subsegment—that is, upper management, lower management, and nonmanagement—by age and sex groups. These norms now serve as reference values in the interpretation of the SCL-90-R scores from individual employee/patients. Capitalizing on this ability to identify individuals with significantly elevated stress levels, and drawing on the conclusions from the aforementioned study and other experience with health promotion program implementation in the work setting, an ongoing program of meditation training was developed and is now being implemented.

Since users of the muscle-relaxing technique (PMR) did not outperform controls in the study, PMR was not included in the final program. The two meditation techniques, CSM and ROM, were combined so that they could be offered as parts of a single instructional system. Trainees in the meditation program are thus given the opportunity to move freely from one meditational approach to the other. This is done to increase the probability that a suitable technique will be adopted by the trainee.

The following summarizes the essential elements of the program. The *long-range goals* are as follows:

1. To provide an additional resource to employees that will assist them in coping with stress.
2. To improve the productivity of employees.

3. To reduce the adverse personal effects of stress, such as anxiety, ineffectiveness, morbidity, and disability.

The program *strategy* is to identify employees who are at a stressful period in their lives and to utilize that situation as a timely point for introducing them to meditation. Based on the findings from the prior studies, under these conditions we anticipate maximum acceptance and very few dropouts.

The *operation* of the program is as follows. It is structured as part of the company medical department's preventive and health maintenance effort. Actual implementation is in the hands of specifically qualified trainers. The trainers initially learn meditation in the same fashion as employee/patients do—by means of cassette recordings and a programmed instruction workbook. They are then trained in supervising the training process by company consultants and the company program coordinator. The trainers work in close collaboration with clinicians in the medical department, who have responsibility for individual case management.

Trainers periodically conduct meetings with the medical staff at various branch medical offices to introduce new staff members to meditation and to reinforce or upgrade subject information for old staff members. At these meetings, a videotape describing the use of meditation in clinical practice is shown, followed by discussion of its contents. The videotape covers meditation within an employee health maintenance program and outlines indications and contraindications for its use. The trainer then acquaints the medical staff with the mechanics for referring employees to the meditation training program and discusses any questions that might be raised.

Employees are referred to the program by the medical staff or by self-referral. The SCL-90-R is used as a measurement for eligibility for those who are self-referred and are not currently under care by the medical department. Once employees have been referred to the program, the trainer contacts them by telephone and informs them of the next orientation meeting, at which they can learn about the meditation program and will have an opportunity to decide whether they wish to participate. The program is offered free of charge.

Orientation meetings are held in groups ranging from 10 to 50 people. Here, employees referred to the program are shown a 25-minute videotape, "Relaxing with Meditation," which depicts Dr. Patricia Carrington (an authority on meditation) being interviewed on the subject. On the videotape, Dr. Carrington presents some of the research that has established meditation as a noncultic, "no-nonsense" procedure and provides answers to most of the questions likely to be asked by those unfamiliar with the technique. When it has been shown to groups of prospective trainees, this videotape has proved to be highly effective in encouraging enrollment in the meditation program. To date, over 95% of the employees who have viewed the videotape have signed up for the program.

At the orientation meeting the trainer answers questions about the method, describes the procedures for meditation training, reviews the workbook and selection of a mantra, and works out schedules for home instruction and follow-up meetings. Participating employees leave the orientation meeting with the training materials they will use (in their homes) to learn the meditation technique.

Two weeks into instruction, trainees, who have been assigned to a group (10 to 20 persons), assemble for their first follow-up training session. Here, they learn to handle any problems encountered and to extend the process of meditation beyond the formal 10- to 20-minute sessions by using "mini-meditations"—short meditation sessions lasting 2 to 3 minutes, which can be used strategically throughout the day in addition to regularly scheduled longer sessions. This meeting affords trainees an opportunity to share their experiences and to help each other solve mutual problems. It also serves as an excellent motivator for continued practice.

The trainer holds two additional follow-up meetings over the course of 3 months. These meetings are scheduled for 6 weeks and 3 months postinstruction. At all of the follow-up meetings, the trainer checks on correctness of the practice; takes up problems of scheduling, interruptions, or resistance; encourages group members to share information on benefits derived from the practice; gives instruction in auxiliary techniques that can be combined with CSM or ROM; and encourages participants' continued meditation practice.

Implementation of this meditation training program was begun 2 years ago. It is now operating in all eight company medical offices and so far has enrolled a total of 619 participants in 36 different groups. Twelve of the groups have now been in existence over a year. The candidates for these groups were symptomatic patients referred by professionals in the company medical department. Of the original 166 referred people, 32 (19%) dropped out before actually getting started and 10 (6%) dropped out after learning the technique. The rest (75%) are actively practicing meditation regularly or intermittently as needed.

Observation of SCL-90-R scores of employees in the program has shown the same marked improvement that was found in preceding studies, and individual anecdotal feedback has been very reassuring. There is no question that many of these individuals have profited substantially in meaningful ways. Moreover, it is not an exaggeration to say that some lives have been literally transformed. Objective measurement of the success of the program—in terms of reduced absenteeism, disability, and morbidity and in terms of increased productivity—is being carried out, but it is too early to have results from these measures.

Operational expense for the first 2 years was $60,000, including the cost of program material for participants and the salary and travel, food, and lodging expenses of trainers.

REFERENCES

Carrington, P.; Collings, G. H., Jr.; Benson, H.; Robinson, H.; Wood, L. W.; Lehrer, P. M.; Wollfolk, R. L.; and Cole, J. W. The use of meditation relaxation techniques for the management of stress in a working population. *Journal of Occupational Medicine,* April 1980 **22**(4), 221–231.

Derogatis, L. R. *The SCL90-R manual I: Scoring, administration, and procedures for the SCL90-R.* Baltimore Clinical Psychometric Research, 1977.

CHAPTER 77

EVALUATING HEALTH PROMOTION IN THE WORKPLACE

ROBERT H. L. FELDMAN

University of Maryland

Many companies have developed health promotion programs, but few of these programs have been evaluated and still fewer have been evaluated properly. Company managers want to know whether programs are effective, and employees want to know whether they are worth their time and effort. A program evaluation measures the effects of a program against the goals it sets out to achieve. This evaluation process can contribute to an improvement in subsequent decision making about the program, including ways of enhancing the program (Edwards, Guttentag, & Snapper, 1975; Weiss, 1972). This chapter examines the process of evaluating health promotion programs in workplace settings, including program planning, program monitoring, assessment of program effectiveness, and economic assessment of costs and benefits.

PROGRAM PLANNING

The first step in program planning is to conduct a needs assessment (Warheit, Bell, & Schwab, 1979): What is the prevalence of alcohol abuse among employees? Are enough employees interested in a weight control program to warrant establishing such a program? Thus, the purpose of a needs assessment is to verify that a problem exists and that a program is desired. Green, Kreuter, Deeds, and Partridge (1980) propose a diagnostic approach to program planning. They recommend that an epidemiological diagnosis be conducted to determine whether a problem exists.

In a workplace setting, such a diagnosis would examine the incidence, prevalence, and distribution of health problems within a particular workplace or a group of similar workplaces. Before instituting a smoking cessation program, for example, a company would want to determine the prevalence and distribution of smoking among its employees. In addition, the employees must be interested and willing to participate in the smoking cessation program for the program to be successful; therefore, a survey of employees' attitudes, beliefs, and intentions is required as part of the needs assessment.

The second step in program planning is setting goals and objectives. The planning process consists of stating overall program goals, specific program objectives, and even more specific behavioral objectives (Green et al., 1980). An overall program goal, for example, is to increase exercise among employees. A specific program objective would be to involve 60% of employees in an exercise program by the end of the first year of the program. A specific behavioral objective would be to have 60% of the employees at company A exercising at least 20 minutes three times a week by the end of the first year of the program. The specific behavioral objective asks: *"Who* is expected to achieve *how much* of *what behavior by when?"* (Green et al., 1980, p. 65). An important factor in setting behavioral objectives is the choice of quantifiable outcome measures (Sechrest & Cohen, 1980). In the above example, the quantifiable outcome measure would be exercising at least 20 minutes three times a week. In a smoking cessation program, the quantifiable outcome measure may be smoking no cigarettes or smoking fewer than five cigarettes a day. In a nutrition program, the quantifiable outcome measure may be an increase in nutrition knowledge (e.g., a 40% increase), a change in nutrition attitudes (e.g., 30% more favorable), or modification in diet (e.g., a 20% decrease in sodium intake).

The final step in program planning is setting priorities. Decisions have to be made concerning which programs are to be developed and which are not. Assuming that employee stress is an important health problem, what is the likelihood that a stress reduction program will succeed? Thus, another factor to be considered in planning a program is the changeability of the recommended health behavior associated with the program. Highest priority should be given to those programs that have both the greatest need and the greatest likelihood of making changes in health behavior.

In summary, to properly plan health promotion programs in workplace settings, a number of steps should be taken. First, a needs assessment is necessary to document that a problem exists and that employees are interested in participating in a program. Second, program goals and objectives, specific behavioral objectives, and quantifiable outcome measures should be clearly stated. Third, once the goals and objectives have been stated, program priorities can be developed according to need and the likelihood that the program will be successful. A complete program planning process increases the probability that a program will be implemented as specified and offers an opportunity for a thorough evaluation of the effectiveness of the program.

PROGRAM EVALUATION

A well-designed program evaluation has several objectives. The first objective is the monitoring of an on-going program. Is the program reaching the appropriate target population? Are overweight employees participating in weight reduction programs? Are smokers signing up for the smoking cessation clinic? Also, program monitoring is needed to determine whether the program is being implemented in the way it was designed. Sometimes a program may fail to have an impact because the wrong type of program is presented, a weak version of the intended program is presented, or unstandardized versions of the program are presented to different participants (Rossi & Freeman, 1982).

A second objective of a program evaluation is to obtain *feedback* about the program from program participants (Posavac & Carey, 1980). How do employees like the program? Was the material and information that was presented useful? Did the program meet the employees' expectations, and would they recommend the program to a co-worker?

A third objective of an evaluation is to assess the *effectiveness* or impact of a program. Is the program achieving its goals? Is there a plausible alternative explanation for the obtained result of the program? Numerous evaluation designs have been developed to assess effectiveness. The following discussion examines three evaluation approaches to measuring program effectiveness: true experimental designs, quasi-experimental designs, and approximate methods.

True Experimental Designs

The best evaluation designs are true experimental designs. Although some have said that it is not possible to implement a true experimental design in a corporate, industrial, or other workplace setting, this is not the case (Boruch, 1976). The use of waiting-list control groups, derived from clinical psychology research, is an ethical and practical way of treating this problem. Consider, for example, a company that announces a weight control program for its employees; 60 employees volunteer to take part, but the program can only accommodate 30 participants. The fairest, most ethical, and most practical manner of solving this problem and at the same time providing the opportunity to conduct a rigorous evaluation is to randomize the 60 volunteers into two groups: 30 program participants and 30 waiting-list individuals (the control group). If a program lasts 8 weeks and a second program is scheduled shortly after the conclusion of the first program, the waiting-list group can remain the control group for the time period prior to the start of the second program. The waiting-list group would then have the opportunity—and first priority—to participate in the second program.

To make a proper comparison between a program group and a waiting-list control group, it is necessary to examine the attrition or dropout rate of the two groups. Attention should be paid to the number of participants who drop out of both groups and the type of individual who drops out, in terms of demographic, psychological, and health factors. Also, consideration should be given to whether an individual drops out of the waiting-list control group in order to join a similar group, such as Weight Watchers. Information about dropouts is important in order to determine whether a self-selection bias is present. If a substantial number of motivated employees in the waiting-list control group leave the group to join another weight control program, for example, then differences between the program group and the control group may be due to this differential dropout. The remaining, less motivated individuals in the control group would be compared to the participants in the program group, and motivation, rather than the program itself, may be the explanation for differences between the groups. Therefore, dropout rates should be examined as part of the evaluation process.

One type of true experimental design is the pretest–posttest control group design (Campbell & Stanley, 1966), described as follows:

$$R \quad O_1 \quad X \quad O_2 \qquad \text{Program group}$$
$$R \quad O_3 \qquad\;\; O_4 \qquad \text{Control group}$$

where the R's refer to the randomization of participants, the O's represent the observations or measurements of the participants, and X refers to the program. The aforementioned weight control program with a waiting-list control group could be evaluated with this design. Volunteers would be randomly assigned either to the program group or to the waiting-list control group. Measurements of weight and other relevant factors would be taken before the beginning of the program and at the end of the program. Determination would be made of whether individuals in the program group lost more weight than individuals in the control group.

A second true experimental design can be instituted without pretest measures, as follows:

$$R \quad X \quad O_1 \qquad \text{Program group}$$
$$R \qquad\; O_2 \qquad \text{Control group}$$

This is the posttest-only control group design (Campbell & Stanley, 1966). There are situations when a pretest measurement may influence the attitudes or the behavior of both the program group and the control group. A pretest questionnaire on stress, for example, may influence the stress beliefs and attitudes of the control group or the program group.

Although true experimental designs are advantageous to implement, they can only be used when the target population is much larger than the number of program participants—that is, when the demand exceeds the supply (Cook & Campbell, 1976). A health promotion program designed to reach all employees cannot be evaluated by these designs, because no one will be available to be assigned to the control group. Also, for health promotion programs that have been conducted at a work setting for some time, it may be difficult to find a sufficient number of volunteers who have not participated in the program to form a control group, thus making it unfeasible to use a true experimental design. In addition, in a small work setting, where experimental and control group participants are likely to interact, contamination of effects may result. Thus, such a setting may be unsuitable for a true experimental design.

Quasi-Experimental Designs

When the use of true experimental design is not possible, quasi-experimental designs (Campbell & Stanley, 1966; Cook & Campbell, 1979) are the next best approach. One type of quasi-experimental design is the nonequivalent control group design. When randomizing volunteers to program and control groups is not possible, it is useful to find a nonrandomized comparison group to compare to the program group. Curtis Wilbur (Note 1) reports that when Johnson & Johnson initiated their Live for Life health promotion program, they found that it was not possible to institute a true experimental design evaluation. It was not feasible when instituting their lifestyle improvement program over an entire factory to keep a randomly assigned control group from being exposed to the program. It was also found that random assignment of sites within a company was not possible. Therefore, from among the Johnson & Johnson family of companies, four companies were chosen as the program group and five other companies were chosen as the control group. All program and control groups were located in the same geographical region.

The nonequivalent control group design is diagrammed as follows:

$$O_1 \quad X \quad O_2 \quad \text{Program group}$$

$$O_3 \quad\quad O_4 \quad \text{Control group}$$

As in the previous design the O's refer to observations or measurements and X is the program. The dashed line indicates that the groups are not randomized. Because the groups are not randomized, it is important that the control group closely resemble the program group in all essential aspects. In the evaluation of the Johnson & Johnson health promotion program, it was important that the companies assigned to the program group be as similar as possible to the companies assigned to the control group. It would be beneficial, for example, to ensure that the employees of companies assigned to the program group were not more health conscious than the employees of companies assigned to the control group. If the program group participants were initially more health conscious, a plausible alternative explanation for an improvement in the health and well-being of the program group would be their health consciousness, rather than the program. Matching for particular characteristics at either the individual or aggregate level reduces bias, but it cannot ensure that a difference between the program group and the control group is due to a program effect rather than to the selection of program and control group participants (selection effect). Therefore, although matching is useful, randomization, if at all possible, is a superior method, since it is not possible to match individuals or groups on every relevant factor.

A second quasi-experimental design is the time series design, which is diagrammed as follows:

$$O_1 \quad O_2 \quad O_3 \quad O_4 \quad X \quad O_5 \quad O_6 \quad O_7 \quad O_8$$

When longitudinal measures are available, program participants can be used as their own controls. If good records of employee absenteeism or work-related injuries are available, for example, a time series design can be used to determine the effect of a new program on subsequent absenteeism or injuries. A word of caution about this design is in order. If another event occurs at the same time as the program (for example, installation of new managers or institution of a community or public health campaign), it is not possible to determine whether the program or the other event is causing the changes in the employees.

One way of improving both the time series design and the nonequivalent control group design is to combine the two quasi-experimental designs to form the multiple time series design (Campbell & Stanley, 1966), diagrammed as follows:

$$O_1 \quad O_2 \quad O_3 \quad X \quad O_4 \quad O_5 \quad O_6$$

$$O_7 \quad O_8 \quad O_9 \qquad O_{10} \quad O_{11} \quad O_{12}$$

If data from another factory, company, or institution are available and has been collected in a similar manner, then the multiple time series design is a very powerful evaluation tool. This design yields greater certainty of interpretation because the effectiveness of a program is, in a sense, demonstrated twice—once against the control group (the nonequivalent control group design) and once against the preprogram measures (the time series design). The multiple time series is an excellent design and has clear advantages over the two previous designs. It is only feasible, however, when (a) preprogram measures are available, (b) a second comparison group is available, and (c) all the measurements have been collected in a similar manner throughout the evaluation process.

Approximate Methods

Although true experimental and quasi-experimental designs are the most appropriate ways of evaluating program effectiveness, there are occasions when less rigorous methods are suitable. Since rigorous methods demand time, resources, and technical knowledge, it may be more appropriate to utilize approximate methods for demonstration programs, small projects, or programs with modest budgets. One approximate method is the before–after design without a control group. It can be used to document whether a program is having an impact, but, it does not offer definitive evidence that the program, and no other factor, is the real cause of any change. A second method is the use of postprogram follow-ups, which supply useful information about how individuals have been affected by their participation in a health promotion program.

A third method is a record-keeping procedure, which monitors the progress of program participants. It can yield graphs and charts that demonstrate how a program is doing (Green, 1982). A record-keeping procedure using periodic data collection over a set time interval provides additional benefits. A fourth method is to make comparisons between the results of a particular program and the results of other programs, national results, and well-established norms. Additional methods of evaluating programs involve obtaining assessments of the program from a variety of sources. Assessments by outside experts, program participants, and program administrators all contribute to an understanding of how well the program is meeting its goals. It should be noted that these approximate methods of evaluating programs should not be used where the program is costly, where there is a high likelihood that the program will be expanded to the regional or national level, or where sensitive issues concerning company policy are involved.

ECONOMIC ASSESSMENT

After a health promotion program has been shown to have an impact on the health and well-being of employees, cost-benefit or cost-effectiveness analyses may be conducted. With the spiraling rise of health care costs, more attention is being paid to the costs, benefits, and efficiency of industrial health promotion programs. If the tangible and intangible benefits and costs of a program can be clearly specified, a cost-benefit analysis can be made. A cost-benefit analysis measures, usually in monetary terms, the economic efficiency of a program as a relationship of costs and benefits (Rossi & Freeman, 1982).

For programs whose benefits or goals cannot be easily converted into monetary units or some other common measure, cost-effectiveness analysis would be more appropriate than cost-benefit analysis. Cost-effectiveness analysis measures the efficacy of a program in achieving its goals in relationship to program costs (Rossi & Freeman, 1982). Benefits derived from a health promotion program may include job satisfaction, greater job involvement, improved morale, greater commitment to the organization, improved ability to handle job stress, a better sense of well-being, and a higher level of wellness. These benefits are not easily converted into monetary terms, so that cost-benefit analysis would not be appropriate. If more than one program is being evaluated, cost-effectiveness analysis allows a comparison and ranking of the magnitude of the effectiveness of each program relative to its costs. A group of programs, for example, may have as their goals reducing sick days, increasing worker satisfaction, and increasing a sense of well-being among workers. Three programs are offered: a comprehensive health promotion program, lecture and discussion groups on health, and health education pamphlets. A cost-effectiveness approach could determine which of the three programs is most effective in terms of program goals relative to program costs.

SUMMARY

Evaluation of health promotion programs in workplace settings requires thorough program planning, careful monitoring of program implementation, accurate feedback from participants, and valid assessments of program effectiveness. Program effectiveness can best be measured by true experimental designs. Quasi-experimental designs can be used when randomization of participants is not feasible. For newly introduced modest programs, approximate evaluation methods would be suitable. Once health promotion programs have been shown to have an impact on employee health, cost-benefit or cost-effectiveness analyses would be used. Thus, the evaluation process provides the necessary information for rational decision making concerning the future of health promotion programs in workplace settings.

REFERENCE NOTE

1. Wilbur, C. S. *Live for Life: An epidemiological evaluation of a comprehensive health promotion program.* Workshop presented at the Annual Meeting of the American Psychological Association, Washington, D.C., August 1982.

REFERENCES

Boruch, R. F. On common contentions about randomized field experiments. In G. V. Glass (Ed.), *Evaluation studies review annual.* Beverly Hills, Calif.: Sage, 1976.

Campbell, D. T., & Stanley, J. C. *Experimental and quasi-experimental designs for research.* Chicago: Rand McNally, 1966.

Cook, T. D., & Campbell, D. T. The design and conduct of quasi-experiments and true experiments in field settings. In M. D. Dunnette (Ed.), *Handbook of industrial and organizational research.* Chicago: Rand McNally, 1976.

Cook, T. D., & Campbell, D. T. *Quasi-experimentation: Design and analysis issues for field settings.* Chicago: Rand McNally, 1979.

Edwards, W., Guttentag, M., & Snapper, J. A. A decision-theoretic approach to evaluation research. In E. L. Struening & M. Guttentag (Eds.), *Handbook of evaluation research* (Vol. 1). Beverly Hills, Calif.: Sage, 1975.

Green L. W. Evaluation. In R. S. Parkinson. *Managing health promotion in the workplace.* Palo Alto, Calif.: Mayfield, 1982.

Green, L. W., Kreuter, M. W., Deeds, S. G., & Partridge, K. B. *Health education planning: A diagnostic approach.* Palo Alto, Calif.: Mayfield, 1980.

Posavac, E. J., & Carey, R. G. *Program evaluation: Methods and case studies.* Englewood Cliffs, N.J.: Prentice-Hall, 1980.

Rossi, P. H., & Freeman, H. E. *Evaluation: A systematic approach* (2nd ed.). Beverly Hills, Calif.: Sage, 1982.

Sechrest, L., & Cohen, R. Y. Evaluating outcomes in health care. In G. C. Stone, F. Cohen, & N. E. Adler. *Health psychology: A handbook. Theories, applications, and challenges to a psychological approach to the health care system.* San Francisco: Jossey-Bass, 1980.

Warheit, G. J., Bell, R. A., & Schwab, J. J. *Needs assessment approaches: Concepts and methods.* DHEW Pub. No. (ADM)79–472. Rockville, Md.: National Institute of Mental Health, 1979.

Weiss, C. H. *Evaluation research: Methods of assessing program effectiveness:* Englewood Cliffs, N.J.: Prentice-Hall, 1972.

CHAPTER 78

COMPREHENSIVE SCHOOL HEALTH EDUCATION PROGRAMS

LLOYD J. KOLBE

University of Texas Health Science Center

DONALD C. IVERSON

Mercy Medical Center, Denver

SCHOOL HEALTH EDUCATION PROGRAMS IN THE UNITED STATES

In recent decades, it has become increasingly true and increasingly evident that the health status of individuals and populations largely is determined by health-related behaviors and lifestyles, leading a noted economist to conclude:

> *The greatest current potential for improving the health of the American people is to be found in what they do and don't do for themselves. Individual decisions about diet, exercise, and smoking are of critical importance, and collective decisions affecting pollution and other aspects of the environment are also relevant. (Fuchs, 1974)*

The potential for the American system of public and private education to provide the increasingly complex knowledge and skills required for individuals to make informed and wise choices about personal behaviors and social actions that will influence their health has been well described by the American Public Health Association (1975):

> *The school, as a social structure, provides an educational setting in which the total health of the child during the impressionable years is a priority concern. No other community setting even approximates the magnitude of the grades K–12 school education enterprise, with an enrollment . . . of 45.5 million in nearly 17,000 school districts comprising more than 115,000 schools with some 2.1 million teachers. . . . Thus, it seems that the school should be regarded as a social unit providing a focal point to which health planning for all other community settings should relate.*

The typology of school health education innovations included in this chapter originally was outlined at the National Conference on Promoting Health through the Schools, sponsored by the U.S. Office of Health Information, Health Promotion and Physical Fitness and Sports Medicine, Denver, August 18, 1980. The chapter was prepared, in part, by Lloyd J. Kolbe during his tenure as Chief of the Evaluation Section, U.S. Office of Disease Prevention and Health Promotion, Office of the Assistant Secretary for Health. However, no official support or endorsement by the U.S. Office of Disease Prevention and Health Promotion is intended or should be inferred.

Indeed, since the early part of this century, virtually all major health and education organizations in the United States have called for the establishment and improvement of health education programs in schools (Johnson, 1969; Means, 1975; National Center for Health Education, Note 1).

In 1973, however, *The Report of the President's Committee on Health Education* concluded that "school health education in most primary and secondary schools is not provided at all, or loses its proper emphasis because of the way it is tacked onto another subject such as physical education or biology, assigned to teachers whose interests and qualifications lie elsewhere" (U.S. Department of Health, Education and Welfare, 1973). Hearings conducted by the President's Committee confirmed the conclusions of an earlier study of health education practices in a national sample of school systems, which found a "majority of situations where health instruction is virtually non-existent or where prevailing practices can be legitimately challenged. What passes for a program in far too many instances is dubious" (Sliepcevich, Note 2). Yet, as John Knowles (1977) has noted:

> The behavior of Americans might be changed if there were adequate programs of health education in primary and secondary schools and even colleges—but there aren't. School health programs are abysmal at best, confining themselves to preemptory sick calls and posters on brushing teeth and eating three meals a day; there are no examinations to determine whether anything's been learned. Awareness of danger to body and mind isn't acquired until the mid-twenties in our culture, and by then patterns of behavior are set which are hard to change.

Indeed, school health education programs that are comprehensive (Kolbe, 1981) can provide the scientific and philosophical foundations necessary for individuals to understand personal and societal health issues; they can increase the competencies of individuals to make decisions about personal behaviors that will influence their own health; they can improve the often complex skills required by individuals to actually engage in behaviors that are conducive to health; and they can increase the skills of individuals to maintain and improve the health of the families for which they will become responsible, and the communities in which they will reside (Kolbe, 1982). In addition, to the extent that comprehensive school health education programs are integrated with coordinated efforts to enable and reinforce targeted behaviors (Kolbe & Iverson, 1983), we can expect them to elicit behaviors that are conducive to health (Kolbe, Iverson, Kreuter, Hochbaum, & Christenson, 1981).

The framers of *Healthy People: The Surgeon General's Report on Health Promotion and Disease Prevention* recognized the proper and essential functions that schools must provide in order to improve the health of the nation's children and future citizenry:

> Many factors affect a child's development—genetics, the home environment, the quality of interactions with parents, teachers, health professionals, other adults, peers. With so many influences, no single course of action will protect the future mental, emotional, and physical health of every child and assure realization of full developmental potential. . . .
> But the special importance of the school should be emphasized here.
> Many hours of a child's life are spent in a classroom. Providing health services through school programs can be of great value; so could effective health education.
> Our children could benefit greatly from a basic understanding of the human body and its functioning, needs, and potential—and from an understanding of what really is involved in health and disease.
> There are a number of school systems which have developed good models for health education.
> For other schools to really take on what could be their highly significant role in

health education and health promotion will require a commitment by school leadership at local, State and national levels to apply these models. (U.S. Department of Health, Education & Welfare, 1979)

INNOVATIONS THAT COMPRISE SCHOOL HEALTH EDUCATION PROGRAMS

To describe the nature and status of health education programs in schools (or in other settings), and to establish a conceptual framework for analyzing and facilitating the implementation of such programs, it is necessary to delineate and differentiate just what is to be implemented. As Schutz and Niedermeyer (Note 3) state:

> *Current thinking on implementation in human service sectors . . . is mushy at best regarding such distinctions. Technical as well as everyday parlance uses the term "program" with great abandon to permit communication to proceed when typically neither the generator nor recipient of the communication is at all clear about the phenomena involved. Thus a program can range from a wish to a world, with all manners and matters of conceptual variation in between.*

To address this enigma, Schutz and Niedermeyer developed a typology that comprises nine categories of educational innovations that are commonly implemented to provide school instruction, including: legislated rights, categorical grants, curricular structures, materials-embodied products, organizational structures, personnel training, professional techniques, specialist personnel assistance, and technical system assistance (Schutz & Niedermeyer, Note 3). An educational innovation may be conceived as any new (i.e., different) policy, process, or organizational practice, even if the innovation is well established for the educational system as a whole but is new only to the particular class, school, or district (Pincus, 1974). A typology of school health education innovations can structure otherwise disparate information about school health education, its organization, and its status; can permit identification of different innovations that school health personnel and decision makers might consider for their own unique situations; and can allow for analysis of relative strengths and weaknesses of innovations within and between categories.

Indeed, to initiate or improve health education programs in schools, those involved should be able to review all potentially available relevant innovations in order to (a) assess the desirability of each; (b) determine the feasibility of implementing those that are desired; (c) anticipate the possible positive and negative effects of implementing those that are feasible in terms of resources, means, constraints, and other influential factors in the specific school and community environment; (d) identify those innovations that seem to hold the most promise; and (e) combine, if possible, those that might provide synergistic effects. For the purposes of such examination, nine categories comprising a typology of health education innovations available for implementation in schools will be described here. Analyses of characteristics that influence the diffusion of the health education innovations delineated in this chapter, and of the social change processes by which they are implemented in schools, have been described elsewhere (Kolbe & Iverson, 1981, Note 4).

CATEGORY ONE: LEGISLATED RIGHTS AND ADMINISTRATIVE REGULATIONS

The roles and functions of federal, state, and local education agencies in the United States have evolved from the broad doctrine that education is a national concern, a state responsibility, and a local function. Educational rights are legislated predominantly by state agencies (Cawelti, 1976; Hall & Brinson, 1978; Phillips & Hawthorne, 1978), although federal and local legislation also influence the nature of school programs. Legislation for school health education (Clifton, Edwards, & Morelle, 1974; Creswell, Tritsch, Jubb, & Hill, 1973; Solleder, 1981; Stein, 1973; Torney, 1981), means to effect the legislative process (Bedworth, 1977; Ervin, 1982; Henderson & Cortese, 1981; Kane, 1982; Kummel, 1973; Leviton, 1977; Lucas, Floss, Madison, & Sova, 1973; Newman & Wilson, 1980; Owens, 1975; Taub, 1980), and analyses of the outcomes of such legislation (Conley & Jackson, 1978; Meeds, 1973; Miller, 1972; Newman & Wilson, 1978) have been addressed by numerous authors.

At the federal level, although the standards were never finalized and implemented, in 1978 the Department of Health, Education and Welfare, in response to requirements of Section 1501 of the National Health Planning and Resources Development Act of 1974 (PL 93–641), proposed the following:

> Health education and promotion programs, under full-time professional direction and having adequate resources (personnel, materiel, funds, and facilities) shall be located in: health departments and federally funded health agencies serving 100,000 or more population, school districts having 10,000 or more students, and Federal agencies having an identifiable employee health program. (U.S. Department of Health, Education and Welfare, 1978) [emphasis added]

In 1981, the Education Commission of the States conducted a nationwide survey to analyze the nature of state policies for school health education (Noak, 1982b) and, with the American School Health Association and the U.S. Center for Health Promotion and Education, published School Health in America: A Survey of State School Health Programs (Castille, Allensworth, & Noak, 1981). In addition to providing similar information about the other two components of the school health program (i.e., school health services and efforts to ensure a healthful school environment), for each state the publication describes the state agency and individual responsible for school health education; the legal basis for school health education; special appropriations; state board of education policy statements; other state board actions; mandatory topics and grade levels; time requirements; health education graduation requirements; the state health education curriculum guide; the school health education specialist; the role of the specialist; other health-related staff; availability of separate or dual certification (most often with physical education) to teach health; certification requirements for elementary health education teachers; certification requirements for secondary school health education teachers; certification requirements for elementary classroom teachers; school health education evaluation projects; and coordination of school health education with voluntary and other health agencies.

The survey revealed that education codes in 43 states addressed health education in some manner (Noak, 1982b). Thirty-seven states required that either some form of generic school health education or some specific health education subject matter (e.g., the effects of alcohol and drugs on health) be included as part of the public school curriculum; six other states strongly recommended and endorsed school health education. Many of these codes, however, specify neither the scope nor the amount of time that should be provided for health education, and many others are disregarded because they are seriously antiquated. Although the inclusion of health education in state education codes is some indication of support, legislative mandates do not guarantee the effectiveness or even the existence of school health education programs (Conley & Jackson, 1978). The effects of these codes depend variably upon the sanctions and incentives included in the legislation and on the support and interest of the state legislature, the state board of education, the chief state school officer, the state education agency, and personnel within each of the regional and local educational agencies established within the state. It is important to note that only 9 legislatures among the 43 states that address health education in their state codes had appropriated specific fiscal resources for the implementation of health education programs in schools (California, Colorado, Florida, Illinois, New York, Nebraska, North Carolina, Utah, and Vermont) (Castille et al., 1981).

In addition to the state legislatures, state boards of education also often are empowered to determine curriculum requirements and to issue guidelines, standards, rules, and regulations for program development and implementation. The state school health education survey revealed that 38 state boards of education addressed school health education in various ways, including policy or position statements, resolutions, guidelines, and administrative regulations or bylaws (Noak, 1982b). Thus, through a combination of various legislated rights and administrative regulations, numerous states have included completion of health education coursework as a requirement for high school graduation; have designated separate certification for health education teachers; have assigned state agency personnel to facilitate and coordinate school health education in the state; have provided for the establishment of a state coordinating group on school health education; and have provided for the generation of a state health education curriculum or planning guide.

The school health education state survey revealed that 24 states have supported health education programs in schools by requiring successful completion of a specified amount of health coursework as a requirement for high school graduation (Noak, 1982b). In addition, since the quality of health education is largely determined by the professional preparation and interest of teachers, 41 states designated a separate certification or endorsement (requiring a certain amount of relevant preservice or in-service training) for health education teachers in the secondary schools (Noak, 1982b). Five states designate certification for elementary school health education, and six states designate combined elementary and secondary certification (K–12), although aspiring elementary teachers in 25 states are required to take some coursework in health education as part of their teacher preparation programs (Castille et al., 1981).

Forty-eight state education agencies employ a professional to facilitate and coordinate school health education within the state. These individuals frequently have backgrounds and assignments as general curriculum, physical education, or health education consultants and, often with other responsibilities, may contribute from 25% to 100% of their time to health education (Noak, 1982b). State school health or health education coordinating groups have been established in 39 states (Noak, 1982b). Functioning in an advisory, coordinating, and/or advocacy capacity, these groups may include representatives of state education and health agencies; institutions of higher education; parent, teacher, and student organizations; local education and health agencies; and voluntary health agencies.

Finally, curriculum or planning guides for school health education have been published by 35 states (Noak, 1982b). These guides are designed to assist personnel in local education agencies in meeting legislated mandates and to help local personnel implement high-quality, up-to-date school health education programs.

Although state agencies may recommend topics to be included in the health education curriculum and may provide technical assistance in program development, personnel in local school systems make the final decisions about specific content to be included, instructional materials, teaching methods, and teacher qualifications. Within a given state, there may be substantial variance in the amount of interest and activity in school health education among various localities, irrespective of state legislation and administrative regulations.

The American Medical Association (Note 5) was one of the first organizations to draft "Model Legislation for Comprehensive School Health Education." Also recognizing the potential role that state policymakers could play in school health education, the American Council of Life Insurance and the Health Insurance Association of America enabled the Education Commission of the States to convene a national task force of leaders in the fields of health and education to develop a policy statement that would provide a model by which states might express an effective commitment to school health education. The resulting "Suggested Policy Statement on School Health Education for State Boards of Education" includes a strong statement of philosophical support that emphasizes the importance of health education within the educational process; a statement of the state school board's intent to assist local agencies in program development; a commitment of state resources; and specific recommendations to guide districts in program planning and development, staffing, curriculum formulation, and assignment of instructional time for health education (Noak, 1981, and 1982a).

CATEGORY TWO: GRANTS

Comprehensive school health education programs, by their very nature, provide for a broad and integrated accumulation of learning and experiences that, more effectively than categorical programs (e.g., drug education, nutrition education), might result in the development of healthy lifestyles (Kolbe & Iverson, 1980).

Yet it is the comprehensive nature of such programs that also serves to diminish their support in the categorically oriented funding arena. Although $10 million was authorized by the U.S. Congress for comprehensive school health education programs in 1979 (U.S. Superintendent of Documents, 1978), and regulations were developed to support state and local education agency activities to plan, implement, and coordinate school health education programs (U.S. Superintendent of Documents, 1979; Conway, 1979a, 1979b, 1979c), program funds never were appropriated (Conway, 1979d, 1979e, 1979f; Conway, 1980a, 1980b, 1980c). Indeed, the Office of Comprehensive School Health, which was established within the U.S. Department of Education to administer the grant program and to provide a federal focal point for school health efforts, was dismantled with the reorganization of the Department of Education in 1982.

In 1980, there were programs in at least 28 federal agencies whose legislative authorizations, objectives, and guidelines clearly provided opportunities for the utilization of funds and resources to implement or improve health education and services in the nation's schools. A description of these programs, agencies, those who are eligible to apply for funds, intended recipients, and other relevant information was prepared by the Director of the Office of Comprehensive School Health in that same year (Cortese, Note 6). Provided an effective rationale and coordination, categorical grants from many of these programs (e.g., Nutrition Education and Training Program, Adolescent Parenting/Pregnancy Initiative, National Diffusion Network) had been used in various ways to stimulate and support health education programs in schools throughout the nation (Kolbe & Iverson, Note 4).

Perhaps most significant among federal categorical grant programs was the Health Education-Risk Reduction Grant Program, established by Congress in 1979 under Section 1703(a) of the Public Health Service Act (U.S. Superintendent of Documents, 1979a). Administered by the Center for Health Promotion and Education at the Centers for Disease Control, the primary purpose of this program was to assist state and local health agencies to initiate, strengthen, and become the focal points for delivery of health education programs (U.S. Center for Health Promotion and Education, 1981a). In 1980, Congress appropriated an additional $10 million for grant programs to deter smoking and the use of alcoholic beverages among children and adolescents, and placed the appropriation within the Health Education-Risk Reduction Grant Program (U.S. Superintendent of Documents, 1980a). Thus, $15.9 million was awarded in 1980 to projects in all 50 state health departments, and in Washington, D.C., Guam, Puerto Rico, and the U.S. Virgin Islands. As part of these 54 state and territorial projects, 21 local intervention projects initiated in 1979 received continued funding and 144 new local intervention projects were funded. . . . Of the total 165 local intervention projects funded in 1980, 78 (47% of the total) were located within a school setting exclusively, while 111 (67% of the total) were located within some combination of a school setting and at least one other setting (i.e., community organization, church, health department, professional organization, hospital/clinic, neighborhood center). A description of each state project and local intervention can be found in the publication *Health Education-Risk Reduction Grant Program* (U.S. Center for Health Promotion and Education, 1981a).

By the inauguration of Ronald Reagan in January 1981, the federal government was funding and operating 534 categorical grant-in-aid programs, most of them delivering some service. The president proposed in March 1981 that a number of health services programs managed at the federal level be consolidated into block grants and transferred to the states, based on the assumption that the states could respond more effectively to the specific health needs of their citizens (Brandt, Note 7). Congress did not accept the entire proposal, but it did shift the authority of some 22 programs back to the states and localities in the *Omnibus Budget Reconciliation Act of 1981* (U.S. Superintendent of Documents, 1981). This law folded together similar categorical grant-in-aid health programs into four block grants to the states: one for preventive services; another for alcohol, drug abuse, and mental health projects; a third for maternal and child health services; and a fourth concerned with primary care. At this writing, although there has been some speculation about the effects that reforging federal categorical health grants into state health block grant programs will have on school health education programs (Duval, 1981), the operational changes required by the health block grants and their attending effects have yet to be analyzed (American Public Health Association, 1982). Similar to the consolidation of federal categorical health grant programs into state health block grants, the *Omnibus Budget Reconciliation Act* channeled together numerous federal categorical educational grant programs into a single educational block grant authorization to the states. Like the health block grant authorization, the educational block grant authorization allows the states to support school health education programs in numerous and varied ways with block grant funds, if they so choose (U.S. Superintendent of Documents, 1981). Given that the total amount of grant-in-aid funds has been reduced by about 25% and given the competition that exists within the states for both health and education funds from the respective block grant programs, without appropriate initiative and organization to secure such funds for school health education programs within each state, it is unlikely that more than a small fraction of these funds will be used to support school health education.

In addition to federal, state, and local government support, philanthropic, community, and voluntary health organizations sometimes provide grant support for school health education. Two documents provide useful information for securing funding for school health education from these six types of sources: "Grantsmanship for School Health Education," first published by the American Alliance for Health Education and then distributed through the National Center for Health Education (Sliepcevich, 1978); and "Locating Funds for Health Promotion," distributed by the U.S. Office of Health Information and Health Promotion (1980).

CATEGORY THREE: CURRICULAR STRUCTURES

Curricular structures often are devised to provide a framework for the scope, sequence, perspective, and scheduling of health education in schools. As described previously, 35 states have published state curriculum or planning guides, although the presence of such a guide does not ensure that it will be referenced for instructional planning. Kupsinel (1980) recently published a descriptive analysis of these state health education curricular structures.

Curricular structures provide conceptual as well as practical frameworks for instructional planning. As such, they may prescribe the format for one or some combination of at least four interrelated facets of curriculum innovation. First, curricular structures often prescribe the scope of content to be included. Health education curricular structures may suggest, for example, that nutrition, drug abuse, exercise, and first aid should be included in instruction and that, by omission from the structure, community health, aging, and environmental health should not.

Second, curricular structures often prescribe the sequence of learning activities. One health education curriculum structure might suggest an in-depth emphasis on drug abuse at the seventh grade level, sex education at the eighth grade, community health at the ninth grade, and so on. Another might call for more superficial learning about a larger number of content areas at lower grade levels, with increasing (spiraling) sophistication of the same content as the students progress developmentally and academically through the upper grades. The *Health Education Curricular Progression Chart* developed by the National Center for Health Education (Note 8), for example, outlines the scope and sequence of health education content that might be included at each grade level from kindergarten through grade twelve.

Third, curricular structures often prescribe pedagogical and metaphysical perspectives from which to reference instructional planning. The School Health Curriculum Study, for example, generated a curriculum structure based on a conceptual approach to teaching and learning (Russell, 1966). Three key concepts (growing and developing, decision making, and interactions) provided a framework for curricula by characterizing the perceived processes underlying health (i.e., the three key concepts). Perspectives from which to reference instructional planning for health were first reviewed by Cushman (1969). Since that review, other perspectives have been advanced, including a conceptual approach (School Health Education Study, 1967), a behavioral objectives approach (Nagel, 1970), an ecological perspective (Hoyman, 1965, 1975, 1977), a life-cycle approach (Hoyman, 1977), a skills approach (Parcel, 1976), a diagnostic approach (Green, Kreuter, Deeds, & Partridge, 1980), and a wellness approach (Bruhn & Cordova, 1977, 1978). Pollock (1969) has claimed, however, that curriculum structures too often result from a "gamesmanship approach."

Fourth, curricular structures often define the manner in which health education should be scheduled into the school program. Direct health education provides for class periods designated solely for the purpose of health instruction, whereas correlated health education provides for the inclusion of health information in related subject matter classes, such as home economics, science, or psychology. In integrated health education, health issues are addressed in several subject matter classes according to a given theme (such as environmental science, social adjustment, or survival skills). With incidental health education, health content is addressed when issues are raised spontaneously by students. It is generally agreed that direct health education is distinctly preferable to correlated, integrated, or incidental health education for several important reasons (Kolbe, 1981).

To serve functions somewhat similar to curriculum guides, several state departments of education and other organizations have published checklists by which to assess the quality of local school health programs, including the school health education component (California Department of Education, Note 9; Indiana Congress of Parents and Teachers, Note 10; Joint Committee on School Health, Note 11; Ohio Department of Education, Note 12; Oregon Department of Education, Note 13; West Virginia School Health Development and Education Project, Note 14).

In addition, several state departments of education and other organizations have published manuals to describe step-by-step procedures by which health education programs can be implemented or improved in schools (Grace, 1978; Michaels, 1978; National PTA, 1981a; Region VII Center for Health Planning, 1979; Schlesinger, 1981; U.S. Center for Health Promotion and Education, 1981; U.S. General Accounting Office, 1982).

CATEGORY FOUR: EDUCATIONAL PRODUCT-SYSTEMS

The term *educational product-system* shall be used here instead of the term coined by Schutz and Niedermeyer (Note 3)—that is, "materials-embodied products"—since product-system portrays more accurately the category of innovations included. Educational product-systems generally are designed to be somewhat self-contained educational packages that can be effectively and efficiently disseminated and used by numerous schools. Product-systems usually result from systematic approaches to curriculum development, characterized by collaboration among subject matter specialists, practitioners, and researchers and by extensive pilot-testing and field-based evaluation. The product-system package generally includes some combination of the following: demonstration and dissemination activities; teacher train-

Table 78.1   School Health Education Product-Systems

Product-System	Description
The Primary Grades Health Curriculum Project (PGHCP) (U.S. Center for Health Promotion and Education, 1980) and the School Health Curriculum Project (SHCP) (U.S. Center for Health Promotion and Education, 1977)	The PGHCP has been designed for students in grades K–3, and the SHCP has been designed for students in grades 4–7. Each project includes a planned sequential curriculum, a variety of teaching methods, a teacher-training program, and strategies for eliciting community support for school health education.
Know Your Body (Williams, Carter, & Eng, 1979)	Designed to motivate children to reduce risk of future disease by providing medical screening for risk factors, by explaining to the students their own results, and by following up with educational activities integrated into existing school curricula.
Quest: Skills for Living (Quest, Note 15)	Designed to provide senior high school students and their parents with information and experiences to clarify and enhance their self-understanding, decision-making skills, self-concept, and values.
Actions for Health (Health Services Research Center, Note 16)	Designed for students in grades K–6, the first two of four modules (decision making, self-reliance, body cues, and balanced living) establish a foundation for decision making. Body cues teaches self-care for the most common health problems of the age group; and balanced living places health needs within the context of other needs.
Feeling Fit (Biological Sciences Curriculum Study, Note 17)	Designed for 10- to 14-year-olds, Feeling Fit is one module of the Human Sciences Program. Characterized as activity-centered, personalized, developmentally based, and interdisciplinary, the 50 activities included address three major questions: What makes me healthy? How does my health depend on others? How does my community protect my health?
An Early Start to Good Health (American Cancer Society, Note 18) and Health Networks (American Cancer Society, Note 19)	An Early Start to Good Health has been designed for students in grades K–3, and Health Networks has been designed for students in grades 4–7. Each multimedia unit is designed to provide positive experiences, to create awareness about what is good and bad for the self, to demonstrate the need for taking personal responsibility for good health, and to teach the skills of making choices.

Table 78.1 (*Continued*)

Product-System	Description
Teenage Health Teaching Modules (Education Development Center, 1981)	Sixteen separate modules have been designed for secondary school teachers to use together, as an introductory survey course on health; or to use separately, as supplements to existing curricula. Each module is a complete teaching package, including a teacher's guide, with some pages designed to be duplicated for student handbooks.
Chicago Heart Health Curriculum Project, (Sunseri, Alberti, Cruc, Kent, Vickers, & Amuwo, 1983; Sunseri, Schoenberger, Beckman, & Cruc, 1980).	Utilizing a humanistic education approach, this program aims to affect lifestyle patterns by influencing the decision-making process.
Health Education Curriculum Guides, (Brooks, Kirkpatrick, & Howard, 1981)	Developed by the United Way of Canton, Ohio, the guides include about 375 activities that comprise health education "cookbooks" for teachers of students in grades K–6.
Putting Your Heart Into the Curriculum (American Heart Association, 1982)	This extensive product-system includes a series of resource guides and teaching modules for teachers of students in grades K–12. Materials referenced are available from local chapters of the American Heart Association.

ing; implementation procedures; curriculum guides; teaching activities, materials, and resources; parental and community involvement activities; and evaluation materials and procedures. Table 78.1 provides a short list and brief description of several school health education product-systems.

More than 100 school health education product-systems that can be replicated in other schools are described in *A Compendium of Health Education Programs Available for Use in Schools* (National Center for Health Education, 1982). For each product-system, the target audience is identified by grade level, goals of the program are stated, a description of the program is offered, materials and implementation requirements are listed, reported evaluation information is summarized, developmental funding sources are identified, and the names, addresses, and telephone numbers of staff to contact for more information about the programs are provided.

CATEGORY FIVE: ORGANIZATIONAL STRUCTURES

The preface to *Comprehensive Health Education Management Model* (Florida Department of Education, 1980) states:

> *A comprehensive school health education program is comprehensive not only in its content, but in its organization and implementation. It requires administrative support, active ongoing management, and community involvement at all levels.*

To facilitate behavioral and environmental adaptations that will maintain or improve health, school health promotion efforts must coordinate and integrate school health education interventions with other organizational, political, and economic interventions, involving

Table 78.2   Organizational Structures for School Health Education

Organizational Structure	Description
Maine School Health Education Project (Walker, Miller, Duby, Topinka, Carney, & Dunham, Note 20)	The project is a cooperative venture of the University of Maine at Farmington's Health Education Resource Center and the Maine Department of Educational and Cultural Services, to develop, implement, and evaluate locally developed K–12 comprehensive health education curricula in Maine's school districts.
Florida Managerial Model (Florida Department of Education, 1980)	The model describes several major management functions to be carried out by agencies operating at state, regional, district, school, or liaison levels. It addresses advocacy for school health education; a clearinghouse activity to acquire, review, and distribute information about available resources; coordination to reduce duplication of efforts and facilitate collaboration; evaluation to gather data on the efficiency and effectiveness of health education; and innovation to foster the adoption of new instructional methods and resources.
Genessee Regional Health Education Program (Sorenson & Sinacore, 1979)	Designed to stimulate and coordinate all health education activities (including school health) in the region, and to realize the synergistic potential provided by integrating existing programs, resources, and expertise.
Youth Gives A Damn (Loya, 1974)	A school-based youth organization designed to generate and sponsor various health-related activities during nonschool hours.
Youth Participation in the Community (National Commission on Resources for Youth, Note 21)	Various programs by which students learn about health by teaching or providing services to others.
New York Academy of Medicine's School Health Education Initiative (New York Academy of Medicine, Note 22)	Convened by the New York Academy of Medicine, a coalition of private, voluntary, and public organizations are providing stimulation, organization, and support for the implementation of health education programs in New York City schools.
Health Systems Agency Efforts (Comprehensive Health Planning of Northwest Illinois, Note 23; Middle Tennessee Health Systems Agency, Note 24; Southeast Nebraska Health Systems Agency, Note 25)	Several health systems agencies have provided various organizational structures by which to implement school health education programs.
Oakland County School Health Curriculum Project (Oakland County Office of Substance Abuse, Note 26)	The Oakland County (Michigan) Office of Substance Abuse Services, within the Oakland County Department of Health, has co-

Table 78.2 *(Continued)*

Organizational Structure	Description
	ordinated the efforts and resources of various state and county governmental agencies and private and voluntary health organizations to implement health education in schools of that county.

legislators, health planners, professional and voluntary health groups, and agencies of government. Thus, in addition to more traditional methods used to organize school health education only within the educational system, several other methods have been used to organize school health education more broadly. These methods are identified and briefly described in Table 78.2.

CATEGORY SIX: PERSONNEL TRAINING

Training in school health education can range from a 2-day in-service workshop on a given topic, such as alcohol education, to the 7 years required to complete a doctoral program in school health education. Colleges and universities, local and state health agencies, local and state education agencies, and voluntary and professional health organizations frequently sponsor in-service seminars and workshops on various issues in school health education. In-service training also is provided as a component of many of the school health education product-systems identified previously.

To provide the professional preparation required to effectively implement, maintain, and improve comprehensive health education programs in schools, the Centers for Disease Control has estimated that, of the 252 institutions of higher education that offer at least one degree program in community or school health education, 227 offer baccalaureate programs, 123 offer master's programs, and 40 offer doctoral programs in school health education (U.S. Bureau of Health Professions, 1982). Indeed, of the estimated 25,000 school, community, patient, and worksite health educators in the United States, school health educators constitute the largest subgroup, comprising probably 20,000 professionals (Hall, Jackson, & Parsons, 1980; National Center for Health Statistics, 1979; Simonds, 1976; U.S. Bureau of Health Professions, 1982). Koski (Note 27) has conducted an analysis of health education professional preparation programs; and listings of institutions that offer degree programs in school health education, and the types of degrees they offer, can be found in *A National Directory of College and University Health Education Programs and Faculties* (Eta Sigma Gamma Professional Health Science Honorary, 1982) and in the *American Association for Health Education Directory of Institutions Offering Specialization in Undergraduate and Graduate Professional Preparation Programs in Health Education* (Association for the Advancement of Health Education, 1979).

With support from the U.S. Bureau of Health Professions (1978), commonalities and differences in the preparation and practice of health educators in school, community, and medical care settings have been analyzed. A plan that could lead to establishment of a credentialing system for health educators among those settings was initiated by the National Center for Health Education with support from the Bureau of Health Professions (Henderson, Wolle, Cortese, & McIntosh, 1981). As a result of implementing part of that plan, specific responsibilities, functions, skills, and knowledge generically required by health educators have been delineated (National Center for Health Education, Note 28) and have been verified and refined (Henderson, 1981). General progress, barriers, and issues in the establishment of such a credentialing system have been described (U.S. Department of Health Information,

1981), and the significance of such a credentialing system for school health education in particular has been addressed (Henderson, 1982).

Training to implement or actually conduct health education programs for schoolchildren is provided for educational administrators, relevant community members, parents, and peers through several different innovations. In one example, initiated by the annual Seaside Conference in Oregon (Dosch & Paxton, 1981; Drolet, Note 29; Passwater, Slater, & Tritsch, Note 30), several states convene annual retreats at which teams of teachers, administrators, and community leaders from various schools experience the elements of a healthy lifestyle, learn about the nature of comprehensive school health education programs, and prepare action plans to implement such programs in their own schools. The Oregon Department of Education (Note 31) has prepared a step-by-step guide that has been used by other state education agencies as a template for planning their own unique state retreats.

As another example, the Maryland School and Community Alcohol and Other Drugs Project (Maryland Department of Education, Note 32) convenes a team of 19 members from a given school-community site to train and assist them in designing and implementing comprehensive programs to reduce the impact of alcohol and drug abuse on school students. Seven members of the team comprise the "school cluster," which includes school administrators, schoolboard members, school guidance and curriculum directors, and students. The "family/parent cluster" includes two parents of students from each of the community elementary, middle, and high schools; and the "community resources cluster" includes one representative each from the clergy, alcohol treatment agencies, drug treatment agencies, legal organizations, local government, and local business agencies.

As a third illustration, recognizing the need expressed by parents, the Centers for Disease Control awarded a contract to Mathtech, Inc., to develop, implement, and evaluate a model program that would help parents in their role as primary sexuality educators of their children (U.S. Center for Health Promotion and Education, 1982a–1982e, Note 33). The contractor identified and reviewed all programs designed to improve parent–child communication about sexuality, assessed the impact of these programs, developed model curricula for use with parents, developed additional curricula for use with parents who simultaneously take a sexuality education course with their adolescent children, and developed methods for establishing community support, training teachers, and designing, implementing, and evaluating programs based on the curricula described.

As a final example, several investigators have shown promising results in using peers to provide health education about a variety of subjects (Newman, 1970; Evans, 1976; Evans, Rozelle, & Mittlemark, 1978; McAlister, Perry, Killen, Slinkard, & Macoby, 1980; Perry, Killen, Telch, Slinkard, & Danaher, 1980; Evans, Rozelle, Maxwell, Raines, Dill, Guthrie, Henderson, & Hill, 1981; Perry, & Murray, 1982).

CATEGORY SEVEN: PROFESSIONAL TECHNIQUES

Professional techniques of school health education indeed are incorporated among many of the previously identified innovations. In general, professional techniques can be dichotomized into two subcategories: models of teaching and teaching methods. Models of teaching essentially are strategies based on the theories and research of educators, psychologists, philosophers, sociologists, and others who have attempted to describe how people learn. Each model is based on a theory of learning and may include a rationale, a series of steps (actions or behaviors) to be taken by the teacher and the learner, a description of necessary support systems, and a method for evaluating the learner's progress (Ellis, 1979). Some models are designed to help students grow in self-awareness or creativity; some foster the development of self-discipline or responsible participation in a group; some stimulate inductive reasoning or theory building; and others provide for mastery of subject matter (Ellis, 1979). Joyce and Weil (1979) have identified more than 80 distinct models of teaching

Table 78.3   Selected Models of Teaching

Category	Representative Models
Social interaction models	Group investigation Social inquiry Laboratory method Jurisprudential Role playing Social simulation
Information-processing models	Inductive thinking model Inquiry-training model Scientific inquiry Concept attainment Cognitive growth Advanced organizer model Memory
Personal models	Nondirective teaching Awareness training Synectics Conceptual systems Social problem solving
Behavior modification/cybernetic models	Programmed instruction Managing behavior Relaxation Anxiety reduction Assertiveness training Simulation Direct training

and have categorized them into four groups. A selection of the models included in each group is given in Table 78.3.

In most cases, many different teaching methods can be used with a given model of teaching. Teaching methods include audiovisual presentations, demonstrations, discussions, experiments, field experiences, games, group work, independent study, individualized instruction, lecture, reading, and simulations. As with teaching models, different teaching methods are variously effective in attaining different types of objectives and should be selected accordingly (Green et al., 1980; Joyce & Weil, 1978).

CATEGORY EIGHT: SPECIALIST PERSONNEL ASSISTANCE

The involvement and assistance of key personnel in planning and implementing health education programs in schools can be critical to the success of such efforts (Nix, 1970). The annual *Directory of the Society of State Directors of Health, Physical Education, and Recreation* includes the names, titles, and addresses of school health education specialists in each state who might be able to provide assistance themselves, and who might identify others in the state with relevant expertise. As listed in Table 78.4, many school and community health and education professionals can provide various types of expertise and support to initiate and improve health education programs in schools. In addition to health and education professionals, parents can and should play an important role in planning and

Table 78.4 Specialist Personnel Assistance

Specialist Personnel	Description
Health educators	In the community, individuals with professional training and experience in school health education, community health education, and sometimes patient education can provide assistance in planning, implementing, and evaluating school health promotion efforts.
School nurses, school physicians, school psychologists	Nurses, physicians, and psychologists, assigned responsibility for the physical and emotional well-being of children in a given school, district, county, or state, can provide assistance.
State Department of Education personnel	Personnel who are assigned responsibility for school health education, school health services, and a healthful school environment can provide assistance.
State Department of Health personnel	Personnel who are assigned responsibility for maternal and child health, drug and alcohol abuse prevention, nutrition, mental health, communicable disease control, and Early and Periodic Screening, Diagnosis, and Treatment Programs (EPSDT) can provide assistance.
Community health and safety personnel	Program planning, implementation, and evaluation assistance can be provided by pediatricians; firemen; emergency medical personnel; traffic safety specialists; alcohol, drug abuse, and mental health counselors; dentists; nutritionists; social workers; staffs of voluntary health agencies; and health planners.
School nutritionists	Those who are responsible for school nutrition programs can provide assistance.
School physical education faculty	Physical education faculty often can provide assistance in planning, implementing, and evaluating exercise and fitness programs.

implementing school health education programs (Berclay, 1977; Berson, 1979; Michigan Department of Education, 1980; Miller & Hammer, 1979; Myren, 1971; Slack, 1979; Spiker, 1978; Nader, Note 34), as should students themselves (National PTA, 1981b).

CATEGORY NINE: TECHNICAL SYSTEM ASSISTANCE

Several documents provide comprehensive information about public and private agencies, organizations, and associations at federal, state, and local levels that can provide technical assistance for school health education programs. *A Guide to Organizations, Agencies and Federal Programs in Health Education* (Conway, 1980a) is published by the staff of *Health Education Reports*. *Locating Funds for Health Promotion Projects* is published by the U.S. Office of Health Information and Health Promotion (1980). *Selected Sources of Instructional Materials: A National Directory of Sources on Instructional Materials in Health Education, Patient Education, and Safety Education* is published by Eta Sigma Gamma Professional Health Science Honorary (1980). *Selected References and Resources in Health Education (Third Edition)* is published by the National Center for Health Education and the U.S. Centers for Disease Control (Beyrer & Solleder, 1983). These four documents describe hundreds of potential sources of technical assistance for school health education programs.

In addition, the National Health Information Clearinghouse has been developed to identify health information resources, to channel requests for information to the appropriate health information resource, and to help community organizations respond to their clientele (U.S. Office of Health Information, Note 35). By providing a data base of resources for health information, an inquiry and referral service, and a source of relevant and timely publications, the National Health Information Clearinghouse serves as an appropriate routing center for requests about technical assistance for school health education programs.

CONCLUSION

Given the mandates for the nation's schools to provide timely and comprehensive health education programs for our young people, and given the wide array and continuing evolution of health education innovations that have been developed for implementation by schools, no child or adolescent should be denied the opportunity to understand how their behaviors will influence the quality of health that they will experience throughout life. Having completed their high school education, no adult should be ignorant about the consequences of individual decisions and social actions that ultimately will influence the health of their families and the communities in which their families reside. To the extent that the educational system fails to gain pace in disseminating and accumulating the complex understandings about health and the human actions that influence it, we can expect that our people will be considerably less healthy than they could be.

REFERENCE NOTES

1. National Center for Health Education. *A compilation of organizational statements that support health education in schools.* San Francisco: National Center for Health Education, 1981. (Mimeographed)

2. Sliepcevich, E. *School Health Education Study: Summary report of a nationwide study of health instruction in the public schools.* Washington, D.C.: School Health Education Study, 1964.

3. Schutz, R., & Niedermeyer, F. *A typology of phenomena commonly implemented in school instruction* (Southwest Regional Laboratory Technical Note No. TN 5–78–04). Los Alamitos, Calif.: Southwest Regional Laboratory, 1978.

4. Kolbe, L., & Iverson, D. Implementing comprehensive school health education. In U.S. Office of Health Information, Health Promotion, and Physical Fitness and Sports Medicine, *Promoting Health through the Schools: A National Conference.* Unpublished conference proceedings, 1980.

5. American Medical Association, Health Education Department. *Model legislation for comprehensive school health education.* Chicago: American Medical Association, no date.

6. Cortese, P. National school health activities: Public sector. In U.S. Office of Health Information, Health Promotion, and Physical Fitness and Sports Medicine, *Promoting*

Health through the Schools: A National Conference. Unpublished conference proceedings, 1980.

7. Brandt, E. *The federal-state partnership in health policy.* Paper presented at the Annual Meeting of the Organization of State Medical Association Presidents, Chicago, June 11, 1982.

8. National Center for Health Education. *Health education curricular progression chart.* San Francisco: National Center for Health Education, 1981.

9. California Department of Education. *Criteria for evaluating the school health education program.* Sacramento: California Department of Education, 1977.

10. Indiana Congress of Parents and Teachers. *An assessment instrument for comprehensive school health.* Indianapolis: Indiana Department of Instruction, no date.

11. Joint Committee on School Health. *Checklist on school health programs for demonstration schools.* Little Rock: Arkansas Department of Education, no date.

12. Ohio Department of Education. *A self-appraisal checklist for school health programs.* Columbus: Ohio Department of Education, no date.

13. Oregon Department of Education. *Planning health education programs in Oregon schools: Administration.* Salem: Oregon Department of Education, 1978.

14. West Virginia School Health Development and Education Project. *Health: School health assessment.* Charleston: West Virginia Department of Education, 1977.

15. Quest, Inc. *A quick look at Quest.* Findlay, Ohio: Quest, Inc., no date.

16. Health Services Research Center. *Actions for Health: A decision-making curriculum for the elementary grades.* Los Angeles: University of California, Health Services Research Center, no date.

17. Biological Sciences Curriculum Study. *Feeling Fit: Overview.* Boulder, Colo.: Biological Sciences Curriculum Study, no date.

18. American Cancer Society. *An Early Start to Good Health.* New York: American Cancer Society, no date.

19. American Cancer Society. *New multimedia teaching units for grades 4, 5, 6.* New York: American Cancer Society, no date.

20. Walker, R., Miller, E., Duby, L., Topinka, S., Carney, W., & Dunham, M. *The Maine School Health Education Project: Implications for the future.* Paper presented at the Annual Meeting of the American Public Health Association, Los Angeles, 1978.

21. National Commission on Resources for Youth. *Youth participation programs in the health field.* New York: National Commission on Resources for Youth, no date.

22. New York Academy of Medicine. *The School Health Curriculum Project in New York City.* New York: Metropolitan Life Insurance Company, no date.

23. Comprehensive Health Planning of Northwest Illinois. *School health coalition.* Rockford: Comprehensive Health Planning of Northwest Illinois, 1980.

24. Middle Tennessee Health Systems Agency. *Annual report: 1979–80.* Nashville: Middle Tennessee Health Systems Agency, 1980.

25. Southeast Nebraska Health Systems Agency. *Southeast Nebraska Health Systems Agency helps to spread the School Health Curriculum Project.* Lincoln: Southeast Nebraska Health Systems Agency, no date.

26. Oakland County Office of Substance Abuse. *Oakland County School Health Curriculum Project.* Pontiac, Mich.: Oakland County Health Division, no date.

27. Koski, A. *A national study of administrative and curricular practices of departments of health, health education, and health science, 1978.* Corvallis: Oregon State University, Department of Health, no date.

28. National Center for Health Education. *Initial role delineation for health education: Final report.* Hyattsville, Md.: Health Resources Administration, 1980.

29. Drolet, J. *Evaluation of the Seaside health education and nutrition education training programs in the Oregon school systems: A summary of the findings, conclusions, and recommendations from a dissertation.* Portland: Oregon Department of Education, 1982.

30. Passwater, D., Slater, S., & Tritsch, L. *Seaside Health Education Conference: Effects of three five-day teacher inservice conferences.* Portland: Oregon Department of Education, 1980.

31. Oregon Department of Education. *Planning materials for a five-day school health promotion/education conference* (Rev.). Portland: Oregon Department of Education, 1982.

32. Maryland Department of Education. *The Maryland School and Community Alcohol and Other Drugs Project: A prevention/intervention approach—Executive summary.* Baltimore: Maryland Department of Education, March 1982.

33. U.S. Center for Health Promotion and Education. *Teaching parents to be the primary sexuality educators of their children: Final report—Executive summary.* Atlanta: Centers for Disease Control, 1982.

34. Nader, P. *Family directed health education.* Unpublished manuscript, University of Texas Medical Branch at Galveston, 1980.

35. U.S. Office of Health Information, Health Promotion, and Physical Fitness and Sports Medicine. *National Health Information Clearinghouse: Fact sheet.* Washington, D.C.: U.S. Department of Health and Human Services, no date.

REFERENCES

American Heart Association, Subcommittee on Health Education of the Young. We've put our heart into the curriculum. *Health Education,* 1982, **13**(1), 20–21.

American Public Health Association. Resolutions and position papers: Education for health in the community setting. *American Journal of Public Health,* 1975, **65**(2), 201.

American Public Health Association. APHA surveys block grants. *Nation's Health,* 1982, June, 1, 13.

Association for the Advancement of Health Education. Association for the Advancement of Health Education directory of institutions offering specialization in undergraduate and graduate professional preparation programs in health education, 1979 edition. *Health Education,* 1979, **9**(6), 35–43.

Bedworth, D. A political action primer for health educators. *Health Education,* 1977, **8**(5), 30–31.

Berclay, G. (Ed.). *Parent involvement in the schools.* Washington, D.C.: National Education Association, 1977.

Berson, M. Tulare cultivates a new crop. *American Education,* 1979, **15**(6), 11–16.

Beyrer, M., & Solleder, M. *Selected references and resources in health education* (3rd ed.). San Francisco: National Center for Health Education, 1983.

Brooks, C., Kirkpatrick, M., & Howard, D. Evaluation of an activity centered child health curriculum using the Health Belief Model. *Journal of School Health,* 1981, **51**(8), 565–569.

Bruhn, J., & Cordova, F. A developmental approach to learning wellness behavior: Part one. Infancy to early adolescence. *Health Values,* 1977, **1**(6), 248–254.

Bruhn, J., & Cordova, F. A developmental approach to learning wellness behavior: Part two. Adolescence to maturity. *Health Values,* 1978, **2**(1), 16–21.

Castille, A., Allensworth, D., & Noak, M. *School health in America: A survey of state school health programs.* Atlanta: U.S. Center for Health Promotion and Education, 1981.

Cawelti, G. Should education groups collaborate to influence legislation? *Educational Leadership,* 1976, **34**(2), 87–89.

Clifton, B., Edwards, E., & Morelle, L. Florida Comprehensive Health Education Act. *Health Education*, 1974, **5**(2), 25.

Conley, J., & Jackson, C. Is a mandated comprehensive health education program a guarantee of successful health education? *Journal of School Health*, 1978, **48**(6), 337–340.

Conway, S. Regulations proposed for funding of school health education. *Health Education Reports*, 1979, **1**(7), 5–6. (a)

Conway, S. Proposed school health rules draw favorable reaction. *Health Education Reports*, 1979, **1**(9), 4–5. (b)

Conway, S. Proposed rules for school health draw comments on funds, timing. *Health Education Reports*, 1979, **1**(11), 5–6. (c)

Conway, S. Two million dollars for school health more than expected. *Health Education Reports*, 1979, **1**(1), 5–6. (d)

Conway, S. School health education funds of $5 million proposed. *Health Education Reports*, 1979, **1**(4), 7. (e)

Conway, S. Congress denies 1980 funds to schools, disease prevention. *Health Education Reports*, 1979, **1**(11), 1–2. (f)

Conway, S. Comprehensive school health education allotted no funds. *Health Education Reports*, 1980, **2**(2), 1–2, 1980. (a)

Conway, S. But supporters of field urged to petition Congress. *Health Education Reports*, 1980, **2**(2), 2–5. (b)

Conway, S. Wide support voiced for funding of school health education. *Health Education Reports*, 1980, **2**(6), 5–6. (c)

Creswell, W., Tritsch, L., Jubb, W., & Hill, P. What's happening in the states. *School Health Review*, 1973, **4**(5), 28.

Cushman, W. An overview of approaches to curricula and course construction in health education. *Journal of School Health*, 1969, **29**(1), 14–21.

Dosch, P., & Paxton, C. Recharging professionally: The Oregon Seaside Conferences. *Health Education*, 1981, **13**(4), 34–35.

Duval, M. Advancing and financing health education in the 1980's. *Health Education*, 1981, **12**(5), 27–29.

Education Development Center, Inc. *Teenage Health Teaching Modules: An introduction to the program.* Atlanta: U.S. Center for Health Promotion and Education, 1981.

Ellis, S. Models of teaching: A solution to the teaching style/learning style dilemma. *Educational Leadership*, 1979, **36**(4), 274–277.

Ervin, T. Up the back stairs for better health legislation. *Health Education*, 1982, **13**(4), 20–23.

Eta Sigma Gamma Professional Health Science Honorary. *Selected sources of instructional materials: A national directory of sources on instructional materials in health education, patient education, and safety education.* Muncie, Ind.: Ball State University, Department of Health Education, 1980.

Eta Sigma Gamma Professional Health Science Honorary. *A national directory of college and university health education programs and faculties, 1982* (8th ed.). Muncie, Ind.: Ball State University, 1982.

Evans, R. Smoking in children: Developing a social psychological strategy of deterrence. *Preventive Medicine*, 1976, **5**, 122–127.

Evans, R., Rozelle, R., Maxwell, S., Raines, B., Dill, C., Guthrie, T., Henderson, A., & Hill, P. Social modeling films to deter smoking in adolescents: Results of a three-year field investigation. *Journal of Applied Psychology*, 1981, **66**(4), 399–414.

Evans, R., Rozelle, R., & Mittlemark, M. Deterring the onset of smoking in children: Knowledge of immediate physiological effects and coping with peer pressure, media pressure, and parent modeling. *Journal of Applied Social Psychology*, 1978, **8**(2), 126–135.

Florida Department of Education. *Comprehensive health education management model.* Atlanta: U.S. Center for Health Promotion and Education, 1980.

Fuchs, V. *Who shall live? Health, economics, and social choice.* New York: Basic Books, 1974.

Grace, H. *Comprehensive health education in New Mexico schools: A community action manual.* Albuquerque: New Mexico PTA, 1978.

Green, L., Kreuter, M., Deeds, S., & Partridge, K. *Health education planning: A diagnostic approach.* Palo Alto, Calif.: Mayfield, 1980.

Hall, K., & Brinson, V. What about curricular reform at the state level? *Educational Leadership,* 1978, **35**(2), 342–349.

Hall, T., Jackson, R., & Parsons, W. *Trends in graduate education: Schools of public health.* Washington, D.C.: U.S. Government Printing Office, 1980.

Henderson, A. *Role refinement and verification for entry level health educators: Final report.* San Francisco: National Center for Health Education, 1981.

Henderson, A. Credentialing: How it applies to school health educators. *Health Values,* 1982, **6**(1), 54–62.

Henderson, A., & Cortese, P. Legislative advocacy in health education. *Health Education,* 1981, **12**(2), 25–27.

Henderson, A., Wolle, J., Cortese, P., & McIntosh, D. The future of the health education profession: Implications for preparation and practice. *Public Health Reports,* 1981, **96**(6), 555–559.

Hoyman, H. An ecologic view of health and health education. *Journal of School Health,* 1965, **35**(3), 110–123.

Hoyman, H. Rethinking an ecologic-system model of man's health, disease, aging, death. *Journal of School Health,* 1975, **45**(9), 509–518.

Hoyman, H. A synthetic health curriculum design in ecologic perspective. *Journal of School Health,* 1977, **47**(1), 17–25.

Johnson, J. *Introduction to the foundations of American education.* Boston: Allyn & Bacon, 1969.

Joyce, B., & Weil, M. *Selecting learning experiences: Linking theory and practice.* Washington, D.C.: Association for Supervision and Curriculum Development, 1978.

Joyce, B., & Weil, M. *Models of teaching* (2nd ed.). Englewood Cliffs, N.J.: Prentice-Hall, 1979.

Kane, W. Advocacy: Political action for school health education. *Health Values,* 1982, **6**(1), 48–53.

Knowles, J. The responsibility of the individual. In *Doing better and feeling worse: Health in the United States. Proceedings of the American Academy of Arts and Sciences,* 1977, **106**(1), 60.

Kolbe, L. *Guidelines for comprehensive school health education programs: Background paper.* San Francisco: National Center for Health Education, 1981.

Kolbe, L. What can we expect from school health education? *Journal of School Health,* 1982, **52**(3), 145–150.

Kolbe, L., & Iverson, D. Research in school health education: A needs assessment. *Health Education,* 1980, **11**(1), 3–8.

Kolbe, L., & Iverson, D. Implementing comprehensive school health education: Educational innovation and social change. *Health Education Quarterly,* 1981, **8**(1), 57–80.

Kolbe, L., & Iverson, D. Integrating school and community efforts to promote health: Strategies, policies, and methods. *Hygie: International Journal of Health Education,* 1983, **2**(3), 40–47.

Kolbe, L., Iverson, D., Kreuter, M., Hochbaum, G., & Christenson, G. Propositions for an alternate and complementary health education paradigm. *Health Education,* 1981, **12**(3), 24–30.

Kummel, W. Support for legislation. *School Health Review,* 1973, **4**(5), 26.

Kupsinel, N. A look at state health curriculum guides. *Health Education,* 1980, **11**(3), 25–27.

Leviton, D. The health educator as legislative witness. *Health Education,* 1977, **8**(5), 33–35.

Loya, R. Youth gives a damn. *Journal of School Health,* 1974, **44**(10), 570–572.

Lucas, P., Floss, D., Madison, J., & Sova, J. Practical advice on tactics for supporting legislation. *School Health Review,* 1973, **4**(5), 26.

McAlister, A., Perry, C., Killen, J., Slinkard, L., & Macoby, N. Pilot study of smoking, alcohol, and drug abuse prevention. *American Journal of Public Health,* 1980, **70**, 719–721.

Means, R. *Historical perspectives on school health.* Thorofare, N.J.: Charles Slack, 1975.

Meeds, L. Legislation as a precipitator of educational development. *School Health Review,* 1973, **4**(5), 21–25.

Michaels, L. *Guidelines for planning and implementing school health education programs.* Pittsburgh: Health Education Center, 1978.

Michigan Department of Education. The health education family handbooks: Grades kindergarten through six. Manistee, Mich.: JB Publications, 1980.

Miller, D. Legislative action, health education and curriculum change. *Journal of School Health*, 1972, **42**(9), 513–515.

Miller, J., & Hammer, S. Parent involvement in child bicycle safety education. *Health Values*, 1979, **3**(2), 113–114.

Myren, J. Health education through parent participation: It's happening now. *Journal of School Health*, 1971, **41**(4), 217–219.

Nagel, C. A behavioral objectives approach to health instruction. *Journal of School Health*, 1970, **40**(5), 255–258.

National Center for Health Education. *A compendium of health education programs available for use by schools*. Atlanta: U.S. Center for Health Promotion and Education, 1982.

National Center for Health Statistics. *Health resources statistics: Health manpower and health facilities, 1976–77 edition*. Washington, D.C.: U.S. Government Printing Office, 1979.

National PTA. *Health education matters: An awareness and action program to promote comprehensive school health education*. Atlanta: U.S. Center for Health Promotion and Education, 1981. (a)

National PTA. *PTA student health education forums*. Atlanta: U.S. Center for Health Promotion and Education, 1981. (b)

Newman, I. Peer pressure hypothesis for adolescent cigarette smoking. *School Health Review*, 1970, **2**, 15.

Newman, I., & Wilson, R. Some lessons learned in legislation. *Health Education*, 1978, **9**(6), 20.

Newman, I., & Wilson, R. Political action and the value of health education: A case study of community attitudes and actions in a legislative hearing. *Health Values*, 1980, **4**(3), 124–129.

Nix, H. *Identification of leaders and their involvement in the planning process*. Washington, D.C.: U.S. Government Printing Office, 1970.

Noak, M. *Recommendations for school health education: A handbook for state policymakers*. Denver: Education Commission of the States, 1981.

Noak, M. Recommendations for state policymakers. *Health Values*, 1982, **6**(2), 44–47. (a)

Noak, M. *State policy support for school health education: A review and analysis*. Denver: Education Commission of the States, 1982. (b)

Owens, M. How legislative resolutions stimulate positive actions. *Health Education*, 1975, **6**(2), 21.

Parcel, G. Skills approach to health education: A framework for integrating cognitive and affective learning. *Journal of School Health*, 1976, **46**(7), 403–412.

Perry, C., Killen, J., Telch, M., Slinkard, L., & Danaher, B. Modifying smoking behavior of teenagers: A school-based intervention. *American Journal of Public Health*, 1980, **70**(7), 722–725.

Perry, C., & Murray, D. Enhancing the transition years: The challenge of adolescent health promotion. *Journal of School Health*, 1982, **52**(5), 307–311.

Phillips, J., & Hawthorne, R. Political dimensions of curriculum decision making. *Educational Leadership*, 1978, **35**(2), 363–366.

Pincus, J. Incentives for innovation in public schools. *Review of Educational Research*, 1974, **44**(1), 115–116.

Pollock, M. Curriculum planning: A gamesmanship approach. *Journal of School Health*, 1969, **39**(8), 523–525.

Porter, E. (Ed.). *Guidelines for improving school health education K-12*. Columbus: Ohio Department of Education, 1980.

Region VII Center for Health Planning. *Starting a comprehensive school health education program (CSHE) in a Missouri school district*. Springfield, Va.: National Technical Information Service, 1979.

Russell, R. Teaching for meaning in health education: The concept approach. *Journal of School Health*, 1966, **36**(1), 12–15.

Schlesinger, L. *School health coordinator's manual*. Augusta: Maine School Health Education Project, 1981.

School Health Education Study. *Health education: A conceptual approach to curriculum design.* St. Paul: Minnesota Mining & Manufacturing, 1967.

Simonds, S. Health education manpower in the United States. *Health Education Monographs,* 1976, **4**(Fall), 208–225.

Slack, G. Dade County wars against rats. *American Education,* 1979, **15**(6), 31–36.

Sliepcevich, E. (Ed.). Special feature: Grantsmanship for school health education. *Health Education,* 1978, **9**(5), 2–30.

Solleder, M. Legislative action for health education: The North Carolina story. *Health Education,* 1981, **12**(6), 26–28.

Sorenson, A., & Sinacore, J. Developing a regional health education program. *Health Values,* 1979, **3**(2), 79–84.

Spiker, C. Parent involvement in cardiovascular disease school health education. *Health Values,* 1978, **2**(5), 257–262.

Stein, B. Summary of the National Conference on Legislative Action for School Health. *School Health Review,* 1973, **4**(5), 26–29.

Sunseri, A., Alberti, J., Cruc, J., Kent, N., Vickers, P., & Amuwo, S. Reading, demographic, and social-normative factors related to pre-adolescent smoking and non-smoking behaviors and attitudes. *Journal of School Health,* 1983, **53**(4), 257–263.

Sunseri, A., Schoenberger, J., Beckman, L., & Cruc, J. Teacher education—The humanistic heart health model. *Health Values,* 1980, **4**(4), 168–171.

Taub, A. Understanding the legislative process: An annotated bibliography of selected references. *Health Education,* 1980, **11**(4), 13–14.

Torney, J. Legislative action for health education: California update. *Health Education,* 1981, **12**(6), 28–30.

U.S. Bureau of Health Professions. *Proceedings of the Workshop on Commonalities and Differences.* Hyattsville, Md.: Health Resources Administration, 1978.

U.S. Bureau of Health Professions. *Public health personnel in the United States, 1980: Second report to the Congress.* Washington, D.C.: U.S. Government Printing Office, 1982.

U.S. Center for Health Promotion and Education. *The School Health Curriculum Project.* Atlanta: Author, 1977.

U.S. Center for Health Promotion and Education. *The Primary Grades Health Curriculum Project.* Atlanta: Author, 1980.

U.S. Center for Health Promotion and Education. *Health Education-Risk Reduction Grant Program.* Washington, D.C.: U.S. Government Printing Office, 1981. (a)

U.S. Center for Health Promotion and Education. *Implementation manual for the Primary Grades Health Curriculum Project and the School Health Curriculum Project.* Atlanta: Author, 1981. (b)

U.S. Center for Health Promotion and Education and U.S. Office of Health Information, Health Promotion, and Physical Fitness and Sports Medicine. Health Education-Risk Reduction Grant Program. *Focal Points,* 1981, May/June, 1–11.

U.S. Center for Health Promotion and Education. *Teaching parents to be the primary sexuality educators of their children: Final report—Volume I, Impact of programs.* Atlanta: Centers for Disease Control, 1982. (a)

U.S. Center for Health Promotion and Education. *Teaching parents to be the primary sexuality educators of their children: Final report—Volume II, Guide to designing and implementing courses.* Atlanta: Centers for Disease Control, 1982. (b)

U.S. Center for Health Promotion and Education. *Teaching parents to be the primary sexuality educators of their children: Final report—Volume III, Curriculum guide to courses for parents.* Atlanta: Centers for Disease Control, 1982. (c)

U.S. Center for Health Promotion and Education. *Teaching parents to be the primary sexuality educators of their children: Final report—Volume IV, Curriculum guide to courses for parents and adolescents together.* Atlanta: Centers for Disease Control, 1982. (d)

U.S. Center for Health Promotion and Education. *Teaching parents to be the primary sexuality educators of their children: Final report—Volume V, National catalogue of programs—1981.* Atlanta: Centers for Disease Control, 1982. (e)

U.S. Department of Health, Education and Welfare. *The report of the President's Committee on Health Education.* Washington, D.C.: U.S. Government Printing Office, 1973.

U.S. Department of Health, Education and Welfare. *Educating the public about health: A planning guide.* Washington, D.C.: U.S. Government Printing Office, 1978.

U.S. Department of Health, Education and Welfare. *Healthy people: The Surgeon General's report on health promotion and disease prevention.* Washington, D.C.: U.S. Government Printing Office, 1979.

U.S. General Accounting Office. *What can be done to improve nutrition education efforts in the schools? Report to the Secretary of Agriculture.* Washington, D.C.: Author, 1982.

U.S. Office of Health Information, Health Promotion, and Physical Fitness and Sports Medicine. *Locating funds for health promotion projects.* Washington, D.C.: Author, 1980.

U.S. Office of Health Information, Health Promotion, and Physical Fitness and Sports Medicine. *Proceedings of the National Conference for Institutions Preparing Health Educators.* Washington, D.C.: Author, 1981.

U.S. Superintendent of Documents. Public Law 95–561: Elementary and Secondary Education Act Amendments of 1978, Title III, Part I—Health Education. Stat. 2221, November 1, 1978, 92.

U.S. Superintendent of Documents. Grants for health education-risk reduction. *Federal Register,* 1979, **44,** 55873. (a)

U.S. Superintendent of Documents. Health education program. *Federal Register,* 1979, **44,** 34024–34031. (b)

U.S. Superintendent of Documents. Grants for health education-risk reduction. *Federal Register,* 1980, **45,** 63845–63849.

U.S. Superintendent of Documents. *Omnibus Budget Reconciliation Act of 1981: Conference report.* Washington, D.C.: U.S. Government Printing Office, 1981.

Williams, C., Carter, B., & Eng, A. *The "Know Your Body" Program: A developmental approach to health education and disease prevention.* New York: American Health Foundation, 1979.

CHAPTER 79

WELLNESS—THE LIFETIME GOAL OF A UNIVERSITY EXPERIENCE

WILLIAM HETTLER

University of Wisconsin

The University of Wisconsin/Stevens Point has been developing and improving its Health Promotion Program since the early 1970s. The program is a cooperative project, involving not only all units within the Student Life Division but also the administration and academic components of the University. The concept of student development is a philosophy shared by the majority of the staff members within the Student Life Division. Although each unit is committed to providing support services within its respective area, each unit also has a commitment to assist the students in developing the skills that will serve them best throughout their lifetime.

The Wellness Program is different from programs with a traditional preventive medicine or health education emphasis. Wellness has been defined at this institution as an active process through which individuals become aware of and make choices toward a more successful existence. We encourage students to take an activated approach toward conducting their lives. We encourage them to view wellness as a six-dimensional paradigm involving the social, occupational, spiritual, physical, intellectual, and emotional dimensions. Through coordinated programming efforts, we attempt to present the concept of interdependence among the various dimensions of wellness. We have assessed, both individually and collectively, each unit of the Student Life Division and have made efforts to identify program opportunities in each of the six dimensions of wellness. Earlier in the development of this program, for example, when deficiencies in program opportunities were identified, additional staff and resources were acquired to assist the students in learning more about that particular dimension.

A significant effort is made from the time students first apply to the university through their entire career at this institution to help them realize that health is not something to be restored after it is lost but, ideally, is something to be pursued on a continuous basis throughout one's life. It is our hope that the students will pursue optimal well-being by developing skills that facilitate that pursuit, rather than simply living their lives as have people from their communities or families for generations—waiting for things to go wrong and then hoping that the disease care system can correct the problems.

Epidemiologic studies in the United States have demonstrated that four major determinants can alter premature death and disability: (a) lifestyle choices, (b) hereditary characteristics, (c) environmental changes, and (d) the disease care system. Tables 79.1 and 79.2 clearly demonstrate that the greatest contributor to premature death and disability in the United States is lifestyle choices. The recognition that decisions made during the college years often end up being lifetime decisions has led the administrators of this institution to

Table 79.1   Leading Causes of Death: Ages 20–24 (1976)

Causes of Death	Rate*a*	Percentage*b*	Chance in 100,000 of the Individual Dying from this Cause
Motor vehicle accidents	40.7	31.0	202.9
All other accidents	21.6	16.5	108.0
Homicide	16.6	12.6	82.5
Suicide	16.4	12.5	81.8
Malignant neoplasms	7.3	5.6	36.7
Diseases of heart	3.3	2.5	16.4
Other external causes	3.1	2.4	15.7
Influenza and pneumonia	1.7	1.3	8.5
Cerebrovascular diseases	1.5	1.1	7.2
Congenital anomalies	1.4	1.0	6.5
All other causes	17.7	13.5	88.3
All causes	131.3	100.0	654.5

Source: Centers for Disease Control, Public Health Service, *Leading Causes of Death and Probabilities of Dying, United States, 1975 and 1976.* Atlanta: Centers for Disease Control, 1979.
a Rates per 100,000 population.
b Percentage of total deaths.

the conclusion that a significant emphasis on health promotion is justified during the college years. It is our hope that students graduating from the University of Wisconsin/Stevens Point will have a selective advantage in terms of quality of life and longevity. The encouragement begins with the initial contact from the university, registrar, and admissions office to the students at the time they apply to matriculate. The letter shown in Figure 79.1 is a sample of the communication that takes place between the university and the students.

Table 79.2   Leading Causes of Death: Ages 40–44 (1976)

Causes of Death	Rate*a*	Percentage*b*	Chance in 100,000 of the Individual Dying from this Cause
Diseases of heart	72.8	23.2	360.9
Malignant neoplasms	68.9	22.0	342.3
Cirrhosis of liver	22.1	7.1	110.5
All other accidents	19.8	6.3	98.0
Motor vehicle accidents	18.3	5.8	90.2
Suicide	16.7	5.3	82.5
Cerebrovascular diseases	15.0	4.8	74.7
Homicide	13.6	4.3	66.9
Influenza and pneumonia	6.4	2.0	31.1
Diabetes	4.6	1.5	23.3
All other causes	55.2	17.7	275.3
All causes	313.4	100.0	1,555.7

Source: Centers for Disease Control, Public Health Service, *Leading Causes of Death and Probabilities of Dying, United States, 1975 and 1976.* Atlanta: Centers for Disease Control, 1979.
a Rates per 100,000 population.
b Percentage of total deaths.

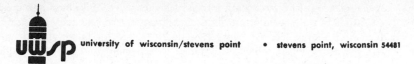

Dear Student:

Welcome to the University of Wisconsin/Stevens Point. We plan to offer you up-to-
date medical care and an opportunity to develop the healthiest lifestyle possible for
you. We expect you to be willing to consider change toward higher levels of wellness
during your career here in Stevens Point. We expect you to be a partner in helping
us provide you with the best care possible. As a first step in forming this partnership,
we require you to provide us with some information about your current health status,
past medical problems, future risks, and possible areas in which you would like to
improve. This partnership is initiated in one of two ways. During the summer
orientation/registration program you may elect one of the following:

1.   You may fill out a Lifestyle Assessment Questionnaire. This is a self-
     administered health and wellness assessment instrument. It is the re-
     commended method for providing us with necessary information about you.
     The cost for the LAQ and related programs is $7.50.

2.   As an alternative, you may request a standard history and physical form
     at orientation or from the University Health Service and have your
     physician fill it out and return it to us. (At an average cost of $25 to
     $40 per physical.)

PLEASE NOTE: IT IS A UNIVERSITY REQUIREMENT TO ACCOMPLISH EITHER NUMBER 1 OR NUMBER 2
AS LISTED ABOVE PRIOR TO REGISTRATION. We recommend the Lifestyle Assessment Questionnaire because it is less expensive, more convenient, and provides us with the most
appropriate information.

The $7.50 charge covers the cost of the computer analysis of you Lifestyle Assessment
Questionnaire and programs that will be offered to you for lifestyle improvement. We
believe that out of 31 possible areas of self-improvement offered, each student will
be able to find at least one topic in which they are interested. If you enter UWSP
at a time when no formal orientation program is offered, you may pick up a Lifestyle
Assessment Questionnaire at the Health Service.

IT IS A UNIVERSITY REQUIREMENT TO SELECT ONE OF THE ABOVE TWO OPTIONS. We feel the
Lifestyle Assessment Questionnaire will give you an accurate measurement of your current
level of wellness, current risks, future risks, and will give you an automated referral
to sources of information or activities that lead to higher levels of wellness. You
may omit any answer you are not sure about or feel is not pertinent. We will process
the forms and return the results to you. This material, as with all of our medical
records, is kept confidential. No one can have access to your records without prior
written permission from you.

Please stop in and see us when you get to campus. We are located on the second floor
of DelzellHall. We have an active Student Health Advisory Committee and we welcome
your input. Thank you for your assistance.

Sincerely yours,

Bill Hettler M.D

Bill Hettler, M.D.
Director   *University Health Service*   •   *(715) 346-4646*

Figure 79.1   Letter sent to new students regarding the university's health promotion efforts.

We emphasize that we are interested in becoming partners with the students, not only to
provide them with the best medical care possible, but also to help them establish the healthiest
lifestyle possible. The first step in forming this partnership is often brought about by the
student's completion of the Lifestyle Assessment Questionnaire (LAQ). The LAQ is divided
into four sections: the Wellness Inventory, Topics for Personal Growth, Risk of Death,
and Medical Alert. The evaluation instrument and the analysis it provides are designed
to encourage the students to record information pertaining to their lifestyle and to show

them how they can make positive modification toward higher levels of wellness and greater longevity. The instrument is designed primarily as an educational tool to assist the students in understanding their current lifestyle, what it is doing to and for them, and to reflect on what they might do to enhance their life and to assess—and exercise—their choices toward becoming more fulfilled individuals.

Students are encouraged to remember that they are their own best health managers. The computerized assessment results will not transform a student's mediocre level of wellness to one of high quality. Rather, LAQ measures outcomes of decisions that students have already made about their lifestyle, but it does provide a base to assist them in their quest for optimal health. Students are encouraged to recognize the value of traditional medical care, but we try to emphasize that traditional medical care very often is less important than lifestyle decisions in improving the quality of life and avoiding premature death. It is our belief that the excellent care provided by the medical care industry should be supplemented by health promotion activities and learning opportunities.

The first section of the Lifestyle Assessment Questionnaire—the Wellness Inventory— is divided into 11 areas, which encompass the six dimensions of wellness. The areas measured in the Wellness Inventory are as follows:

1. *Physical exercise:* Measures your commitment to maintaining physical fitness.

2. *Physical-nutritional:* Measures the degree to which you choose foods that are consistent with the dietary goals of the United States, as published by the Senate Select Committee on Nutrition and Human Needs.

3. *Physical self-care:* Measures the behavior that helps you prevent or detect early illnesses.

4. *Physical vehicle safety:* Measures your safe driving practices that minimize chances of injury or death in a vehicular accident.

5. *Physical drug abuse:* Measures the degree to which you are able to function without the unnecessary use of chemicals.

6. *Social-environmental:* Measures the degree to which you contribute to the common welfare of the community. This emphasizes your interdependence with others and with nature.

7. *Emotional awareness and acceptance:* Measures the degree to which you have an awareness and acceptance of your feelings, including the degree to which you feel positive and enthusiastic about yourself and life.

8. *Emotional management:* Measures your capacity to control your feelings and related behavior appropriately, including realistic assessment of your limitations.

9. *Intellectual:* Measures the degree to which you engage your mind in creative, stimulating mental activities, expanding your knowledge and improving your skills.

10. *Occupational:* Measures the satisfaction gained from your work and the degree to which you are enriched by that work.

11. *Spiritual:* Measures your ongoing involvement in seeking meaning and purpose in human existence. It includes an appreciation of the depth and expanse of life and of the natural forces that exist in the universe.

The students are given a score on each of the 11 sections. They are also given an opportunity to compare their scores with the group average of all people who took this assessment at the same time and with the scores of all people who have ever filled out the questionnaire. This gives the students a chance to compare themselves not only locally but also nationally.

It is our hope that the Wellness Inventory section will stimulate the imagination of the students and create an awareness that there are many possible behaviors or choices that might lead to higher levels of wellness. The next section of the Lifestyle Assessment

Questionnaire is the Topics for Personal Growth section. Students are asked to select from a list of educational topics those for which they might desire information, group activities, or confidential personal assistance. The computer is programmed to print information on up to six topics for personal growth. If the students ask for information concerning one of the 31 possible topics, they will receive, as part of their printout, a listing of courses for credit that would help them learn more about that subject, names and phone numbers of people who are competent to provide assistance in that particular area, media resources available on the campus and where they might be obtained, and names and phone numbers of community agencies that would be able to serve students in that area. It is our hope that the students will pursue improvements in the quality of their lives through these various learning opportunities.

An additional resource available to the students are wellness programs in each of the six dimensions, conducted in the University Center or in the residence halls by upper-class students, who are called Lifestyle Assistants. Lifestyle Assistants offer programs right where the students live. This is one of the differences between a typical health education program and wellness promotion. Rather than sitting in our offices waiting for the consumers to trickle in, we attempt to take the programs to the students in the environment that they find most comfortable. Typical offerings include 6-week programs in smoking cessation, body tune-up and weight control, relaxation, and aerobic dance and 1-hour programs in such areas as the spiritual dimension of wellness, career planning, sex roles and stereotypes, yoga, mature use of alcohol, dealing with shyness, first aid, and physical self-examination.

The third section of the Lifestyle Assessment Questionnaire is the Risk of Death section. This enables the students to identify the most common causes of death that they will face in the next 10 years. It also provides them with an opportunity to identify the most significant lifestyle factors that can improve the quality of their life. If the students have a significant number of risks, the computer can be used to simulate aging to demonstrate to the students what their risk profiles will be like by age 40. The printout provides suggestions on how the students can take steps toward greater longevity. The word *expected* is used to emphasize the fact that all longevity data are determined by predictions based on previous group results. The computer cannot actually tell how long any individual will live or at what age he or she will die, but it will provide a general idea of relative risk.

The last section of the LAQ is the Medical Alert section. This is an abbreviated, problem-oriented medical record. The printout from this section will provide the students with a home medical record of immunizations, current lifestyle improvement suggestions, significant past histories, and known allergies.

The Lifestyle Assessment Questionnaire results are interpreted by the residence hall directors in small group settings. Students are invited to participate on a voluntary basis. Students who do not live in the residence halls are given an opportunity to have their interpretation sessions in the University Center or the University Health Service. Follow-up programs are provided immediately following these interpretation sessions. Through all of our programming, we encourage the students to look at their behaviors and see whether there are behaviors that they would like to change. A behavioral checklist was developed and is made available to the students as part of the health promotion program. Adjunct materials have been purchased and developed to support the program, and these videotapes, audio tapes, self-care modules, and handouts are all useful in assisting the student in making lifestyle changes.

The Fun, Information, and Testing (F.I.T.) Stop, a movable self-testing center for physical fitness, is used throughout the campus. Not only does it move from residence hall to residence hall, it also is used in the academic classroom buildings and the administrative buildings. The F.I.T. Stop is supervised by students who are either interns from other campuses or are taking independent study or practicum credits on this campus. The F.I.T. Stop enables individuals to measure their lung capacity, their blood pressure, their resting pulse, their strength, their flexibility, and their relative tension level, using biofeedback equipment. In

Table 79.3 Student-Selected Topics from Personal Growth Section, LAQ

Type of Assistance Requested	Information		Group Activities		Confidential Personal Assistance	
	1977–78	1978–79	1977–78	1978–79	1977–78	1978–79
1. Responsible alcohol use	432 (7)	408 (10)	120 (18)	81 (21)	0 (25)	0 (26)
2. Stop-smoking programs	280 (20)	285 (20)	120 (18)	96 (16)	24 (19)	18 (14)
3. Sexual dysfunction	272 (23)	285 (20)	104 (23)	42 (24)	32 (13)	36 (4)
4. Contraception	448 (4)	414 (9)	80 (25)	36 (25)	64 (4)	27 (8)
5. Venereal disease	384 (13)	339 (13)	80 (25)	33 (26)	32 (13)	12 (18)
6. Depression	296 (18)	330 (14)	176 (10)	144 (10)	96 (2)	42 (3)
7. Loneliness	280 (20)	261 (24)	224 (5)	177 (6)	80 (3)	21 (10)
8. Exercise programs	544 (3)	594 (2)	554 (1)	507 (1)	32 (13)	3 (24)
9. Weight programs	376 (14)	453 (5)	304 (2)	201 (5)	56 (8)	6 (23)
10. Breast self-examination	320 (16)	321 (16)	64 (26)	3 (27)	64 (4)	15 (16)
11. Medical emergencies	568 (1)	552 (3)	160 (13)	123 (13)	40 (10)	12 (18)
12. Vegetarian diets	440 (5)	441 (8)	112 (21)	69 (23)	8 (24)	9 (21)
13. Relaxation, stress reduction	424 (8)	540 (4)	192 (8)	213 (3)	40 (10)	15 (16)
14. Mate selection	400 (11)	366 (12)	168 (12)	159 (9)	24 (19)	24 (9)
15. Parenting	280 (20)	282 (22)	176 (10)	138 (11)	0 (25)	0 (26)
16. Marital problems	256 (25)	231 (25)	128 (17)	96 (16)	64 (4)	30 (5)
17. Assertiveness training ("How to say no without feeling guilty")	440 (5)	453 (5)	232 (4)	168 (7)	32 (13)	30 (5)
18. Biofeedback for tension headaches	424 (8)	327 (15)	104 (23)	87 (19)	16 (21)	18 (14)
19. Overcoming phobias (example: high places, crowded rooms, etc.)	304 (17)	318 (17)	112 (21)	108 (14)	32 (13)	21 (10)

20. Educational/vocational goal setting/planning	560 (2)	690 (1)	192 (8)	138 (11)	200 (1)	159 (1)
21. Spiritual or philosophical values	272 (23)	312 (19)	216 (16)	168 (7)	32 (13)	21 (10)
22. Interpersonal communication skills	336 (15)	318 (17)	208 (7)	204 (4)	16 (21)	30 (5)
23. Automobile safety	288 (19)	723 (23)	136 (16)	72 (22)	0 (25)	3 (24)
24. Suicide thoughts or attempts	232 (27)	186 (27)	120 (18)	90 (18)	48 (9)	66 (2)
25. Drug abuse	248 (26)	218 (26)	152 (15)	87 (19)	16 (21)	12 (18)
26. Test anxiety reduction	392 (12)	375 (11)	160 (13)	102 (15)	40 (10)	9 (21)
27. Relationships—developing and continuing	424 (8)	447 (7)	288 (3)	243 (2)	64 (4)	21 (10)

Note: The number of incoming freshman students requesting each item is listed by type of assistance requested. The rank-order is given in parentheses.

addition, there is a cardiovascular submaximal step test, which can be done on a self-care basis. The F.I.T. Stop is very popular with the faculty, staff, and student populations. It enhances awareness of relative fitness levels and provides a large sample of health promotion handouts. The F.I.T. Stop is often used to refer people into various lifestyle improvement programs offered on the campus.

Health promotion programs are justified as part of the basic skill offerings of this institution. The university has a four-credit physical education requirement for all students. Cooperative programming elements have been developed between the Physical Education Department and the Student Life Division so that students can take lifestyle improvement classes for credit, substituting them for such activity courses as basketball, volleyball, softball, and so on. There are classes for credit in such subjects as medical self-care, weight control, alcohol awareness, stress management, and diabetic self-care. The diabetic self-care class has been an exciting innovation. Students are encouraged to test their own blood levels, using finger-stick lab tests, and to monitor their own urine. They are encouraged to experiment with a high fiber/high complex carbohydrate diet, and, in one case, a student reduced his daily insulin requirements from 63 units per day to 13 units per day. The diabetic self-care class also emphasizes exercise as a component of self-care. The Health and Physical Education Department has also developed a new wellness major, which helps prepare students for jobs in hospitals, corporations, clinics, and industry.

We have attempted to provide as many open doors as possible, using the hexagonal model of total wellness. It is our hope that each of the six dimensions of wellness can be viewed by the students and the faculty as their doorway to wellness. Once we have people involved in one element of our six-dimensional program, we encourage them by internal referrals to look at other possibilities for lifestyle improvement. We try to be as inclusive as possible, rather than exclusive. There has been tremendous interest on the part of the students in lifestyle improvement programs. Table 79.3 shows the number of students per year who have indicated interest in 31 possible topics in self-improvement. Research on this campus indicates that students are learning significant material through the Health Promotion Program; 23% of them report that they are making lifestyle changes as a result of the Program. It is our belief that every institution of higher learning has, as one of its missions, the responsibility to encourage all students to assess and make improvements in their lifestyles. The leading causes of death at age 20 are mostly accidental, but if we look ahead to age 40, we can see that most of the top killers by age 40 are the result of lifestyle choices. Premature death is not successful living. It seems ludicrous to prepare students for lifetime careers in their areas of interest but not prepare them for the lifetime responsibilities of maintaining their lives. The American culture is changing and is becoming more interested in self-care and lifestyle improvement. Billions of dollars are being spent pursuing positive health. A university that does not address these issues will be seen as regressive or obstructionary. It is our opinion that universities have a responsibility to the public to lead the way in lifestyle improvement endeavors.

CHAPTER 80

HEALTH PROMOTION IN HOSPITALS

PATRICIA H. COTANCH

Duke University Medical Center

You start with the wrong presumption: Once a patient has entered the hospital, you do all his further thinking for him. All thinking is henceforth done for him by your regulations, your daily consultations, your program, the plan and reputation of your medical institution. And I'm just a grain of sand . . . nothing depends on me [the patient speaking to the doctor].

Alexander Solzhenitsyn,
The Cancer Ward

"And I'm just a grain of sand" was a fairly accurate metaphor of patients' feelings toward hospital routine and staff behavior. Fortunately, hospitals mores have changed since Solzhenitsyn wrote *The Cancer Ward,* and patients have more control and input regarding hospital activities. Hospital staffs are increasingly adopting a humanistic approach to patient care and willingly shedding their medical mystique and authoritative behaviors. Indeed, the public is demanding such a change. At present, hospital functions include patient care for the treatment of disease, prevention of disease-related complications, clinical research, education of health professionals, as well as assisting patients and their families in reestablishing as much as possible their premorbid lifestyle or in adjusting as well as possible to a chronic illness. Still, these functions are mostly related to diagnosis, treatment, and rehabilitation of currently ill people. The idea of hospitals as centers for prevention, health promotion, and wellness at first may seem out of place. It has been stated that establishing health promotion programs in hospitals—"disease care centers"—is like setting the fox to guard the chicken coop (Grossman, 1981). Proponents of the wellness movement have a long-term focus that involves altering the current practice of organized medicine. They advocate promotion for the sake of wellness, early intervention in the course of disease, and preventive intervention for the known at-risk population. Wellness proponents are also advocates of medical self-care; the client and health professional develop a working relationship whereby the client takes advantage of the professional's knowledge and information is shared in the decision-making process. The professional supplies an assessment of facts and probabilities, but the decision-making responsibility rests with the client and family (Kemper, 1980).

At present, some wellness advocates are promoting a do-it-yourself health curriculum of nutrition, stress management, and exercise as an implicit alternative for traditional medicine. Ardell (1979), for example, cites overemphasis on physician guidance, physician direction, and continued physician-dependence as shortcomings of traditional medicine. Many supporters of traditional medicine, on the other hand, view the wellness movement as little more than a fad and are skeptical that wellness behavior can create a healthier America and work for the masses, giving lasting benefits. They believe that wellness behavior and health education are destined to minimal success at best (Cohen, 1978).

Rather than considering hospitals and organized medicine at odds with the wellness movement, however, I see a potential marriage and development of a successful long-term partnership. From the traditional medical view, we are slowly reaching a limit in our ability to prolong life to any degree through current medical knowledge and intervention (Robbins, 1980). Knowledgeable health professionals are aware that over half the mortality in the United States is due to unhealthy behavior or lifestyle (Millar, Note 1). Wellness promotors are aware that a significant portion of the money spent for health care is spent during the last year of a person's life, on terminal-stage heroics. They would prefer that these monies be spent on early intervention and health promotion. Both camps agree that health professionals are often left scraping the barrel, trying to preserve life by piecing together individuals who have abused their health for many years. Wellness proponents (especially health psychologists) are aware that a change in behavior is more likely to occur in people who have experienced the dark side of disease and its concomitant stress, or who have had a close call with death as the result of accident or injury. Many patients dealing with altered health states are also willing to learn and are more receptive to adopting new health behaviors. The captive inpatient audience ripe for acquiring new and possibly healthier behaviors has a right to the opportunity to learn about high-level wellness.

Hospitals that have started wellness programs have so far bypassed the typical in-house patient and have concentrated instead on employees and community outreach programs. Perhaps the logic is that employees need to know, understand, and internalize a wellness lifestyle before they can teach, display, and transfer such behavior to patients. I believe there is a need and desire for health professionals—besides adopting wellness lifestyles themselves—to go one step beyond caring for the disease condition of ill people and to assist these people in gaining knowledge about wellness.

This chapter will review the literature concerning the adoption of wellness programs by hospitals in this country. The four major categories of wellness—encouraging self-care, improving nutrition, teaching stress management techniques, and encouraging exercise—will be presented in a manner that is clinically adaptable to patients during an inpatient hospital stay. The chapter will include the philosophy of holistic medicine as it pertains to wellness and health promotion for the patient who is currently ill and receiving inpatient hospital care.

ENCOURAGING SELF-RESPONSIBILITY

Most people, including health professionals, are frightened at the prospect of themselves or family members entering the hospital as patients. This fear is related to the presence of ill health that necessitates hospitalization, but it is surely compounded by the fact that hospitals frequently are dehumanizing, demoralizing, and utterly unhealthy hierarchical institutions, with reams of written and unwritten rules and staffed by a large number of specialized people. Indeed, being admitted to the hospital is a truly intimidating experience. Is it even possible or justifiable to encourage people to attain and assert self-responsibility in such settings? This question remains a personal choice for patients who are conditioned to depend more on doctors than on themselves for their own health care.

Obviously, a well-informed consumer is better prepared to make decisions regarding choice of hospital, selection of physician, assessment of consultants, and application of various diagnostic and treatment procedures. Being armed with the information in such self-help books as *The People's Hospital Book* (Gots & Kaufman, 1978), *The People's Pharmacy* (Graedon, 1976), *Healing from Within* (Jaffe, 1980), and *What Are My Chances?* (Eiseman, 1980) will better prepare patients to relate to the hospital and the health professional bureaucracy. Health professionals should also read the aforementioned books so that they can do their part in encouraging patients to take responsibility for their own care. Patients and health professionals must become active partners in the healing process.

MEDICAL SELF-CARE

One way to assure the development of the active partnership is to provide information to patients about health and illness. Hospital staff members are in a prime position to act as guides and educators in assisting the patients to understand their role in determining their own health status.

Traditionally, health professionals have supplied information to patients under the rubric of patient education, which focuses on a specific disease or illness and provides information on how to deal with the situation. Medical self-care goes beyond a disease intervention treatment plan, because it focuses on how to anticipate common problems, what to do with them when they occur, and when and where to seek appropriate help. Kemper (1980) conceptualizes the overlap of patient education, medical self-care, wellness, and health promotion programs as depicted in Figure 80.1. He states that the areas are interdependent and share the same concepts of self-responsibility and health activation. The same behavior

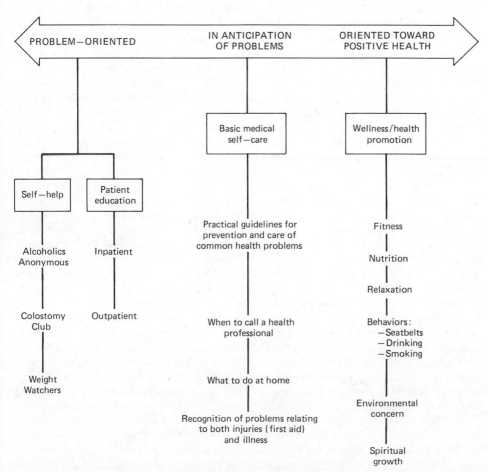

Figure 80.1 Self-care education continuum.

can be part of a rehabilitation program for one person and a wellness activity for another person. Patient education can become the medical self-care practice that eventually allows the patient to see the advantages of the wellness behavior once he or she is discharged from the hospital and has recovered from disease or injury.

A common example encountered on the cancer unit is teaching patients good oral hygiene. Since many patients are receiving chemotherapy, which has the unpleasant side effect of causing mouth sores, scrupulous mouth care is an important aspect of patient education. A great deal of time is spent in demonstrating proper brushing and flossing techniques. The use of mouthwash and gargles after any food is eaten is encouraged. Patients are shown how to inspect their gums, palate, and tongue and how to recognize and record any changes. During treatment, we can be sure that patients expertly clean their teeth and mouth. The oral hygiene behaviors are presented, however, not only as something to do while in the hospital but as a behavior that can be adopted as part of a healthy lifestyle. It is hoped that the oral hygiene behaviors are continued as a medical self-care practice after the course of treatment is completed and the people are home and well.

THE HEALING PARTNERSHIP

The most important prerequisite to effective medical self-care is a change in the health professional–patient relationship. The typical American experiences some type of health problem on an average of 120 days per year (Vickery, Note 2). Since the same typical American visits some type of health professional only four or five times a year, about 96% of the time health problems are dealt with by the person alone or with family and friends. It is incomprehensible for people who are almost totally in charge of their health problems to become submissive, compliant, and unquestioning just because they seek assistance from a health professional. As patients, these same people must maintain or develop confidence in their role as co-decision makers with health professionals, so that they do not regress to a passive state when they interact with a health professional. The health professional needs to come across as a partner and advisor, not as a godlike superior authority (Kemper, 1980). For the successful healing partnership to occur, both partners will have to work on knowing and accepting themselves and each other. This facilitates working effectively toward a common goal of wellness.

The healing partnership is perhaps a necessity for wellness activities in hospitals more than in any other agency or institution. Few people will criticize individuals who purchase Ardell's (1979) *High Level Wellness* for themselves or their families and adapt some of the common "welling" behaviors in their daily activities. Questions remain, however, as to whether a powerful institution such as a hospital and its staff should become involved in such activities. The task of motivating and educating people to take actions to improve their chances for health remains rather fractionated. The various efforts of the many agencies involved in health promotion share one common problem—the low salience of the health-promoting messages to the vast majority of their listeners. It has been stated that patients in hospitals are unusually open to messages that could motivate them to adopt wellness behaviors and that health professionals rank very high in the public's trust as a credible source of health-related information. Yet there is little evidence to suggest that such "teachable moments" of hospitalized patients are exploited in terms of lifestyle change. This may reflect the hospital staff's perception of their appropriate roles. Many health professionals follow the dictum of accepting patients as they are. They believe they would be overstepping their prerogative by encouraging patients to change lifestyles—even those that are life-threatening. They consider it their responsibility to explain the current healthy or unhealthy state and suggest alternatives and likely consequences, but the choice is up to the patient.

The decision not to offer wellness information to patients may result from the assumption that patients who are dealing with daily, ongoing problems at home and work—now compounded by an illness or injury requiring hospitalization—are already overloaded, that information on wellness behavior is a luxury the patients cannot handle. Health professionals who are attuned to the patients' anxiety are accustomed to interfacing at a crisis intervention level, and wellness-related activities may be considered inappropriate or, at best, untimely.

Health professionals have differing perceptions regarding their proper role in encouraging patients to adopt wellness behaviors while they are hospitalized for illness or injury. Although many now see this as overstepping the bounds of their responsibility, it is hoped that health professionals will eventually view wellness interventions as a logical extension of their accustomed injury or illness-related responsibilities. Tostson (1975) states that curricula in medical schools should help students address the problem of how to inform patients about their health in a way that effectively influences behaviors. As more professional health education programs incorporate information on health promotion and wellness, the health–illness dichotomy may fuse. The different dimensions of health promotion versus disease prevention, professionalization versus self-help, sophisticated technology versus simple tools, total care versus a targeted approach, holistic interventions versus allopathic tradition, and incentive/ encouragement versus dissuasion/deterrence (Room, 1981) may become anachronistic. The consumer and the health professional can form a healing partnership, attaining the common goal of wellness. The consumer, as a patient in the hospital, accepts self-responsibility for changing his or her lifestyle and attaining higher levels of health; the health professionals establish a health-promoting hospital environment in which patients and staff are free to learn and participate in high-level wellness behavior.

HOSPITALS AS WELLNESS CENTERS

There is general support for the concept of hospitals increasing their role in promoting wellness, and it is a common belief that health promotion can ultimately contribute to reductions in health care costs. Articles on hospital programmatic developments show a notably increased focus on the effects of health promotion and fitness, holistic health care, wellness, and prevention on the reduction of unhealthy lifestyles (Grubb, 1981). Unless hospitals approach the wellness movement with quality programs, however, they cannot be successful (Behrens, Lee, Jones, & Longe, 1981). Fielding (1980) suggests that hospitals "spend a little money up front" and obtain people with appropriate backgrounds to ensure that the programs will work. Grubb (1981) believes that the proliferation of educational program activities, except for wellness and health promotion programs, will level off because of the cost-benefit challenge. He warns hospital administrators that they should prepare to adopt the health promotion focus properly to ensure that hospitals retain their philosophical and moral position at the hub of health care, or else peripheral groups will take the lead. In addition to the moral and philosophical concerns of hospitals in promoting wellness programs, Ardell (1980) identifies other benefits that may be of interest to hospital administrators and fiscal planners: it is good business, because people will pay for good programs; it is good public relations, because new people will come into the hospital; it enhances patient satisfaction; it improves employee enthusiasm and morale, thereby improving productivity; and it possibly can contribute to changing perceptions held by high-echelon government representatives regarding the institution's contribution to health.

Therefore, the new challenge to health professionals is to educate patients fully, not only about their illness and related activities, but also about optimizing health and wellness. Pelletier (1979) states that health professionals must be involved in patient education efforts that no longer focus primarily on pathology but have an educational approach that recognizes a person's ability to use the experience for positive change. As hospitals change their orientation, it may upset consumers who have learned to expect a certain routine when being hospitalized and who have not readily or willingly embraced the self-care/self-responsibility idea (McKay, 1980). Our sensitivity to such patients is of prime importance. Health care, and its related activities, is an inherently moral concern. No health professional who advocates the wellness philosophy wants to see hospitals change from authoritative "disease museums" run by "biological accountants" (Illich, 1975) to authoritative "Nazi health camps" run by myopic fitness addicts. As always, humanism, personal choice, sensitivity, and even humor are key aspects of therapeutic relationships. I believe one reason for the great success of Ardell's (1979) *High Level Wellness* is the "soft sell, have fun" approach he uses in explaining the wellness philosophy. The successful hospital-based wellness programs have also adopted such an approach.

HEALTH RISK APPRAISAL

One tool that can be easily adapted to a hospital routine and can assist patients through the orientation phase is the health risk appraisal (HRA), used as part of the traditional history taking and patient assessment process. The HRA can actually be a motivational tool for assisting patients to adapt healthier lifestyles because it is a means of presenting an objective measure of risk; eliminating moralistic overtones; offering a time dimension to the immediacy of needed behavioral change; offering some degree of latitude in suggesting that changes could make a difference in outcome; and giving concrete prescriptions for actions (Bauer, 1981). Examples of HRAs are the Health Hazard Appraisal from the Wellness Resource Center in Mill Valley, California; the Life Change Checklist (Holmes & Rahe, 1967); and Project Well Aware About Health at the University of Arizona Health Science Center in Tucson. Risk appraisal systems are currently being evaluated as to cost-effectiveness, feasibility, and applicability. The good risk appraisal systems deliberately avoid arousing fear and give major emphasis to positive rewards associated with good health.

WELLNESS INFORMATION

Once patients are given information about their health risk appraisal, the hospital staff can have appropriate materials and resources available to offer wellness information and health behavior opportunities to the patients. Hospital staff, of course, should practice wellness behavior, use the resources, and function as high-level wellness role models. Unfortunately, health practitioners are less than exemplary in many health habits. Ardell's (1980) comment, "Trust not the counsel of the adipose physician," suggests that patients who are actively involved in their health care will increasingly seek out practitioners who practice what they preach (McKay, 1980).

In addition to self-care and personal responsibility for health, the other common areas addressed by the wellness movement that hospitals can incorporate in patient care are nutrition, physical fitness, and stress management. Carpenter (1980) has proposed a hospital-based health promotion and fitness center that has three major operational divisions: fitness counseling services, fitness facilities, and fitness research. The counseling services could be provided by the health professionals and would include health hazard appraisals, as mentioned earlier; preventive and rehabilitative cardiac clinic services, such as exercise testing and personalized exercise prescriptions; nutritional counseling; selective multiphasic screening programs; behavior modification programs for weight control and smoking; stress management programs; and pain and physical discomfort management programs, incorporating nonpharmacological interventions in addition to traditional analgesia. The fitness facilities could include jogging tracks; racquetball courts; swimming pools; exercise rooms; and gymnasiums that could be used for group exercises. The division of fitness research could study the impact of improved fitness on employees; longitudinal outcomes in disease prevention and rehabilitation of patients with heart and vascular disease; effect of fitness programs on the elderly; and possible psychological benefits of fitness. Carpenter (1980) states that such a hospital fitness center could contract with employers who want on-site fitness programs for employees and could use a mobile van to take the fitness services and information to the work site or into the community. One of the more attractive features of the model is that the fitness services would have immediate access to traditional medical testing services (clinical laboratory, cardiac testing, etc.). More important, the model would provide a "welding together" of medical services, fitness counseling, and recreational facilities.

Several hospitals around the country have already adopted a wellness center focus. Van-Vorst and Root (1980) provide a thorough description of the development of the Wellness Center at St. Vincent Hospital in Carmel, Indiana. They explain the reevaluation of the hospital's mission statement to meet community desire for expanded and centralized health-related services, the planning process, the renovation and furnishing of the wellness facility, the importance of administrative support, the funding mechanisms, and a list of the programs being provided.

Mercy Center for Health Care Services in Aurora, Illinois, is another example of a hospital becoming involved in health promotion and wellness. Sister Rita Meaghir, president of the center, affirmed that the program is relatively inexpensive to operate and has succeeded in encouraging people to take greater responsibility for their own health (1980).

Friedman (1980) describes the seagoing health promotion center called the Floating Hospital. This is a ship, berthed in New York City's South Street Seaport Museum, that provides health education and health-related services to the city's medically underserved residents. There are two unique aspects to the Floating Hospital. One is the lure of the ship, which attracts a large number of people who probably would not be attracted to a land-based facility. The other is the fact that the Floating Hospital specifically serves the medically underserved, poor population of a section of New York. This is particularly refreshing, since most wellness and health promotion literature and services seems to be geared to white middle- and upper-middle-class populations.

In describing the Swedish Medical Center's pioneering wellness program in Englewood, Colorado, Howard and Palmquist (1981) note that, since 1904, the mission of the trustees of the hospital has been to apply funds to "more effectively assist, encourage, and promote the general well-being of mankind." With this statement in the hospital's mission charter, the current trustees set forth the purposes of Swedish Health Resources, Inc., which include:

1. To catalyze, coordinate, and provide high-quality wellness programs for improvement of health and realization of human potential.

2. To provide national leadership in the development of wellness and health promotion efforts.

3. To create supportive environments in hospitals, schools, churches, corporations, physicians' offices, government, and other community groups that aid people in initiating and maintaining healthy lifestyles.

4. To explore innovative roles that a hospital can play in promoting and advancing the health of its community.

5. To establish a cooperative national network of programs that will improve quality, accessibility, and continuity of wellness services.

In addition to the specific objectives of the program, Howard and Palmquist (1981) give sound advice on the administrative planning of hospital-associated wellness centers. They list questions that arise—such as "Why is an illness-oriented institution involved in wellness promotion?"—and comment on the praise that has emanated from persons who have used some or all of the services of the center. They give sound advice to hospital trustees who are interested in wellness programs:

Initiating a new program is never an easy task. It takes commitment, time, dedication, and the allocation of scarce resources. Launching a wellness program takes all of the above, plus a great deal of patience and perseverance. Intense communication with all components of the hospital family is an important ingredient. (Howard & Palmquist, 1981, p. 28)

The Community Hospital in Indianapolis has been involved in a holistic approach to interacting with clients and families, helping them deal with illness and incorporating a wellness model for health promotion. The program is staffed by health resource people, under the direction of the Medical Psychology Department, who are trained in nutrition, fitness, stress control, and vocational guidance (Ardell, 1979).

In 1981, the Michigan Hospital Association published a two-part series in its official publication, *Michigan Hospitals,* on the wellness activities in the various hospitals throughout Michigan (Yenny, 1981a, 1981b). The articles give information about the specific hospital-based wellness programs throughout the state. In addition, they give valuable information concerning administrators' perspectives on such programs, including accountability, accessibility, effectiveness, evaluation, and health staff roles.

The literature on hospital-based wellness programs from 1978 to present is impressive. The trail-blazing activities of the leaders in the aforementioned programs is most commendable. They have shown that hospital-based wellness programs are not only a feasible idea but actually a necessary move "if hospitals are to remain at the hub of health agencies" (Grubb, 1981). The majority of the programs, however, remain community- or employee-based. Even Carpenter's (1980) model stops short of including inpatients in the hospital. It is absurd to think that all patients will be able to participate in many physical activities (tennis, volleyball) while receiving acute hospital care, but it is equally absurd to believe that just because patients are receiving acute care in hospitals, fitness and wellness activities need to be totally absent. Hospitals can be health-promoting environments in which patients are given opportunities to maximize their degree of wellness. A condition of wellness can be reached by progressively limiting negative health-related behaviors and by progressively increasing positive health-related behaviors. (Tager, 1981). This scenario can be accomplished while patients are receiving medical/health care for an illness or injury if wellness information on nutrition, fitness, and stress reduction is made available to them during the course of their hospital stay.

During hospitalization, patients spend time being taken to and from laboratories for various tests and special treatment areas (e.g., X rays, physical therapy, pulmonary function tests). Still, a great deal of patients' time is spent in their hospital rooms, watching television and interacting with other patients, visitors, and hospital staff. Therefore, patients and their families and visitors experience some amount of "down time." It is during this down time that the hospital staff can have wellness material available to be shared with patients and family and to change the down time into "teachable moments."

Nutrition

Most hospitals use a menu that gives three to five choices of foods from which patients select their meals, and most menus offer the possibility of a healthful diet for the patient. Patients are free to select some kind of cake, pie, and the like, or "fresh fruit in season" for a dessert, and many, if not the majority of patients, probably select the cake or pie over the fresh fruit. Would the selection be different if the menu read "Fresh, Crisp Apple," "Fresh, Sweet, Ripe Banana," or "Tasty Juicy Orange" as the forced-choice options for dessert, with a footnoted statement, "Other desserts available on request but not recommended"? The menu could also give options for bread—whole wheat, pumpernickel, or tasty soy/wheat blend, with a footnoted statement, "Plain flat white bread available on request but not recommended." Most hospital menus offer regular brewed coffee or tea and instant decaffeinated coffee (which is now being identified as a cancer risk), but few hospitals give patients a choice of herbal teas, although this might be the only time a person would be curious enough (or bored enough by hospital routine) to try an herbal tea. Most hospitals include mid-morning and/or mid-evening snacks as part of the daily routine. The snacks are usually cookies, canned fruit, fruit-flavored gelatin, and sometimes fresh fruit. Patients and families might be receptive, however, to a cup of fresh yogurt sweetened with fresh fruit or honey and topped with roasted sunflower seeds, attractively served with a card affirming the healthful advantages of each food item and with a sincere wish to "enjoy."

Fitness

Encouraging physical fitness for hospitalized patients is almost routine in hospitals, but it is couched in such terms as "range-of-motion exercises"; preoperative "turn, cough, deep breath"; and "ambulate QID" (four times a day). These are all treatments geared to an illness or injury, and they are necessary. When they are presented only as treatments for illness or injury, however, they lack the positive motivations intrinsic in most fitness programs. When physical therapists are helping patients perform range-of-motion exercises, they could also be explaining basic muscle movement, the formidable recuperative powers of the body, and the good feelings associated with accomplishments, and they could tell stories of the remarkable recovery other patients have achieved. In general, they could inform patients of the inner joys of exercise that most people experience who participate in the fitness experience.

A true wellness activity that occurs on our oncology unit is the use of the mini-gym, which was a joint effort of a nurse clinician and a physical therapist (Morgan & Baker, Note 3). The gym consists of vinyl-covered sandbags, a wooden wand, rubber tubing that people can use for active-resistive arm and leg exercises, hand grips, and a booklet describing the advantages of various exercises. There are plans to purchase two stationary cycles for patients and staff to use. The availability of the exercise equipment for inpatients on the cancer unit not only encourages people to maintain activity and physical muscle strength while being hospitalized but, more important, reinforces the aura of positive thinking that pervades the unit. Although the mini-gym is not considered a specific treatment for patients receiving cancer therapy, it provides an ideal opportunity for ward staff to assure patients that they are valued and capable individuals.

Stress Management

The use of stress management techniques in hospitals is not a new idea. A routine part of hospital evening care was to straighten the bed sheets, offer sleeping medication, give a relaxing back massage, dim the lights, and wish the patient a good night. Unfortunately, during the last 10 years, massage interventions have decreased in frequency, and the use of sedatives has increased. This could be the result of nursing staff shortage and increased work load, but possibly it is because our culture has become more pill-oriented than touch-oriented.

Montague (1975) eloquently describes the importance of touch in the human species. Most health professionals who are knowledgeable about the benefits of massage and therapeutic touch hesitate to use pharmacological methods to induce relaxation and sleep in patients. Massage is a most soothing treatment for bedridden patients and is a frequently used tool in other parts of the world to decrease pain, to aid in healing, and to provide comforting relaxation. Massage therapy is an excellent mode of nonverbal communication that provides reassurance and bridges the gap between caring and therapy (Rosenbaum, 1978). In addition, massage can be a pleasant way for health professionals to encourage families and friends of the patients to participate in the patients' recovery. The families and friends will gain satisfaction from being able to help with health and possibly relieve some of their anxiety surrounding the hospitalization experience. *The Massage Book* by George Downing and Ann Kent-Rush (1972) is an excellent resource for learning about massage therapy.

A vast array of relaxation techniques is available, including meditation, autogenic training, progressive muscle relaxation, visual imagery, hypnosis, and yoga. Selecting a suitable relaxation technique is a very personal matter. Health professionals can assist patients in choosing a technique that is suitable for them. As part of the routine history, physical examination, and health appraisal index, information can be obtained from patients concerning how they hold tension, what their target organs are, and what they do to relax. Many people already have resources to control stress but may not recognize them as stress management techniques. Once such information is obtained, health professionals can help patients continue using their techniques while in the hospital by (a) ensuring quiet time with a "Do not disturb" sign for the door; (b) obtaining the equipment the patients usually use for relaxation (record, tape recorder, exercise mat, etc.), or having the family bring such equipment from home; and (c) providing written information in the form of pamphlets or handouts that explain some of the theory about relaxation and the stress response. If patients practice unhealthy relaxation techniques (consuming alcohol and tranquilizers, etc.), health professionals can capture the moment to educate patients about other relaxation methods and offer them information and instructions. Cheek (1980) states that injured or ill persons frequently are frightened, and he considers them already to be in a hypnotic state when we see them. This makes them very responsive to helpful suggestions, even if they appear apathetic and withdrawn.

A study is under way on our unit in which eligible patients are trained in progressive muscle relaxation as a symptom-management technique for controlling chemotherapy-induced nausea and vomiting. The relaxation procedure is explained in detail and presented as a skill that needs to be learned and can only be learned through practice. Emphasis is placed on the beneficial aspects of learning to relax. Patients are assured that they are learning a self-control technique that they can choose whether or not to use. Although the relaxation technique is taught as a symptom-management technique for decreasing nausea and vomiting, we seize every opportunity to make it a wellness activity. We encourage family (or significant others) to participate in the training and practice sessions; we encourage the people to think of the skill as having extra benefits—aiding sleep, diminishing pain, improving appetite, controlling undesirable habits. Although we have to spend time gathering information on nausea and vomiting and physiological arousal, this is *not* what we emphasize. Relaxation in this case is more patient education than pure wellness activity. A follow-up study is under way, however, to investigate how frequently patients and families use relaxation when they are home and well. The preliminary findings are that most people continue to use relaxation as a stress-management technique in their lives when they are discharged from the hospital and finished with treatment. This is an example of how patient education can become a wellness activity and illustrates the interactive-interdependent properties of health education displayed in Kemper's model (Figure 80.1).

GETTING HOSPITALS TO CHANGE

Change can be effected on many levels. As hospital administrators, physicians, and nurses become informed of the benefits of wellness, change can take place within the institutions, and wellness can become an appropriate goal for hospitals. Medical interests are sensitive and responsive to consumer demands; therefore, change can also occur as a result of consumer feedback. If consumers let it be known that they demand preventive medicine, health education, and an active role in the healing process while hospitalized, there will be a change in both the health professional's self-concept and the role of hospital care in America.

A factor that may hinder hospitals and health professionals from investing in wellness activities is that the benefits of wellness have yet to be evaluated. They may claim that when activities are based on imperfect knowledge, they can quickly become enshrined as conventional wisdom and practice without being clinically tested. Surprisingly few medical practices have been subjected to tight clinical trials to establish proof of efficacy as Bauer (1981) states:

> *Just as lack of perfect knowledge about the causality and most cost effective treatment of most diseases does not justify a moratorium on their diagnosis and therapy, so too, the limitations on the state of the art of risk identification and behavior change does not justify a moratorium on risk appraisal and risk reduction activities. Instead, the challenge in both instances is to make the best use of whatever sound information we have, while systematically adding to our store of knowledge through research and evaluation, and promptly disseminating findings to both practitioners and the public to guide future activities. (p. 170)*

This statement pertains to risk identification and risk reduction activities but is equally applicable to the promotion of wellness activities in hospitals.

Another criticism often put forth, which may impede a hospital's adoption of a wellness focus, is that health promotion is just a fad and that hospitals should therefore not consider extensive or long-term involvement in the wellness movement. There may be some truth in this criticism, but *health* is not a fad. Most people rank health high on the list of the aspects of their lives they most value (Yenny, 1981c). The high-level wellness behaviors and techniques and the semantics used to describe them may appear to be faddish now, or perhaps they are just avant-garde. Health professionals who have personally adopted wellness behaviors can affirm that, rather than being a fad, most wellness activities are actually addicting. Hospital leaders should make decisions about health promotion principles with the faith that health is not going out of style and that wellness activities are a means of increasing a person's chances for health.

REFERENCE NOTES

1. Millar, J. Emerging concepts in preventive medicine. Presented at the Medical Association of Georgia Scientific Assembly, Atlanta, Georgia, 1979.
2. Vickery, D. Promotional letter for: The Center for Consumer Health Education, Inc., Reston, VA, 1978.
3. Morgan, E. & Baker, B. Personal communication, June 21, 1982.

REFERENCES

Ardell, D. *High level wellness.* New York: Bantam Books, 1979.

Ardell, D. And what's in it for the hospitals? *PROmoting HEALTH,* 1980, **1,** 4–6.

Bauer, K. *Improving the chances for health: Lifestyle change and health evaluation.* Hyattsville, Md.: National Center for Health Education Bureau of Health Planning, 1981.

Behrens, R., Lee, E., Jones, L., & Longe, M. Past year saw large increase in number of hospital programs. *Hospitals,* 1981, **55,** 105–108.

Carpenter, D. Hospitals should be fitness centers. *Hospitals,* 1980, **54,** 148–154.

Cheek, D. Hypnosis. In A. Hasting, J. Fadiman, & J. Gordon (Eds.), *Health for the whole person.* New York: Bantam Books, 1980.

Cohen, C. Sounding board—Health education: Panacea, pernicious or pointless? *New England Journal of Medicine,* 1978, **299,** 718–720.

Dowing, G., & Kent-Rush, A. *The massage book.* New York: Random House Book Works, 1972.

Eiseman, B. *What are my chances?* Philadelphia: Saunders, 1980.

Fielding, J. UCLA Center studying why, how, people change health behavior. *PROmoting HEALTH,* 1980, **1,** 4.

Friedman, E. The hospital that's docked at Pier 15. *Hospitals,* 1980, June, 69–72.

Gots, R., & Kaufman, A. *The people's hospital book.* New York: Crown, 1978.

Graedon, J. *The people's pharmacy.* New York: Crown, 1976.

Grossmann, J. The wellness revolution: Will your town be next? *Health,* 1981, January, 43–46.

Grubb, A. Roles, relevance, costs of hospital education, and training debated. *Hospitals,* 1981, 75–79.

Holmes, T., & Rahe, R. The social readjustment rating scale. *Journal of Psychosomatic Research,* 1967, **11**, 213–218.

Howard, W., & Palmquist, L. A hospital that takes care of well people. *Truster,* 1981, March, 25–28.

Illich, I. *Medical nemesis.* London: Calder and Boyars, 1975.

Jaffe, D. *Healing from within.* New York: Knopf, 1980.

Kemper, D. Medical self-care: A stop on the road to high level wellness. *Medical Self-Care,* 1980, **4**, 63–68.

Meaghir, Sister Rita. Healthful living program focuses on wellness. *Hospital Progress,* 1980, September, 6–10.

McKay, S. Holistic health care: Challenge to health professionals. *Journal of Allied Health,* 1980, **9**, 194–201.

Montague, A. *Touching.* New York: Harper & Row, 1978.

Pelletier, K. *Holistic medicine: From stress to optimum health.* New York: Delacorte, 1979.

Robbins, J. Preaching in your practice: What to tell patients to help them live longer. *Primary Care,* 1980, **7**, 549–562.

Room, R. The case for a problem prevention approach to alcohol, drug, and mental problems. *Public Health Reports,* 1981, **96**, 26–33.

Rosenbaum, E. *A Comprehensive Guide for Cancer Patients.* Palo Alto, Calif.: Bull, 1978.

Tager, R. Achieving higher level wellness in the older population. *Health Values,* 1981, **5**, 73–80.

Tostson, D. The right to know: Public education for health. *Journal of Medical Education,* 1975, **50**, 117–123.

Yenny, S. Healthful living program focuses on wellness. *Hospital Progress,* 1980, September, 6; 10.

Yenny, S. Patient education/health promotion—Part I. *Michigan Hospitals,* 1981, January, 20–32.

Yenny, S. Patient education/health promotion—Part II. *Michigan Hospitals,* 1981, February, 22–30.

Yenny, S. Wellness care. *Michigan Hospitals,* 1981, February, 4–6. (c)

CHAPTER 81

COMMUNITY HEALTH PROMOTION DEMONSTRATION PROGRAMS: INTRODUCTION

STEPHEN M. WEISS

National Heart, Lung, and Blood Institute, Bethesda, MD

During the past 20 years, the nations of the industrialized world have been faced with dramatically escalating health care costs, primarily related to the epidemic nature of the three major causes of premature morbidity and mortality—cardiovascular disease, cancer, and stroke. The increasingly sophisticated health care technology available for treatment undoubtedly has had some salutary effect on mortality, but it has probably increased the demand for services and associated costs, having virtually no effect on the supply side in terms of reduced utilization of the health care system. It has therefore become painfully obvious that prevention of disease (reduction in morbidity) may be the only way to contain costs while at the same time improving the health of the population. Such recognition has prompted the development of national health plans in several countries, which seek to address this problem in terms of possible risk factors that might be preventable or at least controllable through public health strategies.

Cardiovascular disease is the single most important cause of death in developed nations. A variety of factors associated with increased risk for disease have been identified, many of them related to our Western, urban-oriented lifestyle. Decreasing the rate of premature cardiovascular mortality through changes in lifestyle will require that individuals assess their behavior patterns regarding smoking, sedentary living, and obesity. Maintaining appropriate blood pressure levels, reducing dietary intake of high-cholesterol foods, animal fats, and sodium, and adopting adequate stress management strategies are also considered desirable methods for maintaining health.

All these risk factors are amenable to lifestyle modification efforts, but the level at which such efforts should be focused has been a source of much speculation and concern. Although initial changes often have been made as a result of medical consultation and therapy, patients have traditionally regressed to their earlier behavior patterns when treatment has ended. Antismoking and weight control programs in clinical settings have been particularly susceptible to compliance (maintenance) problems. Moreover, such programs have proved costly and difficult to apply to large, heterogenous populations.

In an effort to address such problems, recent research and demonstration efforts have adopted a community-based intervention model that combines biomedical, social, and behavioral science approaches to identify effective health behavior change and maintenance strategies that can be used with the population at large. Such models employ "state-of-science" communication and education strategies combined with effective community organization and social support to improve maintenance of health-enhancing behavior across the entire community and to accomplish disease prevention and health promotion objectives in a cost-effective manner. The community model has several important benefits:

1. It uses methods of risk reduction that apply to the real environment in which people live.

2. It enhances opportunities for information exchange and social support among members of the target population.

3. It allows for testing of the efficacy of programs that are more generalizable than clinic-based trials.

4. It allows for observation not only of the efficacy of public health programs but also of related outcomes that might have broader implications for public policy.

5. It obviates the ethical problem of withholding supposedly helpful interventions from a control population.

6. It reduces the unit cost of trials because large groups, rather than individuals, receive educational services.

As a research approach, the community-based model is quasi-experimental. This means that blinding is generally impossible; the model has limited suitability for single-factor tests, and there are limitations on its ability to make causal inference. These limitations can be partially overcome, however, through such methods as matched units, covariance analysis, network analysis, path analysis, time series or trend analysis, ancillary event monitoring, and analysis of unobtrusive measures.

The following five chapters present programs that have been selected to represent the broad spectrum of approaches currently being attempted throughout the world. As Finland and the United States were noted for having the highest cardiovascular disease (CVD) mortality rates in the world in 1970, it is not surprising that two of the earliest efforts were undertaken in North Karelia, the county with the highest CVD mortality in Finland (Puska, 1981) and in northern California, one of the more health-conscious areas of the United States.

Both the North Karelia Project (reported in Chapter 82) and the Stanford Three Community Study began in 1972. The Finnish study has continued without interruption to the present, whereas the Stanford program completed its initial study in 1976 (Farquhar et al., 1977) and embarked upon the Five City Study (reported in Chapter 84) in 1978. The Belgian group had previously participated in the WHO Collaborative Study, begun in 1971, a randomized intervention-control design involving 80 factories located in four countries (United Kingdom, Italy, Poland, and Belgium).

As the Rhode Island and Minnesota community studies (Chapters 85 and 86, respectively) and the current Belgian study (Chapter 83) have only recently gotten under way and are in the midst of data collection, the descriptions of these programs here will be oriented toward theory and methodology. Certain commonalities in design can be observed across programs, which reflect, in part, the willingness of the pioneer programs to share data and methodology with these and other community intervention programs around the world. Each program demonstrates unique characteristics, however, concerning population size and composition, geographic and cultural factors, strategies for health behavior change and maintenance, and community organization and utilization. Collectively, they should provide extensive information on the ability of the community approach to attain critical disease prevention/health promotion public health objectives.

REFERENCES

Farquhar, J. W., Maccoby, N., Wood, P. D., Brietrose, H., Haskell, W. L., Meyer, A. J., Alexander, J. K., Brown, B. W., McAlister, A. L., Nash, J. D., & Stern, M. P. Community education for cardiovascular health. *Lancet,* 1977, **1,** 1192–1195.

Puska, P., Tuomilehto, J., Salonen, J., Nissinen, A., Virtamo, J., Björkqvist, S., Koskela, K., Neittaanmäki, L., Takalo, T., Kottke, T., Mäki, J., Sipila, P., & Varvikko, P. The North Karelia Project: Evaluation of a comprehensive community program for control of cardiovascular diseases in 1972–77 in North Karelia, Finland. Copenhagen: WHO/TURO, 1981.

CHAPTER 82

COMMUNITY-BASED PREVENTION OF CARDIOVASCULAR DISEASE: THE NORTH KARELIA PROJECT

PEKKA PUSKA

National Public Health Institute, Helsinki

The North Karelia Project in Finland has been the first major community-based program for prevention of cardiovascular disease (CVD). Its experiences and results have been analyzed for its original 5-year period (Puska, Tuomilehto, Salonen, Nissinen, A., Virtamo, J., Björkquist, S., Koskela, K., Neittaanmäki, L., Takalo, T., Kohke, T., Maki, J., Sipila, P., & Varvikko, P., 1981). During the last few years, several other community-based programs following this model have been launched in several countries.

The North Karelia Project was started in 1972 after a population petition that asked for urgent action to do something about the incidence of cardiovascular mortality in the area. After the planning phase, a comprehensive community program was initiated, with the main objective of reducing the extremely high cardiovascular mortality and morbidity in the county of North Karelia. The intermediate objectives of the program were to reduce the levels of the established CVD risk factors among the population and to promote secondary prevention among people already affected by CVD.

Since the planning phase, close cooperation has taken place between the project and the World Health Organization and several other international institutions. Within Finland, the project has been an official pilot program of the Finnish health authorities to test the feasibility and effects of such an approach to controlling CVD and related health problems. The original project was to implement and evaluate this program for the 5-year period from 1972 to 1977. After that the project was continued and a 10 year evaluation has recently been carried out.

North Karelia is a mainly rural county in Eastern Finland with 180,000 inhabitants and a rather large geographic area. The implementation of the program was closely integrated with the existing service structure and social organization of the area. Thus, the local project office was established at the county health department. The evaluative research has been carried out at the National Public Health Institute (Helsinki) and at the University of Kuopio.

PROGRAM FORMULATION

During the planning phase, it was realized that, because of the chronic nature of the diseases in question, the potential for their control lay in primary prevention. It was thought, however, that a comprehensive program should also include secondary preventive measures that could contribute to the overall results and could be a useful program component in the community.

The key question in the planning concerned which factors were amenable to intervention. Previous epidemiologic research in Finland and other countries had especially highlighted the role of smoking, elevated serum cholesterol levels, and elevated blood pressure levels. Since the roles of many other possible factors were more controversial and the levels of these conventional risk factors were very high in the North Karelian population, they were naturally chosen as targets for the intervention.

The program strategy was further influenced by some important features of the risk factors that epidemiologic research had discovered. For all these factors, the disease risk increases with an increasing level of the risk factor throughout most of the range of the population. Thus, the North Karelian or Finnish problem was that the general level of these factors was so high. Also, the simultaneous occurrence of the risk factors has a synergistic effect, contributing further to the high community disease rates. Because of the high general levels of the risk factors, it was realized that the disease cases arose from a large segment of the population. Thus, even from the epidemiologic point of view, rather than trying to identify and influence a limited group of people with clearly elevated risk factor levels (the high-risk approach), a more effective strategy would be to influence favorably the entire risk factor distribution (the population approach).

Even from the medical point of view, it was considered that elevated risk characterized most of the people in the community. Furthermore, it was realized that the high community risk factor levels were a consequence of the general lifestyle in the community, and this, in turn, was closely linked with local culture, social organization, and even physical environment. All these considerations formed the basis for adoption of the community model as the strategy of intervention. It was decided to carry out a comprehensive program through the community structure and with the local population. The heart disease problem was seen as a community mass epidemic that needed mass action by the community. "To be in the project" became a slogan of the local people and a symbol of joint effort.

As mentioned earlier, the program that was started in 1972 after the baseline studies in North Karelia was closely integrated with the existing service structure and social organization of the community. Practical subprograms were developed and gradually implemented in the community. The elements of the intervention included intensified mass health communication, organizing of individual and group services, training of local health personnel, and environmental modification. Community involvement was emphasized. The aim was to organize an intensive community action with a systematic service structure as its backbone. A practical information system was developed for monitoring program development and providing feedback to the community about the progress of the program.

The program activities have been primarily educational, aiming to teach the community how people can adopt lifestyles that are likely to reduce cardiovascular disease risks and that otherwise promote good health. Thus, people have been encouraged to stop or reduce smoking and to change to low-fat diets. Local health services have been reorganized for detection and control of hypertension (Tuomilehto, Puska, & Nissinen, 1976) through introduction of a systematic network of hypertension dispensaries, which depend heavily on the work of trained public health nurses. Some important environmental changes have been stimulated, such as smoking restrictions and introduction of low-fat food products and improved availability of these products.

STRATEGIES FOR PROMOTING LIFESTYLE CHANGES

The objective of the project was to carry out a comprehensive program in which a broad range of activities and methods would be used to contribute to a favorable overall change. It was realized that this kind of prevention goes far beyond traditional medicine and health services. The project aim was to become involved in as many components of community life as possible. Existing health services naturally formed an important base for this effort, but the program was to a great extent based on other kinds of activities in the community. The primary strategies used to promote the desired behavioral changes were information, persuasion, training, social support, environmental change, and community organization (McAlister, Puska, Salonen, Tuomilehto, & Koskela, 1982).

Information

Various channels were used to disseminate knowledge about the nature of the problem, the role of the risk factors, and the activities of the project. Different kinds of health education material were prepared and distributed, and the mass media were relied on heavily. Simple messages were used, and interpersonal communication was emphasized.

Persuasion

An important part of the program strategy was persuading people to make the desired behavioral changes. The credibility and expertise of the project was emphasized. Reference was made to the World Health Organization (WHO) and other involved expert groups, and local influential people were also used to maximize the perceived credibility. The background of the project was repeatedly mentioned ("a response to the people's demand. The experts have defined the needed action, but only the people themselves can do it"). The message had a definite affective or emotional component. The project goals were associated with the pride and provincial identity of the population. People were urged to participate, not necessarily for their own benefit, but "for North Karelia." Thus, by personal participation, people knew they could contribute to the success of the project. People felt that the project was their own and that they could be proud of its success, which would be an important demonstration to the rest of Finland and also internationally. The content of the messages was constructed to anticipate and refute counterarguments. Fear was avoided, clear and practical recommendations were given, and the benefits of even small changes were emphasized. Formal opinion leaders were used, and a network of informal lay opinion leaders was trained (Neittaanmäki, Koskela, Puska, & McAlister, 1981).

Training

An important part of the program was to teach and train the people in the practical skills needed to accomplish the desired behavioral change. This was an important principle in communication of the project to the population; people were told not about the dangers of smoking, for example, but about how to stop smoking. Instead of receiving general advice to reduce fat consumption, people were specifically advised that they should switch from fatty milk to low-fat milk, and so on. New cooking and food preparation skills were taught through a strong housewives organization that has over 300 local clubs in the area.

Social support

Lack of social support often makes it difficult for people to adopt a new habit permanently. The project tried to increase social support through several means. The message often emphasized attempting the desired changes jointly. Natural social units, such as families or work groups, were emphasized. Many activities also introduced new social support mechanisms (e.g., smoking cessation groups, dietary education groups, rehabilitation groups). Social support from local nurses and doctors was encouraged. The trained network of local lay leaders provided further support locally and was involved in many kinds of self-help activities.

Environmental change

Since the environment often has a determining influence on behavior, the project attempted to modify the environment as much as possible. With a regional program such possibilities obviously were limited. Smoking restrictions were introduced in various places, and the project distributed antismoking signs in great quantities. The project established close cooperation with the local dairies and the local sausage factory to promote production and sale of low-fat products. Local shopkeepers also were often involved. Several campaigns encouraged people to grow their own vegetables.

Community organization

The central aim of the project was to involve the whole community in a broad effort to fight CVD and to promote health in North Karelia. The project leaders traveled extensively throughout the area, establishing close personal contacts with community leaders, such as political decision makers, local doctors, representatives of the food industry, and local mass media personnel. Their support was requested, and the practical possibilities for expression of such support were discussed. The project was in contact with many existing decision-making bodies in the area, and the project itself had broad local representation on its committees. Natural organizations (e.g., work sites) were emphasized. The trained network of local lay leaders helped to strengthen the community organization on the local level.

EVALUATION DESIGN AND RESULTS

The aim of the evaluative research, according to the original project plan, was to assess the feasibility, costs, process, and other consequences of this program for its first 5-year period, from 1972 to 1977. The evaluation used surveys of large, random, cross-sectional population samples at the outset and, at the end, disease registers (acute myocardial infarction and stroke), other studies, and existing national data sources (death certificates, hospital admission registers, cancer registers, etc.). For evaluation of the effects, a matched reference area (another county in eastern Finland) was chosen, and the surveys were carried out there simultaneously with those in the program area. In this way, a quasi-experimental study design was applied. In both the baseline and the 5-year follow-up survey, random population samples of more than 10,000 people were examined, with participation rates averaging 90%. In addition to a comprehensive questionnaire, physical measurement of risk factors was carried out, using internationally standardized measurement techniques.

A detailed description and the results of this comprehensive evaluation of the first 5 years of the North Karelia project have been published in numerous articles and recently as a WHO monograph (Puska et al., 1981). The 10-year evaluation on risk factor changes was recently published. (Puska, Salonen, Nissinen, Tuomilehto, Vartiainen, Korhonen, Tanskanen, Rommquist, Koskela, & Huttunen, 1983)

The overall feasibility of the program activities was encouraging. Most of the planned activities were well implemented, and the general information effectively reached the population. Approximately 17,000 hypertensives were recruited to the hypertension register for systematic care. The population participation rate was excellent, and the cooperation of health workers and local decision makers was good (Puska et al., 1981).

The surveys showed that health behaviors and risk factors in North Karelia changed clearly during the 5-year period in the desired direction. Changes of a similar kind, but smaller, were also observed in the reference area. These changes were obviously associated partly with the project, reducing the extent to which the intervention could be isolated. However, comparisons of the independent sample surveys in 1972 and 1977 from North Karelia and the reference area (birth cohort aged 25 to 59 in 1972) showed a 17% relative net decrease (i.e., the decrease in North Karelia adjusted for the decrease in the reference area) in estimated CVD risk for the middle-aged male population (Table 82.1). This decrease was composed of an interaction of a 4.1% (11mg/dl) decrease in serum cholesterol, a 3.6% (5.2 mmHg) decrease in systolic blood pressure, a 2.8% decrease (2.6 mmHg) in diastolic blood pressure, and a 9.8% reduction in the average number of cigarettes consumed per day (total sample). The reduction of risk factor levels among the female population resulted in an overall net reduction of 12% in the estimated CVD risk.

Detailed analyses of the behavioral and risk factor changes showed that they took place rather evenly in urban and rural parts of the county and in the different socioeconomic groups, and there was little association with the initial risk of the person—all indicating a rather general change and impact of the program in the community (Salonen, 1980). The

Table 82.1   Mean Risk Factor Levels for Men and Women in North Karelia and the Reference Area, 1972 and 1977, and the Respective Net Changes

Risk Factors	Risk Factor Level		
	1972	1977	Net Change (%)
Men			
Cigarettes/day (total sample)			
North Karelia	9.9	8.1	9.8*
Reference area	8.9	8.1	
Cholesterol			
North Karelia	269.3	259.0	4.1**
Reference area	260.4	261.2	
Systolic BP			
North Karelia	147.3	143.9	3.6**
Reference area	145.0	146.8	
Diastolic BP			
North Karelia	90.8	88.6	2.8**
Reference area	92.4	92.8	
Risk estimate			
North Karelia	4.1	3.4	17.4**
Reference area	3.3	3.7	
Women			
Cigarettes/day (total sample)			
North Karelia	1.3	1.1	8.0
Reference area	1.4	1.3	
Cholesterol			
North Karelia	265.3	258.2	1.2
Systolic BP			
North Karelia	149.4	143.5	4.8**
Reference area	144.1	145.4	
Diastolic BP			
North Karelia	90.7	86.8	3.7**
Reference area	90.0	89.5	
Risk estimate			
North Karelia	3.3	2.9	11.5**
Reference area	3.0	2.9	

* $p < 0.05$.
** $p < 0.001$.

process evaluation showed that the greatest reduction in smoking took place during the first year, the greatest increase in hypertension treatment during the second and third years, and the changes in nutrition habits throughout the whole period under evaluation (Puska et al., 1981).

The recent 10-year evaluation in 1982 showed the risk factor further reduced in North Karelia. The *net* reduction achieved in 1972–1977 was maintained for serum cholesterol and blood pressure, and became greater for smokers (28% for men and 14% for women; Puska, Salonen, Nissinen, Tuomilehto, Vartiainen, Korhonen, Tanskanen, Rommquist, Koskelo, & Huttunen, 1983). Another recent analysis showed that the reduction in age-standardized CHD mortality among men in 1974–1979 was 22% in North Karelia, 12% in the reference area, and 11% in the rest of Finland ($p < .005$ in relation to North Karelia; Salonen, Puska, Kottice, Tuomilehto, & Nissinen, 1983).

Other data were also analyzed as indicators of the effects of the project activities. All pension disability payments (according to diseases) are recorded by county in a national central register. Until 1972–1973, the trends of disability rates were essentially the same in both North Karelia and the reference area. In North Karelia, however, the rate for CVD-related disabilities leveled off in 1974 and began to move downward a year later. By 1977, North Karelia had about a 10% lower payment rate for cardiovascular disabilities. The difference between the two trends was statistically significant and yielded an estimate of more than 15% net savings in rates and payments for disabilities related to cardiovascular diseases. This amounts to approximately $4 million (U.S.) less in payments—a figure more than five times the $0.7 million spent in conducting the intervention. For noncardiovascular disability rates, the trends were virtually the same in the two areas (Puska, Tuomilehto, Salonen, Nissinen, Virtamo, Björkqvist, Koskela, Neittaanmäki, Takalo, Kottke, Maki, Sipilä, & Varvikko, 1981).

Evaluation of possible emotional consequences showed that there was an absolute and a net reduction of emotional problems (psychosomatic symptoms, etc.) in North Karelia during the program, both in general and in high-risk groups only. This indicated that, as a whole, the intervention was not associated with harmful emotional side-effects. It appeared that the practical activities provided more general social support, thus leading to a more general improvement of the health and well-being of the population. This view was further corroborated by softer forms of evaluation, indicating a great general satisfaction with the program among the local population.

DISCUSSION

Only a summary of the results achieved in North Karelia has been given here; full reports of intermediate and primary outcomes are available elsewhere (Puska et al., 1981). Because of the tendency for longitudinal studies of cohorts to exaggerate estimates of change in the entire community (Puska, Virtamo, Tuomilehto, Nissinen, Virtamo, Björkqvist, Koskela, Neittaanmäki, Takalo, Kottke, Maki, Sipila, & Varvikko, 1978), the project evaluation relied on independent surveys of population samples drawn from the national population register. Large samples were used, with high participation rates. These surveys included similarly structured questionnaires and direct risk factor measurement using standardized techniques. Smoking was measured by a set of questions; the reported answers were validated in the follow-up surveys by analyzing the serum thiocyanate levels of the examined subjects. An overall risk score was computed for each subject, using a multiple logistic function based on the subject's smoking, serum cholesterol, and systolic blood pressure values.

Five years is obviously not a long enough period to show a clear effect on cardiovascular morbidity and mortality, especially in situations where a reduction also started in the reference area and even, to a smaller extent, in the whole country. Five years is obviously a long enough period, however, to indicate that individuals' habits and risk factors have changed substantively. The continued follow-up confirmed the impact of the program on the risk factors and also demonstrated a favorable effect on the coronary heart disease rates.

Obviously, the observation of only two statistical units (counties) and the absence of random assignment of the intervention limit the certainty of the inferences that may be drawn. Given the origin of the project, randomization was clearly out of the question, but the reference area was chosen in a "matched" way. Because the possible impact of the project on the reference area was not taken into account, and because a new medical school was opened in the reference area in 1972, the true impact of the project may have been greater than estimated. Socioeconomic conditions and health services development were equivalent in both areas. There was negligible migration in or out among citizens above age 30.

Because the objective was to serve maximally the entire province of North Karelia, different components of intervention were not applied differentially within North Karelia. Thus, we cannot draw meaningful conclusions about the relative contributions of different subprograms or channels of action. The observed changes may have been due to any one or all of the several actions. It is likely, however, that the observed effects were a result of the multiple activities and the naturally occurring interactions in the community. Furthermore, there was obviously also an interaction with the national development. Whereas the implementation of the project could be carried out only because of considerable national interest and readiness, the demonstrations and examples from North Karelia likely influenced the whole country.

A few comments can be made about the feasibility and coverage of different activities. The new preventive services developed gradually and required a fair amount of organizational effort and training of local personnel. Training was extensive, but at times the number of participants was restricted because of conflicts with work duties or other meetings. Environmental changes were certainly effective, but their extent was limited by national legislation, other national rules, or economic realities. The extent and coverage of general antismoking advice certainly matched with initial expectations. Health personnel were attentive to patients' smoking, but the success of more intensive group support in smoking cessation was not great. The nutrition program resembled these experiences. General nutrition information and counseling was extensive and had wide coverage. Less developed was the system to provide intense individual nutrition counseling for the overweight or for those with very high cholesterol levels. On the other hand, it was felt that mass intervention to change nutrition habits was probably a better strategy in the situation where practically everyone had an elevated cholesterol level relative to world norms. The hypertension subprogram succeeded with what proved to be clear and practical programs to screen, treat, and follow the approximately 10% to 15% of the adult population with hypertension. The reorganization of preventive services and the organization of community support and action were probably the most effective aspects of the overall project.

Although some of the final epidemiologic results concerning mortality-reducing effects of the program in North Karelia need still to be confirmed, the goals of health promotion and risk reduction were met in many ways and to the satisfaction of those who initially requested the action. The general perception of success has led to rapid national adoption of innovations that originated in North Karelia. A major risk reduction television program, for example, based on the project experiences and methods, has now been conducted on national television (Puska, McAlister, Koskela, Pallonen, Vartiainen & Homan, 1979; Puska, McAlister, Pekkola, & Koskela, 1981). As mentioned earlier, many of the health education materials and health service models that were developed in North Karelia are now available throughout Finland. The North Karelia Project has become popular as a practical and positive example that health promotion and control of modern chronic disease epidemics is feasible.

REFERENCES

McAlister, A., Puska, P., Salonen, J. T., Tuomilehto, T. & Koskela, K. Theory and action for health promotion: Illustrations from the North Karelia Project. *American Journal of Public Health,* 1982, **72,** 43–50.

Neittaanmäki, L., Koskela, K., Puska, P., & McAlister, A. The role of lay workers in a community health education in the North Karelia Project. *Scandinavian Journal of Social Medicine,* 1981, **8,** 1–7.

Puska, P., McAlister, A., Koskela, K., Pallonen, V., Vartiainen, E. & Homan, K. A comprehensive television smoking cessation program in Finland. *International Journal of Health Education* [*Suppl.*], 1979, **22,** 1–26.

Puska, P., McAlister, A., Pekkola, J., & Koskela, K. Television in health promotion: Evaluation of a national programme in Finland. *International Journal of Health Education* [*Suppl.*], 1981, **24,** 238–250.

Puska, P., Salonen, J., Nissinen, A., Tuomilehto, J., Vartiainen, E., Korhonen, H., Tanskanen, A., Rommquist, P., Koskela, K. & Huttunen, J. Change in risk factors for coronary heart disease during 10 years of a community intervention programme (North Karelia Project). *British Medical Journal,* 1983, **287,** 1840–1844.

Puska, P., Tuomilehto, J., Salonen, J., and others. *The North Karelia Project: Evaluation of a comprehensive community program for control of cardiovascular diseases in 1972–77 in North Karelia, Finland.* Copenhagen: WHO/EURO, 1981.

Puska, P., Virtamo, J., Tuomilehto, J., Nissinen, A., Virtamo, J., Björqvist, S., Koskela, K., Neittaanmäki, L., Takalo, T., Kottke, T., Maki, J., Sipilo, P. & Varvikko, P. Cardiovascular risk factor changes in 5-year follow-up of a cohort in connection with a community program (the North Karelia Project). *Acta Medica Scandinavica,* 1978, **204,** 381–388.

Salonen, J. T. *Smoking and dietary fats in relation to estimated risk of myocardial infarction before and during a preventive community program.* University of Kuopio, Finland, Community Health-Series Original Reports No. 1, 1980.

Salonen, J., Puska, P., Kottke, T., Tuomilehto, J. & Nissinen, A. Decline in mortality from coronary heart disease in Finland from 1969 to 1979. *British Medical Journal,* 1983, 1857–1860.

Tuomilehto, J., Puska, P., & Nissinen, A. Hypertension program of the North Karelia Project. *Scandinavian Journal of Social Medicine,* 1976, **4,** 67–70.

CHAPTER 83

THE INTERUNIVERSITY STUDY ON NUTRITION AND HEALTH*

FRANCE KITTEL

University Libre de Bruxelles

In Belgium, two chronic diseases, cardiovascular diseases and cancer, are responsible for more than 65% of the total mortality. A rational approach to overcoming these lethal diseases is to intervene, before the onset, on the physical, bioclinical, and psychosocial factors that lead to the occurrence of those diseases.

During the 1970s, a controlled, multifactorial intervention trial on cardiovascular diseases in industries was carried out in Belgium (De Backer, Kornitzer, Thilly, & DePoorter, 1977). This trial was an effort of the World Health Organization—European Collaborative Group (WHO, 1980). The urgent need to tackle the problem on the scale of the total community, however, has motivated the Centre International de Recherche sur le Cancer (CIRC) and the Universities of Brussels, Ghent, Leuven, and Liège to set up a collaborative study with the following objectives:

1. To investigate the role of dietary factors in cancers of the digestive tract, using a case-control retrospective study in two provinces of Belgium that differ in nutritional habits and in type of cancer of the digestive tract (Joossens, 1980; Joossens & Geboers, 1981; Ramioul & Tuyns, 1977; Tuyns, Castegnaro, Toussaint, Walker, Griciute, Le Talaer, Loquet, Guerain, & Drilleau, 1980; Tuyns, Pequignot, Gignoux, & Valla, 1982).

2. To gather prevalence data concerning the nutritional characteristics and coronary risk factor distribution in the 43 counties of Belgium (De Backer, Kornitzer, Sobolski, Dramaix, Degre, Marneffe, & Denolin, 1981; Kesteloot, Park, Lee, Brems-Heyns, & Joossens, 1980; Kesteloot, Lee, Park, Kegels, Geboers, Claes, & Joossens, 1982; Kittel, Kornitzer, Zyzanski, Jenkins, Rustin, & Degre, 1978; Kittel, Rustin, Dramaix, De Backer, & Kornitzer, 1978; Reginster-Haneuse, 1979; Reginster-Haneuse, Hullebroeck, 1978).

3. To relate the nutritional habits and other risk factors to the total and cause-specific mortality on a regional basis (Kornitzer, De Backer, Dramaix, & Thilly, 1979; Verdonk, Notte-De Ruyter, Huyghebaert-Deschoolmeester, 1977; Verdonk, Notte-De

---

* The universities involved were Brussels' Free University (French): Prof. M. Graffar, Dr. M. Kornitzer, Dr. C. Thilly, Dr. W. Vanneste, Mrs. M. Dramaix, F. Kittel, L. Ravet, A. Van Hemeldonck; Brussels' Free University (Flemish): Dr. A-M. Depoorter.; Ghent State University: Prof. G. Verdonk, Prof. K. Vuylsteek, Dr. G. De Backer, Dr. G. Haelterman; Leuven Catholic University: Prof. J. V. Joossens, Prof. H. Kesteloot; Liege State University: Dr. G. Reginster-Haneuse; International Agency for Research on Cancer: Dr. A. Tuyns.

Ruyter, Huyghebaert-Deschoolmeester, 1982; Vuylsteek, Maes, De Maeseneer, Heyerick, Everaert, 1980).

4. To implement a program of modification in eating habits and other lifestyle-related behaviors in two communities of more than 200,000 inhabitants in order to reduce the risk of developing cardiovascular diseases and cancer.

The three main parts of the project will be discussed in the following sections.

STUDY OF THE RELATIONSHIP BETWEEN DIETARY BEHAVIOR, SMOKING HABITS, AND CANCERS OF THE DIGESTIVE TRACT

Using a classical case-control design, cancers of the esophagus, stomach, bowel, and rectum that occurred from 1979 to 1982 in the provinces of East Flanders and Liège are being investigated. The morbidity statistics of the Belgian National Work of Cancer predict an annual incidence of 1,200 cases.

From a random sample of the adult population of the two provinces, a control group was drawn, selected for the nationwide cardiovascular study. Individual nutritional habits of cases and controls are being measured by a structured interview designed and validated by the Nutrition Section of the Institut National de la Santé et de la Recherche and by the CIRC. This interview has been specially designed for epidemiologic investigations. The food elements consumed during one week and the dietary history are recorded. On this basis, the average daily consumption of each food element can be computed. Special attention will be paid to the consumption of saturated versus polyunsaturated fats, fiber, alcoholic beverages, and salt—all of which have been shown to be related in one or another way to cancers of the digestive tract. The interview is also directed toward smoking habit history. The first year of the study has been devoted to actualizing the collaboration of several services of the two concerned provinces—gastroenterology, histopathology, surgery and radiotherapy—and to specifying the enrollment methods of the cases and the general operation of the system. The field work has started and is planned to last 3 years. The analysis of the data will take another year.

This research was designed to study the role of dietary factors in the development of cancers of the digestive tract. The nutritional habits of adult populations in Flanders (East Flanders) and Wallonia (Liège) will be compared with cause-specific and total mortality rates observed in those two provinces. In terms of prevention of these diseases, the gathered information will eventually lead to a rational health education program concerning nutrition and smoking behavior.

STUDY OF THE RELATION BETWEEN DIETARY BEHAVIOR, SMOKING HABITS, AND CARDIOVASCULAR DISEASES

Baseline data are recorded concerning nutritional characteristics and coronary risk factors on a national scale. This part of the survey is designed to do the following:

1. To study nationwide representative samples of adults of both sexes (including women and individuals under age 40 for the first time in Belgium).
2. To study the relationship of nutritional characteristics to other coronary risk factors.
3. To study the prevalence of ischemic heart disease, determined by an electrocardiogram and a standardized questionnaire regarding angina (London School of Hygiene) by age and sex in different regions of the country.
4. To study, at the county level, the relationship between regional risk factor distributions and regional total and cause-specific mortality.

5. To record reference baseline data for evaluation of short-term or long-term effects of a structured health education program.

The target sample is calculated to be 21,500 individuals, 500 subjects in each of the 43 counties; the sample is stratified by age and sex.

The screening consists of a medical examination and questionnaires. The medical examination includes the following:

1. Anthropometric measures: height and weight.
2. Blood pressure measurement: two recordings of systolic and diastolic blood pressure.
3. A resting electrocardiogram: 12 standard leads and orthogonal leads.
4. Biological measures:

   a. Serum: cholesterol, HDL-cholesterol, Na, K, Cl, CO_2, proteins, Ca, phosphor, ureum, uric acid, creatinine, bilirubin, alcali-phosphatases.
   b. Urine: 24-hour excretion (in a reduced random sample), Na, K, Ca, Mg, creatinine.

The questionnaires include the following:

1. Medical questionnaire: a standardized questionnaire regarding angina (London School of Hygiene), sociodemographic data, information about smoking habits and medication.
2. For the control subjects of the cancer cases, an interview on their dietary history; for the remaining subjects from seven of the nine provinces, a nutritional questionnaire based on a 24-hour recall.
3. Health education questionnaire concerning knowledge and attitudes.
4. Jenkins Activity Survey (JAS) questionnaire to determine type A behavior pattern: the 1969 JAS for employed people and the 1975 JAS-N for self-employed persons, students, housewives, and retired and unemployed persons.
5. Job-stress questionnaire: a self-constructed questionnaire to determine the perceived subjective stress at work.

This nationwide investigation started in 1980 and should be finished at the end of 1984.

HEALTH EDUCATION PROGRAM

The planned health education program beyond 1984, if approved by the National Fund for Scientific Research, will last for 3 years.

Objectives

The objectives of the program are to modify existing risk factors in the adult population and to prevent or modify their development in adolescents (14 to 18 years). The program also aims to increase the conscientiousness of the population regarding the existence of risk factors and their link with harmful life habits and to motivate people in the total community to change their habits (inoculation techniques). Health education and prevention will have to rely on existing structures.

Methods

An integrated health education package will be used, involving medical and paramedical personnel from the chosen communities, particularly from the medical school, the professional medical and paramedical associations, the Belgian Heart Foundation, the Belgian Red Cross, parents' associations, schoolchildren, and so forth.

Some examples of methods and approaches are as follows:

1. A health education and disease prevention program in industrial settings, based on the experience and results of the Belgian Heart Disease Prevention Project (Kornitzer, De Backer, Dramaix, & Thilly, 1980).
2. A health education and disease prevention program oriented toward youth in general, to be realized in collaboration with school directors, parents associations, health educators, sports associations, and the Red Cross.
3. A health education program for the primary schools (age 5–12), including several health topics (e.g., nutrition, coping with risk factors), has been realized. The program was assessed and evaluated as a pilot study in a representative school sample. It is now implemented in all basic schools of the Flemish community in Belgium (Vuylsteek, 1979).
4. A health education and disease prevention program oriented toward the adult population for detection and control of all cases of hypertension, involving general practitioners as well as hypertensive clinics.

Means

The following means will be used to promote the health education program:

1. Mass media: articles in the daily press and in regional newspapers, regional broadcasting, film presentations in regular movie houses.
2. Posters in industrial settings, schools, public places, storehouses, and consulting rooms, and on public roads.
3. Didactic material and a series of lessons for schoolteachers in the program "Health Is Yours," prepared by the Red Cross, Brussels.
4. Conferences given by medical and paramedical professionals.
5. A 5-day plan against smoking.
6. Face-to-face counseling at various times, such as when consulting the general practitioner.

BEHAVIOR CHANGE TECHNIQUES OF RISK FACTOR MODIFICATION

Fats

For modification of eating habits in the direction of a decrease in the total amount of fat and particularly saturated fats and nutritional cholesterol, the goal will be a maximum of 30% of total caloric intake in fats, including one-third saturated fats, one-third monounsaturated fats, and one-third polyunsaturated fatty acids, with a maximum of 300 g of nutritional cholesterol.

Smoking

The goals are primary prevention of smoking in youth (not to start smoking) and secondary prevention in adults (campaigns against cigarette smoking).

Obesity

The goals are primary prevention (preventing the onset of obesity among young people by promoting sports and well-balanced eating habits) and secondary prevention (reducing obesity by increasing physical activity during leisure time and decreasing total caloric intake).

Blood Pressure

The goals include primary prevention in the total population by reduction of salt intake, with emphasis on young obese individuals at high risk (with a family history of hypertension or stroke) and by treatment of obesity. Secondary prevention will be directed at established hypertensives and will include loss of weight, reduction of salt intake, and prescription of antihypertensive drugs.

Sedentary Lifestyle

The goal is to promote physical activity during leisure time and also in schools and industry.

EVALUATION

The program will be evaluated by screening of subsamples ($N = 1,500$) at regular intervals. In the two communities serving as controls, risk factor status will also be monitored regularly in subsamples of the population. Each chosen subject will be invited (by phone or letter) to a medical examination. Medical, nutritional, and health education questionnaires will be given, and measures of height, weight, and blood pressure will be recorded. Blood samples will be taken in order to determine bioclinical values of, for example, cholesterol and HDL-cholesterol. The health education level and the levels of the various coronary risk factors will be assessed.

REFERENCES

De Backer, G., Kornitzer, M., Thilly, C., & DePoorter, A. The Belgian Multifactor Trial in CVD: I. Design and methodology. *Heart Bulletin* 1977, **8**, 143–146.

De Backer, G., Kornitzer, M., Sobolski, J., Dramaix, M., Degree, S., de Marneffe, M., & Denolin, H. Physical activity and physical fitness levels of Belgian males aged 40–55 years. *Cardiology,* 1981, **67**, 110–128.

Joossens, J. V. Stroke, stomach cancer and salt. A possible clue to the prevention of hypertension. In H. Kesteloot, & J. V. Joossens (Eds.), *Epidemiology of Arterial Blood Pressure,* 1980, 489–508.

Joossens, J. V. & Geboers, J. Nutrition and gastric cancer. *Nutrition and Cancer,* 1981, 2/4, 250–261.

Kesteloot, H., Park, B. C., Lee, C. S., Brems-Heyns, E., & Joossens, J. V. A comparative study of blood pressure and sodium intake in Belgium and in Korea. In H. Kesteloot, & J. V. Joossens (Eds.), *Epidemiology of Arterial Blood Pressure.* 1980, 453–470.

Kesteloot, H., Lee, C. S., Park, H. M., Kegels, C., Geboers, J., Claes, J. H. & Joossens, J. V. A comparative study of serum lipids between Belgium and Korean. *Circulation,* 1982, **65**, 795–799.

Kittel, F., Kornitzer, M., Zyzanski, S. J., Jenkins, C. D., Rustin, R-M., & Degre, C. Two methods of assessing the type A coronary-prone behavior pattern in Belgium. *J. Chron. Dis.,* 1978, **31**, 147–155.

Kittel, F., Rustin, R-M., Dramaix, M., De Backer, G. & Kornitzer, M. Psycho-socio-biological correlates of moderate overweight in an industrial population. *J. Psychosom. Res.,* 1978, **22**, 145–158.

Kornitzer, M., De Backer, G., Dramaix, M. & Thilly, C. Regional differences in risk factor distributions, food habits and coronary heart disease mortality and morbidity in Belgium. *Int. J. of Epid.,* 1979, **8**, 23–31.

Kornitzer, M., De Backer, G., Dramaix, M., Thilly, C. The Belgian Heart Disease Prevention Project. Modification of the risk profile in an industrial population. *Circulation,* 1980, **61**, 18–25.

Reginster-Haneuse, G-M. Consommation de tabac chez les jeunes en Belgique. *Pneumologia Hungarica,* 1979, 32/1, 23–25.

Reginster-Haneuse, G-M., & Hullebroeck, G. Enquêtes auprès d'adolescents belges. Résultats et conclusions pour l'éducation sanitaire. *Arch. belges de Med. Soc., Hyg. Med. du Trav. et Méd. Légale,* 1978, **5**, 296–301.

Ramioul, L., Tuyns, A. J. La distribution géographiques des cancers du tube digestif en Belgique. *Acta gastro-ent. belg.* 1977, **40**, 129–147.

Tuyns, A. J., Castegnaro, M., Toussaint, G., Walker, A., Griciute, L. L., Le Talaer, J. Y., Loquet, G., Guerain, J. & Drilleau, J. F. Recherches concernant les facteurs étiologiques de cancer de l'oesophage dans l'ouest de la France. *Bull. Cancer* (Paris) 1980, 1/67, 15–28.

Tuyns, A. J., Pequignot, G., Gignoux, M., & Valla A. Cancers of the digestive tract, alcohol and tobacco. *Int. J. Cancer,* 1982, **30**, 9–11.

Verdonk, G., Notte-De Ruyter, A., & Huyghebaert-Deschoolmeester, M. J. Nutritional studies of industrial canteens and school meals services in Belgium. *Journal of Human Nutrition,* 1977, **31**, 205–219.

Verdonk, G., Notte-De Ruyter, A., Huyghebaert-Deschoolmeester, M. J. Chemische analyses van collectieve warme maaltijden-nutritionele beoordeling van de resultaten. *Voeding,* 1982, **5**, 161–166.

Vuylsteek, K. Education pour la santé: tabagisme, alcoolisme et drogues. Copenhague, *Rapports et Etudes Euro,* 1979, 10.

Vuylsteek, K., Maes, L., De Maeseneer, J., Heyerick, J-P., & Everaert, J-P. First line health care: facts, problems, solutions. *Arch. Belg. Med. Soc., Hyg. Med. du Trav. et Med. Légale,* 1980, **4**, 197–221.

WHO European Collaborative Group. Multifactorial trial in the prevention of coronary heart disease: 1. Recruitment and initial findings. *Europ. Heart J.,* 1980, **1**, 73–80.

CHAPTER 84

THE STANFORD FIVE CITY PROJECT: AN OVERVIEW

JOHN W. FARQUHAR
STEPHEN P. FORTMANN
NATHAN MACCOBY
PETER D. WOOD
WILLIAM L. HASKELL
C. BARR TAYLOR
JUNE A. FLORA
DOUGLAS S. SOLOMON
TODD ROGERS
ELIZABETH ADLER
PRUDENCE BREITROSE
LINDA WEINER

Stanford University

HISTORY

The Five City Project (FCP) is a major part of the work of the Stanford Heart Disease Prevention Program (SHDPP) in cardiovascular disease risk reduction. The SHDPP, a multidisciplinary group of researchers and education professionals, has conducted numerous studies in this area since 1970. The FCP is a natural outgrowth of our previous work, particularly the Three Community Study (TCS), also funded by the National Heart, Lung, and Blood Institute of the National Institutes of Health and conducted from 1971–1977 (Farquhar, Maccoby, Wood, Brietrose, Haskell, Meyer, Alexander, Brown, McAlister, Nash, & Stern, 1977; Fortmann, Williams, Hulley, Haskell, & Farquhar, 1981; Fortmann, Williams, Hulley, Maccoby, & Farquhar, 1982; Maccoby, Farquhar, Wood, & Alexander, 1977; Stern, Brown, Haskell, Farquhar, & Wood, 1976; Stern, Farquhar, Maccoby, & Russell, 1976; Stern, Haskell, Wood, Osann, King, & Farquhar, 1975; Williams, Fortmann, Farquhar, Varady, & Mellen, 1981).

In the TCS, we were able to demonstrate the potential for community-wide risk reduction by means of a program of education carried out principally through mass media in one town and through mass media supplemented by a face-to-face program of intensive instruction in the second town. The third town served as a reference group. Although there were limitations in the design of that study, and although we were not successful in changing risk in all risk factor areas, we believe the results strongly suggest that health status at the community level can be improved significantly by delivery of an educational program through mediated and interpersonal channels. The design and plans for the FCP grew out of our analysis of the strengths and weaknesses of the TCS. The current project differs, in its broad features, from the TCS in several important ways:

1. The two communities selected for education are much larger and more socially complex than those in the previous study, and the health education campaign is aimed at benefiting the entire population.

2. Three moderate-sized cities, rather than the one town of the TCS, were selected as controls, resulting in a total population size of 350,000 in the five cities as compared to 43,000 in the TCS.

3. The project will run for 9 years, and a community organization method will be devised to create a cost-effective and lasting program of community health promotion.

4. People selected from a broader age range (12–74) are taking part in the surveys. Repeated independent samples will be drawn every 2 years to monitor community-wide changes independent of survey effects, in contrast to the cohort design of the TCS.

5. With the cooperation of local health officials, the FCP will monitor the annual rates of fatal and nonfatal cardiovascular events in the five cities.

Overall, the FCP represents an ambitious new chapter in experimental epidemiology of potential relevance both to etiologic hypothesis testing and to a field application of cardiovascular disease control methods. It also presents a significant opportunity for testing generalizable behavioral health education methods (Hulley & Fortmann, 1981).

OVERALL GOALS AND DESIGN

The major aim of the FCP is to test the hypothesis that a significant decrease in the multiple logistic of risk for the educated communities will lead to a decline in morbidity and mortality from cardiovascular disease beyond that attributable to the secular trend. A 6-year education program is designed to stimulate and maintain the changes in lifestyle that will result in a community-wide reduction in risk of cardiovascular disease. Population surveys, epidemiologic surveillance, and other assessment methods will be combined to evaluate the effects of the education program. The overall design is illustrated in Figure 84.1.

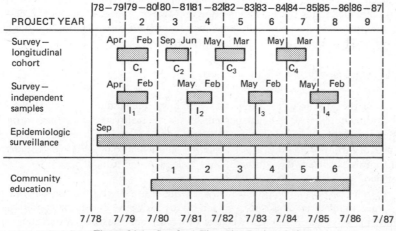

Figure 84.1 Stanford Five City Project design.

Community Education Program

The education program has three goals. The first and broadest goal is to achieve a transformation in the knowledge and skills of individuals and in the educational practices of organizations such that risk factor reduction and decreased morbidity and mortality are achieved. This education program aims to stimulate and to maintain lifestyle changes within the study population so that at least a 10% reduction in overall risk status is achieved after 2 years of intervention. It is estimated that a greater than 20% reduction in overall risk will be achieved if mean changes were to occur in individual risk factors of the following magnitude: (a) smoking—a 9% net change in the proportion of smokers; (b) weight—a 2% net change in relative weight; (c) blood pressure—a 7% change in systolic blood pressure; and (d) blood cholesterol—a 4% change in cholesterol. The education program is to continue for a total of 6 years in order to create changes of approximately this magnitude, which are needed to detect changes in morbidity and mortality.

A second goal is to carry out the education program in a way that creates a self-sustaining health promotion structure, embedded within the organizational fabric of the communities, that continues to function after the project ends.

The third goal is to derive a model for cost-effective community health promotion from the experience and data accumulated in the TCS and in this study, the broad features of which would have general applicability in many other American communities.

Field Trial

The FCP is also a field trial that will evaluate the effectiveness of the overall educational program in achieving the following:

1. Changes in cardiovascular risk factors assessed through repeated longitudinal and cross-sectional population surveys and through unobtrusive assessment of selected aspects of population behavior in the two treatment communities and two of the three reference communities.

2. Changes in cardiovascular morbidity and mortality, assessed through continuous community epidemiologic surveillance of fatal and nonfatal heart attacks and strokes in the two treatment communities and three reference communities.

Community-wide changes in knowledge, behavior, and risk—independent of survey effects—will be determined through comparison of the four biennial cross-sectional sample surveys ($N = 650$) conducted in the two education cities and two of the three reference communities. Studies of the process of change in individuals will be possible by comparing the longitudinal cohort surveys. This cohort was drawn from the first independent sample.

Natural History Study

A final goal of the FCP is to use the survey and surveillance data to analyze the secular trends in cardiovascular risk factors, morbidity, and mortality during a time of declining mortality, the cause of which is uncertain. This will add important epidemiologic information on the causes of cardiovascular disease. The survey data will also be used to explore hypotheses about knowledge, behavior, attitudes, and risk in order to add basic information on health behavior.

This research design is a compromise between the desirable and the feasible. We would prefer a larger number of cities, randomized to treatment and control conditions. Not only would this have increased the expense, however, but the need to isolate the cities from undue influence from each other made randomization impossible (Farquhar, 1978).

The addition of treatment and control units by pooling analyses from the Minnesota and Rhode Island studies is a feasible alternative.

EDUCATION PROGRAM

Risk Factors and Health Behaviors

The major cardiovascular risk factors selected for attention are cigarette use, arterial blood pressure (BP), plasma low-density lipoprotein (LDL) cholesterol, and plasma high-density lipoprotein (HDL) cholesterol. These risk factors have been linked with several health behaviors that therefore become major areas for the intervention: smoking, nutrition, exercise, hypertension (i.e., treatment of high BP), and obesity. Nutrition behavior will affect BP (salt, weight control), LDL cholesterol (dietary saturated fat, cholesterol, and fiber; weight control), and HDL cholesterol (weight control). Exercise will affect BP (weight control), LDL cholesterol (weight control), and HDL cholesterol (weight control, perhaps also directly). Hypertension treatment will affect that proportion of the BP distribution appropriate for drug therapy. The other factors are identified to enable specific plans to be made when appropriate.

Although it is convenient in this presentation, and in planning, to consider each risk factor and health behavior separately, there is a danger of perceiving a fragmentation that is not present. In fact, the educational program planned for the FCP is highly unified. It is most difficult for it to be otherwise. People who attend a smoking cessation class, for example, will be encouraged to begin exercise, to substitute healthy foods for the smoking habit, and so forth. We are presenting a single lifestyle that is most likely to be healthy. It involves being vigorous, active, and self-confident, eating a wide variety of enjoyable foods, and not smoking. It is this basically healthy and happy image that binds together the various elements of the intervention and makes the educational programs and materials coherent and, to an extent, indivisible.

Theoretical Perspectives

A variety of perspectives and theoretical formulations need to be blended to successfully design and carry out the educational program described here. In addition to the clearly relevant field of community organization, which creates a receptive environment for our educational materials and programs, we have also found it necessary to borrow from two additional perspectives to create the blend needed for success. These additional two are the communication–behavior change framework and the social marketing framework. The communication–behavior change framework is based on a social-psychological perspective relevant to the individual and group learning that is needed within the overall community organization method. This perspective is particularly germane to the content of the educational materials produced. The social marketing framework, based on marketing principles, is especially relevant to the practical issues of how to design and distribute the educational products.

The communication–behavior change framework offers a perspective on how individuals and groups change knowledge, attitudes, and behavior. Our picture of the change process draws on the prior work of others: the social learning model of Bandura (1979); the heirarchy of learning model of Ray, Sawyer, Rothschild, Heeler, Strong, and Reed (1973); the communication-persuasion model of McGuire (1969); the attitude change model of Ajzen and Fishbein (1980); and the adoption-diffusion model of Rogers and Shoemaker (1971). The communication–behavior change (CBC) model emphasizes the features that are relevant to community-based education and health promotion. Several underlying assumptions are implicit in these portrayals of the change process:

1. A need for change exists and room for change exists.
2. Initial and final states are measurable.
3. Educating forces have adequate social legitimacy.
4. Adequate time exists within the design for the change to occur.

This approach proposes a series of steps that people go through as they gradually adopt the advocated behavior. The concept of behavior change as an orderly sequence of steps is admittedly an idealized version of real life and may not be a totally accurate portrayal of the process of lifestyle change for all people in all areas. For some people, on some topics, the sequence of steps may vary. On some issues, one or two steps will be much more important than others. One message may perform more than one function. The concept does help us, however, in developing a clearer picture of how to devise a course of action. As we proceed, we can also use it as an evaluation framework to observe the shift of population groups over time in the direction of the intended project goals. The steps are listed and briefly discussed here, and the corresponding communication function is identified for each step.

1. *Become aware* (*gain attention*): The agenda-setting function is to gain the public's attention and focus it on certain specific issues and problems. The existence of the problem must be established in the public's mind, and an awareness of potential solutions must be promoted. In our society, the mass media generally play an important agenda-setting role.

2. *Increase knowledge* (*provide information*): Once a particular topic or subject matter is on the public agenda, an educational program must present information, in layman's terms, that makes the issue interesting and understandable. Messages should be designed that make the issue personally meaningful and that set the stage for action. The messages must be retained in a way that predisposes persons to act in a different way in the future.

3. *Increase motivation* (*provide incentives*): Change is more likely when individuals clearly perceive the personal and social benefits of change, which can be enhanced by appropriate communications.

4. *Learn skills* (*provide training*): Where changes in complex habits of long standing are involved, it may be necessary to provide skills training in how to start making changes, both by providing step-by-step instruction and by promoting the availability of self-help and professional resources.

5. *Take action* (*model*): Ideally, this phase of an overall strategy would provide educational inputs that act as cues to trigger specific actions. Messages would indicate clear action paths to stimulate the trial adoption of new behaviors.

6. *Maintain* (*provide support*): At this stage, inputs are required to provide a sense of social support and approval and as a reminder of both the short-term and the long-term personal and social benefits of the changes undertaken. Gaining self-efficacy and learning self-management methods are important aspects of the maintenance phase.

In health promotion programs with multiple objectives, not everything can be done all at once for everyone. Planners must have a rational basis for making selections from among competing choices and for sequencing actions over time. The communication–behavior change framework can be a general guide, suggesting how to break down the large community health promotion task into manageable pieces.

The concept of social marketing (Kotler & Zaltman, 1973) is that marketing principles and techniques can be usefully applied to social change programs to improve their effectiveness. Kotler (1975) gave this definition of social marketing:

> *Social Marketing is the design, implementation and control of programs seeking to increase the acceptability of a social idea or practice in a target group(s).*

The design and implementation of the FCP education program in general, and the media campaign in particular, can therefore be viewed as an application of social marketing to community health promotion. In social marketing, the focus is on the transaction whereby something of value is exchanged among parties. The marketing process begins with an understanding of the consumer. This understanding directs the creation of products or services with price, promotion, and distribution organized to attract the customer.

The techniques of social marketing are divided by Kotler (1982) into four key elements—the "four P's" of marketing management: "the right PRODUCT backed by the right PROMOTION and put in the right PLACE at the right PRICE."

The *product* element is concerned with designing appropriate educational products in "packages" that target audiences find desirable and are willing to accept or purchase and use. Health promotion products may take a tangible form (such as a low-cholesterol cookbook) or may be quite intangible (a message to reduce blood pressure).

The *promotion* element is concerned with how to make the product familiar, acceptable, and even desirable, usually through some form of communication, such as advertising, personal selling, publicity, or sales promotion.

The *place* element has to do with the provision of adequate and compatible distribution and response channels. Kotler (1975) says that "motivated persons should know where the product can be obtained" and that the activity involved is "arranging for accessible outlets which permit the translation of motivations into actions" through well-established patterns of distribution.

The *price* element, according to Kotler (1975), "represents the costs that the buyer must accept in order to obtain the product." He redefines price to include "money costs, opportunity costs, energy costs, and psychic costs," and in this fashion includes the notion of "transaction" in his formulation of social marketing. He notes that "the marketer's approach to selling a social product is to consider how the rewards for buying the product can be increased relative to the costs, or the costs reduced relative to the rewards."

Although it is clear that semantic analogies can be drawn between social marketing elements and the communication–behavior change elements previously described, it is also clear that the social marketing framework adds to our theory and practice by forcing us to deal more effectively with the practical realities of marketing our products in the complex urban environments of modern America.

The application of social marketing to community health promotion rests on the health promoter's ability to control or arrange the elements of product, promotion, price, and place. It assumes that the social marketer has a clear understanding of consumer attributes and consumer needs and has the requisite flexibility to design and produce needed commodities or services. It further assumes that adequate distribution systems exist for the marketer to reach the target audience. A place where the consumer intersects with the product is required. A marketing model also assumes that transaction is possible within the context of people's lives, and that they can afford and will pay the price of the product. Finally, it requires knowledge of results of prior actions (the equivalent of sales data) as the basis for product design and system management. Examples follow of how the notions of product, promotion, place, and price can apply to FCP methods. These examples will serve to describe many of the methods used in the education program.

Community Organization

We always assumed that community organization would play a significant role in both the initial success and the durability of our program. In accord with this assumption, our educational program is being conducted in a manner that encourages involvement from the outset by local community groups and will eventually lead to local ownership and control.

The following assumptions have been made:

1. Mass media education alone is powerful, but its effects may be augmented by community organization.

2. Interpersonal influence can be enhanced inexpensively through community organization, and this can allow a multiplier effect to occur that will increase behavior change.

3. Organizations can expand our educational program's delivery system in ways that are important for achieving community-wide health education.

4. Organizations can help the process of community adoption of risk reduction programs as their own, thus increasing the likelihood of continuing health education programs and behavior change in their communities.

5. Formation of new organizations can be catalyzed by our external efforts to increase the array of groups concerned with health education and health promotion.

Our general plan for community organization has been to adopt an approach whereby the involvement of SHDPP and the strategies used evolve as the community assumes a greater role in working toward the overall health care goals. Strategies derived from the social work literature (Rothman, 1968; Spergel, Vorwaller, & Switzer, 1972; Warren, 1965) do not adequately encompass our plans.

The novel and highly important aspect of our project is that the need for provision of curricula, training of instructors, and provision of skills training looms large as a dimension that is not covered by the *development* or *maintenance* strategies of Spergel et al. (1972). These terms are synonymous with the *campaign* or *collaborative* strategies of Warren (1965) and with the *social planning* or *locality development* strategies of Rothman (1968). Thus, we propose a new terminology, which includes room for our educational products, in which Rothman's social planning strategy is instead considered "exogenous organization leading to exogenous education." Rothman's locality development strategy is relabeled "exogenous organization leading to endogenous development." We use the terms *exogenous* for those activities originating from Stanford and *endogenous* for activities that require community involvement. We see endogenous development as new development within local organizations as a consequence of Stanford's exogenous organizing. After community groups have "developed," they then engage in collaborative education with Stanford or produce endogenous education without Stanford's continued involvement (see Figure 84.2).

An example of exogenous organizing leading to endogenous development, which in turn leads to collaborative education, is the joint establishment with the County Health Department of smoking classes in the communities (since none existed at the beginning of our project). Stanford helps with training, curriculum development, evaluation, and curriculum revision. An example of exogenous organizing leading to exogenous education is found in our program of supplying columns to newspapers. Our organizing is needed to recruit the newspapers and to remain sensitive to their wishes regarding frequency of columns, and the responsibility for continuation is almost entirely Stanford's.

Our use of community organizing affects all phases of our education program development. The major function of community organization, following the early phases of development, is to provide the environment for the educational products to be used effectively. Regarding the other two frameworks, we rely most heavily on the communication–behavior

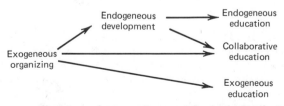

Figure 84.2   Sequence and products of community organizing in the Stanford Five City Project.

change framework to guide our choice of content and on social marketing to improve design and distribution, leaving to community organization the task of creating the environment that will be receptive to our products as well as inducing community groups to create their own educational products.

Formative Evaluation

Formative research, as distinct from summative research, is intended to provide data for use in designing educational strategies, to design particular programs and materials for meeting specific objectives for the target audiences, and to monitor the progress of the educational program. A general criticism of health communication campaigns in the literature (Atkin, 1979) involves their lack of formative research and therefore the resulting design of materials and programs that are not able to meet the objectives of the overall effort. The SHDPP has always been careful to include formative research in health promotion programs. A core element of our education program is our ability to conduct and utilize formative research.

There are numerous areas where formative research is undertaken to assist the design, development, production, and distribution of the education program. Audience segmentation and needs analysis, for example, ask who the appropriate audience is for a given topic and what they need (more information, skills, motivation). Program design and testing evaluate the best place and time for a given program and evaluate an early version to determine what is working and what needs changing. Message design and testing answer analogous questions for media products, such as television spots. Finally, the effectiveness of individual programs and messages is evaluated to the extent possible when they are introduced into general use.

Broadcast Media Programs

The overriding goal of the use of broadcast media in the FCP is the encouragement of lasting behavior change that will result in risk factor modification and, ultimately, in reductions in morbidity and mortality. Underlying this major goal are two subgoals: broadcast media programs must encourage direct behavior change as well as encouraging indirect change through support of community events. Some products are designed to support community programs (particularly by encouraging recruitment), whereas others are designed to create direct changes in knowledge, attitudes, and behavior on the part of the target audience. Some products are hybrids; for example, a smoking cessation television show could encourage cessation as well as recruiting individuals into smoking cessation programs available in the community.

A variety of factors determine the format, content, and time sequence of broadcast media products. Certain products are essential to support programs requested by community groups, and some media products are requested by the mass media outlets themselves. The decision-making process for most of the media productions, however, is highly related to our particular risk factor goals over a certain period of time. Such planning is based on a careful understanding of risk factor goals; on the knowledge, attitudes, behaviors, and desires for change among the majority of adult smokers; and on estimates of the efficacy of various approaches to cessation and maintenance.

Print Media Programs

Print media are able to provide higher information-density messages on a particular topic than broadcast media, which are most capable of presenting relatively low information-density messages. Print messages can be read and reread at the user's own pace. Therefore, they provide a large amount of information in a user-oriented format. With this in mind, the FCP has invested a substantial amount of effort in the use of print media, particularly in topic areas that require more than the superficial amount of information that can be provided in typical broadcast media programs. To this end, formative research efforts of various kinds have been used to design, modify, and distribute printed material. The FCP has conceptualized four types of printed materials: big print, media promotion print, support print, and local print.

Big print is designed to meet the objective of developing effective prototype media products. Big print pieces are developed, written, designed, and produced by the professional staff at Stanford. Their primary purpose is to carry a major message of the project and to have a relatively long time span. There is a reciprocal relationship between big print and community organization; each supports and magnifies the impact of the other. Big print functions largely as an exogenous medium within our previously mentioned classification scheme, but it also plays a role in some collaborative education programs when it is used as text for various groups.

Media promotion print is any print piece whose primary objective is to motivate individuals to attend to the FCP's media events. This form of print is subjected to the same process of formative research as big print, and follow-up evaluation also takes place to assess its effectiveness.

Educational *support print* includes any piece whose purpose is to support classes or workshops. Its purposes include reinforcing the knowledge and skills being taught in an educational program and providing additional information not presented by the instructor or leader.

Local print's purpose is to satisfy the project's objective of developing endogenous print materials. Local print includes any piece needed in the communities where fast turnaround is a central priority, such as print needed for promoting and recruiting for local activities, classes, and groups.

EDUCATION PROGRAM OPERATIONS AND PLANNING

A careful method of planning is essential to any project as complex and extensive as the FCP. Moreover, there are no exact predecessors to the FCP to use as a guide. The planning process actually begins with the creation of a funding proposal and must extend several years into the future. This requires considerable anticipation, so there must also be a mechanism for reevaluating plans periodically according to continuing feedback. We have such a planning mechanism, described as follows.

The planning process begins by setting goals and objectives (using *goals* as a broader term). For this project, this means setting goals for changes in each of the risk factors (e.g., a 7% decline in systolic blood pressure) and then creating a list of objectives that can be expected to achieve the goals (e.g., reducing salt intake by 50%). Goals for the FCP were established in the original grant proposal. These goals were reviewed and confirmed during the first year of the grant by groups of experts in each risk factor area. These groups also created complex lists of health behavior objectives that could reasonably be expected to achieve the goals. The objectives included knowledge, attitude, and behavior changes. These risk factor goals and objectives now constitute the "planning guides" for the project.

The objectives are then turned into plans for various educational projects, each of which has a distinct list of objectives of its own. This enables the project directors to evaluate each project and to set priorities. The next step is to evaluate each project and, periodically, the overall objectives through a process of formative evaluation. One objective, for example, might be to make people aware that exercise is good for the heart as a way to motivate them to begin exercising. In our baseline population survey, however, we learned that this attitude is common but that people with this attitude are still unable to begin exercise.

This knowledge requires a change in the objective and the content of the education program. Thus, planning becomes a data-based management system with continuous feedback from formative evaluation.

The management system in the FCP involves, first, making long-term plans to the end of the project, based on the goals and objectives from the planning guides. These plans have already been modified extensively by the results of our surveys and other specific formative research. Long-term plans for each year are then converted into timelines, and each education group professional translates the master timeline into a personal 6-month timeline. This allows us to evaluate the practicality of each 6-month plan. Priorities are then established by the director of education, the principal investigators, and the education group. Thus the long-term plans are reevaluated every 6 months.

EVALUATION

Health Surveys

Each health survey includes both physiological and behavioral measures. The physiological measures are as follows:

1. Body height and weight.
2. Blood pressure by two methods (mercury manometer and semiautomated machine).
3. Nonfasting venous blood sample analyzed for plasma thiocyanate (as a measure of smoking rate), total cholesterol, triglycerides, and cholesterol content of lipoprotein subfractions.
4. Expired air carbon monoxide.
5. Urinary sodium, potassium, and creatinine (as an index of prior sodium chloride intake).
6. A low-level bicycle exercise test (as a measure of fitness).

Lipid analyses follow long-established methods of the Lipid Research Clinics Program (U.S. DHEW, 1974). Plasma thiocyanate determination follows the procedure of Butts, Kuehneman, and Widdowson (1974), as used in the Multiple Risk Factor Intervention Trial. Expired air carbon monoxide is measured on the Ecolyzer apparatus.

Blood pressure is obtained as indirect brachial artery pressure (systolic and fifth-phase diastolic) on participants sitting at rest for 2 minutes before the first measurement. Pressures are obtained twice, using a Sphygmetrics Infrasonic Automatic Blood Pressure Recorder (SR-2), and this is followed by dual measurements of pressure using a standard mercury sphygmomanometer and auscultation. Urine samples are frozen after collection and shipped to Stanford twice monthly. Standard laboratory procedures are used for determination of urinary sodium and potassium (flame photometry) and creatinine.

The low-level exercise test, using a Schwinn electric-brake stationary cycle ergometer, is performed following blood pressure measurement and blood sampling. Measurements of pulse rate are made using a Quinton Instrument Cardiotachometer. A small proportion of participants is excluded from the test according to very conservative criteria. The test is designed to obtain a pulse rate index of relative fitness after a standard work load that is estimated to be 70% of maximum aerobic capacity.

Behavioral measures include a broad range of attitude and knowledge assessments, behavioral intention measures, self-reported behavior, and dietary and physical activity recalls. In addition, questions are asked for use in formative evaluation, such as attitudes toward different types of educational materials. Of course, standard demographic and medication use data are collected.

Epidemiologic Surveillance

The purpose of community epidemiologic surveillance is to allow calculation of comparable, city-specific rates for total mortality, cardiovascular mortality, fatal myocardial infarction, nonfatal myocardial infarction, fatal stroke, and nonfatal stroke. The mortality rates mentioned are obtainable from vital statistics, but these rely on the unaided interpretation of death certificate diagnoses. A common method for obtaining the morbidity rates is to identify a cohort of individuals and follow them through time with repeated, thorough examinations that discover the occurrence of new events. Such cohort studies are large and expensive. Thus, the needed mortality statistics are available inexpensively, but their accuracy is suspect, and the morbidity data are unobtainable except at great expense. Community surveillance is designed, therefore, to obtain accurate mortality statistics and to obtain morbidity statistics at an acceptable cost (Gillum, 1978).

Potential fatal events are identified from death certificates and nonfatal events from hospital discharge records. Nonclinical or "silent" infarctions are not identified. All potential events are investigated by hospital chart review or family interview. The resulting data are reviewed at Stanford by trained analysts, using standard criteria for each type of event. The analysts are unaware of the community of origin and review the cases independently. A final endpoint is assigned by a computer algorithm applied to the analysts' digest of each case. If the analysts disagree on a case, it is reviewed by a physician.

SUMMARY

A considerable proportion of the chronic disease in the United States could be prevented or delayed. The most important causes of death in the 55-year-old to 74-year-old age group—cardiovascular diseases, cancer, alcoholism, and trauma—have significant environmental and behavioral components. The Stanford Five City Project is an evaluation of a community-wide approach to the control of cardiovascular disease through healthy changes in behavior. This approach may be generalizable to other disease control efforts as we learn to unite the medical, behavioral, communication, and social sciences to solve health problems. The Stanford, Minnesota, and Pawtucket community studies, together with the Multiple Risk Factor Intervention Trial (1983) and the Lipid Research Clinics Program (1984), will determine whether or not we can use the last 40 years of cardiovascular disease epidemiologic research to benefit the general public.

REFERENCES

Ajzen, I., & Fishbein, M. *Understanding attitudes and predicting social behavior.* Englewood Cliffs, N.J.: Prentice-Hall, 1980.

Atkin, C. K. Research evidence on mass mediated health communication campaigns. In D. Nimmo (Ed.), *Communication yearbook 3.* New Brunswick, N.J.: Transaction, 1979.

Bandura, A. *Social learning theory.* Englewood Cliffs, N.J.: Prentice-Hall, 1979.

Butts, W. C., Kuehneman, M., & Widdowson, G. M. Automated method for determining serum thiocyanate to distinguish smokers from non-smokers. *Clinical Chemistry,* 1974, **20**, 1344–1348.

Farquhar, J. W. The community-based model of life-style intervention trials. *American Journal of Epidemiology,* 1978, **108**, 103–111.

Farquhar, J. W., Maccoby, N., Wood, P. D., Brietrose, H., Haskell, W. L., Meyer, A. J., Alexander, J. K., Brown, B. W., McAlister, A. L., Nash, J. D., & Stern, M. P. Community education for cardiovascular health. *Lancet,* 1977, **1**, 1192–1195.

Fortmann, S. P., Williams, P. T., Hulley, S. B., Haskell, W. L., & Farquhar, J. W. Effect of health education on dietary behavior: The Stanford Three Community Study. *American Journal of Clinical Nutrition,* 1981, **34**, 2030–2038.

Fortmann, S. P., Williams, P. T., Hulley, S. B., Maccoby, N., & Farquhar, J. W. Does dietary health education reach only the privileged? An answer from the Stanford Three Community Study. *Circulation,* 1982, **66,** 77–82.

Gillum, R. F. Community surveillance for cardiovascular disease: Methods, problems, applications— A review. *Journal of Chronic Diseases,* 1978, **31,** 87–94.

Hulley, S. B., & Fortmann, S. P. Clinical trials of changing behavior to prevent cardiovascular disease. In S. M. Weiss, J. A. Herd, and B. H. Fox (Eds.), *Perspectives in behavioral medicine.* New York, Academic Press, 1981.

Kotler, P. Social marketing. In *Marketing for nonprofit organizations* (2nd ed). Englewood Cliffs, N.J.: Prentice-Hall.

Kotler, P., & Zaltman, G. Social marketing: an approach to planned social change. In W. Lazer and E. J. Kelley (Eds.), *Social marketing perspectives and viewpoints.* Homewood, IL: Richard D. Irwin, 1973.

Lipid Research Clinics Program. The Lipid Research Clinics coronary primary presention trial results. I. Reduction in incidence of coronary heart disease. *Journal of the American Medical Association,* 1984, **251,** 351–364.

Lipid Research Clinics Program. The Lipid Research Clinics coronary primary prevention trial results. II. The relationship of reduction in incidence of coronary heart disease to cholesterol lowering. *Journal of the American Medical Association,* 1984, **251,** 365–374.

Maccoby, N., Farquhar, J. W., Wood, P. F., & Alexander, J. K. Reducing the risk of cardiovascular disease: Effects of a community-based campaign on knowledge and behavior. *Journal of Community Health,* 1977, **3,** 100–114.

McGuire, W. J. The nature of attitudes and attitude change. In G. Lindsey & E. Aronson (Eds.), *The handbook of social psychology.* Reading, Mass.: Addison-Wesley, 1969.

Multiple Risk Factor Intervention Trial Research Group. Multiple Risk Factor Intervention Trial. Risk factor changes and mortality results. *Journal of the American Medical Association,* 1983, **248,** 1465–1477.

Ray, M. L., Sawyer, A. G., Rothschild, M. L., Heeler, R. M., Strong, E. C., & Reed, J. B. Marketing communication and the hierarchy of effects. In P. Clarke (Ed.), *New models for mass communication research.* Beverly Hills, Calif.: Sage, 1973.

Rogers, E. M., & Shoemaker, F. F. *Communication of innovations: A cross-cultural approach.* New York: Free Press, 1971.

Rothman, J. Three models of community organization practice. In National Conference on Social Welfare, Social work practice. New York: Columbia University Press, 1968.

Spergel, I., Vorwaller, D., & Switzer, E. Community organization from a perspective of social work. In L. Wittmer (Ed.), *Issues in community organization.* Chicago: UC Center for the Study of Religion, 1972.

Stern, M. P., Brown, B. W., Haskell, W. L., Farquhar, J. W., & Wood, P. D. Cardiovascular risk and use of estrogens or estrogen-progestagen combinations: Stanford Three Community Study. *Journal of the American Medical Association,* 1976, **235,** 811–815.

Stern, M. P., Farquhar, J. W., Maccoby, N., & Russell, S. H. Results of a two-year health education campaign on dietary behavior: The Stanford Three Community Study. *Circulation,* 1976, **54,** 826–833.

Stern, M. P., Haskell, W. L., Wood, P. D., Osann, K. E., King, A. B., & Farquhar, J. W. Affluence and cardiovascular risk factors in Mexican-Americans and other whites in three northern California communities. *Journal of Chronic Diseases,* 1975, **28,** 623–636.

U.S. DHEW. Lipid Research Clinics manual of laboratory operations, Vol. 1. Lipid and lipoprotein analysis. Washington, D.C.: U.S. Government Printing Office, DHEW Pub. No. NIH-75-628, 197 .

Warren, R. L. Types of purposive change at the community level. In *Brandeis University papers in social welfare* (No. 11). Waltham, Mass.: Brandeis University, 1965.

Williams, P. T., Fortmann, S. P., Farquhar, J. W., Varady, A., & Mellen, S. A comparison of statistical methods for evaluating risk factor changes in community-based studies: An example from the Stanford Three Community Study. *Journal of Chronic Diseases,* 1981, **34,** 565–571.

CHAPTER 85

LAY VOLUNTEER DELIVERY OF A COMMUNITY-BASED CARDIOVASCULAR RISK FACTOR CHANGE PROGRAM: THE PAWTUCKET EXPERIMENT

T. LASATER
D. ABRAMS
L. ARTZ
P. BEAUDIN
L. CABRERA
J. ELDER
A. FERREIRA
P. KNISLEY
G. PETERSON
A. RODRIGUES
P. ROSENBERG
R. SNOW
R. CARLETON

Memorial Hospital, Pawtucket, and Brown University, Providence

The Pawtucket Heart Health Project (PHHP) was established to develop and assess the effectiveness of a community-based program to prevent atherosclerotic heart disease by modifying behaviors and therefore risk factors that contribute to the development of this disease. The specific risk factor targets include smoking, cholesterol-elevating diets, high blood pressure, obesity, physical inactivity, and stress. Unlike other community heart disease prevention programs, however, the primary deliverers of this change program are volunteers recruited from within the community. This reliance on volunteers has historical as well as theoretical roots.

In the 1970s, it became apparent to the administration of Pawtucket's Memorial Hospital that heart disease was a major problem in this predominantly blue-collar Rhode Island city of 72,000 inhabitants. Professionals from the Brown University system, the State Department of Health, various state and local health-related agencies (e.g., the American Heart

The study reported herein was supported by a grant from the U.S. Public Health Service, National Heart, Lung and Blood Institute, Grant No. HL23639.

Association), and others volunteered their time to help the hospital staff to begin the early design and funding of what was to become the PHHP. By 1978, a group of Pawtucket schoolteachers had formed a school curriculum advisory committee on a volunteer basis and were actively involved in the overall effort. In 1979, a number of community leaders including the mayor, the president of the city council, the school board president, a leading minister and a priest, the president of the Council of Labor Unions, ethnic group leaders (Hispanic, Portuguese, and Cape Verdians), and a number of others were serving on the first committee of non-health professionals—the Leadership Committee.

The commitment and willingness to serve of these community leaders was an important factor in the decision of the National Heart, Lung and Blood Institute to provide a 6-year research and demonstration grant to Memorial Hospital (1980–1986).

THEORETICAL BACKGROUND

The federal funding allowed recruitment of a professional staff, further development of the theory into a theoretical intervention model (Abrams, Elder, & PHHP Staff, Note 1), operationalization of that model into a cohesive community behavior change program, and development of the materials and procedures necessary to implement the program.

The major theoretical underpinnings of the intervention model are provided by social learning theory and the related concept of reciprocal determinism. This concept suggests that there are dynamic relationships among observable behavior, the physical and social environment, and the cognitive personal dimensions (Bandura, 1977). In this construct, a person can be both the agent for and the respondent to change. It follows that changes that are induced simultaneously in both the individual and the environment are more likely to be sustained. Furthermore, self-efficacy theory (Bandura, 1977) suggests that active participation (e.g., participant modeling) enhances efficacy and outcome. According to self-efficacy theory, active participation is likely to be a significantly more effective method for inducing and maintaining behavior change than more traditional health educational approaches based on verbal persuasion or knowledge and attitude change. This theory is obviously compatible with the PHHP volunteer emphasis. The more individuals that are recruited as both change agents and respondents, the more pervasive and simultaneous are the pro-health changes at all levels.

With long-term behavior change and program maintenance as major goals, the concept of reciprocal determinism has been applied to four major levels of the social structure of the community—individual, small group, organization, and community. The intervention model also incorporates a problem-solving technology derived from the self-monitoring, goal-setting, self-evaluation, and self-reinforcement components of Kanfer's (1975) self-control theory. This problem-solving approach is blended with the six stages of Goldfried and D'Zurilla's (1969) model for training in social problem solving: problem orientation, problem definition, generation of alternatives, decision making, solution verification, and corrective feedback. The components lead to change programs designed for each of the four social structure levels, with a combined focus on both the individual and the environment, that are easily grasped and applied by volunteers without prior professional training.

Behavior change itself is conceptualized as a three-phase sequence: promotion (changing antecedent stimuli), skills training (behavior), and maintenance/feedback (consequences). The approach deals with individuals who are at different stages in the change process and recognizes that the promotional variables necessary to motivate an individual are probably different from the skills needed to change a behavior and the skills and supports necessary to maintain change. In summary, operationalization of the intervention model to field application requires attention to a three-dimensional matrix, with the four levels of social structure on one dimension, the three stages of change process on the second dimension, and the six risk factors on the third.

BEHAVIOR CHANGE APPROACH

The behavior change program, which began full implementation in Pawtucket in February 1982, has been developed in keeping with the theoretical intervention model. The practical approaches have also been heavily influenced by principles derived from behavioral community psychology (Fawcett, Mathews, & Fletcher, 1977) and from the locality development model for community organization (Rothman, 1968). Specifically, these principles include emphasis on behavior, cost-containment, flexibility, active involvement, participant control, local ownership, multilevel implementation, simplicity, replicability, evaluation orientation, consistency with local norms, availability, and natural support system orientation.

The principal volunteers at the community level are the Leadership Committee, which was expanded to approximately 70 community leaders, functioning within a variety of sub-committees (e.g., religious, business and industry, youth). During the early implementation stages, these volunteers have provided invaluable guidance regarding both information about and access to the community and the organizations comprising it. Eventually, the Leadership Committee is expected to help organize and assist the community group that will assume governance and maintenance of the programs upon the withdrawal of most of the present PHHP professional staff by late 1985.

ORGANIZATIONAL LEVEL APPROACH

The first step in actually implementing the program was to identify a number of organizations in the city that were sufficiently large to maintain a variety of programs within a single organization and that were likely to provide overlap with other organizations. The program's Leadership Committee assisted in this process, identifying organizations they considered highly visible within the community whose gatekeepers and key decision makers were also known to them personally and were expected to be receptive to the implementation of a heart health program. Then, with the continued assistance of the Leadership Committee, the PHHP staff attempted to collect information about the gatekeepers and their respective organizations. Other sources of information were used during this "homework" phase to attempt to confirm the receptivity of each organization and its gatekeeper and to prepare staff adequately for making gatekeeper contacts. This step not only optimized resources, it also increased the probability of success and helped avoid many potential problems.

Once an organization has been identified as visible and potentially receptive, and home-work information has been collected, a meeting is arranged between the gatekeeper for that organization and a PHHP staff member. A Leadership Committee member who knows the gatekeeper assists in establishing this first contact. At this meeting, the gatekeeper is introduced to the need for heart health programs, the advantages for his or her organization, and the sequence of the PHHP organization approach. After the presentation, gatekeepers are simply asked for permission to proceed with an assessment of the interests and needs of the organization's membership. No other commitment is requested.

If the gatekeeper gives permission for entry, information concerning the PHHP program is distributed throughout the organization. This is followed by a questionnaire assessment of the interest and needs of the organization's membership in regard to heart health. The results of this assessment are used to determine the relative "readiness for change" of the membership and to determine further action. If the readiness for change is low, the gatekeeper is so informed, and the PHHP exits with a promise to return in the future if the situation changes. If the readiness for individual and small group level change (as determined by interests and needs) is high, the appropriate steps are taken to implement individual self-help and small group level programming. If there is also a clear readiness for organizational level change in addition to individual and small group level change, an attempt is made to organize a heart health advisory task force for that organization. Where possible, potential task force members not only have expressed a willingness to participate in such a task force but have also been recommended by others in the organization as potentially effective task force members. This double endorsement procedure is designed to identify the informal or natural support system leaders within the organization and to develop a sense of program ownership.

Prospective heart health task force members are then invited to an introductory meeting at which the functions of a heart health task force are explained in detail. Once a task force is formed, its members are trained to implement individual, small group, and organizational level programming within their organization. Specifically, they are trained to use the results of the interests and needs assessment to prioritize and target health areas for change, to set goals, to design programs for achieving those goals, to implement and evaluate those programs, and then to revise the programming efforts and reset goals as necessary. Programming in such organizations will not be limited to individual and small group level change. Consistent with the principle of reciprocal determinism, heart health task forces will attempt to create organizational environments that duly promote and maintain heart health.

The approach used for schools is essentially the same as that used for other organizations, with slight variations. Organizational membership in schools is considered to include all adults (teachers, staff, and parents) associated with a school, as well as students in the high schools. Heart health task forces in schools may include any mix of these people but willideally include volunteers from each of the groupings. For elementary and junior high school students, specific classroom curricula are available for teachers and school task forces that wish to use it. A cross-aged peer teaching approach that uses high school student volunteers working with elementary and junior high school students (particularly for smoking prevention) has been successfully piloted and is available. Other programs being designed include a parents' correspondence course for self-change and a group program for parents entitled "How to Raise a Heart Healthy Child." Decisions concerning the implementation of any of these programs are made by the heart health task force at each school in the context of the total environment for the school and the interests and needs of its membership.

SMALL GROUP PROGRAMS

It is hoped that organizations that exhibit a readiness for individual and small group level programming only, and do not form heart health task forces initially, will later move up in readiness to the point where sufficient interest in forming an organizational level task force has evolved and task forces can be organized.

Volunteer-led group level programs for each risk factor have been developed by the PHHP staff. These programs include the behavioral intervention techniques of stimulus control and individual self-management methods as well as social skills training. Social skills training was added because a critical reason for the failure of many weight loss, smoking prevention and cessation, and other risk factor interventions to maintain their posttreatment effects over long periods has been related to their lack of focus on specific social network engineering skills (Abrams & Follick, 1983; Brownell, Heckerman, Westlake, Hayes, & Monti, 1978). A major development emphasis has been, and will continue to be, improvement of the technology for enlisting broad-based interpersonal support for health-protective behaviors (Elder, Rodrigues, Fergola, Abrams, & Artz, Note 2). The participants are active partners in this development, first as respondents in behavioral assessment studies, then through trials of specific social network protocols and feedback and refinement of the protocols.

EVALUATION

Inasmuch as the PHHP is a research project, approximately half of its resources are committed to a variety of evaluation efforts—process, formative, and outcome. Process evaluation focuses on such variables as replicability, lay leader usage, delivery of programs, and adequate documentation of the program process and its costs in order to conduct cost-benefit analyses and to facilitate replications in other communities. Behavioral, cognitive, physiological, permanent product, and unobtrusive measures have been developed to answer general and specific formative evaluation questions. Of particular interest is the relationship between social network structure and such factors as promotion, diffusion, and especially maintenance of lifestyle change. As an example, the relative effectiveness of using naturally occurring support groups (e.g., family, worksite, social club) will be compared to artificially created support groups, such as a weight loss program conducted at the local YMCA.

The overall outcome evaluation is based in part on a cross-sectional random sample survey of 1,400 subjects aged 18 through 65 in each of two cities—the intervention city and a comparison community. The baseline samples have been surveyed with follow-up random samples scheduled to be assessed at 2-year intervals. The survey concentrates on risk factor changes and physiological assessment. Blood samples are analyzed, for example, for levels of cholesterol, lipids, and thiocyanate. Expired air is analyzed for carbon monoxide level, blood pressures are taken, and a physical fitness test is accomplished on a stationary bicycle for a one-third subsample. Actual morbidity and mortality surveillance in both cities is a continuous process, based on reabstraction of medical records.

SUMMARY

The major goals of the PHHP are (a) to achieve significant reductions in cardiovascular morbidity and mortality, using public health strategies based on a community voluntarism model; and (b) to develop the community organization framework necessary to maintain the health enhancement programs as the research project professional staff withdraws from the program (by late 1985). Analyses of the data from this program will be available in 1986.

REFERENCE NOTES

1. Abrams, D., Elder, J., & PHHP Staff. *Pawtucket Heart Health Program general theoretical model.* PHHP Technical Report, 1981.

2. Elder, J. P., Rodrigues, A., Fergola, F. D., Abrams, D. B., & Artz, L. M. *Social skills and health protective behaviors: Generating interpersonal support for risk factor reduction.* Paper presented at the annual convention of the Association for Advancement of Behavior Therapy, Toronto, 1981.

REFERENCES

Abrams, D. B., & Follick, M. J. Behavioral weight loss intervention at the worksite: Feasibility and maintenance. *Journal of Consulting and Clinical Psychology,* 1983, **51**, 226–233.

Bandura, A. *Social learning theory.* Englewood Cliffs, N.J.: Prentice-Hall, 1977.

Brownell, K. D., Heckerman, C., Westlake, R., Hayes, S., & Monti, P. The effects of couples training and partner co-operativeness in the behavioral treatment of obesity. *Behavior Research and Therapy,* 1978, **16**, 323–333.

Fawcett, S. B., Mathews, R. W., & Fletcher, R. K. Some promising dimensions for behavioral community technology. *Journal of Applied Behavior Analysis,* 1977, **10**, 501–509.

Goldfried, M., & D'Zurilla, T. A behavior analytic model for assessing competence. In L. Spielberger (Ed.), *Current topics in clinical and community psychology.* New York: Holt, Rinehart & Winston, 1969.

Kanfer, F. H. Self-management methods. In F. H. Kanfer & A. P. Goldstein, *Helping people change.* New York: Pergamon Press, 1975.

Rothman, J. Three models of community organization practice. In National Conference on Social Welfare, *Social work practice.* New York: Columbia University Press, 1968.

CHAPTER 86

THE MINNESOTA HEART HEALTH PROGRAM: A RESEARCH AND DEMONSTRATION PROJECT IN CARDIOVASCULAR DISEASE PREVENTION

HENRY BLACKBURN
RUSSELL LUEPKER
F. G. KLINE
NEIL BRACHT
RAYMOND CARLAW
DAVID JACOBS
MAURICE MITTELMARK
LEE STAUFFER
HENRY L. TAYLOR

University of Minnesota

The Minnesota Heart Health Program (MHHP) is a research and demonstration project of community health education designed to reduce risk of cardiovascular disease (CVD). By multiple strategies, it attempts through education to help three Midwest communities choose and practice more healthy behaviors and to enhance community efforts to support these behaviors. Many years were spent in developing the concepts, assembling the appropriate faculty, and accumulating the needed skills and experience to develop and implement this population-wide approach to primary disease prevention. Approximately 3 years were spent in actual design and preparation of a research proposal and in extensive pretrial studies. A complete surveillance system was established and put in place to measure simultaneously disease and death rates, risk factor distributions, and health behavior in selected Midwest communities. An investigator-initiated research grant proposal was funded in July 1980 by the National Heart, Lung and Blood Institute of the National Institute of Health. The grant is approved for 5 years of a 9-year design and is staffed by 18 faculty, 24 technical and supervisory personnel, and 64 full-time and part-time staff. The purpose of this chapter is to summarize the essentials of the program, the experience and thinking that went into its preparation, the planning that led to its approval, the organization involved in its implementation, the design and the scientific yield it plans to achieve, and its accomplishments and problems in operation.

BACKGROUND

The population-wide approach to cardiovascular disease prevention arose from years of observations in the field and in the laboratory (Blackburn, 1981; Keys, Note 1; WHO, Note 2). From these observations, the concept evolved gradually that mass diseases, such as hypertension and atherosclerosis, are probably the result of powerful and ubiquitous sociocultural factors operating in conjunction with a widespread population susceptibility. This concept provides the causal rationale, while its corollary provides the strategy—that a favorable environment should assure the minimal exhibition of disease among the many suspectible persons. The idea of how best to achieve such a favorable environment is based on theories of how health behavior is learned and how it changes. In addition, abundant practical experience in Minnesota indicated that CVD risk factors can be reduced effectively and safely at group and community levels by direct education, motivation, and skills training in the promotion of health.

The overall research strategy of the MHHP is to bring the needed disciplines together to focus on the major public health issues, using research methods appropriate to the stage of knowledge. In our view, the applied research now needed in prevention of premature heart attacks and strokes requires testing of population-wide strategies to transfer and diffuse the information already available on their cause and preventability.

Within the high-incidence U.S. population, there is much preventive activity in individuals at special risk but not yet manifestly stricken. In time, it has been realized that the bulk of CVD cases in the population and, more important, most of the excess cases attributable to given risk factors come from a large, central part of the distribution of risk characteristics, not just from the tail of high risk (see Figure 86.1). Individuals at high risk who are motivated to change their behavior find it more difficult because their environment is often not supportive. Thus, interest has turned to the spouse, the family, the worksite, and the community influences on health behavior. Finally, it is recognized that prevention of elevated risk in the first place must be an objective of any rational, long-term population approach. Prevention requires changes in risky behaviors among the youth of high-incidence cultures and among entire populations that are now experiencing low cardiovascular disease rates.

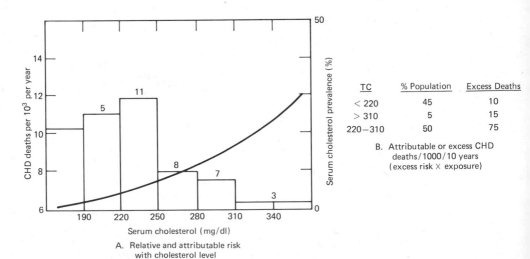

A. Relative and attributable risk
   with cholesterol level

TC	% Population	Excess Deaths
< 220	45	10
> 310	5	15
220–310	50	75

B. Attributable or excess CHD
   deaths/1000/10 years
   (excess risk × exposure)

Figure 86.1 Serum cholesterol. [Source: W. B. Kannel & T. Gordon, eds., "Some Characteristics Related to the Incidence of Cardiovascular Disease and Death," *The Framingham Study, 16-Year Follow-Up* (Washington, D.C.: U.S. Government Printing Office, 1970); WHO Expert Committee, *Prevention of Coronary Heart Disease*, WHO Technical Report Series No. 678, Copenhagen, 1982.]

Such a population view of prevention is now formalized in the recent report of a WHO Expert Committee on Prevention of Coronary Heart Disease (CHD) (WHO, Note 2).

An increasing comprehension of the social learning (and unlearning) of health behaviors, and much encouragement and incentive to develop the MHHP, came from collaborations with Finnish colleagues and Stanford University colleagues whose population view, behavioral strategies, and community projects preceded ours. In eastern Finland, for example, an entire county became activated in the early 1970s as a result of its awareness of its unique status in world health, when we and Finnish collaborators found and reported that the county of North Karelia had the highest rate of CHD measured anywhere. (Keys, Note 1). The entire county soon organized itself and took action to develop the North Karelia Project, now a well-known model community campaign of health promotion (Puska, Tuomilehto, Salonen, Nissinen, Virtamo, Björkqvist, Koskela, Neittaanmäki, Takalo, Kottke, Mäki, Sipilä, & Varvikko, 1981). At about the same time, the Stanford Three Community Study successfully combined advanced concepts of social learning with theories and skills in mass communications, resulting in a systematic campaign for promoting health knowledge and behavior. Its effects were carefully tested over a 3-year period in three small towns. The educated communities changed and, within them, personal changes paralleled the degree of exposure to the campaign (Farquhar, Maccoby, Wood, Brietrose, Haskell, Meyer, Alexander, Brown, McAlister, Nash, & Stern, 1977). All these observations and events contributed to the development of the MHHP—the design, operations, and current status of which are summarized in the following sections.

DESIGN AND EVALUATION

The MHHP is a 9-year research and demonstration project in CVD prevention, the components of which are staged as shown in Figure 86.2. Surveillance is carried out in annual population-based surveys, with periodic cohort studies. The campaigns are staged successively in three progressively larger communities. The MHHP attempts to produce the strongest

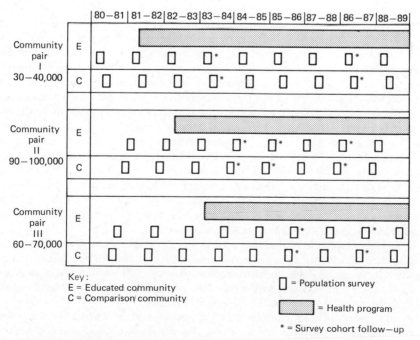

Figure 86.2   Minnesota Heart Health Program schedule of education and surveys.

possible inference about the effects of community education as a valid alternative to a randomized controlled experiment, which was not considered feasible (Cook & Campbell, 1979). Inference is based on deduction from simultaneously measured trends of health behavior, risk factor levels, and morbidity and mortality rates—all linked through evaluation to the educational program and process. The design seeks to strengthen inference about program effects by the following methods:

1. Comparison of educated and noneducated communities that have similar size and complexity.
2. Staggered campaigns in the three educated Midwest communities, adding strength of inference from repetitions.
3. Measurement of differences in risk factors, behavior, and disease trends among samples in the educated communities pooled, versus the comparison populations pooled.
4. "Before and after" analyses of sample cohorts that have particular risk configurations or are exposed to different intensities of the educational message.
5. Standardized outcome measures throughout, so that results from the MHHP and the two other NIH-sponsored programs can be pooled for endpoint events and will be internally consistent for risk factor measurements.
6. A design that incorporates a shakedown period of development, organization, and function before major population exposure.
7. Numerous evaluations of the links between educational efforts, community behavior, and disease risk.

The overall goals of the MHHP evaluation are to measure the change in disease risk and behavioral characteristics of communities and to relate these changes to the effect of the educational program and its specific components. The academic goals are to make original contributions to (a) the design and organization of community research and demonstration programs, (b) evaluation of the educational process, and (c) statistical analysis of time trends in population experiments and demonstrations.

Functional units of evaluation include data processing, morbidity and mortality assessment, education evaluation, quality control, and risk survey. A surveillance system is now in place for measuring mortality from major cardiovascular and noncardiovascular diseases throughout the Midwest states involved and for assessing morbidity from hospital record abstracts in the six project towns. Slopes of disease trends in educated communities are compared with slopes in comparison communities as well as with background mortality data for the states as a whole. Population distributions and changes in relevant cardiovascular risk characteristics are determined by annual population-based surveys of 500 adults, aged 24 to 74, in the education and the reference communities. Cohorts are drawn from the surveyed populations and are followed to measure individual changes over time. The cohorts include a sample of 250 members of the baseline survey and a subsample of those labeled hypertensive to determine the adequacy of subsequent blood pressure control. Community sizes are adequate to demonstrate with confidence a difference of 15% in mortality and morbidity rates (after 8 years), and survey samples are sufficient to detect biologically significant changes in the major risk factors and risk behaviors.

The inference that the educational process is responsible for any community changes and differences found will be based on the magnitude of the differences and trends, the consistency between results in the three community pairs, the coincidence of changes with the annual staged introduction to the educated communities, and short-term evaluations linking specific educational efforts to changes in behavior.

The educational process is evaluated by a special staff and primarily uses telephone interviews to evaluate exposures and the effects of specific campaigns or events on community awareness, knowledge, behavior, norms, and values. School surveys are carried out for changes in youth risk characteristics, health knowledge, and behavior. Samples of individuals exposed to the Health Education Center and to adult classes are surveyed later for behavior change. Significant socioeconomic changes in the community are documented from public records for employment, economic indices, and major community events.

All these evaluations together provide for the measurement of individual, group, and community-wide change. These are linked, in turn, to specific educational strategies and to the degree of individual exposure, from greater to lesser contact with various elements of the program: (a) those surveyed, recruited to the Health Education Center, recruited to special adult classes, and also participating in other community-based programs in the educated communities (these would be among the maximally exposed); (b) those experiencing combinations of three of these four major component exposures in educated towns; (c) those experiencing combinations of two of the exposures in individuals in educated towns; (d) those experiencing exposures to only one of these activities; (e) adults having only their children involved in specific educational strategies; (f) one-time survey participants in educated towns only; (g) those neither surveyed nor participating in direct educational activities; (h) survey cohort participants in noneducated communities; (i) participants only in the final survey (the "after" survey) in noneducated communities.

ADMINISTRATION

The MHHP is directed by a principal investigator, a project officer, a co-principal investigator, and an executive committee and Board. It is advised by a scientific advisory group and overseen by a NIH Project Officer. The MHHP has a central university staff, involved with policy and program development and community liaison, that has three main sections: education, evaluation, and administration. The program is carried out by a local staff and a community advisory board, with campaign task groups in each educated community (separately identified as the Mankato Heart Health Program, the Fargo–Moorhead Heart Health Program, etc.). The central organization is flexible and is administered along functional lines. Its management has sought to recruit section heads, faculty, and local directors with competence, experience, and initiative; to give them great responsibility and authority; and to require from them good communications and accountability. The project is on schedule.

EDUCATION

The educational program of the MHHP involves multiple strategies designed to contribute to changed behaviors and lowered risk factor levels when applied consistently across the whole community and over a substantial time period. Basic assumptions are that there is room for change in the community, that change is feasible within the design period, that the health program itself is credible, that multiple strategies together will contribute more than their individual effects on community behaviors and risk levels, and that the effects can be measured.

The risk factors are measured as (a) the frequency of adult hypertension and the mean population level and distribution of blood pressure, (b) the frequency of hypercholesterolemia and the mean population level and distribution of total and HDL-cholesterol values, (c) the frequency of cigarette smoking and the distribution of smoking habits, and (d) the frequency of regular physical activity and the mean and distribution of energy expenditure measured across the community.

The health behaviors targeted by the educational strategies include habitual eating patterns, physical activity patterns, smoking patterns, and behavior patterns with respect to hypertension detection and control (e.g., pill taking, seeking medical care). Risk factor goals are specified (a) for significant community changes in mean values and in slopes of trends from multiple points measured over the experimental period, (b) for appropriate deflections of these slopes in conjunction with the phased introduction of campaigns into the three educated communities, and (c) for differences in these slopes and trends between the education communities and the reference towns.

Behavioral goals are also specified. They include significant changes in (a) the proportion of people "moving about" and vigorously active; (b) the average calorie expenditure daily; (c) smoking frequency and intensity; (d) the selection, preparation, and consumption of specific foods; and (e) the maintenance of controlled high blood pressure. Disease reduction goals are specified for incidence and death rate differences between the educated towns (combined) and the reference towns and against upper-Midwest mortality experience.

Specific goals for the *average differences* in risk factor level, behaviors, and disease incidence between pooled educated and comparison communities are as follows: 1.5% in systolic or diastolic blood pressure; 2.0% in relative body weight; 3.5% in total serum cholesterol; 20.0% in quit smokers or amount smoked; 50.0% in persons engaged in vigorous activity, and 50 Kcal/day of activity; 15.0% in CHD incidence and deaths. None of these changes and differences is considered essential to a "successful" demonstration; rather, what is essential is the logical occurrence and overall consistency of the observations. Specific quantitative goals are estimated from changes already observed or experimentally demonstrated to be feasible and safe in changing risk behavior, risk factor levels, and disease rates.

The multiple systems for delivery of the educational campaigns are as follows:

1. Mass communications (mass and personalized media).
2. Direct education through the Health Education Center and special adult classes.
3. Professional education through workshops of physicians, dentists, nutritionists, nurses, and other health professionals.
4. Youth education programs through school curricula, 4-H Clubs, youth campaigns, and children's events.
5. Community-based activities implemented by campaign task forces on smoking, exercise, and eating patterns and on special worksite and medical center projects.

The education program develops strategies and materials for each of the risk behavior campaigns and implements delivery through direct education and involvement of community leaders, health professionals, adults, and youth. Community-based efforts are carried out by local educators who staff a community advisory board and its task forces and through community institutions and activities—all coordinated with the intensive media campaigns.

EDUCATION PROGRAM STATUS

Programs began in the fall of 1981 in the first educated community, Mankato, following a year of community analysis, organization of the community advisory board, training of community staff and board members, and professional education activities. Activation of the first community advisory board, now thoroughly involved in the Mankato program, occurred simultaneously with a general awareness campaign and with task forces established for smoking, high blood pressure, physical activity, and eating pattern campaigns. In 1982, for example, intensive Mankato campaigns were staged in January for smoking, in April for physical activity, in May for hypertension, and in September for eating pattern emphasis. Direct public education began with the opening, in October 1981, of the Mankato Health Education Center, offering a unique health education experience that combines measurement of health behavior and a physiological risk factor profile with health messages appropriate to age and risk class. At the screening and education stations, immediate feedback is given for blood pressure and blood cholesterol values, carbon monoxide content of the breath, and physical activity evaluation from an interactive computer program, and audiovisual and printed materials are presented for each risk factor. The visit concludes with a counseling interview and referral to medical sources or to special adult health classes in the community that teach skills in desired behavior changes. Special youth programs were developed by consultation a year in advance, and schoolteacher training occurred in the fall of 1981 in Mankato. Smoking prevention strategies were implemented in all the 7th grades in Mankato in the winter term, 1981–1982, and smoking cessation programs were initiated in the 11th grade in the spring of 1982. Physical activity and eating pattern programs were incorporated into the summer 1982 teacher-training process for implementation in the fall.

Community-based activities include direct contacts with all community health care and related agencies and recruitment of specialists and leaders into task forces of the community advisory Board. In Mankato, a hypertension council was formed of all parties interested in the control and prevention of high blood pressure. It has already made a formal proposal to and received funding from the state health department to develop and implement a detection, control, and prevention protocol appropriate to office and clinic settings. A work-site program in smoking cessation was presented to a leading Mankato industry and included most company smokers, of which one-third were reported to have quit. The emphasis for industry is on direct programs through the union brotherhoods and on environmental programs at the worksite. A fitness training protocol for school systems in collaboration with the local YMCA was developed and implemented in the fall of 1982. An ongoing educational project with grocery retailers includes Mankato Heart Health Program kiosks in four shopping centers as sources of information and menus. Restaurateurs are now actively involved with their own task force, providing alternative menus identified with the Mankato Heart Health Program logo in leading community eateries. Evaluation of the education process has led to improved recruitment to the Health Education Center as well as to intensive planning, staging, and modification of specific risk factor campaigns in Mankato.

Fargo and Moorhead are larger, more complex communities where surveys and community analysis are complete and where community activities got underway in September 1982. The suburban unit in Bloomington opened in September 1983.

EVALUATION PROGRAM STATUS

Baseline and first annual surveys of risk characteristics have been carried out in all communities. The surveys indicate satisfactory comparability of educated and reference communities. Continuous mortality surveillance is ongoing through state health department death certificate records. Morbidity surveillance is under way in all communities through abstraction of hospital charts coded for major cardiovascular diseases, along with a detailed record review of a 10% sample for validation. Ten-year Minnesota mortality trends are analyzed (Gillum, Folsom, Jacobs, Luepker, Prineas, Kottke, Gomez, Taylor, & Blackburn, 1982), and survey data have been presented on risk factor distributions (Luepker, Jacobs, Folsom, Gillum, Taylor, & Blackburn, 1982).

OVERALL MHHP PROBLEMS AND LIMITATIONS

Natural tensions between the university and community groups have arisen in the MHHP. It is thought that these develop from the different expectations of those concerned with the scientific methods and aims of this research demonstration, on the one hand, and of local leaders concerned about services and schedules committed to be performed in their towns, on the other. The very desirable development of a community sense of ownership of the program tends to reduce control of the evaluation on which the research depends. Effective recognition and resolution of these issues have been constructive in developing a true partnership between the community and the university in carrying out the research and service elements.

The more general issue of inherent weaknesses in research demonstrations is acknowledged. Randomized, controlled design, with numerous town units, was not feasible because of the limited numbers of Midwest communities available as well as the prohibitive costs that such an undertaking would involve. Other intrinsic limitations include the difficulty in establishing independence of educational effects, over and above the numerous other changes going on these days in U.S. communities. Although the noneducated communities provide essential comparisons, matching of educated and reference communities is unsure on other than a few general variables (size, socioeconomic status, stability, and political complexity). Thus, interpretation of the relationship between the various steps of education and change in behavior, risk factor levels, and disease rates must be based on inferences from the overall logic and on the several links in the process established by analysis. It cannot depend entirely on disease differences at completion. Finally, community demonstrations are subject to uncontrollable vagaries of economic depression, natural disasters, and unmeasured biases and interactions.

Despite these several issues and limitations, the investigators consider that community health education research and demonstration projects such as the Minnesota Heart Health Program are needed and are important to demonstrate feasibility and effect, to improve educational methods and strategy, and to arrive at crucial inferences and generalizations about the real potential for CVD prevention in the country. This information and these inferences, we believe, cannot be derived from randomized trials among high-risk population segments, as needed for rational preventive practice, or from smaller scale, single-strategy preventive efforts. Such clinical trials or limited health education programs, isolated as they are from community-wide efforts, may have little direct relevance to the transfer of knowledge or the educational strategies required for reduction of chronic disease and improvement of health for entire populations.

REFERENCE NOTES

1. Keys, A. (Ed.). *Coronary heart disease in seven countries.* AHA Monograph No. 29, 1970.
2. WHO Expert Committee. *Prevention of coronary heart disease.* WHO Technical Report Series No. 678, 1982.

REFERENCES

Blackburn, H. Primary prevention of coronary heart disease. In J. A. Spittell, Jr. (Ed.), *Clinical medicine.* Philadelphia: Harper & Row, 1981.

Cook, T. D., & Campbell, D. T. *Quasi-experimentation: Design and analysis issues for field settings.* Chicago: Rand McNally, 1979.

Farquhar, J. W., Maccoby, N., Wood, P. D., Breitrose, H., Haskell, W. L., Meyer, A. J., Alexander, J. K., Brown, B. W., McAlister, A. L., Nash, J. D., & Stern, M. P. Community education for cardiovascular health. *Lancet,* 1977, **1**, 1192–1195.

Gillum, R. F., Folsom, A., Jacobs, D. R., Jr., Luepker, R. V., Prineas, R. J., Kottke, T., Gomez, O., Taylor, H., & Blackburn, H. Myocardial infarction: Hospitalization, case fatality and out-of-hospital coronary deaths in a metropolitan area. *Journal of the American College of Cardiology* 1983, **1**(2, Pt. II), 600.

Luepker, R. V., Jacobs, D. R., Jr., Folsom, A. Gillum, R. F., Taylor, H. L., & Blackburn, H. Trends in cardiovascular disease risk 1973–74 to 1980–81: The Minnesota Heart Survey. *Circulation,* 1982 **66**(4): II-284.

Puska, P., Tuomilehto, J., Salonen, J., Nissinen, A., Virtamo, J., Björkqvist, S., Koskela, K., Neittaanmäki, L., Takalo, T., Kottke, T., Mäki, J., Sipilä, P., Varvikko, P. The North Karelia Project: Community Control of Cardiovascular Diseases. Evaluation of a Comprehensive Programme for Control of Cardiovascular Diseases in 1972–77 in North Karelia, Finland. Copenhagen: World Health Organization, 1981.

CHAPTER 87

THE HEALTH MAINTENANCE ORGANIZATION

NICHOLAS A. CUMMINGS

Biodyne Institute, San Francisco and Honolulu

The concept of preventing disease and keeping the person healthy is inherent in the structure of the health maintenance organization (HMO). The HMO differs strikingly from the traditional health insurance plan, which reimburses the physician for treating illness only—a system that might be more properly termed a "sickness plan." In contrast, the HMO receives a capitation—a set monthly sum per subscriber—and in return agrees to care for all the health needs of that subscriber. No fee is paid the physician each time a patient is seen, and all care must be provided within the economics of the capitation. The incentive is toward keeping the person healthy, thereby avoiding costly medical treatment for disease that might have been prevented. From the beginning, the HMO is free to allocate a significant portion of its resources to the maintenance of health through various approaches, such as behavioral health, consumer education and outreach, preventive services such as periodic health checks, program evaluation and innovation, and the abandonment of traditional techniques and personnel, with concern only for effectiveness. To the extent that these efforts are successful, less money will be required for the treatment of chronic and serious diseases, eventually reducing costs to the consumer.

HISTORICAL PERSPECTIVE

Although the term *health maintenance organization* did not come into use until the Nixon administration, during which federal legislation designed to encourage the establishment of HMOs was enacted, the concept was born in the Mojave Desert of California four decades earlier (Cummings & VandenBos, 1981). After receiving the contract to build the aqueduct to Los Angeles from Boulder Dam (later renamed Hoover Dam), a then unknown builder named Henry J. Kaiser experienced difficulty recruiting and maintaining adequate construction crews on the desert. This problem was due to the total lack of medical care in the desert and the resulting reluctance of workers to move their families there. Upon hearing of this problem, Sidney Garfield, a young physician, offered to provide all the facilities and services necessary for comprehensive health care—not only for the workers, but also for their families. The cost of this package would be a nickel per employee work hour; there would be no fee for service, no matter how adverse the experience. A further unique feature was that a significant portion of effort would be expended to prevent illness, particularly such problems as sun stroke and heat exhaustion, which are perils in the desert.

The arrangement was made and the concept of a capitation to keep people healthy as opposed to a fee to treat the sick was implemented—perhaps out of necessity, perhaps out of Kaiser's ability to recognize a good idea. Seemingly overnight, Kaiser built his shipyards during World War II and brought along Dr. Garfield and a now greatly expanded prepaid health care group. The Kaiser-Permanente Health Plan went public in 1945 and flourished immediately. Its tremendous acceptance was obviously because the Kaiser Plan provided comprehensive treatment without the exclusions, limitations, co-insurance and other troublesome features common to other health plans at the time. Kaiser-Permanente has enjoyed four decades of growth, with nearly 10 million subscribers and 40 hospitals in California, Hawaii, Cleveland, Denver, and Washington, D.C.

As health costs began to escalate alarmingly in the 1970s, Garfield's concept of health maintenance caught the attention of the federal government and led to legislation aimed at encouraging the creation of health maintenance organizations in the United States instead of the traditional fee-for-service health plan reimbursement. Since that time, many HMOs have been established, but on a more modest scale than Kaiser-Permanente. In fact, the subscriber population of the Kaiser Plan still exceeds the combined populations of all other HMOs. For this reason, and because only the Kaiser Plan has existed for sufficient time, this chapter will discuss the Kaiser-Permanente experience.

THE NEW MODEL OF HEALTH CARE DELIVERY

In traditional medical care, developed in the United States over two centuries, demand is regulated by the fee in the marketplace. Because of fees, people tend to put off medical care until they are definitely sick, giving the illusion that well-being is binary—that is, composed of either sick or healthy individuals. As Garfield (1976) has pointed out, however, four groups of individuals comprise an indefinite potential user population for health facilities: the well, the worried well (somatocizers and potential somatocizers), the asymptomatic sick, and the definitely sick. The fee is a regulator of demand, but it is not the only regulator. It tends to keep out the well, the worried well, and the asymptomatic sick. It may also keep out some definitely sick people who cannot afford the fee. For others, entry into the system is economically traumatic. For these reasons, a variety of prepaid health plans have been developed, all designed to reduce or eliminate the personal fee as a barrier to the sick in receiving treatment.

Once "sickness plans" eliminate the personal fee, something very interesting happens. The entire range of potential users enters the arena: the well, the worried well, the asymptomatic sick, and the definitely sick. The well and the worried well begin to compete with the sick on a first-come–first-served basis, causing an inevitable overloading of medical facilities, with reduced quality and efficiency. Physicians, who are trained to find disease, are frustrated as they strive to find sickness in the worried well, who now are beginning to squeeze out the sick in the competition for care.

Garfield, Collen, Feldman, Soghikian, Richardt, and Duncan (1976) identify four serious problems resulting from the impact of the well plus the sick once personal fees have been eliminated as a factor: (a) it overloads the relatively inelastic sick-care delivery system, causing a backlog of unavailable services and the inevitable queuing that has accompanied free care; (b) the large number of well people that get into the system, by usurping the physician's time, act as a barrier to the entry of the sick—the reverse of what was intended by eliminating fees; (c) with this altered demand, instead of caring for the sick, physicians are spending a large portion of their time trying to find something wrong with well people, and they are doing this with techniques they learned for diagnosing sick people; and (d) the impact of the relatively unlimited amount of uncertainty demand on the limited supply of physicians inevitably creates inflationary costs.

To meet these serious problems, Garfield, Collen, Feldman, Soghikian, Richardt, and Duncan (1976) designed a system in which health testing is the key to matching the sick to the sick care system and the well to alternate systems that best meet their needs. This health testing combines a detailed automated medical history with comprehensive panels of physiological and laboratory tests administered by nonphysicians, a physical examination by a nurse practitioner, computer processing of results, and a physician review. This health testing has proved to be an effective way of separating demand into its component parts and matching each user with the appropriate care system, as illustrated in Figure 87.1.

The well and the worried well are directed into the health care system—a new concept designed to enhance health and to keep healthy people well. It is conducted by nonphysician personnel, ranging from educators to nurse practitioners and psychologists. The worried well receive definite guidance on maintaining well-being without overloading physicians by forcing them to try to find something wrong with people who are actually well. Those who have somaticized their concerns and their emotions are directed to the mental health service to see a psychologist. In all instances, the well and the worried well are kept out of the sick care system, where they would be mismatched.

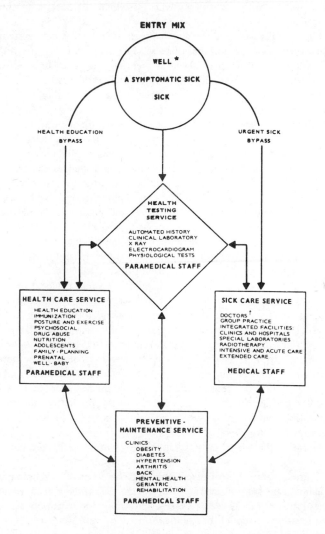

*Includes Worried Well.   †Solo or Group Practice.

Figure 87.1   New medical care delivery system.

The asymptomatic sick are directed to a system of preventive services, again conducted by nonphysician personnel, who are guided by computer-provided advice rules, with follow-up printouts of pertinent data sent to the patients' physicians. This obviously relieves the physician of many routine visits. Finally, the definitely sick are directed to the sick care system, where the physician's techniques to diagnose and treat disease are applied appropriately, and where the physician is now freed to devote the resources of the system only to the sick.

PREVENTION AND MENTAL HEALTH

The startling discovery at Kaiser-Permanente that up to 60% of all physician visits are by patients who have no significant physical abnormality was first thought to be a peculiarity of the HMO (Follette & Cummings, 1967). Eventually, it became clear that this figure is rather constant for all health delivery systems in which the barrier of the fee has been eliminated (Garfield, 1976).

The mismatching of the well and the worried well with the sick care system inadvertently rewards the somaticization of emotional distress. The physician who is overburdened with trying to find disease in well people as well as treating the sick listens only for symptoms of illness. There is no time to heed the patient's emotional distress, so the patient is conditioned to respond with what the physician needs to hear. Consider the man in his mid-fifties who has worked continuously for one boss since his mid-twenties. The boss has retired and has been replaced by his young son, who is impatient to implement a host of new ideas. Frightened and insecure, the middle-aged employee develops a general, vague malaise associated with his underlying anxiety and depression. His physician, finding nothing physically wrong after several visits, grows impatient and ignores the patient's plea, "My new boss is on my back." Several months later, and after several more visits in which both patient and physician feel frustrated, the man complains of a low back pain. Suddenly, the physician's attitude changes, for he has now found a symptom that has medical meaning. X rays are ordered, a referral is made to orthopedics, return visits are scheduled, and both physician and patient have now forgotten that the original complaint was, "My new boss is on my back." If the physician signs sick leave papers, the patient is encouraged to become a chronic somaticizer, for now he is completely relieved of the young boss who does not understand him. A chronic low back pain is a small price to pay.

Follette and Cummings (1967) found that brief, targeted psychological intervention of only a few sessions aided such patients to find more satisfactory solutions to their emotional distress, removed the patient from the sick care system, and reduced medical utilization (defined as all services, including not only physician visits, but also laboratory tests and days in the hospital) by 65% to 75%. Furthermore, the reduction persisted for 8 years without any further recourse to somaticization or recurrence of the emotional distress (Cummings & Follette, 1976). An intensive outreach program designed to transfer the patient with emotional distress from the sick care system to the preventive mental health system did not inundate the mental health system with patients, as had been feared would be the case (Cummings & Follette, 1968). Furthermore, when given a choice, 85% of patients chose short-term rather than long-term psychotherapy, with equally efficacious results (Cummings, 1977b).

The Kaiser-Permanente series of researches into the effect of psychological intervention on medical utilization (as summarized by Cummings, 1977a) have been replicated 24 times, with similar results (Jones & Vischi, 1979), despite the wide variation of delivery systems and geographic locations in which the replications occurred. Mechanic (1966) has demonstrated that emotional distress can have a direct causal relationship to illness, either as a direct contributor or as an inhibitor to recovery. Schlesinger, Mumford, and Glass (1980) found that in the airways diseases, hypertension, ischemic heart disease, and diabetes, psychological intervention reduced medical utilization by increasing compliance to required medical regimens. The conclusion drawn from these studies is that by adding to the somaticizers of emotional distress those patients whose recovery can be enhanced by psychological intervention, up to 90% of physician visits are by persons who could benefit from brief psychotherapy—whether they are the worried well, the early sick, or the definitely sick.

AUTOMATED MULTIPHASIC SCREENING

The heart of the HMO delivery system—which separates at entry the well, the worried well, the asymptomatic sick, and the definitely sick into the health care, preventive care, and sick care systems—is automated multiphasic screening administered as a periodic health check. Breslow (1973), who was the first to use the term *multiphasic screening,* has reviewed its evolution from a single-test procedure to the present complex automatic multiphasic services. In the decade spanning the late 1940s to the late 1950s, three pioneers can be identified: Breslow in California (Canelo, Bissell, Abrams, & Breslow, 1949), Ryder and Getting (1950) in Massachusetts, and Petrie in Georgia (Petrie, Bowdoin, & McLaughlin, 1952). In 1951, Collen first employed multiphasic screening as part of a periodic health examination within an organized group practice—in this case the Kaiser-Permanente HMO (Collen & Linden, 1955). In 1964, that system was computerized into an automated multiphasic screening (Collen, 1966).

The health testing service at Kaiser-Permanente includes a comprehensive automated medical history, 28 computerized laboratory tests, a 155-item automated psychological questionnaire designed to diagnose emotional distress, a physical examination by a nurse practitioner, and follow-up computer printouts to the patient's own physician. The automated test equipment and the computer determine automatically whether there is sufficient likelihood of disease being present to warrant further diagnostic testing. Advice rules, on printouts, determine the assignment of each patient to the health care system, the preventive care system, or the sick care system. Several studies have demonstrated that this automated multiphasic system, using no direct physician services, is as effective in diagnosis as are systems employing varying amounts of costly physician time (Collen, 1973; Cutler, 1973; Dales, 1973; Ramcharan, 1973).

Because the HMO must remain committed to program evaluation and to a constant monitoring of effectiveness in order to survive economically, the automated multiphasic screening service has provided a wealth of research data. Stored in the computer are hundreds of thousands of protocols of well patients who subsequently developed disease. Beyond the importance of early detection, these data provide the opportunity to compare those who develop disease to those who do not. Hundreds of studies have been conducted, with many more in progress or planned, and only a few examples can be cited here. Nonetheless, these studies revealed the importance of psychological, environmental, and lifestyle factors long before it was popular to devote attention to such factors.

In one study, patients who suffered a myocardial infarction were compared with their "normal" multiphasic health checks, which had preceded the infarction by an average of 16.8 months (Friedman, Ury, Klatsky, & Siegelaub, 1974). The automated psychological questionnaire revealed a specific pattern of anxiety and depression, which was absent in the control group and was predictive of myocardial infarction. This pattern was also predictive of whether the person suffering the event would be a slow or fast recoverer. Once the event occurred, however, all patients demonstrated enough emotional distress to render their test protocols indistinguishable. This study illustrates not only the importance of psychological distress in myocardial infarction but also the need to have psychological data before the onset of an illness. Finally, it illustrates the kind of innovative research that is possible with an ongoing program of extensive multiphasic health screening.

By using automated multiphasic screening information Dales, Friedman, Ury, Grossman, and Williams (1978) were able to expand the list of lifestyle patterns that lead to subsequent cancer of the colon. In addition to confirming the importance of high fat and low fiber in the diets of persons developing colorectal cancer, it was found that prolonged cigar smoking in men and nulliparity in women are also risk factors.

Reports that vasectomized men are prone to suffer much more subsequent disease prompted Kaiser-Permanente to reexamine their benefit of providing vasectomies upon request. In a study of 4,385 men who indicated in their multiphasic screening that they had had vasectomies, the computer provided three exact matches for each, or 13,155 men who had not been vasectomized (Petitti, Klein, Kipp, Kahn, Siegelaub, & Friedman, 1982). Comparisons of their health histories over several years revealed no evidence that vasectomy leads to disease in humans. Therefore, provision of vasectomy as a covered benefit continues.

Another study, designed to test side effects and improve effectiveness, investigated the oral contraceptive services. It was found that serum cholesterol levels in women depend on the formulation of the oral contraceptive used (Bradley, Wingerd, Petitti, Krauss, & Ramcharan, 1978). Also, the risk of vascular disease in women taking oral contraceptives was found to be present if the woman smokes cigarettes (Petitti, Wingerd, Pellegrin, & Ramcharan, 1979). Therefore, a program strongly urging such women not to smoke was begun.

Lech, Friedman, and Ury (1975) compared heavy users of prescription drugs with light users and found that the former experienced almost four times the number of adverse reactions. Among the heavy users were many individuals with emotional problems that appeared to contribute to symptoms and requests for drugs. Such patients consult several physicians concurrently and tend to use emergency and drop-in services, where records of prescriptions written by other physicians are not immediately available. As a result of this study, Kaiser-Permanente made the patients' prescription drug histories available to physicians on a computer terminal.

Because of the high cost of alcohol- and tobacco-related illnesses, numerous studies have been conducted on the mortality rate among heavy users of these substances. Besides confirming previous findings, these studies have delineated guidelines for use by physicians and other health personnel in treating such users within a variety of illnesses and conditions. Most notable are the 10-year study of alcohol mortality (Klatsky, Friedman, & Siegelaub, 1981) and another longitudinal study of middle-aged smokers (Friedman, Dales, & Ury, 1979). As a result of these studies, stop-smoking clinics and alcohol and drug abuse programs have been established as part of the HMO.

CONSUMER EDUCATION

Integral to the concept of maintaining subscriber health is the ongoing, effective education of the consumer. This educational effort must respond not only to the immediate concerns of the patient but also to the long-range dissemination of health information. Part of the latter is accomplished by publication of a monthly magazine, attractively prepared and sent to all subscribers. It highlights various health issues and focuses on prevention and early self-detection of disease. Health exhibits provided in the Kaiser-Permanente system's many hospitals are well attended. One study demonstrated that three-dimensional and multimedia presentations that give a positive view of health encourage visitors to accept personal responsibility for their own well-being (Collen & Soghikian, 1974).

Much of the immediate health education is provided through the services of nurse practitioners who provide 24-hour coverage as "advice nurses." Responses are given to telephone inquiries on whether the caller's symptoms warrant coming into the medical center or whether there is something that the patient may more properly do at home. The patient is given practical, effective advice that insures quality care and reassures the worried caller. If the advice nurse on duty is not able to deal with the problem, there is immediate recourse to consultation with the physician specialist on call. In addition to providing quick response to the patient day or night, the use of the nurse practitioner saves costly physician time.

Patients often need to be educated regarding the proper use of medication or the need for cooperation with prescribed regimens. Griffith and Madero (1973) and Soghikian (1978) found that compliance by patients suffering from such conditions as hypertension was increased by a well-structured program of nurse-educator intervention.

In a 4-year study employing nurse practitioners, rather than physicians, to conduct routine physical examinations, it was expected that the substitution of nursing personnel would reduce costs, but the finding that patient compliance was 90% because of the nurses' use of educative techniques was surprising. Also, patient satisfaction equaled that found with physician evaluation. Most important, however, the approach freed the sick care system of the well patients and improved the waiting list for physician appointments from 6 weeks to a few days (Feldman, Taller, Garfield, Collen, Richart, Cella, & Sender, 1977).

In summarizing the educational aspect of the HMO delivery system, Collen, Feldman, Soghikian, and Garfield (1973) state that once the educational need is integrated into the delivery of medical care, it can be handled completely by nonphysician personnel. It has become an essential adjunct to the management of care as prescribed by the physician and an imperative in the health maintenance of all people—sick and well.

REFERENCES

Bradley, D. D., Wingerd, J., Petitti, D. B., Krauss, R. M., & Ramcharan, S. Serum high-density-lipoprotein cholesterol in women using oral contraceptives, estrogens and progestins. *New England Journal of Medicine,* 1978, **299.**

Breslow, L. An historical review of multiphasic screening. *Preventive Medicine,* 1973, **2.**

Canelo, C. K., Bissell, D. M., Abrams, H., & Breslow, L. A. A multiphasic screening survey in San Jose. *California Medicine,* 1949, **71.**

Collen, M. F., Feldman, R., Soghikian, K., & Garfield, S. R. The educational adjunct to multiphasic testing. *Preventive Medicine,* 1973, **2.**

Collen, M. F., & Soghikian, K. Health exhibits accentuate the positive. *Hospitals,* 1974, **48.**

Collen, M. F. Periodic health examinations using an automated multitest laboratory. *Journal of the American Medical Association,* 1966, **195.**

Collen, M. F. Introduction to health testing forum. *Preventive Medicine,* 1973, **2.**

Collen, M. F., & Linden, C. Screening in a group practice prepaid medical care plan. *Journal of Chronic Disability,* 1955, **2.**

Cummings, N. A. The anatomy of psychotherapy under National Health Insurance. *American Psychologist,* 1977, **32.** (a)

Cummings, N. A. Prolonged (ideal) versus short-term (realistic) psychotherapy. *Professional Psychology,* 1977, **8.** (b)

Cummings, N. A., & Follette, W. T. Psychiatric services and medical utilization in a prepaid health plan setting: Part II. *Medical Care,* 1968, **5.**

Cummings, N. A., & Follette, W. T. Brief psychotherapy and medical utilization: An eight-year follow-up. In H. Dörken and Associates (Eds.), *The professional psychologist today: New developments in law, health insurance and health practice.* San Francisco: Jossey-Bass, 1976.

Cummings, N. A., & VandenBos, G. R. The twenty years' Kaiser-Permanente experience with psychotherapy and medical utilization: Implications for national health policy and National Health Insurance. *Health Policy Quarterly,* 1981, **1.**

Cutler, J. L. Multiphasic checkup evaluation study. *Preventive Medicine,* 1973, **2.**

Dales, L. G. Multiphasic checkup evaluation study: Outpatient clinic utilization. *Preventive Medicine,* 1973, **2.**

Dales, L. G., Friedman, G. D., Ury, H. K., Grossman, S., & Williams, S. A case-control study of relationships of diet and other traits to colorectal cancer in American blacks. *American Journal of Epidemiology,* 1978, **109.**

Feldman, R., Taller, S. L., Garfield, S. R., Collen, M. F., Richart, R. H., Cella, R., & Sender, A. J. Nurse practitioner multiphasic health checkups. *Preventive Medicine,* 1977, **6.**

Follette, W. T., & Cummings, N. A. Psychiatric services and medical utilization in a prepaid health plan setting. *Medical Care,* 1967, **5.**

Friedman, G. D., Dales, L. G., & Ury, H. K. Mortality in middle-aged smokers and nonsmokers. *New England Journal of Medicine,* 1979, **300.**

Friedman, G. D., Ury, H. K., Klatsky, A. L., & Siegelaub, A. B. A psychological questionnaire predictive of myocardial infarction: Results from the Kaiser-Permanente epidemiologic study of myocardial infarction. *Psychosomatic Medicine,* 1974, **36.**

Garfield, S. R. Evolving new model for health-care delivery. *Orthopaedic Review,* 1976, **5.**

Garfield, S. R., Collen, M. F., Feldman, R., Soghikian, K., Richardt, R. H., & Duncan, J. H. Evaluation of an ambulatory medical-care delivery system. *New England Journal of Medicine,* 1976, **294.**

Griffith, W. K., & Madero, B. Primary hypertension patients' learning needs. *American Journal of Nursing,* 1973, **73.**

Jones, K. R., & Vischi, T. R. Impact of alcohol, drug abuse and mental health treatment on medical care utilization: A review of the literature. *Medical Care* [*Suppl.*], 1979, **17.**

Klatsky, A. L., Friedman, G. D., & Siegelaub, A. B. Alcohol and mortality: A ten-year Kaiser-Permanente experience. *Annals of Internal Medicine,* 1981, **95.**

Lech, S. V., Friedman, G. D., & Ury, H. K. Characteristics of heavy users of outpatient prescription drugs. *Clinical Toxicology,* 1975, **8.**

Mechanic, D. Response factors in illness: The study of illness behavior. *Social Psychiatry,* 1966, **1.**

Petitti, D. B., Klein, R., Kipp, H., Kahn, W., Siegelaub, A. B., & Friedman, G. D. A survey of personal habits, symptoms of illness, and histories of disease in men with and without vasectomies. *American Journal of Public Health,* 1982, **72.**

Petitti, D. B., Wingerd, J., Pellegrin, F., & Ramcharan, S. Risk of vascular disease in women: Smoking, oral contraceptives, noncontraceptive estrogens, and other factors. *Journal of the American Medical Association,* 1979, **242.**

Petrie, L. M., Bowdoin, C. D., & McLaughlin, C. V. Voluntary multiple health costs. *Journal of the American Medical Association,* 1952, **48.**

Ramcharan, S. Multiphasic checkup evaluation study: Disability and chronic disease after 7 years of multiphasic checkups. *Preventive Medicine,* 1973, **2.**

Ryder, C. F., & Getting, V. A. Preliminary report on the health protection clinic. *New England Journal of Medicine,* 1950, **243.**

Schlesinger, H. J., Mumford, E., & Glass, G. V. Mental health services and medical utilization. In G. R. VandenBos (Ed.), *Psychotherapy: Practice, research, policy.* Beverly Hills, Calif.: Sage, 1980.

Soghikian, K. The role of nurse practitioners in hypertension care. *Clinical Science and Molecular Medicine,* 1978, **55.**

SECTION 12

TRAINING FOR HEALTH PROMOTION

CHAPTER 88

OVERVIEW

GEORGE C. STONE

University of California, San Francisco

Much of the material in this Handbook has to do with promotion of health-enhancing behavior. The issues to be addressed in this section are the definitions of the appropriate roles of several health care professions, a consideration of possible obstacles to the professionals' recognition and performance of those roles, and descriptions of training programs or approaches that can and do facilitate mastery of health-promoting professional behavior. The authors of the chapters that make up the remainder of this section are members of different professions, each of which has recognized, to some degree at least, some responsibility for the promotion of healthy behavior, either for individual clients or patients or through interactions and communications with groups. Each of these authors has taken a significant part in the health-promoting activities of his or her profession. They address the topic from the perspectives of their respective professions. In this introductory overview, I will present an analysis of the health-promoting transaction at a more abstract level, which will provide a basis for comparing the approaches of the several professions represented here.

To set the context, we can consider the persons whose health is at issue (PHAI) to be living in an environment of opportunities for growth and development and of hazards to the integrity of the mind and body. Health-promoting behavior is behavior that minimizes the impact of the hazards on the individual and maximizes exploitation of the opportunities for growth. Persons and organizations that engage in health promotion can do so (a) by reducing or eliminating hazards from the environment and by introducing or enhancing opportunities for growth and development or (b) by influencing the behavior of the PHAI in relation to existing hazards and opportunities. These two approaches to health promotion have been labeled "managerial" and "personal" (Kristein, Arnold, & Wynder, 1977).

PROFESSIONAL ROLES

Within each of these areas—the managerial and the personal—are multiple roles that professionals can play. Basic research can be performed on the nature of hazards or opportunities and on factors that influence their prevalence in the environment. Basic research can also be done on the ways in which social values change and on how these changes find their expression in legislation and in markets. Professionals can engage in applied research and development of methods for altering the prevalence of hazards and opportunities and the behavior of PHAI in relation to them, and they can participate in developing methods for improving health planning. They can appraise the needs of particular individuals or groups, they can apply appropriate techniques directly in performing services for clients, and they can evaluate the impact of their own or others' professional services on the health of those served. Such roles characterize the work of professionals in any domain; the particularities of professional health promotion arise in the interaction of the generic roles with the particular problems of health promotion.

Role definitions and performances are also influenced by the ways in which each profession has developed, the kinds of roles it has played in the past, and the socialization procedures that have been adopted in the training of its members. These influences are reflected in the descriptions of professional roles by the several authors in this section. Public health is a profession that traditionally has been concerned with environmental hazards. Many of the improvements in the health of the world's peoples have resulted from the identification and elimination of hazards by public health workers. For the most part, their interventions have been at the level of the community, the state, or the nation. Only in recent years have public health professionals begun to concern themselves with the behavior of *individuals* in relation to hazards (see Matthews & Avis, 1982). The profession of dietetics/nutrition has traditionally operated at the level of organizations. Schools and hospitals have provided employment for most dieticians and nutritionists. More recently, a counseling role in health care settings has begun to develop. Health educators have also worked mostly through institutional programs, designing curricula, training other professionals, and presenting to groups; only now are they beginning to develop a role in diagnosis, prescription, and delivery of educational interventions to individuals.

By contrast, three other professions represented in this section traditionally have been focused on provision of services to individuals. Physicians do find their way into many situations in which they act at organizational and even political levels. To the extent that they do so, however, they become members of the public health profession, and they often augment their medical education with training in public health. The practice of medicine is based predominantly on work with individuals. The approach has been largely curative, and some spokespersons for the profession have resisted the notion that their professional role could be expanded to include responsibility for patients' adherence to prescribed treatment plans, let alone any responsibility in the matter of patients' lifestyles that might influence future illnesses (Eisenberg, 1977; Spencer, 1978; Thomas, 1978). In the past few years, strong voices have been heard within the medical profession asserting that physicians should make use of the opportunities that come to them, by virtue of their very special relationship with their patients, to attempt to enroll patients in healthier lifestyles (Beck, Blaichman, Scriver, & Clow, 1974; Hess, Liepman, & Ruane, 1983; Steuart, 1975). Physicians are urged to model healthy behaviors (Koop, 1983) and even to take public positions based on their professional knowledge concerning such hazards as nuclear weapons (Executive Committee, 1982; Relman, 1982) and even such issues as traffic safety and handguns (Omenn, 1982).

Although dentists, like physicians, primarily engage in individual curative services, prophylactic and preventive services have been a part of their normal practice for many years. Their professional role has been expanded to include substantial emphasis on prevention through patient education and through support of such public health approaches as fluoridation of water supplies. Despite this commitment to preventive behavior, behavioral scientists have been called upon less in the training of dentists than in the training of physicians. Here again, recent developments have begun to reflect the convergence of the various professions toward a common approach to health promotion—in this case through the addition of behavioral scientists to dental faculties (Cohen, 1981).

The nursing profession developed to engage not primarily in curative services, but in services to support those who are under treatment by others. In nurses' emphasis on support, they were almost inevitably oriented toward dealing with the whole person and toward development of effective ways of communicating with patients and their families. Throughout most of this century, nurses have been the ones who have provided patients with most information about their regimens and with the greatest support in following them. As they expanded their site of action into the community, it was natural for them to develop preventive services that could be delivered to individuals, families, and small community groups.

Psychology, by virtue of its dual nature as basic science and profession, and because of its relatively recent entry into the realm of health promotion, has not developed a single functional role that characterizes its approach. As pointed out by Coates and DeMuth in this section, however, and in a recent statement by Iscoe (1982), psychologists have tended to focus rather narrowly on face-to-face services for individuals seeking treatment, on rehabilitation, or on research, diagnosis, and evaluation that are oriented to supporting and enhancing such services. Now, as health promotion emerges as a major goal in our society, psychologists are responding by expanding their focus to consider behavior in relation to hazards and opportunities and to study the interventions used by other professions so as to become a resource for those who practice out of different traditions.

OBSTACLES TO PROFESSIONAL HEALTH PROMOTION

Thus, we find each of the six professional groups represented in this section embarking, from a position developed historically, on an expansion of their traditional roles toward a convergent emphasis on altering the behavior of individuals, groups, and institutions in relation to hazards to health and opportunities for growth. As they undertake this expansion, they are constrained by various obstacles to changes in their professional roles and activities. Some of these obstacles are specific to the several professions, but some have sufficient generality to warrant mention in this introduction. Two broad, interlocking categories of barriers to expansion can be identified. First, our customary economic practices impede the support of professional activity devoted to health promotion. Second, extension of professional activities into the area of health promotion taxes the ethical norms that we have developed over the years to guide professionals in their work. Each of these issues is extraordinarily complex, and each has been the subject of extended consideration (Klarman, 1981; Kristein et al., 1977; Robison & Pritchard, 1979). I will list here only a few of the most salient aspects.

Economic Obstacles

In the sphere of economics, there are two principal issues. One is our social pattern of supporting health care professionals mostly through payment for services delivered. Given our focus up to this time on curing illness, we have learned to pay our professionals to make us well when we are sick. The effect of such services, when they are successful, is usually apparent quickly, and payment is usually made after the services have had their effect. The increasing emphasis on chronic illnesses in health care has begun to break down that pattern, but it still exists as a basis for expectations that services should cause some observable change in circumstances. Economists have long known that people discount the future. They discount undesirable things as well as desirable things, so that the present subjective value of avoiding an undesirable situation is less than the cost of repair will be when the undesirable event transpires. Health professionals and the public need to become much more aware of this propensity and to factor it in to their behavioral decisions. At the same time, we need to find ways of demonstrating positive results soon after interventions are made and of incorporating health enhancement and growth into our calculus of health economics. Even so positive a thinker as René Dubos (1965) has declared that we cannot construct a workable measure of "positive health" (see Stone, 1979a, for a more extensive discussion), but the emergence of holistic health centers and wellness clinics and the large-scale purchase of vitamins and enrollment in growth-enhancing seminars and workshops indicate that people are willing to pay for health-promoting services and products that promise to enhance their health.

Even if we are successful in developing appropriate methods for paying for the services of health care professionals who engage in health promotion, we must recognize that, in the long run, successful health promotion will lead to less need for activities in the areas of research on and treatment of disease. This is not to say that jobs in the health field will necessarily be lost. As in any sphere of social activity, innovation causes shifts in patterns of employment but often creates more jobs than it eliminates. Nevertheless, there is a conservatism within institutions that generally resists change in goals and methods. If we know how to educate physicians to cure disease, we tend to continue those educational patterns for some time after a case could be made for changing them, simply because people, and particularly organizations, are resistant to change. This conservatism may be a good thing for human society, but it obviously creates obstacles to the introduction of new curricula and new practices aimed at health promotion.

A second economic obstacle to health promotion is our traditional manner of handling the externalities of our industrial world. For many years, industries were allowed to pollute at will, and the short-run economic "benefits" of production and sale of products that were harmful to health were given far greater weight in political decisions than the long-term dollar costs, let alone the costs in human suffering, of the impaired health of those who encountered the pollutants. Health care professionals in policymaking positions, and those whose enterprises depend on the support of organizations that are sensitive to political pressures, have, for whatever reason, been slow to see the implications for health of hazards that arise in the course of economic activities. There are signs of change in this regard, also, but the Reagan administration has turned back from the growing emphasis on improving the quality of the environment in favor of "enhancing the business climate" (see, e.g., "EPA's High-Risk Carcinogen Policy," 1982; "White House Steps into Lead Fight," 1982).

Obstacles Arising from Ethical Considerations

A fundamental ethical dilemma arises in our society out of the conflict of two principles. The first principle is that individuals have a right to free choice of action, so long as they do not bring harm to others. The second is that we have an obligation to look after and protect those who are unable to take care of themselves. Generally, these principles do not come into conflict in the arena of curative health care, because the presence of illness is usually recognized by the occurrence of symptoms that are painful or frightening and that are considered to be threatening by any competent person who suffers or observes them. Thus, people with symptoms seek help and cooperate with the experts who offer to provide it. Such, at least, is the predominant model of health care. The relatively recent recognition of massive noncompliance by patients of all sorts with the regimens prescribed for them has made it apparent that this model is insufficient. Many of the ethical difficulties of preventive health care can already be found in the curative health transaction (Stone, 1979b).

Expert interventions to promote health and prevent illness are generally made in the absence of symptoms. Therefore, the PHAI may be unaware of threat, may value future health less than present pleasure, and may actively resist an intervention that can be rationally shown to have a high probability of benefiting their health. Furthermore, in many cases, the freely chosen action of one person may constitute a hazard to the health of others. In such situations, we know that some societies have claimed for thousands of years the right to require certain sanitary measures. Yet, as indicated earlier, in our society until very recently we have allowed uncontrolled disposal of toxic wastes, and we still permit pollution of the air we breathe by the smoking behavior of others.

Public health measures generally infringe upon the rights of some individuals to free choice of action in the interest of producing a health benefit for others (and perhaps for the infringed-upon person as well). An excellent example of this situation is to be found in the fluoridation of community water supplies. This measure, which has received the widespread support of dentists, has been very clearly demonstrated to reduce the incidence of caries in school-age children (Burt, 1981). In many elections throughout the nation, however, there has nevertheless been passionate and often effective resistance to institution of the measure. The rational essence of this resistance is the question, "Why should the community impose on individuals who are past the age when fluoridation can provide any benefit, on those who believe that the risks outweigh the benefits, and on those who are opposed for other reasons, a treatment for which there are inexpensive and effective alternatives that can be adopted by persons who do want to use the fluoride treatment?" The rational answer to this question is that the people most in need of the protection provided by fluorides are unlikely to make use of them because of ignorance of their availability, irrational prejudices or fears, or general tendencies not to engage in adaptive actions because of their postures of inefficacy, despair, or whatever. The conflict between these viewpoints is heightened because the PHAI in this case are young children, and the people who are making the decision for or against individual treatment are their parents.

Uncertainty and internal conflict over the question of when and to what extent it is appropriate to intrude in order to protect the health of another constitutes an obstacle to the adoption by professionals of techniques that could reduce health risks and promote growth opportunities. Removal or reduction of this obstacle can come about only through a clarification of the ethical issues involved. For some reason, however, many health professionals seem to question the value of spending time in the consideration of such ethical issues. In fact, a crucial issue for training health professionals to participate in health promotion is leading them to the formation of an ethical stance that will provide them with a basis for their work. The health care professions have devoted much thought to their ethical standards over the years. What is needed at this time is a review of those standards in the light of our new technological knowledge about hazards and opportunities in the environment and about methods for behavior change.

The basis of this analysis is the conception of the health care transaction as a joint problem-solving activity involving at least three parties (although perhaps only two persons): the expert, the client, and the target of the professional activity (Stone, 1979b). In some cases, the client and the target are the same individual; in other cases, they are not even personally acquainted (in public health programs, for example). The expert, or professional, is recognized and acknowledged by the client to possess knowledge and skills that are potentially able to alter the circumstances of the target person in a way that the client perceives as having sufficient value so that he or she is willing to pay for professional service—that is, for the application of the knowledge and skills to produce changes. The expert agrees to provide the services, with or without the consent of the target person. Targets, other than young children, generally are asked for their consent when direct services are to be provided, but not when they are to be the targets of educational or public health interventions, for example.

In health care transactions, the circumstances to be changed involve the health status or the risk status of the target. The means whereby this change is to be brought about vary along a scale of invasiveness—from simply providing the target with information, to altering the contingencies in the target's environment (changing the probabilities that certain actions of the target or of others will be followed by particular consequences), to actual manipulations of the target's bodily state by means of drugs, surgery, or other medical procedures. A separate dimension that is descriptive of expert health care is the coerciveness with which it is applied. In most cases, this variable ranges over the portion of the dimension described long ago by Szasz and Hollender (1956)—between the "active expert–passive client" relationship, in which the coercion of expert power is applied to a nonresisting target, and the "collegial" relationship, in which each step of the health care process is presented as an option to the target, with the invitation to approve or disapprove its application with "full knowledge" of the possible outcomes. In most health care transactions, the degree of coerciveness varies according to the expert's perception of the exigencies of the target's need and of the target's capacity to participate effectively in the decision-making process. Coerciveness typically varies also as a function of the stage of the transaction (goal formulation, diagnosis, treatment planning, implementation of treatment, and evaluation). Targets may be given a substantial degree of latitude in the choice of the goals of treatment, but once the treatment is begun, they may be expected to submit without question to the performance of the expert services. The target may accept the degree of coerciveness that the expert attempts to use or may "bargain" in various ways to alter this level (Hayes-Bautista, 1976; Waitzkin & Stoeckle, 1976).

The three variables described—client–expert relationship, invasiveness of treatment, and coerciveness of treatment—create a space within which health care transactions proceed. For the most part, health-promoting activities tend to be noninvasive, although some of the newer forms of massage (such as Rolfing) have as much impact as most curative methods. Other examples of invasive health promotion are immunizations, orthodontics, and some preventive surgery.

Some health care professions are oriented primarily toward the relatively invasive procedures and tend to consider the less invasive activities, talking and persuading, as foreign to their roles. Other professions are restricted by law from the application of highly invasive procedures, and they may find it much easier to incorporate health promotion as a significant component of their professional activity.

In the area of highly invasive procedures, it is customary for the health care expert to proceed only when there is a strong presumption of consent to the procedure by the target person. In the case of young children, parental consent is still the legal basis for providing preventive services such as orthodonture, but more effort would usually be devoted to gaining the child's acquiescence than might be true for restorative procedures. Thus, a major component of preventive treatment may be persuading the target to accept it. Persuading the client to pay the bill is also likely to require more attention and resources in the case of preventive services than when there are symptoms to be relieved. This seems to be true even when a clear case can be made for the cost-effectiveness of preventive care, and insurance companies and governments have been slow to approve expenditures for these purposes.

IMPLICATIONS FOR TRAINING

In this introductory chapter, I have argued that the several professions represented here are variously prepared by their traditional roles to take part in preventive approaches to health care, and that they therefore need, to various degrees, an increasing emphasis in their professional curricula on such questions as the following: What is our profession competent to do in health promotion? How can we persuade clients to pay for preventive services? How can we persuade the PHAI to accept preventive services, or when is it ethical to proceed without their consent? How can professionals facilitate laypersons' taking responsibility for their own health? In the chapters that follow, we will see how prevention-oriented members of six professional groups have formulated and addressed these questions.

REFERENCES

Beck, E., Blaichman, S., Scriver, C. R., & Clow, C. L. Advocacy and compliance in genetic screening. *New England Journal of Medicine,* 1974, **291,** 1166–1172.

Burt, B. A. Fluoridation of public water supplies. In G. L. Slack (Ed.), *Dental public health* (2nd ed.). Bristol, England: Wright, 1981.

Cohen, L. K. Dentistry and the behavioral-social sciences: An historical overview. *Journal of Behavioral Medicine,* 1981, **4,** 247–256.

Dubos, R. J. *Man adapting.* New Haven: Yale University Press, 1965.

Eisenberg, L. The perils of prevention: A cautionary note. *New England Journal of Medicine,* 1977, **297,** 1230–1232.

EPA's high-risk carcinogen policy. *Science,* 1982, **218,** 975–978.

Executive Committee, Physicians for Social Responsibility. Medical care in modern warfare: A look at the Pentagon plan for the civilian sector. *New England Journal of Medicine,* 1982, **306,** 741–743.

Hayes-Bautista, D. E. Modifying the treatment: Patient compliance, patient control and medical care. *Social Science and Medicine,* 1976, **10,** 233–238.

Hess, J. W., Liepman, M. R., & Ruane, T. J. (Eds.). *Family practice and preventive medicine: Health promotion in primary care.* New York: Human Sciences Press, 1983.

Iscoe, I. Toward a viable community health psychology: Caveats from the experience of the mental health movement. *American Psychologist,* 1982, **37,** 961–965.

Klarman, H. E. Economics of health and health care financing. In D. W. Clark & B. MacMahon (Eds.), *Preventive and community medicine* (2nd ed.). Boston: Little, Brown, 1981.

Koop, C. E. Perspectives on future health care. *Health Psychology,* 1983, **2,** 303–312.

Kristein, M. M., Arnold, C. B., & Wynder, E. L. Health economics and preventive care. *Science,* 1977, **195,** 459–462.

Matthews, K. A., & Avis, N. E. Psychologists in schools of public health: Current status, future prospects, and implications for other health settings. *American Psychologist,* 1982, **37,** 949–954.

Omenn, G. S. Preventing injuries, disability, and death at work (starting with vehicles and guns!). *Journal of the American Medical Association,* 1982, **248,** 723–724.

Relman, A. S. Physicians, nuclear war, and politics. *New England Journal of Medicine,* 1982, **307,** 744–745.

Robison, W. L., & Pritchard, M. S. *Medical responsibility: Paternalism, informed consent, and euthanasia.* Clifton, N.J.: HUMANA Press, 1979.

Spencer, F. J. The great preventive life style cop-out. *Virginia Medical Journal,* 1978, **105,** 327.

Steuart, G. W. The people: Motivation, education, and action. *Bulletin of the New York Academy of Medicine,* 1975, **51,** 174–185.

Stone, G. C. Health and the health system: A historical overview and conceptual framework. In G. C. Stone, F. Cohen, N. E. Adler, & Associates, *Health psychology: A handbook.* San Francisco: Jossey-Bass, 1979. (a)

Stone, G. C. Patient compliance and the role of the expert. *Journal of Social Issues,* 1979, **35,** 34–59. (b)

Szasz, T. S., & Hollender, M. H. A contribution to the philosophy of medicine: The basic models of the doctor–patient relationship. *Archives of Internal Medicine,* 1956, **97,** 585–592.

Thomas, L. Notes of a biology watcher: On magic in medicine. *New England Journal of Medicine,* 1978, **299,** 461–463.

Waitzkin, H., & Stoeckle, J. D. Information control and the micropolitics of health care: A summary of an ongoing research project. *Social Science and Medicine,* 1976, **10,** 263–276.

White House steps into lead fight. *Science,* 1982, **217,** 807–808.

CHAPTER 89

AN ANALYSIS OF COMPETENCIES AND TRAINING NEEDS FOR PSYCHOLOGISTS SPECIALIZING IN HEALTH ENHANCEMENT

THOMAS J. COATES

University of California School of Medicine, San Francisco

NANCY MARWICK DEMUTH

The Johns Hopkins School of Hygiene and Public Health, Baltimore

To meet the challenges of health enhancement fully, psychologists must continue to make multiple contributions to scientific research, technological research (e.g., program evaluation and policy research), and clinical practice. The next generation of health psychologists needs a firm grounding in basic psychology plus a good mix of supplementary components (Matarazzo, 1980, in press), such as (a) epidemiology and biostatistics; (b) medical sociology; (c) nontraditional and technological research paradigms (Barlow, 1982; Fishman & Neigher, 1982) as well as traditional research training; (d) physiology, pathophysiology, neurochemistry, and selected aspects of clinical medicine; and (e) organizational/managerial expertise, including analytic techniques drawn from business and economics (e.g., DeMuth & Yates, 1981; Rickard & Clements, 1981; DeMuth & Yates, Note 1).

Just as training—particularly at postdoctoral levels—must expand, psychological interventions must also change in three important directions that extend beyond (a) focusing exclusively on individuals or on individuals within groups, (b) relying primarily on face-to-face contact to deliver services, and (c) giving primary attention to treatment and rehabilitation. Figure 89.1 summarizes this three-way expansion of intervention targets, change methods, and purposes of psychological activity. The figure also underscores psychology's need to abandon its identification with the disease etiology of medicine and to embrace a perspective that recognizes social and ecological determinants of health-related behavior and includes strategies for changing these determinants (Bandura, 1978). By expanding its arenas, psychology enhances its analytical and problem-solving grasp but does not lose its focus on individual human behavior and on problems of improving behavioral coping in specific areas of health and illness (Fox, Barclay, & Rodgers, 1982).

As conceptualized in the figure, specific health enhancement problems can be analyzed for various *intervention targets*, which include individuals, groups, organizations, communi-

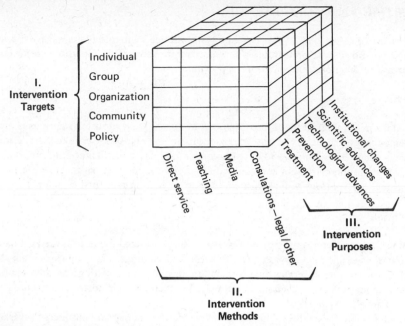

Figure 89.1　Three dimensions of psychological intervention pertaining to health promotion. (Adapted from Morrill, W. H., Oetting, E. R., & Hurst, J. C. Dimensions of counselor functioning. *Personnel and Guidance Journal* 1974, **52**, 354–359.)

ties, and/or social system policies (see Figure 89.1, Axis I). Axis II, *intervention methods*, demonstrates that psychologists must become involved in expanded facets of marketing and delivering their intervention methods. Direct services in the form of clinical activity, mental health, consultation, or psychology teaching are models well known to psychologists. Interventions involving media, economic, legal, or structural systems, however, are not modalities for which psychologists are usually trained. Such approaches are the methods with the greatest potential for reaching large segments of the population. Axis III, *intervention purposes*, shows that contributions to health enhancement require that psychologists expand their activities to simultaneously include prevention (e.g., health education), scientific and technological research advances, and encouragement of institutional reinforcements favoring better health choices (DeMuth & Yates, 1981; Fielding, 1979; Green & Johnson, 1982). Institutional reinforcements, for example, might take the form of corporate financial incentives, such as lower insurance premiums offered to employees who qualify for lower risk classifications by practicing smoking cessation or weight control behaviors.

　　Close examination of Figure 89.1 also highlights unique and unusual ways in which psychologists can contribute to health enhancement. The intersection of community (Axis I), media (Axis II), and prevention (Axis III), for instance, describes the activities of psychologists working in projects such as the Stanford Heart Disease Prevention Program (Farquhar, Maccoby, Wood, Alexander, Breitrose, Brown, Haskell, McAlister, Meyer, Nash, & Stern, 1977). Even more radical, from the viewpoint of traditional psychological activity, is the intersection of policy (Axis I), legal consultation (Axis II), and prevention (Axis III). Psychological interventions might integrate these three dimensions by enhancing the efficacy of the warning and informational content labels on food or drug products; by better understanding the effects of joint versus single custody for children of divorce; and by working with legislators to formulate state policy or, at national levels, to focus attention on health planning, ordering of health priorities, and allocation of resources.

EXPERTISE AND COMPETENCIES

The spectrum of competencies that psychologists will need when they are engaged in health enhancement and disease prevention is summarized in Table 89.1. The three major competency areas are diagnosis, intervention, and evaluation.

Diagnosis

The need for psychological input into diagnosis in medical and industrial settings is increasingly being recognized (e.g., Harper, Wiens, & Hammerstad, 1981; Schenkenberg, Peterson, & DaBell, 1981; Seamonds, 1982). Psychologists can assist in diagnosing environmental and individual problems within and across analytic levels, and can trigger ongoing feedback for adjusting interventions in line with continuing evaluation and further diagnostic inputs.

Intervention

Reductions in excessive primary care utilization can be realized by general medical patients' utilization of psychological services (e.g., Follette & Cummings, 1967; Jones & Vichi, 1979). Beyond a greater direct service involvement in primary care settings as counselors and behavioral change experts, psychologists are also broadening their horizons to include procedural, structural, and policy treatments.

Examples from the state of the art of hypertension management suggest several new roles for psychologists. *Procedural changes* involve modifying methods for accomplishing tasks. Psychologists might help improve methods for disseminating convincing information on hypertension management to providers, patients, and the public. *Structural changes* alter communication channels or modify authority and reporting relations. Switching hypertension control responsibilities from private medical practices to organized settings, such as worksites, schools, or churches, may be more conducive to regularized follow-up and monitoring for hard-to-reach groups, such as young males. *Policy changes* involve alterations in generic approaches to health problems (e.g., endorsing nonpharmacological interventions for treating hypertensives with blood pressure below 96 mmHg). For policy recommendations to be accomplished, practical methods are needed for implementing particular interventions (e.g., lifestyle, diet, exercise changes) for large numbers of people. Opportunities exist for psychologists to assist in identifying optimal policies and methods for reaching specific hypertensive subgroups in divergent settings.

Perhaps most important in the intervention area, psychologists can help contribute to working through and overcoming resistances to planned changes—behavioral, procedural, structural, and/or policy—at all levels. Psychology remains, in our analysis, the only profession that uniquely and "consistently focuses its efforts on solving problems through alterations in patterns of behavioral coping" (Fox et al., 1982, p. 308). This includes sensitivity to and appreciation of the multifaceted ways that change programs can be sabotaged or "stillborn" at the point of implementation, or even earlier. Psychologists can assist in anticipating problems before they develop and can help individuals, organizations, and communities manage change as part of a continuing process.

Evaluation

As psychologists are increasingly thrust into health decision-making roles (e.g., as directors of behavioral medicine or industrial health promotion programs, as private practitioners with organizational consultative roles), there is increasing pressure for them to include economic variables in their analyses (Fishman & Neigher, 1982; Yates, 1980). Unfortunately, most psychologists are little prepared by their training to use the analytical techniques, which are well known in business and economics, to determine cost-effectiveness of alternative therapies, delivery systems, and/or competing health enhancement programs (Almy, 1981). Recently, there has been increased definition and encouragement of the "technological research paradigm" (Fishman & Neigher, 1982), which further leaves many practicing psychologists with limited skills in program evaluation, policy research, and cost-effectiveness analysis. It is clear, however, that to nudge forward the current state of the art of health promotion evaluation efforts, an armamentarium of skills is needed in scientific research, technological research, and other interdisciplinary areas.

TRAINING OPPORTUNITIES AND NEEDS

Our assessment of training assumes (a) that the health care industry is in an era of increasing specialization and (b) that each health psychologist must forge a match between his or her specialty interests and training opportunities. Health psychologists necessarily rely less upon traditional diagnostic and therapeutic skills with individual clients and more upon innovative, consultative, program development, and evaluation skills at organizational, community, and policy levels. As medicine, psychology, and other health professions recognize and address the multifaceted behavioral, attitudinal, and social factors involved in health and behavior change, the training requirements and expertise needed by health psychologists are becoming clearer (Wertlieb & Budman, 1979).

Several industrial and interdisciplinary examples illustrate implications for training and for broadening skill bases. Private industry has become one of the most congenial environments for implementing a variety of lifestyle change programs (e.g., Alderman, Green, & Flynn, 1980). Psychologists—who now have opportunities for worksite diagnosing, intervening, and evaluating—must be equally skilled in assessing organizational norms, sociopolitical realities, and reward systems (e.g., Wilbur & Vermilyea, in press). Psychologists are also assuming consultative roles in the training of other health providers, either on a preservice basis, such as the training of primary care residents or dental students, or on a continuing education basis. Such consultative roles accentuate the need for collaborative acumen and broad knowledge of common as well as "exotic" medical and dental problems.

The sheer variety and breadth of health specialties require considerable expertise that is not currently provided in many training programs. When and from where shall this expertise spring? (Certainly not, like Athena, from the head of Zeus, although many a psychologist would wish for this method of pedagogy.) A recent survey of psychologists in schools of public health suggests that psychological training clearly may be necessary. Matthews and Avis (1982) found that most schools of public health in the United States did not need to be persuaded of the relevance of psychology. Psychologists in those settings, however, experienced difficulty because of their insufficient knowledge of public health perspectives and subject matter. Graduate programs in health psychology appear to be equipped to provide training in psychology, but they may not have the expertise to provide complete training in the broad areas outlined in Table 89.1 and Figure 89.1. These programs must cross disciplinary boundaries and must begin to provide training in the broad spectrum of skills outlined in the figure and the table.

It is no longer novel or iconoclastic to conclude that the "school of hard knocks" or trial-and-error approaches are unsatisfactory vehicles for preparing psychologists to meet complex and expanding roles. This cursory review clearly demonstrates that pockets of training opportunities now exist in behavioral medicine, health psychology, and other interdisciplinary areas to help fill the gap in basic sciences and applied areas for individual psychologists. Psychologists—who have a penchant for augmenting unique and collaborative skills as members of health problem-solving teams—need to be savvy consumers of this expanding training "smorgasbord" and creators of new job–skill matches if psychological insights are to contribute fully to the interdisciplinary health enhancement enterprise.

Table 89.1 Psychologist Competencies Relating to Health Promotion and Disease Prevention

Level of Analysis or Intervention	Major Competency Areas		
	Diagnosis (based on)	Intervention (to produce)	Evaluation (types)
Individual (client)	Interviews/observations related to individual coping styles, problem-solving patterns, characteristic defense mechanisms, lifestyle behaviors (e.g., smoking, alcohol/drug use, exercise habits, stress or anger management)	Behavior change: enhancing frequency of individual behaviors conducive to health by helping persons with changes in coping skills, actions, lifestyle behaviors	Case studies, single-subject designs, controlled clinical trials
Group (single group, such as family, worksite department, school, church)	Interviews/observations related to performance, measured by (a) productivity (e.g., reduced departmental absenteeism) or (b) intragroup/interpersonal processes (e.g., reduced turnover; reduced relitigations by ex-spouses in custody cases)	Behavioral/procedural change: enhancing behaviors conducive to group/subgroup members' health through interventions that may focus on behavioral or procedural changes, including modifying methods for accomplishing group tasks	Pre-and post evaluation, field experiment or quasi-experiment, cost-benefit/cost-effectiveness methods (e.g., is cost-effectiveness greater for group treatment X or Y?)
Organization (multiple groups, including all departments and companies in a corporation)	Interviews/observations related to performance, measured by (a) productivity/efficiency or (b) intergroup and system processes (e.g., company-wide reductions in absenteeism, accidents, turnover)	Behavioral/procedural/structural change: enhancing health-oriented behaviors by all organizational members through changes in individual behaviors, in procedural areas (e.g., changes in methods for accomplishing tasks), and /or in structural areas, including changes in communication channels or in authority and reporting relationships	Pre-and post evaluation, field experiment or quasi-experiment, cost-benefit/cost-effectiveness methods, longitudinal epidemiological study

Community/national/social system policy (multiple organizations and/or communities)

Household surveys, etc., to determine population morbidity/ mortality related to specific health risk factors and to preselect specific behavioral goals (e.g., reductions in uncontrolled hypertension) and consider institutional/national reinforcers, such as taxation or legal policies, to assure enhanced compliance

Behavioral/procedural/structural/ policy change: enhancing health-oriented behaviors by all individuals in the system through behavioral, procedural, structural, and/or policy areas related to national health policy, augmented by institutional and legal reinforcements

Longitudinal epidemiological study, comparison with international statistics, cost-benefit/cost-effectiveness, policy analyses relating specific health goals to national policy implications

REFERENCE NOTE

1. DeMuth, N. M., and Yates, B. T. *The scientist-manager-practitioner web: Training strategies and model implementation.* Paper presented at the Annual Meeting of the American Psychological Association, Washington, D.C., August 1982.

REFERENCES

Alderman, M. H., Green, L. W., & Flynn, B. Hypertension control programs in occupational settings. *Public Health Reports,* 1980, **25,** 158–163.

Almy, T. P. The role of the primary physician in the health-care "industry." *New England Journal of Medicine,* 1981, **304,** 225–228.

Bandura, A. On paradigms and recycled ideologies. *Cognitive Therapy and Research,* 1978, **2,** 79–103.

Barlow, D. H. On the relation of clinical research to clinical practice: Current issues, new directions. *Journal of Consulting and Clinical Psychology,* 1981, **49,** 147–155.

DeMuth, N. M., & Yates, B. T. Improving psychotherapy: Old beliefs, new research and future directions. *Professional Psychology,* 1981, **12,** 587–595.

Farquhar, J. W., Maccoby, N., Wood, P. D., Alexander, J., Breitrose, H., Brown, B. W., Haskell, W. L., McAlister, A. L., Meyer, A. J., Nash, J. D., & Stern, M. P. Community education for cardiovascular health. *Lancet,* 1977, **1,** 1192–1195.

Fielding, J. E. Preventive medicine and the bottom line. *Journal of Occupational Medicine,* 1979, **21**(2), 79–88.

Fishman, D. B., & Neigher, W. D. American psychology in the eighties. Who will buy? *American Psychologist,* 1982, **37,** 533–545.

Follette, W., & Cummings, N. A. Psychiatric services and medical utilization in a prepaid health plan setting. *Medical Care,* 1967, **5,** 25–35.

Fox, R. E., Barclay, A. G., & Rodgers, D. A. The foundations of professional psychology. *American Psychologist,* 1982, **37,** 306–312.

Green, L. W., & Johnson, K. Health education and health promotion. In D. Mechanic (Ed.), *Handbook of health, health care, and health professions.* New York: Wiley, 1982.

Harper, R. G., Wiens, A. N., & Hammerstad, J. Psychologist–physician partnership in a specialty screening clinic. *Professional Psychology,* 1981, **12,** 341–348.

Jones, K., & Vichi, T. Impact of alcohol, drug abuse, and mental health treatment on medical care utilization. *Medical Care,* Special Supplement, December 1979.

Matarazzo, J. D. Behavioral health and behavioral medicine: Frontiers for a new health psychology. *American Psychologist,* 1980, **35,** 807–817.

Matarrazo, J. D. Education in health psychology. *Health Psychology,* in press.

Matthews, K. A., & Avis, M. E. Psychologists in schools of public health: Current status, future prospects and implications for other health settings. *American Psychologist,* 1982, **37,** 949–954.

McAlister, A. L., Perry, C., & Maccoby, N. Adolescent smoking: Onset and prevention. *Pediatrics,* 1979, **63,** 650–658.

Morrill, W. H., Oetting, E. R., & Hurst, J. C. Dimensions of counselor functioning. *Personnel and Guidance Journal,* 1974, **52,** 354–359.

Rickard, H. C., & Clements, C. B. Administrative training for psychologists in APA-approved clinical programs. *Professional Psychology,* 1981, **12,** 349–355.

Schenkenberg, L., Peterson, D. W., & DaBell, R. Psychological consultation/liaison in a medical and neurological setting: Physicians' appraisal. *Professional Psychology,* 1981, **12,** 309–317.

Seamonds, B. C. Stress factors and their effect on absenteeism in a corporate employee group. *Journal of Occupational Medicine,* 1982, **24,** 393–397.

Wertlieb, D., & Budman, S. H. Concluding remarks: Dimensions of role conflict for health care psychologists. *Professional Psychology,* 1979, **10,** 640–644.

Wilbur, C. S., & Vermilyea, C. J. Some business advice to counseling psychologists. *Counseling Psychologist,* in press.

Yates, B. T. The theory and practice of cost-utility, cost-effectiveness, and cost-benefit analysis in behavioral medicine: Toward delivering more health care for less money. In J. Ferguson and C. B. Taylor (Eds.), *The comprehensive handbook of behavioral medicine.* New York: SP Scientific and Technical Books, 1980.

CHAPTER 90

PHYSICIAN EDUCATION IN CLINICAL PREVENTION

ASCHER SEGALL

Boston University

Achievement of a comprehensive preventive approach in medical practice depends on a complex of factors. One key component is the education of physicians in the preventive dimension of clinical care. Although it is clear that factors other than training play a role—such as patient receptivity, physician incentives, and community support—it is equally clear that physicians can act preventively only to the extent that their knowledge and skills enable them to do so. The implication for physician education is that medical students, residents, and practitioners must have access to instruction in preventive medicine if they are to be expected to perform preventively in their practices (*Preventive Medicine USA*, 1975).

Historically, physician education in preventive medicine has been responsive to changes in the patterns of disease, shifts in societal priorities, and progress in health technology. In the early decades of the 20th century, the foremost health problems were those of infectious diseases. Effective control required both clinical intervention and epidemic control at a community level. At the then prevailing state of professional specialization, the practicing physician was expected to play a role at both levels: in clinical practice and as a participant in community programs. There was little ambiguity concerning the scope of the subject matter to be learned and the skills to be acquired; both derived directly from the responsibilities that students would be called upon to assume in their future roles as medical practitioners (Segall, 1974).

As the problem of epidemic diseases receded, with a consequent shift in the age structure of the population, chronic diseases emerged as the major causes of mortality. For the most part, etiology was unknown, and primary prevention was therefore not possible. Practicing physicians were increasingly faced with the problem of managing long-term care within and outside the traditional hospital settings.

Epidemiologists began to turn their attention to the search for etiology of the chronic diseases, often in collaboration with biostatisticians. Clinicians, in small numbers, disenchanted by the restrictive perspective in which patient care was viewed by the post-Flexner academic medical establishment, were attracted to departments of preventive medicine as a possible base from which to experiment with innovative programs for the delivery of comprehensive health services. These departments also provided a hospitable environment for social scientists who were interested in exploring possible application of their disciplines to health problems (Terris, 1981).

Reflecting these developments, the emphasis in teaching preventive medicine shifted from clinical applications to the population-related disciplines of epidemiology, biostatistics, medical sociology, and health care delivery. Concomitantly, the gap between the content of instruction and the needs of practicing physicians tended to increase. In recent years, however, there has been a resurgence of interest in the education of physicians in clinical prevention. The increasing availability of effective methods for clinical prevention and the growing concern with ways in which to contain the cost of health care have contributed to this trend (Arnold, 1981; Barker & Jonas, 1981; Berg, 1982).

The type of training physicians need depends on the range of responsibilities assumed by practitioners in the preventive dimension of clinical medicine and on the competencies needed to meet these responsibilities. In systematic educational planning, summarized in Table 90.1, these professional competencies constitute the basis for formulating educational objectives, for selecting instructional methods to facilitate students' attainment of the objectives, and for designing evaluation instruments to assess their achievement. The educational setting and context of instruction will determine the extent to which the scope of student performance approximates that of professional performance (Segall, Vanderschmidt, Burglass, & Frostman, 1975).

A frame of reference for considering the scope of physician performance in terms of the principal components of clinical prevention is provided by the natural history of disease paradigm, shown in Figure 90.1. The figure shows a temporal continuum in the evolution of the disease process. Intervals along the time axis can be identified during which preventive measures may reduce the risk of progression from an earlier to a later stage of disease. Timely intervention may result in preventing onset of the pathogenic process, reversing the process, or decreasing its rate of progression. The goals, methods, and impact of preventive intervention are therefore specific to each of the sequential stages in the natural history of disease (Segall, 1980).

Reducing the risk of biological onset of disease by decreasing or modifying the consequences of exposure to health hazards is the goal of primary prevention during the prepathogenic stage. Risk factors are most conveniently classified as genetic, environmental (including the physical, biological, and social environment), and behavioral (including diet, exercise, sleep, cigarette smoking, use of alcohol and other mind-altering drugs, and motor vehicle driving) (Stokes, Noren, & Shindell, 1982).

Reducing the risk of clinical onset by reversing or decreasing the rate of progression

Table 90.1   A Systematic Approach to Curriculum Development in Clinical Prevention

Context	Procedures	Product
Professional setting	Identify competencies needed by physicians in the preventive dimension of clinical practice	Specification of professional competencies in clinical prevention
Instructional setting	For each competency, develop a sequence of learner outcomes appropriate to the instructional setting (e.g., medical school, residency training, continuing medical education)	A set of competency-based educational objectives for teaching clinical prevention
Instructional setting	Design learning activities to facilitate student achievement of specified objectives	Instructional syllabus
Instructional and professional settings	Select critical points for evaluation of competencies and develop appropriate testing instruments	Evaluation plan and procedures

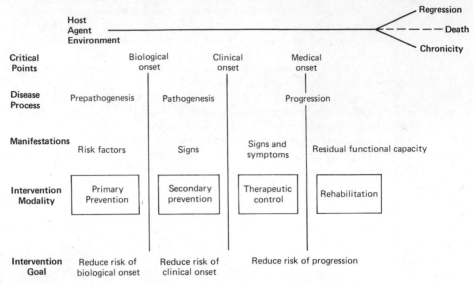

Figure 90.1 The natural history of disease paradigm.

of the pathogenic process is the goal of secondary prevention during the presymptomatic stage. The methods are those of early detection and treatment of unrecognized disease during the interval between biological onset and clinical onset. This period is characterized by the presence of objectively observable manifestations in the absence of symptoms. Examples of early detection include the use of cytology for cancer of the cervix, clinical examination and mammography for breast cancer, and blood pressure determination for hypertension. The impact of secondary prevention depends on the extent to which the prognosis associated with intervention during the presymptomatic stage is more favorable than that which characterizes intervention after the appearance of symptoms (Spitzer, 1979).

Reducing the risk of further progression is a major objective of the preventive dimension of therapeutic intervention during the clinical stage of disease. The preventive component of comprehensive care is also concerned with anticipating and avoiding the occurrence of complications, either of the disease or of contemplated diagnostic or therapeutic measures (Stokes et al., 1982).

Health promotion represents a second dimension of clinical prevention. It is applicable at all stages of the natural history of disease. Health promotion is concerned with augmenting individuals' functional capacity to perform personally valued roles and their reserve capacity to cope with physical, biological, and social stress. The ability to cope with stress reflects functional capacity over and above that required by the demands of day-to-day living.

The emphasis of health promotion is on measures to increase health potential, such as immunization and physical activity, which raise functional and reserve capacities above their current levels. The focus of risk reduction, on the other hand, is on measures such as limiting exposure to carcinogens or counseling at times of emotional crisis, which are designed to prevent a decrease in functional and reserve capacity below their current levels (Segall, Barker, Cobb, Jackson, & Carey, 1981).

Risk reduction and health promotion constitute the principal modalities of health maintenance during successive stages in the natural history of disease. Both reflect a proactive approach by the physician to health care, in contrast to the more familiar stance of simply responding to patient complaints. For this reason, their systematic integration into clinical practice is facilitated by a comprehensive, practice-based preventive program. A coherent, ongoing program can help ensure the continuity of effort that is required for planning and implementing preventive measures of health maintenance for individual patients.

Figure 90.2 summarizes the sequential relationships among three clusters of physician responsibilities in a practice-based program of clinical prevention. Development of a plan for an individual patient (cluster 2) depends, in part, on the program designed for the practice setting (cluster 1). Intervention to assist patients in risk reduction and health promotion (cluster 3) is an outcome of the plan for health maintenance agreed upon by the patient and the physician (cluster 2). Feedback and evaluation procedures are included as an integral part of each cluster (Segall, Jackson, Barker, Cobb, Noren, Shindell, Stokes, & Ericsson, 1983).

The scope of the practice management cluster encompasses planning and implementing a program for risk reduction and health promotion that is responsive to the health needs of the practice population and is compatible with practice resources and constraints. The program should reflect the distribution of risk factors and patterns of health services utilization within the practice population, the type of practice (e.g., solo, group, health maintenance organization), and the availability of community resources for preventive assessment and intervention.

Among the capabilities needed by the physician in program planning are those of an epidemiological nature that relate to assessing the effectiveness of preventive measures and determining the distribution of risk factors in the practice population. In addition, managerial abilities are called for, such as appraising feasibility, formulating goals, and developing a management plan. The requisite knowledge base includes currently available methods for health promotion and risk reduction, basic techniques of descriptive epidemiology, and principles of practice management.

Implementation of the plan involves administrative and interpersonal skills. Among these are the ability to assure access to resources that are necessary to implement the plan, including appropriate personnel, physical facilities, and equipment, and an information sys-

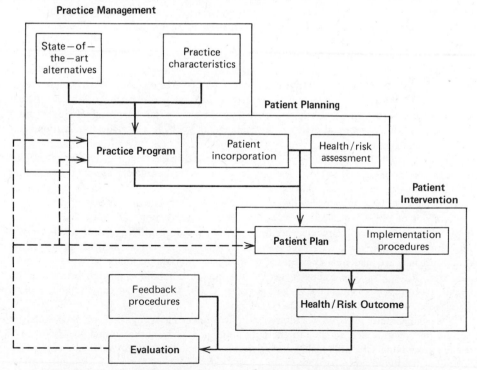

Figure 90.2 Physician performance in a practice-based program of clinical prevention.

tem for patient follow-up. Allocation of responsibilities among members of the practice staff is of particular importance. Although physicians have a leadership role in health promotion and risk reduction, other categories of health personnel, such as nurses, physician assistants, nutritionists, and psychologists, can be expected to assume an increasing role in the actual provision of preventive care. The capacity to identify and ensure optimal utilization of community-based resources (e.g., diagnostic facilities, behavior change programs) may prove critical to the success of a practice-based preventive program.

Once a program is in operation, evaluation competencies are called for. Ability to apply basic epidemiologic methods is needed in analyzing the process and outcomes of patient care as well as in assessing new developments in the field of prevention. Critical judgment is needed in determining whether modification of program goals or methods is warranted on the basis of observed outcomes in the practice population, new developments in the field of clinical prevention, or changes in the local constellation of resources and constraints.

Physicians have few opportunities during the course of their professional studies to acquire the basic managerial skills needed for planning and implementing a practice-based program of clinical prevention. Certain of these competencies can be taught at the medical school level. Others are more appropriately addressed during residency training or as part of continuing medical education.

Effective physician performance in patient planning and intervention calls for clinical competencies in assessing health and risk status, in developing and implementing a health maintenance plan, and in evaluating the outcomes of intervention. Appraisal of health and risk status involves technical skills in the application of screening procedures to assess functional and reserve capacity, exposure to health hazards, and the presence of unrecognized asymptomatic disease. Judgmental capabilities are needed in interpreting the results of these procedures.

Development of a health maintenance plan incorporating measures for health promotion and risk reduction requires judgmental skills in identifying possible modalities of intervention. Interpersonal skills are also needed in communicating the rationale and implications of these intervention options to the patient and in motivating the patient to select those that favor effective prevention.

Modalities of intervention include specific self-limiting measures, such as immunizations, measures to reduce environmental health hazards, and personal interventions to modify patterns of behavior. Control of environmental risks involves changing environments (e.g., air particulate matter) or products (e.g., cigarettes or foods) so that, regardless of personal behavior, exposures are not likely to be at toxic levels. Major hazards include not only chemicals and metals but also dust, physical agents such as noise, heat, radiation, and vibration, and mental stress.

The evidence linking lifestyle with the risk of diverse diseases (e.g., cancer, cardiovascular diseases, oral diseases, and injuries) is growing. As a result, the role of physicians in assisting patients to modify patterns of behavior is receiving increased recognition. In a Delphi survey of primary care practitioners, ability to modify patient behaviors emerged as a critical determinant of physician effectiveness in preventive intervention. The modified behaviors included smoking cessation, reducing abuse of alcohol and drugs, stress control, and improved nutrition, exercise, and fitness. At the same time, respondents indicated a widespread feeling that physicians are inadequately prepared to cope with this responsibility. Providing medical students with appropriate competencies in this domain is therefore of high priority in the teaching of preventive medicine (Segall, Barker, Cobb, Jackson, Noren, Shindell, Stokes, & Ericsson, 1981; U.S. Surgeon General, 1979).

The competencies required of a physician in implementing a program for behavior change depend on the approach adopted for helping patients achieve and maintain successful risk-reducing behavior. One approach, which involves minimal physician technical competency, is limited to encouraging patients to adopt self-care measures for which standard patient guidance materials are available. A second approach is to refer the patient either to another member of the health team in the practice setting or to a community-based facility. A third possibility, requiring far more technical competency in the methodology of behavior change, is for the physician to implement personally an intensive intervention program. In all instances, it is the physician's responsibility to encourage patients to consider risk-reducing behavior change and to secure patients' commitment to attempt such change. It is also incumbent on the physician to monitor the intervention process, to assess its outcomes, and to modify the approach as needed (Greenlick, 1981).

This analysis of physician performance in a practice-based program of health promotion and risk reduction has been used for curriculum development in a collaborative project of the Association of Teachers of Preventive Medicine and the Center for Educational Development in Health at Boston University. A set of competency-based educational objectives relating to the three basic clusters of physician responsibilities was derived, using lifestyle or behavior modification as the modality of individual intervention. A summary of the competency-based goals and objectives is shown in Table 90.2 (Segall, Barker, Cobb, Jackson, Noren, Shindell, Stokes, & Ericsson 1981).

Attitudes toward prevention that are formed during medical school studies and residency training are likely to constitute significant determinants of the extent to which preventive knowledge and skills are applied in subsequent professional practice. Of particular importance is the degree to which health maintenance is perceived as an important goal of health care and personal responsibility for providing preventive services is accepted. For this reason, the attitudinal objectives shown in Table 90.3 were derived from the analysis of physician performance in parallel with the competency-based objectives.

Table 90.2 Competency-based Educational Goals and Objectives in Clinical Prevention

Competency-based Goals	Terminal objectives
Planning a practice-based preventive program	1. Establish priorities for a program of clinical prevention to meet the health needs of a practice population
	2. Set goals for a preventive program based on a specified set of health-related priorities and practice characteristics
	3. Develop an implementation plan to achieve a set of program goals
	4. Develop an evaluation system to assess options for modifying an ongoing program
Assessing health and risk status	5. Acquire data for appraisal of a patient's health and risk status
	6. Determine indications for preventive intervention
Intervening for behavior change	7. Help motivate patients to change behavior patterns appropriately
	8. Develop an individualized plan for health maintenance in collaboration with a patient
	9. Implement the plan within a practice setting or through referral
	10. Monitor the progress of behavior change and support the patient through the vicissitudes of the process
	11. Assess the impact of behavior change on a patient's health status and evaluate the significance of any unintended effects
	12. Work out with a patient appropriate changes in an individualized health maintenance plan

Table 90.3   Attitudinal Educational Goals in Clinical Prevention

1. Belief in the importance of prevention as a goal of health care
2. Acceptance of personal responsibility for providing preventive care in clinical
    practice
3. Recognition of the utility of systematic planning in developing a practice-based preventive
    program
4. Recognition that the nature of physician–patient communication will influence
    patient behavior
5. Sensitivity and responsiveness to the overall potential impact of preventive measures
    on an individual patient
6. Recognition that decisions made jointly with the patient and, if appropriate, with family
    or friends are more likely to be implemented than those made unilaterally by the physician
7. Willingness to persevere in the face of motivational problems on the part of individual
    patients

The objectives shown in Tables 90.2 and 90.3 are generic, in that they are common to and can be applied in a wide range of categorical areas, including specific diseases, conditions, and health hazards. In the spectrum of physician education, generic competencies receive more emphasis in medical school studies, whereas greater weight is attached to more specific categorical competencies during the postgraduate phase of training (i.e., residency, continuing medical education) (Segall, 1980; Segall, Barker, Cobb, Jackson, Noren, Shindell, Stokes, & Ericsson, 1981).

Generic competencies may be taught in various portions of the medical school curriculum. During the preclinical phase, they may be incorporated into a variety of disciplinary or interdisciplinary courses, including epidemiology, pathology, medical sociology, behavioral medicine, preventive medicine, and introduction to clinical medicine. A focus on generic competencies implies that categorical examples will be used for illustrative purposes only.

The epidemiologic basis of health promotion and risk reduction can serve as a central theme in teaching the rationale of clinical prevention during the preclerkship phase of medical studies. Competency-based instruction around this theme relates to (a) using the natural history of disease paradigm to characterize the impact of preventive intervention, (b) evaluating selected categories of epidemiologic evidence to determine options for prevention, and (c) establishing priorities for a program of clinical prevention that reflects the health needs of a defined practice population.

The basic science courses also provide opportunities for students to acquire a knowledge base concerning preventive procedures used in clinical practice. These procedures include methodological aspects of screening as applied in preventive assessment and the rationale and principles that underlie the major modalities of preventive intervention. The knowledge base associated with different approaches to clinical behavior modification might, for example, constitute one component of a course in behavioral medicine or medical psychology. Similar considerations apply to immunization as part of a course in microbiology or certain occupational health hazards within a course in toxicology (Bishop, 1982).

The situation changes when preclerkship categorically oriented courses are considered. These courses may be system-oriented (e.g., cardiovascular, respiratory, gastrointestinal), related to a specific category of pathogenic process (e.g., malignant neoplasms, infectious diseases), or defined in terms of broad categories of health hazards (e.g., environmental medicine, occupational health). It is assumed that, by this point in the curriculum, students will have acquired basic generic competencies in preventive medicine. Objectives for categorically oriented instruction, therefore, stress the application of these generic competencies to specific diseases, conditions, or health hazards.

During the period of clinical clerkships, instruction is specialty-oriented. Within this context, objectives for teaching health maintenance and risk reduction are organized according to the preventable conditions for which patient populations cared for by the respective specialties are at particular risk. Patient contact affords opportunities for students to build on the knowledge base developed in earlier preclerkship studies by acquiring technical and interpersonal skills in performing preventive procedures in practice settings (Andrus, 1982).

A clerkship calls for the development of clinical competencies through student performance under direct supervision. This requires an instructional setting in which there is an ongoing, practice-based program of prevention—one in which procedures for health maintenance and risk reduction are implemented by physicians as an integral part of the health care being delivered. In such a setting, students are able to gain optimal clinical experience and to acquire the requisite skills under the supervision of appropriate role models.

Not all medical schools have access to practice-based teaching facilities that incorporate an ongoing program of clinical prevention. Several approaches to teaching clinical prevention are possible in the absence of such facilities. One approach is to consider creating a suitable instructional environment by adding a preventive component to existing clinical practice. This may be possible, for example, at a university-based student or employee health clinic. Considerations other than those of a pedagogic nature will probably determine the feasibility of this option. A second possibility is to use appropriate community-based health promotion and risk reduction facilities (e.g., smoking cessation, nutritional, blood pressure control clinics) that are not administratively linked with the medical school as sites for clinical clerkships. This option may be exercised more frequently in the future as the number of suitable facilities increases.

Increased responsibility and autonomy mark the transition from the role of student to that of intern and resident. The basic objectives that relate to the preventive dimension of clinical care retain their relevancy, but the postgraduate student is expected to achieve these objectives at a level of performance more closely approximating that of the practicing physician.

Independent performance by the intern or resident, subject to instructor monitoring, is of particular importance in regard to the ability to perform a preventive assessment and to implement appropriate measures for health promotion and risk reduction. Of increasing pertinence at this stage of physician education are competencies in the management of a practice-based preventive program. As the interval between training and practice becomes shorter, increased emphasis on managerial skills is warranted.

The instructional objectives for continuing medical education in preventive medicine continue to underscore those clinical and managerial competencies that are directly applicable to performance in clinical practice. In addition, continuing medical education may be concerned with enabling physicians to achieve more basic learning objectives in areas such as behavior modification, which they have not had the opportunity to address earlier in their professional training.

An important educational goal at all stages of professional education is for the physician/student to engage in a personal program of health promotion and risk reduction. Physicians who do so are more likely to accept responsibility for prevention in caring for their patients. By serving as positive role models, they also increase the likelihood that their patients will adopt and adhere to regimens for health maintenance (Wyshak, Lamb, Lawrence, & Curran, 1980).

Changing morbidity and mortality patterns, rapid progress in the search for more effective methods of clinical prevention, and alterations in the system for health care delivery preclude precise prediction of the competencies that will be needed by today's medical students and residents in their future professional careers. It is therefore essential that, along with knowledge and skills that reflect the state of the art in prevention today, they acquire generic competencies in self-evaluation and self-learning that will facilitate accommodation to changing opportunities for prevention over the next several decades (Jonas, 1982).

The United States has scored some notable achievements in health promotion and disease prevention during the recent past. Age-adjusted death rates for heart disease, stroke, accidents, influenza, and pneumonia have declined sharply. Death rates for cancers of the respiratory system and for homicide and suicide have risen, however. Much more progress can be expected if the pace of reduction of already identified risk factors quickens. This is the challenge that education of physicians in clinical prevention will face during the coming decades (U.S. DHHS, Note 1).

REFERENCE NOTE

1. U.S. Department of Health and Human Services (U.S. DHHS). *Successes, failures, and gaps in prevention and control, United States, 1980, with prevention profile.* DHHS Pub. No. (PHS)81–1232, pp. 291–303.

REFERENCES

Andrus, P. L. Prevention in medical education: Clinical content. *Public Health Reports,* 1982, **97,** 235–238.

Arnold, C. B. Clinical strategies for chronic disease prevention: 1981. In C. B. Arnold (Ed.), *Advances in disease prevention.* New York: Springer, 1981.

Barker, W. H., & Jonas, S. The teaching of preventive medicine in American medical schools, 1940–1980. *Preventive Medicine,* 1981, **10,** 674–688.

Berg, R. L. Prevention: Current status in undergraduate medical education. *Public Health Reports,* 1982, **97,** 205–209.

Bishop, F. M. Prevention in medical education: Preclinical content. *Public Health Reports,* 1982, **97,** 232–234.

Greenlick, M. R. Helping patients achieve risk-reducing behavior change. In C. B. Arnold (Ed.), *Advances in disease prevention.* New York: Springer, 1981.

Jonas, S. A perspective on educating physicians for prevention. *Public Health Reports,* 1982, **97,** 199–204.

Preventive medicine USA: Education and training of health manpower for prevention (A task force report sponsored by the John E. Fogarty International Center for Advanced Study in the Health Sciences, National Institutes of Health, and the American College of Preventive Medicine). New York: Prodist, 1975.

Segall, A. J. Summary of keynote address at the annual meeting, Association of Teachers of Preventive Medicine, November 3, 1973, San Francisco. *ATPM Newsletter,* 1974, **22,** 2.

Segall, A. Generic and specific competence. *Medical Education,* 1980, **14**(Suppl.), 19–22.

Segall, A., Barker, W., Cobb, S., Jackson, G., & Carey, J. A general model for preventive intervention in clinical practice. *Journal of Medical Education,* 1981, **56,** 324–333.

Segall, A., Barker, W., Cobb, S., Jackson, G., Noren, J., Shindell, S., Stokes, J., & Ericsson, S. Development of a competency-based approach to teaching preventive medicine. *Preventive Medicine,* 1981, **10,** 726–735.

Segall, A., Jackson, G., Barker, W., Cobb, S., Noren, J., Shindell, S., Stokes, J., & Ericsson, S. Physician performance objectives: A basis for preventive medicine curriculum development. In W. H. Barker (Ed.), *Teaching preventive medicine in primary care.* New York: Springer, 1983.

Segall, A. J., Vanderschmidt, H., Burglass, R., & Frostman, T. *Systematic course design for the health fields.* New York: Wiley, 1975.

Spitzer, W. O. (Chairman). The periodic health examination: Report of the Canadian Task Force on the Periodic Health Examination. *Canadian Medical Association Journal,* 1979, **121,** 1193–1254.

Stokes, J., Noren, J., & Shindell, S. Definitions of terms and concepts applicable to clinical preventive medicine. *Journal of Community Health,* 1982, **8,** 33–41.

Terris, M. The primacy of prevention. *Preventive Medicine,* 1981, **10,** 689–699.

U.S. Surgeon General. *Healthy people: The Surgeon General's report on health promotion and disease prevention: Background papers, 1979.* DHEW Pub. No. (PHS)79–55071A. Washington, D.C.: U.S. Government Printing Office, 1979.

Wyshak, G. A profile of the health-promoting behaviors of physicians and lawyers. *New England Journal of Medicine,* 1980, **303,** 104–107.

CHAPTER 91

NURSING AND HEALTH EDUCATION

CAROL LINDEMAN

The Oregon Health Sciences University

A frequent theme in today's nursing literature is that nursing is *the* science of health. The American Nurses' Association (1980), for example, in *Nursing: A Social Policy Statement,* defines nursing as "the diagnosis and treatment of human responses to actual or potential health problems." The statement continues:

> *The human responses of people toward which the actions of nurses are directed are of two kinds: (1) reactions of individuals and groups to actual health problems (health-restoring responses), such as the impact of illness-effects upon the self and family, and related self-care needs; and (2) concerns of individuals and groups about potential health problems (health-supporting responses), such as monitoring and teaching in populations or communities at risk in which educative needs for information, skill development, health-oriented attitudes, and related behavioral changes arise.*

Newman (1982), a nationally recognized nursing theorist, states: "The purpose of nursing research is to test theory that describes, explains, and predicts the process whereby nursing facilitates health patterns of behavior in human beings." For Newman, the nursing process is the nurse interacting with the person-environment to facilitate health.

The recognition that the focus of nursing is health, not illness, is not new. In 1893, Florence Nightingale spoke of nursing as putting people into the best possible condition for nature to restore or to preserve health. In 1955, Virginia Henderson defined nursing as assisting the individual, sick or well, in the performance of activities that contribute to health (Henderson, 1966). Henderson also addressed the need to assist individuals in becoming independent of assistance as soon as possible.

Landmark studies of nursing have also emphasized nursing's role in health care in contrast to illness care. The 1923 Goldmark Report emphasized the need for public health nursing as an adjunct to hospital nursing (Goldmark, 1923). The 1970 National Commission for the Study of Nursing and Nursing Education verified through observation what others were saying through intuition—namely, that nursing in the United States involved care of clients on a continuum from well to acutely ill (Lysaught, 1981). The commission also observed the range of settings in which nursing care was delivered and the overall scope and complexity of nursing practice. They were so struck with the difficulties in categorizing nursing practice because of these factors that they proposed that nursing care be thought of as either distributive or episodic. Distributive nursing care, according to the commission, is provided in the community or home setting, is continuous in nature, and is designed for health maintenance or disease prevention. Episodic care, on the other hand, is for ill patients, is offered in the hospital setting, and has a focus of cure and restoration. Lysaught (1981) reported that schools of nursing had moved toward an emphasis on distributive nursing care.

Whether or not nursing is *the* science of health, it is a profession that defines its social significance in terms of its contributions to health care as well as illness care. The generalist in nursing provides health education as an integral component of care for all clients and patients. The term *health education* here refers to educational experiences planned for the client and designed to facilitate voluntary adaptation of behaviors that are conducive to health. This definition of health education is not meant to minimize the value of the unplanned or incidental teaching that is also a part of nursing practice but rather is intended to focus on planned educational programs.

It is easy to agree that a primary nursing intervention linked with health promotion is health education. It is difficult to agree, however, on how to categorize such health education activities because of the multidimensional nature of all nursing practice. Nurses implement health education interventions for individuals, families, and groups. They implement these interventions in every type of health care setting, ranging from the acute-care hospital to the home. They do so with all age groups, with all known illnesses, and with all known motivations regarding health maintenance. Even within a particular setting with a particular client, health education as a nursing intervention occurs along a continuum. In the hospital setting, for instance, nurses provide health education that is specific to the person's needs from admission through discharge. The generalist in nursing routinely uses health education as a primary means of achieving the goal of nursing care—that is, restoring or maintaining health, which includes enabling a client to be an agent for self-care.

Research has substantiated the benefit of health education as a nursing intervention. For hospitalized surgical patients, there is a nursing research base (CURN Project, 1981b) to support structured preoperative teaching as a nursing intervention that leads to beneficial effects in the postoperative period. In fact, the beneficial effects from such nursing intervention were still measurable 33 days after surgery. A second research base (CURN Project, 1981a) supporting the significant benefits of health education as a nursing intervention is in the area of clients' reactions to psychologically threatening health care experiences. The research base shows that preparatory information describing the typical physical sensations that a person may expect to experience during a threatening health care event reduces the amount of distress the person will display. In some studies, people required fewer analgesics and in others patients left the hospital earlier.

The nursing literature contains hundreds of studies describing the beneficial effects of health education as a nursing intervention for diabetics, hypertensives, pregnant women, the young, the old, and those cared for in their homes, the hospital, the school, and so on. It is evident from this literature that nurses both endorse and utilize health education as a primary nursing intervention. It is also evident that the goal of nursing is a concern for health and that the current thought that nursing is the science of health is played out in practice.

Undergraduate nursing programs aimed at preparing the generalist in nursing include formal preparation in health education. Some schools include separate courses in patient education, whereas some distribute the content over a variety of courses. Schools differ in the objectives for classroom teaching and clinical application, but all schools expect the graduate to be able to use health education as a nursing intervention.

The nursing profession also takes pride in the distinct roles that nurses with clinical specialization play in contributing to the nation's goals for health. One can point to the role of the industrial health nurse in health protection, particularly in occupational safety, misuse of alcohol, and control of stress. The school nurse obviously plays a major role in prevention through immunization education and health education programs regarding sexually transmitted diseases. That same nurse implements programs in the school that relate to health protection and health promotion. Women's health care practitioners have contributed to preventive health services, and pediatric nurse practitioners have contributed to health promotion. For the purposes of this chapter, only one of these many roles will be described—one that is linked with the primary federal objective for health promotion and disease prevention.

In 1979, the Public Health Service established as its first goal continuing to improve infant health and, by 1990, reducing infant mortality by at least 35%, to fewer than 9 deaths per 1,000 live births (U.S. Surgeon General, 1979). In its conclusions regarding interventions to reach this goal, the Public Health Service states:

> *The major modality for intervention is prenatal care. Rather than one specific intervention, prenatal care consists of a myriad of interventions that are (or should be) tailored to the individual woman and her pregnancy. Counseling about the effects on the fetus of diet, smoking, and alcohol consumption is a crucial component of prenatal care. Thus, content and quality of prenatal care can vary depending upon the provider as well as the patient.*

Nurse-midwifery is the specialty within nursing that has demonstrated the effectiveness of its educational programs and practices in terms of this national goal. The American College of Nurse-Midwives (ACNM, 1980) describes a certified nurse-midwife as an individual who is educated in the two disciplines of nursing and midwifery. Nurse-midwifery is a practice that involves the independent management of care of essentially normal newborns and women, antepartally, intrapartally, postpartally, and/or gynecologically. The ACNM states:

> *In addition to providing comprehensive prenatal care throughout pregnancy, nurse-midwives teach and counsel about preparation for labor, delivery and parenthood. Formal and individual teaching are an integral part of nurse-midwifery care. Examples of the variety of topics discussed by the certified nurse-midwife with clients are diet evaluation, prenatal, intrapartum and postpartum exercises, sexual adjustments, . . .*

According to the ACNM, the emphasis on nursing along with midwifery leads to a practice that assures a continuing emphasis on education, support, counseling, and family. This is exactly the practice the Public Health Service has identified as necessary to reach one of our nation's major health goals.

Diers (1980) has summarized studies evaluating nurse-midwifery practice, and the data are dramatic. In Madera County, California, for example, prematurity decreased from 11% to 6.6% after nurse-midwives were introduced to care for poor women there. When nurse-midwives were introduced in Holmes County, Mississippi, the mortality rate was reduced from 39.1 per 1,000 live births to 21.3 per 1,000. Comparable data are cited for Kentucky, Texas, and New Mexico.

Although data from across the country substantiate the role of nurse-midwifery, with its emphasis on health promotion, as a major force in reducing infant mortality and premature births, resistance to that practice increases. The resistance stems primarily from the medical profession and, as highlighted by a recent "60 Minutes" television production, takes the form of restrictive practice acts, loss of practice privileges at hospitals, and reimbursement practices. The next decade will see whether the public chooses to view uncomplicated pregnancy as an illness requiring medical treatment or as a condition associated with health promotion. If the latter prevails, nurse-midwives may well be the nation's primary health care providers for normal pregnancies.

As nursing has moved its health care positions forward in the education, practice, research, and legislative arenas, obstacles have emerged. In the education arena, it is difficult to find clinical facilities that offer a health-oriented system of care that can be used as a teaching site. Most students must therefore receive their clinical education in sites that are illness-oriented. This poses a problem, as the students must then try to learn what to do by observing what is *not* done. Learning concepts and skills from negative examples is difficult at best.

To overcome the obstacle of limited health-oriented clinical sites for student education, schools of nursing have become actively involved in establishing and administering new approaches for delivering health care. Schools of nursing, such as the one at Arizona State University, have established nurse-run ambulatory care clinics as a service component of the academic unit. This trend within schools of nursing was encouraged when the Division of Nursing of the Health Resources Administration circulated a request for proposals to further develop such models for care. The Robert Wood Johnson Foundation has invested several million dollars in projects linking schools of nursing with nursing homes as a means of creating excellent care and education sites.

In the practice arena, nurses find few financial rewards for providing health care. The current illness care system links financial rewards to care of the sick. A practice that emphasizes health promotion and health education is simply not financially rewarding. New ideas that might reduce hospital stay or admission are not even encouraged. The data showing the cost-effectiveness of nursing care are all but ignored.

Again, nursing has attempted to overcome this obstacle through positive action. At the state level, nurses have been able to introduce legislation for third-party reimbursement for nursing services and to alter the nature of reimbursable services to include more health-related activities. At the national level, nurses are also using the legislative route to bring about changes in the reimbursement system—not just to open the system to "competition," but to open it to include nonreimbursable and therefore largely unmet health care needs.

The link between the nation's health goals and the nursing profession is clear. The research data support the beneficial effects of nursing interventions directed toward health. The work force is in place, but it is not mobilized. Nurses remain our nation's most underutilized resource. Only with strong leadership both in the community and in the nursing profession will the obstacles of vested interests and traditionalism be overcome.

REFERENCES

American College of Nurse-Midwives (ACNM). *What is a nurse-midwife?* (Pamphlet). Washington, D.C.: American College of Nurse-Midwives, 1980.

American Nurses Association (ANA). *Nursing: A social policy statement.* Kansas City: American Nurses Association, 1980.

CURN Project, Michigan Nurses Association. *Distress reduction through sensory preparation.* New York: Grune & Stratton, 1981. (a)

CURN Project, Michigan Nurses Association. *Structured properative teaching.* New York: Grune & Stratton, 1981. (b)

Diers, Donna. Future of nurse midwives in American health care. In L. Aiken, (Ed.), *Nursing in the 1980's: Crises, opportunities, challenges.* Philadelphia: Lippincott. 1982.

Goldmark, J. *Nursing and nursing education in the United States.* New York: Macmillan, 1923.

Henderson, V. The *nature of nursing.* New York: Macmillan, 1966.

Lysaught, J. P. *Action in affirmation: Toward an unambiguous profession in nursing.* New York: McGraw-Hill, 1981.

Newman, M. What differentiates clinical research? *Image,* 1982, **14,** 86–88.

CHAPTER 92

INNOVATIVE MODELS FOR TEACHING HEALTH PROMOTION TO DENTAL STUDENTS

HOWARD M. FIELD

University of Iowa

Dentistry is a most rewarding profession if one can keep a proper perspective. Dentistry is also fraught with misinformation, confusion, and myths, especially in the area of prevention. There is great satisfaction in assisting people through dental treatment, yet the dentist can inflict more pain and discomfort and create more resistance to treatment than do most other health professionals. The degree to which the practice of dentistry is rewarding for the dentist and for the patient hinges on a point of view: Is dentistry a health profession or is it a profession of health?

All too frequently, dentistry has been oriented to the treatment of a broken body part—oral tissues that need to be replaced, repaired, or restored. All too often, patients ask whether the treatment is really necessary and whether they want to receive it. This situation makes it difficult to enlist patients' cooperation in the dental behaviors that will preserve and restore the dental structures that remain. Even so, the profession has been pressing for an emphasis on prevention of disease, and consumers are slowly beginning to call for this approach.

The problem to be addressed here is how to get the students coming into the profession to think in terms of health promotion. Traditionally, entering dental students have adopted as a model the esteemed dentist, who treats teeth and is respected in the community. As the students apply themselves during their lengthy training, they may pattern themselves after this type of person, and they frequently become disillusioned. They may become lost in clinical detail and bitter from constant negative evaluations regarding the quality of their care. Their confidence can be undermined, and they may find it difficult to project themselves into a private practice of dentistry.

Part of the challenge to dental faculties is to develop curricula that will allow students to discover for themselves early in training some values that can support them throughout their dental education and throughout their careers. In this chapter, I will describe the experience of our faculty—to point out the obstacles that have been faced in gaining the commitment of our students to an attitude of health promotion and the approach we have taken to overcoming them.

The College of Dentistry at the University of Iowa in Iowa City was founded 100 years ago, growing out of an earlier proprietary school. At present, each incoming class has 96 students, of whom about 15% to 20% are women, 5% are members of ethnic minority groups, and 60% to 80% are native Iowans. Most students have completed 4 years of undergraduate education, with a grade-point average of 3.2, and their median age is 23 years.

During the 4 academic years of dental school, our students are exposed to about 5,000 hours of curricular time, most of which is in the clinical environment. In the first 2 years, they take four preventive dentistry courses, beginning on the first day they come to class. These courses, and a course in community dentistry that they take in the third year, provide a basis for evaluating oral health and applying preventive techniques and agents.

We have identified four key areas of attitude and knowledge in which our entering students are deficient:

1. Incoming dental students typically have an incorrect impression of their own oral health. They believe that their mouths are healthy and free of disease and that their usual practices of oral hygiene are adequate.

2. Students have difficulty picturing themselves dealing with patients and providing them with treatment options.

3. They have little understanding of how to go about setting up their own practice of dentistry.

4. They have naive ideas about presenting (marketing) health education to the patient and to the community.

Our curriculum contains programs to help students examine these issues and discover within themselves the values they can bring to their resolution.

GAINING A COMMITMENT TO THE PREVENTIVE APPROACH

Students' lack of commitment to the health behaviors necessary for the prevention of dental disease is reflected in the unhealthy conditions of their own mouths. Although they believe them to be clean, healthy, and free of disease, the sad truth is that, when they are evaluated using the principles and criteria that we set forth, nearly 100% are found to have problems in need of treatment or correction. This insensitivity to the problem of oral health is highly prevalent in our society (Field, Hawkins, Lainson, & Beck, 1982; Hughes & Rozer, Note 1).

We begin our first course in preventive dentistry by asking students to report on their own dental health and then, after listening to a lecture on the healthy mouth, to use a very simple technique on themselves to demonstrate the condition of their gums. They use a bulky type of floss, which, when passed between the teeth, does not cause healthy tissues to bleed. Following the flossing, an intraoral picture is taken of the anterior teeth and gums. Students are guided in examining this photograph for evidence of bleeding and in studying the color, size, and shape of the gum tissues. Over the 9 years we have been using this teaching device, we have consistently found that 98% of our students experience one or more areas of gingival bleeding, indicating the presence of at least an early form of the periodontal disease gingivitis.

Over the next 3 weeks, students are encouraged to practice flossing in their home dental care and to experiment with the other techniques and devices for thorough cleaning of the mouth that are being presented to them in the classroom. In the laboratory, they reevaluate the condition of their mouths, using the techniques learned on the first day. By the end of the second week, 60% are free of gingival bleeding.

In the fourth session, students have their first clinical experience of working with another person's mouth as they floss the teeth of a fellow student and use a hand mirror to examine the condition of the mouth. They discuss with their "patient" the conditions they find and challenge each other to demonstrate how they clean the areas that present the greatest difficulty. An instructor is available to resolve any dispute that might arise. In the next session, students are evaluated by experienced dentists, and they watch an evaluation being performed on another student. This experience provides them the opportunity to see how exacting the discrimination is between health and disease and how difficult it is to achieve optimal gingival health. Gingival disease is graded on a scale of 0 (healthy) to 3 (seriously diseased). On the first day, our students have an average score of 2, declining to 1.3 by the third session, 0.7 by the fifth, and 0.2 to 0.3 by the end of the course (session 14). This change represents great progress and very good health by some standards (Alexander, 1970; Stoner, 1975). The literature has indicated, however (Loe, Thelaide, & Jensen, 1965), that the disease still exists, even when scores are low, and that it is important to persist even into the minutest areas to achieve 100% gingival health.

During the last two-thirds of the course, further learning about examination procedures is coupled with lectures on the epidemiology of dental disease. Students learn to use the dental explorer, the dental mirror, and the periodontal probe and to gather information and calculate indices about decayed, missing, and filled teeth, gingival sulci and bleeding, and plaque coverage. They learn to combine these indices into estimates of overall dental health. These data are collected for each member of the class, and over the winter holiday the instructor combines them to provide a picture of the epidemiology of the class.

Following the winter holiday, as the students begin the second course, they consider their dental health in relation to other classes and to populations of their state, the nation, and many countries of the world. Students are initially defensive about their oral health. By the end of the course, almost 90% of them have a gingival index less than 0.4. They have come to realize that they now have the knowledge, and thus the authority, to ask patients to clean each individual tooth surface thoroughly. They have learned that each mouth and each surface is unique. Some students find it easier than others to achieve clean mouths, but for all persons it requires time, dexterity, and knowledge to achieve and maintain oral health.

Epidemiologic data concerning the state of Iowa are based on a large-scale survey recently completed by the College of Dentistry. In addition to the information on the oral health of the 1,200 families (3,600 individuals) involved in the study, we obtained information regarding their attitudes, values, and behaviors regarding dentistry. This information helps fill out the students' perceptions of the dental needs of the people with whom they will be working in years to come.

The largely didactic second course, in which they learn about dental disease and early prevention, provides the basis for an intense, largely clinical course in the summer term. After reevaluating their own dental health once more, the students provide preventive procedures, as needed, first to a classmate and then to the first actual patients they have engaged as health care providers. They are able to provide an examination, a prophylaxis, diagnosis and removal of calculus, polishing of teeth, application of fluorides and sealants, and presentation of oral hygiene instruction. By this time, most students have developed a thorough appreciation of the role of prevention in dental practice.

DEVELOPING THE STUDENT'S SELF-IMAGE AS A DENTIST

In the summer course, we give students an opportunity to observe their own chairside presence with the aid of a video recorder. They are asked to interview a patient, using criteria established at a previous lecture. When the tape is reviewed (not evaluated) in a group of three or four students and a trained instructor, they have a chance to see the established image of their own person—their body language, their voice projection and articulation, and their rapport with the patient. Most students enjoy this process. They have an opportunity to see themselves operating in a proper way. At the same time, they may see areas in which they want to change, to become more sophisticated or more supportive of the patient. Any observation leading to a desire for change is initially made by the student, although it might then be mutually supported by the other students in the group with the guidance of the instructor.

During the second year's courses in preventive dentistry, students continue to develop their confidence and their competence. By the end of the second year, we expect students to be able to evaluate a patient's oral health, to assist the patient in recognizing both healthy and diseased tissue, to present a treatment plan to the patient, and then to provide the necessary care.

During the third year, largely spent in clinical activities, students learn about treatment planning and the use of record systems to keep track of patients' needs. The college maintains a computer-based clinic management information system, and students follow a group of 20 to 30 patients with the aid of this system. The fourth year is similar, but students are also assigned one patient for whom they provide all care during the year. By the end of this time, most students have confidence in their capacity to provide good care and to follow patients; they have mastered the core competencies of the dentist.

PREPARING STUDENTS TO ESTABLISH THEIR PRACTICES

As students move into their last 2 years in dental school, some of them become apathetic about learning and develop a myopic concentration on finishing school. Curiously, they are reluctant to confront the idea of setting up a practice. It is time for them to begin to think about their futures—where to go, what to look for in a community, what the costs will be, when they should start. If students are experiencing "burnout," however, from sitting in lecture rooms for hours, listening to lectures on pathology, histology, physiology, and the like, they may be reluctant to sit and listen to teachers talking about community programs.

Our third-year course, "The Practice of Dentistry in the Community," attempts to break through this apathy by combining the study of community needs with activities that are relevant to establishing a practice. Working in groups of five to seven, students investigate a community that has said that it needs a dentist, or a community of their choice, to see whether it needs a dentist. They review and analyze the economic and social background of the community—its health values, school systems, government, trade areas, and demographic characteristics. Students are directed to the literature in preparing for this study, and they must present a study plan to a faculty member for approval prior to entering the community. The students spend several weeks interviewing community members and gathering data; then they analyze the data and write up reports that they present to the student body. In gathering and analyzing the data, presenting it to their fellow students, and listening to the reports of others, students become thoroughly engaged in the process.

Much discussion is generated by this process, and many students report that it is the best experience of their dental education to date. As they begin to look at the future, they become excited about their prospects, and we have found that their enthusiasm for dental school increases. Although, in reality, only a small number of students could actually enter practice in the communities studied, it is possible that the students use the process they have learned during their senior year as they move toward their decisions about what they will do following graduation. We have no conclusive data regarding this possibility at this time, but our department is conducting a research program into the factors that influence students' career planning.

TRAINING IN HEALTH EDUCATION

Within the course in community dentistry, we have the opportunity to discuss the values and merits of community health education programs. In the past, students have been lectured about the merits and methods of conducting such programs, but any programs that were initiated as a result usually fell far short of their objectives. Evaluations indicated little or no change in behavior and attitudes as a result of student-generated programs, and we found that student presentations in community schools were unrealistic in terms of the kinds of information presented or that they made use of material that the students had learned in the third or fourth grades.

To break this trend, we have developed an approach that involves students more extensively in the teaching process. Traditionally, schoolteachers in surrounding communities ask us for support in their programs of dental education, and they make time in their classrooms available to us. We now form small groups of students to work with faculty members in developing a curriculum and evaluation plan tailored to the particular group of children to whom they will be presenting. The plan is submitted to the teacher for approval and then implemented in the classroom. Although the teacher and the dental students typically are confident that the presentation will have a major impact on the children's knowledge, evaluation usually reveals that not much has been learned and even less has been applied in the form of changed dental health behavior. Students thus experience failure in presenting traditional materials in traditional ways, but they are then given an opportunity to return with a more realistic approach. They are encouraged to take account of the difficulty they themselves had in learning to care for their own teeth in the first-year course—how sure they were that their mouths were healthy and that they knew all that they needed to know to control and prevent dental disease. Usually, the second presentation is more successful, and the students come away with a recognition of the difficulties of health education and with some confidence that there are methods for overcoming these difficulties.

CONCLUSION

Incoming dental students have some preconceived notions about dentistry, and these notions constitute the principal obstacles to gaining their commitment to a preventive approach in their dental practice. Changing these preconceptions is not easy. The innovative techniques described in this chapter are but a few of the processes conducted at the University of Iowa College of Dentistry to help the students adopt an orientation to health. From this orientation to health, the students can diagnose disease and consider reasonable solutions that they can apply in their practice of dentistry. The stresses and strains of practicing dentistry can be many, but practicing with a health orientation lets the public accept responsibility for their own health, offering techniques to assist and support them in doing so. This attitude will go a long way toward making a dental profession that is healthy and that practices health in a positive manner.

REFERENCE NOTE

1.   Hughes, J. T., & Rozer, R. G. *The survey of dental health in the North Carolina population: Selected findings. Planning for dental care on a statewide basis.* Chapel Hill: Dental Foundation of North Carolina, 1981.

REFERENCES

Alexander, A. G. Dental calculus and bacterial plaque and their relationship to gingival disease in 400 individuals. *British Dental Journal,* 1970, **129,** 116–122.

Field, H. M., Hawkins, B., Lainson, P. A., & Beck, J. A. Iowa Survey of Dental Health: Clinical survey—Periodontal status and treatment needs. *Journal of Dental Research,* 1982, **61,** 179.

Loe, H., Theilade, E., & Jensen, S. B. Experimental gingivitis in man. *Journal of Periodontology,* 1965, **36,** 177–187.

Stoner, J. E. The oral health of a group of dental students. *Australian Dental Journal,* 1975, **20,** 384–387.

CHAPTER 93

HEALTH EDUCATION

SCOTT K. SIMONDS

University of Michigan

The issues involved in the preparation of professionals in health education are wider than simply the preparation of health educators or health education specialists and more complex than initial training of health professionals alone (*Preventive Medicine USA,* 1976; U.S. DHHS, 1979, 1981). According to the U.S. Department of Health and Human Services (Note 1), however, "although many health professionals contribute to health education programs, the professional health educator is the primary specialist in the field and applies skills in education and social change to the planning, organization, implementation, and evaluation of health education programs" (p. 251).

The school as a distinct setting for health education and preparation of school health educators—the largest segment of the health education profession—was recently reviewed by Creswell (Note 2), and the contributions of school health educators to learning and behavior change was reviewed recently by Rothman and Byrne (1981). Although the school is recognized as the single most important place for health education of children and youth, youth organizations and more informal social groups increasingly provide important contact points for health education.

Although many definitions exist of health education, it was defined in the Role Delineation Project as "the process of assisting individuals, acting separately or collectively, to make informed decisions about matters affecting their personal health and that of others" (Henderson & McIntosh, 1981, p. 67). This definition now has the consensus of the major national professional health organizations in the United States.

The basic intent of health education is

> . . . *to bring about behavioral changes in individuals, groups, and larger populations from behaviors that are presumed to be detrimental to health to behaviors that are conducive to present and future health. Thus health educators may address themselves to specific behaviors involving nutrition, immunization, family planning, prenatal care, or compliance with medical regimens, but in the long run health education of the public aims more generally at basic and lasting changes in people's life-styles and living practices by endowing children and adults with a sense of value of health and a responsibility for their own health as well as with the will and capacity to discharge this responsibility persistently and conscientiously within the limits of their ability.* (Simonds, 1976a, p. 107)

HEALTH EDUCATION: ITS HISTORICAL DEVELOPMENT AS A DISCIPLINE

Rosen (1961) has traced health education to the early Greek period and has documented efforts by societies throughout history to encourage individuals to maintain health and prevent illness. So-called hygienic modes of life were then, as now, based on what was known or thought to be known about the human body and the environments in which humans lived.

The modern public health movement, arising around the turn of the century, found public health workers—chiefly physicians, nurses, and sanitarians—serving as the major providers of health knowledge to the public. Selling health through education of the public was recognized as one of the keys to the campaign for public health (Hicks, 1981). Health education as a discipline can trace its contemporary roots in the United States to a nationwide conference on child health held in 1919, where the term *health education* reportedly was used for the first time. The first graduate program for preparing health educators started at the Massachusetts Institute of Technology in 1921, and the first professional organization devoted to health education, the Public Health Education Section of the American Public Health Association, was formed in 1922 (Rosen, 1961).

School health education, partially an outgrowth of the child study movement, with its concern for the health of children and youth, and the temperance movement around the turn of the century, resulted in public campaigns and instruction of pupils in personal hygiene. By the early 1920s, programs for teaching schoolchildren about health matters were well developed (Henderson & McIntosh, 1981; Means, 1962).

It was not until 1937 that the first statement of educational qualifications of health educators appeared (APHA, 1937). Several revisions of the statement appeared over the years under the guidance of the American Public Health Association (APHA, 1943, 1948, 1957). Subsequently, the responsibility for stating criteria for preparation of health educators was carried out by the Society for Public Health Education, which issued its first major report in 1967 and an updated version covering baccalaureate and master's levels preparation in 1977 (SOPHE, 1977, Note 3). These important documents served to clarify the roles and functions of trained public health educators.

Bowman (1976) noted a change over time in the function of health educators from dissemination of health information to more community organization and group work; a greater emphasis on determinants of human behavior and their application to program planning, program development, and program evaluation; and more emphasis on research on health behavior and health education. These early efforts to establish standards for preparation of health educators became the initial basis for the movement within the profession to consider credentialling based essentially on certification by assessment of competencies of entry-level health educators, a process that has been in the developmental stages for several years in the Health Education Role Delineation Project (Henderson & McIntosh, 1981; Henderson, Wolle, Cortese, & McIntosh, 1981).

The numbers of individuals prepared in health education at the baccalaureate, master's, and doctoral levels have been increasing over time—markedly so within recent years (Henderson & McIntosh, 1981; Simonds, 1976b). In 1940, there were fewer than 50 academic programs for preparing health educators, whereas in 1981 more than 260 were identified. The President's Committee on Health Education (Note 4) estimated, on the basis of membership in selected professional health education organizations, that approximately 25,000 health educators were available in 1973. The most complete reviews of human resource data on health educators were completed in 1976 (Simonds, 1976b) and in 1981 (U.S. DHHS, Note 1). The number of qualified health educators is currently estimated to be approximately 25,000 (U.S. DHHS, Note 1), which suggests that the figures provided a decade ago by the President's Committee on Health Education were something of an overestimate.

In any case, it is clear that the health education profession constitutes a manpower resource of considerable size whose preparation is specifically focused on health, health promotion, and prevention of illness or its consequences and whose methods of approach are principally derived from learning theory in the broadest sense and behavioral change at individual, small group, organizational, and community levels (Simonds, 1976a).

APPROPRIATE ROLES OF HEALTH EDUCATORS IN HEALTH PROMOTION

Roles of health educators have been studied extensively, and one can conclude from these studies that although major shifts in these roles have occurred over time, there has been no change in the focus on prevention and health promotion as a "mission" of the profession. There has been a shift to focus more on program planning and evaluation, on training and continuing education of other health personnel, on consultation, on administration and supervision, and on research. One can see the role evolving from work mostly at the grass-roots community or neighborhood levels into a role that includes more administrative responsibility, more assistance to staff in planning programs, and a staff rather than a line function in health agencies. The role in many agencies, however, remains essentially a boundary-spanning role, in which information about the interests, beliefs, and health practices of people in the community are examined, usually involving the people in the community in the process, and then the data are used for program planning with staff in the agency in order to respond to community interests.

There has been a noticeable shift over time in the settings where health educators are employed, from voluntary agencies and public health departments to health care services and, more recently, medical care institutions. Schools have continued to employ significant numbers of health educators, and employment has increased in occupational and industrial settings and in planning organizations and area health education centers. The health educator contributes to health promotion by working closely with client and/or target populations to assess health problems, to assess the behaviors that facilitate maintenance or improvement of health, and to assess behaviors that discourage achievement of health. Program planners are helped to determine which behaviors may be alterable and how voluntary changes might be encouraged. Thus, the three most important contributions health educators make to health promotion programs are in their roles as (a) collaborative diagnosticians, analyzing behaviors affecting health; (b) program planners or designers; and (c) evaluators of educational efforts undertaken separately or as integral parts of wider programs.

Because programs designed to influence health behaviors are increasingly becoming multi-faceted programs, such as the Stanford Heart Disease Prevention Program (Farquhar, Maccoby, and Solomon, 1981) or the North Karelia Project (McAlister, Puska, Koskela, Pallonen, & Maccoby, 1980; McAllister, Puska, Salonen, Tyomilehto, & Koskeld, 1982), health educators increasingly will play coordination and management roles in the application of educational and behavioral change methods to health promotion programs.

OBSTACLES TO ACCEPTANCE AND PERFORMANCE OF THE ROLE OF THE HEALTH EDUCATOR

Although the list of probable obstacles facing health educators is long and varied, there are some groupings of key issues. If the agency employing the health educator does not accept health promotion activities as a part of its mission, then the first task to be faced is organizational change and value clarification to secure the recognition and acceptance of health promotion.

Health promotion efforts developed by health educators in collaboration with others break down for various reasons—program failures, theory failures, measurement failures, or combinations of these factors (Green & Lewis, 1981).

The key obstacle to effective performance likely is the state of the art in health education practice. Health education is closing some important gaps in its knowledge base (Zapka, 1982), and gaps in knowledge about prevention and health promotion are also being closed (McGinnis, Moritsugu, & Roberts, 1982). The state of the art of health education will continue to improve to the extent that attention is focused on improved quality of the design and performance of research and evaluative studies.

Obviously, the barriers to the high-quality practice of individual health educators occur in all the ways they occur in other disciplines. As in all disciplines, there are those who make outstanding contributions, who are able to overcome the problems associated with newness of the profession, and who are able to surmount difficult organizational frameworks and lack of administrative or policy support (Green, Kreuter, Deeds, & Partridge, 1980; Green, Note 5). According to Simonds (1982), however, "there is little doubt that health education has been frequently undertaken as a compromise approach [in society] to deal with health problems, the control of which brings different social values into conflict, i.e. educate the public about the hazards of smoking, but do not make changes in the free market system or tamper with individual liberties" (p. 26). Thus, it is probable that society, acting through its various power groups, sometimes chooses health education as an avoidance response or a low-cost response to major health problems, rather than dealing with basic value conflicts or cost issues.

PROFESSIONAL PREPARATION

What should be abundantly clear to readers of this volume is that the obstacles to effective role performance in any discipline are only partially overcome by upgrading the initial preparation process itself.

If one accepts the oft-stated claim that the half-life of a professional curriculum is 5 years, continued performance analysis and synthesis of research for teaching purposes must proceed at a very rapid rate in health education, disease prevention, and health promotion.

Pressures to raise the quality of teaching programs have increased and, at the same time, the expansion of the number of programs for preparing health educators has created heavy burdens on existing academic faculty members. The Role Delineation Project mentioned earlier has involved hundreds of health educators from all types of employment settings and from universities and colleges throughout the country in defining and comprehensively validating entry-level competencies for health educators (Henderson & McIntosh, 1981) and has inspired academic institutions that prepare health educators to develop competency-based programs in the United States and abroad (Limburg State University, 1982; University of Michigan, Note 6).

Because the academic institution's response to credentialling will rest heavily on health education faculties, it is clear that faculty development is the single most pressing training problem in health education. In-service education and mid-career training of many existing practitioners are required as well (Simmons & Skiff, 1974), which adds to the pressures and responsibilities of faculty members in academic programs. The credentialling of health educators through a national examination system, in order to bring about higher quality preparation and more uniform standards, appears to be the most logical way to upgrade teaching programs and to eliminate obstacles to effective role performance caused by inadequate professional preparation.

The National Conference on Preventive Medicine (*Preventive Medicine USA,* 1976) proposed several ways to upgrade teaching, including the following

1. Greater use of problem-based teaching
2. Teaching from a more holistic viewpoint of people and their health
3. Greater collaboration with agencies and community groups involved with prevention
4. Increased attention to interdisciplinary research
5. Increased preparation in evaluation and program cost-benefit analysis.

The content and methods of teaching of prevention and health promotion in most professions have been found inadequate (McGinnis et al., 1982; *Preventive Medicine USA,* 1976).

These deficiencies affect preparation of health educators as much as preparation in other health disciplines.

SUMMARY

The role of the professionally trained health educator evolved from the original purposes of prevention of illness, encouragement of early treatment and care, and promotion of health. Those purposes are still valid—perhaps even more so today in light of the health needs of our society. Programs that prepare health educators as a separate discipline have been in existence just over 60 years and are only in their third generation of teaching faculties in health education. The health sciences and the theory and research in the social and behavioral sciences on which health education is based are far beyond where they were when the term *health education* was first used in the early 1920s. Since its beginnings, health education has been the subject of a presidential committee—something that happens in a special field such as this probably no more than once in a century. Much progress has been made over the 60 years of its formalized existence, but only the foundations have been laid. Yet, despite the shortcomings both in the profession and in the environments in which it has attempted to grow and develop, many of the major necessary "course corrections" have already been initiated.

The interrelated problems of competency standards, credentialling of health educators in light of those standards, development of curricula that would enable students to meet those standards, development of faculty who can create high-quality teaching programs, and improvement of research and theory and their linkage to teaching programs and to practice, provide an agenda for the future. If training is to contribute to removal of the obstacles to the practice of health education and to the role of professional health educators in health promotion, all these factors will need to be addressed simultaneously.

REFERENCE NOTES

1. U.S. Department of Health and Human Services (U.S. DHHS), Public Health Service. *Public health personnel in the United States, 1980.* DHHS Pub. No. (HRA)82–6, January 8, 1982.
2. Creswell, W. H. Professional preparation: An historical perspective. In *National Conference for Institutions Preparing Health Educators: Proceedings.* DHHS Pub. No. 81,81–50171, 1981.
3. Society for Public Health Education (SOPHE). *State of functions of community health educators and minimum requirements for their professional preparation with recommendations for their implementation.* May 14, 1967 (processed).
4. The President's Committee on Health Education. *Report to the U.S. Department of Health, Education and Welfare.* 1973.
5. Green, L. W. *Determining the impact and effectiveness of health education as it relates to federal policy.* Paper prepared for the Office of the Deputy Assistant Secretary for Planning and Evaluation of Health, U.S. Department of Health, Education and Welfare, April 30, 1976.
6. University of Michigan, Department of Health Behavior and Health Education. *Competency statements and assessment procedures for the Master of Public Health degree.* 1983.

REFERENCES

American Public Health Association (APHA), Committee on Professional Education. Proposed report on educational qualifications of adult health educators. *American Journal of Public Health,* 1937, **27,** 717–721.

American Public Health Association (APHA), Committee on Professional Education. Proposed report on educational qualifications of health educators. *American Journal of Public Health,* 1943, **33,** 998–1002.

American Public Health Association (APHA), Committee on Professional Education. Proposed report on educational qualifications of community health educators. *American Journal of Public Health,* 1948, **38,** 843–850.

American Public Health Association (APHA), Committee on Professional Education. Proposed report on educational qualifications and functions of public health educators. *American Journal of Public Health,* 1957, **47,** 114–120.

Bowman, R. A. Changes in the activities, functions and roles of public health educators. *Health Education Monographs,* 1976, **4,** 3, 226–246.

Farquhar, J. W., Maccoby, N., & Solomon, D. S. Community application of behavioral medicine. In W. D. Gentry (Ed.), *Handbook of behavioral medicine.* New York: Guilford Press, 1981.

Green, L. W., Kreuter, M. W., Deeds, S. G., & Partridge, K. *Health education planning: A diagnostic approach.* Palo Alto: Mayfield, 1980.

Green, L. W., & Lewis, F. M. Issues in relating evaluation to theory, policy, and practice in continuing education and health education. *Mobius,* 1981, **1**(2), 46–47.

Henderson, A. C., Wolle, J., Cortese, P. A., McIntosh, D. V. The future of the health education profession: Implications for preparation and practice. *American Journal of Public Health,* 1981, **95,** 6, 555–559.

Henderson, A. C., & McIntosh, D. V. *Role refinement and verification for entry level health educators: Final report.* San Francisco: National Center for Health Education, 1981.

Hicks, E. *The relationship of job activities and professional preparation of the public health educator at the University of Michigan, 1974–1979.* Unpublished doctoral Dissertation, University of Michigan, 1981.

Limburg State University. *Health education: Philosophy and exit level competencies.* Maastricht, Netherlands: Limburg State University, 1982.

McAlister, A., Puska, P., Koskela, K., Pallonen, U., & Maccoby, N. Psychology in action: Mass communication and community organization for public health education. *American Psychologist,* 1981, **35,** 4, 375–379.

McAlister, A., Puska, P., Salonen, J. T., Tuomilehto, J., & Koskela, K. Theory and action for health promotion: Illustrations from the North Karelia project. *American Journal of Public Health,* 1982, **72,** 43–50.

McGinnis, J. M., Moritsugu, K., & Roberts, C. M. Conference summary and discussion of future directions. Prevention and medical practice: The role of undergraduate medical education. Report of a national symposium. *Public Health Reports,* 1983, **97,** 241–243.

Means, R. K. *A history of health education in the United States.* Philadelphia: Lea and Feibiger, 1962.

Preventive medicine USA: Task Force Reports of the National Conference on Preventive Medicine (National Institutes of Health and the American College of Preventive Medicine). New York: Prodist, 1976.

Rosen, G. Evolving trends in health education. *Canadian Journal of Public Health,* 1961, **52,** 499–506.

Rothman, A. I., & Byrne, N. Health education for children and adolescents. *Review of Educational Research,* 1981, **51,** 85–100.

Simmons, J. and Skiff, A. Report of the committee on manpower education. In *Proceedings: Federal focus on health education.* Atlanta: Bureau of Health Education, Centers for Disease Control, June 1974.

Simonds, S. K. Health education in the mid-1970's: State of the art. In *Preventive Medicine USA.* New York: Prodist, 1976. (a)

Simonds, S. K. Health education manpower in the United States. *Health Education Monographs,* 1976, **4,** 208–225. (b)

Simonds, S. K. Health education: Facing issues of policy, ethics, and social justice. In S. K. Simonds (Ed.), *The SOPHE heritage collection of health education monographs* (Vol. 1). Oakland: Third Party Press, 1982.

Society for Public Health Education (SOPHE). Guidelines for preparation and practice of professional health educators. *Health Education Monographs,* 1977, **5,** 75–89.

U.S. Department of Health and Human Services (U.S. DHHS), Public Health Service. *Healthy people: The Surgeon General's report on disease prevention and health promotion.* DHHS Pub. No. (PHS)79–55071. Washington, D.C.: U.S. Government Printing Office, 1979.

U.S. Department of Health and Human Services (U.S. DHHS), Public Health Service. *Promoting health/preventing disease: Objectives for the nation.* Washington, D.C.: U.S. Government Printing Office, 1981.

Zapka, J. Epilogue. In J. Zapka (Ed.), *The SOPHE heritage collection of health education monographs* (Vol. 3). Oakland: Third Party Press, 1982.

CHAPTER 94

NUTRITION AND DIETETICS

EILEEN B. PECK

Department of Health Services, Sacramento

Behavioral health and health promotion are a natural area for dietitians and nutritionists, and many of them have been involved with health promotion and behavior change for years. The reasons for this are clear. First, nutrition is a body process that supplies the structural material for normal growth and development. Second, nutrition is supported by food intake, and food habits are behaviors that are learned from family and from the culture. Even what is considered acceptable as food is culturally defined; a food that one culture considers a delicacy may be considered an abomination by another. Food habits may be difficult to modify, because they have deep-seated psychological significance, associated with feelings of trust, security, and comfort. Because of these facts, nutritionists and dietitians have considered the inclusion of social and behavioral science essential to their educational programs since the turn of the century, when the first guidelines for programs were published (McCullough, 1906).

The nutritionist/dietitian is a professional who is equipped to teach people of all ages how to make nutritionally sound food choices in a variety of settings, using many methods. The central purpose is to convert nutrient needs into food, by providing either food or the knowledge to select ones own food (Committee on Goals, 1969). The demand for the services of these professionals has increased rapidly in the last few decades as people have become more dependent on the marketplace for food and on social institutions such as schools, adult classes, and health care facilities for knowledge about what to eat and about how to prepare food (Peck, 1970, 1974).

The roles that these related professionals have played include educator, counselor, clinician, consultant, demonstrator, program planner, manager, administrator, and policymaker. The distinction between the dietitian and the nutritionist has frequently been blurred. In 1939, the American Dietetic Association attempted to clarify it by using the term *dietitian* for the clinician and food system administrator and the term *nutritionist* for the educator (Huddleson, 1947). Because of overlapping roles, this dichotomy was never very useful. It has been further confused by the use of the definition of "public health nutritionist" for *nutritionist* in the *Dictionary of Occupational Titles*. The most recent definition views the terms *nutritionist* and *dietitian* as interchangeable, and public health nutrition is viewed as the specialized field of community dietetics practiced in government agencies that are charged with the protection of the health and the public (*Nutrition Personnel*, Note 1).

Historically, as is true of many other health professionals, the nutritionist/dietitian has functioned primarily in the hospital setting and has operated with the medical model of treatment under physician authority. The community or social dietitian emerged, however, over 70 years ago. These professionals operated in a wide variety of settings, such as well-child conferences, schools, and health and welfare agencies, and they began to use a health promotion and disease prevention systems model (Peck, 1974). In recent years, there has been a definite trend to use this latter model as well as behavioral modification techniques in all settings.

The following is a brief examination of the wide variety of roles and settings that have been or could be used effectively by nutritionist/dietitians to affect the ability of people to take responsibility for their own nutritional health. We can view these roles as operating at several levels, as Green (1980) does in his health enhancement model: individual knowledge and motivation, the immediate supporting social and emotional system; and the broader system and society. Most settings involve the use of more than one role and level.

ROLES AND SETTINGS

The school setting is the one that has been in use the longest, although even now the full potential of the role of nutrition education specialists in schools has not been appreciated or reached (Peck, 1974). To promote the nutritional health of children, it is important to provide both nourishing food in the lunchroom and educational experiences with food information in classrooms. The first requires the food service administration skill of the administrative dietitian, whereas the second requires skill as a nutrition education specialist working with the school health program and classroom teachers. Some outstanding programs that have existed for many years include both components (Dwyer, 1981; Gillett, 1932). Only since 1974, however, when federal funds became available, has the nutrition education and training component become more widespread. Some industry-supported nutrition education efforts have been aimed at increasing the ability of teachers and school nurses to be effective in nutrition education in the school. The Big Ideas program of the California Dairy Council is an outstanding example. The full potential of school nutrition programs will probably not be realized until more importance is placed on school health programs by the public and by school administrators.

Community nutrition education is another setting in which nutritionists and dietitians who are interested in behavioral health have become more active in recent years. Programs are sponsored by adult education facilities, by official and voluntary health agencies, by educational organizations sponsored by the food industry, and in group care settings for children and older adults. The Cooperative Extension Service is an agency that has been involved in bringing new knowledge of food and nutrition to the general public in a number of ways. The Expanded Nutrition Education Program of that agency is a unique and effective model that uses indigenous aides supervised by professionals to bring basic nutrition information to low-income homemakers individually and in small groups in their homes.

Group care programs for both preschool children (ADA, 1981; Juhas, 1973) and older adults (ADA, 1978) have provided opportunities to combine feeding programs with educational programs to bring about changes in food habits. The nutritionist/dietitian role in the Head Start program is an especially fortuitous one in health promotion, as it permits work with parents, teachers, other health professionals, and administrators.

Nutritionists and dietitians have been employed by industry in several roles. The food industry has used them in product development and consumer education, where some professionals have been very effective in incorporating health promotion. In addition, industry-sponsored educational organizations such as the National Dairy Council and the American Meat Institute have been active in providing nutrition education for teachers and health professionals as well as for the general public. In a third type of activity, during World War II and for some years after, a number of industries used nutritionists/dietitians in employee health programs to provide both food and educational programs (Comstock, 1940). There is a resurgence of interest in this role in both industry- and labor-sponsored health programs. The potential for effectiveness here is very large.

The media, especially newspapers and women's magazines, have also been a field in which nutritionists and dietitians with a strong interest in health promotion have been able to operate. Nutritionists and dietitians have only recently begun to enter into private practice, but the role of the consulting nutritionist has developed rapidly in the last few years. Most of these professionals are involved in health care, accepting referrals from physicians, clinics, or group practices, but some also consult with industry.

The roles of the nutritionist/dietitian in health care include being a member of the health care team in clinical settings and being a counselor to patients as well as a consultant to and educator of other health care providers regarding the importance of nutrition to health. Although the traditional setting has been in in-patient care, as the importance of ambulatory health care is accepted by the health care team, many more nutritionists and dietitians are now practicing in this setting. The Maternal and Infant Care Projects and the Children and Youth Projects have been particularly influential in demonstrating the cost-effectiveness of utilizing nutritionists in the health care team, providing services to women and children. These professionals can be equally cost-effective in chronic disease settings, especially in relation to diabetics and heart disease (Dahl, 1977).

The role of the nutritionist/dietitian in public health has been to assess the need for nutrition services in the community and to plan, implement, and evaluate programs that provide needed services (Huenemann & Peck, 1971). This does not mean that the services are necessarily provided by these professionals or even the health departments for which they work, since the role is usually that of a catalyst to see that services are available to protect and promote the health of the public.

Nutritionists and dietitians have also been involved in advocacy roles to change the attitudes of decision makers in legislatures, administrative agencies, and the food and health care industries, as well as those of the general public, about nutrition and its importance to health. The advocates come from a variety of settings, including public health, universities, and nonprofit organizations for nutrition education. They realize that the optimal nutritional health for the public is affected by the behavior of industry and government as much as by the behavior of individual citizens.

OBSTACLES TO EFFECTIVENESS

A complex set of factors creates obstacles that have made it difficult for nutritionists and dietitians to be more effective in health promotion. These obstacles include the everyday nature of the subject matter, the undramatic effects of poor nutrition, the attitudes of health professionals and the general public toward the subject, the effect of the profit motive on the food industry and the media, and the actions and attitudes of nutritionists themselves.

Since everyone eats several times a day, there is a tendency for each person to think he or she is an expert in nutrition and knows what is best for himself or herself. In addition, the effects of malnutrition, except in the rapidly growing infant, in severe famine, or in frank deficiency diseases, are long-term and undramatic. This situation produces a lethargic attitude on the part of the public and health professionals toward nutrition. Physicians, especially because of their orientation to disease rather than health, have been slow to appreciate the importance of nutrition to health promotion and the complexity of helping people change food habits.

Only in the past 5 to 10 years has there been general acceptance of the importance of nutrition in any health area except prevention of nutritional deficiency disease. The importance of improved nutrition during pregnancy in the reduction of infant mortality and the incidence of low-birth-weight infants was debated heatedly until the early 1970s, when the publication of a National Academy of Sciences (1970) study reviewing the existing evidence (most of which was 20 years old then) focused attention on this issue and helped bring about a fairly rapid change in policy and attitudes. The relationship of diet and nutrition to heart disease, cancer, stroke, and other leading causes of death has been equally controversial until just recently. An oversimplification of what is required to change food habits has also contributed to the problem. The attitudes that "everyone eats so we are all experts" and that it is impossible to change food habits because people do not act on the knowledge of what they should eat or respond to the physician's admonitions to change have been equally stultifying. Nutrition practitioners who, because of lack of time or knowledge, have been willing to provide diet sheets or dogmatic nutrition education rather than nutrition counseling have only confirmed the truth of such beliefs. The low status of all the allied health professions has plagued nutritionists and dietitians as well.

Another factor has been the generally small importance the medical profession and society have given to health promotion and to public health, the branch of health care that is devoted to it. In addition, educators and school officials have been very slow to see that health and nutrition education can be a respectable subject matter to use in teaching science, mathematics, and language skills.

In some respects, the profession itself has been an obstacle. First, for many years the only avenue to becoming a dietitian was through an internship approved by the American Dietetic Association. Since most of these internships were in hospitals, the medical model and the authority of the physician were used, and the majority of practitioners stayed in the in-patient setting. Second, the Study Commission on Dietetics (1972) recommended that the entry-level dietitian be educated at the bachelor's degree level. The result has been insufficient professionalization of many practitioners, so that they are hesitant to take an equal role on the health care team with professionals who have much more maturity. In addition, the failure of the dietetics profession to secure licensure, and thus a clear-cut legitimization of the field, has led to other problems. The most serious of these is the slowness with which dietetic services have been covered by third-party payment mechanisms.

Another problem related to the lack of exclusive domain for the profession is the ease and willingness of health food store operators and diet fad physicians to promote exorbitant promises for wonder cures through diet supplements and fad diets. Sound nutrition information is not so alluring as a quick cure to all illness. Related to this is the profit motive of the food industry and media, which takes precedence over promoting sound nutrition in the development of new food products and advertising.

Some of these problems are undoubtedly related to the fact that the nutritionist/dietitian is likely to be a woman (about 90% are women) and that the field is still relatively small (45,000 practitioners). Just what effects these factors have had on the slowness with which the profession has moved into private practice and into more assertive roles in health promotion is unclear, but they certainly are factors.

EDUCATING FOR HEALTH PROMOTION

From examination of the wide variety of roles that nutritionists and dietitians can play in health promotion and the obstacles that presently exist, we can gain an idea of the traits these professionals should have and thus the types of education that would produce professionals with a good chance of success in this field.

What is needed are independent professionals who believe that change is necessary in social systems as well as in individuals (Peck, 1976). They should be assertive and should be able to function fully as a member of the health team. They require an understanding of how people behave in relation to health and food and in organizations. They must be able to learn how to apply their knowledge and skills as clinician, counselor, educator, and consultant in a variety of settings. They should be oriented to health, rather than to disease, and to enabling people to take responsibility for their own health and gaining the capacity to make informed decisions about health.

Although undergraduate education for dietetics has always included some course work in basic psychology and sociology, because of the amount of biological and nutritional science required, the behavioral sciences courses usually have not been sufficient to provide depth. With the advent of undergraduate courses in which clinical practice is coordinated with academic work and specialization in either administration, clinical, or community nutrition, there has been increased emphasis on counseling and education skills. There has also been greater emphasis on the role of the dietitian in health promotion and disease prevention. Undergraduates have been exposed to the many opportunities for dietitians in the community. These changes have led to stronger training for community dietetics at the undergraduate level. Students in both the clinical and community options have a better understanding of the role of nutrition in health promotion and of the need for behavioral change methods.

It is at the graduate level, however, that the most education must take place for nutritionists and dietitians who can be effective in health promotion. The components of graduate programs should include the basic preparation for a dietitian, with additional course work in behavioral sciences, the systems approach to the solution of human problems, program planning, and evaluation, as well as some supervised experience in applying this knowledge. This model is basically the one that has been recommended and modified by the faculties of Graduate Programs in Public Health Nutrition for many years (note 1). At one time, these programs accepted only qualified and experienced dietitians. In the early 1960s, however, they began to accept students who had academic nutrition preparation but no experience, and they provided supervised experience as part of the graduate program (Huenemann & Murai, 1972). This model has permitted an expansion of the applicant pool to those with undergraduate majors in behavioral sciences who were willing to acquire the necessary background in nutrition. The result has been that graduates are better prepared to move forward as independent professionals and to assume new roles as necessary.

One shortcoming of the graduate programs in public health has been that most are only 1 year long. This does not permit adequate time to develop the broad knowledge and skills needed plus specialization in ways of reaching a special audience or special techniques such as those needed for media involvement. Recently, some programs have begun to require a 2-year course to permit specialization. The most up-to-date guidelines for these programs have been published in a monograph prepared by a committee with representation from the major organizations of nutritionists (note 1).

Two other models for education have been successful in producing graduates who are especially effective in nutrition counseling and nutrition education and well suited to work in ambulatory health care settings. One combines a master's degree in education with supervised experience in outpatient nutrition counseling. Other programs confer a master's degree in nutrition education, which includes graduate-level nutrition courses with education courses, including courses dealing with behavioral change.

A relatively new model may be an excellent way to combine the two disciplines of behavioral science and nutrition to prepare clinical psychologists, educators, and researchers in areas of mutual interest. A university department of nutritional science has developed an undergraduate community nutrition major, which combines a major in nutrition with one in either anthropology or psychology. Graduates of this program are equipped to pursue a graduate degree program in either nutrition or behavioral science. Their involvement with the subject matter of both disciplines, as well as their exposure to community programs in which the disciplines are utilized, not only provides a strong background for graduate work but permits development of a broad perspective before the necessary narrowing of focus of graduate work.

Still another model for producing educators and researchers is the Nutrition–Behavioral Cardiovascular Disease Prevention Program at Washington University in St. Louis. This is a postdoctoral program aimed at letting both nutritionists and behavioral scientists gain competence in working together.

SUMMARY

Good nutrition is basic to health. Therefore, nutrition is a basic topic for inclusion in health promotion, disease prevention, and health behavior programs. At one time, the knowledge of what foods would support good health and nutrition was common to the public and to healers. Today, the complexity and rapidity of change of the food supply and of lifestyles demand a specialist—the nutritionist/dietitian—to advise the public and other health professionals. Nutritionists and dietitians can be effective in promoting health and in modifying nutrition-related behavior in a wide variety of settings. Education for functioning in these settings can be acquired from several types of programs. The common core of knowledge needed includes adequate knowledge of nutritional science and dietetics and of behavioral science, and supervised practice in applying this knowledge in programs for health promotion and disease prevention.

REFERENCE NOTE

1. Kaufman, M., ed. *Personnel in Public Health Nutrition for the 1980's.* McLean, Va.: Association of State and Territorial Health Officials Foundation, 1982.

REFERENCES

American Dietetic Association (ADA). Position paper on nutrition and aging. *Journal of the American Dietetic Association,* 1972, **61,** 623.

American Dietetic Association (ADA). Position paper on food and nutrition services in child day care centers and day care homes. *Journal of the American Dietetic Association,* 1981, **79,** 464.

Committee on Goals of Education for Dietetics. Goals of the lifetime education of the dietitian. *Journal of the American Dietetic Association,* 1969, **54,** 91–93.

Comstock, L. A nutrition advisor in the industry. *Journal of the American Dietetic Association,* 1940, **16,** 909–913.

Dahl, T. Economics, management and public health nutrition. *Journal of the American Dietetic Association,* 1977, **70,** 144–148.

Dwyer, J. T. Nutrition education and information. In *Better health for our children: A national strategy* (Vol. 4). Washington, D.C.: U.S. Government Printing Office, 1981.

Gillett, L. A. *Nutrition services in the field: White House Conference on Child Health and Protection.* New York: Century, 1932.

Green, L. *Health education planning: A diagnostic approach.* Palo Alto: Mayfield Publishing Co., 1980.

Huddleson, M. P. A new profession is born. *Journal of the American Dietetic Association,* 1947, **23,** 573–578.

Huenemann, R. L., & Murai, M. Philosophy and status of an educational program for public health nutritionists-dietitians. *Journal of the American Dietetic Association,* 1972, **61,** 669–671.

Huenemann, R. L., & Peck, E. B. Who is a public health nutritionist? *Journal of the American Dietetic Association,* 1971, **58,** 327–330.

Juhas, L. Nutrition education in day care programs. *Journal of the American Dietetic Association,* 1973, **61,** 134–137.

McCullough, E. G. The need of and training of the dietitian. *Proceedings of the 8th Lake Placid Conference on Home Economics,* 1906, **7,** 102–107.

National Academy of Sciences. *Nutrition and the outcome of pregnancy.* Washington, D.C.: U.S. Government Printing Office, 1970.

Peck, E. B. The development of a public health profession: The public health nutritionist, 1870–1969. (Doctoral dissertation, University of California, Berkeley, 1970). *Dissertation Abstracts International,* 1970 **31,** 6091. (University Microfilms No. 71–09753)

Peck, E. B. The public health nutritionist-dietitian: An historical prospective. *Journal of the American Dietetic Association,* 1974, **74,** 642–648.

Peck, E. B. The "professional self" and its relation to change processes. *Journal of the American Dietetic Association,* 1976, **69,** 434–537.

Study Commission on Dietetics. *The profession of dietetics.* Chicago: American Dietetic Association, 1972.

SECTION 13

BEHAVIORAL HEALTH IN THE TWENTY-FIRST CENTURY

CHAPTER 95

METAHEALTH: A CHALLENGE FOR THE FUTURE

JOHN J. BURT

University of Maryland

The ultimate test of self-knowledge is whether a person understands the principles and presuppositions operative in his or her thinking and behaving. The ultimate test of education is whether people can work out a personal set of principles and presuppositions wherein they are comfortable in the presence of options. The ultimate test of health education is whether people fully appreciate the health consequences of their options. The ultimate test of behavioral health is the subject of this chapter.

To become an important field of study, behavioral health must first obtain a firm grasp on its fundamental presuppositions, presuppositions that are not a part of behavioral health but rather come before it—metahealth. Such presuppositions are not open to verification or refutation and are never known to be true or false. They are simply presupposed, taken for granted by those concerned with health enhancement and disease prevention—often without realizing it. To uncover these presuppositions and render their consequences clear is the business of a metahealth physician, a professional who does not now exist but whose work is critical to the advancement of behavioral health as an interdisciplinary field of study and practice.

The future of behavioral health and metahealth are inextricably linked; they stand or fall together. The birth of behavioral health—the establishment of orderly thinking about the things people do to or for themselves that may have future health or illness consequences—is also the birth of metahealth—the establishment of orderly thinking about the presupposition operative in behavioral health. So long as either lives, the other lives; if one dies, the other must die with it. Hence, this Handbook would not be complete without a discussion of metahealth.

Prior to a discussion of what underlies behavioral health, it will be useful to define a fundamental or absolute presupposition in its more general sense. According to the English philosopher R. G. Collingwood (1940):

> An absolute presupposition is one which stands, relatively to all questions to which it is related, as a presupposition, never as an answer. Thus if you asked a pathologist about a certain disease "What is the cause of the event E which sometimes happens in this disease?" he would reply "The cause of E is C. That was established by So-and-so." You might go on to ask: "I suppose before So-and-so found out what the cause of E was, he was quite sure it had a cause?" The answer would be "Quite sure, of course." If you now say "Why?" he will probably answer, "Because everything that happens has a cause." If you ask "But how do you know that everything that

happens has a cause?" he will probably blow up right in your face, because you have put your finger on one of his absolute presuppositions, and people are apt to be ticklish in their absolute presuppositions. But if he keeps his temper and gives you a civil and candid answer, it will be to the following effect: "That is a thing we take for granted in my job. We don't question it. We don't try to verify it. It isn't a thing anybody has discovered, like microbes or the circulation of the blood." He is telling you that it is an absolute presupposition of the science he pursues.

Behavioral health also has its ticklish presuppositions, and the letter that follows will introduce us to metahealth by forcing us to confront some of these presuppositions. The fictitious letter, which could be from a citizen of any advanced country in the world, is written to all of us who are defined professionally by a concern for human health, including spiritual health.

To Those Concerned With Health Enhancement and Disease Prevention:

I am writing a single letter to all of you who are closely connected with my physical, mental, and spiritual health. Through this letter I hope to explain why I am, like millions of others in the world, so utterly desperate. You have advised me to put a curb on my pleasures, to resist the desire to engage in behaviors that will jeopardize my health and spiritual rightness. But I do not believe that you are fully aware of the implications of your well-intended advice. That is why I am writing to you. Let me begin by reminding you of a fact that you seem to have forgotten: I am not the maker of my own temperament, which unceasingly invites me to pleasure, an invitation that is more compelling in every sense than your invitation to longevity and spiritual enlightenment. For as long as anyone can remember, those of you in health enhancement and disease prevention have deflected and dispirited people through your teachings and promotion campaigns. I feel certain that this is not your intention; nonetheless, when you go down the list of pleasures known to or available to most people and one by one attach a risk to each and thereafter offer a strategy whereby behavior can be changed to avoid that risk, it is tantamount to saying that pleasure and health are necessarily at odds with each other. Thus, in attempting to promote health, you have simultaneously promoted an attitude—you must choose between health and pleasure—that thwarts the very health you seek to enhance. Intentionally or not, you have caused most of us to think that ill health and bad luck are punishments for pleasure seeking, that it is only just that those who indulge the pleasures of eating should come to look funny (fat funny) and have their arteries clogged, that those who drink too much should be rendered impotent as a warning and develop cirrhosis of the liver if the practice continues, that those who smoke should develop emphysema and lung cancer, that those who have many sex partners should have herpes for life and syphilis and gonorrhea as short-term punishments, that those who eat sweets should have bad teeth, that those who gamble should end up broke, and that those who drive fast should have accidents.

What I am trying to tell you is that the health problems of today's world do not result so much from an ignorance of risk factors or an ignorance of strategies to change behavior as from an ignorance of pleasure options that are not attended by a snag. In the battle for control of the human will—persuader vying against persuader—those of you in health enhancement and disease prevention have not been much of a factor. You have no sensitivity to the positive side of health: you don't understand the affirmative emotions. You don't understand the human will.

To prevent your getting off on another wrong track, let me hasten to add that although my temperament unceasingly invites me to pleasure, this does not negate my free will. This point is worth emphasizing: the invitation from my temperament is in every sense an invitation, nothing more. But I must tell you, with complete honesty, that as a free agent I am interested in pleasure. In truth, I weigh all my options to determine their pleasure content. You seem to have a bias against pleasure, but it is a bias that I do not share. At my very best, I am an intelligent consumer of pleasure options, and a major portion of my mental life is spent evaluating invitations to pleasure. Moreover, I somehow have the feeling that I am far more skillful at this matter than you give me credit for. Because you are preoccupied with promoting longevity and spiritual rightness, you have a tendency to judge my choices as stupid. They are not really; you would understand if you stood in my shoes. The trouble is that, being just a common person, my invitations to pleasure constitute only a short list, and due to your extensive research and teaching nearly every pleasure on my list is now marked: "caution—this may be dangerous to health or spiritual rightness." What I desperately need is an invitation from someone who really understands health enhancement—an invitation to pleasure without a snag, without a caution sign. But it never comes. I have waited and waited—watching you destroy the few pleasures that I have discovered while remaining totally insensitive to my real problem. Don't you care? Can't you see that humanity places little value on longevity and spiritual rightness that is devoid of pleasure? What do you have against pleasure?

I know that you are very busy discovering new risk factors, teaching about old ones, propounding new models of health behavior, and writing books about health enhancement, but would it be asking too much to request that the next time you shoot down one of my pleasure options you replace it with a new one—one without a snag. That is, unless it is true that health and spiritual rightness must forever be at odds with pleasure. In which case, I will just continue weighing pleasure options against longevity options, pleasure against spiritual rightness. Continue asking myself what, if not to enjoy pleasure, is health good for. And wondering—wondering if you are really trying to help me.

Let me end my letter with this observation. The English humorist Josh Billings once suggested that no person who lived to break a hundred years was famous for anything except living to be a hundred. That is not entirely true, but it points to an important presupposition held by people like me: health is something to be used for the accomplishment of goals and pursuing self-selected goals represents one of the highest forms of pleasure seeking. So you must understand that health is a means; the end is pleasure. And if pleasure and health conflict, so much the worse for health. I know that you don't see it that way, but most of us do.

Sincerely,
An Unhealthy Citizen

A thoughtful reading of this letter prompts a number of fundamental questions that must be addressed before behavioral health can be fully established as an interdisciplinary field of study and practice. Among these questions, the most basic is: "To what end should those professionally engaged in behavioral health carry on their business?" Is it the purpose of behavioral health, as the letter from the unhealthy layperson begs, to discover and render lively options in lifestyle that are productive of both pleasure and health? Or will this new field, like the older ones related to health, remain indifferent to this plea? Should behavioral health avoid the difficulties that are certain to be associated with pleasure seeking and pursuit of the affirmative emotions? Should it limit itself to something more solid, such as discovering and promoting lifestyle options that increase longevity and prevent dysfunction? Or should it be even more limited? Perhaps behavioral health should simply limit itself to helping people do what science has demonstrated to be best for them? Or is that too mechanistic? Perhaps the emphasis should be on quality of life. If so, what if the pursuit of quality conflicts with longevity and avoidance of risk factors? Is such a conflict possible? Is it generally the case?

The term *behavioral health* suggests a central focus on health. If so, what is health? Is it a means, as suggested in early Greece, or is it an end? Is it a state of being? Perhaps it is an ideal state of complete mental, physical, and social well-being. Could working to achieve this ideal state be at odds with quality of life? If it is not to enjoy pleasure, what is the worth of health? Was the layperson's question a fair one? Is health an attitude toward life? Who is to say what health is—those associated with behavioral health, outsiders, biomedical science? What if there are differing opinions on what health really is? What if the nature of health is an absolute presupposition? What if each individual has his or her own way of conceptualizing health? Would this make any difference in the professional practice of behavioral health? Could it be that what a person presupposes about the nature of health and the human condition in general plays a major role in longevity and dysfunction and quality of life? Could it be that among all the risks to human well-being, the most important is a metafactor? Could that factor be what a person presupposes about health and human existence in general? If that were so, would it make any difference in the professional practice of behavioral health? Should the first priority of behavioral health be to help people understand the presuppositions operative in their thinking and behaving? Without an understanding of these presuppositions, could any behavior change be by informed consent? Could any change in lifestyle really be self-initiated? If people do not come to understand what they presuppose about health and the human condition, would the professional practice of behavioral health be more than the "good care of cattle," more than a pretense at promoting a philosophy toward health that stresses individual responsibility? If pleasure and health came into conflict, as in the layperson's letter, which would be the greater friend? Would it be wiser to trade, in moderation, a little health for a little pleasure, or the other way around: pleasure for health? Can the question be resolved without reference to some absolute presuppositions? Could a professional in behavioral health help another person work out a conflict between pleasure and health? How?

These questions are critical ones for the future success of behavioral health. Indeed, any attempt to evaluate success presupposes answers to these questions. It is not the purpose of metahealth, however, to answer these questions. The business of the metahealth physician is to uncover and render clear what professionals in behavioral health presuppose when they answer the critical questions—to help professionals understand the presuppositions operative in their behavior.

THE ROLE OF METAHEALTH IN BEHAVIORAL HEALTH

Regarding the field of behavioral health, metahealth has two important roles to play. First there is the business of uncovering the presuppositions operative in the professional behavior of those who constitute this new field. Let us call this Sense I Metahealth. Then there is the study of what people in general presuppose about human well-being and the consequences of such presuppositions for their personal health. Let us call this Sense II Metahealth.

Sense I Metahealth

As practicing professionals in the field of behavioral health, our work is guided by a number of generally accepted principles and presuppositions. These two sets of guides, however, are radically different in nature. Principles are empirically derived and are constantly open to questions regarding their validity. To establish and refine these principles is properly the business of the "science" of behavioral health. Presuppositions, on the other hand, are not open to validation. By labeling something a presupposition, we announce that here is a guide that our best judgment has recommended to us, but it is simply not possible to prove that it represents truth or knowledge. We may presuppose, for example, that health and longevity are more important than certain habits that people find pleasurable, and thereafter we may work for health enhancement and disease prevention at the expense of these pleasures. Despite the fact that many people concerned with human health appear to be guided—knowingly or not—by this presupposition, it is nonetheless one that cannot be demonstrated to be valid or true. It can only be presupposed. Likewise, we might presuppose that behavior change should be by informed consent, but we could never make good on the claim that such a presupposition represents truth or knowledge. This does not mean, of course, that we would not like to demonstrate the validity of our presuppositions— that we would not like to promote them to verified principles. It simply means that, in some matters, if we are totally honest, we must admit that we are limited to presupposing. In fact, it is an overwhelming and at the same time liberating experience to realize how much of our view of the everyday world is shaped by our presuppositions about reality.

My point is that in behavioral health, as in any field, our professional behavior depends on two guides: principles and presuppositions. The former are evolved through the methods of science; the latter, through the methods of metahealth. Both are essential to future success; that is, the great professions and disciplines are those that have become sophisticated about their principles and presuppositions. Physics, for example, is a leading field of study because it pays attention to and constantly reexamines fundamental presuppositions. In my view, the most immediate problem for behavioral health is a problem in Sense I Metahealth—coming to know what it presupposes.

Sense II Metahealth

In addition to the important study of what health professionals presuppose about the nature of their work, there is a second and even more exciting branch of metahealth—a branch that studies what people presuppose, at the personal level, about human well-being and that also studies the consequences of these presuppositions for health enhancement and disease prevention. In my opinion, it is this second branch—metahealth at the personal level—that is most crucial to the future of human health.

Perhaps the best way to introduce the reader to Sense II Metahealth is through a problem in this field. I shall present such a problem here, explain why it is properly a problem in metahealth, and discuss the role of the metahealth physician in diagnosing, preventing, and treating the problem.

THE NEW PLAGUE: A PROBLEM IN METAHEALTH

After more than 25 years of study and practice in the field of health, I am currently of the view that the chief threat to physical, mental, and social well-being in our time is not heart disease or cancer, not an infectious or environmental agent, not poverty or malnutrition, not human exploitation or economic injustice, not prejudice or even thermonuclear war. Rather, the greatest danger to human welfare in our immediate future is a metafactor— what we presuppose about ourselves and the human condition in general. Indeed, two presuppositions that people have concocted about their lives have combined to cause a plague that has spread through much of the world and now threatens to destroy the quality of contemporary lifestyles. This plague constitutes one of the most serious threats to the future that the world has ever known. Many of the afflicted are left passive, apathetic, depressed, and generally pessimistic about their roles in the future. In other cases, the plague changes people into megalomaniacs—people who unrealistically believe they are masters of destiny. In either case, the victims are unable to function effectively.

I have labeled the consequences of these two presuppositions co-creator perception deficiency (CCPD). In CCPD, as in any deficiency disease, some factor or element essential to health is missing. In this new plague, the missing element is the positive presupposition that humans have the capacity to co-create the events that shape their lives. In its place, CCPD victims presuppose that they are controlled by the people and events around them, and they subsequently become dispirited—giving up their hopes and dreams and placing themselves in a "dummy hand," thereby entrusting their success to some outside agent.

Or they accept an equally unhealthy presupposition: If I work hard enough and long enough and don't make too many mistakes, I can become the master of my own destiny. More frequently, they shuttle back and forth between these two presuppositions—sometimes helpless and sometimes megalomaniacal.

Having described CCPD, let me explain why it is a problem in metahealth. At stake are three presuppositions: (a) I am a co-creator of the future; (b) I am fortune's fool, a victim of circumstances beyond my control; and (c) I am the master of my own destiny. None of the three is open to full verification or refutation, and all three must remain presuppositions. What people presuppose, however, can affect their lives as much as or even more than what they know or think they know to be true. Hence, a metahealth physician studies the consequences to health of holding certain presuppositions, even though the presuppositions themselves cannot be validated. It follows, then, that when referenced to its health consequences, a presupposition may be labeled healthy (meaning health-producing) or unhealthy. It is important to emphasize, however, that the labels "healthy presuppositions" or "unhealthy presuppositions" refer only to consequences, not to the rightness or wrongness of what is presupposed. All this to say that the diagnosis of a condition like CCPD is the proper business of a metahealth physician.

Having diagnosed a problem in metahealth, the metahealth physician must turn his or her attention to treatment and to prevention. Here the going is very difficult. Simple replacement therapy won't do. People are not generally open to immediate replacement of unhealthy presuppositions with healthy ones. Moreover, if such a replacement was possible, it is not certain that it would be wise to do so. Rather, the approach to treatment and prevention in metahealth is as follows:

1. To remind people that the presuppositions they hold need not be those of their parents or teachers or friends or society—to remind them that presuppositions may be chosen and discarded and selected again, at will.

2. To teach people that the function of a presupposition is to infuse experience with meaning and coherence.

3. To expand, to examine, and to bring to public awareness a full range of presuppositions about human well-being, thereby ensuring that people are not stuck with a presupposition simply out of ignorance of the existence of alternatives.

SENSE II METAHEALTH AS AN APPROACH TO BEHAVIORAL HEALTH

Behavioral health is the interdisciplinary study of influence on the selection of lifestyle options that have future wellness or illness consequences. The word *influence* comes from the French verb *influere,* which means "to flow in." Accordingly, *Webster's New International Dictionary* gives an early definition of influence as "an ethereal fluid thought to flow from the stars and affect the actions of men." Today, the notion that stars can affect behavior is still very much alive in the world—serving to remind us of the wide range of factors thought by humans to affect their behavior. My point here is simply that health behavior may be influenced by an infinite number of "ethereal fluids," fluids whose source of flow constitutes the principal search of behavioral health.

Looking into the future, it is my guess that among the sources of flow found to influence human health behavior, one of the most significant will be what people presuppose about personal well-being and the human condition. It is my hunch that we shall discover that the health behavior of those who presuppose that they will die "when their time comes" will differ significantly from the behavior of those who feel that they are masters of their own destiny; that the behavior of those who presuppose that health is a means will differ from the behavior of those who see health as an end; that the health behavior of those who presuppose that their stars are crossed will differ from the behavior of those who feel that luck is on their side; that the behavior of those who presuppose that health is more important than pleasure will differ from the behavior of those who put pleasure ahead of health; and that the behavior of those who presuppose that disease is a punishment will differ from the behavior of those who presuppose that disease results from bad luck. Indeed, I believe that we shall discover that all health behavior is influenced, in one way or another, by what we presuppose. Hence, I suggest that if we wish to improve the forecasting efficiency of future models of health behavior, we need to provide for the inclusion of metafactors. In my final glimpse into the future, I see that the inclusion of Sense II Metahealth as a part of the interdisciplinary field of behavioral health has resulted in the reuniting of two estranged friends—psychology and philosophy—in a common-cause marriage.

REFERENCE

Collingwood, R. G. *An essay on metaphysics.* Oxford: Clavendon Press, 1940.

INDEX